VOTER TURNOUT
IN THE UNITED STATES
1788–2009

VOTER TURNOUT
IN THE UNITED STATES
1788–2009

Curtis Gans
with Matthew Mulling

CQ PRESS

A Division of SAGE
Washington, D.C.

CQ Press
2300 N Street, NW, Suite 800
Washington, DC 20037
Phone: 202-729-1900; toll-free, 1-866-4CQ-PRESS (1-866-427-7737)
Web: www.cqpress.com

Cover design: Karen Rasmussen, Archeographics
Interior design and composition: Judy Myers

♾ The paper used in this publication exceeds the requirements of the American National Standard for Information Sciences—Permanence of Paper for Printed Library Materials, ANSI Z39.48-1992.

Printed and bound in the United States of America

14   13   12   3   4   5

ISBN: 978-1-60426-595-8

CONTENTS

CHAPTER CONTENTS

Chapter 4: 1850–1869

Chapter 5: 1870–1889

Chapter 11: 1990–2009

APPENDIX: Voter Turnout 1920–1964, Adjusted for the Disenfranchisement of African Americans in the Southern United States

OVERVIEW

PRESIDENTIAL-YEAR GENERAL ELECTIONS

MIDTERM GENERAL ELECTIONS

CURTIS GANS has been the director since 2005 of American University's Center for the Study of the American Electorate, the successor institution to the independent nonpartisan Committee for the Study of the American Electorate, which he cofounded in 1976. His multiple reports on registration and turnout each election year and his many discrete studies on issues affecting citizen political participation in the United States have established him as a primary source of information and analysis for the media, academics, and institutional and political leaders as well as a contributor to constructive changes in public policy. He has testified frequently before Congress and state legislatures and has appeared on such programs as the *Today Show*, the CBS morning and evening news, *Good Morning America*, the ABC and NBC nightly news programs, and NPR's *Morning Edition* and *All Things Considered*. His writings have appeared in major publications, including the *Atlantic*, *Washington Post*, *New York Times*, *Chicago Tribune*, and *Washington Monthly*. Prior to his work on voter turnout, Gans was perhaps best known for providing the theory for and helping to organize the "Dump Johnson" movement of 1967 and serving as staff director of Sen. Eugene McCarthy's 1968 presidential campaign. He also was a newsman for the *Miami News* and United Press International and helped develop a prototype for community service programs in North Carolina

MATTHEW MULLING was a research assistant at the Center for the Study of the American Electorate for two and a half years, during which he helped compile much of the data in this book. He is pursuing a dual law and master's degree in public policy at American University. Mulling is the 2010–2011 editor-in-chief for the *Legislation and Policy Brief* at the Washington College of Law.

This book is the culmination and continuation of thirty-four years of research and compilation.

I did not start in 1976 to create a book of record on turnout. In March of that year, in the living room of my late friend Maurice Rosenblatt's house, he and I looked at the upcoming election and mused that perhaps the most significant figure that might emerge was not how many people voted Republican or Democratic, but how many eligible Americans didn't go to the polls. The question we were raising was why, despite the fact that the United States had gone through a decade and a half of making it easier for citizens to register and vote, an ever-larger percentage of potential voters were eschewing the ballot box. It seemed to us that what was happening was both symptom and disease—symptom of underlying problems in the polity that were motivating the decline in voting; disease insofar as an ever-declining voting electorate posed serious and discrete threats to the health of American democracy. What I was concerned about, at the time, was ascertaining cause and remedy to this problem.

But that inquiry required research in order to provide supported judgments and reasoned recommendations. To undertake that research, we created a small two-person nonprofit research corporation called the Committee for the Study of the American Electorate. Through that institution, we commissioned two bibliographic inquiries—one international and one domestic—as to what the literature could tell us about the problem. We commissioned Peter Hart to conduct a poll of nonvoters, which garnered sufficient publicity to put the organization on the map. And we began the process of collecting and disseminating registration and voting statistics during and after each election season, which we distributed for free to what turned out to be an eager press and public and an only slightly less eager academic community. This, in turn, allowed the Committee to weigh in with research, articles, testimony, and commentary on a variety of issues that affected both voting and the health of American democracy.

Some of the conclusions reached through the Committee's research (and in some cases its advocacy based on those conclusions) did not square with either conventional wisdom or the herd instincts of some major foundations. The Committee found that the principal source for voter disaffection lay in motivation rather than procedure; that enhanced turnout would not necessarily yield partisan advantage to either major political party; that enhancing the opportunity to vote through registration and voting law liberalization, while desirable, would not necessarily yield higher turnout; that registration law liberalization needed to be accompanied by measures that enhanced the integrity of the voting process; that it has been campaign conduct and particularly demagogic televised advertising rather than campaign finance that had a deleterious effect on turnout; and that voter verification through identification was not necessarily deleterious to the voting process, provided the government picked up the cost and such identification was readily accessible. Our advocacy had one tangible and major positive by-product. Because the Committee was able to demonstrate through data that enhancing turnout would not be detrimental to the Republican Party and because, through the work of a Committee-created bipartisan commission headed by the chairs of the two major political parties, it was possible to provide a process for cleaning the voting lists via methods acceptable to both parties, the Committee had a major role in the passage of the National Voter Registration Act (dubbed the motor voter law because it mandated providing voter registration forms at motor vehicle bureaus and social service agencies).

The staple of the Committee's work has always been its six (midterm election) or seven (presidential election) reports on registration and turnout in both primaries and general elections upon which this book is based. While the basic framework of these reports has been essentially constant, the Committee made some changes over the years. In its early years, in the report it has issued biennially in the two days after each election, the Committee reported the turnout and percentages for states in the Pacific time zone, but both because these states have moved to types of balloting which require weeks of postelection counting and because the immediate posting of turnout gives a distorted picture, the Committee ceased publishing those turnout figures until it released its final report, usually in December or January following the election.

A more important change was launched in 2002. Prior to that year and consonant with the practices of almost every other organization in this field, the Committee published turnout figures based on the Census Bureau's Voting Age Population (VAP) estimates as a denominator. In the notes and commentary section of each of the Committee's reports, the Committee acknowledged that the Census figures included noncitizens in the United States who were not eligible to vote and thus, particularly in states where large numbers of noncitizens resided, the Committee-reported turnout percentages were lower than the actual turnout percentages. The Committee also noted that Dr. Walter Dean Burnham had created a set of denominators for analyzing turnout that eliminated noncitizens in the years from 1860 to the present year.

In the fall of 2000, two academics produced articles that called into question the use of the Census VAP estimates as a denominator for analyzing turnout. Because of those articles, the Committee (and its present incarnation as American University's Center for the Study of the American Electorate) began to use Burnham's methodology to adjust the denominators and resulting turnout percentages from its previous reports and for all its future ones. The Committee made one alteration to the data that Burnham had provided. His figures were based on interpolations of overall eligible population minus noncitizens from census to census (usually April to April). The Committee carried forward the interpolation to November of each year. (A fuller explanation of both the methodology and the reasons for its adoption is included in the introduction to this book.)

This book is an outgrowth of both Burnham's and my calculations. My turnout figures were contained in a custom database program. Burnham's figures were handwritten on numerous individual sheets of paper. Neither were readily available for others to use for their calculations and analysis. The Committee (and now the Center under the auspices of American University) created a turnout database from 1788 to the present. That database had for its numerators the overall votes and partisan votes for president, governor, U.S. senator, and aggregate vote for U.S House of Representatives in general elections, and primary votes for president, governor, and U.S. senator. The data was accumulated for individual states and the nation as a whole. The Committee used Burnham's census-to-census citizen population figures as a denominator for primary elections since the majority of those primaries occur in the spring and early summer. The Committee used its unique November citizen-eligible figures as the denominator for general elections. For the electronic and online version of this book, all of the figures stored in the Committee's database have been turned into electronically accessible and manipulable sets of spreadsheets for those who might wish to use them for their calculations.

ACKNOWLEDGMENTS

Neither the thirty-four years of my institution's existence nor this book would have been possible without the monetary support, research assistance, and helpful guidance of many who deserve acknowledgment here.

The financial support for my work over the years was largely provided by a number of individuals, unions, corporations, and foundations. On the top of the list of individuals were Sophie Engelhard Craighead, Jeffrey and Tondra Lynford, Michael Berman, Bill and Alice Russell-Shapiro, the late Democratic Party Chairman John White, Jerome Kohlberg, and my ex-wife, Shelley Nan Fidler, and her late father, Jay Fidler, who kept me afloat when other sources of money didn't. Union support came from Bill Holayter and the International Association of Machinists; Bill Lucy of the American Federation of State, County, and Municipal Employees; John Perkins of the Committee on Political Education of the AFL-CIO; the National Association of Firefighters; and George Gould of the National Association of Letter Carriers. While corporate support was in the larger scheme of things comparatively minimal, I could count on Bob Healy during the years that he was heading the Atlantic-Richfield Washington office and for many years on Robert Liberatore and the Chrysler Corporation.

My work would not have been possible without the help of a number of individuals in the foundation community, including Craig Kennedy when he was president of the Joyce Foundation, the late David Ramage and the living Colin Greer at the New World Foundation, Geri Mannion at the Carnegie Corporation of New York, Susan Clark of the Columbia Foundation, Mary Stake Hawker of the Deer Creek Foundation, Hodding Carter III as president of the Knight Foundation, Mark Steinmeyer of the Smith Richardson Foundation, Jack Rosenthal and the New York Times Foundation, James Bailey and Richard Cudahy of the Cudahy Fund, and Bill Schambra (with an assist from the Honorable Mitch Daniels) at the Bradley Foundation. We also had some one-time program support from the Field Foundation, the McCormick Foundation, the Herb Block Foundation, and the Bernard and Audre Rapoport Foundation.

Over the years my labors have benefitted from the wise guidance of individuals too numerous to fully tally here. But certain individuals deserve special mention, including the late Senator Terry Sanford, the late Maurice Mitchell, David Cohen, Dorothy Ridings, Josiah Lee Auspitz, David Paletz, Robert Bauer, William Canfield, and Jan Baran. I owe a debt to certain political leaders who believed sufficiently in some of the analysis of the Committee to give it a platform at congressional hearings, including the late Senator Charles Mathias, the Honorable Wendell Ford, the Honorable John Danforth, the Honorable Al Swift, the Honorable Bill Thomas, and the Honorable Paul Kirk. I also owe a debt to the many state election officials and journalists who provided data and information that made my analytic work possible.

Nothing I have done in the past thirty-four years would have been possible without a series of assistants, including Helen Lichtenstein, Kathryn Carroll, Dennis Galvan, Gary Corbin, Laura Lee Guimond, Mark Harvey, Demetra Green, Sean Greene, Rebecca Bond, and Judy Fisher. I also owe a deep debt to Phyllis Doriot Emmett, my accountant extraordinaire who kept the IRS wolves from my door.

While the idea for this book was mine, it would not have been possible without the intervention of Rhodes Cook, who was the matchmaker between CQ Press and myself, and Andrea Pedolsky, who, at CQ Press, decided it was a good idea and commissioned it. I owe a debt to CQ Press for two of its publications—*America Votes* and *A Statistical History of the American Electorate*—from whence some of my voting numbers came. This book would not have been possible without the help and skill of CQ Press editors Doug Goldenberg-Hart and David Arthur and the production assistance of various people at CQ Press and Sage publications, including Anne Stewart, Kathryn Krug, and Gwenda Larsen.

I have saved the best for last, because there were four individuals who made the greatest contributions to this book—Walter Dean Burnham, my friend and mentor; Samuel Schreiber, who served seven years as my research assistant, created the custom and flexible database program that made possible my statistical analyses, and was available for technical support the last six years when I had any problems; Matthew Mulling, who for the last four and a half years at American University has retrieved, entered, and put in legible spreadsheet form the majority of the figures that comprise the heart of this book; and John Martino, whose skill and care as an editor helped ensure that the numbers in this book are accurate and the prose coherent.

I hope this book is a product worthy of all those who helped.

Curtis Gans
August 2010

INTRODUCTION

This is a book of record about the most important, but also the lowest common denominator, political act—voting.

American democracy, or for that matter any democracy, depends upon the consent of the governed for its legitimacy. The broadest measure of that consent is the vote. But because voting is the lowest common denominator political act—citizens who don't vote are unlikely to participate in any other form of sustaining political or civic activity—measuring voting also, to some extent, measures civic health.

The size of the vote in a given election and the margin of victory have an impact on governance. A person elected by a small margin when few people vote theoretically has less latitude in acting than a person who wins office by a large margin in an election where a large percentage of the electorate votes. The level of electoral participation can reflect changes in law, modifications in the structure and institutions of the polity, and the impact of events, public policy, and changing political attitudes.

Who can vote also matters. Since an elected official needs for his or her political survival to be responsive to the desires and views of those who vote, both the shape of the electorate and the portion of that electorate who actually turns out to vote heavily influences the course of public policy. Who can vote is determined, in part, by who is considered an eligible citizen. Today, the threshold enfranchisement issue is whether a convicted felon who has completed his or her jail-time should be allowed to vote. This situation is a long way from the early days of the republic when only propertied (in money or land) males, twenty-one years of age or older, could vote. Even then, some males (Catholics, Jews, and African Americans) could not vote in many places.

Over the years, and in fits and starts, major steps forward, retrenchment, and renewed positive movement, the opportunity to participate in American democracy has been enhanced, creating a more perfect but still imperfect Union. This road is charted in this book through the prism of voter turnout.

This book traces turnout—the percentage of eligible Americans who have cast their ballots—from 1788 through the present. From 1788 until 1902, it traces the votes for president, state governor, and statewide aggregate vote for U.S. House of Representatives—both overall and by party—by state and aggregated nationally. Beginning in 1902, the book traces votes in major party primaries for president and governor. Beginning in 1914, it also traces both the primary and general election overall turnout, and the partisan vote for U.S. Senator, an office that before 1914 had been chosen by state legislatures.

While the book provides raw data on the number of those eligible to vote and on the number who actually cast ballots, it also provides data on turnout percentage trends. The book is divided into twenty-year chapters. The book charts turnout trends within those twenty-year periods and for the entire range of years from 1788 to the present.

This book also longitudinally charts the major changes in voting law and procedures that may have had an effect on levels of voting. And, with a broad brush, it provides some context outlining major world and national events that had an impact on politics during each twenty-year period.

HISTORICAL ANALYSIS

The history of citizen participation in elections, however, does not fall neatly into twenty-year chapters. Rather, it can better be seen through the prism of five eras, each of which had distinctive trends:

1. 1788–1855, or from the beginnings of the republic to the mid-nineteenth century when the two parties still seen in partisan competition today—the Democratic and the Republican—began to emerge.

2. 1856–1875, a period dominated by issues concerning slavery and race.

3. 1876–1927, a period of major changes in the electoral process and sharp declines in the percentage of Americans voting.

4. 1928–1963, two and a half decades of increased political participation, partisan realignment, and minuscule changes in election law.

5. 1964–the present, a period of progressive and generational decline in turnout (except for the high turnout elections of 2004 and 2008 and increased voting in the South and among citizens older than seventy-five years of age), despite changes in society, political competition, and electoral law which should, theoretically, have produced higher levels of voting.

1788–1855: Democracy Defined

The least reliable turnout figures in this compilation are for the period from 1788 through 1855. The only thing consistent among state laws

regarding voting in 1788 was the limitation of the franchise to males and an accepted minimum age of twenty-one. All of the original thirteen states, except Vermont, had some economic qualification for voting—ownership of property, a personal worth threshold, and/or taxpaying. All had a minimal residency requirement of at least six months, and most required a year's residence. In almost all states, African Americans were excluded from voting. In some states Jews and Catholics, among others, couldn't vote. But since the results of the Constitutional Convention left the conduct of elections up to the individual states—except for the broad principles of direct election of members of the U.S. House, indirect election of the president, and legislative election of the U.S. Senate (and the constitutional compromise of counting slaves as three-fifths of a human being for apportionment of U.S. House seats and electors)—there was no uniformity in state statutes as to who could vote and thus no reliable denominator for accurately ascertaining turnout. The one used here—the Census count of male population twenty-one years of age and older—is only a crude way of ascertaining turnout.

While elections for offices in the twentieth century tended to be spaced at regular intervals (every two years in even-numbered years for the U.S. House, a rotating every six years for the U.S. Senate, every four years for president, and every two or four years for governors), elections for U.S. House and governors in the nineteenth century were held in many states in odd-numbered years and at irregular intervals, making trend analysis more difficult.

At the time of the Constitutional Convention, the population of the United States was only four million; by 1855, it was more than twenty million and the nation had grown from thirteen states to thirty-one. By 1855, almost all states that had previously had property and taxpaying qualifications for voting had eliminated them and many new states began to enter the union without such qualifications. But of the thirty-one states, fully twenty-five still didn't grant the vote to African Americans, free or slave. However, three states, Indiana, Michigan, and Wisconsin (a number that would expand in ensuing years) allowed "declarant" aliens to vote—those who were not citizens but declared that they would become citizens.

There were also gradual changes in the political process. In the early days, in some states, voting was by voice. By the end of this period, all elections were by paper ballot, and there was in most states some uniformity imposed on the type of ballot. As political parties grew stronger, better organized, and more disciplined, they produced colored ballots that could be taken into the polls and counted. This helped parties mobilize and keep track of their voters and ensure that they voted in the party-sanctioned manner.

When the Constitution was signed, there were no political parties. Many of the Founding Fathers feared parties, concerned that they would exacerbate faction. Factions were, however, already developing—the federalists, who favored greater power for the central government and its use for the common good, and the anti-federalists, who favored greater power for the individual states and a greater commitment to individual liberty. By the third presidential election in 1796, the Founders' fears had been realized, with the factions loosely arraying themselves as political parties—the Federalists, headed by John Adams, and the Democratic-Republican Party, whose guiding spirit was Thomas Jefferson. Both parties had limited reach and did little to actively increase their memberships. The Federalist Party essentially died during the War of 1812 because of its opposition to that conflict, along with John Adams's enactment of the hugely unpopular Alien and Sedition Acts. By 1815, "The Era of Good Feelings" had taken hold and there was virtually no party competition. This led to an extraordinarily low turnout in the 1820 election. Competition returned in 1824, but it was intraparty competition between John Quincy Adams and Andrew Jackson.

The 1828 election marked the first major effort at nationwide political mobilization. Jackson, who felt that the 1824 election had been stolen from him by elitists in Congress, mounted a populist campaign that both propelled him into office and produced the first electoral turnout in excess of 60 percent of the eligible population. (Prior to this election, presidential turnout had never reached beyond 44 percent of the eligible electorate.) Jackson's policies—inventing the "spoils system" to bring his political supporters with him into paying federal jobs (later called the patronage system), abolishing the national bank, dismantling government subsidies for state programs, supporting slavery, and pursuing a libertarian agenda—led to political schisms. Henry Clay, John C. Calhoun, and Daniel Webster, all U.S. senators, organized a faction which broke from both Jackson's policies and the Democratic-Republican Party, calling themselves the National Republican Party. The National Republicans lost the 1832 election in the face of Jackson's continuing popularity. By 1836, the National Republicans were known as the Whig party, and they narrowly lost that year's presidential election to Democrat (no longer Democratic-Republican) Martin Van Buren. The Whigs did win the succeeding election behind military hero William Henry Harrison, only to have that victory snatched from them by the new president's sudden death on April 4, 1841. The Democratic-leaning views of John Tyler, Harrison's vice president and successor, led him to be drummed out of the Whig party. Tyler was succeeded via the results of the 1844 election by Democrat James Knox Polk, who was, in turn, succeeded by Whig military hero Zachary Taylor, who died after one year in office and was succeeded by his vice president, Millard Fillmore. Fillmore's unpopular presidency yielded to the election of Democrat Franklin Pierce in 1852, who was succeeded by Democrat James Buchanan, via the election of 1856.

By Buchanan's presidency, both parties were shaped, defined, and divided by the seminal political issue of the era—slavery. The issue split the Whigs apart, with the northern anti-slavery wing becoming the Republican Party and the pro-slavery Whigs becoming Democrats. Indeed, by 1855 the Republican and Democratic parties moved toward assuming the composition, character, ideological advocacy, and relative national strength each would retain—except during the Civil War and the Republican split of 1912—until the election of 1932.

Also in place by the mid-nineteenth century was a different concept of party and a modified electoral system. As Jackson and his successor Van Buren had shown, parties could mobilize for victory and sustain themselves in power if they were tightly controlled at the top and highly organized at the bottom, kept faith with their core constituencies, used the patronage system to reward workers, and built a platform (avoiding radical stances) to appeal to the whole electorate. Due to both increased organization within the parties and growing competition, the trend in voter turnout was generally upward from 1828 onward. Well over 50 percent of the electorate was voting in presidential elections, reaching in excess of 70 percent in 1840, 1844, and 1856.

This period produced an expanded electorate, a more competitive playing field, mobilizing institutions, and more liberalized election laws—all of which conspired to produce, after the mid-1820s, enhanced turnout.

1856–1875: The Politics of Race

The election of 1860 was the first major realigning American election—a contest driven by opposing views on slavery, which drew a turnout of nearly 80 percent of those eligible, and which created the underpinnings for a Republican Party political dominance that lasted until the Great Depression of 1929–1940 and the 1932 ascension to the presidency of Democratic Party standard-bearer Franklin Delano Roosevelt.

For almost the entire history of the nation, from the first importation of African slave labor, a central feature of American politics has been its division along lines of race and region. Slaves were imported, largely, for use and abuse to maximize the profits of a southern agrarian plantation system. Slavery faded much more quickly in the northern mercantilist regions. By the mid-nineteenth century a large majority of citizens outside of the South viewed slavery as morally abhorrent. Most within the South, with some notable individual exceptions, defended slavery, the southern way of life, and the region's agrarian and slavery-dependent economic well-being with equal fervor.

In the period between the ratification of the Constitution and the Civil War, there were many attempts to ameliorate the slavery issue, all of which ultimately failed. The constitutional provision to count a slave as three-fifths of a human for the purposes of political apportionment allowed the North and South to have relatively equal say in national governance. In 1820 the Missouri Compromise divided the territory acquired in the Louisiana Purchase by stipulating that new states that were created south of Missouri's southern border would be admitted as slave states, and those to the north as free states. It also allowed Missouri to decide for itself whether to be slave or free. This approach quelled hostilities for a time. Each newly entering free state was balanced by a newly entering slave state.

The tenuous equilibrium over slavery was shattered by the Mexican-American War, the westward growth of the nation, ill-conceived legislative attempts to create balance between slave and non-slave states, and one egregious Supreme Court decision. Democratic Senator Stephen A. Douglas of Illinois (and Lincoln-Douglas debate fame) and Henry Clay (a leader of the soon-to-expire Whig Party) fashioned what came to be called the Compromise of 1850. The compromise was a legislative package of five acts aimed at dealing with the results of the Mexican-American War and westward expansion, but containing elements which would ultimately exacerbate North-South tensions. One part of the package provided that Texas would be admitted as a slave state. Another mandated that when California entered the union, it would be a free state. Still another piece of the package allowed both the territories of New Mexico and Utah to decide for themselves whether to allow slavery when they applied for statehood, thus abrogating the geographical provisions of the Missouri Compromise. But probably the most far-reaching and divisive aspect of this legislative package was the Fugitive Slave Act, which mandated that escaped slaves captured in free states were still the property of their former owners and, by law, had to be returned—a provision that pleased southern slave owners and angered almost everyone else.

Stephen Douglas was also at the heart of another unsuccessful effort to bridge the slavery/anti-slavery divide: the 1854 Kansas-Nebraska Act. The act further vitiated the Missouri Compromise by allowing Kansas and Nebraska to decide for themselves on the issue of slavery. It was an act that satisfied none of the contending parties and led to a series of border skirmishes between pro-slave partisans from Missouri and anti-slavery advocates from Kansas—armed clashes sufficiently violent over a four-year period (1854–1858) to warrant the name "Bleeding Kansas." On a political level, the law bitterly divided the dominant Democratic Party between anti-slave northerners and pro-slavery southerners. What sealed the irreconcilability of the conflict was probably the Dred Scott Supreme Court decision, which, in essence, declared that slaves, former slaves, and descendants of slaves were not human beings and were therefore not entitled to any legal or constitutional protection.

With the Republican Party united against slavery and the Democratic Party divided between pro- and anti-slave factions, the election of 1860 promised to be a deeply emotional and possibly decisive contest. Despite receiving almost no support from the South, Abraham Lincoln was propelled into the presidency (carrying with him Republican majorities in both houses of Congress) in an election which produced the highest voter turnout since the founding of the nation—almost 80 percent of the eligible male population. The decisive nature of the election eliminated any hope the South had of national acceptance of slavery, propelled the southern states toward secession, and established the Republicans as the dominant national party, a position they would retain for nearly seventy-five years.

The best and most stable way of looking at partisan turnout in any one year and over time is the turnout across all U.S. House of Representatives elections. From 1858 until 1930, with the exception of only four elections (two presidential and two midterm), the Republicans drew more House votes than the Democrats. The Republicans became the party of the North and West, of Protestants, and of reform. The power base for the Democrats during this period was largely limited to the South and to urban Catholics, the urban poor, and newly resident immigrants (among the most prominent of whom were the Irish and later those of Italian and Polish descent).

There were two major issues at stake in the Civil War—the preservation of the Union and the end of slavery. In the interest of furthering the former aim, Republicans and those Democrats committed to preserving the Union joined to form the National Union Party during the war. Lincoln ran for reelection as president in 1864 with vice-presidential candidate Andrew Johnson, a Tennessee Democrat, a supporter of maintaining the union of all states, and the only southern Democrat not to resign his senatorial office when war erupted. The ticket

won handily with diminished turnout due to both lack of competition and the large number of adult males who were involved in fighting the war.

But whatever unity existed during the war evaporated after Lincoln's assassination and the end of the war. Andrew Johnson had joined the National Union Party because of his intense feelings about preserving the Union, but he did not have similar feelings about racial equality. Thus, he attempted to swiftly reintegrate the secessionist states with minimal requirements for reforming their racial policies. The Republicans in control of Congress saw in the war victory a mandate to fulfill the promise of Lincoln's Emancipation Proclamation. They had the votes in Congress and, largely, the support of the non-southern nation.

Johnson's advocacy and actions were overcome, overturned, and outvoted. He faced impeachment and, though he was not removed from office, he ended his term in 1869 unpopular and politically emasculated.

Prior to the Civil Rights movement of the mid-twentieth century, it was a widely accepted belief that during Reconstruction "radical" Republicans had imposed an onerous regime on the South which led to the region's later reversion to suppression of African American rights. Scholarly interpretations and public sentiment in the last forty-five years have increasingly rejected this earlier interpretation and instead focused on the postwar Republicans' belief that the Civil War was about the elimination of slavery and the establishment of racial equality. To that end, the Republicans produced and had ratified within three years after the end of the war the Fourteenth and Fifteenth amendments to the Constitution, which theoretically guaranteed racial equality and prohibited denial of the vote on racial grounds by either state or federal governments. When they found that southern leaders were loathe to abide by these amendments, they enacted the Enforcement Act of 1870, which led to the imposition of occupation troops in the South in an attempt to ensure compliance with the amendments. They also refused to permit the secessionist states to rejoin the Union unless they complied with the amendments. During this brief period, southern African Americans both voted and held political office.

Turnout in presidential elections, with the exception of the virtually uncontested reelection of Ulysses S. Grant in 1872, stayed near and above the 80 percent level through the election of 1892. The story of the first ninety years of the republic was one of the expansion of the right to vote, the creation of viable and competitive political parties, some important and emotionally charged issues, strong partisan mobilization, and increasing voter turnout. But the trajectory of increased political participation was about to change, beginning with the disastrous compromise that settled the presidential election of 1876.

1876–1927: Years of Major Changes and Diminishing Turnout

Between 1876 and 1928, turnout in both presidential and midterm elections plummeted. By the 1920s, voter turnout was lower nationally than it had been in 1828. In the southern states, it hit historic lows.

The direct causes of this downturn were fourfold:

1. The progressive and systematic disenfranchisement of African Americans and many lower-class whites in the South.

2. The enfranchisement of women.

3. Changes in the structure, administration, and conduct of politics and elections.

4. The change from an agrarian nation with a relatively homogeneous population to a predominantly industrial nation with successive waves of non-Anglo-Saxon immigrants.

Disenfranchisement of African Americans

While legal barriers to African American voting in the South were first enacted in 1891 in Alabama, it was the resolution of the presidential election impasse of 1876–1877 that fertilized the ground for propagating segregation and disenfranchisement in the postwar South. In that election neither the Democratic candidate Samuel Tilden nor the Republican candidate Rutherford B. Hayes won a popular or electoral vote majority. Both sides claimed victory, bickering over close margins in a few states where the actual vote counts were never resolved. In these states presidential electors selected by different methods vied for legitimacy. Ultimately, after several months of highly partisan political warfare, a compromise was reached. Hayes would be proclaimed president and he would, in turn, yield to the Democratic (and particularly southern Democratic) demand that federal troops stationed in the South to enforce the Fourteenth and Fifteenth amendments be withdrawn. It would take almost ninety years to reverse the damage done by that "compromise."

The decision to withdraw troops from the South, several Supreme Court decisions affirming state rather than federal authority in the interpretation of laws, and the judgment by the Court that it was possible for separate to be considered equal led to the demise of Reconstruction and the rise of a new era of white supremacy in the South. Characteristics of this new era included the segregation of blacks from whites; the enforcement of black legal and de facto inferiority through state court sanctioned intimidation, including lynchings; the economic emasculation of the African American community by the creation of the sharecropper system, in which blacks tilled whites' land for subsistence remuneration while whites excessively profited from black exploitation; the creation of separate and inferior public accommodations and schools for blacks, keeping blacks "in their place" as much as possible; and ultimately the denial to African Americans of the right to vote.

The formal denial of African American voting rights that Alabama started in 1891 was soon emulated by other southern states. Approaches to vote denial included the creation of new state constitutions that grandfathered in voting rights for individuals and their descendants who had been eligible to vote prior to the Civil War, while forcing everyone else (including virtually all African Americans) to register to vote anew. Coupled with the registration requirements were onerous poll taxes and impossible-to-pass literacy tests. While these new voting strictures were aimed at African Americans, they also affected lower-class whites, whom the affluent white leadership believed might some day make common cause with blacks. White southern leaders also established the means by which no black could be elected to office. They created the Democratic Party whites-only primary, which selected candidates for office who would, thereafter, run virtually unopposed in a South dominated by a single political party (the Democratic). And, until the practice was overturned via court decisions in the 1940s, they established the party as a private organization which could legally conduct these primaries, excluding whomever they pleased.

By the 1920s, southern white participation in general elections was under 30 percent and southern black participation was virtually nonexistent.

Women

Though various pioneering women had previously championed the cause of political equality, the first collective manifestation of this demand was the convention held at Seneca Falls, New York, in 1848. The movement for women's suffrage split shortly after that convention, largely over disagreement concerning tactics, but pressure for voting equality grew. By 1912, more than half the states permitted women to vote in school board elections. Between 1913 and 1919, seventeen states passed statutes allowing women to vote in presidential elections, though the southern states of Arkansas and Texas limited that participation to primary elections and party conventions. By 1918, fifteen states, all located (with the exception of New York) west of the Mississippi River, allowed women to vote in all elections.

In 1920, Congress passed, and a sufficient number of states ratified, the Nineteenth Amendment to the Constitution, granting full suffrage to women in all states. But this, in turn, served to depress turnout figures. As a result of almost doubling the eligible electorate (women then constituted slightly less than half the population), but adding a female population which voted at about half the rate of men, turnout percentages were reduced. Women gradually increased their participation, but it would be 1980 before their voting rate equaled that of men.

Changes in Voting Laws and a Diminished Electorate

Many laws enacted or amended just before, and in the immediate aftermath of, the Civil War had a positive impact on voter turnout by expanding the definition of who was qualified to vote. However, most of the changes in the electoral system in the period after 1876 depressed turnout (as, in many cases, they were intended to), by creating obstacles to voting.

The motivations for change were many and varied. Self-styled good government groups, such as the Progressives, wanted a polity free from fraud, corruption, and oligarchical control. Partisanship played a part, as the Republican Party did not want its agrarian and small town base to be overwhelmed by the growing urban lower classes. Fear of succeeding waves of immigrants and their potential to undermine the established order also played a part.

There were major changes involving registration, balloting, the spoils system and civil service, and candidate selection.

Registration. In the earliest days of the republic, voter registration did not exist. Members of a community tended to know one another, and people just showed up to vote (as they still do in North Dakota). As the population grew and as political parties formed and began doing sometimes untoward things in the pursuit of victory, the demand for a list of qualified voters grew. Initially, states and municipalities created lists of those eligible, but between 1876 and 1920, all states moved to personal registration. Under personal registration, a citizen was responsible for registering himself or herself. In almost every state, the citizen would need to re-register if he or she failed to vote in an election or changed residences. This made voting a continuing two-step act, unlike the system in most other advanced democracies, where the state creates the voting list and all the citizen needs to do is vote. Even outside the South, registration was limited. Felons, whether they had served their time or not, generally could not vote, nor could paupers in many places. A few states established literacy tests which, while not as onerous as those in the South, tended to exclude some on the bottom of the income scale. Requiring a citizen to be a resident of a state or locality for up to one year before allowing him or her to register also tended to restrict the franchise. Most often a citizen had to have been resident of a state for a year and of a local jurisdiction for at least six months in order to qualify to vote. Closing dates for the completion of registration tended to be well in advance—as much as six months to a year before an election—making it impossible for those whose interest in an election was kindled late in the process or who had taken up residence in a new state to cast their votes. When and where a citizen could register was left up to the states and localities and, in most places, one could only register in person at a registrar or clerk's office. In some places, one could only register on a few days each year. (In some localities, these days were unadvertised, so strongly did local politicians believe in the principle of electoral continuity or staying in power.) Different states had different rules for naturalized immigrant voting, some requiring a number of years of citizenship-residence after naturalization before a person could register and vote. This was particularly true of those states which had, in the first three decades of the twentieth century, large numbers of immigrants of different stock than long-term residents—such as the Chinese in California and southern and eastern Europeans in the East.

Ballots. Until the late nineteenth century, the most widespread method of balloting was the party ballot. The parties printed up ballots with only their candidates on them. The voter could choose which party ballot to cast, and the ballots were usually color-coded by party. This helped with party mobilization, potentially maximizing a party's vote and providing a straight ticket result. It also led to vote buying and other irregularities. England and some other advanced democracies had adopted the Australian ballot—a ballot prepared by the state of eligible candidates and cast, in most cases, in secret. This reduced, but did not completely eliminate, vote buying, allowed citizens to fend off partisan pressures, and made possible split-ticket voting. But the Australian ballot was among a number of changes which weakened the effectiveness of the political party and its mobilization efforts.

The spoils system and civil service. Beginning with the presidency of Andrew Jackson, the party which won the election claimed the right to install its partisans in appointive offices. The virtue of this system, labeled the "spoils system," was that it put into government administration people likely to carry out the promises and directives of the candidate who won, and it provided incentives and rewards for partisans to maximize their participation and mobilization. The downside was that it often placed unqualified or incompetent people in positions of responsibility and

led to corruption where appointees could buy their way into powerful positions. To remedy the downsides of the spoils system, in 1883 Congress passed the Pendleton Act, which created a civil service system, merit pay, and a partially depoliticized government. (It would become more fully depoliticized via the Hatch Act several decades later.) This reduced governmental corruption and provided a cadre of qualified government workers. The Pendleton Act did not eliminate patronage positions entirely but it sharply reduced their number, also somewhat reducing the political parties' ability to reward their loyal workers and maintain as effective a sustaining grassroots organization as they had previously. However, the Pendleton Act applied only to the federal government. The parties, and particularly the Democratic Party, were still able to build city political machines through local patronage.

Candidate selection. Before the twentieth century, the selection of candidates for most offices was determined by a small group of leaders in each party. These leaders controlled the conventions, which selected national and statewide candidates, and controlled the state legislatures, which had the power to elect U.S. senators. Beginning in 1904 in Wisconsin, and spreading across the nation in subsequent years, the preferred method of choosing candidates became the party primary. This reform spread more slowly in the selection of presidential candidates, but became the rule after the 1968 election. In 1912, via the Seventeenth Amendment, the power to choose U.S. senators was taken from state legislatures and given to citizens via direct elections. These changes did have the salutary effect of reducing both political corruption and oligarchical rule in the major parties, but it also weakened the parties' ability to discipline their candidates, pursue collective party aims, and mobilize the electorate behind them. Parties were still important, but these and other reforms made them less powerful and effective than they had been.

Demographic Changes

Two other changes in the political architecture of the nation also contributed to the decline in voter participation. During this period, the underlying economic shape of the nation changed as the United States went from being a primarily agrarian nation to a predominantly industrial and manufacturing one. This, in turn, produced a working class which would not find its full political voice until the 1930s and the creation of the CIO (Congress of Industrial Organizations), the first effective broad-based trade union movement in America. In addition, and particularly in the first two decades of the twentieth century, there was substantial immigration into the United States. But unlike previous waves of immigration that were largely (but not exclusively) middle class, English-speaking, or northern European, this wave was substantially working class and, with the exception of a substantial number of Irish immigrants, largely came from southern and eastern Europe. These new immigrants had to overcome language barriers, ethnic prejudices, and economic inadequacies before they could feel competent in full political participation. That assimilation took time and helped diminish the rate of voting.

The cumulative effects of all these changes were devastating to political participation nationally and especially in the South. In 1876, presidential election voter turnout was 83 percent of those eligible. In 1896, it was 79 percent of those eligible. In both 1920 and 1924, it was 48 percent. (It rose to about 56 percent in 1928, due largely to the presence of a Catholic candidate at the head of the Democratic ticket and the polarizing effect created by that choice.) Turnout varied narrowly between 66 percent to 68 percent of eligible voters for the aggregate turnout for the U.S. House in midterm elections between 1874 and 1894. Turnout was 32 percent in 1926. Turnout in the 1896 presidential election was 85 percent outside the South, and 61 percent in the South. In 1924, turnout was 56 percent outside the South, and 25 percent in the South. In the midterm election of 1894, turnout was 74 percent of eligible voters outside the South and 54 percent in the South. In 1926, turnout was 42 percent outside the South and less than 15 percent in the South.

Partisan National Turnout for U.S. House Elections during Presidential Election Years, 1856–2008

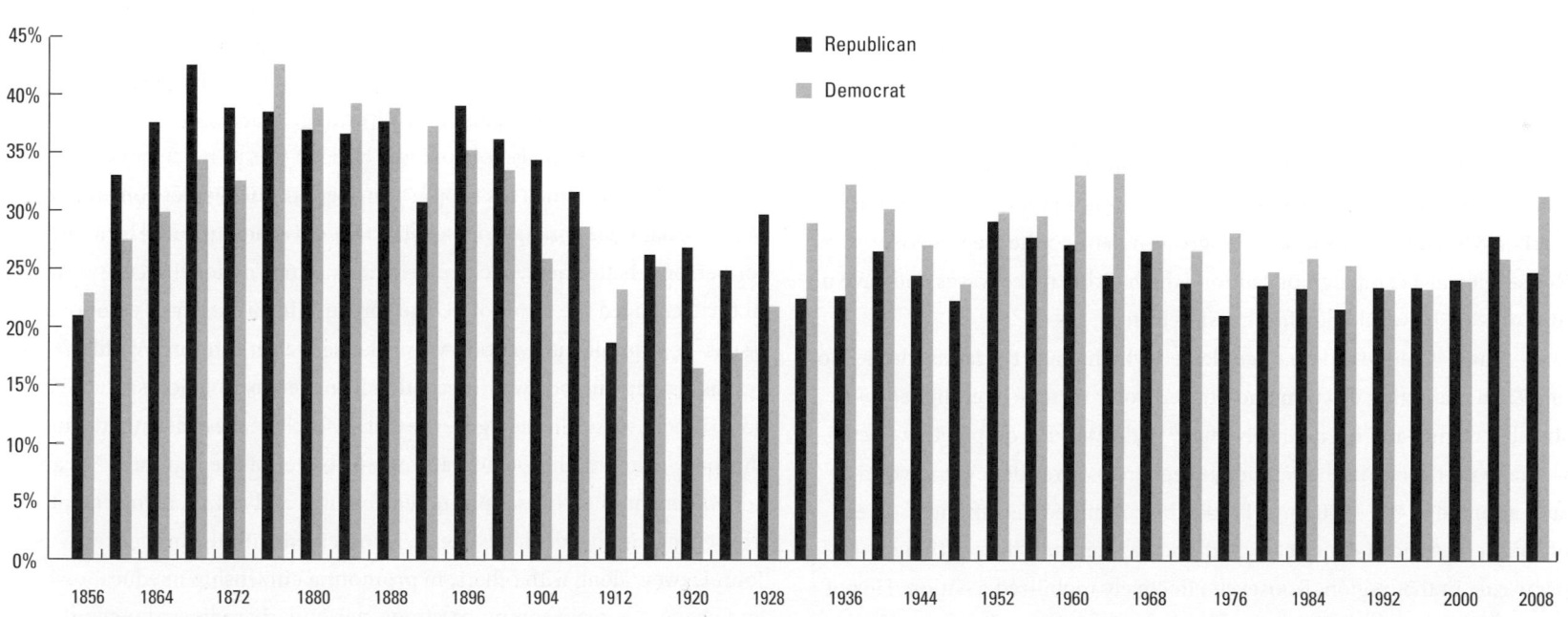

Note: For partisan presidential-year turnout percentages from 1788 to 2008, see graph on page 31

1928–1963: Legal Stasis, Political Realignment, and Turnout Rebound

The paradox of this period is how much happened in national and world events, in politics, and in positive political participation, and yet how little happened in election law. In these three-and-a-half decades, the United States survived a major economic depression, was involved in the Second World War and the Korean War, and witnessed the beginning of the Vietnam War. It launched the nuclear age, was involved in a Cold War, joined a race into space, stirred a civil rights movement, and witnessed the greatest expansion of federal power in the nation's history. During this period, the partisan balance of American politics was overturned and voting rates climbed from their depth in the 1920s, when women were given the right to vote, to their highest post-women's-suffrage level in 1960. Yet a highly restrictive and, in the South, racially exclusionary electoral structure remained virtually intact.

Realignment would not have come about without the Depression and without Franklin Delano Roosevelt. But the election of 1932 that propelled Roosevelt into the presidency was not, in and of itself, a realigning election—even though beginning with that election the Democrats beat the Republicans in the congressional vote in every other presidential or midterm election until 1994 (with the exception of the midterms between 1940 and 1950 and the presidential election year of 1952). The 1932 election was a negative referendum on the incumbent Herbert Hoover and his lack of progress in denting the Depression. Roosevelt ran a campaign of caution which didn't make waves and gave no hint of what he would do after he was elected.

It was what he did do once elected which made the landslide election of 1936 a realigning election and pushed voter turnout ever higher (with a stumble during and immediately after World War II), despite there being virtually no change in the restrictive registration, residency, and voting laws adopted in the 1900s and 1920s, the continued disenfranchisement of southern African Americans and poor whites, and the continued one-party rule in that region. Roosevelt effectively mobilized a nation. He put hundreds of thousands directly to work. He built upon the grievances of the new and more militant Congress of Industrial Organizations and used their grassroots sinew to help mobilize the working class. He poured money into rural electrification and development. He provided urban aid and strengthened the nascent Democratic city political machines. And he was careful to focus on economic issues and avoid race issues, thus keeping southern segregationist Democrats within his large tent, while beginning to break into the Republican allegiance of blacks outside the South. In doing all of this he changed not only the party balance but the content of American politics. The turf was now economic issues and Roosevelt brought together the poor, unions, liberals, big city machines, small plot farmers, rural Americans, northern minorities, urban ethnics—particularly Catholics and Jews—and southern segregationists. Democrats could, in almost every election until the 1970s, count on the South, the industrial Midwest, and Middle Atlantic states as a solid electoral base, a far larger base than the Republicans had. The Roosevelt New Deal coalition kept the Democrats as the dominant party for sixty-two years. The partisan House aggregate turnout figures for 1926 and 1958 tell the story of realignment in graphic detail. In 1926, the Democrats won only five states outside the South: Arizona, Maryland, Missouri, Nebraska, and Nevada; in 1958, the GOP won only five states total: Nebraska, New Hampshire, Utah, Washington, and Wyoming.

What Roosevelt also offered was hope. It was as much hope as programs that sustained his support throughout the Depression and World War II. That hope sprang from a belief that government could be a force for personal betterment, societal benefit, and international security. This, in turn, changed the terms of debate surrounding a variety of emotional issues—economic intervention versus laissez-faire, entering World War II versus staying out, postwar internationalism versus isolationism, activist government versus limited government. In each of these debates during this particular era, the Democrats had the better of the argument. As an added benefit, their causes promoted activism and citizen involvement. This change in the ideological terrain coincided with the influence of John Dewey, along with others, in promoting citizenship in education and changes in mass communications, particularly radio and network

Partisan National Turnout for U.S. House Elections during Midterm Election Years, 1858–2006

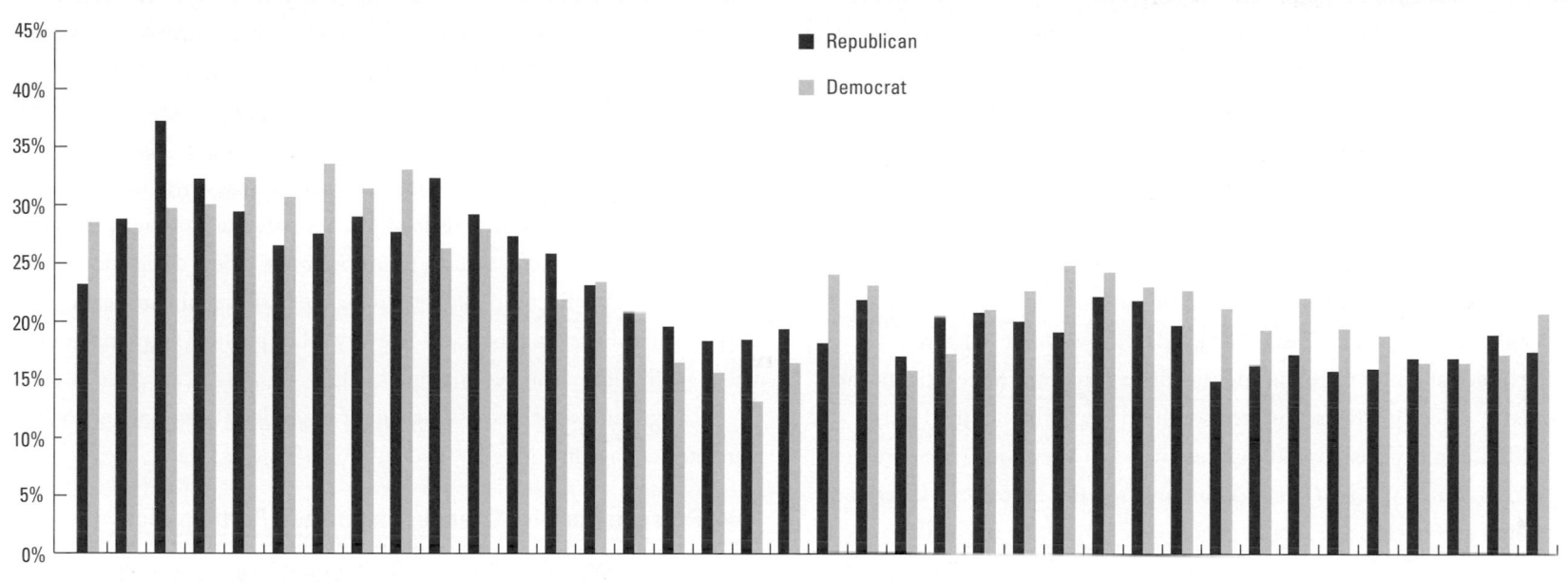

Note: For partisan midterm year turnout percentages from 1790 to 2006, see graph on page 33.

television, which brought shared knowledge and concerns. These are the likely reasons that turnout went up despite the lack of any major changes in voting law and a South whose level of voter turnout remained static until the late 1950s. Overall turnout in presidential elections went from 48 percent of eligible voters in 1924 to over 65 percent in 1960 and stayed over 60 percent from 1952 through 1968. Overall turnout in midterm elections went from 32 percent in 1926 to 47 percent in 1962. Southern turnout stayed between 25 and 32 percent of eligible voters in presidential elections between 1924 and 1948, rising somewhat thereafter as both Republican presidential candidates Dwight Eisenhower and Richard Nixon captured a larger share of the southern vote. (Even so, when southern turnout had risen to 43 percent in 1960, turnout outside the South had reached 73 percent.) In midterm elections from 1922 to 1950, southern turnout never exceeded 19 percent of eligible voters and even in

1962, when the Republicans began making serious inroads in the South, southern turnout at 27 percent of eligible voters was less than half of the 56 percent who turned out in the rest of the nation.

During this period, there were only two changes in voting law of any consequence. During World War II, those involved in military service were given the right to vote and provided the means to do so. This included more than one million African Americans who fought in that war.

Twice during this period the Supreme Court was called upon to rule on the Democratic white-only primaries in the South, and in both cases it ruled against excluding blacks from participating. This, of course, had no substantial effect, since literacy tests, poll taxes, and physical intimidation remained hurdles in the southern states for African Americans to overcome. This decision, however, led southern white leaders to adopt another tactic—to gerrymander districts in such a way as to make it impossible for African Americans to be elected. One such law was struck down by the Supreme Court in 1960, but it would be much later in the decade before all the legal and many of the extra-legal underpinnings of Jim Crow were finally done away with.

Sown, in this period, were the seeds of future change. While there had always been modest support for civil rights and equally modest activist pro-equality movements, civil rights began to take center stage after World War II. At the 1948 Democratic National Convention, then Minneapolis mayor and later Senator and Vice President Hubert H. Humphrey proposed and the convention passed the first civil rights-related platform plank. This, in turn, led to the walkout of J. Strom Thurmond of South Carolina and the formation of the States Rights Party, aimed at defending the segregated southern way of life. In the 1950s, the Montgomery bus boycott captured national attention. The Supreme Court in *Brown v. Board of Education* reversed the 1896 *Plessy v. Ferguson* decision and declared separate schools were inherently unequal. This led to southern defiance initially aimed at blocking the entry of blacks into previously all-white public schools. When that strategy was thwarted by National Guard forces called out by both Presidents Eisenhower and Kennedy, those seeking to preserve the segregated southern order created separate all-white private schools. On February 1, 1960, four African American freshman students from North Carolina A&T College sat in at a Greensboro, North Carolina, Woolworth's lunch counter, were refused service, and returned the next day, and the next—which launched a sit-in movement that spread throughout the South. This led, in turn, to the Freedom Rides and later to voter registration campaigns in the Deep South. And due to the medium of television, the public was able to see well-dressed, peaceful African American protestors being brutally assaulted (and, in some cases, murdered) by whites. When Martin Luther King Jr. proclaimed his dream of equality August 1963 on the steps of the Lincoln Memorial in Washington, D.C., he was speaking for a huge national movement which had, at that time, the substantial backing of the American people. In this period, there were also two civil rights acts passed, in 1957 and 1960, which had little teeth, but which raised the question of voting rights for blacks, established the Civil Rights Commission, and broke a more than eighty-year impasse in Congress on addressing civil rights (an impasse created by the control of Congress by southern Democratic committee chairmen, who held those posts in near-perpetuity because the rules in both houses of Congress anointed the most senior members of congressional committees as their chairs, and the most senior members were invariably from the South, where there were no contests for their election and reelection). Also of note, not for its impact at the time but for its influence on future Supreme Court decisions, the 1962 *Baker v. Carr* decision established for the first time the principle that each person's vote should be equal to every other person's vote—opening a new front in the civil and voting rights battle.

The groundwork was established for major legislative and judicially mandated change in voting law and citizen enfranchisement.

1964–Present: Massive Change, Diminished Participation

The period between 1964 and the present might be seen as a mirror opposite image of the previous three decades. This era featured massive legal and political change, diminished party allegiance, an unsettled political alignment, and declining political participation—except in the South, the elections of 2004 and 2008, and among those at the upper end of the age scale.

In 1963, President John F. Kennedy knew that even at its post-women's-suffrage apex in 1960, American voter participation was lower than most advanced democracies and believed we could do "bettah." He looked at the demography of nonvoters (poorer, less educated, more racial and ethnic minorities, non-unionized, etc.) and thought that expanding the franchise might yield more Democratic voters. As a result, President Kennedy established a Commission on Voter Registration and Participation, directed by Richard Scammon. That commission reported after JFK's death and recommended a series of changes to the electoral process, including abolition of the poll tax and literacy tests, enfranchisement of African Americans, enfranchisement of those young enough to fight for the nation, mail-in registration, bilingual ballots, shortening the time between the close of registration and elections, voter outreach programs, and more. In retrospect, those recommendations seem like a predictive road map to what would follow in the ensuing decades, when almost all of the commission's recommendations became law and were the centerpiece of changes that liberalized voting and registration.

Those changes were hastened by a rapidly swelling civil rights movement and growing national support for its aims. National support also grew from a variety of additional factors including television coverage of white, pro-segregationist brutality during the civil rights movement, and a rapidly expanding southern industry and commerce whose leaders did not want the image of their region as segregated, backward, or violent to undermine their success. Other factors included a liberal Supreme Court, headed by the Eisenhower-appointed Chief Justice Earl Warren, a sequence of elections beginning in 1958 that produced a sufficient number of non-southern congressional Democrats to override their southern committee chairs, the assassination of JFK and the sympathy it generated for turning his idealistic words into public policy deeds, and the deep commitment to equal rights and the enormous behind-the-scenes political skill of President Lyndon Johnson.

In January of 1964, the Twentieth Amendment was ratified, outlawing poll taxes for federal elections. Later that year Johnson proposed and Congress passed the 1964 Civil Rights Act, which outlawed racial discrimination at public accommodations and provided enforcement to ensure compliance.

Johnson's landslide 1964 election victory and a march for voting rights in Alabama, where one marcher was killed and many of the rest were beaten with billy clubs and bullwhips, led to Johnson's introduction and Congress's passage of the 1965 Voting Rights Act aimed at guaranteeing African Americans the right to vote throughout the South and in all other places where discrimination in the registration process and balloting could be demonstrated. The act, in essence, voided all racially discriminatory laws which were in effect in the South, provided enforcement to ensure African Americans could register to vote, and mandated that any changes in laws governing registration and voting in

the covered jurisdictions (those which previously inhibited black voting) would need to be pre-cleared with the Justice Department in Washington, D.C. The registration of citizens in covered jurisdictions, including all of the South, was effectively taken over by the federal government.

In 1966, the Supreme Court extended the ban on poll taxes to cover state and local elections. In a series of Supreme Court decisions from 1969 to 1973, the Court eliminated virtually all economic barriers to voting (lack of property, lack of income) except in very limited situations. In 1970, the Court ruled that literacy tests as a qualification for voting were unconstitutional. In the 1970 reauthorization of the Voting Rights Act, and in part at the behest of the Nixon administration, the maximum residency requirement to register and vote was reduced to thirty days, and it was mandated that those who changed residences after those thirty days must be allowed to vote absentee at their former place of residence. The law only applied to federal elections, but in 1972 the Supreme Court extended this residency requirement limitation to state elections. In 1971, Congress passed, and a sufficient number of states ratified, the Twenty-sixth Amendment to the Constitution extending the franchise to citizens over the age of eighteen. (Prior to this amendment, the voting age had been twenty-one except in four states, which had lowered their voting ages earlier—Georgia during World War II, and later Alaska, Hawaii, and Kentucky.) In the reauthorizations of the Voting Rights Act in 1975 and 1982, Congress added anti-discriminatory provisions for the elderly, the handicapped, and non-English-speakers. And in many states bilingual ballots were mandated and provided.

By far the most complex and difficult issue with which legislators and jurists wrestled, and are still wrestling, is the issue of ensuring that as much as possible, every vote is equal to every other vote in all elections. The exceptions are, of course, races for the U.S. Senate, where each state elects two senators regardless of population size, and the race for president, who is elected by votes cast by electors chosen on a winner-take-all basis of citizen votes cast in each state.[1] After the poll tax and literacy tests were banished and federal protection was implemented against violence and intimidation, the method of last resort for recalcitrant southern leaders was to dilute the black vote and make African American office-holding as difficult as possible via discriminatory drawing of election districts. In some places, cities would annex outlying populations in order to ensure a white majority for at-large elections. In others, they might de-annex a black voting area to ensure white hegemony. In some states, reapportionment was conducted in such a manner as to ensure that rural (mostly white) voters had much greater say than urban (mostly black) voters. In many localities, elections were conducted on an at-large basis or multiple legislative districts were lumped together, both in ways aimed at ensuring the white voters would hold sway and white officeholders would be elected. Slowly and systematically, the courts and the federal government's pre-clearance mechanisms for voting law changes in states that were covered by the Voting Rights Act, using the one-person/one-vote standard, overturned existing apportionment inequalities and blocked new ones from occurring, opposed at-large elections, and mandated single member district elections. Federal authorities tended, in places where there was clear evidence of racially polarized voting, to interpret the Voting Rights Act as favoring voting districts whose population had a majority of minority voters, thus making possible the election of blacks. In some places, the concept of majority/minority districts were supported by a strange coalition of African Americans and Republicans. For the African American, more of these districts meant more African American officeholders. For the Republicans, restricting the majority of blacks to a few districts, given the Democratic leanings of most African Americans after the New Deal and especially after the Civil and Voting Rights Acts, meant that they could create districts where the GOP might more easily win. It is likely that majority/minority districts will remain in place in the Deep South, where there continues to be evidence of politics polarized by race. It is not so clear that these majority/minority districts will or should continue to exist at the same level in the rest of the nation, where the beginnings of a rebellion can be seen against the lack of competitiveness in the overwhelming majority of state legislative and U.S. House districts. Enhancing competitiveness would mean tackling both majority/minority districts and districts gerrymandered to ensure the victory of one party

or the other head-on. Interpreting one-person/one-vote is still a work in progress.

Liberalization of Voter Registration Rules

Prior to the Voting Rights Act, citizens needed to register in person at registrars' offices and re-register each time they moved. Often, registration offices were open for very brief, and sometimes unadvertised, periods. If a citizen didn't vote in a particular election, it was assumed in many states that the person was no longer a voter, and that person had to re-register in order to vote again. In many places, such culling of ineligible voters from the registration lists was done in a partisan manner.

Initially in 1976, four states—Maine, Minnesota, Oregon, and Wisconsin—adopted registration on election day.[2] Many states permitted mail-in registration and/or allowed deputy registrars (citizens who would distribute registration forms and collect completed ones). A few states adopted permanent registration—keeping people on the lists until they were proven to have died or had changed residences. The last two renewals of the Voting Rights Act mandated that registration be open throughout the period between elections. In 1993, the National Voter Registration Act (NVRA) finally was made law after six years of gestation. It mandated that registration be available and solicited when a citizen received or renewed a driver's license, that registration materials be made available at social service agencies, that mail-in registration be available in all states, that no citizen could be purged from the registration lists simply for not voting in a given election, that the names of registrants be kept on the voting lists through two federal elections before a purging process that might affect those names could be undertaken, and that purging be done by state agencies rather than by private, potentially partisan groups.

During this period there were also major changes in the composition and governance of the political parties, particularly the Democratic Party. In 1964, using open caucuses, a democratically selected, racially mixed delegation from Mississippi challenged the all-white delegation chosen to attend the 1964 Democratic Convention via a process in which blacks could not participate. At the convention, this led to the seating of two delegates from the challenging group, the walk-out of the white delegation, and the creation of a commission which resulted in rules mandating that future conventions could not seat any delegation chosen by a racially inequitable process. In 1968, it became apparent, particularly in the case of Senator Eugene J. McCarthy's presidential campaign, that a candidate could win all of the limited number of primaries held that year but still be denied the party's nomination, because the majority of convention delegates were not selected in a democratic manner and remained beholden to party leaders rather than the Democratic electorate as a whole. The perception that this process was both undemocratic and rigid in the preservation of the status quo led to a series of commissions that created a nominating process whereby a large majority of convention delegates were chosen by primaries and caucuses. While the Republican Party made fewer changes to their nominating system than the Democrats, they generally followed the primary and caucus schedule created by the Democrats. The result was that both parties adopted much more open, democratic, and participatory processes than ever before.

In the twenty-six years between 1964 and 2000, virtually all the barriers to African American voter participation were eliminated. Blacks and youths eighteen to twenty years old were fully enfranchised. Registration was made markedly easier. Abuse of the system was dramatically reduced. And the political parties were substantially democratized. But despite these changes, the only place where voter turnout increased significantly was in the South, where a variety of factors contributed to two-party competition where there had previously been none. Newly enfranchised African Americans joined the Democratic Party, which was often credited with liberating them from segregation. In reaction, the older, often racially exclusionary Democratic leadership in the South began defecting to the Republican Party. Because the southern region as a whole was more conservative in outlook than the rest of the nation and because the Republican Party was more conservative than the Democratic, the Republicans made major inroads into the region's historical Democratic political dominance.[3] Those inroads produced competition, and, in 1994, made possible a GOP majority in legislative elections (for U.S. House and state legislative seats) in most southern states and gave the Republicans their first control of both houses of Congress since 1946.

In the presidential election of 1960, turnout in the South was 44 percent of eligible voters and the turnout outside the South was 73 percent. In the presidential election of 2000, southern turnout had increased to 50 percent, while turnout outside the South dropped to 56 percent. Midterm election turnout patterns were similar. In 1962, the average voting rate in the South was 27 percent of eligible voters, while outside the South it was 56. In 2006, southern turnout was 35 percent, while outside the South turnout plunged to 44 percent.

In their 1980 analysis of data from the U.S. Census Bureau aimed at ferreting out which population cohorts voted at the highest rate, Raymond Wolfinger and Steven Rosenstone found that those whose rates were highest were those who were educated, those who were older, those who were residentially stable, and those who were married. Yet census data indicate that more than twice as many citizens attended and graduated college in 2008 than did in 1960, the national population has been aging in the aggregate since 1969, and residential mobility has remained essentially constant. Despite these trends, turnout has gone down when theory suggests it should have increased. Theory does correlate with fact in the area of marriage.

American elections or at least the elections that draw the most voters to the polls—for president, for governor, and for U.S. senator—have also become more competitive because of the elimination of the one-party, whites-only primary system in the South and the emergence of two-party competition. Prior to the enactment of the Voting Rights Act and the subsequent court cases to enforce its principles, there was virtually no competition in general elections for statewide offices in the South. Now statewide elections for major offices are potentially competitive in every state. But except in the South (and with the added exception of the 2004 and 2008 presidential elections), competition has not reversed the four-decade decline in voter participation.

Southern vs. Non-Southern Presidential Election Turnout, 1876–2008

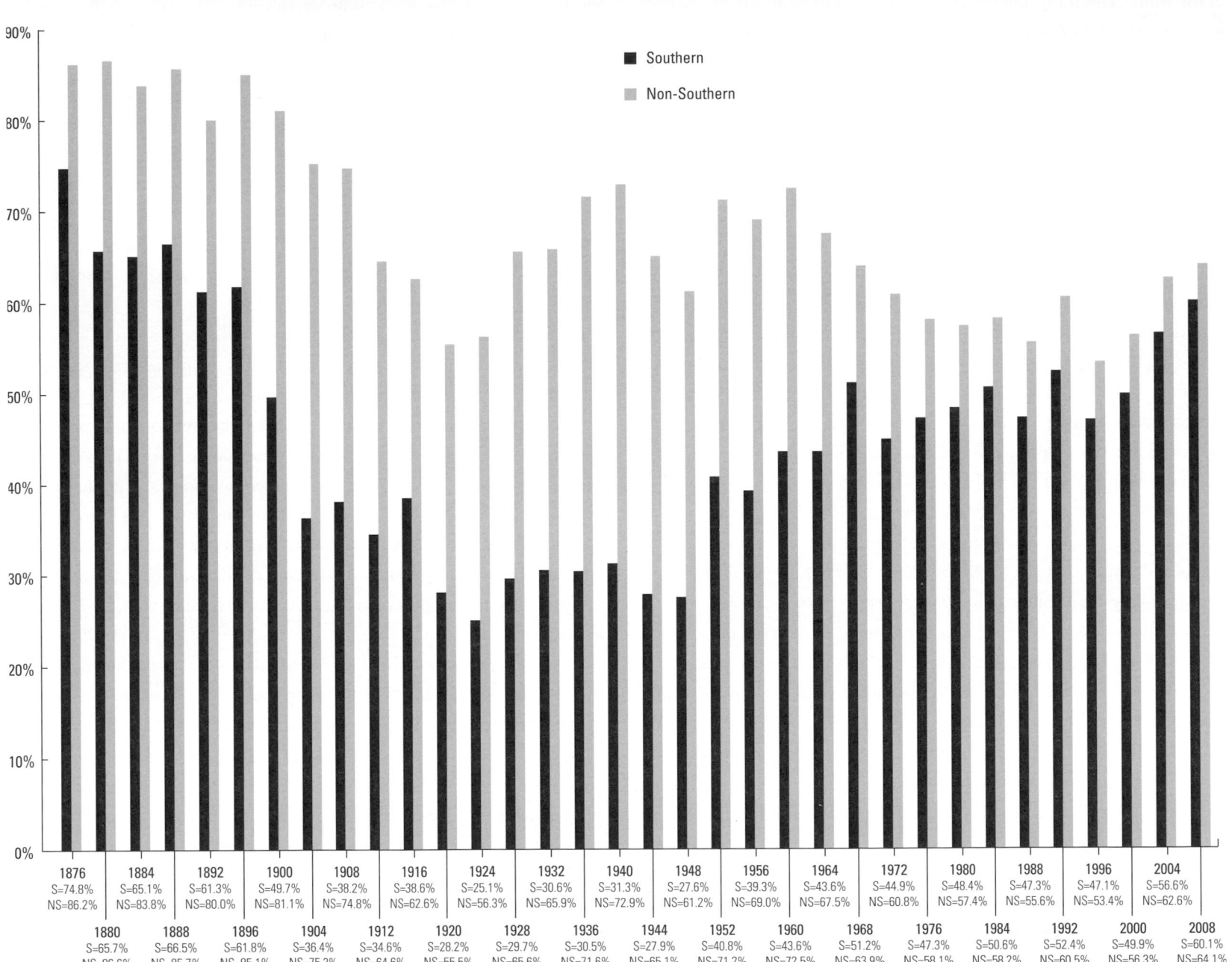

| | Southern |
| | Non-Southern |

1876	1884	1892	1900	1908	1916	1924	1932	1940	1948	1956	1964	1972	1980	1988	1996	2004
S=74.8%	S=65.1%	S=61.3%	S=49.7%	S=38.2%	S=38.6%	S=25.1%	S=30.6%	S=31.3%	S=27.6%	S=39.3%	S=43.6%	S=44.9%	S=48.4%	S=47.3%	S=47.1%	S=56.6%
NS=86.2%	NS=83.8%	NS=80.0%	NS=81.1%	NS=74.8%	NS=62.6%	NS=56.3%	NS=65.9%	NS=72.9%	NS=61.2%	NS=69.0%	NS=67.5%	NS=60.8%	NS=57.4%	NS=55.6%	NS=53.4%	NS=62.6%

1880	1888	1896	1904	1912	1920	1928	1936	1944	1952	1960	1968	1976	1984	1992	2000	2008
S=65.7%	S=66.5%	S=61.8%	S=36.4%	S=34.6%	S=28.2%	S=29.7%	S=30.5%	S=27.9%	S=40.8%	S=43.6%	S=51.2%	S=47.3%	S=50.6%	S=52.4%	S=49.9%	S=60.1%
NS=86.6%	NS=85.7%	NS=85.1%	NS=75.3%	NS=64.6%	NS=55.5%	NS=65.6%	NS=71.6%	NS=65.1%	NS=71.2%	NS=72.5%	NS=63.9%	NS=58.1%	NS=58.2%	NS=60.5%	NS=56.3%	NS=64.1%

Southern vs. Non-Southern Midterm Election Turnout, 1878–2006

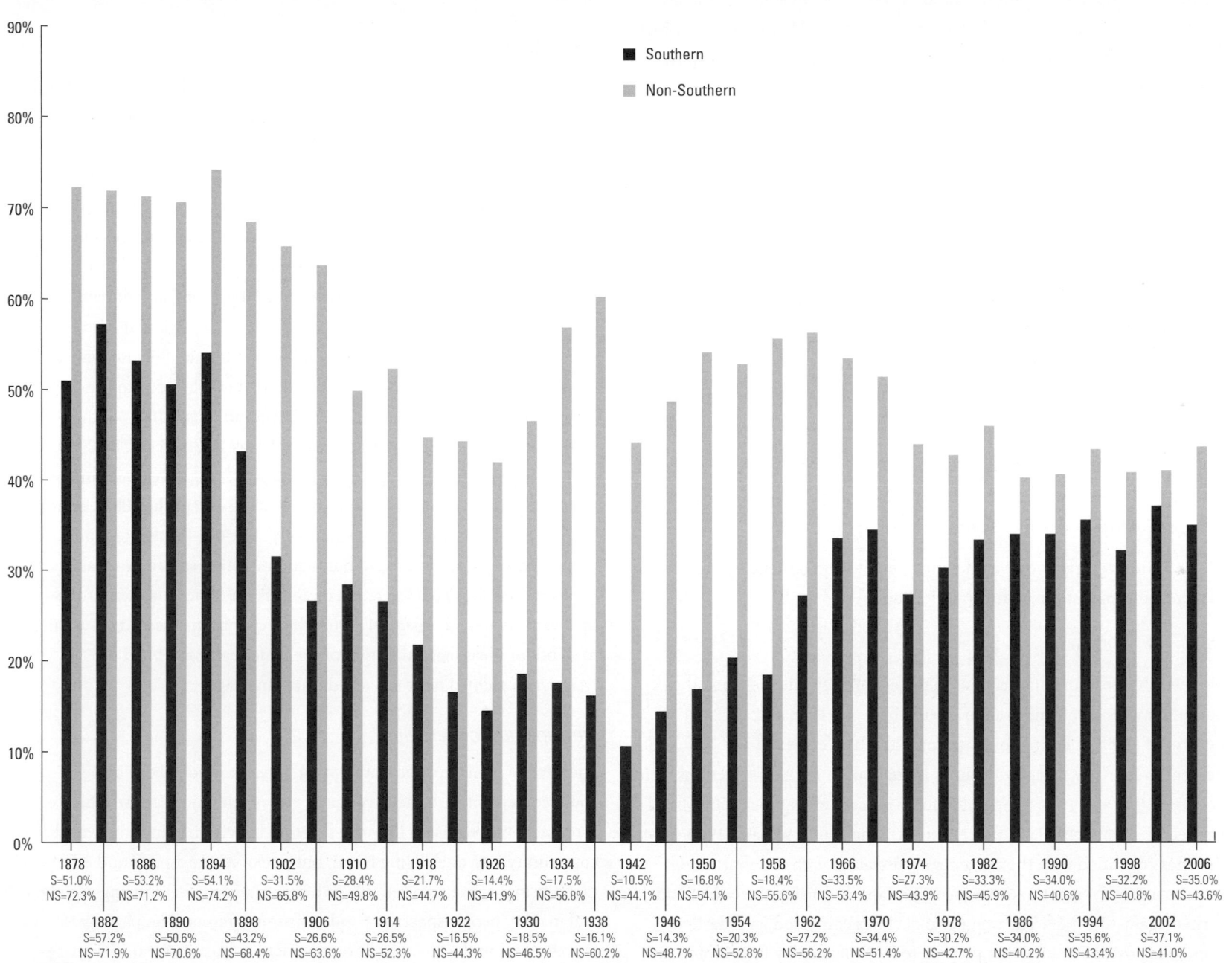

Legend:
- Southern
- Non-Southern

Year	S	NS
1878	S=51.0%	NS=72.3%
1882	S=57.2%	NS=71.9%
1886	S=53.2%	NS=71.2%
1890	S=50.6%	NS=70.6%
1894	S=54.1%	NS=74.2%
1898	S=43.2%	NS=68.4%
1902	S=31.5%	NS=65.8%
1906	S=26.6%	NS=63.6%
1910	S=28.4%	NS=49.8%
1914	S=26.5%	NS=52.3%
1918	S=21.7%	NS=44.7%
1922	S=16.5%	NS=44.3%
1926	S=14.4%	NS=41.9%
1930	S=18.5%	NS=46.5%
1934	S=17.5%	NS=56.8%
1938	S=16.1%	NS=60.2%
1942	S=10.5%	NS=44.1%
1946	S=14.3%	NS=48.7%
1950	S=16.8%	NS=54.1%
1954	S=20.3%	NS=52.8%
1958	S=18.4%	NS=55.6%
1962	S=27.2%	NS=56.2%
1966	S=33.5%	NS=53.4%
1970	S=34.4%	NS=51.4%
1974	S=27.3%	NS=43.9%
1978	S=30.2%	NS=42.7%
1982	S=33.3%	NS=45.9%
1986	S=34.0%	NS=40.2%
1990	S=34.0%	NS=40.6%
1994	S=35.6%	NS=43.4%
1998	S=32.2%	NS=40.8%
2002	S=37.1%	NS=41.0%
2006	S=35.0%	NS=43.6%

All of this is to suggest that the substantial decline in voter participation outside the South cannot be explained by registration law and procedures, all of which have been substantially liberalized and which have produced a modestly higher level of registration; by demography, which should have argued for higher turnout; or by competition, which has increased for the offices which engender the highest turnout. Turnout went up in the period between the 1930s and late 1960s when each of these factors should have restrained turnout, and down in the subsequent period when they should have enhanced turnout—making it clear that the explanation for both increase and decline in turnout lies in motivation and the civic culture.

In his two books on voter participation or lack thereof, Ruy Teixeira found three major changes in attitude and conduct that might help explain the turnout decline:

1. a decline in people's sense of the efficacy of their vote, or whether their vote made any difference;

2. a decline in strong allegiance to either major political party; and

3. a decline in newspaper reading as the principal source of information on politics and public affairs.

Some electoral and related figures tend to corroborate this analysis as a partial explanation for turnout decline.

Sense of Efficacy

The two sharpest turnout declines in presidential elections during the period between 1960 and 2008 occurred between 1968 and 1972 (61 percent of eligibles voting to 56 percent) and between 1992 and 1996 (58 percent to 51). The sharpest declines in turnout in midterm elections were between 1970 and 1974 (47 percent to 39 percent of eligibles voting) and between 1994 and 1998 (41 percent to 38). The 1968/1972 and 1970/1974 declines coincided with the citizenry's frustration with the continuing American involvement in the war in Vietnam, a war that the public had turned against in 1968. The other two declines coincided with dashed hopes for positive change that seemed to be promised by Bill Clinton and

the Democrats in the election of 1992 and the Republicans in the election of 1994.

Party Allegiance

Perhaps the best way of looking at the party allegiance question is through the average aggregate registration figures for the twenty-eight states and the District of Columbia which have partisan registration (figures are available for substantially fewer states in the 1960s). In 1968, Democratic registration stood at 45 percent of eligible voters, Republican registration was 25.6 percent, and registration as either nonaffiliated or for minor parties stood at 3.2 percent. By 2008, Democratic registration was at 39 percent, Republican registration stood at 27.4 percent, and nonaffiliated and minor party registration stood at 23.3 percent. A similar pattern exists for midterm elections. (It should be noted that while Republican registration appears to be slightly increased, it is solely due to the party's inroads in the South. In 1968, GOP registration outside the South was 30 percent, while in southern states, it was 12.2 percent. By 2008, Republican registration outside the South was 25.9 percent and in the South 32 percent.) During most of that period, except the 2008 election for the Democrats and the 2000 and 2004 elections for the Republicans, neither party had attempted to build and maintain sustaining grassroots organizations. Both parties relied on television rather than grassroots involvement and, at least until 2008, the Republicans seemed increasingly to stand for ideas far to the right of the American center and the Democrats seemed not to have a durable message.

Newspaper Readership

The decline in newspaper reading that Teixeira writes about came about coincident with the advent and rise of television. Those who are proponents of television like to assert that television brings the world community into one's living room, but one of its most profound effects is that it brings the citizen into his or her living room—atomizing society and making people spectators and consumers rather than participants and stockholders in the business of democracy. At least in the initial phases of television, there were only three major networks and the nightly news on those networks provided a shared sense of knowledge. But the advent of cable and satellite, with its three hundred channels, more than 90 percent of which offer neither news nor public affairs, has fragmented any semblance of shared community and civic and political knowledge. To this one adds the Internet and its millions of self-selecting websites, personal communities such as Facebook, MySpace, and Twitter, and technologies such as the iPod—all of which contribute to an increasingly fragmented, individualistic society. It is thus not surprising but definitely dismaying that only 35 percent of persons eighteen to twenty-nine years old read any news at all[4] and only 36 percent of incoming college freshmen think it is very important to keep up with political affairs.[5]

The Elections of 2004 and 2008

This analysis has so far left out the elections of 2004 and 2008, advisedly because interpretations differ on what, in terms of turnout, they mean. The figures show that turnout went up substantially in both years. In 2004, turnout was nearly 61 percent of eligible voters, up from 54 percent in 2000, and the highest turnout since 1968. In 2008, it went up again to almost 63 percent, the highest turnout since 1960. Youth turnout (those eighteen to twenty-four) increased to its highest level since 1972, the first year that eighteen- to twenty-year-olds were allowed to vote. Some have claimed that this is the end of a period of turnout decline and that there is a new generation, a "millennial" youth cohort that does not share its predecessors' decreasing interest in politics. The alternative explanation is that the turnout increases in these two elections were due to certain unique factors—the polarization created by the presidency and policies of George W. Bush and the hope engendered by the Barack Obama candidacy among youth and in the African American community, whose turnout increase was greater than any other population cohort. The second explanation has some facts on its side. The deep polarization which produced much higher turnout in the 2004 presidential contest produced only a minuscule increase in turnout in the midterm elections of 2002 and 2006. In the 2008 presidential election, which produced both in the presidential primaries

and the general election the third highest turnout since women were given the vote in 1920, turnout for statewide primaries for governor and U.S. senator, which were not held on the same day as the presidential primaries, produced the lowest aggregate turnout ever. Even with the overall surge in the 2008 presidential general election turnout, there were twelve states with lower turnout than in 2004. Subsequent elections—the 2008 Georgia senatorial runoff, the 2009 Virginia gubernatorial primary, the Virginia and New Jersey 2009 gubernatorial general elections, and the special election for U.S. Senate in Massachusetts—produced youth turnout below 20 percent of eligible voters. The political activism of the so-called "millennial" generation has been limited to the 2004 and 2008 presidential elections and mostly among college educated and college resident youth. The future will tell which interpretation will prove correct.

Observations on Selected Current Issues

Party Alignment

As already noted, there were two historical periods in which one party was dominant—the Republican Party from 1860 until 1930 and the Democratic Party from 1932 until 1994. The election of 1994, in which the Republicans took control of both houses of Congress and maintained that hold until the election of 2006 (when the Democrats reestablished their majorities in both houses), did not usher in a Republican realignment. The period was too short, the GOP hold on power too tenuous. It is possible, if by no means certain, that the Democrats restored their dominance in the election of 2008. In that election, of eight regions—New England, Middle Atlantic, South, industrial Midwest, farm Midwest, Southwest, and West— the GOP had a congressional voting plurality in only two: the South (by one percentage point) and the Southwest (due largely to the population size of Texas and its pro-GOP vote numbers as compared to number of votes in the other states in that region). Perhaps of equal importance is the fact that the core base of Republican support lies among whites in the South and rural areas, and includes virtually no minorities in a nation which will shortly have a population in which nonwhites will be in the majority. Still, the permanence of Democratic dominance rests on the success of the Obama administration and, in particular, its ability to point a way out of the most serious recession since the great Depression of the 1930s. If he succeeds, the Democrats may be back in the saddle again, but if he fails, it is likely that the GOP will enjoy a short period of resurgence, dealignment will be the rule, and the possibility of another major party will be enhanced.

Convenience Voting

The myth that procedural fixes—making it easier to vote—will enhance turnout dies hard. In recent years, some states, acting on the high-minded belief that making voting easier will bring more voters to the polls, and others, on the less high-minded belief that an expanded electorate will enhance their partisan chances, have adopted or urged one or more of four procedural changes: no-excuse absentee voting, mail voting, early voting, and election-day registration. No-excuse absentee voting allows any registered citizen to ask for and receive an absentee ballot without giving reason for its need, and, in some states, a person can be placed on a permanent roll to receive an absentee ballot in every election without making an election-specific request. Oregon has all-mail voting and Washington has nearly an all-mail system. Under a system of early in-person voting, the state and local election officials establish polling places of presumed convenience where citizens can cast their ballots during a period prior to election day. Research indicates that no-excuse absentee voting and mail voting depress turnout in all elections, except some local municipal elections held at times other than the dates of statewide elections. Early voting has a mixed record, producing increased turnout in some elections and decreased turnout in others, without any consistent pattern as to why. Election-day registration, which now is in place in eight states, tends to modestly enhance turnout when first adopted and in elections of high intensity. But election-day registration is an option for only about half the states, those which have experienced no incidents of fraud connected to the registration process. For those states that have experienced the types of fraud which are connected to the registration process (last-minute registration by those who are not entitled to register or registering in the name of someone who has died or moved, to give two examples), election-day registration creates a major dilemma for election officials. They will be faced with a choice of checking the identities of hundred of thousands who might register on election day and thus delay the announcement of results for weeks after election day or they can announce results which after review and checks may prove to be wrong. No-excuse absentee and mail voting undermine the concept of the secret ballot and enhance the possibility of vote buying and other forms of fraud. And no-excuse absentee, mail, and early voting extend the voting period over several days or weeks, creating the possibility that response to a major event occurring near election day may not be possible for millions who have already cast irrevocable ballots. Convenience voting is very popular, but these measures do not enhance—and in two cases (no-excuse absentee and mail voting) undermine—voter turnout and do enhance the possibility of fraud. Both the principle (that ease of voting enhances turnout) and the practice (these laws) are flawed. One hopes there will be a day when they are rolled back.

Larger Procedural Concerns

Despite various measures to make it easier to register and vote, under the present system of personal registration there are fifty million eligible citizens who are not registered, and there are twenty million names on registration rolls which are, for one reason or another, invalid. This has led to repeated multimillion-dollar partisan battles, with the Republicans claiming fraud and the Democrats claiming voter suppression and intimidation. This tit-for-tat undermines confidence in the electoral process and solves none of the problems. If the nation wishes to end this set of problems, it might look to Mexico, where a nationwide biometric ID has eliminated all of them.

Of the 435 members of the House of Representatives, fewer than 75 are elected in competitive districts and a similar percentage of state legislative seats are competitive. This gerrymandering for safe seats takes two forms: (1) If one party controls both houses of the legislature and the governorship in a state, then it draws districts in a manner to enhance that party, putting the opposition party's supporters in a few safe districts while eliminating them from providing competition in the majority of districts. (2) If party control of politics is divided in a state, there tends to be a bipartisan agreement to provide safe seats for incumbents. The result is that for the overwhelming majority of U.S. House and state legislative seats, the relevant election is the primary and not the general election. Turnout for the average statewide Democratic primary (for governor or U.S. senator) is 10 percent of eligible voters; Republican average turnout for similar primaries is between 8 and 9 percent. A smaller percentage vote for U.S. House and an even smaller percentage vote for state legislative seats. This means that an organized minority of less than 4 percent can propel someone to victory in the primary and often in the general election. Because the organized minorities tend to be those with more extreme views, the result of this gerrymandering is a polarized and uncivil politics and legislative gridlock. And the very same polarizing leaders first elected to lower offices become the candidates for higher offices, producing ever-increasing polarization at all levels of government. Citizens might be less hostile to government and might have a higher belief in the efficacy of their vote if more-competitive districts were drawn and a greater number of officeholders came from the pragmatic middle.

There are many other procedural and structural problems worthy of address—the gridlock created in the U.S. Senate by the anonymous "holds," which can keep presidential appointments from being confirmed for months; a Senate in which the same two votes are accorded to a state with a citizen voting age population of 350,000 as to a state with a like population of 22 million, perhaps an extreme form of federalism that the Founding Fathers didn't envision; a U.S. House, the so-called people's branch, in which an individual member now represents, and must campaign within, a district with as great a population as several states and whose campaigns generally get no closer to the "people" than do statewide major office campaigns; the conduct of American politics in thirty-second attack ads that cast aspersions on every candidate, give the public a choice between the bad and the awful, and undermine by inference faith in the political process as a whole. The list is large and not nearly exhausted by this accounting.

Beyond Procedure

Turnout and the Future: From 1930 to 1960, voter turnout increased despite highly restrictive registration laws and procedures and the almost total disenfranchisement of African Americans in the South. Between 1960 and the present (with the exception of the polarization-driven elections of 2004 and 2008), turnout has declined despite major liberalizing steps in registration and voting and the enfranchisement of African Americans. If, as this pattern makes clear, procedure is not primarily responsible for modern-day turnout increases and decreases, then one must look elsewhere for reasons and remedy.

In the era of turnout increase, various aspects of the polity and society likely contributed to rising political participation. The integrating institutions of American society—the churches, unions, schools, and political parties—were strong and active. America's public schools were governed by the teaching of Horace Mann and John Dewey and emphasized the development of thoughtful and active citizens as a primary purpose of education. The nation was united by commonly shared knowledge received through newspapers, radio, and, later, network television, all of which took their role as public educators seriously. Because of this, families discussed politics and public issues over the dinner table. Political parties provided sustaining grassroots organization, separated the wheat from the chaff of interest group advocacy, and presented relatively coherent approaches to governance and non-polarized competition. Through the New and Fair Deals and the successful prosecution of World War II, government was shown to be able to address even the most major of political issues or threats. People, by and large, trusted their leaders and had a positive view of government. In an era of purpose and optimism, the citizenry was happy to participate in self-governance.

During the recent period of turnout decline, a very different political and societal backdrop presented itself. The integrating institutions grew substantially weaker, with the exception of fundamentalist churches. The quality of education measurably declined, particularly in urban America and in such states as California and those that followed California's lead in limiting tax resources, which had been used to sustain high quality education. Education for citizenship declined in both quantity and quality, as schools focused on preparation for employment and international economic competition. Mass media, which had hitherto provided both a commitment to edifying the public and a commons for shared information, grew increasingly diffuse, more profit-driven, and too often less informative. Political parties no longer provided sustaining grassroots organization, separated the wheat from the chaff of interest group advocacy, or provided coherent programmatic choices. Instead they reinvented themselves every two and four years, yielded to interest group advocacy, and served largely as a fundraising adjunct to campaign media consultants. Sprawling growth without governance led to a decline in community. New media and technologies—cable, satellite, the Internet, the iPod, and social media sites—all led to increasingly fragmented, narrowed, and personal communities and diminished involvement in the polity as a whole. And public disillusionment with leadership and government, beginning with the war in Vietnam and through many high profile issues thereafter, increased political pessimism.

This listing is not exhaustive, but it does suggest that durable restoration of an engaged citizenry depends on addressing larger societal issues and, at the outset of the year 2010, there is no indication that such an address will occur.

NOTES ON STATISTICS AND METHODOLOGY

On the surface it would seem that determining turnout would be a relatively simple affair—divide the number of votes cast by the number of Americans eligible to vote. In reality, such calculations are not so simple on either end of the accounting—the numerator of votes and the denominator of those eligible.

Votes Cast in Presidential Elections

In presidential election years, the numerator that is used here and by most others calculating turnout are those votes cast for president. But in every presidential year, there are ballots cast in which a presidential choice has not been made by the voter, although that voter may have voted for other offices. There are also defaced or mutilated ballots and ballots which for a variety of reasons have been disallowed. In any given election year, only some states keep a count of all the ballots cast, but, based on those that do, the difference between ballots cast for president and the total number of ballots cast is usually less than one percentage point.

Votes Cast in Midterm Elections

The numerator for midterm elections is less clear-cut. The midterm elections that typically produce the highest turnout are those for governor and U.S. senator. But in every election there are states which do not hold elections for either of these offices, due to the varying lengths of gubernatorial terms and the fact that only one third of the Senate faces reelection in any election year.

The races used as midterm numerators in this book are those with the highest statewide vote. When there is neither a U.S. Senate nor a gubernatorial race in contention, the aggregate vote across all U.S. House districts in the state is used. As in presidential elections, in midterms there are always a number of ballots cast that do not contain votes for the race with the highest turnout. In midterm elections—and also based on the states which tally total ballots cast—the difference between the race with the highest vote and the total ballots cast tends to be between three quarters of a percentage point and one-and-a-half percentage points.

Eligible Voters

The denominator for assessing turnout—the number of Americans eligible to vote—also poses problems. Throughout American history, the laws concerning eligibility to vote have moved in fits and starts, ultimately resulting in comparatively universal suffrage for adults. More recently, questions have been raised about what is the most accurate denominator of eligible voters for assessing turnout?

The decennial census has been, and remains, the basic source for determining those eligible to vote. Since its inception at the founding of the republic, the census has provided data on population, sorted by, among other things, age, gender, and race. With the publication of each decennial census, it was possible to ascertain who was eligible to vote in accord with the laws governing in any given decade. Thus, until 1920, the census provided a number for those males who were twenty-one years of age and over. By 1920, the figure included females, and by 1971, it included those eighteen years of age and over.[6]

In order to ascertain the age-eligible population in the years between censuses, one could interpolate the census numbers of age-eligible voters based on the rate of change in age-eligible population in each state between the nearest and next-to-nearest censuses. One would then correct, upon the issuance of the results of the ensuing census, for any alteration in that rate of change. One did not have a rate of change in the first census, and the figures for the most recent years—since the most recent census— would need to await the next census, to correct for alterations in each state's rate of change.

Since the first days of the republic, the Census Bureau has attempted to provide an estimate of age-eligible population for each election year. There were, however, many problems with these estimates. By far and away the largest of these was the inclusion in the census estimates of ineligible noncitizens residing within the confines of the United States.

But there were also other problems with these figures. The estimates included those incarcerated and, in some states, released felons and people in mental institutions deemed incompetent, who could not vote. Those figures also did not include the number of Americans living outside the United States who could vote. Nor did these figures adjust for inaccuracies in the census count—undercounting many who could vote in most years, and overcounting in the 2000 census. Two factors were estimated in the projected age-eligible population but could not be accurately ascertained until as much as a year after the election—the number of people of age who were naturalized during the election year and the number of the age-eligible who changed residences.

Correcting for these deficiencies poses problems for all students of voting. No one has been able to come up with a figure for those deemed incompetent in mental institutions. The statistical corrections for under-

and over-counts stretch back only to 1942. It is possible to get an estimate of those living outside the country, but while it is also possible to allocate the nonresidents to states for those in the military and government, it is virtually impossible to accurately and with confidence allocate the rest. Moving and naturalization are, at best, delayed figures for any election year. And while there are estimates for how many convicted felons were in correctional institutions going back to 1915, there is not, at present, any longitudinal data for the laws governing which felons or ex-felons could vote nor for the number of ex-felons who had fulfilled not only their period of incarceration but also their period of parole.

It is, however, possible to correct for the greatest distortion in the age-eligible figures—at least as far back as 1860. Beginning in 1870 and for all censuses thereafter (except 1960), the censuses have counted noncitizens residing in the United States. Thus, it is possible to get a far more accurate estimate of those eligible to vote by taking the age- eligible figure in each census, subtracting the noncitizen population of those ages and interpolating the resulting figures between censuses. This methodology can be applied for all years going back to 1860.

Walter Dean Burnham was the pioneer in using this methodology and creating an age-eligible citizen denominator.[7] His methodology, however, interpolated from census to census or from April to April in most decennial years.[8] The Center for the Study of the American Electorate, whose data is being used in this book, has taken that interpolation one step further, carrying it forward to November of each election year.

Thus, for general elections from 1860 to the present, the denominator in this book for ascertaining turnout in general elections is the Center's November citizen eligible population. For primaries, most of which occur in the spring and early summer, the analysis in this book is based on Burnham's census-to-census April figure (while understanding that some primaries occur in the fall).

Because the laws governing who was eligible to vote in the 1788– 1860 period varied so widely by state and changed so frequently, this book relies on the census's age-eligible figures for denominators for those years. The denominators in this book are, however, corrected for post-1860 franchise changes, such as those in the states that allowed women to vote prior to the 1920 constitutional amendment that enfranchised all women[9] or the states which had a lower voting age than twenty-one, which was almost universal until the 1971 amendment enfranchising eighteen- to twenty-one-year-olds.

While striving for consistency in denominators for estimating turnout, this book also provides an additional set of turnout tables that takes into account the fact that African Americans were considered in the eligible vote estimates but were almost universally disenfranchised in the South. These tables—which exclude southern African Americans from the age-eligible denominator—stretch from the 1920 enfranchisement of women through 1964, the year before the 1965 enactment of the Voting Rights Act, which prohibited the disenfranchisement of any citizen based on race.

Additionally, the book provides graphs for the major trends both within chapters and overall, it provides the share of the eligible vote for every presidential general election candidate who received 1 percent or more of the eligible vote, and it charts major changes in the names and numbers of votes garnered by significant political parties.

Because there tends to be a drop-off of between 10 and 15 percentage points between turnout in presidential election years and midterms (larger in some years and smaller in a few), the charts contained in this book compare only presidential year turnout with presidential year turnout and midterm election turnout with midterm election turnout.

There are also charts in this book for elections held in odd-numbered years, which were plentiful in the early years of the republic but are now limited to a few states—Louisiana, Mississippi, New Jersey, and Virginia.

While there are charts on partisan turnout for all races in this book, the most reliable measure of partisan turnout is the aggregate partisan vote for U.S. House of Representatives, which, particularly in midterm elections, gives a consistent base for analysis, smoothing out the surges and dips in individual statewide high office turnout. It also should be noted that midterm turnout, particularly for the U.S. House, is a better basis of ascertaining what may be called the core electorate, those who will likely be voting in all major elections and whose participation is not subject to the particular climate surrounding an individual national or state election. For instance, there was in both 2004 and 2008 a strong surge in turnout, due largely to the polarizing presidency of George W. Bush and the unique candidacy of Barack Obama. But despite the polarized nature of presidential politics in the first decade of this century, turnout in the 2002 and 2006 midterm elections went up in minute amounts. The midterm turnouts here, as elsewhere, give a better picture of the sustaining level of political participation.

ABOUT THE CHAPTERS AND CHARTS

Structure of the Book

This book is divided into eleven chapters (in addition to the preface, introduction, appendix, and bibliography).

Each chapter covers twenty years of American voter turnout, with the first chapter starting in 1788 and the final chapter concluding in 2009.[10] The chapters are not of equal size. In the early days of the republic, there were fewer states and fewer elections. Presidential electors, for instance, were selected by state legislatures in some states rather than by the vote of the electorate. Many governors were similarly chosen. Only the House of Representatives has always been directly elected by the people. Elections were held in both even and odd numbered years, and there was great variance in terms of office or jurisdictions served, making turnout comparisons difficult, or at least very imprecise.

By Andrew Jackson's populist revolt in 1824, presidential electors were, in the main, elected by the eligible citizenry. In 1875, Congress regularized House of Representatives elections on the first Tuesday after the first Monday in November in even-numbered years. Spurred by the Progressives, selection of nominees by popular primary elections, rather than party caucuses and conventions, began to gain favor at the beginning of the twentieth century. And in 1913, the states ratified the Seventeenth Amendment, which mandated the popular election of U.S. senators.

Structure of Each Chapter

Despite not being of equal size, each chapter is structured similarly. Every chapter begins with material that sets the context for the data: a list of some of the major events that occurred during the time period, which may have had an influence on turnout, followed by a synopsis of the major changes made in election law or court decisions affecting the conduct of elections, and then a listing of the presidential candidates, how many votes they received, and what percentage of the eligible electorate those votes represented.[11] (Candidates who received less than one percent of the eligible vote are excluded.)

In the first seven chapters, spanning 1788–1929, there are additional tables that show the evolution of election law in the individual states with respect to such issues as property and tax requirements for voting, residency requirements, literacy tests, citizenship, gender, and race.

The balance of each chapter is graphs and charts. These are divided into three groups—elections in years in which the president was chosen, midterm elections, and off-year elections (that is, elections held in odd-numbered years). The majority of charts are in the first two groups. The charts are divided in this way because turnout for presidential election years tends to consistently and substantially exceed the turnout for midterm elections. Thus, in its charts, this book compares turnout in presidential elections with other presidential elections and midterm elections with midterm elections.

Turnout, the central focus of this book, is the percentage of eligible voters who actually cast their ballots. Every chapter has two summary graphs at the beginning of the major sections—presidential-year and midterm elections. The summaries are aimed at giving a picture of overall and partisan turnout during the period. In presidential election years, national turnout is estimated by the percentage of eligible voters who cast their vote for president.[12] However, as any single presidential race is often dependent on candidates' individual characteristics or a major national political issue, the presidential election is not a reliable measure for partisan turnout trends. For this reason, to estimate partisan turnout and

generate the second graph, the aggregate vote totals from the U.S. House of Representatives elections are used instead.

The two midterm graphs are found at the beginning of the midterm year section in each chapter. In midterm elections, national turnout is estimated by the national total of the "total highest statewide turnout" from each state. The total highest statewide turnout is the number of votes cast in the statewide race in each state that drew the most voters—whether it be for governor, U.S. senator, or aggregate House vote.[13]

Following the two summary charts in the presidential election year section, there are charts with state-by-state figures for general election turnout in this order: presidential and partisan presidential turnout; presidential-year gubernatorial and partisan gubernatorial turnout; presidential-year overall and partisan turnout for U.S. Senate races (after 1912);[14] and overall and partisan turnout for aggregate statewide vote for U.S. House. The organization is followed for midterm elections without, of course, presidential charts, but adding a set of two charts for highest statewide turnout and partisan turnout. In later chapters, these general election charts are followed by overall turnout and partisan turnout for any primaries held for these offices. One caveat should be noted: the data in the overall primary chart reflects only the states that had primaries in both parties.[15]

The final section(s) of each chapter are off-year (odd-numbered year) elections. All chapters include overall and partisan turnout for off-year gubernatorial elections. In the first five chapters (1788–1889), the off-year elections also include overall and partisan turnout for general elections for the U.S. House of Representatives. Beginning in Chapter 7, off-year gubernatorial primary data follow the general election data.

Structure of the Standard Chart

The basic building block for the charts consists of three columns per year of numbers horizontally aligned with the states in alphabetical order.[16] After the state listing, the first column of numbers, named Voting-Age Population (or VAP), notes the eligible voters for the first election year. In reality, from 1860 on, it is really citizen voting-age population, meaning

Portion of chart for Gubernatorial Turnout (Midterm Years), 1810–1818

STATE GUBERNATORIAL GENERAL ELECTIONS
Election Years 1810–1818

State	1810			1814				1818			
	Voting-age population	Turnout	%	Voting-age population	Turnout	%	Difference from 1810*	Voting-age population	Turnout	%	Difference from 1810
CONNECTICUT	56,000	20,560	**36.7%**	58,000	12,034	**20.7%**	-16.0	59,000	16,432	**27.9%**	-8.9
DELAWARE	11,000	7,257	**66.0%**								
ILLINOIS											
INDIANA											
MAINE											
MASSACHUSETTS	104,000	90,620	**87.1%**	109,000	102,327	**93.9%**	6.7	115,000	69,579	**60.5%**	-26.6
NEW HAMPSHIRE	45,000	31,648	**70.3%**	48,000	38,489	**80.2%**	9.9	51,000	30,543	**59.9%**	-10.4
NEW YORK	196,000	79,578	**40.6%**								
OHIO	48,000	17,655	**36.8%**	75,000	22,050	**29.4%**	-7.4	103,000	38,269	**37.2%**	0.4
PENNSYLVANIA				184,000	80,575	**43.8%**					
RHODE ISLAND				16,000	2,710	**16.9%**		17,000	8,402	**49.4%**	32.5
VERMONT	44,000	23,722	**53.9%**	46,000	34,877	**75.8%**	21.9	49,000	15,243	**31.1%**	-22.8
Total	504,000	271,040	**53.8%**	536,000	293,062	**54.7%**	0.9	394,000	178,468	**45.3%**	-8.5

age-eligible population, excluding non-citizens.[17] The second column of numbers is the number of votes cast for that election in that state in that year. The third column of numbers is the turnout percentage of the eligible vote, which consists of the vote number in the second column divided by the VAP number in the first column.

In a typical presidential-year or midterm year chart, general election or primary, there will be five years of data in four-year intervals running left to right: for example, 1810, 1814, 1818, 1822, 1826.[18] The year furthest to the left will have only the three columns of numbers explained above. For the remaining four election years, there is an additional fourth column of numbers, labeled "Difference from [Year]," which provides the percentage point difference between the year in question and the initial year in the chart. In the chart shown above, 1810 is the initial year for the chart. For example, Connecticut in 1810 has a turnout of 36.7 percent and in 1814, a turnout of 20.7 percent. Hence, for Connecticut in 1814, the

difference from 1810 is -16.0: a decline of sixteen percentage points. In 1818, Connecticut has a turnout of 27.9 percent; hence, for 1818, its difference from 1810 is 27.9 percent minus 36.7 percent, which comes out to: -8.9 percentage points.

If there are no data for the initial year of a given chart, the differences are calculated from the first year that data do appear for that state.[19] For most charts, the bottom of each column is the total voting-age population, turnout, and turnout percentage for that chart. The total percentage and difference from [the initial year] are calculated in the same way as for individual years. For example, in 1810, Rhode Island did not have a gubernatorial election. Therefore, in 1814, Rhode Islsnd's "difference from 1810" column is blank. In 1818, Rhode Island had a turnout of 49.4 percent, and it shows data in the "difference from 1810" column: 32.5 percentage points. Clearly, this number is not calculated using data from 1810. Rather, it is calculated from the first year in which data appeared for Rhode Island: 1814. Thus, 49.4 percent minus 16.9 percent equals 32.5 percentage points, a large increase. If Rhode Island had turnout in 1822 also listed in this chart, the "difference from 1810" column would again be calculated from the first year in which data appeared: 1814.

Variations on the Standard Chart: Partisan and Off-Year Charts

Partisan charts follow the same format as the standard charts: they are essentially three charts in one, showing the turnout for each of the two major parties and then the total for all other candidates. This structure follows the political structure of the republic. While there have been significant splinter parties in American history, some of which had national impact, and others of which were victorious in certain states, the United States has been essentially a two-party democracy. After consensus governance under President George Washington, two parties emerged out of conflicting views on the role and power of the national government— the Democratic-Republican Party and the Federalists. The current Democratic Party is the linear descendant of the Democratic-Republican

Party, founded by Thomas Jefferson and James Madison in 1792. It became the Democratic Party in 1828 and has borne that name ever since, though it splintered on the issue of slavery after 1856. The modern Republican Party is an indirect descendant of the Federalists, a party that was launched, in part, by Alexander Hamilton, but which died after the election of 1816 because of the unpopularity of its antiwar advocacy at the time. It was briefly supplanted in the 1820s by an entity called the National Republicans, which, in turn, morphed into the Whig Party in 1832. The Whig Party became the Republican Party in 1856. The partisan charts in this book reflect this evolution of the two major parties.

The order of the parties in the partisan charts will be Republican (or Federalist–National Republican–Whig) first, Democrat (or Democrat-Republican) second, and Other (including other parties, independents, and write-ins) third. Changes in the major parties during the period are clearly marked in the relevant charts. The total lines are calculated for each of the three parties, not cumulatively across all three.[20] In some cases, as for Other in the example chart, there is no total line due to the paucity of data.

The off-year charts resemble the typical charts but have one difference: they contain ten years of data, spaced two years apart.[21] The first five years run left to right as in a typical chart, but the next five years are directly below it. For example, in the 1831–1849 off-year charts, data for 1831, 1833, 1835, 1837, and 1839 would appear from left to right in the standard format. Then 1841, 1843, 1845, 1847, and 1849 appear below them. The difference from [initial year] column for 1847 refers back to 1831, or whatever year (1833, 1835, etc.) in which data first appears. Partisan off-year charts follow the same format, repeated three times.

Further Observations about the Charts

Please see the Methodology section for more details about the methodology behind the numbers, particularly regarding the calculation of the voter-age population.[22] In addition, a reader using and interpreting the charts may find the following observations helpful:

1. For primary charts, the overall or total primary chart reflects only the states that had primaries in both parties. The primary charts

Portion of chart for Presidential Partisan Turnout, 1788–1796

UNITED STATES PRESIDENTIAL GENERAL ELECTIONS

Federalist Turnout for Election Years 1788–1796

State	1788			1792				1796			
	Voting-age population	Turnout	%	Voting-age population	Turnout	%	Difference from 1788*	Voting-age population	Turnout	%	Difference from 1788
KENTUCKY											
MARYLAND	46,000	7,665	16.7%					46,000	7,029	15.3%	-1.4	4
MASSACHUSETTS	79,000	14,668	18.6%	82,000	19,929	24.3%	5.7				
NEW HAMPSHIRE	30,000	5,909	19.7%	32,000	8,924	27.9%	8.2	35,000	18,274	52.2%	32.5
NEW JERSEY											
NORTH CAROLINA											
OHIO											
PENNSYLVANIA	92,000	6,711	7.3%	99,000	3,358	3.4%	-3.9	113,000	12,229	10.8%	3.5
RHODE ISLAND											
VIRGINIA											
Total	247,000	34,953	14.2%	213,000	32,211	15.1%	1.0	194,000	37,532	19.3%	5.2	2

Democratic-Republican Turnout for Election Years 1788–1796

State	1788			1792				1796			
	Voting-age population	Turnout	%	Voting-age population	Turnout	%	Difference from 1788*	Voting-age population	Turnout	%	Difference from 1788
KENTUCKY											
MARYLAND	46,000	2,280	5.0%					46,000	6,440	14.0%	9.0	4
MASSACHUSETTS											
NEW HAMPSHIRE											
NEW JERSEY											
NORTH CAROLINA											
OHIO											
PENNSYLVANIA	92,000	672	0.7%					113,000	12,516	11.1%	10.3
RHODE ISLAND											
VIRGINIA											
Total	138,000	2,952	2.1%					159,000	18,956	11.9%	9.8	2

Other Turnout for Election Years 1788–1796

State	1788			1792				1796			
	Voting-age population	Turnout	%	Voting-age population	Turnout	%	Difference from 1788*	Voting-age population	Turnout	%	Difference from 1788
DELAWARE	9,000	685	7.6%								
GEORGIA											
MASSACHUSETTS									86,000	15,438	18.0%	
NORTH CAROLINA											

are designed this way so comparisons in the overall charts are between like states. States where only one party holds a primary are a different phenomenon.

2. For states without data in any given election or year, the voting-age population (VAP) is not shown for that year. This means that the total VAP in each chart varies, depending on how many states held a gubernatorial, Senate, or House vote that year. (There were even states ineligible for the presidential vote during and after the Civil War.)

3. The eligible vote for the four summary graphs in each chapter is the total eligible vote for all states for each year. Because in the early years of the republic, some House elections were not held in even-numbered years, the analysis of turnout against the total national eligible vote might not provide the most accurate picture of turnout trends. For this reason, some early chapters of this book also include an alternative partisan turnout chart based only on the eligible votes of the states where there were House elections. In most cases, especially in later chapters, the differences are minimal, and the alternative chart is omitted.

4. There are times when there is more than one Senate race in a given year in a state. The race selected to be included in the charts is the race with the highest turnout. That race will also be the basis of the partisan charts for the state—even if the votes for one party or the other may be higher in the other race held in the same year.

5. If a candidate of a major party has been endorsed by a minor party and receives votes on that party's line, those votes are added to the major party total and are not treated as part of the Other vote.

6. After 1860, the voting-age population is adjusted by removing the non-citizen populations. Due to the rounding of these two figures, a few states with relatively static populations can appear to fluctuate up and down by 1,000 persons from year to year. For instance, the estimated voting-age population of New Hampshire between 1850 and 1859 appears to be 85,000 in even years and 84,000 in odd years. In general, the statistical effect of rounding populations to nearest thousand is negligible, and doing so enhances the intelligibility of the data and protects against a false precision in what remains an inexact estimate.

BIBLIOGRAPHY

Baldino, Thomas J., and Kyle L. Kreider. 2010. *Voting Rights, Disputed Elections, and Electoral Reform: A Documentary and Reference Guide.* Santa Barbara: Greenwood Press.

Burnham, Walter Dean. 1970. *Critical Elections and the Mainsprings of American Politics.* New York: Norton.

Burnham, Walter Dean, with Thomas Ferguson and Louis Ferleger. 2009. *Voting in American Elections: The Shaping of the American Political Universe since 1788.* Palo Alto: Academica Press.

CQ Press. 2010. *Guide to U.S. Elections.* Washington, D.C.: CQ Press.

Dubin, Michael J. 1998. *United States Congressional Elections 1788-1997.* Jefferson, N.C.: McFarland and Company.

Keyssar, Alexander. 2009. *The Right to Vote: The Contested History of Democracy in the United States* Revised Edition. New York: Basic Books.

Kleppner, Paul. 1982. *Who Voted? The Dynamics of Electoral Turnout, 1870–1980.* New York: Praeger.

Patterson, Thomas E. 2003. *The Vanishing Voter: Public Involvement in an Age of Uncertainty.* New York: Knopf.

Rusk, Jerrold G. 2001. *A Statistical History of the American Electorate.* Washington, D.C.: CQ Press.

Scammon, Richard M. 1956–1958. *America Votes: A Handbook of Contemporary Election Statistics. Vols. 1–2.* New York: Macmillan.

——. 1959–1964. *America Votes. Vols. 3–5.* Pittsburgh: University of Pittsburgh.

——. 1966–1975. *America Votes. Vols. 6–11.* Washington, D.C.: Congressional Quarterly.

Scammon, Richard M., Alice V. McGillivray, and Rhodes Cook. 1997–2009. *America Votes. Vols. 22–28.* Washington, D.C.: CQ Press.

Teixeira, Ruy A. 1987. *Why Americans Don't Vote: Turnout Decline in the United States, 1960–1984.* New York: Greenwood Press.

——. 1992. *The Disappearing American Voter.* Washington, D.C.: Brookings.

U.S. Census Bureau, "Census of Population and Housing," http://www.census.gov/prod/www/abs/decennial/.

Wolfinger, Raymond E., and Steven J. Rosenstone. 1980. *Who Votes?* New Haven: Yale University Press.

[1] There are two exceptions to the winner-take-all method of selecting electors. In Maine and Nebraska, the statewide winner of the popular vote receives the votes of the two electors representing the state's number of U.S. senators. The remaining electors are awarded by Congressional district to the winner of the popular vote in each district.

[2] Oregon abandoned election-day registration before the 1992 general election for fear that a cult occupying a portion of the state could use the law to skew the election to its advantage.

[3] Beginning with Richard Nixon's 1972 reelection campaign, the Republicans adopted a "southern strategy," partially formulated by GOP political consultant Lee Atwater. That strategy consisted of using code words such as "state's rights" and "law and order" in speeches aimed at stirring the pot of racial division.

[4] Kristen Purcell, Lee Rainie, Amy Mitchell, Tom Rosenstiel, Kenny Olmstead, "Understanding the Participatory News Consumer," a report by the Pew Internet and American Life Project, Washington, D.C., March 1, 2010, http://www.pewinternet.org/Reports/2010/Online-News.aspx.

[5] CIRP Freshman Survey, Cooperative Institutional Research Program, Higher Education Research Institute, University of California, Los Angeles, press release January 21, 2010; http://www.heri.ucla.edu/PDFs/press/pr012110-09Freshman.pdf or http://www.heri.ucla.edu/pr-display.php?prQry=42.

[6] Georgia allowed citizens eighteen years of age and over to vote beginning in 1943. Kentucky did the same in 1955; Alaska allowed citizens nineteen years of age and older to vote in 1959 when it became a state; and Hawaii allowed citizens twenty years and older to vote when it became a state in 1959.

[7] Statistics using Burnham's methodology were first published in *Historical Statistics of the United States from Colonial Times to 1970,* Bureau of the Census, Washington, D.C., 1975; Part 2, pp. 1067–1069, 1071–1072.

[8] Ibid.

[9] Fifteen states enfranchised women to vote in all elections prior to 1920, beginning with Wyoming in 1889. An additional seventeen states granted women the right to vote in some elections prior to 1920.

[10] The first chapter covers twenty-two years: 1788–1809

[11] The main source for the events chronology is the *Encyclopedia of U.S. Political History* (Andrew Robertson, Washington, D.C.: CQ Press, 2010). The census counts in the events chronology come from the U.S. Census Bureau, "Census of Population and Housing" (http://www.census.gov/prod/www/abs/decennial/ , accessed June 1, 2010). Timelines from the National Humanities Center, "Toolbox Library: Primary Resources in U.S. History and Literature" (http://nationalhumanitiescenter.org/pds/tblibrary.htm/ , accessed June 1, 2010) were also consulted for the chronologies. For Supreme Court cases, see CQ Press Electronic Library, *Guide to the U.S. Supreme Court Online Edition,* "Chronology of Major Decisions of the Court, 1797–2007." Originally published in David G. Savage, *Guide to the U.S. Supreme Court,* 4th ed. (Revised), (Washington: CQ Press, 2008). http://library.cqpress.com/supremecourtguide/search.php (accessed June 18th, 2010).

[12] These are "estimates" for overall turnout because they do not capture voters who produce invalid ballots or voters who decide to vote for another office but not for the presidency. However, based on states that do keep counts of every individual ballot, overall turnout usually differs from presidential turnout by a percentage point or less; the total highest statewide turnout (explained below) may differ from overall turnout by three-quarters to one-and-a-half percentage points.

[13] For example, in Alabama in 1970, 854,952 people voted in the gubernatorial election; 742,072 total people voted in all the U.S. House elections; and there was no U.S. Senate election. Therefore, the highest vote total is 854,952, from the gubernatorial election. In the same year, in Delaware, there was no gubernatorial election, and the highest turnout was seen in the House election, at 161,439 votes. To determine the national estimate for turnout, one adds Alabama's 854,952 to Delaware's 161,439 and so on for all the states in the Union at that time.

[14] The Seventeenth Amendment was passed by Congress in 1912 and ratified in 1913. Some states held popular senatorial elections in 1912 prior to the amendment's ratification.

[15] For example, in 1972, New Jersey had a Democratic presidential primary in which 76,834 voters participated. It held no Republican presidential primary. Because only one party had a primary, there is no data for New Jersey in the overall (or total) primary chart. By contrast, that same year, New Mexico had both a Republican presidential primary (with 55,469 voters) and a Democratic presidential primary (with 153,293 voters). In the overall presidential primary chart, New Mexico has 55,469 + 153,293 = 208,762 voters. The primary charts are designed this way so comparisons in the overall charts are between like states—states that have primaries for both parties—as states that hold only one primary are a different phenomenon.

[16] In the first three chapters, the list includes only states with data in the time period. In later chapters, all fifty states (plus the District of Columbia) are included.

[17] For more explanation on how the population of eligible voters is calculated, please consult pp. 22–24 of the "Methodology" section.

[18] Presidential-year charts in the first chapter have six years of data: 1788, 1792, 1796, 1800, 1804, and 1808. In a handful of cases, a particular chart will have fewer years because that type of election did not occur throughout the twenty-year period.

[19] A blank first column could happen for many reasons. It may be that the state had not entered the union in the first year of the two-decade period of the chapter, or a state may shift when it holds its election from an odd-year election to a presidential-year election. Even in later chapters, for primary races and some gubernatorial and Senate races, there may be no entries for some states in the first column of a given chart.

[20] If a reader adds the three partisan total lines, they will equal the total line in the overall graph. There are two exceptions, however. First, this is not true of primary graphs, for reasons explained earlier. Second, adding the three partisan total lines in the highest statewide chart will typically produce a turnout number higher than the total line in the overall highest statewide chart. To use a simplified example, say a state had two races—gubernatorial and House—and no turnout in the Other category. For governor, the votes were tallied at 4,000 for Republicans and 2,000 for Democrats, while for the House race, the vote tally was 2,000 for Republicans and 3,000 for Democrats. The total highest statewide amount would come from the gubernatorial race: 6,000 votes. The highest turnout for Republicans would be 4,000 (also gubernatorial), but the highest turnout for Democrats would be 3,000 (from the House race). Therefore, in the partisan highest statewide chart, the figures would be 4,000 for Republicans and 3,000 for Democrats, totaling 7,000.

[21] The odd-year charts in Chapter 1 have eleven years of data.

[22] The denominator for turnout—the eligible vote or those who were by law enfranchised to cast ballots—is different for different periods in American history, as there have been changes both in voter eligibility and data availability.

Presidential Turnout, 1788–2008

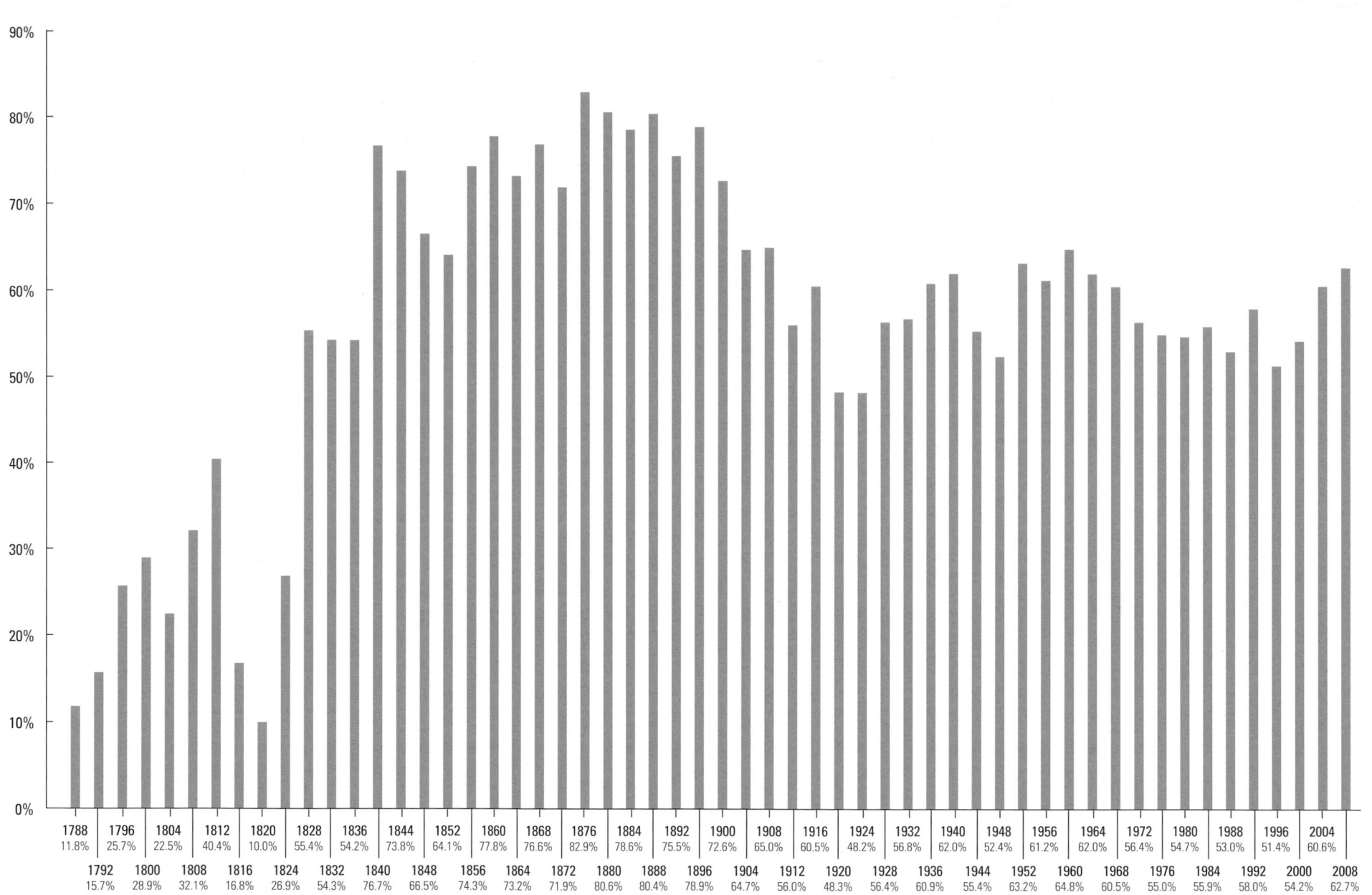

Year	Turnout	Year	Turnout
1788	11.8%	1792	15.7%
1796	25.7%	1800	28.9%
1804	22.5%	1808	32.1%
1812	40.4%	1816	16.8%
1820	10.0%	1824	26.9%
1828	55.4%	1832	54.3%
1836	54.2%	1840	76.7%
1844	73.8%	1848	66.5%
1852	64.1%	1856	74.3%
1860	77.8%	1864	73.2%
1868	76.6%	1872	71.9%
1876	82.9%	1880	80.6%
1884	78.6%	1888	80.4%
1892	75.5%	1896	78.9%
1900	72.6%	1904	64.7%
1908	65.0%	1912	56.0%
1916	60.5%	1920	48.3%
1924	48.2%	1928	56.4%
1932	56.8%	1936	60.9%
1940	62.0%	1944	55.4%
1948	52.4%	1952	63.2%
1956	61.2%	1960	64.8%
1964	62.0%	1968	60.5%
1972	56.4%	1976	55.0%
1980	54.7%	1984	55.9%
1988	53.0%	1992	58.0%
1996	51.4%	2000	54.2%
2004	60.6%	2008	62.7%

Partisan Turnout Presidential Years Based on Aggregate House Turnout, 1788–2008

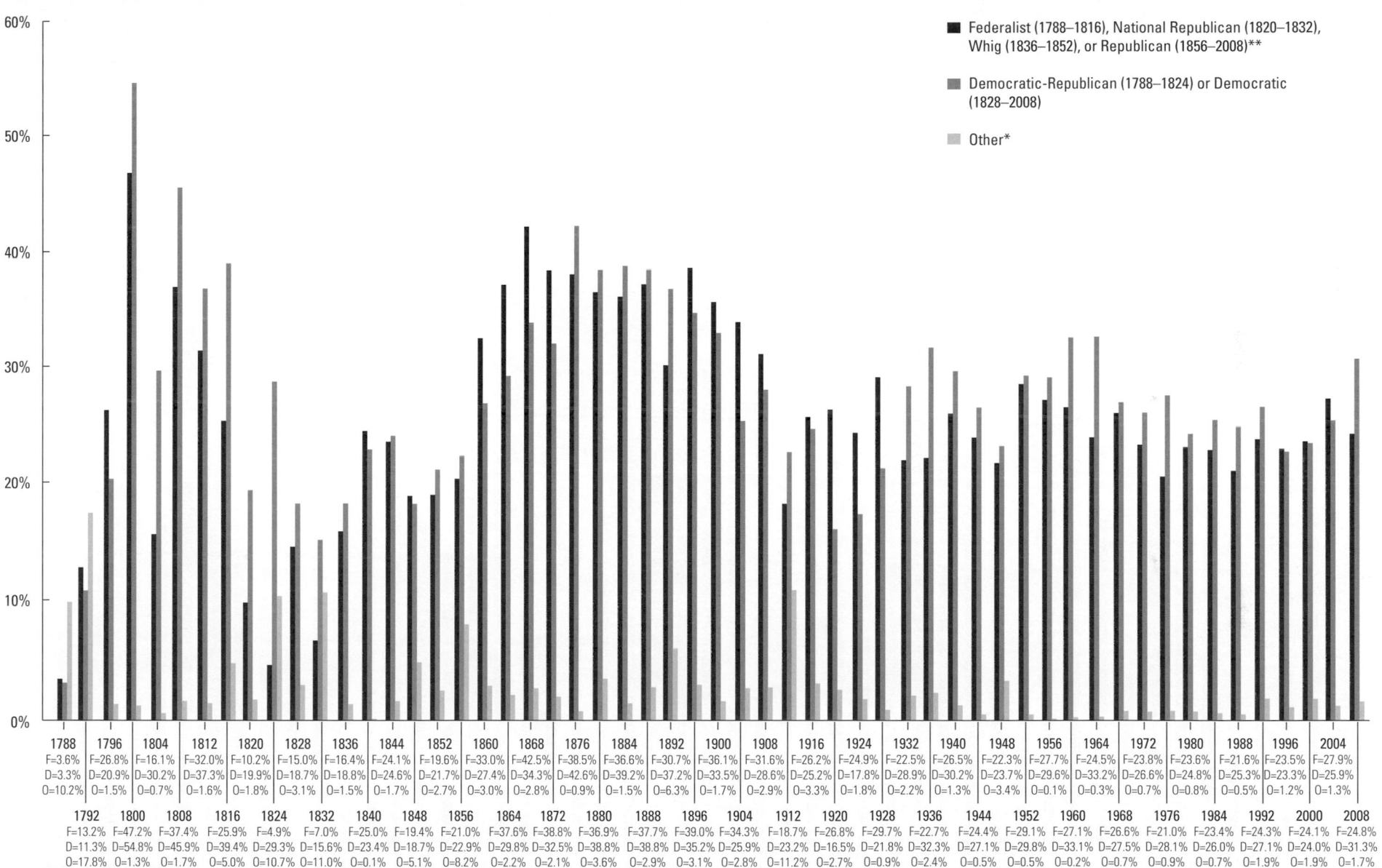

Legend:
- Federalist (1788–1816), National Republican (1820–1832), Whig (1836–1852), or Republican (1856–2008)**
- Democratic-Republican (1788–1824) or Democratic (1828–2008)
- Other*

Year	F	D	O
1788	F=3.6%	D=3.3%	O=10.2%
1792	F=13.2%	D=11.3%	O=17.8%
1796	F=26.8%	D=20.9%	O=1.5%
1800	F=47.2%	D=54.8%	O=1.3%
1804	F=16.1%	D=30.2%	O=0.7%
1808	F=37.4%	D=45.9%	O=1.3%
1812	F=32.0%	D=37.3%	O=1.6%
1816	F=25.9%	D=39.4%	O=5.0%
1820	F=10.2%	D=19.9%	O=1.8%
1824	F=4.9%	D=29.3%	O=10.7%
1828	F=15.0%	D=18.7%	O=3.1%
1832	F=7.0%	D=15.6%	O=11.0%
1836	F=16.4%	D=18.8%	O=1.5%
1840	F=25.0%	D=23.4%	O=0.1%
1844	F=24.1%	D=24.6%	O=1.7%
1848	F=19.4%	D=18.7%	O=5.1%
1852	F=19.6%	D=21.7%	O=2.7%
1856	F=21.0%	D=22.9%	O=8.2%
1860	F=33.0%	D=27.4%	O=3.0%
1864	F=37.6%	D=29.8%	O=2.2%
1868	F=42.5%	D=34.3%	O=2.8%
1872	F=38.8%	D=32.5%	O=2.1%
1876	F=38.5%	D=42.6%	O=0.9%
1880	F=36.9%	D=38.8%	O=3.6%
1884	F=36.6%	D=39.2%	O=1.5%
1888	F=37.7%	D=38.8%	O=3.1%
1892	F=30.7%	D=37.2%	O=6.3%
1896	F=39.0%	D=35.2%	O=2.9%
1900	F=36.1%	D=33.5%	O=1.7%
1904	F=34.3%	D=25.9%	O=3.1%
1908	F=31.6%	D=28.6%	O=2.9%
1912	F=18.7%	D=23.2%	O=11.2%
1916	F=26.2%	D=25.2%	O=3.3%
1920	F=26.8%	D=16.5%	O=2.7%
1924	F=24.9%	D=17.8%	O=1.8%
1928	F=29.7%	D=21.8%	O=2.2%
1932	F=22.5%	D=28.9%	O=2.2%
1936	F=22.7%	D=32.3%	O=1.3%
1940	F=22.3%	D=30.2%	O=3.4%
1944	F=24.4%	D=27.1%	O=0.5%
1948	F=26.5%	D=23.7%	O=0.1%
1952	F=29.1%	D=29.8%	O=0.2%
1956	F=27.7%	D=29.6%	O=0.3%
1960	F=27.1%	D=33.1%	O=0.7%
1964	F=24.5%	D=33.2%	O=0.7%
1968	F=26.6%	D=27.5%	O=0.9%
1972	F=23.8%	D=26.6%	O=0.7%
1976	F=21.0%	D=28.1%	O=0.7%
1980	F=23.6%	D=24.8%	O=0.8%
1984	F=23.4%	D=26.0%	O=1.9%
1988	F=21.6%	D=25.3%	O=0.5%
1992	F=24.3%	D=27.1%	O=1.9%
1996	F=23.5%	D=23.3%	O=1.2%
2000	F=24.1%	D=24.0%	O=1.9%
2004	F=27.9%	D=25.9%	O=1.3%
2008	F=24.8%	D=31.3%	O=1.7%

*1789 and 1792 were elections as the party structure was just forming, and many of these candidates did not formally run on a party slate, including the twice-victorious George Washington.

** The Federalist party was more or less defunct as a national party by 1820. The country briefly had only one national party, the Democratic-Republicans, but the party soon split into factions, one supporting John Adams and one supporting Andrew Jackson. The Adams wing of the party became the National Republicans, and for the purposes of this volume, the National Republicans are dated from 1820 to 1832. The Jackson wing became the Democratic party that continues into the twenty-first century. The Whig party supplanted the National Republicans as a national party in 1834 and were in turn supplanted by the Republicans in 1856.

Midterm Turnout Based on Highest Statewide Turnout, 1810–2006

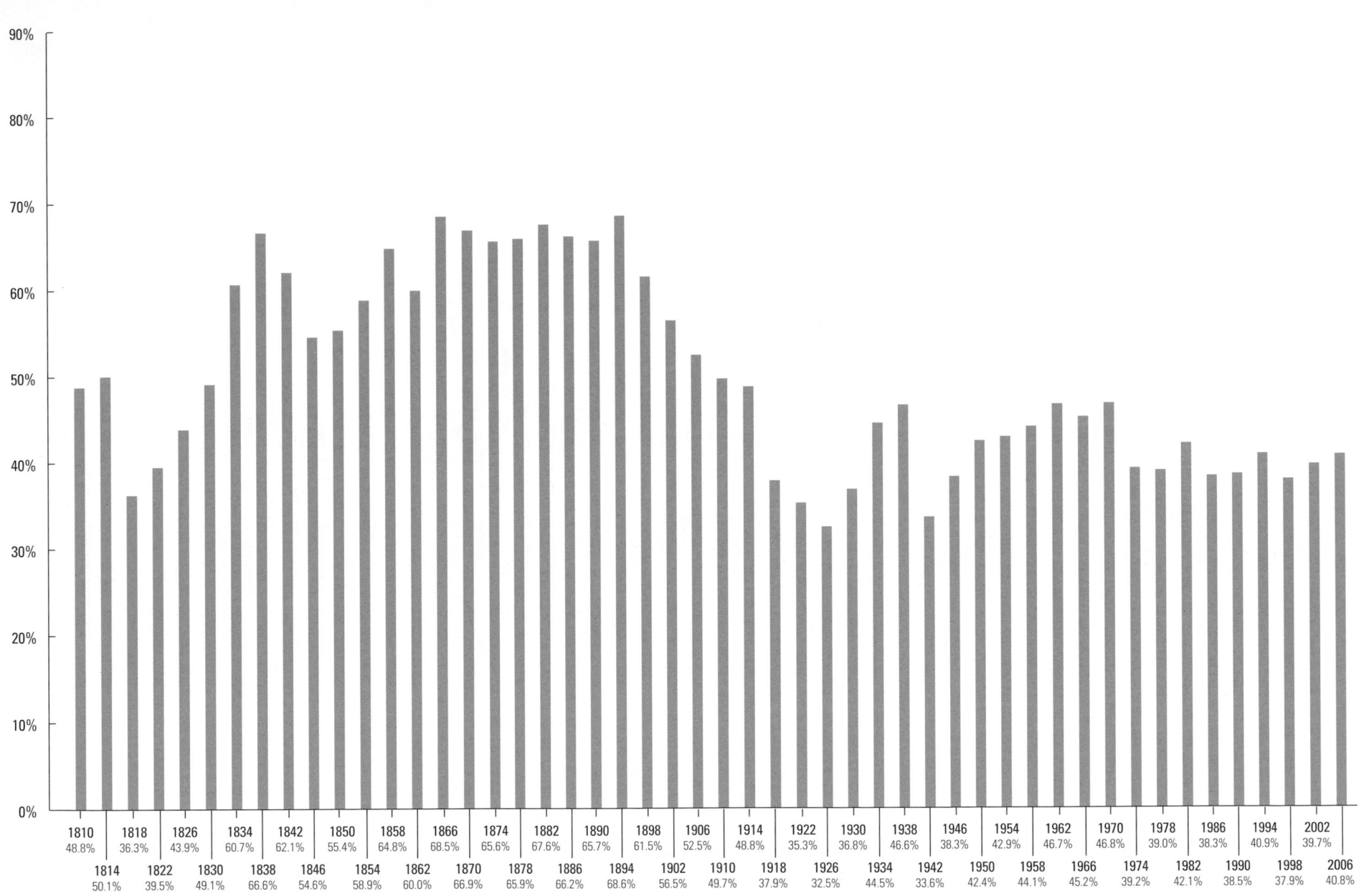

| 1810 | 1814 | 1818 | 1822 | 1826 | 1830 | 1834 | 1838 | 1842 | 1846 | 1850 | 1854 | 1858 | 1862 | 1866 | 1870 | 1874 | 1878 | 1882 | 1886 | 1890 | 1894 | 1898 | 1902 | 1906 | 1910 | 1914 | 1918 | 1922 | 1926 | 1930 | 1934 | 1938 | 1942 | 1946 | 1950 | 1954 | 1958 | 1962 | 1966 | 1970 | 1974 | 1978 | 1982 | 1986 | 1990 | 1994 | 1998 | 2002 | 2006 |

Top row years: 1810 48.8%, 1818 36.3%, 1826 43.9%, 1834 60.7%, 1842 62.1%, 1850 55.4%, 1858 64.8%, 1866 68.5%, 1874 65.6%, 1882 67.6%, 1890 65.7%, 1898 61.5%, 1906 52.5%, 1914 48.8%, 1922 35.3%, 1930 36.8%, 1938 46.6%, 1946 38.3%, 1954 42.9%, 1962 46.7%, 1970 46.8%, 1978 39.0%, 1986 38.3%, 1994 40.9%, 2002 39.7%

Bottom row years: 1814 50.1%, 1822 39.5%, 1830 49.1%, 1838 66.6%, 1846 54.6%, 1854 58.9%, 1862 60.0%, 1870 66.9%, 1878 65.9%, 1886 66.2%, 1894 68.6%, 1902 56.5%, 1910 49.7%, 1918 37.9%, 1926 32.5%, 1934 44.5%, 1942 33.6%, 1950 42.4%, 1958 44.1%, 1966 45.2%, 1974 39.2%, 1982 42.1%, 1990 38.5%, 1998 37.9%, 2006 40.8%

Partisan Turnout Midterm Years Based on Aggregate House Turnout, 1790–2006

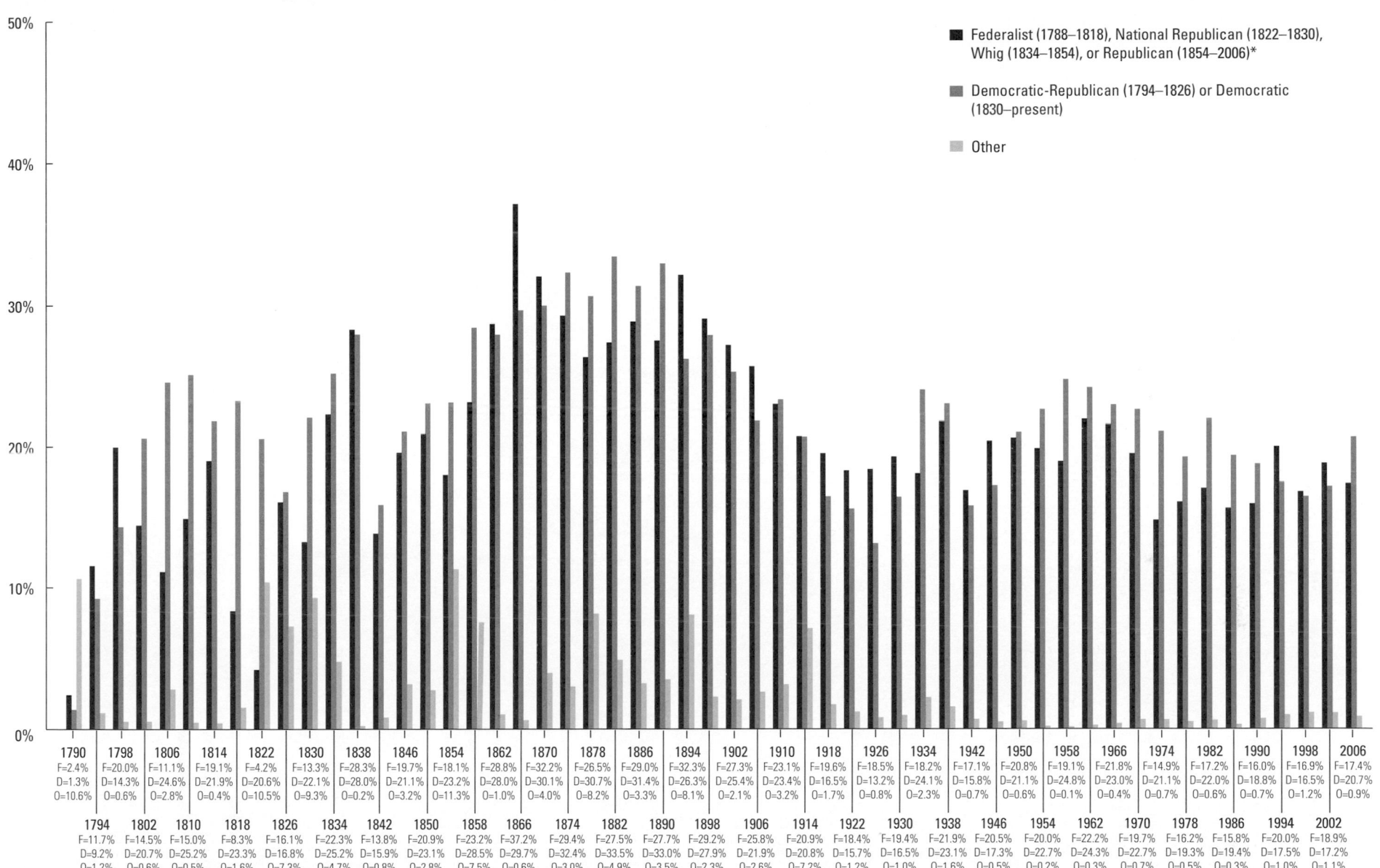

Legend:
- Federalist (1788–1818), National Republican (1822–1830), Whig (1834–1854), or Republican (1854–2006)*
- Democratic-Republican (1794–1826) or Democratic (1830–present)
- Other

Year	F	D	O
1790	2.4%	1.3%	10.6%
1798	20.0%	14.3%	0.6%
1806	11.1%	24.6%	2.8%
1814	19.1%	21.9%	0.4%
1822	4.2%	20.6%	10.5%
1830	13.3%	22.1%	9.3%
1838	28.3%	28.0%	0.2%
1846	19.7%	21.1%	3.2%
1854	18.1%	23.2%	11.3%
1862	28.8%	28.0%	1.0%
1870	32.2%	30.1%	4.0%
1878	26.5%	30.7%	8.2%
1886	29.0%	31.4%	3.3%
1894	32.3%	26.3%	8.1%
1902	27.3%	25.4%	2.1%
1910	23.1%	23.4%	3.2%
1918	19.6%	16.5%	1.7%
1926	18.5%	13.2%	0.8%
1934	18.2%	24.1%	2.3%
1942	17.1%	15.8%	0.7%
1950	20.8%	21.1%	0.6%
1958	19.1%	24.8%	0.1%
1966	21.8%	23.0%	0.4%
1974	14.9%	22.0%	0.7%
1982	17.2%	22.0%	0.6%
1990	16.0%	18.8%	0.7%
1998	16.9%	16.5%	1.2%
2006	17.4%	20.7%	0.9%

Year	F	D	O
1794	11.7%	9.2%	1.2%
1802	14.5%	20.7%	0.6%
1810	15.0%	25.2%	0.5%
1818	8.3%	23.3%	1.6%
1826	16.1%	16.8%	7.3%
1834	22.3%	25.2%	4.7%
1842	13.8%	15.9%	0.8%
1850	20.9%	23.1%	2.8%
1858	23.2%	28.5%	7.5%
1866	37.2%	29.7%	0.6%
1874	29.4%	32.4%	3.0%
1882	27.5%	33.5%	4.9%
1890	27.7%	33.0%	3.5%
1898	29.2%	27.9%	2.3%
1906	25.8%	21.9%	2.6%
1914	20.9%	20.8%	7.2%
1922	18.4%	15.7%	1.2%
1930	19.4%	16.5%	1.0%
1938	21.9%	23.1%	1.6%
1946	20.5%	17.3%	0.5%
1954	20.0%	22.7%	0.2%
1962	22.2%	24.3%	0.3%
1970	19.7%	22.7%	0.7%
1978	16.2%	19.3%	0.5%
1986	15.8%	19.4%	0.3%
1994	20.0%	17.5%	1.0%
2002	18.9%	17.2%	1.1%

* The Federalist party was more or less defunct as a national party by 1820. The country briefly had only one national party, the Democratic-Republicans, but the party soon split into factions, one supporting John Adams and one supporting Andrew Jackson. The Adams wing of the party became the National Republicans, and for the purposes of this volume, the National Republicans are dated from 1820 to 1832. The Jackson wing became the Democratic party that continues into the twenty-first century. The Whig party supplanted the National Republicans as a national party in 1834 and were in turn supplanted by the Republicans in 1856. In 1854, some states (particularly in the Northeast) had a slate of Whig candidates, while other states (particularly in the West) had a slate of Republicans, but few races were contested between Republicans and Whigs. For this reason, Whig and Republican turnout is counted together for 1854 in this volume.

CHAPTER 1
1788–1809

Chronology of Major Events, 1788–1809

1788	U.S. Constitution is ratified by the requisite nine states and replaces the Articles of Confederation.
1789	George Washington becomes first United States president under new Constitution. Ten amendments to the Constitution (Bill of Rights) are adopted by Congress. The Federal Judiciary Act of 1789 establishes federal court system, including a Supreme Court.
1790	Census Act leads to the first census, which counts 3.9 million residents, not including American Indians.
1791	Bill of Rights is ratified by the states.
1792	Washington is re-elected president. Supreme Court hears its first cases.
1793	The cotton gin, invented and produced by Eli Whitney, begins to revitalize southern slave economy. Washington proclaims U.S. neutrality in war pitting France against Britain, Holland, and Spain.
1796	Federalist John Adams defeats Thomas Jefferson in the first contested presidential election.
1798	The Alien and Sedition Acts are passed by Congress and signed into law due to quasi-war with France.
1800	Democratic-Republican Jefferson defeats Adams for the presidency. The second census counts the U.S. population at 5.3 million people.
1803	In his opinion on *Marbury v. Madison*, Supreme Court chief justice John Marshall establishes the Court's right to judicial review of legislation. For $15 million, the Louisiana Purchase from France adds territory that would subsequently become fourteen southern and midwestern states.
1804	Jefferson is re-elected president and sends Lewis and Clark on an expedition to explore the American northwest. Twelfth Amendment to the Constitution makes minor changes to Electoral College in presidential elections.
1807	Robert Fulton debuts the Claremont, the first commercial steamboat. The slave trade is banned.
1808	James Madison is elected president. U.S. economy suffers first depression after enacting a trade embargo against France and Great Britain.

State and Federal Laws Chronology, 1787–1809

1787   *Delaware joins the Union.* It requires the voter to be a "freeholder... And has 50 acres of land or more well seated, and 12 acres or more thereof cleared" or "is otherwise worth 40 pounds money of this government clear estate." [1,2]

Pennsylvania joins the Union. It initially has no property or taxpaying requirements.

New Jersey joins the Union. It requires the voter to be worth fifty pounds proclamation money or clear estate in the same amount worth. [3]

1788   *Georgia joins the Union.* It requires the voter to have ten pounds of personal worth and be liable for state taxes (or be of any "mechanic trade"). [4]

Connecticut joins the Union. It requires the voter to have forty shillings worth of property.

Massachusetts joins the Union. It requires the voter to possess a freehold estate with annual income of three pounds, or any estate worth sixty pounds to vote in a Senate election; in addition, this property must be owned in the same town as residence to be eligible to vote in a House election. [5]

Maryland joins the Union. It requires the voter to possess a freehold of fifty acres or property above thirty pounds in value.

South Carolina joins the Union. It requires the voter to possess a land freehold of fifty acres, owned for a minimum of six months prior to an election, or to have paid a tax the previous year, or to have been eligible for and able to pay a tax equal to what a tax would be for fifty acres of freehold land. It also requires the voter to affirm a belief in God.

New Hampshire joins the Union. It requires the voter to pay a poll tax.

Virginia joins the Union. It requires the voter to possess a "freehold ... in at least 50 acres of land, if no settlement be made upon it, or 25 acres, with a plantation and house thereon, at least 12 feet square," or town lot with house "at least 12 feet square." It also requires the voter to have owned property for at least one year prior to voting in an election. [6]

New York joins the Union. It requires the voter to be a "Freeholder, possessing a freehold of the value of 20 pounds, ... Or have rented a tenement therein of the yearly value of 40 shillings, and been rated and actually paid taxes to this State." It grants an exception to this requirement for "every person who is now a freeman of the city of Albany, or who was made a freeman in the city of New York on or before" October 14, 1775. A voter in a Senate election must further be an owner of one or more freeholds valued at "one hundred pounds, over and above all debts charged thereon." [7]

1789   *North Carolina joins the Union.* It requires the voter to possess a freehold of fifty acres of land to vote in a Senate election. The voter must also pay taxes to vote for any office. [8]

Georgia requires the voter to have paid all taxes for the year preceding the election and be a citizen.

1790   *Rhode Island joins the Union.* It requires the voter to possess a freehold worth forty pounds or forty shillings per year or be the eldest son of a freeholder.

Pennsylvania requires the voter to have paid state or county tax within two years, assessed at least six months before the election. The voter is exempt if under age twenty-two and the son of a qualified voter. A voter must also be citizen.

South Carolina requires the voter to possess a freehold of fifty acres or a town lot, owned six months prior to election. Alternatively, the voter must have paid a tax in the year preceding the election of three shillings sterling and have been a resident for six months. Further, a voter must be a white citizen of the state.

State and Federal Laws Chronology, 1787–1809 (continued)

State and Federal Laws Chronology, 1787–1809 *(continued)*

1791   *Vermont becomes a state.* It enters the Union without any property or taxpaying requirements for suffrage. The voter, however, must be a citizen.

1792   *Kentucky becomes a state.* It enters the Union without any property or taxpaying requirements for suffrage.

Delaware requires the voter to have paid a state or county tax assessed at least six months before the election. The voter is exempt if under twenty-two and the son of a qualified voter. Delaware also abolishes its property requirement but requires voters to be white.

New Hampshire voters who have been excused from paying taxes at their own request are excluded from voting.

1796   Connecticut requires the voter to possess a freehold worth $7 per year or total personal property worth $134.

Tennessee becomes a state. It requires the voter to possess a freehold in the county where he may vote, or to be an inhabitant of any one county in the state for six months.

1799   Kentucky voters must not be "Negroes, mulattos, or Indians."[9]

1801   Maryland drops its freehold requirement but institutes a whites-only suffrage policy.

1803   *Ohio becomes a state.* Voters must have paid or been charged with state or county tax; not applicable to white males above age twenty-one, who are "compelled to labor on the roads" and have resided one year in the state. Voters must be white.[10]

1804   Virginia requires the voter to have owned land for six months prior to election.

New York requires the voter to either rent a tenement worth $25 a year or meet 1777 property requirements. The voter must be a citizen.

1807   New Jersey requires the voter to be worth fifty pounds; any person who paid a state or county tax, or had his name enrolled upon a tax duplicate for the last state or county tax, is deemed to be worth fifty pounds. The voter must also be a white citizen.

1809   Ohio requires the voter to be a U.S. citizen.

Source: Adapted from Alexander Keyssar, *The Right to Vote: The Contested History of Democracy in the United States,* Revised Edition (New York: Basic Books, 2009), 306–319.

[1] As quoted in Keyssar, 306. For sources, see Keyssar 369–379. He does not provide a precise match between quotation and source.

[2] "In order to be categorized as a freehold, an estate must possess the characteristics of (1) immobility—in the sense that the property must be either land, or some interest derived from or affixed to land—and (2) indeterminate duration."—Jeffrey S. Lehman and Shirelle Phelps. *West's Encyclopedia of American Law.* (Detroit, MI: Thomson Gale, 2005). A "clear estate" is "free and clear"; that is, it has no outstanding liens or other claims (such as a mortgage) against it.

[3] "Proclamation money" refers back to a 1704 proclamation by British Queen Anne that fixed the exchange rate for Spanish coins, which were frequently in use in colonial America. Smith, William Roy. *South Carolina as a Royal Province (1719–1776), by W. Roy Smith.* (New York: Macmillan, 1903):230–231.

[4] As quoted in Keyssar, 306. For sources, see Keyssar 369–379.

[5] References to Senate and House refer to state rather than federal offices.

[6] As quoted in Keyssar, 307. For sources, see Keyssar 369–379.

[7] As quoted in Keyssar, 306. For sources, see Keyssar 369–379.

[8] References to Senate and House refer to state rather than federal offices.

[9] As quoted in Keyssar, 316. For sources, see Keyssar 369–379.

[10] As quoted in Keyssar, 311. For sources, see Keyssar 369–379.

National Count of Popular Vote for President, 1792–1808

YEAR	NAME	PARTY	TOTAL[1]	PERCENTAGE[2]
1788	George Washington	(none)	—	—
1792	George Washington	(none)	99,802	12.8%
1796	John Adams	Federalist	37,532	4.8%
	Thomas Jefferson	Democratic-Republican	18,956	2.4%
	Thomas Pinckney	Federalist Independent	15,668	2.0%
1800	Thomas Jefferson	Democratic-Republican	41,516	4.7%
	John Adams	Federalist	25,933	2.9%
1804	Thomas Jefferson	Democratic-Republican	103,931	10.2%
	Charles Pinckney	Federalist	38,690	3.8%
1808	James Madison	Democratic-Republican	123,517	10.9%
	Charles Pinckney	Federalist	62,254	5.5%

[1] In these early years, the legislatures in several states chose the presidential electors rather than the voters.

[2] The percentage figures in this chart are based on the votes cast divided by the eligible voting-age population at the time of the election.

States with Property and Taxpaying Requirements for Suffrage, 1788–1809

STATE	DATE OF STATEHOOD	PROPERTY REQUIREMENT[1]	TAXPAYING REQUIREMENT[1]
CONNECTICUT	1788	1715: Freehold estate worth 40 shillings per year or 40 pounds personal estate 1796: Freehold worth $7 a year or possession of personal property worth $134	None
DELAWARE	1787	1734: "Freeholder … And has 50 acres of land or more well seated, and 12 acres or more thereof cleared." 1792: None	1792: Paid a state or county tax … assessed at least 6 months before the election. Exempt if under age 22 and the son of a qualified voter.
GEORGIA	1788	None	1789: Paid all taxes for the year preceding the election 1798: Paid all taxes for the year preceding the election
KENTUCKY	1792	None	None
MARYLAND	1788	1776: Freehold of 50 acres or property above value of 30 pounds 1801: Freehold requirement dropped	None
MASSACHUSETTS	1788	1780: Freehold estate with annual income of 3 pounds, or any estate worth 60 pounds to vote in the Senate election; property must be owned in same town as residence to vote in the House election.[2]	None
NEW HAMPSHIRE	1788	None	1784: Poll tax 1792: Persons excused from paying taxes at their own request excluded
NEW JERSEY	1787	1776: Worth 50 pounds proclamation money, clear estate in the same 1807: Worth 50 pounds; any person who paid a state or county tax, or had his name enrolled upon a tax duplicate for the last state or county tax deemed to be worth 50 pounds	1776: None 1807: See property requirement

STATE	DATE OF STATEHOOD	PROPERTY REQUIREMENT[1]	TAXPAYING REQUIREMENT[1]
NEW YORK	1788	1777: For Assembly: "freeholder, possessing a freehold of the value of 20 pounds … or have rented a tenement therein of the yearly value of 40 shillings, and been rated and actually paid taxes to this State." Exceptions for "every person who now is a freeman of the city of Albany, or who was made a freeman of the city of New York on or before" October 14th, 1775. For Senate: voters must be owners of freeholds valued at "one hundred pounds, over and above all debts charged thereon."[3] 1804: Those who rent a tenement worth $25 a year or meet 1777 property requirements	1777: See property requirement
NORTH CAROLINA	1789	1776: Freehold of 50 acres of land to vote for Senate; none for House of Commons[4]	1776: Must have paid taxes to vote for House of Commons and governor
OHIO	1803	None	1802: Must have paid or been charged with state or county tax; not applicable to white males above age 21, who are "compelled to labor on the roads" and have resided 1 year in the state.
PENNSYLVANIA	1787	None	1790: Paid state or county tax within 2 years, assessed at least 6 months before the election; exempt if under age 22 and the son of a qualified voter.
RHODE ISLAND	1791	1762: Freehold worth 40 pounds or 40 shillings per year, or the eldest son of a freeholder	None
SOUTH CAROLINA	1788	1790: Freehold of 50 acres or a town lot, owned 6 months prior to election; taxpaying alternative	1790: If resident for 6 months, must have paid tax of 3 shillings sterling the year preceding the election
TENNESSEE	1796	1796: Freehold in the county wherein he may vote, or inhabitant of any one county in the state for 6 months	None
VERMONT	1791	None	None
VIRGINIA	1788	1762: "Freehold … in at least 50 acres of land, if no settlement be made upon it, or 25 acres, with a plantation and house thereon, at least 12 feet square," or town lot with house "at least 12 feet square." 1804: Must own land for 6 months prior to the election	None

Source: Alexander Keyssar, *The Right to Vote: The Contested History of Democracy in the United States,* Revised Edition (New York: Basic Books, 2009), 308–313. Keyssar's table extends from 1790 to 1855. Sources of quotations are found on pp. 369–379.

[1] Dates listed are for the year that the property or tax requirement went into effect. All listed requirements continue into the 1788–1809 date range of this table.
[2] References to Assembly, House, Senate, and House of Commons refer to state rather than federal offices.
[3] References to Assembly, House, Senate, and House of Commons refer to state rather than federal offices.
[4] References to Assembly, House, Senate, and House of Commons refer to state rather than federal offices.

States with Race and Citizenship Requirements for Suffrage, 1788–1809

STATE AND YEAR OF STATEHOOD[1]	DATE OF REQUIREMENT[2]	RACE	CITIZENSHIP	NATIVE AMERICANS
CONNECTICUT	1715	No requirement	No requirement	Not specifically mentioned
DELAWARE	1734	No requirement	No requirement	Not specifically mentioned
	1792	White	No requirement	Not specifically mentioned
GEORGIA	1789	No requirement	Citizen	Not specifically mentioned
KENTUCKY (1792)	1792	No requirement	Citizen	Not specifically mentioned
	1799	"Negroes, mulattos, and Indians" excluded	Citizen	"Indians" specifically excluded
MARYLAND	1776	No requirement	No requirement	Not specifically mentioned
	1801	White	No requirement	Not specifically mentioned
MASSACHUSETTS	1780	No requirement	No requirement	Not specifically mentioned
	1807	No requirement	No requirement	Inhabitants of incorporated plantations not entitled to vote for governor or lieutenant governor; this effectively excluded many Indians
NEW HAMPSHIRE	1792	No requirement	No requirement	Not specifically mentioned
NEW JERSEY	1776	No requirement	No requirement	Not specifically mentioned
	1807	White	Citizen	Not specifically mentioned
NEW YORK	1777	No requirement	No requirement	Not specifically mentioned
	1804	No requirement	Citizen	Not specifically mentioned
NORTH CAROLINA	1776	No requirement	No requirement	Not specifically mentioned
OHIO (1803)	1802	White	No requirement	Not specifically mentioned
	1809	No requirement	U.S. citizen	Not specifically mentioned
PENNSYLVANIA	1790	No requirement	Citizen	Not specifically mentioned
RHODE ISLAND	1762	No requirement	No requirement	Not specifically mentioned
SOUTH CAROLINA	1790	White	Citizen of state	Not specifically mentioned

Source: Alexander Keyssar, *The Right to Vote: The Contested History of Democracy in the United States,* Revised Edition (New York: Basic Books, 2009), 315–319. Keyssar's table extends from 1790 to 1855. Sources of quotations are found on pp. 369–379.
[1] For states after the original thirteen colonies.
[2] Dates listed are for the year that the requirement went into effect. All listed requirements continue into the 1788–1809 date range of this table. States with no requirement are listed for comparison purposes.

United States Presidential Turnout, Election Years 1789–1808

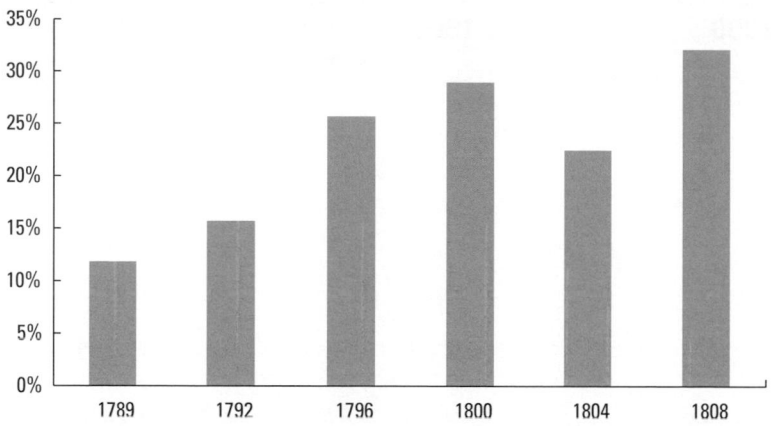

YEAR	VOTING-AGE POPULATION	TURNOUT	%
1789	347,000	41,043	11.8%
1792	213,000	33,472	15.7%
1796	280,000	71,926	25.7%
1800	233,000	67,449	28.9%
1804	635,000	142,621	22.5%
1808	593,000	190,414	32.1%

Partisan Turnout, Presidential Years, Based on Aggregate House Turnout, Election Years 1788–1808

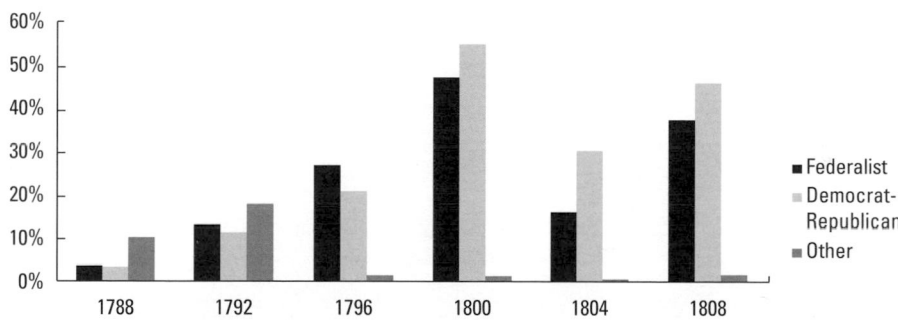

- ■ Federalist
- ▨ Democrat-Republican
- ■ Other

YEAR	VOTING-AGE POPULATION*	FEDERALIST TURNOUT	%	DEMOCRAT-REPUBLICAN TURNOUT	%	OTHER TURNOUT	%
1788	347,000	12,571	3.6%	11,438	3.3%	35,341	10.2%
1792	213,000	28,011	13.2%	24,068	11.3%	37,999	17.8%
1796	280,000	75,135	26.8%	58,390	20.9%	4,154	1.5%
1800	233,000	109,934	47.2%	127,738	54.8%	3,132	1.3%
1804	635,000	102,204	16.1%	191,953	30.2%	4,146	0.7%
1808	593,000	221,592	37.4%	272,173	45.9%	10,051	1.7%

*Voting-age population taken from states with presidential elections

Alternate Graph for Partisan Turnout, Presidential Years, Based on Aggregate House Turnout, 1788–1808

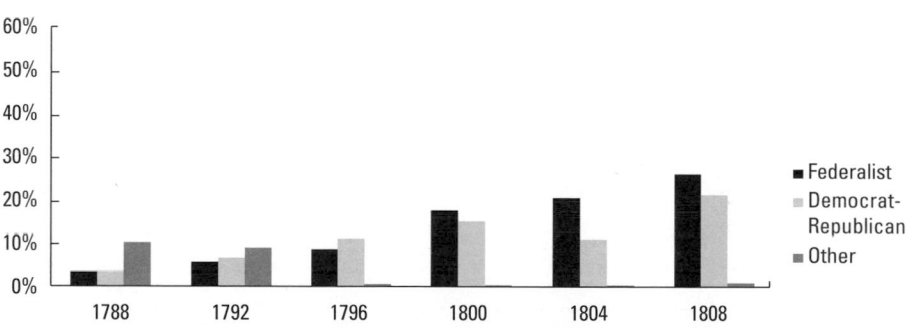

- ■ Federalist
- ▨ Democrat-Republican
- ■ Other

YEAR	VOTING-AGE POPULATION**	FEDERALIST TURNOUT	%	DEMOCRAT-REPUBLICAN TURNOUT	%	OTHER TURNOUT	%
1788	314,000	12,571	3.6%	11,438	4.0%	35,341	11.3%
1792	383,000	28,011	6.3%	24,068	7.3%	37,999	9.9%
1796	611,000	75,135	9.6%	58,390	12.3%	4,154	0.7%
1800	653,000	109,934	19.6%	127,738	16.8%	3,132	0.5%
1804	842,000	102,204	22.8%	191,953	12.1%	4,146	0.5%
1808	941,000	221,592	28.9%	272,173	23.6%	10,051	1.1%

**This is an alternate graph that depicts partisan turnout calculated using voting-age population only from those states that held House elections. For exact percentages, consult the total lines of House partisan charts.

UNITED STATES PRESIDENTIAL GENERAL ELECTIONS

Election Years 1789–1808

State	1789 Voting-age population	Turnout	%	1792 Voting-age population	Turnout	%	Difference from 1789*	1796 Voting-age population	Turnout	%	Difference from 1789	1800 Voting-age population	Turnout	%	Difference from 1789	1804 Voting-age population	Turnout	%	Difference from 1789	1808 Voting-age population	Turnout	%	Difference from 1789
DELAWARE	9,000	685	7.6%																				
KENTUCKY																47,000	5,080	10.8%		58,000	2,733	4.7%	-6.1
MARYLAND	46,000	9,945	21.6%					46,000	13,469	29.3%	7.7	47,000	20,647	43.9%	22.3	49,000	9,762	19.9%	-1.7	51,000	24,219	47.5%	25.9
MASSACHUSETTS	79,000	14,668	18.6%	82,000	19,929	24.3%	5.7	86,000	15,438	18.0%	-0.6					96,000	55,346	57.7%	39.1				
NEW HAMPSHIRE	30,000	5,909	19.7%	32,000	8,924	27.9%	8.2	35,000	18,274	52.2%	32.5					41,000	17,452	42.6%	22.9	43,000	26,750	62.2%	42.5
NEW JERSEY																44,000	13,119	29.8%		47,000	33,172	70.6%	40.8
NORTH CAROLINA												66,000	15,128	22.9%		69,000	1,487	2.2%	-20.8	72,000	18,670	25.9%	3.0
OHIO																23,000	2,866	12.5%		38,000	4,819	12.7%	0.2
PENNSYLVANIA	92,000	7,383	8.0%	99,000	4,619	4.7%	-3.4	113,000	24,745	21.9%	13.9					142,000	23,319	16.4%	8.4	157,000	54,243	34.5%	26.5
RHODE ISLAND												14,000	4,494	32.1%		15,000	1,311	8.7%	-23.4	15,000	5,864	39.1%	7.0
VIRGINIA	91,000	2,453	2.7%									106,000	27,180	25.6%	22.9	109,000	12,879	11.8%	9.1	112,000	19,944	17.8%	15.1
Total	347,000	41,043	11.8%	213,000	33,472	15.7%	3.9	280,000	71,926	25.7%	13.9	233,000	67,449	28.9%	17.1	635,000	142,621	22.5%	10.6	593,000	190,414	32.1%	20.3

*Percentage point difference between turnout in current year and initial year listed in chart. If data do not appear for a state in the initial year listed, the difference is calculated from the first year in which data do appear for that state.

**Georgia cast votes for president in 1796, but the vote tally was 27,000, and the best estimate of eligible population was 16,000, which is why the state's figures are not included for this year.

UNITED STATES PRESIDENTIAL GENERAL ELECTIONS

Federalist Turnout for Election Years 1789–1808

State	1789 Voting-age population	Turnout	%	1792 Voting-age population	Turnout	%	Difference from 1789*	1796 Voting-age population	Turnout	%	Difference from 1789	1800 Voting-age population	Turnout	%	Difference from 1789	1804 Voting-age population	Turnout	%	Difference from 1789	1808 Voting-age population	Turnout	%	Difference from 1789
KENTUCKY																				58,000	54	0.1%	
MARYLAND	46,000	7,665	16.7%					46,000	7,029	15.3%	-1.4	47,000	10,018	21.3%	4.7	49,000	2,461	5.0%	-11.6	51,000	8,873	17.4%	0.7
MASSACHUSETTS	79,000	14,668	18.6%	82,000	19,929	24.3%	5.7									96,000	25,832	26.9%	8.3				
NEW HAMPSHIRE	30,000	5,909	19.7%	32,000	8,924	27.9%	8.2	35,000	18,274	52.2%	32.5					41,000	8,364	20.4%	0.7	43,000	14,006	32.6%	12.9
NEW JERSEY																				47,000	14,684	31.2%	
NORTH CAROLINA												66,000	7,588	11.5%		69,000	431	0.6%	-10.9	72,000	7,798	10.8%	-0.7
OHIO																23,000	384	1.0%		30,000	1,174	3.1%	1.6
PENNSYLVANIA	92,000	6,711	7.3%	99,000	3,358	3.4%	-3.9	113,000	12,229	10.8%	3.5					142,000	1,238	0.9%	-6.4	157,000	11,735	7.5%	0.2
RHODE ISLAND												14,000	2,149	15.4%						15,000	3,172	21.1%	5.8
VIRGINIA												106,000	6,178	5.8%						112,000	758	0.7%	-5.2
Total	247,000	34,953	14.2%	213,000	32,211	15.1%	1.0	194,000	37,532	19.3%	5.2	233,000	25,933	11.1%	-3.0	420,000	38,690	9.2%	-4.9	593,000	62,254	10.5%	-3.7

Democratic-Republican Turnout for Election Years 1789–1808

State	1789 Voting-age population	Turnout	%	1792 Voting-age population	Turnout	%	Difference from 1789*	1796 Voting-age population	Turnout	%	Difference from 1789	1800 Voting-age population	Turnout	%	Difference from 1789	1804 Voting-age population	Turnout	%	Difference from 1789	1808 Voting-age population	Turnout	%	Difference from 1789
KENTUCKY																47,000	5,080	10.8%		58,000	2,679	4.6%	-6.2
MARYLAND	46,000	2,280	5.0%					46,000	6,440	14.0%	9.0	47,000	10,629	22.6%	17.7	49,000	7,301	14.9%	9.9	51,000	15,346	30.1%	25.1
MASSACHUSETTS																96,000	29,514	30.7%					
NEW HAMPSHIRE																41,000	9,088	22.2%		43,000	12,744	29.6%	7.5
NEW JERSEY																44,000	13,119	29.8%		47,000	18,488	39.3%	9.5
NORTH CAROLINA												66,000	7,540	11.4%		69,000	1,056	1.5%	-9.9	72,000	9,733	13.5%	2.1
OHIO																23,000	2,502	10.9%		38,000	3,645	9.6%	-1.3
PENNSYLVANIA	92,000	672	0.7%					113,000	12,516	11.1%	10.3					142,000	22,081	15.6%	14.8	157,000	42,508	27.1%	26.3
RHODE ISLAND												14,000	2,345	16.8%		15,000	1,311	8.7%	-0.0	15,000	2,692	17.9%	1.2
VIRGINIA												106,000	21,002	19.8%		109,000	12,879	11.8%	-8.0	112,000	15,682	14.0%	-5.8
Total	138,000	2,952	2.1%					159,000	18,956	11.9%	9.8	233,000	41,516	17.8%	15.7	635,000	103,931	16.4%	14.2	593,000	123,517	20.8%	18.7

Other Turnout for Election Years 1789–1808

State	1789 Voting-age population	Turnout	%	1792 Voting-age population	Turnout	%	Difference from 1789*	1796 Voting-age population	Turnout	%	Difference from 1789	1800 Voting-age population	Turnout	%	Difference from 1789	1804 Voting-age population	Turnout	%	Difference from 1789	1808 Voting-age population	Turnout	%	Difference from 1789
DELAWARE	9,000	685	7.6%																				
GEORGIA																							
MASSACHUSETTS								86,000	15,438	18.0%													
NORTH CAROLINA																				72,000	1,139	1.6%	
PENNSYLVANIA				99,000	1,261	1.3%																	
VIRGINIA	91,000	2,453	2.7%																	112,000	3,504	3.1%	0.4

*Percentage point difference between turnout in current year and initial year listed in chart. If data do not appear for a state in the initial year listed, the difference is calculated from the first year in which data do appear for that state.

STATE GUBERNATORIAL GENERAL ELECTIONS

Election Years 1788–1808

State	1788 Voting-age population	1788 Turnout	1788 %	1792 Voting-age population	1792 Turnout	1792 %	1792 Difference from 1788*	1796 Voting-age population	1796 Turnout	1796 %	1796 Difference from 1788	1800 Voting-age population	1800 Turnout	1800 %	1800 Difference from 1788	1804 Voting-age population	1804 Turnout	1804 %	1804 Difference from 1788	1808 Voting-age population	1808 Turnout	1808 %	1808 Difference from 1788
CONNECTICUT																54,000	19,312	35.8%		56,000	19,712	35.2%	-0.6
DELAWARE				9,000	4,569	50.8%										10,000	8,441	84.4%	33.6				
KENTUCKY												36,000	21,296	59.2%		47,000	25,917	55.1%	-4.0	58,000	35,996	62.1%	2.9
MASSACHUSETTS	79,000	21,986	27.8%	82,000	15,453	18.8%	-9.0	86,000	26,493	30.8%	3.0	91,000	38,668	42.5%	14.7	96,000	54,007	56.3%	28.4	101,000	80,836	80.0%	52.2
NEW HAMPSHIRE	30,000	8,085	27.0%	32,000	8,092	25.3%	-1.7	35,000	7,809	22.3%	-4.6	38,000	16,401	43.2%	16.2	41,000	24,255	59.2%	32.2	43,000	13,902	32.3%	5.4
NEW YORK				81,000	16,772	20.7%										151,000	52,968	35.1%	14.4				
OHIO																				38,000	16,291	42.9%	
PENNSYLVANIA								113,000	30,020	26.6%										157,000	107,550	68.5%	41.9
VERMONT												32,000	9,683	30.3%		37,000	14,259	38.5%	8.3	42,000	26,409	62.9%	32.6
Total	109,000	30,071	27.6%	204,000	44,886	22.0%	-5.6	234,000	64,322	27.5%	-0.1	197,000	86,048	43.7%	16.1	382,000	179,847	47.1%	19.5	439,000	280,984	64.0%	36.4

*Percentage point difference between turnout in current year and initial year listed in chart. If data do not appear for a state in the initial year listed, the difference is calculated from the first year in which data do appear for that state.

STATE GUBERNATORIAL GENERAL ELECTIONS

Federalist Turnout for Election Years 1788–1808

State	1788 Voting-age population	Turnout	%	1792 Voting-age population	Turnout	%	Difference from 1788*	1796 Voting-age population	Turnout	%	Difference from 1788	1800 Voting-age population	Turnout	%	Difference from 1788	1804 Voting-age population	Turnout	%	Difference from 1788	1808 Voting-age population	Turnout	%	Difference from 1788
CONNECTICUT																54,000	11,398	21.1%		56,000	12,146	21.7%	0.6
DELAWARE																10,000	4,391	43.9%					
MASSACHUSETTS								86,000	11,298	13.1%		91,000	21,649	23.8%	10.7	96,000	30,011	31.3%	18.1	101,000	39,643	39.3%	26.1
NEW HAMPSHIRE								35,000	7,809	22.3%		38,000	10,362	27.3%	5.0	41,000	12,246	29.9%	7.6	43,000	1,261	2.9%	-19.4
NEW YORK				81,000	8,332	10.3%										151,000	30,829	20.4%	10.1				
PENNSYLVANIA																				157,000	39,575	25.2%	
VERMONT												32,000	6,444	20.1%		37,000	8,075	21.8%	1.7	42,000	13,634	32.5%	12.3
Total				81,000	8,332	10.3%		121,000	19,107	15.8%	5.5	161,000	38,455	23.9%	13.6	335,000	85,552	25.5%	15.3	343,000	94,113	27.4%	17.2

Democratic-Republican Turnout for Election Years 1788–1808

State	1788 Voting-age population	Turnout	%	1792 Voting-age population	Turnout	%	Difference from 1788*	1796 Voting-age population	Turnout	%	Difference from 1788	1800 Voting-age population	Turnout	%	Difference from 1788	1804 Voting-age population	Turnout	%	Difference from 1788	1808 Voting-age population	Turnout	%	Difference from 1788
CONNECTICUT																54,000	7,376	13.7%		56,000	7,566	13.5%	-0.1
DELAWARE																10,000	4,050	40.5%					
MASSACHUSETTS												91,000	17,019	18.7%		96,000	23,996	25.0%	6.3	101,000	41,193	40.8%	22.1
NEW HAMPSHIRE												38,000	6,039	15.9%		41,000	12,009	29.3%	13.4	43,000	12,641	29.4%	13.5
NEW YORK				81,000	8,440	10.4%										151,000	22,139	14.7%	4.2				
OHIO																				38,000	16,291	13.5%	
PENNSYLVANIA								113,000	30,020	26.6%										175,000	67,975	38.8%	12.3
VERMONT												32,000	3,239	10.1%		37,000	6,184	16.7%	6.6	42,000	12,775	30.4%	13.7
Total				81,000	8,440	10.4%		113,000	30,020	26.6%	16.1	161,000	26,297	16.3%	5.9	335,000	68,378	20.4%	10.0	399,000	150,875	37.8%	27.4

Other Turnout for Election Years 1788–1808

State	1788 Voting-age population	Turnout	%	1792 Voting-age population	Turnout	%	Difference from 1788*	1796 Voting-age population	Turnout	%	Difference from 1788	1800 Voting-age population	Turnout	%	Difference from 1788	1804 Voting-age population	Turnout	%	Difference from 1788	1808 Voting-age population	Turnout	%	Difference from 1788
DELAWARE				9,000	4,569	50.8%																	
KENTUCKY												36,000	21,296	59.2%		47,000	25,917	55.1%	-4.0	58,000	35,996	62.1%	2.9
MASSACHUSETTS	79,000	21,986	27.8%	82,000	15,453	18.8%	-9.0	86,000	15,195	17.7%	-10.2												
NEW HAMPSHIRE	30,000	8,085	27.0%	32,000	8,092	25.3%	-1.7																

*Percentage point difference between turnout in current year and initial year listed in chart. If data do not appear for a state in the initial year listed, the difference is calculated from the first year in which data do appear for that state.

UNITED STATES HOUSE OF REPRESENTATIVES GENERAL ELECTIONS

Election Years 1788–1808

State	1788 Voting-age population	1788 Turnout	1788 %	1792 Voting-age population	1792 Turnout	1792 %	1792 Difference from 1788*	1796 Voting-age population	1796 Turnout	1796 %	1796 Difference from 1788	1800 Voting-age population	1800 Turnout	1800 %	1800 Difference from 1788	1804 Voting-age population	1804 Turnout	1804 %	1804 Difference from 1788	1808 Voting-age population	1808 Turnout	1808 %	1808 Difference from 1788
CONNECTICUT				51,000	3,344	6.6%		52,000	2,897	5.6%	-1.0	53,000	9,285	17.5%	11.0	54,000	9,956	18.4%	11.9	56,000	13,157	23.5%	16.9
DELAWARE				9,000	4,516	50.2%		10,000	4,071	40.7%	-9.5	10,000	5,014	50.1%	0.0	10,000	8,438	84.4%	34.2	11,000	6,079	55.3%	5.1
GEORGIA				13,000	5,488	42.2%		17,000	10,241	60.2%	18.0	21,000	8,988	42.8%	0.6	24,000	9,903	41.3%	-1.0	28,000	23,883	85.3%	43.1
KENTUCKY																47,000	4,780	10.2%		58,000	9,044	15.6%	5.4
MARYLAND	46,000	7,885	17.1%	46,000	16,733	36.4%	19.2	46,000	12,560	27.3%	10.2					49,000	17,352	35.4%	18.3	51,000	36,451	71.5%	54.3
MASSACHUSETTS	79,000	11,509	14.6%	82,000	10,805	13.2%	-1.4	86,000	17,300	20.1%	5.5	91,000	30,369	33.4%	18.8	96,000	52,829	55.0%	40.5	101,000	68,403	67.7%	53.2
NEW HAMPSHIRE	30,000	5,126	17.1%	32,000	4,462	13.9%	-3.1	35,000	7,291	20.8%	3.7	38,000	9,132	24.0%	6.9	41,000	21,154	51.6%	34.5	43,000	27,293	63.5%	46.4
NEW JERSEY	38,000	17,364	45.7%	38,000	8,577	22.6%	-23.1					41,000	28,903	70.5%	24.8	44,000	13,364	30.4%	-15.3	47,000	33,407	71.1%	25.4
NEW YORK								101,000	27,174	26.9%		121,000	46,632	38.5%	11.6	151,000	69,713	46.2%	19.3	180,000	82,630	45.9%	19.0
NORTH CAROLINA								62,000	11,093	17.9%		66,000	29,485	44.7%	26.8	69,000	28,367	41.1%	23.2	72,000	41,137	57.1%	39.2
OHIO																23,000	5,819	25.3%		38,000	14,794	38.9%	13.6
PENNSYLVANIA	92,000	16,124	17.5%	99,000	35,369	35.7%	18.2	113,000	23,010	20.4%	2.8	127,000	50,781	40.0%	22.5	142,000	36,291	25.6%	8.0	157,000	110,384	70.3%	52.8
RHODE ISLAND				13,000	784	6.0%		13,000	3,716	28.6%	22.6	14,000	3,749	26.8%	20.7	15,000	1,618	10.8%	4.8	15,000	6,175	41.2%	35.1
SOUTH CAROLINA	29,000	1,342	4.6%					35,000	9,798	28.0%	23.4	39,000	7,888	20.2%	15.6	40,000	2,877	7.2%	2.6	42,000	4,699	11.2%	6.6
TENNESSEE								14,000	1,125	8.0%													
VERMONT								27,000	7,403	27.4%		32,000	10,578	33.1%	5.6	37,000	15,842	42.8%	15.4	42,000	26,280	62.6%	35.2
Total	314,000	59,350	18.9%	383,000	90,078	23.5%	4.6	611,000	137,679	22.5%	3.6	653,000	240,804	36.9%	18.0	842,000	298,303	35.4%	16.5	941,000	503,816	53.5%	34.6

*Percentage point difference between turnout in current year and initial year listed in chart. If data do not appear for a state in the initial year listed, the difference is calculated from the first year in which data do appear for that state.

UNITED STATES HOUSE OF REPRESENTATIVES GENERAL ELECTIONS

Federalist Turnout for Election Years 1788–1808

	1788			1792				1796				1800				1804				1808			
State	Voting-age population	Turnout	%	Voting-age population	Turnout	%	Difference from 1788*	Voting-age population	Turnout	%	Difference from 1788	Voting-age population	Turnout	%	Difference from 1788	Voting-age population	Turnout	%	Difference from 1788	Voting-age population	Turnout	%	Difference from 1788
CONNECTICUT								52,000	2,494	4.8%		53,000	6,273	11.8%	7.0	54,000	9,956	18.4%	13.6	56,000	8,949	16.0%	11.2
DELAWARE								10,000	2,292	22.9%		10,000	2,674	26.7%	3.8	10,000	4,398	44.0%	21.1	11,000	3,242	29.5%	6.6
GEORGIA								17,000	3,104	18.3%										28,000	4,838	17.3%	-1.0
MARYLAND	46,000	5,154	11.2%	46,000	10,014	21.8%	10.6	46,000	7,826	17.0%	5.8					49,000	4,514	9.2%	-2.0	51,000	16,209	31.8%	20.6
MASSACHUSETTS								86,000	11,219	13.0%		91,000	15,938	17.5%	4.5	96,000	24,548	25.6%	12.5	101,000	35,895	35.5%	22.5
NEW HAMPSHIRE								35,000	5,822	16.6%		38,000	5,472	14.4%	-2.2	41,000	10,979	26.8%	10.1	43,000	15,022	34.9%	18.3
NEW JERSEY												41,000	14,177	34.6%		44,000	136	0.3%	-34.3	47,000	14,702	31.3%	-3.3
NEW YORK								101,000	16,692	16.5%		121,000	23,401	19.3%	2.8	151,000	25,385	16.8%	0.3	180,000	40,116	22.3%	5.8
NORTH CAROLINA								62,000	5,217	8.4%		66,000	15,411	23.4%	14.9	69,000	6,957	10.1%	1.7	72,000	17,268	24.0%	15.6
OHIO																23,000	1,718	7.5%		38,000	4,485	11.8%	4.3
PENNSYLVANIA	92,000	7,417	8.1%	99,000	17,997	18.2%	10.1	113,000	11,046	9.8%	1.7	127,000	16,929	13.3%	5.3	142,000	6,007	4.2%	-3.8	157,000	44,304	28.2%	20.2
RHODE ISLAND												14,000	1,243	8.9%						15,000	3,272	21.8%	12.9
SOUTH CAROLINA								35,000	5,435	15.5%		39,000	3,525	9.0%	-6.5	40,000	411	1.0%	-14.5	42,000	479	1.1%	-14.4
VERMONT								27,000	3,988	14.8%		32,000	4,891	15.3%	0.5	37,000	7,195	19.4%	4.7	42,000	12,811	30.5%	15.7
Total	138,000	12,571	9.1%	145,000	28,011	19.3%	10.2	584,000	75,135	12.9%	3.8	632,000	109,934	17.4%	8.3	756,000	102,204	13.5%	4.4	883,000	221,592	25.1%	16.0

Democratic-Republican Turnout for Election Years 1788–1808

	1788			1792				1796				1800				1804				1808			
State	Voting-age population	Turnout	%	Voting-age population	Turnout	%	Difference from 1788*	Voting-age population	Turnout	%	Difference from 1788	Voting-age population	Turnout	%	Difference from 1788	Voting-age population	Turnout	%	Difference from 1788	Voting-age population	Turnout	%	Difference from 1788
CONNECTICUT								52,000	403	0.8%		53,000	3,012	5.7%	4.9					56,000	4,208	7.5%	6.7
DELAWARE								10,000	1,779	17.8%		10,000	2,340	23.4%	5.6	10,000	4,040	40.4%	22.6	11,000	2,837	25.8%	8.0
GEORGIA								17,000	5,392	31.7%		21,000	8,988	42.8%	11.1	24,000	9,903	41.3%	9.5	28,000	12,805	45.7%	14.0
KENTUCKY																47,000	4,780	10.2%		57,000	7,581	13.3%	3.1
MARYLAND	46,000	2,731	5.9%	46,000	6,696	14.6%	8.6	46,000	4,734	10.3%	4.4					49,000	12,778	26.1%	20.1	51,000	20,242	39.7%	33.8
MASSACHUSETTS								86,000	4,799	5.6%		91,000	13,630	15.0%	9.4	96,000	27,815	29.0%	23.4	101,000	32,429	32.1%	26.5
NEW HAMPSHIRE								35,000	978	2.8%		38,000	1,777	4.7%	1.9	41,000	10,175	24.8%	22.0	43,000	12,271	28.5%	25.7
NEW JERSEY												41,000	14,726	35.9%		44,000	13,228	30.1%	-5.9	47,000	18,705	39.8%	3.9
NEW YORK								101,000	10,255	10.2%		121,000	23,042	19.0%	8.9	151,000	43,932	29.1%	18.9	180,000	41,290	22.9%	12.8
NORTH CAROLINA								62,000	5,876	9.5%		66,000	14,074	21.3%	11.8	69,000	21,310	30.9%	21.4	72,000	23,869	33.2%	23.7
OHIO																23,000	4,101	17.8%		38,000	10,309	27.1%	9.3
PENNSYLVANIA	92,000	8,707	9.5%	99,000	17,372	17.5%	8.1	113,000	11,887	10.5%	1.1	127,000	33,852	26.7%	17.2	142,000	27,574	19.4%	10.0	157,000	66,080	42.1%	32.6
RHODE ISLAND								13,000	3,716	28.6%		14,000	2,506	17.9%	-10.7	15,000	1,618	10.8%	-7.1	15,000	2,903	19.4%	1.5
SOUTH CAROLINA								35,000	4,363	12.5%		39,000	4,363	11.2%	-1.3	40,000	2,466	6.2%	-6.3	42,000	3,765	9.0%	-3.5

United States House of Representatives General Elections (continued)

United States House of Representatives General Elections (continued)

Democratic-Republican Turnout for Election Years 1788–1808 (continued)

State	1788 Voting-age population	Turnout	%	1792 Voting-age population	Turnout	%	Difference from 1788	1796 Voting-age population	Turnout	%	Difference from 1788	1800 Voting-age population	Turnout	%	Difference from 1788	1804 Voting-age population	Turnout	%	Difference from 1788	1808 Voting-age population	Turnout	%	Difference from 1788
TENNESSEE								14,000	1,113	8.0%													
VERMONT								27,000	3,095	11.5%		32,000	5,428	17.0%	5.5	37,000	8,233	22.3%	10.8	42,000	12,879	30.7%	19.2
Total	138,000	11,438	8.3%	145,000	24,068	16.6%	8.3	611,000	58,390	9.6%	1.3	653,000	127,738	19.6%	11.3	788,000	191,953	24.4%	16.1	940,000	272,173	29.0%	20.7

Other Turnout for Election Years 1788–1808

State	1788 Voting-age population	Turnout	%	1792 Voting-age population	Turnout	%	Difference from 1788*	1796 Voting-age population	Turnout	%	Difference from 1788	1800 Voting-age population	Turnout	%	Difference from 1788	1804 Voting-age population	Turnout	%	Difference from 1788	1808 Voting-age population	Turnout	%	Difference from 1788
CONNECTICUT				51,000	3,344	6.6%																	
DELAWARE				9,000	4,516	50.2%																	
GEORGIA				13,000	5,488	42.2%		17,000	1,745	10.3%	-32.0									28,000	6,240	22.3%	-19.9
KENTUCKY																				58,000	1,463	2.5%	
MARYLAND				46,000	23	0.1%										49,000	60	0.1%	0.1				
MASSACHUSETTS	79,000	11,509	14.6%	82,000	10,805	13.2%	-1.4	86,000	1,282	1.5%	-13.1	91,000	801	0.9%	-13.7	96,000	466	0.5%	-14.1	101,000	79	0.1%	-14.5
NEW HAMPSHIRE	30,000	5,126	17.1%	32,000	4,462	13.9%	-3.1	35,000	491	1.4%	-15.7	38,000	1,883	5.0%	-12.1								
NEW JERSEY	38,000	17,364	45.7%	38,000	8,577	22.6%	-23.1																
NEW YORK								101,000	227	0.2%		121,000	189	0.2%	-0.1	151,000	396	0.3%	0.0	180,000	1,224	0.7%	0.5
NORTH CAROLINA																69,000	100	0.1%					
PENNSYLVANIA								113,000	77	0.1%						142,000	2,710	1.9%	1.8				
RHODE ISLAND				13,000	784	6.0%																	
SOUTH CAROLINA	29,000	1,342	4.6%																	42,000	455	1.1%	-3.5
TENNESSEE								14,000	12	0.1%													
VERMONT								27,000	320	1.2%		32,000	259	0.8%	-0.4	37,000	414	1.1%	-0.1	42,000	590	1.4%	0.2
Total	176,000	35,341	20.1%	284,000	37,999	13.4%	-6.7	393,000	4,154	1.1%	-19.0	282,000	3,132	1.1%	-19.0	544,000	4,146	0.8%	-19.3	451,000	10,051	2.2%	-17.9

*Percentage point difference between turnout in current year and initial year listed in chart. If data do not appear for a state in the initial year listed, the difference is calculated from the first year in which data do appear for that state.

Midterm Turnout Election Based on Aggregate House of Representatives Turnout, Election Years 1790–1806

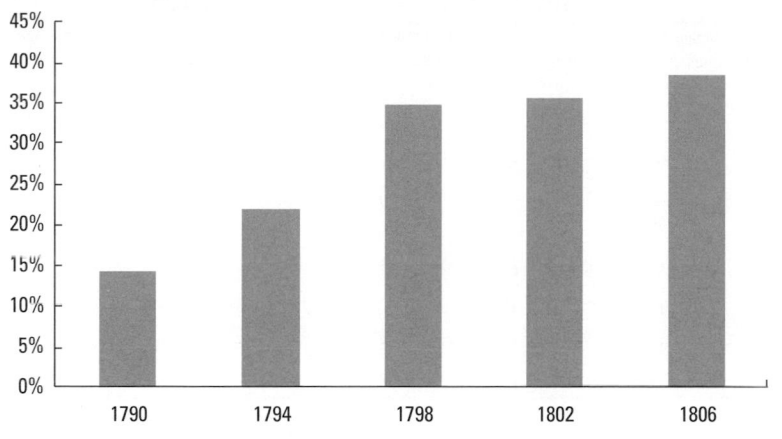

YEAR	VOTING-AGE POPULATION	TOTAL	%
1790	425,000	60,903	14.3%
1794	546,000	120,134	22.0%
1798	667,000	232,711	34.9%
1802	537,000	191,765	35.7%
1806	896,000	345,740	38.6%

Partisan Turnout Midterm Election Based on Aggregate House of Representatives Turnout, Election Years 1790–1806

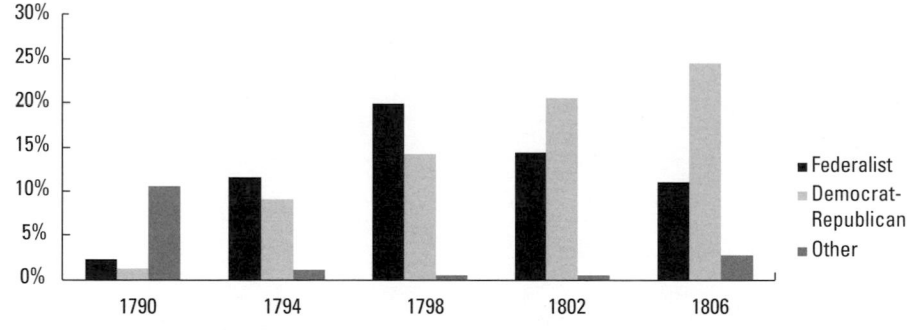

■ Federalist
■ Democrat-Republican
■ Other

YEAR	VOTING AGE POPULATION*	FEDERALIST TURNOUT	%	DEMOCRAT-REPUBLICAN TURNOUT	%	OTHER TURNOUT	%
1790	425,000	10,061	2.4%	5,601	1.3%	45,241	10.6%
1794	546,000	63,666	11.7%	50,081	9.2%	6,387	1.2%
1798	667,000	133,509	20.0%	95,420	14.3%	3,782	0.6%
1802	537,000	77,729	14.5%	110,995	20.7%	3,041	0.6%
1806	896,000	99,613	11.1%	220,612	24.6%	25,515	2.8%

*Voting-age population in all states with House elections in years listed.

STATE GUBERNATORIAL GENERAL ELECTIONS

Election Years 1790–1806

State	1790			1794				1798				1802				1806			
	Voting-age population	Turnout	%	Voting-age population	Turnout	%	Difference from 1790*	Voting-age population	Turnout	%	Difference from 1790	Voting-age population	Turnout	%	Difference from 1790	Voting-age population	Turnout	%	Difference from 1790
CONNECTICUT												54,000	15,921	29.5%		55,000	22,873	41.6%	12.1
DELAWARE								10,000	4,558	45.6%									
MASSACHUSETTS	79,000	16,163	20.5%	84,000	21,624	25.7%	5.3	88,000	20,178	22.9%	2.5	93,000	49,426	53.1%	32.7	99,000	74,849	75.6%	55.1
NEW HAMPSHIRE	30,000	7,234	24.1%	33,000	7,629	23.1%	-1.0	36,000	11,320	31.4%	7.3	39,000	19,130	49.1%	24.9	42,000	18,550	44.2%	20.1
NEW YORK								110,000	29,644	26.9%									
PENNSYLVANIA	92,000	30,527	33.2%									134,000	64,886	48.4%	15.2				
RHODE ISLAND												14,000	5,736	41.0%		15,000	3,853	25.7%	-15.3
VERMONT				24,000	4,643	19.3%		29,000	9,016	31.1%	11.7	34,000	12,908	38.0%	18.6	39,000	16,676	42.8%	23.4
Total	201,000	53,924	26.8%	141,000	33,896	24.0%	-2.8	273,000	74,716	27.4%	0.5	314,000	152,086	48.4%	21.6	195,000	113,928	58.4%	31.6

*Percentage point difference between turnout in current year and initial year listed in chart. If data do not appear for a state in the initial year listed, the difference is calculated from the first year in which data do appear for that state.

STATE GUBERNATORIAL GENERAL ELECTIONS

Federalist Turnout for Election Years 1790–1806

State	1790 Voting-age population	Turnout	%	1794 Voting-age population	Turnout	%	Difference from 1790*	1798 Voting-age population	Turnout	%	Difference from 1790	1802 Voting-age population	Turnout	%	Difference from 1790	1806 Voting-age population	Turnout	%	Difference from 1790
CONNECTICUT												54,000	11,398	**21.1%**		55,000	13,413	**24.4%**	3.3
DELAWARE								10,000	2,490	**24.9%**									
MASSACHUSETTS								88,000	18,245	**20.7%**		93,000	29,983	**32.2%**	11.5	99,000	37,740	**38.1%**	17.4
NEW HAMPSHIRE								36,000	9,397	**26.1%**		39,000	10,377	**26.6%**	0.5	42,000	3,273	**7.8%**	-18.3
NEW YORK								110,000	16,012	**14.6%**									
PENNSYLVANIA	92,000	2,802	**3.0%**									134,000	17,037	**12.7%**	9.7				
RHODE ISLAND																15,000	1,662	**11.1%**	
VERMONT								29,000	6,211	**21.4%**		34,000	7,823	**23.0%**	1.6	39,000	9,435	**24.2%**	2.8
Total	92,000	2,802	**3.0%**					273,000	52,355	**19.2%**	16.1	300,000	65,220	**21.7%**	18.7	195,000	52,110	**26.7%**	23.7

Democratic-Republican Turnout for Election Years 1790–1806

State	1790 Voting-age population	Turnout	%	1794 Voting-age population	Turnout	%	Difference from 1790*	1798 Voting-age population	Turnout	%	Difference from 1790	1802 Voting-age population	Turnout	%	Difference from 1790	1806 Voting-age population	Turnout	%	Difference from 1790
CONNECTICUT												54,000	4,523	**8.4%**		55,000	9,460	**17.2%**	8.8
DELAWARE								10,000	2,068	**20.7%**									
MASSACHUSETTS								88,000	1,933	**2.2%**		93,000	19,443	**20.9%**	18.7	99,000	37,109	**37.5%**	35.3
NEW HAMPSHIRE								36,000	1,189	**3.3%**		39,000	8,753	**22.4%**	19.1	42,000	15,277	**36.4%**	33.1
NEW YORK								110,000	13,632	**12.4%**									
PENNSYLVANIA												134,000	47,849	**35.7%**					
RHODE ISLAND																15,000	2,191	**14.6%**	
VERMONT								29,000	2,805	**9.7%**		34,000	5,085	**15.0%**	5.3	39,000	7,241	**18.6%**	8.9
Total								273,000	21,627	**7.9%**		300,000	81,130	**27.0%**	19.1	195,000	61,818	**31.7%**	23.8

Other Turnout for Election Years 1790–1806

State	1790 Voting-age population	Turnout	%	1794 Voting-age population	Turnout	%	Difference from 1790*	1798 Voting-age population	Turnout	%	Difference from 1790	1802 Voting-age population	Turnout	%	Difference from 1790	1806 Voting-age population	Turnout	%	Difference from 1790
MASSACHUSETTS	79,000	16,163	**20.5%**	84,000	21,624	**25.7%**	5.3												
NEW HAMPSHIRE	30,000	7,234	**24.1%**	33,000	7,629	**23.1%**	-1.0	36,000	734	**2.0%**	-22.1								
PENNSYLVANIA	92,000	27,725	**30.1%**																
RHODE ISLAND												14,000	5,736	**41.0%**					
VERMONT				24,000	4,643	**19.3%**													

*Percentage point difference between turnout in current year and initial year listed in chart. If data do not appear for a state in the initial year listed, the difference is calculated from the first year in which data do appear for that state.

UNITED STATES HOUSE OF REPRESENTATIVES GENERAL ELECTIONS

Election Years 1790–1806

State	1790 Voting-age population	Turnout	%	1794 Voting-age population	Turnout	%	Difference from 1790*	1798 Voting-age population	Turnout	%	Difference from 1790	1802 Voting-age population	Turnout	%	Difference from 1790	1806 Voting-age population	Turnout	%	Difference from 1790
CONNECTICUT	51,000	2,969	5.8%	52,000	3,912	7.5%	1.7	53,000	5,299	10.0%	4.2	54,000	8,743	16.2%	10.4	55,000	15,109	27.5%	21.6
DELAWARE				10,000	4,694	46.9%		10,000	4,564	45.6%	-1.3	10,000	6,827	68.3%	21.3	11,000	3,888	35.3%	-11.6
GEORGIA				15,000	3,780	25.2%		19,000	7,166	37.7%	12.5	23,000	10,677	46.4%	21.2	26,000	12,700	48.8%	23.6
KENTUCKY																52,000	22,464	43.2%	
MARYLAND	46,000	17,173	37.3%	46,000	16,066	34.9%	-2.4	47,000	22,437	47.7%	10.4					50,000	30,836	61.7%	24.3
MASSACHUSETTS	79,000	14,235	18.0%	84,000	16,092	19.2%	1.1	88,000	22,859	26.0%	8.0	93,000	32,824	35.3%	17.3	99,000	38,445	38.8%	20.8
NEW HAMPSHIRE	30,000	3,585	12.0%	33,000	6,957	21.1%	9.1	36,000	7,160	19.9%	7.9	39,000	11,576	29.7%	17.7	42,000	10,177	24.2%	12.3
NEW JERSEY				39,000	8,747	22.4%		40,000	19,167	47.9%	25.5					45,000	20,441	45.4%	23.0
NEW YORK	71,000	10,685	15.0%	91,000	23,642	26.0%	10.9	110,000	36,832	33.5%	18.4	136,000	45,167	33.2%	18.2	165,000	60,517	36.7%	21.6
NORTH CAROLINA	57,000	5,638	9.9%					64,000	27,687	43.3%	33.4					70,000	28,236	40.3%	30.4
OHIO																36,000	9,099	25.3%	
PENNSYLVANIA				106,000	24,705	23.3%		120,000	53,048	44.2%	20.9	134,000	62,209	46.4%	23.1	150,000	60,500	40.3%	17.0
RHODE ISLAND				13,000	3,089	23.8%		14,000	4,095	29.3%	5.5	14,000	4,250	30.4%	6.6	15,000	3,587	23.9%	0.2
SOUTH CAROLINA				33,000	3,732	11.3%		37,000	11,624	31.4%	20.1					41,000	16,456	40.1%	28.8
VERMONT				24,000	4,718	19.7%		29,000	10,773	37.1%	17.5	34,000	9,492	27.9%	8.3	39,000	13,285	34.1%	14.4
VIRGINIA	91,000	6,618	7.3%																
Total	425,000	60,903	14.3%	546,000	120,134	22.0%	7.7	667,000	232,711	34.9%	20.6	537,000	191,765	35.7%	21.4	896,000	345,740	38.6%	24.3

*Percentage point difference between turnout in current year and initial year listed in chart. If data do not appear for a state in the initial year listed, the difference is calculated from the first year in which data do appear for that state.

UNITED STATES HOUSE OF REPRESENTATIVES GENERAL ELECTIONS

Federalist Turnout for Election Years 1790–1806

State	1790			1794				1798				1802				1806			
	Voting-age population	Turnout	%	Voting-age population	Turnout	%	Difference from 1790*	Voting-age population	Turnout	%	Difference from 1790	Voting-age population	Turnout	%	Difference from 1790	Voting-age population	Turnout	%	Difference from 1790
CONNECTICUT				52,000	3,912	7.5%		53,000	5,299	10.0%	2.5	54,000	8,743	16.2%	8.7	55,000	9,326	17.0%	9.4
DELAWARE				10,000	2,285	22.9%		10,000	2,792	27.9%	5.1	10,000	3,406	34.1%	11.2	11,000	2,353	21.4%	-1.5
GEORGIA				15,000	1,150	7.7%		19,000	4,055	21.3%	13.7	23,000	2,539	11.0%	3.4				
MARYLAND				46,000	9,533	20.7%		47,000	11,719	24.9%	4.2					50,000	8,240	16.5%	-4.2
MASSACHUSETTS				84,000	9,426	11.2%		88,000	15,124	17.2%	6.0	93,000	17,790	19.1%	7.9	99,000	18,300	18.5%	7.3
NEW HAMPSHIRE				33,000	3,782	11.5%		36,000	5,776	16.0%	4.6	39,000	6,135	15.7%	4.3	42,000	3,685	8.8%	-2.7
NEW JERSEY				39,000	5,630	14.4%		40,000	9,132	22.8%	8.4					45,000	5,789	12.9%	-1.6
NEW YORK	71,000	7,154	10.1%	91,000	12,124	13.3%	3.2	110,000	20,035	18.2%	8.1	136,000	17,839	13.1%	3.0	165,000	23,160	14.0%	4.0
NORTH CAROLINA	57,000	2,907	5.1%					64,000	14,853	23.2%	18.1					70,000	4,410	6.3%	1.2
OHIO																36,000	2,364	6.6%	
PENNSYLVANIA				106,000	10,167	9.6%		120,000	28,481	23.7%	14.1	133,000	14,265	10.7%	1.1	150,000	11,412	7.6%	-2.0
RHODE ISLAND				13,000	1,911	14.7%		14,000	2,680	19.1%	4.4	14,000	1,644	11.7%	-3.0	15,000	1,483	9.9%	-4.8
SOUTH CAROLINA				33,000	2,591	7.9%		37,000	7,161	19.4%	11.5					41,000	2,993	7.3%	-0.6
VERMONT				24,000	1,155	4.8%		29,000	6,402	22.1%	17.3	34,000	5,368	15.8%	11.0	39,000	6,098	15.6%	10.8
Total	128,000	10,061	7.9%	546,000	63,666	11.7%	3.8	667,000	133,509	20.0%	12.2	536,000	77,729	14.5%	6.6	818,000	99,613	12.2%	4.3

Democratic-Republican Turnout for Election Years 1790–1806

State	1790			1794				1798				1802				1806			
	Voting-age population	Turnout	%	Voting-age population	Turnout	%	Difference from 1790*	Voting-age population	Turnout	%	Difference from 1790	Voting-age population	Turnout	%	Difference from 1790	Voting-age population	Turnout	%	Difference from 1790
CONNECTICUT																55,000	5,783	10.5%	
DELAWARE				10,000	2,409	24.1%		10,000	1,772	17.7%	-6.4	10,000	3,421	34.2%	10.1	11,000	1,212	11.0%	-13.1
GEORGIA				15,000	1,487	9.9%		19,000	3,111	16.4%	6.5	23,000	8,138	35.4%	25.5	26,000	12,700	48.8%	38.9
KENTUCKY																52,000	19,203	36.9%	
MARYLAND				46,000	6,533	14.2%		47,000	10,718	22.8%	8.6					50,000	22,243	44.5%	30.3
MASSACHUSETTS				84,000	6,666	7.9%		88,000	5,832	6.6%	-1.3	93,000	14,887	16.0%	8.1	99,000	20,051	20.3%	12.3
NEW HAMPSHIRE				33,000	3,175	9.6%		36,000	167	0.5%	-9.2	39,000	4,104	10.5%	0.9	42,000	5,773	13.7%	4.1
NEW JERSEY								40,000	10,035	25.1%						45,000	14,652	32.6%	7.5
NEW YORK	71,000	3,132	4.4%	91,000	11,391	12.5%	8.1	110,000	16,788	15.3%	10.9	136,000	25,946	19.1%	14.7	165,000	34,397	20.8%	16.4
NORTH CAROLINA	57,000	2,469	4.3%					64,000	12,834	20.1%	15.7					70,000	23,693	33.8%	29.5
OHIO																36,000	6,735	18.7%	
PENNSYLVANIA				106,000	14,343	13.5%		120,000	24,567	20.5%	6.9	133,000	47,944	36.0%	22.5	150,000	32,928	22.0%	8.4

United States House of Representatives General Elections (continued)

United States House of Representatives General Elections *(continued)*

Democratic-Republican Turnout for Election Years 1790–1806 *(continued)*

State	1790			1794				1798				1802				1806			
	Voting-age population	Turnout	%	Voting-age population	Turnout	%	Difference from 1790	Voting-age population	Turnout	%	Difference from 1790	Voting-age population	Turnout	%	Difference from 1790	Voting-age population	Turnout	%	Difference from 1790
RHODE ISLAND				13,000	1,178	9.1%		14,000	1,415	10.1%	1.0	14,000	2,606	18.6%	9.6	15,000	1,794	12.0%	2.9
SOUTH CAROLINA								37,000	4,463	12.1%						41,000	13,463	32.8%	20.8
VERMONT				24,000	2,899	12.1%		29,000	3,718	12.8%	0.7	34,000	3,949	11.6%	-0.5	39,000	5,985	15.3%	3.3
Total	128,000	5,601	4.4%	422,000	50,081	11.9%	7.5	614,000	95,420	15.5%	11.2	482,000	110,995	23.0%	18.7	896,000	220,612	24.6%	20.2

Other Turnout for Election Years 1790–1806

State	1790			1794				1798				1802				1806			
	Voting-age population	Turnout	%	Voting-age population	Turnout	%	Difference from 1790*	Voting-age population	Turnout	%	Difference from 1790	Voting-age population	Turnout	%	Difference from 1790	Voting-age population	Turnout	%	Difference from 1790
CONNECTICUT	51,000	2,969	5.8%																
DELAWARE																11,000	323	2.9%	
GEORGIA				15,000	1,143	7.6%													
KENTUCKY																52,000	3,261	6.3%	
MARYLAND	46,000	17,173	37.3%													50,000	353	0.7%	-36.6
MASSACHUSETTS	79,000	14,235	18.0%					88,000	1,903	2.2%	-15.9	93,000	147	0.2%	-17.9	99,000	94	0.1%	-17.9
NEW HAMPSHIRE	30,000	3,585	12.0%					36,000	1,217	3.4%	-8.6	39,000	1,337	3.4%	-8.5	42,000	719	1.7%	-10.2
NEW JERSEY				39,000	3,117	8.0%													
NEW YORK	71,000	399	0.6%	91,000	127	0.1%	-0.4	108,000	9	0.0%	-0.6	133,000	1,382	1.0%	0.5	165,000	2,960	1.8%	1.2
NORTH CAROLINA	57,000	262	0.5%													70,000	133	0.2%	-0.3
PENNSYLVANIA				106,000	195	0.2%										150,000	16,160	10.8%	10.6
RHODE ISLAND																15,000	310	2.1%	
SOUTH CAROLINA				33,000	1,141	3.5%													
VERMONT				24,000	664	2.8%		29,000	653	2.3%	-0.5	34,000	175	0.5%	-2.3	39,000	1,202	3.1%	0.3
VIRGINIA	91,000	6,618	7.3%																
Total	425,000	45,241	10.6%	308,000	6,387	2.1%	-8.6	261,000	3,782	1.4%	-9.2	299,000	3,041	1.0%	-9.6	693,000	25,515	3.7%	-7.0

*Percentage point difference between turnout in current year and initial year listed in chart. If data do not appear for a state in the initial year listed, the difference is calculated from the first year in which data do appear for that state.

STATE GUBERNATORIAL GENERAL ELECTIONS
Election Years 1789–1809

State	1789 Voting-age population	Turnout	%	1791 Voting-age population	Turnout	%	Difference from 1789*	1793 Voting-age population	Turnout	%	Difference from 1789	1795 Voting-age population	Turnout	%	Difference from 1789	1797 Voting-age population	Turnout	%	Difference from 1789	1799 Voting-age population	Turnout	%	Difference from 1789
CONNECTICUT																							
DELAWARE												10,000	4,494	44.9%									
MASSACHUSETTS	77,000	20,721	26.9%	80,000	15,996	20.0%	-6.9	83,000	16,428	19.8%	-7.1	85,000	15,976	18.8%	-8.1	87,000	25,218	29.0%	2.1	89,000	32,763	36.8%	9.9
NEW HAMPSHIRE	29,000	8,113	28.0%	31,000	8,679	28.0%	0.0	32,000	9,402	29.4%	1.4	34,000	9,340	27.5%	-0.5	35,000	9,625	27.5%	-0.5	36,000	10,138	28.2%	0.2
NEW YORK	68,000	12,353	18.2%									96,000	25,373	26.4%	8.3								
OHIO																							
PENNSYLVANIA								103,000	29,296	28.4%										123,000	69,887	56.8%	28.4
RHODE ISLAND																14,000	1,204	8.6%					
TENNESSEE																				16,000	5,295	33.1%	
VERMONT								23,000	5,896	25.6%		25,000	6,298	25.2%	-0.4					30,000	11,369	37.9%	12.3
Total	174,000	41,187	23.7%	111,000	24,675	22.2%	-1.4	241,000	61,022	25.3%	1.6	250,000	61,481	24.6%	0.9	136,000	36,047	26.5%	2.8	294,000	129,452	44.0%	20.4

State	1801 Voting-age population	Turnout	%	Difference from 1789	1803 Voting-age population	Turnout	%	Difference from 1789	1805 Voting-age population	Turnout	%	Difference from 1789	1807 Voting-age population	Turnout	%	Difference from 1789	1809 Voting-age population	Turnout	%	Difference from 1789
CONNECTICUT	53,000	12,212	23.0%		54,000	22,223	41.2%	18.1	55,000	21,912	39.8%	16.8	55,000	19,930	36.2%	13.2	56,000	22,809	40.7%	17.7
DELAWARE	10,000	6,932	69.3%	24.4									11,000	6,371	57.9%	13.0				
MASSACHUSETTS	92,000	45,636	49.6%	22.7	95,000	43,109	45.4%	18.5	97,000	68,722	70.8%	43.9	100,000	81,178	81.2%	54.3	103,000	93,034	90.3%	63.4
NEW HAMPSHIRE	38,000	16,147	42.5%	14.5	40,000	21,274	53.2%	25.2	41,000	28,384	69.2%	41.3	43,000	13,912	32.4%	4.4	44,000	30,851	70.1%	42.1
NEW YORK	129,000	45,651	35.4%	17.2									173,000	66,063	38.2%	20.0				
OHIO					19,000	4,060	25.6%		27,000	4,783	17.7%	7.9	34,000	5,616	16.5%	-9.1				
PENNSYLVANIA									146,000	82,477	56.5%	28.0								
RHODE ISLAND	14,000	3,760	26.9%	18.3									15,000	3,832	25.5%	16.9				
TENNESSEE	23,000	8,438	36.7%	3.6	25,000	11,709	46.8%	13.7	29,000	16,148	55.7%	22.6					39,000	22,121	56.7%	23.6
VERMONT					35,000	13,348	38.1%	12.5	38,000	13,738	36.2%	10.5	40,000	18,474	46.2%	20.6	43,000	28,050	65.2%	39.6
Total	359,000	138,776	38.7%	15.0	268,000	116,523	43.5%	19.8	433,000	236,164	54.5%	30.9	471,000	215,376	45.7%	22.1	285,000	196,865	69.1%	45.4

*Percentage point difference between turnout in current year and initial year listed in chart. If data do not appear for a state in the initial year listed, the difference is calculated from the first year in which data do appear for that state.

STATE GUBERNATORIAL GENERAL ELECTIONS

Federalist Turnout for Election Years 1789–1809

State	1789 Voting-age population	Turnout	%	1791 Voting-age population	Turnout	%	1793 Voting-age population	Turnout	%	Difference from 1793*	1795 Voting-age population	Turnout	%	Difference from 1793	1797 Voting-age population	Turnout	%	Difference from 1793	1799 Voting-age population	Turnout	%	Difference from 1793
CONNECTICUT																						
DELAWARE																						
MASSACHUSETTS															87,000	18,093	20.8%		89,000	24,069	27.0%	6.2
NEW HAMPSHIRE															35,000	9,625	27.5%		36,000	10,138	28.2%	0.7
NEW YORK											96,000	13,481	14.0%									
PENNSYLVANIA							103,000	10,706	10.4%										123,000	32,643	26.5%	16.1
VERMONT																			30,000	7,454	24.8%	

State	1801 Voting-age population	Turnout	%	Difference from 1793	1803 Voting-age population	Turnout	%	Difference from 1793	1805 Voting-age population	Turnout	%	Difference from 1793	1807 Voting-age population	Turnout	%	Difference from 1793	1809 Voting-age population	Turnout	%	Difference from 1793
CONNECTICUT					54,000	14,375	26.6%		55,000	13,689	24.9%	-1.7	55,000	11,959	21.7%	-4.9	56,000	14,650	26.2%	-0.5
DELAWARE	10,000	3,457	34.6%										11,000	3,309	30.1%	-4.5				
MASSACHUSETTS	92,000	25,452	27.7%	6.9	95,000	29,199	30.7%	9.9	97,000	35,204	36.3%	15.5	100,000	39,224	39.2%	18.4	103,000	47,916	46.5%	25.7
NEW HAMPSHIRE	38,000	10,898	28.7%	1.2	40,000	12,263	30.7%	3.2	41,000	12,287	30.0%	2.5					44,000	15,610	35.5%	8.0
NEW YORK	129,000	20,843	16.2%	2.1																
PENNSYLVANIA																				
VERMONT					35,000	7,940	22.7%	-2.2	38,000	8,682	22.8%	-2.0	40,000	8,571	21.4%	-3.4	43,000	13,467	31.3%	6.5

Democratic-Republican Turnout for Election Years 1789–1809

State	1789 Voting-age population	Turnout	%	1791 Voting-age population	Turnout	%	1793 Voting-age population	Turnout	%	1795 Voting-age population	Turnout	%	Difference from 1793	1797 Voting-age population	Turnout	%	Difference from 1793	1799 Voting-age population	Turnout	%	Difference from 1793
CONNECTICUT																					
DELAWARE																					
MASSACHUSETTS														87,000	7,125	8.2%		89,000	8,694	9.8%	
NEW HAMPSHIRE																					
NEW YORK										96,000	11,892	12.4%									
OHIO																					
PENNSYLVANIA							103,000	18,590	18.0%									123,000	37,244	30.3%	12.2
VERMONT																		30,000	3,915	13.1%	

State Gubernatorial General Elections (continued)

Democratic-Republican Turnout for Election Years 1789–1809 (continued)

State	1801 Voting-age population	1801 Turnout	1801 %	1801 Difference from 1793	1803 Voting-age population	1803 Turnout	1803 %	1803 Difference from 1793	1805 Voting-age population	1805 Turnout	1805 %	1805 Difference from 1793	1807 Voting-age population	1807 Turnout	1807 %	1807 Difference from 1793	1809 Voting-age population	1809 Turnout	1809 %	1809 Difference from 1793
CONNECTICUT					54,000	7,848	14.5%		55,000	8,223	15.0%	0.4	55,000	7,971	14.5%	0.0	56,000	8,159	14.6%	0.0
DELAWARE	10,000	3,475	34.8%										11,000	3,062	27.8%	-6.9				
MASSACHUSETTS	92,000	20,184	21.9%	13.7	95,000	13,910	14.6%	6.5	97,000	33,518	34.6%	26.4	100,000	41,954	42.0%	33.8	103,000	45,118	43.8%	35.6
NEW HAMPSHIRE	38,000	5,249	13.8%		40,000	9,011	22.5%	8.7	41,000	16,097	39.3%	25.4	43,000	13,912	32.4%	18.5	44,000	15,241	34.6%	20.8
NEW YORK	129,000	24,808	19.2%	6.8									173,000	35,074	20.3%	7.9				
OHIO					19,000	4,860	25.6%		27,000	4,783	17.7%	-7.9	38,000	5,616	14.8%	-10.8				
PENNSYLVANIA									146,000	82,477	56.5%	38.4								
VERMONT					35,000	5,408	15.5%	2.4	38,000	5,056	13.3%	0.3	40,000	9,903	24.8%	11.7	43,000	14,583	33.9%	20.9

Other Turnout for Election Years 1789–1809

State	1789 Voting-age population	1789 Turnout	1789 %	1791 Voting-age population	1791 Turnout	1791 %	1791 Difference from 1789*	1793 Voting-age population	1793 Turnout	1793 %	1793 Difference from 1789	1795 Voting-age population	1795 Turnout	1795 %	1795 Difference from 1789	1797 Voting-age population	1797 Turnout	1797 %	1797 Difference from 1789	1799 Voting-age population	1799 Turnout	1799 %	1799 Difference from 1789
CONNECTICUT																							
DELAWARE												10,000	4,494	44.9%									
MASSACHUSETTS	77,000	20,721	26.9%	80,000	15,996	20.0%	-6.9	83,000	16,428	19.8%	-7.1	85,000	15,976	18.8%	-8.1								
NEW HAMPSHIRE	29,000	8,113	28.0%	31,000	8,679	28.0%	0.0	32,000	9,402	29.4%	1.4	34,000	9,340	27.5%	-0.5								
NEW YORK	68,000	12,353	18.2%																				
RHODE ISLAND																14,000	1,204	8.6%					
TENNESSEE																				16,000	5,295	33.1%	
VERMONT								23,000	5,896	25.6%		25,000	6,298	25.2%	-0.4								

State	1801 Voting-age population	1801 Turnout	1801 %	1801 Difference from 1789	1803 Voting-age population	1803 Turnout	1803 %	1803 Difference from 1789	1805 Voting-age population	1805 Turnout	1805 %	1805 Difference from 1789	1807 Voting-age population	1807 Turnout	1807 %	1807 Difference from 1789	1809 Voting-age population	1809 Turnout	1809 %	1809 Difference from 1789
CONNECTICUT	53,000	12,212	23.0%																	
DELAWARE																				
MASSACHUSETTS																				
NEW HAMPSHIRE																				
NEW YORK													173,000	30,989	17.9%	-0.3				
RHODE ISLAND	14,000	3,760	26.9%	18.3									15,000	3,832	25.5%	16.9				
TENNESSEE	23,000	8,438	36.7%	3.6	25,000	11,709	46.8%	13.7	29,000	16,148	55.7%	22.6					39,000	22,121	56.7%	23.6
VERMONT																				

*Percentage point difference between turnout in current year and initial year listed in chart. If data do not appear for a state in the initial year listed, the difference is calculated from the first year in which data do appear for that state.

UNITED STATES HOUSE OF REPRESENTATIVES GENERAL ELECTIONS

Election Years 1789–1809

State	1789 Voting-age population	Turnout	%	1791 Voting-age population	Turnout	%	Difference from 1789*	1793 Voting-age population	Turnout	%	Difference from 1789	1795 Voting-age population	Turnout	%	Difference from 1789	1797 Voting-age population	Turnout	%	Difference from 1789	1799 Voting-age population	Turnout	%	Difference from 1789
DELAWARE	9,000	2,059	22.9%																				
GEORGIA	10,000	3,974	39.7%	12,000	1,954	16.3%	-23.5																
KENTUCKY																				29,000	9,976	34.4%	
MARYLAND	46,000	7,885	17.1%																				
NEW JERSEY	38,000	13,811	36.3%	38,000	6,435	16.9%	-19.4									40,000	11,178	27.9%	-8.4				
NEW YORK	68,000	9,831	14.5%					86,000	24,175	28.1%	13.7												
NORTH CAROLINA								60,000	4,863	8.1%		61,000	4,241	7.0%	-1.2								
OHIO																							
PENNSYLVANIA				96,000	20,407	21.3%																	
SOUTH CAROLINA								32,000	690	2.2%													
TENNESSEE																				16,000	6,519	40.7%	
VERMONT				20,000	2,061	10.3%		23,000	2,859	12.4%	2.1												
VIRGINIA	89,000	6,271	7.0%					95,000	5,441	5.7%	-1.3	99,000	3,546	3.6%	-3.5	102,000	10,311	10.1%	3.1	102,000	24,357	23.9%	16.8

State	1801 Voting-age population	Turnout	%	Difference from 1789	1803 Voting-age population	Turnout	%	Difference from 1789	1805 Voting-age population	Turnout	%	Difference from 1789	1807 Voting-age population	Turnout	%	Difference from 1789	1809 Voting-age population	Turnout	%	Difference from 1789
DELAWARE																				
GEORGIA																				
KENTUCKY	39,000	21,876	56.1%	21.7	44,000	14,637	33.3%	-1.1												
MARYLAND	47,000	14,903	31.7%	14.6	48,000	30,351	63.2%	46.1												
NEW JERSEY					43,000	14,288	33.2%	-3.1												
NEW YORK																				
NORTH CAROLINA					68,000	41,348	60.8%	52.7												
OHIO					19,000	7,491	39.4%													
PENNSYLVANIA																				
SOUTH CAROLINA					40,000	6,550	16.4%													
TENNESSEE	23,000	9,238	40.2%	-0.6	25,000	10,697	42.8%	2.0	29,000	15,346	52.9%	12.2	34,000	19,889	58.5%	17.8	39,000	8,120	20.8%	-19.9
VERMONT																				
VIRGINIA	107,000	7,172	6.7%	-0.3	108,000	23,212	21.5%	14.4	110,000	14,528	13.2%	6.2	112,000	10,481	9.4%	2.3	113,000	22,494	19.9%	12.9

*Percentage point difference between turnout in current year and initial year listed in chart. If data do not appear for a state in the initial year listed, the difference is calculated from the first year in which data do appear for that state.

UNITED STATES HOUSE OF REPRESENTATIVES GENERAL ELECTIONS

Federalist Turnout for Election Years 1789–1809

State	1789 Voting-age population	Turnout	%	1791 Voting-age population	Turnout	%	1793 Voting-age population	Turnout	%	Difference from 1789*	1795 Voting-age population	Turnout	%	Difference from 1789	1797 Voting-age population	Turnout	%	Difference from 1789	1799 Voting-age population	Turnout	%	Difference from 1789
DELAWARE																						
GEORGIA																						
KENTUCKY																						
MARYLAND	46,000	5,154	11.2%																			
NEW JERSEY															40,000	7,100	17.8%					
NEW YORK	68,000	5,845	8.6%				86,000	12,951	15.1%	6.5												
NORTH CAROLINA							60,000	2,595	4.3%		61,000	1,150	1.9%	-2.4								
OHIO																						
PENNSYLVANIA																						
SOUTH CAROLINA																						
TENNESSEE																						
VERMONT																						
VIRGINIA															102,000	2,922	2.9%		102,000	11,638	11.4%	8.5

State	1801 Voting-age population	Turnout	%	Difference from 1789	1803 Voting-age population	Turnout	%	Difference from 1789	1805 Voting-age population	Turnout	%	Difference from 1789	1807 Voting-age population	Turnout	%	Difference from 1789	1809 Voting-age population	Turnout	%	Difference from 1789
DELAWARE																				
GEORGIA																				
KENTUCKY					44,000	238	0.5%													
MARYLAND	47,000	5,631	12.0%	0.8	48,000	8,705	18.1%	6.9												
NEW JERSEY					43,000	381	0.9%	-16.9												
NEW YORK																				
NORTH CAROLINA					68,000	13,700	20.1%	15.8												
OHIO					19,000	1,960	10.3%													
PENNSYLVANIA																				
SOUTH CAROLINA					40,000	2,323	5.8%													
TENNESSEE													34,000	6,098	17.9%					
VERMONT																				
VIRGINIA	107,000	2,626	2.5%	-0.4	108,000	6,230	5.8%	2.9	110,000	2,991	2.7%	-0.1	112,000	2,131	1.9%	-1.0	113,000	9,854	8.7%	5.9

United States House of Representatives General Elections (continued)

United States House of Representatives General Election (continued)

Democratic-Republican Turnout for Election Years 1789–1809

State	1789 Voting-age population	Turnout	%	1791 Voting-age population	Turnout	%	1793 Voting-age population	Turnout	%	Difference from 1789*	1795 Voting-age population	Turnout	%	Difference from 1789	1797 Voting-age population	Turnout	%	Difference from 1789	1799 Voting-age population	Turnout	%	Difference from 1789
DELAWARE																						
GEORGIA																						
KENTUCKY																			29,000	5,519	19.0%	
MARYLAND	46,000	2,731	5.9%																			
NEW JERSEY															40,000	3,860	9.7%					
NEW YORK	68,000	3,531	5.2%				86,000	11,027	12.8%	7.6												
NORTH CAROLINA							60,000	2,268	3.8%		61,000	2,341	3.8%	0.1								
OHIO																						
PENNSYLVANIA																						
SOUTH CAROLINA																						
TENNESSEE																			16,000	6,519	40.7%	
VERMONT																						
VIRGINIA															102,000	6,858	6.7%		102,000	12,719	12.5%	5.7

State	1801 Voting-age population	Turnout	%	Difference from 1789	1803 Voting-age population	Turnout	%	Difference from 1789	1805 Voting-age population	Turnout	%	Difference from 1789	1807 Voting-age population	Turnout	%	Difference from 1789	1809 Voting-age population	Turnout	%	Difference from 1789
DELAWARE																				
GEORGIA																				
KENTUCKY	39,000	18,124	46.5%	27.4	44,000	14,399	32.7%	13.7												
MARYLAND	47,000	9,272	19.7%	13.8	48,000	21,646	45.1%	39.2												
NEW JERSEY					43,000	13,907	32.3%	22.7												
NEW YORK																				
NORTH CAROLINA					68,000	27,648	40.7%	36.9												
OHIO					19,000	5,531	29.1%													
PENNSYLVANIA																				
SOUTH CAROLINA					40,000	4,227	10.6%													
TENNESSEE	23,000	9,238	40.2%	-0.6	25,000	10,697	42.8%	2.0	28,000	15,346	54.8%	14.1	34,000	12,589	37.0%	-3.7	39,000	7,793	20.0%	-20.8
VERMONT																				
VIRGINIA	107,000	4,546	4.2%	-2.5	108,000	16,962	15.7%	9.0	110,000	11,055	10.1%	3.3	112,000	8,325	7.4%	0.7	113,000	11,382	10.1%	3.3

United States House of Representatives General Election *(continued)*

Other Turnout for Election Years 1789–1809

State	1789 Voting-age population	Turnout	%	1791 Voting-age population	Turnout	%	Difference from 1789*	1793 Voting-age population	Turnout	%	Difference from 1789	1795 Voting-age population	Turnout	%	Difference from 1789	1797 Voting-age population	Turnout	%	Difference from 1789	1799 Voting-age population	Turnout	%	Difference from 1789
DELAWARE	9,000	2,059	22.9%																				
GEORGIA	10,000	3,974	39.7%	12,000	1,954	16.3%	-23.5																
KENTUCKY																				29,000	4,457	15.4%	
MARYLAND																							
NEW JERSEY	38,000	13,811	36.3%	38,000	6,435	16.9%										40,000	218	0.5%	-35.8				
NEW YORK	68,000	455	0.7%					86,000	197	0.2%	-0.4												
NORTH CAROLINA												61,000	750	1.2%									
OHIO																							
PENNSYLVANIA				96,000	20,407	21.3%																	
SOUTH CAROLINA								32,000	690	2.2%													
TENNESSEE																							
VERMONT				20,000	2,061	10.3%		23,000	2,859	12.4%	2.1												
VIRGINIA	89,000	6,271	7.0%					95,000	5,441	5.7%	-1.3	99,000	3,546	3.6%	-3.5	102,000	531	0.5%	-6.5				

State	1801 Voting-age population	Turnout	%	Difference from 1789	1803 Voting-age population	Turnout	%	Difference from 1789	1805 Voting-age population	Turnout	%	Difference from 1789	1807 Voting-age population	Turnout	%	Difference from 1789	1809 Voting-age population	Turnout	%	Difference from 1789
DELAWARE																				
GEORGIA																				
KENTUCKY	39,000	3,752	9.6%	-5.7																
MARYLAND																				
NEW JERSEY																				
NEW YORK																				
NORTH CAROLINA																				
OHIO																				
PENNSYLVANIA																				
SOUTH CAROLINA																				
TENNESSEE													34,000	1,202	3.5%		39,000	327	0.8%	-2.7
VERMONT																				
VIRGINIA					108,000	20	0.0%	-7.0	110,000	482	0.4%	-6.6	112,000	25	0.0%	-7.0	113,000	1,258	1.1%	-5.9

*Percentage point difference between turnout in current year and initial year listed in chart. If data do not appear for a state in the initial year listed, the difference is calculated from the first year in which data do appear for that state.

CHAPTER 2
1810–1829

Chronology of Major Events, 1810–1829

1810	The third census counts the U.S. population at 7.2 million people.
1812	Democratic-Republican James Madison is re-elected. United States pursues its first war as a sovereign nation, the War of 1812 against the British, despite the opposition of the Federalist Party.
1814	British troops burn Washington, D.C. Treaty of Ghent officially ends the War of 1812.
1815	Led by Andrew Jackson, the United States wins the Battle of New Orleans before news of the peace treaty could spread. In the glow of victory, the Federalist Party is discredited.
1816	James Monroe, the Democratic-Republican nominee, is elected with little opposition from the Federalist Party outside New England.
1817	The New York Stock Exchange is founded. The Rush-Bagot treaty is signed, establishing the border between the eastern third of the United States and Canada.
1819	*McCulloch v. Maryland* Supreme Court decision affirms the constitutionality of a national bank and the federal government's "implied powers" beyond those stated in the Constitution. The Bank of the United States cannot prevent a financial panic that same year leading to economic depression.
1820	James Monroe is re-elected president with almost no opposition. The "Era of Good Feelings" is strained over the slavery issue. The Missouri Compromise admits Missouri as a slave state but forbids the practice in any part of the Louisiana Purchase north of the 36° 30' parallel. The fourth census counts the U.S. population at 9.6 million people.
1821	The ratification of a treaty between the United States and Spain is completed, officially ceding Florida to the United States.
1823	The Monroe Doctrine is declared, establishing the basis of U.S. military action against any country that would interfere in the affairs of any country in the Americas.
1824	John Quincy Adams is named president by the U.S. House of Representatives after an election in which none of the four candidates, all from the Democratic-Republican party, garnered a majority of electoral votes. The Adams wing of the party would soon become the National Republicans.
1825	The Erie Canal is completed.
1828	Major protectionist legislation, the Tariff of 1828 (the "Tariff of Abominations" to Southern opponents) is enacted. War hero Andrew Jackson is elected president.
1829	President Jackson introduces the spoils system into national politics.

State and Federal Laws Chronology, 1810–1829

1810   South Carolina drops its taxpaying requirement. The state requires the voter to possess a freehold of fifty acres or a town lot (owned six months prior to election) or to reside in the election district for six months to be eligible to vote.

Maryland adds a requirement that the voter must be a white citizen.

1812   *Louisiana becomes a state.* It enters the Union with a requirement that the voter had paid state taxes in the previous six months, unless he had purchased land from the United States. The voter must also be a white U.S. citizen.

1813   New Hampshire adds the requirement that a voter must be a U.S. citizen.

1816   *Indiana becomes a state.* It enters the Union without any property or taxpaying requirements for suffrage, but the voter must be a white U.S. citizen.

1817   Connecticut drops its freehold requirement but requires that the voter either have paid taxes or served in the militia.

Mississippi becomes a state. It enters the Union without a property requirement, but requires that the voter must have paid state or county tax or enrolled in the local militia, unless exempt from military service. It also requires that the voter be a white U.S. citizen.

1818   *Illinois becomes a state.* It enters the Union without any property or taxpaying requirements for suffrage, but requires the voter to be white.

Connecticut reinstates its original freehold requirement alongside taxpaying and militia service as qualifications to vote. It also requires that the voter be a white U.S. citizen.

1819   *Alabama becomes a state.* It enters the Union without any property or taxpaying requirements for suffrage, but requires the voter to be a white U.S. citizen.

1820   Maine becomes a state. It enters the Union without any property or taxpaying requirements for suffrage, except for Native Americans, as "Indians not taxed" are excluded.[1] Further, the voter must be a U.S. citizen and have resided for three months in the state. There is no loss of residence for soldiers or others traveling on public business, but no residency is gained by military personnel stationed in the state or by students.

Missouri becomes a state. It enters the Union without any property or taxpaying requirements for suffrage. The voter must also be a white U.S. citizen.

1821   Massachusetts drops its property requirement, but requires the voter to be a citizen and to have paid any state or county tax assessed within two years, unless exempted from taxation. The voter must have resided one year in the state and six months in the town or district.

New York drops property requirement for whites but requires that the white voter has "within the year next proceeding the election" paid a state or county tax on real or personal property or be exempted by law from taxation, or "have performed within that year military duty in the militia" or as a fireman; or if meeting special residency requirements, to have labored on public highways. If a "man of color," the voter must have been for one year in possession "of a freehold estate of the value of $250 over and above all debts and encumbrances charged thereon." The voter must be a citizen; if a 'man of color,' he must have been a citizen for three years.[2]

State and Federal Laws Chronology, 1810–1829 *(continued)*

Summary

By 1830, only eight states of the now twenty-four states in the Union had a property requirement for voting. However, as of the same year, fifteen of the twenty-four states excluded blacks from voting, including Louisiana, Indiana, Mississippi, Connecticut, Illinois, Missouri, and, partially, New York, in addition to those mentioned in Chapter One.

Source: Adapted from Alexander Keyssar, *The Right to Vote: The Contested History of Democracy in the United States,* Revised Edition (New York: Basic Books, 2009), 306–319.
[1] As quoted in Keyssar, 316. For sources, see Keyssar 369–379.
[2] As quoted in Keyssar, 310. For sources, see Keyssar 369–379.

National Count of Popular Vote for President, 1812–1828

YEAR	NAME	PARTY	TOTAL	PERCENTAGE[1]
1812	James Madison	Democratic-Republican	138,497	11.0%
	DeWitt Clinton	Federalist	120,475	9.6%
1816	James Monroe	Democratic-Republican	74,696	5.0%
	Rufus King	Federalist	17,611	1.2%
	Other and write-ins		17,589	1.2%
1820	James Monroe	Democratic-Republican	85,613	5.2%
1824[2]	Andrew Jackson	Democratic-Republican	151,271	8.0%
	John Quincy Adams	**Democratic-Republican[3]**	**113,122**	**6.0%**
	Henry Clay	Democratic-Republican	47,531	2.5%
	William Crawford	Democratic-Republican	40,856	2.2%
1828	Andrew Jackson	Democratic	642,553	30.1%
	John Quincy Adams	National Republican	500,897	23.4%

[1] The percentage figures in this chart are based on the votes cast divided by the eligible voting-age population at the time of the election.

[2] John Quincy Adams gained the presidency despite losing both the popular vote and the Electoral College vote to Andrew Jackson. As Jackson received only 99 of the 261 available electoral votes, short of the required majority, the election passed to the House of Representatives, where thirteen of the twenty-four state delegations voted for Adams (Jackson received seven and William Crawford received four).

[3] All presidential candidates in 1824 ran as Democratic-Republicans; however, the faction of the party supporting Adams soon broke away to become the National Republicans; for the purposes of this book, this faction is labeled "National Republicans" from 1820 onward in determining turnout.

States with Property and Taxpaying Requirements for Suffrage, 1810–1829

STATE	DATE OF STATEHOOD[1]	PROPERTY REQUIREMENT[2]	TAXPAYING REQUIREMENT[2]
ALABAMA	1819	None	None
CONNECTICUT		1796: Freehold worth $7 a year or possession of personal property worth $134	1796: None
		1817: Freehold requirement dropped	1817: Paid taxes or served in militia
		1818: Freehold requirement reinstated with taxpaying and militia alternatives	1818: Taxpaying and militia alternatives to freehold requirement
DELAWARE	1788	None	1789: Paid all taxes for the year preceding the election
			1798: Paid all taxes for the year preceding the election
		1734: "Freeholder … and has 50 acres of land or more well seated, and 12 acres or more thereof cleared"	
		1792: None	1792: Paid a state or county tax … assessed at least 6 months before the election. Exempt if under age 22 and the son of a qualified voter.
GEORGIA		None	1798: Paid all taxes for year preceding the election
ILLINOIS	1818	None	None
INDIANA	1816	None	None
KENTUCKY		None	None
LOUISIANA	1812	1812: Exempt from taxpaying requirement if purchased land from U.S.	1812: Paid state tax in last six months or purchased land from U.S.
MAINE	1820	None	None
MARYLAND		None	None
MASSACHUSETTS		1780: To vote for the Senate, freehold estate with annual income of 3 pounds, or any estate worth 60 pounds; to vote for the House, property must be owned in same town as residence.[3]	None
		1821: Property requirement dropped	1821: Paid any state or county tax assessed within 2 years unless exempted from taxation
MISSISSIPPI	1817	None	1817: Paid state or county tax or enrolled in local militia, unless exempt

States with Property and Taxpaying Requirements for Suffrage, 1810–1829 (continued)

States with Property and Taxpaying Requirements for Suffrage, 1810–1829 (continued)

STATE	DATE OF STATEHOOD[1]	PROPERTY REQUIREMENT[2]	TAXPAYING REQUIREMENT[2]
MISSOURI	1820	None	None
NEW HAMPSHIRE		None	1792: Persons excused from paying taxes at their own request excluded
NEW JERSEY		1807: Worth 50 pounds; any person who paid a state or county tax, or had his name enrolled upon a tax duplicate for the last state or county tax deemed to be worth 50 pounds	1807: Worth 50 pounds; any person who paid a state or county tax, or had his name enrolled upon a tax duplicate for the last state or county tax deemed to be worth 50 pounds
NEW YORK		1777: For Assembly: "Freeholder, possessing a freehold of the value of 20 pounds … or have rented a tenement therein of the yearly value of 40 shillings, and been rated and actually paid taxes to this State." Exceptions for "every person who now is a freeman of the city of Albany, or who was made a freeman in the city of New York on or before 14 October 1775." For Senate: owners of freeholds valued at "one hundred pounds, over and above all debts charged thereon." [3]	1777: See property requirement
		1804: Those who rent a tenement worth $25 a year or meet 1777 property requirements	
		1821: Property requirement dropped for whites. If a "man of color," must have been for 1 year seized and possessed of a freehold estate of the value of $250 over and above all debts and debts and encumbrances charged thereon.	1821: If white, "shall have, within the year next preceding the election," paid a state or county tax on real or personal property; or shall by law be exempted from taxation; or "shall have performed within that year military duty in the militia" or as a fireman; or, if meeting special residency requirements, shall have labored on public highways.
		1826: If a "man of color," 1821 property requirements still in effect	
NORTH CAROLINA		1776: Freehold of 50 acres of land to vote for Senate; no property requirement to vote for House of Commons[3]	1776: Must have paid taxes to vote for House of Commons and governor
OHIO		None	1802: Must have paid or been charged with state or county tax; not applicable to white males above age 21, who are "compelled to labor on the roads" and have resided 1 year in the state
PENNSYLVANIA		None	1790: Paid state or county tax within 2 years, assessed at least 6 months before the election; exempt if under age 22 and the son of a qualified voter
RHODE ISLAND		1762: Freehold worth 40 pounds or 40 shillings per year, or the eldest son of a freeholder	None

STATE	DATE OF STATEHOOD[1]	PROPERTY REQUIREMENT[2]	TAXPAYING REQUIREMENT[2]
SOUTH CAROLINA		1810: Freehold of 50 acres or a town lot, owned 6 months prior to election; or residence in the election district for 6 months	1810: Tax requirement dropped
TENNESSEE		1796: Freehold in the county where voting, or inhabitant of any one county in the state for 6 months	None
VERMONT		None	None
VIRGINIA		1762: "Freehold ... in at least 50 acres of land, if no settlement be made upon it, or 25 acres, with a plantation and house thereon, at least 12 feet square," or a town lot with house "at least 12 feet square." 1804: Must own land for 6 months prior to election	None

Source: Alexander Keyssar, *The Right to Vote: The Contested History of Democracy in the United States,* Revised Edition (New York: Basic Books, 2009), 308–313. Keyssar's table extends from 1790 to 1855. Sources of quotations are found on pp. 369–379.

[1] For states whose date of statehood falls within the time period 1810–1829

[2] Dates listed are for the year that the property or tax requirement went into effect. All listed requirements continue into the 1810–1829 date range of this table.

[3] References to Senate, House, and General Assembly refer to state rather than federal offices.

States with Race and Citizenship Requirements for Suffrage, 1810–1829

STATE AND YEAR OF STATEHOOD[1]	DATE OF REQUIREMENT[2]	RACE	CITIZENSHIP	NATIVE AMERICANS
ALABAMA (1819)	1819	White	U.S. citizen	Not specifically mentioned
CONNECTICUT	1715	No requirement	No requirement	Not specifically mentioned
	1818	White	U.S. citizen	Not specifically mentioned
DELAWARE	1792	White	No requirement	Not specifically mentioned
GEORGIA	1789	No requirement	Citizen	Not specifically mentioned
ILLINOIS (1818)	1818	White	No requirement	Not specifically mentioned
INDIANA (1816)	1816	White	U.S. citizen	Not specifically mentioned
KENTUCKY	1799	"Negroes, mulattos, and Indians" excluded	Citizen	"Indians" specifically excluded
LOUISIANA (1812)	1812	White	U.S. citizen	Not specifically mentioned
MAINE (1820)	1819	No requirement	U.S. citizen	"Indians not taxed" excluded
MARYLAND	1810	White	Citizen	Not specifically mentioned
MASSACHUSETTS	1807	No requirement	No requirement	Inhabitants of incorporated plantations not entitled to vote for governor or lieutenant governor; this effectively excluded many Indians.
	1821	No requirement	Citizen	Not specifically mentioned
MISSISSIPPI (1817)	1817	White	U.S. citizen	Not specifically mentioned
MISSOURI (1821)	1820	White	U.S. citizen	Not specifically mentioned
NEW HAMPSHIRE	1792	No requirement	No requirement	Not specifically mentioned
	1813	No requirement	Citizen	Not specifically mentioned
NEW JERSEY	1807	White	Citizen	Not specifically mentioned
NEW YORK	1804	No requirement	Citizen	Not specifically mentioned
	1821	White or "man of color" meeting property and tax requirements	Citizen; if a "man of color," citizen for 3 years	Not specifically mentioned
NORTH CAROLINA	1776	No requirement	No requirement	Not specifically mentioned

States with Race and Citizenship Requirements for Suffrage, 1810–1829 *(continued)*

STATE AND YEAR OF STATEHOOD[1]	DATE OF REQUIREMENT[2]	RACE	CITIZENSHIP	NATIVE AMERICANS
OHIO	1809	No requirement	U.S. citizen	Not specifically mentioned
PENNSYLVANIA	1790	No requirement	Citizen	Not specifically mentioned
RHODE ISLAND	1762	No requirement	No requirement	Not specifically mentioned
SOUTH CAROLINA	1790	White	Citizen of state	Not specifically mentioned

Source: Alexander Keyssar, *The Right to Vote: The Contested History of Democracy in the United States,* Revised Edition (New York. Basic Books, 2009), 315 319. Keyssar's table extends from 1790 to 1855. Sources of quotations are found on pp. 369–379.

[1] For states after the original thirteen colonies.

[2] Dates listed are for the year that the requirement went into effect. All listed requirements continue into the 1788–1809 date range of this table. States with no requirement are listed for comparison purposes.

United States Presidential Turnout, Election Years 1812–1828

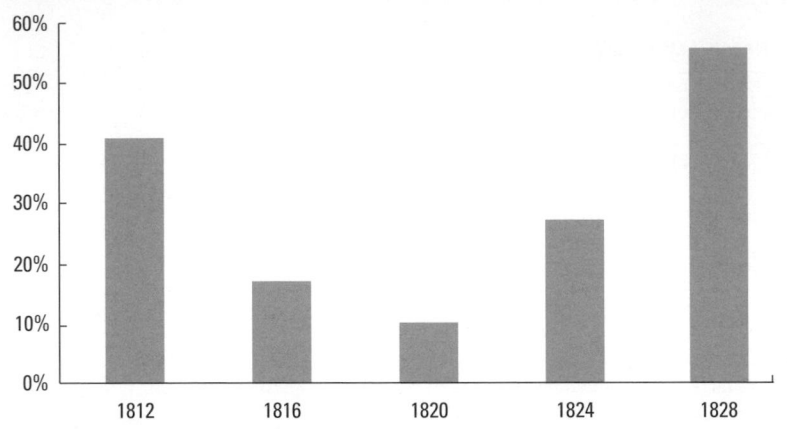

YEAR	VOTING-AGE POPULATION	TURNOUT	%
1812	641,000	258,972	40.4%
1816	654,000	109,896	16.8%
1820	1,054,000	105,487	10.0%
1824	1,362,000	365,833	26.9%
1828	2,074,000	1,148,018	55.4%

Partisan Turnout, Presidential Years, Based on Aggregate House Turnout, Election Years 1812–1828

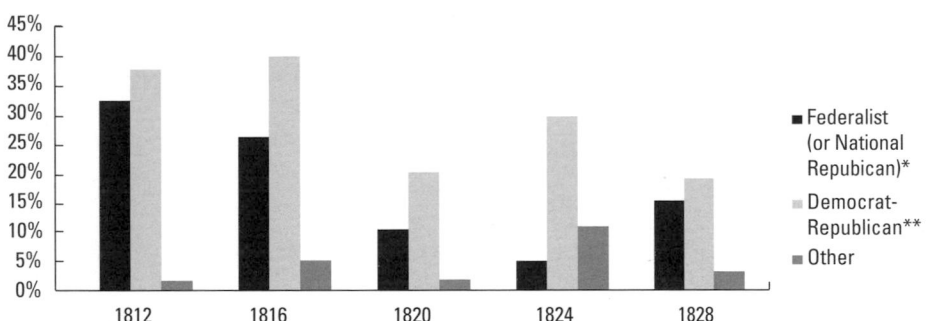

YEAR	VOTING-AGE POPULATION***	FEDERALIST (OR NATIONAL REPUBLICAN)* TURNOUT	%	DEMOCRAT-REPUBLICAN** TURNOUT	%	OTHER TURNOUT	%
1812	641,000	205,033	32.0%	239,016	37.3%	10,503	1.6%
1816	654,000	169,061	25.9%	257,936	39.4%	32,738	5.0%
1820	1,054,000	107,909	10.2%	209,446	19.9%	18,939	1.8%
1824	1,362,000	66,824	4.9%	398,447	29.3%	145,564	10.7%
1828	2,074,000	311,473	15.0%	388,497	18.7%	64,138	3.1%

*In the aftermath of the War of 1812, the Federalist party lost its stature as the second national party. For a brief time, the "Era of Good Feelings," the Democratic-Republican party held sway as the only national party, but the National Republican party developed out of competition within the Democratic-Republicans. For the purposes of this book, the National Republican era begins in 1820 and ends in 1832.

**The Democratic-Republican party finally dropped the "Republican" and became the "Democratic" Party that continues into the 21st century. For the purposes of this book, the Democratic Party is listed from 1826 on.

***Voting-age population taken from states with presidential elections

Alternate Graph for Partisan Turnout, Presidential Years, Based on Aggregate House Turnout, 1812–1828

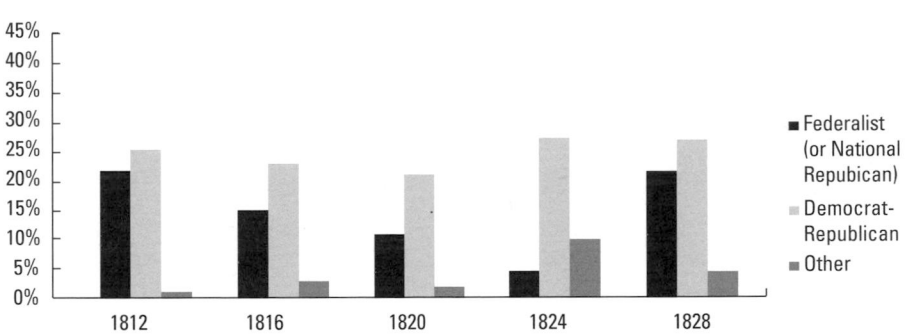

YEAR	VOTING-AGE POPULATION****	FEDERALIST (OR NATIONAL REPUBLICAN) TURNOUT	%	DEMOCRAT-REPUBLICAN TURNOUT	%	OTHER TURNOUT	%
1812	943,000	205,033	21.7%	239,016	25.4%	10,503	1.1%
1816	1,126,000	169,061	15.0%	257,936	22.9%	32,738	2.9%
1820	996,000	107,909	10.8%	209,446	21.0%	18,939	1.9%
1824	1,462,000	66,824	4.6%	398,447	27.3%	145,564	10.0%
1828	1,446,000	311,473	21.5%	388,497	26.9%	64,138	4.4%

****This is an alternate graph that depicts partisan turnout calculated using voting-age population only from those states that held House elections. For percentages, consult the total lines of House partisan charts.

UNITED STATES PRESIDENTIAL GENERAL ELECTIONS

Election Years 1812–1828

State	1812 Voting-age population	Turnout	%	1816 Voting-age population	Turnout	%	Difference from 1812*	1820 Voting-age population	Turnout	%	Difference from 1812	1824 Voting-age population	Turnout	%	Difference from 1812	1828 Voting-age population	Turnout	%	Difference from 1812
ALABAMA												29,000	13,603	46.9%		36,000	18,618	51.7%	4.8
CONNECTICUT								60,000	3,889	6.5%		64,000	10,647	16.6%	10.2	68,000	19,378	28.5%	22.0
GEORGIA																57,000	20,004	35.1%	
ILLINOIS								12,000	1,430	11.9%		20,000	4,671	23.4%	11.4	28,000	14,222	50.8%	38.9
INDIANA												44,000	15,838	36.0%		58,000	39,210	67.6%	31.6
KENTUCKY	67,000	8,645	12.9%					84,000	3,169	3.8%	-9.1	92,000	23,338	25.4%	12.5	101,000	70,776	70.1%	57.2
LOUISIANA																24,000	8,687	36.2%	
MAINE								61,000	5,454	8.9%		72,000	12,625	17.5%	8.6	82,000	34,789	42.4%	33.5
MARYLAND	53,000	29,031	54.8%	55,000	10,483	19.1%	-35.7	58,000	5,105	8.8%	-46.0	62,000	33,214	53.6%	-1.2	66,000	45,796	69.4%	14.6
MASSACHUSETTS	107,000	78,250	73.1%					118,000	24,030	20.4%	-52.8	129,000	42,056	32.6%	-40.5	140,000	39,074	27.9%	-45.2
MISSISSIPPI												12,000	4,894	40.8%		15,000	8,344	55.6%	14.8
MISSOURI												18,000	3,432	19.1%		22,000	11,654	53.0%	33.9
NEW HAMPSHIRE	46,000	26,750	58.2%	49,000	28,527	58.2%	0.1	52,000	9,448	18.2%	-40.0	56,000	10,032	17.9%	-40.2	59,000	44,035	74.6%	16.5
NEW JERSEY				52,000	5,441	10.5%		55,000	4,321	7.9%	-2.6	60,000	19,837	33.1%	22.6	65,000	45,570	70.1%	59.6
NEW YORK																397,000	270,975	68.3%	
NORTH CAROLINA				78,000	10,189	13.1%		81,000	3,300	4.1%	-9.0	86,000	36,109	42.0%	28.9	91,000	51,747	56.9%	43.8
OHIO	61,000	10,721	17.6%	89,000	3,919	4.4%	-13.2	117,000	7,164	6.1%	-11.5	146,000	50,024	34.3%	16.7	176,000	131,049	74.5%	56.9
PENNSYLVANIA	175,000	78,906	45.1%	193,000	43,242	22.4%	-22.7	213,000	32,206	15.1%	-30.0	242,000	47,073	19.5%	-25.6	272,000	152,220	56.0%	10.9
RHODE ISLAND	16,000	6,116	38.2%	17,000	1,236	7.3%	-31.0	17,000	724	4.3%	-34.0	19,000	2,344	12.3%	-25.9	21,000	3,580	17.0%	-21.2
TENNESSEE												78,000	20,725	26.6%		94,000	46,533	49.5%	22.9
VERMONT																61,000	32,833	53.8%	
VIRGINIA	116,000	20,553	17.7%	121,000	6,859	5.7%	-12.0	126,000	5,247	4.2%	-13.6	133,000	15,371	11.6%	-6.2	141,000	38,924	27.6%	9.9
Total	641,000	258,972	40.4%	654,000	109,896	16.8%	-23.6	1,054,000	105,487	10.0%	-30.4	1,362,000	365,833	26.9%	-13.5	2,074,000	1,148,018	55.4%	15.0

*Percentage point difference between turnout in current year and initial year listed in chart. If data do not appear for a state in the initial year listed, the difference is calculated from the first year in which data do appear for that state.

UNITED STATES PRESIDENTIAL GENERAL ELECTIONS

Federalist (or National Republican) Turnout for Election Years 1812–1828*

State	1812 Voting-age population	Turnout	%	1816 Voting-age population	Turnout	%	Difference from 1812**	1820 (National Republicans) Voting-age population	Turnout	%	Difference from 1812	1824 (National Republicans) Voting-age population	Turnout	%	Difference from 1812	1828 (National Republicans) Voting-age population	Turnout	%	Difference from 1812
ALABAMA												29,000	2,422	8.4%		36,000	1,878	5.2%	-3.1
CONNECTICUT												64,000	7,494	11.7%		68,000	13,829	20.3%	8.6
GEORGIA																57,000	642	1.1%	
ILLINOIS												20,000	1,516	7.6%		28,000	4,662	16.7%	9.1
INDIANA												44,000	3,071	7.0%		58,000	17,009	29.3%	22.3
KENTUCKY	67,000	144	0.2%													101,000	31,468	31.2%	30.9
LOUISIANA																24,000	4,082	17.0%	
MAINE												72,000	10,289	14.3%		82,000	20,773	25.3%	11.0
MARYLAND	53,000	14,280	26.9%	55,000	3,048	5.5%	-21.4	58,000	386	0.7%	-26.3	62,000	14,632	23.6%	-3.3	66,000	23,014	34.9%	7.9
MASSACHUSETTS	107,000	49,630	46.4%					118,000	16,341	13.8%	-32.5	129,000	30,687	23.8%	-22.6	140,000	29,836	21.3%	-25.1
MISSISSIPPI												12,000	1,654	13.8%		15,000	1,581	10.5%	-3.2
MISSOURI												18,000	159	0.9%		22,000	3,422	15.6%	14.7
NEW HAMPSHIRE	46,000	14,006	30.4%	49,000	13,330	27.2%	-3.2					56,000	9,389	16.8%	-13.7	59,000	23,823	40.4%	9.9
NEW JERSEY												60,000	8,309	13.8%		65,000	23,753	36.5%	22.7
NEW YORK																397,000	131,563	33.1%	
NORTH CAROLINA				78,000	640	0.8%										91,000	13,918	15.3%	14.5
OHIO	61,000	3,301	5.4%	89,000	593	0.7%	-4.7					146,000	12,280	8.4%	3.0	176,000	63,453	36.1%	30.6
PENNSYLVANIA	175,000	29,509	16.9%									242,000	5,441	2.2%	-14.6	272,000	50,763	18.7%	1.8
RHODE ISLAND	16,000	4,032	25.2%									19,000	2,144	11.3%	-13.9	21,000	2,755	13.1%	-12.1
TENNESSEE												78,000	216	0.3%		94,000	2,240	2.4%	2.1
VERMONT																61,000	24,363	39.9%	
VIRGINIA	116,000	5,573	4.8%									133,000	3,419	2.6%	-2.2	141,000	12,070	8.6%	3.8
Total	641,000	120,475	18.8%	271,000	17,611	6.5%	-12.3	176,000	16,727	9.5%	-9.3	1,184,000	113,122	9.6%	-9.2	2,074,000	500,897	24.2%	5.4

Democratic Turnout for Election Years 1812–1828

State	1812 Voting-age population	Turnout	%	1816 Voting-age population	Turnout	%	Difference from 1812**	1820 Voting-age population	Turnout	%	Difference from 1812	1824 Voting-age population	Turnout	%	Difference from 1812	1828 (Democratic Party) Voting-age population	Turnout	%	Difference from 1812
ALABAMA												29,000	9,429	32.5%		36,000	16,736	46.5%	14.0
CONNECTICUT								60,000	3,889	6.5%						68,000	4,448	6.5%	0.1
GEORGIA																57,000	19,362	34.0%	
ILLINOIS								12,000	938	7.8%		20,000	1,272	6.4%	-1.5	28,000	9,560	34.1%	26.3
INDIANA												44,000	7,444	16.9%		58,000	22,201	38.3%	21.4

United States Presidential General Elections *(continued)*

Democratic Turnout for Election Years 1812–1828 *(continued)*

State	1812 Voting-age population	Turnout	%	1816 Voting-age population	Turnout	%	Difference from 1812	1820 Voting-age population	Turnout	%	Difference from 1812	1824 Voting-age population	Turnout	%	Difference from 1812	1828 (Democratic Party) Voting-age population	Turnout	%	Difference from 1812
KENTUCKY	67,000	8,501	12.7%					84,000	3,169	3.8%	-8.9	92,000	6,356	6.9%	-5.8	101,000	39,308	38.9%	26.2
LOUISIANA																24,000	4,605	19.2%	
MAINE								61,000	4,867	8.0%						82,000	13,927	17.0%	9.0
MARYLAND	53,000	14,751	27.8%	55,000	7,435	13.5%	-14.3	58,000	4,544	7.8%	-20.0	62,000	14,523	23.4%	-4.4	66,000	22,782	34.5%	6.7
MASSACHUSETTS	107,000	28,620	26.7%					118,000	7,689	6.5%	-20.2					140,000	6,012	4.3%	-22.5
MISSISSIPPI												12,000	3,121	26.0%		15,000	6,763	45.1%	19.1
MISSOURI												18,000	1,166	6.5%		22,000	8,232	37.4%	30.9
NEW HAMPSHIRE	46,000	12,744	27.7%	49,000	15,197	31.0%	3.3	52,000	9,448	18.2%	-9.5					59,000	20,212	34.3%	6.6
NEW JERSEY				52,000	5,441	10.5%		55,000	4,321	7.9%	-2.6	60,000	10,332	17.2%	6.8	65,000	21,809	33.6%	23.1
NEW YORK																397,000	139,412	35.1%	
NORTH CAROLINA				78,000	9,549	12.2%		81,000	3,300	4.1%	-8.2	86,000	20,231	23.5%	11.3	91,000	37,814	41.6%	29.3
OHIO	61,000	7,420	12.2%	89,000	3,326	3.7%	-8.4	117,000	7,104	6.1%	6.0	146,000	18,489	12.7%	0.5	176,000	67,596	38.4%	26.2
PENNSYLVANIA	175,000	49,397	28.2%	193,000	25,653	13.3%	-14.9	213,000	30,313	14.2%	-14.0	242,000	35,736	14.8%	-13.5	272,000	101,457	37.3%	9.1
RHODE ISLAND	16,000	2,084	13.0%	17,000	1,236	7.3%	-5.8	17,000	724	4.3%	-8.8					21,000	820	3.9%	-9.1
TENNESSEE												78,000	20,197	25.9%		94,000	44,293	47.1%	21.2
VERMONT																61,000	8,350	13.7%	
VIRGINIA	116,000	14,980	12.9%	121,000	6,859	5.7%	-7.2	126,000	5,247	4.2%	-8.7	133,000	2,975	2.2%	-10.7	141,000	26,854	19.0%	6.1
Total	641,000	138,497	21.6%	654,000	74,696	11.4%	-10.2	1,054,000	85,613	8.1%	-13.5	1,022,000	151,271	14.8%	6.8	2,074,000	642,553	31.0%	9.4

Other Turnout for Election Years 1812–1828

State	1812 Voting-age population	Turnout	%	1816 Voting-age population	Turnout	%	Difference from 1812**	1820 Voting-age population	Turnout	%	Difference from 1812	1824 Voting-age population	Turnout	%	Difference from 1812	1828 Voting-age population	Turnout	%	Difference from 1812
ALABAMA												29,000	1,752	6.0%		36,000	4	0.0%	-6.0
CONNECTICUT												64,000	3,153	4.9%		68,000	1,101	1.6%	-3.3
ILLINOIS								12,000	492	4.1%		20,000	1,883	9.4%	5.3				
INDIANA												44,000	5,323	12.1%					
KENTUCKY												92,000	16,982	18.5%					
MAINE								61,000	587	1.0%		72,000	2,336	3.2%	2.3	82,000	89	0.1%	-0.9
MARYLAND								58,000	175	0.3%		62,000	4,059	6.5%	6.2				
MASSACHUSETTS												129,000	11,369	8.8%		140,000	3,226	2.3%	-6.5
MISSISSIPPI												12,000	119	1.0%					

United States Presidential General Elections (continued)

United States Presidential General Elections *(continued)*

Other Turnout for Election Years 1812–1828 *(continued)*

State	1812			1816				1820				1824				1828			
	Voting-age population	Turnout	%	Voting-age population	Turnout	%	Difference from 1812	Voting-age population	Turnout	%	Difference from 1812	Voting-age population	Turnout	%	Difference from 1812	Voting-age population	Turnout	%	Difference from 1812
MISSOURI												18,000	2,107	11.7%					
NEW HAMPSHIRE												56,000	643	1.1%					
NEW JERSEY												60,000	1,196	2.0%		65,000	8	0.0%	-2.0
NORTH CAROLINA												86,000	15,878	18.5%		91,000	15	0.0%	-18.4
OHIO												146,000	19,255	13.2%					
PENNSYLVANIA				193,000	17,589	9.1%		213,000	1,893	0.9%	-8.2	242,000	5,896	2.4%	-6.7				
RHODE ISLAND												19,000	200	1.1%		21,000	5	0.0%	-1.0
TENNESSEE												78,000	312	0.4%					
VERMONT																61,000	120	0.2%	
VIRGINIA												133,000	8,977	6.7%					
Total				193,000	17,589	9.1%		344,000	3,147	0.9%	-8.2	1,362,000	101,440	7.4%	-1.7	564,000	4,568	0.8%	-8.3

*In the aftermath of the War of 1812, the Federalist party lost its stature as the second national party. For a brief time, the "Era of Good Feelings," the Democratic-Republican party held sway as the only national party, but the National Republican party developed out of competition within the Democratic-Republicans. For the purposes of this book, the National Republican era begins in 1820 and ends in 1832.

**Percentage point difference between turnout in current year and initial year listed in chart. If data do not appear for a state in the initial year listed, the difference is calculated from the first year in which data do appear for that state.

***The Democratic-Republican party finally dropped the "Republican" and became the "Democratic" Party that continues into the 21st century.

STATE GUBERNATORIAL GENERAL ELECTIONS

Election Years 1812–1828

State	1812			1816				1820				1824				1828			
	Voting-age population	Turnout	%	Voting-age population	Turnout	%	Difference from 1812*	Voting-age population	Turnout	%	Difference from 1812	Voting-age population	Turnout	%	Difference from 1812	Voting-age population	Turnout	%	Difference from 1812
CONNECTICUT	57,000	13,208	23.2%	58,000	21,759	37.5%	14.3	60,000	15,738	26.2%	3.1	64,000	7,103	11.1%	-12.1	68,000	9,297	13.7%	-9.5
DELAWARE				11,000	7,525	68.4%		11,000	7,490	68.1%	-0.3								
INDIANA				19,000	9,145	48.1%										58,000	36,927	63.7%	15.5
KENTUCKY	67,000	42,826	63.9%	79,000	47,442	60.1%	-3.9	84,000	62,426	74.3%	10.4	92,000	64,662	70.3%	6.4	101,000	77,171	76.4%	12.5
LOUISIANA	16,000	3,703	23.1%	18,000	4,459	24.8%	1.6	20,000	4,748	23.7%	0.6	22,000	6,105	27.8%	4.6	24,000	7,099	29.6%	6.4
MAINE								61,000	21,083	34.6%		72,000	19,759	27.4%	-7.1	82,000	25,755	31.4%	-3.2
MASSACHUSETTS	107,000	104,022	97.2%	112,000	96,848	86.5%	-10.7	118,000	52,999	44.9%	-52.3	129,000	72,860	56.5%	-40.7	140,000	32,404	23.1%	-74.1
MISSOURI												18,000	10,801	60.0%		22,000	11,958	54.4%	-5.7
NEW HAMPSHIRE	46,000	31,105	67.6%	49,000	38,332	78.2%	10.6	52,000	22,212	42.7%	-24.9	56,000	28,571	51.0%	-16.6	59,000	39,821	67.5%	-0.1
NEW YORK				251,000	84,059	33.5%		290,000	93,437	32.2%	-1.3	344,000	191,721	55.7%	23.5	397,000	276,545	69.7%	36.2
NORTH CAROLINA																			
OHIO	61,000	19,762	32.4%	89,000	30,833	34.6%	2.2	117,000	48,610	41.5%	9.2	146,000	75,197	51.5%	19.1	176,000	105,922	60.2%	27.8
PENNSYLVANIA								213,000	134,205	63.0%									
RHODE ISLAND	16,000	7,996	50.0%	17,000	6,850	40.3%	-9.7	17,000	1,981	11.7%	-38.3	19,000	2,740	14.4%	-35.6	21,000	4,233	20.2%	-29.8
VERMONT	45,000	35,108	78.0%	47,000	31,150	66.3%	-11.7	50,000	13,152	26.3%	-51.7	56,000	15,447	27.6%	-50.4	61,000	17,218	28.2%	-49.8
Total	415,000	257,730	62.1%	750,000	378,402	50.5%	-11.7	1,093,000	478,081	43.7%	-18.4	1,018,000	494,966	48.6%	-13.5	1,209,000	644,350	53.3%	-8.8

*Percentage point difference between turnout in current year and initial year listed in chart. If data do not appear for a state in the initial year listed, the difference is calculated from the first year in which data do appear for that state.

STATE GUBERNATORIAL GENERAL ELECTIONS

Federalist (or National Republican) Turnout for Election Years 1812–1828*

State	1812 Voting-age population	Turnout	%	1816 Voting-age population	Turnout	%	Difference from 1812**	1820 (National Republicans) Voting-age population	Turnout	%	Difference from 1812	1824 (National Republicans) Voting-age population	Turnout	%	Difference from 1812	1828 (National Republicans) Voting-age population	Turnout	%	Difference from 1812
CONNECTICUT	57,000	11,721	20.6%	58,000	11,575	20.0%	-0.6	60,000	15,738	26.2%	5.7	64,000	466	0.7%	-19.8	68,000	9,297	13.7%	-6.9
DELAWARE				11,000	4,008	36.4%		11,000	3,520	32.0%	-4.4								
INDIANA																58,000	26,029	44.9%	
KENTUCKY																101,000	38,940	38.6%	
LOUISIANA																24,000	4,213	17.6%	
MASSACHUSETTS	107,000	52,696	49.2%	112,000	49,527	44.2%	-5.0	118,000	31,072	26.3%	-22.9	129,000	34,210	26.5%	-22.7	140,000	27,981	20.0%	-29.3
NEW HAMPSHIRE	46,000	15,613	33.9%	49,000	17,994	36.7%	2.8									59,000	21,149	35.8%	1.9
NEW YORK				251,000	38,647	15.4%		290,000	45,990	15.9%	0.5					397,000	106,415	26.8%	11.4
NORTH CAROLINA																			
OHIO	61,000	11,859	19.4%	89,000	1,607	1.8%	-17.6					146,000	36,869	25.3%	5.8	176,000	53,971	30.7%	28.9
RHODE ISLAND	16,000	4,122	25.8%	17,000	3,591	21.1%	-4.6												
VERMONT	45,000	15,950	35.4%	47,000	13,888	29.5%	-5.9									61,000	16,285	26.7%	-2.9
Total	332,000	111,961	33.7%	634,000	140,837	22.2%	-11.5	479,000	96,320	20.1%	-13.6	339,000	71,545	21.1%	-12.6	1,084,000	304,280	28.1%	-5.7

Democratic-Republican Turnout for Election Years 1812–1828

State	1812 Voting-age population	Turnout	%	1816 Voting-age population	Turnout	%	Difference from 1812**	1820 Voting-age population	Turnout	%	Difference from 1812	1824 Voting-age population	Turnout	%	Difference from 1812	1828 (Democratic Party)*** Voting-age population	Turnout	%	Difference from 1812
CONNECTICUT	57,000	1,487	2.6%									64,000	6,637	10.4%	7.8				
DELAWARE				11,000	3,517	32.0%		11,000	3,970	36.1%	4.1								
INDIANA																58,000	10,898	18.8%	
KENTUCKY																101,000	38,231	37.9%	
LOUISIANA																			
MAINE								61,000	21,083	34.6%		72,000	19,759	27.4%	-7.1	82,000	25,755	31.4%	-3.2
MASSACHUSETTS	107,000	51,326	48.0%	112,000	47,321	42.3%	-5.7	118,000	21,927	18.6%	-29.4	129,000	38,650	30.0%	-18.0				
MISSOURI																			
NEW HAMPSHIRE	46,000	15,492	33.7%	49,000	20,338	41.5%	7.8	52,000	22,212	42.7%	9.0								
NEW YORK				251,000	45,412	18.1%													
NORTH CAROLINA																			
OHIO	61,000	7,903	13.0%	89,000	29,226	32.8%	19.9	117,000	48,610	41.5%	28.6	146,000	38,328	26.3%	13.3				
PENNSYLVANIA								213,000	134,205	63.0%									
RHODE ISLAND	16,000	3,874	24.2%	17,000	3,259	19.2%	-5.0	17,000	1,981	11.7%	-12.6	19,000	2,740	14.4%	-9.8				
VERMONT	45,000	19,158	42.6%	47,000	17,262	36.7%	-5.8	50,000	13,152	26.3%	-16.3	56,000	13,485	24.1%	-18.5				
Total	332,000	99,240	29.9%	576,000	166,335	28.9%	-1.0	639,000	267,140	41.8%	11.9	486,000	119,599	24.6%	-5.3	241,000	74,884	31.1%	1.2

State Gubernatorial General Elections (continued)

Other Turnout for Election Years 1812–1828

State	1812			1816				1820				1824				1828			
	Voting-age population	Turnout	%	Voting-age population	Turnout	%	Difference from 1812**	Voting-age population	Turnout	%	Difference from 1812	Voting-age population	Turnout	%	Difference from 1812	Voting-age population	Turnout	%	Difference from 1812
CONNECTICUT				58,000	10,184	17.6%													
INDIANA				19,000	9,145	48.1%													
KENTUCKY	67,000	42,826	63.9%	79,000	47,442	60.1%	-3.9	84,000	62,426	74.3%	10.4	92,000	64,662	70.3%	6.4				
LOUISIANA	16,000	3,703	23.1%	18,000	4,459	24.8%	1.6	20,000	4,748	23.7%	0.6	22,000	6,105	27.8%	4.6	24,000	2,886	12.0%	-11.1
MASSACHUSETTS																140,000	4,423	3.2%	
MISSOURI												18,000	10,801	60.0%		22,000	11,958	54.4%	-5.7
NEW HAMPSHIRE												56,000	28,571	51.0%		59,000	18,672	31.6%	-19.4
NEW YORK								290,000	47,447	16.4%		344,000	191,721	55.7%	39.4	397,000	170,130	42.9%	26.5
OHIO																176,000	51,951	29.5%	
RHODE ISLAND																21,000	4,233	20.2%	
VERMONT												56,000	1,962	3.5%		61,000	933	1.5%	-2.0
Total	83,000	46,529	56.1%	174,000	71,230	40.9%	-15.1	394,000	114,621	29.1%	-27.0	588,000	303,822	51.7%	-4.4	900,000	265,186	29.5%	-26.6

*In the aftermath of the War of 1812, the Federalist party lost its stature as the second national party. For a brief time, the "Era of Good Feelings," the Democratic-Republican party held sway as the only national party, but the National Republican party developed out of competition within the Democratic-Republicans. For the purposes of this book, the National Republican era begins in 1820 and ends in 1832.

**Percentage point difference between turnout in current year and initial year listed in chart. If data do not appear for a state in the initial year listed, the difference is calculated from the first year in which data do appear for that state.

***The Democratic-Republican party finally dropped the "Republican" and became the "Democratic" Party that continues into the 21st century.

UNITED STATES HOUSE OF REPRESENTATIVES GENERAL ELECTIONS

Election Years 1812–1828

State	1812			1816				1820				1824				1828			
	Voting-age population	Turnout	%	Voting-age population	Turnout	%	Difference from 1812*	Voting-age population	Turnout	%	Difference from 1812	Voting-age population	Turnout	%	Difference from 1812	Voting-age population	Turnout	%	Difference from 1812
CONNECTICUT	57,000	10,631	18.7%	58,000	9,591	16.5%	-2.1												
DELAWARE	11,000	7,414	67.4%	11,000	7,473	67.9%	0.5	11,000	7,486	68.1%	0.7	12,000	6,550	54.6%	-12.8	12,000	9,116	76.0%	8.6
GEORGIA	31,000	14,580	47.0%	35,000	18,283	52.2%	5.2	39,000	15,574	39.9%	-7.1	48,000	9,812	20.4%	-26.6	57,000	47,978	84.2%	37.1
ILLINOIS								12,000	7,680	64.0%		20,000	12,021	60.1%	-3.9	28,000	16,605	59.3%	-4.7
INDIANA				19,000	6,789	35.7%		30,000	17,954	59.8%	24.1	44,000	18,963	43.1%	7.4	58,000	34,558	59.6%	23.9
KENTUCKY	67,000	28,341	42.3%	75,000	46,997	62.7%	20.4	84,000	4,463	5.3%	-37.0	92,000	16,546	18.0%	-24.3				
LOUISIANA	17,000	2,472	14.5%	18,000	2,644	14.7%	0.1	20,000	4,599	23.0%	8.3					24,000	7,459	31.1%	16.5
MAINE								61,000	9,685	15.9%		72,000	16,789	23.3%	7.4	82,000	27,872	34.0%	18.1
MARYLAND	53,000	34,164	64.5%	55,000	27,843	50.6%	-13.8	58,000	26,319	45.4%	-19.1	62,000	44,418	71.6%	7.2				
MASSACHUSETTS	107,000	69,868	65.3%	112,000	44,096	39.4%	-25.9	118,000	26,383	22.4%	-42.9	129,000	35,916	27.8%	-37.5	140,000	35,360	25.3%	-40.0
MISSISSIPPI												12,000	5,961	49.7%					
MISSOURI								13,000	5,574	42.9%		18,000	10,684	59.4%	16.5	22,000	12,995	59.1%	16.2
NEW HAMPSHIRE	46,000	34,537	75.1%	49,000	29,271	59.7%	-15.3	52,000	11,514	22.1%	-52.9	56,000	17,082	30.5%	-44.6				
NEW JERSEY				52,000	5,538	10.7%		55,000	5,483	10.0%	-0.7	60,000	17,536	29.2%	18.6	65,000	45,797	70.5%	59.8
NEW YORK	214,000	94,153	44.0%	251,000	124,133	49.5%	5.5					344,000	186,795	54.3%	10.3	397,000	281,807	71.0%	27.0
OHIO	61,000	22,944	37.6%	89,000	20,900	23.5%	-14.1	117,000	17,839	15.2%	-22.4	146,000	75,723	51.9%	14.3	176,000	72,400	41.1%	3.5
PENNSYLVANIA	175,000	91,166	52.1%	193,000	57,459	29.8%	-22.3	213,000	139,880	65.7%	13.6	242,000	95,381	39.4%	-12.7	272,000	146,422	53.8%	1.7
RHODE ISLAND	16,000	7,609	47.6%	17,000	2,235	13.1%	-34.4	17,000	6,454	38.0%	-9.6								
SOUTH CAROLINA	43,000	4,923	11.4%	45,000	25,967	57.7%	46.3	46,000	8,125	17.7%	6.2	49,000	18,475	37.7%	26.3	52,000	4,362	8.4%	-3.1
VERMONT	45,000	31,750	70.6%	47,000	30,516	64.9%	-5.6	50,000	21,282	42.6%	-28.0	56,000	22,183	39.6%	-30.9	61,000	21,377	35.0%	-35.5
Total	943,000	454,552	48.2%	1,126,000	459,735	40.8%	-7.4	996,000	336,294	33.8%	-14.4	1,462,000	610,835	41.8%	-6.4	1,446,000	764,108	52.8%	4.6

*Percentage point difference between turnout in current year and initial year listed in chart. If data do not appear for a state in the initial year listed, the difference is calculated from the first year in which data do appear for that state.

UNITED STATES HOUSE OF REPRESENTATIVES GENERAL ELECTIONS

Federalist (or National Republican) Turnout for Election Years 1812–1828*

State	1812 Voting-age population	Turnout	%	1816 Voting-age population	Turnout	%	Difference from 1812**	1820 (National Republicans) Voting-age population	Turnout	%	Difference from 1812	1824 (National Republicans) Voting-age population	Turnout	%	Difference from 1812	1828 (National Republicans) Voting-age population	Turnout	%	Difference from 1812
CONNECTICUT	57,000	10,631	18.7%	58,000	9,591	16.5%	-2.1												
DELAWARE	11,000	4,193	38.1%	11,000	3,945	35.9%	-2.3	11,000	3,709	33.7%	-4.4	12,000	3,387	28.2%	-9.9	12,000	4,769	39.7%	1.6
GEORGIA	31,000	2,699	8.7%																
ILLINOIS																28,000	6,158	22.0%	
INDIANA																58,000	21,780	37.6%	
KENTUCKY				75,000	4,331	5.8%		84,000	1,686	2.0%	-3.8								
LOUISIANA																24,000	3,875	16.1%	
MAINE								61,000	2,185	3.6%		72,000	2,891	4.0%	0.4	82,000	10,231	12.5%	8.9
MARYLAND	53,000	13,074	24.7%	55,000	17,744	32.3%	7.6	58,000	13,001	22.4%	-2.3	62,000	15,460	24.9%	0.3				
MASSACHUSETTS	107,000	42,273	39.5%	112,000	23,869	21.3%	-18.2	118,000	13,986	11.9%	-27.7	129,000	15,326	11.9%	-27.6	140,000	29,623	21.2%	-18.3
MISSOURI																22,000	5,127	23.3%	
NEW HAMPSHIRE	46,000	18,572	40.4%	49,000	13,600	27.8%	-12.6	52,000	1,616	3.1%	-37.3								
NEW JERSEY								55,000	417	0.8%						65,000	23,783	36.6%	35.8
NEW YORK	214,000	50,675	23.7%	251,000	55,525	22.1%	-1.6									397,000	106,499	26.8%	3.1
OHIO	61,000	4,883	8.0%	89,000	937	1.1%	-7.0									176,000	34,545	19.6%	18.6
PENNSYLVANIA	175,000	36,999	21.1%	193,000	18,722	9.7%	-11.4	213,000	62,456	29.3%	8.2	242,000	28,305	11.7%	-9.4	272,000	49,816	18.3%	-2.8
RHODE ISLAND	16,000	4,450	27.8%	17,000	2,235	13.1%	-14.7												
SOUTH CAROLINA	43,000	839	2.0%	45,000	4,715	10.5%	8.5	46,000	1,161	2.5%	0.6								
VERMONT	45,000	15,745	35.0%	47,000	13,847	29.5%	-5.5	50,000	7,692	15.4%	-19.6	56,000	1,455	2.6%	-32.4	61,000	15,267	25.0%	-10.0
Total	859,000	205,033	23.9%	1,002,000	169,061	16.9%	-7.0	748,000	107,909	14.4%	-9.4	573,000	66,824	11.7%	-12.2	1,337,000	311,473	23.3%	-0.6

Democratic-Republican Turnout for Election Years 1812–1828

State	1812 Voting-age population	Turnout	%	1816 Voting-age population	Turnout	%	Difference from 1812**	1820 Voting-age population	Turnout	%	Difference from 1812	1824 Voting-age population	Turnout	%	Difference from 1812	1828 (Democratic Party)*** Voting-age population	Turnout	%	Difference from 1812
DELAWARE	11,000	3,221	29.3%	11,000	3,528	32.1%	2.8	11,000	3,777	34.3%	5.1	12,000	3,163	26.4%	-2.9	12,000	4,347	36.2%	6.9
GEORGIA	31,000	11,881	38.3%	37,000	10,961	29.6%	-8.7	39,000	10,486	26.9%	-11.4	48,000	9,812	20.4%	-17.9	57,000	47,978	84.2%	45.8
ILLINOIS								12,000	5,322	44.4%						28,000	10,447	37.3%	-7.0
INDIANA				19,000	5,160	27.2%		30,000	16,331	54.4%	27.3	44,000	8,961	20.4%	-6.8	58,000	12,778	22.0%	-5.1
KENTUCKY	67,000	25,470	38.0%	75,000	27,216	36.3%	-1.7	83,000	2,651	3.2%	-34.8	92,000	11,014	12.0%	-26.0				
LOUISIANA	17,000	880	5.2%	18,000	2,644	14.7%	9.5	20,000	4,599	23.0%	17.8					24,000	2,450	10.2%	5.0
MAINE								61,000	5,923	9.7%		72,000	10,403	14.4%	4.7	82,000	11,178	13.6%	3.9
MARYLAND	53,000	21,090	39.8%	55,000	10,013	18.2%	-21.6	58,000	13,318	23.0%	-16.8	62,000	25,741	41.5%	1.7				
MASSACHUSETTS	107,000	27,103	25.3%	112,000	18,764	16.8%	-8.6	118,000	9,476	8.0%	-17.3	129,000	14,745	11.4%	-13.9	140,000	4,272	3.1%	-22.3
MISSISSIPPI												12,000	5,961	49.7%					

United States House of Representatives General Elections (continued)

United States House of Representatives General Elections (continued)

Democratic-Republican Turnout for Election Years 1812–1828 (continued)

State	1812 Voting-age population	Turnout	%	1816 Voting-age population	Turnout	%	Difference from 1812	1820 Voting-age population	Turnout	%	Difference from 1812	1824 Voting-age population	Turnout	%	Difference from 1812	1828 (Democratic Party)*** Voting-age population	Turnout	%	Difference from 1812
MISSOURI								13,000	5,574	42.9%		18,000	9,559	53.1%	10.2	22,000	7,868	35.8%	-7.1
NEW HAMPSHIRE	46,000	15,965	34.7%	49,000	15,571	31.8%	-2.9	52,000	9,898	19.0%	-15.7	56,000	11,603	20.7%	-14.0				
NEW JERSEY				52,000	5,538	10.7%		55,000	4,701	8.5%	-2.1	60,000	17,536	29.2%	18.6	65,000	22,014	33.9%	23.2
NEW YORK	210,000	42,433	20.2%	251,000	68,258	27.2%	7.0					344,000	184,474	53.6%	33.4	397,000	141,076	35.5%	15.3
OHIO	61,000	14,856	24.4%	89,000	15,285	17.2%	-7.2	117,000	17,839	15.2%	-9.1					176,000	35,305	20.1%	-4.3
PENNSYLVANIA	175,000	53,793	30.7%	193,000	37,077	19.2%	-11.5	213,000	76,663	36.0%	5.3	242,000	64,919	26.8%	-3.9	272,000	83,229	30.6%	-0.1
RHODE ISLAND	16,000	3,159	19.7%					17,000	2,891	17.0%	-2.7								
SOUTH CAROLINA	43,000	3,160	7.3%	45,000	21,252	47.2%	39.9	46,000	6,964	15.1%	7.8	49,000	5,220	10.7%	3.3	52,000	1,808	3.5%	-3.9
VERMONT	45,000	16,005	35.6%	47,000	16,669	35.5%	-0.1	50,000	13,033	26.1%	-9.5	56,000	15,336	27.4%	-8.2	61,000	3,747	6.1%	-29.4
Total	882,000	239,016	27.1%	1,053,000	257,936	24.5%	-2.6	995,000	209,446	21.0%	-6.0	1,296,000	398,447	30.7%	3.6	1,446,000	388,497	26.9%	-0.2

Other Turnout for Election Years 1812–1828*

State	1812 Voting-age population	Turnout	%	1816 Voting-age population	Turnout	%	Difference from 1812**	1820 Voting-age population	Turnout	%	Difference from 1812	1824 Voting-age population	Turnout	%	Difference from 1812	1828 Voting-age population	Turnout	%	Difference from 1812
GEORGIA				37,000	7,322	19.8%		39,000	5,088	13.0%	-6.7								
ILLINOIS								12,000	2,358	19.7%		20,000	12,021	60.1%	40.5				
INDIANA				19,000	1,629	8.6%		30,000	1,623	5.4%	-3.2	44,000	10,002	22.7%	14.2				
KENTUCKY	66,000	2,871	4.4%	75,000	15,450	20.6%	16.3	83,000	126	0.2%	-4.2	92,000	5,532	6.0%	1.7				
LOUISIANA	17,000	1,592	9.4%													24,000	1,134	4.7%	-4.6
MAINE								61,000	1,577	2.6%		72,000	3,495	4.9%	2.3	81,000	6,463	8.0%	5.4
MARYLAND				55,000	86	0.2%						62,000	3,217	5.2%	5.0				
MASSACHUSETTS	106,000	492	0.5%	112,000	1,463	1.3%	0.8	117,000	2,921	2.5%	2.0	129,000	5,845	4.5%	4.1	139,000	1,465	1.1%	0.6
MISSOURI												18,000	1,125	6.3%					
NEW HAMPSHIRE				49,000	100	0.2%						56,000	5,479	9.8%	9.6				
NEW JERSEY								55,000	365	0.7%									
NEW YORK	210,000	1,045	0.5%	251,000	350	0.1%	-0.4					344,000	2,321	0.7%	0.2	392,000	34,232	8.7%	8.2
OHIO	59,000	3,205	5.4%	89,000	4,678	5.3%	-0.2					146,000	75,723	51.9%	46.4	173,000	2,550	1.5%	-4.0
PENNSYLVANIA	173,000	374	0.2%	193,000	1,660	0.9%	0.6	213,000	761	0.4%	0.1	242,000	2,157	0.9%	0.7	269,000	13,377	5.0%	4.8
RHODE ISLAND								17,000	3,563	21.0%									
SOUTH CAROLINA	43,000	924	2.1%									49,000	13,255	27.1%	24.9	51,000	2,554	5.0%	2.9
VERMONT								50,000	557	1.1%		56,000	5,392	9.6%	8.5	60,000	2,363	3.9%	2.8
Total	674,000	10,503	1.6%	880,000	32,738	3.7%	2.2	677,000	18,939	2.8%	1.2	1,330,000	145,564	10.9%	9.4	1,189,000	64,138	5.4%	3.8

*In the aftermath of the War of 1812, the Federalist party lost its stature as the second national party. For a brief time, the "Era of Good Feelings," the Democratic-Republican party held sway as the only national party, but the National Republican party developed out of competition within the Democratic-Republicans. For the purposes of this book, the National Republican era begins in 1820 and ends in 1832.

**Percentage point difference between turnout in current year and initial year listed in chart. If data do not appear for a state in the initial year listed, the difference is calculated from the first year in which data do appear for that state.

***The Democratic-Republican party finally dropped the "Republican" and became the "Democratic" Party that continues into the 21st century.

Midterm Turnout Election Based on Highest Statewide Turnout, Election Years 1810–1826

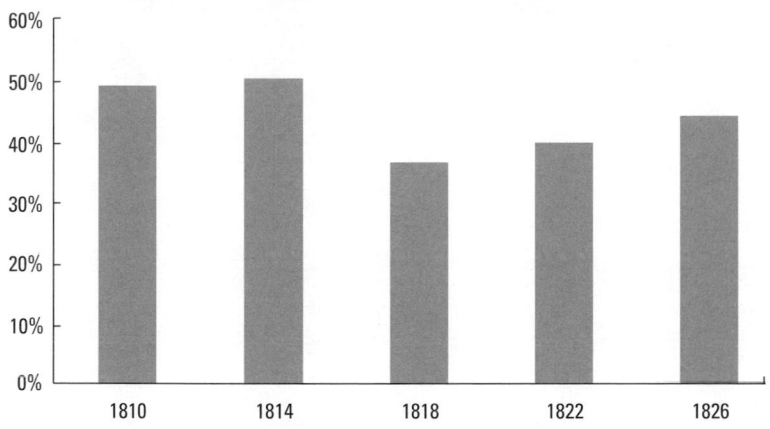

YEAR	VOTING-AGE POPULATION	TOTAL	%
1810	992,000	484,096	48.8%
1814	1,050,000	525,589	50.1%
1818	1,193,000	432,633	36.3%
1822	1,418,000	560,173	39.5%
1826	1,554,000	681,827	43.9%

Partisan Turnout Midterm Election Based on Aggregate House of Representatives Turnout, Election Years 1810–1826

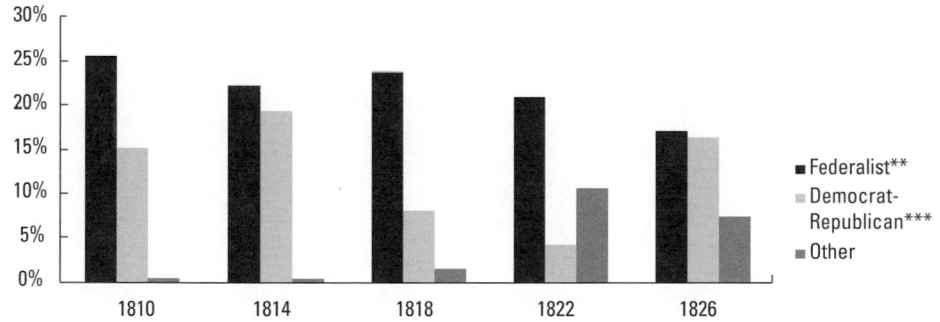

■ Federalist**
■ Democrat-Republican***
■ Other

YEAR	VOTING-AGE POPULATION*	FEDERALIST** TURNOUT	%	DEMOCRAT-REPUBLICAN*** TURNOUT	%	OTHER TURNOUT	%
1810	992,000	148,337	15.0%	249,878	25.2%	4,892	0.5%
1814	1,050,000	200,317	19.1%	230,081	21.9%	4,622	0.4%
1818	1,193,000	99,497	8.3%	278,310	23.3%	18,503	1.6%
1822	1,418,000	60,124	4.2%	292,486	20.6%	148,612	10.5%
1826	1,554,000	250,852	16.1%	261,802	16.8%	114,066	7.3%

*Voting-age population taken from all states with statewide elections. For percentages based on only states with House elections, see House partisan chart.

**In the aftermath of the War of 1812, the Federalist party lost its stature as the second national party. For a brief time, the "Era of Good Feelings," the Democratic-Republican party held sway as the only national party, but the National Republican party developed out of competition within the Democratic-Republicans. For the purposes of this book, the National Republican era begins in 1820 and ends in 1832.

***The Democratic-Republican party finally dropped the "Republican" and became the "Democratic" Party that continues into the 21st century.

STATE GUBERNATORIAL GENERAL ELECTIONS

Election Years 1810–1826

State	1810			1814				1818				1822				1826			
	Voting-age population	Turnout	%	Voting-age population	Turnout	%	Difference from 1810*	Voting-age population	Turnout	%	Difference from 1810	Voting-age population	Turnout	%	Difference from 1810	Voting-age population	Turnout	%	Difference from 1810
CONNECTICUT	56,000	20,560	36.7%	58,000	12,034	20.7%	-16.0	59,000	16,432	27.9%	-8.9	62,000	9,138	14.7%	-22.0	66,000	11,120	16.8%	-19.9
DELAWARE	11,000	7,257	66.0%									12,000	7,546	62.9%	-3.1	12,000	8,582	71.5%	5.5
ILLINOIS												16,000	8,606	53.8%		24,000	12,113	50.5%	-3.3
INDIANA												37,000	18,340	49.6%					
MAINE												67,000	21,271	31.7%		77,000	20,689	26.9%	-4.9
MASSACHUSETTS	104,000	90,620	87.1%	109,000	102,327	93.9%	6.7	115,000	69,579	60.5%	-26.6	124,000	49,664	40.1%	-47.1	135,000	39,140	29.0%	-58.1
NEW HAMPSHIRE	45,000	31,648	70.3%	48,000	38,489	80.2%	9.9	51,000	30,543	59.9%	-10.4	54,000	22,934	42.5%	-27.9	58,000	29,815	51.4%	-18.9
NEW YORK	196,000	79,578	40.6%									317,000	128,493	40.5%	-0.1	370,000	195,888	52.9%	12.3
OHIO	48,000	17,655	36.8%	75,000	22,050	29.4%	-7.4	103,000	38,269	37.2%	0.4	132,000	60,008	45.5%	8.7	161,000	79,449	49.3%	12.6
PENNSYLVANIA				184,000	80,575	43.8%										257,000	72,710	28.3%	-15.5
RHODE ISLAND				16,000	2,710	16.9%		17,000	8,402	49.4%	32.5	18,000	2,092	11.6%	-5.3	20,000	1,731	8.7%	-8.3
VERMONT	44,000	23,722	53.9%	46,000	34,877	75.8%	21.9	49,000	15,243	31.1%	-22.8	53,000	13,152	24.8%	-29.1	58,000	12,123	20.9%	-33.0
Total	504,000	271,040	53.8%	536,000	293,062	54.7%	0.9	394,000	178,468	45.3%	-8.5	892,000	341,244	38.3%	-15.5	1,238,000	483,360	39.0%	-14.7

*Percentage point difference between turnout in current year and initial year listed in chart. If data do not appear for a state in the initial year listed, the difference is calculated from the first year in which data do appear for that state.

STATE GUBERNATORIAL GENERAL ELECTIONS

Federalist (or National Republican) Turnout for Election Years 1810–1826*

State	1810			1814				1818				1822 (National Republicans)				1826 (National Republicans)			
	Voting-age population	Turnout	%	Voting-age population	Turnout	%	Difference from 1810**	Voting-age population	Turnout	%	Difference from 1810	Voting-age population	Turnout	%	Difference from 1810	Voting-age population	Turnout	%	Difference from 1810
CONNECTICUT	56,000	13,375	23.9%	58,000	9,415	16.2%	-7.7					62,000	570	0.9%	-23.0	66,000	4,340	6.6%	-17.3
DELAWARE	11,000	3,593	32.7%									12,000	3,762	31.4%	-1.3	12,000	4,344	36.2%	3.5
ILLINOIS																24,000	6,280	26.2%	
MAINE												67,000	5,795	8.6%					
MASSACHUSETTS	104,000	44,079	42.4%	109,000	56,374	51.7%	9.3	115,000	39,538	34.4%	-8.0	124,000	28,487	23.0%	-19.4	135,000	11,256	8.3%	-34.0
NEW HAMPSHIRE	45,000	15,166	33.7%	48,000	19,695	41.0%	7.3	51,000	11,869	23.3%	-10.4								
NEW YORK																			
OHIO				75,000	6,171	8.2%						132,000	22,889	17.3%	9.1	161,000	70,475	43.8%	35.5
PENNSYLVANIA				184,000	29,566	16.1%													
RHODE ISLAND				16,000	2,710	16.9%		17,000	3,893	22.9%	6.0								
VERMONT	44,000	9,912	22.5%	46,000	17,466	38.0%	15.4												
Total	200,000	66,125	33.1%	606,000	141,307	26.4%	6.7	183,000	55,300	30.2%	2.0	397,000	61,503	15.5%	-17.6	398,000	96,695	24.3%	-8.8

Democratic-Republican Turnout for Election Years 1810–1826

State	1810			1814				1818				1822				1826 (Democratic Party)***			
	Voting-age population	Turnout	%	Voting-age population	Turnout	%	Difference from 1810**	Voting-age population	Turnout	%	Difference from 1810	Voting-age population	Turnout	%	Difference from 1810	Voting-age population	Turnout	%	Difference from 1810
CONNECTICUT	56,000	7,185	12.8%	58,000	2,619	4.5%	-8.3					62,000	8,568	13.8%	1.0	66,000	6,780	10.3%	-2.6
DELAWARE	11,000	3,664	33.3%									11,000	3,784	34.4%	1.1	12,000	4,238	35.3%	2.0
ILLINOIS																24,000	5,833	24.3%	
MAINE												66,000	15,478	23.4%		77,000	20,689	26.9%	3.4
MASSACHUSETTS	104,000	46,541	44.8%	109,000	45,953	42.2%	-2.6	115,000	30,041	26.1%	-18.6	123,000	21,177	17.2%	-27.5				
NEW HAMPSHIRE	45,000	16,482	36.6%	48,000	18,794	39.2%	2.5	51,000	18,674	36.6%	0.0	54,000	22,934	42.5%	5.8				
NEW YORK	196,000	43,094	22.0%																
OHIO	48,000	17,655	36.8%	75,000	15,879	21.2%	-15.6	103,000	38,269	37.2%	0.4	128,000	37,119	29.0%	-7.8				
PENNSYLVANIA				184,000	51,009	27.7%													
RHODE ISLAND								17,000	4,509	26.5%									
VERMONT	44,000	13,810	31.4%	46,000	17,411	37.9%	6.5	49,000	15,243	31.1%	-0.3	53,000	11,520	21.7%	-9.7	58,000	8,966	15.5%	-15.9
Total	504,000	148,431	29.5%	520,000	151,665	29.2%	-0.3	335,000	106,736	31.9%	2.4	497,000	120,578	24.3%	-5.2	237,000	46,506	19.6%	-9.8

State Gubernatorial General Elections (continued)

State Gubernatorial General Elections (continued)

Other Turnout for Election Years 1810–1826

State	1810			1814				1818				1822				1826			
	Voting-age population	Turnout	%	Voting-age population	Turnout	%	Difference from 1810**	Voting-age population	Turnout	%	Difference from 1810	Voting-age population	Turnout	%	Difference from 1810	Voting-age population	Turnout	%	Difference from 1810
CONNECTICUT								59,000	16,432	27.9%									
ILLINOIS												16,000	8,606	53.8%					
INDIANA												37,000	18,340	49.6%					
MASSACHUSETTS																135,000	27,884	20.7%	
NEW HAMPSHIRE																58,000	29,815	51.4%	
NEW YORK	196,000	36,484	18.6%									317,000	128,493	40.5%	21.9	370,000	195,888	52.9%	34.3
OHIO																161,000	8,974	5.6%	
PENNSYLVANIA																257,000	72,710	28.3%	
RHODE ISLAND												18,000	2,092	11.6%		20,000	1,731	8.7%	-3.0
VERMONT												53,000	1,632	3.1%		58,000	3,157	5.4%	2.4

*In the aftermath of the War of 1812, the Federalist party lost its stature as the second national party. For a brief time, the "Era of Good Feelings," the Democratic-Republican party held sway as the only national party, but the National Republican party developed out of competition within the Democratic-Republicans. For the purposes of this book, the National Republican era begins in 1820 and ends in 1832.

**Percentage point difference between turnout in current year and initial year listed in chart. If data do not appear for a state in the initial year listed, the difference is calculated from the first year in which data do appear for that state.

***The Democratic-Republican party finally dropped the "Republican" and became the "Democratic" Party that continues into the 21st century.

UNITED STATES HOUSE OF REPRESENTATIVES GENERAL ELECTIONS

Election Years 1810–1826

State	1810 Voting-age population	Turnout	%	1814 Voting-age population	Turnout	%	Difference from 1810*	1818 Voting-age population	Turnout	%	Difference from 1810	1822 Voting-age population	Turnout	%	Difference from 1810	1826 Voting-age population	Turnout	%	Difference from 1810
CONNECTICUT	56,000	4,744	8.5%					59,000	9,181	15.6%	7.1								
DELAWARE	11,000	7,251	65.9%	11,000	6,511	59.2%	-6.7	11,000	6,105	55.5%	-10.4	12,000	7,576	63.1%	-2.8	12,000	8,561	71.3%	5.4
GEORGIA	29,000	20,285	69.9%	33,000	16,389	49.7%	-20.3	37,000	7,356	19.9%	-50.1	44,000	19,328	43.9%	-26.0	52,000	33,790	65.0%	-5.0
ILLINOIS								9,000	3,978	44.2%		16,000	8,575	53.6%	9.4	24,000	12,765	53.2%	9.0
INDIANA								24,000	11,073	46.1%		37,000	20,614	55.7%	9.6	51,000	31,022	60.8%	14.7
KENTUCKY	63,000	13,272	21.1%	71,000	13,554	19.1%	-2.0	79,000	31,687	40.1%	19.0	88,000	33,644	38.2%	17.2				
LOUISIANA				17,000	2,955	17.4%	.	19,000	4,138	21.8%	4.4	21,000	3,342	15.9%	-1.5	23,000	5,077	22.1%	4.7
MAINE																77,000	21,463	27.9%	
MARYLAND	52,000	18,731	36.0%	54,000	32,207	59.6%	23.6	57,000	32,698	57.4%	21.3	60,000	30,424	50.7%	14.7	64,000	38,986	60.9%	24.9
MASSACHUSETTS	104,000	44,021	42.3%	109,000	53,305	48.9%	6.6	115,000	34,354	29.9%	-12.5	124,000	25,305	20.4%	-21.9	135,000	21,229	15.7%	-26.6
MISSISSIPPI												11,000	7,469	67.9%		14,000	9,541	68.2%	0.2
MISSOURI												16,000	9,906	61.9%		20,000	10,790	54.0%	-8.0
NEW HAMPSHIRE	45,000	24,066	53.5%	48,000	34,737	72.4%	18.9					54,000	15,656	29.0%	-24.5				
NEW JERSEY	48,000	14,257	29.7%	51,000	34,556	67.8%	38.1	54,000	14,404	26.7%	-3.0	58,000	4,769	8.2%	-21.5	62,000	26,443	42.7%	12.9
NEW YORK	196,000	114,192	58.3%	233,000	110,957	47.6%	-10.6	270,000	79,753	29.5%	-28.7	317,000	127,784	40.3%	-18.0	370,000	181,994	49.2%	-9.1
NORTH CAROLINA	73,000	36,281	49.7%																
OHIO	48,000	4,646	9.7%	75,000	12,951	17.3%	7.6	103,000	40,991	39.8%	30.1	132,000	54,089	41.0%	31.3	161,000	85,683	53.2%	43.5
PENNSYLVANIA	165,000	64,780	39.3%	184,000	65,931	35.8%	-3.4	202,000	79,525	39.4%	0.1	228,000	103,540	45.4%	6.2	257,000	104,306	40.6%	1.3
RHODE ISLAND	16,000	7,123	44.5%	16,000	6,724	42.0%	-2.5	17,000	1,933	11.4%	-33.1	18,000	1,432	8.0%	-36.6				
SOUTH CAROLINA	42,000	6,779	16.1%	44,000	9,543	21.7%	5.5	46,000	20,061	43.6%	27.5					50,000	13,978	28.0%	11.8
VERMONT	44,000	22,679	51.5%	46,000	34,700	75.4%	23.9	49,000	19,073	38.9%	-12.6	53,000	27,769	52.4%	0.9	58,000	21,092	36.4%	-15.2
Total	992,000	403,107	40.6%	992,000	435,020	43.9%	3.2	1,151,000	396,310	34.4%	-6.2	1,289,000	501,222	38.9%	-1.8	1,430,000	626,720	43.8%	3.2

*Percentage point difference between turnout in current year and initial year listed in chart. If data do not appear for a state in the initial year listed, the difference is calculated from the first year in which data do appear for that state.

UNITED STATES HOUSE OF REPRESENTATIVES GENERAL ELECTIONS

Federalist (or National Republican) Turnout for Election Years 1810–1826*

State	1810			1814				1818				1822 (National Republicans)				1826 (National Republicans)			
	Voting-age population	Turnout	%	Voting-age population	Turnout	%	Difference from 1810**	Voting-age population	Turnout	%	Difference from 1810	Voting-age population	Turnout	%	Difference from 1810	Voting-age population	Turnout	%	Difference from 1810
CONNECTICUT	56,000	4,744	8.5%					59,000	4,481	7.6%	-0.9								
DELAWARE	11,000	3,634	33.0%	11,000	3,964	36.0%	3.0	11,000	3,098	28.2%	-4.9	12,000	4,110	34.3%	1.2	12,000	4,630	38.6%	5.5
GEORGIA	29,000	2,591	8.9%																
ILLINOIS								9,000	3,978	44.2%						24,000	5,619	23.4%	-20.8
INDIANA								24,000	1,118	4.7%						51,000	18,082	35.5%	30.8
KENTUCKY								79,000	2,663	3.4%									
LOUISIANA				17,000	242	1.4%										23,000	1,412	6.1%	4.7
MAINE																77,000	8,743	11.4%	
MARYLAND	52,000	4,753	9.1%	54,000	20,212	37.4%	28.3	57,000	14,627	25.7%	16.5	60,000	7,181	12.0%	2.8	64,000	8,607	13.4%	4.3
MASSACHUSETTS	104,000	22,441	21.6%	109,000	34,464	31.6%	10.0	115,000	16,745	14.6%	-7.0	124,000	13,257	10.7%	-10.9	135,000	12,725	9.4%	-12.2
MISSISSIPPI																14,000	1,451	10.4%	
NEW HAMPSHIRE	45,000	11,473	25.5%	48,000	18,130	37.8%	12.3												
NEW JERSEY	48,000	523	1.1%	51,000	16,697	32.7%	31.6	54,000	181	0.3%	-0.8					62,000	15,635	25.2%	24.1
NEW YORK	196,000	54,161	27.6%	233,000	51,472	22.1%	-5.5	270,000	19,118	7.1%	-20.6	317,000	678	0.2%	-27.4	370,000	87,369	23.6%	-4.0
NORTH CAROLINA	73,000	12,596	17.3%																
OHIO				75,000	2,806	3.7%		103,000	5,819	5.6%	1.9	132,000	3,896	3.0%	-0.8	161,000	47,335	29.4%	25.7
PENNSYLVANIA	165,000	16,615	10.1%	184,000	28,263	15.4%	5.3	202,000	20,969	10.4%	0.3	228,000	24,230	10.6%	0.6	257,000	25,658	10.0%	-0.1
RHODE ISLAND	16,000	3,648	22.8%	16,000	3,771	23.6%	0.8												
SOUTH CAROLINA	42,000	1,522	3.6%	44,000	2,571	5.8%	2.2	46,000	1,987	4.3%	0.7								
VERMONT	44,000	9,636	21.9%	46,000	17,725	38.5%	16.6	49,000	4,713	9.6%	-12.3	53,000	6,772	12.8%	-9.1	58,000	13,586	23.4%	1.5
Total	881,000	148,337	16.8%	888,000	200,317	22.6%	5.7	1,078,000	99,497	9.2%	-7.6	926,000	60,124	6.5%	-10.3	1,308,000	250,852	19.2%	2.3

Democratic-Republican Turnout for Election Years 1810–1826

State	1810			1814				1818				1822				1826 (Democratic Party)***			
	Voting-age population	Turnout	%	Voting-age population	Turnout	%	Difference from 1810**	Voting-age population	Turnout	%	Difference from 1810	Voting-age population	Turnout	%	Difference from 1810	Voting-age population	Turnout	%	Difference from 1810
CONNECTICUT								59,000	4,700	8.0%									
DELAWARE	11,000	3,617	32.9%	11,000	2,547	23.2%	-9.7	11,000	3,007	27.3%	-5.5	12,000	3,466	28.9%	-4.0	12,000	3,931	32.8%	-0.1
GEORGIA	29,000	17,694	61.0%	33,000	16,389	49.7%	-11.4	37,000	7,356	19.9%	-41.1	44,000	15,487	35.2%	-25.8	52,000	20,785	40.0%	-21.0
ILLINOIS												16,000	4,764	29.8%		24,000	6,322	26.3%	-3.4
INDIANA								24,000	9,955	41.5%						51,000	11,217	22.0%	-19.5
KENTUCKY	63,000	13,272	21.1%	71,000	11,017	15.5%	-5.5	79,000	19,334	24.5%	3.4								

United States House of Representatives General Elections (continued)

Democratic-Republican Turnout for Election Years 1810–1826 (continued)

State	1810			1814				1818				1822				1826 (Democratic Party)***			
	Voting-age population	Turnout	%	Voting-age population	Turnout	%	Difference from 1810	Voting-age population	Turnout	%	Difference from 1810	Voting-age population	Turnout	%	Difference from 1810	Voting-age population	Turnout	%	Difference from 1810
LOUISIANA				17,000	2,684	15.8%		19,000	3,266	17.2%	1.4					23,000	1,567	6.8%	-9.0
MAINE																77,000	6,128	8.0%	
MARYLAND	52,000	13,932	26.8%	54,000	11,995	22.2%	-4.6	57,000	18,071	31.7%	4.9	60,000	22,397	37.3%	10.5	64,000	8,760	13.7%	-13.1
MASSACHUSETTS	104,000	21,108	20.3%	109,000	18,734	17.2%	-3.1	115,000	16,748	14.6%	-5.7	124,000	11,142	9.0%	-11.3				
MISSISSIPPI																14,000	3,236	23.1%	
NEW HAMPSHIRE	45,000	11,558	25.7%	48,000	16,607	34.6%	8.9					54,000	11,654	21.6%	-4.1				
NEW JERSEY	48,000	13,734	28.6%	51,000	17,859	35.0%	6.4	54,000	14,223	26.3%	-2.3	58,000	4,219	7.3%	-21.3	62,000	10,166	16.4%	12.2
NEW YORK	196,000	60,031	30.6%	233,000	59,137	25.4%	-5.2	270,000	60,635	22.5%	-8.2	317,000	127,106	40.1%	9.5	370,000	93,253	25.2%	-5.4
NORTH CAROLINA	73,000	23,685	32.4%																
OHIO	48,000	4,617	9.6%	75,000	8,544	11.4%	1.8	103,000	34,596	33.6%	24.0	132,000	10,311	7.8%	-1.8	161,000	17,784	11.0%	1.4
PENNSYLVANIA	165,000	45,430	27.5%	184,000	37,668	20.5%	-7.1	202,000	52,783	26.1%	-1.4	228,000	63,266	27.7%	0.2	257,000	70,887	27.6%	0.0
RHODE ISLAND	10,000	3,475	21.7%	16,000	2,953	18.5%	-3.3	17,000	1,927	11.3%	-10.4	18,000	1,432	8.0%	-13.8				
SOUTH CAROLINA	42,000	5,141	12.2%	44,000	6,972	15.8%	3.6	46,000	18,074	39.3%	27.1					50,000	7,766	15.5%	3.3
VERMONT	44,000	12,584	28.6%	46,000	16,975	36.9%	8.3	49,000	13,635	27.8%	-0.8	53,000	17,242	32.5%	3.9				
Total	936,000	249,878	26.7%	992,000	230,081	23.2%	-3.5	1,142,000	278,310	24.4%	-2.3	1,116,000	292,486	26.2%	-0.5	1,217,000	261,802	21.5%	-5.2

Other Turnout for Election Years 1810–1826

State	1810			1814				1818				1822				1826			
	Voting-age population	Turnout	%	Voting-age population	Turnout	%	Difference from 1810**	Voting-age population	Turnout	%	Difference from 1810	Voting-age population	Turnout	%	Difference from 1810	Voting-age population	Turnout	%	Difference from 1810
GEORGIA												44,000	3,841	8.7%		52,000	13,005	25.0%	16.3
ILLINOIS												16,000	3,811	23.8%		24,000	824	3.4%	20.4
INDIANA												37,000	20,614	55.7%		51,000	1,723	3.4%	-52.3
KENTUCKY				71,000	2,537	3.6%		79,000	9,690	12.3%	8.7	88,000	33,644	38.2%	34.7				
LOUISIANA				17,000	29	0.2%		19,000	872	4.6%	4.4	21,000	3,342	15.9%	15.7	23,000	2,098	9.1%	9.0
MAINE																77,000	6,592	8.6%	
MARYLAND	52,000	46	0.1%									60,000	846	1.4%	1.3	64,000	21,619	33.8%	33.7
MASSACHUSETTS	104,000	472	0.5%	109,000	107	0.1%	-0.4	115,000	861	0.7%	0.3	124,000	906	0.7%	0.3	135,000	8,504	6.3%	5.8
MISSISSIPPI												11,000	7,469	67.9%		14,000	4,854	34.7%	-33.2
MISSOURI												16,000	9,906	61.9%		20,000	10,790	54.0%	-8.0
NEW HAMPSHIRE	45,000	1,035	2.3%									54,000	4,002	7.4%	5.1				
NEW JERSEY												58,000	550	0.9%		62,000	642	1.0%	0.1

United States House of Representatives General Elections (continued)

United States House of Representatives General Elections *(continued)*

Other Turnout for Election Years 1810–1826 *(continued)*

State	1810 Voting-age population	1810 Turnout	1810 %	1814 Voting-age population	1814 Turnout	1814 %	1814 Difference from 1810	1818 Voting-age population	1818 Turnout	1818 %	1818 Difference from 1810	1822 Voting-age population	1822 Turnout	1822 %	1822 Difference from 1810	1826 Voting-age population	1826 Turnout	1826 %	1826 Difference from 1810
NEW YORK				233,000	348	0.1%										370,000	1,372	0.4%	0.2
OHIO	48,000	29	0.1%	75,000	1,601	2.1%	2.1	103,000	576	0.6%	0.5	132,000	39,882	30.2%	30.2	161,000	20,564	12.8%	12.7
PENNSYLVANIA	165,000	2,735	1.7%					202,000	5,773	2.9%	1.2	228,000	16,044	7.0%	5.4	257,000	7,761	3.0%	1.4
RHODE ISLAND								17,000	6	0.0%									
SOUTH CAROLINA	42,000	116	0.3%													50,000	6,212	12.4%	12.1
VERMONT	44,000	459	1.0%					49,000	725	1.5%	0.4	53,000	3,755	7.1%	6.0	58,000	7,506	12.9%	11.9
Total	500,000	4,892	1.0%	505,000	4,622	0.9%	-0.1	584,000	18,503	3.2%	2.2	942,000	148,612	15.8%	14.8	1,418,000	114,066	8.0%	7.1

*In the aftermath of the War of 1812, the Federalist party lost its stature as the second national party. For a brief time, the "Era of Good Feelings," the Democratic-Republican party held sway as the only national party, but the National Republican party developed out of competition within the Democratic-Republicans. For the purposes of this book, the National Republican era begins in 1820 and ends in 1832.

**Percentage point difference between turnout in current year and initial year listed in chart. If data do not appear for a state in the initial year listed, the difference is calculated from the first year in which data do appear for that state.

***The Democratic-Republican party finally dropped the "Republican" and became the "Democratic" Party that continues into the 21st century.

TOTAL HIGHEST STATEWIDE GENERAL ELECTIONS

Election Years 1810–1826

State	1810			1814				1818				1822				1826			
	Voting-age population	Turnout	%	Voting-age population	Turnout	%	Difference from 1810*	Voting-age population	Turnout	%	Difference from 1810	Voting-age population	Turnout	%	Difference from 1810	Voting-age population	Turnout	%	Difference from 1810
CONNECTICUT	56,000	20,560	36.7%	58,000	12,034	20.7%	-16.0	59,000	16,432	27.9%	-8.9	62,000	8,568	13.8%	-22.9	66,000	11,120	16.8%	-19.9
DELAWARE	11,000	7,257	66.0%	11,000	6,508	59.2%	-6.8	11,000	5,909	53.7%	-12.3	12,000	7,576	63.1%	-2.8	12,000	8,582	71.5%	5.5
GEORGIA	29,000	18,146	62.6%	33,000	16,924	51.3%	-11.3	37,000	7,347	19.9%	-42.7	44,000	19,328	43.9%	-18.6	52,000	33,790	65.0%	2.4
ILLINOIS												16,000	8,606	53.8%		24,000	12,765	53.2%	-0.6
INDIANA								24,000	11,073	46.1%		37,000	20,614	55.7%	9.6	51,000	31,022	60.8%	14.7
KENTUCKY	63,000	14,156	22.5%	71,000	15,224	21.4%	-1.0	79,000	31,687	40.1%	17.6	88,000	33,644	38.2%	15.8				
LOUISIANA				17,000	2,955	17.4%		19,000	4,138	21.8%	4.4	21,000	3,342	15.9%	-1.5	23,000	5,077	22.1%	4.7
MAINE												67,000	21,271	31.7%		77,000	21,463	27.9%	-3.9
MARYLAND	52,000	20,996	40.4%	54,000	29,396	54.4%	14.1	57,000	32,098	57.4%	17.0	60,000	30,424	50.7%	10.3	64,000	36,938	57.7%	17.3
MASSACHUSETTS	104,000	90,620	87.1%	109,000	102,327	93.9%	6.7	115,000	34,354	29.9%	-57.3	124,000	49,664	40.1%	-47.1	135,000	39,140	29.0%	-58.1
MISSISSIPPI												11,000	7,469	67.9%		14,000	9,541	68.2%	0.2
MISSOURI												16,000	9,906	61.9%		20,000	10,790	54.0%	-8.0
NEW HAMPSHIRE	45,000	31,491	70.0%	48,000	38,489	80.2%	10.2	51,000	30,543	59.9%	-10.1	54,000	22,934	42.5%	-27.5	58,000	29,815	51.4%	-18.6
NEW JERSEY	48,000	14,007	29.2%	51,000	34,454	67.6%	38.4	54,000	14,404	26.7%	-2.5	58,000	4,311	7.4%	-21.7	62,000	24,731	39.9%	10.7
NEW YORK	196,000	114,192	58.3%	233,000	111,464	47.8%	-10.4	270,000	76,841	28.5%	-29.8	317,000	128,493	40.5%	-17.7	370,000	181,994	49.2%	-9.1
NORTH CAROLINA	73,000	36,281	49.7%																
OHIO	48,000	17,655	36.8%	75,000	22,050	29.4%	-7.4	103,000	40,991	39.8%	3.0	132,000	60,008	45.5%	8.7	161,000	85,683	53.2%	16.4
PENNSYLVANIA	165,000	61,131	37.0%	184,000	80,671	43.8%	6.8	202,000	79,525	39.4%	2.3	228,000	103,540	45.4%	8.4	257,000	104,306	40.6%	3.5
RHODE ISLAND	16,000	7,103	44.4%	16,000	6,675	41.7%	-2.7	17,000	8,402	49.4%	5.0	18,000	2,092	11.6%	-32.8				
SOUTH CAROLINA	42,000	6,779	16.1%	44,000	11,541	26.2%	10.1	46,000	20,061	43.6%	27.5					50,000	13,978	28.0%	11.8
VERMONT	44,000	23,722	53.9%	46,000	34,877	75.8%	21.9	49,000	18,228	37.2%	-16.7	53,000	18,383	34.7%	-19.2	58,000	21,092	36.4%	-17.5
Total	992,000	484,096	48.8%	1,050,000	525,589	50.1%	1.3	1,193,000	432,633	36.3%	-12.5	1,418,000	560,173	39.5%	-9.3	1,554,000	681,827	43.9%	-4.9

*Percentage point difference between turnout in current year and initial year listed in chart. If data do not appear for a state in the initial year listed, the difference is calculated from the first year in which data do appear for that state.

TOTAL HIGHEST STATEWIDE GENERAL ELECTIONS

Federalist (or National Republican) Turnout for Election Years 1810–1826*

State	1810			1814				1818				1822 (National Republicans)				1826 (National Republicans)			
	Voting-age population	Turnout	%	Voting-age population	Turnout	%	Difference from 1810**	Voting-age population	Turnout	%	Difference from 1810	Voting-age population	Turnout	%	Difference from 1810	Voting-age population	Turnout	%	Difference from 1810
CONNECTICUT	56,000	13,375	23.9%	58,000	9,415	16.2%	-7.7	59,000	4,653	7.9%	-16.0	62,000	570	0.9%	-23.0	66,000	4,340	6.6%	-17.3
DELAWARE	11,000	3,634	33.0%	11,000	3,962	36.0%	3.0	11,000	3,000	27.3%	-5.8	12,000	4,110	34.3%	1.2	12,000	4,630	38.6%	5.5
GEORGIA	29,000	2,591	8.9%																
ILLINOIS																24,000	6,280	26.2%	
INDIANA								24,000	1,118	4.7%						51,000	18,082	35.5%	30.8
KENTUCKY								79,000	2,663	3.4%									
LOUISIANA				17,000	242	1.4%										23,000	1,412	6.1%	4.7
MAINE												67,000	5,795	8.6%		77,000	8,743	11.4%	2.7
MARYLAND	52,000	4,753	9.1%	54,000	17,417	32.3%	23.1	57,000	14,627	25.7%	16.5	60,000	7,181	12.0%	2.8	64,000	8,607	13.4%	4.3
MASSACHUSETTS	104,000	46,541	44.8%	109,000	56,374	51.7%	7.0	115,000	39,538	34.4%	-10.4	124,000	28,487	23.0%	-21.8	135,000	12,725	9.4%	-35.3
MISSISSIPPI																14,000	1,451	10.4%	
NEW HAMPSHIRE	45,000	15,166	33.7%	48,000	19,695	41.0%	7.3	51,000	11,869	23.3%	-10.4	54,000	1,747	3.2%	-30.5				
NEW JERSEY	48,000	359	0.7%	51,000	16,653	32.7%	31.9	54,000	181	0.3%	-0.4	58,000	92	0.2%	-0.6	62,000	16,413	26.5%	25.7
NEW YORK	196,000	54,161	27.6%	233,000	52,433	22.5%	-5.1	270,000	19,197	7.1%	-20.5	317,000	678	0.2%	-27.4	370,000	87,369	23.6%	-4.0
NORTH CAROLINA	73,000	12,596	17.3%																
OHIO				75,000	6,171	8.2%		100,000	5,819	5.8%	-2.4	132,000	22,889	17.3%	9.1	161,000	70,475	43.8%	35.5
PENNSYLVANIA	165,000	16,291	9.9%	184,000	33,632	18.3%	8.4	202,000	20,969	10.4%	0.5	228,000	24,230	10.6%	0.8	257,000	25,658	10.0%	0.1
RHODE ISLAND	16,000	3,460	21.6%	16,000	3,722	23.3%	1.6	17,000	3,893	22.9%	1.3								
SOUTH CAROLINA	42,000	1,522	3.6%	44,000	2,571	5.8%	2.2	46,000	1,987	4.3%	0.7								
VERMONT	44,000	9,912	22.5%	46,000	17,690	38.5%	15.9	49,000	2,573	5.3%	-17.3	53,000	2,158	4.1%	-18.5	58,000	13,586	23.4%	0.9
Total	881,000	184,361	20.9%	946,000	239,977	25.4%	4.4	1,134,000	132,087	11.6%	-9.3	1,167,000	97,937	8.4%	-12.5	1,308,000	275,431	21.1%	0.1

Democratic-Republican Turnout for Election Years 1810–1826

State	1810			1814				1818				1822				1826 (Democratic Party)			
	Voting-age population	Turnout	%	Voting-age population	Turnout	%	Difference from 1810**	Voting-age population	Turnout	%	Difference from 1810	Voting-age population	Turnout	%	Difference from 1810	Voting-age population	Turnout	%	Difference from 1810
CONNECTICUT	56,000	7,185	12.8%	58,000	2,619	4.5%	-8.3	59,000	7,573	12.8%	0.0	62,000	8,568	13.8%	1.0	66,000	6,780	10.3%	-2.6
DELAWARE	11,000	3,664	33.3%	11,000	2,546	23.1%	-10.2	11,000	2,909	26.4%	-6.9	12,000	3,784	31.5%	-1.8	12,000	4,238	35.3%	2.0
GEORGIA	29,000	17,498	60.3%	33,000	16,924	51.3%	-9.1	37,000	7,347	19.9%	-40.5	44,000	15,487	35.2%	-25.1	52,000	20,785	40.0%	-20.4
ILLINOIS												16,000	4,764	29.8%		24,000	6,322	26.3%	-3.4
INDIANA								24,000	9,955	41.5%						51,000	11,217	22.0%	-19.5
KENTUCKY	63,000	13,956	22.2%	71,000	14,123	19.9%	-2.3	79,000	19,334	24.5%	2.3								
LOUISIANA				17,000	2,684	15.8%										23,000	1,567	6.8%	-9.0

Total Highest Statewide General Elections (continued)

Democratic-Republican Turnout for Election Years 1810–1826 (continued)

State	1810			1814				1818				1822				1826 (Democratic Party)			
	Voting-age population	Turnout	%	Voting-age population	Turnout	%	Difference from 1810	Voting-age population	Turnout	%	Difference from 1810	Voting-age population	Turnout	%	Difference from 1810	Voting-age population	Turnout	%	Difference from 1810
MAINE												67,000	15,476	23.1%		77,000	20,689	26.9%	3.8
MARYLAND	52,000	16,197	31.1%	54,000	11,979	22.2%	-9.0	57,000	18,071	31.7%	0.6	60,000	22,397	37.3%	6.2	64,000	6,762	10.6%	-20.6
MASSACHUSETTS	104,000	44,079	42.4%	109,000	45,953	42.2%	-0.2	115,000	30,041	26.1%	-16.3	124,000	21,177	17.1%	-25.3				
MISSISSIPPI																14,000	3,236	23.1%	
NEW HAMPSHIRE	45,000	16,325	36.3%	48,000	18,794	39.2%	2.9	51,000	18,674	36.6%	0.3	54,000	22,934	42.5%	6.2				
NEW JERSEY	48,000	13,648	28.4%	51,000	17,801	34.9%	6.5	54,000	14,223	26.3%	-2.1	58,000	4,219	7.3%	-21.2	62,000	8,110	13.1%	-15.4
NEW YORK	196,000	60,031	30.6%	233,000	59,031	25.3%	-5.3	270,000	57,644	21.3%	-9.3	317,000	128,493	40.5%	9.9	370,000	99,808	27.0%	-3.7
NORTH CAROLINA	73,000	23,685	32.4%																
OHIO	48,000	17,655	36.8%	75,000	15,879	21.2%	-15.6	100,000	38,269	38.3%	1.5	132,000	37,119	28.1%	-8.7	161,000	17,784	11.0%	-25.7
PENNSYLVANIA	165,000	42,105	25.5%	184,000	51,009	27.7%	2.2	202,000	52,783	26.1%	0.6	228,000	63,266	27.7%	2.2	257,000	72,710	28.3%	2.8
RHODE ISLAND	16,000	3,643	22.8%	16,000	2,953	18.5%	-4.3	17,000	4,509	26.5%	3.8	18,000	1,432	8.0%	-14.8				
SOUTH CAROLINA	42,000	5,141	12.2%	44,000	8,970	20.4%	0.1	46,000	18,074	39.3%	27.1					50,000	7,766	15.5%	3.3
VERMONT	44,000	13,810	31.4%	46,000	17,411	37.9%	6.5	49,000	15,534	31.7%	0.3	53,000	14,871	28.1%	-3.3	58,000	8,966		
Total	992,000	298,622	30.1%	1,050,000	288,676	27.5%	2.6	1,171,000	314,940	26.9%	-3.2	1,245,000	363,987	29.2%	-0.9	1,275,000	289,960	22.7%	-7.4

Other Turnout for Election Years 1810–1826

State	1810			1814				1818				1822				1826			
	Voting-age population	Turnout	%	Voting-age population	Turnout	%	Difference from 1810**	Voting-age population	Turnout	%	Difference from 1810	Voting-age population	Turnout	%	Difference from 1810	Voting-age population	Turnout	%	Difference from 1810
CONNECTICUT								59,000	16,432	27.9%									
GEORGIA												44,000	3,841	8.7%		52,000	13,005	25.0%	16.3
ILLINOIS												16,000	8,606	53.8%		24,000	824	3.4%	-50.4
INDIANA												37,000	20,614	55.7%		51,000	1,723	3.4%	-52.3
KENTUCKY	63,000	200	0.3%	71,000	1,101	1.6%	1.2	79,000	9,690	12.3%	11.9	88,000	33,644	38.2%	37.9				
LOUISIANA				17,000	29	0.2%		19,000	872	4.6%	4.4	21,000	3,342	15.9%	15.7	23,000	2,098	9.1%	9.0
MAINE																77,000	6,592	8.6%	
MARYLAND	52,000	46	0.1%									60,000	846	1.4%	1.3	64,000	21,569	33.7%	33.6
MASSACHUSETTS	104,000	472	0.5%	109,000	107	0.1%	-0.4	115,000	861	0.7%	0.3	124,000	906	0.7%	0.3	135,000	27,884	20.7%	20.2
MISSISSIPPI												11,000	7,469	67.9%		14,000	4,854	34.7%	-33.2
MISSOURI												16,000	9,906	61.9%		20,000	10,790	54.0%	-8.0
NEW HAMPSHIRE	45,000	207	0.5%													58,000	29,815	51.4%	50.9
NEW JERSEY																62,000	642	1.0%	
NEW YORK	196,000	36,484	18.6%									317,000	128,493	40.5%	21.9	370,000	96,080	26.0%	7.4

Total Highest Statewide General Elections (continued)

Total Highest Statewide General Elections *(continued)*

Other Turnout for Election Years 1810–1826 *(continued)*

State	1810			1814				1818				1822				1826			
	Voting-age population	Turnout	%	Voting-age population	Turnout	%	Difference from 1810	Voting-age population	Turnout	%	Difference from 1810	Voting-age population	Turnout	%	Difference from 1810	Voting-age population	Turnout	%	Difference from 1810
OHIO	48,000	29	0.1%	75,000	1,601	2.1%	2.1	100,000	576	0.6%	0.5	132,000	39,882	30.2%	30.2	161,000	20,564	12.8%	12.7
PENNSYLVANIA	165,000	2,735	1.7%					202,000	5,773	2.9%	1.2	228,000	16,044	7.0%	5.4	257,000	7,761	3.0%	1.4
RHODE ISLAND												18,000	2,092	11.6%					
SOUTH CAROLINA	42,000	116	0.3%													50,000	6,212	12.4%	12.1
VERMONT	44,000	459	1.0%					49,000	121	0.2%	-0.8	53,000	1,354	2.6%	1.5	58,000	7,506	12.9%	11.9
Total	759,000	40,748	5.4%	272,000	2,838	1.0%	-4.3	623,000	34,325	5.5%	0.1	1,165,000	277,039	23.8%	18.4	1,476,000	257,919	17.5%	12.1

*In the aftermath of the War of 1812, the Federalist party lost its stature as the second national party. For a brief time, the "Era of Good Feelings," the Democratic-Republican party held sway as the only national party, but the National Republican party developed out of competition within the Democratic-Republicans. For the purposes of this book, the National Republican era begins in 1820 and ends in 1832.

**Percentage point difference between turnout in current year and initial year listed in chart. If data do not appear for a state in the initial year listed, the difference is calculated from the first year in which data do appear for that state.

***The Democratic-Republican party finally dropped the "Republican" and became the "Democratic" Party that continues into the 21st century.

STATE GUBERNATORIAL GENERAL ELECTIONS

Election Years 1811–1829

State	1811 Voting-age population	1811 Turnout	1811 %	1813 Voting-age population	1813 Turnout	1813 %	1813 Difference from 1811*	1815 Voting-age population	1815 Turnout	1815 %	1815 Difference from 1811	1817 Voting-age population	1817 Turnout	1817 %	1817 Difference from 1811	1819 Voting-age population	1819 Turnout	1819 %	1819 Difference from 1811
ALABAMA																			
CONNECTICUT	56,000	18,875	33.7%	57,000	19,094	33.5%	-0.2	58,000	13,052	22.5%	-11.2	59,000	26,774	45.4%	11.7	59,000	22,539	38.2%	4.5
DELAWARE				11,000	8,411	76.5%										11,000	7,008	63.7%	-12.8
GEORGIA																			
INDIANA																29,000	11,256	38.8%	
MAINE																			
MASSACHUSETTS	105,000	83,470	79.5%	108,000	99,543	92.2%	12.7	111,000	94,859	85.5%	6.0	114,000	84,289	73.9%	-5.6	116,000	78,152	67.4%	-12.1
MISSISSIPPI																9,000	4,423	49.1%	
MISSOURI																			
NEW HAMPSHIRE	46,000	32,031	69.6%	47,000	35,517	75.6%	5.9	49,000	36,156	73.8%	4.2	50,000	34,724	69.4%	-0.2	52,000	22,421	43.1%	-26.5
NEW YORK				223,000	83,042	37.2%						260,000	43,310	16.7%	-20.6				
PENNSYLVANIA	170,000	55,928	32.9%									198,000	125,603	63.4%	30.5				
RHODE ISLAND	16,000	7,536	47.1%	16,000	3,350	20.9%	-26.2	17,000	5,960	35.1%	-12.0	17,000	7,827	46.0%	-1.1	17,000	2,664	15.7%	-31.4
TENNESSEE	43,000	19,980	46.5%	47,000	21,510	45.8%	-0.7	51,000	34,755	68.1%	21.7	56,000	43,252	77.2%	30.8	60,000	35,244	58.7%	12.3
VERMONT	44,000	25,042	56.9%	46,000	33,360	72.5%	15.6	47,000	34,753	73.9%	17.0	48,000	21,186	44.1%	-12.8	49,000	13,681	27.9%	29.0
Total	480,000	242,862	50.6%	555,000	303,827	54.7%	4.1	333,000	219,535	65.9%	15.3	802,000	386,965	48.3%	-2.3	402,000	197,388	49.1%	-1.5

State	1821 Voting-age population	1821 Turnout	1821 %	1821 Difference from 1811	1823 Voting-age population	1823 Turnout	1823 %	1823 Difference from 1811	1825 Voting-age population	1825 Turnout	1825 %	1825 Difference from 1811	1827 Voting-age population	1827 Turnout	1827 %	1827 Difference from 1811	1829 Voting-age population	1829 Turnout	1829 %	1829 Difference from 1811
ALABAMA	23,000	16,745	72.8%		27,000	23,613	87.5%	14.7	30,000	12,184	40.6%	-32.2	34,000	8,334	24.5%	-48.3	38,000	10,956	28.8%	-44.0
CONNECTICUT	61,000	10,064	16.5%	-17.2	63,000	9,090	14.4%	-19.3	65,000	9,877	15.2%	-18.5	67,000	12,976	19.4%	-14.3	69,000	9,612	13.9%	-19.8
DELAWARE					12,000	8,399	70.0%	-6.5									12,000	8,261	68.8%	-7.6
GEORGIA									50,000	39,412	78.8%		54,000	22,774	42.2%	-36.6	59,000	34,922	59.2%	-19.6
INDIANA									48,000	23,258	48.5%	9.6								
MAINE	64,000	23,577	36.8%		69,000	18,550	26.9%	-10.0	74,000	14,206	19.2%	-17.6	80,000	19,969	25.0%	-11.9	85,000	46,306	54.5%	17.6
MASSACHUSETTS	121,000	48,876	40.4%	-39.1	127,000	64,573	50.8%	-28.7	132,000	35,221	26.7%	-52.8	138,000	36,159	26.2%	-53.3	143,000	32,081	22.4%	-57.1
MISSISSIPPI	11,000	5,999	54.5%	5.4	12,000	9,227	76.9%	27.7	13,000	9,349	71.9%	22.8	14,000	10,740	76.7%	27.6	16,000	11,335	70.8%	21.7
MISSOURI									19,000	5,694	30.0%									
NEW HAMPSHIRE	53,000	22,582	42.6%	-27.0	55,000	29,703	54.0%	-15.6	56,000	29,770	53.2%	-16.5	58,000	26,236	45.2%	-24.4	60,000	42,198	70.3%	0.7
NEW YORK																				
PENNSYLVANIA					235,000	154,139	65.6%	32.7									280,000	129,914	46.4%	13.5
RHODE ISLAND	18,000	6,602	36.7%	-10.4	19,000	1,647	8.7%	-38.4	19,000	1,731	9.1%	-38.0	20,000	2,421	12.1%	-35.0	21,000	3,584	17.1%	-30.0
TENNESSEE	66,000	54,440	82.5%	36.0	74,000	32,597	44.1%	-2.4	82,000	34,284	41.8%	-4.7	90,000	77,172	85.7%	39.3	98,000	58,917	60.1%	13.7
VERMONT	52,000	12,434	23.9%	-33.0	54,000	12,567	23.3%	-33.6	57,000	12,229	21.5%	-35.5	60,000	15,650	26.1%	-30.8	62,000	25,674	41.4%	-15.5
Total	469,000	201,319	42.9%	-7.7	747,000	364,105	48.7%	-1.9	645,000	227,215	35.2%	-15.4	615,000	232,431	37.8%	-12.8	943,000	413,760	43.9%	-6.7

*Percentage point difference between turnout in current year and initial year listed in chart. If data do not appear for a state in the initial year listed, the difference is calculated from the first year in which data do appear for that state.

STATE GUBERNATORIAL GENERAL ELECTIONS

Federalist (or National Republican) Turnout for Election Years 1811–1829*

State	1811 Voting-age population	Turnout	%	1813 Voting-age population	Turnout	%	Difference from 1811**	1815 Voting-age population	Turnout	%	Difference from 1811	1817 Voting-age population	Turnout	%	Difference from 1811	1819 Voting-age population	Turnout	%	Difference from 1811
CONNECTICUT	57,000	18,875	33.1%	57,000	11,893	20.9%	-12.2	58,000	8,176	14.1%	-19.0	59,000	13,119	22.2%	-10.9				
DELAWARE				11,000	4,643	42.2%										11,000	3,823	34.8%	-7.5
INDIANA																			
MAINE																			
MASSACHUSETTS	105,000	40,142	38.2%	108,000	56,754	52.6%	14.3	111,000	50,921	45.9%	7.6	114,000	46,160	40.5%	2.3	116,000	42,875	37.0%	-1.3
MISSISSIPPI																			
MISSOURI																			
NEW HAMPSHIRE	46,000	14,477	31.5%	47,000	18,107	38.5%	7.1	49,000	18,357	37.5%	6.0	50,000	15,636	31.3%	-0.2	52,000	8,660	16.7%	-14.8
NEW YORK				223,000	39,718	17.8%													
PENNSYLVANIA	170,000	3,609	2.1%									198,000	59,272	29.9%	27.8				
RHODE ISLAND	16,000	3,885	24.3%					17,000	3,372	19.8%	-4.4	17,000	3,878	22.8%	-1.5				
VERMONT	44,000	11,214	25.5%	46,000	16,532	35.9%	10.5	47,000	16,698	35.5%	10.0	48,000	7,430	15.5%	-10.0				
Total	438,000	92,202	21.1%	492,000	147,647	30.0%	9.0	282,000	97,524	34.6%	13.5	486,000	145,495	29.9%	8.9	179,000	55,358	30.9%	9.9

State	1821 (National Republicans) Voting-age population	Turnout	%	Difference from 1811	1823 (National Republicans) Voting-age population	Turnout	%	Difference from 1811	1825 (National Republicans) Voting-age population	Turnout	%	Difference from 1811	1827 (National Republicans) Voting-age population	Turnout	%	Difference from 1811	1829 (National Republicans) Voting-age population	Turnout	%	Difference from 1811
CONNECTICUT									65,000	1,342	2.1%	-31.0					69,000	9,612	13.9%	-19.2
DELAWARE					12,000	4,348	36.2%	-6.0												
INDIANA									48,000	10,218	21.3%									
MAINE	64,000	6,811	10.6%														85,000	23,315	27.4%	16.8
MASSACHUSETTS	121,000	28,608	23.6%	-14.6	127,000	30,171	23.8%	-14.5	132,000	35,221	26.7%	-11.5	138,000	29,029	21.0%	-17.2	143,000	25,217	17.6%	-20.6
MISSISSIPPI																	16,000	3,991	24.9%	
MISSOURI									19,000	1,291	6.8%									
NEW HAMPSHIRE									56,000	29,770	53.2%	21.7	58,000	2,541	4.4%	-27.1	60,000	19,583	32.6%	1.2
NEW YORK																				
PENNSYLVANIA					235,000	64,211	27.3%	25.2												
RHODE ISLAND																				
VERMONT																	62,000	14,325	23.1%	-2.4
Total	185,000	35,419	19.1%	-1.9	374,000	98,730	26.4%	5.3	320,000	77,842	24.3%	3.3	196,000	31,570	16.1%	-4.9	435,000	96,043	22.1%	1.0

State Gubernatorial General Elections (continued)

Democratic-Republican Turnout for Election Years 1811–1829

State	1811 Voting-age population	Turnout	%		1813 Voting-age population	Turnout	%	Difference from 1811**	1815 Voting-age population	Turnout	%	Difference from 1811	1817 Voting-age population	Turnout	%	Difference from 1811	1819 Voting-age population	Turnout	%	Difference from 1811
ALABAMA																				
CONNECTICUT					57,000	7,201	12.6%		58,000	4,876	8.4%	-4.2								
DELAWARE					11,000	3,768	34.3%										11,000	3,185	29.0%	-5.3
MAINE																				
MASSACHUSETTS	105,000	43,328	41.3%		100,000	42,780	30.6%	-1.6	111,000	43,938	39.6%	-1.7	114,000	38,129	33.4%	-7.8	116,000	35,277	30.4%	-10.9
MISSISSIPPI																				
MISSOURI																				
NEW HAMPSHIRE	46,000	17,554	38.2%		47,000	17,410	37.0%	-1.1	49,000	17,799	36.3%	-1.8	50,000	19,088	38.2%	0.0	52,000	13,761	26.5%	-11.7
NEW YORK					223,000	43,324	19.4%						260,000	43,310	16.7%	-2.8				
PENNSYLVANIA	170,000	52,319	30.8%										198,000	66,331	33.5%	2.7				
RHODE ISLAND	16,000	3,651	22.8%						17,000	2,588	15.2%	-7.6	17,000	3,949	23.2%	0.4	17,000	2,664	15.7%	-7.1
VERMONT	44,000	13,828	31.4%		46,000	16,828	36.6%	5.2	47,000	18,055	38.4%	7.0	48,000	13,756	28.7%	-2.8	49,000	13,681	27.1%	-3.5
Total	381,000	130,680	34.3%		492,000	131,320	26.7%	-7.6	282,000	87,256	30.9%	-3.4	687,000	184,563	26.9%	-7.4	245,000	68,568	28.0%	-6.3

State	1821 Voting-age population	Turnout	%	Difference from 1811	1823 Voting-age population	Turnout	%	Difference from 1811	1825 Voting-age population	Turnout	%	Difference from 1811	1827 (Democratic Party)*** Voting-age population	Turnout	%	Difference from 1811	1829 (Democratic Party) Voting-age population	Turnout	%	Difference from 1811
ALABAMA	23,000	9,616	41.8%		27,000	13,580	50.3%	8.5	30,000	12,184	40.6%	-1.2	34,000	8,334	24.5%	-17.3	38,000	10,956	28.8%	-13.0
CONNECTICUT	61,000	10,064	16.5%	3.9	63,000	9,090	14.4%	1.8	65,000	7,147	11.0%	-1.6	67,000	12,976	19.4%	6.7				
DELAWARE					12,000	4,051	33.8%	-0.5												
MAINE	64,000	16,766	26.2%		69,000	18,550	26.9%	0.7	74,000	14,206	19.2%	-7.0	80,000	19,969	25.0%	-1.2	85,000	22,991	27.0%	0.9
MASSACHUSETTS	121,000	20,268	16.8%	-24.5	127,000	34,402	27.1%	-14.2												
MISSISSIPPI																	16,000	7,344	45.9%	
MISSOURI									19,000	4,403	23.2%									
NEW HAMPSHIRE	53,000	22,582	42.6%	4.4	55,000	29,703	54.0%	15.8					58,000	23,695	40.9%	2.7	60,000	22,615	37.7%	-0.5
NEW YORK																				
PENNSYLVANIA					235,000	89,928	38.3%	7.5									280,000	78,138	27.9%	-2.9
RHODE ISLAND	18,000	3,801	21.1%	-1.7																
VERMONT	52,000	12,434	23.9%	-7.5	54,000	11,479	21.3%	-10.2	57,000	12,229	21.5%	-10.0	60,000	13,699	22.8%	-8.6	62,000	3,973	6.4%	-25.0
Total	392,000	95,531	24.4%	-9.9	642,000	210,783	32.8%	-1.5	245,000	50,169	20.5%	-13.8	299,000	78,673	26.3%	-8.0	541,000	146,017	27.0%	-7.3

State Gubernatorial General Elections (continued)

State Gubernatorial General Elections (continued)

Other Turnout for Election Years 1811–1829

	1811			1813				1815				1817				1819			
State	Voting-age population	Turnout	%	Voting-age population	Turnout	%	Difference % from 1811**	Voting-age population	Turnout	%	Difference from 1811	Voting-age population	Turnout	%	Difference from 1811	Voting-age population	Turnout	%	Difference from 1811
ALABAMA																			
CONNECTICUT												59,000	13,655	23.1%		59,000	22,539	38.2%	15.1
DELAWARE																			
GEORGIA																			
INDIANA																29,000	11,256	38.8%	
MASSACHUSETTS																			
MISSISSIPPI																9,000	4,423	49.1%	
PENNSYLVANIA																			
RHODE ISLAND				16,000	3,350	20.9%													
TENNESSEE	43,000	19,980	46.5%	47,000	21,510	45.8%	-0.7	51,000	34,755	68.1%	21.7	56,000	43,252	77.2%	30.8	60,000	35,244	58.7%	12.3
VERMONT																			
Total	43,000	19,980	46.5%	63,000	24,860	39.5%	-7.0	51,000	34,755	68.1%	21.7	115,000	56,907	49.5%	3.0	157,000	73,462	46.8%	0.3

	1821				1823				1825				1827 (Democratic Party)***				1829 (Democratic Party)			
State	Voting-age population	Turnout	%	Difference from 1811	Voting-age population	Turnout	%	Difference from 1811	Voting-age population	Turnout	%	Difference from 1811	Voting-age population	Turnout	%	Difference from 1811	Voting-age population	Turnout	%	Difference from 1811
ALABAMA	23,000	7,129	31.0%		27,000	10,033	37.2%	6.2												
CONNECTICUT									65,000	1,388	2.1%	-21.0								
DELAWARE																	12,000	8,261	68.8%	
GEORGIA									50,000	39,412	78.8%		54,000	22,774	42.2%	-36.6	59,000	34,922	59.2%	-19.6
INDIANA									48,000	13,040	27.2%	-11.6								
MASSACHUSETTS													138,000	7,130	5.2%		143,000	6,864	4.8%	-0.4
MISSISSIPPI	11,000	5,999	54.5%	5.4	12,000	9,227	76.9%	27.7	13,000	9,349	71.9%	22.8	14,000	10,740	76.7%	27.6				
PENNSYLVANIA																	280,000	51,776	18.5%	
RHODE ISLAND	18,000	2,801	15.6%	-5.4	19,000	1,647	8.7%	-12.3	19,000	1,731	9.1%	-11.8	20,000	2,421	12.1%	-8.8	21,000	3,584	17.1%	-3.9
TENNESSEE	66,000	54,440	82.5%	36.0	74,000	32,597	44.1%	-2.4	82,000	34,284	41.8%	-4.7	90,000	77,172	85.7%	39.3	98,000	58,917	60.1%	13.7
VERMONT					54,000	1,088	2.0%						60,000	1,951	3.3%	1.2	62,000	7,376	11.9%	9.9
Total	118,000	70,369	59.6%	13.2	186,000	54,592	29.4%	-17.1	277,000	99,204	35.8%	-10.7	376,000	122,188	32.5%	-14.0	675,000	171,700	25.4%	-21.0

*In the aftermath of the War of 1812, the Federalist party lost its stature as the second national party. For a brief time, the "Era of Good Feelings," the Democratic-Republican party held sway as the only national party, but the National Republican party developed out of competition within the Democratic-Republicans. For the purposes of this book, the National Republican era begins in 1820 and ends in 1832.

**Percentage point difference between turnout in current year and initial year listed in chart. If data do not appear for a state in the initial year listed, the difference is calculated from the first year in which data do appear for that state.

***The Democratic-Republican party finally dropped the "Republican" and became the "Democratic" Party that continues into the 21st century.

UNITED STATES HOUSE OF REPRESENTATIVES GENERAL ELECTIONS

Election Years 1811–1829

State	1811 Voting-age population	Turnout	%	1813 Voting-age population	Turnout	%	Difference from 1811*	1815 Voting-age population	Turnout	%	Difference from 1811	1817 Voting-age population	Turnout	%	Difference from 1811	1819 Voting-age population	Turnout	%	Difference from 1811
ALABAMA																			
CONNECTICUT																			
ILLINOIS																			
INDIANA												19,000	9,471	49.8%					
KENTUCKY																			
MAINE																			
MARYLAND																			
MISSISSIPPI																9,000	4,019	44.7%	
NEW HAMPSHIRE																52,000	20,101	38.7%	
NEW JERSEY				50,000	26,325	52.7%													
NEW YORK																			
NORTH CAROLINA				75,000	37,290	49.7%		77,000	47,394	61.6%	11.8	78,000	35,430	45.4%	-4.3	80,000	32,041	40.1%	-9.7
RHODE ISLAND																			
SOUTH CAROLINA																			
TENNESSEE	43,000	19,834	46.1%					51,000	32,791	64.3%	18.2	56,000	43,193	77.1%	31.0	60,000	46,309	77.2%	31.1
VIRGINIA	115,000	11,977	10.4%	117,000	22,336	19.1%	8.7	120,000	20,563	17.1%	6.7	122,000	18,351	15.0%	4.6	124,000	14,902	12.0%	1.6
Total	158,000	31,811	20.1%	242,000	85,951	35.5%	15.4	248,000	100,748	40.6%	20.5	275,000	106,445	38.7%	18.6	325,000	117,372	36.1%	16.0

State	1821 Voting-age population	Turnout	%	Difference from 1811	1823 Voting-age population	Turnout	%	Difference from 1811	1825 Voting-age population	Turnout	%	Difference from 1811	1827 Voting-age population	Turnout	%	Difference from 1811	1829 Voting-age population	Turnout	%	Difference from 1811
ALABAMA	23,000	17,023	74.0%		27,000	15,455	57.2%	-16.8	30,000	18,763	62.5%	-11.5	34,000	11,329	33.3%	-40.7	38,000	31,154	82.0%	8.0
CONNECTICUT	61,000	7,334	12.0%		63,000	5,153	8.2%	-3.8	65,000	7,971	12.3%	0.2	67,000	14,825	22.1%	10.1	69,000	14,981	21.7%	9.7
ILLINOIS																				
INDIANA																				
KENTUCKY													99,000	75,550	76.3%		103,000	60,335	58.6%	-17.7
MAINE					69,000	26,509	38.4%													
MARYLAND																	67,000	38,858	58.0%	
MISSISSIPPI																				
NEW HAMPSHIRE													58,000	29,578	51.0%	12.3	60,000	39,239	65.4%	26.7
NEW JERSEY																				
NEW YORK	303,000	148,867	49.1%																	

United States House of Representatives General Elections (continued)

United States House of Representatives General Elections *(continued)*

Election Years 1811–1829 *(continued)*

State	1821				1823				1825				1827				1829			
	Voting-age population	Turnout	%	Difference from 1811	Voting-age population	Turnout	%	Difference from 1811	Voting-age population	Turnout	%	Difference from 1811	Voting-age population	Turnout	%	Difference from 1811	Voting-age population	Turnout	%	Difference from 1811
NORTH CAROLINA	82,000	37,350	45.5%	-4.2	85,000	40,066	47.1%	-2.6	87,000	56,635	65.1%	15.4	90,000	49,313	54.8%	5.1	93,000	50,391	54.2%	4.5
RHODE ISLAND									19,000	5,278	27.8%		20,000	2,191	11.0%	-16.8	21,000	5,770	27.5%	-0.3
SOUTH CAROLINA					48,000	18,068	37.6%													
TENNESSEE	66,000	38,607	58.5%	12.4	74,000	55,007	74.3%	28.2	82,000	58,325	71.1%	25.0	90,000	78,331	87.0%	40.9	98,000	70,325	71.8%	25.6
VIRGINIA	127,000	21,038	16.6%	6.2	131,000	25,831	19.7%	9.3	135,000	29,387	21.8%	11.4	139,000	30,466	21.9%	11.5	143,000	28,013	19.6%	9.2
Total	662,000	270,219	40.8%	20.7	497,000	186,089	37.4%	17.3	418,000	176,359	42.2%	22.1	597,000	291,583	48.8%	28.7	692,000	339,066	49.0%	28.9

*Percentage point difference between turnout in current year and initial year listed in chart. If data do not appear for a state in the initial year listed, the difference is calculated from the first year in which data do appear for that state.

UNITED STATES HOUSE OF REPRESENTATIVES GENERAL ELECTIONS

Federalist (or National Republican) Turnout for Election Years 1811–1829*

State	1811 Voting-age population	Turnout	%	1813 Voting-age population	Turnout	%	Difference from 1811**	1815 Voting-age population	Turnout	%	Difference from 1811	1817 Voting-age population	Turnout	%	Difference from 1811	1819 Voting-age population	Turnout	%	Difference from 1811
ALABAMA																			
CONNECTICUT																			
INDIANA												19,000	3,778	19.9%					
KENTUCKY																			
MAINE																			
MARYLAND																			
NEW HAMPSHIRE																52,000	6,815	13.1%	
NEW JERSEY				50,000	13,631	27.3%													
NEW YORK																			
NORTH CAROLINA				75,000	20,591	27.5%		77,000	22,155	28.8%	1.3	78,000	12,831	16.5%	-11.0	80,000	10,103	12.6%	-14.8
RHODE ISLAND																			
SOUTH CAROLINA																			
TENNESSEE																			
VIRGINIA	115,000	4,827	4.2%	117,000	8,474	7.2%	3.0	120,000	7,785	6.5%	2.3	122,000	4,114	3.4%	-0.8	124,000	4,790	3.9%	-0.3
Total	115,000	4,827	4.2%	242,000	42,696	17.6%	13.4	197,000	29,940	15.2%	11.0	219,000	20,723	9.5%	5.3	256,000	21,708	8.5%	4.3

State	1821 (National Republicans) Voting-age population	Turnout	%	Difference from 1811	1823 (National Republicans) Voting-age population	Turnout	%	Difference from 1811	1825 (National Republicans) Voting-age population	Turnout	%	Difference from 1811	1827 (National Republicans) Voting-age population	Turnout	%	Difference from 1811	1829 (National Republicans) Voting-age population	Turnout	%	Difference from 1811
ALABAMA																	38,000	3,962	10.4%	
CONNECTICUT	61,000	293	0.5%						65,000	283	0.4%	0.0	67,000	13,614	20.3%	19.8	69,000	8,281	12.0%	11.5
INDIANA																				
KENTUCKY													99,000	17,051	17.2%		103,000	10,215	9.9%	-7.3
MAINE					69,000	5,962	8.6%													
MARYLAND																	67,000	17,871	26.7%	
NEW HAMPSHIRE																	60,000	17,524	29.2%	16.1
NEW JERSEY																				
NEW YORK																				
NORTH CAROLINA	82,000	14,794	18.0%	-9.4	85,000	15,562	18.3%	-9.1	87,000	5,794	6.7%	-20.8	90,000	7,837	8.7%	-18.7	93,000	10,320	11.1%	-16.4
RHODE ISLAND													20,000	2,177	10.9%		21,000	4,218	20.1%	9.2
SOUTH CAROLINA					48,000	1,167	2.4%													
TENNESSEE													90,000	4,878	5.4%					
VIRGINIA	127,000	3,472	2.7%	-1.5	131,000	6,848	5.2%	1.0	135,000	4,969	3.7%	-0.5	139,000	6,368	4.6%	0.4	143,000	6,257	4.4%	0.2
Total	270,000	18,559	6.9%	2.7	333,000	29,539	8.9%	4.7	287,000	11,046	3.8%	-0.3	505,000	51,925	10.3%	6.1	594,000	78,648	13.2%	9.0

United States House of Representatives General Elections (continued)

United States House of Representatives General Elections *(continued)*

Democratic-Republican Turnout for Election Years 1811–1829*

State	1811 Voting-age population	Turnout	%	1813 Voting-age population	Turnout	%	Difference from 1811**	1815 Voting-age population	Turnout	%	Difference from 1811	1817 Voting-age population	Turnout	%	Difference from 1811	1819 Voting-age population	Turnout	%	Difference from 1811
ALABAMA																			
CONNECTICUT																			
ILLINOIS																			
INDIANA												19,000	5,693	30.0%					
KENTUCKY																			
MAINE																			
MARYLAND																			
MISSISSIPPI																9,000	4,019	44.7%	
NEW HAMPSHIRE																52,000	12,814	24.6%	
NEW YORK				50,000	12,537	25.1%													
NORTH CAROLINA				75,000	16,699	22.3%		77,000	24,884	32.3%	10.1	78,000	22,599	29.0%	6.7	80,000	21,922	27.4%	5.1
RHODE ISLAND																			
SOUTH CAROLINA																			
TENNESSEE	43,000	14,674	34.1%	47,000	6,169	13.1%	-21.0	51,000	25,034	49.1%	15.0	56,000	26,534	47.4%	13.3	60,000	25,266	42.1%	8.0
VIRGINIA	115,000	6,069	5.3%	117,000	12,926	11.0%	5.8	120,000	12,690	10.6%	5.3	122,000	14,237	11.7%	6.4	124,000	10,112	8.2%	2.9
Total	158,000	20,743	13.1%	289,000	48,331	16.7%	3.6	248,000	62,608	25.2%	12.1	275,000	69,063	25.1%	12.0	325,000	74,133	22.8%	9.7

State	1821 Voting-age population	Turnout	%	Difference from 1811	1823 Voting-age population	Turnout	%	Difference from 1811	1825 Voting-age population	Turnout	%	Difference from 1811	1827 (Democratic Party)*** Voting-age population	Turnout	%	Difference from 1811	1829 (Democratic Party) Voting-age population	Turnout	%	Difference from 1811
ALABAMA	23,000	10,996	47.8%		27,000	7,817	29.0%	-18.9	30,000	12,576	41.9%	-5.9	34,000	7,924	23.3%	-24.5	38,000	17,563	46.2%	-1.6
CONNECTICUT	61,000	6,577	10.8%		63,000	5,153	8.2%	-2.6	65,000	6,011	9.2%	-1.5					69,000	5,401	7.8%	-3.0
ILLINOIS																				
INDIANA																				
KENTUCKY													99,000	29,171	29.5%		103,000	35,359	34.3%	4.9
MAINE					69,000	14,951	21.7%													
MARYLAND																	67,000	20,716	30.9%	
MISSISSIPPI																				
NEW HAMPSHIRE													58,000	22,680	39.1%	14.5	60,000	21,714	36.2%	11.5
NEW YORK	303,000	148,867	49.1%	24.1																
NORTH CAROLINA	82,000	21,998	26.8%	4.6	85,000	24,504	28.8%	6.6	87,000	25,448	29.3%	7.0					93,000	36,767	39.5%	17.3
RHODE ISLAND									19,000	5,210	27.4%									
SOUTH CAROLINA					48,000	13,385	27.9%													
TENNESSEE	66,000	31,667	48.0%	13.9									90,000	26,810	29.8%	-4.3	98,000	52,182	53.2%	19.1

United States House of Representatives General Elections *(continued)*

Democratic-Republican Turnout for Election Years 1811–1829 *(continued)*

State	1821 Voting-age population	Turnout	%	Difference from 1811	1823 Voting-age population	Turnout	%	Difference from 1811	1825 Voting-age population	Turnout	%	Difference from 1811	1827 Voting-age population	Turnout	%	Difference from 1811	1829 Voting-age population	Turnout	%	Difference from 1811
VIRGINIA	127,000	17,233	13.6%	8.3	131,000	18,681	14.3%	9.0					139,000	2,371	1.7%	-3.6	143,000	15,545	10.9%	5.6
Total	662,000	237,338	35.9%	22.7	423,000	84,491	20.0%	6.8	201,000	49,245	24.5%	11.4	420,000	88,956	21.2%	8.1	671,000	205,247	30.6%	17.5

Other Turnout for Election Years 1811–1829

State	1811 Voting-age population	Turnout	%	1813 Voting-age population	Turnout	%	Difference from 1811**	1815 Voting-age population	Turnout	%	Difference from 1811	1817 Voting-age population	Turnout	%	Difference from 1811	1819 Voting-age population	Turnout	%	Difference from 1811
ALABAMA																			
CONNECTICUT																			
ILLINOIS																			
KENTUCKY																			
MAINE																			
MARYLAND																			
NEW HAMPSHIRE																52,000	472	0.9%	
NEW JERSEY				50,000	74	0.1%													
NEW YORK																			
NORTH CAROLINA								77,000	355	0.5%						80,000	16	0.0%	-0.4
RHODE ISLAND																			
SOUTH CAROLINA																			
TENNESSEE	43,000	5,160	12.0%	47,000	1,255	2.7%	-9.3	51,000	7,757	15.2%	3.2	56,000	16,659	29.7%	17.7	60,000	21,043	35.1%	23.1
VIRGINIA	115,000	1,081	0.9%	117,000	936	0.8%	-0.1	120,000	88	0.1%	-0.9								
Total	158,000	6,241	4.0%	214,000	2,265	1.1%	-2.9	248,000	8,200	3.3%	-0.6	56,000	16,659	29.7%	25.8	192,000	21,531	11.2%	7.3

State	1821 Voting-age population	Turnout	%	Difference from 1811	1823 Voting-age population	Turnout	%	Difference from 1811	1825 Voting-age population	Turnout	%	Difference from 1811	1827 Voting-age population	Turnout	%	Difference from 1811	1829 (Democratic Party)*** Voting-age population	Turnout	%	Difference from 1811
ALABAMA	23,000	6,027	26.2%		27,000	7,638	28.3%	2.1	30,000	6,187	20.6%	-5.6	34,000	3,405	10.0%	-16.2	38,000	9,629	25.3%	-0.9
CONNECTICUT	61,000	293	0.5%										67,000	1,211	1.8%	1.3	69,000	1,299	1.9%	1.4
ILLINOIS																				
KENTUCKY													99,000	29,328	29.6%		103,000	14,761	14.3%	-15.3
MAINE					69,000	5,596	8.1%													
MARYLAND																	67,000	271	0.4%	
NEW HAMPSHIRE													58,000	5,479	9.4%	8.5				
NEW JERSEY																				

United States House of Representatives General Elections (continued)

Other Turnout for Election Years 1811–1829 (continued)

State	1821 Voting-age population	Turnout	%	Difference from 1811	1823 Voting-age population	Turnout	%	Difference from 1811	1825 Voting-age population	Turnout	%	Difference from 1811	1827 Voting-age population	Turnout	%	Difference from 1811	1829 (Democratic Party)*** Voting-age population	Turnout	%	Difference from 1811
NEW YORK	303,000	377	0.1%																	
NORTH CAROLINA	82,000	558	0.7%	0.2					87,000	25,393	29.2%	28.7	90,000	41,476	46.1%	45.6	93,000	3,304	3.6%	3.1
RHODE ISLAND									19,000	136	0.7%		20,000	29	0.1%	-0.6	21,000	1,552	7.4%	6.7
SOUTH CAROLINA					48,000	3,516	7.3%													
TENNESSEE	66,000	6,940	10.5%	-1.5	74,000	55,007	74.3%	62.3	82,000	58,325	71.1%	59.1	90,000	46,643	51.8%	39.8	98,000	18,143	18.5%	6.5
VIRGINIA	127,000	333	0.3%	-0.7	131,000	302	0.2%	-0.7	135,000	24,418	18.1%	17.1	139,000	21,727	15.6%	14.7	143,000	6,211	4.3%	3.4
Total	662,000	14,528	2.2%	-1.8	349,000	72,059	20.6%	16.7	353,000	114,459	32.4%	28.5	597,000	149,298	25.0%	21.1	632,000	55,170	8.7%	4.8

*In the aftermath of the War of 1812, the Federalist party lost its stature as the second national party. For a brief time, the "Era of Good Feelings," the Democratic-Republican party held sway as the only national party, but the National Republican party developed out of competition within the Democratic-Republicans. For the purposes of this book, the National Republican era begins in 1820 and ends in 1832.

**Percentage point difference between turnout in current year and initial year listed in chart. If data do not appear for a state in the initial year listed, the difference is calculated from the first year in which data do appear for that state.

***The Democratic-Republican party finally dropped the "Republican" and became the "Democratic" Party that continues into the 21st century.

CHAPTER 3
1830–1849

Chronology of Major Events, 1830–1849

1830	Senators Daniel Webster of Massachusetts and Robert Hayne of South Carolina debate whether individual states can declare federal laws, such as the Tariff Act of 1828, null. The Baltimore and Ohio becomes the nation's first railroad company. The fifth census counts the U.S. population at 12.9 million people.
1831	William Lloyd Garrison begins publishing *The Liberator*, an evangelical anti-slavery magazine.
1832	Democrat Andrew Jackson is re-elected president. He vetoes rechartering of the U.S. Bank.
	A state convention in South Carolina votes to nullify the Tariff Acts of 1828 and 1832.
	Vice President John C. Calhoun resigns due to differences with President Jackson on the nullification issue.
1833	Jackson removes federal money from the U.S. bank. Whig party begins to become a national party, particularly in opposition to Jackson's banking policy. Senators Calhoun of South Carolina and Henry Clay of Kentucky broker a compromise that averts armed conflict with South Carolina over nullification of tariffs.
1836	Jackson signs an executive order called "Specie circular," aimed at ending currency speculation.
	Texas declares independence from Mexico. Democrat Martin Van Buren is elected president.
1837	Horace Mann begins his career as a major educational influence by being named secretary of the Massachusetts Board of Education. A financial panic and banking controversy solidifies divide between Democrats and Whigs.
1838	Cherokees are forced from Georgia to Oklahoma along the "Trail of Tears."
1840	Whig William Henry Harrison is elected president. The Liberty Party is formed with an abolitionist platform.
	The sixth census counts the U.S. population at 17.1 million people.
1841	Harrison dies in office and is replaced by Vice President John Tyler.
1842	Dorr's Rebellion in Rhode Island leads to liberalized voting requirements.
1844	Democrat James Knox Polk is elected president on a platform of territorial expansion ("manifest destiny"). Samuel Morse sends the first telegram.
1845	Texas annexed by United States as a slave state, days before Tyler leaves office.
	Frederick Douglass, a former slave and abolitionist, publishes his autobiography.
1846	United States declares war on Mexico. Oregon Treaty sets boundaries between the United States from what is now British Columbia east to the Minnesota-Canada line.

1847	The Church of Latter-day Saints (Mormons) founded in Salt Lake City, Utah. Large numbers of refugees from Ireland's potato famine begin to emigrate to the United States.
1848	Whig and former Mexican War general Zachary Taylor is elected president. The Treaty of Guadalupe settles Mexican-American War. A landmark women's rights convention is held in Seneca Falls, New York, which calls for women's suffrage. The antislavery Free-Soil Party is formed, absorbing the Liberty Party.
1849	Cholera erupts in eastern U.S. cities. Many move to California in search of recently discovered gold.

State and Federal Laws Chronology, 1830–1849

1830	Virginia revises its voting requirements to include land-holding and tenancy provisions in values of $25 and $50 and to provide for multiple votes for people based on the amount and value of the land they owned.
1831	Delaware requires the voter to be a citizen and to have paid county tax within two years, assessed at least six months before the election. The voter is exempt if under age twenty-two. The voter must have resided one year in state and six months in the county. No residency is gained by military personnel stationed in state.
1832	Mississippi tax requirement is dropped.
1834	Tennessee property requirement is dropped.
1835	North Carolina requires the voter for Senate to possess a freehold of fifty acres for six months prior to election; to vote for House and governor, there is no land requirement. The voter must also be white.[1]
1836	*Arkansas becomes a state.* It enters the Union without any property or taxpaying requirements for suffrage. The voter must be white, a U.S. citizen, as well as a citizen of the state for six months.
1837	*Michigan becomes a state.* It enters the Union without any property or taxpaying requirements for suffrage. The voter must be a white citizen or inhabitant at the signing of 1835 constitution.
1838	Pennsylvania requires the voter to have paid state or county tax within two years, assessed at least twelve days before the election; the voter is exempt if under age twenty-two. The voter must be a white U.S. citizen and must have resided at least one year in the state and ten days in the election district.
1842	Rhode Island requires the voter to have ownership of real estate worth $134 or the renting an estate for $7 per annum to vote. He must also be a native-born citizen who is a resident of the state for two years and of the city or county for one year. A registry tax of $1 is required, although those who performed at least one day of military duty in the year preceding election and mariners at sea for the year are exempt. The voter must be a U.S. citizen. There is no race requirement, but members of the Narragansett tribe are specifically excluded.
	The Apportionment Act of 1842 mandated single-member districts rather than other combinations for the House of Representatives.
1844	New Jersey drops its taxpaying and property requirements. The voter must be a white U.S. citizen and must have resided for one year in state and five months in county. There is no loss of residence for soldiers or others traveling on public business, but no residency is gained by military personnel stationed in state.
1845	*Florida becomes a state.* It enters the Union without any property or taxpaying requirements for suffrage. The voter must be a white U.S. citizen.
	Texas becomes a state. It enters the Union without any property or taxpaying requirements for suffrage.
	Connecticut and Louisiana drop taxpaying and freeholder requirements.
	Louisiana requires the voter to have been a U.S. citizen for two years.
	Connecticut requires the voter to have resided one year in state and three months in county.

1846   *Iowa becomes a state.* It enters the Union without any property or taxpaying requirements for suffrage. The voter must be a white U.S. citizen.

New York requires the voter to have been a citizen for ten days; if a "man of color," this requirement is lengthened to three years. The voter must have resided one year in the state, four months in the county, and thirty days in the district.

1847   New Hampshire allows voters previously excluded from voting due to excusing themselves from paying taxes to vote after having paid all taxes assessed for a year prior to the election.

1848   *Wisconsin becomes a state.* It enters the Union without any property or taxpaying requirements for suffrage. The declarant alien (a non-citizen who signs a formal declaration of intent to become a citizen) is permitted to vote. The voter must have resided one year in the state.

Illinois requires the voter to be a citizen or to have been an inhabitant of the state on April 1, 1848.

Summary

By 1850, only four states out of thirty-one still had property requirements for voting—New York, North Carolina, Rhode Island and South Carolina. New York's requirements were limited to non-whites; South Carolina offered a length of residency alternative to ownership of property or wealth; and North Carolina would eliminate its property requirement in 1854. In 1850, twenty-five of thirty-one states excluded African Americans from voting. Residency requirements existed in all states, ranging from six months to two years. Many of these requirements also included residency in the locale, county, or town for a minimum duration. Citizenship was a requirement for voting, except in those states (three) that permitted voting for declarant aliens (non-citizens who sign a formal declaration of intent to become a citizen).

Source: Adapted from Alexander Keyssar, *The Right to Vote: The Contested History of Democracy in the United States, Revised Edition* (New York: Basic Books, 2009), 308–313 and 315–319.
[1] References to Senate and House refer to state rather than federal offices.

National Count of Popular Vote for President, 1832–1848

YEAR	NAME	PARTY	TOTAL	PERCENTAGE[1]
1832	Andrew Jackson	Democratic	701,780	28.8%
	Henry Clay	National Republican	484,205	19.9%
	William Wirt	Anti-Masonic	100,715	4.1%
1836	Martin Van Buren	Democratic	764,173	27.1%
	William Harrison	Whig	550,816	19.5%
	Hugh White	Whig	146,107	5.2%
	Daniel Webster	Whig	41,201	1.4%
1840	William Harrison	Whig	1,275,390	39.7%
	Martin Van Buren	Democratic	1,128,854	35.1%
1844	James Knox Polk	Democratic	1,339,494	35.6%
	Henry Clay	Whig	1,300,304	34.6%
	James Birney	Liberty	62,103	1.7%
1848	Zachary Taylor	Whig	1,361,393	31.0%
	Lewis Cass	Democratic	1,223,460	27.9%
	Martin Van Buren	Free-Soil	291,501	6.6%

[1] The percentage figures in this chart are based on the votes cast divided by the eligible voting-age population at the time of the election.

States with Property and Taxpaying Requirements for Suffrage, 1830–1849

STATE	DATE OF STATEHOOD[1]	PROPERTY REQUIREMENT[2]	TAXPAYING REQUIREMENT[2]
ALABAMA		None	None
ARKANSAS	1836	None	None
CONNECTICUT			1817: Paid taxes or served in militia.
		1818: Freehold worth $7 a year or possession of personal property worth $134 with taxpaying and militia alternatives.	1818: Taxpaying and militia alternatives to freehold requirement.
		1845: Freehold requirement dropped.	1845: Taxpaying requirement dropped.
DELAWARE		None	1792: "Paid a State or county tax … assessed at least six months before the election." Exempt if under age 22 and the son of a qualified voter.
			1831: Paid county tax within 2 years, assessed at least 6 months before the election. Exempt if under age 22.
FLORIDA	1845	None	None
GEORGIA		None	1798: Paid all taxes for the year preceding the election.
ILLINOIS		None	None
INDIANA		None	None
IOWA	1846	None	None
KENTUCKY		None	None
LOUISIANA		1812: Exempt from taxpaying requirement if "purchased land from the United States."	1812: Paid state tax in last six months or purchased land from the United States.
		1845: None	1845: None
MAINE		None	None
MARYLAND		1801: Freehold requirement dropped.	None
MASSACHUSETTS		1821: Property requirement dropped.	1821: Paid any state or county tax assessed within 2 years, unless exempted from taxation.
MICHIGAN	1837	None	None
MISSISSIPPI		None	1817: Paid state or county tax or enrolled in local militia, unless exempt from military service.
			1832: Militia/taxpaying requirement dropped.
MISSOURI		None	None

States with Property and Taxpaying Requirements for Suffrage, 1830–1849 (continued)

States with Property and Taxpaying Requirements for Suffrage, 1830–1849 *(continued)*

STATE	DATE OF STATEHOOD[1]	PROPERTY REQUIREMENT[2]	TAXPAYING REQUIREMENT[2]
NEW HAMPSHIRE		None	1784: Poll tax.
			1792: "Persons excused from paying taxes at their own request" excluded.
			1847: Those previously excused from paying taxes can vote after having paid all taxes assessed for a year prior to the election.
NEW JERSEY		1807: Worth 50 pounds; any person who paid a state or county tax, or had his name enrolled upon a tax duplicate for the last state or county tax deemed to be worth 50 pounds.	1807: Worth 50 pounds; any person who paid a state or county tax, or had his name enrolled upon a tax duplicate for the last state or county tax, deemed to be worth 50 pounds.
		1844: Property requirement dropped.	1844: Tax requirement dropped.
NEW YORK		1821: Property requirement dropped for whites. If a "man of color," must have been citizen for one year "seized and possessed of a freehold estate of the value of $250 over and above all debts and debts and encumbrances charged thereon."	1821: If white, "shall have, within the year next preceding the election," paid a state or county tax on real or personal property or shall by law be exempted from taxation; or "shall have performed within that year military duty in the militia" or as a fireman; or if meeting special residency requirements, shall have labored on public highways.
		1826: If a "man of color," must have been citizen for three years.	1826: If a "man of color," must have been citizen for three years.
NORTH CAROLINA		1776: Freehold of 50 acres of land to vote for Senate; no property requirement to vote for House of Commons.[3]	1776: Must have paid taxes to vote for House of Commons.
		1835: To vote for Senate, freehold of 50 acres for 6 months prior to the election; to vote for House of Commons and governor, no property requirement.	1835: Must have paid taxes to vote for House of Commons and governor.
OHIO		None	1802: Must have paid or been charged with state or county tax; not applicable to white males above age 21, who are "compelled to labor on the roads" and have resided 1 year in the state.
PENNSYLVANIA		None	1790: Paid state or county tax within 2 years, assessed at least 6 months before the election; exempt if under age 22 and the son of a qualified voter.
			1838: Paid state or county tax within 2 years, assessed at least 12 days before the election; exempt if under age 22.
RHODE ISLAND		1762: Freehold worth 40 pounds or 40 shillings per year, or voter is the eldest son of a freeholder. *(continued next page)*	None

States with Property and Taxpaying Requirements for Suffrage, 1830–1849 *(continued)*

STATE	DATE OF STATEHOOD[1]	PROPERTY REQUIREMENT[2]	TAXPAYING REQUIREMENT[2]
RHODE ISLAND *(continued)*		1842: Ownership of real estate worth $134 or renting an estate for $7 per annum. Native-born citizen, resident in the state for 2 years and in the city or county for 1 year, may vote if he pays a tax of $1 or performs military duty for at least 1 day in the year preceding the election.	1842: See property requirement. Also a registry tax of $1, or such sum as with his other taxes shall amount to $1. Those performing military duty and mariners at sea for the year are exempt.
SOUTH CAROLINA		1810: Freehold of 50 acres or a town lot, owned 6 months prior to election; or residence in the election district for 6 months.	1810: Tax requirement dropped.
TENNESSEE		1796: Freehold in the county wherein he may vote, or inhabitant of any one county in the state for 6 months 1834: Freehold requirement dropped.	None
TEXAS	1845	None	None
VERMONT		None	None
VIRGINIA		1804: Must own land for 6 months prior to the election. 1830: Must meet the qualifications of previous Constitution and laws or be "possessed, or whose tenant for years, at will, or at sufferance is possessed, of an estate or freehold in land of the value of twenty-five dollars, and so assessed to be if any assessment thereof be required by law" or "possessed as tenant in common, joint tenant, or partner of an interest in or share of land, and having an estate of freehold therein, such interest or share being of the value of twenty-five dollars, and so assessed to be if any assessment thereof be required by law" or persons "entitled to a reversion or vested remainder in fee, expectant on an estate for life or lives, in land of the value of fifty dollars, and so assessed to be if any assessment thereof be required by law . . . each and every such citizen, unless his title shall have come to him by descent, devise, marriage or marriage settlement, having been so possessed or entitled for six months" or "shall own and be himself in actual occupation of a leasehold estate, with the evidence of title recorded two months before he shall offer to vote, of a term originally not less than five years, of the annual value or rent of twenty dollars" or a person "who for twelve months next preceding has been a housekeeper and head of a family within the county, city, town, borough, or election district where he may offer to vote, and shall have been assessed . . . within the preceding year, and actually paid the same" and "in the *(continued next page)*	1804: None 1830: See 1830 property requirements.

States with Property and Taxpaying Requirements for Suffrage, 1830–1849 (continued)

STATE	DATE OF STATEHOOD[1]	PROPERTY REQUIREMENT[2]	TAXPAYING REQUIREMENT[2]
VIRGINIA (continued)		case of two or more tenants in common, joint tenants, or partners in possession, reversion, or remainder, having interest in land, the value whereof shall be insufficient to entitle them all to vote, they shall together have as many votes as the value of the land shall entitle them to; and the legislature shall by law provide the mode in which their vote or votes shall in such case be given."	
WISCONSIN	1848	None	None

Source: Alexander Keyssar, *The Right to Vote: The Contested History of Democracy in the United States, Revised Edition* (New York: Basic Books, 2009), 308–313. Adapted from Keyssar's table, which extends from 1790 to 1855. Sources of quotations are found on pp. 369–379.

[1] For states whose date of statehood falls within the time period 1830–1849.

[2] Dates listed are for the year that the property or tax requirement went into effect. All listed requirements continue into the 1830–1849 date range of this table.

[3] References to Senate and House of Commons refer to state rather than federal offices.

States with Race and Citizenship Requirements for Suffrage, 1830–1849

STATE AND YEAR OF STATEHOOD[1]	DATE OF REQUIREMENT	RACE	CITIZENSHIP	NATIVE AMERICANS
ALABAMA	1819	White	U.S. citizen	Not specifically mentioned
ARKANSAS (1836)	1836	White	U.S. citizen, citizen of state for 6 months	Not specifically mentioned
CONNECTICUT	1818	White	U.S. citizen	Not specifically mentioned
DELAWARE	1792	White	No requirement	Not specifically mentioned
	1831	White	Citizen	Not specifically mentioned
FLORIDA (1845)	1838	White	U.S. citizen	Not specifically mentioned
GEORGIA	1789	No requirement	Citizen of state	Not specifically mentioned
ILLINOIS	1818	White	No requirement	Not specifically mentioned
	1848	White	Citizen or inhabitant of state on April 1, 1848	Not specifically mentioned
INDIANA	1816	White	U.S. citizen	Not specifically mentioned
IOWA (1846)	1846	White	U.S. citizen	Not specifically mentioned
KENTUCKY	1799	"Negroes, mulattos, and Indians" excluded	Citizen	"Indians" specifically excluded
LOUISIANA	1812	White	U.S. citizen	Not specifically mentioned
	1845	White	U.S. citizen for 2 years	Not specifically mentioned
MAINE	1819	No requirement	U.S. citizen	"Indians not taxed" excluded
MARYLAND	1810	White	Citizen	Not specifically mentioned
MASSACHUSETTS	1821	No requirement	Citizen	Not specifically mentioned
MICHIGAN (1837)	1835	White	Citizen or inhabitant of state at time of signing of 1835 constitution.	Not specifically mentioned
MISSISSIPPI	1817	White	U.S. citizen	Not specifically mentioned
MISSOURI	1820	White	U.S. citizen	Not specifically mentioned
NEW HAMPSHIRE	1813	No requirement	Citizen	Not specifically mentioned
NEW JERSEY	1807	White	Citizen	Not specifically mentioned
	1844	White	U.S. citizen	Not specifically mentioned

States with Race and Citizenship Requirements for Suffrage, 1830–1849 (continued)

States with Race and Citizenship Requirements for Suffrage, 1830–1849 (continued)

STATE AND YEAR OF STATEHOOD[1]	DATE OF REQUIREMENT	RACE	CITIZENSHIP	NATIVE AMERICANS
NEW YORK	1821	White or "man of color" meeting property and tax requirements	Citizen; if a "man of color," citizen of state for 1 year	Not specifically mentioned
	1846	Same as 1821	Citizen for 10 days; if "man of color," citizen for 3 years.	Not specifically mentioned
NORTH CAROLINA	1776	No requirement	No requirement	Not specifically mentioned
	1835	White	No requirement	Not specifically mentioned
OHIO	1802	White	No requirement	Not specifically mentioned
	1809	Same as 1802	U.S. citizen	
PENNSYLVANIA	1790	No requirement	Citizen	Not specifically mentioned
	1838	White	U.S. citizen	Not specifically mentioned
RHODE ISLAND	1762	No requirement	No requirement	Not specifically mentioned
	1842	No requirement	U.S. citizen	Members of the Narraganesett tribe excluded
SOUTH CAROLINA	1790	White	Citizen of state	Not specifically mentioned
PENNSYLVANIA	1790	No requirement	Citizen	Not specifically mentioned
RHODE ISLAND	1762	No requirement	No requirement	Not specifically mentioned
SOUTH CAROLINA	1790	White	Citizen of state	Not specifically mentioned

Source: Alexander Keyssar, *The Right to Vote: The Contested History of Democracy in the United States, Revised Edition* (New York: Basic Books, 2009), 315–319. Adapted from Keyssar's table, which extends from 1790 to 1855. Sources of quotations are found on pp. 369–379.

[1] For states whose date of statehood falls within the time period 1830–1849.

United States Presidential Turnout, Election Years 1832–1848

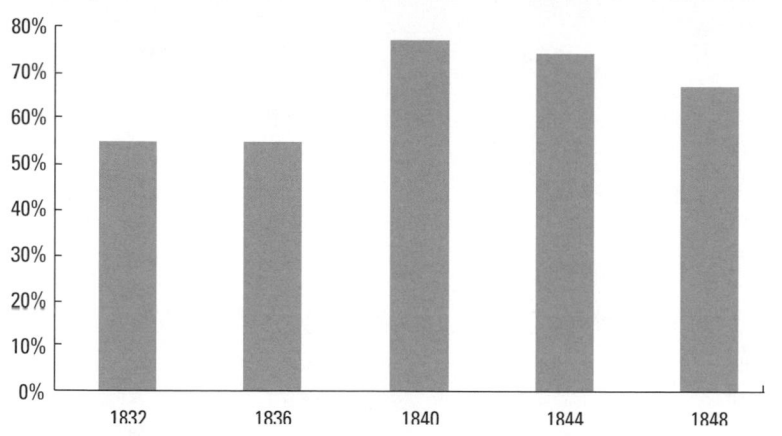

YEAR	VOTING-AGE POPULATION	TURNOUT	%
1832	2,385,000	1,293,973	54.3%
1836	2,772,000	1,503,531	54.2%
1840	3,146,000	2,411,808	76.7%
1844	3,665,000	2,703,659	73.8%
1848	4,328,000	2,879,184	66.5%

Partisan Turnout, Presidential Years, Based on Aggregate House Turnout, Election Years 1832–1848

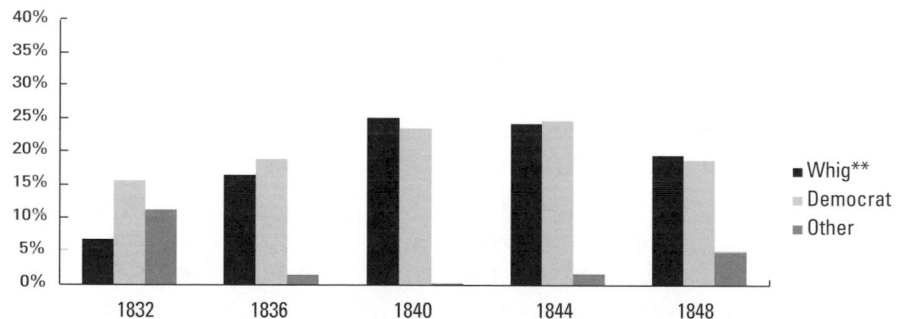

Whig**
Democrat
Other

YEAR	VOTING-AGE POPULATION*	WHIG** TURNOUT	%	DEMOCRAT TURNOUT	%	OTHER TURNOUT	%
1832	2,385,000	166,581	7.0%	371,071	15.6%	262,586	11.0%
1836	2,772,000	454,969	16.4%	520,223	18.8%	41,912	1.5%
1840	3,146,000	786,603	25.0%	736,834	23.4%	2,964	0.1%
1844	3,665,000	885,039	24.1%	901,390	24.6%	62,273	1.7%
1848	4,328,000	840,181	19.4%	808,686	18.7%	221,048	5.1%

*Voting-age population taken from states with presidential elections

**Turnout for 1832 is primarily for the National Republican party. The Whig party supplanted the National Republicans as the Democrats' national opposition by 1834.

Alternate Graph for Partisan Turnout, Presidential Years, Based on Aggregate House Turnout, 1832–1848

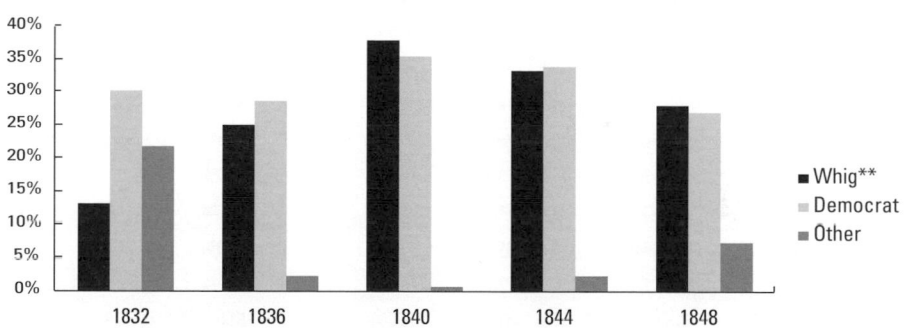

Whig**
Democrat
Other

YEAR	VOTING-AGE POPULATION***	WHIG** TURNOUT	%	DEMOCRAT TURNOUT	%	OTHER TURNOUT	%
1832	1,233,000	166,581	13.5%	371,071	30.1%	262,586	21.3%
1836	1,824,000	454,969	24.9%	520,223	28.5%	41,912	2.3%
1840	2,086,000	786,603	37.7%	736,834	35.3%	2,964	0.1%
1844	2,669,000	885,039	33.2%	901,390	33.8%	62,273	2.3%
1848	3,010,000	840,181	27.9%	808,686	26.9%	221,048	7.3%

**Turnout for 1832 is primarily for the National Republican party. The Whig party supplanted the National Republicans as the Democrats' national opposition by 1834.

***This is an alternate graph that depicts partisan turnout calculated using voting-age population only from those states that held House elections. For percentages, consult the total lines of House partisan charts.

UNITED STATES PRESIDENTIAL GENERAL ELECTIONS

Election Years 1832–1848

State	1832 Voting-age population	1832 Turnout	1832 %	1836 Voting-age population	1836 Turnout	1836 %	1836 Difference from 1832*	1840 Voting-age population	1840 Turnout	1840 %	1840 Difference from 1832	1844 Voting-age population	1844 Turnout	1844 %	1844 Difference from 1832	1848 Voting-age population	1848 Turnout	1848 %	1848 Difference from 1832
ALABAMA	47,000	14,291	30.4%	59,000	37,296	63.2%	32.8	71,000	62,511	88.0%	57.6	79,000	63,403	80.3%	49.9	87,000	61,659	70.9%	40.5
ARKANSAS				13,000	3,714	28.6%		18,000	11,839	65.8%	37.2	25,000	15,150	60.6%	32.0	32,000	16,888	52.8%	24.2
CONNECTICUT	71,000	32,833	46.2%	73,000	38,093	52.2%	5.9	76,000	56,879	74.8%	28.6	86,000	64,616	75.1%	28.9	95,000	62,398	65.7%	19.4
DELAWARE	13,000	8,386	64.5%	13,000	8,892	68.4%	3.9	13,000	10,852	83.5%	19.0	15,000	12,247	81.6%	17.1	16,000	12,432	77.7%	13.2
FLORIDA																11,000	7,203	65.5%	
GEORGIA	65,000	20,750	31.9%	74,000	47,259	63.9%	31.9	82,000	72,322	88.2%	56.3	93,000	86,247	92.7%	60.8	104,000	92,317	88.8%	56.8
ILLINOIS	50,000	21,481	43.0%	81,000	33,589	41.5%	-1.5	112,000	93,175	83.2%	40.2	146,000	109,057	74.7%	31.7	180,000	124,596	69.2%	26.3
INDIANA	81,000	57,152	70.6%	110,000	74,423	67.7%	-2.9	139,000	117,605	84.6%	14.0	168,000	140,157	83.4%	12.9	198,000	152,394	77.0%	6.4
IOWA																38,000	22,271	58.6%	
KENTUCKY	109,000	79,741	73.2%	116,000	70,090	60.4%	-12.7	125,000	91,104	72.9%	-0.3	143,000	113,237	79.2%	6.0	161,000	116,865	72.6%	-0.6
LOUISIANA	30,000	6,337	21.1%	40,000	7,425	18.6%	-2.6	49,000	18,912	38.6%	17.5	61,000	26,865	44.0%	22.9	73,000	33,866	46.4%	25.3
MAINE	93,000	62,153	66.8%	104,000	38,740	37.3%	-29.6	114,000	92,802	81.4%	14.6	127,000	84,933	66.9%	0.0	140,000	87,625	62.6%	-4.2
MARYLAND	69,000	38,316	55.5%	71,000	48,119	67.8%	12.2	75,000	62,280	83.0%	27.5	87,000	68,690	79.0%	23.4	98,000	72,359	73.8%	18.3
MASSACHUSETTS	156,000	67,619	43.3%	174,000	74,732	42.9%	-0.4	194,000	126,825	65.4%	22.0	224,000	132,037	58.9%	15.6	255,000	134,748	52.8%	9.5
MICHIGAN				36,000	12,052	33.5%		54,000	44,029	81.5%	48.1	72,000	55,560	77.2%	43.7	90,000	65,082	72.3%	38.8
MISSISSIPPI	22,000	5,750	26.1%	32,000	20,079	62.7%	36.6	42,000	36,525	87.0%	60.8	52,000	45,004	86.5%	60.4	62,000	52,456	84.6%	58.5
MISSOURI	35,000	5,192	14.8%	54,000	18,332	33.9%	19.1	74,000	52,923	71.5%	56.7	100,000	72,522	72.5%	57.7	126,000	72,748	57.7%	42.9
NEW HAMPSHIRE	62,000	43,793	70.6%	66,000	24,925	37.8%	-32.9	69,000	59,956	86.9%	16.3	76,000	49,187	64.7%	-5.9	82,000	50,104	61.1%	-9.5
NEW JERSEY	70,000	47,760	68.2%	75,000	51,729	69.0%	0.7	81,000	64,454	79.6%	11.3	95,000	75,944	79.9%	11.7	108,000	77,745	72.0%	3.8
NEW YORK	455,000	323,393	71.1%	515,000	305,343	59.3%	-11.8	578,000	441,543	76.4%	5.3	669,000	485,882	72.6%	1.6	761,000	455,944	59.9%	-11.2
NORTH CAROLINA	94,000	29,799	31.7%	95,000	50,153	52.8%	21.1	97,000	80,735	83.2%	51.5	105,000	82,521	78.6%	46.9	113,000	79,826	70.6%	38.9
OHIO	220,000	158,350	72.0%	274,000	202,931	74.1%	2.1	328,000	272,890	83.2%	11.2	379,000	312,300	82.4%	10.4	429,000	328,987	76.7%	4.7
PENNSYLVANIA	305,000	157,679	51.7%	340,000	178,701	52.6%	0.9	378,000	287,695	76.1%	24.4	445,000	331,645	74.5%	22.8	511,000	369,092	72.2%	20.5
RHODE ISLAND	22,000	5,747	26.1%	24,000	5,673	23.6%	-2.5	26,000	8,631	33.2%	7.1	31,000	12,194	39.3%	13.2	36,000	11,049	30.7%	4.6
TENNESSEE	105,000	29,425	28.0%	113,000	62,197	55.0%	27.0	122,000	108,145	88.6%	60.6	135,000	119,957	88.9%	60.8	147,000	122,463	83.3%	55.3
TEXAS																32,000	17,000	53.1%	
VERMONT	64,000	32,344	50.5%	67,000	35,099	52.4%	1.8	69,000	50,782	73.6%	23.1	75,000	48,765	65.0%	14.5	80,000	47,897	59.9%	9.3
VIRGINIA	147,000	45,682	31.1%	153,000	53,945	35.3%	4.2	160,000	86,394	54.0%	22.9	177,000	95,539	54.0%	22.9	193,000	92,004	47.7%	16.6
WISCONSIN																70,000	39,166	56.0%	
Total	2,385,000	1,293,973	54.3%	2,772,000	1,503,531	54.2%	0.0	3,146,000	2,411,808	76.7%	22.4	3,665,000	2,703,659	73.8%	19.5	4,328,000	2,879,184	66.5%	12.3

*Percentage point difference between turnout in current year and initial year listed in chart. If data do not appear for a state in the initial year listed, the difference is calculated from the first year in which data do appear for that state.

UNITED STATES PRESIDENTIAL GENERAL ELECTIONS

Whig Turnout for Election Years 1832–1848

State	1832 (National Republicans)			1836				1840				1844				1848			
	Voting-age population	Turnout	%	Voting-age population	Turnout	%	Difference from 1832*	Voting-age population	Turnout	%	Difference from 1832	Voting-age population	Turnout	%	Difference from 1832	Voting-age population	Turnout	%	Difference from 1832
ALABAMA	47,000	5	0.0%	59,000	16,658	28.2%	28.2	71,000	28,515	40.2%	40.2	79,000	26,002	32.9%	32.9	87,000	30,482	35.0%	35.0
ARKANSAS				13,000	1,334	10.3%		18,000	5,160	28.7%	18.4	25,000	5,604	22.4%	12.2	32,000	7,587	23.7%	13.4
CONNECTICUT	71,000	18,155	25.6%	73,000	18,799	25.8%	0.2	76,000	31,598	41.6%	16.0	86,000	32,832	38.2%	12.6	95,000	30,318	31.9%	6.3
DELAWARE	13,000	4,276	32.9%	13,000	4,736	36.4%	3.5	13,000	5,967	45.9%	13.0	15,000	6,271	41.8%	8.9	16,000	6,440	40.3%	7.4
FLORIDA																11,000	4,120	37.5%	
GEORGIA				74,000	24,481	33.1%		82,000	40,339	49.2%	16.1	93,000	42,100	45.3%	12.2	104,000	47,532	45.7%	12.6
ILLINOIS	50,000	6,745	13.5%	81,000	15,220	18.8%	5.3	112,000	45,574	40.7%	27.2	146,000	45,854	31.4%	17.9	180,000	52,853	29.4%	15.9
INDIANA	81,000	25,473	31.4%	110,000	41,339	37.6%	6.1	139,000	65,280	47.0%	15.5	168,000	67,866	40.4%	8.9	198,000	69,668	35.2%	3.7
IOWA																38,000	9,930	26.1%	
KENTUCKY	109,000	43,449	39.9%	116,000	36,861	31.8%	-8.1	125,000	58,488	46.8%	6.9	143,000	61,249	42.8%	3.0	161,000	67,145	41.7%	1.8
LOUISIANA	30,000	2,429	8.1%	40,000	3,583	9.0%	0.9	49,000	11,296	23.1%	15.0	61,000	13,083	21.4%	13.4	73,000	18,487	25.3%	17.2
MAINE	93,000	27,331	29.4%	104,000	14,803	14.2%	-15.2	114,000	46,612	40.9%	11.5	127,000	34,378	27.1%	-2.3	140,000	35,273	25.2%	4.2
MARYLAND	69,000	19,160	27.8%	71,000	25,852	36.4%	8.6	75,000	33,528	44.7%	16.9	87,000	35,984	41.4%	13.6	98,000	37,702	38.5%	10.7
MASSACHUSETTS	156,000	31,963	20.5%	174,000	41,201	23.7%	3.2	194,000	72,852	37.6%	17.1	224,000	67,062	29.9%	9.4	255,000	61,072	23.9%	3.5
MICHIGAN				36,000	5,545	15.4%		54,000	22,933	42.5%	27.1	72,000	24,185	33.6%	-8.9	90,000	23,947	26.6%	11.2
MISSISSIPPI				32,000	9,782	30.6%		42,000	19,515	46.5%	15.9	52,000	19,158	36.8%	6.3	62,000	25,911	41.8%	11.2
MISSOURI				54,000	7,337	13.6%		74,000	22,954	31.0%	17.4	100,000	31,200	31.2%	0.2	126,000	32,671	25.9%	12.3
NEW HAMPSHIRE	62,000	18,938	30.5%	66,000	6,228	9.4%	-21.1	69,000	26,310	38.1%	7.6	76,000	17,866	23.5%	-7.0	82,000	14,781	18.0%	-12.5
NEW JERSEY	70,000	23,466	33.5%	75,000	26,137	34.8%	1.3	81,000	33,351	41.2%	7.7	95,000	38,318	40.3%	6.8	108,000	40,015	37.1%	3.5
NEW YORK	455,000	154,896	34.0%	515,000	138,548	26.9%	-7.1	578,000	226,001	39.1%	5.1	669,000	232,482	34.8%	0.7	761,000	218,583	28.7%	-5.3
NORTH CAROLINA	94,000	4,538	4.8%	95,000	23,521	24.8%	19.9	97,000	46,567	48.0%	43.2	105,000	43,232	41.2%	36.3	113,000	44,054	39.0%	34.2
OHIO	220,000	76,566	34.8%	274,000	105,809	38.6%	3.8	328,000	148,043	45.1%	10.3	379,000	155,091	40.9%	6.1	429,000	138,656	32.3%	-2.5
PENNSYLVANIA				340,000	87,235	25.7%		378,000	144,023	38.1%	12.4	445,000	161,195	36.2%	-1.9	511,000	185,730	36.3%	10.7
RHODE ISLAND	22,000	2,871	13.1%	24,000	2,710	11.3%	-1.8	26,000	5,213	20.1%	7.0	31,000	7,322	23.6%	10.6	36,000	6,705	18.6%	5.6
TENNESSEE	105,000	1,347	1.3%	113,000	36,027	31.9%	30.6	122,000	60,194	49.3%	48.1	135,000	60,040	44.5%	43.2	147,000	64,321	43.8%	42.5
TEXAS																32,000	5,281	16.5%	
VERMONT	64,000	11,161	17.4%	67,000	20,994	31.3%	13.9	69,000	32,440	47.0%	29.6	75,000	26,770	35.7%	18.3	80,000	23,117	28.9%	11.5
VIRGINIA	147,000	11,436	7.8%	153,000	23,384	15.3%	7.5	160,000	42,637	26.6%	18.9	177,000	44,860	25.3%	17.6	193,000	45,265	23.5%	15.7
WISCONSIN																70,000	13,747	19.6%	
Total	1,958,000	484,205	24.7%	2,772,000	738,124	26.6%	1.9	3,146,000	1,275,390	40.5%	15.8	3,665,000	1,300,004	35.5%	10.7	4,328,000	1,361,393	31.5%	6.7

United States Presidential General Elections (continued)

United States Presidential General Elections (continued)

Democratic Turnout for Election Years 1832–1848

State	1832 Voting-age population	1832 Turnout	1832 %	1836 Voting-age population	1836 Turnout	1836 %	1836 Difference from 1832	1840 Voting-age population	1840 Turnout	1840 %	1840 Difference from 1832	1844 Voting-age population	1844 Turnout	1844 %	1844 Difference from 1832	1848 Voting-age population	1848 Turnout	1848 %	1848 Difference from 1832
ALABAMA	47,000	14,286	30.4%	59,000	20,638	35.0%	4.6	71,000	33,996	47.9%	17.5	79,000	37,401	47.3%	16.9	87,000	31,173	35.8%	5.4
ARKANSAS				13,000	2,380	18.3%		18,000	6,679	37.1%	18.8	25,000	9,546	38.2%	19.9	32,000	9,301	29.1%	10.8
CONNECTICUT	71,000	11,269	15.9%	73,000	19,294	26.4%	10.6	76,000	25,281	33.3%	17.4	86,000	29,841	34.7%	18.8	95,000	27,051	28.5%	12.6
DELAWARE	13,000	4,110	31.6%	13,000	4,151	31.9%	0.3	13,000	4,872	37.5%	5.9	15,000	5,970	39.8%	8.2	16,000	5,910	36.9%	5.3
FLORIDA																11,000	3,083	28.0%	
GEORGIA	65,000	20,750	31.9%	74,000	22,778	30.8%	-1.1	82,000	31,983	39.0%	7.1	93,000	44,147	47.5%	15.5	104,000	44,785	43.1%	11.1
ILLINOIS	50,000	14,609	29.2%	81,000	18,369	22.7%	-6.5	112,000	47,441	42.4%	13.1	146,000	58,795	40.3%	11.1	180,000	55,952	31.1%	1.9
INDIANA	81,000	31,652	39.1%	110,000	33,084	30.1%	-9.0	139,000	51,696	37.2%	-1.9	168,000	70,183	41.8%	2.7	198,000	74,695	37.7%	-1.4
IOWA																38,000	11,238	29.6%	
KENTUCKY	109,000	36,292	33.3%	116,000	33,229	28.6%	-4.6	125,000	32,616	26.1%	-7.2	143,000	51,988	36.4%	3.1	161,000	49,720	30.9%	-2.4
LOUISIANA	30,000	3,908	13.0%	40,000	3,842	9.6%	-3.4	49,000	7,616	15.5%	2.5	61,000	13,782	22.6%	9.6	73,000	15,379	21.1%	8.0
MAINE	93,000	33,978	36.5%	104,000	22,825	21.9%	-14.6	114,000	46,190	40.5%	4.0	127,000	45,719	36.0%	-0.5	140,000	40,195	28.7%	-7.8
MARYLAND	69,000	19,156	27.8%	71,000	22,267	31.4%	3.6	75,000	28,752	38.3%	10.6	87,000	32,706	37.6%	9.8	98,000	34,528	35.2%	7.5
MASSACHUSETTS	156,000	13,933	8.9%	174,000	33,486	19.2%	10.3	194,000	52,355	27.0%	18.1	224,000	53,039	23.7%	14.7	255,000	35,281	13.8%	4.9
MICHIGAN				36,000	6,507	18.1%		54,000	21,096	39.1%	21.0	72,000	27,737	38.5%	20.4	90,000	30,742	34.2%	16.1
MISSISSIPPI	22,000	5,750	26.1%	32,000	10,297	32.2%	6.0	42,000	17,010	40.5%	14.4	52,000	25,846	49.7%	23.6	62,000	26,545	42.8%	16.7
MISSOURI	35,000	5,192	14.8%	54,000	10,995	20.4%	5.5	74,000	29,969	40.5%	25.7	100,000	41,322	41.3%	26.5	126,000	40,077	31.8%	17.0
NEW HAMPSHIRE	62,000	24,855	40.1%	66,000	18,697	28.3%	-11.8	69,000	32,774	47.5%	7.4	76,000	27,160	35.7%	-4.4	82,000	27,763	33.9%	-6.2
NEW JERSEY	70,000	23,826	34.0%	75,000	25,592	34.1%	0.1	81,000	31,034	38.3%	4.3	95,000	37,495	39.5%	5.4	108,000	36,901	34.2%	0.1
NEW YORK	455,000	168,497	37.0%	515,000	166,795	32.4%	-4.6	578,000	212,733	36.8%	-0.2	669,000	237,588	35.5%	-1.5	761,000	114,319	15.0%	-22.0
NORTH CAROLINA	94,000	25,261	26.9%	95,000	26,631	28.0%	1.2	97,000	34,168	35.2%	8.4	105,000	39,287	37.4%	10.5	113,000	35,772	31.7%	4.8
OHIO	220,000	81,246	36.9%	274,000	97,122	35.4%	-1.5	328,000	123,944	37.8%	0.9	379,000	149,127	39.3%	2.4	429,000	154,782	36.1%	-0.9
PENNSYLVANIA	305,000	90,973	29.8%	340,000	91,466	26.9%	-2.9	378,000	143,672	38.0%	8.2	445,000	167,311	37.6%	7.8	511,000	172,186	33.7%	3.9
RHODE ISLAND	22,000	2,051	9.3%	24,000	2,962	12.3%	3.0	26,000	3,263	12.6%	3.2	31,000	4,867	15.7%	6.4	36,000	3,613	10.0%	0.7
TENNESSEE	105,000	28,078	26.7%	113,000	26,170	23.2%	-3.6	122,000	47,951	39.3%	12.6	135,000	59,917	44.4%	17.6	147,000	58,142	39.6%	12.8
TEXAS																32,000	11,644	36.4%	
VERMONT	64,000	7,865	12.3%	67,000	14,040	21.0%	8.7	69,000	18,006	26.1%	13.8	75,000	18,041	24.1%	11.8	80,000	10,943	13.7%	1.4
VIRGINIA	147,000	34,243	23.3%	153,000	30,556	20.0%	-3.3	160,000	43,757	27.3%	4.1	177,000	50,679	28.6%	5.3	193,000	46,739	24.2%	0.9
WISCONSIN																70,000	15,001	21.4%	
Total	2,385,000	701,780	29.4%	2,772,000	764,173	27.6%	-1.9	3,146,000	1,128,854	35.9%	6.5	3,665,000	1,339,494	36.5%	7.1	4,328,000	1,223,460	28.3%	-1.2

United States Presidential General Elections *(continued)*

Other Turnout for Election Years 1832–1848

State	1832				1836				1840				1844				1848			
	Voting-age population	Turnout	%		Voting-age population	Turnout	%	Difference from 1832	Voting-age population	Turnout	%	Difference from 1832	Voting-age population	Turnout	%	Difference from 1832	Voting-age population	Turnout	%	Difference from 1832
ALABAMA																	87,000	4	0.0%	
CONNECTICUT	71,000	3,409	4.8%										86,000	1,943	2.3%	-2.5	95,000	5,029	5.3%	0.5
DELAWARE					13,000	5	0.0%		13,000	13	0.1%	0.1	15,000	6	0.0%	-0.1	16,000	82	0.5%	0.5
ILLINOIS	50,000	127	0.3%						112,000	160	0.1%	-0.1	146,000	4,408	3.0%	2.8	180,000	15,791	8.8%	8.5
INDIANA	81,000	27	0.0%						139,000	629	0.5%	0.4	168,000	2,108	1.3%	1.2	198,000	8,031	4.1%	4.0
IOWA																	38,000	1,103	2.9%	
MAINE	93,000	844	0.9%		104,000	1,112	1.1%	0.2					127,000	4,836	3.8%	2.9	140,000	12,157	8.7%	7.8
MARYLAND																	98,000	129	0.1%	
MASSACHUSETTS	156,000	21,723	13.9%		174,000	45	0.0%	-13.9	194,000	1,618	0.8%	-13.1	224,000	11,936	5.3%	-8.6	255,000	38,395	15.1%	1.1
MICHIGAN													72,000	3,638	5.1%	4.4	90,000	10,393	11.5%	10.9
NEW HAMPSHIRE									69,000	872	1.3%	1.3	76,000	4,161	5.5%	4.2	82,000	7,560	9.2%	9.2
NEW JERSEY	70,000	468	0.7%						81,000	69	0.1%	-0.2	95,000	131	0.1%	-0.1	108,000	829	0.8%	0.5
NEW YORK									578,000	2,809	0.5%	-21.4	669,000	15,812	2.4%	-19.5	761,000	123,042	16.2%	18.2
NORTH CAROLINA					95,000	1	0.0%						105,000	2	0.0%	-3.7				
OHIO	220,000	538	0.2%						328,000	903	0.3%	0.0	379,000	8,082	2.1%	1.9	429,000	35,549	8.3%	8.1
PENNSYLVANIA	305,000	66,706	21.9%										445,000	3,139	0.7%	-21.2	511,000	11,176	2.2%	-19.7
RHODE ISLAND	22,000	825	3.8%		24,000	1	0.0%	-3.7	26,000	155	0.6%	-3.2	31,000	5	0.0%	-3.7	36,000	731	2.0%	-1.7
TEXAS																	32,000	75	0.2%	
VERMONT	64,000	13,318	20.8%		67,000	65	0.1%	-20.7	69,000	336	0.5%	-20.3	75,000	3,954	5.3%	-15.5	80,000	13,837	17.3%	-3.5
VIRGINIA	147,000	3	0.0%		153,000	5	0.0%	0.0												
WISCONSIN																	70,000	10,418	14.9%	
Total	1,279,000	107,988	8.4%		630,000	1,234	0.2%	-8.2	1,609,000	7,564	0.5%	-8.0	2,713,000	64,161	2.4%	-6.1	3,306,000	294,331	8.9%	0.5

*The Whig party supplanted the National Republicans as the Democrats' national opposition by 1834.

**Percentage point difference between turnout in current year and initial year listed in chart. If data do not appear for a state in the initial year listed, the difference is calculated from the first year in which data do appear for that state.

STATE GUBERNATORIAL GENERAL ELECTIONS

Election Years 1832–1848

State	1832 Voting-age population	Turnout	%	1836 Voting-age population	Turnout	%	Difference from 1832*	1840 Voting-age population	Turnout	%	Difference from 1832	1844 Voting-age population	Turnout	%	Difference from 1832	1848 Voting-age population	Turnout	%	Difference from 1832
ARKANSAS				13,000	8,560	65.8%						25,000	18,610	74.4%	8.6				
CONNECTICUT	71,000	16,434	23.1%	73,000	37,753	51.7%	28.6	76,000	55,140	72.6%	49.4	86,000	58,939	68.5%	45.4	95,000	59,242	62.4%	39.2
DELAWARE	13,000	8,386	64.5%	13,000	8,969	69.0%	4.5	13,000	10,879	83.7%	19.2	15,000	12,235	81.6%	17.1				
FLORIDA																11,000	7,891	71.7%	
ILLINOIS																180,000	78,179	43.4%	
INDIANA								139,000	117,267	84.4%									
KENTUCKY	109,000	80,188	73.6%	116,000	69,078	59.6%	-14.0	125,000	95,029	76.0%	2.5	143,000	115,186	80.5%	7.0	161,000	124,511	77.3%	3.8
MAINE	93,000	59,638	64.1%	104,000	54,540	52.4%	-11.7	114,000	91,081	79.9%	15.8	127,000	93,688	73.8%	9.6	140,000	79,314	56.7%	-7.5
MARYLAND												87,000	69,535	79.9%					
MASSACHUSETTS	156,000	63,898	41.0%	174,000	78,152	44.9%	4.0	194,000	126,053	65.0%	24.0	224,000	133,919	59.8%	18.8	255,000	122,974	48.2%	7.3
MISSOURI	35,000	17,273	49.4%	54,000	27,370	50.7%	1.3	74,000	51,861	70.1%	20.7	100,000	68,335	68.3%	19.0	126,000	82,863	65.8%	16.4
NEW HAMPSHIRE	62,000	39,087	63.0%	66,000	29,700	45.0%	-18.0	69,000	50,169	72.7%	9.7	76,000	46,503	61.2%	-1.9	82,000	61,012	74.4%	11.4
NEW JERSEY												95,000	74,540	78.5%					
NEW YORK	455,000	323,082	71.0%	515,000	302,871	58.8%	-12.2	578,000	438,737	75.9%	4.9	669,000	472,147	70.6%	-0.4	761,000	458,398	60.2%	-10.8
NORTH CAROLINA				95,000	63,943	67.3%		97,000	80,942	83.4%	16.1	105,000	82,019	78.1%	10.8	113,000	84,218	74.5%	7.2
OHIO	220,000	134,251	61.0%	274,000	178,362	65.1%	4.1	328,000	274,756	83.8%	22.7	379,000	291,395	76.9%	15.9	429,000	297,218	69.3%	8.3
PENNSYLVANIA	305,000	179,500	58.9%									445,000	316,363	71.1%	12.2	511,000	336,747	65.9%	7.0
RHODE ISLAND	22,000	5,630	25.6%	24,000	7,004	29.2%	3.6	26,000	8,215	31.6%	6.0	31,000	5,560	17.9%	-7.7	36,000	9,378	26.1%	0.5
VERMONT	64,000	41,027	64.1%	67,000	36,505	54.5%	-9.6	69,000	56,653	82.1%	18.0	75,000	54,813	73.1%	9.0	80,000	50,627	63.3%	-0.8
WISCONSIN																70,000	34,496	49.3%	
Total	1,605,000	968,394	60.3%	1,588,000	902,807	56.9%	-3.5	1,902,000	1,456,782	76.6%	16.3	2,682,000	1,913,787	71.4%	11.0	3,050,000	1,887,068	61.9%	1.5

*Percentage point difference between turnout in current year and initial year listed in chart. If data do not appear for a state in the initial year listed, the difference is calculated from the first year in which data do appear for that state.

STATE GUBERNATORIAL GENERAL ELECTIONS

Whig Turnout for Election Years 1832–1848

State	1832 (National Republicans)* Voting-age population	Turnout	%	1836 Voting-age population	Turnout	%	Difference from 1832**	1840 Voting-age population	Turnout	%	Difference from 1832	1844 Voting-age population	Turnout	%	Difference from 1832	1848 Voting-age population	Turnout	%	Difference from 1832
ARKANSAS				13,000	3,222	24.8%						25,000	7,244	29.0%	4.2				
CONNECTICUT	71,000	11,971	16.9%	73,000	17,393	23.8%	7.0	76,000	29,870	39.3%	22.4	86,000	30,093	35.0%	18.1	95,000	30,717	32.3%	15.5
DELAWARE	13,000	4,166	32.0%	13,000	4,693	36.1%	4.1	13,000	5,855	45.0%	13.0	15,000	6,140	40.9%	8.9				
FLORIDA																11,000	4,145	37.7%	
INDIANA								139,000	82,970	45.3%									
KENTUCKY	109,000	39,473	36.2%	116,000	38,587	33.3%	-2.9	125,000	55,370	44.3%	8.1	143,000	59,680	41.7%	5.5	161,000	66,466	41.3%	5.1
MAINE	93,000	27,651	29.7%	104,000	22,703	21.8%	-7.9	114,000	45,574	40.0%	10.2	127,000	48,942	38.5%	8.8	140,000	30,026	21.4%	-8.3
MARYLAND												87,000	35,040	40.3%					
MASSACHUSETTS	156,000	33,946	21.8%	174,000	42,160	24.2%	2.5	194,000	70,884	36.5%	14.8	224,000	69,570	31.1%	9.3	255,000	61,640	24.2%	2.4
MISSOURI								74,000	22,205	30.0%		100,000	31,357	31.4%	1.4	126,000	33,942	26.9%	-3.1
NEW HAMPSHIRE				66,000	2,566	3.9%		69,000	20,700	30.0%	26.1	76,000	14,750	19.4%	15.5	82,000	28,819	35.1%	31.3
NEW JERSEY												95,000	37,949	39.9%					
NEW YORK	455,000	156,672	34.4%	515,000	136,653	26.5%	-7.9	578,000	222,011	38.4%	4.0	669,000	231,060	34.5%	0.1	761,000	218,776	28.7%	-5.7
NORTH CAROLINA				95,000	33,993	35.8%		97,000	44,514	45.9%	10.1	105,000	42,586	40.6%	4.8	113,000	42,536	37.6%	1.9
OHIO	220,000	63,213	28.7%	274,000	92,204	33.7%	4.9	328,000	145,444	44.3%	15.6	379,000	146,333	38.6%	9.9	429,000	148,766	34.7%	5.9
PENNSYLVANIA												445,000	156,041	35.1%		511,000	168,522	33.0%	-2.1
RHODE ISLAND	22,000	2,730	12.4%	24,000	2,984	12.4%	0.0	26,000	4,797	18.5%	6.0					36,000	5,695	15.8%	3.4
VERMONT	64,000	15,499	24.2%	67,000	20,371	30.4%	6.2	69,000	33,653	48.8%	24.6	75,000	28,265	37.7%	13.5	80,000	22,132	27.7%	3.4
WISCONSIN																70,000	14,621	20.9%	
Total	1,203,000	355,321	29.5%	1,534,000	417,529	27.2%	-2.3	1,902,000	763,847	40.2%	10.6	2,651,000	945,050	35.6%	6.1	2,870,000	876,803	30.6%	1.0

Democratic Turnout for Election Years 1832–1848

State	1832 Voting-age population	Turnout	%	1836 Voting-age population	Turnout	%	Difference from 1832	1840 Voting-age population	Turnout	%	Difference from 1832	1844 Voting-age population	Turnout	%	Difference from 1832	1848 Voting-age population	Turnout	%	Difference from 1832
ARKANSAS				13,000	5,338	41.1%						25,000	8,859	35.4%	-5.6				
CONNECTICUT	71,000	4,463	6.3%	73,000	20,360	27.9%	21.6	76,000	25,270	33.3%	27.0	86,000	28,846	33.5%	27.3	95,000	28,525	30.0%	23.7
DELAWARE	13,000	4,220	32.5%	13,000	4,276	32.9%	0.4	13,000	5,024	38.6%	6.2	15,000	6,095	40.6%	8.2				
FLORIDA																11,000	3,746	34.1%	
ILLINOIS																180,000	67,828	37.7%	
INDIANA								139,000	54,297	39.1%									
KENTUCKY	109,000	40,715	37.4%	116,000	30,491	26.3%	-11.1	125,000	39,659	31.7%	-5.6	143,000	55,506	38.8%	1.5	161,000	58,045	36.1%	-1.3
MAINE	93,000	31,987	34.4%	104,000	31,837	30.6%	-3.8	114,000	45,507	39.9%	5.5	127,000	38,501	30.3%	-4.1	140,000	37,310	26.7%	-7.7

State Gubernatorial General Elections (continued)

State Gubernatorial General Elections (continued)

Democratic Turnout for Election Years 1832–1848 (continued)

State	1832 Voting-age population	Turnout	%	1836 Voting-age population	Turnout	%	Difference from 1832	1840 Voting-age population	Turnout	%	Difference from 1832	1844 Voting-age population	Turnout	%	Difference from 1832	1848 Voting-age population	Turnout	%	Difference from 1832
MARYLAND												87,000	34,495	39.6%					
MASSACHUSETTS	156,000	15,197	9.7%	174,000	35,992	20.7%	10.9	194,000	55,169	28.4%	18.7	224,000	54,714	24.4%	14.7	255,000	25,323	9.9%	0.2
MISSOURI	35,000	9,141	26.1%	54,000	14,315	26.5%	0.4	74,000	29,656	40.1%	14.0	100,000	36,978	37.0%	10.9	126,000	48,921	38.8%	12.7
NEW HAMPSHIRE	62,000	24,167	39.0%	66,000	24,904	37.7%	-1.2	69,000	29,469	42.7%	3.7	76,000	25,986	34.2%	-4.8	82,000	32,193	39.3%	0.3
NEW JERSEY												95,000	36,591	38.5%					
NEW YORK	455,000	166,410	36.6%	515,000	166,218	32.3%	-4.3	578,000	216,726	37.5%	0.9	669,000	241,087	36.0%	-0.5	761,000	116,811	15.3%	-21.2
NORTH CAROLINA				95,000	29,950	31.5%		97,000	36,428	37.6%	6.0	105,000	39,433	37.6%	6.0	113,000	41,682	36.9%	5.4
OHIO	220,000	71,038	32.3%	274,000	86,158	31.4%	-0.8	328,000	129,312	39.4%	7.1	379,000	145,062	38.3%	6.0	429,000	148,452	34.6%	2.3
PENNSYLVANIA	305,000	91,385	30.0%									445,000	160,322	36.0%	6.1	511,000	168,225	32.9%	3.0
RHODE ISLAND	22,000	2,290	10.4%	24,000	4,020	16.8%	6.3	26,000	3,418	13.1%	2.7					36,000	3,683	10.2%	-0.2
VERMONT	64,000	8,210	12.8%	67,000	16,134	24.1%	11.3	69,000	23,000	33.3%	20.5	75,000	20,930	27.9%	15.1	80,000	28,495	35.6%	22.8
WISCONSIN																70,000	19,875	28.4%	
Total	1,605,000	469,223	29.2%	1,588,000	469,993	29.6%	0.4	1,902,000	692,935	36.4%	7.2	2,651,000	933,405	35.2%	6.0	3,050,000	829,114	27.2%	-2.1

Other Turnout for Election Years 1832–1848

State	1832 Voting-age population	Turnout	%	1836 Voting-age population	Turnout	%	Difference from 1832	1840 Voting-age population	Turnout	%	Difference from 1832	1844 Voting-age population	Turnout	%	Difference from 1832	1848 Voting-age population	Turnout	%	Difference from 1832
ARKANSAS												25,000	2,507	10.0%					
ILLINOIS																180,000	10,351	5.8%	
MAINE												127,000	6,245	4.9%		140,000	11,978	8.6%	3.6
MASSACHUSETTS	156,000	14,755	9.5%									224,000	9,635	4.3%	-5.2	255,000	36,011	14.1%	4.7
MISSOURI	35,000	8,132	23.2%	54,000	13,055	24.2%	0.9												
NEW HAMPSHIRE	62,000	14,920	24.1%	66,000	2,230	3.4%	-20.7					76,000	5,767	7.6%	-15.6				
NEW YORK																761,000	122,811	16.1%	
PENNSYLVANIA	305,000	88,115	28.9%																
RHODE ISLAND	22,000	610	2.8%									31,000	5,560	17.9%	15.2				
VERMONT	64,000	17,318	27.1%									75,000	5,618	7.5%	-19.6				
Total	644,000	143,850	22.3%	120,000	15,285	12.7%	-9.6					558,000	35,332	6.3%	-16.0	1,336,000	181,151	13.6%	-8.8

*The Whig party supplanted the National Republicans as the Democrats' national opposition by 1834.

**Percentage point difference between turnout in current year and initial year listed in chart. If data do not appear for a state in the initial year listed, the difference is calculated from the first year in which data do appear for that state.

UNITED STATES HOUSE OF REPRESENTATIVES GENERAL ELECTIONS

Election Years 1832–1848

State	1832			1836				1840				1844				1848			
	Voting-age population	Turnout	%	Voting-age population	Turnout	%	Difference from 1832*	Voting-age population	Turnout	%	Difference from 1832	Voting-age population	Turnout	%	Difference from 1832	Voting-age population	Turnout	%	Difference from 1832
ARKANSAS				13,000	8,473	65.2%		18,000	13,664	75.9%	10.7	25,000	18,741	75.0%	9.8	32,000	23,784	74.3%	9.1
DELAWARE	13,000	8,399	64.6%	13,000	8,952	68.9%	4.3	13,000	10,870	83.6%	19.0	15,000	12,252	81.7%	17.1	16,000	12,395	77.5%	12.9
FLORIDA																11,000	8,187	74.4%	
GEORGIA	65,000	61,543	94.7%	74,000	58,603	79.2%	-15.5	82,000	75,191	91.7%	-3.0	93,000	78,488	84.4%	-10.3	104,000	77,559	74.6%	-20.1
ILLINOIS	50,000	25,585	51.2%	81,000	43,981	54.3%	3.1					146,000	98,869	67.7%	16.5	180,000	103,596	57.6%	6.4
IOWA																38,000	24,243	63.8%	
LOUISIANA	30,000	7,881	26.3%	40,000	7,793	19.5%	-6.8	49,000	16,186	33.0%	6.8	61,000	14,697	24.1%	-2.2				
MAINE				104,000	54,696	52.6%		114,000	90,276	79.2%	26.6	127,000	91,536	72.1%	19.5	140,000	81,759	58.4%	5.8
MARYLAND												87,000	49,044	56.4%					
MASSACHUSETTS				174,000	73,623	42.3%		194,000	124,921	64.4%	22.1	224,000	131,506	58.7%	16.4	255,000	123,586	48.5%	6.2
MICHIGAN								54,000	44,223	81.9%		72,000	55,656	77.3%	-4.6	90,000	65,198	72.4%	-9.5
MISSISSIPPI																			
MISSOURI	35,000	18,334	52.4%	54,000	26,755	49.5%	-2.8	74,000	51,086	69.0%	16.7	100,000	65,248	65.2%	12.9	126,000	81,789	64.9%	12.5
NEW JERSEY	70,000	48,062	68.7%	75,000	51,476	68.6%	0.0	81,000	64,548	79.7%	11.0	95,000	69,506	73.2%	4.5	108,000	74,506	69.0%	0.3
NEW YORK	445,000	320,037	71.9%	515,000	302,524	58.7%	-13.2	578,000	440,317	76.2%	4.3	669,000	482,646	72.1%	0.2	761,000	455,769	59.9%	-12.0
OHIO	220,000	134,378	61.1%	274,000	177,188	64.7%	3.6	328,000	273,681	83.4%	22.4	379,000	301,511	79.6%	18.5	429,000	286,700	66.8%	5.7
PENNSYLVANIA	305,000	176,019	57.7%	340,000	169,097	49.7%	-8.0	378,000	255,267	67.5%	9.8	445,000	314,728	70.7%	13.0	511,000	332,723	65.1%	7.4
SOUTH CAROLINA								54,000	12,400	23.0%		56,000	13,228	23.6%	0.7	59,000	32,831	55.6%	32.7
VERMONT				67,000	33,943	50.7%		69,000	53,771	77.9%	27.3	75,000	51,046	68.1%	17.4	80,000	46,900	58.6%	8.0
WISCONSIN																70,000	38,390	54.8%	
Total	1,233,000	800,238	64.9%	1,824,000	1,017,104	55.8%	-9.1	2,086,000	1,526,401	73.2%	8.3	2,669,000	1,848,702	69.3%	4.4	3,010,000	1,869,915	62.1%	-2.8

*Percentage point difference between turnout in current year and initial year listed in chart. If data do not appear for a state in the initial year listed, the difference is calculated from the first year in which data do appear for that state.

UNITED STATES HOUSE OF REPRESENTATIVES GENERAL ELECTIONS

Whig Turnout for Election Years 1832–1848

State	1832 (National Republicans)* Voting-age population	Turnout	%	1836 Voting-age population	Turnout	%	Difference from 1832**	1840 Voting-age population	Turnout	%	Difference from 1832	1844 Voting-age population	Turnout	%	Difference from 1832	1848 Voting-age population	Turnout	%	Difference from 1832
ARKANSAS				13,000	2,379	18.3%		18,000	5,788	32.2%	13.9	25,000	7,516	30.1%	11.8	32,000	9,328	29.2%	10.9
DELAWARE	13,000	4,257	32.7%	13,000	4,705	36.2%	3.4	13,000	5,896	45.4%	12.6	15,000	6,229	41.5%	8.8	16,000	6,369	39.8%	7.1
FLORIDA																11,000	4,382	39.8%	
GEORGIA				74,000	29,003	39.2%		82,000	39,619	48.3%	9.1	93,000	38,111	41.0%	1.8	104,000	38,651	37.2%	-2.0
ILLINOIS	50,000	2,078	4.2%	81,000	15,939	19.7%	15.5					146,000	33,485	22.9%	18.8	180,000	34,387	19.1%	14.9
IOWA																38,000	11,489	30.2%	
LOUISIANA	30,000	5,081	16.9%	40,000	4,725	11.8%	-5.1	49,000	9,137	18.6%	1.7	61,000	4,521	7.4%	-9.5				
MAINE				104,000	23,341	22.4%		114,000	45,238	39.7%	17.2	127,000	39,361	31.0%	8.5	140,000	32,597	23.3%	0.8
MARYLAND												87,000	26,877	30.9%					
MASSACHUSETTS				174,000	41,891	24.1%		194,000	72,041	37.1%	13.1	224,000	68,479	30.6%	6.5	255,000	64,316	25.2%	1.1
MICHIGAN								54,000	22,759	42.1%		72,000	24,611	34.2%	-8.0	90,000	29,391	32.7%	-9.5
MISSOURI				54,000	10,007	18.5%		74,000	21,492	29.0%	10.5	100,000	29,225	29.2%	10.7	126,000	31,427	24.9%	6.4
NEW JERSEY	70,000	23,784	34.0%	75,000	26,006	34.7%	0.7	81,000	33,342	41.2%	7.2	95,000	39,145	41.2%	7.2	108,000	36,668	34.0%	0.0
NEW YORK	455,000	51,030	11.4%	515,000	132,958	25.8%	14.4	578,000	224,021	38.8%	27.4	669,000	249,285	37.3%	25.9	761,000	227,619	29.9%	18.5
OHIO	220,000	60,782	27.6%	274,000	91,814	33.5%	5.9	328,000	145,397	44.3%	16.7	379,000	148,909	39.3%	11.7	429,000	121,173	28.2%	0.6
PENNSYLVANIA	305,000	18,769	6.2%	340,000	53,558	15.8%	9.6	378,000	125,337	33.2%	27.0	445,000	139,542	31.4%	25.2	511,000	158,266	31.0%	24.8
SOUTH CAROLINA								54,000	4,530	8.4%		56,000	2,912	5.2%	-3.2				
VERMONT				67,000	18,643	27.8%		69,000	32,006	46.4%	18.6	75,000	26,831	35.8%	7.9	80,000	20,884	26.1%	-1.7
WISCONSIN																70,000	13,234	18.9%	
Total	1,143,000	166,581	14.6%	1,824,000	454,969	24.9%	10.4	2,086,000	786,603	37.7%	23.1	2,669,000	885,039	33.2%	18.6	2,951,000	840,181	28.5%	13.9

Democratic Turnout for Election Years 1832–1848

State	1832 Voting-age population	Turnout	%	1836 Voting-age population	Turnout	%	Difference from 1832	1840 Voting-age population	Turnout	%	Difference from 1832	1844 Voting-age population	Turnout	%	Difference from 1832	1848 Voting-age population	Turnout	%	Difference from 1832
ARKANSAS				13,000	6,094	46.9%		18,000	7,876	43.8%	-3.1	25,000	11,112	44.4%	-2.4	32,000	14,456	45.2%	-1.7
DELAWARE	13,000	4,142	31.9%	13,000	4,247	32.7%	0.8	13,000	4,974	38.3%	6.4	15,000	6,023	40.2%	8.3	16,000	6,026	37.7%	5.8
FLORIDA																11,000	3,805	34.6%	
GEORGIA				74,000	29,600	40.0%		82,000	35,572	43.4%	3.4	93,000	40,377	43.4%	3.4	104,000	38,908	37.4%	-2.6
ILLINOIS	50,000	18,403	36.8%	81,000	27,899	34.4%	-2.4					146,000	62,305	42.7%	5.9	180,000	64,449	35.8%	-1.0
IOWA																38,000	12,266	32.3%	
LOUISIANA	30,000	2,800	9.3%	40,000	1,800	4.5%	-4.8	49,000	7,049	14.4%	5.1	61,000	10,176	16.7%	7.3				
MAINE				104,000	26,370	25.4%		114,000	44,540	39.1%	13.7	127,000	43,176	34.0%	8.6	140,000	38,491	27.5%	2.1
MARYLAND												87,000	21,960	25.2%					

United States House of Representatives General Elections (continued)

Democratic Turnout for Election Years 1832–1848 (continued)

State	1832 Voting-age population	1832 Turnout	1832 %	1836 Voting-age population	1836 Turnout	1836 %	1836 Difference from 1832	1840 Voting-age population	1840 Turnout	1840 %	1840 Difference from 1832	1844 Voting-age population	1844 Turnout	1844 %	1844 Difference from 1832	1848 Voting-age population	1848 Turnout	1848 %	1848 Difference from 1832
MASSACHUSETTS				174,000	31,366	18.0%		194,000	52,655	27.1%	9.1	224,000	52,827	23.6%	5.6	255,000	26,819	10.5%	-7.5
MICHIGAN								54,000	21,464	39.7%		72,000	27,898	38.7%	-1.0	90,000	31,247	34.7%	-5.0
MISSOURI				54,000	16,468	30.5%		74,000	29,594	40.0%	9.5	100,000	36,023	36.0%	5.5	126,000	50,362	40.0%	9.5
NEW JERSEY	70,000	24,278	34.7%	75,000	25,470	34.0%	-0.7	81,000	31,138	38.4%	3.8	95,000	30,361	32.0%	-2.7	108,000	36,379	33.7%	-1.0
NEW YORK	455,000	166,028	36.5%	515,000	160,652	31.2%	-5.3	578,000	214,559	37.1%	0.6	669,000	232,430	34.7%	-1.7	761,000	106,542	14.0%	-22.5
OHIO	220,000	64,168	29.2%	274,000	85,272	31.1%	2.0	328,000	128,284	39.1%	9.9	379,000	143,950	38.0%	8.8	429,000	143,014	33.3%	4.2
PENNSYLVANIA	305,000	91,252	29.9%	340,000	91,225	26.8%	-3.1	378,000	129,817	34.3%	4.4	445,000	153,274	34.4%	4.5	511,000	167,551	32.8%	2.9
SOUTH CAROLINA								54,000	7,657	14.2%		56,000	10,316	18.4%	4.2	59,000	26,483	44.9%	30.7
VERMONT				67,000	13,760	20.5%		69,000	21,655	31.4%	10.8	75,000	19,182	25.6%	5.0	80,000	26,016	32.5%	12.0
WISCONSIN																70,000	15,872	22.7%	
Total	1,143,000	371,071	32.5%	1,824,000	520,223	28.5%	-3.9	2,086,000	736,834	35.3%	2.9	2,669,000	901,390	33.8%	1.3	3,010,000	808,686	26.9%	-5.6

Other Turnout for Election Years 1832–1848

State	1832 Voting-age population	1832 Turnout	1832 %	1836 Voting-age population	1836 Turnout	1836 %	1836 Difference from 1832	1840 Voting-age population	1840 Turnout	1840 %	1840 Difference from 1832	1844 Voting-age population	1844 Turnout	1844 %	1844 Difference from 1832	1848 Voting-age population	1848 Turnout	1848 %	1848 Difference from 1832
ARKANSAS												25,000	113	0.5%					
GEORGIA***	65,000	61,543	94.7%																
ILLINOIS	50,000	5,104	10.2%	81,000	143	0.2%	-10.0					146,000	3,079	2.1%	-8.1	180,000	4,760	2.6%	-7.6
IOWA																38,000	400	1.3%	
LOUISIANA				40,000	1,268	3.2%													
MAINE				104,000	4,985	4.8%		114,000	498	0.4%	-4.4	127,000	8,999	7.1%	2.3	140,000	10,671	7.6%	2.8
MARYLAND												87,000	207	0.2%					
MASSACHUSETTS				174,000	366	0.2%		194,000	225	0.1%	-0.1	224,000	10,200	4.6%	4.3	255,000	32,451	12.7%	12.5
MICHIGAN												72,000	3,147	4.4%		90,000	4,560	5.1%	0.7
MISSOURI	35,000	18,334	52.4%	54,000	280	0.5%	-51.9												
NEW JERSEY								81,000	68	0.1%						108,000	1,459	1.4%	1.3
NEW YORK	455,000	102,179	22.5%	515,000	8,914	1.7%	-20.7	578,000	1,737	0.3%	-22.2	669,000	931	0.1%	-22.3	761,000	121,608	16.0%	-6.5
OHIO	220,000	9,428	4.3%	274,000	102	0.0%	-4.2					379,000	8,652	2.3%	-2.0	429,000	22,513	5.2%	1.0
PENNSYLVANIA	305,000	65,998	21.6%	340,000	24,314	7.2%	-14.5	378,000	113	0.0%	-21.6	445,000	21,912	4.9%	-16.7	511,000	6,906	1.4%	-20.3
SOUTH CAROLINA								54,000	213	0.4%						59,000	6,348	10.8%	10.4
VERMONT				67,000	1,540	2.3%		69,000	110	0.2%	-2.1	75,000	5,033	6.7%	4.4				
WISCONSIN																70,000	9,284	13.3%	
Total	1,130,000	262,586	23.2%	1,649,000	41,912	2.5%	-20.7	1,468,000	2,964	0.2%	-23.0	2,249,000	62,273	2.8%	-20.5	2,641,000	221,048	8.4%	-14.9

*The Whig party supplanted the National Republicans as the Democrats' national opposition by 1834. This changeover began in two states, Delaware and Louisiana, which fielded Whig candidates for the House in 1832.

**Percentage point difference between turnout in current year and initial year listed in chart. If data do not appear for a state in the initial year listed, the difference is calculated from the first year in which data do appear for that state.

***In 1832, Georgia held an at-large election in which all candidates were entered without party status.

Midterm Turnout, Based on Highest Statewide Turnout, Election Years 1830–1846

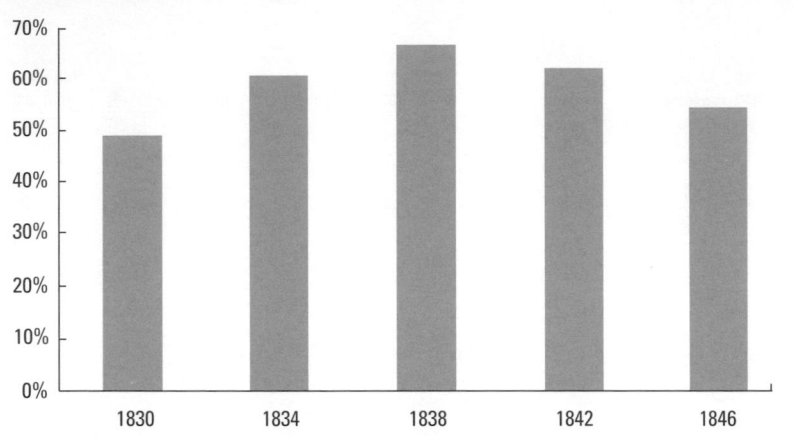

YEAR	VOTING AGE POPULATION	TURNOUT	%
1830	1,625,000	798,239	49.1%
1834	1,990,000	1,207,479	60.7%
1838	2,346,000	1,563,150	66.6%
1842	2,057,000	1,277,174	62.1%
1846	3,337,000	1,821,740	54.6%

Partisan Turnout Midterm Election Based on Aggregate House of Representatives Turnout, Election Years 1830–1846

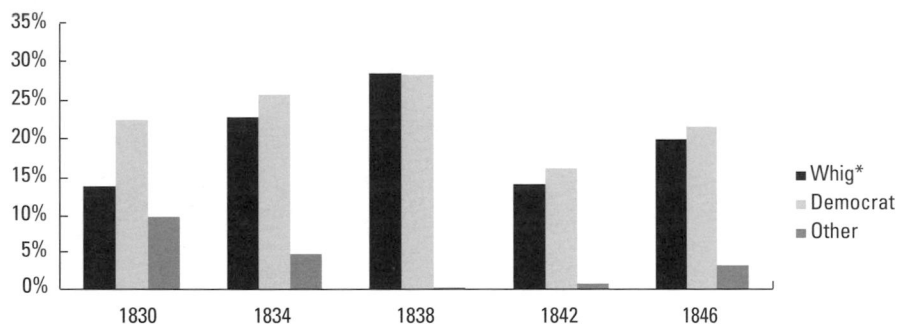

YEAR	VOTING-AGE POPULATION	WHIG* TURNOUT	%	DEMOCRAT TURNOUT	%	OTHER TURNOUT	%
1830	1,625,000	215,493	13.3%	359,081	22.1%	150,669	9.3%
1834	1,990,000	444,198	22.3%	502,191	25.2%	94,175	4.7%
1838	2,346,000	665,036	28.3%	657,043	28.0%	4,759	0.2%
1842	2,057,000	284,684	13.8%	326,722	15.9%	16,625	0.8%
1846	3,337,000	655,857	19.7%	704,421	21.1%	105,128	3.2%

*Turnout for 1830 is for the National Republican party. The Whig party supplanted the National Republicans as the Democrats' national opposition by 1834.

Alternate Graph for Partisan Turnout Midterm Election Based on Aggregate House of Representatives Turnout, Election Years 1830–1846

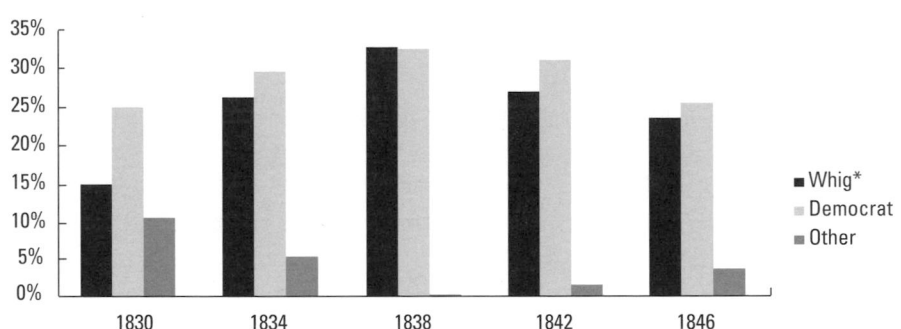

YEAR	VOTING-AGE POPULATION**	WHIG** TURNOUT	%	DEMOCRAT TURNOUT	%	OTHER TURNOUT	%
1830	1,440,000	215,493	15.0%	359,081	24.9%	150,669	10.5%
1834	1,692,000	444,198	26.3%	502,191	29.7%	94,175	5.6%
1838	2,011,000	665,036	33.1%	657,043	32.7%	4,759	0.2%
1842	1,044,000	284,684	27.3%	326,772	31.3%	16,625	1.6%
1846	2,775,000	655,857	23.6%	704,421	25.4%	105,128	3.8%

*Turnout for 1830 is for the National Republican party. The Whig party supplanted the National Republicans as the Democrats' national opposition by 1834.

**This is an alternate graph that depicts changes in partisan turnout percentages using voting-age population only in states that held House elections.

STATE GUBERNATORIAL GENERAL ELECTIONS
Election Years 1830–1846

State	1830 Voting-age population	Turnout	%	1834 Voting-age population	Turnout	%	Difference from 1830*	1838 Voting-age population	Turnout	%	Difference from 1830	1842 Voting-age population	Turnout	%	Difference from 1830	1846 Voting-age population	Turnout	%	Difference from 1830
CONNECTICUT	69,000	12,988	18.8%	72,000	36,643	50.9%	32.1	74,000	48,604	65.7%	46.9	81,000	49,264	60.8%	42.0	90,000	55,025	61.1%	42.3
DELAWARE																15,000	12,160	81.1%	
ILLINOIS	34,000	21,775	64.0%	65,000	31,879	49.0%	-15.0	96,000	60,390	62.9%	-1.1	129,000	85,532	66.3%	2.3	163,000	100,847	61.9%	-2.2
INDIANA				96,000	64,030	66.7%										183,000	124,242	67.9%	1.2
IOWA																32,000	15,005	46.9%	
LOUISIANA				35,000	11,122	31.8%		44,000	14,364	32.6%	0.9	55,000	17,870	32.5%	0.7	67,000	22,767	34.0%	2.2
MAINE	88,000	58,854	66.9%	98,000	72,045	73.5%	6.6	109,000	89,113	81.8%	14.9	121,000	71,680	59.2%	-7.6	134,000	73,365	54.8%	-12.1
MARYLAND								73,000	55,131	75.5%									
MASSACHUSETTS	147,000	45,348	30.8%	165,000	72,600	44.0%	13.2	183,000	93,437	51.1%	20.2	209,000	117,812	56.4%	25.5	239,000	98,009	41.0%	10.2
NEW HAMPSHIRE	61,000	42,254	69.3%	64,000	28,542	44.6%	-24.7	67,000	53,985	80.6%	11.3	72,000	47,746	66.3%	-3.0	79,000	55,080	69.7%	0.5
NEW YORK	425,000	249,614	58.7%	485,000	350,908	72.4%	13.6	545,000	375,343	68.9%	10.1	624,000	394,151	63.2%	4.4	715,000	386,184	54.0%	-4.7
NORTH CAROLINA								96,000	64,482	56.8%		101,000	72,954	71.6%	11.0	100,000	79,113	72.6%	15.8
OHIO	193,000	98,863	51.2%	247,000	138,152	55.9%	4.7	301,000	210,030	69.8%	18.6	353,000	237,676	67.3%	16.1	404,000	235,411	58.3%	7.0
PENNSYLVANIA								358,000	250,146	69.9%									
RHODE ISLAND	21,000	4,248	20.2%	23,000	7,196	31.3%	11.1	25,000	7,488	30.0%	9.7	29,000	7,145	24.6%	4.4	34,000	14,868	43.7%	23.5
VERMONT	63,000	30,684	48.7%	66,000	37,675	57.1%	8.4	68,000	39,585	58.2%	9.5	72,000	51,297	71.2%	22.5	78,000	48,633	62.4%	13.6
Total	1,101,000	564,628	51.3%	1,416,000	850,792	60.1%	8.8	2,039,000	1,352,098	66.3%	15.0	1,846,000	1,152,527	62.4%	11.2	2,342,000	1,320,709	56.4%	5.1

*Percentage point difference between turnout in current year and initial year listed in chart. If data do not appear for a state in the initial year listed, the difference is calculated from the first year in which data do appear for that state.

STATE GUBERNATORIAL GENERAL ELECTIONS

Whig Turnout for Election Years 1830–1846

State	1830 (National Republicans)*			1834				1838				1842				1846			
	Voting-age population	Turnout	%	Voting-age population	Turnout	%	Difference from 1830**	Voting-age population	Turnout	%	Difference from 1830	Voting-age population	Turnout	%	Difference from 1830	Voting-age population	Turnout	%	Difference from 1830
CONNECTICUT	69,000	12,988	18.8%	72,000	18,411	25.6%	6.7	74,000	27,115	36.6%	17.8	81,000	23,700	29.3%	10.4	90,000	27,822	30.9%	12.1
DELAWARE																15,000	6,012	40.1%	
ILLINOIS	34,000	12,837	37.8%	65,000	17,340	26.7%	-11.1	96,000	29,722	31.0%	-6.8	129,000	39,030	30.3%	-7.5	163,000	37,033	22.7%	-15.0
INDIANA				96,000	36,773	38.3%										183,000	60,138	32.9%	-5.4
IOWA																32,000	7,379	23.1%	
LOUISIANA				35,000	6,973	19.9%		44,000	7,588	17.2%	-2.7	55,000	8,204	14.9%	-5.0	67,000	10,138	15.1%	-4.8
MAINE	88,000	28,639	32.5%	98,000	33,912	34.6%	2.1	109,000	42,897	39.4%	6.8	121,000	26,745	22.1%	-10.4	134,000	29,100	21.7%	-10.8
MARYLAND								73,000	27,409	37.5%									
MASSACHUSETTS	147,000	30,908	21.0%	165,000	43,757	26.5%	5.5	183,000	51,642	28.2%	7.2	209,000	54,939	26.3%	5.3	239,000	54,813	22.9%	1.9
NEW HAMPSHIRE	61,000	19,040	31.2%					67,000	25,244	37.7%	6.5	72,000	12,234	17.0%	-14.2	79,000	17,787	22.5%	-8.7
NEW YORK	425,000	120,667	28.4%	485,000	169,008	34.8%	6.5	545,000	192,882	35.4%	7.0	624,000	186,089	29.8%	1.4	715,000	198,878	27.8%	-0.6
NORTH CAROLINA								96,000	34,329	35.8%		101,000	37,943	37.6%	1.8	109,000	43,486	39.9%	4.1
OHIO	193,000	49,677	25.7%	247,000	67,414	27.3%	1.6	301,000	102,146	33.9%	8.2	353,000	117,902	33.4%	7.7	404,000	118,857	29.4%	3.7
RHODE ISLAND				23,000	3,520	15.3%		25,000	3,984	15.9%	0.6	29,000	7,145	24.6%	9.3	34,000	7,477	22.0%	6.7
VERMONT				66,000	10,159	15.4%		68,000	22,169	32.6%	17.2	72,000	27,167	37.7%	22.3	78,000	23,638	30.3%	14.9
Total	1,017,000	274,756	27.0%	1,352,000	407,267	30.1%	3.1	1,681,000	567,127	33.7%	6.7	1,846,000	541,098	29.3%	2.3	2,342,000	642,558	27.4%	0.4

Democratic Turnout for Election Years 1830–1846

State	1830			1834				1838				1842				1846			
	Voting-age population	Turnout	%	Voting-age population	Turnout	%	Difference from 1830	Voting-age population	Turnout	%	Difference from 1830	Voting-age population	Turnout	%	Difference from 1830	Voting-age population	Turnout	%	Difference from 1830
CONNECTICUT				72,000	15,834	22.0%		74,000	21,489	29.0%	7.0	81,000	25,564	31.6%	9.6	90,000	27,203	30.2%	8.2
DELAWARE																15,000	6,148	41.0%	
ILLINOIS	34,000	8,938	26.3%	65,000	10,224	15.7%	-10.6	96,000	30,668	31.9%	5.7	129,000	46,502	36.0%	9.8	163,000	58,660	36.0%	9.7
INDIANA				96,000	27,257	28.4%										183,000	64,104	35.0%	6.6
LOUISIANA				35,000	4,149	11.9%		44,000	6,776	15.4%	3.5	55,000	9,666	17.6%	5.7	67,000	12,629	18.8%	7.0
MAINE	88,000	30,215	34.3%	98,000	38,133	38.9%	4.6	109,000	46,216	42.4%	8.1	121,000	40,855	33.8%	-0.6	134,000	34,715	25.9%	-8.4
MARYLAND								73,000	27,722	38.0%									
MASSACHUSETTS				165,000	18,683	11.3%		183,000	41,795	22.8%	11.5	209,000	56,491	27.0%	15.7	239,000	33,199	13.9%	2.6
NEW HAMPSHIRE	61,000	23,214	38.1%	64,000	28,542	44.6%	6.5	67,000	28,741	42.9%	4.8	72,000	26,831	37.3%	-0.8	79,000	26,914	34.1%	-4.0
NEW YORK	425,000	128,947	30.3%	485,000	181,900	37.5%	7.2	545,000	182,461	33.5%	3.1	624,000	208,062	33.3%	3.0	715,000	187,306	26.2%	-4.1
NORTH CAROLINA								96,000	20,153	21.0%		101,000	34,411	34.1%	13.1	109,000	35,627	32.7%	11.7
OHIO	193,000	49,186	25.5%	247,000	70,738	28.6%	3.2	301,000	107,884	35.8%	10.4	353,000	119,774	33.9%	8.4	404,000	116,554	28.9%	3.4

State Gubernatorial General Elections (continued)

Democratic Turnout for Election Years 1830–1846 (continued)

State	1830			1834				1838				1842				1846			
	Voting-age population	Turnout	%	Voting-age population	Turnout	%	Difference from 1830	Voting-age population	Turnout	%	Difference from 1830	Voting-age population	Turnout	%	Difference from 1830	Voting-age population	Turnout	%	Difference from 1830
PENNSYLVANIA								358,000	127,821	35.7%									
RHODE ISLAND				23,000	3,676	16.0%		25,000	3,504	14.0%	-2.0					34,000	7,391	21.7%	5.8
VERMONT	63,000	6,285	10.0%	66,000	10,385	15.7%	5.8	68,000	17,416	25.6%	15.6	72,000	24,130	33.5%	23.5	78,000	17,877	22.9%	12.9
Total	864,000	246,785	28.6%	1,416,000	409,521	28.9%	0.4	2,039,000	662,646	32.5%	3.9	1,817,000	592,286	32.6%	4.0	2,310,000	628,327	27.2%	-1.4

Other Turnout for Election Years 1830–1846

State	1830			1834				1838				1842				1846			
	Voting-age population	Turnout	%	Voting-age population	Turnout	%	Difference from 1830	Voting-age population	Turnout	%	Difference from 1830	Voting-age population	Turnout	%	Difference from 1830	Voting-age population	Turnout	%	Difference from 1830
CONNECTICUT				72,000	2,398	3.3%													
ILLINOIS				65,000	4,315	6.6%										163,000	5,154	3.2%	-3.5
IOWA																32,000	7,626	23.8%	
MAINE												121,000	4,080	3.4%		134,000	9,550	7.1%	3.8
MASSACHUSETTS	147,000	14,440	9.8%	165,000	10,160	6.2%	-3.7					209,000	6,382	3.1%	-6.8	239,000	9,997	4.2%	-5.6
NEW HAMPSHIRE												72,000	8,681	12.1%		79,000	10,379	13.1%	1.1
PENNSYLVANIA								358,000	122,325	34.2%									
RHODE ISLAND	21,000	4,248	20.2%																
VERMONT	63,000	24,399	38.7%	66,000	17,131	26.0%	-12.8									78,000	7,118	9.1%	-29.6
Total	231,000	43,087	18.7%	368,000	34,004	9.2%	-9.4	358,000	122,325	34.2%	15.5	402,000	19,143	4.8%	-13.9	725,000	49,824	6.9%	-11.8

*The Whig party supplanted the National Republicans as the Democrats' national opposition by 1834.

**Percentage point difference between turnout in current year and initial year listed in chart. If data do not appear for a state in the initial year listed, the difference is calculated from the first year in which data do appear for that state.

UNITED STATES HOUSE OF REPRESENTATIVES GENERAL ELECTIONS

Election Years 1830–1846

State	1830 Voting-age population	Turnout	%	1834 Voting-age population	Turnout	%	Difference from 1830*	1838 Voting-age population	Turnout	%	Difference from 1830	1842 Voting-age population	Turnout	%	Difference from 1830	1846 Voting-age population	Turnout	%	Difference from 1830
ARKANSAS								16,000	10,878	68.0%		22,000	16,414	74.6%	6.6	28,000	16,527	59.0%	-9.0
DELAWARE	12,000	8,100	67.5%	13,000	9,405	72.3%	4.8	13,000	8,816	67.8%	0.3	14,000	10,921	78.0%	10.5	15,000	12,261	81.7%	14.2
FLORIDA																11,000	5,877	53.4%	
GEORGIA	61,000	55,920	91.7%	69,000	61,351	88.9%	-2.8	78,000	64,548	82.8%	-8.9	88,000	69,041	78.5%	-13.2	98,000	59,077	60.3%	-31.4
ILLINOIS				65,000	32,477	50.0%		96,000	58,472	60.9%	10.9					163,000	99,494	61.0%	11.1
IOWA																32,000	15,415	48.2%	
LOUISIANA	26,000	5,086	19.6%	35,000	9,687	27.7%	8.1	44,000	13,308	30.2%	10.7								
MAINE	88,000	50,231	57.1%	98,000	68,694	70.1%	13.0	109,000	87,979	80.7%	23.6					134,000	73,939	55.2%	-1.9
MASSACHUSETTS	147,000	34,525	23.5%	165,000	69,725	42.3%	18.8	183,000	87,599	47.9%	24.4	209,000	115,819	55.4%	31.9	239,000	100,165	41.9%	18.4
MICHIGAN								45,000	32,306	71.8%						81,000	47,673	58.9%	-12.9
MISSISSIPPI	17,000	11,680	68.7%					37,000	34,817	94.1%	25.4								
MISSOURI								64,000	40,598	63.4%		87,000	26,346	30.3%	-33.2	113,000	67,265	59.5%	-3.9
NEW JERSEY	67,000	29,529	44.1%	73,000	53,826	73.7%	29.7									101,000	55,806	55.3%	11.2
NEW YORK	425,000	250,794	59.0%	485,000	349,708	72.1%	13.1	545,000	375,042	68.8%	9.8	624,000	389,540	62.4%	3.4	715,000	398,014	55.7%	-3.3
OHIO	193,000	99,497	51.6%	247,000	135,734	55.0%	3.4	301,000	206,712	68.7%	17.1					404,000	243,132	60.2%	8.6
PENNSYLVANIA	288,000	142,743	49.6%	323,000	184,580	57.1%	7.6	358,000	254,751	71.2%	21.6					478,000	206,491	43.2%	-6.4
SOUTH CAROLINA	53,000	7,974	15.0%	53,000	29,136	55.0%	39.9	54,000	8,026	14.9%	-0.2					58,000	11,272	19.4%	4.4
TEXAS																27,000	6,712	24.9%	
VERMONT	63,000	29,164	46.3%	66,000	36,241	54.9%	8.6	68,000	42,986	63.2%	16.9					78,000	46,286	59.3%	13.0
Total	1,440,000	725,243	50.4%	1,692,000	1,040,564	61.5%	11.1	2,011,000	1,326,838	66.0%	15.6	1,044,000	628,081	60.2%	9.8	2,775,000	1,465,406	52.8%	2.4

*Percentage point difference between turnout in current year and initial year listed in chart. If data do not appear for a state in the initial year listed, the difference is calculated from the first year in which data do appear for that state.

UNITED STATES HOUSE OF REPRESENTATIVES GENERAL ELECTIONS

Whig Turnout for Election Years 1830–1846

| State | 1830 (National Republicans)* | | | 1834 | | | | 1838 | | | | 1842 | | | | 1846 | | | |
	Voting-age population	Turnout	%	Voting-age population	Turnout	%	Difference from 1830**	Voting-age population	Turnout	%	Difference from 1830	Voting-age population	Turnout	%	Difference from 1830	Voting-age population	Turnout	%	Difference from 1830
ARKANSAS								16,000	4,156	26.0%		22,000	5,315	24.2%	-1.8				
DELAWARE	12,000	4,267	35.6%	13,000	4,779	36.8%	1.2	13,000	4,379	33.7%	-1.9	14,000	5,465	39.0%	3.5	15,000	6,254	41.7%	6.1
FLORIDA																11,000	2,990	27.2%	
GEORGIA				69,000	28,417	41.2%		78,000	33,278	42.7%	1.5	88,000	33,580	38.2%	-3.0	98,000	27,350	27.9%	-13.3
ILLINOIS								96,000	23,855	24.8%						163,000	27,828	17.1%	-7.8
IOWA																32,000	7,308	22.8%	
LOUISIANA	26,000	2,442	9.4%	35,000	4,764	13.6%	4.2	44,000	9,090	20.7%	11.3								
MAINE	88,000	23,317	26.5%	98,000	32,098	32.8%	6.3	109,000	42,164	38.7%	12.2					134,000	29,654	22.1%	-4.4
MASSACHUSETTS	147,000	22,672	15.4%	165,000	41,144	24.9%	9.5	183,000	50,473	27.6%	12.2	209,000	53,855	25.8%	10.3	239,000	54,110	22.6%	7.2
MICHIGAN								45,000	16,051	35.7%						81,000	20,904	25.8%	-9.9
MISSISSIPPI	17,000	2,756	16.2%					37,000	16,215	43.8%	27.6								
MISSOURI								64,000	17,193	26.9%						113,000	25,330	22.4%	-4.4
NEW JERSEY	67,000	15,268	22.8%	73,000	26,413	36.2%	13.4									101,000	28,713	28.4%	5.6
NEW YORK	425,000	41,732	9.8%	485,000	167,206	34.5%	24.7	545,000	193,417	35.5%	25.7	624,000	186,469	29.9%	20.1	715,000	187,462	26.2%	16.4
OHIO	193,000	49,998	25.9%	247,000	69,345	28.1%	2.2	301,000	103,242	34.3%	8.4					404,000	123,654	30.6%	4.7
PENNSYLVANIA	288,000	36,077	12.5%	323,000	55,775	17.3%	4.7	358,000	124,342	34.7%	22.2					478,000	91,607	19.2%	6.6
SOUTH CAROLINA								54,000	3,339	6.2%									
VERMONT	63,000	16,964	26.9%	66,000	14,257	21.6%	-5.3	68,000	23,842	35.1%	8.1					78,000	22,693	29.1%	2.2
Total	1,326,000	215,493	16.3%	1,574,000	444,198	28.2%	12.0	2,011,000	665,036	33.1%	16.8	957,000	284,684	29.7%	13.5	2,662,000	655,857	24.6%	8.4

Democratic Turnout for Election Years 1830–1846

| State | 1830 | | | 1834 | | | | 1838 | | | | 1842 | | | | 1846 | | | |
	Voting-age population	Turnout	%	Voting-age population	Turnout	%	Difference from 1830	Voting-age population	Turnout	%	Difference from 1830	Voting-age population	Turnout	%	Difference from 1830	Voting-age population	Turnout	%	Difference from 1830
ARKANSAS								16,000	6,722	42.0%		22,000	9,413	42.8%	0.8	28,000	16,426	58.7%	16.7
DELAWARE	12,000	3,833	31.9%	13,000	4,626	35.6%	3.6	13,000	4,437	34.1%	2.2	14,000	5,456	39.0%	7.0	15,000	6,007	40.0%	8.1
FLORIDA																11,000	2,887	26.2%	
GEORGIA	61,000	50,772	83.2%	69,000	32,934	47.7%	-35.5	78,000	31,270	40.1%	-43.1	88,000	35,461	40.3%	-42.9	98,000	31,606	32.3%	-51.0
ILLINOIS				65,000	20,334	31.3%		96,000	34,617	36.1%	4.8					163,000	61,432	37.7%	6.4
IOWA																32,000	8,107	25.3%	
LOUISIANA				35,000	945	2.7%		44,000	3,796	8.6%	5.9								
MAINE	88,000	25,705	29.2%	98,000	35,998	36.7%	7.5	109,000	45,591	41.8%	12.6					134,000	32,794	24.5%	-4.7

United States House of Representatives General Elections (continued)

United States House of Representatives General Elections *(continued)*

Democratic Turnout for Election Years 1830–1846 *(continued)*

State	1830			1834				1838				1842				1846			
	Voting-age population	Turnout	%	Voting-age population	Turnout	%	Difference from 1830	Voting-age population	Turnout	%	Difference from 1830	Voting-age population	Turnout	%	Difference from 1830	Voting-age population	Turnout	%	Difference from 1830
MASSACHUSETTS	147,000	4,510	3.1%	165,000	20,785	12.6%	9.5	183,000	35,851	19.6%	16.5	209,000	54,898	26.3%	23.2	239,000	32,325	13.5%	10.5
MICHIGAN								45,000	16,255	36.1%						81,000	23,884	29.5%	-6.6
MISSISSIPPI	17,000	8,924	52.5%					37,000	18,602	50.3%	-2.2								
MISSOURI								64,000	23,405	36.6%		84,000	25,658	30.5%	-6.0	113,000	40,363	35.7%	-0.9
NEW JERSEY	67,000	14,261	21.3%	73,000	27,413	37.6%	16.3									101,000	25,662	25.4%	4.1
NEW YORK	425,000	121,495	28.6%	485,000	182,502	37.6%	9.0	545,000	181,625	33.3%	4.7	624,000	195,886	31.4%	2.8	715,000	179,695	25.1%	-3.5
OHIO	193,000	46,116	23.9%	247,000	65,846	26.7%	2.8	301,000	103,470	34.4%	10.5					404,000	116,527	28.8%	4.9
PENNSYLVANIA	288,000	71,731	24.9%	323,000	100,047	31.0%	6.1	358,000	130,409	36.4%	11.5					478,000	96,778	20.2%	-4.7
SOUTH CAROLINA	53,000	3,881	7.3%					54,000	2,358	4.4%	-3.0					58,000	10,582	18.2%	10.9
TEXAS																27,000	2,709	10.0%	
VERMONT	63,000	7,853	12.5%	66,000	10,761	16.3%	3.8	68,000	18,635	27.4%	14.9					78,000	16,637	21.3%	8.9
Total	1,414,000	359,081	25.4%	1,639,000	502,191	30.6%	5.2	2,011,000	657,043	32.7%	7.3	1,041,000	326,772	31.4%	6.0	2,775,000	704,421	25.4%	0.0

Other Turnout for Election Years 1830–1846

State	1830			1834				1838				1842				1846			
	Voting-age population	Turnout	%	Voting-age population	Turnout	%	Difference from 1830	Voting-age population	Turnout	%	Difference from 1830	Voting-age population	Turnout	%	Difference from 1830	Voting-age population	Turnout	%	Difference from 1830
ARKANSAS												22,000	1,686	7.7%		28,000	101	0.4%	-7.3
GEORGIA	61,000	5,148	8.4%													98,000	121	0.1%	-8.3
ILLINOIS				65,000	12,143	18.7%										163,000	10,234	6.3%	-12.4
LOUISIANA	26,000	2,644	10.2%	35,000	3,978	11.4%	1.2	44,000	422	1.0%	-9.2								
MAINE	88,000	1,209	1.4%	98,000	598	0.6%	-0.8	109,000	224	0.2%	-1.2					134,000	11,491	8.6%	7.2
MASSACHUSETTS	147,000	7,343	5.0%	165,000	7,796	4.7%	-0.3	183,000	1,275	0.7%	-4.3	209,000	7,066	3.4%	-1.6	239,000	13,730	5.7%	0.7
MICHIGAN																81,000	2,885	3.6%	
MISSOURI												87,000	688	0.8%		113,000	1,572	1.4%	0.6
NEW JERSEY																101,000	1,431	1.4%	
NEW YORK	425,000	87,567	20.6%									624,000	7,185	1.2%	-19.5	715,000	30,857	4.3%	-16.3
OHIO	193,000	3,383	1.8%	247,000	543	0.2%	-1.5									404,000	2,951	0.7%	-1.0
PENNSYLVANIA	288,000	34,935	12.1%	323,000	28,758	8.9%	-3.2									478,000	18,106	3.8%	-8.3
SOUTH CAROLINA	53,000	4,093	7.7%	53,000	29,136	55.0%	47.3	54,000	2,329	4.3%	-3.4					58,000	690	1.2%	-6.5
TEXAS																27,000	4,003	14.8%	
VERMONT	63,000	4,347	6.9%	66,000	11,223	17.0%	10.1	68,000	509	0.7%	-6.2					78,000	6,956	8.9%	2.0
Total	1,344,000	150,669	11.2%	1,052,000	94,175	9.0%	-2.3	458,000	4,759	1.0%	-10.2	942,000	16,625	1.8%	-9.4	2,717,000	105,128	3.9%	-7.3

*The Whig party supplanted the National Republicans as the Democrats' national opposition by 1834.

**Percentage point difference between turnout in current year and initial year listed in chart. If data do not appear for a state in the initial year listed, the difference is calculated from the first year in which data do appear for that state.

TOTAL HIGHEST STATEWIDE GENERAL ELECTIONS
Election Years 1830–1846

State	1830 Voting-age population	Turnout	%	1834 Voting-age population	Turnout	%	Difference from 1830*	1838 Voting-age population	Turnout	%	Difference from 1830	1842 Voting-age population	Turnout	%	Difference from 1830	1846 Voting-age population	Turnout	%	Difference from 1830
ARKANSAS								16,000	10,878	68.0%		22,000	16,414	74.6%	6.6	28,000	16,527	59.0%	-9.0
CONNECTICUT	69,000	12,988	18.8%	72,000	36,643	50.9%	32.1	74,000	48,604	65.7%	46.9	81,000	49,264	60.8%	42.0	90,000	55,025	61.1%	42.3
DELAWARE	12,000	8,100	67.5%	13,000	9,405	72.3%	4.8	13,000	8,816	67.8%	0.3	14,000	10,921	78.0%	10.5	15,000	12,261	81.7%	14.2
FLORIDA																11,000	5,877	53.4%	
GEORGIA	61,000	32,604	53.4%	69,000	60,379	87.5%	34.1	78,000	63,213	81.0%	27.6	88,000	68,213	77.5%	24.1	98,000	59,077	60.3%	6.8
ILLINOIS	34,000	21,775	64.0%	66,000	32,477	50.0%	-14.1	98,000	60,390	62.9%	-1.1	129,000	85,532	66.3%	2.3	163,000	100,847	61.9%	-2.2
INDIANA				96,000	64,073	66.7%										183,000	124,242	67.9%	1.1
IOWA																32,000	15,313	47.9%	
LOUISIANA	26,000	6,461	24.9%	35,000	10,456	29.9%	5.0	44,000	14,364	32.6%	7.8	55,000	17,920	32.6%	7.7	67,000	24,454	36.5%	11.6
MAINE	88,000	58,854	66.9%	98,000	91,536	93.4%	26.5	109,000	89,113	81.8%	14.9	121,000	71,680	59.2%	-7.6	134,000	73,939	55.2%	-11.7
MARYLAND								73,000	55,131	75.5%									
MASSACHUSETTS	147,000	45,348	30.8%	165,000	72,600	44.0%	13.2	183,000	93,437	51.1%	20.2	209,000	117,812	56.4%	25.5	239,000	100,175	41.9%	11.1
MICHIGAN								45,000	32,306	71.8%						81,000	47,673	58.9%	-12.9
MISSISSIPPI	17,000	11,680	68.7%					37,000	34,235	92.5%	23.8								
MISSOURI								64,000	40,271	62.9%		87,000	26,573	30.5%	-32.4	113,000	67,265	59.5%	-3.4
NEW HAMPSHIRE	61,000	40,992	67.2%	64,000	28,542	44.6%	-22.6	67,000	54,306	81.1%	13.9	72,000	47,944	66.6%	-0.6	79,000	55,024	69.7%	2.5
NEW JERSEY	67,000	28,883	43.1%	73,000	53,770	73.7%	30.5									101,000	55,806	55.3%	12.1
NEW YORK	425,000	250,194	58.9%	485,000	350,908	72.4%	13.5	545,000	375,343	68.9%	10.0	624,000	394,151	63.2%	4.3	715,000	398,014	55.7%	-3.2
NORTH CAROLINA								96,000	59,274	61.7%		101,000	74,620	73.9%	12.1	109,000	79,113	72.6%	10.8
OHIO	193,000	99,497	51.6%	247,000	138,152	55.9%	4.4	301,000	210,030	69.8%	18.2	353,000	237,676	67.3%	15.8	404,000	243,132	60.2%	8.6
PENNSYLVANIA	288,000	138,446	48.1%	323,000	184,531	57.1%	9.1	358,000	254,683	71.1%	23.1					478,000	206,491	43.2%	-4.9
RHODE ISLAND	21,000	4,248	20.2%	53,000	7,196	13.6%	-6.7	25,000	7,488	30.0%	9.7	29,000	7,157	24.7%	4.5	34,000	14,868	43.7%	23.5
SOUTH CAROLINA	53,000	7,485	14.1%	66,000	29,136	44.1%	30.0	54,000	11,683	21.6%	7.5					58,000	11,272	19.4%	5.3
TEXAS																27,000	6,712	24.9%	
VERMONT	63,000	30,684	48.7%	66,000	37,675	57.1%	8.4	68,000	39,585	58.2%	9.5	72,000	51,297	71.2%	22.5	78,000	48,633	62.4%	13.6
Total	1,625,000	798,239	49.1%	1,990,000	1,207,479	60.7%	11.6	2,346,000	1,563,150	66.6%	17.5	2,057,000	1,277,174	62.1%	13.0	3,337,000	1,821,740	54.6%	5.5

*Percentage point difference between turnout in current year and initial year listed in chart. If data do not appear for a state in the initial year listed, the difference is calculated from the first year in which data do appear for that state.

TOTAL HIGHEST STATEWIDE GENERAL ELECTIONS

Whig Turnout for Election Years 1830–1846

State	1830 (National Republicans)*			1834				1838				1842				1846			
	Voting-age population	Turnout	%	Voting-age population	Turnout	%	Difference from 1830**	Voting-age population	Turnout	%	Difference from 1830	Voting-age population	Turnout	%	Difference from 1830	Voting-age population	Turnout	%	Difference from 1830
ARKANSAS								16,000	4,156	26.0%		22,000	5,315	24.2%	-1.8				
CONNECTICUT	69,000	12,988	18.8%	72,000	18,411	25.6%	6.7	74,000	27,115	36.6%	17.8	81,000	23,700	29.3%	10.4	90,000	27,822	30.9%	12.1
DELAWARE	12,000	4,267	35.6%	13,000	4,779	36.8%	1.2	13,000	4,379	33.7%	-1.9	14,000	5,465	39.0%	3.5	15,000	6,254	41.7%	6.1
FLORIDA																11,000	2,990	27.2%	
GEORGIA				69,000	27,796	40.3%		78,000	32,182	41.3%	1.0	88,000	33,094	37.6%	-2.7	98,000	27,350	27.9%	-12.4
ILLINOIS	34,000	12,837	37.8%	65,000	17,340	26.7%	-11.1	96,000	29,722	31.0%	-6.8	129,000	39,030	30.3%	-7.5	163,000	37,033	22.7%	-15.0
INDIANA				96,000	36,797	38.3%										183,000	60,138	32.9%	-5.5
IOWA																32,000	7,379	23.1%	
LOUISIANA	26,000	3,817	14.7%	35,000	6,018	17.2%	2.5	44,000	9,090	20.7%	6.0	55,000	8,204	14.9%	0.2				
MAINE	88,000	28,639	32.5%	98,000	39,361	40.2%	7.6	109,000	42,897	39.4%	6.8	121,000	26,745	22.1%	-10.4	134,000	29,654	22.1%	-10.4
MARYLAND								73,000	27,409	37.5%									
MASSACHUSETTS	147,000	30,908	21.0%	165,000	43,757	26.5%	5.5	183,000	51,642	28.2%	7.2	209,000	54,939	26.3%	5.3	239,000	54,813	22.9%	1.9
MICHIGAN								45,000	16,051	35.7%						81,000	20,904	25.8%	-9.9
MISSISSIPPI	17,000	2,756	16.2%					37,000	15,729	42.5%	26.3								
MISSOURI								64,000	16,946	26.5%						113,000	25,330	22.4%	-4.1
NEW HAMPSHIRE	61,000	18,490	30.3%					67,000	25,565	38.2%	7.8	72,000	12,364	17.2%	-13.1	79,000	17,704	22.4%	-7.9
NEW JERSEY	67,000	15,006	22.4%	73,000	26,377	36.1%	13.7									101,000	28,713	28.4%	6.0
NEW YORK	425,000	120,667	28.4%	485,000	169,008	34.8%	6.5	545,000	193,205	35.5%	7.1	624,000	186,469	29.9%	1.5	715,000	197,627	27.6%	-0.8
NORTH CAROLINA								96,000	38,119	39.7%		101,000	39,596	39.2%	-0.5	109,000	43,486	39.9%	0.2
OHIO	193,000	49,998	25.9%	247,000	69,345	28.1%	2.2	301,000	103,242	34.3%	8.4	353,000	117,902	33.4%	7.5	404,000	118,857	29.4%	3.5
PENNSYLVANIA	288,000	26,614	9.2%	323,000	55,749	17.3%	8.0	358,000	124,304	34.7%	25.5					478,000	91,607	19.2%	9.9
RHODE ISLAND				23,000	3,520	15.3%		25,000	3,984	15.9%	0.6	29,000	7,145	24.6%	9.3				
SOUTH CAROLINA								54,000	3,339	6.2%									
VERMONT	63,000	12,836	20.4%	66,000	14,257	21.6%	1.2	68,000	22,169	32.6%	12.2	72,000	27,167	37.7%	17.4	78,000	23,638	30.3%	9.9
Total	1,490,000	339,823	22.8%	1,830,000	532,515	29.1%	6.3	2,346,000	791,245	33.7%	10.9	1,970,000	587,135	29.8%	7.0	3,123,000	821,299	26.3%	3.5

Democratic Turnout for Election Years 1830–1846

State	1830			1834				1838				1842				1846			
	Voting-age population	Turnout	%	Voting-age population	Turnout	%	Difference from 1830	Voting-age population	Turnout	%	Difference from 1830	Voting-age population	Turnout	%	Difference from 1830	Voting-age population	Turnout	%	Difference from 1830
ARKANSAS								16,000	6,722	42.0%		22,000	9,413	42.8%	0.8	28,000	16,426	58.7%	16.7
CONNECTICUT				72,000	15,834	22.0%		74,000	21,489	29.0%	7.0	81,000	25,564	31.6%	9.6	90,000	27,203	30.2%	8.2

Total Highest Statewide General Elections (continued)

Democratic Turnout for Election Years 1830–1846 (continued)

State	1830 Voting-age population	Turnout	%	1834 Voting-age population	Turnout	%	Difference from 1830	1838 Voting-age population	Turnout	%	Difference from 1830	1842 Voting-age population	Turnout	%	Difference from 1830	1846 Voting-age population	Turnout	%	Difference from 1830
DELAWARE	12,000	3,833	31.9%	13,000	4,626	35.6%	3.6	13,000	4,437	34.1%	2.2	14,000	5,456	39.0%	7.0	15,000	6,148	41.0%	9.0
FLORIDA																11,000	2,887	26.2%	
GEORGIA	61,000	31,869	52.2%	69,000	32,583	47.2%	-5.0	78,000	31,031	39.8%	-12.5	88,000	35,119	39.9%	-12.3	98,000	30,343	31.0%	-21.3
ILLINOIS	34,000	8,938	26.3%	65,000	20,334	31.3%	5.0	96,000	34,617	36.1%	9.8	129,000	46,502	36.0%	9.8	163,000	58,660	36.0%	9.7
INDIANA				96,000	27,276	28.4%										183,000	64,104	35.0%	6.6
IOWA																32,000	8,107	25.3%	
LOUISIANA				35,000	4,438	12.7%		44,000	6,776	15.4%	2.7	55,000	9,716	17.7%	5.0	67,000	13,353	19.9%	7.2
MAINE	88,000	30,215	34.3%	98,000	43,176	44.1%	9.7	109,000	46,216	42.4%	8.1	121,000	40,855	33.8%	-0.6	134,000	33,805	25.2%	-9.1
MARYLAND								73,000	27,722	38.0%									
MASSACHUSETTS	147,000	14,440	9.8%	165,000	20,785	12.6%	2.8	183,000	41,795	22.8%	13.0	209,000	56,491	27.0%	17.2	239,000	33,199	13.9%	4.1
MICHIGAN								45,000	16,255	36.1%						81,000	23,884	29.5%	-6.6
MISSISSIPPI	17,000	8,924	52.5%					37,000	18,506	50.0%	-2.5								
MISSOURI								64,000	23,325	36.4%		87,000	26,350	30.3%	-6.2	113,000	40,363	35.7%	-0.7
NEW HAMPSHIRE	61,000	23,214	38.1%	64,000	28,542	44.6%	6.5	67,000	28,741	42.9%	4.8	72,000	26,830	37.3%	-0.8	79,000	26,914	34.1%	-4.0
NEW JERSEY	67,000	13,877	20.7%	73,000	27,393	37.5%	16.8									101,000	25,662	25.4%	4.7
NEW YORK	425,000	128,947	30.3%	485,000	182,238	37.6%	7.2	545,000	182,461	33.5%	3.1	624,000	208,062	33.3%	3.0	715,000	192,361	26.9%	-3.4
NORTH CAROLINA								96,000	21,155	22.0%		101,000	34,411	34.1%	12.0	109,000	35,627	32.7%	10.6
OHIO	193,000	49,186	25.5%	247,000	70,738	28.6%	3.2	301,000	107,884	35.8%	10.4	353,000	119,774	33.9%	8.4	404,000	116,554	28.9%	3.4
PENNSYLVANIA	288,000	71,472	24.8%	323,000	100,024	31.0%	6.2	358,000	130,379	36.4%	11.6					478,000	91,926	19.2%	-5.6
RHODE ISLAND				23,000	3,676	16.0%		25,000	3,504	14.0%	-2.0					34,000	7,391	21.7%	5.8
SOUTH CAROLINA	53,000	3,881	7.3%					54,000	4,499	8.3%	1.0					58,000	10,582	18.2%	10.9
TEXAS																27,000	2,709	10.0%	
VERMONT	63,000	7,853	12.5%	66,000	10,761	16.3%	3.8	68,000	17,416	25.6%	13.1	72,000	24,130	33.5%	21.0	78,000	17,877	22.9%	10.5
Total	1,509,000	396,649	26.3%	1,894,000	592,424	31.3%	5.0	2,346,000	774,930	33.0%	6.7	2,028,000	668,673	33.0%	6.7	3,337,000	886,085	26.6%	0.3

Other Turnout for Election Years 1830–1846

State	1830 Voting-age population	Turnout	%	1834 Voting-age population	Turnout	%	Difference from 1830	1838 Voting-age population	Turnout	%	Difference from 1830	1842 Voting-age population	Turnout	%	Difference from 1830	1846 Voting-age population	Turnout	%	Difference from 1830
ARKANSAS												22,000	1,686	7.7%		28,000	101	0.4%	-7.3
CONNECTICUT				72,000	2,398	3.3%													
GEORGIA	61,000	735	1.2%													98,000	1,384	1.4%	0.2
ILLINOIS				65,000	12,143	18.7%										163,000	17,302	10.6%	-8.1

Total Highest Statewide General Elections (continued)

Total Highest Statewide General Elections (continued)

Other Turnout for Election Years 1830–1846 (continued)

State	1830			1834				1838				1842				1846			
	Voting-age population	Turnout	%	Voting-age population	Turnout	%	Difference from 1830	Voting-age population	Turnout	%	Difference from 1830	Voting-age population	Turnout	%	Difference from 1830	Voting-age population	Turnout	%	Difference from 1830
IOWA																32,000	7,626	23.8%	
LOUISIANA	26,000	2,644	10.2%	35,000	3,978	11.4%	1.2	44,000	422	1.0%	-9.2								
MAINE	88,000	1,209	1.4%	98,000	8,999	9.2%	7.8	109,000	224	0.2%	-1.2	121,000	4,080	3.4%	2.0	134,000	11,491	8.6%	7.2
MASSACHUSETTS	147,000	7,343	5.0%	165,000	10,160	6.2%	1.2	183,000	1,275	0.7%	-4.3	209,000	7,125	3.4%	-1.6	239,000	13,730	5.7%	0.7
MICHIGAN																81,000	2,885	3.6%	
MISSOURI												87,000	688	0.8%		113,000	1,572	1.4%	0.6
NEW HAMPSHIRE												72,000	8,750	12.2%		79,000	10,406	13.2%	1.0
NEW JERSEY																101,000	1,431	1.4%	
NEW YORK	425,000	87,340	20.6%									624,000	7,185	1.2%	-19.4	715,000	32,058	4.5%	-16.1
OHIO	193,000	3,383	1.8%	247,000	543	0.2%	-1.5									404,000	12,930	3.2%	1.4
PENNSYLVANIA	288,000	40,360	14.0%	323,000	28,758	8.9%	-5.1	358,000	122,325	34.2%	20.2					478,000	22,958	4.8%	-9.2
RHODE ISLAND	21,000	4,248	20.2%																
SOUTH CAROLINA	53,000	3,604	6.8%	53,000	29,136	55.0%	48.2	54,000	3,845	7.1%	0.3	29,000	2,291	7.9%	1.1	58,000	690	1.2%	-5.6
TEXAS																27,000	4,003	14.8%	
VERMONT	63,000	24,399	38.7%	66,000	17,131	26.0%	-12.8	68,000	452	0.7%	-38.1					78,000	7,118	9.1%	-29.6
Total	1,365,000	175,265	12.8%	1,124,000	113,246	10.1%	-2.8	816,000	128,543	15.8%	2.9	1,164,000	31,805	2.7%	-10.1	2,828,000	147,685	5.2%	-7.6

*The Whig party supplanted the National Republicans as the Democrats' national opposition by 1834.

**Percentage point difference between turnout in current year and initial year listed in chart. If data do not appear for a state in the initial year listed, the difference is calculated from the first year in which data do appear for that state.

STATE GUBERNATORIAL GENERAL ELECTIONS

Election Years 1831–1849

State	1831 Voting-age population	Turnout	%	1833 Voting-age population	Turnout	%	Difference from 1831*	1835 Voting-age population	Turnout	%	Difference from 1831	1837 Voting-age population	Turnout	%	Difference from 1831	1839 Voting-age population	Turnout	%	Difference from 1831
ALABAMA	44,000	26,183	59.5%	50,000	9,750	19.5%	-40.0	56,000	35,488	63.4%	3.9	62,000	44,571	71.9%	12.4	68,000	22,159	32.6%	-26.9
ARKANSAS																			
CONNECTICUT	70,000	17,597	25.1%	71,000	21,492	30.3%	5.1	72,000	41,964	58.3%	33.1	74,000	45,313	61.2%	36.1	75,000	50,086	66.8%	41.6
FLORIDA																			
GEORGIA	63,000	52,692	83.6%	67,000	60,054	89.6%	6.0	72,000	59,687	82.9%	-0.7	76,000	67,596	88.9%	5.3	80,000	67,383	84.2%	0.6
INDIANA	74,000	51,504	69.6%									118,000	82,982	70.3%	0.7				
LOUISIANA	28,000	8,318	29.7%																
MAINE	90,000	50,113	55.7%	96,000	46,867	48.8%	-6.9	101,000	44,593	44.2%	-11.5	106,000	68,237	64.4%	8.7	112,000	75,517	67.4%	11.7
MARYLAND																			
MASSACHUSETTS	151,000	53,136	35.2%	160,000	62,375	39.0%	3.8	169,000	62,782	37.1%	2.0	179,000	83,552	46.7%	11.5	188,000	101,759	54.1%	18.9
MICHIGAN								30,000	9,275	30.9%		41,000	30,202	73.7%	42.7	49,000	36,779	75.1%	44.1
MISSISSIPPI	20,000	12,465	62.3%	25,000	12,822	51.3%	-11.0	30,000	19,328	64.4%	2.1	35,000	27,635	79.0%	16.6	40,000	34,766	86.9%	24.6
NEW HAMPSHIRE	62,000	42,184	68.0%	63,000	32,229	51.2%	-16.9	65,000	40,592	62.4%	-5.6	67,000	22,361	33.4%	-34.7	68,000	54,391	80.0%	11.9
NEW JERSEY																			
PENNSYLVANIA								331,000	200,413	60.5%									
RHODE ISLAND	22,000	6,657	30.3%	23,000	7,317	31.8%	1.6	24,000	7,654	31.9%	1.6	25,000	3,662	14.6%	-15.6	25,000	6,136	24.5%	-5.7
TENNESSEE	104,000	64,834	62.3%	107,000	53,224	49.7%	-12.6	111,000	83,041	74.8%	12.5	115,000	87,697	76.3%	13.9	119,000	105,458	88.6%	26.3
TEXAS																			
VERMONT	64,000	34,406	53.8%	65,000	36,248	55.8%	2.0	66,000	34,899	52.9%	-0.9	67,000	39,979	59.7%	5.9	68,000	46,867	68.9%	15.2
WISCONSIN																			
Total	792,000	420,089	53.0%	727,000	342,378	47.1%	-5.9	1,127,000	639,716	56.8%	3.7	965,000	603,787	62.6%	9.5	892,000	601,301	67.4%	14.4

State	1841 Voting-age population	Turnout	%	Difference from 1831	1843 Voting-age population	Turnout	%	Difference from 1831	1845 Voting-age population	Turnout	%	Difference from 1831	1847 Voting-age population	Turnout	%	Difference from 1831	1849 Voting-age population	Turnout	%	Difference from 1831
ALABAMA	73,000	49,193	67.4%	7.9					81,000	55,848	68.9%	9.4	85,000	53,869	63.4%	3.9	89,000	36,350	40.8%	-18.7
ARKANSAS																	34,000	6,518	19.2%	
CONNECTICUT	79,000	48,374	61.2%	36.1	83,000	52,817	63.6%	38.5	88,000	55,766	63.4%	38.2	93,000	57,539	61.9%	36.7	98,000	56,338	57.5%	32.3
FLORIDA									11,000	5,971	54.3%									
GEORGIA	85,000	71,550	84.2%	0.5	90,000	73,984	82.2%	-1.4	96,000	81,276	84.7%	1.0	101,000	85,160	84.3%	0.7	106,000	89,983	84.9%	1.3
INDIANA					161,000	119,739	74.4%	4.8									205,000	144,214	70.3%	0.7
LOUISIANA																	76,000	35,866	47.2%	17.5
MAINE	118,000	84,134	71.3%	15.6	124,000	62,976	50.8%	-4.9	130,000	66,919	51.5%	-4.2	137,000	65,282	47.7%	-8.0	143,000	73,819	51.6%	-4.1

State Gubernatorial General Elections (continued)

State Gubernatorial General Elections (continued)

Election Years 1831–1849 (continued)

State	1841 Voting-age population	Turnout	%	Difference from 1831	1843 Voting-age population	Turnout	%	Difference from 1831	1845 Voting-age population	Turnout	%	Difference from 1831	1847 Voting-age population	Turnout	%	Difference from 1831	1849 Voting-age population	Turnout	%	Difference from 1831
MARYLAND	78,000	57,279	73.4%										96,000	68,098	70.9%	-2.5				
MASSACHUSETTS	201,000	107,341	53.4%	18.2	217,000	121,044	55.8%	20.6	232,000	105,470	45.5%	10.3	247,000	102,297	41.4%	6.2	262,000	109,296	41.7%	6.5
MICHIGAN	58,000	36,450	62.8%	31.9	67,000	39,154	58.4%	27.5	76,000	39,493	52.0%	21.0	85,000	46,214	54.4%	23.5	95,000	51,406	54.1%	23.2
MISSISSIPPI	45,000	35,842	79.6%	17.3	50,000	38,557	77.1%	14.8	55,000	41,162	74.8%	12.5	59,000	40,992	69.5%	7.2	64,000	56,113	87.7%	25.4
NEW HAMPSHIRE	71,000	50,631	71.3%	3.3	74,000	44,526	60.2%	-7.9	77,000	44,353	57.6%	-10.4	80,000	60,446	75.6%	7.5	84,000	56,033	66.7%	-1.3
NEW JERSEY													105,000	67,016	63.8%		110,000	73,777	67.1%	3.2
PENNSYLVANIA	395,000	249,957	63.3%	2.7									495,000	274,229	55.4%	-5.1				
RHODE ISLAND	27,000	2,648	9.8%	-20.5	30,000	16,533	55.1%	24.9	32,000	15,599	48.7%	18.5	35,000	10,650	30.4%	0.2	37,000	8,503	23.0%	-7.3
TENNESSEE	125,000	104,534	83.6%	21.3	131,000	108,827	83.1%	20.7	138,000	115,082	83.4%	21.1	144,000	121,904	84.7%	22.3	151,000	122,080	80.8%	18.5
TEXAS													29,000	13,630	47.0%		34,000	21,288	62.6%	15.6
VERMONT	71,000	47,694	67.2%	13.4	73,000	50,213	68.8%	15.0	76,000	47,895	63.0%	9.3	79,000	48,042	60.8%	7.1	82,000	53,630	65.4%	11.6
WISCONSIN																	77,000	31,779	41.3%	
Total	1,426,000	945,627	66.3%	13.3	1,100,000	728,370	66.2%	13.2	1,092,000	674,834	61.8%	8.8	1,870,000	1,115,368	59.6%	6.6	1,747,000	1,026,993	58.8%	5.7

*Percentage point difference between turnout in current year and initial year listed in chart. If data do not appear for a state in the initial year listed, the difference is calculated from the first year in which data do appear for that state.

STATE GUBERNATORIAL GENERAL ELECTIONS

Whig Turnout for Election Years 1831–1849

State	1831 Voting-age population	Turnout	%	1833* Voting-age population	Turnout	%	Difference from 1831	1835 Voting-age population	Turnout	%	Difference from 1831	1837 Voting-age population	Turnout	%	Difference from 1831	1839 Voting-age population	Turnout	%	Difference from 1831
ALABAMA	44,000	8,137	18.5%					56,000	12,209	21.8%	3.3					68,000	1,708	2.5%	-16.0
ARKANSAS																			
CONNECTICUT	70,000	12,819	18.3%	71,000	9,212	13.0%	-5.3	72,000	19,835	27.5%	9.2	74,000	21,508	29.1%	10.8	75,000	26,358	35.1%	16.8
FLORIDA																			
GEORGIA								72,000	28,497	39.6%		76,000	34,179	45.0%	5.4	80,000	32,715	40.9%	1.3
INDIANA	74,000	23,518	31.8%									118,000	82,982	70.3%	38.5				
LOUISIANA	28,000	5,132	18.3%																
MAINE	90,000	21,821	24.2%	96,000	18,112	18.9%	-5.4	101,000	16,860	16.7%	-7.6	106,000	34,358	32.4%	8.2	112,000	34,749	31.0%	6.8
MARYLAND																			
MASSACHUSETTS	151,000	28,804	19.1%	160,000	25,149	15.7%	-3.4	169,000	37,555	22.2%	3.1	179,000	50,565	28.2%	9.2	188,000	50,725	27.0%	7.9
MICHIGAN								30,000	815	2.7%		41,000	14,884	36.3%	33.6	49,000	19,069	38.9%	36.2
MISSISSIPPI	20,000	3,953	19.8%	25,000	6,117	24.5%	4.7	30,000	9,877	32.9%	13.2	35,000	4,951	14.1%	-5.6	40,000	15,886	39.7%	20.0
NEW HAMPSHIRE	62,000	18,681	30.1%	63,000	3,959	6.3%	-23.8	65,000	14,825	22.8%	-7.3					68,000	23,925	35.2%	5.1
NEW JERSEY																			
PENNSYLVANIA								331,000	65,804	19.9%									
RHODE ISLAND	22,000	3,780	17.2%	23,000	3,292	14.3%	-2.9	24,000	3,774	15.7%	-1.5					25,000	2,908	11.6%	-5.5
TENNESSEE								111,000	41,862	37.7%		115,000	53,385	46.4%	8.7	119,000	51,446	43.2%	5.5
TEXAS																			
VERMONT	64,000	12,990	20.3%					66,000	5,435	8.2%	-12.1	67,000	22,257	33.2%	12.9	68,000	24,611	36.2%	15.9
WISCONSIN																			
Total	625,000	139,635	22.3%	438,000	65,841	15.0%	-7.3	1,127,000	257,348	22.8%	0.5	811,000	319,069	39.3%	17.0	892,000	284,100	31.8%	9.5

State	1841 Voting-age population	Turnout	%	Difference from 1831	1843 Voting-age population	Turnout	%	Difference from 1831	1845 Voting-age population	Turnout	%	Difference from 1831	1847 Voting-age population	Turnout	%	Difference from 1831	1849 Voting-age population	Turnout	%	Difference from 1831
ALABAMA	73,000	21,219	29.1%	10.6									85,000	23,247	27.3%	8.9				
ARKANSAS																	34,000	3,228	9.5%	
CONNECTICUT	79,000	26,986	34.2%	15.8	83,000	25,401	30.6%	12.3	88,000	29,508	33.5%	15.2	93,000	30,137	32.4%	14.1	98,000	27,800	28.4%	10.1
FLORIDA									11,000	2,679	24.4%									
GEORGIA	85,000	33,703	39.7%	0.1	90,000	38,711	43.0%	3.4	96,000	41,523	43.3%	3.7	101,000	41,941	41.5%	1.9	106,000	43,349	40.9%	1.3
INDIANA					161,000	58,809	36.5%	4.7									205,000	67,218	32.8%	1.0
LOUISIANA																	76,000	17,407	22.9%	4.6
MAINE	118,000	36,780	31.2%	6.9	124,000	20,975	16.9%	-7.3	130,000	26,341	20.3%	-4.0	137,000	24,304	17.7%	-6.5	143,000	28,260	19.8%	-4.5

State Gubernatorial General Elections (continued)

State Gubernatorial General Elections (continued)

Whig Turnout for Election Years 1831–1849 (continued)

State	1841				1843				1845				1847				1849			
	Voting-age population	Turnout	%	Difference from 1831	Voting-age population	Turnout	%	Difference from 1831	Voting-age population	Turnout	%	Difference from 1831	Voting-age population	Turnout	%	Difference from 1831	Voting-age population	Turnout	%	Difference from 1831
MARYLAND	78,000	28,320	36.3%										96,000	33,730	35.1%	-1.2				
MASSACHUSETTS	201,000	55,974	27.8%	8.8	217,000	57,899	26.7%	7.6	232,000	51,638	22.3%	3.2	247,000	53,742	21.8%	2.7	262,000	54,009	20.6%	1.5
MICHIGAN	58,000	15,449	26.6%	23.9	67,000	15,024	22.4%	19.7	76,000	16,322	21.5%	18.8	85,000	18,990	22.3%	19.6	95,000	23,561	24.8%	22.1
MISSISSIPPI	45,000	16,783	37.3%	17.5	50,000	17,442	34.9%	15.1	55,000	12,852	23.4%	3.6	59,000	13,997	23.7%	4.0	64,000	22,996	35.9%	16.2
NEW HAMPSHIRE	71,000	21,178	29.8%	-0.3	74,000	12,561	17.0%	-13.2	77,000	15,591	20.2%	-9.9	80,000	21,109	26.4%	-3.7	84,000	18,764	22.3%	-7.8
NEW JERSEY													105,000	32,251	30.7%		110,000	34,054	31.0%	0.2
PENNSYLVANIA	395,000	113,453	28.7%	8.8									495,000	128,148	25.9%	6.0				
RHODE ISLAND	27,000	2,648	9.8%	-7.4	30,000	9,140	30.5%	13.3	32,000	15,599	48.7%	31.6	35,000	6,300	18.0%	0.8	37,000	5,081	13.7%	-3.4
TENNESSEE	125,000	53,829	43.1%	5.3	131,000	57,008	43.5%	5.8	138,000	56,805	41.2%	3.4	144,000	61,450	42.7%	5.0	151,000	60,340	40.0%	2.2
TEXAS																				
VERMONT	71,000	23,353	32.9%	12.6	73,000	24,465	33.5%	13.2	76,000	22,770	30.0%	9.7	79,000	22,455	28.4%	8.1	82,000	26,238	32.0%	11.7
WISCONSIN																	77,000	11,317	14.7%	
Total	1,426,000	449,675	31.5%	9.2	1,100,000	337,435	30.7%	8.3	1,011,000	291,628	28.8%	6.5	1,841,000	511,801	27.8%	5.5	1,624,000	443,622	27.3%	5.0

Democratic Turnout for Election Years 1831–1849

State	1831			1833				1835				1837				1839			
	Voting-age population	Turnout	%	Voting-age population	Turnout	%	Difference from 1831	Voting-age population	Turnout	%	Difference from 1831	Voting-age population	Turnout	%	Difference from 1831	Voting-age population	Turnout	%	Difference from 1831
ALABAMA	44,000	14,403	32.7%	50,000	9,750	19.5%	-13.2	56,000	23,279	41.6%	8.8	62,000	24,419	39.4%	6.7	68,000	20,451	30.1%	-2.7
ARKANSAS																			
CONNECTICUT				71,000	9,030	12.7%		72,000	22,129	30.7%	18.0	74,000	23,805	32.2%	19.5	75,000	23,728	31.6%	18.9
FLORIDA																			
GEORGIA								72,000	31,190	43.3%		76,000	33,417	44.0%	0.7	80,000	34,668	43.3%	0.0
INDIANA	74,000	21,002	28.4%																
LOUISIANA	28,000	3,186	11.4%																
MAINE	90,000	28,292	31.4%	96,000	25,731	26.8%	-4.6	101,000	27,733	27.5%	-4.0	106,000	33,879	32.0%	0.5	112,000	40,768	36.4%	5.0
MARYLAND																			
MASSACHUSETTS	151,000	10,975	7.3%	160,000	15,493	9.7%	2.4	169,000	25,227	14.9%	7.7	179,000	32,987	18.4%	11.2	188,000	51,034	27.1%	19.9
MICHIGAN								30,000	8,461	28.2%		41,000	15,318	37.4%	9.2	49,000	17,710	36.1%	7.9
MISSISSIPPI	20,000	8,512	42.6%	25,000	6,705	26.8%	-15.7	30,000	9,451	31.5%	-11.1	35,000	12,823	36.6%	-5.9	40,000	18,880	47.2%	4.6
NEW HAMPSHIRE	62,000	23,503	37.9%	63,000	28,270	44.9%	7.0	65,000	25,767	39.6%	1.7	66,000	22,361	33.9%	-4.0	68,000	30,466	44.8%	6.9
NEW JERSEY																			
PENNSYLVANIA								331,000	94,023	28.4%									
RHODE ISLAND				23,000	4,025	17.5%		24,000	3,880	16.2%	-1.3	25,000	2,716	10.9%	-6.6	25,000	2,771	11.1%	-6.4

State Gubernatorial General Elections (continued)

Democratic Turnout for Election Years 1831–1849 (continued)

State	1831 Voting-age population	Turnout	%	1833 Voting-age population	Turnout	%	Difference from 1831	1835 Voting-age population	Turnout	%	Difference from 1831	1837 Voting-age population	Turnout	%	Difference from 1831	1839 Voting-age population	Turnout	%	Difference from 1831
TENNESSEE	104,000	64,834	**62.3%**	107,000	53,224	**49.7%**	-12.6	111,000	33,180	**29.9%**	-32.4	115,000	34,312	**29.8%**	-32.5	119,000	54,012	**45.4%**	-17.0
TEXAS																			
VERMONT								66,000	13,254	**20.1%**		67,000	17,722	**26.5%**	6.4	68,000	22,256	**32.7%**	12.6
WISCONSIN																			
Total	573,000	174,707	**30.5%**	595,000	152,228	**25.6%**	-4.9	1,127,000	317,574	**28.2%**	-2.3	846,000	253,759	**30.0%**	-0.5	892,000	316,744	**35.5%**	5.0

State	1841 Voting-age population	Turnout	%	Difference from 1831	1843 Voting-age population	Turnout	%	Difference from 1831	1845 Voting-age population	Turnout	%	Difference from 1831	1847 Voting-age population	Turnout	%	Difference from 1831	1849 Voting-age population	Turnout	%	Difference from 1831
ALABAMA	73,000	27,974	**38.3%**	5.6					81,000	25,587	**31.6%**	-1.1	85,000	30,622	**36.0%**	3.3	89,000	36,350	**40.8%**	8.1
ARKANSAS																	34,000	3,290	**9.7%**	
CONNECTICUT	79,000	21,388	**27.1%**	14.4	83,000	27,416	**33.0%**	20.3	88,000	26,258	**29.8%**	17.1	93,000	27,402	**29.5%**	16.7	98,000	25,018	**25.5%**	12.8
FLORIDA									11,000	3,292	**29.9%**									
GEORGIA	85,000	37,847	**44.5%**	1.2	90,000	35,273	**39.2%**	-4.1	96,000	39,753	**41.4%**	-1.9	101,000	43,219	**42.8%**	-0.5	106,000	46,634	**44.0%**	0.7
INDIANA					161,000	60,930	**37.8%**	9.5									205,000	76,996	**37.6%**	9.2
LOUISIANA																	76,000	18,459	**24.3%**	12.9
MAINE	118,000	47,354	**40.1%**	8.7	124,000	32,034	**25.8%**	-5.6	130,000	34,711	**26.7%**	-4.7	137,000	33,461	**24.4%**	-7.0	143,000	37,534	**26.2%**	-5.2
MARYLAND	78,000	28,959	**37.1%**										96,000	34,368	**35.8%**	-1.3				
MASSACHUSETTS	201,000	51,367	**25.6%**	18.3	217,000	54,242	**25.0%**	17.7	232,000	37,427	**16.1%**	8.9	247,000	39,398	**16.0%**	8.7	262,000	30,040	**11.5%**	4.2
MICHIGAN	58,000	21,001	**36.2%**	8.0	67,000	21,394	**31.9%**	3.7	76,000	20,123	**26.5%**	-1.7	85,000	24,639	**29.0%**	0.8	95,000	27,845	**29.3%**	1.1
MISSISSIPPI	45,000	19,059	**42.4%**	-0.2	50,000	21,115	**42.2%**	-0.3	55,000	28,310	**51.5%**	8.9	59,000	26,995	**45.8%**	3.2	64,000	33,117	**51.7%**	9.2
NEW HAMPSHIRE	71,000	29,453	**41.5%**	3.6	74,000	23,052	**31.2%**	-6.8	77,000	23,298	**30.3%**	-7.7	80,000	30,806	**38.5%**	0.6	84,000	30,107	**35.8%**	-2.1
NEW JERSEY													105,000	34,765	**33.1%**		110,000	39,723	**36.1%**	3.0
PENNSYLVANIA	395,000	136,504	**34.6%**	6.2									495,000	146,081	**29.5%**	1.1				
RHODE ISLAND					30,000	7,393	**24.6%**	7.1					35,000	4,350	**12.4%**	-5.1	37,000	2,964	**8.0%**	-9.5
TENNESSEE	125,000	50,705	**40.6%**	-21.8	131,000	51,819	**39.6%**	-22.8	138,000	58,277	**42.2%**	-20.1	144,000	60,454	**42.0%**	-20.4	151,000	61,740	**40.9%**	-21.5
TEXAS													29,000	12,193	**42.0%**		34,000	10,226	**30.1%**	-12.0
VERMONT	71,000	21,302	**30.0%**	9.9	73,000	21,982	**30.1%**	10.0	76,000	18,591	**24.5%**	4.4	79,000	18,661	**23.6%**	3.5	82,000	4,142	**5.1%**	-15.0
WISCONSIN																	77,000	16,701	**21.7%**	
Total	1,399,000	492,913	**35.2%**	4.7	1,100,000	356,650	**32.4%**	1.9	1,060,000	315,627	**29.8%**	-0.7	1,870,000	567,414	**30.3%**	-0.1	1,747,000	500,886	**28.7%**	-1.8

State Gubernatorial General Elections (continued)

State Gubernatorial General Elections (continued)

Other Turnout for Election Years 1831–1849

State	1831 Voting-age population	Turnout	%	1833 Voting-age population	Turnout	%	Difference from 1831	1835 Voting-age population	Turnout	%	Difference from 1831	1837 Voting-age population	Turnout	%	Difference from 1831	1839 Voting-age population	Turnout	%	Difference from 1831
ALABAMA	44,000	3,643	8.3%									62,000	20,152	32.5%	24.2				
CONNECTICUT	70,000	4,778	6.8%	71,000	3,250	4.6%	-2.2												
GEORGIA	63,000	52,692	83.6%	67,000	60,054	89.6%	6.0												
INDIANA	74,000	6,984	9.4%																
MAINE				96,000	3,024	3.2%													
MASSACHUSETTS	151,000	13,357	8.8%	160,000	21,733	13.6%	4.7												
MICHIGAN																			
MISSISSIPPI												35,000	9,861	28.2%					
NEW HAMPSHIRE																			
PENNSYLVANIA								331,000	40,586	12.3%									
RHODE ISLAND	22,000	2,877	13.1%									25,000	946	3.8%	-9.3	25,000	457	1.8%	-11.2
TENNESSEE								111,000	7,999	7.2%									
TEXAS																			
VERMONT	64,000	21,416	33.5%	65,000	36,248	55.8%	22.3	66,000	16,210	24.6%	-8.9								
WISCONSIN																			
Total	488,000	105,747	21.7%	459,000	124,309	27.1%	5.4	508,000	64,795	12.8%	-8.9	122,000	30,959	25.4%	3.7	25,000	457	1.8%	-19.8

State	1841 Voting-age population	Turnout	%	Difference from 1831	1843 Voting-age population	Turnout	%	Difference from 1831	1845 Voting-age population	Turnout	%	Difference from 1831	1847 Voting-age population	Turnout	%	Difference from 1831	1849 Voting-age population	Turnout	%	Difference from 1831
ALABAMA									81,000	30,261	37.4%	29.1								
CONNECTICUT																	98,000	3,520	3.6%	-3.2
GEORGIA																				
INDIANA																				
MAINE					124,000	9,967	8.0%	4.9	130,000	5,867	4.5%	1.4	137,000	7,517	5.5%	2.3	143,000	8,025	5.6%	2.5
MASSACHUSETTS					217,000	8,903	4.1%	-4.7	232,000	16,405	7.1%	-1.8	247,000	9,157	3.7%	-5.1	262,000	25,247	9.6%	0.8
MICHIGAN					67,000	2,736	4.1%		76,000	3,048	4.0%	-0.1	85,000	2,585	3.0%	-1.0				
MISSISSIPPI																				
NEW HAMPSHIRE					74,000	8,913	12.0%		77,000	5,464	7.1%	-4.9	80,000	8,531	10.7%	-1.4	84,000	7,162	8.5%	-3.5
PENNSYLVANIA																				
RHODE ISLAND																	37,000	458	1.2%	-11.8
TENNESSEE																				
TEXAS													29,000	1,437	5.0%		34,000	11,062	32.5%	27.6
VERMONT	71,000	3,039	4.3%	-29.2	73,000	3,766	5.2%	-28.3	76,000	6,534	8.6%	-24.9	79,000	6,926	8.8%	-24.7	82,000	23,250	28.4%	-5.1
WISCONSIN																	77,000	3,761	4.9%	
Total	71,000	3,039	4.3%	-17.4	555,000	34,285	6.2%	-15.5	672,000	67,579	10.1%	-11.6	657,000	36,153	5.5%	-16.2	817,000	82,485	10.1%	-11.6

*Whigs had supplanted the National Republicans by 1834. In 1833, two states had Whig candidates for governor: Maine and Mississippi. Other states still had National Republican candidates: Connecticut, Massachusetts, New Hampshire, and Rhode Island. In no state did Whigs and National Republicans compete directly.

**Percentage point difference between turnout in current year and initial year listed in chart. If data do not appear for a state in the initial year listed, the difference is calculated from the first year in which data do appear for that state.

UNITED STATES HOUSE OF REPRESENTATIVES GENERAL ELECTIONS

Election Years 1831–1849

State	1831 Voting-age population	Turnout	%	1833 Voting-age population	Turnout	%	Difference from 1831*	1835 Voting-age population	Turnout	%	Difference from 1831	1837 Voting-age population	Turnout	%	Difference from 1831	1839 Voting-age population	Turnout	%	Difference from 1831
ALABAMA	44,000	22,644	51.5%	50,000	22,121	44.2%	-7.2	56,000	9,215	16.5%	-35.0	62,000	28,719	46.3%	-5.1	68,000	35,803	52.7%	1.2
CONNECTICUT	70,000	17,734	25.3%	71,000	20,179	28.4%	3.1	72,000	40,869	56.8%	31.4	74,000	44,769	60.5%	35.2	75,000	50,744	67.7%	42.3
FLORIDA																			
ILLINOIS	42,000	24,123	57.4%																
INDIANA	74,000	51,600	69.7%	80,000	61,188	68.8%	-1.0	103,000	68,667	66.7%	-3.1	118,000	82,656	70.0%	0.3	132,000	100,572	76.2%	6.5
IOWA																			
KENTUCKY	107,000	66,579	62.2%	110,000	58,135	52.9%	-9.4	114,000	65,615	57.6%	-4.7	118,000	70,536	59.8%	-2.4	122,000	44,587	36.5%	-25.7
LOUISIANA																			
MAINE				96,000	47,911	49.9%													
MARYLAND	68,000	40,447	59.5%	70,000	47,562	67.9%	8.5	71,000	42,517	59.9%	0.4	72,000	39,320	54.6%	-4.9	73,000	54,134	74.2%	14.7
MASSACHUSETTS				160,000	42,414	26.5%													
MICHIGAN								30,000	7,432	24.8%		41,000	21,712	53.0%	28.2				
MISSISSIPPI								30,000	18,447	61.5%		35,000	18,346	52.4%	-9.1				
MISSOURI	31,000	12,813	41.3%	40,000	13,253	33.1%	-8.2	50,000	23,682	47.4%	6.0								
NEW HAMPSHIRE	62,000	40,768	65.8%	63,000	31,704	50.3%	-15.4	65,000	38,344	59.0%	-6.8	66,000	23,096	35.0%	-30.8	68,000	55,548	81.7%	15.9
NEW JERSEY																			
NORTH CAROLINA	94,000	27,116	28.8%	94,000	44,924	47.8%	18.9	95,000	60,019	63.2%	34.3	96,000	48,965	51.0%	22.2	96,000	62,534	65.1%	36.3
PENNSYLVANIA																			
RHODE ISLAND	22,000	3,450	15.7%	23,000	5,066	22.0%	6.3	24,000	7,700	32.1%	16.4	25,000	7,615	30.5%	14.8	25,000	7,710	30.8%	15.2
TENNESSEE	104,000	80,377	77.3%	107,000	85,166	79.6%	2.3	111,000	85,919	77.4%	0.1	115,000	93,022	80.9%	3.6	119,000	102,043	85.8%	8.5
TEXAS																			
VERMONT				65,000	22,769	35.0%													
VIRGINIA	147,000	29,202	19.9%	149,000	24,626	16.5%	-3.3	152,000	54,077	35.6%	15.7	154,000	19,193	12.5%	-7.4	157,000	56,425	35.9%	16.1
Total	865,000	416,853	48.2%	1,187,000	527,018	44.4%	-3.8	973,000	522,503	53.7%	5.5	976,000	497,949	51.0%	2.8	935,000	570,100	61.0%	12.8

State	1841 Voting-age population	Turnout	%	Difference from 1831	1843 Voting-age population	Turnout	%	Difference from 1831	1845 Voting-age population	Turnout	%	Difference from 1831	1847 Voting-age population	Turnout	%	Difference from 1831	1849 Voting-age population	Turnout	%	Difference from 1831
ALABAMA	73,000	40,370	55.3%	3.8	77,000	26,378	34.3%	-17.2	81,000	44,654	55.1%	3.7	85,000	44,085	51.9%	0.4	89,000	70,402	79.1%	27.6
CONNECTICUT	79,000	47,968	60.7%	35.4	83,000	54,503	65.7%	40.3	88,000	57,900	65.8%	40.5	93,000	59,412	63.9%	38.5	98,000	56,088	57.2%	31.9
FLORIDA									11,000	5,981	54.4%									
ILLINOIS	120,000	69,631	58.0%	0.6	137,000	93,815	68.5%	11.0												
INDIANA	147,000	88,424	60.2%	-9.6	161,000	119,904	74.5%	4.7	176,000	125,580	71.4%	1.6	190,000	135,254	71.2%	1.5	205,000	140,453	68.5%	-1.2
IOWA													35,000	15,415	44.0%					

United States House of Representatives General Elections (continued)

United States House of Representatives General Elections (continued)

Election Years 1831–1849 (continued)

State	1841 Voting-age population	Turnout	%	Difference from 1831	1843 Voting-age population	Turnout	%	Difference from 1831	1845 Voting-age population	Turnout	%	Difference from 1831	1847 Voting-age population	Turnout	%	Difference from 1831	1849 Voting-age population	Turnout	%	Difference from 1831
KENTUCKY	129,000	40,229	31.2%	-31.0	138,000	102,548	74.3%	12.1	147,000	110,410	75.1%	12.9	156,000	121,645	78.0%	15.8	165,000	103,832	62.9%	0.7
LOUISIANA					58,000	14,729	25.4%						70,000	19,509	27.9%	2.5	76,000	10,671	14.0%	-11.4
MAINE					124,000	63,704	51.4%	1.5												
MARYLAND	78,000	40,677	52.2%	-7.3					90,000	49,044	54.5%	-5.0	96,000	60,137	62.6%	3.2	101,000	57,147	56.6%	-2.9
MASSACHUSETTS																				
MICHIGAN					67,000	38,777	57.9%	33.1												
MISSISSIPPI	45,000	35,498	78.9%	17.4	50,000	38,560	77.1%	15.6	55,000	49,473	90.0%	28.5	59,000	47,274	80.1%	18.6	64,000	55,352	86.5%	25.0
MISSOURI																				
NEW HAMPSHIRE	71,000	50,969	71.8%	6.0	74,000	44,217	59.8%	-6.0	77,000	53,125	69.0%	3.2	80,000	59,907	74.9%	9.1	84,000	55,586	66.2%	0.4
NEW JERSEY					91,000	47,852	52.6%													
NORTH CAROLINA	99,000	40,307	40.7%	11.9	103,000	57,680	56.0%	27.2	107,000	77,376	72.3%	43.5	111,000	63,895	57.6%	28.7	115,000	75,472	65.6%	36.8
PENNSYLVANIA					428,000	200,444	46.8%													
RHODE ISLAND	27,000	2,762	10.2%	-5.5	30,000	11,562	38.5%	22.9	32,000	11,355	35.5%	19.8	35,000	11,143	31.8%	16.2	37,000	8,618	23.3%	7.6
TENNESSEE	125,000	65,725	52.6%	-24.7	131,000	104,443	79.7%	2.4	138,000	104,029	75.4%	-1.9	144,000	114,051	79.2%	1.9	151,000	70,483	46.7%	-30.6
TEXAS																	34,000	19,865	58.4%	
VERMONT					73,000	48,436	66.4%	31.3												
VIRGINIA	164,000	22,015	13.4%	-6.4	172,000	34,706	20.2%	0.3	181,000	18,609	10.3%	-9.6	189,000	66,206	35.0%	15.2	198,000	56,193	28.4%	8.5
Total	1,157,000	544,575	47.1%	-1.1	1,997,000	1,102,258	55.2%	7.0	1,183,000	707,536	59.8%	11.6	1,343,000	817,933	60.9%	12.7	1,417,000	780,162	55.1%	6.9

*Percentage point difference between turnout in current year and initial year listed in chart. If data do not appear for a state in the initial year listed, the difference is calculated from the first year in which data do appear for that state.

UNITED STATES HOUSE OF REPRESENTATIVES GENERAL ELECTIONS

Whig Turnout for Election Years 1831–1849

State	1831 (National Republicans)			1833*				1835				1837				1839			
	Voting-age population	Turnout	%	Voting-age population	Turnout	%	Difference from 1831**	Voting-age population	Turnout	%	Difference from 1831	Voting-age population	Turnout	%	Difference from 1831	Voting-age population	Turnout	%	Difference from 1831
ALABAMA	44,000	4,611	10.5%	50,000	2,023	4.0%	-6.4					62,000	11,731	18.9%	8.4	68,000	14,130	20.8%	10.3
CONNECTICUT	70,000	11,950	17.1%	71,000	10,121	14.3%	-2.8	72,000	19,170	26.6%	9.6	74,000	21,303	28.8%	11.7	75,000	26,471	35.3%	18.2
FLORIDA																			
ILLINOIS																			
INDIANA	74,000	20,260	27.4%	89,000	3,041	3.4%	-24.0	103,000	23,095	22.4%	-5.0	118,000	54,111	45.9%	18.5	132,000	49,582	37.6%	10.2
IOWA																			
KENTUCKY	107,000	32,401	30.3%	110,000	27,197	24.7%	-5.6	114,000	35,920	31.5%	1.2	118,000	41,295	35.0%	4.7	122,000	23,142	19.0%	-11.3
LOUISIANA																			
MAINE				96,000	17,191	17.9%													
MARYLAND	68,000	22,757	33.5%	70,000	23,591	33.7%	0.2	71,000	21,467	30.2%	-3.2	72,000	23,059	32.0%	-1.4	73,000	24,196	33.1%	-0.3
MASSACHUSETTS				160,000	24,559	15.3%													
MICHIGAN												41,000	10,282	25.1%					
MISSISSIPPI								30,000	8,293	27.6%		35,000	7,143	20.4%	-7.2				
MISSOURI	31,000	4,835	15.6%	40,000	4,063	10.2%	-5.4												
NEW HAMPSHIRE	62,000	18,477	29.8%	63,000	6,688	10.6%	-19.2	65,000	14,332	22.0%	-7.8	66,000	1,341	2.0%	-27.8	68,000	23,870	35.1%	5.3
NEW JERSEY																			
NORTH CAROLINA	94,000	2,872	3.1%	94,000	11,093	11.8%	8.7	95,000	37,566	39.5%	36.5	96,000	21,582	22.5%	19.4	96,000	30,117	31.4%	28.3
PENNSYLVANIA																			
RHODE ISLAND	22,000	2,931	13.3%	23,000	3,162	13.7%	0.4	24,000	3,776	15.7%	2.4	25,000	4,282	17.1%	3.8	25,000	4,050	16.2%	2.9
TENNESSEE	104,000	16,959	16.3%	107,000	29,730	27.8%	11.5	111,000	48,938	44.1%	27.8	115,000	63,027	54.8%	38.5	119,000	52,311	44.0%	27.7
TEXAS																			
VERMONT				65,000	8,513	13.1%													
VIRGINIA	147,000	13,502	9.2%	149,000	7,950	5.3%	-3.8	152,000	24,062	15.8%	6.6	154,000	7,450	4.8%	-4.3	157,000	27,388	17.4%	8.3
Total	823,000	151,555	18.4%	1,187,000	178,928	15.1%	-3.3	837,000	236,619	28.3%	9.9	976,000	266,606	27.3%	8.9	935,000	275,257	29.4%	11.0

State	1841				1843				1845				1847				1849			
	Voting-age population	Turnout	%	Difference from 1831	Voting-age population	Turnout	%	Difference from 1831	Voting-age population	Turnout	%	Difference from 1831	Voting-age population	Turnout	%	Difference from 1831	Voting-age population	Turnout	%	Difference from 1831
ALABAMA	73,000	17,306	23.7%	13.2	77,000	12,724	16.5%	6.0	81,000	10,066	12.4%	1.9	85,000	9,420	11.1%	0.6	89,000	38,755	43.5%	33.1
CONNECTICUT	79,000	26,800	33.9%	16.9	83,000	25,669	30.9%	13.9	88,000	29,569	33.6%	16.5	93,000	30,188	32.5%	15.4	98,000	28,023	28.6%	11.5
FLORIDA									11,000	2,373	21.6%									
ILLINOIS	120,000	27,252	22.7%		137,000	42,288	30.9%	8.2												
INDIANA	147,000	49,287	33.5%	6.2	161,000	57,748	35.9%	8.5	176,000	58,816	33.4%	6.0	190,000	67,938	35.8%	8.4	205,000	70,504	34.4%	7.0
IOWA													35,000	7,308	20.9%					

United States House of Representatives General Elections (continued)

United States House of Representatives General Elections (continued)

Whig Turnout for Election Years 1831–1849 (continued)

State	1841				1843				1845				1847				1849			
	Voting-age population	Turnout	%	Difference from 1831	Voting-age population	Turnout	%	Difference from 1831	Voting-age population	Turnout	%	Difference from 1831	Voting-age population	Turnout	%	Difference from 1831	Voting-age population	Turnout	%	Difference from 1831
KENTUCKY	129,000	28,628	22.2%	-8.1	138,000	52,268	37.9%	7.6	147,000	55,107	37.5%	7.2	156,000	64,553	41.4%	11.1	165,000	57,248	34.7%	4.4
LOUISIANA					58,000	6,586	11.4%						70,000	9,223	13.2%	1.8	76,000	5,002	6.6%	-4.8
MAINE					124,000	20,867	16.8%	-1.1												
MARYLAND	78,000	23,766	30.5%	-3.0					90,000	26,877	29.9%	-3.6	96,000	30,005	31.3%	-2.2	101,000	30,699	30.4%	-3.1
MASSACHUSETTS																				
MICHIGAN					67,000	14,704	21.9%	-3.1												
MISSISSIPPI	45,000	16,474	36.6%	9.0					55,000	18,378	33.4%	5.8	59,000	12,526	21.2%	-6.4	64,000	23,620	36.9%	9.3
MISSOURI																				
NEW HAMPSHIRE	71,000	20,833	29.3%	-0.5	74,000	12,901	17.4%	-12.4	77,000	15,177	19.7%	-10.1	80,000	21,001	26.3%	-3.6	84,000	22,068	26.3%	-3.5
NEW JERSEY					91,000	28,404	31.2%													
NORTH CAROLINA	99,000	20,493	20.7%	17.6	103,000	31,642	30.7%	27.7	107,000	43,269	40.4%	37.4	111,000	36,881	33.2%	30.2	115,000	36,412	31.7%	28.6
PENNSYLVANIA					428,000	86,441	20.2%													
RHODE ISLAND	27,000	2,516	9.3%	-4.0	30,000	7,145	23.8%	10.5	32,000	8,180	25.6%	12.2	35,000	5,789	16.5%	3.2	37,000	5,003	13.5%	0.2
TENNESSEE	125,000	34,597	27.7%	11.4	131,000	55,368	42.3%	26.0	138,000	45,849	33.2%	16.9	144,000	55,999	38.9%	22.6	151,000	31,255	20.7%	4.4
TEXAS																				
VERMONT					73,000	23,992	32.9%	19.8												
VIRGINIA	164,000	9,365	5.7%	-3.5	172,000	16,888	9.8%	0.6	181,000	6,843	3.8%	-5.4	189,000	31,030	16.4%	7.2	198,000	28,446	14.4%	5.2
Total	1,157,000	277,317	24.0%	5.6	1,947,000	495,635	25.5%	7.0	1,183,000	320,504	27.1%	8.7	1,343,000	381,861	28.4%	10.0	1,383,000	377,035	27.3%	8.8

Democratic Turnout for Election Years 1831–1849

State	1831			1833				1835				1837				1839			
	Voting-age population	Turnout	%	Voting-age population	Turnout	%	Difference from 1831	Voting-age population	Turnout	%	Difference from 1831	Voting-age population	Turnout	%	Difference from 1831	Voting-age population	Turnout	%	Difference from 1831
ALABAMA	44,000	18,033	41.0%	50,000	14,368	28.7%	-12.2	56,000	9,215	16.5%	-24.5	62,000	16,988	27.4%	-13.6	68,000	21,673	31.9%	-9.1
CONNECTICUT	70,000	5,784	8.3%	71,000	7,469	10.5%	2.3	72,000	21,286	29.6%	21.3	74,000	23,466	31.7%	23.4	75,000	23,829	31.8%	23.5
FLORIDA																			
ILLINOIS	42,000	13,052	31.1%																
INDIANA	74,000	27,669	37.4%	89,000	29,480	33.1%	-4.3	103,000	38,561	37.4%	0.0	118,000	28,545	24.2%	-13.2	132,000	50,990	38.6%	1.2
IOWA																			
KENTUCKY	107,000	34,178	31.9%	110,000	26,214	23.8%	-8.1	114,000	27,123	23.8%	-8.1	118,000	24,105	20.4%	-11.5	122,000	21,445	17.6%	-14.4
LOUISIANA																			
MAINE				96,000	26,710	27.8%													
MARYLAND	68,000	17,424	25.6%	70,000	23,971	34.2%	8.6	71,000	20,774	29.3%	3.6	72,000	16,053	22.3%	-3.3	73,000	27,553	37.7%	12.1

United States House of Representatives General Elections (continued)

Democratic Turnout for Election Years 1831–1849 (continued)

State	1831 Voting-age population	Turnout	%	1833 Voting-age population	Turnout	%	Difference from 1831	1835 Voting-age population	Turnout	%	Difference from 1831	1837 Voting-age population	Turnout	%	Difference from 1831	1839 Voting-age population	Turnout	%	Difference from 1831
MASSACHUSETTS				160,000	6,636	4.1%													
MICHIGAN								30,000	7,130	23.8%		41,000	11,430	27.9%	4.1				
MISSISSIPPI								30,000	9,923	33.1%		35,000	11,203	32.0%	-1.1				
MISSOURI	31,000	7,978	25.7%	40,000	7,060	17.7%	-8.1	50,000	10,856	21.7%	-4.0								
NEW HAMPSHIRE	62,000	22,291	36.0%	63,000	23,141	36.7%	0.8	65,000	24,012	36.9%	1.0	66,000	21,755	33.0%	-3.0	68,000	29,910	44.0%	8.0
NEW JERSEY																			
NORTH CAROLINA	94,000	13,513	14.4%	94,000	21,672	23.1%	8.7	95,000	22,453	23.6%	9.3	96,000	26,718	27.8%	13.5	96,000	32,417	33.8%	19.4
PENNSYLVANIA																			
RHODE ISLAND				23,000	1,904	8.3%		24,000	3,924	16.4%	8.1	25,000	3,261	13.0%	4.8	25,000	3,660	14.6%	6.4
TENNESSEE	104,000	56,378	54.2%	107,000	30,537	28.5%	-25.7	111,000	32,256	29.1%	-25.2	115,000	29,995	26.1%	-28.1	119,000	49,732	41.8%	-12.4
TEXAS																			
VERMONT				65,000	6,249	9.6%													
VIRGINIA	147,000	10,631	7.2%	149,000	13,090	8.8%	1.6	152,000	29,673	19.5%	12.3	154,000	10,803	7.0%	-0.2	157,000	28,912	18.4%	11.2
Total	843,000	226,931	26.9%	1,187,000	238,501	20.1%	-6.8	973,000	257,186	26.4%	-0.5	976,000	224,322	23.0%	-3.9	935,000	290,121	31.0%	4.1

State	1841 Voting-age population	Turnout	%	Difference from 1831	1843 Voting-age population	Turnout	%	Difference from 1831	1845 Voting-age population	Turnout	%	Difference from 1831	1847 Voting-age population	Turnout	%	Difference from 1831	1849 Voting-age population	Turnout	%	Difference from 1831
ALABAMA	73,000	23,064	31.6%	-9.4	77,000	13,462	17.5%	-23.5	81,000	34,180	42.2%	1.2	85,000	32,378	38.1%	-2.9	89,000	31,647	35.6%	-5.4
CONNECTICUT	79,000	21,168	26.8%	18.5	83,000	27,225	32.8%	24.5	88,000	26,199	29.8%	21.5	93,000	27,397	29.5%	21.2	98,000	27,284	27.8%	19.6
FLORIDA									11,000	3,608	32.8%								
ILLINOIS	120,000	41,778	34.8%	3.7	137,000	49,482	36.1%	5.0											
INDIANA	147,000	38,955	26.5%	-10.9	161,000	61,280	38.1%	0.7	176,000	64,995	36.9%	-0.5	190,000	66,737	35.1%	-2.3	205,000	69,949	34.1%	-3.3
IOWA													35,000	8,107	23.2%				
KENTUCKY	129,000	9,565	7.4%	-24.5	138,000	42,623	30.9%	-1.1	147,000	55,115	37.5%	5.6	156,000	53,949	34.6%	2.6	165,000	41,919	25.4%	-6.5
LOUISIANA					58,000	8,143	14.0%						70,000	9,941	14.2%	0.2	76,000	5,669	7.5%	-6.6
MAINE					124,000	31,039	25.0%	-2.8											
MARYLAND	78,000	15,529	19.9%	-5.7					90,000	21,960	24.4%	-1.2	96,000	30,132	31.4%	5.8	101,000	25,976	25.7%	0.1
MASSACHUSETTS																			
MICHIGAN					67,000	21,242	31.7%	7.9											
MISSISSIPPI	45,000	19,024	42.3%	9.2	50,000	38,560	77.1%	44.0	55,000	27,945	50.8%	17.7	59,000	34,694	58.8%	25.7	64,000	31,732	49.6%	16.5
MISSOURI																			
NEW HAMPSHIRE	71,000	28,870	40.7%	4.7	74,000	22,913	31.0%	-5.0	77,000	24,904	32.3%	-3.6	80,000	30,538	38.2%	2.2	84,000	29,969	35.7%	-0.3
NEW JERSEY					91,000	19,448	21.4%												

United States House of Representatives General Elections (continued)

United States House of Representatives General Elections (continued)

Democratic Turnout for Election Years 1831–1849 (continued)

State	1841				1843				1845				1847				1849			
	Voting-age population	Turnout	%	Difference from 1831	Voting-age population	Turnout	%	Difference from 1831	Voting-age population	Turnout	%	Difference from 1831	Voting-age population	Turnout	%	Difference from 1831	Voting-age population	Turnout	%	Difference from 1831
NORTH CAROLINA	99,000	19,703	19.9%	5.5	103,000	26,038	25.3%	10.9	107,000	34,107	31.9%	17.5	111,000	27,014	24.3%	10.0	115,000	37,458	32.6%	18.2
PENNSYLVANIA					428,000	104,138	24.3%													
RHODE ISLAND					30,000	4,417	14.7%	6.4					35,000	4,357	12.4%	4.2	37,000	3,242	8.8%	0.5
TENNESSEE	125,000	30,189	24.2%	-30.1	131,000	49,075	37.5%	-16.7	138,000	55,615	40.3%	-13.9	144,000	57,994	40.3%	-13.9	151,000	35,166	23.3%	-30.9
TEXAS																	34,000	15,531	45.7%	
VERMONT					73,000	20,780	28.5%	18.9												
VIRGINIA	164,000	9,415	5.7%	-1.5	172,000	17,818	10.4%	3.1	181,000	9,446	5.2%	-2.0	189,000	35,176	18.6%	11.4	198,000	27,430	13.9%	6.6
Total	1,130,000	257,260	22.8%	-4.2	1,997,000	557,683	27.9%	1.0	1,151,000	358,074	31.1%	4.2	1,343,000	418,414	31.2%	4.2	1,417,000	382,972	27.0%	0.1

Other Turnout for Election Years 1831–1849

State	1831			1833				1835				1837				1839			
	Voting-age population	Turnout	%	Voting-age population	Turnout	%	Difference from 1831	Voting-age population	Turnout	%	Difference from 1831	Voting-age population	Turnout	%	Difference from 1831	Voting-age population	Turnout	%	Difference from 1831
ALABAMA				50,000	5,730	11.5%													
CONNECTICUT				71,000	2,589	3.6%		72,000	413	0.6%	-3.1					75,000	444	0.6%	-3.1
ILLINOIS	42,000	11,071	26.4%																
INDIANA	74,000	3,671	5.0%	89,000	28,667	32.2%	27.2	103,000	7,011	6.8%	1.8								
KENTUCKY				110,000	4,724	4.3%		114,000	2,572	2.3%	-2.0	118,000	5,136	4.4%	0.1				
MAINE				96,000	4,010	4.2%													
MARYLAND	68,000	266	0.4%					71,000	276	0.4%	0.0	72,000	208	0.3%	-0.1	73,000	2,385	3.3%	2.9
MASSACHUSETTS				160,000	11,219	7.0%													
MICHIGAN								30,000	302	1.0%									
MISSISSIPPI								30,000	231	0.8%									
MISSOURI				40,000	2,130	5.3%		50,000	12,826	25.7%	20.3								
NEW HAMPSHIRE				63,000	1,875	3.0%										68,000	1,768	2.6%	-0.4
NORTH CAROLINA	94,000	10,731	11.4%	94,000	12,159	12.9%	1.5					96,000	665	0.7%	-10.7				
RHODE ISLAND	22,000	519	2.4%									25,000	72	0.3%	-2.1				
TENNESSEE	104,000	7,040	6.8%	107,000	24,893	23.3%	16.5	111,000	4,725	4.3%	-2.5								
TEXAS																			
VERMONT				65,000	8,007	12.3%													
VIRGINIA	147,000	5,069	3.4%	149,000	3,586	2.4%	-1.0	152,000	342	0.2%	-3.2	154,000	940	0.6%	-2.8	157,000	125	0.1%	-3.4
Total	551,000	38,367	7.0%	1,094,000	109,589	10.0%	3.1	733,000	28,698	3.9%	-3.0	465,000	7,021	1.5%	-5.5	373,000	4,722	1.3%	-5.7

United States House of Representatives General Elections (continued)

Other Turnout for Election Years 1831–1849 (continued)

State	1841				1843				1845				1847				1849			
	Voting-age population	Turnout	%	Difference from 1831	Voting-age population	Turnout	%	Difference from 1831	Voting-age population	Turnout	%	Difference from 1831	Voting-age population	Turnout	%	Difference from 1831	Voting-age population	Turnout	%	Difference from 1831
ALABAMA					77,000	192	0.2%	-11.2	81,000	408	0.5%	-11.0	85,000	2,287	2.7%	-8.8				
CONNECTICUT					83,000	1,609	1.9%	-1.7	88,000	2,132	2.4%	-1.2	93,000	1,827	2.0%	-1.7	98,000	781	0.8%	-2.8
ILLINOIS	120,000	601	0.5%	-25.9	137,000	2,045	1.5%	-24.9												
INDIANA	147,000	182	0.1%	-4.8	161,000	876	0.5%	-4.4	176,000	1,769	1.0%	-4.0	190,000	579	0.3%	-4.7				
KENTUCKY	129,000	2,036	1.6%	-2.7	138,000	7,657	5.5%	1.3	147,000	188	0.1%	-4.2	156,000	3,143	2.0%	-2.3	165,000	4,665	2.8%	-1.5
LOUISIANA													70,000	345	0.5%					
MAINE					124,000	11,798	9.5%	5.3												
MARYLAND	78,000	1,382	1.8%	1.4					90,000	207	0.2%	-0.2					101,000	472	0.5%	0.1
MICHIGAN					67,000	2,831	4.2%	3.2												
MISSISSIPPI									55,000	3,150	5.7%	5.0	59,000	54	0.1%	-0.7				
NEW HAMPSHIRE	71,000	1,266	1.8%	-1.2	74,000	8,403	11.4%	8.4	77,000	13,044	16.9%	14.0	80,000	8,368	10.5%	7.5	84,000	3,549	4.2%	1.2
NORTH CAROLINA	99,000	111	0.1%	-11.3													115,000	1,602	1.4%	-10.0
PENNSYLVANIA					428,000	9,865	2.3%													
RHODE ISLAND	27,000	246	0.9%	-1.4					32,000	3,175	9.9%	7.6	35,000	997	2.8%	0.5	37,000	373	1.0%	-1.4
TENNESSEE	125,000	939	0.8%	-6.0					138,000	2,565	1.9%	-4.9	144,000	58	0.0%	-6.7	151,000	4,062	2.7%	-4.1
TEXAS																	34,000	4,334	12.7%	
VERMONT					73,000	3,664	5.0%	-7.3												
VIRGINIA	164,000	3,235	2.0%	-1.5					181,000	2,320	1.3%	-2.2					198,000	317	0.2%	-3.3
Total	960,000	9,998	1.0%	-5.9	1,362,000	48,940	3.6%	-3.4	1,065,000	28,958	2.7%	-4.2	912,000	17,658	1.9%	-5.0	983,000	20,155	2.1%	-4.9

*Whigs had supplanted the National Republicans by 1834. In 1833, some states had a slate of Whig candidates: Alabama, Indiana, Kentucky, Missouri, North Carolina, Rhode Island, and Tennessee. A few states still had a slate of National Republican candidates: Connecticut, Maryland, New Hampshire, and Virginia. In no state did Whigs and National Republicans compete directly.

**Percentage point difference between turnout in current year and initial year listed in chart. If data do not appear for a state in the initial year listed, the difference is calculated from the first year in which data do appear for that state.

CHAPTER 4
1850–1869

Chronology of Major Events, 1850–1869

1850	Whig President Zachary Taylor dies of cholera and Vice President Millard Fillmore becomes president. Congress enacts the Compromise of 1850, balancing concessions to pro- and antislavery factions (satisfying neither), while admitting California as a free state. The seventh census counts the U.S. population at 23.2 million people.
1852	Democrat Franklin Pierce is elected president. *Uncle Tom's Cabin* by Harriet Beecher Stowe is published.
1854	The Kansas-Nebraska Act is enacted by Congress, establishing the territories of Kansas and Nebraska and repealing the Missouri Compromise by permitting new states to decide whether they want to allow slavery. The Act was another unsuccessful effort to reconcile both sides of the slavery issue. The anti-immigrant Know-Nothing Party is founded.
1856	Democrat James Buchanan is elected president. The "Bleeding Kansas" era begins, with deadly skirmishes along the Kansas-Missouri border in reaction to the Kansas-Nebraska Act between pro- and antislavery factions.
1857	In *Dred Scott v. Sanford*, a 7–2 Supreme Court majority rules that blacks, slave or free, are not to be considered U.S. citizens and have no right to sue in federal courts. Chief Justice Roger B. Taney further holds that slaves remained property even in free states, inflaming north-south tensions.
1859	Abolitionist John Brown and his supporters unsuccessfully raid the federal arsenal at Harper's Ferry, but responses further polarize national politics.
1860	The Democratic Party splits regionally over slavery. Republican Abraham Lincoln is elected president. South Carolina secedes from the union. The eighth census counts the U.S. population at 31.4 million people.
1861	The Confederate States of America are formed as ten other states secede. The Civil War begins as the Confederacy takes Fort Sumter, previously held by the Union. The Union loses the first Battle of Bull Run (Manassas).
1862	The Emancipation Proclamation is issued by President Lincoln, declaring slaves free American citizens. Congress passes the Homestead Act for western settlement and creates a national paper currency, two of many extensions of the federal government passed during the war. The Battle of Antietam, Maryland, exacts heavy losses on both sides.
1863	The National Banking Act provides for the federal charters of banks and the regulation of currency. The Union is victorious at Gettysburg and Vicksburg.
1864	Lincoln is re-elected president. Union forces are led by Ulysses S. Grant. Union Major General William T. Sherman captures and burns Atlanta and begins his destructive march to the sea.
1865	General Robert E. Lee surrenders the Confederate Army at Appomattox court house. President Lincoln is assassinated: Vice President Andrew Johnson becomes president. The Thirteenth Amendment to the U.S. Constitution, outlawing slavery, is ratified. The Freedman's Bureau is established to provide medical care, housing, and education for freed slaves.

Chronology of Major Events, 1850–1869 (continued)

Chronology of Major Events, 1850–1869 *(continued)*

| 1866 | The Ku Klux Klan is formed in the South. Congress passes the Civil Rights Act of 1866 over President Johnson's veto, giving all native-born Americans equal rights under the law. |

1867   Congress enacts the Tenure of Office Act, preventing the removal of cabinet and other officials without the consent of the U.S. Senate, denying President Johnson the ability to remove cabinet members opposed to his policies favoring southern whites. Southern states establish Reconstruction governments. Alaska is purchased from Russia.

1868   President Johnson is impeached but is acquitted in a U.S. Senate trial. General Ulysses S. Grant is elected president. The Fourteenth Amendment is ratified, giving equal protection under law to all citizens (except non-tax-paying Native Americans) and denying the right to hold office to those who took an oath against the government of the United States.

1869   The construction of the first transcontinental railroad is completed.

State and Federal Laws Chronology, 1850–1869

1850   *California becomes a state.* It enters the Union without any property or taxpaying requirements for suffrage. The voter must be a white U.S. citizen who has resided for six months in state and thirty days in county or district. There is no loss of residence for soldiers or others traveling on public business, but no residency is gained by military personnel stationed in the state, by students, or by residents of almshouses or other institutions. The legislature may by a two-thirds vote admit "to the right of suffrage, Indians, or the descendants of Indians, in such special cases as such a proportion of the legislative body may deem just and proper."[1]

        Virginia drops property and tax requirements. The voter must have resided for two years in state and twelve months in county, city, or town.

        Kentucky requires the voter to be a white citizen. The voter must also have resided for two years in state or one year in county, town, or city, and sixty days in precinct. There is no loss of residence for soldiers or others traveling on public business.

        Michigan requires the voter to be a white citizen or an inhabitant residing in state on June 24, 1835, or an inhabitant who has declared the intention to become a citizen. "Every civilized male inhabitant of Indian descent, a native of the United States and not a member of any tribe," shall be an elector and entitled to vote.[2] A declarant alien must have been declarant six months prior to election. The voter must have resided six months in state, twenty days in township or ward.

1851   Ohio drops tax requirement. The voter must be a white U.S. citizen and have resided one year in state. No residency is gained by military personnel stationed in state.

        Indiana requires the voter to be a U.S. citizen or declarant alien with one year of U.S. residence. The voter may not be "negro or mulatto."[3] The voter must have residency for six months in state, sixty days in township, thirty days in ward or precinct. There is no loss of residence for soldiers or others traveling on public business, but no residency is gained by military personnel stationed in state.

        Louisiana drops the time period limitation for U.S. citizens.

        Maryland requires the voter to be a white U.S. citizen.

1854   North Carolina drops property requirement but requires the voter to have paid public taxes.

1855   Massachusetts requires naturalized citizens to present naturalization papers when voting.

        Connecticut requires the voter to be able to read any article of the Constitution or any section of the state statutes. Those who could vote before 1855 are exempted.

        Ohio drops tax requirement.

1857   Ohio requires naturalized citizens to present naturalization papers when voting. Voters must have resided one year in state, thirty days in county, twenty days in township, village, or ward of city or village. No residency is gained by students.

        Massachusetts requires the voter to be able to read the Constitution in English and write own name. Those with physical disabilities, "any person who now has the right to vote," and those "who shall be 60 years of age or upwards at the time this amendment shall take effect" are exempted.[4]

        Iowa requires the voter to have resided six months in state and sixty days in county. No residency is gained by military personnel stationed in state.

        Dred Scott v. Sandford, 60 U.S. 393 (1857) Supreme Court decision denies that slaves and their descendants have constitutional rights and affirms that slaves remain property even in states that have banned slavery.

State and Federal Laws Chronology, 1850–1869 (continued)

1858   *Minnesota becomes a state.* It requires the voter to have been a U.S. citizen for three months. The voters must have resided six months in state and thirty days in election district. No residency is gained by military personnel stationed in state. Voting rights affirmed for "persons of mixed white and Indian blood who have adopted the customs and habits of civilization; persons of Indian blood residing in the State, who have adopted the language, customs and habits of civilization, after an examination before any district court of the State, in such manner as may be provided by law."[5]

1859   *Oregon becomes a state.* Declarant aliens are permitted to vote, but must have been declarant one year preceding election. The voter must have been resident six months in state. There is no loss of residence for soldiers or others traveling on public business, but no residency is gained by military personnel stationed in the state, by students, or by residents of almshouses or other institutions.

1860   New Hampshire requires the voter to have resided six months within town.

1861   *Kansas becomes a state.* Declarant aliens are permitted to vote. The voter must have resided for six months in state, thirty days in township or ward. There is no loss of residence for soldiers or others traveling on public business, but no residency is gained by military personnel stationed in state, students, or by residency in almshouse or other institutions.

1863   *West Virginia becomes a state.* The voter must have resided one year in state and thirty days in county.

1864   *Nevada becomes a state.* Nevada has an annual poll tax "and the legislature may, in its discretion, make such a payment a condition to the right of voting."[6] Payment of poll tax is not required for those in the Army or Navy. The voter must have resided six months in state and thirty days in district or county. There is no loss of residence for soldiers or others traveling on public business, but no residency is gained by military personnel stationed in the state, by students, or by residents of almshouses or other institutions.

Rhode Island adds to its requirements that there is no loss of residence for soldiers or others traveling on public business.

1865   Nevada requires every male inhabitant between ages twenty-one and sixty to pay poll tax of $4 unless exempted by law.

Missouri requires the voter to be able to read and write. Those who were qualified electors before January 1, 1876, and those prevented from reading and writing by physical disability are exempted.

1866   Georgia institutes a poll tax of $1.

New York requires naturalized citizens to present naturalization papers when voting.

1867   *Nebraska becomes a state.* The voter must have resided for six months in state, twenty days in county, and ten days in precinct. Declarant aliens are permitted to vote.

Alabama requires the voter to have resided six months in state and six months in county. Declarant aliens are permitted to vote. No residency is gained by military personnel stationed in state.

Maryland requires the voter to have resided for one year in state, six months in legislative district of Baltimore city or of the county.

1868   Georgia requires the voter to have paid taxes for the year preceding election. The voter must have resided six months in state and thirty days in county. No residency is gained by military personnel stationed in state.

1868 *(cont.)*	The Fourteenth Amendment to the Constitution provides a broad definition of citizenship, overriding *Dred Scott v. Sandford* (1857), the ruling that had excluded slaves and their descendants from possessing Constitutional rights. The amendment requires states to provide equal protection under the law to all people within their jurisdictions. Arkansas permits declarant aliens to vote. Florida permits declarant aliens to vote. Naturalized citizens are required to present naturalization papers when voting. Also, the Florida constitution authorizes the use of education qualifications, but none were passed by the legislature. The voter must have resided six months in state and six months in county. No residency is gained by military personnel stationed in state. Georgia permits declarant aliens to vote. Mississippi law declares that "no educational qualification shall ever be required for any person to become an elector."[7] The voter must have resided for six months in state and one month in county. It also excludes from voting Native Americans who are not taxed. Arkansas requires the voter to have resided six months in state. No residency is gained by military personnel stationed in the state, by students, or by residents of almshouses or other institutions. Louisiana requires the voter to have resided one year in state, ten days in parish. North Carolina requires the voter to have resided twelve months in state, thirty days in county. South Carolina requires the voter to have resided one year in state, sixty days in county. No residency is gained by military personnel stationed in state.
1869	Texas permits declarant aliens to vote. The voter must have resided one year in state, sixty days in county. No soldier, seaman, or marine may vote. It also excludes Indians who are not taxed. Nebraska requires the voter to have resided for forty days in county. Massachusetts declares, "Indians and people of color, heretofore known and called Indians … are citizens of the Commonwealth … entitled to all the rights, privileges, and immunities" of citizenship.[8]

Summary

Prior to 1850, there were three states—Indiana, Michigan, and Wisconsin—that permitted declarant aliens (non-citizens who sign a formal declaration of intent to become a citizen) to vote. Oregon, Kansas, Alabama, Nebraska, Arkansas, Florida, and Texas are added to that list between 1850 and 1869. During this period, for the first time, some states enacted a poll tax, tests for literacy and, for naturalized citizens, the need to produce citizenship papers at the polling precinct.

Source: Adapted from Alexander Keyssar, *The Right to Vote: The Contested History of Democracy in the United States, Revised Edition* (New York: Basic Books, 2009), 308–313, 329–335, 342, 363.

[1] As quoted in Keyssar, 315. For sources, see Keyssar 369–379.
[2] As quoted in Keyssar, 363. For sources, see Keyssar 369–379.
[3] As quoted in Keyssar, 315. For sources, see Keyssar 369–379.
[4] As quoted in Keyssar, 363. For sources, see Keyssar 369–379.
[5] As quoted in Keyssar, 363. For sources, see Keyssar 369–379.
[6] As quoted in Keyssar, 334. For sources, see Keyssar 369–379.
[7] As quoted in Keyssar, 342. For sources, see Keyssar 369–379.
[8] As quoted in Keyssar, 363. For sources, see Keyssar 369–379.

National Count of Popular Vote for President, 1852–1868

YEAR	NAME	PARTY	TOTAL	PERCENTAGE[1]
1852	Franklin Pierce	Democratic	1,607,510	32.2%
	Winfield Scott	Whig	1,387,122	27.8%
	John Parker Hale	Free-Soil	155,210	3.1%
1856	James Buchanan	Democratic	1,836,072	33.3%
	John Fremont	Republican	1,342,345	24.3%
	Millard Fillmore	American/Whig	873,053	15.8%
1860	Abraham Lincoln	Republican	1,865,908	30.5%
	Stephen Douglas	Democratic	1,380,202	22.6%
	John Breckinridge	Southern Democratic	848,908	13.9%
	John Bell	Constitutional Union/Whig	590,901	9.7%
1864	Abraham Lincoln	National Union[2]	2,218,388	33.3%
	George McClellan	Democratic	1,812,807	27.2%
1868	Ulysses S. Grant	Republican	3,013,650	37.2%
	Horatio Seymour	Democratic	2,708,744	33.4%

[1] The percentage figures in this chart are based on the votes cast divided by the eligible voting-age population at the time of the election.

[2] The Republican Party briefly reconstituted itself as the National Union Party during the Civil War to form a coalition with pro-war Democrats, including vice presidential nominee Andrew Johnson.

States with Property and Taxpaying Requirements for Suffrage, 1850–1869

STATE	DATE OF STATEHOOD[1]	PROPERTY REQUIREMENT[2]	TAXPAYING REQUIREMENT[2]
ALABAMA		None	None
ARKANSAS		None	None
CALIFORNIA	1850	None	None
CONNECTICUT		None	None
DELAWARE		None	1831: Paid county tax within 2 years, assessed at least 6 months before the election. Exempt if under age 22.
FLORIDA		None	None
GEORGIA		None	1798: Paid all taxes for the year preceding the election 1866: Poll tax of $1
ILLINOIS		None	None
INDIANA		None	None
IOWA		None	None
KANSAS	1861	None	None
KENTUCKY		None	None
LOUISIANA		None	None
MAINE		None	None
MARYLAND		None	None
MASSACHUSETTS		None	1821: Paid any state or county tax assessed within 2 years, unless exempted from taxation.
MICHIGAN		None	None
MISSISSIPPI		None	None
MISSOURI		None	None
MINNESOTA	1858	None	None
NEBRASKA	1867	None	None

States with Property and Taxpaying Requirements for Suffrage, 1850–1869 (continued)

States with Property and Taxpaying Requirements for Suffrage, 1850–1869 *(continued)*

STATE	DATE OF STATEHOOD[1]	PROPERTY REQUIREMENT[2]	TAXPAYING REQUIREMENT[2]
NEVADA	1864	None	1864: Annual poll tax "and the legislature may, in its discretion, make such payment a condition to the right of voting." Payment of poll tax not required for those in army or navy. 1865: Every male inhabitant between ages 21 and 60 must pay poll tax of $4 unless exempted by law.
NEW HAMPSHIRE		None	1784: Poll tax 1792: Persons excused from paying taxes at their own request excluded 1847: Those previously excused from paying taxes can vote after having paid all taxes assessed for a year prior to the election.
NEW JERSEY		None	None
NEW YORK		1821: Property requirement dropped for whites. If a "man of color," must have been for 1 year seized and possessed of a freehold estate of the value of $250 over and above all debts and debts and encumbrances charged thereon. 1826: If a "man of color," property requirements still in effect.	1821: If white, "shall have, within the year next [preceding] the election," paid a state or county tax on real or personal property or shall by law be exempted from taxation, or "shall have performed within that year military duty in the militia" or as a fireman; or if meeting special residency requirements, shall have labored on public highways.
NORTH CAROLINA		1835: To vote for Senate, freehold of 50 acres for 6 months prior to the election; to vote for House of Commons and governor, no property requirements.[3] 1854: Property requirement dropped	1776: Must have paid taxes to vote for House of Commons and governor 1854: Must have paid public taxes
OHIO		None	1802: Must have paid or been charged with state or county tax; not applicable to white males above age 21, who are "compelled to labor on the roads" and have resided 1 year in the state. 1851: Tax requirement dropped
OREGON	1859	None	None
PENNSYLVANIA		None	1838: Paid state or county tax within 2 years, assessed at least 12 days before the election; exempt if under age 22.

States with Property and Taxpaying Requirements for Suffrage, 1850–1869 *(continued)*

STATE	DATE OF STATEHOOD[1]	PROPERTY REQUIREMENT[2]	TAXPAYING REQUIREMENT[2]
RHODE ISLAND		1842: Ownership of real estate worth $134 or renting an estate for $7 per annum. Native-born citizen, resident in the state for two years and in the city or county for one year, may vote if he pays a tax of $1 or performs military duty for at least one day in the year preceding election.	1842: See property requirement. Also a registry tax of $1, or "such sum as with his other taxes shall amount to $1." Those performing military duty and mariners at sea for the year exempt.
SOUTH CAROLINA		1810: Freehold of 50 acres or a town lot, owned 6 months prior to the election, or residence in the election district for 6 months	None
TENNESSEE		None	None
TEXAS		None	None
VERMONT		None	None
VIRGINIA		1850: Property requirement dropped	1850: Tax requirement dropped
WEST VIRGINIA	1863	None	None
WISCONSIN		None	None

Source: Alexander Keyssar, *The Right to Vote: The Contested History of Democracy in the United States, Revised Edition* (New York: Basic Books), 2009, 308–313; 334–335. Adapted from Keyssar's tables, which span 1790–1855 and 1870–1920. Sources for quotations are found on pp. 369–379.

[1] For states whose date of statehood falls within the time period 1850–1869.

[2] Dates listed are for the year that the property or tax requirement went into effect. All listed requirements continue into the 1850–1869 date range of this table.

[3] References to Senate and House of Commons refer to state rather than federal offices.

States with Race and Citizenship Requirements for Suffrage, 1850–1869

STATE AND YEAR OF STATEHOOD[1]	DATE OF REQUIREMENT	RACE	CITIZENSHIP	NATIVE AMERICANS
ALABAMA	1819	White	U.S. citizen	Not specifically mentioned
	1867	*	Declarant aliens permitted to vote[2]	Not specifically mentioned
ARKANSAS	1836	White	U.S. citizen, citizen of the state for 6 months	Not specifically mentioned
	1868	*	Declarant aliens permitted to vote	Not specifically mentioned
CALIFORNIA (1850)	1849	White	U.S. citizen or Mexican citizen who became a U.S. citizen under the Queretaro Treaty of 1848	The legislature may by a two-thirds vote admit "to the right of suffrage, Indians, or the descendants of Indians, in such special cases as such a proportion of the legislative body may deem just and proper."
CONNECTICUT	1818	White	U.S. citizen	Not specifically mentioned
DELAWARE	1831	White	Citizen	Not specifically mentioned
FLORIDA	1838	White	U.S. citizen	Not specifically mentioned
	1868	*	Declarant aliens permitted to vote	Not specifically mentioned
GEORGIA	1789	No requirement	Citizen	Not specifically mentioned
	1868	*	Declarant aliens permitted to vote	Not specifically mentioned
ILLINOIS	1848	White	Citizen or inhabitant of the state on April 1, 1848	Not specifically mentioned
INDIANA	1816	White	U.S. citizen	Not specifically mentioned
	1851	"No negro or mulatto"	U.S. citizen or alien declarant with 1 year of U.S. residence	Not specifically mentioned
IOWA	1846	White	U.S. citizen	Not specifically mentioned
KANSAS (1861)	1861	*	Declarant aliens permitted to vote	Not specifically mentioned
KENTUCKY	1799	"Negros, mulattoes, and Indians excepted"	Citizen	"Indians" specifically excluded
	1850	White	Citizen	Same as 1799
LOUISIANA	1852	White	U.S. citizen	Not specifically mentioned
MAINE	1819	No requirement	U.S. citizen	"Indians not taxed" excluded

States with Race and Citizenship Requirements for Suffrage, 1850–1869 (continued)

STATE AND YEAR OF STATEHOOD[1]	DATE OF REQUIREMENT	RACE	CITIZENSHIP	NATIVE AMERICANS
MARYLAND	1810	White	Citizen of state	Not specifically mentioned
	1851	White	U.S. citizen	Not specifically mentioned
MASSACHUSETTS	1821	No requirement	Citizen	Not specifically mentioned
	1869	*	*	"Indians and people of color, heretofore known and called Indians … are citizens of the Commonwealth … entitled to all the rights, privileges, and immunities" of citizenship.
MICHIGAN	1850	White	U.S. citizen or inhabitant residing in state on June 24, 1835, or inhabitant who had declared his intention to become a citizen.	"Every civilized male inhabitant of Indian descent, a native of the United States and not a member of any tribe, shall be an elector and entitled to vote."
MINNESOTA (1858)	1857	No requirement	*	Voting rights for "persons of mixed white and Indian blood who have adopted the customs and habits of civilization; persons of Indian blood residing in the State, who have adopted the language, customs and habits of civilization, after an examination before any district court of the State, in such manner as may be provided by law."
MISSISSIPPI	1817	White	U.S. citizen	Not specifically mentioned
	1868	*	*	Excludes Indians not taxed
MISSOURI	1820	White	U.S. citizen	Not specifically mentioned
NEBRASKA (1867)	1867	No requirement	Declarant aliens permitted to vote	Not specifically mentioned
NEW HAMPSHIRE	1813	No requirement	Citizen	Not specifically mentioned
NEW JERSEY	1844	White	U.S. citizen	Not specifically mentioned
NEW YORK	1846	White or "man of color" meeting property and tax requirements	Citizen for 10 days; if "man of color," citizen for 3 years.	Not specifically mentioned

States with Race and Citizenship Requirements for Suffrage, 1850–1869 (continued)

States with Race and Citizenship Requirements for Suffrage, 1850–1869 *(continued)*

STATE AND YEAR OF STATEHOOD[1]	DATE OF REQUIREMENT	RACE	CITIZENSHIP	NATIVE AMERICANS
NORTH CAROLINA	1835	White	No requirement	Not specifically mentioned
OHIO	1809	No requirement	U.S. citizen	Not specifically mentioned
	1851	White	U.S. citizen	Not specifically mentioned
OREGON	1857	No requirement	Declarant aliens permitted to vote if declarant 1 year preceding election.	Not specifically mentioned
PENNSYLVANIA	1838	White	U.S. citizen	Not specifically mentioned
RHODE ISLAND	1842	No requirement	U.S. citizen	Members of the Narraganesett tribe excluded
SOUTH CAROLINA	1790	White	Citizen of state	Not specifically mentioned
TENNESSEE	1834	White; "*Provided,* That no person shall be disqualified from voting in any election on account of color, who is now, by the laws of this State, a competent witness in a court of justice against a white man."	U.S. citizen and citizen of the country "wherein he may offer his vote" for 6 months	Not specifically mentioned
TEXAS	1869	No requirement	*	Excludes Indians not taxed
VERMONT	1828	No requirement	U.S. citizen or freeman before the 1828 amendment	Not specifically mentioned
VIRGINIA	1850	White	"Citizen of the commonwealth."	Not specifically mentioned
WISCONSIN	1848	White	U.S. citizen or alien declarant (see also Native American)	"Persons of Indian blood who have once been declared by law of Congress to be citizens of the United States, any subsequent law of Congress notwithstanding" or "civilized persons of Indian descent, not members of any tribe" could vote.

Key: — indicates no requirement at that time
       * indicates that the previous requirement remained in effect
Source: Alexander Keyssar, *The Right to Vote: The Contested History of Democracy in the United States, Revised Edition* (New York: Basic Books, 2009), 315–319, 337–338, 363. Adapted from Keyssar's table, which extends from 1790 to 1855, along with some material from additional tables. Sources of quotations are found on pp. 369–379.
[1] For states whose date of statehood falls within the time period 1830–1849.
[2] A declarant alien is a resident who has formally declared his intention to become a citizen.

United States Presidential Turnout, Election Years 1852–1868

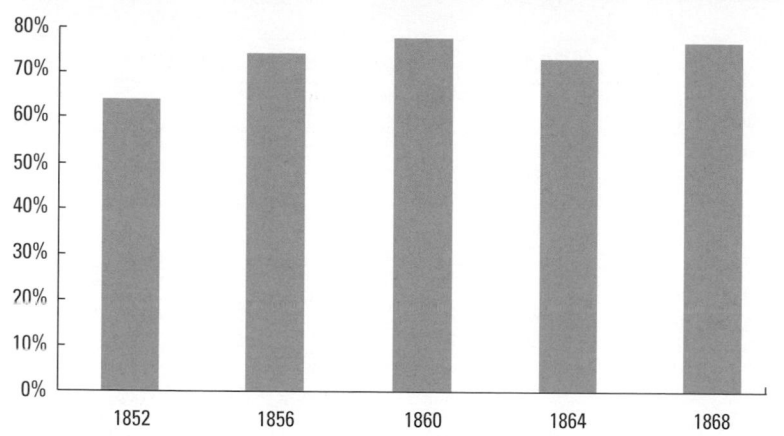

YEAR	VOTING-AGE POPULATION	TURNOUT	%
1852	4,934,000	3,162,010	64.1%
1856	5,458,000	4,054,647	74.3%
1860	6,024,000	4,685,561	77.8%
1864	5,509,000	4,031,887	73.2%
1868	7,472,000	5,722,440	76.6%

Partisan Turnout, Presidential Years, Based on Aggregate House Turnout, Election Years 1852–1868

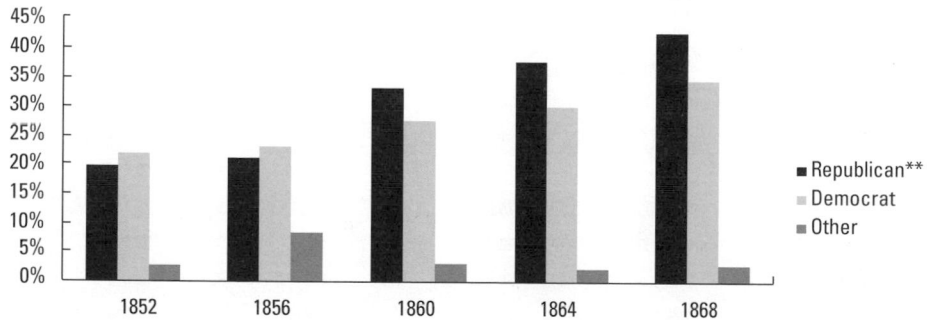

YEAR	VOTING-AGE POPULATION*	REPUBLICAN** TURNOUT	%	DEMOCRAT TURNOUT	%	OTHER TURNOUT	%
1852	4,934,000	964,725	19.6%	1,069,443	21.7%	130,781	2.7%
1856	5,458,000	1,143,878	21.0%	1,249,495	22.9%	449,748	8.2%
1860	6,024,000	1,987,871	33.0%	1,650,435	27.4%	182,484	3.0%
1864***	5,509,000	2,068,921	37.6%	1,643,501	29.8%	119,120	2.2%
1868	7,447,000	3,167,272	42.5%	2,556,754	34.3%	205,915	2.8%

*Voting-age population taken from states with Presidential elections

**Turnout for 1852 is primarily for Whigs, who were supplanted by the Republicans by 1856.

***The Republican Party briefly reconstituted itself as the National Union Party during the Civil War to form a coalition with pro-war Democrats, including vice presidential nominee Andrew Johnson.

Alternate Graph for Partisan Turnout, Presidential Years, Based on Aggregate House Turnout, 1852–1868

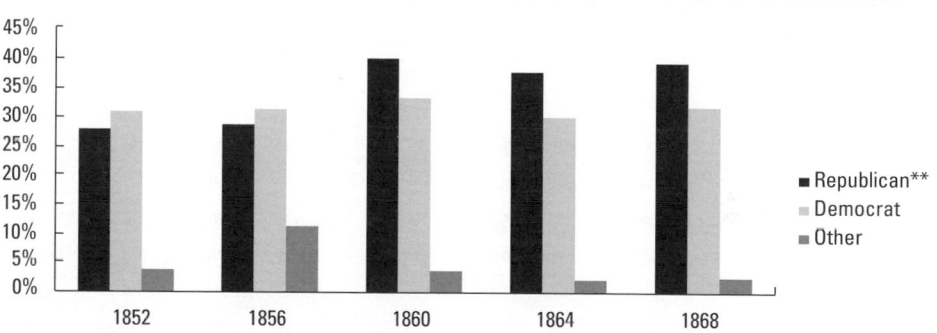

YEAR	VOTING-AGE POPULATION****	REPUBLICAN** TURNOUT	%	DEMOCRAT TURNOUT	%	OTHER TURNOUT	%
1852	3,491,000	964,725	27.6%	1,069,443	30.6%	130,781	3.7%
1856	4,018,000	1,143,878	28.5%	1,249,495	31.1%	449,748	11.2%
1860	4,988,000	1,987,871	39.9%	1,650,435	33.1%	182,484	3.7%
1864	5,509,000	2,068,921	37.6%	1,643,501	29.8%	119,120	2.2%
1868	8,125,000	3,167,272	39.0%	2,556,754	31.5%	205,915	2.5%

**Turnout for 1852 is primarily for Whigs, who were supplanted by the Republicans by 1856.

****This is an alternate graph that depicts partisan turnout calculated using voting-age population only from those states that held House elections. For percentages, consult the total lines of House partisan charts.

UNITED STATES PRESIDENTIAL GENERAL ELECTIONS

Election Years 1852–1868

State	1852 Voting-age population	Turnout	%	1856 Voting-age population	Turnout	%	Difference from 1852*	1860 Voting-age population	Turnout	%	Difference from 1852	1864** Voting-age population	Turnout	%	Difference from 1852	1868*** Voting-age population	Turnout	%	Difference from 1852
ALABAMA	96,000	44,147	46.0%	104,000	75,291	72.4%	26.4	112,000	90,122	80.5%	34.5					203,000	149,594	73.7%	27.7
ALASKA																			
ARIZONA																			
ARKANSAS	42,000	19,577	46.6%	57,000	32,642	57.3%	10.7	69,000	54,152	78.5%	31.9					100,000	41,190	41.2%	-5.4
CALIFORNIA****	85,000	76,810	90.4%	107,000	110,255	103.0%	12.7	128,000	119,827	93.6%	3.3	135,000	105,890	78.4%	-11.9	141,000	108,656	77.1%	-13.3
COLORADO																			
CONNECTICUT	102,000	66,781	65.5%	107,000	80,360	75.1%	9.6	112,000	74,819	66.8%	1.3	118,000	86,958	73.7%	8.2	125,000	98,570	78.9%	13.4
DELAWARE	18,000	12,673	70.4%	19,000	14,598	76.8%	6.4	21,000	16,115	76.7%	6.3	22,000	16,922	76.9%	6.5	27,000	18,571	68.8%	-1.6
DISTRICT OF COLUMBIA																			
FLORIDA	13,000	7,193	55.3%	16,000	11,191	69.9%	14.6	17,000	13,301	78.2%	22.9								
GEORGIA	112,000	62,626	55.9%	119,000	99,020	83.2%	27.3	125,000	106,717	85.4%	29.5					232,000	159,816	68.9%	13.0
HAWAII																			
IDAHO																			
ILLINOIS	239,000	154,974	64.8%	315,000	239,334	76.0%	11.1	392,000	339,666	86.6%	21.8	453,000	348,236	76.9%	12.0	515,000	449,420	87.3%	22.4
INDIANA	230,000	183,176	79.6%	266,000	235,401	88.5%	8.9	302,000	272,143	90.1%	10.5	330,000	280,117	84.9%	5.2	364,000	343,528	94.4%	14.7
IOWA	68,000	35,364	52.0%	109,000	92,310	84.7%	32.7	152,000	128,739	84.7%	32.7	195,000	132,947	68.2%	16.2	237,000	194,439	82.0%	30.0
KANSAS												59,000	21,580	36.6%		88,000	43,630	49.6%	13.0
KENTUCKY	177,000	111,643	63.1%	192,000	142,058	74.0%	10.9	207,000	146,216	70.6%	7.6	220,000	92,088	41.9%	-21.2	277,000	155,455	56.1%	-7.0
LOUISIANA	79,000	35,902	45.4%	81,000	42,873	52.9%	7.5	83,000	50,510	60.9%	15.4					163,000	113,488	69.6%	24.2
MAINE	146,000	82,182	56.3%	149,000	109,689	73.6%	17.3	151,000	100,918	66.8%	10.5	152,000	114,797	75.5%	19.2	153,000	112,962	73.8%	17.5
MARYLAND	106,000	75,120	70.9%	111,000	86,860	78.3%	7.4	116,000	92,502	79.7%	8.9	123,000	72,892	59.3%	-11.6	167,000	92,795	55.6%	-15.3
MASSACHUSETTS	270,000	127,283	47.1%	275,000	170,048	61.8%	14.7	282,000	169,876	60.2%	13.1	293,000	175,493	59.9%	12.8	306,000	195,508	63.9%	16.7
MICHIGAN	116,000	82,939	71.5%	148,000	125,558	84.8%	13.3	181,000	154,758	85.5%	14.0	225,000	165,279	73.5%	2.0	258,000	225,632	87.5%	16.0
MINNESOTA								39,000	34,804	89.2%		66,000	42,433	64.3%	-24.9	92,000	71,620	77.8%	-11.4
MISSISSIPPI	68,000	44,454	65.4%	73,000	59,647	81.7%	16.3	77,000	69,095	89.7%	24.4								
MISSOURI	163,000	68,801	42.2%	206,000	106,486	51.7%	9.5	250,000	165,563	66.2%	24.0	295,000	104,346	35.4%	-6.8	362,000	152,488	42.1%	-0.1
MONTANA																			
NEBRASKA																31,000	15,291	49.3%	
NEVADA												17,000	16,420	96.6%		18,000	11,689	64.9%	-31.6
NEW HAMPSHIRE	85,000	50,535	59.5%	85,000	69,774	82.1%	22.6	84,000	65,943	78.5%	19.1	84,000	69,630	82.9%	23.4	84,000	68,304	81.3%	21.9
NEW JERSEY	120,000	83,926	69.9%	132,000	99,396	75.3%	5.4	146,000	121,215	83.0%	13.1	163,000	128,744	79.0%	9.0	186,000	163,133	87.7%	17.8
NEW MEXICO																			
NEW YORK	818,000	522,294	63.9%	856,000	596,486	69.7%	5.8	892,000	675,156	75.7%	11.8	924,000	730,721	79.1%	15.2	966,000	849,771	88.0%	24.1

United States Presidential General Elections (continued)

Election Years 1852–1868 (continued)

State	1852 Voting-age population	Turnout	%	1856 Voting-age population	Turnout	%	Difference from 1852	1860 Voting-age population	Turnout	%	Difference from 1852	1864 Voting-age population	Turnout	%	Difference from 1852	1868 Voting-age population	Turnout	%	Difference from 1852
NORTH CAROLINA	120,000	78,891	65.7%	128,000	84,963	66.4%	0.6	136,000	96,712	71.1%	5.4					214,000	181,498	84.8%	19.1
NORTH DAKOTA																			
OHIO	465,000	352,903	75.9%	491,000	386,640	78.7%	2.9	516,000	442,866	85.8%	9.9	542,000	471,283	87.0%	11.1	580,000	518,665	89.4%	13.5
OKLAHOMA																			
OREGON								16,000	14,758	92.2%		20,000	18,350	91.8%	-0.5	23,000	22,086	96.0%	3.8
PENNSYLVANIA	559,000	387,920	69.4%	597,000	460,937	77.2%	7.8	635,000	476,442	75.0%	5.6	688,000	573,735	83.4%	14.0	753,000	655,662	87.1%	17.7
RHODE ISLAND	38,000	17,005	44.8%	37,000	19,822	53.6%	8.8	37,000	19,951	53.9%	9.2	39,000	23,067	59.1%	14.4	43,000	19,511	45.4%	0.6
SOUTH CAROLINA																148,000	107,538	72.7%	
SOUTH DAKOTA																			
TENNESSEE	158,000	115,486	73.1%	169,000	133,582	79.0%	6.0	179,000	146,106	81.6%	8.5					255,000	82,757	32.5%	-40.6
TEXAS	52,000	20,223	38.9%	74,000	48,005	64.9%	26.0	95,000	62,855	66.2%	27.3								
UTAH																			
VERMONT	80,000	43,030	54.8%	77,000	50,675	65.8%	11.0	75,000	44,644	59.5%	4.7	74,000	55,740	75.3%	20.5	75,000	56,224	75.0%	20.2
VIRGINIA	208,000	132,604	63.8%	222,000	150,233	67.7%	3.9	229,000	166,891	72.9%	9.1								
WASHINGTON																			
WEST VIRGINIA												88,000	34,877	39.6%		90,000	49,321	54.8%	15.2
WISCONSIN	101,000	64,740	64.1%	136,000	120,513	88.6%	24.5	168,000	152,179	90.6%	26.5	184,000	149,342	81.2%	17.1	196,000	193,628	98.8%	34.7
WYOMING																			
Total	4,934,000	3,162,010	64.1%	5,458,000	4,054,647	74.3%	10.2	6,024,000	4,685,561	77.8%	13.7	5,509,000	4,031,887	73.2%	9.1	7,472,000	5,722,440	76.6%	12.5

*Percentage point difference between turnout in current year and initial year listed in chart. If data do not appear for a state in the initial year listed, the difference is calculated from the first year in which data do appear for that state.

**The eleven Confederate states that had seceded from the Union did not participate in the 1864 presidential election.

***Florida's electoral votes were determined by the state legislature in 1868. Mississippi, Texas, and Virginia did not participate that year due to Reconstruction.

****California 1856 turnout is verified by reliable sources; error is likely with voting-age population, which is an estimate. See "Methodology" section in Introduction.

UNITED STATES PRESIDENTIAL GENERAL ELECTIONS

Republican Turnout for Election Years 1852–1868

State	1852 (Whig) Voting-age population	Turnout	%	1856* Voting-age population	Turnout	%	Difference from 1852**	1860 Voting-age population	Turnout	%	Difference from 1852	1864*** Voting-age population	Turnout	%	Difference from 1852	1868**** Voting-age population	Turnout	%	Difference from 1852
ALABAMA	96,000	15,061	15.7%													203,000	76,667	37.8%	22.1
ALASKA																			
ARIZONA																			
ARKANSAS	42,000	7,404	17.6%													100,000	22,112	22.1%	4.5
CALIFORNIA	85,000	35,972	42.3%	107,000	20,704	19.3%	-23.0	128,000	38,733	30.3%	-12.1	135,000	62,053	46.0%	3.6	141,000	54,588	38.7%	-3.6
COLORADO																			
CONNECTICUT	102,000	30,359	29.8%	107,000	42,717	39.9%	10.2	112,000	43,488	38.8%	9.1	118,000	44,673	37.9%	8.1	125,000	50,789	40.6%	10.9
DELAWARE	18,000	6,293	35.0%	19,000	310	1.6%	-33.3	21,000	3,822	18.2%	-16.8	22,000	8,155	37.1%	2.1	27,000	7,614	28.2%	-6.8
DISTRICT OF COLUMBIA																			
FLORIDA	13,000	2,875	22.1%																
GEORGIA	112,000	16,660	14.9%													232,000	57,109	24.6%	9.7
HAWAII																			
IDAHO																			
ILLINOIS	239,000	64,733	27.1%	315,000	96,275	30.6%	3.5	392,000	172,171	43.9%	16.8	453,000	189,512	41.8%	14.7	515,000	250,304	48.6%	21.5
INDIANA	230,000	80,907	35.2%	266,000	94,375	35.5%	0.3	302,000	139,033	46.0%	10.9	330,000	149,887	45.4%	10.2	364,000	176,548	48.5%	13.3
IOWA	68,000	15,856	23.3%	109,000	45,073	41.4%	18.0	152,000	70,302	46.3%	22.9	195,000	83,858	43.0%	19.7	237,000	120,399	50.8%	27.5
KANSAS												59,000	17,089	29.0%		88,000	30,027	34.1%	5.2
KENTUCKY	177,000	57,428	32.4%					207,000	1,364	0.7%	-31.8	220,000	27,787	12.6%	-19.8	277,000	39,566	14.3%	-18.2
LOUISIANA	79,000	17,255	21.8%													163,000	33,263	20.4%	-1.4
MAINE	146,000	32,543	22.3%	149,000	67,279	45.2%	22.9	151,000	62,811	41.6%	19.3	152,000	67,805	44.6%	22.3	153,000	70,502	46.1%	23.8
MARYLAND	106,000	35,077	33.1%	111,000	285	0.3%	-32.8	116,000	2,294	2.0%	-31.1	123,000	40,153	32.6%	-0.4	167,000	30,438	18.2%	-14.9
MASSACHUSETTS	270,000	52,863	19.6%	275,000	108,172	39.3%	19.8	282,000	106,684	37.8%	18.3	293,000	126,742	43.3%	23.7	306,000	136,379	44.6%	25.0
MICHIGAN	116,000	33,860	29.2%	148,000	71,762	48.5%	19.3	181,000	88,481	48.9%	19.7	225,000	91,133	40.5%	11.3	258,000	128,563	49.8%	20.6
MINNESOTA								39,000	22,069	56.6%		66,000	25,031	37.9%	-18.7	92,000	43,545	47.3%	-9.3
MISSISSIPPI	68,000	17,558	25.8%																
MISSOURI	163,000	29,984	18.4%					250,000	17,028	6.8%	-11.6	295,000	72,750	24.7%	6.3	362,000	86,860	24.0%	5.6
MONTANA																			
NEBRASKA																31,000	9,772	31.5%	
NEVADA												17,000	9,826	57.8%		18,000	6,474	36.0%	-21.8
NEW HAMPSHIRE	85,000	15,486	18.2%	85,000	37,473	44.1%	25.9	84,000	37,519	44.7%	26.4	84,000	36,596	43.6%	25.3	84,000	37,718	44.9%	26.7
NEW JERSEY	120,000	38,551	32.1%	132,000	28,338	21.5%	-10.7	146,000	58,346	40.0%	7.8	163,000	60,724	37.3%	5.1	186,000	80,132	43.1%	11.0
NEW MEXICO																			
NEW YORK	818,000	234,882	28.7%	856,000	276,004	32.2%	3.5	892,000	362,646	40.7%	11.9	924,000	368,735	39.9%	11.2	966,000	419,888	43.5%	14.8

United States Presidential General Elections (continued)

Republican Turnout for Election Years 1852–1868 (continued)

State	1852 (Whig)			1856				1860				1864				1868			
	Voting-age population	Turnout	%	Voting-age population	Turnout	%	Difference from 1852	Voting-age population	Turnout	%	Difference from 1852	Voting-age population	Turnout	%	Difference from 1852	Voting-age population	Turnout	%	Difference from 1852
NORTH CAROLINA	120,000	39,043	32.5%													214,000	96,939	45.3%	12.8
NORTH DAKOTA																			
OHIO	465,000	152,577	32.8%	491,000	187,497	38.2%	5.4	516,000	231,709	44.9%	12.1	542,000	265,674	49.0%	16.2	580,000	280,159	48.3%	15.5
OKLAHOMA																			
OREGON								16,000	5,329	33.3%		20,000	9,888	49.4%	16.1	23,000	10,961	47.7%	14.4
PENNSYLVANIA	559,000	179,182	32.1%	597,000	147,963	24.8%	-7.3	635,000	268,030	42.2%	10.2	688,000	296,292	43.1%	11.0	753,000	342,280	45.5%	13.4
RHODE ISLAND	38,000	7,626	20.1%	37,000	11,467	31.0%	10.9	37,000	12,244	33.1%	13.0	39,000	14,349	36.8%	16.7	43,000	13,017	30.3%	10.2
SOUTH CAROLINA																148,000	62,301	42.1%	
SOUTH DAKOTA																			
TENNESSEE	158,000	58,586	37.1%													255,000	56,628	22.2%	-14.9
TEXAS	52,000	5,356	10.3%																
UTAH																			
VERMONT	80,000	22,173	27.7%	77,000	39,561	51.4%	23.7	75,000	33,808	45.1%	17.4	74,000	42,419	57.3%	29.6	75,000	44,173	58.9%	31.2
VIRGINIA	208,000	58,732	28.2%					229,000	1,887	0.8%	-27.4								
WASHINGTON																			
WEST VIRGINIA												88,000	23,799	27.0%		90,000	29,015	32.2%	5.2
WISCONSIN	101,000	22,240	22.0%	136,000	67,090	49.3%	27.3	168,000	86,110	51.3%	29.2	184,000	83,458	45.4%	23.3	196,000	108,920	55.6%	33.6
WYOMING																			
Total	4,934,000	1,387,122	28.1%	4,017,000	1,342,345	33.4%	5.3	6,024,000	1,865,908	36.4%	8.3	5,509,000	2,218,388	40.3%	12.2	7,472,000	3,013,650	40.3%	12.2

Democratic Turnout for Election Years 1852–1868

State	1852			1856				1860				1864				1868			
	Voting-age population	Turnout	%	Voting-age population	Turnout	%	Difference from 1852	Voting-age population	Turnout	%	Difference from 1852	Voting-age population	Turnout	%	Difference from 1852	Voting-age population	Turnout	%	Difference from 1852
ALABAMA	96,000	26,881	28.0%	104,000	46,739	44.9%	16.9	112,000	13,618	12.2%	-15.8					203,000	72,921	35.9%	7.9
ALASKA																			
ARIZONA																			
ARKANSAS	42,000	12,173	29.0%	57,000	21,910	38.4%	9.5	69,000	5,357	7.8%	-21.2					100,000	19,078	19.1%	-9.9
CALIFORNIA	85,000	40,721	47.9%	107,000	53,342	49.9%	1.9	128,000	37,999	29.7%	-18.2	135,000	43,837	32.5%	-15.4	141,000	54,068	38.3%	-9.6
COLORADO																			
CONNECTICUT	102,000	33,249	32.6%	107,000	35,028	32.7%	0.1	112,000	15,431	13.8%	-18.8	118,000	42,285	35.8%	3.2	125,000	47,781	38.2%	5.6
DELAWARE	18,000	6,318	35.1%	19,000	8,004	42.1%	7.0	21,000	1,066	5.1%	-30.0	22,000	8,767	39.9%	4.8	27,000	10,957	40.6%	5.5
DISTRICT OF COLUMBIA																			
FLORIDA	13,000	4,318	33.2%	16,000	6,358	39.7%	6.5	17,000	223	1.3%	-31.9								

United States Presidential General Elections (continued)

United States Presidential General Elections *(continued)*

Democratic Turnout for Election Years 1852–1868 *(continued)*

State	1852			1856				1860				1864				1868			
	Voting-age population	Turnout	%	Voting-age population	Turnout	%	Difference from 1852	Voting-age population	Turnout	%	Difference from 1852	Voting-age population	Turnout	%	Difference from 1852	Voting-age population	Turnout	%	Difference from 1852
GEORGIA	112,000	40,516	36.2%	119,000	56,581	47.5%	11.4	125,000	11,581	9.3%	-26.9					232,000	102,707	44.3%	8.1
HAWAII																			
IDAHO																			
ILLINOIS	239,000	80,378	33.6%	315,000	105,528	33.5%	-0.1	392,000	160,215	40.9%	7.2	453,000	158,724	35.0%	1.4	515,000	199,116	38.7%	5.0
INDIANA	230,000	95,340	41.5%	266,000	118,670	44.6%	3.2	302,000	115,509	38.2%	-3.2	330,000	130,230	39.5%	-2.0	364,000	166,980	45.9%	4.4
IOWA	68,000	17,763	26.1%	109,000	37,568	34.5%	8.3	152,000	55,639	36.6%	10.5	195,000	49,089	25.2%	-0.9	237,000	74,040	31.2%	5.1
KANSAS												59,000	3,836	6.5%		88,000	13,600	15.5%	9.0
KENTUCKY	177,000	53,949	30.5%	192,000	74,642	38.9%	8.4	207,000	25,651	12.4%	-18.1	220,000	64,301	29.2%	-1.3	277,000	115,889	41.8%	11.4
LOUISIANA	79,000	18,647	23.6%	81,000	22,164	27.4%	3.8	83,000	7,625	9.2%	-14.4					163,000	80,225	49.2%	25.6
MAINE	146,000	41,609	28.5%	149,000	39,140	26.3%	-2.2	151,000	29,693	19.7%	-8.8	152,000	46,992	30.9%	2.4	153,000	42,460	27.8%	-0.7
MARYLAND	106,000	40,022	37.8%	111,000	39,123	35.2%	-2.5	116,000	5,966	5.1%	-32.6	123,000	32,739	26.6%	-11.1	167,000	62,357	37.3%	-0.4
MASSACHUSETTS	270,000	44,569	16.5%	275,000	39,244	14.3%	-2.2	282,000	34,370	12.2%	-4.3	293,000	48,745	16.6%	0.1	306,000	59,103	19.3%	2.8
MICHIGAN	116,000	41,842	36.1%	148,000	52,136	35.2%	-0.8	181,000	65,057	35.9%	-0.1	225,000	74,146	33.0%	-3.1	258,000	97,069	37.6%	1.6
MINNESOTA								39,000	11,920	30.6%		66,000	17,376	26.3%	-4.2	92,000	28,075	30.5%	0.0
MISSISSIPPI	68,000	26,896	39.6%	73,000	35,456	48.6%	9.0	77,000	3,282	4.3%	-35.3								
MISSOURI	163,000	38,817	23.8%	206,000	57,964	28.1%	4.3	250,000	58,801	23.5%	-0.3	295,000	31,596	10.7%	-13.1	362,000	65,628	18.1%	-5.7
MONTANA																			
NEBRASKA																31,000	5,519	17.8%	
NEVADA												17,000	6,594	38.8%		18,000	5,215	29.0%	-9.8
NEW HAMPSHIRE	85,000	28,503	33.5%	85,000	31,891	37.5%	4.0	84,000	25,887	30.8%	-2.7	84,000	33,034	39.3%	5.8	84,000	30,575	36.4%	2.9
NEW JERSEY	120,000	44,301	36.9%	132,000	46,943	35.6%	-1.4	146,000	62,869	43.1%	6.1	163,000	68,020	41.7%	4.8	186,000	83,001	44.6%	7.7
NEW MEXICO																			
NEW YORK	818,000	262,083	32.0%	856,000	195,878	22.9%	-9.2	892,000	312,510	35.0%	3.0	924,000	361,986	39.2%	7.1	966,000	429,883	44.5%	12.5
NORTH CAROLINA	120,000	39,788	33.2%	128,000	48,243	37.7%	4.5	136,000	2,737	2.0%	-31.1					214,000	84,559	39.5%	6.4
NORTH DAKOTA																			
OHIO	465,000	169,193	36.4%	491,000	170,874	34.8%	-1.6	516,000	187,421	36.3%	-0.1	542,000	205,609	37.9%	1.5	580,000	238,506	41.1%	4.7
OKLAHOMA																			
OREGON								16,000	4,136	25.9%		20,000	8,457	42.3%	16.4	23,000	11,125	48.4%	22.5
PENNSYLVANIA	559,000	198,568	35.5%	597,000	230,772	38.7%	3.1	635,000	16,765	2.6%	-32.9	688,000	277,443	40.3%	4.8	753,000	313,382	41.6%	6.1
RHODE ISLAND	38,000	8,735	23.0%	37,000	6,680	18.1%	-4.9	37,000	7,707	20.8%	-2.2	39,000	8,718	22.4%	-0.6	43,000	6,494	15.1%	-7.9
SOUTH CAROLINA																148,000	45,237	30.6%	
SOUTH DAKOTA																			
TENNESSEE	158,000	56,900	36.0%	169,000	69,704	41.2%	5.2	179,000	11,281	6.3%	-29.7					255,000	26,129	10.2%	-25.8

United States Presidential General Elections *(continued)*

Democratic Turnout for Election Years 1852–1868 *(continued)*

State	1852 Voting-age population	1852 Turnout	1852 %	1856 Voting-age population	1856 Turnout	1856 %	1856 Difference from 1852	1860 Voting-age population	1860 Turnout	1860 %	1860 Difference from 1852	1864 Voting-age population	1864 Turnout	1864 %	1864 Difference from 1852	1868 Voting-age population	1868 Turnout	1868 %	1868 Difference from 1852
TEXAS	52,000	14,857	**28.6%**	74,000	31,995	**43.2%**	14.7	95,000	18	**0.0%**	-28.6								
UTAH																			
VERMONT	80,000	13,044	**16.3%**	77,000	10,569	**13.7%**	-2.6	75,000	8,649	**11.5%**	-4.8	74,000	13,321	**18.0%**	1.7	75,000	12,051	**16.1%**	-0.2
VIRGINIA	208,000	73,872	**35.5%**	222,000	90,083	**40.6%**	5.1	229,000	16,198	**7.1%**	-28.4								
WASHINGTON																			
WEST VIRGINIA												88,000	11,078	**12.6%**		90,000	20,306	**22.6%**	10.0
WISCONSIN	101,000	33,658	**33.3%**	136,000	52,843	**38.9%**	5.5	168,000	65,021	**38.7%**	5.4	184,000	65,884	**35.8%**	2.5	196,000	84,708	**43.2%**	9.9
WYOMING																			
Total	4,934,000	1,607,510	**32.6%**	5,458,000	1,836,072	**33.6%**	1.1	6,024,000	1,380,202	**22.9%**	-9.7	5,509,000	1,812,807	**32.9%**	0.3	7,472,000	2,708,744	**36.3%**	3.7

Other Turnout for Election Years 1852–1868

State	1852 Voting-age population	1852 Turnout	1852 %	1856 Voting-age population	1856 Turnout	1856 %	1856 Difference from 1852	1860 Voting-age population	1860 Turnout	1860 %	1860 Difference from 1852	1864 Voting-age population	1864 Turnout	1864 %	1864 Difference from 1852	1868 Voting-age population	1868 Turnout	1868 %	1868 Difference from 1852
ALABAMA	96,000	2,205	**2.3%**	104,000	28,552	**27.5%**	25.2	112,000	76,504	**68.3%**	66.0					203,000	6	**0.0%**	-2.3
ALASKA																			
ARIZONA																			
ARKANSAS				57,000	10,732	**18.8%**		69,000	48,795	**70.7%**	51.9								
CALIFORNIA	85,000	117	**0.1%**	107,000	36,209	**33.8%**	33.7	128,000	43,095	**33.7%**	33.5								
COLORADO																			
CONNECTICUT	102,000	3,173	**3.1%**	107,000	2,615	**2.4%**	-0.7	112,000	15,900	**14.2%**	11.1								
DELAWARE	18,000	62	**0.3%**	19,000	6,284	**33.1%**	32.7	21,000	11,227	**53.5%**	53.1								
DISTRICT OF COLUMBIA																			
FLORIDA				16,000	4,833	**30.2%**		17,000	13,078	**76.9%**	46.7								
GEORGIA	112,000	5,450	**4.9%**	119,000	42,439	**35.7%**	30.8	125,000	95,136	**76.1%**	71.2								
HAWAII																			
IDAHO																			
ILLINOIS	239,000	9,863	**4.1%**	315,000	37,531	**11.9%**	7.8	392,000	7,280	**1.9%**	-2.3								
INDIANA	230,000	6,929	**3.0%**	266,000	22,356	**8.4%**	5.4	302,000	17,601	**5.8%**	2.8								
IOWA	68,000	1,745	**2.6%**	109,000	9,669	**8.9%**	6.3	152,000	2,798	**1.8%**	-0.7								
KANSAS												59,000	655	**1.1%**		88,000	3	**0.0%**	-1.1
KENTUCKY	177,000	266	**0.2%**	192,000	67,416	**35.1%**	35.0	207,000	119,201	**57.6%**	57.4								
LOUISIANA				81,000	20,709	**25.6%**		83,000	42,885	**51.7%**	26.1								
MAINE	146,000	8,030	**5.5%**	149,000	3,270	**2.2%**	-3.3	151,000	8,414	**5.6%**	0.1								

United States Presidential General Elections (continued)

Other Turnout for Election Years 1852–1868 (continued)

State	1852 Voting-age population	Turnout	%	1856 Voting-age population	Turnout	%	Difference from 1852	1860 Voting-age population	Turnout	%	Difference from 1852	1864 Voting-age population	Turnout	%	Difference from 1852	1868 Voting-age population	Turnout	%	Difference from 1852
MARYLAND	106,000	21	0.0%	111,000	47,452	42.7%	42.7	116,000	84,242	72.6%	72.6								
MASSACHUSETTS	270,000	29,851	11.1%	275,000	22,632	8.2%	-2.8	282,000	28,822	10.2%	-0.8	293,000	6	0.0%	-11.1	306,000	26	0.0%	-11.0
MICHIGAN	116,000	7,237	6.2%	148,000	1,660	1.1%	-5.1	181,000	1,220	0.7%	-5.6								
MINNESOTA								39,000	815	2.1%		66,000	26	0.0%	-2.1				
MISSISSIPPI				73,000	24,191	33.1%		77,000	65,813	85.5%	52.3								
MISSOURI				206,000	48,522	23.6%		250,000	89,734	35.9%	12.3								
MONTANA																			
NEBRASKA																			
NEVADA																			
NEW HAMPSHIRE	85,000	6,546	7.7%	85,000	410	0.5%	-7.2	84,000	2,537	3.0%	-4.7					84,000	11	0.0%	-7.7
NEW JERSEY	120,000	1,074	0.9%	132,000	24,115	18.3%	17.4												
NEW MEXICO																			
NEW YORK	818,000	25,329	3.1%	856,000	124,604	14.6%	11.5												
NORTH CAROLINA	120,000	60	0.1%	128,000	36,720	28.7%	28.6	136,000	93,975	69.1%	69.0								
NORTH DAKOTA																			
OHIO	465,000	31,133	6.7%	491,000	28,269	5.8%	-0.9	516,000	23,736	4.6%	-2.1								
OKLAHOMA																			
OREGON								16,000	5,293	33.1%		20,000	5	0.0%	-33.1				
PENNSYLVANIA	559,000	10,170	1.8%	597,000	82,202	13.8%	11.9	635,000	191,647	30.2%	28.4								
RHODE ISLAND	38,000	644	1.7%	37,000	1,675	4.5%	2.8												
SOUTH CAROLINA																			
SOUTH DAKOTA																			
TENNESSEE				169,000	63,878	37.8%		179,000	134,825	75.3%	37.5								
TEXAS	52,000	10	0.0%	74,000	16,010	21.6%	21.6	95,000	62,837	66.1%	66.1								
UTAH																			
VERMONT	80,000	8,621	10.8%	77,000	545	0.7%	-10.1	75,000	2,187	2.9%	-7.9								
VIRGINIA				222,000	60,150	27.1%		229,000	148,806	65.0%	37.9								
WASHINGTON																			
WEST VIRGINIA																			
WISCONSIN	101,000	8,842	8.8%	136,000	580	0.4%	-8.3	168,000	1,048	0.6%	-8.1								
WYOMING																			
Total	4,203,000	167,378	4.0%	5,458,000	876,230	16.1%	12.1	4,949,000	1,439,451	29.1%	25.1	438,000	692	0.2%	-3.8	681,000	46	0.0%	-4.0

*In 1856, the Republicans surpassed the Whigs as receiving the second highest popular vote. Whig-American votes in 1856, which made up 21.5% of the popular vote, are included under "Other."

**Percentage point difference between turnout in current year and initial year listed in chart. If data do not appear for a state in the initial year listed, the difference is calculated from the first year in which data do appear for that state.

***The eleven Confederate states who had succeeded from the Union did not participate in the 1864 presidential election.

****Florida's electoral votes were determined by the state legislature in 1868. Mississippi, Texas, and Virginia did not participate that year due to Reconstruction.

STATE GUBERNATORIAL GENERAL ELECTIONS

Election Years 1852–1868

State	1852 Voting-age population	Turnout	%	1856 Voting-age population	Turnout	%	Difference from 1852*	1860 Voting-age population	Turnout	%	Difference from 1852	1864 Voting-age population	Turnout	%	Difference from 1852	1868 Voting-age population	Turnout	%	Difference from 1852
ALABAMA																203,000	62,067	30.6%	
ALASKA																			
ARIZONA																			
ARKANSAS	42,000	28,887	68.8%	57,000	43,595	76.5%	7.7	69,000	60,200	87.2%	18.5	71,000	12,443	17.5%	-51.3				
CALIFORNIA																			
COLORADO																			
CONNECTICUT	102,000	59,865	58.7%	107,000	65,452	61.2%	2.5	112,000	00,305	78.9%	20.2	118,000	73,988	62.7%	4.0	125,000	99,325	79.5%	20.8
DELAWARE																			
DISTRICT OF COLUMBIA																			
FLORIDA	13,000	8,964	69.0%	16,000	12,102	75.6%	6.7	17,000	12,242	72.0%	3.1					38,000	24,403	64.2%	-4.7
GEORGIA																232,000	159,646	68.8%	
HAWAII																			
IDAHO																			
ILLINOIS	239,000	154,221	64.5%	315,000	237,313	75.3%	10.8	392,000	335,124	85.5%	21.0	453,000	349,077	77.1%	12.5	515,000	449,725	87.3%	22.8
INDIANA	230,000	166,606	72.4%	266,000	230,020	86.5%	14.0	302,000	263,493	87.2%	14.8	330,000	283,475	85.9%	13.5	364,000	342,125	94.0%	21.6
IOWA																			
KANSAS												59,000	21,835	37.0%		88,000	43,604	49.6%	12.5
KENTUCKY																			
LOUISIANA	79,000	33,061	41.8%									78,000	11,355	14.6%	-27.3	163,000	102,389	62.8%	21.0
MAINE	146,000	92,334	63.2%	149,000	121,020	81.2%	18.0	151,000	124,135	82.2%	19.0	152,000	111,986	73.7%	10.4	153,000	131,782	86.1%	22.9
MARYLAND												123,000	72,647	59.1%					
MASSACHUSETTS	270,000	137,736	51.0%	275,000	142,929	52.0%	1.0	282,000	169,609	60.1%	9.1	293,000	174,540	59.6%	8.6	306,000	195,471	63.9%	12.9
MICHIGAN	116,000	83,333	71.8%	148,000	125,487	84.8%	12.9	181,000	155,027	85.7%	13.8	225,000	165,649	73.6%	1.8	258,000	225,341	87.3%	15.5
MINNESOTA																			
MISSISSIPPI																			
MISSOURI	163,000	79,200	48.6%	206,000	115,301	56.0%	7.4	250,000	156,576	62.6%	14.0	295,000	104,674	35.5%	-13.1	362,000	144,887	40.0%	-8.6
MONTANA																			
NEBRASKA																31,000	14,917	48.1%	
NEVADA												17,000	16,389	96.4%					
NEW HAMPSHIRE	85,000	60,080	70.7%	85,000	64,150	75.5%	4.8	84,000	71,603	85.2%	14.6	84,000	68,425	81.5%	10.8	84,000	77,068	91.7%	21.1
NEW JERSEY				132,000	99,049	75.0%													
NEW MEXICO																			
NEW YORK	818,000	505,646	61.8%	856,000	593,886	69.4%	7.6	892,000	672,925	75.4%	13.6	924,000	729,821	79.0%	17.2	966,000	850,656	88.1%	26.2

State Gubernatorial General Elections (continued)

State Gubernatorial General Elections (continued)

Election Years 1852–1868 (continued)

State	1852 Voting-age population	Turnout	%	1856 Voting-age population	Turnout	%	Difference from 1852	1860 Voting-age population	Turnout	%	Difference from 1852	1864 Voting-age population	Turnout	%	Difference from 1852	1868 Voting-age population	Turnout	%	Difference from 1852
NORTH CAROLINA	120,000	91,477	76.2%	128,000	102,668	80.2%	4.0	136,000	112,586	82.8%	6.6	136,000	72,561	53.4%	-22.9	214,000	165,829	77.5%	1.3
NORTH DAKOTA																			
OHIO																			
OKLAHOMA																			
OREGON																			
PENNSYLVANIA								635,000	492,576	77.6%									
RHODE ISLAND	38,000	17,930	47.2%	37,000	17,193	46.5%	-0.7	37,000	23,157	62.6%	15.4	39,000	17,540	45.0%	-2.2	43,000	15,769	36.7%	-10.5
SOUTH CAROLINA																148,000	92,950	62.8%	
SOUTH DAKOTA																			
TENNESSEE																			
TEXAS																			
UTAH																			
VERMONT	80,000	48,241	60.3%	77,000	46,504	60.4%	0.1	75,000	48,101	64.1%	3.8	74,000	44,802	60.5%	0.2	75,000	57,978	77.3%	17.0
VIRGINIA																			
WASHINGTON																			
WEST VIRGINIA												88,000	19,410	22.1%		90,000	49,598	55.1%	33.1
WISCONSIN																			
WYOMING																			
Total	2,541,000	1,567,581	61.7%	2,854,000	2,016,669	70.7%	9.0	3,615,000	2,785,739	77.1%	15.4	3,559,000	2,350,617	66.0%	4.4	4,458,000	3,305,530	74.1%	12.5

*Percentage point difference between turnout in current year and initial year listed in chart. If data do not appear for a state in the initial year listed, the difference is calculated from the first year in which data do appear for that state.

STATE GUBERNATORIAL GENERAL ELECTIONS

Republican Turnout for Election Years 1852–1868

State	1852 (Whig) Voting-age population	Turnout	%	1856* Voting-age population	Turnout	%	Difference from 1852**	1860 Voting-age population	Turnout	%	Difference from 1852	1864 Voting-age population	Turnout	%	Difference from 1852	1868 Voting-age population	Turnout	%	Difference from 1852
ALABAMA																203,000	62,067	30.6%	
ALASKA																			
ARIZONA																			
ARKANSAS	42,000	12,955	30.8%									71,000	12,418	17.5%	-13.4				
CALIFORNIA																			
COLORADO																			
CONNECTICUT	102,000	28,241	27.7%	107,000	6,740	6.3%	-21.4	112,000	44,458	39.7%	12.0	118,000	39,820	33.7%	6.1	125,000	48,777	39.0%	11.3
DELAWARE																			
DISTRICT OF COLUMBIA																			
FLORIDA	13,000	4,336	33.4%													38,000	14,421	38.0%	4.6
GEORGIA																232,000	83,107	35.8%	
HAWAII																			
IDAHO																			
ILLINOIS	239,000	64,408	26.9%	315,000	111,466	35.4%	8.4	392,000	172,196	43.9%	17.0	453,000	190,376	42.0%	15.1	515,000	249,912	48.5%	21.6
INDIANA	230,000	73,647	32.0%	266,000	112,039	42.1%	10.1	302,000	136,725	45.3%	13.3	330,000	152,275	46.1%	14.1	364,000	171,523	47.1%	15.1
IOWA																			
KANSAS												59,000	13,387	22.7%		88,000	29,795	33.9%	11.2
KENTUCKY																			
LOUISIANA	79,000	15,532	19.7%									78,000	6,171	7.9%	-11.7	163,000	64,271	39.4%	19.8
MAINE	146,000	29,129	20.0%	149,000	69,444	46.6%	26.7	151,000	70,030	46.4%	26.4	152,000	65,583	43.1%	23.2	153,000	75,523	49.4%	29.4
MARYLAND												123,000	40,579	33.0%					
MASSACHUSETTS	270,000	62,233	23.0%					282,000	104,527	37.1%	14.0	293,000	125,281	42.8%	19.7	306,000	132,121	43.2%	20.1
MICHIGAN	116,000	34,662	29.9%	148,000	71,402	48.2%	18.4	181,000	87,806	48.5%	18.6	225,000	91,356	40.6%	10.7	258,000	128,051	49.6%	19.8
MINNESOTA																			
MISSISSIPPI																			
MISSOURI	163,000	32,706	20.1%					250,000	6,132	2.5%	-17.6	295,000	73,600	24.9%	4.9	362,000	82,107	22.7%	2.6
MONTANA																			
NEBRASKA																31,000	8,567	27.6%	
NEVADA												17,000	9,834	57.8%					
NEW HAMPSHIRE	85,000	19,850	23.4%					84,000	38,037	45.3%	21.9	84,000	37,006	44.1%	20.7	84,000	39,778	47.4%	24.0
NEW JERSEY																			
NEW MEXICO																			
NEW YORK	818,000	241,525	29.5%	856,000	264,400	30.9%	1.4	892,000	358,272	40.2%	10.6	924,000	368,557	39.9%	10.4	966,000	411,355	42.6%	13.1

State Gubernatorial General Elections (continued)

State Gubernatorial General Elections (continued)

Republican Turnout for Election Years 1852–1868 (continued)

State	1852 (Whig)			1856				1860				1864				1868			
	Voting-age population	Turnout	%	Voting-age population	Turnout	%	Difference from 1852	Voting-age population	Turnout	%	Difference from 1852	Voting-age population	Turnout	%	Difference from 1852	Voting-age population	Turnout	%	Difference from 1852
NORTH CAROLINA	120,000	42,993	**35.8%**													214,000	92,235	**43.1%**	7.3
NORTH DAKOTA																			
OHIO																			
OKLAHOMA																			
OREGON																			
PENNSYLVANIA								635,000	262,346	**41.3%**									
RHODE ISLAND***	38,000	8,746	**23.0%**	37,000	10,035	**27.1%**	4.1	37,000	10,740	**29.0%**	6.0	39,000	8,836	**22.7%**	-0.4	43,000	10,054	**23.4%**	0.4
SOUTH CAROLINA																148,000	69,693	**47.1%**	
SOUTH DAKOTA																			
TENNESSEE																			
TEXAS																			
UTAH																			
VERMONT	80,000	23,795	**29.7%**	77,000	34,757	**45.1%**	15.4	75,000	34,188	**45.6%**	15.8	74,000	32,052	**43.3%**	13.6	75,000	42,615	**56.8%**	27.1
VIRGINIA																			
WASHINGTON																			
WEST VIRGINIA												88,000	19,410	**22.1%**		90,000	27,348	**30.4%**	8.3
WISCONSIN																			
WYOMING																			
Total	2,541,000	694,758	**27.3%**	1,955,000	680,283	**34.8%**	7.5	3,393,000	1,325,457	**39.1%**	11.7	3,423,000	1,286,541	**37.6%**	10.2	4,458,000	1,843,320	**41.3%**	14.0

Democratic Turnout for Election Years 1852–1868

State	1852			1856				1860				1864				1868			
	Voting-age population	Turnout	%	Voting-age population	Turnout	%	Difference from 1852	Voting-age population	Turnout	%	Difference from 1852	Voting-age population	Turnout	%	Difference from 1852	Voting-age population	Turnout	%	Difference from 1852
ALABAMA																			
ALASKA																			
ARIZONA																			
ARKANSAS	42,000	15,932	**37.9%**	57,000	28,159	**49.4%**	11.5	69,000	28,622	**41.5%**	3.5								
CALIFORNIA																			
COLORADO																			
CONNECTICUT	102,000	31,624	**31.0%**	107,000	32,704	**30.6%**	-0.4	112,000	43,917	**39.2%**	8.2	118,000	33,921	**28.7%**	-2.3	125,000	50,541	**40.4%**	9.4
DELAWARE																			
DISTRICT OF COLUMBIA																			
FLORIDA	13,000	4,628	**35.6%**	16,000	6,208	**38.8%**	3.2	17,000	6,994	**41.1%**	5.5					38,000	7,731	**20.3%**	-15.3

State Gubernatorial General Elections (continued)

Democratic Turnout for Election Years 1852–1868 (continued)

State	1852			1856				1860				1864				1868			
	Voting-age population	Turnout	%	Voting-age population	Turnout	%	Difference from 1852	Voting-age population	Turnout	%	Difference from 1852	Voting-age population	Turnout	%	Difference from 1852	Voting-age population	Turnout	%	Difference from 1852
GEORGIA																232,000	76,539	33.0%	
HAWAII																			
IDAHO																			
ILLINOIS	239,000	80,789	33.8%	315,000	106,769	33.9%	0.1	392,000	159,253	40.6%	6.8	453,000	158,701	35.0%	1.2	515,000	199,813	38.8%	5.0
INDIANA	230,000	97,959	40.4%	266,000	117,981	44.4%	3.9	302,000	126,768	42.0%	1.6	330,000	131,200	39.8%	-0.7	364,000	170,602	46.9%	6.5
IOWA																			
KANSAS																88,000	13,809	15.7%	
KENTUCKY																			
LOUISIANA	79,000	17,529	22.2%									78,000	2,959	3.8%	-18.4				
MAINE	146,000	41,616	28.5%	149,000	44,912	30.1%	1.6	151,000	52,350	34.7%	6.2	152,000	46,403	30.5%	2.0	153,000	56,207	36.7%	8.2
MARYLAND												123,000	32,068	26.1%					
MASSACHUSETTS	270,000	38,763	14.4%	276,000	40,077	14.6%	0.2	282,000	35,191	12.5%	1.9	293,000	49,190	16.8%	2.4	306,000	63,266	20.7%	6.3
MICHIGAN	116,000	42,791	36.9%	148,000	54,085	36.5%	-0.3	181,000	67,221	37.1%	0.2	225,000	74,293	33.0%	-3.9	258,000	97,290	37.7%	0.8
MINNESOTA																			
MISSISSIPPI																			
MISSOURI	163,000	46,494	28.5%	206,000	47,066	22.8%	-5.7	250,000	74,446	29.8%	1.3	295,000	31,074	10.5%	-18.0	362,000	62,780	17.3%	-11.2
MONTANA																			
NEBRASKA																31,000	6,349	20.5%	
NEVADA												17,000	6,555	38.6%					
NEW HAMPSHIRE	85,000	30,747	36.2%	85,000	32,031	37.7%	1.5	84,000	33,544	39.9%	3.8	84,000	31,340	37.3%	1.1	84,000	37,260	44.4%	8.2
NEW JERSEY				132,000	48,246	36.6%													
NEW MEXICO																			
NEW YORK	818,000	264,121	32.3%	856,000	198,616	23.2%	-9.1	892,000	294,812	33.1%	0.8	924,000	361,264	39.1%	6.8	966,000	439,301	45.5%	13.2
NORTH CAROLINA	120,000	48,484	40.4%	128,000	57,698	45.1%	4.7	136,000	59,463	43.7%	3.3	136,000	58,070	42.7%	2.3	214,000	73,594	34.4%	-6.0
NORTH DAKOTA																			
OHIO																			
OKLAHOMA																			
OREGON																			
PENNSYLVANIA								635,000	230,230	36.3%									
RHODE ISLAND	38,000	9,184	24.2%	37,000	7,158	19.3%	-4.8	37,000	12,278	33.2%	9.0	39,000	7,312	18.7%	-5.4	43,000	5,709	13.3%	-10.9
SOUTH CAROLINA																148,000	23,087	15.6%	
SOUTH DAKOTA																			
TENNESSEE																			

State Gubernatorial General Elections (continued)

State Gubernatorial General Elections (continued)

Democratic Turnout for Election Years 1852–1868 (continued)

State	1852 Voting-age population	Turnout	%	1856 Voting-age population	Turnout	%	Difference from 1852	1860 Voting-age population	Turnout	%	Difference from 1852	1864 Voting-age population	Turnout	%	Difference from 1852	1868 Voting-age population	Turnout	%	Difference from 1852
TEXAS																			
UTAH																			
VERMONT	80,000	15,001	18.8%	77,000	11,747	15.3%	-3.5	75,000	11,795	15.7%	-3.0	74,000	12,637	17.1%	-1.7	75,000	15,289	20.4%	1.6
VIRGINIA																			
WASHINGTON																			
WEST VIRGINIA																90,000	22,250	24.7%	
WISCONSIN																			
WYOMING																			
Total	2,541,000	780,662	30.7%	2,854,000	833,457	29.2%	-1.5	3,615,000	1,236,884	34.2%	3.5	3,341,000	1,036,987	31.0%	0.3	4,092,000	1,421,417	34.7%	4.0

Other Turnout for Election Years 1852–1868

State	1852 Voting-age population	Turnout	%	1856 Voting-age population	Turnout	%	Difference from 1852	1860 Voting-age population	Turnout	%	Difference from 1852	1864 Voting-age population	Turnout	%	Difference from 1852	1868 Voting-age population	Turnout	%	Difference from 1852
ARKANSAS				57,000	15,436	27.1%		69,000	31,578	45.8%	18.7	71,000	25	0.0%	27.0				
CONNECTICUT				107,000	26,008	24.3%		112,000	10	0.0%	-24.3	118,000	247	0.2%	-24.1	125,000	7	0.0%	-24.3
FLORIDA				16,000	5,894	36.8%		17,000	5,248	30.9%	-6.0					38,000	2,251	5.9%	-30.9
ILLINOIS	239,000	9,024	3.8%	315,000	19,078	6.1%	2.3	392,000	3,675	0.9%	-2.8								
KANSAS												59,000	8,448	14.3%					
LOUISIANA												78,000	2,225	2.9%		163,000	38,118	23.4%	20.5
MAINE	146,000	21,589	14.8%	149,000	6,664	4.5%	-10.3	151,000	1,755	1.2%	-13.6					153,000	52	0.0%	-14.8
MASSACHUSETTS	270,000	36,740	13.6%	275,000	102,852	37.4%	23.8	282,000	29,891	10.6%	-3.0	293,000	69	0.0%	-13.6	306,000	84	0.0%	-13.6
MICHIGAN	116,000	5,880	5.1%																
MISSOURI				206,000	68,235	33.1%		250,000	75,998	30.4%	-2.7								
NEBRASKA																31,000	1	0.0%	
NEW HAMPSHIRE	85,000	9,483	11.2%	85,000	32,119	37.8%	26.6	84,000	22	0.0%	-11.1	84,000	79	0.1%	-11.1	84,000	30	0.0%	-11.1
NEW JERSEY				132,000	50,803	38.5%													
NEW YORK				856,000	130,870	15.3%		892,000	19,841	2.2%	-13.1								
NORTH CAROLINA				128,000	44,970	35.1%		136,000	53,123	39.1%	3.9	136,000	14,491	10.7%	-24.5				
RHODE ISLAND								37,000	139	0.4%		39,000	1,392	3.6%	3.2	43,000	6	0.0%	-0.4
SOUTH CAROLINA																148,000	170	0.1%	
VERMONT	80,000	9,445	11.8%					75,000	2,118	2.8%	-9.0	74,000	113	0.2%	-11.7	75,000	74	0.1%	-11.7
Total	936,000	92,161	9.8%	2,326,000	502,929	21.6%	11.8	2,497,000	223,398	8.9%	-0.9	952,000	27,089	2.8%	-7.0	1,166,000	40,793	3.5%	-6.3

*The Whig party had all but disappeared by 1855 and was replaced by Republicans by 1856. Any Whig votes tallied in 1856 are included in "Other," but the majority of "Other" votes in 1856 are the American ("Know-Nothing") Party.

**Percentage point difference between turnout in current year and initial year listed in chart. If data do not appear for a state in the initial year listed, the difference is calculated from the first year in which data do appear for that state.

***Rhode Island's Whig governor from 1852, William W. Hoppin, changed to the American Party in 1856 but was also listed for the Republican party, whose convention he attended that year.

UNITED STATES HOUSE OF REPRESENTATIVES GENERAL ELECTIONS

Election Years 1852–1868

State	1852 Voting-age population	Turnout	%	1856 Voting-age population	Turnout	%	Difference from 1852*	1860 Voting-age population	Turnout	%	Difference from 1852	1864 Voting-age population	Turnout	%	Difference from 1852	1868 Voting-age population	Turnout	%	Difference from 1852
ALABAMA																203,000	66,125	32.6%	
ALASKA																			
ARIZONA																			
ARKANSAS				57,000	42,096	73.9%		69,000	60,217	87.3%	13.4					100,000	41,115	41.1%	-32.7
CALIFORNIA	85,000	73,780	86.8%	107,000	72,428	67.7%	-19.1	128,000	118,812	92.8%	6.0	135,000	105,084	77.8%	-9.0	141,000	108,421	76.9%	-9.9
COLORADO																			
CONNECTICUT								112,000	83,753	74.8%		118,000	73,183	62.0%	-12.8	125,000	89,293	71.4%	-3.3
DELAWARE	18,000	13,322	74.0%	19,000	14,471	76.2%	2.2	21,000	15,978	76.1%	2.1	22,000	17,015	77.3%	3.3	27,000	18,597	68.9%	-5.1
DISTRICT OF COLUMBIA																			
FLORIDA	13,000	9,158	70.4%	16,000	12,042	75.3%	4.8	17,000	12,894	75.8%	5.4					38,000	17,279	45.5%	-25.0
GEORGIA																232,000	145,371	62.7%	
HAWAII																			
IDAHO																			
ILLINOIS	239,000	151,334	63.3%	315,000	230,531	73.2%	9.9	392,000	334,292	85.3%	22.0	453,000	349,010	77.0%	13.7	515,000	449,283	87.2%	23.9
INDIANA	230,000	167,352	72.8%	266,000	229,580	86.3%	13.5	302,000	262,098	86.8%	14.0	330,000	281,053	85.2%	12.4	364,000	341,326	93.8%	21.0
IOWA	68,000	32,474	47.8%	109,000	73,754	67.7%	19.9	152,000	128,187	84.3%	36.6	195,000	138,304	70.9%	23.2	237,000	194,222	82.0%	34.2
KANSAS												59,000	20,532	34.8%		88,000	43,293	49.2%	14.4
KENTUCKY								207,000	130,131	62.9%		220,000	111,683	50.8%	-12.1	277,000	148,280	53.5%	-9.3
LOUISIANA																163,000	70,683	43.4%	
MAINE	146,000	93,177	63.8%	149,000	119,837	80.4%	16.6	151,000	123,357	81.7%	17.9	152,000	112,140	73.8%	10.0	153,000	131,189	85.7%	21.9
MARYLAND								116,000	67,178	57.9%		123,000	72,370	58.8%	0.9	167,000	91,705	54.9%	-3.0
MASSACHUSETTS	270,000	129,309	47.9%	275,000	161,215	58.6%	10.7	282,000	167,446	59.4%	11.5	293,000	174,414	59.5%	11.6	306,000	193,372	63.2%	15.3
MICHIGAN	116,000	82,038	70.7%	148,000	125,148	84.6%	13.8	181,000	154,779	85.5%	14.8	225,000	164,034	72.9%	2.2	258,000	225,481	87.4%	16.7
MINNESOTA								39,000	35,288	90.5%		66,000	42,142	63.9%	-26.6	92,000	71,404	77.6%	-12.9
MISSISSIPPI																170,000	113,234	66.6%	
MISSOURI	163,000	81,162	49.8%	206,000	121,443	59.0%	9.2	250,000	155,934	62.4%	12.6	295,000	95,543	32.4%	-17.4	362,000	143,818	39.7%	-10.1
MONTANA																			
NEBRASKA																31,000	15,042	48.5%	
NEVADA												17,000	16,328	96.0%		18,000	11,579	64.3%	-31.7
NEW HAMPSHIRE								84,000	66,969	79.7%		84,000	66,268	78.9%	-0.8	84,000	66,973	79.7%	0.0
NEW JERSEY	120,000	83,632	69.7%	132,000	98,804	74.9%	5.2	146,000	121,855	83.5%	13.8	163,000	129,353	79.4%	9.7	186,000	162,489	87.4%	17.7
NEW MEXICO																			
NEW YORK	818,000	517,911	63.3%	856,000	590,560	69.0%	5.7	892,000	670,131	75.1%	11.8	924,000	714,840	77.4%	14.0	966,000	840,082	87.0%	23.7

United States House of Representatives General Elections (continued)

United States House of Representatives General Elections *(continued)*

Election Years 1852–1868 *(continued)*

State	1852			1856				1860				1864				1868			
	Voting-age population	Turnout	%	Voting-age population	Turnout	%	Difference from 1852	Voting-age population	Turnout	%	Difference from 1852	Voting-age population	Turnout	%	Difference from 1852	Voting-age population	Turnout	%	Difference from 1852
NORTH CAROLINA																214,000	160,517	75.0%	
NORTH DAKOTA																			
OHIO	465,000	296,268	63.7%	491,000	354,913	72.3%	8.6	516,000	409,753	79.4%	15.7	542,000	417,517	77.0%	13.3	580,000	515,079	88.8%	25.1
OKLAHOMA																			
OREGON**								16,000	4,250	26.6%		20,000	14,815	74.1%	47.5	23,000	29,946	130.2%	103.6
PENNSYLVANIA	559,000	327,608	58.6%	597,000	421,005	70.5%	11.9	635,000	481,392	75.8%	17.2	688,000	498,103	72.4%	13.8	753,000	652,017	86.6%	28.0
RHODE ISLAND								37,000	21,951	59.3%		39,000	9,712	24.9%	-34.4	43,000	18,691	43.5%	-15.9
SOUTH CAROLINA				62,000	12,796	20.6%										148,000	107,427	72.6%	51.9
SOUTH DAKOTA																			
TENNESSEE																255,000	55,859	21.9%	
TEXAS																163,000	76,107	46.7%	
UTAH																			
VERMONT	80,000	41,997	52.5%	77,000	42,574	55.3%	2.8	75,000	42,221	56.3%	3.8	74,000	42,650	57.6%	5.1	75,000	54,396	72.5%	20.0
VIRGINIA																282,000	217,923	77.3%	
WASHINGTON																			
WEST VIRGINIA												88,000	21,880	24.9%		90,000	48,983	54.4%	29.6
WISCONSIN	101,000	64,427	63.8%	136,000	119,924	88.2%	24.4	168,000	151,924	90.4%	26.6	184,000	143,569	78.0%	14.2	196,000	193,340	98.6%	34.9
WYOMING																			
Total	3,491,000	2,164,949	62.0%	4,018,000	2,843,121	70.8%	8.7	4,988,000	3,820,790	76.6%	14.6	5,509,000	3,831,542	69.6%	7.5	8,125,000	5,929,941	73.0%	11.0

*Overall primary turnout reflects only states with primaries in both parties. To find single party primary results, see partisan primary charts.

**Oregon 1868 turnout is verified by reliable sources; error is likely with voting-age population, which is an estimate. See "Methodology" section in Introduction.

UNITED STATES HOUSE OF REPRESENTATIVES GENERAL ELECTIONS

Republican Turnout for Election Years 1852–1868

State	1852 (Whig) Voting-age population	Turnout	%	1856* Voting-age population	Turnout	%	Difference from 1852**	1860 Voting-age population	Turnout	%	Difference from 1852	1864 Voting-age population	Turnout	%	Difference from 1852	1868 Voting-age population	Turnout	%	Difference from 1852
ALABAMA																203,000	60,605	29.9%	
ALASKA																			
ARIZONA																			
ARKANSAS																100,000	22,030	22.0%	
CALIFORNIA	85,000	34,241	40.3%	107,000	21,575	20.2%	-20.1	128,000	51,651	40.4%	0.1	135,000	62,039	46.0%	5.7	141,000	53,873	38.2%	-2.1
COLORADO																			
CONNECTICUT								112,000	42,465	37.9%		118,000	42,168	35.7%	-2.2	125,000	45,846	36.7%	-1.2
DELAWARE	18,000	6,630	36.8%									22,000	8,253	37.5%	0.7	27,000	7,636	28.3%	-8.6
DISTRICT OF COLUMBIA																			
FLORIDA	13,000	4,568	35.1%													38,000	9,749	25.7%	-9.5
GEORGIA																232,000	81,380	35.1%	
HAWAII																			
IDAHO																			
ILLINOIS	239,000	62,158	26.0%	315,000	118,342	37.6%	11.6	392,000	173,301	44.2%	18.2	453,000	190,226	42.0%	16.0	515,000	249,422	48.4%	22.4
INDIANA	230,000	76,056	33.1%	266,000	111,675	42.0%	8.9	302,000	137,531	45.5%	12.5	330,000	148,748	45.1%	12.0	364,000	170,446	46.8%	13.8
IOWA	68,000	15,651	23.0%	109,000	39,950	36.7%	13.6	152,000	70,741	46.5%	23.5	195,000	88,942	45.6%	22.6	237,000	117,831	49.7%	26.7
KANSAS												59,000	20,532	34.8%		88,000	29,324	33.3%	-1.5
KENTUCKY								207,000	92,365	44.6%						277,000	35,921	13.0%	-31.7
LOUISIANA																163,000	27,563	16.9%	
MAINE	146,000	40,735	27.9%	149,000	69,849	46.9%	19.0	151,000	69,286	45.9%	18.0	152,000	65,502	43.1%	15.2	153,000	74,926	49.0%	21.1
MARYLAND								116,000	50,821	43.8%		123,000	40,448	32.9%	-10.9	167,000	30,079	18.0%	-25.8
MASSACHUSETTS	270,000	57,335	21.2%	275,000	98,716	35.9%	14.7	282,000	103,495	36.7%	15.5	293,000	125,917	43.0%	21.7	306,000	133,494	43.6%	22.4
MICHIGAN	116,000	37,654	32.5%	148,000	71,723	48.5%	16.0	181,000	88,280	48.8%	16.3	225,000	91,052	40.5%	8.0	258,000	126,166	48.9%	16.4
MINNESOTA								39,000	22,333	57.3%		66,000	24,839	37.6%	-19.6	92,000	43,317	47.1%	-10.2
MISSISSIPPI																170,000	73,959	43.5%	
MISSOURI	163,000	35,196	21.6%					250,000	11,453	4.6%	-17.0	295,000	68,881	23.3%	1.8	362,000	81,843	22.6%	1.0
MONTANA																			
NEBRASKA																31,000	8,724	28.1%	
NEVADA												17,000	9,776	57.5%		18,000	6,230	34.6%	-22.9
NEW HAMPSHIRE								84,000	35,596	42.4%		84,000	35,583	42.4%	0.0	84,000	35,512	42.3%	-0.1
NEW JERSEY	120,000	38,270	31.9%	132,000	43,525	33.0%	1.1	146,000	60,403	41.4%	9.5	163,000	61,745	37.9%	6.0	186,000	79,467	42.7%	10.8
NEW MEXICO																			
NEW YORK	818,000	249,589	30.5%	856,000	273,448	31.9%	1.4	892,000	359,067	40.3%	9.7	924,000	360,593	39.0%	8.5	966,000	412,176	42.7%	12.2

United States House of Representatives General Elections (continued)

United States House of Representatives General Elections *(continued)*

Republican Turnout for Election Years 1852–1868 *(continued)*

State	1852 (Whig)			1856				1860				1864				1868			
	Voting-age population	Turnout	%	Voting-age population	Turnout	%	Difference from 1852	Voting-age population	Turnout	%	Difference from 1852	Voting-age population	Turnout	%	Difference from 1852	Voting-age population	Turnout	%	Difference from 1852
NORTH CAROLINA																214,000	86,107	40.2%	
NORTH DAKOTA																			
OHIO	465,000	127,536	27.4%	491,000	178,854	36.4%	9.0	516,000	218,564	42.4%	14.9	542,000	234,804	43.3%	15.9	580,000	264,031	45.5%	18.1
OKLAHOMA																			
OREGON												20,000	8,759	43.8%		23,000	20,187	87.8%	44.0
PENNSYLVANIA	559,000	136,519	24.4%	597,000	16,971	2.8%	-21.6	635,000	260,997	41.1%	16.7	688,000	245,405	35.7%	11.2	753,000	329,736	43.8%	19.4
RHODE ISLAND								37,000	21,951	59.3%		39,000	8,373	21.5%	-37.9	43,000	12,206	28.4%	-30.9
SOUTH CAROLINA																148,000	61,885	41.8%	
SOUTH DAKOTA																			
TENNESSEE																255,000	55,859	21.9%	
TEXAS																163,000	44,138	27.1%	
UTAH																			
VERMONT	80,000	21,388	26.7%	77,000	32,935	42.8%	16.0	75,000	31,149	41.5%	14.8	74,000	30,950	41.8%	15.1	75,000	40,511	54.0%	27.3
VIRGINIA																282,000	100,424	35.6%	
WASHINGTON																			
WEST VIRGINIA												88,000	15,307	17.4%		90,000	26,931	29.9%	12.5
WISCONSIN	101,000	21,199	21.0%	136,000	66,315	48.8%	27.8	168,000	86,422	51.4%	30.5	184,000	80,079	43.5%	22.5	196,000	107,738	55.0%	34.0
WYOMING																			
Total	3,491,000	964,725	27.6%	3,658,000	1,143,878	31.3%	3.6	4,865,000	1,987,871	40.9%	13.2	5,289,000	2,068,921	39.1%	11.5	8,125,000	3,167,272	39.0%	11.3

Democratic Turnout for Election Years 1852–1868

State	1852			1856				1860				1864				1868			
	Voting-age population	Turnout	%	Voting-age population	Turnout	%	Difference from 1852	Voting-age population	Turnout	%	Difference from 1852	Voting-age population	Turnout	%	Difference from 1852	Voting-age population	Turnout	%	Difference from 1852
ALABAMA																			
ALASKA																			
ARIZONA																			
ARKANSAS				57,000	27,234	47.8%		69,000	33,058	47.9%	0.1					100,000	19,085	19.1%	-28.7
CALIFORNIA	85,000	39,539	46.5%	107,000	50,853	47.5%	1.0	128,000	67,161	52.5%	6.0	135,000	43,045	31.9%	-14.6	141,000	54,548	38.7%	-7.8
COLORADO																			
CONNECTICUT								112,000	41,288	36.9%		118,000	31,015	26.3%	-10.6	125,000	43,447	34.8%	-2.1
DELAWARE	18,000	6,692	37.2%	19,000	8,111	42.7%	5.5	21,000	8,246	39.3%	2.1	22,000	8,762	39.8%	2.6	27,000	10,961	40.6%	3.4
DISTRICT OF COLUMBIA																			
FLORIDA	13,000	4,590	35.3%	16,000	6,392	40.0%	4.6	17,000	7,722	45.4%	10.1					38,000	6,653	17.5%	-17.8

United States House of Representatives General Elections *(continued)*

Democratic Turnout for Election Years 1852–1868 *(continued)*

State	1852 Voting-age population	Turnout	%	1856 Voting-age population	Turnout	%	Difference from 1852	1860 Voting-age population	Turnout	%	Difference from 1852	1864 Voting-age population	Turnout	%	Difference from 1852	1868 Voting-age population	Turnout	%	Difference from 1852
GEORGIA																232,000	63,991	27.6%	
HAWAII																			
IDAHO																			
ILLINOIS	239,000	81,734	34.2%	315,000	109,958	34.9%	0.7	392,000	160,832	41.0%	6.8	453,000	158,784	35.1%	0.9	515,000	199,861	38.8%	4.6
INDIANA	230,000	89,778	39.0%	266,000	117,905	44.3%	5.3	302,000	124,259	41.1%	2.1	330,000	132,305	40.1%	1.1	364,000	170,880	46.9%	7.9
IOWA	68,000	16,823	24.7%	109,000	32,978	30.3%	5.5	152,000	57,446	37.8%	13.1	195,000	49,362	25.3%	0.6	237,000	76,242	32.2%	7.4
KANSAS																88,000	13,969	15.9%	
KENTUCKY																277,000	112,066	40.5%	
LOUISIANA																163,000	43,120	26.5%	
MAINE	146,000	47,272	32.4%	149,000	49,988	33.5%	1.2	151,000	52,833	35.0%	2.6	152,000	46,638	30.7%	-1.7	153,000	56,263	36.8%	4.4
MARYLAND												123,000	31,922	26.0%		167,000	61,626	36.9%	10.9
MASSACHUSETTS	270,000	37,766	14.0%	275,000	33,530	12.2%	-1.8	282,000	49,720	17.6%	3.6	293,000	48,497	16.6%	2.6	306,000	59,878	19.6%	5.6
MICHIGAN	116,000	41,662	35.9%	148,000	53,425	36.1%	0.2	181,000	66,172	36.6%	0.6	225,000	72,982	32.4%	-3.5	258,000	99,315	38.5%	2.6
MINNESOTA								39,000	12,955	33.2%		66,000	17,303	26.2%	-7.0	92,000	28,087	30.5%	-2.7
MISSISSIPPI																170,000	35,428	20.8%	
MISSOURI	163,000	45,966	28.2%	206,000	64,772	31.4%	3.2	250,000	86,402	34.6%	6.4	295,000	26,662	9.0%	-19.2	362,000	61,975	17.1%	-11.1
MONTANA																			
NEBRASKA																31,000	6,318	20.4%	
NEVADA												17,000	6,552	38.5%		18,000	5,349	29.7%	-8.8
NEW HAMPSHIRE								84,000	31,373	37.3%		84,000	30,185	35.9%	-1.4	84,000	31,461	37.5%	0.1
NEW JERSEY	120,000	44,323	36.9%	132,000	47,141	35.7%	-1.2	146,000	61,452	42.1%	5.2	163,000	67,608	41.5%	4.5	186,000	83,022	44.6%	7.7
NEW MEXICO																			
NEW YORK	818,000	245,829	30.1%	856,000	203,761	23.8%	-6.2	892,000	310,920	34.9%	4.0	924,000	353,936	38.3%	8.3	966,000	425,323	44.0%	14.0
NORTH CAROLINA																			
NORTH DAKOTA																			
OHIO	465,000	144,063	31.0%	491,000	156,654	31.9%	0.9	516,000	184,921	35.8%	4.9	542,000	182,713	33.7%	2.7	580,000	251,048	43.3%	12.3
OKLAHOMA																			
OREGON								16,000	4,230	26.4%		20,000	6,056	30.3%	3.8	23,000	9,759	42.4%	16.0
PENNSYLVANIA	559,000	177,639	31.8%	597,000	211,480	35.4%	3.6	635,000	212,871	33.5%	1.7	688,000	252,698	36.7%	5.0	753,000	322,281	42.8%	11.0
RHODE ISLAND												39,000	1,286	3.3%		43,000	6,485	15.1%	11.8
SOUTH CAROLINA				62,000	12,454	20.1%										148,000	45,186	30.5%	10.4
SOUTH DAKOTA																			
TENNESSEE																			

United States House of Representatives General Elections *(continued)*

Democratic Turnout for Election Years 1852–1868 *(continued)*

State	1852			1856				1860				1864				1868			
	Voting-age population	Turnout	%	Voting-age population	Turnout	%	Difference from 1852	Voting-age population	Turnout	%	Difference from 1852	Voting-age population	Turnout	%	Difference from 1852	Voting-age population	Turnout	%	Difference from 1852
TEXAS																163,000	31,588	19.4%	
UTAH																			
VERMONT	80,000	11,935	14.9%	77,000	9,250	12.0%	-2.9	75,000	11,072	14.8%	-0.2	74,000	11,700	15.8%	0.9	75,000	13,885	18.5%	3.6
VIRGINIA																			
WASHINGTON																			
WEST VIRGINIA																90,000	22,052	24.5%	
WISCONSIN	101,000	33,832	33.5%	136,000	53,609	39.4%	5.9	168,000	65,502	39.0%	5.5	184,000	63,490	34.5%	1.0	196,000	85,602	43.7%	10.2
WYOMING																			
Total	3,491,000	1,069,443	30.6%	4,018,000	1,249,495	31.1%	0.5	4,628,000	1,650,435	35.7%	5.0	5,142,000	1,643,501	32.0%	1.3	7,171,000	2,556,754	35.7%	5.0

Other Turnout for Election Years 1852–1868

State	1852			1856				1860				1864				1868			
	Voting-age population	Turnout	%	Voting-age population	Turnout	%	Difference from 1852	Voting-age population	Turnout	%	Difference from 1852	Voting-age population	Turnout	%	Difference from 1852	Voting-age population	Turnout	%	Difference from 1852
ALABAMA																203,000	5,520	2.7%	
ALASKA																			
ARIZONA																			
ARKANSAS				57,000	14,862	26.1%		69,000	27,159	39.4%	13.3								
CALIFORNIA																			
COLORADO																			
CONNECTICUT																			
DELAWARE				19,000	6,360	33.5%		21,000	7,732	36.8%	3.3								
DISTRICT OF COLUMBIA																			
FLORIDA				16,000	5,650	35.3%		17,000	5,172	30.4%	-4.9					38,000	877	2.3%	-33.0
GEORGIA																			
HAWAII																			
IDAHO																			
ILLINOIS	239,000	7,442	3.1%	315,000	2,231	0.7%	-2.4	392,000	159	0.0%	-3.1								
INDIANA	230,000	1,518	0.7%					302,000	308	0.1%	-0.6								
IOWA				109,000	826	0.8%										237,000	149	0.1%	-0.7
KANSAS																			
KENTUCKY								207,000	37,766	18.2%		220,000	111,683	50.8%	32.5	277,000	293	0.1%	-18.1
LOUISIANA																			
MAINE	146,000	5,170	3.5%					151,000	1,238	0.8%	-2.7								

United States House of Representatives General Elections (continued)

Other Turnout for Election Years 1852–1868 (continued)

State	1852 Voting-age population	Turnout	%	1856 Voting-age population	Turnout	%	Difference from 1852	1860 Voting-age population	Turnout	%	Difference from 1852	1864 Voting-age population	Turnout	%	Difference from 1852	1868 Voting-age population	Turnout	%	Difference from 1852
MARYLAND								116,000	16,357	14.1%									
MASSACHUSETTS	270,000	34,208	12.7%	275,000	28,969	10.5%	-2.1	282,000	14,231	5.0%	-7.6								
MICHIGAN	116,000	2,722	2.3%					181,000	327	0.2%	-2.2								
MINNESOTA																			
MISSISSIPPI																170,000	3,847	2.3%	
MISSOURI				206,000	56,671	27.5%		250,000	58,079	23.2%	-4.3								
MONTANA																			
NEBRASKA																			
NEVADA																			
NEW HAMPSHIRE												84,000	500	0.6%					
NEW JERSEY	120,000	1,039	0.9%	132,000	8,138	6.2%	5.3												
NEW MEXICO																			
NEW YORK	818,000	22,493	2.7%	856,000	113,351	13.2%	10.5	892,000	144	0.0%	-2.7	924,000	311	0.0%	-2.7	966,000	2,583	0.3%	-2.5
NORTH CAROLINA																214,000	74,410	34.8%	
NORTH DAKOTA																			
OHIO	465,000	24,669	5.3%	491,000	19,405	4.0%	-1.4	516,000	6,268	1.2%	-4.1								
OKLAHOMA																			
OREGON								16,000	20	0.1%									
PENNSYLVANIA	559,000	13,450	2.4%	597,000	192,554	32.3%	29.8	635,000	7,524	1.2%	-1.2								
RHODE ISLAND												39,000	53	0.1%					
SOUTH CAROLINA				62,000	342	0.6%										148,000	356	0.2%	-0.3
SOUTH DAKOTA																			
TENNESSEE																			
TEXAS																163,000	381	0.2%	
UTAH																			
VERMONT	80,000	8,674	10.8%	77,000	389	0.5%	-10.3												
VIRGINIA																282,000	117,499	41.7%	
WASHINGTON																			
WEST VIRGINIA												88,000	6,573	7.5%					
WISCONSIN	101,000	9,396	9.3%																
WYOMING																			
Total	3,240,000	130,781	4.0%	3,212,000	449,748	14.0%	10.0	4,047,000	182,484	4.5%	0.5	1,355,000	119,120	8.8%	4.8	2,698,000	205,915	7.6%	3.6

*By 1856, the Republicans had supplanted the Whigs as the second party opposed to the Democrats. Remaining Whig votes in 1856 are included under "Other," but the majority of "Other" votes in 1856 are the American ("Know-Nothing") Party.

**Percentage point difference between turnout in current year and initial year listed in chart. If data do not appear for a state in the initial year listed, the difference is calculated from the first year in which data do appear for that state.

Midterm Turnout Election Based on Highest Statewide Turnout, Election Years 1850–1866

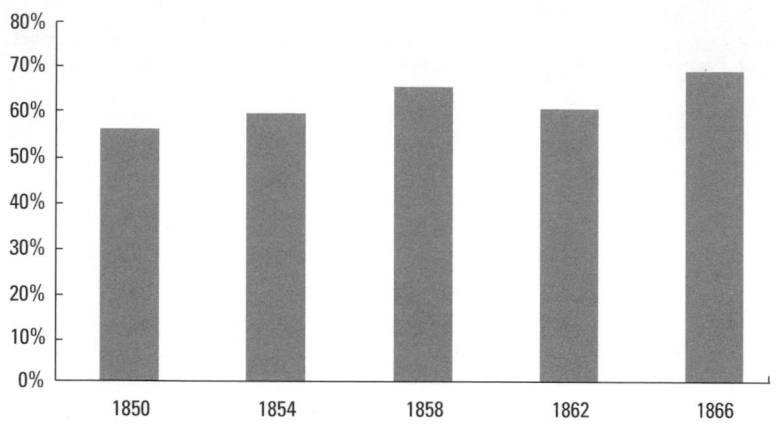

YEAR	VOTING-AGE POPULATION	TOTAL	%
1850	3,464,000	1,919,079	55.4%
1854	4,158,000	2,447,712	58.9%
1858	4,472,000	2,899,053	64.8%
1862	5,526,000	3,315,318	60.0%
1866	6,089,000	4,171,513	68.5%

Partisan Turnout Midterm Election Based on Aggregate House of Representatives Turnout, Election Years 1850–1866

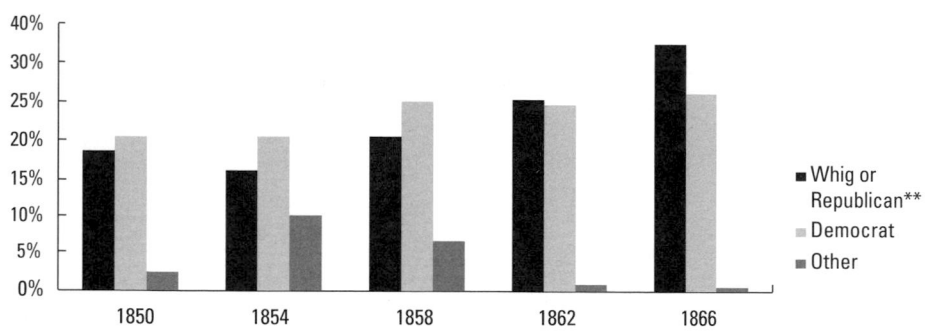

- Whig or Republican**
- Democrat
- Other

YEAR	VOTING-AGE POPULATION*	WHIG OR REPUBLICAN** TURNOUT	%	DEMOCRAT TURNOUT	%	OTHER TURNOUT	%
1850	3,464,000	724,758	20.9%	800,320	23.1%	95,325	2.8%
1854	4,158,000	750,724	18.1%	963,294	23.2%	470,738	11.3%
1858	4,472,000	1,037,192	23.2%	1,273,814	28.5%	335,791	7.5%
1862	5,526,000	1,590,669	28.8%	1,546,915	28.0%	56,430	1.0%
1866	6,089,000	2,265,155	37.2%	1,809,747	29.7%	38,369	0.6%

*Voting-age population taken from all states with statewide elections. For percentages based on only states with House elections, see House partisan chart.

**1850 data is from Whig party; 1858-1866 is from Republican; 1854 is a combination of the two: see House partisan chart for more detail.

STATE GUBERNATORIAL GENERAL ELECTIONS

Election Years 1850–1866

| State | 1850 | | | 1854 | | | | 1858 | | | | 1862 | | | | 1866 | | | |
	Voting-age population	Turnout	%	Voting-age population	Turnout	%	Difference from 1850**	Voting-age population	Turnout	%	Difference from 1852	Voting-age population	Turnout	%	Difference from 1850	Voting-age population	Turnout	%	Difference from 1850
ALABAMA																			
ALASKA																			
ARIZONA																			
ARKANSAS												69,000	26,316	38.1%					
CALIFORNIA																			
COLORADO																			
CONNECTICUT	99,000	57,231	57.8%	104,000	58,675	56.4%	-1.4	109,000	78,616	72.1%	14.3	115,000	70,430	61.2%	3.4	120,000	87,417	72.8%	15.0
DELAWARE	17,000	11,979	70.5%	19,000	13,185	69.4%	-1.1	20,000	15,312	76.6%	6.1	21,000	16,199	77.1%	6.7	22,000	18,408	83.7%	13.2
DISTRICT OF COLUMBIA																			
FLORIDA																			
GEORGIA																			
HAWAII																			
IDAHO																			
ILLINOIS																			
INDIANA																			
IOWA	47,000	24,889	53.0%	88,000	44,504	50.6%	-2.4												
KANSAS												45,000	15,553	34.6%		72,000	27,522	38.2%	3.7
KENTUCKY																			
LOUISIANA																			
MAINE	145,000	80,799	55.7%	148,000	87,116	58.9%	3.1	151,000	113,296	75.0%	19.3	152,000	81,718	53.8%	-2.0	152,000	111,892	73.6%	17.9
MARYLAND	104,000	71,198	68.5%																
MASSACHUSETTS	266,000	120,437	45.3%	272,000	122,524	45.0%	-0.2	278,000	119,082	42.8%	-2.4	287,000	134,155	46.7%	1.5	299,000	118,751	39.7%	-5.6
MICHIGAN				132,000	82,328	62.4%		163,000	121,261	74.4%	12.0	203,000	130,818	64.4%	2.1	246,000	164,454	66.9%	4.5
MINNESOTA																			
MISSISSIPPI																			
MISSOURI																			
MONTANA																			
NEBRASKA																27,000	8,098	30.0%	
NEVADA																18,000	9,230	51.3%	
NEW HAMPSHIRE	85,000	55,626	65.4%	85,000	57,897	68.1%	2.7	85,000	67,905	79.9%	14.4	83,000	62,470	75.3%	9.8	83,000	65,638	79.1%	13.6
NEW JERSEY	114,000	73,777	64.7%																
NEW MEXICO																			
NEW YORK	799,000	428,966	53.7%	837,000	469,431	56.1%	2.4	874,000	539,334	61.7%	8.0	908,000	603,038	66.4%	12.7	939,000	719,195	76.6%	22.9

State Gubernatorial General Elections (continued)

State Gubernatorial General Elections (continued)

Election Years 1850–1866 (continued)

State	1850 Voting-age population	Turnout	%	1854 Voting-age population	Turnout	%	Difference from 1850	1858 Voting-age population	Turnout	%	Difference from 1850	1862 Voting-age population	Turnout	%	Difference from 1850	1866 Voting-age population	Turnout	%	Difference from 1850
NORTH CAROLINA	117,000	87,399	74.7%	125,000	95,349	76.3%	1.6	132,000	96,465	73.1%	-1.6	135,000	76,095	56.4%	-18.3	136,000	45,126	33.2%	-41.5
NORTH DAKOTA																			
OHIO	451,000	267,945	59.4%																
OKLAHOMA																			
OREGON								14,000	9,347	66.8%		18,000	10,479	58.2%	-8.5	23,000	20,355	88.5%	21.7
PENNSYLVANIA				578,000	370,813	64.2%										715,000	597,370	83.5%	19.4
RHODE ISLAND	38,000	4,390	11.6%	37,000	15,596	42.2%	30.6	37,000	11,506	31.1%	19.5	39,000	11,264	28.9%	17.3	41,000	10,681	26.1%	14.5
SOUTH CAROLINA																			
SOUTH DAKOTA																			
TENNESSEE																			
TEXAS*																			
UTAH																			
VERMONT	82,000	48,377	59.0%	79,000	42,941	54.4%	-4.6	76,000	42,998	56.6%	-2.4	75,000	33,392	44.5%	-14.5	74,000	45,412	61.4%	2.4
VIRGINIA												214,000	14,948	7.0%					
WASHINGTON																			
WEST VIRGINIA																89,000	40,960	46.0%	
WISCONSIN																			
WYOMING																			
Total	2,364,000	1,333,013	56.4%	2,504,000	1,460,359	58.3%	1.9	1,939,000	1,215,122	62.7%	6.3	2,364,000	1,286,875	54.4%	-2.0	3,056,000	2,090,509	68.4%	12.0

*Includes elections for states that seceded from the Union during the Civil War, if data are available.

**Percentage point difference between turnout in current year and initial year listed in chart. If data do not appear for a state in the initial year listed, the difference is calculated from the first year in which data do appear for that state.

STATE GUBERNATORIAL GENERAL ELECTIONS

Republican Turnout for Election Years 1850–1866*

State	1850 (Whig)			1854 (Whig)				1858				1862				1866			
	Voting-age population	Turnout	%	Voting-age population	Turnout	%	Difference from 1850**	Voting-age population	Turnout	%	Difference from 1850	Voting-age population	Turnout	%	Difference from 1850	Voting-age population	Turnout	%	Difference from 1850
ALABAMA																			
ALASKA																			
ARIZONA																			
ARKANSAS																			
CALIFORNIA																			
COLORADO																			
CONNECTICUT	99,000	28,209	28.5%	104,000	19,465	18.7%	-9.8	109,000	40,247	36.9%	8.4	115,000	39,702	34.6%	6.1	120,000	43,974	36.6%	8.2
DELAWARE	17,000	5,978	35.2%									21,000	8,155	38.8%	3.7	22,000	8,598	39.1%	3.9
DISTRICT OF COLUMBIA																			
FLORIDA																			
GEORGIA																			
HAWAII																			
IDAHO																			
ILLINOIS																			
INDIANA																			
IOWA	47,000	11,403	24.3%	88,000	23,312	26.5%	2.2												
KANSAS												45,000	10,090	22.4%		72,000	19,370	26.9%	4.5
KENTUCKY																			
LOUISIANA																			
MAINE	145,000	32,308	22.3%	148,000	44,817	30.3%	8.0	151,000	60,599	40.1%	17.9	152,000	42,744	28.1%	5.8	152,000	69,637	45.8%	23.5
MARYLAND	104,000	34,858	33.5%																
MASSACHUSETTS	266,000	56,778	21.3%	272,000	27,279	10.0%	-11.3	278,000	68,700	24.7%	3.4	287,000	79,835	27.8%	6.5	299,000	91,980	30.8%	9.4
MICHIGAN				132,000	43,652	33.1%		163,000	65,201	40.0%	6.9	203,000	68,716	33.9%	0.8	246,000	96,746	39.3%	6.3
MINNESOTA																			
MISSISSIPPI																			
MISSOURI																			
MONTANA																			
NEBRASKA																27,000	4,093	15.2%	
NEVADA																18,000	5,125	28.5%	
NEW HAMPSHIRE	85,000	18,387	21.6%	85,000	17,028	20.0%	-1.6	85,000	36,308	42.7%	21.1	83,000	32,150	38.7%	17.1	83,000	35,136	42.3%	20.7
NEW JERSEY	114,000	34,054	29.9%																
NEW MEXICO																			
NEW YORK	799,000	214,614	26.9%	837,000	156,804	18.7%	-8.1	874,000	247,868	28.4%	1.5	908,000	295,897	32.6%	5.7	939,000	366,315	39.0%	12.2

State Gubernatorial General Elections (continued)

State Gubernatorial General Elections (continued)

Republican Turnout for Election Years 1850–1866 (continued)

State	1850 (Whig)			1854 (Whig)				1858				1862				1866			
	Voting-age population	Turnout	%	Voting-age population	Turnout	%	Difference from 1850	Voting-age population	Turnout	%	Difference from 1850	Voting-age population	Turnout	%	Difference from 1850	Voting-age population	Turnout	%	Difference from 1850
NORTH CAROLINA	117,000	42,341	36.2%	125,000	46,644	37.3%	1.1												
NORTH DAKOTA																			
OHIO	451,000	121,105	26.9%																
OKLAHOMA																			
OREGON												18,000	7,029	39.1%		23,000	10,316	44.9%	5.8
PENNSYLVANIA				578,000	203,822	35.3%										715,000	307,274	43.0%	7.7
RHODE ISLAND	38,000	3,629	9.6%	37,000	9,112	24.6%	15.1	37,000	7,934	21.4%	11.9					41,000	7,725	18.8%	9.3
SOUTH CAROLINA																			
SOUTH DAKOTA																			
TENNESSEE																			
TEXAS																			
UTAH																			
VERMONT	82,000	24,809	30.3%	79,000	27,811	35.2%	4.9	76,000	29,460	38.8%	8.5	75,000	29,543	39.4%	9.1	74,000	34,117	46.1%	15.8
VIRGINIA												214,000	14,824	6.9%					
WASHINGTON																			
WEST VIRGINIA																89,000	23,802	26.7%	
WISCONSIN																			
WYOMING																			
Total	2,364,000	628,473	26.6%	2,485,000	619,746	24.9%	-1.6	1,773,000	556,317	31.4%	4.8	2,121,000	628,765	29.6%	3.1	2,920,000	1,124,208	38.5%	11.9

Democratic Turnout for Election Years 1850–1866

State	1850			1854				1858				1862				1866			
	Voting-age population	Turnout	%	Voting-age population	Turnout	%	Difference from 1850	Voting-age population	Turnout	%	Difference from 1850	Voting-age population	Turnout	%	Difference from 1850	Voting-age population	Turnout	%	Difference from 1850
ALABAMA																			
ALASKA																			
ARIZONA																			
ARKANSAS												69,000	18,189	26.4%					
CALIFORNIA																			
COLORADO																			
CONNECTICUT	99,000	29,022	29.3%	104,000	28,538	27.4%	-1.9	109,000	38,369	35.2%	5.9	115,000	30,634	26.6%	-2.7	120,000	43,433	36.2%	6.9
DELAWARE	17,000	6,001	35.3%	19,000	6,244	32.9%	-2.4	20,000	7,758	38.8%	3.5	21,000	8,044	38.3%	3.0	22,000	9,810	44.6%	9.3
DISTRICT OF COLUMBIA																			
FLORIDA																			

State Gubernatorial General Elections *(continued)*

Democratic Turnout for Election Years 1850–1866 *(continued)*

State	1850 Voting-age population	Turnout	%	1854 Voting-age population	Turnout	%	Difference from 1850	1858 Voting-age population	Turnout	%	Difference from 1850	1862 Voting-age population	Turnout	%	Difference from 1850	1866 Voting-age population	Turnout	%	Difference from 1850
GEORGIA																			
HAWAII																			
IDAHO																			
ILLINOIS																			
INDIANA																			
IOWA	47,000	13,486	28.7%																
KANSAS																			
KENTUCKY																			
LOUISIANA																			
MAINE	145,000	41,220	28.4%	148,000	28,285	19.1%	-9.3	151,000	52,697	34.9%	6.5	152,000	32,108	21.1%	-7.3	152,000	41,947	27.6%	-0.8
MARYLAND	104,000	36,340	34.9%																
MASSACHUSETTS	266,000	36,023	13.5%	272,000	13,742	5.1%	-8.5	278,000	38,298	13.8%	0.2								
MICHIGAN				132,000	38,676	29.3%		163,000	56,060	34.4%	5.1					246,000	67,708	27.5%	-1.8
MINNESOTA																			
MISSISSIPPI																			
MISSOURI																			
MONTANA																			
NEBRASKA																27,000	3,984	14.8%	
NEVADA																18,000	4,105	22.8%	
NEW HAMPSHIRE	85,000	30,683	36.1%	85,000	29,788	35.0%	-1.1	85,000	31,597	37.2%	1.1	83,000	28,566	34.4%	-1.7	83,000	30,484	36.7%	0.6
NEW JERSEY	114,000	39,723	34.8%																
NEW MEXICO																			
NEW YORK	799,000	214,352	26.8%	837,000	190,345	22.7%	-4.1	874,000	230,329	26.4%	-0.5	908,000	306,649	33.8%	6.9	939,000	352,526	37.5%	10.7
NORTH CAROLINA	117,000	45,058	38.5%	125,000	48,705	39.0%	0.5	132,000	56,429	42.7%	4.2	135,000	55,282	40.9%	2.4	136,000	34,250	25.2%	-13.3
NORTH DAKOTA																			
OHIO	451,000	133,093	29.5%																
OKLAHOMA																			
OREGON								14,000	5,134	36.7%		18,000	3,450	19.2%	-17.5	23,000	10,039	43.6%	7.0
PENNSYLVANIA				578,000	166,991	28.9%										715,000	290,096	40.6%	11.7
RHODE ISLAND				37,000	6,484	17.5%		37,000	3,572	9.7%	-7.9	39,000	11,199	28.7%	11.2	41,000	2,796	6.8%	-10.7
SOUTH CAROLINA																			
SOUTH DAKOTA																			
TENNESSEE																			

State Gubernatorial General Elections (continued)

State Gubernatorial General Elections (continued)

Democratic Turnout for Election Years 1850–1866 (continued)

State	1850			1854				1858				1862				1866			
	Voting-age population	Turnout	%	Voting-age population	Turnout	%	Difference from 1850	Voting-age population	Turnout	%	Difference from 1850	Voting-age population	Turnout	%	Difference from 1850	Voting-age population	Turnout	%	Difference from 1850
TEXAS																			
UTAH																			
VERMONT	82,000	23,568	28.7%	79,000	15,130	19.2%	-9.6	76,000	13,538	17.8%	-10.9	75,000	3,772	5.0%	-23.7	74,000	11,292	15.3%	-13.5
VIRGINIA																			
WASHINGTON																			
WEST VIRGINIA																89,000	17,158	19.3%	
WISCONSIN																			
WYOMING																			
Total	2,326,000	648,569	27.9%	2,416,000	572,928	23.7%	-4.2	1,939,000	533,781	27.5%	-0.4	1,615,000	497,893	30.8%	2.9	2,685,000	919,628	34.3%	6.4

Other Turnout for Election Years 1850–1866

State	1850			1854				1858				1862				1866			
	Voting-age population	Turnout	%	Voting-age population	Turnout	%	Difference from 1850	Voting-age population	Turnout	%	Difference from 1850	Voting-age population	Turnout	%	Difference from 1850	Voting-age population	Turnout	%	Difference from 1850
ARKANSAS												69,000	8,127	11.8%					
CONNECTICUT				104,000	10,672	10.3%						115,000	14	0.0%	-10.2	120,000	10	0.0%	-10.3
DELAWARE				19,000	6,941	36.5%		20,000	7,554	37.8%	1.2								
IOWA				88,000	21,192	24.1%													
KANSAS												45,000	5,463	12.1%		72,000	8,152	11.3%	-0.8
MAINE	145,000	7,271	5.0%	148,000	14,014	9.5%	4.5					152,000	6,866	4.5%	-0.5	152,000	308	0.2%	-4.8
MASSACHUSETTS	266,000	27,636	10.4%	272,000	81,503	30.0%	19.6	278,000	12,084	4.3%	-6.0	287,000	54,320	18.9%	8.5	299,000	26,771	9.0%	-1.4
MICHIGAN												203,000	62,102	30.6%					
NEBRASKA																27,000	21	0.1%	
NEW HAMPSHIRE	85,000	6,556	7.7%	85,000	11,081	13.0%	5.3					83,000	1,754	2.1%	-5.6	83,000	18	0.0%	-7.7
NEW YORK				837,000	122,282	14.6%		874,000	61,137	7.0%	-7.6	908,000	492	0.1%	-14.6	939,000	354	0.0%	-14.6
NORTH CAROLINA								132,000	40,036	30.3%		135,000	20,813	15.4%	-14.9	136,000	10,876	8.0%	-22.3
OHIO	451,000	13,747	3.0%																
OREGON								14,000	4,213	30.1%									
RHODE ISLAND	38,000	761	2.0%									39,000	65	0.2%	-1.8	41,000	160	0.4%	-1.6
VERMONT												75,000	77	0.1%		74,000	3	0.0%	-0.1
VIRGINIA												214,000	124	0.1%					
Total	985,000	55,971	5.7%	1,553,000	267,685	17.2%	11.6	1,318,000	125,024	9.5%	3.8	2,325,000	160,217	6.9%	1.2	1,943,000	46,673	2.4%	-3.3

*By 1854, in Iowa, Maine, Michigan, and New York, the Republicans had supplanted the Whigs as the main opposition to the Democrats. The turnout for the handful of Whigs who ran (against Republicans) in those states are included in the "Other" chart. In the Northeast and South, however, the Whigs were not supplanted until 1856 and are included in the 1854 major party data.

**Percentage point difference between turnout in current year and initial year listed in chart. If data do not appear for a state in the initial year listed, the difference is calculated from the first year in which data do appear for that state.

UNITED STATES HOUSE OF REPRESENTATIVES GENERAL ELECTIONS

Election Years 1850–1866

State	1850			1854				1858				1862				1866			
	Voting-age population	Turnout	%	Voting-age population	Turnout	%	Difference from 1850*	Voting-age population	Turnout	%	Difference from 1850	Voting-age population	Turnout	%	Difference from 1850	Voting-age population	Turnout	%	Difference from 1850
ALABAMA																			
ALASKA																			
ARIZONA																			
ARKANSAS				50,000	29,910	59.8%		63,000	43,966	69.8%	10.0								
CALIFORNIA				96,000	82,165	85.6%						132,000	109,065	82.6%	-3.0	139,000	92,782	66.7%	-18.8
COLORADO																			
CONNECTICUT												115,000	79,928	69.5%		120,000	93,874	78.2%	8.7
DELAWARE	17,000	12,294	72.3%	19,000	13,154	69.2%	-3.1	20,000	15,320	76.6%	4.3	21,000	16,065	76.5%	4.2	22,000	18,486	84.0%	11.7
DISTRICT OF COLUMBIA																			
FLORIDA	12,000	8,581	71.5%	15,000	10,202	68.0%	-3.5	16,000	9,745	60.9%	-10.6								
GEORGIA																			
HAWAII																			
IDAHO																			
ILLINOIS	201,000	104,127	51.8%	277,000	140,791	50.8%	-1.0	354,000	251,959	71.2%	19.4	422,000	256,076	60.7%	8.9	483,000	350,500	72.6%	20.8
INDIANA				248,000	190,189	76.7%		284,000	216,385	76.2%	-0.5	317,000	244,810	77.2%	0.5	345,000	324,059	93.9%	17.2
IOWA	47,000	25,365	54.0%	88,000	43,726	49.7%	-4.3	129,000	94,725	73.4%	19.5	174,000	115,340	66.3%	12.3	217,000	147,772	68.1%	14.1
KANSAS												45,000	15,267	33.9%		72,000	27,406	38.1%	4.1
KENTUCKY												213,000	84,136	39.5%		227,000	112,943	49.8%	10.3
LOUISIANA																			
MAINE	145,000	79,348	54.7%	148,000	88,998	60.1%	5.4	151,000	112,699	74.6%	19.9	152,000	85,761	56.4%	1.7	152,000	110,428	72.7%	17.9
MARYLAND												119,000	50,259	42.2%		125,000	68,243	54.6%	12.4
MASSACHUSETTS	266,000	116,295	43.7%	272,000	121,242	44.6%	0.9	278,000	116,296	41.8%	-1.9	287,000	133,952	46.7%	3.0	299,000	116,933	39.1%	-4.6
MICHIGAN	100,000	60,165	60.2%	132,000	81,907	62.1%	1.9	163,000	121,402	74.5%	14.3	203,000	129,592	63.8%	3.7	246,000	164,356	66.8%	6.6
MINNESOTA												53,000	24,651	46.5%		79,000	41,758	52.9%	6.3
MISSISSIPPI																			
MISSOURI	141,000	78,218	55.5%	184,000	100,896	54.8%	-0.6	227,000	127,129	56.0%	0.5	273,000	86,510	31.7%	-23.8	317,000	105,785	33.4%	-22.1
MONTANA																			
NEBRASKA																27,000	8,922	33.0%	
NEVADA																13,000	9,243	71.1%	
NEW HAMPSHIRE												83,000	65,820	79.3%		83,000	68,595	82.6%	3.3
NEW JERSEY	114,000	73,814	64.7%	127,000	78,613	61.9%	-2.8	138,000	95,294	69.1%	4.3	154,000	107,555	69.8%	5.1	172,000	129,596	75.3%	10.6
NEW MEXICO																			
NEW YORK	799,000	425,677	53.3%	837,000	452,085	54.0%	0.7	874,000	537,568	61.5%	8.2	908,000	600,739	66.2%	12.9	939,000	713,442	76.0%	22.7

United States House of Representatives General Elections (continued)

United States House of Representatives General Elections (continued)

Election Years 1850–1866 (continued)

State	1850 Voting-age population	Turnout	%		1854 Voting-age population	Turnout	%	Difference from 1850	1858 Voting-age population	Turnout	%	Difference from 1850	1862 Voting-age population	Turnout	%	Difference from 1850	1866 Voting-age population	Turnout	%	Difference from 1850
NORTH CAROLINA																				
NORTH DAKOTA																				
OHIO	451,000	253,831	56.3%		477,000	292,029	61.2%	4.9	504,000	344,525	68.4%	12.1	529,000	362,205	68.5%	12.2	555,000	468,444	84.4%	28.1
OKLAHOMA																				
OREGON									14,000	10,127	72.3%		18,000	10,432	58.0%	-14.4	23,000	20,170	87.7%	15.4
PENNSYLVANIA	540,000	279,184	51.7%		578,000	340,615	58.9%	7.2	615,000	370,076	60.2%	8.5	662,000	432,525	65.3%	13.6	715,000	596,286	83.4%	31.7
RHODE ISLAND													39,000	18,533	47.5%		41,000	8,561	20.9%	-26.6
SOUTH CAROLINA	60,000	15,962	26.6%		62,000	18,585	30.0%	3.4	64,000	22,726	35.5%	8.9								
SOUTH DAKOTA																				
TENNESSEE																	189,000	96,123	50.9%	
TEXAS																				
UTAH																				
VERMONT	82,000	44,912	54.8%		79,000	40,235	50.9%	-3.8	76,000	40,256	53.0%	-1.8	75,000	38,845	51.8%	-3.0	74,000	43,618	58.9%	4.2
VIRGINIA																				
WASHINGTON																				
WEST VIRGINIA																	89,000	40,156	45.1%	
WISCONSIN	84,000	42,630	50.8%		118,000	59,414	50.4%	-0.4	153,000	116,599	76.2%	25.5	176,000	125,948	71.6%	20.8	191,000	134,790	70.6%	19.8
WYOMING																				
Total	3,059,000	1,620,403	53.0%		3,807,000	2,184,756	57.4%	4.4	4,123,000	2,646,797	64.2%	11.2	5,170,000	3,194,014	61.8%	8.8	5,954,000	4,113,271	69.1%	16.1

*Percentage point difference between turnout in current year and initial year listed in chart. If data do not appear for a state in the initial year listed, the difference is calculated from the first year in which data do appear for that state.

UNITED STATES HOUSE OF REPRESENTATIVES GENERAL ELECTIONS

Republican Turnout for Election Years 1850–1866

State	1850 (Whig)			1854 (Whig or Republican)*				1858				1862				1866			
	Voting-age population	Turnout	%	Voting-age population	Turnout	%	Difference from 1850**	Voting-age population	Turnout	%	Difference from 1850	Voting-age population	Turnout	%	Difference from 1850	Voting-age population	Turnout	%	Difference from 1850
ALABAMA																			
ALASKA																			
ARIZONA																			
ARKANSAS				50,000	4,842	9.7%													
CALIFORNIA				96,000	34,576	36.0%						132,000	65,149	49.4%	13.3	139,000	44,436	32.0%	-4.0
COLORADO																			
CONNECTICUT												115,000	41,048	35.7%		120,000	46,240	38.5%	2.8
DELAWARE	17,000	5,926	34.9%									21,000	8,014	38.2%	3.3	22,000	8,553	38.9%	4.0
DISTRICT OF COLUMBIA																			
FLORIDA	12,000	4,531	37.8%	15,000	4,564	30.4%	-7.3												
GEORGIA																			
HAWAII																			
IDAHO																			
ILLINOIS	201,000	43,204	21.5%	277,000	55,147	19.9%	-1.6	354,000	125,668	35.5%	14.0	422,000	119,819	28.4%	6.9	483,000	203,045	42.0%	20.5
INDIANA								284,000	100,855	35.5%		317,000	116,739	36.8%	1.3	345,000	168,302	48.8%	13.3
IOWA	47,000	11,710	24.9%	88,000	22,466	25.5%	0.6	129,000	49,032	38.0%	13.1	174,000	65,842	37.8%	12.9	217,000	90,930	41.9%	17.0
KANSAS												45,000	14,337	31.9%		72,000	19,200	26.7%	-5.2
KENTUCKY																227,000	28,874	12.7%	
LOUISIANA																			
MAINE	145,000	37,050	25.6%	148,000	51,123	34.5%	9.0	151,000	60,584	40.1%	14.6	152,000	47,041	30.9%	5.4	152,000	68,736	45.2%	19.7
MARYLAND												119,000	37,492	31.5%		125,000	25,918	20.7%	-10.8
MASSACHUSETTS	266,000	54,968	20.7%	272,000	28,838	10.6%	-10.1	278,000	70,154	25.2%	4.6	287,000	85,053	29.6%	9.0	299,000	89,749	30.0%	9.4
MICHIGAN	100,000	30,872	30.9%	132,000	43,660	33.1%	2.2	163,000	65,789	40.4%	9.5	203,000	68,188	33.6%	2.7	246,000	97,009	39.4%	8.6
MINNESOTA												53,000	14,375	27.1%		79,000	25,983	32.9%	5.8
MISSISSIPPI																			
MISSOURI	141,000	31,796	22.6%	184,000	43,769	23.8%	1.2	227,000	6,631	2.9%	-19.6	273,000	41,969	15.4%	-7.2	317,000	62,377	19.7%	-2.9
MONTANA																			
NEBRASKA																27,000	4,820	17.9%	
NEVADA																18,000	5,047	28.0%	
NEW HAMPSHIRE												83,000	33,191	40.0%		83,000	35,797	43.1%	3.1
NEW JERSEY	114,000	33,319	29.2%	127,000	33,996	26.8%	-2.5	138,000	31,505	22.8%	-6.4	154,000	46,964	30.5%	1.3	172,000	65,473	38.1%	8.8
NEW MEXICO																			
NEW YORK	799,000	213,082	26.7%	837,000	202,270	24.2%	-2.5	874,000	248,704	28.5%	1.8	908,000	295,460	32.5%	5.9	939,000	390,182	41.6%	14.9

United States House of Representatives General Elections (continued)

United States House of Representatives General Elections *(continued)*

Republican Turnout for Election Years 1850–1866 *(continued)*

State	1850 (Whig)			1854 (Whig or Republican)				1858				1862				1866			
	Voting-age population	Turnout	%	Voting-age population	Turnout	%	Difference from 1850	Voting-age population	Turnout	%	Difference from 1850	Voting-age population	Turnout	%	Difference from 1850	Voting-age population	Turnout	%	Difference from 1850
NORTH CAROLINA																			
NORTH DAKOTA																			
OHIO	451,000	105,172	**23.3%**					504,000	184,062	**36.5%**	13.2	529,000	180,160	**34.1%**	10.7	555,000	254,043	**45.8%**	22.5
OKLAHOMA																			
OREGON								14,000	4,263	**30.5%**		18,000	6,800	**37.8%**	7.3	23,000	10,362	**45.1%**	14.6
PENNSYLVANIA	540,000	123,473	**22.9%**	578,000	168,290	**29.1%**	6.3					662,000	202,538	**30.6%**	7.7	715,000	303,789	**42.5%**	19.6
RHODE ISLAND												39,000	10,738	**27.5%**		41,000	6,980	**17.0%**	-10.5
SOUTH CAROLINA																			
SOUTH DAKOTA																			
TENNESSEE																189,000	73,617	**39.0%**	
TEXAS																			
UTAH																			
VERMONT	82,000	23,895	**29.1%**	79,000	24,868	**31.5%**	2.3	76,000	28,589	**37.6%**	8.5	75,000	27,923	**37.2%**	8.1	74,000	33,252	**44.9%**	15.8
VIRGINIA																			
WASHINGTON																			
WEST VIRGINIA																89,000	23,271	**26.1%**	
WISCONSIN	84,000	5,752	**6.8%**	118,000	32,315	**27.4%**	20.5	153,000	61,356	**40.1%**	33.3	176,000	61,829	**35.1%**	28.3	191,000	79,170	**41.5%**	34.6
WYOMING																			
Total	2,999,000	724,758	**24.2%**	3,001,000	750,724	**25.0%**	0.8	3,345,000	1,037,192	**31.0%**	6.8	4,957,000	1,590,669	**32.1%**	7.9	5,959,000	2,265,155	**38.0%**	13.8

Democratic Turnout for Election Years 1850–1866

State	1850			1854				1858				1862				1866			
	Voting-age population	Turnout	%	Voting-age population	Turnout	%	Difference from 1850	Voting-age population	Turnout	%	Difference from 1850	Voting-age population	Turnout	%	Difference from 1850	Voting-age population	Turnout	%	Difference from 1850
ALABAMA																			
ALASKA																			
ARIZONA																			
ARKANSAS				50,000	24,752	**49.5%**		63,000	38,009	**60.3%**	10.8								
CALIFORNIA				96,000	47,589	**49.6%**						132,000	43,916	**33.3%**	-16.3	139,000	48,346	**34.8%**	-14.8
COLORADO																			
CONNECTICUT												115,000	38,880	**33.8%**		120,000	47,634	**39.7%**	5.9
DELAWARE	17,000	6,055	**35.6%**	19,000	6,334	**33.3%**	-2.3	20,000	7,868	**39.3%**	3.7	21,000	8,051	**38.3%**	2.7	22,000	9,933	**45.2%**	9.5
DISTRICT OF COLUMBIA																			
FLORIDA	12,000	4,050	**33.8%**	15,000	5,638	**37.6%**	3.8	16,000	9,745	**60.9%**	27.2								

United States House of Representatives General Elections *(continued)*

Democratic Turnout for Election Years 1850–1866 *(continued)*

State	1850 Voting-age population	Turnout	%	1854 Voting-age population	Turnout	%	Difference from 1850	1858 Voting-age population	Turnout	%	Difference from 1850	1862 Voting-age population	Turnout	%	Difference from 1850	1866 Voting-age population	Turnout	%	Difference from 1850
GEORGIA																			
HAWAII																			
IDAHO																			
ILLINOIS	201,000	59,798	29.8%	277,000	70,244	25.4%	-4.4	354,000	126,291	35.7%	5.9	422,000	136,257	32.3%	2.5	483,000	147,455	30.5%	0.8
INDIANA				240,000	07,700	35.4%		284,000	116,630	40.7%	5.3	317,000	128,071	40.4%	5.0	345,000	155,757	45.1%	9.8
IOWA	47,000	13,182	28.0%	88,000	21,086	24.0%	-4.1	129,000	45,693	35.4%	7.4	174,000	49,498	28.4%	0.4	217,000	56,456	26.0%	-2.0
KANSAS												45,000	930	2.1%					
KENTUCKY												213,000	83,926	39.4%		227,000	77,639	34.2%	-5.2
LOUISIANA																			
MAINE	145,000	39,252	27.1%	148,000	31,868	21.5%	-5.5	151,000	52,115	34.5%	7.4	152,000	37,421	24.6%	-2.5	152,000	41,692	27.4%	0.4
MARYLAND												119,000	10,421	8.8%		125,000	42,303	33.8%	25.1
MASSACHUSETTS	266,000	34,723	13.1%	272,000	11,345	4.2%	-8.9	278,000	38,912	14.0%	0.9	207,000	2,762	1.0%	12.1	299,000	26,721	8.9%	-4.1
MICHIGAN	100,000	29,259	29.3%	132,000	38,247	29.0%	-0.3	163,000	55,613	34.1%	4.9	203,000	61,404	30.2%	1.0	246,000	67,347	27.4%	-1.9
MINNESOTA												53,000	10,276	19.4%		79,000	15,775	20.0%	0.6
MISSISSIPPI																			
MISSOURI	141,000	46,422	32.9%	184,000	57,127	31.0%	-1.9	227,000	85,746	37.8%	4.9	273,000	41,675	15.3%	-17.7	317,000	43,400	13.7%	-19.2
MONTANA																			
NEBRASKA																27,000	4,072	15.1%	
NEVADA																18,000	4,196	23.3%	
NEW HAMPSHIRE												83,000	32,629	39.3%		83,000	32,798	39.5%	0.2
NEW JERSEY	114,000	39,368	34.5%	127,000	33,852	26.7%	-7.9	138,000	60,050	43.5%	9.0	154,000	60,591	39.3%	4.8	172,000	63,930	37.2%	2.6
NEW MEXICO																			
NEW YORK	799,000	207,926	26.0%	837,000	206,734	24.7%	-1.3	874,000	213,331	24.4%	-1.6	908,000	301,707	33.2%	7.2	939,000	323,236	34.4%	8.4
NORTH CAROLINA																			
NORTH DAKOTA																			
OHIO	451,000	132,804	29.4%	477,000	105,584	22.1%	-7.3	504,000	159,464	31.6%	2.2	529,000	182,045	34.4%	5.0	555,000	214,401	38.6%	9.2
OKLAHOMA																			
OREGON								14,000	5,864	41.9%		18,000	3,632	20.2%	-21.7	23,000	9,808	42.6%	0.8
PENNSYLVANIA	540,000	143,706	26.6%	578,000	164,152	28.4%	1.8	615,000	175,520	28.5%	1.9	662,000	229,987	34.7%	8.1	715,000	292,497	40.9%	14.3
RHODE ISLAND												39,000	7,795	20.0%		41,000	1,480	3.6%	-16.4
SOUTH CAROLINA	60,000	15,730	26.2%	62,000	13,029	21.0%	-5.2	64,000	17,153	26.8%	0.6								
SOUTH DAKOTA																			
TENNESSEE																			

United States House of Representatives General Elections *(continued)*

Democratic Turnout for Election Years 1850–1866 *(continued)*

State	1850 Voting-age population	1850 Turnout	1850 %	1854 Voting-age population	1854 Turnout	1854 %	1854 Difference from 1850	1858 Voting-age population	1858 Turnout	1858 %	1858 Difference from 1850	1862 Voting-age population	1862 Turnout	1862 %	1862 Difference from 1850	1866 Voting-age population	1866 Turnout	1866 %	1866 Difference from 1850
TEXAS																			
UTAH																			
VERMONT	82,000	9,838	12.0%	79,000	12,920	16.4%	4.4	76,000	11,667	15.4%	3.4	75,000	10,922	14.6%	2.6	74,000	10,366	14.0%	2.0
VIRGINIA																			
WASHINGTON																			
WEST VIRGINIA																89,000	16,885	19.0%	
WISCONSIN	84,000	18,207	21.7%	118,000	25,027	21.2%	-0.5	153,000	55,243	36.1%	14.4	176,000	64,119	36.4%	14.8	191,000	55,620	29.1%	7.4
WYOMING																			
Total	3,059,000	800,320	26.2%	3,807,000	963,294	25.3%	-0.9	4,123,000	1,273,814	30.9%	4.7	5,170,000	1,546,915	29.9%	3.8	5,698,000	1,809,747	31.8%	5.6

Other Turnout for Election Years 1850–1866

State	1850 Voting-age population	1850 Turnout	1850 %	1854 Voting-age population	1854 Turnout	1854 %	1854 Difference from 1850	1858 Voting-age population	1858 Turnout	1858 %	1858 Difference from 1850	1862 Voting-age population	1862 Turnout	1862 %	1862 Difference from 1850	1866 Voting-age population	1866 Turnout	1866 %	1866 Difference from 1850
ARKANSAS				50,000	316	0.6%		63,000	5,957	9.5%	8.8								
DELAWARE	17,000	313	1.8%	19,000	6,820	35.9%	34.1	20,000	7,452	37.3%	35.4								
ILLINOIS	201,000	1,125	0.6%	277,000	15,400	5.6%	5.0												
INDIANA				248,000	102,423	41.3%													
IOWA	47,000	473	1.0%	88,000	174	0.2%	-0.8									217,000	386	0.2%	-0.8
KANSAS																72,000	8,206	11.4%	
KENTUCKY												213,000	210	0.1%		227,000	6,430	2.8%	2.7
MAINE	145,000	3,038	2.1%	148,000	6,007	4.1%	2.0					152,000	1,299	0.9%	-1.2				
MARYLAND												119,000	2,346	2.0%		125,000	22	0.0%	-2.0
MASSACHUSETTS	266,000	26,604	10.0%	272,000	81,059	29.8%	19.8	278,000	7,230	2.6%	-7.4	287,000	46,137	16.1%	6.1	299,000	463	0.2%	-9.8
MICHIGAN	100,000	34	0.0%																
MISSOURI								227,000	34,752	15.3%		273,000	2,866	1.0%	-14.3	317,000	8	0.0%	-15.3
NEBRASKA																27,000	30	0.1%	
NEW JERSEY	114,000	1,127	1.0%	127,000	10,765	8.5%	7.5	138,000	3,739	2.7%	1.7					172,000	193	0.1%	-0.9
NEW MEXICO																			
NEW YORK	799,000	4,669	0.6%	837,000	43,081	5.1%	4.6	874,000	75,533	8.6%	8.1	908,000	3,572	0.4%	-0.2	939,000	24	0.0%	-0.6
OHIO	451,000	15,855	3.5%	477,000	186,445	39.1%	35.6	504,000	999	0.2%	-3.3								
PENNSYLVANIA	540,000	12,005	2.2%	578,000	8,173	1.4%	-0.8	615,000	194,556	31.6%	29.4								
RHODE ISLAND																41,000	101	0.2%	
SOUTH CAROLINA	60,000	232	0.4%	62,000	5,556	9.0%	8.6	64,000	5,573	8.7%	8.3								

United States House of Representatives General Elections (continued)

Other Turnout for Election Years 1850–1866 (continued)

State	1850			1854				1858				1862				1866			
	Voting-age population	Turnout	%	Voting-age population	Turnout	%	Difference from 1850	Voting-age population	Turnout	%	Difference from 1850	Voting-age population	Turnout	%	Difference from 1850	Voting-age population	Turnout	%	Difference from 1850
TENNESSEE																189,000	22,506	11.9%	
VERMONT	82,000	11,179	13.6%	79,000	2,447	3.1%	-10.5												
WISCONSIN	84,000	18,671	22.2%	118,000	2,072	1.8%	-20.5												
Total	2,906,000	95,325	3.3%	3,380,000	470,738	13.9%	10.6	2,783,000	335,791	12.1%	8.8	1,952,000	56,430	2.9%	-0.4	2,625,000	38,369	1.5%	-1.8

*By 1854, in Illinois, Indiana, Iowa, Maine, Ohio, and Wisconsin, the Republicans had supplanted the Whigs as the main opposition to the Democrats. The turnout for the handful of Whigs who ran (against Republicans) in those states are included in the "Other" chart. In the Northeast and South, however, the Whigs were not supplanted until 1856 and are included in the 1854 major party data.

**Percentage point difference between turnout in current year and initial year listed in chart. If data do not appear for a state in the initial year listed, the difference is calculated from the first year in which data do appear for that state.

TOTAL HIGHEST STATEWIDE GENERAL ELECTIONS

Election Years 1850–1866

	1850			1854				1858				1862				1866			
State*	Voting-age population	Turnout	%	Voting-age population	Turnout	%	Difference from 1850**	Voting-age population	Turnout	%	Difference from 1850	Voting-age population	Turnout	%	Difference from 1850	Voting-age population	Turnout	%	Difference from 1850
ALABAMA																			
ALASKA																			
ARIZONA																			
ARKANSAS				50,000	29,910	59.8%		63,000	43,966	69.8%	10.0	69,000	26,316	38.1%	-21.7				
CALIFORNIA				96,000	82,165	85.6%						132,000	109,065	82.6%	-3.0	139,000	92,782	66.7%	-18.8
COLORADO																			
CONNECTICUT	99,000	57,231	57.8%	104,000	58,675	56.4%	-1.4	109,000	78,616	72.1%	14.3	115,000	79,928	69.5%	11.7	120,000	93,874	78.2%	20.4
DELAWARE	17,000	12,294	72.3%	19,000	13,185	69.4%	-2.9	20,000	15,320	76.6%	4.3	21,000	16,199	77.1%	4.8	22,000	18,486	84.0%	11.7
DISTRICT OF COLUMBIA																			
FLORIDA	12,000	8,581	71.5%	15,000	10,202	68.0%	-3.5	16,000	9,745	60.9%	-10.6								
GEORGIA																			
HAWAII																			
IDAHO																			
ILLINOIS	201,000	104,127	51.8%	277,000	140,791	50.8%	-1.0	354,000	251,959	71.2%	19.4	422,000	256,076	60.7%	8.9	483,000	350,500	72.6%	20.8
INDIANA				248,000	190,189	76.7%		284,000	216,385	76.2%	-0.5	317,000	244,810	77.2%	0.5	345,000	324,059	93.9%	17.2
IOWA	47,000	25,365	54.0%	88,000	44,527	50.6%	-3.4	129,000	94,725	73.4%	19.5	174,000	115,340	66.3%	12.3	217,000	147,772	68.1%	14.1
KANSAS												45,000	15,553	34.6%		72,000	27,522	38.2%	3.7
KENTUCKY												213,000	84,136	39.5%		227,000	112,943	49.8%	10.3
LOUISIANA																			
MAINE	145,000	80,799	55.7%	148,000	88,998	60.1%	4.4	151,000	113,296	75.0%	19.3	152,000	85,761	56.4%	0.7	152,000	111,892	73.6%	17.9
MARYLAND	104,000	71,198	68.5%									119,000	50,259	42.2%	-26.2	125,000	68,243	54.6%	-13.9
MASSACHUSETTS	266,000	120,437	45.3%	272,000	122,524	45.0%	-0.2	278,000	119,082	42.8%	-2.4	287,000	133,952	46.7%	1.4	299,000	118,751	39.7%	-5.6
MICHIGAN	100,000	60,165	60.2%	132,000	82,328	62.4%	2.2	163,000	121,402	74.5%	14.3	203,000	130,818	64.4%	4.3	246,000	164,454	66.9%	6.7
MINNESOTA												53,000	24,651	46.5%		79,000	41,758	52.9%	6.3
MISSISSIPPI																			
MISSOURI	141,000	78,218	55.5%	184,000	100,896	54.8%	-0.6	227,000	127,129	56.0%	0.5	273,000	86,510	31.7%	-23.8	317,000	105,785	33.4%	-22.1
MONTANA																			
NEBRASKA																27,000	8,922	33.0%	
NEVADA																18,000	9,243	51.4%	
NEW HAMPSHIRE	85,000	55,626	65.4%	85,000	57,897	68.1%	2.7	85,000	67,905	79.9%	14.4	83,000	65,820	79.3%	13.9	83,000	68,595	82.6%	17.2
NEW JERSEY	114,000	73,814	64.7%	127,000	78,613	61.9%	-2.8	138,000	95,294	69.1%	4.3	154,000	107,555	69.8%	5.1	172,000	129,596	75.3%	10.6
NEW MEXICO																			
NEW YORK	799,000	428,966	53.7%	837,000	452,085	54.0%	0.3	874,000	539,334	61.7%	8.0	908,000	603,038	66.4%	12.7	939,000	719,195	76.6%	22.9

Total Highest Statewide General Elections *(continued)*

Election Years 1850–1866 *(continued)*

State	1850 Voting-age population	Turnout	%	1854 Voting-age population	Turnout	%	Difference from 1850	1858 Voting-age population	Turnout	%	Difference from 1850	1862 Voting-age population	Turnout	%	Difference from 1850	1866 Voting-age population	Turnout	%	Difference from 1850
NORTH CAROLINA	117,000	87,399	**74.7%**	125,000	95,349	**76.3%**	1.6	132,000	96,465	**73.1%**	-1.6	135,000	76,095	**56.4%**	-18.3	136,000	45,126	**33.2%**	-41.5
NORTH DAKOTA																			
OHIO	451,000	267,945	**59.4%**	477,000	292,029	**61.2%**	1.8	504,000	344,525	**68.4%**	8.9	529,000	362,205	**68.5%**	9.1	555,000	468,444	**84.4%**	25.0
OKLAHOMA																			
OREGON												18,000	10,432	**58.0%**		23,000	20,355	**88.5%**	30.5
PENNSYLVANIA	540,000	279,945	**51.8%**	578,000	370,813	**64.2%**	12.3	615,000	370,076	**60.2%**	8.3	662,000	432,525	**65.3%**	13.5	715,000	597,370	**83.5%**	31.7
RHODE ISLAND				37,000	15,596	**42.2%**		37,000	11,506	**31.1%**	-11.1	39,000	18,533	**47.5%**	5.4	41,000	8,561	**20.9%**	-21.3
SOUTH CAROLINA	60,000	15,962	**26.6%**	62,000	18,585	**30.0%**	3.4	64,000	22,726	**35.5%**	8.9								
SOUTH DAKOTA																			
TENNESSEE																189,000	96,123	**50.9%**	
TEXAS																			
UTAH																			
VERMONT	82,000	48,377	**59.0%**	79,000	42,941	**54.4%**	-4.6	76,000	42,998	**56.6%**	-2.4	75,000	38,845	**51.8%**	-7.2	74,000	45,412	**61.4%**	2.4
VIRGINIA												214,000	14,948	**7.0%**					
WASHINGTON																			
WEST VIRGINIA																89,000	40,960	**46.0%**	
WISCONSIN	84,000	42,630	**50.8%**	118,000	59,414	**50.4%**	-0.4	153,000	116,599	**76.2%**	25.5	176,000	125,948	**71.6%**	20.8	191,000	134,790	**70.6%**	19.8
WYOMING																			
Total	3,464,000	1,919,079	**55.4%**	4,158,000	2,447,712	**58.9%**	3.5	4,472,000	2,899,053	**64.8%**	9.4	5,526,000	3,315,318	**60.0%**	4.6	6,089,000	4,171,513	**68.5%**	13.1

*Includes gubernatorial races for states that seceded from the Union during the Civil War, if data are available.

**Percentage point difference between turnout in current year and initial year listed in chart. If data do not appear for a state in the initial year listed, the difference is calculated from the first year in which data do appear for that state.

TOTAL HIGHEST STATEWIDE GENERAL ELECTIONS

Republican Turnout for Election Years 1850–1866

State	1850 (Whig)			1854 (Whig-Republican)*				1858				1862				1866			
	Voting-age population	Turnout	%	Voting-age population	Turnout	%	Difference from 1850**	Voting-age population	Turnout	%	Difference from 1850	Voting-age population	Turnout	%	Difference from 1850	Voting-age population	Turnout	%	Difference from 1850
ALABAMA																			
ALASKA																			
ARIZONA																			
ARKANSAS				50,000	4,842	9.7%													
CALIFORNIA				96,000	34,576	36.0%						132,000	65,149	49.4%	13.3	139,000	44,436	32.0%	-4.0
COLORADO																			
CONNECTICUT	99,000	28,209	28.5%	104,000	19,465	18.7%	-9.8	109,000	40,247	36.9%	8.4	115,000	41,048	35.7%	7.2	120,000	46,240	38.5%	10.0
DELAWARE	17,000	5,978	35.2%									21,000	8,155	38.8%	3.7	22,000	8,598	39.1%	3.9
DISTRICT OF COLUMBIA																			
FLORIDA	12,000	4,531	37.8%	15,000	4,564	30.4%	-7.3												
GEORGIA																			
HAWAII																			
IDAHO																			
ILLINOIS	201,000	43,204	21.5%	277,000	55,147	19.9%	-1.6	354,000	125,668	35.5%	14.0	422,000	119,819	28.4%	6.9	483,000	203,045	42.0%	20.5
INDIANA								284,000	100,855	35.5%		317,000	116,739	36.8%	1.3	345,000	168,302	48.8%	13.3
IOWA	47,000	11,710	24.9%	88,000	22,466	25.5%	0.6	129,000	49,032	38.0%	13.1	174,000	65,842	37.8%	12.9	217,000	90,930	41.9%	17.0
KANSAS												45,000	14,337	31.9%		72,000	19,370	26.9%	-5.0
KENTUCKY																227,000	28,874	12.7%	
LOUISIANA																			
MAINE	145,000	37,058	25.6%	148,000	51,123	34.5%	9.0	151,000	60,599	40.1%	14.6	152,000	47,041	30.9%	5.4	152,000	69,637	45.8%	20.3
MARYLAND	104,000	34,858	33.5%									119,000	37,492	31.5%	-2.0	125,000	25,918	20.7%	-12.8
MASSACHUSETTS	266,000	56,778	21.3%	272,000	28,838	10.6%	-10.7	278,000	70,154	25.2%	3.9	287,000	85,053	29.6%	8.3	299,000	91,980	30.8%	9.4
MICHIGAN	100,000	30,872	30.9%	132,000	43,660	33.1%	2.2	163,000	65,789	40.4%	9.5	203,000	68,716	33.9%	3.0	246,000	97,009	39.4%	8.6
MINNESOTA												53,000	14,375	27.1%		79,000	25,983	32.9%	5.8
MISSISSIPPI																			
MISSOURI	141,000	31,796	22.6%	184,000	43,769	23.8%	1.2	227,000	6,631	2.9%	-19.6	273,000	41,969	15.4%	-7.2	317,000	62,377	19.7%	-2.9
MONTANA																			
NEBRASKA																27,000	4,820	17.9%	
NEVADA																18,000	5,125	28.5%	
NEW HAMPSHIRE	85,000	18,387	21.6%	85,000	17,028	20.0%	-1.6					83,000	33,191	40.0%	18.4	83,000	35,797	43.1%	21.5
NEW JERSEY	114,000	34,054	29.9%	127,000	33,996	26.8%	-3.1	138,000	31,505	22.8%	-7.0	154,000	46,964	30.5%	0.6	172,000	65,473	38.1%	8.2
NEW MEXICO																			
NEW YORK	799,000	214,614	26.9%	837,000	202,270	24.2%	-2.7	874,000	248,704	28.5%	1.6	908,000	295,897	32.6%	5.7	939,000	390,182	41.6%	14.7

Total Highest Statewide General Elections (continued)

Republican Turnout for Election Years 1850–1866 (continued)

State	1850 (Whig)			1854 (Whig-Republican)				1858				1862				1866			
	Voting-age population	Turnout	%	Voting-age population	Turnout	%	Difference from 1850	Voting-age population	Turnout	%	Difference from 1850	Voting-age population	Turnout	%	Difference from 1850	Voting-age population	Turnout	%	Difference from 1850
NORTH CAROLINA	117,000	42,341	36.2%	125,000	46,644	37.3%	1.1									136,000		0.0%	-36.2
NORTH DAKOTA																			
OHIO	451,000	121,105	26.9%					504,000	184,062	36.5%	9.7	529,000	180,160	34.1%	7.2	555,000	254,043	45.8%	18.9
OKLAHOMA																			
OREGON								14,000	4,263	30.5%		18,000	7,029	39.1%	8.6	23,000	10,362	45.1%	14.6
PENNSYLVANIA	540,000	123,473	22.9%	578,000	203,822	35.3%	12.4					662,000	202,530	30.6%	7.7	715,000	307,274	43.0%	20.1
RHODE ISLAND				37,000	9,112	24.6%		37,000	7,934	21.4%	-3.2	39,000	10,738	27.5%	2.9	41,000	7,725	18.8%	-5.8
SOUTH CAROLINA																			
SOUTH DAKOTA																			
TENNESSEE																189,000	73,617	39.0%	
TEXAS																			
UTAH																			
VERMONT	82,000	24,809	30.3%	79,000	27,811	35.2%	4.9	76,000	29,460	38.8%	8.5	75,000	29,543	39.4%	9.1	74,000	34,117	46.1%	15.0
VIRGINIA												214,000	14,824	6.9%					
WASHINGTON																			
WEST VIRGINIA																89,000	23,802	26.7%	
WISCONSIN	84,000	5,752	6.8%	118,000	32,315	27.4%	20.5	153,000	61,356	40.1%	33.3	176,000	61,829	35.1%	28.3	191,000	79,170	41.5%	34.6
WYOMING																			
Total	3,404,000	869,529	25.5%	3,352,000	881,448	26.3%	0.8	3,491,000	1,086,259	31.1%	5.6	5,171,000	1,608,448	31.1%	5.6	6,095,000	2,274,206	37.3%	11.8

Democratic Turnout for Election Years 1850–1866

State	1850			1854				1858				1862				1866			
	Voting-age population	Turnout	%	Voting-age population	Turnout	%	Difference from 1850	Voting-age population	Turnout	%	Difference from 1850	Voting-age population	Turnout	%	Difference from 1850	Voting-age population	Turnout	%	Difference from 1850
ALABAMA																			
ALASKA																			
ARIZONA																			
ARKANSAS				50,000	24,752	49.5%		63,000	38,009	60.3%	10.8	69,000	18,189	26.4%	-23.1				
CALIFORNIA				96,000	47,589	49.6%						132,000	43,916	33.3%	-16.3	139,000	48,346	34.8%	-14.8
COLORADO																			
CONNECTICUT	99,000	29,022	29.3%	104,000	28,538	27.4%	-1.9	109,000	38,369	35.2%	5.9	115,000	38,880	33.8%	4.5	120,000	47,634	39.7%	10.4
DELAWARE	17,000	6,055	35.6%	19,000	6,334	33.3%	-2.3	20,000	7,868	39.3%	3.7	21,000	8,051	38.3%	2.7	22,000	9,933	45.2%	9.5
DISTRICT OF COLUMBIA																			
FLORIDA	12,000	4,050	33.8%	15,000	5,638	37.6%	3.8	16,000	9,745	60.9%	27.2								

Total Highest Statewide General Elections (continued)

Total Highest Statewide General Elections (continued)

Democratic Turnout for Election Years 1850–1866 (continued)

State	1850			1854				1858				1862				1866			
	Voting-age population	Turnout	%	Voting-age population	Turnout	%	Difference from 1850	Voting-age population	Turnout	%	Difference from 1850	Voting-age population	Turnout	%	Difference from 1850	Voting-age population	Turnout	%	Difference from 1850
GEORGIA																			
HAWAII																			
IDAHO																			
ILLINOIS	201,000	59,798	29.8%	277,000	70,244	25.4%	-4.4	354,000	126,291	35.7%	5.9	422,000	136,257	32.3%	2.5	483,000	147,455	30.5%	0.8
INDIANA				248,000	87,766	35.4%		284,000	115,530	40.7%	5.3	317,000	128,071	40.4%	5.0	345,000	155,757	45.1%	9.8
IOWA	47,000	13,486	28.7%	88,000	21,086	24.0%	-4.7	129,000	45,693	35.4%	6.7	174,000	49,498	28.4%	-0.2	217,000	56,456	26.0%	-2.7
KANSAS												45,000	930	2.1%					
KENTUCKY												213,000	83,926	39.4%		227,000	77,639	34.2%	-5.2
LOUISIANA																			
MAINE	145,000	41,220	28.4%	148,000	31,868	21.5%	-6.9	151,000	52,697	34.9%	6.5	152,000	37,421	24.6%	-3.8	152,000	41,947	27.6%	-0.8
MARYLAND	104,000	36,340	34.9%									119,000	10,421	8.8%	-26.2	125,000	42,303	33.8%	-1.1
MASSACHUSETTS	266,000	36,023	13.5%	272,000	13,742	5.1%	-8.5	278,000	38,912	14.0%	0.5	287,000	2,762	1.0%	-12.6	299,000	26,721	8.9%	-4.6
MICHIGAN	100,000	29,259	29.3%	132,000	38,676	29.3%	0.0	163,000	56,060	34.4%	5.1	203,000	61,404	30.2%	1.0	246,000	67,708	27.5%	-1.7
MINNESOTA												53,000	10,276	19.4%		79,000	15,775	20.0%	0.6
MISSISSIPPI																			
MISSOURI	141,000	46,422	32.9%	184,000	57,127	31.0%	-1.9	227,000	85,746	37.8%	4.9	273,000	41,675	15.3%	-17.7	317,000	43,400	13.7%	-19.2
MONTANA																			
NEBRASKA																27,000	4,072	15.1%	
NEVADA																18,000	4,196	23.3%	
NEW HAMPSHIRE	85,000	30,683	36.1%	85,000	29,788	35.0%	-1.1	85,000	31,597	37.2%	1.1	83,000	32,629	39.3%	3.2	83,000	32,798	39.5%	3.4
NEW JERSEY	114,000	39,723	34.8%	127,000	33,852	26.7%	-8.2	138,000	60,050	43.5%	8.7	154,000	60,591	39.3%	4.5	172,000	63,930	37.2%	2.3
NEW MEXICO																			
NEW YORK	799,000	214,352	26.8%	837,000	206,734	24.7%	-2.1	874,000	230,329	26.4%	-0.5	908,000	306,649	33.8%	6.9	939,000	352,526	37.5%	10.7
NORTH CAROLINA	117,000	45,058	38.5%	125,000	48,705	39.0%	0.5	132,000	56,429	42.7%	4.2	135,000	55,282	40.9%	2.4	136,000	34,250	25.2%	-13.3
NORTH DAKOTA																			
OHIO	451,000	133,093	29.5%	477,000	105,584	22.1%	-7.4	504,000	159,464	31.6%	2.1	529,000	182,045	34.4%	4.9	555,000	214,401	38.6%	9.1
OKLAHOMA																			
OREGON												18,000	3,632	20.2%		23,000	10,039	43.6%	23.5
PENNSYLVANIA	540,000	143,706	26.6%	578,000	166,991	28.9%	2.3	615,000	175,520	28.5%	1.9	662,000	229,987	34.7%	8.1	715,000	292,497	40.9%	14.3
RHODE ISLAND				37,000	6,484	17.5%		37,000	3,572	9.7%	-7.9	39,000	11,199	28.7%	11.2	41,000	2,796	6.8%	-10.7
SOUTH CAROLINA	60,000	15,730	26.2%	62,000	13,029	21.0%	-5.2	64,000	17,153	26.8%	0.6								
SOUTH DAKOTA																			
TENNESSEE																			

Total Highest Statewide General Elections *(continued)*

Democratic Turnout for Election Years 1850–1866 *(continued)*

State	1850 Voting-age population	Turnout	%	1854 Voting-age population	Turnout	%	Difference from 1850	1858 Voting-age population	Turnout	%	Difference from 1850	1862 Voting-age population	Turnout	%	Difference from 1850	1866 Voting-age population	Turnout	%	Difference from 1850
TEXAS																			
UTAH																			
VERMONT	82,000	23,568	**28.7%**	79,000	15,130	**19.2%**	-9.6	76,000	13,538	**17.8%**	-10.9	75,000	10,922	**14.6%**	-14.2	74,000	11,292	**15.3%**	-13.5
VIRGINIA																			
WASHINGTON																			
WEST VIRGINIA																89,000	17,158	**19.3%**	
WISCONSIN	84,000	18,207	**21.7%**	118,000	25,027	**21.2%**	-0.5	153,000	55,243	**36.1%**	14.4	176,000	64,119	**36.4%**	14.8	191,000	55,620	**29.1%**	7.4
WYOMING																			
Total	3,464,000	965,795	**27.9%**	4,158,000	1,084,684	**26.1%**	-1.8	4,472,000	1,417,815	**31.7%**	3.8	5,374,000	1,628,732	**30.3%**	2.4	5,834,000	1,876,649	**32.2%**	4.3

Other Turnout for Election Years 1850–1866

State	1850 Voting-age population	Turnout	%	1854 Voting-age population	Turnout	%	Difference from 1850	1858 Voting-age population	Turnout	%	Difference from 1850	1862 Voting-age population	Turnout	%	Difference from 1850	1866 Voting-age population	Turnout	%	Difference from 1850
ALABAMA																			
ALASKA																			
ARIZONA																			
ARKANSAS				50,000	316	**0.6%**		63,000	5,957	**9.5%**	8.8	69,000	8,127	**11.8%**	11.1				
CALIFORNIA																			
COLORADO																			
CONNECTICUT				104,000	10,672	**10.3%**													
DELAWARE	17,000	313	**1.8%**	19,000	6,941	**36.5%**	34.7	20,000	7,554	**37.8%**	35.9								
DISTRICT OF COLUMBIA																			
FLORIDA																			
GEORGIA																			
HAWAII																			
IDAHO																			
ILLINOIS	201,000	1,125	**0.6%**	277,000	15,400	**5.6%**	5.0												
INDIANA				248,000	102,423	**41.3%**													
IOWA	47,000	473	**1.0%**	88,000	21,192	**24.1%**	23.1									217,000	386	**0.2%**	-0.8
KANSAS												45,000	5,463	**12.1%**		72,000	8,206	**11.4%**	-0.7
KENTUCKY												213,000	210	**0.1%**		227,000	6,430	**2.8%**	2.7
LOUISIANA																			
MAINE	145,000	7,271	**5.0%**	148,000	14,014	**9.5%**	4.5					152,000	6,866	**4.5%**	-0.5	152,000	308	**0.2%**	-4.8

Total Highest Statewide General Elections (continued)

Total Highest Statewide General Elections (continued)

Other Turnout for Election Years 1850–1866 (continued)

State	1850 Voting-age population	Turnout	%	1854 Voting-age population	Turnout	%	Difference from 1850	1858 Voting-age population	Turnout	%	Difference from 1850	1862 Voting-age population	Turnout	%	Difference from 1850	1866 Voting-age population	Turnout	%	Difference from 1850
MARYLAND												119,000	2,346	2.0%		125,000	22	0.0%	-2.0
MASSACHUSETTS	266,000	27,636	10.4%	272,000	81,503	30.0%	19.6	278,000	12,084	4.3%	-6.0	287,000	54,320	18.9%	8.5	299,000	26,771	9.0%	-1.4
MICHIGAN	100,000	34	0.0%									203,000	62,102	30.6%	30.6				
MINNESOTA																			
MISSISSIPPI																			
MISSOURI												273,000	2,866	1.0%		317,000	8	0.0%	-1.0
MONTANA																			
NEBRASKA																27,000	30	0.1%	
NEVADA																			
NEW HAMPSHIRE	85,000	6,556	7.7%	85,000	11,081	13.0%	5.3					83,000	1,754	2.1%	-5.6	83,000	18	0.0%	-7.7
NEW JERSEY	114,000	1,127	1.0%	127,000	10,765	8.5%	7.5	138,000	3,739	2.7%	1.7					172,000	193	0.1%	-0.9
NEW MEXICO																			
NEW YORK	799,000	4,669	0.6%	837,000	122,282	14.6%	14.0	874,000	75,533	8.6%	8.1	908,000	3,572	0.4%	-0.2	939,000	354	0.0%	-0.5
NORTH CAROLINA								132,000	40,036	30.3%		135,000	20,813	15.4%	-14.9	136,000	10,876	8.0%	-22.3
NORTH DAKOTA																			
OHIO	451,000	15,855	3.5%	477,000	186,445	39.1%	35.6	504,000	999	0.2%	-3.3								
OKLAHOMA																			
OREGON								14,000	4,213	30.1%									
PENNSYLVANIA	540,000	12,005	2.2%	578,000	8,173	1.4%	-0.8	615,000	194,556	31.6%	29.4								
RHODE ISLAND												39,000	65	0.2%		41,000	160	0.4%	0.2
SOUTH CAROLINA	60,000	232	0.4%	62,000	5,556	9.0%	8.6	64,000	5,573	8.7%	8.3								
SOUTH DAKOTA																			
TENNESSEE																189,000	22,506	11.9%	
TEXAS																			
UTAH																			
VERMONT	82,000	11,179	13.6%	79,000	2,447	3.1%	-10.5					75,000	77	0.1%	-13.5	74,000	3	0.0%	-13.6
VIRGINIA												214,000	124	0.1%					
WASHINGTON																			
WEST VIRGINIA																			
WISCONSIN	84,000	18,671	22.2%	118,000	2,072	1.8%	-20.5												
WYOMING																			
Total	2,991,000	107,146	3.6%	3,569,000	601,282	16.8%	13.3	2,702,000	350,244	13.0%	9.4	2,815,000	168,705	6.0%	2.4	3,070,000	76,271	2.5%	-1.1

*By 1854, in Illinois, Indiana, Iowa, Maine, Michigan, New York, Ohio, and Wisconsin, the Republicans had supplanted the Whigs as the main opposition to the Democrats. The turnout for the handful of Whigs who ran (against Republicans) in those states are included in the "Other" chart. In the Northeast and South, however, the Whigs were not supplanted until 1856 and are included in the 1854 major party data.

**Percentage point difference between turnout in current year and initial year listed in chart. If data do not appear for a state in the initial year listed, the difference is calculated from the first year in which data do appear for that state.

STATE GUBERNATORIAL GENERAL ELECTIONS

Election Years 1851–1869

State*	1851 Voting-age population	Turnout	%	1853 Voting-age population	Turnout	%	Difference from 1851**	1855 Voting-age population	Turnout	%	Difference from 1851	1857 Voting-age population	Turnout	%	Difference from 1851	1859 Voting-age population	Turnout	%	Difference from 1851
ALABAMA	94,000	44,277	47.1%	98,000	47,457	48.4%	1.3	103,000	75,800	73.6%	26.5	107,000	41,871	39.1%	-8.0	111,000	65,363	58.9%	11.8
CALIFORNIA	80,000	45,907	57.4%	91,000	76,394	83.9%	26.6	101,000	97,382	96.4%	39.0	113,000	86,300	76.4%	19.0	124,000	76,669	61.8%	4.4
CONNECTICUT	100,000	58,833	58.8%	102,000	60,411	59.2%	0.4	105,000	64,533	61.5%	2.6	107,000	62,865	58.8%	-0.1	110,000	78,616	71.5%	12.6
FLORIDA																			
GEORGIA	110,000	96,238	87.5%	113,000	94,766	83.9%	-3.6	117,000	103,827	88.7%	1.3	121,000	103,362	85.4%	-2.1	124,000	105,614	85.2%	-2.3
IOWA												119,000	74,586	62.7%		140,000	109,034	70.5%	15.8
KENTUCKY	173,000	108,844	62.9%					188,000	135,440	72.0%	9.1					203,000	143,470	70.7%	7.8
LOUISIANA								81,000	41,799	51.6%						84,000	41,041	48.9%	-2.7
MAINE				147,000	83,437	56.8%		148,000	110,500	74.7%	17.9	150,000	97,623	65.1%	8.3	151,000	102,617	68.0%	11.2
MARYLAND				107,000	74,026	69.2%						113,000	85,822	75.9%	6.8				
MASSACHUSETTS	268,000	136,728	51.0%	271,000	123,330	45.5%	-5.5	274,000	136,236	49.7%	-1.3	276,000	130,153	47.2%	-3.9	279,000	108,479	38.9%	-12.1
MICHIGAN	108,000	40,728	37.7%																
MINNESOTA***																34,000	38,918	114.5%	
MISSISSIPPI	67,000	54,137	80.8%	69,000	56,427	81.8%	1.0	71,000	60,247	84.9%	4.1	74,000	41,461	56.0%	-24.8	76,000	44,967	59.2%	-21.6
MISSOURI												217,000	95,594	44.1%					
NEW HAMPSHIRE	84,000	57,916	68.9%	84,000	56,501	67.3%	-1.7	84,000	63,274	75.3%	6.4	84,000	65,423	77.9%	8.9	84,000	69,128	82.3%	13.3
NEW JERSEY				124,000	72,842	58.7%										142,000	105,029	74.0%	15.2
OHIO	458,000	282,116	61.6%	471,000	283,352	60.2%	-1.4	484,000	302,015	62.4%	0.8	497,000	319,979	64.4%	2.8	510,000	355,768	69.8%	8.2
PENNSYLVANIA	549,000	364,533	66.4%									606,000	363,143	59.9%	-6.5				
RHODE ISLAND	38,000	13,029	34.3%	37,000	18,599	50.3%	16.0	38,000	12,772	33.6%	-0.7	37,000	14,914	40.3%	6.0	37,000	12,474	33.7%	-0.6
SOUTH CAROLINA																			
TENNESSEE	157,000	125,071	79.7%	161,000	124,576	77.4%	-2.3	167,000	132,831	79.5%	-0.1	172,000	130,985	76.2%	-3.5	178,000	144,115	81.0%	1.3
TEXAS	47,000	26,470	56.3%	57,000	35,390	62.1%	5.8	69,000	33,217	48.1%	-8.2	80,000	56,180	70.2%	13.9	91,000	63,727	70.0%	13.7
VERMONT	81,000	44,775	55.3%	79,000	47,775	60.5%	5.2	78,000	42,130	54.0%	-1.3	76,000	39,588	52.1%	-3.2	75,000	45,373	60.5%	5.2
VIRGINIA	205,000	126,550	61.7%					219,000	156,468	71.4%	9.7					233,000	148,656	63.8%	2.1
WEST VIRGINIA																			
WISCONSIN	93,000	44,131	47.5%	110,000	55,659	50.6%	3.1	126,000	72,584	57.6%	10.2	144,000	88,932	61.8%	14.3	161,000	112,538	69.9%	22.4
Total	2,712,000	1,670,283	61.6%	2,121,000	1,310,942	61.8%	0.2	2,453,000	1,641,055	66.9%	5.3	3,093,000	1,898,781	61.4%	-0.2	2,947,000	1,972,396	66.9%	5.3

State	1861 Voting-age population	Turnout	%	Difference from 1851	1863 Voting-age population	Turnout	%	Difference from 1851	1865 Voting-age population	Turnout	%	Difference from 1851	1867 Voting-age population	Turnout	%	Difference from 1851	1869 Voting-age population	Turnout	%	Difference from 1851
ALABAMA	111,000	66,338	59.8%	12.7	110,000	37,865	34.4%	-12.7	108,000	45,548	42.2%	-4.9								
CALIFORNIA	130,000	119,731	92.1%	34.7	134,000	108,905	81.3%	23.9					140,000	90,254	64.5%	7.1				

State Gubernatorial General Elections (continued)

State Gubernatorial General Elections (continued)

Election Years 1851–1869 (continued)

State	1861				1863				1865				1867				1869			
	Voting-age population	Turnout	%	Difference from 1851	Voting-age population	Turnout	%	Difference from 1851	Voting-age population	Turnout	%	Difference from 1851	Voting-age population	Turnout	%	Difference from 1851	Voting-age population	Turnout	%	Difference from 1851
CONNECTICUT	113,000	83,938	74.3%	15.4	116,000	79,427	68.5%	9.6	119,000	73,713	61.9%	3.1	122,000	94,143	77.2%	18.3	127,000	90,575	71.3%	12.5
FLORIDA									19,000	5,873	30.9%									
GEORGIA																				
IOWA	163,000	103,548	63.5%	0.8	184,000	142,276	77.3%	14.6	206,000	124,551	60.5%	-2.2	227,000	153,170	67.5%	4.8	249,000	154,530	62.1%	-0.6
KENTUCKY					217,000	85,925	39.6%	-23.3					230,000	137,322	59.7%	-3.2				
LOUISIANA									77,000	28,829	37.4%	-14.2								
MAINE	151,000	97,957	64.9%	8.1	151,000	118,282	78.3%	21.6	152,000	86,039	56.6%	-0.2	152,000	103,703	68.2%	11.5	153,000	95,240	62.2%	5.5
MARYLAND	118,000	83,584	70.8%	1.7									127,000	85,744	67.5%	-1.7				
MASSACHUSETTS	284,000	96,527	34.0%	-17.0	290,000	99,690	34.4%	-16.6	295,000	91,157	30.9%	-20.1	302,000	168,666	55.8%	4.8	310,000	158,408	51.1%	0.1
MICHIGAN																				
MINNESOTA	46,000	26,722	58.1%	-56.4	60,000	32,367	53.9%	-60.5	72,000	31,155	43.3%	-71.2	86,000	64,385	74.9%	-39.6	98,000	52,989	54.1%	-60.4
MISSISSIPPI	77,000	33,515	43.5%	-37.3	78,000	22,985	29.5%	-51.3	79,000	45,113	57.1%	-23.7					170,000	114,283	67.2%	-13.6
MISSOURI																				
NEW HAMPSHIRE	84,000	66,919	79.7%	10.7	84,000	66,240	78.9%	9.9	84,000	60,902	72.5%	3.6	83,000	68,472	82.5%	13.5	83,000	67,781	81.7%	12.7
NEW JERSEY									167,000	132,231	79.2%	20.4								
OHIO	523,000	358,771	68.6%	7.0	536,000	476,584	88.9%	27.3	549,000	417,433	76.0%	14.4	561,000	484,433	86.4%	24.8	587,000	464,795	79.2%	17.6
PENNSYLVANIA					674,000	523,667	77.7%	11.3									768,000	576,508	75.1%	8.7
RHODE ISLAND	38,000	22,044	58.0%	23.7	39,000	18,365	47.1%	12.8	40,000	10,061	25.2%	-9.1	41,000	10,550	25.7%	-8.6	44,000	10,760	24.5%	-9.8
SOUTH CAROLINA									63,000	18,880	30.0%									
TENNESSEE					184,000	7,050	3.8%	-75.8	188,000	22,814	12.1%	-67.5	191,000	96,924	50.7%	-28.9	258,000	175,369	68.0%	-11.7
TEXAS	97,000	57,294	59.1%	2.7	102,000	29,740	29.2%	-27.2	107,000	61,345	57.3%	1.0					166,000	78,884	47.5%	-8.8
VERMONT	75,000	42,067	56.1%	0.8	75,000	41,575	55.4%	0.2	75,000	36,443	48.6%	-6.7	75,000	43,204	57.6%	2.3	74,000	43,289	58.5%	3.2
VIRGINIA																	272,000	220,739	81.2%	19.4
WEST VIRGINIA					87,000	25,797	29.7%													
WISCONSIN	172,000	99,233	57.7%	10.2	179,000	133,519	74.6%	27.1	188,000	106,662	56.7%	9.3	195,000	142,510	73.1%	25.6	200,000	130,741	65.4%	17.9
Total	2,182,000	1,358,188	62.2%	0.7	3,300,000	2,050,259	62.1%	0.5	2,588,000	1,398,749	54.0%	-7.5	2,532,000	1,743,480	68.9%	7.3	3,559,000	2,434,891	68.4%	6.8

*Includes states that seceded from the Union during the Civil War, if data are available.

**Percentage point difference between turnout in current year and initial year listed in chart. If data do not appear for a state in the initial year listed, the difference is calculated from the first year in which data do appear for that state.

***Minnesota 1859 turnout is verified by reliable sources; error is likely with voting-age population, which is an estimate. See the "Methodology" section in the Introduction for more details on calculation of the eligible number of voters.

STATE GUBERNATORIAL GENERAL ELECTIONS

Republican Turnout for Election Years 1851–1869

State	1851 (Whig) Voting-age population	Turnout	%	1853 (Whig) Voting-age population	Turnout	%	Difference from 1851***	1855 (Whig)** Voting-age population	Turnout	%	Difference from 1851	1857 Voting-age population	Turnout	%	Difference from 1851	1859 Voting-age population	Turnout	%	Difference from 1851
ALABAMA	94,000	5,760	6.1%	98,000	9,499	9.7%	3.6												
CALIFORNIA	80,000	22,732	28.4%	91,000	37,454	41.2%	12.7					113,000	17,723	15.7%	-12.7	124,000	8,466	6.8%	-21.6
CONNECTICUT	100,000	28,756	28.8%	102,000	20,671	20.3%	-8.5	105,000	9,162	8.7%	-20.0	107,000	31,709	29.6%	0.9	110,000	40,247	36.6%	7.8
GEORGIA	110,000	38,824	35.3%	113,000	47,128	41.7%	6.4												
IOWA												119,000	38,498	32.4%		140,000	56,502	40.4%	8.0
KENTUCKY	173,000	54,023	31.2%																
MAINE				147,000	27,259	18.5%		148,000	10,645	7.2%	-11.4	150,000	54,655	36.4%	17.9	151,000	57,230	37.9%	19.4
MARYLAND				107,000	34,939	32.7%													
MASSACHUSETTS	268,000	64,279	24.0%	271,000	59,224	21.9%	-2.1	274,000	13,296	4.9%	-19.1	276,000	60,797	22.0%	2.0	279,000	58,780	21.1%	-2.9
MICHIGAN	108,000	16,901	15.6%																
MINNESOTA****																34,000	21,335	62.8%	
MISSISSIPPI				69,000	25,967	37.6%													
NEW HAMPSHIRE	84,000	18,407	21.9%	84,000	17,580	20.9%	-1.0	84,000	3,436	4.1%	-17.8	84,000	34,214	40.7%	18.8	84,000	36,326	43.2%	21.3
NEW JERSEY				124,000	34,530	27.8%										142,000	53,315	37.5%	9.7
OHIO	458,000	119,550	26.1%	471,000	85,843	18.2%	-7.9	484,000	24,276	5.0%	-21.1	497,000	160,685	32.3%	6.2	510,000	184,502	36.2%	10.1
PENNSYLVANIA	549,000	178,034	32.4%									606,000	146,139	24.1%	-8.3				
RHODE ISLAND	38,000	6,071	16.0%	37,000	8,228	22.2%	6.3	38,000	10,466	27.5%	11.6	37,000	9,591	25.9%	9.9	37,000	8,938	24.2%	8.2
TENNESSEE	157,000	63,423	40.4%	161,000	61,163	38.0%	-2.4												
TEXAS				57,000	9,180	16.1%													
VERMONT	81,000	22,864	20.2%	79,000	21,118	26.7%	-1.5					76,000	26,719	35.2%	6.9	75,000	31,045	41.4%	13.2
VIRGINIA	205,000	59,476	29.0%																
WEST VIRGINIA																			
WISCONSIN	93,000	22,319	24.0%	110,000	25,204	22.9%	-1.1					144,000	44,693	31.0%	7.0	161,000	59,999	37.3%	13.3
Total	2,598,000	721,419	27.8%	2,121,000	524,987	24.8%	-3.0	1,133,000	71,281	6.3%	-21.5	2,209,000	625,423	28.3%	0.5	1,847,000	616,685	33.4%	5.6

State	1861 Voting-age population	Turnout	%	Difference from 1851	1863 Voting-age population	Turnout	%	Difference from 1851	1865 Voting-age population	Turnout	%	Difference from 1851	1867 Voting-age population	Turnout	%	Difference from 1851	1869 Voting-age population	Turnout	%	Difference from 1851
ALABAMA																				
CALIFORNIA	130,000	56,036	43.1%	14.7	134,000	64,283	48.0%	19.6					140,000	40,359	28.8%	0.4				
CONNECTICUT	113,000	43,012	38.1%	9.3	116,000	41,032	35.4%	6.6	119,000	42,374	35.6%	6.9	122,000	46,578	38.2%	9.4	127,000	45,493	35.8%	7.1
GEORGIA																				
IOWA	163,000	60,303	26.5%	4.6									227,000	90,204	39.7%	7.4	249,000	97,243	39.1%	6.7
KENTUCKY					217,000	68,422	31.5%	0.3					230,000	33,939	14.8%	-16.5				

State Gubernatorial General Elections (continued)

State Gubernatorial General Elections (continued)

Republican Turnout for Election Years 1851–1869 (continued)

State	1861 Voting-age population	Turnout	%	Difference from 1851	1863 Voting-age population	Turnout	%	Difference from 1851	1865 Voting-age population	Turnout	%	Difference from 1851	1867 Voting-age population	Turnout	%	Difference from 1851	1869 Voting-age population	Turnout	%	Difference from 1851
MAINE	151,000	57,475	38.1%	19.5	151,000	67,916	45.0%	26.4	152,000	54,430	35.8%	17.3	152,000	57,713	38.0%	19.4	153,000	50,784	33.2%	14.6
MARYLAND	118,000	57,498	48.7%	16.1									127,000	22,050	17.4%	-15.3				
MASSACHUSETTS	284,000	65,261	23.0%	-1.0	290,000	70,483	24.3%	0.3	295,000	69,912	23.7%	-0.3	302,000	98,306	32.6%	8.6	310,000	74,106	23.9%	-0.1
MICHIGAN																				
MINNESOTA	46,000	16,274	35.4%	-27.4	60,000	19,628	32.7%	-30.0	72,000	17,308	24.0%	-38.7	86,000	34,874	40.6%	-22.2	98,000	27,599	28.2%	-34.6
MISSISSIPPI									79,000	15,557	19.7%	-17.9					170,000	76,186	44.8%	7.2
NEW HAMPSHIRE	84,000	35,467	42.2%	20.3	84,000	29,035	34.6%	12.7					83,000	35,809	43.1%	21.2	83,000	35,777	43.1%	21.2
NEW JERSEY									167,000	67,525	40.4%	12.6								
OHIO	523,000	206,997	39.6%	13.5	536,000	288,856	53.9%	27.8	549,000	223,642	40.7%	14.6	561,000	243,811	43.5%	17.4	587,000	236,092	40.2%	14.1
PENNSYLVANIA					674,000	269,496	40.0%	7.6									768,000	290,552	37.8%	5.4
RHODE ISLAND	38,000	10,200	26.8%	10.9	39,000	10,828	27.8%	11.8	40,000	10,061	25.2%	9.2	41,000	7,372	18.0%	2.0	44,000	7,370	16.8%	0.8
TENNESSEE									188,000	22,814	12.1%	-28.3	191,000	74,484	39.0%	-1.4	258,000	175,369	68.0%	27.6
TEXAS									107,000	12,068	11.3%	-4.8					166,000	39,838	24.0%	7.9
VERMONT	75,000	33,155	44.2%	16.0	75,000	29,613	39.5%	11.3	75,000	27,586	36.8%	0.6	75,000	31,694	42.3%	14.0	74,000	31,834	43.0%	14.8
VIRGINIA																	272,000	101,204	37.2%	8.2
WEST VIRGINIA					87,000	25,797	29.7%													
WISCONSIN	172,000	53,777	31.3%	7.3	179,000	78,470	43.8%	19.8	188,000	58,332	31.0%	7.0	195,000	73,637	37.8%	13.8	200,000	69,502	34.8%	10.8
Total	1,897,000	695,455	36.7%	8.9	2,642,000	1,063,859	40.3%	12.5	2,031,000	621,609	30.6%	2.8	2,532,000	890,830	35.2%	7.4	3,559,000	1,358,949	38.2%	10.4

Democratic Turnout for Election Years 1851–1869

State	1851 Voting-age population	Turnout	%	1853 Voting-age population	Turnout	%	Difference from 1851	1855 Voting-age population	Turnout	%	Difference from 1851	1857 Voting-age population	Turnout	%	Difference from 1851	1859 Voting-age population	Turnout	%	Difference from 1851
ALABAMA	94,000	38,517	41.0%	98,000	30,862	31.5%	-9.5	103,000	43,936	42.7%	1.7	107,000	41,871	39.1%	-1.8	111,000	47,293	42.6%	1.6
CALIFORNIA	80,000	23,175	29.0%	91,000	38,940	42.8%	13.8	101,000	46,225	45.8%	16.8	113,000	49,096	43.4%	14.5	124,000	44,023	35.5%	6.5
CONNECTICUT	100,000	30,077	30.1%	102,000	30,814	30.2%	0.1	105,000	27,291	26.0%	-4.1	107,000	31,156	29.1%	-1.0	110,000	38,369	34.9%	4.8
FLORIDA																			
GEORGIA				113,000	47,638	42.2%		117,000	54,136	46.3%	4.1	121,000	57,067	47.2%	5.0	124,000	63,784	51.4%	9.3
IOWA													119,000	36,088	30.3%		140,000	53,332	38.1%	7.8
KENTUCKY	173,000	54,821	31.7%						188,000	65,570	34.9%	3.2					203,000	76,187	37.5%	5.8
LOUISIANA									81,000	22,382	27.6%						84,000	25,454	30.3%	2.7
MAINE				147,000	36,127	24.6%		148,000	48,367	32.7%	8.1	150,000	42,968	28.6%	4.1	151,000	45,387	30.1%	5.5
MARYLAND				107,000	39,087	36.5%						113,000	38,681	34.2%	-2.3				
MASSACHUSETTS	268,000	43,889	16.4%	271,000	35,086	12.9%	-3.4	274,000	34,728	12.7%	-3.7	276,000	31,760	11.5%	-4.9	279,000	35,334	12.7%	-3.7

State Gubernatorial General Elections (continued)

Democratic Turnout for Election Years 1851–1869 (continued)

State	1851 Voting-age population	Turnout	%	Difference from 1851	1853 Voting-age population	Turnout	%	Difference from 1851	1855 Voting-age population	Turnout	%	Difference from 1851	1857 Voting-age population	Turnout	%	Difference from 1851	1859 Voting-age population	Turnout	%	Difference from 1851
MICHIGAN	108,000	23,827	22.1%																	
MINNESOTA****																	34,000	17,583	51.7%	
MISSISSIPPI	67,000	54,137	80.8%		69,000	30,460	44.1%	-36.7	71,000	32,669	46.0%	-34.8	74,000	27,376	37.0%	-43.8	76,000	34,559	45.5%	-35.3
MISSOURI													217,000	47,975	22.1%					
NEW HAMPSHIRE	84,000	27,350	32.6%		84,000	30,924	36.8%	4.3	84,000	27,055	32.2%	-0.4	84,000	31,209	37.2%	4.6	84,000	32,802	39.1%	6.5
NEW JERSEY					124,000	38,312	30.9%										142,000	51,714	36.4%	5.5
OHIO	458,000	145,656	31.8%		471,000	147,663	31.4%	-0.5	484,000	131,019	27.1%	-4.7	497,000	159,294	32.1%	0.2	510,000	171,266	33.6%	1.8
PENNSYLVANIA	549,000	186,499	34.0%										606,000	188,836	31.2%	-2.8				
RHODE ISLAND	38,000	6,958	18.3%		37,000	10,371	28.0%	9.7	38,000	2,306	6.1%	-12.2	37,000	5,323	14.4%	-3.9	37,000	3,536	9.6%	-8.8
TENNESSEE	157,000	61,648	39.3%		161,000	63,413	39.4%	0.1	167,000	67,499	40.4%	1.2	172,000	71,178	41.4%	2.1	178,000	76,073	42.7%	3.5
TEXAS					57,000	26,210	46.0%		69,000	20,136	29.2%	-16.8	80,000	32,552	40.7%	-5.3	91,000	27,500	30.2%	-15.8
VERMONT	81,000	6,790	8.4%		79,000	18,287	23.1%	14.8	78,000	12,800	16.4%	8.0	76,000	12,869	16.9%	8.6	75,000	14,328	19.1%	10.7
VIRGINIA	205,000	67,074	32.7%						219,000	83,224	38.0%	5.3					233,000	77,229	33.1%	0.4
WISCONSIN	93,000	21,812	23.5%		110,000	30,455	27.7%	4.2	126,000	36,387	28.9%	5.4	144,000	44,239	30.7%	7.3	161,000	52,539	32.6%	9.2
Total	2,555,000	792,230	31.0%		2,121,000	654,649	30.9%	-0.1	2,453,000	755,730	30.8%	-0.2	3,093,000	949,538	30.7%	-0.3	2,947,000	988,292	33.5%	2.5

State	1861 Voting-age population	Turnout	%	Difference from 1851	1863 Voting-age population	Turnout	%	Difference from 1851	1865 Voting-age population	Turnout	%	Difference from 1851	1867 Voting-age population	Turnout	%	Difference from 1851	1869 Voting-age population	Turnout	%	Difference from 1851
ALABAMA	111,000	38,221	34.4%	-6.5	110,000	9,664	8.8%	-32.2	108,000	16,380	15.2%	-25.8								
CALIFORNIA	130,000	63,695	49.0%	20.0	134,000	44,622	33.3%	4.3					140,000	49,895	35.6%	6.7				
CONNECTICUT	113,000	40,926	36.2%	6.1	116,000	38,395	33.1%	3.0	119,000	31,339	26.3%	-3.7	122,000	47,565	39.0%	8.9	127,000	45,082	35.5%	5.4
FLORIDA									19,000	5,873	30.9%									
GEORGIA																				
IOWA	163,000	43,245	26.5%	-3.8	184,000	56,169	30.5%	0.2	206,000	54,090	26.3%	-4.1	227,000	62,966	27.7%	-2.6	249,000	57,287	23.0%	-7.3
KENTUCKY					217,000	17,503	8.1%	-23.6					230,000	90,216	39.2%	7.5				
LOUISIANA									77,000	22,532	29.3%	1.6								
MAINE	151,000	21,119	14.0%	-10.6	151,000	50,366	33.4%	8.8	152,000	31,609	20.8%	-3.8	152,000	45,990	30.3%	5.7	153,000	39,428	25.8%	1.2
MARYLAND	118,000	26,086	22.1%	-14.4									127,000	63,694	50.2%	13.6				
MASSACHUSETTS	284,000	31,266	11.0%	-5.4	290,000	29,207	10.1%	-6.3	295,000	21,245	7.2%	-9.2	302,000	70,360	23.3%	6.9	310,000	70,735	22.8%	6.4
MICHIGAN																				
MINNESOTA	46,000	10,448	22.7%	-29.0	60,000	12,739	21.2%	-30.5	72,000	13,847	19.2%	-32.5	86,000	29,511	34.3%	-17.4	98,000	25,390	25.9%	-25.8
MISSISSIPPI																				
MISSOURI																				

State Gubernatorial General Elections (continued)

Democratic Turnout for Election Years 1851–1869 (continued)

State	1861 Voting-age population	Turnout	%	Difference from 1851	1863 Voting-age population	Turnout	%	Difference from 1851	1865 Voting-age population	Turnout	%	Difference from 1851	1867 Voting-age population	Turnout	%	Difference from 1851	1869 Voting-age population	Turnout	%	Difference from 1851
NEW HAMPSHIRE	84,000	31,452	37.4%	4.9	84,000	32,833	39.1%	6.5	84,000	27,735	33.0%	0.5	83,000	32,663	39.4%	6.8	83,000	32,004	38.6%	6.0
NEW JERSEY									167,000	64,706	38.7%	7.8								
OHIO	523,000	151,774	29.0%	-2.8	536,000	187,728	35.0%	3.2	549,000	193,791	35.3%	3.5	561,000	240,622	42.9%	11.1	587,000	228,703	39.0%	7.2
PENNSYLVANIA					674,000	254,171	37.7%	3.7									768,000	285,956	37.2%	3.3
RHODE ISLAND					39,000	7,537	19.3%	1.0					41,000	3,178	7.8%	-10.6	44,000	3,390	7.7%	-10.6
TENNESSEE																				
TEXAS																	166,000	39,046	23.5%	-22.5
VERMONT	75,000	8,912	11.9%	3.5	75,000	11,962	15.9%	7.6	75,000	8,857	11.8%	3.4	75,000	11,510	15.3%	7.0	74,000	11,455	15.5%	7.1
VIRGINIA																				
WISCONSIN	172,000	45,456	26.4%	3.0	179,000	55,049	30.8%	7.3	188,000	48,330	25.7%	2.3	195,000	68,873	35.3%	11.9	200,000	61,239	30.6%	7.2
Total	1,970,000	512,600	26.0%	-5.0	2,849,000	807,945	28.4%	-2.6	2,111,000	540,334	25.6%	-5.4	2,341,000	817,043	34.9%	3.9	2,859,000	899,715	31.5%	0.5

Other Turnout for Election Years 1851–1869

State	1851 Voting-age population	Turnout	%	1853 Voting-age population	Turnout	%	Difference from 1851	1855 Voting-age population	Turnout	%	Difference from 1851	1857 Voting-age population	Turnout	%	Difference from 1851	1859 Voting-age population	Turnout	%	Difference from 1851
ALABAMA				98,000	7,096	7.2%		103,000	31,864	30.9%	23.7					111,000	18,070	16.3%	9.0
CALIFORNIA								101,000	51,157	50.7%		113,000	19,481	17.2%	-33.4	124,000	24,180	19.5%	-31.2
CONNECTICUT				102,000	8,926	8.8%		105,000	28,080	26.7%	18.0								
GEORGIA	110,000	57,414	52.2%					117,000	49,691	42.5%	-9.7	121,000	46,295	38.3%	-13.9	124,000	41,830	33.7%	-18.5
IOWA																			
KENTUCKY								188,000	69,870	37.2%						203,000	67,283	33.1%	-4.0
LOUISIANA								81,000	19,417	24.0%						84,000	15,587	18.6%	-5.4
MAINE				147,000	20,051	13.6%		148,000	51,488	34.8%	21.1								
MARYLAND												113,000	47,141	41.7%					
MASSACHUSETTS	268,000	28,560	10.7%	271,000	29,020	10.7%	0.1	274,000	88,212	32.2%	21.5	276,000	37,596	13.6%	3.0	279,000	14,365	5.1%	-5.6
MINNESOTA																			
MISSISSIPPI								71,000	27,578	38.8%		74,000	14,085	19.0%	-19.8	76,000	10,408	13.7%	-25.1
MISSOURI												217,000	47,619	21.9%					
NEW HAMPSHIRE	84,000	12,159	14.5%	84,000	7,997	9.5%	-5.0	84,000	32,783	39.0%	24.5								
NEW JERSEY																			
OHIO	458,000	16,910	3.7%	471,000	49,846	10.6%	6.9	484,000	146,720	30.3%	26.6								
PENNSYLVANIA												606,000	28,168	4.6%					
RHODE ISLAND																			
SOUTH CAROLINA																			
TENNESSEE								167,000	65,332	39.1%		172,000	59,807	34.8%	-4.3	178,000	68,042	38.2%	-0.9

State Gubernatorial General Elections (continued)

Other Turnout for Election Years 1851–1869 (continued)

State	1851 Voting-age population	Turnout	%	1853 Voting-age population	Turnout	%	Difference from 1851	1855 Voting-age population	Turnout	%	Difference from 1851	1857 Voting-age population	Turnout	%	Difference from 1851	1859 Voting-age population	Turnout	%	Difference from 1851
TEXAS	47,000	26,470	56.3%					69,000	13,081	19.0%	-37.4	80,000	23,628	29.5%	-26.8	91,000	36,227	39.8%	-16.5
VERMONT	81,000	15,121	18.7%	79,000	8,370	10.6%	-8.1	78,000	29,330	37.6%	18.9								
VIRGINIA								219,000	73,244	33.4%						233,000	71,427	30.7%	-2.8
WISCONSIN								126,000	36,198	28.7%									
Total	1,048,000	156,634	14.9%	1,252,000	131,306	10.5%	-4.5	2,415,000	814,045	33.7%	18.8	1,772,000	323,820	18.3%	3.3	1,503,000	367,419	24.4%	9.5

State	1861 Voting-age population	Turnout	%		1863 Voting-age population	Turnout	%	Difference from 1851	1865 Voting-age population	Turnout	%	Difference from 1851	1867 Voting-age population	Turnout	%	Difference from 1851	1869 Voting-age population	Turnout	%	Difference from 1851
ALABAMA	111,000	28,117	25.3%	18.1	110,000	28,201	25.6%	18.4	108,000	29,168	27.0%	19.8								
CALIFORNIA																				
CONNECTICUT																				
GEORGIA																				
IOWA					184,000	86,107	46.8%		206,000	70,461	34.2%	-12.6								
KENTUCKY													230,000	13,167	5.7%	-31.4				
LOUISIANA									77,000	6,297	8.2%	15.8								
MAINE	151,000	19,363	12.8%	-0.8													153,000	5,028	3.3%	-10.4
MARYLAND																				
MASSACHUSETTS																	310,000	13,567	4.4%	-6.3
MINNESOTA																				
MISSISSIPPI	77,000	33,515	43.5%	4.7	78,000	22,985	29.5%	-9.4	79,000	29,556	37.4%	-1.4					170,000	38,097	22.4%	-16.4
MISSOURI																				
NEW HAMPSHIRE					84,000	4,372	5.2%	-9.3	84,000	33,167	39.5%	25.0								
NEW JERSEY																				
OHIO																				
PENNSYLVANIA																				
RHODE ISLAND	38,000	11,844	31.2%																	
SOUTH CAROLINA									63,000	18,880	30.0%									
TENNESSEE					184,000	7,050	3.8%	-35.3					191,000	22,440	11.7%	-27.4				
TEXAS	97,000	57,294	59.1%	2.7	102,000	29,740	29.2%	-27.2	107,000	49,277	46.1%	-10.3								
VERMONT																				
VIRGINIA																	272,000	119,535	43.9%	10.5
WISCONSIN																				
Total	474,000	150,133	31.7%	16.7	742,000	178,455	24.1%	9.1	724,000	236,806	32.7%	17.8	421,000	35,607	8.5%	-6.5	905,000	176,227	19.5%	4.5

*Includes states that seceded from the Union during the Civil War, if data are available.

**1855 gubernatorial races were one of the few moments when Whigs and Republicans competed directly. Republican votes for 1855 are included in "Other." For 1857 and beyond, any Whig votes are included in "Other."

***Percentage point difference between turnout in current year and initial year listed in chart. If data do not appear for a state in the initial year listed, the difference is calculated from the first year in which data do appear for that state.

****Minnesota 1859 turnout is verified by reliable sources; error is likely with voting-age population, which is an estimate. See the "Methodology" section in the Introduction for more details on calculation of the eligible number of voters.

UNITED STATES HOUSE OF REPRESENTATIVES GENERAL ELECTIONS

Election Years 1851–1869

State	1851 Voting-age population	Turnout	%	1853 Voting-age population	Turnout	%	Difference from 1851*	1855 Voting-age population	Turnout	%	Difference from 1851	1857 Voting-age population	Turnout	%	Difference from 1851	1859 Voting-age population	Turnout	%	Difference from 1851
ALABAMA	94,000	67,971	72.3%	98,000	62,038	63.3%	-9.0	103,000	72,793	70.7%	-1.6	107,000	74,328	69.5%	-2.8	111,000	50,799	45.8%	-26.5
ARKANSAS	40,000	20,841	52.1%	46,000	17,329	37.7%	-14.4												
CALIFORNIA	80,000	46,553	58.2%													124,000	101,109	81.5%	23.3
CONNECTICUT	100,000	60,436	60.4%	102,000	59,791	58.6%	-1.8	105,000	63,382	60.4%	-0.1	107,000	62,619	58.5%	-1.9	110,000	78,301	71.2%	10.7
GEORGIA	110,000	93,657	85.1%	113,000	91,688	81.1%	-4.0	117,000	102,598	87.7%	2.5	121,000	99,992	82.6%	-2.5	124,000	97,940	79.0%	-6.2
INDIANA	222,000	148,548	66.9%																
KANSAS																			
KENTUCKY	173,000	101,379	58.6%	181,000	118,238	65.3%	6.7	188,000	135,532	72.1%	13.5	196,000	130,220	66.4%	7.8	203,000	141,212	69.6%	11.0
LOUISIANA	78,000	36,362	46.6%					81,000	41,587	51.3%	4.7	82,000	37,907	46.2%	-0.4	84,000	37,450	44.6%	-2.0
MARYLAND	105,000	53,698	51.1%	107,000	71,696	67.0%	15.9	109,000	81,730	75.0%	23.8	113,000	85,489	75.7%	24.5	115,000	87,028	75.7%	24.5
MINNESOTA**																34,000	38,778	114.1%	
MISSISSIPPI	67,000	57,792	86.3%	69,000	63,645	92.2%	6.0	71,000	60,293	84.9%	-1.3	74,000	37,731	51.0%	-35.3	76,000	39,679	52.2%	-34.0
NEVADA																			
NEW HAMPSHIRE	84,000	53,322	63.5%	84,000	51,466	61.3%	-2.2	84,000	63,964	76.1%	12.7	84,000	63,691	75.8%	12.3	84,000	68,793	81.9%	18.4
NORTH CAROLINA	119,000	47,431	39.9%	122,000	81,098	66.5%	26.6	127,000	91,117	71.7%	31.9	130,000	77,932	59.9%	20.1	135,000	73,787	54.7%	14.8
OREGON																14,000	11,276	80.5%	
RHODE ISLAND	38,000	12,812	33.7%	37,000	15,755	42.6%	8.9	38,000	13,348	35.1%	1.4	37,000	14,765	39.9%	6.2	37,000	12,655	34.2%	0.5
TENNESSEE	157,000	108,513	69.1%	161,000	108,669	67.5%	-1.6	167,000	127,250	76.2%	7.1	172,000	123,396	71.7%	2.6	178,000	137,958	77.5%	8.4
TEXAS	47,000	27,367	58.2%	57,000	33,359	58.5%	0.3	69,000	44,689	64.8%	6.5	80,000	50,116	62.6%	4.4	91,000	58,359	64.1%	5.9
VERMONT																			
VIRGINIA	205,000	47,348	23.1%	212,000	77,908	36.7%	13.7	219,000	129,316	59.0%	36.0	225,000	85,098	37.8%	14.7	233,000	101,813	43.7%	20.6
WEST VIRGINIA																			
Total	1,719,000	984,030	57.2%	1,389,000	852,680	61.4%	4.1	1,478,000	1,027,599	69.5%	12.3	1,528,000	943,284	61.7%	4.5	1,753,000	1,136,937	64.9%	7.6

State	1861 Voting-age population	Turnout	%	Difference from 1851	1863 Voting-age population	Turnout	%	Difference from 1851	1865 Voting-age population	Turnout	%	Difference from 1851	1867 Voting-age population	Turnout	%	Difference from 1851	1869 Voting-age population	Turnout	%	Difference from 1851
ALABAMA									108,000	40,478	37.5%	-34.8					203,000	115,196	56.7%	-15.6
ARKANSAS																				
CALIFORNIA	130,000	111,088	85.5%	27.3	134,000	109,065	81.4%	23.2					140,000	92,782	66.3%	8.1				
CONNECTICUT	113,000	83,753	74.1%	13.7	116,000	79,928	68.9%	8.5	119,000	73,183	61.5%	1.1	122,000	93,874	76.9%	16.5	127,000	89,293	70.3%	9.9
GEORGIA																				
INDIANA																				
KANSAS																				

United States House of Representatives General Elections *(continued)*

Election Years 1851–1869 *(continued)*

State	1861				1863				1865				1867				1869			
	Voting-age population	Turnout	%	Difference from 1851	Voting-age population	Turnout	%	Difference from 1851	Voting-age population	Turnout	%	Difference from 1851	Voting-age population	Turnout	%	Difference from 1851	Voting-age population	Turnout	%	Difference from 1851
KENTUCKY	209,000	130,131	62.3%	3.7	217,000	84,136	38.8%	-19.8	223,000	111,683	50.1%	-8.5	230,000	112,943	49.1%	-9.5				
LOUISIANA																				
MARYLAND	118,000	67,178	56.9%	5.8	120,000	50,259	41.9%	-9.3												
MINNESOTA																				
MISSISSIPPI																	170,000	96,461	56.7%	-29.5
NEVADA									12,000	5,906	49.2%									
NEW HAMPSHIRE	84,000	66,969	79.7%	16.2	84,000	65,820	78.4%	14.9	84,000	66,268	78.9%	15.4	83,000	68,595	82.6%	19.2	83,000	66,973	80.7%	17.2
NORTH CAROLINA																				
OREGON																				
RHODE ISLAND	38,000	21,951	57.8%	24.1	39,000	18,533	47.5%	13.8	40,000	9,712	24.3%	-9.4	41,000	8,561	20.9%	-12.8				
TENNESSEE	181,000	40,817	22.6%	-46.6					188,000	58,622	31.2%	-37.9	191,000	96,123	50.3%	-18.8				
TEXAS																	166,000	76,107	45.8%	-12.4
VERMONT					75,000	38,845	51.8%													
VIRGINIA	221,000	12,990	5.9%	-17.2													272,000	113,234	41.6%	18.5
WEST VIRGINIA					87,000	19,783	22.7%													
Total	1,094,000	534,877	48.9%	-8.4	872,000	466,369	53.5%	-3.8	774,000	365,852	47.3%	-10.0	807,000	472,878	58.6%	1.4	1,021,000	557,264	54.6%	-2.7

*Percentage point difference between turnout in current year and initial year listed in chart. If data do not appear for a state in the initial year listed, the difference is calculated from the first year in which data do appear for that state.

**Minnesota 1859 turnout is verified by reliable sources; error is likely with voting-age population, which is an estimate. See the "Methodology" section in the Introduction for more details on calculation of the eligible number of voters.

UNITED STATES HOUSE OF REPRESENTATIVES GENERAL ELECTIONS

Republican Turnout for Election Years 1851–1869

State	1851 (Whig) Voting-age population	Turnout	%	1853 (Whig) Voting-age population	Turnout	%	Difference from 1851**	1855 (Whig)* Voting-age population	Turnout	%	Difference from 1851	1857 Voting-age population	Turnout	%	Difference from 1851	1859 Voting-age population	Turnout	%	Difference from 1851
ALABAMA	94,000	22,681	24.1%	98,000	19,842	20.2%	-3.9												
ARKANSAS	40,000	8,876	22.2%	46,000	4,143	9.0%	-13.2												
CALIFORNIA	80,000	20,758	25.9%													124,000	20,874	16.8%	-9.1
CONNECTICUT	100,000	28,886	28.9%	102,000	24,947	24.5%	-4.4					107,000	31,785	29.7%	0.8	110,000	39,731	36.1%	7.2
GEORGIA	110,000	55,984	50.9%	113,000	40,589	35.9%	-15.0												
INDIANA	222,000	69,493	31.3%																
KANSAS																			
KENTUCKY	173,000	50,632	29.3%	181,000	61,399	33.9%	4.7												
LOUISIANA	78,000	18,040	23.1%																
MARYLAND	105,000	22,904	21.8%	107,000	23,428	21.9%	0.1												
MINNESOTA																34,000	21,188	62.3%	
MISSISSIPPI	67,000	29,751	44.4%	69,000	29,107	42.2%	-2.2												
NEVADA																			
NEW HAMPSHIRE	84,000	22,656	27.0%	84,000	20,871	24.8%	-2.1					84,000	33,619	40.0%	13.1	84,000	35,844	42.7%	15.7
NORTH CAROLINA	119,000	26,307	22.1%	122,000	32,020	26.2%	4.1	127,000	3,756	3.0%	-19.1					135,000	25,047	18.6%	-3.6
OREGON																14,000	5,630	40.2%	
RHODE ISLAND	38,000	5,895	15.5%	37,000	5,392	14.6%	-0.9					37,000	9,485	25.6%	10.1	37,000	5,552	15.0%	-0.5
TENNESSEE	157,000	55,303	35.2%	161,000	53,969	33.5%	-1.7												
TEXAS	47,000	4,354	9.3%	57,000	2,326	4.1%	-5.2												
VERMONT																			
VIRGINIA	205,000	20,200	9.9%	212,000	27,937	13.2%	3.3												
WEST VIRGINIA																			
Total	1,719,000	462,720	26.9%	1,389,000	345,970	24.9%	-2.0	127,000	3,756	3.0%	-24.0	228,000	74,889	32.8%	5.9	538,000	153,866	28.6%	1.7

State*	1861 Voting-age population	Turnout	%	Difference from 1851	1863 Voting-age population	Turnout	%	Difference from 1851	1865 Voting-age population	Turnout	%	Difference from 1851	1867 Voting-age population	Turnout	%	Difference from 1851	1869 Voting-age population	Turnout	%	Difference from 1851
ALABAMA																	203,000	64,031	31.5%	7.4
ARKANSAS																				
CALIFORNIA	130,000	51,651	39.7%	13.8	134,000	65,149	48.6%	22.7					140,000	44,436	31.7%	5.8				
CONNECTICUT	113,000	42,465	37.6%	8.7	116,000	41,048	35.4%	6.5	119,000	42,168	35.4%	6.5	122,000	46,240	37.9%	9.0	127,000	45,846	36.1%	7.2
GEORGIA																				
INDIANA																				
KANSAS																				

United States House of Representatives General Elections (continued)

Republican Turnout for Election Years 1851–1869 (continued)

State	1861 Voting-age population	Turnout	%	Difference from 1851	1863 Voting-age population	Turnout	%	Difference from 1851	1865 Voting-age population	Turnout	%	Difference from 1851	1867 Voting-age population	Turnout	%	Difference from 1851	1869 Voting-age population	Turnout	%	Difference from 1851
KENTUCKY	209,000	36,845	17.6%	-11.6					223,000	54,008	24.2%	-5.0	230,000	28,874	12.6%	-16.7				
LOUISIANA																				
MARYLAND	118,000	42,397	35.9%	14.1	120,000	37,492	31.2%	9.4												
MINNESOTA																				
MISSISSIPPI																	170,000	57,186	33.6%	-10.8
NEVADA									12,000	2,215	18.5%									
NEW HAMPSHIRE	84,000	35,596	42.4%	15.4	84,000	33,191	39.5%	12.5	84,000	35,583	42.4%	15.4	83,000	35,797	43.1%	16.2	83,000	35,512	42.8%	15.8
NORTH CAROLINA																				
OREGON																				
RHODE ISLAND	38,000	21,951	57.8%	42.3	39,000	10,738	27.5%	12.0	40,000	8,373	20.9%	5.4	41,000	6,980	17.0%	1.5				
TENNESSEE									188,000	24,043	12.8%	-22.4	191,000	73,617	38.5%	3.3				
TEXAS																	166,000	44,138	26.6%	17.3
VERMONT					75,000	27,923	37.2%													
VIRGINIA	221,000	12,937	5.9%	-4.0													272,000	73,959	27.2%	17.3
WEST VIRGINIA					87,000	19,783	22.7%													
Total	913,000	243,842	26.7%	-0.2	655,000	235,324	35.9%	9.0	666,000	166,390	25.0%	-1.9	807,000	235,944	29.2%	2.3	1,021,000	320,672	31.4%	4.5

Democratic Turnout for Election Years 1851–1869

State*	1851 Voting-age population	Turnout	%	1853 Voting-age population	Turnout	%	Difference from 1851*	1855 Voting-age population	Turnout	%	Difference from 1851	1857 Voting-age population	Turnout	%	Difference from 1851	1859 Voting-age population	Turnout	%	Difference from 1851
ALABAMA	94,000	45,290	48.2%	98,000	42,196	43.1%	-5.1	103,000	41,108	39.9%	-8.3	107,000	54,060	50.5%	2.3	111,000	39,207	35.3%	-12.9
ARKANSAS	40,000	11,965	29.9%	46,000	13,186	28.7%	-1.2												
CALIFORNIA	80,000	25,796	32.2%													124,000	80,235	64.7%	32.5
CONNECTICUT	100,000	29,984	30.0%	102,000	31,605	31.0%	1.0	105,000	27,229	25.9%	-4.1	107,000	30,834	28.8%	-1.2	110,000	38,071	34.6%	4.6
GEORGIA	110,000	37,673	34.2%	113,000	46,000	40.7%	6.5	117,000	56,905	48.6%	14.4	121,000	66,612	55.1%	20.8	124,000	61,104	49.3%	15.0
INDIANA	222,000	74,515	33.6%																
KANSAS																			
KENTUCKY	173,000	47,446	27.4%	181,000	56,839	31.4%	4.0	188,000	65,845	35.0%	7.6	196,000	72,681	37.1%	9.7	203,000	76,542	37.7%	10.3
LOUISIANA	78,000	18,322	23.5%					81,000	22,111	27.3%	3.8	82,000	21,962	26.8%	-0.5	84,000	25,638	30.5%	3.2
MARYLAND	105,000	22,949	21.9%	107,000	27,456	25.7%	3.8	109,000	39,786	36.5%	14.6	113,000	38,252	33.9%	12.0	115,000	34,862	30.3%	8.5
MINNESOTA																34,000	17,590	51.7%	
MISSISSIPPI	67,000	28,041	41.9%	69,000	34,538	50.1%	8.2	71,000	32,718	46.1%	4.2	74,000	27,052	36.6%	-5.3	76,000	39,234	51.6%	9.8

United States House of Representatives General Elections (continued)

Democratic Turnout for Election Years 1851–1869 (continued)

State	1851 Voting-age population	Turnout	%	Difference from 1851	1853 Voting-age population	Turnout	%	Difference from 1851	1855 Voting-age population	Turnout	%	Difference from 1851	1857 Voting-age population	Turnout	%	Difference from 1851	1859 Voting-age population	Turnout	%	Difference from 1851
NEVADA																				
NEW HAMPSHIRE	84,000	27,488	32.7%		84,000	28,853	34.3%	1.6	84,000	27,090	32.3%	-0.5	84,000	30,072	35.8%	3.1	84,000	32,949	39.2%	6.5
NORTH CAROLINA	119,000	20,567	17.3%		122,000	49,078	40.2%	22.9	127,000	45,318	35.7%	18.4	130,000	52,624	40.5%	23.2	135,000	45,737	33.9%	16.6
OREGON																	14,000	5,646	40.3%	
RHODE ISLAND	38,000	6,763	17.8%		37,000	9,962	26.9%	9.1	38,000	1,987	5.2%	-12.6	37,000	5,280	14.3%	-3.5	37,000	3,257	8.8%	-9.0
TENNESSEE	157,000	53,210	33.9%		161,000	54,556	33.9%	0.0	167,000	61,824	37.0%	3.1	172,000	70,270	40.9%	7.0	178,000	69,161	38.9%	5.0
TEXAS	47,000	16,928	36.0%		57,000	30,865	54.1%	18.1	69,000	24,910	36.1%	0.1	80,000	35,682	44.6%	8.6	91,000	55,501	61.0%	25.0
VERMONT																				
VIRGINIA	205,000	27,119	13.2%		212,000	48,674	23.0%	9.7	219,000	74,829	34.2%	20.9	225,000	52,567	23.4%	10.1	233,000	84,120	36.1%	22.9
Total	1,719,000	494,056	28.7%		1,389,000	473,808	34.1%	5.4	1,478,000	521,660	35.3%	6.6	1,528,000	557,948	36.5%	7.8	1,753,000	708,854	40.4%	11.7

State*	1861 Voting-age population	Turnout	%	Difference from 1851	1863 Voting-age population	Turnout	%	Difference from 1851	1865 Voting-age population	Turnout	%	Difference from 1851	1867 Voting-age population	Turnout	%	Difference from 1851	1869 Voting-age population	Turnout	%	Difference from 1851
ALABAMA																	203,000	48,380	23.8%	-24.3
ARKANSAS																				
CALIFORNIA	130,000	35,401	27.2%	-5.0	134,000	43,916	32.8%	0.5					140,000	48,346	34.5%	2.3				
CONNECTICUT	113,000	41,288	36.5%	6.6	116,000	38,880	33.5%	3.5	119,000	31,015	26.1%	-3.9	122,000	47,634	39.0%	9.1	127,000	43,447	34.2%	4.2
GEORGIA																				
INDIANA																				
KANSAS																				
KENTUCKY	209,000	92,365	44.2%	16.8	217,000	83,926	38.7%	11.3	223,000	57,675	25.9%	-1.6	230,000	77,639	33.8%	6.3				
LOUISIANA																				
MARYLAND					120,000	10,421	8.7%	-13.2												
MINNESOTA																				
MISSISSIPPI																	170,000	35,428	20.8%	-21.0
NEVADA									12,000	3,691	30.8%									
NEW HAMPSHIRE	84,000	31,373	37.3%	4.6	84,000	32,629	38.8%	6.1	84,000	30,185	35.9%	3.2	83,000	32,798	39.5%	6.8	83,000	31,461	37.9%	5.2
NORTH CAROLINA																				
OREGON																				
RHODE ISLAND					39,000	7,795	20.0%	2.2	40,000	1,286	3.2%	-14.6	41,000	1,480	3.6%	-14.2				
TENNESSEE													191,000	22,506	11.8%	-22.1				
TEXAS																	166,000	31,588	19.0%	-17.0
VERMONT					75,000	10,922	14.6%													

United States House of Representatives General Elections (continued)

Democratic Turnout for Election Years 1851–1869 (continued)

State	1861 Voting-age population	Turnout	%	Difference from 1851	1863 Voting-age population	Turnout	%	Difference from 1851	1865 Voting-age population	Turnout	%	Difference from 1851	1867 Voting-age population	Turnout	%	Difference from 1851	1869 Voting-age population	Turnout	%	Difference from 1851
VIRGINIA																	272,000	35,428	13.0%	-0.2
Total	536,000	200,427	37.4%	8.7	785,000	228,489	29.1%	0.4	478,000	123,852	25.9%	-2.8	807,000	230,403	28.6%	-0.2	1,021,000	225,732	22.1%	-6.6

Other Turnout for Election Years 1851–1869

State*	1851 Voting-age population	Turnout	%	1853 Voting-age population	Turnout	%	Difference from 1851*	1855 Voting-age population	Turnout	%	Difference from 1851	1857 Voting-age population	Turnout	%	Difference from 1851	1859 Voting-age population	Turnout	%	Difference from 1851
ALABAMA								103,000	31,685	30.8%		107,000	20,268	18.9%	-11.8	111,000	11,592	10.4%	-20.3
CALIFORNIA																			
CONNECTICUT	100,000	1,566	1.6%	102,000	3,239	3.2%	1.6	105,000	36,153	34.4%	31.3					110,000	499	0.5%	-1.1
GEORGIA				113,000	5,099	4.5%		117,000	45,693	39.1%	34.5	121,000	33,380	27.6%	23.1	124,000	36,836	29.7%	25.2
INDIANA	222,000	4,540	2.0%																
KENTUCKY	173,000	3,301	1.9%					188,000	69,687	37.1%	35.2	196,000	57,539	29.4%	27.4	203,000	64,670	31.9%	29.9
LOUISIANA								81,000	19,476	24.0%		82,000	15,945	19.4%	-4.6	84,000	11,812	14.1%	-10.0
MARYLAND	105,000	7,845	7.5%	107,000	20,812	19.5%	12.0	109,000	41,944	38.5%	31.0	113,000	47,237	41.8%	34.3	115,000	52,166	45.4%	37.9
MISSISSIPPI								71,000	27,575	38.8%		74,000	10,679	14.4%	-24.4	76,000	445	0.6%	-38.3
NEW HAMPSHIRE	84,000	3,178	3.8%	84,000	1,742	2.1%	-1.7	84,000	36,874	43.9%	40.1								
NORTH CAROLINA	119,000	557	0.5%					127,000	42,043	33.1%	32.6	130,000	25,308	19.5%	19.0	135,000	3,003	2.2%	-30.9
RHODE ISLAND	38,000	154	0.4%	37,000	401	1.1%	0.7	38,000	11,361	29.9%	29.5					37,000	3,846	10.4%	10.0
TENNESSEE				161,000	144	0.1%		167,000	65,426	39.2%	39.1	172,000	53,126	30.9%	30.8	178,000	68,797	38.7%	38.6
TEXAS	47,000	6,085	12.9%	57,000	168	0.3%	-12.7	69,000	19,779	28.7%	15.7	80,000	14,434	18.0%	5.1	91,000	2,858	3.1%	-9.8
VIRGINIA	205,000	29	0.0%	212,000	1,297	0.6%	0.6	219,000	54,487	24.9%	24.9	225,000	32,531	14.5%	14.4	233,000	17,693	7.6%	7.6
Total	4,531,000	984,031	21.7%	3,651,000	852,680	23.4%	1.6	3,083,000	1,027,599	33.3%	11.6	3,056,000	943,284	30.9%	9.1	3,788,000	1,136,937	30.0%	8.3

State*	1861 Voting-age population	Turnout	%	Difference from 1851	1863 Voting-age population	Turnout	%	Difference from 1851	1865 Voting-age population	Turnout	%	Difference from 1851	1867 Voting-age population	Turnout	%	Difference from 1851	1869 Voting-age population	Turnout	%	Difference from 1851
ALABAMA									108,000	40,478	37.5%	6.7					203,000	2,785	1.4%	-29.4
CALIFORNIA	130,000	24,036	18.5%																	
CONNECTICUT																				
GEORGIA																				
INDIANA																				
KENTUCKY	209,000	921	0.4%	-1.5	217,000	210	0.1%	-1.8					230,000	6,430	2.8%	0.9				
LOUISIANA																				

United States House of Representatives General Elections (continued)

United States House of Representatives General Elections *(continued)*

Other Turnout for Election Years 1851–1869 *(continued)*

State	1861				1863				1865				1867				1869			
	Voting-age population	Turnout	%	Difference from 1851	Voting-age population	Turnout	%	Difference from 1851	Voting-age population	Turnout	%	Difference from 1851	Voting-age population	Turnout	%	Difference from 1851	Voting-age population	Turnout	%	Difference from 1851
MARYLAND	118,000	24,781	**21.0%**	13.5	120,000	2,346	**2.0%**	-5.5												
MISSISSIPPI																	170,000	3,847	**2.3%**	-36.6
NEW HAMPSHIRE									84,000	500	**0.6%**	-3.2								
NORTH CAROLINA																				
RHODE ISLAND									40,000	53	**0.1%**	-0.3	41,000	101	**0.2%**	-0.2				
TENNESSEE	181,000	40,817	**22.6%**	22.5					188,000	34,579	**18.4%**	18.3								
TEXAS																	166,000	381	**0.2%**	-12.7
VIRGINIA	221,000	53	**0.0%**	0.0													272,000	3,847	**1.4%**	1.4
Total	2,308,000	534,877	**23.2%**	1.5	1,777,000	466,369	**26.2%**	4.5	1,564,000	365,852	**23.4%**	1.7	1,885,000	472,878	**25.1%**	3.4	2,853,000	557,264	**19.5%**	-2.2

*The Whig party had all but disappeared by 1855 and was replaced by Republicans by 1857. Any Whig votes tallied in 1857 are included in "Other."

**Percentage point difference between turnout in current year and initial year listed in chart. If data do not appear for a state in the initial year listed, the difference is calculated from the first year in which data do appear for that state.

CHAPTER 5
1870–1889

Chronology of Major Events, 1870–1889

1870	The Fifteenth Amendment is ratified, preventing the denial of voting rights "on account of race, color, or previous condition of servitude." The last southern states are fully readmitted to the Union. Congress passes the first of three Enforcement Acts aimed at enforcing the intent of the Fourteenth and Fifteenth amendments. The ninth census counts the U.S. population at 38.6 million people.
1872	Liberal Republicans, a splinter party from the Republicans, nominate Horace Greeley for president but fail to challenge incumbent Ulysses S. Grant. Grant is re-elected president.
1873	The financial Panic of 1873 leads to the depression of 1873–1878.
1875	Several aides to President Grant are indicted on corruption charges.
1876	Democrat Samuel Tilden wins the presidential popular vote but without sufficient electoral votes to be elected president. *U.S. v. Cruikshank* and *U.S. v. Reese* Supreme Court decisions strongly limit the power of the federal government to enforce African American voting rights and permit the establishment of poll taxes and literacy tests as voting requirements.
1877	Unable to resolve the 1876 election in the U.S. House, Democrats and Republican Rutherford B. Hayes reach a compromise that certifies Hayes as president and leads to the removal from the south of remaining federal troops. Without federal enforcement of the Fourteenth and Fifteenth Amendments, African Americans face segregation, serfdom, exploitation, and denial of basic rights; the racially biased Democratic Party gains a stranglehold on the south. Leadership (determined by seniority) of congressional committees comes to be dominated by southern Democrats benefitting from assured re-election, dooming progressive legislation on race until the 1950s. The Great Railroad Strike causes more than one hundred deaths and was brought to a close via armed federal intervention.
1880	Republican James A. Garfield is elected president. The tenth census counts the U.S. population at 50.2 million people.
1881	President Garfield is assassinated. Vice President Chester A. Arthur becomes president.
1882	The Standard Oil Trust is formed, one of many large monopolies in the "Gilded Age." Congress enacts the Chinese Exclusion Act, prohibiting persons of Chinese descent from immigrating for ten years (it would be renewed several times).
1883	Congress passes the Pendleton Civil Service Act, establishing merit appointments for around ten percent of federal government positions and reducing employment by patronage.
1886	Democrat Grover Cleveland is elected president. Labor unrest reaches its zenith in the Haymarket Riot in Chicago. The American Federation of Labor is formed. *Wabash v. Illinois* Supreme Court decision severely restricts states' right to regulate interstate commerce and leads to the creation of the Interstate Commerce Commission the following year.
1887	The Australian balloting method is introduced in Massachusetts and is used in forty-one states by 1891. Adoption of the Australian method involved four parts: 1. the printing of an official ballot by a government at public expense; 2. the ballot would contain the names of all candidates and ballot issues; 3. the ballot would be distributed only at polling places; and 4. votes cast would be secret.
1888	Republican Benjamin Harrison is elected president.

State and Federal Laws Chronology, 1870–1889

1870   The Fifteenth Amendment is passed, which is intended to guarantee black male suffrage. Section One reads, "The right of citizens of the United States to vote shall not be denied or abridged by the United States or by any State on account of race, color, or previous condition of servitude." Section Two reads, "The Congress shall have power to enforce this article by appropriate legislation."

The Enforcement Acts (completed in 1871) are enacted to protect the rights of southern blacks following ratification of the Fourteenth and Fifteenth amendments. One act gave black voters recourse to federal courts, another provided federal supervision of southern elections, and the third strengthened sanctions against those who attacked blacks or prevented them from voting, even allowing the president to use troops to enforce the law and suspend *habeas corpus*.

Tennessee institutes a poll tax; proof of payment of tax is required to vote. The voter must have resided twelve months in the state and six months in the county.

Missouri permits declarant aliens to vote, but voter must have been declarant "not less than one year nor more than five years before he offers to vote."[1] The voter must have resided one year in the state and sixty days in the county, city, or town.

Illinois requires the voter to have resided one year in the state, ninety days in the county, and thirty days in the election district. No residency is gained by military personnel stationed in the state.

Virginia requires the voter to have resided twelve months in the state, three months in the county, city, or town. No residency is gained by military personnel stationed in the state.

1872   California requires naturalized citizens to present naturalization papers before voting.

West Virginia requires the voter to have resided one year in the state and sixty days in the county. No residency is gained by military personnel stationed in the state.

1873   Pennsylvania requires the voter to have paid state or county tax at least one month before the election. The voter must have been a U.S. citizen for one month and have resided for one year in the state, two months in the election district; six months in the state are required for a previously qualified elector or native-born state citizen who is returning after an absence. There is no loss of residence for soldiers or others traveling on public business, but no residency is gained by military personnel stationed in the state, by students, or by residents of almshouses or other institutions.

Arkansas requires the voter to have resided six months in the state and ten days in the county. No residency is gained by military personnel stationed in the state.

1874   New York requires the voter to have been a citizen for twenty days and to have resided one year in the state, four months in the county, and thirty days in the election district. There is no loss of residence for soldiers or others traveling on public business.

Arkansas requires the voter to have resided one year in the state, six months in the county, and one month in the precinct or ward. No residency is gained by military personnel stationed in the state.

Minnesota requires the voter to have resided for three months in the ward (in addition to six months in the state and thirty days in the district). No residency is gained by military personnel stationed in the state.

Chronology of Major Events, 1870–1889 (continued)

1875   *Minor v. Happersett,* 88 U.S. 162 (1875) Supreme Court decision holds that voting is not a privilege of citizenship and states that there are not provisions within the Constitution for women's suffrage.

Alabama implements a constitutional ban on education or property qualifications for suffrage. The voter must have resided one year in the state, three months in the county, and thirty days in precinct, district, or ward. No residency is gained by military personnel stationed in the state. The General Assembly may change residency length in any town with more than five thousand inhabitants.

Nebraska requires declarant aliens to have been declarant at least thirty days prior to election to vote. No residency is gained by military personnel stationed in the state.

Missouri drops its literacy requirement. There is no loss of residence for soldiers or others traveling on public business, but no residency is gained by military personnel stationed in the state, by students, or by residents of almshouses or other institutions.

1876   *United States v. Reese,* 92 U.S. 214 (1876). The Supreme Courts restricts the scope of the Fifteenth Amendment only to discrimination explicitly based on race, color, or previous condition of servitude. It thus upholds such practices as the poll tax, the literacy test, and the grandfather clause (which granted the right of those who were citizen-voters prior to a particular date to avoid literacy tests and poll taxes, thus allowing states to ensure the white vote while erecting the first post-Civil War barriers to the black vote). The Court struck down the Enforcement Act's clauses that made it illegal to interfere with any citizen's voting rights.

United States v. Cruikshank, 92 U.S. 542 (1876). The Supreme Court holds that the Fifteenth Amendment had not conferred federal enforcement of the right to vote unless the actions of those obstructing the right to vote were clearly racially motivated. The right to vote, the Court holds, is a state right. The ruling renders the Enforcement Acts practically moot.

North Carolina institutes a poll tax. The voter must be able to read and write any section of the Constitution in English. Those who were qualified voters on January 1, 1867, and lineal descendants of such persons are exempt from literacy requirement. The voter must have resided two years in the state, six months in the county, and four months in the precinct, ward, or other election district.

Texas requires the voter to have resided one year in the state and six months in the county.

Virginia requires voters to have paid the capitation tax required by law for the year preceding election.

Colorado becomes a state. Declarant aliens are permitted to vote. This right is restricted to declarant aliens who were declarant at least four months prior to election. Also, "the General Assembly may prescribe, by law, an educational qualification for electors, but no such law shall take effect prior to" 1890.[2] The voter must have resided for six months in the state and thirty days in the county. There is no loss of residence for soldiers or others traveling on public business, but no residency is gained by military personnel stationed in the state, students, or by residents of almshouses or other institutions.

1877   Georgia terminates declarant alien voting. The voter must have resided one year in the state and thirty days in the county. No residency is gained by military personnel stationed in the state.

In Illinois, no residency is gained by residents of almshouses or other institutions.

1879   Louisiana permits declarant aliens to vote. The voter must have resided one year in the state and ten days in parish. There is no loss of residence for soldiers or others traveling on public business, but no residency is gained by military personnel stationed in the state or by students.

1879
(cont.)   California requires naturalized citizens to have been naturalized ninety days prior to election in order to vote. The voter must have resided for one year in the state, ninety days in the county, and thirty days in the election district. There is no loss of residence for soldiers or others traveling on public business, but no residency is gained by military personnel stationed in the state, by students, or by residents of almshouses or other institutions.

1881   Massachusetts exempts Civil War veterans who were paupers from paying poll tax.

Colorado requires the voter to have resided for six months in the state, ninety days in the county, thirty days in the city or town, and ten days in the ward or precinct. Other previous restrictions apply.

1882   Wisconsin requires the voter to have resided one year in the state and thirty days in the district.

1883   Texas institutes a $1 poll tax.

Missouri requires naturalized citizens to present naturalization papers when voting. The voter must have resided for one year in the state, sixty days in the city, and twenty days in precinct. There is no loss of residence for soldiers or others traveling on public business but no residency is gained by military personnel stationed in the state, by students, or by residents of almshouses or other institutions.

1885   Florida decrees "the legislature shall have power to make the payment of the capitation tax a prerequisite for voting, and all such taxes received shall go into the school fund."[3]

Massachusetts requires naturalized citizens to have been naturalized more than thirty days before registration.

1887   Under the Electoral Act of 1887, a state's determination of electoral disputes is conclusive in most circumstances. The President of the Senate opens the electoral certificates in the presence of both houses, and hands them to the tellers, two from each house, who are to read them aloud and record the votes. If the same state sends multiple returns to Congress, then whichever return has been certified by the executive of the state is counted, unless both houses of Congress decide otherwise. This was a reaction to the disputed presidential election of 1876.

Massachusetts declares 1885 law requiring thirty days naturalization to be unconstitutional.

1888   Rhode Island repeals the property requirement for state elections, but registry tax of $1 or other tax must be paid. The voter must have resided for two years in the state and six months in the town and city.

1889   Florida institutes a poll tax of $1.

Montana becomes a state. Declarant aliens are permitted to vote for five years after adoption of Constitution. The voter must have resided for six months in the state and thirty days in the county. There is no loss of residence for soldiers or others traveling on public business, but no residency is gained by military personnel stationed in the state, by students, or by residents of almshouses or other institutions. State declares that "[u]pon all questions submitted to the vote of the taxpayers of the State, or any political division thereof, women who are taxpayers and possessed of the qualifications for the right of suffrage required by men by this Constitution equally, with men, have the right to vote."[4]

State and Federal Laws Chronology, 1870–1889 *(continued)*

1889 *(cont.)*	*North Dakota becomes a state.* It permits declarant aliens to vote. This right is restricted to declarant aliens who have been declarant at least one year and at most six years prior to election. The voter must have resided one year in the state, six months in the county, and ninety days in the precinct. There is no loss of residence for soldiers or others traveling on public business, but no residency is gained by military personnel stationed in the state. *South Dakota becomes a state.* It permits declarant aliens to vote. The voter must have resided one year in the United States, six months in the state, thirty days in the county, and ten days in the election precinct. There is no loss of residence for soldiers or others traveling on public business, but no residency is gained by military personnel stationed in the state. *Washington becomes a state.* The voter must have resided one year in the state, ninety days in the county, and thirty days in the city, town, ward, or precinct. There is no loss of residence for soldiers or others traveling on public business, but no residency is gained by military personnel stationed in the state or by students.

Source: Adapted from Alexander Keyssar, *The Right to Vote: The Contested History of Democracy in the United States, Revised Edition* (New York: Basic Books, 2009), 334–355.
[1] As quoted in Keyssar, 337. For sources, see Keyssar 369–379.
[2] As quoted in Keyssar, 340. For sources, see Keyssar 369–379.
[3] As quoted in Keyssar, 334. For sources, see Keyssar 369–379.
[4] As quoted in Keyssar, 334. For sources, see Keyssar 369–379.

National Count of Popular Vote for President, 1872–1888

YEAR	NAME	PARTY	TOTAL	PERCENTAGE[1]
1872	Ulysses Grant	Republican	3,598,235	40.0%
	Horace Greeley	Democratic/Liberal Republican	2,834,761	31.5%
1876[2]	Samuel Tilden	Democratic	4,288,546	42.0%
	Rutherford Hayes	**Republican**	**4,033,497**	**39.5%**
1880	James Garfield	Republican	4,446,158	38.9%
	Winfield Hancock	Democrat	4,444,260	38.9%
	James Weaver	Greenback/Labor	305,997	2.7%
1884	Grover Cleveland	Democratic	4,874,621	38.1%
	James Blaine	Republican	4,848,936	37.9%
	Benjamin Butler	Greenback/Anti-Monopoly	175,096	1.4%
	John St. John	Prohibition	147,482	1.2%
1888[3]	Grover Cleveland	Democratic	5,539,118	39.1%
	Benjamin Harrison	**Republican**	**5,449,825**	**38.4%**
	Clinton Fisk	Prohibition	249,819	1.8%
	Alson Streeter	Union Labor	146,602	1.0%

[1] The percentage figures in this chart are based on the votes cast divided by the eligible voting-age population at the time of the election.
[2] Rutherford B. Hayes gained the presidency in 1877 despite losing the popular vote to Samuel Tilden. The electoral college vote was dependent on disputed vote counts in many southern states; a special electoral commission appointed by Congress awarded Hayes the disputed states and the election by an electoral count of 185 to 184.
[3] Benjamin Harrison won the electoral college 233 to 168, despite losing the popular vote to Grover Cleveland in 1888.

States with Property and Taxpaying Requirements for Suffrage, 1870–1889

STATE	DATE OF STATEHOOD[1]	PROPERTY REQUIREMENT[2]	TAXPAYING REQUIREMENT[2]
ALABAMA		1875: Constitutional ban on education or property qualifications for suffrage	None
FLORIDA		None	1885: "The legislature shall have power to make the payment of the capitation tax a prerequisite for voting, and all such taxes received shall go into the school fund." 1889: Poll tax of $1
GEORGIA		None	1866: Poll tax of $1 1868: Paid taxes required for year preceding election
MASSACHUSETTS		None	1881: Exemption from poll tax for Civil War veterans who were paupers
MONTANA	1889	None	1889: "Upon all questions submitted to the vote of the taxpayers of the State, or any political division thereof, women who are taxpayers and possessed of the qualifications for the right of suffrage required by men by this Constitution equally, with men, have the right to vote."
NEVADA		None	1864: Annual poll tax "and the legislature may, in its discretion, make such a payment a condition to the right of voting." Payment of poll tax not required for those in the army or navy. 1865: Every male inhabitant between ages 21 and 60 must pay poll tax of $4 unless exempted by law.
NORTH CAROLINA		None	1876: Poll tax
PENNSYLVANIA		None	1873: Paid state or county tax at least 1 month before the election
RHODE ISLAND		1888: Property requirement for state elections repealed	1888: Registry tax of $1 or other tax must be paid
TENNESSEE		None	1870: Poll tax; proof of payment required
TEXAS		None	1883: Poll tax of $1
VIRGINIA		None	1876: Paid the capitation tax required by law for year preceding election

Source: Alexander Keyssar, *The Right to Vote: The Contested History of Democracy in the United States,* Revised Edition (New York: Basic Books, 2009), 334–336. Adapted from Keyssar's tables, which extend from 1870 to 1920. Sources of quotations are found on pp. 369–379. Table includes only restrictions that affected statewide elections.

[1] For states whose date of statehood falls within the time period 1870–1889.

[2] Dates listed are for the year that the property or tax requirement went into effect. All listed requirements continue into the 1870–1889 date range of this table.

States with Special Provisions Affecting Aliens and Immigrants, 1870–1889

STATE	DECLARANT ALIENS PERMITTED TO VOTE[1]	TERMINATION OF DECLARANT ALIEN VOTING	NATURALIZED CITIZENS REQUIRED TO PRESENT NATURALIZATION PAPERS	WAITING PERIODS AND OTHER RESTRICTIONS
ALABAMA	1867	—	—	—
ARKANSAS	1868	—	—	—
CALIFORNIA	—	—	1872	1879: Naturalization 90 days prior to election
COLORADO	1876	—	—	1876: Declarant 4 months prior to election
FLORIDA	1868	—	1868	—
GEORGIA	1868	1877	—	—
INDIANA	1851	—	—	—
KANSAS	1861	—	—	—
LOUISIANA	1879	—	—	—
MASSACHUSETTS	—	—	1855	1885: Must be naturalized more than 30 days before registration 1887: 1885 law declared unconstitutional
MICHIGAN	1850	—	—	1850: Declarant 6 months prior to election
MINNESOTA	—	—	—	1857: U.S. citizen for 3 months
MISSOURI	1870	—	1883	1870: Declarant "not less than one year nor more than five years before he offers to vote."
MONTANA	1889: For 5 years after the adoption of constitution	—	—	—
NEBRASKA	1867	—	—	—
NEW YORK	—	—	1866	1875: Declarant at least 30 days prior to election 1846: Citizen for 10 days 1874: Citizen for 20 days
NORTH DAKOTA	1889	—	—	1889: Declarant at least 1 year and not more than 6 years prior to election
OHIO	—	—	1857	—
OREGON	1857	—	—	1857: Declarant 1 year preceding election

States with Special Provisions Affecting Aliens and Immigrants, 1870–1889 (continued)

States with Special Provisions Affecting Aliens and Immigrants, 1870–1889 *(continued)*

STATE	DECLARANT ALIENS PERMITTED TO VOTE[1]	TERMINATION OF DECLARANT ALIEN VOTING	NATURALIZED CITIZENS REQUIRED TO PRESENT NATURALIZATION PAPERS	WAITING PERIODS AND OTHER RESTRICTIONS
PENNSYLVANIA	—	—	—	1873: U.S. citizen for 1 month
SOUTH DAKOTA	1889	—	—	—
TEXAS	1869	—	—	—
WISCONSIN	1848	—	—	—

Key: — indicates no requirement at that time
　　 * indicates that the previous requirement remained in effect
[1] A declarant alien is a resident who has formally declared his intention to become a citizen.

States with Literacy Requirements for Suffrage, 1870–1889

STATE	LITERACY REQUIREMENTS[1]	EXEMPTIONS	ASSISTANCE TO ILLITERATE VOTERS
ALABAMA	1875: "No education qualification for suffrage … shall be made by law"	—	—
COLORADO	1876: "The General Assembly may prescribe, by law, an educational qualification for electors, but no such law shall take effect prior to" 1890	—	—
CONNECTICUT	1855: Must be able to read any article of the Constitution or any section of the state statutes	1855: Those who could vote before 1855	—
FLORIDA	1868: Constitution authorizes education qualifications, but none passed by legislature	—	—
	1885: No requirement		—
MASSACHUSETTS	1857: Must be able to read the Constitution in English and write his name	1857: Those with physical disabilities; also, "any person who now has the right to vote," and those "who shall be 60 years of age or upwards at the time this Amendment shall take effect"	—
MISSISSIPPI	1868: "No educational qualification shall ever be required for any person to become an elector"	—	—
MISSOURI	1865: After 1 January 1876, must be able to read and write	1865: Those who were qualified electors before 1 January 1876, and those prevented from reading and writing by physical disability	—
	1875: No requirement	—	—
NORTH CAROLINA	1876: Must be able to read and write any section of the Constitution in English	1876: Those who were qualified voters on 1 January 1867, and lineal descendants of such persons	—

Key: — indicates no requirement at that time
   * indicates that the previous requirement remained in effect

Source: Alexander Keyssar, *The Right to Vote: The Contested History of Democracy in the United States,* Revised Edition (New York: Basic Books, 2009), 340–345. Adapted from Keyssar's table, which extends from 1870 to 1924. Sources of quotations are found on pp. 369–379.

[1] Dates listed are for the year that the literacy requirement went into effect. All listed requirements continue into the 1870–1889 date range of this table.

States with Residency Requirements for Suffrage, 1870–1889

STATE	LENGTH OF RESIDENCE REQUIRED[1]	NO RESIDENCY GAINED BY MILITARY PERSONNEL STATIONED IN TOWNS AND CITIES	STUDENTS	RESIDENCE IN ALMSHOUSE OR OTHER INSTITUTION	NO LOSS OF RESIDENCE FOR SOLDIERS OR OTHERS TRAVELING ON PUBLIC BUSINESS	OTHER
ALABAMA	1867: 6 months in state, 6 months in county	1867	—	—	—	—
	1875: 1 year in state, 3 months in country, 30 days in precinct, district, or ward	*	—	—	—	1875: General Assembly may change residency length in any town with more than 5,000 inhabitants
ARKANSAS	1868: 6 months in state	1868	—	—	—	—
	1873: 6 months in state, 10 days in county	*	—	—	—	—
	1874: 12 months in state, 6 months in county, 1 month in precinct or ward	*	—	—	—	—
CALIFORNIA	1850: 6 months in state, 30 days in county or district	1850	1850	1850	1850	—
	1879: 1 year in state, 90 days in county, 30 days in election district	*	*	*	*	—
COLORADO	1876: 6 months in state	1876	1876	1876	1876	—
	1877: 30 days in county					
	1881: 6 months in state, 90 days in county, 30 days in city or town, 10 days in ward or precinct	*	*	*	*	—
CONNECTICUT	1845: 1 year in state, 6 months in county	—	—	—	—	—
DELAWARE	1831: 1 year in state, 1 month in county	1831	—	—	—	—
FLORIDA	1868: 1 year in state, 6 months in county	1868	—	—	—	—
GEORGIA	1868: 6 months in state, 30 days in county	1868	—	—	—	—
	1877: 1 year in state, 6 months in county	*	—	—	—	—
ILLINOIS	1870: 1 year in state, 90 days in county, 30 days in election district	1870	—	—	—	—
	*	*	—	1877	—	—
INDIANA	1851: 6 months in state, 60 days in township, 30 days in ward or precinct; for declarants, 1 year in U.S.	1851	—	—	1851	—

STATE	LENGTH OF RESIDENCE REQUIRED[1]	NO RESIDENCY GAINED BY MILITARY PERSONNEL STATIONED IN TOWNS AND CITIES	STUDENTS	RESIDENCE IN ALMSHOUSE OR OTHER INSTITUTION	NO LOSS OF RESIDENCE FOR SOLDIERS OR OTHERS TRAVELING ON PUBLIC BUSINESS	OTHER
IOWA	1857: 6 months in state, 60 days in county	1857	—	—	—	—
KANSAS	1861: 6 months in state, 30 days in township or ward	1861	1861	1861	1861	—
KENTUCKY	1850: 2 years in state or 1 year in county, town, or city, 60 days in precinct	—	—	—	1850	—
LOUISIANA	1868: 1 year in state, 10 days in parish	—	—	—	—	—
	1879: 1 year in state, 6 months in parish, 30 days in ward or precinct	1879	1879	—	1879	—
MAINE	1820: 3 months in state	1820	1820	—	1864	—
MARYLAND	1867: 1 year in state, 6 months in legislative district of Baltimore city or of the county	—	—	—	—	—
MASSACHUSETTS	1821: 1 year in state, 6 months in town or district	—	—	—	—	—
MICHIGAN	1850: 6 months in state, 20 days in township or ward; for declarants, 2 years and 6 months in state prior to 8 November 1894	—	—	—	—	—
MINNESOTA	1857: 6 months in state, 30 days in election district	1857	—	—	—	—
	1874: 3 months in ward	*	—	—	—	1893: No residence for voting purposes can be gained by any "person employed temporarily" cutting timber "or in the construction or repair of any railroad, canal, municipal or other work of public nature"
MISSISSIPPI	1868: 6 months in state, 1 month in county	—	—	—	—	—
MISSOURI	1870: 1 year in state, 60 days in county, city, or town	—	—	—	—	—
	*	1875	1875	1875	1875	—
	1883: 1 year in state, 60 days in city, 20 days in precinct	*	*	*	*	—

States with Residency Requirements for Suffrage, 1870–1889 (continued)

STATE	LENGTH OF RESIDENCE REQUIRED[1]	NO RESIDENCY GAINED BY MILITARY PERSONNEL STATIONED IN TOWNS AND CITIES	STUDENTS	RESIDENCE IN ALMSHOUSE OR OTHER INSTITUTION	NO LOSS OF RESIDENCE FOR SOLDIERS OR OTHERS TRAVELING ON PUBLIC BUSINESS	OTHER
MONTANA	1889: 6 months in state, and 30 days in county	1889	1889	1889	1889	—
NEBRASKA	1866: 6 months in state, 20 days in county, 10 days in precinct	—	—	—	—	—
	1869: 40 days in county	—	—	—	—	—
	*	1875	—	—	—	—
NEW HAMPSHIRE	1860: 6 months within town	—	—	—	—	—
NEW JERSEY	1844: 1 year in state, 5 months in county	1844	—	—	1844	—
NEW YORK	1846: 1 year in state, 4 months in county, 30 days in district; for "man of color," 3 years in state	—	—	—	—	—
	1874: 1 year in state, 4 months in county, 30 days in election district	—	—	—	1874	—
NORTH CAROLINA	1868: 12 months in state, 30 days in county	—	—	—	—	—
	1876: 2 years in state, 6 months in county, 4 months in precinct, ward, or other election district	—	—	—	—	—
NORTH DAKOTA	1889: 1 year in state, 6 months in county, 90 days in precinct	1889	—	—	1889	—
OHIO	1857: 1 year in state, 30 days in county, 20 days in township, village, or ward of city or village	—	1914	—	—	—
OREGON	1859: 6 months in state	1859	1859	1859	1859	—
PENNSYLVANIA	1838: 1 year in state, 10 days in election district	—	—	—	—	—
	1873: 1 year in state, 2 months in election district; 6 months in state for previously qualified elector or native-born state citizen, returning after absence	1873	1873	1873	1873	—

States with Residency Requirements for Suffrage, 1870–1889 *(continued)*

STATE	LENGTH OF RESIDENCE REQUIRED[1]	NO RESIDENCY GAINED BY MILITARY PERSONNEL STATIONED IN TOWNS AND CITIES	STUDENTS	RESIDENCE IN ALMSHOUSE OR OTHER INSTITUTION	NO LOSS OF RESIDENCE FOR SOLDIERS OR OTHERS TRAVELING ON PUBLIC BUSINESS	OTHER
RHODE ISLAND	1842: 1 year in state, 6 months in town or city if owning real estate worth $134 or "which shall rent for seven dollars per annum"; or 2 years in state, 6 months in town or city if taxpayer registered at least 7 days before voting	—	—	—	—	—
	*	—	—	—	1864	—
	1888: 2 years in state, 6 months in town or city	—	—	—	—	—
SOUTH CAROLINA	1868: 1 year in state, 60 days in county	1868	—	—	—	—
SOUTH DAKOTA	1889: 1 year in U.S., 6 months in state, 30 days in county, 10 days in election precinct	1889	—	—	1889	—
TENNESSEE	1870: 12 months in state, 6 months in county	—	—	—	—	—
TEXAS	1869: 1 year in state, 60 days in county	—	—	—	—	No soldier, seaman, or marine may vote
	1876: 1 year in state, 6 months in county	—	—	—	—	—
VERMONT	1793: 1 year in state	—	—	—	—	—
VIRGINIA	1870: 12 months in state, 3 months in county, city, or town	1870	—	—	—	—
WASHINGTON	1889: 1 year in state, 90 days in county, 30 days in city, town, ward, or precinct	1889	1889	—	1889	—
WEST VIRGINIA	1863: 1 year in state, 30 days in county	—	—	—	—	—
	1872: 1 year in state, 60 days in county	1872	—	—	—	—
WISCONSIN	1848: 1 year in state	—	—	—	—	—
	1882: 1 year in state, minimum of 30 days in district	—	—	—	—	—

Key: — indicates no requirement at that time
       * indicates that the previous requirement remained in effect
Source: Alexander Keyssar, *The Right to Vote: The Contested History of Democracy in the United States,* Revised Edition (New York: Basic Books, 2000), 346–355. Adapted from Keyssar's table, which extends from 1870 to 1923. Sources of quotations are found on pp. 369–379.
[1] Dates listed are for the year that the residency requirement went into effect. All listed requirements continue into the 1870–1889 date range of this table.

United States Presidential Turnout, Election Years 1872–1888

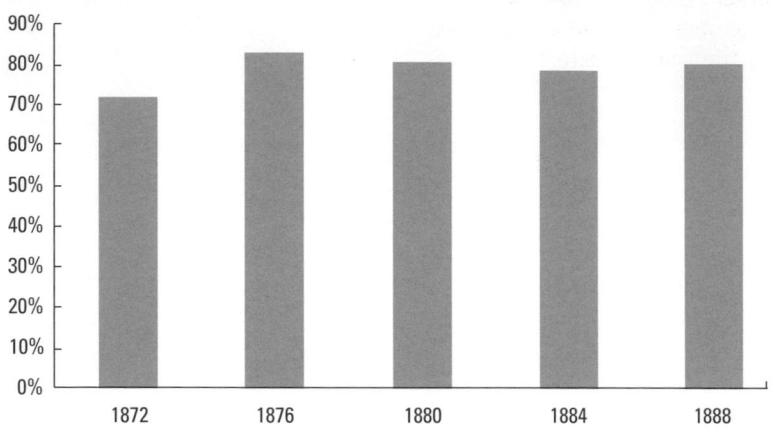

YEAR	VOTING-AGE POPULATION	TOTAL	%
1872	8,996,000	6,467,679	71.9%
1876	10,149,000	8,413,101	82.9%
1880	11,431,000	9,210,420	80.6%
1884	12,794,000	10,049,754	78.6%
1888	14,164,000	11,383,320	80.4%

Partisan Turnout Presidential Years Based on Aggregate House Turnout, Election Years 1872–1888

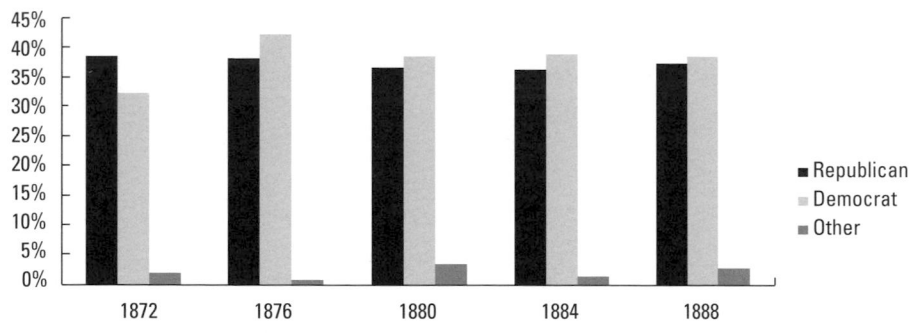

- Republican
- Democrat
- Other

YEAR	VOTING-AGE POPULATION	REPUBLICAN TURNOUT	%	DEMOCRAT TURNOUT	%	OTHER TURNOUT	%
1872	8,996,000	3,491,873	38.8%	2,927,921	32.5%	184,911	2.1%
1876	10,149,000	3,905,401	38.5%	4,322,100	42.6%	90,081	0.9%
1880	11,431,000	4,220,865	36.9%	4,440,239	38.8%	412,051	3.6%
1884	12,794,000	4,682,168	36.6%	5,016,423	39.2%	193,118	1.5%
1888	14,164,000	5,333,964	37.7%	5,499,257	38.8%	413,448	2.9%

UNITED STATES PRESIDENTIAL GENERAL ELECTIONS

Election Years 1872–1888

State	1872 Voting-age population	Turnout	%	1876 Voting-age population	Turnout	%	Difference from 1872*	1880 Voting-age population	Turnout	%	Difference from 1872	1884 Voting-age population	Turnout	%	Difference from 1872	1888 Voting-age population	Turnout	%	Difference from 1872
ALABAMA	215,000	169,716	78.9%	238,000	171,699	72.1%	-6.8	261,000	151,902	58.2%	-20.7	286,000	153,624	53.7%	-25.2	312,000	175,085	56.1%	-22.8
ALASKA																			
ARIZONA																			
ARKANSAS	119,000	79,300	66.6%	152,000	96,946	63.8%	-2.9	183,000	107,772	58.9%	-7.7	213,000	125,779	59.1%	-7.6	243,000	157,058	64.6%	-2.0
CALIFORNIA	164,000	95,785	58.4%	195,000	155,784	79.9%	21.5	227,000	164,218	72.3%	13.9	270,000	196,988	73.0%	14.6	313,000	251,339	80.3%	21.9
COLORADO								88,000	53,546	60.8%		112,000	66,519	59.4%	-1.5	138,000	91,946	66.6%	5.8
CONNECTICUT	132,000	95,992	72.7%	140,000	122,134	87.2%	14.5	147,000	132,798	90.3%	17.6	163,000	137,221	84.2%	11.5	179,000	153,978	86.0%	13.3
DELAWARE	30,000	21,822	72.7%	33,000	24,133	73.1%	0.4	37,000	29,458	79.6%	6.9	40,000	29,984	75.0%	2.2	43,000	29,764	69.2%	-3.5
DISTRICT OF COLUMBIA																			
FLORIDA	43,000	33,190	77.2%	52,000	46,776	90.0%	12.8	60,000	51,618	86.0%	8.8	73,000	59,990	82.2%	5.0	86,000	66,500	77.3%	0.1
GEORGIA	255,000	138,906	54.5%	288,000	180,690	62.7%	8.3	322,000	157,451	48.9%	-5.6	352,000	143,610	40.8%	-13.7	383,000	142,936	37.3%	-17.2
HAWAII																			
IDAHO																			
ILLINOIS	577,000	429,971	74.5%	632,000	554,368	87.7%	13.2	692,000	622,305	89.9%	15.4	789,000	672,670	85.3%	10.7	886,000	747,813	84.4%	9.9
INDIANA	403,000	349,779	86.8%	446,000	431,073	96.7%	9.9	487,000	470,758	96.7%	9.9	525,000	491,649	93.6%	6.9	563,000	536,988	95.4%	8.6
IOWA	284,000	216,365	76.2%	333,000	293,398	88.1%	11.9	379,000	323,140	85.3%	9.1	417,000	393,542	94.4%	18.2	457,000	404,694	88.6%	12.4
KANSAS	135,000	100,512	74.5%	196,000	124,134	63.3%	-11.1	256,000	201,054	78.5%	4.1	300,000	250,991	83.7%	9.2	344,000	331,133	96.3%	21.8
KENTUCKY	303,000	191,135	63.1%	337,000	260,626	77.3%	14.3	371,000	267,104	72.0%	8.9	401,000	274,910	68.6%	5.5	430,000	344,868	80.2%	17.1
LOUISIANA	169,000	128,692	76.1%	188,000	145,823	77.6%	1.4	205,000	104,462	51.0%	-25.2	220,000	113,234	51.5%	-24.7	233,000	115,891	49.7%	-26.4
MAINE	157,000	90,523	57.7%	163,000	117,045	71.8%	14.1	170,000	143,903	84.6%	27.0	174,000	127,114	73.1%	15.4	180,000	128,253	71.3%	13.6
MARYLAND	180,000	134,447	74.7%	198,000	163,759	82.7%	8.0	215,000	172,221	80.1%	5.4	229,000	209,823	91.6%	16.9	243,000	210,941	86.8%	12.1
MASSACHUSETTS	330,000	192,650	58.4%	360,000	259,619	72.1%	13.7	393,000	282,505	71.9%	13.5	446,000	321,253	72.0%	13.7	499,000	344,243	69.0%	10.6
MICHIGAN	304,000	221,569	72.9%	352,000	318,426	90.5%	17.6	414,000	353,076	85.3%	12.4	466,000	364,490	78.2%	5.3	517,000	475,356	91.9%	19.1
MINNESOTA	98,000	91,339	93.2%	134,000	124,160	92.7%	-0.5	186,000	150,806	81.1%	-12.1	242,000	186,434	77.0%	-16.2	299,000	263,162	88.0%	-5.2
MISSISSIPPI	185,000	129,457	70.0%	212,000	164,776	77.7%	7.7	237,000	117,068	49.4%	-20.6	250,000	120,688	48.3%	-21.7	264,000	115,786	43.9%	-26.1
MISSOURI	411,000	273,059	66.4%	462,000	350,610	75.9%	9.5	514,000	397,289	77.3%	10.9	577,000	441,268	76.5%	10.0	641,000	521,359	81.3%	14.9
MONTANA																			
NEBRASKA	55,000	25,932	47.1%	87,000	49,258	56.6%	9.5	121,000	87,355	72.2%	25.0	186,000	134,202	72.2%	25.0	250,000	202,630	81.1%	33.9
NEVADA	20,000	14,649	73.2%	23,000	19,691	85.6%	12.4	24,000	18,343	76.4%	3.2	21,000	12,779	60.9%	-12.4	18,000	12,573	69.9%	-3.4
NEW HAMPSHIRE	85,000	68,906	81.1%	90,000	80,143	89.0%	8.0	94,000	86,361	91.9%	10.8	97,000	84,586	87.2%	6.1	101,000	90,770	89.9%	8.8
NEW JERSEY	208,000	168,112	80.8%	232,000	220,193	94.9%	14.1	257,000	245,928	95.7%	14.9	298,000	260,853	87.5%	6.7	340,000	303,634	89.3%	8.5
NEW MEXICO																			
NEW YORK	1,031,000	828,020	80.3%	1,112,000	1,015,503	91.3%	11.0	1,199,000	1,103,945	92.1%	11.8	1,325,000	1,167,003	88.1%	7.8	1,451,000	1,319,748	91.0%	10.6

United States Presidential General Elections (continued)

United States Presidential General Elections (continued)

Election Years 1872–1888 (continued)

State	1872			1876				1880				1884				1888			
	Voting-age population	Turnout	%	Voting-age population	Turnout	%	Difference from 1872	Voting-age population	Turnout	%	Difference from 1872	Voting-age population	Turnout	%	Difference from 1872	Voting-age population	Turnout	%	Difference from 1872
NORTH CAROLINA	233,000	165,163	70.9%	264,000	233,911	88.6%	17.7	295,000	240,946	81.7%	10.8	314,000	268,356	85.5%	14.6	334,000	285,563	85.5%	14.6
NORTH DAKOTA																			
OHIO	636,000	529,435	83.2%	706,000	658,650	93.3%	10.0	777,000	724,984	93.3%	10.1	850,000	784,620	92.3%	9.1	922,000	839,357	91.0%	7.8
OKLAHOMA																			
OREGON	30,000	20,107	67.0%	41,000	29,873	72.9%	5.8	51,000	40,841	80.1%	13.1	70,000	52,683	75.3%	8.2	87,000	61,889	71.1%	4.1
PENNSYLVANIA	820,000	561,629	68.5%	891,000	758,973	85.2%	16.7	970,000	874,783	90.2%	21.7	1,098,000	899,710	81.9%	13.4	1,226,000	997,568	81.4%	12.9
RHODE ISLAND	47,000	18,994	40.4%	52,000	26,499	51.0%	10.5	58,000	29,235	50.4%	10.0	65,000	32,771	50.4%	10.0	72,000	40,775	56.6%	16.2
SOUTH CAROLINA	161,000	95,452	59.3%	184,000	182,683	99.3%	40.0	206,000	169,793	82.4%	23.1	218,000	92,812	42.6%	-16.7	230,000	79,997	34.8%	-24.5
SOUTH DAKOTA																			
TENNESSEE	275,000	179,046	65.1%	302,000	222,743	73.8%	8.6	329,000	243,263	73.9%	8.8	358,000	259,978	72.6%	7.5	386,000	303,694	78.7%	13.6
TEXAS	215,000	115,700	53.8%	289,000	151,431	52.4%	-1.4	362,000	233,632	64.5%	10.7	420,000	321,242	76.5%	22.7	478,000	354,412	74.1%	20.3
UTAH																			
VERMONT	77,000	52,408	68.1%	80,000	64,460	80.6%	12.5	83,000	65,098	78.4%	10.4	86,000	59,409	69.1%	1.0	90,000	63,476	70.5%	2.5
VIRGINIA	282,000	185,195	65.7%	308,000	236,288	76.7%	11.0	332,000	211,616	63.7%	-1.9	350,000	284,977	81.4%	15.8	368,000	304,087	82.6%	17.0
WASHINGTON																			
WEST VIRGINIA	104,000	62,467	60.1%	121,000	99,647	82.4%	22.3	138,000	112,641	81.6%	21.6	155,000	132,145	85.3%	25.2	172,000	159,440	92.7%	32.6
WISCONSIN**	223,000	192,255	86.2%	256,000	257,176	100.5%	14.2	291,000	267,202	91.8%	5.6	338,000	319,847	94.6%	8.4	386,000	354,614	91.9%	5.7
WYOMING																			
Total	8,996,000	6,467,679	71.9%	10,149,000	8,413,101	82.9%	11.0	11,431,000	9,210,420	80.6%	8.7	12,794,000	10,049,754	78.6%	6.7	14,164,000	11,383,320	80.4%	8.5

*Percentage point difference between turnout in current year and initial year listed in chart. If data do not appear for a state in the initial year listed, the difference is calculated from the first year in which data do appear for that state.

**Wisconsin 1876 turnout is verified by reliable sources; error is likely with voting-age population, which is an estimate. See "About the Charts" in introduction.

UNITED STATES PRESIDENTIAL GENERAL ELECTIONS

Republican Turnout for Election Years 1872–1888

State	1872 Voting-age population	1872 Turnout	1872 %	1876 Voting-age population	1876 Turnout	1876 %	1876 Difference from 1872*	1880 Voting-age population	1880 Turnout	1880 %	1880 Difference from 1872	1884 Voting-age population	1884 Turnout	1884 %	1884 Difference from 1872	1888 Voting-age population	1888 Turnout	1888 %	1888 Difference from 1872
ALABAMA	215,000	90,272	42.0%	238,000	68,708	28.9%	-13.1	261,000	56,350	21.6%	-20.4	286,000	59,444	20.8%	-21.2	312,000	57,177	18.3%	-23.7
ALASKA																			
ARIZONA																			
ARKANSAS	119,000	41,373	34.8%	152,000	38,649	25.4%	-9.3	183,000	41,661	22.8%	-12.0	213,000	51,198	24.0%	-10.7	243,000	59,752	24.6%	-10.2
CALIFORNIA	164,000	54,007	32.9%	195,000	79,258	40.6%	7.7	227,000	80,282	35.4%	2.4	270,000	102,369	37.9%	5.0	313,000	124,816	39.9%	6.9
COLORADO								88,000	27,450	31.2%		112,000	36,084	32.2%	1.0	138,000	50,772	36.8%	5.6
CONNECTICUT	132,000	50,307	38.1%	140,000	59,033	42.2%	4.1	147,000	67,071	45.6%	7.5	163,000	65,879	40.4%	2.3	179,000	74,584	41.7%	3.6
DELAWARE	30,000	11,129	37.1%	33,000	10,752	32.6%	-4.5	37,000	14,148	38.2%	1.1	40,000	12,953	32.4%	-4.7	43,000	12,950	30.1%	-7.0
DISTRICT OF COLUMBIA																			
FLORIDA	43,000	17,763	41.3%	52,000	23,849	45.9%	4.6	60,000	23,654	39.4%	-1.9	73,000	28,031	38.4%	-2.9	86,000	26,529	30.8%	-10.5
GEORGIA	255,000	62,550	24.5%	288,000	50,533	17.5%	-7.0	322,000	54,470	16.9%	-7.6	352,000	48,603	13.8%	-10.7	383,000	40,499	10.6%	-14.0
HAWAII																			
IDAHO																			
ILLINOIS	577,000	241,936	41.9%	632,000	278,232	44.0%	2.1	692,000	318,036	46.0%	4.0	789,000	337,469	42.8%	0.8	886,000	370,475	41.8%	-0.1
INDIANA	403,000	186,147	46.2%	446,000	208,011	46.6%	0.4	487,000	232,169	47.7%	1.5	525,000	238,466	45.4%	-0.8	563,000	263,366	46.8%	0.6
IOWA	284,000	131,566	46.3%	333,000	171,326	51.4%	5.1	379,000	183,904	48.5%	2.2	417,000	197,089	47.3%	0.9	457,000	211,607	46.3%	0.0
KANSAS	135,000	66,805	49.5%	196,000	78,324	40.0%	-9.5	256,000	121,520	47.5%	-2.0	300,000	154,410	51.5%	2.0	344,000	182,845	53.2%	3.7
KENTUCKY	303,000	88,766	29.3%	337,000	97,568	29.0%	-0.3	371,000	106,490	28.7%	-0.6	401,000	118,690	29.6%	0.3	430,000	155,138	36.1%	6.8
LOUISIANA	169,000	71,663	42.4%	188,000	75,315	40.1%	-2.3	205,000	38,978	19.0%	-23.4	220,000	46,347	21.1%	-21.3	233,000	30,660	13.2%	-29.2
MAINE	157,000	61,426	39.1%	163,000	66,300	40.7%	1.6	170,000	74,052	43.6%	4.4	174,000	72,217	41.5%	2.4	180,000	73,730	41.0%	1.8
MARYLAND	180,000	66,760	37.1%	198,000	71,980	36.4%	-0.7	215,000	78,515	36.5%	-0.6	229,000	85,748	37.4%	0.4	243,000	99,986	41.1%	4.1
MASSACHUSETTS	330,000	133,455	40.4%	360,000	150,063	41.7%	1.2	393,000	165,198	42.0%	1.6	446,000	146,724	32.9%	-7.5	499,000	183,892	36.9%	-3.6
MICHIGAN	304,000	138,768	45.6%	352,000	166,901	47.4%	1.8	414,000	185,335	44.8%	-0.9	466,000	192,669	41.3%	-4.3	517,000	236,387	45.7%	0.1
MINNESOTA	98,000	56,040	57.2%	134,000	72,962	54.4%	-2.7	186,000	93,939	50.5%	-6.7	242,000	111,685	46.2%	-11.0	299,000	142,492	47.7%	-9.5
MISSISSIPPI	185,000	82,175	44.4%	212,000	52,603	24.8%	-19.6	237,000	34,844	14.7%	-29.7	250,000	43,035	17.2%	-27.2	264,000	30,095	11.4%	-33.0
MISSOURI	411,000	119,196	29.0%	462,000	145,027	31.4%	2.4	514,000	153,647	29.9%	0.9	577,000	203,081	35.2%	6.2	641,000	236,252	36.9%	7.9
MONTANA																			
NEBRASKA	55,000	18,329	33.3%	87,000	31,915	36.7%	3.4	121,000	54,979	45.4%	12.1	186,000	76,912	41.4%	8.0	250,000	108,417	43.4%	10.0
NEVADA	20,000	8,413	42.1%	23,000	10,383	45.1%	3.1	24,000	8,732	36.4%	-5.7	21,000	7,176	34.2%	-7.9	18,000	7,229	40.2%	-1.9
NEW HAMPSHIRE	85,000	37,168	43.7%	90,000	41,540	46.2%	2.4	94,000	44,856	47.7%	4.0	97,000	43,254	44.6%	0.9	101,000	45,734	45.3%	1.6
NEW JERSEY	208,000	91,656	44.1%	232,000	103,517	44.6%	0.6	257,000	120,555	46.9%	2.8	298,000	123,436	41.4%	-2.6	340,000	144,347	42.5%	-1.6
NEW MEXICO																			
NEW YORK	1,031,000	440,738	42.7%	1,112,000	489,207	44.0%	1.2	1,199,000	555,544	46.3%	3.6	1,325,000	562,001	42.4%	-0.3	1,451,000	650,338	44.8%	2.1

United States Presidential General Elections (continued)

United States Presidential General Elections (continued)

Republican Turnout for Election Years 1872–1888 (continued)

State	1872 Voting-age population	Turnout	%	1876 Voting-age population	Turnout	%	Difference from 1872	1880 Voting-age population	Turnout	%	Difference from 1872	1884 Voting-age population	Turnout	%	Difference from 1872	1888 Voting-age population	Turnout	%	Difference from 1872
NORTH CAROLINA	233,000	94,772	40.7%	264,000	108,484	41.1%	0.4	295,000	115,616	39.2%	-1.5	314,000	125,021	39.8%	-0.9	334,000	134,784	40.4%	-0.3
NORTH DAKOTA																			
OHIO	636,000	281,852	44.3%	706,000	330,698	46.8%	2.5	777,000	375,048	48.3%	4.0	850,000	400,092	47.1%	2.8	922,000	416,054	45.1%	0.8
OKLAHOMA																			
OREGON	30,000	11,818	39.4%	41,000	15,207	37.1%	-2.3	51,000	20,619	40.4%	1.0	70,000	26,845	38.4%	-1.0	87,000	33,291	38.3%	-1.1
PENNSYLVANIA	820,000	349,589	42.6%	891,000	384,157	43.1%	0.5	970,000	444,704	45.8%	3.2	1,098,000	472,792	43.1%	0.4	1,226,000	526,091	42.9%	0.3
RHODE ISLAND	47,000	13,665	29.1%	52,000	15,787	30.4%	1.3	58,000	18,195	31.4%	2.3	65,000	19,030	29.3%	0.2	72,000	21,969	30.5%	1.4
SOUTH CAROLINA	161,000	72,290	44.9%	184,000	91,786	49.9%	5.0	206,000	57,954	28.1%	-16.8	218,000	21,730	10.0%	-34.9	230,000	13,736	6.0%	-38.9
SOUTH DAKOTA																			
TENNESSEE	275,000	85,655	31.1%	302,000	89,566	29.7%	-1.5	329,000	107,677	32.7%	1.6	358,000	124,101	34.7%	3.5	386,000	138,978	36.0%	4.9
TEXAS	215,000	47,910	22.3%	289,000	45,013	15.6%	-6.7	362,000	50,217	13.9%	-8.4	420,000	91,234	21.7%	-0.6	478,000	88,604	18.5%	-3.7
UTAH																			
VERMONT	77,000	41,481	53.9%	80,000	44,092	55.1%	1.2	83,000	45,567	54.9%	1.0	86,000	39,514	45.9%	-7.9	90,000	45,193	50.2%	-3.7
VIRGINIA	282,000	93,463	33.1%	308,000	95,518	31.0%	-2.1	332,000	83,533	25.2%	-8.0	350,000	139,356	39.8%	6.7	368,000	150,399	40.9%	7.7
WASHINGTON																			
WEST VIRGINIA	104,000	32,320	31.1%	121,000	41,997	34.7%	3.6	138,000	46,243	33.5%	2.4	155,000	63,096	40.7%	9.6	172,000	78,171	45.4%	14.4
WISCONSIN	223,000	105,012	47.1%	256,000	130,050	50.8%	3.7	291,000	144,406	49.6%	2.5	338,000	161,155	47.7%	0.6	386,000	176,553	45.7%	-1.4
WYOMING																			
Total	8,996,000	3,598,235	40.0%	10,149,000	4,034,311	39.8%	-0.2	11,431,000	4,446,158	38.9%	-1.1	12,794,000	4,848,936	37.9%	-2.1	14,164,000	5,443,892	38.4%	-1.6

Democratic Turnout for Election Years 1872–1888

State	1872 Voting-age population	Turnout	%	1876 Voting-age population	Turnout	%	Difference from 1872*	1880 Voting-age population	Turnout	%	Difference from 1872	1884 Voting-age population	Turnout	%	Difference from 1872	1888 Voting-age population	Turnout	%	Difference from 1872
ALABAMA	215,000	79,444	37.0%	238,000	102,989	43.3%	6.3	261,000	91,130	34.9%	-2.0	286,000	92,736	32.4%	-4.5	312,000	117,314	37.6%	0.6
ALASKA																			
ARIZONA																			
ARKANSAS	119,000	37,927	31.9%	152,000	58,086	38.2%	6.3	183,000	60,489	33.1%	1.2	213,000	72,734	34.1%	2.3	243,000	86,062	35.4%	3.5
CALIFORNIA	164,000	40,717	24.8%	195,000	76,460	39.2%	14.4	227,000	80,426	35.4%	10.6	270,000	89,288	33.1%	8.2	313,000	117,729	37.6%	12.8
COLORADO								88,000	24,647	28.0%		112,000	27,723	24.8%	-3.3	138,000	37,549	27.2%	-0.8
CONNECTICUT	132,000	45,685	34.6%	140,000	61,927	44.2%	9.6	147,000	64,411	43.8%	9.2	163,000	67,167	41.2%	6.6	179,000	74,920	41.9%	7.2
DELAWARE	30,000	10,205	34.0%	33,000	13,381	40.5%	6.5	37,000	15,181	41.0%	7.0	40,000	16,957	42.4%	8.4	43,000	16,414	38.2%	4.2
DISTRICT OF COLUMBIA																			
FLORIDA	43,000	15,427	35.9%	52,000	22,927	44.1%	8.2	60,000	27,964	46.6%	10.7	73,000	31,769	43.5%	7.6	86,000	39,557	46.0%	10.1

United States Presidential General Elections *(continued)*

Democratic Turnout for Election Years 1872–1888 *(continued)*

State	1872 Voting-age population	Turnout	%	1876 Voting-age population	Turnout	%	Difference from 1872	1880 Voting-age population	Turnout	%	Difference from 1872	1884 Voting-age population	Turnout	%	Difference from 1872	1888 Voting-age population	Turnout	%	Difference from 1872
GEORGIA	255,000	76,356	29.9%	288,000	130,157	45.2%	15.2	322,000	102,981	32.0%	2.0	352,000	94,667	26.9%	-3.0	383,000	100,493	26.2%	-3.7
HAWAII																			
IDAHO																			
ILLINOIS	577,000	184,884	32.0%	632,000	258,611	40.9%	8.9	692,000	277,321	40.1%	8.0	789,000	312,351	39.6%	7.5	886,000	348,351	39.3%	7.3
INDIANA	403,000	163,632	40.6%	446,000	213,529	47.9%	7.3	487,000	225,523	46.3%	5.7	525,000	244,989	46.7%	6.1	563,000	260,990	46.4%	5.8
IOWA	284,000	71,189	25.1%	333,000	112,121	33.7%	8.6	379,000	105,845	27.9%	2.9	417,000	177,316	42.5%	17.5	457,000	179,876	39.4%	14.3
KANSAS	135,000	32,970	24.4%	196,000	37,902	19.3%	-5.1	256,000	59,789	23.4%	-1.1	300,000	90,111	30.0%	5.6	344,000	102,739	29.9%	5.4
KENTUCKY	303,000	99,995	33.0%	337,000	160,060	47.5%	14.5	371,000	148,875	40.1%	7.1	401,000	152,961	38.1%	5.1	430,000	183,830	42.8%	9.7
LOUISIANA	169,000	57,029	33.7%	188,000	70,508	37.5%	3.8	205,000	65,047	31.7%	-2.0	220,000	62,594	20.5%	5.3	233,000	85,032	36.5%	2.7
MAINE	157,000	29,097	18.5%	163,000	49,917	30.6%	12.1	170,000	65,211	38.4%	19.8	174,000	52,153	30.0%	11.4	180,000	50,472	28.0%	9.5
MARYLAND	180,000	67,687	37.6%	198,000	91,779	46.4%	8.7	215,000	93,706	43.6%	6.0	229,000	96,866	42.3%	4.7	243,000	106,188	43.7%	6.1
MASSACHUSETTS	330,000	59,195	17.9%	360,000	108,777	30.2%	12.3	393,000	111,960	28.5%	10.6	446,000	122,352	27.4%	9.5	499,000	151,590	30.4%	12.4
MICHIGAN	304,000	78,651	25.9%	352,000	141,665	40.2%	14.4	414,000	131,596	31.8%	5.9	466,000	149,835	32.2%	6.3	517,000	213,469	41.3%	15.4
MINNESOTA	98,000	35,131	35.8%	134,000	48,799	36.4%	0.6	186,000	53,314	28.7%	-7.2	242,000	70,065	29.0%	-6.9	299,000	104,372	34.9%	-0.9
MISSISSIPPI	185,000	47,282	25.6%	212,000	112,173	52.9%	27.4	237,000	75,750	32.0%	6.4	250,000	77,653	31.1%	5.5	264,000	85,451	32.4%	6.8
MISSOURI	411,000	151,434	36.8%	462,000	202,086	43.7%	6.9	514,000	208,600	40.6%	3.7	577,000	236,023	40.9%	4.1	641,000	261,943	40.9%	4.0
MONTANA																			
NEBRASKA	55,000	7,603	13.8%	87,000	17,343	19.9%	6.1	121,000	28,523	23.6%	9.7	186,000	54,391	29.2%	15.4	250,000	80,552	32.2%	18.4
NEVADA	20,000	6,236	31.2%	23,000	9,308	40.5%	9.3	24,000	9,611	40.0%	8.9	21,000	5,577	26.6%	-4.6	18,000	5,303	29.5%	-1.7
NEW HAMPSHIRE	85,000	31,425	37.0%	90,000	38,510	42.8%	5.8	94,000	40,797	43.4%	6.4	97,000	39,198	40.4%	3.4	101,000	43,382	43.0%	6.0
NEW JERSEY	208,000	76,456	36.8%	232,000	115,962	50.0%	13.2	257,000	122,565	47.7%	10.9	298,000	127,747	42.9%	6.1	340,000	151,493	44.6%	7.8
NEW MEXICO																			
NEW YORK	1,031,000	387,282	37.6%	1,112,000	521,949	46.9%	9.4	1,199,000	534,511	44.6%	7.0	1,325,000	563,048	42.5%	4.9	1,451,000	635,965	43.8%	6.3
NORTH CAROLINA	233,000	70,130	30.1%	264,000	125,427	47.5%	17.4	295,000	124,204	42.1%	12.0	314,000	142,905	45.5%	15.4	334,000	147,902	44.3%	14.2
NORTH DAKOTA																			
OHIO	636,000	244,320	38.4%	706,000	323,182	45.8%	7.4	777,000	340,867	43.9%	5.5	850,000	368,280	43.3%	4.9	922,000	395,456	42.9%	4.5
OKLAHOMA																			
OREGON	30,000	7,742	25.8%	41,000	14,157	34.5%	8.7	51,000	19,955	39.1%	13.3	70,000	24,598	35.1%	9.3	87,000	26,518	30.5%	4.7
PENNSYLVANIA	820,000	212,040	25.9%	891,000	366,204	41.1%	15.2	970,000	407,428	42.0%	16.1	1,098,000	394,772	36.0%	10.1	1,226,000	446,633	36.4%	10.6
RHODE ISLAND	47,000	5,329	11.3%	52,000	10,712	20.6%	9.3	58,000	10,779	18.6%	7.2	65,000	12,391	19.1%	7.7	72,000	17,530	24.3%	13.0
SOUTH CAROLINA	161,000	22,699	14.1%	184,000	90,897	49.4%	35.3	206,000	111,236	54.0%	39.9	218,000	69,845	32.0%	17.9	230,000	65,824	28.6%	14.5
SOUTH DAKOTA																			
TENNESSEE	275,000	93,391	34.0%	302,000	133,177	44.1%	10.1	329,000	129,569	39.4%	5.4	358,000	133,770	37.4%	3.4	386,000	158,699	41.1%	7.2

United States Presidential General Elections (continued)

United States Presidential General Elections *(continued)*

Democratic Turnout for Election Years 1872–1888 *(continued)*

State	1872 Voting-age population	Turnout	%	1876 Voting-age population	Turnout	%	Difference from 1872	1880 Voting-age population	Turnout	%	Difference from 1872	1884 Voting-age population	Turnout	%	Difference from 1872	1888 Voting-age population	Turnout	%	Difference from 1872
TEXAS	215,000	67,675	31.5%	289,000	106,372	36.8%	5.3	362,000	156,010	43.1%	11.6	420,000	223,209	53.1%	21.7	478,000	232,189	48.6%	17.1
UTAH																			
VERMONT	77,000	10,927	14.2%	80,000	20,254	25.3%	11.1	83,000	18,316	22.1%	7.9	86,000	17,331	20.2%	6.0	90,000	16,788	18.7%	4.5
VIRGINIA	282,000	91,647	32.5%	308,000	140,770	45.7%	13.2	332,000	128,083	38.6%	6.1	350,000	145,491	41.6%	9.1	368,000	152,004	41.3%	8.8
WASHINGTON																			
WEST VIRGINIA	104,000	29,532	28.4%	121,000	56,546	46.7%	18.3	138,000	57,390	41.6%	13.2	155,000	67,311	43.4%	15.0	172,000	78,677	45.7%	17.3
WISCONSIN	223,000	86,390	38.7%	256,000	123,922	48.4%	9.7	291,000	114,650	39.4%	0.7	338,000	146,447	43.3%	4.6	386,000	155,232	40.2%	1.5
WYOMING																			
Total	8,996,000	2,834,761	31.5%	10,149,000	4,288,546	42.3%	10.7	11,431,000	4,444,260	38.9%	7.4	12,794,000	4,874,621	38.1%	6.6	14,164,000	5,534,488	39.1%	7.6

Other Turnout for Election Years 1872–1888

State	1872 Voting-age population	Turnout	%	1876 Voting-age population	Turnout	%	Difference from 1872*	1880 Voting-age population	Turnout	%	Difference from 1872	1884 Voting-age population	Turnout	%	Difference from 1872	1888 Voting-age population	Turnout	%	Difference from 1872
ALABAMA				238,000	2	0.0%		261,000	4,422	1.7%	1.7	286,000	1,444	0.5%	0.5	312,000	594	0.2%	0.2
ALASKA																			
ARIZONA																			
ARKANSAS				152,000	211	0.1%		183,000	5,622	3.1%	2.9	213,000	1,847	0.9%	0.7	243,000	11,244	4.6%	4.5
CALIFORNIA	164,000	1,061	0.6%	195,000	66	0.0%	-0.6	227,000	3,510	1.5%	0.9	270,000	5,331	2.0%	1.3	313,000	8,794	2.8%	2.2
COLORADO								88,000	1,449	1.6%		112,000	2,712	2.4%	0.8	138,000	3,625	2.6%	1.0
CONNECTICUT				140,000	1,174	0.8%		147,000	1,316	0.9%	0.1	163,000	4,175	2.6%	1.7	179,000	4,474	2.5%	1.7
DELAWARE	30,000	488	1.6%					37,000	129	0.3%	-1.3	40,000	74	0.2%	-1.4	43,000	400	0.9%	-0.7
DISTRICT OF COLUMBIA																			
FLORIDA												73,000	190	0.3%		86,000	414	0.5%	0.2
GEORGIA												352,000	340	0.1%		383,000	1,944	0.5%	0.4
HAWAII																			
IDAHO																			
ILLINOIS	577,000	3,151	0.5%	632,000	17,525	2.8%	2.2	692,000	26,948	3.9%	3.3	789,000	22,850	2.9%	2.3	886,000	28,987	3.3%	2.7
INDIANA				446,000	9,533	2.1%		487,000	13,066	2.7%	0.5	525,000	8,194	1.6%	-0.6	563,000	12,632	2.2%	0.1
IOWA	284,000	13,610	4.8%	333,000	9,951	3.0%	-1.8	379,000	33,391	8.8%	4.0	417,000	19,137	4.6%	-0.2	457,000	13,211	2.9%	-1.9
KANSAS	135,000	737	0.5%	196,000	7,908	4.0%	3.5	256,000	19,745	7.7%	7.2	300,000	6,470	2.2%	1.6	344,000	45,549	13.2%	12.7
KENTUCKY	303,000	2,374	0.8%	337,000	2,998	0.9%	0.1	371,000	11,739	3.2%	2.4	401,000	3,259	0.8%	0.0	430,000	5,900	1.4%	0.6
LOUISIANA								205,000	437	0.2%		220,000	4,293	2.0%	1.7	233,000	199	0.1%	-0.1
MAINE				163,000	828	0.5%		170,000	4,640	2.7%	2.2	174,000	2,744	1.6%	1.1	180,000	4,051	2.3%	1.7

United States Presidential General Elections (continued)

Other Turnout for Election Years 1872–1888 (continued)

State	1872 Voting-age population	Turnout	%	1876 Voting-age population	Turnout	%	Difference from 1872	1880 Voting-age population	Turnout	%	Difference from 1872	1884 Voting-age population	Turnout	%	Difference from 1872	1888 Voting-age population	Turnout	%	Difference from 1872
MARYLAND												229,000	27,209	11.9%		243,000	4,767	2.0%	-9.9
MASSACHUSETTS				360,000	779	0.2%		393,000	5,347	1.4%	1.1	446,000	52,177	11.7%	11.5	499,000	8,761	1.8%	1.5
MICHIGAN	304,000	4,150	1.4%	352,000	9,860	2.8%	1.4	414,000	36,145	8.7%	7.4	466,000	21,986	4.7%	3.4	517,000	25,500	4.9%	3.6
MINNESOTA	98,000	168	0.2%	134,000	2,399	1.8%	1.6	186,000	3,553	1.9%	1.7	242,000	4,684	1.9%	1.8	299,000	16,298	5.5%	5.3
MISSISSIPPI								237,000	6,474	2.7%						264,000	240	0.1%	2.6
MISSOURI	411,000	2,429	0.6%	462,000	3,497	0.8%	0.2	514,000	35,042	6.8%	6.2	577,000	2,164	0.4%	-0.2	641,000	23,164	3.6%	3.0
MONTANA																			
NEBRASKA								121,000	3,853	3.2%		186,000	2,899	1.6%	-1.6	250,000	13,661	5.5%	2.3
NEVADA												21,000	26	0.1%		18,000	41	0.2%	0.1
NEW HAMPSHIRE	85,000	313	0.4%	90,000	93	0.1%	-0.3	94,000	708	0.8%	0.4	97,000	2,134	2.2%	1.8	101,000	1,654	1.6%	1.3
NEW JERSEY				232,000	714	0.3%		257,000	2,808	1.1%	0.8	298,000	9,670	3.2%	2.9	340,000	7,794	2.3%	2.0
NEW MEXICO																			
NEW YORK				1,112,000	4,347	0.4%		1,199,000	13,890	1.2%	0.8	1,325,000	41,954	3.2%	2.8	1,451,000	33,445	2.3%	1.9
NORTH CAROLINA	233,000	261	0.1%					295,000	1,126	0.4%	0.3	314,000	430	0.1%	0.0	334,000	2,877	0.9%	0.7
NORTH DAKOTA																			
OHIO	636,000	3,263	0.5%	706,000	4,770	0.7%	0.2	777,000	9,069	1.2%	0.7	850,000	16,248	1.9%	1.4	922,000	27,847	3.0%	2.5
OKLAHOMA																			
OREGON	30,000	547	1.8%	41,000	509	1.2%	-0.6	51,000	267	0.5%	-1.3	70,000	1,240	1.8%	-0.1	87,000	2,080	2.4%	0.6
PENNSYLVANIA				891,000	8,612	1.0%		970,000	22,651	2.3%	1.4	1,098,000	32,146	2.9%	2.0	1,226,000	24,844	2.0%	1.1
RHODE ISLAND								58,000	261	0.5%		65,000	1,350	2.1%	1.6	72,000	1,276	1.8%	1.3
SOUTH CAROLINA	161,000	463	0.3%					206,000	603	0.3%	0.0	218,000	1,237	0.6%	0.3	230,000	437	0.2%	-0.1
SOUTH DAKOTA																			
TENNESSEE								329,000	6,017	1.8%		358,000	2,107	0.6%	-1.2	386,000	6,017	1.6%	-0.3
TEXAS	215,000	115	0.1%	289,000	46	0.0%	0.0	362,000	27,405	7.6%	7.5	420,000	6,799	1.6%	1.6	478,000	33,619	7.0%	7.0
UTAH																			
VERMONT				80,000	114	0.1%		83,000	1,215	1.5%	1.3	86,000	2,564	3.0%	2.8	90,000	1,495	1.7%	1.5
VIRGINIA	282,000	85	0.0%									350,000	130	0.0%	0.0	368,000	1,684	0.5%	0.4
WASHINGTON																			
WEST VIRGINIA	104,000	615	0.6%	121,000	1,104	0.9%	0.3	138,000	9,008	6.5%	5.9	155,000	1,738	1.1%	0.5	172,000	2,592	1.5%	0.9
WISCONSIN	223,000	853	0.4%	256,000	3,204	1.3%	0.9	291,000	8,146	2.8%	2.4	338,000	12,245	3.6%	3.2	386,000	22,829	5.9%	5.5
WYOMING																			
Total	4,275,000	34,683	0.8%	7,958,000	90,244	1.1%	0.3	10,478,000	320,002	3.1%	2.2	12,544,000	326,197	2.6%	1.8	14,164,000	404,940	2.9%	2.0

*Percentage point difference between turnout in current year and initial year listed in chart. If data do not appear for a state in the initial year listed, the difference is calculated from the first year in which data do appear for that state.

STATE GUBERNATORIAL GENERAL ELECTIONS

Election Years 1872–1888

State	1872 Voting-age population	1872 Turnout	1872 %	1876 Voting-age population	1876 Turnout	1876 %	1876 Difference from 1872*	1880 Voting-age population	1880 Turnout	1880 %	1880 Difference from 1872	1884 Voting-age population	1884 Turnout	1884 %	1884 Difference from 1872	1888 Voting-age population	1888 Turnout	1888 %	1888 Difference from 1872
ALABAMA	215,000	171,239	79.6%	238,000	152,083	63.9%	-15.7	261,000	177,268	67.9%	-11.7	286,000	143,644	50.2%	-29.4	312,000	200,991	64.4%	-15.2
ALASKA																			
ARIZONA																			
ARKANSAS	119,000	80,717	67.8%	152,000	106,336	70.0%	2.1	183,000	115,609	63.2%	-4.7	213,000	156,263	73.4%	5.5	243,000	183,502	75.5%	7.7
CALIFORNIA																			
COLORADO				60,000	27,470	45.8%		88,000	53,421	60.7%	14.9	112,000	66,709	59.6%	13.8	138,000	91,920	66.6%	20.8
CONNECTICUT	132,000	93,098	70.5%	140,000	98,620	70.4%	-0.1	147,000	132,763	90.3%	19.8	163,000	137,723	84.5%	14.0	179,000	153,648	85.8%	15.3
DELAWARE																			
DISTRICT OF COLUMBIA																			
FLORIDA	43,000	33,607	78.2%	52,000	48,163	92.6%	14.5	60,000	51,626	86.0%	7.9	73,000	59,932	82.1%	3.9	86,000	66,740	77.6%	-0.6
GEORGIA	255,000	151,014	59.2%	288,000	144,839	50.3%	-8.9	322,000	182,353	56.6%	-2.6					383,000	121,999	31.9%	-27.4
HAWAII																			
IDAHO																			
ILLINOIS	577,000	418,043	72.5%	632,000	552,093	87.4%	14.9	692,000	622,070	89.9%	17.4	789,000	673,489	85.4%	12.9	886,000	748,447	84.5%	12.0
INDIANA	403,000	377,911	93.8%	446,000	434,495	97.4%	3.6	487,000	470,738	96.7%	2.9	525,000	495,084	94.3%	0.5	563,000	536,816	95.3%	1.6
IOWA																			
KANSAS	135,000	101,323	75.1%	196,000	121,827	62.2%	-12.9	256,000	200,636	78.4%	3.3	300,000	265,248	88.4%	13.4	344,000	331,602	96.4%	21.3
KENTUCKY																			
LOUISIANA	169,000	127,025	75.2%	188,000	160,963	85.6%	10.5					220,000	132,282	60.1%	-15.0	233,000	188,740	81.0%	5.8
MAINE	157,000	127,266	81.1%	163,000	136,823	83.9%	2.9	170,000	147,802	86.9%	5.9	174,000	142,107	81.7%	0.6	180,000	145,404	80.8%	-0.3
MARYLAND																			
MASSACHUSETTS	330,000	193,780	58.7%	360,000	256,904	71.4%	12.6	393,000	282,346	71.8%	13.1	446,000	304,115	68.2%	9.5	499,000	343,114	68.8%	10.0
MICHIGAN	304,000	222,511	73.2%	352,000	317,678	90.2%	17.1	414,000	349,034	84.3%	11.1	466,000	400,398	85.9%	12.7	517,000	474,777	91.8%	18.6
MINNESOTA																299,000	261,632	87.5%	
MISSISSIPPI																			
MISSOURI	411,000	278,666	67.8%	462,000	350,236	75.8%	8.0	514,000	397,644	77.4%	9.6	577,000	437,353	75.8%	8.0	641,000	518,122	80.8%	13.0
MONTANA																			
NEBRASKA	55,000	27,775	50.5%	87,000	52,224	60.0%	9.5	121,000	87,345	72.2%	21.7	186,000	133,555	71.8%	21.3	250,000	202,865	81.1%	30.6
NEVADA																			
NEW HAMPSHIRE	85,000	76,232	89.7%	90,000	80,319	89.2%	-0.4	94,000	86,164	91.7%	2.0	97,000	84,470	87.1%	-2.6	101,000	90,623	89.7%	0.0
NEW JERSEY																			
NEW MEXICO																			
NEW YORK	1,031,000	838,151	81.3%	1,112,000	1,014,050	91.2%	9.9									1,451,000	1,315,663	90.7%	9.4

State Gubernatorial General Elections *(continued)*

Election Years 1872–1888 *(continued)*

State	1872 Voting-age population	Turnout	%	1876 Voting-age population	Turnout	%	Difference from 1872	1880 Voting-age population	Turnout	%	Difference from 1872	1884 Voting-age population	Turnout	%	Difference from 1872	1888 Voting-age population	Turnout	%	Difference from 1872
NORTH CAROLINA	233,000	194,366	**83.4%**	264,000	233,326	**88.4%**	5.0	295,000	237,421	**80.5%**	-2.9	314,000	266,163	**84.8%**	1.3	334,000	285,561	**85.5%**	2.1
NORTH DAKOTA																			
OHIO																			
OKLAHOMA																			
OREGON																			
PENNSYLVANIA	820,000	672,237	**82.0%**																
RHODE ISLAND	47,000	17,851	**38.0%**	52,000	19,037	**36.6%**	-1.4	58,000	22,809	**39.3%**	1.3	65,000	25,541	**39.3%**	1.3	72,000	39,563	**54.9%**	17.0
SOUTH CAROLINA	161,000	106,722	**66.3%**	184,000	183,388	**99.7%**	33.4	206,000	121,801	**59.1%**	-7.2	218,000	67,895	**31.1%**	-35.1	230,000	58,746	**25.5%**	-40.7
SOUTH DAKOTA																			
TENNESSEE	275,000	181,789	**66.1%**	302,000	210,632	**69.7%**	3.6	329,000	243,286	**73.9%**	7.8	358,000	257,996	**72.1%**	6.0	386,000	301,745	**78.2%**	12.1
TEXAS				289,000	198,300	**68.6%**		362,000	264,204	**73.0%**	4.4	420,000	326,241	**77.7%**	9.1	478,000	348,785	**73.0%**	4.4
UTAH																			
VERMONT	77,000	58,573	**76.1%**	80,000	65,704	**82.2%**	6.2	83,000	70,684	**85.2%**	9.1	86,000	63,198	**73.5%**	-2.6	90,000	69,426	**77.1%**	1.1
VIRGINIA																			
WASHINGTON																			
WEST VIRGINIA	104,000	83,193	**80.0%**	121,000	100,015	**82.7%**	2.7	138,000	118,873	**86.1%**	6.1	155,000	137,587	**88.8%**	8.8	172,000	159,594	**92.8%**	12.8
WISCONSIN												338,000	319,997	**94.7%**		386,000	354,714	**91.9%**	-2.8
WYOMING																			
Total	6,138,000	4,633,089	**75.5%**	6,310,000	5,065,605	**80.3%**	4.8	5,673,000	4,435,897	**78.2%**	2.7	6,581,000	5,096,990	**77.5%**	2.0	9,453,000	7,594,739	**80.3%**	4.9

*Percentage point difference between turnout in current year and initial year listed in chart. If data do not appear for a state in the initial year listed, the difference is calculated from the first year in which data do appear for that state.

STATE GUBERNATORIAL GENERAL ELECTIONS

Republican Turnout for Election Years 1872–1888

State	1872 Voting-age population	1872 Turnout	1872 %	1876 Voting-age population	1876 Turnout	1876 %	1876 Difference from 1872*	1880 Voting-age population	1880 Turnout	1880 %	1880 Difference from 1872	1884 Voting-age population	1884 Turnout	1884 %	1884 Difference from 1872	1888 Voting-age population	1888 Turnout	1888 %	1888 Difference from 1872
ALABAMA	215,000	89,868	41.8%	238,000	55,682	23.4%	-18.4									312,000	44,707	14.3%	-27.5
ALASKA																			
ARIZONA																			
ARKANSAS	119,000	41,808	35.1%	152,000	36,272	23.9%	-11.3					213,000	55,388	26.0%	-9.1				
CALIFORNIA																			
COLORADO				60,000	14,154	23.6%		88,000	28,465	32.3%	8.8	112,000	33,845	30.2%	6.6	138,000	49,490	35.9%	12.3
CONNECTICUT	132,000	46,563	35.3%	140,000	43,510	31.1%	-4.2	147,000	67,070	45.6%	10.4	163,000	66,274	40.7%	5.4	179,000	73,659	41.2%	5.9
DELAWARE																			
DISTRICT OF COLUMBIA																			
FLORIDA	43,000	17,603	40.9%	52,000	23,984	46.1%	5.2	60,000	23,285	38.8%	-2.1					86,000	26,485	30.8%	-10.1
GEORGIA	255,000	46,475	18.2%	288,000	33,444	11.6%	-6.6												
HAWAII																			
IDAHO																			
ILLINOIS	577,000	237,774	41.2%	632,000	279,263	44.2%	3.0	692,000	314,565	45.5%	4.2	789,000	334,234	42.4%	1.2	886,000	367,860	41.5%	0.3
INDIANA	403,000	188,276	46.7%	446,000	208,080	46.7%	-0.1	487,000	231,405	47.5%	0.8	525,000	237,748	45.3%	-1.4	563,000	263,194	46.7%	0.0
IOWA																			
KANSAS	135,000	66,715	49.4%	196,000	69,173	35.3%	-14.1	256,000	115,204	45.0%	-4.4	300,000	146,777	48.9%	-0.5	344,000	181,841	52.9%	3.4
KENTUCKY																			
LOUISIANA	169,000	72,890	43.1%	188,000	76,476	40.7%	-2.5					220,000	43,502	19.8%	-23.4	233,000	51,993	22.3%	-20.8
MAINE	157,000	71,888	45.8%	163,000	75,867	46.5%	0.8	170,000	73,544	43.3%	-2.5	174,000	78,318	45.0%	-0.8	180,000	79,401	44.1%	-1.7
MARYLAND																			
MASSACHUSETTS	330,000	133,900	40.6%	360,000	137,665	38.2%	-2.3	393,000	164,926	42.0%	1.4	446,000	159,345	35.7%	-4.8	499,000	180,849	36.2%	-4.3
MICHIGAN	304,000	137,602	45.3%	352,000	165,926	47.1%	1.9	414,000	178,944	43.2%	-2.0	466,000	190,840	41.0%	-4.3	517,000	233,580	45.2%	-0.1
MINNESOTA																299,000	134,355	44.9%	
MISSISSIPPI																			
MISSOURI	411,000	121,889	29.7%	462,000	147,694	32.0%	2.3	514,000	153,636	29.9%	0.2					641,000	242,531	37.8%	8.2
MONTANA																			
NEBRASKA	55,000	16,543	30.1%	87,000	31,947	36.7%	6.6	121,000	55,237	45.7%	15.6	186,000	72,835	39.2%	9.1	250,000	103,983	41.6%	11.5
NEVADA																			
NEW HAMPSHIRE	85,000	38,752	45.6%	90,000	41,761	46.4%	0.8	94,000	44,432	47.3%	1.7	97,000	42,514	43.8%	-1.8	101,000	44,809	44.4%	-1.2
NEW JERSEY																			
NEW MEXICO																			
NEW YORK	1,031,000	445,801	43.2%	1,112,000	489,371	44.0%	0.8									1,451,000	631,293	43.5%	0.3

State Gubernatorial General Elections *(continued)*

Republican Turnout for Election Years 1872–1888 *(continued)*

State	1872			1876				1880				1884				1888			
	Voting-age population	Turnout	%	Voting-age population	Turnout	%	Difference from 1872	Voting-age population	Turnout	%	Difference from 1872	Voting-age population	Turnout	%	Difference from 1872	Voting-age population	Turnout	%	Difference from 1872
NORTH CAROLINA	233,000	98,132	42.1%	264,000	110,061	41.7%	-0.4	295,000	115,589	39.2%	-2.9	314,000	122,914	39.1%	-3.0	334,000	134,026	40.1%	-2.0
NORTH DAKOTA																			
OHIO																			
OKLAHOMA																			
OREGON																			
PENNSYLVANIA	820,000	353,287	43.1%																
RHODE ISLAND	47,000	9,463	20.1%	52,000	8,689	16.7%	-3.4	58,000	10,224	17.6%	-2.5	65,000	15,936	24.5%	4.4	72,000	20,698	28.7%	8.6
SOUTH CAROLINA	161,000	69,838	43.4%	184,000	91,127	49.5%	6.1	206,000	4,277	2.1%	-41.3								
SOUTH DAKOTA																			
TENNESSEE	275,000	84,089	30.6%	302,000	10,436	3.5%	-27.1	329,000	103,964	31.6%	1.0	358,000	125,246	35.0%	4.4	386,000	139,014	36.0%	5.4
TEXAS				289,000	47,719	16.5%		362,000	64,382	17.8%	1.3	420,000	25,557	6.1%	-10.4				
UTAH																			
VERMONT	77,000	41,946	54.5%	80,000	44,723	55.9%	1.4	83,000	47,848	57.6%	3.2	86,000	42,524	49.4%	-5.0	90,000	48,522	53.9%	0.6
VIRGINIA																			
WASHINGTON																			
WEST VIRGINIA				121,000	43,477	35.9%		138,000	44,855	32.5%	-3.4	155,000	66,149	42.7%	6.7	172,000	78,460	45.6%	9.7
WISCONSIN												338,000	163,214	48.3%		386,000	175,696	45.5%	-2.8
WYOMING																			
Total	6,034,000	2,431,102	40.3%	6,310,000	2,286,501	36.2%	-4.1	4,907,000	1,841,852	37.5%	-2.8	5,427,000	2,023,160	37.3%	-3.0	8,119,000	3,306,446	40.7%	0.4

Democratic Turnout for Election Years 1872–1888

State	1872			1876				1880				1884				1888			
	Voting-age population	Turnout	%	Voting-age population	Turnout	%	Difference from 1872*	Voting-age population	Turnout	%	Difference from 1872	Voting-age population	Turnout	%	Difference from 1872	Voting-age population	Turnout	%	Difference from 1872
ALABAMA	215,000	81,371	37.8%	238,000	96,401	40.5%	2.7	261,000	134,905	51.7%	13.8	286,000	143,229	50.1%	12.2	312,000	155,973	50.0%	12.1
ALASKA																			
ARIZONA																			
ARKANSAS				152,000	69,775	45.9%		183,000	84,185	46.0%	0.1	213,000	100,875	47.4%	1.5	243,000	99,229	40.8%	-5.1
CALIFORNIA																			
COLORADO				60,000	13,316	22.2%		88,000	23,547	26.8%	4.6	112,000	30,743	27.4%	5.3	138,000	39,197	28.4%	6.2
CONNECTICUT	132,000	44,562	33.8%	140,000	51,138	36.5%	2.8	147,000	64,293	43.7%	10.0	163,000	67,910	41.7%	7.9	179,000	75,074	41.9%	8.2
DELAWARE																			
DISTRICT OF COLUMBIA																			
FLORIDA	43,000	16,004	37.2%	52,000	24,179	46.5%	9.3	60,000	28,341	47.2%	10.0	73,000	32,087	44.0%	6.7	86,000	40,255	46.8%	9.6

State Gubernatorial General Elections (continued)

State Gubernatorial General Elections (continued)

Democratic Turnout for Election Years 1872–1888 (continued)

State	1872			1876				1880				1884				1888			
	Voting-age population	Turnout	%	Voting-age population	Turnout	%	Difference from 1872	Voting-age population	Turnout	%	Difference from 1872	Voting-age population	Turnout	%	Difference from 1872	Voting-age population	Turnout	%	Difference from 1872
GEORGIA	255,000	104,539	41.0%	288,000	111,297	38.6%	-2.4	322,000	118,349	36.8%	-4.2					383,000	121,999	31.9%	-9.1
HAWAII																			
IDAHO																			
ILLINOIS								692,000	277,532	40.1%		789,000	319,635	40.5%	0.4	886,000	355,313	40.1%	0.0
INDIANA	403,000	189,424	47.0%	446,000	213,164	47.8%	0.8	487,000	224,452	46.1%	-0.9	525,000	245,130	46.7%	-0.3	563,000	260,994	46.4%	-0.6
IOWA																			
KANSAS				196,000	46,204	23.6%		256,000	63,557	24.8%	1.3	300,000	108,284	36.1%	12.5	344,000	107,480	31.2%	7.7
KENTUCKY																			
LOUISIANA	169,000	54,079	32.0%	188,000	84,487	44.9%	12.9					220,000	88,780	40.4%	8.4	233,000	136,747	58.7%	26.7
MAINE	157,000	55,343	35.3%	163,000	60,423	37.1%	1.8					174,000	58,954	33.9%	-1.4	180,000	61,348	34.1%	-1.2
MARYLAND																			
MASSACHUSETTS				360,000	106,850	29.7%		393,000	111,410	28.3%	-1.3	446,000	111,829	25.1%	-4.6	499,000	152,780	30.6%	0.9
MICHIGAN	304,000	2,720	0.9%	352,000	142,585	40.5%	39.6	414,000	137,671	33.3%	32.4					517,000	216,450	41.9%	41.0
MINNESOTA																299,000	110,251	36.9%	
MISSISSIPPI																			
MISSOURI	411,000	156,777	38.1%	462,000	199,580	43.2%	5.1	514,000	207,670	40.4%	2.3	577,000	218,885	37.9%	-0.2	641,000	255,764	39.9%	1.8
MONTANA																			
NEBRASKA	55,000	11,227	20.4%	87,000	17,219	19.8%	-0.6	121,000	28,167	23.3%	2.9	186,000	57,634	31.0%	10.6	250,000	85,420	34.2%	13.8
NEVADA																			
NEW HAMPSHIRE	85,000	36,584	43.0%	90,000	38,133	42.4%	-0.7	94,000	40,813	43.4%	0.4	97,000	39,637	40.9%	-2.2	101,000	44,217	43.8%	0.7
NEW JERSEY																			
NEW MEXICO																			
NEW YORK	1,031,000	392,350	38.1%	1,112,000	519,831	46.7%	8.7									1,451,000	650,464	44.8%	6.8
NORTH CAROLINA	233,000	96,234	41.3%	264,000	123,265	46.7%	5.4	295,000	121,832	41.3%	0.0	314,000	143,249	45.6%	4.3	334,000	148,406	44.4%	3.1
NORTH DAKOTA																			
OHIO																			
OKLAHOMA																			
OREGON																			
PENNSYLVANIA	820,000	317,700	38.7%																
RHODE ISLAND	47,000	8,308	17.7%	52,000	3,599	6.9%	-10.8	58,000	7,440	12.8%	-4.8	65,000	9,592	14.8%	-2.9	72,000	17,525	24.3%	6.7
SOUTH CAROLINA				184,000	92,261	50.1%		206,000	117,432	57.0%	6.9	218,000	67,895	31.1%	-19.0	230,000	58,730	25.5%	-24.6
SOUTH DAKOTA																			
TENNESSEE	275,000	97,700	35.5%	302,000	123,740	41.0%	5.4	329,000	78,783	23.9%	-11.6	358,000	132,201	36.9%	1.4	386,000	155,888	40.4%	4.9

Democratic Turnout for Election Years 1872–1888 *(continued)*

State	1872 Voting-age population	1872 Turnout	1872 %	1876 Voting-age population	1876 Turnout	1876 %	1876 Difference from 1872	1880 Voting-age population	1880 Turnout	1880 %	1880 Difference from 1872	1884 Voting-age population	1884 Turnout	1884 %	1884 Difference from 1872	1888 Voting-age population	1888 Turnout	1888 %	1888 Difference from 1872
TEXAS				289,000	150,581	52.1%		362,000	166,101	45.9%	-6.2	420,000	212,234	50.5%	-1.6	478,000	250,338	52.4%	0.3
UTAH																			
VERMONT				80,000	20,988	26.2%		83,000	21,245	25.6%	-0.6	86,000	19,820	23.0%	-3.2	90,000	19,527	21.7%	-4.5
VIRGINIA																			
WASHINGTON																			
WEST VIRGINIA	104,000	40,305	38.8%	121,000	56,206	46.5%	7.7	138,000	60,991	44.2%	5.4	155,000	71,438	46.1%	7.3	172,000	78,097	45.0%	7.0
WISCONSIN												338,000	143,945	42.6%		386,000	155,423	40.3%	-2.3
WYOMING																			
Total	4,739,000	1,705,227	36.0%	5,678,000	2,365,222	41.7%	5.7	5,503,000	2,118,716	38.5%	2.5	6,115,000	2,423,986	39.6%	3.7	9,453,000	3,853,489	40.8%	4.8

Other Turnout for Election Years 1872–1888

State	1872 Voting-age population	1872 Turnout	1872 %	1876 Voting-age population	1876 Turnout	1876 %	1876 Difference from 1872*	1880 Voting-age population	1880 Turnout	1880 %	1880 Difference from 1872	1884 Voting-age population	1884 Turnout	1884 %	1884 Difference from 1872	1888 Voting-age population	1888 Turnout	1888 %	1888 Difference from 1872
ALABAMA								261,000	42,363	16.2%		286,000	415	0.1%	-16.1	312,000	311	0.1%	-16.1
ALASKA																			
ARIZONA																			
ARKANSAS	119,000	38,909	32.7%	152,000	289	0.2%	-32.5	183,000	31,424	17.2%	-15.5					243,000	84,273	34.7%	2.0
CALIFORNIA																			
COLORADO								88,000	1,409	1.6%		112,000	2,121	1.9%	0.3	138,000	3,233	2.3%	0.7
CONNECTICUT	132,000	1,973	1.5%	140,000	3,972	2.8%	1.3	147,000	1,400	1.0%	-0.5	163,000	3,539	2.2%	0.7	179,000	4,915	2.7%	1.3
DELAWARE																			
DISTRICT OF COLUMBIA																			
FLORIDA												73,000	27,845	38.1%					
GEORGIA				288,000	98	0.0%		322,000	64,004	19.9%	19.8								
HAWAII																			
IDAHO																			
ILLINOIS	577,000	180,269	31.2%	632,000	272,830	43.2%	11.9	692,000	29,973	4.3%	-26.9	789,000	19,620	2.5%	-28.8	886,000	25,274	2.9%	-28.4
INDIANA	403,000	211	0.1%	446,000	13,251	3.0%	2.9	487,000	14,881	3.1%	3.0	525,000	12,206	2.3%	2.3	563,000	12,628	2.2%	2.2
IOWA																			
KANSAS	135,000	34,608	25.6%	196,000	6,450	3.3%	-22.3	256,000	21,875	8.5%	-17.1	300,000	10,187	3.4%	-22.2	344,000	42,281	12.3%	-13.3
KENTUCKY																			
LOUISIANA	169,000	56	0.0%																
MAINE	157,000	35	0.0%	163,000	533	0.3%	0.3	170,000	74,258	43.7%	43.7	174,000	4,835	2.8%	2.8	180,000	4,655	2.6%	2.6

State Gubernatorial General Elections (continued)

State Gubernatorial General Elections (continued)

Other Turnout for Election Years 1872–1888 (continued)

State	1872 Voting-age population	Turnout	%	1876 Voting-age population	Turnout	%	Difference from 1872	1880 Voting-age population	Turnout	%	Difference from 1872	1884 Voting-age population	Turnout	%	Difference from 1872	1888 Voting-age population	Turnout	%	Difference from 1872
MARYLAND																			
MASSACHUSETTS	330,000	59,880	18.1%	360,000	12,389	3.4%	-14.7	393,000	6,010	1.5%	-16.6	446,000	32,941	7.4%	-10.8	499,000	9,485	1.9%	-16.2
MICHIGAN	304,000	82,189	27.0%	352,000	9,167	2.6%	-24.4	414,000	32,419	7.8%	-19.2	466,000	209,558	45.0%	17.9	517,000	24,747	4.8%	-22.2
MINNESOTA																299,000	17,026	5.7%	
MISSISSIPPI																			
MISSOURI				462,000	2,962	0.6%		514,000	36,338	7.1%	6.4	577,000	218,468	37.9%	37.2	641,000	19,827	3.1%	2.5
MONTANA																			
NEBRASKA	55,000	5	0.0%	87,000	3,058	3.5%	3.5	121,000	3,941	3.3%	3.2	186,000	3,086	1.7%	1.7	250,000	13,462	5.4%	5.4
NEVADA																			
NEW HAMPSHIRE	85,000	896	1.1%	90,000	425	0.5%	-0.6	94,000	919	1.0%	-0.1	97,000	2,319	2.4%	1.3	101,000	1,597	1.6%	0.5
NEW JERSEY																			
NEW MEXICO																			
NEW YORK				1,112,000	4,848	0.4%										1,451,000	33,906	2.3%	1.9
NORTH CAROLINA																334,000	3,129	0.9%	
NORTH DAKOTA																			
OHIO																			
OKLAHOMA																			
OREGON																			
PENNSYLVANIA	820,000	1,250	0.2%																
RHODE ISLAND	47,000	80	0.2%	52,000	6,749	13.0%	12.8	58,000	5,145	8.9%	8.7	65,000	13	0.0%	-0.2	72,000	1,340	1.9%	1.7
SOUTH CAROLINA	161,000	36,884	22.9%					206,000	92	0.0%	-22.9					230,000	16	0.0%	-22.9
SOUTH DAKOTA																			
TENNESSEE				302,000	76,456	25.3%		329,000	60,539	18.4%	-6.9	358,000	549	0.2%	-25.2	386,000	6,843	1.8%	-23.5
TEXAS								362,000	33,721	9.3%		420,000	88,450	21.1%	11.7	478,000	98,447	20.6%	11.3
UTAH																			
VERMONT	77,000	16,627	21.6%	80,000	73	0.1%	-21.5	83,000	1,591	1.9%	-19.7	86,000	854	1.0%	-20.6	90,000	1,377	1.5%	-20.1
VIRGINIA																			
WASHINGTON																			
WEST VIRGINIA	104,000	42,888	41.2%	121,000	332	0.3%	-41.0	138,000	13,027	9.4%	-31.8					172,000	2,437	1.4%	-39.8
WISCONSIN												338,000	12,838	3.8%		386,000	23,595	6.1%	2.3
WYOMING																			
Total	3,675,000	496,760	13.5%	5,035,000	413,882	8.2%	-5.3	5,318,000	475,329	8.9%	-4.6	5,461,000	649,844	11.9%	-1.6	8,751,000	434,804	5.0%	-8.5

*Percentage point difference between turnout in current year and initial year listed in chart. If data do not appear for a state in the initial year listed, the difference is calculated from the first year in which data do appear for that state.

UNITED STATES HOUSE OF REPRESENTATIVES GENERAL ELECTIONS

Election Years 1872–1888

State	1872 Voting-age population	Turnout	%	1876 Voting-age population	Turnout	%	Difference from 1872*	1880 Voting-age population	Turnout	%	Difference from 1872	1884 Voting-age population	Turnout	%	Difference from 1872	1888 Voting-age population	Turnout	%	Difference from 1872
ALABAMA	215,000	171,061	79.6%	238,000	158,181	66.5%	-13.1	261,000	141,257	54.1%	-25.4	286,000	141,310	49.4%	-30.2	312,000	173,224	55.5%	-24.0
ALASKA																			
ARIZONA																			
ARKANSAS	119,000	79,620	66.9%	152,000	85,572	56.3%	-10.6	183,000	105,686	57.8%	-9.2	213,000	124,533	58.5%	-8.4	243,000	156,376	64.4%	-2.6
CALIFORNIA	164,000	95,980	58.5%	195,000	155,271	79.6%	21.1	227,000	163,602	72.1%	13.5	270,000	195,428	72.4%	13.9	313,000	249,083	79.6%	21.1
COLORADO				60,000	26,022	43.4%		88,000	53,236	60.5%	17.1	112,000	66,655	59.5%	16.1	138,000	92,009	66.7%	23.3
CONNECTICUT	132,000	86,282	65.4%	140,000	121,391	86.7%	21.3	147,000	132,527	90.2%	24.8	163,000	137,486	84.3%	19.0	179,000	153,615	85.8%	20.5
DELAWARE				33,000	23,997	72.7%		37,000	29,434	79.6%	6.8	40,000	29,932	74.8%	2.1	43,000	29,718	69.1%	-3.6
DISTRICT OF COLUMBIA																			
FLORIDA	43,000	33,418	77.7%	52,000	48,872	94.0%	16.3	60,000	51,238	85.4%	7.7	73,000	59,838	82.0%	4.3	86,000	66,970	77.9%	0.2
GEORGIA	255,000	146,086	57.3%	288,000	172,970	60.1%	2.8	322,000	147,814	45.9%	-11.4	352,000	126,687	36.0%	-21.3	383,000	129,991	33.9%	-23.3
HAWAII																			
IDAHO																			
ILLINOIS	577,000	435,200	75.4%	632,000	550,141	87.0%	11.6	692,000	620,353	89.6%	14.2	789,000	680,216	86.2%	10.8	886,000	745,653	84.2%	8.7
INDIANA	403,000	377,262	93.6%	446,000	431,891	96.8%	3.2	487,000	469,538	96.4%	2.8	525,000	492,133	93.7%	0.1	563,000	533,598	94.8%	1.2
IOWA	284,000	206,901	72.9%	333,000	292,252	87.8%	14.9	379,000	320,472	84.6%	11.7	417,000	375,852	90.1%	17.3	457,000	402,875	88.2%	15.3
KANSAS	135,000	101,790	75.4%	196,000	121,795	62.1%	-13.3	256,000	200,625	78.4%	3.0	300,000	259,538	86.5%	11.1	344,000	327,972	95.3%	19.9
KENTUCKY	303,000	161,142	53.2%	337,000	252,975	75.1%	21.9	371,000	256,670	69.2%	16.0	401,000	252,840	63.1%	9.9	430,000	340,479	79.2%	26.0
LOUISIANA	169,000	128,077	75.8%	188,000	160,773	85.5%	9.7	205,000	101,735	49.6%	-26.2	220,000	106,458	48.4%	-27.4	233,000	113,496	48.7%	-27.1
MAINE	157,000	126,244	80.4%	163,000	135,836	83.3%	2.9	170,000	146,802	86.4%	5.9	174,000	141,295	81.2%	0.8	180,000	144,918	80.5%	0.1
MARYLAND	180,000	134,747	74.9%	198,000	162,620	82.1%	7.3	215,000	172,270	80.1%	5.3	229,000	184,285	80.5%	5.6	243,000	210,284	86.5%	11.7
MASSACHUSETTS	330,000	192,955	58.5%	360,000	253,967	70.5%	12.1	393,000	280,676	71.4%	12.9	446,000	302,198	67.8%	9.3	499,000	342,028	68.5%	10.1
MICHIGAN	304,000	222,872	73.3%	352,000	316,404	89.9%	16.6	414,000	352,114	85.1%	11.7	466,000	399,403	85.7%	12.4	517,000	473,846	91.7%	18.3
MINNESOTA	98,000	89,677	91.5%	134,000	123,214	92.0%	0.4	186,000	150,104	80.7%	-10.8	242,000	188,941	78.1%	-13.4	299,000	261,786	87.6%	-4.0
MISSISSIPPI	185,000	124,232	67.2%	212,000	164,572	77.6%	10.5	237,000	114,292	48.2%	-18.9	250,000	111,655	44.7%	-22.5	264,000	115,643	43.8%	-23.3
MISSOURI	411,000	274,759	66.9%	462,000	342,278	74.1%	7.2	514,000	375,676	73.1%	6.2	577,000	436,835	75.7%	8.9	641,000	516,672	80.6%	13.8
MONTANA																			
NEBRASKA	55,000	27,536	50.1%	87,000	51,685	59.4%	9.3	121,000	84,409	69.8%	19.7	186,000	132,573	71.3%	21.2	250,000	201,952	80.8%	30.7
NEVADA	20,000	14,993	75.0%	23,000	19,571	85.1%	10.1	24,000	18,393	76.6%	1.7	21,000	12,799	60.9%	-14.0	18,000	12,603	70.0%	-4.9
NEW HAMPSHIRE	85,000	67,433	79.3%	90,000	77,890	86.5%	7.2	94,000	86,301	91.8%	12.5	97,000	82,567	85.1%	5.8	101,000	90,623	89.7%	10.4
NEW JERSEY	208,000	170,649	82.0%	232,000	219,167	94.5%	12.4	257,000	245,300	95.4%	13.4	298,000	260,134	87.3%	5.3	340,000	303,350	89.2%	7.2
NEW MEXICO																			
NEW YORK	1,031,000	839,153	81.4%	1,112,000	990,358	89.1%	7.7	1,199,000	1,079,879	90.1%	8.7	1,325,000	1,129,695	85.3%	3.9	1,451,000	1,265,551	87.2%	5.8

United States House of Representatives General Elections (continued)

United States House of Representatives General Elections (continued)

Election Years 1872–1888 (continued)

State	1872			1876				1880				1884				1888			
	Voting-age population	Turnout	%	Voting-age population	Turnout	%	Difference from 1872	Voting-age population	Turnout	%	Difference from 1872	Voting-age population	Turnout	%	Difference from 1872	Voting-age population	Turnout	%	Difference from 1872
NORTH CAROLINA	233,000	195,126	83.7%	264,000	226,049	85.6%	1.9	295,000	229,549	77.8%	-5.9	314,000	260,342	82.9%	-0.8	334,000	279,263	83.6%	-0.1
NORTH DAKOTA																			
OHIO	636,000	518,008	81.4%	706,000	629,486	89.2%	7.7	777,000	711,201	91.5%	10.1	850,000	780,865	91.9%	10.4	922,000	837,772	90.9%	9.4
OKLAHOMA																			
OREGON	30,000	25,485	85.0%	41,000	29,586	72.2%	-12.8	51,000	38,059	74.6%	-10.3	70,000	49,351	70.5%	-14.4	87,000	60,207	69.2%	-15.7
PENNSYLVANIA	820,000	671,440	81.9%	891,000	753,054	84.5%	2.6	970,000	866,783	89.4%	7.5	1,098,000	899,337	81.9%	0.0	1,226,000	983,018	80.2%	-1.7
RHODE ISLAND	47,000	18,930	40.3%	52,000	26,125	50.2%	10.0	58,000	28,895	49.8%	9.5	65,000	32,276	49.7%	9.4	72,000	40,336	56.0%	15.7
SOUTH CAROLINA	161,000	89,631	55.7%	184,000	182,702	99.3%	43.6	206,000	178,094	86.5%	30.8	218,000	89,550	41.1%	-14.6	230,000	76,248	33.2%	-22.5
SOUTH DAKOTA																			
TENNESSEE	275,000	183,913	66.9%	302,000	216,934	71.8%	5.0	329,000	235,061	71.4%	4.6	358,000	252,646	70.6%	3.7	386,000	299,449	77.6%	10.7
TEXAS	215,000	116,203	54.0%	289,000	145,187	50.2%	-3.8	362,000	249,163	68.8%	14.8	420,000	305,777	72.8%	18.8	478,000	339,994	71.1%	17.1
UTAH																			
VERMONT	77,000	49,274	64.0%	80,000	59,063	73.8%	9.8	83,000	66,049	79.6%	15.6	86,000	54,386	63.2%	-0.8	90,000	68,244	75.8%	11.8
VIRGINIA	282,000	190,523	67.6%	308,000	235,495	76.5%	8.9	332,000	193,718	58.3%	-9.2	350,000	285,895	81.7%	14.1	368,000	303,161	82.4%	14.8
WASHINGTON																			
WEST VIRGINIA	104,000	44,905	43.2%	121,000	99,419	82.2%	39.0	138,000	111,129	80.5%	37.4	155,000	131,365	84.8%	41.6	172,000	151,188	87.9%	44.7
WISCONSIN	223,000	193,198	86.6%	256,000	254,817	99.5%	12.9	291,000	265,051	91.1%	4.4	338,000	318,633	94.3%	7.6	386,000	353,474	91.6%	4.9
WYOMING																			
Total	8,966,000	6,604,705	73.7%	10,209,000	8,317,582	81.5%	7.8	11,431,000	9,073,155	79.4%	5.7	12,794,000	9,891,709	77.3%	3.7	14,164,000	11,246,669	79.4%	5.7

*Percentage point difference between turnout in current year and initial year listed in chart. If data do not appear for a state in the initial year listed, the difference is calculated from the first year in which data do appear for that state.

UNITED STATES HOUSE OF REPRESENTATIVES GENERAL ELECTIONS

Republican Turnout for Election Years 1872–1888

State	1872 Voting-age population	1872 Turnout	1872 %	1876 Voting-age population	1876 Turnout	1876 %	1876 Difference from 1872*	1880 Voting-age population	1880 Turnout	1880 %	1880 Difference from 1872	1884 Voting-age population	1884 Turnout	1884 %	1884 Difference from 1872	1888 Voting-age population	1888 Turnout	1888 %	1888 Difference from 1872
ALABAMA	215,000	89,500	**41.6%**	238,000	38,154	**16.0%**	-25.6	261,000	33,927	**13.0%**	-28.6	286,000	46,951	**16.4%**	-25.2	312,000	54,547	**17.5%**	-24.1
ALASKA																			
ARIZONA																			
ARKANSAS	119,000	39,687	**33.4%**	152,000	26,522	**17.4%**	-15.9	183,000	40,597	**22.2%**	-11.2	213,000	51,042	**24.0%**	-9.4	243,000	17,011	**7.0%**	-26.4
CALIFORNIA	164,000	49,237	**30.0%**	195,000	81,043	**41.6%**	11.5	227,000	79,796	**35.2%**	5.1	270,000	101,572	**37.6%**	7.6	313,000	126,646	**40.5%**	10.4
COLORADO				60,000	13,438	**22.4%**		88,000	27,069	**30.8%**	8.4	112,000	35,446	**31.6%**	9.3	138,000	50,620	**36.7%**	14.3
CONNECTICUT	132,000	43,352	**32.8%**	140,000	58,951	**42.1%**	9.3	147,000	67,695	**46.1%**	13.2	163,000	67,235	**41.2%**	8.4	179,000	75,129	**42.0%**	9.1
DELAWARE				33,000	10,592	**32.1%**		37,000	14,336	**38.7%**	6.6	40,000	12,878	**32.2%**	0.1	43,000	12,935	**30.1%**	-2.0
DISTRICT OF COLUMBIA																			
FLORIDA	43,000	17,537	**40.8%**	52,000	24,139	**46.4%**	5.6	60,000	23,035	**38.4%**	-2.4	73,000	27,971	**38.3%**	-2.5	86,000	27,134	**31.6%**	-9.2
GEORGIA	255,000	61,655	**24.2%**	288,000	38,573	**13.4%**	-10.8	322,000	25,060	**7.8%**	-16.4	352,000	28,617	**8.1%**	-16.0	383,000	23,625	**6.2%**	-18.0
HAWAII																			
IDAHO																			
ILLINOIS	577,000	240,374	**41.7%**	632,000	274,518	**43.4%**	1.8	692,000	317,962	**45.9%**	4.3	789,000	350,246	**44.4%**	2.7	886,000	372,138	**42.0%**	0.3
INDIANA	403,000	188,760	**46.8%**	446,000	206,535	**46.3%**	-0.5	487,000	229,620	**47.1%**	0.3	525,000	238,233	**45.4%**	-1.5	563,000	264,365	**47.0%**	0.1
IOWA	284,000	127,094	**44.8%**	333,000	168,289	**50.5%**	5.8	379,000	181,841	**48.0%**	3.2	417,000	196,980	**47.2%**	2.5	457,000	212,090	**46.4%**	1.7
KANSAS	135,000	67,400	**49.9%**	196,000	76,611	**39.1%**	-10.8	256,000	120,451	**47.1%**	-2.9	300,000	155,148	**51.7%**	1.8	344,000	182,375	**53.0%**	3.1
KENTUCKY	303,000	49,392	**16.3%**	337,000	93,825	**27.8%**	11.5	371,000	97,744	**26.3%**	10.0	401,000	97,104	**24.2%**	7.9	430,000	154,413	**35.9%**	19.6
LOUISIANA	169,000	68,947	**40.8%**	188,000	76,385	**40.6%**	-0.2	205,000	35,691	**17.4%**	-23.4	220,000	35,509	**16.1%**	-24.7	233,000	26,817	**11.5%**	-29.3
MAINE	157,000	72,094	**45.9%**	163,000	74,772	**45.9%**	0.0	170,000	73,630	**43.3%**	-2.6	174,000	78,115	**44.9%**	-1.0	180,000	79,744	**44.3%**	-1.6
MARYLAND	180,000	67,024	**37.2%**	198,000	72,627	**36.7%**	-0.6	215,000	80,313	**37.4%**	0.1	229,000	86,360	**37.7%**	0.5	243,000	99,975	**41.1%**	3.9
MASSACHUSETTS	330,000	131,733	**39.9%**	360,000	143,987	**40.0%**	0.1	393,000	164,280	**41.8%**	1.9	446,000	157,728	**35.4%**	-4.6	499,000	179,841	**36.0%**	-3.9
MICHIGAN	304,000	135,829	**44.7%**	352,000	165,626	**47.1%**	2.4	414,000	183,796	**44.4%**	-0.3	466,000	189,282	**40.6%**	-4.1	517,000	236,898	**45.8%**	1.1
MINNESOTA	98,000	55,291	**56.4%**	134,000	68,563	**51.2%**	-5.3	186,000	90,984	**48.9%**	-7.5	242,000	108,412	**44.8%**	-11.6	299,000	139,466	**46.6%**	-9.8
MISSISSIPPI	185,000	80,535	**43.5%**	212,000	50,917	**24.0%**	-19.5	237,000	30,512	**12.9%**	-30.7	250,000	29,723	**11.9%**	-31.6	264,000	26,904	**10.2%**	-33.3
MISSOURI	411,000	117,961	**28.7%**	462,000	135,643	**29.4%**	0.7	514,000	134,075	**26.1%**	-2.6	577,000	198,527	**34.4%**	5.7	641,000	235,668	**36.8%**	8.1
MONTANA																			
NEBRASKA	55,000	17,124	**31.1%**	87,000	30,900	**35.5%**	4.4	121,000	52,642	**43.5%**	12.4	186,000	69,811	**37.5%**	6.4	250,000	106,073	**42.4%**	11.3
NEVADA	20,000	7,146	**35.7%**	23,000	10,241	**44.5%**	8.8	24,000	8,578	**35.7%**	0.0	21,000	6,797	**32.4%**	-3.4	18,000	6,921	**38.5%**	2.7
NEW HAMPSHIRE	85,000	33,178	**39.0%**	90,000	39,771	**44.2%**	5.2	94,000	44,651	**47.5%**	8.5	97,000	42,670	**44.0%**	5.0	101,000	45,271	**44.8%**	5.8
NEW JERSEY	208,000	94,341	**45.4%**	232,000	91,579	**39.5%**	-5.9	257,000	120,114	**46.7%**	1.4	298,000	124,800	**41.9%**	-3.5	340,000	146,035	**43.0%**	-2.4
NEW MEXICO																			
NEW YORK	1,031,000	438,456	**42.5%**	1,112,000	478,597	**43.0%**	0.5	1,199,000	533,655	**44.5%**	2.0	1,325,000	525,102	**39.6%**	-2.9	1,451,000	650,763	**44.8%**	2.3

United States House of Representatives General Elections (continued)

United States House of Representatives General Elections (continued)

Republican Turnout for Election Years 1872–1888 (continued)

State	1872 Voting-age population	Turnout	%	1876 Voting-age population	Turnout	%	Difference from 1872	1880 Voting-age population	Turnout	%	Difference from 1872	1884 Voting-age population	Turnout	%	Difference from 1872	1888 Voting-age population	Turnout	%	Difference from 1872
NORTH CAROLINA	233,000	99,400	42.7%	264,000	104,534	39.6%	-3.1	295,000	100,179	34.0%	-8.7	314,000	119,448	38.0%	-4.6	334,000	130,680	39.1%	-3.5
NORTH DAKOTA																			
OHIO	636,000	253,482	39.9%	706,000	314,519	44.5%	4.7	777,000	362,040	46.6%	6.7	850,000	394,578	46.4%	6.6	922,000	416,520	45.2%	5.3
OKLAHOMA																			
OREGON	30,000	13,168	43.9%	41,000	15,347	37.4%	-6.5	51,000	19,578	38.4%	-5.5	70,000	25,699	36.7%	-7.2	87,000	32,820	37.7%	-6.2
PENNSYLVANIA	820,000	359,485	43.8%	891,000	379,475	42.6%	-1.2	970,000	456,828	47.1%	3.3	1,098,000	478,140	43.5%	-0.3	1,226,000	515,791	42.1%	-1.8
RHODE ISLAND	47,000	13,287	28.3%	52,000	15,700	30.2%	1.9	58,000	18,017	31.1%	2.8	65,000	17,992	27.7%	-0.6	72,000	22,032	30.6%	2.3
SOUTH CAROLINA	161,000	88,862	55.2%	184,000	91,143	49.5%	-5.7	206,000	60,796	29.5%	-25.7	218,000	20,369	9.3%	-45.9	230,000	10,105	4.4%	-50.8
SOUTH DAKOTA																			
TENNESSEE	275,000	80,825	29.4%	302,000	83,207	27.6%	-1.8	329,000	104,818	31.9%	2.5	358,000	117,679	32.9%	3.5	386,000	136,914	35.5%	6.1
TEXAS	215,000	47,125	21.9%	289,000	42,655	14.8%	-7.2					420,000	41,917	10.0%	-11.9	478,000	63,379	13.3%	-8.7
UTAH																			
VERMONT	77,000	39,534	51.3%	80,000	40,900	51.1%	-0.2	83,000	44,775	53.9%	2.6	86,000	38,925	45.3%	-6.1	90,000	48,111	53.5%	2.1
VIRGINIA	282,000	78,371	27.8%	308,000	95,823	31.1%	3.3	332,000	49,094	14.8%	-13.0	350,000	140,789	40.2%	12.4	368,000	150,807	41.0%	13.2
WASHINGTON																			
WEST VIRGINIA	104,000	19,544	18.8%	121,000	43,069	35.6%	16.8	138,000	49,012	35.5%	16.7	155,000	63,884	41.2%	22.4	172,000	73,798	42.9%	24.1
WISCONSIN	223,000	105,143	47.1%	256,000	128,231	50.1%	2.9	291,000	143,665	49.4%	2.2	338,000	160,489	47.5%	0.3	386,000	179,603	46.5%	-0.6
WYOMING																			
Total	8,966,000	3,491,873	38.9%	10,209,000	3,905,401	38.3%	-0.7	11,069,000	4,220,865	38.1%	-0.8	12,794,000	4,682,168	36.6%	-2.3	14,164,000	5,333,964	37.7%	-1.3

Democratic Turnout for Election Years 1872–1888

State	1872 Voting-age population	Turnout	%	1876 Voting-age population	Turnout	%	Difference from 1872*	1880 Voting-age population	Turnout	%	Difference from 1872	1884 Voting-age population	Turnout	%	Difference from 1872	1888 Voting-age population	Turnout	%	Difference from 1872
ALABAMA	215,000	81,561	37.9%	238,000	120,027	50.4%	12.5	261,000	91,421	35.0%	-2.9	286,000	93,404	32.7%	-5.3	312,000	117,673	37.7%	-0.2
ALASKA																			
ARIZONA																			
ARKANSAS	119,000	39,933	33.6%	152,000	57,965	38.1%	4.6	183,000	61,169	33.4%	-0.1	213,000	73,491	34.5%	0.9	243,000	89,576	36.9%	3.3
CALIFORNIA	164,000	46,743	28.5%	195,000	74,228	38.1%	9.6	227,000	79,184	34.9%	6.4	270,000	90,954	33.7%	5.2	313,000	116,069	37.1%	8.6
COLORADO				60,000	12,584	21.0%		88,000	24,476	27.8%	6.8	112,000	28,720	25.6%	4.7	138,000	37,725	27.3%	6.4
CONNECTICUT	132,000	41,498	31.4%	140,000	61,797	44.1%	12.7	147,000	63,788	43.4%	12.0	163,000	66,658	40.9%	9.5	179,000	74,340	41.5%	10.1
DELAWARE				33,000	13,169	39.9%		37,000	14,966	40.4%	0.5	40,000	17,054	42.6%	2.7	43,000	16,396	38.1%	-1.8
DISTRICT OF COLUMBIA																			
FLORIDA				52,000	24,733	47.6%		60,000	28,076	46.8%	-0.8	73,000	31,867	43.7%	-3.9	86,000	39,836	46.3%	-1.2

United States House of Representatives General Elections *(continued)*

Democratic Turnout for Election Years 1872–1888 *(continued)*

State	1872 Voting-age population	1872 Turnout	1872 %	1876 Voting-age population	1876 Turnout	1876 %	1876 Difference from 1872	1880 Voting-age population	1880 Turnout	1880 %	1880 Difference from 1872	1884 Voting-age population	1884 Turnout	1884 %	1884 Difference from 1872	1888 Voting-age population	1888 Turnout	1888 %	1888 Difference from 1872
GEORGIA	255,000	84,431	33.1%	288,000	133,989	46.5%	13.4	322,000	122,754	38.1%	5.0	352,000	97,984	27.8%	-5.3	383,000	96,046	25.1%	-8.0
HAWAII																			
IDAHO																			
ILLINOIS	577,000	194,217	33.7%	632,000	266,341	42.1%	8.5	692,000	279,242	40.4%	6.7	789,000	318,224	40.3%	6.7	886,000	347,562	39.2%	5.6
INDIANA	403,000	188,502	46.8%	446,000	212,619	47.7%	0.9	487,000	224,750	46.1%	-0.6	525,000	248,521	47.3%	0.6	563,000	257,987	45.8%	-1.0
IOWA	284,000	79,716	28.1%	333,000	118,414	35.6%	7.5	379,000	102,618	27.1%	-1.0	417,000	178,740	42.9%	14.8	457,000	184,304	40.3%	12.3
KANSAS	135,000	34,390	25.5%	196,000	15,649	8.0%	-17.5	256,000	63,460	24.8%	-0.7	300,000	96,624	32.2%	6.7	344,000	103,629	30.1%	4.7
KENTUCKY	303,000	105,719	34.9%	337,000	158,441	47.0%	12.1	371,000	147,918	39.9%	5.0	401,000	155,075	38.7%	3.8	430,000	182,037	42.3%	7.4
LOUISIANA	169,000	59,130	35.0%	188,000	84,388	44.9%	9.9	205,000	66,044	32.2%	-2.8	220,000	70,949	32.2%	-2.7	233,000	86,435	37.1%	2.1
MAINE	157,000	54,150	34.5%	163,000	60,514	37.1%	2.6	170,000	72,799	42.8%	8.3	174,000	59,706	34.3%	-0.2	180,000	60,970	33.9%	-0.6
MARYLAND	180,000	67,723	37.6%	198,000	89,993	45.5%	7.8	215,000	91,131	42.4%	4.8	229,000	96,749	42.2%	4.6	243,000	106,095	43.7%	6.0
MASSACHUSETTS	330,000	61,222	18.6%	360,000	109,980	30.6%	12.0	393,000	111,833	28.5%	9.9	446,000	115,587	25.9%	7.4	499,000	150,917	30.2%	11.7
MICHIGAN	304,000	86,355	28.4%	352,000	146,802	41.7%	13.3	414,000	131,122	31.7%	3.3	466,000	191,614	41.1%	12.7	517,000	215,090	41.6%	13.2
MINNESOTA	98,000	34,386	35.1%	134,000	51,772	38.6%	3.5	186,000	56,279	30.3%	-4.8	242,000	77,310	31.9%	-3.1	299,000	108,010	36.1%	1.0
MISSISSIPPI	185,000	40,838	22.1%	212,000	113,655	53.6%	31.5	237,000	76,125	32.1%	10.0	250,000	81,932	32.8%	10.7	264,000	88,632	33.6%	11.5
MISSOURI	411,000	156,680	38.1%	462,000	204,082	44.2%	6.1	514,000	214,905	41.8%	3.7	577,000	234,673	40.7%	2.5	641,000	261,196	40.7%	2.6
MONTANA																			
NEBRASKA	55,000	10,412	18.9%	87,000	17,206	19.8%	0.8	121,000	23,634	19.5%	0.6	186,000	59,990	32.3%	13.3	250,000	81,838	32.7%	13.8
NEVADA	20,000	7,847	39.2%	23,000	9,330	40.6%	1.3	24,000	9,815	40.9%	1.7	21,000	6,002	28.6%	-10.7	18,000	5,682	31.6%	-7.7
NEW HAMPSHIRE	85,000	33,131	39.0%	90,000	37,866	42.1%	3.1	94,000	40,943	43.6%	4.6	97,000	38,085	39.3%	0.3	101,000	43,935	43.5%	4.5
NEW JERSEY	208,000	76,308	36.7%	232,000	127,068	54.8%	18.1	257,000	122,169	47.5%	10.9	298,000	127,614	42.8%	6.1	340,000	149,239	43.9%	7.2
NEW MEXICO																			
NEW YORK	1,031,000	400,697	38.9%	1,112,000	507,909	45.7%	6.8	1,199,000	530,758	44.3%	5.4	1,325,000	576,394	43.5%	4.6	1,451,000	576,435	39.7%	0.9
NORTH CAROLINA	233,000	95,726	41.1%	264,000	121,515	46.0%	4.9	295,000	120,479	40.8%	-0.2	314,000	140,894	44.9%	3.8	334,000	148,344	44.4%	3.3
NORTH DAKOTA																			
OHIO	636,000	263,479	41.4%	706,000	309,098	43.8%	2.4	777,000	340,562	43.8%	2.4	850,000	374,934	44.1%	2.7	922,000	395,649	42.9%	1.5
OKLAHOMA																			
OREGON	30,000	12,317	41.1%	41,000	14,239	34.7%	-6.3	51,000	18,181	35.6%	-5.4	70,000	23,652	33.8%	-7.3	87,000	25,413	29.2%	-11.8
PENNSYLVANIA	820,000	311,036	37.9%	891,000	369,226	41.4%	3.5	970,000	389,822	40.2%	2.3	1,098,000	401,042	36.5%	-1.4	1,226,000	446,464	36.4%	-1.5
RHODE ISLAND	47,000	5,643	12.0%	52,000	10,371	19.9%	7.9	58,000	10,616	18.3%	6.3	65,000	11,971	18.4%	6.4	72,000	17,033	23.7%	11.7
SOUTH CAROLINA				184,000	91,559	49.8%		206,000	116,884	56.7%	7.0	218,000	67,804	31.1%	-18.7	230,000	65,915	28.7%	-21.1
SOUTH DAKOTA																			
TENNESSEE	275,000	65,188	23.7%	302,000	133,727	44.3%	20.6	329,000	126,776	38.5%	14.8	358,000	134,551	37.6%	13.9	386,000	159,506	41.3%	17.6

United States House of Representatives General Elections (continued)

United States House of Representatives General Elections (continued)

Democratic Turnout for Election Years 1872–1888 (continued)

State	1872 Voting-age population	1872 Turnout	1872 %	1876 Voting-age population	1876 Turnout	1876 %	1876 Difference from 1872	1880 Voting-age population	1880 Turnout	1880 %	1880 Difference from 1872	1884 Voting-age population	1884 Turnout	1884 %	1884 Difference from 1872	1888 Voting-age population	1888 Turnout	1888 %	1888 Difference from 1872
TEXAS	215,000	69,078	32.1%	289,000	102,532	35.5%	3.3	362,000	176,172	48.7%	16.5	420,000	251,128	59.8%	27.7	478,000	239,711	50.1%	18.0
UTAH																			
VERMONT	77,000	6,797	8.8%	80,000	18,163	22.7%	13.9	83,000	19,660	23.7%	14.9	86,000	15,073	17.5%	8.7	90,000	19,351	21.5%	12.7
VIRGINIA				308,000	139,642	45.3%		332,000	96,532	29.1%	-16.3	350,000	145,106	41.5%	-3.9	368,000	152,087	41.3%	-4.0
WASHINGTON																			
WEST VIRGINIA	104,000	25,013	24.1%	121,000	56,350	46.6%	22.5	138,000	57,114	41.4%	17.3	155,000	67,481	43.5%	19.5	172,000	75,484	43.9%	19.8
WISCONSIN	223,000	88,055	39.5%	256,000	125,157	48.9%	9.4	291,000	116,062	39.9%	0.4	338,000	148,866	44.0%	4.6	386,000	156,566	40.6%	1.1
WYOMING																			
Total	8,480,000	2,927,921	34.5%	10,209,000	4,322,100	42.3%	7.8	11,431,000	4,440,239	38.8%	4.3	12,794,000	5,016,423	39.2%	4.7	14,164,000	5,499,257	38.8%	4.3

Other Turnout for Election Years 1872–1888

State	1872 Voting-age population	1872 Turnout	1872 %	1876 Voting-age population	1876 Turnout	1876 %	1876 Difference from 1872*	1880 Voting-age population	1880 Turnout	1880 %	1880 Difference from 1872	1884 Voting-age population	1884 Turnout	1884 %	1884 Difference from 1872	1888 Voting-age population	1888 Turnout	1888 %	1888 Difference from 1872
ALABAMA								261,000	15,909	6.1%		286,000	955	0.3%	-5.8	312,000	1,004	0.3%	-5.8
ALASKA																			
ARIZONA																			
ARKANSAS				152,000	1,085	0.7%		183,000	3,920	2.1%	1.4					243,000	49,789	20.5%	19.8
CALIFORNIA								227,000	4,622	2.0%		270,000	2,902	1.1%	-1.0	313,000	6,368	2.0%	0.0
COLORADO								88,000	1,691	1.9%		112,000	2,489	2.2%	0.3	138,000	3,664	2.7%	0.7
CONNECTICUT	132,000	1,432	1.1%	140,000	643	0.5%	-0.6	147,000	1,044	0.7%	-0.4	163,000	3,593	2.2%	1.1	179,000	4,146	2.3%	1.2
DELAWARE				33,000	236	0.7%		37,000	132	0.4%	-0.4					43,000	387	0.9%	0.2
DISTRICT OF COLUMBIA																			
FLORIDA	43,000	15,881	36.9%					60,000	127	0.2%	-36.7								
GEORGIA				288,000	408	0.1%						352,000	86	0.0%	-0.1	383,000	10,320	2.7%	2.6
HAWAII																			
IDAHO																			
ILLINOIS	577,000	609	0.1%	632,000	9,282	1.5%	1.4	692,000	23,149	3.3%	3.2	789,000	11,746	1.5%	1.4	886,000	25,953	2.9%	2.8
INDIANA				446,000	12,737	2.9%		487,000	15,168	3.1%	0.3	525,000	5,379	1.0%	-1.8	563,000	11,246	2.0%	-0.9
IOWA	284,000	91	0.0%	333,000	5,549	1.7%	1.6	379,000	36,013	9.5%	9.5	417,000	132	0.0%	0.0	457,000	6,401	1.4%	1.4
KANSAS				196,000	29,535	15.1%		256,000	16,714	6.5%	-8.5	300,000	7,766	2.6%	-12.5	344,000	41,968	12.2%	-2.9
KENTUCKY	303,000	6,031	2.0%	337,000	709	0.2%	-1.8	371,000	11,008	3.0%	1.0	401,000	661	0.2%	-1.8	430,000	4,029	0.9%	-1.1
LOUISIANA																233,000	244	0.1%	
MAINE				163,000	550	0.3%		170,000	364	0.2%	-0.1	174,000	3,474	2.0%	1.7	180,000	4,204	2.3%	2.0

United States House of Representatives General Elections (continued)

Other Turnout for Election Years 1872–1888 (continued)

State	1872 Voting-age population	Turnout	%	1876 Voting-age population	Turnout	%	Difference from 1872	1880 Voting-age population	Turnout	%	Difference from 1872	1884 Voting-age population	Turnout	%	Difference from 1872	1888 Voting-age population	Turnout	%	Difference from 1872
MARYLAND								215,000	826	0.4%		229,000	1,176	0.5%	0.1	243,000	4,214	1.7%	1.3
MASSACHUSETTS								393,000	4,563	1.2%		446,000	28,883	6.5%	5.3	499,000	11,270	2.3%	1.1
MICHIGAN	304,000	688	0.2%	352,000	3,976	1.1%	0.9	414,000	37,196	9.0%	8.8	466,000	18,507	4.0%	3.7	517,000	21,858	4.2%	4.0
MINNESOTA				134,000	2,879	2.1%		186,000	2,841	1.5%	-0.6	242,000	3,219	1.3%	-0.8	299,000	14,310	4.8%	2.6
MISSISSIPPI	185,000	2,050	1.5%					237,000	7,655	3.2%	1.7					264,000	107	0.0%	-1.5
MISSOURI	411,000	118	0.0%	462,000	2,553	0.6%	0.5	514,000	26,696	5.2%	5.2	577,000	3,635	0.6%	0.6	641,000	10,008	3.1%	3.1
MONTANA																			
NEBRASKA				87,000	3,579	4.1%		121,000	8,133	6.7%	2.6	186,000	2,772	1.5%	-2.6	250,000	14,041	5.6%	1.5
NEVADA																			
NEW HAMPSHIRE	85,000	1,124	1.3%	90,000	253	0.3%	-1.0	94,000	707	0.8%	-0.6	97,000	1,812	1.9%	0.5	101,000	1,417	1.4%	0.1
NEW JERSEY				232,000	520	0.2%		257,000	3,017	1.2%	0.9	298,000	7,720	2.6%	2.4	340,000	8,076	2.4%	2.2
NEW MEXICO																			
NEW YORK				1,112,000	3,852	0.3%		1,199,000	15,466	1.3%	0.9	1,325,000	28,199	2.1%	1.8	1,451,000	38,353	2.6%	2.3
NORTH CAROLINA								295,000	8,891	3.0%						334,000	239	0.1%	-2.9
NORTH DAKOTA																			
OHIO	636,000	1,047	0.2%	706,000	5,869	0.8%	0.7	777,000	8,599	1.1%	0.9	850,000	11,353	1.3%	1.2	922,000	25,603	2.8%	2.6
OKLAHOMA																			
OREGON								51,000	300	0.6%						87,000	1,974	2.3%	1.7
PENNSYLVANIA	820,000	919	0.1%	891,000	4,353	0.5%	0.4	970,000	20,133	2.1%	2.0	1,098,000	20,155	1.8%	1.7	1,226,000	20,763	1.7%	1.6
RHODE ISLAND				52,000	54	0.1%		50,000	262	0.5%	0.3	65,000	2,313	3.6%	3.5	72,000	1,271	1.8%	1.7
SOUTH CAROLINA	161,000	769	0.5%					206,000	414	0.2%	-0.3	218,000	1,377	0.6%	0.2	230,000	228	0.1%	-0.4
SOUTH DAKOTA																			
TENNESSEE	275,000	37,900	13.8%					329,000	3,467	1.1%	-12.7	358,000	416	0.1%	-13.7	386,000	3,029	0.8%	-13.0
TEXAS								362,000	72,991	20.2%		420,000	12,732	3.0%	-17.1	478,000	36,904	7.7%	-12.4
UTAH																			
VERMONT	77,000	2,943	3.8%					83,000	1,614	1.9%	-1.9	86,000	388	0.5%	-3.4	90,000	782	0.9%	-3.0
VIRGINIA	282,000	112,152	39.8%	308,000	30	0.0%	-39.8	332,000	48,092	14.5%	-25.3					368,000	267	0.1%	-39.7
WASHINGTON																			
WEST VIRGINIA	104,000	348	0.3%					138,000	5,003	3.6%	3.3					172,000	1,906	1.1%	0.8
WISCONSIN				256,000	1,429	0.6%		291,000	5,324	1.8%	1.3	338,000	9,278	2.7%	2.2	386,000	17,305	4.5%	3.9
WYOMING																			
Total	4,679,000	184,911	4.0%	7,402,000	90,081	1.2%	-2.7	10,880,000	412,051	3.8%	-0.2	11,088,000	193,118	1.7%	-2.2	14,060,000	413,448	2.9%	-1.0

Midterm Turnout Election Based on Highest Statewide Turnout, Election Years 1870–1886

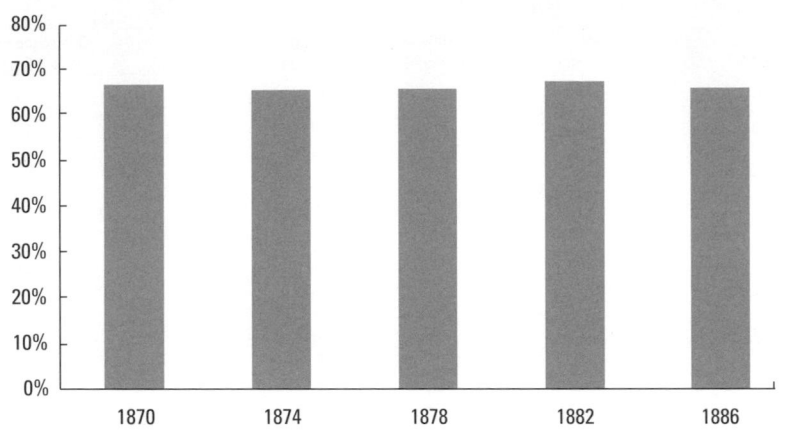

YEAR	VOTING-AGE POPULATION	TOTAL	%
1870	8,256,000	5,523,739	66.9%
1874	9,574,000	6,283,510	65.6%
1878	10,794,000	7,116,410	65.9%
1882	12,116,000	8,185,432	67.6%
1886	13,473,000	8,919,126	66.2%

Partisan Turnout Midterm Election Based on Aggregate House of Representatives Turnout, Election Years 1870–1886

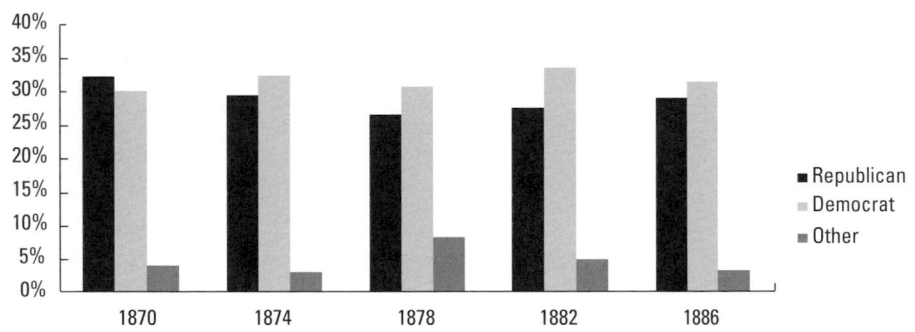

- Republican
- Democrat
- Other

YEAR	VOTING-AGE POPULATION	REPUBLICAN TURNOUT	%	DEMOCRAT TURNOUT	%	OTHER TURNOUT	%
1870	8,256,000	2,661,573	32.2%	2,481,531	30.1%	329,923	4.0%
1874	9,574,000	2,817,263	29.4%	3,099,918	32.4%	289,839	3.0%
1878	10,794,000	2,862,571	26.5%	3,313,147	30.7%	887,109	8.2%
1882	12,116,000	3,336,406	27.5%	4,062,716	33.5%	596,152	4.9%
1886	13,473,000	3,906,416	29.0%	4,233,021	31.4%	438,610	3.3%

STATE GUBERNATORIAL GENERAL ELECTIONS

Election Years 1870–1886

State	1870 Voting-age population	Turnout	%	1874 Voting-age population	Turnout	%	Difference from 1870*	1878 Voting-age population	Turnout	%	Difference from 1870	1882 Voting-age population	Turnout	%	Difference from 1870	1886 Voting-age population	Turnout	%	Difference from 1870
ALABAMA	205,000	154,005	75.1%	226,000	201,046	89.0%	13.8	249,000	88,255	35.4%	-39.7	273,000	149,388	54.7%	-20.4	299,000	182,667	61.1%	-14.0
ALASKA																			
ARIZONA																			
ARKANSAS				136,000	76,503	56.3%		167,000	88,726	53.1%	-3.1	198,000	147,183	74.3%	18.1	228,000	163,882	71.9%	15.6
CALIFORNIA												249,000	164,673	66.1%		292,000	195,653	67.0%	0.9
COLORADO								73,000	28,626	39.2%		100,000	61,441	61.4%	22.2	125,000	58,868	47.1%	7.9
CONNECTICUT	129,000	87,415	67.8%	135,000	91,701	67.9%	0.2	143,000	104,741	73.2%	5.5	156,000	115,638	74.1%	6.4	170,000	123,243	72.5%	4.7
DELAWARE	28,000	20,594	73.6%	32,000	23,747	74.2%	0.7	35,000	13,565	38.8%	-34.8	39,000	31,178	79.9%	6.4	41,000	21,918	53.5%	-20.1
DISTRICT OF COLUMBIA																			
FLORIDA																			
GEORGIA												337,000	152,542	45.3%		368,000	101,974	27.7%	-17.6
HAWAII																			
IDAHO																			
ILLINOIS																			
INDIANA																			
IOWA																			
KANSAS	105,000	61,243	58.3%	166,000	86,293	52.0%	-6.3	227,000	138,296	60.9%	2.6	278,000	179,384	64.5%	6.2	321,000	273,417	85.2%	26.8
KENTUCKY																			
LOUISIANA																			
MAINE	154,000	99,790	64.8%	161,000	95,300	59.2%	-5.6	167,000	126,169	75.6%	10.8	173,000	138,475	80.0%	15.2	177,000	128,171	72.4%	7.6
MARYLAND																			
MASSACHUSETTS	316,000	150,237	47.5%	345,000	185,990	53.9%	6.4	375,000	256,332	68.4%	20.8	420,000	256,277	61.0%	13.5	473,000	243,769	51.5%	4.0
MICHIGAN	279,000	186,507	66.8%	328,000	221,006	67.4%	0.5	377,000	281,565	74.7%	7.8	440,000	312,169	70.9%	4.1	491,000	380,885	77.6%	10.7
MINNESOTA																271,000	220,558	81.4%	
MISSISSIPPI																			
MISSOURI	386,000	167,709	43.4%	436,000	261,670	60.0%	16.6												
MONTANA																			
NEBRASKA	40,000	19,774	49.4%	71,000	36,019	50.7%	1.3	102,000	52,417	51.4%	2.0	154,000	89,075	57.8%	8.4	218,000	138,239	63.4%	14.0
NEVADA	19,000	13,347	70.2%	21,000	18,093	86.2%	15.9	24,000	18,829	78.5%	8.2	23,000	14,305	62.2%	-8.1	19,000	12,332	64.9%	-5.3
NEW HAMPSHIRE	84,000	68,442	81.5%	88,000	71,891	81.7%	0.2	92,000	77,788	84.6%	3.1	95,000	76,287	80.3%	-1.2	99,000	77,391	78.2%	-3.3
NEW JERSEY																			
NEW MEXICO																			
NEW YORK	990,000	769,280	77.7%	1,071,000	795,059	74.2%	-3.5					1,262,000	915,539	72.5%	-5.2				

State Gubernatorial General Elections (continued)

State Gubernatorial General Elections (continued)

Election Years 1870–1886 (continued)

State	1870 Voting-age population	Turnout	%	1874 Voting-age population	Turnout	%	Difference from 1870	1878 Voting-age population	Turnout	%	Difference from 1870	1882 Voting-age population	Turnout	%	Difference from 1870	1886 Voting-age population	Turnout	%	Difference from 1870
NORTH CAROLINA																			
NORTH DAKOTA																			
OHIO																			
OKLAHOMA																			
OREGON	26,000	22,822	87.8%	35,000	25,408	72.6%	-15.2	46,000	33,767	73.4%	-14.4	60,000	41,513	69.2%	-18.6	78,000	54,832	70.3%	-17.5
PENNSYLVANIA								928,000	702,038	75.7%		1,034,000	743,803	71.9%	-3.7	1,161,000	819,212	70.6%	-5.1
RHODE ISLAND	45,000	16,880	37.5%	50,000	14,101	28.2%	-9.3	55,000	19,709	35.8%	-1.7	61,000	15,523	25.4%	-12.1	69,000	26,875	38.9%	1.4
SOUTH CAROLINA	149,000	136,620	91.7%	173,000	149,240	86.3%	-5.4	196,000	119,763	61.1%	-30.6	212,000	84,477	39.8%	-51.8	224,000	33,114	14.8%	-76.9
SOUTH DAKOTA																			
TENNESSEE	262,000	120,479	46.0%	289,000	161,130	55.8%	9.8	316,000	147,397	46.6%	0.7	344,000	228,279	66.4%	20.4	373,000	235,988	63.3%	17.3
TEXAS								326,000	237,436	72.8%		391,000	253,644	64.9%	-8.0	449,000	313,300	69.8%	-3.1
UTAH																			
VERMONT	75,000	45,429	60.6%	78,000	46,861	60.1%	-0.5	81,000	57,956	71.6%	11.0	84,000	51,848	61.7%	1.2	89,000	56,602	63.6%	3.0
VIRGINIA																			
WASHINGTON																			
WEST VIRGINIA	95,000	55,983	58.9%																
WISCONSIN																361,000	286,368	79.3%	
WYOMING																			
Total	3,387,000	2,196,556	64.9%	3,841,000	2,561,058	66.7%	1.8	3,979,000	2,593,375	65.2%	0.3	6,383,000	4,222,641	66.2%	1.3	6,396,000	4,149,258	64.9%	0.0

*Percentage point difference between turnout in current year and initial year listed in chart. If data do not appear for a state in the initial year listed, the difference is calculated from the first year in which data do appear for that state.

STATE GUBERNATORIAL GENERAL ELECTIONS

Republican Turnout for Election Years 1870–1886

State	1870			1874				1878				1882				1886			
	Voting-age population	Turnout	%	Voting-age population	Turnout	%	Difference from 1870*	Voting-age population	Turnout	%	Difference from 1870	Voting-age population	Turnout	%	Difference from 1870	Voting-age population	Turnout	%	Difference from 1870
ALABAMA	205,000	76,282	37.2%	226,000	93,928	41.6%	4.4									299,000	36,792	12.3%	-24.9
ALASKA																			
ARIZONA																			
ARKANSAS												198,000	49,372	24.9%		228,000	54,063	23.7%	-1.2
CALIFORNIA												249,000	67,175	27.0%		292,000	84,316	28.9%	1.9
COLORADO								73,000	14,308	19.6%		100,000	28,820	28.8%	9.2	125,000	26,816	21.5%	1.9
CONNECTICUT	129,000	43,285	33.6%	135,000	39,761	29.5%	-4.1	143,000	40,067	34.2%	0.6	156,000	54,853	35.2%	1.6	170,000	56,920	33.5%	-0.1
DELAWARE	28,000	9,130	32.6%	32,000	11,259	35.2%	2.6					39,000	14,620	37.5%	4.9				
DISTRICT OF COLUMBIA																			
FLORIDA																			
GEORGIA																			
HAWAII																			
IDAHO																			
ILLINOIS																			
INDIANA																			
IOWA																			
KANSAS	105,000	40,666	38.7%	166,000	48,594	29.3%	-9.5	227,000	74,020	32.6%	-6.1	278,000	75,158	27.0%	-11.7	321,000	149,615	46.6%	7.9
KENTUCKY																			
LOUISIANA																			
MAINE	154,000	54,019	35.1%	161,000	52,958	32.9%	-2.2	167,000	56,554	33.9%	-1.2	173,000	72,481	41.9%	6.8	177,000	68,991	39.0%	3.9
MARYLAND																			
MASSACHUSETTS	316,000	79,549	25.2%	345,000	89,344	25.9%	0.7	375,000	134,725	35.9%	10.8	420,000	119,997	28.6%	3.4	473,000	122,346	25.9%	0.7
MICHIGAN	279,000	100,176	35.9%	328,000	111,519	34.0%	-1.9	377,000	126,280	33.5%	-2.4	440,000	149,697	34.0%	-1.9	491,000	181,474	37.0%	1.1
MINNESOTA																271,000	107,064	39.5%	
MISSISSIPPI																			
MISSOURI	386,000	63,336	16.4%	436,000	112,104	25.7%	9.3												
MONTANA																			
NEBRASKA	40,000	11,126	27.8%	71,000	21,568	30.4%	2.6	102,000	29,469	28.9%	1.1	154,000	43,495	28.2%	0.4	218,000	75,956	34.8%	7.0
NEVADA	19,000	6,147	32.4%	21,000	7,754	36.9%	4.6	24,000	9,678	40.3%	8.0	23,000	6,535	28.4%	-3.9	19,000	6,463	34.0%	1.7
NEW HAMPSHIRE	84,000	34,847	41.5%	88,000	34,143	38.8%	-2.7	92,000	39,372	42.8%	1.3	95,000	38,402	40.4%	-1.1	99,000	37,796	38.2%	-3.3
NEW JERSEY																			
NEW MEXICO																			
NEW YORK	990,000	366,424	37.0%	1,071,000	366,074	34.2%	-2.8					1,262,000	342,464	27.1%	-9.9				

State Gubernatorial General Elections (continued)

State Gubernatorial General Elections (continued)

Republican Turnout for Election Years 1870–1886 (continued)

State	1870			1874				1878				1882				1886			
	Voting-age population	Turnout	%	Voting-age population	Turnout	%	Difference from 1870	Voting-age population	Turnout	%	Difference from 1870	Voting-age population	Turnout	%	Difference from 1870	Voting-age population	Turnout	%	Difference from 1870
NORTH CAROLINA																			
NORTH DAKOTA																			
OHIO																			
OKLAHOMA																			
OREGON	26,000	11,096	42.7%	35,000	9,163	26.2%	-16.5	46,000	16,132	35.1%	-7.6	60,000	21,481	35.8%	-6.9	78,000	24,199	31.0%	-11.7
PENNSYLVANIA								928,000	319,567	34.4%		1,034,000	315,589	30.5%	-3.9	1,161,000	412,285	35.5%	1.1
RHODE ISLAND	45,000	10,337	23.0%	50,000	12,335	24.7%	1.7	55,000	11,454	20.8%	-2.1	61,000	10,056	16.5%	-6.5	69,000	14,340	20.8%	-2.2
SOUTH CAROLINA	149,000	85,071	57.1%	173,000	80,403	46.5%	-10.6					212,000	17,319	8.2%	-48.9				
SOUTH DAKOTA																			
TENNESSEE	262,000	41,500	15.8%	289,000	55,847	19.3%	3.5	316,000	42,284	13.4%	-2.5	344,000	93,168	27.1%	11.2	373,000	109,837	29.4%	13.6
TEXAS								326,000	23,402	7.2%						449,000	65,236	14.5%	7.4
UTAH																			
VERMONT	75,000	33,367	44.5%	78,000	33,582	43.1%	-1.4	81,000	37,312	46.1%	1.6	84,000	35,839	42.7%	-1.8	89,000	37,709	42.4%	-2.1
VIRGINIA																			
WASHINGTON																			
WEST VIRGINIA	95,000	26,924	28.3%																
WISCONSIN																361,000	133,247	36.9%	
WYOMING																			
Total	3,387,000	1,093,282	32.3%	3,705,000	1,180,336	31.9%	-0.4	3,332,000	983,424	29.5%	-2.8	5,382,000	1,556,521	28.9%	-3.4	5,763,000	1,805,465	31.3%	-1.0

Democratic Turnout for Election Years 1870–1886

State	1870			1874				1878				1882				1886			
	Voting-age population	Turnout	%	Voting-age population	Turnout	%	Difference from 1870*	Voting-age population	Turnout	%	Difference from 1870	Voting-age population	Turnout	%	Difference from 1870	Voting-age population	Turnout	%	Difference from 1870
ALABAMA	205,000	77,723	37.9%	226,000	107,118	47.4%	9.5	249,000	88,255	35.4%	-2.5	273,000	102,617	37.6%	-0.3	299,000	145,095	48.5%	10.6
ALASKA																			
ARIZONA																			
ARKANSAS				136,000	76,453	56.2%		167,000	88,726	53.1%	-3.1	198,000	87,669	44.3%	-11.9	228,000	90,650	39.8%	-16.5
CALIFORNIA												249,000	90,694	36.4%		292,000	84,965	29.1%	-7.3
COLORADO								73,000	11,535	15.8%		100,000	31,375	31.4%	15.6	125,000	29,234	23.4%	7.6
CONNECTICUT	129,000	44,128	34.2%	135,000	46,755	34.6%	0.4	143,000	46,385	32.4%	-1.8	156,000	59,014	37.8%	3.6	170,000	58,818	34.6%	0.4
DELAWARE	28,000	11,464	40.9%	32,000	12,488	39.0%	-1.9	35,000	10,730	30.7%	-10.3	39,000	16,558	42.5%	1.5	41,000	13,942	34.0%	-6.9
DISTRICT OF COLUMBIA																			
FLORIDA																			

State Gubernatorial General Elections *(continued)*

Democratic Turnout for Election Years 1870–1886 *(continued)*

State	1870 Voting-age population	Turnout	%	1874 Voting-age population	Turnout	%	Difference from 1870	1878 Voting-age population	Turnout	%	Difference from 1870	1882 Voting-age population	Turnout	%	Difference from 1870	1886 Voting-age population	Turnout	%	Difference from 1870
GEORGIA												337,000	107,649	31.9%		368,000	101,159	27.5%	-4.5
HAWAII																			
IDAHO																			
ILLINOIS																			
INDIANA																			
IOWA																			
KANSAS	105,000	20,469	19.5%	166,000	35,301	21.3%	1.8	227,000	37,208	16.4%	-3.1	278,000	83,237	29.9%	10.4	321,000	115,697	36.0%	16.5
KENTUCKY																			
LOUISIANA																			
MAINE	154,000	45,733	29.7%	161,000	41,898	26.0%	-3.7	167,000	28,208	16.9%	-12.8					177,000	55,289	31.2%	1.5
MARYLAND																			
MASSACHUSETTS	316,000	48,536	15.4%	345,000	96,376	27.9%	12.6	375,000	109,435	29.2%	13.8	420,000	133,946	31.9%	16.5	473,000	112,883	23.9%	8.5
MICHIGAN	279,000	83,391	29.9%	328,000	105,550	32.2%	2.3	377,000	78,503	20.8%	9.1								
MINNESOTA																271,000	104,464	38.5%	
MISSISSIPPI																			
MISSOURI				436,000	149,566	34.3%													
MONTANA																			
NEBRASKA	40,000	8,648	21.6%	71,000	8,946	12.6%	-9.0	102,000	13,473	13.2%	-8.4	154,000	28,562	18.5%	-3.1	218,000	52,656	24.2%	2.5
NEVADA	19,000	7,200	37.9%	21,000	10,339	49.2%	11.3	24,000	9,151	38.1%	0.2	23,000	7,770	33.8%	-4.1	19,000	5,869	30.9%	-7.0
NEW HAMPSHIRE	84,000	25,058	29.8%	88,000	35,608	40.5%	10.6	92,000	37,860	41.2%	11.3	95,000	36,916	38.9%	9.0	99,000	37,338	37.7%	7.9
NEW JERSEY																			
NEW MEXICO																			
NEW YORK	990,000	399,490	40.4%	1,071,000	416,391	38.9%	-1.5					1,262,000	535,318	42.4%	2.1				
NORTH CAROLINA																			
NORTH DAKOTA																			
OHIO																			
OKLAHOMA																			
OREGON	26,000	11,726	45.1%	35,000	9,713	27.8%	-17.3	46,000	16,201	35.2%	-9.9	60,000	20,029	33.4%	-11.7	78,000	27,901	35.8%	-9.3
PENNSYLVANIA								928,000	297,060	32.0%		1,034,000	355,791	34.4%	2.4	1,161,000	369,634	31.8%	-0.2
RHODE ISLAND	45,000	6,295	14.0%	50,000	1,589	3.2%	-10.8	55,000	7,639	13.9%	-0.1	61,000	5,311	8.7%	-5.3	69,000	9,944	14.4%	0.4
SOUTH CAROLINA								196,000	119,550	61.0%		212,000	67,158	31.7%	-29.3	224,000	33,114	14.8%	-46.2
SOUTH DAKOTA																			
TENNESSEE	262,000	78,979	30.1%	289,000	105,061	36.4%	6.2	316,000	89,958	28.5%	-1.7	344,000	120,637	35.1%	4.9	373,000	126,151	33.8%	3.7

State Gubernatorial General Elections (continued)

State Gubernatorial General Elections (continued)

Democratic Turnout for Election Years 1870–1886 (continued)

State	1870 Voting-age population	Turnout	%	1874 Voting-age population	Turnout	%	Difference from 1870	1878 Voting-age population	Turnout	%	Difference from 1870	1882 Voting-age population	Turnout	%	Difference from 1870	1886 Voting-age population	Turnout	%	Difference from 1870
TEXAS								326,000	158,933	48.8%		391,000	150,809	38.6%	-10.2	449,000	228,776	51.0%	2.2
UTAH																			
VERMONT	75,000	12,058	16.1%	78,000	13,258	17.0%	0.9	81,000	17,247	21.3%	5.2	84,000	14,466	17.2%	1.1	89,000	17,187	19.3%	3.2
VIRGINIA																			
WASHINGTON																			
WEST VIRGINIA	95,000	29,059	30.6%																
WISCONSIN																361,000	114,529	31.7%	
WYOMING																			
Total	2,852,000	909,957	31.9%	3,668,000	1,272,410	34.7%	2.8	3,979,000	1,266,057	31.8%	-0.1	5,770,000	2,055,526	35.6%	3.7	5,905,000	1,935,295	32.8%	0.9

Other Turnout for Election Years 1870–1886

State	1870 Voting-age population	Turnout	%	1874 Voting-age population	Turnout	%	Difference from 1870*	1878 Voting-age population	Turnout	%	Difference from 1870	1882 Voting-age population	Turnout	%	Difference from 1870	1886 Voting-age population	Turnout	%	Difference from 1870
ALABAMA												273,000	46,771	17.1%		299,000	780	0.3%	-16.9
ARKANSAS				136,000	50	0.0%						198,000	10,142	5.1%	5.1	228,000	19,169	8.4%	8.4
CALIFORNIA												249,000	6,804	2.7%		292,000	26,372	9.0%	6.3
COLORADO								73,000	2,783	3.8%		100,000	1,246	1.2%	-2.6	125,000	2,818	2.3%	-1.6
CONNECTICUT	129,000	2	0.0%	135,000	5,185	3.8%	3.8	143,000	9,489	6.6%	6.6	156,000	1,771	1.1%	1.1	170,000	7,505	4.4%	4.4
DELAWARE								35,000	2,835	8.1%						41,000	7,976	19.5%	11.4
GEORGIA												337,000	44,893	13.3%		368,000	815	0.2%	-13.1
KANSAS	105,000	108	0.1%	166,000	2,398	1.4%	1.3	227,000	27,068	11.9%	11.8	278,000	20,989	7.6%	7.4	321,000	8,105	2.5%	2.4
MAINE	154,000	38	0.0%	161,000	444	0.3%	0.3	167,000	41,407	24.8%	24.8	173,000	65,994	38.1%	38.1	177,000	3,891	2.2%	2.2
MASSACHUSETTS	316,000	22,152	7.0%	345,000	270	0.1%	-6.9	375,000	12,172	3.2%	-3.8	420,000	2,334	0.6%	-6.5	473,000	8,540	1.8%	-5.2
MICHIGAN	279,000	2,940	1.1%	328,000	3,937	1.2%	0.1	377,000	76,782	20.4%	19.3	440,000	162,472	36.9%	35.9	491,000	199,411	40.6%	39.6
MINNESOTA																271,000	9,030	3.3%	
MISSOURI	386,000	104,373	27.0%																
NEBRASKA				71,000	5,505	7.8%		102,000	9,475	9.3%	1.5	154,000	17,018	11.1%	3.3	218,000	9,627	4.4%	-3.3
NEW HAMPSHIRE	84,000	8,537	10.2%	88,000	2,140	2.4%	-7.7	92,000	556	0.6%	-9.6	95,000	969	1.0%	-9.1	99,000	2,257	2.3%	-7.9
NEW YORK	990,000	3,366	0.3%	1,071,000	12,594	1.2%	0.8					1,262,000	37,757	3.0%	2.7				
OREGON				35,000	6,532	18.7%		46,000	1,434	3.1%	-15.5	60,000	3	0.0%	-18.7	78,000	2,732	3.5%	-15.2
PENNSYLVANIA								928,000	85,411	9.2%		1,034,000	72,423	7.0%	-2.2	1,161,000	37,293	3.2%	-6.0

State Gubernatorial General Elections *(continued)*

Other Turnout for Election Years 1870–1886 *(continued)*

State	1870			1874				1878				1882				1886			
	Voting-age population	Turnout	%	Voting-age population	Turnout	%	Difference from 1870	Voting-age population	Turnout	%	Difference from 1870	Voting-age population	Turnout	%	Difference from 1870	Voting-age population	Turnout	%	Difference from 1870
RHODE ISLAND	45,000	248	0.6%	50,000	177	0.4%	-0.2	55,000	616	1.1%	0.6	61,000	156	0.3%	-0.3	69,000	2,591	3.8%	3.2
SOUTH CAROLINA	149,000	51,549	34.6%	173,000	68,837	39.8%	5.2	196,000	213	0.1%	-34.5								
TENNESSEE				289,000	222	0.1%		316,000	15,155	4.8%	4.7	344,000	14,474	4.2%	4.1				
TEXAS								326,000	55,101	16.9%		391,000	102,835	26.3%	9.4	449,000	19,288	4.3%	-12.6
VERMONT	75,000	4	0.0%	78,000	21	0.0%	0.0	81,000	3,397	4.2%	4.2	84,000	1,543	1.8%	1.8	89,000	1,706	1.9%	1.9
WISCONSIN																361,000	38,592	10.7%	
Total	2,712,000	193,317	7.1%	3,126,000	108,312	3.5%	-3.7	3,539,000	343,894	9.7%	2.6	6,109,000	610,594	10.0%	2.9	5,780,000	408,498	7.1%	-0.1

*Percentage point difference between turnout in current year and initial year listed in chart. If data do not appear for a state in the initial year listed, the difference is calculated from the first year in which data do appear for that state.

UNITED STATES HOUSE OF REPRESENTATIVES GENERAL ELECTIONS

Election Years 1870–1886

State	1870 Voting-age population	Turnout	%	1874 Voting-age population	Turnout	%	Difference from 1870*	1878 Voting-age population	Turnout	%	Difference from 1870	1882 Voting-age population	Turnout	%	Difference from 1870	1886 Voting-age population	Turnout	%	Difference from 1870
ALABAMA	205,000	152,862	74.6%	226,000	195,932	86.7%	12.1	249,000	88,243	35.4%	-39.1	273,000	120,644	44.2%	-30.4	299,000	86,663	29.0%	-45.6
ALASKA																			
ARIZONA																			
ARKANSAS	103,000	52,716	51.2%	136,000	63,983	47.0%	-4.1	167,000	77,824	46.6%	-4.6	198,000	65,041	32.8%	-18.3	228,000	55,488	24.3%	-26.8
CALIFORNIA	150,000	119,604	79.7%	179,000	122,273	68.3%	-11.4	210,000	156,774	74.7%	-5.1	249,000	164,821	66.2%	-13.5	292,000	193,966	66.4%	-13.3
COLORADO								73,000	28,626	39.2%		100,000	61,122	61.1%	21.9	125,000	58,258	46.6%	7.4
CONNECTICUT	129,000	93,990	72.9%	135,000	100,624	74.5%	1.7	143,000	104,361	73.0%	0.1	156,000	115,105	73.8%	0.9	170,000	123,005	72.4%	-0.5
DELAWARE	28,000	22,435	80.1%	32,000	23,626	73.8%	-6.3	35,000	13,542	38.7%	-41.4	39,000	31,203	80.0%	-0.1	41,000	22,229	54.2%	-25.9
DISTRICT OF COLUMBIA																			
FLORIDA	40,000	24,251	60.6%	48,000	35,063	73.0%	12.4	55,000	39,562	71.9%	11.3	66,000	47,704	72.3%	11.7	79,000	56,955	72.1%	11.5
GEORGIA	238,000	169,149	71.1%	272,000	126,571	46.5%	-24.5	305,000	125,621	41.2%	-29.9	337,000	106,373	31.6%	-39.5	368,000	27,546	7.5%	-63.6
HAWAII																			
IDAHO																			
ILLINOIS	548,000	316,958	57.8%	604,000	367,751	60.9%	3.0	660,000	450,017	68.2%	10.3	741,000	526,172	71.0%	13.2	838,000	564,390	67.3%	9.5
INDIANA	381,000	315,083	82.7%	424,000	361,711	85.3%	2.6	467,000	407,367	87.2%	4.5	507,000	439,281	86.6%	3.9	543,000	469,104	86.4%	3.7
IOWA	261,000	162,272	62.2%	308,000	184,631	59.9%	-2.2	356,000	260,337	73.1%	11.0	399,000	289,187	72.5%	10.3	437,000	345,052	79.0%	16.8
KANSAS	105,000	61,318	58.4%	166,000	87,181	52.5%	-5.9	227,000	137,802	60.7%	2.3	278,000	210,000	75.5%	17.1	321,000	273,162	85.1%	26.7
KENTUCKY	286,000	147,901	51.7%	320,000	125,429	39.2%	-12.5	354,000	160,156	45.2%	-6.5	386,000	190,709	49.4%	-2.3	415,000	208,702	50.3%	-1.4
LOUISIANA	161,000	104,218	64.7%	179,000	144,968	81.0%	16.3	196,000	117,555	60.0%	-4.8	212,000	77,882	36.7%	-28.0	226,000	84,697	37.5%	-27.3
MAINE	154,000	99,217	64.4%	161,000	94,499	58.7%	-5.7	167,000	124,478	74.5%	10.1	173,000	138,086	79.8%	15.4	177,000	128,294	72.5%	8.1
MARYLAND	172,000	134,322	78.1%	189,000	120,880	64.0%	-14.1	207,000	121,713	58.8%	-19.3	222,000	157,109	70.8%	-7.3	236,000	146,008	61.9%	-16.2
MASSACHUSETTS	316,000	137,981	43.7%	345,000	182,101	52.8%	9.1	375,000	252,399	67.3%	23.6	420,000	256,531	61.1%	17.4	473,000	243,212	51.4%	7.8
MICHIGAN	279,000	184,507	66.1%	328,000	216,777	66.1%	0.0	377,000	281,140	74.6%	8.4	440,000	312,434	71.0%	4.9	491,000	379,495	77.3%	11.2
MINNESOTA	79,000	66,134	83.7%	115,000	91,740	79.8%	-3.9	152,000	100,185	65.9%	-17.8	215,000	145,925	67.9%	-15.8	271,000	215,473	79.5%	-4.2
MISSISSIPPI				199,000	158,061	79.4%		224,000	52,550	23.5%	-56.0	243,000	79,202	32.6%	-46.8	256,000	46,734	18.3%	-61.2
MISSOURI	386,000	176,640	45.8%	436,000	253,473	58.1%	12.4	487,000	321,953	66.1%	20.3	546,000	367,533	67.3%	21.6	609,000	418,773	68.8%	23.0
MONTANA																			
NEBRASKA	40,000	20,342	50.9%	71,000	35,938	50.6%	-0.2	102,000	50,093	49.1%	-1.7	154,000	88,036	57.2%	6.3	218,000	136,456	62.6%	11.7
NEVADA	19,000	13,312	70.1%	21,000	17,867	85.1%	15.0	24,000	18,794	78.3%	8.2	23,000	14,182	61.7%	-8.4	19,000	12,370	65.1%	-5.0
NEW HAMPSHIRE	84,000	69,479	82.7%	88,000	78,806	89.6%	6.8	92,000	75,492	82.1%	-0.7	95,000	76,875	80.9%	-1.8	99,000	77,073	77.9%	-4.9
NEW JERSEY	197,000	157,429	79.9%	220,000	180,493	82.0%	2.1	244,000	195,837	80.3%	0.3	278,000	205,977	74.1%	-5.8	319,000	231,369	72.5%	-7.4
NEW MEXICO																			
NEW YORK	990,000	759,820	76.7%	1,071,000	780,543	72.9%	-3.9	1,153,000	827,507	71.8%	-5.0	1,262,000	923,467	73.2%	-3.6	1,387,000	930,238	67.1%	-9.7

United States House of Representatives General Elections *(continued)*

Election Years 1870–1886 *(continued)*

State	1870 Voting-age population	Turnout	%	1874 Voting-age population	Turnout	%	Difference from 1870	1878 Voting-age population	Turnout	%	Difference from 1870	1882 Voting-age population	Turnout	%	Difference from 1870	1886 Voting-age population	Turnout	%	Difference from 1870
NORTH CAROLINA	217,000	146,044	67.3%	249,000	190,944	76.7%	9.4	281,000	129,895	46.2%	-21.1	304,000	223,083	73.4%	6.1	324,000	212,419	65.6%	-1.7
NORTH DAKOTA																			
OHIO	600,000	426,975	71.2%	671,000	463,854	69.1%	-2.0	742,000	586,299	79.0%	7.9	813,000	629,335	77.4%	6.2	886,000	692,905	78.2%	7.0
OKLAHOMA																			
OREGON	26,000	22,833	87.8%	35,000	25,332	72.4%	-15.4	46,000	33,523	72.9%	-14.9	60,000	41,669	69.4%	-18.4	78,000	53,992	69.2%	-18.6
PENNSYLVANIA	783,000	535,071	68.3%	856,000	551,084	64.4%	-4.0	928,000	696,454	75.0%	6.7	1,034,000	742,140	71.0%	3.4	1,161,000	817,865	70.4%	2.1
RHODE ISLAND	45,000	12,183	27.1%	50,000	6,770	13.5%	-13.5	55,000	18,299	33.3%	6.2	61,000	10,186	16.7%	-10.4	69,000	17,887	25.9%	-1.2
SOUTH CAROLINA	149,000	120,413	80.8%	173,000	141,297	81.7%	0.9	196,000	161,950	82.6%	1.8	212,000	121,399	57.3%	-23.6	224,000	38,988	17.4%	-63.4
SOUTH DAKOTA																			
TENNESSEE	262,000	120,662	46.1%	289,000	154,578	53.5%	7.4	316,000	146,360	46.3%	0.3	344,000	219,592	63.8%	17.8	373,000	232,344	62.3%	16.2
TEXAS	177,000	106,703	60.3%	252,000	48,683	19.3%	-41.0	326,000	217,561	66.7%	6.5	391,000	243,369	62.2%	2.0	449,000	288,548	64.3%	4.0
UTAH																			
VERMONT	75,000	41,807	55.7%	78,000	41,967	53.8%	-1.9	81,000	55,038	67.9%	12.2	84,000	47,102	56.1%	0.3	89,000	48,362	54.3%	-1.4
VIRGINIA	269,000	175,953	65.4%	295,000	178,282	60.4%	-5.0	321,000	126,318	39.4%	-26.1	341,000	198,518	58.2%	-7.2	359,000	225,049	62.7%	-2.7
WASHINGTON																			
WEST VIRGINIA	95,000	55,229	58.1%	113,000	66,697	59.0%	0.9	129,000	94,884	73.6%	15.4	146,000	91,404	62.6%	4.5	163,000	131,445	80.6%	22.5
WISCONSIN	207,000	147,214	71.1%	240,000	186,611	77.8%	6.6	272,000	206,318	75.9%	4.7	314,000	216,868	69.1%	-2.1	361,000	283,531	78.5%	7.4
WYOMING																			
Total	8,256,000	5,473,027	66.3%	9,574,000	6,207,020	64.8%	-1.5	10,794,000	7,062,827	65.4%	-0.9	12,116,000	7,995,274	66.0%	-0.3	13,473,000	8,578,047	63.7%	-2.6

*Percentage point difference between turnout in current year and initial year listed in chart. If data do not appear for a state in the initial year listed, the difference is calculated from the first year in which data do appear for that state.

UNITED STATES HOUSE OF REPRESENTATIVES GENERAL ELECTIONS

Republican Turnout for Election Years 1870–1886

State	1870 Voting-age population	Turnout	%	1874 Voting-age population	Turnout	%	Difference from 1870*	1878 Voting-age population	Turnout	%	Difference from 1870	1882 Voting-age population	Turnout	%	Difference from 1870	1886 Voting-age population	Turnout	%	Difference from 1870
ALABAMA	205,000	74,405	36.3%	226,000	89,909	39.8%	3.5	249,000	13,185	5.3%	-31.0	273,000	35,512	13.0%	-23.3	299,000	24,436	8.2%	-28.1
ALASKA																			
ARIZONA																			
ARKANSAS	103,000	27,278	26.5%	136,000	22,808	16.8%	-9.7	167,000	21,162	12.7%	-13.8	198,000	21,422	10.8%	-15.7	228,000	8,549	3.7%	-22.7
CALIFORNIA	150,000	62,539	41.7%	179,000	39,789	22.2%	-19.5	210,000	74,651	35.5%	-6.1	249,000	73,647	29.6%	-12.1	292,000	93,921	32.2%	-9.5
COLORADO								73,000	14,294	19.6%		100,000	30,847	30.8%	11.3	125,000	27,732	22.2%	2.6
CONNECTICUT	129,000	47,272	36.6%	135,000	47,418	35.1%	-1.5	143,000	51,763	36.2%	-0.4	156,000	55,722	35.7%	-0.9	170,000	57,234	33.7%	-3.0
DELAWARE	28,000	10,001	35.7%	32,000	11,024	34.5%	-1.3					39,000	14,640	37.5%	1.8				
DISTRICT OF COLUMBIA																			
FLORIDA	40,000	12,439	31.1%	48,000	18,267	38.1%	7.0	55,000	18,393	33.4%	2.3	66,000	23,645	35.8%	4.7	79,000	23,152	29.3%	-1.8
GEORGIA	238,000	73,170	30.7%	272,000	33,149	12.2%	-18.6	305,000	8,674	2.8%	-27.9	337,000	24,930	7.4%	-23.3	368,000	17	0.0%	-30.7
HAWAII																			
IDAHO																			
ILLINOIS	548,000	168,801	30.8%	604,000	172,301	28.5%	-2.3	660,000	194,470	29.5%	-1.3	741,000	233,799	31.6%	0.7	838,000	276,579	33.0%	2.2
INDIANA	381,000	154,581	40.6%	424,000	168,902	39.8%	-0.7	467,000	180,729	38.7%	-1.9	507,000	207,174	40.9%	0.3	543,000	226,604	41.7%	1.2
IOWA	261,000	98,636	37.8%	308,000	104,815	34.0%	-3.8	356,000	131,790	37.0%	-0.8	399,000	141,795	35.5%	-2.3	437,000	189,993	43.5%	5.7
KANSAS	105,000	40,368	38.4%	166,000	48,908	29.5%	-9.0	227,000	74,714	32.9%	-5.5	278,000	99,866	35.9%	-2.5	321,000	154,194	48.0%	9.6
KENTUCKY	286,000	57,551	20.1%	320,000	28,128	8.8%	-11.3	354,000	50,720	14.3%	-5.8	386,000	79,080	20.5%	0.4	415,000	83,258	20.1%	-0.1
LOUISIANA	161,000	65,992	41.0%	179,000	68,505	38.3%	-2.7	196,000	21,997	11.2%	-29.8	212,000	29,012	13.7%	-27.3	226,000	21,450	9.5%	-31.5
MAINE	154,000	54,454	35.4%	161,000	53,240	33.1%	-2.3	167,000	56,296	33.7%	-1.6	173,000	73,076	42.2%	6.9	177,000	69,126	39.1%	3.7
MARYLAND	172,000	57,727	33.6%	189,000	53,377	28.2%	-5.3	207,000	40,856	19.7%	-13.8	222,000	74,520	33.6%	0.0	236,000	51,703	21.9%	-11.7
MASSACHUSETTS	316,000	78,721	24.9%	345,000	87,599	25.4%	0.5	375,000	136,116	36.3%	11.4	420,000	130,220	31.0%	6.1	473,000	119,100	25.2%	0.3
MICHIGAN	279,000	96,598	34.6%	328,000	111,965	34.1%	-0.5	377,000	126,461	33.5%	-1.1	440,000	157,519	35.8%	1.2	491,000	183,134	37.3%	2.7
MINNESOTA	79,000	36,739	46.5%	115,000	48,637	42.3%	-4.2	152,000	53,298	35.1%	-11.4	215,000	92,802	43.2%	-3.3	271,000	126,000	46.5%	0.0
MISSISSIPPI				199,000	74,095	37.2%		224,000	8,396	3.7%	-33.5	243,000	20,525	8.4%	-28.8	256,000	10,998	4.3%	-32.9
MISSOURI	386,000	60,022	15.5%	436,000	65,270	15.0%	-0.6	487,000	62,789	12.9%	-2.7	546,000	122,164	22.4%	6.8	609,000	172,628	28.3%	12.8
MONTANA																			
NEBRASKA	40,000	12,375	30.9%	71,000	22,532	31.7%	0.8	102,000	28,341	27.8%	-3.2	154,000	41,283	26.8%	-4.1	218,000	66,463	30.5%	-0.4
NEVADA	19,000	6,491	34.2%	21,000	9,240	44.0%	9.8	24,000	9,747	40.6%	6.4	23,000	6,462	28.1%	-6.1	19,000	6,700	35.3%	1.1
NEW HAMPSHIRE	84,000	33,758	40.2%	88,000	38,950	44.3%	4.1	92,000	38,195	41.5%	1.3	95,000	41,111	43.3%	3.1	99,000	37,980	38.4%	-1.8
NEW JERSEY	197,000	80,426	40.8%	220,000	85,455	38.8%	-2.0	244,000	90,514	37.1%	-3.7	278,000	97,869	35.2%	-5.6	319,000	102,766	32.2%	-8.6
NEW MEXICO																			
NEW YORK	990,000	363,291	36.7%	1,071,000	354,258	33.1%	-3.6	1,153,000	392,567	34.0%	-2.6	1,262,000	394,232	31.2%	-5.5	1,387,000	440,915	31.8%	-4.9

United States House of Representatives General Elections *(continued)*

Republican Turnout for Election Years 1870–1886 *(continued)*

State	1870 Voting-age population	Turnout	%	1874 Voting-age population	Turnout	%	Difference from 1870	1878 Voting-age population	Turnout	%	Difference from 1870	1882 Voting-age population	Turnout	%	Difference from 1870	1886 Voting-age population	Turnout	%	Difference from 1870
NORTH CAROLINA	217,000	69,776	32.2%	249,000	74,271	29.8%	-2.3	281,000	60,554	21.5%	-10.6					324,000	60,552	18.7%	-13.5
NORTH DAKOTA																			
OHIO	600,000	219,341	36.6%	671,000	218,550	32.6%	-4.0	742,000	277,875	37.4%	0.9	813,000	296,574	36.5%	-0.1	886,000	336,063	37.9%	1.4
OKLAHOMA																			
OREGON	26,000	11,245	43.3%	35,000	9,340	26.7%	-16.6	46,000	15,593	33.9%	-9.4	60,000	22,517	37.5%	-5.7	78,000	26,018	33.4%	-9.9
PENNSYLVANIA	783,000	276,380	35.3%	856,000	248,017	29.0%	-6.3	928,000	313,265	33.8%	-1.5	1,034,000	323,255	31.3%	-4.0	1,161,000	415,166	35.8%	0.5
RHODE ISLAND	45,000	9,589	21.3%	50,000	4,678	9.4%	-12.0	55,000	11,541	21.0%	-0.3	61,000	6,864	11.3%	-10.1	69,000	8,485	12.3%	-9.0
SOUTH CAROLINA	149,000	80,017	53.7%	173,000	109,508	63.3%	9.6	196,000	45,031	23.0%	-30.7	212,000	53,188	25.1%	-28.6	224,000	5,961	2.7%	-51.0
SOUTH DAKOTA																			
TENNESSEE	262,000	42,595	16.3%	289,000	51,561	17.8%	1.6	316,000	34,413	10.9%	-5.4	344,000	95,294	27.7%	11.4	373,000	99,164	26.6%	10.3
TEXAS	177,000	43,771	24.7%	252,000	10,095	4.0%	-20.7					391,000	42,190	10.8%	-13.9	449,000	34,407	7.7%	-17.1
UTAH																			
VERMONT	75,000	31,879	42.5%	78,000	33,764	43.3%	0.8	81,000	40,679	50.2%	7.7	84,000	33,475	39.9%	-2.7	89,000	34,317	38.6%	-3.9
VIRGINIA				295,000	77,371	26.2%		321,000	27,217	8.5%	-17.7	341,000	4,342	1.3%	-25.0	359,000	102,145	28.5%	2.2
WASHINGTON																			
WEST VIRGINIA	95,000	26,769	28.2%	113,000	28,440	25.2%	-3.0	129,000	36,248	28.1%	-0.1	146,000	41,227	28.2%	0.1	163,000	64,749	39.7%	11.5
WISCONSIN	207,000	76,576	37.0%	240,000	93,127	38.8%	1.8	272,000	100,037	36.8%	-0.2	314,000	94,606	30.1%	-6.9	361,000	144,757	40.1%	3.1
WYOMING																			
Total	7,987,000	2,661,573	33.3%	9,574,000	2,817,263	29.4%	-3.9	10,433,000	2,862,571	27.4%	-5.9	11,812,000	3,336,406	28.2%	-5.1	13,432,000	3,906,416	29.1%	-4.2

Democratic Turnout for Election Years 1870–1886

State	1870 Voting-age population	Turnout	%	1874 Voting-age population	Turnout	%	Difference from 1870*	1878 Voting-age population	Turnout	%	Difference from 1870	1882 Voting-age population	Turnout	%	Difference from 1870	1886 Voting-age population	Turnout	%	Difference from 1870
ALABAMA	205,000	78,457	38.3%	226,000	106,023	46.9%	8.6	249,000	54,775	22.0%	-16.3	273,000	82,539	30.2%	-8.0	299,000	62,211	20.8%	-17.5
ALASKA																			
ARIZONA																			
ARKANSAS	103,000	25,438	24.7%	136,000	41,175	30.3%	5.6	167,000	47,294	28.3%	3.6	198,000	43,619	22.0%	-2.7	228,000	36,673	16.1%	-8.6
CALIFORNIA	150,000	57,065	38.0%	179,000	58,688	32.8%	-5.3	210,000	47,915	22.8%	-15.2	249,000	87,259	35.0%	-3.0	292,000	91,710	31.4%	-6.6
COLORADO								73,000	12,003	16.4%		100,000	29,080	29.1%	12.6	125,000	26,929	21.5%	5.1
CONNECTICUT	129,000	46,718	36.2%	135,000	51,197	37.9%	1.7	143,000	48,905	34.2%	-2.0	156,000	58,004	37.2%	1.0	170,000	58,581	34.5%	-1.8
DELAWARE	28,000	12,434	44.4%	32,000	12,602	39.4%	-5.0	35,000	10,576	30.2%	-14.2	39,000	16,563	42.5%	-1.9	41,000	13,837	33.7%	-10.7
DISTRICT OF COLUMBIA																			
FLORIDA	40,000	11,812	29.5%	48,000	16,796	35.0%	5.5	55,000	21,169	38.5%	9.0	66,000	24,059	36.5%	6.9	79,000	33,383	42.3%	12.7

United States House of Representatives General Elections (continued)

United States House of Representatives General Elections (continued)

Democratic Turnout for Election Years 1870–1886 (continued)

State	1870 Voting-age population	1870 Turnout	1870 %	1874 Voting-age population	1874 Turnout	1874 %	1874 Difference from 1870	1878 Voting-age population	1878 Turnout	1878 %	1878 Difference from 1870	1882 Voting-age population	1882 Turnout	1882 %	1882 Difference from 1870	1886 Voting-age population	1886 Turnout	1886 %	1886 Difference from 1870
GEORGIA	238,000	95,979	**40.3%**	272,000	93,347	**34.3%**	-6.0	305,000	108,336	**35.5%**	-4.8	337,000	81,443	**24.2%**	-16.2	368,000	25,492	**6.9%**	-33.4
HAWAII																			
IDAHO																			
ILLINOIS	548,000	145,191	**26.5%**	604,000	182,060	**30.1%**	3.6	660,000	174,150	**26.4%**	-0.1	741,000	266,569	**36.0%**	9.5	838,000	242,185	**28.9%**	2.4
INDIANA	381,000	160,502	**42.1%**	424,000	183,201	**43.2%**	1.1	467,000	194,233	**41.6%**	-0.5	507,000	220,920	**43.6%**	1.4	543,000	231,826	**42.7%**	0.6
IOWA	261,000	63,636	**24.4%**					356,000	87,836	**24.7%**	0.3	399,000	115,463	**28.9%**	4.6	437,000	146,099	**33.4%**	9.1
KANSAS	105,000	20,950	**20.0%**	166,000	11,225	**6.8%**	-13.2	227,000	36,355	**16.0%**	-3.9	278,000	83,433	**30.0%**	10.1	321,000	110,009	**34.3%**	14.3
KENTUCKY	286,000	90,350	**31.6%**	320,000	82,649	**25.8%**	-5.8	354,000	100,895	**28.5%**	-3.1	386,000	110,801	**28.7%**	-2.9	415,000	119,720	**28.8%**	-2.7
LOUISIANA	161,000	38,226	**23.7%**	179,000	76,463	**42.7%**	19.0	196,000	82,327	**42.0%**	18.3	212,000	48,827	**23.0%**	-0.7	226,000	63,097	**27.9%**	4.2
MAINE	154,000	44,467	**28.9%**	161,000	41,103	**25.5%**	-3.3	167,000	33,658	**20.2%**	-8.7	173,000	63,366	**36.6%**	7.8	177,000	52,656	**29.7%**	0.9
MARYLAND	172,000	76,595	**44.5%**	189,000	67,503	**35.7%**	-8.8	207,000	71,965	**34.8%**	-9.8	222,000	82,301	**37.1%**	-7.5	236,000	88,606	**37.5%**	-7.0
MASSACHUSETTS	316,000	49,781	**15.8%**	345,000	72,976	**21.2%**	5.4	375,000	89,548	**23.9%**	8.1	420,000	119,776	**28.5%**	12.8	473,000	114,155	**24.1%**	8.4
MICHIGAN	279,000	85,733	**30.7%**	328,000	102,273	**31.2%**	0.5	377,000	77,642	**20.6%**	-10.1	440,000	148,242	**33.7%**	3.0	491,000	173,376	**35.3%**	4.6
MINNESOTA	79,000	29,395	**37.2%**	115,000	43,103	**37.5%**	0.3	152,000	45,241	**29.8%**	-7.4	215,000	46,653	**21.7%**	-15.5	271,000	81,573	**30.1%**	-7.1
MISSISSIPPI				199,000	83,966	**42.2%**		224,000	37,128	**16.6%**	-25.6	243,000	48,479	**20.0%**	-22.2	256,000	35,560	**13.9%**	-28.3
MISSOURI	386,000	63,626	**16.5%**	436,000	163,609	**37.5%**	21.0	487,000	176,763	**36.3%**	19.8	546,000	214,753	**39.3%**	22.8	609,000	234,414	**38.5%**	22.0
MONTANA																			
NEBRASKA	40,000	7,967	**19.9%**	71,000	8,360	**11.8%**	-8.1	102,000	21,752	**21.3%**	1.4	154,000	25,692	**16.7%**	-3.2	218,000	60,654	**27.8%**	7.9
NEVADA	19,000	6,821	**35.9%**	21,000	8,627	**41.1%**	5.2	24,000	9,047	**37.7%**	1.8	23,000	7,720	**33.6%**	-2.3	19,000	5,670	**29.8%**	-6.1
NEW HAMPSHIRE	84,000	35,098	**41.8%**	88,000	39,231	**44.6%**	2.8	92,000	31,442	**34.2%**	-7.6	95,000	35,091	**36.9%**	-4.8	99,000	36,919	**37.3%**	-4.5
NEW JERSEY	197,000	77,003	**39.1%**	220,000	95,038	**43.2%**	4.1	244,000	80,051	**32.8%**	-6.3	278,000	100,054	**36.0%**	-3.1	319,000	104,932	**32.9%**	-6.2
NEW MEXICO																			
NEW YORK	990,000	393,409	**39.7%**	1,071,000	419,906	**39.2%**	-0.5	1,153,000	362,573	**31.4%**	-8.3	1,262,000	503,954	**39.9%**	0.2	1,387,000	446,237	**32.2%**	-7.6
NORTH CAROLINA				249,000	102,317	**41.1%**		281,000	68,263	**24.3%**	-16.8	304,000	111,763	**36.8%**	-4.3	324,000	123,496	**38.1%**	-3.0
NORTH DAKOTA																			
OHIO	600,000	205,947	**34.3%**	671,000	238,899	**35.6%**	1.3	742,000	266,877	**36.0%**	1.6	813,000	316,975	**39.0%**	4.7	886,000	325,639	**36.8%**	2.4
OKLAHOMA																			
OREGON	26,000	11,588	**44.6%**	35,000	9,642	**27.5%**	-17.0	46,000	16,744	**36.4%**	-8.2	60,000	19,152	**31.9%**	-12.6	78,000	25,221	**32.3%**	-12.2
PENNSYLVANIA	783,000	256,334	**32.7%**	856,000	277,351	**32.4%**	-0.3	928,000	280,949	**30.3%**	-2.5	1,034,000	352,855	**34.1%**	1.4	1,161,000	367,551	**31.7%**	-1.1
RHODE ISLAND	45,000	2,327	**5.2%**	50,000	2,092	**4.2%**	-1.0	55,000	5,872	**10.7%**	5.5	61,000	3,322	**5.4%**	0.3	69,000	7,803	**11.3%**	6.1
SOUTH CAROLINA	149,000	39,064	**26.2%**	173,000	27,328	**15.8%**	-10.4	196,000	116,919	**59.7%**	33.4	212,000	61,360	**28.9%**	2.7	224,000	32,969	**14.7%**	-11.5
SOUTH DAKOTA																			
TENNESSEE	262,000	78,067	**29.8%**	289,000	102,574	**35.5%**	5.7	316,000	95,099	**30.1%**	0.3	344,000	120,332	**35.0%**	5.2	373,000	133,161	**35.7%**	5.9

United States House of Representatives General Elections *(continued)*

Democratic Turnout for Election Years 1870–1886 *(continued)*

State	1870 Voting-age population	Turnout	%	1874 Voting-age population	Turnout	%	Difference from 1870	1878 Voting-age population	Turnout	%	Difference from 1870	1882 Voting-age population	Turnout	%	Difference from 1870	1886 Voting-age population	Turnout	%	Difference from 1870
TEXAS	177,000	62,525	35.3%	252,000	38,368	15.2%	-20.1	326,000	166,958	51.2%	15.9	391,000	156,930	40.1%	4.8	449,000	213,836	47.6%	12.3
UTAH																			
VERMONT	75,000	9,928	13.2%	78,000	8,203	10.5%	-2.7	81,000	14,359	17.7%	4.5	84,000	12,372	14.7%	1.5	89,000	13,831	15.5%	2.3
VIRGINIA				295,000	100,716	34.1%		321,000	73,957	23.0%	-11.1	341,000	94,184	27.6%	-6.5	359,000	113,306	31.6%	-2.6
WASHINGTON																			
WEST VIRGINIA	95,000	28,460	30.0%	113,000	37,823	33.5%	3.5	129,000	50,318	39.0%	9.0	146,000	45,171	30.9%	1.0	183,000	85,194	40.0%	10.0
WISCONSIN	207,000	70,638	34.1%	240,000	93,484	39.0%	4.8	272,000	93,253	34.3%	0.2	314,000	103,640	33.0%	-1.1	361,000	114,510	31.7%	-2.4
WYOMING																			
Total	7,770,000	2,481,531	31.9%	9,266,000	3,099,918	33.5%	1.5	10,794,000	3,313,147	30.7%	-1.2	12,116,000	4,062,716	33.5%	1.6	13,473,000	4,233,021	31.4%	-0.5

Other Turnout for Election Years 1870–1886

State	1870 Voting-age population	Turnout	%	1874 Voting-age population	Turnout	%	Difference from 1870*	1878 Voting-age population	Turnout	%	Difference from 1870	1882 Voting-age population	Turnout	%	Difference from 1870	1886 Voting-age population	Turnout	%	Difference from 1870
ALABAMA								249,000	20,283	8.1%		273,000	2,593	0.9%	-7.2	299,000	16	0.0%	-8.1
ALASKA																			
ARIZONA																			
ARKANSAS								167,000	9,368	5.6%						228,000	10,266	4.5%	-1.1
CALIFORNIA				179,000	23,796	13.3%		210,000	34,208	16.3%	3.0	249,000	3,915	1.6%	-11.7	292,000	8,335	2.9%	-10.4
COLORADO								73,000	2,329	3.2%		100,000	1,195	1.2%	-2.0	125,000	3,597	2.9%	-0.3
CONNECTICUT				135,000	2,009	1.5%		143,000	3,693	2.6%	1.1	156,000	1,379	0.9%	-0.6	170,000	7,190	4.2%	2.7
DELAWARE								35,000	2,966	8.5%						41,000	8,392	20.5%	12.0
DISTRICT OF COLUMBIA																			
FLORIDA																79,000	420	0.5%	
GEORGIA				272,000	75	0.0%		305,000	8,611	2.8%	2.8					368,000	2,037	0.6%	0.5
HAWAII																			
IDAHO																			
ILLINOIS	548,000	2,966	0.5%	604,000	13,390	2.2%	1.7	660,000	81,397	12.3%	11.8	741,000	25,804	3.5%	2.9	838,000	45,626	5.4%	4.9
INDIANA				424,000	9,608	2.3%		467,000	32,405	6.9%	4.7	507,000	11,187	2.2%	-0.1	543,000	10,674	2.0%	-0.3
IOWA				308,000	79,816	25.9%		356,000	40,711	11.4%	-14.5	399,000	31,929	8.0%	-17.9	437,000	8,960	2.1%	-23.9
KANSAS				166,000	27,048	16.3%		227,000	26,733	11.8%	-4.5	278,000	26,701	9.6%	-6.7	321,000	8,959	2.8%	-13.5
KENTUCKY				320,000	14,652	4.6%		354,000	8,541	2.4%	-2.2	386,000	828	0.2%	-4.4	415,000	5,724	1.4%	-3.2
LOUISIANA								196,000	13,231	6.8%		212,000	43	0.0%	-6.7	226,000	150	0.1%	-6.7
MAINE	154,000	296	0.2%	161,000	156	0.1%	-0.1	167,000	34,524	20.7%	20.5	173,000	1,644	1.0%	0.8	177,000	6,512	3.7%	3.5

United States House of Representatives General Elections (continued)

United States House of Representatives General Elections (continued)

Other Turnout for Election Years 1870–1886 (continued)

State	1870 Voting-age population	Turnout	%	1874 Voting-age population	Turnout	%	Difference from 1870	1878 Voting-age population	Turnout	%	Difference from 1870	1882 Voting-age population	Turnout	%	Difference from 1870	1886 Voting-age population	Turnout	%	Difference from 1870
MARYLAND								207,000	8,892	4.3%		222,000	288	0.1%	-4.2	236,000	5,699	2.4%	-1.9
MASSACHUSETTS	316,000	9,479	3.0%	345,000	21,526	6.2%	3.2	375,000	26,735	7.1%	4.1	420,000	6,535	1.6%	-1.4	473,000	9,957	2.1%	-0.9
MICHIGAN	279,000	2,176	0.8%	328,000	2,539	0.8%	0.0	377,000	77,037	20.4%	19.7	440,000	6,673	1.5%	0.7	491,000	22,985	4.7%	3.9
MINNESOTA								152,000	1,646	1.1%		215,000	6,470	3.0%	1.9	271,000	7,900	2.9%	1.8
MISSISSIPPI								224,000	7,026	3.1%		243,000	10,198	4.2%	1.1	256,000	176	0.1%	-3.1
MISSOURI	386,000	52,992	13.7%	436,000	24,594	5.6%	-8.1	487,000	82,401	16.9%	3.2	546,000	30,616	5.6%	-8.1	609,000	11,731	1.9%	-11.8
MONTANA																			
NEBRASKA				71,000	5,046	7.1%						154,000	21,061	13.7%	6.6	218,000	9,339	4.3%	-2.8
NEVADA																			
NEW HAMPSHIRE	84,000	623	0.7%	88,000	625	0.7%	0.0	92,000	5,855	6.4%	5.6	95,000	673	0.7%	0.0	99,000	2,174	2.2%	1.5
NEW JERSEY								244,000	25,272	10.4%		278,000	8,054	2.9%	-7.5	319,000	23,671	7.4%	-2.9
NEW MEXICO																			
NEW YORK	990,000	3,120	0.3%	1,071,000	6,379	0.6%	0.3	1,153,000	72,367	6.3%	6.0	1,262,000	25,281	2.0%	1.7	1,387,000	43,086	3.1%	2.8
NORTH CAROLINA	217,000	76,268	35.1%	249,000	14,356	5.8%	-29.4	281,000	1,078	0.4%	-34.8	304,000	111,320	36.6%	1.5	324,000	28,371	8.8%	-26.4
NORTH DAKOTA																			
OHIO	600,000	1,687	0.3%	671,000	6,405	1.0%	0.7	742,000	41,547	5.6%	5.3	813,000	15,786	1.9%	1.7	886,000	31,203	3.5%	3.2
OKLAHOMA																			
OREGON				35,000	6,350	18.1%		46,000	1,186	2.6%	-15.6					78,000	2,753	3.5%	-14.6
PENNSYLVANIA	783,000	2,357	0.3%	856,000	25,716	3.0%	2.7	928,000	102,240	11.0%	10.7	1,034,000	66,038	6.4%	6.1	1,161,000	35,148	3.0%	2.7
RHODE ISLAND	45,000	267	0.6%					55,000	886	1.6%	1.0					69,000	1,599	2.3%	1.7
SOUTH CAROLINA	149,000	1,332	0.9%	173,000	4,461	2.6%	1.7					212,000	6,851	3.2%	2.3	224,000	58	0.0%	-0.9
SOUTH DAKOTA																			
TENNESSEE				289,000	443	0.2%		316,000	16,848	5.3%	5.2	344,000	3,966	1.2%	1.0	373,000	19	0.0%	-0.1
TEXAS	177,000	407	0.2%	252,000	220	0.1%	-0.1	326,000	50,603	15.5%	15.3	391,000	44,249	11.3%	11.1	449,000	40,305	9.0%	8.7
UTAH																			
VERMONT												84,000	1,255	1.5%		89,000	214	0.2%	-1.3
VIRGINIA**	269,000	175,953	65.4%	295,000	195	0.1%	-65.3	321,000	25,144	7.8%	-57.6	341,000	99,992	29.3%	-36.1	359,000	9,598	2.7%	-62.7
WASHINGTON																			
WEST VIRGINIA				113,000	434	0.4%		129,000	8,318	6.4%	6.1	146,000	5,006	3.4%	3.0	163,000	1,502	0.9%	0.5
WISCONSIN								272,000	13,028	4.8%		314,000	18,622	5.9%	1.1	361,000	24,264	6.7%	1.9
WYOMING																			
Total	4,997,000	329,923	6.6%	7,841,000	289,839	3.7%	-2.9	10,336,000	887,109	8.6%	2.0	11,332,000	596,152	5.3%	-1.3	13,454,000	438,610	3.3%	-3.3

*Percentage point difference between turnout in current year and initial year listed in chart. If data do not appear for a state in the initial year listed, the difference is calculated from the first year in which data do appear for that state.

**Virginia officially re-entered the Union in 1870. Its election that year featured the "Conservatives" and the "Radicals."

TOTAL HIGHEST STATEWIDE GENERAL ELECTIONS

Election Years 1870–1886

State	1870 Voting-age population	Turnout	%	1874 Voting-age population	Turnout	%	Difference from 1870*	1878 Voting-age population	Turnout	%	Difference from 1870	1882 Voting-age population	Turnout	%	Difference from 1870	1886 Voting-age population	Turnout	%	Difference from 1870
ALABAMA	205,000	154,005	75.1%	226,000	201,046	89.0%	13.8	249,000	88,255	35.4%	-39.7	273,000	149,388	54.7%	-20.4	299,000	182,667	61.1%	-14.0
ALASKA																			
ARIZONA																			
ARKANSAS	103,000	52,716	51.2%	136,000	76,503	56.3%	5.1	167,000	88,726	53.1%	1.9	198,000	147,183	74.3%	23.2	228,000	163,882	71.9%	20.7
CALIFORNIA	150,000	119,604	79.7%	179,000	122,273	68.3%	-11.4	210,000	156,774	74.7%	-5.1	249,000	164,821	66.2%	-13.5	292,000	195,653	67.0%	-12.7
COLORADO								73,000	28,626	39.2%		100,000	61,441	61.4%	22.2	125,000	58,868	47.1%	7.9
CONNECTICUT	129,000	93,990	72.9%	135,000	100,624	74.5%	1.7	143,000	104,741	73.2%	0.4	156,000	115,638	74.1%	1.3	170,000	123,243	72.5%	-0.4
DELAWARE	28,000	22,435	80.1%	32,000	23,747	74.2%	-5.9	35,000	13,565	38.8%	-41.4	39,000	31,203	80.0%	-0.1	41,000	22,229	54.2%	-25.9
DISTRICT OF COLUMBIA																			
FLORIDA	40,000	24,251	60.6%	48,000	35,063	73.0%	12.4	55,000	39,562	71.9%	11.3	66,000	47,704	72.3%	11.7	79,000	56,955	72.1%	11.5
GEORGIA	238,000	169,149	71.1%	272,000	126,571	46.5%	-24.5	305,000	125,621	41.2%	-29.9	337,000	152,542	45.3%	-25.8	368,000	101,974	27.7%	-43.4
HAWAII																			
IDAHO																			
ILLINOIS	548,000	316,958	57.8%	604,000	367,751	60.9%	3.0	660,000	450,017	68.2%	10.3	741,000	526,172	71.0%	13.2	838,000	564,390	67.3%	9.5
INDIANA	381,000	315,083	82.7%	424,000	361,711	85.3%	2.6	467,000	407,367	87.2%	4.5	507,000	439,281	86.6%	3.9	543,000	469,104	86.4%	3.7
IOWA	261,000	162,272	62.2%	308,000	184,631	59.9%	-2.2	356,000	260,337	73.1%	11.0	399,000	289,187	72.5%	10.3	437,000	345,052	79.0%	16.8
KANSAS	105,000	61,318	58.4%	166,000	87,181	52.5%	-5.9	227,000	138,296	60.9%	2.5	278,000	210,000	75.5%	17.1	321,000	273,417	85.2%	26.8
KENTUCKY	286,000	147,901	51.7%	320,000	125,429	39.2%	-12.5	354,000	160,156	45.2%	-6.5	386,000	190,709	49.4%	-2.3	415,000	208,702	50.3%	-1.4
LOUISIANA	161,000	104,218	64.7%	179,000	144,968	81.0%	16.3	196,000	117,555	60.0%	-4.8	212,000	77,882	36.7%	-28.0	226,000	84,697	37.5%	-27.3
MAINE	154,000	99,790	64.8%	161,000	95,300	59.2%	-5.6	167,000	126,169	75.6%	10.8	173,000	138,475	80.0%	15.2	177,000	128,294	72.5%	7.7
MARYLAND	172,000	134,322	78.1%	189,000	120,880	64.0%	-14.1	207,000	121,713	58.8%	-19.3	222,000	157,109	70.8%	-7.3	236,000	146,008	61.9%	-16.2
MASSACHUSETTS	316,000	150,237	47.5%	345,000	185,990	53.9%	6.4	375,000	256,332	68.4%	20.8	420,000	256,531	61.1%	13.5	473,000	243,769	51.5%	4.0
MICHIGAN	279,000	186,507	66.8%	328,000	221,006	67.4%	0.5	377,000	281,565	74.7%	7.8	440,000	312,434	71.0%	4.2	491,000	380,885	77.6%	10.7
MINNESOTA	79,000	66,134	83.7%	115,000	91,740	79.8%	-3.9	152,000	100,185	65.9%	-17.8	215,000	145,925	67.9%	-15.8	271,000	220,558	81.4%	-2.3
MISSISSIPPI				199,000	158,061	79.4%		224,000	52,550	23.5%	-56.0	243,000	79,202	32.6%	-46.8	256,000	46,734	18.3%	-61.2
MISSOURI	386,000	176,640	45.8%	436,000	261,670	60.0%	14.3	487,000	321,953	66.1%	20.3	546,000	367,533	67.3%	21.6	609,000	418,773	68.8%	23.0
MONTANA																			
NEBRASKA	40,000	20,342	50.9%	71,000	36,019	50.7%	-0.1	102,000	52,417	51.4%	0.5	154,000	89,075	57.8%	7.0	218,000	138,239	63.4%	12.6
NEVADA	19,000	13,312	70.1%	21,000	18,093	86.2%	16.1	24,000	18,829	78.5%	8.4	23,000	14,305	62.2%	-7.9	19,000	12,370	65.1%	-5.0
NEW HAMPSHIRE	84,000	69,479	82.7%	88,000	78,806	89.6%	6.8	92,000	77,788	84.6%	1.8	95,000	76,875	80.9%	-1.8	99,000	77,073	77.9%	-4.9
NEW JERSEY	197,000	157,429	79.9%	220,000	180,493	82.0%	2.1	244,000	195,837	80.3%	0.3	278,000	205,977	74.1%	-5.8	319,000	231,369	72.5%	-7.4
NEW MEXICO																			
NEW YORK	990,000	769,280	77.7%	1,071,000	795,059	74.2%	-3.5	1,153,000	827,507	71.8%	-5.9	1,262,000	923,467	73.2%	-4.5	1,387,000	930,238	67.1%	-10.6

Total Highest Statewide General Elections (continued)

Total Highest Statewide General Elections (continued)

Election Years 1870–1886 (continued)

State	1870 Voting-age population	Turnout	%	1874 Voting-age population	Turnout	%	Difference from 1870	1878 Voting-age population	Turnout	%	Difference from 1870	1882 Voting-age population	Turnout	%	Difference from 1870	1886 Voting-age population	Turnout	%	Difference from 1870
NORTH CAROLINA	217,000	146,044	67.3%	249,000	190,944	76.7%	9.4	281,000	129,895	46.2%	-21.1	304,000	223,083	73.4%	6.1	324,000	212,419	65.6%	-1.7
NORTH DAKOTA																			
OHIO	600,000	426,975	71.2%	671,000	463,854	69.1%	-2.0	742,000	586,299	79.0%	7.9	813,000	629,335	77.4%	6.2	886,000	692,905	78.2%	7.0
OKLAHOMA																			
OREGON	26,000	22,833	87.8%	35,000	25,408	72.6%	-15.2	46,000	33,767	73.4%	-14.4	60,000	41,669	69.4%	-18.4	78,000	54,832	70.3%	-17.5
PENNSYLVANIA	783,000	535,071	68.3%	856,000	551,084	64.4%	-4.0	928,000	702,038	75.7%	7.3	1,034,000	743,803	71.9%	3.6	1,161,000	819,212	70.6%	2.2
RHODE ISLAND	45,000	16,880	37.5%	50,000	14,101	28.2%	-9.3	55,000	19,709	35.8%	-1.7	61,000	15,523	25.4%	-12.1	69,000	26,875	38.9%	1.4
SOUTH CAROLINA	149,000	136,620	91.7%	173,000	149,240	86.3%	-5.4	196,000	161,950	82.6%	-9.1	212,000	121,399	57.3%	-34.4	224,000	38,988	17.4%	-74.3
SOUTH DAKOTA																			
TENNESSEE	262,000	120,662	46.1%	289,000	161,130	55.8%	9.7	316,000	147,397	46.6%	0.6	344,000	228,279	66.4%	20.3	373,000	235,988	63.3%	17.2
TEXAS	177,000	106,703	60.3%	252,000	48,683	19.3%	-41.0	326,000	237,436	72.8%	12.5	391,000	253,644	64.9%	4.6	449,000	313,300	69.8%	9.5
UTAH																			
VERMONT	75,000	45,429	60.6%	78,000	46,861	60.1%	-0.5	81,000	57,956	71.6%	11.0	84,000	51,848	61.7%	1.2	89,000	56,602	63.6%	3.0
VIRGINIA	269,000	175,953	65.4%	295,000	178,282	60.4%	-5.0	321,000	126,318	39.4%	-26.1	341,000	198,518	58.2%	-7.2	359,000	225,049	62.7%	-2.7
WASHINGTON																			
WEST VIRGINIA	95,000	55,983	58.9%	113,000	66,697	59.0%	0.1	129,000	94,884	73.6%	14.6	146,000	91,404	62.6%	3.7	163,000	131,445	80.6%	21.7
WISCONSIN	207,000	147,214	71.1%	240,000	186,611	77.8%	6.6	272,000	206,318	75.9%	4.7	314,000	216,868	69.1%	-2.1	361,000	286,368	79.3%	8.2
WYOMING																			
Total	8,256,000	5,523,739	66.9%	9,574,000	6,283,510	65.6%	-1.3	10,794,000	7,116,410	65.9%	-1.0	12,116,000	8,185,432	67.6%	0.7	13,473,000	8,919,126	66.2%	-0.7

*Percentage point difference between turnout in current year and initial year listed in chart. If data do not appear for a state in the initial year listed, the difference is calculated from the first year in which data do appear for that state.

TOTAL HIGHEST STATEWIDE GENERAL ELECTIONS

Republican Turnout for Election Years 1870–1886

State	1870 Voting-age population	Turnout	%	1874 Voting-age population	Turnout	%	Difference from 1870*	1878 Voting-age population	Turnout	%	Difference from 1870	1882 Voting-age population	Turnout	%	Difference from 1870	1886 Voting-age population	Turnout	%	Difference from 1870
ALABAMA	205,000	76,282	37.2%	226,000	93,928	41.6%	4.4	249,000	13,185	5.3%	-31.9	273,000	35,512	13.0%	-24.2	299,000	36,792	12.3%	-24.9
ALASKA																			
ARIZONA																			
ARKANSAS	103,000	27,278	26.5%	136,000	22,808	16.8%	-9.7	167,000	21,162	12.7%	-13.8	198,000	49,372	24.9%	-1.5	228,000	54,063	23.7%	-2.8
CALIFORNIA	150,000	62,539	41.7%	179,000	39,789	22.2%	-19.5	210,000	74,651	35.5%	-6.1	249,000	73,647	29.6%	-12.1	292,000	93,921	32.2%	-9.5
COLORADO								73,000	14,308	19.6%		100,000	30,847	30.8%	11.2	125,000	27,732	22.2%	2.6
CONNECTICUT	129,000	47,272	36.6%	135,000	47,418	35.1%	-1.5	143,000	51,763	36.2%	-0.4	156,000	55,722	35.7%	-0.9	170,000	57,234	33.7%	-3.0
DELAWARE	28,000	10,001	35.7%	32,000	11,259	35.2%	-0.5					39,000	14,640	37.5%	1.8				
DISTRICT OF COLUMBIA																			
FLORIDA	40,000	12,439	31.1%	48,000	18,267	38.1%	7.0	55,000	18,393	33.4%	2.3	66,000	23,645	35.8%	4.7	79,000	23,152	29.3%	-1.8
GEORGIA	238,000	73,170	30.7%	272,000	33,149	12.2%	-18.6	305,000	8,674	2.8%	-27.9	337,000	24,930	7.4%	-23.3	368,000	17	0.0%	-30.7
HAWAII																			
IDAHO																			
ILLINOIS	548,000	168,801	30.8%	604,000	172,301	28.5%	-2.3	660,000	194,470	29.5%	-1.3	741,000	233,799	31.6%	0.7	838,000	276,579	33.0%	2.2
INDIANA	381,000	154,581	40.6%	424,000	168,902	39.8%	-0.7	467,000	180,729	38.7%	-1.9	507,000	207,174	40.9%	0.3	543,000	226,604	41.7%	1.2
IOWA	261,000	98,636	37.8%	308,000	104,815	34.0%	-3.8	356,000	131,790	37.0%	-0.8	399,000	141,795	35.5%	-2.3	437,000	189,993	43.5%	5.7
KANSAS	105,000	40,666	38.7%	166,000	48,908	29.5%	-9.3	227,000	74,714	32.9%	-5.8	278,000	99,866	35.9%	-2.8	321,000	154,194	48.0%	9.3
KENTUCKY	286,000	57,551	20.1%	320,000	28,128	8.8%	-11.3	354,000	50,720	14.3%	-5.8	386,000	79,080	20.5%	0.4	415,000	83,258	20.1%	-0.1
LOUISIANA	161,000	65,992	41.0%	179,000	68,505	38.3%	-2.7	196,000	21,997	11.2%	-29.8	212,000	29,012	13.7%	-27.3	226,000	21,450	9.5%	-31.5
MAINE	154,000	54,454	35.4%	161,000	53,240	33.1%	-2.3	167,000	56,554	33.9%	-1.5	173,000	73,076	42.2%	6.9	177,000	69,126	39.1%	3.7
MARYLAND	172,000	57,727	33.6%	189,000	53,377	28.2%	-5.3	207,000	40,856	19.7%	-13.8	222,000	74,520	33.6%	0.0	236,000	51,703	21.9%	-11.7
MASSACHUSETTS	316,000	79,549	25.2%	345,000	89,344	25.9%	0.7	375,000	136,116	36.3%	11.1	420,000	130,220	31.0%	5.8	473,000	122,346	25.9%	0.7
MICHIGAN	279,000	100,176	35.9%	328,000	111,965	34.1%	-1.8	377,000	126,461	33.5%	-2.4	440,000	157,519	35.8%	-0.1	491,000	183,134	37.3%	1.4
MINNESOTA	79,000	36,739	46.5%	115,000	48,637	42.3%	-4.2	152,000	53,298	35.1%	-11.4	215,000	92,802	43.2%	-3.3	271,000	126,000	46.5%	0.0
MISSISSIPPI				199,000	74,095	37.2%		224,000	8,396	3.7%	-33.5	243,000	20,525	8.4%	-28.8	256,000	10,998	4.3%	-32.9
MISSOURI	386,000	63,336	16.4%	436,000	112,104	25.7%	9.3	487,000	62,789	12.9%	-3.5	546,000	122,164	22.4%	6.0	609,000	172,628	28.3%	11.9
MONTANA																			
NEBRASKA	40,000	12,375	30.9%	71,000	22,532	31.7%	0.8	102,000	29,469	28.9%	-2.0	154,000	43,495	28.2%	-2.7	218,000	75,956	34.8%	3.9
NEVADA	19,000	6,491	34.2%	21,000	9,240	44.0%	9.8	24,000	9,747	40.6%	6.4	23,000	6,535	28.4%	-5.8	19,000	6,700	35.3%	1.1
NEW HAMPSHIRE	84,000	34,847	41.5%	88,000	38,950	44.3%	2.8	92,000	39,372	42.8%	1.3	95,000	41,111	43.3%	1.8	99,000	37,980	38.4%	-3.1
NEW JERSEY	197,000	80,426	40.8%	220,000	85,455	38.8%	-2.0	244,000	90,514	37.1%	-3.7	278,000	97,869	35.2%	-5.6	319,000	102,766	32.2%	-8.6
NEW MEXICO																			
NEW YORK	990,000	366,424	37.0%	1,071,000	366,074	34.2%	-2.8	1,153,000	392,567	34.0%	-3.0	1,262,000	394,232	31.2%	-5.8	1,387,000	440,915	31.8%	-5.2

Total Highest Statewide General Elections (continued)

Total Highest Statewide General Elections (continued)

Republican Turnout for Election Years 1870–1886 (continued)

State	1870 Voting-age population	Turnout	%	1874 Voting-age population	Turnout	%	Difference from 1870	1878 Voting-age population	Turnout	%	Difference from 1870	1882 Voting-age population	Turnout	%	Difference from 1870	1886 Voting-age population	Turnout	%	Difference from 1870
NORTH CAROLINA	217,000	69,776	32.2%	249,000	74,271	29.8%	-2.3	281,000	60,554	21.5%	-10.6					324,000	60,552	18.7%	-13.5
NORTH DAKOTA																			
OHIO	600,000	219,341	36.6%	671,000	218,550	32.6%	-4.0	742,000	277,875	37.4%	0.9	813,000	296,574	36.5%	-0.1	886,000	336,063	37.9%	1.4
OKLAHOMA																			
OREGON	26,000	11,245	43.3%	35,000	9,340	26.7%	-16.6	46,000	16,132	35.1%	-8.2	60,000	22,517	37.5%	-5.7	78,000	26,018	33.4%	-9.9
PENNSYLVANIA	783,000	276,380	35.3%	856,000	248,017	29.0%	-6.3	928,000	319,567	34.4%	-0.9	1,034,000	323,255	31.3%	-4.0	1,161,000	415,166	35.8%	0.5
RHODE ISLAND	45,000	10,337	23.0%	50,000	12,335	24.7%	1.7	55,000	11,541	21.0%	-2.0	61,000	10,056	16.5%	-6.5	69,000	14,340	20.8%	-2.2
SOUTH CAROLINA	149,000	85,071	57.1%	173,000	109,508	63.3%	6.2	196,000	45,031	23.0%	-34.1	212,000	53,188	25.1%	-32.0	224,000	5,961	2.7%	-54.4
SOUTH DAKOTA																			
TENNESSEE	262,000	42,595	16.3%	289,000	55,847	19.3%	3.1	316,000	23,402	7.4%	-8.9	344,000	42,190	12.3%	-4.0	373,000	65,236	17.5%	1.2
TEXAS	177,000	43,771	24.7%	252,000	10,095	4.0%	-20.7												
UTAH																			
VERMONT	75,000	33,367	44.5%	78,000	33,764	43.3%	-1.2	81,000	40,679	50.2%	5.7	84,000	35,839	42.7%	-1.8	89,000	37,709	42.4%	-2.1
VIRGINIA				295,000	77,371	26.2%		321,000	27,217	8.5%	-17.7	341,000	4,342	1.3%	-25.0	359,000	102,145	28.5%	2.2
WASHINGTON																			
WEST VIRGINIA	95,000	26,924	28.3%	113,000	28,440	25.2%	-3.2	129,000	36,248	28.1%	-0.2	146,000	41,227	28.2%	-0.1	163,000	64,749	39.7%	11.4
WISCONSIN	207,000	76,576	37.0%	240,000	93,127	38.8%	1.8	272,000	100,037	36.8%	-0.2	314,000	94,606	30.1%	-6.9	361,000	144,757	40.1%	3.1
WYOMING																			
Total	7,987,000	2,683,135	33.6%	9,574,000	2,893,855	30.2%	-3.4	10,433,000	2,860,978	27.4%	-6.2	11,421,000	3,276,903	28.7%	-4.9	12,983,000	3,917,937	30.2%	-3.4

Democratic Turnout for Election Years 1870–1886

State	1870 Voting-age population	Turnout	%	1874 Voting-age population	Turnout	%	Difference from 1870*	1878 Voting-age population	Turnout	%	Difference from 1870	1882 Voting-age population	Turnout	%	Difference from 1870	1886 Voting-age population	Turnout	%	Difference from 1870
ALABAMA	205,000	78,457	38.3%	226,000	107,118	47.4%	9.1	249,000	88,255	35.4%	-2.8	273,000	102,617	37.6%	-0.7	299,000	145,095	48.5%	10.3
ALASKA																			
ARIZONA																			
ARKANSAS	103,000	25,438	24.7%	136,000	76,453	56.2%	31.5	167,000	88,726	53.1%	28.4	198,000	87,669	44.3%	19.6	228,000	90,650	39.8%	15.1
CALIFORNIA	150,000	57,065	38.0%	179,000	58,688	32.8%	-5.3	210,000	47,915	22.8%	-15.2	249,000	90,694	36.4%	-1.6	292,000	91,710	31.4%	-6.6
COLORADO								73,000	12,003	16.4%		100,000	31,375	31.4%	14.9	125,000	29,234	23.4%	6.9
CONNECTICUT	129,000	46,718	36.2%	135,000	51,197	37.9%	1.7	143,000	48,905	34.2%	-2.0	156,000	59,014	37.8%	1.6	170,000	58,818	34.6%	-1.6
DELAWARE	28,000	12,434	44.4%	32,000	12,602	39.4%	-5.0	35,000	10,730	30.7%	-13.8	39,000	16,563	42.5%	-1.9	41,000	13,942	34.0%	-10.4
DISTRICT OF COLUMBIA																			
FLORIDA	40,000	11,812	29.5%	48,000	16,796	35.0%	5.5	55,000	21,169	38.5%	9.0	66,000	24,059	36.5%	6.9	79,000	33,383	42.3%	12.7

Total Highest Statewide General Elections (continued)

Democratic Turnout for Election Years 1870–1886 (continued)

State	1870			1874				1878				1882				1886			
	Voting-age population	Turnout	%	Voting-age population	Turnout	%	Difference from 1870	Voting-age population	Turnout	%	Difference from 1870	Voting-age population	Turnout	%	Difference from 1870	Voting-age population	Turnout	%	Difference from 1870
GEORGIA	238,000	95,979	40.3%	272,000	93,347	34.3%	-6.0	305,000	108,336	35.5%	-4.8	337,000	107,649	31.9%	-8.4	368,000	101,159	27.5%	-12.8
HAWAII																			
IDAHO																			
ILLINOIS	548,000	145,191	26.5%	604,000	182,060	30.1%	3.6	660,000	174,150	26.4%	-0.1	741,000	266,569	36.0%	9.5	838,000	242,185	28.9%	2.4
INDIANA	381,000	160,502	42.1%	424,000	183,201	43.2%	1.1	467,000	194,233	41.6%	-0.5	507,000	220,920	43.6%	1.4	543,000	231,826	42.7%	0.6
IOWA	261,000	63,636	24.4%					356,000	87,836	24.7%	0.3	399,000	115,463	28.9%	4.6	437,000	146,099	33.4%	9.1
KANSAS	105,000	20,950	20.0%	166,000	35,301	21.3%	1.3	227,000	37,208	16.4%	-3.6	278,000	83,433	30.0%	10.1	321,000	115,697	36.0%	16.1
KENTUCKY	286,000	90,350	31.6%	320,000	82,649	25.8%	-5.8	354,000	100,895	28.5%	-3.1	386,000	110,801	28.7%	-2.9	415,000	119,720	28.8%	-2.7
LOUISIANA	161,000	38,226	23.7%	179,000	76,463	42.7%	19.0	196,000	82,327	42.0%	18.3	212,000	48,827	23.0%	-0.7	226,000	63,097	27.9%	4.2
MAINE	154,000	45,733	29.7%	161,000	41,898	26.0%	-3.7	167,000	33,658	20.2%	-9.5	173,000	63,366	36.6%	6.9	177,000	55,289	31.2%	1.5
MARYLAND	172,000	76,595	44.5%	189,000	67,503	35.7%	-8.8	207,000	71,965	34.8%	-9.8	222,000	82,301	37.1%	-7.5	236,000	88,606	37.5%	-7.0
MASSACHUSETTS	316,000	49,781	15.8%	345,000	96,376	27.9%	12.2	375,000	109,435	29.2%	13.4	420,000	133,946	31.9%	16.1	473,000	114,155	24.1%	8.4
MICHIGAN	279,000	85,733	30.7%	328,000	105,660	32.2%	1.5	377,000	78,503	20.8%	-9.9	440,000	148,242	33.7%	3.0	491,000	173,376	35.3%	4.6
MINNESOTA	79,000	29,395	37.2%	115,000	43,103	37.5%	0.3	152,000	45,241	29.8%	-7.4	215,000	46,653	21.7%	-15.5	271,000	104,464	38.5%	1.3
MISSISSIPPI				199,000	83,966	42.2%		224,000	37,128	16.6%	-25.6	243,000	48,479	20.0%	-22.2	256,000	35,560	13.9%	-28.3
MISSOURI	386,000	63,626	16.5%	436,000	163,609	37.5%	21.0	487,000	176,763	36.3%	19.8	546,000	214,753	39.3%	22.8	609,000	234,414	38.5%	22.0
MONTANA																			
NEBRASKA	40,000	8,648	21.6%	71,000	8,946	12.6%	-9.0	102,000	21,752	21.3%	-0.3	154,000	28,562	18.5%	-3.1	218,000	60,654	27.8%	6.2
NEVADA	19,000	7,200	37.9%	21,000	10,339	49.2%	11.3	24,000	9,151	38.1%	0.2	23,000	7,770	33.8%	-4.1	19,000	5,869	30.9%	-7.0
NEW HAMPSHIRE	84,000	35,098	41.8%	88,000	39,231	44.6%	2.8	92,000	37,860	41.2%	-0.6	95,000	36,916	38.9%	-2.9	99,000	37,338	37.7%	-4.1
NEW JERSEY	197,000	77,003	39.1%	220,000	95,038	43.2%	4.1	244,000	80,051	32.8%	-6.3	278,000	100,054	36.0%	-3.1	319,000	104,932	32.9%	-6.2
NEW MEXICO																			
NEW YORK	990,000	399,490	40.4%	1,071,000	419,906	39.2%	-1.1	1,153,000	362,573	31.4%	-8.9	1,262,000	535,318	42.4%	2.1	1,387,000	446,237	32.2%	-8.2
NORTH CAROLINA				249,000	102,317	41.1%		281,000	68,263	24.3%	-16.8	304,000	111,763	36.8%	-4.3	324,000	123,496	38.1%	-3.0
NORTH DAKOTA																			
OHIO	600,000	205,947	34.3%	671,000	238,899	35.6%	1.3	742,000	266,877	36.0%	1.6	813,000	316,975	39.0%	4.7	886,000	325,639	36.8%	2.4
OKLAHOMA																			
OREGON	26,000	11,726	45.1%	35,000	9,713	27.8%	-17.3	46,000	16,744	36.4%	-8.7	60,000	20,029	33.4%	-11.7	78,000	27,901	35.8%	-9.3
PENNSYLVANIA	783,000	256,334	32.7%	856,000	277,351	32.4%	-0.3	928,000	297,060	32.0%	-0.7	1,034,000	355,791	34.4%	1.7	1,161,000	369,634	31.8%	-0.9
RHODE ISLAND	45,000	6,295	14.0%	50,000	2,092	4.2%	-9.8	55,000	7,639	13.9%	-0.1	61,000	5,311	8.7%	-5.3	69,000	9,944	14.4%	0.4
SOUTH CAROLINA	149,000	39,064	26.2%	173,000	27,328	15.8%	-10.4	196,000	119,550	61.0%	34.8	212,000	67,158	31.7%	5.5	224,000	33,114	14.8%	-11.4
SOUTH DAKOTA																			
TENNESSEE	262,000	78,979	30.1%	289,000	105,061	36.4%	6.2	316,000	95,099	30.1%	-0.1	344,000	156,930	45.6%	15.5	373,000	228,776	61.3%	31.2

Total Highest Statewide General Elections (continued)

Total Highest Statewide General Elections (continued)

Democratic Turnout for Election Years 1870–1886 (continued)

State	1870 Voting-age population	Turnout	%	1874 Voting-age population	Turnout	%	Difference from 1870	1878 Voting-age population	Turnout	%	Difference from 1870	1882 Voting-age population	Turnout	%	Difference from 1870	1886 Voting-age population	Turnout	%	Difference from 1870
TEXAS	177,000	62,525	35.3%	252,000	38,368	15.2%	-20.1	326,000	166,958	51.2%	15.9								
UTAH																			
VERMONT	75,000	12,058	16.1%	78,000	13,258	17.0%	0.9	81,000	17,247	21.3%	5.2	84,000	14,466	17.2%	1.1	89,000	17,187	19.3%	3.2
VIRGINIA				295,000	100,716	34.1%		321,000	73,957	23.0%	-11.1	341,000	94,184	27.6%	-6.5	359,000	113,306	31.6%	-2.6
WASHINGTON																			
WEST VIRGINIA	95,000	29,059	30.6%	113,000	37,823	33.5%	2.9	129,000	50,318	39.0%	8.4	146,000	45,171	30.9%	0.4	163,000	65,194	40.0%	9.4
WISCONSIN	207,000	70,638	34.1%	240,000	93,484	39.0%	4.8	272,000	93,253	34.3%	0.2	314,000	103,640	33.0%	-1.1	361,000	114,529	31.7%	-2.4
WYOMING																			
Total	7,770,000	2,497,685	32.1%	9,266,000	3,197,750	34.5%	2.4	10,794,000	3,439,733	31.9%	-0.3	11,725,000	4,103,431	35.0%	2.9	13,024,000	4,372,229	33.6%	1.4

Other Turnout for Election Years 1870–1886

State	1870 Voting-age population	Turnout	%	1874 Voting-age population	Turnout	%	Difference from 1870*	1878 Voting-age population	Turnout	%	Difference from 1870	1882 Voting-age population	Turnout	%	Difference from 1870	1886 Voting-age population	Turnout	%	Difference from 1870
ALABAMA								249,000	20,283	8.1%		273,000	46,771	17.1%	9.0	299,000	780	0.3%	-7.9
ALASKA																			
ARIZONA																			
ARKANSAS				136,000	50	0.0%		167,000	9,368	5.6%	5.6	198,000	10,142	5.1%	5.1	228,000	19,169	8.4%	8.4
CALIFORNIA				179,000	23,796	13.3%		210,000	34,208	16.3%	3.0	249,000	6,804	2.7%	-10.6	292,000	26,372	9.0%	-4.3
COLORADO								73,000	2,783	3.8%		100,000	1,246	1.2%	-2.6	125,000	3,597	2.9%	-0.9
CONNECTICUT	129,000	2	0.0%	135,000	5,185	3.8%	3.8	143,000	9,489	6.6%	6.6	156,000	1,771	1.1%	1.1	170,000	7,505	4.4%	4.4
DELAWARE								35,000	2,966	8.5%		39,000	44,893	115.1%	106.6	41,000	8,392	20.5%	12.0
DISTRICT OF COLUMBIA																			
FLORIDA																79,000	420	0.5%	
GEORGIA				272,000	75	0.0%		305,000	8,611	2.8%	2.8					368,000	2,037	0.6%	0.5
HAWAII																			
IDAHO																			
ILLINOIS	548,000	2,966	0.5%	604,000	13,390	2.2%	1.7	660,000	81,397	12.3%	11.8	741,000	25,804	3.5%	2.9	838,000	45,626	5.4%	4.9
INDIANA				424,000	9,608	2.3%		467,000	32,405	6.9%	4.7	507,000	11,187	2.2%	-0.1	543,000	10,674	2.0%	-0.3
IOWA				308,000	79,816	25.9%		356,000	40,711	11.4%	-14.5	399,000	31,929	8.0%	-17.9	437,000	8,960	2.1%	-23.9
KANSAS	105,000	108	0.1%	166,000	27,048	16.3%	16.2	227,000	27,068	11.9%	11.8	278,000	26,701	9.6%	9.5	321,000	8,959	2.8%	2.7
KENTUCKY				320,000	14,652	4.6%		354,000	8,541	2.4%	-2.2	386,000	828	0.2%	-4.4	415,000	5,724	1.4%	-3.2
LOUISIANA								196,000	13,231	6.8%		212,000	43	0.0%	-6.7	226,000	150	0.1%	-6.7
MAINE	154,000	296	0.2%	161,000	444	0.3%	0.1	167,000	41,407	24.8%	24.6	173,000	65,994	38.1%	38.0	177,000	6,512	3.7%	3.5

Total Highest Statewide General Elections (continued)

Other Turnout for Election Years 1870–1886 (continued)

State	1870 Voting-age population	Turnout	%	1874 Voting-age population	Turnout	%	Difference from 1870	1878 Voting-age population	Turnout	%	Difference from 1870	1882 Voting-age population	Turnout	%	Difference from 1870	1886 Voting-age population	Turnout	%	Difference from 1870
MARYLAND								207,000	8,892	4.3%		222,000	288	0.1%	-4.2	236,000	5,699	2.4%	-1.9
MASSACHUSETTS	316,000	22,152	7.0%	345,000	21,526	6.2%	-0.8	375,000	26,735	7.1%	0.1	420,000	6,535	1.6%	-5.5	473,000	9,957	2.1%	-4.9
MICHIGAN	279,000	2,940	1.1%	328,000	3,937	1.2%	0.1	377,000	77,037	20.4%	19.4	440,000	162,472	36.9%	35.9	491,000	199,411	40.6%	39.6
MINNESOTA								152,000	1,646	1.1%		215,000	6,470	3.0%	1.9	271,000	9,030	3.3%	2.2
MISSISSIPPI								224,000	7,026	3.1%		243,000	10,198	4.2%	1.1	256,000	176	0.1%	-3.1
MISSOURI	386,000	104,373	27.0%	436,000	24,594	5.6%	-21.4	487,000	82,401	16.9%	-10.1	546,000	30,616	5.6%	-21.4	609,000	11,731	1.9%	-25.1
MONTANA																			
NEBRASKA				71,000	5,505	7.8%		102,000	9,475	9.3%	1.5	154,000	21,061	13.7%	5.9	218,000	9,627	4.4%	-3.3
NEVADA																			
NEW HAMPSHIRE	84,000	8,537	10.2%	88,000	2,140	2.4%	-7.7	92,000	5,855	6.4%	-3.8	95,000	969	1.0%	-9.1	99,000	2,257	2.3%	-7.9
NEW JERSEY								244,000	25,272	10.4%		278,000	8,054	2.9%	-7.5	319,000	23,671	7.4%	-2.9
NEW MEXICO																			
NEW YORK	990,000	3,366	0.3%	1,071,000	12,594	1.2%	0.8					1,262,000	37,757	3.0%	2.7	1,387,000	43,086	3.1%	2.0
NORTH CAROLINA	217,000	76,268	35.1%	249,000	14,356	5.8%	-29.4	281,000	1,078	0.4%	-34.8	304,000	111,320	36.6%	1.5	324,000	28,371	8.8%	-26.4
NORTH DAKOTA																			
OHIO	600,000	1,687	0.3%	671,000	6,405	1.0%	0.7	742,000	41,547	5.6%	5.3	813,000	15,786	1.9%	1.7	886,000	31,203	3.5%	3.2
OKLAHOMA																			
OREGON				35,000	6,532	18.7%		46,000	1,434	3.1%	-15.5	60,000	3	0.0%	-18.7	78,000	2,753	3.5%	-15.1
PENNSYLVANIA	783,000	2,357	0.3%	856,000	25,716	3.0%	2.7	928,000	102,240	11.0%	10.7	1,034,000	72,423	7.0%	6.7	1,161,000	37,293	3.2%	2.9
RHODE ISLAND	45,000	267	0.6%	50,000	177	0.4%	-0.2	55,000	886	1.6%	1.0	61,000	156	0.3%	-0.3	69,000	2,591	3.8%	3.2
SOUTH CAROLINA	149,000	51,549	34.6%	173,000	68,837	39.8%	5.2	190,000	213	0.1%	-34.5	212,000	6,851	3.2%	-31.4	224,000	58	0.0%	-34.6
SOUTH DAKOTA																			
TENNESSEE				289,000	443	0.2%		316,000	55,101	17.4%	17.3	344,000	102,835	29.9%	29.7	373,000	40,305	10.8%	10.7
TEXAS	177,000	407	0.2%	252,000	220	0.1%	-0.1												
UTAH																			
VERMONT	75,000	4	0.0%	78,000	21	0.0%	0.0	81,000	3,397	4.2%	4.2	84,000	1,543	1.8%	1.8	89,000	1,706	1.9%	1.9
VIRGINIA**	269,000	175,953	65.4%	295,000	195	0.1%	-65.3	321,000	25,144	7.8%	-57.6	341,000	99,992	29.3%	-36.1	359,000	9,598	2.7%	-62.7
WASHINGTON																			
WEST VIRGINIA				113,000	434	0.4%		129,000	8,318	6.4%	6.1	146,000	5,006	3.4%	3.0	163,000	1,502	0.9%	0.5
WISCONSIN								272,000	13,028	4.8%		314,000	18,622	5.9%	1.1	361,000	38,592	10.7%	5.9
WYOMING																			
Total	5,306,000	453,232	8.5%	8,105,000	367,696	4.5%	-4.0	9,236,000	829,193	9.0%	0.4	11,299,000	993,070	8.8%	0.2	13,005,000	663,494	5.1%	-3.4

*Percentage point difference between turnout in current year and initial year listed in chart. If data do not appear for a state in the initial year listed, the difference is calculated from the first year in which data do appear for that state.

**Virginia officially re-entered the Union in 1870. Its election that year featured the "Conservatives" and the "Radicals."

STATE GUBERNATORIAL GENERAL ELECTIONS

Election Years 1871–1889

State	1871 Voting-age population	Turnout	%	1873 Voting-age population	Turnout	%	Difference from 1871*	1875 Voting-age population	Turnout	%	Difference from 1871	1877 Voting-age population	Turnout	%	Difference from 1871	1879 Voting-age population	Turnout	%	Difference from 1871
CALIFORNIA	157,000	120,101	76.5%					188,000	122,583	65.2%	-11.3					218,000	160,114	73.4%	-3.1
CONNECTICUT	130,000	94,843	73.0%	134,000	84,305	62.9%	-10.0	138,000	98,024	71.0%	-1.9								
IOWA	273,000	177,527	65.0%	297,000	187,688	63.2%	-1.8	320,000	218,125	68.2%	3.1	344,000	234,936	68.3%	3.3	368,000	288,446	78.4%	13.4
KENTUCKY	295,000	215,743	73.1%					328,000	217,771	66.4%	-6.7					363,000	226,234	62.3%	-10.8
LOUISIANA																201,000	114,038	56.7%	
MAINE	155,000	105,823	68.3%	159,000	78,163	49.2%	-19.1	162,000	111,619	68.9%	0.6	165,000	101,186	61.3%	-6.9	168,000	138,039	82.2%	13.9
MARYLAND	176,000	132,783	75.4%					193,000	157,991	81.9%	6.4					211,000	159,350	75.5%	0.1
MASSACHUSETTS	323,000	129,702	40.2%	338,000	131,543	38.9%	-1.2	353,000	171,096	48.5%	8.3	368,000	180,794	49.1%	9.0	383,000	231,900	60.5%	20.4
MINNESOTA	88,000	77,881	88.5%	106,000	75,986	71.7%	-16.8	124,000	80,348	64.8%	-23.7	143,000	96,218	67.3%	-21.2	161,000	99,366	61.7%	-26.8
MISSISSIPPI				192,000	126,181	65.7%						218,000	96,376	44.2%	-21.5				
MONTANA																			
NEW HAMPSHIRE	85,000	68,592	80.7%	87,000	66,039	75.9%	-4.8	89,000	78,414	88.1%	7.4	90,000	77,483	86.1%	5.4	92,000	75,817	82.4%	1.7
NEW JERSEY	203,000	158,745	78.2%									238,000	182,931	76.9%	-1.3				
NEW YORK																1,173,000	871,923	74.3%	
NORTH DAKOTA																			
OHIO	617,000	456,378	74.0%	653,000	428,491	65.6%	-8.3	688,000	590,000	85.8%	11.8	724,000	520,747	71.9%	-2.0	760,000	655,453	86.2%	12.3
PENNSYLVANIA								874,000	596,311	68.2%									
RHODE ISLAND	46,000	14,205	30.9%	49,000	13,442	27.4%	-3.4	52,000	22,258	42.8%	11.9	54,000	24,238	44.9%	14.0	57,000	15,223	26.7%	-4.2
SOUTH DAKOTA																			
TEXAS				233,000	149,955	64.4%		270,000	199,968	74.1%	9.7								
VIRGINIA				289,000	213,085	73.7%						315,000	101,873	32.3%	-41.4				
WASHINGTON																			
WISCONSIN	215,000	147,221	68.5%	231,000	147,823	64.0%	-4.5	247,000	169,539	68.6%	0.2	264,000	175,352	66.4%	-2.1	281,000	188,563	67.1%	-1.4
Total	2,763,000	1,899,544	68.7%	2,768,000	1,702,701	61.5%	-7.2	4,026,000	2,834,047	70.4%	1.6	2,923,000	1,792,134	61.3%	-7.4	4,436,000	3,224,466	72.7%	3.9

State	1881 Voting-age population	Turnout	%	Difference from 1871	1883 Voting-age population	Turnout	%	Difference from 1871	1885 Voting-age population	Turnout	%	Difference from 1871	1887 Voting-age population	Turnout	%	Difference from 1871	1889 Voting-age population	Turnout	%	Difference from 1871
CALIFORNIA																				
CONNECTICUT																				
IOWA	388,000	234,784	60.5%	-4.5	408,000	327,196	80.2%	15.2	428,000	344,189	80.4%	15.4	447,000	323,302	72.3%	7.3	466,000	353,556	75.9%	10.8
KENTUCKY					394,000	222,796	56.5%	-16.6					423,000	270,220	63.9%	-9.3				
LOUISIANA																				
MAINE																				

State Gubernatorial General Elections *(continued)*

Election Years 1871–1889 *(continued)*

State	1881				1883				1885				1887				1889			
	Voting-age population	Turnout	%	Difference from 1871	Voting-age population	Turnout	%	Difference from 1871	Voting-age population	Turnout	%	Difference from 1871	Voting-age population	Turnout	%	Difference from 1871	Voting-age population	Turnout	%	Difference from 1871
MARYLAND					225,000	173,406	77.1%	1.6					240,000	185,660	77.4%	1.9				
MASSACHUSETTS	407,000	151,195	37.1%	-3.0	433,000	310,320	71.7%	31.5	460,000	202,589	44.0%	3.9	486,000	254,394	52.3%	12.2	513,000	263,047	51.3%	11.1
MINNESOTA	201,000	102,193	50.8%	-37.7	229,000	130,707	57.1%	-31.4												
MISSISSIPPI	240,000	128,799	53.7%	-12.1					253,000	88,783	35.1%	-30.6					267,000	84,929	31.8%	-33.9
MONTANA																	54,000	38,726	71.7%	
NEW HAMPSHIRE																				
NEW JERSEY					288,000	200,903	69.8%	-8.4									350,000	262,237	74.9%	-3.3
NEW YORK									1,356,000	991,787	73.1%	-1.2								
NORTH DAKOTA																	43,000	38,980	90.7%	
OHIO	795,000	601,211	75.6%	1.7	831,000	706,857	85.1%	11.1	868,000	701,111	80.8%	6.8	904,000	689,739	76.3%	2.3	940,000	747,974	79.6%	5.6
PENNSYLVANIA																				
RHODE ISLAND	60,000	15,605	26.0%	-4.9	64,000	23,279	36.4%	5.5	67,000	22,443	33.5%	2.6	71,000	35,101	49.4%	18.6	75,000	41,755	55.7%	24.8
SOUTH DAKOTA																	86,000	77,804	90.5%	
TEXAS																				
VIRGINIA	337,000	214,221	63.6%	10.2					354,000	289,055	81.7%	7.9					371,000	284,420	76.7%	2.9
WASHINGTON																	117,000	58,443	50.0%	
WISCONSIN	303,000	164,776	54.4%	-14.1																
Total	2,731,000	1,612,784	59.1%	-9.7	2,872,000	2,095,464	73.0%	4.2	3,786,000	2,639,957	69.7%	1.0	2,571,000	1,758,416	68.4%	-0.4	3,282,000	2,251,871	68.6%	-0.1

*Percentage point difference between turnout in current year and initial year listed in chart. If data do not appear for a state in the initial year listed, the difference is calculated from the first year in which data do appear for that state.

STATE GUBERNATORIAL GENERAL ELECTIONS

Republican Turnout for Election Years 1871–1889

State	1871			1873				1875				1877				1879			
	Voting-age population	Turnout	%	Voting-age population	Turnout	%	Difference from 1871*	Voting-age population	Turnout	%	Difference from 1871	Voting-age population	Turnout	%	Difference from 1871	Voting-age population	Turnout	%	Difference from 1871
CALIFORNIA	157,000	62,581	39.9%					188,000	31,322	16.7%	-23.2					218,000	67,965	31.2%	-8.7
CONNECTICUT	130,000	47,473	36.5%	134,000	39,245	29.3%	-7.2	138,000	44,272	32.1%	-4.4								
IOWA	273,000	109,328	40.0%	297,000	105,132	35.4%	-4.6	320,000	124,855	39.0%	-1.0	344,000	121,316	35.3%	-4.8	368,000	157,408	42.8%	2.7
KENTUCKY	295,000	89,298	30.3%					328,000	90,795	27.7%	-2.6					363,000	81,881	22.6%	-7.7
LOUISIANA																201,000	40,415	20.1%	
MAINE	155,000	58,285	37.6%	159,000	45,239	28.5%	-9.2	162,000	57,782	35.7%	-1.9	165,000	53,584	32.5%	-5.1	168,000	68,527	40.8%	3.2
MARYLAND	176,000	58,824	33.4%					193,000	72,544	37.6%	4.2					211,000	68,619	32.5%	-0.9
MASSACHUSETTS	323,000	75,129	23.3%	338,000	72,183	21.4%	-1.9	353,000	83,639	23.7%	0.4	368,000	91,255	24.8%	1.5	383,000	122,751	32.0%	8.8
MINNESOTA	88,000	46,669	53.0%	106,000	40,741	38.4%	-14.6	124,000	45,073	36.3%	-16.7	143,000	57,071	39.9%	-13.1	161,000	57,522	35.7%	-17.3
MISSISSIPPI				192,000	73,324	38.2%													
MONTANA																			
NEW HAMPSHIRE	85,000	33,892	39.9%	87,000	34,023	39.1%	-0.8	89,000	39,293	44.1%	4.3	90,000	40,757	45.3%	5.4	92,000	38,175	41.5%	1.6
NEW JERSEY	203,000	76,383	37.6%									238,000	85,094	35.8%	-1.9				
NEW YORK																1,173,000	418,567	35.7%	
NORTH DAKOTA																			
OHIO	617,000	238,273	38.6%	653,000	213,837	32.7%	-5.9	688,000	297,817	43.3%	4.7	724,000	249,105	34.4%	-4.2	760,000	336,321	44.3%	5.6
PENNSYLVANIA								874,000	304,175	34.8%									
RHODE ISLAND	46,000	8,838	19.2%	49,000	9,656	19.7%	0.5	52,000	8,368	16.1%	-3.1	54,000	12,455	23.1%	3.9	57,000	9,717	17.0%	-2.2
SOUTH DAKOTA																			
TEXAS				233,000	51,049	21.9%		270,000	49,994	18.5%	-3.4								
VIRGINIA				289,000	93,413	32.3%													
WASHINGTON																			
WISCONSIN	215,000	78,301	36.4%	231,000	66,224	28.7%	-7.8	247,000	85,165	34.5%	-1.9	264,000	78,750	29.8%	-6.6	281,000	100,537	35.8%	-0.6
Total	2,763,000	983,274	35.6%	2,768,000	844,066	30.5%	-5.1	4,026,000	1,335,094	33.2%	-2.4	2,390,000	789,387	33.0%	-2.6	4,436,000	1,568,405	35.4%	-0.2

State	1881				1883				1885				1887				1889			
	Voting-age population	Turnout	%	Difference from 1871	Voting-age population	Turnout	%	Difference from 1871	Voting-age population	Turnout	%	Difference from 1871	Voting-age population	Turnout	%	Difference from 1871	Voting-age population	Turnout	%	Difference from 1871
CALIFORNIA																				
CONNECTICUT																				
IOWA	388,000	133,328	34.4%	-5.7	408,000	164,095	40.2%	0.2	428,000	175,605	41.0%	1.0	447,000	169,596	37.9%	-2.1	466,000	173,450	37.2%	-2.8
KENTUCKY					394,000	89,181	22.6%	-7.6					423,000	126,754	30.0%	-0.3				
LOUISIANA																				
MAINE																				

State Gubernatorial General Elections (continued)

Republican Turnout for Election Years 1871–1889 (continued)

State	1881 Voting-age population	Turnout	%	Difference from 1871	1883 Voting-age population	Turnout	%	Difference from 1871	1885 Voting-age population	Turnout	%	Difference from 1871	1887 Voting-age population	Turnout	%	Difference from 1871	1889 Voting-age population	Turnout	%	Difference from 1871
MARYLAND					225,000	80,712	35.9%	2.4					240,000	86,622	36.1%	2.7				
MASSACHUSETTS	407,000	96,609	23.7%	0.5	433,000	160,092	37.0%	13.7	460,000	112,243	24.4%	1.1	486,000	136,000	28.0%	4.7	513,000	127,357	24.8%	1.6
MINNESOTA	201,000	65,025	32.4%	-20.7	219,000	72,462	33.1%	-19.9												
MISSISSIPPI	240,000	51,994	21.7%	-16.5																
MONTANA																	54,000	18,991	35.2%	
NEW HAMPSHIRE																				
NEW JERSEY					288,000	97,047	33.7%	-3.9									350,000	123,992	35.4%	-2.2
NEW YORK									1,356,000	490,331	36.2%	0.5								
NORTH DAKOTA																	43,000	25,365	59.0%	
OHIO	795,000	312,785	39.3%	0.7	831,000	347,164	41.8%	3.2	868,000	359,281	41.4%	2.8	904,000	356,534	39.4%	0.8	940,000	368,551	39.2%	0.6
PENNSYLVANIA																				
RHODE ISLAND	60,000	10,849	18.1%	-1.1	64,000	13,078	20.4%	1.2	67,000	12,563	18.8%	-0.5	71,000	15,111	21.3%	2.1	75,000	16,870	22.5%	3.3
SOUTH DAKOTA																	86,000	53,964	62.7%	
TEXAS																				
VIRGINIA									354,000	136,508	38.6%	6.2					371,000	121,240	32.7%	0.4
WASHINGTON																	117,000	33,711	28.8%	
WISCONSIN	303,000	81,754	27.0%	-9.4																
Total	2,394,000	752,344	31.4%	-4.2	2,862,000	1,023,831	35.8%	0.2	3,533,000	1,286,531	36.4%	0.8	2,571,000	890,617	34.6%	-0.9	3,015,000	1,063,491	35.3%	-0.3

Democratic Turnout for Election Years 1871–1889

State	1871 Voting-age population	Turnout	%	1873 Voting-age population	Turnout	%	Difference from 1871*	1875 Voting-age population	Turnout	%	Difference from 1871	1877 Voting-age population	Turnout	%	Difference from 1871	1879 Voting-age population	Turnout	%	Difference from 1871
CALIFORNIA	157,000	57,520	36.6%					188,000	61,509	32.7%	-3.9					218,000	47,667	21.9%	-14.8
CONNECTICUT	130,000	47,370	36.4%	134,000	45,060	33.6%	-2.8	138,000	53,752	39.0%	2.5								
IOWA	273,000	68,199	25.0%					320,000	93,270	29.1%	4.2	344,000	79,304	23.1%	-1.9	368,000	85,364	23.2%	-1.8
KENTUCKY	295,000	126,445	42.9%					328,000	126,976	38.7%	-4.2					363,000	125,399	34.5%	-8.3
LOUISIANA																201,000	73,623	36.6%	
MAINE	155,000	47,538	30.7%	159,000	32,924	20.7%	-10.0	162,000	53,837	33.2%	2.6	165,000	42,311	25.6%	-5.0	168,000	21,525	12.8%	-17.9
MARYLAND	176,000	73,959	42.0%					193,000	85,447	44.3%	2.3					211,000	90,731	43.0%	1.0
MASSACHUSETTS	323,000	47,725	14.8%	338,000	59,360	17.6%	2.8	353,000	78,333	22.2%	7.4	368,000	73,185	19.9%	5.1	383,000	109,149	28.5%	13.7
MINNESOTA	88,000	31,212	35.5%	106,000	35,245	33.3%	-2.2	124,000	35,275	28.4%	-7.0	143,000	39,147	27.4%	-8.1	161,000	41,844	26.0%	-9.5
MISSISSIPPI												218,000	96,376	44.2%					
MONTANA																			

State Gubernatorial General Elections (continued)

Democratic Turnout for Election Years 1871–1889 (continued)

State	1871 Voting-age population	Turnout	%	Difference from 1871	1873 Voting-age population	Turnout	%	Difference from 1871	1875 Voting-age population	Turnout	%	Difference from 1871	1877 Voting-age population	Turnout	%	Difference from 1871	1879 Voting-age population	Turnout	%	Difference from 1871
NEW HAMPSHIRE	85,000	34,700	40.8%		87,000	32,016	36.8%	-4.0	89,000	39,121	44.0%	3.1	90,000	36,726	40.8%	0.0	92,000	31,135	33.8%	-7.0
NEW JERSEY	203,000	82,362	40.6%										238,000	97,837	41.1%	0.5				
NEW YORK																	1,173,000	453,356	38.6%	
NORTH DAKOTA																				
OHIO	617,000	218,105	35.3%		653,000	214,654	32.9%	-2.5	688,000	292,279	42.5%	7.1	724,000	271,642	37.5%	2.2	760,000	319,132	42.0%	6.6
PENNSYLVANIA									874,000	292,136	33.4%									
RHODE ISLAND	46,000	5,367	11.7%		49,000	3,786	7.7%	-3.9	52,000	5,166	9.9%	-1.7	54,000	11,783	21.8%	10.2	57,000	5,506	9.7%	-2.0
SOUTH DAKOTA																				
TEXAS					233,000	98,906	42.4%		270,000	149,974	55.5%	13.1								
VIRGINIA					289,000	119,672	41.4%						315,000	101,873	32.3%	-9.1				
WASHINGTON																				
WISCONSIN	215,000	68,920	32.1%		231,000	81,599	35.3%	3.3	247,000	84,374	34.2%	2.1	264,000	70,486	26.7%	-5.4	281,000	75,030	26.7%	-5.4
Total	2,763,000	909,422	32.9%		2,279,000	723,222	31.7%	-1.2	4,026,000	1,451,449	36.1%	3.1	2,923,000	920,670	31.5%	-1.4	4,436,000	1,479,461	33.4%	0.4

State	1881 Voting-age population	Turnout	%	Difference from 1871	1883 Voting-age population	Turnout	%	Difference from 1871	1885 Voting-age population	Turnout	%	Difference from 1871	1887 Voting-age population	Turnout	%	Difference from 1871	1889 Voting-age population	Turnout	%	Difference from 1871
CALIFORNIA																				
CONNECTICUT																				
IOWA	388,000	73,344	18.9%	-6.1	408,000	140,012	34.3%	9.3	428,000	168,584	39.4%	14.4	447,000	153,706	34.4%	9.4	466,000	180,106	38.6%	13.7
KENTUCKY					394,000	133,615	33.9%	-9.0					423,000	143,466	33.9%	-8.9				
LOUISIANA																				
MAINE																				
MARYLAND					225,000	92,694	41.2%	-0.8					240,000	99,038	41.3%	-0.8				
MASSACHUSETTS	407,000	54,586	13.4%	-1.4	433,000	150,228	34.7%	19.9	460,000	90,346	19.6%	4.9	486,000	118,394	24.4%	9.6	513,000	120,582	23.5%	8.7
MINNESOTA	201,000	37,168	18.5%	-17.0	219,000	58,245	26.6%	-8.9												
MISSISSIPPI	240,000	76,805	32.0%	-12.2					253,000	88,783	35.1%	-9.1					267,000	84,929	31.8%	-12.4
MONTANA																	54,000	19,735	36.5%	
NEW HAMPSHIRE																				
NEW JERSEY					288,000	103,856	36.1%	-4.5									350,000	138,245	39.5%	-1.1
NEW YORK									1,356,000	501,456	37.0%	-1.7								
NORTH DAKOTA																	43,000	12,733	29.6%	
OHIO	795,000	288,426	36.3%	0.9	831,000	359,693	43.3%	7.9	868,000	341,830	39.4%	4.0	904,000	333,205	36.9%	1.5	940,000	379,423	40.4%	5.0
PENNSYLVANIA																				
RHODE ISLAND	60,000	4,756	7.9%	-3.7	64,000	10,201	15.9%	4.3	67,000	8,674	12.9%	1.3	71,000	18,095	25.5%	13.8	75,000	21,289	28.4%	16.7

State Gubernatorial General Elections (continued)

Democratic Turnout for Election Years 1871–1889 (continued)

State	1881 Voting-age population	Turnout	%	Difference from 1871	1883 Voting-age population	Turnout	%	Difference from 1871	1885 Voting-age population	Turnout	%	Difference from 1871	1887 Voting-age population	Turnout	%	Difference from 1871	1889 Voting-age population	Turnout	%	Difference from 1871
SOUTH DAKOTA																	86,000	23,840	27.7%	
TEXAS																				
VIRGINIA	337,000	100,757	29.9%	-11.5					354,000	152,547	43.1%	1.7					371,000	163,180	44.0%	2.6
WASHINGTON																	117,000	24,732	21.1%	
WISCONSIN	303,000	69,797	23.0%	-9.0																
Total	2,731,000	705,639	25.8%	-7.1	2,862,000	1,048,544	36.6%	3.7	3,786,000	1,352,220	35.7%	2.8	2,671,000	005,904	33.7%	0.8	3,282,000	1,168,794	35.6%	2.7

Other Turnout for Election Years 1871–1889

State	1871 Voting-age population	Turnout	%	1873 Voting-age population	Turnout	%	Difference from 1871*	1875 Voting-age population	Turnout	%	Difference from 1871	1877 Voting-age population	Turnout	%	Difference from 1871	1879 Voting-age population	Turnout	%	Difference from 1871
CALIFORNIA								188,000	29,752	15.8%						218,000	44,482	20.4%	4.6
IOWA				297,000	82,556	27.8%						344,000	34,316	10.0%	-17.8	368,000	45,674	12.4%	-15.4
KENTUCKY																363,000	18,954	5.2%	
MAINE												165,000	5,291	3.2%		168,000	47,987	28.6%	25.4
MASSACHUSETTS	323,000	6,848	2.1%					353,000	9,124	2.6%	0.5	368,000	16,354	4.4%	2.3				
MISSISSIPPI				192,000	52,857	27.5%													
NEW HAMPSHIRE																92,000	6,507	7.1%	
RHODE ISLAND								52,000	8,724	16.8%									
VIRGINIA																			
WISCONSIN												264,000	26,116	9.9%		281,000	12,996	4.6%	-5.3

State	1881 Voting-age population	Turnout	%	Difference from 1871	1883 Voting-age population	Turnout	%	Difference from 1871	1885 Voting-age population	Turnout	%	Difference from 1871	1887 Voting-age population	Turnout	%	Difference from 1871	1889 Voting-age population	Turnout	%	Difference from 1871
CALIFORNIA																				
IOWA	388,000	28,112	7.2%	-20.6	408,000	23,089	5.7%	-22.1												
KENTUCKY																				
MAINE																				
MASSACHUSETTS																	513,000	15,108	2.9%	0.8
MISSISSIPPI																				
NEW HAMPSHIRE																				
RHODE ISLAND									67,000	1,206	1.8%	-15.0	71,000	1,895	2.7%	-14.1	75,000	3,596	4.8%	-12.0
VIRGINIA	337,000	113,464	33.7%																	
WISCONSIN	303,000	13,225	4.4%	-5.5																

*Percentage point difference between turnout in current year and initial year listed in chart. If data do not appear for a state in the initial year listed, the difference is calculated from the first year in which data do appear for that state.

UNITED STATES HOUSE OF REPRESENTATIVES GENERAL ELECTIONS

Election Years 1871–1889

State	1871 Voting-age population	Turnout	%	1873 Voting-age population	Turnout	%	Difference from 1871*	1875 Voting-age population	Turnout	%	Difference from 1871	1877 Voting-age population	Turnout	%	Difference from 1871	1879 Voting-age population	Turnout	%	Difference from 1871
CALIFORNIA	157,000	119,604	76.2%					188,000	122,273	65.0%	-11.1					218,000	156,774	71.9%	-4.3
CONNECTICUT	130,000	93,990	72.3%	134,000	86,282	64.4%	-7.9	138,000	100,624	72.9%	0.6								
MISSISSIPPI								205,000	158,061	77.1%									
MONTANA																			
NEW HAMPSHIRE	85,000	69,479	81.7%	87,000	67,433	77.5%	-4.2	89,000	78,806	88.5%	6.8	90,000	77,890	86.5%	4.8				
NORTH DAKOTA																			
SOUTH DAKOTA																			
TEXAS	196,000	106,703	54.4%																
WASHINGTON																			

State	1881 Voting-age population	Turnout	%	Difference from 1871	1883 Voting-age population	Turnout	%	Difference from 1871	1885 Voting-age population	Turnout	%	Difference from 1871	1887 Voting-age population	Turnout	%	Difference from 1871	1889 Voting-age population	Turnout	%	Difference from 1871
CALIFORNIA																				
CONNECTICUT																				
MISSISSIPPI																				
MONTANA																	54,000	38,176	70.7%	
NEW HAMPSHIRE																				
NORTH DAKOTA																	43,000	38,143	88.7%	
SOUTH DAKOTA																	86,000	77,524	90.1%	
TEXAS																				
WASHINGTON																	117,000	58,531	50.0%	

*Percentage point difference between turnout in current year and initial year listed in chart. If data do not appear for a state in the initial year listed, the difference is calculated from the first year in which data do appear for that state.

UNITED STATES HOUSE OF REPRESENTATIVES GENERAL ELECTIONS

Republican Turnout for Election Years 1871–1889

State	1871 Voting-age population	Turnout	%	1873 Voting-age population	Turnout	%	Difference from 1871*	1875 Voting-age population	Turnout	%	Difference from 1871	1877 Voting-age population	Turnout	%	Difference from 1871	1879 Voting-age population	Turnout	%	Difference from 1871
CALIFORNIA	157,000	62,539	39.8%					188,000	39,789	21.2%	-18.7					218,000	74,651	34.2%	-5.6
CONNECTICUT	130,000	47,272	36.4%	134,000	43,352	32.4%	-4.0	138,000	47,418	34.4%	-2.0								
MISSISSIPPI								205,000	74,095	36.1%									
MONTANA																			
NEW HAMPSHIRE	85,000	33,758	39.7%	87,000	33,178	38.1%	-1.6	89,000	38,950	43.8%	4.0	90,000	39,771	44.2%	4.5				
NORTH DAKOTA																			
SOUTH DAKOTA																			
TEXAS	196,000	43,771	22.3%																
WASHINGTON																			

State	1881 Voting-age population	Turnout	%	Difference from 1871	1883 Voting-age population	Turnout	%	Difference from 1871	1885 Voting-age population	Turnout	%	Difference from 1871	1887 Voting-age population	Turnout	%	Difference from 1871	1889 Voting-age population	Turnout	%	Difference from 1871
CALIFORNIA																				
CONNECTICUT																				
MISSISSIPPI																				
MONTANA																	54,000	19,912	36.9%	
NEW HAMPSHIRE																				
NORTH DAKOTA																	43,000	26,077	60.6%	
SOUTH DAKOTA																	86,000	54,983	63.9%	
TEXAS																				
WASHINGTON																	117,000	34,039	29.1%	

United States House of Representatives General Elections (continued)

United States House of Representatives General Elections (continued)

Democratic Turnout for Election Years 1871–1889

State	1871 Voting-age population	Turnout	%	1873 Voting-age population	Turnout	%	Difference from 1871*	1875 Voting-age population	Turnout	%	Difference from 1871	1877 Voting-age population	Turnout	%	Difference from 1871	1879 Voting-age population	Turnout	%	Difference from 1871
CALIFORNIA	157,000	57,065	36.3%					188,000	58,688	31.2%	-5.1					218,000	47,915	22.0%	-14.4
CONNECTICUT	130,000	46,718	35.9%	134,000	41,498	31.0%	-5.0	138,000	51,197	37.1%	1.2								
MISSISSIPPI								205,000	83,966	41.0%									
MONTANA																			
NEW HAMPSHIRE	85,000	35,098	41.3%	87,000	33,131	38.1%	-3.2	89,000	39,231	44.1%	2.8	90,000	37,866	42.1%	0.8				
NORTH DAKOTA																			
SOUTH DAKOTA																			
TEXAS	196,000	62,525	31.9%																
WASHINGTON																			

State	1881 Voting-age population	Turnout	%	Difference from 1871	1883 Voting-age population	Turnout	%	Difference from 1871	1885 Voting-age population	Turnout	%	Difference from 1871	1887 Voting-age population	Turnout	%	Difference from 1871	1889 Voting-age population	Turnout	%	Difference from 1871
CALIFORNIA																				
CONNECTICUT																				
MISSISSIPPI																				
MONTANA																	54,000	18,264	33.8%	
NEW HAMPSHIRE																				
NORTH DAKOTA																	43,000	12,066	28.1%	
SOUTH DAKOTA																	86,000	22,541	26.2%	
TEXAS																				
WASHINGTON																	117,000	24,492	20.9%	

Other Turnout for Election Years 1871–1879**

State	1871 Voting-age population	Turnout	%	1873 Voting-age population	Turnout	%	Difference from 1871*	1875 Voting-age population	Turnout	%	Difference from 1871	1877 Voting-age population	Turnout	%	Difference from 1871	1879 Voting-age population	Turnout	%	Difference from 1871
CALIFORNIA								188,000	23,796	12.7%						218,000	34,208	15.7%	3.0
CONNECTICUT				134,000	1,432	1.1%		138,000	2,009	1.5%	0.4								
NEW HAMPSHIRE	85,000	623	0.7%	87,000	1,124	1.3%	0.6	89,000	625	0.7%	0.0	90,000	253	0.3%	-0.5				
TEXAS	196,000	407	0.2%																

*Percentage point difference between turnout in current year and initial year listed in chart. If data do not appear for a state in the initial year listed, the difference is calculated from the first year in which data do appear for that state.

**No Other turnout from 1881-1889

CHAPTER 6
1890–1909

MIDTERM GENERAL ELECTIONS

MIDTERM PRIMARY ELECTIONS

OFF-YEAR GENERAL ELECTIONS

Chronology of Major Events, 1890–1909

1890	Congress passes the Sherman Antitrust Act, providing a legal basis for reining in monopoly power. While the act was ostensibly aimed at corporations, it was also used as a tool against unions. Native American armed resistance is crushed in the Battle of Wounded Knee. The eleventh census counts the U.S. population at 62.9 million people, and the director of the census proclaims the end of the American frontier.
1891	The Populist (or People's) Party is formed as an alliance of farmers and other grassroots reformers.
1892	Democrat Grover Cleveland is elected president. The first Populist Party Convention is held in Omaha, Nebraska. A union-busting attempt by Carnegie Steel Company leads to the Homestead Strike, in which violence between workers and guards is broken up by the Pennsylvania militia.
1893	The Panic of 1893 leads to an economic depression from 1893–1897 and a national debate on the gold standard that divides the Democratic Party.
1894	Ohio businessman Jacob Coxey leads a well-publicized march of unemployed workers ("Coxey's Army") to Washington but without success. The Pullman rail strike pits the American Railway Union against railroad owner George Pullman and federal troops, on the grounds of interrupting U.S. mail service. ARU leaders, including Eugene Debs, are jailed for six months. A small federal income tax is reinstated (it had been a temporary measure during the Civil War). *In re Saito* Supreme Court decision holds that only whites and blacks, not Asian Americans or others, could become citizens.
1895	*Pollock v. Farmers' Loan and Trust Co.* Supreme Court decision strikes down federal income tax as unconstitutional.
1896	Republican William T. McKinley defeats Democrat William Jennings Bryan for president. *Plessy v. Ferguson* Supreme Court decision upholds "separate but equal" principle, reinforcing segregation in the South.
1897	Congress passes the Dingley Tariff, raising tariffs on foreign goods to forty-five percent.
1898	The sinking of the USS *Maine* leads to the Spanish-American War. Hawaii is annexed by the United States.
1899	Congress ratifies the Treaty of Paris, which enables United States control over Guam, Puerto Rico, the Philippines, and (temporarily) Cuba and sparks debate over U.S. imperialism. A Filipino insurgency begins that last two years.
1900	McKinley is re-elected, again defeating William Jennings Bryan. The twelfth census counts the U.S. population at 76.0 million people.
1901	President McKinley is assassinated. Vice President Theodore Roosevelt becomes president. Congress authorizes the building of the Panama Canal and passes the Platt Amendment, authorizing long-term U.S. interference in Cuban foreign affairs and maintaining U.S. naval bases in Cuba, including Guantanamo Bay.
1904	Theodore Roosevelt is re-elected president.
1906	Upton Sinclair's *The Jungle* is published, exposing the unsavory practices of the meat industry. Partially as a result, Congress creates the Food and Drug Administration, establishing the principle of federal regulation for public health and safety. The Naturalization Act standardizes requirements for citizenship, including English language.
1908	Republican William Howard Taft is elected president.

State and Federal Laws Chronology, 1890–1909

1890   *Davis v. Beason*, 130 U.S. 333 (1890). Supreme Court unanimously upholds Utah's law requiring voters to neither practice polygamy nor belong to a sect that promoted this "crime."

Idaho becomes a state. The state constitutionally bans property requirements for voting except in certain types of local elections. Citizens must have resided six months in the state and thirty days in the county in order to vote. There is no loss of residence for soldiers or others traveling on public business, but no residency is gained by military personnel stationed in the state, by students, or by residents of almshouses or other institutions.

Mississippi requires that "on or after the first day of January, 1892, every elector shall ... Be able to read any section of the Constitution of this State; or he shall be able to understand the same when read to him, or give a reasonable interpretation thereof."[1] It requires the voter to have paid all taxes for the two preceding years by February 1 of the election year. Ministers with six months' residence in the district are exempt. There is also a $2 poll tax, except for persons who are "deaf and dumb or blind, or who are maimed by loss of hand or foot; said tax to be a lien only upon taxable property."[2] The voter must have resided for two years in the state and one year in the election district or incorporated city or town.

Kentucky constitutionally declares that the legislature shall "provide that persons illiterate, blind, or in any way disabled, may have their ballots marked as herein required."[3]

Wyoming becomes a state. It enters the Union without any property or taxpaying requirements. Women are fully enfranchised, and declarant aliens are permitted to vote until 1895. The voter must be able to read state constitution; those prevented from reading by physical disability are exempted. The voter must have resided one year in the state and sixty days in the county. There is no residency gained by military personnel stationed in the state.

1891   Colorado naturalized citizens are required to present naturalization papers before voting, if challenged. Also, assistance will be provided for any voter who declares under oath that he cannot read or write. Interpreters will be provided for those who cannot speak or understand English.

Arkansas permits election judges to assist illiterate voters.

Illinois stipulates that any voter who declares under oath that he cannot read the English language shall be assisted in marking his ballot. Ohio declares that assistance may be given to voters for any reason.

Kentucky requires the voter to have resided one year in the state, six months in the county, and sixty days in the precinct. There is no residency gained by military personnel stationed in the state.

Massachusetts repeals its 1821 tax requirement for voting.

1892   Massachusetts requires the voter to be able to read the state constitution in English and write his name. "Those who cannot read or write because of physical disability or ... those who had the right to vote on May 1, 1857" are exempted.[4]

1893   Colorado fully enfranchises women.

Arkansas institutes a poll tax. The voter must present receipt or other evidence that the tax has been paid.

1893 (cont.) Maine requires the voter to be able to read the Constitution in English and write his name. Those prevented from reading or writing by physical infirmities or those sixty years or older at the time of the amendment are exempted from the literacy requirement.

Minnesota stipulates that no residence for voting purposes can be gained by any "person employed temporarily" cutting timber "or in the construction or repair of any railroad, canal, municipal or other work of public nature." [5]

Montana requires the voter to have resided for one year in the state and thirty days in the county. There is no loss of residence for soldiers or others traveling on public business, but no residency is gained by military personnel stationed in the state, by students, or by residents in almshouses or other institutions.

1894 Michigan terminates declarant alien voting.

New York requires the voter to have been a citizen for ninety days.

California requires the voter to have resided for one year in the state and thirty days in the election precinct. There is no loss of residence for soldiers or others traveling on public business, but no residency is gained by military personnel stationed in the state, by students, or by residents of almshouses or other institutions.

Montana terminates declarant alien voting.

1895 South Carolina institutes a poll tax. If registering for the first time after January 1, 1898, all property taxes collectible during the previous year must be paid and proof of payment is required. Until January 1, 1898, the voter must be able to read any section of the state constitution submitted by the registration officer, or understand and explain it when read by registration officer. After January 1, 1898, the voter must be able to read and write any section of the state constitution submitted to him by the registration officer. There is a property/taxpaying alternative to the literacy test if all taxes collectible during previous year on property assessed at $300 or more were paid. The voter must have resided two years in the state, one year in the county, and four months in polling district; six months in the state for ministers and public school teachers. There is no loss of residence for soldiers or others traveling on public business, but no residency is gained by military personnel stationed in the state or by students.

Florida terminates declarant alien voting.

Wyoming terminates declarant alien voting.

1896 Idaho fully enfranchises women.

Utah becomes a state. Women are fully enfranchised. Also, "Except in elections levying a special tax or creating indebtedness, no property qualification shall be required for any person to vote or hold office." [6] The voter must have been a U.S. citizen for ninety days, and must have resided one year in the state or territory, four months in the county, and sixty days in the precinct.

Rhode Island exempts property owners from its registration requirement.

Texas declarant aliens must have been declarant not less than six months prior to voting date.

New York declares that any voter who has made an oath of illiteracy shall be assisted in filling out his ballot.

Ohio restricts the acceptable reasons for voter assistance to physical infirmity only.

Washington requires the voter to be able to read and speak English.

1897   Delaware 1831 tax requirement is repealed. Also, the voter must be able to read the Constitution and write his name if becoming eligible to vote after January 1, 1900. Those who cannot read or write due to physical disability are exempted. The voter must have resided for one year in the state, three months in the county, and thirty days in the election district. No residency is gained by military personnel stationed in the state.

1898   *Williams v. Mississippi,* 170 U.S. 213 (1898). Supreme Court upholds literacy tests and poll taxes paid retroactively from one's twenty-first birthday as prerequisites for voter registration. Because the provisions are not discriminatory on their face, the Court upholds them, although in practice the provisions prevent African Americans and poor whites from both voting and serving on juries.

Louisiana requires the voter, if younger than sixty, to have paid a poll tax of $1 per annum for two years. Declarant alien voting is terminated. The voter must demonstrate the ability to read or write in English or mother tongue. Exempted from this requirement are those who could vote on or before January 1, 1867, and their sons and grandsons; foreign-born males naturalized prior to January 1, 1898, if registered prior to September 1, 1898, and if a resident for five years preceding registration; and owners of property worth $300 on which all taxes were paid. The voter must have resided two years in the state, one year in the parish, and six months in the district. There is no loss of residence for soldiers or others traveling on public business, but no residency is gained by military personnel stationed in the state or by students.

Wisconsin requires the voter to have resided one year in the state and ten days in the election district.

1899   North Dakota constitutionally declares "the legislature shall by law establish an educational test as a qualification," but the legislature declines to do so.[7]

1901   Alabama institutes a poll tax of $1.50 for those between the ages of twenty-one and forty-five; the legislature is constitutionally authorized to increase maximum age to sixty, at most. Declarant alien voting is terminated. After January 1, 1903, the voter must be able to "read or write any article of the Constitution of the United States in the English Language."[8] The voter is exempt from literacy requirement if unable to read or write due to physical disability. The voter is exempt from literacy requirement if owning forty acres of land or real estate assessed at $300. After January 1, 1903, if the voter is using the property alternative to the literacy requirement, all taxes must be paid on that property. The voter must have resided for two years in the state, one year in the county, and three months in the precinct or ward. No residency is gained by military personnel stationed in the state. The residency requirement, until December 20, 1902, is not applicable to veterans, their descendants, and "all persons who are of good character and who understand the duties and obligations of citizenship under a republican form of government."[9] After January 1, 1903, the residency requirement is not applied to those who meet literacy requirements or are owners of land worth $300.

1902   New Hampshire excludes from voting those who are excused from paying taxes at their own request. The voter must be able to read the Constitution in English and to write. Those already enfranchised are exempted, along with those age sixty or more on January 1, 1903, and those with physical disabilities that prevent them from meeting the requirement.

Texas requires the voter to have paid poll tax and produced a receipt by February 1 of election year.

Virginia declares that through 1903, the voter must be able to read any section of the state constitution "and to give a reasonable explanation of the same; or, if unable to read such a section, able to understand and give a reasonable explanation thereof when read to him by the officers."[10] After 1904, the voter must apply for registration in own handwriting. War veterans and their descendants are exempted. Property is another alternative to the literacy requirements: the General Assembly may prescribe a property qualification not exceeding $250 for county, city, or town elections. If using property alternative to literacy requirement between 1902 and 1903, the voter must have paid "state taxes aggregating at least one dollar" on the property.[11] If registered after January 1, 1904, voter must have paid poll taxes for the three years preceding

1902 (cont.) registration at least six months prior to the election. Civil War veterans are exempted from the poll tax. The voter must have resided two years in the state, one year in the county, city, or town, and thirty days in the precinct. There is no loss of residence for soldiers or others traveling on public business, but no residency is gained by military personnel stationed in the state, by students, or by residents of almshouses or other institutions.

Colorado terminates declarant alien voting.

Connecticut naturalized citizens are required to present naturalization papers when voting. Also, the voter must "read at least three lines of the Constitution or of the statutes of this State, other than the title or enacting clause, in such manner as to show that he is not prompted nor reciting from memory." [12] No one will be held ineligible by reason of blindness or defective sight.

1903 Colorado requires the voter to have resided for one year in the state, ninety days in the county, thirty days in the city or town, and ten days in the ward or precinct. There is no loss of residence for soldiers or others traveling on public business, but no residency is gained by military personnel stationed in the state, by students, or by residents of almshouses or other institutions.

1904 *Pope v. Williams,* 193 U.S. 621 (1904). Supreme Court upholds Maryland's one-year residency requirement, confirming its previous doctrine that the qualifications for voting are the states' discretion, provided that they do not commit the forms of discrimination prohibited by the federal Constitution.

1907 Georgia requires the voter to have paid all taxes since the 1877 constitution, at least six months prior to election. Also, the voter must be able to read in English any paragraph of the state or U.S. Constitution and write the same in English. Exemptions include all veterans of all wars and their descendants; "all persons who are of good character, and understand the duties and obligations of citizenship under a republican form of government"; those who are prevented from reading and writing due to physical disability but can understand and give a reasonable interpretation of the state or U.S. Constitution; and owners of at least forty acres of land assessed for taxation at the value of $500. [13]

Oklahoma becomes a state. It enters the Union without any property or taxpaying requirements, except on certain types of local elections. The voter must be able to read and write any section of the state constitution. Those who were qualified as voters on January 1, 1866, and lineal descendants of such persons are exempted. The voter must have resided one year in the state, six months in the county, and thirty days in the precinct. No residency is gained by military personnel stationed in the state.

1908 Michigan requires the voter to have resided six months in the state and thirty days in the city or township. There is no loss of residence for soldiers or others traveling on public business, but no residency is gained by military personnel stationed in the state, by students, or by residents of almshouses or other institutions.

Wisconsin terminates declarant alien voting.

West Virginia requires naturalized citizens to present naturalization papers when voting.

1909 Montana requires naturalized citizens to present naturalization papers when voting.

Source: Adapted from Alexander Keyssar, *The Right to Vote: The Contested History of Democracy in the United States,* Revised Edition (New York: Basic Books, 2009), 334–355.

[1] As quoted in Keyssar, 348. For sources, see Keyssar 369–379.
[2] As quoted in Keyssar, 334. For sources, see Keyssar 369–379.
[3] As quoted in Keyssar, 341. For sources, see Keyssar 369–379.
[4] As quoted in Keyssar, 342. For sources, see Keyssar 369–379.
[5] As quoted in Keyssar, 348. For sources, see Keyssar 369–379.
[6] As quoted in Keyssar, 336. For sources, see Keyssar 369–379.
[7] As quoted in Keyssar, 344. For sources, see Keyssar 369–379.
[8] As quoted in Keyssar, 340. For sources, see Keyssar 369–379.
[9] As quoted in Keyssar, 346. For sources, see Keyssar 369–379.
[10] As quoted in Keyssar, 345. For sources, see Keyssar 369–379.
[11] As quoted in Keyssar, 335. For sources, see Keyssar 369–379.
[12] As quoted in Keyssar, 340. For sources, see Keyssar 369–379.
[13] As quoted in Keyssar, 341. For sources, see Keyssar 369–379.

National Count of Popular Vote for President, 1892–1908

YEAR	NAME	PARTY	TOTAL	PERCENTAGE[1]
1892	Grover Cleveland	Democratic	5,554,617	34.8%
	Benjamin Harrison	Republican	5,186.793	32.4%
	James Weaver	Populist	1,024,280	6.4%
	John Bidwell	Prohibition	270,979	1.7%
1896	William McKinley	Republican	7,105,144	40.2%
	William Bryan	Democratic	6,370,897	36.8%
	Other and write-ins		315,763	1.8%
1900	William McKinley	Republican	7,219,193	37.6%
	William Bryan	Democratic	6,357,698	33.1%
	John Woolley	Prohibition	210,864	1.1%
1904	Theodore Roosevelt	Republican	7,625,599	36.5%
	Alton Parker	Democratic	5,083,501	24.3%
	Eugene Debs	Socialist	402,490	1.9%
	Silas Swallow	Prohibition	258,596	1.2%
1908	William Taft	Republican	7,676,598	33.5%
	William Bryan	Democratic	6,406,874	28.0%
	Eugene Debs	Socialist	420,436	1.8%
	Eugene Chafin	Prohibition	253,428	1.1%

[1] The percentage figures in this chart are based on the votes cast divided by the eligible voting-age population at the time of the election.

States with Property and Taxpaying Requirements for Suffrage, 1890–1909

STATE	DATE OF STATEHOOD[1]	PROPERTY REQUIREMENT[2]	TAXPAYING REQUIREMENT[2]
ALABAMA		1875: Constitutional ban on education or property qualifications for suffrage	None
		1901: Exempt from literacy requirement if owning 40 acres of land or real estate assessed at $300	1901: Poll tax of $1.50 for those ages 21 to 45; legislature authorized to increase maximum age to "not more than 60 years." After January 1, 1903, if using property alternative to literacy requirement, paid all taxes on that property.
ARKANSAS		None	1893: Poll tax; must present receipt or other evidence that tax has been paid
DELAWARE		None	1897: 1831 tax requirement repealed
FLORIDA		None	1885: "The legislature shall have power to make the payment of the capitation tax a prerequisite for voting, and all such taxes received shall go into the school fund."
			1889: Poll tax of $1
GEORGIA			1868: Paid taxes required for year preceding election
		1907: Owners of at least 40 acres of land assessed for taxation at $500 exempt from literacy requirement	1907: Paid all taxes since the 1877 constitution at least 6 months prior to election
IDAHO	1890	1890: Constitutional ban on property qualifications for voting except in school elections, elections creating indebtedness, or irrigation district elections	None
LOUISIANA		1898: Owners of property worth $300 on which all taxes paid exempt from literacy requirement	1898: If younger than 60, paid poll tax of $1 per annum for two years. If using property alternative to literacy requirement, paid all taxes on that property.
MASSACHUSETTS		None	1881: Exemption from poll tax for Civil War veterans who were paupers
			1891: 1821 tax requirement repealed
MISSISSIPPI		None	1890: Paid all taxes for 2 preceding years by February 1 of the election year. Exemption for ministers with 6 months residence in district. Also, $2 poll tax, except for persons who are "deaf and dumb or blind, or who are maimed by loss of hand or foot; said tax to be a lien only upon taxable property."
MONTANA		None	1889 : "Upon all questions submitted to the vote of the taxpayers of the State, or any political division thereof, women who are taxpayers and possessed of the qualifications for the right of suffrage required by men in this Constitution equally, with men have the right to vote."

States with Property and Taxpaying Requirements for Suffrage, 1890–1909 (continued)

States with Property and Taxpaying Requirements for Suffrage, 1890–1909 *(continued)*

STATE	DATE OF STATEHOOD[1]	PROPERTY REQUIREMENT[2]	TAXPAYING REQUIREMENT[2]
NEVADA		None	1865: Every male inhabitant between ages 21 and 60 must pay poll tax of $4 unless exempted by law
NEW HAMPSHIRE		None	1902: Excludes persons excused from paying taxes at their own request
NORTH CAROLINA		None	1876: Poll tax
OKLAHOMA	1907	None	1907: Taxpayers only may vote to authorize incurring of debts by city or town
PENNSYLVANIA		None	1873: Paid state or county tax at least 1 month before the election
RHODE ISLAND		1888: Property requirement for state elections repealed	1888: Registry tax of $1 or other tax must be paid
		1896: Property owners exempt from registration requirement	None
SOUTH CAROLINA		1895: If registered after January 1, 1898, property/taxpaying alternative to literacy test: paid all taxes collectible during previous year on property assessed at $300 or more.	1895: Poll tax; if registering for the first time after January 1, 1898, paid all property taxes collectible during the previous year. Proof of payment required. In addition, property/taxpaying alternative to literacy test: see 1895 property requirement.
TENNESSEE		None	1870: Poll tax; proof of payment required
TEXAS		None	1883: Poll tax of $1
			1902: Paid poll tax and produced receipt by February 1 of election year
UTAH	1896	1896: "Except in elections levying a special tax or creating indebtedness, no property qualification shall be required for any person to vote or hold office."	None
VIRGINIA			1876: Paid the capitation tax required by law for year preceding election
		1902: In 1902 and 1903 a property alternative to literacy requirement. General Assembly may prescribe property qualification not exceeding $250 for county, city, or town elections.	1902: If using property alternative to literacy requirement between 1902 and 1903, paid "state taxes aggregating at least one dollar" on the property. If registered after January 1, 1904, paid poll taxes for the 3 years preceding registration at least 6 months prior to the election. Exemption for Civil War veterans.
WYOMING	1890	None	None

Source: Alexander Keyssar, *The Right to Vote: The Contested History of Democracy in the United States,* Revised Edition (New York: Basic Books, 2009), 334–336. Adapted from Keyssar's tables, which extend from 1870 to 1920. Sources of quotations are found on pp. 369–379. Table includes only restrictions that affected statewide elections.

[1] For states whose date of statehood falls within the time period 1890–1909

[2] Dates listed are for the year that the property or tax requirement went into effect. All listed requirements continue into the 1890–1909 date range of this table.

States with Special Provisions Affecting Aliens and Immigrants, 1890–1909

STATE	DECLARANT ALIENS PERMITTED TO VOTE[1]	TERMINATION OF DECLARANT ALIEN VOTING	NATURALIZED CITIZENS REQUIRED TO PRESENT NATURALIZATION PAPERS	WAITING PERIODS AND OTHER RESTRICTIONS
ALABAMA	1867	1901	—	—
ARKANSAS	1868	—	—	—
CALIFORNIA	—	—	1872	1879: Naturalization 90 days prior to election
COLORADO	1876	1902	1891: If challenged	1876: Aliens must have declared intention to be citizen 4 months prior to election
CONNECTICUT	—	—	1902	—
FLORIDA	1868	1895	1868	—
INDIANA	1851	—	—	—
KANSAS	1859	—	—	—
LOUISIANA	1879	1898	—	—
MASSACHUSETTS	—	—	1855	—
MICHIGAN	1850	1894	—	1850: Aliens must have declared intention to be citizen 6 months prior to election
MINNESOTA	—	—	—	1857: U.S. citizen for 3 months
MISSOURI	1870	—	1883	1870: Aliens must have declared intention to be citizen "not less than one year nor more than five years before he offers to vote"
MONTANA	1889: For 5 years after adoption of state constitution	1894	1909	—
NEBRASKA	1867	—	—	1875: Aliens must have declared intention to be citizen at least 30 days prior to election
NEW YORK	—	—	1866	1874: Citizen for 20 days 1894: Citizen for 90 days
NORTH DAKOTA	1889	—	—	1889: Aliens must have declared intention to be citizen at least 1 year and not more than 6 years prior to election
OHIO	—	—	1857	—

States with Special Provisions Affecting Aliens and Immigrants, 1890–1909 (continued)

STATE	DECLARANT ALIENS PERMITTED TO VOTE[1]	TERMINATION OF DECLARANT ALIEN VOTING	NATURALIZED CITIZENS REQUIRED TO PRESENT NATURALIZATION PAPERS	WAITING PERIODS AND OTHER RESTRICTIONS
OREGON	1859	—	—	1859: Aliens must have declared intention to be citizen 1 year preceding election
PENNSYLVANIA	—	—	—	1873: U.S. citizen for 1 month
SOUTH DAKOTA	1889	—	—	—
TEXAS	1869	—	—	1896: Aliens must have declared intention to be citizen not less than 6 months prior to election.
UTAH	—	—	—	1896: U.S. citizen for 90 days
WEST VIRGINIA	—	—	1908	—
WISCONSIN	1848	1908	—	—
WYOMING	1890: Provides for expiration of alien voting in 1895	1895	—	—

Key: — indicates no requirement at that time
       * indicates that the previous requirement remained in effect

Source: Alexander Keyssar, *The Right to Vote: The Contested History of Democracy in the United States,* Revised Edition (New York: Basic Books, 2009), 337–339. Adapted from Keyssar's table, which extends from 1870 to 1920. Sources of quotations are found on pp. 369–379.
[1] A declarant alien is a resident who has formally declared his intention to become a citizen.

States with Literacy Requirements for Suffrage, 1890–1909

STATE	LITERACY REQUIREMENTS[1]	EXEMPTIONS	ASSISTANCE TO ILLITERATE VOTERS
ALABAMA	1875: No education qualification for suffrage	—	—
	1901: After January 1, 1903, must be able to "read or write any article of the Constitution of the United States in the English Language."	1901: Those unable to read or write due to physical disability; owners of 40 acres of property or real estate assessed for taxation at $300	—
ARKANSAS	—	—	1891: Election judges may assist illiterate voters.
COLORADO	1876: "The General Assembly may prescribe, by law, an educational qualification for electors, but no such law shall take effect prior to" 1890.	—	—
		—	1891: Assistance provided for any voter who declares under oath that he cannot read or write. Interpreters provided for those who cannot speak or understand English.
CONNECTICUT	1855: Must be able to read any article of the Constitution or any section of the state statutes	1855: Those who could vote before 1855	—
	1902: Must "read at least three lines of the Constitution or of the statutes of this State, other than the title or enacting clause, in such manner as to show that he is not prompted nor reciting from memory."	1902: No one will be held ineligible by reason of blindness or defective sight	—
DELAWARE	1897: Must be able to read Constitution and write name if becoming eligible to vote after January 1, 1900.	1897: Those who cannot read or write due to physical disability	—
FLORIDA	—	—	—
GEORGIA	1907: Must be able to read in English any paragraph of state or U.S. Constitution and write the same in English	1907: All veterans of all wars and their descendants; "all persons who are of good character, and understand the duties and obligations of citizenship under a republican form of government"; those who are prevented from reading and writing due to physical disability but can understand and give a reasonable interpretation of state or U.S. Constitution; owners of at least 40 acres of land assessed for taxation at the value of $500.	—

States with Literacy Requirements for Suffrage, 1890–1909 (continued)

States with Literacy Requirements for Suffrage, 1890–1909 (continued)

STATE	LITERACY REQUIREMENTS[1]	EXEMPTIONS	ASSISTANCE TO ILLITERATE VOTERS
ILLINOIS	—	—	1891: Any voter who declares under oath that he cannot read the English language shall be assisted in marking his ballot.
KENTUCKY	—	—	1890: The legislature shall "provide that persons illiterate, blind, or in any way disabled, may have their ballots marked as herein required."
LOUISIANA	1898: Must demonstrate ability to read or write in English or mother tongue	1898: Owners of property worth $300 on which all taxes were paid; those who could vote on or before January 1, 1867, and their sons and grandsons; foreign-born males naturalized prior to January 1, 1898, if registered prior to September 1, 1898, and if resident for five years preceding registration.	—
MAINE	1893: Must be able to read the Constitution in English and write his name	1893: Those prevented from reading or writing by physical infirmities; those 60 years or older at time of amendment	—
MASSACHUSETTS	1857: Must be able to read the Constitution in English and write his name.	1857: Those with physical disabilities; also, "any person who now has the right to vote," and those "who shall be 60 years of age or upwards at the time this Amendment shall take effect.	—
	1892: Must be able to read the state constitution in English and write his name	1892: "Those who cannot read or write because of physical disability or … those who had the right to vote on May 1, 1857."	
MISSISSIPPI	1890: "On or after the first day of January, AD, 1892, every elector shall … be able to read any section of the Constitution of this State; or he shall be able to understand the same when read to him, or give a reasonable interpretation thereof."	—	—
NEW HAMPSHIRE	1902: Must be able to read the Constitution in English and to write	1902: Those currently enfranchised; those age 60 or more on January 1, 1903, and those with physical disabilities that prevent them from meeting requirement.	—
NEW YORK	—	—	1896: Any voter who has made an oath of illiteracy shall be assisted in filling his ballot

States with Literacy Requirements for Suffrage, 1890–1909 *(continued)*

STATE	LITERACY REQUIREMENTS[1]	EXEMPTIONS	ASSISTANCE TO ILLITERATE VOTERS
NORTH CAROLINA	1876: Must be able to read and write any section of the Constitution in English	1876: Those who were qualified voters on January 1, 1867, and lineal descendants of such persons.	—
NORTH DAKOTA	1899: "The legislature shall by law establish an educational test as a qualification." Legislature declined to do so.	—	
OHIO	—	—	1891: Assistance may be given to voters for any reason 1896: Assistance may be given only for reasons of physical infirmity
OKLAHOMA	1907: Must be able to read and write any section of the state constitution	1907: Those who were qualified voters on January 1, 1866, and lineal descendants of such persons	—
SOUTH CAROLINA	1895: Until January 1, 1898, must be able to read any section of the state constitution submitted by the registration officer, or understand and explain it when read by registration officer. After January 1, 1898, must be able to read and write any section of this constitution submitted to him by the registration officer.	1895: Those who have paid all taxes during the previous year on property assessed at $300 or more	—
VIRGINIA	1902: In 1902 and 1903, must be able to read any section of the state constitution "and to give a reasonable explanation of the same; or, if unable to read such a section, able to understand and give a reasonable explanation thereof when read to him by the officers." After 1904, must apply for registration in own handwriting.	1902: Property owners; wartime veterans and their descendants	—
WASHINGTON	1896: Must be able to read and speak English	—	—
WYOMING	1890: Must be able to read state constitution	1890: Those prevented from reading by physical disability	—

Key: — indicates no requirement at that time
    * indicates that the previous requirement remained in effect

Source: Alexander Keyssar, *The Right to Vote: The Contested History of Democracy in the United States,* Revised Edition (New York: Basic Books, 2009), 340–345. Adapted from Keyssar's table, which extends from 1870 to 1924. Sources of quotations are found on pp. 369–379.

[1] Dates listed are for the year that the literacy requirement went into effect. All listed requirements continue into the 1890–1909 date range of this table.

States with Residency Requirements for Suffrage, 1890–1909

STATE	LENGTH OF RESIDENCE REQUIRED[1]	NO RESIDENCY GAINED BY MILITARY PERSONNEL STATIONED IN TOWNS AND CITIES	STUDENTS	RESIDENCE IN ALMSHOUSE OR OTHER INSTITUTION	NO LOSS OF RESIDENCE FOR SOLDIERS OR OTHERS TRAVELING ON PUBLIC BUSINESS	OTHER
ALABAMA	1875: 1 year in state, 3 months in county, 30 days in precinct, district, or ward	1867	—	—	—	1875: General Assembly may change residency length in any town with more than 5,000 inhabitants.
	1901: 2 years in state, 1 year in county, 3 months in precinct or ward	*	—	—	—	1901: Residency requirement, until December 20, 1902, not applicable to veterans, their decendants, and "all persons who are of good character and who understand the duties and obligations of citizenship under a republican form of government." After January 1, 1903, not applied to those who meet literacy requirements or are owners of land worth $300.
ARKANSAS	1874: 12 months in state, 6 months in county, 1 month in precinct or ward	1868	—	—	—	—
CALIFORNIA	1879: 1 year in state, 90 days in county, 30 days in election district	1850	1850	1850	1850	—
	1894: 1 year in state, 30 days in election precinct	*	*	*	*	—
COLORADO	1881: 6 months in state, 90 days in county, 30 days in city or town, 10 days in ward or precinct	1876	1876	1876	1876	—
	1903: 1 year in state, 90 days in county, 30 days in city or town, 10 days in ward or precinct	*	*	*	*	—
CONNECTICUT	1845: 1 year in state, 6 months in county	—	—	—	—	—
DELAWARE	1831: 1 year in state, 1 month in county	1831	—	—	—	—
	1897: 1 year in state, 3 months in county, 30 days in election district	*	—	—	—	—
FLORIDA	1868: 1 year in state, 6 months in county	1868	—	—	—	—

States with Residency Requirements for Suffrage, 1890–1909 *(continued)*

STATE	LENGTH OF RESIDENCE REQUIRED[1]	NO RESIDENCY GAINED BY MILITARY PERSONNEL STATIONED IN TOWNS AND CITIES	STUDENTS	RESIDENCE IN ALMSHOUSE OR OTHER INSTITUTION	NO LOSS OF RESIDENCE FOR SOLDIERS OR OTHERS TRAVELING ON PUBLIC BUSINESS	OTHER
GEORGIA	1877: 1 year in state, 6 months in county	1868	—	—	—	—
IDAHO	1890: 6 months in state, 30 days in county	1890	1890	1890	1890	—
ILLINOIS	1870: 1 year in state, 90 days in county, 30 days in election district	1870	—	1877	—	—
INDIANA	1851: 6 months in state, 60 days in township, 30 days in ward or precinct; for declarants, 1 year in U.S.	1851	—	—	1851	—
IOWA	1857: 6 months in state, 60 days in county	1857	—	—	—	—
KANSAS	1861: 6 months in state, 30 days in township or ward	1861	1861	1861	1861	—
KENTUCKY	1850: 2 years in state or 1 year in county, town, or city, 60 days in precinct	—	—	—	1850	—
	1891: 1 year in state, 6 months in county, 60 days in precinct	1891	—	—	1891: No provision	—
LOUISIANA	1879: 1 year in state, 6 months in parish, 30 days in ward or precinct	1879	1879	—	1879	—
	1898: 2 years in state, 1 year in parish, 6 months in precinct	—	—	—	—	—
MAINE	1820: 3 months in state	1820	1820	—	1864	—
MARYLAND	1867: 1 year in state, 6 months in legislative district of Baltimore city or of the county	—	—	—	—	—
MASSACHUSETTS	1821: 1 year in state, 6 months in town or district	—	—	—	—	—
MICHIGAN	1850: 6 months in state, 20 days in township or ward; for declarants, 2 years and 6 months in state prior to November 8, 1894	—	—	—	—	—
	1908: 6 months in state, 30 days in city or township	1908	1908	1908	1908	1908

States with Residency Requirements for Suffrage, 1890–1909 (continued)

States with Residency Requirements for Suffrage, 1890–1909 *(continued)*

STATE	LENGTH OF RESIDENCE REQUIRED[1]	NO RESIDENCY GAINED BY MILITARY PERSONNEL STATIONED IN TOWNS AND CITIES	STUDENTS	RESIDENCE IN ALMSHOUSE OR OTHER INSTITUTION	NO LOSS OF RESIDENCE FOR SOLDIERS OR OTHERS TRAVELING ON PUBLIC BUSINESS	OTHER
MINNESOTA	1874: 3 months in ward	1857	—	—	—	1893: No residence for voting purposes can be gained by any "person employed temporarily" cutting timber "or in the construction or repair of any railroad, canal, municipal or other work of public nature."
MISSISSIPPI	1890: 2 years in state, 1 year in election district or incorporated city or town	—	—	—	—	—
MISSOURI	1883: 1 year in state, 60 days in city, 20 days in precinct	1875	1875	1875	1875	—
MONTANA	1889: 6 months in state, and 30 days in county	1889	1889	1889	1889	—
	1893: 1 year in state, and 30 days in county	—	—	—	—	—
NEBRASKA	1869: 40 days in county	1875	—	—	—	—
NEVADA	1864: 6 months in state, 30 days in district or county	1864	1864	1864	1864	—
NEW HAMPSHIRE	1860: 6 months within town	—	—	—	—	—
NEW JERSEY	1844: 1 year in state, 5 months in county	1844	—	—	1844	—
NEW YORK	1874: 1 year in state, 4 months in county, 30 days in election district	—	—	—	1874	—
NORTH CAROLINA	1876: 2 years in state, 6 months in county, 4 months in precinct, ward, or other election district	—	—	—	—	—
NORTH DAKOTA	1889: 1 year in state, 6 months in county, 90 days in precinct	1889	—	—	1889	—
OHIO	1857: 1 year in state, 30 days in county, 20 days in township, village, or ward of city or village	—	—	—	—	—
OKLAHOMA	1907: 1 year in state, 6 months in county, 30 days in precinct	1907	—	—	—	—
OREGON	1859: 6 months in state	1859	1859	1859	1859	—

States with Residency Requirements for Suffrage, 1890–1909 *(continued)*

STATE	LENGTH OF RESIDENCE REQUIRED[1]	NO RESIDENCY GAINED BY MILITARY PERSONNEL STATIONED IN TOWNS AND CITIES	STUDENTS	RESIDENCE IN ALMSHOUSE OR OTHER INSTITUTION	NO LOSS OF RESIDENCE FOR SOLDIERS OR OTHERS TRAVELING ON PUBLIC BUSINESS	OTHER
PENNSYLVANIA	1873: 1 year in state, 2 months in election district; 6 months in state for previously qualified elector or native-born state citizen, returning after absence	1873	1873	1873	1873	—
RHODE ISLAND	1888: 2 years in state, 6 months in town and city	—	—	—	1864	—
SOUTH CAROLINA	1895: 2 years in state, 1 year in county, 4 months in polling district; 6 months in state for ministers and public school teachers	1895	1895	—	1895	—
SOUTH DAKOTA	1889: 1 year in U.S., 6 months in state, 30 days in county, 10 days in election precinct	1889	—	—	1889	—
TENNESSEE	1870: 12 months in state, 6 months in county	—	—	—	—	—
TEXAS	1876: 1 year in state, 6 months in county	1876	—	—	—	—
UTAH	1896: 1 year in state, 4 months in county, 60 days in precinct	—	—	—	—	—
VERMONT	1793: 1 year in state	—	—	—	—	—
VIRGINIA	1870: 12 months in state, 3 months in county, city, or town	1870	—	—	—	—
	1902: 2 years in state, 1 year in county, city, or town, 30 days in precinct	*	1902	1902	1902	—
WASHINGTON	1889: 1 year in state, 90 days in county, 30 days in city, town, ward, or precinct	1889	1889	—	1889	—
WEST VIRGINIA	1872: 1 year in state, 60 days in county	1872	—	—	—	—
WISCONSIN	1898: 1 year in state, 10 days in election district	—	—	—	—	—
WYOMING	1890: 1 year in state, 60 days in county	1890	—	—	—	—

Key: — indicates no requirement at that time
  * indicates that the previous requirement remained in effect

Source: Alexander Keyssar, *The Right to Vote: The Contested History of Democracy in the United States,* Revised Edition (New York: Basic Books, 2000), 346–355. Adapted from Keyssar's table, which extends from 1870 to 1923. Sources of quotations are found on pp. 369–379.

[1] Dates listed are for the year that the residency requirement went into effect. All listed requirements continue into the 1890–1909 date range of this table.

States Fully Enfranchising Women Prior to 1910

STATE	DATE IN EFFECT
Wyoming	1890
Colorado	1893
Utah	1896
Idaho	1896

Source: Adapted from Alexander Keyssar, *The Right to Vote: The Contested History of Democracy in the United States,* Revised Edition (New York: Basic Books, 2009), 368.

United States Presidential Turnout, Election Years 1892–1908

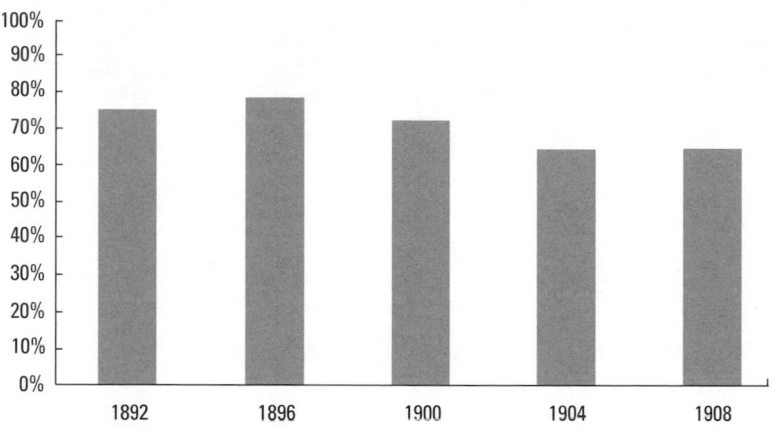

YEAR	VOTING-AGE POPULATION	TOTAL	%
1892	15,967,000	12,056,097	75.5%
1896	17,671,000	13,935,738	78.8%
1900	19,231,000	13,970,470	72.6%
1904	20,004,000	13,518,964	64.7%
1908	22,901,000	14,882,734	65.0%

Partisan Turnout Presidential Years Based on Aggregate House Turnout, Election Years 1892–1908

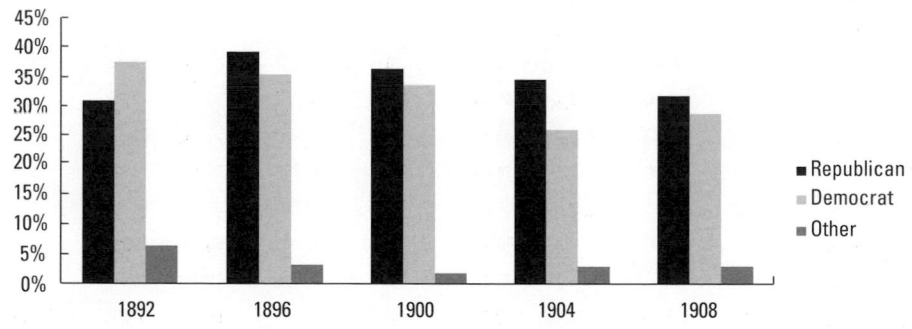

■ Republican
■ Democrat
■ Other

YEAR	VOTING-AGE POPULATION	REPUBLICAN TURNOUT	%	DEMOCRAT TURNOUT	%	OTHER TURNOUT	%
1892	15,967,000	4,902,506	30.7%	5,946,971	37.2%	998,532	6.3%
1896	17,671,000	6,893,934	39.0%	6,218,664	35.2%	544,431	3.1%
1900	19,231,000	6,948,459	36.1%	6,434,532	33.5%	326,304	1.7%
1904	20,884,000	7,172,968	34.3%	5,400,170	25.9%	589,846	2.8%
1908	22,901,000	7,237,227	31.6%	6,551,965	28.6%	656,310	2.9%

UNITED STATES PRESIDENTIAL GENERAL ELECTIONS

Election Years 1892–1908

State	1892			1896				1900				1904				1908			
	Voting-age population	Turnout	%	Voting-age population	Turnout	%	Difference from 1892*	Voting-age population	Turnout	%	Difference from 1892	Voting-age population	Turnout	%	Difference from 1892	Voting-age population	Turnout	%	Difference from 1892
ALABAMA	343,000	232,543	67.8%	379,000	194,580	51.3%	-16.5	415,000	159,692	38.5%	-29.3	454,000	108,785	24.0%	-43.8	494,000	105,152	21.3%	-46.5
ALASKA																			
ARIZONA																			
ARKANSAS	268,000	148,117	55.3%	291,000	149,396	51.3%	-3.9	314,000	127,966	40.8%	-14.5	348,000	116,328	33.4%	-21.8	380,000	151,845	40.0%	-15.3
CALIFORNIA	355,000	269,585	75.9%	397,000	298,598	75.2%	-0.7	444,000	302,318	68.1%	-7.8	547,000	331,768	60.7%	-15.3	650,000	386,625	59.5%	-16.5
COLORADO	153,000	93,881	61.4%	273,000	189,539	69.4%	8.1	296,000	220,895	74.6%	13.3	354,000	243,667	68.8%	7.5	413,000	263,858	63.9%	2.5
CONNECTICUT	195,000	164,593	84.4%	211,000	174,394	82.7%	-1.8	227,000	180,195	79.4%	-5.0	240,000	191,136	79.6%	-4.8	251,000	189,903	75.7%	-8.7
DELAWARE	47,000	37,235	79.2%	49,000	38,456	78.5%	-0.7	51,000	41,989	82.3%	3.1	54,000	43,856	81.2%	2.0	56,000	48,007	85.7%	6.5
DISTRICT OF COLUMBIA																			
FLORIDA	102,000	35,471	34.8%	119,000	46,488	39.1%	4.3	136,000	39,649	29.2%	-5.6	164,000	38,705	23.6%	-11.2	192,000	49,360	25.7%	-9.1
GEORGIA	420,000	223,126	53.1%	461,000	162,480	35.2%	-17.9	503,000	121,410	24.1%	-29.0	551,000	130,986	23.8%	-29.4	599,000	132,504	22.1%	-31.0
HAWAII																			
IDAHO	47,000	19,407	41.3%	62,000	29,631	47.8%	6.5	105,000	57,984	55.2%	13.9	129,000	72,577	56.3%	15.0	152,000	97,293	64.0%	22.7
ILLINOIS	1,006,000	873,667	86.8%	1,140,000	1,090,766	95.7%	8.8	1,268,000	1,131,898	89.3%	2.4	1,348,000	1,076,495	79.9%	-7.0	1,428,000	1,155,254	80.9%	-5.9
INDIANA	607,000	553,613	91.2%	656,000	637,089	97.1%	5.9	705,000	664,094	94.2%	3.0	741,000	682,206	92.1%	0.9	777,000	721,117	92.8%	1.6
IOWA	501,000	443,159	88.5%	551,000	521,550	94.7%	6.2	596,000	530,345	89.0%	0.5	600,000	485,703	81.0%	-7.5	606,000	494,770	81.6%	-6.8
KANSAS	373,000	323,591	86.8%	385,000	336,085	87.3%	0.5	399,000	353,766	88.7%	1.9	433,000	329,047	76.0%	-10.8	468,000	376,043	80.4%	-6.4
KENTUCKY	465,000	340,864	73.3%	504,000	445,928	88.5%	15.2	540,000	468,265	86.7%	13.4	564,000	435,946	77.3%	4.0	588,000	490,719	83.5%	10.2
LOUISIANA	258,000	114,889	44.5%	287,000	101,046	35.2%	-9.3	317,000	67,906	21.4%	-23.1	351,000	53,908	15.4%	-29.2	386,000	75,117	19.5%	-25.1
MAINE	184,000	116,451	63.3%	189,000	118,419	62.7%	-0.6	192,000	105,693	55.0%	-8.2	197,000	97,023	49.3%	-14.0	201,000	106,335	52.9%	-10.4
MARYLAND	263,000	213,275	81.1%	287,000	250,249	87.2%	6.1	310,000	264,386	85.3%	4.2	325,000	224,229	69.0%	-12.1	339,000	238,531	70.4%	-10.7
MASSACHUSETTS	550,000	391,028	71.1%	602,000	401,269	66.7%	-4.4	652,000	414,804	63.6%	-7.5	697,000	445,100	63.9%	-7.2	741,000	456,905	61.7%	-9.4
MICHIGAN	538,000	466,917	86.8%	577,000	545,583	94.6%	7.8	616,000	543,789	88.3%	1.5	667,000	520,443	78.0%	-8.8	718,000	538,124	74.9%	-11.8
MINNESOTA	352,000	267,841	76.1%	403,000	341,762	84.8%	8.7	452,000	316,311	70.0%	-6.1	482,000	292,860	60.8%	-15.3	513,000	330,254	64.4%	-11.7
MISSISSIPPI	288,000	52,519	18.2%	319,000	69,591	21.8%	3.6	350,000	59,055	16.9%	-1.4	381,000	58,721	15.4%	-2.8	413,000	66,904	16.2%	-2.0
MISSOURI	708,000	541,583	76.5%	772,000	674,032	87.3%	10.8	832,000	683,658	82.2%	5.7	873,000	643,861	73.8%	-2.7	913,000	715,841	78.4%	1.9
MONTANA	63,000	44,461	70.6%	77,000	53,330	69.3%	-1.3	86,000	63,856	74.3%	3.7	102,000	63,568	62.3%	-8.3	117,000	69,233	59.2%	-11.4
NEBRASKA	276,000	200,205	72.5%	277,000	223,181	80.6%	8.0	280,000	241,430	86.2%	13.7	300,000	225,732	75.2%	2.7	320,000	266,799	83.4%	10.8
NEVADA	15,000	10,826	72.2%	15,000	10,286	68.6%	-3.6	15,000	10,196	68.0%	-4.2	23,000	12,115	52.7%	-19.5	30,000	24,526	81.8%	9.6
NEW HAMPSHIRE	104,000	89,328	85.9%	107,000	83,670	78.2%	-7.7	110,000	92,364	84.0%	-1.9	111,000	90,151	81.2%	-4.7	111,000	89,595	80.7%	-5.2
NEW JERSEY	383,000	337,485	88.1%	428,000	371,014	86.7%	-1.4	472,000	401,050	85.0%	-3.1	524,000	432,247	82.5%	-5.6	575,000	467,111	81.2%	-6.9
NEW MEXICO																			
NEW YORK	1,580,000	1,336,793	84.6%	1,711,000	1,423,876	83.2%	-1.4	1,842,000	1,548,043	84.0%	-0.6	1,959,000	1,617,765	82.6%	-2.0	2,076,000	1,638,350	78.9%	-5.7

United States Presidential General Elections (continued)

Election Years 1892–1908 (continued)

State	1892			1896				1900				1904				1908			
	Voting-age population	Turnout	%	Voting-age population	Turnout	%	Difference from 1892	Voting-age population	Turnout	%	Difference from 1892	Voting-age population	Turnout	%	Difference from 1892	Voting-age population	Turnout	%	Difference from 1892
NORTH CAROLINA	360,000	280,270	77.9%	390,000	331,337	85.0%	7.1	420,000	292,518	69.6%	-8.2	456,000	207,818	45.6%	-32.3	491,000	252,554	51.4%	-26.4
NORTH DAKOTA	53,000	36,118	68.1%	68,000	47,391	69.7%	1.5	84,000	57,783	68.8%	0.6	109,000	70,014	64.2%	-3.9	133,000	94,524	71.1%	2.9
OHIO	998,000	850,164	85.2%	1,075,000	1,014,295	94.4%	9.2	1,151,000	1,040,073	90.4%	5.2	1,222,000	1,004,395	82.2%	-3.0	1,293,000	1,121,552	86.7%	1.6
OKLAHOMA																373,000	254,260	68.2%	
OREGON	103,000	78,378	76.1%	116,000	97,335	83.9%	7.8	132,000	83,251	63.1%	-13.0	174,000	89,656	51.5%	-24.6	216,000	110,539	51.2%	-24.9
PENNSYLVANIA	1,346,000	1,003,000	74.5%	1,461,000	1,194,355	81.7%	7.2	1,575,000	1,173,210	74.5%	0.0	1,678,000	1,236,738	73.7%	-0.8	1,780,000	1,267,450	71.2%	-3.3
RHODE ISLAND	82,000	53,196	64.9%	91,000	54,785	60.2%	-4.7	102,000	56,548	55.4%	-9.4	110,000	68,656	62.4%	-2.5	118,000	72,317	61.3%	-3.6
SOUTH CAROLINA	246,000	70,504	28.7%	265,000	68,938	26.0%	-2.6	285,000	50,698	17.8%	-10.9	306,000	55,890	18.3%	-10.4	326,000	66,379	20.4%	-8.3
SOUTH DAKOTA	92,000	70,160	76.3%	97,000	82,937	85.5%	9.2	104,000	96,169	92.5%	16.2	130,000	101,395	78.0%	1.7	155,000	114,775	74.0%	-2.2
TENNESSEE	419,000	265,732	63.4%	453,000	320,903	70.8%	7.4	486,000	273,860	56.3%	-7.1	513,000	242,750	47.3%	-16.1	538,000	257,180	47.8%	-15.6
TEXAS	554,000	410,860	74.2%	632,000	541,018	85.6%	11.4	714,000	424,334	59.4%	-14.7	810,000	233,609	28.8%	-45.3	907,000	292,913	32.3%	-41.9
UTAH				99,000	78,098	78.9%		112,000	93,071	83.1%	4.2	133,000	101,626	76.4%	-2.5	154,000	108,757	70.6%	-8.3
VERMONT	92,000	55,793	60.6%	95,000	63,568	66.9%	6.3	98,000	56,212	57.4%	3.3	99,000	51,888	52.4%	-0.2	100,000	52,680	52.7%	-8.0
VIRGINIA	390,000	292,238	74.9%	418,000	294,674	70.5%	-4.4	446,000	264,208	59.2%	-15.7	476,000	130,410	27.4%	-47.5	505,000	137,065	27.1%	-47.8
WASHINGTON	130,000	87,968	67.7%	149,000	93,583	62.8%	-4.9	174,000	107,523	61.8%	-5.9	254,000	145,151	57.1%	-10.5	335,000	183,570	54.8%	-12.9
WEST VIRGINIA	193,000	171,079	88.6%	219,000	201,757	92.1%	3.5	245,000	220,796	90.1%	1.5	273,000	239,986	87.9%	-0.7	301,000	258,098	85.7%	-2.9
WISCONSIN	430,000	371,481	86.4%	473,000	447,409	94.6%	8.2	516,000	442,501	85.8%	-0.6	553,000	443,440	80.2%	-6.2	591,000	454,438	76.9%	-9.5
WYOMING	35,000	16,703	47.7%	41,000	21,067	51.4%	3.7	62,000	24,708	39.9%	-7.9	69,000	30,614	44.4%	-3.4	78,000	37,608	48.2%	0.5
Total	15,967,000	12,056,097	75.5%	17,671,000	13,935,738	78.9%	3.4	19,231,000	13,970,470	72.6%	-2.9	20,884,000	13,518,964	64.7%	-10.8	22,901,000	14,882,734	65.0%	-10.5

*Percentage point difference between turnout in current year and initial year listed in chart. If data do not appear for a state in the initial year listed, the difference is calculated from the first year in which data do appear for that state.

UNITED STATES PRESIDENTIAL GENERAL ELECTIONS

Republican Turnout for Election Years 1892–1908

State	1892 Voting-age population	1892 Turnout	1892 %	1896 Voting-age population	1896 Turnout	1896 %	1896 Difference from 1892*	1900 Voting-age population	1900 Turnout	1900 %	1900 Difference from 1892	1904 Voting-age population	1904 Turnout	1904 %	1904 Difference from 1892	1908 Voting-age population	1908 Turnout	1908 %	1908 Difference from 1892
ALABAMA	343,000	9,184	2.7%	379,000	55,673	14.7%	12.0	415,000	55,612	13.4%	10.7	454,000	22,472	4.9%	2.3	494,000	25,561	5.2%	2.5
ALASKA																			
ARIZONA																			
ARKANSAS	268,000	47,072	17.6%	291,000	37,512	12.9%	-4.7	314,000	44,800	14.3%	-3.3	348,000	46,760	13.4%	-4.1	380,000	56,684	14.9%	-2.6
CALIFORNIA	355,000	118,027	33.2%	397,000	146,756	37.0%	3.7	444,000	164,755	37.1%	3.9	547,000	205,226	37.5%	4.3	650,000	214,398	33.0%	-0.3
COLORADO	153,000	38,620	25.2%	273,000	26,271	9.6%	-15.6	296,000	92,701	31.3%	6.1	354,000	134,661	38.0%	12.8	413,000	123,693	29.9%	4.7
CONNECTICUT	195,000	77,030	39.5%	211,000	110,285	52.3%	12.8	227,000	102,572	45.2%	5.7	240,000	111,089	46.3%	6.8	251,000	112,815	44.9%	5.4
DELAWARE	47,000	18,077	38.5%	49,000	20,450	41.7%	3.3	51,000	22,535	44.2%	5.7	54,000	23,705	43.9%	5.4	56,000	25,014	44.7%	6.2
DISTRICT OF COLUMBIA																			
FLORIDA				119,000	11,298	9.5%		136,000	7,355	5.4%	-4.1	164,000	8,314	5.1%	-4.4	192,000	10,654	5.5%	-3.9
GEORGIA	420,000	48,408	11.5%	461,000	59,395	12.9%	1.4	503,000	34,260	6.8%	-4.7	551,000	24,004	4.4%	-7.2	599,000	41,355	6.9%	-4.6
HAWAII																			
IDAHO	47,000	8,599	18.3%	62,000	6,324	10.2%	-8.1	105,000	27,198	25.9%	7.6	129,000	47,783	37.0%	18.7	152,000	52,621	34.6%	16.3
ILLINOIS	1,006,000	399,308	39.7%	1,140,000	607,130	53.3%	13.6	1,268,000	597,985	47.2%	7.5	1,348,000	632,645	46.9%	7.2	1,428,000	629,932	44.1%	4.4
INDIANA	607,000	255,615	42.1%	656,000	323,754	49.4%	7.2	705,000	336,063	47.7%	5.6	741,000	368,289	49.7%	7.6	777,000	348,993	44.9%	2.8
IOWA	501,000	219,795	43.9%	551,000	289,293	52.5%	8.6	596,000	307,799	51.6%	7.8	600,000	307,907	51.3%	7.4	606,000	275,210	45.4%	1.5
KANSAS	373,000	156,134	41.9%	385,000	159,484	41.4%	-0.4	399,000	185,955	46.6%	4.7	433,000	213,455	49.3%	7.4	468,000	197,316	42.2%	0.3
KENTUCKY	465,000	135,462	29.1%	504,000	218,171	43.3%	14.2	540,000	227,132	42.1%	12.9	564,000	205,457	36.4%	7.3	588,000	235,711	40.1%	11.0
LOUISIANA	258,000	26,963	10.5%	287,000	22,037	7.7%	-2.8	317,000	14,234	4.5%	-6.0	351,000	5,205	1.5%	-9.0	386,000	8,958	2.3%	-8.1
MAINE	184,000	62,936	34.2%	189,000	80,403	42.5%	8.3	192,000	65,412	34.1%	-0.1	197,000	65,432	33.2%	-1.0	201,000	66,987	33.3%	-0.9
MARYLAND	263,000	92,736	35.3%	287,000	136,959	47.7%	12.5	310,000	136,151	43.9%	8.7	325,000	109,497	33.7%	-1.6	339,000	116,513	34.4%	-0.9
MASSACHUSETTS	550,000	202,814	36.9%	602,000	278,976	46.3%	9.5	652,000	238,866	36.6%	-0.2	697,000	257,813	37.0%	0.1	741,000	265,966	35.9%	-1.0
MICHIGAN	538,000	222,708	41.4%	577,000	293,336	50.8%	9.4	616,000	316,014	51.3%	9.9	667,000	361,863	54.3%	12.9	718,000	333,313	46.4%	5.0
MINNESOTA	352,000	122,736	34.9%	403,000	193,503	48.0%	13.1	452,000	190,461	42.1%	7.3	482,000	216,651	44.9%	10.1	513,000	195,843	38.2%	3.3
MISSISSIPPI	288,000	1,398	0.5%	319,000	4,819	1.5%	1.0	350,000	5,707	1.6%	1.1	381,000	3,280	0.9%	0.4	413,000	4,363	1.1%	0.6
MISSOURI	708,000	227,646	32.2%	772,000	304,940	39.5%	7.3	832,000	314,092	37.8%	5.6	873,000	321,449	36.8%	4.7	913,000	347,203	38.0%	5.9
MONTANA	63,000	18,871	30.0%	77,000	10,509	13.6%	-16.3	86,000	25,409	29.5%	-0.4	102,000	33,994	33.3%	3.4	117,000	32,471	27.8%	-2.2
NEBRASKA	276,000	87,213	31.6%	277,000	103,064	37.2%	5.6	280,000	121,835	43.5%	11.9	300,000	138,558	46.2%	14.6	320,000	126,997	39.7%	8.1
NEVADA	15,000	2,811	18.7%	15,000	1,938	12.9%	-5.8	15,000	3,849	25.7%	6.9	23,000	6,864	29.8%	11.1	30,000	10,775	35.9%	17.2
NEW HAMPSHIRE	104,000	45,658	43.9%	107,000	57,444	53.7%	9.8	110,000	54,799	49.8%	5.9	111,000	54,157	48.8%	4.9	111,000	53,144	47.9%	4.0
NEW JERSEY	383,000	156,059	40.7%	428,000	221,367	51.7%	11.0	472,000	221,707	47.0%	6.2	524,000	245,164	46.8%	6.0	575,000	265,298	46.1%	5.4
NEW MEXICO																			
NEW YORK	1,580,000	609,350	38.6%	1,711,000	819,838	47.9%	9.3	1,842,000	822,013	44.6%	6.1	1,959,000	859,533	43.9%	5.3	2,076,000	870,070	41.9%	3.3

United States Presidential General Elections *(continued)*

Republican Turnout for Election Years 1892–1908 *(continued)*

State	1892 Voting-age population	Turnout	%	1896 Voting-age population	Turnout	%	Difference from 1892	1900 Voting-age population	Turnout	%	Difference from 1892	1904 Voting-age population	Turnout	%	Difference from 1892	1908 Voting-age population	Turnout	%	Difference from 1892
NORTH CAROLINA	360,000	100,346	27.9%	390,000	155,122	39.8%	11.9	420,000	132,997	31.7%	3.8	456,000	82,442	18.1%	-9.8	491,000	114,887	23.4%	-4.5
NORTH DAKOTA	53,000	17,519	33.1%	68,000	26,335	38.7%	5.7	84,000	35,898	42.7%	9.7	109,000	52,595	48.3%	15.2	133,000	57,680	43.4%	10.3
OHIO	998,000	405,187	40.6%	1,075,000	525,991	48.9%	8.3	1,151,000	543,918	47.3%	6.7	1,222,000	600,095	49.1%	8.5	1,293,000	572,312	44.3%	3.7
OKLAHOMA																373,000	110,473	29.6%	
OREGON	103,000	35,002	34.0%	116,000	48,700	42.0%	8.0	132,000	46,172	35.0%	1.0	174,000	60,309	34.7%	0.7	216,000	62,454	28.9%	-5.1
PENNSYLVANIA	1,346,000	516,011	38.3%	1,461,000	728,300	49.8%	11.5	1,575,000	712,665	45.2%	0.9	1,078,000	840,949	50.1%	11.8	1,780,000	745,779	41.9%	3.6
RHODE ISLAND	82,000	26,975	32.9%	91,000	37,437	41.1%	8.2	102,000	33,784	33.1%	0.2	110,000	41,605	37.8%	4.9	118,000	43,942	37.2%	4.3
SOUTH CAROLINA	246,000	13,345	5.4%	265,000	9,313	3.5%	-1.9	285,000	3,525	1.2%	-4.2	306,000	2,570	0.8%	-4.6	326,000	3,945	1.2%	-4.2
SOUTH DAKOTA	92,000	34,714	37.7%	97,000	41,040	42.3%	4.6	104,000	54,574	52.5%	14.7	130,000	72,083	55.4%	17.7	155,000	67,536	43.6%	5.8
TENNESSEE	419,000	100,537	24.0%	453,000	148,683	32.8%	8.8	486,000	123,108	25.3%	1.3	513,000	105,363	20.5%	-3.5	538,000	117,977	21.9%	-2.1
TEXAS	554,000	70,982	12.8%	632,000	163,894	25.9%	13.1	714,000	131,174	18.4%	5.6	810,000	51,307	6.3%	-6.5	907,000	65,605	7.2%	-5.6
UTAH				99,000	13,491	13.6%		112,000	47,089	42.0%	28.4	133,000	62,446	47.0%	33.3	154,000	61,165	39.7%	26.1
VERMONT	92,000	37,992	41.3%	95,000	51,127	53.8%	12.5	98,000	42,569	43.4%	2.1	99,000	40,459	40.9%	-0.4	100,000	39,552	39.6%	-1.7
VIRGINIA	390,000	113,098	29.0%	418,000	135,379	32.4%	3.4	446,000	115,769	26.0%	-3.0	476,000	48,180	10.1%	-18.9	505,000	52,572	10.4%	-18.6
WASHINGTON	130,000	36,459	28.0%	149,000	39,153	26.3%	-1.8	174,000	57,455	33.0%	5.0	254,000	101,540	40.0%	11.9	335,000	106,062	31.7%	3.6
WEST VIRGINIA	193,000	80,292	41.6%	219,000	105,379	48.1%	6.5	245,000	119,829	48.9%	7.3	273,000	132,620	48.6%	7.0	301,000	137,869	45.8%	4.2
WISCONSIN	430,000	171,101	39.8%	473,000	268,135	56.7%	16.9	516,000	265,760	51.5%	11.7	553,000	280,314	50.7%	10.9	591,000	247,744	41.9%	2.1
WYOMING	35,000	8,454	24.2%	41,000	10,072	24.6%	0.4	62,000	14,482	23.4%	-0.8	69,000	20,489	29.7%	5.5	78,000	20,846	26.7%	2.6
Total	15,865,000	5,179,244	32.6%	17,671,000	7,108,480	40.2%	7.6	19,231,000	7,218,039	37.5%	4.9	20,884,000	7,626,593	36.5%	3.9	22,901,000	7,676,258	33.5%	0.9

Democratic Turnout for Election Years 1892–1908

State	1892 Voting-age population	Turnout	%	1896 Voting-age population	Turnout	%	Difference from 1892*	1900 Voting-age population	Turnout	%	Difference from 1892	1904 Voting-age population	Turnout	%	Difference from 1892	1908 Voting-age population	Turnout	%	Difference from 1892
ALABAMA	343,000	138,135	40.3%	379,000	130,298	34.4%	-5.9	415,000	97,129	23.4%	-16.9	454,000	79,797	17.6%	-22.7	494,000	74,391	15.1%	-25.2
ALASKA																			
ARIZONA																			
ARKANSAS	268,000	87,834	32.8%	291,000	110,103	37.8%	5.1	314,000	81,242	25.9%	-6.9	348,000	64,434	18.5%	-14.3	380,000	87,020	22.9%	-9.9
CALIFORNIA	355,000	118,151	33.3%	397,000	144,877	36.5%	3.2	444,000	124,985	28.1%	-5.1	547,000	89,294	16.3%	-17.0	650,000	127,492	19.6%	-13.7
COLORADO				273,000	161,005	59.0%		296,000	122,705	41.5%	-17.5	354,000	100,105	28.3%	-30.7	413,000	126,644	30.7%	-28.3
CONNECTICUT	195,000	82,395	42.3%	211,000	56,740	26.9%	-15.4	227,000	74,014	32.6%	-9.6	240,000	72,909	30.4%	-11.9	251,000	68,255	27.2%	-15.1
DELAWARE	47,000	18,581	39.5%	49,000	16,574	33.8%	-5.7	51,000	18,852	37.0%	-2.6	54,000	19,347	35.8%	-3.7	56,000	22,055	39.4%	-0.2
DISTRICT OF COLUMBIA																			
FLORIDA	102,000	30,153	29.6%	119,000	32,756	27.5%	-2.0	136,000	28,273	20.8%	-8.8	164,000	26,449	16.1%	-13.4	192,000	31,104	16.2%	-13.4

United States Presidential General Elections (continued)

United States Presidential General Elections (continued)

Democratic Turnout for Election Years 1892–1908 (continued)

State	1892 Voting-age population	Turnout	%	1896 Voting-age population	Turnout	%	Difference from 1892	1900 Voting-age population	Turnout	%	Difference from 1892	1904 Voting-age population	Turnout	%	Difference from 1892	1908 Voting-age population	Turnout	%	Difference from 1892
GEORGIA	420,000	129,446	30.8%	461,000	93,885	20.4%	-10.5	503,000	81,180	16.1%	-14.7	551,000	83,466	15.1%	-15.7	599,000	72,350	12.1%	-18.7
HAWAII																			
IDAHO				62,000	23,135	37.3%		105,000	29,484	28.1%	-9.2	129,000	18,480	14.3%	-23.0	152,000	36,162	23.8%	-13.5
ILLINOIS	1,006,000	426,281	42.4%	1,140,000	465,593	40.8%	-1.5	1,268,000	503,061	39.7%	-2.7	1,348,000	327,606	24.3%	-18.1	1,428,000	450,810	31.6%	-10.8
INDIANA	607,000	262,740	43.3%	656,000	305,538	46.6%	3.3	705,000	309,584	43.9%	0.6	741,000	274,356	37.0%	-6.3	777,000	338,262	43.5%	0.2
IOWA	501,000	196,367	39.2%	551,000	223,744	40.6%	1.4	596,000	209,261	35.1%	-4.1	600,000	149,141	24.9%	-14.3	606,000	200,771	33.1%	-6.1
KANSAS				385,000	173,049	44.9%		399,000	162,601	40.8%	-4.2	433,000	86,164	19.9%	-25.0	468,000	161,209	34.4%	-10.5
KENTUCKY	465,000	175,461	37.7%	504,000	217,894	43.2%	5.5	540,000	235,126	43.5%	5.8	564,000	217,170	38.5%	0.8	588,000	244,092	41.5%	3.8
LOUISIANA	258,000	87,926	34.1%	287,000	77,175	26.9%	-7.2	317,000	53,668	16.9%	-17.1	351,000	47,708	13.6%	-20.5	386,000	63,568	16.5%	-17.6
MAINE	184,000	48,049	26.1%	189,000	34,587	18.3%	-7.8	192,000	36,822	19.2%	-6.9	197,000	27,642	14.0%	-12.1	201,000	35,403	17.6%	-8.5
MARYLAND	263,000	113,866	43.3%	287,000	104,150	36.3%	-7.0	310,000	122,237	39.4%	-3.9	325,000	109,446	33.7%	-9.6	339,000	115,908	34.2%	-9.1
MASSACHUSETTS	550,000	176,813	32.1%	602,000	105,414	17.5%	-14.6	652,000	156,997	24.1%	-8.1	697,000	165,746	23.8%	-8.4	741,000	155,533	21.0%	-11.2
MICHIGAN	538,000	202,396	37.6%	577,000	237,164	41.1%	3.5	616,000	211,432	34.3%	-3.3	667,000	134,163	20.1%	-17.5	718,000	174,619	24.3%	-13.3
MINNESOTA	352,000	100,589	28.6%	403,000	139,735	34.7%	6.1	452,000	112,901	25.0%	-3.6	482,000	55,187	11.4%	-17.1	513,000	109,401	21.3%	-7.3
MISSISSIPPI	288,000	40,030	13.9%	319,000	63,355	19.9%	6.0	350,000	51,706	14.8%	0.9	381,000	53,480	14.0%	0.1	413,000	60,287	14.6%	0.7
MISSOURI	708,000	268,400	37.9%	772,000	363,667	47.1%	9.2	832,000	351,922	42.3%	4.4	873,000	296,312	33.9%	-4.0	913,000	346,574	38.0%	0.1
MONTANA	63,000	17,690	28.1%	77,000	42,628	55.4%	27.3	86,000	37,311	43.4%	15.3	102,000	21,816	21.4%	-6.7	117,000	29,511	25.2%	-2.9
NEBRASKA	276,000	24,956	9.0%	277,000	115,007	41.5%	32.5	280,000	114,013	40.7%	31.7	300,000	52,921	17.6%	8.6	320,000	131,099	41.0%	31.9
NEVADA	15,000	703	4.7%	15,000	8,348	55.7%	51.0	15,000	6,347	42.3%	37.6	23,000	3,982	17.3%	12.6	30,000	11,212	37.4%	32.7
NEW HAMPSHIRE	104,000	42,081	40.5%	107,000	21,650	20.2%	-20.2	110,000	35,489	32.3%	-8.2	111,000	34,071	30.7%	-9.8	111,000	33,655	30.3%	-10.1
NEW JERSEY	383,000	170,987	44.6%	428,000	133,675	31.2%	-13.4	472,000	164,808	34.9%	-9.7	524,000	164,566	31.4%	-13.2	575,000	182,522	31.7%	-12.9
NEW MEXICO																			
NEW YORK	1,580,000	654,868	41.4%	1,711,000	551,369	32.2%	-9.2	1,842,000	678,462	36.8%	-4.6	1,959,000	683,981	34.9%	-6.5	2,076,000	667,468	32.2%	-9.3
NORTH CAROLINA	360,000	132,951	36.9%	390,000	174,408	44.7%	7.8	420,000	157,733	37.6%	0.6	456,000	124,091	27.2%	-9.7	491,000	136,928	27.9%	-9.0
NORTH DAKOTA				68,000	20,686	30.4%		84,000	20,524	24.4%	-6.0	109,000	14,273	13.1%	-17.3	133,000	32,884	24.7%	-5.7
OHIO	998,000	404,115	40.5%	1,075,000	477,497	44.4%	3.9	1,151,000	474,882	41.3%	0.8	1,222,000	344,674	28.2%	-12.3	1,293,000	502,721	38.9%	-1.6
OKLAHOMA																373,000	122,362	32.8%	
OREGON	103,000	14,243	13.8%	116,000	46,739	40.3%	26.5	132,000	32,810	24.9%	11.0	174,000	17,327	10.0%	-3.9	216,000	37,792	17.5%	3.7
PENNSYLVANIA	1,346,000	452,264	33.6%	1,461,000	433,228	29.7%	-3.9	1,575,000	424,232	26.9%	-6.7	1,678,000	337,998	20.1%	-13.5	1,780,000	448,782	25.2%	-8.4
RHODE ISLAND	82,000	24,336	29.7%	91,000	14,459	15.9%	-13.8	102,000	19,812	19.4%	-10.3	110,000	24,839	22.6%	-7.1	118,000	24,706	20.9%	-8.7
SOUTH CAROLINA	246,000	54,680	22.2%	265,000	58,801	22.2%	0.0	285,000	47,173	16.6%	-5.7	306,000	53,320	17.4%	-4.8	326,000	62,288	19.1%	-3.1
SOUTH DAKOTA	92,000	8,894	9.7%	97,000	41,225	42.5%	32.8	104,000	39,538	38.0%	28.3	130,000	21,969	16.9%	7.2	155,000	40,266	26.0%	16.3
TENNESSEE	419,000	136,468	32.6%	453,000	167,168	36.9%	4.3	486,000	145,240	29.9%	-2.7	513,000	131,653	25.7%	-6.9	538,000	135,608	25.2%	-7.4

United States Presidential General Elections *(continued)*

Democratic Turnout for Election Years 1892–1908 *(continued)*

State	1892 Voting-age population	Turnout	%	1896 Voting-age population	Turnout	%	Difference from 1892	1900 Voting-age population	Turnout	%	Difference from 1892	1904 Voting-age population	Turnout	%	Difference from 1892	1908 Voting-age population	Turnout	%	Difference from 1892
TEXAS	554,000	236,979	42.8%	632,000	370,308	58.6%	15.8	714,000	267,945	37.5%	-5.2	810,000	167,088	20.6%	-22.1	907,000	216,662	23.9%	-18.9
UTAH				99,000	64,607	65.3%		112,000	44,949	40.1%	-25.1	133,000	33,413	25.1%	-40.1	154,000	42,610	27.7%	-37.6
VERMONT	92,000	16,325	17.7%	95,000	10,367	10.9%	-6.8	98,000	12,849	13.1%	-4.6	99,000	9,777	9.9%	-7.9	100,000	11,496	11.5%	-6.2
VIRGINIA	390,000	164,136	42.1%	418,000	154,708	37.0%	-5.1	446,000	146,079	32.8%	-9.3	476,000	80,649	16.9%	-25.1	505,000	82,946	16.4%	-25.7
WASHINGTON	130,000	29,802	22.9%	149,000	53,314	35.8%	12.9	174,000	44,833	25.8%	2.8	254,000	28,098	11.1%	-11.9	335,000	58,383	17.4%	-5.5
WEST VIRGINIA	193,000	84,467	43.8%	219,000	94,480	43.1%	-0.6	245,000	98,807	40.3%	-3.4	273,000	100,855	36.9%	-6.8	301,000	111,410	37.0%	-6.8
WISCONSIN	430,000	177,325	41.2%	473,000	165,523	35.0%	-6.2	516,000	159,163	30.8%	-10.4	553,000	124,205	22.5%	-18.8	591,000	166,662	28.2%	-13.0
WYOMING				41,000	10,862	26.5%		62,000	10,164	16.4%	-10.1	69,000	8,930	12.9%	-13.6	78,000	14,918	19.1%	-7.4
Total	15,306,000	5,551,883	36.3%	17,671,000	6,511,495	36.8%	0.6	19,231,000	6,358,345	33.1%	-3.2	20,884,000	5,082,898	24.3%	-11.9	22,901,000	6,406,801	28.0%	-8.3

Other Turnout for Election Years 1892–1908

State	1892 Voting-age population	Turnout	%	1896 Voting-age population	Turnout	%	Difference from 1892*	1900 Voting-age population	Turnout	%	Difference from 1892	1904 Voting-age population	Turnout	%	Difference from 1892	1908 Voting-age population	Turnout	%	Difference from 1892
ALABAMA	343,000	85,224	24.8%	379,000	8,609	2.3%	-22.6	415,000	6,951	1.7%	-23.2	454,000	6,516	1.4%	-23.4	494,000	5,200	1.1%	-23.8
ALASKA																			
ARIZONA																			
ARKANSAS	268,000	13,211	4.9%	291,000	1,781	0.6%	-4.3	314,000	1,924	0.6%	-4.3	348,000	5,134	1.5%	-3.5	380,000	8,141	2.1%	-2.8
CALIFORNIA	355,000	33,407	9.4%	397,000	6,965	1.8%	-7.7	444,000	12,578	2.8%	-6.6	547,000	37,248	6.8%	-2.6	650,000	44,735	6.9%	-2.5
COLORADO	153,000	55,261	36.1%	273,000	2,263	0.8%	-35.3	296,000	5,489	1.9%	-34.3	354,000	8,901	2.5%	-33.6	413,000	13,521	3.3%	-32.8
CONNECTICUT	195,000	5,168	2.7%	211,000	7,369	3.5%	0.8	227,000	3,609	1.6%	-1.1	240,000	7,138	3.0%	0.3	251,000	8,833	3.5%	0.9
DELAWARE	47,000	577	1.2%	49,000	1,432	2.9%	1.7	51,000	602	1.2%	0.0	54,000	804	1.5%	0.3	56,000	938	1.7%	0.4
DISTRICT OF COLUMBIA																			
FLORIDA	102,000	5,318	5.2%	119,000	2,434	2.0%	-3.2	136,000	4,021	3.0%	-2.3	164,000	3,942	2.4%	-2.8	192,000	7,602	4.0%	-1.3
GEORGIA	420,000	45,272	10.8%	461,000	9,200	2.0%	-8.8	503,000	5,970	1.2%	-9.6	551,000	23,516	4.3%	-6.5	599,000	18,799	3.1%	-7.6
HAWAII																			
IDAHO	47,000	10,808	23.0%	62,000	172	0.3%	-22.7	105,000	1,302	1.2%	-21.8	129,000	6,314	4.9%	-18.1	152,000	8,510	5.6%	-17.4
ILLINOIS	1,006,000	48,078	4.8%	1,140,000	18,043	1.6%	-3.2	1,268,000	30,852	2.4%	-2.3	1,348,000	116,244	8.6%	3.8	1,428,000	74,512	5.2%	0.4
INDIANA	607,000	35,258	5.8%	656,000	7,797	1.2%	-4.6	705,000	18,447	2.6%	-3.2	741,000	39,561	5.3%	-0.5	777,000	33,862	4.4%	-1.5
IOWA	501,000	26,997	5.4%	551,000	8,513	1.5%	-3.8	596,000	13,285	2.2%	-3.2	600,000	28,655	4.8%	-0.6	606,000	18,789	3.1%	-2.3
KANSAS	373,000	167,457	44.9%	385,000	3,552	0.9%	-44.0	399,000	5,210	1.3%	-43.6	433,000	29,428	6.8%	-38.1	468,000	17,518	3.7%	-41.2
KENTUCKY	465,000	29,941	6.4%	504,000	9,863	2.0%	-4.5	540,000	6,007	1.1%	-5.3	564,000	13,319	2.4%	-4.1	588,000	10,916	1.9%	-4.6
LOUISIANA				287,000	1,834	0.6%		317,000	4	0.0%	-0.6	351,000	995	0.3%	-0.4	386,000	2,591	0.7%	0.0
MAINE	184,000	5,466	3.0%	189,000	3,429	1.8%	-1.2	192,000	3,459	1.8%	-1.2	197,000	3,949	2.0%	-1.0	201,000	3,945	2.0%	-1.0

United States Presidential General Elections (continued)

United States Presidential General Elections *(continued)*

Other Turnout for Election Years 1892–1908 *(continued)*

State	1892 Voting-age population	Turnout	%	1896 Voting-age population	Turnout	%	Difference from 1892	1900 Voting-age population	Turnout	%	Difference from 1892	1904 Voting-age population	Turnout	%	Difference from 1892	1908 Voting-age population	Turnout	%	Difference from 1892
MARYLAND	263,000	6,673	2.5%	287,000	9,140	3.2%	0.6	310,000	5,998	1.9%	-0.6	325,000	5,286	1.6%	-0.9	339,000	6,110	1.8%	-0.7
MASSACHUSETTS	550,000	11,401	2.1%	602,000	16,879	2.8%	0.7	652,000	18,941	2.9%	0.8	697,000	21,541	3.1%	1.0	741,000	35,406	4.8%	2.7
MICHIGAN	538,000	41,813	7.8%	577,000	15,083	2.6%	-5.2	616,000	16,343	2.7%	-5.1	667,000	24,417	3.7%	-4.1	718,000	30,192	4.2%	-3.6
MINNESOTA	352,000	44,516	12.6%	403,000	8,524	2.1%	-10.5	452,000	12,949	2.9%	-9.8	482,000	21,022	4.4%	-8.3	513,000	25,010	4.9%	-7.8
MISSISSIPPI	288,000	11,091	3.9%	319,000	1,417	0.4%	-3.4	350,000	1,642	0.5%	-3.4	381,000	1,961	0.5%	-3.3	413,000	2,254	0.5%	-3.3
MISSOURI	708,000	45,537	6.4%	772,000	5,425	0.7%	-5.7	832,000	17,644	2.1%	-4.3	873,000	26,100	3.0%	-3.4	913,000	22,064	2.4%	-4.0
MONTANA	63,000	7,900	12.5%	77,000	193	0.3%	-12.3	86,000	1,136	1.3%	-11.2	102,000	7,758	7.6%	-4.9	117,000	7,251	6.2%	-6.3
NEBRASKA	276,000	88,036	31.9%	277,000	5,110	1.8%	-30.1	280,000	5,582	2.0%	-29.9	300,000	34,253	11.4%	-20.5	320,000	8,703	2.7%	-29.2
NEVADA	15,000	7,312	48.7%									23,000	1,269	5.5%	-43.2	30,000	2,539	8.5%	-40.3
NEW HAMPSHIRE	104,000	1,589	1.5%	107,000	4,576	4.3%	2.7	110,000	2,076	1.9%	0.4	111,000	1,923	1.7%	0.2	111,000	2,796	2.5%	1.0
NEW JERSEY	383,000	10,439	2.7%	428,000	15,972	3.7%	1.0	472,000	14,535	3.1%	0.4	524,000	22,517	4.3%	1.6	575,000	19,291	3.4%	0.6
NEW MEXICO																			
NEW YORK	1,580,000	72,575	4.6%	1,711,000	52,669	3.1%	-1.5	1,842,000	47,568	2.6%	-2.0	1,959,000	74,251	3.8%	-0.8	2,076,000	100,812	4.9%	0.3
NORTH CAROLINA	360,000	46,973	13.0%	390,000	1,807	0.5%	-12.6	420,000	1,788	0.4%	-12.6	456,000	1,285	0.3%	-12.8	491,000	739	0.2%	-12.9
NORTH DAKOTA	53,000	18,599	35.1%	68,000	370	0.5%	-34.5	84,000	1,361	1.6%	-33.5	109,000	3,146	2.9%	-32.2	133,000	3,960	3.0%	-32.1
OHIO	998,000	40,862	4.1%	1,075,000	10,807	1.0%	-3.1	1,151,000	21,273	1.8%	-2.2	1,222,000	59,626	4.9%	0.8	1,293,000	46,519	3.6%	-0.5
OKLAHOMA																373,000	21,425	5.7%	
OREGON	103,000	29,133	28.3%	116,000	1,896	1.6%	-26.6	132,000	4,269	3.2%	-25.1	174,000	12,020	6.9%	-21.4	216,000	10,293	4.8%	-23.5
PENNSYLVANIA	1,346,000	34,725	2.6%	1,461,000	32,827	2.2%	-0.3	1,575,000	36,313	2.3%	-0.3	1,678,000	57,791	3.4%	0.9	1,780,000	72,889	4.1%	1.5
RHODE ISLAND	82,000	1,885	2.3%	91,000	2,889	3.2%	0.9	102,000	2,952	2.9%	0.6	110,000	2,212	2.0%	-0.3	118,000	3,669	3.1%	0.8
SOUTH CAROLINA	246,000	2,479	1.0%	265,000	824	0.3%	-0.7									326,000	146	0.0%	-1.0
SOUTH DAKOTA	92,000	26,552	28.9%	97,000	672	0.7%	-28.2	104,000	2,057	2.0%	-26.9	130,000	7,343	5.6%	-23.2	155,000	6,973	4.5%	-24.4
TENNESSEE	419,000	28,727	6.9%	453,000	5,052	1.1%	-5.7	486,000	5,512	1.1%	-5.7	513,000	5,734	1.1%	-5.7	538,000	3,595	0.7%	-6.2
TEXAS	554,000	102,899	18.6%	632,000	6,816	1.1%	-17.5	714,000	25,215	3.5%	-15.0	810,000	15,214	1.9%	-16.7	907,000	10,646	1.2%	-17.4
UTAH								112,000	1,033	0.9%		133,000	5,767	4.3%	3.4	154,000	4,982	3.2%	2.3
VERMONT	92,000	1,476	1.6%	95,000	2,074	2.2%	0.6	98,000	794	0.8%	-0.8	99,000	1,652	1.7%	0.1	100,000	1,632	1.6%	0.0
VIRGINIA	390,000	15,004	3.8%	418,000	4,587	1.1%	-2.7	446,000	2,360	0.5%	-3.3	476,000	1,581	0.3%	-3.5	505,000	1,547	0.3%	-3.5
WASHINGTON	130,000	21,707	16.7%	149,000	1,116	0.7%	-15.9	174,000	5,235	3.0%	-13.7	254,000	15,513	6.1%	-10.6	335,000	19,125	5.7%	-11.0
WEST VIRGINIA	193,000	6,320	3.3%	219,000	1,898	0.9%	-2.4	245,000	2,160	0.9%	-2.4	273,000	6,511	2.4%	-0.9	301,000	8,819	2.9%	-0.3
WISCONSIN	430,000	23,055	5.4%	473,000	13,751	2.9%	-2.5	516,000	17,578	3.4%	-2.0	553,000	38,921	7.0%	1.7	591,000	40,032	6.8%	1.4
WYOMING	35,000	8,249	23.6%	41,000	133	0.3%	-23.2	62,000	62	0.1%	-23.5	69,000	1,195	1.7%	-21.8	78,000	1,844	2.4%	-21.2
Total	15,709,000	1,324,970	8.4%	17,557,000	315,763	1.8%	-6.6	18,931,000	394,086	2.1%	-6.4	20,578,000	809,473	3.9%	-4.5	22,901,000	799,675	3.5%	-4.9

*Percentage point difference between turnout in current year and initial year listed in chart. If data do not appear for a state in the initial year listed, the difference is calculated from the first year in which data do appear for that state.

STATE GUBERNATORIAL GENERAL ELECTIONS

Election Years 1892–1908

State	1892 Voting-age population	Turnout	%	1896 Voting-age population	Turnout	%	Difference from 1892*	1900 Voting-age population	Turnout	%	Difference from 1892	1904 Voting-age population	Turnout	%	Difference from 1892	1908 Voting-age population	Turnout	%	Difference from 1892
ALABAMA	343,000	243,028	70.9%	379,000	210,843	55.6%	-15.2	415,000	162,465	39.1%	-31.7								
ALASKA																			
ARIZONA																			
ARKANSAS	268,000	156,185	58.3%	291,000	111,889	38.4%	-19.8	314,000	132,978	42.3%	-15.9	348,000	148,050	42.5%	-15.7	380,000	162,197	42.7%	-15.6
CALIFORNIA																			
COLORADO	153,000	92,856	60.7%	273,000	189,072	69.3%	8.6	206,000	220,020	74.5%	13.8	354,000	243,066	68.7%	8.0	413,000	263,380	63.8%	3.1
CONNECTICUT	195,000	164,551	84.4%	211,000	174,019	82.5%	-1.9	227,000	180,723	79.6%	-4.8	240,000	190,831	79.5%	4.9	251,000	189,085	75.3%	-9.1
DELAWARE				49,000	37,346	76.2%		51,000	41,867	82.1%	5.9	54,000	43,833	81.2%	5.0	56,000	47,924	85.6%	9.4
DISTRICT OF COLUMBIA																			
FLORIDA	102,000	40,670	39.9%	119,000	40,732	34.2%	-5.6	136,000	36,120	26.6%	-13.3	164,000	36,598	22.3%	-17.6	192,000	41,916	21.8%	-18.0
GEORGIA	420,000	209,392	49.9%	461,000	206,659	44.8%	-5.0	503,000	118,014	23.5%	-26.4	551,000	67,523	12.3%	-37.6	599,000	124,038	20.7%	-29.1
HAWAII																			
IDAHO	47,000	20,076	42.7%	62,000	28,776	46.4%	3.7	105,000	56,373	53.7%	11.0	129,000	71,298	55.3%	12.6	152,000	96,474	63.5%	20.8
ILLINOIS	1,006,000	873,145	86.8%	1,140,000	1,086,372	95.3%	8.5	1,268,000	1,126,828	88.9%	2.1	1,348,000	1,072,934	79.6%	-7.2	1,428,000	1,154,612	80.9%	-5.9
INDIANA	607,000	549,020	90.4%	656,000	630,189	96.1%	5.6	705,000	655,987	93.0%	2.6	741,000	671,543	90.6%	0.2	777,000	712,699	91.7%	1.3
IOWA																606,000	470,653	77.7%	
KANSAS	373,000	324,770	87.1%	385,000	331,360	86.1%	-1.0	399,000	350,611	87.9%	0.8	433,000	322,407	74.5%	-12.6	468,000	374,758	80.1%	-7.0
KENTUCKY																			
LOUISIANA	258,000	178,302	69.1%	287,000	206,530	72.0%	2.9	317,000	76,870	24.2%	-44.9	351,000	53,622	15.3%	-53.8	386,000	68,930	17.9%	-51.3
MAINE	184,000	130,082	70.7%	189,000	123,564	65.4%	-5.3	192,000	117,878	61.4%	-9.3	197,000	131,512	66.8%	-3.9	201,000	142,666	71.0%	0.3
MARYLAND																			
MASSACHUSETTS	550,000	380,137	69.1%	602,000	385,064	64.0%	-5.2	652,000	386,154	59.2%	-9.9	697,000	450,107	64.6%	-4.5	741,000	442,549	59.7%	-9.4
MICHIGAN	538,000	468,637	87.1%	577,000	547,802	94.9%	7.8	616,000	548,214	89.0%	1.9	667,000	524,721	78.7%	-8.4	718,000	541,767	75.5%	-11.7
MINNESOTA	352,000	255,921	72.7%	403,000	337,229	83.7%	11.0	452,000	314,181	69.5%	-3.2	482,000	303,802	63.0%	-9.7	513,000	337,266	65.7%	-7.0
MISSISSIPPI																			
MISSOURI	708,000	541,082	76.4%	772,000	663,945	86.0%	9.6	832,000	684,291	82.2%	5.8	873,000	643,969	73.8%	-2.7	913,000	715,717	78.4%	2.0
MONTANA	63,000	44,174	70.1%	77,000	51,681	67.1%	-3.0	86,000	63,803	74.2%	4.1	102,000	65,765	64.5%	-5.6	117,000	68,186	58.3%	-11.8
NEBRASKA	276,000	197,474	71.5%	277,000	217,763	78.6%	7.1	280,000	232,981	83.2%	11.7	300,000	224,895	75.0%	3.4	320,000	266,469	83.3%	11.7
NEVADA																			
NEW HAMPSHIRE	104,000	86,980	83.6%	107,000	78,791	73.6%	-10.0	110,000	90,793	82.5%	-1.1	111,000	88,482	79.7%	-3.9	111,000	88,549	79.8%	-3.9
NEW JERSEY																			
NEW MEXICO																			
NEW YORK				1,711,000	1,424,549	83.3%		1,842,000	1,548,551	84.1%	0.8	1,959,000	1,617,786	82.6%	-0.7	2,076,000	1,639,503	79.0%	-4.3

State Gubernatorial General Elections (continued)

State Gubernatorial General Elections (continued)

Election Years 1892–1908 (continued)

State	1892 Voting-age population	Turnout	%	1896 Voting-age population	Turnout	%	Difference from 1892	1900 Voting-age population	Turnout	%	Difference from 1892	1904 Voting-age population	Turnout	%	Difference from 1892	1908 Voting-age population	Turnout	%	Difference from 1892
NORTH CAROLINA	360,000	280,505	77.9%	390,000	330,997	84.9%	7.0	420,000	313,313	74.6%	-3.3	456,000	208,615	45.7%	-32.2	491,000	253,175	51.6%	-26.4
NORTH DAKOTA	53,000	36,231	68.4%	68,000	46,609	68.5%	0.2	84,000	57,525	68.5%	0.1	109,000	67,920	62.3%	-6.0	133,000	96,737	72.7%	4.4
OHIO																1,293,000	1,123,198	86.9%	
OKLAHOMA																			
OREGON																			
PENNSYLVANIA																			
RHODE ISLAND	82,000	54,679	66.7%	91,000	50,485	55.5%	-11.2	102,000	47,660	46.7%	-20.0	110,000	69,078	62.8%	-3.9	118,000	73,509	62.3%	-4.4
SOUTH CAROLINA	246,000	56,729	23.1%	265,000	66,678	25.2%	2.1	285,000	46,475	16.3%	-6.8	306,000	51,097	16.7%	-6.4	326,000	61,060	18.7%	-4.3
SOUTH DAKOTA	92,000	70,410	76.5%	97,000	82,777	85.3%	8.8	104,000	95,541	91.9%	15.3	130,000	100,491	77.3%	0.8	155,000	113,607	73.3%	-3.2
TENNESSEE	419,000	263,867	63.0%	453,000	320,467	70.7%	7.8	486,000	270,336	55.6%	-7.4	513,000	236,021	46.0%	-17.0	538,000	247,821	46.1%	-16.9
TEXAS	554,000	435,467	78.6%	632,000	539,778	85.4%	6.8	714,000	449,624	63.0%	-15.6	810,000	279,874	34.6%	-44.1	907,000	300,743	33.2%	-45.4
UTAH								112,000	92,047	82.2%		133,000	101,735	76.5%	-5.7	154,000	111,519	72.4%	-9.8
VERMONT	92,000	59,880	65.1%	95,000	69,922	73.6%	8.5	98,000	67,099	68.5%	3.4	99,000	66,622	67.3%	2.2	100,000	64,379	64.4%	-0.7
VIRGINIA																			
WASHINGTON	130,000	89,928	69.2%	149,000	91,545	61.4%	-7.7	174,000	106,461	61.2%	-8.0	254,000	144,669	57.0%	-12.2	335,000	176,141	52.6%	-16.6
WEST VIRGINIA	193,000	171,324	88.8%	219,000	201,472	92.0%	3.2	245,000	220,825	90.1%	1.4	273,000	239,356	87.7%	-1.1	301,000	257,991	85.7%	-3.1
WISCONSIN	430,000	371,559	86.4%	473,000	444,110	93.9%	7.5	516,000	441,900	85.6%	-0.8	553,000	446,570	80.8%	-5.7	591,000	449,656	76.1%	-10.3
WYOMING	35,000	17,256	49.3%									69,000	30,909	44.8%	-4.5				
Total	9,233,000	6,864,317	74.3%	11,960,000	9,329,015	78.0%	3.7	13,138,000	9,355,108	71.2%	-3.1	13,916,000	9,015,701	64.8%	-9.6	16,860,000	11,278,874	66.9%	-7.4

*Percentage point difference between turnout in current year and initial year listed in chart. If data do not appear for a state in the initial year listed, the difference is calculated from the first year in which data do appear for that state.

STATE GUBERNATORIAL GENERAL ELECTIONS

Republican Turnout for Election Years 1892–1908

State	1892 Voting-age population	Turnout	%	1896 Voting-age pop.	Turnout	%	Difference from 1892*	1900 Voting-age population	Turnout	%	Difference from 1892	1904 Voting-age population	Turnout	%	Difference from 1892	1908 Voting-age population	Turnout	%	Difference from 1892
ALABAMA								415,000	28,305	6.8%									
ALASKA																			
ARIZONA																			
ARKANSAS	268,000	33,634	12.6%	291,000	27,524	9.5%	-3.1	314,000	40,701	13.0%	0.4	348,000	53,898	15.5%	2.9	380,000	44,863	11.8%	-0.7
CALIFORNIA																			
COLORADO	153,000	38,806	25.4%	273,000	23,945	8.8%	-16.6	296,000	96,027	32.4%	7.1	364,000	113,754	32.1%	0.8	413,000	118,953	28.8%	3.4
CONNECTICUT	195,000	76,745	39.4%	211,000	108,807	51.6%	12.2	227,000	95,822	42.2%	2.9	240,000	104,736	43.6%	4.3	251,000	98,179	39.1%	-0.2
DELAWARE				49,000	12,235	25.0%		51,000	22,421	44.0%	19.0	54,000	22,532	41.7%	16.8	56,000	24,905	44.5%	19.5
DISTRICT OF COLUMBIA																			
FLORIDA				119,000	8,290	7.0%		136,000	6,238	4.6%	-2.4	164,000	6,357	3.9%	-3.1	192,000	6,453	3.4%	-3.6
GEORGIA																			
HAWAII																			
IDAHO	47,000	8,178	17.4%	62,000	6,441	10.4%	7.0	105,000	26,460	25.2%	7.8	129,000	41,877	32.5%	15.1	152,000	47,864	31.5%	14.1
ILLINOIS	1,006,000	402,676	40.0%	1,140,000	587,637	51.5%	11.5	1,268,000	580,199	45.8%	5.7	1,348,000	634,029	47.0%	7.0	1,428,000	550,076	38.5%	-1.5
INDIANA	607,000	253,625	41.8%	656,000	320,936	48.9%	7.1	705,000	331,531	47.0%	5.2	741,000	359,362	48.5%	6.7	777,000	334,040	43.0%	1.2
IOWA																606,000	256,980	42.4%	
KANSAS	373,000	158,075	42.4%	385,000	160,507	41.7%	-0.7	399,000	181,897	45.6%	3.2	433,000	186,731	43.1%	0.7	468,000	196,692	42.0%	-0.4
KENTUCKY																			
LOUISIANA	258,000	29,648	11.5%					317,000	2,449	0.8%	-10.7	351,000	5,877	1.7%	-9.8	386,000	7,617	2.0%	-9.5
MAINE	184,000	67,900	36.9%	189,000	82,596	43.7%	6.8	192,000	73,470	38.3%	1.4	197,000	76,962	39.1%	2.2	201,000	73,551	36.6%	-0.3
MARYLAND																			
MASSACHUSETTS	550,000	183,843	33.4%	602,000	258,204	42.9%	9.5	652,000	228,054	35.0%	1.6	697,000	198,681	28.5%	-4.9	741,000	228,318	30.8%	-2.6
MICHIGAN	538,000	221,228	41.1%	577,000	304,431	52.8%	11.6	616,000	305,612	49.6%	8.5	667,000	283,799	42.5%	1.4	718,000	262,141	36.5%	-4.6
MINNESOTA	352,000	109,220	31.0%	403,000	165,806	41.1%	10.1	452,000	152,905	33.8%	2.8	482,000	140,130	29.1%	-2.0	513,000	147,997	28.8%	-2.2
MISSISSIPPI																			
MISSOURI	708,000	235,383	33.2%	772,000	307,729	39.9%	6.6	832,000	317,905	38.2%	5.0	873,000	296,552	34.0%	0.7	913,000	355,932	39.0%	5.7
MONTANA	63,000	18,187	28.9%	77,000	14,993	19.5%	-9.4	86,000	22,691	26.4%	-2.5	102,000	26,957	26.4%	-2.4	117,000	30,792	26.3%	-2.6
NEBRASKA	276,000	78,426	28.4%	277,000	94,723	34.2%	5.8	280,000	113,879	40.7%	12.3	300,000	111,711	37.2%	8.8	320,000	125,976	39.4%	11.0
NEVADA																			
NEW HAMPSHIRE	104,000	43,676	42.0%	107,000	48,387	45.2%	3.2	110,000	53,891	49.0%	7.0	111,000	51,171	46.1%	4.1	111,000	44,630	40.2%	-1.8
NEW JERSEY																			
NEW MEXICO																			
NEW YORK				1,711,000	787,516	46.0%		1,842,000	804,859	43.7%	-2.3	1,959,000	813,264	41.5%	-4.5	2,076,000	804,651	38.8%	-7.3

State Gubernatorial General Elections (continued)

State Gubernatorial General Elections (continued)

Republican Turnout for Election Years 1892–1908 (continued)

State	1892 Voting-age population	Turnout	%	1896 Voting-age pop.	Turnout	%	Difference from 1892	1900 Voting-age population	Turnout	%	Difference from 1892	1904 Voting-age population	Turnout	%	Difference from 1892	1908 Voting-age population	Turnout	%	Difference from 1892
NORTH CAROLINA	360,000	94,684	26.3%	390,000	153,787	39.4%	13.1	420,000	126,296	30.1%	3.8	456,000	79,505	17.4%	-8.9	491,000	107,760	21.9%	-4.4
NORTH DAKOTA	53,000	17,236	32.5%	68,000	25,918	38.1%	5.6	84,000	34,052	40.5%	8.0	109,000	48,026	44.1%	11.5	133,000	46,849	35.2%	2.7
OHIO																1,293,000	533,197	41.2%	
OKLAHOMA																			
OREGON																			
PENNSYLVANIA																			
RHODE ISLAND	82,000	27,461	33.5%	91,000	28,472	31.3%	-2.2	102,000	26,043	25.5%	-8.0	110,000	33,821	30.7%	-2.7	118,000	38,676	32.8%	-0.7
SOUTH CAROLINA				265,000	2,780	1.0%													
SOUTH DAKOTA	92,000	33,414	36.3%	97,000	40,868	42.1%	5.8	104,000	53,803	51.7%	15.4	130,000	68,561	52.7%	16.4	155,000	62,989	40.6%	4.3
TENNESSEE	419,000	100,577	24.0%	453,000	149,374	33.0%	9.0	486,000	119,831	24.7%	0.7	513,000	103,409	20.2%	-3.8	538,000	113,233	21.0%	-3.0
TEXAS								714,000	112,864	15.8%		810,000	56,865	7.0%	-8.8	907,000	73,305	8.1%	-7.7
UTAH								112,000	47,600	42.5%		133,000	50,837	38.2%	-4.3	154,000	52,913	34.4%	-8.1
VERMONT	92,000	38,918	42.3%	95,000	53,426	56.2%	13.9	98,000	48,441	49.4%	7.1	99,000	48,115	48.6%	6.3	100,000	45,598	45.6%	3.3
VIRGINIA																			
WASHINGTON	130,000	33,281	25.6%	149,000	38,154	25.6%	0.0	174,000	49,860	28.7%	3.1	254,000	74,278	29.2%	3.6	335,000	110,190	32.9%	7.3
WEST VIRGINIA	193,000	80,658	41.8%	219,000	105,588	48.2%	6.4	245,000	118,798	48.5%	6.7	273,000	121,540	44.5%	2.7	301,000	130,807	43.5%	1.7
WISCONSIN	430,000	170,497	39.7%	473,000	264,981	56.0%	16.4	516,000	264,419	51.2%	11.6	553,000	227,253	41.1%	1.4	591,000	242,935	41.1%	1.5
WYOMING	35,000	7,509	21.5%									69,000	17,765	25.7%	4.3				
Total	7,568,000	2,563,485	33.9%	10,201,000	4,184,055	41.0%	7.1	12,350,000	4,487,331	36.3%	2.5	13,059,000	4,458,355	34.1%	0.3	15,935,000	5,319,062	33.4%	-0.5

Democratic Turnout for Election Years 1892–1908

State	1892 Voting-age population	Turnout	%	1896 Voting-age population	Turnout	%	Difference from 1892*	1900 Voting-age population	Turnout	%	Difference from 1892	1904 Voting-age population	Turnout	%	Difference from 1892	1908 Voting-age population	Turnout	%	Difference from 1892
ALABAMA	343,000	126,954	37.0%	379,000	128,549	33.9%	-3.1	415,000	115,167	27.8%	-9.3								
ALASKA																			
ARIZONA																			
ARKANSAS	268,000	90,115	33.6%	291,000	75,354	25.9%	-7.7	314,000	88,636	28.2%	-5.4	348,000	90,263	25.9%	-7.7	380,000	110,418	29.1%	-4.6
CALIFORNIA																			
COLORADO	153,000	8,944	5.8%	273,000	87,387	32.0%	26.2	296,000	118,647	40.1%	34.2	354,000	123,092	34.8%	28.9	413,000	130,141	31.5%	25.7
CONNECTICUT	195,000	82,787	42.5%	211,000	56,524	26.8%	-15.7	227,000	81,421	35.9%	-6.6	240,000	79,164	33.0%	-9.5	251,000	82,260	32.8%	-9.7
DELAWARE				49,000	16,219	33.1%		51,000	18,808	36.9%	3.8	54,000	19,780	36.6%	3.5	56,000	22,794	40.7%	7.6
DISTRICT OF COLUMBIA																			
FLORIDA	102,000	32,064	31.4%	119,000	27,172	22.8%	-8.6	136,000	29,251	21.5%	-9.9	164,000	28,971	17.7%	-13.8	192,000	33,036	17.2%	-14.2

State Gubernatorial General Elections (continued)

Democratic Turnout for Election Years 1892–1908 (continued)

State	1892			1896				1900				1904				1908			
	Voting-age population	Turnout	%	Voting-age population	Turnout	%	Difference from 1892	Voting-age population	Turnout	%	Difference from 1892	Voting-age population	Turnout	%	Difference from 1892	Voting-age population	Turnout	%	Difference from 1892
GEORGIA	420,000	140,492	33.5%	461,000	120,827	26.2%	-7.2	503,000	92,729	18.4%	-15.0	551,000	67,523	12.3%	-21.2	599,000	112,292	18.7%	-14.7
HAWAII																			
IDAHO	47,000	6,769	14.4%	62,000	22,096	35.6%	21.2	105,000	28,628	27.3%	12.9	129,000	24,252	18.8%	4.4	152,000	40,145	26.4%	12.0
ILLINOIS	1,006,000	425,558	42.3%	1,140,000	474,256	41.6%	-0.7	1,268,000	518,966	40.9%	-1.4	1,348,000	334,880	24.8%	-17.5	1,428,000	526,912	36.9%	-5.4
INDIANA	607,000	260,601	42.9%	656,000	294,855	44.9%	2.0	705,000	306,368	43.5%	0.5	741,000	274,998	37.1%	-5.8	777,000	348,843	44.9%	2.0
IOWA																606,000	196,929	32.5%	
KANSAS												433,000	116,991	27.0%		468,000	162,385	34.7%	7.7
KENTUCKY																			
LOUISIANA	258,000	47,046	18.2%	287,000	116,216	40.5%	22.3	317,000	60,206	19.0%	0.8	351,000	47,745	13.6%	-4.6	386,000	60,066	15.6%	-2.7
MAINE	184,000	55,397	30.1%	189,000	34,350	18.2%	-11.9	192,000	40,086	20.9%	-9.2	197,000	50,146	25.5%	-4.7	201,000	66,278	33.0%	2.9
MARYLAND																			
MASSACHUSETTS	550,000	186,377	33.9%	602,000	103,662	17.2%	-16.7	652,000	130,078	20.0%	-13.9	697,000	234,670	33.7%	-0.2	741,000	168,162	22.7%	-11.2
MICHIGAN	538,000	205,138	38.1%	577,000	221,022	38.3%	0.2	616,000	226,228	36.7%	-1.4	667,000	223,571	33.5%	-4.6	718,000	252,611	35.2%	-2.9
MINNESOTA	352,000	94,600	26.9%	403,000	162,254	40.3%	13.4	452,000	150,651	33.3%	6.5	482,000	147,992	30.7%	3.8	513,000	175,136	34.1%	7.3
MISSISSIPPI																			
MISSOURI	708,000	265,044	37.4%	772,000	351,062	45.5%	8.0	832,000	350,045	42.1%	4.6	873,000	326,652	37.4%	0.0	913,000	340,053	37.2%	-0.2
MONTANA	63,000	17,650	28.0%					86,000	31,419	36.5%	8.5	102,000	35,377	34.7%	6.7	117,000	32,282	27.6%	-0.4
NEBRASKA	276,000	44,195	16.0%													320,000	132,960	41.6%	25.5
NEVADA																			
NEW HAMPSHIRE	104,000	41,501	39.9%	107,000	28,333	26.5%	-13.4	110,000	34,956	31.8%	-8.1	111,000	35,437	31.9%	-8.0	111,000	41,386	37.3%	-2.6
NEW JERSEY																			
NEW MEXICO																			
NEW YORK				1,711,000	574,524	33.6%		1,842,000	693,733	37.7%	4.1	1,959,000	732,704	37.4%	3.8	2,076,000	735,189	35.4%	1.8
NORTH CAROLINA	360,000	135,519	37.6%	390,000	145,266	37.2%	-0.4	420,000	186,650	44.4%	6.8	456,000	128,761	28.2%	-9.4	491,000	145,102	29.6%	-8.1
NORTH DAKOTA								84,000	22,275	26.5%		109,000	16,744	15.4%	-11.2	133,000	49,398	37.1%	10.6
OHIO																1,293,000	552,569	42.7%	
OKLAHOMA																			
OREGON																			
PENNSYLVANIA																			
RHODE ISLAND	82,000	25,433	31.0%	91,000	17,061	18.7%	-12.3	102,000	17,184	16.8%	-14.2	110,000	32,965	30.0%	-1.0	118,000	31,406	26.6%	-4.4
SOUTH CAROLINA	246,000	56,673	23.0%	265,000	59,424	22.4%	-0.6	285,000	46,457	16.3%	-6.7	306,000	51,097	16.7%	-6.3	326,000	61,060	18.7%	-4.3
SOUTH DAKOTA	92,000	14,472	15.7%					104,000	40,091	38.5%	22.8	130,000	24,772	19.1%	3.3	155,000	44,837	28.9%	13.2
TENNESSEE	419,000	126,348	30.2%	453,000	156,228	34.5%	4.3	486,000	145,708	30.0%	-0.2	513,000	131,503	25.6%	-4.5	538,000	133,166	24.8%	-5.4

State Gubernatorial General Elections (continued)

State Gubernatorial General Elections (continued)

Democratic Turnout for Election Years 1892–1908 (continued)

State	1892			1896				1900				1904				1908			
	Voting-age population	Turnout	%	Voting-age population	Turnout	%	Difference from 1892	Voting-age population	Turnout	%	Difference from 1892	Voting-age population	Turnout	%	Difference from 1892	Voting-age population	Turnout	%	Difference from 1892
TEXAS	554,000	190,486	34.4%	632,000	298,528	47.2%	12.9	714,000	303,586	42.5%	8.1	810,000	206,160	25.5%	-8.9	907,000	218,956	24.1%	-10.2
UTAH								112,000	44,447	39.7%		133,000	38,047	28.6%	-11.1	154,000	43,266	28.1%	-11.6
VERMONT	92,000	19,216	20.9%	95,000	14,855	15.6%	-5.3	98,000	17,129	17.5%	-3.4	99,000	16,556	16.7%	-4.2	100,000	15,953	16.0%	-4.9
VIRGINIA																			
WASHINGTON	130,000	28,960	22.3%									254,000	59,119	23.3%	1.0	335,000	58,126	17.4%	-4.9
WEST VIRGINIA	193,000	84,585	43.8%	219,000	93,558	42.7%	-1.1	245,000	100,233	40.9%	-2.9	273,000	112,538	41.2%	-2.6	301,000	118,909	39.5%	-4.3
WISCONSIN	430,000	178,095	41.4%	473,000	169,257	35.8%	-5.6	516,000	160,674	31.1%	-10.3	553,000	173,301	31.3%	-10.1	591,000	165,977	28.1%	-13.3
WYOMING	35,000	9,290	26.5%									69,000	12,137	17.6%	-9.0				
Total	8,807,000	3,000,309	34.1%	10,907,000	3,848,839	35.3%	1.2	12,285,000	4,200,457	34.2%	0.1	13,616,000	3,997,908	29.4%	-4.7	16,860,000	5,409,003	32.1%	-2.0

Other Turnout for Election Years 1892–1908

State	1892			1896				1900				1904				1908			
	Voting-age population	Turnout	%	Voting-age population	Turnout	%	Difference from 1892*	Voting-age population	Turnout	%	Difference from 1892	Voting-age population	Turnout	%	Difference from 1892	Voting-age population	Turnout	%	Difference from 1892
ALABAMA	343,000	116,074	33.8%	379,000	82,294	21.7%	-12.1	415,000	18,993	4.6%	-29.3								
ALASKA																			
ARIZONA																			
ARKANSAS	268,000	32,436	12.1%	291,000	9,011	3.1%	-9.0	314,000	3,641	1.2%	-10.9	348,000	3,889	1.1%	-11.0	380,000	6,916	1.8%	-10.3
CALIFORNIA																			
COLORADO	153,000	45,106	29.5%	273,000	77,740	28.5%	-1.0	296,000	5,946	2.0%	-27.5	354,000	6,220	1.8%	-27.7	413,000	14,286	3.5%	-26.0
CONNECTICUT	195,000	5,019	2.6%	211,000	8,688	4.1%	1.5	227,000	3,480	1.5%	-1.0	240,000	6,931	2.9%	0.3	251,000	8,646	3.4%	0.9
DELAWARE				49,000	8,892	18.1%		51,000	638	1.3%	-16.9	54,000	1,521	2.8%	-15.3	56,000	225	0.4%	-17.7
DISTRICT OF COLUMBIA																			
FLORIDA	102,000	8,606	8.4%	119,000	5,270	4.4%	-4.0	136,000	631	0.5%	-8.0	164,000	1,270	0.8%	-7.7	192,000	2,427	1.3%	-7.2
GEORGIA	420,000	68,900	16.4%	461,000	85,832	18.6%	2.2	503,000	25,285	5.0%	-11.4	551,000		0.0%	-16.4	599,000	11,746	2.0%	-14.4
HAWAII																			
IDAHO	47,000	5,129	10.9%	62,000	239	0.4%	-10.5	105,000	1,277	1.2%	-9.7	129,000	5,169	4.0%	-6.9	152,000	8,465	5.6%	-5.3
ILLINOIS	1,006,000	44,911	4.5%	1,140,000	24,479	2.1%	-2.3	1,268,000	27,663	2.2%	-2.3	1,348,000	104,025	7.7%	3.3	1,428,000	77,624	5.4%	1.0
INDIANA	607,000	34,794	5.7%	656,000	14,398	2.2%	-3.5	705,000	18,088	2.6%	-3.2	741,000	37,183	5.0%	-0.7	777,000	29,816	3.8%	-1.9
IOWA																606,000	16,744	2.8%	
KANSAS	373,000	166,695	44.7%	385,000	170,853	44.4%	-0.3	399,000	168,714	42.3%	-2.4	433,000	18,685	4.3%	-40.4	468,000	15,681	3.4%	-41.3
KENTUCKY																			
LOUISIANA	258,000	101,608	39.4%	287,000	90,314	31.5%	-7.9	317,000	14,215	4.5%	-34.9					386,000	1,247	0.3%	-39.1
MAINE	184,000	6,785	3.7%	189,000	6,618	3.5%	-0.2	192,000	4,322	2.3%	-1.4	197,000	4,404	2.2%	-1.5	201,000	2,837	1.4%	-2.3

State Gubernatorial General Elections (continued)

Other Turnout for Election Years 1892–1908 (continued)

State	1892 Voting-age population	Turnout	%	1896 Voting-age population	Turnout	%	Difference from 1892	1900 Voting-age population	Turnout	%	Difference from 1892	1904 Voting-age population	Turnout	%	Difference from 1892	1908 Voting-age population	Turnout	%	Difference from 1892
MARYLAND																			
MASSACHUSETTS	550,000	9,917	1.8%	602,000	23,198	3.9%	2.1	652,000	28,022	4.3%	2.5	697,000	16,756	2.4%	0.6	741,000	46,069	6.2%	4.4
MICHIGAN	538,000	42,271	7.9%	577,000	22,349	3.9%	-4.0	616,000	16,374	2.7%	-5.2	667,000	17,351	2.6%	-5.3	718,000	27,015	3.8%	-4.1
MINNESOTA	352,000	52,101	14.8%	403,000	9,169	2.3%	-12.5	452,000	10,625	2.4%	-12.5	482,000	15,680	3.3%	-11.5	513,000	14,133	2.8%	-12.0
MISSISSIPPI																			
MISSOURI	708,000	40,655	5.7%	772,000	5,154	0.7%	-5.1	832,000	16,341	2.0%	-3.8	873,000	20,765	2.4%	-3.4	913,000	19,732	2.2%	-3.6
MONTANA	63,000	8,337	13.2%	77,000	36,688	47.6%	34.4	86,000	9,693	11.3%	-2.0	102,000	3,431	3.4%	-9.9	117,000	5,112	4.4%	-8.9
NEBRASKA	276,000	74,853	27.1%	277,000	123,040	44.4%	17.3	280,000	119,102	42.5%	15.4	300,000	113,184	37.7%	10.6	320,000	7,533	2.4%	-24.8
NEVADA																			
NEW HAMPSHIRE	104,000	1,803	1.7%	107,000	2,071	1.9%	0.2	110,000	1,946	1.8%	0.0	111,000	1,874	1.7%	0.0	111,000	2,533	2.3%	0.5
NEW JERSEY																			
NEW MEXICO																			
NEW YORK				1,711,000	62,509	3.7%		1,842,000	49,959	2.7%	-0.9	1,959,000	71,818	3.7%	0.0	2,076,000	99,663	4.8%	1.1
NORTH CAROLINA	360,000	50,302	14.0%	390,000	31,944	8.2%	-5.8	420,000	367	0.1%	-13.9	456,000	349	0.1%	-13.9	491,000	313	0.1%	-13.9
NORTH DAKOTA	53,000	18,995	35.8%	68,000	20,691	30.4%	-5.4	84,000	1,198	1.4%	-34.4	109,000	3,150	2.9%	-32.9	133,000	490	0.4%	-35.5
OHIO																1,293,000	37,432	2.9%	
OKLAHOMA																			
OREGON																			
PENNSYLVANIA																			
RHODE ISLAND	82,000	1,785	2.2%	91,000	4,952	5.4%	3.3	102,000	4,433	4.3%	2.2	110,000	2,292	2.1%	-0.1	118,000	3,427	2.9%	0.7
SOUTH CAROLINA	246,000	56	0.0%	265,000	4,474	1.7%	1.7	285,000	18	0.0%	0.0					326,000		0.0%	0.0
SOUTH DAKOTA	92,000	22,524	24.5%	97,000	41,909	43.2%	18.7	104,000	1,647	1.6%	-22.9	130,000	7,158	5.5%	-19.0	155,000	5,781	3.7%	-20.8
TENNESSEE	419,000	36,942	8.8%	453,000	14,865	3.3%	-5.5	486,000	4,797	1.0%	-7.8	513,000	1,109	0.2%	-8.6	538,000	1,422	0.3%	-8.6
TEXAS	554,000	244,981	44.2%	632,000	241,250	38.2%	-6.0	714,000	33,174	4.6%	-39.6	810,000	16,849	2.1%	-42.1	907,000	8,482	0.9%	-43.3
UTAH												133,000	12,851	9.7%		154,000	15,340	10.0%	0.3
VERMONT	92,000	1,746	1.9%	95,000	1,641	1.7%	-0.2	98,000	1,529	1.6%	-0.3	99,000	1,951	2.0%	0.1	100,000	2,828	2.8%	0.9
VIRGINIA																			
WASHINGTON	130,000	27,687	21.3%	149,000	53,391	35.8%	14.5	174,000	56,601	32.5%	11.2	254,000	11,272	4.4%	-16.9	335,000	7,825	2.3%	-19.0
WEST VIRGINIA	193,000	6,081	3.2%	219,000	2,326	1.1%	-2.1	245,000	1,794	0.7%	-2.4	273,000	5,278	1.9%	-1.2	301,000	8,275	2.7%	-0.4
WISCONSIN	430,000	22,967	5.3%	473,000	9,872	2.1%	-3.3	516,000	16,807	3.3%	-2.1	553,000	46,016	8.3%	3.0	591,000	40,744	6.9%	1.6
WYOMING	35,000	457	1.3%									69,000	1,007	1.5%	0.2				
Total	9,233,000	1,300,523	14.1%	11,960,000	1,296,121	10.8%	-3.2	13,026,000	667,320	5.1%	-9.0	13,259,000	559,438	4.2%	-9.9	16,860,000	550,809	3.3%	-10.8

*Percentage point difference between turnout in current year and initial year listed in chart. If data do not appear for a state in the initial year listed, the difference is calculated from the first year in which data do appear for that state.

UNITED STATES HOUSE OF REPRESENTATIVES GENERAL ELECTIONS

Election Years 1892–1908

State	1892 Voting-age population	Turnout	%	1896 Voting-age population	Turnout	%	Difference from 1892*	1900 Voting-age population	Turnout	%	Difference from 1892	1904 Voting-age population	Turnout	%	Difference from 1892	1908 Voting-age population	Turnout	%	Difference from 1892
ALABAMA	343,000	232,551	67.8%	379,000	185,310	48.9%	-18.9	415,000	141,190	34.0%	-33.8	454,000	102,803	22.6%	-45.2	494,000	101,106	20.5%	-47.3
ALASKA																			
ARIZONA																			
ARKANSAS	268,000	137,162	51.2%	291,000	151,374	52.0%	0.8	314,000	126,969	40.4%	-10.7	348,000	109,977	31.6%	-19.6	380,000	152,942	40.2%	-10.9
CALIFORNIA	355,000	240,406	67.7%	397,000	278,096	70.0%	2.3	444,000	292,064	65.8%	-1.9	547,000	328,126	60.0%	-7.7	650,000	371,567	57.2%	-10.6
COLORADO	153,000	92,535	60.5%	273,000	179,381	65.7%	5.2	296,000	217,200	73.4%	12.9	354,000	241,532	68.2%	7.7	413,000	262,548	63.6%	3.1
CONNECTICUT	195,000	163,949	84.1%	211,000	174,376	82.6%	-1.4	227,000	181,018	79.7%	-4.3	240,000	190,924	79.6%	-4.5	251,000	190,248	75.8%	-8.3
DELAWARE	47,000	37,143	79.0%	49,000	34,995	71.4%	-7.6	51,000	42,112	82.6%	3.5	54,000	43,814	81.1%	2.1	56,000	47,997	85.7%	6.7
DISTRICT OF COLUMBIA																			
FLORIDA	102,000	35,556	34.9%	119,000	42,345	35.6%	0.7	136,000	31,705	23.3%	-11.5	164,000	32,759	20.0%	-14.9	192,000	39,017	20.3%	-14.5
GEORGIA	420,000	216,275	51.5%	461,000	170,647	37.0%	-14.5	503,000	105,734	21.0%	-30.5	551,000	116,453	21.1%	-30.4	599,000	96,653	16.1%	-35.4
HAWAII																			
IDAHO	47,000	19,367	41.2%	62,000	28,875	46.6%	5.4	105,000	54,939	52.3%	11.1	129,000	70,395	54.6%	13.4	152,000	96,039	63.2%	22.0
ILLINOIS	1,006,000	872,173	86.7%	1,140,000	1,080,652	94.8%	8.1	1,268,000	1,118,786	88.2%	1.5	1,348,000	1,059,156	78.6%	-8.1	1,428,000	1,141,218	79.9%	-6.8
INDIANA	607,000	549,615	90.5%	656,000	630,652	96.1%	5.6	705,000	655,361	93.0%	2.4	741,000	671,162	90.6%	0.0	777,000	711,831	91.6%	1.1
IOWA	501,000	441,465	88.1%	551,000	517,137	93.9%	5.7	596,000	525,015	88.1%	0.0	600,000	477,280	79.5%	-8.6	606,000	464,445	76.6%	-11.5
KANSAS	373,000	324,577	87.0%	385,000	328,068	85.2%	-1.8	399,000	344,662	86.4%	-0.6	433,000	311,628	72.0%	-15.0	468,000	381,817	81.6%	-5.4
KENTUCKY	465,000	321,613	69.2%	504,000	436,585	86.6%	17.5	540,000	463,155	85.8%	16.6	564,000	429,620	76.2%	7.0	588,000	478,973	81.5%	12.3
LOUISIANA	258,000	113,754	44.1%	287,000	97,278	33.9%	-10.2	317,000	67,279	21.2%	-22.9	351,000	52,432	14.9%	-29.2	386,000	70,755	18.3%	-25.8
MAINE	184,000	127,681	69.4%	189,000	124,221	65.7%	-3.7	192,000	117,498	61.2%	-8.2	197,000	129,094	65.5%	-3.9	201,000	142,601	70.9%	1.6
MARYLAND	263,000	211,767	80.5%	287,000	248,489	86.6%	6.1	310,000	263,611	85.0%	4.5	325,000	208,090	64.0%	-16.5	339,000	212,269	62.6%	-17.9
MASSACHUSETTS	550,000	372,249	67.7%	602,000	373,933	62.1%	-5.6	652,000	392,035	60.1%	-7.6	697,000	411,632	59.1%	-8.6	741,000	422,366	57.0%	-10.7
MICHIGAN	538,000	465,811	86.6%	577,000	534,440	92.6%	6.0	616,000	541,281	87.9%	1.3	667,000	514,866	77.2%	-9.4	718,000	530,820	73.9%	-12.7
MINNESOTA	352,000	259,740	73.8%	403,000	339,697	84.3%	10.5	452,000	317,936	70.3%	-3.4	482,000	284,151	59.0%	-14.8	513,000	311,473	60.7%	-13.1
MISSISSIPPI	288,000	50,777	17.6%	319,000	66,364	20.8%	3.2	350,000	51,524	14.7%	-2.9	381,000	53,337	14.0%	-3.6	413,000	59,701	14.5%	-3.2
MISSOURI	708,000	532,728	75.2%	772,000	664,677	86.1%	10.9	832,000	673,148	80.9%	5.7	873,000	631,249	72.3%	-2.9	913,000	711,105	77.9%	2.6
MONTANA	63,000	43,324	68.8%	77,000	43,424	56.4%	-12.4	86,000	61,393	71.4%	2.6	102,000	63,711	62.5%	-6.3	117,000	67,169	57.4%	-11.4
NEBRASKA	276,000	196,263	71.1%	277,000	216,437	78.1%	7.0	280,000	227,762	81.3%	10.2	300,000	224,278	74.8%	3.6	320,000	264,084	82.5%	11.4
NEVADA	15,000	9,888	65.9%	15,000	9,696	64.6%	-1.3	15,000	10,165	67.8%	1.8	23,000	11,398	49.6%	-16.4	30,000	23,801	79.3%	13.4
NEW HAMPSHIRE	104,000	85,553	82.3%	107,000	82,252	76.9%	-5.4	110,000	90,227	82.0%	-0.2	111,000	87,145	78.5%	-3.8	111,000	86,803	78.2%	-4.1
NEW JERSEY	383,000	334,882	87.4%	428,000	369,070	86.2%	-1.2	472,000	399,387	84.6%	-2.8	524,000	430,786	82.2%	-5.2	575,000	462,251	80.4%	-7.0
NEW MEXICO																			
NEW YORK	1,580,000	1,300,558	82.3%	1,711,000	1,369,303	80.0%	-2.3	1,842,000	1,513,082	82.1%	-0.2	1,959,000	1,566,895	80.0%	-2.3	2,076,000	1,631,528	78.6%	-3.7

United States House of Representatives General Elections (continued)

Election Years 1892–1908 (continued)

State	1892 Voting-age population	Turnout	%	1896 Voting-age population	Turnout	%	Difference from 1892	1900 Voting-age population	Turnout	%	Difference from 1892	1904 Voting-age population	Turnout	%	Difference from 1892	1908 Voting-age population	Turnout	%	Difference from 1892
NORTH CAROLINA	360,000	270,875	75.2%	390,000	327,832	84.1%	8.8	420,000	291,767	69.5%	-5.8	456,000	208,851	45.8%	-29.4	491,000	252,854	51.5%	-23.7
NORTH DAKOTA	53,000	36,150	68.2%	68,000	46,754	68.8%	0.5	84,000	57,181	68.1%	-0.1	109,000	67,454	61.9%	-6.3	133,000	87,374	65.7%	-2.5
OHIO	998,000	841,571	84.3%	1,075,000	1,004,680	93.5%	9.1	1,151,000	1,029,122	89.4%	5.1	1,222,000	985,568	80.7%	-3.7	1,293,000	1,117,509	86.4%	2.1
OKLAHOMA																373,000	252,983	67.8%	
OREGON	103,000	75,648	73.4%	116,000	89,454	77.1%	3.7	132,000	82,947	62.8%	-10.6	174,000	93,906	54.0%	-19.5	216,000	110,252	51.0%	-22.4
PENNSYLVANIA	1,346,000	989,188	73.5%	1,461,000	1,160,245	79.4%	5.9	1,575,000	1,127,783	71.6%	-1.9	1,678,000	1,105,549	65.9%	-7.6	1,780,000	1,106,575	62.2%	-11.3
RHODE ISLAND	82,000	50,659	61.8%	91,000	53,429	58.7%	-3.1	102,000	52,943	51.9%	-9.9	110,000	63,595	57.8%	-4.0	118,000	72,641	61.6%	-0.2
SOUTH CAROLINA	246,000	68,585	27.9%	265,000	68,579	25.9%	-2.0	285,000	51,107	17.9%	-9.9	306,000	57,144	18.7%	-9.2	326,000	65,414	20.1%	-7.8
SOUTH DAKOTA	92,000	73,431	79.8%	97,000	82,791	85.4%	5.5	104,000	95,771	92.1%	12.3	130,000	100,037	77.0%	-2.9	155,000	112,856	72.8%	-7.0
TENNESSEE	419,000	256,321	61.2%	453,000	315,093	69.6%	8.4	486,000	265,920	54.7%	-6.5	513,000	228,572	44.6%	-16.6	538,000	232,359	43.2%	-18.0
TEXAS	554,000	414,173	74.8%	632,000	535,247	84.7%	9.9	714,000	411,864	57.7%	-17.1	810,000	249,829	30.8%	-43.9	907,000	286,874	31.6%	-43.1
UTAH				99,000	77,548	78.3%		112,000	92,829	82.9%	4.6	133,000	101,739	76.5%	-1.8	154,000	111,452	72.4%	-6.0
VERMONT	92,000	54,321	59.0%	95,000	66,931	70.5%	11.4	98,000	64,155	65.5%	6.4	99,000	64,789	65.4%	6.4	100,000	61,412	61.4%	2.4
VIRGINIA	390,000	284,195	72.9%	418,000	301,576	72.1%	-0.7	446,000	269,653	60.5%	-12.4	476,000	132,020	27.7%	-45.1	505,000	140,011	27.7%	-45.1
WASHINGTON	130,000	88,588	68.1%	149,000	90,917	61.0%	-7.1	174,000	105,956	60.9%	-7.3	254,000	142,410	56.1%	-12.1	335,000	167,850	50.1%	-18.0
WEST VIRGINIA	193,000	170,397	88.3%	219,000	199,548	91.1%	2.8	245,000	219,720	89.7%	1.4	273,000	239,079	87.6%	-0.7	301,000	257,473	85.5%	-2.7
WISCONSIN	430,000	367,296	85.4%	473,000	437,649	92.5%	7.1	516,000	439,783	85.2%	-0.2	553,000	437,008	79.0%	-6.4	591,000	438,926	74.3%	-11.1
WYOMING	35,000	17,249	49.3%	41,000	20,982	51.2%	1.9	62,000	24,556	39.6%	-9.7	69,000	30,741	44.6%	-4.7	78,000	37,560	48.2%	-1.1
Total	15,967,000	11,848,009	74.2%	17,671,000	13,657,029	77.3%	3.1	19,231,000	13,709,295	71.3%	-2.9	20,884,000	13,162,984	63.0%	-11.2	22,901,000	14,445,502	63.1%	-11.1

*Percentage point difference between turnout in current year and initial year listed in chart. If data do not appear for a state in the initial year listed, the difference is calculated from the first year in which data do appear for that state.

UNITED STATES HOUSE OF REPRESENTATIVES GENERAL ELECTIONS

Republican Turnout for Election Years 1892–1908

State	1892 Voting-age population	1892 Turnout	1892 %	1896 Voting-age population	1896 Turnout	1896 %	1896 Difference from 1892*	1900 Voting-age population	1900 Turnout	1900 %	1900 Difference from 1892	1904 Voting-age population	1904 Turnout	1904 %	1904 Difference from 1892	1908 Voting-age population	1908 Turnout	1908 %	1908 Difference from 1892
ALABAMA	343,000	11,269	3.3%	379,000	36,980	9.8%	6.5	415,000	36,303	8.7%	5.5	454,000	19,551	4.3%	1.0	494,000	19,118	3.9%	0.6
ALASKA																			
ARIZONA																			
ARKANSAS	268,000	15,451	5.8%	291,000	41,725	14.3%	8.6	314,000	42,650	13.6%	7.8	348,000	32,517	9.3%	3.6	380,000	48,081	12.7%	6.9
CALIFORNIA	355,000	101,080	28.5%	397,000	128,941	32.5%	4.0	444,000	157,440	35.5%	7.0	547,000	186,427	34.1%	5.6	650,000	202,309	31.1%	2.7
COLORADO	153,000	37,181	24.3%	273,000	24,010	8.8%	-15.5	296,000	92,805	31.4%	7.1	354,000	121,236	34.2%	9.9	413,000	121,265	29.4%	5.1
CONNECTICUT	195,000	77,031	39.5%	211,000	109,494	51.9%	12.4	227,000	102,559	45.2%	5.7	240,000	108,918	45.4%	5.9	251,000	111,557	44.4%	4.9
DELAWARE	47,000	18,080	38.5%	49,000	18,282	37.3%	-1.2	51,000	22,353	43.8%	5.4	54,000	23,512	43.5%	5.1	56,000	24,314	43.4%	4.9
DISTRICT OF COLUMBIA																			
FLORIDA				119,000	9,431	7.9%		136,000	5,254	3.9%	-4.1	164,000	6,010	3.7%	-4.3	192,000	6,254	3.3%	-4.7
GEORGIA	420,000	10,046	2.4%	461,000	35,908	7.8%	5.4	503,000	11,605	2.3%	-0.1	551,000	20,078	3.6%	1.3	599,000	427	0.1%	-2.3
HAWAII																			
IDAHO	47,000	8,549	18.2%	62,000	15,088	24.3%	6.1	105,000	26,860	25.6%	7.4	129,000	44,813	34.7%	16.5	152,000	49,983	32.9%	14.7
ILLINOIS	1,006,000	399,307	39.7%	1,140,000	600,667	52.7%	13.0	1,268,000	591,886	46.7%	7.0	1,348,000	613,866	45.5%	5.8	1,428,000	614,396	43.0%	3.3
INDIANA	607,000	253,588	41.8%	656,000	321,250	49.0%	7.2	705,000	330,813	46.9%	5.1	741,000	353,087	47.7%	5.9	777,000	334,224	43.0%	1.2
IOWA	501,000	219,214	43.8%	551,000	287,951	52.3%	8.5	596,000	304,302	51.1%	7.3	600,000	295,258	49.2%	5.5	606,000	253,826	41.9%	-1.9
KANSAS	373,000	155,791	41.8%	385,000	158,147	41.1%	-0.7	399,000	180,162	45.2%	3.4	433,000	187,983	43.4%	1.6	468,000	199,561	42.6%	0.9
KENTUCKY	465,000	121,960	26.2%	504,000	193,577	38.4%	12.2	540,000	228,676	42.3%	16.1	564,000	204,484	36.3%	10.0	588,000	230,988	39.3%	13.1
LOUISIANA	258,000	20,736	8.0%	287,000	21,940	7.6%	-0.4	317,000	14,554	4.6%	-3.4	351,000	4,632	1.3%	-6.7	386,000	5,341	1.4%	-6.7
MAINE	184,000	65,637	35.7%	189,000	83,947	44.4%	8.7	192,000	72,947	38.0%	2.3	197,000	76,519	38.8%	3.2	201,000	75,307	37.5%	1.8
MARYLAND	263,000	91,762	34.9%	287,000	135,423	47.2%	12.3	310,000	135,546	43.7%	8.8	325,000	104,435	32.1%	-2.8	339,000	100,611	29.7%	-5.2
MASSACHUSETTS	550,000	187,046	34.0%	602,000	249,384	41.4%	7.4	652,000	222,299	34.1%	0.1	697,000	235,365	33.8%	-0.2	741,000	249,206	33.6%	-0.4
MICHIGAN	538,000	222,783	41.4%	577,000	291,697	50.6%	9.1	616,000	312,911	50.8%	9.4	667,000	344,043	51.6%	10.2	718,000	323,403	45.0%	3.6
MINNESOTA	352,000	115,637	32.9%	403,000	187,566	46.5%	13.7	452,000	180,356	39.9%	7.1	482,000	205,639	42.7%	9.8	513,000	195,812	38.2%	5.3
MISSISSIPPI	288,000	512	0.2%	319,000	4,353	1.4%	1.2	350,000	2,565	0.7%	0.6	381,000	91	0.0%	-0.2	413,000	384	0.1%	-0.1
MISSOURI	708,000	227,652	32.2%	772,000	304,101	39.4%	7.2	832,000	313,563	37.7%	5.5	873,000	317,003	36.3%	4.2	913,000	347,362	38.0%	5.9
MONTANA	63,000	17,934	28.5%	77,000	43,424	56.4%	27.9	86,000	23,207	27.0%	-1.5	102,000	32,957	32.3%	3.8	117,000	32,819	28.1%	-0.4
NEBRASKA	276,000	82,842	30.0%	277,000	100,076	36.1%	6.1	280,000	113,191	40.4%	10.4	300,000	123,986	41.3%	11.3	320,000	128,896	40.3%	10.3
NEVADA	15,000	2,295	15.3%	15,000	1,319	8.8%	-6.5	15,000	4,190	27.9%	12.6	23,000	5,301	23.0%	7.7	30,000	7,552	25.2%	9.9
NEW HAMPSHIRE	104,000	42,456	40.8%	107,000	52,360	48.9%	8.1	110,000	53,502	48.6%	7.8	111,000	52,112	46.9%	6.1	111,000	50,420	45.4%	4.6
NEW JERSEY	383,000	158,191	41.3%	428,000	220,471	51.5%	10.2	472,000	220,350	46.7%	5.4	524,000	236,218	45.1%	3.8	575,000	241,619	42.0%	0.7
NEW MEXICO																			
NEW YORK	1,580,000	605,021	38.3%	1,711,000	786,417	46.0%	7.7	1,842,000	805,574	43.7%	5.4	1,959,000	841,418	43.0%	4.7	2,076,000	827,619	39.9%	1.6

United States House of Representatives General Elections (continued)

Republican Turnout for Election Years 1892–1908 (continued)

State	1892			1896				1900				1904				1908			
	Voting-age population	Turnout	%	Voting-age population	Turnout	%	Difference from 1892	Voting-age population	Turnout	%	Difference from 1892	Voting-age population	Turnout	%	Difference from 1892	Voting-age population	Turnout	%	Difference from 1892
NORTH CAROLINA	360,000	70,332	19.5%	390,000	177,552	45.5%	26.0	420,000	115,634	27.5%	8.0	456,000	78,693	17.3%	-2.3	491,000	108,592	22.1%	2.6
NORTH DAKOTA	53,000	17,695	33.4%	68,000	25,233	37.1%	3.7	84,000	34,887	41.5%	8.1	109,000	49,111	45.1%	11.7	133,000	57,357	43.1%	9.7
OHIO	998,000	397,200	39.8%	1,075,000	524,682	48.8%	9.0	1,151,000	541,265	47.0%	7.2	1,222,000	581,376	47.6%	7.8	1,293,000	532,914	41.2%	1.4
OKLAHOMA																373,000	109,413	29.3%	
OREGON	103,000	34,588	33.6%	116,000	31,972	27.6%	-6.0	132,000	43,300	32.8%	-0.8	174,000	51,096	29.4%	-4.2	216,000	67,468	31.2%	-2.3
PENNSYLVANIA	1,346,000	512,557	38.1%	1,461,000	711,246	48.7%	10.6	1,575,000	683,941	43.4%	5.3	1,678,000	729,760	43.5%	5.4	1,780,000	641,047	36.1%	-2.0
RHODE ISLAND	82,000	25,088	30.6%	91,000	33,990	37.4%	6.8	102,000	30,961	30.4%	-0.2	110,000	33,662	30.6%	0.0	118,000	39,596	33.6%	3.0
SOUTH CAROLINA	246,000	9,713	3.9%	265,000	8,627	3.3%	-0.7	285,000	3,178	1.1%	-2.8	306,000	2,473	0.8%	-3.1	326,000	1,682	0.5%	-3.4
SOUTH DAKOTA	92,000	33,769	36.7%	97,000	40,943	42.2%	5.5	104,000	53,583	51.5%	14.8	130,000	70,002	53.8%	17.1	155,000	67,582	43.6%	6.9
TENNESSEE	419,000	81,159	19.4%	453,000	129,220	28.5%	9.2	486,000	109,278	22.5%	3.1	513,000	99,439	19.4%	0.0	538,000	104,887	19.5%	0.1
TEXAS	554,000	73,108	13.2%	632,000	121,018	19.1%	6.0	714,000	83,291	11.7%	-1.5	810,000	43,124	5.3%	-7.9	907,000	46,001	5.1%	-8.1
UTAH				99,000	27,813	28.1%		112,000	46,180	41.2%	13.1	133,000	52,675	39.6%	11.5	154,000	57,544	37.4%	9.3
VERMONT	92,000	34,995	38.0%	97,000	52,464	54.1%	16.0	98,000	46,118	47.1%	9.0	99,000	46,989	47.5%	9.4	100,000	45,058	45.1%	7.0
VIRGINIA	390,000	47,343	12.1%	418,000	125,235	30.0%	17.8	446,000	98,728	22.1%	10.0	476,000	44,873	9.4%	-2.7	505,000	49,370	9.8%	-2.4
WASHINGTON	130,000	35,434	27.3%	149,000	38,196	25.6%	-1.6	174,000	55,393	31.8%	4.6	254,000	93,328	36.7%	9.5	335,000	107,862	32.2%	4.9
WEST VIRGINIA	193,000	80,538	41.7%	219,000	104,544	47.7%	6.0	245,000	118,223	48.3%	6.5	273,000	128,437	47.0%	5.3	301,000	135,674	45.1%	3.3
WISCONSIN	430,000	171,542	39.9%	473,000	267,226	56.5%	16.6	516,000	261,537	50.7%	10.8	553,000	250,609	45.3%	5.4	591,000	240,195	40.6%	0.7
WYOMING	35,000	8,394	24.0%	41,000	10,044	24.5%	0.5	62,000	14,539	23.5%	-0.5	69,000	19,862	28.8%	4.8	78,000	21,431	27.5%	3.5
Total	15,865,000	4,902,506	30.9%	17,673,000	6,893,934	39.0%	8.1	19,231,000	6,948,459	36.1%	5.2	20,884,000	7,172,968	34.3%	3.4	22,901,000	7,237,227	31.6%	0.7

Democratic Turnout for Election Years 1892–1908

State	1892			1896				1900				1904				1908			
	Voting-age population	Turnout	%	Voting-age population	Turnout	%	Difference from 1892*	Voting-age population	Turnout	%	Difference from 1892	Voting-age population	Turnout	%	Difference from 1892	Voting-age population	Turnout	%	Difference from 1892
ALABAMA	343,000	221,109	64.5%	379,000	123,939	32.7%	-31.8	415,000	104,626	25.2%	-39.3	454,000	82,826	18.2%	-46.2	494,000	81,629	16.5%	-47.9
ALASKA																			
ARIZONA																			
ARKANSAS	268,000	94,513	35.3%	291,000	109,649	37.7%	2.4	314,000	84,319	26.9%	-8.4	348,000	77,460	22.3%	-13.0	380,000	104,861	27.6%	-7.7
CALIFORNIA	355,000	117,427	33.1%	397,000	129,789	32.7%	-0.4	444,000	120,411	27.1%	-6.0	547,000	112,587	20.6%	-12.5	650,000	134,699	20.7%	-12.4
COLORADO	153,000	53,833	35.2%	273,000	151,839	55.6%	20.4	296,000	121,598	41.1%	5.9	354,000	112,373	31.7%	-3.4	413,000	126,934	30.7%	-4.5
CONNECTICUT	195,000	82,004	42.1%	211,000	61,825	29.3%	-12.8	227,000	74,989	33.0%	-9.0	240,000	75,212	31.3%	-10.7	251,000	70,029	27.9%	-14.2
DELAWARE	47,000	18,554	39.5%	49,000	16,251	33.2%	-6.3	51,000	19,157	37.6%	-1.9	54,000	19,552	36.2%	-3.3	56,000	22,515	40.2%	0.7
DISTRICT OF COLUMBIA																			
FLORIDA	102,000	30,781	30.2%	119,000	30,355	25.5%	-4.7	136,000	26,451	19.4%	-10.7	164,000	25,592	15.6%	-14.6	192,000	30,011	15.6%	-14.5

United States House of Representatives General Elections (continued)

United States House of Representatives General Elections (continued)

Democratic Turnout for Election Years 1892–1908 (continued)

State	1892 Voting-age population	Turnout	%	1896 Voting-age population	Turnout	%	Difference from 1892	1900 Voting-age population	Turnout	%	Difference from 1892	1904 Voting-age population	Turnout	%	Difference from 1892	1908 Voting-age population	Turnout	%	Difference from 1892
GEORGIA	420,000	137,197	32.7%	461,000	99,816	21.7%	-11.0	503,000	83,504	16.6%	-16.1	551,000	95,979	17.4%	-15.2	599,000	96,226	16.1%	-16.6
HAWAII																			
IDAHO	47,000	6,029	12.8%	62,000	13,787	22.2%	9.4	105,000	28,079	26.7%	13.9	129,000	20,146	15.6%	2.8	152,000	37,605	24.7%	11.9
ILLINOIS	1,006,000	425,336	42.3%	1,140,000	464,354	40.7%	-1.5	1,268,000	502,227	39.6%	-2.7	1,348,000	344,266	25.5%	-16.7	1,428,000	458,117	32.1%	-10.2
INDIANA	607,000	259,190	42.7%	656,000	304,525	46.4%	3.7	705,000	312,014	44.3%	1.6	741,000	288,706	39.0%	-3.7	777,000	351,658	45.3%	2.6
IOWA	501,000	201,925	40.3%	551,000	226,246	41.1%	0.8	596,000	212,649	35.7%	-4.6	600,000	161,801	27.0%	-13.3	606,000	198,031	32.7%	-7.6
KANSAS	373,000	164,624	44.1%	385,000	168,420	43.7%	-0.4	399,000	160,980	40.3%	-3.8	433,000	105,479	24.4%	-19.8	468,000	166,452	35.6%	-8.6
KENTUCKY	465,000	174,359	37.5%	504,000	223,777	44.4%	6.9	540,000	232,937	43.1%	5.6	564,000	219,749	39.0%	1.5	588,000	242,589	41.3%	3.8
LOUISIANA	258,000	92,966	36.0%	287,000	64,509	22.5%	-13.6	317,000	52,725	16.6%	-19.4	351,000	47,388	13.5%	-22.5	386,000	63,891	16.6%	-19.5
MAINE	184,000	55,758	30.3%	189,000	34,404	18.2%	-12.1	192,000	40,485	21.1%	-9.2	197,000	50,383	25.6%	-4.7	201,000	64,493	32.1%	1.8
MARYLAND	263,000	113,931	43.3%	287,000	106,832	37.2%	-6.1	310,000	123,492	39.8%	-3.5	325,000	99,180	30.5%	-12.8	339,000	106,792	31.5%	-11.8
MASSACHUSETTS	550,000	174,289	31.7%	602,000	123,556	20.5%	-11.2	652,000	151,388	23.2%	-8.5	697,000	152,142	21.8%	-9.9	741,000	147,778	19.9%	-11.7
MICHIGAN	538,000	210,692	39.2%	577,000	240,563	41.7%	2.5	616,000	216,664	35.2%	-4.0	667,000	158,146	23.7%	-15.5	718,000	192,437	26.8%	-12.4
MINNESOTA	352,000	96,432	27.4%	403,000	146,574	36.4%	9.0	452,000	127,947	28.3%	0.9	482,000	73,260	15.2%	-12.2	513,000	87,768	17.1%	-10.3
MISSISSIPPI	288,000	37,571	13.0%	319,000	50,873	15.9%	2.9	350,000	47,849	13.7%	0.6	381,000	52,797	13.9%	0.8	413,000	59,317	14.4%	1.3
MISSOURI	708,000	266,865	37.7%	772,000	339,139	43.9%	6.2	832,000	354,180	42.6%	4.9	873,000	304,391	34.9%	-2.8	913,000	349,047	38.2%	0.5
MONTANA	63,000	17,762	28.2%					86,000	37,573	43.7%	15.5	102,000	26,729	26.2%	-2.0	117,000	29,032	24.8%	-3.4
NEBRASKA	276,000	65,482	23.7%	277,000	112,998	40.8%	17.1	280,000	110,119	39.3%	15.6	300,000	89,959	30.0%	6.3	320,000	131,027	40.9%	17.2
NEVADA	15,000	345	2.3%	15,000	6,429	42.9%	40.6	15,000	5,975	39.8%	37.5	23,000	5,525	24.0%	21.7	30,000	11,253	37.5%	35.2
NEW HAMPSHIRE	104,000	41,408	39.8%	107,000	27,805	26.0%	-13.8	110,000	34,908	31.7%	-8.1	111,000	33,328	30.0%	-9.8	111,000	34,066	30.7%	-9.1
NEW JERSEY	383,000	166,796	43.5%	428,000	138,538	32.4%	-11.2	472,000	165,370	35.0%	-8.5	524,000	173,217	33.1%	-10.5	575,000	206,808	36.0%	-7.6
NEW MEXICO																			
NEW YORK	1,580,000	633,621	40.1%	1,711,000	544,172	31.8%	-8.3	1,842,000	666,943	36.2%	-3.9	1,959,000	661,896	33.8%	-6.3	2,076,000	707,542	34.1%	-6.0
NORTH CAROLINA	360,000	132,844	36.9%	390,000	146,970	37.7%	0.8	420,000	162,260	38.6%	1.7	456,000	130,038	28.5%	-8.4	491,000	143,840	29.3%	-7.6
NORTH DAKOTA	53,000	11,021	20.8%	68,000	21,172	31.1%	10.3	84,000	21,175	25.2%	4.4	109,000	15,622	14.3%	-6.5	133,000	29,426	22.1%	1.3
OHIO	998,000	407,230	40.8%	1,075,000	472,986	44.0%	3.2	1,151,000	479,168	41.6%	0.8	1,222,000	354,803	29.0%	-11.8	1,293,000	524,086	40.5%	-0.3
OKLAHOMA																373,000	122,804	32.9%	
OREGON	103,000	25,139	24.4%	116,000	15,013	12.9%	-11.5	132,000	34,285	26.0%	1.6	174,000	29,930	17.2%	-7.2	216,000	28,706	13.3%	-11.1
PENNSYLVANIA	1,346,000	448,714	33.3%	1,461,000	413,800	28.3%	-5.0	1,575,000	411,552	26.1%	-7.2	1,678,000	319,647	19.0%	-14.3	1,780,000	403,098	22.6%	-10.7
RHODE ISLAND	82,000	23,430	28.6%	91,000	16,630	18.3%	-10.3	102,000	18,751	18.4%	-10.2	110,000	28,861	26.2%	-2.3	118,000	30,775	26.1%	-2.5
SOUTH CAROLINA	246,000	56,929	23.1%	265,000	59,930	22.6%	-0.5	285,000	47,929	16.8%	-6.3	306,000	54,671	17.9%	-5.3	326,000	63,732	19.5%	-3.6
SOUTH DAKOTA	92,000	14,218	15.5%	97,000	41,125	42.4%	26.9	104,000	40,560	39.0%	23.5	130,000	22,692	17.5%	2.0	155,000	38,758	25.0%	9.6
TENNESSEE	419,000	142,902	34.1%	453,000	167,327	36.9%	2.8	486,000	143,930	29.6%	-4.5	513,000	128,452	25.0%	-9.1	538,000	126,142	23.4%	-10.7

United States House of Representatives General Elections *(continued)*

Democratic Turnout for Election Years 1892–1908 *(continued)*

State	1892 Voting-age population	Turnout	%	1896 Voting-age population	Turnout	%	Difference from 1892	1900 Voting-age population	Turnout	%	Difference from 1892	1904 Voting-age population	Turnout	%	Difference from 1892	1908 Voting-age population	Turnout	%	Difference from 1892
TEXAS	554,000	238,908	43.1%	632,000	296,251	46.9%	3.8	714,000	307,202	43.0%	-0.1	810,000	204,772	25.3%	-17.8	907,000	235,846	26.0%	-17.1
UTAH				99,000	47,456	47.9%		112,000	45,939	41.0%	-6.9	133,000	37,445	28.2%	-19.8	154,000	35,981	23.4%	-24.6
VERMONT	92,000	18,045	19.6%	97,000	13,895	14.3%	-5.3	98,000	16,732	17.1%	-2.5	99,000	15,934	16.1%	-3.5	100,000	14,942	14.9%	-4.7
VIRGINIA	390,000	165,629	42.5%	418,000	174,765	41.8%	-0.7	446,000	165,705	37.2%	-5.3	476,000	86,361	18.1%	-24.3	505,000	90,401	17.9%	-24.6
WASHINGTON	130,000	30,659	23.6%					174,000	45,448	26.1%	2.5	254,000	35,698	14.1%	-9.5	335,000	56,322	16.8%	-6.8
WEST VIRGINIA	193,000	85,808	44.5%	219,000	94,743	43.3%	-1.2	245,000	100,496	41.0%	-3.4	273,000	104,896	38.4%	-6.0	301,000	113,579	37.7%	-6.7
WISCONSIN	430,000	175,841	40.9%	473,000	165,327	35.0%	-5.9	516,000	163,824	31.7%	-9.1	553,000	150,376	27.2%	-13.7	591,000	167,277	28.3%	-12.6
WYOMING	35,000	8,855	25.3%	41,000	10,310	25.1%	-0.2	62,000	10,017	16.2%	-9.1	69,000	9,903	14.4%	-10.9	78,000	13,643	17.5%	-7.8
Total	15,967,000	5,946,971	37.2%	17,447,000	6,218,664	35.6%	-1.6	19,231,000	6,434,532	33.5%	-3.8	20,884,000	5,400,170	25.9%	-11.4	22,901,000	6,551,965	28.6%	-8.6

Other Turnout for Election Years 1892–1908

State	1892 Voting-age population	Turnout	%	1896 Voting-age population	Turnout	%	Difference from 1892	1900 Voting-age population	Turnout	%	Difference from 1892	1904 Voting-age population	Turnout	%	Difference from 1892	1908 Voting-age population	Turnout	%	Difference from 1892
ALABAMA	343,000	173	0.1%	379,000	24,391	6.4%	6.4	415,000	261	0.1%	0.0	454,000	426	0.1%	0.0	494,000	359	0.1%	0.0
ALASKA																			
ARIZONA																			
ARKANSAS	268,000	27,198	10.1%																
CALIFORNIA	355,000	21,899	6.2%	397,000	19,366	4.9%	-1.3	444,000	14,213	3.2%	-3.0	547,000	29,112	5.3%	-0.8	650,000	34,559	5.3%	-0.9
COLORADO	153,000	1,521	1.0%	273,000	3,532	1.3%	0.3	296,000	2,797	0.9%	0.0	354,000	7,923	2.2%	1.2	413,000	14,349	3.5%	2.5
CONNECTICUT	195,000	4,914	2.5%	211,000	3,057	1.4%	-1.1	227,000	3,470	1.5%	-1.0	240,000	6,794	2.8%	0.3	251,000	8,662	3.5%	0.9
DELAWARE	47,000	509	1.1%	49,000	462	0.9%	-0.1	51,000	602	1.2%	0.1	54,000	750	1.4%	0.3	56,000	1,168	2.1%	1.0
DISTRICT OF COLUMBIA																			
FLORIDA	102,000	4,775	4.7%	119,000	2,559	2.2%	-2.5					164,000	1,157	0.7%	-4.0	192,000	2,752	1.4%	-3.2
GEORGIA	420,000	69,032	16.4%	461,000	34,923	7.6%	-8.9	503,000	10,625	2.1%	-14.3	551,000	396	0.1%	-16.4				
HAWAII																			
IDAHO	47,000	4,789	10.2%									129,000	5,436	4.2%	-6.0	152,000	8,451	5.6%	-4.6
ILLINOIS	1,006,000	47,530	4.7%	1,140,000	15,631	1.4%	-3.4	1,268,000	24,673	1.9%	-2.8	1,348,000	101,024	7.5%	2.8	1,428,000	68,705	4.8%	0.1
INDIANA	607,000	36,837	6.1%	656,000	4,877	0.7%	-5.3	705,000	12,534	1.8%	-4.3	741,000	29,369	4.0%	-2.1	777,000	25,949	3.3%	-2.7
IOWA	501,000	20,326	4.1%	551,000	2,940	0.5%	-3.5	596,000	8,064	1.4%	-2.7	600,000	20,221	3.4%	-0.7	606,000	12,588	2.1%	-2.0
KANSAS	373,000	4,162	1.1%	385,000	1,501	0.4%	-0.7	399,000	3,520	0.9%	-0.2	433,000	18,166	4.2%	3.1	468,000	15,804	3.4%	2.3
KENTUCKY	465,000	25,294	5.4%	504,000	19,231	3.8%	-1.6	540,000	1,542	0.3%	-5.2	564,000	5,387	1.0%	-4.5	588,000	5,396	0.9%	-4.5
LOUISIANA	258,000	52	0.0%	287,000	10,829	3.8%	3.8					351,000	412	0.1%	0.1	386,000	1,523	0.4%	0.4
MAINE	184,000	6,286	3.4%	189,000	5,870	3.1%	-0.3	192,000	4,066	2.1%	-1.3	197,000	2,192	1.1%	-2.3	201,000	2,801	1.4%	-2.0

United States House of Representatives General Elections (continued)

United States House of Representatives General Elections (continued)

Other Turnout for Election Years 1892–1908 (continued)

State	1892 Voting-age population	Turnout	%	1896 Voting-age population	Turnout	%	Difference from 1892	1900 Voting-age population	Turnout	%	Difference from 1892	1904 Voting-age population	Turnout	%	Difference from 1892	1908 Voting-age population	Turnout	%	Difference from 1892
MARYLAND	263,000	6,074	2.3%	287,000	6,234	2.2%	-0.1	310,000	4,573	1.5%	-0.8	325,000	4,475	1.4%	-0.9	339,000	4,866	1.4%	-0.9
MASSACHUSETTS	550,000	10,914	2.0%	602,000	993	0.2%	-1.8	652,000	18,348	2.8%	0.8	697,000	24,125	3.5%	1.5	741,000	25,382	3.4%	1.4
MICHIGAN	538,000	32,336	6.0%	577,000	2,180	0.4%	-5.6	616,000	11,706	1.9%	-4.1	667,000	12,677	1.9%	-4.1	718,000	14,980	2.1%	-3.9
MINNESOTA	352,000	47,671	13.5%	403,000	5,557	1.4%	-12.2	452,000	9,633	2.1%	-11.4	482,000	5,252	1.1%	-12.5	513,000	27,893	5.4%	-8.1
MISSISSIPPI	288,000	12,694	4.4%	319,000	11,138	3.5%	-0.9	350,000	1,110	0.3%	-4.1	381,000	449	0.1%	-4.3				
MISSOURI	708,000	38,211	5.4%	772,000	21,437	2.8%	-2.6	832,000	5,405	0.6%	-4.7	873,000	9,855	1.1%	-4.3	913,000	14,696	1.6%	-3.8
MONTANA	63,000	7,628	12.1%					86,000	613	0.7%	-11.4	102,000	4,025	3.9%	-8.2	117,000	5,318	4.5%	-7.6
NEBRASKA	276,000	47,939	17.4%	277,000	3,363	1.2%	-16.2	280,000	4,452	1.6%	-15.8	300,000	10,333	3.4%	-13.9	320,000	4,161	1.3%	-16.1
NEVADA	15,000	7,248	48.3%	15,000	1,948	13.0%	-35.3					23,000	572	2.5%	-45.8	30,000	4,996	16.7%	-31.7
NEW HAMPSHIRE	104,000	1,689	1.6%	107,000	2,087	2.0%	0.3	110,000	1,817	1.7%	0.0	111,000	1,705	1.5%	-0.1	111,000	2,317	2.1%	0.5
NEW JERSEY	383,000	9,895	2.6%	428,000	10,061	2.4%	-0.2	472,000	13,667	2.9%	0.3	524,000	21,351	4.1%	1.5	575,000	13,824	2.4%	-0.2
NEW MEXICO																			
NEW YORK	1,580,000	61,916	3.9%	1,711,000	38,714	2.3%	-1.7	1,842,000	40,565	2.2%	-1.7	1,959,000	63,581	3.2%	-0.7	2,076,000	96,367	4.6%	0.7
NORTH CAROLINA	360,000	67,699	18.8%	390,000	3,310	0.8%	-18.0	420,000	13,873	3.3%	-15.5	456,000	120	0.0%	-18.8	491,000	422	0.1%	-18.7
NORTH DAKOTA	53,000	7,434	14.0%	68,000	349	0.5%	-13.5	84,000	1,119	1.3%	-12.7	109,000	2,721	2.5%	-11.5	133,000	591	0.4%	-13.6
OHIO	998,000	37,141	3.7%	1,075,000	7,012	0.7%	-3.1	1,151,000	8,689	0.8%	-3.0	1,222,000	49,389	4.0%	0.3	1,293,000	60,509	4.7%	1.0
OKLAHOMA																373,000	20,766	5.6%	
OREGON	103,000	15,921	15.5%	116,000	42,469	36.6%	21.2	132,000	5,362	4.1%	-11.4	174,000	12,880	7.4%	-8.1	216,000	14,078	6.5%	-8.9
PENNSYLVANIA	1,346,000	27,917	2.1%	1,461,000	35,199	2.4%	0.3	1,575,000	32,290	2.1%	0.0	1,678,000	56,142	3.3%	1.3	1,780,000	61,530	3.5%	1.4
RHODE ISLAND	82,000	2,141	2.6%	91,000	2,809	3.1%	0.5	102,000	3,231	3.2%	0.6	110,000	1,072	1.0%	-1.6	118,000	2,270	1.9%	-0.7
SOUTH CAROLINA	246,000	1,943	0.8%	265,000	22	0.0%	-0.8												
SOUTH DAKOTA	92,000	25,444	27.7%	97,000	723	0.7%	-26.9	104,000	1,628	1.6%	-26.1	130,000	7,343	5.6%	-22.0	155,000	6,516	4.2%	-23.5
TENNESSEE	419,000	32,260	7.7%	453,000	18,546	4.1%	-3.6	486,000	12,712	2.6%	-5.1	513,000	681	0.1%	-7.6	538,000	1,330	0.2%	-7.5
TEXAS	554,000	102,157	18.4%	632,000	117,978	18.7%	0.2	714,000	21,371	3.0%	-15.4	810,000	1,933	0.2%	-18.2	907,000	5,027	0.6%	-17.9
UTAH				99,000	2,279	2.3%		112,000	710	0.6%	-1.7	133,000	11,619	8.7%	6.4	154,000	17,927	11.6%	9.3
VERMONT	92,000	1,281	1.4%	97,000	572	0.6%	-0.8	98,000	1,305	1.3%	-0.1	99,000	1,866	1.9%	0.5	100,000	1,412	1.4%	0.0
VIRGINIA	390,000	71,223	18.3%	418,000	1,576	0.4%	-17.9	446,000	5,220	1.2%	-17.1	476,000	786	0.2%	-18.1	505,000	240	0.0%	-18.2
WASHINGTON	130,000	22,495	17.3%	149,000	52,721	35.4%	18.1	174,000	5,115	2.9%	-14.4	254,000	13,384	5.3%	-12.0	335,000	3,666	1.1%	-16.2
WEST VIRGINIA	193,000	4,051	2.1%	219,000	261	0.1%	-2.0	245,000	1,001	0.4%	-1.7	273,000	5,746	2.1%	0.0	301,000	8,220	2.7%	0.6
WISCONSIN	430,000	19,913	4.6%	473,000	5,096	1.1%	-3.6	516,000	14,422	2.8%	-1.8	553,000	36,023	6.5%	1.9	591,000	31,454	5.3%	0.7
WYOMING				41,000	628	1.5%						69,000	976	1.4%	-0.1	78,000	2,486	3.2%	1.7
Total	15,932,000	998,532	6.3%	17,243,000	544,431	3.2%	-3.1	17,997,000	326,304	1.8%	-4.5	20,230,000	589,846	2.9%	-3.4	21,183,000	656,310	3.1%	-3.2

*Percentage point difference between turnout in current year and initial year listed in chart. If data do not appear for a state in the initial year listed, the difference is calculated from the first year in which data do appear for that state.

STATE GUBERNATORIAL PRIMARY ELECTIONS

Republican Turnout for Election Year 1908

State	1908 Voting-age population	Turnout	%
IOWA	605,000	181,863	30.1%
MISSOURI	908,000	163,618	18.0%
NORTH DAKOTA	130,000	62,871	48.4%
SOUTH DAKOTA	153,000	62,884	41.1%
WASHINGTON	326,000	101,995	31.3%
Total	2,122,000	573,231	27.0%

Democrat Turnout for Election Year 1908

State	1908 Voting-age population	Turnout	%
IOWA	605,000	50,065	8.3%
MISSOURI	908,000	245,527	27.0%
NORTH DAKOTA	130,000	12,068	9.3%
WASHINGTON	326,000	12,920	4.0%
Total	1,969,000	320,580	16.3%

Other Turnout for Election Year 1908

State	1908 Voting-age population	Turnout	%
IOWA	605,000	1,325	0.2%

Midterm Turnout Election Based on Highest Statewide Turnout, Election Years 1890–1906

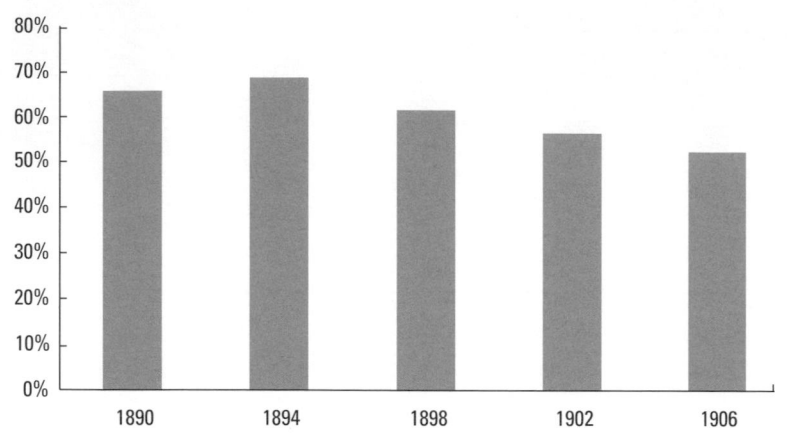

YEAR	VOTING-AGE POPULATION	TOTAL	%
1890	15,222,000	9,999,571	65.7%
1894	16,815,000	11,528,941	68.6%
1898	18,427,000	11,340,566	61.5%
1902	20,048,000	11,324,518	56.5%
1906	21,701,000	11,387,436	52.5%

Partisan Turnout Midterm Election Based on Aggregate House of Representatives Turnout, Election Years 1890–1906

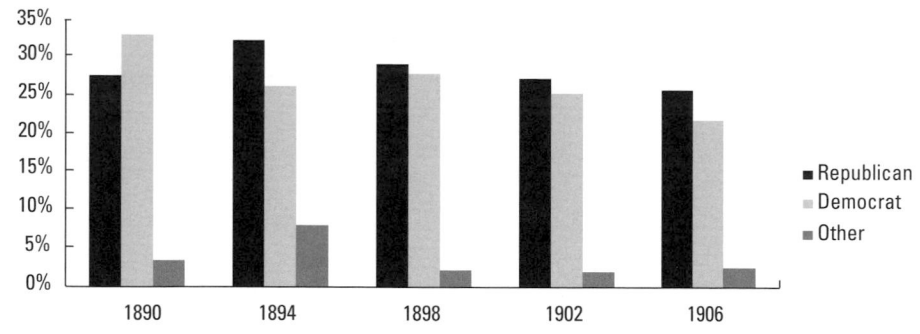

■ Republican
▨ Democrat
■ Other

YEAR	VOTING-AGE POPULATION	REPUBLICAN TURNOUT	%	DEMOCRAT TURNOUT	%	OTHER TURNOUT	%
1890	15,222,000	4,212,903	27.7%	5,029,443	33.0%	540,032	3.5%
1894	16,815,000	5,433,787	32.3%	4,418,849	26.3%	1,369,840	8.1%
1898	18,427,000	5,380,574	29.2%	5,149,719	27.9%	423,452	2.3%
1902	20,048,000	5,478,660	27.3%	5,088,122	25.4%	421,138	2.1%
1906	21,701,000	5,606,363	25.8%	4,755,595	21.9%	574,284	2.6%

STATE GUBERNATORIAL GENERAL ELECTIONS

Election Years 1890–1906

State	1890 Voting-age population	1890 Turnout	1890 %	1894 Voting-age population	1894 Turnout	1894 %	1894 Difference from 1890*	1898 Voting-age population	1898 Turnout	1898 %	1898 Difference from 1890	1902 Voting-age population	1902 Turnout	1902 %	1902 Difference from 1890	1906 Voting-age population	1906 Turnout	1906 %	1906 Difference from 1890
ALABAMA	326,000	183,797	56.4%	361,000	194,170	53.8%	-2.6	397,000	165,064	41.6%	-14.8	435,000	91,922	21.1%	-35.2	475,000	71,621	15.1%	-41.3
ALASKA																			
ARIZONA																			
ARKANSAS	257,000	191,448	74.5%	280,000	126,626	45.2%	-29.3	302,000	111,889	37.0%	-37.4	331,000	119,741	36.2%	-38.3	363,000	152,753	42.1%	-32.4
CALIFORNIA	335,000	252,457	75.4%	376,000	284,546	75.7%	0.3	417,000	286,996	68.8%	-6.5	496,000	304,473	61.4%	-14.0	599,000	311,975	52.1%	-23.3
COLORADO	148,000	83,465	56.4%	259,000	179,969	69.5%	13.1	287,000	149,524	52.1%	-4.3	325,000	186,781	57.5%	1.1	383,000	203,135	53.0%	-3.4
CONNECTICUT	186,000	135,298	72.7%	203,000	154,981	76.3%	3.6	219,000	149,568	68.3%	-4.4	233,000	159,702	68.5%	-4.2	245,000	161,193	65.8%	-6.9
DELAWARE	45,000	35,197	78.2%	47,000	39,128	83.3%	5.0												
DISTRICT OF COLUMBIA																			
FLORIDA																			
GEORGIA	399,000	105,365	26.4%	440,000	217,937	49.5%	23.1	482,000	170,137	35.3%	8.9	527,000	86,091	16.3%	-10.1	575,000	77,110	13.4%	-13.0
HAWAII																			
IDAHO	41,000	18,210	44.4%	55,000	24,591	44.7%	0.3	70,000	39,747	56.8%	12.4	117,000	60,257	51.5%	7.1	140,000	73,569	52.5%	8.1
ILLINOIS																			
INDIANA																			
IOWA																603,000	432,405	71.7%	
KANSAS	367,000	294,588	80.3%	379,000	299,232	79.0%	-1.3	391,000	288,219	73.7%	-6.6	416,000	287,168	69.0%	-11.2	451,000	315,379	69.9%	-10.3
KENTUCKY																			
LOUISIANA																			
MAINE	182,000	113,902	62.6%	186,000	107,776	57.9%	-4.6	191,000	86,720	45.4%	-17.2	195,000	107,877	55.3%	-7.3	198,000	133,499	67.4%	4.8
MARYLAND																			
MASSACHUSETTS	525,000	285,526	54.4%	576,000	335,354	58.2%	3.8	627,000	317,735	50.7%	-3.7	674,000	398,689	59.2%	4.8	719,000	428,278	59.6%	5.2
MICHIGAN	519,000	397,856	76.7%	558,000	416,988	74.7%	-1.9	595,000	421,164	70.8%	-5.9	642,000	402,226	62.7%	-14.0	692,000	373,806	54.0%	-22.6
MINNESOTA	326,000	240,892	73.9%	377,000	296,249	78.6%	4.7	428,000	252,562	59.0%	-14.9	466,000	270,888	58.1%	-15.8	497,000	276,511	55.6%	-18.3
MISSISSIPPI																			
MISSOURI																			
MONTANA																			
NEBRASKA	275,000	214,090	77.9%	277,000	204,017	73.7%	-4.2	278,000	190,668	68.6%	-9.3	290,000	194,143	66.9%	-10.9	309,000	190,853	61.8%	-16.1
NEVADA	16,000	12,392	77.5%	16,000	10,473	65.5%	-12.0	14,000	10,008	71.5%	-6.0	19,000	11,318	59.6%	-17.9	26,000	14,837	57.1%	-20.4
NEW HAMPSHIRE	103,000	86,240	83.7%	106,000	83,056	78.4%	-5.4	109,000	82,475	75.7%	-8.1	110,000	79,173	72.0%	-11.8	111,000	81,513	73.4%	-10.3
NEW JERSEY																			
NEW MEXICO																			
NEW YORK				1,645,000	1,269,172	77.2%		1,777,000	1,349,974	76.0%	-1.2	1,900,000	1,383,167	72.8%	-4.4	2,017,000	1,482,485	73.5%	-3.7

State Gubernatorial General Elections (continued)

State Gubernatorial General Elections (continued)

Election Years 1890–1906 (continued)

State	1890 Voting-age population	Turnout	%	1894 Voting-age population	Turnout	%	Difference from 1890	1898 Voting-age population	Turnout	%	Difference from 1890	1902 Voting-age population	Turnout	%	Difference from 1890	1906 Voting-age population	Turnout	%	Difference from 1890
NORTH CAROLINA																			
NORTH DAKOTA	47,000	36,478	77.6%	61,000	42,548	69.8%	-7.9	76,000	47,804	62.9%	-14.7	96,000	50,434	52.5%	-25.1	121,000	66,280	54.8%	-22.8
OHIO																			
OKLAHOMA																			
OREGON	96,000	72,685	75.7%	109,000	87,109	79.9%	4.2	122,000	84,714	69.4%	-6.3	153,000	90,662	59.3%	-16.5	195,000	96,715	49.6%	-26.1
PENNSYLVANIA	1,288,000	928,196	72.1%	1,404,000	953,017	67.9%	-4.2	1,519,000	971,742	64.0%	-8.1	1,626,000	1,094,771	67.3%	-4.7	1,729,000	1,006,577	58.2%	-13.8
RHODE ISLAND	76,000	42,141	55.4%	87,000	54,863	63.1%	7.6	97,000	42,856	44.2%	-11.3	105,000	59,757	56.9%	1.5	113,000	66,501	58.9%	3.4
SOUTH CAROLINA	237,000	74,124	31.3%	256,000	56,785	22.2%	-9.1	275,000	28,225	10.3%	-21.0	295,000	31,817	10.8%	-20.5	315,000	30,283	9.6%	-21.7
SOUTH DAKOTA	88,000	77,572	88.2%	94,000	76,716	81.6%	-6.5	99,000	75,204	76.0%	-12.2	117,000	74,463	63.6%	-24.5	142,000	74,572	52.5%	-35.6
TENNESSEE	401,000	200,712	50.1%	436,000	209,978	48.2%	-1.9	470,000	182,384	38.8%	-11.2	499,000	160,102	32.1%	-18.0	526,000	205,485	39.1%	-11.0
TEXAS	514,000	342,409	66.6%	593,000	422,726	71.3%	4.7	673,000	409,554	60.9%	-5.8	762,000	309,150	40.6%	-26.0	859,000	185,840	21.6%	-45.0
UTAH																			
VERMONT	92,000	54,226	58.9%	94,000	58,015	61.7%	2.8	96,000	54,337	56.6%	-2.3	98,000	69,935	71.4%	12.4	100,000	70,493	70.5%	11.6
VIRGINIA																			
WASHINGTON																			
WEST VIRGINIA																			
WISCONSIN	408,000	309,254	75.8%	452,000	375,449	83.1%	7.3	494,000	329,430	66.7%	-9.1	534,000	365,776	68.5%	-7.3	572,000	320,003	55.9%	-19.9
WYOMING	31,000	16,032	51.7%	38,000	19,290	50.8%	-1.0	45,000	19,803	44.0%	-7.7	66,000	25,052	38.0%	-13.8	74,000	27,103	36.6%	-15.1
Total	7,328,000	4,804,552	65.6%	9,765,000	6,600,761	67.6%	2.2	10,550,000	6,318,503	59.9%	-5.5	11,527,000	6,475,535	56.2%	-9.2	13,149,000	6,930,774	52.7%	-12.7

*Percentage point difference between turnout in current year and initial year listed in chart. If data do not appear for a state in the initial year listed, the difference is calculated from the first year in which data do appear for that state.

STATE GUBERNATORIAL GENERAL ELECTIONS

Republican Turnout for Election Years 1890–1906

	1890			1894				1898				1902				1906			
State	Voting-age population	Turnout	%	Voting-age population	Turnout	%	Difference from 1890*	Voting-age population	Turnout	%	Difference from 1890	Voting-age population	Turnout	%	Difference from 1890	Voting-age population	Turnout	%	Difference from 1890
ALABAMA	326,000	42,391	13.0%					397,000	3,134	0.8%	-12.2	435,000	24,150	5.6%	-7.5	475,000	9,981	2.1%	-10.9
ALASKA																			
ARIZONA																			
ARKANSAS				280,000	26,085	9.3%		302,000	27,524	9.1%	-0.2	331,000	29,251	8.8%	-0.5	363,000	41,689	11.5%	2.2
CALIFORNIA	335,000	125,129	37.4%	376,000	110,738	29.5%	-7.9	417,000	148,334	35.6%	-1.8	496,000	146,332	29.5%	-7.8	599,000	125,887	21.0%	-16.3
COLORADO	148,000	41,827	28.3%	259,000	93,502	36.1%	7.8	287,000	51,051	17.8%	-10.5	325,000	87,684	27.0%	-1.3	383,000	92,602	24.2%	-4.1
CONNECTICUT	186,000	63,975	34.4%	203,000	83,975	41.4%	7.0	219,000	81,015	37.0%	2.6	233,000	85,338	36.6%	2.2	245,000	88,384	36.1%	1.7
DELAWARE	45,000	17,258	38.4%	47,000	19,880	42.3%	3.9												
DISTRICT OF COLUMBIA																			
FLORIDA																			
GEORGIA																			
HAWAII																			
IDAHO	41,000	10,262	25.0%	55,000	10,208	18.6%	0.0	70,000	13,794	19.7%	-5.3	117,000	31,874	27.2%	2.2	140,000	38,386	27.4%	2.4
ILLINOIS																			
INDIANA																			
IOWA																603,000	216,995	36.0%	
KANSAS	367,000	115,025	31.3%	379,000	148,697	39.2%	7.9	391,000	149,312	38.2%	6.8	416,000	159,242	38.3%	6.9	451,000	152,147	33.7%	2.4
KENTUCKY																			
LOUISIANA																			
MAINE	182,000	64,259	35.3%	186,000	69,322	37.3%	2.0	191,000	53,900	28.2%	-7.1	195,000	63,354	32.5%	-2.8	198,000	69,427	35.1%	-0.2
MARYLAND																			
MASSACHUSETTS	525,000	131,454	25.0%	576,000	189,307	32.9%	7.8	627,000	191,146	30.5%	5.4	674,000	196,276	29.1%	4.1	719,000	222,528	30.9%	5.9
MICHIGAN	519,000	172,205	33.2%	558,000	237,215	42.5%	9.3	595,000	243,239	40.9%	7.7	642,000	211,261	32.9%	-0.3	692,000	227,567	32.9%	-0.3
MINNESOTA	326,000	88,111	27.0%	377,000	147,943	39.2%	12.2	428,000	111,796	26.1%	-0.9	466,000	155,849	33.4%	6.4	497,000	96,162	19.3%	-7.7
MISSISSIPPI																			
MISSOURI																			
MONTANA																			
NEBRASKA	275,000	68,878	25.0%	277,000	94,613	34.2%	9.1	278,000	92,982	33.4%	8.4	290,000	96,471	33.3%	8.2	309,000	97,858	31.7%	6.6
NEVADA	16,000	6,601	41.3%	16,000	3,861	24.1%	-17.1	14,000	3,548	25.3%	-15.9	19,000	4,778	25.1%	-16.1	26,000	5,336	20.5%	-20.7
NEW HAMPSHIRE	103,000	42,479	41.2%	106,000	46,491	43.9%	2.6	109,000	44,730	41.0%	-0.2	110,000	42,115	38.3%	-3.0	111,000	40,581	36.6%	-4.7
NEW JERSEY																			
NEW MEXICO																			
NEW YORK				1,645,000	673,818	41.0%		1,777,000	661,707	37.2%	-3.7	1,900,000	665,150	35.0%	-6.0	2,017,000	749,002	37.1%	-3.8

State Gubernatorial General Elections (continued)

State Gubernatorial General Elections (continued)

Republican Turnout for Election Years 1890–1906 (continued)

State	1890 Voting-age population	Turnout	%	1894 Voting-age population	Turnout	%	Difference from 1890	1898 Voting-age population	Turnout	%	Difference from 1890	1902 Voting-age population	Turnout	%	Difference from 1890	1906 Voting-age population	Turnout	%	Difference from 1890
NORTH CAROLINA																			
NORTH DAKOTA	47,000	19,053	40.5%	61,000	23,723	38.9%	-1.6	76,000	28,308	37.2%	-3.3	96,000	31,613	32.9%	-7.6	121,000	29,309	24.2%	-16.3
OHIO																			
OKLAHOMA																			
OREGON	96,000	33,765	35.2%	109,000	41,139	37.7%	2.6	122,000	45,093	37.0%	1.8	153,000	41,611	27.2%	-8.0	195,000	43,508	22.3%	-12.9
PENNSYLVANIA	1,288,000	447,655	34.8%	1,404,000	574,801	40.9%	6.2	1,519,000	476,206	31.3%	-3.4	1,626,000	593,328	36.5%	1.7	1,729,000	506,418	29.3%	-5.5
RHODE ISLAND	76,000	18,988	25.0%	87,000	29,157	33.5%	8.5	97,000	24,743	25.5%	0.5	105,000	24,541	23.4%	-1.6	113,000	31,877	28.2%	3.2
SOUTH CAROLINA																			
SOUTH DAKOTA	88,000	34,497	39.2%	94,000	40,381	43.0%	3.8	99,000	36,994	37.4%	-1.8	117,000	48,196	41.2%	2.0	142,000	48,709	34.3%	-4.9
TENNESSEE	401,000	76,081	19.0%	436,000	92,266	21.2%	2.2	470,000	72,611	15.4%	-3.5	499,000	59,007	11.8%	-7.1	526,000	92,809	17.6%	-1.3
TEXAS	514,000	77,742	15.1%	593,000	54,520	9.2%	-5.9					762,000	65,706	8.6%	-6.5	859,000	23,711	2.8%	-12.4
UTAH																			
VERMONT	92,000	33,462	36.4%	94,000	42,663	45.4%	9.0	96,000	38,555	40.2%	3.8	98,000	31,864	32.5%	-3.9	100,000	42,332	42.3%	6.0
VIRGINIA																			
WASHINGTON																			
WEST VIRGINIA																			
WISCONSIN	408,000	132,068	32.4%	452,000	196,150	43.4%	11.0	494,000	173,137	35.0%	2.7	534,000	193,417	36.2%	3.9	572,000	183,558	32.1%	-0.3
WYOMING	31,000	8,879	28.6%	38,000	10,149	26.7%	-1.9	45,000	10,383	23.1%	-5.6	66,000	14,483	21.9%	-6.7	74,000	16,317	22.1%	-6.6
Total	6,435,000	1,872,044	29.1%	8,708,000	3,060,604	35.1%	6.1	9,120,000	2,783,242	30.5%	1.4	10,705,000	3,102,891	29.0%	-0.1	12,259,000	3,293,080	26.9%	-2.2

Democratic Turnout for Election Years 1890–1906

State	1890 Voting-age population	Turnout	%	1894 Voting-age population	Turnout	%	Difference from 1890*	1898 Voting-age population	Turnout	%	Difference from 1890	1902 Voting-age population	Turnout	%	Difference from 1890	1906 Voting-age population	Turnout	%	Difference from 1890
ALABAMA	326,000	139,912	42.9%	361,000	110,875	30.7%	-12.2	397,000	110,551	27.8%	-15.1	435,000	67,748	15.6%	-27.3	475,000	61,223	12.9%	-30.0
ALASKA																			
ARIZONA																			
ARKANSAS	257,000	106,267	41.3%	280,000	74,809	26.7%	-14.6	302,000	75,354	25.0%	-16.4	331,000	77,354	23.4%	-18.0	363,000	105,586	29.1%	-12.3
CALIFORNIA	335,000	117,184	35.0%	376,000	111,942	29.8%	-5.2	417,000	129,255	31.0%	-4.0	496,000	143,783	29.0%	-6.0	599,000	117,645	19.6%	-15.3
COLORADO	148,000	35,359	23.9%	259,000	8,327	3.2%	-20.7	287,000	93,966	32.7%	8.8	325,000	80,727	24.8%	0.9	383,000	74,416	19.4%	-4.5
CONNECTICUT	186,000	67,658	36.4%	203,000	66,287	32.7%	-3.7	219,000	64,227	29.3%	-7.0	233,000	69,330	29.8%	-6.6	245,000	67,776	27.7%	-8.7
DELAWARE	45,000	17,801	39.6%	47,000	18,659	39.7%	0.1												
DISTRICT OF COLUMBIA																			
FLORIDA																			

State Gubernatorial General Elections (continued)

Democratic Turnout for Election Years 1890–1906 (continued)

State	1890 Voting-age population	1890 Turnout	1890 %	1894 Voting-age population	1894 Turnout	1894 %	1894 Difference from 1890	1898 Voting-age population	1898 Turnout	1898 %	1898 Difference from 1890	1902 Voting-age population	1902 Turnout	1902 %	1902 Difference from 1890	1906 Voting-age population	1906 Turnout	1906 %	1906 Difference from 1890
GEORGIA	399,000	105,365	26.4%	440,000	121,049	27.5%	1.1	482,000	118,557	24.6%	-1.8	527,000	81,344	15.4%	-11.0	575,000	76,962	13.4%	-13.0
HAWAII																			
IDAHO	41,000	7,948	19.4%	55,000	7,057	12.8%	-6.6	70,000	19,407	27.7%	8.3	117,000	26,021	22.2%	2.9	140,000	29,496	21.1%	1.7
ILLINOIS																			
INDIANA																			
IOWA																803,000	198,123	32.5%	
KANSAS	367,000	71,357	19.4%	379,000	26,709	7.0%	-12.4					416,000	117,148	28.2%	8.7	451,000	150,024	33.3%	13.8
KENTUCKY																			
LOUISIANA																			
MAINE	182,000	45,360	24.9%	186,000	30,405	16.3%	-8.6	191,000	29,485	15.4%	-9.5	195,000	38,107	19.5%	-5.4	198,000	61,362	31.0%	6.1
MARYLAND																			
MASSACHUSETTS	525,000	140,507	26.8%	576,000	123,930	21.5%	-5.2	627,000	107,960	17.2%	-9.5	674,000	159,156	23.6%	-3.1	719,000	192,295	26.7%	0.0
MICHIGAN	519,000	183,725	35.4%	558,000	130,823	23.4%	-12.0	595,000	168,142	28.3%	-7.1	642,000	174,077	27.1%	-8.3	692,000	130,018	18.8%	-16.6
MINNESOTA	326,000	85,844	26.3%	377,000	53,584	14.2%	-12.1	428,000	131,980	30.8%	4.5	466,000	99,362	21.3%	-5.0	497,000	168,480	33.9%	7.6
MISSISSIPPI																			
MISSOURI																			
MONTANA																			
NEBRASKA	275,000	71,331	25.9%	277,000	6,985	2.5%	-23.4					290,000	91,116	31.4%	5.5	309,000	84,885	27.5%	1.5
NEVADA	16,000	5,791	36.2%	16,000	678	4.2%	-32.0	14,000	2,057	14.7%	-21.5	19,000	6,540	34.4%	-1.8	26,000	8,686	33.4%	-2.8
NEW HAMPSHIRE	103,000	42,386	41.2%	106,000	33,959	32.0%	-9.1	109,000	35,653	32.7%	-8.4	110,000	33,844	30.8%	-10.4	111,000	37,672	33.9%	-7.2
NEW JERSEY																			
NEW MEXICO																			
NEW YORK				1,645,000	517,710	31.5%		1,777,000	643,921	36.2%	4.8	1,900,000	656,347	34.5%	3.1	2,017,000	691,105	34.3%	2.8
NORTH CAROLINA																			
NORTH DAKOTA	47,000	12,604	26.8%	61,000	8,188	13.4%	-13.4	76,000	19,496	25.7%	-1.2	96,000	17,576	18.3%	-8.5	121,000	34,424	28.4%	1.6
OHIO																			
OKLAHOMA																			
OREGON	96,000	38,920	40.5%	109,000	17,865	16.4%	-24.2					153,000	41,857	27.4%	-13.2	195,000	46,002	23.6%	-17.0
PENNSYLVANIA	1,288,000	464,209	36.0%	1,404,000	333,404	23.7%	-12.3	1,519,000	358,300	23.6%	-12.5	1,626,000	450,978	27.7%	-8.3	1,729,000	458,054	26.5%	-9.5
RHODE ISLAND	76,000	20,548	27.0%	87,000	22,650	26.0%	-1.0	97,000	13,224	13.6%	-13.4	105,000	32,279	30.7%	3.7	113,000	33,195	29.4%	2.3
SOUTH CAROLINA	237,000	59,159	25.0%	256,000	39,507	15.4%	-9.5	275,000	28,225	10.3%	-14.7	295,000	31,817	10.8%	-14.2	315,000	30,251	9.6%	-15.4
SOUTH DAKOTA	88,000	18,484	21.0%	94,000	8,756	9.3%	-11.7					117,000	21,396	18.3%	-2.7	142,000	19,923	14.0%	-7.0
TENNESSEE	401,000	113,549	28.3%	436,000	94,620	21.7%	-6.6	470,000	105,640	22.5%	-5.8	499,000	98,902	19.8%	-8.5	526,000	111,776	21.3%	-7.1

State Gubernatorial General Elections (continued)

State Gubernatorial General Elections (continued)

Democratic Turnout for Election Years 1890–1906 (continued)

State	1890 Voting-age population	Turnout	%	1894 Voting-age population	Turnout	%	Difference from 1890	1898 Voting-age population	Turnout	%	Difference from 1890	1902 Voting-age population	Turnout	%	Difference from 1890	1906 Voting-age population	Turnout	%	Difference from 1890
TEXAS	514,000	262,432	51.1%	593,000	207,167	34.9%	-16.1	673,000	291,548	43.3%	-7.7	762,000	219,076	28.8%	-22.3	859,000	148,264	17.3%	-33.8
UTAH																			
VERMONT	92,000	19,299	21.0%	94,000	14,142	15.0%	-5.9	96,000	14,686	15.3%	-5.7	98,000	7,364	7.5%	-13.5	100,000	26,912	26.9%	5.9
VIRGINIA																			
WASHINGTON																			
WEST VIRGINIA																			
WISCONSIN	408,000	160,388	39.3%	452,000	142,250	31.5%	-7.8	494,000	135,353	27.4%	-11.9	534,000	145,818	27.3%	-12.0	572,000	103,311	18.1%	-21.2
WYOMING	31,000	7,153	23.1%	38,000	6,965	18.3%	-4.7	45,000	8,989	20.0%	-3.1	66,000	10,017	15.2%	-7.9	74,000	9,444	12.8%	-10.3
Total	7,328,000	2,420,540	33.0%	9,765,000	2,339,302	24.0%	-9.1	9,660,000	2,705,976	28.0%	-5.0	11,527,000	2,999,084	26.0%	-7.0	13,149,000	3,275,310	24.9%	-8.1

Other Turnout for Election Years 1890–1906

State	1890 Voting-age population	Turnout	%	1894 Voting-age population	Turnout	%	Difference from 1890*	1898 Voting-age population	Turnout	%	Difference from 1890	1902 Voting-age population	Turnout	%	Difference from 1890	1906 Voting-age population	Turnout	%	Difference from 1890
ALABAMA	326,000	1,494	0.5%	361,000	83,295	23.1%	22.6	397,000	51,379	12.9%	12.5	435,000	24	0.0%	-0.5	475,000	417	0.1%	-0.4
ALASKA																			
ARIZONA																			
ARKANSAS	257,000	85,181	33.1%	280,000	25,732	9.2%	-24.0	302,000	9,011	3.0%	-30.2	331,000	13,136	4.0%	-29.2	363,000	5,478	1.5%	-31.6
CALIFORNIA	335,000	10,144	3.0%	376,000	61,866	16.5%	13.4	417,000	9,407	2.3%	-0.8	496,000	14,358	2.9%	-0.1	599,000	68,443	11.4%	8.4
COLORADO	148,000	6,279	4.2%	259,000	78,140	30.2%	25.9	287,000	4,507	1.6%	-2.7	325,000	18,370	5.7%	1.4	383,000	36,117	9.4%	5.2
CONNECTICUT	186,000	3,665	2.0%	203,000	4,719	2.3%	0.4	219,000	4,326	2.0%	0.0	233,000	5,034	2.2%	0.2	245,000	5,033	2.1%	0.1
DELAWARE	45,000	138	0.3%	47,000	589	1.3%	0.9												
DISTRICT OF COLUMBIA																			
FLORIDA																			
GEORGIA				440,000	96,888	22.0%		482,000	51,580	10.7%	-11.3	527,000	4,747	0.9%	-21.1	575,000	148	0.0%	-22.0
HAWAII																			
IDAHO				55,000	7,326	13.3%		70,000	6,546	9.4%	-4.0	117,000	2,362	2.0%	-11.3	140,000	5,687	4.1%	-9.3
ILLINOIS																			
INDIANA																			
IOWA																603,000	19,287	3.2%	
KANSAS	367,000	108,206	29.5%	379,000	123,826	32.7%	3.2	391,000	138,907	35.5%	6.0	416,000	10,778	2.6%	-26.9	451,000	13,208	2.9%	-26.6
KENTUCKY																			
LOUISIANA																			
MAINE	182,000	4,283	2.4%	186,000	8,049	4.3%	2.0	191,000	3,335	1.7%	-0.6	195,000	6,416	3.3%	0.9	198,000	2,710	1.4%	-1.0

State Gubernatorial General Elections (continued)

Other Turnout for Election Years 1890–1906 (continued)

State	1890 Voting-age population	1890 Turnout	1890 %	1894 Voting-age population	1894 Turnout	1894 %	1894 Difference from 1890	1898 Voting-age population	1898 Turnout	1898 %	1898 Difference from 1890	1902 Voting-age population	1902 Turnout	1902 %	1902 Difference from 1890	1906 Voting-age population	1906 Turnout	1906 %	1906 Difference from 1890
MARYLAND																			
MASSACHUSETTS	525,000	13,565	2.6%	576,000	22,117	3.8%	1.3	627,000	18,629	3.0%	0.4	674,000	43,257	6.4%	3.8	719,000	13,455	1.9%	-0.7
MICHIGAN	519,000	41,926	8.1%	558,000	48,950	8.8%	0.7	595,000	9,783	1.6%	-6.4	642,000	16,888	2.6%	-5.4	692,000	16,221	2.3%	-5.7
MINNESOTA	326,000	66,937	20.5%	377,000	94,722	25.1%	4.6	428,000	8,786	2.1%	-18.5	466,000	15,677	3.4%	-17.2	497,000	11,869	2.4%	-18.1
MISSISSIPPI																			
MISSOURI																			
MONTANA																			
NEBRASKA	275,000	73,881	26.9%	277,000	102,419	37.0%	10.1	278,000	97,686	35.1%	8.3	290,000	6,556	2.3%	-24.6	309,000	8,110	2.6%	-24.2
NEVADA				16,000	5,934	37.1%		14,000	4,403	31.5%	-5.6					26,000	815	3.1%	-34.0
NEW HAMPSHIRE	103,000	1,375	1.3%	106,000	2,606	2.5%	1.1	109,000	2,092	1.9%	0.6	110,000	3,214	2.9%	1.6	111,000	3,260	2.9%	1.6
NEW JERSEY																			
NEW MEXICO																			
NEW YORK				1,645,000	77,644	4.7%		1,777,000	44,346	2.5%	-2.2	1,900,000	61,670	3.2%	-1.5	2,017,000	42,378	2.1%	-2.6
NORTH CAROLINA																			
NORTH DAKOTA	47,000	4,821	10.3%	61,000	10,637	17.4%	7.2					96,000	1,245	1.3%	-9.0	121,000	2,547	2.1%	-8.2
OHIO																			
OKLAHOMA																			
OREGON				109,000	28,105	25.8%		122,000	39,621	32.5%	6.7	153,000	7,194	4.7%	-21.1	195,000	7,205	3.7%	-22.1
PENNSYLVANIA	1,288,000	16,332	1.3%	1,404,000	44,812	3.2%	1.9	1,519,000	137,236	9.0%	7.8	1,626,000	50,465	3.1%	1.8	1,729,000	42,105	2.4%	1.2
RHODE ISLAND	76,000	2,605	3.4%	87,000	3,056	3.5%	0.1	97,000	4,889	5.0%	1.6	105,000	2,937	2.8%	-0.6	113,000	1,429	1.3%	-2.2
SOUTH CAROLINA	237,000	14,965	6.3%	256,000	17,278	6.7%	0.4									315,000	32	0.0%	-6.3
SOUTH DAKOTA	88,000	24,591	27.9%	94,000	27,579	29.3%	1.4	99,000	38,210	38.6%	10.7	117,000	4,871	4.2%	-23.8	142,000	5,940	4.2%	-23.8
TENNESSEE	401,000	11,082	2.8%	436,000	23,092	5.3%	2.5	470,000	4,133	0.9%	-1.9	499,000	2,193	0.4%	-2.3	526,000	900	0.2%	-2.6
TEXAS	514,000	2,235	0.4%	593,000	161,039	27.2%	26.7	673,000	118,006	17.5%	17.1	762,000	24,368	3.2%	2.8	859,000	13,865	1.6%	1.2
UTAH																			
VERMONT	92,000	1,465	1.6%	94,000	1,210	1.3%	-0.3	96,000	1,096	1.1%	-0.5	98,000	30,707	31.3%	29.7	100,000	1,249	1.2%	-0.3
VIRGINIA																			
WASHINGTON																			
WEST VIRGINIA																			
WISCONSIN	408,000	16,798	4.1%	452,000	37,049	8.2%	4.1	494,000	20,940	4.2%	0.1	534,000	26,541	5.0%	0.9	572,000	33,134	5.8%	1.7
WYOMING				38,000	2,176	5.7%		45,000	431	1.0%	-4.8	66,000	552	0.8%	-4.9	74,000	1,342	1.8%	-3.9
Total	6,745,000	511,968	7.6%	9,765,000	1,200,855	12.3%	4.7	10,199,000	829,285	8.1%	0.5	11,213,000	373,560	3.3%	-4.3	13,149,000	362,384	2.8%	-4.8

*Percentage point difference between turnout in current year and initial year listed in chart. If data do not appear for a state in the initial year listed, the difference is calculated from the first year in which data do appear for that state.

UNITED STATES HOUSE OF REPRESENTATIVES GENERAL ELECTIONS

Election Years 1890–1906

State	1890 Voting-age population	Turnout	%	1894 Voting-age population	Turnout	%	Difference from 1890*	1898 Voting-age population	Turnout	%	Difference from 1890	1902 Voting-age population	Turnout	%	Difference from 1890	1906 Voting-age population	Turnout	%	Difference from 1890
ALABAMA	326,000	118,389	36.3%	361,000	127,544	35.3%	-1.0	397,000	90,810	22.9%	-13.4	435,000	91,486	21.0%	-15.3	475,000	65,541	13.8%	-22.5
ALASKA																			
ARIZONA																			
ARKANSAS	257,000	112,704	43.9%	280,000	52,283	18.7%	-25.2	302,000	27,179	9.0%	-34.9	331,000	39,417	11.9%	-31.9	363,000	51,014	14.1%	-29.8
CALIFORNIA	335,000	251,535	75.1%	376,000	268,453	71.4%	-3.7	417,000	273,061	65.5%	-9.6	496,000	291,027	58.7%	-16.4	599,000	285,331	47.6%	-27.5
COLORADO	148,000	84,115	56.8%	259,000	178,506	68.9%	12.1	287,000	144,488	50.3%	-6.5	325,000	185,047	56.9%	0.1	383,000	196,212	51.2%	-5.6
CONNECTICUT	186,000	134,839	72.5%	203,000	154,309	76.0%	3.5	219,000	149,224	68.1%	-4.4	233,000	159,188	68.3%	-4.2	245,000	160,899	65.7%	-6.8
DELAWARE	45,000	35,285	78.4%	47,000	38,932	82.8%	4.4	50,000	33,073	66.1%	-12.3	53,000	38,207	72.1%	-6.3	55,000	38,244	69.5%	-8.9
DISTRICT OF COLUMBIA																			
FLORIDA	93,000	44,476	47.8%	110,000	26,095	23.7%	-24.1	127,000	32,972	26.0%	-21.9	150,000	16,724	11.1%	-36.7	178,000	22,949	12.9%	-34.9
GEORGIA	399,000	106,952	26.8%	440,000	201,935	45.9%	19.1	482,000	68,612	14.2%	-12.6	527,000	41,347	7.8%	-19.0	575,000	33,344	5.8%	-21.0
HAWAII																			
IDAHO	41,000	18,156	44.3%	55,000	23,937	43.5%	-0.8	70,000	39,092	55.8%	11.6	117,000	59,636	51.0%	6.7	140,000	71,915	51.4%	7.1
ILLINOIS	938,000	675,625	72.0%	1,073,000	851,389	79.3%	7.3	1,206,000	873,723	72.4%	0.4	1,307,000	815,412	62.4%	-9.6	1,387,000	825,486	59.5%	-12.5
INDIANA	582,000	471,146	81.0%	632,000	559,057	88.5%	7.5	681,000	566,040	83.1%	2.2	722,000	585,809	81.1%	0.2	759,000	583,068	76.8%	-4.1
IOWA	477,000	389,075	81.6%	526,000	419,534	79.8%	-1.8	575,000	419,994	73.0%	-8.5	598,000	393,673	65.8%	-15.7	603,000	406,136	67.4%	-14.2
KANSAS	367,000	290,705	79.2%	379,000	293,298	77.4%	-1.8	391,000	281,143	71.9%	-7.3	416,000	281,981	67.8%	-11.4	451,000	305,428	67.7%	-11.5
KENTUCKY	446,000	194,947	43.7%	484,000	340,146	70.3%	26.6	522,000	273,714	52.4%	8.7	552,000	291,849	52.9%	9.2	576,000	288,593	50.1%	6.4
LOUISIANA	244,000	74,233	30.4%	273,000	114,045	41.8%	11.4	302,000	33,275	11.0%	-19.4	334,000	26,265	7.9%	-22.6	369,000	37,266	10.1%	-20.3
MAINE	182,000	112,112	61.6%	186,000	107,918	58.0%	-3.6	191,000	83,755	43.9%	-17.7	195,000	107,220	55.0%	-6.6	198,000	133,402	67.4%	5.8
MARYLAND	251,000	181,625	72.4%	274,000	204,373	74.6%	2.2	299,000	216,500	72.4%	0.0	317,000	197,183	62.2%	-10.2	332,000	199,155	60.0%	-12.4
MASSACHUSETTS	525,000	280,032	53.3%	576,000	327,147	56.8%	3.5	627,000	312,511	49.8%	-3.5	674,000	389,716	57.8%	4.5	719,000	403,116	56.1%	2.7
MICHIGAN	519,000	394,762	76.1%	558,000	408,008	73.1%	-2.9	595,000	415,770	69.9%	-6.2	642,000	392,891	61.2%	-14.9	692,000	327,680	47.4%	-28.7
MINNESOTA	326,000	235,635	72.3%	377,000	287,509	76.3%	4.0	428,000	249,673	58.3%	-13.9	466,000	264,969	56.9%	-15.4	497,000	252,706	50.8%	-21.4
MISSISSIPPI	272,000	62,117	22.8%	304,000	39,739	13.1%	-9.8	335,000	27,313	8.2%	-14.7	366,000	18,058	4.9%	-17.9	397,000	20,273	5.1%	-17.7
MISSOURI	677,000	463,097	68.4%	739,000	498,792	67.5%	-0.9	803,000	551,076	68.6%	0.2	852,000	510,035	59.9%	-8.5	893,000	585,376	65.6%	-2.9
MONTANA	57,000	31,090	54.5%	70,000	49,268	70.4%	15.8	83,000	49,787	60.0%	5.4	94,000	53,324	56.7%	2.2	110,000	56,161	51.1%	-3.5
NEBRASKA	275,000	211,499	76.9%	277,000	198,456	71.6%	-5.3	278,000	188,443	67.8%	-9.1	290,000	192,915	66.5%	-10.4	309,000	187,547	60.7%	-16.2
NEVADA	16,000	12,346	77.2%	16,000	10,106	63.2%	-14.0	14,000	8,877	63.4%	-13.8	19,000	10,921	57.5%	-19.7	26,000	14,236	54.8%	-22.4
NEW HAMPSHIRE	103,000	85,431	82.9%	106,000	81,948	77.3%	-5.6	109,000	81,241	74.5%	-8.4	110,000	76,987	70.0%	-13.0	111,000	79,034	71.2%	-11.7
NEW JERSEY	360,000	251,650	69.9%	405,000	296,216	73.1%	3.2	449,000	332,078	74.0%	4.1	498,000	360,682	72.4%	2.5	550,000	358,356	65.2%	-4.7
NEW MEXICO																			
NEW YORK	1,514,000	965,485	63.8%	1,645,000	1,218,506	74.1%	10.3	1,777,000	1,324,064	74.5%	10.7	1,900,000	1,364,835	71.8%	8.1	2,017,000	1,450,274	71.9%	8.1

United States House of Representatives General Elections *(continued)*

Election Years 1890–1906 *(continued)*

State	1890 Voting-age population	Turnout	%	1894 Voting-age population	Turnout	%	Difference from 1890	1898 Voting-age population	Turnout	%	Difference from 1890	1902 Voting-age population	Turnout	%	Difference from 1890	1906 Voting-age population	Turnout	%	Difference from 1890
NORTH CAROLINA	345,000	255,493	74.1%	375,000	277,191	73.9%	-0.1	405,000	331,622	81.9%	7.8	438,000	196,771	44.9%	-29.1	473,000	202,631	42.8%	-31.2
NORTH DAKOTA	47,000	36,195	77.0%	61,000	38,997	63.9%	-13.1	76,000	45,620	60.0%	-17.0	96,000	48,946	51.0%	-26.0	121,000	61,424	50.8%	-26.2
OHIO	960,000	739,386	77.0%	1,036,000	755,800	73.0%	-4.1	1,113,000	770,590	69.2%	-7.8	1,186,000	809,988	68.3%	-8.7	1,258,000	771,612	61.3%	-15.7
OKLAHOMA																			
OREGON	96,000	73,322	76.4%	109,000	86,167	79.1%	2.7	122,000	82,875	67.9%	-8.4	153,000	88,264	57.7%	-18.7	195,000	93,461	47.9%	-28.4
PENNSYLVANIA	1,288,000	924,414	71.8%	1,404,000	942,626	67.1%	-4.6	1,519,000	941,847	62.0%	9.8	1,626,000	1,002,475	61.7%	-10.1	1,729,000	959,122	55.5%	-16.3
RHODE ISLAND	76,000	36,765	48.4%	87,000	38,509	44.3%	-4.1	97,000	38,093	39.3%	-9.1	105,000	58,255	55.5%	7.1	113,000	65,500	58.0%	9.6
SOUTH CAROLINA	237,000	73,359	31.0%	256,000	63,616	24.9%	-6.1	275,000	31,771	11.6%	-19.4	295,000	32,090	10.9%	-20.1	315,000	29,330	9.3%	-21.6
SOUTH DAKOTA	88,000	77,290	87.8%	94,000	77,040	82.0%	-5.9	99,000	71,956	72.7%	-15.1	117,000	74,624	63.8%	-24.0	142,000	73,817	52.0%	-35.8
TENNESSEE	401,000	194,860	48.6%	436,000	227,800	52.2%	3.7	470,000	176,925	37.6%	-10.9	499,000	152,433	30.5%	-18.0	526,000	200,093	38.0%	-10.6
TEXAS	514,000	319,677	62.2%	593,000	432,284	72.9%	10.7	673,000	407,026	60.5%	-1.7	762,000	342,731	45.0%	-17.2	859,000	175,590	20.4%	-41.8
UTAH								106,000	68,127	64.3%		122,000	84,844	69.5%	5.3	143,000	84,057	58.8%	-5.5
VERMONT	92,000	52,793	57.4%	94,000	55,528	59.1%	1.7	96,000	52,071	54.2%	-3.1	98,000	44,125	45.0%	-12.4	100,000	59,529	59.5%	2.1
VIRGINIA	377,000	188,626	50.0%	404,000	214,745	53.2%	3.1	432,000	173,563	40.2%	-9.9	460,000	123,123	26.8%	-23.3	490,000	86,057	17.6%	-32.5
WASHINGTON	121,000	54,797	45.3%	139,000	77,188	55.5%	10.2	158,000	78,314	49.6%	4.3	214,000	100,921	47.2%	1.9	295,000	114,747	38.9%	-6.4
WEST VIRGINIA	180,000	149,517	83.1%	206,000	169,925	82.5%	-0.6	231,000	174,409	75.5%	-7.6	258,000	192,100	74.5%	-8.6	287,000	182,631	63.6%	-19.4
WISCONSIN	408,000	301,214	73.8%	452,000	368,485	81.5%	7.7	494,000	341,777	69.2%	-4.6	534,000	354,726	66.4%	-7.4	572,000	310,850	54.3%	-19.5
WYOMING	31,000	15,607	50.3%	38,000	19,126	50.3%	0.0	45,000	19,671	43.7%	-6.6	66,000	24,700	37.4%	-12.9	74,000	27,049	36.6%	-13.8
Total	15,222,000	9,782,378	64.3%	16,815,000	11,222,476	66.7%	2.5	18,427,000	10,953,745	59.4%	-4.8	20,048,000	10,987,920	54.8%	-9.5	21,701,000	10,936,242	50.4%	-13.9

*Percentage point difference between turnout in current year and initial year listed in chart. If data do not appear for a state in the initial year listed, the difference is calculated from the first year in which data do appear for that state.

UNITED STATES HOUSE OF REPRESENTATIVES GENERAL ELECTIONS

Republican Turnout for Election Years 1890–1906

State	1890			1894				1898				1902				1906			
	Voting-age population	Turnout	%	Voting-age population	Turnout	%	Difference from 1890*	Voting-age population	Turnout	%	Difference from 1890	Voting-age population	Turnout	%	Difference from 1890	Voting-age population	Turnout	%	Difference from 1890
ALABAMA	326,000	24,390	7.5%	361,000	15,473	4.3%	-3.2	397,000	24,254	6.1%	-1.4	435,000	21,380	4.9%	-2.6	475,000	5,982	1.3%	-6.2
ALASKA																			
ARIZONA																			
ARKANSAS	257,000	27,429	10.7%	280,000	10,389	3.7%	-7.0	302,000	2,706	0.9%	-9.8	331,000	6,587	2.0%	-8.7	363,000	12,511	3.4%	-7.2
CALIFORNIA	335,000	128,061	38.2%	376,000	110,542	29.4%	-8.8	417,000	139,382	33.4%	-4.8	496,000	152,373	30.7%	-7.5	599,000	159,897	26.7%	-11.5
COLORADO	148,000	43,118	29.1%	259,000	90,079	34.8%	5.6	287,000	46,163	16.1%	-13.0	325,000	85,217	26.2%	-2.9	383,000	102,426	26.7%	-2.4
CONNECTICUT	186,000	63,701	34.2%	203,000	85,178	42.0%	7.7	219,000	81,747	37.3%	3.1	233,000	83,666	35.9%	1.7	245,000	88,115	36.0%	1.7
DELAWARE	45,000	17,180	38.2%	47,000	19,789	42.1%	3.9	50,000	17,566	35.1%	-3.0	53,000	21,026	39.7%	1.5	55,000	20,210	36.7%	-1.4
DISTRICT OF COLUMBIA																			
FLORIDA	93,000	15,209	16.4%					127,000	7,316	5.8%	-10.6					178,000	1,179	0.7%	-15.7
GEORGIA	399,000	16,737	4.2%					482,000	7,037	1.5%	-2.7					575,000	429	0.1%	-4.1
HAWAII																			
IDAHO	41,000	10,130	24.7%	55,000	10,383	18.9%	-5.8	70,000	30,750	43.9%	19.2	117,000	32,384	27.7%	3.0	140,000	42,134	30.1%	5.4
ILLINOIS	938,000	311,320	33.2%	1,073,000	448,075	41.8%	8.6	1,206,000	463,298	38.4%	5.2	1,307,000	406,582	31.1%	-2.1	1,387,000	435,985	31.4%	-1.8
INDIANA	582,000	216,209	37.1%	632,000	284,447	45.0%	7.9	681,000	283,306	41.6%	4.5	722,000	291,459	40.4%	3.2	759,000	282,827	37.3%	0.1
IOWA	477,000	185,785	38.9%	526,000	230,702	43.9%	4.9	575,000	233,456	40.6%	1.7	598,000	223,021	37.3%	-1.7	603,000	224,341	37.2%	-1.7
KANSAS	367,000	122,682	33.4%	379,000	147,858	39.0%	5.6	391,000	147,691	37.8%	4.3	416,000	158,307	38.1%	4.6	451,000	165,210	36.6%	3.2
KENTUCKY	446,000	66,925	15.0%	484,000	158,395	32.7%	17.7	522,000	131,126	25.1%	10.1	552,000	124,953	22.6%	7.6	576,000	124,044	21.5%	6.5
LOUISIANA	244,000	12,873	5.3%	273,000	27,056	9.9%	4.6	302,000	3,920	1.3%	-4.0	334,000	4,047	1.2%	-4.1	369,000	3,962	1.1%	-4.2
MAINE	182,000	63,489	34.9%	186,000	69,457	37.3%	2.5	191,000	54,981	28.8%	-6.1	195,000	65,491	33.6%	-1.3	198,000	70,022	35.4%	0.5
MARYLAND	251,000	77,800	31.0%	274,000	99,224	36.2%	5.2	299,000	106,927	35.8%	4.8	317,000	100,054	31.6%	0.6	332,000	99,266	29.9%	-1.1
MASSACHUSETTS	525,000	133,189	25.4%	576,000	189,329	32.9%	7.5	627,000	176,674	28.2%	2.8	674,000	191,770	28.5%	3.1	719,000	228,536	31.8%	6.4
MICHIGAN	519,000	177,021	34.1%	558,000	234,329	42.0%	7.9	595,000	232,535	39.1%	5.0	642,000	228,399	35.6%	1.5	692,000	232,662	33.6%	-0.5
MINNESOTA	326,000	98,316	30.2%	377,000	149,963	39.8%	9.6	428,000	136,797	32.0%	1.8	466,000	158,962	34.1%	4.0	497,000	171,349	34.5%	4.3
MISSISSIPPI	272,000	13,884	5.1%	304,000	165	0.1%	-5.1	335,000	1,316	0.4%	-4.7								
MISSOURI	677,000	184,337	27.2%	739,000	231,783	31.4%	4.1	803,000	256,434	31.9%	4.7	852,000	230,649	27.1%	-0.2	893,000	286,132	32.0%	4.8
MONTANA	57,000	15,128	26.5%	70,000	23,140	33.1%	6.5	83,000	26,436	31.9%	5.3	94,000	24,626	26.2%	-0.3	110,000	28,368	25.8%	-0.8
NEBRASKA	275,000	72,879	26.5%	277,000	98,241	35.5%	9.0	278,000	93,509	33.6%	7.1	290,000	98,367	33.9%	7.4	309,000	98,903	32.0%	5.5
NEVADA	16,000	6,610	41.3%	16,000	2,774	17.3%	-24.0					19,000	5,073	26.7%	-14.6	26,000	5,665	21.8%	-19.5
NEW HAMPSHIRE	103,000	41,375	40.2%	106,000	46,146	43.5%	3.4	109,000	43,768	40.2%	0.0	110,000	44,629	40.6%	0.4	111,000	45,774	41.2%	1.1
NEW JERSEY	360,000	114,808	31.9%	405,000	163,823	40.5%	8.6	449,000	165,120	36.8%	4.9	498,000	183,576	36.9%	5.0	550,000	172,261	31.3%	-0.6
NEW MEXICO																			
NEW YORK	1,514,000	426,224	28.2%	1,645,000	663,844	40.4%	12.2	1,777,000	658,934	37.1%	8.9	1,900,000	661,243	34.8%	6.7	2,017,000	700,000	34.7%	6.6

United States House of Representatives General Elections *(continued)*

Republican Turnout for Election Years 1890–1906 *(continued)*

State	1890 Voting-age population	Turnout	%	1894 Voting-age population	Turnout	%	Difference from 1890	1898 Voting-age population	Turnout	%	Difference from 1890	1902 Voting-age population	Turnout	%	Difference from 1890	1906 Voting-age population	Turnout	%	Difference from 1890
NORTH CAROLINA	345,000	104,771	**30.4%**	375,000	87,624	**23.4%**	-7.0	405,000	143,085	**35.3%**	5.0	438,000	59,166	**13.5%**	-16.9	473,000	77,747	**16.4%**	-13.9
NORTH DAKOTA	47,000	21,365	**45.5%**	61,000	21,615	**35.4%**	-10.0	76,000	27,776	**36.5%**	-8.9	96,000	32,986	**34.4%**	-11.1	121,000	38,923	**32.2%**	-13.3
OHIO	960,000	362,624	**37.8%**	1,036,000	409,245	**39.5%**	1.7	1,113,000	404,659	**36.4%**	-1.4	1,186,000	439,765	**37.1%**	-0.7	1,258,000	407,698	**32.4%**	-5.4
OKLAHOMA																			
OREGON	96,000	40,176	**41.9%**	109,000	41,140	**37.7%**	-4.1	122,000	42,615	**34.9%**	-6.9	153,000	46,982	**30.7%**	-11.1	195,000	51,435	**26.4%**	-15.5
PENNSYLVANIA	1,288,000	468,519	**36.4%**	1,404,000	571,124	**40.7%**	4.3	1,519,000	532,898	**35.1%**	-1.3	1,626,000	619,753	**38.1%**	1.7	1,729,000	561,090	**32.5%**	-3.9
RHODE ISLAND	76,000	16,868	**22.2%**	87,000	22,691	**26.1%**	3.9	97,000	21,309	**22.0%**	-0.2	105,000	28,215	**26.9%**	4.7	113,000	33,009	**29.2%**	7.0
SOUTH CAROLINA	237,000	14,554	**6.1%**	256,000	14,322	**5.6%**	-0.5	275,000	2,804	**1.0%**	-5.1	295,000	742	**0.3%**	-5.9	315,000	436	**0.1%**	-6.0
SOUTH DAKOTA	88,000	34,856	**39.6%**	94,000	40,683	**43.3%**	3.7	99,000	38,760	**39.2%**	-0.5	117,000	48,454	**41.4%**	1.8	142,000	48,010	**33.8%**	-5.8
TENNESSEE	401,000	81,037	**20.2%**	436,000	101,060	**23.2%**	3.0	470,000	63,923	**13.6%**	-6.6	499,000	53,646	**10.8%**	-9.5	526,000	87,043	**16.5%**	-3.7
TEXAS	514,000	59,597	**11.6%**	593,000	46,886	**7.9%**	-3.7	673,000	68,945	**10.2%**	-1.4	762,000	57,721	**7.6%**	-4.0	859,000	20,359	**2.4%**	-9.2
UTAH								106,000	29,603	**27.9%**		122,000	43,710	**35.8%**	7.9	143,000	42,565	**29.8%**	1.8
VERMONT	92,000	35,228	**38.3%**	94,000	41,883	**44.6%**	6.3	96,000	38,078	**39.7%**	1.4	98,000	33,639	**34.2%**	-4.1	100,000	41,398	**41.4%**	3.1
VIRGINIA	377,000	49,351	**13.1%**	404,000	88,846	**22.0%**	8.9	432,000	63,100	**14.6%**	1.5	460,000	39,514	**8.6%**	-4.5	490,000	30,558	**6.2%**	-6.9
WASHINGTON	121,000	29,153	**24.1%**	139,000	35,981	**25.9%**	1.8	158,000	39,835	**25.2%**	1.1	214,000	59,366	**27.7%**	3.6	295,000	71,921	**24.4%**	0.3
WEST VIRGINIA	180,000	70,729	**39.3%**	206,000	89,518	**43.5%**	4.2	231,000	87,999	**38.1%**	-1.2	258,000	100,356	**38.9%**	-0.4	287,000	98,275	**34.2%**	-5.1
WISCONSIN	408,000	128,179	**31.4%**	452,000	200,517	**44.4%**	12.9	494,000	191,274	**38.7%**	7.3	534,000	195,096	**36.5%**	5.1	572,000	170,893	**29.9%**	-1.5
WYOMING	31,000	9,087	**29.3%**	38,000	10,068	**26.5%**	-2.8	45,000	10,762	**23.9%**	-5.4	66,000	15,808	**24.0%**	-5.4	74,000	16,813	**22.7%**	-6.6
Total	15,222,000	4,212,903	**27.7%**	16,815,000	5,433,787	**32.3%**	4.6	18,413,000	5,380,574	**29.2%**	1.5	19,005,000	5,478,660	**28.8%**	1.2	21,304,000	5,606,363	**26.3%**	-1.4

Democratic Turnout for Election Years 1890–1906

State	1890 Voting-age population	Turnout	%	1894 Voting-age population	Turnout	%	Difference from 1890*	1898 Voting-age population	Turnout	%	Difference from 1890	1902 Voting-age population	Turnout	%	Difference from 1890	1906 Voting-age population	Turnout	%	Difference from 1890
ALABAMA	326,000	82,150	**25.2%**	361,000	73,299	**20.3%**	-4.9	397,000	66,556	**16.8%**	-8.4	435,000	69,867	**16.1%**	-9.1	475,000	59,548	**12.5%**	-12.7
ALASKA																			
ARIZONA																			
ARKANSAS	257,000	69,768	**27.1%**	280,000	37,584	**13.4%**	-13.7	302,000	24,473	**8.1%**	-19.0	331,000	32,821	**9.9%**	-17.2	363,000	38,472	**10.6%**	-16.5
CALIFORNIA	335,000	116,361	**34.7%**	376,000	96,152	**25.6%**	-9.2	417,000	128,700	**30.9%**	-3.9	496,000	126,290	**25.5%**	-9.3	599,000	100,330	**16.7%**	-18.0
COLORADO	148,000	34,736	**23.5%**	259,000	49,550	**19.1%**	-4.3	287,000	95,483	**33.3%**	9.8	325,000	84,367	**26.0%**	2.5	383,000	76,792	**20.1%**	-3.4
CONNECTICUT	186,000	67,888	**36.5%**	203,000	64,542	**31.8%**	-4.7	219,000	63,337	**28.9%**	-7.6	233,000	70,590	**30.3%**	-6.2	245,000	67,747	**27.7%**	-8.8
DELAWARE	45,000	17,848	**39.7%**	47,000	18,492	**39.3%**	-0.3	50,000	15,053	**30.1%**	-9.6	53,000	16,396	**30.9%**	-8.7	55,000	17,118	**31.1%**	-8.5
DISTRICT OF COLUMBIA																			
FLORIDA	93,000	29,267	**31.5%**	110,000	21,626	**19.7%**	-11.8	127,000	25,656	**20.2%**	-11.3	150,000	16,724	**11.1%**	-20.3	178,000	20,419	**11.5%**	-20.0

United States House of Representatives General Elections (continued)

United States House of Representatives General Elections (continued)

Democratic Turnout for Election Years 1890–1906 (continued)

State	1890 Voting-age population	Turnout	%	1894 Voting-age population	Turnout	%	Difference from 1890	1898 Voting-age population	Turnout	%	Difference from 1890	1902 Voting-age population	Turnout	%	Difference from 1890	1906 Voting-age population	Turnout	%	Difference from 1890
GEORGIA	399,000	86,128	21.6%	440,000	125,178	28.4%	6.9	482,000	55,962	11.6%	-10.0	527,000	40,467	7.7%	-13.9	575,000	32,912	5.7%	-15.9
HAWAII																			
IDAHO	41,000	8,026	19.6%	55,000	5,834	10.6%	-9.0					117,000	24,878	21.3%	1.7	140,000	23,818	17.0%	-2.6
ILLINOIS	938,000	342,042	36.5%	1,073,000	312,837	29.2%	-7.3	1,206,000	390,887	32.4%	-4.1	1,307,000	373,490	28.6%	-7.9	1,387,000	312,082	22.5%	-14.0
INDIANA	582,000	239,204	41.1%	632,000	238,874	37.8%	-3.3	681,000	273,097	40.1%	-1.0	722,000	273,246	37.8%	-3.3	759,000	276,163	36.4%	-4.7
IOWA	477,000	194,832	40.8%	526,000	168,193	32.0%	-8.9	575,000	177,797	30.9%	-9.9	598,000	158,849	26.6%	-14.3	603,000	168,844	28.0%	-12.8
KANSAS	367,000	27,010	7.4%	379,000	26,113	6.9%	-0.5	391,000	130,801	33.5%	26.1	416,000	115,342	27.7%	20.4	451,000	127,715	28.3%	21.0
KENTUCKY	446,000	125,485	28.1%	484,000	160,407	33.1%	5.0	522,000	138,344	26.5%	-1.6	552,000	157,471	28.5%	0.4	576,000	155,815	27.1%	-1.1
LOUISIANA	244,000	59,801	24.5%	273,000	77,650	28.4%	3.9	302,000	27,728	9.2%	-15.3	334,000	22,218	6.7%	-17.9	369,000	32,701	8.9%	-15.6
MAINE	182,000	45,313	24.9%	186,000	30,502	16.4%	-8.5	191,000	26,455	13.9%	-11.0	195,000	38,631	19.8%	-5.1	198,000	61,196	30.9%	6.0
MARYLAND	251,000	99,848	39.8%	274,000	96,628	35.3%	-4.5	299,000	101,448	33.9%	-5.9	317,000	91,546	28.9%	-10.9	332,000	92,366	27.8%	-12.0
MASSACHUSETTS	525,000	137,079	26.1%	576,000	122,807	21.3%	-4.8	627,000	128,640	20.5%	-5.6	674,000	160,064	23.7%	-2.4	719,000	159,382	22.2%	-3.9
MICHIGAN	519,000	186,649	36.0%	558,000	130,489	23.4%	-12.6	595,000	176,863	29.7%	-6.2	642,000	155,732	24.3%	-11.7	692,000	83,432	12.1%	-23.9
MINNESOTA	326,000	107,249	32.9%	377,000	73,525	19.5%	-13.4	428,000	102,842	24.0%	-8.9	466,000	91,291	19.6%	-13.3	497,000	64,944	13.1%	-19.8
MISSISSIPPI	272,000	48,233	17.7%	304,000	27,062	8.9%	-8.8	335,000	23,802	7.1%	-10.6	366,000	18,058	4.9%	-12.8	397,000	20,100	5.1%	-12.7
MISSOURI	677,000	253,736	37.5%	739,000	220,217	29.8%	-7.7	803,000	285,019	35.5%	-2.0	852,000	274,220	32.2%	-5.3	893,000	291,276	32.6%	-4.9
MONTANA	57,000	15,411	27.0%	70,000	10,369	14.8%	-12.2	83,000	23,351	28.1%	1.1	94,000	19,560	20.8%	-6.2	110,000	22,894	20.8%	-6.2
NEBRASKA	275,000	90,833	33.0%	277,000	79,746	28.8%	-4.2	278,000	94,884	34.1%	1.1	290,000	89,234	30.8%	-2.3	309,000	84,449	27.3%	-5.7
NEVADA	16,000	5,736	35.9%					14,000	5,766	41.2%	5.3	19,000	5,848	30.8%	-5.1	26,000	8,571	33.0%	-2.9
NEW HAMPSHIRE	103,000	42,870	41.6%	106,000	33,629	31.7%	-9.9	109,000	35,784	32.8%	-8.8	110,000	30,204	27.5%	-14.2	111,000	31,270	28.2%	-13.5
NEW JERSEY	360,000	128,417	35.7%	405,000	115,345	28.5%	-7.2	449,000	154,658	34.4%	-1.2	498,000	164,199	33.0%	-2.7	550,000	169,068	30.7%	-4.9
NEW MEXICO																			
NEW YORK	1,514,000	499,955	33.0%	1,645,000	504,199	30.7%	-2.4	1,777,000	621,646	35.0%	2.0	1,900,000	651,325	34.3%	1.3	2,017,000	638,932	31.7%	-1.3
NORTH CAROLINA	345,000	149,266	43.3%	375,000	126,692	33.8%	-9.5	405,000	171,070	42.2%	-1.0	438,000	135,277	30.9%	-12.4	473,000	124,696	26.4%	-16.9
NORTH DAKOTA	47,000	14,830	31.6%					76,000	17,844	23.5%	-8.1	96,000	14,765	15.4%	-16.2	121,000	21,350	17.6%	-13.9
OHIO	960,000	351,528	36.6%	1,036,000	274,628	26.5%	-10.1	1,113,000	356,169	32.0%	-4.6	1,186,000	337,758	28.5%	-8.1	1,258,000	333,465	26.5%	-10.1
OKLAHOMA																			
OREGON	96,000	30,263	31.5%	109,000	19,803	18.2%	-13.4	122,000	33,921	27.8%	-3.7	153,000	31,811	20.8%	-10.7	195,000	31,491	16.1%	-15.4
PENNSYLVANIA	1,288,000	441,119	34.2%	1,404,000	328,677	23.4%	-10.8	1,519,000	350,213	23.1%	-11.2	1,626,000	335,607	20.6%	-13.6	1,729,000	331,717	19.2%	-15.1
RHODE ISLAND	76,000	18,706	24.6%	87,000	13,619	15.7%	-9.0	97,000	13,206	13.6%	-11.0	105,000	27,855	26.5%	1.9	113,000	31,439	27.8%	3.2
SOUTH CAROLINA	237,000	58,805	24.8%	256,000	48,628	19.0%	-5.8	275,000	28,967	10.5%	-14.3	295,000	31,343	10.6%	-14.2	315,000	28,874	9.2%	-15.6
SOUTH DAKOTA	88,000	17,527	19.9%	94,000	8,102	8.6%	-11.3	99,000	32,314	32.6%	12.7	117,000	21,113	18.0%	-1.9	142,000	19,976	14.1%	-5.8
TENNESSEE	401,000	105,185	26.2%	436,000	95,750	22.0%	-4.3	470,000	106,638	22.7%	-3.5	499,000	98,787	19.8%	-6.4	526,000	111,480	21.2%	-5.0

United States House of Representatives General Elections *(continued)*

Democratic Turnout for Election Years 1890–1906 *(continued)*

State	1890 Voting-age population	1890 Turnout	1890 %	1894 Voting-age population	1894 Turnout	1894 %	1894 Difference from 1890	1898 Voting-age population	1898 Turnout	1898 %	1898 Difference from 1890	1902 Voting-age population	1902 Turnout	1902 %	1902 Difference from 1890	1906 Voting-age population	1906 Turnout	1906 %	1906 Difference from 1890
TEXAS	514,000	257,393	50.1%	593,000	223,660	37.7%	-12.4	673,000	256,091	38.1%	-12.0	762,000	283,196	37.2%	-12.9	859,000	152,885	17.8%	-32.3
UTAH								106,000	35,646	33.6%		122,000	38,196	31.3%	-2.3	143,000	27,021	18.9%	-14.7
VERMONT	92,000	17,565	19.1%	94,000	13,645	14.5%	-4.6	96,000	13,993	14.6%	-4.5	98,000	8,544	8.7%	-10.4	100,000	17,114	17.1%	-2.0
VIRGINIA	377,000	136,435	36.2%	404,000	113,439	28.1%	-8.1	432,000	108,485	25.1%	-11.1	460,000	82,526	17.9%	-18.2	490,000	55,259	11.3%	-24.9
WASHINGTON	121,000	22,825	18.9%	139,000	14,602	10.5%	-8.4					214,000	34,315	16.0%	-2.8	295,000	31,811	10.8%	-8.1
WEST VIRGINIA	180,000	77,700	43.2%	206,000	76,057	36.9%	-6.2	231,000	85,407	37.0%	-6.2	258,000	88,350	34.2%	-8.9	287,000	77,167	26.9%	-16.3
WISCONSIN	408,000	161,901	39.7%	452,000	134,546	29.8%	-9.9	494,000	136,257	27.6%	-12.1	534,000	136,859	25.6%	-14.1	572,000	112,560	19.7%	-20.0
WYOMING	31,000	6,520	21.0%	38,000	6,152	16.2%	-4.8	45,000	8,466	18.8%	-2.2	66,000	8,892	13.5%	-7.6	74,000	8,944	12.1%	-8.9
Total	15,222,000	5,029,443	33.0%	16,738,000	4,418,849	26.4%	-6.6	18,199,000	5,149,719	28.3%	-4.7	20,048,000	5,088,122	25.4%	-7.7	21,701,000	4,755,595	21.9%	-11.1

Other Turnout for Election Years 1890–1906

State	1890 Voting-age population	1890 Turnout	1890 %	1894 Voting-age population	1894 Turnout	1894 %	1894 Difference from 1890*	1898 Voting-age population	1898 Turnout	1898 %	1898 Difference from 1890	1902 Voting-age population	1902 Turnout	1902 %	1902 Difference from 1890	1906 Voting-age population	1906 Turnout	1906 %	1906 Difference from 1890
ALABAMA	326,000	11,849	3.6%	361,000	38,772	10.7%	7.1					435,000	239	0.1%	-3.6	475,000	11	0.0%	-3.6
ALASKA																			
ARIZONA																			
ARKANSAS	257,000	15,507	6.0%	280,000	4,310	1.5%	-4.5					331,000	9	0.0%	-6.0	363,000	31	0.0%	-6.0
CALIFORNIA	335,000	7,113	2.1%	376,000	61,759	16.4%	14.3	417,000	4,979	1.2%	-0.9	496,000	12,364	2.5%	0.4	599,000	25,104	4.2%	2.1
COLORADO	140,000	6,261	4.2%	259,000	38,877	15.0%	10.8	287,000	2,842	1.0%	-3.2	325,000	15,463	4.8%	0.5	383,000	16,994	4.4%	0.2
CONNECTICUT	186,000	3,250	1.7%	203,000	4,589	2.3%	0.5	219,000	4,140	1.9%	0.1	233,000	4,932	2.1%	0.4	245,000	5,037	2.1%	0.3
DELAWARE	45,000	257	0.6%	47,000	651	1.4%	0.8	50,000	454	0.9%	0.3	53,000	785	1.5%	0.9	55,000	916	1.7%	1.1
DISTRICT OF COLUMBIA																			
FLORIDA				110,000	4,469	4.1%										178,000	1,351	0.8%	-3.3
GEORGIA	399,000	4,087	1.0%	440,000	76,757	17.4%	16.4	482,000	5,613	1.2%	0.1	527,000	880	0.2%	-0.9	575,000	3	0.0%	-1.0
HAWAII																			
IDAHO				55,000	7,720	14.0%		70,000	8,342	11.9%	-2.1	117,000	2,374	2.0%	-12.0	140,000	5,963	4.3%	-9.8
ILLINOIS	938,000	22,263	2.4%	1,073,000	90,477	8.4%	6.1	1,206,000	19,538	1.6%	-0.8	1,307,000	35,340	2.7%	0.3	1,387,000	77,419	5.6%	3.2
INDIANA	582,000	15,733	2.7%	632,000	35,736	5.7%	3.0	681,000	9,637	1.4%	-1.3	722,000	21,104	2.9%	0.2	759,000	24,078	3.2%	0.5
IOWA	477,000	8,458	1.8%	526,000	20,639	3.9%	2.2	575,000	8,741	1.5%	-0.3	598,000	11,803	2.0%	0.2	603,000	12,951	2.1%	0.4
KANSAS	367,000	141,013	38.4%	379,000	119,327	31.5%	-6.9	391,000	2,651	0.7%	-37.7	416,000	8,332	2.0%	-36.4	451,000	12,503	2.8%	-35.7
KENTUCKY	446,000	2,537	0.6%	484,000	21,344	4.4%	3.8	522,000	4,244	0.8%	0.2	552,000	9,425	1.7%	1.1	576,000	8,734	1.5%	0.9
LOUISIANA	244,000	1,559	0.6%	273,000	9,339	3.4%	2.8	302,000	1,627	0.5%	-0.1					369,000	603	0.2%	-0.5
MAINE	182,000	3,310	1.8%	186,000	7,959	4.3%	2.5	191,000	2,319	1.2%	-0.6	195,000	3,098	1.6%	-0.2	198,000	2,184	1.1%	-0.7

United States House of Representatives General Elections (continued)

United States House of Representatives General Elections (continued)

Other Turnout for Election Years 1890–1906 (continued)

State	1890			1894				1898				1902				1906			
	Voting-age population	Turnout	%	Voting-age population	Turnout	%	Difference from 1890	Voting-age population	Turnout	%	Difference from 1890	Voting-age population	Turnout	%	Difference from 1890	Voting-age population	Turnout	%	Difference from 1890
MARYLAND	251,000	3,977	1.6%	274,000	8,521	3.1%	1.5	299,000	8,125	2.7%	1.1	317,000	5,583	1.8%	0.2	332,000	7,523	2.3%	0.7
MASSACHUSETTS	525,000	9,764	1.9%	576,000	15,011	2.6%	0.7	627,000	7,197	1.1%	-0.7	674,000	37,882	5.6%	3.8	719,000	15,198	2.1%	0.3
MICHIGAN	519,000	31,092	6.0%	558,000	43,190	7.7%	1.7	595,000	6,372	1.1%	-4.9	642,000	8,760	1.4%	-4.6	692,000	11,586	1.7%	-4.3
MINNESOTA	326,000	30,070	9.2%	377,000	64,021	17.0%	7.8	428,000	10,034	2.3%	-6.9	466,000	14,716	3.2%	-6.1	497,000	16,413	3.3%	-5.9
MISSISSIPPI				304,000	12,512	4.1%		335,000	2,195	0.7%	-3.5					397,000	173	0.0%	-4.1
MISSOURI	677,000	25,024	3.7%	739,000	46,792	6.3%	2.6	803,000	9,623	1.2%	-2.5	852,000	5,166	0.6%	-3.1	893,000	7,968	0.9%	-2.8
MONTANA	57,000	551	1.0%	70,000	15,759	22.5%	21.5					94,000	9,138	9.7%	8.8	110,000	4,899	4.5%	3.5
NEBRASKA	275,000	47,787	17.4%	277,000	20,469	7.4%	-10.0	278,000	50	0.0%	-17.4	290,000	5,314	1.8%	-15.5	309,000	4,195	1.4%	-16.0
NEVADA				16,000	7,332	45.8%		14,000	3,111	22.2%	-23.6								
NEW HAMPSHIRE	103,000	1,186	1.2%	106,000	2,173	2.1%	0.9	109,000	1,689	1.5%	0.4	110,000	2,154	2.0%	0.8	111,000	1,990	1.8%	0.6
NEW JERSEY	360,000	8,425	2.3%	405,000	17,048	4.2%	1.9	449,000	12,300	2.7%	0.4	498,000	12,907	2.6%	0.3	550,000	17,027	3.1%	0.8
NEW MEXICO																			
NEW YORK	1,514,000	39,306	2.6%	1,645,000	50,463	3.1%	0.5	1,777,000	43,484	2.4%	-0.1	1,900,000	52,267	2.8%	0.2	2,017,000	111,342	5.5%	2.9
NORTH CAROLINA	345,000	1,456	0.4%	375,000	62,875	16.8%	16.3	405,000	17,467	4.3%	3.9	438,000	2,328	0.5%	0.1	473,000	188	0.0%	-0.4
NORTH DAKOTA				61,000	17,382	28.5%						96,000	1,195	1.2%	-27.3	121,000	1,151	1.0%	-27.5
OHIO	960,000	25,234	2.6%	1,036,000	71,927	6.9%	4.3	1,113,000	9,762	0.9%	-1.8	1,186,000	32,465	2.7%	0.1	1,258,000	30,449	2.4%	-0.2
OKLAHOMA																			
OREGON	96,000	2,883	3.0%	109,000	25,224	23.1%	20.1	122,000	6,339	5.2%	2.2	153,000	9,471	6.2%	3.2	195,000	10,535	5.4%	2.4
PENNSYLVANIA	1,288,000	14,776	1.1%	1,404,000	42,825	3.1%	1.9	1,519,000	58,736	3.9%	2.7	1,626,000	47,115	2.9%	1.8	1,729,000	66,315	3.8%	2.7
RHODE ISLAND	76,000	1,191	1.6%	87,000	2,199	2.5%	1.0	97,000	3,578	3.7%	2.1	105,000	2,185	2.1%	0.5	113,000	1,052	0.9%	-0.6
SOUTH CAROLINA				256,000	666	0.3%						295,000	5	0.0%	-0.3	315,000	20	0.0%	-0.3
SOUTH DAKOTA	88,000	24,907	28.3%	94,000	28,255	30.1%	1.8	99,000	882	0.9%	-27.4	117,000	5,057	4.3%	-24.0	142,000	5,831	4.1%	-24.2
TENNESSEE	401,000	8,638	2.2%	436,000	30,990	7.1%	5.0	470,000	6,364	1.4%	-0.8					526,000	1,570	0.3%	-1.9
TEXAS	514,000	2,687	0.5%	593,000	161,738	27.3%	26.8	673,000	81,990	12.2%	11.7	762,000	1,814	0.2%	-0.3	859,000	2,346	0.3%	-0.2
UTAH								106,000	2,878	2.7%		122,000	2,938	2.4%	-0.3	143,000	14,471	10.1%	7.4
VERMONT												98,000	2,042	2.1%		100,000	1,017	1.0%	-1.1
VIRGINIA	377,000	2,840	0.8%	404,000	12,460	3.1%	2.3	432,000	1,978	0.5%	-0.3	460,000	1,083	0.2%	-0.5	490,000	240	0.0%	-0.7
WASHINGTON	121,000	2,819	2.3%	139,000	26,605	19.1%	16.8	158,000	38,479	24.4%	22.0	214,000	7,240	3.4%	1.1	295,000	11,015	3.7%	1.4
WEST VIRGINIA	180,000	1,088	0.6%	206,000	4,350	2.1%	1.5	231,000	1,003	0.4%	-0.2	258,000	3,394	1.3%	0.7	287,000	7,199	2.5%	1.9
WISCONSIN	408,000	11,134	2.7%	452,000	33,422	7.4%	4.7	494,000	14,246	2.9%	0.2	534,000	22,771	4.3%	1.5	572,000	27,397	4.8%	2.1
WYOMING				38,000	2,906	7.6%		45,000	443	1.0%	-6.7					74,000	1,292	1.7%	-5.9
Total	14,393,000	540,032	3.8%	16,721,000	1,369,840	8.2%	4.4	17,071,000	423,452	2.5%	-1.3	18,614,000	421,138	2.3%	-1.5	21,675,000	574,284	2.6%	-1.1

*Percentage point difference between turnout in current year and initial year listed in chart. If data do not appear for a state in the initial year listed, the difference is calculated from the first year in which data do appear for that state.

TOTAL HIGHEST STATEWIDE GENERAL ELECTIONS

Election Years 1890–1906

State	1890 Voting-age population	1890 Turnout	1890 %	1894 Voting-age population	1894 Turnout	1894 %	1894 Difference from 1890*	1898 Voting-age population	1898 Turnout	1898 %	1898 Difference from 1890	1902 Voting-age population	1902 Turnout	1902 %	1902 Difference from 1890	1906 Voting-age population	1906 Turnout	1906 %	1906 Difference from 1890
ALABAMA	326,000	183,797	56.4%	361,000	194,170	53.8%	-2.6	397,000	165,064	41.6%	-14.8	435,000	91,922	21.1%	-35.2	475,000	71,621	15.1%	-41.3
ALASKA																			
ARIZONA																			
ARKANSAS	257,000	191,448	74.5%	280,000	126,626	45.2%	-29.3	302,000	111,889	37.0%	-37.4	331,000	119,741	36.2%	-38.3	363,000	152,753	42.1%	-32.4
CALIFORNIA	335,000	252,457	75.4%	376,000	284,546	75.7%	0.3	417,000	286,996	68.8%	-6.5	496,000	304,473	61.4%	-14.0	599,000	311,975	52.1%	-23.3
COLORADO	148,000	84,115	56.8%	259,000	179,969	69.5%	12.7	287,000	149,524	52.1%	-4.7	325,000	186,781	57.5%	0.6	383,000	203,135	53.0%	-3.8
CONNECTICUT	186,000	135,298	72.7%	203,000	154,981	76.3%	3.6	219,000	149,568	68.3%	-4.4	233,000	159,702	68.5%	-4.2	245,000	161,193	65.8%	-6.9
DELAWARE	45,000	35,285	78.4%	47,000	39,128	83.3%	4.8	50,000	33,073	66.1%	-12.3	53,000	38,207	72.1%	-6.3	55,000	38,244	69.5%	-8.9
DISTRICT OF COLUMBIA																			
FLORIDA	93,000	44,476	47.8%	110,000	26,095	23.7%	-24.1	127,000	32,972	26.0%	-21.9	150,000	16,724	11.1%	-36.7	178,000	22,949	12.9%	-34.9
GEORGIA	399,000	106,952	26.8%	440,000	217,937	49.5%	22.7	482,000	170,137	35.3%	8.5	527,000	86,091	16.3%	-10.5	575,000	77,110	13.4%	-13.4
HAWAII																			
IDAHO	41,000	18,210	44.4%	55,000	24,591	44.7%	0.3	70,000	39,747	56.8%	12.4	117,000	60,257	51.5%	7.1	140,000	73,569	52.5%	8.1
ILLINOIS	938,000	675,625	72.0%	1,073,000	851,389	79.3%	7.3	1,206,000	873,723	72.4%	0.4	1,307,000	815,412	62.4%	-9.6	1,387,000	825,486	59.5%	-12.5
INDIANA	582,000	471,146	81.0%	632,000	559,057	88.5%	7.5	681,000	566,040	83.1%	2.2	722,000	585,809	81.1%	0.2	759,000	583,068	76.8%	-4.1
IOWA	477,000	389,075	81.6%	526,000	419,534	79.8%	-1.8	575,000	419,994	73.0%	-8.5	598,000	393,673	65.8%	-15.7	603,000	432,405	71.7%	-9.9
KANSAS	367,000	294,588	80.3%	379,000	299,232	79.0%	-1.3	391,000	288,219	73.7%	-6.6	416,000	287,168	69.0%	-11.2	451,000	315,379	69.9%	-10.3
KENTUCKY	446,000	194,947	43.7%	484,000	340,146	70.3%	26.6	522,000	273,714	52.4%	8.7	552,000	291,849	52.9%	9.2	576,000	288,593	50.1%	6.4
LOUISIANA	244,000	74,233	30.4%	273,000	114,045	41.8%	11.4	302,000	33,275	11.0%	-19.4	334,000	26,265	7.9%	-22.6	369,000	37,266	10.1%	-20.3
MAINE	182,000	113,902	62.6%	186,000	107,918	58.0%	-4.6	191,000	86,720	45.4%	-17.2	195,000	107,877	55.3%	-7.3	198,000	133,499	67.4%	4.8
MARYLAND	251,000	181,625	72.4%	274,000	204,373	74.6%	2.2	299,000	216,500	72.4%	0.0	317,000	197,183	62.2%	-10.2	332,000	199,155	60.0%	-12.4
MASSACHUSETTS	525,000	285,526	54.4%	576,000	335,354	58.2%	3.8	627,000	317,735	50.7%	-3.7	674,000	398,689	59.2%	4.8	719,000	428,278	59.6%	5.2
MICHIGAN	519,000	397,856	76.7%	558,000	416,988	74.7%	-1.9	595,000	421,164	70.8%	-5.9	642,000	402,226	62.7%	-14.0	692,000	373,806	54.0%	-22.6
MINNESOTA	326,000	240,892	73.9%	377,000	296,249	78.6%	4.7	428,000	252,562	59.0%	-14.9	466,000	270,888	58.1%	-15.8	497,000	276,511	55.6%	-18.3
MISSISSIPPI	272,000	62,117	22.8%	304,000	39,739	13.1%	-9.8	335,000	27,313	8.2%	-14.7	366,000	18,058	4.9%	-17.9	397,000	20,273	5.1%	-17.7
MISSOURI	677,000	463,097	68.4%	739,000	498,792	67.5%	-0.9	803,000	551,076	68.6%	0.2	852,000	510,035	59.9%	-8.5	893,000	585,376	65.6%	-2.9
MONTANA	57,000	31,090	54.5%	70,000	49,268	70.4%	15.8	83,000	49,787	60.0%	5.4	94,000	53,324	56.7%	2.2	110,000	56,161	51.1%	-3.5
NEBRASKA	275,000	214,090	77.9%	277,000	204,017	73.7%	-4.2	278,000	190,668	68.6%	-9.3	290,000	194,143	66.9%	-10.9	309,000	190,853	61.8%	-16.1
NEVADA	16,000	12,346	77.2%	16,000	10,473	65.5%	-11.7	14,000	10,008	71.5%	-5.7	19,000	11,318	59.6%	-17.6	26,000	14,837	57.1%	-20.1
NEW HAMPSHIRE	103,000	86,240	83.7%	106,000	83,056	78.4%	-5.4	109,000	82,475	75.7%	-8.1	110,000	79,173	72.0%	-11.8	111,000	81,513	73.4%	-10.3
NEW JERSEY	360,000	251,650	69.9%	405,000	296,216	73.1%	3.2	449,000	332,078	74.0%	4.1	498,000	360,682	72.4%	2.5	550,000	358,356	65.2%	-4.7
NEW MEXICO																			
NEW YORK	1,514,000	965,485	63.8%	1,645,000	1,269,172	77.2%	13.4	1,777,000	1,349,974	76.0%	12.2	1,900,000	1,383,167	72.8%	9.0	2,017,000	1,482,485	73.5%	9.7

Total Highest Statewide General Elections (continued)

Total Highest Statewide General Elections (continued)

Election Years 1890–1906 (continued)

State	1890 Voting-age population	Turnout	%	1894 Voting-age population	Turnout	%	Difference from 1890	1898 Voting-age population	Turnout	%	Difference from 1890	1902 Voting-age population	Turnout	%	Difference from 1890	1906 Voting-age population	Turnout	%	Difference from 1890
NORTH CAROLINA	345,000	255,493	74.1%	375,000	277,191	73.9%	-0.1	405,000	331,622	81.9%	7.8	438,000	196,771	44.9%	-29.1	473,000	202,631	42.8%	-31.2
NORTH DAKOTA	47,000	36,478	77.6%	61,000	42,548	69.8%	-7.9	76,000	47,804	62.9%	-14.7	96,000	50,434	52.5%	-25.1	121,000	66,280	54.8%	-22.8
OHIO	960,000	739,386	77.0%	1,036,000	755,800	73.0%	-4.1	1,113,000	770,590	69.2%	-7.8	1,186,000	809,988	68.3%	-8.7	1,258,000	771,612	61.3%	-15.7
OKLAHOMA																			
OREGON	96,000	73,322	76.4%	109,000	87,109	79.9%	3.5	122,000	84,714	69.4%	-6.9	153,000	90,662	59.3%	-17.1	195,000	96,715	49.6%	-26.8
PENNSYLVANIA	1,288,000	928,196	72.1%	1,404,000	953,017	67.9%	-4.2	1,519,000	971,742	64.0%	-8.1	1,626,000	1,094,771	67.3%	-4.7	1,729,000	1,006,577	58.2%	-13.8
RHODE ISLAND	76,000	42,141	55.4%	87,000	54,863	63.1%	7.6	97,000	42,856	44.2%	-11.3	105,000	59,757	56.9%	1.5	113,000	66,501	58.9%	3.4
SOUTH CAROLINA	237,000	74,124	31.3%	256,000	63,616	24.9%	-6.4	275,000	31,771	11.6%	-19.7	295,000	32,090	10.9%	-20.4	315,000	30,283	9.6%	-21.7
SOUTH DAKOTA	88,000	77,290	87.8%	94,000	77,040	82.0%	-5.9	99,000	75,204	76.0%	-11.9	117,000	74,624	63.8%	-24.0	142,000	74,572	52.5%	-35.3
TENNESSEE	401,000	200,712	50.1%	436,000	227,800	52.2%	2.2	470,000	182,384	38.8%	-11.2	499,000	160,102	32.1%	-18.0	526,000	205,485	39.1%	-11.0
TEXAS	514,000	342,409	66.6%	593,000	432,284	72.9%	6.3	673,000	409,554	60.9%	-5.8	762,000	342,731	45.0%	-21.6	859,000	185,840	21.6%	-45.0
UTAH								106,000	68,127	64.3%		122,000	84,844	69.5%	5.3	143,000	84,057	58.8%	-5.5
VERMONT	92,000	54,226	58.9%	94,000	58,015	61.7%	2.8	96,000	54,337	56.6%	-2.3	98,000	69,935	71.4%	12.4	100,000	70,493	70.5%	11.6
VIRGINIA	377,000	188,626	50.0%	404,000	214,745	53.2%	3.1	432,000	173,563	40.2%	-9.9	460,000	123,123	26.8%	-23.3	490,000	86,057	17.6%	-32.5
WASHINGTON	121,000	54,797	45.3%	139,000	77,188	55.5%	10.2	158,000	78,314	49.6%	4.3	214,000	100,921	47.2%	1.9	295,000	114,747	38.9%	-6.4
WEST VIRGINIA	180,000	149,517	83.1%	206,000	169,925	82.5%	-0.6	231,000	174,409	75.5%	-7.6	258,000	192,100	74.5%	-8.6	287,000	182,631	63.6%	-19.4
WISCONSIN	408,000	309,254	75.8%	452,000	375,449	83.1%	7.3	494,000	341,777	69.2%	-6.6	534,000	365,776	68.5%	-7.3	572,000	320,003	55.9%	-19.9
WYOMING	31,000	16,032	51.7%	38,000	19,290	50.8%	-1.0	45,000	19,803	44.0%	-7.7	66,000	25,052	38.0%	-13.8	74,000	27,103	36.6%	-15.1
Total	15,222,000	9,999,571	65.7%	16,815,000	11,528,941	68.6%	2.9	18,427,000	11,340,566	61.5%	-4.1	20,048,000	11,324,518	56.5%	-9.2	21,701,000	11,387,436	52.5%	-13.2

*Percentage point difference between turnout in current year and initial year listed in chart. If data do not appear for a state in the initial year listed, the difference is calculated from the first year in which data do appear for that state.

TOTAL HIGHEST STATEWIDE GENERAL ELECTIONS

Republican Turnout for Election Years 1890–1906

State	1890 Voting-age population	1890 Turnout	1890 %	1894 Voting-age population	1894 Turnout	1894 %	1894 Difference from 1890*	1898 Voting-age population	1898 Turnout	1898 %	1898 Difference from 1890	1902 Voting-age population	1902 Turnout	1902 %	1902 Difference from 1890	1906 Voting-age population	1906 Turnout	1906 %	1906 Difference from 1890
ALABAMA	326,000	42,391	13.0%	361,000	15,473	4.3%	-8.7	397,000	24,254	6.1%	-6.9	435,000	24,150	5.6%	-7.5	475,000	9,981	2.1%	-10.9
ALASKA																			
ARIZONA																			
ARKANSAS	257,000	27,429	10.7%	280,000	26,085	9.3%	-1.4	302,000	27,524	9.1%	-1.6	331,000	29,251	8.8%	-1.8	363,000	41,689	11.5%	0.8
CALIFORNIA	335,000	128,061	38.2%	376,000	110,738	29.5%	-8.8	417,000	148,334	35.6%	-2.7	496,000	152,373	30.7%	-7.5	599,000	159,897	26.7%	-11.5
COLORADO	148,000	43,118	29.1%	259,000	93,502	36.1%	7.0	287,000	51,051	17.8%	-11.3	325,000	87,684	27.0%	-2.2	383,000	102,426	26.7%	-2.4
CONNECTICUT	186,000	63,975	34.4%	203,000	85,178	42.0%	7.6	219,000	81,747	37.3%	2.9	233,000	85,338	36.6%	2.2	245,000	88,384	36.1%	1.7
DELAWARE	45,000	17,258	38.4%	47,000	19,880	42.3%	3.9	50,000	17,566	35.1%	-3.2	53,000	21,026	39.7%	1.3	55,000	20,210	36.7%	-1.6
DISTRICT OF COLUMBIA																			
FLORIDA	93,000	15,209	16.4%					127,000	7,316	5.8%	-10.6					178,000	1,179	0.7%	-15.7
GEORGIA	399,000	16,737	4.2%					482,000	7,037	1.5%	-2.7					575,000	429	0.1%	-4.1
HAWAII																			
IDAHO	41,000	10,262	25.0%	55,000	10,383	18.9%	-6.2	70,000	30,750	43.9%	18.9	117,000	32,384	27.7%	2.6	140,000	42,134	30.1%	5.1
ILLINOIS	938,000	311,320	33.2%	1,073,000	448,075	41.8%	8.6	1,206,000	463,298	38.4%	5.2	1,307,000	406,582	31.1%	-2.1	1,387,000	435,985	31.4%	-1.8
INDIANA	582,000	216,209	37.1%	632,000	284,447	45.0%	7.9	681,000	283,306	41.6%	4.5	722,000	291,459	40.4%	3.2	759,000	282,827	37.3%	0.1
IOWA	477,000	185,785	38.9%	526,000	230,702	43.9%	4.9	575,000	233,456	40.6%	1.7	598,000	223,021	37.3%	-1.7	603,000	224,341	37.2%	-1.7
KANSAS	367,000	122,682	33.4%	379,000	148,697	39.2%	5.8	391,000	149,312	38.2%	4.8	416,000	159,242	38.3%	4.9	451,000	165,210	36.6%	3.2
KENTUCKY	446,000	66,925	15.0%	484,000	158,395	32.7%	17.7	522,000	131,126	25.1%	10.1	552,000	124,953	22.6%	7.6	576,000	124,044	21.5%	6.5
LOUISIANA	244,000	12,873	5.3%	273,000	27,056	9.9%	4.6	302,000	3,920	1.3%	-4.0	334,000	4,047	1.2%	-4.1	369,000	3,962	1.1%	-4.2
MAINE	182,000	64,259	35.3%	186,000	69,457	37.3%	2.0	191,000	54,981	28.8%	-6.5	195,000	65,491	33.6%	-1.7	198,000	70,022	35.4%	0.1
MARYLAND	251,000	77,800	31.0%	274,000	99,224	36.2%	5.2	299,000	106,927	35.8%	4.8	317,000	100,054	31.6%	0.6	332,000	99,266	29.9%	-1.1
MASSACHUSETTS	525,000	133,189	25.4%	576,000	189,329	32.9%	7.5	627,000	191,146	30.5%	5.1	674,000	196,276	29.1%	3.8	719,000	228,536	31.8%	6.4
MICHIGAN	519,000	177,021	34.1%	558,000	237,215	42.5%	8.4	595,000	243,239	40.9%	6.8	642,000	228,399	35.6%	1.5	692,000	232,662	33.6%	-0.5
MINNESOTA	326,000	98,316	30.2%	377,000	149,963	39.8%	9.6	428,000	136,797	32.0%	1.8	466,000	158,962	34.1%	4.0	484,000	171,349	35.4%	5.2
MISSISSIPPI	272,000	13,884	5.1%	304,000	165	0.1%	-5.1	335,000	1,316	0.4%	-4.7								
MISSOURI	677,000	184,337	27.2%	739,000	231,783	31.4%	4.1	803,000	256,434	31.9%	4.7	852,000	230,649	27.1%	-0.2	893,000	286,132	32.0%	4.8
MONTANA	57,000	15,128	26.5%	70,000	23,140	33.1%	6.5	83,000	26,436	31.9%	5.3	94,000	24,626	26.2%	-0.3	110,000	28,368	25.8%	-0.8
NEBRASKA	275,000	72,879	26.5%	277,000	98,241	35.5%	9.0	278,000	93,509	33.6%	7.1	290,000	98,367	33.9%	7.4	309,000	98,903	32.0%	5.5
NEVADA	16,000	6,610	41.3%	16,000	3,861	24.1%	-17.2	14,000	3,548	25.3%	-16.0	19,000	5,073	26.7%	-14.6	26,000	8,686	33.4%	-7.9
NEW HAMPSHIRE	103,000	42,479	41.2%	106,000	46,491	43.9%	2.6	109,000	44,730	41.0%	-0.2	110,000	44,629	40.6%	-0.7	111,000	45,774	41.2%	0.0
NEW JERSEY	360,000	114,808	31.9%	405,000	163,823	40.5%	8.6	449,000	165,120	36.8%	4.9	498,000	183,576	36.9%	5.0	550,000	172,261	31.3%	-0.6
NEW MEXICO																			
NEW YORK	1,514,000	426,224	28.2%	1,645,000	673,818	41.0%	12.8	1,777,000	661,707	37.2%	9.1	1,900,000	665,150	35.0%	6.9	2,017,000	407,698	20.2%	-7.9

Total Highest Statewide General Elections (continued)

Total Highest Statewide General Elections (continued)

Republican Turnout for Election Years 1890–1906 (continued)

State	1890 Voting-age population	Turnout	%	1894 Voting-age population	Turnout	%	Difference from 1890	1898 Voting-age population	Turnout	%	Difference from 1890	1902 Voting-age population	Turnout	%	Difference from 1890	1906 Voting-age population	Turnout	%	Difference from 1890
NORTH CAROLINA	345,000	104,771	30.4%	375,000	87,624	23.4%	-7.0	405,000	143,085	35.3%	5.0	438,000	59,166	13.5%	-16.9	473,000	77,747	16.4%	-13.9
NORTH DAKOTA	47,000	21,365	45.5%	61,000	23,723	38.9%	-6.6	76,000	28,308	37.2%	-8.2	96,000	32,986	34.4%	-11.1	121,000	38,923	32.2%	-13.3
OHIO	960,000	362,624	37.8%	1,036,000	409,245	39.5%	1.7	1,113,000	404,659	36.4%	-1.4	1,186,000	439,765	37.1%	-0.7	1,258,000	101,668	8.1%	-29.7
OKLAHOMA																			
OREGON	96,000	40,176	41.9%	109,000	41,140	37.7%	-4.1	122,000	45,093	37.0%	-4.9	153,000	46,982	30.7%	-11.1	195,000	51,435	26.4%	-15.5
PENNSYLVANIA	1,288,000	468,519	36.4%	1,404,000	574,801	40.9%	4.6	1,519,000	532,898	35.1%	-1.3	1,626,000	619,753	38.1%	1.7	1,729,000	561,090	32.5%	-3.9
RHODE ISLAND	76,000	18,988	25.0%	87,000	29,157	33.5%	8.5	97,000	24,743	25.5%	0.5	105,000	28,215	26.9%	1.9	113,000	33,009	29.2%	4.2
SOUTH CAROLINA	237,000	14,554	6.1%	256,000	14,322	5.6%	-0.5	275,000	2,804	1.0%	-5.1	295,000	742	0.3%	-5.9	315,000	436	0.1%	-6.0
SOUTH DAKOTA	88,000	34,856	39.6%	94,000	40,683	43.3%	3.7	99,000	38,760	39.2%	-0.5	117,000	48,454	41.4%	1.8	142,000	48,709	34.3%	-5.3
TENNESSEE	401,000	81,037	20.2%	436,000	101,060	23.2%	3.0	470,000	72,611	15.4%	-4.8	499,000	59,007	11.8%	-8.4	526,000	92,809	17.6%	-2.6
TEXAS	514,000	77,742	15.1%	593,000	54,520	9.2%	-5.9	673,000	68,945	10.2%	-4.9	762,000	65,706	8.6%	-6.5	859,000	23,711	2.8%	-12.4
UTAH								106,000	29,603	27.9%		122,000	43,710	35.8%	7.9	143,000	42,565	29.8%	1.8
VERMONT	92,000	35,228	38.3%	94,000	42,663	45.4%	7.1	96,000	38,555	40.2%	1.9	98,000	33,539	34.2%	-4.1	100,000	42,332	42.3%	4.0
VIRGINIA	377,000	49,351	13.1%	404,000	88,846	22.0%	8.9	432,000	63,100	14.6%	1.5	460,000	39,514	8.6%	-4.5	490,000	30,558	6.2%	-6.9
WASHINGTON	121,000	29,153	24.1%	139,000	35,981	25.9%	1.8	158,000	39,835	25.2%	1.1	214,000	59,366	27.7%	3.6	295,000	71,921	24.4%	0.3
WEST VIRGINIA	180,000	70,729	39.3%	206,000	89,518	43.5%	4.2	231,000	87,999	38.1%	-1.2	258,000	100,356	38.9%	-0.4	287,000	98,275	34.2%	-5.1
WISCONSIN	408,000	132,068	32.4%	452,000	200,517	44.4%	12.0	494,000	191,274	38.7%	6.3	534,000	195,096	36.5%	4.2	572,000	183,558	32.1%	-0.3
WYOMING	31,000	9,087	29.3%	38,000	10,149	26.7%	-2.6	45,000	10,762	23.9%	-5.4	66,000	15,808	24.0%	-5.4	74,000	16,813	22.7%	-6.6
Total	15,222,000	4,257,416	28.0%	16,265,000	5,489,070	33.7%	5.8	18,427,000	5,468,921	29.7%	1.7	19,005,000	5,530,927	29.1%	1.1	21,291,000	5,067,914	23.8%	-4.2

Democratic Turnout for Election Years 1890–1906

State	1890 Voting-age population	Turnout	%	1894 Voting-age population	Turnout	%	Difference from 1890*	1898 Voting-age population	Turnout	%	Difference from 1890	1902 Voting-age population	Turnout	%	Difference from 1890	1906 Voting-age population	Turnout	%	Difference from 1890
ALABAMA	326,000	139,912	42.9%	361,000	110,875	30.7%	-12.2	397,000	110,551	27.8%	-15.1	435,000	69,867	16.1%	-26.9	475,000	61,223	12.9%	-30.0
ALASKA																			
ARIZONA																			
ARKANSAS	257,000	106,267	41.3%	280,000	74,809	26.7%	-14.6	302,000	75,354	25.0%	-16.4	331,000	77,354	23.4%	-18.0	363,000	105,586	29.1%	-12.3
CALIFORNIA	335,000	117,184	35.0%	376,000	111,942	29.8%	-5.2	417,000	129,255	31.0%	-4.0	496,000	143,783	29.0%	-6.0	599,000	117,645	19.6%	-15.3
COLORADO	148,000	35,359	23.9%	259,000	49,550	19.1%	-4.8	287,000	95,483	33.3%	9.4	325,000	84,367	26.0%	2.1	383,000	76,792	20.1%	-3.8
CONNECTICUT	186,000	67,888	36.5%	203,000	66,287	32.7%	-3.8	219,000	64,227	29.3%	-7.2	233,000	70,590	30.3%	-6.2	245,000	67,776	27.7%	-8.8
DELAWARE	45,000	17,848	39.7%	47,000	18,659	39.7%	0.0	50,000	15,053	30.1%	-9.6	53,000	16,396	30.9%	-8.7	55,000	17,118	31.1%	-8.5
DISTRICT OF COLUMBIA																			
FLORIDA	93,000	29,267	31.5%	110,000	21,626	19.7%	-11.8	127,000	25,656	20.2%	-11.3	150,000	16,724	11.1%	-20.3	178,000	20,419	11.5%	-20.0

Total Highest Statewide General Elections *(continued)*

Democratic Turnout for Election Years 1890–1906 *(continued)*

State	1890 Voting-age population	Turnout	%	1894 Voting-age population	Turnout	%	Difference from 1890	1898 Voting-age population	Turnout	%	Difference from 1890	1902 Voting-age population	Turnout	%	Difference from 1890	1906 Voting-age population	Turnout	%	Difference from 1890
GEORGIA	399,000	105,365	26.4%	440,000	125,178	28.4%	2.0	482,000	118,557	24.6%	-1.8	527,000	81,344	15.4%	-11.0	575,000	76,962	13.4%	-13.0
HAWAII																			
IDAHO	41,000	8,026	19.6%	55,000	7,057	12.8%	-6.7	70,000	19,407	27.7%	8.1	117,000	26,021	22.2%	2.7	140,000	29,496	21.1%	1.5
ILLINOIS	938,000	342,042	36.5%	1,073,000	312,837	29.2%	-7.3	1,206,000	390,887	32.4%	-4.1	1,307,000	373,490	28.6%	-7.9	1,387,000	312,082	22.5%	-14.0
INDIANA	582,000	239,204	41.1%	632,000	238,874	37.8%	-3.3	681,000	273,097	40.1%	-1.0	722,000	273,246	37.8%	-3.3	759,000	276,163	36.4%	-4.7
IOWA	477,000	194,832	40.8%	526,000	168,193	32.0%	-8.9	575,000	177,797	30.9%	-9.9	608,000	168,840	26.6%	-14.3	603,000	190,123	32.5%	-8.3
KANSAS	367,000	71,357	19.4%	379,000	26,709	7.0%	-12.4	391,000	130,801	33.5%	14.0	416,000	117,148	28.2%	8.7	451,000	150,024	33.3%	13.8
KENTUCKY	446,000	125,485	28.1%	484,000	160,407	33.1%	5.0	522,000	138,344	26.5%	-1.6	552,000	157,471	28.5%	0.4	576,000	155,815	27.1%	-1.1
LOUISIANA	244,000	59,801	24.5%	273,000	77,650	28.4%	3.9	302,000	27,728	9.2%	-15.3	334,000	22,218	6.7%	-17.9	369,000	32,701	8.9%	-15.6
MAINE	182,000	45,360	24.9%	186,000	30,502	16.4%	-8.5	191,000	29,485	15.4%	-9.5	195,000	38,631	19.8%	-5.1	198,000	61,362	31.0%	6.1
MARYLAND	251,000	99,848	39.8%	274,000	96,628	35.3%	-4.5	299,000	101,448	33.9%	-5.9	317,000	91,546	28.9%	-10.9	332,000	92,366	27.8%	-12.0
MASSACHUSETTS	525,000	140,507	26.8%	576,000	123,930	21.5%	-5.2	627,000	128,640	20.5%	-6.2	674,000	160,064	23.7%	-3.0	719,000	192,295	26.7%	0.0
MICHIGAN	519,000	186,649	36.0%	558,000	130,823	23.4%	12.6	595,000	176,063	29.7%	-6.2	642,000	174,077	27.1%	-8.8	692,000	130,018	18.8%	-17.2
MINNESOTA	326,000	107,249	32.9%	377,000	73,525	19.5%	-13.4	428,000	131,980	30.8%	-2.1	466,000	99,362	21.3%	-11.6	484,000	168,480	34.8%	1.9
MISSISSIPPI	272,000	48,233	17.7%	304,000	27,062	8.9%	-8.8	335,000	23,802	7.1%	-10.6	366,000	18,058	4.9%	-12.8	397,000	20,100	5.1%	-12.7
MISSOURI	677,000	253,736	37.5%	739,000	220,217	29.8%	-7.7	803,000	285,019	35.5%	-2.0	852,000	274,220	32.2%	-5.3	893,000	291,276	32.6%	-4.9
MONTANA	57,000	15,411	27.0%	70,000	10,369	14.8%	-12.2	83,000	23,351	28.1%	1.1	94,000	19,560	20.8%	-6.2	110,000	22,894	20.8%	-6.2
NEBRASKA	275,000	90,833	33.0%	277,000	79,746	28.8%	-4.2	278,000	94,884	34.1%	1.1	290,000	91,116	31.4%	-1.6	309,000	84,885	27.5%	-5.6
NEVADA	16,000	5,791	36.2%	16,000	678	4.2%	-32.0	14,000	5,766	41.2%	5.0	19,000	6,540	34.4%	-1.8	26,000	5,336	20.5%	-15.7
NEW HAMPSHIRE	103,000	42,870	41.6%	106,000	33,959	32.0%	-9.6	109,000	35,784	32.8%	-8.8	110,000	33,844	30.8%	-10.9	111,000	37,672	33.9%	-7.7
NEW JERSEY	360,000	120,417	35.7%	405,000	115,345	28.5%	-7.2	449,000	154,658	34.4%	-1.2	498,000	164,199	33.0%	-2.7	550,000	169,068	30.7%	-4.9
NEW MEXICO																			
NEW YORK	1,514,000	499,955	33.0%	1,645,000	517,710	31.5%	-1.6	1,777,000	643,921	36.2%	3.2	1,900,000	656,347	34.5%	1.5	2,017,000	333,465	16.5%	-16.5
NORTH CAROLINA	345,000	149,266	43.3%	375,000	126,692	33.8%	-9.5	405,000	171,070	42.2%	-1.0	438,000	135,277	30.9%	-12.4	473,000	124,696	26.4%	-16.9
NORTH DAKOTA	47,000	14,830	31.6%	61,000	8,188	13.4%	-18.1	76,000	19,496	25.7%	-5.9	96,000	17,576	18.3%	-13.2	121,000	34,424	28.4%	-3.1
OHIO	960,000	351,528	36.6%	1,036,000	274,628	26.5%	-10.1	1,113,000	356,169	32.0%	-4.6	1,186,000	337,758	28.5%	-8.1	1,258,000	136,096	10.8%	-25.8
OKLAHOMA																			
OREGON	96,000	38,920	40.5%	109,000	19,803	18.2%	-22.4	122,000	33,921	27.8%	-12.7	153,000	41,857	27.4%	-13.2	195,000	46,002	23.6%	-17.0
PENNSYLVANIA	1,288,000	464,209	36.0%	1,404,000	333,404	23.7%	-12.3	1,519,000	358,300	23.6%	-12.5	1,626,000	450,978	27.7%	-8.3	1,729,000	458,054	26.5%	-9.5
RHODE ISLAND	76,000	20,548	27.0%	87,000	22,650	26.0%	-1.0	97,000	13,224	13.6%	-13.4	105,000	32,279	30.7%	3.7	113,000	33,195	29.4%	2.3
SOUTH CAROLINA	237,000	59,159	25.0%	256,000	48,628	19.0%	-6.0	275,000	28,967	10.5%	-14.4	295,000	31,817	10.8%	-14.2	315,000	30,251	9.6%	-15.4
SOUTH DAKOTA	88,000	18,484	21.0%	94,000	8,756	9.3%	-11.7	99,000	32,314	32.6%	11.6	117,000	21,396	18.3%	-2.7	142,000	19,976	14.1%	-6.9
TENNESSEE	401,000	113,549	28.3%	436,000	95,750	22.0%	-6.4	470,000	106,638	22.7%	-5.6	499,000	98,902	19.8%	-8.5	526,000	111,776	21.3%	-7.1

Total Highest Statewide General Elections (continued)

Total Highest Statewide General Elections (continued)

Democratic Turnout for Election Years 1890–1906 (continued)

State	1890 Voting-age population	1890 Turnout	1890 %	1894 Voting-age population	1894 Turnout	1894 %	1894 Difference from 1890	1898 Voting-age population	1898 Turnout	1898 %	1898 Difference from 1890	1902 Voting-age population	1902 Turnout	1902 %	1902 Difference from 1890	1906 Voting-age population	1906 Turnout	1906 %	1906 Difference from 1890
TEXAS	514,000	262,432	51.1%	593,000	223,660	37.7%	-13.3	673,000	291,548	43.3%	-7.7	762,000	283,196	37.2%	-13.9	859,000	152,885	17.8%	-33.3
UTAH								106,000	35,646	33.6%		122,000	38,196	31.3%	-2.3	143,000	27,021	18.9%	-14.7
VERMONT	92,000	19,299	21.0%	94,000	14,142	15.0%	-5.9	96,000	14,686	15.3%	-5.7	98,000	8,544	8.7%	-12.3	100,000	26,912	26.9%	5.9
VIRGINIA	377,000	136,435	36.2%	404,000	113,439	28.1%	-8.1	432,000	108,485	25.1%	-11.1	460,000	82,526	17.9%	-18.2	490,000	55,259	11.3%	-24.9
WASHINGTON	121,000	22,825	18.9%	139,000	14,602	10.5%	-8.4					214,000	34,315	16.0%	-2.8	295,000	31,811	10.8%	-8.1
WEST VIRGINIA	180,000	77,700	43.2%	206,000	76,057	36.9%	-6.2	231,000	85,407	37.0%	-6.2	258,000	88,350	34.2%	-8.9	287,000	77,157	26.9%	-16.3
WISCONSIN	408,000	161,901	39.7%	452,000	142,250	31.5%	-8.2	494,000	136,257	27.6%	-12.1	534,000	145,818	27.3%	-12.4	572,000	112,560	19.7%	-20.0
WYOMING	31,000	7,153	23.1%	38,000	6,965	18.3%	-4.7	45,000	8,989	20.0%	-3.1	66,000	10,017	15.2%	-7.9	74,000	9,444	12.8%	-10.3
Total	15,222,000	5,242,934	34.4%	16,815,000	4,560,761	27.1%	-7.3	18,269,000	5,428,915	29.7%	-4.7	20,048,000	5,375,234	26.8%	-7.6	21,688,000	4,792,661	22.1%	-12.3

Other Turnout for Election Years 1890–1906

State	1890 Voting-age population	1890 Turnout	1890 %	1894 Voting-age population	1894 Turnout	1894 %	1894 Difference from 1890*	1898 Voting-age population	1898 Turnout	1898 %	1898 Difference from 1890	1902 Voting-age population	1902 Turnout	1902 %	1902 Difference from 1890	1906 Voting-age population	1906 Turnout	1906 %	1906 Difference from 1890
ALABAMA	326,000	11,849	3.6%	361,000	83,295	23.1%	19.4	397,000	51,379	12.9%	9.3	435,000	239	0.1%	-3.6	475,000	417	0.1%	-3.5
ALASKA																			
ARIZONA																			
ARKANSAS	257,000	85,181	33.1%	280,000	25,732	9.2%	-24.0	302,000	9,011	3.0%	-30.2	331,000	13,136	4.0%	-29.2	363,000	5,478	1.5%	-31.6
CALIFORNIA	335,000	10,144	3.0%	376,000	61,866	16.5%	13.4	417,000	9,407	2.3%	-0.8	496,000	14,358	2.9%	-0.1	599,000	68,443	11.4%	8.4
COLORADO	148,000	6,279	4.2%	259,000	78,140	30.2%	25.9	287,000	4,507	1.6%	-2.7	325,000	18,370	5.7%	1.4	383,000	36,117	9.4%	5.2
CONNECTICUT	186,000	3,665	2.0%	203,000	4,719	2.3%	0.4	219,000	4,326	2.0%	0.0	233,000	5,034	2.2%	0.2	245,000	5,037	2.1%	0.1
DELAWARE	45,000	257	0.6%	47,000	651	1.4%	0.8	50,000	454	0.9%	0.3	53,000	785	1.5%	0.9	55,000	916	1.7%	1.1
DISTRICT OF COLUMBIA																			
FLORIDA				110,000	4,469	4.1%										178,000	1,351	0.8%	-3.3
GEORGIA	399,000	4,087	1.0%	440,000	96,888	22.0%	21.0	482,000	51,580	10.7%	9.7	527,000	4,747	0.9%	-0.1	575,000	148	0.0%	-1.0
HAWAII																			
IDAHO				55,000	7,720	14.0%		70,000	8,342	11.9%	-2.1	117,000	2,374	2.0%	-12.0	140,000	5,963	4.3%	-9.8
ILLINOIS	938,000	22,263	2.4%	1,073,000	90,477	8.4%	6.1	1,206,000	19,538	1.6%	-0.8	1,307,000	35,340	2.7%	0.3	1,387,000	77,419	5.6%	3.2
INDIANA	582,000	15,733	2.7%	632,000	35,736	5.7%	3.0	681,000	9,637	1.4%	-1.3	722,000	21,104	2.9%	0.2	759,000	24,078	3.2%	0.5
IOWA	477,000	8,458	1.8%	526,000	20,639	3.9%	2.2	575,000	8,741	1.5%	-0.3	598,000	11,803	2.0%	0.2	603,000	19,287	3.2%	1.4
KANSAS	367,000	141,013	38.4%	379,000	123,826	32.7%	-5.8	391,000	138,907	35.5%	-2.9	416,000	10,778	2.6%	-35.8	451,000	13,208	2.9%	-35.5
KENTUCKY	446,000	2,537	0.6%	484,000	21,344	4.4%	3.8	522,000	4,244	0.8%	0.2	552,000	9,425	1.7%	1.1	576,000	8,734	1.5%	0.9
LOUISIANA	244,000	1,559	0.6%	273,000	9,339	3.4%	2.8	302,000	1,627	0.5%	-0.1					369,000	603	0.2%	-0.5
MAINE	182,000	4,283	2.4%	186,000	8,049	4.3%	2.0	191,000	3,335	1.7%	-0.6	195,000	6,416	3.3%	0.9	198,000	2,710	1.4%	-1.0

Total Highest Statewide General Elections *(continued)*

Other Turnout for Election Years 1890–1906 *(continued)*

State	1890 Voting-age population	Turnout	%	1894 Voting-age population	Turnout	%	Difference from 1890	1898 Voting-age population	Turnout	%	Difference from 1890	1902 Voting-age population	Turnout	%	Difference from 1890	1906 Voting-age population	Turnout	%	Difference from 1890
MARYLAND	251,000	3,977	1.6%	274,000	8,521	3.1%	1.5	299,000	8,125	2.7%	1.1	317,000	5,583	1.8%	0.2	332,000	7,523	2.3%	0.7
MASSACHUSETTS	525,000	13,565	2.6%	576,000	22,117	3.8%	1.3	627,000	18,629	3.0%	0.4	674,000	43,257	6.4%	3.8	719,000	15,198	2.1%	-0.5
MICHIGAN	519,000	41,926	8.1%	558,000	48,950	8.8%	0.7	595,000	9,783	1.6%	-6.4	642,000	16,888	2.6%	-5.4	692,000	16,221	2.3%	-5.7
MINNESOTA	326,000	66,937	20.5%	377,000	94,722	25.1%	4.6	428,000	10,034	2.3%	-18.2	466,000	15,677	3.4%	-17.2	484,000	16,413	3.4%	-17.1
MISSISSIPPI				304,000	12,512	4.1%		335,000	2,195	0.7%	-3.5					397,000	173	0.0%	-4.1
MISSOURI	677,000	25,024	3.7%	739,000	46,792	6.3%	2.6	803,000	9,623	1.2%	-2.5	852,000	5,166	0.6%	-3.1	893,000	7,968	0.9%	-2.8
MONTANA	57,000	551	1.0%	70,000	15,759	22.5%	21.5					94,000	9,138	9.7%	8.8	110,000	4,899	4.5%	3.5
NEBRASKA	275,000	73,881	26.9%	277,000	102,419	37.0%	10.1	278,000	97,686	35.1%	8.3	290,000	6,556	2.3%	-24.6	309,000	8,110	2.6%	-24.2
NEVADA				16,000	7,332	45.8%		14,000	4,403	31.5%	-14.4					26,000	815	3.1%	-42.7
NEW HAMPSHIRE	103,000	1,375	1.3%	106,000	2,606	2.5%	1.1	109,000	2,092	1.9%	0.6	110,000	3,214	2.9%	1.6	111,000	3,260	2.9%	1.6
NEW JERSEY	360,000	8,425	2.3%	405,000	17,048	4.2%	1.9	449,000	12,300	2.7%	0.4	498,000	12,907	2.6%	0.3	550,000	17,027	3.1%	0.8
NEW MEXICO																			
NEW YORK	1,514,000	39,306	2.6%	1,645,000	77,644	4.7%	2.1	1,777,000	44,346	2.5%	-0.1	1,900,000	61,670	3.2%	0.6	2,017,000	30,449	1.5%	-1.1
NORTH CAROLINA	345,000	1,456	0.4%	375,000	62,875	16.8%	16.3	405,000	17,467	4.3%	3.9	438,000	2,328	0.5%	0.1	473,000	188	0.0%	-0.4
NORTH DAKOTA	47,000	4,821	10.3%	61,000	17,382	28.5%	18.2					96,000	1,245	1.3%	-9.0	121,000	2,547	2.1%	-8.2
OHIO	960,000	25,234	2.6%	1,036,000	71,927	6.9%	4.3	1,113,000	9,762	0.9%	-1.8	1,186,000	32,465	2.7%	0.1	1,258,000	5,083	0.4%	-2.2
OKLAHOMA																			
OREGON	96,000	2,883	3.0%	109,000	28,105	25.8%	22.8	122,000	39,621	32.5%	29.5	153,000	9,471	6.2%	3.2	195,000	10,535	5.4%	2.4
PENNSYLVANIA	1,288,000	16,332	1.3%	1,404,000	44,812	3.2%	1.9	1,519,000	137,236	9.0%	7.8	1,626,000	50,465	3.1%	1.8	1,729,000	66,315	3.8%	2.6
RHODE ISLAND	76,000	2,605	3.4%	87,000	3,056	3.5%	0.1	97,000	4,889	5.0%	1.6	105,000	2,937	2.8%	-0.6	113,000	1,429	1.3%	-2.2
SOUTH CAROLINA	237,000	14,965	6.3%	256,000	17,278	6.7%	0.4					295,000	5	0.0%	-6.3	315,000	32	0.0%	-6.3
SOUTH DAKOTA	88,000	24,907	28.3%	94,000	28,255	30.1%	1.8	99,000	38,210	38.6%	10.3	117,000	5,057	4.3%	-24.0	142,000	5,940	4.2%	-24.1
TENNESSEE	401,000	11,082	2.8%	436,000	30,990	7.1%	4.3	470,000	6,364	1.4%	-1.4	499,000	2,193	0.4%	-2.3	526,000	1,570	0.3%	-2.5
TEXAS	514,000	2,687	0.5%	593,000	161,738	27.3%	26.8	673,000	118,006	17.5%	17.0	762,000	24,368	3.2%	2.7	859,000	13,865	1.6%	1.1
UTAH								106,000	2,878	2.7%		122,000	2,938	2.4%	-0.3	143,000	14,471	10.1%	7.4
VERMONT	92,000	1,465	1.6%	94,000	1,210	1.3%	-0.3	96,000	1,096	1.1%	-0.5	98,000	30,707	31.3%	29.7	100,000	1,249	1.2%	-0.3
VIRGINIA	377,000	2,840	0.8%	404,000	12,460	3.1%	2.3	432,000	1,978	0.5%	-0.3	460,000	1,083	0.2%	-0.5	490,000	240	0.0%	-0.7
WASHINGTON	121,000	2,819	2.3%	139,000	26,605	19.1%	16.8	158,000	38,479	24.4%	22.0	214,000	7,240	3.4%	1.1	295,000	11,015	3.7%	1.4
WEST VIRGINIA	180,000	1,088	0.6%	206,000	4,350	2.1%	1.5	231,000	1,003	0.4%	-0.2	258,000	3,394	1.3%	0.7	287,000	7,199	2.5%	1.9
WISCONSIN	408,000	16,798	4.1%	452,000	37,049	8.2%	4.1	494,000	20,940	4.2%	0.1	534,000	26,541	5.0%	0.9	572,000	33,134	5.8%	1.7
WYOMING				38,000	2,906	7.6%		45,000	443	1.0%	-6.7	66,000	552	0.8%	-6.8	74,000	1,342	1.8%	-5.8
Total	14,769,000	724,257	4.9%	16,815,000	1,680,310	10.0%	5.1	17,866,000	982,623	5.5%	0.6	19,179,000	536,954	2.8%	-2.1	21,688,000	574,119	2.6%	-2.3

*Percentage point difference between turnout in current year and initial year listed in chart. If data do not appear for a state in the initial year listed, the difference is calculated from the first year in which data do appear for that state.

STATE GUBERNATORIAL PRIMARY ELECTIONS

Election Year 1906

	1906		
State	Voting-age population	Turnout	%
WISCONSIN -- Republican	569,000	170,814	**30.0%**
WISCONSIN -- Democratic	569,000	29,844	**5.2%**
WISCONSIN -- Other	569,000	5,687	**1.0%**
WISCONSIN -- Total	569,000	206,345	**36.3%**

STATE GUBERNATORIAL GENERAL ELECTIONS

Election Years 1891–1909

State	1891 Voting-age population	Turnout	%	1893 Voting-age population	Turnout	%	Difference from 1891*	1895 Voting-age population	Turnout	%	Difference from 1891	1897 Voting-age population	Turnout	%	Difference from 1891	1899 Voting-age population	Turnout	%	Difference from 1891
IOWA	490,000	406,975	83.1%	514,000	405,457	78.9%	-4.2	539,000	390,325	72.4%	-10.6	563,000	419,582	74.5%	-8.5	588,000	422,765	71.9%	-11.2
KENTUCKY	455,000	285,886	62.8%					493,000	335,960	68.1%	5.3					532,000	385,058	72.4%	9.5
MARYLAND	257,000	186,927	72.7%					280,000	231,105	82.5%	9.8					304,000	244,695	80.5%	7.8
MASSACHUSETTS	538,000	309,497	57.5%	563,000	349,529	62.1%	4.6	589,000	307,879	52.3%	-5.3	614,000	258,526	42.1%	-15.4	640,000	272,704	42.6%	-14.9
MISSISSIPPI								311,000	65,037	20.9%						343,000	48,370	14.1%	-6.8
NEW JERSEY								416,000	298,900	71.9%									
NEW YORK	1,547,000	1,117,849	72.3%																
OHIO	978,000	751,967	76.9%	1,017,000	785,689	77.3%	0.4	1,056,000	814,285	77.1%	0.2	1,094,000	831,665	76.0%	-0.9	1,132,000	892,096	78.8%	1.9
OKLAHOMA																			
RHODE ISLAND	79,000	43,244	54.7%	84,000	47,110	56.1%	1.3	89,000	42,011	47.2%	-7.5	94,000	40,080	42.6%	-12.1	100,000	41,851	41.9%	0.9
VIRGINIA				397,000	207,797	52.3%						425,000	166,992	39.3%	-13.0				
Total	4,344,000	3,102,345	71.4%	2,575,000	1,795,582	69.7%	-1.7	3,773,000	2,485,502	65.9%	-5.5	2,790,000	1,716,845	61.5%	-9.9	3,639,000	2,307,539	63.4%	0.9

State	1901 Voting-age population	Turnout	%	Difference from 1891	1903 Voting-age population	Turnout	%	Difference from 1891	1905 Voting-age population	Turnout	%	Difference from 1891	1907 Voting-age population	Turnout	%	Difference from 1891	1909 Voting-age population	Turnout	%	Difference from 1891
IOWA	596,000	370,685	62.2%	-20.9	599,000	398,529	66.5%	-16.5												
KENTUCKY					558,000	431,876	77.4%	14.6					582,000	410,906	70.6%	7.8				
MARYLAND					321,000	204,471	63.7%	-9.0					336,000	196,353	58.4%	-14.3				
MASSACHUSETTS	663,000	300,171	45.3%	-12.3	685,000	388,635	56.7%	-0.8	708,000	372,380	52.6%	-4.9	730,000	347,946	47.7%	-9.9	752,000	372,438	49.5%	-8.0
MISSISSIPPI					374,000	32,191	8.6%	-12.3					405,000	29,528	7.3%	-13.6				
NEW JERSEY	485,000	350,495	72.3%	0.4									563,000	380,613	67.6%	-4.2				
NEW YORK																				
OHIO	1,168,000	804,617	68.9%	-8.0	1,204,000	837,308	69.5%	-7.3	1,240,000	903,881	72.9%	-4.0								
OKLAHOMA													328,000	247,929	75.6%					
RHODE ISLAND	103,000	44,613	43.3%	-11.4	108,000	59,853	55.4%	0.7	111,000	57,127	51.5%	-3.3	115,000	64,305	55.9%	1.2	119,000	62,445	52.5%	-2.3
VIRGINIA	454,000	198,057	43.6%	-8.7					483,000	130,050	26.9%	-25.4					512,000	111,116	21.7%	-30.6
Total	3,469,000	2,068,638	59.6%	-11.8	3,849,000	2,352,863	61.1%	-10.3	2,542,000	1,463,438	57.6%		3,059,000	1,677,580	54.8%	-16.6	1,383,000	545,999	39.5%	-31.9

*Percentage point difference between turnout in current year and initial year listed in chart. If data do not appear for a state in the initial year listed, the difference is calculated from the first year in which data do appear for that state.

STATE GUBERNATORIAL GENERAL ELECTIONS

Republican Turnout for Election Years 1891–1909

State	1891 Voting-age population	Turnout	%	1893 Voting-age population	Turnout	%	Difference from 1891*	1895 Voting-age population	Turnout	%	Difference from 1891	1897 Voting-age population	Turnout	%	Difference from 1891	1899 Voting-age population	Turnout	%	Difference from 1891
IOWA	490,000	199,381	40.7%	514,000	206,821	40.2%	-0.5	539,000	208,708	38.7%	-2.0	563,000	224,729	39.9%	-0.8	588,000	239,464	40.7%	0.0
KENTUCKY	455,000	116,087	25.5%					493,000	172,436	35.0%	9.5					532,000	193,727	36.4%	10.9
MARYLAND	257,000	78,388	30.5%					280,000	124,936	44.6%	14.1					304,000	116,286	38.3%	7.8
MASSACHUSETTS	538,000	151,515	28.2%	563,000	192,613	34.2%	6.0	589,000	186,280	31.6%	3.5	614,000	165,095	26.9%	-1.3	640,000	168,902	26.4%	-1.8
NEW JERSEY								416,000	162,900	39.2%									
NEW YORK	1,547,000	534,956	34.6%																
OHIO	978,000	386,739	39.5%	1,017,000	433,342	42.6%	3.1	1,056,000	427,141	40.4%	0.9	1,094,000	429,915	39.3%	-0.2	1,132,000	417,199	36.9%	-2.7
OKLAHOMA																			
RHODE ISLAND	79,000	20,995	26.6%	84,000	21,830	26.0%	-0.6	89,000	25,098	28.2%	1.6	94,000	24,309	25.9%	-0.7	100,000	24,308	24.3%	0.9
VIRGINIA												425,000	56,739	13.4%					
Total	4,344,000	1,488,061	34.3%	2,178,000	854,606	39.2%	5.0	3,462,000	1,307,499	37.8%	3.5	2,790,000	900,787	32.3%	-2.0	3,296,000	1,159,886	35.2%	0.9

State	1901 Voting-age population	Turnout	%		1903 Voting-age population	Turnout	%	Difference from 1891*	1905 Voting-age population	Turnout	%	Difference from 1891	1907 Voting-age population	Turnout	%	Difference from 1891	1909 Voting-age population	Turnout	%	Difference from 1891
IOWA	596,000	226,902	38.1%	-2.6	599,000	238,804	39.9%	-0.8												
KENTUCKY					558,000	202,862	36.4%	10.8					582,000	214,478	36.9%	11.3				
MARYLAND					321,000	95,923	29.9%	-0.6					336,000	94,302	28.1%	-2.4				
MASSACHUSETTS	663,000	185,809	28.0%	-0.1	685,000	199,684	29.2%	1.0	708,000	197,469	27.9%	-0.3	730,000	188,068	25.8%	-2.4	752,000	190,186	25.3%	-2.9
NEW JERSEY	485,000	183,814	37.9%	-1.3									563,000	194,313	34.5%	-4.6				
NEW YORK																				
OHIO	1,168,000	436,092	37.3%	-2.2	1,204,000	475,560	39.5%	0.0	1,240,000	430,617	34.7%	-4.8								
OKLAHOMA													328,000	110,296	33.6%					
RHODE ISLAND	103,000	25,575	24.8%	-1.7	108,000	29,275	27.1%	0.5	111,000	31,311	28.2%	1.6	115,000	31,005	27.0%	0.4	119,000	37,107	31.2%	4.6
VIRGINIA	454,000	81,366	17.9%	4.6					483,000	45,815	9.5%	-3.9					512,000	40,357	7.9%	-5.5
Total	3,469,000	1,139,558	32.8%	-1.4	3,475,000	1,242,108	35.7%	2.9	2,542,000	705,212	27.7%	-5.1	2,654,000	832,462	31.4%	-1.5	1,383,000	267,650	19.4%	-13.5

Democratic Turnout for Election Years 1891–1909

State	1891 Voting-age population	Turnout	%	1893 Voting-age population	Turnout	%	Difference from 1891*	1895 Voting-age population	Turnout	%	Difference from 1891	1897 Voting-age population	Turnout	%	Difference from 1891	1899 Voting-age population	Turnout	%	Difference from 1891
IOWA	490,000	207,594	42.4%	514,000	174,656	34.0%	-8.4	539,000	149,428	27.7%	-14.6	563,000	194,853	34.6%	-7.8	588,000	183,301	31.2%	-11.2
KENTUCKY	455,000	144,168	31.7%					493,000	163,524	33.2%	1.5					532,000	191,331	36.0%	4.3
MARYLAND	257,000	108,539	42.2%					280,000	106,169	37.9%	-4.3					304,000	128,409	42.2%	0.0
MASSACHUSETTS	538,000	157,982	29.4%	563,000	156,916	27.9%	-1.5	589,000	121,599	20.6%	-8.7	614,000	79,552	13.0%	-16.4	640,000	103,802	16.2%	-13.1

State Gubernatorial General Elections (continued)

Democratic Turnout for Election Years 1891–1909 (continued)

State	1891 Voting-age population	Turnout	%	1893 Voting-age population	Turnout	%	Difference from 1891	1895 Voting-age population	Turnout	%	Difference from 1891	1897 Voting-age population	Turnout	%	Difference from 1891	1899 Voting-age population	Turnout	%	Difference from 1891
MISSISSIPPI								311,000	46,870	15.1%						343,000	42,273	12.3%	-2.7
NEW JERSEY								416,000	136,000	32.7%									
NEW YORK	1,547,000	582,893	37.7%																
OHIO	978,000	365,228	37.3%	1,017,000	352,347	34.6%	-2.7	1,056,000	334,519	31.7%	-5.7	1,094,000	401,750	36.7%	-0.6	1,132,000	368,176	32.5%	-4.8
OKLAHOMA																			
RHODE ISLAND	79,000	22,249	28.2%	84,000	22,015	26.2%	-2.0	89,000	14,289	16.1%	-12.1	94,000	13,675	14.5%	-13.6	100,000	14,602	14.6%	0.9
VIRGINIA				397,000	128,144	32.3%						425,000	110,253	25.9%	-6.3				
Total	4,344,000	1,588,653	36.6%	2,575,000	834,078	32.4%	-4.2	3,773,000	1,072,398	28.4%	-8.1	2,790,000	800,083	28.7%	-7.9	3,639,000	1,031,894	28.4%	-8.2

State	1901 Voting-age population	Turnout	%	Difference from 1891	1903 Voting-age population	Turnout	%	Difference from 1891	1905 Voting-age population	Turnout	%	Difference from 1891	1907 Voting-age population	Turnout	%	Difference from 1891	1909 Voting-age population	Turnout	%	Difference from 1891
IOWA	596,000	143,783	24.1%	-18.2	599,000	159,725	26.7%	-15.7												
KENTUCKY					558,000	229,014	41.0%	9.4					582,000	196,428	33.8%	2.1				
MARYLAND					321,000	108,548	33.8%	-8.4					336,000	102,051	30.4%	-11.9				
MASSACHUSETTS	663,000	114,362	17.2%	-12.1	685,000	163,700	23.9%	-5.5	708,000	174,911	24.7%	-4.7	730,000	84,379	11.6%	-17.8	752,000	182,252	24.2%	-5.1
MISSISSIPPI					374,000	32,191	8.6%	-6.5					405,000	29,528	7.3%	-7.8				
NEW JERSEY	485,000	166,681	34.4%	1.7									563,000	186,300	33.1%	0.4				
NEW YORK																				
OHIO	1,168,000	368,525	31.6%	-5.8	1,204,000	361,748	30.0%	-7.3	1,240,000	473,264	38.2%	0.8								
OKLAHOMA													328,000	137,633	42.0%					
RHODE ISLAND	103,000	19,038	18.5%	-9.7	108,000	30,578	28.3%	0.1	111,000	25,816	23.3%	-4.9	115,000	33,300	29.0%	0.8	119,000	25,338	21.3%	-6.9
VIRGINIA	454,000	116,691	25.7%	-6.6					483,000	84,235	17.4%	-14.8					512,000	70,759	13.8%	-18.5
Total	3,469,000	929,080	26.8%	-9.8	3,849,000	1,085,504	28.2%	1.4	2,542,000	758,226	29.8%	3.0	3,059,000	769,619	25.2%	-1.6	1,383,000	278,349	20.1%	-6.7

State Gubernatorial General Elections (continued)

State Gubernatorial General Elections (continued)

Other Turnout for Election Years 1891–1909

State	1891 Voting-age population	Turnout	%	1893 Voting-age population	Turnout	%	Difference from 1891*	1895 Voting-age population	Turnout	%	Difference from 1891	1897 Voting-age population	Turnout	%	Difference from 1891	1899 Voting-age population	Turnout	%	Difference from 1891
IOWA				514,000	23,980	4.7%		539,000	32,189	6.0%	1.3								
KENTUCKY	455,000	25,631	5.6%																
MASSACHUSETTS												614,000	13,879	2.3%					
MISSISSIPPI								311,000	18,167	5.8%						343,000	6,097	1.8%	-4.1
OHIO								1,056,000	52,625	5.0%						1,132,000	106,721	9.4%	4.4
RHODE ISLAND				84,000	3,265	3.9%		89,000	2,624	2.9%	-0.9	94,000	2,096	2.2%	-1.7	100,000	2,941	2.9%	-0.9
VIRGINIA				397,000	79,653	20.1%													

State	1901 Voting-age population	Turnout	%	1903 Voting-age population	Turnout	%	Difference from 1891	1905 Voting-age population	Turnout	%	Difference from 1891	1907 Voting-age population	Turnout	%	Difference from 1891	1909 Voting-age population	Turnout	%	Difference from 1891
IOWA																			
KENTUCKY																			
MASSACHUSETTS				685,000	25,251	3.7%	1.4					730,000	75,499	10.3%	8.1				
MISSISSIPPI																			
OHIO																			
RHODE ISLAND																			
VIRGINIA																			

*Percentage point difference between turnout in current year and initial year listed in chart. If data do not appear for a state in the initial year listed, the difference is calculated from the first year in which data do appear for that state.

CHAPTER 7
1910–1929

Chronology of Major Events, 1910–1929

1910	The thirteenth census counts the U.S. population at 62.9 million people.
1911	*Standard Oil of NJ v. United States.* The Supreme Court orders the breakup of Standard Oil Trust under the Sherman Antitrust Act, one of ninety antitrust prosecutions during President William Taft's four years in office.
1912	Democrat Woodrow Wilson wins the presidency. Theodore Roosevelt creates the Progressive (Bull Moose) Party, effectively splitting the Republican vote between himself and Taft. Eugene Debs garners 900,000 votes as a Socialist.
1913	The Sixteenth Amendment (permitting a federal income tax) and Seventeenth Amendment (providing for the direct election of U.S. Senators) are both ratified. The Federal Reserve Board is created to oversee a regional reserve banking system.
1914	World War I begins in Europe. The Panama Canal opens. The creation of the Federal Trade Commission and the passage of the Clayton Antitrust Act strengthen antitrust enforcement and safeguard unions from antitrust prosecution.
1916	Wilson is re-elected president. United States remains neutral in the war despite the sinking of an American merchant ship by Germany. Three-year "Great Migration" of nearly half a million African Americans to northern industrial cities begins.
1917	Renewed German submarine attacks on American merchant ships and a possible German-Mexican alliance lead to the United States entering the war. Congress passes the Selective Service Act providing for the conscription of young men for military service.
1918	Wilson signs the Sedition Act, declaring words spoken or written against the war effort a criminal offense. Many activists, including Socialist Eugene Debs, are jailed. Wilson outlines war aims and post-war policies in his "Fourteen Points" speech. Active fighting in Europe is halted in December.
1919	The Treaty of Versailles formally ends World War I. The Senate rejects the entry of the United States into the League of Nations. The Eighteenth Amendment prohibits the sale of "intoxicating liquors;" the subsequent Volstead Act includes beer and wine in this prohibition. In *Schenck v. United States*, the Supreme Court unanimously upholds a conviction for speech posing a "clear and present danger" to national interests.
1920	Republican Warren Harding is elected president. The Nineteenth Amendment is ratified, granting women the right to vote. The second "Palmer raid," named after the U.S. attorney general, headlines government crackdowns on the left in response to the Big Red Scare that follows the 1917 Bolshevik revolution. The fourteenth census counts the U.S. population at 105.7 million people.
1921	Congress enacts its first immigration quotas.
1922	Southern senators filibuster the Dyer antilynching bill, leading to its abandonment.
1923	Harding dies in office, succeeded by Vice President Calvin Coolidge. The Teapot Dome oil reserve scandal is one of several scandals involving Harding's administration.

Chronology of Major Events, 1910–1929 (continued)

Chronology of Major Events, 1910–1929 *(continued)*

1924	Coolidge is re-elected president. Democrats are divided by a failed resolution to condemn the Ku Klux Klan in their platform. Former Republican Robert LaFollette garners almost five million votes. The National Origins Act excludes all Asians and defines smaller immigration quotas favoring northwestern Europeans. Ethnic minorities mobilize in response, with most joining the Democratic Party and opposing Prohibition.
1925	Judiciary Act grants the Supreme Court the power to limit the cases it hears.
1927	Anarchists Sacco and Vanzetti are executed for robbery and murder after a trial in which their procedural rights were violated.
1928	Republican Herbert Hoover defeats Al Smith, the first Catholic candidate for president.
1929	U.S. stock market crashes, creating conditions for the Great Depression.

State and Federal Laws Chronology, 1910–1929

1910   Washington fully enfranchises women.

Texas institutes exemptions from poll tax for the following groups: those over the age of sixty, Native Americans, insane persons, blind persons, deaf and dumb persons, persons who have lost a hand, persons who have lost a foot, and persons permanently disabled.

1911   California fully enfranchises women. The voter must be able to read the Constitution in the English language and write his or her name. Those with physical disabilities, those currently enfranchised, and those over the age of fifty-nine at the time the amendment takes effect are exempted.

Wyoming requires the voter to have resided one year in the state, sixty days in the county, and ten days in the district. There is no loss of residence for soldiers or others traveling on public business, but no residency is gained by military personnel stationed in the state.

1912   Kansas and Oregon fully enfranchise women.

New Mexico becomes a state. "The right of any citizen of the state to vote … shall never be restricted, abridged, or impaired on account of … inability to speak, read, or write the English or Spanish languages, except as may otherwise be provided by this Constitution."[1] Voters must have resided twelve months in the state, ninety days in the county, and thirty days in the precinct. There is no loss of residence for soldiers or others traveling on public business, but no residency is gained by military personnel stationed in the state, by students, or by residents of almshouses or other institutions.

Rhode Island requires naturalized citizens to present naturalization papers when voting.

Washington requires naturalized citizens to be able to read and speak English language. Exemptions are provided for those incapacitated who can prove previous English aptitude and for those qualified to vote at act's passage.

Arizona becomes a state. The voter must be able to "read the Constitution of the United States in the English language in such manner as to show he is neither prompted nor reciting from memory, and to write his name."[2] Several provisions enacted in 1910 take effect: women are fully enfranchised. The voter must have resided for one year in the state. There is no loss of residence for soldiers or others traveling on public business, but no residency is gained by military personnel stationed in the state, by students, or by residents of almshouses or other institutions.

1913   Illinois permits women to vote in presidential elections.

The Seventeenth Amendment is ratified by the states, mandating the direct election of U.S. Senators by popular vote rather than by state legislatures.

New Hampshire institutes a poll tax of $2 for every male inhabitant between the ages of twenty-one and seventy except paupers, insane persons, or others exempt by law.

Pennsylvania requires the voter to have paid taxes on or before the last day of registration.

North Dakota terminates declarant alien voting.

Nevada requires naturalized citizens to present naturalization papers when voting.

1914   Montana and Nevada fully enfranchise women.

United States Code Title 2 Section 1 (1914) requires states to hold their U.S. House and U.S. Senate elections on the same day.

Oregon terminates declarant alien voting.

State and Federal Laws Chronology, 1910–1929 (continued)

1915	*Guinn v. United States*, 238 U.S. 347 (1915). Supreme Court upholds Oklahoma's literacy test to vote but rules "grandfather clause" exemptions in violation of Fifteenth Amendment's prohibition of discrimination based on race. In *United States v. Mosley*, 238 U.S. 383 (1915), the Court upholds the right of Congress to intervene in elections in cases of fraud and/or corruption.
	Pennsylvania requires naturalized citizens to present naturalization papers when voting.
1917	New York fully enfranchises women.
	Indiana, Michigan, Nebraska, North Dakota, Rhode Island, and Ohio permit women to vote in presidential elections. The Indiana law is declared unconstitutional the same year by the Indiana Supreme Court. Ohio's law is suspended from operation by the filing of a referendum petition and subsequently is defeated by voters on November 6, 1917.
	Arkansas permits women to vote in presidential primary elections.
	Kansas terminates declarant alien voting.
	Missouri requires the voter to have resided one year in the state and sixty days in the county. There is no loss of residence for soldiers or others traveling on public business, but no residency is gained by military personnel stationed in the state, by students, or by residents of almshouses or other institutions. No military personnel are permitted to vote.
1918	Michigan and Oklahoma fully enfranchise women.
	Texas permits women to vote in primary elections and nominating conventions. Women are exempt from the poll tax required of men in the 1918 election but are required to pay the poll tax beginning on January 1, 1919. Also, no interpreters are permitted at polls and no assistance is allowed for naturalized citizens from election judges unless the individual has been a citizen for twenty-one years. The state terminates declarant alien voting for primary elections.
	Nebraska terminates declarant alien voting.
	South Dakota terminates declarant alien voting and fully enfranchises women.
1919	Indiana, Iowa, Maine, Minnesota, Missouri, Ohio, Tennessee, and Wisconsin permit women to vote in presidential elections.
1920	The Nineteenth Amendment is passed nationally enfranchising women: "The right of citizens of the United States to vote shall not be denied or abridged by the United States or by any State on account of sex. Congress shall have power to enforce this article by appropriate legislation."
1921	Louisiana poll taxpaying requirement is repealed. Those physically disabled or of "good character and reputation, attached to the principles of the Constitution of the United States and of the State of Louisiana, and … able to understand and give a reasonable interpretation of any section of either Constitution when read to him by the registrar and well disposed to the good order and happiness of the State of Louisiana and of the United States and must understand the duties and obligations of citizenship under a republican form of government" can be exempted from the literacy requirement.[3] Also, assistance to illiterate voters is permissible if an individual is disabled. Property exemption to literacy test is eliminated. Louisiana requires the voter to have resided for two years in the state, one year in the parish, four months in the municipality, and three months in the precinct. There is no loss of residence for soldiers or others traveling on public business, but no residency is gained by military personnel stationed in the state or by residents of almshouses or other institutions.

1921 *(cont.)*	Indiana terminates declarant alien voting.
	Texas terminates declarant alien voting for all elections.
	New York declares that after January 1, 1922, no person could become entitled to vote by attaining majority, by naturalization, or otherwise, unless such person is also able to read and write in the English language. Those with physical infirmities preventing them from reading or writing are exempt, as well as those who were electors before January 1, 1922.
	North Dakota requires the voter to have resided one year in the state, ninety days in the county, and thirty days in the precinct.
	Indian Citizenship Act of 1924 grants Native Americans U.S. citizenship, although they remain disenfranchised in many states until the 1960s.
	Missouri terminates declarant alien voting.
1924	Oregon requires the voter to be able to write name and read the Constitution in English.
1926	Arkansas terminates declarant alien voting.
1927	*Nixon v. Herndon,* 273 U.S. 536 (1927). Supreme Court unanimously rules that "white primary" in Texas is a violation of the Fourteenth Amendment's equal protection clause. African Americans must have access to primary elections.

Source: Adapted from Alexander Keyssar, *The Right to Vote: The Contested History of Democracy in the United States,* Revised Edition (New York: Basic Books, 2009), 334–355.
[1] As quoted in Keyssar, 343. For sources, see Keyssar 369–379.
[2] As quoted in Keyssar, 340. For sources, see Keyssar 369–379.
[3] As quoted in Keyssar, 342. For sources, see Keyssar 369–379.

National Count of Popular Vote for President, 1912–1928

YEAR	NAME	PARTY	TOTAL	PERCENTAGE[1]
1912	Woodrow Wilson	Democratic	6,293,152	23.4%
	Theodore Roosevelt	Progressive	4,122,722	15.4%
	William Taft	Republican	3,486,333	13.0%
	Eugene Debs	Socialist	901,551	3.4%
1916	Woodrow Wilson	Democratic	9,126,300	29.8%
	Charles Hughes	Republican	8,546,789	27.9%
	Allan Benson	Socialist	590,524	1.9%
1920	Warren Harding	Republican	16,153,115	29.1%
	James Cox	Democratic	9,133,092	16.5%
	Eugene Debs	Socialist	913,693	1.7%
	Other and write-ins		568,713	1.0%
1924	Calvin Coolidge	Republican	15,719,921	26.0%
	John Smith	Democratic	8,386,704	13.9%
	Robert LaFollette	Progressive	4,831,706	8.0%
1928	Herbert Hoover	Republican	21,437,277	32.8%
	Al Smith	Democratic	15,007,698	23.0%

[1] The percentage figures in this chart are based on the votes cast divided by the eligible voting-age population at the time of the election.

States with Property and Taxpaying Requirements for Suffrage, 1910–1929

STATE	DATE OF STATEHOOD[1]	PROPERTY REQUIREMENT[2]	TAXPAYING REQUIREMENT[2]
ALABAMA		1875: Constitutional ban on education or property qualifications for suffrage	
		1901: Exempt from literacy requirement if owning 40 acres of land or real estate assessed at $300	1901: Poll tax of $1.50 for those age 21 to 45; legislature authorized to increase maximum age to "not more than 60 years." After January 1, 1903, if using property alternative to literacy requirement, paid all taxes on that property.
ARKANSAS		None	1893: Poll tax; must present receipt or other evidence that tax has been paid.
ARIZONA	1912	1912: "Questions upon bond issue or special assessments shall be submitted to the vote of real property taxpayers."	1912: "Questions upon bond issues or special assessments shall be submitted to the vote of real property tax payers."
DELAWARE		None	1897: 1831 tax requirement repealed
FLORIDA		None	1885: "The legislature shall have power to make the payment of the capitation tax a prerequisite for voting, and all such taxes received shall go into the school fund."
			1889: Poll tax of $1
GEORGIA		1907: Owners of at least 40 acres of land assessed for taxation at $500 exempt from literacy requirement	1907: Paid all taxes since the 1877 constitution at least 6 months prior to election
IDAHO		1890: Constitutional ban on property qualifications for voting except in school elections, elections creating indebtedness, or irrigation district elections	None
LOUISIANA		1898: Owners of property worth $300 on which all taxes paid exempt from literacy requirement	1898: If younger than 60, paid poll tax of $1 per annum for two years. If using property alternative to literacy requirement, paid all taxes on that property.
		1921: No requirement	1921: Poll tax repealed
MISSISSIPPI		None	1890: Paid all taxes for 2 preceding years by February 1 of the election year. Exemption for ministers with 6 months residence in district. Also $2 poll tax, except for persons who are "deaf and dumb or blind, or who are maimed by loss of hand or foot; said tax to be a lien only upon taxable property."
MONTANA		None	1889 : "Upon all questions submitted to the vote of the taxpayers of the State, or any political division thereof, women who are taxpayers and possessed of the qualifications for the right of suffrage required by men in this Constitution equally, with men have the right to vote."
NEVADA		None	1865: Every male inhabitant between ages 21 and 60 must pay poll tax of $4 unless exempted by law

States with Property and Taxpaying Requirements for Suffrage, 1910–1929 (continued)

States with Property and Taxpaying Requirements for Suffrage, 1910–1929 *(continued)*

STATE	DATE OF STATEHOOD[1]	PROPERTY REQUIREMENT[2]	TAXPAYING REQUIREMENT[2]
NEW HAMPSHIRE		None	1902: Excludes persons excused from paying taxes at their own request 1913: Poll tax of $2 for every male inhabitant between age 21 and 70 except paupers, insane persons, or others exempt by law
NEW MEXICO	1912	None	None
NORTH CAROLINA		None	1876: Poll tax
PENNSYLVANIA		None	1873: Paid state or county tax at least 1 month before the election 1913: Paid taxes on or before the last day of registration
RHODE ISLAND		1888: Property requirement for state elections repealed 1896: Property owners exempt from registration requirement	1888: Registry tax of $1 or other tax must be paid
SOUTH CAROLINA		1895: If registered after January 1, 1898, property/taxpaying alternative to literacy test: paid all taxes collectible during previous year on property assessed at $300 or more	1895: Poll tax; if registering for the first time after January 1, 1898, paid all property taxes collectible during the previous year. Proof of payment required. In addition, property/taxpaying alternative to literacy test: see 1895 property requirement.
TENNESSEE		None	1870: Poll tax; proof of payment required
TEXAS		None	1883: Poll tax of $1 1902: Paid poll tax and produced receipt by February 1 of election year 1910: Exemptions from poll tax for those over 60, Indians not taxed, insane persons, blind persons, deaf and dumb persons, persons who have lost a hand, persons who have lost a foot, persons permanently disabled
UTAH		1896: "Except in elections levying a special tax or creating indebtedness, no property qualification shall be required for any person to vote or hold office."	None
VIRGINIA		1902: In 1902 and 1903 a property alternative to literacy requirement. General Assembly may prescribe property qualification not exceeding $250 for county, city, or town elections.	1902: If using property alternative to literacy requirement between 1902 and 1903, paid "state taxes aggregating at least one dollar" on the property. If registered after January 1, 1904, paid poll taxes for the 3 years preceding registration at least 6 months prior to the election. Exemption for Civil War veterans.

Source: Alexander Keyssar, *The Right to Vote: The Contested History of Democracy in the United States,* Revised Edition (New York: Basic Books, 2009), 334–336. Adapted from Keyssar's tables, which extend from 1870 to 1920. Sources of quotations are found on pp. 369–379. Table includes only restrictions that affected statewide elections.

[1] For states whose date of statehood falls within the time period 1910–1929

[2] Dates listed are for the year that the property or tax requirement went into effect. All listed requirements continue into the 1910–1929 date range of this table.

States with Special Provisions Affecting Aliens and Immigrants, 1910–1929

STATE	DECLARANT ALIENS PERMITTED TO VOTE[1]	TERMINATION OF DECLARANT ALIEN VOTING	NATURALIZED CITIZENS REQUIRED TO PRESENT NATURALIZATION PAPERS	WAITING PERIODS AND OTHER RESTRICTIONS
ARKANSAS	1868	1926	—	—
CALIFORNIA	—	—	1872	1879: Naturalization 90 days prior to election
COLORADO	1876	1902	1891: If challenged	1876: Alien must have declared intention to be citizen 4 months prior to election
CONNECTICUT	—	—	1902	—
FLORIDA	—	—	1868	—
INDIANA	1851	1921	—	—
KANSAS	1861	1917	—	—
MASSACHUSETTS	—	—	1855	—
MINNESOTA	—	—	—	1858: U.S. citizen for 3 months
MISSOURI	1870	1924	1883	1870: Alien must have declared intention to be citizen "not less than one year nor more than five years before he offers to vote"
MONTANA	—	—	1909	—
NEBRASKA	1867	1918	—	1875: Alien must have declared intention to be citizen at least 30 days prior to election
NEVADA	—	—	1913	—
NEW JERSEY	—	—	1888	—
NEW YORK	—	—	1866	1894: Citizen for 90 days
NORTH DAKOTA	1889	1913	—	1889: Alien must have declared intention to be citizen at least 1 year and not more than 6 years prior to election
OHIO	—	—	1857	—
OREGON	1859	1914	—	1857: Alien must have declared intention to be citizen 1 year preceding election
PENNSYLVANIA	—	—	1915	1873: U.S. citizen for 1 month
RHODE ISLAND	—	—	1912	—
SOUTH DAKOTA	1889	1918	—	—

States with Special Provisions Affecting Aliens and Immigrants, 1910–1929 (continued)

States with Special Provisions Affecting Aliens and Immigrants, 1910–1929 (continued)

STATE	DECLARANT ALIENS PERMITTED TO VOTE[1]	TERMINATION OF DECLARANT ALIEN VOTING	NATURALIZED CITIZENS REQUIRED TO PRESENT NATURALIZATION PAPERS	WAITING PERIODS AND OTHER RESTRICTIONS
TEXAS	1869		—	1869: Aliens must have declared intention to be citizen not less than 6 months prior to election
		1918: Repealed for primaries		1918: No interpreters at polls. No assistance from election judges unless citizen for 21 years
		1921: Repealed for all elections		
UTAH	—	—	—	1895: U.S. citizen for 90 days
WASHINGTON	—	—	—	1912: Naturalized citizens must be able to read and speak English language, unless incapacitated
WEST VIRGINIA	—	—	1908	—
WISCONSIN	1848	1908	—	—

Key: — indicates no requirement at that time
   * indicates that the previous requirement remained in effect

Source: Alexander Keyssar, *The Right to Vote: The Contested History of Democracy in the United States,* Revised Edition (New York: Basic Books, 2009), 337–339. Adapted from Keyssar's table, which extends from 1870 to 1920. Sources of quotations are found on pp. 369–379.

[1] A declarant alien is a resident who has formally declared his or her intention to become a citizen.

States with Literacy Requirements for Suffrage, 1910–1929

STATE	LITERACY REQUIREMENTS[1]	EXEMPTIONS	ASSISTANCE TO ILLITERATE VOTERS
ALABAMA	1901: After January 1, 1903, must be able to "read or write any article of the Constitution of the United States in the English language."	1901: Those unable to read or write due to physical disability; owners of 40 acres of property or real estate assessed for taxation at $300	—
ARIZONA	1912: Must be able to "read the Constitution of the United States in the English language in such manner as to show he is neither prompted nor reciting from memory, and to write his name."	—	—
ARKANSAS	—	—	1891: Election Judges may assist illiterate voters.
CALIFORNIA	1911: Excludes those "who shall not be able to read the Constitution in the English language and write his or her name."	1911: Those with physical disabilities, those enfranchised in 1911, and those over age 59 at the time amendment took effect	—
COLORADO	1876: "The General Assembly may prescribe, by law, an educational qualification for electors, but no such law shall take effect prior to" 1890.	—	—
	*	—	1891: Assistance provided for any voter who declares under oath that he cannot read or write. Interpreters provided for those who cannot speak or understand English.
CONNECTICUT	—	1855: Those who could vote before 1855	—
	1902: Must "read at least three lines of the Constitution or of the statutes of this State, other than the title or enacting clause, in such manner as to show that he is not prompted nor reciting from memory."	1902: No one will be held ineligible by reason of blindness or defective sight	—
DELAWARE	1897: Must be able to read Constitution and write name if becoming eligible to vote after January 1, 1900	1897: Those who cannot read or write due to physical disability	—
GEORGIA	1907: Must be able to read in English any paragraph of state or U.S. Constitution and write the same in English	1907: All veterans of all wars and their descendants; "all persons who are of good character, and understand the duties and obligations of citizenship under a republican form of government"; those who are prevented from reading and writing due to physical disability but can understand and give a reasonable interpretation of state or U.S. Constitution; owners of at least 40 acres of land assessed for taxation at the value of $500	—

States with Literacy Requirements for Suffrage, 1910–1929 (continued)

States with Literacy Requirements for Suffrage, 1910–1929 *(continued)*

STATE	LITERACY REQUIREMENTS¹	EXEMPTIONS	ASSISTANCE TO ILLITERATE VOTERS
ILLINOIS	—	—	1891: Any voter who declares under oath that he cannot read the English language shall be assisted in marking his ballot.
KENTUCKY	—	—	1890: The legislature shall "provide that persons illiterate, blind, or in any way disabled, may have their ballots marked as herein required."
LOUISIANA	1898: Must demonstrate ability to read or write in English or mother tongue	1898: Owners of property; those who could vote on or before January 1, 1867, and their sons and grandsons; foreign-born males naturalized prior to January 1, 1898, if registered prior to September 1, 1898, and if resident in state for five years preceding registration	—
	*	1921: Those physically disabled; also those "of good character and reputation, attached to the principles of the Constitution of the United States and of the State of Louisiana, and … able to understand and give a reasonable interpretation of any section of either Constitution when read to him by the registrar, and he must be well disposed to the good order and happiness of the State of Louisiana and of the United States and must understand the duties and obligations of citizenship under a republican form of government."	1921: Assistance provided for the disabled
MAINE	1893: Must be able to read the Constitution in English and write his name	1893: Those prevented from reading or writing by physical infirmities; those 60 years or older at time of amendment	—
MASSACHUSETTS	1892: Must be able to read the state Constitution in English and write his name	1892: "Those who cannot read or write because of physical disability or … those who had the right to vote on May 1, 1857."	—
MISSISSIPPI	1890: "On or after the first day of January, AD, 1892, every elector shall … be able to read any section of the Constitution of this State; or he shall be able to understand the same when read to him, or give a reasonable interpretation thereof."	—	—

States with Literacy Requirements for Suffrage, 1910–1929 *(continued)*

STATE	LITERACY REQUIREMENTS[1]	EXEMPTIONS	ASSISTANCE TO ILLITERATE VOTERS
MISSOURI	—	1865: Those who were qualified electors before January 1, 1876, and those prevented from reading and writing by physical disability	*
	1875: No requirement		—
NEW HAMPSHIRE	1902: Must be able to read the Constitution in English and to write	1902: Those currently enfranchised; those age 60 or more on January 1, 1903, and those with physical disabilities that prevent them from meeting requirement	—
NEW MEXICO	1912: "The right of any citizen of the State to vote … shall never be restricted, abridged, or impaired on account of … inability to speak, read, or write the English or Spanish languages, except as may otherwise be provided by this Constitution."	—	—
NEW YORK	—	—	1896: Any voter who has made an oath of illiteracy shall be assisted in filling out his ballot
	1921: After January 1, 1922, no person shall become entitled to vote by attaining majority, by naturalization, or otherwise, unless such person is also able to read and write in English.	1921: Those with physical infirmities preventing them from reading or writing; those who were electors before January 1, 1922	—
NORTH CAROLINA	1876: Must be able to read and write any section of the Constitution in English	1876: Those who were qualified voters on January 1, 1867, and lineal descendants of such persons	—
NORTH DAKOTA	1899: "The legislature shall by law establish an educational test as a qualification." Legislature declined to do so.	—	—
OHIO	—	—	1896: Assistance may be given to voters only for reasons of physical infirmity.
OKLAHOMA	1907: Must be able to read and write any section of the state constitution	1907: Those who were qualified voters on January 1, 1866, and lineal descendants of such persons.	—
OREGON	1924: Must be able to read the Constitution in English and write name	—	—

States with Literacy Requirements for Suffrage, 1910–1929 (continued)

States with Literacy Requirements for Suffrage, 1910–1929 *(continued)*

STATE	LITERACY REQUIREMENTS[1]	EXEMPTIONS	ASSISTANCE TO ILLITERATE VOTERS
SOUTH CAROLINA	1895: Until January 1, 1898, must be able to read and write any section of the state constitution submitted by the registration officer, or understand and explain it when read by registration officer; after January 1, 1898, must be able to read and write any section of this constitution submitted to him by registration officer	1895: Those who have paid all taxes collectable during the previous year on property assessed at $300 or more	—
VIRGINIA	1902: After 1904, must apply for registration in own handwriting	1902: Property owners; wartime veterans and their descendants	—
WASHINGTON	1896: Must be able to read and speak English	—	—
	1912: "If naturalized, must furnish satisfactory evidence that he is capable of reading and speaking the English language so as to comprehend the meaning of ordinary English prose."	1912: Those qualified to vote at time act takes effect; also those incapacitated through physical infirmity, if they present evidence of literacy in English prior to incapacity	—
WYOMING	1890: Must be able to read state constitution	1890: Those prevented from reading by physical disability	—

Key: — indicates no requirement at that time
     * indicates that the previous requirement remained in effect
Source: Alexander Keyssar, *The Right to Vote: The Contested History of Democracy in the United States,* Revised Edition (New York: Basic Books, 2009), 340–345. Adapted from Keyssar's table, which extends from 1870 to 1924. Sources of quotations are found on pp. 369–379.
[1] Dates listed are for the year that the literacy requirement went into effect. All listed requirements continue into the 1910–1929 date range of this table.

States with Residency Requirements for Suffrage, 1910–1929

STATE	LENGTH OF RESIDENCE REQUIRED[1]	NO RESIDENCY GAINED BY MILITARY PERSONNEL STATIONED IN TOWNS AND CITIES	STUDENTS	RESIDENCE IN ALMSHOUSE OR OTHER INSTITUTION	NO LOSS OF RESIDENCE FOR SOLDIERS OR OTHERS TRAVELING ON PUBLIC BUSINESS	OTHER
ALABAMA	1901: 2 years in state, 1 year in county, 3 months in precinct or ward	*	—	—	—	After January 1, 1903, residency requirement not applied to those who meet literacy requirements or are owners of land worth $300
ARIZONA	1912: 1 year in state	1912	1912	1912	1912	—
ARKANSAS	1874: 12 months in state, 6 months in county, 1 month in precinct or ward	1868	—	—	—	—
CALIFORNIA	1894: 1 year in state, 30 days in election precinct	1850	1850	1850	1850	—
COLORADO	1903: 1 year in state, 90 days in county, 30 days in city or town, 10 days in ward or precinct	1876	1876	1876	1876	—
CONNECTICUT	1845: 1 year in state, 6 months in county	—		—	—	—
DELAWARE	1897: 1 year in state, 3 months in county, 30 days in election district	1831	—	—	—	—
FLORIDA	1868: 1 year in state, 6 months in county	1868	—	—	—	—
GEORGIA	1877: 1 year in state, 6 months in county	1868	—	—	—	—
IDAHO	1890: 6 months in state, 30 days in county	1889	1889	1889	1889	—
ILLINOIS	1870: 1 year in state, 90 days in county, 30 days in election district	1870	—	1877	—	—
INDIANA	1851: 6 months in state, 60 days in township, 30 days in ward or precinct; for declarants, 1 year in U.S.	1851	—	—	1851	—
IOWA	1857: 6 months in state, 60 days in county	1857	—	—	—	—
KANSAS	1861: 6 months in state, 30 days in township or ward	1861	1861	1861	1861	—
KENTUCKY	1891: 1 year in state, 6 months in county, 60 days in precinct	1891	—	—	1891: No provision	—

States with Residency Requirements for Suffrage, 1910–1929 (continued)

States with Residency Requirements for Suffrage, 1910–1929 *(continued)*

STATE	LENGTH OF RESIDENCE REQUIRED[1]	NO RESIDENCY GAINED BY MILITARY PERSONNEL STATIONED IN TOWNS AND CITIES	STUDENTS	RESIDENCE IN ALMSHOUSE OR OTHER INSTITUTION	NO LOSS OF RESIDENCE FOR SOLDIERS OR OTHERS TRAVELING ON PUBLIC BUSINESS	OTHER
LOUISIANA	1898: 2 years in state, 1 year in parish, 6 months in precinct	1879	1879	—	1879	—
	1921: 2 years in state, 1 year in parish, 4 months in municipality, 3 months in precinct	*	*	—	*	—
MAINE	1820: 3 months in state	1820	1820	—	1864	—
MARYLAND	1867: 1 year in state, 6 months in legislative district of Baltimore city or of the county	—	—	—	—	—
MASSACHUSETTS	1821: 1 year in state, 6 months in town or district	—	—	—	—	—
MICHIGAN	1908: 6 months in state, 30 days in city or township	1908	1908	1908	1908	1908
MINNESOTA	1874: 3 months in ward	1857	—	—	—	
		—	—	—	—	1893: No residence for voting purposes can be gained by any "person employed temporarily" cutting timber "or in the construction or repair of any railroad, canal, municipal or other work of public nature."
MISSISSIPPI	1890: 2 years in state, 1 year in election district or incorporated city or town	—	—	—	—	—
MISSOURI	1883: 1 year in state, 60 days in city, 20 days in precinct	1875	1875	1875	1875	—
	1917: 1 year in state, 60 days in county	*	*	*	*	1917: No military personnel permitted to vote
MONTANA	1893: 1 year in state, and 30 days in county	1889	1889	1889	1889	—
NEBRASKA	1869: 40 days in county	1875	—	—	—	—
NEVADA	1864: 6 months in state, 30 days in district or county	1864	1864	1864	1864	—

STATE	LENGTH OF RESIDENCE REQUIRED[1]	NO RESIDENCY GAINED BY MILITARY PERSONNEL STATIONED IN TOWNS AND CITIES	STUDENTS	RESIDENCE IN ALMSHOUSE OR OTHER INSTITUTION	NO LOSS OF RESIDENCE FOR SOLDIERS OR OTHERS TRAVELING ON PUBLIC BUSINESS	OTHER
NEW HAMPSHIRE	1860: 6 months within town	—	—	—	—	—
NEW JERSEY	1844: 1 year in state, 5 months in county	1844	—	—	1844	—
NEW MEXICO	1912: 12 months in state, 90 days in county, 30 days in precinct	1912	1912	—	1912	—
NEW YORK	1874: 1 year in state, 4 months in county, 30 days in election district	—	—	—	1874	—
NORTH CAROLINA	1876: 2 years in state, 6 months in county, 4 months in precinct, ward, or other election district	—	—	—	—	—
NORTH DAKOTA	1889: 1 year in state, 6 months in county, 90 days in precinct	1889	—	—	1889	—
	1923: 1 year in state, 90 days in county, 30 days in precinct					
OHIO	1857: 1 year in state, 30 days in county, 20 days in township, village, or ward of city or village	—	1914	—	—	—
OKLAHOMA	1907: 1 year in state, 6 months in county, 30 days in precinct	1907	—	—	—	—
OREGON	1859: 6 months in state	1859	1859	1859	1859	—
PENNSYLVANIA	1873: 1 year in state, 2 months in election district; 6 months in state for previously qualified elector or native-born state citizen, returning after absence	1873	1873	1873	1873	—
RHODE ISLAND	1888: 2 years in state, 6 months in town and city	—	—	—	—	—
SOUTH CAROLINA	1895: 2 years in state, 1 year in county, 4 months in polling district; 6 months in state for ministers and public school teachers	1895	1895	—	1895	—
SOUTH DAKOTA	1889: 1 year in U.S., 6 months in state, 30 days in county, 10 days in election precinct	1889	—	—	1889	—
TENNESSEE	1870: 12 months in state, 6 months in county	—	—	—	—	—

States with Residency Requirements for Suffrage, 1910–1929 (continued)

States with Residency Requirements for Suffrage, 1910–1929 *(continued)*

STATE	LENGTH OF RESIDENCE REQUIRED[1]	NO RESIDENCY GAINED BY MILITARY PERSONNEL STATIONED IN TOWNS AND CITIES	STUDENTS	RESIDENCE IN ALMSHOUSE OR OTHER INSTITUTION	NO LOSS OF RESIDENCE FOR SOLDIERS OR OTHERS TRAVELING ON PUBLIC BUSINESS	OTHER
TEXAS	1876: 1 year in state, 6 months in county	—	—	—	—	—
UTAH	1896: 1 year in state, 4 months in county, 60 days in precinct	—	—	—	—	—
VERMONT	1793: 1 year in state	—	—	—	—	—
VIRGINIA	1902: 2 years in state, 1 year in county, city, or town, 30 days in precinct	1870	1902	1902	1902	—
WASHINGTON	1889: 1 year in state, 90 days in county, 30 days in city, town, ward, or precinct	1889	1889	—	1889	—
WEST VIRGINIA	1872: 1 year in state, 60 days in county	1872	—	—	—	—
WISCONSIN	1898: 1 year in state, 10 days in election district	—	—	—	—	—
WYOMING	1890: 1 year in state, 60 days in county	1890	—	—	—	—
	1911: 1 year in state, 60 days in county, 10 days in district	*	—	—	1911	—

Key: — indicates no requirement at that time
      * indicates that the previous requirement remained in effect

Source: Alexander Keyssar, *The Right to Vote: The Contested History of Democracy in the United States,* Revised Edition (New York: Basic Books, 2009), 346–355. Adapted from Keyssar's table, which extends from 1870 to 1923. Sources of quotations are found on pp. 369–379.

[1] Dates listed are for the year that the residency requirement went into effect. All listed requirements continue into the 1910–1929 date range of this table.

States Fully Enfranchising Women Prior to the Nineteenth Amendment

STATE	DATE IN FORCE
Wyoming	1890
Colorado	1893
Utah	1896
Idaho	1896
Washington	1910
California	1911
Arizona	1912
Kansas	1912
Oregon	1912
Montana	1914
Nevada	1914
New York	1917
Michigan	1918
Oklahoma	1918
South Dakota	1918

Source: Adapted from Alexander Keyssar, *The Right to Vote: The Contested History of Democracy in the United States,* Revised Edition (New York: Basic Books, 2009), 368.

States Permitting Women to Vote in Presidential Elections Prior to the Nineteenth Amendment

STATE[1]	DATE ENACTED
Illinois	1913
Arkansas	1917: Primary elections
Indiana	1917[2]
Michigan	1917
Nebraska	1917
North Dakota	1917
Rhode Island	1917
Ohio	1917[3]
Texas	1918: Primary elections and nominating conventions[4]
Indiana	1919
Iowa	1919
Maine	1919
Minnesota	1919
Missouri	1919
Ohio	1919
Tennessee	1919
Wisconsin	1919

Source: Alexander Keyssar, *The Right to Vote: The Contested History of Democracy in the United States,* Revised Edition (New York: Basic Books, 2009), 367.
[1] Does not include states with full suffrage for women.
[2] Declared unconstitutional by Indiana Supreme Court the same year.
[3] Law was suspended from operation by the filing of a referendum petition and subsequently was defeated by voters on November 6, 1917.
[4] Women were exempt from the poll tax required of men in 1918 election but were required to pay the poll tax beginning January 1, 1919.

United States Presidential Turnout, Election Years 1912–1928

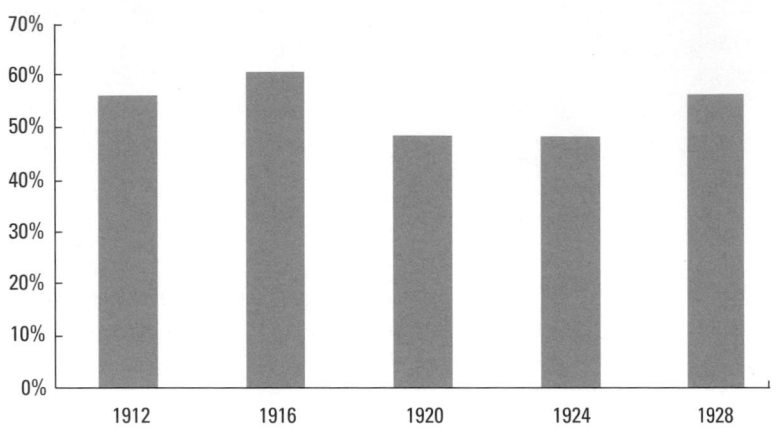

YEAR	VOTING-AGE POPULATION	TOTAL	%
1912	26,839,000	15,040,963	**56.0%**
1916	30,618,000	18,535,022	**60.5%**
1920	55,442,000	26,768,613	**48.3%**
1924	60,351,000	29,095,023	**48.2%**
1928	65,267,000	36,805,951	**56.4%**

Partisan Turnout Presidential Years Based on Aggregate House Turnout, Election Years 1912–1928

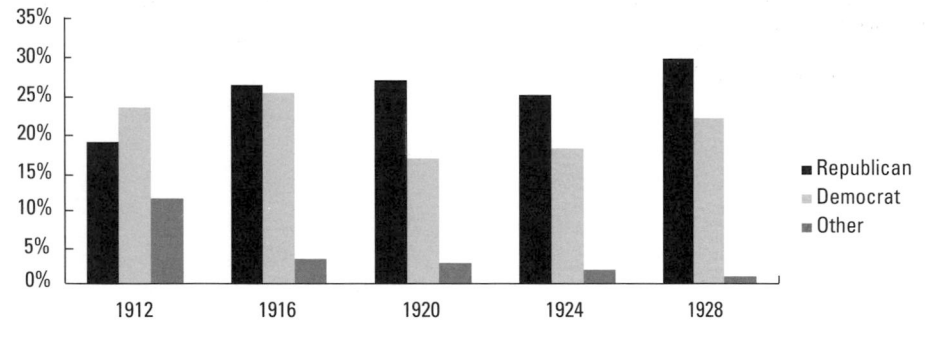

YEAR	VOTING-AGE POPULATION	REPUBLICAN TURNOUT	%	DEMOCRAT TURNOUT	%	OTHER TURNOUT	%
1912	26,839,000	5,012,684	**18.7%**	6,233,325	**23.2%**	3,012,030	**11.2%**
1916	30,618,000	8,025,364	**26.2%**	7,709,350	**25.2%**	998,077	**3.3%**
1920	55,442,000	14,874,251	**26.8%**	9,150,957	**16.5%**	1,503,303	**2.7%**
1924	60,351,000	15,009,086	**24.9%**	10,746,697	**17.8%**	1,098,383	**1.8%**
1928	65,267,000	19,369,186	**29.7%**	14,216,500	**21.8%**	616,272	**0.9%**

UNITED STATES PRESIDENTIAL GENERAL ELECTIONS

Election Years 1912–1928

State	1912 Voting-age population	Turnout	%	1916 Voting-age population	Turnout	%	Difference from 1912*	1920 Voting-age population	Turnout	%	Difference from 1912	1924 Voting-age population	Turnout	%	Difference from 1912	1928 Voting-age population	Turnout	%	Difference from 1912
ALABAMA	523,000	117,959	22.6%	549,000	130,435	23.8%	1.2	1,155,000	233,951	20.3%	-2.3	1,238,000	164,563	13.3%	-9.3	1,321,000	248,981	18.8%	-3.7
ALASKA																			
ARIZONA	92,000	23,687	25.7%	120,000	58,019	48.3%	22.6	145,000	66,803	46.1%	20.3	153,000	73,961	48.3%	22.6	161,000	91,254	56.7%	30.9
ARKANSAS	407,000	125,104	30.7%	431,000	170,104	39.5%	8.7	872,000	183,871	21.1%	-9.7	913,000	138,540	15.2%	-15.6	954,000	197,726	20.7%	-10.0
CALIFORNIA	1,530,000	677,877	44.3%	1,791,000	999,250	55.8%	11.5	2,110,000	943,463	44.7%	0.4	2,603,000	1,281,778	49.2%	4.9	3,096,000	1,796,656	58.0%	13.7
COLORADO	466,000	265,954	57.1%	496,000	292,037	58.9%	1.8	526,000	292,053	55.5%	-1.5	546,000	342,261	62.7%	5.6	564,000	392,242	69.5%	12.5
CONNECTICUT	270,000	190,404	70.5%	292,000	213,874	73.2%	2.7	648,000	365,518	56.4%	-14.1	714,000	400,396	56.1%	14.4	780,000	553,118	70.9%	0.4
DELAWARE	59,000	48,690	82.5%	62,000	51,810	83.6%	1.0	128,000	94,875	74.1%	-8.4	134,000	90,885	67.8%	-14.7	140,000	104,602	74.7%	-7.8
DISTRICT OF COLUMBIA																			
FLORIDA	220,000	50,837	23.1%	246,000	80,734	32.8%	9.7	544,000	145,684	26.8%	3.7	675,000	109,158	16.2%	-6.9	805,000	252,068	31.3%	8.2
GEORGIA	641,000	121,470	19.0%	677,000	160,681	23.7%	4.8	1,423,000	149,558	10.5%	-8.4	1,453,000	166,635	11.5%	-7.5	1,485,000	231,592	15.6%	-3.4
HAWAII																			
IDAHO	177,000	105,754	59.7%	202,000	134,615	66.6%	6.9	223,000	138,281	62.0%	2.3	228,000	147,690	64.8%	5.0	233,000	151,541	65.0%	5.3
ILLINOIS	1,535,000	1,146,173	74.7%	3,285,000	2,192,707	66.7%	-7.9	3,553,000	2,094,714	59.0%	-15.7	3,938,000	2,470,067	62.7%	-11.9	4,322,000	3,107,489	71.9%	-2.8
INDIANA	808,000	654,474	81.0%	833,000	718,853	86.3%	5.3	1,725,000	1,262,974	73.2%	-7.8	1,822,000	1,272,390	69.8%	-11.2	1,918,000	1,421,314	74.1%	-6.9
IOWA	632,000	492,353	77.9%	670,000	518,738	77.4%	-0.5	1,377,000	894,959	65.0%	-12.9	1,419,000	976,770	68.8%	-9.1	1,461,000	1,009,189	69.1%	-8.8
KANSAS	936,000	365,560	39.1%	962,000	629,813	65.5%	26.4	995,000	570,243	57.3%	18.3	1,042,000	662,456	63.6%	24.5	1,091,000	713,200	65.4%	26.3
KENTUCKY	611,000	452,714	74.1%	633,000	520,078	82.2%	8.1	1,291,000	918,636	71.2%	-2.9	1,346,000	813,843	60.5%	-13.6	1,401,000	940,521	67.1%	-7.0
LOUISIANA	413,000	79,248	19.2%	435,000	92,974	21.4%	2.2	918,000	126,397	13.8%	-5.4	1,006,000	121,951	12.1%	-7.1	1,093,000	215,833	19.7%	0.6
MAINE	204,000	129,641	63.5%	208,000	136,314	65.5%	2.0	423,000	197,840	46.8%	-16.8	430,000	192,192	44.7%	-18.9	437,000	262,170	60.0%	-3.6
MARYLAND	361,000	231,981	64.3%	388,000	262,039	67.5%	3.3	832,000	428,443	51.5%	-12.8	888,000	358,630	40.4%	-23.9	943,000	528,348	56.0%	-8.2
MASSACHUSETTS	793,000	488,056	61.5%	848,000	531,822	62.7%	1.2	1,895,000	993,718	52.4%	-9.1	2,031,000	1,129,837	55.6%	-5.9	2,166,000	1,577,823	72.8%	11.3
MICHIGAN	830,000	547,971	66.0%	976,000	646,873	66.3%	0.3	1,947,000	1,048,411	53.8%	-12.2	2,221,000	1,160,419	52.2%	-13.8	2,497,000	1,372,082	54.9%	-11.1
MINNESOTA	598,000	334,219	55.9%	623,000	387,367	62.2%	6.3	1,257,000	735,838	58.5%	2.6	1,345,000	822,146	61.1%	5.2	1,432,000	970,976	67.8%	11.9
MISSISSIPPI	428,000	64,483	15.1%	434,000	86,679	20.0%	4.9	886,000	82,351	9.3%	-5.8	949,000	112,442	11.8%	-3.2	1,011,000	151,568	15.0%	-0.1
MISSOURI	949,000	698,566	73.6%	984,000	786,773	80.0%	6.3	1,993,000	1,332,140	66.8%	-6.8	2,093,000	1,310,095	62.6%	-11.0	2,194,000	1,500,845	68.4%	-5.2
MONTANA	143,000	80,256	56.1%	258,000	178,009	69.0%	12.9	291,000	179,006	61.5%	5.4	292,000	174,425	59.7%	3.6	292,000	194,108	66.5%	10.4
NEBRASKA	335,000	249,483	74.5%	344,000	287,315	83.5%	9.0	696,000	382,743	55.0%	-19.5	734,000	463,559	63.2%	-11.3	772,000	547,128	70.9%	-3.6
NEVADA	31,000	20,115	64.9%	44,000	33,314	75.7%	10.8	45,000	27,194	60.4%	-4.5	47,000	26,921	57.3%	-7.6	50,000	32,417	64.8%	-0.1
NEW HAMPSHIRE	113,000	87,961	77.8%	115,000	89,127	77.5%	-0.3	237,000	159,092	67.1%	-10.7	246,000	164,769	67.0%	-10.9	255,000	196,757	77.2%	-0.7
NEW JERSEY	637,000	433,663	68.1%	703,000	494,442	70.3%	2.3	1,588,000	910,251	57.3%	-10.8	1,849,000	1,088,054	58.8%	-9.2	2,110,000	1,549,381	73.4%	5.4
NEW MEXICO	87,000	48,807	56.1%	85,000	66,879	78.7%	22.6	170,000	105,412	62.0%	5.9	172,000	112,830	65.6%	9.5	174,000	118,077	67.9%	11.8
NEW YORK	2,472,000	1,588,315	64.3%	2,656,000	1,706,305	64.2%	0.0	5,294,000	2,898,513	54.8%	-9.5	5,965,000	3,263,939	54.7%	-9.5	6,635,000	4,405,626	66.4%	2.1

United States Presidential General Elections (continued)

United States Presidential General Elections (continued)

Election Years 1912–1928 (continued)

State	1912 Voting-age population	Turnout	%	1916 Voting-age population	Turnout	%	Difference from 1912	1920 Voting-age population	Turnout	%	Difference from 1912	1924 Voting-age population	Turnout	%	Difference from 1912	1928 Voting-age population	Turnout	%	Difference from 1912
NORTH CAROLINA	529,000	243,776	46.1%	568,000	289,837	51.0%	4.9	1,237,000	538,649	43.5%	-2.5	1,368,000	481,608	35.2%	-10.9	1,497,000	635,150	42.4%	-3.7
NORTH DAKOTA	145,000	86,474	59.6%	152,000	115,390	75.9%	16.3	297,000	205,786	69.3%	9.7	314,000	199,081	63.4%	3.8	332,000	239,845	72.2%	12.6
OHIO	1,403,000	1,037,114	73.9%	1,535,000	1,165,091	75.9%	2.0	3,289,000	2,021,653	61.5%	-12.5	3,551,000	2,016,296	56.8%	-17.1	3,811,000	2,508,346	65.8%	-8.1
OKLAHOMA	456,000	253,694	55.6%	498,000	292,327	58.7%	3.1	1,026,000	485,678	47.3%	-8.3	1,118,000	527,828	47.2%	-8.4	1,211,000	618,427	51.1%	-4.6
OREGON	392,000	137,040	35.0%	428,000	261,650	61.1%	26.2	467,000	238,522	51.1%	16.1	514,000	279,488	54.4%	19.4	563,000	319,942	56.8%	21.9
PENNSYLVANIA	1,907,000	1,217,736	63.9%	2,048,000	1,297,189	63.3%	-0.5	4,412,000	1,851,248	42.0%	-21.9	4,766,000	2,144,850	45.0%	-18.9	5,121,000	3,150,612	61.5%	-2.3
RHODE ISLAND	125,000	77,894	62.3%	134,000	87,816	65.5%	3.2	296,000	167,981	56.8%	-5.6	323,000	210,115	65.1%	2.7	351,000	237,194	67.6%	5.3
SOUTH CAROLINA	347,000	50,403	14.5%	370,000	63,950	17.3%	2.8	781,000	66,808	8.6%	-6.0	796,000	50,755	6.4%	-8.1	813,000	68,605	8.4%	-6.1
SOUTH DAKOTA	172,000	116,327	67.6%	179,000	128,942	72.0%	4.4	326,000	182,237	55.9%	-11.7	342,000	203,868	59.6%	-8.0	359,000	261,857	72.9%	5.3
TENNESSEE	563,000	251,933	44.7%	587,000	272,190	46.4%	1.6	1,228,000	428,036	34.9%	-9.9	1,309,000	301,030	23.0%	-21.8	1,391,000	353,192	25.4%	-19.4
TEXAS	1,004,000	300,961	30.0%	1,101,000	373,310	33.9%	3.9	2,304,000	486,109	21.1%	-8.9	2,558,000	657,054	25.7%	-4.3	2,811,000	717,733	25.5%	-4.4
UTAH	174,000	112,272	64.5%	194,000	143,145	73.8%	9.3	213,000	145,828	68.5%	3.9	227,000	156,990	69.2%	4.6	243,000	176,603	72.7%	8.2
VERMONT	101,000	62,804	62.2%	101,000	64,475	63.8%	1.7	199,000	89,961	45.2%	-17.0	201,000	102,917	51.2%	-11.0	203,000	135,191	66.6%	4.4
VIRGINIA	538,000	136,975	25.5%	575,000	152,025	26.4%	1.0	1,203,000	231,000	19.2%	-6.3	1,242,000	223,603	18.0%	-7.5	1,282,000	305,364	23.8%	-1.6
WASHINGTON	640,000	322,799	50.4%	707,000	380,994	53.9%	3.5	774,000	398,715	51.5%	1.1	833,000	421,549	50.6%	0.2	892,000	500,840	56.1%	5.7
WEST VIRGINIA	328,000	268,728	81.9%	353,000	289,671	82.1%	0.1	726,000	509,936	70.2%	-11.7	791,000	583,662	73.8%	-8.1	857,000	642,752	75.0%	-6.9
WISCONSIN	627,000	399,975	63.8%	643,000	447,134	69.5%	5.7	1,371,000	701,281	51.2%	-12.6	1,493,000	840,827	56.3%	-7.5	1,617,000	1,016,831	62.9%	-0.9
WYOMING	87,000	42,283	48.6%	95,000	51,906	54.6%	6.0	106,000	56,253	53.1%	4.5	113,000	79,900	70.7%	22.1	120,000	82,835	69.0%	20.4
Total	26,839,000	15,040,963	56.0%	30,618,000	18,535,022	60.5%	4.5	55,442,000	26,768,613	48.3%	-7.8	60,351,000	29,095,023	48.2%	-7.8	65,267,000	36,805,951	56.4%	0.4

*Percentage point difference between turnout in current year and initial year listed in chart. If data do not appear for a state in the initial year listed, the difference is calculated from the first year in which data do appear for that state.

UNITED STATES PRESIDENTIAL GENERAL ELECTIONS

Republican Turnout for Election Years 1912–1928

State	1912 Voting-age population	1912 Turnout	1912 %	1916 Voting-age population	1916 Turnout	1916 %	1916 Difference from 1912*	1920 Voting-age population	1920 Turnout	1920 %	1920 Difference from 1912	1924 Voting-age population	1924 Turnout	1924 %	1924 Difference from 1912	1928 Voting-age population	1928 Turnout	1928 %	1928 Difference from 1912
ALABAMA	523,000	9,807	1.9%	549,000	28,662	5.2%	3.3	1,155,000	74,719	6.5%	4.6	1,238,000	42,823	3.5%	1.6	1,321,000	120,725	9.1%	7.3
ALASKA																			
ARIZONA	92,000	2,986	3.2%	120,000	20,522	17.1%	13.9	145,000	37,016	25.5%	22.3	153,000	30,516	19.9%	16.7	161,000	52,533	32.6%	29.4
ARKANSAS	407,000	25,585	6.3%	431,000	48,879	11.3%	5.1	872,000	72,316	8.3%	2.0	913,000	40,583	4.4%	-1.8	954,000	77,784	8.2%	1.9
CALIFORNIA	1,530,000	3,847	0.3%	1,791,000	462,516	25.8%	25.6	2,110,000	624,992	29.6%	29.4	2,603,000	733,250	28.2%	27.9	3,096,000	1,162,323	37.5%	37.3
COLORADO	466,000	58,386	12.5%	496,000	101,388	20.4%	7.9	526,000	173,248	32.9%	20.4	546,000	195,171	35.7%	23.2	664,000	263,872	45.0%	32.5
CONNECTICUT	270,000	68,324	25.3%	292,000	106,514	36.5%	11.2	648,000	229,238	35.4%	10.1	714,000	246,322	34.5%	9.2	780,000	296,641	38.0%	12.7
DELAWARE	59,000	15,997	27.1%	62,000	26,011	42.0%	14.8	128,000	52,858	41.3%	14.2	134,000	52,441	39.1%	12.0	140,000	68,860	49.2%	22.1
DISTRICT OF COLUMBIA																			
FLORIDA	220,000	4,279	1.9%	246,000	14,611	5.9%	4.0	544,000	44,853	8.2%	6.3	675,000	30,633	4.5%	2.6	805,000	145,860	18.1%	16.2
GEORGIA	641,000	5,191	0.8%	677,000	11,294	1.7%	0.9	1,423,000	42,981	3.0%	2.2	1,453,000	30,300	2.1%	1.3	1,485,000	101,800	6.9%	6.0
HAWAII																			
IDAHO	177,000	32,810	18.5%	202,000	55,368	27.4%	8.9	223,000	91,351	41.0%	22.4	228,000	60,701	30.6%	12.1	233,000	97,322	41.8%	23.2
ILLINOIS	1,535,000	253,593	16.5%	3,285,000	1,152,549	35.1%	18.6	3,553,000	1,420,480	40.0%	23.5	3,938,000	1,453,321	36.9%	20.4	4,322,000	1,769,141	40.9%	24.4
INDIANA	808,000	151,267	18.7%	833,000	341,005	40.9%	22.2	1,725,000	696,370	40.4%	21.6	1,822,000	703,042	38.6%	19.9	1,918,000	848,290	44.2%	25.5
IOWA	632,000	119,805	19.0%	670,000	280,439	41.9%	22.9	1,377,000	634,674	46.1%	27.1	1,419,000	537,458	37.9%	18.9	1,461,000	623,570	42.7%	23.7
KANSAS	936,000	74,845	8.0%	962,000	277,658	28.9%	20.9	995,000	369,268	37.1%	29.1	1,042,000	407,671	39.1%	31.1	1,091,000	513,672	47.1%	39.1
KENTUCKY	611,000	115,510	18.9%	633,000	241,854	38.2%	19.3	1,291,000	452,480	35.0%	16.1	1,346,000	396,758	29.5%	10.6	1,401,000	558,064	39.8%	20.9
LOUISIANA	413,000	3,833	0.9%	435,000	6,466	1.5%	0.6	918,000	38,539	4.2%	3.3	1,006,000	24,670	2.5%	1.5	1,093,000	51,160	4.7%	3.8
MAINE	204,000	26,545	13.0%	208,000	69,508	33.4%	20.4	423,000	136,355	32.2%	19.2	430,000	138,440	32.2%	19.2	437,000	179,923	41.2%	28.2
MARYLAND	361,000	54,956	15.2%	388,000	117,347	30.2%	15.0	832,000	236,117	28.4%	13.2	888,000	162,414	18.3%	3.1	943,000	301,479	32.0%	16.7
MASSACHUSETTS	793,000	155,948	19.7%	848,000	268,784	31.7%	12.0	1,895,000	681,153	35.9%	16.3	2,031,000	703,476	34.6%	15.0	2,166,000	775,566	35.8%	16.1
MICHIGAN	830,000	151,434	18.2%	976,000	337,952	34.6%	16.4	1,947,000	762,865	39.2%	20.9	2,221,000	874,631	39.4%	21.1	2,497,000	965,396	38.7%	20.4
MINNESOTA	598,000	64,334	10.8%	623,000	179,544	28.8%	18.1	1,257,000	519,421	41.3%	30.6	1,345,000	420,759	31.3%	20.5	1,432,000	560,977	39.2%	28.4
MISSISSIPPI	428,000	1,560	0.4%	434,000	4,253	1.0%	0.6	886,000	11,576	1.3%	0.9	949,000	8,494	0.9%	0.5	1,011,000	27,030	2.7%	2.3
MISSOURI	949,000	207,821	21.9%	984,000	369,339	37.5%	15.6	1,993,000	727,252	36.5%	14.6	2,093,000	648,488	31.0%	9.1	2,194,000	834,080	38.0%	16.1
MONTANA	143,000	18,575	13.0%	258,000	66,933	25.9%	13.0	291,000	109,430	37.6%	24.6	292,000	74,138	25.4%	12.4	292,000	113,300	38.8%	25.8
NEBRASKA	335,000	54,226	16.2%	344,000	117,771	34.2%	18.0	696,000	247,498	35.6%	19.4	734,000	218,985	29.8%	13.6	772,000	345,745	44.8%	28.6
NEVADA	31,000	3,196	10.3%	44,000	12,127	27.6%	17.3	45,000	15,479	34.4%	24.1	47,000	11,243	23.9%	13.6	50,000	18,327	36.7%	26.3
NEW HAMPSHIRE	113,000	32,927	29.1%	115,000	43,725	38.0%	8.9	237,000	95,196	40.2%	11.0	246,000	98,575	40.1%	10.9	255,000	115,404	45.3%	16.1
NEW JERSEY	637,000	89,066	14.0%	703,000	268,982	38.3%	24.3	1,588,000	615,333	38.7%	24.8	1,849,000	676,277	36.6%	22.6	2,110,000	926,050	43.9%	29.9
NEW MEXICO	87,000	17,164	19.7%	85,000	31,097	36.6%	16.9	170,000	57,634	33.9%	14.2	172,000	54,745	31.8%	12.1	174,000	69,708	40.1%	20.3
NEW YORK	2,472,000	455,487	18.4%	2,656,000	879,238	33.1%	14.7	5,294,000	1,871,167	35.3%	16.9	5,965,000	1,820,058	30.5%	12.1	6,635,000	2,193,344	33.1%	14.6

United States Presidential General Elections (continued)

United States Presidential General Elections (continued)

Republican Turnout for Election Years 1912–1928 (continued)

State	1912 Voting-age population	Turnout	%	1916 Voting-age population	Turnout	%	Difference from 1912	1920 Voting-age population	Turnout	%	Difference from 1912	1924 Voting-age population	Turnout	%	Difference from 1912	1928 Voting-age population	Turnout	%	Difference from 1912
NORTH CAROLINA	529,000	29,129	5.5%	568,000	120,890	21.3%	15.8	1,237,000	232,819	18.8%	13.3	1,368,000	190,754	13.9%	8.4	1,497,000	348,923	23.3%	17.8
NORTH DAKOTA	145,000	22,990	15.9%	152,000	53,471	35.2%	19.3	297,000	160,082	53.9%	38.0	314,000	94,931	30.2%	14.4	332,000	131,419	39.6%	23.7
OHIO	1,403,000	278,168	19.8%	1,535,000	514,753	33.5%	13.7	3,289,000	1,182,022	35.9%	16.1	3,551,000	1,176,130	33.1%	13.3	3,811,000	1,627,546	42.7%	22.9
OKLAHOMA	456,000	90,726	19.9%	498,000	97,233	19.5%	-0.4	1,026,000	243,840	23.8%	3.9	1,118,000	225,756	20.2%	0.3	1,211,000	394,046	32.5%	12.6
OREGON	392,000	34,673	8.8%	428,000	126,813	29.6%	20.8	467,000	143,592	30.7%	21.9	514,000	142,579	27.7%	18.9	563,000	205,341	36.5%	27.6
PENNSYLVANIA	1,907,000	273,360	14.3%	2,048,000	703,823	34.4%	20.0	4,412,000	1,218,215	27.6%	13.3	4,766,000	1,401,481	29.4%	15.1	5,121,000	2,055,382	40.1%	25.8
RHODE ISLAND	125,000	27,703	22.2%	134,000	44,858	33.5%	11.3	296,000	107,463	36.3%	14.1	323,000	125,286	38.8%	16.6	351,000	117,522	33.5%	11.3
SOUTH CAROLINA	347,000	536	0.2%	370,000	1,550	0.4%	0.3	781,000	2,610	0.3%	0.2	796,000	1,123	0.1%	0.0	813,000	5,858	0.7%	0.6
SOUTH DAKOTA				179,000	64,217	35.9%		326,000	110,692	34.0%	-1.9	342,000	101,299	29.6%	-6.3	359,000	157,603	43.9%	8.0
TENNESSEE	563,000	60,475	10.7%	587,000	116,223	19.8%	9.1	1,228,000	219,229	17.9%	7.1	1,309,000	130,831	10.0%	-0.7	1,391,000	195,388	14.0%	3.3
TEXAS	1,004,000	28,310	2.8%	1,101,000	64,999	5.9%	3.1	2,304,000	114,658	5.0%	2.2	2,558,000	130,794	5.1%	2.3	2,811,000	372,324	13.2%	10.4
UTAH	174,000	42,013	24.1%	194,000	54,137	27.9%	3.8	213,000	81,555	38.3%	14.1	227,000	77,327	34.1%	9.9	243,000	94,618	38.9%	14.8
VERMONT	101,000	23,303	23.1%	101,000	40,250	39.9%	16.8	199,000	68,212	34.3%	11.2	201,000	80,498	40.0%	17.0	203,000	90,404	44.5%	21.5
VIRGINIA	538,000	23,288	4.3%	575,000	48,384	8.4%	4.1	1,203,000	87,456	7.3%	2.9	1,242,000	73,328	5.9%	1.6	1,282,000	164,609	12.8%	8.5
WASHINGTON	640,000	70,445	11.0%	707,000	167,208	23.7%	12.6	774,000	223,137	28.8%	17.8	833,000	220,224	26.4%	15.4	892,000	335,844	37.7%	26.6
WEST VIRGINIA	328,000	56,754	17.3%	353,000	143,124	40.5%	23.2	726,000	282,007	38.8%	21.5	791,000	288,635	36.5%	19.2	857,000	375,551	43.8%	26.5
WISCONSIN	627,000	130,596	20.8%	643,000	220,822	34.3%	13.5	1,371,000	498,576	36.4%	15.5	1,493,000	311,614	20.9%	0.0	1,617,000	544,205	33.7%	12.8
WYOMING	87,000	14,560	16.7%	95,000	21,698	22.8%	6.1	106,000	35,091	33.1%	16.4	113,000	41,858	37.0%	20.3	120,000	52,748	44.0%	27.2
Total	26,667,000	3,486,333	13.1%	30,618,000	8,546,789	27.9%	14.8	55,442,000	16,153,115	29.1%	16.1	60,351,000	15,719,921	26.0%	13.0	65,267,000	21,437,277	32.8%	19.8

Democratic Turnout for Election Years 1912–1928

State	1912 Voting-age population	Turnout	%	1916 Voting-age population	Turnout	%	Difference from 1912*	1920 Voting-age population	Turnout	%	Difference from 1912	1924 Voting-age population	Turnout	%	Difference from 1912	1928 Voting-age population	Turnout	%	Difference from 1912
ALABAMA	523,000	82,438	15.8%	549,000	99,116	18.1%	2.3	1,155,000	156,064	13.5%	-2.3	1,238,000	113,138	9.1%	-6.6	1,321,000	127,796	9.7%	-6.1
ALASKA																			
ARIZONA	92,000	10,324	11.2%	120,000	33,170	27.6%	16.4	145,000	29,546	20.4%	9.2	153,000	26,235	17.1%	5.9	161,000	38,537	23.9%	12.7
ARKANSAS	407,000	68,814	16.9%	431,000	112,211	26.0%	9.1	872,000	106,427	12.2%	-4.7	913,000	84,790	9.3%	-7.6	954,000	119,196	12.5%	-4.4
CALIFORNIA	1,530,000	283,436	18.5%	1,791,000	465,936	26.0%	7.5	2,110,000	229,191	10.9%	-7.7	2,603,000	105,514	4.1%	-14.5	3,096,000	614,365	19.8%	1.3
COLORADO	466,000	113,912	24.4%	496,000	177,496	35.8%	11.3	526,000	104,936	19.9%	-4.5	546,000	75,238	13.8%	-10.7	564,000	133,131	23.6%	-0.8
CONNECTICUT	270,000	74,561	27.6%	292,000	99,786	34.2%	6.6	648,000	120,721	18.6%	-9.0	714,000	110,184	15.4%	-12.2	780,000	252,085	32.3%	4.7
DELAWARE	59,000	22,631	38.4%	62,000	24,753	39.9%	1.6	128,000	39,911	31.2%	-7.2	134,000	33,445	25.0%	-13.4	140,000	35,354	25.3%	-13.1
DISTRICT OF COLUMBIA																			
FLORIDA	220,000	35,343	16.1%	246,000	55,984	22.8%	6.7	544,000	90,515	16.6%	0.6	675,000	62,083	9.2%	-6.9	805,000	101,764	12.6%	-3.4

United States Presidential General Elections (continued)

Democratic Turnout for Election Years 1912–1928 (continued)

State	1912 Voting-age population	Turnout	%	1916 Voting-age population	Turnout	%	Difference from 1912	1920 Voting-age population	Turnout	%	Difference from 1912	1924 Voting-age population	Turnout	%	Difference from 1912	1928 Voting-age population	Turnout	%	Difference from 1912
GEORGIA	641,000	93,087	**14.5%**	677,000	127,754	**18.9%**	4.3	1,423,000	106,112	**7.5%**	-7.1	1,453,000	123,262	**8.5%**	-6.0	1,485,000	129,604	**8.7%**	-5.8
HAWAII																			
IDAHO	177,000	33,921	**19.2%**	202,000	70,054	**34.7%**	15.5	223,000	46,930	**21.0%**	1.9	228,000	23,951	**10.5%**	-8.7	233,000	52,926	**22.7%**	3.6
ILLINOIS	1,535,000	405,048	**26.4%**	3,285,000	950,229	**28.9%**	2.5	3,553,000	534,395	**15.0%**	-11.3	3,938,000	576,975	**14.7%**	-11.7	4,322,000	1,313,817	**30.4%**	4.0
INDIANA	808,000	281,890	**34.9%**	833,000	334,063	**40.1%**	5.2	1,725,000	511,364	**29.6%**	-5.2	1,822,000	492,245	**27.0%**	-7.9	1,918,000	562,691	**29.3%**	-5.5
IOWA	632,000	185,322	**29.3%**	670,000	221,699	**33.1%**	3.8	1,377,000	227,804	**16.5%**	-12.8	1,419,000	160,382	**11.3%**	-18.0	1,461,000	379,011	**25.9%**	-3.4
KANSAS	936,000	143,663	**15.3%**	962,000	314,588	**32.7%**	17.4	995,000	185,464	**18.6%**	3.3	1,042,000	156,320	**15.0%**	-0.3	1,091,000	193,003	**17.7%**	2.3
KENTUCKY	611,000	219,484	**35.9%**	633,000	269,990	**42.7%**	6.7	1,291,000	456,497	**35.4%**	-0.6	1,346,000	375,593	**27.9%**	-8.0	1,401,000	381,070	**27.2%**	-8.7
LOUISIANA	413,000	60,871	**14.7%**	435,000	79,875	**18.4%**	3.6	918,000	87,519	**9.5%**	-5.2	1,006,000	93,218	**9.3%**	-5.5	1,093,000	164,655	**15.1%**	0.3
MAINE	204,000	51,113	**25.1%**	208,000	64,033	**30.8%**	5.7	423,000	58,961	**13.9%**	-11.1	430,000	41,964	**9.8%**	-15.3	437,000	81,179	**18.6%**	-6.5
MARYLAND	361,000	112,674	**31.2%**	388,000	138,359	**35.7%**	4.4	832,000	180,626	**21.7%**	-9.5	888,000	148,072	**16.7%**	-14.5	943,000	223,626	**23.7%**	-7.5
MASSACHUSETTS	793,000	173,408	**21.9%**	848,000	247,885	**29.2%**	7.4	1,895,000	276,691	**14.6%**	-7.3	2,031,000	280,831	**13.8%**	-8.0	2,166,000	792,758	**36.6%**	14.7
MICHIGAN	830,000	150,201	**18.1%**	976,000	283,993	**29.1%**	11.0	1,947,000	233,450	**12.0%**	-6.1	2,221,000	152,359	**6.9%**	-11.2	2,497,000	396,762	**15.9%**	-2.2
MINNESOTA	598,000	106,426	**17.8%**	623,000	179,155	**28.8%**	11.0	1,257,000	142,994	**11.4%**	-6.4	1,345,000	55,913	**4.2%**	-13.6	1,432,000	396,451	**27.7%**	9.9
MISSISSIPPI	428,000	57,324	**13.4%**	434,000	80,422	**18.5%**	5.1	886,000	69,136	**7.8%**	-5.6	949,000	100,474	**10.6%**	-2.8	1,011,000	124,538	**12.3%**	-1.1
MISSOURI	949,000	330,746	**34.9%**	984,000	398,032	**40.5%**	5.6	1,993,000	574,699	**28.8%**	-6.0	2,093,000	574,962	**27.5%**	-7.4	2,194,000	662,684	**30.2%**	-4.6
MONTANA	143,000	28,129	**19.7%**	258,000	101,104	**39.2%**	19.5	291,000	57,372	**19.7%**	0.0	292,000	33,805	**11.6%**	-8.1	292,000	78,578	**26.9%**	7.2
NEBRASKA	335,000	109,008	**32.5%**	344,000	158,827	**46.2%**	13.6	696,000	119,608	**17.2%**	-15.4	734,000	137,299	**18.7%**	-13.8	772,000	197,950	**25.6%**	-6.9
NEVADA	31,000	7,986	**25.8%**	44,000	17,776	**40.4%**	14.6	45,000	9,851	**21.9%**	-3.9	47,000	5,909	**12.6%**	-13.2	50,000	14,090	**28.2%**	2.4
NEW HAMPSHIRE	113,000	34,724	**30.7%**	115,000	43,781	**38.1%**	7.3	237,000	62,662	**26.4%**	-4.3	246,000	57,201	**23.3%**	-7.5	255,000	80,715	**31.7%**	0.9
NEW JERSEY	637,000	178,638	**28.0%**	703,000	211,018	**30.0%**	2.0	1,588,000	258,761	**16.3%**	-11.7	1,849,000	298,043	**16.1%**	-11.9	2,110,000	616,517	**29.2%**	1.2
NEW MEXICO	87,000	20,437	**23.5%**	85,000	33,693	**39.6%**	16.1	170,000	46,668	**27.5%**	4.0	172,000	48,542	**28.2%**	4.7	174,000	48,211	**27.7%**	4.2
NEW YORK	2,472,000	655,573	**26.5%**	2,656,000	759,426	**28.6%**	2.1	5,294,000	781,238	**14.8%**	-11.8	5,965,000	950,796	**15.9%**	-10.6	6,635,000	2,089,863	**31.5%**	5.0
NORTH CAROLINA	529,000	144,407	**27.3%**	568,000	168,383	**29.6%**	2.3	1,237,000	305,367	**24.7%**	-2.6	1,368,000	284,190	**20.8%**	-6.5	1,497,000	286,227	**19.1%**	-8.2
NORTH DAKOTA	145,000	29,549	**20.4%**	152,000	55,206	**36.3%**	15.9	297,000	37,422	**12.6%**	-7.8	314,000	13,858	**4.4%**	-16.0	332,000	106,648	**32.1%**	11.7
OHIO	1,403,000	424,834	**30.3%**	1,535,000	604,161	**39.4%**	9.1	3,289,000	780,037	**23.7%**	-6.6	3,551,000	477,887	**13.5%**	-16.8	3,811,000	864,210	**22.7%**	-7.6
OKLAHOMA	456,000	119,143	**26.1%**	498,000	148,123	**29.7%**	3.6	1,026,000	216,122	**21.1%**	-5.1	1,118,000	255,798	**22.9%**	-3.2	1,211,000	219,174	**18.1%**	-8.0
OREGON	392,000	47,064	**12.0%**	428,000	120,087	**28.1%**	16.1	467,000	80,019	**17.1%**	5.1	514,000	67,589	**13.1%**	1.1	563,000	109,223	**19.4%**	7.4
PENNSYLVANIA	1,907,000	395,637	**20.7%**	2,048,000	521,784	**25.5%**	4.7	4,412,000	503,202	**11.4%**	-9.3	4,766,000	409,192	**8.6%**	-12.2	5,121,000	1,067,586	**20.8%**	0.1
RHODE ISLAND	125,000	30,412	**24.3%**	134,000	40,394	**30.1%**	5.8	296,000	55,062	**18.6%**	-5.7	323,000	76,606	**23.7%**	-0.6	351,000	118,973	**33.9%**	9.6
SOUTH CAROLINA	347,000	48,355	**13.9%**	370,000	61,845	**16.7%**	2.8	781,000	64,170	**8.2%**	-5.7	796,000	49,008	**6.2%**	-7.8	813,000	62,700	**7.7%**	-6.2
SOUTH DAKOTA	172,000	48,942	**28.5%**	179,000	59,191	**33.1%**	4.6	326,000	35,938	**11.0%**	-17.4	342,000	27,214	**8.0%**	-20.5	359,000	102,660	**28.6%**	0.1
TENNESSEE	563,000	133,021	**23.6%**	587,000	153,280	**26.1%**	2.5	1,228,000	206,558	**16.8%**	-6.8	1,309,000	159,339	**12.2%**	-11.5	1,391,000	157,143	**11.3%**	-12.3

United States Presidential General Elections (continued)

United States Presidential General Elections (continued)

Democratic Turnout for Election Years 1912–1928 (continued)

State	1912 Voting-age population	Turnout	%	1916 Voting-age population	Turnout	%	Difference from 1912	1920 Voting-age population	Turnout	%	Difference from 1912	1924 Voting-age population	Turnout	%	Difference from 1912	1928 Voting-age population	Turnout	%	Difference from 1912
TEXAS	1,004,000	218,921	21.8%	1,101,000	287,415	26.1%	4.3	2,304,000	287,920	12.5%	-9.3	2,558,000	483,381	18.9%	-2.9	2,811,000	344,542	12.3%	-9.5
UTAH	174,000	36,576	21.0%	194,000	84,145	43.4%	22.4	213,000	56,639	26.6%	5.6	227,000	47,001	20.7%	-0.3	243,000	80,985	33.3%	12.3
VERMONT	101,000	15,350	15.2%	101,000	22,708	22.5%	7.3	199,000	20,919	10.5%	-4.7	201,000	16,124	8.0%	-7.2	203,000	44,440	21.9%	6.7
VIRGINIA	538,000	90,332	16.8%	575,000	101,840	17.7%	0.9	1,203,000	141,670	11.8%	-5.0	1,242,000	139,717	11.2%	-5.5	1,282,000	140,146	10.9%	-5.9
WASHINGTON	640,000	86,840	13.6%	707,000	183,388	25.9%	12.4	774,000	84,298	10.9%	-2.7	833,000	42,842	5.1%	-8.4	892,000	156,772	17.6%	4.0
WEST VIRGINIA	328,000	113,097	34.5%	353,000	140,403	39.8%	5.3	726,000	220,785	30.4%	-4.1	791,000	257,232	32.5%	-2.0	857,000	263,784	30.8%	-3.7
WISCONSIN	627,000	164,230	26.2%	643,000	191,363	29.8%	3.6	1,371,000	113,422	8.3%	-17.9	1,493,000	68,115	4.6%	-21.6	1,617,000	450,259	27.8%	1.7
WYOMING	87,000	15,310	17.6%	95,000	28,376	29.9%	12.3	106,000	17,429	16.4%	-1.2	113,000	12,868	11.4%	-6.2	120,000	29,299	24.4%	6.8
Total	26,839,000	6,293,152	23.4%	30,618,000	9,126,300	29.8%	6.4	55,442,000	9,133,092	16.5%	-7.0	60,351,000	8,386,704	13.9%	-9.6	65,267,000	15,007,698	23.0%	-0.5

Other Turnout for Election Years 1912–1928

State	1912 Voting-age population	Turnout	%	1916 Voting-age population	Turnout	%	Difference from 1912*	1920 Voting-age population	Turnout	%	Difference from 1912	1924 Voting-age population	Turnout	%	Difference from 1912	1928 Voting-age population	Turnout	%	Difference from 1912
ALABAMA	523,000	25,714	4.9%	549,000	2,657	0.5%	-4.4	1,155,000	3,168	0.3%	-4.6	1,238,000	8,602	0.7%	-4.2	1,321,000	460	0.0%	-4.9
ALASKA																			
ARIZONA	92,000	10,377	11.3%	120,000	4,327	3.6%	-7.7	145,000	241	0.2%	-11.1	153,000	17,210	11.2%	0.0	161,000	184	0.1%	-11.2
ARKANSAS	407,000	30,705	7.5%	431,000	9,014	2.1%	-5.5	872,000	5,128	0.6%	-7.0	913,000	13,167	1.4%	-6.1	954,000	746	0.1%	-7.5
CALIFORNIA	1,530,000	390,594	25.5%	1,791,000	70,798	4.0%	-21.6	2,110,000	89,280	4.2%	-21.3	2,603,000	443,014	17.0%	-8.5	3,096,000	19,968	0.6%	-24.9
COLORADO	466,000	93,656	20.1%	496,000	13,153	2.7%	-17.4	526,000	13,869	2.6%	-17.5	546,000	71,852	13.2%	-6.9	564,000	5,239	0.9%	-19.2
CONNECTICUT	270,000	47,519	17.6%	292,000	7,574	2.6%	-15.0	648,000	15,559	2.4%	-15.2	714,000	43,890	6.1%	-11.5	780,000	4,392	0.6%	-17.0
DELAWARE	59,000	10,062	17.1%	62,000	1,046	1.7%	-15.4	128,000	2,106	1.6%	-15.4	134,000	4,999	3.7%	-13.3	140,000	388	0.3%	-16.8
DISTRICT OF COLUMBIA																			
FLORIDA	220,000	11,215	5.1%	246,000	10,139	4.1%	-1.0	544,000	10,316	1.9%	-3.2	675,000	16,442	2.4%	-2.7	805,000	4,444	0.6%	-4.5
GEORGIA	641,000	23,192	3.6%	677,000	21,633	3.2%	-0.4	1,423,000	465	0.0%	-3.6	1,453,000	13,073	0.9%	-2.7	1,485,000	188	0.0%	-3.6
HAWAII																			
IDAHO	177,000	39,023	22.0%	202,000	9,193	4.6%	-17.5					228,000	53,948	23.7%	1.6	233,000	1,293	0.6%	-21.5
ILLINOIS	1,535,000	487,532	31.8%	3,285,000	89,929	2.7%	-29.0	3,553,000	139,839	3.9%	-27.8	3,938,000	439,771	11.2%	-20.6	4,322,000	24,531	0.6%	-31.2
INDIANA	808,000	221,317	27.4%	833,000	43,785	5.3%	-22.1	1,725,000	55,240	3.2%	-24.2	1,822,000	77,103	4.2%	-23.2	1,918,000	10,333	0.5%	-26.9
IOWA	632,000	187,226	29.6%	670,000	16,600	2.5%	-27.1	1,377,000	32,481	2.4%	-27.3	1,419,000	278,930	19.7%	-10.0	1,461,000	6,608	0.5%	-29.2
KANSAS	936,000	147,052	15.7%	962,000	37,567	3.9%	-11.8	995,000	15,511	1.6%	-14.2	1,042,000	98,465	9.4%	-6.3	1,091,000	6,525	0.6%	-15.1
KENTUCKY	611,000	117,720	19.3%	633,000	8,234	1.3%	-18.0	1,291,000	9,659	0.7%	-18.5	1,346,000	41,492	3.1%	-16.2	1,401,000	1,387	0.1%	-19.2
LOUISIANA	413,000	14,544	3.5%	435,000	6,633	1.5%	-2.0	918,000	339	0.0%	-3.5	1,006,000	4,063	0.4%	-3.1	1,093,000	18	0.0%	-3.5
MAINE	204,000	51,983	25.5%	208,000	2,773	1.3%	-24.1	423,000	2,524	0.6%	-24.9	430,000	11,788	2.7%	-22.7	437,000	1,068	0.2%	-25.2

United States Presidential General Elections *(continued)*

Other Turnout for Election Years 1912–1928 *(continued)*

State	1912 Voting-age population	1912 Turnout	1912 %	1916 Voting-age population	1916 Turnout	1916 %	1916 Difference from 1912	1920 Voting-age population	1920 Turnout	1920 %	1920 Difference from 1912	1924 Voting-age population	1924 Turnout	1924 %	1924 Difference from 1912	1928 Voting-age population	1928 Turnout	1928 %	1928 Difference from 1912
MARYLAND	361,000	64,351	17.8%	388,000	6,333	1.6%	-16.2	832,000	11,700	1.4%	-16.4	888,000	48,144	5.4%	-12.4	943,000	3,243	0.3%	-17.5
MASSACHUSETTS	793,000	158,700	20.0%	848,000	15,153	1.8%	-18.2	1,895,000	35,874	1.9%	-18.1	2,031,000	145,530	7.2%	-12.8	2,166,000	9,499	0.4%	-19.6
MICHIGAN	830,000	246,336	29.7%	976,000	24,928	2.6%	-27.1	1,947,000	52,096	2.7%	-27.0	2,221,000	133,429	6.0%	-23.7	2,497,000	9,924	0.4%	-29.3
MINNESOTA	598,000	163,459	27.3%	623,000	28,668	4.6%	-22.7	1,257,000	73,423	5.8%	-21.5	1,345,000	345,474	25.7%	-1.6	1,432,000	13,548	0.9%	-26.4
MISSISSIPPI	428,000	5,599	1.3%	434,000	2,004	0.5%	-0.8	886,000	1,639	0.2%	-1.1	949,000	3,474	0.4%	-0.9				
MISSOURI	949,000	159,999	16.9%	984,000	19,402	2.0%	-14.9	1,993,000	30,189	1.5%	-15.3	2,093,000	86,645	4.1%	-12.7	2,194,000	4,081	0.2%	-16.7
MONTANA	143,000	33,552	23.5%	258,000	9,972	3.9%	-19.6	291,000	12,204	4.2%	-19.3	292,000	66,482	22.8%	-0.7	292,000	2,230	0.8%	-22.7
NEBRASKA	335,000	86,249	25.7%	344,000	10,717	3.1%	-22.6	696,000	15,637	2.2%	-23.5	734,000	107,275	14.6%	-11.1	772,000	3,433	0.4%	-25.3
NEVADA	31,000	8,933	28.8%	44,000	3,411	7.8%	-21.1	45,000	1,864	4.1%	-24.7	47,000	9,769	20.8%	-8.0				
NEW HAMPSHIRE	113,000	20,310	18.0%	115,000	1,621	1.4%	-16.6	237,000	1,234	0.5%	-17.5	246,000	8,993	3.7%	-14.3	255,000	638	0.3%	-17.7
NEW JERSEY	637,000	165,959	26.1%	703,000	14,442	2.1%	-24.0	1,588,000	36,157	2.3%	-23.8	1,849,000	113,734	6.2%	-19.9	2,110,000	6,814	0.3%	-25.7
NEW MEXICO	87,000	11,206	12.9%	85,000	2,089	2.5%	-10.4	170,000	1,110	0.7%	-12.2	172,000	9,543	5.5%	-7.3	174,000	158	0.1%	-12.8
NEW YORK	2,472,000	477,255	19.3%	2,656,000	67,641	2.5%	-16.8	5,294,000	246,108	4.6%	-14.7	5,965,000	493,085	8.3%	-11.0	6,635,000	122,419	1.8%	-17.5
NORTH CAROLINA	529,000	70,240	13.3%	568,000	564	0.1%	-13.2	1,237,000	463	0.0%	-13.2	1,368,000	6,664	0.5%	-12.8				
NORTH DAKOTA	145,000	33,935	23.4%	152,000	6,713	4.4%	-19.0	297,000	8,282	2.8%	-20.6	314,000	90,292	28.8%	5.4	332,000	1,778	0.5%	-22.9
OHIO	1,403,000	334,112	23.8%	1,535,000	46,177	3.0%	-20.8	3,289,000	59,594	1.8%	-22.0	3,551,000	362,279	10.2%	-13.6	3,811,000	16,590	0.4%	-23.4
OKLAHOMA	456,000	43,825	9.6%	498,000	46,971	9.4%	-0.2	1,026,000	25,716	2.5%	-7.1	1,118,000	46,274	4.1%	-5.5	1,211,000	5,207	0.4%	-9.2
OREGON	392,000	55,303	14.1%	428,000	14,750	3.4%	-10.7	467,000	14,911	3.2%	-10.9	514,000	69,320	13.5%	-0.6	563,000	5,378	1.0%	-13.2
PENNSYLVANIA	1,907,000	548,739	28.8%	2,048,000	71,582	3.5%	-25.3	4,412,000	129,831	2.9%	-25.8	4,766,000	334,177	7.0%	-21.8	5,121,000	27,644	0.5%	-28.2
RHODE ISLAND	125,000	19,779	15.8%	134,000	2,564	1.9%	-13.9	296,000	5,456	1.8%	-14.0	323,000	8,223	2.5%	-13.3	351,000	699	0.2%	-15.6
SOUTH CAROLINA	347,000	1,512	0.4%	370,000	555	0.2%	-0.3	781,000	28	0.0%	-0.4	796,000	624	0.1%	-0.4	813,000	47	0.0%	-0.4
SOUTH DAKOTA	172,000	67,385	39.2%	179,000	5,534	3.1%	-36.1	326,000	35,607	10.9%	-28.3	342,000	75,355	22.0%	-17.1	359,000	1,594	0.4%	-38.7
TENNESSEE	563,000	58,437	10.4%	587,000	2,687	0.5%	-9.9	1,228,000	2,249	0.2%	-10.2	1,309,000	10,860	0.8%	-9.5	1,391,000	661	0.0%	-10.3
TEXAS	1,004,000	53,730	5.4%	1,101,000	20,896	1.9%	-3.5	2,304,000	83,531	3.6%	-1.7	2,558,000	42,879	1.7%	-3.7	2,811,000	867	0.0%	-5.3
UTAH	174,000	33,683	19.4%	194,000	4,863	2.5%	-16.9	213,000	7,634	3.6%	-15.8	227,000	32,662	14.4%	-5.0	243,000	1,000	0.4%	-18.9
VERMONT	101,000	24,151	23.9%	101,000	1,517	1.5%	-22.4	199,000	830	0.4%	-23.5	201,000	6,295	3.1%	-20.8	203,000	347	0.2%	-23.7
VIRGINIA	538,000	23,355	4.3%	575,000	1,801	0.3%	-4.0	1,203,000	1,874	0.2%	-4.2	1,242,000	10,558	0.9%	-3.5	1,282,000	609	0.0%	-4.3
WASHINGTON	640,000	165,514	25.9%	707,000	30,398	4.3%	-21.6	774,000	91,280	11.8%	-14.1	833,000	158,483	19.0%	-6.8	892,000	8,224	0.9%	-24.9
WEST VIRGINIA	328,000	98,877	30.1%	353,000	6,144	1.7%	-28.4	726,000	7,144	1.0%	-29.2	791,000	37,795	4.8%	-25.4	857,000	3,417	0.4%	-29.7
WISCONSIN	627,000	105,149	16.8%	643,000	34,949	5.4%	-11.3	1,371,000	89,283	6.5%	-10.3	1,493,000	461,098	30.9%	14.1	1,617,000	22,367	1.4%	-15.4
WYOMING	87,000	12,413	14.3%	95,000	1,832	1.9%	-12.3	106,000	3,733	3.5%	-10.7	113,000	25,174	22.3%	8.0	120,000	788	0.7%	-13.6
Total	26,839,000	5,261,478	19.6%	30,618,000	861,933	2.8%	-16.8	55,442,000	1,482,406	2.7%	-16.9	60,351,000	4,988,398	8.3%	-11.3	65,267,000	360,976	0.6%	-19.1

*Percentage point difference between turnout in current year and initial year listed in chart. If data do not appear for a state in the initial year listed, the difference is calculated from the first year in which data do appear for that state.

STATE GUBERNATORIAL GENERAL ELECTIONS

Election Years 1912–1928

State	1912 Voting-age population	1912 Turnout	1912 %	1916 Voting-age population	1916 Turnout	1916 %	1916 Difference from 1912*	1920 Voting-age population	1920 Turnout	1920 %	1920 Difference from 1912	1924 Voting-age population	1924 Turnout	1924 %	1924 Difference from 1912	1928 Voting-age population	1928 Turnout	1928 %	1928 Difference from 1912
ALABAMA																			
ALASKA																			
ARIZONA				120,000	58,516	48.8%		145,000	68,445	47.2%	-1.6	153,000	75,943	49.6%	0.9	161,000	92,504	57.5%	8.7
ARKANSAS	407,000	169,603	41.7%	431,000	175,734	40.8%	-0.9	872,000	190,148	21.8%	-19.9	913,000	124,750	13.7%	-28.0	954,000	196,336	20.6%	-21.1
CALIFORNIA																			
COLORADO	466,000	265,786	57.0%	496,000	285,163	57.5%	0.5	526,000	293,030	55.7%	-1.3	546,000	342,962	62.8%	5.8	564,000	388,265	68.8%	11.8
CONNECTICUT	270,000	190,394	70.5%	292,000	213,807	73.2%	2.7	648,000	366,088	56.5%	-14.0	714,000	372,312	52.1%	-18.4	780,000	552,974	70.9%	0.4
DELAWARE	59,000	48,441	82.1%	62,000	51,207	82.6%	0.5	128,000	93,957	73.4%	-8.7	134,000	88,939	66.4%	-15.7	140,000	94,209	67.3%	-14.8
DISTRICT OF COLUMBIA																			
FLORIDA	220,000	48,465	22.0%	246,000	82,885	33.7%	11.7	544,000	132,672	24.4%	2.4	675,000	101,680	15.1%	-7.0	805,000	243,473	30.2%	8.2
GEORGIA				677,000	59,526	8.8%						1,453,000	152,367	10.5%	1.7	1,485,000	202,035	13.6%	4.8
HAWAII																			
IDAHO	177,000	105,513	59.6%	202,000	134,503	66.6%	7.0	223,000	143,009	64.1%	4.5	228,000	148,973	65.3%	5.7	233,000	151,635	65.1%	5.5
ILLINOIS	1,535,000	1,162,880	75.8%	1,657,000	1,322,553	79.8%	4.1	3,553,000	2,111,605	59.4%	-16.3	3,938,000	2,409,115	61.2%	-14.6	4,322,000	3,012,203	69.7%	-6.1
INDIANA	808,000	642,306	79.5%	833,000	706,728	84.8%	5.3	1,725,000	1,250,595	72.5%	-7.0	1,822,000	1,236,279	67.9%	-11.6	1,918,000	1,421,000	74.1%	-5.4
IOWA	632,000	461,206	73.0%	670,000	513,848	76.7%	3.7	1,377,000	874,810	63.5%	-9.4	1,419,000	831,474	58.6%	-14.4	1,461,000	942,492	64.5%	-8.5
KANSAS	936,000	359,684	38.4%	962,000	581,126	60.4%	22.0	995,000	547,399	55.0%	16.6	1,042,000	659,681	63.3%	24.9	1,091,000	660,646	60.6%	22.1
KENTUCKY																			
LOUISIANA	413,000	56,526	13.7%	435,000	129,249	29.7%	16.0	918,000	55,188	6.0%	-7.7	1,006,000	67,623	6.7%	-7.0	1,093,000	96,674	8.8%	-4.8
MAINE	204,000	141,940	69.6%	208,000	151,410	72.8%	3.2	423,000	205,440	48.6%	-21.0	430,000	253,907	59.0%	-10.5	437,000	213,625	48.9%	-20.7
MARYLAND																			
MASSACHUSETTS	793,000	475,793	60.0%	848,000	526,421	62.1%	2.1	1,895,000	960,697	50.7%	-9.3	2,031,000	1,161,510	57.2%	-2.8	2,166,000	1,536,890	71.0%	11.0
MICHIGAN	830,000	548,921	66.1%	976,000	651,518	66.8%	0.6	1,947,000	1,058,538	54.4%	-11.8	2,221,000	1,160,918	52.3%	-13.9	2,497,000	1,374,341	55.0%	-11.1
MINNESOTA	598,000	318,447	53.3%	623,000	390,819	62.7%	9.5	1,257,000	783,624	62.3%	9.1	1,345,000	835,002	62.1%	8.8	1,432,000	999,823	69.8%	16.6
MISSISSIPPI																			
MISSOURI	949,000	699,210	73.7%	984,000	785,998	79.9%	6.2	1,993,000	1,330,822	66.8%	-6.9	2,093,000	1,296,119	61.9%	-11.8	2,194,000	1,519,136	69.2%	-4.4
MONTANA	143,000	79,778	55.8%	258,000	173,572	67.3%	11.5	291,000	185,988	63.9%	8.1	292,000	174,059	59.6%	3.8	292,000	194,193	66.5%	10.7
NEBRASKA	335,000	251,678	75.1%	344,000	291,406	84.7%	9.6	696,000	378,245	54.3%	-20.8	734,000	448,370	61.1%	-14.0	772,000	540,997	70.1%	-5.1
NEVADA																			
NEW HAMPSHIRE	113,000	83,279	73.7%	115,000	86,239	75.0%	1.3	237,000	156,527	66.0%	-7.7	246,000	164,341	66.8%	-6.9	255,000	188,562	73.9%	0.2
NEW JERSEY																2,110,000	1,495,733	70.9%	
NEW MEXICO				85,000	66,373	78.1%		170,000	106,185	62.5%	-15.6	172,000	115,093	66.9%	-11.2	174,000	118,616	68.2%	-9.9
NEW YORK	2,472,000	1,567,236	63.4%	2,656,000	1,615,155	60.8%	-2.6	5,294,000	2,867,948	54.2%	-9.2	5,965,000	3,257,383	54.6%	-8.8	6,635,000	4,351,635	65.6%	2.2

State Gubernatorial General Elections (continued)

Election Years 1912–1928 (continued)

State	1912 Voting-age population	Turnout	%	1916 Voting-age population	Turnout	%	Difference from 1912	1920 Voting-age population	Turnout	%	Difference from 1912	1924 Voting-age population	Turnout	%	Difference from 1912	1928 Voting-age population	Turnout	%	Difference from 1912
NORTH CAROLINA	529,000	244,474	46.2%	568,000	288,508	50.8%	4.6	1,237,000	538,326	43.5%	-2.7	1,368,000	480,068	35.1%	-11.1	1,497,000	651,424	43.5%	-2.7
NORTH DAKOTA	145,000	87,596	60.4%	152,000	110,631	72.8%	12.4	297,000	229,606	77.3%	16.9	314,000	187,584	59.7%	-0.7	332,000	232,222	69.9%	9.5
OHIO	1,403,000	1,036,731	73.9%	1,535,000	1,174,075	76.5%	2.6	3,289,000	2,003,183	60.9%	-13.0	3,551,000	1,973,364	55.6%	-18.3	3,811,000	2,473,952	64.9%	-9.0
OKLAHOMA																			
OREGON																			
PENNSYLVANIA																			
RHODE ISLAND	125,000	78,166	62.5%	134,000	88,568	66.1%	3.6	296,000	168,842	57.0%	-5.5	323,000	209,604	64.9%	2.4	351,000	235,496	67.1%	4.6
SOUTH CAROLINA	347,000	44,330	12.8%	370,000	61,675	16.7%	3.9	781,000	58,050	7.4%	-5.3	796,000	53,545	6.7%	-6.0	813,000	259,168	31.9%	19.1
SOUTH DAKOTA	172,000	117,828	68.5%	179,000	128,520	71.8%	3.3	326,000	183,888	56.4%	-12.1	342,000	203,943	59.6%	-8.9				
TENNESSEE	563,000	248,787	44.2%	587,000	266,648	45.4%	1.2	1,228,000	417,146	34.0%	-10.2	1,309,000	283,230	21.6%	-22.6	1,391,000	320,279	23.0%	-21.2
TEXAS	1,004,000	301,157	30.0%	1,101,000	363,565	33.0%	3.0	2,304,000	481,731	20.9%	-9.1	2,558,000	717,528	28.1%	-1.9	2,811,000	707,201	25.2%	-4.8
UTAH	174,000	111,386	64.0%	194,000	142,415	73.4%	9.4	213,000	143,574	67.4%	3.4	227,000	153,435	67.6%	3.6	243,000	175,999	72.4%	8.4
VERMONT	101,000	84,839	84.2%	101,000	80,854	80.3%	-3.9	199,000	86,762	43.6%	-20.6	201,000	95,285	47.4%	-16.8	203,000	129,173	63.6%	-0.6
VIRGINIA																			
WASHINGTON	640,000	318,359	49.7%	707,000	377,602	53.4%	3.7	774,000	403,198	52.1%	2.3	833,000	390,304	46.9%	-2.9	892,000	501,628	56.2%	6.5
WEST VIRGINIA	328,000	268,275	81.8%	353,000	289,292	82.0%	0.2	726,000	511,114	70.4%	-11.4	791,000	572,651	72.4%	-9.4	857,000	643,670	75.1%	-6.7
WISCONSIN	627,000	393,849	62.8%	643,000	434,340	67.5%	4.7	1,371,000	691,294	50.4%	-12.4	1,493,000	796,432	53.3%	-9.5	1,617,000	989,143	61.2%	-1.6
WYOMING												113,000	78,598	69.6%					
Total	18,518,000	10,992,863	59.4%	20,804,000	12,840,449	61.7%	2.4	38,898,000	20,077,674	51.6%	-7.7	43,791,000	21,674,371	49.5%	-9.9	48,789,000	27,907,352	57.2%	-2.2

*Percentage point difference between turnout in current year and initial year listed in chart. If data do not appear for a state in the initial year listed, the difference is calculated from the first year in which data do appear for that state.

STATE GUBERNATORIAL GENERAL ELECTIONS

Republican Turnout for Election Years 1912–1928

State	1912			1916				1920				1924				1928			
	Voting-age population	Turnout	%	Voting-age population	Turnout	%	Difference from 1912*	Voting-age population	Turnout	%	Difference from 1912	Voting-age population	Turnout	%	Difference from 1912	Voting-age population	Turnout	%	Difference from 1912
ALABAMA																			
ALASKA																			
ARIZONA				120,000	28,051	23.4%		145,000	37,060	25.6%	2.2	153,000	37,571	24.6%	1.2	161,000	47,829	29.7%	6.3
ARKANSAS	407,000	46,440	11.4%	431,000	43,963	10.2%	-1.2	872,000	46,350	5.3%	-6.1	913,000	25,152	2.8%	-8.7	954,000	44,565	4.7%	-6.7
CALIFORNIA																			
COLORADO	466,000	63,061	13.5%	496,000	117,723	23.7%	10.2	526,000	174,488	33.2%	19.6	546,000	178,078	32.6%	19.1	564,000	144,167	25.6%	12.0
CONNECTICUT	270,000	67,531	25.0%	292,000	109,293	37.4%	12.4	648,000	230,792	35.6%	10.6	714,000	246,336	34.5%	9.5	780,000	296,216	38.0%	13.0
DELAWARE	59,000	22,745	38.6%	62,000	26,664	43.0%	4.5	128,000	51,895	40.5%	2.0	134,000	53,046	39.6%	1.0	140,000	63,215	45.2%	6.6
DISTRICT OF COLUMBIA																			
FLORIDA	220,000	2,646	1.2%	246,000	10,333	4.2%	3.0	544,000	23,788	4.4%	3.2	675,000	17,499	2.6%	1.4	805,000	95,018	11.8%	10.6
GEORGIA																			
HAWAII																			
IDAHO	177,000	35,074	19.8%	202,000	63,305	31.3%	11.5	223,000	75,748	34.0%	14.2	228,000	65,408	28.7%	8.9	233,000	87,681	37.6%	17.8
ILLINOIS	1,535,000	318,469	20.7%	1,657,000	696,535	42.0%	21.3	3,553,000	1,243,148	35.0%	14.2	3,938,000	1,366,436	34.7%	14.0	4,322,000	1,709,818	39.6%	18.8
INDIANA	808,000	142,850	17.7%	833,000	337,831	40.6%	22.9	1,725,000	683,253	39.6%	21.9	1,822,000	654,184	35.9%	18.2	1,918,000	728,203	38.0%	20.3
IOWA	632,000	184,148	29.1%	670,000	313,586	46.8%	17.7	1,377,000	513,118	37.3%	8.1	1,419,000	604,624	42.6%	13.5	1,461,000	591,770	40.5%	11.4
KANSAS	936,000	167,408	17.9%	962,000	353,169	36.7%	18.8	995,000	319,914	32.2%	14.3	1,042,000	323,403	31.0%	13.2	1,091,000	433,395	39.7%	21.8
KENTUCKY																			
LOUISIANA	413,000	4,961	1.2%					918,000	1,396	0.2%	-1.0	1,006,000	1,420	0.1%	-1.1	1,093,000	3,733	0.3%	-0.9
MAINE	204,000	70,931	34.8%	208,000	81,760	39.3%	4.5	423,000	135,393	32.0%	-2.8	430,000	145,281	33.8%	-1.0	437,000	148,053	33.9%	-0.9
MARYLAND																			
MASSACHUSETTS	793,000	143,597	18.1%	848,000	276,123	32.6%	14.5	1,895,000	643,869	34.0%	15.9	2,031,000	650,817	32.0%	13.9	2,166,000	769,372	35.5%	17.4
MICHIGAN	830,000	169,963	20.5%	976,000	363,724	37.3%	16.8	1,947,000	703,180	36.1%	15.6	2,221,000	799,225	36.0%	15.5	2,497,000	961,179	38.5%	18.0
MINNESOTA	598,000	129,688	21.7%	623,000	245,841	39.5%	17.8	1,257,000	415,805	33.1%	11.4	1,345,000	406,692	30.2%	8.6	1,432,000	549,857	38.4%	16.7
MISSISSIPPI																			
MISSOURI	949,000	217,819	23.0%	984,000	380,092	38.6%	15.7	1,993,000	722,020	36.2%	13.3	2,093,000	640,135	30.6%	7.6	2,194,000	784,293	35.7%	12.8
MONTANA	143,000	22,950	16.0%	258,000	76,547	29.7%	13.6	291,000	111,113	38.2%	22.1	292,000	74,126	25.4%	9.3	292,000	79,777	27.3%	11.3
NEBRASKA	335,000	114,075	34.1%	344,000	136,811	39.8%	5.7	696,000	152,863	22.0%	-12.1	734,000	229,067	31.2%	-2.8	772,000	308,262	39.9%	5.9
NEVADA																			
NEW HAMPSHIRE	113,000	32,504	28.8%	115,000	45,899	39.9%	11.1	237,000	93,273	39.4%	10.6	246,000	88,650	36.0%	7.3	255,000	108,431	42.5%	13.8
NEW JERSEY																2,110,000	824,005	39.1%	
NEW MEXICO				85,000	31,524	37.1%		170,000	54,426	32.0%	-5.1	172,000	55,984	32.5%	-4.5	174,000	65,967	37.9%	0.8
NEW YORK	2,472,000	444,105	18.0%	2,656,000	850,020	32.0%	14.0	5,294,000	1,335,878	25.2%	7.3	5,965,000	1,518,552	25.5%	7.5	6,635,000	2,104,629	31.7%	13.8

State Gubernatorial General Elections (continued)

Republican Turnout for Election Years 1912–1928 (continued)

State	1912 Voting-age population	1912 Turnout	1912 %	1916 Voting-age population	1916 Turnout	1916 %	1916 Difference from 1912	1920 Voting-age population	1920 Turnout	1920 %	1920 Difference from 1912	1924 Voting-age population	1924 Turnout	1924 %	1924 Difference from 1912	1928 Voting-age population	1928 Turnout	1928 %	1928 Difference from 1912
NORTH CAROLINA	529,000	43,625	8.2%	568,000	120,157	21.2%	12.9	1,237,000	230,175	18.6%	10.4	1,368,000	185,627	13.6%	5.3	1,497,000	289,415	19.3%	11.1
NORTH DAKOTA	145,000	39,811	27.5%	152,000	87,665	57.7%	30.2	297,000	117,118	39.4%	12.0	314,000	101,170	32.2%	4.8	332,000	131,193	39.5%	12.1
OHIO	1,403,000	272,500	19.4%	1,535,000	561,602	36.6%	17.2	3,289,000	1,039,835	31.6%	12.2	3,551,000	888,139	25.0%	5.6	3,811,000	1,355,526	35.6%	16.1
OKLAHOMA																			
OREGON																			
PENNSYLVANIA																			
RHODE ISLAND	125,000	34,133	27.3%	134,000	49,524	37.0%	9.7	296,000	109,138	36.9%	9.6	323,000	122,749	38.0%	10.7	351,000	121,442	34.6%	7.3
SOUTH CAROLINA																813,000	121,643	15.0%	
SOUTH DAKOTA	172,000	57,160	33.2%	179,000	72,789	40.7%	7.4	326,000	103,592	31.8%	-1.5	342,000	109,894	32.1%	-1.1				
TENNESSEE	563,000	124,641	22.1%	587,000	117,819	20.1%	-2.1	1,228,000	229,143	18.7%	-3.5	1,309,000	121,228	9.3%	-12.9	1,391,000	124,733	9.0%	-13.2
TEXAS	1,004,000	23,089	2.3%	1,101,000	49,118	4.5%	2.2	2,304,000	90,217	3.9%	1.6	2,558,000	294,970	11.5%	9.2	2,811,000	123,337	4.4%	2.1
UTAH	174,000	42,552	24.5%	194,000	59,522	30.7%	6.2	213,000	83,518	39.2%	14.8	227,000	72,127	31.8%	7.3	243,000	72,306	29.8%	5.3
VERMONT	101,000	26,237	26.0%	101,000	43,265	42.8%	16.9	199,000	67,674	34.0%	8.0	201,000	75,510	37.6%	11.6	203,000	94,974	46.8%	20.8
VIRGINIA																			
WASHINGTON	640,000	96,629	15.1%	707,000	167,809	23.7%	8.6	774,000	210,662	27.2%	12.1	833,000	220,162	26.4%	11.3	892,000	281,991	31.6%	16.5
WEST VIRGINIA	328,000	128,062	39.0%	353,000	140,569	39.8%	0.8	726,000	242,327	33.4%	-5.7	791,000	303,587	38.4%	-0.7	857,000	345,909	40.4%	1.3
WISCONSIN	627,000	179,360	28.6%	643,000	229,889	35.8%	7.1	1,371,000	366,247	26.7%	-1.9	1,493,000	412,255	27.6%	-1.0	1,617,000	547,738	33.9%	5.3
WYOMING												113,000	35,275	31.2%					
Total	18,171,000	3,468,764	19.1%	19,322,000	6,288,522	32.5%	13.5	38,117,000	10,658,416	28.0%	8.9	41,542,000	11,124,379	26.8%	7.7	47,304,000	14,559,642	30.8%	11.7

Democratic Turnout for Election Years 1912–1928

State	1912 Voting-age population	1912 Turnout	1912 %	1916 Voting-age population	1916 Turnout	1916 %	1916 Difference from 1912*	1920 Voting-age population	1920 Turnout	1920 %	1920 Difference from 1912	1924 Voting-age population	1924 Turnout	1924 %	1924 Difference from 1912	1928 Voting-age population	1928 Turnout	1928 %	1928 Difference from 1912
ALABAMA																			
ALASKA																			
ARIZONA				120,000	28,094	23.4%		145,000	31,385	21.6%	-1.8	153,000	38,372	25.1%	1.7	161,000	44,553	27.7%	4.3
ARKANSAS	407,000	109,825	27.0%	431,000	122,041	28.3%	1.3	872,000	123,637	14.2%	-12.8	913,000	99,598	10.9%	-16.1	954,000	151,771	15.9%	-11.1
CALIFORNIA																			
COLORADO	466,000	114,044	24.5%	496,000	151,912	30.6%	6.2	526,000	108,738	20.7%	-3.8	546,000	151,041	27.7%	3.2	564,000	240,160	42.6%	18.1
CONNECTICUT	270,000	78,264	29.0%	292,000	96,787	33.1%	4.2	648,000	121,729	18.8%	-10.2	714,000	118,676	16.6%	-12.4	780,000	252,209	32.3%	3.3
DELAWARE	59,000	21,460	36.4%	62,000	24,053	38.8%	2.4	128,000	41,038	32.1%	-4.3	134,000	34,830	26.0%	-10.4	140,000	30,994	22.1%	-14.2
DISTRICT OF COLUMBIA																			
FLORIDA	220,000	38,977	17.7%	246,000	30,343	12.3%	-5.4	544,000	103,407	19.0%	1.3	675,000	84,181	12.5%	-5.2	805,000	148,455	18.4%	0.7

State Gubernatorial General Elections (continued)

State Gubernatorial General Elections (continued)

Democratic Turnout for Election Years 1912–1928 (continued)

State	1912 Voting-age population	Turnout	%	1916 Voting-age population	Turnout	%	Difference from 1912	1920 Voting-age population	Turnout	%	Difference from 1912	1924 Voting-age population	Turnout	%	Difference from 1912	1928 Voting-age population	Turnout	%	Difference from 1912
GEORGIA				677,000	59,526	8.8%						1,453,000	152,367	10.5%	1.7	1,485,000	202,035	13.6%	4.8
HAWAII																			
IDAHO	177,000	33,992	19.2%	202,000	63,877	31.6%	12.4	223,000	38,509	17.3%	-1.9	228,000	25,081	11.0%	-8.2	233,000	63,046	27.1%	7.9
ILLINOIS	1,535,000	443,120	28.9%	1,657,000	556,654	33.6%	4.7	3,553,000	731,551	20.6%	-8.3	3,938,000	1,021,408	25.9%	-2.9	4,322,000	1,284,897	29.7%	0.9
INDIANA	808,000	275,357	34.1%	833,000	325,060	39.0%	4.9	1,725,000	515,253	29.9%	-4.2	1,822,000	572,303	31.4%	-2.7	1,918,000	683,545	35.6%	1.6
IOWA	632,000	182,449	28.9%	670,000	186,832	27.9%	-1.0	1,377,000	338,108	24.6%	-4.3	1,419,000	226,850	16.0%	-12.9	1,461,000	350,722	24.0%	-4.9
KANSAS	936,000	167,437	17.9%	962,000	192,037	20.0%	2.1	995,000	214,940	21.6%	3.7	1,042,000	182,861	17.5%	-0.3	1,091,000	219,327	20.1%	2.2
KENTUCKY																			
LOUISIANA	413,000	50,581	12.2%	435,000	80,807	18.6%	6.3	918,000	53,792	5.9%	-6.4	1,006,000	66,203	6.6%	-5.7	1,093,000	92,941	8.5%	-3.7
MAINE	204,000	67,702	33.2%	208,000	67,930	32.7%	-0.5	423,000	70,047	16.6%	-16.6	430,000	108,626	25.3%	-7.9	437,000	65,572	15.0%	-18.2
MARYLAND																			
MASSACHUSETTS	793,000	193,184	24.4%	848,000	229,883	27.1%	2.7	1,895,000	290,350	15.3%	-9.0	2,031,000	490,010	24.1%	-0.2	2,166,000	750,137	34.6%	10.3
MICHIGAN	830,000	194,017	23.4%	976,000	264,440	27.1%	3.7	1,947,000	310,566	16.0%	-7.4	2,221,000	343,577	15.5%	-7.9	2,497,000	404,546	16.2%	-7.2
MINNESOTA	598,000	99,659	16.7%	623,000	93,112	14.9%	-1.7	1,257,000	81,293	6.5%	-10.2	1,345,000	49,353	3.7%	-13.0	1,432,000	213,734	14.9%	-1.7
MISSISSIPPI																			
MISSOURI	949,000	337,019	35.5%	984,000	382,355	38.9%	3.3	1,993,000	580,716	29.1%	-6.4	2,093,000	634,263	30.3%	-5.2	2,194,000	731,783	33.4%	-2.2
MONTANA	143,000	25,381	17.7%	258,000	85,683	33.2%	15.5	291,000	74,875	25.7%	8.0	292,000	88,801	30.4%	12.7	292,000	113,635	38.9%	21.2
NEBRASKA	335,000	123,997	37.0%	344,000	143,564	41.7%	4.7	696,000	130,433	18.7%	-18.3	734,000	183,709	25.0%	-12.0	772,000	230,640	29.9%	-7.1
NEVADA																			
NEW HAMPSHIRE	113,000	34,203	30.3%	115,000	38,853	33.8%	3.5	237,000	62,174	26.2%	-4.0	246,000	75,691	30.8%	0.5	255,000	79,798	31.3%	1.0
NEW JERSEY																2,110,000	671,728	31.8%	
NEW MEXICO				85,000	32,732	38.5%		170,000	50,755	29.9%	-8.7	172,000	56,183	32.7%	-5.8	174,000	52,550	30.2%	-8.3
NEW YORK	2,472,000	649,559	26.3%	2,656,000	686,862	25.9%	-0.4	5,294,000	1,261,812	23.8%	-2.4	5,965,000	1,627,111	27.3%	1.0	6,635,000	2,130,193	32.1%	5.8
NORTH CAROLINA	529,000	149,975	28.4%	568,000	167,761	29.5%	1.2	1,237,000	308,151	24.9%	-3.4	1,368,000	294,441	21.5%	-6.8	1,497,000	362,009	24.2%	-4.2
NORTH DAKOTA	145,000	31,544	21.8%	152,000	20,351	13.4%	-8.4	297,000	112,488	37.9%	16.1	314,000	86,414	27.5%	5.8	332,000	100,205	30.2%	8.4
OHIO	1,403,000	439,323	31.3%	1,535,000	568,218	37.0%	5.7	3,289,000	918,962	27.9%	-3.4	3,551,000	1,064,981	30.0%	-1.3	3,811,000	1,106,739	29.0%	-2.3
OKLAHOMA																			
OREGON																			
PENNSYLVANIA																			
RHODE ISLAND	125,000	32,725	26.2%	134,000	36,158	27.0%	0.8	296,000	55,963	18.9%	-7.3	323,000	85,942	26.6%	0.4	351,000	113,391	32.3%	6.1
SOUTH CAROLINA	347,000	44,122	12.7%	370,000	60,396	16.3%	3.6	781,000	58,050	7.4%	-5.3	796,000	53,545	6.7%	-6.0	813,000	136,016	16.7%	4.0
SOUTH DAKOTA	172,000	53,850	31.3%	179,000	50,545	28.2%	-3.1	326,000	31,870	9.8%	-21.5	342,000	46,663	13.6%	-17.7				
TENNESSEE	563,000	116,610	20.7%	587,000	146,759	25.0%	4.3	1,228,000	185,890	15.1%	-5.6	1,309,000	162,002	12.4%	-8.3	1,391,000	195,546	14.1%	-6.7

State Gubernatorial General Elections (continued)

Democratic Turnout for Election Years 1912–1928 (continued)

State	1912 Voting-age population	Turnout	%	1916 Voting-age population	Turnout	%	Difference from 1912	1920 Voting-age population	Turnout	%	Difference from 1912	1924 Voting-age population	Turnout	%	Difference from 1912	1928 Voting-age population	Turnout	%	Difference from 1912
TEXAS	1,004,000	234,352	23.3%	1,101,000	296,667	26.9%	3.6	2,304,000	289,188	12.6%	-10.8	2,558,000	422,558	16.5%	-6.8	2,811,000	582,968	20.7%	-2.6
UTAH	174,000	36,076	20.7%	194,000	78,502	40.5%	19.7	213,000	54,913	25.8%	5.0	227,000	81,308	35.8%	15.1	243,000	102,953	42.4%	21.6
VERMONT	101,000	20,001	19.8%	101,000	15,789	15.6%	-4.2	199,000	18,917	9.5%	-10.3	201,000	18,263	9.1%	-10.7	203,000	33,563	16.5%	-3.3
VIRGINIA																			
WASHINGTON	640,000	97,251	15.2%	707,000	181,645	25.7%	10.5	774,000	66,079	8.5%	-6.7	833,000	126,447	15.2%	0.0	892,000	214,334	24.0%	8.8
WEST VIRGINIA	328,000	119,292	36.4%	353,000	143,324	40.6%	4.2	726,000	184,762	25.4%	10.8	701,000	261,846	33.1%	3.3	857,000	296,037	34.6%	-1.0
WISCONSIN	627,000	167,316	26.7%	643,000	164,555	25.6%	-1.1	1,371,000	247,746	18.1%	-8.6	1,493,000	317,550	21.3%	-5.4	1,617,000	394,368	24.4%	-2.3
WYOMING												113,000	43,323	38.3%					
Total	18,518,000	4,782,664	25.8%	20,804,000	5,874,107	28.2%	2.4	38,898,000	7,868,087	20.2%	-5.6	43,791,000	9,496,378	21.7%	-4.1	48,789,000	12,847,700	26.3%	0.5

Other Turnout for Election Years 1912–1928

State	1912 Voting-age population	Turnout	%	1916 Voting-age population	Turnout	%	Difference from 1912*	1920 Voting-age population	Turnout	%	Difference from 1912	1924 Voting-age population	Turnout	%	Difference from 1912	1928 Voting-age population	Turnout	%	Difference from 1912
ALABAMA																			
ALASKA																			
ARIZONA				120,000	2,371	2.0%										161,000	122	0.1%	-1.9
ARKANSAS	407,000	13,338	3.3%	431,000	9,730	2.3%	-1.0	872,000	20,161	2.3%	-1.0								
CALIFORNIA																			
COLORADO	466,000	88,681	19.0%	496,000	15,528	3.1%	-15.9	526,000	9,804	1.9%	-17.2	546,000	13,843	2.5%	-16.5	564,000	3,938	0.7%	-18.3
CONNECTICUT	270,000	44,599	16.5%	292,000	7,727	2.6%	-13.9	648,000	13,567	2.1%	-14.4	714,000	7,300	1.0%	-15.5	780,000	4,549	0.6%	-15.9
DELAWARE	59,000	4,236	7.2%	62,000	490	0.0%	-0.4	128,000	1,024	0.8%	-8.4	134,000	1,063	0.8%	-6.4				
DISTRICT OF COLUMBIA																			
FLORIDA	220,000	6,842	3.1%	246,000	42,209	17.2%	14.0	544,000	5,477	1.0%	-2.1								
GEORGIA																			
HAWAII																			
IDAHO	177,000	36,447	20.6%	202,000	7,321	3.6%	-17.0	223,000	28,752	12.9%	-7.7	228,000	58,484	25.7%	5.1	233,000	908	0.4%	-20.2
ILLINOIS	1,535,000	401,291	26.1%	1,657,000	69,364	4.2%	-22.0	3,553,000	136,906	3.9%	-22.3	3,938,000	21,271	0.5%	-25.6	4,322,000	17,488	0.4%	-25.7
INDIANA	808,000	224,099	27.7%	833,000	43,837	5.3%	-22.5	1,725,000	52,089	3.0%	-24.7	1,822,000	9,792	0.5%	-27.2	1,918,000	9,252	0.5%	-27.3
IOWA	632,000	94,609	15.0%	670,000	13,430	2.0%	-13.0	1,377,000	23,584	1.7%	-13.3								
KANSAS	936,000	24,839	2.7%	962,000	35,920	3.7%	1.1	995,000	12,545	1.3%	-1.4	1,042,000	153,417	14.7%	12.1	1,091,000	7,924	0.7%	-1.9
KENTUCKY																			
LOUISIANA	413,000	984	0.2%	435,000	48,442	11.1%	10.9												
MAINE	204,000	3,307	1.6%	208,000	1,720	0.8%	-0.8												

State Gubernatorial General Elections (continued)

State Gubernatorial General Elections (continued)

Other Turnout for Election Years 1912–1928 (continued)

State	1912 Voting-age population	Turnout	%	1916 Voting-age population	Turnout	%	Difference from 1912	1920 Voting-age population	Turnout	%	Difference from 1912	1924 Voting-age population	Turnout	%	Difference from 1912	1928 Voting-age population	Turnout	%	Difference from 1912
MARYLAND																			
MASSACHUSETTS	793,000	139,012	17.5%	848,000	20,415	2.4%	-15.1	1,895,000	26,478	1.4%	-16.1	2,031,000	20,683	1.0%	-16.5	2,166,000	17,381	0.8%	-16.7
MICHIGAN	830,000	184,941	22.3%	976,000	23,354	2.4%	-19.9	1,947,000	44,792	2.3%	-20.0	2,221,000	18,116	0.8%	-21.5	2,497,000	8,616	0.3%	-21.9
MINNESOTA	598,000	89,100	14.9%	623,000	51,866	8.3%	-6.6	1,257,000	286,526	22.8%	7.9	1,345,000	378,957	28.2%	13.3	1,432,000	236,232	16.5%	1.6
MISSISSIPPI																			
MISSOURI	949,000	144,372	15.2%	984,000	23,551	2.4%	-12.8	1,993,000	28,086	1.4%	-13.8	2,093,000	21,721	1.0%	-14.2	2,194,000	3,060	0.1%	-15.1
MONTANA	143,000	31,447	22.0%	258,000	11,342	4.4%	-17.6					292,000	11,132	3.8%	-18.2	292,000	781	0.3%	-21.7
NEBRASKA	335,000	13,606	4.1%	344,000	11,031	3.2%	-0.9	696,000	94,949	13.6%	9.6	734,000	35,594	4.8%	0.8	772,000	2,095	0.3%	-3.8
NEVADA																			
NEW HAMPSHIRE	113,000	16,572	14.7%	115,000	1,487	1.3%	-13.4	237,000	1,080	0.5%	-14.2					255,000	333	0.1%	-14.5
NEW JERSEY																			
NEW MEXICO				85,000	2,117	2.5%		170,000	1,004	0.6%	-1.9	172,000	2,926	1.7%	-0.8	174,000	99	0.1%	-2.4
NEW YORK	2,472,000	473,572	19.2%	2,656,000	78,273	2.9%	-16.2	5,294,000	270,258	5.1%	-14.1	5,965,000	111,720	1.9%	-17.3	6,635,000	116,813	1.8%	-17.4
NORTH CAROLINA	529,000	50,874	9.6%	568,000	590	0.1%	-9.5												
NORTH DAKOTA	145,000	16,241	11.2%	152,000	2,615	1.7%	-9.5									332,000	824	0.2%	-11.0
OHIO	1,403,000	324,908	23.2%	1,535,000	44,255	2.9%	-20.3	3,289,000	44,386	1.3%	-21.8	3,551,000	20,244	0.6%	-22.6	3,811,000	11,687	0.3%	-22.9
OKLAHOMA																			
OREGON																			
PENNSYLVANIA																			
RHODE ISLAND	125,000	11,308	9.0%	134,000	2,886	2.2%	-6.9	296,000	3,741	1.3%	-7.8	323,000	913	0.3%	-8.8	351,000	663	0.2%	-8.9
SOUTH CAROLINA	347,000	208	0.1%	370,000	1,279	0.3%	0.3									813,000	1,509	0.2%	0.1
SOUTH DAKOTA	172,000	6,818	4.0%	179,000	5,186	2.9%	-1.1	326,000	48,426	14.9%	10.9	342,000	47,386	13.9%	9.9				
TENNESSEE	563,000	7,536	1.3%	587,000	2,070	0.4%	-1.0	1,228,000	2,113	0.2%	-1.2								
TEXAS	1,004,000	43,716	4.4%	1,101,000	17,780	1.6%	-2.7	2,304,000	102,326	4.4%	0.1					2,811,000	896	0.0%	-4.3
UTAH	174,000	32,758	18.8%	194,000	4,391	2.3%	-16.6	213,000	5,143	2.4%	-16.4					243,000	740	0.3%	-18.5
VERMONT	101,000	18,601	18.4%	101,000	1,800	1.8%	-16.6	199,000	171	0.1%	-18.3	201,000	1,512	0.8%	-17.7	203,000	636	0.3%	-18.1
VIRGINIA																			
WASHINGTON	640,000	124,479	19.4%	707,000	28,148	4.0%	-15.5	774,000	126,457	16.3%	-3.1	833,000	43,695	5.2%	-14.2	892,000	5,303	0.6%	-18.9
WEST VIRGINIA	328,000	20,921	6.4%	353,000	5,399	1.5%	-4.8	726,000	84,025	11.6%	5.2	791,000	7,218	0.9%	-5.5	857,000	1,124	0.1%	-6.2
WISCONSIN	627,000	47,173	7.5%	643,000	39,896	6.2%	-1.3	1,371,000	77,301	5.6%	-1.9	1,493,000	66,627	4.5%	-3.1	1,617,000	47,037	2.9%	-4.6
WYOMING																			
Total	18,518,000	2,741,435	14.8%	20,127,000	677,820	3.4%	-11.4	34,806,000	1,551,171	4.5%	-10.3	30,811,000	1,053,614	3.4%	-11.4	37,416,000	500,010	1.3%	-13.5

*Percentage point difference between turnout in current year and initial year listed in chart. If data do not appear for a state in the initial year listed, the difference is calculated from the first year in which data do appear for that state.

UNITED STATES SENATE GENERAL ELECTIONS

Election Years 1912–1928

State	1912* Voting-age population	Turnout	%	1916 Voting-age population	Turnout	%	Difference from 1912**	1920 Voting-age population	Turnout	%	Difference from 1912	1924 Voting-age population	Turnout	%	Difference from 1912	1928 Voting-age population	Turnout	%	Difference from 1912
ALABAMA								1,155,000	228,982	19.8%		1,238,000	159,640	12.9%	-6.9				
ALASKA																			
ARIZONA				120,000	53,970	45.0%		145,000	65,062	44.9%	-0.1					161,000	86,664	53.8%	8.9
ARKANSAS								872,000	191,958	22.0%		913,000	136,571	15.0%	-7.1				
CALIFORNIA				1,791,000	940,956	52.5%		2,110,000	913,769	43.3%	-9.2					3,096,000	1,549,796	50.1%	-2.5
COLORADO	466,000	249,806	53.6%					526,000	287,200	54.6%	1.0	545,000	318,169	58.4%	4.8				
CONNECTICUT				292,000	213,344	73.1%		648,000	365,188	56.4%	-16.7					780,000	551,401	70.7%	-2.4
DELAWARE				62,000	51,210	82.6%						134,000	88,816	66.3%	-16.3	140,000	104,553	74.7%	-7.9
DISTRICT OF COLUMBIA																			
FLORIDA				246,000	70,469	28.6%		544,000	133,260	24.5%	-4.1					805,000	224,451	27.9%	-0.8
GEORGIA								1,423,000	131,330	9.2%		1,453,000	155,497	10.7%	1.5				
HAWAII																			
IDAHO								223,000	140,498	63.0%		228,000	126,699	66.1%	7.0				
ILLINOIS								3,553,000	2,067,045	58.2%		3,938,000	2,280,847	57.9%	-0.3	4,322,000	2,909,369	67.3%	9.1
INDIANA				833,000	705,667	84.7%		1,725,000	1,249,567	72.4%	-12.3					1,918,000	1,414,440	73.7%	-11.0
IOWA								1,377,000	860,470	62.5%		1,419,000	894,434	63.0%	0.5				
KANSAS	936,000	350,033	37.4%					995,000	510,933	51.4%	14.0	1,042,000	611,290	58.7%	21.3				
KENTUCKY								1,291,000	903,470	70.0%		1,346,000	787,728	58.5%	-11.5				
LOUISIANA								918,000	94,944	10.3%		1,006,000	94,939	9.4%	-0.9				
MAINE				208,000	151,116	72.7%						430,000	246,211	57.3%	-15.4	437,000	208,930	47.8%	-24.8
MARYLAND				388,000	230,460	59.4%		832,000	391,210	47.0%	-12.4					943,000	474,067	50.3%	-9.1
MASSACHUSETTS				848,000	516,999	61.0%						2,031,000	1,126,526	55.5%	-5.5	2,166,000	1,524,953	70.4%	9.4
MICHIGAN				976,000	647,278	66.3%						2,221,000	1,156,726	52.1%	-14.2	2,497,000	1,362,148	54.6%	-11.8
MINNESOTA	598,000	275,765	46.1%	623,000	381,125	61.2%	15.1					1,345,000	836,563	62.2%	16.1	1,432,000	1,017,541	71.1%	24.9
MISSISSIPPI				434,000	74,290	17.1%						949,000	97,257	10.2%	-6.9	1,011,000	111,210	11.0%	-6.1
MISSOURI				984,000	783,492	79.6%		1,993,000	1,325,519	66.5%	-13.1					2,194,000	1,516,923	69.1%	-10.5
MONTANA	143,000	69,032	48.3%	258,000	167,630	65.0%	16.7					292,000	169,866	58.2%	9.9	292,000	194,840	66.7%	18.5
NEBRASKA				344,000	286,295	83.2%						734,000	440,010	59.9%	-23.3	772,000	528,751	68.5%	-14.7
NEVADA				44,000	32,890	74.8%		45,000	27,427	60.9%	-13.8					50,000	32,929	65.9%	-8.9
NEW HAMPSHIRE								237,000	156,212	65.9%		246,000	158,028	64.2%	-1.7				
NEW JERSEY				703,000	437,096	62.2%						1,849,000	983,175	53.2%	-9.0	2,110,000	1,454,627	68.9%	6.8
NEW MEXICO				85,000	66,797	78.6%						172,000	115,041	66.9%	-11.7	174,000	117,987	67.8%	-10.8
NEW YORK				2,656,000	1,545,189	58.2%		5,294,000	2,739,317	51.7%	-6.4					6,635,000	4,246,998	64.0%	5.8

United States Senate General Elections (continued)

United States Senate General Elections (continued)

Election Years 1912–1928 (continued)

State	1912 Voting-age population	Turnout	%	1916 Voting-age population	Turnout	%	Difference from 1912	1920 Voting-age population	Turnout	%	Difference from 1912	1924 Voting-age population	Turnout	%	Difference from 1912	1928 Voting-age population	Turnout	%	Difference from 1912
NORTH CAROLINA								1,237,000	539,847	43.6%		1,368,000	479,837	35.1%	-8.6				
NORTH DAKOTA				152,000	107,174	70.5%		297,000	218,379	73.5%	3.0					332,000	200,843	60.5%	-10.0
OHIO				1,535,000	1,160,091	75.6%		3,289,000	1,920,250	58.4%	-17.2					3,811,000	2,326,205	61.0%	-14.5
OKLAHOMA	456,000	250,731	55.0%					1,026,000	489,755	47.7%	-7.3	1,118,000	553,884	49.5%	-5.4				
OREGON	392,000	133,578	34.1%					467,000	230,007	49.3%	15.2	514,000	264,803	51.5%	17.4				
PENNSYLVANIA				2,048,000	1,208,457	59.0%		4,412,000	1,783,339	40.4%	-18.6					5,121,000	3,026,869	59.1%	0.1
RHODE ISLAND				134,000	88,877	66.3%						323,000	209,626	64.9%	-1.4	351,000	235,775	67.2%	0.8
SOUTH CAROLINA								781,000	64,389	8.2%		796,000	49,060	6.2%	-2.1				
SOUTH DAKOTA								326,000	184,179	56.5%		342,000	183,132	53.5%	-2.9				
TENNESSEE				587,000	264,075	45.0%						1,309,000	257,931	19.7%	-25.3	1,391,000	295,720	21.3%	-23.7
TEXAS				1,101,000	372,761	33.9%						2,558,000	693,309	27.1%	-6.8	2,811,000	697,115	24.8%	-9.1
UTAH				194,000	142,416	73.4%		213,000	145,858	68.5%	-4.9					243,000	175,507	72.2%	-1.2
VERMONT				101,000	63,798	63.2%		199,000	89,271	44.9%	-18.3					203,000	130,177	64.1%	1.0
VIRGINIA				575,000	133,203	23.2%						1,242,000	207,185	16.7%	-6.5	1,282,000	276,048	21.5%	-1.6
WASHINGTON				707,000	365,189	51.7%		774,000	384,866	49.7%	-1.9					892,000	489,605	54.9%	3.2
WEST VIRGINIA				353,000	287,705	81.5%						791,000	569,564	72.0%	-9.5	857,000	645,805	75.4%	-6.1
WISCONSIN				643,000	423,883	65.9%		1,371,000	677,149	49.4%	-16.5					1,617,000	742,553	45.9%	-20.0
WYOMING				95,000	51,147	53.8%						113,000	77,858	68.9%	15.1	120,000	80,441	67.0%	13.2
Total	2,991,000	1,328,945	44.4%	20,120,000	12,025,049	59.8%	15.3	40,298,000	19,510,650	48.4%	4.0	34,005,000	14,529,122	42.7%	-1.7	50,966,000	28,955,241	56.8%	12.4

*A handful of states held popular elections for Senate in 1912 even before the Seventeenth Amendment was ratified in 1913.

**Percentage point difference between turnout in current year and initial year listed in chart. If data do not appear for a state in the initial year listed, the difference is calculated from the first year in which data do appear for that state.

UNITED STATES SENATE GENERAL ELECTIONS

Republican Turnout for Election Years 1912–1928

State	1912*			1916				1920				1924				1928			
	Voting-age population	Turnout	%	Voting-age population	Turnout	%	Difference from 1912**	Voting-age population	Turnout	%	Difference from 1912	Voting-age population	Turnout	%	Difference from 1912	Voting-age population	Turnout	%	Difference from 1912
ALABAMA								1,155,000	71,334	6.2%		1,238,000	39,623	3.2%	-3.0				
ALASKA																			
ARIZONA				120,000	21,261	17.7%		145,000	35,893	24.8%	7.0					161,000	39,651	24.6%	6.9
ARKANSAS								872,000	65,381	7.5%		913,000	36,163	4.0%	-3.5				
CALIFORNIA				1,791,000	574,667	32.1%		2,110,000	447,835	21.2%	-10.9					3,096,000	1,148,397	37.1%	5.0
COLORADO	466,000	66,949	14.4%					526,000	156,577	29.8%	15.4	546,000	159,698	29.2%	14.9				
CONNECTICUT				292,000	107,020	36.7%		648,000	216,792	33.5%	-3.2					780,000	296,958	38.1%	1.4
DELAWARE				62,000	22,925	37.0%						134,000	52,731	39.4%	2.4	140,000	63,725	45.5%	8.5
DISTRICT OF COLUMBIA																			
FLORIDA				246,000	8,774	3.6%		544,000	30,761	5.7%	2.1					805,000	70,633	8.8%	5.2
GEORGIA																			
HAWAII																			
IDAHO								223,000	75,985	34.1%		228,000	99,846	43.8%	9.7				
ILLINOIS								3,553,000	1,381,384	38.9%		3,938,000	1,449,180	36.8%	-2.1	4,322,000	1,594,031	36.9%	-2.0
INDIANA				833,000	337,089	40.5%		1,725,000	681,854	39.5%	-0.9					1,918,000	782,144	40.8%	0.3
IOWA								1,377,000	528,499	38.4%		1,419,000	447,594	31.5%	-6.8				
KANSAS	936,000	151,647	16.2%					995,000	327,072	32.9%	16.7	1,042,000	428,494	41.1%	24.9				
KENTUCKY								1,291,000	454,226	35.2%		1,346,000	406,123	30.2%	-5.0				
LOUISIANA																			
MAINE				208,000	79,841	38.4%						430,000	148,783	34.6%	-3.8	437,000	145,501	33.3%	-5.1
MARYLAND				388,000	113,662	29.3%		832,000	184,999	22.2%	-7.1					943,000	256,224	27.2%	-2.1
MASSACHUSETTS				848,000	267,177	31.5%						2,031,000	566,188	27.9%	-3.6	2,166,000	693,563	32.0%	0.5
MICHIGAN				976,000	364,657	37.4%						2,221,000	858,934	38.7%	1.3	2,497,000	977,893	39.2%	1.8
MINNESOTA	598,000	173,074	28.9%	623,000	185,159	29.7%	0.8					1,345,000	388,594	28.9%	-0.1	1,432,000	342,992	24.0%	-5.0
MISSISSIPPI																			
MISSOURI				984,000	371,710	37.8%		1,993,000	711,161	35.7%	-2.1					2,194,000	787,499	35.9%	-1.9
MONTANA	143,000	18,450	12.9%	258,000	72,753	28.2%	15.3					292,000	72,005	24.7%	11.8	292,000	91,185	31.2%	18.3
NEBRASKA				344,000	131,359	38.2%						734,000	274,640	37.4%	-0.8	772,000	324,014	42.0%	3.8
NEVADA				44,000	10,618	24.1%		45,000	11,550	25.7%	1.5					50,000	13,414	26.8%	2.7
NEW HAMPSHIRE								237,000	90,173	38.0%		246,000	94,432	38.4%	0.3				
NEW JERSEY				703,000	244,715	34.8%						1,849,000	608,020	32.9%	-1.9	2,110,000	841,752	39.9%	5.1
NEW MEXICO				05,000	30,622	36.0%						172,000	54,558	31.7%	-4.3	174,000	68,070	39.1%	3.1
NEW YORK				2,656,000	839,314	31.6%		5,294,000	1,434,393	27.1%	-4.5					6,635,000	2,034,014	30.7%	-0.9

United States Senate General Elections (continued)

United States Senate General Elections (continued)

Republican Turnout for Election Years 1912–1928 (continued)

State	1912 Voting-age population	Turnout	%	1916 Voting-age population	Turnout	%	Difference from 1912	1920 Voting-age population	Turnout	%	Difference from 1912	1924 Voting-age population	Turnout	%	Difference from 1912	1928 Voting-age population	Turnout	%	Difference from 1912
NORTH CAROLINA								1,237,000	229,343	18.5%		1,368,000	184,493	13.5%	-5.1				
NORTH DAKOTA				152,000	57,714	38.0%		297,000	130,614	44.0%	6.0					332,000	159,940	48.2%	10.2
OHIO				1,535,000	535,391	34.9%		3,289,000	1,134,953	34.5%	-0.4					3,811,000	1,412,805	37.1%	2.2
OKLAHOMA	456,000	83,448	18.3%					1,026,000	247,721	24.1%	5.8	1,118,000	341,720	30.6%	12.3				
OREGON	392,000	38,453	9.8%					467,000	116,696	25.0%	15.2	514,000	174,672	34.0%	24.2				
PENNSYLVANIA				2,048,000	680,451	33.2%		4,412,000	1,068,985	24.2%	-9.0					5,121,000	1,948,646	38.1%	4.8
RHODE ISLAND				134,000	39,211	29.3%						323,000	120,815	37.4%	8.1	351,000	119,228	34.0%	4.7
SOUTH CAROLINA																			
SOUTH DAKOTA								326,000	92,267	28.3%		342,000	90,006	26.3%	-2.0				
TENNESSEE				587,000	118,174	20.1%						1,309,000	109,863	8.4%	-11.7	1,391,000	120,289	8.6%	-11.5
TEXAS				1,101,000	48,788	4.4%						2,558,000	101,252	4.0%	-0.5	2,811,000	130,172	4.6%	0.2
UTAH				194,000	56,862	29.3%		213,000	82,566	38.8%	9.5					243,000	77,073	31.7%	2.4
VERMONT				101,000	47,362	46.9%		199,000	69,650	35.0%	-11.9					203,000	93,136	45.9%	-1.0
VIRGINIA												1,242,000	5,594	0.5%					
WASHINGTON				707,000	202,287	28.6%		774,000	217,069	28.0%	-0.6					892,000	227,415	25.5%	-3.1
WEST VIRGINIA				353,000	144,243	40.9%						791,000	290,004	36.7%	-4.2	857,000	327,266	38.2%	-2.7
WISCONSIN				643,000	251,303	39.1%		1,371,000	281,576	20.5%	-18.5					1,617,000	716,678	44.3%	5.2
WYOMING				95,000	23,258	24.5%						113,000	41,293	36.5%	12.1	120,000	37,076	30.9%	6.4
Total	2,991,000	532,021	17.8%	19,111,000	5,988,367	31.3%	13.5	37,176,000	10,577,309	28.5%	10.7	29,802,000	7,645,318	25.7%	7.9	48,673,000	15,941,384	32.8%	15.0

Democratic Turnout for Election Years 1912–1928

State	1912* Voting-age population	Turnout	%	1916 Voting-age population	Turnout	%	Difference from 1912**	1920 Voting-age population	Turnout	%	Difference from 1912	1924 Voting-age population	Turnout	%	Difference from 1912	1928 Voting-age population	Turnout	%	Difference from 1912
ALABAMA								1,155,000	155,664	13.5%		1,238,000	120,017	9.7%	-3.8				
ALASKA																			
ARIZONA				120,000	29,882	24.9%		145,000	29,169	20.1%	-4.8					161,000	47,013	29.2%	4.3
ARKANSAS								872,000	126,577	14.5%		913,000	100,408	11.0%	-3.5				
CALIFORNIA				1,791,000	277,852	15.5%		2,110,000	371,580	17.6%	2.1					3,096,000	282,411	9.1%	-6.4
COLORADO	466,000	118,260	25.4%					526,000	112,890	21.5%	-3.9	546,000	139,660	25.6%	0.2				
CONNECTICUT				292,000	98,649	33.8%		648,000	131,824	20.3%	-13.4					780,000	251,429	32.2%	-1.5
DELAWARE				62,000	25,434	41.0%										140,000	40,828	29.2%	-11.9
DISTRICT OF COLUMBIA																			
FLORIDA				246,000	58,391	23.7%		544,000	98,966	18.2%	-5.5					805,000	153,816	19.1%	-4.6

United States Senate General Elections (continued)

Democratic Turnout for Election Years 1912–1928 (continued)

State	1912 Voting-age population	Turnout	%	1916 Voting-age population	Turnout	%	Difference from 1912	1920 Voting-age population	Turnout	%	Difference from 1912	1924 Voting-age population	Turnout	%	Difference from 1912	1928 Voting-age population	Turnout	%	Difference from 1912
GEORGIA								1,423,000	124,630	8.8%		1,453,000	155,497	10.7%	1.9				
HAWAII																			
IDAHO								223,000	64,513	28.9%		228,000	25,199	11.1%	-17.9				
ILLINOIS								3,553,000	554,372	15.6%		3,938,000	806,702	20.5%	4.9	4,322,000	1,315,338	30.4%	14.8
INDIANA				833,000	325,588	39.1%		1,725,000	514,191	29.8%	-9.3					1,918,000	623,996	32.5%	-6.6
IOWA								1,377,000	322,015	23.4%		1,419,000	446,840	31.5%	8.1				
KANSAS	936,000	172,601	18.4%					995,000	170,443	17.1%	-1.3	1,042,000	154,189	14.8%	-3.6				
KENTUCKY								1,291,000	449,244	34.8%		1,346,000	381,605	28.4%	-6.4				
LOUISIANA								918,000	94,944	10.3%		1,006,000	94,939	9.4%	-0.9				
MAINE				208,000	69,486	33.4%						430,000	97,428	22.7%	-10.7	437,000	63,429	14.5%	-18.9
MARYLAND				388,000	109,740	28.3%		832,000	169,200	20.3%	-7.9					943,000	214,447	22.7%	-5.5
MASSACHUSETTS				848,000	234,238	27.6%						2,031,000	547,600	27.0%	-0.7	2,166,000	818,055	37.8%	10.1
MICHIGAN				976,000	257,954	28.4%						2,221,000	284,609	12.8%	-13.6	2,497,000	376,592	15.1%	-11.3
MINNESOTA	598,000	102,691	17.2%	623,000	117,541	18.9%	1.7					1,345,000	53,709	4.0%	-13.2				
MISSISSIPPI				434,000	74,290	17.1%						949,000	97,257	10.2%	-6.9	1,011,000	111,210	11.0%	-6.1
MISSOURI				984,000	396,166	40.3%		1,993,000	589,498	29.6%	-10.7					2,194,000	726,322	33.1%	-7.2
MONTANA	143,000	28,421	19.9%	258,000	85,585	33.2%	13.3					292,000	89,681	30.7%	10.8	292,000	103,655	35.5%	15.6
NEBRASKA				344,000	143,082	41.6%						734,000	165,370	22.5%	-19.1	772,000	204,737	26.5%	-15.1
NEVADA				44,000	12,765	29.0%		45,000	10,402	23.1%	-5.9					50,000	19,515	39.0%	10.0
NEW HAMPSHIRE								237,000	65,035	27.4%		246,000	63,596	25.9%	-1.6				
NEW JERSEY				703,000	170,019	24.2%						1,849,000	331,034	17.9%	-6.3	2,110,000	608,623	28.8%	4.7
NEW MEXICO				85,000	34,142	40.2%						172,000	57,355	33.3%	-6.8	174,000	49,913	28.7%	-11.5
NEW YORK				2,656,000	605,933	22.8%		5,294,000	901,310	17.0%	-5.8					6,635,000	2,084,273	31.4%	8.6
NORTH CAROLINA								1,237,000	310,504	25.1%		1,368,000	295,344	21.6%	-3.5				
NORTH DAKOTA				152,000	40,988	27.0%		297,000	87,765	29.6%	2.6					332,000	38,856	11.7%	-15.3
OHIO				1,535,000	571,488	37.2%		3,289,000	782,650	23.8%	-13.4					3,811,000	908,952	23.9%	-13.4
OKLAHOMA	456,000	126,407	27.7%					1,026,000	218,371	21.3%	-6.4	1,118,000	196,527	17.6%	-10.1				
OREGON	392,000	40,172	10.2%					467,000	100,124	21.4%	11.2	514,000	65,340	12.7%	2.5				
PENNSYLVANIA				2,048,000	450,112	22.0%		4,412,000	484,862	11.0%	-11.0					5,121,000	1,029,055	20.1%	-1.9
RHODE ISLAND				134,000	47,048	35.1%						323,000	87,620	27.1%	-8.0	351,000	116,234	33.1%	-2.0
SOUTH CAROLINA								781,000	64,388	8.2%		796,000	49,060	6.2%	-2.1				
SOUTH DAKOTA								326,000	36,833	11.3%		342,000	63,548	18.6%	7.3				
TENNESSEE				587,000	143,718	24.5%						1,309,000	147,821	11.3%	-13.2	1,391,000	175,431	12.6%	-11.9

United States Senate General Elections (continued)

United States Senate General Elections (continued)

Democratic Turnout for Election Years 1912–1928 (continued)

State	1912 Voting-age population	Turnout	%	1916 Voting-age population	Turnout	%	Difference from 1912	1920 Voting-age population	Turnout	%	Difference from 1912	1924 Voting-age population	Turnout	%	Difference from 1912	1928 Voting-age population	Turnout	%	Difference from 1912
TEXAS				1,101,000	303,035	27.5%						2,558,000	592,057	23.1%	-4.4	2,811,000	566,139	20.1%	-7.4
UTAH				194,000	81,057	41.8%		213,000	56,280	26.4%	-15.4					243,000	97,436	40.1%	-1.7
VERMONT				101,000	14,956	14.8%		199,000	19,580	9.8%	-5.0					203,000	37,030	18.2%	3.4
VIRGINIA				575,000	133,091	23.1%						1,242,000	151,498	12.2%	-10.9	1,282,000	275,425	21.5%	-1.7
WASHINGTON				707,000	135,339	19.1%		774,000	68,488	8.8%	-10.3					892,000	261,524	29.3%	10.2
WEST VIRGINIA				353,000	138,585	39.3%						791,000	271,809	34.4%	-4.9	857,000	317,620	37.1%	-2.2
WISCONSIN				643,000	135,144	21.0%		1,371,000	89,265	6.5%	-14.5								
WYOMING				95,000	26,324	27.7%						113,000	33,536	29.7%	2.0	120,000	43,032	35.9%	8.2
Total	2,991,000	588,552	19.7%	20,120,000	5,347,622	26.6%	6.9	40,298,000	7,375,577	18.3%	-1.4	29,802,000	7,645,318	25.7%	7.9	47,917,000	11,962,336	25.0%	5.3

Other Turnout for Election Years 1892–1908

State	1912* Voting-age population	Turnout	%	1916 Voting-age population	Turnout	%	Difference from 1912**	1920 Voting-age population	Turnout	%	Difference from 1912	1924 Voting-age population	Turnout	%	Difference from 1912	1928 Voting-age population	Turnout	%	Difference from 1912
ALABAMA								1,155,000	1,984	0.2%									
ALASKA																			
ARIZONA				120,000	2,827	2.4%													
ARKANSAS																			
CALIFORNIA				1,791,000	88,437	4.9%		2,110,000	94,354	4.5%	-0.5					3,096,000	118,988	3.8%	-1.1
COLORADO	466,000	64,597	13.9%					526,000	17,733	3.4%	-10.5	545,000	18,811	3.5%	-10.4				
CONNECTICUT				292,000	7,675	2.6%		648,000	16,572	2.6%	-0.1					780,000	3,014	0.4%	-2.2
DELAWARE				62,000	2,851	4.6%						134,000	36,085	26.9%	22.3				
DISTRICT OF COLUMBIA																			
FLORIDA				246,000	3,304	1.3%		544,000	3,533	0.6%	-0.7					805,000	2	0.0%	-1.3
GEORGIA								1,423,000	6,700	0.5%									
HAWAII																			
IDAHO												228,000	554	0.2%					
ILLINOIS								3,553,000	131,289	3.7%		3,938,000	24,965	0.6%	-3.1				
INDIANA				833,000	42,990	5.2%		1,725,000	53,522	3.1%	-2.1					1,918,000	8,300	0.4%	-4.7
IOWA								1,377,000	9,956	0.7%									
KANSAS	936,000	25,785	2.8%					995,000	13,418	1.3%	-1.4	1,042,000	28,607	2.7%	0.0				
KENTUCKY																			
LOUISIANA																			
MAINE				208,000	1,789	0.9%													

United States Senate General Elections (continued)

Other Turnout for Election Years 1912–1928 (continued)

State	1912 Voting-age population	Turnout	%	1916 Voting-age population	Turnout	%	Difference from 1912	1920 Voting-age population	Turnout	%	Difference from 1912	1924 Voting-age population	Turnout	%	Difference from 1912	1928 Voting-age population	Turnout	%	Difference from 1912
MARYLAND				388,000	7,058	1.8%		832,000	37,011	4.4%	2.6					943,000	3,396	0.4%	-1.5
MASSACHUSETTS				848,000	15,584	1.8%						2,031,000	12,738	0.6%	-1.2	2,166,000	13,335	0.6%	-1.2
MICHIGAN				976,000	24,667	2.5%						2,221,000	13,183	0.6%	-1.9	2,497,000	7,663	0.3%	-2.2
MINNESOTA				623,000	78,425	12.6%						1,345,000	394,260	29.3%	16.7	1,432,000	674,549	47.1%	34.5
MISSISSIPPI																			
MISSOURI				984,000	15,010	1.6%		1,993,000	24,880	1.2%	-0.3					2,194,000	3,102	0.1%	-1.4
MONTANA	143,000	22,161	15.5%	258,000	9,292	3.6%	-11.9					292,000	8,180	2.8%	-12.7				
NEBRASKA				344,000	11,854	3.4%													
NEVADA				44,000	9,507	21.6%		45,000	5,475	12.2%	-9.4								
NEW HAMPSHIRE								237,000	1,004	0.4%									
NEW JERSEY				703,000	22,362	3.2%						1,849,000	44,121	2.4%	-0.8	2,110,000	4,252	0.2%	-3.0
NEW MEXICO				85,000	2,033	2.4%						172,000	3,128	1.8%	-0.6	174,000	4	0.0%	-2.4
NEW YORK				2,656,000	99,942	3.8%		5,294,000	403,614	7.6%	3.9					6,635,000	128,711	1.9%	-1.8
NORTH CAROLINA																			
NORTH DAKOTA				152,000	8,472	5.6%										332,000	2,047	0.6%	-5.0
OHIO				1,535,000	53,212	3.5%		3,289,000	2,647	0.1%	-3.4					3,811,000	4,448	0.1%	-3.3
OKLAHOMA	456,000	40,876	9.0%					1,026,000	23,663	2.3%	-6.7	1,118,000	15,637	1.4%	-7.6				
OREGON	392,000	54,953	14.0%					467,000	13,187	2.8%	-11.2	514,000	24,791	4.8%	-9.2				
PENNSYLVANIA				2,048,000	77,894	3.8%		4,412,000	229,492	5.2%	1.4					5,121,000	49,168	1.0%	-2.8
RHODE ISLAND				134,000	2,618	2.0%						323,000	1,191	0.4%	-1.6	351,000	313	0.1%	-1.9
SOUTH CAROLINA								781,000	1	0.0%									
SOUTH DAKOTA								326,000	55,079	16.9%		342,000	29,578	8.6%	-8.2				
TENNESSEE				587,000	2,183	0.4%						1,309,000	247	0.0%	-0.4				
TEXAS				1,101,000	20,938	1.9%										2,811,000	804	0.0%	-1.9
UTAH				194,000	4,497	2.3%		213,000	7,012	3.3%	1.0					243,000	998	0.4%	-1.9
VERMONT				101,000	1,480	1.5%		199,000	41	0.0%	-1.4					203,000	11	0.0%	-1.5
VIRGINIA				575,000	112	0.0%						1,242,000	50,093	4.0%	4.0	1,282,000	623	0.0%	0.0
WASHINGTON				707,000	27,563	3.9%		774,000	99,309	12.8%	8.9					892,000	666	0.1%	-3.8
WEST VIRGINIA				353,000	4,877	1.4%						791,000	7,751	1.0%	-0.4	857,000	919	0.1%	-1.3
WISCONSIN				643,000	37,436	5.8%		1,371,000	306,308	22.3%	16.5					1,617,000	25,875	1.6%	-4.2
WYOMING				95,000	1,565	1.6%						113,000	3,029	2.7%	1.0	120,000	333	0.3%	-1.4
Total	2,393,000	208,372	8.7%	19,686,000	689,060	3.5%	-5.2	35,315,000	1,557,764	4.4%	-4.3	19,550,000	716,949	3.7%	-5.0	42,390,000	1,051,521	2.5%	-6.2

*A handful of states held popular elections for Senate in 1912 even before the 17th Amendment was ratified in 1913.

**Percentage point difference between turnout in current year and initial year listed in chart. If data do not appear for a state in the initial year listed, the difference is calculated from the first year in which data do appear for that state.

UNITED STATES HOUSE OF REPRESENTATIVES GENERAL ELECTIONS

Election Years 1912–1928

State	1912 Voting-age population	Turnout	%	1916 Voting-age population	Turnout	%	Difference from 1912*	1920 Voting-age population	Turnout	%	Difference from 1912	1924 Voting-age population	Turnout	%	Difference from 1912	1928 Voting-age population	Turnout	%	Difference from 1912
ALABAMA	523,000	99,641	19.1%	549,000	123,085	22.4%	3.4	1,155,000	224,255	19.4%	0.4	1,238,000	151,589	12.2%	-6.8	1,321,000	200,636	15.2%	-3.9
ALASKA																			
ARIZONA	92,000	23,545	25.6%	120,000	52,344	43.6%	18.0	145,000	61,238	42.2%	16.6	153,000	48,957	32.0%	6.4	161,000	81,613	50.7%	25.1
ARKANSAS	407,000	116,171	28.5%	431,000	172,914	40.1%	11.6	872,000	190,189	21.8%	-6.7	913,000	136,386	14.9%	-13.6	954,000	199,942	21.0%	-7.6
CALIFORNIA	1,530,000	622,778	40.7%	1,791,000	882,469	49.3%	8.6	2,110,000	811,790	38.5%	-2.2	2,603,000	997,897	38.3%	-2.4	3,096,000	1,326,287	42.8%	2.1
COLORADO	466,000	265,653	57.0%	496,000	260,221	52.5%	-4.5	526,000	277,192	52.7%	-4.3	546,000	319,276	58.5%	1.5	564,000	352,792	62.6%	5.5
CONNECTICUT	270,000	189,492	70.2%	292,000	213,309	73.1%	2.9	648,000	362,969	56.0%	-14.2	714,000	373,355	52.3%	-17.9	780,000	551,394	70.7%	0.5
DELAWARE	59,000	48,707	82.6%	62,000	51,211	82.6%	0.0	128,000	93,610	73.1%	-9.4	134,000	87,998	65.7%	-16.9	140,000	104,406	74.6%	-8.0
DISTRICT OF COLUMBIA																			
FLORIDA	220,000	44,359	20.2%	246,000	67,290	27.4%	7.2	544,000	123,119	22.6%	2.5	675,000	96,763	14.3%	-5.8	805,000	218,014	27.1%	6.9
GEORGIA	641,000	116,458	18.2%	677,000	134,218	19.8%	1.7	1,423,000	278,747	19.6%	1.4	1,453,000	158,431	10.9%	-7.3	1,485,000	200,188	13.5%	-4.7
HAWAII																			
IDAHO	177,000	108,349	61.2%	202,000	128,534	63.6%	2.4	223,000	137,249	61.5%	0.3	228,000	135,152	59.3%	-1.9	233,000	146,531	62.9%	1.7
ILLINOIS	1,535,000	1,144,496	74.6%	1,657,000	1,315,630	79.4%	4.8	3,553,000	2,088,468	58.8%	-15.8	3,938,000	2,211,976	56.2%	-18.4	4,322,000	2,899,411	67.1%	-7.5
INDIANA	808,000	640,827	79.3%	833,000	706,382	84.8%	5.5	1,725,000	1,251,673	72.6%	-6.7	1,822,000	1,246,772	68.4%	-10.9	1,918,000	1,413,893	73.7%	-5.6
IOWA	632,000	429,917	68.0%	670,000	478,255	71.4%	3.4	1,377,000	717,303	52.1%	-15.9	1,419,000	825,986	58.2%	-9.8	1,461,000	810,388	55.5%	-12.6
KANSAS	936,000	350,652	37.5%	962,000	568,368	59.1%	21.6	995,000	527,432	53.0%	15.5	1,042,000	593,830	57.0%	19.5	1,091,000	593,682	54.4%	17.0
KENTUCKY	611,000	400,559	65.6%	633,000	510,049	80.6%	15.0	1,291,000	852,352	66.0%	0.5	1,346,000	694,353	51.6%	-14.0	1,401,000	938,728	67.0%	1.4
LOUISIANA	413,000	65,513	15.9%	435,000	86,290	19.8%	4.0	918,000	92,052	10.0%	-5.8	1,006,000	93,311	9.3%	-6.6	1,093,000	167,477	15.3%	-0.5
MAINE	204,000	141,669	69.4%	208,000	151,156	72.7%	3.2	423,000	202,745	47.9%	-21.5	430,000	246,200	57.3%	-12.2	437,000	207,845	47.6%	-21.9
MARYLAND	361,000	179,928	49.8%	388,000	224,768	57.9%	8.1	832,000	377,516	45.4%	-4.5	888,000	311,523	35.1%	-14.8	943,000	463,278	49.1%	-0.7
MASSACHUSETTS	793,000	469,586	59.2%	848,000	504,742	59.5%	0.3	1,895,000	936,683	49.4%	-9.8	2,031,000	1,076,480	53.0%	-6.2	2,166,000	1,445,243	66.7%	7.5
MICHIGAN	830,000	541,750	65.3%	976,000	642,975	65.9%	0.6	1,947,000	1,009,759	51.9%	-13.4	2,221,000	1,115,730	50.2%	-15.0	2,497,000	1,338,588	53.6%	-11.7
MINNESOTA	598,000	279,865	46.8%	623,000	380,197	61.0%	14.2	1,257,000	747,070	59.4%	12.6	1,345,000	812,605	60.4%	13.6	1,432,000	971,757	67.9%	21.1
MISSISSIPPI	428,000	49,099	11.5%	434,000	78,378	18.1%	6.6	886,000	70,448	8.0%	-3.5	949,000	99,127	10.4%	-1.0	1,011,000	112,546	11.1%	-0.3
MISSOURI	949,000	686,147	72.3%	984,000	779,359	79.2%	6.9	1,993,000	1,319,463	66.2%	-6.1	2,093,000	1,277,782	61.1%	-11.3	2,194,000	1,516,299	69.1%	-3.2
MONTANA	143,000	76,311	53.4%	258,000	170,433	66.1%	12.7	291,000	175,007	60.1%	6.8	292,000	158,896	54.4%	1.1	292,000	181,955	62.3%	8.9
NEBRASKA	335,000	250,294	74.7%	344,000	283,163	82.3%	7.6	696,000	360,324	51.8%	-22.9	734,000	438,088	59.7%	-15.0	772,000	522,993	67.7%	-7.0
NEVADA	31,000	19,774	63.8%	44,000	32,331	73.5%	9.7	45,000	26,870	59.7%	-4.1	47,000	25,987	55.3%	-8.5	50,000	32,102	64.2%	0.4
NEW HAMPSHIRE	113,000	82,276	72.8%	115,000	85,535	74.4%	1.6	237,000	154,644	65.3%	-7.6	246,000	158,532	64.4%	-8.4	255,000	184,313	72.3%	-0.5
NEW JERSEY	637,000	358,144	56.2%	703,000	440,000	62.6%	6.4	1,588,000	837,063	52.7%	-3.5	1,849,000	973,035	52.6%	-3.6	2,110,000	1,436,418	68.1%	11.9
NEW MEXICO	87,000	48,557	55.8%	85,000	66,684	78.5%	22.6	170,000	105,388	62.0%	6.2	172,000	112,788	65.6%	9.8	174,000	117,253	67.4%	11.6
NEW YORK	2,472,000	1,545,619	62.5%	2,656,000	1,526,821	57.5%	-5.0	5,294,000	2,707,972	51.2%	-11.4	5,965,000	3,078,152	51.6%	-10.9	6,635,000	4,212,691	63.5%	1.0

United States House of Representatives General Elections (continued)

Election Years 1912–1928 (continued)

State	1912 Voting-age population	Turnout	%	1916 Voting-age population	Turnout	%	Difference from 1912	1920 Voting-age population	Turnout	%	Difference from 1912	1924 Voting-age population	Turnout	%	Difference from 1912	1928 Voting-age population	Turnout	%	Difference from 1912
NORTH CAROLINA	529,000	225,972	42.7%	568,000	286,458	50.4%	7.7	1,237,000	532,287	43.0%	0.3	1,368,000	469,361	34.3%	-8.4	1,497,000	644,693	43.1%	0.3
NORTH DAKOTA	145,000	79,896	55.1%	152,000	96,855	63.7%	8.6	297,000	208,938	70.3%	15.2	314,000	170,689	54.4%	-0.7	332,000	200,552	60.4%	5.3
OHIO	1,403,000	1,016,528	72.5%	1,535,000	1,119,017	72.9%	0.4	3,289,000	1,938,231	58.9%	-13.5	3,551,000	1,861,578	52.4%	-20.0	3,811,000	2,376,252	62.4%	-10.1
OKLAHOMA	456,000	249,840	54.8%	498,000	288,830	58.0%	3.2	1,026,000	485,098	47.3%	-7.5	1,118,000	504,425	45.1%	-9.7	1,211,000	592,893	49.0%	-5.8
OREGON	392,000	129,910	33.1%	428,000	224,850	52.5%	19.4	467,000	199,548	42.7%	9.6	514,000	256,359	49.9%	16.7	563,000	293,567	52.1%	19.0
PENNSYLVANIA	1,907,000	1,101,606	57.8%	2,048,000	1,246,141	60.8%	3.1	4,412,000	1,792,936	40.6%	-17.1	4,766,000	2,008,857	42.1%	-15.8	5,121,000	3,005,004	58.7%	0.9
RHODE ISLAND	125,000	74,888	59.9%	134,000	86,930	64.9%	5.0	296,000	167,036	56.4%	-3.5	323,000	207,318	64.2%	4.3	351,000	234,815	66.9%	7.0
SOUTH CAROLINA	347,000	49,530	14.3%	370,000	63,073	17.0%	2.8	781,000	65,736	8.4%	-5.9	796,000	49,491	6.2%	-8.1	813,000	61,347	7.5%	-6.7
SOUTH DAKOTA	172,000	115,109	66.9%	179,000	126,346	70.6%	3.7	326,000	182,056	55.8%	-11.1	342,000	195,844	57.3%	-9.7	359,000	248,715	69.3%	2.4
TENNESSEE	563,000	230,520	40.9%	587,000	242,687	41.3%	0.4	1,228,000	395,947	32.2%	-8.7	1,309,000	225,238	17.2%	-23.7	1,391,000	294,923	21.2%	-19.7
TEXAS	1,004,000	299,943	29.9%	1,101,000	365,541	33.2%	3.3	2,304,000	405,838	17.6%	-12.3	2,558,000	674,230	26.4%	-3.5	2,811,000	649,740	23.1%	-6.8
UTAH	174,000	112,159	64.5%	194,000	142,136	73.3%	8.8	213,000	144,373	67.8%	3.3	227,000	148,460	65.4%	0.9	243,000	175,901	72.4%	7.9
VERMONT	101,000	48,853	48.4%	101,000	62,448	61.8%	13.5	199,000	88,478	44.5%	-3.9	201,000	97,313	48.4%	0.0	203,000	129,362	63.7%	15.4
VIRGINIA	538,000	134,813	25.1%	575,000	156,011	27.1%	2.1	1,203,000	246,417	20.5%	-4.6	1,242,000	229,759	18.5%	-6.6	1,282,000	306,000	23.9%	-1.2
WASHINGTON	640,000	303,752	47.5%	707,000	357,951	50.6%	3.2	774,000	375,156	48.5%	1.0	833,000	347,874	41.8%	-5.7	892,000	427,710	47.9%	0.5
WEST VIRGINIA	328,000	266,928	81.4%	353,000	282,957	80.2%	-1.2	726,000	499,306	68.8%	-12.6	791,000	561,795	71.0%	-10.4	857,000	639,261	74.6%	-6.8
WISCONSIN	627,000	380,452	60.7%	643,000	417,079	64.9%	4.2	1,371,000	624,119	45.5%	-15.2	1,493,000	717,055	48.0%	-12.7	1,617,000	896,720	55.5%	-5.2
WYOMING	87,000	41,204	47.4%	95,000	50,370	53.0%	5.7	106,000	56,421	53.2%	5.9	113,000	71,563	63.3%	16.0	120,000	75,240	62.7%	15.3
Total	26,839,000	14,258,039	53.1%	28,990,000	16,732,791	57.7%	4.6	55,442,000	25,528,511	46.0%	-7.1	60,351,000	26,854,166	44.5%	-8.6	65,267,000	34,201,958	52.4%	-0.7

*Percentage point difference between turnout in current year and initial year listed in chart. If data do not appear for a state in the initial year listed, the difference is calculated from the first year in which data do appear for that state.

UNITED STATES HOUSE OF REPRESENTATIVES GENERAL ELECTIONS

Republican Turnout for Election Years 1912–1928

State	1912 Voting-age population	1912 Turnout	1912 %	1916 Voting-age population	1916 Turnout	1916 %	1916 Difference from 1912*	1920 Voting-age population	1920 Turnout	1920 %	1920 Difference from 1912	1924 population	1924 Turnout	1924 %	1924 Difference from 1912	1928 Voting-age population	1928 Turnout	1928 %	1928 Difference from 1912
ALABAMA	523,000	9,589	1.8%	549,000	23,515	4.3%	2.4	1,155,000	62,095	5.4%	3.5	1,238,000	31,368	2.5%	0.7	1,321,000	35,613	2.7%	0.9
ALASKA																			
ARIZONA	92,000	3,110	3.4%	120,000	14,907	12.4%	9.0	145,000	25,841	17.8%	14.4	153,000	8,628	5.6%	2.3	161,000	31,382	19.5%	16.1
ARKANSAS	407,000	26,453	6.5%	431,000	29,626	6.9%	0.4	872,000	61,924	7.1%	0.6	913,000	36,899	4.0%	-2.5	954,000	42,581	4.5%	-2.0
CALIFORNIA	1,530,000	287,222	18.8%	1,791,000	433,078	24.2%	5.4	2,110,000	556,025	26.4%	7.6	2,603,000	682,037	26.2%	7.4	3,096,000	1,127,910	36.4%	17.7
COLORADO	466,000	63,714	13.7%	496,000	113,320	22.8%	9.2	526,000	167,587	31.9%	18.2	546,000	169,546	31.1%	17.4	564,000	210,838	37.4%	23.7
CONNECTICUT	270,000	70,048	25.9%	292,000	106,930	36.6%	10.7	648,000	227,635	35.1%	9.2	714,000	245,089	34.3%	8.4	780,000	297,651	38.2%	12.2
DELAWARE	59,000	16,740	28.4%	62,000	24,202	39.0%	10.7	128,000	52,145	40.7%	12.4	134,000	51,536	38.5%	10.1	140,000	66,361	47.4%	19.0
DISTRICT OF COLUMBIA																			
FLORIDA	220,000	2,942	1.3%	246,000	10,995	4.5%	3.1	544,000	22,632	4.2%	2.8	675,000	21,525	3.2%	1.9	805,000	69,469	8.6%	7.3
GEORGIA	641,000	356	0.1%	677,000	6,964	1.0%	1.0	1,423,000	99,890	7.0%	7.0	1,453,000	3,500	0.2%	0.2				
HAWAII																			
IDAHO	177,000	53,542	30.2%	202,000	64,648	32.0%	1.8	223,000	84,296	37.8%	7.6	228,000	77,712	34.1%	3.8	233,000	97,006	41.6%	11.4
ILLINOIS	1,535,000	313,608	20.4%	1,657,000	707,958	42.7%	22.3	3,553,000	1,369,673	38.5%	18.1	3,938,000	1,519,773	38.6%	18.2	4,322,000	1,711,651	39.6%	19.2
INDIANA	808,000	166,698	20.6%	833,000	342,806	41.2%	20.5	1,725,000	695,041	40.3%	19.7	1,822,000	690,066	37.9%	17.2	1,918,000	770,317	40.2%	19.5
IOWA	632,000	184,776	29.2%	670,000	282,179	42.1%	12.9	1,377,000	605,532	44.0%	14.7	1,419,000	566,978	40.0%	10.7	1,461,000	575,061	39.4%	10.1
KANSAS	936,000	159,248	17.0%	962,000	261,622	27.2%	10.2	995,000	325,686	32.7%	15.7	1,042,000	325,550	31.2%	14.2	1,091,000	375,500	34.4%	17.4
KENTUCKY	611,000	86,975	14.2%	633,000	237,106	37.5%	23.2	1,291,000	409,165	31.7%	17.5	1,346,000	289,123	21.5%	7.2	1,401,000	526,194	37.6%	23.3
LOUISIANA				435,000	359	0.1%										1,093,000	14,661	1.3%	1.3
MAINE	204,000	71,850	35.2%	208,000	80,998	38.9%	3.7	423,000	135,230	32.0%	-3.3	430,000	148,345	34.5%	-0.7	437,000	145,955	33.4%	-1.8
MARYLAND	361,000	62,382	17.3%	388,000	105,627	27.2%	9.9	832,000	189,937	22.8%	5.5	888,000	149,226	16.8%	-0.5	943,000	234,848	24.9%	7.6
MASSACHUSETTS	793,000	180,850	22.8%	848,000	281,546	33.2%	10.4	1,895,000	618,132	32.6%	9.8	2,031,000	647,535	31.9%	9.1	2,166,000	753,391	34.8%	12.0
MICHIGAN	830,000	185,657	22.4%	976,000	355,298	36.4%	14.0	1,947,000	761,334	39.1%	16.7	2,221,000	882,889	39.8%	17.4	2,497,000	979,071	39.2%	16.8
MINNESOTA	598,000	154,308	25.8%	623,000	209,611	33.6%	7.8	1,257,000	447,297	35.6%	9.8	1,345,000	422,182	31.4%	5.6	1,432,000	525,511	36.7%	10.9
MISSISSIPPI								886,000	2,154	0.2%		949,000	579	0.1%	0.1				
MISSOURI	949,000	223,341	23.5%	984,000	368,832	37.5%	13.9	1,993,000	713,264	35.8%	12.3	2,093,000	644,762	30.8%	7.3	2,194,000	790,062	36.0%	12.5
MONTANA	143,000	23,505	16.4%	258,000	76,932	29.8%	13.4	291,000	108,215	37.2%	20.8	292,000	79,202	27.1%	10.7	292,000	103,478	35.4%	19.0
NEBRASKA	335,000	118,922	35.5%	344,000	140,430	40.8%	5.3	696,000	222,060	31.9%	-3.6	734,000	219,470	29.9%	-5.6	772,000	289,899	37.6%	2.1
NEVADA	31,000	7,380	23.8%	44,000	14,106	32.1%	8.3	45,000	13,149	29.2%	5.4	47,000	13,107	27.9%	4.1	50,000	18,815	37.6%	13.8
NEW HAMPSHIRE	113,000	35,324	31.3%	115,000	44,122	38.4%	7.1	237,000	93,326	39.4%	8.1	246,000	92,346	37.5%	6.3	255,000	108,284	42.5%	11.2
NEW JERSEY	637,000	112,499	17.7%	703,000	225,858	32.1%	14.5	1,588,000	517,659	32.6%	14.9	1,849,000	600,352	32.5%	14.8	2,110,000	870,883	41.3%	23.6
NEW MEXICO	87,000	17,892	20.6%	85,000	32,042	37.7%	17.1	170,000	54,672	32.2%	11.6	172,000	53,860	31.3%	10.7	174,000	61,208	35.2%	14.6
NEW YORK	2,472,000	482,874	19.5%	2,656,000	805,826	30.3%	10.8	5,294,000	1,566,205	29.6%	10.1	5,965,000	1,595,143	26.7%	7.2	6,635,000	2,072,853	31.2%	11.7

United States House of Representatives General Elections *(continued)*

Republican Turnout for Election Years 1912–1928 *(continued)*

State	1912 Voting-age population	Turnout	%	1916 Voting-age population	Turnout	%	Difference from 1912	1920 Voting-age population	Turnout	%	Difference from 1912	1924 population	Turnout	%	Difference from 1912	1928 Voting-age population	Turnout	%	Difference from 1912
NORTH CAROLINA	529,000	67,980	12.9%	568,000	120,246	21.2%	8.3	1,237,000	225,368	18.2%	5.4	1,368,000	179,607	13.1%	0.3	1,497,000	289,333	19.3%	6.5
NORTH DAKOTA	145,000	47,003	32.4%	152,000	63,329	41.7%	9.2	297,000	119,788	40.3%	7.9	314,000	113,890	36.3%	3.9	332,000	149,005	44.9%	12.5
OHIO	1,403,000	297,355	21.2%	1,535,000	543,941	35.4%	14.2	3,289,000	1,125,574	34.2%	13.0	3,551,000	1,055,925	29.7%	8.5	3,811,000	1,442,859	37.9%	16.7
OKLAHOMA	456,000	87,409	19.2%	498,000	98,594	19.8%	0.6	1,026,000	232,306	22.6%	3.5	1,118,000	203,869	18.2%	-0.9	1,211,000	293,876	24.3%	5.1
OREGON	392,000	58,829	15.0%	428,000	132,421	30.9%	15.9	467,000	143,136	30.7%	15.6	514,000	153,681	29.9%	14.9	563,000	196,539	34.9%	19.9
PENNSYLVANIA	1,907,000	618,537	32.4%	2,048,000	668,571	32.6%	0.2	4,412,000	1,140,836	25.9%	-6.6	4,766,000	1,353,365	28.4%	-4.0	5,121,000	2,068,355	40.4%	8.0
RHODE ISLAND	125,000	31,716	25.4%	134,000	43,259	32.3%	6.9	296,000	105,692	35.7%	10.3	323,000	122,775	38.0%	12.6	351,000	120,361	34.3%	8.9
SOUTH CAROLINA	347,000	85	0.0%	370,000	1,117	0.3%	0.3	781,000	834	0.1%	0.1	796,000	253	0.0%	0.0				
SOUTH DAKOTA	172,000	63,809	37.1%	179,000	69,243	38.7%	1.6	326,000	103,325	31.7%	-5.4	342,000	112,157	32.8%	-4.3	359,000	142,552	39.7%	2.6
TENNESSEE	563,000	82,726	14.7%	587,000	97,142	16.5%	1.9	1,228,000	202,668	16.5%	1.8	1,309,000	75,113	5.7%	-9.0	1,391,000	116,447	8.4%	-6.3
TEXAS	1,004,000	22,795	2.3%	1,101,000	46,467	4.2%	2.0	2,304,000	70,997	3.1%	0.8	2,558,000	86,793	3.4%	1.1	2,811,000	81,283	2.9%	0.6
UTAH	174,000	43,133	24.8%	194,000	57,680	29.7%	4.9	213,000	80,984	38.0%	13.2	227,000	82,771	36.5%	11.7	243,000	97,140	40.0%	15.2
VERMONT	101,000	28,785	28.5%	101,000	44,722	44.3%	15.8	199,000	67,891	34.1%	5.6	201,000	77,377	38.5%	10.0	203,000	91,223	44.9%	16.4
VIRGINIA	538,000	23,856	4.4%	575,000	47,654	8.3%	3.9	1,203,000	91,594	7.6%	3.2	1,242,000	63,051	5.1%	0.6	1,282,000	97,686	7.6%	3.2
WASHINGTON	640,000	87,613	13.7%	707,000	184,117	26.0%	12.4	774,000	218,655	28.3%	14.6	833,000	223,883	26.9%	13.2	892,000	291,977	32.7%	19.0
WEST VIRGINIA	328,000	132,733	40.5%	353,000	142,188	40.3%	-0.2	726,000	273,288	37.6%	-2.8	791,000	287,992	36.4%	-4.1	857,000	347,085	40.5%	0.0
WISCONSIN	627,000	177,385	28.3%	643,000	238,537	37.1%	8.8	1,371,000	428,825	31.3%	3.0	1,493,000	505,230	33.8%	5.5	1,617,000	598,077	37.0%	8.7
WYOMING	87,000	19,130	22.0%	95,000	24,693	26.0%	4.0	106,000	34,689	32.7%	10.7	113,000	43,026	38.1%	16.1	120,000	38,935	32.4%	10.5
Total	25,998,000	5,012,684	19.3%	28,556,000	8,025,364	28.1%	8.8	54,524,000	14,874,251	27.3%	8.0	59,345,000	15,009,086	25.3%	6.0	61,958,000	19,369,186	31.3%	12.0

Democratic Turnout for Election Years 1912–1928

State	1912 Voting-age population	Turnout	%	1916 Voting-age population	Turnout	%	Difference from 1912*	1920 Voting-age population	Turnout	%	Difference from 1912	1924 Voting-age population	Turnout	%	Difference from 1912	1928 Voting-age population	Turnout	%	Difference from 1912
ALABAMA	523,000	87,519	16.7%	549,000	98,780	18.0%	1.3	1,155,000	161,243	14.0%	-2.8	1,238,000	120,221	9.7%	-7.0	1,321,000	165,023	12.5%	-4.2
ALASKA																			
ARIZONA	92,000	11,389	12.4%	120,000	34,377	28.6%	16.3	145,000	35,397	24.4%	12.0	153,000	40,329	26.4%	14.0	161,000	50,231	31.2%	18.8
ARKANSAS	407,000	89,718	22.0%	431,000	143,288	33.2%	11.2	872,000	128,265	14.7%	-7.3	913,000	99,487	10.9%	-11.1	954,000	157,361	16.5%	-5.5
CALIFORNIA	1,530,000	196,610	12.9%	1,791,000	282,994	15.8%	3.0	2,110,000	160,693	7.6%	-5.2	2,603,000	226,445	8.7%	-4.2	3,096,000	152,591	4.9%	-7.9
COLORADO	466,000	115,143	24.7%	496,000	130,589	26.3%	1.6	526,000	109,605	20.8%	-3.9	546,000	139,135	25.5%	0.8	564,000	141,005	25.0%	0.3
CONNECTICUT	270,000	76,148	28.2%	292,000	98,652	33.8%	5.6	648,000	122,321	18.9%	-9.3	714,000	123,776	17.3%	-10.9	780,000	250,526	32.1%	3.9
DELAWARE	59,000	22,485	38.1%	62,000	24,395	39.3%	1.2	128,000	40,206	31.4%	-6.7	134,000	35,943	26.8%	-11.3	140,000	38,045	27.2%	-10.9
DISTRICT OF COLUMBIA																			
FLORIDA	220,000	34,324	15.6%	246,000	52,389	21.3%	5.7	544,000	97,082	17.8%	2.2	675,000	72,243	10.7%	-4.9	805,000	148,528	18.5%	2.8

United States House of Representatives General Elections (continued)

United States House of Representatives General Elections *(continued)*

Democratic Turnout for Election Years 1912–1928 *(continued)*

State	1912 Voting-age population	Turnout	%	1916 Voting-age population	Turnout	%	Difference from 1912	1920 Voting-age population	Turnout	%	Difference from 1912	1924 Voting-age population	Turnout	%	Difference from 1912	1928 Voting-age population	Turnout	%	Difference from 1912
GEORGIA	641,000	116,102	18.1%	677,000	126,555	18.7%	0.6	1,423,000	170,252	12.0%	-6.1	1,453,000	154,915	10.7%	-7.5	1,485,000	200,188	13.5%	-4.6
HAWAII																			
IDAHO	177,000	30,172	17.0%	202,000	55,807	27.6%	10.6	223,000	44,348	19.9%	2.8	228,000	33,704	14.8%	-2.3	233,000	48,486	20.8%	3.8
ILLINOIS	1,535,000	415,386	27.1%	1,657,000	546,471	33.0%	5.9	3,553,000	579,799	16.3%	-10.7	3,938,000	669,555	17.0%	-10.1	4,322,000	1,171,520	27.1%	0.0
INDIANA	808,000	291,288	36.1%	833,000	321,751	38.6%	2.6	1,725,000	516,083	29.9%	-6.1	1,822,000	544,259	29.9%	-6.2	1,918,000	641,498	33.4%	-2.6
IOWA	632,000	182,969	29.0%	670,000	186,358	27.8%	-1.1	1,377,000	88,857	6.5%	-22.5	1,419,000	258,181	18.2%	-10.8	1,461,000	235,327	16.1%	-12.8
KANSAS	936,000	163,926	17.5%	962,000	261,589	27.2%	9.7	995,000	192,262	19.3%	1.8	1,042,000	262,385	25.2%	7.7	1,091,000	218,182	20.0%	2.5
KENTUCKY	611,000	210,685	34.5%	633,000	266,712	42.1%	7.7	1,291,000	431,913	33.5%	-1.0	1,346,000	389,168	28.9%	-5.6	1,401,000	412,421	29.4%	-5.0
LOUISIANA	413,000	62,672	15.2%	435,000	78,607	18.1%	2.9	918,000	92,037	10.0%	-5.1	1,006,000	93,311	9.3%	-5.9	1,093,000	152,816	14.0%	-1.2
MAINE	204,000	66,894	32.8%	208,000	68,569	33.0%	0.2	423,000	67,515	16.0%	-16.8	430,000	97,855	22.8%	-10.0	437,000	61,890	14.2%	-18.6
MARYLAND	361,000	107,476	29.8%	388,000	109,318	28.2%	-1.6	832,000	163,920	19.7%	-10.1	888,000	158,272	17.8%	-11.9	943,000	226,116	24.0%	-5.8
MASSACHUSETTS	793,000	188,633	23.8%	848,000	197,772	23.3%	-0.5	1,895,000	291,740	15.4%	-8.4	2,031,000	415,710	20.5%	-3.3	2,166,000	686,700	31.7%	7.9
MICHIGAN	830,000	152,188	18.3%	976,000	270,365	27.7%	9.4	1,947,000	228,583	11.7%	-6.6	2,221,000	232,180	10.5%	-7.9	2,497,000	357,065	14.3%	-4.0
MINNESOTA	598,000	69,652	11.6%	623,000	108,572	17.4%	5.8	1,257,000	104,458	8.3%	-3.3	1,345,000	53,388	4.0%	-7.7	1,432,000	174,383	12.2%	0.5
MISSISSIPPI	428,000	48,797	11.4%	434,000	76,513	17.6%	6.2	886,000	66,306	7.5%	-3.9	949,000	98,548	10.4%	-1.0	1,011,000	112,546	11.1%	-0.3
MISSOURI	949,000	337,702	35.6%	984,000	396,617	40.3%	4.7	1,993,000	583,378	29.3%	-6.3	2,093,000	620,546	29.6%	-5.9	2,194,000	726,050	33.1%	-2.5
MONTANA	143,000	25,891	18.1%	258,000	84,499	32.8%	14.6	291,000	66,792	23.0%	4.8	292,000	72,847	24.9%	6.8	292,000	77,651	26.6%	8.5
NEBRASKA	335,000	114,044	34.0%	344,000	134,367	39.1%	5.0	696,000	116,512	16.7%	-17.3	734,000	200,974	27.4%	-6.7	772,000	233,094	30.2%	-3.8
NEVADA	31,000	7,311	23.6%	44,000	13,100	29.8%	6.2	45,000	9,167	20.4%	-3.2	47,000	12,880	27.4%	3.8	50,000	13,287	26.6%	3.0
NEW HAMPSHIRE	113,000	40,682	36.0%	115,000	39,951	34.7%	-1.3	237,000	60,730	25.6%	-10.4	246,000	66,186	26.9%	-9.1	255,000	75,843	29.7%	-6.3
NEW JERSEY	637,000	169,540	26.6%	703,000	186,792	26.6%	0.0	1,588,000	295,260	18.6%	-8.0	1,849,000	353,700	19.1%	-7.5	2,110,000	564,621	26.8%	0.1
NEW MEXICO	87,000	22,139	25.4%	85,000	32,592	38.3%	12.9	170,000	49,426	29.1%	3.6	172,000	57,802	33.6%	8.2	174,000	56,045	32.2%	6.8
NEW YORK	2,472,000	647,635	26.2%	2,656,000	626,913	23.6%	-2.6	5,294,000	899,198	17.0%	-9.2	5,965,000	1,335,228	22.4%	-3.8	6,635,000	1,989,414	30.0%	3.8
NORTH CAROLINA	529,000	149,569	28.3%	568,000	165,954	29.2%	0.9	1,237,000	306,919	24.8%	-3.5	1,368,000	289,754	21.2%	-7.1	1,497,000	355,360	23.7%	-4.5
NORTH DAKOTA	145,000	24,341	16.8%	152,000	29,167	19.2%	2.4	297,000	24,460	8.2%	-8.6	314,000	28,241	9.0%	-7.8	332,000	51,547	15.5%	-1.3
OHIO	1,403,000	423,301	30.2%	1,535,000	545,975	35.6%	5.4	3,289,000	798,981	24.3%	-5.9	3,551,000	769,751	21.7%	-8.5	3,811,000	931,103	24.4%	-5.7
OKLAHOMA	456,000	121,202	26.6%	498,000	142,031	28.5%	1.9	1,026,000	227,642	22.2%	-4.4	1,118,000	283,432	25.4%	-1.2	1,211,000	296,574	24.5%	-2.1
OREGON	392,000	35,285	9.0%	428,000	48,925	11.4%	2.4	467,000	44,902	9.6%	0.6	514,000	83,676	16.3%	7.3	563,000	85,553	15.2%	6.2
PENNSYLVANIA	1,907,000	357,562	18.7%	2,048,000	471,308	23.0%	4.3	4,412,000	466,564	10.6%	-8.2	4,766,000	551,102	11.6%	-7.2	5,121,000	912,317	17.8%	-0.9
RHODE ISLAND	125,000	33,626	26.9%	134,000	41,630	31.1%	4.2	296,000	58,927	19.9%	-7.0	323,000	84,543	26.2%	-0.7	351,000	114,454	32.6%	5.7
SOUTH CAROLINA	347,000	49,292	14.2%	370,000	61,869	16.7%	2.5	781,000	64,400	8.2%	-6.0	796,000	49,238	6.2%	-8.0	813,000	61,347	7.5%	-6.7
SOUTH DAKOTA	172,000	44,487	25.9%	179,000	52,769	29.5%	3.6	326,000	39,799	12.2%	-13.7	342,000	37,973	11.1%	-14.8	359,000	104,419	29.1%	3.2
TENNESSEE	563,000	141,400	25.1%	587,000	139,293	23.7%	-1.4	1,228,000	190,153	15.5%	-9.6	1,309,000	144,534	11.0%	-14.1	1,391,000	178,476	12.8%	-12.3

United States House of Representatives General Elections (continued)

Democratic Turnout for Election Years 1912–1928 (continued)

State	1912 Voting-age population	1912 Turnout	1912 %	1916 Voting-age population	1916 Turnout	1916 %	1916 Difference from 1912	1920 Voting-age population	1920 Turnout	1920 %	1920 Difference from 1912	1924 Voting-age population	1924 Turnout	1924 %	1924 Difference from 1912	1928 Voting-age population	1928 Turnout	1928 %	1928 Difference from 1912
TEXAS	1,004,000	235,065	23.4%	1,101,000	298,966	27.2%	3.7	2,304,000	311,565	13.5%	-9.9	2,558,000	587,437	23.0%	-0.4	2,811,000	568,457	20.2%	-3.2
UTAH	174,000	37,192	21.4%	194,000	79,882	41.2%	19.8	213,000	56,175	26.4%	5.0	227,000	65,689	28.9%	7.6	243,000	77,914	32.1%	10.7
VERMONT	101,000	17,422	17.2%	101,000	15,955	15.8%	-1.5	199,000	20,587	10.3%	-6.9	201,000	19,936	9.9%	-7.3	203,000	36,451	18.0%	0.7
VIRGINIA	538,000	99,053	18.4%	575,000	105,646	18.4%	0.0	1,203,000	154,402	12.8%	-5.6	1,242,000	166,708	13.4%	-5.0	1,282,000	206,533	16.1%	-2.3
WASHINGTON	640,000	73,133	11.4%	707,000	152,410	21.6%	10.1	774,000	63,390	8.2%	-3.2	833,000	90,308	10.8%	-0.6	892,000	134,910	15.1%	3.7
WEST VIRGINIA	328,000	114,578	34.9%	353,000	140,769	39.9%	4.9	726,000	226,017	31.1%	3.8	791,000	270,683	34.2%	0.7	867,000	202,061	34.1%	0.0
WISCONSIN	627,000	156,977	25.0%	643,000	137,391	21.4%	-3.7	1,371,000	107,774	7.9%	-17.2	1,493,000	155,982	10.4%	-14.6	1,617,000	234,599	14.5%	-10.5
WYOMING	87,000	14,720	16.9%	95,000	24,156	25.4%	8.5	106,000	14,952	14.1%	-2.8	113,000	28,537	25.3%	8.3	120,000	35,972	30.0%	13.1
Total	26,839,000	6,233,325	23.2%	28,990,000	7,709,350	26.6%	3.4	55,442,000	9,150,957	16.5%	-6.7	60,351,000	10,746,697	17.8%	-5.4	65,267,000	14,216,500	21.8%	-1.4

Other Turnout for Election Years 1912–1928

State	1912 Voting-age population	1912 Turnout	1912 %	1916 Voting-age population	1916 Turnout	1916 %	1916 Difference from 1912*	1920 Voting-age population	1920 Turnout	1920 %	1920 Difference from 1912	1924 Voting-age population	1924 Turnout	1924 %	1924 Difference from 1912	1928 Voting-age population	1928 Turnout	1928 %	1928 Difference from 1912
ALABAMA	523,000	2,533	0.5%	549,000	790	0.1%	-0.3	1,155,000	917	0.1%	-0.4								
ALASKA																			
ARIZONA	92,000	9,046	9.8%	120,000	3,060	2.6%	-7.3												
ARKANSAS																			
CALIFORNIA	1,530,000	138,946	9.1%	1,791,000	166,397	9.3%	0.2	2,110,000	95,072	4.5%	-4.6	2,603,000	89,415	3.4%	-5.6	3,096,000	45,786	1.5%	-7.6
COLORADO	466,000	86,796	18.6%	496,000	16,312	3.3%	-15.3					546,000	10,595	1.9%	-16.7	564,000	949	0.2%	-18.5
CONNECTICUT	270,000	43,296	16.0%	292,000	7,727	2.6%	-13.4	648,000	13,013	2.0%	-14.0	714,000	4,490	0.6%	-15.4	780,000	3,217	0.4%	-15.6
DELAWARE	59,000	9,482	16.1%	62,000	2,614	4.2%	-11.9	128,000	1,259	1.0%	-15.1	134,000	519	0.4%	-15.7				
DISTRICT OF COLUMBIA																			
FLORIDA	220,000	7,093	3.2%	246,000	3,906	1.6%	-1.6	544,000	3,405	0.6%	-2.6	675,000	2,995	0.4%	-2.8	805,000	17	0.0%	-3.2
GEORGIA				677,000	699	0.1%		1,423,000	8,605	0.6%	0.5	1,453,000	16	0.0%	-0.1				
HAWAII																			
IDAHO	177,000	24,635	13.9%	202,000	8,079	4.0%	-9.9	223,000	8,605	3.9%	-10.1	228,000	23,736	10.4%	-3.5	233,000	1,039	0.4%	-13.5
ILLINOIS	1,535,000	415,502	27.1%	1,657,000	61,201	3.7%	-23.4	3,553,000	138,996	3.9%	-23.2	3,938,000	22,648	0.6%	-26.5	4,322,000	16,240	0.4%	-26.7
INDIANA	808,000	182,841	22.6%	833,000	41,825	5.0%	-17.6	1,725,000	40,549	2.4%	-20.3	1,822,000	12,447	0.7%	-21.9	1,918,000	2,078	0.1%	-22.5
IOWA	632,000	62,172	9.8%	670,000	9,718	1.5%	-8.4	1,377,000	22,914	1.7%	-8.2	1,419,000	827	0.1%	-9.8				
KANSAS	936,000	27,478	2.9%	962,000	45,157	4.7%	1.8	995,000	9,484	1.0%	-2.0	1,042,000	5,895	0.6%	-2.4				
KENTUCKY	611,000	102,899	16.8%	633,000	6,231	1.0%	-15.9	1,291,000	11,274	0.9%	-16.0	1,346,000	16,062	1.2%	-15.6	1,401,000	113	0.0%	-16.8
LOUISIANA	413,000	2,841	0.7%	435,000	7,324	1.7%	1.0	918,000	15	0.0%	-0.7								
MAINE	204,000	2,925	1.4%	208,000	1,589	0.8%	-0.7												

United States House of Representatives General Elections (continued)

Other Turnout for Election Years 1912–1928 (continued)

State	1912 Voting-age population	Turnout	%	1916 Voting-age population	Turnout	%	Difference from 1912	1920 Voting-age population	Turnout	%	Difference from 1912	1924 Voting-age population	Turnout	%	Difference from 1912	1928 Voting-age population	Turnout	%	Difference from 1912
MARYLAND	361,000	10,070	2.8%	388,000	9,823	2.5%	-0.3	832,000	23,659	2.8%	0.1	888,000	4,025	0.5%	-2.3	943,000	2,314	0.2%	-2.5
MASSACHUSETTS	793,000	100,103	12.6%	848,000	25,424	3.0%	-9.6	1,895,000	26,811	1.4%	-11.2	2,031,000	13,235	0.7%	-12.0	2,166,000	5,152	0.2%	-12.4
MICHIGAN	830,000	203,905	24.6%	976,000	17,312	1.8%	-22.8	1,947,000	19,842	1.0%	-23.5	2,221,000	661	0.0%	-24.5	2,497,000	2,452	0.1%	-24.5
MINNESOTA	598,000	55,905	9.3%	623,000	62,014	10.0%	0.6	1,257,000	195,315	15.5%	6.2	1,345,000	337,035	25.1%	15.7	1,432,000	271,863	19.0%	9.6
MISSISSIPPI	428,000	302	0.1%	434,000	1,865	0.4%	0.4	886,000	1,988	0.2%	0.2								
MISSOURI	949,000	125,104	13.2%	984,000	13,910	1.4%	-11.8	1,993,000	22,821	1.1%	-12.0	2,093,000	12,474	0.6%	-12.6	2,194,000	187	0.0%	-13.2
MONTANA	143,000	26,915	18.8%	258,000	9,002	3.5%	-15.3					292,000	6,847	2.3%	-16.5	292,000	826	0.3%	-18.5
NEBRASKA	335,000	17,328	5.2%	344,000	8,366	2.4%	-2.7	696,000	21,752	3.1%	-2.0	734,000	17,644	2.4%	-2.8				
NEVADA	31,000	5,083	16.4%	44,000	5,125	11.6%	-4.7	45,000	4,554	10.1%	-6.3								
NEW HAMPSHIRE	113,000	6,270	5.5%	115,000	1,462	1.3%	-4.3	237,000	588	0.2%	-5.3					255,000	186	0.1%	-5.5
NEW JERSEY	637,000	76,105	11.9%	703,000	27,350	3.9%	-8.1	1,588,000	24,144	1.5%	-10.4	1,849,000	18,983	1.0%	-10.9	2,110,000	914	0.0%	-11.9
NEW MEXICO	87,000	8,526	9.8%	85,000	2,050	2.4%	-7.4	170,000	1,290	0.8%	-9.0	172,000	1,126	0.7%	-9.1				
NEW YORK	2,472,000	415,110	16.8%	2,656,000	94,082	3.5%	-13.3	5,294,000	242,569	4.6%	-12.2	5,965,000	147,781	2.5%	-14.3	6,635,000	150,424	2.3%	-14.5
NORTH CAROLINA	529,000	8,423	1.6%	568,000	258	0.0%	-1.5												
NORTH DAKOTA	145,000	8,552	5.9%	152,000	4,359	2.9%	-3.0	297,000	64,690	21.8%	15.9	314,000	28,558	9.1%	3.2				
OHIO	1,403,000	295,872	21.1%	1,535,000	29,101	1.9%	-19.2	3,289,000	13,676	0.4%	-20.7	3,551,000	35,902	1.0%	-20.1	3,811,000	2,290	0.1%	-21.0
OKLAHOMA	456,000	41,229	9.0%	498,000	48,205	9.7%	0.6	1,026,000	25,150	2.5%	-6.6	1,118,000	17,124	1.5%	-7.5	1,211,000	2,443	0.2%	-8.8
OREGON	392,000	35,796	9.1%	428,000	43,504	10.2%	1.0	467,000	11,510	2.5%	-6.7	514,000	19,002	3.7%	-5.4	563,000	11,475	2.0%	-7.1
PENNSYLVANIA	1,907,000	125,507	6.6%	2,048,000	106,262	5.2%	-1.4	4,412,000	185,536	4.2%	-2.4	4,766,000	104,390	2.2%	-4.4	5,121,000	24,932	0.5%	-6.1
RHODE ISLAND	125,000	9,546	7.6%	134,000	2,041	1.5%	-6.1	296,000	2,417	0.8%	-6.8								
SOUTH CAROLINA	347,000	153	0.0%	370,000	87	0.0%	0.0	781,000	502	0.1%	0.0								
SOUTH DAKOTA	172,000	6,813	4.0%	179,000	4,334	2.4%	-1.5	326,000	38,932	11.9%	8.0	342,000	45,714	13.4%	9.4	359,000	1,744	0.5%	-3.5
TENNESSEE	563,000	6,394	1.1%	587,000	6,252	1.1%	-0.1	1,228,000	3,126	0.3%	-0.9	1,309,000	5,591	0.4%	-0.7				
TEXAS	1,004,000	42,083	4.2%	1,101,000	20,108	1.8%	-2.4	2,304,000	23,276	1.0%	-3.2								
UTAH	174,000	31,834	18.3%	194,000	4,574	2.4%	-15.9	213,000	7,214	3.4%	-14.9					243,000	847	0.3%	-17.9
VERMONT	101,000	2,646	2.6%	101,000	1,771	1.8%	-0.9									203,000	1,688	0.8%	-1.8
VIRGINIA	538,000	11,904	2.2%	575,000	2,711	0.5%	-1.7	1,203,000	421	0.0%	-2.2					1,282,000	1,781	0.1%	-2.1
WASHINGTON	640,000	143,006	22.3%	707,000	21,424	3.0%	-19.3	774,000	93,111	12.0%	-10.3	833,000	33,683	4.0%	-18.3	892,000	823	0.1%	-22.3
WEST VIRGINIA	328,000	19,617	6.0%					726,000	1	0.0%	-6.0	791,000	3,120	0.4%	-5.6	857,000	115	0.0%	-6.0
WISCONSIN	627,000	46,090	7.4%	643,000	41,151	6.4%	-1.0	1,371,000	87,520	6.4%	-1.0	1,493,000	55,843	3.7%	-3.6	1,617,000	64,044	4.0%	-3.4
WYOMING	87,000	7,354	8.5%	95,000	1,521	1.6%	-6.9	106,000	6,780	6.4%	-2.1					120,000	333	0.3%	-8.2
Total	25,791,000	3,012,030	11.7%	28,205,000	998,077	3.5%	-8.1	51,749,000	1,503,303	2.9%	-8.8	48,541,000	1,098,383	2.3%	-9.4	47,922,000	616,272	1.3%	-10.4

*Percentage point difference between turnout in current year and initial year listed in chart. If data do not appear for a state in the initial year listed, the difference is calculated from the first year in which data do appear for that state.

UNITED STATES PRESIDENTIAL PRIMARY ELECTIONS

Election Years 1912–1928

State*	1912 Voting-age population	Turnout	%	1916 Voting-age population	Turnout	%	Difference from 1912**	1920 Voting-age population	Turnout	%	Difference from 1912	1924 Voting-age population	Turnout	%	Difference from 1912	1928 Voting-age population	Turnout	%	Difference from 1912
ALABAMA																			
ALASKA																			
ARIZONA																			
ARKANSAS																			
CALIFORNIA	1,503,000	314,161	20.9%	1,764,000	311,362	17.7%	-3.3	2,033,000	602,693	29.6%	8.7	2,526,000	701,005	27.8%	6.8	3,020,000	815,727	27.0%	6.1
COLORADO																			
CONNECTICUT																			
DELAWARE																			
DISTRICT OF COLUMBIA																			
FLORIDA																			
GEORGIA																			
HAWAII																			
IDAHO																			
ILLINOIS	1,523,000	731,100	48.0%	1,645,000	310,040	18.8%	-29.2	3,499,000	485,252	13.9%	-34.1	3,883,000	1,101,585	28.4%	-19.6	4,266,000	1,228,979	28.8%	-19.2
INDIANA				834,000	336,501	40.3%										1,905,000	579,008	30.4%	-10.0
IOWA				666,000	71,704	10.8%													
KANSAS																			
KENTUCKY																			
LOUISIANA																			
MAINE																			
MARYLAND	359,000	117,700	32.8%																
MASSACHUSETTS	707,000	222,182	28.2%	843,000	125,159	14.8%	-13.4	1,877,000	114,582	6.1%	-22.1	2,012,000	115,181	5.7%	-22.5	2,148,000	156,535	7.3%	-20.9
MICHIGAN				960,000	260,266	27.1%		1,906,000	497,651	26.1%	-1.0	2,181,000	442,272	20.3%	-6.8	2,457,000	368,458	15.0%	-12.1
MINNESOTA				621,000	115,753	18.6%													
MISSISSIPPI																			
MISSOURI																			
MONTANA				254,000	29,548	11.6%		291,000	43,134	14.8%	3.2	292,000	29,258	10.0%	-1.6				
NEBRASKA	334,000	129,226	38.7%	343,000	167,857	48.9%	10.2	691,000	192,329	27.8%	-10.9	729,000	141,645	19.4%	-19.3	767,000	161,157	21.0%	-17.7
NEVADA																			
NEW HAMPSHIRE				115,000	15,371	13.4%		236,000	23,298	9.9%	-3.5	246,000	23,857	9.7%	-3.7	254,000	35,319	13.9%	0.5
NEW JERSEY	630,000	157,653	25.0%	697,000	26,866	3.9%	-21.2	1,550,000	110,050	7.1%	-17.9	1,812,000	161,794	8.9%	-16.1	2,073,000	411,413	19.8%	-5.2
NEW MEXICO																			
NEW YORK				2,636,000	259,576	9.8%		5,197,000	312,449	6.0%	-3.8								

United States Presidential Primary Elections (continued)

United States Presidential Primary Elections (continued)

Election Years 1912–1928 (continued)

State	1912			1916				1920				1924				1928			
	Voting-age population	Turnout	%	Voting-age population	Turnout	%	Difference from 1912	Voting-age population	Turnout	%	Difference from 1912	Voting-age population	Turnout	%	Difference from 1912	Voting-age population	Turnout	%	Difference from 1912
NORTH CAROLINA																			
NORTH DAKOTA	145,000	69,025	47.6%	152,000	45,566	30.0%	-17.6	295,000	32,214	10.9%	-36.7	312,000	136,703	43.8%	-3.8	330,000	106,679	32.3%	-15.3
OHIO	1,390,000	485,857	35.0%	1,522,000	225,780	14.8%	-20.1	3,253,000	346,849	10.7%	-24.3	3,513,000	304,641	8.7%	-26.3	3,775,000	383,325	10.2%	-24.8
OKLAHOMA																			
OREGON	389,000	90,027	23.1%	424,000	122,813	29.0%	5.8	459,000	145,383	31.7%	8.5	508,000	162,893	32.1%	8.9	555,000	138,408	24.9%	1.8
PENNSYLVANIA	1,893,000	572,032	30.2%	2,033,000	414,246	20.4%	-9.8	4,365,000	388,509	8.9%	-21.3	4,719,000	157,100	3.3%	-26.9				
RHODE ISLAND																			
SOUTH CAROLINA																			
SOUTH DAKOTA	172,000	82,356	47.9%	177,000	39,997	22.6%	-25.3	323,000	92,303	28.6%	-19.3	340,000	89,749	26.4%	-21.5	357,000	40,485	11.3%	-36.5
TENNESSEE																			
TEXAS																			
UTAH																			
VERMONT				100,000	11,568	11.6%		199,000	5,659	2.8%	-8.7								
VIRGINIA																			
WASHINGTON																			
WEST VIRGINIA																847,000	401,056	47.4%	
WISCONSIN	624,000	264,696	42.4%	640,000	221,092	34.5%	-7.9	1,354,000	33,566	2.5%	-39.9	1,476,000	145,684	9.9%	-32.5	1,600,000	268,281	16.8%	-25.7
WYOMING																			
Total	9,749,000	3,236,015	33.2%	16,426,000	3,111,065	18.9%	-14.3	27,528,000	3,425,921	12.4%	-20.7	24,549,000	3,713,367	15.1%	-18.1	24,354,000	5,094,830	20.9%	-12.3

*Overall primary turnout reflects only states with primaries in both parties. To find single party primary results, see partisan primary charts.

**Percentage point difference between turnout in current year and initial year listed in chart. If data do not appear for a state in the initial year listed, the difference is calculated from the first year in which data do appear for that state.

UNITED STATES PRESIDENTIAL PRIMARY ELECTIONS

Republican Turnout for Election Years 1912–1928

State	1912 Voting-age population	Turnout	%	1916 Voting-age population	Turnout	%	Difference from 1912*	1920 Voting-age population	Turnout	%	Difference from 1912	1924 Voting-age population	Turnout	%	Difference from 1912	1928 Voting-age population	Turnout	%	Difference from 1912
ALABAMA																			
ALASKA																			
ARIZONA																			
ARKANSAS																			
CALIFORNIA	1,503,000	253,784	25.8%	1,764,000	236,277	13.4%	-3.5	2,033,000	578,862	28.5%	11.6	2,526,000	572,184	22.7%	5.8	3,020,000	567,219	18.8%	1.9
COLORADO																			
CONNECTICUT																			
DELAWARE																			
DISTRICT OF COLUMBIA																			
FLORIDA																			
GEORGIA																			
HAWAII																			
IDAHO																			
ILLINOIS	1,523,000	437,090	28.7%	1,645,000	172,982	10.5%	-18.2	3,499,000	463,797	13.3%	-15.4	3,883,000	919,082	23.7%	-5.0	4,266,000	1,180,768	27.7%	-1.0
INDIANA				834,000	176,078	21.1%		1,711,000	225,957	13.2%	-7.9	1,808,000	392,648	21.7%	0.6	1,905,000	432,074	22.7%	1.6
IOWA				666,000	40,257	6.0%													
KANSAS																			
KENTUCKY																			
LOUISIANA																			
MAINE																			
MARYLAND	359,000	55,119	15.4%					823,000	23,959	2.9%	-12.4	880,000	20,986	2.4%	-13.0	936,000	32,554	3.5%	-11.9
MASSACHUSETTS	787,000	171,978	21.9%	843,000	105,579	12.5%	-9.3	1,877,000	93,356	5.0%	-16.9	2,012,000	84,840	4.2%	-17.6	2,148,000	117,722	5.5%	-16.4
MICHIGAN				960,000	175,294	18.3%		1,906,000	409,157	21.5%	3.2	2,181,000	351,242	16.1%	-2.2	2,457,000	289,824	11.8%	-6.5
MINNESOTA				621,000	70,617	11.4%													
MISSISSIPPI																			
MISSOURI																			
MONTANA				254,000	11,588	4.6%		291,000	40,140	13.8%	9.2	292,000	19,200	6.6%	2.0				
NEBRASKA	334,000	77,957	23.3%	343,000	88,607	25.8%	2.5	691,000	136,647	19.8%	-3.6	729,000	125,335	17.2%	-6.1	767,000	105,383	13.7%	-9.6
NEVADA																			
NEW HAMPSHIRE				115,000	9,687	8.4%		236,000	16,195	6.9%	-1.6	246,000	17,170	7.0%	-1.4	254,000	25,603	10.1%	1.7
NEW JERSEY	630,000	108,795	17.3%	697,000	1,459	0.2%	-17.1	1,550,000	105,494	6.8%	-10.5	1,812,000	125,365	6.9%	-10.4	2,073,000	382,907	18.5%	1.2
NEW MEXICO																			
NEW YORK				2,636,000	147,038	5.6%		5,197,000	199,149	3.8%	-1.7								

United States Presidential Primary Elections (continued)

United States Presidential Primary Elections (continued)

Republican Turnout for Election Years 1912–1928 (continued)

State	1912 Voting-age population	Turnout	%	1916 Voting-age population	Turnout	%	Difference from 1912	1920 Voting-age population	Turnout	%	Difference from 1912	1924 population	Turnout	%	Difference from 1912	1928 Voting-age population	Turnout	%	Difference from 1912
NORTH CAROLINA								1,218,000	20,978	1.7%									
NORTH DAKOTA	145,000	59,668	41.2%	152,000	33,225	21.9%	-19.3	295,000	31,825	10.8%	-30.4	312,000	125,430	40.2%	-0.9	330,000	95,857	29.0%	-12.1
OHIO	1,390,000	299,741	21.6%	1,522,000	140,677	9.2%	-12.3	3,253,000	259,072	8.0%	-13.6	3,513,000	201,191	5.7%	-15.8	3,775,000	319,068	8.5%	-13.1
OKLAHOMA																			
OREGON	389,000	71,927	18.5%	424,000	94,915	22.4%	3.9	459,000	120,071	26.2%	7.7	508,000	129,229	25.4%	6.9	555,000	102,451	18.5%	0.0
PENNSYLVANIA	1,893,000	474,032	25.0%	2,033,000	270,205	13.3%	-11.8	4,365,000	279,472	6.4%	-18.6	4,719,000	133,354	2.8%	-22.2				
RHODE ISLAND																			
SOUTH CAROLINA																			
SOUTH DAKOTA	172,000	69,010	40.1%	177,000	29,656	16.8%	-23.4	323,000	85,691	26.5%	-13.6	340,000	80,726	23.7%	-16.4	357,000	34,264	9.6%	-30.5
TENNESSEE																			
TEXAS																			
UTAH																			
VERMONT				100,000	7,834	7.8%		199,000	5,223	2.6%	-5.2								
VIRGINIA																			
WASHINGTON																			
WEST VIRGINIA								716,000	61,104	8.5%		782,000	162,042	20.7%	12.2	847,000	237,732	28.1%	19.5
WISCONSIN	624,000	182,139	29.2%	640,000	111,399	17.4%	-11.8	1,354,000	30,099	2.2%	-27.0	1,476,000	65,161	4.4%	-24.8	1,600,000	186,862	11.7%	-17.5
WYOMING																			
Total	9,749,000	2,261,240	23.2%	16,426,000	1,923,374	11.7%	-11.5	31,996,000	3,186,248	10.0%	-13.2	28,019,000	3,525,185	12.6%	-10.6	25,290,000	4,110,288	16.3%	-6.9

Democratic Turnout for Election Years 1912–1928

State	1912 Voting-age population	Turnout	%	1916 Voting-age population	Turnout	%	Difference from 1912*	1920 Voting-age population	Turnout	%	Difference from 1912	1924 Voting-age population	Turnout	%	Difference from 1912	1928 Voting-age population	Turnout	%	Difference from 1912
ALABAMA																1,308,000	138,957	10.6%	
ALASKA																			
ARIZONA																			
ARKANSAS																			
CALIFORNIA	1,503,000	60,377	4.0%	1,764,000	75,085	4.3%	0.2	2,033,000	23,831	1.2%	-2.8	2,526,000	128,821	5.1%	1.1	3,020,000	248,508	8.2%	4.2
COLORADO																			
CONNECTICUT																			
DELAWARE																			
DISTRICT OF COLUMBIA																			
FLORIDA																786,000	108,167	13.8%	

United States Presidential Primary Elections *(continued)*

Democratic Turnout for Election Years 1912–1928 *(continued)*

State	1912 Voting-age population	Turnout	%	1916 Voting-age population	Turnout	%	Difference from 1912	1920 Voting-age population	Turnout	%	Difference from 1912	1924 Voting-age population	Turnout	%	Difference from 1912	1928 Voting-age population	Turnout	%	Difference from 1912
GEORGIA																			
HAWAII																			
IDAHO																			
ILLINOIS	1,523,000	294,010	19.3%	1,645,000	137,058	8.3%	-11.0	3,499,000	21,455	0.6%	-18.7	3,883,000	182,503	4.7%	-14.6	4,266,000	48,211	1.1%	-18.2
INDIANA				834,000	160,423	19.2%										1,905,000	146,934	7.7%	-11.5
IOWA				666,000	31,447	4.7%													
KANSAS																			
KENTUCKY																			
LOUISIANA																			
MAINE																			
MARYLAND	359,000	62,581	17.4%																
MASSACHUSETTS	787,000	50,204	6.4%	843,000	19,580	2.3%	-4.1	1,877,000	21,226	1.1%	-5.2	2,012,000	30,341	1.5%	-4.9	2,148,000	38,813	1.8%	-4.6
MICHIGAN				960,000	84,972	8.9%		1,906,000	88,494	4.6%	-4.2	2,181,000	91,030	4.2%	-4.7	2,457,000	78,634	3.2%	-5.7
MINNESOTA				621,000	45,136	7.3%													
MISSISSIPPI																			
MISSOURI																			
MONTANA				254,000	17,960	7.1%		291,000	2,994	1.0%	-6.0	292,000	10,058	3.4%	-3.6				
NEBRASKA	334,000	51,269	15.4%	343,000	79,250	23.1%	7.8	691,000	55,682	8.1%	-7.3	729,000	16,310	2.2%	-13.1	767,000	55,774	7.3%	-8.1
NEVADA																			
NEW HAMPSHIRE				115,000	5,684	4.9%		236,000	7,103	3.0%	-1.9	246,000	6,687	2.7%	-2.2	254,000	9,716	3.8%	-1.1
NEW JERSEY	630,000	48,858	7.8%	697,000	25,407	3.6%	-4.1	1,550,000	4,556	0.3%	-7.5	1,812,000	36,429	2.0%	-5.7	2,073,000	28,506	1.4%	-6.4
NEW MEXICO																			
NEW YORK				2,636,000	112,538	4.3%		5,197,000	113,300	2.2%	-2.1								
NORTH CAROLINA																			
NORTH DAKOTA	145,000	9,357	6.5%	152,000	12,341	8.1%	1.7	295,000	389	0.1%	-6.3	312,000	11,273	3.6%	-2.8	330,000	10,822	3.3%	-3.2
OHIO	1,390,000	186,116	13.4%	1,522,000	85,103	5.6%	-7.8	3,253,000	87,777	2.7%	-10.7	3,513,000	103,450	2.9%	-10.4	3,775,000	64,257	1.7%	-11.7
OKLAHOMA																			
OREGON	389,000	18,100	4.7%	424,000	27,898	6.6%	1.9	459,000	25,312	5.5%	0.9	508,000	33,664	6.6%	2.0	555,000	35,957	6.5%	1.8
PENNSYLVANIA	1,893,000	98,000	5.2%	2,033,000	144,041	7.1%	1.9	4,365,000	109,037	2.5%	-2.7	4,719,000	23,746	0.5%	-4.7				
RHODE ISLAND																			
SOUTH CAROLINA																			
SOUTH DAKOTA	172,000	13,346	7.8%	177,000	10,341	5.8%	-1.9	323,000	6,612	2.0%	-5.7	340,000	9,023	2.7%	-5.1	357,000	6,221	1.7%	-6.0
TENNESSEE																			

United States Presidential Primary Elections (continued)

Democratic Turnout for Election Years 1912–1928 *(continued)*

State	1912 Voting-age population	Turnout	%	1916 Voting-age population	Turnout	%	Difference from 1912	1920 Voting-age population	Turnout	%	Difference from 1912	1924 Voting-age population	Turnout	%	Difference from 1912	1928 Voting-age population	Turnout	%	Difference from 1912
TEXAS																			
UTAH																			
VERMONT				100,000	3,734	3.7%		199,000	436	0.2%	-3.5								
VIRGINIA																			
WASHINGTON																			
WEST VIRGINIA																847,000	163,324	19.3%	
WISCONSIN	624,000	82,557	13.2%	640,000	109,693	17.1%	3.9	1,354,000	3,467	0.3%	-13.0	1,476,000	80,523	5.5%	-7.8	1,600,000	81,419	5.1%	-8.1
WYOMING																			
Total	9,749,000	974,775	10.0%	16,426,000	1,187,691	7.2%	-2.8	27,528,000	571,671	2.1%	-7.9	24,549,000	763,858	3.1%	-6.9	26,448,000	1,264,220	4.8%	-5.2

*Percentage point difference between turnout in current year and initial year listed in chart. If data do not appear for a state in the initial year listed, the difference is calculated from the first year in which data do appear for that state.

STATE GUBERNATORIAL PRIMARY ELECTIONS
Election Years 1912–1928

State*	1912 Voting-age population	Turnout	%	1916 Voting-age population	Turnout	%	Difference from 1912**	1920 Voting-age population	Turnout	%	Difference from 1912	1924 Voting-age population	Turnout	%	Difference from 1912	1928 Voting-age population	Turnout	%	Difference from 1912
ALABAMA																			
ALASKA																			
ARIZONA																			
ARKANSAS																			
CALIFORNIA																			
COLORADO	463,000	104,995	22.7%	492,000	120,450	24.5%	1.8	523,000	120,658	23.1%	0.4	542,000	160,000	29.5%	6.8	562,000	124,180	22.1%	-0.6
CONNECTICUT																			
DELAWARE																			
DISTRICT OF COLUMBIA																			
FLORIDA																			
GEORGIA																			
HAWAII																			
IDAHO	175,000	52,927	30.2%	199,000	58,751	29.5%	-0.7												
ILLINOIS	1,523,000	751,208	49.3%	1,645,000	662,515	40.3%	-9.0	3,499,000	993,353	28.4%	-20.9	3,883,000	1,301,150	33.5%	-15.8	4,266,000	1,907,517	44.7%	-4.6
INDIANA								1,711,000	317,335	18.5%		1,808,000	690,841	38.2%	19.7				
IOWA	628,000	241,630	38.5%	666,000	305,062	45.8%	7.3	1,371,000	252,040	18.4%	-20.1	1,413,000	402,300	28.5%	-10.0				
KANSAS	933,000	181,268	19.4%	960,000	189,611	19.8%	0.3	988,000	203,784	20.6%	1.2	1,036,000	317,793	30.7%	11.2	1,084,000	347,063	32.0%	12.6
KENTUCKY																			
LOUISIANA																			
MAINE																			
MARYLAND																			
MASSACHUSETTS																			
MICHIGAN																			
MINNESOTA																			
MISSISSIPPI																			
MISSOURI	947,000	377,965	39.9%	980,000	429,270	43.8%	3.9	1,979,000	378,069	19.1%	-20.8	2,079,000	655,017	31.5%	-8.4	2,179,000	694,426	31.9%	-8.0
MONTANA				254,000	91,500	36.0%		291,000	110,312	37.9%	1.9	292,000	149,780	51.3%	15.3	292,000	115,499	39.6%	3.5
NEBRASKA																			
NEVADA																			
NEW HAMPSHIRE	113,000	25,193	22.3%	115,000	30,241	26.3%	4.0	236,000	62,242	26.4%	4.1	246,000	48,161	19.6%	-2.7	254,000	71,294	28.1%	5.8
NEW JERSEY																2,073,000	661,435	31.9%	
NEW MEXICO																			
NEW YORK																			

State Gubernatorial Primary Elections (continued)

State Gubernatorial Primary Elections (continued)

Election Years 1912–1928 (continued)

State	1912 Voting-age population	Turnout	%	1916 Voting-age population	Turnout	%	Difference from 1912	1920 Voting-age population	Turnout	%	Difference from 1912	1924 Voting-age population	Turnout	%	Difference from 1912	1928 Voting-age population	Turnout	%	Difference from 1912
NORTH CAROLINA																			
NORTH DAKOTA	145,000	67,563	46.6%	152,000	88,515	58.2%	11.6	295,000	121,216	41.1%	-5.5	312,000	161,608	51.8%	5.2	330,000	192,755	58.4%	11.8
OHIO				1,522,000	470,821	30.9%		3,253,000	465,974	14.3%	-16.6	3,513,000	785,900	22.4%	-8.6	3,775,000	889,762	23.6%	-7.4
OKLAHOMA																			
OREGON																			
PENNSYLVANIA																			
RHODE ISLAND																			
SOUTH CAROLINA																			
SOUTH DAKOTA				177,000	67,346	38.0%													
TENNESSEE																			
TEXAS																			
UTAH																			
VERMONT				100,000	36,848	36.8%		199,000	63,898	32.1%	-4.7	201,000	43,526	21.7%	-15.2	203,000	60,127	29.6%	-7.2
VIRGINIA																			
WASHINGTON	633,000	121,725	19.2%	700,000	219,672	31.4%	12.2	765,000	227,649	29.8%	10.5	824,000	263,364	32.0%	12.7	883,000	320,765	36.3%	17.1
WEST VIRGINIA																			
WISCONSIN	624,000	181,094	29.0%	640,000	226,336	35.4%	6.3	1,354,000	436,574	32.2%	3.2	1,476,000	466,021	31.6%	2.6	1,600,000	565,514	35.3%	6.3
WYOMING																			
Total	6,174,000	2,105,568	34.1%	8,602,000	2,996,938	34.8%	0.8	16,464,000	3,753,104	22.8%	-11.3	17,625,000	5,445,461	30.9%	-3.2	17,501,000	5,950,317	34.0%	-0.1

*Overall primary turnout reflects only states with primaries in both parties. To find single party primary results, see partisan primary charts.

**Percentage point difference between turnout in current year and initial year listed in chart. If data do not appear for a state in the initial year listed, the difference is calculated from the first year in which data do appear for that state.

STATE GUBERNATORIAL PRIMARY ELECTIONS

Republican Turnout for Election Years 1912–1928

State	1912 Voting-age population	Turnout	%	1916 Voting-age population	Turnout	%	Difference from 1912*	1920 Voting-age population	Turnout	%	Difference from 1912	1924 Voting-age population	Turnout	%	Difference from 1912	1928 Voting-age population	Turnout	%	Difference from 1912
ALABAMA																			
ALASKA																			
ARIZONA																			
ARKANSAS																			
CALIFORNIA																			
COLORADO	463,000	39,923	8.6%	492,000	80,881	16.4%	7.8	523,000	66,692	12.8%	4.1	542,000	116,840	21.6%	12.9	562,000	81,223	14.5%	5.8
CONNECTICUT																			
DELAWARE																			
DISTRICT OF COLUMBIA																			
FLORIDA																			
GEORGIA																			
HAWAII																			
IDAHO	175,000	38,134	21.8%	199,000	45,790	23.0%	1.2												
ILLINOIS	1,523,000	439,662	28.9%	1,645,000	420,959	25.6%	-3.3	3,499,000	810,950	23.2%	-5.7	3,883,000	995,824	25.6%	-3.2	4,266,000	1,663,422	39.0%	10.1
INDIANA								1,711,000	214,655	12.5%		1,808,000	413,222	22.9%	10.3				
IOWA	628,000	181,219	28.9%	666,000	227,863	34.2%	5.4	1,371,000	213,186	15.5%	-13.3	1,413,000	350,089	24.8%	-4.1	1,455,000	369,094	25.4%	-3.5
KANSAS	993,000	115,770	11.7%	960,000	138,916	14.5%	2.8	988,000	164,224	16.6%	5.0	1,036,000	236,392	22.8%	11.2	1,084,000	291,884	26.9%	15.3
KENTUCKY																			
LOUISIANA																			
MAINE																			
MARYLAND																			
MASSACHUSETTS																			
MICHIGAN																			
MINNESOTA												1,333,000	236,283	17.7%		1,421,000	271,648	19.1%	1.4
MISSISSIPPI																			
MISSOURI	947,000	145,234	15.3%	980,000	191,654	19.6%	4.2	1,979,000	197,719	10.0%	-5.3	2,079,000	292,919	14.1%	-1.2	2,179,000	347,947	16.0%	0.6
MONTANA				254,000	49,128	19.3%		291,000	52,868	18.2%	-1.2	292,000	72,506	24.8%	5.5	292,000	47,969	16.4%	-2.9
NEBRASKA																			
NEVADA																			
NEW HAMPSHIRE	113,000	18,209	16.1%	115,000	22,407	19.5%	3.4	236,000	52,633	22.3%	6.2	246,000	38,719	15.7%	-0.4	254,000	58,439	23.0%	6.9
NEW JERSEY																2,073,000	426,061	20.6%	
NEW MEXICO																			
NEW YORK																			

State Gubernatorial Primary Elections (continued)

State Gubernatorial Primary Elections (continued)

Republican Turnout for Election Years 1912–1928 (continued)

State	1912			1916				1920				1924				1928			
	Voting-age population	Turnout	%	Voting-age population	Turnout	%	Difference from 1912	Voting-age population	Turnout	%	Difference from 1912	Voting-age population	Turnout	%	Difference from 1912	Voting-age population	Turnout	%	Difference from 1912
NORTH CAROLINA																			
NORTH DAKOTA	145,000	57,503	39.7%	152,000	75,369	49.6%	9.9	295,000	113,296	38.4%	-1.3	312,000	150,327	48.2%	8.5	330,000	181,219	54.9%	15.3
OHIO				1,522,000	282,478	18.6%		3,253,000	335,065	10.3%	-8.3	3,513,000	560,670	16.0%	-2.6	3,775,000	656,376	17.4%	-1.2
OKLAHOMA																			
OREGON																			
PENNSYLVANIA																			
RHODE ISLAND																			
SOUTH CAROLINA																			
SOUTH DAKOTA	172,000	74,717	43.4%	177,000	53,878	30.4%	-13.0												
TENNESSEE																			
TEXAS																			
UTAH																			
VERMONT				100,000	33,281	33.3%		199,000	60,480	30.4%	-2.9	201,000	41,141	20.5%	-12.8	203,000	57,117	28.1%	-5.1
VIRGINIA																			
WASHINGTON	633,000	89,694	14.2%	700,000	186,933	26.7%	12.5	765,000	204,897	26.8%	12.6	824,000	233,763	28.4%	14.2	883,000	281,163	31.8%	17.7
WEST VIRGINIA																			
WISCONSIN	624,000	81,412	13.0%	640,000	172,386	26.9%	13.9	1,354,000	378,263	27.9%	14.9	1,476,000	424,789	28.8%	15.7	1,600,000	514,065	32.1%	19.1
WYOMING																			
Total	6,416,000	1,281,477	20.0%	8,602,000	1,981,923	23.0%	3.1	16,464,000	2,864,928	17.4%	-2.6	18,958,000	4,163,484	22.0%	2.0	20,377,000	5,247,627	25.8%	5.8

Democratic Turnout for Election Years 1912–1928

State	1912			1916				1920				1924				1928			
	Voting-age population	Turnout	%	Voting-age population	Turnout	%	Difference from 1912*	Voting-age population	Turnout	%	Difference from 1912	Voting-age population	Turnout	%	Difference from 1912	Voting-age population	Turnout	%	Difference from 1912
ALABAMA																			
ALASKA																			
ARIZONA																			
ARKANSAS								866,000	141,816	16.4%		907,000	207,003	22.8%	6.4	948,000	217,966	23.0%	6.6
CALIFORNIA																			
COLORADO	463,000	65,072	14.1%	492,000	39,569	8.0%	-6.0	523,000	53,966	10.3%	-3.7	542,000	43,160	8.0%	-6.1	562,000	42,937	7.6%	-6.4
CONNECTICUT																			
DELAWARE																			
DISTRICT OF COLUMBIA																			
FLORIDA								526,000	88,422	16.8%		655,000	145,288	22.2%	5.4	786,000	251,706	32.0%	15.2

State Gubernatorial Primary Elections (continued)

Democratic Turnout for Election Years 1912–1928 (continued)

State	1912 Voting-age population	Turnout	%	1916 Voting-age population	Turnout	%	Difference from 1912	1920 Voting-age population	Turnout	%	Difference from 1912	1924 Voting-age population	Turnout	%	Difference from 1912	1928 Voting-age population	Turnout	%	Difference from 1912
GEORGIA								1,418,000	227,905	16.1%						1,481,000	234,769	15.9%	-0.2
HAWAII																			
IDAHO	175,000	14,793	8.5%	199,000	12,961	6.5%	-1.9												
ILLINOIS	1,523,000	299,645	19.7%	1,645,000	238,507	14.5%	-5.2	3,499,000	180,544	5.2%	-14.5	3,883,000	304,401	7.8%	-11.8	4,266,000	244,095	5.7%	-14.0
INDIANA								1,711,000	102,680	6.0%		1,808,000	277,619	15.4%	9.4				
IOWA	628,000	57,370	9.1%	668,000	74,794	11.2%	2.1	1,371,000	38,083	2.8%	-6.4	1,413,000	52,211	3.7%	-5.4				
KANSAS	993,000	60,798	6.1%	960,000	47,435	4.9%	-1.2	988,000	38,739	3.9%	-2.2	1,036,000	81,098	7.8%	1.7	1,084,000	54,982	5.1%	-1.1
KENTUCKY																			
LOUISIANA								905,000	143,553	15.9%		993,000	239,529	24.1%	8.3	1,081,000	288,915	26.7%	10.9
MAINE																			
MARYLAND																			
MASSACHUSETTS																			
MICHIGAN																			
MINNESOTA																			
MISSISSIPPI																			
MISSOURI	947,000	225,387	23.8%	980,000	234,812	24.0%	0.2	1,979,000	178,719	9.0%	-14.8	2,079,000	362,098	17.4%	-6.4	2,179,000	346,343	15.9%	-7.9
MONTANA				254,000	40,001	15.7%		291,000	57,444	19.7%	4.0	292,000	74,638	25.6%	9.8	292,000	67,530	23.1%	7.4
NEBRASKA																			
NEVADA																			
NEW HAMPSHIRE	113,000	6,984	6.2%	115,000	7,834	6.8%	0.6	236,000	9,609	4.1%	-2.1	246,000	9,442	3.8%	-2.3	254,000	12,855	5.1%	-1.1
NEW JERSEY												2,073,000	158,655	7.7%					
NEW MEXICO																			
NEW YORK																			
NORTH CAROLINA								1,218,000	128,233	10.5%		1,348,000	234,770	17.4%	6.9				
NORTH DAKOTA	145,000	10,060	6.9%	152,000	11,420	7.5%	0.6	295,000	7,920	2.7%	-4.3	312,000	11,264	3.6%	-3.3	330,000	11,355	3.4%	-3.5
OHIO				1,522,000	188,343	12.4%		3,253,000	130,909	4.0%	-8.4	3,513,000	225,230	6.4%	-6.0	3,775,000	233,386	6.2%	-6.2
OKLAHOMA																			
OREGON																			
PENNSYLVANIA																			
RHODE ISLAND																			
SOUTH CAROLINA												794,000	175,511	22.1%					
SOUTH DAKOTA				177,000	12,243	6.9%						340,000	10,186	3.0%	-3.9				
TENNESSEE								1,215,000	112,719	9.3%		1,297,000	158,230	12.2%	2.9	1,379,000	217,129	15.7%	6.5

State Gubernatorial Primary Elections (continued)

State Gubernatorial Primary Elections (continued)

Democratic Turnout for Election Years 1912–1928 (continued)

State	1912 Voting-age population	Turnout	%	1916 Voting-age population	Turnout	%	Difference from 1912	1920 Voting-age population	Turnout	%	Difference from 1912	1924 Voting-age population	Turnout	%	Difference from 1912	1928 Voting-age population	Turnout	%	Difference from 1912
TEXAS								2,264,000	449,800	19.9%		2,518,000	606,151	24.1%	4.2	2,772,000	687,588	24.8%	4.9
UTAH																			
VERMONT				100,000	3,563	3.6%		199,000	3,418	1.7%	-1.8	201,000	2,385	1.2%	-2.4	203,000	3,010	1.5%	-2.1
VIRGINIA																			
WASHINGTON	633,000	22,243	3.5%	700,000	32,414	4.6%	1.1	765,000	22,752	3.0%	-0.5	824,000	22,415	2.7%	-0.8	883,000	39,602	4.5%	1.0
WEST VIRGINIA																			
WISCONSIN	624,000	84,572	13.6%	640,000	40,124	6.3%	-7.3	1,354,000	22,435	1.7%	-11.9	1,476,000	21,347	1.4%	-12.1	1,600,000	38,432	2.4%	-11.2
WYOMING																			
Total	6,244,000	846,924	13.6%	8,602,000	984,020	11.4%	-2.1	24,876,000	2,139,646	8.6%	-5.0	26,477,000	3,263,976	12.3%	-1.2	25,948,000	3,151,255	12.1%	-1.4

Other Turnout for Election Years 1912–1928

State	1912 Voting-age population	Turnout	%	1916 Voting-age population	Turnout	%	Difference from 1912*	1920 Voting-age population	Turnout	%	Difference from 1912	1924 Voting-age population	Turnout	%	Difference from 1912	1928 Voting-age population	Turnout	%	Difference from 1912
ILLINOIS	1,523,000	11,901	0.8%	1,645,000	3,049	0.2%	-0.6	3,499,000	1,859	0.1%	-0.7	3,883,000	925	0.0%	-0.8				
IOWA	628,000	3,041	0.5%	666,000	2,405	0.4%	-0.1	1,371,000	791	0.1%	-0.4								
KANSAS	993,000	4,700	0.5%	960,000	3,260	0.3%	-0.1	988,000	821	0.1%	-0.4	1,036,000	303	0.0%	-0.4	1,084,000	197	0.0%	-0.5
MINNESOTA												1,333,000	198,434	14.9%		1,421,000	86,722	6.1%	-8.8
MISSOURI	947,000	7,344	0.8%	980,000	2,804	0.3%	-0.5	1,979,000	1,631	0.1%	-0.7					2,179,000	136	0.0%	-0.8
MONTANA				254,000	2,371	0.9%						292,000	2,636	0.9%	0.0				
NEW JERSEY												2,073,000	76,719	3.7%					
NORTH DAKOTA				152,000	1,726	1.1%						312,000	17	0.0%	-1.1	330,000	181	0.1%	-1.1
SOUTH DAKOTA				177,000	1,225	0.7%						340,000	4,192	1.2%	0.5				
VERMONT				100,000	4	0.0%													
WASHINGTON	633,000	9,788	1.5%	700,000	325	0.0%	-1.5					824,000	7,186	0.9%	-0.7				
WISCONSIN	624,000	15,110	2.4%	640,000	13,826	2.2%	-0.3	1,354,000	35,876	2.6%	0.2	1,476,000	19,885	1.3%	-1.1	1,600,000	13,017	0.8%	-1.6
Total	5,348,000	51,884	1.0%	6,274,000	30,995	0.5%	-0.5	9,191,000	40,978	0.4%	-0.5	9,496,000	233,578	2.5%	1.5	8,687,000	176,972	2.0%	1.1

*Percentage point difference between turnout in current year and initial year listed in chart. If data do not appear for a state in the initial year listed, the difference is calculated from the first year in which data do appear for that state.

UNITED STATES SENATE PRIMARY ELECTIONS

Election Years 1912–1928

State*	1912** Voting-age population	Turnout	%	1916 Voting-age population	Turnout	%	Difference % from 1912***	1920 Voting-age population	Turnout	%	Difference from 1912	1924 Voting-age population	Turnout	%	Difference from 1912	1928 Voting-age population	Turnout	%	Difference from 1912
ALABAMA																			
ALASKA																			
ARIZONA																			
ARKANSAS																			
CALIFORNIA				1,764,000	422,093	23.9%										3,020,000	621,384	20.6%	-3.4
COLORADO	463,000	106,434	23.0%					523,000	129,483	24.8%	1.8	542,000	180,903	29.7%	8.7				
CONNECTICUT																			
DELAWARE																			
DISTRICT OF COLUMBIA																			
FLORIDA																			
GEORGIA																			
HAWAII																			
IDAHO																			
ILLINOIS								3,499,000	972,682	27.8%		3,883,000	1,128,450	29.1%	1.3	4,266,000	1,715,149	40.2%	12.4
INDIANA								1,711,000	239,796	14.0%									
IOWA								1,371,000	250,846	18.3%		1,413,000	417,936	29.6%	11.3				
KANSAS	933,000	175,200	18.8%					988,000	192,881	19.5%	0.7	1,036,000	301,265	29.1%	10.3				
KENTUCKY												1,338,000	239,387	17.9%					
LOUISIANA																			
MAINE																			
MARYLAND																			
MASSACHUSETTS																			
MICHIGAN																			
MINNESOTA																			
MISSISSIPPI																			
MISSOURI				980,000	386,201	39.4%		1,979,000	370,266	18.7%	-20.7					2,179,000	684,582	31.4%	-8.0
MONTANA				254,000	87,101	34.3%						292,000	107,981	37.0%	2.7	292,000	117,300	40.2%	5.9
NEBRASKA																			
NEVADA																			
NEW HAMPSHIRE								236,000	62,549	26.5%		246,000	39,655	16.1%	-10.4				
NEW JERSEY												1,812,000	545,767	30.1%		2,073,000	782,155	37.7%	7.6
NEW MEXICO																			
NEW YORK																			

United States Senate Primary Elections (continued)

United States Senate Primary Elections (continued)

Election Years 1912–1928 (continued)

State	1912 Voting-age population	Turnout	%	1916 Voting-age population	Turnout	%	Difference from 1912	1920 Voting-age population	Turnout	%	Difference from 1912	1924 Voting-age population	Turnout	%	Difference from 1912	1928 Voting-age population	Turnout	%	Difference from 1912
NORTH CAROLINA																			
NORTH DAKOTA				152,000	84,168	55.4%		295,000	119,814	40.6%	-14.8					330,000	196,008	59.4%	4.0
OHIO				1,522,000	433,607	28.5%		3,253,000	449,449	13.8%	-14.7					3,775,000	727,317	19.3%	-9.2
OKLAHOMA	451,000	149,322	33.1%					1,012,000	260,033	25.7%	-7.4	1,105,000	406,583	36.8%	3.7				
OREGON																			
PENNSYLVANIA																5,074,000	925,679	18.2%	
RHODE ISLAND																			
SOUTH CAROLINA																			
SOUTH DAKOTA												340,000	92,253	27.1%					
TENNESSEE																			
TEXAS																			
UTAH																			
VERMONT				100,000	47,707	47.7%		199,000	62,098	31.2%	-16.5					203,000	56,982	28.1%	-19.6
VIRGINIA																			
WASHINGTON				700,000	216,150	30.9%		765,000	206,254	27.0%	-3.9					883,000	281,813	31.9%	1.0
WEST VIRGINIA																			
WISCONSIN				640,000	216,371	33.8%		1,354,000	423,268	31.3%	-1.7					1,600,000	523,394	32.7%	-0.3
WYOMING				94,000	16,922	18.0%						112,000	37,507	33.5%	15.5	119,000	42,670	35.9%	17.9
Total	1,847,000	430,956	23.3%	6,206,000	1,910,320	30.8%	7.4	17,185,000	3,739,419	21.8%	-2.5	12,119,000	3,477,687	28.7%		23,814,000	6,674,433	28.0%	-1.1

*Overall primary turnout reflects only states with primaries in both parties. To find single party primary results, see partisan primary charts.

**A handful of states held popular elections for Senate in 1912 even before the Seventeenth Amendment was ratified in 1913.

***Percentage point difference between turnout in current year and initial year listed in chart. If data do not appear for a state in the initial year listed, the difference is calculated from the first year in which data do appear for that state.

UNITED STATES SENATE PRIMARY ELECTIONS

Republican Turnout for Election Years 1912–1928

State	1912* Voting-age population	Turnout	%	1916 Voting-age population	Turnout	%	Difference from 1912**	1920 Voting-age population	Turnout	%	Difference from 1912	1924 Voting-age population	Turnout	%	Difference from 1912	1928 Voting-age population	Turnout	%	Difference from 1912
ALABAMA																			
ALASKA																			
ARIZONA																			
ARKANSAS																			
CALIFORNIA				1,764,000	307,793	17.4%										3,020,000	512,929	17.0%	-0.5
COLORADO	463,000	104,995	22.7%					523,000	76,800	14.7%	6.1	542,000	113,336	20.9%	12.3				
CONNECTICUT																			
DELAWARE																			
DISTRICT OF COLUMBIA																			
FLORIDA																			
GEORGIA																			
HAWAII																			
IDAHO																			
ILLINOIS								3,499,000	799,402	22.8%		3,883,000	857,360	22.1%	-0.8	4,266,000	1,467,331	34.4%	11.5
INDIANA								1,711,000	158,931	9.3%									
IOWA								1,371,000	212,331	15.5%		1,413,000	363,241	25.7%	10.2				
KANSAS	933,000	115,922	12.4%					988,000	156,301	15.8%	3.4	1,036,000	236,524	22.8%	10.4				
KENTUCKY												1,338,000	89,151	6.7%					
LOUISIANA																			
MAINE																			
MARYLAND																			
MASSACHUSETTS																			
MICHIGAN																			
MINNESOTA												1,333,000	230,390	17.3%		1,421,000	263,210	18.5%	1.2
MISSISSIPPI																			
MISSOURI				980,000	189,555	19.3%		1,979,000	192,749	9.7%	-9.6					2,179,000	339,409	15.6%	-3.8
MONTANA				254,000	48,985	19.3%						292,000	70,125	24.0%	4.7	292,000	67,618	23.2%	3.9
NEBRASKA																			
NEVADA								45,000	7,111	15.8%									
NEW HAMPSHIRE								236,000	53,240	22.6%		246,000	31,373	12.8%	-9.8				
NEW JERSEY												1,812,000	431,744	23.8%		2,073,000	574,294	27.7%	3.9
NEW MEXICO																			
NEW YORK																			

United States Senate Primary Elections (continued)

United States Senate Primary Elections (continued)

Republican Turnout for Election Years 1912–1928 (continued)

State	1912			1916				1920				1924				1928			
	Voting-age population	Turnout	%	Voting-age population	Turnout	%	Difference from 1912	Voting-age population	Turnout	%	Difference from 1912	Voting-age population	Turnout	%	Difference from 1912	Voting-age population	Turnout	%	Difference from 1912
NORTH CAROLINA																			
NORTH DAKOTA				152,000	68,885	45.3%		295,000	111,576	37.8%	-7.5					330,000	184,725	56.0%	10.7
OHIO				1,522,000	271,994	17.9%		3,253,000	320,906	9.9%	-8.0					3,775,000	539,678	14.3%	-3.6
OKLAHOMA	451,000	13,529	3.0%					1,012,000	69,091	6.8%	3.8	1,105,000	107,847	9.8%	6.8				
OREGON																			
PENNSYLVANIA																5,074,000	815,387	16.1%	
RHODE ISLAND																			
SOUTH CAROLINA																			
SOUTH DAKOTA	172,000	73,981	43.0%									340,000	77,505	22.8%	-20.2				
TENNESSEE																			
TEXAS																			
UTAH																			
VERMONT				100,000	43,885	43.9%		199,000	52,711	26.5%	-17.4					203,000	53,908	26.6%	-17.3
VIRGINIA																			
WASHINGTON				700,000	186,224	26.6%		765,000	186,250	24.3%	-2.3					883,000	247,857	28.1%	1.5
WEST VIRGINIA																			
WISCONSIN				640,000	166,296	26.0%		1,354,000	368,690	27.2%	1.9					1,600,000	484,135	30.3%	4.9
WYOMING				94,000	14,045	14.9%						112,000	22,721	20.3%	5.3	119,000	30,225	25.4%	10.5
Total	2,019,000	243,398	12.1%	6,206,000	1,297,662	20.9%	8.9	17,230,000	2,766,089	16.1%	3.9	13,452,000	2,631,317	19.6%	7.4	25,235,000	5,580,706	22.1%	10.0

Democratic Turnout for Election Years 1912–1928

State	1912*			1916				1920				1924				1928			
	Voting-age population	Turnout	%	Voting-age population	Turnout	%	Difference from 1912**	Voting-age population	Turnout	%	Difference from 1912	Voting-age population	Turnout	%	Difference from 1912	Voting-age population	Turnout	%	Difference from 1912
ALABAMA								1,143,000	130,814	11.4%									
ALASKA																			
ARIZONA																			
ARKANSAS																			
CALIFORNIA				1,764,000	77,830	4.4%										3,020,000	97,442	3.2%	-1.2
COLORADO	463,000	104,995	22.7%					526,000	52,683	10.0%	-4.3	542,000	47,567	8.8%	-5.6				
CONNECTICUT																			
DELAWARE																			
DISTRICT OF COLUMBIA																			
FLORIDA																786,000	238,988	30.4%	

United States Senate Primary Elections (continued)

Democratic Turnout for Election Years 1912–1928 (continued)

State	1912 Voting-age population	Turnout	%	1916 Voting-age population	Turnout	%	Difference from 1912	1920 Voting-age population	Turnout	%	Difference from 1912	1924 Voting-age population	Turnout	%	Difference from 1912	1928 Voting-age population	Turnout	%	Difference from 1912
GEORGIA												1,449,000	220,453	15.2%					
HAWAII																			
IDAHO																			
ILLINOIS								3,499,000	171,267	4.9%		3,823,000	270,144	7.1%	2.2	4,266,000	247,818	5.8%	0.9
INDIANA								1,711,000	80,865	4.7%									
IOWA								1,371,000	38,515	2.8%		1,413,000	54,605	3.9%	1.1				
KANSAS	933,000	54,667	5.9%					988,000	35,834	3.6%	-2.2	1,036,000	64,469	6.2%	0.4				
KENTUCKY												1,338,000	150,236	11.2%					
LOUISIANA												993,000	189,859	19.1%					
MAINE																			
MARYLAND																			
MASSACHUSETTS																			
MICHIGAN																			
MINNESOTA																			
MISSISSIPPI																1,002,000	119,491	11.9%	
MISSOURI				980,000	194,255	19.8%		1,979,000	176,002	8.9%	-10.9					2,179,000	345,035	15.8%	-4.0
MONTANA				254,000	35,796	14.1%						292,000	35,029	12.0%	-2.1	292,000	49,682	17.0%	2.9
NEBRASKA																			
NEVADA																			
NEW HAMPSHIRE								236,000	9,309	3.9%		246,000	8,282	3.4%	-0.6				
NEW JERSEY												1,812,000	114,023	6.3%		2,073,000	207,861	10.0%	3.7
NEW MEXICO																			
NEW YORK																			
NORTH CAROLINA																			
NORTH DAKOTA				152,000	13,436	8.8%		295,000	8,238	2.8%	-6.0					330,000	11,086	3.4%	-5.5
OHIO				1,522,000	161,613	10.6%		3,253,000	128,543	4.0%	-6.7					3,775,000	187,639	5.0%	-5.6
OKLAHOMA	451,000	124,687	27.6%					1,012,000	186,697	18.4%	-9.2	1,105,000	298,536	27.0%	-0.6				
OREGON																			
PENNSYLVANIA																5,074,000	106,904	2.1%	
RHODE ISLAND																			
SOUTH CAROLINA												794,000	195,890	24.7%					
SOUTH DAKOTA												340,000	10,379	3.1%					
TENNESSEE																1,379,000	184,768	13.4%	

United States Senate Primary Elections (continued)

Democratic Turnout for Election Years 1912–1928 (continued)

State	1912 Voting-age population	Turnout	%	1916 Voting-age population	Turnout	%	Difference from 1912	1920 Voting-age population	Turnout	%	Difference from 1912	1924 Voting-age population	Turnout	%	Difference from 1912	1928 Voting-age population	Turnout	%	Difference from 1912
TEXAS																2,772,000	636,850	23.0%	
UTAH																			
VERMONT				100,000	3,822	3.8%		199,000	9,387	4.7%	0.9					203,000	3,074	1.5%	-2.3
VIRGINIA																			
WASHINGTON				700,000	29,630	4.2%		765,000	20,004	2.6%	-1.6					883,000	33,956	3.8%	-0.4
WEST VIRGINIA																			
WISCONSIN				640,000	36,795	5.7%		1,354,000	19,952	1.5%	-4.1					1,600,000	38,432	2.4%	-3.2
WYOMING				94,000	2,877	3.1%						113,000	14,786	13.1%	10.0	119,000	12,445	10.5%	7.4
Total	2,019,000	243,398	12.1%	6,206,000	556,054	9.0%	-4.3	18,331,000	1,068,110	5.8%	-7.6	15,296,000	1,674,348	10.9%	-2.4	29,753,000	2,521,471	8.5%	-4.9

Other Turnout for Election Years 1912–1928

State	1912* Voting-age population	Turnout	%	1916 Voting-age population	Turnout	%	Difference from 1912**	1920 Voting-age population	Turnout	%	Difference from 1912	1924 Voting-age population	Turnout	%	Difference from 1912	1928 Voting-age population	Turnout	%	Difference from 1912
CALIFORNIA				1,764,000	36,470	2.1%										3,020,000	11,013	0.4%	-1.7
ILLINOIS								3,499,000	2,013	0.1%		3,883,000	946	0.0%	0.0				
KANSAS	933,000	4,611	0.5%					988,000	746	0.1%	-0.4	1,036,000	272	0.0%	-0.5				
MINNESOTA												1,333,000	197,145	14.8%		1,421,000	95,622	6.7%	-8.1
MISSOURI				980,000	2,391	0.2%		1,979,000	1,515	0.1%	-0.2					2,179,000	138	0.0%	-0.2
MONTANA				254,000	2,320	0.9%						292,000	2,827	1.0%	0.1				
NORTH DAKOTA				152,000	1,847	1.2%										330,000	197	0.1%	-1.2
OKLAHOMA	451,000	11,106	2.5%					1,012,000	4,245	0.4%	-2.0	1,105,000	200	0.0%	-2.4				
PENNSYLVANIA																5,074,000	3,388	0.1%	
SOUTH DAKOTA												340,000	4,369	1.3%					
WASHINGTON				700,000	296	0.0%													
WISCONSIN				640,000	13,280	2.1%		1,354,000	34,626	2.6%	0.5					1,600,000	827	0.1%	-2.0
Total	1,384,000	15,717	1.1%	4,490,000	56,604	1.3%	0.1	8,832,000	43,145	0.5%	-0.6	7,989,000	205,759	2.6%	1.4	13,624,000	111,185	0.8%	-0.3

*A handful of states held popular elections for Senate in 1912 even before the Seventeenth Amendment was ratified in 1913.

**Percentage point difference between turnout in current year and initial year listed in chart. If data do not appear for a state in the initial year listed, the difference is calculated from the first year in which data do appear for that state.

Midterm Turnout Election Based on Highest Statewide Turnout, Election Years 1910–1926

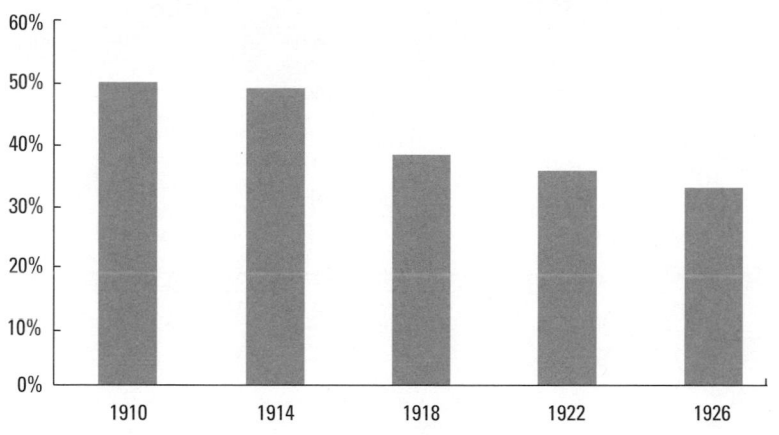

YEAR	VOTING-AGE POPULATION	TOTAL	%
1910	24,388,000	12,127,397	49.7%
1914	27,974,000	13,646,100	48.8%
1918	33,725,000	12,768,082	37.9%
1922	57,897,000	20,410,828	35.3%
1926	62,807,000	20,398,829	32.5%

Partisan Turnout Midterm Election Based on Aggregate House of Representatives Turnout, Election Years 1910–1926

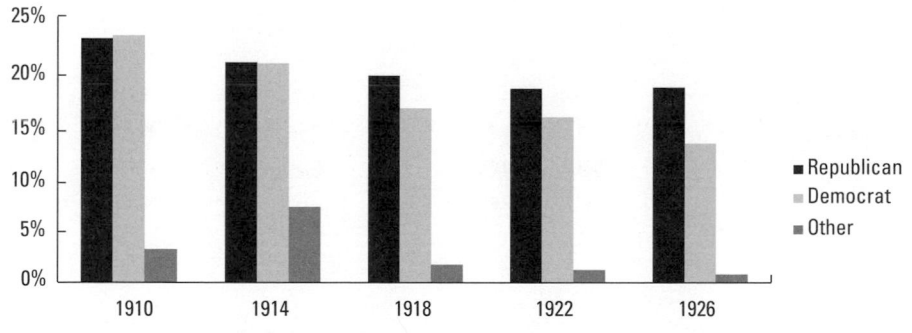

- ■ Republican
- ■ Democrat
- ■ Other

YEAR	VOTING-AGE POPULATION	REPUBLICAN TURNOUT	%	DEMOCRAT TURNOUT	%	OTHER TURNOUT	%
1910	24,388,000	5,643,621	23.1%	5,709,136	23.4%	774,640	3.2%
1914	27,974,000	5,832,617	20.9%	5,806,505	20.8%	2,006,978	7.2%
1918	33,725,000	6,610,510	19.6%	5,568,265	16.5%	589,307	1.7%
1922	57,897,000	10,633,303	18.4%	9,062,740	15.7%	714,785	1.2%
1926	62,807,000	11,610,611	18.5%	8,271,764	13.2%	516,454	0.8%

STATE GUBERNATORIAL GENERAL ELECTIONS

Election Years 1910–1926

State	1910 Voting-age population	1910 Turnout	1910 %	1914 Voting-age population	1914 Turnout	1914 %	1914 Difference from 1910*	1918 Voting-age population	1918 Turnout	1918 %	1918 Difference from 1910	1922 Voting-age population	1922 Turnout	1922 %	1922 Difference from 1910	1926 Voting-age population	1926 Turnout	1926 %	1926 Difference from 1910
ALABAMA	512,000	98,772	19.3%	537,000	77,877	14.5%	-4.8	562,000	68,243	12.1%	-7.1	1,196,000	146,477	12.2%	-7.0	1,279,000	115,037	9.0%	-10.3
ALASKA																			
ARIZONA				106,000	51,007	48.1%		132,000	51,959	39.4%	-8.8	148,000	67,909	45.9%	-2.2	157,000	79,559	50.7%	2.6
ARKANSAS	395,000	150,678	38.1%	419,000	135,524	32.3%	-5.8	442,000	72,984	16.5%	-21.6	892,000	128,042	14.4%	-23.8	933,000	152,704	16.4%	-21.8
CALIFORNIA	715,000	385,713	53.9%	1,660,000	946,776	57.0%	3.1	1,921,000	688,670	35.8%	-18.1	2,357,000	965,777	41.0%	-13.0	2,850,000	1,149,029	40.3%	-13.6
COLORADO	452,000	225,605	49.9%	481,000	265,229	55.1%	5.2	509,000	220,341	43.3%	-6.6	536,000	278,215	51.9%	2.0	555,000	306,402	55.2%	5.3
CONNECTICUT	258,000	166,181	64.4%	281,000	181,107	64.5%	0.0	303,000	167,436	55.3%	-9.2	680,000	325,073	47.8%	-16.6	746,000	302,668	40.6%	-23.8
DELAWARE																			
DISTRICT OF COLUMBIA																			
FLORIDA																			
GEORGIA								696,000	70,621	10.1%		1,438,000	75,019	5.2%	-4.9	1,470,000	47,267	3.2%	-6.9
HAWAII																			
IDAHO	165,000	86,159	52.2%	190,000	107,913	56.8%	4.6	215,000	96,125	44.7%	-7.5	226,000	127,864	56.6%	4.4	231,000	120,620	52.2%	0.0
ILLINOIS																			
INDIANA																			
IOWA	613,000	412,964	67.4%	651,000	422,579	64.9%	-2.5	689,000	381,107	55.3%	-12.1	1,398,000	594,900	42.6%	-24.8	1,439,000	527,858	36.7%	-30.7
KANSAS	497,000	325,954	65.6%	950,000	528,207	55.6%	-10.0	976,000	433,743	44.4%	-21.1	1,019,000	532,803	52.3%	-13.3	1,067,000	507,901	47.6%	-18.0
KENTUCKY																			
LOUISIANA																			
MAINE	203,000	140,948	69.4%	206,000	141,666	68.8%	-0.7	209,000	123,119	58.9%	-10.5	427,000	178,969	41.9%	-27.5	433,000	181,524	41.9%	-27.5
MARYLAND																915,000	358,075	39.1%	
MASSACHUSETTS	766,000	440,831	57.5%	821,000	458,504	55.8%	-1.7	876,000	422,370	48.2%	-9.3	1,963,000	889,543	45.3%	-12.2	2,099,000	1,012,166	48.2%	-9.3
MICHIGAN	757,000	383,762	50.7%	903,000	440,448	48.8%	-1.9	1,827,000	434,376	23.8%	-26.9	2,084,000	583,661	28.0%	-22.7	2,359,000	630,752	26.7%	-24.0
MINNESOTA	585,000	294,607	50.4%	611,000	343,255	56.2%	5.8	636,000	369,698	58.1%	7.8	1,302,000	685,138	52.6%	2.3	1,389,000	700,632	50.4%	0.1
MISSISSIPPI																			
MISSOURI																			
MONTANA																			
NEBRASKA	329,000	237,109	72.1%	341,000	238,717	70.0%	-2.1	354,000	222,183	62.8%	-9.3	715,000	391,440	54.7%	-17.3	754,000	413,745	54.9%	-17.2
NEVADA	32,000	20,626	64.5%	44,000	21,551	49.0%	-15.5	44,000	24,720	56.2%	-8.3	46,000	28,652	62.3%	-2.2	48,000	30,895	64.4%	-0.1
NEW HAMPSHIRE	111,000	84,167	75.8%	114,000	84,108	73.8%	-2.0	116,000	71,077	61.3%	-14.6	242,000	131,686	54.4%	-21.4	251,000	129,630	51.6%	-24.2
NEW JERSEY																			
NEW MEXICO								88,000	47,032	53.4%		170,000	110,537	65.0%	11.6	173,000	109,091	63.1%	9.6
NEW YORK	2,381,000	1,437,041	60.4%	2,564,000	1,440,012	56.2%	-4.2	5,038,000	2,132,448	42.3%	-18.0	5,630,000	2,531,775	45.0%	-15.4	6,300,000	2,913,776	46.3%	-14.1

State Gubernatorial General Elections *(continued)*

Election Years 1910–1926 *(continued)*

State	1910 Voting-age population	1910 Turnout	1910 %	1914 Voting-age population	1914 Turnout	1914 %	1914 Difference from 1910	1918 Voting-age population	1918 Turnout	1918 %	1918 Difference from 1910	1922 Voting-age population	1922 Turnout	1922 %	1922 Difference from 1910	1926 Voting-age population	1926 Turnout	1926 %	1926 Difference from 1910
NORTH CAROLINA																			
NORTH DAKOTA	142,000	94,084	66.3%	149,000	89,307	59.9%	-6.3	156,000	91,250	58.5%	-7.8	306,000	191,369	62.5%	-3.7	323,000	160,264	49.6%	-16.6
OHIO	1,337,000	924,463	69.1%	1,469,000	1,129,223	76.9%	7.7	1,601,000	960,862	60.0%	-9.1	3,420,000	1,625,799	47.5%	-21.6	3,680,000	1,396,272	37.9%	-31.2
OKLAHOMA	434,000	247,666	57.1%	477,000	253,687	53.2%	-3.9	973,000	194,435	20.0%	-37.1	1,072,000	514,616	48.0%	-9.1	1,165,000	387,308	33.2%	-23.8
OREGON	230,000	117,690	51.2%	410,000	248,052	60.5%	9.3	446,000	152,987	34.3%	-16.9	491,000	232,556	47.4%	-3.8	538,000	225,945	42.0%	-9.2
PENNSYLVANIA	1,837,000	931,441	50.7%	1,977,000	1,110,752	56.2%	5.5	2,118,000	905,025	42.7%	-8.0	4,589,000	1,464,672	31.9%	-18.8	4,943,000	1,503,668	30.4%	-20.3
RHODE ISLAND	121,000	67,622	55.9%	129,000	78,023	60.5%	4.6	137,000	80,361	58.7%	2.8	310,000	158,410	51.1%	4.8	337,000	166,190	49.3%	-6.6
SOUTH CAROLINA	336,000	30,902	9.2%	359,000	34,690	9.7%	0.5	381,000	25,267	6.6%	-2.6	788,000	34,065	4.3%	-4.9	805,000	16,589	2.1%	-7.1
SOUTH DAKOTA	170,000	105,812	62.2%	174,000	99,141	57.0%	-5.3	316,000	96,160	30.4%	-31.8	334,000	175,426	52.5%	-9.7	350,000	183,832	52.5%	-9.7
TENNESSEE	551,000	256,475	46.5%	575,000	256,004	44.5%	-2.0	599,000	158,147	26.4%	-20.1	1,268,000	243,588	19.2%	-27.3	1,350,000	131,368	9.7%	-36.8
TEXAS	955,000	230,341	24.1%	1,052,000	214,781	20.4%	-3.7	1,150,000	177,355	15.4%	-8.7	2,431,000	407,526	16.8%	-7.4	2,685,000	265,507	9.9%	-14.2
UTAH																			
VERMONT	100,000	54,828	54.8%	100,000	55,163	55.2%	0.3	100,000	42,323	42.3%	-12.5	200,000	69,307	34.7%	-20.2	202,000	73,272	36.3%	-18.6
VIRGINIA																			
WASHINGTON																			
WEST VIRGINIA																			
WISCONSIN	610,000	319,522	52.4%	644,000	325,430	50.5%	-1.8	676,000	331,582	49.1%	-3.3	1,432,000	481,828	33.6%	-18.7	1,554,000	552,912	35.6%	-16.8
WYOMING	82,000	37,926	46.3%	92,000	43,377	47.1%	0.9	102,000	42,465	41.6%	-4.6	110,000	62,184	56.5%	10.3	117,000	70,041	59.9%	13.6
Total	15,676,000	8,309,889	53.0%	18,486,000	9,822,110	53.1%	0.3	24,388,000	9,356,471	38.4%	-14.5	39,220,000	14,434,826	36.8%	-16.0	43,497,000	14,922,508	34.3%	-18.5

*Percentage point difference between turnout in current year and initial year listed in chart. If data do not appear for a state in the initial year listed, the difference is calculated from the first year in which data do appear for that state.

STATE GUBERNATORIAL GENERAL ELECTIONS

Republican Turnout for Election Years 1910–1926

State	1910			1914				1918				1922				1926			
	Voting-age population	Turnout	%	Voting-age population	Turnout	%	Difference from 1910*	Voting-age population	Turnout	%	Difference from 1910	Voting-age population	Turnout	%	Difference from 1910	Voting-age population	Turnout	%	Difference from 1910
ALABAMA	512,000	19,210	3.8%	537,000	11,773	2.2%	-1.6	562,000	13,497	2.4%	-1.4	1,196,000	31,175	2.6%	-1.1	1,279,000	21,605	1.7%	-2.1
ALASKA																			
ARIZONA				106,000	17,602	16.6%		132,000	25,927	19.6%	3.0	148,000	30,599	20.7%	4.1	157,000	39,580	25.2%	8.6
ARKANSAS	395,000	39,870	10.1%	419,000	30,947	7.4%	-2.7					892,000	28,055	3.1%	-6.9	933,000	35,969	3.9%	-6.2
CALIFORNIA	715,000	177,191	24.8%	1,660,000	291,990	17.6%	-7.2	1,921,000	387,547	20.2%	-4.6	2,357,000	576,445	24.5%	-0.3	2,850,000	814,815	28.6%	3.8
COLORADO	452,000	97,648	21.6%	481,000	129,096	26.8%	5.2	509,000	112,693	22.1%	0.5	536,000	134,353	25.1%	3.5	555,000	116,756	21.0%	-0.6
CONNECTICUT	258,000	73,528	28.5%	281,000	91,262	32.5%	4.0	303,000	84,891	28.0%	-0.5	680,000	170,231	25.0%	-3.5	746,000	192,425	25.8%	-2.7
DELAWARE																			
DISTRICT OF COLUMBIA																			
FLORIDA																			
GEORGIA																			
HAWAII																			
IDAHO	165,000	39,961	24.2%	190,000	40,349	21.2%	-3.0	215,000	57,626	26.8%	2.6	226,000	50,538	22.4%	-1.9	231,000	61,575	26.7%	2.4
ILLINOIS																			
INDIANA																			
IOWA	613,000	205,678	33.6%	651,000	207,881	31.9%	-1.6	689,000	192,662	28.0%	-5.6	1,398,000	419,648	30.0%	-3.5	1,439,000	377,443	26.2%	-7.3
KANSAS	497,000	162,181	32.6%	950,000	209,543	22.1%	-10.6	976,000	287,957	29.5%	-3.1	1,019,000	252,602	24.8%	-7.8	1,067,000	321,540	30.1%	-2.5
KENTUCKY																			
LOUISIANA																			
MAINE	203,000	64,644	31.8%	206,000	58,887	28.6%	-3.3	209,000	64,069	30.7%	-1.2	427,000	103,713	24.3%	-7.6	433,000	100,776	23.3%	-8.6
MARYLAND																915,000	148,145	16.2%	
MASSACHUSETTS	766,000	194,173	25.3%	821,000	198,627	24.2%	-1.2	876,000	214,863	24.5%	-0.8	1,963,000	464,873	23.7%	-1.7	2,099,000	595,006	28.3%	3.0
MICHIGAN	757,000	202,803	26.8%	903,000	176,254	19.5%	-7.3	1,827,000	266,738	14.6%	-12.2	2,084,000	356,933	17.1%	-9.7	2,331,000	399,564	17.1%	-9.6
MINNESOTA	585,000	164,185	28.1%	611,000	143,730	23.5%	-4.5	636,000	166,515	26.2%	-1.9	1,302,000	309,756	23.8%	-4.3	1,389,000	395,779	28.5%	0.4
MISSISSIPPI																			
MISSOURI																			
MONTANA																			
NEBRASKA	329,000	123,070	37.4%	341,000	101,229	29.7%	-7.7	354,000	120,888	34.1%	-3.3	715,000	163,935	22.9%	-14.5	754,000	206,120	27.3%	-10.1
NEVADA	32,000	10,435	32.6%	44,000	8,537	19.4%	-13.2	44,000	11,845	26.9%	-5.7	46,000	13,215	28.7%	-3.9	48,000	16,374	34.1%	1.5
NEW HAMPSHIRE	111,000	44,908	40.5%	114,000	46,413	40.7%	0.3	116,000	38,465	33.2%	-7.3	242,000	61,526	25.4%	-15.0	251,000	77,394	30.8%	-9.6
NEW JERSEY																			
NEW MEXICO								88,000	23,752	27.0%		170,000	49,363	29.0%	2.0	173,000	56,294	32.5%	5.5
NEW YORK	2,381,000	622,299	26.1%	2,564,000	686,701	26.8%	0.6	5,038,000	995,094	19.8%	-6.4	5,630,000	1,011,725	18.0%	-8.2	6,300,000	1,276,137	20.3%	-5.9

State Gubernatorial General Elections *(continued)*

Republican Turnout for Election Years 1910–1926 *(continued)*

State	1910 Voting-age population	Turnout	%	1914 Voting-age population	Turnout	%	Difference from 1910	1918 Voting-age population	Turnout	%	Difference from 1910	1922 Voting-age population	Turnout	%	Difference from 1910	1926 Voting-age population	Turnout	%	Difference from 1910
NORTH CAROLINA																			
NORTH DAKOTA	142,000	44,555	31.4%	149,000	44,279	29.7%	-1.7	156,000	54,517	34.9%	3.6	306,000	110,321	36.1%	4.7	323,000	131,003	40.6%	9.2
OHIO	1,337,000	376,700	28.2%	1,469,000	523,074	35.6%	7.4	1,601,000	474,459	29.6%	1.5	3,420,000	803,300	23.5%	-4.7	3,680,000	685,957	18.6%	-9.5
OKLAHOMA	434,000	99,527	22.9%	477,000	95,904	20.1%	-2.8	973,000	82,865	8.5%	-14.4	1,072,000	230,469	21.5%	-1.4	1,165,000	170,714	14.7%	-8.3
OREGON	230,000	48,751	21.2%	410,000	121,037	29.5%	8.3	446,000	81,067	18.2%	-3.0	491,000	99,164	20.2%	-1.0	538,000	120,073	22.3%	1.1
PENNSYLVANIA	1,837,000	415,614	22.6%	1,077,000	688,706	20.8%	7.2	2,118,000	552,537	26.1%	3.5	4,500,000	831,006	10.1%	-4.5	4,943,000	1,102,023	22.3%	-0.3
RHODE ISLAND	121,000	33,540	27.7%	129,000	41,996	32.6%	4.8	137,000	42,682	31.2%	3.4	310,000	74,724	24.1%	-3.6	337,000	89,574	26.6%	-1.1
SOUTH CAROLINA																			
SOUTH DAKOTA	170,000	61,744	36.3%	174,000	49,138	28.2%	-8.1	316,000	51,175	16.2%	-20.1	334,000	78,984	23.6%	-12.7	350,000	74,101	21.2%	-15.1
TENNESSEE	551,000	133,074	24.2%	575,000	116,677	20.3%	-3.9	599,000	59,519	9.9%	-14.2	1,268,000	102,586	8.1%	-16.1	1,350,000	46,238	3.4%	-20.7
TEXAS	955,000	26,191	2.7%	1,052,000	11,411	1.1%	-1.7	1,150,000	26,713	2.3%	-0.4	2,431,000	73,327	3.0%	0.3	2,685,000	31,531	1.2%	-1.6
UTAH																			
VERMONT	100,000	35,263	35.3%	100,000	36,972	37.0%	1.7	100,000	28,358	28.4%	-6.9	200,000	52,104	26.1%	-9.2	202,000	44,564	22.1%	-13.2
VIRGINIA																			
WASHINGTON																			
WEST VIRGINIA																			
WISCONSIN	610,000	161,619	26.5%	644,000	140,787	21.9%	-4.6	676,000	155,799	23.0%	-3.4	1,432,000	367,929	25.7%	-0.8	1,554,000	350,927	22.6%	-3.9
WYOMING	82,000	15,235	18.6%	92,000	19,174	20.8%	2.3	102,000	23,825	23.4%	4.8	110,000	30,387	27.6%	9.0	117,000	35,651	30.5%	11.9
Total	15,340,000	3,693,597	24.1%	18,127,000	4,239,975	23.4%	-0.6	22,869,000	4,698,545	20.5%	-3.4	36,994,000	7,083,676	19.1%	-4.8	41,194,000	8,136,453	19.8%	-4.2

Democratic Turnout for Election Years 1910–1926

State	1910 Voting-age population	Turnout	%	1914 Voting-age population	Turnout	%	Difference from 1910*	1918 Voting-age population	Turnout	%	Difference from 1910	1922 Voting-age population	Turnout	%	Difference from 1910	1926 Voting-age population	Turnout	%	Difference from 1910
ALABAMA	512,000	77,694	15.2%	537,000	61,307	11.4%	-3.8	562,000	54,746	9.7%	-5.4	1,196,000	113,605	9.5%	-5.7	1,279,000	93,432	7.3%	-7.9
ALASKA																			
ARIZONA				106,000	25,226	23.8%		132,000	25,588	19.4%	-4.4	148,000	37,310	25.2%	1.4	157,000	39,979	25.5%	1.7
ARKANSAS	395,000	101,612	25.7%	419,000	94,143	22.5%	-3.3	442,000	68,192	15.4%	-10.3	892,000	99,987	11.2%	-14.5	933,000	116,735	12.5%	-13.2
CALIFORNIA	715,000	154,835	21.7%	1,660,000	116,121	7.0%	-14.7	1,921,000	20,605	1.1%	-20.6	2,357,000	347,520	14.7%	-6.9	2,850,000	282,451	9.9%	-11.7
COLORADO	452,000	115,627	25.6%	481,000	90,640	18.8%	-6.7	509,000	102,397	20.1%	-5.5	536,000	138,098	25.8%	0.2	555,000	183,342	33.0%	7.5
CONNECTICUT	258,000	77,243	29.9%	281,000	73,888	26.3%	-3.6	303,000	76,849	25.4%	-4.6	680,000	148,641	21.9%	-8.1	746,000	107,045	14.3%	-15.6
DELAWARE																			
DISTRICT OF COLUMBIA																			
FLORIDA																			

State Gubernatorial General Elections (continued)

State Gubernatorial General Elections (continued)

Democratic Turnout for Election Years 1910–1926 (continued)

State	1910 Voting-age population	Turnout	%	1914 Voting-age population	Turnout	%	Difference from 1910	1918 Voting-age population	Turnout	%	Difference from 1910	1922 Voting-age population	Turnout	%	Difference from 1910	1926 Voting-age population	Turnout	%	Difference from 1910
GEORGIA								696,000	70,621	10.1%		1,438,000	75,019	5.2%	-4.9	1,470,000	47,267	3.2%	-6.9
HAWAII																			
IDAHO	165,000	40,856	24.8%	190,000	47,618	25.1%	0.3	215,000	38,499	17.9%	-6.9	226,000	36,810	16.3%	-8.5	231,000	24,837	10.8%	-14.0
ILLINOIS																			
INDIANA																			
IOWA	613,000	187,353	30.6%	651,000	182,036	28.0%	-2.6	689,000	178,815	26.0%	-4.6	1,398,000	175,252	12.5%	-18.0	1,439,000	150,415	10.5%	-20.1
KANSAS	482,000	146,014	30.3%	950,000	161,696	17.0%	-13.3	976,000	133,054	13.6%	-16.7	1,019,000	271,058	26.6%	-3.7	1,067,000	179,308	16.8%	-13.5
KENTUCKY																			
LOUISIANA																			
MAINE	203,000	73,304	36.1%	206,000	62,076	30.1%	-6.0	209,000	59,050	28.3%	-7.9	427,000	75,256	17.6%	-18.5	433,000	80,748	18.6%	-17.5
MARYLAND																915,000	207,435	22.7%	
MASSACHUSETTS	766,000	229,352	29.9%	821,000	210,442	25.6%	-4.3	876,000	197,828	22.6%	-7.4	1,963,000	404,192	20.6%	-9.4	2,099,000	407,389	19.4%	-10.5
MICHIGAN	757,000	159,770	21.1%	903,000	212,063	23.5%	2.4	1,827,000	158,142	8.7%	-12.4	2,084,000	218,252	10.5%	-10.6	2,359,000	227,155	9.6%	-11.5
MINNESOTA	585,000	103,779	17.7%	611,000	156,304	25.6%	7.8	636,000	76,793	12.1%	-5.7	1,302,000	79,903	6.1%	-11.6	1,389,000	38,008	2.7%	-15.0
MISSISSIPPI																			
MISSOURI																			
MONTANA																			
NEBRASKA	329,000	107,760	32.8%	341,000	120,206	35.3%	2.5	354,000	97,886	27.7%	-5.1	715,000	214,070	29.9%	-2.8	754,000	202,688	26.9%	-5.9
NEVADA	32,000	8,798	27.5%	44,000	9,623	21.9%	-5.6	44,000	12,875	29.3%	1.8	46,000	15,437	33.6%	6.1	48,000	14,521	30.3%	2.8
NEW HAMPSHIRE	111,000	37,737	34.0%	114,000	33,674	29.5%	-4.5	116,000	32,605	28.1%	-5.9	242,000	70,160	29.0%	-5.0	251,000	52,236	20.8%	-13.2
NEW JERSEY																			
NEW MEXICO								88,000	22,433	25.5%		170,000	60,317	35.5%	10.0	173,000	52,523	30.4%	4.9
NEW YORK	2,381,000	689,700	29.0%	2,564,000	541,269	21.1%	-7.9	5,038,000	1,009,936	20.0%	-8.9	5,630,000	1,397,657	24.8%	-4.1	6,300,000	1,523,813	24.2%	-4.8
NORTH CAROLINA																			
NORTH DAKOTA	142,000	47,005	33.1%	149,000	34,746	23.3%	-9.8	156,000	36,733	23.5%	-9.6					323,000	24,287	7.5%	-25.6
OHIO	1,337,000	477,077	35.7%	1,469,000	493,804	33.6%	-2.1	1,601,000	486,403	30.4%	-5.3	3,420,000	821,948	24.0%	-11.6	3,680,000	702,733	19.1%	-16.6
OKLAHOMA	434,000	120,218	27.7%	477,000	100,597	21.1%	-6.6	973,000	104,132	10.7%	-17.0	1,072,000	280,206	26.1%	-1.6	1,165,000	213,167	18.3%	-9.4
OREGON	230,000	54,853	23.8%	410,000	94,594	23.1%	-0.8	446,000	65,440	14.7%	-9.2	491,000	133,392	27.2%	3.3	538,000	93,470	17.4%	-6.5
PENNSYLVANIA	1,837,000	129,395	7.0%	1,977,000	453,380	22.9%	15.9	2,118,000	305,315	14.4%	7.4	4,589,000	581,625	12.7%	5.6	4,943,000	365,280	7.4%	0.3
RHODE ISLAND	121,000	32,400	26.8%	129,000	32,182	24.9%	-1.8	137,000	36,031	26.3%	-0.5	310,000	81,935	26.4%	-0.3	337,000	75,882	22.5%	-4.3
SOUTH CAROLINA	336,000	30,832	9.2%	359,000	34,606	9.6%	0.5	381,000	25,267	6.6%	-2.5	788,000	34,065	4.3%	-4.9	805,000	16,589	2.1%	-7.1
SOUTH DAKOTA	170,000	37,983	22.3%	174,000	35,542	20.4%	-1.9	316,000	17,858	5.7%	-16.7	334,000	50,409	15.1%	-7.3	350,000	87,136	24.9%	2.6
TENNESSEE	551,000	121,694	22.1%	575,000	137,656	23.9%	1.9	599,000	98,628	16.5%	-5.6	1,268,000	141,002	11.1%	-11.0	1,350,000	84,979	6.3%	-15.8

State Gubernatorial General Elections (continued)

Democratic Turnout for Election Years 1910–1926 (continued)

State	1910 Voting-age population	Turnout	%	1914 Voting-age population	Turnout	%	Difference from 1910	1918 Voting-age population	Turnout	%	Difference from 1910	1922 Voting-age population	Turnout	%	Difference from 1910	1926 Voting-age population	Turnout	%	Difference from 1910
TEXAS	955,000	174,596	18.3%	1,052,000	176,599	16.8%	-1.5	1,150,000	148,982	13.0%	-5.3	2,431,000	334,199	13.7%	-4.5	2,685,000	233,068	8.7%	-9.6
UTAH																			
VERMONT	100,000	17,425	17.4%	100,000	16,191	16.2%	-1.2	100,000	13,859	13.9%	-3.6	200,000	17,059	8.5%	-8.9	202,000	28,672	14.2%	-3.2
VIRGINIA																			
WASHINGTON																			
WEST VIRGINIA																			
WISCONSIN	610,000	110,442	18.1%	644,000	119,509	18.6%	0.5	676,000	112,576	16.7%	-1.5	1,432,000	51,061	3.6%	-14.5	1,554,000	72,627	4.7%	-13.4
WYOMING				92,000	22,387	24.3%		102,000	18,640	18.3%	-6.1	110,000	31,110	28.3%	3.9	117,000	34,286	29.3%	5.0
Total	15,579,000	3,665,354	23.5%	18,486,000	3,950,125	21.4%	-2.1	24,388,000	3,906,778	16.0%	-7.4	38,914,000	6,536,555	16.8%	-6.6	43,497,000	6,063,503	13.9%	-9.5

Other Turnout for Election Years 1910–1926

State	1910 Voting-age population	Turnout	%	1914 Voting-age population	Turnout	%	Difference from 1910*	1918 Voting-age population	Turnout	%	Difference from 1910	1922 Voting-age population	Turnout	%	Difference from 1910	1926 Voting-age population	Turnout	%	Difference from 1910
ALABAMA	512,000	1,868	0.4%	537,000	4,797	0.9%	0.5					1,196,000	1,697	0.1%	-0.2				
ALASKA																			
ARIZONA				106,000	8,179	7.7%		132,000	444	0.3%	-7.4								
ARKANSAS	395,000	9,196	2.3%	419,000	10,434	2.5%	0.2	442,000	4,792	1.1%	-1.2								
CALIFORNIA	715,000	177,191	24.8%	1,660,000	538,665	32.4%	-7.7	1,921,000	280,518	14.6%	-4.6	2,357,000	41,812	1.8%	-0.3	2,850,000	51,763	1.8%	-3.8
COLORADO	452,000	12,330	2.7%	481,000	45,493	9.5%	6.7	509,000	5,251	1.0%	-1.7	536,000	5,764	1.1%	-1.7	555,000	6,304	1.1%	-1.6
CONNECTICUT	258,000	15,410	6.0%	281,000	15,957	5.7%	-0.3	303,000	5,696	1.9%	-4.1	680,000	6,201	0.9%	-5.1	746,000	3,198	0.4%	-5.5
DELAWARE																			
DISTRICT OF COLUMBIA																			
FLORIDA																			
GEORGIA																			
HAWAII																			
IDAHO	165,000	5,342	3.2%	190,000	19,946	10.5%	7.3					226,000	40,516	17.9%	14.7	231,000	34,208	14.8%	11.6
ILLINOIS																			
INDIANA																			
IOWA	613,000	19,933	3.3%	651,000	32,662	5.0%	1.8	689,000	9,630	1.4%	-1.9								
KANSAS	497,000	17,759	3.6%	950,000	156,968	16.5%	12.9	976,000	12,732	1.3%	-2.3	1,019,000	9,143	0.9%	-2.7	1,067,000	7,053	0.7%	-2.9
KENTUCKY																			
LOUISIANA																			
MAINE	203,000	3,000	1.5%	206,000	20,703	10.1%	8.6												

State Gubernatorial General Elections (continued)

State Gubernatorial General Elections (continued)

Other Turnout for Election Years 1910–1926 (continued)

State	1910 Voting-age population	Turnout	%	1914 Voting-age population	Turnout	%	Difference from 1910	1918 Voting-age population	Turnout	%	Difference from 1910	1922 Voting-age population	Turnout	%	Difference from 1910	1926 Voting-age population	Turnout	%	Difference from 1910
MARYLAND																915,000	2,495	0.3%	
MASSACHUSETTS	766,000	17,306	2.3%	821,000	49,435	6.0%	3.8	876,000	9,679	1.1%	-1.2	1,963,000	20,478	1.0%	-1.2	2,099,000	9,771	0.5%	-1.8
MICHIGAN	757,000	21,189	2.8%	903,000	52,131	5.8%	3.0	1,827,000	9,496	0.5%	-2.3	2,084,000	8,476	0.4%	-2.4	2,359,000	4,033	0.2%	-2.6
MINNESOTA	585,000	26,643	4.6%	611,000	43,221	7.1%	2.5	636,000	126,390	19.9%	15.3	1,302,000	295,479	22.7%	18.1	1,389,000	266,845	19.2%	14.7
MISSISSIPPI																			
MISSOURI																			
MONTANA																			
NEBRASKA	329,000	6,279	1.9%	341,000	17,282	5.1%	3.2	354,000	3,409	1.0%	-0.9	715,000	13,435	1.9%	0.0	754,000	4,937	0.7%	-1.3
NEVADA	32,000	1,393	4.4%	44,000	3,391	7.7%	3.4												
NEW HAMPSHIRE	111,000	1,522	1.4%	114,000	4,021	3.5%	2.2	116,000	7	0.0%	-1.4								
NEW JERSEY																			
NEW MEXICO								88,000	847	1.0%		170,000	857	0.5%	-0.5	173,000	274	0.2%	-0.8
NEW YORK	2,381,000	125,042	5.3%	2,564,000	212,042	8.3%	3.0	5,038,000	127,418	2.5%	-2.7	5,630,000	122,393	2.2%	-3.1	6,300,000	113,826	1.8%	-3.4
NORTH CAROLINA																			
NORTH DAKOTA	142,000	2,524	1.8%	149,000	10,282	6.9%	5.1					306,000	81,048	26.5%	24.7	323,000	4,974	1.5%	-0.2
OHIO	1,337,000	70,686	5.3%	1,469,000	112,345	7.6%	2.4					3,420,000	551	0.0%	-5.3	3,680,000	7,582	0.2%	-5.1
OKLAHOMA	434,000	27,921	6.4%	477,000	57,186	12.0%	5.6	973,000	7,438	0.8%	-5.7	1,072,000	3,941	0.4%	-6.1	1,165,000	3,427	0.3%	-6.1
OREGON	230,000	14,086	6.1%	410,000	32,421	7.9%	1.8	446,000	6,480	1.5%	-4.7					538,000	12,402	2.3%	-3.8
PENNSYLVANIA	1,837,000	386,432	21.0%	1,977,000	68,667	3.5%	-17.6	2,118,000	47,173	2.2%	-18.8	4,589,000	51,351	1.1%	-19.9	4,943,000	35,565	0.7%	-20.3
RHODE ISLAND	121,000	1,682	1.4%	129,000	3,845	3.0%	1.6	137,000	1,648	1.2%	-0.2	310,000	1,751	0.6%	-0.8	337,000	743	0.2%	-1.2
SOUTH CAROLINA	336,000	70	0.0%	359,000	84	0.0%	0.0												
SOUTH DAKOTA	170,000	6,085	3.6%	174,000	14,461	8.3%	4.7	316,000	27,127	8.6%	5.0	334,000	46,033	13.8%	10.2	350,000	22,595	6.5%	2.9
TENNESSEE	551,000	1,707	0.3%	575,000	1,671	0.3%	0.0	599,000		0.0%	-0.3					1,350,000	151	0.0%	-0.3
TEXAS	955,000	29,554	3.1%	1,052,000	26,771	2.5%	-0.5	1,150,000	1,660	0.1%	-3.0					2,685,000	908	0.0%	-3.1
UTAH																			
VERMONT	100,000	2,140	2.1%	100,000	2,000	2.0%	-0.1	100,000	106	0.1%	-2.0	200,000	144	0.1%	-2.1	202,000	36	0.0%	-2.1
VIRGINIA																			
WASHINGTON																			
WEST VIRGINIA																			
WISCONSIN	610,000	47,461	7.8%	644,000	65,134	10.1%	2.3	676,000	63,207	9.4%	1.6	1,432,000	62,838	4.4%	-3.4	1,554,000	129,358	8.3%	0.5
WYOMING	82,000	22,691	27.7%	92,000	1,816	2.0%	-25.7					110,000	687	0.6%	-27.0	117,000	104	0.1%	-27.6
Total	15,340,000	3,693,597	24.1%	18,486,000	1,632,010	8.8%	2.8	20,422,000	751,148	3.7%	-2.4	29,651,000	814,595	2.7%	-3.3	36,682,000	722,552	2.0%	-4.1

*Percentage point difference between turnout in current year and initial year listed in chart. If data do not appear for a state in the initial year listed, the difference is calculated from the first year in which data do appear for that state.

UNITED STATES SENATE GENERAL ELECTIONS

Election Years 1910–1926

State	1910 Voting-age population	1910 Turnout	1910 %	1914* Voting-age population	1914* Turnout	1914* %	1918 Voting-age population	1918 Turnout	1918 %	1918 Difference from 1914**	1922 Voting-age population	1922 Turnout	1922 %	1922 Difference from 1914	1926 Voting-age population	1926 Turnout	1926 %	1926 Difference from 1914
ALABAMA				537,000	81,090	15.1%	562,000	54,880	9.8%	-5.3					1,279,000	113,565	8.9%	-6.2
ALASKA																		
ARIZONA				106,000	48,465	45.7%					148,000	61,080	41.3%	-4.5	157,000	76,436	48.7%	3.0
ARKANSAS				419,000	44,671	10.7%	442,000	78,386	17.7%	7.1					933,000	33,912	3.6%	-7.0
CALIFORNIA				1,660,000	886,055	53.4%					2,357,000	908,095	38.5%	-14.8	2,850,000	1,061,854	37.3%	-16.1
COLORADO				481,000	253,213	52.6%	509,000	217,679	42.8%	-9.9					555,000	297,695	53.6%	1.0
CONNECTICUT				281,000	180,814	64.3%					680,000	323,906	47.6%	-16.7	746,000	302,327	40.5%	-23.8
DELAWARE							64,000	42,052	65.7%		131,000	74,891	57.2%	-8.5				
DISTRICT OF COLUMBIA																		
FLORIDA				232,000	22,871	9.9%					610,000	51,950	8.5%	-1.3	741,000	65,568	8.8%	-1.0
GEORGIA				658,000	89,924	13.7%	696,000	60,809	8.7%	-4.9					1,470,000	47,446	3.2%	-10.4
HAWAII																		
IDAHO				190,000	108,198	56.9%	215,000	94,605	44.0%	-12.9					231,000	125,179	54.2%	-2.8
ILLINOIS				1,596,000	1,015,808	63.6%	1,719,000	950,486	55.3%	-8.4					4,130,000	1,797,359	43.5%	-20.1
INDIANA				823,000	646,059	78.5%					1,773,000	1,097,362	61.9%	-16.6	1,870,000	1,044,717	55.9%	-22.6
IOWA				651,000	427,102	65.6%	689,000	352,094	51.1%	-14.5	1,398,000	352,094	25.2%	-40.4	1,439,000	572,186	39.8%	-25.8
KANSAS				950,000	508,894	53.6%	976,000	442,654	45.4%	-8.2					1,067,000	484,878	45.4%	-8.1
KENTUCKY				622,000	339,755	54.6%	644,000	363,182	56.4%	1.8					1,373,000	553,564	40.3%	-14.3
LOUISIANA							447,000	44,224	9.9%						1,050,000	54,193	5.2%	-4.7
MAINE							209,000	120,318	57.6%		427,000	175,685	41.1%	-16.4				
MARYLAND				375,000	216,133	57.6%					860,000	305,915	35.6%	-22.1	915,000	339,064	37.1%	-20.6
MASSACHUSETTS							876,000	417,842	47.7%		1,963,000	870,157	44.3%	-3.4				
MICHIGAN							1,827,000	438,452	24.0%		2,084,000	582,970	28.0%	4.0				
MINNESOTA							636,000	343,981	54.1%		1,302,000	690,829	53.1%	-1.0				
MISSISSIPPI							437,000	31,624	7.2%		917,000	68,271	7.4%	0.2				
MISSOURI				967,000	618,227	63.9%	1,002,000	570,077	56.9%	-7.0	2,043,000	976,365	47.8%	-16.1	2,143,000	986,486	46.0%	-17.9
MONTANA							280,000	112,402	40.1%		292,000	159,214	54.5%	14.4				
NEBRASKA							354,000	219,182	61.9%		715,000	387,691	54.2%	-7.7				
NEVADA				44,000	21,567	49.0%	44,000	24,853	56.5%	7.5	46,000	28,971	63.0%	14.0	48,000	31,246	65.1%	16.1
NEW HAMPSHIRE				114,000	81,528	71.5%	116,000	70,550	60.8%	-10.7					251,000	127,214	50.7%	-20.8
NEW JERSEY							738,000	355,608	48.2%		1,718,000	823,438	47.9%	-0.3				
NEW MEXICO							88,000	47,323	53.8%		170,000	110,508	65.0%	11.2				
NEW YORK				2,564,000	1,358,685	53.0%					5,630,000	2,427,214	43.1%	-9.9	6,300,000	2,842,830	45.1%	-7.9

United States Senate General Elections (continued)

United States Senate General Elections *(continued)*

Election Years 1910–1926 *(continued)*

State	1910 Voting-age population	1910 Turnout	1910 %	1914 Voting-age population	1914 Turnout	1914 %	1918 Voting-age population	1918 Turnout	1918 %	1918 Difference from 1914	1922 Voting-age population	1922 Turnout	1922 %	1922 Difference from 1914	1926 Voting-age population	1926 Turnout	1926 %	1926 Difference from 1914
NORTH CAROLINA				549,000	208,868	38.0%	588,000	237,226	40.3%	2.3					1,432,000	361,825	25.3%	-12.8
NORTH DAKOTA				149,000	87,310	58.6%					306,000	193,776	63.3%	4.7	323,000	155,106	48.0%	-10.6
OHIO				1,469,000	1,070,169	72.9%					3,420,000	1,560,221	45.6%	-27.2	3,680,000	1,337,426	36.3%	-36.5
OKLAHOMA				477,000	248,995	52.2%	973,000	189,497	19.5%	-32.7					1,165,000	356,527	30.6%	-21.6
OREGON				410,000	245,580	59.9%	446,000	152,036	34.1%	-25.8					538,000	223,699	41.6%	-18.3
PENNSYLVANIA				1,977,000	1,111,826	56.2%					4,589,000	1,431,485	31.2%	-25.0	4,943,000	1,504,698	30.4%	-25.8
RHODE ISLAND							137,000	81,251	59.3%		310,000	158,889	51.3%	-8.1				
SOUTH CAROLINA				359,000	33,039	9.2%	381,000	25,792	6.8%	-2.4					805,000	14,560	1.8%	-7.4
SOUTH DAKOTA				174,000	99,096	57.0%	316,000	92,968	29.4%	-27.5					350,000	177,681	50.8%	-6.2
TENNESSEE							599,000	158,594	26.5%		1,268,000	222,722	17.6%	-8.9				
TEXAS							1,150,000	179,050	15.6%		2,431,000	391,794	16.1%	0.5				
UTAH				184,000	114,666	62.3%					220,000	120,823	54.9%	-7.4	234,000	143,225	61.2%	-1.1
VERMONT				100,000	62,705	62.7%					200,000	66,659	33.3%	-29.4	202,000	71,216	35.3%	-27.4
VIRGINIA							594,000	40,534	6.8%		1,222,000	161,923	13.3%	6.4				
WASHINGTON				674,000	345,279	51.2%					804,000	294,677	36.7%	-14.6	862,000	319,872	37.1%	-14.1
WEST VIRGINIA							366,000	215,219	58.8%		759,000	388,794	51.2%	-7.6				
WISCONSIN				644,000	317,278	49.3%	676,000	423,181	62.6%	13.3	1,432,000	470,818	32.9%	-16.4	1,554,000	546,638	35.2%	-14.1
WYOMING							102,000	41,503	40.7%		110,000	62,973	57.2%	16.6				
Total				20,436,000	10,893,870	53.3%	19,898,000	7,290,114	36.6%	-16.7	42,335,000	16,002,160	37.8%	-15.5	45,636,000	16,170,192	35.4%	-17.9

*The Seventeenth Amendment, ratified in 1913, instituted direct election of U.S. Senators.

**Percentage point difference between turnout in current year and initial year listed in chart. If data do not appear for a state in the initial year listed, the difference is calculated from the first year in which data do appear for that state.

UNITED STATES SENATE GENERAL ELECTIONS

Republican Turnout for Election Years 1910–1926

State	1910 Voting-age population	1910 Turnout	1910 %	1914* Voting-age population	1914* Turnout	1914* %	1918 Voting-age population	1918 Turnout	1918 %	1918 Difference from 1914**	1922 Voting-age population	1922 Turnout	1922 %	1922 Difference from 1914	1926 Voting-age population	1926 Turnout	1926 %	1926 Difference from 1914
ALABAMA				537,000	12,328	2.3%									1,279,000	21,722	1.7%	-0.6
ALASKA																		
ARIZONA				106,000	9,182	8.7%					148,000	21,358	14.4%	5.8	157,000	31,845	20.3%	11.6
ARKANSAS				419,000	11,222	2.7%									933,000	5,848	0.6%	-2.1
CALIFORNIA				1,060,000	254,159	15.3%					2,357,000	564,422	23.9%	8.6	2,850,000	670,128	23.5%	8.2
COLORADO				481,000	98,728	20.5%	509,000	107,726	21.2%	0.6					555,000	149,585	27.0%	6.4
CONNECTICUT				281,000	89,983	32.0%					680,000	169,524	24.9%	-7.1	746,000	191,401	25.7%	-6.4
DELAWARE							64,000	21,519	33.6%		131,000	36,979	28.2%	-5.4				
DISTRICT OF COLUMBIA																		
FLORIDA											610,000	6,074	1.0%		741,000	14,514	2.0%	1.0
GEORGIA							696,000	7,078	1.0%									
HAWAII																		
IDAHO				190,000	47,486	25.0%	215,000	63,587	29.6%	4.6					231,000	56,847	24.6%	-0.4
ILLINOIS				1,596,000	390,661	24.5%	1,719,000	479,957	27.9%	3.4					4,130,000	998,518	24.2%	-0.3
INDIANA				823,000	226,766	27.6%					1,773,000	524,558	29.6%	2.0	1,870,000	522,737	28.0%	0.4
IOWA				651,000	205,832	31.6%	689,000	230,264	33.4%	1.8	1,398,000	389,751	27.9%	-3.7	1,439,000	323,409	22.5%	-9.1
KANSAS				950,000	180,823	19.0%	976,000	281,931	28.9%	9.9					1,067,000	308,222	28.9%	9.9
KENTUCKY				622,000	144,758	23.3%	644,000	178,797	27.8%	4.5					1,373,000	266,567	19.4%	-3.9
LOUISIANA																		
MAINE							209,000	66,858	32.0%		427,000	101,026	23.7%	-8.3				
MARYLAND				375,000	94,864	25.3%					860,000	139,581	16.2%	-9.1	915,000	139,995	15.3%	-10.0
MASSACHUSETTS							876,000	188,287	21.5%		1,963,000	414,130	21.1%	-0.4				
MICHIGAN							1,827,000	220,054	12.0%		2,084,000	281,843	13.5%	1.5				
MINNESOTA							636,000	206,687	32.5%		1,302,000	241,833	18.6%	-13.9				
MISSISSIPPI											917,000	1,273	0.1%					
MISSOURI				967,000	257,054	26.6%	1,002,000	302,680	30.2%	3.6	2,043,000	462,009	22.6%	-4.0	2,143,000	470,654	22.0%	-4.6
MONTANA							280,000	40,229	14.4%		292,000	69,464	23.8%	9.4				
NEBRASKA							354,000	119,486	33.8%		715,000	220,350	30.8%	-2.9				
NEVADA				44,000	8,038	18.3%	44,000	8,053	18.3%	0.0	46,000	10,770	23.4%	5.1	48,000	17,430	36.3%	18.0
NEW HAMPSHIRE				114,000	42,113	36.9%	116,000	37,787	32.6%	-4.4					251,000	79,279	31.6%	-5.4
NEW JERSEY							738,000	179,022	24.3%		1,718,000	362,699	21.1%	-3.1				
NEW MEXICO							88,000	24,322	27.6%		170,000	48,721	28.7%	1.0				
NEW YORK				2,564,000	639,112	24.9%					5,630,000	995,421	17.7%	-7.2	6,300,000	1,437,152	22.8%	-2.1

United States Senate General Elections (continued)

United States Senate General Elections (continued)

Republican Turnout for Election Years 1910–1926 (continued)

State	1910 Voting-age population	Turnout	%	1914 Voting-age population	Turnout	%	1918 Voting-age population	Turnout	%	Difference from 1914	1922 Voting-age population	Turnout	%	Difference from 1914	1926 Voting-age population	Turnout	%	Difference from 1914
NORTH CAROLINA				549,000	87,101	15.9%	588,000	93,707	15.9%	0.1					1,432,000	142,891	10.0%	-5.9
NORTH DAKOTA				149,000	48,732	32.7%					306,000	101,312	33.1%	0.4	323,000	117,659	36.4%	3.7
OHIO				1,469,000	526,115	35.8%					3,420,000	794,149	23.2%	-12.6	3,680,000	711,359	19.3%	-16.5
OKLAHOMA				477,000	73,292	15.4%	973,000	77,188	7.9%	-7.4					1,165,000	159,287	13.7%	-1.7
OREGON				410,000	88,297	21.5%	446,000	82,360	18.5%	-3.1					538,000	89,007	16.5%	-5.0
PENNSYLVANIA				1,977,000	519,801	26.3%					4,589,000	802,146	17.5%	-8.8	4,943,000	822,187	16.6%	-9.7
RHODE ISLAND							137,000	42,055	30.7%		310,000	68,930	22.2%	-8.5				
SOUTH CAROLINA																		
SOUTH DAKOTA				174,000	44,244	25.4%	316,000	51,198	16.2%	-9.2					350,000	105,756	30.2%	4.8
TENNESSEE							599,000	59,989	10.0%		1,268,000	71,199	5.6%	-4.4				
TEXAS							1,150,000	22,214	1.9%		2,431,000	130,731	5.4%	3.4				
UTAH				184,000	56,282	30.6%					220,000	58,188	26.4%	-4.1	234,000	88,101	37.7%	7.1
VERMONT				100,000	35,137	35.1%					200,000	45,284	22.6%	-12.5	202,000	52,286	25.9%	-9.3
VIRGINIA											1,222,000	42,903	3.5%					
WASHINGTON				674,000	130,479	19.4%					804,000	126,556	15.7%	-3.6	862,000	164,130	19.0%	-0.3
WEST VIRGINIA							366,000	115,216	31.5%		759,000	185,046	24.4%	-7.1				
WISCONSIN				644,000	133,969	20.8%	676,000	163,980	24.3%	3.5	1,432,000	379,494	26.5%	5.7	1,554,000	411,881	26.5%	5.7
WYOMING							102,000	23,975	23.5%		110,000	26,627	24.2%	0.7				
Total				19,187,000	4,456,558	23.2%	17,035,000	3,496,206	20.5%	-2.7	42,335,000	7,894,351	18.6%	-4.6	42,311,000	8,570,397	20.3%	-3.0

Democratic Turnout for Election Years 1910–1926

State	1910 Voting-age population	Turnout	%	1914* Voting-age population	Turnout	%	1918 Voting-age population.	Turnout	%	Difference from 1914**	1922 Voting-age population	Turnout	%	Difference from 1914	1926 Voting-age population	Turnout	%	Difference from 1914
ALABAMA				537,000	63,338	11.8%	562,000	54,880	9.8%	-2.0					1,279,000	91,843	7.2%	-4.6
ALASKA																		
ARIZONA				106,000	25,800	24.3%					148,000	39,722	26.8%	2.5	157,000	44,591	28.4%	4.1
ARKANSAS				419,000	33,449	8.0%	442,000	78,386	17.7%	9.8					933,000	28,064	3.0%	-5.0
CALIFORNIA				1,660,000	279,896	16.9%					2,357,000	215,748	9.2%	-7.7	2,850,000	391,599	13.7%	-3.1
COLORADO				481,000	102,037	21.2%	509,000	104,347	20.5%	-0.7					555,000	138,113	24.9%	3.7
CONNECTICUT				281,000	76,081	27.1%					680,000	147,276	21.7%	-5.4	746,000	107,753	14.4%	-12.6
DELAWARE							64,000	20,113	31.4%		131,000	37,304	28.5%	-3.0				
DISTRICT OF COLUMBIA																		
FLORIDA				232,000	22,761	9.8%					610,000	45,707	7.5%	-2.3	741,000	51,054	6.9%	-2.9

United States Senate General Elections (continued)

Democratic Turnout for Election Years 1910–1926 (continued)

State	1910 Voting-age population	1910 Turnout	1910 %	1914 Voting-age population	1914 Turnout	1914 %	1918 Voting-age population.	1918 Turnout	1918 %	1918 Difference from 1914	1922 Voting-age population	1922 Turnout	1922 %	1922 Difference from 1914	1926 Voting-age population	1926 Turnout	1926 %	1926 Difference from 1914
GEORGIA				658,000	61,489	9.3%	696,000	53,731	7.7%	-1.6					1,470,000	47,446	3.2%	-6.1
HAWAII																		
IDAHO				190,000	41,266	21.7%	215,000	31,018	14.4%	-7.3					231,000	31,285	13.5%	-8.2
ILLINOIS				1,596,000	373,403	23.4%	1,719,000	426,943	24.8%	1.4					4,130,000	779,146	18.9%	-4.5
INDIANA				823,000	272,249	33.1%					1,773,000	558,169	31.5%	-1.6	1,870,000	511,454	27.4%	-5.7
IOWA				651,000	167,251	25.7%	689,000	121,830	17.7%	-8.0	1,398,000	227,833	16.3%	-9.4	1,439,000	247,869	17.2%	-8.5
KANSAS				950,000	176,929	18.6%	976,000	149,300	15.3%	-3.3					1,067,000	168,446	15.8%	-2.8
KENTUCKY				622,000	175,999	28.3%	644,000	184,385	28.6%	0.3					1,373,000	286,997	20.9%	-7.4
LOUISIANA							447,000	44,224	9.9%						1,050,000	54,180	5.2%	-4.7
MAINE							209,000	53,460	25.6%		427,000	74,659	17.5%	-8.1				
MARYLAND				375,000	110,204	29.4%					860,000	160,947	18.7%	-10.7	915,000	195,410	21.4%	-8.0
MASSACHUSETTS							876,000	207,478	23.7%		1,963,000	406,776	20.7%	-3.0				
MICHIGAN							1,827,000	212,487	11.6%		2,084,000	294,932	14.2%	2.5				
MINNESOTA											1,302,000	123,624	9.5%					
MISSISSIPPI							437,000	30,055	6.9%		917,000	63,636	6.9%	0.1				
MISSOURI				967,000	311,616	32.2%	1,002,000	267,397	26.7%	-5.5	2,043,000	506,267	24.8%	-7.4	2,143,000	506,015	23.6%	-8.6
MONTANA							280,000	46,160	16.5%		292,000	88,205	30.2%	13.7				
NEBRASKA							354,000	99,696	28.2%		715,000	148,265	20.7%	-7.4				
NEVADA				44,000	8,078	18.4%	44,000	12,917	29.4%	11.0	46,000	18,201	39.6%	21.2	48,000	13,273	27.7%	9.3
NEW HAMPSHIRE				114,000	36,382	31.9%	116,000	32,763	28.2%	-3.7					251,000	47,935	19.1%	-12.8
NEW JERSEY							738,000	153,743	20.8%		1,718,000	451,832	26.3%	5.5				
NEW MEXICO							88,000	22,470	25.5%		170,000	60,969	35.9%	10.3				
NEW YORK				2,564,000	571,419	22.3%					5,630,000	1,276,667	22.7%	0.4	6,300,000	1,321,463	21.0%	-1.3
NORTH CAROLINA				549,000	121,342	22.1%	588,000	143,519	24.4%	2.3					1,432,000	218,934	15.3%	-6.8
NORTH DAKOTA				149,000	29,640	19.9%					306,000	92,464	30.2%	10.3	323,000	13,519	4.2%	-15.7
OHIO				1,469,000	423,742	28.8%					3,420,000	744,558	21.8%	-7.1	3,680,000	623,221	16.9%	-11.9
OKLAHOMA				477,000	119,443	25.0%	973,000	105,050	10.8%	-14.2					1,165,000	195,307	16.8%	-8.3
OREGON				410,000	111,748	27.3%	446,000	64,303	14.4%	-12.8					538,000	81,301	15.1%	-12.1
PENNSYLVANIA				1,977,000	266,415	13.5%					4,589,000	423,583	9.2%	-4.2	4,943,000	648,680	13.1%	-0.4
RHODE ISLAND							137,000	37,573	27.4%		310,000	82,889	26.7%	-0.7				
SOUTH CAROLINA				359,000	32,950	9.2%	381,000	25,792	6.8%	-2.4					805,000	14,560	1.8%	-7.4
SOUTH DAKOTA				174,000	47,668	27.4%	316,000	36,210	11.5%	-15.9					350,000	71,925	20.6%	-6.8
TENNESSEE							599,000	98,605	16.5%		1,268,000	151,523	11.9%	-4.5				

United States Senate General Elections *(continued)*

Democratic Turnout for Election Years 1910–1926 *(continued)*

State	1910 Voting-age population	Turnout	%	1914 Voting-age population	Turnout	%	1918 Voting-age population.	Turnout	%	Difference from 1914	1922 Voting-age population	Turnout	%	Difference from 1914	1926 Voting-age population	Turnout	%	Difference from 1914
TEXAS							1,150,000	155,178	**13.5%**		2,431,000	261,063	**10.7%**	-2.8				
UTAH				184,000	53,127	**28.9%**					220,000	58,749	**26.7%**	-2.2	234,000	53,809	**23.0%**	-5.9
VERMONT				100,000	26,776	**26.8%**					200,000	21,375	**10.7%**	-16.1	202,000	18,878	**9.3%**	-17.4
VIRGINIA							594,000	40,403	**6.8%**		1,222,000	116,393	**9.5%**	2.7				
WASHINGTON				674,000	91,733	**13.6%**					804,000	130,375	**16.2%**	2.6	862,000	152,229	**17.7%**	4.0
WEST VIRGINIA							366,000	97,715	**26.7%**		759,000	198,853	**26.2%**	-0.5				
WISCONSIN				644,000	134,925	**21.0%**	676,000	148,714	**22.0%**	1.0	1,432,000	78,029	**5.4%**	-15.5	1,554,000	66,672	**4.3%**	-16.7
WYOMING							102,000	17,528	**17.2%**		110,000	35,734	**32.5%**	15.3				
Total				20,436,000	4,369,156	**21.4%**	19,262,000	3,378,373	**17.5%**	-3.8	42,335,000	7,342,327	**17.3%**	-4.0	45,636,000	7,222,971	**15.8%**	-5.6

Other Turnout for Election Years 1910–1926

State	1910 Voting-age population	Turnout	%	1914* Voting-age population	Turnout	%	1918 Voting-age population	Turnout	%	Difference from 1914**	1922 Voting-age population	Turnout	%	Difference from 1914	1926 Voting-age population	Turnout	%	Difference from 1914
ALABAMA				537,000	5,424	**1.0%**												
ALASKA																		
ARIZONA				106,000	13,483	**12.7%**												
ARKANSAS																		
CALIFORNIA				1,660,000	352,000	**21.2%**					2,357,000	127,925	**5.4%**	-15.8	2,850,000	127	**0.0%**	-21.2
COLORADO				481,000	52,448	**10.9%**	509,000	5,606	**1.1%**	-9.8					555,000	9,997	**1.8%**	-9.1
CONNECTICUT				281,000	14,750	**5.2%**					680,000	7,106	**1.0%**	-4.2	746,000	3,173	**0.4%**	-4.8
DELAWARE							64,000	420	**0.7%**		131,000	608	**0.5%**	-0.2				
DISTRICT OF COLUMBIA																		
FLORIDA				232,000	110	**0.0%**					610,000	169	**0.0%**	0.0				
GEORGIA				658,000	28,435	**4.3%**												
HAWAII																		
IDAHO				190,000	19,446	**10.2%**									231,000	37,047	**16.0%**	5.8
ILLINOIS				1,596,000	251,744	**15.8%**	1,719,000	43,586	**2.5%**	-13.2					4,130,000	19,695	**0.5%**	-15.3
INDIANA				823,000	147,044	**17.9%**					1,773,000	14,635	**0.8%**	-17.0	1,870,000	10,526	**0.6%**	-17.3
IOWA				651,000	54,019	**8.3%**									1,439,000	908	**0.1%**	-8.2
KANSAS				950,000	151,142	**15.9%**	976,000	11,423	**1.2%**	-14.7					1,067,000	8,210	**0.8%**	-15.1
KENTUCKY				622,000	18,998	**3.1%**												
LOUISIANA															1,050,000	13	**0.0%**	
MAINE																		

United States Senate General Elections (continued)

Other Turnout for Election Years 1910–1926 (continued)

State	1910 Voting-age population	Turnout	%	1914 Voting-age population	Turnout	%	1918 Voting-age population	Turnout	%	Difference from 1914	1922 Voting-age population	Turnout	%	Difference from 1914	1926 Voting-age population	Turnout	%	Difference from 1914
MARYLAND				375,000	11,065	3.0%					860,000	5,387	0.6%	-2.3	915,000	3,659	0.4%	-2.6
MASSACHUSETTS							876,000	22,077	2.5%		1,963,000	49,251	2.5%	0.0				
MICHIGAN							1,827,000	5,911	0.3%		2,084,000	6,195	0.3%	0.0				
MINNESOTA							636,000	137,294	21.6%		1,302,000	325,372	25.0%	3.4				
MISSISSIPPI							437,000	1,569	0.4%		917,000	3,362	0.4%	0.0				
MISSOURI				967,000	49,557	5.1%					2,043,000	8,089	0.4%	-4.7	2,143,000	9,817	0.5%	-4.7
MONTANA							280,000	26,013	9.3%		292,000	1,545	0.5%	-8.8				
NEBRASKA											715,000	19,076	2.7%					
NEVADA				44,000	5,451	12.4%	44,000	4,603	10.5%	-1.9					48,000	543	1.1%	-11.3
NEW HAMPSHIRE				114,000	3,033	2.7%												
NEW JERSEY							738,000	22,843	3.1%		1,718,000	8,907	0.5%	-2.6				
NEW MEXICO							88,000	531	0.6%		170,000	818	0.5%	-0.1				
NEW YORK				2,564,000	148,154	5.8%					5,630,000	155,126	2.8%	-3.0	6,300,000	84,215	1.3%	4.4
NORTH CAROLINA				549,000	425	0.1%												
NORTH DAKOTA				149,000	8,938	6.0%									323,000	23,928	7.4%	1.4
OHIO				1,469,000	120,312	8.2%					3,420,000	21,514	0.6%	-7.6	3,680,000	2,846	0.1%	-8.1
OKLAHOMA				477,000	56,260	11.8%	973,000	7,259	0.7%	-11.0					1,165,000	1,933	0.2%	-11.6
OREGON				410,000	45,535	11.1%	446,000	5,373	1.2%	9.9					538,000	53,391	9.9%	-1.2
PENNSYLVANIA				1,977,000	325,610	16.5%					4,589,000	205,756	4.5%	-12.0	4,943,000	33,831	0.7%	-15.8
RHODE ISLAND							137,000	1,623	1.2%		310,000	7,070	2.3%	1.1				
SOUTH CAROLINA				359,000	89	0.0%												
SOUTH DAKOTA				174,000	7,184	4.1%	316,000	5,560	1.8%	-2.4								
TENNESSEE																		
TEXAS							1,150,000	1,658	0.1%									
UTAH				184,000	5,257	2.9%					220,000	3,886	1.8%	-1.1	234,000	1,315	0.6%	-2.3
VERMONT				100,000	792	0.8%									202,000	52	0.0%	-0.8
VIRGINIA							594,000	131	0.0%		1,222,000	2,627	0.2%	0.2				
WASHINGTON				674,000	123,067	18.3%					804,000	37,746	4.7%	-13.6	862,000	3,513	0.4%	-17.9
WEST VIRGINIA							366,000	2,288	0.6%		759,000	4,895	0.6%	0.0				
WISCONSIN				644,000	48,384	7.5%					1,432,000	13,295	0.9%	-6.6	1,554,000	68,085	4.4%	-3.1
WYOMING											110,000	612	0.6%					
Total				20,017,000	2,068,156	10.3%	12,176,000	305,768	2.5%	-7.8	36,111,000	1,030,972	2.9%	-7.5	36,845,000	376,824	1.0%	-9.3

*The Seventeenth Amendment, ratified in 1913, instituted direct election of U.S. Senators.

**Percentage point difference between turnout in current year and initial year listed in chart. If data do not appear for a state in the initial year listed, the difference is calculated from the first year in which data do appear for that state.

UNITED STATES HOUSE OF REPRESENTATIVES GENERAL ELECTIONS

Election Years 1910–1926

State	1910 Voting-age population	1910 Turnout	1910 %	1914 Voting-age population	1914 Turnout	1914 %	1914 Difference from 1910*	1918 Voting-age population	1918 Turnout	1918 %	1918 Difference from 1910	1922 Voting-age population	1922 Turnout	1922 %	1922 Difference from 1910	1926 Voting-age population	1926 Turnout	1926 %	1926 Difference from 1910
ALABAMA	512,000	97,322	19.0%	537,000	80,547	15.0%	-4.0	562,000	62,345	11.1%	-7.9	1,196,000	139,792	11.7%	-7.3	1,279,000	107,095	8.4%	-10.6
ALASKA																			
ARIZONA				106,000	44,665	42.1%		132,000	44,381	33.6%	-8.5	148,000	51,863	35.0%	-7.1	157,000	68,227	43.5%	1.3
ARKANSAS	395,000	40,763	10.3%	419,000	43,100	10.3%	0.0	442,000	78,573	17.8%	7.5	892,000	34,581	3.9%	-6.4	933,000	33,712	3.6%	-6.7
CALIFORNIA	715,000	362,948	50.8%	1,660,000	855,747	51.6%	0.8	1,921,000	626,422	32.6%	-18.2	2,357,000	781,889	33.2%	-17.6	2,850,000	954,418	33.5%	-17.3
COLORADO	452,000	220,731	48.8%	481,000	247,506	51.5%	2.6	509,000	215,319	42.3%	-6.5	536,000	265,636	49.6%	0.7	555,000	291,275	52.5%	3.6
CONNECTICUT	258,000	166,153	64.4%	281,000	181,355	64.5%	0.1	303,000	166,994	55.1%	-9.3	680,000	323,590	47.6%	-16.8	746,000	301,458	40.4%	-24.0
DELAWARE	57,000	44,022	77.2%	60,000	45,719	76.2%	-1.0	64,000	41,298	64.5%	-12.7	131,000	72,611	55.4%	-21.8	137,000	68,333	49.9%	-27.4
DISTRICT OF COLUMBIA																			
FLORIDA	206,000	37,552	18.2%	232,000	24,076	10.4%	-7.9	260,000	31,813	12.2%	-6.0	610,000	50,883	8.3%	-9.9	741,000	64,684	8.7%	-9.5
GEORGIA	622,000	45,760	7.4%	658,000	81,177	12.3%	5.0	696,000	60,105	8.6%	1.3	1,438,000	78,679	5.5%	-1.9	1,470,000	47,003	3.2%	-4.2
HAWAII																			
IDAHO	165,000	83,696	50.7%	190,000	102,818	54.1%	3.4	215,000	93,857	43.7%	-7.1	226,000	121,143	53.6%	2.9	231,000	114,740	49.7%	-1.1
ILLINOIS	1,474,000	903,573	61.3%	1,596,000	930,416	58.3%	-3.0	1,719,000	903,459	52.6%	-8.7	3,746,000	1,679,173	44.8%	-16.5	4,130,000	1,630,610	39.5%	-21.8
INDIANA	794,000	621,633	78.3%	823,000	630,342	76.6%	-1.7	852,000	567,411	66.6%	-11.7	1,773,000	1,082,088	61.0%	-17.3	1,870,000	1,027,407	54.9%	-23.3
IOWA	613,000	374,693	61.1%	651,000	408,536	62.8%	1.6	689,000	348,816	50.6%	-10.5	1,398,000	585,590	41.9%	-19.2	1,439,000	504,925	35.1%	-26.0
KANSAS	497,000	295,149	59.4%	950,000	483,633	50.9%	-8.5	976,000	429,108	44.0%	-15.4	1,019,000	524,858	51.5%	-7.9	1,067,000	480,161	45.0%	-14.4
KENTUCKY	600,000	328,992	54.8%	622,000	323,255	52.0%	-2.9	644,000	356,432	55.3%	0.5	1,318,000	352,858	26.8%	-28.1	1,373,000	503,216	36.7%	-18.2
LOUISIANA	402,000	51,013	12.7%	425,000	50,910	12.0%	-0.7	447,000	44,795	10.0%	-2.7	962,000	44,198	4.6%	-8.1	1,050,000	54,192	5.2%	-7.5
MAINE	203,000	140,674	69.3%	206,000	140,899	68.4%	-0.9	209,000	121,836	58.3%	-11.0	427,000	175,351	41.1%	-28.2	433,000	173,039	40.0%	-29.3
MARYLAND	348,000	204,540	58.8%	375,000	216,869	57.8%	-0.9	401,000	160,074	39.9%	-18.9	860,000	303,859	35.3%	-23.4	915,000	336,098	36.7%	-22.0
MASSACHUSETTS	766,000	426,237	55.6%	821,000	447,689	54.5%	-1.1	876,000	394,427	45.0%	-10.6	1,963,000	824,713	42.0%	-13.6	2,099,000	933,091	44.5%	-11.2
MICHIGAN	757,000	374,887	49.5%	903,000	429,861	47.6%	-1.9	1,827,000	406,861	22.3%	-27.3	2,084,000	546,333	26.2%	-23.3	2,359,000	561,713	23.8%	-25.7
MINNESOTA	585,000	265,205	45.3%	611,000	322,820	52.8%	7.5	636,000	333,051	52.4%	7.0	1,302,000	636,896	48.9%	3.6	1,389,000	658,762	47.4%	2.1
MISSISSIPPI	425,000	23,888	5.6%	431,000	36,954	8.6%	3.0	437,000	32,311	7.4%	1.8	917,000	68,152	7.4%	1.8	980,000	26,917	2.7%	-2.9
MISSOURI	932,000	670,739	72.0%	967,000	600,589	62.1%	-9.9	1,002,000	551,105	55.0%	-17.0	2,043,000	976,529	47.8%	-24.2	2,143,000	987,831	46.1%	-25.9
MONTANA	135,000	65,774	48.7%	238,000	82,108	34.5%	-14.2	280,000	103,835	37.1%	-11.6	292,000	149,795	51.3%	2.6	292,000	153,452	52.6%	3.8
NEBRASKA	329,000	234,468	71.3%	341,000	233,627	68.5%	-2.8	354,000	217,026	61.3%	-10.0	715,000	375,541	52.5%	-18.7	754,000	389,400	51.6%	-19.6
NEVADA	32,000	20,163	63.0%	44,000	21,240	48.3%	-14.7	44,000	24,707	56.2%	-6.9	46,000	28,075	61.0%	-2.0	48,000	30,508	63.6%	0.5
NEW HAMPSHIRE	111,000	80,846	72.8%	114,000	81,125	71.2%	-1.7	116,000	70,046	60.4%	-12.4	242,000	127,037	52.5%	-20.3	251,000	124,151	49.5%	-23.4
NEW JERSEY	603,000	430,560	71.4%	670,000	389,979	58.2%	-13.2	738,000	349,137	47.3%	-24.1	1,718,000	792,271	46.1%	-25.3	1,980,000	791,603	40.0%	-31.4
NEW MEXICO				87,000	46,422	53.4%		88,000	47,053	53.5%	0.1	170,000	109,760	64.6%	11.2	173,000	107,805	62.3%	9.0
NEW YORK	2,381,000	1,421,929	59.7%	2,564,000	1,349,693	52.6%	-7.1	5,038,000	2,039,585	40.5%	-19.2	5,630,000	2,427,949	43.1%	-16.6	6,300,000	2,789,657	44.3%	-15.4

United States House of Representatives General Elections (continued)

Election Years 1910–1926 (continued)

State	1910 Voting-age population	Turnout	%	1914 Voting-age population	Turnout	%	Difference from 1910	1918 Voting-age population	Turnout	%	Difference from 1910	1922 Voting-age population	Turnout	%	Difference from 1910	1926 Voting-age population	Turnout	%	Difference from 1910
NORTH CAROLINA	510,000	235,922	46.3%	549,000	202,744	36.9%	-9.3	588,000	234,616	39.9%	-6.4	1,302,000	364,443	28.0%	-18.3	1,432,000	358,917	25.1%	-21.2
NORTH DAKOTA	142,000	80,661	56.8%	149,000	84,131	56.5%	-0.3	156,000	83,913	53.8%	-3.0	306,000	150,492	49.2%	-7.6	323,000	146,183	45.3%	-11.5
OHIO	1,337,000	902,433	67.5%	1,469,000	1,067,540	72.7%	5.2	1,601,000	905,541	56.6%	-10.9	3,420,000	1,589,363	46.5%	-21.0	3,680,000	1,286,478	35.0%	-32.5
OKLAHOMA	434,000	234,454	54.0%	477,000	245,636	51.5%	-2.5	973,000	189,630	19.5%	-34.5	1,072,000	469,827	43.8%	-10.2	1,165,000	362,544	31.1%	-22.9
OREGON	230,000	113,210	49.2%	410,000	236,372	57.7%	8.4	446,000	141,891	31.8%	-17.4	491,000	180,292	36.7%	-12.5	538,000	208,259	38.7%	-10.5
PENNSYLVANIA	1,837,000	941,598	51.3%	1,977,000	1,062,609	53.7%	2.5	2,118,000	878,002	41.5%	-9.8	4,589,000	1,446,417	31.5%	-19.7	4,943,000	1,468,782	29.7%	-21.5
RHODE ISLAND	121,000	67,352	55.7%	129,000	77,753	60.3%	4.6	137,000	79,608	58.1%	2.4	310,000	155,450	50.1%	-5.5	337,000	164,080	48.7%	-7.0
SOUTH CAROLINA	336,000	31,175	9.3%	359,000	33,376	9.3%	0.0	381,000	25,456	6.7%	-2.6	788,000	35,130	4.5%	-4.8	805,000	14,322	1.8%	-7.5
SOUTH DAKOTA	170,000	103,212	60.7%	174,000	96,725	55.6%	-5.1	316,000	87,424	27.7%	-33.0	334,000	159,776	47.8%	-12.9	350,000	168,001	48.0%	-12.7
TENNESSEE	551,000	226,469	41.1%	575,000	214,816	37.4%	-3.7	599,000	120,688	20.1%	-21.0	1,268,000	219,494	17.3%	-23.8	1,350,000	102,679	7.6%	-33.5
TEXAS	955,000	207,253	21.7%	1,052,000	209,639	19.9%	-1.8	1,150,000	165,145	14.4%	-7.3	2,431,000	400,403	16.5%	-5.2	2,685,000	237,026	8.8%	-12.9
UTAH	164,000	102,243	62.3%	184,000	113,670	61.8%	-0.6	204,000	86,937	42.6%	-19.7	220,000	119,613	54.4%	-8.0	234,000	141,546	60.5%	-1.9
VERMONT	100,000	52,414	52.4%	100,000	61,466	61.5%	9.1	100,000	43,143	43.1%	-9.3	200,000	70,351	35.2%	17.2	202,000	72,426	35.9%	-16.6
VIRGINIA	520,000	100,811	19.4%	557,000	84,885	15.2%	-4.1	594,000	42,357	7.1%	-12.3	1,222,000	166,234	13.6%	-5.8	1,262,000	107,893	8.5%	-10.8
WASHINGTON	606,000	138,243	22.8%	674,000	335,190	49.7%	26.9	741,000	201,395	27.2%	4.4	804,000	260,085	32.3%	9.5	862,000	270,757	31.4%	8.6
WEST VIRGINIA	314,000	209,584	66.7%	340,000	235,351	69.2%	2.5	366,000	213,803	58.4%	-8.3	759,000	381,490	50.3%	-16.5	824,000	427,463	51.9%	-14.9
WISCONSIN	610,000	309,327	50.7%	644,000	308,911	48.0%	-2.7	676,000	305,468	45.2%	-5.5	1,432,000	452,373	31.6%	-19.1	1,554,000	481,216	31.0%	-19.7
WYOMING	82,000	37,126	45.3%	92,000	41,609	45.2%	0.0	102,000	40,083	40.1%	-5.2	110,000	57,902	52.6%	7.4	117,000	64,774	55.4%	10.1
Total	24,388,000	12,127,397	49.7%	27,974,000	13,646,100	48.8%	-0.9	33,725,000	12,768,082	37.9%	-11.9	57,897,000	20,410,828	35.3%	-14.5	62,807,000	20,398,829	32.5%	-17.2

*Percentage point difference between turnout in current year and initial year listed in chart. If data do not appear for a state in the initial year listed, the difference is calculated from the first year in which data do appear for that state.

UNITED STATES HOUSE OF REPRESENTATIVES GENERAL ELECTIONS

Republican Turnout for Election Years 1910–1926

State	1910 Voting-age population	1910 Turnout	1910 %	1914 Voting-age population	1914 Turnout	1914 %	1914 Difference from 1910*	1918 Voting-age population	1918 Turnout	1918 %	1918 Difference from 1910	1922 Voting-age population	1922 Turnout	1922 %	1922 Difference from 1910	1926 Voting-age population	1926 Turnout	1926 %	1926 Difference from 1910
ALABAMA	512,000	14,976	2.9%	537,000	12,832	2.4%	-0.5	562,000	8,856	1.6%	-1.3	1,196,000	26,182	2.2%	-0.7	1,279,000	16,729	1.3%	-1.6
ALASKA																			
ARIZONA				106,000	7,586	7.2%		132,000	16,822	12.7%	5.6	148,000	14,601	9.9%	2.7	157,000	24,502	15.6%	8.4
ARKANSAS	395,000	9,236	2.3%	419,000	4,087	1.0%	-1.4					892,000	4,207	0.5%	-1.9	933,000	4,801	0.5%	-1.8
CALIFORNIA	715,000	204,014	28.5%	1,660,000	380,493	22.9%	-5.6	1,921,000	355,004	18.5%	-10.1	2,357,000	596,084	25.3%	-3.2	2,850,000	752,546	26.4%	-2.1
COLORADO	452,000	101,722	22.5%	481,000	99,900	20.8%	-1.7	509,000	112,787	22.2%	-0.3	536,000	136,926	25.5%	3.0	555,000	158,396	28.5%	6.0
CONNECTICUT	258,000	79,585	30.8%	281,000	89,000	31.7%	0.8	303,000	82,983	27.4%	-3.5	680,000	170,194	25.0%	-5.8	746,000	192,082	25.7%	-5.1
DELAWARE	57,000	22,410	39.3%	60,000	22,922	38.2%	-1.1	64,000	21,226	33.2%	-6.2	131,000	32,577	24.9%	-14.4	137,000	38,909	28.4%	-10.9
DISTRICT OF COLUMBIA																			
FLORIDA	206,000	1,372	0.7%									610,000	6,323	1.0%	0.4	741,000	15,189	2.0%	1.4
GEORGIA	622,000	2,285	0.4%					696,000	2,831	0.4%	0.0	1,438,000	1,261	0.1%	-0.3				
HAWAII																			
IDAHO	165,000	46,401	28.1%	190,000	45,365	23.9%	-4.2	215,000	59,358	27.6%	-0.5	226,000	57,373	25.4%	-2.7	231,000	72,210	31.3%	3.1
ILLINOIS	1,474,000	424,466	28.8%	1,596,000	388,896	24.4%	-4.4	1,719,000	501,974	29.2%	0.4	3,746,000	943,684	25.2%	-3.6	4,130,000	987,968	23.9%	-4.9
INDIANA	794,000	277,636	35.0%	823,000	233,140	28.3%	-6.6	852,000	306,807	36.0%	1.0	1,773,000	546,595	30.8%	-4.1	1,870,000	546,605	29.2%	-5.7
IOWA	613,000	207,272	33.8%	651,000	212,865	32.7%	-1.1	689,000	223,381	32.4%	-1.4	1,398,000	357,174	25.5%	-8.3	1,439,000	348,727	24.2%	-9.6
KANSAS	497,000	162,880	32.8%	950,000	188,056	19.8%	-13.0	976,000	244,374	25.0%	-7.7	1,019,000	284,687	27.9%	-4.8	1,067,000	283,890	26.6%	-6.2
KENTUCKY	600,000	147,372	24.6%	622,000	123,518	19.9%	-4.7	644,000	170,218	26.4%	1.9	1,318,000	138,239	10.5%	-14.1	1,373,000	239,909	17.5%	-7.1
LOUISIANA	402,000	3,874	1.0%	425,000	615	0.1%	-0.8									1,050,000	869	0.1%	-0.9
MAINE	203,000	67,563	33.3%	206,000	60,264	29.3%	-4.0	209,000	68,061	32.6%	-0.7	427,000	101,064	23.7%	-9.6	433,000	106,707	24.6%	-8.6
MARYLAND	348,000	95,230	27.4%	375,000	95,586	25.5%	-1.9	401,000	76,077	19.0%	-8.4	860,000	145,314	16.9%	-10.5	915,000	146,659	16.0%	-11.3
MASSACHUSETTS	766,000	203,136	26.5%	821,000	222,850	27.1%	0.6	876,000	233,809	26.7%	0.2	1,963,000	475,942	24.2%	-2.3	2,099,000	553,632	26.4%	-0.1
MICHIGAN	757,000	212,663	28.1%	903,000	218,445	24.2%	-3.9	1,827,000	265,334	14.5%	-13.6	2,084,000	365,970	17.6%	-10.5	2,359,000	438,653	18.6%	-9.5
MINNESOTA	585,000	180,124	30.8%	611,000	181,482	29.7%	-1.1	636,000	216,579	34.1%	3.3	1,302,000	385,030	29.6%	-1.2	1,389,000	386,448	27.8%	-3.0
MISSISSIPPI												917,000	1,621	0.2%					
MISSOURI	932,000	318,587	34.2%	967,000	240,897	24.9%	-9.3	1,002,000	256,555	25.6%	-8.6	2,043,000	476,109	23.3%	-10.9	2,143,000	487,173	22.7%	-11.4
MONTANA	135,000	32,519	24.1%	238,000	26,161	11.0%	-13.1	280,000	47,358	16.9%	-7.2	292,000	73,183	25.1%	1.0	292,000	74,515	25.5%	1.4
NEBRASKA	329,000	115,065	35.0%	341,000	110,839	32.5%	-2.5	354,000	121,476	34.3%	-0.7	715,000	179,070	25.0%	-9.9	754,000	187,963	24.9%	-10.0
NEVADA	32,000	10,066	31.5%	44,000	8,915	20.3%	-11.2	44,000	10,660	24.2%	-7.2	46,000	12,084	26.3%	-5.2	48,000	17,598	36.7%	5.2
NEW HAMPSHIRE	111,000	42,580	38.4%	114,000	42,450	37.2%	-1.1	116,000	38,001	32.8%	-5.6	242,000	62,264	25.7%	-12.6	251,000	77,264	30.8%	-7.6
NEW JERSEY	603,000	187,842	31.2%	670,000	183,475	27.4%	-3.8	738,000	173,228	23.5%	-7.7	1,718,000	393,269	22.9%	-8.3	1,980,000	448,038	22.6%	-8.5
NEW MEXICO				87,000	23,812	27.4%		88,000	23,862	27.1%	-0.3	170,000	49,635	29.2%	1.8	173,000	52,075	30.1%	2.7
NEW YORK	2,381,000	650,334	27.3%	2,564,000	619,650	24.2%	-3.1	5,038,000	985,960	19.6%	-7.7	5,630,000	1,120,920	19.9%	-7.4	6,300,000	1,372,957	21.8%	-5.5

United States House of Representatives General Elections *(continued)*

Republican Turnout for Election Years 1910–1926 *(continued)*

State	1910 Voting-age population	1910 Turnout	1910 %	1914 Voting-age population	1914 Turnout	1914 %	1914 Difference from 1910	1918 Voting-age population	1918 Turnout	1918 %	1918 Difference from 1910	1922 Voting-age population	1922 Turnout	1922 %	1922 Difference from 1910	1926 Voting-age population	1926 Turnout	1926 %	1926 Difference from 1910
NORTH CAROLINA	510,000	94,430	18.5%	549,000	79,842	14.5%	-4.0	588,000	92,809	15.8%	-2.7	1,302,000	138,522	10.6%	-7.9	1,432,000	138,762	9.7%	-8.8
NORTH DAKOTA	142,000	51,556	36.3%	149,000	50,792	34.1%	-2.2	156,000	54,508	34.9%	-1.4	306,000	115,986	37.9%	1.6	323,000	113,856	35.2%	-1.1
OHIO	1,337,000	383,745	28.7%	1,469,000	480,482	32.7%	4.0	1,601,000	495,616	31.0%	2.3	3,420,000	854,380	25.0%	-3.7	3,680,000	722,876	19.6%	-9.1
OKLAHOMA	434,000	93,206	21.5%	477,000	75,784	15.9%	-5.6	973,000	78,351	8.1%	-13.4	1,072,000	180,203	16.8%	-4.7	1,165,000	157,345	13.5%	-8.0
OREGON	230,000	56,898	24.7%	410,000	102,107	24.9%	0.2	446,000	98,834	22.2%	-2.6	491,000	123,124	25.1%	0.3	538,000	148,266	27.6%	2.8
PENNSYLVANIA	1,837,000	478,276	26.0%	1,977,000	514,270	26.0%	0.0	2,118,000	546,373	25.8%	-0.2	4,589,000	857,453	18.7%	-7.4	4,943,000	1,043,281	21.1%	-4.9
RHODE ISLAND	121,000	34,664	28.6%	129,000	39,001	30.2%	1.6	137,000	43,225	31.6%	2.9	310,000	73,688	23.8%	-4.9	337,000	95,367	28.3%	-0.3
SOUTH CAROLINA	336,000	370	0.1%	359,000	30	0.0%	-0.1	381,000	176	0.0%	-0.1	788,000	679	0.1%	0.0				
SOUTH DAKOTA	170,000	64,777	38.1%	174,000	52,844	30.4%	-7.7	316,000	48,905	15.5%	-22.6	334,000	87,277	26.1%	-12.0	350,000	96,070	27.4%	-10.7
TENNESSEE	551,000	73,640	13.4%	575,000	47,932	8.3%	-5.0	599,000	27,620	4.6%	-8.8	1,268,000	77,461	6.1%	-7.3	1,350,000	30,828	2.3%	-11.1
TEXAS	955,000	17,260	1.8%	1,052,000	10,605	1.0%	-0.8	1,150,000	6,113	0.5%	-1.3	2,431,000	60,926	2.5%	0.7	2,685,000	6,563	0.2%	-1.6
UTAH	164,000	50,614	30.9%	184,000	54,940	29.9%	1.0	204,000	36,612	17.9%	-12.9	220,000	61,779	28.1%	-2.8	234,000	86,080	36.8%	5.9
VERMONT	100,000	37,136	37.1%	100,000	36,980	37.0%	-0.2	100,000	32,446	32.4%	-4.7	200,000	45,340	22.7%	-14.5	202,000	55,130	27.3%	9.8
VIRGINIA	520,000	31,610	6.1%	557,000	23,654	4.2%	-1.8	594,000	8,555	1.4%	-4.6	1,222,000	53,231	4.4%	-1.7	1,262,000	32,801	2.6%	-3.5
WASHINGTON	606,000	78,291	12.9%	674,000	128,001	19.0%	6.1	741,000	112,166	15.1%	2.2	804,000	161,646	20.1%	7.2	862,000	190,797	22.1%	9.2
WEST VIRGINIA	314,000	94,457	30.1%	340,000	110,520	32.5%	2.4	366,000	112,022	30.6%	0.5	759,000	185,090	24.4%	-5.7	824,000	221,016	26.8%	-3.3
WISCONSIN	610,000	161,169	26.4%	644,000	159,370	24.7%	-1.7	676,000	166,354	24.6%	-1.8	1,432,000	368,051	25.7%	-0.7	1,554,000	399,167	25.7%	-0.7
WYOMING	82,000	20,312	24.8%	92,000	21,362	23.2%	-1.6	102,000	26,244	25.7%	1.0	110,000	30,885	28.1%	3.3	117,000	39,392	33.7%	8.9
Total	23,963,000	5,643,621	23.6%	26,653,000	5,832,617	21.9%	-1.7	32,139,000	6,610,510	20.6%	-3.0	56,935,000	10,633,303	18.7%	-4.9	59,552,000	11,610,611	19.5%	-4.1

Democratic Turnout for Election Years 1910–1926

State	1910 Voting-age population	1910 Turnout	1910 %	1914 Voting-age population	1914 Turnout	1914 %	1914 Difference from 1910*	1918 Voting-age population	1918 Turnout	1918 %	1918 Difference from 1910	1922 Voting-age population	1922 Turnout	1922 %	1922 Difference from 1910	1926 Voting-age population	1926 Turnout	1926 %	1926 Difference from 1910
ALABAMA	512,000	82,278	16.1%	537,000	62,830	11.7%	-4.4	562,000	53,489	9.5%	-6.6	1,196,000	113,610	9.5%	-6.6	1,279,000	90,366	7.1%	-9.0
ALASKA																			
ARIZONA				106,000	33,306	31.4%		132,000	26,805	20.3%	-11.1	148,000	37,262	25.2%	-6.2	157,000	43,725	27.9%	-3.6
ARKANSAS	395,000	31,527	8.0%	419,000	37,266	8.9%	0.9	442,000	78,573	17.8%	9.8	892,000	30,374	3.4%	-4.6	933,000	28,911	3.1%	-4.9
CALIFORNIA	715,000	111,620	15.6%	1,660,000	220,279	13.3%	-2.3	1,921,000	216,921	11.3%	-4.3	2,357,000	154,615	6.6%	-9.1	2,850,000	168,972	5.9%	-9.7
COLORADO	452,000	105,700	23.4%	481,000	118,211	24.6%	1.2	509,000	93,906	18.4%	-4.9	536,000	127,751	23.8%	0.4	555,000	130,377	23.5%	0.1
CONNECTICUT	258,000	73,221	28.4%	281,000	78,110	27.8%	-0.6	303,000	78,373	25.9%	-2.5	680,000	147,760	21.7%	-6.7	746,000	106,571	14.3%	-14.1
DELAWARE	57,000	20,281	35.6%	60,000	20,681	34.5%	-1.1	64,000	19,652	30.7%	-4.9	131,000	39,126	29.9%	-5.7	137,000	29,424	21.5%	-14.1
DISTRICT OF COLUMBIA																			
FLORIDA	206,000	30,995	15.0%	232,000	23,951	10.3%	-4.7	260,000	31,813	12.2%	-2.8	610,000	44,544	7.3%	-7.7	741,000	49,495	6.7%	-8.4

United States House of Representatives General Elections (continued)

United States House of Representatives General Elections (continued)

Democratic Turnout for Election Years 1910–1926 (continued)

State	1910 Voting-age population	1910 Turnout	1910 %	1914 Voting-age population	1914 Turnout	1914 %	1914 Difference from 1910	1918 Voting-age population	1918 Turnout	1918 %	1918 Difference from 1910	1922 Voting-age population	1922 Turnout	1922 %	1922 Difference from 1910	1926 Voting-age population	1926 Turnout	1926 %	1926 Difference from 1910
GEORGIA	622,000	43,361	7.0%	658,000	80,537	12.2%	5.3	696,000	57,274	8.2%	1.3	1,438,000	77,071	5.4%	-1.6	1,470,000	47,003	3.2%	-3.8
HAWAII																			
IDAHO	165,000	31,832	19.3%	190,000	39,736	20.9%	1.6	215,000	34,499	16.0%	-3.2	226,000	33,647	14.9%	-4.4	231,000	27,162	11.8%	-7.5
ILLINOIS	1,474,000	412,333	28.0%	1,596,000	375,465	23.5%	-4.4	1,719,000	361,505	21.0%	-6.9	3,746,000	666,583	17.8%	-10.2	4,130,000	631,708	15.3%	-12.7
INDIANA	794,000	312,153	39.3%	823,000	275,891	33.5%	-5.8	852,000	251,331	29.5%	-9.8	1,773,000	524,183	29.6%	-9.7	1,870,000	480,579	25.7%	-13.6
IOWA	613,000	157,504	25.7%	651,000	162,982	25.0%	-0.7	689,000	121,994	17.7%	-8.0	1,398,000	225,821	16.2%	-9.5	1,439,000	155,579	10.8%	-14.9
KANSAS	497,000	116,225	23.4%	950,000	195,830	20.6%	-2.8	976,000	171,897	17.6%	-5.8	1,019,000	233,706	22.9%	-0.5	1,067,000	196,084	18.4%	-5.0
KENTUCKY	600,000	175,574	29.3%	622,000	173,374	27.9%	-1.4	644,000	186,214	28.9%	-0.3	1,318,000	195,141	14.8%	-14.5	1,373,000	263,307	19.2%	-10.1
LOUISIANA	402,000	46,069	11.5%	425,000	40,545	9.5%	-1.9	447,000	44,794	10.0%	-1.4	962,000	44,180	4.6%	-6.9	1,050,000	53,320	5.1%	-6.4
MAINE	203,000	70,542	34.7%	206,000	60,649	29.4%	-5.3	209,000	53,775	25.7%	-9.0	427,000	74,287	17.4%	-17.4	433,000	66,332	15.3%	-19.4
MARYLAND	348,000	101,663	29.2%	375,000	111,410	29.7%	0.5	401,000	81,485	20.3%	-8.9	860,000	151,408	17.6%	-11.6	915,000	186,890	20.4%	-8.8
MASSACHUSETTS	766,000	213,656	27.9%	821,000	189,197	23.0%	-4.8	876,000	150,774	17.2%	-10.7	1,963,000	347,203	17.7%	-10.2	2,099,000	379,424	18.1%	-9.8
MICHIGAN	757,000	146,701	19.4%	903,000	149,762	16.6%	-2.8	1,827,000	135,987	7.4%	-11.9	2,084,000	178,633	8.6%	-10.8	2,359,000	122,395	5.2%	-14.2
MINNESOTA	585,000	67,474	11.5%	611,000	87,305	14.3%	2.8	636,000	82,619	13.0%	1.5	1,302,000	133,482	10.3%	-1.3	1,389,000	37,807	2.7%	-8.8
MISSISSIPPI	425,000	23,865	5.6%	431,000	35,830	8.3%	2.7	437,000	31,599	7.2%	1.6	917,000	66,482	7.2%	1.6	980,000	26,917	2.7%	-2.9
MISSOURI	932,000	328,216	35.2%	967,000	318,587	32.9%	-2.3	1,002,000	287,840	28.7%	-6.5	2,043,000	494,376	24.2%	-11.0	2,143,000	499,807	23.3%	-11.9
MONTANA	135,000	28,071	20.8%	238,000	37,011	15.6%	-5.2	280,000	48,356	17.3%	-3.5	292,000	75,736	25.9%	5.1	292,000	75,833	26.0%	5.2
NEBRASKA	329,000	113,505	34.5%	341,000	112,309	32.9%	-1.6	354,000	94,538	26.7%	-7.8	715,000	173,384	24.2%	-10.3	754,000	193,307	25.6%	-8.9
NEVADA	32,000	7,688	24.0%	44,000	8,031	18.3%	-5.8	44,000	12,670	28.8%	4.8	46,000	15,991	34.8%	10.7	48,000	12,910	26.9%	2.9
NEW HAMPSHIRE	111,000	37,006	33.3%	114,000	35,241	30.9%	-2.4	116,000	32,045	27.6%	-5.7	242,000	64,773	26.8%	-6.6	251,000	46,887	18.7%	-14.7
NEW JERSEY	603,000	225,817	37.4%	670,000	175,355	26.2%	-11.3	738,000	158,899	21.5%	-15.9	1,718,000	393,350	22.9%	-14.6	1,980,000	339,937	17.2%	-20.3
NEW MEXICO				87,000	19,805	22.8%		88,000	22,627	25.7%	2.9	170,000	59,254	34.9%	12.1	173,000	55,433	32.0%	9.3
NEW YORK	2,381,000	695,543	29.2%	2,564,000	542,166	21.1%	-8.1	5,038,000	870,236	17.3%	-11.9	5,630,000	1,162,206	20.6%	-8.6	6,300,000	1,330,850	21.1%	-8.1
NORTH CAROLINA	510,000	141,049	27.7%	549,000	122,129	22.2%	-5.4	588,000	141,807	24.1%	-3.5	1,302,000	225,921	17.4%	-10.3	1,432,000	220,155	15.4%	-12.3
NORTH DAKOTA	142,000	25,880	18.2%	149,000	26,684	17.9%	-0.3	156,000	29,405	18.8%	0.6	306,000	34,506	11.3%	-6.9	323,000	25,731	8.0%	-10.3
OHIO	1,337,000	454,224	34.0%	1,469,000	484,348	33.0%	-1.0	1,601,000	392,581	24.5%	-9.5	3,420,000	713,974	20.9%	-13.1	3,680,000	561,206	15.3%	-18.7
OKLAHOMA	434,000	118,348	27.3%	477,000	112,161	23.5%	-3.8	973,000	104,238	10.7%	-16.6	1,072,000	285,581	26.6%	-0.6	1,165,000	204,335	17.5%	-9.7
OREGON	230,000	37,709	16.4%	410,000	67,349	16.4%	0.0	446,000	26,189	5.9%	-10.5	491,000	52,479	10.7%	-5.7	538,000	59,993	11.2%	-5.2
PENNSYLVANIA	1,837,000	312,803	17.0%	1,977,000	281,154	14.2%	-2.8	2,118,000	276,836	13.1%	-4.0	4,589,000	533,664	11.6%	-5.4	4,943,000	376,747	7.6%	-9.4
RHODE ISLAND	121,000	31,236	25.8%	129,000	35,190	27.3%	1.5	137,000	34,646	25.3%	-0.5	310,000	81,762	26.4%	0.6	337,000	68,713	20.4%	-5.4
SOUTH CAROLINA	336,000	30,787	9.2%	359,000	33,077	9.2%	0.1	381,000	25,280	6.6%	-2.5	788,000	34,451	4.4%	-4.8	805,000	14,322	1.8%	-7.4
SOUTH DAKOTA	170,000	32,655	19.2%	174,000	37,842	21.7%	2.5	316,000	34,165	10.8%	-8.4	334,000	31,229	9.4%	-9.9	350,000	67,854	19.4%	0.2
TENNESSEE	551,000	147,887	26.8%	575,000	155,058	27.0%	0.1	599,000	92,890	15.5%	-11.3	1,268,000	142,033	11.2%	-15.6	1,350,000	71,851	5.3%	-21.5

United States House of Representatives General Elections *(continued)*

Democratic Turnout for Election Years 1910–1926 *(continued)*

State	1910 Voting-age population	Turnout	%	1914 Voting-age population	Turnout	%	Difference from 1910	1918 Voting-age population	Turnout	%	Difference from 1910	1922 Voting-age population	Turnout	%	Difference from 1910	1926 Voting-age population	Turnout	%	Difference from 1910
TEXAS	955,000	182,187	19.1%	1,052,000	173,177	16.5%	-2.6	1,150,000	159,032	13.8%	-5.2	2,431,000	339,477	14.0%	-5.1	2,685,000	230,463	8.6%	-10.5
UTAH	164,000	32,730	20.0%	184,000	53,057	28.8%	8.9	204,000	49,258	24.1%	4.2	220,000	53,946	24.5%	4.6	234,000	54,204	23.2%	3.2
VERMONT	100,000	14,441	14.4%	100,000	13,685	13.7%	-0.8	100,000	10,697	10.7%	-3.7	200,000	24,989	12.5%	-1.9	202,000	17,282	8.6%	-5.9
VIRGINIA	520,000	67,570	13.0%	557,000	58,320	10.5%	-2.5	594,000	33,802	5.7%	-7.3	1,222,000	112,906	9.2%	-3.8	1,262,000	74,365	5.9%	-7.1
WASHINGTON	606,000	44,827	7.4%	674,000	96,652	14.3%	6.9	741,000	81,350	11.0%	3.6	804,000	58,882	7.3%	-0.1	862,000	79,434	9.2%	1.8
WEST VIRGINIA	314,000	103,293	32.9%	340,000	102,223	30.1%	-2.8	366,000	99,917	27.3%	-5.6	759,000	194,525	25.6%	-7.3	824,000	206,284	25.0%	-7.9
WISCONSIN	610,000	106,431	17.4%	644,000	115,501	17.9%	0.5	676,000	69,043	10.2%	-7.2	1,432,000	29,459	2.1%	-15.4	1,554,000	36,431	2.3%	-15.1
WYOMING	82,000	14,659	17.9%	92,000	17,246	18.7%	0.9	102,000	14,639	14.4%	-3.5	110,000	27,017	24.6%	6.7	117,000	25,082	21.4%	3.6
Total	24,388,000	5,709,136	23.4%	27,974,000	5,806,505	20.8%	-2.7	33,725,000	5,568,285	16.5%	-6.9	57,897,000	9,062,740	15.7%	-7.8	62,807,000	8,271,764	13.2%	-10.2

Other Turnout for Election Years 1910–1926

State	1910 Voting-age population	Turnout	%	1914 Voting age population	Turnout	%	Difference from 1910*	1918 Voting-age population	Turnout	%	Difference from 1910	1922 Voting age population	Turnout	%	Difference from 1910	1926 Voting-age population	Turnout	%	Difference from 1910
ALABAMA	512,000	68	0.0%	537,000	4,885	0.9%	0.9												
ALASKA																			
ARIZONA				106,000	3,773	3.6%		132,000	754	0.6%	-3.0								
ARKANSAS				419,000	1,747	0.4%													
CALIFORNIA	715,000	47,314	6.6%	1,660,000	254,975	15.4%	8.7	1,921,000	54,497	2.8%	-3.8	2,357,000	31,190	1.3%	-5.3	2,850,000	32,900	1.2%	-5.5
COLORADO	452,000	13,309	2.9%	481,000	29,395	6.1%	3.2	509,000	8,626	1.7%	-1.2	536,000	959	0.2%	-2.8	555,000	2,502	0.5%	-2.5
CONNECTICUT	258,000	13,347	5.2%	281,000	14,245	5.1%	-0.1	303,000	5,638	1.9%	-3.3	680,000	5,636	0.8%	-4.3	746,000	2,805	0.4%	-4.8
DELAWARE	57,000	1,331	2.3%	60,000	2,116	3.5%	1.2	64,000	420	0.7%	-1.7	131,000	908	0.7%	-1.6				
DISTRICT OF COLUMBIA																			
FLORIDA	206,000	5,185	2.5%	232,000	125	0.1%	-2.5					610,000	16	0.0%	-2.5				
GEORGIA	622,000	114	0.0%	658,000	640	0.1%	0.1					1,438,000	347	0.0%	0.0				
HAWAII																			
IDAHO	165,000	5,463	3.3%	190,000	17,717	9.3%	6.0					226,000	30,123	13.3%	10.0	231,000	15,368	6.7%	3.3
ILLINOIS	1,474,000	66,774	4.5%	1,596,000	166,055	10.4%	5.9	1,719,000	39,980	2.3%	-2.2	3,746,000	68,906	1.8%	-2.7	4,130,000	10,934	0.3%	-4.3
INDIANA	794,000	31,844	4.0%	823,000	121,311	14.7%	10.7	852,000	9,273	1.1%	-2.9	1,773,000	11,310	0.6%	-3.4	1,870,000	223	0.0%	-4.0
IOWA	613,000	9,917	1.6%	651,000	32,689	5.0%	3.4	689,000	3,441	0.5%	-1.1	1,398,000	2,595	0.2%	-1.4	1,439,000	619	0.0%	-1.6
KANSAS	497,000	16,044	3.2%	950,000	99,747	10.5%	7.3	976,000	12,837	1.3%	-1.9	1,019,000	6,465	0.6%	-2.6	1,067,000	187	0.0%	-3.2
KENTUCKY	600,000	6,046	1.0%	622,000	26,363	4.2%	3.2					1,318,000	19,478	1.5%	0.5				
LOUISIANA	402,000	1,070	0.3%	425,000	9,750	2.3%	2.0	447,000	1	0.0%	-0.3	962,000	18	0.0%	-0.3	1,050,000	3	0.0%	-0.3
MAINE	203,000	2,569	1.3%	206,000	19,986	9.7%	8.4												

United States House of Representatives General Elections (continued)

United States House of Representatives General Elections *(continued)*

Other Turnout for Election Years 1910–1926 *(continued)*

State	1910 Voting-age population	Turnout	%	1914 Voting-age population	Turnout	%	Difference from 1910	1918 Voting-age population	Turnout	%	Difference from 1910	1922 Voting-age population	Turnout	%	Difference from 1910	1926 Voting-age population	Turnout	%	Difference from 1910
MARYLAND	348,000	7,647	2.2%	375,000	9,873	2.6%	0.4	401,000	2,512	0.6%	-1.6	860,000	7,137	0.8%	-1.4	915,000	2,549	0.3%	-1.9
MASSACHUSETTS	766,000	9,445	1.2%	821,000	35,642	4.3%	3.1	876,000	9,844	1.1%	-0.1	1,963,000	1,568	0.1%	-1.2	2,099,000	35	0.0%	-1.2
MICHIGAN	757,000	15,523	2.1%	903,000	61,654	6.8%	4.8	1,827,000	5,540	0.3%	-1.7	2,084,000	1,730	0.1%	-2.0	2,359,000	665	0.0%	-2.0
MINNESOTA	585,000	17,607	3.0%	611,000	54,033	8.8%	5.8	636,000	33,853	5.3%	2.3	1,302,000	118,384	9.1%	6.1	1,389,000	234,507	16.9%	13.9
MISSISSIPPI	425,000	23	0.0%	431,000	1,124	0.3%	0.3	437,000	712	0.2%	0.2	917,000	49	0.0%	0.0				
MISSOURI	932,000	23,936	2.6%	967,000	41,105	4.3%	1.7	1,002,000	6,710	0.7%	-1.9	2,043,000	6,044	0.3%	-2.3	2,143,000	851	0.0%	-2.5
MONTANA	135,000	5,184	3.8%	238,000	18,936	8.0%	4.1	280,000	8,121	2.9%	-0.9	292,000	876	0.3%	-3.5	292,000	3,104	1.1%	-2.8
NEBRASKA	329,000	5,898	1.8%	341,000	10,479	3.1%	1.3	354,000	1,012	0.3%	-1.5	715,000	23,087	3.2%	1.4	754,000	8,130	1.1%	-0.7
NEVADA	32,000	2,409	7.5%	44,000	4,294	9.8%	2.2	44,000	1,377	3.1%	-4.4								
NEW HAMPSHIRE	111,000	1,260	1.1%	114,000	3,434	3.0%	1.9												
NEW JERSEY	603,000	16,901	2.8%	670,000	31,149	4.6%	1.8	738,000	17,010	2.3%	-0.5	1,718,000	5,652	0.3%	-2.5	1,980,000	3,628	0.2%	-2.6
NEW MEXICO				87,000	2,805	3.2%		88,000	564	0.6%	-2.6	170,000	871	0.5%	-2.7	173,000	297	0.2%	-3.1
NEW YORK	2,381,000	76,052	3.2%	2,564,000	187,877	7.3%	4.1	5,038,000	183,389	3.6%	0.4	5,630,000	144,823	2.6%	-0.6	6,300,000	85,850	1.4%	-1.8
NORTH CAROLINA	510,000	443	0.1%	549,000	773	0.1%	0.1												
NORTH DAKOTA	142,000	3,225	2.3%	149,000	6,655	4.5%	2.2									323,000	6,596	2.0%	-0.2
OHIO	1,337,000	64,464	4.8%	1,469,000	102,710	7.0%	2.2	1,601,000	17,344	1.1%	-3.7	3,420,000	21,009	0.6%	-4.2	3,680,000	2,396	0.1%	-4.8
OKLAHOMA	434,000	22,900	5.3%	477,000	57,691	12.1%	6.8	973,000	7,041	0.7%	-4.6	1,072,000	4,043	0.4%	-4.9	1,165,000	864	0.1%	-5.2
OREGON	230,000	18,603	8.1%	410,000	66,916	16.3%	8.2	446,000	16,868	3.8%	-4.3	491,000	4,689	1.0%	-7.1				
PENNSYLVANIA	1,837,000	150,519	8.2%	1,977,000	267,185	13.5%	5.3	2,118,000	54,793	2.6%	-5.6	4,589,000	55,300	1.2%	-7.0	4,943,000	48,754	1.0%	-7.2
RHODE ISLAND	121,000	1,452	1.2%	129,000	3,562	2.8%	1.6	137,000	1,737	1.3%	0.1								
SOUTH CAROLINA	336,000	18	0.0%	359,000	269	0.1%	0.1												
SOUTH DAKOTA	170,000	5,780	3.4%	174,000	6,039	3.5%	0.1	316,000	4,354	1.4%	-2.0	334,000	41,270	12.4%	9.0	350,000	4,077	1.2%	-2.2
TENNESSEE	551,000	4,942	0.9%	575,000	11,826	2.1%	1.2	599,000	178	0.0%	-0.9								
TEXAS	955,000	7,806	0.8%	1,052,000	25,857	2.5%	1.6												
UTAH	164,000	18,899	11.5%	184,000	5,673	3.1%	-8.4	204,000	1,067	0.5%	-11.0	220,000	3,888	1.8%	-9.8	234,000	1,262	0.5%	-11.0
VERMONT	100,000	837	0.8%	100,000	10,801	10.8%	10.0					200,000	22	0.0%	-0.8	202,000	14	0.0%	-0.8
VIRGINIA	520,000	1,631	0.3%	557,000	2,911	0.5%	0.2					1,222,000	97	0.0%	-0.3	1,262,000	727	0.1%	-0.3
WASHINGTON	606,000	15,125	2.5%	674,000	110,537	16.4%	13.9	741,000	7,879	1.1%	-1.4	804,000	39,557	4.9%	2.4	862,000	526	0.1%	-2.4
WEST VIRGINIA	314,000	11,834	3.8%	340,000	22,608	6.6%	2.9	366,000	1,864	0.5%	-3.3	759,000	1,875	0.2%	-3.5	824,000	163	0.0%	-3.7
WISCONSIN	610,000	41,727	6.8%	644,000	34,040	5.3%	-1.6	676,000	70,071	10.4%	3.5	1,432,000	54,863	3.8%	-3.0	1,554,000	45,618	2.9%	-3.9
WYOMING	82,000	2,155	2.6%	92,000	3,001	3.3%	0.6									117,000	300	0.3%	-2.4
Total	23,993,000	774,640	3.2%	27,974,000	2,006,978	7.2%	3.9	27,510,000	589,307	2.1%	-1.1	48,431,000	714,785	1.5%	-1.8	47,858,000	516,454	1.1%	-2.1

*Percentage point difference between turnout in current year and initial year listed in chart. If data do not appear for a state in the initial year listed, the difference is calculated from the first year in which data do appear for that state.

TOTAL HIGHEST STATEWIDE GENERAL ELECTIONS

Election Years 1910–1926

State	1910 Voting-age population	Turnout	%	1914 Voting-age population	Turnout	%	Difference from 1910*	1918 Voting-age population	Turnout	%	Difference from 1910	1922 Voting-age population	Turnout	%	Difference from 1910	1926 Voting-age population	Turnout	%	Difference from 1910
ALABAMA	512,000	97,322	19.0%	537,000	80,547	15.0%	-4.0	562,000	62,345	11.1%	-7.9	1,196,000	139,792	11.7%	-7.3	1,279,000	107,095	8.4%	-10.6
ALASKA																			
ARIZONA				106,000	44,665	42.1%		132,000	44,381	33.6%	-8.5	148,000	51,863	35.0%	-7.1	157,000	68,227	43.5%	1.3
ARKANSAS	395,000	40,763	10.3%	419,000	43,100	10.3%	0.0	442,000	78,573	17.8%	7.5	892,000	34,581	3.9%	-6.4	933,000	33,712	3.6%	-6.7
CALIFORNIA	715,000	362,948	50.8%	1,000,000	866,747	51.6%	0.8	1,921,000	626,422	32.6%	-18.2	2,357,000	781,889	33.2%	-17.6	2,850,000	954,418	33.5%	-17.3
COLORADO	452,000	220,731	48.8%	481,000	247,506	51.5%	2.6	509,000	215,319	42.3%	-6.5	536,000	265,030	49.6%	0.7	555,000	291,275	52.5%	3.6
CONNECTICUT	258,000	166,153	64.4%	281,000	181,355	64.5%	0.1	303,000	166,994	55.1%	-9.3	680,000	323,590	47.6%	-16.8	746,000	301,458	40.4%	-24.0
DELAWARE	57,000	44,022	77.2%	60,000	45,719	76.2%	-1.0	64,000	41,298	64.5%	-12.7	131,000	72,611	55.4%	-21.8	137,000	68,333	49.9%	-27.4
DISTRICT OF COLUMBIA																			
FLORIDA	206,000	37,552	18.2%	232,000	24,076	10.4%	-7.9	260,000	31,813	12.2%	-6.0	610,000	50,883	8.3%	-9.9	741,000	64,684	8.7%	-9.5
GEORGIA	622,000	45,760	7.4%	658,000	81,177	12.3%	5.0	696,000	60,105	8.6%	1.3	1,438,000	78,679	5.5%	-1.9	1,470,000	47,003	3.2%	-4.2
HAWAII																			
IDAHO	165,000	83,696	50.7%	190,000	102,818	54.1%	3.4	215,000	93,857	43.7%	-7.1	226,000	121,143	53.6%	2.9	231,000	114,740	49.7%	-1.1
ILLINOIS	1,474,000	903,573	61.3%	1,596,000	930,416	58.3%	-3.0	1,719,000	903,459	52.6%	-8.7	3,746,000	1,679,173	44.8%	-16.5	4,130,000	1,630,610	39.5%	-21.8
INDIANA	794,000	621,633	78.3%	823,000	630,342	76.6%	-1.7	852,000	567,411	66.6%	-11.7	1,773,000	1,082,088	61.0%	-17.3	1,870,000	1,027,407	54.9%	-23.3
IOWA	613,000	374,693	61.1%	651,000	408,536	62.8%	1.6	689,000	348,816	50.6%	-10.5	1,398,000	585,590	41.9%	-19.2	1,439,000	504,925	35.1%	-26.0
KANSAS	497,000	295,149	59.4%	950,000	483,633	50.9%	-8.5	976,000	429,108	44.0%	-15.4	1,019,000	524,858	51.5%	-7.9	1,067,000	480,161	45.0%	-14.4
KENTUCKY	600,000	328,992	54.8%	622,000	323,255	52.0%	-2.9	644,000	356,432	55.3%	0.5	1,318,000	352,858	26.8%	-28.1	1,373,000	503,216	36.7%	-18.2
LOUISIANA	402,000	51,013	12.7%	425,000	50,910	12.0%	-0.7	447,000	44,795	10.0%	-2.7	962,000	44,198	4.6%	-8.1	1,050,000	54,192	5.2%	7.5
MAINE	203,000	140,674	69.3%	206,000	140,899	68.4%	-0.9	209,000	121,836	58.3%	-11.0	427,000	175,351	41.1%	-28.2	433,000	173,039	40.0%	-29.3
MARYLAND	348,000	204,540	58.8%	375,000	216,869	57.8%	-0.9	401,000	160,074	39.9%	-18.9	860,000	303,859	35.3%	-23.4	915,000	336,098	36.7%	-22.0
MASSACHUSETTS	766,000	426,237	55.6%	821,000	447,689	54.5%	-1.1	876,000	394,427	45.0%	-10.6	1,963,000	824,713	42.0%	-13.6	2,099,000	933,091	44.5%	-11.2
MICHIGAN	757,000	374,887	49.5%	903,000	429,861	47.6%	-1.9	1,827,000	406,861	22.3%	-27.3	2,084,000	546,333	26.2%	-23.3	2,359,000	561,713	23.8%	-25.7
MINNESOTA	585,000	265,205	45.3%	611,000	322,820	52.8%	7.5	636,000	333,051	52.4%	7.0	1,302,000	636,896	48.9%	3.6	1,389,000	658,762	47.4%	2.1
MISSISSIPPI	425,000	23,888	5.6%	431,000	36,954	8.6%	3.0	437,000	32,311	7.4%	1.8	917,000	68,152	7.4%	1.8	980,000	26,917	2.7%	-2.9
MISSOURI	932,000	670,739	72.0%	967,000	600,589	62.1%	-9.9	1,002,000	551,105	55.0%	-17.0	2,043,000	976,529	47.8%	-24.2	2,143,000	987,831	46.1%	-25.9
MONTANA	135,000	65,774	48.7%	238,000	82,108	34.5%	-14.2	280,000	103,835	37.1%	-11.6	292,000	149,795	51.3%	2.6	292,000	153,452	52.6%	3.8
NEBRASKA	329,000	234,468	71.3%	341,000	233,627	68.5%	-2.8	354,000	217,026	61.3%	-10.0	715,000	375,541	52.5%	-18.7	754,000	389,400	51.6%	-19.6
NEVADA	32,000	20,163	63.0%	44,000	21,240	48.3%	-14.7	44,000	24,707	56.2%	-6.9	46,000	28,075	61.0%	-2.0	48,000	30,508	63.6%	0.5
NEW HAMPSHIRE	111,000	80,846	72.8%	114,000	81,125	71.2%	-1.7	116,000	70,046	60.4%	-12.4	242,000	127,037	52.5%	-20.3	251,000	124,151	49.5%	-23.4
NEW JERSEY	603,000	430,560	71.4%	670,000	389,979	58.2%	-13.2	738,000	349,137	47.3%	-24.1	1,718,000	792,271	46.1%	-25.3	1,980,000	791,603	40.0%	-31.4
NEW MEXICO				87,000	46,422	53.4%		88,000	47,053	53.5%	0.1	170,000	109,760	64.6%	11.2	173,000	107,805	62.3%	9.0
NEW YORK	2,381,000	1,421,929	59.7%	2,564,000	1,349,693	52.6%	-7.1	5,038,000	2,039,585	40.5%	-19.2	5,630,000	2,427,949	43.1%	-16.6	6,300,000	2,789,657	44.3%	-15.4

Total Highest Statewide General Elections (continued)

Total Highest Statewide General Elections (continued)

Election Years 1910–1926 (continued)

State	1910 Voting-age population	Turnout	%	1914 Voting-age population	Turnout	%	Difference from 1910	1918 Voting-age population	Turnout	%	Difference from 1910	1922 Voting-age population	Turnout	%	Difference from 1910	1926 Voting-age population	Turnout	%	Difference from 1910
NORTH CAROLINA	510,000	235,922	46.3%	549,000	202,744	36.9%	-9.3	588,000	234,616	39.9%	-6.4	1,302,000	364,443	28.0%	-18.3	1,432,000	358,917	25.1%	-21.2
NORTH DAKOTA	142,000	80,661	56.8%	149,000	84,131	56.5%	-0.3	156,000	83,913	53.8%	-3.0	306,000	150,492	49.2%	-7.6	323,000	146,183	45.3%	-11.5
OHIO	1,337,000	902,433	67.5%	1,469,000	1,067,540	72.7%	5.2	1,601,000	905,541	56.6%	-10.9	3,420,000	1,589,363	46.5%	-21.0	3,680,000	1,286,478	35.0%	-32.5
OKLAHOMA	434,000	234,454	54.0%	477,000	245,636	51.5%	-2.5	973,000	189,630	19.5%	-34.5	1,072,000	469,827	43.8%	-10.2	1,165,000	362,544	31.1%	-22.9
OREGON	230,000	113,210	49.2%	410,000	236,372	57.7%	8.4	446,000	141,891	31.8%	-17.4	491,000	180,292	36.7%	-12.5	538,000	208,259	38.7%	-10.5
PENNSYLVANIA	1,837,000	941,598	51.3%	1,977,000	1,062,609	53.7%	2.5	2,118,000	878,002	41.5%	-9.8	4,589,000	1,446,417	31.5%	-19.7	4,943,000	1,468,782	29.7%	-21.5
RHODE ISLAND	121,000	67,352	55.7%	129,000	77,753	60.3%	4.6	137,000	79,608	58.1%	2.4	310,000	155,450	50.1%	-5.5	337,000	164,080	48.7%	-7.0
SOUTH CAROLINA	336,000	31,175	9.3%	359,000	33,376	9.3%	0.0	381,000	25,456	6.7%	-2.6	788,000	35,130	4.5%	-4.8	805,000	14,322	1.8%	-7.5
SOUTH DAKOTA	170,000	103,212	60.7%	174,000	96,725	55.6%	-5.1	316,000	87,424	27.7%	-33.0	334,000	159,776	47.8%	-12.9	350,000	168,001	48.0%	-12.7
TENNESSEE	551,000	226,469	41.1%	575,000	214,816	37.4%	-3.7	599,000	120,688	20.1%	-21.0	1,268,000	219,494	17.3%	-23.8	1,350,000	102,679	7.6%	-33.5
TEXAS	955,000	207,253	21.7%	1,052,000	209,639	19.9%	-1.8	1,150,000	165,145	14.4%	-7.3	2,431,000	400,403	16.5%	-5.2	2,685,000	237,026	8.8%	-12.9
UTAH	164,000	102,243	62.3%	184,000	113,670	61.8%	-0.6	204,000	86,937	42.6%	-19.7	220,000	119,613	54.4%	-8.0	234,000	141,546	60.5%	-1.9
VERMONT	100,000	52,414	52.4%	100,000	61,466	61.5%	9.1	100,000	43,143	43.1%	-9.3	200,000	70,351	35.2%	-17.2	202,000	72,426	35.9%	-16.6
VIRGINIA	520,000	100,811	19.4%	557,000	84,885	15.2%	-4.1	594,000	42,357	7.1%	-12.3	1,222,000	166,234	13.6%	-5.8	1,262,000	107,893	8.5%	-10.8
WASHINGTON	606,000	138,243	22.8%	674,000	335,190	49.7%	26.9	741,000	201,395	27.2%	4.4	804,000	260,085	32.3%	9.5	862,000	270,757	31.4%	8.6
WEST VIRGINIA	314,000	209,584	66.7%	340,000	235,351	69.2%	2.5	366,000	213,803	58.4%	-8.3	759,000	381,490	50.3%	-16.5	824,000	427,463	51.9%	-14.9
WISCONSIN	610,000	309,327	50.7%	644,000	308,911	48.0%	-2.7	676,000	305,468	45.2%	-5.5	1,432,000	452,373	31.6%	-19.1	1,554,000	481,216	31.0%	-19.7
WYOMING	82,000	37,126	45.3%	92,000	41,609	45.2%	0.0	102,000	40,883	40.1%	-5.2	110,000	57,902	52.6%	7.4	117,000	64,774	55.4%	10.1
Total	24,388,000	12,127,397	49.7%	27,974,000	13,646,100	48.8%	-0.9	33,725,000	12,768,082	37.9%	-11.9	57,897,000	20,410,828	35.3%	-14.5	62,807,000	20,398,829	32.5%	-17.2

*Percentage point difference between turnout in current year and initial year listed in chart. If data do not appear for a state in the initial year listed, the difference is calculated from the first year in which data do appear for that state.

TOTAL HIGHEST STATEWIDE GENERAL ELECTIONS

Republican Turnout for Election Years 1910–1926

State	1910 Voting-age population	Turnout	%	1914 Voting-age population	Turnout	%	Difference from 1910*	1918 Voting-age population	Turnout	%	Difference from 1910	1922 Voting-age population	Turnout	%	Difference from 1910	1926 Voting-age population	Turnout	%	Difference from 1910
ALABAMA	512,000	19,210	3.8%	537,000	12,832	2.4%	-1.4	562,000	13,497	2.4%	-1.4	1,196,000	31,175	2.6%	-1.1	1,279,000	21,722	1.7%	-2.1
ALASKA																			
ARIZONA				106,000	17,602	16.6%		132,000	25,927	19.6%	3.0	148,000	30,599	20.7%	4.1	157,000	39,580	25.2%	8.6
ARKANSAS	395,000	39,870	10.1%	419,000	30,947	7.4%	-2.7					892,000	28,055	3.1%	-6.9	933,000	35,969	3.9%	-6.2
CALIFORNIA	715,000	204,014	28.5%	1,000,000	380,493	22.9%	-5.6	1,921,000	387,547	20.2%	-8.4	2,357,000	596,084	25.3%	-3.2	2,850,000	814,815	28.6%	0.1
COLORADO	452,000	101,722	22.5%	481,000	129,096	26.8%	4.3	509,000	112,787	22.2%	-0.3	530,000	136,026	25.5%	3.0	555,000	158,396	28.5%	6.0
CONNECTICUT	258,000	79,585	30.8%	281,000	91,262	32.5%	1.6	303,000	84,891	28.0%	-2.8	680,000	170,231	25.0%	-5.8	746,000	192,425	25.8%	-5.1
DELAWARE	57,000	22,410	39.3%	60,000	22,922	38.2%	-1.1	64,000	21,519	33.6%	-5.7	131,000	36,979	28.2%	-11.1	137,000	38,909	28.4%	-10.9
DISTRICT OF COLUMBIA																			
FLORIDA	206,000	1,372	0.7%									610,000	6,323	1.0%	0.4	741,000	15,189	2.0%	1.4
GEORGIA	622,000	2,285	0.4%					696,000	7,078	1.0%	0.6	1,438,000	1,261	0.1%	-0.3				
HAWAII																			
IDAHO	165,000	46,401	28.1%	190,000	47,486	25.0%	-3.1	215,000	63,587	29.6%	1.5	226,000	57,373	25.4%	-2.7	231,000	72,210	31.3%	3.1
ILLINOIS	1,474,000	424,466	28.8%	1,596,000	390,661	24.5%	-4.3	1,719,000	501,974	29.2%	0.4	3,746,000	943,684	25.2%	3.6	4,130,000	998,518	24.2%	-4.6
INDIANA	794,000	277,636	35.0%	823,000	233,140	28.3%	-6.6	852,000	306,807	36.0%	1.0	1,773,000	546,595	30.8%	-4.1	1,870,000	546,605	29.2%	-5.7
IOWA	613,000	207,272	33.8%	651,000	212,865	32.7%	-1.1	689,000	230,264	33.4%	-0.4	1,398,000	419,648	30.0%	-3.8	1,439,000	377,443	26.2%	-7.6
KANSAS	497,000	162,880	32.8%	950,000	209,543	22.1%	-10.7	976,000	287,957	29.5%	-3.3	1,019,000	284,687	27.9%	-4.8	1,067,000	321,540	30.1%	-2.6
KENTUCKY	600,000	147,372	24.6%	622,000	144,758	23.3%	-1.3	644,000	178,797	27.8%	3.2	1,318,000	138,239	10.5%	-14.1	1,373,000	266,567	19.4%	-5.1
LOUISIANA	402,000	3,874	1.0%	425,000	615	0.1%	-0.8									1,050,000	869	0.1%	-0.9
MAINE	203,000	67,563	33.3%	206,000	60,264	29.3%	-4.0	209,000	68,061	32.6%	-0.7	427,000	103,713	24.3%	-9.0	433,000	106,707	24.6%	-8.6
MARYLAND	348,000	95,230	27.4%	375,000	95,586	25.5%	-1.9	401,000	76,077	19.0%	-8.4	860,000	145,314	16.9%	-10.5	915,000	148,145	16.2%	-11.2
MASSACHUSETTS	766,000	203,136	26.5%	821,000	222,850	27.1%	0.6	876,000	233,809	26.7%	0.2	1,963,000	475,942	24.2%	-2.3	2,099,000	595,006	28.3%	1.8
MICHIGAN	757,000	212,663	28.1%	903,000	218,445	24.2%	-3.9	1,827,000	266,738	14.6%	-13.5	2,084,000	365,970	17.6%	-10.5	2,359,000	438,653	18.6%	-9.5
MINNESOTA	585,000	180,124	30.8%	611,000	181,482	29.7%	-1.1	636,000	216,579	34.1%	3.3	1,302,000	385,030	29.6%	-1.2	1,389,000	395,779	28.5%	-2.3
MISSISSIPPI												917,000	1,621	0.2%					
MISSOURI	932,000	318,587	34.2%	967,000	257,054	26.6%	-7.6	1,002,000	256,555	25.6%	-8.6	2,043,000	476,109	23.3%	-10.9	2,143,000	487,173	22.7%	-11.4
MONTANA	135,000	32,519	24.1%	238,000	26,161	11.0%	-13.1	280,000	47,358	16.9%	-7.2	292,000	73,183	25.1%	1.0	292,000	74,515	25.5%	1.4
NEBRASKA	329,000	123,070	37.4%	341,000	110,839	32.5%	-4.9	354,000	121,476	34.3%	-3.1	715,000	220,350	30.8%	-6.6	754,000	206,120	27.3%	-10.1
NEVADA	32,000	10,435	32.6%	44,000	8,915	20.3%	-12.3	44,000	11,845	26.9%	-5.7	46,000	13,215	28.7%	-3.9	48,000	17,598	36.7%	4.1
NEW HAMPSHIRE	111,000	44,908	40.5%	114,000	46,413	40.7%	0.3	116,000	38,465	33.2%	-7.3	242,000	62,264	25.7%	-14.7	251,000	79,279	31.6%	-8.9
NEW JERSEY	603,000	187,842	31.2%	670,000	183,475	27.4%	-3.8	738,000	179,022	24.3%	-6.9	1,718,000	393,269	22.9%	-8.3	1,980,000	448,038	22.6%	-8.5
NEW MEXICO				87,000	23,812	27.4%		88,000	24,322	27.6%	0.3	170,000	49,635	29.2%	1.8	173,000	56,294	32.5%	5.2
NEW YORK	2,381,000	650,334	27.3%	2,564,000	686,701	26.8%	-0.5	5,038,000	995,094	19.8%	-7.6	5,630,000	1,120,920	19.9%	-7.4	6,300,000	1,437,152	22.8%	-4.5

Total Highest Statewide General Elections (continued)

Total Highest Statewide General Elections *(continued)*

Republican Turnout for Election Years 1910–1926 *(continued)*

State	1910 Voting-age population	Turnout	%	1914 Voting-age population	Turnout	%	Difference from 1910	1918 Voting-age population	Turnout	%	Difference from 1910	1922 Voting-age population	Turnout	%	Difference from 1910	1926 Voting-age population	Turnout	%	Difference from 1910
NORTH CAROLINA	510,000	94,430	18.5%	549,000	87,101	15.9%	-2.7	588,000	93,707	15.9%	-2.6	1,302,000	138,522	10.6%	-7.9	1,432,000	142,891	10.0%	-8.5
NORTH DAKOTA	142,000	51,556	36.3%	149,000	50,792	34.1%	-2.2	156,000	54,517	34.9%	-1.4	306,000	115,986	37.9%	1.6	323,000	131,003	40.6%	4.3
OHIO	1,337,000	383,745	28.7%	1,469,000	526,115	35.8%	7.1	1,601,000	495,616	31.0%	2.3	3,420,000	854,380	25.0%	-3.7	3,680,000	722,876	19.6%	-9.1
OKLAHOMA	434,000	99,527	22.9%	477,000	95,904	20.1%	-2.8	973,000	82,865	8.5%	-14.4	1,072,000	230,469	21.5%	-1.4	1,165,000	170,714	14.7%	-8.3
OREGON	230,000	56,898	24.7%	410,000	121,037	29.5%	4.8	446,000	98,834	22.2%	-2.6	491,000	123,124	25.1%	0.3	538,000	148,266	27.6%	2.8
PENNSYLVANIA	1,837,000	478,276	26.0%	1,977,000	588,705	29.8%	3.7	2,118,000	552,537	26.1%	0.1	4,589,000	857,453	18.7%	-7.4	4,943,000	1,102,823	22.3%	-3.7
RHODE ISLAND	121,000	34,664	28.6%	129,000	41,996	32.6%	3.9	137,000	43,225	31.6%	2.9	310,000	74,724	24.1%	-4.5	337,000	95,367	28.3%	-0.3
SOUTH CAROLINA	336,000	370	0.1%	359,000	30	0.0%	-0.1	381,000	176	0.0%	-0.1	788,000	679	0.1%	0.0				
SOUTH DAKOTA	170,000	64,777	38.1%	174,000	52,844	30.4%	-7.7	316,000	51,198	16.2%	-21.9	334,000	87,277	26.1%	-12.0	350,000	105,756	30.2%	-7.9
TENNESSEE	551,000	133,074	24.2%	575,000	116,677	20.3%	-3.9	599,000	59,989	10.0%	-14.1	1,268,000	102,586	8.1%	-16.1	1,350,000	46,238	3.4%	-20.7
TEXAS	955,000	26,191	2.7%	1,052,000	11,411	1.1%	-1.7	1,150,000	26,713	2.3%	-0.4	2,431,000	130,731	5.4%	2.6	2,685,000	31,531	1.2%	-1.6
UTAH	164,000	50,614	30.9%	184,000	56,282	30.6%	-0.3	204,000	36,612	17.9%	-12.9	220,000	61,779	28.1%	-2.8	234,000	88,101	37.7%	6.8
VERMONT	100,000	37,136	37.1%	100,000	36,980	37.0%	-0.2	100,000	32,446	32.4%	-4.7	200,000	52,104	26.1%	-11.1	202,000	55,130	27.3%	-9.8
VIRGINIA	520,000	31,610	6.1%	557,000	23,654	4.2%	-1.8	594,000	8,555	1.4%	-4.6	1,222,000	53,231	4.4%	-1.7	1,262,000	32,801	2.6%	-3.5
WASHINGTON	606,000	78,291	12.9%	674,000	130,479	19.4%	6.4	741,000	112,166	15.1%	2.2	804,000	161,646	20.1%	7.2	862,000	190,797	22.1%	9.2
WEST VIRGINIA	314,000	94,457	30.1%	340,000	110,520	32.5%	2.4	366,000	115,216	31.5%	1.4	759,000	185,090	24.4%	-5.7	824,000	221,016	26.8%	-3.3
WISCONSIN	610,000	161,619	26.5%	644,000	159,370	24.7%	-1.7	676,000	166,354	24.6%	-1.9	1,432,000	379,494	26.5%	0.0	1,554,000	411,881	26.5%	0.0
WYOMING	82,000	20,312	24.8%	92,000	21,362	23.2%	-1.6	102,000	26,244	25.7%	1.0	110,000	30,885	28.1%	3.3	117,000	39,392	33.7%	8.9
Total	23,963,000	5,764,327	24.1%	26,653,000	6,277,478	23.6%	-0.5	32,139,000	6,815,003	21.2%	-2.9	56,935,000	10,954,554	19.2%	-4.8	59,552,000	12,127,799	20.4%	-3.7

Democratic Turnout for Election Years 1910–1926

State	1910 Voting-age population	Turnout	%	1914 Voting-age population	Turnout	%	Difference from 1910*	1918 Voting-age population	Turnout	%	Difference from 1910	1922 Voting-age population	Turnout	%	Difference from 1910	1926 Voting-age population	Turnout	%	Difference from 1910
ALABAMA	512,000	82,278	16.1%	537,000	63,338	11.8%	-4.3	562,000	54,880	9.8%	-6.3	1,196,000	113,610	9.5%	-6.6	1,279,000	93,432	7.3%	-8.8
ALASKA																			
ARIZONA				106,000	33,306	31.4%		132,000	26,805	20.3%	-11.1	148,000	39,722	26.8%	-4.6	157,000	44,591	28.4%	-3.0
ARKANSAS	395,000	101,612	25.7%	419,000	94,143	22.5%	-3.3	442,000	78,573	17.8%	-7.9	892,000	99,987	11.2%	-14.5	933,000	116,735	12.5%	-13.2
CALIFORNIA	715,000	154,835	21.7%	1,660,000	279,896	16.9%	-4.8	1,921,000	216,921	11.3%	-10.4	2,357,000	347,520	14.7%	-6.9	2,850,000	391,599	13.7%	-7.9
COLORADO	452,000	115,627	25.6%	481,000	118,211	24.6%	-1.0	509,000	104,347	20.5%	-5.1	536,000	138,098	25.8%	0.2	555,000	183,342	33.0%	7.5
CONNECTICUT	258,000	77,243	29.9%	281,000	78,110	27.8%	-2.1	303,000	78,373	25.9%	-4.1	680,000	148,641	21.9%	-8.1	746,000	107,753	14.4%	-15.5
DELAWARE	57,000	20,281	35.6%	60,000	20,681	34.5%	-1.1	64,000	20,113	31.4%	-4.2	131,000	39,126	29.9%	-5.7	137,000	29,424	21.5%	-14.1
DISTRICT OF COLUMBIA																			
FLORIDA	206,000	30,995	15.0%	232,000	23,951	10.3%	-4.7	260,000	31,813	12.2%	-2.8	610,000	45,707	7.5%	-7.6	741,000	51,054	6.9%	-8.2

Total Highest Statewide General Elections (continued)

Democratic Turnout for Election Years 1910–1926 (continued)

State	1910 Voting-age population	Turnout	%	1914 Voting-age population	Turnout	%	Difference from 1910	1918 Voting-age population	Turnout	%	Difference from 1910	1922 Voting-age population	Turnout	%	Difference from 1910	1926 Voting-age population	Turnout	%	Difference from 1910
GEORGIA	622,000	43,361	7.0%	658,000	80,537	12.2%	5.3	696,000	70,621	10.1%	3.2	1,438,000	77,071	5.4%	-1.6	1,470,000	47,446	3.2%	-3.7
HAWAII																			
IDAHO	165,000	40,856	24.8%	190,000	47,618	25.1%	0.3	215,000	38,499	17.9%	-6.9	226,000	36,810	16.3%	-8.5	231,000	31,285	13.5%	-11.2
ILLINOIS	1,474,000	412,333	28.0%	1,596,000	375,465	23.5%	-4.4	1,719,000	426,943	24.8%	-3.1	3,746,000	666,583	17.8%	-10.2	4,130,000	779,146	18.9%	-9.1
INDIANA	794,000	312,153	39.3%	823,000	275,891	33.5%	-5.8	852,000	251,331	29.5%	-9.8	1,773,000	558,169	31.5%	-7.8	1,870,000	511,454	27.4%	-12.0
IOWA	613,000	187,353	30.6%	651,000	182,036	28.0%	-2.6	689,000	178,815	26.0%	-4.6	1,398,000	225,821	16.2%	-14.4	1,439,000	247,869	17.2%	-13.3
KANSAS	497,000	146,014	29.4%	950,000	195,830	20.6%	-8.8	976,000	171,897	17.6%	-11.8	1,019,000	271,058	26.6%	-2.8	1,067,000	196,084	18.4%	-11.0
KENTUCKY	600,000	175,574	29.3%	622,000	175,999	28.3%	-1.0	644,000	186,214	28.9%	-0.3	1,318,000	195,141	14.8%	-14.5	1,373,000	286,997	20.9%	-8.4
LOUISIANA	402,000	46,069	11.5%	425,000	40,545	9.5%	-1.9	447,000	44,794	10.0%	-1.4	962,000	44,180	4.6%	-6.9	1,050,000	54,180	5.2%	-6.3
MAINE	203,000	73,304	36.1%	206,000	62,076	30.1%	-6.0	209,000	59,050	28.3%	-7.9	427,000	75,256	17.6%	-18.5	433,000	80,748	18.6%	-17.5
MARYLAND	348,000	101,663	29.2%	375,000	111,410	29.7%	0.5	401,000	81,485	20.3%	-8.9	860,000	160,947	18.7%	-10.5	915,000	207,435	22.7%	-6.5
MASSACHUSETTS	766,000	229,352	29.9%	821,000	210,442	25.6%	-4.3	876,000	207,478	23.7%	-6.3	1,963,000	406,776	20.7%	-9.2	2,099,000	407,389	19.4%	-10.5
MICHIGAN	757,000	159,770	21.1%	903,000	212,063	23.5%	2.4	1,827,000	212,487	11.6%	-9.5	2,084,000	294,932	14.2%	-7.0	2,359,000	227,155	9.6%	11.5
MINNESOTA	585,000	103,779	17.7%	611,000	156,304	25.6%	7.8	636,000	82,619	13.0%	-4.7	1,302,000	133,482	10.3%	-7.5	1,389,000	38,008	2.7%	-15.0
MISSISSIPPI	425,000	23,865	5.6%	431,000	35,830	8.3%	2.7	437,000	31,599	7.2%	1.6	917,000	66,482	7.2%	1.6	980,000	26,917	2.7%	-2.9
MISSOURI	932,000	328,216	35.2%	967,000	318,587	32.9%	-2.3	1,002,000	287,840	28.7%	-6.5	2,043,000	506,267	24.8%	-10.4	2,143,000	506,015	23.6%	-11.6
MONTANA	135,000	28,071	20.8%	238,000	37,011	15.6%	-5.2	280,000	48,356	17.3%	-3.5	292,000	88,205	30.2%	9.4	292,000	75,833	26.0%	5.2
NEBRASKA	329,000	113,505	34.5%	341,000	120,206	35.3%	0.8	354,000	99,696	28.2%	-6.3	715,000	214,070	29.9%	-4.6	754,000	202,688	26.9%	-7.6
NEVADA	32,000	8,798	27.5%	44,000	9,623	21.9%	-5.6	44,000	12,875	29.3%	1.8	46,000	18,201	39.6%	12.1	48,000	14,521	30.3%	2.8
NEW HAMPSHIRE	111,000	37,737	34.0%	114,000	36,382	31.9%	-2.1	116,000	32,763	28.2%	-5.8	242,000	70,160	29.0%	-5.0	251,000	52,236	20.8%	-13.2
NEW JERSEY	603,000	225,817	37.4%	670,000	175,355	26.2%	-11.3	738,000	158,899	21.5%	-15.9	1,718,000	451,832	26.3%	-11.1	1,980,000	339,937	17.2%	-20.3
NEW MEXICO				87,000	19,805	22.8%		88,000	22,627	25.7%	2.9	170,000	60,969	35.9%	13.1	173,000	55,433	32.0%	9.3
NEW YORK	2,381,000	695,543	29.2%	2,564,000	571,419	22.3%	-6.9	5,038,000	1,009,936	20.0%	-9.2	5,630,000	1,397,657	24.8%	-4.4	6,300,000	1,523,813	24.2%	-5.0
NORTH CAROLINA	510,000	141,049	27.7%	549,000	122,129	22.2%	-5.4	588,000	143,519	24.4%	-3.2	1,302,000	225,921	17.4%	-10.3	1,432,000	220,155	15.4%	-12.3
NORTH DAKOTA	142,000	47,005	33.1%	149,000	34,746	23.3%	-9.8	156,000	36,733	23.5%	-9.6	306,000	92,464	30.2%	-2.9	323,000	25,731	8.0%	-25.1
OHIO	1,337,000	477,077	35.7%	1,469,000	493,804	33.6%	-2.1	1,601,000	486,403	30.4%	-5.3	3,420,000	821,948	24.0%	-11.6	3,680,000	702,733	19.1%	-16.6
OKLAHOMA	434,000	120,218	27.7%	477,000	119,443	25.0%	-2.7	973,000	105,050	10.8%	-16.9	1,072,000	285,581	26.6%	-1.1	1,165,000	213,167	18.3%	-9.4
OREGON	230,000	54,853	23.8%	410,000	111,748	27.3%	3.4	446,000	65,440	14.7%	-9.2	491,000	133,392	27.2%	3.3	538,000	93,470	17.4%	-6.5
PENNSYLVANIA	1,837,000	312,803	17.0%	1,977,000	453,380	22.9%	5.9	2,118,000	305,315	14.4%	-2.6	4,589,000	581,625	12.7%	-4.4	4,943,000	648,680	13.1%	-3.9
RHODE ISLAND	121,000	32,400	26.8%	129,000	35,190	27.3%	0.5	137,000	37,573	27.4%	0.6	310,000	82,889	26.7%	0.0	337,000	75,882	22.5%	-4.3
SOUTH CAROLINA	336,000	30,832	9.2%	359,000	34,606	9.6%	0.5	381,000	25,792	6.8%	-2.4	788,000	34,451	4.4%	-4.8	805,000	16,589	2.1%	-7.1
SOUTH DAKOTA	170,000	37,983	22.3%	174,000	47,668	27.4%	5.1	316,000	36,210	11.5%	-10.9	334,000	50,409	15.1%	-7.3	350,000	87,136	24.9%	2.6
TENNESSEE	551,000	147,887	26.8%	575,000	155,058	27.0%	0.1	599,000	98,628	16.5%	-10.4	1,268,000	151,523	11.9%	-14.9	1,350,000	84,979	6.3%	-20.5

Total Highest Statewide General Elections (continued)

Total Highest Statewide General Elections (continued)

Democratic Turnout for Election Years 1910–1926 (continued)

State	1910 Voting-age population	1910 Turnout	1910 %	1914 Voting-age population	1914 Turnout	1914 %	1914 Difference from 1910	1918 Voting-age population	1918 Turnout	1918 %	1918 Difference from 1910	1922 Voting-age population	1922 Turnout	1922 %	1922 Difference from 1910	1926 Voting-age population	1926 Turnout	1926 %	1926 Difference from 1910
TEXAS	955,000	182,187	19.1%	1,052,000	176,599	16.8%	-2.3	1,150,000	159,032	13.8%	-5.2	2,431,000	339,477	14.0%	-5.1	2,685,000	233,068	8.7%	-10.4
UTAH	164,000	32,730	20.0%	184,000	53,127	28.9%	8.9	204,000	49,258	24.1%	4.2	220,000	58,749	26.7%	6.7	234,000	54,204	23.2%	3.2
VERMONT	100,000	17,425	17.4%	100,000	26,776	26.8%	9.4	100,000	13,859	13.9%	-3.6	200,000	24,989	12.5%	-4.9	202,000	28,672	14.2%	-3.2
VIRGINIA	520,000	67,570	13.0%	557,000	58,320	10.5%	-2.5	594,000	40,403	6.8%	-6.2	1,222,000	116,393	9.5%	-3.5	1,262,000	74,365	5.9%	-7.1
WASHINGTON	606,000	44,827	7.4%	674,000	96,652	14.3%	6.9	741,000	81,350	11.0%	3.6	804,000	130,375	16.2%	8.8	862,000	152,229	17.7%	10.3
WEST VIRGINIA	314,000	103,293	32.9%	340,000	102,223	30.1%	-2.8	366,000	99,917	27.3%	-5.6	759,000	198,853	26.2%	-6.7	824,000	206,284	25.0%	-7.9
WISCONSIN	610,000	110,442	18.1%	644,000	134,925	21.0%	2.8	676,000	112,576	16.7%	-1.5	1,432,000	78,029	5.4%	-12.7	1,554,000	72,627	4.7%	-13.4
WYOMING	82,000	14,659	17.9%	92,000	22,387	24.3%	6.5	102,000	18,640	18.3%	0.4	110,000	35,734	32.5%	14.6	117,000	34,286	29.3%	11.4
Total	24,388,000	6,051,244	24.8%	27,974,000	6,440,851	23.0%	-1.8	33,725,000	6,244,347	18.5%	-6.3	57,897,000	10,435,282	18.0%	-6.8	62,807,000	9,954,776	15.8%	-9.0

Other Turnout for Election Years 1910–1926

State	1910 Voting-age population	1910 Turnout	1910 %	1914 Voting-age population	1914 Turnout	1914 %	1914 Difference from 1910*	1918 Voting-age population	1918 Turnout	1918 %	1918 Difference from 1910	1922 Voting-age population	1922 Turnout	1922 %	1922 Difference from 1910	1926 Voting-age population	1926 Turnout	1926 %	1926 Difference from 1910
ALABAMA	512,000	1,868	0.4%	537,000	5,424	1.0%	0.6					1,196,000	1,697	0.1%	-0.2				
ALASKA																			
ARIZONA				106,000	13,483	12.7%		132,000	754	0.6%	-12.1								
ARKANSAS	395,000	9,196	2.3%	419,000	10,434	2.5%	0.2	442,000	4,792	1.1%	-1.2								
CALIFORNIA	715,000	53,687	7.5%	1,660,000	538,665	32.4%	24.9	1,921,000	280,518	14.6%	7.1	2,357,000	127,925	5.4%	-2.1	2,850,000	51,763	1.8%	-5.7
COLORADO	452,000	13,309	2.9%	481,000	52,448	10.9%	8.0	509,000	8,626	1.7%	-1.2	536,000	5,764	1.1%	-1.9	555,000	9,997	1.8%	-1.1
CONNECTICUT	258,000	15,410	6.0%	281,000	15,957	5.7%	-0.3	303,000	5,696	1.9%	-4.1	680,000	7,106	1.0%	-4.9	746,000	3,198	0.4%	-5.5
DELAWARE	57,000	1,331	2.3%	60,000	2,116	3.5%	1.2	64,000	420	0.7%	-1.7	131,000	908	0.7%	-1.6				
DISTRICT OF COLUMBIA																			
FLORIDA	206,000	5,185	2.5%	232,000	125	0.1%	-2.5					610,000	169	0.0%	-2.5				
GEORGIA	622,000	114	0.0%	658,000	28,435	4.3%	4.3					1,438,000	347	0.0%	0.0				
HAWAII																			
IDAHO	165,000	5,463	3.3%	190,000	19,946	10.5%	7.2					226,000	40,516	17.9%	14.6	231,000	37,047	16.0%	12.7
ILLINOIS	1,474,000	66,774	4.5%	1,596,000	251,744	15.8%	11.2	1,719,000	43,586	2.5%	-2.0	3,746,000	68,906	1.8%	-2.7	4,130,000	19,695	0.5%	-4.1
INDIANA	794,000	31,844	4.0%	823,000	147,044	17.9%	13.9	852,000	9,273	1.1%	-2.9	1,773,000	14,635	0.8%	-3.2	1,870,000	10,526	0.6%	-3.4
IOWA	613,000	19,933	3.3%	651,000	54,019	8.3%	5.0	689,000	9,630	1.4%	-1.9	1,398,000	2,595	0.2%	-3.1	1,439,000	908	0.1%	-3.2
KANSAS	497,000	17,759	3.6%	950,000	156,968	16.5%	12.9	976,000	12,837	1.3%	-2.3	1,019,000	9,143	0.9%	-2.7	1,067,000	8,210	0.8%	-2.8
KENTUCKY	600,000	6,046	1.0%	622,000	26,363	4.2%	3.2					1,318,000	19,478	1.5%	0.5				
LOUISIANA	402,000	1,070	0.3%	425,000	9,750	2.3%	2.0	447,000	1	0.0%	-0.3	962,000	18	0.0%	-0.3	1,050,000	13	0.0%	-0.3
MAINE	203,000	3,000	1.5%	206,000	20,703	10.1%	8.6												

Total Highest Statewide General Elections (continued)

Other Turnout for Election Years 1910–1926 (continued)

State	1910 Voting-age population	Turnout	%	1914 Voting-age population	Turnout	%	Difference from 1910	1918 Voting-age population	Turnout	%	Difference from 1910	1922 Voting-age population	Turnout	%	Difference from 1910	1926 Voting-age population	Turnout	%	Difference from 1910
MARYLAND	348,000	7,647	2.2%	375,000	11,065	3.0%	0.8	401,000	2,512	0.6%	-1.6	860,000	7,137	0.8%	-1.4	915,000	3,659	0.4%	-1.8
MASSACHUSETTS	766,000	17,306	2.3%	821,000	49,435	6.0%	3.8	876,000	22,077	2.5%	0.3	1,963,000	49,251	2.5%	0.2	2,099,000	9,771	0.5%	-1.8
MICHIGAN	757,000	21,189	2.8%	903,000	61,654	6.8%	4.0	1,827,000	9,496	0.5%	-2.3	2,084,000	8,476	0.4%	-2.4	2,359,000	4,033	0.2%	-2.6
MINNESOTA	585,000	26,643	4.6%	611,000	54,033	8.8%	4.3	636,000	137,294	21.6%	17.0	1,302,000	325,372	25.0%	20.4	1,389,000	266,845	19.2%	14.7
MISSISSIPPI	425,000	23	0.0%	431,000	1,124	0.3%	0.3	437,000	1,569	0.4%	0.4	917,000	3,362	0.4%	0.4				
MISSOURI	932,000	23,936	2.6%	967,000	49,557	5.1%	2.6	1,002,000	6,710	0.7%	-1.9	2,043,000	8,089	0.4%	-2.2	2,143,000	9,817	0.5%	-2.1
MONTANA	135,000	5,184	3.8%	238,000	18,936	8.0%	4.1	280,000	26,013	9.3%	5.5	292,000	1,545	0.5%	-3.3	292,000	3,104	1.1%	-2.8
NEBRASKA	329,000	6,279	1.9%	341,000	17,282	5.1%	3.2	354,000	3,409	1.0%	-0.9	715,000	23,087	3.2%	1.3	754,000	8,130	1.1%	-0.8
NEVADA	32,000	2,409	7.5%	44,000	5,451	12.4%	4.9	44,000	1,377	3.1%	-4.4					48,000	543	1.1%	-6.4
NEW HAMPSHIRE	111,000	1,522	1.4%	114,000	4,021	3.5%	2.2	116,000	7	0.0%	-1.4								
NEW JERSEY	603,000	16,901	2.8%	670,000	31,149	4.6%	1.8	738,000	22,843	3.1%	0.3	1,718,000	8,907	0.5%	-2.3	1,980,000	3,628	0.2%	-2.6
NEW MEXICO				87,000	2,805	3.2%		88,000	847	1.0%	-2.3	170,000	871	0.5%	-2.7	173,000	297	0.2%	-3.1
NEW YORK	2,381,000	125,042	5.3%	2,564,000	212,042	8.3%	3.0	5,038,000	183,389	3.6%	-1.6	5,630,000	155,126	2.8%	-2.5	6,300,000	113,826	1.8%	-3.4
NORTH CAROLINA	510,000	443	0.1%	549,000	773	0.1%	0.1												
NORTH DAKOTA	142,000	3,225	2.3%	149,000	10,282	6.9%	4.6					306,000	81,048	26.5%	24.2	323,000	23,928	7.4%	5.1
OHIO	1,337,000	70,686	5.3%	1,469,000	120,312	8.2%	2.9	1,601,000	17,344	1.1%	-4.2	3,420,000	21,514	0.6%	-4.7	3,680,000	7,582	0.2%	-5.1
OKLAHOMA	434,000	27,921	6.4%	477,000	57,691	12.1%	5.7	973,000	7,438	0.8%	-5.7	1,072,000	4,043	0.4%	-6.1	1,165,000	3,427	0.3%	-6.1
OREGON	230,000	18,603	8.1%	410,000	66,916	16.3%	8.2	446,000	16,868	3.8%	-4.3	491,000	4,689	1.0%	-7.1	538,000	53,391	9.9%	1.8
PENNSYLVANIA	1,837,000	386,432	21.0%	1,977,000	325,610	16.5%	-4.6	2,118,000	54,793	2.6%	-18.4	4,589,000	205,756	4.5%	-16.6	4,943,000	48,754	1.0%	-20.0
RHODE ISLAND	121,000	1,682	1.4%	129,000	3,845	3.0%	1.6	137,000	1,737	1.3%	-0.1	310,000	7,070	2.3%	0.9	337,000	743	0.2%	-1.2
SOUTH CAROLINA	336,000	70	0.0%	359,000	269	0.1%	0.1												
SOUTH DAKOTA	170,000	6,085	3.6%	174,000	14,461	8.3%	4.7	316,000	27,127	8.6%	5.0	334,000	46,033	13.8%	10.2	350,000	22,595	6.5%	2.9
TENNESSEE	551,000	4,942	0.9%	575,000	11,826	2.1%	1.2	599,000	178	0.0%	-0.9					1,350,000	151	0.0%	-0.9
TEXAS	955,000	29,554	3.1%	1,052,000	26,771	2.5%	-0.5	1,150,000	1,660	0.1%	-3.0					2,685,000	908	0.0%	-3.1
UTAH	164,000	18,899	11.5%	184,000	5,673	3.1%	-8.4	204,000	1,067	0.5%	-11.0	220,000	3,888	1.8%	-9.8	234,000	1,315	0.6%	-11.0
VERMONT	100,000	2,140	2.1%	100,000	10,801	10.8%	8.7	100,000	106	0.1%	-2.0	200,000	144	0.1%	-2.1	202,000	52	0.0%	-2.1
VIRGINIA	520,000	1,631	0.3%	557,000	2,911	0.5%	0.2	594,000	131	0.0%	-0.3	1,222,000	2,627	0.2%	-0.1	1,262,000	727	0.1%	-0.3
WASHINGTON	606,000	15,125	2.5%	674,000	123,067	18.3%	15.8	741,000	7,879	1.1%	-1.4	804,000	39,557	4.9%	2.4	862,000	3,513	0.4%	-2.1
WEST VIRGINIA	314,000	11,834	3.8%	340,000	22,608	6.6%	2.9	366,000	2,288	0.6%	-3.1	759,000	4,895	0.6%	-3.1	824,000	163	0.0%	-3.7
WISCONSIN	610,000	47,461	7.8%	644,000	65,134	10.1%	2.3	676,000	70,071	10.4%	2.6	1,432,000	62,838	4.4%	-3.4	1,554,000	129,358	8.3%	0.5
WYOMING	82,000	22,691	27.7%	92,000	3,001	3.3%	-24.4					110,000	687	0.6%	-27.0	117,000	300	0.3%	-27.4
Total	24,388,000	1,175,494	4.8%	27,974,000	2,744,129	9.8%	5.0	29,912,000	1,002,363	3.4%	-1.5	50,353,000	1,375,219	2.7%	-2.1	52,816,000	861,917	1.6%	-3.2

*Percentage point difference between turnout in current year and initial year listed in chart. If data do not appear for a state in the initial year listed, the difference is calculated from the first year in which data do appear for that state.

STATE GUBERNATORIAL PRIMARY ELECTIONS

Election Years 1910–1926

State*	1910			1914				1918				1922				1926			
	Voting-age population	Turnout	%	Voting-age population	Turnout	%	Difference from 1910**	Voting-age population	Turnout	%	Difference from 1910	Voting-age population	Turnout	%	Difference from 1910	Voting-age population	Turnout	%	Difference from 1910
ALABAMA																			
ALASKA																			
ARIZONA																			
ARKANSAS																			
CALIFORNIA																			
COLORADO				478,000	95,034	19.9%		508,000	105,379	20.7%	0.9	532,000	119,420	22.4%	2.6	552,000	171,583	31.1%	11.2
CONNECTICUT																			
DELAWARE																			
DISTRICT OF COLUMBIA																			
FLORIDA																			
GEORGIA																			
HAWAII																			
IDAHO	162,000	70,380	43.4%	186,000	59,051	31.7%	-11.7	211,000	66,194	31.4%	-12.1								
ILLINOIS																			
INDIANA																			
IOWA	609,000	224,451	36.9%	647,000	224,060	34.6%	-2.2	685,000	166,914	24.4%	-12.5								
KANSAS	496,000	181,859	36.7%	946,000	197,672	20.9%	-15.8	974,000	200,901	20.6%	-16.0	1,012,000	258,147	25.5%	-11.2	1,060,000	294,965	27.8%	-8.8
KENTUCKY																			
LOUISIANA																			
MAINE																			
MARYLAND																			
MASSACHUSETTS																			
MICHIGAN																			
MINNESOTA																			
MISSISSIPPI																			
MISSOURI																			
MONTANA																			
NEBRASKA																			
NEVADA	32,000	12,604	39.4%					44,000	16,761	38.1%	-1.3	46,000	16,922	36.8%	-2.6				
NEW HAMPSHIRE	111,000	38,767	34.9%	114,000	30,003	26.3%	-8.6	115,000	21,704	18.9%	-16.1					249,000	65,208	26.2%	-8.7
NEW JERSEY																			
NEW MEXICO																			
NEW YORK																			

State Gubernatorial Primary Elections *(continued)*

Election Years 1910–1926 *(continued)*

State	1910 Voting-age population	Turnout	%	1914 Voting-age population	Turnout	%	Difference from 1910	1918 Voting-age population	Turnout	%	Difference from 1910	1922 Voting-age population	Turnout	%	Difference from 1910	1926 Voting-age population	Turnout	%	Difference from 1910
NORTH CAROLINA																			
NORTH DAKOTA	141,000	66,146	46.9%	148,000	77,132	52.1%	5.2	154,000	102,969	66.9%	20.0	303,000	190,703	62.9%	16.0	321,000	168,637	52.5%	5.6
OHIO				1,455,000	434,716	29.9%		1,587,000	371,588	23.4%	-6.5	3,383,000	716,092	21.2%	-8.7	3,644,000	685,502	18.8%	-11.1
OKLAHOMA	430,000	221,301	51.5%	472,000	181,502	38.5%	-13.0	965,000	155,114	16.1%	-35.4	1,059,000	308,533	29.1%	-22.3	1,151,000	306,620	26.6%	-24.8
OREGON																			
PENNSYLVANIA																4,896,000	1,596,750	32.6%	
RHODE ISLAND																			
SOUTH CAROLINA																			
SOUTH DAKOTA								314,000	44,354	14.1%						348,000	87,252	25.1%	10.9
TENNESSEE																			
TEXAS																2,645,000	1,581,981	59.8%	
UTAH																			
VERMONT								100,000	35,077	35.1%		200,000	48,386	24.2%	-10.5	201,000	52,528	26.1%	-8.6
VIRGINIA																			
WASHINGTON																			
WEST VIRGINIA																			
WISCONSIN				640,000	212,187	33.2%						1,415,000	538,340	38.0%	4.9	1,538,000	311,724	20.3%	-12.9
WYOMING								100,000	22,306	22.3%		109,000	44,349	40.7%	18.6	116,000	43,571	37.6%	15.5
Total	1,981,000	815,508	41.2%	5,086,000	1,511,357	29.7%	-11.5	5,757,000	1,309,261	22.7%	-18.4	8,059,000	2,240,892	27.8%	-13.4	16,721,000	5,366,321	32.1%	-9.1

*Overall primary turnout reflects only states with primaries in both parties. To find single party primary results, see partisan primary charts.

**Percentage point difference between turnout in current year and initial year listed in chart. If data do not appear for a state in the initial year listed, the difference is calculated from the first year in which data do appear for that state.

STATE GUBERNATORIAL PRIMARY ELECTIONS

Republican Turnout for Election Years 1910–1926

State	1910			1914				1918				1922				1926			
	Voting-age population	Turnout	%	Voting-age population	Turnout	%	Difference from 1910*	Voting-age population	Turnout	%	Difference from 1910	Voting-age population	Turnout	%	Difference from 1910	Voting-age population	Turnout	%	Difference from 1910
ALABAMA																			
ALASKA																			
ARIZONA																			
ARKANSAS																			
CALIFORNIA																			
COLORADO				478,000	43,089	9.0%		508,000	45,963	9.0%	0.0	532,000	54,101	10.2%	1.2	552,000	118,032	21.4%	12.4
CONNECTICUT																			
DELAWARE																			
DISTRICT OF COLUMBIA																			
FLORIDA																			
GEORGIA																			
HAWAII																			
IDAHO	162,000	59,592	36.8%	186,000	40,803	21.9%	-14.8	211,000	29,339	13.9%	-22.9								
ILLINOIS																			
INDIANA																			
IOWA	609,000	176,899	29.0%	647,000	142,596	22.0%	-7.0	685,000	127,753	18.7%	-10.4								
KANSAS	496,000	137,184	27.7%	946,000	105,800	11.2%	-16.5	974,000	162,683	16.7%	-11.0	1,012,000	200,431	19.8%	-7.9	1,060,000	232,571	21.9%	-5.7
KENTUCKY																			
LOUISIANA																			
MAINE																			
MARYLAND																			
MASSACHUSETTS																			
MICHIGAN																			
MINNESOTA																1,376,000	410,176	29.8%	
MISSISSIPPI																			
MISSOURI																			
MONTANA																			
NEBRASKA																			
NEVADA	32,000	6,059	18.9%					44,000	6,573	14.9%	-4.0	46,000	8,303	18.1%	-0.9				
NEW HAMPSHIRE	111,000	29,877	26.9%	114,000	19,293	16.9%	-10.0	115,000	16,497	14.3%	-12.6					249,000	56,423	22.7%	-4.3
NEW JERSEY																			
NEW MEXICO																			
NEW YORK																			

State Gubernatorial Primary Elections *(continued)*

Republican Turnout for Election Years 1910–1926 *(continued)*

State	1910 Voting-age population	Turnout	%	1914 Voting-age population	Turnout	%	Difference from 1910	1918 Voting-age population	Turnout	%	Difference from 1910	1922 Voting-age population	Turnout	%	Difference from 1910	1926 Voting-age population	Turnout	%	Difference from 1910
NORTH CAROLINA																			
NORTH DAKOTA	141,000	56,376	40.0%	148,000	61,201	41.4%	1.4	154,000	92,064	59.8%	19.8	303,000	180,368	59.5%	19.5	321,000	162,225	50.5%	10.6
OHIO				1,455,000	230,696	15.9%		1,587,000	238,153	15.0%	-0.8	3,383,000	464,539	13.7%	-2.1	3,644,000	472,987	13.0%	-2.9
OKLAHOMA	430,000	84,158	19.6%	472,000	31,770	6.7%	-12.8	965,000	41,404	4.3%	-15.3	1,059,000	37,809	3.6%	-16.0	1,151,000	68,859	6.0%	-13.6
OREGON																			
PENNSYLVANIA																4,896,000	1,415,967	28.9%	
RHODE ISLAND																			
SOUTH CAROLINA																			
SOUTH DAKOTA	169,000	68,153	40.3%	174,000	45,935	26.4%	-13.9	314,000	35,752	11.4%	-28.9					348,000	78,898	22.7%	-17.7
TENNESSEE																			
TEXAS																2,645,000	766,318	29.0%	
UTAH																			
VERMONT								100,000	32,587	32.6%		200,000	45,401	22.7%	9.9	201,000	50,301	25.0%	-7.6
VIRGINIA																			
WASHINGTON																			
WEST VIRGINIA																			
WISCONSIN				640,000	124,617	19.5%						1,415,000	500,548	35.4%	15.9	1,538,000	282,590	18.4%	-1.1
WYOMING				91,000	10,039	11.0%		100,000	14,587	14.6%	3.6	109,000	31,777	29.2%	18.1	116,000	30,396	26.2%	15.2
Total	2,150,000	618,298	28.8%	5,351,000	855,839	16.0%	-12.8	5,757,000	843,355	14.6%	-14.1	8,059,000	1,523,277	18.9%	-9.9	18,097,000	4,145,743	22.9%	-5.8

Democratic Turnout for Election Years 1910–1926

State	1910 Voting-age population	Turnout	%	1914 Voting-age population	Turnout	%	Difference from 1910*	1918 Voting-age population	Turnout	%	Difference from 1910	1922 Voting-age population	Turnout	%	Difference from 1910	1926 Voting-age population	Turnout	%	Difference from 1910
ALABAMA												1,184,000	207,368	17.5%		1,267,000	222,675	17.6%	0.1
ALASKA																			
ARIZONA																			
ARKANSAS												886,000	181,300	20.5%		927,000	219,213	23.6%	3.2
CALIFORNIA																			
COLORADO				478,000	45,832	9.6%		508,000	59,416	11.7%	2.1	532,000	65,319	12.3%	2.7	552,000	53,551	9.7%	0.1
CONNECTICUT																			
DELAWARE																			
DISTRICT OF COLUMBIA																			
FLORIDA																			

State Gubernatorial Primary Elections (continued)

State Gubernatorial Primary Elections (continued)

Democratic Turnout for Election Years 1910–1926 (continued)

State	1910 Voting-age population	Turnout	%	1914 Voting-age population	Turnout	%	Difference from 1910	1918 Voting-age population	Turnout	%	Difference from 1910	1922 Voting-age population	Turnout	%	Difference from 1910	1926 Voting-age population	Turnout	%	Difference from 1910
GEORGIA												1,434,000	210,173	14.7%		1,465,000	193,025	13.2%	-1.5
HAWAII																			
IDAHO	162,000	10,788	6.7%	186,000	15,147	8.1%	1.5	211,000	36,855	17.5%	10.8								
ILLINOIS																			
INDIANA																			
IOWA	609,000	47,552	7.8%	647,000	73,776	11.4%	3.6	685,000	39,161	5.7%	-2.1								
KANSAS	496,000	40,914	8.2%	946,000	72,736	7.7%	-0.6	974,000	36,976	3.8%	-4.5	1,012,000	57,206	5.7%	-2.6	1,060,000	62,235	5.9%	-2.4
KENTUCKY																			
LOUISIANA																			
MAINE																			
MARYLAND																			
MASSACHUSETTS																			
MICHIGAN																			
MINNESOTA																			
MISSISSIPPI																			
MISSOURI																			
MONTANA																			
NEBRASKA																			
NEVADA	32,000	6,545	20.5%	45,000	7,784	17.3%	-3.2	44,000	10,188	23.2%	2.7	46,000	8,619	18.7%	-1.7				
NEW HAMPSHIRE	111,000	8,890	8.0%	114,000	10,710	9.4%	1.4	115,000	5,207	4.5%	-3.5					249,000	8,354	3.4%	-4.7
NEW JERSEY																			
NEW MEXICO																			
NEW YORK																			
NORTH CAROLINA																			
NORTH DAKOTA	141,000	9,770	6.9%	148,000	12,881	8.7%	1.8	154,000	10,905	7.1%	0.2	303,000	10,335	3.4%	-3.5	321,000	6,141	1.9%	-5.0
OHIO				1,455,000	204,020	14.0%		1,587,000	133,435	8.4%	-5.6	3,383,000	251,553	7.4%	-6.6	3,644,000	212,515	5.8%	-8.2
OKLAHOMA	430,000	123,734	28.8%	472,000	131,291	27.8%	-1.0	965,000	107,919	11.2%	-17.6	1,059,000	269,538	25.5%	-3.3	1,151,000	237,580	20.6%	-8.1
OREGON																			
PENNSYLVANIA																4,896,000	172,871	3.5%	
RHODE ISLAND																			
SOUTH CAROLINA												786,000	166,730	21.2%		803,000	165,042	20.6%	-0.7
SOUTH DAKOTA								314,000	8,361	2.7%						348,000	8,354	2.4%	-0.3
TENNESSEE												1,256,000	163,061	13.0%		1,339,000	185,033	13.8%	0.8

State Gubernatorial Primary Elections (continued)

Democratic Turnout for Election Years 1910–1926 (continued)

State	1910 Voting-age population	Turnout	%	1914 Voting-age population	Turnout	%	Difference from 1910	1918 Voting-age population	Turnout	%	Difference from 1910	1922 Voting-age population	Turnout	%	Difference from 1910	1926 Voting-age population	Turnout	%	Difference from 1910
TEXAS												2,391,000	571,558	23.9%		2,645,000	815,663	30.8%	6.9
UTAH																			
VERMONT								100,000	2,490	2.5%		200,000	2,985	1.5%	-1.0	201,000	2,227	1.1%	-1.4
VIRGINIA																			
WASHINGTON																			
WEST VIRGINIA																			
WISCONSIN				640,000	72,952	11.4%						1,415,000	18,897	1.3%	-10.1	1,538,000	16,358	1.1%	-10.3
WYOMING								100,000	7,719	7.7%		109,000	12,572	11.5%	3.8	116,000	13,175	11.4%	3.6
Total	1,981,000	248,193	12.5%	5,131,000	647,129	12.6%	0.1	5,757,000	458,632	8.0%	-4.6	15,996,000	2,197,214	13.7%	1.2	22,522,000	2,594,012	11.5%	-1.0

Other Turnout for Election Years 1910–1926

State	1910 Voting-age population	Turnout	%	1914 Voting-age population	Turnout	%	Difference from 1910*	1918 Voting-age population	Turnout	%	Difference from 1910	1922 Voting-age population	Turnout	%	Difference from 1910	1926 Voting-age population	Turnout	%	Difference from 1910
COLORADO				478,000	6,113	1.3%													
IDAHO				186,000	3,101	1.7%													
IOWA				647,000	7,688	1.2%													
KANSAS	496,000	3,761	0.8%	946,000	19,136	2.0%	1.3	974,000	1,242	0.1%	-0.6	1,012,000	510	0.1%	-0.7	1,060,000	159	0.0%	-0.7
MINNESOTA																1,376,000	152,436	11.1%	
NORTH DAKOTA				148,000	3,050	2.1%										321,000	271	0.1%	-2.0
OKLAHOMA	430,000	13,409	3.1%	472,000	18,441	3.9%	0.8	965,000	5,791	0.6%	-2.5	1,059,000	1,186	0.1%	-3.0	1,151,000	181	0.0%	-3.1
PENNSYLVANIA																4,896,000	7,912	0.2%	
SOUTH DAKOTA								314,000	241	0.1%									
WISCONSIN				640,000	14,618	2.3%		673,000	239,585	35.6%	33.3	1,415,000	18,895	1.3%	-0.9	1,538,000	12,776	0.8%	-1.5
WYOMING				91,000	366	0.4%													
Total	926,000	17,170	1.9%	3,608,000	72,513	2.0%	0.2	2,926,000	246,859	8.4%	6.6	3,486,000	20,591	0.6%	-1.3	10,342,000	173,735	1.7%	-0.2

*Percentage point difference between turnout in current year and initial year listed in chart. If data do not appear for a state in the initial year listed, the difference is calculated from the first year in which data do appear for that state.

UNITED STATES SENATE PRIMARY ELECTIONS

Election Years 1910–1926

State*	1910 Voting-age population	Turnout	%	1914** Voting-age population	Turnout	%	1918 Voting-age population	Turnout	%	Difference from 1914***	1922 Voting-age population	Turnout	%	Difference from 1914	1926 Voting-age population	Turnout	%	Difference from 1914
ALABAMA																		
ALASKA																		
ARIZONA																		
ARKANSAS																		
CALIFORNIA																		
COLORADO				478,000	75,758	15.8%	508,000	89,436	17.6%	1.8					552,000	169,257	30.7%	14.8
CONNECTICUT																		
DELAWARE																		
DISTRICT OF COLUMBIA																		
FLORIDA																		
GEORGIA																		
HAWAII																		
IDAHO				186,000	68,052	36.6%	211,000	61,546	29.2%	-7.4								
ILLINOIS				1,583,000	542,587	34.3%	1,705,000	609,547	35.8%	1.5					4,075,000	1,443,141	35.4%	1.1
INDIANA											1,760,000	657,999	37.4%					
IOWA				647,000	227,686	35.2%	685,000	164,778	24.1%	-11.1					1,434,000	438,856	30.6%	-4.6
KANSAS				946,000	206,912	21.9%	974,000	213,306	21.9%	0.0					1,060,000	271,560	25.6%	3.7
KENTUCKY																		
LOUISIANA																		
MAINE																		
MARYLAND																		
MASSACHUSETTS																		
MICHIGAN																		
MINNESOTA																		
MISSISSIPPI																		
MISSOURI				963,000	385,459	40.0%	998,000	309,814	31.0%	-9.0	2,029,000	664,872	32.8%	-7.3	2,129,000	608,070	28.6%	-11.5
MONTANA							275,000	73,982	26.9%		291,000	108,643	37.3%	10.4				
NEBRASKA																		
NEVADA															48,000	21,904	45.6%	
NEW HAMPSHIRE				114,000	29,019	25.5%	115,000	24,523	21.3%	-4.1					249,000	65,351	26.2%	0.8
NEW JERSEY																		
NEW MEXICO																		
NEW YORK																		

United States Senate Primary Elections *(continued)*

Election Years 1910–1926 *(continued)*

	1910			1914			1918				1922				1926			
State	Voting-age population	Turnout	%	Voting-age population	Turnout	%	Voting-age population	Turnout	%	Difference from 1914	Voting-age population	Turnout	%	Difference from 1914	Voting-age population	Turnout	%	Difference from 1914
NORTH CAROLINA																		
NORTH DAKOTA				148,000	74,134	50.1%					303,000	189,177	62.4%	12.3	321,000	168,538	52.5%	2.4
OHIO				1,455,000	403,939	27.8%					3,383,000	602,358	17.8%	-10.0	3,644,000	614,988	16.9%	-10.9
OKLAHOMA				472,000	158,568	33.6%	965,000	135,558	14.0%	-19.5					1,151,000	257,194	22.3%	-11.2
OREGON																		
PENNSYLVANIA															4,896,000	1,612,012	32.9%	
RHODE ISLAND																		
SOUTH CAROLINA																		
SOUTH DAKOTA							314,000	48,435	15.4%									
TENNESSEE																		
TEXAS																		
UTAH																		
VERMONT											200,000	45,080	22.5%		201,000	46,701	23.2%	0.7
VIRGINIA																		
WASHINGTON											795,000	218,560	27.5%		854,000	224,665	26.3%	-1.2
WEST VIRGINIA																		
WISCONSIN				640,000	219,220	34.3%	673,000	253,588	37.7%	3.4	1,415,000	519,717	36.7%	2.5	1,538,000	494,714	32.2%	-2.1
WYOMING							100,000	16,895	16.9%		109,000	37,837	34.7%	17.8				
Total				7,632,000	2,391,334	31.3%	7,523,000	2,001,408	26.6%	-4.7	10,285,000	3,044,243	29.6%	-1.7	22,152,000	6,436,951	29.1%	-2.3

*Overall primary turnout reflects only states with primaries in both parties. To find single party primary results, see partisan primary charts.

**The Seventeenth Amendment, ratified in 1913, instituted direct election of U.S. Senators.

***Percentage point difference between turnout in current year and initial year listed in chart. If data do not appear for a state in the initial year listed, the difference is calculated from the first year in which data do appear for that state.

UNITED STATES SENATE PRIMARY ELECTIONS

Republican Turnout for Election Years 1910–1926

State	1910 Voting-age population	1910 Turnout	1910 %	1914* Voting-age population	1914* Turnout	1914* %	1918 Voting-age population	1918 Turnout	1918 %	1918 Difference from 1914**	1922 Voting-age population	1922 Turnout	1922 %	1922 Difference from 1914	1926 Voting-age population	1926 Turnout	1926 %	1926 Difference from 1914
ALABAMA																		
ALASKA																		
ARIZONA																		
ARKANSAS																		
CALIFORNIA																		
COLORADO				478,000	38,726	8.1%	508,000	46,772	9.2%	1.1					552,000	115,494	20.9%	12.8
CONNECTICUT																		
DELAWARE																		
DISTRICT OF COLUMBIA																		
FLORIDA																		
GEORGIA																		
HAWAII																		
IDAHO				186,000	46,671	25.1%	211,000	27,979	13.3%	-11.8								
ILLINOIS				1,583,000	216,077	13.6%	1,705,000	399,383	23.4%	9.8					4,075,000	1,146,794	28.1%	14.5
INDIANA											1,760,000	390,670	22.2%					
IOWA				647,000	141,707	21.9%	685,000	127,960	18.7%	-3.2	1,403,000	323,622	23.1%	1.2	1,434,000	422,333	29.5%	7.5
KANSAS				946,000	113,818	12.0%	974,000	173,471	17.8%	5.8					1,060,000	217,217	20.5%	8.5
KENTUCKY																		
LOUISIANA																		
MAINE																		
MARYLAND																		
MASSACHUSETTS																		
MICHIGAN																		
MINNESOTA																		
MISSISSIPPI																		
MISSOURI				963,000	118,600	12.3%	998,000	112,746	11.3%	-1.0	2,029,000	267,735	13.2%	0.9	2,129,000	308,914	14.5%	2.2
MONTANA							275,000	45,263	16.5%		291,000	70,383	24.2%	7.7				
NEBRASKA																		
NEVADA							44,000	6,426	14.6%		46,000	8,758	19.0%	4.4	48,000	12,414	25.9%	11.3
NEW HAMPSHIRE				114,000	17,796	15.6%	115,000	19,200	16.7%	1.1					249,000	56,456	22.7%	7.1
NEW JERSEY																		
NEW MEXICO																		
NEW YORK																		

United States Senate Primary Elections (continued)

Republican Turnout for Election Years 1910–1926 (continued)

State	1910 Voting-age population	Turnout	%	1914 Voting-age population	Turnout	%	1918 Voting-age population	Turnout	%	Difference from 1914	1922 Voting-age population	Turnout	%	Difference from 1914	1926 Voting-age population	Turnout	%	Difference from 1914
NORTH CAROLINA																		
NORTH DAKOTA				148,000	58,272	39.4%					303,000	177,471	58.6%	19.2	321,000	161,958	50.5%	11.1
OHIO				1,455,000	218,594	15.0%					3,383,000	385,147	11.4%	-3.6	3,644,000	419,479	11.5%	-3.5
OKLAHOMA				472,000	25,438	5.4%	965,000	35,490	3.7%	-1.7					1,151,000	56,351	4.9%	-0.5
OREGON																		
PENNSYLVANIA															4,896,000	1,451,557	29.6%	
RHODE ISLAND																		
SOUTH CAROLINA																		
SOUTH DAKOTA				174,000	45,193	26.0%	314,000	38,780	12.4%	-13.6					348,000	77,208	22.2%	-3.8
TENNESSEE																		
TEXAS																		
UTAH																		
VERMONT											200,000	42,103	21.1%		201,000	44,508	22.2%	1.1
VIRGINIA																		
WASHINGTON											795,000	196,752	24.7%		854,000	215,142	25.2%	0.4
WEST VIRGINIA																		
WISCONSIN				640,000	115,178	18.0%	673,000	143,958	21.4%	3.4	1,415,000	501,772	35.5%	17.5	1,538,000	466,637	30.3%	12.3
WYOMING							100,000	12,709	12.7%		109,000	25,055	23.0%	10.3				
Total				7,806,000	1,156,070	14.8%	7,567,000	1,190,137	15.7%	0.9	11,734,000	2,389,468	20.4%	5.6	22,500,000	5,172,542	23.0%	8.2

Democratic Turnout for Election Years 1910–1926

State	1910 Voting-age population	Turnout	%	1914* Voting-age population	Turnout	%	1918 Voting-age population	Turnout	%	Difference from 1914**	1922 Voting-age population	Turnout	%	Difference from 1914	1926 Voting-age population	Turnout	%	Difference from 1914
ALABAMA																		
ALASKA																		
ARIZONA																		
ARKANSAS																		
CALIFORNIA																		
COLORADO				478,000	37,032	7.7%	508,000	42,664	8.4%	0.7					552,000	53,763	9.7%	2.0
CONNECTICUT																		
DELAWARE																		
DISTRICT OF COLUMBIA																		
FLORIDA											591,000	88,759	15.0%					

United States Senate Primary Elections (continued)

United States Senate Primary Elections *(continued)*

Democratic Turnout for Election Years 1910–1926 *(continued)*

State	1910 Voting-age population	1910 Turnout	1910 %	1914 Voting-age population	1914 Turnout	1914 %	1914 Difference from 1910	1918 Voting-age population	1918 Turnout	1918 %	1918 Difference from 1910	1922 Voting-age population	1922 Turnout	1922 %	1922 Difference from 1910	1926 Voting-age population	1926 Turnout	1926 %	1926 Difference from 1910
GEORGIA																			
HAWAII																			
IDAHO				186,000	18,539	10.0%		211,000	33,567	15.9%	5.9								
ILLINOIS				1,583,000	297,337	18.8%		1,705,000	208,363	12.2%	-6.6					4,075,000	295,852	7.3%	-11.5
INDIANA												1,760,000	267,329	15.2%					
IOWA				647,000	78,995	12.2%		685,000	36,818	5.4%	-6.8					1,434,000	16,523	1.2%	-11.1
KANSAS				946,000	73,942	7.8%		974,000	38,590	4.0%	-3.9					1,060,000	54,183	5.1%	-2.7
KENTUCKY																			
LOUISIANA																			
MAINE																			
MARYLAND																			
MASSACHUSETTS																			
MICHIGAN																			
MINNESOTA																			
MISSISSIPPI												908,000	158,880	17.5%					
MISSOURI				963,000	256,984	26.7%		998,000	195,606	19.6%	-7.1	2,029,000	395,947	19.5%	-7.2	2,129,000	299,052	14.0%	-12.6
MONTANA								275,000	28,719	10.4%		291,000	38,260	13.1%	2.7				
NEBRASKA																			
NEVADA																48,000	9,490	19.8%	
NEW HAMPSHIRE				114,000	10,479	9.2%		115,000	5,323	4.6%	-4.6					249,000	8,895	3.6%	-5.6
NEW JERSEY																			
NEW MEXICO																			
NEW YORK																			
NORTH CAROLINA																			
NORTH DAKOTA				148,000	12,809	8.7%						303,000	11,706	3.9%	-4.8	321,000	6,263	2.0%	-6.7
OHIO				1,455,000	185,345	12.7%						3,383,000	217,211	6.4%	-6.3	3,644,000	195,509	5.4%	-7.4
OKLAHOMA				472,000	115,848	24.5%		965,000	94,514	9.8%	-14.7					1,151,000	200,675	17.4%	-7.1
OREGON																			
PENNSYLVANIA																4,896,000	153,750	3.1%	
RHODE ISLAND																			
SOUTH CAROLINA																			
SOUTH DAKOTA								314,000	9,403	3.0%									
TENNESSEE												1,256,000	159,799	12.7%					

United States Senate Primary Elections *(continued)*

Democratic Turnout for Election Years 1910–1926 *(continued)*

State	1910 Voting-age population	Turnout	%	1914 Voting-age population	Turnout	%	Difference from 1910	1918 Voting-age population	Turnout	%	Difference from 1910	1922 Voting-age population	Turnout	%	Difference from 1910	1926 Voting-age population	Turnout	%	Difference from 1910
TEXAS												2,391,000	572,288	23.9%					
UTAH																			
VERMONT												200,000	2,977	1.5%		201,000	2,113	1.1%	-0.4
VIRGINIA												1,217,000	139,716	11.5%					
WASHINGTON												795,000	14,991	1.9%		854,000	9,523	1.1%	-0.8
WEST VIRGINIA																			
WISCONSIN				640,000	65,469	10.2%		673,000	71,066	10.6%	0.3	1,415,000	16,663	1.2%	-9.1	1,538,000	16,003	1.0%	-9.2
WYOMING								100,000	4,186	4.2%		109,000	12,782	11.7%	7.5				
Total				7,632,000	1,152,779	15.1%		7,523,000	768,819	10.2%	-4.9	16,648,000	2,097,308	12.6%	-2.5	22,152,000	1,321,594	6.0%	-9.1

Other Turnout for Election Years 1910–1926

State	1910 Voting-age population	Turnout	%	1914* Voting-age population	Turnout	%	1918 Voting-age population	Turnout	%	Difference from 1914**	1922 Voting-age population	Turnout	%	Difference from 1914	1926 Voting-age population	Turnout	%	Difference from 1914
IDAHO				186,000	2,842	1.5%												
ILLINOIS				1,583,000	29,173	1.8%	1,705,000	1,801	0.1%	-1.7					4,075,000	495	0.0%	-1.8
IOWA				647,000	6,984	1.1%												
KANSAS				946,000	19,152	2.0%	974,000	1,245	0.1%	-1.9					1,060,000	160	0.0%	-2.0
MISSOURI				963,000	9,875	1.0%	998,000	1,462	0.1%	-0.9	2,029,000	1,190	0.1%	-1.0	2,129,000	104	0.0%	-1.0
NEW HAMPSHIRE				114,000	744	0.7%												
NORTH DAKOTA				148,000	3,053	2.1%									321,000	317	0.1%	-2.0
OKLAHOMA				472,000	17,282	3.7%	965,000	5,554	0.6%	-3.1					1,151,000	168	0.0%	-3.6
PENNSYLVANIA															4,896,000	6,705	0.1%	
SOUTH DAKOTA							314,000	252	0.1%									
WASHINGTON											795,000	6,817	0.9%					
WISCONSIN				640,000	38,573	6.0%	673,000	38,564	5.7%	-0.3	1,415,000	1,282	0.1%	-5.9	1,538,000	12,074	0.8%	-5.2
Total				5,699,000	127,678	2.2%	5,629,000	48,878	0.9%	-1.4	4,239,000	9,289	0.2%	-2.0	15,170,000	20,023	0.1%	-2.1

*The Seventeenth Amendment, ratified in 1913, instituted direct election of U.S. Senators.

**Percentage point difference between turnout in current year and initial year listed in chart. If data do not appear for a state in the initial year listed, the difference is calculated from the first year in which data do appear for that state.

STATE GUBERNATORIAL GENERAL ELECTIONS

Election Years 1911–1929

State	1911 Voting-age population	Turnout	%	1913 Voting-age population	Turnout	%	Difference from 1911*	1915 Voting-age population	Turnout	%	Difference from 1911	1917 Voting-age population	Turnout	%	Difference from 1911	1919 Voting-age population	Turnout	%	Difference from 1911
ARKANSAS				413,000	83,504	20.2%													
KENTUCKY	605,000	422,221	69.8%					628,000	439,511	70.0%	0.2					650,000	468,606	72.1%	2.3
MARYLAND	355,000	209,787	59.1%					382,000	235,453	61.6%	2.5					408,000	224,315	55.0%	-4.1
MASSACHUSETTS	779,000	421,692	54.1%	807,000	427,727	53.0%	-1.1	835,000	465,413	55.7%	1.6	862,000	361,821	42.0%	-12.2	890,000	510,447	57.4%	3.2
MISSISSIPPI	426,000	40,471	9.5%					432,000	54,587	12.6%	3.1					438,000	39,239	9.0%	-0.5
NEW JERSEY				654,000	354,578	54.2%										755,000	420,462	55.7%	1.5
NEW MEXICO	87,000	59,055	67.9%																
RHODE ISLAND	123,000	68,544	55.7%																
VIRGINIA				548,000	70,307	12.8%						585,000	89,183	15.2%	2.4				
Total	2,375,000	1,221,770	51.4%	2,422,000	936,116	38.7%	-12.8	2,277,000	1,194,964	52.5%	1.0	1,447,000	451,004	31.2%	-20.3	3,141,000	1,663,069	52.9%	1.5

State	1921 Voting-age population	Turnout	%	Difference from 1911	1923 Voting-age population	Turnout	%	Difference from 1911	1925 Voting-age population	Turnout	%	Difference from 1911	1927 Voting-age population	Turnout	%	Difference from 1911	1929 Voting-age population	Turnout	%	Difference from 1911
ARKANSAS																				
KENTUCKY					1,333,000	662,322	49.7%	-20.1					1,388,000	767,274	55.3%	-14.5				
MARYLAND					873,000	315,342	36.1%	-23.0												
MASSACHUSETTS																				
MISSISSIPPI					933,000	29,138	3.1%	-6.4					995,000	31,717	3.2%	-6.3				
NEW JERSEY									1,914,000	904,670	47.3%	-7.0								
NEW MEXICO																				
RHODE ISLAND																				
VIRGINIA	1,212,000	205,249	16.9%	4.1					1,253,000	144,970	11.6%	-1.3					1,293,000	268,979	20.8%	8.0
Total	1,212,000	205,249	16.9%	-34.5	3,139,000	1,006,802	32.1%	-19.4	3,167,000	1,049,640	33.1%	-18.3	2,383,000	798,991	33.5%	-17.9	1,293,000	268,979	20.8%	-30.6

*Percentage point difference between turnout in current year and initial year listed in chart. If data do not appear for a state in the initial year listed, the difference is calculated from the first year in which data do appear for that state.

STATE GUBERNATORIAL GENERAL ELECTIONS

Republican Turnout for Election Years 1911–1929

State	1911 Voting-age population	Turnout	%	1913 Voting-age population	Turnout	%	Difference from 1911*	1915 Voting-age population	Turnout	%	Difference from 1911	1917 Voting-age population	Turnout	%	Difference from 1911	1919 Voting-age population	Turnout	%	Difference from 1911
ARKANSAS				413,000	17,040	4.1%													
KENTUCKY	605,000	195,672	32.3%					628,000	219,520	35.0%	2.6					650,000	254,472	39.1%	6.8
MARYLAND	355,000	106,392	30.0%					382,000	116,136	30.4%	0.4					408,000	112,075	27.5%	-2.5
MASSACHUSETTS	779,000	206,795	26.5%	807,000	116,705	14.5%	-12.1	835,000	235,863	28.2%	1.7	862,000	226,145	26.2%	-0.3	890,000	317,774	35.7%	9.2
NEW JERSEY				654,000	140,298	21.5%										755,000	202,976	26.9%	5.4
NEW MEXICO	87,000	28,019	32.2%																
RHODE ISLAND	123,000	37,969	30.9%																
VIRGINIA												585,000	24,957	4.3%					
Total	1,949,000	574,847	29.5%	1,874,000	274,043	14.6%	-14.9	1,845,000	571,519	31.0%	1.5	1,447,000	251,102	17.4%	-12.1	2,703,000	887,297	32.8%	3.3

State	1921 Voting-age population	Turnout	%	Difference from 1911	1923 Voting-age population	Turnout	%	Difference from 1911	1925 Voting-age population	Turnout	%	Difference from 1911	1927 Voting-age population	Turnout	%	Difference from 1911	1929 Voting-age population	Turnout	%	Difference from 1911
ARKANSAS																				
KENTUCKY					1,333,000	306,277	23.0%	-9.4					1,388,000	399,090	28.8%	-3.5				
MARYLAND					873,000	137,471	15.7%	-14.2												
MASSACHUSETTS																				
NEW JERSEY									1,914,000	433,121	22.6%	1.2								
NEW MEXICO																				
RHODE ISLAND																				
VIRGINIA	1,212,000	65,833	5.4%	1.2					1,253,000	37,592	3.0%	-1.3					1,293,000	99,650	7.7%	3.4
Total	1,212,000	65,833	5.4%	-24.1	2,206,000	443,748	20.1%	-9.4	3,167,000	470,713	14.9%	-14.6	1,388,000	399,698	28.8%	-0.7	1,293,000	99,650	7.7%	-21.8

Democratic Turnout for Election Years 1911–1929

State	1911 Voting-age population	Turnout	%	1913 Voting-age population	Turnout	%	Difference from 1911*	1915 Voting-age population	Turnout	%	Difference from 1911	1917 Voting-age population	Turnout	%	Difference from 1911	1919 Voting-age population	Turnout	%	Difference from 1911
ARKANSAS				413,000	53,655	13.0%													
KENTUCKY	605,000	226,549	37.4%					628,000	219,991	35.0%	-2.4					650,000	214,134	32.9%	-4.5
MARYLAND	355,000	103,395	29.1%					382,000	119,317	31.2%	2.1					408,000	112,240	27.5%	-1.6
MASSACHUSETTS	779,000	206,795	26.5%	807,000	183,267	22.7%	-4.9	835,000	229,550	27.5%	-0.1	862,000	135,676	15.7%	-11.8	890,000	192,673	21.6%	-5.9
MISSISSIPPI	426,000	40,471	9.5%					432,000	50,541	11.7%	2.2					438,000	39,239	9.0%	-0.5
NEW JERSEY				654,000	173,148	26.5%										755,000	217,486	28.8%	2.3
NEW MEXICO	87,000	31,036	35.7%																
RHODE ISLAND	123,000	30,575	24.9%																

State Gubernatorial General Elections (continued)

State Gubernatorial General Elections *(continued)*

Democratic Turnout for Election Years 1911–1929 *(continued)*

State	1911 Voting-age population	Turnout	%	1913 Voting-age population	Turnout	%	Difference from 1911	1915 Voting-age population	Turnout	%	Difference from 1911	1917 Voting-age population	Turnout	%	Difference from 1911	1919 Voting-age population	Turnout	%	Difference from 1911
VIRGINIA				548,000	66,518	12.1%						585,000	64,226	11.0%	-1.2				
Total	1,949,000	574,847	29.5%	2,422,000	476,588	19.7%	-7.6	2,277,000	619,399	27.2%	0.0	1,447,000	199,902	13.8%	-13.4	3,141,000	775,772	24.7%	-2.5

State	1921 Voting-age population	Turnout	%	Difference from 1911	1923 Voting-age population	Turnout	%	Difference from 1911	1925 Voting-age population	Turnout	%	Difference from 1911	1927 Voting-age population	Turnout	%	Difference from 1911	1929 Voting-age population	Turnout	%	Difference from 1911
ARKANSAS																				
KENTUCKY					1,333,000	356,045	26.7%	-10.7					1,388,000	367,576	26.5%	-11.0				
MARYLAND					873,000	177,871	20.4%	-8.8												
MASSACHUSETTS																				
MISSISSIPPI					933,000	29,138	3.1%	-6.4					995,000	31,717	3.2%	-6.3				
NEW JERSEY									1,914,000	471,549	24.6%	-1.8								
NEW MEXICO																				
RHODE ISLAND																				
VIRGINIA	1,212,000	139,416	11.5%	-0.6					1,253,000	107,378	8.6%	-3.6					1,293,000	169,329	13.1%	1.0
Total	1,212,000	139,416	11.5%	-15.7	3,139,000	563,054	17.9%	-9.3	3,167,000	578,927	18.3%	-9.0	2,383,000	399,293	16.8%	-10.5	1,293,000	169,329	13.1%	-14.1

Other Turnout for Election Years 1911–1929

State	1911 Voting-age population	Turnout	%	1913 Voting-age population	Turnout	%	1915 Voting-age population	Turnout	%	1917 Voting-age population	Turnout	%	Difference from 1911	1919 Voting-age population	Turnout	%	Difference from 1911
ARKANSAS				413,000	12,809	3.1%											
MASSACHUSETTS				807,000	127,755	15.8%											
MISSISSIPPI							432,000	4,046	0.9%								
NEW JERSEY				654,000	41,132	6.3%											
VIRGINIA				548,000	3,789	0.7%											

State	1921 Voting-age population	Turnout	%	Difference from 1911	1923 Voting-age population	Turnout	%	Difference from 1911	1925 Voting-age population	Turnout	%	Difference from 1911	1927 Voting-age population	Turnout	%	Difference from 1911	1929 Voting-age population	Turnout	%	Difference from 1911
ARKANSAS																				
MASSACHUSETTS																				
MISSISSIPPI																				
NEW JERSEY																				
VIRGINIA																				

*Percentage point difference between turnout in current year and initial year listed in chart. If data do not appear for a state in the initial year listed, the difference is calculated from the first year in which data do appear for that state.

STATE GUBERNATORIAL PRIMARY ELECTIONS

Democratic Turnout, Election Years 1911–1929*

State	1911 Voting-age population	Turnout	%	1913 Voting-age population	Turnout	%	1915 Voting-age population	Turnout	%	1917 Voting-age population	Turnout	%	1919 Voting-age population	Turnout	%
MISSISSIPPI													437,000	148,411	**34.0%**
VIRGINIA															

State	1921 Voting-age population	Turnout	%	1923 Voting-age population	Turnout	%	Difference from 1919**	1925 Voting-age population	Turnout	%	Difference from 1921	1927 Voting-age population	Turnout	%	Difference from 1919	1929 Voting-age population	Turnout	%	Difference from 1921
MISSISSIPPI				924,000	254,141	**27.5%**	-6.5					986,000	287,831	**29.2%**	-4.8				
VIRGINIA	1,207,000	151,098	**12.5%**					1,246,000	174,896	**14.0%**	1.5					1,284,000	133,696	**10.4%**	-2.1

*Only Democratic primaries were held in this time period.

**Percentage point difference between turnout in current year and initial year listed in chart. If data do not appear for a state in the initial year listed, the difference is calculated from the first year in which data do appear for that state.

CHAPTER 8
1930–1949

Chronology of Major Events, 1930–1949

1930	The Smoot-Hawley tariff bill raises tariffs on foreign goods, touching off trade conflict that helps to plunge world economy into the Depression. The fifteenth census counts the U.S. population at 122.8 million people.
1932	Democrat Franklin D. Roosevelt defeats incumbent Herbert Hoover for president. Prompted by Hoover, Congress creates the Reconstruction Finance Corporation to provide funds for banks to help overcome the Depression.
1933	The Twenty-first Amendment repeals Prohibition. In his first hundred days, Roosevelt initiates his "New Deal," a panoply of legislation responding to the Depression, including the National Industrial Recovery Act (imposing price controls and other stabilizing measures), the Emergency Banking Act, and the Agricultural Adjustment Act (increasing the prices of food products to make agriculture profitable again). This legislative burst also creates the Federal Deposit Insurance Corporation; the Rural Electrification Administration and the Tennessee Valley Authority; and the Civilian Conservation Corps and Works Progress Administration, which employ millions in public works.
1934	The Securities and Exchange Commission is established to oversee investment trading. The first House committee on Un-American Activities is established.
1935	The Supreme Court invalidates the National Industrial Recovery Act. The first Neutrality Act is passed to keep the United States out of European conflicts. The Social Security Act creates a national pension program.
1936	Roosevelt is re-elected easily. The Supreme Court invalidates the Agricultural Adjustment Act for paying farmers with agricultural taxes to keep land out of production. The Spanish Civil War begins; the United States remains neutral, but U.S. businesses aid the right-wing Nationalists while the American left supports the Republicans.
1937	Roosevelt unsuccessfully attempts to "pack" the Supreme Court with additional members who support his New Deal, hurting his reputation. Roosevelt also raises interest rates and cuts federal spending, leading to the "Roosevelt Recession."
1938	Roosevelt calls for quarantining the aggressor nations of Germany, Italy, and Japan—an idea that flops among both isolationists and interventionists. The Soviet Union and Germany sign a non-aggression pact.
1939	Germany invades Poland; World War II officially begins.
1940	Roosevelt is re-elected to an unprecedented third term. Axis powers Germany, Italy and Japan sign tripartite agreement of mutual support. Congress passes the Selective Service Act, providing for the registration and drafting of citizens into the military. The sixteenth census counts the U.S. population at 131.7 million people.
1941	The Roosevelt-backed Lend-Lease Act enables the president to provide monetary and supply aid to Great Britain and other Allied powers. The Atlantic Charter is signed by Roosevelt and British Prime Minister Winston Churchill, outlining principles by which to govern a post-war world. Germany invades the Soviet Union. In response to the Japanese attack on Pearl Harbor, the United States declares war on Axis powers.
1942	Japan occupies the Philippines. The Allied North African campaign is launched. The United States wins the naval battle of Midway. The Manhattan Project to produce the atom bomb begins. Congress lowers the draft age to eighteen, prompting proposals to lower the voting age as well. Japanese-Americans on the West Coast are ordered into internment camps.
1943	The United States takes Guadalcanal. The Soviet Union deals Germany a costly defeat in the Battle of Stalingrad. The Allies invade Italy.

1944 Roosevelt is re-elected for an unprecedented fourth term. The Allies successfully land at Normandy and march across France. The United States retakes the Philippines. The Supreme Court upholds the constitutionality of Japanese internment in *Korematsu v. United States*.

1945 Roosevelt dies, succeeded by Vice President Harry S. Truman. Germany and Italy surrender. The United States drops atomic bombs on Hiroshima and Nagasaki, and Japan surrenders. The United Nations is founded to organize post-war world politics.

1946 Republicans capture congressional majorities for first time since 1930.

1947 Truman Doctrine of containing communist expansion is formulated. The Marshall Plan for European recovery is initiated. The House Un-American Activities Committee intensifies investigations of alleged communists, particularly in the film industry.

1948 Truman is re-elected president. Strom Thurmond forms the segregationist States' Rights Party in response to the Democrats' new civil rights platform advanced by Minneapolis mayor Hubert Humphrey. Former vice president and Agriculture Secretary Henry Wallace leaves the Democratic Party to run for president with the Progressive Party. The United States airlifts food and other supplies to West Berlin in response to Soviet occupation. Israel is established by the United Nations.

1949 Mao Tse-tung completes his revolutionary campaign, installing the Communist People's Republic of China government and ousting Chiang Kai-shek's Nationalist government. The Soviet Union explodes its own atomic bomb. In light of the communist threat, the North American Treaty Organization (NATO) is established.

State and Federal Laws Chronology, 1930–1949

1932   *Nixon v. Condon*, 286 U.S. 73 (1932). Supreme Court 5–4 decision holds that political party regulations excluding blacks from primary elections are unconstitutional. The Texas legislature had delegated primary qualifications to parties to evade the *Nixon v. Herndon* (1927) decision that prohibited states from passing laws eliminating blacks from primaries, but the Court rules that parties in such cases act as agents of the state.[1]

       Wood v. Broom, 287 U.S. 1 (1932). The Supreme Court's 5–4 decision holds that electoral districts need not be contiguous, compact, and equal, as the Congress left such language out of the Apportionment Act of 1929 after including it previously. This decision removes federal power to address claims of gerrymandering.

1935   *Grovey v. Townsend*, 295 U.S. 45 (1935). The Supreme Court unanimously declares that the restriction of Texas Democratic Party membership to whites is constitutional, as the party is a private organization. This ruling effectively negates the force of *Nixon v. Condon* (1932), allowing the "white primary" to continue.

1937   *Breedlove v. Suttles*, 302 U.S. 277 (1937). The Supreme Court deems the state of Georgia's poll tax of one dollar to be constitutional.

1939   *Lane v. Wilson*, 307 U.S. 268 (1939). The Supreme Court rules that Oklahoma's revised grandfather clause is still unconstitutional. The grandfather clauses were exemptions to other requirements (in Oklahoma, a literacy test) that were enacted in the South to ensure the enfranchisement of whites whose ancestors were enfranchised prior to the Civil War. After *Guinn v. United States* (1915) outlawed such clauses, Oklahoma responded by offering an exemption for those who had voted in 1914 (when the grandfather clause was in effect), with only a brief window for new voters to register. The Court reaffirmed *Guinn* in rejecting this ploy.

1941   *United States v. Classic*, 313 U.S. 299 (1940). The Supreme Court rules that congressional power extends to primary elections, a decision consistent with *Nixon v. Condon* (1932), but overturns *Newberry v. United States* (1921), which had ruled that Congress did not have the authority under the Constitution to regulate political party primaries and nominating processes along with overturning campaign spending limits.

1942   Soldiers Voting Act of 1942 (P.L. 712-561) guaranteed federal voting rights for members of the armed forces during wartime. The law allowed members of the armed forces to vote for presidential electors and candidates for the U.S. Senate and House, whether or not they were previously registered and regardless of poll tax requirements. The law provided for the use of a postage-free, federal postcard application to request an absentee ballot; it also required the preparation of an appropriate number of "official war ballots" that listed federal office candidates and candidates for state and local office if authorized by the state legislature.

1943   Georgia lowers the voting age to eighteen years. Numerous other states reject such a proposed move during the war.

1944   *Smith v. Allwright*, 321 U.S. 649 (1944). The Supreme Court negates the Texas Democratic Party's restriction of membership to whites, insofar as this restriction prevented African Americans from voting in primary elections integral to the selection of state and national candidates. The ruling puts an end to all-white primaries in Texas and other states, overturning *Grovey v. Townsend* (1935).

       The Soldiers Voting Act is amended in September, reducing the procedural requirements of the 1942 law to recommendations and giving little time to prepare for the November 1944 election.

1946   *Colegrove v. Green*, 328 U.S. 549 (1946). In a 4–3 decision, the Supreme Court demurs from requiring the state of Illinois to redraw its legislative districts, which were badly out of date and favored rural areas.

---

[1] For Supreme Court cases, see CQ Press Electronic Library, *Guide to the U.S. Supreme Court Online Edition*, "Chronology of Major Decisions of the Court, 1797–2007." Originally published in David G. Savage, *Guide to the U.S. Supreme Court, 4th ed. (rev.)*, (Washington: CQ Press, 2008). http://library.cqpress.com/supremecourtguide/search.php (accessed June 18th, 2010).

National Count of Popular Vote for President, 1932–1948

YEAR	NAME	PARTY	TOTAL	PERCENTAGE[1]
1932	Franklin Roosevelt	Democratic	22,829,501	32.6%
	Herbert Hoover	Republican	15,760,684	22.5%
	Norman Thomas	Socialist	884,885	1.3%
1936	Franklin Roosevelt	Democratic	27,757,333	37.0%
	Alf Landon	Republican	16,684,231	22.2%
	William Lemke	Union	892,378	1.2%
1940	Franklin Roosevelt	Democratic	27,313,041	33.9%
	Wendell Willkie	Republican	22,348,480	27.8%
1944	Franklin Roosevelt	Democratic	25,612,610	29.6%
	Thomas Dewey	Republican	22,017,617	25.4%
1948	Harry Truman	Democratic	24,105,812	26.0%
	Thomas Dewcy	Republican	21,970,065	23.6%
	J. Strom Thurmond	States Rights	1,175,930	1.3%
	Henry Wallace	Progressive/American Labor	1,157,328	1.3%

[1] The percentage figures in this chart are based on the votes cast divided by the eligible voting-age population at the time of the election.

United States Presidential Turnout, Election Years 1932–1948

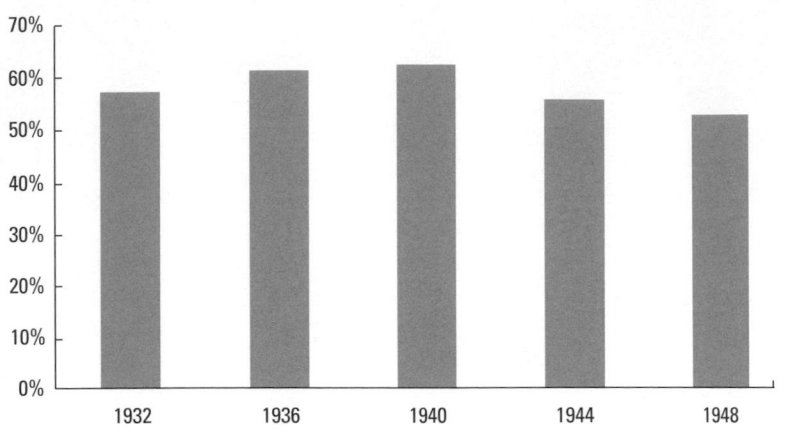

YEAR	VOTING-AGE POPULATION	TOTAL	%
1932	70,022,000	39,758,759	56.8%
1936	75,005,000	45,654,763	60.9%
1940	80,471,000	49,900,418	62.0%
1944	86,671,000	47,976,670	55.4%
1948	92,869,000	48,690,956	52.4%

Partisan Turnout Presidential Years Based on Aggregate House Turnout, Election Years 1932–1948

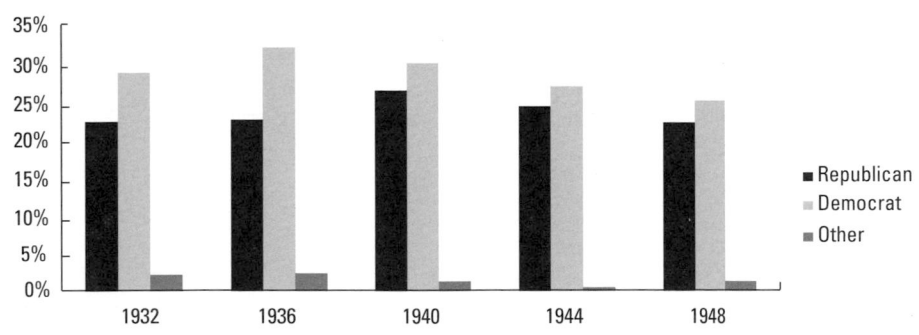

■ Republican
▫ Democrat
▪ Other

YEAR	VOTING-AGE POPULATION	REPUBLICAN TURNOUT	%	DEMOCRAT TURNOUT	%	OTHER TURNOUT	%
1932	70,022,000	15,726,307	22.5%	20,267,306	28.9%	1,532,449	2.2%
1936	75,005,000	17,025,266	22.7%	24,196,344	32.3%	1,774,968	2.4%
1940	80,471,000	21,346,565	26.5%	24,266,432	30.2%	1,046,162	1.3%
1944	86,671,000	21,183,304	24.4%	23,458,538	27.1%	421,802	0.5%
1948	92,869,000	20,923,293	22.5%	23,778,858	25.6%	1,197,689	1.3%

UNITED STATES PRESIDENTIAL GENERAL ELECTIONS

Election Years 1932–1948

State	1932 Voting-age population	1932 Turnout	1932 %	1936 Voting-age population	1936 Turnout	1936 %	1936 Difference from 1932*	1940 Voting-age population	1940 Turnout	1940 %	1940 Difference from 1932	1944 Voting-age population	1944 Turnout	1944 %	1944 Difference from 1932	1948 Voting-age population	1948 Turnout	1948 %	1948 Difference from 1932
ALABAMA	1,402,000	245,303	17.5%	1,486,000	275,744	18.6%	1.1	1,572,000	294,219	18.7%	1.2	1,648,000	244,743	14.9%	-2.6	1,723,000	214,980	12.5%	-5.0
ALASKA																			
ARIZONA	184,000	118,251	64.3%	213,000	124,163	58.3%	-6.0	253,000	150,039	59.3%	-5.0	328,000	137,634	42.0%	-22.3	401,000	177,065	44.2%	-20.1
ARKANSAS	1,002,000	216,569	21.6%	1,055,000	179,431	17.0%	-4.6	1,100,000	200,429	18.2%	-3.4	1,104,000	212,954	19.3%	-2.3	1,109,000	242,475	21.9%	0.3
CALIFORNIA	3,535,000	2,266,972	64.1%	3,979,000	2,638,882	66.3%	2.2	4,569,000	3,268,791	71.5%	7.4	5,572,000	3,520,875	63.2%	-0.9	6,575,000	4,021,538	61.2%	-3.0
COLORADO	601,000	457,696	76.2%	649,000	488,685	75.3%	-0.9	699,000	549,004	78.5%	2.4	755,000	505,039	66.9%	-9.3	812,000	515,237	63.5%	-12.7
CONNECTICUT	857,000	594,183	69.3%	942,000	690,723	73.3%	4.0	1,037,000	781,502	75.4%	6.0	1,152,000	831,990	72.2%	2.9	1,266,000	883,518	69.8%	0.5
DELAWARE	151,000	112,901	74.8%	162,000	127,603	78.8%	4.0	175,000	136,374	77.9%	3.2	189,000	125,361	66.3%	-8.4	203,000	139,073	68.5%	-6.3
DISTRICT OF COLUMBIA																			
FLORIDA	936,000	276,943	29.6%	1,075,000	327,436	30.5%	0.9	1,243,000	485,640	39.1%	9.5	1,484,000	482,803	32.5%	2.9	1,725,000	577,643	33.5%	3.9
GEORGIA	1,570,000	255,590	16.3%	1,680,000	293,170	17.5%	1.2	1,806,000	312,686	17.3%	1.0	1,969,000	328,129	16.7%	0.4	2,131,000	418,764	19.7%	3.4
HAWAII																			
IDAHO	254,000	186,520	73.4%	280,000	199,617	71.3%	-2.1	306,000	235,168	76.9%	3.4	323,000	208,321	64.5%	-8.9	339,000	214,816	63.4%	-10.1
ILLINOIS	4,615,000	3,407,926	73.8%	4,891,000	3,956,522	80.9%	7.0	5,179,000	4,217,935	81.4%	7.6	5,453,000	4,036,061	74.0%	0.2	5,727,000	3,984,046	69.6%	-4.3
INDIANA	2,014,000	1,576,927	78.3%	2,116,000	1,650,897	78.0%	-0.3	2,229,000	1,782,747	80.0%	1.7	2,362,000	1,672,091	70.8%	-7.5	2,496,000	1,656,214	66.4%	-11.9
IOWA	1,510,000	1,036,687	68.7%	1,564,000	1,142,737	73.1%	4.4	1,614,000	1,215,432	75.3%	6.7	1,641,000	1,052,599	64.1%	-4.5	1,669,000	1,038,264	62.2%	-6.4
KANSAS	1,115,000	791,978	71.0%	1,131,000	865,507	76.5%	5.5	1,152,000	860,297	74.7%	3.6	1,187,000	733,776	61.8%	-9.2	1,222,000	788,819	64.6%	-6.5
KENTUCKY	1,475,000	983,059	66.6%	1,561,000	926,214	59.3%	-7.3	1,654,000	970,163	58.7%	-8.0	1,754,000	867,924	49.5%	-17.2	1,854,000	822,658	44.4%	-22.3
LOUISIANA	1,185,000	268,804	22.7%	1,284,000	329,778	25.7%	3.0	1,383,000	372,305	26.9%	4.2	1,468,000	349,383	23.8%	1.1	1,554,000	416,326	26.8%	4.1
MAINE	454,000	298,444	65.7%	475,000	304,240	64.1%	-1.7	498,000	320,840	64.4%	-1.3	522,000	296,400	56.8%	-9.0	546,000	264,787	48.5%	-17.2
MARYLAND	1,012,000	511,054	50.5%	1,090,000	624,896	57.3%	6.8	1,185,000	660,104	55.7%	5.2	1,324,000	608,439	46.0%	-4.5	1,463,000	596,708	40.8%	-9.7
MASSACHUSETTS	2,305,000	1,580,114	68.6%	2,454,000	1,840,357	75.0%	6.4	2,617,000	2,026,993	77.5%	8.9	2,802,000	1,960,665	70.0%	1.4	2,988,000	2,107,146	70.5%	2.0
MICHIGAN	2,724,000	1,664,765	61.1%	2,947,000	1,805,098	61.3%	0.1	3,204,000	2,085,929	65.1%	4.0	3,538,000	2,205,223	62.3%	1.2	3,872,000	2,109,609	54.5%	-6.6
MINNESOTA	1,529,000	1,002,843	65.6%	1,637,000	1,129,975	69.0%	3.4	1,738,000	1,251,188	72.0%	6.4	1,798,000	1,125,504	62.6%	-3.0	1,857,000	1,212,226	65.3%	-0.3
MISSISSIPPI	1,073,000	146,034	13.6%	1,140,000	162,142	14.2%	0.6	1,195,000	175,824	14.7%	1.1	1,199,000	180,234	15.0%	1.4	1,204,000	192,190	16.0%	2.4
MISSOURI	2,287,000	1,609,894	70.4%	2,384,000	1,828,635	76.7%	6.3	2,477,000	1,833,729	74.0%	3.6	2,540,000	1,571,697	61.9%	-8.5	2,603,000	1,578,628	60.6%	-9.7
MONTANA	304,000	216,479	71.2%	321,000	230,502	71.8%	0.6	338,000	247,873	73.3%	2.1	349,000	207,355	59.4%	-11.8	361,000	224,278	62.1%	-9.1
NEBRASKA	792,000	570,135	72.0%	805,000	608,023	75.5%	3.5	818,000	615,878	75.3%	3.3	830,000	563,126	67.8%	-4.1	843,000	488,940	58.0%	-14.0
NEVADA	55,000	41,430	75.3%	62,000	43,848	70.7%	-4.6	70,000	53,174	76.0%	0.6	85,000	54,234	63.8%	-11.5	100,000	62,117	62.1%	-13.2
NEW HAMPSHIRE	268,000	205,520	76.7%	283,000	218,114	77.1%	0.4	300,000	235,419	78.5%	1.8	317,000	229,625	72.4%	-4.2	333,000	231,440	69.5%	-7.2
NEW JERSEY	2,294,000	1,630,063	71.1%	2,459,000	1,820,437	74.0%	3.0	2,649,000	1,972,552	74.5%	3.4	2,899,000	1,963,761	67.7%	-3.3	3,150,000	1,949,555	61.9%	-9.2
NEW MEXICO	197,000	151,606	77.0%	231,000	169,135	73.2%	-3.7	270,000	183,258	67.9%	-9.1	312,000	152,225	48.8%	-28.2	356,000	186,853	52.5%	-24.5
NEW YORK	7,228,000	4,688,614	64.9%	7,826,000	5,596,398	71.5%	6.6	8,447,000	6,301,596	74.6%	9.7	9,042,000	6,316,790	69.9%	5.0	9,635,000	6,177,337	64.1%	-0.8

United States Presidential General Elections (continued)

United States Presidential General Elections (continued)

Election Years 1932–1948 (continued)

State	1932 Voting-age population	Turnout	%	1936 Voting-age population	Turnout	%	Difference from 1932	1940 Voting-age population	Turnout	%	Difference from 1932	1944 Voting-age population	Turnout	%	Difference from 1932	1948 Voting-age population	Turnout	%	Difference from 1932
NORTH CAROLINA	1,638,000	711,498	43.4%	1,791,000	839,475	46.9%	3.4	1,952,000	822,648	42.1%	-1.3	2,107,000	790,554	37.5%	-5.9	2,263,000	791,209	35.0%	-8.5
NORTH DAKOTA	341,000	256,290	75.2%	348,000	273,716	78.7%	3.5	354,000	280,775	79.3%	4.2	356,000	220,182	61.8%	-13.3	358,000	220,716	61.7%	-13.5
OHIO	4,025,000	2,609,728	64.8%	4,234,000	3,012,660	71.2%	6.3	4,475,000	3,319,912	74.2%	9.4	4,786,000	3,153,056	65.9%	1.0	5,097,000	2,936,071	57.6%	-7.2
OKLAHOMA	1,263,000	704,633	55.8%	1,301,000	749,740	57.6%	1.8	1,335,000	826,212	61.9%	6.1	1,354,000	722,636	53.4%	-2.4	1,372,000	721,599	52.6%	-3.2
OREGON	612,000	368,751	60.3%	667,000	414,021	62.1%	1.8	735,000	481,240	65.5%	5.2	843,000	480,147	57.0%	-3.3	951,000	524,080	55.1%	-5.1
PENNSYLVANIA	5,441,000	2,859,021	52.5%	5,766,000	4,138,105	71.8%	19.2	6,103,000	4,078,714	66.8%	14.3	6,423,000	3,794,793	59.1%	6.5	6,743,000	3,735,148	55.4%	2.8
RHODE ISLAND	377,000	266,170	70.6%	403,000	310,278	77.0%	6.4	433,000	321,152	74.2%	3.6	469,000	299,276	63.8%	-6.8	504,000	327,702	65.0%	-5.6
SOUTH CAROLINA	865,000	104,407	12.1%	934,000	115,437	12.4%	0.3	1,004,000	99,830	9.9%	-2.1	1,068,000	103,382	9.7%	-2.4	1,131,000	142,571	12.6%	0.5
SOUTH DAKOTA	364,000	288,438	79.2%	366,000	296,452	81.0%	1.8	370,000	308,427	83.4%	4.1	382,000	232,076	60.8%	-18.5	394,000	250,105	63.5%	-15.8
TENNESSEE	1,493,000	390,273	26.1%	1,609,000	477,086	29.7%	3.5	1,728,000	522,823	30.3%	4.1	1,836,000	510,692	27.8%	1.7	1,944,000	550,283	28.3%	2.2
TEXAS	3,104,000	874,382	28.2%	3,437,000	849,701	24.7%	-3.4	3,789,000	1,124,437	29.7%	1.5	4,141,000	1,150,334	27.8%	-0.4	4,492,000	1,147,245	25.5%	-2.6
UTAH	260,000	206,578	79.5%	279,000	216,679	77.7%	-1.8	303,000	247,819	81.8%	2.3	337,000	248,319	73.7%	-5.8	371,000	276,305	74.5%	-5.0
VERMONT	207,000	136,980	66.2%	211,000	143,689	68.1%	1.9	216,000	143,062	66.2%	0.1	222,000	125,361	56.5%	-9.7	228,000	123,382	54.1%	-12.1
VIRGINIA	1,362,000	297,942	21.9%	1,463,000	334,590	22.9%	1.0	1,588,000	346,608	21.8%	0.0	1,775,000	388,485	21.9%	0.0	1,962,000	419,256	21.4%	-0.5
WASHINGTON	962,000	614,814	63.9%	1,042,000	692,338	66.4%	2.5	1,144,000	793,833	69.4%	5.5	1,304,000	856,328	65.7%	1.8	1,465,000	905,059	61.8%	-2.1
WEST VIRGINIA	922,000	743,774	80.7%	990,000	829,945	83.8%	3.2	1,056,000	868,076	82.2%	1.5	1,102,000	715,596	64.9%	-15.7	1,148,000	748,750	65.2%	-15.4
WISCONSIN	1,729,000	1,114,814	64.5%	1,842,000	1,258,560	68.3%	3.8	1,958,000	1,405,522	71.8%	7.3	2,058,000	1,339,152	65.1%	0.6	2,157,000	1,276,800	59.2%	-5.3
WYOMING	129,000	96,962	75.2%	140,000	103,382	73.8%	-1.3	151,000	112,240	74.3%	-0.8	162,000	101,340	62.6%	-12.6	172,000	101,425	59.0%	-16.2
Total	70,022,000	39,758,759	56.8%	75,005,000	45,654,763	60.9%	4.1	80,471,000	49,900,418	62.0%	5.2	86,671,000	47,976,670	55.4%	-1.4	92,869,000	48,690,956	52.4%	-4.4

*Percentage point difference between turnout in current year and initial year listed in chart. If data do not appear for a state in the initial year listed, the difference is calculated from the first year in which data do appear for that state.

UNITED STATES PRESIDENTIAL GENERAL ELECTIONS

Republican Turnout for Election Years 1932–1948

State	1932 Voting-age population	Turnout	%	1936 Voting-age population	Turnout	%	Difference from 1932*	1940 Voting-age population	Turnout	%	Difference from 1932	1944 Voting-age population	Turnout	%	Difference from 1932	1948 Voting-age population	Turnout	%	Difference from 1932
ALABAMA	1,402,000	34,675	2.5%	1,486,000	35,358	2.4%	-0.1	1,572,000	42,184	2.7%	0.2	1,648,000	44,540	2.7%	0.2	1,723,000	40,930	2.4%	-0.1
ALASKA																			
ARIZONA	184,000	36,104	19.6%	213,000	33,433	15.7%	-3.9	253,000	54,030	21.4%	1.7	328,000	56,287	17.2%	-2.5	401,000	77,597	19.4%	-0.3
ARKANSAS	1,002,000	27,465	2.7%	1,055,000	32,049	3.0%	0.3	1,100,000	42,122	3.8%	1.1	1,104,000	63,551	5.8%	3.0	1,109,000	50,959	4.6%	1.9
CALIFORNIA	3,535,000	847,902	24.0%	3,979,000	836,431	21.0%	-3.0	4,569,000	1,351,419	29.6%	5.6	5,572,000	1,512,965	27.2%	3.2	6,575,000	1,895,269	28.8%	4.8
COLORADO	601,000	189,617	31.6%	649,000	181,267	27.9%	-3.6	699,000	279,576	40.0%	8.4	755,000	268,731	35.6%	4.0	812,000	239,714	29.5%	-2.0
CONNECTICUT	857,000	288,420	33.7%	942,000	278,685	29.6%	-4.1	1,037,000	361,819	34.9%	1.2	1,152,000	390,527	33.9%	0.2	1,266,000	437,754	34.6%	0.0
DELAWARE	151,000	57,073	37.8%	162,000	57,236	35.3%	-2.5	175,000	61,440	35.1%	-2.7	189,000	56,747	30.0%	-7.8	203,000	69,588	34.3%	-3.5
DISTRICT OF COLUMBIA																			
FLORIDA	936,000	69,170	7.4%	1,075,000	78,248	7.3%	-0.1	1,243,000	126,158	10.1%	2.8	1,484,000	143,215	9.7%	2.3	1,725,000	194,280	11.3%	3.9
GEORGIA	1,570,000	19,863	1.3%	1,680,000	36,943	2.2%	0.9	1,806,000	46,495	2.6%	1.3	1,969,000	59,900	3.0%	1.8	2,131,000	76,691	3.6%	2.3
HAWAII																			
IDAHO	254,000	71,312	28.1%	280,000	66,256	23.7%	-4.4	306,000	106,553	34.8%	6.7	323,000	100,137	31.0%	2.9	339,000	101,514	29.9%	1.9
ILLINOIS	4,615,000	1,432,756	31.0%	4,891,000	1,570,393	32.1%	1.1	5,179,000	2,047,240	39.5%	8.5	5,453,000	1,939,314	35.6%	4.5	5,727,000	1,961,103	34.2%	3.2
INDIANA	2,014,000	677,184	33.6%	2,116,000	691,570	32.7%	-0.9	2,229,000	899,466	40.4%	6.7	2,362,000	875,891	37.1%	3.5	2,496,000	821,079	32.9%	-0.7
IOWA	1,510,000	414,433	27.4%	1,564,000	487,977	31.2%	3.8	1,614,000	632,370	39.2%	11.7	1,641,000	547,267	33.3%	5.9	1,669,000	494,018	29.6%	2.2
KANSAS	1,115,000	349,498	31.3%	1,131,000	397,727	35.2%	3.8	1,152,000	489,169	42.5%	11.1	1,187,000	442,096	37.2%	5.9	1,222,000	423,039	34.6%	3.3
KENTUCKY	1,475,000	394,716	26.8%	1,561,000	369,702	23.7%	3.1	1,654,000	410,384	24.8%	-1.9	1,754,000	392,448	22.4%	-4.4	1,854,000	341,210	18.4%	-8.4
LOUISIANA	1,185,000	18,853	1.6%	1,284,000	36,791	2.9%	1.3	1,383,000	52,446	3.8%	2.2	1,468,000	67,750	4.6%	3.0	1,554,000	72,657	4.7%	3.1
MAINE	454,000	166,631	36.7%	475,000	168,823	35.5%	-1.2	498,000	163,951	32.9%	-3.8	522,000	155,434	29.8%	-6.9	546,000	150,234	27.5%	-9.2
MARYLAND	1,012,000	184,184	18.2%	1,090,000	231,435	21.2%	3.0	1,185,000	269,534	22.7%	4.5	1,324,000	292,949	22.1%	3.9	1,463,000	294,814	20.2%	2.0
MASSACHUSETTS	2,305,000	736,959	32.0%	2,454,000	768,613	31.3%	-0.7	2,617,000	939,700	35.9%	3.9	2,802,000	921,350	32.9%	0.9	2,988,000	909,370	30.4%	-1.5
MICHIGAN	2,724,000	739,894	27.2%	2,947,000	699,733	23.7%	-3.4	3,204,000	1,039,917	32.5%	5.3	3,538,000	1,084,423	30.7%	3.5	3,872,000	1,038,595	26.8%	-0.3
MINNESOTA	1,529,000	363,959	23.8%	1,637,000	350,461	21.4%	-2.4	1,738,000	596,274	34.3%	10.5	1,798,000	527,416	29.3%	5.5	1,857,000	483,617	26.0%	2.2
MISSISSIPPI	1,073,000	5,180	0.5%	1,140,000	4,467	0.4%	-0.1	1,195,000	7,364	0.6%	0.1	1,199,000	11,613	1.0%	0.5	1,204,000	5,043	0.4%	-0.1
MISSOURI	2,287,000	564,713	24.7%	2,384,000	697,891	29.3%	4.6	2,477,000	871,009	35.2%	10.5	2,540,000	761,175	30.0%	5.3	2,603,000	655,039	25.2%	0.5
MONTANA	304,000	78,078	25.7%	321,000	63,598	19.8%	-5.9	338,000	99,579	29.5%	3.8	349,000	93,163	26.7%	1.0	361,000	96,770	26.8%	1.1
NEBRASKA	792,000	201,177	25.4%	805,000	247,731	30.8%	5.4	818,000	352,201	43.1%	17.7	830,000	329,880	39.7%	14.3	843,000	264,774	31.4%	6.0
NEVADA	55,000	12,674	23.0%	62,000	11,923	19.2%	-3.8	70,000	21,229	30.3%	7.3	85,000	24,611	29.0%	5.9	100,000	29,357	29.4%	6.3
NEW HAMPSHIRE	268,000	103,629	38.7%	283,000	104,642	37.0%	-1.7	300,000	110,127	36.7%	-2.0	317,000	109,916	34.7%	-4.0	333,000	121,299	36.4%	-2.2
NEW JERSEY	2,294,000	775,684	33.8%	2,459,000	720,322	29.3%	-4.5	2,649,000	945,475	35.7%	1.9	2,899,000	961,335	33.2%	-0.7	3,150,000	981,124	31.1%	-2.7
NEW MEXICO	197,000	54,217	27.5%	231,000	61,727	26.7%	-0.8	270,000	79,315	29.4%	1.9	312,000	70,688	22.7%	-4.9	356,000	80,303	22.6%	-5.0
NEW YORK	7,228,000	1,937,963	26.8%	7,826,000	2,180,670	27.9%	1.1	8,447,000	3,027,478	35.8%	9.0	9,042,000	2,987,647	33.0%	6.2	9,635,000	2,841,163	29.5%	2.7

United States Presidential General Elections (continued)

United States Presidential General Elections (continued)

Republican Turnout for Election Years 1932–1948 (continued)

State	1932 Voting-age population	Turnout	%	1936 Voting-age population	Turnout	%	Difference from 1932	1940 Voting-age population	Turnout	%	Difference from 1932	1944 Voting-age population	Turnout	%	Difference from 1932	1948 Voting-age population	Turnout	%	Difference from 1932
NORTH CAROLINA	1,638,000	208,344	12.7%	1,791,000	223,294	12.5%	-0.3	1,952,000	213,633	10.9%	-1.8	2,107,000	263,155	12.5%	-0.2	2,263,000	258,572	11.4%	-1.3
NORTH DAKOTA	341,000	71,772	21.0%	348,000	72,751	20.9%	-0.1	354,000	154,590	43.7%	22.6	356,000	118,535	33.3%	12.2	358,000	115,139	32.2%	11.1
OHIO	4,025,000	1,227,319	30.5%	4,234,000	1,127,855	26.6%	-3.9	4,475,000	1,586,773	35.5%	5.0	4,786,000	1,582,293	33.1%	2.6	5,097,000	1,445,684	28.4%	-2.1
OKLAHOMA	1,263,000	188,165	14.9%	1,301,000	245,122	18.8%	3.9	1,335,000	348,872	26.1%	11.2	1,354,000	319,424	23.6%	8.7	1,372,000	268,817	19.6%	4.7
OREGON	612,000	136,019	22.2%	667,000	122,706	18.4%	-3.8	735,000	219,555	29.9%	7.6	843,000	225,365	26.7%	4.5	951,000	260,904	27.4%	5.2
PENNSYLVANIA	5,441,000	1,453,540	26.7%	5,766,000	1,690,300	29.3%	2.6	6,103,000	1,889,848	31.0%	4.3	6,423,000	1,835,054	28.6%	1.9	6,743,000	1,902,197	28.2%	1.5
RHODE ISLAND	377,000	115,266	30.6%	403,000	125,031	31.0%	0.5	433,000	138,654	32.0%	1.4	469,000	123,487	26.3%	-4.2	504,000	135,787	26.9%	-3.6
SOUTH CAROLINA	865,000	1,978	0.2%	934,000	1,646	0.2%	-0.1	1,004,000	4,360	0.4%	0.2	1,068,000	4,617	0.4%	0.2	1,131,000	5,386	0.5%	0.2
SOUTH DAKOTA	364,000	99,212	27.3%	366,000	125,977	34.4%	7.2	370,000	177,065	47.9%	20.6	382,000	135,365	35.4%	8.2	394,000	129,651	32.9%	5.7
TENNESSEE	1,493,000	126,752	8.5%	1,609,000	147,055	9.1%	0.6	1,728,000	169,153	9.8%	1.3	1,836,000	200,311	10.9%	2.4	1,944,000	202,914	10.4%	1.9
TEXAS	3,104,000	98,218	3.2%	3,437,000	104,661	3.0%	-0.1	3,789,000	212,692	5.6%	2.4	4,141,000	191,423	4.6%	1.5	4,492,000	282,240	6.3%	3.1
UTAH	260,000	84,795	32.6%	279,000	64,555	23.1%	-9.5	303,000	93,151	30.7%	-1.9	337,000	97,891	29.0%	-3.6	371,000	124,402	33.5%	0.9
VERMONT	207,000	78,984	38.2%	211,000	81,023	38.4%	0.2	216,000	78,371	36.3%	-1.9	222,000	71,527	32.2%	-5.9	228,000	75,926	33.3%	-4.9
VIRGINIA	1,362,000	89,637	6.6%	1,463,000	98,336	6.7%	0.1	1,588,000	109,363	6.9%	0.3	1,775,000	145,243	8.2%	1.6	1,962,000	172,070	8.8%	2.2
WASHINGTON	962,000	208,645	21.7%	1,042,000	206,892	19.9%	-1.8	1,144,000	322,123	28.2%	6.5	1,304,000	361,689	27.7%	6.0	1,465,000	386,315	26.4%	4.7
WEST VIRGINIA	922,000	330,731	35.9%	990,000	325,358	32.9%	-3.0	1,056,000	372,414	35.3%	-0.6	1,102,000	322,819	29.3%	-6.6	1,148,000	316,251	27.5%	-8.3
WISCONSIN	1,729,000	347,741	20.1%	1,842,000	380,828	20.7%	0.6	1,958,000	679,206	34.7%	14.6	2,058,000	674,532	32.8%	12.7	2,157,000	590,959	27.4%	7.3
WYOMING	129,000	39,583	30.7%	140,000	38,739	27.7%	-3.0	151,000	52,633	34.9%	4.2	162,000	51,921	32.1%	1.4	172,000	47,947	27.9%	-2.8
Total	70,022,000	15,760,684	22.5%	75,005,000	16,684,231	22.2%	-0.3	80,471,000	22,348,480	27.8%	5.3	86,671,000	22,017,617	25.4%	2.9	92,869,000	21,970,065	23.7%	1.1

Democratic Turnout for Election Years 1932–1948

State	1932 Voting-age population	Turnout	%	1936 Voting-age population	Turnout	%	Difference from 1932*	1940 Voting-age population	Turnout	%	Difference from 1932	1944 Voting-age population	Turnout	%	Difference from 1932	1948 Voting-age population	Turnout	%	Difference from 1932
ALABAMA	1,402,000	207,910	14.8%	1,486,000	238,196	16.0%	1.2	1,572,000	250,726	15.9%	1.1	1,648,000	198,918	12.1%	-2.8				
ALASKA																			
ARIZONA	184,000	79,264	43.1%	213,000	86,722	40.7%	-2.4	253,000	95,267	37.7%	-5.4	328,000	80,926	24.7%	-18.4	401,000	95,251	23.8%	-19.3
ARKANSAS	1,002,000	186,829	18.6%	1,055,000	146,765	13.9%	-4.7	1,100,000	157,213	14.3%	-4.4	1,104,000	148,965	13.5%	-5.2	1,109,000	149,659	13.5%	-5.2
CALIFORNIA	3,535,000	1,324,157	37.5%	3,979,000	1,766,836	44.4%	6.9	4,569,000	1,877,618	41.1%	3.6	5,572,000	1,988,564	35.7%	-1.8	6,575,000	1,913,134	29.1%	-8.4
COLORADO	601,000	250,877	41.7%	649,000	295,021	45.5%	3.7	699,000	265,554	38.0%	-3.8	755,000	234,331	31.0%	-10.7	812,000	267,288	32.9%	-8.8
CONNECTICUT	857,000	281,632	32.9%	942,000	382,129	40.6%	7.7	1,037,000	417,621	40.3%	7.4	1,152,000	435,146	37.8%	4.9	1,266,000	423,297	33.4%	0.6
DELAWARE	151,000	54,319	36.0%	162,000	69,702	43.0%	7.1	175,000	74,599	42.6%	6.7	189,000	68,166	36.1%	0.1	203,000	67,813	33.4%	-2.6
DISTRICT OF COLUMBIA																			
FLORIDA	936,000	206,307	22.0%	1,075,000	249,117	23.2%	1.1	1,243,000	359,334	28.9%	6.9	1,484,000	339,377	22.9%	0.8	1,725,000	281,988	16.3%	-5.7

United States Presidential General Elections *(continued)*

Democratic Turnout for Election Years 1932–1948 *(continued)*

State	1932 Voting-age population	Turnout	%	1936 Voting-age population	Turnout	%	Difference from 1932	1940 Voting-age population	Turnout	%	Difference from 1932	1944 Voting-age population	Turnout	%	Difference from 1932	1948 Voting-age population	Turnout	%	Difference from 1932
GEORGIA	1,570,000	234,118	14.9%	1,680,000	255,363	15.2%	0.3	1,806,000	265,194	14.7%	-0.2	1,969,000	268,187	13.6%	-1.3	2,131,000	254,646	11.9%	-3.0
HAWAII																			
IDAHO	254,000	109,479	43.1%	280,000	125,683	44.9%	1.8	306,000	127,842	41.8%	-1.3	323,000	107,399	33.3%	-9.9	339,000	107,370	31.7%	-11.4
ILLINOIS	4,615,000	1,882,304	40.8%	4,891,000	2,282,999	46.7%	5.9	5,179,000	2,149,934	41.5%	0.7	5,453,000	2,079,479	38.1%	-2.7	5,727,000	1,994,715	34.8%	-6.0
INDIANA	2,014,000	862,054	42.8%	2,116,000	934,974	44.2%	1.4	2,229,000	874,063	39.2%	-3.6	2,362,000	781,403	33.1%	-9.7	2,496,000	807,833	32.4%	-10.4
IOWA	1,510,000	598,019	39.6%	1,564,000	621,756	39.8%	0.2	1,614,000	578,802	35.9%	-3.7	1,641,000	499,876	30.5%	0.1	1,669,000	522,380	31.3%	-8.3
KANSAS	1,115,000	424,204	38.0%	1,131,000	464,520	41.1%	3.0	1,152,000	364,725	31.7%	-6.4	1,187,000	287,458	24.2%	-13.8	1,222,000	351,902	28.8%	-9.2
KENTUCKY	1,475,000	580,574	39.4%	1,561,000	541,944	34.7%	-4.6	1,654,000	557,322	33.7%	-5.7	1,754,000	472,589	26.9%	-12.4	1,854,000	466,756	25.2%	-14.2
LOUISIANA	1,185,000	249,418	21.0%	1,284,000	292,894	22.8%	1.8	1,383,000	319,751	23.1%	2.1	1,468,000	281,564	19.2%	-1.9	1,554,000	136,344	8.8%	-12.3
MAINE	454,000	128,907	28.4%	475,000	126,333	26.6%	-1.8	498,000	156,478	31.4%	3.0	522,000	140,631	26.9%	-1.5	546,000	111,916	20.5%	-7.9
MARYLAND	1,012,000	314,314	31.1%	1,090,000	389,612	35.7%	4.7	1,185,000	384,546	32.5%	1.4	1,324,000	315,490	23.8%	-7.2	1,463,000	286,521	19.6%	-11.5
MASSACHUSETTS	2,305,000	800,148	34.7%	2,454,000	942,716	38.4%	3.7	2,617,000	1,076,522	41.1%	6.4	2,802,000	1,035,296	36.9%	2.2	2,988,000	1,151,788	38.5%	3.8
MICHIGAN	2,724,000	871,700	32.0%	2,947,000	1,016,794	34.5%	2.5	3,204,000	1,032,991	32.2%	0.2	3,538,000	1,106,899	31.3%	-0.7	3,872,000	1,003,448	25.9%	-6.1
MINNESOTA	1,529,000	600,806	39.3%	1,637,000	698,811	42.7%	3.4	1,738,000	644,196	37.1%	-2.2	1,798,000	589,864	32.8%	-6.5	1,857,000	692,966	37.3%	-2.0
MISSISSIPPI	1,073,000	140,168	13.1%	1,140,000	157,333	13.8%	0.7	1,195,000	168,267	14.1%	1.0	1,199,000	168,621	14.1%	1.0	1,204,000	19,384	1.6%	-11.5
MISSOURI	2,287,000	1,025,406	44.8%	2,384,000	1,111,043	46.6%	1.8	2,477,000	958,476	38.7%	-6.1	2,540,000	807,356	31.8%	-13.1	2,603,000	917,315	35.2%	-9.6
MONTANA	304,000	127,286	41.9%	321,000	159,690	49.7%	7.9	338,000	145,698	43.1%	1.2	349,000	112,556	32.3%	-9.6	361,000	119,071	33.0%	-8.9
NEBRASKA	792,000	359,082	45.3%	805,000	347,445	43.2%	-2.2	818,000	263,677	32.2%	13.1	830,000	233,246	28.1%	-17.2	843,000	224,165	26.6%	-18.7
NEVADA	55,000	28,756	52.3%	62,000	31,925	51.5%	-0.8	70,000	31,945	45.6%	-6.6	85,000	29,623	34.9%	-17.4	100,000	31,291	31.3%	-21.0
NEW HAMPSHIRE	268,000	100,680	37.6%	283,000	108,460	38.3%	0.8	300,000	125,292	41.8%	4.2	317,000	119,663	37.7%	0.2	333,000	107,995	32.4%	-5.1
NEW JERSEY	2,294,000	806,630	35.2%	2,459,000	1,083,850	44.1%	8.9	2,649,000	1,016,808	38.4%	3.2	2,899,000	987,874	34.1%	-1.1	3,150,000	895,455	28.4%	-6.7
NEW MEXICO	197,000	95,089	48.3%	231,000	106,037	45.9%	-2.4	270,000	103,699	38.4%	-9.9	312,000	81,389	26.1%	-22.2	356,000	105,464	29.6%	-18.6
NEW YORK	7,228,000	2,534,959	35.1%	7,826,000	3,293,222	42.1%	7.0	8,447,000	3,251,918	38.5%	3.4	9,042,000	3,304,238	36.5%	1.5	9,635,000	2,780,204	28.9%	-6.2
NORTH CAROLINA	1,638,000	497,566	30.4%	1,791,000	616,141	34.4%	4.0	1,952,000	609,015	31.2%	0.8	2,107,000	527,399	25.0%	-5.3	2,263,000	459,070	20.3%	-10.1
NORTH DAKOTA	341,000	178,350	52.3%	348,000	163,148	46.9%	-5.4	354,000	124,036	35.0%	-17.3	356,000	100,144	28.1%	-24.2	358,000	95,812	26.8%	-25.5
OHIO	4,025,000	1,301,695	32.3%	4,234,000	1,747,140	41.3%	8.9	4,475,000	1,733,139	38.7%	6.4	4,786,000	1,570,763	32.8%	0.5	5,097,000	1,452,791	28.5%	-3.8
OKLAHOMA	1,263,000	516,468	40.9%	1,301,000	501,069	38.5%	-2.4	1,335,000	474,313	35.5%	-5.4	1,354,000	401,549	29.7%	-11.2	1,372,000	452,782	33.0%	-7.9
OREGON	612,000	213,871	34.9%	667,000	266,733	40.0%	5.0	735,000	258,415	35.2%	0.2	843,000	248,635	29.5%	-5.5	951,000	243,147	25.6%	-9.4
PENNSYLVANIA	5,441,000	1,295,948	23.8%	5,766,000	2,353,788	40.8%	17.0	6,103,000	2,171,035	35.6%	11.8	6,423,000	1,940,479	30.2%	6.4	6,743,000	1,752,426	26.0%	2.2
RHODE ISLAND	377,000	146,604	38.9%	403,000	164,338	40.8%	1.9	433,000	182,181	42.1%	3.2	469,000	175,356	37.4%	-1.5	504,000	188,736	37.4%	-1.4
SOUTH CAROLINA	865,000	102,347	11.8%	934,000	113,791	12.2%	0.4	1,004,000	95,470	9.5%	-2.3	1,068,000	90,601	8.5%	-3.3	1,131,000	34,423	3.0%	-8.8
SOUTH DAKOTA	364,000	183,515	50.4%	366,000	160,137	43.8%	-6.7	370,000	131,362	35.5%	-14.9	382,000	96,711	25.3%	-25.1	394,000	117,653	29.9%	-20.6
TENNESSEE	1,493,000	259,473	17.4%	1,609,000	328,083	20.4%	3.0	1,728,000	351,601	20.3%	3.0	1,836,000	308,707	16.8%	-0.6	1,944,000	270,402	13.9%	-3.5

United States Presidential General Elections (continued)

United States Presidential General Elections (continued)

Democratic Turnout for Election Years 1932–1948 (continued)

State	1932 Voting-age population	1932 Turnout	1932 %	1936 Voting-age population	1936 Turnout	1936 %	1936 Difference from 1932	1940 Voting-age population	1940 Turnout	1940 %	1940 Difference from 1932	1944 Voting-age population	1944 Turnout	1944 %	1944 Difference from 1932	1948 Voting-age population	1948 Turnout	1948 %	1948 Difference from 1932
TEXAS	3,104,000	771,109	24.8%	3,437,000	739,952	21.5%	-3.3	3,789,000	909,974	24.0%	-0.8	4,141,000	821,605	19.8%	-5.0	4,492,000	750,700	16.7%	-8.1
UTAH	260,000	116,750	44.9%	279,000	150,248	53.9%	8.9	303,000	154,277	50.9%	6.0	337,000	150,088	44.5%	-0.4	371,000	149,151	40.2%	-4.7
VERMONT	207,000	56,266	27.2%	211,000	62,124	29.4%	2.3	216,000	64,269	29.8%	2.6	222,000	53,820	24.2%	-2.9	228,000	45,557	20.0%	-7.2
VIRGINIA	1,362,000	203,979	15.0%	1,463,000	234,980	16.1%	1.1	1,588,000	235,961	14.9%	-0.1	1,775,000	242,276	13.6%	-1.3	1,962,000	200,786	10.2%	-4.7
WASHINGTON	962,000	353,260	36.7%	1,042,000	459,579	44.1%	7.4	1,144,000	462,145	40.4%	3.7	1,304,000	486,774	37.3%	0.6	1,465,000	476,165	32.5%	-4.2
WEST VIRGINIA	922,000	405,124	43.9%	990,000	502,582	50.8%	6.8	1,056,000	495,662	46.9%	3.0	1,102,000	392,777	35.6%	-8.3	1,148,000	429,188	37.4%	-6.6
WISCONSIN	1,729,000	707,410	40.9%	1,842,000	802,984	43.6%	2.7	1,958,000	704,821	36.0%	-4.9	2,058,000	650,413	31.6%	-9.3	2,157,000	647,310	30.0%	-10.9
WYOMING	129,000	54,370	42.1%	140,000	62,624	44.7%	2.6	151,000	59,287	39.3%	-2.9	162,000	49,419	30.5%	-11.6	172,000	52,354	30.4%	-11.7
Total	70,022,000	22,829,501	32.6%	75,005,000	27,757,333	37.0%	4.4	80,471,000	27,313,041	33.9%	1.3	86,671,000	25,612,610	29.6%	-3.1	91,146,000	24,105,812	26.4%	-6.2

Other Turnout for Election Years 1932–1948

State	1932 Voting-age population	1932 Turnout	1932 %	1936 Voting-age population	1936 Turnout	1936 %	1936 Difference from 1932*	1940 Voting-age population	1940 Turnout	1940 %	1940 Difference from 1932	1944 Voting-age population	1944 Turnout	1944 %	1944 Difference from 1932	1948 Voting-age population	1948 Turnout	1948 %	1948 Difference from 1932
ALABAMA	1,402,000	2,718	0.2%	1,486,000	2,190	0.1%	0.0	1,572,000	1,309	0.1%	-0.1	1,648,000	1,285	0.1%	-0.1	1,723,000	174,050	10.1%	9.9
ALASKA																			
ARIZONA	184,000	2,883	1.6%	213,000	4,008	1.9%	0.3	253,000	742	0.3%	-1.3	328,000	421	0.1%	-1.4	401,000	4,217	1.1%	-0.5
ARKANSAS	1,002,000	2,275	0.2%	1,055,000	617	0.1%	-0.2	1,100,000	1,094	0.1%	-0.1	1,104,000	438	0.0%	-0.2	1,109,000	41,857	3.8%	3.5
CALIFORNIA	3,535,000	94,913	2.7%	3,979,000	35,615	0.9%	-1.8	4,569,000	39,754	0.9%	-1.8	5,572,000	19,346	0.3%	-2.3	6,575,000	213,135	3.2%	0.6
COLORADO	601,000	17,202	2.9%	649,000	12,397	1.9%	-1.0	699,000	3,874	0.6%	-2.3	755,000	1,977	0.3%	-2.6	812,000	8,235	1.0%	-1.8
CONNECTICUT	857,000	24,131	2.8%	942,000	29,909	3.2%	0.4	1,037,000	2,062	0.2%	-2.6	1,152,000	6,317	0.5%	-2.3	1,266,000	22,467	1.8%	-1.0
DELAWARE	151,000	1,509	1.0%	162,000	665	0.4%	-0.6	175,000	335	0.2%	-0.8	189,000	448	0.2%	-0.8	203,000	1,672	0.8%	-0.2
DISTRICT OF COLUMBIA																			
FLORIDA	936,000	1,466	0.2%	1,075,000	71	0.0%	-0.2	1,243,000	148	0.0%	-0.1	1,484,000	211	0.0%	-0.1	1,725,000	101,375	5.9%	5.7
GEORGIA	1,570,000	1,609	0.1%	1,680,000	864	0.1%	-0.1	1,806,000	997	0.1%	0.0	1,969,000	42	0.0%	-0.1	2,131,000	87,427	4.1%	4.0
HAWAII																			
IDAHO	254,000	5,729	2.3%	280,000	7,678	2.7%	0.5	306,000	773	0.3%	-2.0	323,000	785	0.2%	-2.0	339,000	5,932	1.7%	-0.5
ILLINOIS	4,615,000	92,866	2.0%	4,891,000	103,130	2.1%	0.1	5,179,000	20,761	0.4%	-1.6	5,453,000	17,268	0.3%	-1.7	5,727,000	28,228	0.5%	-1.5
INDIANA	2,014,000	37,689	1.9%	2,116,000	24,353	1.2%	-0.7	2,229,000	9,218	0.4%	-1.5	2,362,000	14,797	0.6%	-1.2	2,496,000	27,302	1.1%	-0.8
IOWA	1,510,000	24,235	1.6%	1,564,000	33,004	2.1%	0.5	1,614,000	4,260	0.3%	-1.3	1,641,000	5,456	0.3%	-1.3	1,669,000	21,866	1.3%	-0.3
KANSAS	1,115,000	18,276	1.6%	1,131,000	3,260	0.3%	-1.4	1,152,000	6,403	0.6%	-1.1	1,187,000	4,222	0.4%	-1.3	1,222,000	13,878	1.1%	-0.5
KENTUCKY	1,475,000	7,769	0.5%	1,561,000	14,568	0.9%	0.4	1,654,000	2,457	0.1%	-0.4	1,754,000	2,887	0.2%	-0.4	1,854,000	14,692	0.8%	0.3
LOUISIANA	1,185,000	533	0.0%	1,284,000	93	0.0%	0.0	1,383,000	108	0.0%	0.0	1,468,000	69	0.0%	0.0	1,554,000	207,325	13.3%	13.3
MAINE	454,000	2,906	0.6%	475,000	9,084	1.9%	1.3	498,000	411	0.1%	-0.6	522,000	335	0.1%	-0.6	546,000	2,637	0.5%	-0.2

United States Presidential General Elections (continued)

Other Turnout for Election Years 1932–1948 (continued)

State	1932 Voting-age population	Turnout	%	1936 Voting-age population	Turnout	%	Difference from 1932	1940 Voting-age population	Turnout	%	Difference from 1932	1944 Voting-age population	Turnout	%	Difference from 1932	1948 Voting-age population	Turnout	%	Difference from 1932
MARYLAND	1,012,000	12,556	1.2%	1,090,000	3,849	0.4%	-0.9	1,185,000	6,024	0.5%	-0.7					1,463,000	15,373	1.1%	-0.2
MASSACHUSETTS	2,305,000	43,007	1.9%	2,454,000	129,028	5.3%	3.4	2,617,000	10,771	0.4%	-1.5	2,802,000	4,019	0.1%	-1.7	2,988,000	45,988	1.5%	-0.3
MICHIGAN	2,724,000	53,171	2.0%	2,947,000	88,571	3.0%	1.1	3,204,000	13,021	0.4%	-1.5	3,538,000	13,901	0.4%	-1.6	3,872,000	67,566	1.7%	-0.2
MINNESOTA	1,529,000	38,078	2.5%	1,637,000	80,703	4.9%	2.4	1,738,000	10,718	0.6%	-1.9	1,798,000	8,224	0.5%	-2.0	1,857,000	35,643	1.9%	-0.6
MISSISSIPPI	1,073,000	686	0.1%	1,140,000	342	0.0%	0.0	1,195,000	193	0.0%	0.0					1,204,000	167,763	13.9%	13.9
MISSOURI	2,287,000	19,775	0.9%	2,384,000	19,701	0.8%	0.0	2,477,000	4,244	0.2%	0.7	2,540,000	3,166	0.1%	-0.7	2,603,000	6,274	0.2%	-0.6
MONTANA	304,000	11,115	3.7%	321,000	7,214	2.2%	-1.4	338,000	2,596	0.8%	-2.9	349,000	1,636	0.5%	-3.2	361,000	8,437	2.3%	-1.3
NEBRASKA	792,000	9,876	1.2%	805,000	12,847	1.6%	0.3									843,000	1	0.0%	-1.2
NEVADA																100,000	1,469	1.5%	
NEW HAMPSHIRE	268,000	1,211	0.5%	283,000	5,012	1.8%	1.3					317,000	46	0.0%	0.4	333,000	2,146	0.6%	0.2
NEW JERSEY	2,294,000	47,749	2.1%	2,459,000	16,265	0.7%	-1.4	2,649,000	10,269	0.4%	-1.7	2,899,000	14,552	0.5%	-1.6	3,150,000	72,976	2.3%	0.2
NEW MEXICO	197,000	2,300	1.2%	231,000	1,371	0.6%	-0.6	270,000	244	0.1%	-1.1	312,000	148	0.0%	-1.1	356,000	1,086	0.3%	-0.9
NEW YORK	7,228,000	215,692	3.0%	7,826,000	122,506	1.6%	-1.4	8,447,000	22,200	0.3%	-2.7	9,042,000	24,905	0.3%	-2.7	9,635,000	555,970	5.8%	2.8
NORTH CAROLINA	1,638,000	5,588	0.3%	1,791,000	40	0.0%	-0.3									2,263,000	73,587	3.3%	2.9
NORTH DAKOTA	341,000	6,168	1.8%	348,000	37,817	10.9%	9.1	354,000	2,149	0.6%	-1.2	356,000	1,503	0.4%	-1.4	358,000	9,765	2.7%	0.9
OHIO	4,025,000	80,714	2.0%	4,234,000	137,665	3.3%	1.2									5,097,000	37,596	0.7%	1.3
OKLAHOMA				1,301,000	3,549	0.3%		1,335,000	3,027	0.2%	0.0	1,354,000	1,663	0.1%	-0.1				
OREGON	612,000	18,861	3.1%	667,000	24,582	3.7%	0.6	735,000	3,270	0.4%	-2.6	843,000	6,147	0.7%	-2.4	951,000	20,029	2.1%	-1.0
PENNSYLVANIA	5,441,000	109,533	2.0%	5,766,000	94,017	1.6%	-0.4	6,103,000	17,831	0.3%	-1.7	6,423,000	19,260	0.3%	-1.7	6,743,000	80,525	1.2%	-0.8
RHODE ISLAND	377,000	4,300	1.1%	403,000	20,909	5.2%	4.0	433,000	317	0.1%	-1.1	469,000	433	0.1%	-1.0	504,000	3,179	0.6%	-0.5
SOUTH CAROLINA	865,000	82	0.0%									1,068,000	8,164	0.8%	0.8	1,131,000	102,762	9.1%	9.1
SOUTH DAKOTA	364,000	5,711	1.6%	366,000	10,338	2.8%	1.3									394,000	2,801	0.7%	-0.9
TENNESSEE	1,493,000	4,048	0.3%	1,609,000	1,948	0.1%	-0.2	1,728,000	2,069	0.1%	-0.2	1,836,000	1,674	0.1%	-0.2	1,944,000	76,967	4.0%	3.7
TEXAS	3,104,000	5,055	0.2%	3,437,000	5,088	0.1%	0.0	3,789,000	1,771	0.0%	-0.1	4,141,000	137,306	3.3%	3.2	4,492,000	114,305	2.5%	2.4
UTAH	260,000	5,033	1.9%	279,000	1,876	0.7%	-1.3	303,000	391	0.1%	-1.8	337,000	340	0.1%	-1.8	371,000	2,752	0.7%	-1.2
VERMONT	207,000	1,730	0.8%	211,000	542	0.3%	-0.6	216,000	422	0.2%	-0.6	222,000	14	0.0%	-0.8	228,000	1,899	0.8%	0.0
VIRGINIA	1,362,000	4,326	0.3%	1,463,000	1,274	0.1%	-0.2	1,588,000	1,284	0.1%	-0.2	1,775,000	966	0.1%	-0.3	1,962,000	46,400	2.4%	2.0
WASHINGTON	962,000	52,909	5.5%	1,042,000	25,867	2.5%	-3.0	1,144,000	9,565	0.8%	-4.7	1,304,000	7,865	0.6%	-4.9	1,465,000	42,579	2.9%	-2.6
WEST VIRGINIA	922,000	7,919	0.9%	990,000	2,005	0.2%	-0.7									1,148,000	3,311	0.3%	-0.6
WISCONSIN	1,729,000	59,663	3.5%	1,842,000	74,748	4.1%	0.6	1,958,000	21,495	1.1%	-2.4	2,058,000	14,207	0.7%	-2.8	2,157,000	38,531	1.8%	-1.7
WYOMING	129,000	3,009	2.3%	140,000	2,019	1.4%	-0.9	151,000	320	0.2%	-2.1					172,000	1,124	0.7%	-1.7
Total	68,704,000	1,168,574	1.7%	74,009,000	1,213,199	1.6%	-0.1	70,426,000	238,897	0.3%	-1.4	74,694,000	346,443	0.5%	-1.2	91,497,000	2,615,079	2.9%	1.2

*Percentage point difference between turnout in current year and initial year listed in chart. If data do not appear for a state in the initial year listed, the difference is calculated from the first year in which data do appear for that state.

STATE GUBERNATORIAL GENERAL ELECTIONS

Election Years 1932–1948

State	1932 Voting-age population	Turnout	%	1936 Voting-age population	Turnout	%	Difference from 1932*	1940 Voting-age population	Turnout	%	Difference from 1932	1944 Voting-age population	Turnout	%	Difference from 1932	1948 Voting-age population	Turnout	%	Difference from 1932
ALABAMA																			
ALASKA																			
ARIZONA	184,000	119,124	64.7%	213,000	124,052	58.2%	-6.5	253,000	148,967	58.9%	-5.9	328,000	128,642	39.2%	-25.5	401,000	175,767	43.8%	-20.9
ARKANSAS	1,002,000	221,871	22.1%	1,055,000	184,460	17.5%	-4.7	1,100,000	202,044	18.4%	-3.8	1,104,000	216,843	19.6%	-2.5	1,109,000	249,301	22.5%	0.3
CALIFORNIA																			
COLORADO	601,000	449,369	74.8%	649,000	482,535	74.4%	-0.4	699,000	545,636	78.1%	3.3	755,000	495,948	65.7%	-9.1	812,000	501,680	61.8%	-13.0
CONNECTICUT	857,000	596,547	69.6%	942,000	674,523	71.6%	2.0	1,037,000	784,013	75.6%	6.0	1,152,000	828,579	71.9%	2.3	1,266,000	875,170	69.1%	-0.5
DELAWARE	151,000	112,314	74.4%	162,000	126,987	78.4%	4.0	175,000	135,187	77.2%	2.9	189,000	126,355	66.9%	-7.5	203,000	140,335	69.1%	-5.2
DISTRICT OF COLUMBIA																			
FLORIDA	936,000	279,593	29.9%	1,075,000	313,470	29.2%	-0.7	1,243,000	334,152	26.9%	-3.0	1,484,000	454,328	30.6%	0.7	1,725,000	457,638	26.5%	-3.3
GEORGIA	1,570,000	240,242	15.3%	1,680,000	264,013	15.7%	0.4	1,806,000	291,050	16.1%	0.8					2,131,000	363,763	17.1%	1.8
HAWAII																			
IDAHO	254,000	189,002	74.4%	280,000	201,244	71.9%	-2.5	306,000	238,537	78.0%	3.5	323,000	208,059	64.4%	-10.0				
ILLINOIS	4,615,000	3,350,310	72.6%	4,891,000	3,891,976	79.6%	7.0	5,179,000	4,152,622	80.2%	7.6	5,453,000	3,966,765	72.7%	0.1	5,727,000	3,940,257	68.8%	-3.8
INDIANA	2,014,000	1,566,909	77.8%	2,116,000	1,641,074	77.6%	-0.2	2,229,000	1,782,252	80.0%	2.2	2,362,000	1,666,239	70.5%	-7.3	2,496,000	1,652,321	66.2%	-11.6
IOWA	1,510,000	963,718	63.8%	1,564,000	1,079,492	69.0%	5.2	1,614,000	1,176,940	72.9%	9.1	1,641,000	1,003,158	61.1%	-2.7	1,669,000	994,833	59.6%	-4.2
KANSAS	1,115,000	800,026	71.8%	1,131,000	848,083	75.0%	3.2	1,152,000	858,289	74.5%	2.8	1,187,000	705,597	59.4%	-12.3	1,222,000	760,407	62.2%	-9.5
KENTUCKY																			
LOUISIANA	1,185,000	110,252	9.3%	1,284,000	131,999	10.3%	1.0	1,383,000	227,208	16.4%	7.1	1,468,000	51,604	3.5%	-5.8	1,554,000	76,566	4.9%	-4.4
MAINE	454,000	241,095	53.1%	475,000	310,044	65.3%	12.2	498,000	255,047	51.2%	-1.9	522,000	187,632	35.9%	-17.2	546,000	222,500	40.8%	-12.4
MARYLAND																			
MASSACHUSETTS	2,305,000	1,564,561	67.9%	2,454,000	1,822,257	74.3%	6.4	2,617,000	2,008,820	76.8%	8.9	2,802,000	1,954,324	69.7%	1.9	2,988,000	2,099,250	70.3%	2.4
MICHIGAN	2,724,000	1,616,262	59.3%	2,947,000	1,747,698	59.3%	0.0	3,204,000	2,030,069	63.4%	4.0	3,538,000	2,210,246	62.5%	3.1	3,872,000	2,113,102	54.6%	-4.8
MINNESOTA	1,529,000	1,033,009	67.6%	1,637,000	1,120,179	68.4%	0.9	1,738,000	1,257,491	72.4%	4.8	1,798,000	1,138,468	63.3%	-4.2	1,857,000	1,210,894	65.2%	-2.4
MISSISSIPPI																			
MISSOURI	2,287,000	1,609,794	70.4%	2,384,000	1,817,596	76.2%	5.9	2,477,000	1,821,207	73.5%	3.1	2,540,000	1,557,844	61.3%	-9.1	2,603,000	1,567,338	60.2%	-10.2
MONTANA	304,000	216,381	71.2%	321,000	226,353	70.5%	-0.7	338,000	245,601	72.7%	1.5	349,000	206,645	59.2%	-12.0	361,000	222,964	61.8%	-9.4
NEBRASKA	792,000	563,738	71.2%	805,000	596,425	74.1%	2.9	818,000	600,805	73.4%	2.3	830,000	538,896	64.9%	-6.3	843,000	476,352	56.5%	-14.7
NEVADA																			
NEW HAMPSHIRE	268,000	197,024	73.5%	283,000	208,806	73.8%	0.3	300,000	221,479	73.8%	0.3	317,000	218,031	68.8%	-4.7	333,000	222,571	66.8%	-6.7
NEW JERSEY																			
NEW MEXICO	197,000	152,536	77.4%	231,000	170,671	73.9%	-3.5	270,000	185,341	68.6%	-8.8	312,000	147,556	47.3%	-30.1	356,000	189,992	53.4%	-24.1
NEW YORK	7,228,000	4,691,650	64.9%	7,826,000	5,557,338	71.0%	6.1												

State Gubernatorial General Elections (continued)

Election Years 1932–1948 (continued)

State	1932 Voting-age population	Turnout	%	1936 Voting-age population	Turnout	%	Difference from 1932	1940 Voting-age population	Turnout	%	Difference from 1932	1944 Voting-age population	Turnout	%	Difference from 1932	1948 Voting-age population	Turnout	%	Difference from 1932
NORTH CAROLINA	1,638,000	710,218	43.4%	1,791,000	812,982	45.4%	2.0	1,952,000	804,146	41.2%	-2.2	2,107,000	759,993	36.1%	-7.3	2,263,000	960,525	42.4%	-0.9
NORTH DAKOTA	341,000	244,785	71.8%	348,000	276,813	79.5%	7.8	354,000	274,565	77.6%	5.8	356,000	207,360	58.2%	-13.5	358,000	214,858	60.0%	-11.8
OHIO	4,025,000	2,568,447	63.8%	4,234,000	2,959,606	69.9%	6.1	4,475,000	3,285,259	73.4%	9.6	4,786,000	3,095,259	64.7%	0.9	5,097,000	3,018,289	59.2%	-4.6
OKLAHOMA																			
OREGON																951,000	509,633	53.6%	
PENNSYLVANIA																			
RHODE ISLAND	377,000	265,354	70.4%	403,000	299,624	74.3%	4.0	433,000	318,668	73.6%	3.2	469,000	295,168	62.9%	-7.5	504,000	323,863	64.3%	-6.1
SOUTH CAROLINA																			
SOUTH DAKOTA	364,000	284,115	78.1%	366,000	293,914	80.3%	2.3	370,000	304,114	82.2%	4.1	382,000	226,924	59.4%	-18.6	394,000	245,372	62.3%	-15.8
TENNESSEE	1,493,000	398,120	26.7%	1,609,000	414,601	25.8%	-0.9	1,728,000	448,720	26.0%	-0.7	1,836,000	441,191	24.0%	-2.6	1,944,000	543,001	28.0%	1.3
TEXAS	3,104,000	849,538	27.4%	3,437,000	842,170	24.5%	-2.9	3,789,000	1,079,489	28.5%	1.1	4,141,000	1,108,113	26.8%	-0.6	4,492,000	1,208,860	26.9%	-0.5
UTAH	260,000	205,751	79.1%	279,000	215,231	77.1%	-2.0	303,000	246,812	81.5%	2.3	337,000	246,758	73.2%	-5.9	371,000	275,067	74.1%	-5.0
VERMONT	207,000	132,373	63.9%	211,000	137,291	65.1%	1.1	216,000	136,416	63.2%	-0.8	222,000	119,747	53.9%	-10.0	228,000	120,183	52.7%	-11.2
VIRGINIA																			
WASHINGTON	962,000	614,768	63.9%	1,042,000	672,607	64.5%	0.6	1,144,000	781,328	68.3%	4.4	1,304,000	832,483	63.8%	-0.1	1,465,000	883,141	60.3%	-3.6
WEST VIRGINIA	922,000	748,225	81.2%	990,000	831,040	83.9%	2.8	1,056,000	879,726	83.3%	2.2	1,102,000	725,771	65.9%	-15.3	1,148,000	768,061	66.9%	-14.2
WISCONSIN	1,729,000	1,124,502	65.0%	1,842,000	1,237,095	67.2%	2.1	1,958,000	1,373,754	70.2%	5.1	2,058,000	1,320,483	64.2%	-0.9	2,157,000	1,266,139	58.7%	-6.3
WYOMING	129,000	94,649	73.4%																
Total	49,633,000	29,126,172	58.7%	52,957,000	32,534,249	61.4%	2.8	48,214,000	29,435,754	61.1%	2.4	49,554,000	27,391,009	55.3%	-3.4	55,446,000	20,050,873	52.0%	-6.6

*Percentage point difference between turnout in current year and initial year listed in chart. If data do not appear for a state in the initial year listed, the difference is calculated from the first year in which data do appear for that state.

STATE GUBERNATORIAL GENERAL ELECTIONS

Republican Turnout for Election Years 1932–1948

State	1932 Voting-age population	Turnout	%	1936 Voting-age population	Turnout	%	Difference from 1932*	1940 Voting-age population	Turnout	%	Difference from 1932	1944 Voting-age population	Turnout	%	Difference from 1932	1948 Voting-age population	Turnout	%	Difference from 1932
ALABAMA																			
ALASKA																			
ARIZONA	184,000	42,202	22.9%	213,000	36,114	17.0%	-6.0	253,000	50,358	19.9%	-3.0	328,000	27,261	8.3%	-14.6	401,000	70,419	17.6%	-5.4
ARKANSAS	1,002,000	19,713	2.0%	1,055,000	26,875	2.5%	0.6	1,100,000	16,600	1.5%	-0.5	1,104,000	30,442	2.8%	0.8	1,109,000	26,500	2.4%	0.4
CALIFORNIA																			
COLORADO	601,000	183,258	30.5%	649,000	210,614	32.5%	2.0	699,000	296,671	42.4%	12.0	755,000	259,862	34.4%	3.9	812,000	168,928	20.8%	-9.7
CONNECTICUT	857,000	277,853	32.4%	942,000	277,190	29.4%	-3.0	1,037,000	374,581	36.1%	3.7	1,152,000	418,289	36.3%	3.9	1,266,000	429,071	33.9%	1.5
DELAWARE	151,000	60,903	40.3%	162,000	52,782	32.6%	-7.8	175,000	70,909	40.5%	0.2	189,000	63,829	33.8%	-6.6	203,000	64,996	32.0%	-8.3
DISTRICT OF COLUMBIA																			
FLORIDA	936,000	93,323	10.0%	1,075,000	59,832	5.6%	-4.4					1,484,000	93,321	6.3%	-3.7	1,725,000	76,153	4.4%	-5.6
GEORGIA																			
HAWAII																			
IDAHO	254,000	68,863	27.1%	280,000	83,430	29.8%	2.7	306,000	118,117	38.6%	11.5	323,000	98,532	30.5%	3.4				
ILLINOIS	4,615,000	1,364,043	29.6%	4,891,000	1,682,685	34.4%	4.8	5,179,000	2,197,778	42.4%	12.9	5,453,000	2,013,270	36.9%	7.4	5,727,000	1,678,007	29.3%	-0.3
INDIANA	2,014,000	669,797	33.3%	2,116,000	727,526	34.4%	1.1	2,229,000	885,657	39.7%	6.5	2,362,000	849,346	36.0%	2.7	2,496,000	745,892	29.9%	-3.4
IOWA	1,510,000	455,145	30.1%	1,564,000	521,747	33.4%	3.2	1,614,000	620,480	38.4%	8.3	1,641,000	561,827	34.2%	4.1	1,669,000	553,900	33.2%	3.0
KANSAS	1,115,000	278,581	25.0%	1,131,000	411,446	36.4%	11.4	1,152,000	425,928	37.0%	12.0	1,187,000	464,110	39.1%	14.1	1,222,000	433,396	35.5%	10.5
KENTUCKY																			
LOUISIANA								1,383,000	1,367	0.1%									
MAINE	454,000	118,800	26.2%	475,000	173,716	36.6%	10.4	498,000	162,719	32.7%	6.5	522,000	131,849	25.3%	-0.9	546,000	145,956	26.7%	0.6
MARYLAND																			
MASSACHUSETTS	2,305,000	704,576	30.6%	2,454,000	839,740	34.2%	3.7	2,617,000	999,223	38.2%	7.6	2,802,000	897,708	32.0%	1.5	2,988,000	849,895	28.4%	-2.1
MICHIGAN	2,724,000	696,935	25.6%	2,947,000	843,855	28.6%	3.0	3,204,000	945,784	29.5%	3.9	3,538,000	1,208,859	34.2%	8.6	3,872,000	964,810	24.9%	-0.7
MINNESOTA	1,529,000	334,081	21.8%	1,637,000	431,841	26.4%	4.5	1,738,000	654,686	37.7%	15.8	1,798,000	701,185	39.0%	17.1	1,857,000	643,572	34.7%	12.8
MISSISSIPPI																			
MISSOURI	2,287,000	629,428	27.5%	2,384,000	772,934	32.4%	4.9	2,477,000	911,530	36.8%	9.3	2,540,000	762,908	30.0%	2.5	2,603,000	670,064	25.7%	-1.8
MONTANA	304,000	101,105	33.3%	321,000	108,914	33.9%	0.7	338,000	124,435	36.8%	3.6	349,000	116,461	33.4%	0.1	361,000	97,792	27.1%	-6.2
NEBRASKA	792,000	260,888	32.9%	805,000	257,267	32.0%	-1.0	818,000	365,638	44.7%	11.8	830,000	410,136	49.4%	16.5	843,000	286,119	33.9%	1.0
NEVADA																			
NEW HAMPSHIRE	268,000	106,777	39.8%	283,000	118,178	41.8%	1.9	300,000	112,386	37.5%	-2.4	317,000	115,799	36.5%	-3.3	333,000	116,212	34.9%	-4.9
NEW JERSEY																			
NEW MEXICO	197,000	67,406	34.2%	231,000	72,511	31.4%	-2.8	270,000	82,306	30.5%	-3.7	312,000	71,113	22.8%	-11.4	356,000	86,023	24.2%	-10.1
NEW YORK	7,228,000	1,812,080	25.1%	7,826,000	2,450,104	31.3%	6.2												

State Gubernatorial General Elections (continued)

Republican Turnout for Election Years 1932–1948 (continued)

State	1932 Voting-age population	Turnout	%	1936 Voting-age population	Turnout	%	Difference from 1932	1940 Voting-age population	Turnout	%	Difference from 1932	1944 Voting-age population	Turnout	%	Difference from 1932	1948 Voting-age population	Turnout	%	Difference from 1932
NORTH CAROLINA	1,638,000	212,561	13.0%	1,791,000	270,843	15.1%	2.1	1,952,000	195,402	10.0%	-3.0	2,107,000	230,998	11.0%	-2.0	2,263,000	206,166	9.1%	-3.9
NORTH DAKOTA	341,000	134,231	39.4%	348,000	95,697	27.5%	-11.9	354,000	101,287	28.6%	-10.8	356,000	107,863	30.3%	-9.1	358,000	131,764	36.8%	-2.6
OHIO	4,025,000	1,151,933	28.6%	4,234,000	1,412,773	33.4%	4.7	4,475,000	1,824,863	40.8%	12.2	4,786,000	1,491,450	31.2%	2.5	5,097,000	1,398,514	27.4%	-1.2
OKLAHOMA																			
OREGON																951,000	271,295	28.5%	
PENNSYLVANIA																			
RHODE ISLAND	377,000	115,438	30.6%	403,000	137,369	34.1%	3.5	433,000	140,474	32.4%	1.8	469,000	116,158	24.8%	-5.9	504,000	124,441	24.7%	-5.9
SOUTH CAROLINA																			
SOUTH DAKOTA	364,000	120,473	33.1%	366,000	151,659	41.4%	8.3	370,000	167,686	45.3%	12.2	382,000	148,646	38.9%	5.8	394,000	149,883	38.0%	4.9
TENNESSEE	1,493,000	121,397	8.1%	1,609,000	78,292	4.9%	-3.3	1,728,000	125,254	7.2%	-0.9	1,836,000	158,742	8.6%	0.5	1,944,000	170,957	9.3%	1.1
TEXAS	3,104,000	317,807	10.2%	3,437,000	58,842	1.7%	-8.5	3,789,000	59,885	1.6%	-8.7	4,141,000	100,287	2.4%	-7.8	4,492,000	177,399	3.9%	-6.3
UTAH	260,000	85,913	33.0%	279,000	80,118	28.7%	-4.3	303,000	117,713	38.8%	5.8	337,000	122,851	36.5%	3.4	371,000	151,253	40.8%	7.7
VERMONT	207,000	81,656	39.4%	211,000	83,602	39.6%	0.2	216,000	87,346	40.4%	1.0	222,000	70,907	35.5%	-3.9	228,000	86,394	37.9%	-1.6
VIRGINIA																			
WASHINGTON	962,000	207,497	21.6%	1,042,000	189,141	18.2%	-3.4	1,144,000	392,522	34.3%	12.7	1,304,000	400,604	30.7%	9.2	1,465,000	445,958	30.4%	8.9
WEST VIRGINIA	922,000	342,660	37.2%	990,000	338,555	34.2%	-3.0	1,056,000	383,698	36.3%	-0.8	1,102,000	330,649	30.0%	-7.2	1,148,000	329,309	28.7%	-8.5
WISCONSIN	1,729,000	470,805	27.2%	1,842,000	363,973	19.8%	-7.5	1,958,000	558,678	28.5%	1.3	2,058,000	697,740	33.9%	6.7	2,157,000	684,839	31.7%	4.5
WYOMING	129,000	44,692	34.6%																
Total	46,878,000	11,752,820	25.1%	49,993,000	13,420,165	26.8%	1.8	45,165,000	13,571,961	30.0%	5.0	48,086,000	13,281,002	27.6%	2.5	51,761,000	12,444,877	24.0%	-1.0

Democratic Turnout for Election Years 1932–1948

State	1932 Voting-age population	Turnout	%	1936 Voting-age population	Turnout	%	Difference from 1932*	1940 Voting-age population	Turnout	%	Difference from 1932	1944 Voting-age population	Turnout	%	Difference from 1932	1948 Voting-age population	Turnout	%	Difference from 1932
ALABAMA																			
ALASKA																			
ARIZONA	184,000	75,314	40.9%	213,000	87,678	41.2%	0.2	253,000	97,606	38.6%	-2.4	328,000	100,220	30.6%	-10.4	401,000	104,008	25.9%	-15.0
ARKANSAS	1,002,000	200,612	20.0%	1,055,000	156,852	14.9%	-5.2	1,100,000	184,578	16.8%	-3.2	1,104,000	186,401	16.9%	-3.1	1,109,000	222,801	20.1%	0.1
CALIFORNIA																			
COLORADO	601,000	257,188	42.8%	649,000	263,311	40.6%	-2.2	699,000	245,292	35.1%	-7.7	755,000	236,086	31.3%	-11.5	812,000	332,752	41.0%	-1.8
CONNECTICUT	857,000	288,633	33.7%	942,000	372,953	39.6%	5.9	1,037,000	388,361	37.5%	3.8	1,152,000	392,417	34.1%	0.4	1,266,000	431,296	34.1%	0.4
DELAWARE	151,000	50,401	33.4%	162,000	65,437	40.4%	7.0	175,000	61,303	35.0%	1.7	189,000	62,156	32.9%	-0.5	203,000	75,339	37.1%	3.7
DISTRICT OF COLUMBIA																			
FLORIDA	936,000	186,270	19.9%	1,075,000	253,638	23.6%	3.7	1,243,000	334,152	26.9%	7.0	1,484,000	361,007	24.3%	4.4	1,725,000	381,459	22.1%	2.2

State Gubernatorial General Elections (continued)

State Gubernatorial General Elections (continued)

Democratic Turnout for Election Years 1932–1948 (continued)

State	1932 Voting-age population	Turnout	%	1936 Voting-age population	Turnout	%	Difference from 1932	1940 Voting-age population	Turnout	%	Difference from 1932	1944 Voting-age population	Turnout	%	Difference from 1932	1948 Voting-age population	Turnout	%	Difference from 1932
GEORGIA	1,570,000	240,242	15.3%	1,680,000	263,140	15.7%	0.4	1,806,000	289,879	16.1%	0.7					2,131,000	354,711	16.6%	1.3
HAWAII																			
IDAHO	254,000	116,663	45.9%	280,000	115,098	41.1%	-4.8	306,000	120,420	39.4%	-6.6	323,000	109,527	33.9%	-12.0				
ILLINOIS	4,615,000	1,930,330	41.8%	4,891,000	2,067,861	42.3%	0.5	5,179,000	1,940,833	37.5%	-4.4	5,453,000	1,940,999	35.6%	-6.2	5,727,000	2,250,074	39.3%	-2.5
INDIANA	2,014,000	862,127	42.8%	2,116,000	908,494	42.9%	0.1	2,229,000	889,620	39.9%	-2.9	2,362,000	802,765	34.0%	-8.8	2,496,000	884,995	35.5%	-7.4
IOWA	1,510,000	508,573	33.7%	1,564,000	524,178	33.5%	-0.2	1,614,000	553,941	34.3%	0.6	1,641,000	437,684	26.7%	-7.0	1,669,000	434,432	26.0%	-7.7
KANSAS	1,115,000	272,944	24.5%	1,131,000	433,319	38.3%	13.8	1,152,000	425,498	36.9%	12.5	1,187,000	231,410	19.5%	-5.0	1,222,000	307,485	25.2%	0.7
KENTUCKY																			
LOUISIANA	1,185,000	110,193	9.3%	1,284,000	131,999	10.3%	1.0	1,383,000	225,841	16.3%	7.0	1,468,000	51,604	3.5%	-5.8	1,554,000	76,566	4.9%	-4.4
MAINE	454,000	121,158	26.7%	475,000	130,466	27.5%	0.8	498,000	92,003	18.5%	-8.2	522,000	55,783	10.7%	-16.0	546,000	76,544	14.0%	-12.7
MARYLAND																			
MASSACHUSETTS	2,305,000	825,479	35.8%	2,454,000	867,743	35.4%	-0.5	2,617,000	993,635	38.0%	2.2	2,802,000	1,048,284	37.4%	1.6	2,988,000	1,239,247	41.5%	5.7
MICHIGAN	2,724,000	887,672	32.6%	2,947,000	892,774	30.3%	-2.3	3,204,000	1,077,065	33.6%	1.0	3,538,000	989,307	28.0%	-4.6	3,872,000	1,128,644	29.1%	-3.4
MINNESOTA	1,529,000	169,859	11.1%					1,738,000	140,021	8.1%	-3.1	1,798,000	430,132	23.9%	12.8	1,857,000	545,766	29.4%	18.3
MISSISSIPPI																			
MISSOURI	2,287,000	968,551	42.4%	2,384,000	1,037,133	43.5%	1.2	2,477,000	907,917	36.7%	-5.7	2,540,000	793,490	31.2%	-11.1	2,603,000	893,092	34.3%	-8.0
MONTANA	304,000	104,949	34.5%	321,000	115,310	35.9%	1.4	338,000	119,453	35.3%	0.8	349,000	89,224	25.6%	-9.0	361,000	124,267	34.4%	-0.1
NEBRASKA	792,000	296,117	37.4%	805,000	333,412	41.4%	4.0	818,000	235,167	28.7%	-8.6	830,000	128,760	15.5%	-21.9	843,000	190,214	22.6%	-14.8
NEVADA																			
NEW HAMPSHIRE	268,000	89,487	33.4%	283,000	89,011	31.5%	-1.9	300,000	109,093	36.4%	3.0	317,000	102,232	32.2%	-1.1	333,000	105,207	31.6%	-1.8
NEW JERSEY																			
NEW MEXICO	197,000	83,612	42.4%	231,000	98,089	42.5%	0.0	270,000	103,035	38.2%	-4.3	312,000	76,443	24.5%	-17.9	356,000	103,969	29.2%	-13.2
NEW YORK	7,228,000	2,659,519	36.8%	7,826,000	2,970,595	38.0%	1.2												
NORTH CAROLINA	1,638,000	497,657	30.4%	1,791,000	542,139	30.3%	-0.1	1,952,000	608,744	31.2%	0.8	2,107,000	528,995	25.1%	-5.3	2,263,000	750,995	33.2%	2.8
NORTH DAKOTA	341,000	109,863	32.2%	348,000	80,726	23.2%	-9.0	354,000	173,278	48.9%	16.7	356,000	59,961	16.8%	-15.4	358,000	80,555	22.5%	-9.7
OHIO	4,025,000	1,356,518	33.7%	4,234,000	1,539,461	36.4%	2.7	4,475,000	1,460,396	32.6%	-1.1	4,786,000	1,603,809	33.5%	-0.2	5,097,000	1,619,775	31.8%	-1.9
OKLAHOMA																			
OREGON																951,000	226,958	23.9%	
PENNSYLVANIA																			
RHODE ISLAND	377,000	146,474	38.9%	403,000	160,776	39.9%	1.0	433,000	177,937	41.1%	2.2	469,000	179,010	38.2%	-0.7	504,000	198,056	39.3%	0.4
SOUTH CAROLINA																			
SOUTH DAKOTA	364,000	158,058	43.4%	366,000	142,255	38.9%	-4.6	370,000	136,428	36.9%	-6.6	382,000	78,278	20.5%	-22.9	394,000	95,489	24.2%	-19.2
TENNESSEE	1,493,000	168,075	11.3%	1,609,000	332,523	20.7%	9.4	1,728,000	323,466	18.7%	7.5	1,836,000	275,746	15.0%	3.8	1,944,000	363,903	18.7%	7.5

State Gubernatorial General Elections (continued)

Democratic Turnout for Election Years 1932–1948 (continued)

State	1932 Voting-age population	Turnout	%	1936 Voting-age population	Turnout	%	Difference from 1932	1940 Voting-age population	Turnout	%	Difference from 1932	1944 Voting-age population	Turnout	%	Difference from 1932	1948 Voting-age population	Turnout	%	Difference from 1932
TEXAS	3,104,000	528,986	17.0%	3,437,000	782,083	22.8%	5.7	3,789,000	1,019,338	26.9%	9.9	4,141,000	1,007,826	24.3%	7.3	4,492,000	1,024,160	22.8%	5.8
UTAH	260,000	116,031	44.6%	279,000	109,656	39.3%	-5.3	303,000	128,519	42.4%	-2.2	337,000	123,907	36.8%	-7.9	371,000	123,814	33.4%	-11.3
VERMONT	207,000	49,247	23.8%	211,000	53,218	25.2%	1.4	216,000	49,068	22.7%	-1.1	222,000	40,835	18.4%	-5.4	228,000	33,588	14.7%	-9.1
VIRGINIA																			
WASHINGTON	962,000	352,215	36.6%	1,042,000	466,550	44.8%	8.2	1,144,000	386,706	33.8%	-2.8	1,304,000	428,834	32.9%	-3.7	1,465,000	417,035	28.5%	-8.1
WEST VIRGINIA	922,000	402,325	43.6%	990,000	492,485	49.7%	6.1	1,056,000	496,028	47.0%	3.3	1,102,000	395,122	35.9%	-7.8	1,148,000	438,752	38.2%	-5.4
WISCONSIN	1,729,000	590,114	34.1%	1,842,000	268,530	14.6%	-19.6	1,958,000	264,985	13.5%	-20.6	2,058,000	536,357	26.1%	-8.1	2,157,000	558,497	25.9%	-8.2
WYOMING	129,000	48,130	37.3%																
Total	49,633,000	15,829,586	31.9%	51,320,000	17,148,893	33.4%	1.5	48,214,000	14,759,606	30.6%	-1.3	49,554,000	13,884,611	28.0%	-3.9	55,446,000	16,194,445	29.2%	-2.7

Other Turnout for Election Years 1932–1948

State	1932 Voting-age population	Turnout	%	1936 Voting-age population	Turnout	%	Difference from 1932*	1940 Voting-age population	Turnout	%	Difference from 1932	1944 Voting-age population	Turnout	%	Difference from 1932	1948 Voting-age population	Turnout	%	Difference from 1932
ALABAMA																			
ALASKA																			
ARIZONA	184,000	1,608	0.9%	213,000	260	0.1%	-0.8	253,000	1,003	0.4%	-0.5	328,000	1,161	0.4%	-0.5	401,000	1,340	0.3%	-0.5
ARKANSAS	1,002,000	1,546	0.2%	1,055,000	733	0.1%	-0.1	1,100,000	866	0.1%	-0.1								
CALIFORNIA																			
COLORADO	601,000	8,923	1.5%	649,000	8,610	1.3%	-0.2	699,000	3,673	0.5%	-1.0								
CONNECTICUT	857,000	30,061	3.5%	942,000	24,380	2.6%	-0.9	1,037,000	21,071	2.0%	-1.5	1,152,000	17,873	1.6%	-2.0	1,266,000	14,803	1.2%	-2.3
DELAWARE	151,000	1,010	0.7%	162,000	8,768	5.4%	4.7	175,000	2,975	1.7%	1.0	189,000	370	0.2%	-0.5				
DISTRICT OF COLUMBIA																			
FLORIDA																1,725,000	26	0.0%	
GEORGIA				1,680,000	873	0.1%		1,806,000	1,171	0.1%	0.0					2,131,000	9,052	0.4%	0.4
HAWAII																			
IDAHO	254,000	3,476	1.4%	280,000	2,716	1.0%	-0.4												
ILLINOIS	4,615,000	55,937	1.2%	4,891,000	141,430	2.9%	1.7	5,179,000	14,011	0.3%	-0.9	5,453,000	12,496	0.2%	-1.0	5,727,000	12,176	0.2%	-1.0
INDIANA	2,014,000	34,985	1.7%	2,116,000	5,054	0.2%	-1.5	2,229,000	6,975	0.3%	-1.4	2,362,000	14,128	0.6%	-1.1	2,496,000	21,434	0.9%	-0.9
IOWA				1,564,000	33,567	2.1%		1,614,000	2,519	0.2%	-2.0	1,641,000	3,647	0.2%	-1.9	1,669,000	6,501	0.4%	-1.8
KANSAS	1,115,000	248,501	22.3%	1,131,000	3,318	0.3%	-22.0	1,152,000	6,863	0.6%	-21.7	1,187,000	10,077	0.8%	-21.4	1,222,000	19,526	1.6%	-20.7
KENTUCKY																			
LOUISIANA	1,185,000	59	0.0%																
MAINE	454,000	1,137	0.3%	475,000	5,862	1.2%	1.0	498,000	325	0.1%	-0.2								

State Gubernatorial General Elections *(continued)*

Other Turnout for Election Years 1932–1948 *(continued)*

State	1932			1936				1940				1944				1948			
	Voting-age population	Turnout	%	Voting-age population	Turnout	%	Difference from 1932	Voting-age population	Turnout	%	Difference from 1932	Voting-age population	Turnout	%	Difference from 1932	Voting-age population	Turnout	%	Difference from 1932
MARYLAND																			
MASSACHUSETTS	2,305,000	34,506	1.5%	2,454,000	114,774	4.7%	3.2	2,617,000	15,962	0.6%	-0.9	2,802,000	8,332	0.3%	-1.2	2,988,000	10,108	0.3%	-1.2
MICHIGAN	2,724,000	31,655	1.2%	2,947,000	11,069	0.4%	-0.8	3,204,000	7,220	0.2%	-0.9	3,538,000	12,080	0.3%	-0.8	3,872,000	19,648	0.5%	-0.7
MINNESOTA	1,529,000	529,069	34.6%	1,637,000	688,338	42.0%	7.4	1,738,000	462,784	26.6%	-8.0	1,798,000	7,151	0.4%	-34.2	1,857,000	21,556	1.2%	-33.4
MISSISSIPPI																			
MISSOURI	2,287,000	11,815	0.5%	2,384,000	7,529	0.3%	-0.2	2,477,000	1,760	0.1%	-0.4	2,540,000	1,446	0.1%	-0.5	2,603,000	4,182	0.2%	-0.4
MONTANA	304,000	10,327	3.4%	321,000	2,129	0.7%	-2.7	338,000	1,713	0.5%	-2.9	349,000	960	0.3%	-3.1	361,000	905	0.3%	-3.1
NEBRASKA	792,000	6,733	0.9%	805,000	5,746	0.7%	-0.1									843,000	19	0.0%	-0.8
NEVADA																			
NEW HAMPSHIRE	268,000	760	0.3%	283,000	1,617	0.6%	0.3									333,000	1,152	0.3%	0.1
NEW JERSEY																			
NEW MEXICO	197,000	1,518	0.8%	231,000	71	0.0%	-0.7												
NEW YORK	7,228,000	220,051	3.0%	7,826,000	136,639	1.7%	-1.3												
NORTH CAROLINA																2,263,000	3,364	0.1%	
NORTH DAKOTA	341,000	691	0.2%	348,000	100,390	28.8%	28.6					356,000	39,536	11.1%	10.9	358,000	2,539	0.7%	0.5
OHIO	4,025,000	59,996	1.5%	4,234,000	7,372	0.2%	-1.3												
OKLAHOMA																			
OREGON																951,000	11,380	1.2%	
PENNSYLVANIA																			
RHODE ISLAND	377,000	3,442	0.9%	403,000	1,479	0.4%	-0.5	433,000	257	0.1%	-0.9					504,000	1,366	0.3%	-0.6
SOUTH CAROLINA																			
SOUTH DAKOTA	364,000	5,584	1.5%																
TENNESSEE	1,493,000	108,648	7.3%	1,609,000	3,786	0.2%	-7.0					1,836,000	6,703	0.4%	-6.9	1,944,000	21	0.0%	-7.3
TEXAS	3,104,000	2,745	0.1%	3,437,000	1,245	0.0%	-0.1	3,789,000	266	0.0%	-0.1					4,492,000	7,301	0.2%	0.1
UTAH	260,000	3,807	1.5%	279,000	25,457	9.1%	7.7	303,000	580	0.2%	-1.3								
VERMONT	207,000	1,470	0.7%	211,000	471	0.2%	-0.5	216,000	2	0.0%	-0.7	222,000	5	0.0%	-0.7	228,000	201	0.1%	-0.6
VIRGINIA																			
WASHINGTON	962,000	55,056	5.7%	1,042,000	16,916	1.6%	-4.1	1,144,000	2,100	0.2%	-5.5	1,304,000	3,045	0.2%	-5.5	1,465,000	20,148	1.4%	-4.3
WEST VIRGINIA	922,000	3,240	0.4%																
WISCONSIN	1,729,000	63,583	3.7%	1,842,000	604,592	32.8%	29.1	1,958,000	550,091	28.1%	24.4	2,058,000	86,386	4.2%	0.5	2,157,000	22,803	1.1%	-2.6
WYOMING	129,000	1,827	1.4%																
Total	43,979,000	1,543,766	3.5%	47,451,000	1,965,191	4.1%	0.6	33,959,000	1,104,187	3.3%	-0.3	29,115,000	225,396	0.8%	-2.7	43,856,000	211,551	0.5%	-3.0

*Percentage point difference between turnout in current year and initial year listed in chart. If data do not appear for a state in the initial year listed, the difference is calculated from the first year in which data do appear for that state.

UNITED STATES SENATE GENERAL ELECTIONS

Election Years 1932–1948

State	1932 Voting-age population	Turnout	%	1936 Voting-age population	Turnout	%	Difference from 1932*	1940 Voting-age population	Turnout	%	Difference from 1932	1944 Voting-age population	Turnout	%	Difference from 1932	1948 Voting-age population	Turnout	%	Difference from 1932
ALABAMA	1,402,000	243,040	17.3%	1,486,000	275,353	18.5%	1.2					1,648,000	247,749	15.0%	-2.3	1,723,000	220,875	12.8%	-4.5
ALASKA																			
ARIZONA	184,000	111,463	60.6%					253,000	141,731	56.0%	-4.6	328,000	130,226	39.7%	-20.9				
ARKANSAS	1,002,000	205,392	20.5%	1,055,000	189,497	18.0%	-2.5					1,104,000	214,471	19.4%	-1.1	1,109,000	231,922	20.9%	0.4
CALIFORNIA	3,535,000	2,173,834	61.5%					4,569,000	2,713,865	59.4%	-2.1	5,572,000	3,305,234	59.3%	-2.2				
COLORADO	601,000	436,339	72.6%	649,000	471,827	72.7%	0.1					755,000	494,800	65.5%	-7.1	812,000	510,121	62.8%	-9.8
CONNECTICUT	857,000	594,402	69.4%					1,037,000	784,067	75.6%	6.3	1,152,000	828,497	71.9%	2.6				
DELAWARE				162,000	126,729	78.2%		175,000	134,879	77.1%	-1.2					203,000	141,362	69.6%	-8.6
DISTRICT OF COLUMBIA																			
FLORIDA	936,000	205,110	21.9%	1,075,000	313,470	29.2%	7.2	1,243,000	323,216	26.0%	4.1	1,484,000	470,943	31.7%	9.8				
GEORGIA	1,570,000	252,741	16.1%	1,680,000	263,468	15.7%	-0.4					1,969,000	272,545	13.8%	-2.3	2,131,000	362,504	17.0%	0.9
HAWAII																			
IDAHO	254,000	185,046	72.9%	280,000	203,167	72.6%	-0.3	306,000	235,199	76.9%	4.0	323,000	209,469	64.9%	8.0	339,000	214,188	63.2%	-9.7
ILLINOIS	4,615,000	3,198,135	69.3%	4,891,000	3,794,596	77.6%	8.3	5,179,000	4,071,021	78.6%	9.3	5,453,000	3,913,925	71.8%	2.5	5,727,000	3,900,285	68.1%	-1.2
INDIANA	2,014,000	1,565,750	77.7%					2,229,000	1,760,245	79.0%	1.2	2,362,000	1,651,385	69.9%	-7.8				
IOWA	1,510,000	994,296	65.8%	1,564,000	1,071,716	68.5%	2.7					1,641,000	1,021,697	62.3%	-3.6	1,669,000	1,000,412	59.9%	-5.9
KANSAS	1,115,000	720,408	64.6%	1,131,000	819,368	72.4%	7.8					1,187,000	669,200	56.4%	-8.2	1,222,000	716,342	58.6%	-6.0
KENTUCKY	1,475,000	972,133	65.9%	1,561,000	918,327	58.8%	-7.1					1,754,000	846,626	48.3%	-17.6	1,854,000	794,441	42.9%	-23.1
LOUISIANA	1,185,000	249,192	21.0%	1,284,000	293,263	22.8%	1.8					1,468,000	286,391	19.5%	-1.5	1,554,000	330,124	21.2%	0.2
MAINE				475,000	311,488	65.6%		498,000	256,194	51.4%	-14.1					546,000	223,256	40.9%	-24.7
MARYLAND	1,012,000	443,068	43.8%					1,185,000	608,975	51.4%	7.6	1,324,000	558,430	42.2%	-1.6				
MASSACHUSETTS				2,454,000	1,803,357	73.5%		2,617,000	1,957,089	74.8%	1.3					2,988,000	2,055,798	68.8%	-4.7
MICHIGAN				2,947,000	1,709,564	58.0%		3,204,000	2,000,343	62.4%	4.4					3,872,000	2,062,097	53.3%	-4.8
MINNESOTA				1,637,000	1,065,767	65.1%		1,738,000	1,209,599	69.6%	4.5					1,857,000	1,220,250	65.7%	0.6
MISSISSIPPI				1,140,000	140,570	12.3%		1,195,000	143,333	12.0%	-0.3					1,204,000	151,478	12.6%	0.3
MISSOURI	2,287,000	1,609,748	70.4%					2,477,000	1,819,016	73.4%	3.0	2,540,000	1,557,793	61.3%	-9.1				
MONTANA				321,000	221,462	69.0%		338,000	240,694	71.2%	2.2					361,000	221,003	61.2%	-7.8
NEBRASKA				805,000	590,367	73.3%		818,000	596,891	73.0%	-0.4					843,000	471,895	56.0%	-17.4
NEVADA	55,000	41,104	74.7%					70,000	51,839	74.1%	-0.7	85,000	52,411	61.7%	-13.1				
NEW HAMPSHIRE	268,000	196,176	73.2%	283,000	208,107	73.5%	0.3					317,000	217,057	68.5%	-4.7	333,000	222,898	66.9%	-6.3
NEW JERSEY	2,294,000	1,467,245	64.0%	2,459,000	1,669,291	67.9%		2,649,000	1,867,775	70.5%	2.6	2,899,000	1,850,083	63.8%	-0.1	3,150,000	1,869,882	59.4%	-8.5
NEW MEXICO				231,000	169,443	73.4%		270,000	184,451	68.3%	-5.0					356,000	189,200	53.1%	-20.2
NEW YORK	7,228,000	4,541,380	62.8%					8,447,000	6,148,574	72.8%	10.0	9,042,000	6,209,317	68.7%	5.8				

United States Senate General Elections (continued)

United States Senate General Elections *(continued)*

Election Years 1932–1948 *(continued)*

State	1932 Voting-age population	Turnout	%	1936 Voting-age population	Turnout	%	Difference from 1932	1940 Voting-age population	Turnout	%	Difference from 1932	1944 Voting-age population	Turnout	%	Difference from 1932	1948 Voting-age population	Turnout	%	Difference from 1932
NORTH CAROLINA	1,638,000	697,440	42.6%	1,791,000	797,088	44.5%	1.9					2,107,000	759,850	36.1%	-6.5	2,263,000	764,559	33.8%	-8.8
NORTH DAKOTA	341,000	238,914	70.1%					354,000	264,101	74.6%	4.5	356,000	210,422	59.1%	-11.0				
OHIO	4,025,000	2,458,992	61.1%					4,475,000	3,059,926	68.4%	7.3	4,786,000	2,983,878	62.3%	1.3				
OKLAHOMA	1,263,000	649,504	51.4%	1,301,000	725,921	55.8%	4.4					1,354,000	702,394	51.9%	0.4	1,372,000	708,931	51.7%	0.2
OREGON	612,000	353,139	57.7%	667,000	401,130	60.1%	2.4					843,000	443,235	52.6%	-5.1	951,000	498,570	52.4%	-5.3
PENNSYLVANIA	5,441,000	2,781,031	51.1%					6,103,000	3,997,020	65.5%	14.4	6,423,000	3,730,392	58.1%	7.0				
RHODE ISLAND				403,000	306,832	76.1%		433,000	315,159	72.8%	-3.4					504,000	320,952	63.7%	-12.5
SOUTH CAROLINA	865,000	106,448	12.3%	934,000	115,359	12.4%	0.0					1,068,000	101,736	9.5%	-2.8	1,131,000	141,006	12.5%	0.2
SOUTH DAKOTA	364,000	282,092	77.5%	366,000	289,786	79.2%	1.7					382,000	227,447	59.5%	-18.0	394,000	242,833	61.6%	-15.9
TENNESSEE				1,609,000	357,679	22.2%		1,728,000	417,264	24.1%	1.9					1,944,000	499,138	25.7%	3.4
TEXAS				3,437,000	835,796	24.3%		3,789,000	1,054,431	27.8%	3.5					4,492,000	1,061,563	23.6%	-0.7
UTAH	260,000	206,322	79.4%					303,000	247,430	81.7%	2.3	337,000	248,280	73.7%	-5.7				
VERMONT	207,000	134,793	65.1%					216,000	140,388	65.0%	-0.1	222,000	123,248	55.5%	-9.6				
VIRGINIA				1,463,000	266,666	18.2%		1,588,000	293,881	18.5%	0.3					1,962,000	387,017	19.7%	1.5
WASHINGTON	962,000	603,805	62.8%					1,144,000	747,307	65.3%	2.6	1,304,000	819,879	62.9%	0.1				
WEST VIRGINIA				990,000	828,923	83.7%		1,056,000	874,219	82.8%	-0.9					1,148,000	763,888	66.5%	-17.2
WISCONSIN	1,729,000	1,070,996	61.9%					1,958,000	1,338,135	68.3%	6.4	2,058,000	1,256,374	61.0%	-0.9				
WYOMING				140,000	100,172	71.6%		151,000	110,704	73.3%	1.8					172,000	101,480	59.0%	-12.6
Total	53,106,000	29,989,478	56.5%	42,671,000	21,655,549	50.8%	-5.7	63,795,000	40,108,961	62.9%	6.4	65,647,000	36,615,472	55.8%	-0.7	50,186,000	22,600,270	45.0%	-11.4

*Percentage point difference between turnout in current year and initial year listed in chart. If data do not appear for a state in the initial year listed, the difference is calculated from the first year in which data do appear for that state.

UNITED STATES SENATE GENERAL ELECTIONS

Republican Turnout for Election Years 1932–1948

State	1932 Voting-age population	1932 Turnout	1932 %	1936 Voting-age population	1936 Turnout	1936 %	1936 Difference from 1932*	1940 Voting-age population	1940 Turnout	1940 %	1940 Difference from 1932	1944 Voting-age population	1944 Turnout	1944 %	1944 Difference from 1932	1948 Voting-age population	1948 Turnout	1948 %	1948 Difference from 1932
ALABAMA	1,402,000	33,425	2.4%	1,486,000	33,698	2.3%	-0.1					1,648,000	41,983	2.5%	0.2	1,723,000	35,341	2.1%	-0.3
ALASKA																			
ARIZONA	184,000	35,737	19.4%					253,000	39,657	15.7%	-3.7	328,000	39,891	12.2%	-7.3				
ARKANSAS	1,002,000	21,597	2.2%	1,055,000	30,997	2.9%	0.8					1,104,000	31,942	2.9%	0.7				
CALIFORNIA	3,535,000	669,878	10.9%					4,569,000	2,238,899	49.0%	30.1	5,572,000	1,576,553	28.3%	9.4				
COLORADO	601,000	198,519	33.0%	649,000	166,308	25.6%	-7.4					766,000	277,410	36.7%	3.7	812,000	165,069	20.3%	-12.7
CONNECTICUT	857,000	288,682	33.7%					1,037,000	358,313	34.6%	0.9	1,152,000	391,748	34.0%	0.3				
DELAWARE				162,000	52,460	32.4%		175,000	63,799	36.5%	4.1					203,000	68,246	33.6%	1.2
DISTRICT OF COLUMBIA																			
FLORIDA				1,075,000	59,832	5.6%						1,484,000	135,258	9.1%	3.5				
GEORGIA	1,570,000	18,151	1.2%																
HAWAII																			
IDAHO	254,000	78,225	30.8%	280,000	128,723	46.0%	15.2	306,000	124,535	40.7%	9.9	323,000	102,373	31.7%	0.9	339,000	103,868	30.6%	-0.2
ILLINOIS	4,615,000	1,471,841	31.9%	4,891,000	1,545,160	31.6%	-0.3	5,179,000	2,045,924	39.5%	7.6	5,453,000	1,841,793	33.8%	1.9	5,727,000	1,740,026	30.4%	-1.5
INDIANA	2,014,000	661,750	32.9%					2,229,000	888,070	39.8%	7.0	2,362,000	829,489	35.1%	2.3				
IOWA	1,510,000	399,929	26.5%	1,564,000	503,635	32.2%	5.7					1,641,000	523,963	31.9%	5.4	1,669,000	415,778	24.9%	-1.6
KANSAS	1,115,000	302,809	27.2%	1,131,000	417,873	36.9%	9.8					1,187,000	387,090	32.6%	5.5	1,222,000	393,412	32.2%	5.0
KENTUCKY	1,475,000	393,865	26.7%	1,561,000	365,850	23.4%	-3.3					1,754,000	380,425	21.7%	-5.0	1,854,000	383,776	20.7%	-6.0
LOUISIANA																			
MAINE				475,000	158,068	33.3%		498,000	150,149	30.2%	-3.1					546,000	159,182	29.2%	-4.1
MARYLAND	1,012,000	138,266	13.7%					1,185,000	203,912	17.2%	3.5	1,324,000	213,705	16.1%	2.5				
MASSACHUSETTS				2,454,000	875,160	35.7%		2,617,000	838,122	32.0%	-3.6					2,988,000	1,088,475	36.4%	0.8
MICHIGAN				2,947,000	714,602	24.2%		3,204,000	1,053,104	32.9%	8.6					3,872,000	1,045,156	27.0%	2.7
MINNESOTA				1,637,000	402,404	24.6%		1,738,000	641,049	36.9%	12.3					1,857,000	485,801	26.2%	1.6
MISSISSIPPI																			
MISSOURI	2,287,000	577,184	25.2%					2,477,000	886,376	35.8%	10.5	2,540,000	779,029	30.7%	5.4				
MONTANA				321,000	60,038	18.7%		338,000	63,941	18.9%	0.2					361,000	94,458	26.2%	7.5
NEBRASKA				805,000	223,276	27.7%		818,000	340,250	41.6%	13.9					843,000	267,575	31.7%	4.0
NEVADA	55,000	19,706	35.8%					70,000	20,488	29.3%	-6.6	85,000	21,816	25.7%	-10.2				
NEW HAMPSHIRE	268,000	96,649	36.1%	283,000	107,923	38.1%	-3.3					317,000	110,549	34.9%	-1.2	333,000	129,600	38.9%	2.9
NEW JERSEY	2,294,000	741,734	32.3%	2,459,000	740,088	30.1%	-2.2	2,649,000	1,029,331	38.9%	6.5	2,899,000	939,987	32.4%	0.1	3,150,000	934,720	29.7%	-2.7
NEW MEXICO				231,000	64,817	28.1%		270,000	81,257	30.1%	2.0					356,000	80,226	22.5%	-5.5
NEW YORK	7,228,000	1,751,186	24.2%					8,447,000	2,868,852	34.0%	9.7	9,042,000	2,899,497	32.1%	7.8				

United States Senate General Elections (continued)

Republican Turnout for Election Years 1932–1948 *(continued)*

State	1932 Voting-age population	1932 Turnout	1932 %	1936 Voting-age population	1936 Turnout	1936 %	1936 Difference from 1932	1940 Voting-age population	1940 Turnout	1940 %	1940 Difference from 1932	1944 Voting-age population	1944 Turnout	1944 %	1944 Difference from 1932	1948 Voting-age population	1948 Turnout	1948 %	1948 Difference from 1932
NORTH CAROLINA	1,638,000	221,392	**13.5%**	1,791,000	233,000	**13.0%**	-0.5					2,107,000	226,037	**10.7%**	-2.8	2,263,000	220,307	**9.7%**	-3.8
NORTH DAKOTA	341,000	172,796	**50.7%**					354,000	100,647	**28.4%**	-22.2	356,000	114,126	**32.1%**	-18.6				
OHIO	4,025,000	1,126,830	**28.0%**					4,475,000	1,602,567	**35.8%**	7.8	4,786,000	1,500,809	**31.4%**	3.4				
OKLAHOMA	1,263,000	218,854	**17.3%**	1,301,000	229,004	**17.6%**	0.3					1,354,000	309,222	**22.8%**	5.5	1,372,000	265,169	**19.3%**	2.0
OREGON	612,000	186,210	**30.4%**	667,000	199,332	**29.9%**	-0.5					843,000	269,095	**31.9%**	1.5	951,000	299,295	**31.5%**	1.0
PENNSYLVANIA	5,441,000	1,371,844	**25.2%**					6,103,000	1,893,104	**31.0%**	5.8	6,423,000	1,840,943	**28.7%**	3.4				
RHODE ISLAND				403,000	136,174	**33.8%**		433,000	141,312	**32.6%**	-1.2					504,000	130,668	**25.9%**	-7.9
SOUTH CAROLINA	865,000	1,976	**0.2%**	934,000	1,663	**0.2%**	-0.1					1,068,000	3,214	**0.3%**	0.1	1,131,000	5,008	**0.4%**	0.2
SOUTH DAKOTA	364,000	151,845	**41.7%**	366,000	135,461	**37.0%**	-4.7					382,000	145,248	**38.0%**	-3.7	394,000	144,084	**36.6%**	-5.1
TENNESSEE				1,609,000	67,238	**4.2%**		1,728,000	121,790	**7.0%**	2.9					1,944,000	166,947	**8.6%**	4.4
TEXAS				3,437,000	59,491	**1.7%**		3,789,000	60,051	**1.6%**	-0.1					4,492,000	349,665	**7.8%**	6.1
UTAH	260,000	86,066	**33.1%**					303,000	91,931	**30.3%**	-2.8	337,000	99,532	**29.5%**	-3.6				
VERMONT	207,000	74,319	**35.9%**					216,000	93,283	**43.2%**	7.3	222,000	81,094	**36.5%**	0.6				
VIRGINIA				1,463,000	12,473	**0.9%**										1,962,000	119,366	**6.1%**	5.2
WASHINGTON	962,000	197,450	**20.5%**					1,144,000	342,589	**29.9%**	9.4	1,304,000	364,356	**27.9%**	7.4				
WEST VIRGINIA				990,000	338,363	**34.2%**		1,056,000	381,806	**36.2%**	2.0					1,148,000	328,534	**28.6%**	-5.6
WISCONSIN	1,729,000	387,668	**22.4%**					1,958,000	553,692	**28.3%**	5.9	2,058,000	634,513	**30.8%**	8.4				
WYOMING				140,000	45,483	**32.5%**		151,000	45,682	**30.3%**	-2.2					172,000	43,527	**25.3%**	-7.2
Total	50,985,000	12,096,181	**23.7%**	38,567,000	8,108,594	**21.0%**	-2.7	59,769,000	19,364,482	**32.4%**	8.7	62,210,000	17,112,690	**27.5%**	3.8	44,188,000	9,663,279	**21.9%**	-1.9

Democratic Turnout for Election Years 1932–1948

State	1932 Voting-age population	1932 Turnout	1932 %	1936 Voting-age population	1936 Turnout	1936 %	1936 Difference from 1932*	1940 Voting-age population	1940 Turnout	1940 %	1940 Difference from 1932	1944 Voting-age population	1944 Turnout	1944 %	1944 Difference from 1932	1948 Voting-age population	1948 Turnout	1948 %	1948 Difference from 1932
ALABAMA	1,402,000	209,614	**15.0%**	1,486,000	239,632	**16.1%**	1.2					1,648,000	202,604	**12.3%**	-2.7	1,723,000	185,534	**10.8%**	-4.2
ALASKA																			
ARIZONA	184,000	74,310	**40.4%**					253,000	101,495	**40.1%**	-0.3	328,000	90,335	**27.5%**	-12.8				
ARKANSAS	1,002,000	183,795	**18.3%**	1,055,000	155,075	**14.7%**	-3.6					1,104,000	182,529	**16.5%**	-1.8	1,109,000	216,401	**19.5%**	1.2
CALIFORNIA	3,535,000	943,164	**26.7%**									5,572,000	1,728,155	**31.0%**	4.3				
COLORADO	601,000	226,516	**37.7%**	649,000	299,376	**46.1%**	8.4					755,000	214,335	**28.4%**	-9.3	812,000	340,719	**42.0%**	4.3
CONNECTICUT	857,000	282,327	**32.9%**					1,037,000	416,740	**40.2%**	7.2	1,152,000	430,716	**37.4%**	4.4				
DELAWARE				162,000	67,136	**41.4%**		175,000	71,080	**40.6%**	-0.8					203,000	71,888	**35.4%**	-6.0
DISTRICT OF COLUMBIA																			
FLORIDA	936,000	204,651	**21.9%**	1,075,000	253,638	**23.6%**	1.7	1,243,000	323,216	**26.0%**	4.1	1,484,000	335,685	**22.6%**	0.8				

United States Senate General Elections (continued)

Democratic Turnout for Election Years 1932–1948 (continued)

State	1932 Voting-age population	Turnout	%	1936 Voting-age population	Turnout	%	Difference from 1932	1940 Voting-age population	Turnout	%	Difference from 1932	1944 Voting-age population	Turnout	%	Difference from 1932	1948 Voting-age population	Turnout	%	Difference from 1932
GEORGIA	1,570,000	234,590	14.9%	1,680,000	263,468	15.7%	0.7					1,969,000	272,541	13.8%	-1.1	2,131,000	362,104	17.0%	2.1
HAWAII																			
IDAHO	254,000	103,020	40.6%	280,000	74,444	26.6%	-14.0	306,000	110,664	36.2%	-4.4	323,000	107,096	33.2%	-7.4	339,000	107,000	31.6%	-9.0
ILLINOIS	4,615,000	1,670,466	36.2%	4,891,000	2,142,887	43.8%	7.6	5,179,000	2,025,097	39.1%	2.9	5,453,000	2,059,023	37.8%	1.6	5,727,000	2,147,754	37.5%	1.3
INDIANA	2,014,000	870,053	43.2%					2,229,000	864,803	38.8%	-4.4	2,362,000	807,766	34.2%	-9.0				
IOWA	1,510,000	538,422	35.7%	1,564,000	539,555	34.5%	-1.2					1,641,000	494,229	30.1%	-5.5	1,669,000	578,226	34.6%	-1.0
KANSAS	1,115,000	328,992	29.5%	1,131,000	396,685	35.1%	5.6					1,187,000	272,053	22.9%	-6.6	1,222,000	305,987	25.0%	-4.5
KENTUCKY	1,475,000	574,977	39.0%	1,561,000	539,968	34.6%	-4.4					1,754,000	464,053	26.5%	-12.5	1,854,000	408,256	22.0%	-17.0
LOUISIANA	1,185,000	249,189	21.0%	1,284,000	293,256	22.8%	1.8					1,468,000	286,365	19.5%	-1.5	1,554,000	330,115	21.2%	0.2
MAINE				475,000	153,420	32.3%		498,000	105,740	21.2%	-11.1					546,000	64,074	11.7%	20.6
MARYLAND	1,012,000	293,389	29.0%					1,185,000	394,239	33.3%	4.3	1,324,000	344,725	26.0%	-3.0				
MASSACHUSETTS				2,454,000	739,751	30.1%		2,617,000	1,088,838	41.6%	11.5					2,988,000	954,398	31.9%	1.8
MICHIGAN				2,947,000	910,937	30.9%		3,204,000	939,740	29.3%	-1.6					3,872,000	1,000,329	25.8%	-5.1
MINNESOTA								1,738,000	248,658	14.3%						1,857,000	729,494	39.3%	25.0
MISSISSIPPI				1,140,000	140,570	12.3%		1,195,000	143,333	12.0%	-0.3					1,204,000	151,478	12.6%	0.3
MISSOURI	2,287,000	1,017,046	44.5%					2,477,000	930,775	37.6%	-6.9	2,540,000	777,229	30.6%	-13.9				
MONTANA				321,000	121,769	37.9%		338,000	176,753	52.3%	14.4					361,000	125,193	34.7%	-3.3
NEBRASKA				805,000	108,391	13.5%		818,000	247,659	30.3%	16.8					843,000	204,320	24.2%	10.8
NEVADA	55,000	21,398	38.9%					70,000	31,351	44.8%	5.9	85,000	30,595	36.0%	-2.9				
NEW HAMPSHIRE	268,000	98,766	36.9%	283,000	99,195	35.1%	-1.8					317,000	106,508	33.6%	-3.3	333,000	91,760	27.6%	-9.3
NEW JERSEY	2,294,000	725,511	31.6%	2,459,000	916,414	37.3%	5.6	2,649,000	823,893	31.1%	-0.5	2,899,000	910,096	31.4%	-0.2	3,150,000	884,414	28.1%	-3.5
NEW MEXICO				231,000	104,550	45.3%		270,000	103,194	38.2%	-7.0					356,000	108,269	30.4%	-14.8
NEW YORK	7,228,000	2,532,905	35.0%					8,447,000	3,274,766	38.8%	3.7	9,042,000	3,294,576	36.4%	1.4				
NORTH CAROLINA	1,638,000	476,048	29.1%	1,791,000	564,088	31.5%	2.4					2,107,000	533,813	25.3%	-3.7	2,263,000	540,762	23.9%	-5.2
NORTH DAKOTA	341,000	65,575	19.2%					354,000	69,847	19.7%	0.5	356,000	95,102	26.7%	7.5				
OHIO	4,025,000	1,290,175	32.1%					4,475,000	1,457,359	32.6%	0.5	4,786,000	1,483,069	31.0%	-1.1				
OKLAHOMA	1,263,000	426,130	33.7%	1,301,000	493,407	37.9%	4.2					1,354,000	390,851	28.9%	-4.9	1,372,000	441,654	32.2%	-1.5
OREGON	612,000	137,237	22.4%	667,000	193,822	29.1%	6.6					843,000	174,140	20.7%	-1.8	951,000	199,275	21.0%	-1.5
PENNSYLVANIA	5,441,000	1,200,767	22.1%					6,103,000	2,069,980	33.9%	11.8	6,423,000	1,864,735	29.0%	7.0				
RHODE ISLAND				403,000	149,157	37.0%		433,000	173,847	40.1%	3.1					504,000	190,284	37.8%	0.7
SOUTH CAROLINA	865,000	104,472	12.1%	934,000	113,696	12.2%	0.1					1,068,000	98,363	9.2%	-2.9	1,131,000	135,998	12.0%	-0.1
SOUTH DAKOTA	364,000	125,731	34.5%	366,000	141,509	38.7%	4.1					382,000	82,199	21.5%	-13.0	394,000	98,749	25.1%	-9.5
TENNESSEE				1,609,000	273,298	17.0%		1,728,000	295,440	17.1%	0.1					1,944,000	326,062	16.8%	-0.2

United States Senate General Elections (continued)

United States Senate General Elections (continued)

Democratic Turnout for Election Years 1932–1948 (continued)

	1932			1936				1940				1944				1948			
State	Voting-age population	Turnout	%	Voting-age population	Turnout	%	Difference from 1932	Voting-age population	Turnout	%	Difference from 1932	Voting-age population	Turnout	%	Difference from 1932	Voting-age population	Turnout	%	Difference from 1932
TEXAS				3,437,000	773,574	22.5%		3,789,000	993,974	26.2%	3.7					4,492,000	702,985	15.6%	-6.9
UTAH	260,000	116,909	45.0%					303,000	155,499	51.3%	6.4	337,000	148,748	44.1%	-0.8				
VERMONT	207,000	60,453	29.2%					216,000	47,101	21.8%	-7.4	222,000	42,136	19.0%	-10.2				
VIRGINIA				1,463,000	244,987	16.7%		1,588,000	274,260	17.3%	0.5					1,962,000	253,865	12.9%	-3.8
WASHINGTON	962,000	365,949	38.0%					1,144,000	404,718	35.4%	-2.7	1,304,000	452,013	34.7%	-3.4				
WEST VIRGINIA				990,000	488,620	49.4%		1,056,000	492,413	46.6%	-2.7					1,148,000	435,354	37.9%	-11.4
WISCONSIN	1,729,000	610,236	35.3%					1,958,000	176,688	9.0%	-26.3	2,058,000	537,144	26.1%	-9.2				
WYOMING				140,000	53,919	38.5%		151,000	65,022	43.1%	4.5					172,000	57,953	33.7%	-4.8
Total	53,106,000	16,362,783	30.8%	41,034,000	12,050,194	29.4%	-1.4	59,226,000	19,098,182	32.2%	1.4	65,647,000	19,313,527	29.4%	-1.4	50,186,000	12,750,654	25.4%	-5.4

Other Turnout for Election Years 1932–1948

	1932			1936				1940				1944				1948			
State	Voting-age population	Turnout	%	Voting-age population	Turnout	%	Difference from 1932*	Voting-age population	Turnout	%	Difference from 1932	Voting-age population	Turnout	%	Difference from 1932	Voting-age population	Turnout	%	Difference from 1932
ALABAMA	1,402,000	1	0.0%	1,486,000	2,023	0.1%	0.1					1,648,000	3,162	0.2%	0.2				
ALASKA																			
ARIZONA	184,000	1,416	0.8%					253,000	579	0.2%	-0.5								
ARKANSAS				1,055,000	3,425	0.3%										1,109,000	15,521	1.4%	1.1
CALIFORNIA	3,535,000	560,994	15.9%					4,569,000	474,966	10.4%	-5.5	5,572,000	526	0.0%	-15.9				
COLORADO	601,000	11,304	1.9%	649,000	6,143	0.9%	-0.9					755,000	3,143	0.4%	-1.5	812,000	4,333	0.5%	-1.3
CONNECTICUT	857,000	23,393	2.7%					1,037,000	9,014	0.9%	-1.9	1,152,000	6,033	0.5%	-2.2				
DELAWARE				162,000	7,133	4.4%										203,000	1,228	0.6%	-3.8
DISTRICT OF COLUMBIA																			
FLORIDA	936,000	459	0.0%																
GEORGIA												1,969,000	4	0.0%		2,131,000	400	0.0%	0.0
HAWAII																			
IDAHO	254,000	3,801	1.5%													339,000	3,320	1.0%	-0.5
ILLINOIS	4,615,000	55,828	1.2%	4,891,000	106,549	2.2%	1.0					5,453,000	13,109	0.2%	-1.0	5,727,000	12,505	0.2%	-1.0
INDIANA	2,014,000	33,947	1.7%					2,229,000	7,372	0.3%	-1.4	2,362,000	14,130	0.6%	-1.1				
IOWA	1,510,000	55,945	3.7%	1,564,000	28,526	1.8%	-1.9					1,641,000	3,505	0.2%	-3.5	1,669,000	6,408	0.4%	-3.3
KANSAS	1,115,000	88,607	7.9%	1,131,000	4,810	0.4%	-7.5					1,187,000	10,057	0.8%	-7.1	1,222,000	16,943	1.4%	-6.6
KENTUCKY	1,475,000	3,291	0.2%	1,561,000	12,509	0.8%	0.6					1,754,000	2,148	0.1%	-0.1	1,854,000	2,409	0.1%	-0.1
LOUISIANA	1,185,000	3	0.0%	1,284,000	7	0.0%	0.0					1,468,000	26	0.0%	0.0	1,554,000	9	0.0%	0.0
MAINE								498,000	305	0.1%									

United States Senate General Elections *(continued)*

Other Turnout for Election Years 1932–1948 *(continued)*

State	1932 Voting-age population	Turnout	%	1936 Voting-age population	Turnout	%	Difference from 1932	1940 Voting-age population	Turnout	%	Difference from 1932	1944 Voting-age population	Turnout	%	Difference from 1932	1948 Voting-age population	Turnout	%	Difference from 1932
MARYLAND	1,012,000	11,413	1.1%					1,185,000	10,824	0.9%	-0.2								
MASSACHUSETTS				2,454,000	188,446	7.7%		2,617,000	30,129	1.2%	-6.5					2,988,000	12,925	0.4%	-7.2
MICHIGAN				2,947,000	84,025	2.9%		3,204,000	7,499	0.2%	-2.6					3,872,000	16,612	0.4%	-2.4
MINNESOTA				1,637,000	663,363	40.5%		1,738,000	319,892	18.4%	-22.1					1,857,000	4,955	0.3%	-40.3
MISSISSIPPI																			
MISSOURI	2,287,000	15,518	0.7%					2,477,000	1,865	0.1%	-0.6	2,540,000	1,535	0.1%	-0.6				
MONTANA				321,000	39,655	12.4%										361,000	1,352	0.4%	-12.0
NEBRASKA				805,000	258,700	32.1%		818,000	8,982	1.1%	-31.0								
NEVADA																			
NEW HAMPSHIRE	268,000	761	0.3%	283,000	989	0.3%	0.1									333,000	1,538	0.5%	0.2
NEW JERSEY				2,459,000	12,789	0.5%		2,649,000	14,551	0.5%	0.0					3,150,000	50,748	1.6%	1.1
NEW MEXICO				231,000	76	0.0%										356,000	705	0.2%	0.2
NEW YORK	7,228,000	257,289	3.6%					8,447,000	4,956	0.1%	-3.5	9,042,000	15,244	0.2%	-3.4				
NORTH CAROLINA																2,263,000	3,490	0.2%	
NORTH DAKOTA	341,000	543	0.2%					354,000	93,607	26.4%	26.3	356,000	1,194	0.3%	0.2				
OHIO	4,025,000	41,987	1.0%																
OKLAHOMA	1,263,000	4,520	0.4%	1,301,000	3,510	0.3%	-0.1					1,354,000	2,321	0.2%	-0.2	1,372,000	2,108	0.2%	-0.2
OREGON	612,000	29,692	4.9%	667,000	7,976	1.2%	-3.7												
PENNSYLVANIA	5,441,000	208,420	3.8%					6,103,000	33,936	0.6%	-3.3	6,423,000	24,714	0.4%	-3.4				
RHODE ISLAND				403,000	21,501	5.3%													
SOUTH CAROLINA												1,068,000	159	0.0%					
SOUTH DAKOTA	364,000	4,516	1.2%	366,000	12,816	3.5%	2.3												
TENNESSEE				1,609,000	17,143	1.1%		1,728,000	34	0.0%	-1.1					1,944,000	6,129	0.3%	-0.8
TEXAS				3,437,000	2,731	0.1%		3,789,000	406	0.0%	-0.1					4,492,000	8,913	0.2%	0.1
UTAH	260,000	3,347	1.3%																
VERMONT	207,000	21	0.0%					216,000	4	0.0%	0.0	222,000	18	0.0%	0.0				
VIRGINIA				1,463,000	9,206	0.6%		1,588,000	19,621	1.2%	0.6					1,962,000	13,786	0.7%	0.1
WASHINGTON	962,000	40,406	4.2%									1,304,000	3,510	0.3%	-3.9				
WEST VIRGINIA				990,000	1,940	0.2%													
WISCONSIN	1,729,000	73,092	4.2%					1,958,000	607,755	31.0%	26.8	2,058,000	84,717	4.1%	-0.1				
WYOMING				140,000	770	0.6%													
Total	45,682,000	1,530,514	3.4%	35,296,000	1,496,761	4.2%	0.9	47,457,000	1,646,297	3.5%	0.1	49,328,000	189,255	0.4%	-3.0	41,570,000	186,337	0.4%	-2.9

*Percentage point difference between turnout in current year and initial year listed in chart. If data do not appear for a state in the initial year listed, the difference is calculated from the first year in which data do appear for that state.

UNITED STATES HOUSE OF REPRESENTATIVES GENERAL ELECTIONS

Election Years 1932–1948

State	1932 Voting-age population	Turnout	%	1936 Voting-age population	Turnout	%	Difference from 1932*	1940 Voting-age population	Turnout	%	Difference from 1932	1944 Voting-age population	Turnout	%	Difference from 1932	1948 Voting-age population	Turnout	%	Difference from 1932
ALABAMA	1,402,000	231,634	**16.5%**	1,486,000	255,052	**17.2%**	0.6	1,572,000	269,644	**17.2%**	0.6	1,648,000	222,338	**13.5%**	-3.0	1,723,000	197,083	**11.4%**	-5.1
ALASKA																			
ARIZONA	184,000	106,584	**57.9%**	213,000	108,750	**51.1%**	-6.9	253,000	139,784	**55.3%**	-2.7	328,000	128,036	**39.0%**	-18.9	401,000	158,975	**39.6%**	-18.3
ARKANSAS	1,002,000	218,185	**21.8%**	1,055,000	174,298	**16.5%**	-5.3	1,100,000	208,890	**19.0%**	-2.8	1,104,000	217,215	**19.7%**	-2.1	1,109,000	251,032	**22.6%**	0.9
CALIFORNIA	3,535,000	1,874,331	**53.0%**	3,979,000	2,240,495	**56.3%**	3.3	4,569,000	2,770,550	**60.6%**	7.6	5,572,000	3,004,942	**53.9%**	0.9	6,575,000	3,558,500	**54.1%**	1.1
COLORADO	601,000	429,515	**71.5%**	649,000	457,759	**70.5%**	-0.9	699,000	525,026	**75.1%**	3.6	755,000	493,862	**65.4%**	-6.1	812,000	497,411	**61.3%**	-10.2
CONNECTICUT	857,000	592,776	**69.2%**	942,000	689,512	**73.2%**	4.0	1,037,000	782,593	**75.5%**	6.3	1,152,000	827,745	**71.9%**	2.7	1,266,000	879,351	**69.5%**	0.3
DELAWARE	151,000	112,096	**74.2%**	162,000	126,663	**78.2%**	4.0	175,000	134,778	**77.0%**	2.8	189,000	126,440	**66.9%**	-7.3	203,000	140,535	**69.2%**	-5.0
DISTRICT OF COLUMBIA																			
FLORIDA	936,000	247,596	**26.5%**	1,075,000	284,937	**26.5%**	0.1	1,243,000	380,248	**30.6%**	4.1	1,484,000	412,753	**27.8%**	1.4	1,725,000	351,133	**20.4%**	-6.1
GEORGIA	1,570,000	246,831	**15.7%**	1,680,000	276,274	**16.4%**	0.7	1,806,000	271,399	**15.0%**	-0.7	1,969,000	274,905	**14.0%**	-1.8	2,131,000	365,410	**17.1%**	1.4
HAWAII																			
IDAHO	254,000	183,575	**72.3%**	280,000	194,972	**69.6%**	-2.6	306,000	231,636	**75.7%**	3.4	323,000	205,579	**63.6%**	-8.6	339,000	212,169	**62.6%**	-9.7
ILLINOIS	4,615,000	3,150,133	**68.3%**	4,891,000	3,728,850	**76.2%**	8.0	5,179,000	4,032,799	**77.9%**	9.6	5,453,000	3,882,659	**71.2%**	2.9	5,727,000	3,848,640	**67.2%**	-1.1
INDIANA	2,014,000	1,546,772	**76.8%**	2,116,000	1,629,116	**77.0%**	0.2	2,229,000	1,761,617	**79.0%**	2.2	2,362,000	1,651,217	**69.9%**	-6.9	2,496,000	1,633,401	**65.4%**	-11.4
IOWA	1,510,000	941,650	**62.4%**	1,564,000	1,054,364	**67.4%**	5.1	1,614,000	1,114,969	**69.1%**	6.7	1,641,000	972,759	**59.3%**	-3.1	1,669,000	949,744	**56.9%**	-5.5
KANSAS	1,115,000	719,095	**64.5%**	1,131,000	799,850	**70.7%**	6.2	1,152,000	788,662	**68.5%**	4.0	1,187,000	664,192	**56.0%**	-8.5	1,222,000	703,910	**57.6%**	-6.9
KENTUCKY	1,475,000	970,573	**65.8%**	1,561,000	917,647	**58.8%**	-7.0	1,654,000	893,233	**54.0%**	-11.8	1,754,000	843,843	**48.1%**	-17.7	1,854,000	740,527	**39.9%**	-25.9
LOUISIANA	1,185,000	244,681	**20.6%**	1,284,000	291,963	**22.7%**	2.1	1,383,000	321,044	**23.2%**	2.6	1,468,000	282,569	**19.2%**	-1.4	1,554,000	321,676	**20.7%**	0.1
MAINE	454,000	235,245	**51.8%**	475,000	301,048	**63.4%**	11.6	498,000	246,673	**49.5%**	-2.3	522,000	183,771	**35.2%**	-16.6	546,000	213,894	**39.2%**	-12.6
MARYLAND	1,012,000	453,836	**44.8%**	1,090,000	543,381	**49.9%**	5.0	1,185,000	585,418	**49.4%**	4.6	1,324,000	550,940	**41.6%**	-3.2	1,463,000	533,916	**36.5%**	-8.4
MASSACHUSETTS	2,305,000	1,500,704	**65.1%**	2,454,000	1,780,290	**72.5%**	7.4	2,617,000	1,954,738	**74.7%**	9.6	2,802,000	1,889,750	**67.4%**	2.3	2,988,000	1,946,475	**65.1%**	0.0
MICHIGAN	2,724,000	1,576,032	**57.9%**	2,947,000	1,697,944	**57.6%**	-0.2	3,204,000	1,987,358	**62.0%**	4.2	3,538,000	2,163,387	**61.1%**	3.3	3,872,000	2,064,536	**53.3%**	-4.5
MINNESOTA	1,529,000	1,146,800	**75.0%**	1,637,000	1,091,195	**66.7%**	-8.3	1,738,000	1,205,753	**69.4%**	-5.6	1,798,000	1,109,109	**61.7%**	-13.3	1,857,000	1,181,726	**63.6%**	-11.4
MISSISSIPPI	1,073,000	134,688	**12.6%**	1,140,000	148,440	**13.0%**	0.5	1,195,000	146,219	**12.2%**	-0.3	1,199,000	152,702	**12.7%**	0.2	1,204,000	152,537	**12.7%**	0.1
MISSOURI	2,287,000	1,635,377	**71.5%**	2,384,000	1,810,975	**76.0%**	4.5	2,477,000	1,816,729	**73.3%**	1.8	2,540,000	1,521,399	**59.9%**	-11.6	2,603,000	1,560,112	**59.9%**	-11.6
MONTANA	304,000	208,871	**68.7%**	321,000	208,467	**64.9%**	-3.8	338,000	237,975	**70.4%**	1.7	349,000	197,217	**56.5%**	-12.2	361,000	214,549	**59.4%**	-9.3
NEBRASKA	792,000	546,201	**69.0%**	805,000	569,336	**70.7%**	1.8	818,000	575,316	**70.3%**	1.4	830,000	514,666	**62.0%**	-7.0	843,000	460,451	**54.6%**	-14.3
NEVADA	55,000	41,112	**74.7%**	62,000	43,764	**70.6%**	-4.2	70,000	50,746	**72.5%**	-2.3	85,000	51,744	**60.9%**	-13.9	100,000	58,705	**58.7%**	-16.0
NEW HAMPSHIRE	268,000	193,083	**72.0%**	283,000	203,736	**72.0%**	-0.1	300,000	218,206	**72.7%**	0.7	317,000	215,847	**68.1%**	-4.0	333,000	220,363	**66.2%**	-5.9
NEW JERSEY	2,294,000	1,501,770	**65.5%**	2,459,000	1,688,241	**68.7%**	3.2	2,649,000	1,862,440	**70.3%**	4.8	2,899,000	1,849,478	**63.8%**	-1.7	3,150,000	1,853,513	**58.8%**	-6.6
NEW MEXICO	197,000	149,568	**75.9%**	231,000	168,373	**72.9%**	-3.0	270,000	182,057	**67.4%**	-8.5	312,000	151,553	**48.6%**	-27.3	356,000	186,029	**52.3%**	-23.7
NEW YORK	7,228,000	4,373,733	**60.5%**	7,826,000	5,264,203	**67.3%**	6.8	8,447,000	6,035,215	**71.4%**	10.9	9,042,000	6,024,597	**66.6%**	6.1	9,635,000	5,997,449	**62.2%**	1.7

United States House of Representatives General Elections *(continued)*

Election Years 1932–1948 *(continued)*

State	1932 Voting-age population	Turnout	%	1936 Voting-age population	Turnout	%	Difference from 1932	1940 Voting-age population	Turnout	%	Difference from 1932	1944 Voting-age population	Turnout	%	Difference from 1932	1948 Voting-age population	Turnout	%	Difference from 1932
NORTH CAROLINA	1,638,000	706,072	43.1%	1,791,000	798,884	44.6%	1.5	1,952,000	797,655	40.9%	-2.2	2,107,000	754,658	35.8%	-7.3	2,263,000	763,513	33.7%	-9.4
NORTH DAKOTA	341,000	217,688	63.8%	348,000	235,576	67.7%	3.9	354,000	235,288	66.5%	2.6	356,000	200,729	56.4%	-7.5	358,000	190,803	53.3%	-10.5
OHIO	4,025,000	2,347,868	58.3%	4,234,000	2,788,251	65.9%	7.5	4,475,000	3,003,562	67.1%	8.8	4,786,000	2,905,265	60.7%	2.4	5,097,000	2,798,360	54.9%	-3.4
OKLAHOMA	1,263,000	642,102	50.8%	1,301,000	672,360	51.7%	0.8	1,335,000	729,723	54.7%	3.8	1,354,000	684,560	50.6%	-0.3	1,372,000	679,761	49.5%	-1.3
OREGON	612,000	347,634	56.8%	607,000	380,040	58.5%	1.7	735,000	461,902	62.8%	6.0	843,000	442,476	52.5%	-4.3	951,000	491,142	51.6%	-5.2
PENNSYLVANIA	5,441,000	2,785,218	51.2%	5,766,000	4,070,599	70.6%	19.4	6,103,000	3,847,614	63.0%	11.9	6,423,000	3,712,030	67.8%	6.6	6,743,000	3,657,029	54.2%	3.0
RHODE ISLAND	377,000	260,684	69.1%	403,000	305,402	75.8%	6.6	433,000	314,388	72.6%	3.5	469,000	293,481	62.6%	-6.6	504,000	318,512	63.2%	-6.0
SOUTH CAROLINA	865,000	106,633	12.3%	934,000	115,249	12.3%	0.0	1,004,000	99,668	9.9%	-2.4	1,068,000	100,855	9.4%	-2.9	1,131,000	140,639	12.4%	0.1
SOUTH DAKOTA	364,000	273,361	75.1%	366,000	286,449	78.3%	3.2	370,000	298,601	80.7%	5.6	382,000	225,738	59.1%	-16.0	394,000	240,720	61.1%	-14.0
TENNESSEE	1,493,000	340,601	22.8%	1,609,000	392,553	24.4%	1.6	1,728,000	417,157	24.1%	1.3	1,836,000	398,632	21.7%	-1.1	1,944,000	448,966	23.1%	0.3
TEXAS	3,104,000	857,602	27.6%	3,437,000	819,673	23.8%	-3.8	3,789,000	1,027,554	27.1%	-0.5	4,141,000	1,063,351	25.7%	-2.0	4,492,000	1,051,803	23.4%	-4.2
UTAH	260,000	205,595	79.1%	279,000	215,706	77.3%	-1.7	303,000	246,881	81.5%	2.4	337,000	247,681	73.5%	-5.6	371,000	274,333	73.9%	-5.1
VERMONT	207,000	133,801	64.6%	211,000	140,395	66.5%	1.9	216,000	140,477	65.0%	0.4	222,000	123,038	55.4%	-9.2	228,000	121,968	53.5%	-11.1
VIRGINIA	1,362,000	364,525	26.8%	1,463,000	322,276	22.0%	-4.7	1,588,000	316,576	19.9%	-6.8	1,775,000	342,980	19.3%	-7.4	1,962,000	383,160	19.5%	-7.2
WASHINGTON	962,000	553,538	57.5%	1,042,000	646,856	62.1%	4.5	1,144,000	744,286	65.1%	7.5	1,304,000	803,093	61.6%	4.0	1,465,000	817,578	55.8%	-1.7
WEST VIRGINIA	922,000	735,788	79.8%	990,000	825,466	83.4%	3.6	1,056,000	870,115	82.4%	2.6	1,102,000	718,509	65.2%	-14.6	1,148,000	758,631	66.1%	-13.7
WISCONSIN	1,729,000	1,044,114	60.4%	1,842,000	1,122,655	60.9%	0.6	1,958,000	1,269,109	64.8%	4.4	2,058,000	1,162,654	56.5%	-3.9	2,157,000	1,211,168	56.2%	-4.2
WYOMING	129,000	90,191	69.9%	140,000	98,313	70.2%	0.3	151,000	106,888	70.8%	0.9	162,000	96,102	59.3%	-10.6	172,000	97,464	56.7%	-13.3
Total	70,022,000	37,526,062	53.6%	75,005,000	42,996,578	57.3%	3.7	80,471,000	46,659,159	58.0%	4.4	86,671,000	45,063,644	52.0%	-1.6	92,869,000	45,899,302	49.4%	-4.2

*Percentage point difference between turnout in current year and initial year listed in chart. If data do not appear for a state in the initial year listed, the difference is calculated from the first year in which data do appear for that state.

UNITED STATES HOUSE OF REPRESENTATIVES GENERAL ELECTIONS

Republican Turnout for Election Years 1932–1948

State	1932 Voting-age population	Turnout	%	1936 Voting-age population	Turnout	%	Difference from 1932*	1940 Voting-age population	Turnout	%	Difference from 1932	1944 Voting-age population	Turnout	%	Difference from 1932	1948 Voting-age population	Turnout	%	Difference from 1932
ALABAMA	1,402,000	22,669	1.6%	1,486,000	16,044	1.1%	-0.5	1,572,000	14,877	0.9%	-0.7	1,648,000	21,876	1.3%	-0.3	1,723,000	13,564	0.8%	-0.8
ALASKA																			
ARIZONA	184,000	29,710	16.1%	213,000	20,383	9.6%	-6.6	253,000	40,360	16.0%	-0.2	328,000	39,035	11.9%	-4.2	401,000	60,004	15.0%	-1.2
ARKANSAS	1,002,000	4,996	0.5%	1,055,000	13,993	1.3%	0.8	1,100,000	8,566	0.8%	0.3	1,104,000	16,515	1.5%	1.0	1,109,000	21,629	2.0%	1.5
CALIFORNIA	3,535,000	941,668	26.6%	3,979,000	965,728	24.3%	-2.4	4,569,000	1,473,115	32.2%	5.6	5,572,000	1,479,443	26.6%	-0.1	6,575,000	1,974,748	30.0%	3.4
COLORADO	601,000	191,903	31.9%	649,000	169,765	26.2%	-5.8	699,000	237,254	33.9%	2.0	755,000	281,578	37.3%	5.4	812,000	224,927	27.7%	-4.2
CONNECTICUT	857,000	289,509	33.8%	942,000	282,618	30.0%	-3.8	1,037,000	365,851	35.3%	1.5	1,152,000	397,725	34.5%	0.7	1,266,000	433,311	34.2%	0.4
DELAWARE	151,000	48,841	32.3%	162,000	61,002	37.7%	5.3	175,000	64,384	36.8%	4.4	189,000	62,378	33.0%	0.7	203,000	71,127	35.0%	2.7
DISTRICT OF COLUMBIA																			
FLORIDA	936,000	61,300	6.5%	1,075,000	51,532	4.8%	-1.8	1,243,000	52,411	4.2%	-2.3	1,484,000	63,183	4.3%	-2.3	1,725,000	55,803	3.2%	-3.3
GEORGIA	1,570,000	12,872	0.8%	1,680,000	15,765	0.9%	0.1	1,806,000	9,817	0.5%	-0.3								
HAWAII																			
IDAHO	254,000	78,838	31.0%	280,000	68,793	24.6%	-6.5	306,000	107,803	35.2%	4.2	323,000	99,749	30.9%	-0.2	339,000	103,094	30.4%	-0.6
ILLINOIS	4,615,000	1,421,221	30.8%	4,891,000	1,568,552	32.1%	1.3	5,179,000	2,050,493	39.6%	8.8	5,453,000	1,839,518	33.7%	2.9	5,727,000	1,823,266	31.8%	1.0
INDIANA	2,014,000	683,517	33.9%	2,116,000	706,988	33.4%	-0.5	2,229,000	896,841	40.2%	6.3	2,362,000	872,721	36.9%	3.0	2,496,000	782,346	31.3%	-2.6
IOWA	1,510,000	439,783	29.1%	1,564,000	510,875	32.7%	3.5	1,614,000	610,378	37.8%	8.7	1,641,000	552,046	33.6%	4.5	1,669,000	517,207	31.0%	1.9
KANSAS	1,115,000	350,332	31.4%	1,131,000	412,041	36.4%	5.0	1,152,000	454,866	39.5%	8.1	1,187,000	418,332	35.2%	3.8	1,222,000	404,432	33.1%	1.7
KENTUCKY	1,475,000	391,868	26.6%	1,561,000	368,576	23.6%	-3.0	1,654,000	335,241	20.3%	-6.3	1,754,000	381,552	21.8%	-4.8	1,854,000	320,691	17.3%	-9.3
LOUISIANA								1,383,000	13,933	1.0%						1,554,000	13,437	0.9%	-0.1
MAINE	454,000	116,641	25.7%	475,000	170,431	35.9%	10.2	498,000	159,387	32.0%	6.3	522,000	129,910	24.9%	-0.8	546,000	141,780	26.0%	0.3
MARYLAND	1,012,000	150,552	14.9%	1,090,000	215,236	19.7%	4.9	1,185,000	228,745	19.3%	4.4	1,324,000	240,129	18.1%	3.3	1,463,000	230,733	15.8%	0.9
MASSACHUSETTS	2,305,000	769,317	33.4%	2,454,000	884,243	36.0%	2.7	2,617,000	1,024,746	39.2%	5.8	2,802,000	1,001,682	35.7%	2.4	2,988,000	970,179	32.5%	-0.9
MICHIGAN	2,724,000	773,318	28.4%	2,947,000	765,887	26.0%	-2.4	3,204,000	1,013,774	31.6%	3.3	3,538,000	1,126,956	31.9%	3.5	3,872,000	1,024,507	26.5%	-1.9
MINNESOTA	1,529,000	337,110	22.0%	1,637,000	420,321	25.7%	3.6	1,738,000	644,608	37.1%	15.0	1,798,000	653,150	36.3%	14.3	1,857,000	593,088	31.9%	9.9
MISSISSIPPI	1,073,000	4,734	0.4%	1,140,000	1,929	0.2%	-0.3					1,199,000	5,133	0.4%	0.0	1,204,000	252	0.0%	-0.4
MISSOURI	2,287,000	609,268	26.6%	2,384,000	715,403	30.0%	3.4	2,477,000	864,919	34.9%	8.3	2,540,000	722,889	28.5%	1.8	2,603,000	641,851	24.7%	-2.0
MONTANA	304,000	87,223	28.7%	321,000	73,685	23.0%	-5.7	338,000	106,326	31.5%	2.8	349,000	77,513	22.2%	-6.5	361,000	91,061	25.2%	-3.5
NEBRASKA	792,000	208,954	26.4%	805,000	262,155	32.6%	6.2	818,000	320,175	39.1%	12.8	830,000	336,400	40.5%	14.1	843,000	268,620	31.9%	5.5
NEVADA	55,000	16,133	29.3%	62,000	11,745	18.9%	-10.4	70,000	18,032	25.8%	-3.6	85,000	19,096	22.5%	-6.9	100,000	28,972	29.0%	-0.4
NEW HAMPSHIRE	268,000	97,802	36.5%	283,000	105,526	37.3%	0.8	300,000	113,512	37.8%	1.3	317,000	113,448	35.8%	-0.7	333,000	124,299	37.3%	0.8
NEW JERSEY	2,294,000	751,130	32.7%	2,459,000	766,595	31.2%	-1.6	2,649,000	979,158	37.0%	4.2	2,899,000	988,108	34.1%	1.3	3,150,000	937,820	29.8%	-3.0
NEW MEXICO	197,000	52,905	26.9%	231,000	62,375	27.0%	0.1	270,000	75,085	27.8%	1.0	312,000	66,309	21.3%	-5.6	356,000	76,695	21.5%	-5.3
NEW YORK	7,228,000	1,756,343	24.3%	7,826,000	2,078,803	26.6%	2.3	8,447,000	2,830,517	33.5%	9.2	9,042,000	2,780,038	30.7%	6.4	9,635,000	2,658,309	27.6%	3.3

United States House of Representatives General Elections (continued)

Republican Turnout for Election Years 1932–1948 (continued)

State	1932 Voting-age population	Turnout	%	1936 Voting-age population	Turnout	%	Difference from 1932	1940 Voting-age population	Turnout	%	Difference from 1932	1944 Voting-age population	Turnout	%	Difference from 1932	1948 Voting-age population	Turnout	%	Difference from 1932
NORTH CAROLINA	1,638,000	214,022	13.1%	1,791,000	230,402	12.9%	-0.2	1,952,000	195,683	10.0%	-3.0	2,107,000	230,384	10.9%	-2.1	2,263,000	219,295	9.7%	-3.4
NORTH DAKOTA	341,000	144,339	42.3%	348,000	131,117	37.7%	-4.7	354,000	148,227	41.9%	-0.5	356,000	140,895	39.6%	-2.8	358,000	132,343	37.0%	-5.4
OHIO	4,025,000	1,109,562	27.6%	4,234,000	1,226,247	29.0%	1.4	4,475,000	1,519,628	34.0%	6.4	4,786,000	1,542,422	32.2%	4.7	5,097,000	1,342,388	26.3%	-1.2
OKLAHOMA	1,263,000	171,415	13.6%	1,301,000	193,487	14.9%	1.3	1,335,000	245,384	18.4%	4.8	1,354,000	282,279	20.8%	7.3	1,372,000	222,390	16.2%	2.6
OREGON	612,000	148,202	24.2%	667,000	181,758	27.3%	3.0	735,000	263,479	35.8%	11.6	843,000	272,212	32.3%	8.1	951,000	296,387	31.2%	6.9
PENNSYLVANIA	5,441,000	1,536,791	28.2%	5,766,000	1,718,625	29.8%	1.6	6,103,000	1,834,084	30.1%	1.8	6,420,000	1,827,055	28.4%	0.2	6,743,000	1,864,385	27.6%	-0.6
RHODE ISLAND	377,000	116,406	30.9%	403,000	134,180	33.3%	2.4	433,000	139,526	32.2%	1.3	469,000	118,011	25.2%	-5.7	504,000	124,881	24.8%	-6.1
SOUTH CAROLINA	865,000	1,987	0.2%	934,000	910	0.1%	-0.1	1,004,000	1,492	0.1%	-0.1	1,068,000	3,495	0.3%	0.1	1,131,000	6,907	0.6%	0.4
SOUTH DAKOTA	364,000	121,128	33.3%	366,000	143,071	39.1%	5.8	370,000	182,457	49.3%	16.0	382,000	146,888	38.5%	5.2	394,000	135,775	34.5%	1.2
TENNESSEE	1,493,000	88,686	5.9%	1,609,000	105,819	6.6%	0.6	1,728,000	107,495	6.2%	0.3	1,836,000	131,714	7.2%	1.2	1,944,000	150,778	7.8%	1.8
TEXAS	3,104,000	60,360	1.9%	3,437,000	52,201	1.5%	-0.4	3,789,000	33,271	0.9%	-1.1	4,141,000	63,341	1.5%	-0.4	4,492,000	65,410	1.5%	-0.5
UTAH	260,000	91,746	35.3%	279,000	65,270	23.4%	-11.9	303,000	97,353	32.1%	-3.2	337,000	98,082	29.1%	-6.2	371,000	114,922	31.0%	-4.3
VERMONT	207,000	86,194	41.6%	211,000	83,091	39.4%	-2.3	216,000	89,637	41.5%	-0.1	222,000	76,800	34.6%	-7.0	228,000	74,076	32.5%	-9.2
VIRGINIA	1,362,000	92,586	6.8%	1,463,000	86,040	5.9%	-0.9	1,588,000	60,731	3.8%	-3.0	1,775,000	80,623	4.5%	-2.3	1,962,000	121,474	6.2%	-0.6
WASHINGTON	962,000	186,571	19.4%	1,042,000	219,024	21.0%	1.6	1,144,000	313,614	27.4%	8.0	1,304,000	375,554	28.8%	9.4	1,465,000	401,334	27.4%	8.0
WEST VIRGINIA	922,000	341,170	37.0%	990,000	329,833	33.3%	-3.7	1,056,000	370,103	35.0%	-2.0	1,102,000	328,771	29.8%	-7.2	1,148,000	316,077	27.5%	-9.5
WISCONSIN	1,729,000	469,809	27.2%	1,842,000	315,040	17.1%	-10.1	1,958,000	579,526	29.6%	2.4	2,058,000	624,833	30.4%	3.2	2,157,000	676,501	31.4%	4.2
WYOMING	129,000	44,816	34.7%	140,000	41,362	29.5%	-5.2	151,000	49,701	32.9%	-1.8	162,000	53,533	33.0%	-1.7	172,000	50,218	29.2%	-5.5
Total	68,837,000	15,726,307	22.8%	73,721,000	17,025,266	23.1%	0.2	79,276,000	21,346,565	26.9%	4.1	83,234,000	21,183,304	25.5%	2.6	90,738,000	20,923,293	23.1%	0.3

Democratic Turnout for Election Years 1932–1948

State	1932 Voting-age population	Turnout	%	1936 Voting-age population	Turnout	%	Difference from 1932*	1940 Voting-age population	Turnout	%	Difference from 1932	1944 Voting-age population	Turnout	%	Difference from 1932	1948 Voting-age population	Turnout	%	Difference from 1932
ALABAMA	1,402,000	207,489	14.8%	1,486,000	238,558	16.1%	1.3	1,572,000	254,425	16.2%	1.4	1,648,000	200,462	12.2%	-2.6	1,723,000	183,519	10.7%	-4.1
ALASKA																			
ARIZONA	184,000	75,469	41.0%	213,000	84,343	39.6%	-1.4	253,000	99,424	39.3%	-1.7	328,000	88,532	27.0%	-14.0	401,000	96,631	24.1%	-16.9
ARKANSAS	1,002,000	213,189	21.3%	1,055,000	160,305	15.2%	-6.1	1,100,000	200,324	18.2%	-3.1	1,104,000	200,700	18.2%	-3.1	1,109,000	229,403	20.7%	-0.6
CALIFORNIA	3,535,000	849,270	24.0%	3,979,000	1,199,206	30.1%	6.1	4,569,000	1,183,943	25.9%	1.9	5,572,000	1,519,190	27.3%	3.2	6,575,000	1,348,098	20.5%	-3.5
COLORADO	601,000	234,843	39.1%	649,000	283,147	43.6%	4.6	699,000	286,104	40.9%	1.9	755,000	210,275	27.9%	-11.2	812,000	272,484	33.6%	-5.5
CONNECTICUT	857,000	282,557	33.0%	942,000	371,572	39.4%	6.5	1,037,000	407,868	39.3%	6.4	1,152,000	424,146	36.8%	3.8	1,266,000	429,348	33.9%	0.9
DELAWARE	151,000	51,698	34.2%	162,000	65,485	40.4%	6.2	175,000	70,394	40.2%	6.0	189,000	63,649	33.7%	-0.6	203,000	68,909	33.9%	-0.3
DISTRICT OF COLUMBIA																			
FLORIDA	936,000	186,284	19.9%	1,075,000	233,405	21.7%	1.8	1,243,000	327,837	26.4%	6.5	1,484,000	349,570	23.6%	3.7	1,725,000	295,330	17.1%	-2.8

United States House of Representatives General Elections (continued)

United States House of Representatives General Elections (continued)

Democratic Turnout for Election Years 1932–1948 (continued)

State	1932 Voting-age population	Turnout	%	1936 Voting-age population	Turnout	%	Difference from 1932	1940 Voting-age population	Turnout	%	Difference from 1932	1944 Voting-age population	Turnout	%	Difference from 1932	1948 Voting-age population	Turnout	%	Difference from 1932
GEORGIA	1,570,000	233,915	14.9%	1,680,000	260,509	15.5%	0.6	1,806,000	260,783	14.4%	-0.5	1,969,000	271,976	13.8%	-1.1	2,131,000	365,176	17.1%	2.2
HAWAII																			
IDAHO	254,000	100,922	39.7%	280,000	126,179	45.1%	5.3	306,000	123,833	40.5%	0.7	323,000	105,830	32.8%	-7.0	339,000	105,852	31.2%	-8.5
ILLINOIS	4,615,000	1,675,274	36.3%	4,891,000	2,062,886	42.2%	5.9	5,179,000	1,968,143	38.0%	1.7	5,453,000	2,030,755	37.2%	0.9	5,727,000	2,001,650	35.0%	-1.3
INDIANA	2,014,000	850,181	42.2%	2,116,000	910,851	43.0%	0.8	2,229,000	864,576	38.8%	-3.4	2,362,000	767,157	32.5%	-9.7	2,496,000	836,852	33.5%	-8.7
IOWA	1,510,000	495,732	32.8%	1,564,000	520,085	33.3%	0.4	1,614,000	504,371	31.2%	-1.6	1,641,000	420,340	25.6%	-7.2	1,669,000	429,048	25.7%	-7.1
KANSAS	1,115,000	357,154	32.0%	1,131,000	377,432	33.4%	1.3	1,152,000	333,796	29.0%	-3.1	1,187,000	245,860	20.7%	-11.3	1,222,000	299,478	24.5%	-7.5
KENTUCKY	1,475,000	575,191	39.0%	1,561,000	539,598	34.6%	-4.4	1,654,000	557,992	33.7%	-5.3	1,754,000	459,936	26.2%	-12.8	1,854,000	416,014	22.4%	-16.6
LOUISIANA	1,185,000	244,681	20.6%	1,284,000	291,930	22.7%	2.1	1,383,000	307,102	22.2%	1.6	1,468,000	282,569	19.2%	-1.4	1,554,000	308,239	19.8%	-0.8
MAINE	454,000	118,391	26.1%	475,000	119,195	25.1%	-1.0	498,000	87,286	17.5%	-8.6	522,000	53,861	10.3%	-15.8	546,000	72,114	13.2%	-12.9
MARYLAND	1,012,000	299,954	29.6%	1,090,000	321,447	29.5%	-0.1	1,185,000	356,667	30.1%	0.5	1,324,000	310,811	23.5%	-6.2	1,463,000	291,011	19.9%	-9.7
MASSACHUSETTS	2,305,000	716,971	31.1%	2,454,000	816,131	33.3%	2.2	2,617,000	925,462	35.4%	4.3	2,802,000	887,957	31.7%	0.6	2,988,000	976,241	32.7%	1.6
MICHIGAN	2,724,000	769,088	28.2%	2,947,000	887,874	30.1%	1.9	3,204,000	969,328	30.3%	2.0	3,538,000	1,028,071	29.1%	0.8	3,872,000	1,022,761	26.4%	-1.8
MINNESOTA	1,529,000	321,949	21.1%	1,637,000	190,367	11.6%	-9.4	1,738,000	262,895	15.1%	-5.9	1,798,000	452,945	25.2%	4.1	1,857,000	588,628	31.7%	10.6
MISSISSIPPI	1,073,000	129,954	12.1%	1,140,000	146,511	12.9%	0.7	1,195,000	146,219	12.2%	0.1	1,199,000	147,569	12.3%	0.2	1,204,000	152,285	12.6%	0.5
MISSOURI	2,287,000	1,013,824	44.3%	2,384,000	1,093,138	45.9%	1.5	2,477,000	951,656	38.4%	-5.9	2,540,000	798,374	31.4%	-12.9	2,603,000	914,886	35.1%	-9.2
MONTANA	304,000	115,262	37.9%	321,000	134,006	41.7%	3.8	338,000	130,453	38.6%	0.7	349,000	118,131	33.8%	-4.1	361,000	122,987	34.1%	-3.8
NEBRASKA	792,000	296,256	37.4%	805,000	289,381	35.9%	-1.5	818,000	231,873	28.3%	-9.1	830,000	165,489	19.9%	-17.5	843,000	191,831	22.8%	-14.7
NEVADA	55,000	24,979	45.4%	62,000	25,575	41.3%	-4.2	70,000	32,714	46.7%	1.3	85,000	32,648	38.4%	-7.0	100,000	29,733	29.7%	-15.7
NEW HAMPSHIRE	268,000	94,765	35.4%	283,000	96,807	34.2%	-1.2	300,000	104,694	34.9%	-0.5	317,000	102,364	32.3%	-3.1	333,000	94,551	28.4%	-7.0
NEW JERSEY	2,294,000	724,572	31.6%	2,459,000	901,234	36.7%	5.1	2,649,000	870,406	32.9%	1.3	2,899,000	860,326	29.7%	-1.9	3,150,000	880,881	28.0%	-3.6
NEW MEXICO	197,000	94,764	48.1%	231,000	105,937	45.9%	-2.2	270,000	106,972	39.6%	-8.5	312,000	85,244	27.3%	-20.8	356,000	108,529	30.5%	-17.6
NEW YORK	7,228,000	2,363,627	32.7%	7,826,000	3,013,931	38.5%	5.8	8,447,000	3,199,019	37.9%	5.2	9,042,000	3,052,178	33.8%	1.1	9,635,000	2,607,312	27.1%	-5.6
NORTH CAROLINA	1,638,000	492,050	30.0%	1,791,000	568,482	31.7%	1.7	1,952,000	601,972	30.8%	0.8	2,107,000	524,274	24.9%	-5.2	2,263,000	540,873	23.9%	-6.1
NORTH DAKOTA	341,000	72,659	21.3%	348,000	100,609	28.9%	7.6	354,000	63,662	18.0%	-3.3	356,000	56,699	15.9%	-5.4	358,000	56,702	15.8%	-5.5
OHIO	4,025,000	1,206,631	30.0%	4,234,000	1,553,059	36.7%	6.7	4,475,000	1,483,934	33.2%	3.2	4,786,000	1,362,843	28.5%	-1.5	5,097,000	1,455,972	28.6%	-1.4
OKLAHOMA	1,263,000	467,644	37.0%	1,301,000	475,567	36.6%	-0.5	1,335,000	479,433	35.9%	-1.1	1,354,000	401,232	29.6%	-7.4	1,372,000	457,371	33.3%	-3.7
OREGON	612,000	164,582	26.9%	667,000	184,824	27.7%	0.8	735,000	189,702	25.8%	-1.1	843,000	170,264	20.2%	-6.7	951,000	176,014	18.5%	-8.4
PENNSYLVANIA	5,441,000	1,109,136	20.4%	5,766,000	2,252,229	39.1%	18.7	6,103,000	1,993,546	32.7%	12.3	6,423,000	1,880,777	29.3%	8.9	6,743,000	1,782,985	26.4%	6.1
RHODE ISLAND	377,000	143,652	38.1%	403,000	149,957	37.2%	-0.9	433,000	174,862	40.4%	2.3	469,000	175,368	37.4%	-0.7	504,000	193,631	38.4%	0.3
SOUTH CAROLINA	865,000	104,646	12.1%	934,000	113,651	12.2%	0.1	1,004,000	98,176	9.8%	-2.3	1,068,000	97,360	9.1%	-3.0	1,131,000	133,732	11.8%	-0.3
SOUTH DAKOTA	364,000	146,886	40.4%	366,000	143,378	39.2%	-1.2	370,000	116,144	31.4%	-9.0	382,000	78,850	20.6%	-19.7	394,000	104,945	26.6%	-13.7
TENNESSEE	1,493,000	217,905	14.6%	1,609,000	281,664	17.5%	2.9	1,728,000	282,337	16.3%	1.7	1,836,000	260,694	14.2%	-0.4	1,944,000	283,231	14.6%	0.0

United States House of Representatives General Elections *(continued)*

Democratic Turnout for Election Years 1932–1948 *(continued)*

State	1932 Voting-age population	Turnout	%	1936 Voting-age population	Turnout	%	Difference from 1932	1940 Voting-age population	Turnout	%	Difference from 1932	1944 Voting-age population	Turnout	%	Difference from 1932	1948 Voting-age population	Turnout	%	Difference from 1932
TEXAS	3,104,000	794,520	25.6%	3,437,000	765,362	22.3%	-3.3	3,789,000	994,207	26.2%	0.6	4,141,000	1,000,010	24.1%	-1.4	4,492,000	984,944	21.9%	-3.7
UTAH	260,000	110,176	42.4%	279,000	149,996	53.8%	11.4	303,000	149,528	49.3%	7.0	337,000	149,599	44.4%	2.0	371,000	159,411	43.0%	0.6
VERMONT	207,000	47,591	23.0%	211,000	56,334	26.7%	3.7	216,000	50,804	23.5%	0.5	222,000	46,230	20.8%	-2.2	228,000	47,767	21.0%	-2.0
VIRGINIA	1,362,000	206,631	15.2%	1,463,000	233,462	16.0%	0.8	1,588,000	253,562	16.0%	0.8	1,775,000	250,366	14.1%	-1.1	1,962,000	255,176	13.0%	-2.2
WASHINGTON	962,000	327,702	34.1%	1,042,000	425,985	40.9%	6.8	1,144,000	430,442	37.6%	3.6	1,304,000	426,036	32.7%	-1.4	1,465,000	402,505	27.5%	-6.6
WEST VIRGINIA	922,000	392,924	42.6%	990,000	495,633	50.1%	7.4	1,056,000	500,012	47.3%	4.7	1,102,000	300,738	35.4%	-7.3	1,148,000	442,554	38.6%	-4.1
WISCONSIN	1,729,000	500,710	29.0%	1,842,000	322,923	17.5%	-11.4	1,958,000	220,520	11.3%	-17.7	2,058,000	408,714	19.9%	-9.1	2,157,000	514,018	23.8%	-5.1
WYOMING	129,000	43,056	33.4%	140,000	56,204	40.1%	6.8	151,000	57,030	37.8%	4.4	162,000	42,569	26.3%	-7.1	172,000	47,246	27.5%	-5.9
Total	70,022,000	20,267,306	28.9%	75,005,000	24,196,344	32.3%	3.3	80,471,000	24,266,432	30.2%	1.2	86,671,000	23,458,538	27.1%	-1.9	92,869,000	23,778,858	25.6%	-3.3

Other Turnout for Election Years 1932–1948

State	1932 Voting-age population	Turnout	%	1936 Voting-age pop.	Turnout	%	Difference from 1932*	1940 Voting-age population	Turnout	%	Difference from 1932	1944 Voting-age population	Turnout	%	Difference from 1932	1948 Voting-age population	Turnout	%	Difference from 1932
ALABAMA	1,402,000	1,476	0.1%	1,486,000	450	0.0%	-0.1	1,572,000	342	0.0%	-0.1								
ALASKA																			
ARIZONA	184,000	1,405	0.8%	213,000	4,024	1.9%	1.1					328,000	469	0.1%	-0.6	401,000	2,340	0.6%	-0.2
ARKANSAS																			
CALIFORNIA	3,535,000	83,393	2.4%	3,979,000	75,561	1.9%	-0.5	4,569,000	113,492	2.5%	0.1	5,572,000	6,309	0.1%	-2.2	6,575,000	235,654	3.6%	1.2
COLORADO	601,000	2,769	0.5%	649,000	4,847	0.7%	0.3	699,000	1,668	0.2%	-0.2	755,000	2,009	0.3%	-0.2				
CONNECTICUT	857,000	20,710	2.4%	942,000	35,322	3.7%	1.3	1,037,000	8,874	0.9%	-1.6	1,152,000	5,874	0.5%	-1.9	1,266,000	16,692	1.3%	-1.1
DELAWARE	151,000	11,557	7.7%	162,000	176	0.1%	-7.5					189,000	413	0.2%	-7.4	203,000	499	0.2%	-7.4
DISTRICT OF COLUMBIA																			
FLORIDA	936,000	12	0.0%																
GEORGIA	1,570,000	44	0.0%					1,806,000	799	0.0%	0.0	1,969,000	2,929	0.1%	0.1	2,131,000	234	0.0%	0.0
HAWAII																			
IDAHO	254,000	3,815	1.5%													339,000	3,223	1.0%	-0.6
ILLINOIS	4,615,000	53,638	1.2%	4,891,000	97,412	2.0%	0.8	5,179,000	14,163	0.3%	-0.9	5,453,000	12,386	0.2%	-0.9	5,727,000	23,724	0.4%	-0.7
INDIANA	2,014,000	13,074	0.6%	2,116,000	11,277	0.5%	-0.1	2,229,000	200	0.0%	-0.6	2,362,000	11,339	0.5%	-0.2	2,496,000	14,203	0.6%	-0.1
IOWA	1,510,000	6,135	0.4%	1,564,000	23,404	1.5%	1.1	1,614,000	220	0.0%	-0.4	1,641,000	373	0.0%	-0.4	1,669,000	3,489	0.2%	-0.2
KANSAS	1,115,000	11,609	1.0%	1,131,000	10,377	0.9%	-0.1												
KENTUCKY	1,475,000	3,514	0.2%	1,561,000	9,473	0.6%	0.4					1,754,000	2,355	0.1%	-0.1	1,854,000	3,822	0.2%	0.0
LOUISIANA				1,284,000	33	0.0%		1,383,000	9	0.0%	0.0								
MAINE	454,000	213	0.0%	475,000	11,422	2.4%	2.4												

United States House of Representatives General Elections (continued)

Other Turnout for Election Years 1932–1948 (continued)

State	1932 Voting-age population	Turnout	%	1936 Voting-age population	Turnout	%	Difference from 1932	1940 Voting-age population	Turnout	%	Difference from 1932	1944 Voting-age population	Turnout	%	Difference from 1932	1948 Voting-age population	Turnout	%	Difference from 1932
MARYLAND	1,012,000	3,330	0.3%	1,090,000	6,698	0.6%	0.3	1,185,000	6	0.0%	-0.3					1,463,000	12,172	0.8%	0.5
MASSACHUSETTS	2,305,000	14,416	0.6%	2,454,000	79,916	3.3%	2.6	2,617,000	4,530	0.2%	-0.5	2,802,000	111	0.0%	-0.6	2,988,000	55	0.0%	-0.6
MICHIGAN	2,724,000	33,626	1.2%	2,947,000	44,183	1.5%	0.3	3,204,000	4,256	0.1%	-1.1	3,538,000	8,360	0.2%	-1.0	3,872,000	17,268	0.4%	-0.8
MINNESOTA	1,529,000	487,741	31.9%	1,637,000	480,507	29.4%	-2.5	1,738,000	298,250	17.2%	-14.7	1,798,000	3,014	0.2%	-31.7	1,857,000	10	0.0%	-31.9
MISSISSIPPI																			
MISSOURI	2,287,000	12,285	0.5%	2,384,000	2,434	0.1%	-0.4	2,477,000	154	0.0%	-0.5	2,540,000	136	0.0%	-0.5	2,603,000	3,375	0.1%	-0.4
MONTANA	304,000	6,386	2.1%	321,000	776	0.2%	-1.9	338,000	1,196	0.4%	-1.7	349,000	1,573	0.5%	-1.6	361,000	501	0.1%	-2.0
NEBRASKA	792,000	40,991	5.2%	805,000	17,800	2.2%	-3.0	818,000	23,268	2.8%	-2.3	830,000	12,777	1.5%	-3.6				
NEVADA				62,000	6,444	10.4%													
NEW HAMPSHIRE	268,000	516	0.2%	283,000	1,403	0.5%	0.3					317,000	35	0.0%	-0.2	333,000	1,513	0.5%	0.3
NEW JERSEY	2,294,000	26,068	1.1%	2,459,000	20,412	0.8%	-0.3	2,649,000	12,876	0.5%	-0.7	2,899,000	1,044	0.0%	-1.1	3,150,000	34,812	1.1%	0.0
NEW MEXICO	197,000	1,899	1.0%	231,000	61	0.0%	-0.9									356,000	805	0.2%	-0.7
NEW YORK	7,228,000	253,763	3.5%	7,826,000	171,469	2.2%	-1.3	8,447,000	5,679	0.1%	-3.4	9,042,000	192,381	2.1%	-1.4	9,635,000	732,366	7.6%	4.1
NORTH CAROLINA																2,263,000	3,345	0.1%	
NORTH DAKOTA	341,000	690	0.2%	348,000	3,850	1.1%	0.9	354,000	23,399	6.6%	6.4	356,000	3,135	0.9%	0.7	358,000	1,758	0.5%	0.3
OHIO	4,025,000	31,675	0.8%	4,234,000	8,945	0.2%	-0.6												
OKLAHOMA	1,263,000	3,043	0.2%	1,301,000	3,306	0.3%	0.0	1,335,000	4,906	0.4%	0.1	1,354,000	1,049	0.1%	-0.2				
OREGON	612,000	34,790	5.7%	667,000	23,358	3.5%	-2.2	735,000	8,721	1.2%	-4.5					951,000	18,741	2.0%	-3.7
PENNSYLVANIA	5,441,000	139,291	2.6%	5,766,000	99,745	1.7%	-0.8	6,103,000	19,984	0.3%	-2.2	6,423,000	4,798	0.1%	-2.5	6,743,000	9,659	0.1%	-2.4
RHODE ISLAND	377,000	626	0.2%	403,000	21,265	5.3%	5.1					469,000	102	0.0%	-0.1				
SOUTH CAROLINA				934,000	688	0.1%													
SOUTH DAKOTA	364,000	5,347	1.5%																
TENNESSEE	1,493,000	34,010	2.3%	1,609,000	5,070	0.3%	-2.0	1,728,000	27,325	1.6%	-0.7	1,836,000	6,224	0.3%	-1.9	1,944,000	14,957	0.8%	-1.5
TEXAS	3,104,000	2,722	0.1%	3,437,000	2,110	0.1%	0.0	3,789,000	76	0.0%	-0.1					4,492,000	1,449	0.0%	-0.1
UTAH	260,000	3,673	1.4%	279,000	520	0.2%	-1.2												
VERMONT	207,000	16	0.0%	211,000	970	0.5%	0.5	216,000	36	0.0%	0.0	222,000	6	0.0%	0.0	228,000	125	0.1%	0.0
VIRGINIA	1,362,000	65,308	4.8%	1,463,000	1,974	0.1%	-4.7	1,588,000	2,283	0.1%	-4.7	1,775,000	11,991	0.7%	-4.1	1,962,000	6,510	0.3%	-4.5
WASHINGTON	962,000	39,265	4.1%	1,042,000	1,847	0.2%	-3.9	1,144,000	230	0.0%	-4.1	1,304,000	1,503	0.1%	-4.0	1,465,000	13,739	0.9%	-3.1
WEST VIRGINIA	922,000	1,694	0.2%																
WISCONSIN	1,729,000	73,595	4.3%	1,842,000	484,692	26.3%	22.1	1,958,000	469,063	24.0%	19.7	2,058,000	129,107	6.3%	2.0	2,157,000	20,649	1.0%	-3.3
WYOMING	129,000	2,319	1.8%	140,000	747	0.5%	-1.3	151,000	157	0.1%	-1.7								
Total	64,204,000	1,532,449	2.4%	66,628,000	1,774,968	2.7%	0.3	62,662,000	1,046,162	1.7%	-0.7	61,087,000	421,802	0.7%	-1.7	71,842,000	1,197,689	1.7%	-0.7

*Percentage point difference between turnout in current year and initial year listed in chart. If data do not appear for a state in the initial year listed, the difference is calculated from the first year in which data do appear for that state.

UNITED STATES PRESIDENTIAL PRIMARY ELECTIONS

Election Years 1932–1948

State*	1932 Voting-age population	Turnout	%	1936 Voting-age population	Turnout	%	Difference from 1932**	1940 Voting-age population	Turnout	%	Difference from 1932	1944 Voting-age population	Turnout	%	Difference from 1932	1948 Voting-age population	Turnout	%	Difference from 1932
ALABAMA																			
ALASKA																			
ARIZONA																			
ARKANSAS																			
CALIFORNIA	3,471,000	1,190,330	34.6%	3,914,000	1,568,781	40.1%	5.6	4,465,000	1,515,543	33.9%	-0.5	5,467,000	1,364,661	25.0%	-9.5	6,470,000	1,581,440	24.4%	-10.0
COLORADO																			
CONNECTICUT																			
DELAWARE																			
DISTRICT OF COLUMBIA																			
FLORIDA																			
GEORGIA																			
HAWAII																			
IDAHO																			
ILLINOIS	4,575,000	941,547	20.6%	4,851,000	2,331,597	48.1%	27.5	5,151,000	2,345,144	45.5%	24.9	5,424,000	645,972	11.9%	-8.7	5,699,000	354,354	6.2%	-14.4
INDIANA																			
IOWA																			
KANSAS																			
KENTUCKY																			
LOUISIANA																			
MAINE																			
MARYLAND																			
MASSACHUSETTS	2,283,000	267,453	11.7%	2,431,000	155,896	6.4%	-5.3	2,597,000	175,894	6.8%	-4.9	2,783,000	110,810	4.0%	-7.7	2,969,000	123,398	4.2%	-7.6
MICHIGAN																			
MINNESOTA																			
MISSISSIPPI																			
MISSOURI																			
MONTANA																			
NEBRASKA	790,000	198,381	25.1%	803,000	234,073	29.1%	4.0	817,000	286,615	35.1%	10.0	829,000	116,623	14.1%	-11.0	842,000	254,573	30.2%	5.1
NEVADA																			
NEW HAMPSHIRE	266,000	38,304	14.4%	281,000	48,744	17.3%	2.9	298,000	45,117	15.1%	0.7	315,000	23,495	7.5%	-6.9	332,000	33,263	10.0%	-4.4
NEW JERSEY	2,270,000	159,899	7.0%	2,434,000	499,826	20.5%	13.5	2,624,000	397,120	15.1%	8.1	2,873,000	37,113	1.3%	-5.8	3,123,000	10,165	0.3%	-6.7
NEW MEXICO																			
NEW YORK																			

United States Presidential Primary Elections (continued)

United States Presidential Primary Elections *(continued)*

Election Years 1932–1948 *(continued)*

State	1932 Voting-age population	Turnout	%	1936 Voting-age population	Turnout	%	Difference from 1932	1940 Voting-age population	Turnout	%	Difference from 1932	1944 Voting-age population	Turnout	%	Difference from 1932	1948 Voting-age population	Turnout	%	Difference from 1932
NORTH CAROLINA																			
NORTH DAKOTA	340,000	145,000	42.6%																
OHIO	3,995,000	245,508	6.1%	4,204,000	714,063	17.0%	10.8	4,443,000	796,429	17.9%	11.8	4,753,000	525,054	11.0%	4.9	5,064,000	697,913	13.8%	7.6
OKLAHOMA																			
OREGON	605,000	167,041	27.6%	659,000	190,486	28.9%	1.3	724,000	265,303	36.6%	9.0	832,000	144,834	17.4%	-10.2	940,000	347,372	37.0%	9.3
PENNSYLVANIA	5,393,000	613,672	11.4%	5,718,000	1,215,642	21.3%	9.9	6,070,000	803,633	13.2%	1.9	6,390,000	498,477	7.8%	-3.6	6,709,000	600,814	9.0%	-2.4
RHODE ISLAND																			
SOUTH CAROLINA																			
SOUTH DAKOTA	364,000	134,967	37.1%	366,000	137,041	37.4%	0.4	369,000	80,202	21.7%	-15.3	380,000	69,773	18.4%	-18.7	392,000	64,672	16.5%	-20.6
TENNESSEE																			
TEXAS																			
UTAH																			
VERMONT																			
VIRGINIA																			
WASHINGTON																			
WEST VIRGINIA	911,000	331,229	36.4%	980,000	421,802	43.0%	6.7	1,052,000	208,852	19.9%	-16.5	1,098,000	150,884	13.7%	-22.6	1,143,000	290,287	25.4%	-11.0
WISCONSIN	1,712,000	391,346	22.9%	1,826,000	592,621	32.5%	9.6	1,948,000	525,344	27.0%	4.1	2,047,000	193,777	9.5%	-13.4	2,147,000	193,071	9.0%	-13.9
WYOMING																			
Total	26,975,000	4,830,677	17.9%	28,467,000	8,110,572	28.5%	10.6	30,558,000	7,445,196	24.4%	6.5	33,191,000	3,881,473	11.7%	-6.2	35,830,000	4,551,322	12.7%	-5.2

*Overall primary turnout reflects only states with primaries in both parties. To find single party primary results, see partisan primary charts.

**Percentage point difference between turnout in current year and initial year listed in chart. If data do not appear for a state in the initial year listed, the difference is calculated from the first year in which data do appear for that state.

UNITED STATES PRESIDENTIAL PRIMARY ELECTIONS

Republican Turnout for Election Years 1932–1948

State	1932 Voting-age population	1932 Turnout	1932 %	1936 Voting-age population	1936 Turnout	1936 %	1936 Difference from 1932*	1940 Voting-age population	1940 Turnout	1940 %	1940 Difference from 1932	1944 Voting-age population	1944 Turnout	1944 %	1944 Difference from 1932	1948 Voting-age population	1948 Turnout	1948 %	1948 Difference from 1932
ALABAMA																			
ALASKA																			
ARIZONA																			
ARKANSAS																			
CALIFORNIA	3,471,000	657,420	18.9%	3,914,000	611,087	15.6%	-3.3	4,465,000	538,112	12.1%	-6.9	5,467,000	594,439	10.9%	-8.1	6,470,000	769,520	11.9%	-7.0
COLORADO																			
CONNECTICUT																			
DELAWARE																			
DISTRICT OF COLUMBIA																			
FLORIDA																			
GEORGIA																			
HAWAII																			
IDAHO																			
ILLINOIS	4,575,000	349,995	7.7%	4,851,000	914,775	18.9%	11.2	5,151,000	977,777	19.0%	11.3	5,424,000	598,068	11.0%	3.4	5,699,000	334,406	5.9%	-1.8
INDIANA																			
IOWA																			
KANSAS																			
KENTUCKY																			
LOUISIANA																			
MAINE																			
MARYLAND	1,001,000	45,568	4.6%					1,171,000	54,802	4.7%	0.1	1,309,000	22,301	1.7%	-2.8				
MASSACHUSETTS	2,283,000	57,534	2.5%	2,431,000	95,416	3.9%	1.4	2,597,000	98,975	3.8%	1.3	2,783,000	53,511	1.9%	-0.6	2,969,000	72,191	2.4%	-0.1
MICHIGAN																			
MINNESOTA																			
MISSISSIPPI																			
MISSOURI																			
MONTANA																			
NEBRASKA	790,000	54,415	6.9%	803,000	94,330	11.7%	4.9	817,000	174,713	21.4%	14.5	829,000	78,899	9.5%	2.6	842,000	186,007	22.1%	15.2
NEVADA																			
NEW HAMPSHIRE	266,000	22,903	8.6%	281,000	32,992	11.7%	3.1	298,000	34,616	11.6%	3.0	315,000	16,723	5.3%	-3.3	332,000	28,854	8.7%	0.1
NEW JERSEY	2,270,000	151,446	6.7%	2,434,000	438,194	18.0%	11.3	2,624,000	362,842	13.8%	7.2	2,873,000	20,169	0.7%	-6.0	3,123,000	8,976	0.3%	-6.4
NEW MEXICO																			
NEW YORK																			

United States Presidential Primary Elections (continued)

United States Presidential Primary Elections (continued)

Republican Turnout for Election Years 1932–1948 (continued)

State	1932 Voting-age population	Turnout	%	1936 Voting-age population	Turnout	%	Difference from 1932	1940 Voting-age population	Turnout	%	Difference from 1932	1944 population	Turnout	%	Difference from 1932	1948 Voting-age population	Turnout	%	Difference from 1932
NORTH CAROLINA																			
NORTH DAKOTA	340,000	61,000	17.9%																
OHIO	3,995,000	128,851	3.2%	4,204,000	166,747	4.0%	0.7	4,443,000	512,477	11.5%	8.3	4,753,000	360,139	7.6%	4.4	5,064,000	426,767	8.4%	5.2
OKLAHOMA																			
OREGON	605,000	105,280	17.4%	659,000	101,973	15.5%	-1.9	724,000	139,205	19.2%	1.8	832,000	63,944	7.7%	-9.7	940,000	226,974	24.1%	6.7
PENNSYLVANIA	5,393,000	378,880	7.0%	5,718,000	459,982	8.0%	1.0	6,070,000	78,976	1.3%	-5.7	6,390,000	175,047	2.7%	-4.3	6,709,000	258,162	3.8%	-3.2
RHODE ISLAND																			
SOUTH CAROLINA																			
SOUTH DAKOTA	364,000	99,597	27.4%	366,000	88,779	24.3%	-3.1	369,000	52,566	14.2%	-13.1	380,000	55,632	14.6%	-12.7	392,000	45,463	11.6%	-15.8
TENNESSEE																			
TEXAS																			
UTAH																			
VERMONT																			
VIRGINIA																			
WASHINGTON																			
WEST VIRGINIA	911,000	88,005	9.7%	980,000	124,841	12.7%	3.1	1,052,000	106,123	10.1%	0.4	1,098,000	91,602	8.3%	-1.3	1,143,000	133,185	11.7%	2.0
WISCONSIN	1,712,000	146,102	8.5%	1,826,000	190,694	10.4%	1.9	1,948,000	96,691	5.0%	-3.6	2,047,000	141,131	6.9%	-1.6	2,147,000	162,750	7.6%	-1.0
WYOMING																			
Total	27,976,000	2,346,996	8.4%	28,467,000	3,319,810	11.7%	3.3	31,729,000	3,227,875	10.2%	1.8	34,500,000	2,271,605	6.6%	-1.8	35,830,000	2,653,255	7.4%	-1.0

Democratic Turnout for Election Years 1932–1948

State	1932 Voting-age population	Turnout	%	1936 Voting-age population	Turnout	%	Difference from 1932*	1940 Voting-age population	Turnout	%	Difference from 1932	1944 Voting-age population	Turnout	%	Difference from 1932	1948 Voting-age population	Turnout	%	Difference from 1932
ALABAMA	1,389,000	134,781	9.7%					1,564,000	196,508	12.6%	2.9	1,640,000	116,922	7.1%	-2.6				
ALASKA																			
ARIZONA																			
ARKANSAS																			
CALIFORNIA	3,471,000	538,910	15.5%	3,914,000	957,694	24.5%	8.9	4,465,000	977,431	21.9%	6.4	5,467,000	770,222	14.1%	-1.4	6,470,000	811,920	12.5%	-3.0
COLORADO																			
CONNECTICUT																			
DELAWARE																			
DISTRICT OF COLUMBIA																			
FLORIDA	916,000	231,864	25.3%	1,055,000	270,888	25.7%	0.4					1,459,000	118,518	8.1%	-17.2	1,700,000	92,169	5.4%	-19.9

United States Presidential Primary Elections (continued)

Democratic Turnout for Election Years 1932–1948 (continued)

State	1932 Voting-age population	Turnout	%	1936 Voting-age population	Turnout	%	Difference from 1932	1940 Voting-age population	Turnout	%	Difference from 1932	1944 Voting-age population	Turnout	%	Difference from 1932	1948 Voting-age population	Turnout	%	Difference from 1932
GEORGIA	1,554,000	57,039	3.7%																
HAWAII																			
IDAHO																			
ILLINOIS	4,575,000	591,552	12.9%	4,851,000	1,416,822	29.2%	16.3	5,151,000	1,367,367	26.5%	13.6	5,424,000	47,904	0.9%	-12.0	5,699,000	19,948	0.4%	-12.6
INDIANA																			
IOWA																			
KANSAS																			
KENTUCKY																			
LOUISIANA																			
MAINE																			
MARYLAND				1,078,000	120,158	11.1%													
MASSACHUSETTS	2,283,000	209,919	9.2%	2,431,000	60,480	2.5%	-6.7	2,597,000	76,919	3.0%	-6.2	2,783,000	57,299	2.1%	-7.1	2,969,000	51,207	1.7%	-7.5
MICHIGAN																			
MINNESOTA																			
MISSISSIPPI																			
MISSOURI																			
MONTANA																			
NEBRASKA	790,000	143,966	18.2%	803,000	139,743	17.4%	-0.8	817,000	111,902	13.7%	-4.5	829,000	37,724	4.6%	-13.7	842,000	68,566	8.1%	-10.1
NEVADA																			
NEW HAMPSHIRE	266,000	15,401	5.8%	281,000	15,752	5.6%	-0.2	298,000	10,501	3.5%	-2.3	315,000	6,772	2.1%	-3.6	332,000	4,409	1.3%	-4.5
NEW JERSEY	2,270,000	8,453	0.4%	2,434,000	61,632	2.5%	2.2	2,624,000	34,278	1.3%	0.9	2,873,000	16,944	0.6%	0.2	3,123,000	1,189	0.0%	-0.3
NEW MEXICO																			
NEW YORK																			
NORTH CAROLINA																			
NORTH DAKOTA	340,000	84,000	24.7%																
OHIO	3,995,000	116,657	2.9%	4,204,000	547,316	13.0%	10.1	4,443,000	283,952	6.4%	3.5	4,753,000	164,915	3.5%	0.5	5,064,000	271,146	5.4%	2.4
OKLAHOMA																			
OREGON	605,000	61,761	10.2%	659,000	88,513	13.4%	3.2	724,000	126,098	17.4%	7.2	832,000	80,890	9.7%	-0.5	940,000	120,398	12.8%	2.6
PENNSYLVANIA	5,393,000	234,792	4.4%	5,718,000	755,660	13.2%	8.9	6,070,000	724,657	11.9%	7.6	6,390,000	323,430	5.1%	0.7	6,709,000	342,652	5.1%	0.8
RHODE ISLAND																			
SOUTH CAROLINA																			
SOUTH DAKOTA	364,000	35,370	9.7%	366,000	48,262	13.2%	3.5	369,000	27,636	7.5%	-2.2	380,000	14,141	3.7%	-6.0	392,000	19,209	4.9%	-4.8
TENNESSEE																			

United States Presidential Primary Elections (continued)

Democratic Turnout for Election Years 1932–1948 *(continued)*

State	1932 Voting-age population	Turnout	%	1936 Voting-age population	Turnout	%	Difference from 1932	1940 Voting-age population	Turnout	%	Difference from 1932	1944 Voting-age population	Turnout	%	Difference from 1932	1948 Voting-age population	Turnout	%	Difference from 1932
TEXAS																			
UTAH																			
VERMONT																			
VIRGINIA																			
WASHINGTON																			
WEST VIRGINIA	911,000	243,224	**26.7%**	980,000	296,961	**30.3%**	3.6	1,052,000	102,729	**9.8%**	-16.9	1,098,000	59,282	**5.4%**	-21.3	1,143,000	157,102	**13.7%**	-13.0
WISCONSIN	1,712,000	245,244	**14.3%**	1,826,000	401,927	**22.0%**	7.7	1,948,000	428,653	**22.0%**	7.7	2,047,000	52,646	**2.6%**	-11.8	2,147,000	30,321	**1.4%**	-12.9
WYOMING																			
Total	30,834,000	2,952,933	**9.6%**	30,600,000	5,181,808	**16.9%**	7.4	32,122,000	4,468,631	**13.9%**	4.3	36,290,000	1,867,609	**5.1%**	-4.4	37,530,000	1,990,236	**5.3%**	-4.3

*Percentage point difference between turnout in current year and initial year listed in chart. If data do not appear for a state in the initial year listed, the difference is calculated from the first year in which data do appear for that state.

STATE GUBERNATORIAL PRIMARY ELECTIONS

Election Years 1932–1948

State*	1932 Voting-age population	Turnout	%	1936 Voting-age population	Turnout	%	Difference from 1932**	1940 Voting-age population	Turnout	%	Difference from 1932	1944 Voting-age population	Turnout	%	Difference from 1932	1948 Voting-age population	Turnout	%	Difference from 1932
ALABAMA																			
ALASKA																			
ARIZONA																			
ARKANSAS																			
CALIFORNIA																			
COLORADO	595,000	231,012	38.8%	641,000	213,364	33.3%	-5.5	694,000	227,405	32.8%	-6.1	750,000	77,308	10.3%	-28.5	806,000	187,423	23.3%	-15.6
CONNECTICUT																			
DELAWARE																			
DISTRICT OF COLUMBIA																			
FLORIDA												1,459,000	415,797	28.5%		1,700,000	561,021	33.0%	4.5
GEORGIA																			
HAWAII																			
IDAHO	249,000	83,845	33.7%	277,000	95,644	34.5%	0.9	305,000	110,494	36.2%	2.6	321,000	71,365	22.2%	-11.4	338,000	65,968	19.5%	-14.2
ILLINOIS	4,575,000	2,132,018	46.6%	4,851,000	2,518,139	51.9%	5.3	5,151,000	2,433,108	47.2%	0.6	5,424,000	1,252,252	23.1%	-23.5	5,699,000	1,322,750	23.2%	-23.4
INDIANA																			
IOWA	1,502,000	497,466	33.1%	1,556,000	383,398	24.6%	-8.5	1,612,000	453,955	28.2%	-5.0	1,639,000	213,202	13.0%	-20.1	1,666,000	373,904	22.4%	-10.7
KANSAS	1,112,000	437,286	39.3%	1,129,000	386,394	34.2%	-5.1	1,149,000	372,022	32.4%	-6.9	1,183,000	180,544	15.3%	-24.1	1,218,000	272,963	22.4%	-16.9
KENTUCKY																			
LOUISIANA																			
MAINE																			
MARYLAND																			
MASSACHUSETTS																			
MICHIGAN																			
MINNESOTA	1,514,000	352,106	23.3%	1,622,000	517,063	31.9%	8.6												
MISSISSIPPI																			
MISSOURI	2,273,000	980,949	43.2%	2,370,000	1,035,082	43.7%	0.5	2,471,000	949,685	38.4%	-4.7	2,533,000	645,723	25.5%	-17.7	2,596,000	713,849	27.5%	-15.7
MONTANA	301,000	146,038	48.5%	319,000	155,781	48.8%	0.3	336,000	154,971	46.1%	-2.4	348,000	105,262	30.2%	-18.3	360,000	136,402	37.9%	-10.6
NEBRASKA																			
NEVADA																			
NEW HAMPSHIRE	266,000	81,491	30.6%	281,000	98,701	35.1%	4.5	298,000	76,062	25.5%	-5.1	315,000	63,672	20.2%	-10.4	332,000	66,566	20.1%	-10.6
NEW JERSEY								2,624,000	788,171	30.0%									
NEW MEXICO								265,000	127,278	48.0%		308,000	52,353	17.0%	-31.0	351,000	95,015	27.1%	-21.0
NEW YORK																			

State Gubernatorial Primary Elections (continued)

State Gubernatorial Primary Elections (continued)

Election Years 1932–1948 (continued)

State	1932			1936				1940				1944				1948			
	Voting-age population	Turnout	%	Voting-age population	Turnout	%	Difference from 1932	Voting-age population	Turnout	%	Difference from 1932	Voting-age population	Turnout	%	Difference from 1932	Voting-age population	Turnout	%	Difference from 1932
NORTH CAROLINA								1,935,000	479,413	24.8%									
NORTH DAKOTA	340,000	200,472	59.0%	347,000	222,245	64.0%	5.1	354,000	178,359	50.4%	-8.6	356,000	124,023	34.8%	-24.1	358,000	199,304	55.7%	-3.3
OHIO	3,995,000	1,044,105	26.1%	4,204,000	1,026,211	24.4%	-1.7	4,443,000	1,199,854	27.0%	0.9	4,753,000	803,336	16.9%	-9.2	5,064,000	1,155,513	22.8%	-3.3
OKLAHOMA																			
OREGON																			
PENNSYLVANIA																			
RHODE ISLAND																			
SOUTH CAROLINA																			
SOUTH DAKOTA	364,000	169,933	46.7%					369,000	160,659	43.5%	-3.1								
TENNESSEE												1,825,000	195,210	10.7%		1,933,000	536,529	27.8%	17.1
TEXAS																			
UTAH								300,000	121,536	40.5%		333,000	77,218	23.2%	-17.3	368,000	122,928	33.4%	-7.1
VERMONT	206,000	79,355	38.5%	210,000	61,306	29.2%	-9.3	215,000	64,096	29.8%	-8.7	221,000	38,189	17.3%	-21.2	227,000	74,960	33.0%	-5.5
VIRGINIA																			
WASHINGTON	951,000	403,231	42.4%	1,030,000	503,197	48.9%	6.5	1,126,000	537,191	47.7%	5.3	1,287,000	352,547	27.4%	-15.0	1,447,000	540,266	37.3%	-5.1
WEST VIRGINIA																			
WISCONSIN	1,712,000	899,558	52.5%	1,826,000	491,056	26.9%	-25.7	1,948,000	658,912	33.8%	-18.7	2,047,000	451,348	22.0%	-30.5	2,147,000	597,580	27.8%	-24.7
WYOMING	128,000	65,711	51.3%																
Total	20,083,000	7,804,576	38.9%	20,663,000	7,707,581	37.3%	-1.6	25,595,000	9,093,171	35.5%	-3.3	25,102,000	5,119,349	20.4%	-18.5	26,610,000	7,022,941	26.4%	-12.5

*Overall primary turnout reflects only states with primaries in both parties. To find single party primary results, see partisan primary charts.

**Percentage point difference between turnout in current year and initial year listed in chart. If data do not appear for a state in the initial year listed, the difference is calculated from the first year in which data do appear for that state.

STATE GUBERNATORIAL PRIMARY ELECTIONS

Republican Turnout for Election Years 1932–1948

State	1932 Voting-age population	Turnout	%	1936 Voting-age population	Turnout	%	Difference from 1932*	1940 Voting-age population	Turnout	%	Difference from 1932	1944 Voting-age population	Turnout	%	Difference from 1932	1948 Voting-age population	Turnout	%	Difference from 1932
ALABAMA																			
ALASKA																			
ARIZONA																			
ARKANSAS																			
CALIFORNIA																			
COLORADO	595,000	113,004	19.0%	641,000	77,323	12.1%	-6.9	694,000	95,521	13.8%	-5.2	750,000	43,227	5.8%	-13.2	806,000	81,267	10.1%	-8.9
CONNECTICUT																			
DELAWARE																			
DISTRICT OF COLUMBIA																			
FLORIDA												1,459,000	9,720	0.7%		1,700,000	16,886	1.0%	0.3
GEORGIA																			
HAWAII																			
IDAHO	249,000	43,644	17.5%	277,000	38,730	14.0%	-3.5	305,000	55,171	18.1%	0.6	321,000	39,849	12.4%	-5.1	338,000	41,911	12.4%	-5.1
ILLINOIS	4,575,000	1,315,245	28.7%	4,851,000	1,010,004	20.8%	-7.9	5,151,000	1,067,668	20.7%	-8.0	5,424,000	721,117	13.3%	-15.5	5,699,000	744,360	13.1%	-15.7
INDIANA																			
IOWA	1,502,000	400,239	26.6%	1,556,000	246,421	15.8%	-10.8	1,612,000	332,610	20.6%	-6.0	1,639,000	175,116	10.7%	-16.0	1,666,000	317,709	19.1%	-7.6
KANSAS	1,112,000	289,820	26.1%	1,129,000	232,516	20.6%	-5.5	1,149,000	252,709	22.0%	-4.1	1,183,000	143,886	12.2%	-13.9	1,218,000	210,707	17.3%	-8.8
KENTUCKY																			
LOUISIANA																			
MAINE																			
MARYLAND																			
MASSACHUSETTS																			
MICHIGAN																			
MINNESOTA	1,514,000	253,774	16.8%	1,622,000	202,011	12.5%	-4.3												
MISSISSIPPI																			
MISSOURI	2,273,000	361,613	15.9%	2,370,000	314,369	13.3%	-2.6	2,471,000	297,104	12.0%	-3.9	2,533,000	309,154	12.2%	-3.7	2,596,000	316,059	12.2%	-3.7
MONTANA	301,000	70,541	23.4%	319,000	39,989	12.5%	-10.9	336,000	49,652	14.8%	-8.7	348,000	45,132	13.0%	-10.5	360,000	57,327	15.9%	-7.5
NEBRASKA																			
NEVADA																			
NEW HAMPSHIRE	266,000	56,291	21.2%	281,000	74,277	26.4%	5.3	298,000	58,430	19.6%	-1.6	315,000	49,465	15.7%	-5.5	332,000	46,767	14.1%	-7.1
NEW JERSEY								2,624,000	531,163	20.2%									
NEW MEXICO								265,000	27,838	10.5%		308,000	15,969	5.2%	-5.3	351,000	24,345	6.9%	-3.6
NEW YORK																			

State Gubernatorial Primary Elections (continued)

State Gubernatorial Primary Elections (continued)

Republican Turnout for Election Years 1932–1948 (continued)

State	1932 Voting-age population	Turnout	%	1936 Voting-age population	Turnout	%	Difference from 1932	1940 Voting-age population	Turnout	%	Difference from 1932	1944 Voting-age population	Turnout	%	Difference from 1932	1948 Voting-age population	Turnout	%	Difference from 1932
NORTH CAROLINA								1,935,000	27,810	1.4%									
NORTH DAKOTA	340,000	174,406	51.3%	347,000	180,881	52.1%	0.8	354,000	143,490	40.5%	-10.8	356,000	110,340	31.0%	-20.3	358,000	176,581	49.3%	-2.0
OHIO	3,995,000	687,810	17.2%	4,204,000	485,390	11.5%	-5.7	4,443,000	612,610	13.8%	-3.4	4,753,000	475,686	10.0%	-7.2	5,064,000	660,238	13.0%	-4.2
OKLAHOMA																			
OREGON																			
PENNSYLVANIA																			
RHODE ISLAND																501,000	51,315	10.2%	
SOUTH CAROLINA																			
SOUTH DAKOTA	364,000	127,653	35.1%					369,000	108,369	29.4%	-5.7								
TENNESSEE												1,825,000	51,085	2.8%		1,933,000	111,905	5.8%	3.0
TEXAS																			
UTAH								300,000	42,983	14.3%		333,000	36,170	10.9%	-3.5	368,000	67,834	18.4%	4.1
VERMONT	206,000	75,416	36.6%	210,000	55,893	26.6%	-10.0	215,000	58,452	27.2%	-9.4	221,000	35,981	16.3%	-20.3	227,000	72,209	31.8%	-4.8
VIRGINIA																			
WASHINGTON	951,000	218,288	23.0%	1,030,000	100,498	9.8%	-13.2	1,126,000	183,181	16.3%	-6.7	1,287,000	254,355	19.8%	-3.2	1,447,000	256,571	17.7%	-5.2
WEST VIRGINIA																			
WISCONSIN	1,712,000	734,459	42.9%	1,826,000	166,155	9.1%	-33.8	1,948,000	366,654	18.8%	-24.1	2,047,000	312,588	15.3%	-27.6	2,147,000	476,898	22.2%	-20.7
WYOMING	128,000	40,614	31.7%																
Total	20,083,000	4,962,817	24.7%	20,663,000	3,224,457	15.6%	-9.1	25,595,000	4,311,415	16.8%	-7.9	25,102,000	2,828,840	11.3%	-13.4	27,111,000	3,730,889	13.8%	-10.9

Democratic Turnout for Election Years 1932–1948

State	1932 Voting-age population	Turnout	%	1936 Voting-age population	Turnout	%	Difference from 1932*	1940 Voting-age population	Turnout	%	Difference from 1932	1944 Voting-age population	Turnout	%	Difference from 1932	1948 Voting-age population	Turnout	%	Difference from 1932
ALABAMA																			
ALASKA																			
ARIZONA																			
ARKANSAS	994,000	253,586	25.5%	1,048,000	232,520	22.2%	-3.3	1,099,000	252,860	23.0%	-2.5	1,104,000	184,104	16.7%	-8.8	1,108,000	253,846	22.9%	-2.6
CALIFORNIA																			
COLORADO	595,000	118,008	19.8%	641,000	136,041	21.2%	1.4	694,000	131,884	19.0%	-0.8	750,000	34,081	4.5%	-15.3	806,000	106,156	13.2%	-6.7
CONNECTICUT																			
DELAWARE																			
DISTRICT OF COLUMBIA																			
FLORIDA	916,000	254,002	27.7%	1,055,000	311,372	29.5%	1.8	1,218,000	443,871	36.4%	8.7	1,459,000	406,077	27.8%	0.1	1,700,000	544,135	32.0%	4.3

State Gubernatorial Primary Elections (continued)

Democratic Turnout for Election Years 1932–1948 (continued)

State	1932 Voting-age population	Turnout	%	1936 Voting-age population	Turnout	%	Difference from 1932	1940 Voting-age population	Turnout	%	Difference from 1932	1944 Voting-age population	Turnout	%	Difference from 1932	1948 Voting-age population	Turnout	%	Difference from 1932
GEORGIA	1,554,000	249,918	16.1%	1,664,000	389,313	23.4%	7.3	1,789,000	355,068	19.8%	3.8					2,114,000	669,900	31.7%	15.6
HAWAII																			
IDAHO	249,000	40,201	16.1%	277,000	56,914	20.5%	4.4	305,000	55,323	18.1%	2.0	321,000	31,516	9.8%	-6.3	338,000	24,057	7.1%	-9.0
ILLINOIS	4,575,000	816,773	17.9%	4,851,000	1,508,135	31.1%	13.2	5,151,000	1,365,440	26.5%	8.7	5,424,000	531,135	9.8%	-8.1	5,699,000	578,390	10.1%	-7.7
INDIANA																			
IOWA	1,502,000	97,227	6.5%	1,556,000	135,272	8.7%	2.2	1,612,000	121,345	7.5%	1.1	1,030,000	38,086	2.3%	-4.1	1,666,000	56,195	3.4%	-3.1
KANSAS	1,112,000	147,281	13.2%	1,129,000	153,704	13.6%	0.4	1,149,000	119,190	10.4%	-2.9	1,183,000	36,494	3.1%	-10.2	1,218,000	61,614	5.1%	-8.2
KENTUCKY																			
LOUISIANA	1,170,000	378,503	32.4%	1,269,000	538,652	42.4%	10.1	1,375,000	546,128	39.7%	7.4	1,459,000	449,924	30.8%	-1.5	1,545,000	643,905	41.7%	9.3
MAINE																			
MARYLAND																			
MASSACHUSETTS																			
MICHIGAN																			
MINNESOTA	1,514,000	98,332	6.5%	1,622,000	124,404	7.7%	1.2												
MISSISSIPPI																			
MISSOURI	2,273,000	618,772	27.2%	2,370,000	720,713	30.4%	3.2	2,471,000	652,581	26.4%	-0.8	2,533,000	336,569	13.3%	-13.9	2,596,000	397,790	15.3%	-11.9
MONTANA	301,000	75,497	25.1%	319,000	115,792	36.3%	11.2	336,000	105,319	31.3%	6.3	348,000	60,130	17.3%	-7.8	360,000	79,075	22.0%	-3.1
NEBRASKA																			
NEVADA																			
NEW HAMPSHIRE	266,000	25,200	9.5%	281,000	24,424	8.7%	-0.8	298,000	17,632	5.9%	-3.6	315,000	14,207	4.5%	-5.0	332,000	19,799	6.0%	-3.5
NEW JERSEY								2,624,000	257,008	9.8%									
NEW MEXICO								265,000	99,440	37.5%		308,000	36,384	11.8%	-25.7	351,000	70,670	20.1%	-17.4
NEW YORK																			
NORTH CAROLINA	1,616,000	379,657	23.5%	1,769,000	510,258	28.8%	5.4	1,935,000	451,603	23.3%	-0.2	2,091,000	319,688	15.3%	-8.2	2,247,000	407,715	18.1%	-5.3
NORTH DAKOTA	340,000	26,066	7.7%	347,000	41,364	11.9%	4.3	354,000	34,869	9.9%	2.2	356,000	13,683	3.8%	-3.8	358,000	22,723	6.3%	-1.3
OHIO	3,995,000	356,295	8.9%	4,204,000	540,821	12.9%	3.9	4,443,000	587,244	13.2%	4.3	4,753,000	327,650	6.9%	-2.0	5,064,000	495,275	9.8%	0.9
OKLAHOMA																			
OREGON																			
PENNSYLVANIA																			
RHODE ISLAND																			
SOUTH CAROLINA																			
SOUTH DAKOTA	364,000	42,280	11.6%					369,000	52,290	14.2%	2.6								
TENNESSEE	1,476,000	281,385	19.1%	1,592,000	352,633	22.2%	3.1	1,717,000	284,549	16.6%	-2.5	1,825,000	144,125	7.9%	-11.2	1,933,000	424,624	22.0%	2.9

State Gubernatorial Primary Elections (continued)

Democratic Turnout for Election Years 1932–1948 (continued)

State	1932 Voting-age population	1932 Turnout	1932 %	1936 Voting-age population	1936 Turnout	1936 %	1936 Difference from 1932	1940 Voting-age population	1940 Turnout	1940 %	1940 Difference from 1932	1944 Voting-age population	1944 Turnout	1944 %	1944 Difference from 1932	1948 Voting-age population	1948 Turnout	1948 %	1948 Difference from 1932
TEXAS	3,056,000	919,012	30.1%	3,389,000	1,019,726	30.1%	0.0	3,752,000	1,183,664	31.5%	1.5	4,104,000	744,625	18.1%	-11.9	4,456,000	1,109,285	24.9%	-5.2
UTAH								300,000	78,553	26.2%		333,000	41,048	12.3%	-13.9	368,000	55,094	15.0%	-11.2
VERMONT	206,000	3,939	1.9%	210,000	5,413	2.6%	0.7	215,000	5,644	2.6%	0.7	221,000	2,208	1.0%	-0.9	227,000	2,751	1.2%	-0.7
VIRGINIA																			
WASHINGTON	951,000	184,943	19.4%	1,030,000	402,699	39.1%	19.6	1,126,000	354,010	31.4%	12.0	1,287,000	98,192	7.6%	-11.8	1,447,000	283,695	19.6%	0.2
WEST VIRGINIA																			
WISCONSIN	1,712,000	131,930	7.7%	1,826,000	146,767	8.0%	0.3	1,948,000	138,860	7.1%	-0.6	2,047,000	106,965	5.2%	-2.5	2,147,000	110,359	5.1%	-2.6
WYOMING	128,000	25,097	19.6%																
Total	30,865,000	5,523,904	17.9%	32,449,000	7,466,937	23.0%	5.1	36,545,000	7,694,375	21.1%	3.2	33,860,000	3,956,891	11.7%	-6.2	38,080,000	6,417,053	16.9%	-1.0

Other Turnout for Election Years 1932–1948

State	1932 Voting-age population	1932 Turnout	1932 %	1936 Voting-age population	1936 Turnout	1936 %	1936 Difference from 1932*	1940 Voting-age population	1940 Turnout	1940 %	1940 Difference from 1932	1944 Voting-age population	1944 Turnout	1944 %	1944 Difference from 1932	1948 Voting-age population	1948 Turnout	1948 %	1948 Difference from 1932
IOWA				1,556,000	1,705	0.1%													
KANSAS	1,112,000	185	0.0%	1,129,000	174	0.0%	0.0	1,149,000	123	0.0%	0.0	1,183,000	164	0.0%	0.0	1,218,000	642	0.1%	0.0
MINNESOTA				1,622,000	190,648	11.8%													
MISSOURI	2,273,000	564	0.0%																
WISCONSIN	1,712,000	33,169	1.9%	1,826,000	178,134	9.8%	7.8	1,948,000	153,398	7.9%	5.9	2,047,000	31,795	1.6%	-0.4	2,147,000	10,323	0.5%	-1.5

*Percentage point difference between turnout in current year and initial year listed in chart. If data do not appear for a state in the initial year listed, the difference is calculated from the first year in which data do appear for that state.

UNITED STATES SENATE PRIMARY ELECTIONS

Election Years 1932–1948

State*	1932 Voting-age population	1932 Turnout	1932 %	1936 Voting-age population	1936 Turnout	1936 %	1936 Difference from 1932**	1940 Voting-age population	1940 Turnout	1940 %	1940 Difference from 1932	1944 Voting-age population	1944 Turnout	1944 %	1944 Difference from 1932	1948 Voting-age population	1948 Turnout	1948 %	1948 Difference from 1932
ALABAMA																			
ALASKA																			
ARIZONA																			
ARKANSAS																			
CALIFORNIA	3,471,000	1,390,711	40.1%					4,465,000	1,763,565	39.5%	-0.6	5,467,000	1,650,569	30.2%	-9.9				
COLORADO	595,000	237,898	40.0%	641,000	211,469	33.0%	-7.0					750,000	72,493	9.7%	-30.3	806,000	209,949	26.0%	-13.9
CONNECTICUT																			
DELAWARE																			
DISTRICT OF COLUMBIA																			
FLORIDA																			
GEORGIA																			
HAWAII																			
IDAHO	249,000	88,955	35.7%	277,000	94,200	34.0%	-1.7	305,000	107,022	35.1%	-0.6	321,000	71,926	22.4%	-13.3				
ILLINOIS	4,575,000	1,738,224	38.0%	4,851,000	2,193,615	45.2%	7.2	5,151,000	2,345,439	45.5%	7.5	5,424,000	1,210,729	22.3%	-15.7	5,699,000	1,374,017	24.1%	-13.9
INDIANA																			
IOWA	1,502,000	549,008	36.6%	1,556,000	403,246	25.9%	-10.6					1,639,000	200,952	12.3%	-24.3	1,666,000	335,873	20.2%	-16.4
KANSAS	1,112,000	422,286	38.0%	1,129,000	415,438	36.8%	-1.2					1,183,000	194,767	16.5%	-21.5	1,218,000	274,578	22.5%	-15.4
KENTUCKY				1,549,000	643,513	41.5%													
LOUISIANA																			
MAINE																			
MARYLAND								1,171,000	354,193	30.2%		1,309,000	131,815	10.1%	-20.2				
MASSACHUSETTS																			
MICHIGAN																			
MINNESOTA				1,622,000	511,318	31.5%													
MISSISSIPPI																			
MISSOURI	2,273,000	952,754	41.9%					2,471,000	944,285	38.2%	-3.7	2,533,000	625,243	24.7%	-17.2				
MONTANA				319,000	149,125	46.7%		336,000	146,354	43.6%	-3.2					360,000	133,742	37.2%	-9.6
NEBRASKA																			
NEVADA												84,000	29,936	35.6%					
NEW HAMPSHIRE	266,000	70,995	26.7%	281,000	105,352	37.5%	10.8					315,000	60,388	19.2%	-7.5	332,000	63,774	19.2%	-7.5
NEW JERSEY	2,270,000	751,841	33.1%	2,434,000	897,887	36.9%	3.8	2,624,000	913,538	34.8%	1.7	2,873,000	453,862	15.8%	-17.3	3,123,000	555,067	17.8%	-15.3
NEW MEXICO								265,000	125,237	47.3%						351,000	90,383	25.8%	-21.5
NEW YORK																			

United States Senate Primary Elections (continued)

United States Senate Primary Elections (continued)

Election Years 1932–1948 (continued)

State	1932			1936				1940				1944				1948			
	Voting-age population	Turnout	%	Voting-age population	Turnout	%	Difference from 1932	Voting-age population	Turnout	%	Difference from 1932	Voting-age population	Turnout	%	Difference from 1932	Voting-age population	Turnout	%	Difference from 1932
NORTH CAROLINA																			
NORTH DAKOTA	340,000	223,420	65.7%					354,000	183,961	52.0%	-13.7	356,000	127,047	35.7%	-30.0				
OHIO	3,995,000	839,802	21.0%					4,443,000	1,016,449	22.9%	1.9	4,753,000	640,669	13.5%	-7.5				
OKLAHOMA	1,257,000	420,386	33.4%	1,295,000	580,741	44.8%	11.4					1,351,000	279,481	20.7%	-12.8	1,369,000	406,573	29.7%	-3.7
OREGON																			
PENNSYLVANIA								6,070,000	1,747,297	28.8%		6,390,000	876,879	13.7%	-15.1				
RHODE ISLAND																			
SOUTH CAROLINA																			
SOUTH DAKOTA	364,000	169,742	46.6%																
TENNESSEE																			
TEXAS																			
UTAH								300,000	119,029	39.7%									
VERMONT	206,000	72,667	35.3%					215,000	66,041	30.7%	-4.6	221,000	35,987	16.3%	-19.0				
VIRGINIA																			
WASHINGTON	951,000	376,647	39.6%					1,126,000	500,181	44.4%	4.8	1,287,000	340,231	26.4%	-13.2				
WEST VIRGINIA																			
WISCONSIN	1,712,000	830,109	48.5%					1,948,000	623,547	32.0%	-16.5	2,047,000	398,124	19.4%	-29.0				
WYOMING				138,000	66,136	47.9%		150,000	60,226	40.2%	-7.8					171,000	46,667	27.3%	-20.6
Total	25,138,000	9,135,445	36.3%	16,092,000	6,272,040	39.0%	2.6	31,394,000	11,016,364	35.1%	-1.3	38,303,000	7,401,098	19.3%	-17.0	15,095,000	3,490,623	23.1%	-13.2

*Overall primary turnout reflects only states with primaries in both parties. To find single party primary results, see partisan primary charts.

**Percentage point difference between turnout in current year and initial year listed in chart. If data do not appear for a state in the initial year listed, the difference is calculated from the first year in which data do appear for that state.

UNITED STATES SENATE PRIMARY ELECTIONS

Republican Turnout for Election Years 1932–1948

State	1932 Voting-age population	Turnout	%	1936 Voting-age population	Turnout	%	Difference from 1932*	1940 Voting-age population	Turnout	%	Difference from 1932	1944 Voting-age population	Turnout	%	Difference from 1932	1948 Voting-age population	Turnout	%	Difference from 1932
ALABAMA																			
ALASKA																			
ARIZONA																			
ARKANSAS																			
CALIFORNIA	3,471,000	866,225	25.0%					4,465,000	746,847	16.7%	-8.2	5,467,000	718,010	13.1%	-11.8				
COLORADO	595,000	113,259	19.0%	641,000	71,875	11.2%	-7.8					750,000	40,868	5.4%	-13.6	806,000	91,768	11.4%	-7.6
CONNECTICUT																			
DELAWARE																			
DISTRICT OF COLUMBIA																			
FLORIDA																			
GEORGIA																			
HAWAII																			
IDAHO	249,000	49,230	19.8%	277,000	41,941	15.1%	-4.6	305,000	53,958	17.7%	2.5	321,000	39,698	12.4%	-7.4				
ILLINOIS	4,575,000	1,067,446	23.3%	4,851,000	900,546	18.6%	-4.8	5,151,000	1,038,172	20.2%	-3.2	5,424,000	678,368	12.5%	10.8	5,699,000	776,300	13.6%	-9.7
INDIANA																			
IOWA	1,502,000	415,902	27.7%	1,556,000	260,204	16.7%	-11.0					1,639,000	156,431	9.5%	-18.1	1,666,000	270,617	16.2%	-11.4
KANSAS	1,112,000	285,010	25.6%	1,129,000	263,842	23.4%	-2.3					1,183,000	154,057	13.0%	-12.6	1,218,000	207,107	17.0%	-8.6
KENTUCKY				1,549,000	189,540	12.2%						1,743,000	82,486	4.7%	-7.5				
LOUISIANA																			
MAINE																			
MARYLAND								1,171,000	79,882	6.8%		1,309,000	27,193	2.1%	-4.7				
MASSACHUSETTS																			
MICHIGAN																			
MINNESOTA				1,622,000	203,708	12.6%													
MISSISSIPPI																			
MISSOURI	2,273,000	342,038	15.0%					2,471,000	287,784	11.6%	-3.4	2,533,000	298,008	11.8%	-3.3				
MONTANA				319,000	37,679	11.8%		336,000	42,728	12.7%	0.9					360,000	56,980	15.8%	4.0
NEBRASKA																			
NEVADA								69,000	9,877	14.3%		84,000	8,873	10.6%	-3.8				
NEW HAMPSHIRE	266,000	45,443	17.1%	281,000	81,118	28.9%	11.8					315,000	47,590	15.1%	-2.0	332,000	44,616	13.4%	-3.6
NEW JERSEY	2,270,000	514,079	22.6%	2,434,000	567,072	23.3%	0.7	2,624,000	588,246	22.4%	-0.9	2,873,000	271,192	9.4%	-13.2	3,123,000	402,666	12.9%	-9.8
NEW MEXICO								265,000	27,922	10.5%						351,000	21,184	6.0%	-4.5
NEW YORK																			

United States Senate Primary Elections (continued)

Republican Turnout for Election Years 1932–1948 (continued)

State	1932 Voting-age population	Turnout	%	1936 Voting-age population	Turnout	%	Difference from 1932	1940 Voting-age population	Turnout	%	Difference from 1932	1944 Voting-age population	Turnout	%	Difference from 1932	1948 Voting-age population	Turnout	%	Difference from 1932
NORTH CAROLINA																			
NORTH DAKOTA	340,000	197,241	58.0%					354,000	152,250	43.0%	-15.0	356,000	112,397	31.6%	-26.4				
OHIO	3,995,000	569,968	14.3%					4,443,000	573,941	12.9%	-1.3	4,753,000	392,722	8.3%	-6.0				
OKLAHOMA	1,257,000	74,666	5.9%	1,295,000	72,599	5.6%	-0.3					1,351,000	43,482	3.2%	-2.7	1,369,000	43,349	3.2%	-2.8
OREGON																			
PENNSYLVANIA								6,070,000	973,957	16.0%		6,390,000	603,486	9.4%	-6.6				
RHODE ISLAND																501,000	51,709	10.3%	
SOUTH CAROLINA																			
SOUTH DAKOTA	364,000	128,508	35.3%	366,000	95,248	26.0%	-9.3					380,000	64,012	16.8%	-18.5	392,000	77,617	19.8%	-15.5
TENNESSEE																			
TEXAS																			
UTAH								300,000	40,857	13.6%		333,000	35,601	10.7%	-2.9				
VERMONT	206,000	68,623	33.3%					215,000	60,668	28.2%	-5.1	221,000	33,751	15.3%	-18.0				
VIRGINIA																			
WASHINGTON	951,000	197,215	20.7%					1,126,000	233,913	20.8%	0.0	1,287,000	185,943	14.4%	-6.3				
WEST VIRGINIA																			
WISCONSIN	1,712,000	687,033	40.1%					1,948,000	349,935	18.0%	-22.2	2,047,000	291,193	14.2%	-25.9				
WYOMING				138,000	34,723	25.2%		150,000	32,065	21.4%	-3.8					171,000	23,129	13.5%	-11.6
Total	25,138,000	5,621,886	22.4%	16,458,000	2,820,095	17.1%	-5.2	31,463,000	5,293,002	16.8%	-5.5	40,759,000	4,285,361	10.5%	-11.9	15,988,000	2,067,042	12.9%	-9.4

Democratic Turnout for Election Years 1932–1948

State	1932 Voting-age population	Turnout	%	1936 Voting-age population	Turnout	%	Difference from 1932*	1940 Voting-age population	Turnout	%	Difference from 1932	1944 Voting-age population	Turnout	%	Difference from 1932	1948 Voting-age population	Turnout	%	Difference from 1932
ALABAMA				1,474,000	220,173	14.9%										1,716,000	296,772	17.3%	2.4
ALASKA																			
ARIZONA																			
ARKANSAS				1,048,000	234,249	22.4%													
CALIFORNIA	3,471,000	513,298	14.8%					4,465,000	1,007,926	22.6%	7.8	5,467,000	931,630	17.0%	2.3				
COLORADO	595,000	124,639	20.9%	641,000	139,594	21.8%	0.8					750,000	31,625	4.2%	-16.7	806,000	118,181	14.7%	-6.3
CONNECTICUT																			
DELAWARE																			
DISTRICT OF COLUMBIA																			
FLORIDA				1,055,000	129,917	12.3%		1,218,000	433,598	35.6%	23.3								

United States Senate Primary Elections *(continued)*

Democratic Turnout for Election Years 1932–1948 *(continued)*

State	1932 Voting-age population	Turnout	%	1936 Voting-age population	Turnout	%	Difference from 1932	1940 Voting-age population	Turnout	%	Difference from 1932	1944 Voting-age population	Turnout	%	Difference from 1932	1948 Voting-age population	Turnout	%	Difference from 1932
GEORGIA	1,554,000	281,938	**18.1%**	1,664,000	390,849	**23.5%**	5.3									2,114,000	703,048	**33.3%**	15.1
HAWAII																			
IDAHO	249,000	39,725	**16.0%**	277,000	52,259	**18.9%**	2.9	305,000	53,064	**17.4%**	-1.5	321,000	32,228	**10.0%**	-5.9				
ILLINOIS	4,575,000	670,778	**14.7%**	4,851,000	1,293,069	**26.7%**	12.0	5,151,000	1,307,267	**25.4%**	10.7	5,424,000	532,361	**9.8%**	-4.8	5,699,000	597,717	**10.5%**	-4.2
INDIANA																			
IOWA	1,502,000	133,106	**8.9%**	1,556,000	141,372	**9.1%**	0.2					1,639,000	44,521	**2.7%**	-6.1	1,666,000	65,256	**3.9%**	-4.9
KANSAS	1,112,000	137,087	**12.3%**	1,129,000	151,421	**13.4%**	1.1					1,183,000	40,568	**3.4%**	-8.9	1,218,000	66,898	**5.5%**	-6.8
KENTUCKY	1,463,000	187,420	**12.8%**	1,549,000	453,973	**29.3%**	16.5	1,643,000	222,906	**13.6%**	0.8					1,843,000	205,462	**11.1%**	-1.7
LOUISIANA				1,269,000	532,402	**42.0%**										1,545,000	403,752	**26.1%**	-15.8
MAINE																			
MARYLAND								1,171,000	274,311	**23.4%**		1,309,000	104,622	**8.0%**	-15.4				
MASSACHUSETTS																			
MICHIGAN																			
MINNESOTA				1,622,000	118,006	**7.3%**													
MISSISSIPPI								1,194,000	153,975	**12.9%**									
MISSOURI	2,273,000	610,716	**26.9%**					2,471,000	656,501	**26.6%**	-0.3	2,533,000	327,235	**12.9%**	-13.9				
MONTANA				319,000	111,446	**34.9%**		336,000	103,626	**30.8%**	-4.1					360,000	76,762	**21.3%**	-13.6
NEBRASKA																			
NEVADA												84,000	21,063	**25.1%**					
NEW HAMPSHIRE	266,000	25,552	**9.6%**	281,000	24,234	**8.6%**	-1.0					315,000	12,798	**4.1%**	-5.5	332,000	19,158	**5.8%**	-3.8
NEW JERSEY	2,270,000	237,762	**10.5%**	2,434,000	330,815	**13.6%**	3.1	2,624,000	325,292	**12.4%**	-1.2	2,873,000	182,670	**6.4%**	-4.1	3,123,000	152,401	**4.9%**	-5.6
NEW MEXICO								265,000	97,315	**36.7%**						351,000	69,199	**19.7%**	-17.0
NEW YORK																			
NORTH CAROLINA				1,769,000	457,733	**25.9%**										2,247,000	391,846	**17.4%**	-8.4
NORTH DAKOTA	340,000	26,179	**7.7%**					354,000	31,711	**9.0%**	1.3	356,000	14,650	**4.1%**	-3.6				
OHIO	3,995,000	269,834	**6.8%**					4,443,000	442,508	**10.0%**	3.2	4,753,000	247,947	**5.2%**	-1.5				
OKLAHOMA	1,257,000	345,720	**27.5%**	1,295,000	508,142	**39.2%**	11.7					1,351,000	235,999	**17.5%**	-10.0	1,369,000	363,224	**26.5%**	-1.0
OREGON																			
PENNSYLVANIA								6,070,000	773,340	**12.7%**		6,390,000	273,307	**4.3%**	-8.5				
RHODE ISLAND																			
SOUTH CAROLINA				924,000	282,919	**30.6%**										1,124,000	318,931	**28.4%**	-2.2
SOUTH DAKOTA	364,000	41,234	**11.3%**																
TENNESSEE								1,717,000	244,616	**14.2%**									

United States Senate Primary Elections (continued)

Democratic Turnout for Election Years 1932–1948 *(continued)*

State	1932			1936				1940				1944				1948			
	Voting-age population	Turnout	%	Voting-age population	Turnout	%	Difference from 1932	Voting-age population	Turnout	%	Difference from 1932	Voting-age population	Turnout	%	Difference from 1932	Voting-age population	Turnout	%	Difference from 1932
TEXAS								3,752,000	1,088,306	29.0%									
UTAH								300,000	78,172	26.1%									
VERMONT	206,000	4,044	2.0%					215,000	5,373	2.5%	0.5	221,000	2,236	1.0%	-1.0				
VIRGINIA																			
WASHINGTON	951,000	179,432	18.9%					1,126,000	266,268	23.6%	4.8	1,287,000	154,288	12.0%	-6.9				
WEST VIRGINIA																			
WISCONSIN	1,712,000	110,548	6.5%					1,948,000	128,920	6.6%	0.2	2,047,000	80,277	3.9%	-2.5				
WYOMING				138,000	31,413	22.8%		150,000	28,161	18.8%	-4.0					171,000	23,538	13.8%	-9.0
Total	28,155,000	3,939,012	14.0%	25,295,000	5,603,986	22.2%	8.2	40,918,000	7,723,156	18.9%	4.9	38,303,000	3,270,025	8.5%	-5.5	25,684,000	3,872,145	15.1%	1.1

Other Turnout for Election Years 1932–1948

State	1932			1936				1940				1944				1948			
	Voting-age population	Turnout	%	Voting-age population	Turnout	%	Difference from 1932*	Voting-age population	Turnout	%	Difference from 1932	Voting-age population	Turnout	%	Difference from 1932	Voting-age population	Turnout	%	Difference from 1932
CALIFORNIA	3,471,000	11,188	0.3%					4,465,000	8,792	0.2%	-0.1	5,467,000	929	0.0%	-0.3				
ILLINOIS																			
IOWA				1,556,000	1,670	0.1%													
KANSAS	1,112,000	189	0.0%	1,129,000	175	0.0%	0.0					1,183,000	142	0.0%	0.0	1,218,000	573	0.0%	0.0
MINNESOTA				1,622,000	189,604	11.7%													
PENNSYLVANIA												6,390,000	86	0.0%					
WISCONSIN	1,712,000	32,528	1.9%					1,948,000	144,692	7.4%	5.5	2,047,000	26,654	1.3%	-0.6				

*Percentage point difference between turnout in current year and initial year listed in chart. If data do not appear for a state in the initial year listed, the difference is calculated from the first year in which data do appear for that state.

Midterm Turnout Election Based on Highest Statewide Turnout, Election Years 1930–1946

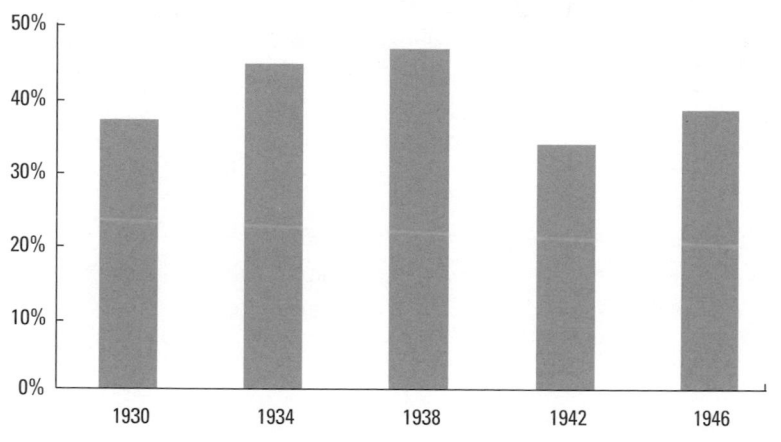

YEAR	VOTING-AGE POPULATION	TOTAL	%
1930	67,322,000	24,800,840	36.8%
1934	72,507,000	32,279,984	44.5%
1938	77,495,000	36,128,468	46.6%
1942	83,574,000	28,077,247	33.6%
1946	89,772,000	34,364,954	38.3%

Partisan Turnout Midterm Election Based on Aggregate House of Representatives Turnout, Election Years 1930–1946

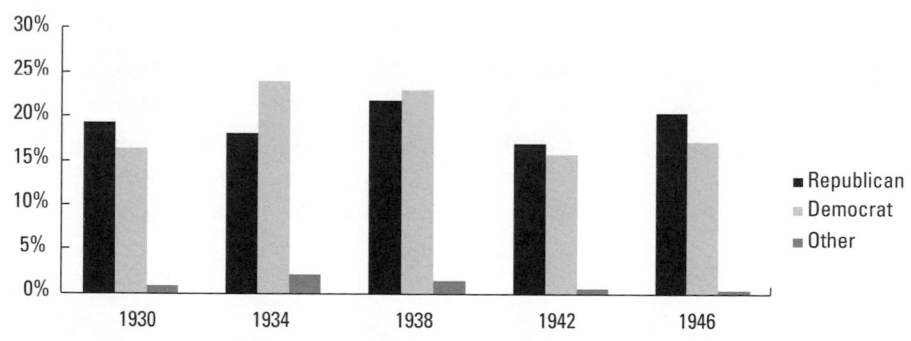

■ Republican
▨ Democrat
■ Other

YEAR	VOTING-AGE POPULATION	REPUBLICAN TURNOUT	%	DEMOCRAT TURNOUT	%	OTHER TURNOUT	%
1930	67,322,000	13,051,778	19.4%	11,087,763	16.5%	661,299	1.0%
1934	72,507,000	13,185,721	18.2%	17,457,671	24.1%	1,636,592	2.3%
1938	77,495,000	16,972,061	21.9%	17,927,403	23.1%	1,228,960	1.6%
1942	83,574,000	14,253,793	17.1%	13,239,668	15.8%	583,786	0.7%
1946	89,772,000	18,409,852	20.5%	15,496,218	17.3%	458,884	0.5%

STATE GUBERNATORIAL GENERAL ELECTIONS

Election Years 1930–1946

State	1930			1934				1938				1942				1946			
	Voting-age population	Turnout	%	Voting-age population	Turnout	%	Difference from 1930*	Voting-age population	Turnout	%	Difference from 1930	Voting-age population	Turnout	%	Difference from 1930	Voting-age population	Turnout	%	Difference from 1930
ALABAMA	1,356,000	250,779	18.5%	1,444,000	178,530	12.4%	-6.1	1,528,000	132,517	8.7%	-9.8	1,611,000	77,621	4.8%	-13.7	1,686,000	197,321	11.7%	-6.8
ALASKA																			
ARIZONA	168,000	95,106	56.6%	198,000	102,855	51.9%	-4.7	228,000	117,219	51.4%	-5.2	291,000	87,583	30.1%	-26.5	365,000	122,462	33.6%	-23.1
ARKANSAS	973,000	141,735	14.6%	1,029,000	138,870	13.5%	-1.1	1,082,000	139,266	12.9%	-1.7	1,102,000	98,871	9.0%	-5.6	1,106,000	152,162	13.8%	-0.8
CALIFORNIA	3,295,000	1,383,846	42.0%	3,756,000	2,329,722	62.0%	20.0	4,201,000	2,651,463	63.1%	21.1	5,070,000	2,234,490	44.1%	2.1	6,074,000	2,558,399	42.1%	0.1
COLORADO	577,000	326,206	56.5%	624,000	407,892	65.4%	8.8	672,000	457,123	68.0%	11.5	727,000	344,135	47.3%	-9.2	783,000	335,087	42.8%	-13.7
CONNECTICUT	810,000	430,902	53.2%	899,000	552,296	61.4%	8.2	985,000	632,083	64.2%	11.0	1,095,000	575,001	52.5%	-0.7	1,210,000	683,831	56.5%	3.3
DELAWARE																			
DISTRICT OF COLUMBIA																			
FLORIDA																			
GEORGIA				1,625,000	53,101	3.3%		1,735,000	70,919	4.1%	0.8	1,887,000	64,608	3.4%	0.2	2,050,000	145,403	7.1%	3.8
HAWAII																			
IDAHO	239,000	131,898	55.2%	267,000	170,973	64.0%	8.8	294,000	185,459	63.1%	7.9	314,000	144,086	45.9%	-9.3	331,000	181,364	54.8%	-0.4
ILLINOIS																			
INDIANA																			
IOWA	1,480,000	548,948	37.1%	1,536,000	906,167	59.0%	21.9	1,592,000	848,133	53.3%	16.2	1,628,000	698,939	42.9%	5.8	1,656,000	631,681	38.1%	1.1
KANSAS	1,106,000	621,235	56.2%	1,123,000	788,651	70.2%	14.1	1,139,000	756,698	66.4%	10.3	1,169,000	507,929	43.4%	-12.7	1,205,000	577,694	47.9%	-8.2
KENTUCKY																			
LOUISIANA																			
MAINE	442,000	149,482	33.8%	464,000	290,649	62.6%	28.8	486,000	297,238	61.2%	27.3	510,000	176,605	34.6%	0.8	533,000	179,951	33.8%	-0.1
MARYLAND	970,000	506,894	52.3%	1,052,000	512,614	48.7%	-3.5	1,129,000	564,540	50.0%	-2.3	1,254,000	377,692	30.1%	-22.1	1,394,000	489,836	35.1%	-17.1
MASSACHUSETTS	2,224,000	1,225,016	55.1%	2,379,000	1,483,229	62.3%	7.3	2,527,000	1,765,758	69.9%	14.8	2,709,000	1,401,718	51.7%	-3.3	2,895,000	1,683,452	58.2%	3.1
MICHIGAN	2,604,000	850,892	32.7%	2,836,000	1,258,925	44.4%	11.7	3,058,000	1,605,241	52.5%	19.8	3,371,000	1,226,774	36.4%	3.7	3,706,000	1,665,475	44.9%	12.3
MINNESOTA	1,471,000	797,385	54.2%	1,583,000	1,050,887	66.4%	12.2	1,690,000	1,132,876	67.0%	12.8	1,768,000	794,228	44.9%	-9.3	1,827,000	880,348	48.2%	-6.0
MISSISSIPPI																			
MISSOURI																			
MONTANA																			
NEBRASKA	785,000	436,776	55.6%	798,000	558,794	70.0%	14.4	812,000	496,943	61.2%	5.6	825,000	378,502	45.9%	-9.8	837,000	380,835	45.5%	-10.1
NEVADA	51,000	34,634	67.9%	58,000	42,806	73.8%	5.9	65,000	46,114	70.9%	3.0	78,000	40,669	52.1%	-15.8	92,000	49,902	54.2%	-13.7
NEW HAMPSHIRE	260,000	130,247	50.1%	276,000	177,022	64.1%	14.0	291,000	188,925	64.9%	14.8	308,000	160,548	52.1%	2.0	324,000	163,451	50.4%	0.4
NEW JERSEY				2,376,000	1,360,626	57.3%										3,024,000	1,393,338	46.1%	-11.2
NEW MEXICO	179,000	118,089	66.0%	215,000	151,055	70.3%	4.3	249,000	157,631	63.3%	-2.7	291,000	108,638	37.3%	-28.6	334,000	132,930	39.8%	-26.2
NEW YORK	6,904,000	3,153,923	45.7%	7,527,000	3,795,499	50.4%	4.7	8,124,000	4,746,584	58.4%	12.7	8,745,000	4,123,838	47.2%	1.5	9,339,000	4,964,552	53.2%	7.5

State Gubernatorial General Elections (continued)

Election Years 1930–1946 (continued)

State	1930			1934				1938				1942				1946			
	Voting-age population	Turnout	%	Voting-age population	Turnout	%	Difference from 1930	Voting-age population	Turnout	%	Difference from 1930	Voting-age population	Turnout	%	Difference from 1930	Voting-age population	Turnout	%	Difference from 1930
NORTH CAROLINA																			
NORTH DAKOTA	338,000	181,006	53.6%	345,000	274,419	79.5%	26.0	351,000	263,516	75.1%	21.5	355,000	175,967	49.6%	-4.0	357,000	169,391	47.4%	-6.1
OHIO	3,913,000	1,956,706	50.0%	4,130,000	2,187,026	53.0%	2.9	4,338,000	2,412,871	55.6%	5.6	4,631,000	1,796,570	38.8%	-11.2	4,941,000	2,303,750	46.6%	-3.4
OKLAHOMA	1,242,000	511,320	41.2%	1,281,000	628,331	49.1%	7.9	1,319,000	507,956	38.5%	-2.7	1,344,000	378,781	28.2%	-13.0	1,362,000	494,599	36.3%	-4.9
OREGON	584,000	248,795	42.6%	640,000	302,521	47.3%	4.7	693,000	372,863	53.8%	11.2	789,000	282,762	35.8%	-6.8	897,000	344,155	38.4%	-4.2
PENNSYLVANIA	5,264,000	2,131,846	40.5%	5,603,000	2,950,446	52.7%	12.2	5,928,000	2,812,567	47.4%	6.9	6,263,000	2,548,071	40.7%	0.2	6,583,000	3,123,991	47.5%	7.0
RHODE ISLAND	362,000	221,796	61.3%	389,000	247,730	63.7%	2.4	417,000	311,289	74.6%	13.4	451,000	238,148	52.8%	-8.5	486,000	275,341	56.7%	-4.6
SOUTH CAROLINA	827,000	17,790	2.2%	899,000	23,177	2.6%	0.4	968,000	49,292	5.1%	2.9	1,036,000	23,859	2.3%	0.2	1,100,000	26,520	2.4%	0.3
SOUTH DAKOTA	364,000	203,217	55.8%	365,000	293,895	80.5%	24.7	367,000	276,847	75.4%	19.6	376,000	178,492	47.5%	-8.4	387,000	162,292	41.9%	-13.9
TENNESSEE	1,430,000	240,235	16.8%	1,551,000	321,708	20.7%	3.9	1,668,000	293,598	17.6%	0.8	1,782,000	171,266	9.6%	-7.2	1,890,000	229,456	12.1%	-4.7
TEXAS	2,923,000	316,022	10.8%	3,270,000	444,558	13.6%	2.8	3,605,000	370,741	10.3%	-0.5	3,965,000	289,939	7.3%	-3.5	4,316,000	378,744	8.8%	-2.0
UTAH																			
VERMONT	204,000	74,440	36.5%	208,000	128,565	61.8%	25.3	213,000	112,502	52.8%	16.3	219,000	57,513	26.3%	-10.2	225,000	72,044	32.0%	-4.5
VIRGINIA																			
WASHINGTON																			
WEST VIRGINIA																			
WISCONSIN	1,666,000	606,825	36.4%	1,785,000	953,797	53.4%	17.0	1,899,000	981,560	51.7%	15.3	2,008,000	800,985	39.9%	3.5	2,108,000	1,040,444	49.4%	12.9
WYOMING	123,000	75,246	61.2%	135,000	93,780	69.5%	8.3	146,000	95,789	65.6%	4.4	156,000	77,167	49.5%	-11.7	166,000	81,353	49.0%	-12.2
Total	45,134,000	18,119,237	40.1%	52,666,000	25,161,116	47.8%	7.6	53,799,000	25,854,121	48.1%	7.9	58,128,000	20,641,995	35.5%	-4.6	65,589,000	26,271,557	40.1%	-0.1

*Percentage point difference between turnout in current year and initial year listed in chart. If data do not appear for a state in the initial year listed, the difference is calculated from the first year in which data do appear for that state.

STATE GUBERNATORIAL GENERAL ELECTIONS

Republican Turnout for Election Years 1930–1946

State	1930 Voting-age population	1930 Turnout	1930 %	1934 Voting-age population	1934 Turnout	1934 %	1934 Difference from 1930*	1938 Voting-age population	1938 Turnout	1938 %	1938 Difference from 1930	1942 Voting-age population	1942 Turnout	1942 %	1942 Difference from 1930	1946 Voting-age population	1946 Turnout	1946 %	1946 Difference from 1930
ALABAMA				1,444,000	22,621	1.6%		1,528,000	16,513	1.1%	-0.5	1,611,000	8,167	0.5%	-1.1	1,686,000	22,362	1.3%	-0.2
ALASKA																			
ARIZONA	168,000	46,231	27.5%	198,000	39,242	19.8%	-7.7	228,000	32,055	14.1%	-13.5	291,000	23,562	8.1%	-19.4	365,000	48,867	13.4%	-14.1
ARKANSAS	973,000	26,161	2.7%	1,029,000	13,083	1.3%	-1.4	1,082,000	6,729	0.6%	-2.1					1,106,000	24,133	2.2%	-0.5
CALIFORNIA	3,295,000	999,393	30.3%	3,756,000	1,138,620	30.3%	0.0	4,201,000	1,171,019	27.9%	-2.5	5,070,000	1,275,237	25.2%	-5.2	6,074,000	2,344,542	38.6%	8.3
COLORADO	577,000	124,164	21.5%	624,000	162,791	26.1%	4.6	672,000	255,159	38.0%	16.5	727,000	193,501	26.6%	5.1	783,000	160,483	20.5%	-1.0
CONNECTICUT	810,000	209,607	25.9%	899,000	249,397	27.7%	1.9	985,000	230,237	23.4%	-2.5	1,095,000	281,362	25.7%	-0.2	1,210,000	371,852	30.7%	4.9
DELAWARE																			
DISTRICT OF COLUMBIA																			
FLORIDA																			
GEORGIA																			
HAWAII																			
IDAHO	239,000	58,002	24.3%	267,000	75,659	28.3%	4.1	294,000	106,268	36.1%	11.9	314,000	72,260	23.0%	-1.3	331,000	102,233	30.9%	6.6
ILLINOIS																			
INDIANA																			
IOWA	1,480,000	364,024	24.6%	1,536,000	394,634	25.7%	1.1	1,592,000	446,959	28.1%	3.5	1,628,000	438,556	26.9%	2.3	1,656,000	362,592	21.9%	-2.7
KANSAS	1,106,000	216,920	19.6%	1,123,000	422,030	37.6%	18.0	1,139,000	393,989	34.6%	15.0	1,169,000	287,895	24.6%	5.0	1,205,000	309,064	25.6%	6.0
KENTUCKY																			
LOUISIANA																			
MAINE	442,000	82,310	18.6%	464,000	133,418	28.8%	10.1	486,000	157,206	32.3%	13.7	510,000	118,047	23.1%	4.5	533,000	110,327	20.7%	2.1
MARYLAND	970,000	216,864	22.4%	1,052,000	253,813	24.1%	1.8	1,129,000	242,095	21.4%	-0.9	1,254,000	179,204	14.3%	-8.1	1,394,000	221,752	15.9%	-6.4
MASSACHUSETTS	2,224,000	590,238	26.5%	2,379,000	627,413	26.4%	-0.2	2,527,000	941,465	37.3%	10.7	2,709,000	758,402	28.0%	1.5	2,895,000	911,152	31.5%	4.9
MICHIGAN	2,604,000	483,990	18.6%	2,836,000	659,743	23.3%	4.7	3,058,000	847,245	27.7%	9.1	3,371,000	645,335	19.1%	0.6	3,706,000	1,003,878	27.1%	8.5
MINNESOTA	1,471,000	289,528	19.7%	1,583,000	396,359	25.0%	5.4	1,690,000	678,839	40.2%	20.5	1,768,000	409,800	23.2%	3.5	1,827,000	519,067	28.4%	8.7
MISSISSIPPI																			
MISSOURI																			
MONTANA																			
NEBRASKA	785,000	215,615	27.5%	798,000	266,707	33.4%	6.0	812,000	201,898	24.9%	-2.6	825,000	283,271	34.3%	6.9	837,000	249,468	29.8%	2.3
NEVADA	51,000	18,442	36.2%	58,000	14,778	25.5%	-10.7	65,000	17,586	27.1%	-9.1	78,000	16,164	20.7%	-15.4	92,000	21,247	23.1%	-13.1
NEW HAMPSHIRE	260,000	75,518	29.0%	276,000	89,481	32.4%	3.4	291,000	107,841	37.1%	8.0	308,000	83,766	27.2%	-1.8	324,000	103,204	31.9%	2.8
NEW JERSEY				2,376,000	686,530	28.9%										3,024,000	807,378	26.7%	-2.2
NEW MEXICO	179,000	55,026	30.7%	215,000	71,899	33.4%	2.7	249,000	75,017	30.1%	-0.6	291,000	49,380	17.0%	-13.8	334,000	62,875	18.8%	-11.9
NEW YORK	6,904,000	1,045,341	15.1%	7,527,000	1,393,638	18.5%	3.4	8,124,000	2,326,892	28.6%	13.5	8,745,000	2,148,546	24.6%	9.4	9,339,000	2,825,633	30.3%	15.1

State Gubernatorial General Elections *(continued)*

Republican Turnout for Election Years 1930–1946 *(continued)*

State	1930 Voting-age population	Turnout	%	1934 Voting-age population	Turnout	%	Difference from 1930	1938 Voting-age population	Turnout	%	Difference from 1930	1942 Voting-age population	Turnout	%	Difference from 1930	1946 Voting-age population	Turnout	%	Difference from 1930
NORTH CAROLINA																			
NORTH DAKOTA	338,000	133,264	39.4%	345,000	127,954	37.1%	-2.3	351,000	125,246	35.7%	-3.7	355,000	74,577	21.0%	-18.4	357,000	116,672	32.7%	-6.7
OHIO	3,913,000	923,538	23.6%	4,130,000	1,052,851	25.5%	1.9	4,338,000	1,265,548	29.2%	5.6	4,631,000	1,086,937	23.5%	-0.1	4,941,000	1,166,550	23.6%	0.0
OKLAHOMA	1,242,000	208,575	16.8%	1,281,000	243,841	19.0%	2.2	1,319,000	148,861	11.3%	-5.5	1,344,000	180,454	13.4%	-3.4	1,362,000	227,426	16.7%	-0.1
OREGON	584,000	46,840	8.0%	640,000	86,923	13.0%	6.6	693,000	214,062	30.9%	22.9	789,000	220,188	27.9%	19.9	897,000	237,681	26.5%	18.5
PENNSYLVANIA	5,264,000	1,068,874	20.3%	5,603,000	1,410,138	25.2%	4.9	5,928,000	1,035,340	17.5%	-2.8	6,263,000	1,367,531	21.8%	1.5	6,683,000	1,828,462	27.8%	7.5
RHODE ISLAND	362,000	112,070	31.0%	389,000	105,139	27.0%	-3.9	417,000	167,003	40.0%	9.1	451,000	98,741	21.9%	-9.1	486,000	126,456	26.0%	-4.9
SOUTH CAROLINA								968,000	283	0.0%									
SOUTH DAKOTA	364,000	107,643	29.6%	365,000	119,477	32.7%	3.2	367,000	149,362	40.7%	11.1	376,000	109,786	29.2%	-0.4	387,000	108,998	28.2%	-1.4
TENNESSEE	1,430,000	85,598	6.0%					1,668,000	83,031	5.0%	-1.0	1,782,000	51,120	2.9%	-3.1	1,890,000	73,222	3.9%	-2.1
TEXAS	2,923,000	62,224	2.1%	3,270,000	13,703	0.4%	-1.7	3,605,000	11,309	0.3%	-1.8	3,965,000	9,204	0.2%	-1.9	4,316,000	33,231	0.8%	-1.4
UTAH																			
VERMONT	204,000	52,836	25.9%	208,000	73,620	35.4%	9.5	213,000	75,098	35.3%	9.4	219,000	44,804	20.5%	-5.4	225,000	57,849	25.7%	-0.2
VIRGINIA																			
WASHINGTON																			
WEST VIRGINIA																			
WISCONSIN	1,666,000	392,958	23.6%	1,785,000	172,980	9.7%	-13.9	1,899,000	543,675	28.6%	5.0	2,008,000	291,945	14.5%	-9.0	2,108,000	621,970	29.5%	5.9
WYOMING	123,000	38,058	30.9%	135,000	38,792	28.7%	-2.2	146,000	57,288	39.2%	8.3	156,000	37,568	24.1%	-6.9	166,000	38,333	23.1%	-7.8
Total	42,951,000	8,349,852	19.4%	48,591,000	10,557,274	21.7%	2.3	52,064,000	12,131,118	23.3%	3.9	54,103,000	10,845,310	20.0%	0.6	62,439,000	15,218,959	24.4%	4.9

Democratic Turnout for Election Years 1930–1946

State	1930 Voting-age population	Turnout	%	1934 Voting-age population	Turnout	%	Difference from 1930*	1938 Voting-age population	Turnout	%	Difference from 1930	1942 Voting-age population	Turnout	%	Difference from 1930	1946 Voting-age population	Turnout	%	Difference from 1930
ALABAMA	1,356,000	155,034	11.4%	1,444,000	155,197	10.7%	-0.7	1,528,000	115,761	7.6%	-3.9	1,611,000	69,048	4.3%	-7.1	1,686,000	174,959	10.4%	-1.1
ALASKA																			
ARIZONA	168,000	48,875	29.1%	198,000	61,355	31.0%	1.9	228,000	80,350	35.2%	6.1	291,000	63,484	21.8%	-7.3	365,000	73,595	20.2%	-8.9
ARKANSAS	973,000	115,574	11.9%	1,029,000	123,918	12.0%	0.2	1,082,000	120,563	11.1%	-0.7	1,102,000	98,871	9.0%	-2.9	1,106,000	128,029	11.6%	-0.3
CALIFORNIA	3,295,000	333,973	10.1%	3,756,000	879,537	23.4%	13.3	4,201,000	1,391,734	33.1%	23.0	5,070,000	932,995	18.4%	8.3				
COLORADO	577,000	197,067	34.2%	624,000	237,026	38.0%	3.8	672,000	199,562	29.7%	-4.5	727,000	149,402	20.6%	-13.6	783,000	174,604	22.3%	-11.9
CONNECTICUT	810,000	215,072	26.6%	899,000	257,996	28.7%	2.1	985,000	227,549	23.1%	-3.5	1,095,000	255,166	23.3%	-3.2	1,210,000	276,335	22.8%	-3.7
DELAWARE																			
DISTRICT OF COLUMBIA																			
FLORIDA																			

State Gubernatorial General Elections (continued)

State Gubernatorial General Elections *(continued)*

Democratic Turnout for Election Years 1930–1946 *(continued)*

State	1930 Voting-age population	Turnout	%	1934 Voting-age population	Turnout	%	Difference from 1930	1938 Voting-age population	Turnout	%	Difference from 1930	1942 Voting-age population	Turnout	%	Difference from 1930	1946 Voting-age population	Turnout	%	Difference from 1930
GEORGIA				1,625,000	53,101	3.3%		1,735,000	66,863	3.9%	0.6	1,887,000	62,220	3.3%	0.0	2,050,000	143,279	7.0%	3.7
HAWAII																			
IDAHO	239,000	73,896	30.9%	267,000	93,313	34.9%	4.0	294,000	77,697	26.4%	-4.5	314,000	71,826	22.9%	-8.0	331,000	79,131	23.9%	-7.0
ILLINOIS																			
INDIANA																			
IOWA	1,480,000	184,924	12.5%	1,536,000	468,921	30.5%	18.0	1,592,000	387,783	24.4%	11.9	1,628,000	258,310	15.9%	3.4	1,656,000	266,190	16.1%	3.6
KANSAS	1,106,000	217,171	19.6%	1,123,000	359,877	32.0%	12.4	1,139,000	341,271	30.0%	10.3	1,169,000	212,071	18.1%	-1.5	1,205,000	254,283	21.1%	1.5
KENTUCKY																			
LOUISIANA																			
MAINE	442,000	67,172	15.2%	464,000	156,917	33.8%	18.6	486,000	139,745	28.8%	13.6	510,000	58,558	11.5%	-3.7	533,000	69,624	13.1%	-2.1
MARYLAND	970,000	283,639	29.2%	1,052,000	247,664	23.5%	-5.7	1,129,000	308,372	27.3%	-1.9	1,254,000	198,488	15.8%	-13.4	1,394,000	268,084	19.2%	-10.0
MASSACHUSETTS	2,224,000	606,902	27.3%	2,379,000	736,463	31.0%	3.7	2,527,000	793,884	31.4%	4.1	2,709,000	630,265	23.3%	-4.0	2,895,000	762,743	26.3%	-0.9
MICHIGAN	2,604,000	357,664	13.7%	2,836,000	577,044	20.3%	6.6	3,058,000	753,752	24.6%	10.9	3,371,000	573,314	17.0%	3.3	3,706,000	644,540	17.4%	3.7
MINNESOTA	1,471,000	29,109	2.0%	1,583,000	176,928	11.2%	9.2	1,690,000	65,875	3.9%	1.9	1,768,000	75,151	4.3%	2.3	1,827,000	349,565	19.1%	17.2
MISSISSIPPI																			
MISSOURI																			
MONTANA																			
NEBRASKA	785,000	221,161	28.2%	798,000	284,095	35.6%	7.4	812,000	218,787	26.9%	-1.2	825,000	95,231	11.5%	-16.6	837,000	131,367	15.7%	-12.5
NEVADA	51,000	16,192	31.7%	58,000	23,088	39.8%	8.1	65,000	28,528	43.9%	12.1	78,000	24,505	31.4%	-0.3	92,000	28,655	31.1%	-0.6
NEW HAMPSHIRE	260,000	54,441	20.9%	276,000	87,019	31.5%	10.6	291,000	80,847	27.8%	6.8	308,000	76,782	24.9%	4.0	324,000	60,247	18.6%	-2.3
NEW JERSEY				2,376,000	674,096	28.4%										3,024,000	585,960	19.4%	-9.0
NEW MEXICO	179,000	62,789	35.1%	215,000	78,390	36.5%	1.4	249,000	82,344	33.1%	-2.0	291,000	59,258	20.4%	-14.7	334,000	70,055	21.0%	-14.1
NEW YORK	6,904,000	1,770,342	25.6%	7,527,000	2,201,729	29.3%	3.6	8,124,000	2,391,286	29.4%	3.8	8,745,000	1,501,039	17.2%	-8.5	9,339,000	2,138,482	22.9%	-2.7
NORTH CAROLINA																			
NORTH DAKOTA	338,000	41,988	12.4%	345,000	145,333	42.1%	29.7	351,000	138,270	39.4%	27.0	355,000	101,390	28.6%	16.1	357,000	52,719	14.8%	2.3
OHIO	3,913,000	1,033,168	26.4%	4,130,000	1,118,257	27.1%	0.7	4,338,000	1,147,323	26.4%	0.0	4,631,000	709,599	15.3%	-11.1	4,941,000	1,125,997	22.8%	-3.6
OKLAHOMA	1,242,000	301,921	24.3%	1,281,000	365,992	28.6%	4.3	1,319,000	355,740	27.0%	2.7	1,344,000	196,565	14.6%	-9.7	1,362,000	259,491	19.1%	-5.3
OREGON	584,000	62,434	10.7%	640,000	116,677	18.2%	7.5	693,000	158,744	22.9%	12.2	789,000	62,561	7.9%	-2.8	897,000	106,474	11.9%	1.2
PENNSYLVANIA	5,264,000	1,036,605	19.7%	5,603,000	1,476,467	26.4%	6.7	5,928,000	1,756,792	29.6%	9.9	6,263,000	1,149,897	18.4%	-1.3	6,583,000	1,270,947	19.3%	-0.4
RHODE ISLAND	362,000	108,558	30.0%	389,000	140,258	36.1%	6.1	417,000	129,603	31.1%	1.1	451,000	139,407	30.9%	0.9	486,000	148,885	30.6%	0.6
SOUTH CAROLINA	827,000	17,790	2.2%	899,000	23,177	2.6%	0.4	968,000	49,009	5.1%	2.9	1,036,000	23,859	2.3%	0.2	1,100,000	26,520	2.4%	0.3
SOUTH DAKOTA	364,000	93,954	25.8%	365,000	172,228	47.2%	21.4	367,000	127,485	34.7%	8.9	376,000	68,706	18.3%	-7.5	387,000	53,294	13.8%	-12.0
TENNESSEE	1,430,000	153,341	10.7%	1,551,000	198,743	12.8%	2.1	1,668,000	210,567	12.6%	1.9	1,782,000	120,146	6.7%	-4.0	1,890,000	149,937	7.9%	-2.8

State Gubernatorial General Elections (continued)

Democratic Turnout for Election Years 1930–1946 (continued)

State	1930 Voting-age population	Turnout	%	1934 Voting-age population	Turnout	%	Difference from 1930	1938 Voting-age population	Turnout	%	Difference from 1930	1942 Voting-age population	Turnout	%	Difference from 1930	1946 Voting-age population	Turnout	%	Difference from 1930
TEXAS	2,923,000	252,738	8.6%	3,270,000	428,734	13.1%	4.5	3,605,000	358,943	10.0%	1.3	3,965,000	280,735	7.1%	-1.6	4,316,000	345,513	8.0%	-0.6
UTAH																			
VERMONT	204,000	21,540	10.6%	208,000	54,159	26.0%	15.5	213,000	37,404	17.6%	7.0	219,000	12,708	5.8%	-4.8	225,000	14,096	6.3%	-4.3
VIRGINIA																			
WASHINGTON																			
WEST VIRGINIA																			
WISCONSIN	1,666,000	170,020	10.2%	1,785,000	359,467	20.1%	9.9	1,899,000	78,446	4.1%	-6.1	2,008,000	98,153	4.9%	-5.3	2,108,000	406,499	19.3%	9.1
WYOMING	123,000	37,188	30.2%	135,000	54,305	40.2%	10.0	146,000	38,501	26.4%	-3.9	156,000	39,599	25.4%	-4.9	166,000	43,020	25.9%	-4.3
Total	45,134,000	8,342,242	18.5%	52,666,000	12,587,471	23.9%	5.4	53,799,000	12,459,380	23.2%	4.7	58,128,000	8,469,309	14.6%	-3.9	59,515,000	10,683,119	18.0%	-0.5

Other Turnout for Election Years 1930–1946

State	1930 Voting-age population	Turnout	%	1934 Voting-age population	Turnout	%	Difference from 1930*	1938 Voting-age population	Turnout	%	Difference from 1930	1942 Voting-age population	Turnout	%	Difference from 1930	1946 Voting-age population	Turnout	%	Difference from 1930
ALABAMA	1,356,000	95,745	7.1%	1,444,000	712	0.0%	-7.0	1,528,000	243	0.0%	-7.0	1,611,000	406	0.0%	-7.0				
ALASKA																			
ARIZONA				198,000	2,258	1.1%		228,000	4,814	2.1%	1.0	291,000	537	0.2%	-1.0				
ARKANSAS				1,029,000	1,869	0.2%		1,082,000	11,974	1.1%	0.9								
CALIFORNIA	3,295,000	50,480	1.5%	3,756,000	311,565	8.3%	6.8	4,201,000	88,710	2.1%	0.6	5,070,000	26,258	0.5%	-1.0	6,074,000	213,857	3.5%	2.0
COLORADO	577,000	4,975	0.9%	624,000	8,075	1.3%	0.4	672,000	2,402	0.4%	-0.5	727,000	1,232	0.2%	-0.7				
CONNECTICUT	810,000	6,223	0.8%	899,000	44,903	5.0%	4.2	985,000	174,297	17.7%	16.9	1,095,000	38,473	3.5%	2.7	1,210,000	35,644	2.9%	2.2
DELAWARE																			
DISTRICT OF COLUMBIA																			
FLORIDA																			
GEORGIA								1,735,000	4,056	0.2%		1,887,000	2,388	0.1%	-0.1	2,050,000	2,124	0.1%	-0.1
HAWAII																			
IDAHO				267,000	2,001	0.7%		294,000	1,494	0.5%	-0.2								
ILLINOIS																			
INDIANA																			
IOWA				1,536,000	42,612	2.8%		1,592,000	13,391	0.8%	-1.9	1,628,000	2,073	0.1%	-2.6	1,656,000	2,899	0.2%	-2.6
KANSAS	1,106,000	187,144	16.9%	1,123,000	6,744	0.6%	-16.3	1,139,000	21,438	1.9%	-15.0	1,169,000	7,963	0.7%	-16.2	1,205,000	14,347	1.2%	-15.7
KENTUCKY																			
LOUISIANA																			
MAINE				464,000	314	0.1%		486,000	287	0.1%	0.0								

State Gubernatorial General Elections (continued)

State Gubernatorial General Elections (continued)

Other Turnout for Election Years 1930–1946 (continued)

State	1930 Voting-age population	Turnout	%	1934 Voting-age population	Turnout	%	Difference from 1930	1938 Voting-age population	Turnout	%	Difference from 1930	1942 Voting-age population	Turnout	%	Difference from 1930	1946 Voting-age population	Turnout	%	Difference from 1930
MARYLAND	970,000	6,391	0.7%	1,052,000	11,137	1.1%	0.4	1,129,000	14,073	1.2%	0.6								
MASSACHUSETTS	2,224,000	27,876	1.3%	2,379,000	119,353	5.0%	3.8	2,527,000	30,409	1.2%	-0.1	2,709,000	13,051	0.5%	-0.8	2,895,000	9,557	0.3%	-0.9
MICHIGAN	2,604,000	9,238	0.4%	2,836,000	22,138	0.8%	0.4	3,058,000	4,244	0.1%	-0.2	3,371,000	8,125	0.2%	-0.1	3,706,000	17,057	0.5%	0.1
MINNESOTA	1,471,000	478,748	32.5%	1,583,000	477,600	30.2%	-2.4	1,690,000	388,162	23.0%	-9.6	1,768,000	309,277	17.5%	-15.1	1,827,000	11,716	0.6%	-31.9
MISSISSIPPI																			
MISSOURI																			
MONTANA																			
NEBRASKA				798,000	7,992	1.0%		812,000	76,258	9.4%	8.4								
NEVADA				58,000	4,940	8.5%													
NEW HAMPSHIRE	260,000	288	0.1%	276,000	522	0.2%	0.1	291,000	237	0.1%	0.0								
NEW JERSEY																			
NEW MEXICO	179,000	274	0.2%	215,000	766	0.4%	0.2	249,000	270	0.1%	0.0								
NEW YORK	6,904,000	338,240	4.9%	7,527,000	200,132	2.7%	-2.2	8,124,000	28,406	0.3%	-4.5	8,745,000	474,253	5.4%	0.5	9,339,000	437	0.0%	-4.9
NORTH CAROLINA																			
NORTH DAKOTA	338,000	5,754	1.7%	345,000	1,132	0.3%	-1.4												
OHIO				4,130,000	15,918	0.4%						4,631,000	34	0.0%	-0.4	4,941,000	11,203	0.2%	-0.2
OKLAHOMA	1,242,000	824	0.1%	1,281,000	18,498	1.4%	1.4	1,319,000	3,355	0.3%	0.2	1,344,000	1,762	0.1%	0.1	1,362,000	7,682	0.6%	0.5
OREGON	584,000	139,521	23.9%	640,000	98,921	15.5%	-8.4	693,000	57	0.0%	-23.9	789,000	13	0.0%	-23.9				
PENNSYLVANIA	5,264,000	26,367	0.5%	5,603,000	63,841	1.1%	0.6	5,928,000	20,435	0.3%	-0.2	6,263,000	30,643	0.5%	0.0	6,583,000	24,585	0.4%	-0.1
RHODE ISLAND	362,000	1,168	0.3%	389,000	2,333	0.6%	0.3	417,000	14,683	3.5%	3.2								
SOUTH CAROLINA																			
SOUTH DAKOTA	364,000	1,620	0.4%	365,000	2,190	0.6%	0.2												
TENNESSEE	1,430,000	1,296	0.1%	1,551,000	122,965	7.9%	7.8									1,890,000	6,297	0.3%	0.2
TEXAS	2,923,000	1,060	0.0%	3,270,000	2,121	0.1%	0.0	3,605,000	489	0.0%	0.0								
UTAH																			
VERMONT	204,000	64	0.0%	208,000	786	0.4%	0.3					219,000	1	0.0%	0.0	225,000	99	0.0%	0.0
VIRGINIA																			
WASHINGTON																			
WEST VIRGINIA																			
WISCONSIN	1,666,000	43,847	2.6%	1,785,000	421,350	23.6%	21.0	1,899,000	359,439	18.9%	16.3	2,008,000	410,887	20.5%	17.8	2,108,000	11,975	0.6%	-2.1
WYOMING				135,000	683	0.5%													
Total	36,133,000	1,427,143	3.9%	47,766,000	2,016,371	4.2%	0.3	45,683,000	1,263,623	2.8%	-1.2	45,325,000	1,327,376	2.9%	-1.0	47,071,000	369,479	0.8%	-3.2

*Percentage point difference between turnout in current year and initial year listed in chart. If data do not appear for a state in the initial year listed, the difference is calculated from the first year in which data do appear for that state.

UNITED STATES SENATE GENERAL ELECTIONS
Election Years 1930–1946

State	1930 Voting-age population	1930 Turnout	1930 %	1934 Voting-age population	1934 Turnout	1934 %	1934 Difference from 1930*	1938 Voting-age population	1938 Turnout	1938 %	1938 Difference from 1930	1942 Voting-age population	1942 Turnout	1942 %	1942 Difference from 1930	1946 Voting-age population	1946 Turnout	1946 %	1946 Difference from 1930
ALABAMA	1,356,000	252,847	18.6%					1,528,000	131,298	8.6%	-10.1	1,611,000	69,216	4.3%	-14.4				
ALASKA																			
ARIZONA				198,000	93,920	47.4%		228,000	108,092	47.4%	0.0					365,000	116,239	31.8%	-15.6
ARKANSAS	973,000	141,806	14.6%					1,082,000	137,111	12.7%	-1.9	1,102,000	99,126	9.0%	-5.6				
CALIFORNIA				3,756,000	2,050,940	54.8%		4,201,000	2,522,142	60.0%	5.2					6,074,000	2,639,465	43.5%	-11.4
COLORADO	577,000	322,348	55.9%					672,000	451,229	67.1%	11.3	727,000	347,596	47.8%	0.1				
CONNECTICUT				899,000	548,525	61.0%		985,000	630,433	64.0%	3.0					1,210,000	682,921	56.4%	-4.6
DELAWARE	143,000	87,925	61.5%	156,000	99,166	63.6%	2.1					182,000	85,308	46.9%	-14.6	197,000	113,513	57.6%	-3.9
DISTRICT OF COLUMBIA																			
FLORIDA				1,006,000	131,780	13.1%		1,145,000	176,792	15.4%	2.3					1,605,000	198,645	12.4%	-0.7
GEORGIA	1,511,000	55,607	3.7%					1,735,000	70,339	4.1%	0.4	1,887,000	61,762	3.3%	-0.4				
HAWAII																			
IDAHO	239,000	131,100	54.9%					294,000	182,585	62.1%	7.3	314,000	142,342	45.3%	-9.5	331,000	180,152	54.4%	-0.4
ILLINOIS	4,466,000	2,237,104	50.1%					5,029,000	3,191,443	63.5%	13.4	5,316,000	2,973,229	55.9%	5.8				
INDIANA				2,065,000	1,474,612	71.4%		2,167,000	1,581,790	73.0%	1.6					2,429,000	1,347,434	55.5%	-15.9
IOWA	1,480,000	546,514	36.9%					1,592,000	831,839	52.3%	15.3	1,628,000	707,809	43.5%	6.6				
KANSAS	1,106,000	596,709	54.0%					1,139,000	746,405	65.5%	11.6	1,169,000	497,359	42.5%	-11.4				
KENTUCKY	1,429,000	645,928	45.2%					1,604,000	559,001	34.9%	10.4	1,704,000	392,039	23.0%	-22.2	1,804,000	613,481	34.0%	-11.2
LOUISIANA	1,131,000	130,560	11.5%					1,333,000	151,835	11.4%	-0.2	1,426,000	85,488	6.0%	-5.5				
MAINE	442,000	144,823	32.8%	464,000	278,768	60.1%	27.3					510,000	167,274	32.8%	0.0	533,000	175,014	32.8%	0.1
MARYLAND				1,052,000	471,112	44.8%		1,129,000	523,238	46.3%	1.6					1,394,000	472,232	33.9%	-10.9
MASSACHUSETTS	2,224,000	1,207,036	54.3%	2,379,000	1,435,932	60.4%	6.1					2,709,000	1,375,444	50.8%	-3.5	2,895,000	1,662,063	57.4%	3.1
MICHIGAN	2,604,000	812,007	31.2%	2,836,000	1,219,734	43.0%	11.8					3,371,000	1,189,966	35.3%	4.1	3,706,000	1,618,720	43.7%	12.5
MINNESOTA	1,471,000	780,629	53.1%	1,583,000	1,009,457	63.8%	10.7					1,768,000	758,452	42.9%	-10.2	1,827,000	878,731	48.1%	-5.0
MISSISSIPPI	1,037,000	33,953	3.3%	1,106,000	51,709	4.7%	1.4					1,197,000	51,355	4.3%	1.0	1,202,000	46,747	3.9%	0.6
MISSOURI				2,336,000	1,321,876	56.6%		2,432,000	1,248,277	51.3%	-5.3					2,571,000	1,086,241	42.2%	-14.3
MONTANA	295,000	176,161	59.7%	312,000	203,626	65.3%	5.5					344,000	170,514	49.6%	-10.1	355,000	190,566	53.7%	-6.0
NEBRASKA	785,000	434,797	55.4%	798,000	553,155	69.3%	13.9					825,000	380,169	46.1%	-9.3	837,000	382,959	45.8%	-9.6
NEVADA				58,000	42,755	73.7%		65,000	46,484	71.5%	-2.2	78,000	40,540	52.0%	-21.7	92,000	50,354	54.7%	-19.0
NEW HAMPSHIRE	260,000	124,791	48.0%					291,000	185,553	63.8%	15.8	308,000	162,257	52.7%	4.7				
NEW JERSEY	2,205,000	1,028,223	46.6%	2,376,000	1,357,409	57.1%	10.5	2,540,000	1,028,223	40.5%	-6.2	2,774,000	1,222,132	44.1%	-2.6	3,024,000	1,367,155	45.2%	-1.4
NEW MEXICO	179,000	118,309	66.1%	215,000	151,862	70.6%	4.5					291,000	107,005	36.8%	-29.3	334,000	133,282	39.9%	-26.2
NEW YORK				7,527,000	3,697,818	49.1%		8,124,000	4,583,059	56.4%	7.3					9,339,000	4,867,477	52.1%	3.0

United States Senate General Elections (continued)

United States Senate General Elections (continued)

Election Years 1930–1946 (continued)

State	1930 Voting-age population	1930 Turnout	1930 %	1934 Voting-age population	1934 Turnout	1934 %	1934 Difference from 1930	1938 Voting-age population	1938 Turnout	1938 %	1938 Difference from 1930	1942 Voting-age population	1942 Turnout	1942 %	1942 Difference from 1930	1946 Voting-age population	1946 Turnout	1946 %	1946 Difference from 1930
NORTH CAROLINA	1,555,000	535,054	34.4%					1,868,000	496,146	26.6%	-7.8	2,029,000	349,592	17.2%	-17.2				
NORTH DAKOTA				345,000	259,607	75.2%		351,000	263,158	75.0%	-0.3					357,000	165,382	46.3%	-28.9
OHIO	3,913,000	1,910,505	48.8%	4,130,000	2,128,843	51.5%		4,338,000	2,344,227	54.0%	2.5					4,941,000	2,237,269	45.3%	-6.3
OKLAHOMA	1,242,000	489,259	39.4%					1,319,000	471,066	35.7%	-3.7	1,344,000	372,365	27.7%	-11.7				
OREGON	584,000	236,371	40.5%					693,000	370,261	53.4%	13.0	789,000	278,704	35.3%	-5.2				
PENNSYLVANIA	5,264,000	1,985,524	37.7%	5,603,000	2,942,277	52.5%		5,928,000	3,815,019	64.4%	11.8					6,583,000	3,127,860	47.5%	-5.0
RHODE ISLAND	362,000	223,084	61.6%	389,000	246,313	63.3%	1.7					451,000	238,475	52.9%	-8.7	486,000	273,528	56.3%	-5.3
SOUTH CAROLINA	827,000	16,213	2.0%					968,000	46,261	4.8%	2.8	1,036,000	23,358	2.3%	0.3				
SOUTH DAKOTA	364,000	205,912	56.6%					367,000	279,877	76.3%	19.7	376,000	181,649	48.3%	-8.3				
TENNESSEE	1,430,000	216,013	15.1%	1,551,000	308,274	19.9%	4.8					1,782,000	159,522	9.0%	-6.2	1,890,000	218,710	11.6%	-3.5
TEXAS	2,923,000	306,715	10.5%	3,270,000	452,259	13.8%	3.3					3,965,000	274,658	6.9%	-3.6	4,316,000	380,550	8.8%	-1.7
UTAH				269,000	180,792	67.2%		289,000	183,424	63.5%	-3.7					354,000	197,399	55.8%	-11.4
VERMONT				208,000	131,552	63.2%		213,000	112,667	52.9%	-10.4					225,000	73,340	32.6%	-30.7
VIRGINIA	1,308,000	146,096	11.2%	1,413,000	144,750	10.2%	-0.9					1,682,000	87,152	5.2%	-6.0	1,869,000	252,863	13.5%	2.4
WASHINGTON				1,002,000	496,688	49.6%		1,081,000	593,292	54.9%	5.3					1,384,000	660,342	47.7%	-1.9
WEST VIRGINIA	884,000	553,187	62.6%	956,000	634,571	66.4%	3.8					1,079,000	463,861	43.0%	-19.6	1,125,000	542,768	48.2%	-14.3
WISCONSIN				1,785,000	921,926	51.6%		1,899,000	937,503	49.4%	-2.3					2,108,000	1,012,504	48.0%	-3.6
WYOMING	123,000	73,885	60.1%	135,000	95,026	70.4%	10.3					156,000	75,989	48.7%	-11.4	166,000	81,557	49.1%	-10.9
Total	46,692,000	16,906,995	36.2%	52,178,000	25,145,034	48.2%	12.0	58,629,000	29,000,069	49.5%	13.3	45,930,000	13,591,707	29.6%	-6.6	67,928,000	28,047,463	41.3%	5.1

*Percentage point difference between turnout in current year and initial year listed in chart. If data do not appear for a state in the initial year listed, the difference is calculated from the first year in which data do appear for that state.

UNITED STATES SENATE GENERAL ELECTIONS

Republican Turnout for Election Years 1930–1946

State	1930 Voting-age population	Turnout	%	1934 Voting-age population	Turnout	%	Difference from 1930*	1938 Voting-age population	Turnout	%	Difference from 1930	1942 Voting-age population	Turnout	%	Difference from 1930	1946 Voting-age population	Turnout	%	Difference from 1930
ALABAMA								1,528,000	17,885	1.2%									
ALASKA																			
ARIZONA				198,000	24,075	12.2%		228,000	25,378	11.1%	-1.0					365,000	35,022	9.6%	-2.6
ARKANSAS								1,082,000	14,240	1.3%									
CALIFORNIA				3,756,000	1,946,572	51.8%		4,201,000	1,126,240	26.8%	-25.0					6,074,000	1,428,067	23.5%	-28.3
COLORADO	577,000	137,487	23.8%					672,000	181,297	27.0%	3.2	727,000	170,970	23.5%	-0.3				
CONNECTICUT				899,000	247,623	27.5%		985,000	270,413	27.5%	-0.1					1,210,000	381,328	31.5%	4.0
DELAWARE	143,000	47,909	33.5%	156,000	52,829	33.9%	0.4					182,000	46,210	25.4%	-8.1	197,000	62,603	31.8%	-1.7
DISTRICT OF COLUMBIA																			
FLORIDA								1,145,000	31,035	2.7%						1,605,000	42,413	2.6%	-0.1
GEORGIA																			
HAWAII																			
IDAHO	239,000	94,938	39.7%					294,000	81,939	27.9%	-11.9	314,000	73,353	23.4%	16.4	331,000	105,523	31.9%	-7.8
ILLINOIS	4,466,000	786,954	17.6%					5,029,000	1,542,574	30.7%	13.1	5,316,000	1,582,887	29.8%	12.2				
INDIANA				2,065,000	700,103	33.9%		2,167,000	783,189	36.1%	2.2					2,429,000	739,809	30.5%	-3.4
IOWA	1,480,000	307,613	20.8%					1,592,000	410,983	25.8%	5.0	1,628,000	410,333	25.2%	4.4				
KANSAS	1,106,000	364,548	33.0%					1,139,000	419,532	36.8%	3.9	1,169,000	284,059	24.3%	-8.7				
KENTUCKY	1,429,000	309,180	21.6%					1,604,000	212,266	13.2%	-8.4	1,704,000	175,081	10.3%	-11.4	1,804,000	327,652	18.2%	-3.5
LOUISIANA																			
MAINE	442,000	88,262	20.0%	464,000	139,773	30.1%	10.2					510,000	111,520	21.9%	1.9	533,000	111,215	20.9%	0.9
MARYLAND				1,052,000	197,643	18.8%		1,129,000	153,253	13.6%	-5.2					1,394,000	235,000	16.9%	-1.9
MASSACHUSETTS	2,224,000	539,226	24.2%	2,379,000	536,692	22.6%	-1.7					2,709,000	721,239	26.6%	2.4	2,895,000	989,736	34.2%	9.9
MICHIGAN	2,604,000	634,577	24.4%	2,836,000	626,017	22.1%	-2.3					3,371,000	621,825	18.4%	-5.9	3,706,000	1,085,570	29.3%	4.9
MINNESOTA	1,471,000	293,626	20.0%	1,583,000	200,083	12.6%	-7.3					1,768,000	356,297	20.2%	0.2	1,827,000	517,775	28.3%	8.4
MISSISSIPPI																			
MISSOURI				2,336,000	524,954	22.5%		2,432,000	488,687	20.1%	-2.4					2,571,000	572,556	22.3%	-0.2
MONTANA	295,000	66,724	22.6%	312,000	59,900	19.2%	-3.4					344,000	82,461	24.0%	1.4	355,000	101,901	28.7%	6.1
NEBRASKA	785,000	247,118	31.5%	798,000	237,126	29.7%	-1.8					825,000	186,207	22.6%	-8.9	837,000	271,208	32.4%	0.9
NEVADA				58,000	14,273	24.6%		65,000	19,078	29.4%	4.7	78,000	16,735	21.5%	-3.2	92,000	27,801	30.2%	5.6
NEW HAMPSHIRE	260,000	72,225	27.8%					291,000	100,633	34.6%	6.8	308,000	88,601	28.8%	1.0				
NEW JERSEY	2,205,000	601,497	27.3%	2,376,000	554,483	23.3%	-3.9	2,540,000	601,497	23.7%	-3.6	2,774,000	648,855	23.4%	-3.9	3,024,000	799,808	26.4%	-0.8
NEW MEXICO	179,000	48,699	27.2%	215,000	76,228	35.5%	8.2					291,000	43,704	15.0%	-12.2	334,000	64,632	19.4%	-7.9
NEW YORK				7,527,000	1,363,440	18.1%		8,124,000	2,058,615	25.3%	7.2					9,339,000	2,559,365	27.4%	9.3

United States Senate General Elections (continued)

United States Senate General Elections (continued)

Republican Turnout for Election Years 1930–1946 (continued)

State	1930 Voting-age population	Turnout	%	1934 Voting-age population	Turnout	%	Difference from 1930	1938 Voting-age population	Turnout	%	Difference from 1930	1942 Voting-age population	Turnout	%	Difference from 1930	1946 Voting-age population	Turnout	%	Difference from 1930
NORTH CAROLINA	1,555,000	210,761	13.6%					1,868,000	179,461	9.6%	-3.9	2,029,000	119,165	5.9%	-7.7				
NORTH DAKOTA				345,000	151,205	43.8%		351,000	131,907	37.6%	-6.2					357,000	88,210	24.7%	-19.1
OHIO	3,913,000	863,944	22.1%	4,130,000	839,068	20.3%		4,338,000	1,257,412	29.0%	8.7					4,941,000	1,275,774	25.8%	5.5
OKLAHOMA	1,242,000	232,589	18.7%					1,319,000	159,734	12.1%	-6.6	1,344,000	204,163	15.2%	-3.5				
OREGON	584,000	137,231	23.5%					693,000	203,120	29.3%	5.8	789,000	214,755	27.2%	3.7				
PENNSYLVANIA	5,264,000	1,462,186	27.8%	5,603,000	1,366,877	24.4%		5,928,000	2,086,932	35.2%	10.8					6,583,000	1,853,458	28.2%	3.8
RHODE ISLAND	362,000	112,202	31.0%	389,000	105,545	27.1%	-3.9					451,000	100,236	22.2%	-8.8	486,000	122,780	25.3%	-5.7
SOUTH CAROLINA								968,000	508	0.1%									
SOUTH DAKOTA	364,000	99,595	27.4%					367,000	146,813	40.0%	12.6	376,000	106,704	28.4%	1.0				
TENNESSEE	1,430,000	58,550	4.1%	1,551,000	110,401	7.1%	3.0					1,782,000	34,324	1.9%	-2.2	1,890,000	57,237	3.0%	-1.1
TEXAS	2,923,000	39,053	1.3%	3,270,000	12,859	0.4%	-0.9					3,965,000	12,054	0.3%	-1.0	4,316,000	43,619	1.0%	-0.3
UTAH				269,000	82,154	30.5%		289,000	81,071	28.1%	-2.5					354,000	101,142	28.6%	-2.0
VERMONT				208,000	67,146	32.3%		213,000	73,990	34.7%	2.5					225,000	54,729	24.3%	-8.0
VIRGINIA				1,413,000	30,289	2.1%										1,869,000	77,005	4.1%	2.0
WASHINGTON				1,002,000	168,994	16.9%		1,081,000	220,204	20.4%	3.5					1,384,000	358,847	25.9%	9.1
WEST VIRGINIA	884,000	209,427	23.7%	956,000	281,756	29.5%	5.8					1,079,000	256,816	23.8%	0.1	1,125,000	269,617	24.0%	0.3
WISCONSIN				1,785,000	210,569	11.8%		1,899,000	454,021	23.9%	12.1					2,108,000	620,430	29.4%	17.6
WYOMING	123,000	43,626	35.5%	135,000	40,819	30.2%	-5.2					156,000	41,486	26.6%	-8.9	166,000	35,714	21.5%	-14.0
Total	38,549,000	8,109,747	21.0%	50,066,000	10,969,496	21.9%	0.9	55,561,000	13,533,907	24.4%	3.3	35,989,000	6,710,040	18.6%	-2.4	66,726,000	15,417,546	23.1%	2.1

Democratic Turnout for Election Years 1930–1946

State	1930 Voting-age population	Turnout	%	1934 Voting-age population	Turnout	%	Difference from 1930*	1938 Voting-age population	Turnout	%	Difference from 1930	1942 Voting-age population	Turnout	%	Difference from 1930	1946 Voting-age population	Turnout	%	Difference from 1930
ALABAMA	1,356,000	150,985	11.1%					1,528,000	113,413	7.4%	-3.7	1,611,000	69,212	4.3%	-6.8				
ALASKA																			
ARIZONA				198,000	67,648	34.2%		228,000	82,714	36.3%	2.1					365,000	80,415	22.0%	-12.1
ARKANSAS	973,000	141,806	14.6%					1,082,000	122,871	11.4%	-3.2	1,102,000	99,126	9.0%	-5.6				
CALIFORNIA								4,201,000	1,372,314	32.7%						6,074,000	1,167,161	19.2%	-13.5
COLORADO	577,000	180,028	31.2%					672,000	262,806	39.1%	7.9	727,000	174,612	24.0%	-7.2				
CONNECTICUT				899,000	265,552	29.5%		985,000	252,426	25.6%	-3.9					1,210,000	276,424	22.8%	-6.7
DELAWARE	143,000	39,881	27.9%	156,000	45,771	29.3%	1.5					182,000	38,322	21.1%	-6.8	197,000	50,910	25.8%	-2.0
DISTRICT OF COLUMBIA																			
FLORIDA				1,006,000	131,780	13.1%		1,145,000	145,757	12.7%	-0.4					1,605,000	156,232	9.7%	-3.4

United States Senate General Elections (continued)

Democratic Turnout for Election Years 1930–1946 (continued)

State	1930 Voting-age population	1930 Turnout	1930 %	1934 Voting-age population	1934 Turnout	1934 %	1934 Difference from 1930	1938 Voting-age population	1938 Turnout	1938 %	1938 Difference from 1930	1942 Voting-age population	1942 Turnout	1942 %	1942 Difference from 1930	1946 Voting-age population	1946 Turnout	1946 %	1946 Difference from 1930
GEORGIA	1,511,000	55,606	3.7%					1,735,000	66,897	3.9%	0.2	1,887,000	59,870	3.2%	-0.5				
HAWAII																			
IDAHO	239,000	36,162	15.1%					294,000	99,801	33.9%	18.8	314,000	68,989	22.0%	6.8	331,000	74,629	22.5%	7.4
ILLINOIS	4,466,000	1,432,216	32.1%					5,029,000	1,638,162	32.6%	0.5	5,316,000	1,380,011	26.0%	-6.1				
INDIANA				2,065,000	758,801	36.7%		2,167,000	788,386	36.4%	-0.4					2,429,000	584,288	24.1%	-12.7
IOWA	1,480,000	235,186	15.9%					1,592,000	413,788	26.0%	10.1	1,020,000	295,194	18.1%	2.2				
KANSAS	1,106,000	232,161	21.0%					1,139,000	326,774	28.7%	7.7	1,169,000	200,437	17.1%	-3.8				
KENTUCKY	1,429,000	336,748	23.6%					1,604,000	346,735	21.6%	-1.9	1,704,000	216,958	12.7%	-10.8	1,804,000	285,829	15.8%	-7.7
LOUISIANA	1,131,000	130,536	11.5%					1,333,000	151,585	11.4%	-0.2	1,426,000	85,488	6.0%	-5.5				
MAINE	442,000	56,561	12.8%	464,000	138,573	29.9%	17.1					510,000	55,754	10.9%	-1.9	533,000	63,799	12.0%	-0.8
MARYLAND				1,052,000	264,279	25.1%		1,129,000	357,245	31.6%	6.5					1,394,000	237,232	17.0%	-8.1
MASSACHUSETTS	2,224,000	651,939	29.3%	2,379,000	852,776	35.8%	6.5					2,709,000	641,042	23.7%	-5.7	2,895,000	660,200	22.8%	-6.5
MICHIGAN	2,604,000	169,757	6.5%	2,836,000	573,574	20.2%	13.7					3,371,000	561,505	16.7%	10.1	3,706,000	517,923	14.0%	7.5
MINNESOTA	1,471,000	282,018	19.2%	1,583,000	294,757	18.6%	-0.6					1,768,000	78,959	4.5%	-14.7	1,827,000	349,520	19.1%	0.0
MISSISSIPPI	1,037,000	33,953	3.3%	1,106,000	51,709	4.7%	1.4					1,197,000	51,355	4.3%	1.0	1,202,000	46,747	3.9%	0.6
MISSOURI				2,336,000	787,110	33.7%		2,432,000	757,587	31.2%	-2.5					2,571,000	511,544	19.9%	-13.8
MONTANA	295,000	106,274	36.0%	312,000	142,823	45.8%	9.8					344,000	83,673	24.3%	-11.7	355,000	86,476	24.4%	-11.7
NEBRASKA	785,000	172,795	22.0%	798,000	305,858	38.3%	16.3					825,000	83,763	10.2%	-11.9	837,000	111,751	13.4%	-8.7
NEVADA				58,000	27,581	47.6%		65,000	27,406	42.2%	-5.4	78,000	23,805	30.5%	-17.0	92,000	22,553	24.5%	-23.0
NEW HAMPSHIRE	260,000	52,284	20.1%					291,000	84,920	29.2%	9.1	308,000	73,656	23.9%	3.8				
NEW JERSEY	2,205,000	401,007	18.2%	2,376,000	785,971	33.1%	14.9	2,540,000	401,007	15.8%	-2.4	2,774,000	559,851	20.2%	2.0	3,024,000	548,458	18.1%	0.0
NEW MEXICO	179,000	69,356	38.7%	215,000	74,944	34.9%	-3.9					291,000	63,301	21.8%	-17.0	334,000	68,650	20.6%	-18.2
NEW YORK				7,527,000	2,046,377	27.2%		8,124,000	2,497,029	30.7%	3.5					9,339,000	2,308,112	24.7%	-2.5
NORTH CAROLINA	1,555,000	324,293	20.9%					1,868,000	316,685	17.0%	-3.9	2,029,000	230,427	11.4%	-9.5				
NORTH DAKOTA				345,000	104,477	30.3%		351,000	19,244	5.5%	-24.8					357,000	38,368	10.7%	-19.5
OHIO	3,913,000	1,046,561	26.7%	4,130,000	1,276,206	30.9%		4,338,000	1,086,815	25.1%	-5.8					4,941,000	947,610	19.2%	-11.7
OKLAHOMA	1,242,000	255,838	20.6%					1,319,000	307,936	23.3%	2.7	1,344,000	166,653	12.4%	-8.2				
OREGON	584,000	66,028	11.3%					693,000	167,135	24.1%	12.8	789,000	63,946	8.1%	-3.2				
PENNSYLVANIA	5,262,000	523,338	9.9%	5,603,000	1,494,001	26.7%		5,928,000	1,694,464	28.6%	1.9					6,583,000	1,245,338	18.9%	-7.7
RHODE ISLAND	362,000	109,687	30.3%	389,000	140,700	36.2%	5.9					451,000	138,239	30.7%	0.4	486,000	150,748	31.0%	0.7
SOUTH CAROLINA	827,000	16,213	2.0%					968,000	45,751	4.7%	2.8	1,036,000	23,356	2.3%	0.3				
SOUTH DAKOTA	364,000	106,317	29.2%					367,000	133,064	36.3%	7.0	376,000	74,945	19.9%	-9.3				
TENNESSEE	1,430,000	154,071	10.8%	1,551,000	195,430	12.6%	1.8					1,782,000	109,881	6.2%	-4.6	1,890,000	145,654	7.7%	-3.1

United States Senate General Elections (continued)

United States Senate General Elections (continued)

Democratic Turnout for Election Years 1930–1946 (continued)

State	1930 Voting-age population	Turnout	%	1934 Voting-age population	Turnout	%	Difference from 1930	1938 Voting-age population	Turnout	%	Difference from 1930	1942 Voting-age population	Turnout	%	Difference from 1930	1946 Voting-age population	Turnout	%	Difference from 1930
TEXAS	2,923,000	266,562	9.1%	3,270,000	437,254	13.4%	4.3					3,965,000	260,629	6.6%	-2.5	4,316,000	336,931	7.8%	-1.3
UTAH				269,000	95,931	35.7%		289,000	102,353	35.4%	-0.2					354,000	96,257	27.2%	-8.5
VERMONT				208,000	63,632	30.6%		213,000	38,673	18.2%	-12.4					225,000	18,594	8.3%	-22.3
VIRGINIA	1,308,000	112,002	8.6%	1,413,000	109,963	7.8%	-0.8					1,682,000	79,421	4.7%	-3.8	1,869,000	163,960	8.8%	0.2
WASHINGTON				1,002,000	302,606	30.2%		1,081,000	371,535	34.4%	4.2					1,384,000	298,683	21.6%	-8.6
WEST VIRGINIA	884,000	342,467	38.7%	956,000	349,882	36.6%	-2.1					1,079,000	207,045	19.2%	-19.6	1,125,000	273,151	24.3%	-14.5
WISCONSIN				1,785,000	223,438	12.5%		1,899,000	231,976	12.2%	-0.3					2,108,000	378,772	18.0%	5.5
WYOMING	123,000	30,259	24.6%	135,000	53,806	39.9%	15.3					156,000	34,503	22.1%	-2.5	166,000	45,843	27.6%	3.0
Total	46,690,000	8,320,895	17.8%	48,422,000	12,463,210	25.7%	7.9	58,629,000	14,825,254	25.3%	7.5	45,930,000	6,354,018	13.8%	-4.0	67,928,000	12,348,762	18.2%	0.4

Other Turnout for Election Years 1930–1946

State	1930 Voting-age population	Turnout	%	1934 Voting-age population	Turnout	%	Difference from 1930*	1938 Voting-age population	Turnout	%	Difference from 1930	1942 Voting-age population	Turnout	%	Difference from 1930	1946 Voting-age population	Turnout	%	Difference from 1930
ALABAMA	1,356,000	101,862	7.5%									1,611,000	4	0.0%	-7.5				
ALASKA																			
ARIZONA				198,000	2,197	1.1%										365,000	802	0.2%	-0.9
ARKANSAS																			
CALIFORNIA				3,756,000	112,368	3.0%		4,201,000	23,588	0.6%	-2.4					6,074,000	44,237	0.7%	-2.3
COLORADO	577,000	4,833	0.8%					672,000	7,126	1.1%	0.2	727,000	2,014	0.3%	-0.6				
CONNECTICUT				899,000	35,350	3.9%		985,000	107,594	10.9%	7.0					1,210,000	25,169	2.1%	-1.9
DELAWARE	143,000	135	0.1%	156,000	566	0.4%	0.3					182,000	776	0.4%	0.3				
DISTRICT OF COLUMBIA																			
FLORIDA																			
GEORGIA	1,511,000	1	0.0%					1,735,000	3,442	0.2%	0.2	1,887,000	1,892	0.1%	0.1				
HAWAII																			
IDAHO								294,000	845	0.3%									
ILLINOIS	4,466,000	17,934	0.4%					5,029,000	10,707	0.2%	-0.2	5,316,000	10,331	0.2%	-0.2				
INDIANA				2,065,000	15,708	0.8%		2,167,000	10,215	0.5%	-0.3					2,429,000	23,337	1.0%	0.2
IOWA	1,480,000	3,715	0.3%					1,592,000	7,068	0.4%	0.2	1,628,000	2,282	0.1%	-0.1				
KANSAS								1,139,000	99	0.0%		1,169,000	12,863	1.1%	1.1				
KENTUCKY																			
LOUISIANA	1,131,000	24	0.0%					1,333,000	250	0.0%	0.0								
MAINE				464,000	422	0.1%													

United States Senate General Elections (continued)

Other Turnout for Election Years 1930–1946 (continued)

State	1930 Voting-age population	Turnout	%	1934 Voting-age population	Turnout	%	Difference from 1930	1938 Voting-age population	Turnout	%	Difference from 1930	1942 Voting-age population	Turnout	%	Difference from 1930	1946 Voting-age population	Turnout	%	Difference from 1930
MARYLAND				1,052,000	9,190	0.9%		1,129,000	12,740	1.1%	0.3								
MASSACHUSETTS	2,224,000	15,871	0.7%	2,379,000	46,464	2.0%	1.2					2,709,000	13,163	0.5%	-0.2	2,895,000	12,127	0.4%	-0.3
MICHIGAN	2,604,000	7,673	0.3%	2,836,000	20,143	0.7%	0.4					3,371,000	6,546	0.2%	-0.1	3,706,000	15,227	0.4%	0.1
MINNESOTA	1,471,000	204,985	13.9%	1,583,000	514,617	32.5%	18.6					1,768,000	323,196	18.3%	4.3	1,827,000	11,436	0.6%	-13.3
MISSISSIPPI																			
MISSOURI				2,336,000	9,812	0.4%		2,432,000	2,003	0.1%	-0.3					2,671,000	2,141	0.1%	-0.3
MONTANA	295,000	3,163	1.1%	312,000	903	0.3%	-0.8					344,000	4,380	1.3%	0.2	355,000	2,189	0.6%	-0.5
NEBRASKA	785,000	14,884	1.9%	798,000	10,171	1.3%	-0.6					825,000	110,199	13.4%	11.5				
NEVADA				58,000	901	1.6%													
NEW HAMPSHIRE	260,000	282	0.1%																
NEW JERSEY	2,205,000	25,719	1.2%	2,376,000	16,955	0.7%	-0.5	2,540,000	25,719	1.0%	-0.2	2,774,000	13,426	0.5%	-0.7	3,024,000	18,889	0.6%	-0.5
NEW MEXICO	179,000	254	0.1%	215,000	690	0.3%	0.2												
NEW YORK				7,527,000	288,001	3.8%		8,124,000	27,415	0.3%	-3.5								
NORTH CAROLINA																			
NORTH DAKOTA				345,000	3,925	1.1%		351,000	112,007	31.9%	30.8					357,000	38,804	10.9%	9.7
OHIO				4,130,000	13,569	0.3%										4,941,000	13,885	0.3%	0.0
OKLAHOMA	1,242,000	832	0.1%					1,319,000	3,396	0.3%	0.2	1,344,000	1,549	0.1%	0.0				
OREGON	584,000	33,112	5.7%					693,000	6	0.0%	-5.7	789,000	3	0.0%	-5.7				
PENNSYLVANIA				5,603,000	81,399	1.5%		5,928,000	33,623	0.6%	-0.9					6,583,000	29,064	0.4%	-1.0
RHODE ISLAND	362,000	1,195	0.3%	389,000	68	0.0%	-0.3												
SOUTH CAROLINA								968,000	2	0.0%		1,036,000	2	0.0%	0.0				
SOUTH DAKOTA																			
TENNESSEE	1,430,000	3,392	0.2%	1,551,000	2,443	0.2%	-0.1					1,782,000	15,317	0.9%	0.6	1,890,000	15,819	0.8%	0.6
TEXAS	2,923,000	1,100	0.0%	3,270,000	2,146	0.1%	0.0					3,965,000	1,975	0.0%	0.0				
UTAH				269,000	2,707	1.0%													
VERMONT				208,000	774	0.4%		213,000	4	0.0%	-0.4					225,000	17	0.0%	-0.4
VIRGINIA	1,308,000	34,094	2.6%	1,413,000	4,498	0.3%	-2.3					1,682,000	7,731	0.5%	-2.1	1,869,000	11,898	0.6%	-2.0
WASHINGTON				1,002,000	25,088	2.5%		1,081,000	1,553	0.1%	-2.4					1,384,000	2,812	0.2%	-2.3
WEST VIRGINIA	884,000	1,293	0.1%	956,000	2,933	0.3%	0.2												
WISCONSIN				1,785,000	487,919	27.3%		1,899,000	251,506	13.2%	-14.1					2,108,000	13,302	0.6%	-26.7
WYOMING				135,000	401	0.3%													
Total	29,420,000	476,353	1.6%	50,066,000	1,712,328	3.4%	1.8	45,824,000	640,908	1.4%	-0.2	34,909,000	527,649	1.5%	-0.1	43,813,000	281,155	0.6%	-1.0

*Percentage point difference between turnout in current year and initial year listed in chart. If data do not appear for a state in the initial year listed, the difference is calculated from the first year in which data do appear for that state.

UNITED STATES HOUSE OF REPRESENTATIVES GENERAL ELECTIONS

Election Years 1930–1946

State	1930 Voting-age population	Turnout	%	1934 Voting-age population	Turnout	%	Difference from 1930*	1938 Voting-age population	Turnout	%	Difference from 1930	1942 Voting-age population	Turnout	%	Difference from 1930	1946 Voting-age population	Turnout	%	Difference from 1930
ALABAMA	1,356,000	198,433	14.6%	1,444,000	164,890	11.4%	-3.2	1,528,000	123,876	8.1%	-6.5	1,611,000	69,131	4.3%	-10.3	1,686,000	179,488	10.6%	-4.0
ALASKA																			
ARIZONA	168,000	52,342	31.2%	198,000	96,044	48.5%	17.4	228,000	104,058	45.6%	14.5	291,000	79,747	27.4%	-3.8	365,000	112,812	30.9%	-0.2
ARKANSAS	973,000	145,124	14.9%	1,029,000	139,895	13.6%	-1.3	1,082,000	143,956	13.3%	-1.6	1,102,000	98,346	8.9%	-6.0	1,106,000	151,333	13.7%	-1.2
CALIFORNIA	3,295,000	1,096,598	33.3%	3,756,000	2,028,658	54.0%	20.7	4,201,000	2,389,227	56.9%	23.6	5,070,000	1,899,109	37.5%	4.2	6,074,000	2,334,522	38.4%	5.2
COLORADO	577,000	314,643	54.5%	624,000	395,698	63.4%	8.9	672,000	449,537	66.9%	12.4	727,000	342,396	47.1%	-7.4	783,000	331,982	42.4%	-12.1
CONNECTICUT	810,000	428,179	52.9%	899,000	551,778	61.4%	8.5	985,000	630,132	64.0%	11.1	1,095,000	569,005	52.0%	-0.9	1,210,000	679,766	56.2%	3.3
DELAWARE	143,000	87,011	60.8%	156,000	98,857	63.4%	2.5	168,000	108,571	64.6%	3.8	182,000	84,726	46.6%	-14.3	197,000	112,621	57.2%	-3.7
DISTRICT OF COLUMBIA																			
FLORIDA	861,000	95,943	11.1%	1,006,000	125,263	12.5%	1.3	1,145,000	153,061	13.4%	2.2	1,364,000	91,120	6.7%	-4.5	1,605,000	186,763	11.6%	0.5
GEORGIA	1,511,000	56,458	3.7%	1,625,000	52,683	3.2%	-0.5	1,735,000	68,065	3.9%	0.2	1,887,000	61,879	3.3%	-0.5	2,050,000	161,539	7.9%	4.1
HAWAII																			
IDAHO	239,000	126,528	52.9%	267,000	163,376	61.2%	8.2	294,000	178,684	60.8%	7.8	314,000	139,287	44.4%	-8.6	331,000	178,758	54.0%	1.1
ILLINOIS	4,466,000	2,065,436	46.2%	4,753,000	2,750,326	57.9%	11.6	5,029,000	3,054,847	60.7%	14.5	5,316,000	2,887,632	54.3%	8.1	5,591,000	3,458,882	61.9%	15.6
INDIANA	1,960,000	1,214,387	62.0%	2,065,000	1,456,301	70.5%	8.6	2,167,000	1,572,649	72.6%	10.6	2,296,000	1,286,734	56.0%	-5.9	2,429,000	1,332,634	54.9%	-7.1
IOWA	1,480,000	530,250	35.8%	1,536,000	829,427	54.0%	18.2	1,592,000	802,637	50.4%	14.6	1,628,000	664,747	40.8%	5.0	1,656,000	593,031	35.8%	0.0
KANSAS	1,106,000	565,252	51.1%	1,123,000	757,234	67.4%	16.3	1,139,000	737,021	64.7%	13.6	1,169,000	493,692	42.2%	-8.9	1,205,000	554,860	46.0%	-5.1
KENTUCKY	1,429,000	548,582	38.4%	1,518,000	469,470	30.9%	-7.5	1,604,000	533,968	33.3%	-5.1	1,704,000	342,605	20.1%	-18.3	1,804,000	583,302	32.3%	-6.1
LOUISIANA	1,131,000	132,293	11.7%	1,234,000	186,112	15.1%	3.4	1,333,000	152,410	11.4%	-0.3	1,426,000	84,987	6.0%	-5.7	1,512,000	106,009	7.0%	-4.7
MAINE	442,000	143,541	32.5%	464,000	279,295	60.2%	27.7	486,000	281,619	57.9%	25.5	510,000	160,841	31.5%	-0.9	533,000	174,248	32.7%	0.2
MARYLAND	970,000	466,056	48.0%	1,052,000	455,630	43.3%	-4.7	1,129,000	486,473	43.1%	-5.0	1,254,000	337,436	26.9%	-21.1	1,394,000	444,955	31.9%	-16.1
MASSACHUSETTS	2,224,000	1,176,585	52.9%	2,379,000	1,381,425	58.1%	5.2	2,527,000	1,719,677	68.1%	15.1	2,709,000	1,327,242	49.0%	-3.9	2,895,000	1,617,314	55.9%	3.0
MICHIGAN	2,604,000	744,429	28.6%	2,836,000	1,212,526	42.8%	14.2	3,058,000	1,547,211	50.6%	22.0	3,371,000	1,170,694	34.7%	6.1	3,706,000	1,604,732	43.3%	14.7
MINNESOTA	1,471,000	759,763	51.6%	1,583,000	995,605	62.9%	11.2	1,690,000	1,070,927	63.4%	11.7	1,768,000	761,274	43.1%	-8.6	1,827,000	875,005	47.9%	-3.8
MISSISSIPPI	1,037,000	34,897	3.4%	1,106,000	57,327	5.2%	1.8	1,173,000	35,439	3.0%	-0.3	1,197,000	51,698	4.3%	1.0	1,202,000	49,957	4.2%	0.8
MISSOURI	2,234,000	947,063	42.4%	2,336,000	1,320,343	56.5%	14.1	2,432,000	1,245,034	51.2%	8.8	2,509,000	925,319	36.9%	-5.5	2,571,000	1,084,276	42.2%	-0.2
MONTANA	295,000	170,147	57.7%	312,000	196,739	63.1%	5.4	329,000	208,710	63.4%	5.8	344,000	169,508	49.3%	-8.4	355,000	190,088	53.5%	-4.1
NEBRASKA	785,000	415,601	52.9%	798,000	519,339	65.1%	12.1	812,000	477,715	58.8%	5.9	825,000	357,569	43.3%	-9.6	837,000	372,040	44.4%	-8.5
NEVADA	51,000	33,622	65.9%	58,000	41,683	71.9%	5.9	65,000	45,441	69.9%	4.0	78,000	39,389	50.5%	-15.4	92,000	49,046	53.3%	-12.6
NEW HAMPSHIRE	260,000	123,829	47.6%	276,000	170,213	61.7%	14.0	291,000	181,273	62.3%	14.7	308,000	156,215	50.7%	3.1	324,000	161,092	49.7%	2.1
NEW JERSEY	2,205,000	990,834	44.9%	2,376,000	1,328,407	55.9%	11.0	2,540,000	1,531,121	60.3%	15.3	2,774,000	1,203,455	43.4%	-1.6	3,024,000	1,381,993	45.7%	0.8
NEW MEXICO	179,000	117,398	65.6%	215,000	148,268	69.0%	3.4	249,000	155,157	62.3%	-3.3	291,000	105,947	36.4%	-29.2	334,000	126,939	38.0%	-27.6
NEW YORK	6,904,000	3,025,182	43.8%	7,527,000	3,613,973	48.0%	4.2	8,124,000	4,511,005	55.5%	11.7	8,745,000	3,953,789	45.2%	1.4	9,339,000	4,712,410	50.5%	6.6

United States House of Representatives General Elections *(continued)*

Election Years 1930–1946 *(continued)*

State	1930 Voting-age population	Turnout	%	1934 Voting-age population	Turnout	%	Difference from 1930	1938 Voting-age population	Turnout	%	Difference from 1930	1942 Voting-age population	Turnout	%	Difference from 1930	1946 Voting-age population	Turnout	%	Difference from 1930
NORTH CAROLINA	1,555,000	532,686	34.3%	1,715,000	493,703	28.8%	-5.5	1,868,000	479,267	25.7%	-8.6	2,029,000	314,827	15.5%	-18.7	2,185,000	452,222	20.7%	-13.6
NORTH DAKOTA	338,000	182,500	54.0%	345,000	276,680	80.2%	26.2	351,000	216,340	61.6%	7.6	355,000	182,380	51.4%	-2.6	357,000	144,394	40.4%	-13.5
OHIO	3,913,000	1,880,085	48.0%	4,130,000	1,981,089	48.0%	-0.1	4,338,000	2,246,898	51.8%	3.7	4,631,000	1,663,687	35.9%	-12.1	4,941,000	2,153,524	43.6%	-4.5
OKLAHOMA	1,242,000	456,730	36.8%	1,281,000	530,356	41.4%	4.6	1,319,000	445,824	33.8%	-3.0	1,344,000	351,727	26.2%	-10.6	1,362,000	492,141	36.1%	-0.6
OREGON	584,000	228,525	39.1%	640,000	285,389	44.6%	5.5	693,000	365,943	52.8%	13.7	789,000	276,425	35.0%	-4.1	897,000	334,670	37.3%	-1.8
PENNSYLVANIA	5,264,000	2,019,307	38.4%	5,603,000	2,926,338	52.2%	13.9	5,928,000	3,783,751	63.8%	25.5	6,263,000	2,489,357	39.7%	1.4	6,583,000	3,111,987	47.3%	8.9
RHODE ISLAND	362,000	219,322	60.6%	389,000	244,560	62.9%	2.3	417,000	300,220	72.0%	11.4	451,000	236,604	52.5%	-8.1	486,000	272,450	56.1%	-4.5
SOUTH CAROLINA	827,000	16,163	2.0%	899,000	22,156	2.5%	0.5	968,000	46,190	4.8%	2.8	1,036,000	23,356	2.3%	0.3	1,100,000	26,358	2.4%	0.4
SOUTH DAKOTA	364,000	170,073	46.7%	365,000	277,593	76.1%	29.3	367,000	274,425	74.8%	28.1	376,000	178,111	47.4%	0.6	387,000	162,804	42.1%	-4.7
TENNESSEE	1,430,000	197,870	13.8%	1,551,000	275,242	17.7%	3.9	1,668,000	264,404	15.9%	2.0	1,782,000	156,211	8.8%	-5.1	1,890,000	193,444	10.2%	-3.6
TEXAS	2,923,000	293,733	10.0%	3,270,000	445,883	13.6%	3.6	3,605,000	366,541	10.2%	0.1	3,965,000	278,419	7.0%	-3.0	4,316,000	349,659	8.1%	-1.9
UTAH	249,000	154,754	62.2%	269,000	170,977	66.9%	4.8	289,000	182,532	63.2%	1.0	320,000	150,493	47.0%	-15.1	354,000	196,672	55.6%	-6.6
VERMONT	204,000	72,822	35.7%	208,000	129,725	62.4%	26.7	213,000	114,473	53.7%	18.0	219,000	58,070	26.5%	-9.2	225,000	73,066	32.5%	-3.2
VIRGINIA	1,308,000	164,832	12.6%	1,413,000	148,124	10.5%	-2.1	1,513,000	126,043	8.3%	-4.3	1,682,000	90,014	5.4%	-7.3	1,869,000	253,855	13.6%	1.0
WASHINGTON	920,000	289,378	31.5%	1,002,000	479,365	47.8%	16.4	1,081,000	586,493	54.3%	22.8	1,224,000	428,186	35.0%	3.5	1,384,000	644,930	46.6%	15.1
WEST VIRGINIA	884,000	537,836	60.8%	956,000	619,947	64.8%	4.0	1,025,000	622,821	60.8%	-0.1	1,079,000	460,287	42.7%	-18.2	1,125,000	537,357	47.8%	-13.1
WISCONSIN	1,666,000	509,409	30.6%	1,785,000	885,689	49.6%	19.0	1,899,000	912,302	48.0%	17.5	2,008,000	748,717	37.3%	6.7	2,108,000	983,566	46.7%	16.1
WYOMING	123,000	68,409	55.6%	135,000	91,383	67.7%	12.1	146,000	94,500	64.7%	9.1	156,000	74,857	48.0%	-7.6	166,000	79,458	47.9%	-7.8
Total	67,322,000	24,800,840	36.8%	72,507,000	32,279,984	44.5%	7.7	77,495,000	36,128,468	46.6%	9.8	83,574,000	28,077,247	33.6%	-3.2	89,772,000	34,364,954	38.3%	1.4

*Percentage point difference between turnout in current year and initial year listed in chart. If data do not appear for a state in the initial year listed, the difference is calculated from the first year in which data do appear for that state.

UNITED STATES HOUSE OF REPRESENTATIVES GENERAL ELECTIONS

Republican Turnout for Election Years 1930–1946

State	1930 Voting-age population	1930 Turnout	1930 %	1934 Voting-age population	1934 Turnout	1934 %	1934 Difference from 1930*	1938 Voting-age population	1938 Turnout	1938 %	1938 Difference from 1930	1942 Voting-age population	1942 Turnout	1942 %	1942 Difference from 1930	1946 Voting-age population	1946 Turnout	1946 %	1946 Difference from 1930
ALABAMA	1,356,000	33,030	2.4%	1,444,000	10,200	0.7%	-1.7	1,528,000	9,573	0.6%	-1.8	1,611,000	378	0.0%	-2.4	1,686,000	14,105	0.8%	-1.6
ALASKA																			
ARIZONA				198,000	28,283	14.3%		228,000	20,502	9.0%	-5.3	291,000	23,015	7.9%	-6.4	365,000	37,033	10.1%	-4.1
ARKANSAS				1,029,000	10,158	1.0%										1,106,000	8,081	0.7%	-0.3
CALIFORNIA	3,295,000	964,690	29.3%	3,756,000	862,566	23.0%	-6.3	4,201,000	1,112,189	26.5%	-2.8	5,070,000	936,042	18.5%	-10.8	6,074,000	1,203,346	19.8%	-9.5
COLORADO	577,000	167,227	29.0%	624,000	140,202	22.5%	-6.5	672,000	181,829	27.1%	-1.9	727,000	199,365	27.4%	-1.6	783,000	184,429	23.6%	-5.4
CONNECTICUT	810,000	216,418	26.7%	899,000	249,146	27.7%	1.0	985,000	271,329	27.5%	0.8	1,095,000	283,280	25.9%	-0.8	1,210,000	377,972	31.2%	4.5
DELAWARE	143,000	48,493	33.9%	156,000	52,468	33.6%	-0.3	168,000	61,477	36.6%	2.7	182,000	45,376	24.9%	-9.0	197,000	63,516	32.2%	-1.7
DISTRICT OF COLUMBIA																			
FLORIDA	861,000	11,819	1.4%					1,145,000	6,705	0.6%	-0.8					1,605,000	35,640	2.2%	0.8
GEORGIA	1,511,000	1,526	0.1%	1,625,000	240	0.0%	-0.1												
HAWAII																			
IDAHO	239,000	80,869	33.8%	267,000	63,169	23.7%	-10.2	294,000	83,167	28.3%	-5.5	314,000	71,367	22.7%	-11.1	331,000	101,018	30.5%	-3.3
ILLINOIS	4,466,000	991,083	22.2%	4,753,000	1,201,373	25.3%	3.1	5,029,000	1,472,638	29.3%	7.1	5,316,000	1,481,419	27.9%	5.7	5,591,000	1,906,717	34.1%	11.9
INDIANA	1,960,000	572,082	29.2%	2,065,000	686,598	33.2%	4.1	2,167,000	799,455	36.9%	7.7	2,296,000	713,831	31.1%	1.9	2,429,000	725,622	29.9%	0.7
IOWA	1,480,000	321,706	21.7%	1,536,000	385,862	25.1%	3.4	1,592,000	445,939	28.0%	6.3	1,628,000	410,472	25.2%	3.5	1,656,000	364,992	22.0%	0.3
KANSAS	1,106,000	322,775	29.2%	1,123,000	380,037	33.8%	4.7	1,139,000	434,692	38.2%	9.0	1,169,000	299,015	25.6%	-3.6	1,205,000	328,642	27.3%	-1.9
KENTUCKY	1,429,000	253,903	17.8%	1,518,000	206,118	13.6%	-4.2	1,604,000	218,331	13.6%	-4.2	1,704,000	145,391	8.5%	-9.2	1,804,000	311,502	17.3%	-0.5
LOUISIANA	1,131,000	2,207	0.2%													1,512,000	5,651	0.4%	0.2
MAINE	442,000	88,070	19.9%	464,000	136,859	29.5%	9.6	486,000	164,845	33.9%	14.0	510,000	111,918	21.9%	2.0	533,000	110,388	20.7%	0.8
MARYLAND	970,000	189,815	19.6%	1,052,000	180,493	17.2%	-2.4	1,129,000	192,168	17.0%	-2.5	1,254,000	147,628	11.8%	-7.8	1,394,000	212,457	15.2%	-4.3
MASSACHUSETTS	2,224,000	629,821	28.3%	2,379,000	728,261	30.6%	2.3	2,527,000	925,853	36.6%	8.3	2,709,000	713,423	26.3%	-2.0	2,895,000	863,274	29.8%	1.5
MICHIGAN	2,604,000	567,205	21.8%	2,836,000	605,047	21.3%	-0.4	3,058,000	830,394	27.2%	5.4	3,371,000	629,679	18.7%	-3.1	3,706,000	975,363	26.3%	4.5
MINNESOTA	1,471,000	412,888	28.1%	1,583,000	323,189	20.4%	-7.7	1,690,000	537,465	31.8%	3.7	1,768,000	452,192	25.6%	-2.5	1,827,000	514,784	28.2%	0.1
MISSISSIPPI																			
MISSOURI	2,234,000	468,853	21.0%	2,336,000	515,268	22.1%	1.1	2,432,000	505,605	20.8%	-0.2	2,509,000	476,994	19.0%	-2.0	2,571,000	566,296	22.0%	1.0
MONTANA	295,000	82,736	28.0%	312,000	59,270	19.0%	-9.0	329,000	103,885	31.6%	3.5	344,000	73,654	21.4%	-6.6	355,000	93,265	26.3%	-1.8
NEBRASKA	785,000	199,196	25.4%	798,000	232,620	29.2%	3.8	812,000	247,996	30.5%	5.2	825,000	228,024	27.6%	2.3	837,000	248,724	29.7%	4.3
NEVADA	51,000	18,279	35.8%	58,000	11,992	20.7%	-15.2	65,000	15,285	23.5%	-12.3	78,000	18,289	23.4%	-12.4	92,000	28,859	31.4%	-4.5
NEW HAMPSHIRE	260,000	71,506	27.5%	276,000	84,131	30.5%	3.0	291,000	102,140	35.1%	7.6	308,000	85,999	27.9%	0.4	324,000	99,872	30.8%	3.3
NEW JERSEY	2,205,000	558,925	25.3%	2,376,000	638,424	26.9%	1.5	2,540,000	794,609	31.3%	5.9	2,774,000	648,359	23.4%	-2.0	3,024,000	815,261	27.0%	1.6
NEW MEXICO	179,000	51,655	28.9%	215,000	70,659	32.9%	4.0	249,000	64,281	25.8%	-3.0	291,000	43,627	15.0%	-13.9	334,000	60,519	18.1%	-10.7
NEW YORK	6,904,000	1,304,010	18.9%	7,527,000	1,417,271	18.8%	-0.1	8,124,000	2,011,567	24.8%	5.9	8,745,000	1,967,218	22.5%	3.6	9,339,000	2,540,526	27.2%	8.3

United States House of Representatives General Elections (continued)

Republican Turnout for Election Years 1930–1946 (continued)

State	1930 Voting-age population	Turnout	%	1934 Voting-age population	Turnout	%	Difference from 1930	1938 Voting-age population	Turnout	%	Difference from 1930	1942 Voting-age population	Turnout	%	Difference from 1930	1946 Voting-age population	Turnout	%	Difference from 1930
NORTH CAROLINA	1,555,000	198,310	12.8%	1,715,000	173,447	10.1%	-2.6	1,868,000	160,458	8.6%	-4.2	2,029,000	85,847	4.2%	-8.5	2,185,000	174,945	8.0%	-4.7
NORTH DAKOTA	338,000	126,678	37.5%	345,000	144,605	41.9%	4.4	351,000	153,106	43.6%	6.1	355,000	134,408	37.9%	0.4	357,000	103,205	28.9%	-8.6
OHIO	3,913,000	955,686	24.4%	4,130,000	905,233	21.9%	-2.5	4,338,000	1,177,982	27.2%	2.7	4,631,000	945,995	20.4%	-4.0	4,941,000	1,281,864	25.9%	1.5
OKLAHOMA	1,242,000	173,944	14.0%	1,281,000	162,991	12.7%	-1.3	1,319,000	137,733	10.4%	-3.6	1,344,000	147,764	11.0%	-3.0	1,362,000	204,163	15.0%	1.0
OREGON	584,000	116,642	20.0%	640,000	132,441	20.7%	0.7	603,000	214,571	31.0%	11.0	789,000	160,904	20.4%	0.4	897,000	217,005	24.2%	4.2
PENNSYLVANIA	5,264,000	1,429,675	27.2%	5,603,000	1,242,101	22.2%	-5.0	5,928,000	2,003,483	33.8%	6.6	6,263,000	1,360,664	21.7%	-5.4	6,583,000	1,795,552	27.3%	0.1
RHODE ISLAND	362,000	113,354	31.3%	389,000	104,278	26.8%	-4.5	417,000	161,328	38.7%	7.4	451,000	98,951	21.9%	-9.4	486,000	122,887	25.3%	-6.0
SOUTH CAROLINA				899,000	54	0.0%		968,000	310	0.0%	0.0					1,100,000	243	0.0%	0.0
SOUTH DAKOTA	364,000	106,429	29.2%	365,000	116,935	32.0%	2.8	367,000	153,140	41.7%	12.5	376,000	111,762	29.7%	0.5	387,000	104,731	27.1%	-2.2
TENNESSEE	1,430,000	72,347	5.1%	1,551,000	69,454	4.5%	-0.6	1,668,000	64,062	3.8%	-1.2	1,782,000	52,367	2.9%	-2.1	1,890,000	55,031	2.9%	-2.1
TEXAS	2,923,000	45,281	1.5%	3,270,000	5,643	0.2%	-1.4	3,605,000	3,815	0.1%	-1.4	3,965,000	2,949	0.1%	-1.5	4,316,000	16,998	0.4%	-1.2
UTAH	249,000	80,981	32.5%	269,000	63,885	23.7%	-8.8	289,000	71,149	24.6%	7.9	320,000	70,614	22.1%	-10.5	354,000	101,186	28.6%	-3.9
VERMONT	204,000	49,074	24.1%	208,000	73,809	35.5%	11.4	213,000	73,990	34.7%	10.7	219,000	40,751	18.6%	-5.4	225,000	46,985	20.9%	-3.2
VIRGINIA	1,308,000	55,634	4.3%	1,413,000	34,178	2.4%	-1.8	1,513,000	26,144	1.7%	-2.5	1,682,000	12,015	0.7%	-3.5	1,869,000	83,638	4.5%	0.2
WASHINGTON	920,000	205,937	22.4%	1,002,000	151,655	15.1%	-7.2	1,081,000	227,958	21.1%	-1.3	1,224,000	202,332	16.5%	-5.9	1,384,000	375,715	27.1%	4.8
WEST VIRGINIA	884,000	265,857	30.1%	956,000	272,011	28.5%	-1.6	1,025,000	279,487	27.3%	-2.8	1,079,000	231,738	21.5%	-8.6	1,125,000	268,051	23.8%	-6.2
WISCONSIN	1,666,000	380,272	22.8%	1,785,000	215,605	12.1%	-10.7	1,899,000	399,451	21.0%	-1.8	2,008,000	350,812	17.5%	-5.4	2,108,000	615,287	29.2%	6.4
WYOMING	123,000	44,890	36.5%	135,000	37,492	27.8%	-8.7	146,000	49,975	34.2%	-2.3	156,000	37,965	24.3%	-12.2	166,000	44,512	26.8%	-9.7
Total	64,317,000	13,051,778	20.3%	69,161,000	13,185,721	19.1%	-1.2	72,172,000	16,972,061	23.5%	3.2	75,562,000	14,253,793	18.9%	-1.4	86,520,000	18,409,852	21.3%	1.0

Democratic Turnout for Election Years 1930–1946

State	1930 Voting-age population	Turnout	%	1934 Voting-age population	Turnout	%	Difference from 1930*	1938 Voting-age population	Turnout	%	Difference from 1930	1942 Voting-age population	Turnout	%	Difference from 1930	1946 Voting-age population	Turnout	%	Difference from 1930
ALABAMA	1,356,000	165,403	12.2%	1,444,000	149,104	10.3%	-1.9	1,528,000	114,253	7.5%	-4.7	1,611,000	68,724	4.3%	-7.9	1,686,000	165,383	9.8%	-2.4
ALASKA																			
ARIZONA	168,000	52,342	31.2%	198,000	65,914	33.3%	2.1	228,000	83,556	36.6%	5.5	291,000	56,357	19.4%	-11.8	365,000	74,948	20.5%	-10.6
ARKANSAS	973,000	145,124	14.9%	1,029,000	129,124	12.5%	-2.4	1,082,000	143,956	13.3%	-1.6	1,102,000	98,346	8.9%	-6.0	1,106,000	143,252	13.0%	-2.0
CALIFORNIA	3,295,000	131,859	4.0%	3,756,000	993,600	26.5%	22.5	4,201,000	1,104,772	26.3%	22.3	5,070,000	906,614	17.9%	13.9	6,074,000	1,105,646	18.2%	14.2
COLORADO	577,000	146,192	25.3%	624,000	237,491	38.1%	12.7	672,000	265,297	39.5%	14.1	727,000	141,761	19.5%	-5.8	783,000	145,692	18.6%	-6.7
CONNECTICUT	810,000	208,202	25.7%	899,000	265,427	29.5%	3.8	985,000	250,013	25.4%	-0.3	1,095,000	257,941	23.6%	-2.1	1,210,000	277,872	23.0%	-2.7
DELAWARE	143,000	38,391	26.8%	156,000	45,927	29.4%	2.6	168,000	46,989	28.0%	1.1	182,000	38,791	21.3%	-5.5	197,000	49,105	24.9%	-1.9
DISTRICT OF COLUMBIA																			
FLORIDA	861,000	84,070	9.8%	1,006,000	125,263	12.5%	2.7	1,145,000	146,356	12.8%	3.0	1,364,000	91,120	6.7%	-3.1	1,605,000	151,123	9.4%	-0.3

United States House of Representatives General Elections (continued)

United States House of Representatives General Elections *(continued)*

Democratic Turnout for Election Years 1930–1946 *(continued)*

State	1930 Voting-age population	1930 Turnout	1930 %	1934 Voting-age population	1934 Turnout	1934 %	1934 Difference from 1930	1938 Voting-age population	1938 Turnout	1938 %	1938 Difference from 1930	1942 Voting-age population	1942 Turnout	1942 %	1942 Difference from 1930	1946 Voting-age population	1946 Turnout	1946 %	1946 Difference from 1930
GEORGIA	1,511,000	54,563	3.6%	1,625,000	52,443	3.2%	-0.4	1,735,000	67,252	3.9%	0.3	1,887,000	58,352	3.1%	-0.5	2,050,000	141,961	6.9%	3.3
HAWAII																			
IDAHO	239,000	45,659	19.1%	267,000	99,770	37.4%	18.3	294,000	95,517	32.5%	13.4	314,000	67,920	21.6%	2.5	331,000	77,740	23.5%	4.4
ILLINOIS	4,466,000	1,062,606	23.8%	4,753,000	1,507,714	31.7%	7.9	5,029,000	1,572,870	31.3%	7.5	5,316,000	1,395,053	26.2%	2.4	5,591,000	1,539,248	27.5%	3.7
INDIANA	1,960,000	641,406	32.7%	2,065,000	759,795	36.8%	4.1	2,167,000	773,121	35.7%	3.0	2,296,000	572,903	25.0%	-7.8	2,429,000	588,639	24.2%	-8.5
IOWA	1,480,000	207,686	14.0%	1,536,000	443,565	28.9%	14.8	1,592,000	352,516	22.1%	8.1	1,628,000	252,570	15.5%	1.5	1,656,000	228,039	13.8%	-0.3
KANSAS	1,106,000	242,477	21.9%	1,123,000	367,747	32.7%	10.8	1,139,000	302,329	26.5%	4.6	1,169,000	194,677	16.7%	-5.3	1,205,000	223,173	18.5%	-3.4
KENTUCKY	1,429,000	288,354	20.2%	1,518,000	254,584	16.8%	-3.4	1,604,000	315,427	19.7%	-0.5	1,704,000	193,181	11.3%	-8.8	1,804,000	271,480	15.0%	-5.1
LOUISIANA	1,131,000	130,086	11.5%	1,234,000	186,063	15.1%	3.6	1,333,000	152,366	11.4%	-0.1	1,426,000	84,987	6.0%	-5.5	1,512,000	100,357	6.6%	-4.9
MAINE	442,000	55,471	12.6%	464,000	142,436	30.7%	18.1	486,000	116,774	24.0%	11.5	510,000	48,923	9.6%	-3.0	533,000	63,860	12.0%	-0.6
MARYLAND	970,000	275,461	28.4%	1,052,000	267,204	25.4%	-3.0	1,129,000	290,342	25.7%	-2.7	1,254,000	189,808	15.1%	-13.3	1,394,000	232,498	16.7%	-11.7
MASSACHUSETTS	2,224,000	529,268	23.8%	2,379,000	641,349	27.0%	3.2	2,527,000	792,848	31.4%	7.6	2,709,000	611,714	22.6%	-1.2	2,895,000	744,765	25.7%	1.9
MICHIGAN	2,604,000	171,402	6.6%	2,836,000	590,620	20.8%	14.2	3,058,000	714,988	23.4%	16.8	3,371,000	534,682	15.9%	9.3	3,706,000	619,318	16.7%	10.1
MINNESOTA	1,471,000	65,490	4.5%	1,583,000	256,001	16.2%	11.7	1,690,000	190,036	11.2%	6.8	1,768,000	156,748	8.9%	4.4	1,827,000	357,758	19.6%	15.1
MISSISSIPPI	1,037,000	34,897	3.4%	1,106,000	57,327	5.2%	1.8	1,173,000	35,439	3.0%	-0.3	1,197,000	51,698	4.3%	1.0	1,202,000	49,957	4.2%	0.8
MISSOURI	2,234,000	477,467	21.4%	2,336,000	797,975	34.2%	12.8	2,432,000	737,851	30.3%	9.0	2,509,000	448,078	17.9%	-3.5	2,571,000	517,980	20.1%	-1.2
MONTANA	295,000	84,604	28.7%	312,000	135,733	43.5%	14.8	329,000	104,825	31.9%	3.2	344,000	93,243	27.1%	-1.6	355,000	95,982	27.0%	-1.6
NEBRASKA	785,000	216,405	27.6%	798,000	277,028	34.7%	7.1	812,000	218,116	26.9%	-0.7	825,000	122,279	14.8%	-12.7	837,000	118,800	14.2%	-13.4
NEVADA	51,000	15,343	30.1%	58,000	29,691	51.2%	21.1	65,000	30,156	46.4%	16.3	78,000	21,100	27.1%	-3.0	92,000	20,187	21.9%	-8.1
NEW HAMPSHIRE	260,000	52,323	20.1%	276,000	85,690	31.0%	10.9	291,000	79,133	27.2%	7.1	308,000	70,216	22.8%	2.7	324,000	61,220	18.9%	-1.2
NEW JERSEY	2,205,000	425,352	19.3%	2,376,000	676,016	28.5%	9.2	2,540,000	719,301	28.3%	9.0	2,774,000	546,134	19.7%	0.4	3,024,000	553,964	18.3%	-1.0
NEW MEXICO	179,000	65,444	36.6%	215,000	76,833	35.7%	-0.8	249,000	90,608	36.4%	-0.2	291,000	62,320	21.4%	-15.1	334,000	66,420	19.9%	-16.7
NEW YORK	6,904,000	1,532,413	22.2%	7,527,000	1,978,670	26.3%	4.1	8,124,000	2,363,463	29.1%	6.9	8,745,000	1,912,114	21.9%	-0.3	9,339,000	1,942,166	20.8%	-1.4
NORTH CAROLINA	1,555,000	334,376	21.5%	1,715,000	320,256	18.7%	-2.8	1,868,000	318,809	17.1%	-4.4	2,029,000	228,980	11.3%	-10.2	2,185,000	277,277	12.7%	-8.8
NORTH DAKOTA	338,000	52,284	15.5%	345,000	85,771	24.9%	9.4	351,000	55,125	15.7%	0.2	355,000	47,972	13.5%	-2.0	357,000	41,189	11.5%	-3.9
OHIO	3,913,000	910,931	23.3%	4,130,000	1,061,857	25.7%	2.4	4,338,000	1,068,916	24.6%	1.4	4,631,000	717,692	15.5%	-7.8	4,941,000	871,660	17.6%	-5.6
OKLAHOMA	1,242,000	282,620	22.8%	1,281,000	354,542	27.7%	4.9	1,319,000	306,241	23.2%	0.5	1,344,000	202,284	15.1%	-7.7	1,362,000	287,978	21.1%	-1.6
OREGON	584,000	107,187	18.4%	640,000	121,846	19.0%	0.7	693,000	151,364	21.8%	3.5	789,000	115,519	14.6%	-3.7	897,000	117,665	13.1%	-5.2
PENNSYLVANIA	5,264,000	567,838	10.8%	5,603,000	1,591,616	28.4%	17.6	5,928,000	1,756,157	29.6%	18.8	6,263,000	1,105,992	17.7%	6.9	6,583,000	1,306,723	19.8%	9.1
RHODE ISLAND	362,000	105,968	29.3%	389,000	140,281	36.1%	6.8	417,000	138,892	33.3%	4.0	451,000	137,653	30.5%	1.2	486,000	148,673	30.6%	1.3
SOUTH CAROLINA	827,000	16,163	2.0%	899,000	21,921	2.4%	0.5	968,000	45,806	4.7%	2.8	1,036,000	23,356	2.3%	0.3	1,100,000	26,067	2.4%	0.4
SOUTH DAKOTA	364,000	55,718	15.3%	365,000	158,399	43.4%	28.1	367,000	121,285	33.0%	17.7	376,000	66,349	17.6%	2.3	387,000	58,073	15.0%	-0.3
TENNESSEE	1,430,000	123,615	8.6%	1,551,000	194,312	12.5%	3.9	1,668,000	170,493	10.2%	1.6	1,782,000	102,143	5.7%	-2.9	1,890,000	126,530	6.7%	-1.9

United States House of Representatives General Elections *(continued)*

Democratic Turnout for Election Years 1930–1946 *(continued)*

State	1930 Voting-age population	1930 Turnout	1930 %	1934 Voting-age population	1934 Turnout	1934 %	1934 Difference from 1930	1938 Voting-age population	1938 Turnout	1938 %	1938 Difference from 1930	1942 Voting-age population	1942 Turnout	1942 %	1942 Difference from 1930	1946 Voting-age population	1946 Turnout	1946 %	1946 Difference from 1930
TEXAS	2,923,000	248,450	**8.5%**	3,270,000	439,685	**13.4%**	4.9	3,605,000	362,689	**10.1%**	1.6	3,965,000	275,101	**6.9%**	-1.6	4,316,000	332,661	**7.7%**	-0.8
UTAH	249,000	62,828	**25.2%**	269,000	113,975	**42.4%**	17.1	289,000	111,383	**38.5%**	13.3	320,000	79,879	**25.0%**	-0.3	354,000	95,486	**27.0%**	1.7
VERMONT	204,000	23,741	**11.6%**	208,000	54,967	**26.4%**	14.8	213,000	40,483	**19.0%**	7.4	219,000	17,304	**7.9%**	-3.7	225,000	26,056	**11.6%**	-0.1
VIRGINIA	1,308,000	109,013	**8.3%**	1,413,000	108,655	**7.7%**	-0.6	1,513,000	97,531	**6.4%**	-1.9	1,682,000	77,087	**4.6%**	-3.8	1,869,000	167,919	**9.0%**	0.7
WASHINGTON	920,000	75,424	**8.2%**	1,002,000	314,685	**31.4%**	23.2	1,081,000	357,686	**33.1%**	24.9	1,224,000	225,025	**18.4%**	10.2	1,384,000	267,187	**19.3%**	11.1
WEST VIRGINIA	884,000	271,979	**30.8%**	956,000	345,144	**36.1%**	5.3	1,025,000	343,334	**33.5%**	2.7	1,079,000	228,549	**21.2%**	-9.6	1,125,000	269,306	**23.9%**	-6.8
WISCONSIN	1,666,000	70,349	**4.2%**	1,785,000	280,367	**15.7%**	11.5	1,899,000	166,214	**8.8%**	4.5	2,008,000	203,537	**10.1%**	5.9	2,108,000	312,289	**14.8%**	10.6
WYOMING	123,000	23,519	**19.1%**	135,000	53,288	**39.5%**	20.4	146,000	44,525	**30.5%**	11.4	156,000	36,892	**23.6%**	4.5	166,000	34,946	**21.1%**	1.9
Total	67,322,000	11,087,763	**16.5%**	72,507,000	17,457,671	**24.1%**	7.6	77,495,000	17,927,403	**23.1%**	6.7	83,574,000	13,239,668	**15.8%**	-0.6	89,772,000	15,496,218	**17.3%**	0.8

Other Turnout for Election Years 1930–1946

State	1930 Voting-age population	1930 Turnout	1930 %	1934 Voting-age population	1934 Turnout	1934 %	1934 Difference from 1930*	1938 Voting-age population	1938 Turnout	1938 %	1938 Difference from 1930	1942 Voting-age population	1942 Turnout	1942 %	1942 Difference from 1930	1946 Voting-age population	1946 Turnout	1946 %	1946 Difference from 1930
ALABAMA				1,444,000	5,586	**0.4%**		1,528,000	50	**0.0%**	-0.4	1,611,000	29	**0.0%**	-0.4				
ALASKA																			
ARIZONA				198,000	1,847	**0.9%**						291,000	375	**0.1%**	-0.8	365,000	831	**0.2%**	-0.7
ARKANSAS				1,029,000	613	**0.1%**													
CALIFORNIA	3,295,000	49	**0.0%**	3,756,000	172,492	**4.6%**	4.6	4,201,000	172,266	**4.1%**	4.1	5,070,000	56,453	**1.1%**	1.1	6,074,000	25,530	**0.4%**	0.4
COLORADO	577,000	1,224	**0.2%**	624,000	18,005	**2.9%**	2.7	672,000	2,411	**0.4%**	0.1	727,000	1,270	**0.2%**	0.0	783,000	1,861	**0.2%**	0.0
CONNECTICUT	810,000	3,559	**0.4%**	899,000	37,205	**4.1%**	3.7	985,000	108,790	**11.0%**	10.6	1,095,000	27,784	**2.5%**	2.1	1,210,000	23,922	**2.0%**	1.5
DELAWARE	143,000	127	**0.1%**	156,000	462	**0.3%**	0.2	168,000	105	**0.1%**	0.0	182,000	559	**0.3%**	0.2				
DISTRICT OF COLUMBIA																			
FLORIDA	861,000	54	**0.0%**																
GEORGIA	1,511,000	369	**0.0%**					1,735,000	813	**0.0%**	0.0	1,887,000	3,527	**0.2%**	0.2	2,050,000	19,578	**1.0%**	0.9
HAWAII																			
IDAHO				267,000	437	**0.2%**													
ILLINOIS	4,466,000	11,747	**0.3%**	4,753,000	41,239	**0.9%**	0.6	5,029,000	9,339	**0.2%**	-0.1	5,316,000	11,160	**0.2%**	-0.1	5,591,000	12,917	**0.2%**	0.0
INDIANA	1,960,000	899	**0.0%**	2,065,000	9,908	**0.5%**	0.4	2,167,000	73	**0.0%**	0.0					2,429,000	18,373	**0.8%**	0.7
IOWA	1,480,000	858	**0.1%**					1,592,000	4,182	**0.3%**	0.2	1,628,000	1,705	**0.1%**	0.0				
KANSAS				1,123,000	9,450	**0.8%**										1,205,000	3,045	**0.3%**	-0.6
KENTUCKY	1,429,000	6,325	**0.4%**	1,518,000	8,768	**0.6%**	0.1	1,604,000	210	**0.0%**	-0.4	1,704,000	4,033	**0.2%**	-0.2	1,804,000	320	**0.0%**	-0.4
LOUISIANA				1,234,000	49	**0.0%**										1,512,000	1	**0.0%**	0.0
MAINE																			

United States House of Representatives General Elections (continued)

United States House of Representatives General Elections (continued)

Other Turnout for Election Years 1930–1946 (continued)

State	1930 Voting-age population	Turnout	%	1934 Voting-age population	Turnout	%	Difference from 1930	1938 Voting-age population	Turnout	%	Difference from 1930	1942 Voting-age population	Turnout	%	Difference from 1930	1946 Voting-age population	Turnout	%	Difference from 1930
MARYLAND	970,000	780	0.1%	1,052,000	7,933	0.8%	0.7	1,129,000	3,963	0.4%	0.3								
MASSACHUSETTS	2,224,000	17,496	0.8%	2,379,000	11,815	0.5%	-0.3	2,527,000	976	0.0%	-0.7	2,709,000	2,105	0.1%	-0.7	2,895,000	9,275	0.3%	-0.5
MICHIGAN	2,604,000	5,822	0.2%	2,836,000	16,859	0.6%	0.4	3,058,000	1,829	0.1%	-0.2	3,371,000	6,333	0.2%	0.0	3,706,000	10,051	0.3%	0.0
MINNESOTA	1,471,000	281,385	19.1%	1,583,000	416,415	26.3%	7.2	1,690,000	343,426	20.3%	1.2	1,768,000	152,334	8.6%	-10.5	1,827,000	2,463	0.1%	-19.0
MISSISSIPPI																			
MISSOURI	2,234,000	743	0.0%	2,336,000	7,100	0.3%	0.3	2,432,000	1,578	0.1%	0.0	2,509,000	247	0.0%	0.0				
MONTANA	295,000	2,807	1.0%	312,000	1,736	0.6%	-0.4					344,000	2,611	0.8%	-0.2	355,000	841	0.2%	-0.7
NEBRASKA				798,000	9,691	1.2%		812,000	11,603	1.4%	0.2	825,000	7,266	0.9%	-0.3	837,000	4,516	0.5%	-0.7
NEVADA																			
NEW HAMPSHIRE				276,000	392	0.1%													
NEW JERSEY	2,205,000	6,557	0.3%	2,376,000	13,967	0.6%	0.3	2,540,000	17,211	0.7%	0.4	2,774,000	8,962	0.3%	0.0	3,024,000	12,768	0.4%	0.1
NEW MEXICO	179,000	299	0.2%	215,000	776	0.4%	0.2	249,000	268	0.1%	-0.1								
NEW YORK	6,904,000	188,759	2.7%	7,527,000	218,032	2.9%	0.2	8,124,000	135,975	1.7%	-1.1	8,745,000	74,457	0.9%	-1.9	9,339,000	229,718	2.5%	-0.3
NORTH CAROLINA																			
NORTH DAKOTA	338,000	3,538	1.0%	345,000	46,304	13.4%	12.4	351,000	8,109	2.3%	1.3								
OHIO	3,913,000	13,468	0.3%	4,130,000	13,999	0.3%	0.0												
OKLAHOMA	1,242,000	166	0.0%	1,281,000	12,823	1.0%	1.0	1,319,000	1,850	0.1%	0.1	1,344,000	1,679	0.1%	0.1				
OREGON	584,000	4,696	0.8%	640,000	31,102	4.9%	4.1	693,000	8	0.0%	-0.8	789,000	2	0.0%	-0.8				
PENNSYLVANIA	5,264,000	21,794	0.4%	5,603,000	92,621	1.7%	1.2	5,928,000	24,111	0.4%	0.0	6,263,000	22,701	0.4%	-0.1	6,583,000	9,712	0.1%	-0.3
RHODE ISLAND				389,000	1	0.0%										486,000	890	0.2%	0.2
SOUTH CAROLINA				899,000	181	0.0%		968,000	74	0.0%	0.0					1,100,000	48	0.0%	0.0
SOUTH DAKOTA	364,000	7,926	2.2%	365,000	2,259	0.6%	-1.6												
TENNESSEE	1,430,000	1,908	0.1%	1,551,000	11,476	0.7%	0.6	1,668,000	29,849	1.8%	1.7	1,782,000	1,701	0.1%	0.0	1,890,000	11,883	0.6%	0.5
TEXAS	2,923,000	2	0.0%	3,270,000	555	0.0%	0.0	3,605,000	37	0.0%	0.0	3,965,000	369	0.0%	0.0				
UTAH	249,000	10,945	4.4%	269,000	2,117	0.8%	-3.6												
VERMONT	204,000	7	0.0%	208,000	949	0.5%	0.5					219,000	15	0.0%	0.0	225,000	25	0.0%	0.0
VIRGINIA	1,308,000	185	0.0%	1,413,000	5,291	0.4%	0.4	1,513,000	2,368	0.2%	0.1	1,682,000	912	0.1%	0.0	1,869,000	2,298	0.1%	0.1
WASHINGTON	920,000	8,017	0.9%	1,002,000	13,025	1.3%	0.4	1,081,000	849	0.1%	-0.8	1,224,000	829	0.1%	-0.8	1,384,000	2,028	0.1%	-0.7
WEST VIRGINIA				956,000	2,792	0.3%													
WISCONSIN	1,666,000	58,788	3.5%	1,785,000	389,717	21.8%	18.3	1,899,000	346,637	18.3%	14.7	2,008,000	194,368	9.7%	6.2	2,108,000	55,990	2.7%	-0.9
WYOMING				135,000	603	0.4%													
Total	56,023,000	661,299	1.2%	64,997,000	1,636,592	2.5%	1.3	61,267,000	1,228,960	2.0%	0.8	61,832,000	583,786	0.9%	-0.2	60,651,000	458,884	0.8%	-0.4

*Percentage point difference between turnout in current year and initial year listed in chart. If data do not appear for a state in the initial year listed, the difference is calculated from the first year in which data do appear for that state.

TOTAL HIGHEST STATEWIDE GENERAL ELECTIONS

Election Years 1930–1946

State	1930 Voting-age population	1930 Turnout	1930 %	1934 Voting-age population	1934 Turnout	1934 %	1934 Difference from 1930*	1938 Voting-age population	1938 Turnout	1938 %	1938 Difference from 1930	1942 Voting-age population	1942 Turnout	1942 %	1942 Difference from 1930	1946 Voting-age population	1946 Turnout	1946 %	1946 Difference from 1930
ALABAMA	1,356,000	198,433	14.6%	1,444,000	164,890	11.4%	-3.2	1,528,000	123,876	8.1%	-6.5	1,611,000	69,131	4.3%	-10.3	1,686,000	179,488	10.6%	-4.0
ALASKA																			
ARIZONA	168,000	52,342	31.2%	198,000	96,044	48.5%	17.4	228,000	104,058	45.6%	14.5	291,000	79,747	27.4%	-3.8	365,000	112,812	30.9%	-0.2
ARKANSAS	973,000	145,124	14.9%	1,029,000	139,895	13.6%	-1.3	1,082,000	143,956	13.3%	-1.6	1,102,000	98,346	8.9%	-6.0	1,106,000	151,333	13.7%	-1.2
CALIFORNIA	3,295,000	1,090,500	33.3%	3,756,000	2,028,658	54.0%	20.7	4,201,000	2,389,227	56.9%	23.6	5,070,000	1,899,109	37.5%	4.2	6,074,000	2,334,522	38.4%	5.2
COLORADO	577,000	314,643	54.5%	624,000	395,698	63.4%	8.9	672,000	449,537	66.9%	12.4	727,000	342,396	47.1%	-7.4	783,000	331,982	42.4%	-12.1
CONNECTICUT	810,000	428,179	52.9%	899,000	551,778	61.4%	8.5	985,000	630,132	64.0%	11.1	1,095,000	569,005	52.0%	-0.9	1,210,000	679,766	56.2%	3.3
DELAWARE	143,000	87,011	60.8%	156,000	98,857	63.4%	2.5	168,000	108,571	64.6%	3.8	182,000	84,726	46.6%	-14.3	197,000	112,621	57.2%	-3.7
DISTRICT OF COLUMBIA																			
FLORIDA	861,000	95,943	11.1%	1,006,000	125,263	12.5%	1.3	1,145,000	153,061	13.4%	2.2	1,364,000	91,120	6.7%	-4.5	1,605,000	186,763	11.6%	0.5
GEORGIA	1,511,000	56,458	3.7%	1,625,000	52,683	3.2%	-0.5	1,735,000	68,065	3.9%	0.2	1,887,000	61,879	3.3%	-0.5	2,050,000	161,539	7.9%	4.1
HAWAII																			
IDAHO	239,000	126,528	52.9%	267,000	163,376	61.2%	8.2	294,000	178,684	60.8%	7.8	314,000	139,287	44.4%	-8.6	331,000	178,758	54.0%	1.1
ILLINOIS	4,466,000	2,065,436	46.2%	4,753,000	2,750,326	57.9%	11.6	5,029,000	3,054,847	60.7%	14.5	5,316,000	2,887,632	54.3%	8.1	5,591,000	3,458,882	61.9%	15.6
INDIANA	1,960,000	1,214,387	62.0%	2,065,000	1,456,301	70.5%	8.6	2,167,000	1,572,649	72.6%	10.6	2,296,000	1,286,734	56.0%	-5.9	2,429,000	1,332,634	54.9%	-7.1
IOWA	1,480,000	530,250	35.8%	1,536,000	829,427	54.0%	18.2	1,592,000	802,637	50.4%	14.6	1,628,000	664,747	40.8%	5.0	1,656,000	593,031	35.8%	0.0
KANSAS	1,106,000	565,252	51.1%	1,123,000	757,234	67.4%	16.3	1,139,000	737,021	64.7%	13.6	1,169,000	493,692	42.2%	-8.9	1,205,000	554,860	46.0%	-5.1
KENTUCKY	1,429,000	548,582	38.4%	1,518,000	469,470	30.9%	-7.5	1,604,000	533,968	33.3%	-5.1	1,704,000	342,605	20.1%	-18.3	1,804,000	583,302	32.3%	-6.1
LOUISIANA	1,131,000	132,293	11.7%	1,234,000	186,112	15.1%	3.4	1,333,000	152,410	11.4%	-0.3	1,426,000	84,987	6.0%	-5.7	1,512,000	106,009	7.0%	-4.7
MAINE	442,000	143,541	32.5%	464,000	279,295	60.2%	27.7	486,000	281,619	57.9%	25.5	510,000	160,841	31.5%	-0.9	533,000	174,248	32.7%	0.2
MARYLAND	970,000	466,056	48.0%	1,052,000	455,630	43.3%	-4.7	1,129,000	486,473	43.1%	-5.0	1,254,000	337,436	26.9%	-21.1	1,394,000	444,955	31.9%	-16.1
MASSACHUSETTS	2,224,000	1,176,585	52.9%	2,379,000	1,381,425	58.1%	5.2	2,527,000	1,719,677	68.1%	15.1	2,709,000	1,327,242	49.0%	-3.9	2,895,000	1,617,314	55.9%	3.0
MICHIGAN	2,604,000	744,429	28.6%	2,836,000	1,212,526	42.8%	14.2	3,058,000	1,547,211	50.6%	22.0	3,371,000	1,170,694	34.7%	6.1	3,706,000	1,604,732	43.3%	14.7
MINNESOTA	1,471,000	759,763	51.6%	1,583,000	995,605	62.9%	11.2	1,690,000	1,070,927	63.4%	11.7	1,768,000	761,274	43.1%	-8.6	1,827,000	875,005	47.9%	-3.8
MISSISSIPPI	1,037,000	34,897	3.4%	1,106,000	57,327	5.2%	1.8	1,173,000	35,439	3.0%	-0.3	1,197,000	51,698	4.3%	1.0	1,202,000	49,957	4.2%	0.8
MISSOURI	2,234,000	947,063	42.4%	2,336,000	1,320,343	56.5%	14.1	2,432,000	1,245,034	51.2%	8.8	2,509,000	925,319	36.9%	-5.5	2,571,000	1,084,276	42.2%	-0.2
MONTANA	295,000	170,147	57.7%	312,000	196,739	63.1%	5.4	329,000	208,710	63.4%	5.8	344,000	169,508	49.3%	-8.4	355,000	190,088	53.5%	-4.1
NEBRASKA	785,000	415,601	52.9%	798,000	519,339	65.1%	12.1	812,000	477,715	58.8%	5.9	825,000	357,569	43.3%	-9.6	837,000	372,040	44.4%	-8.5
NEVADA	51,000	33,622	65.9%	58,000	41,683	71.9%	5.9	65,000	45,441	69.9%	4.0	78,000	39,389	50.5%	-15.4	92,000	49,046	53.3%	-12.6
NEW HAMPSHIRE	260,000	123,829	47.6%	276,000	170,213	61.7%	14.0	291,000	181,273	62.3%	14.7	308,000	156,215	50.7%	3.1	324,000	161,092	49.7%	2.1
NEW JERSEY	2,205,000	990,834	44.9%	2,376,000	1,328,407	55.9%	11.0	2,540,000	1,531,121	60.3%	15.3	2,774,000	1,203,455	43.4%	-1.6	3,024,000	1,381,993	45.7%	0.8
NEW MEXICO	179,000	117,398	65.6%	215,000	148,268	69.0%	3.4	249,000	155,157	62.3%	-3.3	291,000	105,947	36.4%	-29.2	334,000	126,939	38.0%	-27.6
NEW YORK	6,904,000	3,025,182	43.8%	7,527,000	3,613,973	48.0%	4.2	8,124,000	4,511,005	55.5%	11.7	8,745,000	3,953,789	45.2%	1.4	9,339,000	4,712,410	50.5%	6.6

Total Highest Statewide General Elections (continued)

Election Years 1930–1946 (continued)

State	1930			1934				1938				1942				1946			
	Voting-age population	Turnout	%	Voting-age population	Turnout	%	Difference from 1930	Voting-age population	Turnout	%	Difference from 1930	Voting-age population	Turnout	%	Difference from 1930	Voting-age population	Turnout	%	Difference from 1930
NORTH CAROLINA	1,555,000	532,686	34.3%	1,715,000	493,703	28.8%	-5.5	1,868,000	479,267	25.7%	-8.6	2,029,000	314,827	15.5%	-18.7	2,185,000	452,222	20.7%	-13.6
NORTH DAKOTA	338,000	182,500	54.0%	345,000	276,680	80.2%	26.2	351,000	216,340	61.6%	7.6	355,000	182,380	51.4%	-2.6	357,000	144,394	40.4%	-13.5
OHIO	3,913,000	1,880,085	48.0%	4,130,000	1,981,089	48.0%	-0.1	4,338,000	2,246,898	51.8%	3.7	4,631,000	1,663,687	35.9%	-12.1	4,941,000	2,153,524	43.6%	-4.5
OKLAHOMA	1,242,000	456,730	36.8%	1,281,000	530,356	41.4%	4.6	1,319,000	445,824	33.8%	-3.0	1,344,000	351,727	26.2%	-10.6	1,362,000	492,141	36.1%	-0.6
OREGON	584,000	228,525	39.1%	640,000	285,389	44.6%	5.5	693,000	365,943	52.8%	13.7	789,000	276,425	35.0%	-4.1	897,000	334,670	37.3%	-1.8
PENNSYLVANIA	5,264,000	2,019,307	38.4%	5,603,000	2,926,338	52.2%	13.9	5,928,000	3,783,751	63.8%	25.5	6,263,000	2,489,357	39.7%	1.4	6,583,000	3,111,987	47.3%	8.9
RHODE ISLAND	362,000	219,322	60.6%	389,000	244,560	62.9%	2.3	417,000	300,220	72.0%	11.4	451,000	236,604	52.5%	-8.1	486,000	272,450	56.1%	-4.5
SOUTH CAROLINA	827,000	16,163	2.0%	899,000	22,156	2.5%	0.5	968,000	46,190	4.8%	2.8	1,036,000	23,356	2.3%	0.3	1,100,000	26,358	2.4%	0.4
SOUTH DAKOTA	364,000	170,073	46.7%	365,000	277,593	76.1%	29.3	367,000	274,425	74.8%	28.1	376,000	178,111	47.4%	0.6	387,000	162,804	42.1%	-4.7
TENNESSEE	1,430,000	197,870	13.8%	1,551,000	275,242	17.7%	3.9	1,668,000	264,404	15.9%	2.0	1,782,000	156,211	8.8%	-5.1	1,890,000	193,444	10.2%	-3.6
TEXAS	2,923,000	293,733	10.0%	3,270,000	445,883	13.6%	3.6	3,605,000	366,541	10.2%	0.1	3,965,000	278,419	7.0%	-3.0	4,316,000	349,659	8.1%	-1.9
UTAH	249,000	154,754	62.2%	269,000	179,977	66.9%	4.8	289,000	182,532	63.2%	1.0	320,000	150,493	47.0%	-15.1	354,000	196,672	55.6%	-6.6
VERMONT	204,000	72,822	35.7%	208,000	129,725	62.4%	26.7	213,000	114,473	53.7%	18.0	219,000	58,070	26.5%	-9.2	225,000	73,066	32.5%	-3.2
VIRGINIA	1,308,000	164,832	12.6%	1,413,000	148,124	10.5%	-2.1	1,513,000	126,043	8.3%	-4.3	1,682,000	90,014	5.4%	-7.3	1,869,000	253,855	13.6%	1.0
WASHINGTON	920,000	289,378	31.5%	1,002,000	479,365	47.8%	16.4	1,081,000	586,493	54.3%	22.8	1,224,000	428,186	35.0%	3.5	1,384,000	644,930	46.6%	15.1
WEST VIRGINIA	884,000	537,836	60.8%	956,000	619,947	64.8%	4.0	1,025,000	622,821	60.8%	-0.1	1,079,000	460,287	42.7%	-18.2	1,125,000	537,357	47.8%	-13.1
WISCONSIN	1,666,000	509,409	30.6%	1,785,000	885,689	49.6%	19.0	1,899,000	912,302	48.0%	17.5	2,008,000	748,717	37.3%	6.7	2,108,000	983,566	46.7%	16.1
WYOMING	123,000	68,409	55.6%	135,000	91,383	67.7%	12.1	146,000	94,500	64.7%	9.1	156,000	74,857	48.0%	-7.6	166,000	79,458	47.9%	-7.8
Total	67,322,000	24,800,840	36.8%	72,507,000	32,279,984	44.5%	7.7	77,495,000	36,128,468	46.6%	9.8	83,574,000	28,077,247	33.6%	-3.2	89,772,000	34,364,954	38.3%	1.4

*Percentage point difference between turnout in current year and initial year listed in chart. If data do not appear for a state in the initial year listed, the difference is calculated from the first year in which data do appear for that state.

TOTAL HIGHEST STATEWIDE GENERAL ELECTIONS

Republican Turnout for Election Years 1930–1946

State	1930			1934				1938				1942				1946			
	Voting-age population	Turnout	%	Voting-age population	Turnout	%	Difference from 1930*	Voting-age population	Turnout	%	Difference from 1930	Voting-age population	Turnout	%	Difference from 1930	Voting-age population	Turnout	%	Difference from 1930
ALABAMA	1,356,000	33,030	2.4%	1,444,000	22,621	1.6%	-0.9	1,528,000	17,885	1.2%	-1.3	1,611,000	8,167	0.5%	-1.9	1,686,000	22,362	1.3%	-1.1
ALASKA																			
ARIZONA	168,000	46,231	27.5%	198,000	39,242	19.8%	-7.7	228,000	32,055	14.1%	-13.5	291,000	23,562	8.1%	-19.4	365,000	48,867	13.4%	-14.1
ARKANSAS	973,000	26,161	2.7%	1,029,000	13,083	1.3%	-1.4	1,082,000	14,240	1.3%	-1.4					1,106,000	24,133	2.2%	-0.5
CALIFORNIA	3,295,000	999,393	30.3%	3,756,000	1,946,572	51.8%	21.5	4,201,000	1,171,019	27.9%	-2.5	5,070,000	1,275,237	25.2%	-5.2	6,074,000	2,344,542	38.6%	8.3
COLORADO	577,000	167,227	29.0%	624,000	162,791	26.1%	-2.9	672,000	255,159	38.0%	9.0	727,000	199,365	27.4%	-1.6	783,000	184,429	23.6%	-5.4
CONNECTICUT	810,000	216,418	26.7%	899,000	249,397	27.7%	1.0	985,000	271,329	27.5%	0.8	1,095,000	283,280	25.9%	-0.8	1,210,000	381,328	31.5%	4.8
DELAWARE	143,000	48,493	33.9%	156,000	52,829	33.9%	0.0	168,000	61,477	36.6%	2.7	182,000	46,210	25.4%	-8.5	197,000	63,516	32.2%	-1.7
DISTRICT OF COLUMBIA																			
FLORIDA	861,000	11,819	1.4%					1,145,000	31,035	2.7%	1.3					1,605,000	42,413	2.6%	1.3
GEORGIA	1,511,000	1,526	0.1%	1,625,000	240	0.0%	-0.1												
HAWAII																			
IDAHO	239,000	94,938	39.7%	267,000	75,659	28.3%	-11.4	294,000	106,268	36.1%	-3.6	314,000	73,353	23.4%	-16.4	331,000	102,233	30.9%	-0.8
ILLINOIS	4,466,000	991,083	22.2%	4,753,000	1,201,373	25.3%	3.1	5,029,000	1,542,574	30.7%	8.5	5,316,000	1,582,887	29.8%	7.6	5,591,000	1,906,717	34.1%	11.9
INDIANA	1,960,000	572,082	29.2%	2,065,000	700,103	33.9%	4.7	2,167,000	799,455	36.9%	7.7	2,296,000	713,831	31.1%	1.9	2,429,000	739,809	30.5%	1.3
IOWA	1,480,000	364,024	24.6%	1,536,000	394,634	25.7%	1.1	1,592,000	446,959	28.1%	3.5	1,628,000	438,556	26.9%	2.3	1,656,000	364,992	22.0%	-2.6
KANSAS	1,106,000	364,548	33.0%	1,123,000	422,030	37.6%	4.6	1,139,000	434,692	38.2%	5.2	1,169,000	299,015	25.6%	-7.4	1,205,000	328,642	27.3%	-5.7
KENTUCKY	1,429,000	309,180	21.6%	1,518,000	206,118	13.6%	-8.1	1,604,000	218,331	13.6%	8.0	1,704,000	175,081	10.3%	-11.4	1,804,000	311,502	17.3%	-4.4
LOUISIANA	1,131,000	2,207	0.2%													1,512,000	5,651	0.4%	0.2
MAINE	442,000	88,262	20.0%	464,000	139,773	30.1%	10.2	486,000	164,845	33.9%	13.9	510,000	118,047	23.1%	3.2	533,000	111,215	20.9%	0.9
MARYLAND	970,000	216,864	22.4%	1,052,000	253,813	24.1%	1.8	1,129,000	242,095	21.4%	-0.9	1,254,000	179,204	14.3%	-8.1	1,394,000	235,000	16.9%	-5.5
MASSACHUSETTS	2,224,000	629,821	28.3%	2,379,000	728,261	30.6%	2.3	2,527,000	941,465	37.3%	8.9	2,709,000	758,402	28.0%	-0.3	2,895,000	989,736	34.2%	5.9
MICHIGAN	2,604,000	634,577	24.4%	2,836,000	659,743	23.3%	-1.1	3,058,000	847,245	27.7%	3.3	3,371,000	645,335	19.1%	-5.2	3,706,000	1,085,570	29.3%	4.9
MINNESOTA	1,471,000	412,888	28.1%	1,583,000	396,359	25.0%	-3.0	1,690,000	678,839	40.2%	12.1	1,768,000	452,192	25.6%	-2.5	1,827,000	519,067	28.4%	0.3
MISSISSIPPI																			
MISSOURI	2,234,000	468,853	21.0%	2,336,000	524,954	22.5%	1.5	2,432,000	505,605	20.8%	-0.2	2,509,000	476,994	19.0%	-2.0	2,571,000	572,556	22.3%	1.3
MONTANA	295,000	82,736	28.0%	312,000	59,900	19.2%	-8.8	329,000	103,885	31.6%	3.5	344,000	82,461	24.0%	-4.1	355,000	101,901	28.7%	0.7
NEBRASKA	785,000	247,118	31.5%	798,000	266,707	33.4%	1.9	812,000	247,996	30.5%	-0.9	825,000	283,271	34.3%	2.9	837,000	271,208	32.4%	0.9
NEVADA	51,000	18,442	36.2%	58,000	14,778	25.5%	-10.7	65,000	19,078	29.4%	-6.8	78,000	18,289	23.4%	-12.7	92,000	28,859	31.4%	-4.8
NEW HAMPSHIRE	260,000	75,518	29.0%	276,000	89,481	32.4%	3.4	291,000	107,841	37.1%	8.0	308,000	88,601	28.8%	-0.3	324,000	103,204	31.9%	2.8
NEW JERSEY	2,205,000	601,497	27.3%	2,376,000	638,424	26.9%	-0.4	2,540,000	794,609	31.3%	4.0	2,774,000	648,855	23.4%	-3.9	3,024,000	815,261	27.0%	-0.3
NEW MEXICO	179,000	55,026	30.7%	215,000	76,228	35.5%	4.7	249,000	75,017	30.1%	-0.6	291,000	49,380	17.0%	-13.8	334,000	64,632	19.4%	-11.4
NEW YORK	6,904,000	1,304,010	18.9%	7,527,000	1,417,271	18.8%	-0.1	8,124,000	2,326,892	28.6%	9.8	8,745,000	2,148,546	24.6%	5.7	9,339,000	2,825,633	30.3%	11.4

Total Highest Statewide General Elections (continued)

Total Highest Statewide General Elections *(continued)*

Republican Turnout for Election Years 1930–1946 *(continued)*

State	1930 Voting-age population	1930 Turnout	1930 %	1934 Voting-age population	1934 Turnout	1934 %	1934 Difference from 1930	1938 Voting-age population	1938 Turnout	1938 %	1938 Difference from 1930	1942 Voting-age population	1942 Turnout	1942 %	1942 Difference from 1930	1946 Voting-age population	1946 Turnout	1946 %	1946 Difference from 1930
NORTH CAROLINA	1,555,000	210,761	13.6%	1,715,000	173,447	10.1%	-3.4	1,868,000	179,461	9.6%	-3.9	2,029,000	119,165	5.9%	-7.7	2,185,000	174,945	8.0%	-5.5
NORTH DAKOTA	338,000	133,264	39.4%	345,000	151,205	43.8%	4.4	351,000	153,106	43.6%	4.2	355,000	134,408	37.9%	-1.6	357,000	116,672	32.7%	-6.7
OHIO	3,913,000	955,686	24.4%	4,130,000	1,052,851	25.5%	1.1	4,338,000	1,265,548	29.2%	4.8	4,631,000	1,086,937	23.5%	-1.0	4,941,000	1,281,864	25.9%	1.5
OKLAHOMA	1,242,000	232,589	18.7%	1,281,000	243,841	19.0%	0.3	1,319,000	159,734	12.1%	-6.6	1,344,000	204,163	15.2%	-3.5	1,362,000	227,426	16.7%	-2.0
OREGON	584,000	137,231	23.5%	640,000	132,441	20.7%	-2.8	693,000	214,571	31.0%	7.5	789,000	220,188	27.9%	4.4	897,000	237,681	26.5%	3.0
PENNSYLVANIA	5,264,000	1,429,675	27.2%	5,603,000	1,410,138	25.2%	-2.0	5,928,000	2,086,932	35.2%	8.0	6,263,000	1,367,531	21.8%	-5.3	6,583,000	1,853,458	28.2%	1.0
RHODE ISLAND	362,000	113,354	31.3%	389,000	105,545	27.1%	-4.2	417,000	167,003	40.0%	8.7	451,000	100,236	22.2%	-9.1	486,000	126,456	26.0%	-5.3
SOUTH CAROLINA				899,000	54	0.0%		968,000	508	0.1%	0.0					1,100,000	243	0.0%	0.0
SOUTH DAKOTA	364,000	107,643	29.6%	365,000	119,477	32.7%	3.2	367,000	153,140	41.7%	12.2	376,000	111,762	29.7%	0.2	387,000	108,998	28.2%	-1.4
TENNESSEE	1,430,000	85,598	6.0%	1,551,000	110,401	7.1%	1.1	1,668,000	83,031	5.0%	-1.0	1,782,000	52,367	2.9%	-3.0	1,890,000	73,222	3.9%	-2.1
TEXAS	2,923,000	62,224	2.1%	3,270,000	13,703	0.4%	-1.7	3,605,000	11,309	0.3%	-1.8	3,965,000	12,054	0.3%	-1.8	4,316,000	43,619	1.0%	-1.1
UTAH	249,000	80,981	32.5%	269,000	82,154	30.5%	-2.0	289,000	81,071	28.1%	-4.5	320,000	70,614	22.1%	-10.5	354,000	101,186	28.6%	-3.9
VERMONT	204,000	52,836	25.9%	208,000	73,809	35.5%	9.6	213,000	75,098	35.3%	9.4	219,000	44,804	20.5%	-5.4	225,000	57,849	25.7%	-0.2
VIRGINIA	1,308,000	55,634	4.3%	1,413,000	34,178	2.4%	-1.8	1,513,000	26,144	1.7%	-2.5	1,682,000	12,015	0.7%	-3.5	1,869,000	83,638	4.5%	0.2
WASHINGTON	920,000	205,937	22.4%	1,002,000	168,994	16.9%	-5.5	1,081,000	227,958	21.1%	-1.3	1,224,000	202,332	16.5%	-5.9	1,384,000	375,715	27.1%	4.8
WEST VIRGINIA	884,000	265,857	30.1%	956,000	281,756	29.5%	-0.6	1,025,000	279,487	27.3%	-2.8	1,079,000	256,816	23.8%	-6.3	1,125,000	269,617	24.0%	-6.1
WISCONSIN	1,666,000	392,958	23.6%	1,785,000	215,605	12.1%	-11.5	1,899,000	543,675	28.6%	5.0	2,008,000	350,812	17.5%	-6.1	2,108,000	621,970	29.5%	5.9
WYOMING	123,000	44,890	36.5%	135,000	40,819	30.2%	-6.3	146,000	57,288	39.2%	2.7	156,000	41,486	26.6%	-9.9	166,000	44,512	26.8%	-9.7
Total	65,458,000	13,651,090	20.9%	69,161,000	15,162,802	21.9%	1.1	73,254,000	18,222,954	24.9%	4.0	75,562,000	15,455,811	20.5%	-0.4	86,520,000	20,394,049	23.6%	2.7

Democratic Turnout for Election Years 1930–1946

State	1930 Voting-age population	1930 Turnout	1930 %	1934 Voting-age population	1934 Turnout	1934 %	1934 Difference from 1930*	1938 Voting-age population	1938 Turnout	1938 %	1938 Difference from 1930	1942 Voting-age population	1942 Turnout	1942 %	1942 Difference from 1930	1946 Voting-age population	1946 Turnout	1946 %	1946 Difference from 1930
ALABAMA	1,356,000	165,403	12.2%	1,444,000	155,197	10.7%	-1.5	1,528,000	115,761	7.6%	-4.6	1,611,000	69,212	4.3%	-7.9	1,686,000	174,959	10.4%	-1.8
ALASKA																			
ARIZONA	168,000	52,342	31.2%	198,000	67,648	34.2%	3.0	228,000	83,556	36.6%	5.5	291,000	63,484	21.8%	-9.3	365,000	80,415	22.0%	-9.1
ARKANSAS	973,000	145,124	14.9%	1,029,000	129,124	12.5%	-2.4	1,082,000	143,956	13.3%	-1.6	1,102,000	99,126	9.0%	-5.9	1,106,000	143,252	13.0%	-2.0
CALIFORNIA	3,295,000	333,973	10.1%	3,756,000	993,600	26.5%	16.3	4,201,000	1,391,734	33.1%	23.0	5,070,000	932,995	18.4%	8.3	6,074,000	1,167,161	19.2%	9.1
COLORADO	577,000	197,067	34.2%	624,000	237,491	38.1%	3.9	672,000	265,297	39.5%	5.3	727,000	174,612	24.0%	-10.1	783,000	174,604	22.3%	-11.9
CONNECTICUT	810,000	215,072	26.6%	899,000	265,552	29.5%	3.0	985,000	252,426	25.6%	-0.9	1,095,000	257,941	23.6%	-3.0	1,210,000	277,872	23.0%	-3.6
DELAWARE	143,000	39,881	27.9%	156,000	45,927	29.4%	1.6	168,000	46,989	28.0%	0.1	182,000	38,791	21.3%	-6.6	197,000	50,910	25.8%	-2.0
DISTRICT OF COLUMBIA																			
FLORIDA	861,000	84,070	9.8%	1,006,000	131,780	13.1%	3.3	1,145,000	146,356	12.8%	3.0	1,364,000	91,120	6.7%	-3.1	1,605,000	156,232	9.7%	0.0

Total Highest Statewide General Elections (continued)

Democratic Turnout for Election Years 1930–1946 (continued)

State	1930 Voting-age population	1930 Turnout	1930 %	1934 Voting-age population	1934 Turnout	1934 %	1934 Difference from 1930	1938 Voting-age population	1938 Turnout	1938 %	1938 Difference from 1930	1942 Voting-age population	1942 Turnout	1942 %	1942 Difference from 1930	1946 Voting-age population	1946 Turnout	1946 %	1946 Difference from 1930
GEORGIA	1,511,000	55,606	3.7%	1,625,000	53,101	3.3%	-0.4	1,735,000	67,252	3.9%	0.2	1,887,000	62,220	3.3%	-0.4	2,050,000	143,279	7.0%	3.3
HAWAII																			
IDAHO	239,000	73,896	30.9%	267,000	99,770	37.4%	6.4	294,000	99,801	33.9%	3.0	314,000	71,826	22.9%	-8.0	331,000	79,131	23.9%	-7.0
ILLINOIS	4,466,000	1,432,216	32.1%	4,753,000	1,507,714	31.7%	-0.3	5,029,000	1,638,162	32.6%	0.5	5,316,000	1,395,053	26.2%	-5.8	5,591,000	1,539,248	27.5%	-4.5
INDIANA	1,960,000	641,406	32.7%	2,065,000	759,795	36.8%	4.1	2,167,000	788,386	36.4%	3.7	2,296,000	572,903	25.0%	-7.8	2,429,000	588,639	24.2%	-8.5
IOWA	1,480,000	235,186	15.9%	1,536,000	468,921	30.5%	14.6	1,592,000	413,788	20.0%	10.1	1,628,000	295,194	18.1%	2.2	1,656,000	266,190	16.1%	0.2
KANSAS	1,106,000	242,477	21.9%	1,123,000	367,747	32.7%	10.8	1,139,000	341,271	30.0%	8.0	1,169,000	212,071	18.1%	-3.8	1,205,000	254,283	21.1%	0.8
KENTUCKY	1,429,000	336,748	23.6%	1,518,000	254,584	16.8%	-6.8	1,604,000	346,735	21.6%	-1.9	1,704,000	216,958	12.7%	-10.8	1,804,000	271,480	15.0%	-8.5
LOUISIANA	1,131,000	130,536	11.5%	1,234,000	186,063	15.1%	3.5	1,333,000	152,366	11.4%	-0.1	1,426,000	85,488	6.0%	-5.5	1,512,000	100,357	6.6%	-4.9
MAINE	442,000	67,172	15.2%	464,000	156,917	33.8%	18.6	486,000	139,745	28.8%	13.6	510,000	58,558	11.5%	-3.7	533,000	69,624	13.1%	-2.1
MARYLAND	970,000	283,639	29.2%	1,052,000	267,204	25.4%	-3.8	1,129,000	357,245	31.6%	2.4	1,254,000	198,488	15.8%	-13.4	1,394,000	268,084	19.2%	-10.0
MASSACHUSETTS	2,224,000	651,939	29.3%	2,379,000	852,776	35.8%	6.5	2,527,000	793,884	31.4%	2.1	2,709,000	641,042	23.7%	-5.7	2,895,000	762,743	26.3%	-3.0
MICHIGAN	2,604,000	357,664	13.7%	2,836,000	590,620	20.8%	7.1	3,058,000	753,752	24.6%	10.9	3,371,000	573,314	17.0%	3.3	3,706,000	644,540	17.4%	3.7
MINNESOTA	1,471,000	282,018	19.2%	1,583,000	294,757	18.6%	-0.6	1,690,000	190,036	11.2%	-7.9	1,768,000	156,748	8.9%	-10.3	1,827,000	357,758	19.6%	0.4
MISSISSIPPI	1,037,000	34,897	3.4%	1,106,000	57,327	5.2%	1.8	1,173,000	35,439	3.0%	-0.3	1,197,000	51,698	4.3%	1.0	1,202,000	49,957	4.2%	0.8
MISSOURI	2,234,000	477,467	21.4%	2,336,000	797,975	34.2%	12.8	2,432,000	757,587	31.2%	9.8	2,509,000	448,078	17.9%	-3.5	2,571,000	517,980	20.1%	-1.2
MONTANA	295,000	106,274	36.0%	312,000	142,823	45.8%	9.8	329,000	104,825	31.9%	-4.2	344,000	93,243	27.1%	-8.9	355,000	95,982	27.0%	-9.0
NEBRASKA	785,000	221,161	28.2%	798,000	305,858	38.3%	10.2	812,000	218,787	26.9%	-1.2	825,000	122,279	14.8%	-13.4	837,000	131,367	15.7%	-12.5
NEVADA	51,000	16,192	31.7%	58,000	29,691	51.2%	19.4	65,000	30,156	46.4%	14.6	78,000	24,505	31.4%	-0.3	92,000	28,655	31.1%	-0.6
NEW HAMPSHIRE	260,000	54,441	20.9%	276,000	87,019	31.5%	10.6	291,000	84,920	29.2%	8.2	308,000	76,782	24.9%	4.0	324,000	61,220	18.9%	-2.0
NEW JERSEY	2,205,000	425,352	19.3%	2,376,000	785,971	33.1%	13.8	2,540,000	719,301	28.3%	9.0	2,774,000	559,851	20.2%	0.9	3,024,000	553,964	18.3%	-1.0
NEW MEXICO	179,000	69,356	38.7%	215,000	78,390	36.5%	-2.3	249,000	90,608	36.4%	-2.4	291,000	63,301	21.8%	-17.0	334,000	70,055	21.0%	-17.8
NEW YORK	6,904,000	1,770,342	25.6%	7,527,000	2,201,729	29.3%	3.6	8,124,000	2,497,029	30.7%	5.1	8,745,000	1,912,114	21.9%	-3.8	9,339,000	2,308,112	24.7%	-0.9
NORTH CAROLINA	1,555,000	334,376	21.5%	1,715,000	320,256	18.7%	-2.8	1,868,000	318,809	17.1%	-4.4	2,029,000	230,427	11.4%	-10.1	2,185,000	277,277	12.7%	-8.8
NORTH DAKOTA	338,000	52,284	15.5%	345,000	145,333	42.1%	26.7	351,000	138,270	39.4%	23.9	355,000	101,390	28.6%	13.1	357,000	52,719	14.8%	-0.7
OHIO	3,913,000	1,033,168	26.4%	4,130,000	1,276,206	30.9%	4.5	4,338,000	1,147,323	26.4%	0.0	4,631,000	717,692	15.5%	-10.9	4,941,000	1,125,997	22.8%	-3.6
OKLAHOMA	1,242,000	301,921	24.3%	1,281,000	365,992	28.6%	4.3	1,319,000	355,740	27.0%	2.7	1,344,000	202,284	15.1%	-9.3	1,362,000	287,978	21.1%	-3.2
OREGON	584,000	107,187	18.4%	640,000	121,846	19.0%	0.7	693,000	167,135	24.1%	5.8	789,000	115,519	14.6%	-3.7	897,000	117,665	13.1%	-5.2
PENNSYLVANIA	5,264,000	1,036,605	19.7%	5,603,000	1,591,616	28.4%	8.7	5,928,000	1,756,792	29.6%	9.9	6,263,000	1,149,897	18.4%	-1.3	6,583,000	1,306,723	19.8%	0.2
RHODE ISLAND	362,000	109,687	30.3%	389,000	140,700	36.2%	5.9	417,000	138,892	33.3%	3.0	451,000	139,407	30.9%	0.6	486,000	150,748	31.0%	0.7
SOUTH CAROLINA	827,000	17,790	2.2%	899,000	23,177	2.6%	0.4	968,000	49,009	5.1%	2.9	1,036,000	23,859	2.3%	0.2	1,100,000	26,520	2.4%	0.3
SOUTH DAKOTA	364,000	106,317	29.2%	365,000	172,228	47.2%	18.0	367,000	133,064	36.3%	7.0	376,000	74,945	19.9%	-9.3	387,000	58,073	15.0%	-14.2
TENNESSEE	1,430,000	154,071	10.8%	1,551,000	198,743	12.8%	2.0	1,668,000	210,567	12.6%	1.8	1,782,000	120,146	6.7%	-4.0	1,890,000	149,937	7.9%	-2.8

Total Highest Statewide General Elections (continued)

Total Highest Statewide General Elections *(continued)*

Democratic Turnout for Election Years 1930–1946 *(continued)*

State	1930 Voting-age population	Turnout	%	1934 Voting-age population	Turnout	%	Difference from 1930	1938 Voting-age population	Turnout	%	Difference from 1930	1942 Voting-age population	Turnout	%	Difference from 1930	1946 Voting-age population	Turnout	%	Difference from 1930
TEXAS	2,923,000	266,562	9.1%	3,270,000	439,685	13.4%	4.3	3,605,000	362,689	10.1%	0.9	3,965,000	280,735	7.1%	-2.0	4,316,000	345,513	8.0%	-1.1
UTAH	249,000	62,828	25.2%	269,000	113,975	42.4%	17.1	289,000	111,383	38.5%	13.3	320,000	79,879	25.0%	-0.3	354,000	96,257	27.2%	2.0
VERMONT	204,000	23,741	11.6%	208,000	63,632	30.6%	19.0	213,000	40,483	19.0%	7.4	219,000	17,304	7.9%	-3.7	225,000	26,056	11.6%	-0.1
VIRGINIA	1,308,000	112,002	8.6%	1,413,000	109,963	7.8%	-0.8	1,513,000	97,531	6.4%	-2.1	1,682,000	79,421	4.7%	-3.8	1,869,000	167,919	9.0%	0.4
WASHINGTON	920,000	75,424	8.2%	1,002,000	314,685	31.4%	23.2	1,081,000	371,535	34.4%	26.2	1,224,000	225,025	18.4%	10.2	1,384,000	298,683	21.6%	13.4
WEST VIRGINIA	884,000	342,467	38.7%	956,000	349,882	36.6%	-2.1	1,025,000	343,334	33.5%	-5.2	1,079,000	228,549	21.2%	-17.6	1,125,000	273,151	24.3%	-14.5
WISCONSIN	1,666,000	170,020	10.2%	1,785,000	359,467	20.1%	9.9	1,899,000	231,976	12.2%	2.0	2,008,000	203,537	10.1%	-0.1	2,108,000	406,499	19.3%	9.1
WYOMING	123,000	37,188	30.2%	135,000	54,305	40.2%	10.0	146,000	44,525	30.5%	0.3	156,000	39,599	25.4%	-4.9	166,000	45,843	27.6%	-2.6
Total	67,322,000	13,542,555	20.1%	72,507,000	18,534,762	25.6%	5.4	77,495,000	19,086,207	24.6%	4.5	83,574,000	13,648,610	16.3%	-3.8	89,772,000	16,601,611	18.5%	-1.6

Other Turnout for Election Years 1930–1946

State	1930 Voting-age population	Turnout	%	1934 Voting-age population	Turnout	%	Difference from 1930*	1938 Voting-age population	Turnout	%	Difference from 1930	1942 Voting-age population	Turnout	%	Difference from 1930	1946 Voting-age population	Turnout	%	Difference from 1930
ALABAMA	1,356,000	101,862	7.5%	1,444,000	5,586	0.4%	-7.1	1,528,000	243	0.0%	-7.5	1,611,000	406	0.0%	-7.5				
ALASKA																			
ARIZONA				198,000	2,258	1.1%		228,000	4,814	2.1%	1.0	291,000	537	0.2%	-1.0	365,000	831	0.2%	-0.9
ARKANSAS				1,029,000	1,869	0.2%		1,082,000	11,974	1.1%	0.9								
CALIFORNIA	3,295,000	50,480	1.5%	3,756,000	311,565	8.3%	6.8	4,201,000	172,266	4.1%	2.6	5,070,000	56,453	1.1%	-0.4	6,074,000	213,857	3.5%	2.0
COLORADO	577,000	4,975	0.9%	624,000	18,005	2.9%	2.0	672,000	7,126	1.1%	0.2	727,000	2,014	0.3%	-0.6	783,000	1,861	0.2%	-0.6
CONNECTICUT	810,000	6,223	0.8%	899,000	44,903	5.0%	4.2	985,000	174,297	17.7%	16.9	1,095,000	38,473	3.5%	2.7	1,210,000	35,644	2.9%	2.2
DELAWARE	143,000	135	0.1%	156,000	566	0.4%	0.3	168,000	105	0.1%	0.0	182,000	776	0.4%	0.3				
DISTRICT OF COLUMBIA																			
FLORIDA	861,000	54	0.0%																
GEORGIA	1,511,000	369	0.0%					1,735,000	4,056	0.2%	0.2	1,887,000	3,527	0.2%	0.2	2,050,000	19,578	1.0%	0.9
HAWAII																			
IDAHO				267,000	2,001	0.7%		294,000	1,494	0.5%	-0.2								
ILLINOIS	4,466,000	17,934	0.4%	4,753,000	41,239	0.9%	0.5	5,029,000	10,707	0.2%	-0.2	5,316,000	11,160	0.2%	-0.2	5,591,000	12,917	0.2%	-0.2
INDIANA	1,960,000	899	0.0%	2,065,000	15,708	0.8%	0.7	2,167,000	10,215	0.5%	0.4					2,429,000	23,337	1.0%	0.9
IOWA	1,480,000	3,715	0.3%	1,536,000	42,612	2.8%	2.5	1,592,000	13,391	0.8%	0.6	1,628,000	2,282	0.1%	-0.1	1,656,000	2,899	0.2%	-0.1
KANSAS	1,106,000	187,144	16.9%	1,123,000	9,450	0.8%	-16.1	1,139,000	21,438	1.9%	-15.0	1,169,000	12,863	1.1%	-15.8	1,205,000	14,347	1.2%	-15.7
KENTUCKY	1,429,000	6,325	0.4%	1,518,000	8,768	0.6%	0.1	1,604,000	210	0.0%	-0.4	1,704,000	4,033	0.2%	-0.2	1,804,000	320	0.0%	-0.4
LOUISIANA	1,131,000	24	0.0%	1,234,000	49	0.0%	0.0	1,333,000	250	0.0%	0.0					1,512,000	1	0.0%	0.0
MAINE				464,000	422	0.1%		486,000	287	0.1%	0.0								

Total Highest Statewide General Elections (continued)

Other Turnout for Election Years 1930–1946 (continued)

State	1930 Voting-age population	1930 Turnout	1930 %	1934 Voting-age population	1934 Turnout	1934 %	1934 Difference from 1930	1938 Voting-age population	1938 Turnout	1938 %	1938 Difference from 1930	1942 Voting-age population	1942 Turnout	1942 %	1942 Difference from 1930	1946 Voting-age population	1946 Turnout	1946 %	1946 Difference from 1930
MARYLAND	970,000	6,391	0.7%	1,052,000	11,137	1.1%	0.4	1,129,000	14,073	1.2%	0.6								
MASSACHUSETTS	2,224,000	27,876	1.3%	2,379,000	119,353	5.0%	3.8	2,527,000	30,409	1.2%	-0.1	2,709,000	13,163	0.5%	-0.8	2,895,000	12,127	0.4%	-0.8
MICHIGAN	2,604,000	9,238	0.4%	2,836,000	22,138	0.8%	0.4	3,058,000	4,244	0.1%	-0.2	3,371,000	8,125	0.2%	-0.1	3,706,000	17,057	0.5%	0.1
MINNESOTA	1,471,000	478,748	32.5%	1,583,000	514,617	32.5%	0.0	1,690,000	388,162	23.0%	-9.6	1,768,000	323,196	18.3%	-14.3	1,827,000	11,716	0.6%	-31.9
MISSISSIPPI																			
MISSOURI	2,234,000	743	0.0%	2,336,000	9,812	0.4%	0.4	2,432,000	2,003	0.1%	0.0	2,509,000	247	0.0%	0.0	2,571,000	2,141	0.1%	0.1
MONTANA	295,000	3,163	1.1%	312,000	1,736	0.6%	-0.5					344,000	4,380	1.3%	0.2	355,000	2,189	0.6%	-0.5
NEBRASKA	785,000	14,884	1.9%	798,000	10,171	1.3%	-0.6	812,000	76,258	9.4%	7.5	825,000	110,199	13.4%	11.5	837,000	4,516	0.5%	-1.4
NEVADA				58,000	4,940	8.5%													
NEW HAMPSHIRE	260,000	288	0.1%	276,000	522	0.2%	0.1	291,000	237	0.1%	0.0								
NEW JERSEY	2,205,000	25,719	1.2%	2,376,000	16,955	0.7%	-0.5	2,540,000	17,211	0.7%	-0.5	2,774,000	13,426	0.5%	-0.7	3,024,000	18,889	0.6%	-0.5
NEW MEXICO	179,000	299	0.2%	215,000	776	0.4%	0.2	249,000	270	0.1%	-0.1								
NEW YORK	6,904,000	338,240	4.9%	7,527,000	288,001	3.8%	-1.1	8,124,000	135,975	1.7%	-3.2	8,745,000	474,253	5.4%	0.5	9,339,000	229,718	2.5%	-2.4
NORTH CAROLINA																			
NORTH DAKOTA	338,000	5,754	1.7%	345,000	46,304	13.4%	11.7	351,000	112,007	31.9%	30.2					357,000	38,804	10.9%	9.2
OHIO	3,913,000	13,468	0.3%	4,130,000	15,918	0.4%	0.0					4,631,000	34	0.0%	-0.3	4,941,000	13,885	0.3%	-0.1
OKLAHOMA	1,242,000	832	0.1%	1,281,000	18,498	1.4%	1.4	1,319,000	3,396	0.3%	0.2	1,344,000	1,762	0.1%	0.1	1,362,000	7,682	0.6%	0.5
OREGON	584,000	139,521	23.9%	640,000	98,921	15.5%	-8.4	693,000	57	0.0%	-23.9	789,000	13	0.0%	-23.9				
PENNSYLVANIA	5,264,000	26,367	0.5%	5,603,000	92,621	1.7%	1.2	5,928,000	33,623	0.6%	0.1	6,263,000	30,643	0.5%	0.0	6,583,000	29,064	0.4%	-0.1
RHODE ISLAND	362,000	1,195	0.3%	389,000	2,333	0.6%	0.3	417,000	14,683	3.5%	3.2					486,000	890	0.2%	-0.1
SOUTH CAROLINA				899,000	181	0.0%		968,000	74	0.0%	0.0	1,036,000	2	0.0%	0.0	1,100,000	48	0.0%	0.0
SOUTH DAKOTA	364,000	7,926	2.2%	365,000	2,259	0.6%	-1.6												
TENNESSEE	1,430,000	3,392	0.2%	1,551,000	122,965	7.9%	7.7	1,668,000	29,849	1.8%	1.6	1,782,000	15,317	0.9%	0.6	1,890,000	15,819	0.8%	0.6
TEXAS	2,923,000	1,100	0.0%	3,270,000	2,146	0.1%	0.0	3,605,000	489	0.0%	0.0	3,965,000	1,975	0.0%	0.0				
UTAH	249,000	10,945	4.4%	269,000	2,707	1.0%	-3.4												
VERMONT	204,000	64	0.0%	208,000	949	0.5%	0.4	213,000	4	0.0%	0.0	219,000	15	0.0%	0.0	225,000	99	0.0%	0.0
VIRGINIA	1,308,000	34,094	2.6%	1,413,000	5,291	0.4%	-2.2	1,513,000	2,368	0.2%	-2.5	1,682,000	7,731	0.5%	-2.1	1,869,000	11,898	0.6%	-2.0
WASHINGTON	920,000	8,017	0.9%	1,002,000	25,088	2.5%	1.6	1,081,000	1,553	0.1%	-0.7	1,224,000	829	0.1%	-0.8	1,384,000	2,812	0.2%	-0.7
WEST VIRGINIA	884,000	1,293	0.1%	956,000	2,933	0.3%	0.2												
WISCONSIN	1,666,000	58,788	3.5%	1,785,000	487,919	27.3%	23.8	1,899,000	359,439	18.9%	15.4	2,008,000	410,887	20.5%	16.9	2,108,000	55,990	2.7%	-0.9
WYOMING				135,000	683	0.5%													
Total	61,907,000	1,598,484	2.6%	67,055,000	2,432,875	3.6%	1.0	66,750,000	1,659,257	2.5%	-0.1	68,668,000	1,548,721	2.3%	-0.3	71,538,000	800,936	1.1%	-1.5

*Percentage point difference between turnout in current year and initial year listed in chart. If data do not appear for a state in the initial year listed, the difference is calculated from the first year in which data do appear for that state.

STATE GUBERNATORIAL PRIMARY ELECTIONS

Election Years 1930–1946

State*	1930 Voting-age population	Turnout	%	1934 Voting-age population	Turnout	%	Difference from 1930**	1938 Voting-age population	Turnout	%	Difference from 1930	1942 Voting-age population	Turnout	%	Difference from 1930	1946 Voting-age population	Turnout	%	Difference from 1930
ALABAMA																			
ALASKA																			
ARIZONA																			
ARKANSAS																			
CALIFORNIA	3,248,000	1,166,939	35.9%	3,692,000	1,685,223	45.6%	9.7	4,136,000	1,914,695	46.3%	10.4	4,966,000	1,669,796	33.6%	-2.3	5,969,000	1,995,019	33.4%	-2.5
COLORADO	572,000	131,812	23.0%	618,000	201,612	32.6%	9.6	664,000	170,664	25.7%	2.7	722,000	112,689	15.6%	-7.4	778,000	84,750	10.9%	-12.2
CONNECTICUT																			
DELAWARE																			
DISTRICT OF COLUMBIA																			
FLORIDA																			
GEORGIA																			
HAWAII																			
IDAHO				263,000	92,037	35.0%		290,000	117,253	40.4%	5.4	313,000	61,085	19.5%	-15.5	329,000	77,195	23.5%	-11.5
ILLINOIS																			
INDIANA																			
IOWA				1,529,000	485,195	31.7%		1,584,000	369,674	23.3%	-8.4	1,625,000	309,938	19.1%	-12.7	1,652,000	271,999	16.5%	-15.3
KANSAS	1,105,000	354,416	32.1%	1,120,000	448,599	40.1%	8.0	1,137,000	380,614	33.5%	1.4	1,166,000	252,626	21.7%	-10.4	1,200,000	237,384	19.8%	-12.3
KENTUCKY																			
LOUISIANA																			
MAINE																			
MARYLAND				1,040,000	348,462	33.5%		1,117,000	439,870	39.4%	5.9	1,240,000	221,532	17.9%	-15.6				
MASSACHUSETTS																			
MICHIGAN																			
MINNESOTA				1,568,000	695,533	44.4%													
MISSISSIPPI																			
MISSOURI																			
MONTANA																			
NEBRASKA																			
NEVADA	50,000	23,220	46.4%					64,000	32,960	51.5%	5.1					91,000	33,993	37.4%	-9.1
NEW HAMPSHIRE	259,000	69,553	26.9%	273,000	85,454	31.3%	4.4	288,000	109,144	37.9%	11.0	306,000	58,194	19.0%	-7.8	323,000	61,798	19.1%	-7.7
NEW JERSEY				2,352,000	762,479	32.4%										2,998,000	648,866	21.6%	-10.8
NEW MEXICO												286,000	74,260	26.0%		330,000	79,300	24.0%	-1.9
NEW YORK																			

State Gubernatorial Primary Elections (continued)

Election Years 1930–1946 (continued)

State	1930 Voting-age population	Turnout	%	1934 Voting-age population	Turnout	%	Difference from 1930	1938 Voting-age population	Turnout	%	Difference from 1930	1942 Voting-age population	Turnout	%	Difference from 1930	1946 Voting-age population	Turnout	%	Difference from 1930
NORTH CAROLINA																			
NORTH DAKOTA	337,000	182,628	54.2%	343,000	236,932	69.1%	14.9	350,000	214,940	61.4%	7.2	355,000	135,273	38.1%	-16.1	357,000	139,605	39.1%	-15.1
OHIO	3,891,000	645,196	16.6%	4,099,000	1,232,472	30.1%	13.5	4,308,000	1,452,170	33.7%	17.1	4,598,000	669,377	14.6%	-2.0	4,909,000	668,695	13.6%	-3.0
OKLAHOMA	1,237,000	416,876	33.7%	1,275,000	582,556	45.7%	12.0	1,313,000	646,243	49.2%	15.5	1,342,000	430,305	32.1%	-1.6	1,361,000	427,091	31.4%	-2.3
OREGON																			
PENNSYLVANIA	5,230,000	1,655,814	31.7%	5,555,000	1,796,850	32.3%	0.7	5,881,000	2,710,922	46.1%	14.4	6,230,000	1,499,129	24.1%	-7.6	6,549,000	1,330,052	20.3%	-11.4
RHODE ISLAND																			
SOUTH CAROLINA																			
SOUTH DAKOTA	364,000	138,116	37.9%	365,000	174,836	47.9%	10.0	367,000	167,178	45.6%	7.6					387,000	91,783	23.7%	-14.2
TENNESSEE												1,879,000	340,923	18.1%					
TEXAS	2,889,000	831,785	28.8%	3,222,000	1,009,015	31.3%	2.5												
UTAH																			
VERMONT	204,000	63,038	30.9%	208,000	67,828	32.6%	1.7	213,000	53,071	24.9%	-6.0	218,000	31,855	14.6%	-16.3	224,000	58,500	26.1%	-4.8
VIRGINIA																			
WASHINGTON																			
WEST VIRGINIA																			
WISCONSIN	1,654,000	606,401	36.7%	1,769,000	561,864	31.8%	-4.9	1,883,000	525,478	27.9%	-8.8	1,998,000	390,328	19.5%	-17.1	2,097,000	531,970	25.4%	-11.3
WYOMING	122,000	51,476	42.2%	133,000	65,911	49.6%	7.4	143,000	65,852	46.1%	3.9	155,000	27,103	17.5%	-24.7	165,000	43,598	26.4%	-15.8
Total	21,162,000	6,337,270	29.9%	29,424,000	10,532,858	35.8%	5.9	23,738,000	9,370,728	39.5%	9.5	25,520,000	5,943,490	23.3%	-6.7	31,598,000	7,122,521	22.5%	-7.4

*Overall primary turnout reflects only states with primaries in both parties. To find single party primary results, see partisan primary charts.

**Percentage point difference between turnout in current year and initial year listed in chart. If data do not appear for a state in the initial year listed, the difference is calculated from the first year in which data do appear for that state.

STATE GUBERNATORIAL PRIMARY ELECTIONS

Republican Turnout for Election Years 1930–1946

State	1930			1934				1938				1942				1946			
	Voting-age population	Turnout	%	Voting-age population	Turnout	%	Difference from 1930*	Voting-age population	Turnout	%	Difference from 1930	Voting-age population	Turnout	%	Difference from 1930	Voting-age population	Turnout	%	Difference from 1930
ALABAMA																			
ALASKA																			
ARIZONA																			
ARKANSAS																			
CALIFORNIA	3,248,000	1,044,051	32.1%	3,692,000	825,800	22.4%	-9.8	4,136,000	739,003	17.9%	-14.3	4,966,000	674,164	13.6%	-18.6	5,969,000	850,192	14.2%	-17.9
COLORADO	572,000	87,223	15.2%	618,000	62,265	10.1%	-5.2	664,000	61,724	9.3%	-6.0	722,000	48,395	6.7%	-8.5	778,000	39,646	5.1%	-10.2
CONNECTICUT																			
DELAWARE																			
DISTRICT OF COLUMBIA																			
FLORIDA																			
GEORGIA																			
HAWAII																			
IDAHO				263,000	33,512	12.7%		290,000	30,398	10.5%	-2.3	313,000	31,046	9.9%	-2.8	329,000	38,316	11.6%	-1.1
ILLINOIS																			
INDIANA																			
IOWA	1,474,000	467,417	31.7%	1,529,000	341,457	22.3%	-9.4	1,584,000	229,571	14.5%	-17.2	1,625,000	231,473	14.2%	-17.5	1,652,000	221,614	13.4%	-18.3
KANSAS	1,105,000	290,101	26.3%	1,120,000	292,939	26.2%	-0.1	1,137,000	256,834	22.6%	-3.7	1,166,000	176,521	15.1%	-11.1	1,200,000	168,951	14.1%	-12.2
KENTUCKY																			
LOUISIANA																			
MAINE																			
MARYLAND				1,040,000	104,602	10.1%		1,117,000	99,089	8.9%	-1.2	1,240,000	45,988	3.7%	-6.3				
MASSACHUSETTS																			
MICHIGAN																			
MINNESOTA	1,460,000	439,280	30.1%	1,568,000	160,395	10.2%	-19.9												
MISSISSIPPI																			
MISSOURI																			
MONTANA																			
NEBRASKA																			
NEVADA	50,000	13,929	27.9%					64,000	8,695	13.6%	-14.3					91,000	23,484	25.8%	-2.1
NEW HAMPSHIRE	259,000	60,024	23.2%	273,000	52,478	19.2%	-4.0	288,000	81,770	28.4%	5.2	306,000	41,464	13.6%	-9.6	323,000	46,024	14.2%	-8.9
NEW JERSEY				2,352,000	474,553	20.2%										2,998,000	162,845	5.4%	-14.7
NEW MEXICO												286,000	10,171	3.6%		330,000	16,440	5.0%	1.4
NEW YORK																			

State Gubernatorial Primary Elections (continued)

Republican Turnout for Election Years 1930–1946 (continued)

State	1930 Voting-age population	1930 Turnout	1930 %	1934 Voting-age population	1934 Turnout	1934 %	1934 Difference from 1930	1938 Voting-age population	1938 Turnout	1938 %	1938 Difference from 1930	1942 Voting-age population	1942 Turnout	1942 %	1942 Difference from 1930	1946 Voting-age population	1946 Turnout	1946 %	1946 Difference from 1930
NORTH CAROLINA																			
NORTH DAKOTA	337,000	174,620	51.8%	343,000	198,341	57.8%	6.0	350,000	173,228	49.5%	-2.3	355,000	100,825	28.4%	-23.4	357,000	124,856	35.0%	-16.8
OHIO	3,891,000	429,432	11.0%	4,099,000	624,124	15.2%	4.2	4,308,000	581,326	13.5%	2.5	4,598,000	350,730	7.6%	-3.4	4,909,000	341,791	7.0%	-4.1
OKLAHOMA	1,237,000	76,137	6.2%	1,275,000	69,070	5.4%	-0.7	1,313,000	52,548	4.0%	-2.2	1,342,000	35,913	2.7%	-3.5	1,361,000	41,139	3.0%	-3.1
OREGON																			
PENNSYLVANIA	5,230,000	1,534,657	29.3%	5,555,000	1,221,590	22.0%	-7.4	5,881,000	1,429,047	24.3%	-5.0	6,230,000	938,730	15.1%	-14.3	6,549,000	942,199	14.4%	-15.0
RHODE ISLAND																			
SOUTH CAROLINA																			
SOUTH DAKOTA	364,000	117,170	32.2%	365,000	97,315	26.7%	-5.5	367,000	98,800	26.9%	-5.3	374,000	82,201	22.0%	-10.2	387,000	72,092	18.6%	-13.6
TENNESSEE																1,879,000	33,269	1.8%	
TEXAS	2,889,000	9,574	0.3%	3,222,000	13,043	0.4%	0.1												
UTAH																			
VERMONT	204,000	61,257	30.0%	208,000	60,420	29.0%	-1.0	213,000	48,077	22.6%	-7.5	218,000	29,548	13.6%	-16.5	224,000	56,391	25.2%	-4.9
VIRGINIA																			
WASHINGTON																			
WEST VIRGINIA																			
WISCONSIN	1,654,000	392,958	23.8%	1,769,000	148,838	8.4%	-15.3	1,883,000	227,159	12.1%	-11.7	1,998,000	265,628	13.3%	-10.5	2,097,000	455,173	21.7%	-2.1
WYOMING	122,000	41,849	34.3%	133,000	34,489	25.9%	-8.4	143,000	32,055	22.4%	-11.9	155,000	5,220	3.4%	-30.9	165,000	26,142	15.8%	-18.5
Total	24,096,000	5,239,679	21.7%	29,424,000	4,815,231	16.4%	-5.4	23,738,000	4,149,324	17.5%	-4.3	25,894,000	3,068,017	11.8%	-9.9	31,598,000	3,660,564	11.6%	-10.2

Democratic Turnout for Election Years 1930–1946

State	1930 Voting-age population	1930 Turnout	1930 %	1934 Voting-age population	1934 Turnout	1934 %	1934 Difference from 1930*	1938 Voting-age population	1938 Turnout	1938 %	1938 Difference from 1930	1942 Voting-age population	1942 Turnout	1942 %	1942 Difference from 1930	1946 Voting-age population	1946 Turnout	1946 %	1946 Difference from 1930
ALABAMA	1,347,000	186,356	13.8%	1,431,000	305,178	21.3%	7.5	1,516,000	297,701	19.6%	5.8	1,603,000	272,552	17.0%	3.2	1,678,000	365,513	21.8%	7.9
ALASKA																			
ARIZONA																			
ARKANSAS	967,000	242,544	25.1%	1,021,000	254,811	25.0%	-0.1	1,074,000	278,263	25.9%	0.8	1,102,000	165,115	15.0%	-10.1	1,106,000	189,045	17.1%	-8.0
CALIFORNIA	3,248,000	114,936	3.5%	3,692,000	844,117	22.9%	19.3	4,136,000	1,151,863	27.8%	24.3	4,966,000	988,235	19.9%	16.4	5,969,000	1,142,188	19.1%	15.6
COLORADO	572,000	44,589	7.8%	618,000	139,347	22.5%	14.8	664,000	108,940	16.4%	8.6	722,000	64,294	8.9%	1.1	778,000	45,104	5.8%	-2.0
CONNECTICUT																			
DELAWARE																			
DISTRICT OF COLUMBIA																			
FLORIDA																			

State Gubernatorial Primary Elections (continued)

State Gubernatorial Primary Elections (continued)

Democratic Turnout for Election Years 1930–1946 (continued)

State	1930 Voting-age population	1930 Turnout	1930 %	1934 Voting-age population	1934 Turnout	1934 %	1934 Difference from 1930	1938 Voting-age population	1938 Turnout	1938 %	1938 Difference from 1930	1942 Voting-age population	1942 Turnout	1942 %	1942 Difference from 1930	1946 Voting-age population	1946 Turnout	1946 %	1946 Difference from 1930
GEORGIA	1,499,000	199,467		1,609,000	265,458	16.5%	3.2	1,719,000	314,117	18.3%	1.8	1,870,000	303,151	16.2%	-0.3	2,033,000	680,123	33.5%	17.0
HAWAII																			
IDAHO				263,000	58,525	22.3%		290,000	86,855	30.0%	7.7	313,000	30,039	9.6%	-12.7	329,000	38,879	11.8%	-10.4
ILLINOIS																			
INDIANA																			
IOWA				1,529,000	143,738	9.4%		1,584,000	139,280	8.8%	-0.6	1,625,000	78,465	4.8%	-4.6	1,652,000	50,385	3.0%	-6.4
KANSAS	1,105,000	64,209	5.8%	1,120,000	155,355	13.9%	8.1	1,137,000	123,649	10.9%	5.1	1,166,000	75,932	6.5%	0.7	1,200,000	68,109	5.7%	-0.1
KENTUCKY																			
LOUISIANA																			
MAINE																			
MARYLAND				1,040,000	243,860	23.4%		1,117,000	340,781	30.5%	7.1	1,240,000	175,544	14.2%	-9.3				
MASSACHUSETTS																			
MICHIGAN																			
MINNESOTA				1,568,000	263,049	16.8%													
MISSISSIPPI																			
MISSOURI																			
MONTANA																			
NEBRASKA																			
NEVADA	50,000	9,291	18.6%	57,000	18,672	32.8%	14.2	64,000	24,265	37.9%	19.3	76,000	21,458	28.2%	9.7	91,000	10,509	11.5%	-7.0
NEW HAMPSHIRE	259,000	9,529	3.7%	273,000	32,976	12.1%	8.4	288,000	27,374	9.5%	5.8	306,000	16,730	5.5%	1.8	323,000	15,774	4.9%	1.2
NEW JERSEY				2,352,000	287,926	12.2%										2,998,000	486,021	16.2%	4.0
NEW MEXICO												286,000	64,089	22.4%		330,000	62,860	19.0%	-3.4
NEW YORK																			
NORTH CAROLINA																			
NORTH DAKOTA	337,000	8,008	2.4%	343,000	38,591	11.3%	8.9	350,000	41,680	11.9%	9.5	355,000	34,448	9.7%	7.3	357,000	14,749	4.1%	1.8
OHIO	3,891,000	215,764	5.5%	4,099,000	608,348	14.8%	9.3	4,308,000	870,844	20.2%	14.7	4,598,000	318,647	6.9%	1.4	4,909,000	326,904	6.7%	1.1
OKLAHOMA	1,237,000	340,569	27.5%	1,275,000	513,486	40.3%	12.7	1,313,000	593,695	45.2%	17.7	1,342,000	394,392	29.4%	1.9	1,361,000	385,952	28.4%	0.8
OREGON																			
PENNSYLVANIA	5,230,000	121,157	2.3%	5,555,000	571,067	10.3%	8.0	5,881,000	1,281,694	21.8%	19.5	6,230,000	560,399	9.0%	6.7	6,549,000	386,841	5.9%	3.6
RHODE ISLAND																			
SOUTH CAROLINA	820,000	224,359	27.4%	889,000	282,689	31.8%	4.4	958,000	387,337	40.4%	13.1	1,029,000	234,479	22.8%	-4.6	1,093,000	271,492	24.8%	-2.5
SOUTH DAKOTA	364,000	20,946	5.8%	365,000	77,521	21.2%	15.5	367,000	68,378	18.6%	12.9					387,000	19,691	5.1%	-0.7
TENNESSEE	1,418,000	246,175	17.4%	1,534,000	328,713	21.4%	4.1	1,650,000	396,707	24.0%	6.7	1,770,000	295,296	16.7%	-0.7	1,879,000	307,654	16.4%	-1.0

State Gubernatorial Primary Elections (continued)

Democratic Turnout for Election Years 1930–1946 (continued)

State	1930 Voting-age population	Turnout	%	1934 Voting-age population	Turnout	%	Difference from 1930	1938 Voting-age population	Turnout	%	Difference from 1930	1942 Voting-age population	Turnout	%	Difference from 1930	1946 Voting-age population	Turnout	%	Difference from 1930
TEXAS	2,889,000	822,211	28.5%	3,222,000	995,972	30.9%	2.5	3,556,000	1,074,708	30.2%	1.8	3,929,000	923,687	23.5%	-5.0	4,280,000	1,103,578	25.8%	-2.7
UTAH																			
VERMONT	204,000	1,781	0.9%	208,000	7,408	3.6%	2.7	213,000	4,994	2.3%	1.5	218,000	2,307	1.1%	0.2	224,000	2,109	0.9%	0.1
VIRGINIA																			
WASHINGTON																			
WEST VIRGINIA																			
WISCONSIN	1,654,000	170,020	10.3%	1,769,000	222,175	12.6%	2.3	1,883,000	125,844	6.7%	-3.6	1,998,000	64,526	3.2%	-7.0	2,097,000	72,991	3.5%	-6.8
WYOMING	122,000	9,627	7.9%	133,000	31,422	23.6%	15.7	143,000	33,797	23.6%	15.7	155,000	21,883	14.1%	6.2	165,000	17,456	10.6%	2.7
Total	27,213,000	3,051,538	11.2%	35,965,000	6,690,404	18.6%	7.4	34,211,000	7,772,766	22.7%	11.5	36,899,000	5,105,668	13.8%	2.6	41,788,000	6,063,927	14.5%	3.3

Other Turnout for Election Years 1930–1946

State	1930 Voting-age population	Turnout	%	1934 Voting-age population	Turnout	%	Difference from 1930*	1938 Voting-age population	Turnout	%	Difference from 1930	1942 Voting-age population	Turnout	%	Difference from 1930	1946 Voting-age population	Turnout	%	Difference from 1930
CALIFORNIA	3,248,000	7,952	0.2%	3,692,000	15,306	0.4%	0.2	4,136,000	23,829	0.6%	0.3	4,966,000	7,397	0.1%	-0.1	5,969,000	2,639	0.0%	-0.2
KANSAS	1,105,000	106	0.0%	1,120,000	305	0.0%	0.0	1,137,000	131	0.0%	0.0	1,166,000	173	0.0%	0.0	1,200,000	324	0.0%	0.0
MINNESOTA	1,460,000	72,246	4.9%	1,568,000	272,089	17.4%	12.4												
NORTH DAKOTA								350,000	32	0.0%									
OKLAHOMA	1,237,000	170	0.0%																
PENNSYLVANIA				5,555,000	4,193	0.1%		5,881,000	181	0.0%	-0.1					6,549,000	1,012	0.0%	-0.1
WISCONSIN	1,654,000	43,423	2.6%	1,769,000	190,851	10.8%	8.2	1,883,000	172,475	9.2%	6.5	1,998,000	60,174	3.0%	0.4	2,097,000	3,806	0.2%	-2.4
Total	8,704,000	123,897	1.4%	13,704,000	482,744	3.5%	2.1	13,387,000	196,648	1.5%	0.0	8,130,000	67,744	0.8%	-0.6	15,815,000	7,781	0.0%	-1.4

*Percentage point difference between turnout in current year and initial year listed in chart. If data do not appear for a state in the initial year listed, the difference is calculated from the first year in which data do appear for that state.

UNITED STATES SENATE PRIMARY ELECTIONS

Election Years 1930–1946

State*	1930 Voting-age population	Turnout	%	1934 Voting-age population	Turnout	%	Difference from 1930**	1938 Voting-age population	Turnout	%	Difference from 1930	1942 Voting-age population	Turnout	%	Difference from 1930	1946 Voting-age population	Turnout	%	Difference from 1930
ALABAMA																			
ALASKA																			
ARIZONA																			
ARKANSAS																			
CALIFORNIA				3,692,000	1,502,155	40.7%		4,136,000	1,800,419	43.5%	2.8								
COLORADO	572,000	160,009	28.0%					664,000	149,416	22.5%	-5.5	722,000	110,950	15.4%	-12.6				
CONNECTICUT																			
DELAWARE																			
DISTRICT OF COLUMBIA																			
FLORIDA																			
GEORGIA																			
HAWAII																			
IDAHO								290,000	113,878	39.3%		313,000	62,082	19.8%	-19.4	329,000	76,886	23.4%	-15.9
ILLINOIS	4,437,000	1,737,849	39.2%					4,990,000	2,294,171	46.0%	6.8	5,287,000	1,770,481	33.5%	-5.7				
INDIANA																			
IOWA								1,584,000	414,667	26.2%		1,625,000	314,542	19.4%	-6.8				
KANSAS	1,105,000	324,350	29.4%					1,137,000	385,223	33.9%	4.5	1,166,000	245,205	21.0%	-8.3				
KENTUCKY								1,592,000	585,022	36.7%		1,693,000	230,796	13.6%	-23.1	1,793,000	182,717	10.2%	-26.6
LOUISIANA																			
MAINE																			
MARYLAND				1,040,000	299,592	28.8%		1,117,000	408,285	36.6%	7.7								
MASSACHUSETTS																			
MICHIGAN																			
MINNESOTA				1,568,000	664,253	42.4%													
MISSISSIPPI																			
MISSOURI				2,321,000	938,949	40.5%		2,419,000	924,826	38.2%	-2.2					2,565,000	501,589	19.6%	-20.9
MONTANA	292,000	98,854	33.9%	309,000	133,098	43.1%	9.2					342,000	118,478	34.6%	0.8	354,000	127,889	36.1%	2.3
NEBRASKA																			
NEVADA				57,000	30,304	53.2%										91,000	35,028	38.5%	-14.7
NEW HAMPSHIRE	259,000	53,357	20.6%					288,000	100,927	35.0%	14.4	306,000	64,326	21.0%	0.4				
NEW JERSEY	2,187,000	784,239	35.9%	2,352,000	733,736	31.2%	-4.7	2,516,000	794,216	31.6%	0.4	2,748,000	468,276	17.0%	-18.8	2,998,000	530,371	17.7%	-18.2
NEW MEXICO												286,000	70,438	24.6%		330,000	79,828	24.2%	-0.4
NEW YORK																			

United States Senate Primary Elections *(continued)*

Election Years 1930–1946 *(continued)*

State	1930 Voting-age population	Turnout	%	1934 Voting-age population	Turnout	%	Difference from 1930	1938 Voting-age population	Turnout	%	Difference from 1930	1942 Voting-age population	Turnout	%	Difference from 1930	1946 Voting-age population	Turnout	%	Difference from 1930
NORTH CAROLINA	1,539,000	367,779	23.9%																
NORTH DAKOTA				343,000	219,622	64.0%		350,000	216,764	61.9%	-2.1					357,000	136,826	38.3%	-25.7
OHIO	3,891,000	554,585	14.3%	4,099,000	1,140,265	27.8%	13.6	4,308,000	1,296,972	30.1%	15.9					4,909,000	514,597	10.5%	-3.8
OKLAHOMA	1,237,000	353,433	28.6%					1,313,000	614,390	46.8%	18.2	1,342,000	389,238	29.0%	0.4				
OREGON																			
PENNSYLVANIA	5,230,000	1,628,255	31.1%	5,555,000	1,770,514	31.9%	0.7	5,881,000	2,512,894	42.7%	11.0					6,549,000	1,304,494	19.9%	-11.2
RHODE ISLAND																			
SOUTH CAROLINA																			
SOUTH DAKOTA								367,000	179,038	48.8%		374,000	122,071	32.6%	-16.1				
TENNESSEE																1,879,000	327,122	17.4%	
TEXAS				3,222,000	924,250	28.7%													
UTAH																			
VERMONT				208,000	67,181	32.3%		213,000	52,453	24.6%	-7.7					224,000	58,223	26.0%	-6.3
VIRGINIA																			
WASHINGTON				990,000	333,795	33.7%		1,069,000	440,558	41.2%	7.5					1,367,000	361,446	26.4%	-7.3
WEST VIRGINIA																			
WISCONSIN				1,769,000	509,185	28.8%		1,883,000	473,744	25.2%	-3.6					2,097,000	507,149	24.2%	-4.6
WYOMING	122,000	53,767	44.1%	133,000	59,474	44.7%	0.6					155,000	49,110	31.7%	-12.4	165,000	40,346	24.5%	-19.6
Total	20,871,000	6,116,477	29.3%	27,658,000	9,326,373	33.7%	4.4	36,117,000	13,757,863	38.1%	8.8	16,359,000	4,015,993	24.5%	-4.8	26,007,000	4,784,511	18.4%	-10.9

*Overall primary turnout reflects only states with primaries in both parties. To find single party primary results, see partisan primary charts.

**Percentage point difference between turnout in current year and initial year listed in chart. If data do not appear for a state in the initial year listed, the difference is calculated from the first year in which data do appear for that state.

UNITED STATES SENATE PRIMARY ELECTIONS

Republican Turnout for Election Years 1930–1946

State	1930 Voting-age population	Turnout	%	1934 Voting-age population	Turnout	%	Difference from 1930*	1938 Voting-age population	Turnout	%	Difference from 1930	1942 Voting-age population	Turnout	%	Difference from 1930	1946 Voting-age population	Turnout	%	Difference from 1930
ALABAMA																			
ALASKA																			
ARIZONA																			
ARKANSAS																			
CALIFORNIA				3,692,000	741,537	20.1%		4,136,000	659,299	15.9%	-4.1								
COLORADO	572,000	112,155	19.6%					664,000	57,410	8.6%	-11.0	722,000	44,683	6.2%	-13.4				
CONNECTICUT																			
DELAWARE																			
DISTRICT OF COLUMBIA																			
FLORIDA																			
GEORGIA																			
HAWAII																			
IDAHO								290,000	29,416	10.1%		313,000	29,984	9.6%	-0.6	329,000	37,221	11.3%	1.2
ILLINOIS	4,437,000	1,410,538	31.8%					4,990,000	687,925	13.8%	-18.0	5,287,000	865,621	16.4%	-15.4				
INDIANA																			
IOWA	1,474,000	353,112	24.0%					1,584,000	257,611	16.3%	-7.7	1,625,000	235,176	14.5%	-9.5				
KANSAS	1,105,000	268,375	24.3%					1,137,000	248,169	21.8%	-2.5	1,166,000	173,354	14.9%	-9.4				
KENTUCKY								1,592,000	59,468	3.7%		1,693,000	43,249	2.6%	-1.2	1,793,000	56,019	3.1%	-0.6
LOUISIANA																			
MAINE																			
MARYLAND				1,040,000	89,531	8.6%		1,117,000	85,941	7.7%	-0.9								
MASSACHUSETTS																			
MICHIGAN																			
MINNESOTA	1,460,000	464,699	31.8%	1,568,000	156,413	10.0%	-21.9												
MISSISSIPPI																			
MISSOURI				2,321,000	270,689	11.7%		2,419,000	195,782	8.1%	-3.6					2,565,000	216,523	8.4%	-3.2
MONTANA	292,000	65,877	22.6%	309,000	54,175	17.5%	-5.0					342,000	41,943	12.3%	-10.3	354,000	33,957	9.6%	-13.0
NEBRASKA																			
NEVADA				57,000	11,443	20.1%		64,000	24,107	37.7%	17.6					91,000	10,848	11.9%	-8.2
NEW HAMPSHIRE	259,000	45,217	17.5%					288,000	75,299	26.1%	8.7	306,000	40,085	13.1%	-4.4				
NEW JERSEY	2,187,000	665,745	30.4%	2,352,000	438,776	18.7%	-11.8	2,516,000	437,962	17.4%	-13.0	2,748,000	297,655	10.8%	-19.6	2,998,000	369,157	12.3%	-18.1
NEW MEXICO												286,000	10,275	3.6%		330,000	14,920	4.5%	0.9
NEW YORK																			

United States Senate Primary Elections *(continued)*

Republican Turnout for Election Years 1930–1946 *(continued)*

State	1930			1934				1938				1942				1946			
	Voting-age population	Turnout	%	Voting-age population	Turnout	%	Difference from 1930	Voting-age population	Turnout	%	Difference from 1930	Voting-age population	Turnout	%	Difference from 1930	Voting-age population	Turnout	%	Difference from 1930
NORTH CAROLINA	1,539,000	37,662	2.4%																
NORTH DAKOTA				343,000	183,961	53.6%		350,000	177,869	50.8%	-2.8					357,000	75,998	21.3%	-32.3
OHIO	3,891,000	341,055	8.8%	4,099,000	542,965	13.2%	4.5	4,308,000	568,319	13.2%	-0.1					4,909,000	293,985	6.0%	-2.8
OKLAHOMA	1,237,000	70,232	5.7%					1,313,000	49,018	3.7%	-1.9	1,342,000	36,056	2.7%	-3.0				
OREGON																			
PENNSYLVANIA	5,230,000	1,504,601	28.8%	5,555,000	1,190,198	21.4%	-7.3	5,881,000	1,306,011	22.2%	0.8					6,549,000	928,603	14.2%	-14.6
RHODE ISLAND																			
SOUTH CAROLINA																			
SOUTH DAKOTA								367,000	105,605	28.8%		374,000	82,667	22.1%	-6.7				
TENNESSEE																1,879,000	30,954	1.6%	
TEXAS				3,222,000	1,148	0.0%													
UTAH								286,000	26,073	9.1%						350,000	19,862	5.7%	-3.4
VERMONT				208,000	59,295	28.5%		213,000	47,516	22.3%	-6.2					224,000	55,697	24.9%	-3.6
VIRGINIA																			
WASHINGTON				990,000	128,335	13.0%		1,069,000	137,612	12.9%	-0.1					1,367,000	179,613	13.1%	0.2
WEST VIRGINIA																			
WISCONSIN				1,769,000	126,034	7.1%		1,883,000	213,936	11.4%	4.2					2,097,000	440,115	21.0%	13.9
WYOMING	122,000	44,051	36.1%	133,000	34,462	25.9%	-10.2					155,000	29,272	18.9%	-17.2	165,000	22,757	13.8%	-22.3
Total	23,805,000	5,383,319	22.6%	27,658,000	4,028,962	14.6%	-8.0	36,467,000	5,450,348	14.9%	-7.7	16,359,000	1,930,020	11.8%	-10.8	26,357,000	2,786,229	10.6%	-12.0

Democratic Turnout for Election Years 1930–1946

State	1930			1934				1938				1942				1946			
	Voting-age population	Turnout	%	Voting-age population	Turnout	%	Difference from 1930*	Voting-age population	Turnout	%	Difference from 1930	Voting-age population	Turnout	%	Difference from 1930	Voting-age population	Turnout	%	Difference from 1930
ALABAMA**	1,347,000	160,271	11.9%													1,678,000	167,833	10.0%	-1.9
ALASKA																			
ARIZONA																			
ARKANSAS	967,000	218,252	22.6%									1,102,000	169,089	15.3%	-7.2				
CALIFORNIA				3,692,000	750,800	20.3%		4,136,000	1,111,644	26.9%	6.5								
COLORADO	572,000	47,854	8.4%					664,000	92,006	13.9%	5.5	722,000	66,267	9.2%	0.8				
CONNECTICUT																			
DELAWARE																			
DISTRICT OF COLUMBIA																			
FLORIDA				985,000	205,730	20.9%										1,595,000	204,352	12.8%	-8.1

United States Senate Primary Elections (continued)

United States Senate Primary Elections (continued)

Democratic Turnout for Election Years 1930–1946 (continued)

State	1930 Voting-age population	Turnout	%	1934 Voting-age population	Turnout	%	Difference from 1930	1938 Voting-age population	Turnout	%	Difference from 1930	1942 Voting-age population	Turnout	%	Difference from 1930	1946 Voting-age population	Turnout	%	Difference from 1930
GEORGIA	1,499,000	208,264	13.9%									1,870,000	287,929	15.4%	1.5				
HAWAII																			
IDAHO								290,000	84,462	29.1%		313,000	32,098	10.3%	-18.9	329,000	39,665	12.1%	-17.1
ILLINOIS	4,437,000	327,311	7.4%					4,990,000	1,606,246	32.2%	24.8	5,287,000	904,860	17.1%	9.7				
INDIANA																			
IOWA								1,584,000	157,056	9.9%		1,625,000	79,366	4.9%	-5.0				
KANSAS	1,105,000	55,873	5.1%					1,137,000	137,054	12.1%	7.0	1,166,000	71,695	6.1%	1.1				
KENTUCKY								1,592,000	525,554	33.0%		1,693,000	187,547	11.1%	-21.9	1,793,000	126,698	7.1%	-25.9
LOUISIANA	1,121,000	261,091	23.3%									1,417,000	321,041	22.7%	-0.6				
MAINE																			
MARYLAND				1,040,000	210,061	20.2%		1,117,000	322,344	28.9%	8.7								
MASSACHUSETTS																			
MICHIGAN																			
MINNESOTA				1,568,000	237,717	15.2%													
MISSISSIPPI				1,097,000	169,996	15.5%										1,202,000	190,420	15.8%	0.3
MISSOURI				2,321,000	668,260	28.8%		2,419,000	729,044	30.1%	1.3					2,565,000	285,066	11.1%	-17.7
MONTANA	292,000	32,977	11.3%	309,000	78,923	25.5%	14.2					342,000	76,535	22.4%	11.1	354,000	93,932	26.5%	15.2
NEBRASKA																			
NEVADA				57,000	18,861	33.1%						76,000	21,776	28.7%	-4.4	91,000	24,180	26.6%	-6.5
NEW HAMPSHIRE	259,000	8,140	3.1%					288,000	25,628	8.9%	5.8	306,000	24,241	7.9%	4.8				
NEW JERSEY	2,187,000	118,494	5.4%	2,352,000	294,960	12.5%	7.1	2,516,000	356,254	14.2%	8.7	2,748,000	170,621	6.2%	0.8	2,998,000	161,214	5.4%	0.0
NEW MEXICO												286,000	60,163	21.0%		330,000	64,908	19.7%	-1.4
NEW YORK																			
NORTH CAROLINA	1,539,000	330,117	21.5%									2,014,000	305,619	15.2%	-6.3				
NORTH DAKOTA				343,000	35,661	10.4%		350,000	38,861	11.1%	0.7					357,000	37,507	10.5%	0.1
OHIO	3,891,000	213,530	5.5%	4,099,000	597,300	14.6%	9.1	4,308,000	728,653	16.9%	2.3					4,909,000	220,612	4.5%	-10.1
OKLAHOMA	1,237,000	283,201	22.9%					1,313,000	565,205	43.0%	20.2	1,342,000	353,182	26.3%	3.4				
OREGON																			
PENNSYLVANIA	5,230,000	123,654	2.4%	5,555,000	575,998	10.4%	8.0	5,881,000	1,206,722	20.5%	10.1					6,549,000	375,626	5.7%	-4.6
RHODE ISLAND																			
SOUTH CAROLINA	820,000	245,743	30.0%									1,029,000	234,972	22.8%	-7.1				
SOUTH DAKOTA								367,000	73,433	20.0%		374,000	39,404	10.5%	-9.5				
TENNESSEE				1,534,000	252,689	16.5%										1,879,000	296,168	15.8%	-0.7

United States Senate Primary Elections (continued)

Democratic Turnout for Election Years 1930–1946 (continued)

State	1930 Voting-age population	Turnout	%	1934 Voting-age population	Turnout	%	Difference from 1930	1938 Voting-age population	Turnout	%	Difference from 1930	1942 Voting-age population	Turnout	%	Difference from 1930	1946 Voting-age population	Turnout	%	Difference from 1930
TEXAS				3,222,000	923,102	28.6%										4,280,000	1,050,309	24.5%	-4.1
UTAH																			
VERMONT				208,000	7,886	3.8%		213,000	4,937	2.3%	-1.5					224,000	2,526	1.1%	-2.7
VIRGINIA																1,861,000	223,528	12.0%	
WASHINGTON				990,000	205,460	20.8%		1,069,000	302,946	28.3%	7.6					1,367,000	181,833	13.3%	-7.5
WEST VIRGINIA																			
WISCONSIN				1,769,000	200,492	11.3%		1,883,000	109,129	5.8%	-5.5					2,097,000	63,361	3.0%	-8.3
WYOMING	122,000	9,716	8.0%	133,000	25,012	18.8%	10.8					155,000	19,838	12.8%	4.8	165,000	17,589	10.7%	2.7
Total	26,625,000	2,644,488	9.9%	31,274,000	5,458,908	17.5%	7.5	36,117,000	8,177,178	22.6%	12.7	23,867,000	3,426,243	14.4%	4.4	36,623,000	3,827,327	10.5%	0.5

Other Turnout for Election Years 1930–1946

State	1930 Voting-age population	Turnout	%	1934 Voting-age population	Turnout	%	Difference from 1930*	1938 Voting-age population	Turnout	%	Difference from 1930	1942 Voting-age population	Turnout	%	Difference from 1930	1946 Voting-age population	Turnout	%	Difference from 1930
CALIFORNIA				3,692,000	9,818	0.3%		4,136,000	29,476	0.7%	0.4								
KANSAS	1,105,000	102	0.0%									1,166,000	156	0.0%	0.0				
MINNESOTA	1,460,000	67,250	4.6%	1,568,000	270,123	17.2%	12.6												
NORTH DAKOTA								350,000	34	0.0%						357,000	23,321	6.5%	6.5
OKLAHOMA								1,313,000	167	0.0%									
PENNSYLVANIA				5,555,000	4,318	0.1%		5,881,000	161	0.0%	-0.1					6,549,000	265	0.0%	-0.1
WISCONSIN				1,769,000	182,659	10.3%		1,883,000	150,679	8.0%	-2.3					2,097,000	3,673	0.2%	-10.2

*Percentage point difference between turnout in current year and initial year listed in chart. If data do not appear for a state in the initial year listed, the difference is calculated from the first year in which data do appear for that state.

**ALABAMA 1946—Democratic primary winner ran unopposed in general election

STATE GUBERNATORIAL GENERAL ELECTIONS

Election Years 1931–1949

| | 1931 | | | 1933 | | | 1935 | | | | 1937 | | | | 1939 | | | |
State	Voting-age population	Turnout	%	Voting-age population	Turnout	%	Voting-age population	Turnout	%	Difference from 1931*	Voting-age population	Turnout	%	Difference from 1931	Voting-age population	Turnout	%	Difference from 1931
KENTUCKY	1,454,000	805,495	55.4%				1,539,000	1,017,366	66.1%	10.7					1,625,000	815,538	50.2%	-5.2
MISSISSIPPI	1,057,000	45,942	4.3%				1,123,000	45,881	4.1%	-0.3					1,189,000	61,614	5.2%	0.8
NEW JERSEY	2,253,000	1,240,955	55.1%								2,499,000	1,446,800	57.9%	2.8				
VIRGINIA				1,387,000	163,197	11.8%					1,488,000	147,815	9.9%	-1.8				

| | 1941 | | | | 1943 | | | | 1945 | | | | 1947 | | | | 1949 | | | |
State	Voting-age population	Turnout	%	Difference from 1931	Voting-age population	Turnout	%	Difference from 1931	Voting-age population	Turnout	%	Difference from 1931	Voting-age population	Turnout	%	Difference from 1931	Voting-age population	Turnout	%	Difference from 1931
KENTUCKY					1,729,000	549,669	31.8%	-23.6					1,829,000	675,551	36.9%	-18.5				
MISSISSIPPI					1,198,000	50,488	4.2%	-0.1					1,203,000	161,993	13.5%	9.1				
NEW JERSEY					2,837,000	1,140,968	40.2%	-14.9									3,212,000	1,695,904	52.8%	-2.3
VIRGINIA	1,635,000	120,576	7.4%	-4.4					1,822,000	164,741	9.0%	-2.7					2,009,000	256,763	12.8%	1.0

*Percentage point difference between turnout in current year and initial year listed in chart. If data do not appear for a state in the initial year listed, the difference is calculated from the first year in which data do appear for that state.

STATE GUBERNATORIAL GENERAL ELECTIONS

Republican Turnout for Election Years 1931–1949

State	1931 Voting-age population	Turnout	%	1933 Voting-age population	Turnout	%	1935 Voting-age population	Turnout	%	Difference from 1931*	1937 Voting-age population	Turnout	%	Difference from 1931	1939 Voting-age population	Turnout	%	Difference from 1931
KENTUCKY	1,454,000	366,982	**25.2%**				1,539,000	461,104	**30.0%**	4.7					1,625,000	354,704	**21.8%**	-3.4
NEW JERSEY	2,253,000	505,451	**22.4%**								2,499,000	700,767	**28.0%**	5.6				
VIRGINIA				1,387,000	40,377	**2.9%**												

State	1941 Voting-age population	Turnout	%	Difference from 1931	1943 Voting-age population	Turnout	%	Difference from 1931	1945 Voting-age population	Turnout	%	Difference from 1931	1947 Voting-age population	Turnout	%	Difference from 1931	1949 Voting-age population	Turnout	%	Difference from 1931
KENTUCKY					1,729,000	279,144	16.1%	-9.1					1,829,000	287,756	**15.7%**	-9.5				
NEW JERSEY					2,837,000	634,364	**22.4%**	-0.1									3,212,000	885,882	27.6%	5.1
VIRGINIA																	2,009,000	71,991	**3.6%**	0.7

Democratic Turnout for Election Years 1931–1949

State	1931 Voting-age population	Turnout	%	1933 Voting-age population	Turnout	%	1935 Voting-age population	Turnout	%	Difference from 1931*	1937 Voting-age population	Turnout	%	Difference from 1931	1939 Voting-age population	Turnout	%	Difference from 1931
KENTUCKY	1,454,000	438,513	**30.2%**				1,539,000	556,262	**36.1%**	6.0					1,625,000	460,834	**28.4%**	-1.8
MISSISSIPPI	1,057,000	45,942	**4.3%**				1,123,000	45,881	**4.1%**	-0.3					1,189,000	61,614	**5.2%**	0.8
NEW JERSEY	2,253,000	735,504	**32.6%**								2,499,000	746,033	**29.9%**	-2.8				
VIRGINIA				1,387,000	122,820	**8.9%**					1,488,000	124,145	**8.3%**	-0.5				

State	1941 Voting-age population	Turnout	%	Difference from 1931	1943 Voting-age population	Turnout	%	Difference from 1931	1945 Voting-age population	Turnout	%	Difference from 1931	1947 Voting-age population	Turnout	%	Difference from 1931	1949 Voting-age population	Turnout	%	Difference from 1931
KENTUCKY					1,729,000	270,525	**15.6%**	-14.5					1,829,000	387,795	**21.2%**	-9.0				
MISSISSIPPI					1,198,000	50,488	**4.2%**	-0.1					1,203,000	161,993	**13.5%**	9.1				
NEW JERSEY					2,837,000	506,604	**17.9%**	-14.8									3,212,000	810,022	**25.2%**	-7.4
VIRGINIA	1,635,000	98,680	**6.0%**	-2.8					1,822,000	112,355	**6.2%**	-2.7					2,009,000	184,772	**9.2%**	0.3

Other Turnout for Election Years 1931–1949

State	1931 Voting-age population	Turnout	%	1933 Voting-age population	Turnout	%	1935 Voting-age population	Turnout	%	1937 Voting-age population	Turnout	%	1939 Voting-age population	Turnout	%	Difference from 1931*
VIRGINIA										1,488,000	23,670	**1.6%**				

State	1941 Voting-age population	Turnout	%	Difference from 1931	1943 Voting-age population	Turnout	%	1945 Voting-age population	Turnout	%	Difference from 1931	1947 Voting-age population	Turnout	%	Difference from 1931	1949 Voting-age population	Turnout	%	Difference from 1931
VIRGINIA	1,635,000	21,896	**1.3%**	-0.3				1,822,000	52,386	**2.9%**	1.3								

*Percentage point difference between turnout in current year and initial year listed in chart. If data do not appear for a state in the initial year listed, the difference is calculated from the first year in which data do appear for that state.

STATE GUBERNATORIAL PRIMARY ELECTIONS

Democratic Turnout Election Years 1931–1949*

State	1931 Voting-age population	Turnout	%	1933 Voting-age population	Turnout	%	Difference from 1931**	1935 Voting-age population	Turnout	%	Difference from 1931	1937 Voting-age population	Turnout	%	Difference from 1931	1939 Voting-age population	Turnout	%	Difference from 1931
MISSISSIPPI	1,047,000	312,981	29.9%					1,113,000	350,045	31.5%	1.6					1,180,000	297,480	25.2%	-4.7
VIRGINIA				1,373,000	189,623	13.8%						1,474,000	193,274	13.1%	-0.7				

State	1941 Voting-age population	Turnout	%	Difference from 1931	1943 Voting-age population	Turnout	%	Difference from 1931	1945 Voting-age population	Turnout	%	Difference from 1931	1947 Voting-age population	Turnout	%	Difference from 1931	1949 Voting-age population	Turnout	%	Difference from 1931
MISSISSIPPI					1,197,000	285,630	23.9%	-6.0					1,202,000	352,134	29.3%	-0.6				
VIRGINIA	1,615,000	137,974	8.5%	-5.3					1,803,000	138,788	7.7%	-6.1					1,974,000	316,612	16.0%	2.2

*Only Democratic primaries were held in this time period

**Percentage point difference between turnout in current year and initial year listed in chart. If data do not appear for a state in the initial year listed, the difference is calculated from the first year in which data do appear for that state.

CHAPTER 9
1950–1969

Chronology of Major Events, 1950–1969

1950 North Korea invades South Korea. The United Nations (with the Soviet Union boycotting) authorizes a multilateral defense of South Korea. After allied offense and Chinese response, Korea remains at war and divided. Senator Joseph McCarthy gains fame for denouncing individuals as communists. The trial of Julius and Ethel Rosenberg begins, which would end with both found guilty of espionage and executed. The seventeenth census counts the U.S. population at 150.7 million people.

1952 President Harry S. Truman chooses not to seek re-election. Republican Dwight D. Eisenhower, the commander of allied forces in Europe during World War II, is elected president. The United States ends its postwar Japanese occupation.

1953 The Korean War ends, facilitated by the death of Soviet leader Joseph Stalin.

1954 Joseph McCarthy launches hearings about possible communist subversion in the U.S. Army; his claims are discredited, and he is censured by the U.S. Senate. In *Brown v Topeka Board of Education*, the Supreme Court overturns *Plessy v. Ferguson*, ruling that racially separate educational facilities are inherently unequal.

1956 Eisenhower is reelected president, defeating Democrat Adlai Stevenson a second time. Montgomery bus boycott leads to local bus desegregation and national attention to segregation.

1957 The Soviet Union launches Sputnik, the first space vehicle to orbit the earth, igniting the space race. President Eisenhower orders troops to assist in the integration of Little Rock, Arkansas, schools over the resistance of Governor Orval Faubus.

1958 Democrats score large midterm election congressional victory, establishing sufficient control of Congress to offer the hope that the southern Democratic-conservative Republican coalition, which had blocked much progressive legislation since the New Deal, could be outvoted.

1959 Fidel Castro's revolutionary forces are victorious in Cuba.

1960 A sit-in movement is begun by Greensboro, North Carolina, college students and sweeps across the south. Senator John F. Kennedy and Eisenhower's vice president, Richard Nixon, participate in the first televised presidential debates. Democrat Kennedy is elected president by a very narrow margin. The eighteenth census counts the U.S. population at 179.3 million people.

1961 Cuban exiles, supported and trained by the United States, launch an unsuccessful invasion of Cuba at the Bay of Pigs. Berlin Wall is erected, partitioning East and West Berlin. The Peace Corps is created.

1962 Americans fear a nuclear war during a ten-day standoff over the Soviet placement of ballistic missiles in Cuba. The Cuban Missile Crisis ends as Soviets withdraw their missiles, and, later, the United States withdraws missiles from Turkey. The University of Mississippi is integrated.

1963 Gov. George Wallace of Alabama unsuccessfully tries to block the integration of the University of Alabama. Martin Luther King Jr. delivers his "I Have a Dream" speech during the March on Washington. President Kennedy is assassinated in Dallas; Vice President Lyndon B. Johnson becomes president.

1964 Congress passes the Civil Rights Act, ending segregation in public accommodations. Freedom Summer campaign registers voters in the Deep South and meets violent opposition, including the murder of three civil rights workers in Philadelphia, Mississippi. President Johnson announces a "War on Poverty." Congress passes the Gulf of Tonkin resolution, creating a pretext for the president to escalate American military involvement in Vietnam. Johnson is reelected president.

Chronology of Major Events, 1950–1969 (continued)

1965	Congress passes the Voting Rights Act, following a bloody march in Selma, Alabama, and Johnson's subsequent "We Shall Overcome" speech. The Act in effect enfranchises previously disenfranchised southern African Americans and abolishes poll taxes and literacy tests as a prerequisite for voting. Race riots occur in the Watts district of Los Angeles. Johnson sends combat troops to Vietnam. Congress passes many social welfare and regulatory acts in response to Johnson's Great Society vision.
1966	The war in Vietnam becomes a deeply divisive issue, stirring anti-war campaigns and limiting resources for Johnson's Great Society social programs.
1967	Johnson sends more troops to Vietnam and casualties mount.
1968	Public perception of the Vietcong's February Tet offensive fuels anti-war sentiment, helping Senator Eugene McCarthy surprise Johnson in the New Hampshire primary. Johnson withdraws from the presidential race three days before he would have been trounced in the Wisconsin primary. Martin Luther King Jr. is assassinated in Memphis. Presidential candidate Robert Kennedy is assassinated immediately after victory statement on his narrow California primary win. Race riots occur in New York, Detroit, and other major cities. Democratic convention nominates Vice President Hubert Humphrey, while new left demonstrators and Chicago police have a bloody confrontation in Grant Park. Republican Richard Nixon is elected president.
1969	Nixon intensifies bombing of North Vietnam but begins small troop withdrawals. Neil Armstrong and Buzz Aldrin walk on the moon.

State and Federal Laws Chronology, 1950–1969

1951   The Twenty-second Amendment is ratified, limiting a president to two elected terms.

1953   *Terry v. Adams*, 345 U.S. 461 (1953). The Supreme Court invalidates another version of the whites-only primary: a primary held by an all-white "party" which typically determines the outcome of the official Democratic primary. As before, when a primary constitutes an integral part of the election process, the Court requires equal access for black voters.[1]

1955   The state of Kentucky lowers its legal voting age to eighteen years.

1959   *Alaska becomes a state.* It allows citizens over the age of nineteen to vote.

        Hawaii becomes a state. It allows citizens over the age of twenty to vote.

        Lassiter v. Northampton Election Board, 360 U.S. 45 (1959). The Supreme Court unanimously upholds the North Carolina literacy test to vote, ruling that literacy tests are not necessarily violations of the Equal Protection Clause of either the Fourteenth or Fifteenth Amendments.

1960   The Civil Rights Act of 1960 establishes the federal inspection of local voter registration polls and introduces penalties for obstructing any person's attempts either to register to vote or to actually vote.

        Gomillion v. Lightfoot, 364 U.S. 339 (1960). The Supreme Court finds that an electoral district created to disenfranchise black voters violates the Fifteenth Amendment.

1961   The Twenty-third Amendment is ratified, allowing citizens of the District of Columbia to vote for electors for president and vice president.

1962   *Baker v. Carr*, 369 U.S. 186 (1962). The Supreme Court holds that attempts to alter the delineation of voting districts present questions that enable federal courts to intervene in and decide reapportionment cases. This decision overturns *Colegrove v. Green* (1946), which had considered reapportionment to be a "political" rather than judicial question.

1963   *Gray v. Sanders*, 372 U.S. 368 (1963). The Supreme Court formulates the "one-person, one-vote" standard for legislative districting, holding that each individual must be weighted equally in legislative apportionment.

1964   The Twenty-fourth Amendment is ratified, abolishing the poll tax for federal elections.

        Wesberry v. Sanders, 376 U.S. 1 (1964). The Supreme Court rules that voting districts must be approximately equal in population.

        Wright v. Rockefeller, 376 U.S. 52 (1964). The Supreme Court affirms that racial gerrymandering is improper but sets a high bar for the evidence needed to show that a state legislature is motivated by racial considerations.

        Reynolds v. Sims, 377 U.S. 533 (1964). The Supreme Court holds that seats in both houses of a bicameral state legislature must, under the Equal Protection Clause, represent districts as equal in population as practicably possible. The U.S Senate is unaffected, as the U.S. Constitution explicitly grants each state two senators.

        The Civil Rights Act of 1964 outlaws racial segregation in schools, public places, and employment.

State and Federal Laws Chronology, 1950–1969 (continued)

1965 *Carrington v. Rash*, 380 U.S. 89 (1965). The Supreme Court rules that a state cannot prohibit service personnel stationed in the state from establishing residency to vote in the state.

Louisiana v. United States, 380 U.S. 145 (1965). The Supreme Court holds as unconstitutional provisions of the Louisiana Constitution requiring the voter to "give a reasonable interpretation" of any clause in the Louisiana Constitution or the Constitution of the United States. The Court observed that the implementation of the test conflicted with prohibitions against voter discrimination due to race found both in the Fifteenth Amendment and in statutes. The test had given complete discretion to registrars to deny an applicant the ability to register to vote, and history had shown this discretion had been used as a basis for racial discrimination.

Harman v. Forssenius, 380 U.S. 538 (1965). The Supreme Courts finds unconstitutional a Virginia law that created special registration requirements to vote in federal elections for voters who failed to pay the state poll tax. The Court holds these provisions are violations of the Twenty-fourth Amendment's abolition of poll taxes in federal elections.

The Voting Rights Act of 1965 bans any law or action that might deprive a citizen of his or her right to vote and establishes ongoing enforcement of the right to vote, particularly in the South, placing states and jurisdictions with any history of discriminatory electoral practices under U.S. Justice Department supervision. This gives discretion to the federal government to decide when a state is in compliance with the act and can be removed from supervision and also helps to enfranchise Native Americans and African Americans who had in several states been denied the right to vote. Literacy tests are suspended in districts where voter turnout is historically low.

1966 *South Carolina v. Katzenbach*, 383 U.S. 301 (1966). The Supreme Court rejects a challenge by the state of South Carolina to powers of federal electoral supervision granted by the Voting Rights Act of 1965. In his opinion for the Court, Chief Justice Earl Warren writes that the Voting Rights Act was a valid exercise of Congress's power under the enforcement clause of the Fifteenth Amendment to the United States Constitution.

Harper v. Virginia Board of Elections, 383 U.S. 663 (1966). The Supreme Court extends the prohibition of poll taxes to state elections on the basis of the Fourteenth Amendment, as a poll tax discriminates based upon income.

Katzenbach v. Morgan, 384 U.S. 641 (1966). The Supreme Court finds that the provision of the Voting Rights Act of 1965 banning literacy tests is constitutional. The Court holds that even though the banning of literacy tests is not required by the Fifteenth Amendment, the ban is consistent with congressional power under the enforcement clause of the Amendment.

1969 *Gaston County (NC) v. the United States,* 395 U.S. 285 (1969). The Supreme Court again affirms that Section 4 of the Voting Rights Act banning literacy tests is constitutional. It holds that a literacy test is *de facto* racial discrimination because African Americans are more likely to be illiterate due to poor quality segregated schools.

Federal Contested Election Act of 1969 (83 U.S.C. §284) establishes procedures by which a House committee would be empowered to review any claim involving the result of a contested House election and report its findings to the full House for action, should it be deemed necessary.

[1] For Supreme Court cases, see CQ Press Electronic Library, *Guide to the U.S. Supreme Court Online Edition*, "Chronology of Major Decisions of the Court, 1797–2007." Originally published in David G. Savage, *Guide to the U.S. Supreme Court,* 4th ed. (Revised), (Washington, D.C.: CQ Press, 2008). http://library.cqpress.com/supremecourtguide/search.php (accessed June 18th, 2010).

National Count of Popular Vote for President, 1952–1968

YEAR	NAME	PARTY	TOTAL	PERCENTAGE[1]
1952	Dwight Eisenhower	Republican	33,936,234	34.9%
	Adlai Stevenson	Democratic	27,314,992	28.1%
1956	Dwight Eisenhower	Republican	35,590,472	35.1%
	Adlai Stevenson	Democratic	26,029,752	25.7%
1960	John Kennedy	Democratic	34,226,731	32.2%
	Richard Nixon	Republican	34,108,157	32.1%
1964	Lyndon Johnson	Democratic	43,340,299	38.2%
	Barry Goldwater	Republican	27,178,188	23.9%
1968	Richard Nixon	Republican	31,785,480	26.3%
	Hubert Humphrey	Democratic	31,275,166	25.8%
	George Wallace	American Independent	9,901,118	8.2%

[1] The percentage figures in this chart are based on the votes cast divided by the eligible voting-age population at the time of the election.

United States Presidential Turnout, Election Years 1952–1968

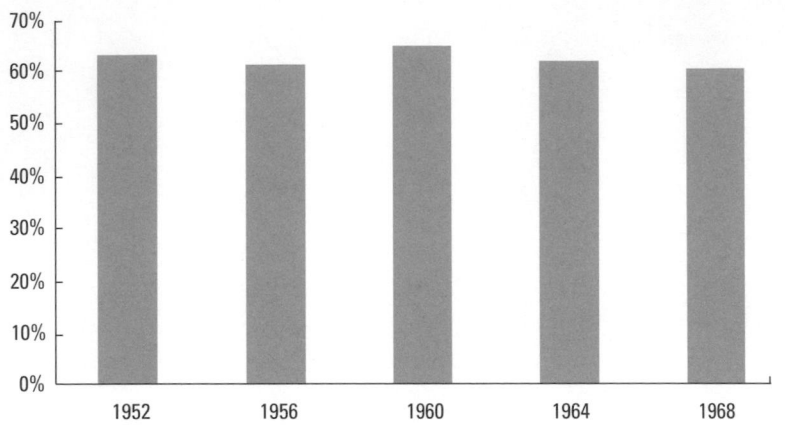

YEAR	VOTING-AGE POPULATION	TOTAL	%
1952	97,344,000	61,550,918	63.2%
1956	101,295,000	62,033,908	61.2%
1960	106,188,000	68,838,219	64.8%
1964	113,979,000	70,644,592	62.0%
1968	120,988,000	73,211,875	60.5%

Partisan Turnout Presidential Years Based on Aggregate House Turnout, Election Years 1952–1968

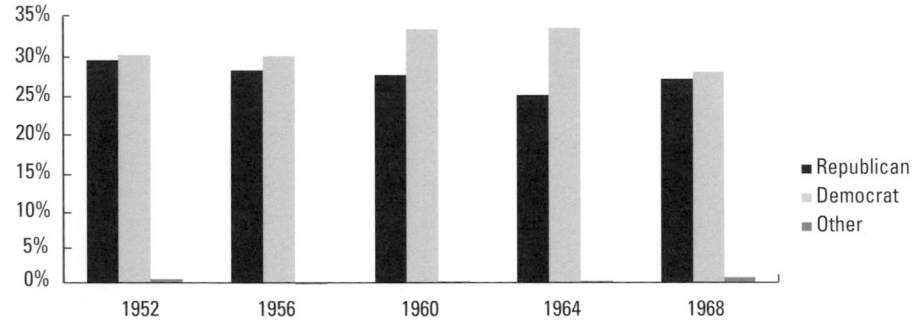

- Republican
- Democrat
- Other

YEAR	VOTING-AGE POPULATION	REPUBLICAN TURNOUT	%	DEMOCRAT TURNOUT	%	OTHER TURNOUT	%
1952	97,344,000	28,320,766	29.1%	28,994,253	29.8%	530,478	0.5%
1956	101,295,000	28,074,609	27.7%	29,956,895	29.6%	139,619	0.1%
1960	106,188,000	28,758,621	27.1%	35,110,913	33.1%	263,185	0.2%
1964	113,979,000	27,892,438	24.5%	37,861,363	33.2%	316,619	0.3%
1968	120,988,000	32,141,899	26.6%	33,243,510	27.5%	899,932	0.7%

UNITED STATES PRESIDENTIAL GENERAL ELECTIONS

Election Years 1952–1968

State	1952 Voting-age population	1952 Turnout	1952 %	1956 Voting-age population	1956 Turnout	1956 %	1956 Difference from 1952*	1960 Voting-age population	1960 Turnout	1960 %	1960 Difference from 1952	1964 Voting-age population	1964 Turnout	1964 %	1964 Difference from 1952	1968 Voting-age population	1968 Turnout	1968 %	1968 Difference from 1952
ALABAMA	1,768,000	426,120	24.1%	1,801,000	496,861	27.6%	3.5	1,840,000	570,225	31.0%	6.9	1,920,000	689,818	35.9%	11.8	1,997,000	1,049,922	52.6%	28.5
ALASKA								135,000	60,762	45.0%		154,000	67,259	43.7%	-1.3	170,000	83,035	48.8%	3.8
ARIZONA	501,000	260,570	52.0%	615,000	290,173	47.2%	-4.8	728,000	398,491	54.7%	2.7	863,000	480,770	55.7%	3.7	990,000	486,936	49.2%	-2.8
ARKANSAS	1,091,000	404,800	37.1%	1,062,000	406,572	38.3%	1.2	1,046,000	428,509	41.0%	3.9	1,100,000	560,426	50.9%	13.8	1,153,000	619,969	53.8%	16.7
CALIFORNIA	7,453,000	5,141,849	69.0%	8,335,000	5,466,355	65.6%	-3.4	9,239,000	6,506,578	70.4%	1.4	10,572,000	7,057,586	66.8%	-2.2	11,852,000	7,251,587	61.2%	-7.8
COLORADO	875,000	630,103	72.0%	946,000	664,074	70.2%	-1.8	1,020,000	736,236	72.2%	0.2	1,145,000	776,986	67.9%	-4.2	1,264,000	811,199	64.2%	-7.8
CONNECTICUT	1,358,000	1,096,911	80.8%	1,445,000	1,117,121	77.3%	-3.5	1,537,000	1,222,883	79.6%	-1.2	1,683,000	1,218,578	72.4%	-8.4	1,824,000	1,256,232	68.9%	-11.9
DELAWARE	221,000	174,025	78.7%	241,000	177,988	73.9%	-4.9	261,000	196,683	75.4%	-3.4	289,000	201,320	69.7%	-9.1	315,000	214,367	68.1%	-10.7
DISTRICT OF COLUMBIA												483,000	198,597	41.1%		489,000	170,578	34.9%	-6.2
FLORIDA	2,115,000	989,337	46.8%	2,587,000	1,125,762	43.5%	-3.3	3,051,000	1,544,176	50.6%	3.8	3,629,000	1,854,481	51.1%	4.3	4,184,000	2,187,805	52.3%	5.5
GEORGIA	2,238,000	655,785	29.3%	2,329,000	669,655	28.8%	-0.5	2,433,000	733,349	30.1%	0.8	2,654,000	1,139,335	42.9%	13.6	2,867,000	1,250,266	43.6%	14.3
HAWAII								345,000	184,705	53.5%		383,000	207,271	54.1%	0.6	418,000	236,218	56.5%	3.0
IDAHO	350,000	276,254	78.9%	360,000	272,989	75.8%	-3.1	371,000	300,450	81.0%	2.1	388,000	292,477	75.4%	-3.5	405,000	291,183	71.9%	-7.0
ILLINOIS	5,889,000	4,481,058	76.1%	6,016,000	4,407,407	73.3%	-2.8	6,155,000	4,757,409	77.3%	1.2	6,422,000	4,702,841	73.2%	-2.9	6,677,000	4,619,749	69.2%	-6.9
INDIANA	2,593,000	1,955,049	75.4%	2,682,000	1,974,607	73.6%	-1.8	2,773,000	2,135,360	77.0%	1.6	2,906,000	2,091,606	72.0%	-3.4	3,032,000	2,123,597	70.0%	-5.4
IOWA	1,669,000	1,268,773	76.0%	1,659,000	1,234,564	74.4%	-1.6	1,654,000	1,273,810	77.0%	1.0	1,674,000	1,184,539	70.8%	-5.3	1,693,000	1,167,931	69.0%	-7.0
KANSAS	1,253,000	896,166	71.5%	1,286,000	866,243	67.4%	-4.2	1,316,000	928,825	70.6%	-0.9	1,341,000	857,901	64.0%	-7.5	1,365,000	872,783	63.9%	-7.6
KENTUCKY	1,884,000	993,148	52.7%	1,889,000	1,053,005	55.8%	3.1	1,905,000	1,124,462	59.0%	6.3	1,991,000	1,046,105	52.5%	-0.2	2,074,000	1,055,893	50.9%	-1.8
LOUISIANA	1,637,000	651,952	39.8%	1,722,000	617,544	35.9%	-4.0	1,807,000	807,891	44.7%	4.9	1,911,000	896,293	46.9%	7.1	2,012,000	1,097,450	54.5%	14.7
MAINE	555,000	351,786	63.4%	560,000	351,706	62.8%	-0.6	565,000	421,767	74.6%	11.3	578,000	380,965	65.9%	2.5	592,000	392,936	66.4%	3.0
MARYLAND	1,586,000	902,074	56.9%	1,711,000	932,827	54.5%	-2.4	1,842,000	1,055,349	57.3%	0.4	2,064,000	1,116,457	54.1%	-2.8	2,277,000	1,235,039	54.2%	-2.6
MASSACHUSETTS	3,056,000	2,383,398	78.0%	3,082,000	2,348,506	76.2%	-1.8	3,126,000	2,469,480	79.0%	1.0	3,296,000	2,344,798	71.1%	-6.9	3,457,000	2,331,752	67.5%	-10.5
MICHIGAN	4,099,000	2,798,592	68.3%	4,297,000	3,080,468	71.7%	3.4	4,498,000	3,318,097	73.8%	5.5	4,786,000	3,203,102	66.9%	-1.3	5,062,000	3,306,250	65.3%	-3.0
MINNESOTA	1,901,000	1,379,483	72.6%	1,942,000	1,340,005	69.0%	-3.6	1,988,000	1,541,887	77.6%	5.0	2,091,000	1,554,462	74.3%	1.8	2,189,000	1,588,506	72.6%	0.0
MISSISSIPPI	1,195,000	285,532	23.9%	1,180,000	248,104	21.0%	-2.9	1,172,000	298,171	25.4%	1.5	1,203,000	409,146	34.0%	10.1	1,234,000	654,509	53.0%	29.1
MISSOURI	2,636,000	1,892,062	71.8%	2,658,000	1,832,562	68.9%	-2.8	2,687,000	1,934,422	72.0%	0.2	2,772,000	1,817,879	65.6%	-6.2	2,854,000	1,809,502	63.4%	-8.4
MONTANA	370,000	265,037	71.6%	378,000	271,171	71.7%	0.1	386,000	277,579	71.9%	0.3	394,000	278,628	70.7%	-0.9	402,000	274,404	68.3%	-3.4
NEBRASKA	847,000	609,660	72.0%	848,000	577,137	68.1%	-3.9	851,000	613,095	72.0%	0.1	870,000	584,154	67.1%	-4.8	889,000	536,851	60.4%	-11.6
NEVADA	122,000	82,190	67.4%	148,000	96,689	65.3%	-2.0	177,000	107,267	60.6%	-6.8	230,000	135,433	58.9%	-8.5	281,000	154,218	54.9%	-12.5
NEW HAMPSHIRE	344,000	272,950	79.3%	353,000	266,994	75.6%	-3.7	365,000	295,761	81.0%	1.7	400,000	288,093	72.0%	-7.3	432,000	297,298	68.8%	-10.5
NEW JERSEY	3,354,000	2,418,554	72.1%	3,552,000	2,484,312	69.9%	-2.2	3,758,000	2,773,111	73.8%	1.7	4,069,000	2,847,663	70.0%	-2.1	4,368,000	2,875,395	65.8%	-6.3
NEW MEXICO	402,000	238,608	59.4%	452,000	253,926	56.2%	-3.2	497,000	311,107	62.6%	3.2	522,000	328,645	63.0%	3.6	547,000	327,350	59.8%	0.5
NEW YORK	9,944,000	7,128,239	71.7%	10,059,000	7,095,971	70.5%	-1.1	10,402,000	7,291,079	70.1%	-1.6	10,893,000	7,166,275	65.8%	-5.9	11,364,000	6,791,688	59.8%	-11.9

United States Presidential General Elections (continued)

United States Presidential General Elections (continued)

Election Years 1952–1968 (continued)

State	1952 Voting-age population	Turnout	%	1956 Voting-age population	Turnout	%	Difference from 1952	1960 Voting-age population	Turnout	%	Difference from 1952	1964 Voting-age population	Turnout	%	Difference from 1952	1968 Voting-age population	Turnout	%	Difference from 1952
NORTH CAROLINA	2,372,000	1,210,910	51.1%	2,469,000	1,165,592	47.2%	-3.8	2,575,000	1,368,556	53.1%	2.1	2,765,000	1,424,983	51.5%	0.5	2,947,000	1,587,493	53.9%	2.8
NORTH DAKOTA	356,000	270,127	75.9%	353,000	253,991	72.0%	-3.9	350,000	278,431	79.6%	3.7	352,000	258,389	73.4%	-2.5	355,000	247,882	69.8%	-6.1
OHIO	5,339,000	3,700,758	69.3%	5,567,000	3,702,265	66.5%	-2.8	5,790,000	4,161,859	71.9%	2.6	6,040,000	3,969,196	65.7%	-3.6	6,281,000	3,959,698	63.0%	-6.3
OKLAHOMA	1,385,000	948,984	68.5%	1,399,000	859,350	61.4%	-7.1	1,420,000	903,150	63.6%	-4.9	1,493,000	932,499	62.5%	-6.1	1,562,000	943,086	60.4%	-8.1
OREGON	1,000,000	695,059	69.5%	1,030,000	736,132	71.5%	2.0	1,068,000	776,421	72.7%	3.2	1,164,000	786,305	67.6%	-2.0	1,256,000	819,622	65.3%	-4.2
PENNSYLVANIA	6,870,000	4,580,969	66.7%	6,928,000	4,576,503	66.1%	-0.6	6,998,000	5,006,541	71.5%	4.9	7,157,000	4,822,690	67.4%	0.7	7,311,000	4,747,928	64.9%	-1.7
RHODE ISLAND	516,000	414,498	80.3%	518,000	387,609	74.8%	-5.5	524,000	405,535	77.4%	-2.9	554,000	390,091	70.4%	-9.9	582,000	385,000	66.2%	-14.2
SOUTH CAROLINA	1,180,000	341,087	28.9%	1,225,000	300,583	24.5%	-4.4	1,274,000	386,688	30.4%	1.4	1,360,000	524,779	38.6%	9.7	1,441,000	666,978	46.3%	17.4
SOUTH DAKOTA	395,000	294,283	74.5%	392,000	293,857	75.0%	0.5	388,000	306,487	79.0%	4.5	388,000	293,118	75.5%	1.0	387,000	281,264	72.7%	-1.8
TENNESSEE	2,005,000	892,553	44.5%	2,050,000	939,404	45.8%	1.3	2,104,000	1,051,792	50.0%	5.5	2,226,000	1,143,946	51.4%	6.9	2,342,000	1,248,617	53.3%	8.8
TEXAS	4,809,000	2,075,946	43.2%	5,131,000	1,955,168	38.1%	-5.1	5,462,000	2,311,084	42.3%	-0.9	5,952,000	2,626,811	44.1%	1.0	6,422,000	3,079,216	47.9%	4.8
UTAH	400,000	329,554	82.4%	429,000	333,995	77.9%	-4.5	461,000	374,709	81.3%	-1.1	510,000	401,413	78.7%	-3.7	556,000	422,568	76.0%	-6.4
VERMONT	228,000	153,557	67.3%	226,000	152,978	67.7%	0.3	226,000	167,324	74.0%	6.7	241,000	163,089	67.7%	0.3	256,000	161,404	63.0%	-4.3
VIRGINIA	2,090,000	619,689	29.7%	2,202,000	697,978	31.7%	2.0	2,323,000	771,449	33.2%	3.6	2,530,000	1,042,267	41.2%	11.5	2,729,000	1,361,491	49.9%	20.2
WASHINGTON	1,553,000	1,102,708	71.0%	1,617,000	1,150,889	71.2%	0.2	1,692,000	1,241,572	73.4%	2.4	1,854,000	1,258,556	67.9%	-3.1	2,009,000	1,304,281	64.9%	-6.1
WEST VIRGINIA	1,138,000	873,548	76.8%	1,103,000	830,831	75.3%	-1.4	1,076,000	837,781	77.9%	1.1	1,073,000	792,040	73.8%	-2.9	1,070,000	754,206	70.5%	-6.3
WISCONSIN	2,223,000	1,607,370	72.3%	2,278,000	1,550,558	68.1%	-4.2	2,338,000	1,729,082	74.0%	1.6	2,452,000	1,691,815	69.0%	-3.3	2,559,000	1,691,538	66.1%	-6.2
WYOMING	179,000	129,253	72.2%	183,000	124,127	67.8%	-4.4	189,000	140,782	74.5%	2.3	192,000	142,716	74.3%	2.1	194,000	127,205	65.6%	-6.6
Total	97,344,000	61,550,918	63.2%	101,295,000	62,033,908	61.2%	-2.0	106,188,000	68,838,219	64.8%	1.6	113,979,000	70,644,592	62.0%	-1.2	120,988,000	73,211,875	60.5%	-2.7

*Percentage point difference between turnout in current year and initial year listed in chart. If data do not appear for a state in the initial year listed, the difference is calculated from the first year in which data do appear for that state.

UNITED STATES PRESIDENTIAL GENERAL ELECTIONS

Republican Turnout for Election Years 1952–1968

State	1952 Voting-age population	Turnout	%	1956 Voting-age population	Turnout	%	Difference from 1952*	1960 Voting-age population	Turnout	%	Difference from 1952	1964 Voting-age population	Turnout	%	Difference from 1952	1968 Voting-age population	Turnout	%	Difference from 1952
ALABAMA	1,768,000	149,231	8.4%	1,801,000	195,694	10.9%	2.4	1,840,000	237,981	12.9%	4.5	1,920,000	479,085	25.0%	16.5	1,997,000	146,923	7.4%	-1.1
ALASKA								135,000	30,953	22.9%		154,000	22,930	14.9%	-8.0	170,000	37,600	22.1%	-0.8
ARIZONA	501,000	152,042	30.3%	615,000	176,990	28.8%	-1.6	728,000	221,241	30.4%	0.0	863,000	242,535	28.1%	-2.2	990,000	266,721	26.9%	-3.4
ARKANSAS	1,091,000	177,155	16.2%	1,062,000	186,287	17.5%	1.3	1,046,000	184,508	17.6%	1.4	1,100,000	243,264	22.1%	5.9	1,153,000	190,759	16.5%	0.3
CALIFORNIA	7,453,000	2,897,310	38.9%	8,336,000	3,027,668	36.3%	-2.5	9,239,000	3,259,722	35.3%	-3.6	10,572,000	2,879,108	27.2%	-11.6	11,852,000	3,467,664	29.3%	-9.6
COLORADO	875,000	379,782	43.4%	946,000	394,479	41.7%	-1.7	1,020,000	402,242	39.4%	-4.0	1,145,000	290,707	25.9%	-17.5	1,264,000	409,345	32.4%	-11.0
CONNECTICUT	1,358,000	611,012	45.0%	1,445,000	711,837	49.3%	4.3	1,537,000	565,813	36.8%	8.2	1,683,000	390,996	23.2%	-21.8	1,824,000	556,721	30.5%	-14.5
DELAWARE	221,000	90,059	40.8%	241,000	98,057	40.7%	-0.1	261,000	96,373	36.9%	-3.8	289,000	78,078	27.0%	-13.7	315,000	96,714	30.7%	-10.0
DISTRICT OF COLUMBIA												483,000	28,801	6.0%		489,000	31,012	6.3%	0.4
FLORIDA	2,115,000	544,036	25.7%	2,587,000	643,849	24.9%	-0.8	3,051,000	795,476	26.1%	0.3	3,629,000	905,941	25.0%	-0.8	4,184,000	886,804	21.2%	4.5
GEORGIA	2,238,000	198,961	8.9%	2,329,000	222,778	9.6%	0.7	2,433,000	274,472	11.3%	2.4	2,654,000	616,584	23.2%	14.3	2,867,000	380,111	13.3%	4.4
HAWAII								345,000	92,295	26.8%		383,000	44,022	11.5%	-15.3	418,000	91,425	21.9%	-4.9
IDAHO	350,000	180,707	51.6%	360,000	166,979	46.4%	-5.2	371,000	161,597	43.6%	-8.1	388,000	143,557	37.0%	-14.6	405,000	165,369	40.8%	-10.8
ILLINOIS	5,889,000	2,457,327	41.7%	6,016,000	2,623,327	43.6%	1.9	6,155,000	2,368,988	38.5%	-3.2	6,422,000	1,905,946	29.7%	-12.0	6,677,000	2,174,774	32.6%	-9.2
INDIANA	2,593,000	1,136,259	43.8%	2,682,000	1,182,811	44.1%	0.3	2,773,000	1,175,120	42.4%	-1.4	2,906,000	911,118	31.4%	-12.5	3,032,000	1,067,885	35.2%	-8.6
IOWA	1,669,000	808,906	48.5%	1,659,000	729,187	44.0%	-4.5	1,654,000	722,381	43.7%	-4.8	1,674,000	449,148	26.8%	-21.6	1,693,000	619,106	36.6%	-11.9
KANSAS	1,253,000	616,302	49.2%	1,286,000	566,878	44.1%	-5.1	1,316,000	561,474	42.7%	-6.5	1,341,000	386,579	28.8%	-20.4	1,365,000	478,674	35.1%	-14.1
KENTUCKY	1,884,000	495,029	26.3%	1,889,000	572,192	30.3%	4.0	1,905,000	602,607	31.6%	5.4	1,991,000	372,977	18.7%	-7.5	2,074,000	462,411	22.3%	-4.0
LOUISIANA	1,637,000	306,925	18.7%	1,722,000	329,047	19.1%	0.4	1,807,000	230,980	12.8%	-6.0	1,911,000	509,225	26.6%	7.9	2,012,000	257,535	12.8%	-5.9
MAINE	555,000	232,353	41.9%	560,000	249,238	44.5%	2.6	565,000	240,608	42.6%	0.7	578,000	118,701	20.5%	-21.3	592,000	169,254	28.6%	-13.3
MARYLAND	1,586,000	499,424	31.5%	1,711,000	559,738	32.7%	1.2	1,842,000	489,538	26.6%	-4.9	2,064,000	385,495	18.7%	-12.8	2,277,000	517,995	22.7%	-8.7
MASSACHUSETTS	3,056,000	1,292,325	42.3%	3,082,000	1,393,197	45.2%	2.9	3,126,000	976,750	31.2%	-11.0	3,296,000	549,727	16.7%	-25.6	3,457,000	766,844	22.2%	-20.1
MICHIGAN	4,099,000	1,551,529	37.9%	4,297,000	1,713,647	39.9%	2.0	4,498,000	1,620,428	36.0%	-1.8	4,786,000	1,060,152	22.2%	-15.7	5,062,000	1,370,665	27.1%	-10.8
MINNESOTA	1,901,000	763,211	40.1%	1,942,000	719,302	37.0%	-3.1	1,988,000	757,915	38.1%	-2.0	2,091,000	559,624	26.8%	-13.4	2,189,000	658,643	30.1%	-10.1
MISSISSIPPI	1,195,000	112,966	9.5%	1,180,000	60,685	5.1%	-4.3	1,172,000	73,561	6.3%	-3.2	1,203,000	356,528	29.6%	20.2	1,234,000	88,516	7.2%	-2.3
MISSOURI	2,636,000	959,429	36.4%	2,658,000	914,289	34.4%	-2.0	2,687,000	962,221	35.8%	-0.6	2,772,000	653,535	23.6%	-12.8	2,854,000	811,932	28.4%	-7.9
MONTANA	370,000	157,394	42.5%	378,000	154,933	41.0%	-1.6	386,000	141,841	36.7%	-5.8	394,000	113,032	28.7%	-13.9	402,000	138,835	34.5%	-8.0
NEBRASKA	847,000	421,603	49.8%	848,000	378,108	44.6%	-5.2	851,000	380,553	44.7%	-5.1	870,000	276,847	31.8%	-18.0	889,000	321,163	36.1%	-13.6
NEVADA	122,000	50,502	41.4%	148,000	56,049	37.9%	-3.5	177,000	52,387	29.6%	-11.8	230,000	56,094	24.4%	-17.0	281,000	73,188	26.0%	-15.3
NEW HAMPSHIRE	344,000	166,287	48.3%	353,000	176,519	50.0%	1.7	365,000	157,989	43.3%	-5.1	400,000	104,029	26.0%	-22.3	432,000	154,903	35.9%	-12.5
NEW JERSEY	3,354,000	1,373,613	41.0%	3,552,000	1,606,942	45.2%	4.3	3,758,000	1,363,324	36.3%	-4.7	4,069,000	964,174	23.7%	-17.3	4,368,000	1,325,467	30.3%	-10.6
NEW MEXICO	402,000	132,170	32.9%	452,000	146,788	32.5%	-0.4	497,000	153,733	30.9%	-1.9	522,000	132,838	25.4%	-7.4	547,000	169,692	31.0%	-1.9
NEW YORK	9,944,000	3,952,813	39.8%	10,059,000	4,345,506	43.2%	3.4	10,402,000	3,446,419	33.1%	-6.6	10,893,000	2,243,559	20.6%	-19.2	11,364,000	3,007,932	26.5%	-13.3

United States Presidential General Elections (continued)

United States Presidential General Elections (continued)

Republican Turnout for Election Years 1952–1968 (continued)

State	1952 Voting-age population	1952 Turnout	1952 %	1956 Voting-age population	1956 Turnout	1956 %	1956 Difference from 1952	1960 Voting-age population	1960 Turnout	1960 %	1960 Difference from 1952	1964 Voting-age population	1964 Turnout	1964 %	1964 Difference from 1952	1968 Voting-age population	1968 Turnout	1968 %	1968 Difference from 1952
NORTH CAROLINA	2,372,000	558,107	23.5%	2,469,000	575,062	23.3%	-0.2	2,575,000	655,420	25.5%	1.9	2,765,000	624,844	22.6%	-0.9	2,947,000	627,192	21.3%	-2.2
NORTH DAKOTA	356,000	191,712	53.9%	353,000	156,766	44.4%	-9.4	350,000	154,310	44.1%	-9.8	352,000	108,207	30.7%	-23.1	355,000	138,669	39.1%	-14.8
OHIO	5,339,000	2,100,391	39.3%	5,567,000	2,262,610	40.6%	1.3	5,790,000	2,217,611	38.3%	-1.0	6,040,000	1,470,865	24.4%	-15.0	6,281,000	1,791,014	28.5%	-10.8
OKLAHOMA	1,385,000	518,045	37.4%	1,399,000	473,769	33.9%	-3.5	1,420,000	533,039	37.5%	0.1	1,493,000	412,665	27.6%	-9.8	1,562,000	449,697	28.8%	-8.6
OREGON	1,000,000	420,815	42.1%	1,030,000	406,393	39.5%	-2.6	1,068,000	408,060	38.2%	-3.9	1,164,000	282,779	24.3%	-17.8	1,256,000	408,433	32.5%	-9.6
PENNSYLVANIA	6,870,000	2,415,789	35.2%	6,928,000	2,585,252	37.3%	2.2	6,998,000	2,439,956	34.9%	-0.3	7,157,000	1,673,657	23.4%	-11.8	7,311,000	2,090,017	28.6%	-6.6
RHODE ISLAND	516,000	210,935	40.9%	518,000	225,819	43.6%	2.7	524,000	147,502	28.1%	-12.7	554,000	74,615	13.5%	-27.4	582,000	122,359	21.0%	-19.9
SOUTH CAROLINA	1,180,000	168,082	14.2%	1,225,000	75,700	6.2%	-8.1	1,274,000	188,558	14.8%	0.6	1,360,000	309,048	22.7%	8.5	1,441,000	254,062	17.6%	3.4
SOUTH DAKOTA	395,000	203,857	51.6%	392,000	171,569	43.8%	-7.8	388,000	178,417	46.0%	-5.6	388,000	130,108	33.5%	-18.1	387,000	149,841	38.7%	-12.9
TENNESSEE	2,005,000	446,147	22.3%	2,050,000	462,288	22.6%	0.3	2,104,000	556,577	26.5%	4.2	2,226,000	508,965	22.9%	0.6	2,342,000	472,592	20.2%	-2.1
TEXAS	4,809,000	1,102,878	22.9%	5,131,000	1,080,619	21.1%	-1.9	5,462,000	1,121,310	20.5%	-2.4	5,952,000	958,566	16.1%	-6.8	6,422,000	1,227,844	19.1%	-3.8
UTAH	400,000	194,190	48.5%	429,000	215,631	50.3%	1.7	461,000	205,361	44.5%	-4.0	510,000	181,785	35.6%	-12.9	556,000	238,728	42.9%	-5.6
VERMONT	228,000	109,717	48.1%	226,000	110,390	48.8%	0.7	226,000	98,131	43.4%	-4.7	241,000	54,942	22.8%	-25.3	256,000	85,142	33.3%	-14.9
VIRGINIA	2,090,000	349,037	16.7%	2,202,000	386,459	17.6%	0.9	2,323,000	404,521	17.4%	0.7	2,530,000	481,334	19.0%	2.3	2,729,000	590,319	21.6%	4.9
WASHINGTON	1,553,000	599,107	38.6%	1,617,000	620,430	38.4%	-0.2	1,692,000	629,273	37.2%	-1.4	1,854,000	470,366	25.4%	-13.2	2,009,000	588,510	29.3%	-9.3
WEST VIRGINIA	1,138,000	419,970	36.9%	1,103,000	449,297	40.7%	3.8	1,076,000	395,995	36.8%	-0.1	1,073,000	253,953	23.7%	-13.2	1,070,000	307,555	28.7%	-8.2
WISCONSIN	2,223,000	979,744	44.1%	2,278,000	954,844	41.9%	-2.2	2,338,000	895,175	38.3%	-5.8	2,452,000	638,495	26.0%	-18.0	2,559,000	809,997	31.7%	-12.4
WYOMING	179,000	81,049	45.3%	183,000	74,573	40.8%	-4.5	189,000	77,451	41.0%	-4.3	192,000	61,998	32.3%	-13.0	194,000	70,927	36.6%	-8.7
Total	97,344,000	33,936,234	34.9%	101,295,000	35,590,472	35.1%	0.3	106,188,000	34,108,157	32.1%	-2.7	113,979,000	27,178,188	23.8%	-11.0	120,988,000	31,785,480	26.3%	-8.6

Democratic Turnout for Election Years 1952–1968

State	1952 Voting-age population	1952 Turnout	1952 %	1956 Voting-age population	1956 Turnout	1956 %	1956 Difference from 1952*	1960 Voting-age population	1960 Turnout	1960 %	1960 Difference from 1952	1964 Voting-age population	1964 Turnout	1964 %	1964 Difference from 1952	1968 Voting-age population	1968 Turnout	1968 %	1968 Difference from 1952
ALABAMA	1,768,000	275,075	15.6%	1,801,000	280,844	15.6%	0.0	1,840,000	324,050	17.6%	2.1	1,920,000	210,733	11.0%	-4.6	1,997,000	196,579	9.8%	-5.7
ALASKA								135,000	29,809	22.1%		154,000	44,329	28.8%	6.7	170,000	35,411	20.8%	-1.3
ARIZONA	501,000	108,528	21.7%	615,000	112,880	18.4%	-3.3	728,000	176,781	24.3%	2.6	863,000	237,753	27.5%	5.9	990,000	170,514	17.2%	-4.4
ARKANSAS	1,091,000	226,300	20.7%	1,062,000	213,277	20.1%	-0.7	1,046,000	215,049	20.6%	-0.2	1,100,000	314,197	28.6%	7.8	1,153,000	188,228	16.3%	-4.4
CALIFORNIA	7,453,000	2,197,548	29.5%	8,335,000	2,420,135	29.0%	-0.4	9,239,000	3,224,099	34.9%	5.4	10,572,000	4,171,877	39.5%	10.0	11,852,000	3,244,318	27.4%	-2.1
COLORADO	875,000	245,504	28.1%	946,000	264,997	28.0%	0.0	1,020,000	330,629	32.4%	4.4	1,145,000	476,024	41.6%	13.5	1,264,000	335,174	26.5%	-1.5
CONNECTICUT	1,358,000	481,649	35.5%	1,445,000	405,079	28.0%	-7.4	1,537,000	657,055	42.7%	7.3	1,683,000	826,269	49.1%	13.6	1,824,000	621,561	34.1%	-1.4
DELAWARE	221,000	83,315	37.7%	241,000	79,421	33.0%	-4.7	261,000	99,590	38.2%	0.5	289,000	122,704	42.5%	4.8	315,000	89,194	28.3%	-9.4
DISTRICT OF COLUMBIA												483,000	169,796	35.2%		489,000	139,566	28.5%	-6.6
FLORIDA	2,115,000	444,950	21.0%	2,587,000	480,371	18.6%	-2.5	3,051,000	748,700	24.5%	3.5	3,629,000	948,540	26.1%	5.1	4,184,000	676,794	16.2%	-4.9

United States Presidential General Elections *(continued)*

Democratic Turnout for Election Years 1952–1968 *(continued)*

State	1952 Voting-age population	Turnout	%	1956 Voting-age population	Turnout	%	Difference from 1952	1960 Voting-age population	Turnout	%	Difference from 1952	1964 Voting-age population	Turnout	%	Difference from 1952	1968 Voting-age population	Turnout	%	Difference from 1952
GEORGIA	2,238,000	456,823	20.4%	2,329,000	444,688	19.1%	-1.3	2,433,000	458,638	18.9%	-1.6	2,654,000	522,556	19.7%	-0.7	2,867,000	334,440	11.7%	-8.7
HAWAII								345,000	92,410	26.8%		383,000	163,249	42.6%	15.8	418,000	141,324	33.8%	7.0
IDAHO	350,000	95,081	27.2%	360,000	105,868	29.4%	2.2	371,000	138,853	37.4%	10.3	388,000	148,920	38.4%	11.2	405,000	89,273	22.0%	-5.1
ILLINOIS	5,889,000	2,013,920	34.2%	6,016,000	1,775,682	29.5%	-4.7	6,155,000	2,377,846	38.6%	4.4	6,422,000	2,796,833	43.6%	9.4	6,677,000	2,039,814	30.5%	-3.6
INDIANA	2,593,000	801,530	30.9%	2,682,000	783,908	29.2%	-1.7	2,773,000	952,358	34.3%	3.4	2,906,000	1,170,848	40.3%	9.4	3,032,000	806,659	26.6%	-4.3
IOWA	1,669,000	451,513	27.1%	1,659,000	501,858	30.3%	3.2	1,654,000	550,565	33.3%	6.2	1,674,000	733,030	43.8%	16.7	1,693,000	476,699	28.2%	1.1
KANSAS	1,253,000	273,296	21.8%	1,286,000	296,317	23.0%	1.2	1,316,000	363,213	27.6%	5.8	1,341,000	464,028	34.6%	12.8	1,365,000	302,996	22.2%	0.4
KENTUCKY	1,884,000	495,729	26.3%	1,889,000	476,453	25.2%	-1.1	1,905,000	521,855	27.4%	1.1	1,991,000	669,659	33.6%	7.3	2,074,000	397,541	19.2%	-7.1
LOUISIANA	1,637,000	345,027	21.1%	1,722,000	243,977	14.2%	-6.9	1,807,000	407,339	22.5%	1.5	1,911,000	387,068	20.3%	-0.8	2,012,000	309,615	15.4%	-5.7
MAINE	555,000	118,806	21.4%	560,000	102,468	18.3%	-3.1	565,000	181,159	32.1%	10.7	578,000	262,264	45.4%	24.0	592,000	217,312	36.7%	15.3
MARYLAND	1,586,000	395,337	24.9%	1,711,000	372,613	21.8%	-3.1	1,842,000	565,808	30.7%	5.8	2,064,000	730,912	35.4%	10.5	2,277,000	538,310	23.6%	-1.3
MASSACHUSETTS	3,056,000	1,083,525	35.5%	3,082,000	948,190	30.8%	-4.7	3,126,000	1,487,174	47.6%	12.1	3,296,000	1,786,422	54.2%	18.7	3,457,000	1,469,218	42.5%	7.0
MICHIGAN	4,099,000	1,230,657	30.0%	4,297,000	1,359,898	31.6%	1.6	4,498,000	1,687,269	37.5%	7.5	4,786,000	2,136,615	44.6%	14.6	5,062,000	1,593,082	31.5%	1.4
MINNESOTA	1,901,000	608,458	32.0%	1,942,000	617,525	31.8%	-0.2	1,908,000	779,933	39.2%	7.2	2,091,000	991,117	47.4%	15.4	2,189,000	857,738	39.2%	7.2
MISSISSIPPI	1,195,000	172,566	14.4%	1,180,000	144,453	12.2%	-2.2	1,172,000	108,362	9.2%	-5.2	1,203,000	52,618	4.4%	-10.1	1,234,000	150,644	12.2%	-2.2
MISSOURI	2,636,000	929,830	35.3%	2,658,000	918,273	34.5%	-0.7	2,687,000	972,201	36.2%	0.9	2,772,000	1,164,344	42.0%	6.7	2,854,000	791,444	27.7%	-7.5
MONTANA	370,000	106,213	28.7%	378,000	116,238	30.8%	2.0	386,000	134,891	34.9%	6.2	394,000	164,246	41.7%	13.0	402,000	114,117	28.4%	-0.3
NEBRASKA	847,000	188,057	22.2%	848,000	199,029	23.5%	1.3	851,000	232,542	27.3%	5.1	870,000	307,307	35.3%	13.1	889,000	170,784	19.2%	-3.0
NEVADA	122,000	31,688	26.0%	148,000	40,640	27.5%	1.5	177,000	54,880	31.0%	5.0	230,000	79,339	34.5%	8.5	281,000	60,598	21.6%	-4.4
NEW HAMPSHIRE	344,000	106,663	31.0%	353,000	90,364	25.6%	-5.4	365,000	137,772	37.7%	6.7	400,000	184,064	46.0%	15.0	432,000	130,589	30.2%	-0.8
NEW JERSEY	3,354,000	1,015,902	30.3%	3,552,000	850,337	23.9%	-6.3	3,758,000	1,385,415	36.9%	6.6	4,069,000	1,868,231	45.9%	15.6	4,368,000	1,264,206	28.9%	-1.3
NEW MEXICO	402,000	105,661	26.3%	452,000	106,098	23.5%	-2.8	497,000	156,027	31.4%	5.1	522,000	194,015	37.2%	10.9	547,000	130,081	23.8%	-2.5
NEW YORK	9,944,000	3,104,601	31.2%	10,059,000	2,747,944	27.3%	-3.9	10,402,000	3,830,085	36.8%	5.6	10,893,000	4,913,102	45.1%	13.9	11,364,000	3,378,470	29.7%	-1.5
NORTH CAROLINA	2,372,000	652,803	27.5%	2,469,000	590,530	23.9%	-3.6	2,575,000	713,136	27.7%	0.2	2,765,000	800,139	28.9%	1.4	2,947,000	464,113	15.7%	-11.8
NORTH DAKOTA	356,000	76,694	21.5%	353,000	96,742	27.4%	5.9	350,000	123,963	35.4%	13.9	352,000	149,784	42.6%	21.0	355,000	94,769	26.7%	5.2
OHIO	5,339,000	1,600,367	30.0%	5,567,000	1,439,655	25.9%	-4.1	5,790,000	1,944,248	33.6%	3.6	6,040,000	2,498,331	41.4%	11.4	6,281,000	1,700,586	27.1%	-2.9
OKLAHOMA	1,385,000	430,939	31.1%	1,399,000	385,581	27.6%	-3.6	1,420,000	370,111	26.1%	-5.1	1,493,000	519,834	34.8%	3.7	1,562,000	301,658	19.3%	-11.8
OREGON	1,000,000	270,579	27.1%	1,030,000	329,204	32.0%	4.9	1,068,000	367,402	34.4%	7.3	1,164,000	501,017	43.0%	16.0	1,256,000	358,866	28.6%	1.5
PENNSYLVANIA	6,870,000	2,146,269	31.2%	6,928,000	1,981,769	28.6%	-2.6	6,998,000	2,556,282	36.5%	5.3	7,157,000	3,130,954	43.7%	12.5	7,311,000	2,259,405	30.9%	-0.3
RHODE ISLAND	516,000	203,293	39.4%	518,000	161,790	31.2%	-8.2	524,000	258,032	49.2%	9.8	554,000	315,463	56.9%	17.5	582,000	246,518	42.4%	3.0
SOUTH CAROLINA	1,180,000	173,004	14.7%	1,225,000	136,372	11.1%	-3.5	1,274,000	198,129	15.6%	0.9	1,360,000	215,723	15.9%	1.2	1,441,000	197,486	13.7%	-1.0
SOUTH DAKOTA	395,000	90,426	22.9%	392,000	122,288	31.2%	8.3	388,000	128,070	33.0%	10.1	388,000	163,010	42.0%	19.1	387,000	118,023	30.5%	7.6
TENNESSEE	2,005,000	443,710	22.1%	2,050,000	456,507	22.3%	0.1	2,104,000	481,453	22.9%	0.8	2,226,000	634,947	28.5%	6.4	2,342,000	351,233	15.0%	-7.1

United States Presidential General Elections (continued)

United States Presidential General Elections *(continued)*

Democratic Turnout for Election Years 1952–1968 *(continued)*

	1952			1956				1960				1964				1968			
State	Voting-age population	Turnout	%	Voting-age population	Turnout	%	Difference from 1952	Voting-age population	Turnout	%	Difference from 1952	Voting-age population	Turnout	%	Difference from 1952	Voting-age population	Turnout	%	Difference from 1952
TEXAS	4,809,000	969,228	20.2%	5,131,000	859,958	16.8%	-3.4	5,462,000	1,167,567	21.4%	1.2	5,952,000	1,663,185	27.9%	7.8	6,422,000	1,266,804	19.7%	-0.4
UTAH	400,000	135,364	33.8%	429,000	118,364	27.6%	-6.3	461,000	169,248	36.7%	2.9	510,000	219,628	43.1%	9.2	556,000	156,665	28.2%	-5.7
VERMONT	228,000	43,355	19.0%	226,000	42,549	18.8%	-0.2	226,000	69,186	30.6%	11.6	241,000	108,127	44.9%	25.9	256,000	70,255	27.4%	8.4
VIRGINIA	2,090,000	268,677	12.9%	2,202,000	267,760	12.2%	-0.7	2,323,000	362,327	15.6%	2.7	2,530,000	558,038	22.1%	9.2	2,729,000	442,387	16.2%	3.4
WASHINGTON	1,553,000	492,845	31.7%	1,617,000	523,002	32.3%	0.6	1,692,000	599,298	35.4%	3.7	1,854,000	779,881	42.1%	10.3	2,009,000	616,037	30.7%	-1.1
WEST VIRGINIA	1,138,000	453,578	39.9%	1,103,000	381,534	34.6%	-5.3	1,076,000	441,786	41.1%	1.2	1,073,000	538,087	50.1%	10.3	1,070,000	374,091	35.0%	-4.9
WISCONSIN	2,223,000	622,175	28.0%	2,278,000	586,768	25.8%	-2.2	2,338,000	830,805	35.5%	7.5	2,452,000	1,050,424	42.8%	14.9	2,559,000	748,804	29.3%	1.3
WYOMING	179,000	47,934	26.8%	183,000	49,554	27.1%	0.3	189,000	63,331	33.5%	6.7	192,000	80,718	42.0%	15.3	194,000	45,173	23.3%	-3.5
Total	97,344,000	27,314,992	28.1%	101,295,000	26,029,752	25.7%	-2.4	106,188,000	34,226,731	32.2%	4.2	113,979,000	43,340,299	38.0%	10.0	120,988,000	31,275,166	25.8%	-2.2

Other Turnout for Election Years 1952–1968

	1952			1956				1960				1964				1968			
State	Voting-age population	Turnout	%	Voting-age population	Turnout	%	Difference from 1952*	Voting-age population	Turnout	%	Difference from 1952	Voting-age population	Turnout	%	Difference from 1952	Voting-age population	Turnout	%	Difference from 1952
ALABAMA	1,768,000	1,814	0.1%	1,801,000	20,323	1.1%	1.0	1,840,000	8,194	0.4%	0.3					1,997,000	706,420	35.4%	35.3
ALASKA																170,000	10,024	5.9%	
ARIZONA				615,000	303	0.0%		728,000	469	0.1%	0.0	863,000	482	0.1%	0.0	990,000	49,701	5.0%	5.0
ARKANSAS	1,091,000	1,345	0.1%	1,062,000	7,008	0.7%	0.5	1,046,000	28,952	2.8%	2.6	1,100,000	2,965	0.3%	0.1	1,153,000	240,982	20.9%	20.8
CALIFORNIA	7,453,000	46,991	0.6%	8,335,000	18,552	0.2%	-0.4	9,239,000	22,757	0.2%	-0.4	10,572,000	6,601	0.1%	-0.6	11,852,000	539,605	4.6%	3.9
COLORADO	875,000	4,817	0.6%	946,000	4,598	0.5%	-0.1	1,020,000	3,365	0.3%	-0.2	1,145,000	4,195	0.4%	-0.2	1,264,000	66,680	5.3%	4.7
CONNECTICUT	1,358,000	4,250	0.3%	1,445,000	205	0.0%	-0.3	1,537,000	15	0.0%	-0.3	1,683,000	1,313	0.1%	-0.2	1,824,000	77,950	4.3%	4.0
DELAWARE	221,000	651	0.3%	241,000	510	0.2%	-0.1	261,000	720	0.3%	0.0	289,000	538	0.2%	-0.1	315,000	28,459	9.0%	8.7
DISTRICT OF COLUMBIA																			
FLORIDA	2,115,000	351	0.0%	2,587,000	1,542	0.1%	0.0									4,184,000	624,207	14.9%	14.9
GEORGIA	2,238,000	1	0.0%	2,329,000	2,189	0.1%	0.1	2,433,000	239	0.0%	0.0	2,654,000	195	0.0%	0.0	2,867,000	535,715	18.7%	18.7
HAWAII																418,000	3,469	0.8%	
IDAHO	350,000	466	0.1%	360,000	142	0.0%	-0.1									405,000	36,541	9.0%	8.9
ILLINOIS	5,889,000	9,811	0.2%	6,016,000	8,398	0.1%	0.0	6,155,000	10,575	0.2%	0.0	6,422,000	62	0.0%	-0.2	6,677,000	405,161	6.1%	5.9
INDIANA	2,593,000	17,260	0.7%	2,682,000	7,888	0.3%	-0.4	2,773,000	7,882	0.3%	-0.4	2,906,000	9,640	0.3%	-0.3	3,032,000	249,053	8.2%	7.5
IOWA	1,669,000	8,354	0.5%	1,659,000	3,519	0.2%	-0.3	1,654,000	864	0.1%	-0.4	1,674,000	2,361	0.1%	-0.4	1,693,000	72,126	4.3%	3.8
KANSAS	1,253,000	6,568	0.5%	1,286,000	3,048	0.2%	-0.3	1,316,000	4,138	0.3%	-0.2	1,341,000	7,294	0.5%	0.0	1,365,000	91,113	6.7%	6.2
KENTUCKY	1,884,000	2,390	0.1%	1,889,000	5,160	0.3%	0.1					1,991,000	3,469	0.2%	0.0	2,074,000	195,941	9.4%	9.3
LOUISIANA				1,722,000	44,520	2.6%		1,807,000	169,572	9.4%	6.8					2,012,000	530,300	26.4%	23.8
MAINE	555,000	627	0.1%													592,000	6,370	1.1%	1.0

United States Presidential General Elections *(continued)*

Other Turnout for Election Years 1952–1968 *(continued)*

State	1952 Voting-age population	1952 Turnout	1952 %	1956 Voting-age population	1956 Turnout	1956 %	1956 Difference from 1952	1960 Voting-age population	1960 Turnout	1960 %	1960 Difference from 1952	1964 Voting-age population	1964 Turnout	1964 %	1964 Difference from 1952	1968 Voting-age population	1968 Turnout	1968 %	1968 Difference from 1952
MARYLAND	1,586,000	7,313	0.5%	1,711,000	476	0.0%	-0.4	1,842,000	3	0.0%	-0.5	2,064,000	50	0.0%	-0.5	2,277,000	178,734	7.8%	7.4
MASSACHUSETTS	3,056,000	7,548	0.2%	3,082,000	7,119	0.2%	0.0	3,126,000	5,556	0.2%	-0.1	3,296,000	8,649	0.3%	0.0	3,457,000	95,690	2.8%	2.5
MICHIGAN	4,099,000	16,406	0.4%	4,297,000	6,923	0.2%	-0.2	4,498,000	10,400	0.2%	-0.2	4,786,000	6,335	0.1%	-0.3	5,062,000	342,503	6.8%	6.4
MINNESOTA	1,901,000	7,814	0.4%	1,942,000	3,178	0.2%	-0.2	1,988,000	4,039	0.2%	-0.2	2,091,000	3,721	0.2%	-0.2	2,189,000	72,125	3.3%	2.9
MISSISSIPPI				1,180,000	42,966	3.6%		1,172,000	116,248	9.9%	6.3					1,234,000	415,349	33.7%	30.0
MISSOURI	2,636,000	2,803	0.1%													2,854,000	206,126	7.2%	7.1
MONTANA	370,000	1,430	0.4%					386,000	847	0.2%	-0.2	394,000	1,350	0.3%	0.0	402,000	21,452	5.3%	4.9
NEBRASKA																889,000	44,904	5.1%	
NEVADA																281,000	20,432	7.3%	
NEW HAMPSHIRE				353,000	111	0.0%										432,000	11,806	2.7%	2.7
NEW JERSEY	3,354,000	29,039	0.9%	3,552,000	27,033	0.8%	-0.1	3,758,000	24,372	0.6%	-0.2	4,069,000	15,258	0.4%	-0.5	4,368,000	285,722	6.5%	5.7
NEW MEXICO	402,000	777	0.2%	452,000	1,040	0.2%	0.0	497,000	1,347	0.3%	0.1	522,000	1,792	0.3%	0.2	547,000	27,577	5.0%	4.8
NEW YORK	9,944,000	70,825	0.7%	10,059,000	2,521	0.0%	-0.7	10,402,000	14,575	0.1%	-0.6	10,893,000	9,614	0.1%	-0.6	11,364,000	405,286	3.6%	2.9
NORTH CAROLINA																2,947,000	496,188	16.8%	
NORTH DAKOTA	356,000	1,721	0.5%	353,000	483	0.1%	-0.3	350,000	158	0.0%	-0.4	352,000	398	0.1%	-0.4	355,000	14,444	4.1%	3.6
OHIO																6,281,000	468,098	7.5%	
OKLAHOMA																1,562,000	191,731	12.3%	
OREGON	1,000,000	3,665	0.4%	1,030,000	535	0.1%	-0.3	1,068,000	959	0.1%	-0.3	1,164,000	2,509	0.2%	-0.2	1,256,000	52,323	4.2%	3.8
PENNSYLVANIA	6,870,000	18,911	0.3%	6,928,000	9,482	0.1%	-0.1	6,998,000	10,303	0.1%	0.1	7,157,000	18,079	0.3%	0.0	7,311,000	398,506	5.5%	5.2
RHODE ISLAND	516,000	270	0.1%					524,000	1	0.0%	-0.1	554,000	13	0.0%	0.0	582,000	16,123	2.8%	2.7
SOUTH CAROLINA	1,180,000	1	0.0%	1,225,000	88,511	7.2%	7.2	1,274,000	1	0.0%	0.0	1,360,000	8	0.0%	0.0	1,441,000	215,430	15.0%	14.9
SOUTH DAKOTA																387,000	13,400	3.5%	
TENNESSEE	2,005,000	2,696	0.1%	2,050,000	20,609	1.0%	0.9	2,104,000	13,762	0.7%	0.5	2,226,000	34	0.0%	-0.1	2,342,000	424,792	18.1%	18.0
TEXAS	4,809,000	3,840	0.1%	5,131,000	14,591	0.3%	0.2	5,462,000	22,207	0.4%	0.3	5,952,000	5,060	0.1%	0.0	6,422,000	584,568	9.1%	9.0
UTAH								461,000	100	0.0%						556,000	27,175	4.9%	4.9
VERMONT	228,000	485	0.2%	226,000	39	0.0%	-0.2	226,000	7	0.0%	-0.2	241,000	20	0.0%	-0.2	256,000	6,007	2.3%	2.1
VIRGINIA	2,090,000	1,975	0.1%	2,202,000	43,759	2.0%	1.9	2,323,000	4,601	0.2%	0.1	2,530,000	2,895	0.1%	0.0	2,729,000	328,785	12.0%	12.0
WASHINGTON	1,553,000	10,756	0.7%	1,617,000	7,457	0.5%	-0.2	1,692,000	13,001	0.8%	0.1	1,854,000	8,309	0.4%	-0.2	2,009,000	99,734	5.0%	4.3
WEST VIRGINIA																1,070,000	72,560	6.8%	
WISCONSIN	2,223,000	5,451	0.2%	2,278,000	8,946	0.4%	0.1	2,338,000	3,102	0.1%	-0.1	2,452,000	2,896	0.1%	-0.1	2,559,000	132,737	5.2%	4.9
WYOMING	179,000	270	0.2%													194,000	11,105	5.7%	5.6
Total	81,669,000	299,692	0.4%	84,643,000	413,684	0.5%	0.1	84,298,000	503,331	0.6%	0.2	86,597,000	126,105	0.1%	-0.2	120,499,000	10,151,229	8.4%	8.1

*Percentage point difference between turnout in current year and initial year listed in chart. If data do not appear for a state in the initial year listed, the difference is calculated from the first year in which data do appear for that state.

STATE GUBERNATORIAL GENERAL ELECTIONS

Election Years 1952–1968

State	1952 Voting-age population	Turnout	%	1956 Voting-age population	Turnout	%	Difference from 1952*	1960 Voting-age population	Turnout	%	Difference from 1952	1964 Voting-age population	Turnout	%	Difference from 1952	1968 Voting-age population	Turnout	%	Difference from 1952
ALABAMA																			
ALASKA																			
ARIZONA	501,000	260,285	52.0%	615,000	288,592	46.9%	-5.0	728,000	397,107	54.5%	2.6	863,000	473,502	54.9%	2.9	990,000	483,998	48.9%	-3.1
ARKANSAS	1,091,000	391,592	35.9%	1,062,000	399,012	37.6%	1.7	1,046,000	421,985	40.3%	4.4	1,100,000	592,113	53.8%	17.9	1,153,000	615,595	53.4%	17.5
CALIFORNIA																			
COLORADO	875,000	613,034	70.1%	946,000	645,233	68.2%	-1.9												
CONNECTICUT																			
DELAWARE	221,000	170,749	77.3%	241,000	177,012	73.4%	-3.8	261,000	194,835	74.6%	-2.6	289,000	200,171	69.3%	-8.0	315,000	206,834	65.7%	-11.6
DISTRICT OF COLUMBIA																			
FLORIDA	2,115,000	834,518	39.5%	2,587,000	1,014,733	39.2%	-0.2	3,051,000	1,419,343	46.5%	7.1	3,629,000	1,663,481	45.8%	6.4				
GEORGIA																			
HAWAII																			
IDAHO																			
ILLINOIS	5,889,000	4,415,864	75.0%	6,016,000	4,314,611	71.7%	-3.3	6,155,000	4,674,187	75.9%	1.0	6,422,000	4,657,500	72.5%	-2.5	6,677,000	4,506,000	67.5%	-7.5
INDIANA	2,593,000	1,931,869	74.5%	2,682,000	1,954,290	72.9%	-1.6	2,773,000	2,128,965	76.8%	2.3	2,906,000	2,072,915	71.3%	-3.2	3,032,000	2,049,072	67.6%	-6.9
IOWA	1,669,000	1,230,045	73.7%	1,659,000	1,204,235	72.6%	-1.1	1,654,000	1,237,089	74.8%	1.1	1,674,000	1,167,734	69.8%	-3.9	1,693,000	1,136,489	67.1%	-6.6
KANSAS	1,253,000	872,139	69.6%	1,286,000	864,935	67.3%	-2.3	1,316,000	922,522	70.1%	0.5	1,341,000	850,414	63.4%	-6.2	1,365,000	862,473	63.2%	-6.4
KENTUCKY																			
LOUISIANA	1,637,000	123,681	7.6%	1,722,000	172,291	10.0%	2.4	1,807,000	506,562	28.0%	20.5	1,911,000	773,390	40.5%	32.9	2,012,000	372,762	18.5%	11.0
MAINE	555,000	248,441	44.8%	560,000	218,695	39.1%	-5.7	565,000	417,315	73.9%	29.1								
MARYLAND																			
MASSACHUSETTS	3,056,000	2,356,298	77.1%	3,082,000	2,339,884	75.9%	-1.2	3,126,000	2,417,133	77.3%	0.2	3,296,000	2,340,130	71.0%	-6.1				
MICHIGAN	4,099,000	2,865,980	69.9%	4,297,000	3,049,651	71.0%	1.1	4,498,000	3,255,991	72.4%	2.5	4,786,000	3,158,102	66.0%	-3.9				
MINNESOTA	1,901,000	1,418,869	74.6%	1,942,000	1,422,161	73.2%	-1.4	1,988,000	1,550,265	78.0%	3.3								
MISSISSIPPI																			
MISSOURI	2,636,000	1,871,095	71.0%	2,658,000	1,808,338	68.0%	-2.9	2,687,000	1,887,331	70.2%	-0.7	2,772,000	1,789,600	64.6%	-6.4	2,854,000	1,764,602	61.8%	-9.2
MONTANA	370,000	263,792	71.3%	378,000	270,366	71.5%	0.2	386,000	279,881	72.5%	1.2	394,000	280,975	71.3%	0.0	402,000	278,112	69.2%	-2.1
NEBRASKA	847,000	595,714	70.3%	848,000	563,933	66.5%	-3.8	851,000	598,971	70.4%	0.1	870,000	578,090	66.4%	-3.9				
NEVADA																			
NEW HAMPSHIRE	344,000	265,715	77.2%	353,000	258,695	73.3%	-4.0	365,000	290,527	79.6%	2.4	400,000	285,863	71.5%	-5.8	432,000	285,342	66.1%	-11.2
NEW JERSEY																			
NEW MEXICO	402,000	240,150	59.7%	452,000	251,751	55.7%	-4.0	497,000	305,542	61.5%	1.7	522,000	318,042	60.9%	1.2	547,000	318,975	58.3%	-1.4
NEW YORK																			

Election Years 1952–1968 *(continued)*

State	1952 Voting-age population	Turnout	%	1956 Voting-age population	Turnout	%	Difference from 1952	1960 Voting-age population	Turnout	%	Difference from 1952	1964 Voting-age population	Turnout	%	Difference from 1952	1968 Voting-age population	Turnout	%	Difference from 1952
NORTH CAROLINA	2,372,000	1,179,635	49.7%	2,469,000	1,135,859	46.0%	-3.7	2,575,000	1,350,360	52.4%	2.7	2,765,000	1,396,508	50.5%	0.8	2,947,000	1,558,308	52.9%	3.1
NORTH DAKOTA	356,000	253,934	71.3%	353,000	252,435	71.5%	0.2	350,000	275,375	78.7%	7.3	352,000	262,661	74.6%	3.3	355,000	248,000	69.9%	-1.5
OHIO	5,339,000	3,605,168	67.5%	5,567,000	3,542,091	63.6%	-3.9												
OKLAHOMA																			
OREGON				1,030,000	731,279	71.0%													
PENNSYLVANIA																			
RHODE ISLAND	516,000	409,689	79.4%	518,000	383,919	74.1%	-5.3	524,000	401,362	76.6%	-2.8	554,000	391,668	70.7%	-8.7	582,000	383,725	65.9%	-13.5
SOUTH CAROLINA																			
SOUTH DAKOTA	395,000	289,515	73.3%	392,000	292,017	74.5%	1.2	388,000	304,625	78.5%	5.2	388,000	290,570	74.9%	1.6	387,000	276,906	71.6%	-1.7
TENNESSEE	2,005,000	806,771	40.2%																
TEXAS	4,809,000	1,881,202	39.1%	5,131,000	1,828,161	35.6%	-3.5	5,462,000	2,250,718	41.2%	2.1	5,952,000	2,544,753	42.8%	3.6	6,422,000	2,916,509	45.4%	6.3
UTAH	400,000	327,704	81.9%	429,000	332,889	77.6%	-4.3	461,000	371,489	80.6%	-1.3	510,000	398,256	78.1%	-3.8	556,000	421,012	75.7%	-6.2
VERMONT	228,000	150,862	66.2%	226,000	153,809	68.1%	1.9	226,000	164,632	72.8%	6.7	241,000	164,199	68.1%	2.0	256,000	161,089	62.9%	-3.2
VIRGINIA																			
WASHINGTON	1,553,000	1,078,497	69.4%	1,617,000	1,128,977	69.8%	0.4	1,692,000	1,215,748	71.9%	2.4	1,854,000	1,250,274	67.4%	-2.0	2,009,000	1,265,355	63.0%	-6.5
WEST VIRGINIA	1,138,000	882,527	77.6%	1,103,000	817,623	74.1%	-3.4	1,076,000	827,420	76.9%	-0.7	1,073,000	788,582	73.5%	-4.1	1,070,000	743,845	69.5%	-8.0
WISCONSIN	2,223,000	1,615,214	72.7%	2,278,000	1,557,788	68.4%	-4.3	2,338,000	1,728,009	73.9%	1.3	2,452,000	1,694,887	69.1%	-3.5	2,559,000	1,689,738	66.0%	-6.6
WYOMING																			
Total	53,388,000	33,450,548	62.7%	54,499,000	33,375,265	61.2%	-1.4	48,846,000	31,795,289	65.1%	2.4	49,316,000	30,384,380	61.6%	-1.0	38,615,000	22,544,741	58.4%	-4.3

*Percentage point difference between turnout in current year and initial year listed in chart. If data do not appear for a state in the initial year listed, the difference is calculated from the first year in which data do appear for that state.

STATE GUBERNATORIAL GENERAL ELECTIONS

Republican Turnout for Election Years 1952–1968

State	1952 Voting-age population	Turnout	%	1956 Voting-age population	Turnout	%	Difference from 1952*	1960 Voting-age population	Turnout	%	Difference from 1952	1964 Voting-age population	Turnout	%	Difference from 1952	1968 Voting-age population	Turnout	%	Difference from 1952
ALABAMA																			
ALASKA																			
ARIZONA	501,000	156,592	31.3%	615,000	116,744	19.0%	-12.3	728,000	235,502	32.3%	1.1	863,000	221,404	25.7%	-5.6	990,000	279,923	28.3%	-3.0
ARKANSAS	1,091,000	49,292	4.5%	1,062,000	77,215	7.3%	2.8	1,046,000	129,921	12.4%	7.9	1,100,000	254,561	23.1%	18.6	1,153,000	322,782	28.0%	23.5
CALIFORNIA																			
COLORADO	875,000	349,924	40.0%	946,000	313,950	33.2%	-6.8												
CONNECTICUT																			
DELAWARE	221,000	88,977	40.3%	241,000	91,965	38.2%	-2.1	261,000	94,043	36.0%	-4.2	289,000	97,374	33.7%	-6.6	315,000	104,474	33.2%	-7.1
DISTRICT OF COLUMBIA																			
FLORIDA	2,115,000	210,009	9.9%	2,587,000	266,980	10.3%	0.4	3,051,000	569,936	18.7%	8.8	3,629,000	686,297	18.9%	9.0				
GEORGIA																			
HAWAII																			
IDAHO																			
ILLINOIS	5,889,000	2,317,363	39.4%	6,016,000	2,171,786	36.1%	-3.3	6,155,000	2,070,479	33.6%	-5.7	6,422,000	2,239,095	34.9%	-4.5	6,677,000	2,307,295	34.6%	-4.8
INDIANA	2,593,000	1,075,685	41.5%	2,682,000	1,086,868	40.5%	-1.0	2,773,000	1,049,540	37.8%	-3.6	2,906,000	901,342	31.0%	-10.5	3,032,000	1,080,271	35.6%	-5.9
IOWA	1,669,000	638,388	38.2%	1,659,000	587,383	35.4%	-2.8	1,654,000	645,026	39.0%	0.7	1,674,000	365,131	21.8%	-16.4	1,693,000	614,328	36.3%	-2.0
KANSAS	1,253,000	491,338	39.2%	1,286,000	364,340	28.3%	-10.9	1,316,000	511,534	38.9%	-0.3	1,341,000	432,667	32.3%	-6.9	1,365,000	410,673	30.1%	-9.1
KENTUCKY																			
LOUISIANA	1,637,000	4,958	0.3%					1,807,000	86,135	4.8%	4.5	1,911,000	297,753	15.6%	15.3				
MAINE	555,000	128,532	23.2%	560,000	124,395	22.2%	-0.9	565,000	219,768	38.9%	15.7								
MARYLAND																			
MASSACHUSETTS	3,056,000	1,175,955	38.5%	3,082,000	1,096,759	35.6%	-2.9	3,126,000	1,269,295	40.6%	2.1	3,296,000	1,176,462	35.7%	-2.8				
MICHIGAN	4,099,000	1,423,275	34.7%	4,297,000	1,376,376	32.0%	-2.7	4,498,000	1,602,022	35.6%	0.9	4,786,000	1,764,355	36.9%	2.1				
MINNESOTA	1,901,000	785,125	41.3%	1,942,000	685,196	35.3%	-6.0	1,988,000	783,813	39.4%	-1.9								
MISSISSIPPI																			
MISSOURI	2,636,000	886,370	33.6%	2,658,000	866,810	32.6%	-1.0	2,687,000	792,131	29.5%	-4.1	2,772,000	678,949	24.5%	-9.1	2,854,000	691,797	24.2%	-9.4
MONTANA	370,000	134,423	36.3%	378,000	138,878	36.7%	0.4	386,000	154,230	40.0%	3.6	394,000	144,113	36.6%	0.2	402,000	116,432	29.0%	-7.4
NEBRASKA	847,000	366,009	43.2%	848,000	308,293	36.4%	-6.9	851,000	287,302	33.8%	-9.5	870,000	231,029	26.6%	-16.7				
NEVADA																			
NEW HAMPSHIRE	344,000	167,791	48.8%	353,000	141,578	40.1%	-8.7	365,000	161,123	44.1%	-4.6	400,000	94,824	23.7%	-25.1	432,000	149,902	34.7%	-14.1
NEW JERSEY																			
NEW MEXICO	402,000	129,116	32.1%	452,000	131,488	29.1%	-3.0	497,000	153,765	30.9%	-1.2	522,000	126,540	24.2%	-7.9	547,000	160,140	29.3%	-2.8
NEW YORK																			

State Gubernatorial General Elections (continued)

Republican Turnout for Election Years 1952–1968 (continued)

State	1952 Voting-age population	Turnout	%	1956 Voting-age population	Turnout	%	Difference from 1952	1960 Voting-age population	Turnout	%	Difference from 1952	1964 Voting-age population	Turnout	%	Difference from 1952	1968 Voting-age population	Turnout	%	Difference from 1952
NORTH CAROLINA	2,372,000	383,329	16.2%	2,469,000	375,379	15.2%	-1.0	2,575,000	613,975	23.8%	7.7	2,765,000	606,165	21.9%	5.8	2,947,000	737,075	25.0%	8.9
NORTH DAKOTA	356,000	199,944	56.2%	353,000	147,566	41.8%	-14.4	350,000	122,486	35.0%	-21.2	352,000	116,247	33.0%	-23.1	355,000	108,382	30.5%	-25.6
OHIO	5,339,000	1,590,058	29.8%	5,567,000	1,984,988	35.7%	5.9												
OKLAHOMA																			
OREGON				1,030,000	361,840	35.1%													
PENNSYLVANIA																			
RHODE ISLAND	516,000	194,102	37.6%	518,000	191,604	37.0%	-0.6	524,000	174,044	33.2%	-4.4	554,000	239,501	43.2%	5.6	582,000	187,958	32.3%	-5.3
SOUTH CAROLINA																			
SOUTH DAKOTA	395,000	203,102	51.4%	392,000	158,819	40.5%	-10.9	388,000	154,530	39.8%	-11.6	388,000	150,151	38.7%	-12.7	387,000	159,646	41.3%	-10.2
TENNESSEE	2,005,000	166,377	8.3%																
TEXAS				5,131,000	271,088	5.3%		5,462,000	612,963	11.2%	5.9	5,952,000	661,675	11.1%	5.8	6,422,000	1,254,333	19.5%	14.2
UTAH	400,000	180,516	45.1%	429,000	127,164	29.6%	-15.5	461,000	195,634	42.4%	-2.7	510,000	171,300	33.6%	-11.5	556,000	131,729	23.7%	-21.4
VERMONT	228,000	78,338	34.4%	226,000	88,379	39.1%	4.7	226,000	92,861	41.1%	6.7	241,000	57,576	23.9%	-10.5	256,000	89,387	34.9%	0.6
VIRGINIA																			
WASHINGTON	1,553,000	567,822	36.6%	1,617,000	508,041	31.4%	-5.1	1,692,000	594,122	35.1%	-1.4	1,854,000	697,256	37.6%	1.0	2,009,000	692,378	34.5%	-2.1
WEST VIRGINIA	1,138,000	427,629	37.6%	1,103,000	440,502	39.9%	2.4	1,076,000	380,665	35.4%	-2.2	1,073,000	355,559	33.1%	-4.4	1,070,000	378,315	35.4%	-2.2
WISCONSIN	2,223,000	1,009,171	45.4%	2,278,000	808,273	35.5%	-9.9	2,338,000	837,123	35.8%	-9.6	2,452,000	856,779	34.9%	-10.5	2,559,000	893,463	34.9%	-10.5
WYOMING																			
Total	48,579,000	15,579,510	32.1%	52,777,000	15,410,647	29.2%	-2.9	48,846,000	14,593,968	29.9%	-2.2	49,316,000	13,624,105	27.6%	-4.4	36,603,000	10,870,683	29.7%	-2.4

Democratic Turnout for Election Years 1952–1968

State	1952 Voting-age population	Turnout	%	1956 Voting-age population	Turnout	%	Difference from 1952*	1960 Voting-age population	Turnout	%	Difference from 1952	1964 Voting-age population	Turnout	%	Difference from 1952	1968 Voting-age population	Turnout	%	Difference from 1952
ALABAMA																			
ALASKA																			
ARIZONA	501,000	103,693	20.7%	615,000	171,848	27.9%	7.2	728,000	161,605	22.2%	1.5	863,000	252,098	29.2%	8.5	990,000	204,075	20.6%	-0.1
ARKANSAS	1,091,000	342,292	31.4%	1,062,000	321,797	30.3%	-1.1	1,046,000	292,064	27.9%	-3.5	1,100,000	337,489	30.7%	-0.7	1,153,000	292,813	25.4%	-6.0
CALIFORNIA																			
COLORADO	875,000	260,044	29.7%	946,000	331,283	35.0%	5.3												
CONNECTICUT																			
DELAWARE	221,000	81,772	37.0%	241,000	85,047	35.3%	-1.7	261,000	100,792	38.6%	1.6	289,000	102,797	35.6%	-1.4	315,000	102,360	32.5%	-4.5
DISTRICT OF COLUMBIA																			
FLORIDA	2,115,000	624,463	29.5%	2,587,000	747,753	28.9%	-0.6	3,051,000	849,407	27.8%	-1.7	3,629,000	933,554	25.7%	-3.8				

State Gubernatorial General Elections (continued)

State Gubernatorial General Elections *(continued)*

Democratic Turnout for Election Years 1952–1968 *(continued)*

State	1952 Voting-age population	1952 Turnout	1952 %	1956 Voting-age population	1956 Turnout	1956 %	1956 Difference from 1952	1960 Voting-age population	1960 Turnout	1960 %	1960 Difference from 1952	1964 Voting-age population	1964 Turnout	1964 %	1964 Difference from 1952	1968 Voting-age population	1968 Turnout	1968 %	1968 Difference from 1952
GEORGIA																			
HAWAII																			
IDAHO																			
ILLINOIS	5,889,000	2,089,721	35.5%	6,016,000	2,134,909	35.5%	0.0	6,155,000	2,594,731	42.2%	6.7	6,422,000	2,418,394	37.7%	2.2	6,677,000	2,179,501	32.6%	-2.8
INDIANA	2,593,000	841,984	32.5%	2,682,000	859,393	32.0%	-0.4	2,773,000	1,072,717	38.7%	6.2	2,906,000	1,164,620	40.1%	7.6	3,032,000	965,816	31.9%	-0.6
IOWA	1,669,000	587,671	35.2%	1,659,000	616,852	37.2%	2.0	1,654,000	592,063	35.8%	0.6	1,674,000	794,610	47.5%	12.3	1,693,000	521,216	30.8%	-4.4
KANSAS	1,253,000	363,482	29.0%	1,286,000	479,701	37.3%	8.3	1,316,000	402,261	30.6%	1.6	1,341,000	400,264	29.8%	0.8	1,365,000	447,269	32.8%	3.8
KENTUCKY																			
LOUISIANA	1,637,000	118,723	7.3%	1,722,000	172,291	10.0%	2.8	1,807,000	407,907	22.6%	15.3	1,911,000	469,589	24.6%	17.3	2,012,000	372,762	18.5%	11.3
MAINE	555,000	82,538	14.9%	560,000	94,300	16.8%	2.0	565,000	197,547	35.0%	20.1								
MARYLAND																			
MASSACHUSETTS	3,056,000	1,161,499	38.0%	3,082,000	1,234,618	40.1%	2.1	3,126,000	1,130,810	36.2%	-1.8	3,296,000	1,153,416	35.0%	-3.0				
MICHIGAN	4,099,000	1,431,893	34.9%	4,297,000	1,666,689	38.8%	3.9	4,498,000	1,643,634	36.5%	1.6	4,786,000	1,381,442	28.9%	-6.1				
MINNESOTA	1,901,000	624,480	32.9%	1,942,000	731,180	37.7%	4.8	1,988,000	760,934	38.3%	5.4								
MISSISSIPPI																			
MISSOURI	2,636,000	983,166	37.3%	2,658,000	941,528	35.4%	-1.9	2,687,000	1,095,200	40.8%	3.5	2,772,000	1,110,651	40.1%	2.8	2,854,000	1,072,805	37.6%	0.3
MONTANA	370,000	129,369	35.0%	378,000	131,488	34.8%	-0.2	386,000	125,651	32.6%	-2.4	394,000	136,862	34.7%	-0.2	402,000	150,481	37.4%	2.5
NEBRASKA	847,000	229,700	27.1%	848,000	224,048	26.4%	-0.7	851,000	311,344	36.6%	9.5	870,000	347,026	39.9%	12.8				
NEVADA																			
NEW HAMPSHIRE	344,000	97,924	28.5%	353,000	117,117	33.2%	4.7	365,000	129,404	35.5%	7.0	400,000	190,863	47.7%	19.2	432,000	135,378	31.3%	2.9
NEW JERSEY																			
NEW MEXICO	402,000	111,034	27.6%	452,000	120,263	26.6%	-1.0	497,000	151,777	30.5%	2.9	522,000	191,497	36.7%	9.1	547,000	157,230	28.7%	1.1
NEW YORK																			
NORTH CAROLINA	2,372,000	796,306	33.6%	2,469,000	760,480	30.8%	-2.8	2,575,000	735,248	28.6%	-5.0	2,765,000	790,343	28.6%	-5.0	2,947,000	821,233	27.9%	-5.7
NORTH DAKOTA	356,000	53,990	15.2%	353,000	104,869	29.7%	14.5	350,000	136,148	38.9%	23.7	352,000	146,414	41.6%	26.4	355,000	135,955	38.3%	23.1
OHIO	5,339,000	2,015,110	37.7%	5,567,000	1,557,103	28.0%	-9.8												
OKLAHOMA																			
OREGON				1,030,000	369,439	35.9%													
PENNSYLVANIA																			
RHODE ISLAND	516,000	215,587	41.8%	518,000	192,315	37.1%	-4.7	524,000	227,318	43.4%	1.6	554,000	152,165	27.5%	-14.3	582,000	195,766	33.6%	-8.1
SOUTH CAROLINA																			
SOUTH DAKOTA	395,000	86,413	21.9%	392,000	133,198	34.0%	12.1	388,000	150,095	38.7%	16.8	388,000	140,419	36.2%	14.3	387,000	117,260	30.3%	8.4
TENNESSEE	2,005,000	640,290	31.9%																

State Gubernatorial General Elections *(continued)*

Democratic Turnout for Election Years 1952–1968 *(continued)*

State	1952 Voting-age population	Turnout	%	1956 Voting-age population	Turnout	%	Difference from 1952	1960 Voting-age population	Turnout	%	Difference from 1952	1964 Voting-age population	Turnout	%	Difference from 1952	1968 Voting-age population	Turnout	%	Difference from 1952
TEXAS	4,809,000	1,844,530	38.4%	5,131,000	1,433,051	27.9%	-10.4	5,462,000	1,637,755	30.0%	-8.4	5,952,000	1,877,793	31.5%	-6.8	6,422,000	1,662,019	25.9%	-12.5
UTAH	400,000	147,188	36.8%	429,000	111,297	25.9%	-10.9	461,000	175,855	38.1%	1.3	510,000	226,956	44.5%	7.7	556,000	289,283	52.0%	15.2
VERMONT	228,000	60,051	26.3%	226,000	65,420	28.9%	2.6	226,000	71,755	31.8%	5.4	241,000	106,611	44.2%	17.9	256,000	71,656	28.0%	1.7
VIRGINIA																			
WASHINGTON	1,553,000	510,675	32.9%	1,617,000	616,773	38.1%	5.3	1,692,000	611,987	36.2%	3.3	1,854,000	548,692	29.6%	-3.3	2,009,000	560,262	27.9%	-5.0
WEST VIRGINIA	1,138,000	454,898	40.0%	1,103,000	377,121	34.2%	-5.8	1,076,000	446,755	41.5%	1.5	1,073,000	433,023	40.4%	0.4	1,070,000	365,530	34.2%	-5.8
WISCONSIN	2,223,000	601,844	27.1%	2,278,000	749,421	32.9%	5.8	2,338,000	890,868	38.1%	11.0	2,452,000	837,901	34.2%	7.1	2,559,000	791,100	30.9%	3.8
WYOMING																			
Total	53,388,000	17,692,330	33.1%	54,499,000	17,652,592	32.4%	-0.7	48,846,000	17,103,632	35.0%	1.9	49,316,000	16,645,489	33.8%	0.6	38,615,000	11,611,770	30.1%	-3.1

Other Turnout for Election Years 1952–1968

State	1952 Voting-age population	Turnout	%	1956 Voting-age population	Turnout	%	Difference from 1952*	1960 Voting-age population	Turnout	%	Difference from 1952	1964 Voting-age population	Turnout	%	Difference from 1952	1968 Voting-age population	Turnout	%	Difference from 1952
ALABAMA																			
ALASKA																			
ARIZONA																			
ARKANSAS	1,091,000	8	0.0%									1,100,000	63	0.0%	0.0				
CALIFORNIA																			
COLORADO	875,000	3,066	0.4%																
CONNECTICUT																			
DELAWARE																			
DISTRICT OF COLUMBIA																			
FLORIDA	2,115,000	46	0.0%									3,629,000	43,630	1.2%	1.2				
GEORGIA																			
HAWAII																			
IDAHO																			
ILLINOIS	5,889,000	8,780	0.1%	6,016,000	7,916	0.1%	0.0	6,155,000	8,977	0.1%	0.0	6,422,000	11	0.0%	-0.1	6,677,000	19,204	0.3%	0.1
INDIANA	2,593,000	14,200	0.5%	2,682,000	8,029	0.3%	-0.2	2,773,000	6,708	0.2%	-0.3	2,906,000	6,953	0.2%	-0.3	3,032,000	2,985	0.1%	-0.4
IOWA	1,669,000	3,986	0.2%									1,674,000	7,993	0.5%	0.2	1,693,000	945	0.1%	-0.2
KANSAS	1,253,000	17,319	1.4%	1,286,000	20,894	1.6%	0.2	1,316,000	8,727	0.7%	-0.7	1,341,000	17,483	1.3%	-0.1	1,365,000	4,531	0.3%	-1.1
KENTUCKY																			
LOUISIANA								1,807,000	12,520	0.7%		1,911,000	6,048	0.3%	-0.4				
MAINE	555,000	37,371	6.7%																

State Gubernatorial General Elections (continued)

State Gubernatorial General Elections (continued)

Other Turnout for Election Years 1952–1968 (continued)

State	1952 Voting-age population	Turnout	%	1956 Voting-age population	Turnout	%	Difference from 1952	1960 Voting-age population	Turnout	%	Difference from 1952	1964 Voting-age population	Turnout	%	Difference from 1952	1968 Voting-age population	Turnout	%	Difference from 1952
MARYLAND																			
MASSACHUSETTS	3,056,000	18,844	0.6%	3,082,000	8,507	0.3%	-0.3	3,126,000	17,028	0.5%	-0.1	3,296,000	10,252	0.3%	-0.3				
MICHIGAN	4,099,000	10,812	0.3%	4,297,000	6,586	0.2%	-0.1	4,498,000	10,335	0.2%	0.0	4,786,000	12,305	0.3%	0.0				
MINNESOTA	1,901,000	9,264	0.5%	1,942,000	5,785	0.3%	-0.2	1,988,000	5,518	0.3%	-0.2								
MISSISSIPPI																			
MISSOURI	2,636,000	1,559	0.1%																
MONTANA																402,000	11,199	2.8%	
NEBRASKA	847,000	5	0.0%	848,000	31,592	3.7%	3.7	851,000	325	0.0%	0.0	870,000	35	0.0%	0.0				
NEVADA																			
NEW HAMPSHIRE												400,000	176	0.0%		432,000	62	0.0%	0.0
NEW JERSEY																			
NEW MEXICO												522,000	5	0.0%		547,000	1,605	0.3%	0.3
NEW YORK																			
NORTH CAROLINA								2,575,000	1,137	0.0%									
NORTH DAKOTA								350,000	16,741	4.8%						355,000	3,663	1.0%	-3.8
OHIO																			
OKLAHOMA																			
OREGON																			
RHODE ISLAND												554,000	2	0.0%		582,000	1	0.0%	0.0
SOUTH CAROLINA																			
SOUTH DAKOTA																			
TENNESSEE	2,005,000	104	0.0%																
TEXAS	4,809,000	36,672	0.8%	5,131,000	124,022	2.4%	1.7					5,952,000	5,285	0.1%	-0.7	6,422,000	157	0.0%	-0.8
UTAH				429,000	94,428	22.0%													
VERMONT	228,000	12,473	5.5%	226,000	10	0.0%	-5.5	226,000	16	0.0%	-5.5	241,000	12	0.0%	-5.5	256,000	46	0.0%	-5.5
VIRGINIA																			
WASHINGTON				1,617,000	4,163	0.3%		1,692,000	9,639	0.6%	0.3	1,854,000	4,326	0.2%	0.0	2,009,000	12,715	0.6%	0.4
WEST VIRGINIA																			
WISCONSIN	2,223,000	4,199	0.2%	2,278,000	94	0.0%	-0.2	2,338,000	18	0.0%	-0.2	2,452,000	207	0.0%	-0.2	2,559,000	5,175	0.2%	0.0
WYOMING																			
Total	37,844,000	178,708	0.5%	29,834,000	312,026	1.0%	0.6	29,695,000	97,689	0.3%	-0.1	39,910,000	114,786	0.3%	-0.2	26,331,000	62,288	0.2%	-0.2

*Percentage point difference between turnout in current year and initial year listed in chart. If data do not appear for a state in the initial year listed, the difference is calculated from the first year in which data do appear for that state.

UNITED STATES SENATE GENERAL ELECTIONS

Election Years 1952–1968

State	1952 Voting-age population	Turnout	%	1956 Voting-age population	Turnout	%	Difference from 1952*	1960 Voting-age population	Turnout	%	Difference from 1952	1964 Voting-age population	Turnout	%	Difference from 1952	1968 Voting-age population	Turnout	%	Difference from 1952
ALABAMA				1,801,000	330,182	18.3%		1,840,000	554,081	30.1%	11.8					1,997,000	912,708	45.7%	27.4
ALASKA								135,000	59,978	44.4%						170,000	80,931	47.6%	3.2
ARIZONA	501,000	257,401	51.4%	615,000	278,263	45.2%	-6.1					863,000	468,801	54.3%	2.9	990,000	479,945	48.5%	-2.9
ARKANSAS				1,062,000	399,695	37.6%										1,153,000	591,704	51.3%	13.7
CALIFORNIA	7,453,000	4,542,540	60.0%	8,335,000	5,361,467	64.3%	3.4					10,572,000	7,041,821	66.6%	5.7	11,852,000	7,102,465	59.9%	-1.0
COLORADO				946,000	636,974	67.3%		1,020,000	727,633	71.3%	4.0					1,264,000	785,536	62.1%	-5.2
CONNECTICUT	1,358,000	1,093,467	80.5%	1,445,000	1,113,786	77.1%	-3.4					1,683,000	1,208,163	71.8%	-8.7	1,824,000	1,206,537	66.1%	-14.4
DELAWARE	221,000	170,705	77.2%					261,000	194,964	74.7%	-2.5	289,000	200,703	69.4%	-7.8				
DISTRICT OF COLUMBIA																			
FLORIDA	2,115,000	617,800	29.2%	2,587,000	655,418	25.3%	-3.9					3,629,000	1,560,337	43.0%	13.8	4,184,000	2,024,136	48.4%	19.2
GEORGIA				2,329,000	541,267	23.2%		2,433,000	576,495	23.7%	0.5					2,867,000	1,141,889	39.8%	16.6
HAWAII												383,000	208,814	54.5%		418,000	226,927	54.3%	-0.2
IDAHO				360,000	265,292	73.7%		371,000	292,096	78.7%	5.0					405,000	287,876	71.1%	-2.6
ILLINOIS				6,016,000	4,264,830	70.9%		6,155,000	4,632,796	75.3%	4.4					6,677,000	4,449,757	66.6%	-4.2
INDIANA	2,593,000	1,946,118	75.1%	2,682,000	1,963,986	73.2%	-1.8					2,906,000	2,076,963	71.5%	-3.6	3,032,000	2,053,118	67.7%	-7.3
IOWA				1,659,000	1,178,655	71.0%		1,654,000	1,237,582	74.8%	3.8					1,693,000	1,144,086	67.6%	-3.5
KANSAS				1,286,000	825,280	64.2%		1,316,000	888,592	67.5%	3.3					1,365,000	817,096	59.9%	-4.3
KENTUCKY				1,889,000	1,006,825	53.3%		1,905,000	1,088,377	57.1%	3.8					2,074,000	942,865	45.5%	-7.8
LOUISIANA				1,722,000	335,564	19.5%		1,807,000	541,919	30.0%	10.5					2,012,000	510,586	25.8%	6.3
MAINE	555,000	237,164	42.7%					565,000	416,699	73.8%	31.0	578,000	380,551	65.8%	23.1				
MARYLAND	1,586,000	856,193	54.0%	1,711,000	892,167	52.1%	-1.8					2,064,000	1,081,049	52.4%	-1.6	2,277,000	1,133,727	49.8%	-4.2
MASSACHUSETTS	3,056,000	2,360,425	77.2%					3,126,000	2,417,813	77.3%	0.1	3,296,000	2,312,028	70.1%	-7.1				
MICHIGAN	4,099,000	2,821,131	68.8%					4,498,000	3,226,647	71.7%	2.9	4,786,000	3,101,667	64.8%	-4.0				
MINNESOTA	1,901,000	1,387,419	73.0%					1,988,000	1,536,839	77.3%	4.3	2,091,000	1,543,590	73.8%	0.8				
MISSISSIPPI	1,195,000	233,919	19.6%					1,172,000	266,148	22.7%	3.1	1,203,000	343,364	28.5%	9.0				
MISSOURI	2,636,000	1,868,101	70.9%	2,658,000	1,800,984	67.8%	-3.1	2,687,000	1,880,232	70.0%	-0.9	2,772,000	1,783,003	64.3%	-6.5	2,854,000	1,737,958	60.9%	-10.0
MONTANA	370,000	262,297	70.9%					386,000	276,612	71.7%	0.8	394,000	280,010	71.1%	0.2				
NEBRASKA	847,000	591,718	69.9%					851,000	598,585	70.3%	0.5	870,000	563,401	64.8%	-5.1				
NEVADA	122,000	81,090	66.5%	148,000	96,389	65.1%	-1.3					230,000	134,564	58.5%	-8.0	281,000	152,690	54.3%	-12.1
NEW HAMPSHIRE				353,000	251,943	71.4%		365,000	287,545	78.8%	7.4					432,000	286,989	66.4%	-4.9
NEW JERSEY	3,354,000	2,318,232	69.1%					3,758,000	2,664,556	70.9%	1.8	4,069,000	2,710,441	66.6%	-2.5				
NEW MEXICO	402,000	239,711	59.6%					497,000	300,551	60.5%	0.8	522,000	325,774	62.4%	2.8				
NEW YORK	9,944,000	6,980,259	70.2%	10,059,000	6,991,136	69.5%	-0.7					10,893,000	7,151,686	65.7%	-4.5	11,364,000	6,581,587	57.9%	-12.3

United States Senate General Elections (continued)

United States Senate General Elections (continued)

Election Years 1952–1968 (continued)

State	1952 Voting-age population	1952 Turnout	1952 %	1956 Voting-age population	1956 Turnout	1956 %	1956 Difference from 1952	1960 Voting-age population	1960 Turnout	1960 %	1960 Difference from 1952	1964 Voting-age population	1964 Turnout	1964 %	1964 Difference from 1952	1968 Voting-age population	1968 Turnout	1968 %	1968 Difference from 1952
NORTH CAROLINA				2,469,000	1,098,828	44.5%		2,575,000	1,291,485	50.2%	5.6					2,947,000	1,437,340	48.8%	4.3
NORTH DAKOTA	356,000	237,995	66.9%	353,000	244,161	69.2%	2.3	350,000	210,349	60.1%	-6.8	352,000	258,945	73.6%	6.7	355,000	239,776	67.5%	0.7
OHIO	5,339,000	3,442,291	64.5%	5,567,000	3,525,499	63.3%	-1.1					6,040,000	3,830,389	63.4%	-1.1	6,281,000	3,743,121	59.6%	-4.9
OKLAHOMA				1,399,000	831,142	59.4%		1,420,000	864,475	60.9%	1.5	1,493,000	912,174	61.1%	1.7	1,562,000	909,119	58.2%	-1.2
OREGON				1,030,000	732,254	71.1%		1,068,000	755,875	70.8%	-0.3					1,256,000	814,176	64.8%	-6.3
PENNSYLVANIA	6,870,000	4,519,761	65.8%	6,928,000	4,529,874	65.4%	-0.4					7,157,000	4,803,835	67.1%	1.3	7,311,000	4,624,218	63.3%	-2.5
RHODE ISLAND	516,000	410,978	79.6%					524,000	399,983	76.3%	-3.3	554,000	386,322	69.7%	-9.9				
SOUTH CAROLINA				1,225,000	279,845	22.8%		1,274,000	330,266	25.9%	3.1					1,441,000	652,855	45.3%	22.5
SOUTH DAKOTA				392,000	290,622	74.1%		388,000	305,442	78.7%	4.6					387,000	279,912	72.3%	-1.8
TENNESSEE	2,005,000	735,219	36.7%					2,104,000	828,519	39.4%	2.7	2,226,000	1,091,093	49.0%	12.3				
TEXAS	4,809,000	1,895,192	39.4%					5,462,000	2,253,784	41.3%	1.9	5,952,000	2,603,856	43.7%	4.3				
UTAH	400,000	327,033	81.8%	429,000	330,381	77.0%	-4.7					510,000	397,384	77.9%	-3.8	556,000	419,262	75.4%	-6.4
VERMONT	228,000	154,052	67.6%	226,000	155,289	68.7%	1.1					241,000	164,350	68.2%	0.6	256,000	157,375	61.5%	-6.1
VIRGINIA	2,090,000	543,516	26.0%					2,323,000	622,820	26.8%	0.8	2,530,000	928,363	36.7%	10.7				
WASHINGTON	1,553,000	1,058,735	68.2%	1,617,000	1,122,217	69.4%	1.2					1,854,000	1,213,088	65.4%	-2.7	2,009,000	1,236,063	61.5%	-6.6
WEST VIRGINIA	1,138,000	876,573	77.0%					1,076,000	828,292	77.0%	0.0	1,073,000	761,087	70.9%	-6.1				
WISCONSIN	2,223,000	1,605,167	72.2%	2,278,000	1,523,121	66.9%	-5.3					2,452,000	1,673,776	68.3%	-3.9	2,559,000	1,654,861	64.7%	-7.5
WYOMING	179,000	130,097	72.7%					189,000	138,550	73.3%	0.6	192,000	141,670	73.8%	1.1				
Total	72,014,000	44,802,307	62.2%	73,576,000	43,853,336	59.6%	-2.6	57,543,000	33,496,580	58.2%	-4.0	86,719,000	53,643,062	61.9%	-0.4	88,105,000	50,827,191	57.7%	-4.5

*Percentage point difference between turnout in current year and initial year listed in chart. If data do not appear for a state in the initial year listed, the difference is calculated from the first year in which data do appear for that state.

UNITED STATES SENATE GENERAL ELECTIONS

Republican Turnout for Election Years 1952–1968

State	1952 Voting-age population	Turnout	%	1956 Voting-age population	Turnout	%	Difference from 1952*	1960 Voting-age population	Turnout	%	Difference from 1952	1964 Voting-age population	Turnout	%	Difference from 1952	1968 Voting-age population	Turnout	%	Difference from 1952
ALABAMA								1,840,000	164,868	9.0%						1,997,000	201,227	10.1%	1.1
ALASKA								135,000	21,937	16.2%						170,000	30,286	17.8%	1.6
ARIZONA	501,000	132,063	26.4%	615,000	107,447	17.5%	-8.9					863,000	241,089	27.9%	1.6	990,000	274,607	27.7%	1.4
ARKANSAS				1,062,000	68,016	6.4%										1,153,000	241,739	21.0%	14.6
CALIFORNIA	7,453,000	3,902,440	53.1%	8,335,000	2,892,918	34.7%	-18.7					10,572,000	3,628,555	34.3%	-19.1	11,852,000	3,329,148	28.1%	-25.3
COLORADO				946,000	317,102	33.5%		1,020,000	389,428	38.2%	4.7					1,264,000	459,952	36.4%	2.9
CONNECTICUT	1,358,000	596,122	43.9%	1,445,000	621,028	43.0%	-0.9					1,683,000	426,939	25.4%	-18.5	1,824,000	551,455	30.2%	-13.7
DELAWARE	221,000	93,020	42.1%					261,000	98,874	37.9%	-4.2	289,000	103,782	35.9%	-6.2				
DISTRICT OF COLUMBIA																			
FLORIDA												3,629,000	562,212	15.5%		4,184,000	1,131,499	27.0%	11.6
GEORGIA																2,867,000	256,796	9.0%	
HAWAII												383,000	110,747	28.9%		418,000	34,008	8.1%	-20.8
IDAHO				360,000	102,781	28.6%		371,000	152,648	41.1%	12.6					405,000	114,394	28.2%	-0.3
ILLINOIS				6,016,000	2,307,352	38.4%		6,155,000	2,093,846	34.0%	-4.3					6,677,000	2,358,947	35.3%	-3.0
INDIANA	2,593,000	1,020,605	39.4%	2,682,000	1,084,262	40.4%	1.1					2,906,000	941,519	32.4%	-7.0	3,032,000	988,571	32.6%	-6.8
IOWA				1,659,000	635,499	38.3%		1,654,000	642,463	38.8%	0.5					1,693,000	568,469	33.6%	-4.7
KANSAS				1,286,000	477,822	37.2%		1,316,000	485,499	36.9%	-0.3					1,365,000	490,911	36.0%	-1.2
KENTUCKY				1,889,000	506,903	26.8%		1,905,000	644,087	33.8%	7.0					2,074,000	484,260	23.3%	-3.5
LOUISIANA								1,807,000	109,689	6.1%									
MAINE	555,000	139,205	25.1%					565,000	256,890	45.5%	20.4	578,000	127,040	22.0%	-3.1				
MARYLAND	1,586,000	449,823	28.4%	1,711,000	473,059	27.6%	-0.7					2,064,000	402,393	19.5%	-8.9	2,277,000	541,893	23.8%	-4.6
MASSACHUSETTS	3,056,000	1,141,247	37.3%					3,126,000	1,358,556	43.5%	6.1	3,296,000	587,663	17.8%	-19.5				
MICHIGAN	4,099,000	1,428,352	34.8%					4,498,000	1,548,873	34.4%	-0.4	4,786,000	1,096,272	22.9%	-11.9				
MINNESOTA	1,901,000	785,649	41.3%					1,988,000	648,586	32.6%	-8.7	2,091,000	605,933	29.0%	-12.4				
MISSISSIPPI								1,172,000	21,807	1.9%									
MISSOURI	2,636,000	858,170	32.6%	2,658,000	785,048	29.5%	-3.0	2,687,000	880,576	32.8%	0.2	2,772,000	596,337	21.5%	-11.0	2,854,000	850,544	29.8%	-2.8
MONTANA	370,000	127,360	34.4%					386,000	136,281	35.3%	0.9	394,000	99,367	25.2%	-9.2				
NEBRASKA	847,000	408,971	48.3%					851,000	352,748	41.5%	-6.8	870,000	345,772	39.7%	-8.5				
NEVADA	122,000	41,906	34.3%	148,000	45,712	30.9%	-3.5					230,000	67,228	29.2%	-5.1	281,000	69,068	24.6%	-9.8
NEW HAMPSHIRE				353,000	161,424	45.7%		365,000	173,521	47.5%	1.8					432,000	170,163	39.4%	-6.3
NEW JERSEY	3,354,000	1,286,782	38.4%					3,758,000	1,483,832	39.5%	1.1	4,069,000	1,011,610	24.9%	-13.5				
NEW MEXICO	402,000	117,168	29.1%					497,000	109,897	22.1%	-7.0	522,000	147,562	28.3%	-0.9				
NEW YORK	9,944,000	3,853,934	38.8%	10,059,000	3,723,933	37.0%	-1.7					10,893,000	3,104,056	28.5%	-10.3	11,364,000	3,269,772	28.8%	-10.0

United States Senate General Elections (continued)

United States Senate General Elections *(continued)*

Republican Turnout for Election Years 1952–1968 *(continued)*

State	1952 Voting-age population	Turnout	%	1956 Voting-age population	Turnout	%	Difference from 1952	1960 Voting-age population	Turnout	%	Difference from 1952	1964 Voting-age population	Turnout	%	Difference from 1952	1968 Voting-age population	Turnout	%	Difference from 1952
NORTH CAROLINA				2,469,000	367,475	14.9%		2,575,000	497,964	19.3%	4.5					2,947,000	566,934	19.2%	4.4
NORTH DAKOTA	356,000	157,907	44.4%	353,000	155,305	44.0%	-0.4	350,000	103,475	29.6%	-14.8	352,000	109,681	31.2%	-13.2	355,000	154,968	43.7%	-0.7
OHIO	5,339,000	1,878,961	35.2%	5,567,000	1,660,910	29.8%	-5.4					6,040,000	1,906,781	31.6%	-3.6	6,281,000	1,928,964	30.7%	-4.5
OKLAHOMA				1,399,000	371,146	26.5%		1,420,000	385,646	27.2%	0.6	1,493,000	445,392	29.8%	3.3	1,562,000	470,120	30.1%	3.6
OREGON				1,030,000	335,405	32.6%		1,068,000	343,009	32.1%	-0.4					1,256,000	408,646	32.5%	0.0
PENNSYLVANIA	6,870,000	2,331,034	33.9%	6,928,000	2,250,671	32.5%	-1.4					7,157,000	2,429,858	34.0%	0.0	7,311,000	2,399,762	32.8%	-1.1
RHODE ISLAND	516,000	185,850	36.0%					524,000	124,408	23.7%	-12.3	554,000	66,715	12.0%	-24.0				
SOUTH CAROLINA				1,225,000	49,695	4.1%										1,441,000	248,780	17.3%	13.2
SOUTH DAKOTA				392,000	147,621	37.7%		388,000	160,181	41.3%	3.6					387,000	120,951	31.3%	-6.4
TENNESSEE	2,005,000	153,479	7.7%					2,104,000	234,053	11.1%	3.5	2,226,000	517,330	23.2%	15.6				
TEXAS								5,462,000	926,653	17.0%		5,952,000	1,134,337	19.1%	2.1				
UTAH	400,000	177,435	44.4%	429,000	178,261	41.6%	-2.8					510,000	169,562	33.2%	-11.1	556,000	225,075	40.5%	-3.9
VERMONT	228,000	111,406	48.9%	226,000	103,101	45.6%	-3.2					241,000	87,879	36.5%	-12.4	256,000	157,154	61.4%	12.5
VIRGINIA												2,530,000	176,624	7.0%					
WASHINGTON	1,553,000	460,884	29.7%	1,617,000	436,652	27.0%	-2.7					1,854,000	337,138	18.2%	-11.5	2,009,000	435,894	21.7%	-8.0
WEST VIRGINIA	1,138,000	406,554	35.7%					1,076,000	369,935	34.4%	-1.3	1,073,000	246,072	22.9%	-12.8				
WISCONSIN	2,223,000	870,444	39.2%	2,278,000	892,473	39.2%	0.0					2,452,000	780,116	31.8%	-7.3	2,559,000	633,910	24.8%	-14.4
WYOMING	179,000	67,176	37.5%					189,000	78,103	41.3%	3.8	192,000	65,185	34.0%	-3.6				
Total	61,805,000	23,263,955	37.6%	65,137,000	21,259,021	32.6%	-5.0	51,513,000	14,998,333	29.1%	-8.5	85,516,000	22,678,746	26.5%	-11.1	86,093,000	24,168,867	28.1%	-9.6

Democratic Turnout for Election Years 1952–1968

State	1952 Voting-age population	Turnout	%	1956 Voting-age population	Turnout	%	Difference from 1952*	1960 Voting-age population	Turnout	%	Difference from 1952	1964 Voting-age population	Turnout	%	Difference from 1952	1968 Voting-age population	Turnout	%	Difference from 1952
ALABAMA				1,801,000	330,182	18.3%		1,840,000	389,196	21.2%	2.8					1,997,000	638,774	32.0%	13.7
ALASKA								135,000	38,041	28.2%						170,000	36,527	21.5%	-6.7
ARIZONA	501,000	125,338	25.0%	615,000	170,816	27.8%	2.8					863,000	227,712	26.4%	1.4	990,000	205,338	20.7%	-4.3
ARKANSAS				1,062,000	331,679	31.2%										1,153,000	349,965	30.4%	-0.9
CALIFORNIA				8,335,000	2,445,816	29.3%						10,572,000	3,411,912	32.3%	2.9	11,852,000	3,680,352	31.1%	1.7
COLORADO				946,000	319,872	33.8%		1,020,000	334,854	32.8%	-1.0					1,264,000	325,584	25.8%	-8.1
CONNECTICUT	1,358,000	485,066	35.7%	1,445,000	479,460	33.2%	-2.5					1,683,000	781,008	46.4%	10.7	1,824,000	655,043	35.9%	0.2
DELAWARE	221,000	77,685	35.2%					261,000	96,090	36.8%	1.7	289,000	96,850	33.5%	-1.6				
DISTRICT OF COLUMBIA																			
FLORIDA	2,115,000	616,665	29.2%	2,587,000	655,418	25.3%	-3.8					3,629,000	997,585	27.5%	-1.7	4,184,000	892,637	21.3%	-7.8

United States Senate General Elections (continued)

Democratic Turnout for Election Years 1952–1968 (continued)

State	1952 Voting-age population	1952 Turnout	1952 %	1956 Voting-age population	1956 Turnout	1956 %	1956 Difference from 1952	1960 Voting-age population	1960 Turnout	1960 %	1960 Difference from 1952	1964 Voting-age population	1964 Turnout	1964 %	1964 Difference from 1952	1968 Voting-age population	1968 Turnout	1968 %	1968 Difference from 1952
GEORGIA				2,329,000	541,094	23.2%		2,433,000	576,140	23.7%	0.4					2,867,000	885,093	30.9%	7.6
HAWAII												383,000	96,789	25.3%		418,000	189,248	45.3%	20.0
IDAHO				360,000	149,096	41.4%		371,000	139,448	37.6%	-3.8					405,000	173,482	42.8%	1.4
ILLINOIS				6,016,000	1,949,883	32.4%		6,155,000	2,530,943	41.1%	8.7					6,677,000	2,073,242	31.1%	-1.4
INDIANA	2,593,000	911,169	35.1%	2,002,000	871,781	32.5%	-2.6					2,906,000	1,128,505	38.8%	3.7	3,032,000	1,060,456	35.0%	-0.2
IOWA				1,659,000	543,156	32.7%		1,654,000	595,119	36.0%	3.2					1,693,000	574,884	34.0%	1.2
KANSAS				1,286,000	333,939	26.0%		1,316,000	388,895	29.6%	3.6					1,365,000	315,911	23.1%	-2.8
KENTUCKY				1,889,000	499,922	26.5%		1,905,000	444,290	23.3%	-3.1					2,074,000	448,960	21.6%	-4.8
LOUISIANA				1,722,000	335,564	19.5%		1,807,000	432,228	23.9%	4.4					2,012,000	518,586	25.8%	6.3
MAINE	555,000	97,959	17.7%					565,000	159,809	28.3%	10.6	578,000	253,511	43.9%	26.2				
MARYLAND	1,586,000	406,370	25.6%	1,711,000	419,108	24.5%	-1.1					2,064,000	678,649	32.9%	7.3	2,277,000	443,367	19.5%	-6.2
MASSACHUSETTS	3,056,000	1,211,984	39.7%					3,126,000	1,050,725	33.6%	-6.0	3,296,000	1,716,907	52.1%	12.4				
MICHIGAN	4,099,000	1,383,416	33.8%					4,498,000	1,669,179	37.1%	3.4	4,786,000	1,996,912	41.7%	8.0				
MINNESOTA	1,901,000	590,011	31.0%					1,988,000	884,168	44.5%	13.4	2,091,000	931,353	44.5%	13.5				
MISSISSIPPI	1,195,000	233,919	19.6%					1,172,000	244,341	20.8%	1.3	1,203,000	343,364	28.5%	9.0				
MISSOURI	2,636,000	1,008,523	38.3%	2,658,000	1,015,936	38.2%	0.0	2,687,000	999,656	37.2%	-1.1	2,772,000	1,186,666	42.8%	4.5	2,854,000	887,414	31.1%	-7.2
MONTANA	370,000	133,109	36.0%					386,000	140,331	36.4%	0.4	394,000	180,643	45.8%	9.9				
NEBRASKA	847,000	164,660	19.4%					851,000	245,837	28.9%	9.4	870,000	217,605	25.0%	5.6				
NEVADA	122,000	39,184	32.1%	148,000	50,677	34.2%	2.1					230,000	67,336	29.3%	-2.8	281,000	83,622	29.8%	-2.4
NEW HAMPSHIRE				353,000	90,519	25.6%		365,000	114,024	31.2%	5.6					432,000	116,816	27.0%	1.4
NEW JERSEY	3,354,000	1,011,187	30.1%					3,758,000	1,151,385	30.6%	0.5	4,069,000	1,678,051	41.2%	11.1				
NEW MEXICO	402,000	122,543	30.5%					497,000	190,654	38.4%	7.9	522,000	178,209	34.1%	3.7				
NEW YORK	9,944,000	3,011,511	30.3%	10,059,000	3,265,159	32.5%	2.2					10,893,000	3,823,749	35.1%	4.8	11,364,000	2,150,695	18.9%	-11.4
NORTH CAROLINA				2,469,000	731,353	29.6%		2,575,000	793,521	30.8%	1.2					2,947,000	870,406	29.5%	-0.1
NORTH DAKOTA	356,000	55,347	15.5%	353,000	87,919	24.9%	9.4	350,000	104,593	29.9%	14.3	352,000	149,264	42.4%	26.9	355,000	80,815	22.8%	7.2
OHIO	5,339,000	1,563,330	29.3%	5,567,000	1,864,589	33.5%	4.2					6,040,000	1,923,608	31.8%	2.6	6,281,000	1,814,152	28.9%	-0.4
OKLAHOMA				1,399,000	459,996	32.9%		1,420,000	474,116	33.4%	0.5	1,493,000	466,782	31.3%	-1.6	1,562,000	419,658	26.9%	-6.0
OREGON				1,030,000	396,849	38.5%		1,068,000	412,757	38.6%	0.1					1,256,000	405,353	32.3%	-6.3
PENNSYLVANIA	6,870,000	2,168,546	31.6%	6,928,000	2,268,641	32.7%	1.2					7,157,000	2,359,223	33.0%	1.4	7,311,000	2,117,662	29.0%	-2.6
RHODE ISLAND	516,000	225,128	43.6%					524,000	275,575	52.6%	9.0	554,000	319,607	57.7%	14.1				
SOUTH CAROLINA				1,225,000	230,150	18.8%		1,274,000	330,164	25.9%	7.1					1,441,000	404,060	28.0%	9.3
SOUTH DAKOTA				392,000	143,001	36.5%		388,000	145,261	37.4%	1.0					387,000	158,961	41.1%	4.6
TENNESSEE	2,005,000	545,432	27.2%					2,104,000	594,460	28.3%	1.1	2,226,000	568,905	25.6%	-1.6				

United States Senate General Elections (continued)

United States Senate General Elections *(continued)*

Democratic Turnout for Election Years 1952–1968 *(continued)*

State	1952 Voting-age population	Turnout	%	1956 Voting-age population	Turnout	%	Difference from 1952	1960 Voting-age population	Turnout	%	Difference from 1952	1964 Voting-age population	Turnout	%	Difference from 1952	1968 Voting-age population	Turnout	%	Difference from 1952
TEXAS	4,809,000	1,895,192	39.4%					5,462,000	1,306,625	23.9%	-15.5	5,952,000	1,463,958	24.6%	-14.8				
UTAH	400,000	149,598	37.4%	429,000	152,120	35.5%	-1.9					510,000	227,822	44.7%	7.3	556,000	192,168	34.6%	-2.8
VERMONT	228,000	42,630	18.7%	226,000	52,184	23.1%	4.4					241,000	76,457	31.7%	13.0				
VIRGINIA	2,090,000	467,810	22.4%					2,323,000	506,169	21.8%	-0.6	2,530,000	592,260	23.4%	1.0				
WASHINGTON	1,553,000	595,288	38.3%	1,617,000	685,565	42.4%	4.1					1,854,000	875,950	47.2%	8.9	2,009,000	796,183	39.6%	1.3
WEST VIRGINIA	1,138,000	470,019	41.3%					1,076,000	458,355	42.6%	1.3	1,073,000	515,015	48.0%	6.7				
WISCONSIN	2,223,000	731,402	32.9%	2,278,000	627,903	27.6%	-5.3					2,452,000	892,013	36.4%	3.5	2,559,000	1,020,931	39.9%	7.0
WYOMING	179,000	62,921	35.2%					189,000	60,447	32.0%	-3.2	192,000	76,485	39.8%	4.7				
Total	64,561,000	20,602,942	31.9%	73,576,000	22,499,347	30.6%	-1.3	57,543,000	18,277,396	31.8%	-0.1	86,719,000	30,500,665	35.2%	3.3	87,849,000	24,986,345	28.4%	-3.5

Other Turnout for Election Years 1952–1968

State	1952 Voting-age population	Turnout	%	1956 Voting-age population	Turnout	%	Difference from 1952*	1960 Voting-age population	Turnout	%	Difference from 1952	1964 Voting-age population	Turnout	%	Difference from 1952	1968 Voting-age population	Turnout	%	Difference from 1952
ALABAMA								1,840,000	17	0.0%						1,997,000	72,707	3.6%	3.6
ALASKA																170,000	14,118	8.3%	
ARIZONA																			
ARKANSAS																			
CALIFORNIA	7,453,000	560,100	7.5%	8,335,000	22,733	0.3%	-7.2					10,572,000	1,354	0.0%	-7.5	11,852,000	92,965	0.8%	-6.7
COLORADO								1,020,000	3,351	0.3%									
CONNECTICUT	1,358,000	12,279	0.9%	1,445,000	13,298	0.9%	0.0					1,683,000	216	0.0%	-0.9	1,824,000	39	0.0%	-0.9
DELAWARE												289,000	71	0.0%					
DISTRICT OF COLUMBIA																			
FLORIDA	2,115,000	1,135	0.1%									3,629,000	540	0.0%	0.0				
GEORGIA				2,329,000	173	0.0%		2,433,000	355	0.0%	0.0								
HAWAII												383,000	1,278	0.3%		418,000	3,671	0.9%	0.5
IDAHO				360,000	13,415	3.7%													
ILLINOIS				6,016,000	7,595	0.1%		6,155,000	8,007	0.1%	0.0					6,677,000	17,568	0.3%	0.1
INDIANA	2,593,000	14,344	0.6%	2,682,000	7,943	0.3%	-0.3					2,906,000	6,939	0.2%	-0.3	3,032,000	4,091	0.1%	-0.4
IOWA																1,693,000	733	0.0%	
KANSAS				1,286,000	13,519	1.1%		1,316,000	14,198	1.1%	0.0					1,365,000	10,274	0.8%	-0.3
KENTUCKY																2,074,000	9,645	0.5%	
LOUISIANA								1,807,000	2	0.0%									
MAINE																			

United States Senate General Elections (continued)

Other Turnout for Election Years 1952–1968 (continued)

State	1952 Voting-age population	Turnout	%	1956 Voting-age population	Turnout	%	Difference from 1952	1960 Voting-age population	Turnout	%	Difference from 1952	1964 Voting-age population	Turnout	%	Difference from 1952	1968 Voting-age population	Turnout	%	Difference from 1952
MARYLAND												2,064,000	7	0.0%		2,277,000	148,467	6.5%	6.5
MASSACHUSETTS	3,056,000	7,194	0.2%					3,126,000	8,532	0.3%	0.0	3,296,000	7,458	0.2%	0.0				
MICHIGAN	4,099,000	9,363	0.2%					4,498,000	8,595	0.2%	0.0	4,786,000	8,483	0.2%	-0.1				
MINNESOTA	1,901,000	11,759	0.6%					1,988,000	4,085	0.2%	-0.4	2,091,000	6,304	0.3%	-0.3				
MISSISSIPPI																			
MISSOURI	2,636,000	1,408	0.1%																
MONTANA	370,000	1,828	0.5%																
NEBRASKA	847,000	18,087	2.1%									870,000	24	0.0%	-2.1				
NEVADA																			
NEW HAMPSHIRE																432,000	10	0.0%	
NEW JERSEY	3,354,000	20,263	0.6%					3,758,000	29,339	0.8%	0.2	4,069,000	20,780	0.5%	-0.1				
NEW MEXICO												522,000	3	0.0%					
NEW YORK	9,944,000	114,814	1.2%	10,059,000	2,044	0.0%	-1.1					10,893,000	223,881	2.1%	0.9	11,364,000	1,161,120	10.2%	9.1
NORTH CAROLINA																			
NORTH DAKOTA	356,000	24,741	6.9%	353,000	937	0.3%	-6.7	350,000	2,281	0.7%	-6.3					355,000	3,993	1.1%	-5.8
OHIO												6,281,000	5	0.0%					
OKLAHOMA								1,420,000	4,713	0.3%						1,562,000	19,341	1.2%	0.9
OREGON								1,068,000	109	0.0%						1,256,000	177	0.0%	0.0
PENNSYLVANIA	6,870,000	20,181	0.3%	6,928,000	10,562	0.2%	-0.1					7,157,000	14,754	0.2%	-0.1	7,311,000	106,794	1.5%	1.2
RHODE ISLAND																			
SOUTH CAROLINA								1,274,000	102	0.0%						1,441,000	15	0.0%	0.0
SOUTH DAKOTA																			
TENNESSEE	2,005,000	36,308	1.8%					2,104,000	6	0.0%	-1.8	2,226,000	4,858	0.2%	-1.6				
TEXAS								5,462,000	20,506	0.4%		5,952,000	5,561	0.1%	-0.3				
UTAH																556,000	2,019	0.4%	
VERMONT	228,000	16	0.0%	226,000	4	0.0%	0.0					241,000	14	0.0%	0.0	256,000	221	0.1%	0.1
VIRGINIA	2,090,000	75,706	3.6%					2,323,000	116,651	5.0%	1.4	2,530,000	159,479	6.3%	2.7				
WASHINGTON	1,553,000	2,563	0.2%													2,009,000	3,986	0.2%	0.0
WEST VIRGINIA								1,076,000	2	0.0%									
WISCONSIN	2,223,000	3,321	0.1%	2,278,000	2,745	0.1%	0.0					2,452,000	1,647	0.1%	-0.1	2,559,000	20	0.0%	-0.1
WYOMING																			
Total	55,051,000	935,410	1.7%	42,297,000	94,968	0.2%	-1.5	43,018,000	220,851	0.5%	-1.2	68,611,000	463,651	0.7%	-1.0	68,761,000	1,671,979	2.4%	0.7

*Percentage point difference between turnout in current year and initial year listed in chart. If data do not appear for a state in the initial year listed, the difference is calculated from the first year in which data do appear for that state.

UNITED STATES HOUSE OF REPRESENTATIVES GENERAL ELECTIONS

Election Years 1952–1968

State	1952 Voting-age population	Turnout	%	1956 Voting-age population	Turnout	%	Difference from 1952*	1960 Voting-age population	Turnout	%	Difference from 1952	1964 Voting-age population	Turnout	%	Difference from 1952	1968 Voting-age population	Turnout	%	Difference from 1952
ALABAMA	1,768,000	342,826	19.4%	1,801,000	382,955	21.3%	1.9	1,840,000	437,713	23.8%	4.4	1,920,000	717,130	37.4%	18.0	1,997,000	919,143	46.0%	26.6
ALASKA								135,000	59,063	43.8%		154,000	67,146	43.6%	-0.1	170,000	80,362	47.3%	3.5
ARIZONA	501,000	248,400	49.6%	615,000	280,509	45.6%	-4.0	728,000	376,562	51.7%	2.1	863,000	460,824	53.4%	3.8	990,000	463,630	46.8%	-2.7
ARKANSAS	1,091,000	361,923	33.2%	1,062,000	259,763	24.5%	-8.7	1,046,000	69,671	6.7%	-26.5	1,100,000	130,112	11.8%	-21.3	1,153,000	297,986	25.8%	-7.3
CALIFORNIA	7,453,000	4,560,156	61.2%	8,335,000	5,177,320	62.1%	0.9	9,239,000	6,192,548	67.0%	5.8	10,572,000	6,823,729	64.5%	3.4	11,852,000	7,001,986	59.1%	-2.1
COLORADO	875,000	606,566	69.3%	946,000	628,554	66.4%	-2.9	1,020,000	715,279	70.1%	0.8	1,145,000	757,595	66.2%	-3.2	1,264,000	780,442	61.7%	-7.6
CONNECTICUT	1,358,000	1,093,948	80.6%	1,445,000	1,112,096	77.0%	-3.6	1,537,000	1,218,503	79.3%	-1.3	1,683,000	1,209,379	71.9%	-8.7	1,824,000	1,206,941	66.2%	-14.4
DELAWARE	221,000	170,015	76.9%	241,000	176,182	73.1%	-3.8	261,000	194,564	74.5%	-2.4	289,000	198,691	68.8%	-8.2	315,000	200,820	63.8%	-13.2
DISTRICT OF COLUMBIA																			
FLORIDA	2,115,000	741,685	35.1%	2,587,000	941,723	36.4%	1.3	3,051,000	1,247,774	40.9%	5.8	3,629,000	1,415,353	39.0%	3.9	4,184,000	1,769,684	42.3%	7.2
GEORGIA	2,238,000	547,274	24.5%	2,329,000	592,270	25.4%	1.0	2,433,000	574,272	23.6%	-0.9	2,654,000	835,524	31.5%	7.0	2,867,000	944,833	33.0%	8.5
HAWAII								345,000	182,639	52.9%		383,000	229,649	60.0%	7.0	418,000	243,119	58.2%	5.2
IDAHO	350,000	264,602	75.6%	360,000	260,434	72.3%	-3.3	371,000	290,290	78.2%	2.6	388,000	284,531	73.3%	-2.3	405,000	276,534	68.3%	-7.3
ILLINOIS	5,889,000	4,353,358	73.9%	6,016,000	4,240,100	70.5%	-3.4	6,155,000	4,604,573	74.8%	0.9	6,422,000	4,574,607	71.2%	-2.7	6,677,000	4,422,223	66.2%	-7.7
INDIANA	2,593,000	1,935,563	74.6%	2,682,000	1,961,321	73.1%	-1.5	2,773,000	2,123,201	76.6%	1.9	2,906,000	2,073,281	71.3%	-3.3	3,032,000	2,039,136	67.3%	-7.4
IOWA	1,669,000	1,143,062	68.5%	1,659,000	1,170,214	70.5%	2.0	1,654,000	1,226,222	74.1%	5.6	1,674,000	1,141,571	68.2%	-0.3	1,693,000	1,123,411	66.4%	-2.1
KANSAS	1,253,000	823,939	65.8%	1,286,000	827,381	64.3%	-1.4	1,316,000	870,887	66.2%	0.4	1,341,000	813,688	60.7%	-5.1	1,365,000	817,288	59.9%	-5.9
KENTUCKY	1,884,000	950,795	50.5%	1,889,000	965,052	51.1%	0.6	1,905,000	913,026	47.9%	-2.5	1,991,000	955,185	48.0%	-2.5	2,074,000	865,240	41.7%	-8.7
LOUISIANA	1,637,000	416,403	25.4%	1,722,000	387,655	22.5%	-2.9	1,807,000	520,011	28.8%	3.3	1,911,000	600,704	31.4%	6.0	2,012,000	629,381	31.3%	5.8
MAINE	555,000	234,125	42.2%	560,000	292,456	52.2%	10.0	565,000	408,694	72.3%	30.2	578,000	369,502	63.9%	21.7	592,000	384,217	64.9%	22.7
MARYLAND	1,586,000	841,338	53.0%	1,711,000	865,800	50.6%	-2.4	1,842,000	980,805	53.2%	0.2	2,064,000	1,012,192	49.0%	-4.0	2,277,000	1,019,648	44.8%	-8.3
MASSACHUSETTS	3,056,000	2,288,715	74.9%	3,082,000	2,249,506	73.0%	-1.9	3,126,000	2,259,012	72.3%	-2.6	3,296,000	2,108,334	64.0%	-10.9	3,457,000	2,057,445	59.5%	-15.4
MICHIGAN	4,099,000	2,781,934	67.9%	4,297,000	2,994,674	69.7%	1.8	4,498,000	3,211,545	71.4%	3.5	4,786,000	3,059,650	63.9%	-3.9	5,062,000	3,043,679	60.1%	-7.7
MINNESOTA	1,901,000	1,388,188	73.0%	1,942,000	1,388,510	71.5%	-1.5	1,988,000	1,515,122	76.2%	3.2	2,091,000	1,521,308	72.8%	-0.3	2,189,000	1,534,044	70.1%	-2.9
MISSISSIPPI	1,195,000	240,752	20.1%	1,180,000	205,532	17.4%	-2.7	1,172,000	257,777	22.0%	1.8	1,203,000	361,227	30.0%	9.9	1,234,000	448,704	36.4%	16.2
MISSOURI	2,636,000	1,861,436	70.6%	2,658,000	1,692,781	63.7%	-6.9	2,687,000	1,843,371	68.6%	-2.0	2,772,000	1,772,274	63.9%	-6.7	2,854,000	1,733,086	60.7%	-9.9
MONTANA	370,000	256,066	69.2%	378,000	263,204	69.6%	0.4	386,000	272,212	70.5%	1.3	394,000	276,610	70.2%	1.0	402,000	263,476	65.5%	-3.7
NEBRASKA	847,000	566,281	66.9%	848,000	546,402	64.4%	-2.4	851,000	580,537	68.2%	1.4	870,000	561,088	64.5%	-2.4	889,000	522,171	58.7%	-8.1
NEVADA	122,000	80,595	66.1%	148,000	94,254	63.7%	-2.4	177,000	103,602	58.5%	-7.5	230,000	130,737	56.8%	-9.2	281,000	144,345	51.4%	-14.7
NEW HAMPSHIRE	344,000	257,669	74.9%	353,000	253,145	71.7%	-3.2	365,000	284,681	78.0%	3.1	400,000	279,302	69.8%	-5.1	432,000	282,783	65.5%	-9.4
NEW JERSEY	3,354,000	2,315,577	69.0%	3,552,000	2,387,402	67.2%	-1.8	3,758,000	2,659,025	70.8%	1.7	4,069,000	2,720,526	66.9%	-2.2	4,368,000	2,698,040	61.8%	-7.3
NEW MEXICO	402,000	233,774	58.2%	452,000	244,344	54.1%	-4.1	497,000	301,048	60.6%	2.4	522,000	319,646	61.2%	3.1	547,000	309,852	56.6%	-1.5
NEW YORK	9,944,000	6,910,388	69.5%	10,159,000	6,886,811	67.8%	-1.7	10,402,000	7,055,887	67.8%	-1.7	10,893,000	6,763,308	62.1%	-7.4	11,364,000	6,118,920	53.8%	-15.6

United States House of Representatives General Elections *(continued)*

Election Years 1952–1968 *(continued)*

State	1952 Voting-age population	1952 Turnout	1952 %	1956 Voting-age population	1956 Turnout	1956 %	1956 Difference from 1952	1960 Voting-age population	1960 Turnout	1960 %	1960 Difference from 1952	1964 Voting-age population	1964 Turnout	1964 %	1964 Difference from 1952	1968 Voting-age population	1968 Turnout	1968 %	1968 Difference from 1952
NORTH CAROLINA	2,372,000	1,122,198	47.3%	2,469,000	1,025,272	41.5%	-5.8	2,575,000	1,302,471	50.6%	3.3	2,765,000	1,304,242	47.2%	-0.1	2,947,000	1,398,077	47.4%	0.1
NORTH DAKOTA	356,000	231,047	64.9%	353,000	229,257	64.9%	0.0	350,000	256,352	73.2%	8.3	352,000	249,071	70.8%	5.9	355,000	238,115	67.1%	2.2
OHIO	5,339,000	3,382,285	63.4%	5,567,000	3,381,367	60.7%	-2.6	5,790,000	3,846,632	66.4%	3.1	6,040,000	2,732,361	45.2%	-18.1	6,281,000	3,636,278	57.9%	-5.5
OKLAHOMA	1,385,000	933,336	67.4%	1,399,000	812,715	58.1%	-9.3	1,420,000	838,594	59.1%	-8.3	1,493,000	840,291	56.3%	-11.1	1,562,000	809,861	51.8%	-15.5
OREGON	1,000,000	666,092	66.6%	1,030,000	718,694	69.8%	3.2	1,068,000	761,837	71.3%	4.7	1,164,000	767,757	66.0%	-0.7	1,256,000	787,224	62.7%	-3.9
PENNSYLVANIA	6,870,000	4,517,725	65.8%	6,928,000	4,518,779	65.2%	-0.5	6,998,000	4,954,095	70.8%	5.0	7,157,000	4,522,083	63.2%	-2.6	7,311,000	4,577,373	62.6%	-3.2
RHODE ISLAND	516,000	407,289	78.9%	518,000	375,510	72.5%	-6.4	524,000	392,238	74.9%	-4.1	554,000	373,088	67.3%	-11.6	582,000	364,781	62.7%	-16.3
SOUTH CAROLINA	1,180,000	283,822	24.1%	1,225,000	262,004	21.4%	-2.7	1,274,000	328,438	25.8%	1.7	1,360,000	438,209	32.2%	8.2	1,441,000	627,838	43.6%	19.5
SOUTH DAKOTA	395,000	287,475	72.8%	392,000	288,016	73.5%	0.7	388,000	301,004	77.6%	4.8	388,000	287,713	74.2%	1.4	387,000	271,640	70.2%	-2.6
TENNESSEE	2,005,000	700,395	34.9%	2,050,000	681,278	33.2%	-1.7	2,104,000	642,827	30.6%	-4.4	2,226,000	1,034,798	46.5%	11.6	2,342,000	1,013,422	43.3%	8.3
TEXAS	4,809,000	1,979,811	41.2%	5,131,000	1,459,698	28.4%	-12.7	5,462,000	2,040,041	37.3%	-3.8	5,952,000	3,732,361	62.7%	21.5	6,422,000	2,395,982	37.3%	-3.9
UTAH	400,000	326,823	81.7%	429,000	329,293	76.8%	-4.9	461,000	369,462	80.1%	-1.6	510,000	396,020	77.7%	-4.1	556,000	415,796	74.8%	-6.9
VERMONT	228,000	153,060	67.1%	226,000	154,533	68.4%	1.2	226,000	166,035	73.5%	6.3	241,000	163,452	67.8%	0.7	256,000	157,133	61.4%	-5.8
VIRGINIA	2,090,000	446,840	21.4%	2,202,000	696,785	31.6%	10.3	2,323,000	639,947	27.5%	6.2	2,530,000	928,732	36.7%	15.3	2,729,000	1,268,874	46.5%	25.1
WASHINGTON	1,553,000	1,020,513	65.7%	1,617,000	1,061,014	65.6%	-0.1	1,692,000	1,124,725	66.5%	0.8	1,854,000	1,197,523	64.6%	-1.1	2,009,000	1,204,081	59.9%	-5.8
WEST VIRGINIA	1,138,000	874,602	76.9%	1,103,000	806,394	73.1%	-3.7	1,076,000	820,481	76.3%	-0.6	1,073,000	770,385	71.8%	-5.1	1,070,000	712,065	66.5%	-10.3
WISCONSIN	2,223,000	1,568,111	70.5%	2,278,000	1,522,036	66.8%	-3.7	2,338,000	1,663,093	71.1%	0.6	2,452,000	1,648,756	67.2%	-3.3	2,559,000	1,640,919	64.1%	-6.4
WYOMING	179,000	126,720	70.8%	183,000	120,128	65.6%	-5.1	189,000	134,331	71.1%	0.3	192,000	139,175	72.5%	1.7	194,000	123,313	63.6%	-7.2
Total	97,344,000	57,845,497	59.4%	101,395,000	58,171,123	57.4%	-2.1	106,188,000	64,132,719	60.4%	1.0	113,496,000	66,070,420	58.2%	-1.2	120,499,000	66,205,341	55.0%	-4.4

*Percentage point difference between turnout in current year and initial year listed in chart. If data do not appear for a state in the initial year listed, the difference is calculated from the first year in which data do appear for that state.

UNITED STATES HOUSE OF REPRESENTATIVES GENERAL ELECTIONS

Republican Turnout for Election Years 1952–1968

State	1952 Voting-age population	1952 Turnout	1952 %	1956 Voting-age population	1956 Turnout	1956 %	1956 Difference from 1952*	1960 Voting-age population	1960 Turnout	1960 %	1960 Difference from 1952	1964 Voting-age population	1964 Turnout	1964 %	1964 Difference from 1952	1968 Voting-age population	1968 Turnout	1968 %	1968 Difference from 1952
ALABAMA	1,768,000	18,673	1.1%	1,801,000	51,818	2.9%	1.8	1,840,000	48,117	2.6%	1.6	1,920,000	317,160	16.5%	15.5	1,997,000	247,438	12.4%	11.3
ALASKA								135,000	25,517	18.9%		154,000	32,556	21.1%	2.2	170,000	43,577	25.6%	6.7
ARIZONA	501,000	120,533	24.1%	615,000	133,594	21.7%	-2.3	728,000	197,374	27.1%	3.1	863,000	230,091	26.7%	2.6	990,000	260,663	26.3%	2.3
ARKANSAS	1,091,000	51,889	4.8%	1,062,000	24,318	2.3%	-2.5	1,046,000	12,054	1.2%	-3.6	1,100,000	58,884	5.4%	0.6	1,153,000	158,055	13.7%	9.0
CALIFORNIA	7,453,000	2,382,921	32.0%	8,335,000	2,466,620	29.6%	-2.4	9,239,000	2,855,115	30.9%	-1.1	10,572,000	3,213,828	30.4%	-1.6	11,852,000	3,808,934	32.1%	0.2
COLORADO	875,000	335,394	38.3%	946,000	296,502	31.3%	-7.0	1,020,000	344,792	33.8%	-4.5	1,145,000	316,322	27.6%	-10.7	1,264,000	392,779	31.1%	-7.3
CONNECTICUT	1,358,000	601,238	44.3%	1,445,000	683,387	47.3%	3.0	1,537,000	566,246	36.8%	-7.4	1,683,000	456,233	27.1%	-17.2	1,824,000	569,957	31.2%	-13.0
DELAWARE	221,000	88,285	39.9%	241,000	91,538	38.0%	-2.0	261,000	96,337	36.9%	-3.0	289,000	86,254	29.8%	-10.1	315,000	117,827	37.4%	-2.5
DISTRICT OF COLUMBIA																			
FLORIDA	2,115,000	191,582	9.1%	2,587,000	352,149	13.6%	4.6	3,051,000	386,513	12.7%	3.6	3,629,000	420,856	11.6%	2.5	4,184,000	757,907	18.1%	9.1
GEORGIA				2,329,000	58,966	2.5%		2,433,000	24,285	1.0%	-1.5	2,654,000	248,024	9.3%	6.8	2,867,000	194,129	6.8%	4.2
HAWAII								345,000	46,812	13.6%		383,000	89,425	23.3%	9.8	418,000	78,733	18.8%	5.3
IDAHO	350,000	157,181	44.9%	360,000	139,712	38.8%	-6.1	371,000	131,266	35.4%	-9.5	388,000	144,306	37.2%	-7.7	405,000	155,899	38.5%	-6.4
ILLINOIS	5,889,000	2,348,725	39.9%	6,016,000	2,272,995	37.8%	-2.1	6,155,000	2,235,048	36.3%	-3.6	6,422,000	2,082,167	32.4%	-7.5	6,677,000	2,368,310	35.5%	-4.4
INDIANA	2,593,000	1,093,589	42.2%	2,682,000	1,092,367	40.7%	-1.4	2,773,000	1,088,328	39.2%	-2.9	2,906,000	977,548	33.6%	-8.5	3,032,000	1,094,964	36.1%	-6.1
IOWA	1,669,000	762,310	45.7%	1,659,000	636,573	38.4%	-7.3	1,654,000	662,864	40.1%	-5.6	1,674,000	516,929	30.9%	-14.8	1,693,000	609,875	36.0%	-9.7
KANSAS	1,253,000	489,661	39.1%	1,286,000	438,868	34.1%	-5.0	1,316,000	471,995	35.9%	-3.2	1,341,000	451,526	33.7%	-5.4	1,365,000	507,733	37.2%	-1.9
KENTUCKY	1,884,000	454,802	24.1%	1,889,000	461,644	24.4%	0.3	1,905,000	373,773	19.6%	-4.5	1,991,000	336,696	16.9%	-7.2	2,074,000	421,010	20.3%	-3.8
LOUISIANA	1,637,000	36,161	2.2%	1,722,000	57,385	3.3%	1.1	1,807,000	78,478	4.3%	2.1	1,911,000	171,137	9.0%	6.7	2,012,000	118,026	5.9%	3.7
MAINE	555,000	156,727	28.2%	560,000	150,415	26.9%	-1.4	565,000	230,834	40.9%	12.6	578,000	163,376	28.3%	0.0	592,000	168,347	28.4%	0.2
MARYLAND	1,586,000	436,113	27.5%	1,711,000	421,382	24.6%	-2.9	1,842,000	398,490	21.6%	-5.9	2,064,000	375,746	18.2%	-9.3	2,277,000	483,829	21.2%	-6.2
MASSACHUSETTS	3,056,000	1,209,742	39.6%	3,082,000	1,156,137	37.5%	-2.1	3,126,000	880,079	28.2%	-11.4	3,296,000	787,292	23.9%	-15.7	3,457,000	971,190	28.1%	-11.5
MICHIGAN	4,099,000	1,457,342	35.6%	4,297,000	1,500,172	34.9%	-0.6	4,498,000	1,567,845	34.9%	-0.7	4,786,000	1,289,291	26.9%	-8.6	5,062,000	1,506,972	29.8%	-5.8
MINNESOTA	1,901,000	749,415	39.4%	1,942,000	676,104	34.8%	-4.6	1,988,000	749,770	37.7%	-1.7	2,091,000	693,118	33.1%	-6.3	2,189,000	801,209	36.6%	-2.8
MISSISSIPPI	1,195,000	6,024	0.5%					1,172,000	5,036	0.4%	-0.1	1,203,000	35,277	2.9%	2.4	1,234,000	33,683	2.7%	2.2
MISSOURI	2,636,000	890,237	33.8%	2,658,000	681,724	25.6%	-8.1	2,687,000	780,432	29.0%	-4.7	2,772,000	664,561	24.0%	-9.8	2,854,000	763,399	26.7%	-7.0
MONTANA	370,000	144,296	39.0%	378,000	116,755	30.9%	-8.1	386,000	133,624	34.6%	-4.4	394,000	139,658	35.4%	-3.6	402,000	148,750	37.0%	-2.0
NEBRASKA	847,000	386,432	45.6%	848,000	323,641	38.2%	-7.5	851,000	327,606	38.5%	-7.1	870,000	288,153	33.1%	-12.5	889,000	309,218	34.8%	-10.8
NEVADA	122,000	40,683	33.3%	148,000	43,154	29.2%	-4.2	177,000	43,986	24.9%	-8.5	230,000	47,989	20.9%	-12.5	281,000	40,209	14.3%	-19.0
NEW HAMPSHIRE	344,000	162,550	47.3%	353,000	155,215	44.0%	-3.3	365,000	165,819	45.4%	-1.8	400,000	138,016	34.5%	-12.7	432,000	188,878	43.7%	-3.5
NEW JERSEY	3,354,000	1,317,404	39.3%	3,552,000	1,391,335	39.2%	-0.1	3,758,000	1,361,844	36.2%	-3.0	4,069,000	1,228,000	30.2%	-9.1	4,368,000	1,364,409	31.2%	-8.0
NEW MEXICO	402,000	112,297	27.9%	452,000	114,719	25.4%	-2.6	497,000	123,683	24.9%	-3.0	522,000	154,780	29.7%	1.7	547,000	160,374	29.3%	1.4
NEW YORK	9,944,000	3,613,153	36.3%	10,059,000	3,745,821	37.2%	0.9	10,402,000	3,281,208	31.5%	-4.8	10,893,000	2,718,154	25.0%	-11.4	11,364,000	2,812,889	24.8%	-11.6

United States House of Representatives General Elections *(continued)*

Republican Turnout for Election Years 1952–1968 *(continued)*

State	1952 Voting-age population	Turnout	%	1956 Voting-age population	Turnout	%	Difference from 1952	1960 Voting-age population	Turnout	%	Difference from 1952	1964 Voting-age population	Turnout	%	Difference from 1952	1968 Voting-age population	Turnout	%	Difference from 1952
NORTH CAROLINA	2,372,000	358,810	15.1%	2,469,000	309,071	12.5%	-2.6	2,575,000	515,488	20.0%	4.9	2,765,000	516,340	18.7%	3.5	2,947,000	633,012	21.5%	6.4
NORTH DAKOTA	356,000	181,218	50.9%	353,000	143,514	40.7%	-10.2	350,000	135,579	38.7%	-12.2	352,000	124,453	35.4%	-15.5	355,000	140,076	39.5%	-11.4
OHIO	5,339,000	1,836,354	34.4%	5,567,000	1,936,662	34.8%	0.4	5,790,000	2,080,270	35.9%	1.5	6,040,000	845,598	14.0%	-20.4	6,281,000	2,207,658	35.1%	0.8
OKLAHOMA	1,385,000	383,859	27.7%	1,399,000	326,993	23.4%	-4.3	1,420,000	379,131	26.7%	-1.0	1,493,000	310,563	20.8%	-6.9	1,562,000	364,866	23.4%	-4.4
OREGON	1,000,000	408,349	40.8%	1,030,000	338,303	32.8%	-8.0	1,068,000	372,187	34.8%	-6.0	1,164,000	305,682	26.3%	-14.6	1,256,000	417,107	33.2%	-7.6
PENNSYLVANIA	6,870,000	2,363,167	34.4%	6,928,000	2,386,657	34.4%	0.1	6,998,000	2,396,322	34.2%	-0.2	7,157,000	2,000,222	20.0%	-6.4	7,311,000	2,230,052	30.5%	-3.9
RHODE ISLAND	516,000	186,828	36.2%	518,000	173,282	33.5%	-2.8	524,000	123,532	23.6%	-12.6	554,000	94,657	17.1%	-19.1	582,000	140,896	24.2%	-12.0
SOUTH CAROLINA	1,180,000	5,642	0.5%	1,225,000	12,278	1.0%	0.5					1,360,000	48,970	3.6%	3.1	1,441,000	203,902	14.2%	13.7
SOUTH DAKOTA	395,000	197,137	49.9%	392,000	142,516	36.4%	-13.6	388,000	168,503	43.4%	-6.5	388,000	164,448	42.4%	-7.5	387,000	159,219	41.1%	-8.8
TENNESSEE	2,005,000	203,766	10.2%	2,050,000	279,903	13.7%	3.5	2,104,000	202,711	9.6%	-0.5	2,226,000	416,750	18.7%	8.6	2,342,000	507,996	21.7%	11.5
TEXAS								5,462,000	297,230	5.4%		5,952,000	1,845,598	31.0%	25.6	6,422,000	672,767	10.5%	5.0
UTAH	400,000	181,841	45.5%	429,000	193,790	45.2%	-0.3	461,000	182,752	39.6%	-5.8	510,000	186,498	36.6%	-8.9	556,000	269,583	48.5%	3.0
VERMONT	228,000	109,871	48.2%	226,000	103,736	45.9%	-2.3	226,000	94,905	42.0%	-6.2	241,000	92,252	38.3%	9.9	256,000	156,956	61.3%	13.1
VIRGINIA	2,090,000	138,604	6.6%	2,202,000	279,660	12.7%	6.1	2,323,000	199,656	8.6%	2.0	2,530,000	298,888	11.8%	5.2	2,729,000	551,889	20.2%	13.6
WASHINGTON	1,553,000	504,783	32.5%	1,617,000	439,896	27.2%	-5.3	1,692,000	646,517	38.2%	5.7	1,854,000	583,765	31.5%	-1.0	2,009,000	576,072	28.7%	-3.8
WEST VIRGINIA	1,138,000	403,427	35.5%	1,103,000	378,130	34.3%	-1.2	1,076,000	352,353	32.7%	-2.7	1,073,000	320,183	29.8%	-5.6	1,070,000	277,925	26.0%	-9.5
WISCONSIN	2,223,000	965,590	43.4%	2,278,000	825,305	36.2%	-7.2	2,338,000	845,994	36.2%	-7.3	2,452,000	789,736	32.2%	-11.2	2,559,000	895,388	35.0%	-8.4
WYOMING	179,000	76,161	42.5%	183,000	69,903	38.2%	-4.3	189,000	70,241	37.2%	-5.4	192,000	68,482	35.7%	-6.9	194,000	77,363	39.9%	-2.7
Total	90,297,000	28,320,766	31.4%	94,984,000	28,074,609	29.6%	-1.8	104,914,000	28,758,621	27.4%	-4.0	113,496,000	27,892,438	24.6%	-6.8	120,499,000	32,141,899	26.7%	-4.7

Democratic Turnout for Election Years 1952–1968

State	1952 Voting-age population	Turnout	%	1956 Voting-age population	Turnout	%	Difference from 1952*	1960 Voting-age population	Turnout	%	Difference from 1952	1964 Voting-age population	Turnout	%	Difference from 1952	1968 Voting-age population	Turnout	%	Difference from 1952
ALABAMA	1,768,000	324,153	18.3%	1,801,000	331,137	18.4%	0.1	1,840,000	389,567	21.2%	2.8	1,920,000	397,951	20.7%	2.4	1,997,000	555,026	27.8%	9.5
ALASKA								135,000	33,546	24.8%		154,000	34,590	22.5%	-2.4	170,000	36,785	21.6%	-3.2
ARIZONA	501,000	127,867	25.5%	615,000	146,915	23.9%	-1.6	728,000	179,188	24.6%	-0.9	863,000	230,733	26.7%	1.2	990,000	202,967	20.5%	-5.0
ARKANSAS	1,091,000	308,838	28.3%	1,062,000	235,445	22.2%	-6.1	1,046,000	57,617	5.5%	-22.8	1,100,000	71,228	6.5%	-21.8	1,153,000	139,931	12.1%	-16.2
CALIFORNIA	7,453,000	2,030,549	27.2%	8,335,000	2,710,700	32.5%	5.3	9,239,000	3,336,709	36.1%	8.9	10,572,000	3,609,315	34.1%	6.9	11,852,000	3,085,320	26.0%	-1.2
COLORADO	875,000	269,865	30.8%	946,000	332,051	35.1%	4.3	1,020,000	370,487	36.3%	5.5	1,145,000	440,090	38.4%	7.6	1,264,000	362,164	28.7%	-2.2
CONNECTICUT	1,358,000	489,645	36.1%	1,445,000	428,709	29.7%	-6.4	1,537,000	649,907	42.3%	6.2	1,683,000	752,983	44.7%	8.7	1,824,000	625,278	34.3%	-1.8
DELAWARE	221,000	81,730	37.0%	241,000	84,644	35.1%	-1.9	261,000	98,227	37.6%	0.7	289,000	112,361	38.9%	1.9	315,000	82,993	26.3%	-10.6
DISTRICT OF COLUMBIA																			
FLORIDA	2,115,000	550,103	26.0%	2,587,000	589,574	22.8%	-3.2	3,051,000	861,261	28.2%	2.2	3,629,000	991,897	27.3%	1.3	4,184,000	1,011,749	24.2%	-1.8

United States House of Representatives General Elections (continued)

United States House of Representatives General Elections *(continued)*

Democratic Turnout for Election Years 1952–1968 *(continued)*

State	1952 Voting-age population	Turnout	%	1956 Voting-age population	Turnout	%	Difference from 1952	1960 Voting-age population	Turnout	%	Difference from 1952	1964 Voting-age population	Turnout	%	Difference from 1952	1968 Voting-age population	Turnout	%	Difference from 1952
GEORGIA	2,238,000	547,095	24.4%	2,329,000	522,072	22.4%	-2.0	2,433,000	549,405	22.6%	-1.9	2,654,000	562,422	21.2%	-3.3	2,867,000	750,538	26.2%	1.7
HAWAII								345,000	135,827	39.4%		383,000	140,224	36.6%	-2.8	418,000	161,954	38.7%	-0.6
IDAHO	350,000	107,417	30.7%	360,000	120,722	33.5%	2.8	371,000	159,024	42.9%	12.2	388,000	140,225	36.1%	5.4	405,000	116,258	28.7%	-2.0
ILLINOIS	5,889,000	2,004,628	34.0%	6,016,000	1,967,104	32.7%	-1.3	6,155,000	2,369,523	38.5%	4.5	6,422,000	2,492,433	38.8%	4.8	6,677,000	2,053,892	30.8%	-3.3
INDIANA	2,593,000	830,758	32.0%	2,682,000	864,351	32.2%	0.2	2,773,000	1,033,166	37.3%	5.2	2,906,000	1,094,999	37.7%	5.6	3,032,000	943,806	31.1%	-0.9
IOWA	1,669,000	378,763	22.7%	1,659,000	533,641	32.2%	9.5	1,654,000	563,358	34.1%	11.4	1,674,000	622,844	37.2%	14.5	1,693,000	513,529	30.3%	7.6
KANSAS	1,253,000	334,278	26.7%	1,286,000	387,096	30.1%	3.4	1,316,000	398,892	30.3%	3.6	1,341,000	362,162	27.0%	0.3	1,365,000	309,551	22.7%	-4.0
KENTUCKY	1,884,000	495,420	26.3%	1,889,000	503,295	26.6%	0.3	1,905,000	539,253	28.3%	2.0	1,991,000	618,489	31.1%	4.8	2,074,000	440,974	21.3%	-5.0
LOUISIANA	1,637,000	380,242	23.2%	1,722,000	330,270	19.2%	-4.0	1,807,000	441,533	24.4%	1.2	1,911,000	429,567	22.5%	-0.7	2,012,000	511,355	25.4%	2.2
MAINE	555,000	77,398	13.9%	560,000	142,041	25.4%	11.4	565,000	177,442	31.4%	17.5	578,000	206,126	35.7%	21.7	592,000	215,870	36.5%	22.5
MARYLAND	1,586,000	405,225	25.6%	1,711,000	444,418	26.0%	0.4	1,842,000	582,315	31.6%	6.1	2,064,000	636,445	30.8%	5.3	2,277,000	535,819	23.5%	-2.0
MASSACHUSETTS	3,056,000	1,064,454	34.8%	3,082,000	1,092,697	35.5%	0.6	3,126,000	1,378,382	44.1%	9.3	3,296,000	1,313,448	39.8%	5.0	3,457,000	1,032,731	29.9%	-5.0
MICHIGAN	4,099,000	1,316,374	32.1%	4,297,000	1,490,834	34.7%	2.6	4,498,000	1,638,588	36.4%	4.3	4,786,000	1,767,716	36.9%	4.8	5,062,000	1,532,693	30.3%	-1.8
MINNESOTA	1,901,000	638,773	33.6%	1,942,000	712,406	36.7%	3.1	1,988,000	759,893	38.2%	4.6	2,091,000	826,879	39.5%	5.9	2,189,000	731,536	33.4%	-0.2
MISSISSIPPI	1,195,000	234,728	19.6%	1,180,000	205,532	17.4%	-2.2	1,172,000	252,741	21.6%	1.9	1,203,000	325,950	27.1%	7.5	1,234,000	415,021	33.6%	14.0
MISSOURI	2,636,000	971,199	36.8%	2,658,000	1,011,057	38.0%	1.2	2,687,000	1,062,939	39.6%	2.7	2,772,000	1,107,512	40.0%	3.1	2,854,000	968,693	33.9%	-2.9
MONTANA	370,000	110,882	30.0%	378,000	146,449	38.7%	8.8	386,000	138,588	35.9%	5.9	394,000	136,308	34.6%	4.6	402,000	114,726	28.5%	-1.4
NEBRASKA	847,000	179,849	21.2%	848,000	220,372	26.0%	4.8	851,000	252,931	29.7%	8.5	870,000	272,922	31.4%	10.1	889,000	208,356	23.4%	2.2
NEVADA	122,000	39,912	32.7%	148,000	51,100	34.5%	1.8	177,000	59,616	33.7%	1.0	230,000	82,748	36.0%	3.3	281,000	104,136	37.1%	4.3
NEW HAMPSHIRE	344,000	95,119	27.7%	353,000	97,930	27.7%	0.1	365,000	118,862	32.6%	4.9	400,000	141,282	35.3%	7.7	432,000	93,901	21.7%	-5.9
NEW JERSEY	3,354,000	977,914	29.2%	3,552,000	972,620	27.4%	-1.8	3,758,000	1,275,882	34.0%	4.8	4,069,000	1,483,125	36.4%	7.3	4,368,000	1,288,447	29.5%	0.3
NEW MEXICO	402,000	121,477	30.2%	452,000	129,625	28.7%	-1.5	497,000	176,514	35.5%	5.3	522,000	164,863	31.6%	1.4	547,000	147,975	27.1%	-3.2
NEW YORK	9,944,000	3,086,262	31.0%	10,059,000	3,072,860	30.5%	-0.5	10,402,000	3,648,347	35.1%	4.0	10,893,000	3,919,002	36.0%	4.9	11,364,000	2,998,439	26.4%	-4.7
NORTH CAROLINA	2,372,000	763,388	32.2%	2,469,000	716,201	29.0%	-3.2	2,575,000	786,983	30.6%	-1.6	2,765,000	787,902	28.5%	-3.7	2,947,000	765,065	26.0%	-6.2
NORTH DAKOTA	356,000	49,829	14.0%	353,000	85,743	24.3%	10.3	350,000	120,773	34.5%	20.5	352,000	123,959	35.2%	21.2	355,000	94,347	26.6%	12.6
OHIO	5,339,000	1,471,110	27.6%	5,567,000	1,444,705	26.0%	-1.6	5,790,000	1,766,362	30.5%	3.0	6,040,000	1,886,763	31.2%	3.7	6,281,000	1,428,021	22.7%	-4.8
OKLAHOMA	1,385,000	545,713	39.4%	1,399,000	485,321	34.7%	-4.7	1,420,000	459,463	32.4%	-7.0	1,493,000	529,728	35.5%	-3.9	1,562,000	444,995	28.5%	-10.9
OREGON	1,000,000	257,743	25.8%	1,030,000	380,391	36.9%	11.2	1,068,000	389,569	36.5%	10.7	1,164,000	461,690	39.7%	13.9	1,256,000	370,036	29.5%	3.7
PENNSYLVANIA	6,870,000	2,151,247	31.3%	6,928,000	2,131,833	30.8%	-0.5	6,998,000	2,554,885	36.5%	5.2	7,157,000	2,515,861	35.2%	3.8	7,311,000	2,286,363	31.3%	0.0
RHODE ISLAND	516,000	220,461	42.7%	518,000	202,228	39.0%	-3.7	524,000	268,706	51.3%	8.6	554,000	278,430	50.3%	7.5	582,000	221,989	38.1%	-4.6
SOUTH CAROLINA	1,180,000	278,180	23.6%	1,225,000	249,591	20.4%	-3.2	1,274,000	328,326	25.8%	2.2	1,360,000	386,738	28.4%	4.9	1,441,000	416,181	28.9%	5.3
SOUTH DAKOTA	395,000	90,338	22.9%	392,000	145,500	37.1%	14.2	388,000	132,421	34.1%	11.3	388,000	123,265	31.8%	8.9	387,000	112,421	29.0%	6.2
TENNESSEE	2,005,000	479,641	23.9%	2,050,000	401,375	19.6%	-4.3	2,104,000	440,111	20.9%	-3.0	2,226,000	581,011	26.1%	2.2	2,342,000	485,833	20.7%	-3.2

United States House of Representatives General Elections *(continued)*

Democratic Turnout for Election Years 1952–1968 *(continued)*

State	1952 Voting-age population	1952 Turnout	1952 %	1956 Voting-age population	1956 Turnout	1956 %	1956 Difference from 1952	1960 Voting-age population	1960 Turnout	1960 %	1960 Difference from 1952	1964 Voting-age population	1964 Turnout	1964 %	1964 Difference from 1952	1968 Voting-age population	1968 Turnout	1968 %	1968 Difference from 1952
TEXAS	4,809,000	1,979,811	41.2%	5,131,000	1,437,830	28.0%	-13.1	5,462,000	1,681,305	30.8%	-10.4	5,952,000	1,886,763	31.7%	-9.5	6,422,000	1,720,408	26.8%	-14.4
UTAH	400,000	144,982	36.2%	429,000	135,503	31.6%	-4.7	461,000	186,710	40.5%	4.3	510,000	209,522	41.1%	4.8	556,000	146,213	26.3%	-9.9
VERMONT	228,000	43,187	18.9%	226,000	50,797	22.5%	3.5	226,000	71,111	31.5%	12.5	241,000	71,193	29.5%	10.6				
VIRGINIA	2,090,000	298,238	14.3%	2,202,000	415,872	18.9%	4.6	2,323,000	411,015	17.7%	3.4	2,530,000	536,527	21.2%	6.9	2,729,000	613,844	22.5%	8.2
WASHINGTON	1,553,000	515,213	33.2%	1,017,000	621,118	38.4%	5.2	1,692,000	478,208	28.3%	-4.9	1,854,000	613,421	33.1%	-0.1	2,009,000	623,630	31.0%	-2.1
WEST VIRGINIA	1,138,000	471,175	41.4%	1,103,000	428,264	38.8%	-2.6	1,076,000	468,128	43.5%	2.1	1,073,000	450,202	42.0%	0.6	1,070,000	434,140	40.6%	-0.8
WISCONSIN	2,223,000	602,521	27.1%	2,278,000	696,731	30.6%	3.5	2,338,000	813,217	34.8%	7.7	2,452,000	858,856	35.0%	7.9	2,559,000	741,661	29.0%	1.9
WYOMING	179,000	50,559	28.2%	183,000	50,225	27.4%	-0.8	189,000	64,090	33.9%	5.7	192,000	70,693	36.8%	8.6	194,000	45,950	23.7%	-4.6
Total	97,344,000	28,994,253	29.8%	101,295,000	29,956,895	29.6%	-0.2	106,188,000	35,110,913	33.1%	3.3	113,496,000	37,861,363	33.4%	3.6	120,243,000	33,243,510	27.6%	-2.1

Other Turnout for Election Years 1952–1968

State	1952 Voting-age population	1952 Turnout	1952 %	1956 Voting-age population	1956 Turnout	1956 %	1956 Difference from 1952*	1960 Voting-age population	1960 Turnout	1960 %	1960 Difference from 1952	1964 Voting-age population	1964 Turnout	1964 %	1964 Difference from 1952	1968 Voting-age population	1968 Turnout	1968 %	1968 Difference from 1952
ALABAMA								1,840,000	29	0.0%		1,920,000	2,019	0.1%	0.1	1,997,000	116,679	5.8%	5.8
ALASKA																			
ARIZONA																			
ARKANSAS	1,091,000	1,196	0.1%																
CALIFORNIA	7,453,000	146,686	2.0%					9,239,000	724	0.0%	-2.0	10,572,000	586	0.0%	-2.0	11,852,000	107,732	0.9%	-1.1
COLORADO	875,000	1,307	0.1%	946,000	1	0.0%	-0.1					1,145,000	1,183	0.1%	0.0	1,264,000	25,499	2.0%	1.9
CONNECTICUT	1,358,000	3,065	0.2%					1,537,000	2,350	0.2%	-0.1	1,683,000	163	0.0%	-0.2	1,824,000	11,706	0.6%	0.4
DELAWARE												289,000	76	0.0%					
DISTRICT OF COLUMBIA																			
FLORIDA												3,629,000	2,600	0.1%		4,184,000	28	0.0%	-0.1
GEORGIA	2,238,000	179	0.0%	2,329,000	11,232	0.5%	0.5	2,433,000	582	0.0%	0.0	2,654,000	25,078	0.9%	0.9	2,867,000	166	0.0%	0.0
HAWAII																418,000	2,432	0.6%	
IDAHO	350,000	4	0.0%													405,000	4,377	1.1%	1.1
ILLINOIS	5,889,000	5	0.0%	6,016,000	1	0.0%	0.0	6,155,000	2	0.0%	0.0	6,422,000	7	0.0%	0.0	6,677,000	21	0.0%	0.0
INDIANA	2,593,000	11,216	0.4%	2,682,000	4,603	0.2%	-0.3	2,773,000	1,707	0.1%	-0.4	2,906,000	734	0.0%	-0.4	3,032,000	366	0.0%	-0.4
IOWA	1,669,000	1,989	0.1%									1,674,000	1,798	0.1%	0.0	1,693,000	7	0.0%	-0.1
KANSAS				1,286,000	1,417	0.1%										1,365,000	4	0.0%	-0.1
KENTUCKY	1,884,000	573	0.0%	1,889,000	113	0.0%	0.0									2,074,000	3,256	0.2%	0.1
LOUISIANA																			
MAINE								565,000	418	0.1%									

United States House of Representatives General Elections (continued)

Other Turnout for Election Years 1952–1968 (continued)

State	1952 Voting-age population	Turnout	%	1956 Voting-age population	Turnout	%	Difference from 1952	1960 Voting-age population	Turnout	%	Difference from 1952	1964 Voting-age population	Turnout	%	Difference from 1952	1968 Voting-age population	Turnout	%	Difference from 1952
MARYLAND												2,064,000	1	0.0%					
MASSACHUSETTS	3,056,000	14,519	0.5%	3,082,000	672	0.0%	-0.5	3,126,000	551	0.0%	-0.5	3,296,000	7,594	0.2%	-0.2	3,457,000	53,524	1.5%	1.1
MICHIGAN	4,099,000	8,218	0.2%	4,297,000	3,668	0.1%	-0.1	4,498,000	5,112	0.1%	-0.1	4,786,000	2,643	0.1%	-0.1	5,062,000	4,014	0.1%	-0.1
MINNESOTA								1,988,000	5,459	0.3%		2,091,000	1,311	0.1%	-0.2	2,189,000	1,299	0.1%	-0.2
MISSISSIPPI																			
MISSOURI												2,772,000	201	0.0%		2,854,000	994	0.0%	0.0
MONTANA	370,000	888	0.2%									394,000	644	0.2%	-0.1				
NEBRASKA				848,000	2,389	0.3%						870,000	13	0.0%	-0.3	889,000	4,597	0.5%	0.2
NEVADA																			
NEW HAMPSHIRE												400,000	4	0.0%		432,000	4	0.0%	0.0
NEW JERSEY	3,354,000	20,259	0.6%	3,552,000	23,447	0.7%	0.1	3,758,000	21,299	0.6%	0.0	4,069,000	9,401	0.2%	-0.4	4,368,000	45,184	1.0%	0.4
NEW MEXICO								497,000	851	0.2%		522,000	3	0.0%	-0.2	547,000	1,503	0.3%	0.1
NEW YORK	9,944,000	210,973	2.1%	10,059,000	68,130	0.7%	-1.4	10,402,000	126,332	1.2%	-0.9	10,893,000	126,152	1.2%	-1.0	11,364,000	307,592	2.7%	0.6
NORTH CAROLINA																			
NORTH DAKOTA												352,000	659	0.2%		355,000	3,692	1.0%	0.9
OHIO	5,339,000	74,821	1.4%													6,281,000	599	0.0%	-1.4
OKLAHOMA	1,385,000	3,764	0.3%	1,399,000	401	0.0%	-0.2												
OREGON								1,068,000	81	0.0%		1,164,000	385	0.0%	0.0	1,256,000	81	0.0%	0.0
PENNSYLVANIA	6,870,000	3,311	0.0%	6,928,000	289	0.0%	0.0	6,998,000	2,888	0.0%	0.0					7,311,000	60,958	0.8%	0.8
RHODE ISLAND												554,000	1	0.0%		582,000	1,896	0.3%	0.3
SOUTH CAROLINA				1,225,000	135	0.0%		1,274,000	112	0.0%	0.0	1,360,000	2,501	0.2%	0.2	1,441,000	7,755	0.5%	0.5
SOUTH DAKOTA																			
TENNESSEE	2,005,000	16,988	0.8%					2,104,000	5	0.0%	-0.8	2,226,000	37,037	1.7%	0.8	2,342,000	19,593	0.8%	0.0
TEXAS				5,131,000	21,868	0.4%		5,462,000	61,506	1.1%	0.7					6,422,000	2,807	0.0%	-0.4
UTAH																			
VERMONT	228,000	2	0.0%					226,000	19	0.0%	0.0	241,000	7	0.0%	0.0	256,000	177	0.1%	0.1
VIRGINIA	2,090,000	9,998	0.5%	2,202,000	1,253	0.1%	-0.4	2,323,000	29,276	1.3%	0.8	2,530,000	93,317	3.7%	3.2	2,729,000	103,141	3.8%	3.3
WASHINGTON	1,553,000	517	0.0%									1,854,000	337	0.0%	0.0	2,009,000	4,379	0.2%	0.2
WEST VIRGINIA																			
WISCONSIN								2,338,000	3,882	0.2%		2,452,000	164	0.0%	-0.2	2,559,000	3,870	0.2%	0.0
WYOMING																			
Total	65,693,000	530,478	0.8%	53,871,000	139,619	0.3%	-0.5	70,604,000	263,185	0.4%	-0.4	77,784,000	316,619	0.4%	-0.4	104,357,000	899,932	0.9%	0.1

*Percentage point difference between turnout in current year and initial year listed in chart. If data do not appear for a state in the initial year listed, the difference is calculated from the first year in which data do appear for that state.

UNITED STATES PRESIDENTIAL PRIMARY ELECTIONS

Election Years 1952–1968

State*	1952 Voting-age population	Turnout	%	1956 Voting-age population	Turnout	%	Difference from 1952**	1960 Voting-age population	Turnout	%	Difference from 1952	1964 Voting-age population	Turnout	%	Difference from 1952	1968 Voting-age population	Turnout	%	Difference from 1952
ALABAMA																			
ALASKA																			
ARIZONA																			
ARKANSAS																			
CALIFORNIA	7,324,000	3,192,022	**43.6%**	8,207,000	3,175,450	**38.7%**	-4.9					10,386,000	4,664,700	**44.9%**	1.3	11,665,000	4,706,844	**40.4%**	-3.2
COLORADO																			
CONNECTICUT																			
DELAWARE																			
DISTRICT OF COLUMBIA																			
FLORIDA				2,518,000	489,981	**19.5%**										4,102,000	563,866	**13.7%**	-5.7
GEORGIA																			
HAWAII																			
IDAHO																			
ILLINOIS	5,870,000	1,872,435	**31.9%**	5,997,000	1,577,173	**26.3%**	-5.6					6,384,000	917,314	**14.4%**	-17.5				
INDIANA				2,669,000	608,065	**22.8%**						2,886,000	978,716	**33.9%**	11.1	3,014,000	1,284,875	**42.6%**	19.8
IOWA																			
KANSAS																			
KENTUCKY																			
LOUISIANA																			
MAINE																			
MARYLAND				1,692,000	241,169	**14.3%**						2,032,000	600,605	**29.6%**	15.3				
MASSACHUSETTS	3,053,000	417,636	**13.7%**	3,078,000	109,163	**3.5%**	-10.1	3,110,000	161,008	**5.2%**	-8.5	3,272,000	175,343	**5.4%**	-8.3	3,434,000	355,424	**10.4%**	-3.3
MICHIGAN																			
MINNESOTA	1,895,000	420,419	**22.2%**	1,935,000	634,027	**32.8%**	10.6												
MISSISSIPPI																			
MISSOURI																			
MONTANA				376,000	115,407	**30.7%**													
NEBRASKA	847,000	326,199	**38.5%**	847,000	161,627	**19.1%**	-19.4	849,000	169,949	**20.0%**	-18.5	867,000	199,792	**23.0%**	-15.5	886,000	363,087	**41.0%**	2.5
NEVADA																			
NEW HAMPSHIRE	342,000	128,525	**37.6%**	352,000	82,710	**23.5%**	-14.1	362,000	123,930	**34.2%**	-3.3	395,000	123,630	**31.3%**	-6.3	428,000	159,402	**37.2%**	-0.3
NEW JERSEY	3,325,000	798,030	**24.0%**	3,524,000	479,375	**13.6%**	-10.4					4,025,000	24,842	**0.6%**	-23.4	4,324,000	116,038	**2.7%**	-21.3
NEW MEXICO																			
NEW YORK																			

United States Presidential Primary Elections (continued)

United States Presidential Primary Elections *(continued)*

Election Years 1952–1968 *(continued)*

State	1952 Voting-age population	Turnout	%	1956 Voting-age population	Turnout	%	Difference from 1952	1960 Voting-age population	Turnout	%	Difference from 1952	1964 Voting-age population	Turnout	%	Difference from 1952	1968 Voting-age population	Turnout	%	Difference from 1952
NORTH CAROLINA																			
NORTH DAKOTA																			
OHIO	5,305,000	1,333,402	25.1%	5,535,000	755,123	13.6%	-11.5									6,246,000	1,163,632	18.6%	-6.5
OKLAHOMA																			
OREGON	996,000	464,212	46.6%	1,026,000	394,423	38.4%	-8.2	1,058,000	514,130	48.6%	2.0					1,242,000	685,229	55.2%	8.6
PENNSYLVANIA	6,862,000	1,448,068	21.1%	6,920,000	1,682,622	24.3%	3.2	6,982,000	1,243,644	17.8%	-3.3	7,135,000	706,096	9.9%	-11.2	7,289,000	884,662	12.1%	-9.0
RHODE ISLAND																			
SOUTH CAROLINA																			
SOUTH DAKOTA	395,000	163,127	41.3%	392,000	90,314	23.0%	-18.3									386,000	132,400	34.3%	-7.0
TENNESSEE																			
TEXAS																			
UTAH																			
VERMONT																			
VIRGINIA																			
WASHINGTON																			
WEST VIRGINIA	1,143,000	369,534	32.3%	1,108,000	224,715	20.3%	-12.0												
WISCONSIN	2,214,000	1,018,149	46.0%	2,270,000	786,497	34.6%	-11.3					2,436,000	1,088,969	44.7%	-1.3	2,543,000	1,222,855	48.1%	2.1
WYOMING																			
Total	39,571,000	11,951,758	30.2%	48,446,000	11,607,841	24.0%	-6.2	12,361,000	2,212,661	17.9%	-12.3	39,818,000	9,480,007	23.8%	-6.4	45,559,000	11,638,314	25.5%	-4.7

*Overall primary turnout reflects only states with primaries in both parties. To find single party primary results, see partisan primary charts.

**Percentage point difference between turnout in current year and initial year listed in chart. If data do not appear for a state in the initial year listed, the difference is calculated from the first year in which data do appear for that state.

UNITED STATES PRESIDENTIAL PRIMARY ELECTIONS

Republican Turnout for Election Years 1952–1968

State	1952 Voting-age population	Turnout	%	1956 Voting-age population	Turnout	%	Difference from 1952*	1960 Voting-age population	Turnout	%	Difference from 1952	1964 Voting-age population	Turnout	%	Difference from 1952	1968 Voting-age population	Turnout	%	Difference from 1952
ALABAMA																			
ALASKA																			
ARIZONA																			
ARKANSAS																			
CALIFORNIA	7,324,000	1,550,605	21.2%	8,207,000	1,354,764	16.5%	-4.7					10,386,000	2,172,456	20.9%	-0.3	11,665,000	1,525,091	13.1%	-8.1
COLORADO																			
CONNECTICUT																			
DELAWARE																			
DISTRICT OF COLUMBIA																			
FLORIDA				2,518,000	43,147	1.7%						3,548,000	100,704	2.8%	1.1	4,102,000	51,509	1.3%	-0.5
GEORGIA																			
HAWAII																			
IDAHO																			
ILLINOIS	5,870,000	1,272,321	21.7%	5,997,000	823,699	13.7%	-7.9					6,384,000	827,791	13.0%	-8.7				
INDIANA				2,669,000	365,223	13.7%						2,886,000	399,680	13.8%	0.2	3,014,000	508,362	16.9%	3.2
IOWA																			
KANSAS																			
KENTUCKY																			
LOUISIANA																			
MAINE																			
MARYLAND				1,692,000	70,035	4.1%						2,032,000	97,998	4.8%	0.7				
MASSACHUSETTS	3,053,000	365,086	12.0%	3,078,000	54,639	1.8%	-10.2	3,110,000	61,845	2.0%	-10.0	3,272,000	92,134	2.8%	9.1	3,434,000	106,521	3.1%	-8.9
MICHIGAN																			
MINNESOTA	1,895,000	292,323	15.4%	1,935,000	201,371	10.4%	-5.0												
MISSISSIPPI																			
MISSOURI																			
MONTANA				376,000	38,179	10.2%													
NEBRASKA	847,000	219,201	25.9%	847,000	102,806	12.1%	-13.7	849,000	79,257	9.3%	-16.5	867,000	138,522	16.0%	-9.9	886,000	200,476	22.6%	-3.3
NEVADA																			
NEW HAMPSHIRE	342,000	92,530	27.1%	352,000	57,064	16.2%	-10.8	362,000	73,031	20.2%	-6.9	395,000	92,853	23.5%	-3.5	428,000	103,938	24.3%	-2.8
NEW JERSEY	3,325,000	643,066	19.3%	3,524,000	357,089	10.1%	-9.2					4,025,000	18,933	0.5%	-18.9	4,324,000	88,592	2.0%	-17.3
NEW MEXICO																			
NEW YORK																			

United States Presidential Primary Elections (continued)

United States Presidential Primary Elections (continued)

Republican Turnout for Election Years 1952–1968 (continued)

State	1952 Voting-age population	Turnout	%	1956 Voting-age population	Turnout	%	Difference from 1952	1960 Voting-age population	Turnout	%	Difference from 1952	1964 Voting-age population	Turnout	%	Difference from 1952	1968 Voting-age population	Turnout	%	Difference from 1952
NORTH CAROLINA																			
NORTH DAKOTA																			
OHIO	5,305,000	842,530	15.9%	5,535,000	478,453	8.6%	-7.2									6,246,000	614,492	9.8%	-6.0
OKLAHOMA																			
OREGON	996,000	267,197	26.8%	1,026,000	231,418	22.6%	-4.3	1,058,000	227,033	21.5%	-5.4	1,150,000	285,486	24.8%	-2.0	1,242,000	312,159	25.1%	-1.7
PENNSYLVANIA	6,862,000	1,273,293	18.6%	6,920,000	996,416	14.4%	-4.2	6,982,000	986,831	14.1%	-4.4	7,135,000	452,868	6.3%	-12.2	7,289,000	287,573	3.9%	-14.6
RHODE ISLAND																			
SOUTH CAROLINA																			
SOUTH DAKOTA	395,000	128,574	32.6%	392,000	59,374	15.1%	-17.4					387,000	84,729	21.9%	-10.7	386,000	68,113	17.6%	-14.9
TENNESSEE																			
TEXAS																			
UTAH																			
VERMONT																			
VIRGINIA																			
WASHINGTON																			
WEST VIRGINIA	1,143,000	178,063	15.6%	1,108,000	111,883	10.1%	-5.5												
WISCONSIN	2,214,000	776,624	35.1%	2,270,000	455,832	20.1%	-15.0					2,436,000	300,428	12.3%	-22.7	2,543,000	489,853	19.3%	-15.8
WYOMING																			
Total	39,571,000	7,901,413	20.0%	48,446,000	5,801,392	12.0%	-8.0	12,361,000	1,427,997	11.6%	-8.4	44,903,000	5,064,582	11.3%	-8.7	45,559,000	4,356,679	9.6%	-10.4

Democratic Turnout for Election Years 1952–1968

State	1952 Voting-age population	Turnout	%	1956 Voting-age population	Turnout	%	Difference from 1952*	1960 Voting-age population	Turnout	%	Difference from 1952	1964 Voting-age population	Turnout	%	Difference from 1952	1968 Voting-age population	Turnout	%	Difference from 1952
ALABAMA																			
ALASKA																			
ARIZONA																			
ARKANSAS																			
CALIFORNIA	7,324,000	1,641,417	22.4%	8,207,000	1,820,686	22.2%	-0.2	9,106,000	2,000,418	22.0%	-0.4	10,386,000	2,492,244	24.0%	1.6	11,665,000	3,181,753	27.3%	4.9
COLORADO																			
CONNECTICUT																			
DELAWARE																			
DISTRICT OF COLUMBIA																			
FLORIDA	2,046,000	674,634	33.0%	2,518,000	446,834	17.7%	-15.2									4,102,000	512,357	12.5%	-5.3

United States Presidential Primary Elections (continued)

Democratic Turnout for Election Years 1952–1968 (continued)

State	1952 Voting-age population	Turnout	%	1956 Voting-age population	Turnout	%	Difference from 1952	1960 Voting-age population	Turnout	%	Difference from 1952	1964 Voting-age population	Turnout	%	Difference from 1952	1968 Voting-age population	Turnout	%	Difference from 1952
GEORGIA																			
HAWAII																			
IDAHO																			
ILLINOIS	5,870,000	600,114	10.2%	5,997,000	753,474	12.6%	2.3					6,384,000	89,523	1.4%	-8.8				
INDIANA				2,669,000	242,842	9.1%						2,886,000	579,036	20.1%	11.0	3,014,000	776,513	25.8%	16.7
IOWA																			
KANSAS																			
KENTUCKY																			
LOUISIANA																			
MAINE																			
MARYLAND	1,568,000	184,246	11.8%	1,692,000	171,134	10.1%	-1.6	1,820,000	286,956	15.8%	4.0	2,032,000	502,607	24.7%	14.6				
MASSACHUSETTS	3,053,000	52,550	1.7%	3,070,000	54,524	1.8%	0.1	3,110,000	99,163	3.2%	1.5	3,272,000	83,209	2.5%	0.8	3,434,000	248,903	7.2%	5.5
MICHIGAN																			
MINNESOTA	1,895,000	128,096	6.8%	1,935,000	432,656	22.4%	15.6												
MISSISSIPPI																			
MISSOURI																			
MONTANA				376,000	77,228	20.5%													
NEBRASKA	847,000	106,998	12.6%	847,000	58,821	6.9%	-5.7	849,000	90,692	10.7%	-2.0	867,000	61,270	7.1%	-5.6	886,000	162,611	18.4%	5.7
NEVADA																			
NEW HAMPSHIRE	342,000	35,995	10.5%	352,000	25,646	7.3%	-3.2	362,000	50,899	14.1%	3.5	395,000	30,777	7.8%	-2.7	428,000	55,464	13.0%	2.4
NEW JERSEY	3,325,000	154,964	4.7%	3,524,000	122,286	3.5%	-1.2					4,025,000	5,909	0.1%	-4.5	4,324,000	27,446	0.6%	-4.0
NEW MEXICO																			
NEW YORK																			
NORTH CAROLINA																			
NORTH DAKOTA																			
OHIO	5,305,000	490,872	9.3%	5,535,000	276,670	5.0%	-4.3									6,246,000	549,140	8.8%	-0.5
OKLAHOMA																			
OREGON	996,000	197,015	19.8%	1,026,000	163,005	15.9%	-3.9	1,058,000	287,097	27.1%	7.4					1,242,000	373,070	30.0%	10.3
PENNSYLVANIA	6,862,000	174,775	2.5%	6,920,000	686,206	9.9%	7.4	6,982,000	256,813	3.7%	1.1	7,135,000	253,228	3.5%	1.0	7,289,000	597,089	8.2%	5.6
RHODE ISLAND																			
SOUTH CAROLINA																			
SOUTH DAKOTA	395,000	34,553	8.7%	392,000	30,940	7.9%	-0.9									386,000	64,287	16.7%	7.9
TENNESSEE																			

United States Presidential Primary Elections *(continued)*

Democratic Turnout for Election Years 1952–1968 *(continued)*

State	1952 Voting-age population	Turnout	%	1956 Voting-age population	Turnout	%	Difference from 1952	1960 Voting-age population	Turnout	%	Difference from 1952	1964 Voting-age population	Turnout	%	Difference from 1952	1968 Voting-age population	Turnout	%	Difference from 1952
TEXAS																			
UTAH																			
VERMONT																			
VIRGINIA																			
WASHINGTON																			
WEST VIRGINIA	1,143,000	191,471	16.8%	1,108,000	112,832	10.2%	-6.6	1,076,000	388,697	36.1%	19.4								
WISCONSIN	2,214,000	241,525	10.9%	2,270,000	330,665	14.6%	3.7	2,327,000	842,777	36.2%	25.3	2,436,000	788,541	32.4%	21.5	2,543,000	733,002	28.8%	17.9
WYOMING																			
Total	43,185,000	4,909,225	11.4%	48,446,000	5,806,449	12.0%	0.6	26,690,000	4,303,512	16.1%	4.8	39,818,000	4,886,344	12.3%	0.9	45,559,000	7,281,635	16.0%	4.6

*Percentage point difference between turnout in current year and initial year listed in chart. If data do not appear for a state in the initial year listed, the difference is calculated from the first year in which data do appear for that state.

STATE GUBERNATORIAL PRIMARY ELECTIONS

Election Years 1952–1968

State*	1952				1956				1960				1964				1968			
	Voting-age population	Turnout	%		Voting-age population	Turnout	%	Difference from 1952**	Voting-age population	Turnout	%	Difference from 1952	Voting-age population	Turnout	%	Difference from 1952	Voting-age population	Turnout	%	Difference from 1952
ALABAMA																				
ALASKA																				
ARIZONA													843,000	292,937	34.7%					
ARKANSAS																	1,145,000	444,122	38.8%	
CALIFORNIA																				
COLORADO																				
CONNECTICUT																				
DELAWARE																				
DISTRICT OF COLUMBIA																				
FLORIDA	2,046,000	701,344	34.3%						2,993,000	1,026,753	34.3%	0.0	3,548,000	1,266,790	35.7%	1.4				
GEORGIA																				
HAWAII																				
IDAHO																				
ILLINOIS					5,997,000	1,620,861	27.0%		6,130,000	1,910,956	31.2%	4.1								
INDIANA																				
IOWA									1,652,000	347,037	21.0%									
KANSAS					1,281,000	432,966	33.8%						1,337,000	438,259	32.8%	-1.0				
KENTUCKY																				
LOUISIANA																				
MAINE																				
MARYLAND																				
MASSACHUSETTS																				
MICHIGAN																				
MINNESOTA																				
MISSISSIPPI																				
MISSOURI					2,654,000	625,346	23.6%		2,679,000	739,495	27.6%	4.0	2,761,000	858,001	31.1%	7.5	2,842,000	804,504	28.3%	4.7
MONTANA									385,000	193,735	50.3%						401,000	193,240	48.2%	-2.1
NEBRASKA					847,000	166,338	19.6%		849,000	269,374	31.7%	12.1	867,000	233,834	27.0%	7.3				
NEVADA																				
NEW HAMPSHIRE									362,000	139,304	38.5%						428,000	122,548	28.6%	-9.8
NEW JERSEY																				
NEW MEXICO	395,000	113,902	28.8%						494,000	162,612	32.9%	4.1					544,000	184,955	34.0%	5.2
NEW YORK																				

State Gubernatorial Primary Elections (continued)

State Gubernatorial Primary Elections (continued)

Election Years 1952–1968 (continued)

State	1952			1956				1960				1964				1968			
	Voting-age population	Turnout	%	Voting-age population	Turnout	%	Difference from 1952	Voting-age population	Turnout	%	Difference from 1952	Voting-age population	Turnout	%	Difference from 1952	Voting-age population	Turnout	%	Difference from 1952
NORTH CAROLINA												2,738,000	832,905	30.4%		2,920,000	857,167	29.4%	-1.1
NORTH DAKOTA	357,000	194,341	54.4%																
OHIO				5,535,000	1,052,189	19.0%													
OKLAHOMA																			
OREGON				1,026,000	469,183	45.7%													
PENNSYLVANIA																			
RHODE ISLAND																			
SOUTH CAROLINA																			
SOUTH DAKOTA												387,000	135,266	35.0%					
TENNESSEE																			
TEXAS																6,354,000	1,855,493	29.2%	
UTAH				426,000	196,061	46.0%		456,000	193,063	42.3%	-3.7	503,000	211,364	42.0%	-4.0				
VERMONT																			
VIRGINIA																			
WASHINGTON				1,608,000	707,765	44.0%		1,676,000	705,917	42.1%	-1.9	1,831,000	826,259	45.1%	1.1	1,986,000	704,718	35.5%	-8.5
WEST VIRGINIA				1,108,000	534,377	48.2%		1,076,000	553,133	51.4%	3.2	1,073,000	519,776	48.4%	0.2	1,071,000	513,902	48.0%	-0.2
WISCONSIN	2,214,000	877,215	39.6%									2,436,000	686,417	28.2%	-11.4				
WYOMING																			
Total	5,012,000	1,886,802	37.6%	20,482,000	5,805,086	28.3%	-9.3	18,752,000	6,241,379	33.3%	-4.4	18,324,000	6,301,808	34.4%	-3.3	17,691,000	5,680,649	32.1%	-5.5

*Overall primary turnout reflects only states with primaries in both parties. To find single party primary results, see partisan primary charts.

**Percentage point difference between turnout in current year and initial year listed in chart. If data do not appear for a state in the initial year listed, the difference is calculated from the first year in which data do appear for that state.

STATE GUBERNATORIAL PRIMARY ELECTIONS

Republican Turnout for Election Years 1952–1968

State	1952 Voting-age population	1952 Turnout	1952 %	1956 Voting-age population	1956 Turnout	1956 %	1956 Difference from 1952*	1960 Voting-age population	1960 Turnout	1960 %	1960 Difference from 1952	1964 Voting-age population	1964 Turnout	1964 %	1964 Difference from 1952	1968 Voting-age population	1968 Turnout	1968 %	1968 Difference from 1952
ALABAMA																			
ALASKA																			
ARIZONA				600,000	44,528	7.4%						843,000	102,441	12.2%	4.7				
ARKANSAS																1,145,000	29,245	2.6%	
CALIFORNIA																			
COLORADO																			
CONNECTICUT																			
DELAWARE																			
DISTRICT OF COLUMBIA																			
FLORIDA	2,046,000	25,926	1.3%					2,993,000	89,686	3.0%	1.7	3,548,000	130,951	3.7%	2.4				
GEORGIA																			
HAWAII																			
IDAHO																			
ILLINOIS				5,997,000	797,590	13.3%		6,130,000	844,707	13.8%	0.5	6,384,000	1,038,622	16.3%	3.0	6,639,000	706,600	10.6%	-2.7
INDIANA																			
IOWA								1,652,000	225,505	13.7%						1,691,000	251,900	14.9%	1.2
KANSAS				1,281,000	279,874	21.8%		1,313,000	262,975	20.0%	-1.8	1,337,000	282,164	21.1%	-0.7	1,361,000	272,968	20.1%	-1.8
KENTUCKY																			
LOUISIANA																			
MAINE				558,000	84,167	15.1%													
MARYLAND																			
MASSACHUSETTS																			
MICHIGAN				4,269,000	505,474	11.8%						4,746,000	663,981	14.0%	2.1				
MINNESOTA																			
MISSISSIPPI																			
MISSOURI				2,654,000	203,909	7.7%		2,679,000	198,978	7.4%	-0.3	2,761,000	213,163	7.7%	0.0	2,842,000	222,971	7.8%	0.2
MONTANA								385,000	65,637	17.0%						401,000	91,419	22.8%	5.7
NEBRASKA				847,000	104,370	12.3%		849,000	162,396	19.1%	6.8	867,000	139,930	16.1%	3.8				
NEVADA																			
NEW HAMPSHIRE				352,000	72,142	20.5%		362,000	98,513	27.2%	6.7	395,000	62,683	15.9%	-4.6	428,000	85,772	20.0%	-0.5
NEW JERSEY																			
NEW MEXICO	395,000	28,980	7.3%					494,000	38,817	7.9%	0.5					544,000	51,066	9.4%	2.1
NEW YORK																			

State Gubernatorial Primary Elections (continued)

State Gubernatorial Primary Elections (continued)

Republican Turnout for Election Years 1952–1968 (continued)

State	1952 Voting-age population	Turnout	%	1956 Voting-age population	Turnout	%	Difference from 1952	1960 Voting-age population	Turnout	%	Difference from 1952	1964 Voting-age population	Turnout	%	Difference from 1952	1968 Voting-age population	Turnout	%	Difference from 1952
NORTH CAROLINA												2,738,000	63,815	2.3%		2,920,000	156,067	5.3%	3.0
NORTH DAKOTA	357,000	182,211	51.0%	353,000	103,445	29.3%	-21.7	350,000	112,032	32.0%	-19.0	352,000	78,358	22.3%	-28.8	355,000	90,169	25.4%	-25.6
OHIO				5,335,000	587,773	11.0%													
OKLAHOMA																			
OREGON				1,026,000	248,054	24.2%													
PENNSYLVANIA																			
RHODE ISLAND																			
SOUTH CAROLINA																			
SOUTH DAKOTA												387,000	94,144	24.3%					
TENNESSEE																			
TEXAS																6,354,000	104,765	1.6%	
UTAH				426,000	117,355	27.5%		456,000	87,594	19.2%	-8.3	503,000	119,046	23.7%	-3.9	549,000	133,542	24.3%	-3.2
VERMONT								224,000	59,050	26.4%		239,000	44,692	18.7%	-7.7	254,000	58,540	23.0%	-3.3
VIRGINIA																			
WASHINGTON				1,608,000	291,520	18.1%		1,676,000	408,337	24.4%	6.2	1,831,000	539,665	29.5%	11.3	1,986,000	342,212	17.2%	-0.9
WEST VIRGINIA				1,108,000	189,432	17.1%		1,076,000	185,646	17.3%	0.2	1,073,000	170,012	15.8%	-1.3	1,071,000	186,479	17.4%	0.3
WISCONSIN	2,214,000	699,082	31.6%									2,436,000	343,181	14.1%	-17.5				
WYOMING																			
Total	5,012,000	936,199	18.7%	26,414,000	3,629,633	13.7%	-4.9	20,639,000	2,839,873	13.8%	-4.9	30,440,000	4,086,848	13.4%	-5.3	28,540,000	2,783,715	9.8%	-8.9

Democratic Turnout for Election Years 1952–1968

State	1952 Voting-age population	Turnout	%	1956 Voting-age population	Turnout	%	Difference from 1952*	1960 Voting-age population	Turnout	%	Difference from 1952	1964 Voting-age population	Turnout	%	Difference from 1952	1968 Voting-age population	Turnout	%	Difference from 1952
ALABAMA																			
ALASKA																			
ARIZONA												843,000	190,496	22.6%		972,000	153,898	15.8%	-6.8
ARKANSAS	1,095,000	329,050	30.1%	1,066,000	324,599	30.5%	0.4	1,040,000	406,817	39.1%	9.1	1,093,000	365,037	33.4%	3.3	1,145,000	414,877	36.2%	6.2
CALIFORNIA																			
COLORADO																			
CONNECTICUT																			
DELAWARE																			
DISTRICT OF COLUMBIA																			
FLORIDA	2,046,000	675,418	33.0%	2,518,000	831,752	33.0%	0.0	2,993,000	937,067	31.3%	-1.7	3,548,000	1,135,839	32.0%	-1.0				

State Gubernatorial Primary Elections *(continued)*

Democratic Turnout for Election Years 1952–1968 *(continued)*

State	1952 Voting-age population	Turnout	%	1956 Voting-age population	Turnout	%	Difference from 1952	1960 Voting-age population	Turnout	%	Difference from 1952	1964 Voting-age population	Turnout	%	Difference from 1952	1968 Voting-age population	Turnout	%	Difference from 1952
GEORGIA																			
HAWAII																			
IDAHO																			
ILLINOIS				5,977,000	823,271	13.8%		6,130,000	1,066,249	17.4%	3.6								
INDIANA																			
IOWA				1,661,000	110,309	6.6%		1,652,000	121,532	7.4%	0.7								
KANSAS				1,281,000	153,092	12.0%						1,337,000	156,095	11.7%	-0.3				
KENTUCKY																			
LOUISIANA	1,624,000	750,199	46.2%	1,710,000	819,709	47.9%	1.7	1,797,000	842,609	46.9%	0.7	1,896,000	906,475	47.8%	1.6				
MAINE																			
MARYLAND																			
MASSACHUSETTS				3,078,000	489,547	15.9%		3,110,000	598,294	19.2%	3.3	3,272,000	733,073	22.4%	6.5				
MICHIGAN								4,470,000	540,743	12.1%									
MINNESOTA								1,978,000	298,023	15.1%									
MISSISSIPPI																			
MISSOURI				2,654,000	421,437	15.9%		2,679,000	540,517	20.2%	4.3	2,761,000	644,838	23.4%	7.5	2,842,000	581,533	20.5%	4.6
MONTANA				376,000	121,352	32.3%		385,000	128,098	33.3%	1.0	393,000	128,677	32.7%	0.5	401,000	101,821	25.4%	-6.9
NEBRASKA				847,000	61,968	7.3%		849,000	106,978	12.6%	5.3	867,000	93,904	10.8%	3.5				
NEVADA																			
NEW HAMPSHIRE								362,000	40,791	11.3%						428,000	36,776	8.6%	-2.7
NEW JERSEY																			
NEW MEXICO	395,000	84,922	21.5%	445,000	96,726	21.7%	0.2	494,000	123,795	25.1%	3.6					544,000	133,889	24.6%	3.1
NEW YORK																			
NORTH CAROLINA	2,357,000	559,845	23.8%	2,456,000	454,746	18.5%	-5.2	2,556,000	653,060	25.6%	1.8	2,738,000	769,090	28.1%	4.3	2,920,000	701,100	24.0%	0.3
NORTH DAKOTA	357,000	12,130	3.4%																
OHIO				5,535,000	464,416	8.4%													
OKLAHOMA																			
OREGON				1,026,000	221,129	21.6%													
PENNSYLVANIA																			
RHODE ISLAND								522,000	130,807	25.1%		549,000	97,454	17.8%	-7.3				
SOUTH CAROLINA																			
SOUTH DAKOTA												387,000	41,122	10.6%					
TENNESSEE	1,998,000	622,926	31.2%																

State Gubernatorial Primary Elections (continued)

Democratic Turnout for Election Years 1952–1968 *(continued)*

State	1952			1956				1960				1964				1968			
	Voting-age population	Turnout	%	Voting-age population	Turnout	%	Difference from 1952	Voting-age population	Turnout	%	Difference from 1952	Voting-age population	Turnout	%	Difference from 1952	Voting-age population	Turnout	%	Difference from 1952
TEXAS	4,762,000	1,322,206	27.8%	5,085,000	1,528,859	30.1%	2.3	5,413,000	1,528,834	28.2%	0.5	5,884,000	1,630,351	27.7%	-0.1	6,354,000	1,750,728	27.6%	-0.2
UTAH				426,000	78,706	18.5%		456,000	105,469	23.1%	4.7	503,000	92,318	18.4%	-0.1				
VERMONT																			
VIRGINIA																			
WASHINGTON				1,608,000	416,245	25.9%		1,676,000	297,580	17.8%	-8.1	1,831,000	286,594	15.7%	-10.2	1,986,000	362,506	18.3%	-7.6
WEST VIRGINIA				1,108,000	344,945	31.1%		1,076,000	367,487	34.2%	3.0	1,073,000	349,764	32.6%	1.5	1,071,000	327,423	30.6%	-0.6
WISCONSIN	2,214,000	178,133	8.0%									2,436,000	343,236	14.1%	6.0	2,543,000	205,546	8.1%	0.0
WYOMING																			
Total	16,848,000	4,534,829	26.9%	38,857,000	7,762,808	20.0%	-6.9	39,638,000	8,834,750	22.3%	-4.6	31,411,000	7,964,363	25.4%	-1.6	21,206,000	4,770,097	22.5%	-4.4

*Percentage point difference between turnout in current year and initial year listed in chart. If data do not appear for a state in the initial year listed, the difference is calculated from the first year in which data do appear for that state.

UNITED STATES SENATE PRIMARY ELECTIONS

Election Years 1952–1968

State*	1952 Voting-age population	Turnout	%	1956 Voting-age population	Turnout	%	Difference from 1952**	1960 Voting-age population	Turnout	%	Difference from 1952	1964 Voting-age population	Turnout	%	Difference from 1952	1968 Voting-age population	Turnout	%	Difference from 1952
ALABAMA																			
ALASKA																168,000	53,417	31.8%	
ARIZONA				600,000	160,622	26.8%													
ARKANSAS																			
CALIFORNIA				8,207,000	3,354,960	40.9%						10,386,000	4,732,256	45.6%	4.7	11,665,000	5,074,992	43.5%	2.6
COLORADO																			
CONNECTICUT																			
DELAWARE																			
DISTRICT OF COLUMBIA																			
FLORIDA																4,102,000	1,072,715	26.2%	
GEORGIA																2,836,000	939,207	33.1%	
HAWAII												377,000	144,811	38.4%					
IDAHO				358,000	136,772	38.2%													
ILLINOIS																			
INDIANA																			
IOWA				1,661,000	334,701	20.2%										1,691,000	364,614	21.6%	1.4
KANSAS				1,281,000	401,615	31.4%		1,313,000	401,396	30.6%	-0.8					1,361,000	416,092	30.6%	-0.8
KENTUCKY				1,888,000	418,098	22.1%		1,896,000	247,377	13.0%	-9.1					2,062,000	321,070	15.6%	-6.6
LOUISIANA																			
MAINE																			
MARYLAND	1,568,000	370,496	23.6%	1,692,000	367,142	21.7%	-1.9					2,032,000	588,533	29.0%	5.3	2,246,000	306,583	13.7%	-10.0
MASSACHUSETTS																			
MICHIGAN																			
MINNESOTA																			
MISSISSIPPI																			
MISSOURI				2,654,000	611,295	23.0%						2,761,000	823,450	29.8%	6.8	2,842,000	838,469	29.5%	6.5
MONTANA								385,000	196,210	51.0%		393,000	182,323	46.4%	-4.6				
NEBRASKA																			
NEVADA	118,000	52,313	44.3%									223,000	88,831	39.8%	-4.5				
NEW HAMPSHIRE								362,000	134,556	37.2%									
NEW JERSEY	3,325,000	679,118	20.4%					3,727,000	579,781	15.6%	-4.9								
NEW MEXICO	395,000	116,436	29.5%					494,000	156,155	31.6%	2.1								
NEW YORK																			

United States Senate Primary Elections (continued)

United States Senate Primary Elections (continued)

Election Years 1952–1968 (continued)

State	1952 Voting-age population	Turnout	%	1956 Voting-age population	Turnout	%	Difference from 1952	1960 Voting-age population	Turnout	%	Difference from 1952	1964 Voting-age population	Turnout	%	Difference from 1952	1968 Voting-age population	Turnout	%	Difference from 1952
NORTH CAROLINA																2,920,000	770,255	26.4%	
NORTH DAKOTA	357,000	199,124	55.8%																
OHIO												6,005,000	1,549,986	25.8%		6,246,000	1,682,164	26.9%	1.1
OKLAHOMA				1,397,000	389,371	27.9%		1,413,000	439,871	31.1%	3.3	1,482,000	718,251	48.5%	20.6				
OREGON				1,026,000	484,015	47.2%		1,058,000	506,826	47.9%	0.7					1,242,000	651,815	52.5%	5.3
PENNSYLVANIA												7,135,000	1,993,277	27.9%					
RHODE ISLAND																			
SOUTH CAROLINA																			
SOUTH DAKOTA																			
TENNESSEE								2,092,000	746,351	35.7%		2,208,000	760,024	34.4%	-1.3				
TEXAS												5,884,000	1,720,325	29.2%					
UTAH																549,000	229,121	41.7%	
VERMONT																254,000	60,254	23.7%	
VIRGINIA																			
WASHINGTON												1,831,000	795,423	43.4%		1,986,000	688,663	34.7%	-8.8
WEST VIRGINIA				1,108,000	507,683	45.8%													
WISCONSIN	2,214,000	877,215	39.6%	2,270,000	705,896	31.1%	-8.5												
WYOMING								188,000	86,587	46.1%		191,000	88,475	46.3%	0.3				
Total	7,977,000	2,294,702	28.8%	24,142,000	7,872,170	32.6%	3.8	12,928,000	3,495,110	27.0%	-1.7	40,908,000	14,185,965	34.7%	5.9	42,170,000	13,469,431	31.9%	3.2

*Overall primary turnout reflects only states with primaries in both parties. To find single party primary results, see partisan primary charts.

**Percentage point difference between turnout in current year and initial year listed in chart. If data do not appear for a state in the initial year listed, the difference is calculated from the first year in which data do appear for that state.

UNITED STATES SENATE PRIMARY ELECTIONS

Republican Turnout for Election Years 1952–1968

State	1952			1956				1960				1964				1968			
	Voting-age population	Turnout	%	Voting-age population	Turnout	%	Difference from 1952*	Voting-age population	Turnout	%	Difference from 1952	Voting-age population	Turnout	%	Difference from 1952	Voting-age population	Turnout	%	Difference from 1952
ALABAMA																			
ALASKA								133,000	12,998	9.8%						168,000	19,431	11.6%	1.8
ARIZONA				600,000	39,393	6.6%													
ARKANSAS																			
CALIFORNIA				8,207,000	1,472,746	17.9%						10,386,000	2,071,950	19.9%	2.0	11,665,000	2,223,782	19.1%	1.1
COLORADO																			
CONNECTICUT																			
DELAWARE																			
DISTRICT OF COLUMBIA																			
FLORIDA																4,102,000	212,152	5.2%	
GEORGIA																2,836,000	34,121	1.2%	
HAWAII												377,000	33,356	8.8%					
IDAHO				358,000	62,754	17.5%													
ILLINOIS								6,130,000	792,548	12.9%						6,639,000	675,796	10.2%	-2.7
INDIANA																			
IOWA				1,661,000	232,916	14.0%		1,652,000	215,786	13.1%	-1.0					1,691,000	244,905	14.5%	0.5
KANSAS				1,281,000	276,417	21.6%		1,313,000	252,260	19.2%	-2.4					1,361,000	278,583	20.5%	-1.1
KENTUCKY				1,888,000	59,509	3.2%		1,896,000	52,874	2.8%	-0.4					2,062,000	118,033	5.7%	2.6
LOUISIANA								1,797,000	1,040	0.1%									
MAINE																			
MARYLAND	1,568,000	102,265	6.5%	1,692,000	67,714	4.0%	-2.5					2,032,000	115,297	5.7%	-0.8	2,246,000	83,494	3.7%	-2.8
MASSACHUSETTS																			
MICHIGAN								4,470,000	477,612	10.7%		4,746,000	564,225	11.9%	1.2				
MINNESOTA								1,978,000	286,883	14.5%									
MISSISSIPPI																			
MISSOURI				2,654,000	204,685	7.7%						2,761,000	211,078	7.6%	-0.1	2,842,000	227,192	8.0%	0.3
MONTANA								385,000	67,265	17.5%		393,000	53,789	13.7%	-3.8				
NEBRASKA																			
NEVADA	118,000	20,960	17.8%									223,000	27,933	12.5%	-5.2	274,000	38,841	14.2%	-3.6
NEW HAMPSHIRE				352,000	68,937	19.6%		362,000	94,310	26.1%	6.5					428,000	84,484	19.7%	0.2
NEW JERSEY	3,325,000	484,706	14.6%					3,727,000	362,218	9.7%	-4.9								
NEW MEXICO	395,000	31,853	8.1%					494,000	35,609	7.2%	-0.9								
NEW YORK																			

United States Senate Primary Elections (continued)

United States Senate Primary Elections (continued)

Republican Turnout for Election Years 1952–1968 (continued)

State	1952 Voting-age population	1952 Turnout	1952 %	1956 Voting-age population	1956 Turnout	1956 %	1956 Difference from 1952	1960 Voting-age population	1960 Turnout	1960 %	1960 Difference from 1952	1964 Voting-age population	1964 Turnout	1964 %	1964 Difference from 1952	1968 Voting-age population	1968 Turnout	1968 %	1968 Difference from 1952
NORTH CAROLINA																2,920,000	132,018	4.5%	
NORTH DAKOTA	357,000	186,264	52.2%	353,000	100,136	28.4%	-23.8												
OHIO												6,005,000	767,207	12.8%		6,246,000	698,762	11.2%	-1.6
OKLAHOMA				1,397,000	44,031	3.2%		1,413,000	53,251	3.8%	0.6	1,482,000	126,925	8.6%	5.4				
OREGON				1,026,000	249,272	24.3%		1,058,000	234,647	22.2%	-2.1					1,242,000	274,271	22.1%	-2.2
PENNSYLVANIA				6,920,000	945,791	13.7%						7,135,000	977,868	13.7%	0.0				
RHODE ISLAND																			
SOUTH CAROLINA																			
SOUTH DAKOTA																			
TENNESSEE								2,092,000	28,300	1.4%		2,208,000	109,844	5.0%	3.6				
TEXAS												5,884,000	142,918	2.4%					
UTAH												503,000	120,565	24.0%		549,000	134,634	24.5%	0.6
VERMONT																254,000	58,062	22.9%	
VIRGINIA																			
WASHINGTON												1,831,000	266,770	14.6%		1,986,000	286,677	14.4%	-0.1
WEST VIRGINIA				1,108,000	190,475	17.2%													
WISCONSIN	2,214,000	699,082	31.6%	2,270,000	451,905	19.9%	-11.7									2,543,000	262,165	10.3%	-21.3
WYOMING								188,000	45,741	24.3%		191,000	44,800	23.5%	-0.9				
Total	7,977,000	1,525,130	19.1%	31,767,000	4,466,680	14.1%	-5.1	29,088,000	3,013,342	10.4%	-8.8	46,157,000	5,634,525	12.2%	-6.9	52,054,000	6,087,403	11.7%	-7.4

Democratic Turnout for Election Years 1952–1968

State	1952 Voting-age population	1952 Turnout	1952 %	1956 Voting-age population	1956 Turnout	1956 %	1956 Difference from 1952*	1960 Voting-age population	1960 Turnout	1960 %	1960 Difference from 1952	1964 Voting-age population	1964 Turnout	1964 %	1964 Difference from 1952	1968 Voting-age population	1968 Turnout	1968 %	1968 Difference from 1952
ALABAMA				1,796,000	362,959	20.2%		1,832,000	404,085	22.1%	1.8					1,986,000	535,992	27.0%	6.8
ALASKA																168,000	33,986	20.2%	
ARIZONA				600,000	121,229	20.2%						843,000	185,225	22.0%	1.8	972,000	151,689	15.6%	-4.6
ARKANSAS				1,066,000	331,689	31.1%										1,145,000	417,023	36.4%	5.3
CALIFORNIA				8,207,000	1,882,215	22.9%						10,386,000	2,660,306	25.6%	2.7	11,665,000	2,851,210	24.4%	1.5
COLORADO				936,000	123,389	13.2%										1,247,000	157,597	12.6%	-0.5
CONNECTICUT																			
DELAWARE																			
DISTRICT OF COLUMBIA																			
FLORIDA	2,046,000	576,526	28.2%	2,518,000	702,188	27.9%	-0.3					3,548,000	965,468	27.2%	-1.0	4,102,000	860,563	21.0%	-7.2

United States Senate Primary Elections *(continued)*

Democratic Turnout for Election Years 1952–1968 *(continued)*

State	1952 Voting-age population	Turnout	%	1956 Voting-age population	Turnout	%	Difference from 1952	1960 Voting-age population	Turnout	%	Difference from 1952	1964 Voting-age population	Turnout	%	Difference from 1952	1968 Voting-age population	Turnout	%	Difference from 1952
GEORGIA				2,315,000	620,492	26.8%										2,836,000	905,086	31.9%	
HAWAII												377,000	111,455	29.6%		413,000	126,961	30.7%	1.2
IDAHO				358,000	74,018	20.7%		368,000	69,647	18.9%	-1.7								
ILLINOIS																			
INDIANA																			
IOWA				1,661,000	101,785	6.1%										1,691,000	119,709	7.1%	1.0
KANSAS				1,281,000	125,198	9.8%		1,313,000	149,136	11.4%	1.6					1,361,000	137,509	10.1%	0.3
KENTUCKY				1,888,000	358,589	19.0%		1,896,000	194,503	10.3%	-8.7					2,062,000	203,037	9.8%	-9.1
LOUISIANA																1,997,000	568,258	28.5%	
MAINE																			
MARYLAND	1,568,000	268,231	17.1%	1,692,000	299,428	17.7%	0.6					2,032,000	473,236	23.3%	6.2	2,246,000	223,089	9.9%	-7.2
MASSACHUSETTS								3,110,000	558,798	18.0%									
MICHIGAN																			
MINNESOTA												2,076,000	270,897	13.0%					
MISSISSIPPI	1,197,000	214,182	17.9%					1,169,000	145,132	12.4%	-5.5	1,199,000	178,467	14.9%	-3.0				
MISSOURI				2,654,000	406,610	15.3%						2,761,000	612,372	22.2%	6.9	2,842,000	611,277	21.5%	6.2
MONTANA								385,000	128,945	33.5%		393,000	128,534	32.7%	-0.8				
NEBRASKA								849,000	98,663	11.6%									
NEVADA	118,000	31,353	26.6%	145,000	39,283	27.1%	0.5					223,000	60,898	27.3%	0.7				
NEW HAMPSHIRE								362,000	40,246	11.1%									
NEW JERSEY	3,325,000	194,412	5.8%					3,727,000	217,563	5.8%	0.0								
NEW MEXICO	395,000	84,583	21.4%					494,000	120,546	24.4%	3.0								
NEW YORK																11,295,000	763,409	6.8%	
NORTH CAROLINA				2,456,000	426,479	17.4%		2,556,000	597,538	23.4%	6.0					2,920,000	638,237	21.9%	4.5
NORTH DAKOTA	357,000	12,860	3.6%																
OHIO												6,005,000	782,779	13.0%		6,246,000	983,402	15.7%	2.7
OKLAHOMA				1,397,000	345,340	24.7%		1,413,000	386,620	27.4%	2.6	1,482,000	591,326	39.9%	15.2	1,552,000	369,121	23.8%	-0.9
OREGON				1,026,000	234,743	22.9%		1,058,000	272,179	25.7%	2.8					1,242,000	377,544	30.4%	7.5
PENNSYLVANIA												7,135,000	1,015,409	14.2%		7,289,000	863,179	11.8%	-2.4
RHODE ISLAND								522,000	135,643	26.0%									
SOUTH CAROLINA								1,266,000	305,931	24.2%						1,429,000	392,780	27.5%	3.3
SOUTH DAKOTA				392,000	38,563	9.8%													
TENNESSEE	1,998,000	580,011	29.0%					2,092,000	718,051	34.3%	5.3	2,208,000	650,180	29.4%	0.4				

United States Senate Primary Elections (continued)

United States Senate Primary Elections (continued)

Democratic Turnout for Election Years 1952–1968 (continued)

State	1952 Voting-age population	Turnout	%	1956 Voting-age population	Turnout	%	Difference from 1952	1960 Voting-age population	Turnout	%	Difference from 1952	1964 Voting-age population	Turnout	%	Difference from 1952	1968 Voting-age population	Turnout	%	Difference from 1952
TEXAS	4,762,000	1,296,744	27.2%									5,884,000	1,577,407	26.8%	-0.4				
UTAH				426,000	79,226	18.6%										549,000	94,487	17.2%	-1.4
VERMONT												239,000	17,435	7.3%		254,000	2,192	0.9%	-6.4
VIRGINIA	2,074,000	345,307	16.6%																
WASHINGTON												1,831,000	528,653	28.9%		1,986,000	401,986	20.2%	-8.6
WEST VIRGINIA				1,108,000	317,208	28.6%						1,073,000	314,106	29.3%	0.6				
WISCONSIN	2,214,000	178,133	8.0%	2,270,000	253,991	11.2%	3.1					2,436,000	333,031	13.7%	5.6				
WYOMING								188,000	40,846	21.7%		191,000	43,675	22.9%	1.1				
Total	20,054,000	3,782,342	18.9%	36,192,000	7,244,622	20.0%	1.2	24,600,000	4,584,072	18.6%	-0.2	52,322,000	11,500,859	22.0%	3.1	71,495,000	12,789,323	17.9%	-1.0

Other Turnout for Election Years 1952–1968

State	1952 Voting-age population	Turnout	%	1956 Voting-age population	Turnout	%	Difference from 1952*	1960 Voting-age population	Turnout	%	Difference from 1952	1964 Voting-age population	Turnout	%	Difference from 1952	1968 Voting-age population	Turnout	%	Difference from 1952
NEW YORK																11,295,000	14,246	0.1%	

*Percentage point difference between turnout in current year and initial year listed in chart. If data do not appear for a state in the initial year listed, the difference is calculated from the first year in which data do appear for that state.

Midterm Turnout Election Based on Highest Statewide Turnout, Election Years 1950–1966

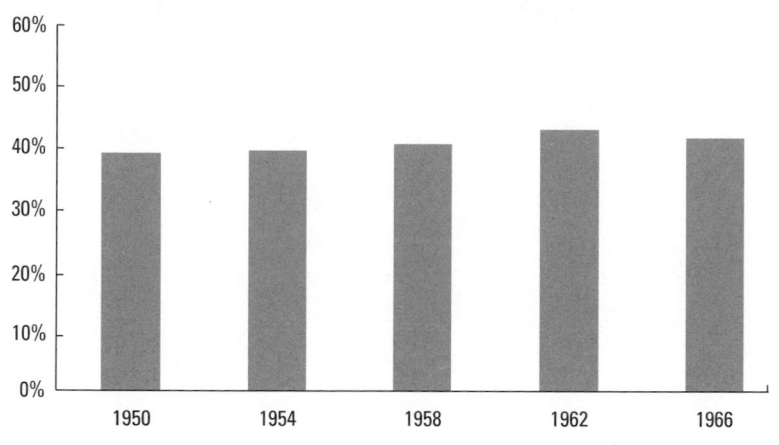

YEAR	VOTING-AGE POPULATION	TOTAL	%
1950	94,998,000	40,311,778	42.4%
1954	99,232,000	42,585,072	42.9%
1958	103,892,000	45,816,549	44.1%
1962	109,984,000	51,350,966	46.7%
1966	116,993,000	52,892,122	45.2%

Partisan Turnout Midterm Election Based on Aggregate House of Representatives Turnout, Election Years 1950–1966

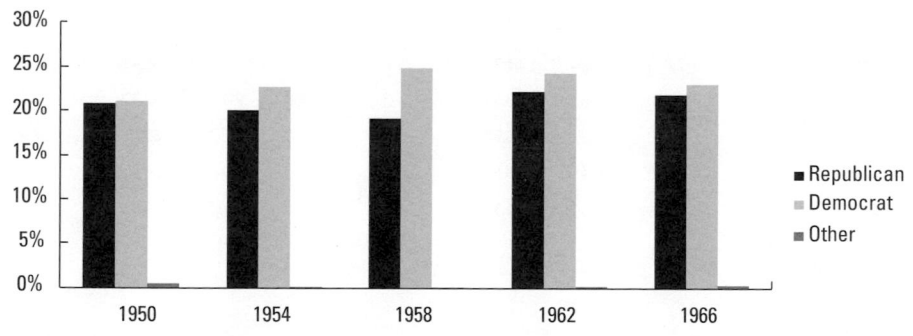

■ Republican
■ Democrat
■ Other

YEAR	VOTING-AGE POPULATION	REPUBLICAN TURNOUT	%	DEMOCRAT TURNOUT	%	OTHER TURNOUT	%
1950	94,998,000	19,763,965	20.8%	19,998,288	21.1%	549,525	0.6%
1954	99,232,000	19,895,605	20.0%	22,490,589	22.7%	198,878	0.2%
1958	103,892,000	19,875,549	19.1%	25,788,016	24.8%	152,984	0.1%
1962	109,984,000	24,384,312	22.2%	26,674,299	24.3%	292,355	0.3%
1966	116,993,000	25,524,531	21.8%	26,904,131	23.0%	463,460	0.4%

STATE GUBERNATORIAL GENERAL ELECTIONS

Election Years 1950–1966

State	1950 Voting-age population	1950 Turnout	1950 %.	1954 Voting-age population	1954 Turnout	1954 %.	1954 Difference from 1950*	1958 Voting-age population	1958 Turnout	1958 %	1958 Difference from 1950	1962 Voting-age population	1962 Turnout	1962 %	1962 Difference from 1950	1966 Voting-age population	1966 Turnout	1966 %.	1966 Difference from 1950
ALABAMA	1,749,000	170,591	**9.8%**	1,785,000	333,090	**18.7%**	8.9	1,819,000	270,952	**14.9%**	5.1	1,882,000	315,776	**16.8%**	7.0	1,958,000	848,101	**43.3%**	33.6
ALASKA								127,000	48,968	**38.6%**		144,000	56,681	**39.4%**	0.8	162,000	66,294	**40.9%**	2.4
ARIZONA	438,000	195,227	**44.6%**	559,000	243,970	**43.6%**	-0.9	673,000	290,465	**43.2%**	-1.4	798,000	365,841	**45.8%**	1.3	926,000	378,342	**40.9%**	-3.7
ARKANSAS	1,106,000	317,087	**28.7%**	1,076,000	335,176	**31.2%**	2.5	1,047,000	286,886	**27.4%**	-1.3	1,075,000	308,092	**28.7%**	0.0	1,126,000	563,527	**50.0%**	21.4
CALIFORNIA	6,975,000	3,796,090	**54.4%**	7,895,000	4,030,368	**51.0%**	-3.4	8,777,000	5,255,777	**59.9%**	5.5	9,933,000	5,853,270	**58.9%**	4.5	11,212,000	6,503,445	**58.0%**	3.6
COLORADO	838,000	450,994	**53.8%**	910,000	489,540	**53.8%**	0.0	981,000	609,808	**62.2%**	8.3	1,086,000	616,481	**56.8%**	2.9	1,205,000	660,063	**54.8%**	1.0
CONNECTICUT	1,311,000	878,735	**67.0%**	1,401,000	936,753	**66.9%**	-0.2	1,488,000	974,509	**65.5%**	-1.5	1,612,000	1,031,902	**64.0%**	-3.0	1,753,000	1,008,557	**57.5%**	-9.5
DELAWARE																			
DISTRICT OF COLUMBIA																			
FLORIDA				2,351,000	357,783	**15.2%**										3,906,000	1,489,661	**38.1%**	22.9
GEORGIA	2,189,000	234,430	**10.7%**	2,283,000	331,966	**14.5%**	3.8	2,373,000	168,497	**7.1%**	-3.6	2,548,000	311,691	**12.2%**	1.5	2,760,000	975,019	**35.3%**	24.6
HAWAII												364,000	196,015	**53.9%**		401,000	213,164	**53.2%**	-0.7
IDAHO	345,000	204,792	**59.4%**	355,000	228,685	**64.4%**	5.1	365,000	239,046	**65.5%**	6.1	380,000	255,454	**67.2%**	7.9	397,000	252,593	**63.6%**	4.3
ILLINOIS																			
INDIANA																			
IOWA	1,675,000	857,213	**51.2%**	1,664,000	848,592	**51.0%**	-0.2	1,654,000	859,095	**51.9%**	0.8	1,665,000	819,854	**49.2%**	-1.9	1,684,000	893,175	**53.0%**	1.9
KANSAS	1,236,000	619,310	**50.1%**	1,269,000	622,633	**49.1%**	-1.0	1,302,000	735,939	**56.5%**	6.4	1,329,000	638,798	**48.1%**	-2.0	1,353,000	692,955	**51.2%**	1.1
KENTUCKY																			
LOUISIANA																			
MAINE	553,000	241,177	**43.6%**	557,000	189,842	**34.1%**	-9.5	561,000	280,245	**50.0%**	6.3	572,000	292,725	**51.2%**	7.6	585,000	323,838	**55.4%**	11.7
MARYLAND	1,519,000	645,631	**42.5%**	1,648,000	700,484	**42.5%**	0.0	1,772,000	763,234	**43.1%**	0.6	1,958,000	775,101	**39.6%**	-2.9	2,170,000	918,761	**42.3%**	-0.2
MASSACHUSETTS	3,042,000	1,910,180	**62.8%**	3,070,000	1,903,774	**62.0%**	-0.8	3,095,000	1,899,117	**61.4%**	-1.4	3,214,000	2,109,089	**65.6%**	2.8	3,377,000	2,041,177	**60.4%**	-2.4
MICHIGAN	3,992,000	1,879,382	**47.1%**	4,199,000	2,187,027	**52.1%**	5.0	4,396,000	2,312,184	**52.6%**	5.5	4,648,000	2,764,839	**59.5%**	12.4	4,923,000	2,461,909	**50.0%**	2.9
MINNESOTA	1,879,000	1,046,632	**55.7%**	1,922,000	1,151,417	**59.9%**	4.2	1,962,000	1,186,915	**60.5%**	4.8	2,041,000	1,246,904	**61.1%**	5.4	2,140,000	1,295,058	**60.5%**	4.8
MISSISSIPPI																			
MISSOURI																			
MONTANA																			
NEBRASKA	846,000	449,720	**53.2%**	847,000	414,841	**49.0%**	-4.2	849,000	421,067	**49.6%**	-3.6	861,000	464,585	**54.0%**	0.8	880,000	486,396	**55.3%**	2.1
NEVADA	107,000	61,773	**57.7%**	136,000	78,462	**57.7%**	0.0	162,000	84,889	**52.4%**	-5.3	205,000	96,929	**47.3%**	-10.4	256,000	137,677	**53.8%**	-4.0
NEW HAMPSHIRE	339,000	191,239	**56.4%**	348,000	194,631	**55.9%**	-0.5	357,000	206,745	**57.9%**	1.5	383,000	230,048	**60.1%**	3.7	416,000	233,642	**56.2%**	-0.2
NEW JERSEY																			
NEW MEXICO	375,000	180,205	**48.1%**	427,000	193,956	**45.4%**	-2.6	477,000	205,048	**43.0%**	-5.1	509,000	247,135	**48.6%**	0.5	534,000	260,232	**48.7%**	0.7
NEW YORK	9,827,000	5,308,889	**54.0%**	10,051,000	5,161,942	**51.4%**	-2.7	10,266,000	5,712,665	**55.6%**	1.6	10,657,000	5,805,631	**54.5%**	0.5	11,128,000	6,031,585	**54.2%**	0.2

State Gubernatorial General Elections *(continued)*

Election Years 1950–1966 *(continued)*

State	1950 Voting-age population	1950 Turnout	1950 %.	1954 Voting-age population	1954 Turnout	1954 %.	1954 Difference from 1950	1958 Voting-age population	1958 Turnout	1958 %	1958 Difference from 1950	1962 Voting-age population	1962 Turnout	1962 %	1962 Difference from 1950	1966 Voting-age population	1966 Turnout	1966 %.	1966 Difference from 1950
NORTH CAROLINA																			
NORTH DAKOTA	358,000	183,772	51.3%	354,000	193,501	54.7%	3.3	351,000	210,599	60.0%	8.7	351,000	228,509	65.1%	13.8				
OHIO	5,214,000	2,892,819	55.5%	5,454,000	2,597,790	47.6%	-7.9	5,682,000	3,284,134	57.8%	2.3	5,920,000	3,116,711	52.6%	-2.8	6,161,000	2,887,331	46.9%	-8.6
OKLAHOMA	1,378,000	644,276	46.8%	1,392,000	609,194	43.8%	-3.0	1,406,000	538,839	38.3%	-8.4	1,457,000	709,763	48.7%	2.0	1,528,000	677,258	44.3%	-2.4
OREGON	985,000	505,910	51.4%	1,010,000	566,701	55.8%	4.4	1,045,000	599,994	57.4%	6.1	1,117,000	637,407	57.1%	5.7	1,210,000	682,862	56.4%	5.1
PENNSYLVANIA	6,838,000	3,540,059	51.8%	6,899,000	3,720,457	53.9%	2.2	6,958,000	3,986,918	57.3%	5.5	7,081,000	4,378,042	61.8%	10.1	7,234,000	4,050,668	56.0%	4.2
RHODE ISLAND	514,000	296,808	57.7%	517,000	328,670	63.6%	5.8	520,000	346,780	66.7%	8.9	540,000	327,506	60.6%	2.9	568,000	332,064	58.5%	0.7
SOUTH CAROLINA	1,155,000	50,642	4.4%	1,203,000	214,212	17.8%	13.4	1,248,000	77,740	6.2%	1.8	1,319,000	253,721	19.2%	14.9	1,401,000	439,942	31.4%	27.0
SOUTH DAKOTA	396,000	253,316	64.0%	393,000	236,255	60.1%	-3.9	390,000	258,281	66.2%	2.3	388,000	256,120	66.0%	2.0	387,000	228,214	59.0%	-5.0
TENNESSEE	1,980,000	236,194	11.9%	2,027,000	322,586	15.9%	4.0	2,073,000	432,545	20.9%	8.9	2,166,000	621,064	28.7%	16.7	2,284,000	656,566	28.7%	16.8
TEXAS	4,635,000	374,747	8.1%	4,970,000	636,892	12.8%	4.7	5,293,000	789,133	14.9%	6.8	5,717,000	1,569,181	27.4%	19.4	6,187,000	1,425,861	23.0%	15.0
UTAH																			
VERMONT	229,000	87,155	38.1%	227,000	114,360	50.4%	12.3	225,000	123,728	55.0%	16.9	234,000	121,422	51.9%	13.8	240,000	136,262	54.7%	16.7
VIRGINIA																			
WASHINGTON																			
WEST VIRGINIA																			
WISCONSIN	2,192,000	1,138,148	51.9%	2,250,000	1,158,666	51.5%	-0.4	2,306,000	1,202,219	52.1%	0.2	2,397,000	1,265,900	52.8%	0.9	2,505,000	1,170,173	46.7%	-5.2
WYOMING	176,000	96,959	55.1%	181,000	111,438	61.6%	6.5	186,000	112,537	60.5%	5.4	190,000	119,268	62.8%	7.7	193,000	120,873	62.6%	7.5
Total	66,391,000	29,940,102	45.1%	71,636,000	31,745,654	44.3%	-0.8	72,186,000	34,775,498	48.2%	3.1	76,741,000	38,407,455	50.0%	5.0	85,159,000	41,543,245	48.8%	3.7

*Percentage point difference between turnout in current year and initial year listed in chart. If data do not appear for a state in the initial year listed, the difference is calculated from the first year in which data do appear for that state.

STATE GUBERNATORIAL GENERAL ELECTIONS

Republican Turnout for Election Years 1950–1966

State	1950 Voting-age population	1950 Turnout	1950 %	1954 Voting-age population	1954 Turnout	1954 %	1954 Difference from 1950*	1958 Voting-age population	1958 Turnout	1958 %	1958 Difference from 1950	1962 Voting-age population	1962 Turnout	1962 %	1962 Difference from 1950	1966 Voting-age population	1966 Turnout	1966 %	1966 Difference from 1950
ALABAMA	1,749,000	15,177	0.9%	1,785,000	88,688	5.0%	4.1	1,819,000	30,415	1.7%	0.8					1,958,000	262,943	13.4%	12.6
ALASKA								127,000	19,299	15.2%		144,000	27,054	18.8%	3.6	162,000	33,145	20.5%	5.3
ARIZONA	438,000	99,109	22.6%	559,000	115,866	20.7%	-1.9	673,000	160,136	23.8%	1.2	798,000	200,578	25.1%	2.5	926,000	203,438	22.0%	-0.7
ARKANSAS	1,106,000	50,309	4.5%	1,076,000	127,004	11.8%	7.3	1,047,000	50,288	4.8%	0.3	1,075,000	82,349	7.7%	3.1	1,126,000	306,324	27.2%	22.7
CALIFORNIA	6,975,000	2,461,754	35.3%	7,895,000	2,290,519	29.0%	-6.3	8,777,000	2,110,911	24.1%	-11.2	9,933,000	2,740,351	27.6%	-7.7	11,212,000	3,742,913	33.4%	-1.9
COLORADO	838,000	236,472	28.2%	910,000	227,335	25.0%	-3.2	981,000	288,643	29.4%	1.2	1,086,000	349,342	32.2%	3.9	1,205,000	356,730	29.6%	1.4
CONNECTICUT	1,311,000	436,418	33.3%	1,401,000	460,528	32.9%	-0.4	1,488,000	360,644	24.2%	-9.1	1,612,000	482,852	30.0%	-3.3	1,753,000	446,536	25.5%	-7.8
DELAWARE																			
DISTRICT OF COLUMBIA																			
FLORIDA				2,351,000	69,852	3.0%										3,906,000	821,190	21.0%	18.1
GEORGIA																2,760,000	453,665	16.4%	
HAWAII												364,000	81,707	22.4%		401,000	104,324	26.0%	3.6
IDAHO	345,000	107,642	31.2%	355,000	124,038	34.9%		365,000	121,810	33.4%	2.2	380,000	139,578	36.7%	5.5	397,000	104,586	26.3%	-4.9
ILLINOIS																			
INDIANA																			
IOWA	1,675,000	506,642	30.2%	1,664,000	435,944	26.2%	-4.0	1,654,000	394,071	23.8%	-6.4	1,665,000	388,955	23.4%	-6.9	1,684,000	394,518	23.4%	-6.8
KANSAS	1,236,000	333,001	26.9%	1,269,000	329,868	26.0%	-0.9	1,302,000	313,036	24.0%	-2.9	1,329,000	341,257	25.7%	-1.3	1,353,000	304,325	22.5%	-4.4
KENTUCKY																			
LOUISIANA																			
MAINE	553,000	145,823	26.4%	557,000	113,298	20.3%	-6.0	561,000	134,572	24.0%	-2.4	572,000	146,604	25.6%	-0.7	585,000	151,802	25.9%	-0.4
MARYLAND	1,519,000	369,807	24.3%	1,648,000	381,451	23.1%	-1.2	1,772,000	278,173	15.7%	-8.6	1,958,000	343,051	17.5%	-6.8	2,170,000	455,318	21.0%	-3.4
MASSACHUSETTS	3,042,000	824,069	27.1%	3,070,000	985,339	32.1%	5.0	3,095,000	818,463	26.4%	-0.6	3,214,000	1,047,891	32.6%	5.5	3,377,000	1,277,358	37.8%	10.7
MICHIGAN	3,992,000	933,998	23.4%	4,199,000	963,300	22.9%	-0.5	4,396,000	1,078,089	24.5%	1.1	4,648,000	1,420,086	30.6%	7.2	4,923,000	1,490,430	30.3%	6.9
MINNESOTA	1,879,000	635,800	33.8%	1,922,000	538,865	28.0%	-5.8	1,962,000	490,731	25.0%	-8.8	2,041,000	619,751	30.4%	-3.5	2,140,000	680,593	31.8%	-2.0
MISSISSIPPI																			
MISSOURI																			
MONTANA																			
NEBRASKA	846,000	247,081	29.2%	847,000	250,080	29.5%	0.3	849,000	209,705	24.7%	-4.5	861,000	221,885	25.8%	-3.4	880,000	299,245	34.0%	4.8
NEVADA	107,000	35,609	33.3%	136,000	41,665	30.6%	-2.6	162,000	34,025	21.0%	-12.3	205,000	32,145	15.7%	-17.6	256,000	71,807	28.0%	-5.2
NEW HAMPSHIRE	339,000	108,907	32.1%	348,000	107,287	30.8%	-1.3	357,000	106,790	29.9%	-2.2	383,000	94,567	24.7%	-7.4	416,000	107,259	25.8%	-6.3
NEW JERSEY																			
NEW MEXICO	375,000	96,846	25.8%	427,000	83,373	19.5%	-6.3	477,000	101,567	21.3%	-4.5	509,000	116,184	22.8%	-3.0	534,000	134,625	25.2%	-0.6
NEW YORK	9,827,000	2,819,523	28.7%	10,051,000	2,549,613	25.4%	-3.3	10,266,000	3,126,929	30.5%	1.8	10,657,000	3,081,587	28.9%	0.2	11,128,000	2,690,626	24.2%	-4.5

State Gubernatorial General Elections (continued)

Republican Turnout for Election Years 1950–1966 (continued)

State	1950 Voting-age population	Turnout	%	1954 Voting-age population	Turnout	%	Difference from 1950	1958 Voting-age population	Turnout	%	Difference from 1950	1962 Voting-age population	Turnout	%	Difference from 1950	1966 Voting-age population	Turnout	%	Difference from 1950
NORTH CAROLINA																			
NORTH DAKOTA	358,000	121,822	34.0%	354,000	124,253	35.1%	1.1	351,000	111,836	31.9%	-2.2	351,000	113,251	32.3%	-1.8				
OHIO	5,214,000	1,370,570	26.3%	5,454,000	1,192,528	21.9%	-4.4	5,682,000	1,414,874	24.9%	-1.4	5,920,000	1,836,190	31.0%	4.7	6,161,000	1,795,277	29.1%	2.9
OKLAHOMA	1,378,000	313,205	22.7%	1,392,000	251,808	18.1%	-4.6	1,406,000	107,495	7.6%	-15.1	1,457,000	392,316	26.9%	4.2	1,528,000	377,078	24.7%	1.9
OREGON	985,000	334,160	33.9%	1,010,000	322,622	31.7%	-2.2	1,045,000	331,900	31.8%	-2.2	1,117,000	345,497	30.9%	-3.0	1,210,000	377,346	31.2%	-2.7
PENNSYLVANIA	6,838,000	1,796,119	26.3%	6,899,000	1,717,070	24.9%	-1.4	6,958,000	1,948,769	28.0%	1.7	7,081,000	2,424,918	34.2%	8.0	7,234,000	2,110,349	29.2%	2.9
RHODE ISLAND	514,000	120,683	23.5%	517,000	137,131	26.5%	3.0	520,000	176,505	33.9%	10.5	540,000	163,952	30.4%	6.9	568,000	210,202	37.0%	13.5
SOUTH CAROLINA																1,401,000	184,088	13.1%	
SOUTH DAKOTA	396,000	154,254	39.0%	393,000	133,878	34.1%	-4.9	390,000	125,520	32.2%	-6.8	388,000	143,682	37.0%	-1.9	387,000	131,710	34.0%	-4.9
TENNESSEE								2,073,000	35,938	1.7%		2,166,000	100,190	4.6%	2.9				
TEXAS	4,635,000	39,737	0.9%	4,970,000	66,154	1.3%	0.5	5,293,000	94,098	1.8%	0.9	5,717,000	715,025	12.5%	11.6	6,187,000	368,025	5.9%	5.1
UTAH																			
VERMONT	229,000	64,915	28.3%	227,000	59,778	26.3%	-2.0	225,000	62,222	27.7%	-0.7	234,000	60,035	25.7%	-2.7	240,000	57,577	23.1%	-5.2
VIRGINIA																			
WASHINGTON																			
WEST VIRGINIA																			
WISCONSIN	2,192,000	605,649	27.6%	2,250,000	596,158	26.5%	-1.1	2,306,000	556,391	24.1%	-3.5	2,397,000	625,536	26.1%	-1.5	2,505,000	626,041	25.0%	-2.6
WYOMING	176,000	54,441	30.9%	181,000	56,275	31.1%	0.2	186,000	52,488	28.2%	-2.7	190,000	64,970	34.2%	3.3	193,000	65,624	34.0%	3.1
Total	61,067,000	15,439,542	25.3%	66,123,000	14,941,468	22.6%	-2.7	68,565,000	15,246,333	22.2%	-3.0	70,992,000	18,943,336	26.7%	1.4	82,875,000	21,197,017	25.6%	0.3

Democratic Turnout for Election Years 1950–1966

State	1950 Voting-age population	Turnout	%	1954 Voting-age population	Turnout	%	Difference from 1950*	1958 Voting-age population	Turnout	%	Difference from 1950	1962 Voting-age population	Turnout	%	Difference from 1950	1966 Voting-age population	Turnout	%	Difference from 1950
ALABAMA	1,749,000	155,414	8.9%	1,785,000	244,401	13.7%	4.8	1,819,000	239,633	13.2%	4.3	1,882,000	303,987	16.2%	7.3	1,958,000	537,505	27.5%	18.6
ALASKA								127,000	29,189	23.0%		144,000	29,627	20.6%	-2.4	162,000	32,065	19.8%	-3.2
ARIZONA	438,000	96,118	21.9%	559,000	128,104	22.9%	1.0	673,000	130,329	19.4%	-2.6	798,000	165,263	20.7%	-1.2	926,000	174,904	18.9%	-3.1
ARKANSAS	1,106,000	266,778	24.1%	1,076,000	208,121	19.3%	-4.8	1,047,000	236,598	22.6%	-1.5	1,075,000	225,743	21.0%	-3.1	1,126,000	257,203	22.8%	-1.3
CALIFORNIA	6,975,000	1,333,856	19.1%	7,895,000	1,739,368	22.0%	2.9	8,777,000	3,140,076	35.8%	16.7	9,933,000	3,037,109	30.6%	11.5	11,212,000	2,749,174	24.5%	5.4
COLORADO	838,000	212,976	25.4%	910,000	262,205	28.8%	3.4	981,000	321,165	32.7%	7.3	1,086,000	262,890	24.2%	-1.2	1,205,000	287,132	23.8%	-1.6
CONNECTICUT	1,311,000	419,404	32.0%	1,401,000	463,643	33.1%	1.1	1,488,000	607,012	40.8%	8.8	1,612,000	549,027	34.1%	2.1	1,753,000	561,599	32.0%	0.0
DELAWARE																			
DISTRICT OF COLUMBIA																			
FLORIDA				2,351,000	287,769	12.2%										3,906,000	668,233	17.1%	4.9

State Gubernatorial General Elections (continued)

State Gubernatorial General Elections *(continued)*

Democratic Turnout for Election Years 1950–1966 *(continued)*

State	1950 Voting-age population	1950 Turnout	1950 %	1954 Voting-age population	1954 Turnout	1954 %	1954 Difference from 1950	1958 Voting-age population	1958 Turnout	1958 %	1958 Difference from 1950	1962 Voting-age population	1962 Turnout	1962 %	1962 Difference from 1950	1966 Voting-age population	1966 Turnout	1966 %	1966 Difference from 1950
GEORGIA	2,189,000	230,771	10.5%	2,283,000	331,899	14.5%	4.0	2,373,000	168,414	7.1%	-3.4	2,548,000	311,524	12.2%	1.7	2,760,000	450,626	16.3%	5.8
HAWAII												364,000	114,308	31.4%		401,000	108,840	27.1%	-4.3
IDAHO	345,000	97,150	28.2%	355,000	104,647	29.5%		365,000	117,236	32.1%	4.0	380,000	115,876	30.5%	2.3	397,000	93,744	23.6%	-4.5
ILLINOIS																			
INDIANA																			
IOWA	1,675,000	347,176	20.7%	1,664,000	410,255	24.7%	3.9	1,654,000	465,024	28.1%	7.4	1,665,000	430,899	25.9%	5.2	1,684,000	494,259	29.4%	8.6
KANSAS	1,236,000	275,494	22.3%	1,269,000	286,218	22.6%	0.3	1,302,000	415,506	31.9%	9.6	1,329,000	291,285	21.9%	-0.4	1,353,000	380,030	28.1%	5.8
KENTUCKY																			
LOUISIANA																			
MAINE	553,000	94,300	17.1%	557,000	76,544	13.7%	-3.3	561,000	145,673	26.0%	8.9	572,000	146,121	25.5%	8.5	585,000	172,036	29.4%	12.4
MARYLAND	1,519,000	275,824	18.2%	1,648,000	319,033	19.4%	1.2	1,772,000	485,061	27.4%	9.2	1,958,000	432,045	22.1%	3.9	2,170,000	373,543	17.2%	-0.9
MASSACHUSETTS	3,042,000	1,074,570	35.3%	3,070,000	910,087	29.6%	-5.7	3,095,000	1,067,020	34.5%	-0.8	3,214,000	1,053,322	32.8%	-2.6	3,377,000	752,720	22.3%	-13.0
MICHIGAN	3,992,000	935,152	23.4%	4,199,000	1,216,308	29.0%	5.5	4,396,000	1,225,533	27.9%	4.5	4,648,000	1,339,513	28.8%	5.4	4,923,000	963,383	19.6%	-3.9
MINNESOTA	1,879,000	400,637	21.3%	1,922,000	607,099	31.6%	10.3	1,962,000	685,326	34.9%	13.6	2,041,000	619,842	30.4%	9.0	2,140,000	607,943	28.4%	7.1
MISSISSIPPI																			
MISSOURI																			
MONTANA																			
NEBRASKA	846,000	202,638	24.0%	847,000	164,753	19.5%	-4.5	849,000	211,345	24.9%	0.9	861,000	242,669	28.2%	4.2	880,000	186,985	21.2%	-2.7
NEVADA	107,000	26,164	24.5%	136,000	36,797	27.1%	2.6	162,000	50,864	31.4%	6.9	205,000	64,784	31.6%	7.1	256,000	65,870	25.7%	1.3
NEW HAMPSHIRE	339,000	82,258	24.3%	348,000	87,344	25.1%	0.8	357,000	99,955	28.0%	3.7	383,000	135,481	35.4%	11.1	416,000	125,882	30.3%	6.0
NEW JERSEY																			
NEW MEXICO	375,000	83,359	22.2%	427,000	110,583	25.9%	3.7	477,000	103,481	21.7%	-0.5	509,000	130,933	25.7%	3.5	534,000	125,587	23.5%	1.3
NEW YORK	9,827,000	2,246,855	22.9%	10,051,000	2,560,738	25.5%	2.6	10,266,000	2,553,895	24.9%	2.0	10,657,000	2,552,418	24.0%	1.1	11,128,000	2,298,363	20.7%	-2.2
NORTH CAROLINA																			
NORTH DAKOTA	358,000	61,950	17.3%	354,000	69,248	19.6%	2.3	351,000	98,763	28.1%	10.8	351,000	115,258	32.8%	15.5				
OHIO	5,214,000	1,522,249	29.2%	5,454,000	1,405,262	25.8%	-3.4	5,682,000	1,869,260	32.9%	3.7	5,920,000	1,280,521	21.6%	-7.6	6,161,000	1,092,054	17.7%	-11.5
OKLAHOMA	1,378,000	329,308	23.9%	1,392,000	357,386	25.7%	1.8	1,406,000	399,504	28.4%	4.5	1,457,000	315,357	21.6%	-2.3	1,528,000	296,328	19.4%	-4.5
OREGON	985,000	171,750	17.4%	1,016,000	244,179	24.0%	6.6	1,045,000	267,934	25.6%	8.2	1,117,000	265,359	23.8%	6.3	1,210,000	305,008	25.2%	7.8
PENNSYLVANIA	6,838,000	1,710,355	25.0%	6,899,000	1,996,266	28.9%	3.9	6,958,000	2,024,852	29.1%	4.1	7,081,000	1,938,627	27.4%	2.4	7,234,000	1,868,719	25.8%	0.8
RHODE ISLAND	514,000	176,125	34.3%	517,000	189,595	36.7%	2.4	520,000	170,275	32.7%	-1.5	540,000	163,554	30.3%	-4.0	568,000	121,862	21.5%	-12.8
SOUTH CAROLINA	1,155,000	50,633	4.4%	1,203,000	214,204	17.8%	13.4	1,248,000	77,714	6.2%	1.8	1,319,000	253,704	19.2%	14.9	1,401,000	255,854	18.3%	13.9
SOUTH DAKOTA	396,000	99,062	25.0%	393,000	102,377	26.1%	1.0	390,000	132,761	34.0%	9.0	388,000	112,438	29.0%	4.0	387,000	96,504	24.9%	-0.1
TENNESSEE	1,980,000	184,437	9.3%	2,027,000	281,291	13.9%	4.6	2,073,000	248,874	12.0%	2.7	2,166,000	315,648	14.6%	5.3	2,284,000	532,998	23.3%	14.0

State Gubernatorial General Elections (continued)

Democratic Turnout for Election Years 1950–1966 (continued)

State	1950 Voting-age population	Turnout	%	1954 Voting-age population	Turnout	%	Difference from 1950	1958 Voting-age population	Turnout	%	Difference from 1950	1962 Voting-age population	Turnout	%	Difference from 1950	1966 Voting-age population	Turnout	%	Difference from 1950
TEXAS	4,635,000	335,010	**7.2%**	4,970,000	569,533	**11.5%**	4.2	5,293,000	695,035	**13.1%**	5.9	5,717,000	847,036	**14.8%**	7.6	6,187,000	1,037,517	**16.8%**	9.5
UTAH																			
VERMONT	229,000	22,227	**9.7%**	227,000	54,554	**24.0%**	14.3	225,000	61,503	**27.3%**	17.6	234,000	61,383	**26.2%**	16.5	249,000	78,669	**31.6%**	21.9
VIRGINIA																			
WASHINGTON																			
WEST VIRGINIA																			
WISCONSIN	2,192,000	525,319	**24.0%**	2,250,000	560,747	**24.9%**	1.0	2,306,000	644,296	**27.9%**	4.0	2,397,000	637,491	**26.6%**	2.6	2,505,000	539,258	**21.5%**	-2.4
WYOMING	176,000	42,518	**24.2%**	181,000	55,163	**30.5%**	6.3	186,000	55,070	**29.6%**	5.4	190,000	54,298	**28.6%**	4.4	193,000	55,249	**28.6%**	4.5
Total	66,391,000	14,087,837	**21.2%**	71,636,000	16,655,721	**23.3%**	2.0	72,186,000	19,244,176	**26.7%**	5.4	76,741,000	18,915,340	**24.6%**	3.4	85,159,000	18,747,646	**22.0%**	0.8

Other Turnout for Election Years 1950–1966

State	1950 Voting-age population	Turnout	%	1954 Voting-age population	Turnout	%	Difference from 1950*	1958 Voting-age population	Turnout	%	Difference from 1950	1962 Voting-age population	Turnout	%	Difference from 1950	1966 Voting-age population	Turnout	%	Difference from 1950
ALABAMA				1,785,000	1	**0.0%**		1,819,000	904	**0.0%**	0.0	1,882,000	11,789	**0.6%**	0.6	1,958,000	47,653	**2.4%**	2.4
ALASKA								127,000	480	**0.4%**						162,000	1,084	**0.7%**	0.3
ARIZONA																			
ARKANSAS				1,076,000	51	**0.0%**													
CALIFORNIA	6,975,000	480	**0.0%**	7,895,000	481	**0.0%**	0.0	8,777,000	4,790	**0.1%**	0.0	9,933,000	75,010	**0.8%**	0.8	11,212,000	11,358	**0.1%**	0.1
COLORADO	838,000	1,546	**0.2%**									1,086,000	4,249	**0.4%**	0.2	1,205,000	16,201	**1.3%**	1.2
CONNECTICUT	1,311,000	22,913	**1.7%**	1,401,000	12,582	**0.9%**	-0.8	1,488,000	6,853	**0.5%**	-1.3	1,612,000	23	**0.0%**	-1.7	1,753,000	422	**0.0%**	-1.7
DELAWARE																			
DISTRICT OF COLUMBIA																			
FLORIDA				2,351,000	162	**0.0%**										3,906,000	238	**0.0%**	0.0
GEORGIA	2,189,000	3,659	**0.2%**	2,283,000	67	**0.0%**	-0.2	2,373,000	83	**0.0%**	-0.2	2,548,000	167	**0.0%**	-0.2	2,760,000	70,728	**2.6%**	2.4
HAWAII																			
IDAHO																397,000	54,263	**13.7%**	
ILLINOIS																			
INDIANA																			
IOWA	1,675,000	3,395	**0.2%**	1,664,000	2,393	**0.1%**	-0.1									1,684,000	4,398	**0.3%**	0.1
KANSAS	1,236,000	10,815	**0.9%**	1,269,000	6,547	**0.5%**	-0.4	1,302,000	7,397	**0.6%**	-0.3	1,329,000	6,256	**0.5%**	-0.4	1,353,000	8,600	**0.6%**	-0.2
KENTUCKY																			
LOUISIANA																			
MAINE	553,000	1,054	**0.2%**																

State Gubernatorial General Elections (continued)

Other Turnout for Election Years 1950–1966 (continued)

State	1950 Voting-age population	Turnout	%	1954 Voting-age population	Turnout	%	Difference from 1950	1958 Voting-age population	Turnout	%	Difference from 1950	1962 Voting-age population	Turnout	%	Difference from 1950	1966 Voting-age population	Turnout	%	Difference from 1950
MARYLAND												1,958,000	5	0.0%		2,170,000	89,900	4.1%	4.1
MASSACHUSETTS	3,042,000	11,541	0.4%	3,070,000	8,348	0.3%	-0.1	3,095,000	13,634	0.4%	0.1	3,214,000	7,876	0.2%	-0.1	3,377,000	11,099	0.3%	-0.1
MICHIGAN	3,992,000	10,232	0.3%	4,199,000	7,419	0.2%	-0.1	4,396,000	8,562	0.2%	-0.1	4,648,000	5,240	0.1%	-0.1	4,923,000	8,096	0.2%	-0.1
MINNESOTA	1,879,000	10,195	0.5%	1,922,000	5,453	0.3%	-0.3	1,962,000	10,858	0.6%	0.0	2,041,000	7,311	0.4%	-0.2	2,140,000	6,522	0.3%	-0.2
MISSISSIPPI																			
MISSOURI																			
MONTANA																			
NEBRASKA	846,000	1	0.0%	847,000	8	0.0%	0.0	849,000	17	0.0%	0.0	861,000	31	0.0%	0.0	880,000	166	0.0%	0.0
NEVADA																			
NEW HAMPSHIRE	339,000	74	0.0%													416,000	501	0.1%	0.1
NEW JERSEY																			
NEW MEXICO												509,000	18	0.0%					
NEW YORK	9,827,000	242,511	2.5%	10,051,000	51,591	0.5%	-2.0	10,266,000	31,841	0.3%	-2.2	10,657,000	171,626	1.6%	-0.9	11,128,000	1,042,596	9.4%	6.9
NORTH CAROLINA																			
NORTH DAKOTA																			
OHIO																			
OKLAHOMA	1,378,000	1,763	0.1%					1,406,000	31,840	2.3%	2.1	1,457,000	2,090	0.1%	0.0	1,528,000	3,852	0.3%	0.1
OREGON								1,045,000	160	0.0%		1,117,000	26,551	2.4%	2.4	1,210,000	508	0.0%	0.0
PENNSYLVANIA	6,838,000	33,585	0.5%	6,899,000	7,121	0.1%	-0.4	6,958,000	13,297	0.2%	-0.3	7,081,000	14,497	0.2%	-0.3	7,234,000	71,600	1.0%	0.5
RHODE ISLAND				517,000	1,944	0.4%													
SOUTH CAROLINA	1,155,000	9	0.0%	1,203,000	8	0.0%	0.0	1,248,000	26	0.0%	0.0	1,319,000	17	0.0%	0.0				
SOUTH DAKOTA																			
TENNESSEE	1,980,000	51,757	2.6%	2,027,000	41,295	2.0%	-0.6	2,073,000	147,733	7.1%	4.5	2,166,000	205,226	9.5%	6.9	2,284,000	123,568	5.4%	2.8
TEXAS				4,970,000	1,205	0.0%						5,717,000	7,120	0.1%	0.1	6,187,000	20,319	0.3%	0.3
UTAH																			
VERMONT	229,000	13	0.0%	227,000	28	0.0%	0.0	225,000	3	0.0%	0.0	234,000	4	0.0%	0.0	249,000	16	0.0%	0.0
VIRGINIA																			
WASHINGTON																			
WEST VIRGINIA																			
WISCONSIN	2,192,000	7,180	0.3%	2,250,000	1,761	0.1%	-0.2	2,306,000	1,532	0.1%	-0.3	2,397,000	2,873	0.1%	-0.2	2,505,000	4,874	0.2%	-0.1
WYOMING								186,000	4,979	2.7%									
Total	48,474,000	412,723	0.9%	57,906,000	148,465	0.3%	-0.6	51,901,000	284,989	0.5%	-0.3	63,766,000	548,779	0.9%	0.0	72,621,000	1,598,562	2.2%	1.3

*Percentage point difference between turnout in current year and initial year listed in chart. If data do not appear for a state in the initial year listed, the difference is calculated from the first year in which data do appear for that state.

UNITED STATES SENATE GENERAL ELECTIONS

Election Years 1950–1966

State	1950 Voting-age population	Turnout	%	1954 Voting-age population	Turnout	%	Difference from 1950*	1958 Voting-age population	Turnout	%	Difference from 1950	1962 Voting-age population	Turnout	%	Difference from 1950	1966 Voting-age population	Turnout	%	Difference from 1950
ALABAMA	1,749,000	164,011	9.4%	1,785,000	314,459	17.6%	8.2					1,882,000	397,079	21.1%	11.7	1,958,000	802,608	41.0%	31.6
ALASKA								127,000	49,525	39.0%		144,000	58,181	40.4%	1.4	162,000	65,250	40.3%	1.3
ARIZONA	438,000	185,092	42.3%					673,000	293,623	43.6%	1.4	798,000	362,605	45.4%	3.2				
ARKANSAS	1,106,000	302,582	27.4%	1,076,000	291,058	27.1%	-0.3					1,075,000	312,880	29.1%	1.7				
CALIFORNIA	6,975,000	3,686,315	52.9%					8,777,000	5,135,221	58.5%	5.7	9,933,000	5,647,952	56.9%	4.0				
COLORADO	838,000	450,176	53.7%	910,000	484,188	53.2%	-0.5					1,086,000	613,444	56.6%	2.8	1,205,000	634,898	52.7%	-0.5
CONNECTICUT	1,311,000	877,827	67.0%					1,488,000	968,506	65.1%	-1.9	1,612,000	1,029,301	63.9%	-3.1				
DELAWARE				231,000	144,900	62.7%		251,000	154,432	61.5%	-1.2					302,000	164,549	54.5%	-8.2
DISTRICT OF COLUMBIA																			
FLORIDA	1,859,000	313,487	16.9%					2,822,000	542,069	19.2%	2.3	3,351,000	939,207	28.0%	11.2				
GEORGIA	2,189,000	261,293	11.9%	2,283,000	333,936	14.6%	2.7					2,548,000	306,250	12.0%	0.1	2,760,000	622,371	22.5%	10.6
HAWAII								337,000	164,808	48.9%		364,000	196,361	53.9%	5.0				
IDAHO	345,000	201,417	58.4%	355,000	226,408	63.8%	5.4					380,000	258,786	68.1%	9.7	397,000	252,456	63.6%	5.2
ILLINOIS	5,820,000	3,622,673	62.2%	5,953,000	3,368,025	56.6%	-5.7					6,295,000	3,709,216	58.9%	-3.3	6,549,000	3,822,725	58.4%	-3.9
INDIANA	2,545,000	1,598,724	62.8%					2,727,000	1,724,598	63.2%	0.4	2,842,000	1,800,038	63.3%	0.5				
IOWA	1,675,000	858,523	51.3%	1,664,000	847,355	50.9%	-0.3					1,665,000	807,972	48.5%	-2.7	1,684,000	857,496	50.9%	-0.3
KANSAS	1,236,000	619,104	50.1%	1,269,000	618,063	48.7%	-1.4					1,329,000	622,232	46.8%	-3.3	1,353,000	671,345	49.6%	-0.5
KENTUCKY	1,739,000	617,113	35.5%	1,748,000	797,057	45.6%	10.1					1,950,000	820,088	42.1%	6.6	2,032,000	749,884	36.9%	1.4
LOUISIANA	1,590,000	251,838	15.8%	1,679,000	207,115	12.3%	-3.5					1,861,000	421,904	22.7%	6.8	1,961,000	437,695	22.3%	6.5
MAINE				557,000	246,605	44.3%		561,000	284,364	50.7%	6.4					585,000	319,535	54.6%	10.3
MARYLAND	1,519,000	615,614	40.5%					1,772,000	749,291	42.3%	1.8	1,958,000	714,248	36.5%	-4.0				
MASSACHUSETTS				3,070,000	1,892,710	61.7%		3,095,000	1,862,041	60.2%	-1.5	3,214,000	2,097,085	65.2%	3.6	3,377,000	1,999,949	59.2%	-2.4
MICHIGAN				4,199,000	2,144,840	51.1%		4,396,000	2,271,644	51.7%	0.6					4,923,000	2,439,365	49.6%	-1.5
MINNESOTA				1,922,000	1,138,952	59.3%		1,962,000	1,150,883	58.7%	-0.6					2,140,000	1,271,426	59.4%	0.2
MISSISSIPPI				1,187,000	105,526	8.9%		1,172,000	61,039	5.2%	-3.7					1,218,000	393,900	32.3%	23.4
MISSOURI	2,623,000	1,279,631	48.8%					2,669,000	1,173,930	44.0%	-4.8	2,731,000	1,222,259	44.8%	-4.0				
MONTANA				374,000	227,454	60.8%		382,000	229,483	60.1%	-0.7					399,000	259,863	65.1%	4.3
NEBRASKA				847,000	418,685	49.4%		849,000	417,379	49.2%	-0.3					880,000	485,101	55.1%	5.7
NEVADA	107,000	61,762	57.7%					162,000	84,492	52.2%	-5.6	205,000	97,192	47.4%	-10.3				
NEW HAMPSHIRE	339,000	190,573	56.2%	348,000	194,536	55.9%	-0.3					383,000	224,479	58.6%	2.4	416,000	229,305	55.1%	-1.1
NEW JERSEY				3,453,000	1,770,557	51.3%		3,652,000	1,881,329	51.5%	0.2					4,218,000	2,131,188	50.5%	-0.7
NEW MEXICO				427,000	194,422	45.5%		477,000	203,323	42.6%	-2.9					534,000	258,203	48.4%	2.8
NEW YORK	9,827,000	5,228,403	53.2%					10,266,000	5,601,979	54.6%	1.4	10,657,000	5,700,186	53.5%	0.3				

United States Senate General Elections (continued)

United States Senate General Elections (continued)

Election Years 1950–1966 (continued)

State	1950 Voting-age population	1950 Turnout	1950 %	1954 Voting-age population	1954 Turnout	1954 %	1954 Difference from 1950	1958 Voting-age population	1958 Turnout	1958 %	1958 Difference from 1950	1962 Voting-age population	1962 Turnout	1962 %	1962 Difference from 1950	1966 Voting-age population	1966 Turnout	1966 %	1966 Difference from 1950
NORTH CAROLINA	2,319,000	548,277	23.6%	2,421,000	619,634	25.6%	2.0					2,674,000	813,155	30.4%	6.8	2,856,000	901,978	31.6%	7.9
NORTH DAKOTA	358,000	186,716	52.2%					351,000	204,635	58.3%	6.1	351,000	223,737	63.7%	11.6				
OHIO	5,214,000	2,860,102	54.9%					5,682,000	3,149,410	55.4%	0.6	5,920,000	2,994,986	50.6%	-4.3				
OKLAHOMA	1,378,000	631,177	45.8%	1,392,000	600,120	43.1%	-2.7					1,457,000	664,712	45.6%	-0.2	1,528,000	638,742	41.8%	-4.0
OREGON	985,000	503,455	51.1%	1,016,000	569,088	56.0%	4.9					1,117,000	636,558	57.0%	5.9	1,210,000	685,067	56.6%	5.5
PENNSYLVANIA	6,838,000	3,548,642	51.9%					6,958,000	3,988,622	57.3%	5.4	7,081,000	4,383,475	61.9%	10.0				
RHODE ISLAND				517,000	326,624	63.2%		520,000	344,519	66.3%	3.1					568,000	324,173	57.1%	-6.1
SOUTH CAROLINA	1,155,000	50,277	4.4%	1,203,000	227,232	18.9%	14.5					1,319,000	312,647	23.7%	19.4	1,401,000	436,252	31.1%	26.8
SOUTH DAKOTA	396,000	251,362	63.5%	393,000	235,745	60.0%	-3.5					388,000	254,319	65.5%	2.1	387,000	227,080	58.7%	-4.8
TENNESSEE				2,027,000	356,092	17.6%		2,073,000	401,666	19.4%	1.8					2,284,000	866,961	38.0%	20.4
TEXAS				4,970,000	636,475	12.8%		5,293,000	787,128	14.9%	2.1					6,187,000	1,493,182	24.1%	11.3
UTAH	384,000	264,440	68.9%					445,000	291,311	65.5%	-3.4	486,000	318,411	65.5%	-3.3				
VERMONT	229,000	89,171	38.9%					225,000	124,442	55.3%	16.4	234,000	121,571	52.0%	13.0				
VIRGINIA				2,147,000	306,510	14.3%		2,259,000	457,640	20.3%	6.0					2,629,000	733,879	27.9%	13.6
WASHINGTON	1,518,000	744,783	49.1%					1,650,000	886,822	53.7%	4.7	1,777,000	943,229	53.1%	4.0				
WEST VIRGINIA				1,120,000	593,329	53.0%		1,086,000	644,917	59.4%	6.4					1,072,000	491,216	45.8%	-7.2
WISCONSIN	2,192,000	1,116,077	50.9%					2,306,000	1,194,678	51.8%	0.9	2,397,000	1,260,168	52.6%	1.7				
WYOMING				181,000	112,252	62.0%		186,000	114,157	61.4%	-0.6	190,000	119,372	62.8%	0.8	193,000	122,689	63.6%	1.6
Total	68,796,000	32,180,637	46.8%	52,724,000	20,549,952	39.0%	-7.8	77,651,000	37,593,906	48.4%	1.6	83,654,000	41,405,285	49.5%	2.7	59,368,000	25,790,331	43.4%	-3.3

*Percentage point difference between turnout in current year and initial year listed in chart. If data do not appear for a state in the initial year listed, the difference is calculated from the first year in which data do appear for that state.

UNITED STATES SENATE GENERAL ELECTIONS

Republican Turnout for Election Years 1950–1966

State	1950 Voting-age population	Turnout	%	1954 Voting-age population	Turnout	%	Difference from 1950*	1958 Voting-age population	Turnout	%	Difference from 1950	1962 Voting-age population	Turnout	%	Difference from 1950	1966 Voting-age population	Turnout	%	Difference from 1950
ALABAMA				1,785,000	55,110	3.1%						1,882,000	195,134	10.4%	7.3	1,958,000	313,018	16.0%	12.9
ALASKA								127,000	23,462	18.5%		144,000	24,354	16.9%	-1.6	162,000	15,961	9.9%	-8.6
ARIZONA	438,000	68,846	15.7%					673,000	164,593	24.5%	8.7	798,000	163,388	20.5%	4.8				
ARKANSAS												1,075,000	98,013	9.1%					
CALIFORNIA	6,975,000	2,183,454	31.3%					8,777,000	2,204,337	25.1%	-6.2	9,933,000	3,180,483	32.0%	0.7				
COLORADO	838,000	239,734	28.6%	910,000	248,502	27.3%	-1.3					1,086,000	320,055	30.3%	1.7	1,205,000	368,307	30.6%	3.3
CONNECTICUT	1,311,000	409,053	31.2%					1,488,000	410,622	27.6%	3.6	1,612,000	501,694	31.1%	-0.1				
DELAWARE				231,000	62,389	27.0%		251,000	82,280	32.8%	5.8					302,000	97,268	32.2%	5.2
DISTRICT OF COLUMBIA																			
FLORIDA	1,859,000	74,228	4.0%					2,822,000	155,956	5.5%	1.5	3,351,000	281,381	8.4%	4.4				
GEORGIA																			
HAWAII								337,000	87,161	25.9%		364,000	60,067	16.5%	-9.4				
IDAHO	345,000	124,237	36.0%	355,000	142,269	40.1%	4.1					380,000	117,129	30.8%	6.2	397,000	139,819	35.2%	-0.8
ILLINOIS	5,820,000	1,951,984	33.5%	5,953,000	1,563,683	26.3%	-7.3					6,295,000	1,961,202	31.2%	-2.4	6,549,000	2,100,449	32.1%	-1.5
INDIANA	2,545,000	844,303	33.2%					2,727,000	731,635	26.8%	-6.3	2,842,000	894,547	31.5%	-1.7				
IOWA	1,675,000	470,613	28.1%	1,664,000	442,409	26.6%	-1.5					1,665,000	431,364	25.9%	-2.2	1,684,000	522,339	31.0%	2.9
KANSAS	1,236,000	335,880	27.2%	1,269,000	348,144	27.4%	0.3					1,329,000	388,500	29.2%	2.1	1,353,000	350,077	25.9%	-1.3
KENTUCKY	1,739,000	278,368	16.0%	1,748,000	362,948	20.8%	4.8					1,950,000	432,648	22.2%	6.2	2,032,000	483,805	23.8%	7.8
LOUISIANA	1,590,000	30,931	1.9%									1,861,000	103,066	5.5%	3.6				
MAINE				557,000	144,530	25.9%		561,000	111,522	19.9%	-6.1					585,000	188,291	32.2%	6.2
MARYLAND	1,519,000	326,291	21.5%					1,772,000	382,021	21.6%	0.1	1,958,000	270,312	13.8%	-7.7				
MASSACHUSETTS				3,070,000	956,605	31.2%		3,095,000	488,318	15.8%	-15.4	3,214,000	877,669	27.3%	-3.9	3,377,000	1,213,473	35.9%	4.8
MICHIGAN				4,199,000	1,049,420	25.0%		4,396,000	1,046,963	23.8%	-1.2					4,923,000	1,363,530	27.7%	2.7
MINNESOTA				1,922,000	479,619	25.0%		1,962,000	536,629	27.4%	2.4					2,140,000	574,868	26.9%	1.9
MISSISSIPPI				1,187,000	4,678	0.4%										1,218,000	105,150	8.6%	8.2
MISSOURI	2,623,000	593,139	22.6%					2,669,000	393,847	14.8%	-7.9	2,731,000	555,330	20.3%	-2.3				
MONTANA				374,000	112,863	30.2%		382,000	54,573	14.3%	-15.9					399,000	121,697	30.5%	0.3
NEBRASKA				847,000	255,695	30.2%		849,000	232,227	27.4%	-2.8					880,000	296,116	33.6%	3.5
NEVADA	107,000	25,933	24.2%					162,000	35,760	22.1%	-2.2	205,000	33,749	16.5%	-7.8				
NEW HAMPSHIRE	339,000	106,142	31.3%	348,000	117,150	33.7%	2.4					383,000	134,035	35.0%	3.7	416,000	105,241	25.3%	-6.0
NEW JERSEY				3,453,000	861,528	25.0%		3,652,000	882,287	24.2%	-0.8					4,218,000	1,279,343	30.3%	5.4
NEW MEXICO				427,000	83,071	19.5%		477,000	75,827	15.9%	-3.6					534,000	120,988	22.7%	3.2
NEW YORK	9,827,000	2,367,353	24.1%					10,266,000	2,842,942	27.7%	3.6	10,657,000	3,269,417	30.7%	6.6				

United States Senate General Elections (continued)

United States Senate General Elections (continued)

Republican Turnout for Election Years 1950–1946 (continued)

State	1950 Voting-age population	Turnout	%	1954 Voting-age population	Turnout	%	Difference from 1950	1958 Voting-age population	Turnout	%	Difference from 1950	1962 Voting-age population	Turnout	%	Difference from 1950	1966 Voting-age population	Turnout	%	Difference from 1950
NORTH CAROLINA	2,319,000	171,804	7.4%	2,421,000	211,322	8.7%	1.3					2,674,000	321,635	12.0%	4.6	2,856,000	400,502	14.0%	6.6
NORTH DAKOTA	358,000	126,209	35.3%					351,000	117,070	33.4%	-1.9	351,000	135,705	38.7%	3.4				
OHIO	5,214,000	1,645,643	31.6%					5,682,000	1,497,199	26.3%	-5.2	5,920,000	1,151,173	19.4%	-12.1				
OKLAHOMA	1,378,000	285,224	20.7%	1,392,000	262,013	18.8%	-1.9					1,457,000	307,966	21.1%	0.4	1,528,000	295,585	19.3%	-1.4
OREGON	985,000	376,510	38.2%	1,016,000	283,313	27.9%	-10.3					1,117,000	291,587	26.1%	-12.1	1,210,000	354,391	29.3%	-8.9
PENNSYLVANIA	6,838,000	1,820,400	26.6%					6,958,000	2,042,586	29.4%	2.7	7,081,000	2,134,649	30.1%	3.5				
RHODE ISLAND				517,000	132,970	25.7%		520,000	122,353	23.5%	-2.2					568,000	104,838	18.5%	-7.3
SOUTH CAROLINA												1,319,000	133,930	10.2%		1,401,000	271,297	19.4%	9.2
SOUTH DAKOTA	396,000	160,670	40.6%	393,000	135,071	34.4%	-6.2					388,000	126,861	32.7%	-7.9	387,000	150,517	38.9%	-1.7
TENNESSEE				2,027,000	106,971	5.3%		2,073,000	76,371	3.7%	-1.6					2,284,000	483,063	21.1%	15.9
TEXAS				4,970,000	94,131	1.9%		5,293,000	185,926	3.5%	1.6					6,187,000	842,501	13.6%	11.7
UTAH	384,000	142,427	37.1%					445,000	101,471	22.8%	-14.3	486,000	166,755	34.3%	-2.8				
VERMONT	229,000	69,543	30.4%					225,000	64,900	28.8%	-1.5	234,000	81,241	34.7%	4.4				
VIRGINIA																2,629,000	245,681	9.3%	
WASHINGTON	1,518,000	342,464	22.6%					1,650,000	278,271	16.9%	-5.7	1,777,000	446,204	25.1%	2.5				
WEST VIRGINIA				1,120,000	268,066	23.9%		1,086,000	263,172	24.2%	0.3					1,072,000	198,891	18.6%	-5.4
WISCONSIN	2,192,000	595,283	27.2%					2,306,000	510,398	22.1%	-5.0	2,397,000	594,846	24.8%	-2.3				
WYOMING				181,000	54,407	30.1%		186,000	56,122	30.2%	0.1	190,000	69,043	36.3%	6.3	193,000	63,548	32.9%	2.9
Total	62,597,000	16,166,666	25.8%	44,336,000	8,838,877	19.9%	-5.9	74,220,000	16,258,801	21.9%	-3.9	81,106,000	20,263,732	25.0%	-0.8	54,647,000	13,170,554	24.1%	-1.7

Democratic Turnout for Election Years 1950–1966

State	1950 Voting-age population	Turnout	%	1954 Voting-age population	Turnout	%	Difference from 1950*	1958 Voting-age population	Turnout	%	Difference from 1950	1962 Voting-age population	Turnout	%	Difference from 1950	1966 Voting-age population	Turnout	%	Difference from 1950
ALABAMA	1,749,000	125,534	7.2%	1,785,000	259,348	14.5%	7.4					1,882,000	201,937	10.7%	3.6	1,958,000	482,138	24.6%	17.4
ALASKA								127,000	26,063	20.5%		144,000	33,827	23.5%	3.0	162,000	49,289	30.4%	9.9
ARIZONA	438,000	116,246	26.5%					673,000	129,030	19.2%	-7.4	798,000	199,217	25.0%	-1.6				
ARKANSAS	1,106,000	302,582	27.4%	1,076,000	291,058	27.1%	-0.3					1,075,000	214,867	20.0%	-7.4				
CALIFORNIA	6,975,000	1,502,507	21.5%					8,777,000	2,927,693	33.4%	11.8	9,933,000	2,452,839	24.7%	3.2				
COLORADO	838,000	210,442	25.1%	910,000	235,686	25.9%	0.8					1,086,000	279,586	25.7%	0.6	1,205,000	266,259	22.1%	-3.8
CONNECTICUT	1,311,000	453,646	34.6%					1,488,000	554,841	37.3%	2.7	1,612,000	527,522	32.7%	-1.9				
DELAWARE				231,000	82,511	35.7%		251,000	72,152	28.7%	-7.0					302,000	67,281	22.3%	-13.4
DISTRICT OF COLUMBIA																			
FLORIDA	1,859,000	238,987	12.9%					2,822,000	386,113	13.7%	0.8	3,351,000	657,633	19.6%	6.8				

United States Senate General Elections (continued)

Democratic Turnout for Election Years 1950–1966 (continued)

State	1950 Voting-age population	Turnout	%	1954 Voting-age population	Turnout	%	Difference from 1950	1958 Voting-age population	Turnout	%	Difference from 1950	1962 Voting-age population	Turnout	%	Difference from 1950	1966 Voting-age population	Turnout	%	Difference from 1950
GEORGIA	2,189,000	261,290	11.9%	2,283,000	333,917	14.6%	2.7					2,548,000	306,250	12.0%	0.1	2,760,000	622,043	22.5%	10.6
HAWAII								337,000	77,647	23.0%		364,000	136,294	37.4%	14.4				
IDAHO	345,000	77,180	22.4%	355,000	84,139	23.7%	1.3					380,000	141,657	37.3%	14.9	397,000	112,637	28.4%	6.0
ILLINOIS	5,820,000	1,657,630	28.5%	5,953,000	1,804,338	30.3%	1.8					6,295,000	1,748,007	27.8%	-0.7	6,549,000	1,678,147	25.6%	-2.9
INDIANA	2,545,000	741,025	29.1%					2,727,000	973,636	35.7%	6.6	2,842,000	905,491	31.9%	2.7				
IOWA	1,675,000	384,337	22.9%	1,664,000	402,712	24.2%	1.3					1,665,000	370,002	22.6%	-0.3	1,684,000	324,114	19.2%	-3.7
KANSAS	1,236,000	271,365	22.0%	1,269,000	258,575	20.4%	-1.6					1,329,000	223,630	16.8%	-5.1	1,353,000	303,223	22.4%	0.5
KENTUCKY	1,739,000	334,249	19.2%	1,748,000	434,109	24.8%	5.6					1,950,000	387,440	19.9%	0.6	2,032,000	266,079	13.1%	-6.1
LOUISIANA	1,590,000	220,907	13.9%	1,679,000	207,115	12.3%	-1.6					1,861,000	318,838	17.1%	3.2	1,961,000	437,695	22.3%	8.4
MAINE				557,000	102,075	18.3%		561,000	172,842	30.8%	12.5					585,000	131,136	22.4%	4.1
MARYLAND	1,519,000	283,180	18.6%					1,772,000	367,270	20.7%	2.1	1,958,000	443,935	22.7%	4.0				
MASSACHUSETTS				3,070,000	927,899	30.2%		3,095,000	1,362,926	44.0%	13.8	3,214,000	1,162,611	36.2%	5.9	3,377,000	774,761	22.9%	-7.3
MICHIGAN				4,199,000	1,088,550	25.9%		4,396,000	1,216,966	27.7%	1.8					4,923,000	1,069,484	21.7%	-4.2
MINNESOTA				1,922,000	642,193	33.4%		1,962,000	608,847	31.0%	-2.4					2,140,000	685,840	32.0%	-1.4
MISSISSIPPI				1,187,000	100,848	8.5%		1,172,000	61,039	5.2%	-3.3					1,218,000	258,248	21.2%	12.7
MISSOURI	2,623,000	685,732	26.1%					2,669,000	780,083	29.2%	3.1	2,731,000	666,929	24.4%	-1.7				
MONTANA				374,000	114,591	30.6%		382,000	174,910	45.8%	15.1					399,000	138,166	34.6%	4.0
NEBRASKA				847,000	162,990	19.2%		849,000	185,152	21.8%	2.6					880,000	187,950	21.4%	2.1
NEVADA	107,000	35,829	33.5%					162,000	48,732	30.1%	-3.4	205,000	63,443	30.9%	-2.5				
NEW HAMPSHIRE	339,000	72,473	21.4%	348,000	77,386	22.2%	0.9					383,000	90,444	23.6%	2.2	416,000	123,888	29.8%	8.4
NEW JERSEY				3,453,000	858,158	24.9%		3,652,000	966,832	26.5%	1.6					4,218,000	788,021	18.7%	-6.2
NEW MEXICO				427,000	111,351	26.1%		477,000	127,496	26.7%	0.7					534,000	137,205	25.7%	-0.4
NEW YORK	9,827,000	2,632,313	26.8%					10,266,000	2,709,950	26.4%	-0.4	10,657,000	2,289,341	21.5%	-5.3				
NORTH CAROLINA	2,319,000	376,473	16.2%	2,421,000	408,312	16.9%	0.6					2,674,000	491,520	18.4%	2.1	2,856,000	501,440	17.6%	1.3
NORTH DAKOTA	358,000	60,507	16.9%					351,000	84,892	24.2%	7.3	351,000	88,032	25.1%	8.2				
OHIO	5,214,000	1,214,459	23.3%					5,682,000	1,652,211	29.1%	5.8	5,920,000	1,843,813	31.1%	7.9				
OKLAHOMA	1,378,000	345,953	25.1%	1,392,000	335,127	24.1%	-1.0					1,457,000	353,890	24.3%	-0.8	1,528,000	343,157	22.5%	-2.6
OREGON	985,000	116,780	11.9%	1,016,000	285,775	28.1%	16.3					1,117,000	344,716	30.9%	19.0	1,210,000	330,374	27.3%	15.4
PENNSYLVANIA	6,838,000	1,694,076	24.8%					6,958,000	1,929,821	27.7%	3.0	7,081,000	2,238,383	31.6%	6.8				
RHODE ISLAND				517,000	193,654	37.5%		520,000	222,166	42.7%	5.3					568,000	219,331	38.6%	1.2
SOUTH CAROLINA	1,155,000	50,240	4.3%	1,203,000	83,525	6.9%	2.6					1,319,000	178,712	13.5%	9.2	1,401,000	164,955	11.8%	7.4
SOUTH DAKOTA	396,000	90,692	22.9%	393,000	100,674	25.6%	2.7					388,000	127,458	32.9%	9.9	387,000	76,563	19.8%	-3.1
TENNESSEE				2,027,000	249,121	12.3%		2,073,000	317,324	15.3%	3.0					2,284,000	383,843	16.8%	4.5

United States Senate General Elections (continued)

United States Senate General Elections *(continued)*

Democratic Turnout for Election Years 1950–1966 *(continued)*

State	1950 Voting-age population	1950 Turnout	1950 %	1954 Voting-age population	1954 Turnout	1954 %	1954 Difference from 1950	1958 Voting-age population	1958 Turnout	1958 %	1958 Difference from 1950	1962 Voting-age population	1962 Turnout	1962 %	1962 Difference from 1950	1966 Voting-age population	1966 Turnout	1966 %	1966 Difference from 1950
TEXAS				4,970,000	539,319	10.9%		5,293,000	587,030	11.1%	0.2					6,187,000	643,855	10.4%	-0.4
UTAH	384,000	121,198	31.6%					445,000	112,827	25.4%	-6.2	486,000	151,656	31.2%	-0.4				
VERMONT	229,000	19,608	8.6%					225,000	59,536	26.5%	17.9	234,000	40,134	17.2%	8.6				
VIRGINIA				2,147,000	277,525	12.9%		2,259,000	317,221	14.0%	1.1					2,629,000	429,855	16.4%	3.4
WASHINGTON	1,518,000	397,719	26.2%					1,650,000	597,040	36.2%	10.0	1,777,000	491,365	27.7%	1.5				
WEST VIRGINIA				1,120,000	325,263	29.0%		1,086,000	381,745	35.2%	6.1					1,072,000	292,325	27.3%	-1.8
WISCONSIN	2,192,000	515,539	23.5%					2,306,000	682,440	29.6%	6.1	2,397,000	662,342	27.6%	4.1				
WYOMING				181,000	57,845	32.0%		186,000	58,035	31.2%	-0.8	190,000	50,329	26.5%	-5.5	193,000	59,141	30.6%	-1.3
Total	68,796,000	15,610,698	22.7%	52,724,000	11,435,689	21.7%	-1.0	77,651,000	20,932,508	27.0%	4.3	83,654,000	20,890,690	25.0%	2.3	59,368,000	12,348,443	20.8%	-1.9

Other Turnout for Election Years 1950–1966

State	1950 Voting-age population	1950 Turnout	1950 %	1954 Voting-age population	1954 Turnout	1954 %	1954 Difference from 1950*	1958 Voting-age population	1958 Turnout	1958 %	1958 Difference from 1950	1962 Voting-age population	1962 Turnout	1962 %	1962 Difference from 1950	1966 Voting-age population	1966 Turnout	1966 %	1966 Difference from 1950
ALABAMA	1,749,000	38,477	2.2%	1,785,000	1	0.0%	-2.2					1,882,000	8	0.0%	-2.2	1,958,000	7,452	0.4%	-1.8
ALASKA																			
ARIZONA																			
ARKANSAS																			
CALIFORNIA	6,975,000	354	0.0%					8,777,000	3,191	0.0%	0.0	9,933,000	14,630	0.1%	0.1				
COLORADO												1,086,000	5,203	0.5%		1,205,000	332	0.0%	-0.5
CONNECTICUT	1,311,000	15,128	1.2%					1,488,000	3,043	0.2%	-0.9	1,612,000	85	0.0%	-1.1				
DELAWARE																			
DISTRICT OF COLUMBIA																			
FLORIDA	1,859,000	272	0.0%									3,351,000	193	0.0%	0.0				
GEORGIA	2,189,000	3	0.0%	2,283,000	19	0.0%	0.0									2,760,000	328	0.0%	0.0
HAWAII																			
IDAHO																			
ILLINOIS	5,820,000	13,059	0.2%	5,953,000	4	0.0%	-0.2					6,295,000	7	0.0%	-0.2	6,549,000	44,129	0.7%	0.4
INDIANA	2,545,000	13,396	0.5%					2,727,000	19,327	0.7%	0.2								
IOWA	1,675,000	3,573	0.2%	1,664,000	2,234	0.1%	-0.1					1,665,000	6	0.0%	-0.2	1,684,000	11,043	0.7%	0.4
KANSAS	1,236,000	11,859	1.0%	1,269,000	11,344	0.9%	-0.1					1,329,000	10,102	0.8%	-0.2	1,353,000	18,045	1.3%	0.4
KENTUCKY	1,739,000	4,496	0.3%																
LOUISIANA																			
MAINE																585,000	108	0.0%	

United States Senate General Elections *(continued)*

Other Turnout for Election Years 1950–1966 *(continued)*

State	1950 Voting-age population	Turnout	%	1954 Voting-age population	Turnout	%	Difference from 1950	1958 Voting-age population	Turnout	%	Difference from 1950	1962 Voting-age population	Turnout	%	Difference from 1950	1966 Voting-age population	Turnout	%	Difference from 1950
MARYLAND	1,519,000	6,143	0.4%									1,958,000	1	0.0%	-0.4				
MASSACHUSETTS				3,070,000	8,206	0.3%		3,095,000	10,797	0.3%	0.1	3,214,000	56,805	1.8%	1.5	3,377,000	11,715	0.3%	0.1
MICHIGAN				4,199,000	6,870	0.2%		4,396,000	7,715	0.2%	0.0					4,923,000	6,351	0.1%	0.0
MINNESOTA				1,922,000	17,140	0.9%		1,962,000	5,407	0.3%	-0.6					2,140,000	10,718	0.5%	-0.4
MISSISSIPPI																1,218,000	30,502	2.5%	
MISSOURI	2,623,000	760	0.0%																
MONTANA																			
NEBRASKA																880,000	1,035	0.1%	
NEVADA																			
NEW HAMPSHIRE	339,000	11,958	3.5%													416,000	176	0.0%	-3.5
NEW JERSEY				3,453,000	50,871	1.5%		3,652,000	32,210	0.9%	-0.6					4,218,000	63,824	1.5%	0.0
NEW MEXICO																534,000	10	0.0%	
NEW YORK	9,827,000	228,737	2.3%					10,266,000	49,087	0.5%	-1.8	10,657,000	141,428	1.3%	-1.0				
NORTH CAROLINA																2,856,000	36	0.0%	
NORTH DAKOTA								351,000	2,673	0.8%									
OHIO																			
OKLAHOMA				1,392,000	2,980	0.2%						1,457,000	2,856	0.2%	0.0				
OREGON	985,000	10,165	1.0%									1,117,000	255	0.0%	-1.0	1,210,000	302	0.0%	-1.0
PENNSYLVANIA	6,838,000	34,166	0.5%					6,958,000	16,215	0.2%	-0.3	7,081,000	10,443	0.1%	-0.4				
RHODE ISLAND																568,000	4	0.0%	
SOUTH CAROLINA	1,155,000	37	0.0%	1,203,000	143,707	11.9%	11.9					1,319,000	5	0.0%	0.0				
SOUTH DAKOTA																			
TENNESSEE								2,073,000	7,971	0.4%						2,284,000	55	0.0%	-0.4
TEXAS				4,970,000	3,025	0.1%		5,293,000	14,172	0.3%	0.2					6,187,000	6,826	0.1%	0.0
UTAH	384,000	815	0.2%					445,000	77,013	17.3%	17.1								
VERMONT	229,000	20	0.0%					225,000	6	0.0%	0.0	234,000	196	0.1%	0.1				
VIRGINIA				2,147,000	28,985	1.4%		2,259,000	140,419	6.2%	4.9					2,629,000	58,343	2.2%	0.9
WASHINGTON	1,518,000	4,600	0.3%					1,650,000	11,511	0.7%	0.4	1,777,000	5,660	0.3%	0.0				
WEST VIRGINIA																			
WISCONSIN	2,192,000	5,255	0.2%					2,306,000	1,840	0.1%	-0.2	2,397,000	2,980	0.1%	-0.1				
WYOMING																			
Total	54,707,000	403,273	0.7%	35,310,000	275,386	0.8%	0.0	57,923,000	402,597	0.7%	0.0	58,364,000	250,863	0.4%	-0.3	49,534,000	271,334	0.5%	-0.2

*Percentage point difference between turnout in current year and initial year listed in chart. If data do not appear for a state in the initial year listed, the difference is calculated from the first year in which data do appear for that state.

UNITED STATES HOUSE OF REPRESENTATIVES GENERAL ELECTIONS

Election Years 1950–1966

State	1950 Voting-age population	Turnout	%	1954 Voting-age population	Turnout	%	Difference from 1950*	1958 Voting-age population	Turnout	%	Difference from 1950	1962 Voting-age population	Turnout	%	Difference from 1950	1966 Voting-age population	Turnout	%	Difference from 1950
ALABAMA	1,749,000	152,192	8.7%	1,785,000	279,789	15.7%	7.0	1,819,000	237,162	13.0%	4.3	1,882,000	477,858	25.4%	16.7	1,958,000	705,261	36.0%	27.3
ALASKA								127,000	48,644	38.3%		144,000	58,591	40.7%	2.4	162,000	65,907	40.7%	2.4
ARIZONA	438,000	177,667	40.6%	559,000	223,402	40.0%	-0.6	673,000	277,566	41.2%	0.7	798,000	349,024	43.7%	3.2	926,000	364,423	39.4%	-1.2
ARKANSAS	1,106,000	295,802	26.7%	1,076,000	280,274	26.0%	-0.7	1,047,000	60,222	5.8%	-21.0	1,075,000	181,592	16.9%	-9.9	1,126,000	291,638	25.9%	-0.8
CALIFORNIA	6,975,000	3,357,704	48.1%	7,895,000	3,873,075	49.1%	0.9	8,777,000	4,953,137	56.4%	8.3	9,933,000	5,573,346	56.1%	8.0	11,212,000	6,278,601	56.0%	7.9
COLORADO	838,000	442,892	52.9%	910,000	480,054	52.8%	-0.1	981,000	534,019	54.4%	1.6	1,086,000	596,596	54.9%	2.1	1,205,000	640,485	53.2%	0.3
CONNECTICUT	1,311,000	878,388	67.0%	1,401,000	932,410	66.6%	-0.4	1,488,000	967,767	65.0%	-2.0	1,612,000	1,032,244	64.0%	-3.0	1,753,000	1,003,617	57.3%	-9.7
DELAWARE	210,000	129,404	61.6%	231,000	144,236	62.4%	0.8	251,000	152,896	60.9%	-0.7	275,000	153,356	55.8%	-5.9	302,000	163,103	54.0%	-7.6
DISTRICT OF COLUMBIA																			
FLORIDA	1,859,000	253,049	13.6%	2,351,000	326,287	13.9%	0.3	2,822,000	494,361	17.5%	3.9	3,351,000	940,839	28.1%	14.5	3,906,000	1,053,775	27.0%	13.4
GEORGIA	2,189,000	290,008	13.2%	2,283,000	352,743	15.5%	2.2	2,373,000	158,638	6.7%	-6.6	2,548,000	333,374	13.1%	-0.2	2,760,000	850,788	30.8%	17.6
HAWAII								337,000	163,717	48.6%		364,000	194,529	53.4%	4.9	401,000	208,161	51.9%	3.3
IDAHO	345,000	200,084	58.0%	355,000	226,012	63.7%	5.7	365,000	239,028	65.5%	7.5	380,000	254,329	66.9%	8.9	397,000	248,228	62.5%	4.5
ILLINOIS	5,820,000	3,509,695	60.3%	5,953,000	3,257,722	54.7%	-5.6	6,079,000	3,229,864	53.1%	-7.2	6,295,000	3,625,309	57.6%	-2.7	6,549,000	3,735,310	57.0%	-3.3
INDIANA	2,545,000	1,587,309	62.4%	2,638,000	1,586,631	60.1%	-2.2	2,727,000	1,721,464	63.1%	0.8	2,842,000	1,790,709	63.0%	0.6	2,968,000	1,678,037	56.5%	-5.8
IOWA	1,675,000	819,959	49.0%	1,664,000	817,253	49.1%	0.2	1,654,000	829,916	50.2%	1.2	1,665,000	802,847	48.2%	-0.7	1,684,000	878,968	52.2%	3.2
KANSAS	1,236,000	604,746	48.9%	1,269,000	614,989	48.5%	-0.5	1,302,000	717,694	55.1%	6.2	1,329,000	625,282	47.0%	-1.9	1,353,000	660,530	48.8%	-0.1
KENTUCKY	1,739,000	488,614	28.1%	1,748,000	668,488	38.2%	10.1	1,891,000	475,818	25.2%	-2.9	1,950,000	631,453	32.4%	4.3	2,032,000	677,124	33.3%	5.2
LOUISIANA	1,590,000	227,075	14.3%	1,679,000	216,323	12.9%	-1.4	1,766,000	182,124	10.3%	-4.0	1,861,000	346,232	18.6%	4.3	1,961,000	546,258	27.9%	13.6
MAINE	553,000	237,632	43.0%	557,000	241,443	43.3%	0.4	561,000	274,962	49.0%	6.0	572,000	285,501	49.9%	6.9	585,000	312,816	53.5%	10.5
MARYLAND	1,519,000	572,927	37.7%	1,648,000	638,875	38.8%	1.0	1,772,000	712,126	40.2%	2.5	1,958,000	718,772	36.7%	-1.0	2,170,000	765,423	35.3%	-2.4
MASSACHUSETTS	3,042,000	1,859,396	61.1%	3,070,000	1,782,659	58.1%	-3.1	3,095,000	1,776,218	57.4%	-3.7	3,214,000	1,970,481	61.3%	0.2	3,377,000	1,811,584	53.6%	-7.5
MICHIGAN	3,992,000	1,804,724	45.2%	4,199,000	2,133,390	50.8%	5.6	4,396,000	2,253,810	51.3%	6.1	4,648,000	2,679,253	57.6%	12.4	4,923,000	2,367,440	48.1%	2.9
MINNESOTA	1,879,000	1,018,267	54.2%	1,922,000	1,131,492	58.9%	4.7	1,962,000	1,131,127	57.7%	3.5	2,041,000	1,204,753	59.0%	4.8	2,140,000	1,220,376	57.0%	2.8
MISSISSIPPI	1,203,000	87,756	7.3%	1,187,000	99,342	8.4%	1.1	1,172,000	61,464	5.2%	-2.1	1,188,000	161,615	13.6%	6.3	1,218,000	382,547	31.4%	24.1
MISSOURI	2,623,000	1,250,150	47.7%	2,646,000	1,184,813	44.8%	-2.9	2,669,000	1,166,817	43.7%	-3.9	2,731,000	1,212,324	44.4%	-3.3	2,813,000	1,045,210	37.2%	-10.5
MONTANA	365,000	210,527	57.7%	374,000	224,587	60.1%	2.4	382,000	228,470	59.8%	2.1	390,000	248,441	63.7%	6.0	399,000	258,371	64.8%	7.1
NEBRASKA	846,000	436,330	51.6%	847,000	406,690	48.0%	-3.6	849,000	415,590	49.0%	-2.6	861,000	445,032	51.7%	0.1	880,000	471,145	53.5%	2.0
NEVADA	107,000	60,328	56.4%	136,000	77,639	57.1%	0.7	162,000	82,328	50.8%	-5.6	205,000	93,324	45.5%	-10.9	256,000	127,850	49.9%	-6.4
NEW HAMPSHIRE	339,000	185,247	54.6%	348,000	191,818	55.1%	0.5	357,000	197,501	55.3%	0.7	383,000	221,252	57.8%	3.1	416,000	228,766	55.0%	0.3
NEW JERSEY	3,246,000	1,571,263	48.4%	3,453,000	1,786,853	51.7%	3.3	3,652,000	1,906,452	52.2%	3.8	3,920,000	1,958,960	50.0%	1.6	4,218,000	2,097,991	49.7%	1.3
NEW MEXICO	375,000	172,634	46.0%	427,000	188,862	44.2%	-1.8	477,000	197,846	41.5%	-4.6	509,000	244,913	48.1%	2.1	534,000	251,657	47.1%	1.1
NEW YORK	9,827,000	5,051,889	51.4%	10,051,000	5,002,181	49.8%	-1.6	10,266,000	5,522,916	53.8%	2.4	10,657,000	5,559,864	52.2%	0.8	11,128,000	5,513,336	49.5%	-1.9

United States House of Representatives General Elections *(continued)*

Election Years 1950–1966 *(continued)*

State	1950 Voting-age population	Turnout	%	1954 Voting-age population	Turnout	%	Difference from 1950	1958 Voting-age population	Turnout	%	Difference from 1950	1962 Voting-age population	Turnout	%	Difference from 1950	1966 Voting-age population	Turnout	%	Difference from 1950
NORTH CAROLINA	2,319,000	522,200	**22.5%**	2,421,000	604,179	**25.0%**	2.4	2,518,000	608,853	**24.2%**	1.7	2,674,000	818,529	**30.6%**	8.1	2,856,000	916,449	**32.1%**	9.6
NORTH DAKOTA	358,000	181,369	**50.7%**	354,000	188,934	**53.4%**	2.7	351,000	197,424	**56.2%**	5.6	351,000	216,282	**61.6%**	11.0	353,000	197,499	**55.9%**	5.3
OHIO	5,214,000	2,684,563	**51.5%**	5,454,000	2,498,837	**45.8%**	-5.7	5,682,000	3,110,579	**54.7%**	3.3	5,920,000	3,000,610	**50.7%**	-0.8	6,161,000	2,795,641	**45.4%**	-6.1
OKLAHOMA	1,378,000	606,786	**44.0%**	1,392,000	545,789	**39.2%**	-4.8	1,406,000	529,775	**37.7%**	-6.4	1,457,000	624,613	**42.9%**	-1.2	1,528,000	636,389	**41.6%**	-2.4
OREGON	985,000	499,489	**50.7%**	1,016,000	564,494	**55.6%**	4.9	1,045,000	595,111	**56.9%**	6.2	1,117,000	630,865	**56.5%**	5.8	1,210,000	664,879	**54.9%**	4.2
PENNSYLVANIA	6,838,000	3,511,889	**51.4%**	6,899,000	3,695,910	**53.6%**	2.2	6,958,000	3,961,198	**56.9%**	5.6	7,081,000	4,354,207	**61.5%**	10.1	7,234,000	3,973,740	**54.9%**	3.6
RHODE ISLAND	514,000	295,591	**57.5%**	517,000	326,059	**63.1%**	5.6	520,000	340,642	**65.5%**	8.0	540,000	318,658	**59.0%**	1.5	568,000	322,022	**56.7%**	-0.8
SOUTH CAROLINA	1,155,000	50,400	**4.4%**	1,203,000	213,335	**17.7%**	13.4	1,248,000	76,647	**6.1%**	1.8	1,319,000	262,554	**19.9%**	15.5	1,401,000	364,314	**26.0%**	21.6
SOUTH DAKOTA	396,000	248,426	**62.7%**	393,000	231,167	**58.8%**	-3.9	390,000	257,989	**66.2%**	3.4	388,000	252,731	**65.1%**	2.4	387,000	225,046	**58.2%**	-4.6
TENNESSEE	1,980,000	262,608	**13.3%**	2,027,000	344,796	**17.0%**	3.7	2,073,000	371,803	**17.9%**	4.7	2,166,000	605,907	**28.0%**	14.7	2,284,000	799,871	**35.0%**	21.8
TEXAS	4,635,000	360,442	**7.8%**	4,970,000	630,918	**12.7%**	4.9	5,293,000	768,847	**14.5%**	6.7	5,717,000	1,551,699	**27.1%**	19.4	6,187,000	1,258,471	**20.3%**	12.6
UTAH	384,000	263,847	**68.7%**	415,000	263,031	**63.4%**	-5.3	445,000	286,323	**64.3%**	-4.4	486,000	317,010	**65.2%**	-3.5	532,000	307,437	**57.8%**	-10.9
VERMONT	229,000	88,822	**38.8%**	227,000	114,284	**50.3%**	11.6	225,000	122,667	**54.5%**	15.7	234,000	121,381	**51.9%**	13.1	249,000	135,748	**54.5%**	15.7
VIRGINIA	2,030,000	211,830	**10.4%**	2,147,000	342,344	**15.9%**	5.5	2,259,000	431,609	**19.1%**	8.7	2,430,000	448,952	**18.5%**	8.0	2,629,000	682,737	**26.0%**	15.5
WASHINGTON	1,518,000	723,605	**47.7%**	1,584,000	809,795	**51.1%**	3.5	1,650,000	876,826	**53.1%**	5.5	1,777,000	881,150	**49.6%**	1.9	1,932,000	939,441	**48.6%**	1.0
WEST VIRGINIA	1,156,000	662,836	**57.3%**	1,120,000	591,402	**52.8%**	-4.5	1,086,000	615,787	**56.7%**	-0.6	1,073,000	613,018	**57.1%**	-0.2	1,072,000	494,345	**46.1%**	-11.2
WISCONSIN	2,192,000	1,110,069	**50.6%**	2,250,000	1,140,695	**50.7%**	0.1	2,306,000	1,181,025	**51.2%**	0.6	2,397,000	1,244,331	**51.9%**	1.3	2,505,000	1,153,941	**46.1%**	-4.6
WYOMING	176,000	93,348	**53.0%**	181,000	108,771	**60.1%**	7.1	186,000	111,780	**60.1%**	7.1	190,000	116,474	**61.3%**	8.3	193,000	119,426	**61.9%**	8.8
Total	94,998,000	40,311,778	**42.4%**	99,232,000	42,585,072	**42.9%**	0.5	103,892,000	45,816,549	**44.1%**	1.7	109,984,000	51,350,966	**46.7%**	4.3	116,993,000	52,892,122	**45.2%**	2.8

*Percentage point difference between turnout in current year and initial year listed in chart. If data do not appear for a state in the initial year listed, the difference is calculated from the first year in which data do appear for that state.

UNITED STATES HOUSE OF REPRESENTATIVES GENERAL ELECTIONS

Republican Turnout for Election Years 1950–1966

State	1950 Voting-age population	1950 Turnout	1950 %	1954 Voting-age population	1954 Turnout	1954 %	1954 Difference from 1950*	1958 Voting-age population	1958 Turnout	1958 %	1958 Difference from 1950	1962 Voting-age population	1962 Turnout	1962 %	1962 Difference from 1950	1966 Voting-age population	1966 Turnout	1966 %	1966 Difference from 1950
ALABAMA	1,749,000	980	0.1%	1,785,000	11,236	0.6%	0.6	1,819,000	6,050	0.3%	0.3	1,882,000	141,202	7.5%	7.4	1,958,000	275,482	14.1%	14.0
ALASKA								127,000	20,699	16.3%		144,000	26,638	18.5%	2.2	162,000	34,040	21.0%	4.7
ARIZONA	438,000	62,150	14.2%	559,000	102,010	18.2%	4.1	673,000	138,099	20.5%	6.3	798,000	179,392	22.5%	8.3	926,000	204,478	22.1%	7.9
ARKANSAS				1,076,000	4	0.0%						1,075,000	47,805	4.4%	4.4	1,126,000	130,742	11.6%	11.6
CALIFORNIA	6,975,000	1,754,001	25.1%	7,895,000	1,876,626	23.8%	-1.4	8,777,000	1,981,276	22.6%	-2.6	9,933,000	2,679,662	27.0%	1.8	11,212,000	3,336,943	29.8%	4.6
COLORADO	838,000	225,986	27.0%	910,000	240,074	26.4%	-0.6	981,000	222,971	22.7%	-4.2	1,086,000	314,122	28.9%	2.0	1,205,000	298,472	24.8%	-2.2
CONNECTICUT	1,311,000	433,912	33.1%	1,401,000	474,585	33.9%	0.8	1,488,000	425,452	28.6%	-4.5	1,612,000	473,659	29.4%	-3.7	1,753,000	443,319	25.3%	-7.8
DELAWARE	210,000	73,313	34.9%	231,000	65,035	28.2%	-6.8	251,000	76,099	30.3%	-4.6	275,000	71,934	26.2%	-8.8	302,000	90,961	30.1%	-4.8
DISTRICT OF COLUMBIA																			
FLORIDA	1,859,000	24,263	1.3%	2,351,000	71,137	3.0%	1.7	2,822,000	139,419	4.9%	3.6	3,351,000	351,954	10.5%	9.2	3,906,000	368,976	9.4%	8.1
GEORGIA				2,283,000	29,911	1.3%						2,548,000	59,514	2.3%	1.0	2,760,000	292,150	10.6%	9.3
HAWAII								337,000	51,058	15.2%		364,000	70,880	19.5%	4.3	401,000	67,281	16.8%	1.6
IDAHO	345,000	108,789	31.5%	355,000	123,117	34.7%	3.1	365,000	114,731	31.4%	-0.1	380,000	119,755	31.5%	0.0	397,000	149,434	37.6%	6.1
ILLINOIS	5,820,000	1,891,177	32.5%	5,953,000	1,621,278	27.2%	-5.3	6,079,000	1,468,590	24.2%	-8.3	6,295,000	1,820,824	28.9%	-3.6	6,549,000	2,027,714	31.0%	-1.5
INDIANA	2,545,000	850,357	33.4%	2,638,000	833,304	31.6%	-1.8	2,727,000	798,850	29.3%	-4.1	2,842,000	911,596	32.1%	-1.3	2,968,000	897,086	30.2%	-3.2
IOWA	1,675,000	500,426	29.9%	1,664,000	478,322	28.7%	-1.1	1,654,000	412,798	25.0%	-4.9	1,665,000	432,483	26.0%	-3.9	1,684,000	458,948	27.3%	-2.6
KANSAS	1,236,000	355,849	28.8%	1,269,000	347,458	27.4%	-1.4	1,302,000	354,732	27.2%	-1.5	1,329,000	375,726	28.3%	-0.5	1,353,000	416,610	30.8%	2.0
KENTUCKY	1,739,000	180,778	10.4%	1,748,000	236,194	13.5%	3.1	1,891,000	164,425	8.7%	-1.7	1,950,000	258,182	13.2%	2.8	2,032,000	319,636	15.7%	5.3
LOUISIANA				1,679,000	8,212	0.5%		1,766,000	4,160	0.2%	-0.3	1,861,000	42,419	2.3%	1.8	1,961,000	99,252	5.1%	4.6
MAINE	553,000	136,901	24.8%	557,000	132,895	23.9%	-0.9	561,000	128,606	22.9%	-1.8	572,000	158,213	27.7%	2.9	585,000	138,460	23.7%	-1.1
MARYLAND	1,519,000	285,957	18.8%	1,648,000	295,426	17.9%	-0.9	1,772,000	248,238	14.0%	-4.8	1,958,000	315,533	16.1%	-2.7	2,170,000	336,043	15.5%	-3.3
MASSACHUSETTS	3,042,000	930,280	30.6%	3,070,000	835,165	27.2%	-3.4	3,095,000	754,373	24.4%	-6.2	3,214,000	808,240	25.1%	-5.4	3,377,000	713,144	21.1%	-9.5
MICHIGAN	3,992,000	956,497	24.0%	4,199,000	1,028,093	24.5%	0.5	4,396,000	1,054,854	24.0%	0.0	4,648,000	1,282,082	27.6%	3.6	4,923,000	1,216,202	24.7%	0.7
MINNESOTA	1,879,000	538,973	28.7%	1,922,000	531,376	27.6%	-1.0	1,962,000	534,870	27.3%	-1.4	2,041,000	605,054	29.6%	1.0	2,140,000	630,049	29.4%	0.8
MISSISSIPPI	1,203,000	2,861	0.2%													1,218,000	61,514	5.1%	4.8
MISSOURI	2,623,000	552,014	21.0%	2,646,000	519,091	19.6%	-1.4	2,669,000	429,940	16.1%	-4.9	2,731,000	528,447	19.3%	-1.7	2,813,000	484,098	17.2%	-3.8
MONTANA	365,000	99,948	27.4%	374,000	107,478	28.7%	1.4	382,000	80,744	21.1%	-6.2	390,000	129,075	33.1%	5.7	399,000	140,940	35.3%	7.9
NEBRASKA	846,000	271,840	32.1%	847,000	250,347	29.6%	-2.6	849,000	220,140	25.9%	-6.2	861,000	271,777	31.6%	-0.6	880,000	292,603	33.3%	1.1
NEVADA	107,000	28,485	26.6%	136,000	42,321	31.1%	4.5	162,000	27,275	16.8%	-9.8	205,000	26,458	12.9%	-13.7	256,000	41,383	16.2%	-10.5
NEW HAMPSHIRE	339,000	112,487	33.2%	348,000	104,905	30.1%	-3.0	357,000	115,370	32.3%	-0.9	383,000	121,803	31.8%	-1.4	416,000	139,048	33.4%	0.2
NEW JERSEY	3,246,000	859,145	26.5%	3,453,000	903,839	26.2%	-0.3	3,652,000	944,349	25.9%	-0.6	3,920,000	964,280	24.6%	-1.9	4,218,000	1,045,641	24.8%	-1.7
NEW MEXICO	375,000	75,447	20.1%	427,000	77,151	18.1%	-2.1	477,000	72,922	15.3%	-4.8	509,000	116,262	22.8%	2.7	534,000	124,536	23.3%	3.2
NEW YORK	9,827,000	2,369,182	24.1%	10,051,000	2,489,275	24.8%	0.7	10,266,000	2,686,818	26.2%	2.1	10,657,000	2,686,334	25.2%	1.1	11,128,000	2,494,847	22.4%	-1.7

United States House of Representatives General Elections (continued)

Republican Turnout for Election Years 1950–1966 (continued)

State	1950 Voting-age population	1950 Turnout	1950 %	1954 Voting-age population	1954 Turnout	1954 %	1954 Difference from 1950	1958 Voting-age population	1958 Turnout	1958 %	1958 Difference from 1950	1962 Voting-age population	1962 Turnout	1962 %	1962 Difference from 1950	1966 Voting-age population	1966 Turnout	1966 %	1966 Difference from 1950
NORTH CAROLINA	2,319,000	156,602	6.8%	2,421,000	214,012	8.8%	2.1	2,518,000	177,651	7.1%	0.3	2,674,000	336,383	12.6%	5.8	2,856,000	432,036	15.1%	8.4
NORTH DAKOTA	358,000	119,047	33.3%	354,000	124,845	35.3%	2.0	351,000	97,862	27.9%	-5.4	351,000	117,533	33.5%	0.2	353,000	116,812	33.1%	-0.2
OHIO	5,214,000	1,447,154	27.8%	5,454,000	1,340,847	24.6%	-3.2	5,682,000	1,529,565	26.9%	-0.8	5,920,000	1,676,274	28.3%	0.6	6,161,000	1,599,492	26.0%	-1.8
OKLAHOMA	1,378,000	243,334	17.7%	1,392,000	191,450	13.8%	-3.9	1,406,000	159,168	11.3%	-6.3	1,457,000	242,876	16.7%	-1.0	1,528,000	302,792	19.8%	2.2
OREGON	985,000	288,355	29.3%	1,010,000	307,386	30.3%	1.0	1,045,000	256,253	24.5%	-4.8	1,117,000	288,571	25.8%	-3.4	1,210,000	349,902	28.9%	-0.4
PENNSYLVANIA	6,838,000	1,834,128	26.8%	6,899,000	1,824,186	26.4%	-0.4	6,958,000	1,940,666	27.9%	1.1	7,081,000	2,217,431	31.3%	4.5	7,234,000	2,070,037	28.6%	1.8
RHODE ISLAND	514,000	112,488	21.9%	517,000	130,859	25.3%	3.4	520,000	125,523	24.1%	2.3	540,000	111,141	20.6%	-1.3	568,000	124,531	21.9%	0.0
SOUTH CAROLINA				1,203,000	2,711	0.2%						1,319,000	34,947	2.6%	2.4	1,401,000	106,775	7.6%	7.4
SOUTH DAKOTA	396,000	150,706	38.1%	393,000	137,273	34.9%	-3.1	390,000	125,296	32.1%	-5.9	388,000	151,067	38.9%	0.9	387,000	143,655	37.1%	-0.9
TENNESSEE	1,980,000	97,203	4.9%	2,027,000	112,272	5.5%	0.6	2,073,000	92,999	4.5%	-0.4	2,166,000	212,362	9.8%	4.9	2,284,000	382,824	16.8%	11.9
TEXAS	4,635,000	34,314	0.7%	4,970,000	75,472	1.5%	0.8	5,293,000	91,287	1.7%	1.0	5,717,000	680,839	11.9%	11.2	6,187,000	206,419	3.3%	2.6
UTAH	384,000	125,403	32.7%	415,000	146,406	35.3%	2.6	445,000	145,375	32.7%	0.0	486,000	167,390	34.4%	1.8	532,000	196,176	36.9%	4.2
VERMONT	229,000	65,248	28.5%	227,000	70,143	30.9%	2.4	225,000	59,536	26.5%	-2.0	234,000	68,822	29.4%	0.9	249,000	89,097	35.8%	7.3
VIRGINIA	2,030,000	51,493	2.5%	2,147,000	128,315	6.0%	3.4	2,259,000	86,211	3.8%	1.3	2,430,000	178,913	7.4%	4.8	2,629,000	268,094	10.2%	7.7
WASHINGTON	1,518,000	378,419	24.9%	1,584,000	342,089	21.6%	-3.3	1,650,000	467,678	28.3%	3.4	1,777,000	543,318	30.6%	5.6	1,932,000	449,765	23.3%	-1.6
WEST VIRGINIA	1,156,000	287,915	24.9%	1,120,000	251,444	22.5%	-2.5	1,086,000	234,804	21.6%	-3.3	1,073,000	269,744	25.1%	0.2	1,072,000	232,322	21.7%	-3.2
WISCONSIN	2,192,000	639,293	29.2%	2,250,000	598,919	26.6%	-2.5	2,306,000	547,873	23.8%	-5.4	2,397,000	623,907	26.0%	-3.1	2,505,000	620,786	24.8%	-4.4
WYOMING	176,000	50,865	28.9%	181,000	61,111	33.8%	4.9	186,000	59,094	32.2%	3.3	190,000	71,489	37.6%	8.7	193,000	62,984	32.6%	3.7
Total	88,958,000	19,763,965	22.2%	98,045,000	19,895,605	20.3%	-1.9	98,052,000	19,875,549	20.3%	-1.9	108,796,000	24,384,312	22.4%	0.2	116,993,000	25,524,531	21.8%	-0.4

Democratic Turnout for Election Years 1950–1966

State	1950 Voting-age population	1950 Turnout	1950 %	1954 Voting-age population	1954 Turnout	1954 %	1954 Difference from 1950*	1958 Voting-age population	1958 Turnout	1958 %	1958 Difference from 1950	1962 Voting-age population	1962 Turnout	1962 %	1962 Difference from 1950	1966 Voting-age population	1966 Turnout	1966 %	1966 Difference from 1950
ALABAMA	1,749,000	151,212	8.6%	1,785,000	268,552	15.0%	6.4	1,819,000	231,112	12.7%	4.1	1,882,000	304,210	16.2%	7.5	1,958,000	429,770	21.9%	13.3
ALASKA								127,000	27,945	22.0%		144,000	31,953	22.2%	0.2	162,000	31,867	19.7%	-2.3
ARIZONA	438,000	115,517	26.4%	559,000	121,392	21.7%	-4.7	673,000	139,467	20.7%	-5.7	798,000	169,632	21.3%	-5.1	926,000	159,945	17.3%	-9.1
ARKANSAS	1,106,000	295,802	26.7%	1,076,000	280,264	26.0%	-0.7	1,047,000	60,222	5.8%	-21.0	1,075,000	133,758	12.4%	-14.3	1,126,000	160,896	14.3%	-12.5
CALIFORNIA	6,975,000	1,480,639	21.2%	7,895,000	1,991,169	25.2%	4.0	8,777,000	2,971,861	33.9%	12.6	9,933,000	2,891,518	29.1%	7.9	11,212,000	2,937,862	26.2%	5.0
COLORADO	838,000	214,385	25.6%	910,000	239,565	26.3%	0.7	981,000	309,873	31.6%	6.0	1,086,000	282,474	26.0%	0.4	1,205,000	339,750	28.2%	2.6
CONNECTICUT	1,311,000	426,485	32.5%	1,401,000	455,887	32.5%	0.0	1,488,000	542,315	36.4%	3.9	1,612,000	556,907	34.5%	2.0	1,753,000	543,149	31.0%	-1.5
DELAWARE	210,000	56,091	26.7%	231,000	79,201	34.3%	7.6	251,000	76,797	30.6%	3.9	275,000	81,166	29.5%	2.8	302,000	72,142	23.9%	-2.8
DISTRICT OF COLUMBIA																			
FLORIDA	1,859,000	228,786	12.3%	2,351,000	255,150	10.9%	-1.5	2,822,000	354,942	12.6%	0.3	3,351,000	588,719	17.6%	5.3	3,906,000	680,466	17.4%	5.1

United States House of Representatives General Elections (continued)

United States House of Representatives General Elections *(continued)*

Democratic Turnout for Election Years 1950–1966 *(continued)*

State	1950 Voting-age population	1950 Turnout	1950 %	1954 Voting-age population	1954 Turnout	1954 %	1954 Difference from 1950	1958 Voting-age population	1958 Turnout	1958 %	1958 Difference from 1950	1962 Voting-age population	1962 Turnout	1962 %	1962 Difference from 1950	1966 Voting-age population	1966 Turnout	1966 %	1966 Difference from 1950
GEORGIA	2,189,000	289,931	13.2%	2,283,000	317,703	13.9%	0.7	2,373,000	158,636	6.7%	-6.6	2,548,000	272,494	10.7%	-2.6	2,760,000	557,886	20.2%	7.0
HAWAII								337,000	111,727	33.2%		364,000	123,649	34.0%	0.8	401,000	140,880	35.1%	2.0
IDAHO	345,000	91,295	26.5%	355,000	102,895	29.0%	2.5	365,000	124,297	34.1%	7.6	380,000	134,574	35.4%	9.0	397,000	98,794	24.9%	-1.6
ILLINOIS	5,820,000	1,617,000	27.8%	5,953,000	1,636,443	27.5%	-0.3	6,079,000	1,754,248	28.9%	1.1	6,295,000	1,802,063	28.6%	0.8	6,549,000	1,707,576	26.1%	-1.7
INDIANA	2,545,000	727,467	28.6%	2,638,000	747,800	28.3%	-0.2	2,727,000	921,795	33.8%	5.2	2,842,000	878,311	30.9%	2.3	2,968,000	779,588	26.3%	-2.3
IOWA	1,675,000	317,369	18.9%	1,664,000	338,931	20.4%	1.4	1,654,000	417,118	25.2%	6.3	1,665,000	370,362	22.2%	3.3	1,684,000	417,740	24.8%	5.9
KANSAS	1,236,000	248,897	20.1%	1,269,000	267,531	21.1%	0.9	1,302,000	359,763	27.6%	7.5	1,329,000	249,556	18.8%	-1.4	1,353,000	241,571	17.9%	-2.3
KENTUCKY	1,739,000	307,836	17.7%	1,748,000	431,992	24.7%	7.0	1,891,000	309,771	16.4%	-1.3	1,950,000	372,378	19.1%	1.4	2,032,000	357,345	17.6%	-0.1
LOUISIANA	1,590,000	227,075	14.3%	1,679,000	208,111	12.4%	-1.9	1,766,000	177,963	10.1%	-4.2	1,861,000	303,813	16.3%	2.0	1,961,000	447,006	22.8%	8.5
MAINE	553,000	100,731	18.2%	557,000	108,548	19.5%	1.3	561,000	146,356	26.1%	7.9	572,000	127,288	22.3%	4.0	585,000	167,258	28.6%	10.4
MARYLAND	1,519,000	283,727	18.7%	1,648,000	342,115	20.8%	2.1	1,772,000	463,888	26.2%	7.5	1,958,000	403,239	20.6%	1.9	2,170,000	429,380	19.8%	1.1
MASSACHUSETTS	3,042,000	920,988	30.3%	3,070,000	947,494	30.9%	0.6	3,095,000	1,021,174	33.0%	2.7	3,214,000	1,146,884	35.7%	5.4	3,377,000	1,098,362	32.5%	2.2
MICHIGAN	3,992,000	838,752	21.0%	4,199,000	1,100,939	26.2%	5.2	4,396,000	1,193,696	27.2%	6.1	4,648,000	1,392,221	30.0%	8.9	4,923,000	1,150,400	23.4%	2.4
MINNESOTA	1,879,000	473,710	25.2%	1,922,000	600,116	31.2%	6.0	1,962,000	596,257	30.4%	5.2	2,041,000	599,124	29.4%	4.1	2,140,000	590,327	27.6%	2.4
MISSISSIPPI	1,203,000	82,696	6.9%	1,187,000	99,342	8.4%	1.5	1,172,000	61,464	5.2%	-1.6	1,188,000	157,154	13.2%	6.4	1,218,000	282,574	23.2%	16.3
MISSOURI	2,623,000	697,542	26.6%	2,646,000	665,722	25.2%	-1.4	2,669,000	736,877	27.6%	1.0	2,731,000	683,877	25.0%	-1.6	2,813,000	561,112	19.9%	-6.6
MONTANA	365,000	108,248	29.7%	374,000	117,109	31.3%	1.7	382,000	147,726	38.7%	9.0	390,000	119,366	30.6%	0.9	399,000	117,431	29.4%	-0.2
NEBRASKA	846,000	164,490	19.4%	847,000	156,343	18.5%	-1.0	849,000	195,450	23.0%	3.6	861,000	164,403	19.1%	-0.3	880,000	178,518	20.3%	0.8
NEVADA	107,000	31,843	29.8%	136,000	35,318	26.0%	-3.8	162,000	55,053	34.0%	4.2	205,000	66,866	32.6%	2.9	256,000	86,467	33.8%	4.0
NEW HAMPSHIRE	339,000	72,760	21.5%	348,000	86,913	25.0%	3.5	357,000	81,263	22.8%	1.3	383,000	99,449	26.0%	4.5	416,000	89,575	21.5%	0.1
NEW JERSEY	3,246,000	689,814	21.3%	3,453,000	862,382	25.0%	3.7	3,652,000	938,603	25.7%	4.4	3,920,000	980,509	25.0%	3.8	4,218,000	1,020,779	24.2%	2.9
NEW MEXICO	375,000	97,187	25.9%	427,000	111,711	26.2%	0.2	477,000	124,924	26.2%	0.3	509,000	128,651	25.3%	-0.6	534,000	126,984	23.8%	-2.1
NEW YORK	9,827,000	2,368,221	24.1%	10,051,000	2,416,963	24.0%	-0.1	10,266,000	2,763,883	26.9%	2.8	10,657,000	2,778,105	26.1%	2.0	11,128,000	2,763,837	24.8%	0.7
NORTH CAROLINA	2,319,000	365,598	15.8%	2,421,000	390,167	16.1%	0.4	2,518,000	431,202	17.1%	1.4	2,674,000	482,146	18.0%	2.3	2,856,000	484,413	17.0%	1.2
NORTH DAKOTA	358,000	62,322	17.4%	354,000	64,089	18.1%	0.7	351,000	99,562	28.4%	11.0	351,000	98,749	28.1%	10.7	353,000	80,687	22.9%	5.4
OHIO	5,214,000	1,237,409	23.7%	5,454,000	1,113,334	20.4%	-3.3	5,682,000	1,581,014	27.8%	4.1	5,920,000	1,318,741	22.3%	-1.5	6,161,000	1,196,149	19.4%	-4.3
OKLAHOMA	1,378,000	363,452	26.4%	1,392,000	354,339	25.5%	-0.9	1,406,000	369,271	26.3%	-0.1	1,457,000	381,737	26.2%	-0.2	1,528,000	333,597	21.8%	-4.5
OREGON	985,000	201,096	20.4%	1,016,000	257,108	25.3%	4.9	1,045,000	338,858	32.4%	12.0	1,117,000	342,209	30.6%	10.2	1,210,000	314,881	26.0%	5.6
PENNSYLVANIA	6,838,000	1,672,788	24.5%	6,899,000	1,871,625	27.1%	2.7	6,958,000	2,019,994	29.0%	4.6	7,081,000	2,135,717	30.2%	5.7	7,234,000	1,897,161	26.2%	1.8
RHODE ISLAND	514,000	183,103	35.6%	517,000	195,200	37.8%	2.1	520,000	214,931	41.3%	5.7	540,000	207,517	38.4%	2.8	568,000	196,957	34.7%	-0.9
SOUTH CAROLINA	1,155,000	50,381	4.4%	1,203,000	210,624	17.5%	13.1	1,248,000	76,632	6.1%	1.8	1,319,000	225,714	17.1%	12.8	1,401,000	257,193	18.4%	14.0
SOUTH DAKOTA	396,000	97,720	24.7%	393,000	93,894	23.9%	-0.8	390,000	132,693	34.0%	9.3	388,000	101,664	26.2%	1.5	387,000	81,391	21.0%	-3.6
TENNESSEE	1,980,000	165,405	8.4%	2,027,000	232,524	11.5%	3.1	2,073,000	278,694	13.4%	5.1	2,166,000	297,310	13.7%	5.4	2,284,000	382,296	16.7%	8.4

United States House of Representatives General Elections *(continued)*

Democratic Turnout for Election Years 1950–1966 *(continued)*

State	1950 Voting-age population	Turnout	%	1954 Voting-age population	Turnout	%	Difference from 1950	1958 Voting-age population	Turnout	%	Difference from 1950	1962 Voting-age population	Turnout	%	Difference from 1950	1966 Voting-age population	Turnout	%	Difference from 1950
TEXAS	4,635,000	326,128	7.0%	4,970,000	555,446	11.2%	4.1	5,293,000	673,771	12.7%	5.7	5,717,000	870,860	15.2%	8.2	6,187,000	1,037,344	16.8%	9.7
UTAH	384,000	138,444	36.1%	415,000	116,625	28.1%	-8.0	445,000	140,948	31.7%	-4.4	486,000	149,620	30.8%	-5.3	532,000	111,261	20.9%	-15.1
VERMONT	229,000	22,709	9.9%	227,000	44,141	19.4%	9.5	225,000	63,131	28.1%	18.1	234,000	52,535	22.5%	12.5	249,000	46,643	18.7%	8.8
VIRGINIA	2,030,000	155,396	7.7%	2,147,000	204,433	9.5%	1.9	2,259,000	318,633	14.1%	6.5	2,430,000	268,699	11.1%	3.4	2,629,000	391,538	14.9%	7.2
WASHINGTON	1,518,000	342,182	22.5%	1,684,000	464,045	29.3%	6.8	1,650,000	406,195	24.6%	2.1	1,777,000	337,832	19.0%	-3.5	1,932,000	474,021	24.5%	2.0
WEST VIRGINIA	1,156,000	374,921	32.4%	1,120,000	339,958	30.4%	-2.1	1,086,000	380,983	35.1%	2.6	1,073,000	343,274	32.0%	-0.4	1,072,000	262,023	24.4%	-8.0
WISCONSIN	2,192,000	470,275	21.5%	2,250,000	541,776	24.1%	2.6	2,306,000	633,152	27.5%	6.0	2,397,000	620,317	25.9%	4.4	2,505,000	532,897	21.3%	-0.2
WYOMING	176,000	42,483	24.1%	181,000	47,660	26.3%	2.2	186,000	51,886	27.9%	3.8	190,000	44,985	23.7%	-0.5	193,000	56,442	29.2%	5.1
Total	94,998,000	19,998,288	21.1%	99,232,000	22,490,589	22.7%	1.6	103,892,000	25,700,016	24.8%	3.8	109,984,000	26,674,299	24.3%	3.2	116,993,000	26,904,131	23.0%	1.9

Other Turnout for Election Years 1950–1966

State	1950 Voting-age population	Turnout	%	1954 Voting-age population	Turnout	%	Difference from 1950[x]	1958 Voting-age population	Turnout	%	Difference from 1950	1962 Voting-age population	Turnout	%	Difference from 1950	1966 Voting-age population	Turnout	%	Difference from 1950
ALABAMA				1,785,000	1	0.0%						1,882,000	32,446	1.7%	1.7	1,958,000	9	0.0%	0.0
ALASKA																			
ARIZONA																			
ARKANSAS				1,076,000	6	0.0%						1,075,000	29	0.0%	0.0				
CALIFORNIA	6,975,000	123,064	1.8%	7,895,000	5,280	0.1%	-1.7					9,933,000	2,166	0.0%	-1.7	11,212,000	3,796	0.0%	-1.7
COLORADO	838,000	2,521	0.3%	910,000	415	0.0%	-0.3	981,000	1,175	0.1%	-0.2					1,205,000	2,263	0.2%	-0.1
CONNECTICUT	1,311,000	17,991	1.4%	1,401,000	1,938	0.1%	-1.2					1,612,000	1,678	0.1%	-1.3	1,753,000	17,149	1.0%	-0.4
DELAWARE												275,000	256	0.1%					
DISTRICT OF COLUMBIA																			
FLORIDA												3,351,000	166	0.0%		3,906,000	4,333	0.1%	0.1
GEORGIA	2,189,000	77	0.0%	2,283,000	5,129	0.2%	0.2	2,373,000	2	0.0%	0.0	2,548,000	1,366	0.1%	0.1	2,760,000	752	0.0%	0.0
HAWAII								337,000	932	0.3%									
IDAHO																			
ILLINOIS	5,820,000	1,518	0.0%	5,953,000	1	0.0%	0.0	6,079,000	7,026	0.1%	0.1	6,295,000	2,422	0.0%	0.0	6,549,000	20	0.0%	0.0
INDIANA	2,545,000	9,485	0.4%	2,638,000	5,527	0.2%	-0.2	2,727,000	819	0.0%	-0.3	2,842,000	802	0.0%	-0.3	2,968,000	1,363	0.0%	-0.3
IOWA	1,675,000	2,164	0.1%									1,665,000	2	0.0%	-0.1	1,684,000	2,280	0.1%	0.0
KANSAS								1,302,000	3,199	0.2%						1,353,000	2,349	0.2%	-0.1
KENTUCKY				1,748,000	302	0.0%		1,891,000	1,622	0.1%	0.1	1,950,000	893	0.0%	0.0	2,032,000	143	0.0%	0.0
LOUISIANA								1,766,000	1	0.0%									
MAINE																585,000	7,098	1.2%	

United States House of Representatives General Elections (continued)

United States House of Representatives General Elections (continued)

Other Turnout for Election Years 1950–1966 (continued)

State	1950 Voting-age population	Turnout	%	1954 Voting-age population	Turnout	%	Difference from 1950	1958 Voting-age population	Turnout	%	Difference from 1950	1962 Voting-age population	Turnout	%	Difference from 1950	1966 Voting-age population	Turnout	%	Difference from 1950
MARYLAND	1,519,000	3,243	0.2%	1,648,000	1,334	0.1%	-0.1												
MASSACHUSETTS	3,042,000	8,128	0.3%					3,095,000	671	0.0%	-0.2	3,214,000	15,357	0.5%	0.2	3,377,000	78	0.0%	-0.3
MICHIGAN	3,992,000	9,475	0.2%	4,199,000	4,358	0.1%	-0.1	4,396,000	5,260	0.1%	-0.1	4,648,000	4,950	0.1%	-0.1	4,923,000	838	0.0%	-0.2
MINNESOTA	1,879,000	5,584	0.3%									2,041,000	575	0.0%	-0.3				
MISSISSIPPI	1,203,000	2,199	0.2%									1,188,000	4,461	0.4%	0.2	1,218,000	38,459	3.2%	3.0
MISSOURI	2,623,000	594	0.0%																
MONTANA	365,000	2,331	0.6%																
NEBRASKA												861,000	8,852	1.0%		880,000	24	0.0%	-1.0
NEVADA																			
NEW HAMPSHIRE								357,000	868	0.2%						416,000	143	0.0%	-0.2
NEW JERSEY	3,246,000	22,304	0.7%	3,453,000	20,632	0.6%	-0.1	3,652,000	23,500	0.6%	0.0	3,920,000	14,171	0.4%	-0.3	4,218,000	31,571	0.7%	0.1
NEW MEXICO																534,000	137	0.0%	
NEW YORK	9,827,000	314,486	3.2%	10,051,000	95,943	1.0%	-2.2	10,266,000	72,215	0.7%	-2.5	10,657,000	95,425	0.9%	-2.3	11,128,000	254,652	2.3%	-0.9
NORTH CAROLINA																			
NORTH DAKOTA																			
OHIO				5,454,000	44,656	0.8%						5,920,000	5,595	0.1%	-0.7				
OKLAHOMA								1,406,000	1,336	0.1%									
OREGON	985,000	10,038	1.0%									1,117,000	85	0.0%	-1.0	1,210,000	96	0.0%	-1.0
PENNSYLVANIA	6,838,000	4,973	0.1%	6,899,000	99	0.0%	-0.1	6,958,000	538	0.0%	-0.1	7,081,000	1,059	0.0%	-0.1	7,234,000	6,542	0.1%	0.0
RHODE ISLAND								520,000	188	0.0%						568,000	534	0.1%	0.1
SOUTH CAROLINA	1,155,000	19	0.0%					1,248,000	15	0.0%	0.0	1,319,000	1,893	0.1%	0.1	1,401,000	346	0.0%	0.0
SOUTH DAKOTA																			
TENNESSEE								2,073,000	110	0.0%		2,166,000	96,235	4.4%	4.4	2,284,000	34,751	1.5%	1.5
TEXAS								5,293,000	3,789	0.1%						6,187,000	14,708	0.2%	0.2
UTAH																			
VERMONT	229,000	865	0.4%					225,000	0	0.0%	-0.4	234,000	24	0.0%	-0.4	249,000	8	0.0%	-0.4
VIRGINIA	2,030,000	4,941	0.2%	2,147,000	9,596	0.4%	0.2	2,259,000	26,765	1.2%	0.9	2,430,000	1,340	0.1%	-0.2	2,629,000	23,105	0.9%	0.6
WASHINGTON	1,518,000	3,024	0.2%	1,584,000	3,661	0.2%	0.0	1,650,000	2,953	0.2%	0.0					1,932,000	15,655	0.8%	0.6
WEST VIRGINIA																			
WISCONSIN	2,192,000	501	0.0%									2,397,000	107	0.0%	0.0	2,505,000	258	0.0%	0.0
WYOMING																			
Total	63,996,000	549,525	0.9%	61,124,000	198,878	0.3%	-0.5	60,854,000	152,984	0.3%	-0.6	82,621,000	292,355	0.4%	-0.5	90,858,000	463,460	0.5%	-0.3

*Percentage point difference between turnout in current year and initial year listed in chart. If data do not appear for a state in the initial year listed, the difference is calculated from the first year in which data do appear for that state.

TOTAL HIGHEST STATEWIDE GENERAL ELECTIONS

Election Years 1950–1966

State	1950 Voting-age population	1950 Turnout	1950 %	1954 Voting-age population	1954 Turnout	1954 %	1954 Difference from 1950*	1958 Voting-age population	1958 Turnout	1958 %	1958 Difference from 1950	1962 Voting-age population	1962 Turnout	1962 %	1962 Difference from 1950	1966 Voting-age population	1966 Turnout	1966 %	1966 Difference from 1950
ALABAMA	1,749,000	152,192	8.7%	1,785,000	279,789	15.7%	7.0	1,819,000	237,162	13.0%	4.3	1,882,000	477,858	25.4%	16.7	1,958,000	705,261	36.0%	27.3
ALASKA								127,000	48,644	38.3%		144,000	58,591	40.7%	2.4	162,000	65,907	40.7%	2.4
ARIZONA	438,000	177,667	40.6%	559,000	223,402	40.0%	-0.6	673,000	277,566	41.2%	0.7	798,000	349,024	43.7%	3.2	926,000	364,423	39.4%	-1.2
ARKANSAS	1,106,000	295,802	26.7%	1,076,000	280,274	26.0%	-0.7	1,047,000	60,222	5.8%	-21.0	1,075,000	181,592	16.9%	-9.9	1,126,000	291,638	25.9%	-0.8
CALIFORNIA	6,975,000	3,357,704	48.1%	7,895,000	3,073,076	49.1%	0.9	8,777,000	4,953,137	56.4%	8.3	9,933,000	5,573,346	56.1%	8.0	11,212,000	6,278,601	56.0%	7.9
COLORADO	838,000	442,892	52.9%	910,000	480,054	52.8%	-0.1	981,000	534,019	54.4%	1.6	1,086,000	596,596	54.9%	2.1	1,205,000	640,485	53.2%	0.3
CONNECTICUT	1,311,000	878,388	67.0%	1,401,000	932,410	66.6%	-0.4	1,488,000	967,767	65.0%	-2.0	1,612,000	1,032,244	64.0%	-3.0	1,753,000	1,003,617	57.3%	-9.7
DELAWARE	210,000	129,404	61.6%	231,000	144,236	62.4%	0.8	251,000	152,896	60.9%	-0.7	275,000	153,356	55.8%	-5.9	302,000	163,103	54.0%	-7.6
DISTRICT OF COLUMBIA																			
FLORIDA	1,859,000	253,049	13.6%	2,351,000	326,287	13.9%	0.3	2,822,000	494,361	17.5%	3.9	3,351,000	940,839	28.1%	14.5	3,906,000	1,053,775	27.0%	13.4
GEORGIA	2,189,000	290,008	13.2%	2,283,000	352,743	15.5%	2.2	2,373,000	158,638	6.7%	-6.6	2,548,000	333,374	13.1%	-0.2	2,760,000	850,788	30.8%	17.6
HAWAII								337,000	163,717	48.6%		364,000	194,529	53.4%	4.9	401,000	208,161	51.9%	3.3
IDAHO	345,000	200,084	58.0%	355,000	226,012	63.7%	5.7	365,000	239,028	65.5%	7.5	380,000	254,329	66.9%	8.9	397,000	248,228	62.5%	4.5
ILLINOIS	5,820,000	3,509,695	60.3%	5,953,000	3,257,722	54.7%	-5.6	6,079,000	3,229,864	53.1%	-7.2	6,295,000	3,625,309	57.6%	-2.7	6,549,000	3,735,310	57.0%	-3.3
INDIANA	2,545,000	1,587,309	62.4%	2,638,000	1,586,631	60.1%	-2.2	2,727,000	1,721,464	63.1%	0.8	2,842,000	1,790,709	63.0%	0.6	2,968,000	1,678,037	56.5%	-5.8
IOWA	1,675,000	819,959	49.0%	1,664,000	817,253	49.1%	0.2	1,654,000	829,916	50.2%	1.2	1,665,000	802,847	48.2%	-0.7	1,684,000	878,968	52.2%	3.2
KANSAS	1,236,000	604,746	48.9%	1,269,000	614,989	48.5%	-0.5	1,302,000	717,694	55.1%	6.2	1,329,000	625,282	47.0%	-1.9	1,353,000	660,530	48.8%	-0.1
KENTUCKY	1,739,000	488,614	28.1%	1,748,000	668,488	38.2%	10.1	1,891,000	475,818	25.2%	-2.9	1,950,000	631,453	32.4%	4.3	2,032,000	677,124	33.3%	5.2
LOUISIANA	1,590,000	227,075	14.3%	1,679,000	216,323	12.9%	-1.4	1,766,000	182,124	10.3%	-4.0	1,861,000	346,232	18.6%	4.3	1,961,000	546,258	27.9%	13.6
MAINE	553,000	237,632	43.0%	557,000	241,443	43.3%	0.4	561,000	274,962	49.0%	6.0	572,000	285,501	49.9%	6.9	585,000	312,816	53.5%	10.5
MARYLAND	1,519,000	572,927	37.7%	1,648,000	638,875	38.8%	1.0	1,772,000	712,126	40.2%	2.5	1,958,000	718,772	36.7%	-1.0	2,170,000	765,423	35.3%	-2.4
MASSACHUSETTS	3,042,000	1,859,396	61.1%	3,070,000	1,782,659	58.1%	-3.1	3,095,000	1,776,218	57.4%	-3.7	3,214,000	1,970,481	61.3%	0.2	3,377,000	1,811,584	53.6%	-7.5
MICHIGAN	3,992,000	1,804,724	45.2%	4,199,000	2,133,390	50.8%	5.6	4,396,000	2,253,810	51.3%	6.1	4,648,000	2,679,253	57.6%	12.4	4,923,000	2,367,440	48.1%	2.9
MINNESOTA	1,879,000	1,018,267	54.2%	1,922,000	1,131,492	58.9%	4.7	1,962,000	1,131,127	57.7%	3.5	2,041,000	1,204,753	59.0%	4.8	2,140,000	1,220,376	57.0%	2.8
MISSISSIPPI	1,203,000	87,756	7.3%	1,187,000	99,342	8.4%	1.1	1,172,000	61,464	5.2%	-2.1	1,188,000	161,615	13.6%	6.3	1,218,000	382,547	31.4%	24.1
MISSOURI	2,623,000	1,250,150	47.7%	2,646,000	1,184,813	44.8%	-2.9	2,669,000	1,166,817	43.7%	-3.9	2,731,000	1,212,324	44.4%	-3.3	2,813,000	1,045,210	37.2%	-10.5
MONTANA	365,000	210,527	57.7%	374,000	224,587	60.1%	2.4	382,000	228,470	59.8%	2.1	390,000	248,441	63.7%	6.0	399,000	258,371	64.8%	7.1
NEBRASKA	846,000	436,330	51.6%	847,000	406,690	48.0%	-3.6	849,000	415,590	49.0%	-2.6	861,000	445,032	51.7%	0.1	880,000	471,145	53.5%	2.0
NEVADA	107,000	60,328	56.4%	136,000	77,639	57.1%	0.7	162,000	82,328	50.8%	-5.6	205,000	93,324	45.5%	-10.9	256,000	127,850	49.9%	-6.4
NEW HAMPSHIRE	339,000	185,247	54.6%	348,000	191,818	55.1%	0.5	357,000	197,501	55.3%	0.7	383,000	221,252	57.8%	3.1	416,000	228,766	55.0%	0.3
NEW JERSEY	3,246,000	1,571,263	48.4%	3,453,000	1,786,853	51.7%	3.3	3,652,000	1,906,452	52.2%	3.8	3,920,000	1,958,960	50.0%	1.6	4,218,000	2,097,991	49.7%	1.3
NEW MEXICO	375,000	172,634	46.0%	427,000	188,862	44.2%	-1.8	477,000	197,846	41.5%	-4.6	509,000	244,913	48.1%	2.1	534,000	251,657	47.1%	1.1
NEW YORK	9,827,000	5,051,889	51.4%	10,051,000	5,002,181	49.8%	-1.6	10,266,000	5,522,916	53.8%	2.4	10,657,000	5,559,864	52.2%	0.8	11,128,000	5,513,336	49.5%	-1.9

Total Highest Statewide General Elections (continued)

Total Highest Statewide General Elections *(continued)*

Election Years 1950–1966 *(continued)*

State	1950 Voting-age population	1950 Turnout	1950 %	1954 Voting-age population	1954 Turnout	1954 %	1954 Difference from 1950	1958 Voting-age population	1958 Turnout	1958 %	1958 Difference from 1950	1962 Voting-age population	1962 Turnout	1962 %	1962 Difference from 1950	1966 Voting-age population	1966 Turnout	1966 %	1966 Difference from 1950
NORTH CAROLINA	2,319,000	522,200	22.5%	2,421,000	604,179	25.0%	2.4	2,518,000	608,853	24.2%	1.7	2,674,000	818,529	30.6%	8.1	2,856,000	916,449	32.1%	9.6
NORTH DAKOTA	358,000	181,369	50.7%	354,000	188,934	53.4%	2.7	351,000	197,424	56.2%	5.6	351,000	216,282	61.6%	11.0	353,000	197,499	55.9%	5.3
OHIO	5,214,000	2,684,563	51.5%	5,454,000	2,498,837	45.8%	-5.7	5,682,000	3,110,579	54.7%	3.3	5,920,000	3,000,610	50.7%	-0.8	6,161,000	2,795,641	45.4%	-6.1
OKLAHOMA	1,378,000	606,786	44.0%	1,392,000	545,789	39.2%	-4.8	1,406,000	529,775	37.7%	-6.4	1,457,000	624,613	42.9%	-1.2	1,528,000	636,389	41.6%	-2.4
OREGON	985,000	499,489	50.7%	1,016,000	564,494	55.6%	4.9	1,045,000	595,111	56.9%	6.2	1,117,000	630,865	56.5%	5.8	1,210,000	664,879	54.9%	4.2
PENNSYLVANIA	6,838,000	3,511,889	51.4%	6,899,000	3,695,910	53.6%	2.2	6,958,000	3,961,198	56.9%	5.6	7,081,000	4,354,207	61.5%	10.1	7,234,000	3,973,740	54.9%	3.6
RHODE ISLAND	514,000	295,591	57.5%	517,000	326,059	63.1%	5.6	520,000	340,642	65.5%	8.0	540,000	318,658	59.0%	1.5	568,000	322,022	56.7%	-0.8
SOUTH CAROLINA	1,155,000	50,400	4.4%	1,203,000	213,335	17.7%	13.4	1,248,000	76,647	6.1%	1.8	1,319,000	262,554	19.9%	15.5	1,401,000	364,314	26.0%	21.6
SOUTH DAKOTA	396,000	248,426	62.7%	393,000	231,167	58.8%	-3.9	390,000	257,989	66.2%	3.4	388,000	252,731	65.1%	2.4	387,000	225,046	58.2%	-4.6
TENNESSEE	1,980,000	262,608	13.3%	2,027,000	344,796	17.0%	3.7	2,073,000	371,803	17.9%	4.7	2,166,000	605,907	28.0%	14.7	2,284,000	799,871	35.0%	21.8
TEXAS	4,635,000	360,442	7.8%	4,970,000	630,918	12.7%	4.9	5,293,000	768,847	14.5%	6.7	5,717,000	1,551,699	27.1%	19.4	6,187,000	1,258,471	20.3%	12.6
UTAH	384,000	263,847	68.7%	415,000	263,031	63.4%	-5.3	445,000	286,323	64.3%	-4.4	486,000	317,010	65.2%	-3.5	532,000	307,437	57.8%	-10.9
VERMONT	229,000	88,822	38.8%	227,000	114,284	50.3%	11.6	225,000	122,667	54.5%	15.7	234,000	121,381	51.9%	13.1	249,000	135,748	54.5%	15.7
VIRGINIA	2,030,000	211,830	10.4%	2,147,000	342,344	15.9%	5.5	2,259,000	431,609	19.1%	8.7	2,430,000	448,952	18.5%	8.0	2,629,000	682,737	26.0%	15.5
WASHINGTON	1,518,000	723,605	47.7%	1,584,000	809,795	51.1%	3.5	1,650,000	876,826	53.1%	5.5	1,777,000	881,150	49.6%	1.9	1,932,000	939,441	48.6%	1.0
WEST VIRGINIA	1,156,000	662,836	57.3%	1,120,000	591,402	52.8%	-4.5	1,086,000	615,787	56.7%	-0.6	1,073,000	613,018	57.1%	-0.2	1,072,000	494,345	46.1%	-11.2
WISCONSIN	2,192,000	1,110,069	50.6%	2,250,000	1,140,695	50.7%	0.1	2,306,000	1,181,025	51.2%	0.6	2,397,000	1,244,331	51.9%	1.3	2,505,000	1,153,941	46.1%	-4.6
WYOMING	176,000	93,348	53.0%	181,000	108,771	60.1%	7.1	186,000	111,780	60.1%	7.1	190,000	116,474	61.3%	8.3	193,000	119,426	61.9%	8.8
Total	94,998,000	40,311,778	42.4%	99,232,000	42,585,072	42.9%	0.5	103,892,000	45,816,549	44.1%	1.7	109,984,000	51,350,966	46.7%	4.3	116,993,000	52,892,122	45.2%	2.8

*Percentage point difference between turnout in current year and initial year listed in chart. If data do not appear for a state in the initial year listed, the difference is calculated from the first year in which data do appear for that state.

TOTAL HIGHEST STATEWIDE GENERAL ELECTIONS

Republican Turnout for Election Years 1950–1966

State	1950 Voting-age population	Turnout	%	1954 Voting-age population	Turnout	%	Difference from 1950*	1958 Voting-age population	Turnout	%	Difference from 1950	1962 Voting-age population	Turnout	%	Difference from 1950	1966 Voting-age population	Turnout	%	Difference from 1950
ALABAMA	1,749,000	15,177	0.9%	1,785,000	88,688	5.0%	4.1	1,819,000	30,415	1.7%	0.8	1,882,000	195,134	10.4%	9.5	1,958,000	313,018	16.0%	15.1
ALASKA								127,000	23,462	18.5%		144,000	27,054	18.8%	0.3	162,000	34,040	21.0%	2.5
ARIZONA	438,000	99,109	22.6%	559,000	115,866	20.7%	-1.9	673,000	164,593	24.5%	1.8	798,000	200,578	25.1%	2.5	926,000	204,478	22.1%	-0.5
ARKANSAS	1,100,000	50,309	4.5%	1,076,000	127,004	11.8%	7.3	1,047,000	50,288	4.8%	0.3	1,075,000	98,013	9.1%	4.6	1,126,000	306,324	27.2%	22.7
CALIFORNIA	6,975,000	2,461,754	35.3%	7,895,000	2,290,519	29.0%	-0.3	8,777,000	2,204,337	25.1%	-10.2	9,933,000	3,180,483	32.0%	-3.3	11,212,000	3,742,913	33.4%	-1.9
COLORADO	838,000	239,734	28.6%	910,000	248,502	27.3%	-1.3	981,000	288,643	29.4%	0.8	1,086,000	349,342	32.2%	3.6	1,205,000	368,307	30.6%	2.0
CONNECTICUT	1,311,000	436,418	33.3%	1,401,000	474,585	33.9%	0.6	1,488,000	425,452	28.6%	-4.7	1,612,000	501,694	31.1%	-2.2	1,753,000	446,536	25.5%	-7.8
DELAWARE	210,000	73,313	34.9%	231,000	65,035	28.2%	-6.8	251,000	82,280	32.8%	-2.1	275,000	71,934	26.2%	-8.8	302,000	97,268	32.2%	-2.7
DISTRICT OF COLUMBIA																			
FLORIDA	1,859,000	74,228	4.0%	2,351,000	71,137	3.0%	-1.0	2,822,000	155,956	5.5%	1.5	3,351,000	351,954	10.5%	6.5	3,906,000	821,190	21.0%	17.0
GEORGIA				2,283,000	29,911	1.3%						2,548,000	59,514	2.3%	1.0	2,760,000	453,665	16.4%	15.1
HAWAII								337,000	87,161	25.9%		364,000	81,707	22.4%	-3.4	401,000	104,324	26.0%	0.2
IDAHO	345,000	124,237	36.0%	355,000	142,269	40.1%	4.1	365,000	121,810	33.4%	-2.6	380,000	139,578	36.7%	0.7	397,000	149,434	37.6%	1.6
ILLINOIS	5,820,000	1,951,984	33.5%	5,953,000	1,621,278	27.2%	-6.3	6,079,000	1,468,590	24.2%	-9.4	6,295,000	1,961,202	31.2%	-2.4	6,549,000	2,100,449	32.1%	-1.5
INDIANA	2,545,000	850,357	33.4%	2,638,000	833,304	31.6%	-1.8	2,727,000	798,850	29.3%	-4.1	2,842,000	911,596	32.1%	-1.3	2,968,000	897,086	30.2%	-3.2
IOWA	1,675,000	506,642	30.2%	1,664,000	478,322	28.7%	-1.5	1,654,000	412,798	25.0%	-5.3	1,665,000	432,483	26.0%	-4.3	1,684,000	522,339	31.0%	0.8
KANSAS	1,236,000	355,849	28.8%	1,269,000	348,144	27.4%	-1.4	1,302,000	354,732	27.2%	-1.5	1,329,000	388,500	29.2%	0.4	1,353,000	416,610	30.8%	2.0
KENTUCKY	1,739,000	278,368	16.0%	1,748,000	362,948	20.8%	4.8	1,891,000	164,425	8.7%	-7.3	1,950,000	432,648	22.2%	6.2	2,032,000	483,805	23.8%	7.8
LOUISIANA	1,590,000	30,931	1.9%	1,679,000	8,212	0.5%	-1.5	1,766,000	4,160	0.2%	-1.7	1,861,000	103,066	5.5%	3.6	1,961,000	99,252	5.1%	3.1
MAINE	553,000	145,823	26.4%	557,000	144,530	25.9%	-0.4	561,000	134,572	24.0%	-2.4	572,000	158,213	27.7%	1.3	585,000	188,291	32.2%	5.8
MARYLAND	1,519,000	369,807	24.3%	1,648,000	381,451	23.1%	-1.2	1,772,000	382,021	21.6%	-2.8	1,958,000	343,051	17.5%	-6.8	2,170,000	455,318	21.0%	-3.4
MASSACHUSETTS	3,042,000	930,280	30.6%	3,070,000	985,339	32.1%	1.5	3,095,000	818,463	26.4%	-4.1	3,214,000	1,047,891	32.6%	2.0	3,377,000	1,277,358	37.8%	7.2
MICHIGAN	3,992,000	956,497	24.0%	4,199,000	1,049,420	25.0%	1.0	4,396,000	1,078,089	24.5%	0.6	4,648,000	1,420,086	30.6%	6.6	4,923,000	1,490,430	30.3%	6.3
MINNESOTA	1,879,000	635,800	33.8%	1,922,000	538,865	28.0%	-5.8	1,962,000	536,629	27.4%	-6.5	2,041,000	619,751	30.4%	-3.5	2,140,000	680,593	31.8%	-2.0
MISSISSIPPI	1,203,000	2,861	0.2%	1,187,000	4,678	0.4%	0.2									1,218,000	105,150	8.6%	8.4
MISSOURI	2,623,000	593,139	22.6%	2,646,000	519,091	19.6%	-3.0	2,669,000	429,940	16.1%	-6.5	2,731,000	555,330	20.3%	-2.3	2,813,000	484,098	17.2%	-5.4
MONTANA	365,000	99,948	27.4%	374,000	112,863	30.2%	2.8	382,000	80,744	21.1%	-6.2	390,000	129,075	33.1%	5.7	399,000	140,940	35.3%	7.9
NEBRASKA	846,000	271,840	32.1%	847,000	255,695	30.2%	-1.9	849,000	232,227	27.4%	-4.8	861,000	271,777	31.6%	-0.6	880,000	299,245	34.0%	1.9
NEVADA	107,000	35,609	33.3%	136,000	42,321	31.1%	-2.2	162,000	35,760	22.1%	-11.2	205,000	33,749	16.5%	-16.8	256,000	71,807	28.0%	-5.2
NEW HAMPSHIRE	339,000	112,487	33.2%	348,000	117,150	33.7%	0.5	357,000	115,370	32.3%	-0.9	383,000	134,035	35.0%	1.8	416,000	139,048	33.4%	0.2
NEW JERSEY	3,246,000	859,145	26.5%	3,453,000	903,839	26.2%	-0.3	3,652,000	944,349	25.9%	-0.6	3,920,000	964,280	24.6%	-1.9	4,218,000	1,279,343	30.3%	3.9
NEW MEXICO	375,000	96,846	25.8%	427,000	83,373	19.5%	-6.3	477,000	101,567	21.3%	-4.5	509,000	116,262	22.8%	-3.0	534,000	134,625	25.2%	-0.6
NEW YORK	9,827,000	2,819,523	28.7%	10,051,000	2,549,613	25.4%	-3.3	10,266,000	3,126,929	30.5%	1.8	10,657,000	3,269,417	30.7%	2.0	11,128,000	2,690,626	24.2%	-4.5

Total Highest Statewide General Elections (continued)

Total Highest Statewide General Elections (continued)

Republican Turnout for Election Years 1950–1966 (continued)

State	1950 Voting-age population	Turnout	%	1954 Voting-age population	Turnout	%	Difference from 1950	1958 Voting-age population	Turnout	%	Difference from 1950	1962 Voting-age population	Turnout	%	Difference from 1950	1966 Voting-age population	Turnout	%	Difference from 1950
NORTH CAROLINA	2,319,000	171,804	7.4%	2,421,000	214,012	8.8%	1.4	2,518,000	177,651	7.1%	-0.4	2,674,000	336,383	12.6%	5.2	2,856,000	432,036	15.1%	7.7
NORTH DAKOTA	358,000	126,209	35.3%	354,000	124,845	35.3%	0.0	351,000	117,070	33.4%	-1.9	351,000	135,705	38.7%	3.4	353,000	116,812	33.1%	-2.2
OHIO	5,214,000	1,645,643	31.6%	5,454,000	1,340,847	24.6%	-7.0	5,682,000	1,529,565	26.9%	-4.6	5,920,000	1,836,190	31.0%	-0.5	6,161,000	1,795,277	29.1%	-2.4
OKLAHOMA	1,378,000	313,205	22.7%	1,392,000	262,013	18.8%	-3.9	1,406,000	159,168	11.3%	-11.4	1,457,000	392,316	26.9%	4.2	1,528,000	377,078	24.7%	1.9
OREGON	985,000	376,510	38.2%	1,016,000	322,522	31.7%	-6.5	1,045,000	331,900	31.8%	-6.5	1,117,000	345,497	30.9%	-7.3	1,210,000	377,346	31.2%	-7.0
PENNSYLVANIA	6,838,000	1,834,128	26.8%	6,899,000	1,824,186	26.4%	-0.4	6,958,000	2,042,586	29.4%	2.5	7,081,000	2,424,918	34.2%	7.4	7,234,000	2,110,349	29.2%	2.4
RHODE ISLAND	514,000	120,683	23.5%	517,000	137,131	26.5%	3.0	520,000	176,505	33.9%	10.5	540,000	163,952	30.4%	6.9	568,000	210,202	37.0%	13.5
SOUTH CAROLINA				1,203,000	2,711	0.2%						1,319,000	133,930	10.2%	9.9	1,401,000	271,297	19.4%	19.1
SOUTH DAKOTA	396,000	160,670	40.6%	393,000	137,273	34.9%	-5.6	390,000	125,520	32.2%	-8.4	388,000	151,067	38.9%	-1.6	387,000	150,517	38.9%	-1.7
TENNESSEE	1,980,000	97,203	4.9%	2,027,000	112,272	5.5%	0.6	2,073,000	92,999	4.5%	-0.4	2,166,000	212,362	9.8%	4.9	2,284,000	483,063	21.1%	16.2
TEXAS	4,635,000	39,737	0.9%	4,970,000	94,131	1.9%	1.0	5,293,000	185,926	3.5%	2.7	5,717,000	715,025	12.5%	11.6	6,187,000	842,501	13.6%	12.8
UTAH	384,000	142,427	37.1%	415,000	146,406	35.3%	-1.8	445,000	145,375	32.7%	-4.4	486,000	167,390	34.4%	-2.6	532,000	196,176	36.9%	-0.2
VERMONT	229,000	69,543	30.4%	227,000	70,143	30.9%	0.5	225,000	64,900	28.8%	-1.5	234,000	81,241	34.7%	4.4	249,000	89,097	35.8%	5.4
VIRGINIA	2,030,000	51,493	2.5%	2,147,000	128,315	6.0%	3.4	2,259,000	86,211	3.8%	1.3	2,430,000	178,913	7.4%	4.8	2,629,000	268,094	10.2%	7.7
WASHINGTON	1,518,000	378,419	24.9%	1,584,000	342,089	21.6%	-3.3	1,650,000	467,678	28.3%	3.4	1,777,000	543,318	30.6%	5.6	1,932,000	449,765	23.3%	-1.6
WEST VIRGINIA	1,156,000	287,915	24.9%	1,120,000	268,066	23.9%	-1.0	1,086,000	263,172	24.2%	-0.7	1,073,000	269,744	25.1%	0.2	1,072,000	232,322	21.7%	-3.2
WISCONSIN	2,192,000	639,293	29.2%	2,250,000	598,919	26.6%	-2.5	2,306,000	556,391	24.1%	-5.0	2,397,000	625,536	26.1%	-3.1	2,505,000	626,041	25.0%	-4.2
WYOMING	176,000	54,441	30.9%	181,000	61,111	33.8%	2.8	186,000	59,894	32.2%	1.3	190,000	71,489	37.6%	6.7	193,000	65,624	34.0%	3.1
Total	91,654,000	21,987,338	24.0%	99,232,000	21,180,944	21.3%	-2.6	99,099,000	21,437,123	21.6%	-2.4	108,796,000	27,334,373	25.1%	1.1	116,993,000	30,091,507	25.7%	1.7

Democratic Turnout for Election Years 1950–1966

State	1950 Voting-age population	Turnout	%	1954 Voting-age population	Turnout	%	Difference from 1950*	1958 Voting-age population.	Turnout	%	Difference from 1950	1962 Voting-age population	Turnout	%	Difference from 1950	1966 Voting-age population	Turnout	%	Difference from 1950
ALABAMA	1,749,000	155,414	8.9%	1,785,000	268,552	15.0%	6.2	1,819,000	239,633	13.2%	4.3	1,882,000	304,210	16.2%	7.3	1,958,000	537,505	27.5%	18.6
ALASKA								127,000	29,189	23.0%		144,000	33,827	23.5%	0.5	162,000	49,289	30.4%	7.4
ARIZONA	438,000	116,246	26.5%	559,000	128,104	22.9%	-3.6	673,000	139,467	20.7%	-5.8	798,000	199,217	25.0%	-1.6	926,000	174,904	18.9%	-7.7
ARKANSAS	1,106,000	302,582	27.4%	1,076,000	291,058	27.1%	-0.3	1,047,000	236,598	22.6%	-4.8	1,075,000	225,743	21.0%	-6.4	1,126,000	257,203	22.8%	-4.5
CALIFORNIA	6,975,000	1,502,507	21.5%	7,895,000	1,991,169	25.2%	3.7	8,777,000	3,140,076	35.8%	14.2	9,933,000	3,037,109	30.6%	9.0	11,212,000	2,937,862	26.2%	4.7
COLORADO	838,000	214,385	25.6%	910,000	262,205	28.8%	3.2	981,000	321,165	32.7%	7.2	1,086,000	282,474	26.0%	0.4	1,205,000	339,750	28.2%	2.6
CONNECTICUT	1,311,000	453,646	34.6%	1,401,000	463,643	33.1%	-1.5	1,488,000	607,012	40.8%	6.2	1,612,000	556,907	34.5%	-0.1	1,753,000	561,599	32.0%	-2.6
DELAWARE	210,000	56,091	26.7%	231,000	82,511	35.7%	9.0	251,000	76,797	30.6%	3.9	275,000	81,166	29.5%	2.8	302,000	72,142	23.9%	-2.8
DISTRICT OF COLUMBIA																			
FLORIDA	1,859,000	238,987	12.9%	2,351,000	287,769	12.2%	-0.6	2,822,000	386,113	13.7%	0.8	3,351,000	657,633	19.6%	6.8	3,906,000	680,466	17.4%	4.6

Total Highest Statewide General Elections (continued)

Democratic Turnout for Election Years 1950–1966 (continued)

State	1950 Voting-age population	Turnout	%	1954 Voting-age population	Turnout	%	Difference from 1950	1958 Voting-age population.	Turnout	%	Difference from 1950	1962 Voting-age population	Turnout	%	Difference from 1950	1966 Voting-age population	Turnout	%	Difference from 1950
GEORGIA	2,189,000	289,931	13.2%	2,283,000	333,917	14.6%	1.4	2,373,000	168,414	7.1%	-6.1	2,548,000	311,524	12.2%	-1.0	2,760,000	622,043	22.5%	9.3
HAWAII								337,000	111,727	33.2%		364,000	136,294	37.4%	4.3	401,000	140,880	35.1%	2.0
IDAHO	345,000	97,150	28.2%	355,000	104,647	29.5%	1.3	365,000	124,297	34.1%	5.9	380,000	141,657	37.3%	9.1	397,000	112,637	28.4%	0.2
ILLINOIS	5,820,000	1,657,630	28.5%	5,953,000	1,804,338	30.3%	1.8	0,070,000	1,754,248	28.9%	0.4	6,295,000	1,802,063	28.6%	0.1	6,549,000	1,707,576	26.1%	-2.4
INDIANA	2,545,000	741,025	29.1%	2,638,000	747,800	28.3%	-0.8	2,727,000	973,636	35.7%	6.6	2,842,000	905,491	31.9%	2.7	2,968,000	779,588	26.3%	-2.9
IOWA	1,675,000	384,337	22.9%	1,664,000	410,255	24.7%	1.7	1,654,000	465,024	28.1%	5.2	1,665,000	430,899	25.9%	2.9	1,684,000	404,259	29.4%	6.4
KANSAS	1,236,000	275,494	22.3%	1,269,000	286,218	22.6%	0.3	1,302,000	415,506	31.9%	9.6	1,329,000	291,285	21.9%	-0.4	1,353,000	380,030	28.1%	5.8
KENTUCKY	1,739,000	334,249	19.2%	1,748,000	434,109	24.8%	5.6	1,891,000	309,771	16.4%	-2.8	1,950,000	387,440	19.9%	0.6	2,032,000	357,345	17.6%	-1.6
LOUISIANA	1,590,000	227,075	14.3%	1,679,000	208,111	12.4%	-1.9	1,766,000	177,963	10.1%	-4.2	1,861,000	318,838	17.1%	2.9	1,961,000	447,006	22.8%	8.5
MAINE	553,000	100,731	18.2%	557,000	108,548	19.5%	1.3	561,000	172,842	30.8%	12.6	572,000	146,121	25.5%	7.3	585,000	172,036	29.4%	11.2
MARYLAND	1,519,000	283,727	18.7%	1,648,000	342,115	20.8%	2.1	1,772,000	485,061	27.4%	8.7	1,958,000	443,935	22.7%	4.0	2,170,000	429,380	19.8%	1.1
MASSACHUSETTS	3,042,000	1,074,570	35.3%	3,070,000	947,494	30.9%	-4.5	3,095,000	1,362,926	44.0%	8.7	3,214,000	1,162,611	36.2%	0.8	3,377,000	1,098,362	32.5%	-2.8
MICHIGAN	3,992,000	935,152	23.4%	4,199,000	1,216,308	29.0%	5.5	4,396,000	1,225,533	27.9%	4.5	4,648,000	1,392,221	30.0%	6.5	4,923,000	1,150,400	23.4%	-0.1
MINNESOTA	1,879,000	473,710	25.2%	1,922,000	642,193	33.4%	8.2	1,962,000	685,326	34.9%	9.7	2,041,000	619,842	30.4%	5.2	2,140,000	685,840	32.0%	6.8
MISSISSIPPI	1,203,000	82,696	6.9%	1,187,000	100,848	8.5%	1.6	1,172,000	61,464	5.2%	-1.6	1,188,000	157,154	13.2%	6.4	1,218,000	282,574	23.2%	16.3
MISSOURI	2,623,000	697,542	26.6%	2,646,000	665,722	25.2%	-1.4	2,669,000	780,083	29.2%	2.6	2,731,000	683,877	25.0%	-1.6	2,813,000	561,112	19.9%	-6.6
MONTANA	365,000	108,248	29.7%	374,000	117,109	31.3%	1.7	382,000	174,910	45.8%	16.1	390,000	119,366	30.6%	0.9	399,000	138,166	34.6%	5.0
NEBRASKA	846,000	202,638	24.0%	847,000	164,753	19.5%	-4.5	849,000	211,345	24.9%	0.9	861,000	242,669	28.2%	4.2	880,000	187,950	21.4%	-2.6
NEVADA	107,000	35,829	33.5%	136,000	36,797	27.1%	-6.4	162,000	55,053	34.0%	0.5	205,000	66,866	32.6%	-0.9	256,000	86,467	33.8%	0.3
NEW HAMPSHIRE	339,000	82,258	24.3%	348,000	87,344	25.1%	0.8	357,000	99,955	28.0%	3.7	383,000	135,481	35.4%	11.1	416,000	125,882	30.3%	6.0
NEW JERSEY	3,246,000	689,814	21.3%	3,453,000	862,382	25.0%	3.7	3,652,000	966,832	26.5%	5.2	3,920,000	980,509	25.0%	3.8	4,218,000	1,020,779	24.2%	2.9
NEW MEXICO	375,000	97,187	25.9%	427,000	111,711	26.2%	0.2	477,000	127,496	26.7%	0.8	509,000	130,933	25.7%	-0.2	534,000	137,205	25.7%	-0.2
NEW YORK	9,827,000	2,632,313	26.8%	10,051,000	2,560,738	25.5%	-1.3	10,266,000	2,763,883	26.9%	0.1	10,657,000	2,778,105	26.1%	-0.7	11,128,000	2,763,837	24.8%	-1.9
NORTH CAROLINA	2,319,000	376,473	16.2%	2,421,000	408,312	16.9%	0.6	2,518,000	431,202	17.1%	0.9	2,674,000	491,520	18.4%	2.1	2,856,000	501,440	17.6%	1.3
NORTH DAKOTA	358,000	62,322	17.4%	354,000	69,248	19.6%	2.2	351,000	99,562	28.4%	11.0	351,000	115,258	32.8%	15.4	353,000	80,687	22.9%	5.4
OHIO	5,214,000	1,522,249	29.2%	5,454,000	1,405,262	25.8%	-3.4	5,682,000	1,869,260	32.9%	3.7	5,920,000	1,843,813	31.1%	2.0	6,161,000	1,196,149	19.4%	-9.8
OKLAHOMA	1,378,000	363,452	26.4%	1,392,000	357,386	25.7%	-0.7	1,406,000	399,504	28.4%	2.0	1,457,000	381,737	26.2%	-0.2	1,528,000	343,157	22.5%	-3.9
OREGON	985,000	201,096	20.4%	1,016,000	285,775	28.1%	7.7	1,045,000	338,858	32.4%	12.0	1,117,000	344,716	30.9%	10.4	1,210,000	330,374	27.3%	6.9
PENNSYLVANIA	6,838,000	1,710,355	25.0%	6,899,000	1,996,266	28.9%	3.9	6,958,000	2,024,852	29.1%	4.1	7,081,000	2,238,383	31.6%	6.6	7,234,000	1,897,161	26.2%	1.2
RHODE ISLAND	514,000	183,103	35.6%	517,000	195,200	37.8%	2.1	520,000	222,166	42.7%	7.1	540,000	207,517	38.4%	2.8	568,000	219,331	38.6%	3.0
SOUTH CAROLINA	1,155,000	50,633	4.4%	1,203,000	214,204	17.8%	13.4	1,248,000	77,714	6.2%	1.8	1,319,000	253,704	19.2%	14.9	1,401,000	257,193	18.4%	14.0
SOUTH DAKOTA	396,000	99,062	25.0%	393,000	102,377	26.1%	1.0	390,000	132,761	34.0%	9.0	388,000	127,458	32.9%	7.8	387,000	96,504	24.9%	-0.1
TENNESSEE	1,980,000	184,437	9.3%	2,027,000	281,291	13.9%	4.6	2,073,000	317,324	15.3%	6.0	2,166,000	315,648	14.6%	5.3	2,284,000	532,998	23.3%	14.0

Total Highest Statewide General Elections (continued)

Total Highest Statewide General Elections *(continued)*

Democratic Turnout for Election Years 1950–1966 *(continued)*

State	1950 Voting-age population	1950 Turnout	1950 %	1954 Voting-age population	1954 Turnout	1954 %	1954 Difference from 1950	1958 Voting-age population.	1958 Turnout	1958 %	1958 Difference from 1950	1962 Voting-age population	1962 Turnout	1962 %	1962 Difference from 1950	1966 Voting-age population	1966 Turnout	1966 %	1966 Difference from 1950
TEXAS	4,635,000	335,010	7.2%	4,970,000	569,533	11.5%	4.2	5,293,000	695,035	13.1%	5.9	5,717,000	870,860	15.2%	8.0	6,187,000	1,037,517	16.8%	9.5
UTAH	384,000	138,444	36.1%	415,000	116,625	28.1%	-8.0	445,000	140,948	31.7%	-4.4	486,000	151,656	31.2%	-4.8	532,000	111,261	20.9%	-15.1
VERMONT	229,000	22,709	9.9%	227,000	54,554	24.0%	14.1	225,000	63,131	28.1%	18.1	234,000	61,383	26.2%	16.3	249,000	78,669	31.6%	21.7
VIRGINIA	2,030,000	155,396	7.7%	2,147,000	277,525	12.9%	5.3	2,259,000	318,633	14.1%	6.5	2,430,000	268,699	11.1%	3.4	2,629,000	429,855	16.4%	8.7
WASHINGTON	1,518,000	397,719	26.2%	1,584,000	464,045	29.3%	3.1	1,650,000	597,040	36.2%	10.0	1,777,000	491,365	27.7%	1.5	1,932,000	474,021	24.5%	-1.7
WEST VIRGINIA	1,156,000	374,921	32.4%	1,120,000	339,958	30.4%	-2.1	1,086,000	381,745	35.2%	2.7	1,073,000	343,274	32.0%	-0.4	1,072,000	292,325	27.3%	-5.2
WISCONSIN	2,192,000	525,319	24.0%	2,250,000	560,747	24.9%	1.0	2,306,000	682,440	29.6%	5.6	2,397,000	662,342	27.6%	3.7	2,505,000	539,258	21.5%	-2.4
WYOMING	176,000	42,518	24.2%	181,000	57,845	32.0%	7.8	186,000	58,035	31.2%	7.0	190,000	54,298	28.6%	4.4	193,000	59,141	30.6%	6.5
Total	94,998,000	21,288,382	22.4%	99,232,000	23,824,621	24.0%	1.6	103,892,000	27,699,555	26.7%	4.3	109,984,000	28,387,098	25.8%	3.4	116,993,000	27,969,115	23.9%	1.5

Other Turnout for Election Years 1950–1966

State	1950 Voting-age population	1950 Turnout	1950 %	1954 Voting-age population	1954 Turnout	1954 %	1954 Difference from 1950*	1958 Voting-age population	1958 Turnout	1958 %	1958 Difference from 1950	1962 Voting-age population	1962 Turnout	1962 %	1962 Difference from 1950	1966 Voting-age population	1966 Turnout	1966 %	1966 Difference from 1950
ALABAMA	1,749,000	38,477	2.2%	1,785,000	1	0.0%	-2.2	1,819,000	904	0.0%	-2.2	1,882,000	32,446	1.7%	-0.5	1,958,000	47,653	2.4%	0.2
ALASKA								127,000	480	0.4%						162,000	1,084	0.7%	0.3
ARIZONA																			
ARKANSAS				1,076,000	51	0.0%						1,075,000	29	0.0%	0.0				
CALIFORNIA	6,975,000	123,064	1.8%	7,895,000	5,280	0.1%	-1.7	8,777,000	4,790	0.1%	-1.7	9,933,000	75,810	0.8%	-1.0	11,212,000	11,358	0.1%	-1.7
COLORADO	838,000	2,521	0.3%	910,000	415	0.0%	-0.3	981,000	1,175	0.1%	-0.2	1,086,000	5,203	0.5%	0.2	1,205,000	16,201	1.3%	1.0
CONNECTICUT	1,311,000	22,913	1.7%	1,401,000	12,582	0.9%	-0.8	1,488,000	6,853	0.5%	-1.3	1,612,000	1,678	0.1%	-1.6	1,753,000	17,149	1.0%	-0.8
DELAWARE												275,000	256	0.1%					
DISTRICT OF COLUMBIA																			
FLORIDA	1,859,000	272	0.0%	2,351,000	162	0.0%	0.0					3,351,000	193	0.0%	0.0	3,906,000	4,333	0.1%	0.1
GEORGIA	2,189,000	3,659	0.2%	2,283,000	5,129	0.2%	0.1	2,373,000	83	0.0%	-0.2	2,548,000	1,366	0.1%	-0.1	2,760,000	70,728	2.6%	2.4
HAWAII								337,000	932	0.3%									
IDAHO																397,000	54,263	13.7%	
ILLINOIS	5,820,000	13,059	0.2%	5,953,000	4	0.0%	-0.2	6,079,000	7,026	0.1%	-0.1	6,295,000	2,422	0.0%	-0.2	6,549,000	44,129	0.7%	0.4
INDIANA	2,545,000	13,396	0.5%	2,638,000	5,527	0.2%	-0.3	2,727,000	19,327	0.7%	0.2	2,842,000	802	0.0%	-0.5	2,968,000	1,363	0.0%	-0.5
IOWA	1,675,000	3,573	0.2%	1,664,000	2,393	0.1%	-0.1					1,665,000	6	0.0%	-0.2	1,684,000	11,043	0.7%	0.4
KANSAS	1,236,000	11,859	1.0%	1,269,000	11,344	0.9%	-0.1	1,302,000	7,397	0.6%	-0.4	1,329,000	10,102	0.8%	-0.2	1,353,000	18,045	1.3%	0.4
KENTUCKY	1,739,000	4,496	0.3%	1,748,000	302	0.0%	-0.2	1,891,000	1,622	0.1%	-0.2	1,950,000	893	0.0%	-0.2	2,032,000	143	0.0%	-0.3
LOUISIANA								1,766,000	1	0.0%									
MAINE	553,000	1,054	0.2%													585,000	7,098	1.2%	1.0

Total Highest Statewide General Elections (continued)

Other Turnout for Election Years 1950–1966 (continued)

State	1950 Voting-age population	Turnout	%	1954 Voting-age population	Turnout	%	Difference from 1950	1958 Voting-age population	Turnout	%	Difference from 1950	1962 Voting-age population	Turnout	%	Difference from 1950	1966 Voting-age population	Turnout	%	Difference from 1950
MARYLAND	1,519,000	6,143	0.4%	1,648,000	1,334	0.1%	-0.3					1,958,000	5	0.0%	-0.4	2,170,000	89,900	4.1%	3.7
MASSACHUSETTS	3,042,000	11,541	0.4%	3,070,000	8,348	0.3%	-0.1	3,095,000	13,634	0.4%	0.1	3,214,000	56,805	1.8%	1.4	3,377,000	11,715	0.3%	0.0
MICHIGAN	3,992,000	10,232	0.3%	4,199,000	7,419	0.2%	-0.1	4,396,000	8,562	0.2%	-0.1	4,648,000	5,240	0.1%	-0.1	4,923,000	8,096	0.2%	-0.1
MINNESOTA	1,879,000	10,195	0.5%	1,922,000	17,140	0.9%	0.3	1,962,000	10,858	0.6%	0.0	2,041,000	7,311	0.4%	-0.2	2,140,000	10,718	0.5%	0.0
MISSISSIPPI	1,203,000	2,199	0.2%									1,188,000	4,461	0.4%	0.2	1,218,000	38,459	3.2%	3.0
MISSOURI	2,623,000	760	0.0%																
MONTANA	365,000	2,331	0.6%																
NEBRASKA	846,000	1	0.0%	847,000	8	0.0%	0.0	849,000	17	0.0%	0.0	861,000	8,852	1.0%	1.0	880,000	1,035	0.1%	0.1
NEVADA																			
NEW HAMPSHIRE	339,000	11,958	3.5%					357,000	868	0.2%	-3.3					416,000	501	0.1%	-3.4
NEW JERSEY	3,246,000	22,304	0.7%	3,453,000	50,871	1.5%	0.8	3,652,000	32,210	0.9%	0.2	3,920,000	14,171	0.4%	-0.3	4,218,000	63,824	1.5%	0.8
NEW MEXICO												509,000	18	0.0%		534,000	137	0.0%	0.0
NEW YORK	9,827,000	314,486	3.2%	10,051,000	95,943	1.0%	-2.2	10,266,000	72,715	0.7%	-2.5	10,657,000	171,626	1.6%	-1.6	11,128,000	1,042,596	9.4%	6.2
NORTH CAROLINA																2,856,000	36	0.0%	
NORTH DAKOTA								351,000	2,673	0.8%									
OHIO				5,454,000	44,656	0.8%						5,920,000	5,595	0.1%	-0.7				
OKLAHOMA	1,378,000	1,763	0.1%	1,392,000	2,980	0.2%	0.1	1,406,000	31,840	2.3%	2.1	1,457,000	2,856	0.2%	0.1	1,528,000	3,852	0.3%	0.1
OREGON	985,000	10,165	1.0%					1,045,000	160	0.0%	1.0	1,117,000	26,551	2.4%	1.3	1,210,000	508	0.0%	-1.0
PENNSYLVANIA	6,838,000	34,166	0.5%	6,899,000	7,121	0.1%	-0.4	6,958,000	16,215	0.2%	-0.3	7,081,000	14,497	0.2%	-0.3	7,234,000	71,600	1.0%	0.5
RHODE ISLAND				517,000	1,944	0.4%		520,000	188	0.0%	-0.3					568,000	534	0.1%	-0.3
SOUTH CAROLINA	1,155,000	37	0.0%	1,203,000	143,707	11.9%	11.9	1,248,000	26	0.0%	0.0	1,319,000	1,893	0.1%	0.1	1,401,000	346	0.0%	0.0
SOUTH DAKOTA																			
TENNESSEE	1,980,000	51,757	2.6%	2,027,000	41,295	2.0%	-0.6	2,073,000	147,733	7.1%	4.5	2,166,000	205,226	9.5%	6.9	2,284,000	123,568	5.4%	2.8
TEXAS				4,970,000	3,025	0.1%		5,293,000	14,172	0.3%	0.2	5,717,000	7,120	0.1%	0.1	6,187,000	20,319	0.3%	0.3
UTAH	384,000	815	0.2%					445,000	77,013	17.3%	17.1								
VERMONT	229,000	865	0.4%	227,000	28	0.0%	-0.4	225,000	6	0.0%	-0.4	234,000	196	0.1%	-0.3	249,000	16	0.0%	-0.4
VIRGINIA	2,030,000	4,941	0.2%	2,147,000	28,985	1.4%	1.1	2,259,000	140,419	6.2%	6.0	2,430,000	1,340	0.1%	-0.2	2,629,000	58,343	2.2%	2.0
WASHINGTON	1,518,000	4,600	0.3%	1,584,000	3,661	0.2%	-0.1	1,650,000	11,511	0.7%	0.4	1,777,000	5,660	0.3%	0.0	1,932,000	15,655	0.8%	0.5
WEST VIRGINIA																			
WISCONSIN	2,192,000	7,180	0.3%	2,250,000	1,761	0.1%	-0.2	2,306,000	1,840	0.1%	-0.2	2,397,000	2,980	0.1%	-0.2				
WYOMING								186,000	4,979	2.7%									
Total	76,059,000	746,782	1.0%	84,833,000	503,416	0.6%	-0.4	80,209,000	637,729	0.8%	-0.2	96,454,000	673,609	0.7%	-0.3	97,606,000	1,866,348	1.9%	0.9

*Percentage point difference between turnout in current year and initial year listed in chart. If data do not appear for a state in the initial year listed, the difference is calculated from the first year in which data do appear for that state.

STATE GUBERNATORIAL PRIMARY ELECTIONS

Election Years 1950–1966

State*	1950 Voting-age population	1950 Turnout	1950 %	1954 Voting-age population	1954 Turnout	1954 %	1954 Difference from 1950**	1958 Voting-age population	1958 Turnout	1958 %	1958 Difference from 1950	1962 Voting-age population	1962 Turnout	1962 %	1962 Difference from 1950	1966 Voting-age population	1966 Turnout	1966 %	1966 Difference from 1950
ALABAMA																			
ALASKA												142,000	38,826	27.3%		160,000	51,591	32.2%	5.3
ARIZONA																908,000	225,244	24.8%	
ARKANSAS								1,052,000	388,324	36.9%						1,119,000	440,021	39.3%	2.4
CALIFORNIA								8,648,000	3,868,992	44.7%		9,746,000	4,101,048	42.1%	-2.7	11,025,000	4,802,626	43.6%	-1.2
COLORADO	830,000	146,850	17.7%																
CONNECTICUT																			
DELAWARE																			
DISTRICT OF COLUMBIA																			
FLORIDA				2,282,000	702,341	30.8%										3,826,000	1,178,446	30.8%	0.0
GEORGIA																			
HAWAII												359,000	156,798	43.7%		396,000	145,227	36.7%	-6.4
IDAHO	344,000	127,569	37.1%									377,000	148,470	39.4%	2.3	394,000	157,628	40.0%	2.9
ILLINOIS																			
INDIANA																			
IOWA	1,676,000	332,190	19.8%									1,662,000	282,374	17.0%	-2.8				
KANSAS	1,233,000	337,683	27.4%									1,325,000	312,892	23.6%	-3.8	1,349,000	305,692	22.7%	-4.7
KENTUCKY																			
LOUISIANA																			
MAINE								560,000	142,326	25.4%						583,000	149,200	25.6%	0.2
MARYLAND												1,927,000	534,932	27.8%		2,139,000	609,747	28.5%	1.2
MASSACHUSETTS																			
MICHIGAN																			
MINNESOTA								1,956,000	616,574	31.5%						2,126,000	790,236	37.2%	5.6
MISSISSIPPI																			
MISSOURI																			
MONTANA																			
NEBRASKA								848,000	156,955	18.5%		858,000	256,192	29.9%	11.4	876,000	292,539	33.4%	14.9
NEVADA	104,000	46,838	45.0%									198,000	70,049	35.4%	-9.7	248,000	104,518	42.1%	-2.9
NEW HAMPSHIRE	338,000	98,557	29.2%					356,000	103,141	29.0%	-0.2	378,000	128,906	34.1%	4.9				
NEW JERSEY																			
NEW MEXICO	369,000	117,692	31.9%													531,000	176,778	33.3%	1.4
NEW YORK																			

State Gubernatorial Primary Elections (continued)

Election Years 1950–1966 (continued)

State	1950 Voting-age population	1950 Turnout	1950 %	1954 Voting-age population	1954 Turnout	1954 %	1954 Difference from 1950	1958 Voting-age population	1958 Turnout	1958 %	1958 Difference from 1950	1962 Voting-age population	1962 Turnout	1962 %	1962 Difference from 1950	1966 Voting-age population	1966 Turnout	1966 %	1966 Difference from 1950
NORTH CAROLINA																			
NORTH DAKOTA	358,000	168,558	**47.1%**																
OHIO	5,191,000	986,343	**19.0%**					5,649,000	1,181,833	**20.9%**	1.9	5,884,000	1,239,194	**21.1%**	2.1	6,126,000	1,209,080	**19.7%**	0.7
OKLAHOMA	1,377,000	563,347	**40.9%**					1,404,000	532,390	**37.9%**	-3.0	1,448,000	596,171	**41.2%**	0.3	1,518,000	603,541	**39.8%**	-1.2
OREGON								1,040,000	420,323	**40.4%**		1,104,000	437,944	**39.7%**	-0.7	1,196,000	488,203	**40.8%**	0.4
PENNSYLVANIA	6,832,000	2,003,385	**29.3%**					6,949,000	2,041,494	**29.4%**	0.1	7,058,000	1,845,534	**26.1%**	-3.2	7,212,000	2,189,030	**30.4%**	1.0
RHODE ISLAND												536,000	121,024	**22.6%**					
SOUTH CAROLINA																			
SOUTH DAKOTA																			
TENNESSEE								2,066,000	710,168	**34.4%**									
TEXAS												5,649,000	1,562,389	**27.7%**					
UTAH																			
VERMONT	229,000	74,817	**32.7%**																
VIRGINIA																			
WASHINGTON																			
WEST VIRGINIA																			
WISCONSIN	2,187,000	593,211	**27.1%**																
WYOMING												189,000	87,901	**46.5%**		192,000	89,573	**46.7%**	0.4
Total	21,068,000	5,597,040	**26.6%**	2,282,000	702,341	**30.8%**	4.2	30,528,000	10,162,520	**33.3%**	6.7	38,840,000	11,920,644	**30.7%**	4.1	41,924,000	14,008,920	**33.4%**	6.8

*Overall primary turnout reflects only states with primaries in both parties. To find single party primary results, see partisan primary charts.

**Percentage point difference between turnout in current year and initial year listed in chart. If data do not appear for a state in the initial year listed, the difference is calculated from the first year in which data do appear for that state.

STATE GUBERNATORIAL PRIMARY ELECTIONS

Republican Turnout for Election Years 1950–1966

State	1950 Voting-age population	Turnout	%	1954 Voting-age population	Turnout	%	Difference from 1950*	1958 Voting-age population	Turnout	%	Difference from 1950	1962 Voting-age population	Turnout	%	Difference from 1950	1966 Voting-age population	Turnout	%	Difference from 1950
ALABAMA																			
ALASKA												142,000	16,832	11.9%		160,000	19,130	12.0%	0.1
ARIZONA																908,000	84,506	9.3%	
ARKANSAS								1,052,000	4,420	0.4%						1,119,000	19,956	1.8%	1.4
CALIFORNIA								8,648,000	1,664,985	19.3%		9,746,000	1,964,298	20.2%	0.9	11,025,000	2,191,750	19.9%	0.6
COLORADO	830,000	80,165	9.7%									1,068,000	110,720	10.4%	0.7				
CONNECTICUT																			
DELAWARE																			
DISTRICT OF COLUMBIA																			
FLORIDA				2,282,000	35,981	1.6%										3,826,000	124,791	3.3%	1.7
GEORGIA																			
HAWAII												359,000	77,477	21.6%		396,000	36,001	9.1%	-12.5
IDAHO	344,000	63,022	18.3%									377,000	65,995	17.5%	-0.8	394,000	86,644	22.0%	3.7
ILLINOIS																			
INDIANA																			
IOWA	1,676,000	238,686	14.2%					1,656,000	198,650	12.0%	-2.2	1,662,000	197,980	11.9%	-2.3	1,681,000	173,113	10.3%	-3.9
KANSAS	1,233,000	228,951	18.6%					1,297,000	177,879	13.7%	-4.9	1,325,000	196,109	14.8%	-3.8	1,349,000	192,893	14.3%	-4.3
KENTUCKY																			
LOUISIANA																			
MAINE								560,000	102,289	18.3%						583,000	93,689	16.1%	-2.2
MARYLAND												1,927,000	92,267	4.8%		2,139,000	118,482	5.5%	0.8
MASSACHUSETTS								3,091,000	181,975	5.9%									
MICHIGAN																			
MINNESOTA								1,956,000	237,711	12.2%						2,126,000	282,230	13.3%	1.1
MISSISSIPPI																			
MISSOURI																			
MONTANA																			
NEBRASKA								848,000	117,918	13.9%		858,000	153,346	17.9%	4.0	876,000	178,024	20.3%	6.4
NEVADA	104,000	15,579	15.0%									198,000	25,714	13.0%	-2.0	248,000	34,602	14.0%	-1.0
NEW HAMPSHIRE	338,000	74,442	22.0%					356,000	79,126	22.2%	0.2	378,000	98,934	26.2%	4.1	411,000	75,668	18.4%	-3.6
NEW JERSEY																			
NEW MEXICO	369,000	14,829	4.0%													531,000	34,424	6.5%	2.5
NEW YORK																			

State Gubernatorial Primary Elections (continued)

Republican Turnout for Election Years 1950–1966 (continued)

State	1950				1954				1958				1962				1966			
	Voting-age population	Turnout	%		Voting-age population	Turnout	%	Difference from 1950	Voting-age population	Turnout	%	Difference from 1950	Voting-age population	Turnout	%	Difference from 1950	Voting-age population	Turnout	%	Difference from 1950
NORTH CAROLINA																				
NORTH DAKOTA	358,000	138,211	38.6%																	
OHIO	5,191,000	540,130	10.4%						5,649,000	544,833	9.6%	-0.8	5,884,000	580,784	9.9%	-0.5	6,126,000	651,255	10.6%	0.2
OKLAHOMA	1,377,000	55,411	4.0%						1,404,000	58,618	4.2%	0.2	1,448,000	61,873	4.3%	0.2	1,518,000	94,002	6.2%	2.2
OREGON									1,040,000	212,356	20.4%		1,104,000	212,717	19.3%	-1.2	1,196,000	236,245	19.8%	-0.7
PENNSYLVANIA	6,832,000	1,430,829	20.9%						6,949,000	1,060,613	15.3%	-5.7	7,058,000	953,020	13.5%	-7.4	7,712,000	1,071,284	14.9%	-6.1
RHODE ISLAND													536,000	28,429	5.3%					
SOUTH CAROLINA																				
SOUTH DAKOTA	396,000	100,751	25.4%						390,000	80,751	20.7%	-4.7								
TENNESSEE									2,066,000	30,888	1.5%									
TEXAS													5,649,000	115,274	2.0%					
UTAH																				
VERMONT	229,000	71,547	31.2%														246,000	37,413	15.2%	-16.0
VIRGINIA																				
WASHINGTON																				
WEST VIRGINIA																				
WISCONSIN	2,187,000	422,454	19.3%										2,381,000	465,138	19.5%	0.2				
WYOMING									105,000	37,043	20.0%		189,000	49,975	26.4%	6.4	192,000	47,269	24.6%	4.6
Total	21,464,000	3,475,007	16.2%		2,282,000	35,981	1.6%	-14.6	37,147,000	4,790,055	12.9%	-3.3	42,289,000	5,466,891	12.9%	-3.3	44,262,000	5,883,371	13.3%	-2.9

Democratic Turnout for Election Years 1950–1966

State	1950				1954				1958				1962				1966			
	Voting-age population	Turnout	%		Voting-age population	Turnout	%	Difference from 1950*	Voting-age population	Turnout	%	Difference from 1950	Voting-age population	Turnout	%	Difference from 1950	Voting-age population	Turnout	%	Difference from 1950
ALABAMA	1,745,000	348,542	20.0%		1,780,000	566,808	31.8%	11.9	1,813,000	549,001	30.3%	10.3	1,871,000	637,237	34.1%	14.1	1,947,000	888,838	45.7%	25.7
ALASKA									124,000	37,236	30.0%		142,000	21,994	15.5%	-14.5	160,000	32,461	20.3%	-9.7
ARIZONA									657,000	154,752	23.6%		779,000	153,156	19.7%	-3.9	908,000	140,738	15.5%	-8.1
ARKANSAS	1,109,000	322,210	29.1%		1,080,000	324,599	30.1%	1.0	1,052,000	383,904	36.5%	7.4	1,067,000	405,112	38.0%	8.9	1,119,000	420,065	37.5%	8.5
CALIFORNIA									8,648,000	2,204,007	25.5%		9,746,000	2,136,750	21.9%	-3.6	11,025,000	2,610,876	23.7%	-1.8
COLORADO	830,000	66,685	8.0%																	
CONNECTICUT																				
DELAWARE																				
DISTRICT OF COLUMBIA																				
FLORIDA					2,282,000	666,360	29.2%										3,826,000	1,053,655	27.5%	-1.7

State Gubernatorial Primary Elections (continued)

State Gubernatorial Primary Elections *(continued)*

Democratic Turnout for Election Years 1950–1966 *(continued)*

State	1950 Voting-age population	Turnout	%	1954 Voting-age population	Turnout	%	Difference from 1950	1958 Voting-age population	Turnout	%	Difference from 1950	1962 Voting-age population	Turnout	%	Difference from 1950	1966 Voting-age population	Turnout	%	Difference from 1950
GEORGIA	2,179,000	566,774	26.0%	2,270,000	635,835	28.0%	2.0	2,360,000	620,406	26.3%	0.3	2,517,000	852,350	33.9%	7.9	2,730,000	787,952	28.9%	2.9
HAWAII												359,000	79,321	22.1%		396,000	109,226	27.6%	5.5
IDAHO	344,000	64,547	18.8%					363,000	72,283	19.9%	1.1	377,000	82,475	21.9%	3.1	394,000	70,984	18.0%	-0.7
ILLINOIS																			
INDIANA																			
IOWA	1,676,000	93,504	5.6%									1,662,000	84,394	5.1%	-0.5				
KANSAS	1,233,000	108,319	8.8%									1,325,000	116,783	8.8%	0.0	1,349,000	112,799	8.4%	-0.4
KENTUCKY																			
LOUISIANA																			
MAINE								560,000	40,037	7.1%		570,000	36,241	6.4%	-0.8	583,000	55,511	9.5%	2.4
MARYLAND								1,755,000	318,842	18.2%		1,927,000	442,665	23.0%	4.8	2,139,000	491,265	23.0%	4.8
MASSACHUSETTS												3,191,000	746,062	23.4%		3,353,000	622,936	18.6%	-4.8
MICHIGAN								4,367,000	451,478	10.3%									
MINNESOTA								1,956,000	378,863	19.4%		2,028,000	293,860	14.5%	-4.9	2,126,000	508,006	23.9%	4.5
MISSISSIPPI																			
MISSOURI																			
MONTANA																			
NEBRASKA								848,000	39,037	4.6%		858,000	102,846	12.0%	7.4	876,000	114,515	13.1%	8.5
NEVADA	104,000	31,259	30.1%					158,000	45,258	28.6%	-1.4	198,000	44,335	22.4%	-7.7	248,000	69,916	28.2%	-1.9
NEW HAMPSHIRE	338,000	24,115	7.1%					356,000	24,015	6.7%	-0.4	378,000	29,972	7.9%	0.8				
NEW JERSEY																			
NEW MEXICO	369,000	102,863	27.9%					470,000	61,986	13.2%	-14.7	506,000	123,624	24.4%	-3.4	531,000	142,354	26.8%	-1.1
NEW YORK																			
NORTH CAROLINA																			
NORTH DAKOTA	358,000	30,347	8.5%					352,000	47,718	13.6%	5.1								
OHIO	5,191,000	446,213	8.6%					5,649,000	637,000	11.3%	2.7	5,884,000	658,410	11.2%	2.6	6,126,000	557,825	9.1%	0.5
OKLAHOMA	1,377,000	507,936	36.9%					1,404,000	473,772	33.7%	-3.1	1,448,000	534,298	36.9%	0.0	1,518,000	509,539	33.6%	-3.3
OREGON								1,040,000	207,967	20.0%		1,104,000	225,227	20.4%	0.4	1,196,000	251,958	21.1%	1.1
PENNSYLVANIA	6,832,000	572,277	8.4%					6,949,000	980,881	14.1%	5.7	7,058,000	892,505	12.6%	4.3	7,212,000	1,117,746	15.5%	7.1
RHODE ISLAND								518,000	94,657	18.3%		536,000	92,595	17.3%	-1.0				
SOUTH CAROLINA	1,150,000	340,834	29.6%	1,196,000	302,483	25.3%	-4.3	1,241,000	377,239	30.4%	0.8	1,307,000	328,291	25.1%	-4.5				
SOUTH DAKOTA																			
TENNESSEE	1,975,000	476,489	24.1%	2,020,000	676,964	33.5%	9.4	2,066,000	679,280	32.9%	8.8	2,150,000	727,202	33.8%	9.7	2,267,000	774,064	34.1%	10.0

State Gubernatorial Primary Elections (continued)

Democratic Turnout for Election Years 1950–1966 (continued)

State	1950 Voting-age population	1950 Turnout	1950 %	1954 Voting-age population	1954 Turnout	1954 %	1954 Difference from 1950	1958 Voting-age population	1958 Turnout	1958 %	1958 Difference from 1950	1962 Voting-age population	1962 Turnout	1962 %	1962 Difference from 1950	1966 Voting-age population	1966 Turnout	1966 %	1966 Difference from 1950
TEXAS	4,601,000	1,025,727	22.3%	4,923,000	1,314,907	26.7%	4.4	5,245,000	1,283,843	24.5%	2.2	5,649,000	1,447,115	25.6%	3.3	6,119,000	1,225,400	20.0%	-2.3
UTAH																			
VERMONT	229,000	3,270	1.4%																
VIRGINIA																			
WASHINGTON																			
WEST VIRGINIA																			
WISCONSIN	2,187,000	167,522	7.7%													2,490,000	283,889	11.4%	3.7
WYOMING												189,000	37,926	20.1%		192,000	42,304	22.0%	2.0
Total	33,827,000	5,299,433	15.7%	15,551,000	4,487,956	28.9%	13.2	49,951,000	10,163,462	20.3%	4.7	54,826,000	11,332,746	20.7%	5.0	60,830,000	12,994,822	21.4%	5.7

Other Turnout for Election Years 1950–1966

State	1950 Voting-age population	1950 Turnout	1950 %	1954 Voting-age population	1954 Turnout	1954 %	1954 Difference from 1950*	1958 Voting-age population	1958 Turnout	1958 %	1958 Difference from 1950	1962 Voting-age population	1962 Turnout	1962 %	1962 Difference from 1950	1966 Voting-age population	1966 Turnout	1966 %	1966 Difference from 1950
KANSAS	1,233,000	413	0.0%																
PENNSYLVANIA	6,832,000	279	0.0%																
WISCONSIN	2,187,000	3,235	0.1%																

*Percentage point difference between turnout in current year and initial year listed in chart. If data do not appear for a state in the initial year listed, the difference is calculated from the first year in which data do appear for that state.

UNITED STATES SENATE PRIMARY ELECTIONS

Election Years 1950–1966

State*	1950 Voting-age population	Turnout	%	1954** Voting-age population	Turnout	%	Difference from 1950***	1958 Voting-age population	Turnout	%	Difference from 1950	1962 Voting-age population	Turnout	%	Difference from 1950	1966 Voting-age population	Turnout	%	Difference from 1950
ALABAMA																			
ALASKA												142,000	36,646	25.8%		160,000	48,769	30.5%	4.7
ARIZONA												779,000	222,111	28.5%					
ARKANSAS																			
CALIFORNIA								8,648,000	3,816,114	44.1%		9,746,000	3,837,308	39.4%	-4.8				
COLORADO	830,000	137,460	16.6%																
CONNECTICUT																			
DELAWARE																			
DISTRICT OF COLUMBIA																			
FLORIDA																			
GEORGIA																			
HAWAII																			
IDAHO	344,000	131,798	38.3%																
ILLINOIS	5,807,000	1,510,792	26.0%									6,257,000	1,815,849	29.0%	3.0				
INDIANA																			
IOWA	1,676,000	355,888	21.2%	1,666,000	274,725	16.5%	-4.7									1,681,000	247,659	14.7%	-6.5
KANSAS												1,325,000	298,000	22.5%		1,349,000	305,804	22.7%	0.2
KENTUCKY	1,881,000	209,456	11.1%									1,938,000	211,339	10.9%	-0.2	2,020,000	165,010	8.2%	-3.0
LOUISIANA																			
MAINE																			
MARYLAND								1,755,000	435,757	24.8%		1,927,000	439,543	22.8%	-2.0				
MASSACHUSETTS												3,191,000	1,248,132	39.1%					
MICHIGAN				4,169,000	763,804	18.3%													
MINNESOTA				1,915,000	599,357	31.3%		1,956,000	592,179	30.3%	-1.0					2,126,000	711,849	33.5%	2.2
MISSISSIPPI																			
MISSOURI	2,621,000	641,583	24.5%					2,665,000	534,446	20.1%	-4.4	2,720,000	607,410	22.3%	-2.1				
MONTANA								381,000	145,462	38.2%									
NEBRASKA																			
NEVADA	104,000	46,550	44.8%									198,000	75,683	38.2%	-6.5				
NEW HAMPSHIRE	338,000	97,191	28.8%																
NEW JERSEY								3,623,000	709,028	19.6%									
NEW MEXICO				420,000	91,149	21.7%		470,000	124,861	26.6%	4.9								
NEW YORK																			

United States Senate Primary Elections *(continued)*

Election Years 1950–1966 *(continued)*

State	1950			1954				1958				1962				1966			
	Voting-age population	Turnout	%	Voting-age population	Turnout	%	Difference from 1950	Voting-age population	Turnout	%	Difference from 1950	Voting-age population	Turnout	%	Difference from 1950	Voting-age population	Turnout	%	Difference from 1950
NORTH CAROLINA																			
NORTH DAKOTA	358,000	168,880	47.2%					352,000	151,380	43.0%	-4.2								
OHIO	5,191,000	877,622	16.9%									5,884,000	1,096,506	18.6%	1.7				
OKLAHOMA	1,377,000	490,070	35.6%													1,518,000	515,301	33.9%	-1.6
OREGON												1,104,000	442,871	40.1%		1,196,000	494,693	41.4%	1.2
PENNSYLVANIA	6,832,000	1,916,423	28.1%					6,949,000	2,012,251	29.0%	0.9								
RHODE ISLAND																			
SOUTH CAROLINA																			
SOUTH DAKOTA	396,000	134,185	33.9%																
TENNESSEE																2,267,000	899,086	39.7%	
TEXAS																			
UTAH								441,000	118,754	26.9%		479,000	191,417	40.0%	13.0				
VERMONT																			
VIRGINIA	2,018,000	72,859	3.6%																
WASHINGTON	1,511,000	458,431	30.3%									1,754,000	517,205	29.5%	-0.9				
WEST VIRGINIA																			
WISCONSIN	2,187,000	564,859	25.8%																
WYOMING																			
Total	33,471,000	7,814,047	23.3%	8,170,000	1,729,035	21.2%	-2.2	27,240,000	8,640,232	31.7%	8.4	37,444,000	11,040,020	29.5%	6.1	12,317,000	3,388,171	27.5%	4.2

*Overall primary turnout reflects only states with primaries in both parties. To find single party primary results, see partisan primary charts.

**1954 Senate primary data are not complete.

***Percentage point difference between turnout in current year and initial year listed in chart. If data do not appear for a state in the initial year listed, the difference is calculated from the first year in which data do appear for that state.

UNITED STATES SENATE PRIMARY ELECTIONS

Republican Turnout for Election Years 1950–1966

State	1950 Voting-age population	Turnout	%	1954* Voting-age population	Turnout	%	Difference from 1950**	1958 Voting-age population	Turnout	%	Difference from 1950	1962 Voting-age population	Turnout	%	Difference from 1950	1966 Voting-age population	Turnout	%	Difference from 1950
ALABAMA																			
ALASKA												142,000	15,175	10.7%		160,000	16,668	10.4%	-0.3
ARIZONA												779,000	68,265	8.8%					
ARKANSAS																			
CALIFORNIA								8,648,000	1,616,223	18.7%		9,746,000	1,810,143	18.6%	-0.1				
COLORADO	830,000	70,953	8.5%																
CONNECTICUT																			
DELAWARE																			
DISTRICT OF COLUMBIA																			
FLORIDA																			
GEORGIA																			
HAWAII																			
IDAHO	344,000	64,353	18.7%									377,000	63,433	16.8%	-1.9				
ILLINOIS	5,807,000	741,984	12.8%									6,257,000	852,549	13.6%	0.8	6,512,000	668,363	10.3%	-2.5
INDIANA																			
IOWA	1,676,000	287,915	17.2%	1,666,000	185,907	11.2%	-6.0					1,662,000	192,632	11.6%	-5.6	1,681,000	168,148	10.0%	-7.2
KANSAS												1,325,000	192,666	14.5%		1,349,000	201,923	15.0%	0.4
KENTUCKY	1,881,000	47,934	2.5%									1,938,000	45,940	2.4%	-0.2	2,020,000	70,070	3.5%	0.9
LOUISIANA																			
MAINE								560,000	98,581	17.6%									
MARYLAND								1,755,000	74,406	4.2%		1,927,000	90,214	4.7%	0.4				
MASSACHUSETTS												3,191,000	441,400	13.8%					
MICHIGAN				4,169,000	410,758	9.9%													
MINNESOTA				1,915,000	271,290	14.2%		1,956,000	222,307	11.4%	-2.8					2,126,000	260,223	12.2%	-1.9
MISSISSIPPI																			
MISSOURI	2,621,000	236,645	9.0%					2,665,000	137,760	5.2%	-3.9	2,720,000	178,764	6.6%	-2.5				
MONTANA								381,000	39,484	10.4%									
NEBRASKA																			
NEVADA	104,000	14,987	14.4%									198,000	25,081	12.7%	-1.7				
NEW HAMPSHIRE	338,000	77,096	22.8%									378,000	99,003	26.2%	3.4	411,000	77,059	18.7%	-4.1
NEW JERSEY								3,623,000	355,532	9.8%									
NEW MEXICO				420,000	23,820	5.7%		470,000	20,245	4.3%	-1.4								
NEW YORK																			

United States Senate Primary Elections (continued)

Republican Turnout for Election Years 1950–1966 (continued)

State	1950 Voting-age population	1950 Turnout	1950 %	1954 Voting-age population	1954 Turnout	1954 %	1954 Difference from 1950	1958 Voting-age population	1958 Turnout	1958 %	1958 Difference from 1950	1962 Voting-age population	1962 Turnout	1962 %	1962 Difference from 1950	1966 Voting-age population	1966 Turnout	1966 %	1966 Difference from 1950
NORTH CAROLINA												2,647,000	52,002	2.0%					
NORTH DAKOTA	358,000	138,263	38.6%					352,000	104,606	29.7%	-8.9	351,000	73,667	21.0%	-17.6				
OHIO	5,191,000	473,343	9.1%									5,884,000	504,452	8.6%	-0.5				
OKLAHOMA	1,377,000	37,655	2.7%													1,518,000	84,790	5.6%	2.9
OREGON												1,104,000	213,128	19.3%		1,196,000	235,542	19.7%	0.4
PENNSYLVANIA	6,832,000	1,378,676	20.2%					6,949,000	1,035,138	14.9%	-5.3								
RHODE ISLAND																563,000	18,814	3.3%	
SOUTH CAROLINA																			
SOUTH DAKOTA	396,000	102,137	25.8%									388,000	68,997	17.8%	-8.0	387,000	81,351	21.0%	-4.8
TENNESSEE																2,267,000	148,682	6.6%	
TEXAS																			
UTAH	381,000	48,610	12.8%					441,000	58,156	13.2%	0.4	479,000	119,125	24.9%	12.1				
VERMONT								225,000	49,338	21.9%									
VIRGINIA	2,018,000	69,534	3.4%																
WASHINGTON	1,511,000	245,853	16.3%									1,754,000	217,375	12.4%	-3.9				
WEST VIRGINIA																1,072,000	97,009	9.0%	
WISCONSIN	2,187,000	396,465	18.1%									2,381,000	432,332	18.2%	0.0				
WYOMING												189,000	50,507	26.7%		192,000	46,570	24.3%	-2.5
Total	33,852,000	4,432,403	13.1%	8,170,000	891,775	10.9%	-2.2	28,025,000	3,811,776	13.6%	0.5	45,817,000	5,806,850	12.7%	-0.4	21,454,000	2,175,212	10.1%	-3.0

Democratic Turnout for Election Years 1950–1966

State	1950 Voting-age population	1950 Turnout	1950 %	1954* Voting-age population	1954* Turnout	1954* %	1954* Difference from 1950**	1958 Voting-age population	1958 Turnout	1958 %	1958 Difference from 1950	1962 Voting-age population	1962 Turnout	1962 %	1962 Difference from 1950	1966 Voting-age population	1966 Turnout	1966 %	1966 Difference from 1950
ALABAMA				1,780,000	532,043	29.9%						1,871,000	493,290	26.4%	-3.5	1,947,000	663,945	34.1%	4.2
ALASKA												142,000	21,471	15.1%		160,000	32,101	20.1%	4.9
ARIZONA								657,000	153,628	23.4%		779,000	153,846	19.7%	-3.6				
ARKANSAS												1,067,000	383,738	36.0%		1,119,000	402,272	35.9%	0.0
CALIFORNIA								8,648,000	2,165,575	25.0%		9,746,000	2,027,165	20.8%	-4.2				
COLORADO	830,000	66,507	8.0%																
CONNECTICUT																			
DELAWARE																			
DISTRICT OF COLUMBIA																			
FLORIDA								2,754,000	729,461	26.5%		3,271,000	697,959	21.3%	-5.1				

United States Senate Primary Elections (continued)

Democratic Turnout for Election Years 1950–1966 (continued)

State	1950 Voting-age population	Turnout	%	1954 Voting-age population	Turnout	%	Difference from 1950	1958 Voting-age population	Turnout	%	Difference from 1950	1962 Voting-age population	Turnout	%	Difference from 1950	1966 Voting-age population	Turnout	%	Difference from 1950
GEORGIA				2,270,000	619,129	27.3%						2,517,000	765,446	30.4%	3.1	2,730,000	658,131	24.1%	-3.2
HAWAII								334,000	78,175	23.4%		359,000	86,183	24.0%	0.6				
IDAHO	344,000	67,445	19.6%																
ILLINOIS	5,807,000	768,808	13.2%									6,257,000	963,300	15.4%	2.2				
INDIANA																			
IOWA	1,676,000	67,973	4.1%	1,666,000	88,818	5.3%	1.3									1,681,000	79,511	4.7%	0.7
KANSAS												1,325,000	105,334	7.9%		1,349,000	103,881	7.7%	-0.2
KENTUCKY	1,881,000	161,522	8.6%									1,938,000	165,399	8.5%	-0.1	2,020,000	94,940	4.7%	-3.9
LOUISIANA				1,666,000	430,839	25.9%						1,847,000	508,005	27.5%	1.6	1,947,000	666,810	34.2%	8.4
MAINE												583,000	51,489	8.8%					
MARYLAND								1,755,000	361,351	20.6%		1,927,000	349,329	18.1%	-2.5				
MASSACHUSETTS												3,191,000	806,732	25.3%		3,353,000	637,430	19.0%	-6.3
MICHIGAN				4,169,000	353,046	8.5%		4,367,000	371,114	8.5%	0.0					4,883,000	727,905	14.9%	6.4
MINNESOTA				1,915,000	328,067	17.1%		1,956,000	369,872	18.9%	1.8					2,126,000	451,626	21.2%	4.1
MISSISSIPPI																1,214,000	289,085	23.8%	
MISSOURI	2,621,000	404,938	15.4%					2,665,000	396,686	14.9%	-0.6	2,720,000	428,646	15.8%	0.3				
MONTANA								381,000	105,978	27.8%									
NEBRASKA								848,000	68,431	8.1%						876,000	116,933	13.3%	5.3
NEVADA	104,000	31,563	30.3%					158,000	44,106	27.9%	-2.4	198,000	50,602	25.6%	-4.8				
NEW HAMPSHIRE	338,000	20,095	5.9%																
NEW JERSEY								3,623,000	353,496	9.8%						4,175,000	271,442	6.5%	-3.3
NEW MEXICO				420,000	67,329	16.0%		470,000	104,616	22.3%	6.2								
NEW YORK																			
NORTH CAROLINA	2,309,000	612,579	26.5%	2,406,000	598,783	24.9%	-1.6									2,829,000	562,002	19.9%	-6.7
NORTH DAKOTA	358,000	30,617	8.6%					352,000	46,774	13.3%	4.7								
OHIO	5,191,000	404,279	7.8%	5,420,000	480,464	8.9%	1.1					5,884,000	592,054	10.1%	2.3				
OKLAHOMA	1,377,000	452,415	32.9%									1,448,000	452,083	31.2%	-1.6	1,518,000	430,511	28.4%	-4.5
OREGON												1,104,000	229,743	20.8%		1,196,000	259,151	21.7%	0.9
PENNSYLVANIA	6,832,000	537,708	7.9%					6,949,000	977,113	14.1%	6.2								
RHODE ISLAND																			
SOUTH CAROLINA												1,307,000	320,941	24.6%		1,388,000	323,000	23.3%	-1.3
SOUTH DAKOTA	396,000	32,048	8.1%																
TENNESSEE				2,020,000	645,590	32.0%		2,066,000	636,341	30.8%	-1.2					2,267,000	750,404	33.1%	2.3

United States Senate Primary Elections *(continued)*

Democratic Turnout for Election Years 1950–1966 *(continued)*

State	1950 Voting-age population	Turnout	%	1954 Voting-age population	Turnout	%	Difference from 1950	1958 Voting-age population	Turnout	%	Difference from 1950	1962 Voting-age population	Turnout	%	Difference from 1950	1966 Voting-age population	Turnout	%	Difference from 1950
TEXAS								5,245,000	1,296,933	**24.7%**						6,119,000	1,126,129	**18.4%**	-6.3
UTAH								441,000	60,598	**13.7%**		479,000	72,292	**15.1%**	1.4				
VERMONT												232,000	10,472	**4.5%**					
VIRGINIA	2,018,000	3,325	**0.2%**													2,601,000	434,217	**16.7%**	16.5
WASHINGTON	1,511,000	212,578	**14.1%**					1,641,000	390,062	**23.8%**	9.7	1,754,000	299,830	**17.1%**	3.0				
WEST VIRGINIA								1,092,000	217,427	**19.9%**									
WISCONSIN	2,187,000	166,392	**7.6%**					2,297,000	257,128	**11.2%**	3.6								
WYOMING								185,000	37,122	**20.1%**									
Total	35,780,000	4,040,792	**11.3%**	23,732,000	4,144,108	**17.5%**	6.2	48,884,000	9,221,987	**18.9%**	7.6	51,363,000	9,983,860	**19.4%**	8.1	48,081,000	9,132,915	**19.0%**	7.7

Other Turnout for Election Years 1950–1966

State	1950 Voting-age population	Turnout	%	1954* Voting-age population	Turnout	%	Difference from 1950**	1958 Voting-age population	Turnout	%	Difference from 1950	1962 Voting-age population	Turnout	%	Difference from 1950	1966 Voting-age population	Turnout	%	Difference from 1950
PENNSYLVANIA	6,832,000	39	**0.0%**																
WISCONSIN	2,187,000	2,002	**0.1%**																
Total	9,019,000	2,041	**0.0%**																

*1954 Senate primary data are not complete.

**Percentage point difference between turnout in current year and initial year listed in chart. If data do not appear for a state in the initial year listed, the difference is calculated from the first year in which data do appear for that state.

STATE GUBERNATORIAL GENERAL ELECTIONS

Election Years 1951–1969

State	1951 Voting-age population	Turnout	%		1953 Voting-age population	Turnout	%	Difference from 1951*	1955 Voting-age population	Turnout	%	Difference from 1951	1957 Voting-age population	Turnout	%	Difference from 1951	1959 Voting-age population	Turnout	%	Difference from 1951
HAWAII																	341,000	168,287	49.4%	
KENTUCKY	1,883,000	634,359	33.7%						1,888,000	774,318	41.0%	7.3					1,893,000	853,005	45.1%	11.4
MISSISSIPPI	1,198,000	43,422	3.6%						1,183,000	40,707	3.4%	-0.2					1,168,000	57,671	4.9%	1.3
NEW JERSEY					3,403,000	1,771,778	52.1%						3,602,000	1,998,451	55.5%	3.4				
VIRGINIA					2,118,000	410,326	19.4%						2,231,000	515,549	23.1%	3.7				

State	1961 Voting-age population	Turnout	%	Difference from 1951	1963 Voting-age population	Turnout	%	Difference from 1951	1965 Voting-age population	Turnout	%	Difference from 1951	1967 Voting-age population	Turnout	%	Difference from 1951	1969 Voting-age population	Turnout	%	Difference from 1951
HAWAII																				
KENTUCKY					1,970,000	886,047	45.0%	11.3					2,053,000	879,797	42.9%	9.2				
MISSISSIPPI					1,196,000	364,061	30.4%	26.8					1,226,000	448,697	36.6%	33.0				
NEW JERSEY	3,845,000	2,133,468	55.5%	3.4					4,144,000	2,195,564	53.0%	0.9					4,442,000	2,322,908	52.3%	0.2
VIRGINIA	2,381,000	394,428	16.6%	-2.8					2,580,000	557,040	21.6%	2.2					2,779,000	896,564	32.3%	12.9

*Percentage point difference between turnout in current year and initial year listed in chart. If data do not appear for a state in the initial year listed, the difference is calculated from the first year in which data do appear for that state.

STATE GUBERNATORIAL GENERAL ELECTIONS

Republican Turnout for Election Years 1951–1969

State	1951 Voting-age population	Turnout	%	1953 Voting-age population	Turnout	%	1955 Voting-age population	Turnout	%	Difference from 1951*	1957 Voting-age population	Turnout	%	Difference from 1951	1959 Voting-age population	Turnout	%	Difference from 1951
HAWAII															341,000	86,213	25.3%	
KENTUCKY	1,883,000	288,014	15.3%				1,888,000	322,671	17.1%	1.8					1,893,000	336,456	17.8%	2.5
MISSISSIPPI																		
NEW JERSEY				3,403,000	809,068	23.8%					3,602,000	897,321	24.9%	1.1				
VIRGINIA				2,118,000	183,328	8.7%					2,231,000	188,628	8.5%	-0.2				

State	1961 Voting-age population	Turnout	%	Difference from 1951	1963 Voting-age population	Turnout	%	Difference from 1951	1965 Voting-age population	Turnout	%	Difference from 1951	1967 Voting-age population	Turnout	%	Difference from 1951	1969 Voting-age population	Turnout	%	Difference from 1951
HAWAII																				
KENTUCKY					1,970,000	436,496	22.2%	6.9					2,053,000	454,123	22.1%	6.8				
MISSISSIPPI					1,196,000	138,605	11.6%						1,226,000	133,379	10.9%	-0.7				
NEW JERSEY	3,845,000	1,049,274	27.3%	3.5					4,144,000	915,996	22.1%	-1.7					4,442,000	911,003	20.5%	-3.3
VIRGINIA	2,381,000	142,567	6.0%	-2.2					2,580,000	212,207	8.2%	0.4					2,779,000	480,869	17.3%	8.6

Democratic Turnout for Election Years 1951–1969

State	1951 Voting-age population	Turnout	%	1953 Voting-age population	Turnout	%	1955 Voting-age population	Turnout	%	Difference from 1951*	1957 Voting-age population	Turnout	%	Difference from 1951	1959 Voting-age population	Turnout	%	Difference from 1951
HAWAII															341,000	82,074	24.1%	
KENTUCKY	1,883,000	346,345	18.4%				1,888,000	451,647	23.9%	5.5					1,893,000	516,549	27.3%	8.9
MISSISSIPPI	1,198,000	43,422	3.6%				1,183,000	40,707	3.4%	-0.2					1,168,000	57,671	4.9%	1.3
NEW JERSEY				3,403,000	962,710	28.3%					3,602,000	1,101,130	30.6%	2.3				
VIRGINIA				2,118,000	226,998	10.7%					2,231,000	326,921	14.7%	3.9				

State	1961 Voting-age population	Turnout	%	Difference from 1951	1963 Voting-age population	Turnout	%	Difference from 1951	1965 Voting-age population	Turnout	%	Difference from 1951	1967 Voting-age population	Turnout	%	Difference from 1951	1969 Voting-age population	Turnout	%	Difference from 1951
HAWAII																				
KENTUCKY					1,970,000	449,551	22.8%	4.4					2,053,000	425,674	20.7%	2.3				
MISSISSIPPI					1,196,000	225,456	18.9%	15.2					1,226,000	315,318	25.7%	22.1				
NEW JERSEY	3,845,000	1,084,194	28.2%	-0.1					4,144,000	1,279,568	30.9%	2.6					4,442,000	1,411,905	31.8%	3.5
VIRGINIA	2,381,000	251,861	10.6%	0.4					2,580,000	269,526	10.4%	-0.3					2,779,000	415,695	15.0%	0.3

State Gubernatorial General Elections (continued)

State Gubernatorial General Elections (continued)

Other Turnout for Election Years 1951–1969

State	1951 Voting-age population	Turnout	%	1953 Voting-age population	Turnout	%	Difference from 1951*	1955 Voting-age population	Turnout	%	Difference from 1951	1957 Voting-age population	Turnout	%	Difference from 1951	1959 Voting-age population	Turnout	%	Difference from 1951
VIRGINIA																			

State	1961 Voting-age population	Turnout	%	Difference from 1951	1963 Voting-age population	Turnout	%	Difference from 1951	1965 Voting-age population	Turnout	%	1967 Voting-age population	Turnout	%	Difference from 1951	1969 Voting-age population	Turnout	%	Difference from 1951
VIRGINIA									2,580,000	75,307	**2.9%**								

*Percentage point difference between turnout in current year and initial year listed in chart. If data do not appear for a state in the initial year listed, the difference is calculated from the first year in which data do appear for that state.

STATE GUBERNATORIAL PRIMARY ELECTIONS

Republican Turnout for Election Years 1951–1969*

State	1951 Voting-age population	Turnout	%	1953 Voting-age population	Turnout	%	1955 Voting-age population	Turnout	%	1957 Voting-age population	Turnout	%	1959 Voting-age population	Turnout	%
HAWAII															
KENTUCKY													1,892,000	73,140	3.9%
MISSISSIPPI															
NEW JERSEY										3,573,000	340,027	9.5%			
VIRGINIA															

State	1961 Voting-age population	Turnout	%	Difference from 1957**	1963 Voting-age population	Turnout	%	Difference from 1951	1965 Voting-age population	Turnout	%	Difference from 1951	1967 Voting-age population	Turnout	%	Difference from 1951	1969 Voting-age population	Turnout	%	Difference from 1951
HAWAII																				
KENTUCKY					1,958,000	87,494	4.5%	0.6					2,041,000	176,613	8.7%	4.8				
MISSISSIPPI																				
NEW JERSEY	3,801,000	458,502	12.1%	2.5					4,100,000	321,893	7.9%	-1.7					4,399,000	386,138	8.8%	-0.7
VIRGINIA																				

Democratic Turnout for Election Years 1951–1969

State	1951 Voting-age population	Turnout	%	1953 Voting-age population	Turnout	%	1955 Voting-age population	Turnout	% Difference from 1951**	1957 Voting-age population	Turnout	%	Difference from 1951	1959 Voting-age population	Turnout	%	Difference from 1951
HAWAII														338,000	76,980	22.8%	
KENTUCKY														1,892,000	551,923	29.2%	
MISSISSIPPI	1,201,000	394,634	32.9%				1,186,000	436,227	36.8% 3.9					1,171,000	438,343	37.4%	4.6
NEW JERSEY																	
VIRGINIA				2,102,000	228,214	10.9%				2,214,000	150,101	6.8%	-4.1				

State	1961 Voting-age population	Turnout	%	Difference from 1951	1963 Voting-age population	Turnout	%	Difference from 1951	1965 Voting-age population	Turnout	%	Difference from 1951	1967 Voting-age population	Turnout	%	Difference from 1951	1969 Voting-age population	Turnout	%	Difference from 1951
HAWAII																				
KENTUCKY					1,958,000	575,309	29.4%	0.2					2,041,000	362,162	17.7%	-11.4				
MISSISSIPPI					1,191,000	471,157	39.6%	6.7					1,221,000	680,283	55.7%	22.9				
NEW JERSEY	3,801,000	264,561	7.0%						4,100,000	260,240	6.3%	-0.6					4,399,000	381,890	8.7%	1.7
VIRGINIA	2,352,000	352,158	15.0%	4.1													2,749,000	408,630	14.9%	4.0

*Due to the paucity of data, no overall primary chart is included for this time period.

**Percentage point difference between turnout in current year and initial year listed in chart. If data do not appear for a state in the initial year listed, the difference is calculated from the first year in which data do appear for that state.

CHAPTER 10
1970–1989

Chronology of Major Events, 1970–1989

1970   U.S. troops invade Cambodia. Four student anti-war demonstrators are killed by police at Kent State University. Congress passes the National Environmental Policy Act and creates the Environmental Protection Agency. The nineteenth census counts the U.S. population at 203.3 million people.

1971   The Pentagon Papers, an expansive Department of Defense study on the progress of the Vietnam conflict, are leaked and published by the *New York Times*. Among other things, the papers show that the conflict was misrepresented prior to the Gulf of Tonkin Resolution; Congress repeals the resolution. The Twenty-sixth Amendment is ratified, lowering the voting age for federal elections to eighteen. In October, United Nations seats People's Republic of China in General Assembly and Security Council, expelling the Taiwan/Nationalist government.

1972   President Nixon goes to China to ease tensions, putting the United States on the path towards recognition of the People's Republic of China as the sole government of China. Nixon operatives break into the Democratic National Committee headquarters in the Watergate office complex and steal documents. Nixon is re-elected by a landslide.

1973   *Roe v. Wade* Supreme Court decision legalizes most abortions and fans the flames of a growing "culture war." Vice President Spiro Agnew resigns in a corruption scandal; U.S. House minority leader Gerald Ford is chosen as vice president. American troops leave Vietnam as peace accords are signed. Congress passes the War Powers Act, limiting presidential discretion over the deployment of troops. The draft is officially ended and replaced by voluntary enlistment. War in the Middle East leads to an oil crisis as Arab states embargo Israel's allies; price controls lead to massive shortages at gas stations across the United States.

1974   The final Americans leave Vietnam. The Watergate inquiry reveals secret tapes of White House conversations, which the Supreme Court orders the White House to turn over to Congress. Nixon resigns as impeachment proceedings begin in the U.S. House. Vice President Ford succeeds him and pardons Nixon, forestalling what would have been a deeply divisive trial.

1975   South Vietnam is defeated by the North, and the country is unified under North Vietnamese Premier Ho Chi Minh.

1976   Democrat Jimmy Carter is elected president, narrowly defeating Ford. Chinese revolutionary leader, Communist Party chair and premier Mao Tse-tung dies.

1977   In his first presidential act, Carter pardons those who evaded the draft during the war in Vietnam. Fifteen countries, including the United States and Soviet Union, sign a nuclear nonproliferation pact.

1978   Israel and Egypt sign the U.S.-brokered Camp David Accords.

1979   Soviets invade Afghanistan. The United States normalizes diplomatic ties with China. Iran's Shah is deposed by Islamic revolutionaries; radical students storm U.S. Embassy in Iran and hold fifty-three hostages. Uncertainty causes a second oil crisis as prices spike.

1980   The United States boycotts Moscow summer Olympics in protest of the Soviet invasion of Afghanistan. Iran hostage crisis and double-digit inflation doom Carter's campaign, and Republican Ronald Reagan is elected president. The twentieth census counts the U.S. population at 226.5 million people.

1981   The hostages in Iran are released as Reagan takes office. Reagan fires air traffic controllers after they stage illegal strike. Sandra Day O'Connor becomes first female Supreme Court justice. The Federal Reserve, under the leadership of Paul Volcker and with the acquiescence of President Reagan, sharply raises interest rates to deliberately create a mild recession in order to bring double-digit inflation under control. Congress passes the largest tax cut in American history.

1982	The Equal Rights Amendment for women's equality, passed by Congress in 1971, falls three states short of ratification. The economy begins to rebound.
1983	Two hundred forty-one U.S. Marines killed in suicide bombing of barracks in Lebanon. Marine forces are withdrawn from Lebanon. America immediately invades Grenada and topples the leftist government.
1984	Soviets boycott Los Angeles Olympics. Democrat Geraldine Ferraro becomes first woman vice-presidential candidate. Reagan is reelected in a landslide.
1986	A nuclear accident at Chernobyl, a Russian power plant, kills 1700 people. Iran-Contra—the selling of arms covertly to funnel money to one side of the civil war in Nicaragua—becomes a national scandal, leading to the resignation and indictment of Reagan Administration officials. Soviet premier Mikhail Gorbachev outlines and launches reforms of the Soviet Union under the names of *glasnost* (openness) and *perestroika* (restructuring).
1987	The third of three Reagan-Gorbachev summits yields agreement on nuclear reduction and peaceful relations. October 19th marks the largest one-day stock market decline since Black Friday in 1929.
1988	The Soviets are driven from Afghanistan. Republican Vice President George H. W. Bush is elected president.
1989	The United States invades Panama; General Manuel Noriega flees rather than face arrest on drug distribution charges. The Berlin Wall is torn down. Gorbachev is elected Soviet president in first multi-candidate elections in 75 years.

State and Federal Laws Chronology, 1970–1989

1970   Voting Rights Act (VRA) Amendment restricts residency requirements for presidential elections to thirty days. Congress renews the VRA for five years.

Evans v. Cornman, 398 U.S. 419 (1970). The Supreme Court holds that residents of federal enclaves are treated as state residents to such an extent that it is a violation of the Fourteenth Amendment for the state to deny them the right to vote.[1]

Oregon v. Mitchell, Texas v. Mitchell, United States v. Idaho, United States v. Arizona, 400 U.S. 112 (1970). In a decision considering several cases at once, the Supreme Court rules that Congress can restrict residency requirements to thirty days for presidential elections and ban literacy tests for all elections, but that it can only set age limits for federal elections (not state or local elections).

1971   The Twenty-sixth Amendment passes, in which "the right of citizens of the United States, who are eighteen years of age or older, to vote shall not be denied or abridged by the United States or by any state on account of age."

1972   *Dunn v. Blumstein*, 405 U.S. 330 (1972). The Supreme Court holds that one-year residency requirements to vote are impermissible and violate equal protection as granted under the Fourteenth Amendment.

1973   *Mahan v. Howell, City of Virginia Beach v. Howell, Weinberg v. Prichard*, 410 U.S. 315 (1973). The Supreme Court relaxes the requirement that state legislative districts be as equal as possible, allowing them to be more divergent than federal districts.

Marston v. Lewis, 410 U.S. 679 (1973); *Burns v. Fortson*, 410 U.S. 686 (1973). The Supreme Court upholds an Arizona requirement that voters register fifty days before a primary election, as the party shows that the period is necessary to prepare an accurate voting list.

1974   *Richardson v. Ramirez*, 418 U.S. 24 (1974). The Supreme Court holds that convicted felons can be barred from voting without violating the Fourteenth Amendment.

1975   Congress renews the Voting Rights Act for seven more years.

1977   *United Jewish Organizations of Williamsburg, Inc. v. Carey*, 430 U.S. 144 (1977). The Supreme Court rejects the claim of New York's Hasidic Jewish community that a revision of the state legislative districts to create districts with African American majorities is discriminatory against the Hasidic Jews. The case marks the acceptance of racial criteria for redistricting under the Voting Rights Act; the eight justices affirming the decision are evenly divided as to whether the inclusion of racial criteria requires past discrimination.

1980   *Mobile v. Bolden*, 446 U.S. 55 (1980). The Supreme Court finds that an at-large system of voting, such as that used by Mobile, Alabama, to elect city commissioners, is not discriminatory merely because it has produced no electoral victories for racial minorities.

City of Rome v. United States (1980). The Supreme Court again upholds the Voting Rights Act's Section 5 "preclearance" requirement that requires states to present prospective changes in election districts to the U.S. Attorney General. The city of Rome argues unsuccessfully that recent case law had undermined *South Carolina v. Katzenbach* (1966).

1982   The Voting Rights Act of 1982 renews the previous act for twenty-five years. In one amendment, Congress responds to *Mobile v. Bolden* by amending the act to prohibit voting systems that deny minorities the likelihood of representation, even if the system is not intentionally discriminatory.

1984   Voting Accessibility for the Elderly and Handicapped Act of 1984 (28 U.S.C. §1973) promotes the fundamental right to vote by providing improved access for handicapped and elderly individuals to registration facilities and polling places for federal elections.

1986   *Davis v. Bandemer,* 478 U.S. 109 (1986). The Supreme Court holds that political gerrymandering is reviewable by federal courts even if the disputed districts meet the "one person, one vote" test.

Thornburg v. Gingles, 478 U.S. 30 (1986). The Supreme Court applies the 1982 amendment to the Voting Rights Act to reject a districting plan that "dilutes" the minority vote into districts with white majorities.

Uniformed and Overseas Citizens Absentee Voting Act of 1986 requires that all U.S. states and incorporated territories allow U.S. citizens residing overseas, including members of the armed forces and their families, to register to vote and vote by absentee ballot in federal elections.

---

[1] For Supreme Court cases, see CQ Press Electronic Library, *Guide to the U.S. Supreme Court Online Edition,* "Chronology of Major Decisions of the Court, 1797–2007." Originally published in David G. Savage, *Guide to the U.S. Supreme Court,* 4th ed., (Revised), (Washington, D.C.: CQ Press, 2008). http://library.cqpress.com/supremecourtguide/search.php (accessed June 18th, 2010).

National Count of Popular Vote for President, 1972–1988

YEAR	NAME	PARTY	TOTAL	PERCENTAGE[1]
1972	Richard Nixon	Republican	47,169,911	34.2%
	George McGovern	Democratic	29,170,383	21.2%
	Other and write-ins		1,378,260	1.0%
1976	Jimmy Carter	Democratic	40,830,763	27.5%
	Gerald Ford	Republican	39,147,793	26.4%
	Other and write-ins		1,577,333	1.1%
1980	Ronald Reagan	Republican	43,904,153	27.8%
	Jimmy Carter	Democratic	35,483,883	22.4%
	John Anderson	Independent	5,719,850	3.6%
1984	Ronald Reagan	Republican	54,455,075	32.9%
	Walter Mondale	Democratic	37,577,185	22.7%
1988	George H. W. Bush	Republican	48,886,097	28.3%
	Michael Dukakis	Democratic	41,809,074	24.2%

[1] The percentage figures in this chart are based on the votes cast divided by the eligible voting-age population at the time of the election.

United States Presidential Turnout, Election Years 1972–1988

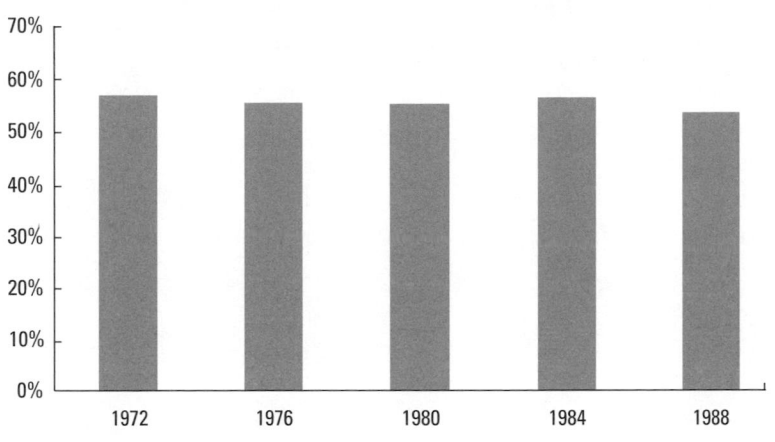

YEAR	VOTING-AGE POPULATION	TOTAL	%
1972	137,787,000	77,718,554	56.4%
1976	148,418,000	81,555,080	55.0%
1980	158,111,000	86,515,221	54.7%
1984	165,727,000	92,652,842	55.9%
1988	172,777,000	91,594,809	53.0%

Partisan Turnout Presidential Years Based on Aggregate House Turnout, Election Years 1972–1988

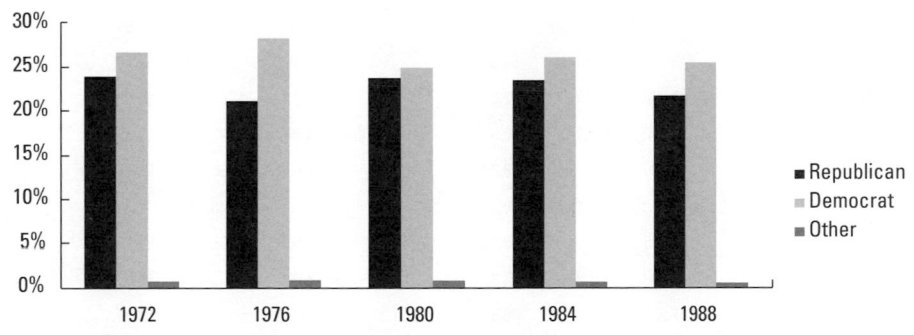

■ Republican
■ Democrat
■ Other

YEAR	VOTING-AGE POPULATION	REPUBLICAN TURNOUT	%	DEMOCRAT TURNOUT	%	OTHER TURNOUT	%
1972	137,787,000	32,822,920	23.8%	36,599,592	26.6%	994,807	0.7%
1976	148,418,000	31,241,822	21.0%	41,742,193	28.1%	1,279,705	0.9%
1980	158,111,000	37,348,291	23.6%	39,195,884	24.8%	1,270,214	0.8%
1984	165,727,000	38,716,885	23.4%	43,018,851	26.0%	1,092,283	0.7%
1988	172,777,000	37,327,901	21.6%	43,775,709	25.3%	927,205	0.5%

UNITED STATES PRESIDENTIAL GENERAL ELECTIONS

Election Years 1972–1988

State	1972 Voting-age population	Turnout	%	1976 Voting-age population	Turnout	%	Difference from 1972*	1980 Voting-age population	Turnout	%	Difference from 1972	1984 Voting-age population	Turnout	%	Difference from 1972	1988 Voting-age population	Turnout	%	Difference from 1972
ALABAMA	2,346,000	1,006,111	42.9%	2,552,000	1,182,850	46.3%	3.5	2,732,000	1,341,929	49.1%	6.2	2,833,000	1,441,713	50.9%	8.0	2,931,000	1,378,476	47.0%	4.1
ALASKA	202,000	95,219	47.1%	237,000	123,574	52.1%	5.0	271,000	158,445	58.5%	11.3	314,000	207,605	66.1%	19.0	355,000	200,116	56.4%	9.2
ARIZONA	1,312,000	622,926	47.5%	1,615,000	742,719	46.0%	-1.5	1,902,000	873,945	45.9%	-1.5	2,187,000	1,025,897	46.9%	-0.6	2,460,000	1,171,873	47.6%	0.2
ARKANSAS	1,357,000	651,320	48.0%	1,495,000	767,535	51.3%	3.3	1,614,000	837,582	51.9%	3.9	1,660,000	884,406	53.3%	5.3	1,704,000	827,738	48.6%	0.6
CALIFORNIA	13,275,000	8,367,862	63.0%	14,481,000	7,867,117	54.3%	-8.7	15,629,000	8,587,063	54.9%	-8.1	16,816,000	9,505,423	56.5%	-6.5	17,957,000	9,887,065	55.1%	-8.0
COLORADO	1,570,000	953,884	60.8%	1,829,000	1,081,554	59.1%	-1.6	2,058,000	1,184,415	57.6%	-3.2	2,196,000	1,295,380	59.0%	-1.8	2,328,000	1,372,394	59.0%	-1.8
CONNECTICUT	2,011,000	1,384,277	68.8%	2,114,000	1,381,526	65.4%	-3.5	2,210,000	1,406,285	63.6%	-5.2	2,299,000	1,466,900	63.8%	-5.0	2,392,000	1,443,394	60.3%	-8.5
DELAWARE	367,000	235,516	64.2%	398,000	235,834	59.3%	-4.9	426,000	235,900	55.4%	-8.8	457,000	254,572	55.7%	-8.5	486,000	249,891	51.4%	-12.8
DISTRICT OF COLUMBIA	504,000	163,421	32.4%	487,000	168,830	34.7%	2.2	472,000	175,237	37.1%	4.7	464,000	211,288	45.5%	13.1	456,000	192,877	42.3%	9.9
FLORIDA	5,163,000	2,583,283	50.0%	6,159,000	3,150,631	51.2%	1.1	7,102,000	3,686,930	51.9%	1.9	8,053,000	4,180,051	51.9%	1.9	8,966,000	4,302,313	48.0%	-2.0
GEORGIA	3,167,000	1,174,772	37.1%	3,506,000	1,467,458	41.9%	4.8	3,832,000	1,596,695	41.7%	4.6	4,197,000	1,776,120	42.3%	5.2	4,548,000	1,809,672	39.8%	2.7
HAWAII	504,000	270,274	53.6%	572,000	291,301	50.9%	-2.7	636,000	303,287	47.7%	-5.9	692,000	335,846	48.5%	-5.1	747,000	354,461	47.5%	-6.2
IDAHO	495,000	310,379	62.7%	568,000	344,071	60.6%	-2.1	631,000	437,431	69.3%	6.6	655,000	411,144	62.8%	0.1	677,000	408,968	60.4%	-2.3
ILLINOIS	7,333,000	4,723,236	64.4%	7,613,000	4,718,914	62.0%	-2.4	7,851,000	4,749,721	60.5%	-3.9	7,928,000	4,819,088	60.8%	-3.6	8,000,000	4,559,120	57.0%	-7.4
INDIANA	3,469,000	2,125,529	61.3%	3,672,000	2,220,362	60.5%	-0.8	3,850,000	2,242,033	58.2%	-3.0	3,937,000	2,233,069	56.7%	-4.6	4,021,000	2,168,621	53.9%	-7.3
IOWA	1,905,000	1,225,944	64.4%	1,996,000	1,279,306	64.1%	-0.3	2,070,000	1,317,661	63.7%	-0.7	2,055,000	1,319,805	64.2%	-0.1	2,042,000	1,225,614	60.0%	-4.3
KANSAS	1,547,000	916,095	59.2%	1,629,000	957,845	58.8%	-0.4	1,701,000	979,795	57.6%	-1.6	1,739,000	1,021,991	58.8%	-0.4	1,774,000	993,044	56.0%	-3.2
KENTUCKY	2,228,000	1,067,499	47.9%	2,413,000	1,167,142	48.4%	0.5	2,574,000	1,294,627	50.3%	2.4	2,636,000	1,369,345	51.9%	4.0	2,696,000	1,322,517	49.1%	1.1
LOUISIANA	2,406,000	1,051,491	43.7%	2,646,000	1,278,439	48.3%	4.6	2,847,000	1,548,591	54.4%	10.7	2,892,000	1,706,822	59.0%	15.3	2,935,000	1,628,202	55.5%	11.8
MAINE	678,000	417,042	61.5%	740,000	483,216	65.3%	3.8	797,000	523,011	65.6%	4.1	845,000	553,144	65.5%	4.0	890,000	555,035	62.4%	0.9
MARYLAND	2,628,000	1,353,812	51.5%	2,817,000	1,439,897	51.1%	-0.4	2,999,000	1,540,496	51.4%	-0.1	3,202,000	1,675,873	52.3%	0.8	3,398,000	1,714,358	50.5%	-1.1
MASSACHUSETTS	3,798,000	2,458,756	64.7%	3,952,000	2,547,558	64.5%	-0.3	4,096,000	2,524,298	61.6%	-3.1	4,228,000	2,559,453	60.5%	-4.2	4,355,000	2,632,805	60.5%	-4.3
MICHIGAN	5,755,000	3,489,727	60.6%	6,100,000	3,653,749	59.9%	-0.7	6,399,000	3,909,725	61.1%	0.5	6,529,000	3,801,658	58.2%	-2.4	6,654,000	3,669,163	55.1%	-5.5
MINNESOTA	2,533,000	1,741,652	68.8%	2,719,000	1,949,931	71.7%	3.0	2,887,000	2,051,980	71.1%	2.3	3,007,000	2,084,449	69.3%	0.6	3,121,000	2,096,790	67.2%	-1.6
MISSISSIPPI	1,460,000	645,963	44.2%	1,590,000	769,361	48.4%	4.1	1,703,000	892,620	52.4%	8.2	1,753,000	941,104	53.7%	9.4	1,802,000	931,527	51.7%	7.5
MISSOURI	3,222,000	1,855,803	57.6%	3,390,000	1,953,600	57.6%	0.0	3,541,000	2,099,824	59.3%	1.7	3,642,000	2,122,783	58.3%	0.7	3,738,000	2,093,713	56.0%	-1.6
MONTANA	471,000	317,603	67.4%	515,000	328,734	63.8%	-3.6	552,000	363,952	65.9%	-1.5	561,000	384,377	68.5%	1.1	569,000	365,674	64.3%	-3.2
NEBRASKA	1,009,000	576,289	57.1%	1,067,000	607,668	57.0%	-0.2	1,115,000	640,854	57.5%	0.4	1,125,000	652,090	58.0%	0.8	1,135,000	661,465	58.3%	1.2
NEVADA	381,000	181,766	47.7%	480,000	201,876	42.1%	-5.7	578,000	247,885	42.9%	-4.8	701,000	286,667	40.9%	-6.8	818,000	350,067	42.8%	-4.9
NEW HAMPSHIRE	522,000	334,055	64.0%	593,000	339,618	57.3%	-6.7	660,000	383,990	58.2%	-5.8	728,000	389,066	53.4%	-10.6	793,000	451,074	56.9%	-7.1
NEW JERSEY	4,754,000	2,997,229	63.0%	4,951,000	3,014,472	60.9%	-2.2	5,133,000	2,975,684	58.0%	-5.1	5,298,000	3,217,862	60.7%	-2.3	5,455,000	3,099,553	56.8%	-6.2
NEW MEXICO	675,000	386,241	57.2%	780,000	418,409	53.6%	-3.6	875,000	456,971	52.2%	-5.0	942,000	514,370	54.6%	-2.6	1,008,000	521,287	51.7%	-5.5
NEW YORK	11,891,000	7,165,919	60.3%	11,949,000	6,534,170	54.7%	-5.6	12,020,000	6,201,959	51.6%	-8.7	12,182,000	6,806,810	55.9%	-4.4	12,337,000	6,485,683	52.6%	-7.7

United States Presidential General Elections *(continued)*

Election Years 1972–1988 *(continued)*

State	1972 Voting-age population	1972 Turnout	1972 %	1976 Voting-age population	1976 Turnout	1976 %	1976 Difference from 1972	1980 Voting-age population	1980 Turnout	1980 %	1980 Difference from 1972	1984 Voting-age population	1984 Turnout	1984 %	1984 Difference from 1972	1988 Voting-age population	1988 Turnout	1988 %	1988 Difference from 1972
NORTH CAROLINA	3,553,000	1,518,612	**42.7%**	3,907,000	1,678,914	**43.0%**	0.2	4,239,000	1,855,833	**43.8%**	1.0	4,560,000	2,175,361	**47.7%**	5.0	4,867,000	2,134,370	**43.9%**	1.1
NORTH DAKOTA	409,000	280,514	**68.6%**	436,000	297,188	**68.2%**	-0.4	458,000	301,545	**65.8%**	-2.7	458,000	308,971	**67.5%**	-1.1	459,000	297,261	**64.8%**	-3.8
OHIO	7,053,000	4,094,787	**58.1%**	7,365,000	4,111,873	**55.8%**	-2.2	7,638,000	4,283,603	**56.1%**	-2.0	7,776,000	4,547,619	**58.5%**	0.4	7,909,000	4,393,699	**55.6%**	-2.5
OKLAHOMA	1,833,000	1,029,900	**56.2%**	2,005,000	1,092,251	**54.5%**	-1.7	2,152,000	1,149,708	**53.4%**	-2.8	2,208,000	1,255,676	**56.9%**	0.7	2,260,000	1,171,036	**51.8%**	-4.4
OREGON	1,511,000	927,946	**61.4%**	1,709,000	1,029,070	**60.3%**	-1.2	1,879,000	1,181,516	**62.9%**	1.5	1,954,000	1,226,527	**62.8%**	1.4	2,027,000	1,201,694	**59.3%**	-2.1
PENNSYLVANIA	8,073,000	4,592,106	**56.9%**	8,383,000	4,620,787	**55.1%**	-1.8	8,653,000	4,561,501	**52.7%**	-4.2	8,786,000	4,844,903	**55.1%**	-1.7	9,014,000	4,536,251	**50.9%**	-6.0
RHODE ISLAND	642,000	415,808	**64.8%**	660,000	411,170	**62.3%**	-2.5	677,000	416,072	**61.5%**	-3.3	702,000	410,492	**58.5%**	-6.3	726,000	404,620	**55.7%**	-9.0
SOUTH CAROLINA	1,776,000	673,960	**37.9%**	1,990,000	802,583	**40.3%**	2.4	2,186,000	894,071	**40.9%**	3.0	2,344,000	968,529	**41.3%**	3.4	2,495,000	986,009	**39.5%**	1.6
SOUTH DAKOTA	440,000	307,415	**69.9%**	463,000	300,678	**64.9%**	-4.9	483,000	327,703	**67.8%**	-2.0	488,000	317,867	**65.1%**	-4.7	492,000	312,991	**63.6%**	-6.3
TENNESSEE	2,778,000	1,201,182	**43.2%**	3,051,000	1,476,345	**48.4%**	5.1	3,295,000	1,617,616	**49.1%**	5.9	3,444,000	1,711,994	**49.7%**	6.5	3,538,000	1,636,250	**46.2%**	3.0
TEXAS	7,729,000	3,471,281	**44.9%**	8,708,000	4,071,884	**46.8%**	1.8	9,608,000	4,541,636	**47.3%**	2.4	10,358,000	5,397,571	**52.1%**	7.2	11,077,000	5,427,410	**49.0%**	4.1
UTAH	701,000	478,476	**68.3%**	813,000	541,198	**66.6%**	1.7	912,000	604,222	**66.3%**	-2.0	980,000	629,656	**64.3%**	-4.0	1,046,000	647,008	**61.9%**	-6.4
VERMONT	303,000	186,947	**61.7%**	334,000	187,765	**56.2%**	-5.5	363,000	213,299	**58.8%**	-2.9	385,000	234,561	**60.9%**	-0.8	408,000	243,328	**59.9%**	-1.0
VIRGINIA	3,243,000	1,457,019	**44.9%**	3,549,000	1,697,094	**47.8%**	2.9	3,841,000	1,866,032	**48.6%**	3.7	4,144,000	2,146,635	**51.8%**	6.9	4,434,000	2,191,609	**49.4%**	4.5
WASHINGTON	2,396,000	1,470,847	**61.4%**	2,677,000	1,555,534	**58.1%**	-3.3	2,937,000	1,742,394	**59.3%**	-2.1	3,170,000	1,883,910	**59.4%**	-2.0	3,392,000	1,865,253	**55.0%**	6.4
WEST VIRGINIA	1,221,000	762,399	**62.4%**	1,310,000	750,964	**57.3%**	-5.1	1,381,000	737,715	**53.4%**	-9.0	1,365,000	735,742	**53.9%**	-8.5	1,348,000	653,311	**48.5%**	-14.0
WISCONSIN	2,947,000	1,852,890	**62.9%**	3,149,000	2,104,175	**66.8%**	3.9	3,326,000	2,273,221	**68.3%**	5.5	3,427,000	2,211,689	**64.5%**	1.7	3,523,000	2,191,608	**62.2%**	-0.7
WYOMING	241,000	145,570	**60.4%**	284,000	156,343	**55.1%**	-5.4	320,000	176,713	**55.2%**	5.2	318,000	188,968	**59.4%**	-1.0	316,000	176,551	**55.9%**	-4.5
Total	137,787,000	77,718,554	**56.4%**	148,418,000	81,555,889	**55.0%**	-1.5	158,111,000	86,515,221	**54.7%**	-1.7	165,620,000	92,652,842	**55.9%**	-0.5	172,777,000	91,594,809	**53.0%**	-3.4

*Percentage point difference between turnout in current year and initial year listed in chart. If data do not appear for a state in the initial year listed, the difference is calculated from the first year in which data do appear for that state.

UNITED STATES PRESIDENTIAL GENERAL ELECTIONS

Republican Turnout for Election Years 1972–1988

State	1972 Voting-age population	Turnout	%	1976 Voting-age population	Turnout	%	Difference from 1972*	1980 Voting-age population	Turnout	%	Difference from 1972	1984 Voting-age population	Turnout	%	Difference from 1972	1988 Voting-age population	Turnout	%	Difference from 1972
ALABAMA	2,346,000	728,701	31.1%	2,552,000	504,070	19.8%	-11.3	2,732,000	654,192	23.9%	-7.1	2,833,000	872,849	30.8%	-0.3	2,931,000	815,576	27.8%	-3.2
ALASKA	202,000	55,349	27.4%	237,000	71,555	30.2%	2.8	271,000	86,112	31.8%	4.4	314,000	138,377	44.1%	16.7	355,000	119,251	33.6%	6.2
ARIZONA	1,312,000	402,812	30.7%	1,615,000	418,642	25.9%	-4.8	1,902,000	529,688	27.8%	-2.9	2,187,000	681,416	31.2%	0.5	2,460,000	702,541	28.6%	-2.1
ARKANSAS	1,357,000	448,541	33.1%	1,495,000	267,903	17.9%	-15.1	1,614,000	403,164	25.0%	-8.1	1,660,000	534,774	32.2%	-0.8	1,704,000	466,578	27.4%	-5.7
CALIFORNIA	13,275,000	4,602,096	34.7%	14,481,000	3,882,244	26.8%	-7.9	15,629,000	4,524,858	29.0%	-5.7	16,816,000	5,467,009	32.5%	-2.2	17,957,000	5,054,917	28.2%	-6.5
COLORADO	1,570,000	597,189	38.0%	1,829,000	584,367	32.0%	-6.1	2,058,000	652,264	31.7%	-6.3	2,196,000	821,817	37.4%	-0.6	2,328,000	728,177	31.3%	-6.8
CONNECTICUT	2,011,000	810,763	40.3%	2,114,000	719,261	34.0%	-6.3	2,210,000	677,210	30.6%	-9.7	2,299,000	890,877	38.8%	-1.6	2,392,000	750,241	31.4%	-9.0
DELAWARE	367,000	140,357	38.2%	398,000	109,831	27.6%	-10.6	426,000	111,252	26.1%	-12.1	457,000	152,190	33.3%	-4.9	486,000	139,639	28.7%	-9.5
DISTRICT OF COLUMBIA	504,000	35,226	7.0%	487,000	27,873	5.7%	-1.3	472,000	23,545	5.0%	-2.0	464,000	29,009	6.3%	-0.7	456,000	27,590	6.1%	-0.9
FLORIDA	5,163,000	1,857,759	36.0%	6,159,000	1,469,531	23.9%	-12.1	7,102,000	2,046,951	28.8%	-7.2	8,053,000	2,730,350	33.9%	-2.1	8,966,000	2,618,885	29.2%	-6.8
GEORGIA	3,167,000	881,496	27.8%	3,506,000	483,743	13.8%	-14.0	3,832,000	654,168	17.1%	-10.8	4,197,000	1,068,722	25.5%	-2.4	4,548,000	1,081,331	23.8%	-4.1
HAWAII	504,000	168,865	33.5%	572,000	140,003	24.5%	-9.0	636,000	130,112	20.5%	-13.0	692,000	185,050	26.7%	-6.8	747,000	158,625	21.2%	-12.3
IDAHO	495,000	199,384	40.3%	568,000	204,151	35.9%	-4.3	631,000	290,699	46.1%	5.8	655,000	297,523	45.4%	5.1	677,000	253,881	37.5%	-2.8
ILLINOIS	7,333,000	2,788,179	38.0%	7,613,000	2,364,269	31.1%	-7.0	7,851,000	2,358,049	30.0%	-8.0	7,928,000	2,707,103	34.1%	-3.9	8,000,000	2,310,939	28.9%	-9.1
INDIANA	3,469,000	1,405,154	40.5%	3,672,000	1,183,958	32.2%	-8.3	3,850,000	1,255,656	32.6%	-7.9	3,937,000	1,377,230	35.0%	-5.5	4,021,000	1,297,763	32.3%	-8.2
IOWA	1,905,000	706,207	37.1%	1,996,000	632,863	31.7%	-5.4	2,070,000	676,026	32.7%	-4.4	2,055,000	703,088	34.2%	-2.9	2,042,000	545,355	26.7%	-10.4
KANSAS	1,547,000	619,812	40.1%	1,629,000	502,752	30.9%	-9.2	1,701,000	566,812	33.3%	-6.7	1,739,000	677,296	38.9%	-1.1	1,774,000	554,049	31.2%	-8.8
KENTUCKY	2,228,000	676,446	30.4%	2,413,000	531,852	22.0%	-8.3	2,574,000	635,274	24.7%	-5.7	2,636,000	821,702	31.2%	0.8	2,696,000	734,281	27.2%	-3.1
LOUISIANA	2,406,000	686,852	28.5%	2,646,000	587,446	22.2%	-6.3	2,847,000	792,853	27.8%	-0.7	2,892,000	1,037,299	35.9%	7.3	2,935,000	883,702	30.1%	1.6
MAINE	678,000	256,458	37.8%	740,000	236,320	31.9%	-5.9	797,000	238,522	29.9%	-7.9	845,000	336,500	39.8%	2.0	890,000	307,131	34.5%	-3.3
MARYLAND	2,628,000	829,305	31.6%	2,817,000	672,661	23.9%	-7.7	2,999,000	680,606	22.7%	-8.9	3,202,000	879,918	27.5%	-4.1	3,398,000	876,167	25.8%	-5.8
MASSACHUSETTS	3,798,000	1,112,078	29.3%	3,952,000	1,030,276	26.1%	-3.2	4,096,000	1,057,631	25.8%	-3.5	4,228,000	1,310,936	31.0%	1.7	4,355,000	1,194,635	27.4%	-1.8
MICHIGAN	5,755,000	1,961,721	34.1%	6,100,000	1,893,742	31.0%	-3.0	6,399,000	1,915,225	29.9%	-4.2	6,529,000	2,251,571	34.5%	0.4	6,654,000	1,965,486	29.5%	-4.5
MINNESOTA	2,533,000	898,269	35.5%	2,719,000	819,395	30.1%	-5.3	2,887,000	873,268	30.2%	-5.2	3,007,000	1,032,603	34.3%	-1.1	3,121,000	962,337	30.8%	-4.6
MISSISSIPPI	1,460,000	505,125	34.6%	1,590,000	366,846	23.1%	-11.5	1,703,000	441,089	25.9%	-8.7	1,753,000	582,377	33.2%	-1.4	1,802,000	557,890	31.0%	-3.6
MISSOURI	3,222,000	1,153,852	35.8%	3,390,000	927,443	27.4%	-8.5	3,541,000	1,074,181	30.3%	-5.5	3,642,000	1,274,188	35.0%	-0.8	3,738,000	1,084,953	29.0%	-6.8
MONTANA	471,000	183,976	39.1%	515,000	173,703	33.7%	-5.3	552,000	206,814	37.5%	-1.6	561,000	232,450	41.4%	2.4	569,000	190,412	33.5%	-5.6
NEBRASKA	1,009,000	406,298	40.3%	1,067,000	359,705	33.7%	-6.6	1,115,000	419,937	37.7%	-2.6	1,125,000	460,054	40.9%	0.6	1,135,000	397,956	35.1%	-5.2
NEVADA	381,000	115,750	30.4%	480,000	101,273	21.1%	-9.3	578,000	155,017	26.8%	-3.6	701,000	188,770	26.9%	-3.5	818,000	206,040	25.2%	-5.2
NEW HAMPSHIRE	522,000	213,724	40.9%	593,000	185,935	31.4%	-9.6	660,000	221,705	33.6%	-7.4	728,000	267,051	36.7%	-4.3	793,000	281,537	35.5%	-5.4
NEW JERSEY	4,754,000	1,845,502	38.8%	4,951,000	1,509,688	30.5%	-8.3	5,133,000	1,546,557	30.1%	-8.7	5,298,000	1,933,630	36.5%	-2.3	5,455,000	1,743,192	32.0%	-6.9
NEW MEXICO	675,000	235,606	34.9%	780,000	211,419	27.1%	-7.8	875,000	250,779	28.7%	-6.2	942,000	307,101	32.6%	-2.3	1,008,000	270,341	26.8%	-8.1
NEW YORK	11,891,000	4,192,778	35.3%	11,949,000	3,100,791	26.0%	-9.3	12,020,000	2,893,831	24.1%	-11.2	12,182,000	3,664,763	30.1%	-5.2	12,337,000	3,081,871	25.0%	-10.3

United States Presidential General Elections (continued)

Republican Turnout for Election Years 1972–1988 (continued)

State	1972 Voting-age population	1972 Turnout	1972 %	1976 Voting-age population	1976 Turnout	1976 %	1976 Difference from 1972	1980 Voting-age population	1980 Turnout	1980 %	1980 Difference from 1972	1984 Voting-age population	1984 Turnout	1984 %	1984 Difference from 1972	1988 Voting-age population	1988 Turnout	1988 %	1988 Difference from 1972
NORTH CAROLINA	3,553,000	1,054,889	29.7%	3,907,000	741,960	19.0%	-10.7	4,239,000	915,018	21.6%	-8.1	4,560,000	1,346,481	29.5%	-0.2	4,867,000	1,237,258	25.4%	-4.3
NORTH DAKOTA	409,000	174,109	42.6%	436,000	153,470	35.2%	-7.4	458,000	193,695	42.3%	-0.3	458,000	200,336	43.7%	1.2	459,000	166,559	36.3%	-6.3
OHIO	7,053,000	2,441,827	34.6%	7,365,000	2,000,505	27.2%	-7.5	7,638,000	2,206,545	28.9%	-5.7	7,776,000	2,678,560	34.4%	-0.2	7,909,000	2,416,549	30.6%	-4.1
OKLAHOMA	1,833,000	759,025	41.4%	2,005,000	545,708	27.2%	-14.2	2,152,000	695,570	32.3%	-9.1	2,208,000	861,530	39.0%	-2.4	2,260,000	678,367	30.0%	-11.4
OREGON	1,511,000	486,686	32.2%	1,700,000	492,120	28.8%	-3.4	1,879,000	571,044	30.4%	-1.8	1,954,000	685,700	35.1%	2.9	2,027,000	560,126	27.6%	-4.6
PENNSYLVANIA	8,073,000	2,714,521	33.6%	8,383,000	2,205,604	26.3%	-7.3	8,653,000	2,261,872	26.1%	-7.5	8,786,000	2,504,323	28.4%	-4.2	8,914,000	2,300,087	25.8%	-7.8
RHODE ISLAND	642,000	220,383	34.3%	660,000	181,249	27.5%	-6.9	677,000	154,793	22.9%	-11.5	702,000	212,080	30.2%	-4.1	726,000	177,761	24.5%	-9.8
SOUTH CAROLINA	1,776,000	477,044	26.9%	1,990,000	346,149	17.4%	-9.5	2,186,000	441,841	20.2%	-6.6	2,344,000	615,539	26.3%	-0.6	2,495,000	606,443	24.3%	-2.6
SOUTH DAKOTA	440,000	166,476	37.8%	463,000	151,505	32.7%	-5.1	483,000	198,343	41.1%	3.2	488,000	200,267	41.0%	3.2	492,000	165,415	33.6%	-4.2
TENNESSEE	2,778,000	813,147	29.3%	3,051,000	633,969	20.8%	-8.5	3,295,000	787,761	23.9%	-5.4	3,444,000	990,212	28.8%	-0.5	3,538,000	947,233	26.8%	2.5
TEXAS	7,729,000	2,298,896	29.7%	8,708,000	1,953,300	22.4%	-7.3	9,608,000	2,510,705	26.1%	-3.6	10,358,000	3,433,428	33.1%	3.4	11,077,000	3,036,829	27.4%	-2.3
UTAH	701,000	323,643	46.2%	813,000	337,908	41.6%	-4.6	912,000	439,687	48.2%	2.0	980,000	469,105	47.9%	1.7	1,046,000	428,442	41.0%	-5.2
VERMONT	303,000	117,149	38.7%	334,000	102,085	30.6%	-8.1	363,000	94,628	26.1%	-12.6	385,000	135,865	35.3%	-3.4	406,000	124,331	30.6%	-8.0
VIRGINIA	3,243,000	988,493	30.5%	3,549,000	836,554	23.6%	-6.9	3,841,000	989,609	25.8%	-4.7	4,144,000	1,337,078	32.3%	1.8	4,434,000	1,309,162	29.5%	-1.0
WASHINGTON	2,396,000	837,135	34.9%	2,677,000	777,732	29.1%	-5.9	2,937,000	865,244	29.5%	-5.5	3,170,000	1,051,670	33.2%	-1.8	3,392,000	903,835	26.6%	-8.3
WEST VIRGINIA	1,221,000	484,964	39.7%	1,310,000	314,760	24.0%	-15.7	1,381,000	334,206	24.2%	-15.5	1,365,000	405,483	29.7%	-10.0	1,348,000	310,065	23.0%	-16.7
WISCONSIN	2,947,000	989,430	33.6%	3,149,000	1,004,987	31.9%	-1.7	3,326,000	1,088,845	32.7%	-0.8	3,427,000	1,198,584	35.0%	1.4	3,523,000	1,047,499	29.7%	-3.8
WYOMING	241,000	100,464	41.7%	284,000	92,717	32.6%	-9.0	320,000	110,700	34.6%	-7.1	318,000	133,241	41.9%	0.2	316,000	106,867	33.8%	-7.9
Total	137,787,000	47,169,911	34.2%	148,418,000	39,147,793	26.4%	-7.9	158,111,000	43,904,153	27.8%	-6.5	165,620,000	54,455,075	32.9%	-1.4	172,777,000	48,886,097	28.3%	-5.9

Democratic Turnout for Election Years 1972–1988

State	1972 Voting-age population	1972 Turnout	1972 %	1976 Voting-age population	1976 Turnout	1976 %	1976 Difference from 1972*	1980 Voting-age population	1980 Turnout	1980 %	1980 Difference from 1972	1984 Voting-age population	1984 Turnout	1984 %	1984 Difference from 1972	1988 Voting-age population	1988 Turnout	1988 %	1988 Difference from 1972
ALABAMA	2,346,000	256,923	11.0%	2,552,000	659,170	25.8%	14.9	2,732,000	636,730	23.3%	12.4	2,833,000	551,899	19.5%	8.5	2,931,000	549,506	18.7%	7.8
ALASKA	202,000	32,967	16.3%	237,000	44,058	18.6%	2.3	271,000	41,842	15.4%	-0.9	314,000	62,007	19.7%	3.4	355,000	72,584	20.4%	4.1
ARIZONA	1,312,000	198,540	15.1%	1,615,000	295,602	18.3%	3.2	1,902,000	246,843	13.0%	-2.2	2,187,000	333,854	15.3%	0.1	2,460,000	454,029	18.5%	3.3
ARKANSAS	1,357,000	199,892	14.7%	1,495,000	498,604	33.4%	18.6	1,614,000	398,041	24.7%	9.9	1,660,000	338,646	20.4%	5.7	1,704,000	349,237	20.5%	5.8
CALIFORNIA	13,275,000	3,475,847	26.2%	14,481,000	3,742,284	25.8%	-0.3	15,629,000	3,083,661	19.7%	-6.5	16,816,000	3,922,519	23.3%	-2.9	17,957,000	4,702,233	26.2%	0.0
COLORADO	1,570,000	329,980	21.0%	1,829,000	460,353	25.2%	4.2	2,058,000	367,973	17.9%	-3.1	2,196,000	454,975	20.7%	-0.3	2,328,000	621,453	26.7%	5.7
CONNECTICUT	2,011,000	555,498	27.6%	2,114,000	647,895	30.6%	3.0	2,210,000	541,732	24.5%	-3.1	2,299,000	569,597	24.8%	-2.8	2,392,000	676,584	28.3%	0.7
DELAWARE	367,000	92,283	25.1%	398,000	122,596	30.8%	5.7	426,000	105,754	24.8%	-0.3	457,000	101,656	22.2%	-2.9	486,000	108,647	22.4%	-2.8
DISTRICT OF COLUMBIA	504,000	127,627	25.3%	487,000	137,818	28.3%	3.0	472,000	131,113	27.8%	2.5	464,000	180,408	38.9%	13.6	456,000	159,407	35.0%	9.6
FLORIDA	5,163,000	718,117	13.9%	6,159,000	1,636,000	26.6%	12.7	7,102,000	1,419,475	20.0%	6.1	8,053,000	1,448,816	18.0%	4.1	8,966,000	1,656,701	18.5%	4.6

United States Presidential General Elections (continued)

United States Presidential General Elections (continued)

Democratic Turnout for Election Years 1972–1988 (continued)

State	1972 Voting-age population	1972 Turnout	1972 %	1976 Voting-age population	1976 Turnout	1976 %	1976 Difference from 1972	1980 Voting-age population	1980 Turnout	1980 %	1980 Difference from 1972	1984 Voting-age population	1984 Turnout	1984 %	1984 Difference from 1972	1988 Voting-age population	1988 Turnout	1988 %	1988 Difference from 1972
GEORGIA	3,167,000	289,529	9.1%	3,506,000	979,409	27.9%	18.8	3,832,000	890,733	23.2%	14.1	4,197,000	706,628	16.8%	7.7	4,548,000	714,792	15.7%	6.6
HAWAII	504,000	101,409	20.1%	572,000	147,375	25.8%	5.6	636,000	135,879	21.4%	1.2	692,000	147,154	21.3%	1.1	747,000	192,364	25.8%	5.6
IDAHO	495,000	80,826	16.3%	568,000	126,549	22.3%	6.0	631,000	110,192	17.5%	1.1	655,000	108,510	16.6%	0.2	677,000	147,272	21.8%	5.4
ILLINOIS	7,333,000	1,913,472	26.1%	7,613,000	2,271,295	29.8%	3.7	7,851,000	1,981,413	25.2%	-0.9	7,928,000	2,086,499	26.3%	0.2	8,000,000	2,215,940	27.7%	1.6
INDIANA	3,469,000	708,568	20.4%	3,672,000	1,014,714	27.6%	7.2	3,850,000	844,197	21.9%	1.5	3,937,000	841,481	21.4%	0.9	4,021,000	860,643	21.4%	1.0
IOWA	1,905,000	496,206	26.0%	1,996,000	619,931	31.1%	5.0	2,070,000	508,672	24.6%	-1.5	2,055,000	605,620	29.5%	3.4	2,042,000	670,557	32.8%	6.8
KANSAS	1,547,000	270,287	17.5%	1,629,000	430,421	26.4%	9.0	1,701,000	326,150	19.2%	1.7	1,739,000	333,149	19.2%	1.7	1,774,000	422,636	23.8%	6.4
KENTUCKY	2,228,000	371,159	16.7%	2,413,000	615,717	25.5%	8.9	2,574,000	616,417	23.9%	7.3	2,636,000	539,539	20.5%	3.8	2,696,000	580,368	21.5%	4.9
LOUISIANA	2,406,000	298,142	12.4%	2,646,000	661,365	25.0%	12.6	2,847,000	708,453	24.9%	12.5	2,892,000	651,586	22.5%	10.1	2,935,000	717,460	24.4%	12.1
MAINE	678,000	160,584	23.7%	740,000	232,279	31.4%	7.7	797,000	220,974	27.7%	4.0	845,000	214,515	25.4%	1.7	890,000	243,569	27.4%	3.7
MARYLAND	2,628,000	505,781	19.2%	2,817,000	759,612	27.0%	7.7	2,999,000	726,161	24.2%	5.0	3,202,000	787,935	24.6%	5.4	3,398,000	826,304	24.3%	5.1
MASSACHUSETTS	3,798,000	1,332,540	35.1%	3,952,000	1,429,475	36.2%	1.1	4,096,000	1,053,802	25.7%	-9.4	4,228,000	1,239,606	29.3%	-5.8	4,355,000	1,401,415	32.2%	-2.9
MICHIGAN	5,755,000	1,459,435	25.4%	6,100,000	1,696,714	27.8%	2.5	6,399,000	1,661,532	26.0%	0.6	6,529,000	1,529,638	23.4%	-1.9	6,654,000	1,675,783	25.2%	-0.2
MINNESOTA	2,533,000	802,346	31.7%	2,719,000	1,070,440	39.4%	7.7	2,887,000	954,174	33.1%	1.4	3,007,000	1,036,364	34.5%	2.8	3,121,000	1,109,471	35.5%	3.9
MISSISSIPPI	1,460,000	126,782	8.7%	1,590,000	381,309	24.0%	15.3	1,703,000	429,281	25.2%	16.5	1,753,000	352,192	20.1%	11.4	1,802,000	363,921	20.2%	11.5
MISSOURI	3,222,000	697,147	21.6%	3,390,000	998,387	29.5%	7.8	3,541,000	931,182	26.3%	4.7	3,642,000	848,583	23.3%	1.7	3,738,000	1,001,619	26.8%	5.2
MONTANA	471,000	120,197	25.5%	515,000	149,259	29.0%	3.5	552,000	118,032	21.4%	-4.1	561,000	146,742	26.2%	0.6	569,000	168,936	29.7%	4.2
NEBRASKA	1,009,000	169,991	16.8%	1,067,000	233,692	21.9%	5.1	1,115,000	166,851	15.0%	-1.9	1,125,000	187,866	16.7%	-0.1	1,135,000	259,235	22.8%	6.0
NEVADA	381,000	66,016	17.3%	480,000	92,479	19.3%	1.9	578,000	66,666	11.5%	-5.8	701,000	91,655	13.1%	-4.3	818,000	132,738	16.2%	-1.1
NEW HAMPSHIRE	522,000	116,435	22.3%	593,000	147,635	24.9%	2.6	660,000	108,864	16.5%	-5.8	728,000	120,395	16.5%	-5.8	793,000	163,696	20.6%	-1.7
NEW JERSEY	4,754,000	1,102,211	23.2%	4,951,000	1,444,653	29.2%	6.0	5,133,000	1,147,364	22.4%	-0.8	5,298,000	1,261,323	23.8%	0.6	5,455,000	1,320,352	24.2%	1.0
NEW MEXICO	675,000	141,084	20.9%	780,000	201,148	25.8%	4.9	875,000	167,826	19.2%	-1.7	942,000	201,769	21.4%	0.5	1,008,000	244,497	24.3%	3.4
NEW YORK	11,891,000	2,951,084	24.8%	11,949,000	3,389,558	28.4%	3.5	12,020,000	2,728,372	22.7%	-2.1	12,182,000	3,119,609	25.6%	0.8	12,337,000	3,347,882	27.1%	2.3
NORTH CAROLINA	3,553,000	438,705	12.3%	3,907,000	927,365	23.7%	11.4	4,239,000	875,635	20.7%	8.3	4,560,000	824,287	18.1%	5.7	4,867,000	890,167	18.3%	5.9
NORTH DAKOTA	409,000	100,384	24.5%	436,000	136,078	31.2%	6.7	458,000	79,189	17.3%	-7.3	458,000	104,429	22.8%	-1.7	459,000	127,739	27.8%	3.3
OHIO	7,053,000	1,558,889	22.1%	7,365,000	2,011,621	27.3%	5.2	7,638,000	1,752,414	22.9%	0.8	7,776,000	1,825,440	23.5%	1.4	7,909,000	1,939,629	24.5%	2.4
OKLAHOMA	1,833,000	247,147	13.5%	2,005,000	532,442	26.6%	13.1	2,152,000	402,026	18.7%	5.2	2,208,000	385,080	17.4%	4.0	2,260,000	483,423	21.4%	7.9
OREGON	1,511,000	392,760	26.0%	1,709,000	490,407	28.7%	2.7	1,879,000	456,890	24.3%	-1.7	1,954,000	536,479	27.5%	1.5	2,027,000	616,206	30.4%	4.4
PENNSYLVANIA	8,073,000	1,796,951	22.3%	8,383,000	2,328,677	27.8%	5.5	8,653,000	1,937,540	22.4%	0.1	8,786,000	2,228,131	25.4%	3.1	8,914,000	2,194,944	24.6%	2.4
RHODE ISLAND	642,000	194,645	30.3%	660,000	227,636	34.5%	4.2	677,000	198,342	29.3%	-1.0	702,000	197,106	28.1%	-2.2	726,000	225,123	31.0%	0.7
SOUTH CAROLINA	1,776,000	186,824	10.5%	1,990,000	450,807	22.7%	12.1	2,186,000	430,385	19.7%	9.2	2,344,000	344,459	14.7%	4.2	2,495,000	370,554	14.9%	4.3
SOUTH DAKOTA	440,000	139,945	31.8%	463,000	147,068	31.8%	0.0	483,000	103,855	21.5%	-10.3	488,000	116,113	23.8%	-8.0	492,000	145,560	29.6%	-2.2
TENNESSEE	2,778,000	357,293	12.9%	3,051,000	825,879	27.1%	14.2	3,295,000	783,051	23.8%	10.9	3,444,000	711,714	20.7%	7.8	3,538,000	679,794	19.2%	6.4

United States Presidential General Elections *(continued)*

Democratic Turnout for Election Years 1972–1988 *(continued)*

State	1972 Voting-age population	Turnout	%	1976 Voting-age population	Turnout	%	Difference from 1972	1980 Voting-age population	Turnout	%	Difference from 1972	1984 Voting-age population	Turnout	%	Difference from 1972	1988 Voting-age population	Turnout	%	Difference from 1972
TEXAS	7,729,000	1,154,289	**14.9%**	8,708,000	2,082,319	**23.9%**	9.0	9,608,000	1,881,147	**19.6%**	4.6	10,358,000	1,949,276	**18.8%**	3.9	11,077,000	2,352,748	**21.2%**	6.3
UTAH	701,000	126,284	**18.0%**	813,000	182,110	**22.4%**	4.4	912,000	124,266	**13.6%**	-4.4	980,000	155,369	**15.9%**	-2.2	1,046,000	207,343	**19.8%**	1.8
VERMONT	303,000	68,174	**22.5%**	334,000	80,954	**24.2%**	1.7	363,000	81,952	**22.6%**	0.1	385,000	95,730	**24.9%**	2.4	406,000	115,775	**28.5%**	6.0
VIRGINIA	3,243,000	438,887	**13.5%**	3,549,000	813,896	**22.9%**	9.4	3,841,000	752,174	**19.6%**	6.0	4,144,000	796,250	**19.2%**	5.7	4,434,000	859,799	**19.4%**	5.9
WASHINGTON	2,396,000	568,334	**23.7%**	2,677,000	717,323	**26.8%**	3.1	2,937,000	650,193	**22.1%**	-1.6	3,170,000	807,352	**25.5%**	1.7	3,392,000	933,516	**27.5%**	3.8
WEST VIRGINIA	1,221,000	277,435	**22.7%**	1,310,000	435,914	**33.3%**	10.6	1,381,000	367,462	**26.6%**	3.9	1,365,000	328,125	**24.0%**	1.3	1,348,000	341,016	**25.3%**	2.6
WISCONSIN	2,947,000	810,174	**27.5%**	3,149,000	1,040,232	**33.0%**	5.5	3,326,000	981,584	**29.5%**	2.0	3,427,000	995,740	**29.1%**	1.6	3,523,000	1,126,794	**32.0%**	4.5
WYOMING	241,000	44,358	**18.4%**	284,000	62,239	**21.9%**	3.5	320,000	49,427	**15.4%**	-3.0	318,000	53,370	**16.8%**	-1.6	316,000	67,113	**21.2%**	2.8
Total	137,787,000	29,170,383	**21.2%**	148,418,000	40,830,763	**27.5%**	6.3	158,111,000	35,483,883	**22.4%**	1.3	165,620,000	37,577,185	**22.7%**	1.5	172,777,000	41,809,074	**24.2%**	3.0

Other Turnout for Election Years 1972–1988

State	1972 Voting-age population	Turnout	%	1976 Voting-age population	Turnout	%	Difference from 1972*	1980 Voting-age population	Turnout	%	Difference from 1972	1984 Voting-age population	Turnout	%	Difference from 1972	1988 Voting-age population	Turnout	%	Difference from 1972
ALABAMA	2,346,000	20,487	**0.9%**	2,552,000	19,610	**0.8%**	-0.1	2,732,000	51,007	**1.9%**	1.0	2,833,000	16,965	**0.6%**	-0.3	2,931,000	13,394	**0.5%**	-0.4
ALASKA	202,000	6,903	**3.4%**	237,000	7,961	**3.4%**	-0.1	271,000	30,491	**11.3%**	7.8	314,000	7,221	**2.3%**	-1.1	355,000	8,281	**2.3%**	-1.1
ARIZONA	1,312,000	21,574	**1.6%**	1,615,000	28,475	**1.8%**	0.1	1,902,000	97,414	**5.1%**	3.5	2,187,000	10,627	**0.5%**	-1.2	2,460,000	15,303	**0.6%**	-1.0
ARKANSAS	1,357,000	2,887	**0.2%**	1,495,000	1,028	**0.1%**	-0.1	1,614,000	36,377	**2.3%**	2.0	1,660,000	10,986	**0.7%**	0.4	1,704,000	11,923	**0.7%**	0.5
CALIFORNIA	13,275,000	289,919	**2.2%**	14,481,000	242,589	**1.7%**	-0.5	15,629,000	978,544	**6.3%**	4.1	16,816,000	115,895	**0.7%**	-1.5	17,957,000	129,915	**0.7%**	-1.5
COLORADO	1,570,000	26,715	**1.7%**	1,829,000	36,834	**2.0%**	0.3	2,058,000	164,178	**8.0%**	6.3	2,196,000	18,588	**0.8%**	-0.9	2,328,000	22,764	**1.0%**	-0.7
CONNECTICUT	2,011,000	18,016	**0.9%**	2,114,000	14,370	**0.7%**	-0.2	2,210,000	187,343	**8.5%**	7.6	2,299,000	6,426	**0.3%**	-0.6	2,392,000	16,569	**0.7%**	-0.2
DELAWARE	367,000	2,876	**0.8%**	398,000	3,407	**0.9%**	0.1	426,000	18,894	**4.4%**	3.7	457,000	726	**0.2%**	-0.6	486,000	1,605	**0.3%**	-0.5
DISTRICT OF COLUMBIA	504,000	568	**0.1%**	487,000	137,818	**28.3%**	3.0	472,000	20,579	**4.4%**	4.2	464,000	1,871	**0.4%**	0.3	456,000	5,880	**1.3%**	1.2
FLORIDA	5,163,000	7,407	**0.1%**	6,159,000	45,100	**0.7%**	0.6	7,102,000	220,504	**3.1%**	3.0	8,053,000	885	**0.0%**	-0.1	8,966,000	26,727	**0.3%**	0.2
GEORGIA	3,167,000	3,747	**0.1%**	3,506,000	4,306	**0.1%**	0.0	3,832,000	51,794	**1.4%**	1.2	4,197,000	770	**0.0%**	-0.1	4,548,000	13,549	**0.3%**	0.2
HAWAII				572,000	3,923	**0.7%**		636,000	37,296	**5.9%**	5.2	692,000	3,642	**0.5%**	-0.2	747,000	3,472	**0.5%**	-0.2
IDAHO	495,000	30,169	**6.1%**	568,000	13,371	**2.4%**	-3.7	631,000	36,540	**5.8%**	-0.3	655,000	5,111	**0.8%**	-5.3	677,000	7,815	**1.2%**	-4.9
ILLINOIS	7,333,000	21,585	**0.3%**	7,613,000	83,350	**1.1%**	0.8	7,851,000	410,259	**5.2%**	4.9	7,928,000	25,486	**0.3%**	0.0	8,000,000	32,241	**0.4%**	0.1
INDIANA	3,469,000	11,807	**0.3%**	3,672,000	21,690	**0.6%**	0.3	3,850,000	142,180	**3.7%**	3.4	3,937,000	14,358	**0.4%**	0.0	4,021,000	10,215	**0.3%**	-0.1
IOWA	1,905,000	23,531	**1.2%**	1,996,000	26,512	**1.3%**	0.1	2,070,000	132,963	**6.4%**	5.2	2,055,000	11,097	**0.5%**	-0.7	2,042,000	9,702	**0.5%**	-0.8
KANSAS	1,547,000	25,996	**1.7%**	1,629,000	24,672	**1.5%**	-0.2	1,701,000	86,833	**5.1%**	3.4	1,739,000	11,546	**0.7%**	-1.0	1,774,000	16,359	**0.9%**	-0.8
KENTUCKY	2,228,000	19,894	**0.9%**	2,413,000	19,573	**0.8%**	-0.1	2,574,000	42,936	**1.7%**	0.8	2,636,000	8,104	**0.3%**	-0.6	2,696,000	7,868	**0.3%**	-0.6
LOUISIANA	2,406,000	66,497	**2.8%**	2,646,000	29,628	**1.1%**	-1.6	2,847,000	47,285	**1.7%**	-1.1	2,892,000	17,937	**0.6%**	-2.1	2,935,000	27,040	**0.9%**	-1.8
MAINE				740,000	14,617	**2.0%**		797,000	63,515	**8.0%**	6.0	845,000	2,129	**0.3%**	-1.7	890,000	4,335	**0.5%**	-1.5

United States Presidential General Elections (continued)

United States Presidential General Elections (continued)

Other Turnout for Election Years 1972–1988 (continued)

State	1972 Voting-age population	Turnout	%	1976 Voting-age population	Turnout	%	Difference from 1972	1980 Voting-age population	Turnout	%	Difference from 1972	1984 Voting-age population	Turnout	%	Difference from 1972	1988 Voting-age population	Turnout	%	Difference from 1972
MARYLAND	2,628,000	18,726	0.7%	2,817,000	7,624	0.3%	-0.4	2,999,000	133,729	4.5%	3.7	3,202,000	8,020	0.3%	-0.5	3,398,000	11,887	0.3%	-0.4
MASSACHUSETTS	3,798,000	14,138	0.4%	3,952,000	87,807	2.2%	1.8	4,096,000	412,865	10.1%	9.7	4,228,000	8,911	0.2%	-0.2	4,355,000	36,755	0.8%	0.5
MICHIGAN	5,755,000	68,571	1.2%	6,100,000	63,293	1.0%	-0.2	6,399,000	332,968	5.2%	4.0	6,529,000	20,449	0.3%	-0.9	6,654,000	27,894	0.4%	-0.8
MINNESOTA	2,533,000	41,037	1.6%	2,719,000	60,096	2.2%	0.6	2,887,000	224,538	7.8%	6.2	3,007,000	15,482	0.5%	-1.1	3,121,000	24,982	0.8%	-0.8
MISSISSIPPI	1,460,000	14,056	1.0%	1,590,000	21,206	1.3%	0.4	1,703,000	22,250	1.3%	0.3	1,753,000	6,535	0.4%	-0.6	1,802,000	9,716	0.5%	-0.4
MISSOURI	3,222,000	4,804	0.1%	3,390,000	27,770	0.8%	0.7	3,541,000	94,461	2.7%	2.5	3,642,000	12	0.0%	-0.1	3,738,000	7,141	0.2%	0.0
MONTANA	471,000	13,430	2.9%	515,000	5,772	1.1%	-1.7	552,000	39,106	7.1%	4.2	561,000	5,185	0.9%	-1.9	569,000	6,326	1.1%	-1.7
NEBRASKA				1,067,000	14,271	1.3%		1,115,000	54,066	4.8%	3.5	1,125,000	4,170	0.4%	-1.0	1,135,000	4,274	0.4%	-1.0
NEVADA				480,000	8,124	1.7%		578,000	26,202	4.5%	2.8	701,000	6,242	0.9%	-0.8	818,000	11,289	1.4%	-0.3
NEW HAMPSHIRE	522,000	3,896	0.7%	593,000	6,048	1.0%	0.3	660,000	53,421	8.1%	7.3	728,000	1,620	0.2%	-0.5	793,000	5,841	0.7%	0.0
NEW JERSEY	4,754,000	49,516	1.0%	4,951,000	60,131	1.2%	0.2	5,133,000	281,763	5.5%	4.4	5,298,000	22,909	0.4%	-0.6	5,455,000	36,009	0.7%	-0.4
NEW MEXICO	675,000	9,551	1.4%	780,000	5,842	0.7%	-0.7	875,000	38,366	4.4%	3.0	942,000	5,500	0.6%	-0.8	1,008,000	6,449	0.6%	-0.8
NEW YORK	11,891,000	22,057	0.2%	11,949,000	43,821	0.4%	0.2	12,020,000	579,756	4.8%	4.6	12,182,000	22,438	0.2%	0.0	12,337,000	55,930	0.5%	0.3
NORTH CAROLINA	3,553,000	25,018	0.7%	3,907,000	9,589	0.2%	-0.5	4,239,000	65,180	1.5%	0.8	4,560,000	4,593	0.1%	-0.6	4,867,000	6,945	0.1%	-0.6
NORTH DAKOTA	409,000	6,021	1.5%	436,000	7,640	1.8%	0.3	458,000	28,661	6.3%	4.8	458,000	4,206	0.9%	-0.6	459,000	2,963	0.6%	-0.8
OHIO	7,053,000	94,071	1.3%	7,365,000	99,747	1.4%	0.0	7,638,000	324,644	4.3%	2.9	7,776,000	43,619	0.6%	-0.8	7,909,000	37,521	0.5%	-0.9
OKLAHOMA	1,833,000	23,728	1.3%	2,005,000	14,101	0.7%	-0.6	2,152,000	52,112	2.4%	1.1	2,208,000	9,066	0.4%	-0.9	2,260,000	9,246	0.4%	-0.9
OREGON	1,511,000	48,500	3.2%	1,709,000	47,349	2.8%	-0.4	1,879,000	153,582	8.2%	5.0	1,954,000	4,348	0.2%	-3.0	2,027,000	25,362	1.3%	-2.0
PENNSYLVANIA	8,073,000	80,634	1.0%	8,383,000	86,506	1.0%	0.0	8,653,000	362,089	4.2%	3.2	8,786,000	32,449	0.4%	-0.6	8,914,000	41,220	0.5%	-0.5
RHODE ISLAND	642,000	780	0.1%	660,000	2,285	0.3%	0.2	677,000	62,937	9.3%	9.2	702,000	1,306	0.2%	0.1	726,000	1,736	0.2%	0.1
SOUTH CAROLINA	1,776,000	10,092	0.6%	1,990,000	5,627	0.3%	-0.3	2,186,000	21,845	1.0%	0.4	2,344,000	8,531	0.4%	-0.2	2,495,000	9,012	0.4%	-0.2
SOUTH DAKOTA	440,000	994	0.2%	463,000	2,105	0.5%	0.2	483,000	25,505	5.3%	5.1	488,000	1,487	0.3%	0.1	492,000	2,016	0.4%	0.2
TENNESSEE	2,778,000	30,742	1.1%	3,051,000	16,497	0.5%	-0.6	3,295,000	46,804	1.4%	0.3	3,444,000	10,068	0.3%	-0.8	3,538,000	9,223	0.3%	-0.8
TEXAS	7,729,000	18,096	0.2%	8,708,000	36,265	0.4%	0.2	9,608,000	149,784	1.6%	1.3	10,358,000	14,867	0.1%	-0.1	11,077,000	37,833	0.3%	0.1
UTAH	701,000	28,549	4.1%	813,000	21,180	2.6%	-1.5	912,000	40,269	4.4%	0.3	980,000	5,182	0.5%	-3.5	1,046,000	11,223	1.1%	-3.0
VERMONT	303,000	1,624	0.5%	334,000	4,726	1.4%	0.9	363,000	36,719	10.1%	9.6	385,000	2,966	0.8%	0.2	406,000	3,222	0.8%	0.3
VIRGINIA	3,243,000	29,639	0.9%	3,549,000	46,644	1.3%	0.4	3,841,000	124,249	3.2%	2.3	4,144,000	13,307	0.3%	-0.6	4,434,000	22,648	0.5%	-0.4
WASHINGTON	2,396,000	65,378	2.7%	2,677,000	60,479	2.3%	-0.5	2,937,000	226,957	7.7%	5.0	3,170,000	24,888	0.8%	-1.9	3,392,000	27,902	0.8%	-1.9
WEST VIRGINIA				1,310,000	290	0.0%		1,381,000	36,047	2.6%	2.6	1,365,000	2,134	0.2%	0.1	1,348,000	2,230	0.2%	0.1
WISCONSIN	2,947,000	53,286	1.8%	3,149,000	58,956	1.9%	0.1	3,326,000	202,792	6.1%	4.3	3,427,000	17,365	0.5%	-1.3	3,523,000	17,315	0.5%	-1.3
WYOMING	241,000	748	0.3%	284,000	1,387	0.5%	0.2	320,000	16,586	5.2%	4.9	318,000	2,357	0.7%	0.4	316,000	2,571	0.8%	0.5
Total	133,994,000	1,378,260	1.0%	148,418,000	40,830,763	27.5%	6.3	158,111,000	7,127,185	4.5%	3.5	165,620,000	620,582	0.4%	-0.7	172,777,000	899,638	0.5%	-0.5

*Percentage point difference between turnout in current year and initial year listed in chart. If data do not appear for a state in the initial year listed, the difference is calculated from the first year in which data do appear for that state.

STATE GUBERNATORIAL GENERAL ELECTIONS

Election Years 1972–1988

State	1972 Voting-age population	Turnout	%	1976 Voting-age population	Turnout	%	Difference from 1972*	1980 Voting-age population	Turnout	%	Difference from 1972	1984 Voting-age population	Turnout	%	Difference from 1972	1988 Voting-age population	Turnout	%	Difference from 1972
ALABAMA																			
ALASKA																			
ARIZONA																			
ARKANSAS	1,357,000	648,069	47.8%	1,495,000	726,949	48.6%	0.9	1,614,000	838,925	52.0%	4.2	1,660,000	886,548	53.4%	5.6				
CALIFORNIA																			
COLORADO																			
CONNECTICUT																			
DELAWARE	367,000	228,722	62.3%	398,000	229,563	57.7%	-4.6	426,000	225,081	52.8%	-9.5	457,000	243,565	53.3%	-9.0	486,000	239,969	49.4%	-12.9
DISTRICT OF COLUMBIA																			
FLORIDA																			
GEORGIA																			
HAWAII																			
IDAHO																			
ILLINOIS	7,333,000	4,678,804	63.8%	7,613,000	4,638,997	60.9%	-2.9												
INDIANA	3,469,000	2,120,847	61.1%	3,672,000	2,175,324	59.2%	-1.9	3,850,000	2,178,403	56.6%	-4.6	3,937,000	2,197,898	55.8%	-5.3	4,021,000	2,140,781	53.2%	-7.9
IOWA	1,905,000	1,210,222	63.5%																
KANSAS	1,547,000	921,552	59.6%																
KENTUCKY																			
LOUISIANA	2,406,000	1,121,570	46.6%																
MAINE																			
MARYLAND																			
MASSACHUSETTS																			
MICHIGAN																			
MINNESOTA																			
MISSISSIPPI																			
MISSOURI	3,222,000	1,865,683	57.9%	3,390,000	1,933,575	57.0%	-0.9	3,541,000	2,088,028	59.0%	1.1	3,642,000	2,108,208	57.9%	0.0	3,738,000	2,085,928	55.8%	-2.1
MONTANA	471,000	318,754	67.7%	515,000	316,720	61.5%	-6.2	552,000	360,466	65.3%	-2.4	561,000	378,970	67.6%	-0.1	569,000	367,021	64.5%	-3.2
NEBRASKA																			
NEVADA																			
NEW HAMPSHIRE	522,000	323,102	61.9%	593,000	342,669	57.8%	-4.1	660,000	384,031	58.2%	-3.7	728,000	383,910	52.7%	-9.2	793,000	441,923	55.7%	-6.2
NEW JERSEY																			
NEW MEXICO																			
NEW YORK																			

State Gubernatorial General Elections (continued)

State Gubernatorial General Elections (continued)

Election Years 1972–1988 (continued)

State	1972 Voting-age population	Turnout	%	1976 Voting-age population	Turnout	%	Difference from 1972	1980 Voting-age population	Turnout	%	Difference from 1972	1984 Voting-age population	Turnout	%	Difference from 1972	1988 Voting-age population	Turnout	%	Difference from 1972
NORTH CAROLINA	3,553,000	1,504,785	42.4%	3,907,000	1,663,824	42.6%	0.2	4,239,000	1,847,432	43.6%	1.2	4,560,000	2,226,727	48.8%	6.5	4,867,000	2,180,025	44.8%	2.4
NORTH DAKOTA	409,000	281,931	68.9%	436,000	297,249	68.2%	-0.8	458,000	302,621	66.1%	-2.9	458,000	314,382	68.6%	-0.3	459,000	299,080	65.2%	-3.8
OHIO																			
OKLAHOMA																			
OREGON																			
PENNSYLVANIA																			
RHODE ISLAND	642,000	412,866	64.3%	660,000	398,683	60.4%	-3.9	677,000	405,916	60.0%	-4.4	702,000	408,375	58.2%	-6.1	726,000	400,516	55.2%	-9.1
SOUTH CAROLINA																			
SOUTH DAKOTA	440,000	308,147	70.0%																
TENNESSEE																			
TEXAS	7,729,000	3,410,128	44.1%																
UTAH	701,000	476,447	68.0%	813,000	539,649	66.4%	-1.6	912,000	600,019	65.8%	-2.2	980,000	629,619	64.2%	-3.7	1,046,000	649,114	62.1%	-5.9
VERMONT	303,000	189,237	62.5%	334,000	185,929	55.7%	-6.8	363,000	210,381	58.0%	-4.5	385,000	233,753	60.7%	-1.7	406,000	242,879	59.8%	-2.6
VIRGINIA																			
WASHINGTON	2,396,000	1,472,542	61.5%	2,677,000	1,546,382	57.8%	-3.7	2,937,000	1,730,896	58.9%	-2.5	3,170,000	1,888,987	59.6%	-1.9	3,392,000	1,874,929	55.3%	-6.2
WEST VIRGINIA	1,221,000	774,279	63.4%	1,310,000	749,270	57.2%	-6.2	1,381,000	742,150	53.7%	-9.7	1,365,000	741,502	54.3%	-9.1	1,348,000	649,593	48.2%	-15.2
WISCONSIN																			
WYOMING																			
Total	39,993,000	22,267,687	55.7%	27,813,000	15,744,783	56.6%	0.9	21,610,000	11,914,349	55.1%	-0.5	22,605,000	12,642,444	55.9%	24.9%	21,851,000	11,571,758	53.0%	-2.7

*Percentage point difference between turnout in current year and initial year listed in chart. If data do not appear for a state in the initial year listed, the difference is calculated from the first year in which data do appear for that state.

STATE GUBERNATORIAL GENERAL ELECTIONS

Republican Turnout for Election Years 1972–1988

State	1972 Voting-age population	1972 Turnout	1972 %	1976 Voting-age population	1976 Turnout	1976 %	1976 Difference from 1972*	1980 Voting-age population	1980 Turnout	1980 %	1980 Difference from 1972	1984 Voting-age population	1984 Turnout	1984 %	1984 Difference from 1972	1988 Voting-age population	1988 Turnout	1988 %	1988 Difference from 1972
ALABAMA																			
ALASKA																			
ARIZONA																			
ARKANSAS	1,357,000	159,177	11.7%	1,495,000	121,716	8.1%	-3.6	1,614,000	435,684	27.0%	15.3	1,660,000	331,987	20.0%	8.3				
CALIFORNIA																			
COLORADO																			
CONNECTICUT																			
DELAWARE	367,000	109,583	29.9%	398,000	130,531	32.8%	2.9	426,000	159,004	37.3%	7.5	457,000	135,250	29.6%	-0.3	486,000	169,733	34.9%	5.1
DISTRICT OF COLUMBIA																			
FLORIDA																			
GEORGIA																			
HAWAII																			
IDAHO																			
ILLINOIS	7,333,000	2,293,809	31.3%	7,613,000	3,000,395	39.4%	8.1												
INDIANA	3,469,000	1,203,903	34.7%	3,672,000	1,236,555	33.7%	-1.0	3,850,000	1,257,383	32.7%	-2.0	3,937,000	1,146,497	29.1%	-5.6	4,021,000	1,002,207	24.9%	-9.8
IOWA	1,905,000	707,177	37.1%																
KANSAS	1,547,000	341,440	22.1%																
KENTUCKY																			
LOUISIANA	2,406,000	480,424	20.0%																
MAINE																			
MARYLAND																			
MASSACHUSETTS																			
MICHIGAN																			
MINNESOTA																			
MISSISSIPPI																			
MISSOURI	3,222,000	1,029,451	32.0%	3,390,000	958,110	28.3%	-3.7	3,541,000	1,098,950	31.0%	-0.9	3,642,000	1,194,504	32.8%	0.8	3,738,000	1,339,531	35.8%	3.9
MONTANA	471,000	146,231	31.0%	515,000	115,848	22.5%	-8.6	552,000	160,892	29.1%	-1.9	561,000	100,070	17.8%	-13.2	569,000	190,604	33.5%	2.5
NEBRASKA																			
NEVADA																			
NEW HAMPSHIRE	522,000	133,702	25.6%	593,000	197,589	33.3%	7.7	660,000	156,178	23.7%	-2.0	728,000	256,574	35.2%	9.6	793,000	267,064	33.7%	8.1
NEW JERSEY																			
NEW MEXICO																			
NEW YORK																			

State Gubernatorial General Elections (continued)

State Gubernatorial General Elections (continued)

Republican Turnout for Election Years 1972–1988 (continued)

State	1972 Voting-age population	Turnout	%	1976 Voting-age population	Turnout	%	Difference from 1972	1980 Voting-age population	Turnout	%	Difference from 1972	1984 Voting-age population	Turnout	%	Difference from 1972	1988 Voting-age population	Turnout	%	Difference from 1972
NORTH CAROLINA	3,553,000	767,470	21.6%	3,907,000	564,102	14.4%	-7.2	4,239,000	691,449	16.3%	-5.3	4,560,000	1,208,167	26.5%	4.9	4,867,000	1,222,338	25.1%	3.5
NORTH DAKOTA	409,000	138,032	33.7%	436,000	138,321	31.7%	-2.0	458,000	162,230	35.4%	1.7	458,000	140,460	30.7%	-3.1	459,000	119,986	26.1%	-7.6
OHIO																			
OKLAHOMA																			
OREGON																			
PENNSYLVANIA																			
RHODE ISLAND	642,000	194,315	30.3%	660,000	178,254	27.0%	-3.3	677,000	106,729	15.8%	-14.5	702,000	245,059	34.9%	4.6	726,000	203,550	28.0%	-2.2
SOUTH CAROLINA																			
SOUTH DAKOTA	440,000	123,135	28.0%																
TENNESSEE																			
TEXAS	7,729,000	1,534,060	19.8%																
UTAH	701,000	144,449	20.6%	813,000	248,027	30.5%	9.9	912,000	266,578	29.2%	8.6	980,000	351,792	35.9%	15.3	1,046,000	260,462	24.9%	4.3
VERMONT	303,000	82,491	27.2%	334,000	99,268	29.7%	2.5	363,000	123,229	33.9%	6.7	385,000	113,264	29.4%	2.2	406,000	105,191	25.9%	-1.3
VIRGINIA																			
WASHINGTON	2,396,000	747,825	31.2%	2,677,000	687,039	25.7%	-5.5	2,937,000	981,083	33.4%	2.2	3,170,000	881,994	27.8%	-3.4	3,392,000	708,481	20.9%	-10.3
WEST VIRGINIA	1,221,000	423,817	34.7%	1,310,000	253,420	19.3%	-15.4	1,381,000	337,240	24.4%	-10.3	1,365,000	394,937	28.9%	-5.8	1,348,000	267,172	19.8%	-14.9
WISCONSIN																			
WYOMING																			
Total	39,993,000	10,760,491	26.9%	27,813,000	7,929,175	28.5%	1.6	21,610,000	5,936,629	27.5%	0.6	22,605,000	6,500,555	28.8%	1.9	21,851,000	5,856,319	26.8%	-0.1

Democratic Turnout for Election Years 1972–1988

State	1972 Voting-age population	Turnout	%	1976 Voting-age population	Turnout	%	Difference from 1972*	1980 Voting-age population	Turnout	%	Difference from 1972	1984 Voting-age population	Turnout	%	Difference from 1972	1988 Voting-age population	Turnout	%	Difference from 1972
ALABAMA																			
ALASKA																			
ARIZONA																			
ARKANSAS	1,357,000	488,892	36.0%	1,495,000	605,083	40.5%	4.4	1,614,000	403,241	25.0%	-11.0	1,660,000	554,561	33.4%	-2.6				
CALIFORNIA																			
COLORADO																			
CONNECTICUT																			
DELAWARE	367,000	117,274	32.0%	398,000	97,480	24.5%	-7.5	426,000	64,217	15.1%	-16.9	457,000	108,315	23.7%	-8.3	486,000	70,236	14.5%	-17.5
DISTRICT OF COLUMBIA																			
FLORIDA																			

State Gubernatorial General Elections *(continued)*

Democratic Turnout for Election Years 1972–1988 *(continued)*

State	1972 Voting-age population	Turnout	%	1976 Voting-age population	Turnout	%	Difference from 1972	1980 Voting-age population	Turnout	%	Difference from 1972	1984 Voting-age population	Turnout	%	Difference from 1972	1988 Voting-age population	Turnout	%	Difference from 1972
GEORGIA																			
HAWAII																			
IDAHO																			
ILLINOIS	7,333,000	2,371,303	32.3%	7,613,000	1,610,258	21.2%	-11.2												
INDIANA	3,469,000	900,489	26.0%	3,672,000	927,243	25.3%	-0.7	3,850,000	913,116	23.7%	-2.2	3,937,000	1,036,832	26.3%	0.4	4,021,000	1,138,574	28.3%	2.4
IOWA	1,905,000	487,282	25.6%																
KANSAS	1,547,000	571,256	36.9%																
KENTUCKY																			
LOUISIANA	2,406,000	641,146	26.6%																
MAINE																			
MARYLAND																			
MASSACHUSETTS																			
MICHIGAN																			
MINNESOTA																			
MISSISSIPPI																			
MISSOURI	3,222,000	832,751	25.8%	3,390,000	971,184	28.6%	2.8	3,541,000	981,884	27.7%	1.9	3,642,000	913,700	25.1%	-0.8	3,738,000	724,919	19.4%	-6.5
MONTANA	471,000	172,523	36.6%	515,000	195,420	37.9%	1.3	552,000	199,574	36.2%	-0.5	561,000	266,578	47.5%	10.9	569,000	169,313	29.8%	-6.9
NEBRASKA																			
NEVADA																			
NEW HAMPSHIRE	522,000	126,107	24.2%	593,000	145,015	24.5%	0.3	660,000	226,436	34.3%	10.2	728,000	127,156	17.5%	-6.7	793,000	172,543	21.8%	-2.4
NEW JERSEY																			
NEW MEXICO																			
NEW YORK																			
NORTH CAROLINA	3,553,000	729,104	20.5%	3,907,000	1,081,293	27.7%	7.2	4,239,000	1,143,145	27.0%	6.4	4,560,000	1,011,209	22.2%	1.7	4,867,000	957,687	19.7%	-0.8
NORTH DAKOTA	409,000	143,899	35.2%	436,000	153,309	35.2%	0.0	458,000	140,391	30.7%	-4.5	458,000	173,922	38.0%	2.8	459,000	179,094	39.0%	3.8
OHIO																			
OKLAHOMA																			
OREGON																			
PENNSYLVANIA																			
RHODE ISLAND	642,000	216,953	33.8%	660,000	218,561	33.1%	-0.7	677,000	299,174	44.2%	10.4	702,000	163,311	23.3%	-10.5	726,000	196,936	27.1%	-6.7
SOUTH CAROLINA																			
SOUTH DAKOTA	440,000	185,012	42.0%																
TENNESSEE																			

State Gubernatorial General Elections (continued)

State Gubernatorial General Elections *(continued)*

Democratic Turnout for Election Years 1972–1988 *(continued)*

State	1972 Voting-age population	1972 Turnout	1972 %	1976 Voting-age population	1976 Turnout	1976 %	1976 Difference from 1972	1980 Voting-age population	1980 Turnout	1980 %	1980 Difference from 1972	1984 Voting-age population	1984 Turnout	1984 %	1984 Difference from 1972	1988 Voting-age population	1988 Turnout	1988 %	1988 Difference from 1972
TEXAS	7,729,000	1,633,970	21.1%																
UTAH	701,000	331,998	47.4%	813,000	280,706	34.5%	-12.8	912,000	330,974	36.3%	-11.1	980,000	275,669	28.1%	-19.2	1,046,000	249,321	23.8%	-23.5
VERMONT	303,000	104,533	34.5%	334,000	75,262	22.5%	-12.0	363,000	77,363	21.3%	-13.2	385,000	116,938	30.4%	-4.1	406,000	134,438	33.1%	-1.4
VIRGINIA																			
WASHINGTON	2,396,000	630,613	26.3%	2,677,000	821,797	30.7%	4.4	2,937,000	749,813	25.5%	-0.8	3,170,000	1,006,993	31.8%	5.4	3,392,000	1,166,448	34.4%	8.1
WEST VIRGINIA	1,221,000	350,462	28.7%	1,310,000	495,661	37.8%	9.1	1,381,000	401,863	29.1%	0.4	1,365,000	346,565	25.4%	-3.3	1,348,000	382,421	28.4%	-0.3
WISCONSIN																			
WYOMING																			
Total	39,993,000	11,035,567	27.6%	27,813,000	7,678,272	27.6%	0.0	21,610,000	5,931,191	27.4%	-0.1	22,605,000	6,101,749	27.0%	-0.6	21,851,000	5,541,930	25.4%	-2.2

Other Turnout for Election Years 1972–1988

State	1972 Voting-age population	1972 Turnout	1972 %	1976 Voting-age population	1976 Turnout	1976 %	1976 Difference from 1972*	1980 Voting-age population	1980 Turnout	1980 %	1980 Difference from 1972	1984 Voting-age population	1984 Turnout	1984 %	1984 Difference from 1972	1988 Voting-age population	1988 Turnout	1988 %	1988 Difference from 1972
ARKANSAS				1,495,000	150	0.0%													
DELAWARE	367,000	1,865	0.5%	398,000	1,552	0.4%	-0.1	426,000	1,860	0.4%	-0.1								
ILLINOIS	7,333,000	13,692	0.2%	7,613,000	28,344	0.4%	0.2												
INDIANA	3,469,000	16,455	0.5%	3,672,000	11,526	0.3%	-0.2	3,850,000	7,904	0.2%	-0.3	3,937,000	14,569	0.4%	-0.1				
IOWA	1,905,000	15,763	0.8%																
KANSAS	1,547,000	8,856	0.6%																
MISSOURI	3,222,000	3,481	0.1%	3,390,000	4,281	0.1%	0.0	3,541,000	7,194	0.2%	0.1	3,642,000	4	0.0%	-0.1	3,738,000	21,478	0.6%	0.5
MONTANA				515,000	5,452	1.1%						561,000	12,322	2.2%	1.1	569,000	7,104	1.2%	0.2
NEW HAMPSHIRE	522,000	63,293	12.1%	593,000	65	0.0%	-12.1	660,000	1,417	0.2%	-11.9	728,000	180	0.0%	-12.1	793,000	2,316	0.3%	-11.8
NORTH CAROLINA	3,553,000	8,211	0.2%	3,907,000	18,429	0.5%	0.2	4,239,000	12,838	0.3%	0.1	4,560,000	7,351	0.2%	-0.1				
NORTH DAKOTA				436,000	5,619	1.3%													
RHODE ISLAND	642,000	1,598	0.2%	660,000	1,868	0.3%	0.0	677,000	13	0.0%	-0.2	702,000	5	0.0%	-0.2	726,000	30	0.0%	-0.2
UTAH				813,000	10,916	1.3%		912,000	2,467	0.3%	-1.1	980,000	2,158	0.2%	-1.1	1,046,000	139,331	13.3%	12.0
VERMONT	303,000	2,213	0.7%	334,000	11,399	3.4%	2.7	363,000	9,789	2.7%	2.0	385,000	3,551	0.9%	0.2	406,000	3,250	0.8%	0.1
WASHINGTON	2,396,000	94,104	3.9%	2,677,000	37,546	1.4%	-2.5												
WEST VIRGINIA				1,310,000	189	0.0%		1,381,000	3,047	0.2%	0.2								
WISCONSIN																			
WYOMING																			
Total	25,259,000	229,531	0.9%	27,813,000	137,336	0.5%	-0.4	16,049,000	46,529	0.3%	-0.6	15,495,000	40,140	0.3%	-0.6	7,278,000	173,509	2.4%	1.5

*Percentage point difference between turnout in current year and initial year listed in chart. If data do not appear for a state in the initial year listed, the difference is calculated from the first year in which data do appear for that state.

UNITED STATES SENATE GENERAL ELECTIONS

Election Years 1972–1988

State	1972 Voting-age population	Turnout	%	1976 Voting-age population	Turnout	%	Difference from 1972*	1980 Voting-age population	Turnout	%	Difference from 1972	1984 Voting-age population	Turnout	%	Difference from 1972	1988 Voting-age population	Turnout	%	Difference from 1972
ALABAMA	2,346,000	1,051,099	44.8%					2,732,000	1,296,757	47.5%	2.7	2,833,000	1,371,238	48.4%	3.6				
ALASKA	202,000	96,007	47.5%					271,000	156,762	57.8%	10.3	314,000	206,888	65.9%	18.4				
ARIZONA				1,615,000	741,210	45.9%		1,902,000	874,238	46.0%	0.1					2,460,000	1,164,539	47.3%	1.4
ARKANSAS	1,357,000	634,636	46.8%					1,614,000	808,812	50.1%	3.3								
CALIFORNIA				14,481,000	7,472,268	51.6%		15,629,000	8,327,481	53.3%	1.7					17,957,000	9,743,598	54.3%	2.7
COLORADO	1,570,000	926,093	59.0%					2,058,000	1,173,646	57.0%	-2.0	2,196,000	1,297,809	59.1%	0.1				
CONNECTICUT				2,114,000	1,361,666	64.4%		2,210,000	1,356,075	61.4%	-3.1					2,392,000	1,383,526	57.8%	-6.6
DELAWARE	367,000	229,828	62.6%	398,000	224,859	56.5%	-6.1					457,000	245,932	53.8%	-8.8	486,000	243,493	50.1%	-12.5
DISTRICT OF COLUMBIA																			
FLORIDA				6,159,000	2,857,534	46.4%		7,102,000	3,528,028	49.7%	3.3					8,966,000	4,068,209	45.4%	-1.0
GEORGIA	3,167,000	1,178,708	37.2%					3,832,000	1,580,340	41.2%	4.0	4,197,000	1,681,300	40.1%	2.8				
HAWAII				572,000	302,092	52.0%		636,000	288,006	45.3%	-7.5					747,000	323,876	43.4%	-9.5
IDAHO	495,000	309,602	62.5%					631,000	439,647	69.7%	7.1	655,000	406,168	62.0%	-0.5				
ILLINOIS	7,333,000	4,608,380	62.8%					7,051,000	4,580,029	58.3%	-4.5	7,928,000	4,787,473	60.4%	-2.5				
INDIANA				3,672,000	2,171,187	59.1%		3,850,000	2,198,376	57.1%	-2.0					4,021,000	2,099,303	52.2%	-6.9
IOWA	1,905,000	1,203,333	63.2%					2,070,000	1,277,034	61.7%	-1.5	2,055,000	1,292,700	62.9%	-0.3				
KANSAS	1,547,000	871,722	56.3%					1,701,000	938,957	55.2%	-1.1	1,739,000	996,729	57.3%	1.0				
KENTUCKY	2,228,000	1,037,861	46.6%					2,574,000	1,106,890	43.0%	-3.6	2,636,000	1,292,407	49.0%	2.4				
LOUISIANA**	2,406,000	1,084,904	45.1%					2,847,000	841,013	29.5%	-15.6	2,892,000	977,473	33.8%	-11.3				
MAINE	678,000	421,310	62.1%	740,000	486,254	65.7%	3.6					845,000	551,406	65.3%	3.1	890,000	557,375	62.6%	0.5
MARYLAND				2,817,000	1,365,568	48.5%		2,999,000	1,286,088	42.9%	-5.6					3,398,000	1,617,065	47.6%	-0.9
MASSACHUSETTS	3,798,000	2,370,676	62.4%	3,952,000	2,491,255	63.0%	0.6					4,228,000	2,530,195	59.8%	-2.6	4,355,000	2,606,225	59.8%	-2.6
MICHIGAN	5,755,000	3,406,906	59.2%	6,100,000	3,490,664	57.2%	-2.0					6,529,000	3,700,938	56.7%	-2.5	6,654,000	3,505,985	52.7%	-6.5
MINNESOTA	2,533,000	1,731,653	68.4%	2,719,000	1,912,068	70.3%	2.0					3,007,000	2,066,143	68.7%	0.3	3,121,000	2,093,953	67.1%	-1.3
MISSISSIPPI	1,460,000	645,746	44.2%	1,590,000	554,433	34.9%	-9.4					1,753,000	952,240	54.3%	10.1	1,802,000	946,719	52.5%	8.3
MISSOURI				3,390,000	1,914,777	56.5%		3,541,000	2,066,965	58.4%	1.9					3,738,000	2,078,875	55.6%	-0.9
MONTANA	471,000	314,925	66.9%	515,000	321,445	62.4%	-4.4					561,000	379,155	67.6%	0.7	569,000	365,254	64.2%	-2.7
NEBRASKA	1,009,000	568,580	56.4%	1,067,000	598,314	56.1%	-0.3					1,125,000	639,668	56.9%	0.5	1,135,000	667,860	58.8%	2.5
NEVADA				480,000	201,980	42.1%		578,000	246,436	42.6%	0.6					818,000	349,649	42.7%	0.7
NEW HAMPSHIRE	522,000	324,354	62.1%					660,000	375,060	56.8%	-5.3	728,000	384,406	52.8%	-9.3				
NEW JERSEY	4,754,000	2,791,907	58.7%	4,951,000	2,771,390	56.0%	-2.8					5,298,000	3,096,456	58.4%	-0.3	5,455,000	2,987,634	54.8%	-4.0
NEW MEXICO	675,000	378,330	56.0%	780,000	413,141	53.0%	-3.1					942,000	502,634	53.4%	-2.7	1,008,000	508,598	50.5%	-5.6
NEW YORK				11,949,000	6,319,755	52.9%		12,020,000	6,014,914	50.0%	-2.8					12,337,000	6,040,980	49.0%	-3.9

United States Senate General Elections (continued)

United States Senate General Elections *(continued)*

Election Years 1972–1988 *(continued)*

State	1972 Voting-age population	1972 Turnout	1972 %	1976 Voting-age population	1976 Turnout	1976 %	1976 Difference from 1972	1980 Voting-age population	1980 Turnout	1980 %	1980 Difference from 1972	1984 Voting-age population	1984 Turnout	1984 %	1984 Difference from 1972	1988 Voting-age population	1988 Turnout	1988 %	1988 Difference from 1972
NORTH CAROLINA	3,553,000	1,472,541	41.4%					4,239,000	1,797,665	42.4%	1.0	4,560,000	2,239,051	49.1%	7.7				
NORTH DAKOTA				436,000	283,062	64.9%		458,000	299,272	65.3%	0.4					459,000	289,170	63.0%	-1.9
OHIO				7,365,000	3,920,613	53.2%		7,638,000	4,027,303	52.7%	-0.5					7,909,000	4,352,905	55.0%	1.8
OKLAHOMA	1,833,000	1,005,148	54.8%					2,152,000	1,098,294	51.0%	-3.8	2,208,000	1,197,937	54.3%	-0.6				
OREGON	1,511,000	920,833	60.9%					1,879,000	1,140,494	60.7%	-0.2	1,954,000	1,214,735	62.2%	1.2				
PENNSYLVANIA				8,383,000	4,546,353	54.2%		8,653,000	4,418,042	51.1%	-3.2					8,914,000	4,366,598	49.0%	-5.2
RHODE ISLAND	642,000	413,432	64.4%	660,000	398,906	60.4%	-4.0					702,000	395,285	56.3%	-8.1	726,000	397,996	54.8%	-9.6
SOUTH CAROLINA	1,776,000	672,246	37.9%					2,186,000	870,594	39.8%	2.0	2,344,000	965,130	41.2%	3.3				
SOUTH DAKOTA	440,000	306,386	69.6%					483,000	327,478	67.8%	-1.8	488,000	315,713	64.7%	-4.9				
TENNESSEE	2,778,000	1,164,195	41.9%	3,051,000	1,432,046	46.9%	5.0					3,444,000	1,648,036	47.9%	5.9	3,538,000	1,567,181	43.7%	2.4
TEXAS	7,729,000	3,413,903	44.2%	8,708,000	3,874,516	44.5%	0.3					10,358,000	5,319,178	51.4%	7.2	11,077,000	5,323,606	48.1%	3.9
UTAH				813,000	540,108	66.4%		912,000	594,298	65.2%	-1.3					1,046,000	640,702	61.3%	-5.2
VERMONT	303,000	71,348	23.5%	334,000	189,060	56.6%	33.1	363,000	209,124	57.6%	34.1					406,000	240,108	59.1%	35.6
VIRGINIA	3,243,000	1,396,268	43.1%	3,549,000	1,557,500	43.9%	0.8					4,144,000	2,007,487	48.4%	5.4	4,434,000	2,068,897	46.7%	3.6
WASHINGTON				2,677,000	1,491,111	55.7%		2,937,000	1,728,369	58.8%	3.1					3,392,000	1,848,542	54.5%	-1.2
WEST VIRGINIA	1,221,000	731,841	59.9%	1,310,000	566,790	43.3%	-16.7					1,365,000	722,212	52.9%	-7.0	1,348,000	634,547	47.1%	-12.9
WISCONSIN				3,149,000	1,935,183	61.5%		3,326,000	2,204,202	66.3%	4.8					3,523,000	2,168,190	61.5%	0.1
WYOMING	241,000	142,067	58.9%	284,000	155,368	54.7%	-4.2					318,000	186,898	58.8%	-0.2	316,000	180,964	57.3%	-1.7
Total	71,848,000	37,896,768	52.7%	110,780,000	58,862,476	53.1%	0.4	114,534,000	59,476,689	51.9%	-1.2	84,803,000	45,571,020	53.7%	1.0	129,397,000	67,432,122	52.1%	-0.6

*Percentage point difference between turnout in current year and initial year listed in chart. If data do not appear for a state in the initial year listed, the difference is calculated from the first year in which data do appear for that state.

**In 1978 Louisiana eliminated the partisan primary for senator and instituted an open primary with candidates from all parties running on the same ballot. Any candidate who received a majority appeared in the general election unopposed. If no candidate received fifty percent, a runoff was held between the top two finishers. In 2008 Louisiana returned to a partisan primary system.

UNITED STATES SENATE GENERAL ELECTIONS

Republican Turnout for Election Years 1972–1988

State	1972 Voting-age population	1972 Turnout	1972 %	1976 Voting-age population	1976 Turnout	1976 %	1976 Difference from 1972*	1980 Voting-age population	1980 Turnout	1980 %	1980 Difference from 1972	1984 Voting-age population	1984 Turnout	1984 %	1984 Difference from 1972	1988 Voting-age population	1988 Turnout	1988 %	1988 Difference from 1972
ALABAMA	2,346,000	347,523	14.8%					2,732,000	650,362	23.8%	9.0	2,833,000	498,508	17.6%	2.8				
ALASKA	202,000	74,216	36.7%					271,000	84,159	31.1%	-5.7	314,000	59,108	18.8%	-17.9				
ARIZONA				1,615,000	321,236	19.9%		1,902,000	432,371	22.7%	2.8					2,460,000	478,060	19.4%	-0.5
ARKANSAS	1,357,000	248,238	18.3%					1,614,000	330,576	20.5%	2.2								
CALIFORNIA				14,481,000	3,748,973	25.9%		15,629,000	3,093,426	19.8%	-6.1					17,957,000	5,143,409	28.6%	2.8
COLORADO	1,570,000	447,957	28.5%					2,058,000	571,295	27.8%	-0.8	2,196,000	833,821	38.0%	9.4				
CONNECTICUT				2,114,000	785,683	37.2%		2,210,000	581,884	26.3%	-10.8					2,392,000	678,454	28.4%	-8.8
DELAWARE	367,000	112,844	30.7%	398,000	125,502	31.5%	0.8					457,000	98,101	21.5%	-9.3	486,000	151,115	31.1%	0.3
DISTRICT OF COLUMBIA																			
FLORIDA				6,159,000	1,057,886	17.2%		7,102,000	1,822,460	25.7%	8.5					8,966,000	2,051,071	22.9%	5.7
GEORGIA	3,167,000	542,331	17.1%					3,832,000	803,686	21.0%	3.8	4,197,000	337,196	8.0%	-9.1				
HAWAII				572,000	122,724	21.5%		636,000	53,068	8.3%	-13.1					747,000	66,987	9.0%	-12.5
IDAHO	495,000	161,804	32.7%					631,000	210,701	34.7%	2.0	655,000	293,193	44.8%	12.1				
ILLINOIS	7,333,000	2,867,078	39.1%					7,851,000	1,946,296	24.8%	-14.3	7,928,000	2,308,039	29.1%	-10.0				
INDIANA				3,672,000	1,275,833	34.7%		3,850,000	1,182,414	30.7%	-4.0					4,021,000	1,430,525	35.6%	0.8
IOWA	1,905,000	530,525	27.8%					2,070,000	683,014	33.0%	5.1	2,055,000	564,381	27.5%	-0.4				
KANSAS	1,547,000	622,591	40.2%					1,701,000	598,686	35.2%	-5.0	1,739,000	757,402	43.6%	3.3				
KENTUCKY	2,228,000	494,337	22.2%					2,574,000	386,029	15.0%	-7.2	2,636,000	644,990	24.5%	2.3				
LOUISIANA**	2,406,000	206,846	8.6%					2,847,000	23,947	0.8%	-7.8	2,892,000	139,292	4.8%	-3.8				
MAINE	678,000	197,040	29.1%	740,000	193,489	26.1%	-2.9					845,000	404,414	47.9%	18.8	890,000	104,758	11.8%	-17.3
MARYLAND				2,817,000	530,439	18.8%		2,999,000	850,970	28.4%	9.5					3,398,000	617,537	18.2%	-0.7
MASSACHUSETTS	3,798,000	1,505,932	39.7%	3,952,000	722,641	18.3%	-21.4					4,228,000	1,136,806	26.9%	-12.8	4,355,000	884,267	20.3%	-19.3
MICHIGAN	5,755,000	1,781,065	30.9%	6,100,000	1,635,087	26.8%	-4.1					6,529,000	1,745,302	26.7%	-4.2	6,654,000	1,348,219	20.3%	-10.7
MINNESOTA	2,533,000	742,121	29.3%	2,719,000	478,611	17.6%	-11.7					3,007,000	1,199,926	39.9%	10.6	3,121,000	1,176,210	37.7%	8.4
MISSISSIPPI	1,460,000	249,779	17.1%									1,753,000	580,314	33.1%	16.0	1,802,000	510,380	28.3%	11.2
MISSOURI				3,390,000	1,090,067	32.2%		3,541,000	985,399	27.8%	-4.3					3,738,000	1,407,416	37.7%	5.5
MONTANA	471,000	151,316	32.1%	515,000	115,213	22.4%	-9.8					561,000	154,308	27.5%	-4.6	569,000	189,445	33.3%	1.2
NEBRASKA	1,009,000	301,841	29.9%	1,067,000	284,284	26.6%	-3.3					1,125,000	307,147	27.3%	-2.6	1,135,000	278,250	24.5%	-5.4
NEVADA				480,000	63,471	13.2%		578,000	144,224	25.0%	11.7					818,000	161,336	19.7%	6.5
NEW HAMPSHIRE	522,000	139,852	26.8%					660,000	195,559	29.6%	2.8	728,000	225,828	31.0%	4.2				
NEW JERSEY	4,754,000	1,743,854	36.7%	4,951,000	1,054,508	21.3%	-15.4					5,298,000	1,080,100	20.4%	-16.3	5,455,000	1,349,937	24.7%	-11.9
NEW MEXICO	675,000	204,253	30.3%	780,000	234,681	30.1%	-0.2					942,000	361,371	38.4%	8.1	1,008,000	186,579	18.5%	-11.7
NEW YORK				11,949,000	2,836,633	23.7%		12,020,000	2,699,652	22.5%	-1.3					12,337,000	1,875,784	15.2%	-8.5

United States Senate General Elections (continued)

United States Senate General Elections *(continued)*

Republican Turnout for Election Years 1972–1988 *(continued)*

State	1972 Voting-age population	1972 Turnout	1972 %	1976 Voting-age population	1976 Turnout	1976 %	1976 Difference from 1972	1980 Voting-age population	1980 Turnout	1980 %	1980 Difference from 1972	1984 Voting-age population	1984 Turnout	1984 %	1984 Difference from 1972	1988 Voting-age population	1988 Turnout	1988 %	1988 Difference from 1972
NORTH CAROLINA	3,553,000	795,248	22.4%					4,239,000	898,064	21.2%	-1.2	4,560,000	1,156,768	25.4%	3.0				
NORTH DAKOTA				436,000	103,466	23.7%		458,000	210,347	45.9%	22.2					459,000	112,937	24.6%	0.9
OHIO				7,365,000	1,823,774	24.8%		7,638,000	1,137,695	14.9%	-9.9					7,909,000	1,872,716	23.7%	-1.1
OKLAHOMA	1,833,000	516,934	28.2%					2,152,000	587,252	27.3%	-0.9	2,208,000	280,638	12.7%	-15.5				
OREGON	1,511,000	494,671	32.7%					1,879,000	594,290	31.6%	-1.1	1,954,000	808,152	41.4%	8.6				
PENNSYLVANIA				8,383,000	2,381,891	28.4%		8,653,000	2,230,404	25.8%	-2.6					8,914,000	2,901,715	32.6%	4.1
RHODE ISLAND	642,000	188,990	29.4%	660,000	230,329	34.9%	5.5					702,000	108,492	15.5%	-14.0	726,000	217,273	29.9%	0.5
SOUTH CAROLINA	1,776,000	426,601	24.0%					2,186,000	257,946	11.8%	-12.2	2,344,000	644,815	27.5%	3.5				
SOUTH DAKOTA	440,000	131,613	29.9%					483,000	190,594	39.5%	9.5	488,000	235,176	48.2%	18.3				
TENNESSEE	2,778,000	716,539	25.8%	3,051,000	673,231	22.1%	-3.7					3,444,000	557,016	16.2%	-9.6	3,538,000	541,033	15.3%	-10.5
TEXAS	7,729,000	1,822,877	23.6%	8,708,000	1,636,370	18.8%	-4.8					10,358,000	3,116,348	30.1%	6.5	11,077,000	2,129,228	19.2%	-4.4
UTAH				813,000	290,221	35.7%		912,000	437,675	48.0%	12.3					1,046,000	430,089	41.1%	5.4
VERMONT	303,000	45,888	15.1%	334,000	94,481	28.3%	13.1	363,000	101,421	27.9%	12.8					406,000	163,183	40.2%	25.0
VIRGINIA	3,243,000	718,337	22.2%									4,144,000	1,406,194	33.9%	11.8	4,434,000	593,652	13.4%	-8.8
WASHINGTON				2,677,000	361,546	13.5%		2,937,000	936,317	31.9%	18.4					3,392,000	944,359	27.8%	14.3
WEST VIRGINIA	1,221,000	245,531	20.1%									1,365,000	344,680	25.3%	5.1	1,348,000	223,564	16.6%	-3.5
WISCONSIN				3,149,000	521,902	16.6%		3,326,000	1,106,311	33.3%	16.7					3,523,000	1,030,440	29.2%	12.7
WYOMING	241,000	101,314	42.0%	284,000	84,810	29.9%	-12.2					318,000	146,373	46.0%	4.0	316,000	91,143	28.8%	-13.2
Total	71,848,000	19,877,886	27.7%	104,331,000	24,878,982	23.8%	-3.8	114,534,000	27,026,494	23.6%	-4.1	84,803,000	22,534,199	26.6%	-1.1	129,397,000	31,341,071	24.2%	-3.4

Democratic Turnout for Election Years 1972–1988

State	1972 Voting-age population	1972 Turnout	1972 %	1976 Voting-age population	1976 Turnout	1976 %	1976 Difference from 1972*	1980 Voting-age population	1980 Turnout	1980 %	1980 Difference from 1972	1984 Voting-age population	1984 Turnout	1984 %	1984 Difference from 1972	1988 Voting-age population	1988 Turnout	1988 %	1988 Difference from 1972
ALABAMA	2,346,000	654,491	27.9%					2,732,000	610,175	22.3%	-5.6	2,833,000	860,535	30.4%	2.5				
ALASKA	202,000	21,791	10.8%					271,000	72,007	26.6%	15.8	314,000	146,942	46.8%	36.0				
ARIZONA				1,615,000	400,334	24.8%		1,902,000	422,972	22.2%	-2.6					2,460,000	660,403	26.8%	2.1
ARKANSAS	1,357,000	386,398	28.5%					1,614,000	477,905	29.6%	1.1								
CALIFORNIA				14,481,000	3,502,862	24.2%		15,629,000	4,705,399	30.1%	5.9					17,957,000	4,287,253	23.9%	-0.3
COLORADO	1,570,000	457,545	29.1%					2,058,000	590,501	28.7%	-0.5	2,196,000	449,327	20.5%	-8.7				
CONNECTICUT				2,114,000	561,018	26.5%		2,210,000	763,969	34.6%	8.0					2,392,000	688,499	28.8%	2.2
DELAWARE	367,000	116,006	31.6%	398,000	98,055	24.6%	-7.0					457,000	147,831	32.3%	0.7	486,000	92,378	19.0%	-12.6
DISTRICT OF COLUMBIA																			
FLORIDA				6,159,000	1,799,518	29.2%		7,102,000	1,705,409	24.0%	-5.2					8,966,000	2,016,553	22.5%	-6.7

United States Senate General Elections (continued)

Democratic Turnout for Election Years 1972–1988 (continued)

State	1972 Voting-age population	1972 Turnout	1972 %	1976 Voting-age population	1976 Turnout	1976 %	1976 Difference from 1972	1980 Voting-age population	1980 Turnout	1980 %	1980 Difference from 1972	1984 Voting-age population	1984 Turnout	1984 %	1984 Difference from 1972	1988 Voting-age population	1988 Turnout	1988 %	1988 Difference from 1972
GEORGIA	3,167,000	635,970	20.1%					3,832,000	776,143	20.3%	0.2	4,197,000	1,344,104	32.0%	11.9				
HAWAII				572,000	162,305	28.4%		636,000	224,485	35.3%	6.9					747,000	247,941	33.2%	4.8
IDAHO	495,000	140,913	28.5%					631,000	214,439	34.0%	5.5	655,000	105,591	16.1%	-12.3				
ILLINOIS	7,333,000	1,721,031	23.5%					7,851,000	2,565,302	32.7%	9.2	7,928,000	2,397,303	30.2%	6.8				
INDIANA				3,672,000	878,522	23.9%		3,860,000	1,015,962	26.4%	2.5					4,021,000	668,778	16.6%	-7.3
IOWA	1,905,000	662,637	34.8%					2,070,000	581,545	28.1%	-6.7	2,055,000	716,883	34.9%	0.1				
KANSAS	1,547,000	200,764	13.0%					1,701,000	340,271	20.0%	7.0	1,739,000	211,664	12.2%	-0.8				
KENTUCKY	2,228,000	528,550	23.7%					2,574,000	720,861	28.0%	4.3	2,636,000	639,721	24.3%	0.5				
LOUISIANA**	2,406,000	598,987	24.9%					2,847,000	810,692	28.5%	3.6	2,892,000	830,181	29.0%	4.1				
MAINE	678,000	224,270	33.1%	740,000	292,704	39.6%	6.5					845,000	142,626	16.9%	-16.2	890,000	452,590	50.9%	17.8
MARYLAND				2,817,000	772,101	27.4%		2,999,000	435,118	14.5%	-12.9					3,398,000	999,166	29.4%	2.0
MASSACHUSETTS	3,798,000	823,278	21.7%	3,952,000	1,726,657	43.7%	22.0					4,228,000	1,392,981	32.9%	11.3	4,355,000	1,693,344	38.9%	17.2
MICHIGAN	5,755,000	1,577,178	27.4%	6,100,000	1,831,031	30.0%	2.6					6,529,000	1,915,831	29.3%	1.9	6,654,000	2,116,865	31.8%	4.4
MINNESOTA	2,533,000	981,340	38.7%	2,719,000	1,290,736	47.5%	8.7					3,007,000	852,844	28.4%	-10.4	3,121,000	856,694	27.4%	-11.3
MISSISSIPPI	1,460,000	375,102	25.7%	1,590,000	554,433	34.9%	9.2					1,753,000	371,926	21.2%	-4.5	1,802,000	436,339	24.2%	-1.5
MISSOURI				3,390,000	813,571	24.0%		3,541,000	1,074,859	30.4%	6.4					3,738,000	660,045	17.7%	-6.3
MONTANA	471,000	163,609	34.7%	515,000	206,232	40.0%	5.3					561,000	215,704	38.4%	3.7	569,000	175,809	30.9%	-3.8
NEBRASKA	1,009,000	265,922	26.4%	1,067,000	313,809	29.4%	3.1					1,125,000	332,217	29.5%	3.2	1,135,000	378,717	33.4%	7.0
NEVADA				480,000	127,295	26.5%		578,000	92,129	15.9%	-10.6					818,000	175,548	21.5%	-5.1
NEW HAMPSHIRE	522,000	184,495	35.3%					660,000	179,455	27.2%	-8.2	728,000	157,447	21.6%	-13.7				
NEW JERSEY	4,754,000	963,573	20.3%	4,951,000	1,681,140	34.0%	13.7					5,298,000	1,986,644	37.5%	17.2	5,455,000	1,599,905	29.3%	9.1
NEW MEXICO	675,000	173,815	25.8%	780,000	176,382	22.6%	-3.1					942,000	141,253	15.0%	-10.8	1,008,000	321,983	31.9%	6.2
NEW YORK				11,949,000	3,422,594	28.6%		12,020,000	2,618,661	21.8%	-6.9					12,337,000	4,048,649	32.8%	4.2
NORTH CAROLINA	3,553,000	677,293	19.1%					4,239,000	887,653	20.9%	1.9	4,560,000	1,070,488	23.5%	4.4				
NORTH DAKOTA				436,000	175,772	40.3%		458,000	86,658	18.9%	-21.4					459,000	171,899	37.5%	-2.9
OHIO				7,365,000	1,941,113	26.4%		7,638,000	2,770,786	36.3%	9.9					7,909,000	2,480,038	31.4%	5.0
OKLAHOMA	1,833,000	478,212	26.1%					2,152,000	478,283	22.2%	-3.9	2,208,000	906,131	41.0%	14.9				
OREGON	1,511,000	425,036	28.1%					1,879,000	501,963	26.7%	-1.4	1,954,000	406,122	20.8%	-7.3				
PENNSYLVANIA				8,383,000	2,126,977	25.4%		8,653,000	2,122,391	24.5%	-0.8					8,914,000	1,416,764	15.9%	-9.5
RHODE ISLAND	642,000	221,942	34.6%	660,000	167,665	25.4%	-9.2					702,000	286,780	40.9%	6.3	726,000	180,717	24.9%	-9.7
SOUTH CAROLINA	1,776,000	245,457	13.8%					2,186,000	612,554	28.0%	14.2	2,344,000	306,982	13.1%	-0.7				
SOUTH DAKOTA	440,000	174,773	39.7%					483,000	129,018	26.7%	-13.0	488,000	80,537	16.5%	-23.2				
TENNESSEE	2,778,000	440,599	15.9%	3,051,000	751,180	24.6%	8.8					3,444,000	1,000,607	29.1%	13.2	3,538,000	1,020,061	28.8%	13.0

United States Senate General Elections (continued)

Democratic Turnout for Election Years 1972–1988 (continued)

State	1972 Voting-age population	1972 Turnout	1972 %	1976 Voting-age population	1976 Turnout	1976 %	1976 Difference from 1972	1980 Voting-age population	1980 Turnout	1980 %	1980 Difference from 1972	1984 Voting-age population	1984 Turnout	1984 %	1984 Difference from 1972	1988 Voting-age population	1988 Turnout	1988 %	1988 Difference from 1972
TEXAS	7,729,000	1,511,985	19.6%	8,708,000	2,199,956	25.3%	5.7					10,358,000	2,202,557	21.3%	1.7	11,077,000	3,149,806	28.4%	8.9
UTAH				813,000	241,948	29.8%		912,000	151,454	16.6%	-13.2					1,046,000	203,364	19.4%	-10.3
VERMONT	303,000	23,842	7.9%	334,000	85,682	25.7%	17.8	363,000	104,176	28.7%	20.8					406,000	71,460	17.6%	9.7
VIRGINIA	3,243,000	643,963	19.9%	3,549,000	596,009	16.8%	-3.1					4,144,000	601,142	14.5%	-5.4	4,434,000	1,474,086	33.2%	13.4
WASHINGTON				2,677,000	1,071,219	40.0%		2,937,000	792,052	27.0%	-13.0					3,392,000	904,183	26.7%	-13.4
WEST VIRGINIA	1,221,000	486,310	39.8%	1,310,000	566,423	43.2%	3.4					1,365,000	374,233	27.4%	-12.4	1,348,000	410,983	30.5%	-9.3
WISCONSIN				3,149,000	1,396,970	44.4%		3,326,000	1,065,487	32.0%	-12.3					3,523,000	1,128,625	32.0%	-12.3
WYOMING	241,000	40,753	16.9%	284,000	70,558	24.8%	7.9					318,000	40,525	12.7%	-4.2	316,000	89,821	28.4%	11.5
Total	71,848,000	17,227,830	24.0%	110,780,000	32,002,771	28.9%	4.9	114,534,000	30,700,734	26.8%	2.8	84,803,000	22,643,659	26.7%	2.7	129,397,000	35,279,266	27.3%	3.3

Other Turnout for Election Years 1972–1988

State	1972 Voting-age population	1972 Turnout	1972 %	1976 Voting-age population	1976 Turnout	1976 %	1976 Difference from 1972*	1980 Voting-age population	1980 Turnout	1980 %	1980 Difference from 1972	1984 Voting-age population	1984 Turnout	1984 %	1984 Difference from 1972	1988 Voting-age population	1988 Turnout	1988 %	1988 Difference from 1972
ALABAMA	2,346,000	49,085	2.1%					2,732,000	36,220	1.3%	-0.8	2,833,000	12,195	0.4%	-1.7				
ALASKA								271,000	596	0.2%		314,000	838	0.3%	0.0				
ARIZONA				1,615,000	19,640	1.2%		1,902,000	18,895	1.0%	-0.2					2,460,000	26,076	1.1%	-0.2
ARKANSAS								1,614,000	331	0.0%									
CALIFORNIA				14,481,000	220,433	1.5%		15,629,000	528,656	3.4%	1.9					17,957,000	312,936	1.7%	0.2
COLORADO	1,570,000	20,591	1.3%					2,058,000	11,850	0.6%	-0.7	2,196,000	14,661	0.7%	-0.6				
CONNECTICUT				2,114,000	14,965	0.7%		2,210,000	10,222	0.5%	-0.2					2,392,000	16,573	0.7%	0.0
DELAWARE	367,000	978	0.3%	398,000	1,302	0.3%	0.1												
DISTRICT OF COLUMBIA																			
FLORIDA				6,159,000	130	0.0%		7,102,000	159	0.0%	0.0					8,966,000	585	0.0%	0.0
GEORGIA	3,167,000	407	0.0%					3,832,000	511	0.0%	0.0								
HAWAII				572,000	17,063	3.0%		636,000	10,453	1.6%	-1.3					747,000	8,948	1.2%	-1.8
IDAHO	495,000	6,885	1.4%					631,000	6,507	1.0%	-0.4	655,000	7,384	1.1%	-0.3				
ILLINOIS	7,333,000	20,271	0.3%					7,851,000	68,431	0.9%	0.6	7,928,000	82,131	1.0%	0.8				
INDIANA				3,672,000	16,832	0.5%													
IOWA	1,905,000	10,171	0.5%					2,070,000	12,475	0.6%	0.1	2,055,000	11,436	0.6%	0.0				
KANSAS	1,547,000	48,367	3.1%									1,739,000	27,663	1.6%	-1.5				
KENTUCKY	2,228,000	14,974	0.7%									2,636,000	7,696	0.3%	-0.4				
LOUISIANA**	2,406,000	279,071	11.6%					2,847,000	6,374	0.2%	-11.4								
MAINE				740,000	61	0.0%						845,000	4,366	0.5%	0.5	890,000	27	0.0%	0.0

United States Senate General Elections (continued)

Other Turnout for Election Years 1972–1988 (continued)

State	1972 Voting-age population	Turnout	%	1976 Voting-age population	Turnout	%	Difference from 1972	1980 Voting-age population	Turnout	%	Difference from 1972	1984 Voting-age population	Turnout	%	Difference from 1972	1988 Voting-age population	Turnout	%	Difference from 1972
MARYLAND				2,817,000	63,028	2.2%										3,398,000	362	0.0%	-2.2
MASSACHUSETTS	3,798,000	41,466	1.1%	3,952,000	41,957	1.1%	0.0					4,228,000	408	0.0%	-1.1	4,355,000	28,614	0.7%	-0.4
MICHIGAN	5,755,000	48,663	0.8%	6,100,000	24,546	0.4%	-0.4					6,529,000	39,805	0.6%	-0.2	6,654,000	40,901	0.6%	-0.2
MINNESOTA	2,533,000	8,192	0.3%	2,719,000	142,721	5.2%	4.9					3,007,000	13,373	0.4%	0.1	3,121,000	61,049	2.0%	1.6
MISSISSIPPI	1,460,000	20,865	1.4%																
MISSOURI				3,390,000	11,139	0.3%		3,541,000	6,707	0.2%	-0.1					3,738,000	11,414	0.3%	0.0
MONTANA												561,000	9,143	1.6%					
NEBRASKA	1,009,000	817	0.1%	1,067,000	221	0.0%	-0.1					1,125,000	304	0.0%	-0.1	1,135,000	10,893	1.0%	0.9
NEVADA				480,000	11,214	2.3%		578,000	10,083	1.7%	0.6					818,000	12,765	1.6%	-0.8
NEW HAMPSHIRE	522,000	7	0.0%					660,000	46	0.0%	0.0	728,000	1,131	0.2%	0.2				
NEW JERSEY	4,754,000	84,480	1.8%	4,951,000	35,742	0.7%	-1.1					5,298,000	29,712	0.6%	-1.2	5,455,000	37,792	0.7%	-1.1
NEW MEXICO	675,000	262	0.0%	780,000	2,078	0.3%	0.2					942,000	10	0.0%	0.0	1,008,000	36	0.0%	0.0
NEW YORK				11,949,000	60,528	0.5%		12,020,000	696,601	5.8%	5.3					12,337,000	116,547	0.9%	0.4
NORTH CAROLINA								4,239,000	11,948	0.3%		4,560,000	11,795	0.3%	0.0				
NORTH DAKOTA				436,000	3,824	0.9%		458,000	2,267	0.5%	-0.4					459,000	4,334	0.9%	0.1
OHIO				7,365,000	155,726	2.1%		7,638,000	118,822	1.6%	-0.6					7,909,000	151	0.0%	-2.1
OKLAHOMA	1,833,000	10,002	0.5%					2,152,000	32,759	1.5%	1.0	2,208,000	11,168	0.5%	0.0				
OREGON	1,511,000	1,126	0.1%					1,879,000	44,241	2.4%	2.3	1,054,000	461	0.0%	-0.1				
PENNSYLVANIA				8,383,000	37,485	0.4%		8,653,000	65,247	0.8%	0.3					8,914,000	48,119	0.5%	0.1
RHODE ISLAND	642,000	2,500	0.4%	660,000	912	0.1%	-0.3					702,000	13	0.0%	-0.4	726,000	6	0.0%	-0.4
SOUTH CAROLINA	1,776,000	188	0.0%					2,186,000	94	0.0%	0.0	2,344,000	13,333	0.6%	0.6				
SOUTH DAKOTA								483,000	7,866	1.6%									
TENNESSEE	2,778,000	7,057	0.3%	3,051,000	7,635	0.3%	0.0					3,444,000	90,413	2.6%	2.4	3,538,000	6,087	0.2%	-0.1
TEXAS	7,729,000	79,041	1.0%	8,708,000	38,190	0.4%	-0.6					10,358,000	273	0.0%	-1.0	11,077,000	44,572	0.4%	-0.6
UTAH				813,000	7,939	1.0%		912,000	5,169	0.6%	-0.4					1,046,000	7,249	0.7%	-0.3
VERMONT	303,000	1,618	0.5%	334,000	8,897	2.7%	2.1	363,000	3,527	1.0%	0.4					406,000	5,465	1.3%	0.8
VIRGINIA	3,243,000	33,968	1.0%	3,549,000	961,491	27.1%	26.0					4,144,000	151	0.0%	-1.0	4,434,000	1,159	0.0%	-1.0
WASHINGTON				2,677,000	58,346	2.2%													
WEST VIRGINIA				1,310,000	367	0.0%						1,365,000	3,299	0.2%	0.2				
WISCONSIN				3,149,000	16,311	0.5%		3,326,000	32,404	1.0%	0.5					3,523,000	9,125	0.3%	-0.3
WYOMING																			
Total	63,685,000	791,052	1.2%	108,391,000	1,980,723	1.8%	0.6	100,473,000	1,749,461	1.7%	0.5	74,698,000	393,162	0.5%	-0.7	117,463,000	811,785	0.7%	-0.6

*Percentage point difference between turnout in current year and initial year listed in chart. If data do not appear for a state in the initial year listed, the difference is calculated from the first year in which data do appear for that state.

**In 1978 Louisiana eliminated the partisan primary for senator and instituted an open primary with candidates from all parties running on the same ballot. Any candidate who received a majority appeared in the general election unopposed. If no candidate received fifty percent, a runoff was held between the top two finishers. In 2008 Louisiana returned to a partisan primary system.

UNITED STATES HOUSE OF REPRESENTATIVES GENERAL ELECTIONS

Election Years 1972–1988

State	1972 Voting-age population	1972 Turnout	1972 %	1976 Voting-age population	1976 Turnout	1976 %	1976 Difference from 1972*	1980 Voting-age population	1980 Turnout	1980 %	1980 Difference from 1972	1984 Voting-age population	1984 Turnout	1984 %	1984 Difference from 1972	1988 Voting-age population	1988 Turnout	1988 %	1988 Difference from 1972
ALABAMA	2,346,000	972,629	41.5%	2,552,000	984,181	38.6%	-2.9	2,732,000	1,011,676	37.0%	-4.4	2,833,000	1,148,574	40.5%	-0.9	2,931,000	1,178,298	40.2%	-1.3
ALASKA	202,000	95,401	47.2%	237,000	118,208	49.9%	2.6	271,000	154,618	57.1%	9.8	314,000	206,437	65.7%	18.5	355,000	192,955	54.4%	7.1
ARIZONA	1,312,000	593,907	45.3%	1,615,000	729,002	45.1%	-0.1	1,902,000	853,952	44.9%	-0.4	2,187,000	943,123	43.1%	-2.1	2,460,000	1,124,816	45.7%	0.5
ARKANSAS	1,357,000	187,052	13.8%	1,495,000	336,389	22.5%	8.7	1,614,000	201,655	12.5%	-1.3	1,660,000	463,246	27.9%	14.1	1,704,000	605,920	35.6%	21.8
CALIFORNIA	13,275,000	8,116,591	61.1%	14,481,000	7,453,946	51.5%	-9.7	15,629,000	8,179,742	52.3%	-8.8	16,816,000	8,953,334	53.2%	-7.9	17,957,000	9,381,240	52.2%	-8.9
COLORADO	1,570,000	912,880	58.1%	1,829,000	1,022,245	55.9%	-2.3	2,058,000	1,150,090	55.9%	-2.3	2,196,000	1,247,634	56.8%	-1.3	2,328,000	1,315,471	56.5%	-1.6
CONNECTICUT	2,011,000	1,351,001	67.2%	2,114,000	1,348,472	63.8%	-3.4	2,210,000	1,339,245	60.6%	-6.6	2,299,000	1,432,288	62.3%	-4.9	2,392,000	1,340,610	56.0%	-11.1
DELAWARE	367,000	225,851	61.5%	398,000	214,799	54.0%	-7.6	426,000	216,629	50.9%	-10.7	457,000	243,014	53.2%	-8.4	486,000	234,517	48.3%	-13.3
DISTRICT OF COLUMBIA																			
FLORIDA	5,163,000	1,931,510	37.4%	6,159,000	2,082,530	33.8%	-3.6	7,102,000	3,094,362	43.6%	6.2	8,053,000	2,435,596	30.2%	-7.2	8,966,000	3,047,042	34.0%	-3.4
GEORGIA	3,167,000	891,826	28.2%	3,506,000	1,253,090	35.7%	7.6	3,832,000	1,354,801	35.4%	7.2	4,197,000	1,520,825	36.2%	8.1	4,548,000	1,672,178	36.8%	8.6
HAWAII	504,000	274,863	54.5%	572,000	293,701	51.3%	-3.2	636,000	280,561	44.1%	-10.4	692,000	275,606	39.8%	-14.7	747,000	339,828	45.5%	-9.0
IDAHO	495,000	301,554	60.9%	568,000	341,907	60.2%	-0.7	631,000	415,102	65.8%	4.9	655,000	405,075	61.8%	0.9	677,000	407,434	60.2%	-0.7
ILLINOIS	7,333,000	4,385,023	59.8%	7,613,000	4,366,051	57.3%	-2.4	7,851,000	4,472,601	57.0%	-2.8	7,928,000	4,579,081	57.8%	-2.0	8,000,000	4,343,949	54.3%	-5.5
INDIANA	3,469,000	2,110,236	60.8%	3,672,000	2,103,138	57.3%	-3.6	3,850,000	2,159,460	56.1%	-4.7	3,937,000	2,179,955	55.4%	-5.5	4,021,000	2,119,958	52.7%	-8.1
IOWA	1,905,000	1,195,736	62.8%	1,996,000	1,242,141	62.2%	-0.5	2,070,000	1,257,036	60.7%	-2.0	2,055,000	1,268,759	61.7%	-1.0	2,042,000	1,188,758	58.2%	-4.6
KANSAS	1,547,000	878,365	56.8%	1,629,000	909,291	55.8%	-1.0	1,701,000	933,114	54.9%	-1.9	1,739,000	1,010,646	58.1%	1.3	1,774,000	932,307	52.6%	-4.2
KENTUCKY	2,228,000	985,977	44.3%	2,413,000	988,948	41.0%	-3.3	2,574,000	1,056,092	41.0%	-3.2	2,636,000	1,187,722	45.1%	0.8	2,696,000	1,104,951	41.0%	-3.3
LOUISIANA	2,406,000	678,428	28.2%	2,646,000	1,014,337	38.3%	10.1	2,847,000	729,806	25.6%	-2.6	2,892,000	641,850	22.2%	-6.0	2,935,000	620,228	21.1%	-7.1
MAINE	678,000	413,411	61.0%	740,000	473,213	63.9%	3.0	797,000	512,939	64.4%	3.4	845,000	541,538	64.1%	3.1	890,000	554,887	62.3%	1.4
MARYLAND	2,628,000	1,218,946	46.4%	2,817,000	1,315,871	46.7%	0.3	2,999,000	1,403,047	46.8%	0.4	3,202,000	1,495,280	46.7%	0.3	3,398,000	1,560,984	45.9%	-0.4
MASSACHUSETTS	3,798,000	2,158,701	56.8%	3,952,000	2,345,384	59.3%	2.5	4,096,000	2,256,192	55.1%	-1.8	4,228,000	2,346,047	55.5%	-1.3	4,355,000	2,370,882	54.4%	-2.4
MICHIGAN	5,755,000	3,273,174	56.9%	6,100,000	3,431,890	56.3%	-0.6	6,399,000	3,588,154	56.1%	-0.8	6,529,000	3,452,365	52.9%	-4.0	6,654,000	3,456,393	51.9%	-4.9
MINNESOTA	2,533,000	1,689,786	66.7%	2,719,000	1,794,504	66.0%	-0.7	2,887,000	1,904,913	66.0%	-0.7	3,007,000	1,739,997	57.9%	-8.8	3,121,000	1,969,090	63.1%	-3.6
MISSISSIPPI	1,460,000	588,073	40.3%	1,590,000	636,538	40.0%	-0.2	1,703,000	788,517	46.3%	6.0	1,753,000	868,852	49.6%	9.3	1,802,000	918,119	51.0%	10.7
MISSOURI	3,222,000	1,832,628	56.9%	3,390,000	1,905,016	56.2%	-0.7	3,541,000	2,050,570	57.9%	1.0	3,642,000	2,039,577	56.0%	-0.9	3,738,000	2,070,186	55.4%	-1.5
MONTANA	471,000	315,033	66.9%	515,000	320,905	62.3%	-4.6	552,000	338,541	61.3%	-5.6	561,000	370,829	66.1%	-0.8	569,000	365,217	64.2%	-2.7
NEBRASKA	1,009,000	568,846	56.4%	1,067,000	601,812	56.4%	0.0	1,115,000	625,261	56.1%	-0.3	1,125,000	650,061	57.8%	1.4	1,135,000	656,278	57.8%	1.4
NEVADA	381,000	180,462	47.4%	480,000	199,863	41.6%	-5.7	578,000	244,587	42.3%	-5.0	701,000	270,624	38.6%	-8.8	818,000	344,173	42.1%	-5.3
NEW HAMPSHIRE	522,000	317,034	60.7%	593,000	325,174	54.8%	-5.9	660,000	364,325	55.2%	-5.5	728,000	372,897	51.2%	-9.5	793,000	429,499	54.2%	-6.6
NEW JERSEY	4,754,000	2,831,909	59.6%	4,951,000	2,810,793	56.8%	-2.8	5,133,000	2,741,395	53.4%	-6.2	5,298,000	2,991,937	56.5%	-3.1	5,455,000	2,776,104	50.9%	-8.7
NEW MEXICO	675,000	373,653	55.4%	780,000	401,305	51.4%	-3.9	875,000	408,805	46.7%	-8.6	942,000	499,620	53.0%	-2.3	1,008,000	449,178	44.6%	-10.8
NEW YORK	11,891,000	6,137,203	51.6%	11,949,000	5,990,741	50.1%	-1.5	12,020,000	5,617,366	46.7%	-4.9	12,182,000	6,218,792	51.0%	-0.6	12,337,000	5,505,904	44.6%	-7.0

United States House of Representatives General Elections (continued)

Election Years 1972–1988 (continued)

State	1972 Voting-age population	1972 Turnout	1972 %	1976 Voting-age population	1976 Turnout	1976 %	1976 Difference from 1972	1980 Voting-age population	1980 Turnout	1980 %	1980 Difference from 1972	1984 Voting-age population	1984 Turnout	1984 %	1984 Difference from 1972	1988 Voting-age population	1988 Turnout	1988 %	1988 Difference from 1972
NORTH CAROLINA	3,553,000	1,406,497	39.6%	3,907,000	1,571,678	40.2%	0.6	4,239,000	1,736,797	41.0%	1.4	4,560,000	2,157,655	47.3%	7.7	4,867,000	1,984,673	40.8%	1.2
NORTH DAKOTA	409,000	268,721	65.7%	436,000	289,881	66.5%	0.8	458,000	293,076	64.0%	-1.7	458,000	308,729	67.4%	1.7	459,000	299,982	65.4%	-0.3
OHIO	7,053,000	3,835,541	54.4%	7,365,000	3,841,754	52.2%	-2.2	7,638,000	3,951,679	51.7%	-2.6	7,776,000	4,332,479	55.7%	1.3	7,909,000	4,154,961	52.5%	-1.8
OKLAHOMA	1,833,000	817,081	44.6%	2,005,000	1,067,924	53.3%	8.7	2,152,000	835,582	38.8%	-5.7	2,208,000	1,110,884	50.3%	5.7	2,260,000	767,203	33.9%	-10.6
OREGON	1,511,000	869,730	57.6%	1,709,000	926,664	54.2%	-3.3	1,879,000	1,106,440	58.9%	1.3	1,954,000	1,203,491	61.6%	4.0	2,027,000	1,023,596	50.5%	-7.1
PENNSYLVANIA	8,073,000	4,462,789	55.3%	8,383,000	4,434,255	52.9%	-2.4	8,653,000	4,320,756	49.9%	-5.3	8,786,000	4,642,977	52.8%	2.4	8,914,000	4,197,174	47.1%	-8.2
RHODE ISLAND	642,000	387,992	60.4%	660,000	388,914	58.9%	-1.5	677,000	386,633	57.1%	-3.3	702,000	390,031	55.6%	-4.9	726,000	391,004	53.9%	-6.6
SOUTH CAROLINA	1,776,000	630,657	35.5%	1,990,000	783,524	39.4%	3.9	2,186,000	830,069	38.0%	2.5	2,344,000	927,602	39.6%	4.1	2,495,000	991,372	39.7%	4.2
SOUTH DAKOTA	440,000	300,992	68.4%	463,000	294,971	63.7%	-4.7	483,000	319,503	66.1%	-2.3	488,000	316,222	64.8%	-3.6	492,000	311,916	63.4%	-5.0
TENNESSEE	2,778,000	663,171	23.9%	3,051,000	1,251,060	41.0%	17.1	3,295,000	1,304,197	39.6%	15.7	3,444,000	1,315,735	38.2%	14.3	3,538,000	1,409,321	39.8%	16.0
TEXAS	7,729,000	2,885,949	37.3%	8,708,000	3,663,455	42.1%	4.7	9,608,000	4,068,532	42.3%	5.0	10,358,000	4,680,385	45.2%	7.8	11,077,000	4,669,690	42.2%	4.8
UTAH	701,000	473,068	67.5%	813,000	543,031	66.9%	-0.6	912,000	592,335	64.9%	-2.5	980,000	601,082	61.3%	-6.1	1,046,000	608,668	58.2%	-9.3
VERMONT	303,000	186,028	61.4%	334,000	184,783	55.3%	-6.1	363,000	194,697	53.6%	-7.8	385,000	226,297	58.8%	-2.6	406,000	240,131	59.1%	-2.2
VIRGINIA	3,243,000	1,270,988	39.2%	3,549,000	1,462,822	41.2%	2.0	3,841,000	1,552,835	40.4%	1.2	4,144,000	1,837,605	44.3%	5.2	4,434,000	1,890,028	42.6%	3.5
WASHINGTON	2,396,000	1,301,833	54.3%	2,677,000	1,425,602	53.3%	-1.1	2,937,000	1,626,245	55.4%	1.0	3,170,000	1,808,033	57.0%	2.7	3,392,000	1,731,230	51.0%	-3.3
WEST VIRGINIA	1,221,000	721,200	59.1%	1,310,000	663,094	50.6%	-8.4	1,381,000	685,832	49.7%	-9.4	1,365,000	704,369	51.6%	-7.5	1,348,000	568,579	42.2%	-16.9
WISCONSIN	2,947,000	1,801,094	61.1%	3,149,000	1,962,255	62.3%	1.2	3,326,000	2,134,328	64.2%	3.1	3,427,000	2,075,358	60.6%	-0.6	3,523,000	2,035,482	57.8%	-3.3
WYOMING	241,000	146,299	60.7%	284,000	151,868	53.5%	-7.2	320,000	169,699	53.0%	-7.7	318,000	187,904	59.1%	-1.6	316,000	177,651	56.2%	-4.5
Total	137,283,000	70,417,319	51.3%	147,931,000	74,263,720	50.2%	-1.1	157,639,000	77,814,389	49.4%	-1.9	165,156,000	82,828,019	50.2%	-1.1	172,321,000	82,030,815	47.6%	-3.7

*Percentage point difference between turnout in current year and initial year listed in chart. If data do not appear for a state in the initial year listed, the difference is calculated from the first year in which data do appear for that state.

UNITED STATES HOUSE OF REPRESENTATIVES GENERAL ELECTIONS

Republican Turnout for Election Years 1972–1988

State	1972 Voting-age population	1972 Turnout	1972 %	1976 Voting-age population	1976 Turnout	1976 %	1976 Difference from 1972*	1980 Voting-age population	1980 Turnout	1980 %	1980 Difference from 1972	1984 Voting-age population	1984 Turnout	1984 %	1984 Difference from 1972	1988 Voting-age population	1988 Turnout	1988 %	1988 Difference from 1972
ALABAMA	2,346,000	383,623	16.4%	2,552,000	314,970	12.3%	-4.0	2,732,000	354,224	13.0%	-3.4	2,833,000	308,182	10.9%	-5.5	2,931,000	432,232	14.7%	-1.6
ALASKA	202,000	41,750	20.7%	237,000	83,722	35.3%	14.7	271,000	114,089	42.1%	21.4	314,000	113,582	36.2%	15.5	355,000	120,595	34.0%	13.3
ARIZONA	1,312,000	309,862	23.6%	1,615,000	340,478	21.1%	-2.5	1,902,000	434,024	22.8%	-0.8	2,187,000	602,737	27.6%	3.9	2,460,000	766,111	31.1%	7.5
ARKANSAS	1,357,000	144,571	10.7%	1,495,000	75,384	5.0%	-5.6	1,614,000	159,148	9.9%	-0.8	1,660,000	90,841	5.5%	-5.2	1,704,000	252,756	14.8%	4.2
CALIFORNIA	13,275,000	3,760,095	28.3%	14,481,000	3,220,418	22.2%	-6.1	15,629,000	4,178,626	26.7%	-1.6	16,816,000	4,423,734	26.3%	-2.0	17,957,000	4,173,715	23.2%	-5.1
COLORADO	1,570,000	480,059	30.6%	1,829,000	536,781	29.3%	-1.2	2,058,000	619,461	30.1%	-0.5	2,196,000	779,700	35.5%	4.9	2,328,000	667,091	28.7%	-1.9
CONNECTICUT	2,011,000	690,839	34.4%	2,114,000	651,250	30.8%	-3.5	2,210,000	640,177	29.0%	-5.4	2,299,000	761,647	33.1%	-1.2	2,392,000	676,817	28.3%	-6.1
DELAWARE	367,000	141,237	38.5%	398,000	110,677	27.8%	-10.7	426,000	133,842	31.4%	-7.1	457,000	100,650	22.0%	-16.5	486,000	76,179	15.7%	-22.8
DISTRICT OF COLUMBIA																			
FLORIDA	5,163,000	900,683	17.4%	6,159,000	937,257	15.2%	-2.2	7,102,000	1,275,718	18.0%	0.5	8,053,000	1,190,228	14.8%	-2.7	8,966,000	1,615,567	18.0%	0.6
GEORGIA	3,167,000	252,901	8.0%	3,506,000	321,891	9.2%	1.2	3,832,000	381,174	9.9%	2.0	4,197,000	430,143	10.2%	2.3	4,548,000	556,817	12.2%	4.3
HAWAII	504,000	121,181	24.0%	572,000	77,662	13.6%	-10.5	636,000	19,819	3.1%	-20.9	692,000	40,608	5.9%	-18.2	747,000	96,848	13.0%	-11.1
IDAHO	495,000	187,807	37.9%	568,000	180,008	31.7%	-6.2	631,000	233,041	36.9%	-1.0	655,000	240,218	36.7%	-1.3	677,000	203,447	30.1%	-7.9
ILLINOIS	7,333,000	2,223,305	30.3%	7,613,000	2,112,868	27.8%	-2.6	7,851,000	2,417,747	30.8%	0.5	7,928,000	2,203,506	27.8%	-2.5	8,000,000	2,022,568	25.3%	-5.0
INDIANA	3,469,000	1,133,646	32.7%	3,672,000	931,902	25.4%	-7.3	3,850,000	1,099,991	28.6%	-4.1	3,937,000	1,146,505	29.1%	-3.6	4,021,000	1,023,124	25.4%	-7.2
IOWA	1,905,000	577,425	30.3%	1,996,000	526,677	26.4%	-3.9	2,070,000	609,478	29.4%	-0.9	2,055,000	673,343	32.8%	2.5	2,042,000	606,647	29.7%	-0.6
KANSAS	1,547,000	581,900	37.6%	1,629,000	545,240	33.5%	-4.1	1,701,000	519,874	30.6%	-7.1	1,739,000	541,986	31.2%	-6.4	1,774,000	565,308	31.9%	-5.7
KENTUCKY	2,228,000	487,820	21.9%	2,413,000	374,086	15.5%	-6.4	2,574,000	442,309	17.2%	-4.7	2,636,000	528,862	20.1%	-1.8	2,696,000	564,433	20.9%	-1.0
LOUISIANA	2,406,000	86,607	3.6%	2,646,000	364,582	13.8%	10.2	2,847,000	289,889	10.2%	6.6	2,892,000	238,794	8.3%	4.7	2,935,000	270,056	9.2%	5.6
MAINE	678,000	194,868	28.7%	740,000	314,815	42.5%	13.8	797,000	375,073	47.1%	18.3	845,000	374,951	44.4%	15.6	890,000	278,354	31.3%	2.5
MARYLAND	2,628,000	584,859	22.3%	2,817,000	473,316	16.8%	-5.5	2,999,000	537,078	17.9%	-4.3	3,202,000	535,915	16.7%	-5.5	3,398,000	624,021	18.4%	-3.9
MASSACHUSETTS	3,798,000	808,394	21.3%	3,952,000	723,119	18.3%	-3.0	4,096,000	757,738	18.5%	-2.8	4,228,000	703,945	16.6%	-4.6	4,355,000	509,360	11.7%	-9.6
MICHIGAN	5,755,000	1,710,177	29.7%	6,100,000	1,503,114	24.6%	-5.1	6,399,000	1,659,101	25.9%	-3.8	6,529,000	1,566,916	24.0%	-5.7	6,654,000	1,604,946	24.1%	-5.6
MINNESOTA	2,533,000	760,620	30.0%	2,719,000	729,577	26.8%	-3.2	2,887,000	987,147	34.2%	4.2	3,007,000	839,626	27.9%	-2.1	3,121,000	809,624	25.9%	-4.1
MISSISSIPPI	1,460,000	184,598	12.6%	1,590,000	256,608	16.1%	3.5	1,703,000	304,472	17.9%	5.2	1,753,000	326,826	18.6%	6.0	1,802,000	307,555	17.1%	4.4
MISSOURI	3,222,000	737,377	22.9%	3,390,000	812,238	24.0%	1.1	3,541,000	940,510	26.6%	3.7	3,642,000	903,035	24.8%	1.9	3,738,000	909,599	24.3%	1.4
MONTANA	471,000	124,436	26.4%	515,000	140,446	27.3%	0.9	552,000	162,305	29.4%	3.0	561,000	178,726	31.9%	5.4	569,000	171,870	30.2%	3.8
NEBRASKA	1,009,000	375,065	37.2%	1,067,000	385,630	36.1%	-1.0	1,115,000	451,328	40.5%	3.3	1,125,000	482,121	42.9%	5.7	1,135,000	425,726	37.5%	0.3
NEVADA	381,000	94,113	24.7%	480,000	24,124	5.0%	-19.7	578,000	63,163	10.9%	-13.8	701,000	155,166	22.1%	-2.6	818,000	159,569	19.5%	-5.2
NEW HAMPSHIRE	522,000	222,753	42.7%	593,000	148,998	25.1%	-17.5	660,000	186,869	28.3%	-14.4	728,000	250,602	34.4%	-8.2	793,000	251,566	31.7%	-10.9
NEW JERSEY	4,754,000	1,416,485	29.8%	4,951,000	1,217,932	24.6%	-5.2	5,133,000	1,368,981	26.7%	-3.1	5,298,000	1,470,836	27.8%	-2.0	5,455,000	1,411,840	25.9%	-3.9
NEW MEXICO	675,000	163,187	24.2%	780,000	214,718	27.5%	3.4	875,000	187,474	21.4%	-2.8	942,000	294,165	31.2%	7.1	1,008,000	236,263	23.4%	-0.7
NEW YORK	11,891,000	2,851,265	24.0%	11,949,000	2,341,925	19.6%	-4.4	12,020,000	2,706,661	22.5%	-1.5	12,182,000	2,722,510	22.3%	-1.6	12,337,000	2,463,459	20.0%	-4.0

United States House of Representatives General Elections (continued)

Republican Turnout for Election Years 1972–1988 (continued)

State	1972 Voting-age population	Turnout	%	1976 Voting-age population	Turnout	%	Difference from 1972	1980 Voting-age population	Turnout	%	Difference from 1972	1984 Voting-age population	Turnout	%	Difference from 1972	1988 Voting-age population	Turnout	%	Difference from 1972
NORTH CAROLINA	3,553,000	609,926	17.2%	3,907,000	549,410	14.1%	-3.1	4,239,000	769,144	18.1%	1.0	4,560,000	1,026,391	22.5%	5.3	4,867,000	876,362	18.0%	0.8
NORTH DAKOTA	409,000	195,360	47.8%	436,000	181,018	41.5%	-6.2	458,000	124,707	27.2%	-20.5	458,000	65,761	14.4%	-33.4	459,000	84,475	18.4%	-29.4
OHIO	7,053,000	2,071,040	29.4%	7,365,000	1,917,322	26.0%	-3.3	7,638,000	2,135,669	28.0%	-1.4	7,776,000	2,159,354	27.8%	-1.6	7,909,000	2,067,595	26.1%	-3.2
OKLAHOMA	1,833,000	310,180	16.9%	2,005,000	372,221	18.6%	1.6	2,152,000	391,209	18.2%	1.3	2,208,000	458,053	20.7%	3.8	2,260,000	361,538	16.0%	-0.9
OREGON	1,511,000	390,138	25.0%	1,700,000	262,514	15.4%	-10.5	1,879,000	438,738	23.3%	-2.5	1,954,000	548,201	28.1%	2.2	2,027,000	357,701	17.6%	-8.2
PENNSYLVANIA	8,073,000	2,281,484	28.3%	8,383,000	2,006,856	23.9%	-4.3	8,653,000	2,161,638	25.0%	-3.3	8,786,000	2,111,871	24.0%	-4.2	8,914,000	2,069,885	23.2%	-5.0
RHODE ISLAND	642,000	138,786	21.6%	660,000	113,518	17.2%	-4.4	677,000	172,901	25.5%	3.9	702,000	195,077	27.8%	6.2	726,000	250,724	34.5%	12.9
SOUTH CAROLINA	1,776,000	301,695	17.0%	1,990,000	279,390	14.0%	-2.9	2,186,000	399,039	18.3%	1.3	2,344,000	441,256	18.8%	1.8	2,495,000	439,476	17.6%	0.6
SOUTH DAKOTA	440,000	141,135	32.1%	463,000	221,188	47.8%	15.7	483,000	146,146	30.3%	-1.8	488,000	134,821	27.6%	-4.4	492,000	88,157	17.9%	-14.2
TENNESSEE	2,778,000	380,110	13.7%	3,051,000	452,877	14.8%	1.2	3,295,000	618,876	18.8%	5.1	3,444,000	589,118	17.1%	3.4	3,538,000	536,480	15.2%	1.5
TEXAS	7,729,000	835,185	10.8%	8,708,000	1,277,165	14.7%	3.9	9,608,000	1,608,636	16.7%	5.9	10,358,000	1,981,823	19.1%	8.3	11,077,000	1,834,135	16.6%	5.8
UTAH	701,000	203,481	29.0%	813,000	251,403	30.9%	1.9	912,000	351,996	38.6%	9.6	980,000	387,410	39.5%	10.5	1,046,000	341,056	32.6%	3.6
VERMONT	303,000	120,924	39.9%	334,000	124,458	37.3%	-2.6	363,000	154,274	42.5%	2.6	385,000	148,025	38.4%	-1.5	406,000	90,937	24.4%	-15.5
VIRGINIA	3,243,000	589,573	18.2%	3,549,000	670,400	18.9%	0.7	3,841,000	1,005,272	26.2%	8.0	4,144,000	1,003,211	24.2%	6.0	4,434,000	1,076,895	24.3%	6.1
WASHINGTON	2,396,000	438,683	18.3%	2,677,000	585,719	21.9%	3.6	2,937,000	792,836	27.0%	8.7	3,170,000	799,565	25.2%	6.9	3,392,000	742,844	21.9%	3.6
WEST VIRGINIA	1,221,000	243,906	20.0%	1,310,000	157,063	12.0%	-8.0	1,381,000	294,846	21.4%	1.4	1,365,000	275,160	20.2%	0.2	1,348,000	131,963	9.8%	-10.2
WISCONSIN	2,947,000	767,139	26.0%	3,149,000	760,740	24.2%	-1.9	3,326,000	1,055,472	31.7%	5.7	3,427,000	1,032,948	30.1%	4.1	3,523,000	997,265	28.3%	2.3
WYOMING	241,000	70,667	29.3%	284,000	66,147	23.3%	-6.0	320,000	116,361	36.4%	7.0	318,000	138,234	43.5%	14.1	316,000	118,350	37.5%	8.1
Total	137,283,000	32,822,920	23.9%	147,931,000	31,241,822	21.1%	-2.8	157,639,000	37,348,291	23.7%	-0.2	165,156,000	38,716,885	23.4%	-0.5	172,321,000	37,327,901	21.7%	-2.2

Democratic Turnout for Election Years 1972–1988

State	1972 Voting-age population	Turnout	%	1976 Voting-age population	Turnout	%	Difference from 1972*	1980 Voting-age population	Turnout	%	Difference from 1972	1984 Voting-age population	Turnout	%	Difference from 1972	1988 Voting-age population	Turnout	%	Difference from 1972
ALABAMA	2,346,000	544,070	23.2%	2,552,000	667,052	26.1%	2.9	2,732,000	628,133	23.0%	-0.2	2,833,000	821,773	29.0%	5.8	2,931,000	722,200	24.6%	1.4
ALASKA	202,000	53,651	26.6%	237,000	34,194	14.4%	-12.1	271,000	39,922	14.7%	-11.8	314,000	86,052	27.4%	0.8	355,000	71,881	20.2%	-6.3
ARIZONA	1,312,000	284,045	21.6%	1,615,000	355,747	22.0%	0.4	1,902,000	394,275	20.7%	-0.9	2,187,000	319,560	14.6%	-7.0	2,460,000	321,815	13.1%	-8.6
ARKANSAS	1,357,000	42,481	3.1%	1,495,000	260,997	17.5%	14.3	1,614,000	42,278	2.6%	-0.5	1,660,000	341,335	20.6%	17.4	1,704,000	353,164	20.7%	17.6
CALIFORNIA	13,275,000	4,209,586	31.7%	14,481,000	4,144,324	28.6%	-3.1	15,629,000	3,665,518	23.5%	-8.3	16,816,000	4,327,237	25.7%	-6.0	17,957,000	4,944,646	27.5%	-4.2
COLORADO	1,570,000	428,259	27.3%	1,829,000	456,103	24.9%	-2.3	2,058,000	505,654	24.6%	-2.7	2,196,000	436,041	19.9%	-7.4	2,328,000	645,469	27.7%	0.4
CONNECTICUT	2,011,000	657,265	32.7%	2,114,000	681,730	32.2%	-0.4	2,210,000	695,255	31.5%	-1.2	2,299,000	667,668	29.0%	-3.6	2,392,000	660,360	27.6%	-5.1
DELAWARE	367,000	83,230	22.7%	398,000	102,431	25.7%	3.1	426,000	81,227	19.1%	-3.6	457,000	142,070	31.1%	8.4	486,000	158,338	32.6%	9.9
DISTRICT OF COLUMBIA																			
FLORIDA	5,163,000	1,030,817	20.0%	6,159,000	1,125,782	18.3%	-1.7	7,102,000	1,813,164	25.5%	5.6	8,053,000	1,244,180	15.4%	-4.5	8,966,000	1,430,881	16.0%	-4.0

United States House of Representatives General Elections (continued)

United States House of Representatives General Elections *(continued)*

Democratic Turnout for Election Years 1972–1988 *(continued)*

State	1972 Voting-age population	1972 Turnout	1972 %	1976 Voting-age population	1976 Turnout	1976 %	1976 Difference from 1972	1980 Voting-age population	1980 Turnout	1980 %	1980 Difference from 1972	1984 Voting-age population	1984 Turnout	1984 %	1984 Difference from 1972	1988 Voting-age population	1988 Turnout	1988 %	1988 Difference from 1972
GEORGIA	3,167,000	638,826	20.2%	3,506,000	930,621	26.5%	6.4	3,832,000	973,540	25.4%	5.2	4,197,000	1,090,682	26.0%	5.8	4,548,000	1,115,343	24.5%	4.4
HAWAII	504,000	153,682	30.5%	572,000	184,166	32.2%	1.7	636,000	239,733	37.7%	7.2	692,000	227,261	32.8%	2.3	747,000	221,196	29.6%	-0.9
IDAHO	495,000	108,187	21.9%	568,000	161,899	28.5%	6.6	631,000	182,061	28.9%	7.0	655,000	164,857	25.2%	3.3	677,000	198,284	29.3%	7.4
ILLINOIS	7,333,000	2,146,823	29.3%	7,613,000	2,246,614	29.5%	0.2	7,851,000	2,048,658	26.1%	-3.2	7,928,000	2,367,383	29.9%	0.6	8,000,000	2,317,444	29.0%	-0.3
INDIANA	3,469,000	973,706	28.1%	3,672,000	1,166,368	31.8%	3.7	3,850,000	1,057,115	27.5%	-0.6	3,937,000	1,022,262	26.0%	-2.1	4,021,000	1,096,834	27.3%	-0.8
IOWA	1,905,000	616,378	32.4%	1,996,000	709,435	35.5%	3.2	2,070,000	642,763	31.1%	-1.3	2,055,000	595,265	29.0%	-3.4	2,042,000	580,200	28.4%	-3.9
KANSAS	1,547,000	280,653	18.1%	1,629,000	348,621	21.4%	3.3	1,701,000	404,549	23.8%	5.6	1,739,000	435,071	25.0%	6.9	1,774,000	366,757	20.7%	2.5
KENTUCKY	2,228,000	493,795	22.2%	2,413,000	605,680	25.1%	2.9	2,574,000	610,411	23.7%	1.6	2,636,000	656,661	24.9%	2.7	2,696,000	534,313	19.8%	-2.3
LOUISIANA	2,406,000	573,977	23.9%	2,646,000	624,098	23.6%	-0.3	2,847,000	437,416	15.4%	-8.5	2,892,000	402,430	13.9%	-9.9	2,935,000	350,172	11.9%	-11.9
MAINE	678,000	218,543	32.2%	740,000	151,255	20.4%	-11.8	797,000	137,845	17.3%	-14.9	845,000	162,319	19.2%	-13.0	890,000	276,335	31.0%	-1.2
MARYLAND	2,628,000	634,087	24.1%	2,817,000	789,029	28.0%	3.9	2,999,000	865,969	28.9%	4.7	3,202,000	954,873	29.8%	5.7	3,398,000	936,963	27.6%	3.4
MASSACHUSETTS	3,798,000	1,243,753	32.7%	3,952,000	1,509,521	38.2%	5.4	4,096,000	1,473,289	36.0%	3.2	4,228,000	1,618,131	38.3%	5.5	4,355,000	1,787,467	41.0%	8.3
MICHIGAN	5,755,000	1,535,707	26.7%	6,100,000	1,898,241	31.1%	4.4	6,399,000	1,877,335	29.3%	2.7	6,529,000	1,861,442	28.5%	1.8	6,654,000	1,824,103	27.4%	0.7
MINNESOTA	2,533,000	896,854	35.4%	2,719,000	1,039,999	38.2%	2.8	2,887,000	905,793	31.4%	-4.0	3,007,000	895,725	29.8%	-5.6	3,121,000	1,148,700	36.8%	1.4
MISSISSIPPI	1,460,000	387,389	26.5%	1,590,000	375,328	23.6%	-2.9	1,703,000	427,773	25.1%	-1.4	1,753,000	523,161	29.8%	3.3	1,802,000	606,715	33.7%	7.1
MISSOURI	3,222,000	1,092,405	33.9%	3,390,000	1,080,807	31.9%	-2.0	3,541,000	1,110,060	31.3%	-2.6	3,642,000	1,129,691	31.0%	-2.9	3,738,000	1,148,292	30.7%	-3.2
MONTANA	471,000	190,597	40.5%	515,000	180,459	35.0%	-5.4	552,000	176,236	31.9%	-8.5	561,000	187,443	33.4%	-7.1	569,000	193,347	34.0%	-6.5
NEBRASKA	1,009,000	193,644	19.2%	1,067,000	211,011	19.8%	0.6	1,115,000	167,415	15.0%	-4.2	1,125,000	167,617	14.9%	-4.3	1,135,000	229,524	20.2%	1.0
NEVADA	381,000	86,349	22.7%	480,000	153,996	32.1%	9.4	578,000	165,107	28.6%	5.9	701,000	109,372	15.6%	-7.1	818,000	176,927	21.6%	-1.0
NEW HAMPSHIRE	522,000	94,255	18.1%	593,000	173,598	29.3%	11.2	660,000	177,411	26.9%	8.8	728,000	119,111	16.4%	-1.7	793,000	176,300	22.2%	4.2
NEW JERSEY	4,754,000	1,390,869	29.3%	4,951,000	1,538,658	31.1%	1.8	5,133,000	1,316,100	25.6%	-3.6	5,298,000	1,508,599	28.5%	-0.8	5,455,000	1,336,325	24.5%	-4.8
NEW MEXICO	675,000	210,391	31.2%	780,000	185,363	23.8%	-7.4	875,000	175,988	20.1%	-11.1	942,000	201,131	21.4%	-9.8	1,008,000	209,076	20.7%	-10.4
NEW YORK	11,891,000	3,047,213	25.6%	11,949,000	3,501,443	29.3%	3.7	12,020,000	2,771,427	23.1%	-2.6	12,182,000	3,072,707	25.2%	-0.4	12,337,000	2,923,488	23.7%	-1.9
NORTH CAROLINA	3,553,000	734,627	20.7%	3,907,000	1,010,630	25.9%	5.2	4,239,000	964,493	22.8%	2.1	4,560,000	1,130,979	24.8%	4.1	4,867,000	1,108,311	22.8%	2.1
NORTH DAKOTA	409,000	72,850	17.8%	436,000	104,263	23.9%	6.1	458,000	166,437	36.3%	18.5	458,000	242,968	53.0%	35.2	459,000	212,583	46.3%	28.5
OHIO	7,053,000	1,684,303	23.9%	7,365,000	1,817,528	24.7%	0.8	7,638,000	1,788,410	23.4%	-0.5	7,776,000	2,134,198	27.4%	3.6	7,909,000	2,086,756	26.4%	2.5
OKLAHOMA	1,833,000	496,657	27.1%	2,005,000	683,293	34.1%	7.0	2,152,000	439,651	20.4%	-6.7	2,208,000	645,537	29.2%	2.1	2,260,000	405,665	17.9%	-9.1
OREGON	1,511,000	479,024	31.7%	1,709,000	599,135	35.1%	3.4	1,879,000	656,737	35.0%	3.2	1,954,000	655,092	33.5%	1.8	2,027,000	664,564	32.8%	1.1
PENNSYLVANIA	8,073,000	2,172,844	26.9%	8,383,000	2,410,267	28.8%	1.8	8,653,000	2,055,590	23.8%	-3.2	8,786,000	2,513,946	28.6%	1.7	8,914,000	2,117,078	23.8%	-3.2
RHODE ISLAND	642,000	243,444	37.9%	660,000	271,127	41.1%	3.2	677,000	213,726	31.6%	-6.4	702,000	194,942	27.8%	-10.2	726,000	140,270	19.3%	-18.6
SOUTH CAROLINA	1,776,000	328,860	18.5%	1,990,000	501,943	25.2%	6.7	2,186,000	408,296	18.7%	0.2	2,344,000	470,567	20.1%	1.6	2,495,000	549,652	22.0%	3.5
SOUTH DAKOTA	440,000	159,857	36.3%	463,000	72,501	15.7%	-20.7	483,000	173,357	35.9%	-0.4	488,000	181,401	37.2%	0.8	492,000	223,759	45.5%	9.1
TENNESSEE	2,778,000	277,869	10.0%	3,051,000	775,027	25.4%	15.4	3,295,000	663,796	20.1%	10.1	3,444,000	726,462	21.1%	11.1	3,538,000	844,210	23.9%	13.9

United States House of Representatives General Elections (continued)

Democratic Turnout for Election Years 1972–1988 (continued)

State	1972 Voting-age population	Turnout	%	1976 Voting-age population	Turnout	%	Difference from 1972	1980 Voting-age population	Turnout	%	Difference from 1972	1984 Voting-age population	Turnout	%	Difference from 1972	1988 Voting-age population	Turnout	%	Difference from 1972
TEXAS	7,729,000	2,032,183	26.3%	8,708,000	2,368,543	27.2%	0.9	9,608,000	2,405,026	25.0%	-1.3	10,358,000	2,695,028	26.0%	-0.3	11,077,000	2,735,940	24.7%	-1.6
UTAH	701,000	259,859	37.1%	813,000	266,562	32.8%	-4.3	912,000	232,426	25.5%	-11.6	980,000	208,223	21.2%	-15.8	1,046,000	260,123	24.9%	-12.2
VERMONT	303,000	65,062	21.5%	334,000	60,202	18.0%	-3.4					385,000	60,360	15.7%	-5.8	406,000	45,330	11.2%	-10.3
VIRGINIA	3,243,000	627,298	19.3%	3,549,000	666,082	18.8%	-0.6	3,841,000	486,084	12.7%	-6.7	4,144,000	795,009	19.2%	-0.2	4,434,000	801,831	18.1%	-1.3
WASHINGTON	2,396,000	857,621	35.8%	2,677,000	817,018	30.6%	-5.2	2,937,000	816,133	27.8%	-8.0	3,170,000	996,950	31.4%	-4.3	3,392,000	988,386	29.1%	-6.7
WEST VIRGINIA	1,221,000	477,294	39.1%	1,310,000	446,564	34.1%	-5.0	1,381,000	390,986	28.3%	-10.8	1,365,000	429,209	31.4%	-7.0	1,340,000	436,616	32.4%	-6.7
WISCONSIN	2,947,000	1,012,821	34.4%	3,149,000	1,190,287	37.8%	3.4	3,326,000	1,071,978	32.2%	-2.1	3,427,000	1,033,013	30.1%	-4.2	3,523,000	1,035,249	29.4%	-5.0
WYOMING	241,000	75,632	31.4%	284,000	85,721	30.2%	-1.2	320,000	53,338	16.7%	-14.7	318,000	45,857	14.4%	-17.0	316,000	56,527	17.9%	-13.5
Total	137,283,000	36,599,592	26.7%	147,931,000	41,742,193	28.2%	1.6	157,276,000	39,195,884	24.9%	-1.7	165,156,000	43,018,851	26.0%	-0.6	172,321,000	43,775,709	25.4%	-1.3

Other Turnout for Election Years 1972–1988

State	1972 Voting-age population	Turnout	%	1976 Voting-age population	Turnout	%	Difference from 1972*	1980 Voting-age population	Turnout	%	Difference from 1972	1984 Voting-age population	Turnout	%	Difference from 1972	1988 Voting-age population	Turnout	%	Difference from 1972
ALABAMA	2,346,000	44,936	1.9%	2,552,000	2,159	0.1%	-1.8	2,732,000	29,319	1.1%	-0.8	2,833,000	18,619	0.7%	-1.3	2,931,000	23,866	0.8%	1.1
ALASKA				237,000	292	0.1%		271,000	607	0.2%	0.1	314,000	6,803	2.2%	2.0	355,000	479	0.1%	0.0
ARIZONA				1,615,000	32,777	2.0%		1,902,000	25,653	1.3%	-0.7	2,187,000	20,826	1.0%	-1.1	2,460,000	36,890	1.5%	-0.5
ARKANSAS				1,495,000	8	0.0%		1,614,000	229	0.0%	0.0	1,660,000	31,070	1.9%	1.9				
CALIFORNIA	13,275,000	146,910	1.1%	14,481,000	89,204	0.6%	-0.5	15,629,000	335,598	2.1%	1.0	16,816,000	202,363	1.2%	0.1	17,957,000	262,879	1.5%	0.4
COLORADO	1,570,000	4,562	0.3%	1,829,000	29,361	1.6%	1.3	2,058,000	24,975	1.2%	0.9	2,196,000	31,893	1.5%	1.2	2,328,000	2,911	0.1%	-0.2
CONNECTICUT	2,011,000	2,897	0.1%	2,114,000	15,492	0.7%	0.6	2,210,000	3,813	0.2%	0.0	2,299,000	2,973	0.1%	0.0	2,392,000	3,433	0.1%	0.0
DELAWARE	367,000	1,384	0.4%	398,000	1,691	0.4%	0.0	426,000	1,560	0.4%	0.0	457,000	294	0.1%	-0.3				
DISTRICT OF COLUMBIA																			
FLORIDA	5,163,000	10	0.0%	6,159,000	19,491	0.3%	0.3	7,102,000	5,480	0.1%	0.1	8,053,000	1,188	0.0%	0.0	8,966,000	594	0.0%	0.0
GEORGIA	3,167,000	99	0.0%	3,506,000	578	0.0%	0.0	3,832,000	87	0.0%	0.0					4,548,000	18	0.0%	0.0
HAWAII				572,000	31,873	5.6%		636,000	21,009	3.3%	-2.3	692,000	7,737	1.1%	-4.5	747,000	21,784	2.9%	-2.7
IDAHO	495,000	5,560	1.1%													677,000	5,703	0.8%	-0.3
ILLINOIS	7,333,000	14,895	0.2%	7,613,000	6,569	0.1%	-0.1	7,851,000	6,196	0.1%	-0.1	7,928,000	8,192	0.1%	-0.1	8,000,000	3,937	0.0%	-0.2
INDIANA	3,469,000	2,884	0.1%	3,672,000	4,868	0.1%	0.0	3,850,000	2,354	0.1%	0.0	3,937,000	11,188	0.3%	0.2				
IOWA	1,905,000	1,933	0.1%	1,996,000	6,029	0.3%	0.2	2,070,000	4,795	0.2%	0.1	2,055,000	151	0.0%	-0.1	2,042,000	1,911	0.1%	0.0
KANSAS	1,547,000	15,812	1.0%	1,629,000	15,430	0.9%	-0.1	1,701,000	8,691	0.5%	-0.5	1,739,000	33,589	1.9%	0.9	1,774,000	242	0.0%	-1.0
KENTUCKY	2,228,000	4,362	0.2%	2,413,000	9,182	0.4%	0.2	2,574,000	3,372	0.1%	-0.1	2,636,000	2,199	0.1%	-0.1	2,696,000	6,205	0.2%	0.0
LOUISIANA	2,406,000	17,844	0.7%	2,646,000	25,657	1.0%	0.2	2,847,000	2,501	0.1%	-0.7	2,892,000	626	0.0%	-0.7				
MAINE				740,000	7,143	1.0%		797,000	21	0.0%	-1.0	845,000	4,268	0.5%	-0.5	890,000	198	0.0%	-0.9

United States House of Representatives General Elections (continued)

United States House of Representatives General Elections (continued)

Other Turnout for Election Years 1972–1988 (continued)

State	1972 Voting-age population	Turnout	%	1976 Voting-age population	Turnout	%	Difference from 1972	1980 Voting-age population	Turnout	%	Difference from 1972	1984 Voting-age population	Turnout	%	Difference from 1972	1988 Voting-age population	Turnout	%	Difference from 1972
MARYLAND				2,817,000	53,526	1.9%						3,202,000	4,492	0.1%	-1.8				
MASSACHUSETTS	3,798,000	106,554	2.8%	3,952,000	112,744	2.9%	0.0	4,096,000	25,165	0.6%	-2.2	4,228,000	23,971	0.6%	-2.2	4,355,000	74,055	1.7%	-1.1
MICHIGAN	5,755,000	27,290	0.5%	6,100,000	30,535	0.5%	0.0	6,399,000	51,718	0.8%	0.3	6,529,000	24,007	0.4%	-0.1	6,654,000	27,344	0.4%	-0.1
MINNESOTA	2,533,000	32,312	1.3%	2,719,000	24,928	0.9%	-0.4	2,887,000	11,973	0.4%	-0.9	3,007,000	4,646	0.2%	-1.1	3,121,000	10,766	0.3%	-0.9
MISSISSIPPI	1,460,000	16,086	1.1%	1,590,000	4,602	0.3%	-0.8	1,703,000	56,272	3.3%	2.2	1,753,000	18,865	1.1%	0.0	1,802,000	3,849	0.2%	-0.9
MISSOURI	3,222,000	2,846	0.1%	3,390,000	11,971	0.4%	0.3	3,541,000	0	0.0%	-0.1	3,642,000	6,851	0.2%	0.1	3,738,000	12,295	0.3%	0.2
MONTANA												561,000	4,660	0.8%					
NEBRASKA	1,009,000	137	0.0%	1,067,000	5,171	0.5%	0.5	1,115,000	6,518	0.6%	0.6	1,125,000	323	0.0%	0.0	1,135,000	1,028	0.1%	0.1
NEVADA				480,000	21,743	4.5%		578,000	16,317	2.8%	-1.7	701,000	6,086	0.9%	-3.7	818,000	7,677	0.9%	-3.6
NEW HAMPSHIRE	522,000	26	0.0%	593,000	2,578	0.4%	0.4	660,000	45	0.0%	0.0	728,000	3,184	0.4%	0.4	793,000	1,633	0.2%	0.2
NEW JERSEY	4,754,000	24,555	0.5%	4,951,000	54,203	1.1%	0.6	5,133,000	56,314	1.1%	0.6	5,298,000	12,502	0.2%	-0.3	5,455,000	27,939	0.5%	0.0
NEW MEXICO	675,000	75	0.0%	780,000	1,224	0.2%	0.1	875,000	45,343	5.2%	5.2	942,000	4,324	0.5%	0.4	1,008,000	3,839	0.4%	0.4
NEW YORK	11,891,000	238,725	2.0%	11,949,000	147,373	1.2%	-0.8	12,020,000	139,278	1.2%	-0.8	12,182,000	423,575	3.5%	1.5	12,337,000	118,957	1.0%	-1.0
NORTH CAROLINA	3,553,000	61,944	1.7%	3,907,000	11,638	0.3%	-1.4	4,239,000	3,160	0.1%	-1.7	4,560,000	285	0.0%	-1.7				
NORTH DAKOTA	409,000	511	0.1%	436,000	4,600	1.1%	0.9	458,000	1,932	0.4%	0.3					459,000	2,924	0.6%	0.5
OHIO	7,053,000	80,198	1.1%	7,365,000	106,904	1.5%	0.3	7,638,000	27,600	0.4%	-0.8	7,776,000	38,927	0.5%	-0.6	7,909,000	610	0.0%	-1.1
OKLAHOMA	1,833,000	10,244	0.6%	2,005,000	12,410	0.6%	0.1	2,152,000	4,722	0.2%	-0.3	2,208,000	7,294	0.3%	-0.2				
OREGON	1,511,000	568	0.0%	1,709,000	65,015	3.8%	3.8	1,879,000	10,965	0.6%	0.5	1,954,000	198	0.0%	0.0	2,027,000	1,331	0.1%	0.0
PENNSYLVANIA	8,073,000	8,461	0.1%	8,383,000	17,132	0.2%	0.1	8,653,000	103,528	1.2%	1.1	8,786,000	17,160	0.2%	0.1	8,914,000	10,211	0.1%	0.0
RHODE ISLAND	642,000	5,762	0.9%	660,000	4,269	0.6%	-0.3	677,000	6	0.0%	-0.9	702,000	12	0.0%	-0.9	726,000	10	0.0%	-0.9
SOUTH CAROLINA	1,776,000	102	0.0%	1,990,000	2,191	0.1%	0.1	2,186,000	22,734	1.0%	1.0	2,344,000	15,779	0.7%	0.7	2,495,000	2,244	0.1%	0.1
SOUTH DAKOTA				463,000	1,282	0.3%													
TENNESSEE	2,778,000	5,192	0.2%	3,051,000	23,156	0.8%	0.6	3,295,000	21,525	0.7%	0.5	3,444,000	155	0.0%	-0.2	3,538,000	28,631	0.8%	0.6
TEXAS	7,729,000	18,581	0.2%	8,708,000	17,747	0.2%	0.0	9,608,000	54,870	0.6%	0.3	10,358,000	3,534	0.0%	-0.2	11,077,000	99,615	0.9%	0.7
UTAH	701,000	9,728	1.4%	813,000	25,866	3.2%	1.8	912,000	7,913	0.9%	-0.5	980,000	5,449	0.6%	-0.8	1,046,000	7,489	0.7%	-0.7
VERMONT	303,000	42	0.0%	334,000	123	0.0%	0.0	363,000	40,423	11.1%	11.1	385,000	17,912	4.7%	4.6	406,000	95,864	23.6%	23.6
VIRGINIA	3,243,000	54,117	1.7%	3,549,000	126,340	3.6%	1.9	3,841,000	61,479	1.6%	-0.1	4,144,000	39,385	1.0%	-0.7	4,434,000	12,102	0.3%	-1.4
WASHINGTON	2,396,000	5,529	0.2%	2,677,000	21,935	0.8%	0.6	2,937,000	17,276	0.6%	0.4	3,170,000	11,518	0.4%	0.1				
WEST VIRGINIA				1,310,000	59,467	4.5%													
WISCONSIN	2,947,000	21,134	0.7%	3,149,000	11,228	0.4%	-0.4	3,326,000	6,878	0.2%	-0.5	3,427,000	9,397	0.3%	-0.4	3,523,000	2,968	0.1%	-0.6
WYOMING												318,000	3,813	1.2%		316,000	2,774	0.9%	-0.3
Total	127,848,000	994,807	0.8%	146,564,000	1,279,705	0.9%	0.1	151,273,000	1,270,214	0.8%	0.1	157,993,000	1,092,283	0.7%	-0.1	146,849,000	927,205	0.6%	-0.1

*Percentage point difference between turnout in current year and initial year listed in chart. If data do not appear for a state in the initial year listed, the difference is calculated from the first year in which data do appear for that state.

UNITED STATES PRESIDENTIAL PRIMARY ELECTIONS

Election Years 1972–1988

State*	1972 Voting-age population	Turnout	%	1976 Voting-age population	Turnout	%	Difference from 1972**	1980 Voting-age population	Turnout	%	Difference from 1972	1984 Voting-age population	Turnout	%	Difference from 1972	1988 Voting-age population	Turnout	%	Difference from 1972
ALABAMA								2,722,000	448,817	16.5%						2,917,000	619,207	21.2%	4.7
ALASKA																			
ARIZONA																			
ARKANSAS				1,475,000	534,251	36.2%										1,698,000	565,849	33.3%	-2.9
CALIFORNIA	13,100,000	5,048,440	44.6%	14,305,000	5,860,212	41.0%	-3.7	15,510,000	5,928,041	38.2%	-6.4	16,650,000	4,845,878	29.1%	-15.5	17,790,000	5,282,743	29.7%	-14.9
COLORADO																			
CONNECTICUT								2,201,000	392,559	17.8%						2,379,000	345,566	14.5%	-3.3
DELAWARE																			
DISTRICT OF COLUMBIA								473,000	71,679	15.2%		465,000	108,423	23.3%	8.2	456,000	92,772	20.3%	5.2
FLORIDA	5,017,000	1,678,761	33.5%	6,013,000	1,910,149	31.8%	-1.7	7,007,000	1,712,998	24.4%	-9.0	7,919,000	1,526,340	19.3%	-14.2	8,832,000	2,174,520	24.6%	-0.8
GEORGIA				3,457,000	690,943	20.0%		3,795,000	584,951	15.4%	-4.6	4,147,000	735,334	17.7%	-2.3	4,497,000	1,023,680	22.8%	2.8
HAWAII																			
IDAHO				557,000	164,198	29.5%		628,000	185,361	29.5%	0.0	651,000	160,409	24.6%	-4.8	674,000	119,645	17.8%	-11.7
ILLINOIS	7,293,000	1,258,713	17.3%	7,572,000	2,087,807	27.6%	10.3	7,843,000	2,331,148	29.7%	12.5	7,917,000	2,254,503	28.5%	11.2	7,990,000	2,362,184	29.6%	12.3
INDIANA	3,440,000	1,168,527	34.0%	3,643,000	1,245,681	34.2%	0.2	3,841,000	1,157,754	30.1%	-3.8	3,925,000	1,145,514	29.2%	-4.8	4,009,000	1,083,363	27.0%	-6.9
IOWA																			
KANSAS								1,696,000	479,316	28.3%									
KENTUCKY				2,387,000	439,534	18.4%		2,568,000	335,126	13.1%	-5.4					2,687,000	440,123	16.4%	-2.0
LOUISIANA								2,842,000	400,424	14.1%		2,885,000	335,497	11.6%	-2.5	2,929,000	769,231	26.3%	12.2
MAINE																			
MARYLAND	2,600,000	683,380	26.3%	2,790,000	757,717	27.2%	0.9	2,978,000	644,393	21.6%	-4.6	3,174,000	580,549	18.3%	-8.0	3,369,000	732,089	21.7%	-4.6
MASSACHUSETTS	3,774,000	740,655	19.6%	3,930,000	924,270	23.5%	3.9	4,084,000	1,308,149	32.0%	12.4	4,210,000	696,899	16.6%	-3.1	4,336,000	953,534	22.0%	2.4
MICHIGAN	5,705,000	1,924,816	33.7%	6,050,000	1,771,480	29.3%	-4.5	6,385,000	673,600	10.5%	-23.2								
MINNESOTA																			
MISSISSIPPI																1,795,000	517,943	28.9%	
MISSOURI																3,724,000	928,705	24.9%	
MONTANA				509,000	196,620	38.6%		551,000	209,482	38.0%	-0.6	560,000	106,101	18.9%	-19.7	568,000	206,830	36.4%	-2.2
NEBRASKA	1,001,000	386,409	38.6%	1,058,000	383,427	36.2%	-2.4	1,114,000	359,084	32.2%	-6.4	1,124,000	295,503	26.3%	-12.3	1,133,000	373,057	32.9%	-5.7
NEVADA				466,000	122,991	26.4%		567,000	114,343	20.2%	-6.2								
NEW HAMPSHIRE	512,000	206,062	40.2%	583,000	194,055	33.3%	-7.0	654,000	259,087	39.6%	-0.6	718,000	176,701	24.6%	-15.6	783,000	279,717	35.7%	-4.5
NEW JERSEY				4,922,000	602,961	12.3%		5,117,000	838,885	16.4%	4.1	5,274,000	916,615	17.4%	5.1	5,432,000	878,647	16.2%	3.9
NEW MEXICO	658,000	208,762	31.7%					867,000	218,910	25.2%	-6.5	933,000	230,397	24.7%	-7.0	998,000	264,588	26.5%	-5.2
NEW YORK																			

United States Presidential Primary Elections (continued)

United States Presidential Primary Elections *(continued)*

Election Years 1972–1988 *(continued)*

State	1972 Voting-age population	1972 Turnout	1972 %	1976 Voting-age population	1976 Turnout	1976 %	1976 Difference from 1972	1980 Voting-age population	1980 Turnout	1980 %	1980 Difference from 1972	1984 Voting-age population	1984 Turnout	1984 %	1984 Difference from 1972	1988 Voting-age population	1988 Turnout	1988 %	1988 Difference from 1972
NORTH CAROLINA	3,501,000	989,309	28.3%	3,856,000	798,559	20.7%	-7.5	4,207,000	905,653	21.5%	-6.7					4,822,000	953,759	19.8%	-8.5
NORTH DAKOTA												458,000	77,664	17.0%		459,000	42,839	9.3%	-7.6
OHIO	7,007,000	1,905,158	27.2%	7,319,000	2,070,131	28.3%	1.1	7,623,000	2,043,183	26.8%	-0.4	7,757,000	2,105,405	27.1%	0.0	7,890,000	2,233,436	28.3%	1.1
OKLAHOMA																2,252,000	601,665	26.7%	
OREGON	1,482,000	690,654	46.6%	1,680,000	731,167	43.5%	-3.1	1,872,000	683,688	36.5%	-10.1	1,944,000	643,025	33.1%	-13.5	2,017,000	658,069	32.6%	-14.0
PENNSYLVANIA	8,028,000	1,559,640	19.4%	8,338,000	2,181,702	26.2%	6.7	8,639,000	2,854,962	33.0%	13.6	8,768,000	2,277,500	26.0%	6.5	8,895,000	2,378,239	26.7%	7.3
RHODE ISLAND	640,000	43,475	6.8%	657,000	74,700	11.4%	4.6	675,000	43,662	6.5%	-0.3	699,000	46,746	6.7%	-0.1	722,000	65,064	9.0%	2.2
SOUTH CAROLINA																			
SOUTH DAKOTA	437,000	80,837	18.5%	459,000	142,748	31.1%	12.6	482,000	151,668	31.5%	13.0					492,000	165,011	33.5%	15.0
TENNESSEE	2,738,000	607,210	22.2%	3,011,000	576,613	19.2%	-3.0	3,279,000	489,890	14.9%	-7.2	3,423,000	404,984	11.8%	-10.3	3,568,000	830,489	23.3%	1.1
TEXAS								9,533,000	1,904,123	20.0%						10,972,000	2,782,001	25.4%	5.4
UTAH																			
VERMONT				330,000	70,871	21.5%		360,000	105,314	29.3%	7.8	382,000	107,702	28.2%	6.7	403,000	98,623	24.5%	3.0
VIRGINIA																4,391,000	599,041	13.6%	
WASHINGTON																			
WEST VIRGINIA				1,297,000	528,269	40.7%		1,382,000	455,950	33.0%	-7.7	1,367,000	506,241	37.0%	-3.7	1,351,000	450,197	33.3%	-7.4
WISCONSIN	2,917,000	1,415,028	48.5%	3,119,000	1,332,340	42.7%	-5.8	3,317,000	1,537,472	46.4%	-2.2	3,413,000	930,581	27.3%	-21.2	3,509,000	1,374,076	39.2%	-9.4
WYOMING																			
Total	69,850,000	21,395,836	30.6%	89,783,000	26,393,396	29.4%	-1.2	114,812,000	29,829,672	26.0%	-4.6	88,763,000	21,214,511	23.9%	-6.7	130,739,000	33,246,502	25.4%	-5.2

*Overall primary turnout reflects only states with primaries in both parties. To find single party primary results, see partisan primary charts.

**Percentage point difference between turnout in current year and initial year listed in chart. If data do not appear for a state in the initial year listed, the difference is calculated from the first year in which data do appear for that state.

UNITED STATES PRESIDENTIAL PRIMARY ELECTIONS

Republican Turnout for Election Years 1972–1988

State	1972 Voting-age population	Turnout	%	1976 Voting-age population	Turnout	%	Difference from 1972*	1980 Voting-age population	Turnout	%	Difference from 1972	1984 Voting-age population	Turnout	%	Difference from 1972	1988 Voting-age population	Turnout	%	Difference from 1972
ALABAMA								2,722,000	211,353	7.8%						2,917,000	213,565	7.3%	-0.4
ALASKA																			
ARIZONA																			
ARKANSAS				1,475,000	32,451	2.2%										1,698,000	68,305	4.0%	1.8
CALIFORNIA	13,100,000	2,203,022	17.4%	14,305,000	2,450,511	17.1%	-0.3	15,510,000	3,363,969	21.7%	4.3	16,650,000	1,874,975	11.3%	-6.2	17,790,000	2,193,579	12.3%	-5.1
COLORADO																			
CONNECTICUT								2,201,000	182,284	8.3%						2,379,000	104,171	4.4%	-3.9
DELAWARE																			
DISTRICT OF COLUMBIA								473,000	7,529	1.6%		465,000	5,692	1.2%	-0.4	456,000	6,720	1.5%	-0.1
FLORIDA	5,017,000	414,207	8.3%	6,013,000	609,819	10.1%	1.9	7,007,000	614,995	8.8%	0.5	7,919,000	344,150	4.3%	-3.9	8,832,000	901,222	10.2%	1.9
GEORGIA				3,457,000	188,472	5.5%		3,795,000	200,171	5.3%	-0.2	4,147,000	50,793	1.2%	-4.2	4,497,000	400,928	8.9%	3.5
HAWAII																			
IDAHO				557,000	89,793	16.1%		628,000	134,879	21.5%	5.4	651,000	105,687	16.2%	0.1	674,000	68,275	10.1%	-6.0
ILLINOIS	7,293,000	33,569	0.5%	7,572,000	775,893	10.2%	9.8	7,843,000	1,130,081	14.4%	13.9	7,917,000	595,078	7.5%	7.1	7,990,000	861,256	10.8%	10.3
INDIANA	3,440,000	417,069	12.1%	3,643,000	631,292	17.3%	5.2	3,841,000	568,313	14.8%	2.7	3,925,000	428,559	10.9%	-1.2	4,009,000	437,655	10.9%	-1.2
IOWA																			
KANSAS								1,696,000	285,398	16.8%									
KENTUCKY				2,387,000	133,528	5.6%		2,568,000	94,795	3.7%	-1.9					2,687,000	121,402	4.5%	-1.1
LOUISIANA								2,842,000	41,683	1.5%		2,885,000	16,687	0.6%	-0.9	2,929,000	144,781	4.9%	3.5
MAINE																			
MARYLAND	2,600,000	115,249	4.4%	2,790,000	165,971	5.9%	1.5	2,978,000	167,303	5.6%	1.2	3,174,000	73,663	2.3%	-2.1	3,369,000	200,754	6.0%	1.5
MASSACHUSETTS	3,774,000	122,139	3.2%	3,930,000	188,449	4.8%	1.6	4,084,000	400,826	9.8%	6.6	4,210,000	65,937	1.6%	-1.7	4,336,000	240,945	5.6%	2.3
MICHIGAN	5,705,000	336,743	5.9%	6,050,000	1,062,814	17.6%	11.7	6,385,000	595,176	9.3%	3.4								
MINNESOTA																			
MISSISSIPPI								1,698,000	25,751	1.5%						1,795,000	158,526	8.8%	7.3
MISSOURI																3,724,000	400,300	10.7%	
MONTANA				509,000	89,779	17.6%		551,000	79,423	14.4%	-3.2	560,000	71,887	12.8%	-4.8	568,000	85,896	15.1%	-2.5
NEBRASKA	1,001,000	194,272	19.4%	1,058,000	208,414	19.7%	0.3	1,114,000	205,203	18.4%	-1.0	1,124,000	146,648	13.0%	-6.4	1,133,000	204,049	18.0%	-1.4
NEVADA				466,000	47,749	10.2%		567,000	47,395	8.4%	-1.9								
NEW HAMPSHIRE	512,000	117,208	22.9%	583,000	111,674	19.2%	-3.7	654,000	147,157	22.5%	-0.4	718,000	75,570	10.5%	-12.4	783,000	157,556	20.1%	-2.8
NEW JERSEY				4,922,000	242,122	4.9%		5,117,000	277,977	5.4%	0.5	5,274,000	240,054	4.6%	-0.4	5,432,000	239,235	4.4%	-0.5
NEW MEXICO	658,000	55,469	8.4%					867,000	59,546	6.9%	-1.6	933,000	42,994	4.6%	-3.8	998,000	85,842	8.6%	0.2
NEW YORK																			

United States Presidential Primary Elections (continued)

United States Presidential Primary Elections (continued)

Republican Turnout for Election Years 1972–1988 (continued)

State	1972 Voting-age population	Turnout	%	1976 Voting-age population	Turnout	%	Difference from 1972	1980 Voting-age population	Turnout	%	Difference from 1972	1984 Voting-age population	Turnout	%	Difference from 1972	1988 Voting-age population	Turnout	%	Difference from 1972
NORTH CAROLINA	3,501,000	167,899	4.8%	3,856,000	193,727	5.0%	0.2	4,207,000	168,391	4.0%	-0.8					4,822,000	273,801	5.7%	0.9
NORTH DAKOTA												458,000	44,109	9.6%		459,000	39,434	8.6%	-1.0
OHIO	7,007,000	692,828	9.9%	7,319,000	935,757	12.8%	2.9	7,623,000	856,773	11.2%	1.4	7,757,000	658,169	8.5%	-1.4	7,890,000	794,904	10.1%	0.2
OKLAHOMA																2,252,000	208,938	9.3%	
OREGON	1,482,000	282,010	19.0%	1,680,000	298,535	17.8%	-1.3	1,872,000	315,366	16.8%	-2.2	1,944,000	243,346	12.5%	-6.5	2,017,000	270,278	13.4%	-5.6
PENNSYLVANIA	8,028,000	184,801	2.3%	8,338,000	796,660	9.6%	7.3	8,639,000	1,241,411	14.4%	12.1	8,768,000	621,206	7.1%	4.8	8,895,000	870,549	9.8%	7.5
RHODE ISLAND	640,000	5,611	0.9%	657,000	14,352	2.2%	1.3	675,000	5,335	0.8%	-0.1	699,000	2,235	0.3%	-0.6	722,000	16,035	2.2%	1.3
SOUTH CAROLINA								2,170,000	145,501	6.7%						2,474,000	195,292	7.9%	1.2
SOUTH DAKOTA	437,000	52,820	12.1%	459,000	84,077	18.3%	6.2	482,000	82,905	17.2%	5.1					492,000	93,405	19.0%	6.9
TENNESSEE	2,738,000	114,489	4.2%	3,011,000	242,535	8.1%	3.9	3,279,000	195,210	6.0%	1.8	3,423,000	82,921	2.4%	-1.8	3,568,000	254,231	7.1%	2.9
TEXAS								9,533,000	526,769	5.5%		10,253,000	319,839	3.1%	-2.4	10,972,000	1,014,956	9.3%	3.7
UTAH																			
VERMONT				330,000	32,157	9.7%		360,000	65,611	18.2%	8.5	382,000	33,643	8.8%	-0.9	403,000	47,832	11.9%	2.1
VIRGINIA																4,391,000	234,142	5.3%	
WASHINGTON																			
WEST VIRGINIA				1,297,000	155,692	12.0%		1,382,000	138,016	10.0%	-2.0	1,367,000	136,996	10.0%	-2.0	1,351,000	134,803	10.0%	-2.0
WISCONSIN	2,917,000	286,444	9.8%	3,119,000	591,812	19.0%	9.2	3,317,000	907,853	27.4%	17.5	3,413,000	294,813	8.6%	-1.2	3,509,000	359,294	10.2%	0.4
WYOMING																			
Total	69,850,000	5,876,749	8.4%	89,783,000	10,374,035	11.6%	3.1	118,680,000	13,490,348	11.4%	3.0	99,016,000	6,575,651	6.6%	-1.8	133,213,000	12,102,856	9.1%	0.7

Democratic Turnout for Election Years 1972–1988

State	1972 Voting-age population	Turnout	%	1976 Voting-age population	Turnout	%	Difference from 1972*	1980 Voting-age population	Turnout	%	Difference from 1972	1984 Voting-age population	Turnout	%	Difference from 1972	1988 Voting-age population	Turnout	%	Difference from 1972
ALABAMA								2,722,000	237,464	8.7%		2,820,000	428,283	15.2%	6.5	2,917,000	405,642	13.9%	5.2
ALASKA																			
ARIZONA																			
ARKANSAS				1,475,000	501,800	34.0%		1,609,000	448,290	27.9%	-6.2					1,698,000	497,544	29.3%	-4.7
CALIFORNIA	13,100,000	3,564,518	27.2%	14,305,000	3,409,701	23.8%	-3.4	15,510,000	2,564,072	16.5%	-10.7	16,650,000	2,970,903	17.8%	-9.4	17,790,000	3,089,164	17.4%	-9.8
COLORADO																			
CONNECTICUT								2,201,000	210,275	9.6%		2,290,000	220,842	9.6%	0.1	2,379,000	241,395	10.1%	0.6
DELAWARE																			
DISTRICT OF COLUMBIA	505,000	29,560	5.9%	489,000	33,291	6.8%	1.0	473,000	64,150	13.6%	7.7	465,000	102,731	22.1%	16.2	456,000	86,052	18.9%	13.0
FLORIDA	5,017,000	1,264,554	25.2%	6,013,000	1,300,330	21.6%	-3.6	7,007,000	1,098,003	15.7%	-9.5	7,919,000	1,182,190	14.9%	-10.3	8,832,000	1,273,298	14.4%	-10.8

United States Presidential Primary Elections (continued)

Democratic Turnout for Election Years 1972–1988 (continued)

State	1972 Voting-age population	Turnout	%	1976 Voting-age population	Turnout	%	Difference from 1972	1980 Voting-age population	Turnout	%	Difference from 1972	1984 Voting-age population	Turnout	%	Difference from 1972	1988 Voting-age population	Turnout	%	Difference from 1972
GEORGIA				3,457,000	502,471	14.5%		3,795,000	384,780	10.1%	-4.4	4,147,000	684,541	16.5%	2.0	4,497,000	622,752	13.8%	-0.7
HAWAII																			
IDAHO				557,000	74,405	13.4%		628,000	50,482	8.0%	-5.3	651,000	54,722	8.4%	-5.0	674,000	51,370	7.6%	-5.7
ILLINOIS	7,293,000	1,225,144	16.8%	7,572,000	1,311,914	17.3%	0.5	7,843,000	1,201,067	15.3%	-1.5	7,917,000	1,659,425	21.0%	4.2	7,990,000	1,500,928	18.8%	2.0
INDIANA	3,440,000	731,458	21.0%	3,643,000	614,389	16.9%	-5.0	3,841,000	589,441	15.3%	-6.5	3,925,000	716,955	18.3%	-3.6	4,009,000	645,708	16.1%	-5.7
IOWA																			
KANSAS								1,696,000	193,918	11.4%									
KENTUCKY				2,387,000	306,006	12.8%		2,568,000	240,331	9.4%	-3.5					2,687,000	318,721	11.9%	-1.0
LOUISIANA								2,842,000	350,741	12.6%		2,885,000	318,810	11.1%	-1.6	2,929,000	624,450	21.3%	8.7
MAINE																			
MARYLAND	2,600,000	568,131	21.9%	2,790,000	591,746	21.2%	-0.6	2,978,000	477,090	16.0%	-5.8	3,174,000	506,886	16.0%	-5.9	3,369,000	531,335	15.8%	-6.1
MASSACHUSETTS	3,774,000	618,516	16.4%	3,930,000	735,821	18.7%	2.3	4,084,000	907,323	22.2%	5.8	4,210,000	630,962	15.0%	-1.4	4,336,000	712,589	16.4%	0.0
MICHIGAN	5,705,000	1,588,073	27.8%	6,050,000	708,666	11.7%	-16.1	6,385,000	78,424	1.2%	-26.6								
MINNESOTA																			
MISSISSIPPI																1,795,000	359,417	20.0%	
MISSOURI																3,724,000	528,405	14.2%	
MONTANA				509,000	106,841	21.0%		551,000	130,059	23.6%	2.6	560,000	34,214	6.1%	-14.9	568,000	120,934	21.3%	0.3
NEBRASKA	1,001,000	192,137	19.2%	1,058,000	175,013	16.5%	-2.7	1,114,000	153,881	13.8%	-5.4	1,124,000	148,855	13.2%	-6.0	1,133,000	169,008	14.9%	-4.3
NEVADA				466,000	75,242	16.1%		567,000	66,948	11.8%	-4.3								
NEW HAMPSHIRE	512,000	88,854	17.4%	583,000	82,381	14.1%	-3.2	654,000	111,930	17.1%	-0.2	718,000	101,131	14.1%	-3.3	783,000	122,161	15.6%	-1.8
NEW JERSEY	4,724,000	76,834	1.6%	4,922,000	360,839	7.3%	5.7	5,117,000	560,908	11.0%	9.3	5,274,000	676,561	12.8%	11.2	5,432,000	639,412	11.8%	10.1
NEW MEXICO	658,000	153,793	23.3%					867,000	159,364	18.4%	-4.9	933,000	187,403	20.1%	-3.2	998,000	178,746	17.9%	-5.4
NEW YORK								12,004,000	989,062	8.2%		12,160,000	1,387,950	11.4%	3.2	12,315,000	1,575,186	12.8%	4.6
NORTH CAROLINA	3,501,000	821,410	23.5%	3,856,000	604,832	15.7%	-7.8	4,207,000	737,262	17.5%	-5.9	4,515,000	960,857	21.3%	-2.2	4,822,000	679,958	14.1%	-9.4
NORTH DAKOTA												458,000	33,555	7.3%		459,000	3,405	0.7%	-6.6
OHIO	7,007,000	1,212,330	17.3%	7,319,000	1,134,374	15.5%	-1.8	7,623,000	1,186,410	15.6%	-1.7	7,757,000	1,447,236	18.7%	1.4	7,890,000	1,438,532	18.2%	0.9
OKLAHOMA																2,252,000	392,727	17.4%	
OREGON	1,482,000	408,644	27.6%	1,680,000	432,632	25.8%	-1.8	1,872,000	368,322	19.7%	-7.9	1,944,000	399,679	20.6%	-7.0	2,017,000	387,791	19.2%	-8.3
PENNSYLVANIA	8,028,000	1,374,839	17.1%	8,338,000	1,385,042	16.6%	-0.5	8,639,000	1,613,551	18.7%	1.6	8,768,000	1,656,294	18.9%	1.8	8,895,000	1,507,690	16.9%	-0.2
RHODE ISLAND	640,000	37,864	5.9%	657,000	60,348	9.2%	3.3	675,000	38,327	5.7%	-0.2	699,000	44,511	6.4%	0.5	722,000	49,029	6.8%	0.9
SOUTH CAROLINA																			
SOUTH DAKOTA	437,000	28,017	6.4%	459,000	58,671	12.8%	6.4	482,000	68,763	14.3%	7.9	488,000	52,561	10.8%	4.4	492,000	71,606	14.6%	8.1
TENNESSEE	2,738,000	492,721	18.0%	3,011,000	334,078	11.1%	-6.9	3,279,000	294,680	9.0%	-9.0	3,423,000	322,063	9.4%	-8.6	3,568,000	576,258	16.2%	-1.8

United States Presidential Primary Elections (continued)

United States Presidential Primary Elections *(continued)*

Democratic Turnout for Election Years 1972–1988 *(continued)*

State	1972 Voting-age population	Turnout	%	1976 Voting-age population	Turnout	%	Difference from 1972	1980 Voting-age population	Turnout	%	Difference from 1972	1984 Voting-age population	Turnout	%	Difference from 1972	1988 Voting-age population	Turnout	%	Difference from 1972
TEXAS								9,533,000	1,377,354	14.4%						10,972,000	1,767,045	16.1%	1.7
UTAH																			
VERMONT				330,000	38,714	11.7%		360,000	39,703	11.0%	-0.7	382,000	74,059	19.4%	7.7	403,000	50,791	12.6%	0.9
VIRGINIA																4,391,000	364,899	8.3%	
WASHINGTON																			
WEST VIRGINIA	1,208,000	368,484	30.5%	1,297,000	372,577	28.7%	-1.8	1,382,000	317,934	23.0%	-7.5	1,367,000	369,245	27.0%	-3.5	1,351,000	315,394	23.3%	-7.2
WISCONSIN	2,917,000	1,128,584	38.7%	3,119,000	740,528	23.7%	-14.9	3,317,000	629,619	19.0%	-19.7	3,413,000	635,768	18.6%	-20.1	3,509,000	1,014,782	28.9%	-9.8
WYOMING																			
Total	76,287,000	15,993,965	21.0%	90,272,000	16,052,652	17.8%	-3.2	128,425,000	17,947,928	14.0%	-7.0	111,036,000	18,009,192	16.2%	-4.7	143,054,000	22,914,124	16.0%	-4.9

Other Turnout for Election Years 1972–1988

State	1972 Voting-age population	Turnout	%	1976 Voting-age population	Turnout	%	Difference from 1972*	1980 Voting-age population	Turnout	%	Difference from 1972	1984 Voting-age population	Turnout	%	Difference from 1972	1988 Voting-age population	Turnout	%	Difference from 1972
TENNESSEE												3,423,000	630	0.0%					

*Percentage point difference between turnout in current year and initial year listed in chart. If data do not appear for a state in the initial year listed, the difference is calculated from the first year in which data do appear for that state.

STATE GUBERNATORIAL PRIMARY ELECTIONS

Election Years 1972–1988

State*	1972 Voting-age population	1972 Turnout	1972 %	1976 Voting-age population	1976 Turnout	1976 %	1976 Difference from 1972**	1980 Voting-age population	1980 Turnout	1980 %	1980 Difference from 1972	1984 Voting-age population	1984 Turnout	1984 %	1984 Difference from 1972	1988 Voting-age population	1988 Turnout	1988 %	1988 Difference from 1972
ALABAMA																			
ALASKA																			
ARIZONA																			
ARKANSAS				1,475,000	548,758	37.2%		1,609,000	453,572	28.2%	9.0	1,654,000	511,726	30.9%	6.3				
CALIFORNIA																			
COLORADO																			
CONNECTICUT																			
DELAWARE																			
DISTRICT OF COLUMBIA																			
FLORIDA																			
GEORGIA																			
HAWAII																			
IDAHO																			
ILLINOIS	7,293,000	2,015,694	27.6%	7,572,000	2,231,910	29.5%	1.8												
INDIANA												3,925,000	1,054,928	26.9%					
IOWA																			
KANSAS																			
KENTUCKY																			
LOUISIANA	2,371,000	1,184,614	50.0%																
MAINE																			
MARYLAND																			
MASSACHUSETTS																			
MICHIGAN																			
MINNESOTA																			
MISSISSIPPI																			
MISSOURI	3,197,000	1,003,191	31.4%	3,365,000	1,144,605	34.0%	2.6	3,530,000	1,017,636	28.8%	-2.6	3,627,000	878,483	24.2%	-7.2				
MONTANA	465,000	224,098	48.2%					551,000	207,930	37.7%	-10.5					568,000	179,152	31.5%	16.7
NEBRASKA																			
NEVADA																			
NEW HAMPSHIRE	512,000	138,842	27.1%	583,000	134,171	23.0%	-4.1	654,000	144,888	22.2%	-5.0	718,000	108,845	15.2%	-12.0				
NEW JERSEY																			
NEW MEXICO																			
NEW YORK																			

State Gubernatorial Primary Elections (continued)

State Gubernatorial Primary Elections (continued)

Election Years 1972–1988 (continued)

State	1972 Voting-age population	1972 Turnout	1972 %	1976 Voting-age population	1976 Turnout	1976 %	1976 Difference from 1972	1980 Voting-age population	1980 Turnout	1980 %	1980 Difference from 1972	1984 Voting-age population	1984 Turnout	1984 %	1984 Difference from 1972	1988 Voting-age population	1988 Turnout	1988 %	1988 Difference from 1972
NORTH CAROLINA	3,501,000	978,688	28.0%	3,856,000	783,673	20.3%	-7.6	4,207,000	901,293	21.4%	-6.5	4,515,000	1,096,153	24.3%	-3.7				
NORTH DAKOTA	405,000	129,632	32.0%																
OHIO																			
OKLAHOMA																			
OREGON																			
PENNSYLVANIA																			
RHODE ISLAND																			
SOUTH CAROLINA																			
SOUTH DAKOTA																			
TENNESSEE																			
TEXAS	7,586,000	2,306,910	30.4%																
UTAH				796,000	249,049	31.3%						971,000	250,010	25.7%	5.5				
VERMONT				330,000	76,414	23.2%		360,000	76,248	21.2%	2.0								
VIRGINIA																			
WASHINGTON	2,355,000	912,083	38.7%	2,637,000	851,930	32.3%	-6.4	2,915,000	969,527	33.3%	-5.5	3,137,000	914,001	29.1%	-9.6	3,360,000	929,685	27.7%	-11.1
WEST VIRGINIA				1,297,000	567,927	43.8%										1,351,000	496,354	36.7%	7.0
WISCONSIN																			
WYOMING																			
Total	27,685,000	8,893,752	32.1%	21,911,000	6,588,437	30.1%	-2.1	13,826,000	3,771,094	27.3%	-4.8	18,547,000	4,814,146	26.0%	-6.2	5,279,000	1,605,191	30.4%	-1.7

*Overall primary turnout reflects only states with primaries in both parties. To find single party primary results, see partisan primary charts.

**Percentage point difference between turnout in current year and initial year listed in chart. If data do not appear for a state in the initial year listed, the difference is calculated from the first year in which data do appear for that state.

STATE GUBERNATORIAL PRIMARY ELECTIONS

Republican Turnout for Election Years 1972–1988

State	1972 Voting-age population	Turnout	%	1976 Voting-age population	Turnout	%	Difference from 1972*	1980 Voting-age population	Turnout	%	Difference from 1972	1984 Voting-age population	Turnout	%	Difference from 1972	1988 Voting-age population	Turnout	%	Difference from 1972
ALABAMA																			
ALASKA																			
ARIZONA																			
ARKANSAS				1,475,000	22,797	1.5%		1,609,000	8,177	0.5%	1.0	1,654,000	19,040	1.2%	-0.4				
CALIFORNIA																			
COLORADO																			
CONNECTICUT																			
DELAWARE	363,000	44,067	12.1%																
DISTRICT OF COLUMBIA																			
FLORIDA																			
GEORGIA																			
HAWAII																			
IDAHO																			
ILLINOIS	7,293,000	585,577	8.0%	7,572,000	723,564	9.6%	1.5												
INDIANA												3,925,000	443,667	11.3%					
IOWA																			
KANSAS	1,536,000	297,939	19.4%																
KENTUCKY																			
LOUISIANA	2,371,000	10,571	0.4%																
MAINE																			
MARYLAND																			
MASSACHUSETTS																			
MICHIGAN																			
MINNESOTA																			
MISSISSIPPI																			
MISSOURI	3,197,000	353,298	11.1%	3,365,000	311,352	9.3%	-1.8	3,530,000	352,079	10.0%	-1.1	3,627,000	363,638	10.0%	-1.0				
MONTANA	465,000	97,304	20.9%	509,000	84,049	16.5%	-4.4	551,000	71,566	13.0%	-7.9					568,000	87,921	15.5%	-5.4
NEBRASKA																			
NEVADA																			
NEW HAMPSHIRE	512,000	91,059	17.8%	583,000	81,953	14.1%	-3.7	654,000	98,413	15.0%	-2.7	718,000	62,689	8.7%	-9.1	783,000	83,271	10.6%	-7.2
NEW JERSEY																			
NEW MEXICO																			
NEW YORK																			

State Gubernatorial Primary Elections (continued)

State Gubernatorial Primary Elections *(continued)*

Republican Turnout for Election Years 1972–1988 *(continued)*

State	1972 Voting-age population	Turnout	%	1976 Voting-age population	Turnout	%	Difference from 1972	1980 Voting-age population	Turnout	%	Difference from 1972	1984 Voting-age population	Turnout	%	Difference from 1972	1988 Voting-age population	Turnout	%	Difference from 1972
NORTH CAROLINA	3,501,000	170,583	4.9%	3,856,000	115,852	3.0%	-1.9	4,207,000	147,609	3.5%	-1.4	4,515,000	140,354	3.1%	-1.8				
NORTH DAKOTA	405,000	97,422	24.1%	432,000	66,440	15.4%	-8.7	458,000	79,322	17.3%	-6.7								
OHIO																			
OKLAHOMA																			
OREGON																			
PENNSYLVANIA																			
RHODE ISLAND																			
SOUTH CAROLINA																			
SOUTH DAKOTA	437,000	90,513	20.7%																
TENNESSEE																			
TEXAS	7,586,000	114,007	1.5%																
UTAH				796,000	163,390	20.5%						971,000	167,287	17.2%	-3.3				
VERMONT	298,000	61,271	20.6%	330,000	34,287	10.4%	-10.2	360,000	44,992	12.5%	-2.1	382,000	49,985	13.1%	-7.5				
VIRGINIA																			
WASHINGTON	2,355,000	331,235	14.1%	2,637,000	306,484	11.6%	-2.4	2,915,000	399,577	13.7%	-0.4	3,137,000	250,656	8.0%	-6.1	3,360,000	334,441	10.0%	-4.1
WEST VIRGINIA				1,297,000	151,764	11.7%										1,351,000	147,468	10.9%	-0.8
WISCONSIN																			
WYOMING																			
Total	30,319,000	2,344,846	7.7%	22,852,000	2,061,932	9.0%	1.3	14,284,000	1,201,735	8.4%	0.7	18,929,000	1,497,316	7.9%	0.2	6,062,000	653,101	10.8%	3.0

Democratic Turnout for Election Years 1972–1988

State	1972 Voting-age population	Turnout	%	1976 Voting-age population	Turnout	%	Difference from 1972*	1980 Voting-age population	Turnout	%	Difference from 1972	1984 Voting-age population	Turnout	%	Difference from 1972	1988 Voting-age population	Turnout	%	Difference from 1972
ALABAMA																			
ALASKA																			
ARIZONA																			
ARKANSAS	1,336,000	494,851	37.0%	1,475,000	525,961	35.7%	-1.4	1,609,000	445,395	27.7%	8.0	1,654,000	492,686	29.8%	5.9				
CALIFORNIA																			
COLORADO																			
CONNECTICUT																			
DELAWARE												452,000	34,658	7.7%				
DISTRICT OF COLUMBIA																			
FLORIDA																			

State Gubernatorial Primary Elections *(continued)*

Democratic Turnout for Election Years 1972–1988 *(continued)*

State	1972 Voting-age population	Turnout	%	1976 Voting-age population	Turnout	%	Difference from 1972	1980 Voting-age population	Turnout	%	Difference from 1972	1984 Voting-age population	Turnout	%	Difference from 1972	1988 Voting-age population	Turnout	%	Difference from 1972
GEORGIA																			
HAWAII																			
IDAHO																			
ILLINOIS	7,293,000	1,430,117	19.6%	7,572,000	1,508,346	19.9%	0.3												
INDIANA				3,643,000	555,992	15.3%		3,841,000	541,961	14.1%	1.2	3,925,000	611,261	15.6%	0.3				
IOWA	1,891,000	149,103	7.9%																
KANSAS																			
KENTUCKY																			
LOUISIANA	2,371,000	1,174,043	49.5%																
MAINE																			
MARYLAND																			
MASSACHUSETTS																			
MICHIGAN																			
MINNESOTA																			
MISSISSIPPI																			
MISSOURI	3,197,000	649,893	20.3%	3,365,000	833,253	24.8%	4.4	3,530,000	665,557	18.9%	-1.5	3,627,000	514,845	14.2%	-6.1	3,724,000	460,973	12.4%	-7.9
MONTANA	465,000	126,794	27.3%					551,000	136,364	24.7%	-2.5	560,000	99,056	17.7%	-9.6	568,000	91,231	16.1%	-11.2
NEBRASKA																			
NEVADA																			
NEW HAMPSHIRE	512,000	47,783	9.3%	583,000	52,218	9.0%	-0.4	654,000	46,475	7.1%	-2.2	718,000	46,156	6.4%	-2.9				
NEW JERSEY																			
NEW MEXICO																			
NEW YORK																			
NORTH CAROLINA	3,501,000	808,105	23.1%	3,856,000	667,821	17.3%	-5.8	4,207,000	753,684	17.9%	-5.2	4,515,000	955,799	21.2%	-1.9				
NORTH DAKOTA	405,000	32,210	8.0%									458,000	41,641	9.1%	1.1				
OHIO																			
OKLAHOMA																			
OREGON																			
PENNSYLVANIA																			
RHODE ISLAND				657,000	137,939	21.0%						699,000	126,131	18.0%	-3.0	722,000	75,393	10.4%	-10.6
SOUTH CAROLINA																			
SOUTH DAKOTA																			
TENNESSEE																			

State Gubernatorial Primary Elections *(continued)*

Democratic Turnout for Election Years 1972–1988 *(continued)*

State	1972 Voting-age population	1972 Turnout	1972 %	1976 Voting-age population	1976 Turnout	1976 %	1976 Difference from 1972	1980 Voting-age population	1980 Turnout	1980 %	1980 Difference from 1972	1984 Voting-age population	1984 Turnout	1984 %	1984 Difference from 1972	1988 Voting-age population	1988 Turnout	1988 %	1988 Difference from 1972
TEXAS	7,586,000	2,192,903	28.9%																
UTAH				796,000	85,659	10.8%						971,000	82,723	8.5%	-2.2				
VERMONT				330,000	42,127	12.8%		360,000	31,256	8.7%	4.1								
VIRGINIA																			
WASHINGTON	2,355,000	580,848	24.7%	2,637,000	545,446	20.7%	-4.0	2,915,000	569,950	19.6%	-5.1	3,137,000	654,221	20.9%	-3.8	3,360,000	595,244	17.7%	-6.9
WEST VIRGINIA	1,208,000	363,743	30.1%	1,297,000	416,163	32.1%	2.0	1,382,000	321,002	23.2%	-6.9	1,367,000	365,609	26.7%	-3.4	1,351,000	348,886	25.8%	-4.3
WISCONSIN																			
WYOMING																			
Total	32,120,000	8,050,393	25.1%	26,211,000	5,370,925	20.5%	-4.6	19,049,000	3,511,644	18.4%	-6.6	22,083,000	4,024,786	18.2%	-6.8	9,725,000	1,571,727	16.2%	-8.9

Other Turnout for Election Years 1972–1988

State	1972 Voting-age population	1972 Turnout	1972 %	1976 Voting-age population	1976 Turnout	1976 %	1976 Difference from 1972*	1980 Voting-age population	1980 Turnout	1980 %	1980 Difference from 1972	1984 Voting-age population	1984 Turnout	1984 %	1984 Difference from 1972	1988 Voting-age population	1988 Turnout	1988 %	1988 Difference from 1972
INDIANA								3,841,000	413,477	10.8%									
WASHINGTON												3,137,000	9,124	0.3%					

*Percentage point difference between turnout in current year and initial year listed in chart. If data do not appear for a state in the initial year listed, the difference is calculated from the first year in which data do appear for that state.

UNITED STATES SENATE PRIMARY ELECTIONS

Election Years 1972–1988

State*	1972 Voting-age population	Turnout	%	1976 Voting-age population	Turnout	%	Difference from 1972**	1980 Voting-age population	Turnout	%	Difference from 1972	1984 Voting-age population	Turnout	%	Difference from 1972	1988 Voting-age population	Turnout	%	Difference from 1972
ALABAMA	2,316,000	711,530	30.7%					2,722,000	573,111	21.1%	-9.7	2,820,000	524,579	18.6%	-12.1				
ALASKA								267,000	99,990	37.4%		308,000	94,651	30.7%	-6.7				
ARIZONA				1,571,000	423,177	26.9%													
ARKANSAS																			
CALIFORNIA				14,305,000	5,619,712	39.3%		15,510,000	5,600,832	36.1%	-3.2								
COLORADO																			
CONNECTICUT																			
DELAWARE																			
DISTRICT OF COLUMBIA																			
FLORIDA								7,007,000	1,625,455	23.2%						8,832,000	1,665,701	18.9%	-4.3
GEORGIA	3,117,000	795,059	25.5%					3,795,000	1,076,438	28.4%	2.9	4,147,000	955,438	23.0%	-2.5				
HAWAII				562,000	241,388	43.0%		630,000	235,001	37.3%	-5.6					739,000	245,453	33.2%	-9.7
IDAHO	485,000	195,455	40.3%																
ILLINOIS								7,843,000	2,028,955	25.9%		7,917,000	2,216,628	28.0%	2.1				
INDIANA				3,643,000	1,173,462	32.2%													
IOWA																			
KANSAS								1,696,000	391,467	23.1%									
KENTUCKY	2,200,000	230,522	10.5%					2,568,000	277,529	10.8%	0.3								
LOUISIANA***								2,842,000	841,013	29.6%		2,885,000	977,473	33.9%	4.3				
MAINE	669,000	183,493	27.4%																
MARYLAND								2,978,000	502,492	16.9%						3,369,000	511,232	15.2%	-1.7
MASSACHUSETTS												4,210,000	1,068,504	25.4%					
MICHIGAN				6,050,000	1,208,254	20.0%													
MINNESOTA				2,692,000	487,663	18.1%						2,990,000	482,224	16.1%	-2.0	3,105,000	290,058	9.3%	-8.8
MISSISSIPPI	1,440,000	313,484	21.8%																
MISSOURI				3,365,000	1,188,996	35.3%		3,530,000	965,593	27.4%	-8.0								
MONTANA	465,000	209,796	45.1%	509,000	180,963	35.6%	-9.6					560,000	167,995	30.0%	-15.1	568,000	193,426	34.1%	-11.1
NEBRASKA	1,001,000	372,897	37.3%	1,058,000	357,046	33.7%	-3.5									1,133,000	385,394	34.0%	-3.2
NEVADA				466,000	110,075	23.6%										801,000	145,896	18.2%	-5.4
NEW HAMPSHIRE								654,000	146,014	22.3%									
NEW JERSEY	4,724,000	579,803	12.3%	4,922,000	722,444	14.7%	2.4					5,274,000	617,250	11.7%	-0.6				
NEW MEXICO	658,000	212,495	32.3%	764,000	192,418	25.2%	-7.1												
NEW YORK				11,941,000	1,260,769	10.6%		12,004,000	1,510,179	12.6%	2.0								

United States Senate Primary Elections (continued)

United States Senate Primary Elections (continued)

Election Years 1972–1988 (continued)

State	1972 Voting-age population	Turnout	%	1976 Voting-age population	Turnout	%	Difference from 1972	1980 Voting-age population	Turnout	%	Difference from 1972	1984 Voting-age population	Turnout	%	Difference from 1972	1988 Voting-age population	Turnout	%	Difference from 1972
NORTH CAROLINA	3,501,000	921,380	26.3%									4,515,000	994,520	22.0%	-4.3				
NORTH DAKOTA																			
OHIO																			
OKLAHOMA	1,808,000	545,154	30.2%					2,147,000	598,007	27.9%	-2.3	2,200,000	599,710	27.3%	-2.9				
OREGON	1,482,000	676,793	45.7%					1,872,000	643,976	34.4%	-11.3	1,944,000	603,694	31.1%	-14.6				
PENNSYLVANIA				8,338,000	2,060,736	24.7%		8,639,000	2,600,693	30.1%	5.4								
RHODE ISLAND																			
SOUTH CAROLINA								2,170,000	361,610	16.7%		2,322,000	345,671	14.9%	-1.8				
SOUTH DAKOTA	437,000	158,915	36.4%					482,000	165,290	34.3%	-2.1								
TENNESSEE	2,738,000	632,474	23.1%																
TEXAS				8,565,000	1,885,475	22.0%						10,253,000	1,800,263	17.6%	-4.5	10,972,000	2,359,888	21.5%	-0.5
UTAH																			
VERMONT				330,000	76,517	23.2%													
VIRGINIA																			
WASHINGTON				2,637,000	804,869	30.5%		2,915,000	940,562	32.3%	1.7					3,360,000	932,151	27.7%	-2.8
WEST VIRGINIA												1,367,000	491,033	35.9%		1,351,000	428,512	31.7%	-4.2
WISCONSIN																3,509,000	899,866	25.6%	
WYOMING												318,000	114,198	35.9%		316,000	116,178	36.8%	0.9
Total	27,041,000	6,739,250	24.9%	71,718,000	17,993,964	25.1%	0.2	82,271,000	21,184,207	25.7%	0.8	54,030,000	12,053,831	22.3%	-2.6	38,055,000	8,173,755	21.5%	-3.4

*Overall primary turnout reflects only states with primaries in both parties. To find single party primary results, see partisan primary charts.

**Percentage point difference between turnout in current year and initial year listed in chart. If data do not appear for a state in the initial year listed, the difference is calculated from the first year in which data do appear for that state.

***In 1978 Louisiana eliminated the partisan primary for senator and instituted an open primary with candidates from all parties running on the same ballot. Any candidate who received a majority appeared in the general election unopposed. If no candidate received fifty percent, a runoff was held between the top two finishers. In 2008 Louisiana returned to a partisan primary system.

UNITED STATES SENATE PRIMARY ELECTIONS

Republican Turnout for Election Years 1972–1988

State	1972			1976				1980				1984				1988			
	Voting-age population	Turnout	%	Voting-age population	Turnout	%	Difference from 1972*	Voting-age population	Turnout	%	Difference from 1972	Voting-age population	Turnout	%	Difference from 1972	Voting-age population	Turnout	%	Difference from 1972
ALABAMA	2,316,000	51,210	2.2%					2,722,000	115,533	4.2%	2.0	2,820,000	44,186	1.6%	-0.6				
ALASKA								267,000	27,622	10.3%		308,000	65,522	21.3%	10.9				
ARIZONA				1,571,000	195,876	12.5%													
ARKANSAS																			
CALIFORNIA				14,305,000	2,319,787	16.2%		15,510,000	2,336,190	15.1%	-1.2								
COLORADO								2,044,000	213,339	10.4%									
CONNECTICUT								2,201,000	115,058	5.2%									
DELAWARE																			
DISTRICT OF COLUMBIA																			
FLORIDA				6,013,000	302,046	5.0%		7,007,000	476,511	6.8%	1.8					8,832,000	656,026	7.4%	2.4
GEORGIA	3,117,000	78,418	2.5%					3,795,000	47,138	1.2%	-1.3	4,147,000	67,053	1.6%	-0.9				
HAWAII				562,000	34,228	6.1%		630,000	8,243	1.3%	-4.8					739,000	37,240	5.0%	-1.1
IDAHO	485,000	129,013	26.6%																
ILLINOIS								7,843,000	1,024,581	13.1%		7,917,000	654,133	8.3%	-4.8				
INDIANA				3,643,000	600,596	16.5%		3,841,000	515,546	13.4%	-3.1								
IOWA	1,891,000	202,208	10.7%					2,071,000	259,529	12.5%	1.8								
KANSAS	1,536,000	279,733	18.2%					1,696,000	246,158	14.5%									
KENTUCKY	2,200,000	82,269	3.7%					2,568,000	61,200	2.4%	-1.4								
LOUISIANA**								2,842,000	23,947	0.8%		2,885,000	139,292	4.8%	4.0				
MAINE	669,000	115,309	17.2%	731,000	77,776	10.6%	-6.6												
MARYLAND								2,978,000	149,973	5.0%						3,369,000	149,931	4.5%	-0.6
MASSACHUSETTS												4,210,000	278,682	6.6%					
MICHIGAN				6,050,000	473,111	7.8%						6,511,000	522,700	8.0%	0.2	6,636,000	401,259	6.0%	-1.8
MINNESOTA				2,692,000	139,769	5.2%						2,990,000	168,294	5.6%	0.4	3,105,000	120,256	3.9%	-1.3
MISSISSIPPI	1,440,000	23,228	1.6%																
MISSOURI				3,365,000	303,821	9.0%		3,530,000	320,244	9.1%	0.0								
MONTANA	465,000	86,576	18.6%	509,000	79,957	15.7%	-2.9					560,000	66,290	11.8%	-6.8	568,000	74,757	13.2%	-5.5
NEBRASKA	1,001,000	190,721	19.1%	1,058,000	192,373	18.2%	-0.9					1,124,000	150,801	13.4%	-5.6	1,133,000	214,225	18.9%	-0.1
NEVADA				466,000	38,527	8.3%		567,000	50,767	9.0%	0.7					801,000	67,551	8.4%	0.2
NEW HAMPSHIRE	512,000	89,302	17.4%					654,000	99,595	15.2%	-2.2								
NEW JERSEY	4,724,000	267,034	5.7%	4,922,000	277,713	5.6%	0.0					5,274,000	182,269	3.5%	-2.2				
NEW MEXICO	658,000	59,030	9.0%	764,000	47,520	6.2%	-2.8									998,000	82,438	8.3%	-0.7
NEW YORK				11,941,000	344,156	2.9%		12,004,000	580,901	4.8%	2.0								

United States Senate Primary Elections (continued)

United States Senate Primary Elections (continued)

Republican Turnout for Election Years 1972–1988 (continued)

State	1972 Voting-age population	Turnout	%	1976 Voting-age population	Turnout	%	Difference from 1972	1980 Voting-age population	Turnout	%	Difference from 1972	1984 Voting-age population	Turnout	%	Difference from 1972	1988 Voting-age population	Turnout	%	Difference from 1972
NORTH CAROLINA	3,501,000	153,831	4.4%									4,515,000	148,574	3.3%	-1.1				
NORTH DAKOTA																			
OHIO																			
OKLAHOMA	1,808,000	101,964	5.6%					2,147,000	137,855	6.4%	0.8	2,200,000	118,415	5.4%	-0.3				
OREGON	1,482,000	280,589	18.9%					1,872,000	306,136	16.4%	-2.6	1,944,000	273,537	14.1%	-4.9				
PENNSYLVANIA				8,338,000	950,681	11.4%		8,639,000	1,152,059	13.3%	1.9								
RHODE ISLAND								·											
SOUTH CAROLINA								2,170,000	33,045	1.5%		2,322,000	47,355	2.0%	0.5				
SOUTH DAKOTA	437,000	99,821	22.8%					482,000	93,510	19.4%	-3.4								
TENNESSEE	2,738,000	249,954	9.1%									3,423,000	168,540	4.9%	-4.2	3,568,000	158,123	4.4%	-4.7
TEXAS				8,565,000	356,307	4.2%						10,253,000	336,814	3.3%	-0.9	10,972,000	749,347	6.8%	2.7
UTAH				796,000	161,739	20.3%													
VERMONT				330,000	35,427	10.7%		360,000	46,820	13.0%	2.3					403,000	50,276	12.5%	1.7
VIRGINIA																			
WASHINGTON				2,637,000	175,866	6.7%		2,915,000	563,586	19.3%	12.7					3,360,000	393,582	11.7%	5.0
WEST VIRGINIA												1,367,000	128,337	9.4%		1,351,000	115,559	8.6%	-0.8
WISCONSIN								3,317,000	366,080	11.0%						3,509,000	366,862	10.5%	-0.6
WYOMING				278,000	54,137	19.5%						318,000	75,315	23.7%	4.2	316,000	67,001	21.2%	1.7
Total	30,980,000	2,540,210	8.2%	79,536,000	7,161,413	9.0%	0.8	96,672,000	9,371,246	9.7%	1.5	65,088,000	3,636,109	5.6%	-2.6	49,660,000	3,704,433	7.5%	-0.7

Democratic Turnout for Election Years 1972–1988

State	1972 Voting-age population	Turnout	%	1976 Voting-age population	Turnout	%	Difference from 1972*	1980 Voting-age population	Turnout	%	Difference from 1972	1984 Voting-age population	Turnout	%	Difference from 1972	1988 Voting-age population	Turnout	%	Difference from 1972
ALABAMA	2,316,000	660,320	28.5%					2,722,000	457,578	16.8%	-11.7	2,820,000	480,393	17.0%	-11.5				
ALASKA								267,000	72,368	27.1%		308,000	29,129	9.5%	-17.6				
ARIZONA				1,571,000	227,301	14.5%		1,873,000	176,158	9.4%	-5.1								
ARKANSAS	1,336,000	493,470	36.9%																
CALIFORNIA				14,305,000	3,299,925	23.1%		15,510,000	3,264,642	21.0%	-2.0					17,790,000	2,897,587	16.3%	-6.8
COLORADO	1,534,000	131,872	8.6%									2,176,000	153,525	7.1%	-1.5				
CONNECTICUT																			
DELAWARE																481,000	40,379	8.4%	
DISTRICT OF COLUMBIA																			
FLORIDA								7,007,000	1,148,944	16.4%						8,832,000	1,009,675	11.4%	-5.0

United States Senate Primary Elections (continued)

Democratic Turnout for Election Years 1972–1988 (continued)

State	1972 Voting-age population	1972 Turnout	1972 %	1976 Voting-age population	1976 Turnout	1976 %	1976 Difference from 1972	1980 Voting-age population	1980 Turnout	1980 %	1980 Difference from 1972	1984 Voting-age population	1984 Turnout	1984 %	1984 Difference from 1972	1988 Voting-age population	1988 Turnout	1988 %	1988 Difference from 1972
GEORGIA	3,117,000	716,641	23.0%					3,795,000	1,029,300	27.1%	4.1	4,147,000	888,385	21.4%	-1.6				
HAWAII				562,000	207,160	36.9%		630,000	226,758	36.0%	-0.9					739,000	208,213	28.2%	-8.7
IDAHO	485,000	66,442	13.7%									651,000	44,936	6.9%	-6.8				
ILLINOIS	7,293,000	1,217,705	16.7%					7,843,000	1,004,374	12.8%	-3.9	7,917,000	1,562,495	19.7%	3.0				
INDIANA				3,643,000	572,866	15.7%										4,009,000	593,800	14.8%	-0.9
IOWA																			
KANSAS								1,696,000	145,309	8.6%									
KENTUCKY	2,200,000	148,253	6.7%					2,568,000	216,249	8.4%	1.7								
LOUISIANA**	2,371,000	784,362	33.1%					2,842,000	810,692	28.5%	-4.6	2,885,000	838,181	29.1%	-4.0				
MAINE	669,000	68,184	10.2%																
MARYLAND				2,790,000	547,754	19.6%		2,978,000	352,519	11.8%	-7.8					3,369,000	361,301	10.7%	-8.9
MASSACHUSETTS	3,774,000	478,459	12.7%	3,030,000	693,988	17.7%	5.0					4,210,000	789,822	18.8%	6.1				
MICHIGAN				6,050,000	735,143	12.2%													
MINNESOTA	2,506,000	256,641	10.2%	2,692,000	347,894	12.9%	2.7					2,990,000	313,930	10.5%	0.3	3,105,000	169,802	5.5%	-4.8
MISSISSIPPI	1,440,000	290,256	20.2%	1,572,000	184,959	11.8%	-8.4					1,746,000	127,857	7.3%	-12.8	1,795,000	355,356	19.8%	-0.4
MISSOURI				3,365,000	885,175	26.3%		3,530,000	645,349	18.3%	-8.0								
MONTANA	465,000	123,220	26.5%	509,000	101,006	19.8%	-6.7					560,000	101,705	18.2%	-8.3	568,000	118,669	20.9%	-5.6
NEBRASKA	1,001,000	182,176	18.2%	1,058,000	164,673	15.6%	-2.6									1,133,000	171,169	15.1%	-3.1
NEVADA				466,000	71,548	15.4%										801,000	78,345	9.8%	-5.6
NEW HAMPSHIRE								654,000	46,419	7.1%									
NEW JERSEY	4,724,000	312,769	6.6%	4,922,000	444,731	9.0%	2.4					5,274,000	434,981	8.2%	1.6	5,432,000	455,313	8.4%	1.8
NEW MEXICO	658,000	153,465	23.3%	764,000	144,898	19.0%	-4.4					933,000	148,850	16.0%	-7.4				
NEW YORK				11,941,000	916,613	7.7%		12,004,000	929,278	7.7%	0.1								
NORTH CAROLINA	3,501,000	767,549	21.9%									4,515,000	845,946	18.7%	-3.2	4,822,000	506,073	10.5%	-11.4
NORTH DAKOTA								458,000	39,802	8.7%									
OHIO				7,319,000	1,078,177	14.7%		7,623,000	1,087,006	14.3%	-0.5					7,890,000	1,281,442	16.2%	1.5
OKLAHOMA	1,808,000	443,190	24.5%					2,147,000	460,152	21.4%	-3.1	2,200,000	481,295	21.9%	-2.6				
OREGON	1,482,000	396,204	26.7%					1,872,000	337,840	18.0%	-8.7	1,944,000	330,157	17.0%	-9.8				
PENNSYLVANIA				8,338,000	1,110,055	13.3%		8,639,000	1,448,634	16.8%	3.5					8,895,000	1,085,230	12.2%	-1.1
RHODE ISLAND				657,000	158,695	24.2%													
SOUTH CAROLINA	1,745,000	342,928	19.7%					2,170,000	328,565	15.1%	-4.5	2,322,000	298,316	12.8%	-6.8				
SOUTH DAKOTA	437,000	59,094	13.5%					482,000	71,780	14.9%	1.4	488,000	46,021	9.4%	-4.1				
TENNESSEE	2,738,000	382,520	14.0%	3,011,000	553,849	18.4%	4.4												

United States Senate Primary Elections (continued)

United States Senate Primary Elections (continued)

Democratic Turnout for Election Years 1972–1988 (continued)

State	1972 Voting-age population	Turnout	%	1976 Voting-age population	Turnout	%	Difference from 1972	1980 Voting-age population	Turnout	%	Difference from 1972	1984 Voting-age population	Turnout	%	Difference from 1972	1988 Voting-age population	Turnout	%	Difference from 1972
TEXAS	7,586,000	2,065,748	27.2%	8,565,000	1,529,168	17.9%	-9.4					10,253,000	1,463,449	14.3%	-13.0	10,972,000	1,610,541	14.7%	-12.6
UTAH								904,000	57,573	6.4%									
VERMONT				330,000	41,090	12.5%													
VIRGINIA																			
WASHINGTON				2,637,000	629,003	23.9%		2,915,000	376,976	12.9%	-10.9					3,360,000	538,569	16.0%	-7.8
WEST VIRGINIA												1,367,000	362,696	26.5%		1,351,000	312,953	23.2%	-3.4
WISCONSIN																3,509,000	533,004	15.2%	
WYOMING	234,000	30,736	13.1%									318,000	38,883	12.2%	-0.9	316,000	49,177	15.6%	2.4
Total	55,420,000	10,572,204	19.1%	90,997,000	14,645,671	16.1%	-3.0	93,129,000	14,734,265	15.8%	-3.3	60,024,000	9,780,952	16.3%	-2.8	89,169,000	12,376,598	13.9%	-5.2

Other Turnout for Election Years 1972–1988

State	1972 Voting-age population	Turnout	%	1976 Voting-age population	Turnout	%	Difference from 1972*	1980 Voting-age population	Turnout	%	Difference from 1972	1984 Voting-age population	Turnout	%	Difference from 1972	1988 Voting-age population	Turnout	%	Difference from 1972
CALIFORNIA																17,790,000	6,324	0.0%	
IDAHO								628,000	153	0.0%									
LOUISIANA								2,842,000	6,374	0.2%									
NEVADA																801,000	13,495	1.7%	

*Percentage point difference between turnout in current year and initial year listed in chart. If data do not appear for a state in the initial year listed, the difference is calculated from the first year in which data do appear for that state.

**In 1978 Louisiana eliminated the partisan primary for senator and instituted an open primary with candidates from all parties running on the same ballot. Any candidate who received a majority appeared in the general election unopposed. If no candidate received fifty percent, a runoff was held between the top two finishers. In 2008 Louisiana returned to a partisan primary system.

Midterm Turnout Election Based on Highest Statewide Turnout, Election Years 1970–1986

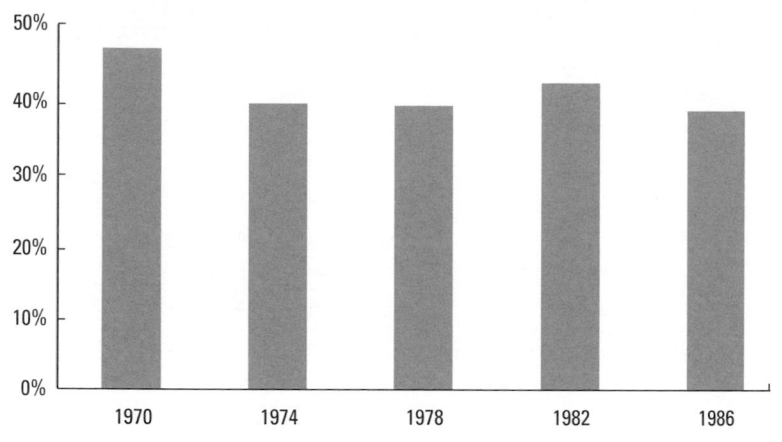

YEAR	VOTING-AGE POPULATION	TOTAL	%
1970	124,000,000	58,015,926	46.8%
1974	142,608,000	55,955,269	39.2%
1978	153,258,000	59,711,116	39.0%
1982	161,552,000	68,014,910	42.1%
1986	168,768,000	64,671,044	38.3%

Partisan Turnout Midterm Election Based on Aggregate House of Representatives Turnout, Election Years 1970–1986

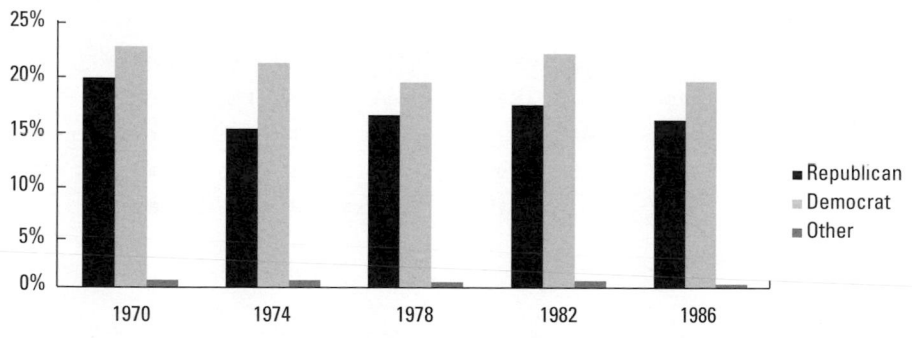

■ Republican
■ Democrat
■ Other

YEAR	VOTING-AGE POPULATION	REPUBLICAN TURNOUT	%	DEMOCRAT TURNOUT	%	OTHER TURNOUT	%
1970	124,000,000	24,414,855	19.7%	28,132,340	22.7%	835,016	0.7%
1974	142,608,000	21,285,562	14.9%	30,154,752	21.1%	957,195	0.7%
1978	153,258,000	24,867,105	16.2%	29,582,062	19.3%	788,187	0.5%
1982	161,552,000	27,782,036	17.2%	35,602,088	22.0%	1,017,800	0.6%
1986	168,768,000	26,620,667	15.8%	32,758,722	19.4%	547,967	0.3%

STATE GUBERNATORIAL GENERAL ELECTIONS

Election Years 1970–1986

State	1970 Voting-age population	Turnout	%	1974 Voting-age population	Turnout	%	Difference from 1970*	1978 Voting-age population	Turnout	%	Difference from 1970	1982 Voting-age population	Turnout	%	Difference from 1970	1986 Voting-age population	Turnout	%	Difference from 1970
ALABAMA	2,035,000	854,952	42.0%	2,449,000	598,305	24.4%	-17.6	2,654,000	760,474	28.7%	-13.4	2,785,000	1,128,725	40.5%	-1.5	2,882,000	1,236,230	42.9%	0.9
ALASKA	179,000	80,779	45.1%	220,000	96,163	43.7%	-1.4	255,000	126,910	49.8%	4.6	294,000	194,885	66.3%	21.2	334,000	179,555	53.8%	8.6
ARIZONA	1,055,000	411,409	39.0%	1,463,000	552,202	37.7%	-1.3	1,767,000	538,556	30.5%	-8.5	2,050,000	726,364	35.4%	-3.6	2,324,000	866,984	37.3%	-1.7
ARKANSAS	1,179,000	609,198	51.7%	1,426,000	545,974	38.3%	-13.4	1,564,000	528,912	33.8%	-17.9	1,638,000	789,351	48.2%	-3.5	1,682,000	688,551	40.9%	-10.7
CALIFORNIA	12,492,000	6,510,072	52.1%	13,878,000	6,248,070	45.0%	-7.1	15,085,000	6,922,378	45.9%	-6.2	16,246,000	7,876,698	48.5%	-3.6	17,387,000	7,443,551	42.8%	-9.3
COLORADO	1,324,000	668,496	50.5%	1,700,000	828,968	48.8%	-1.7	1,957,000	823,807	42.1%	-8.4	2,129,000	956,021	44.9%	-5.6	2,262,000	1,058,928	46.8%	-3.7
CONNECTICUT	1,895,000	1,082,797	57.1%	2,063,000	1,102,773	53.5%	-3.7	2,165,000	1,036,608	47.9%	-9.3	2,258,000	1,084,156	48.0%	-9.1	2,347,000	993,692	42.3%	-14.8
DELAWARE																			
DISTRICT OF COLUMBIA																			
FLORIDA	4,461,000	1,730,813	38.8%	5,661,000	1,828,392	32.3%	-6.5	6,657,000	2,530,468	38.0%	-0.8	7,597,000	2,688,566	35.4%	-3.4	8,509,000	3,386,171	39.8%	1.0
GEORGIA	2,973,000	1,046,663	35.2%	3,336,000	936,438	28.1%	-7.1	3,675,000	662,862	18.0%	-17.2	4,022,000	1,169,041	29.1%	-6.1	4,373,000	1,175,114	26.9%	-8.3
HAWAII	436,000	239,061	54.8%	538,000	249,650	46.4%	-8.4	607,000	281,587	46.4%	-8.4	665,000	311,853	46.9%	-7.9	720,000	334,115	46.4%	-8.4
IDAHO	413,000	245,112	59.3%	532,000	259,632	48.8%	-10.5	605,000	288,566	47.7%	-11.7	643,000	326,522	50.8%	-8.6	666,000	387,426	58.2%	-1.2
ILLINOIS								7,753,000	3,150,095	40.6%		7,891,000	3,673,681	46.6%	5.9	7,965,000	3,143,978	39.5%	-1.2
INDIANA																			
IOWA	1,703,000	791,241	46.5%	1,951,000	920,458	47.2%	0.7	2,043,000	843,190	41.3%	-5.2	2,063,000	1,038,229	50.3%	3.9	2,048,000	910,623	44.5%	-2.0
KANSAS	1,377,000	745,196	54.1%	1,588,000	783,875	49.4%	-4.8	1,670,000	736,246	44.1%	-10.0	1,720,000	763,263	44.4%	-9.7	1,757,000	840,605	47.8%	-6.3
KENTUCKY																			
LOUISIANA																			
MAINE	598,000	325,386	54.4%	709,000	363,945	51.3%	-3.1	771,000	370,258	48.0%	-6.4	822,000	460,295	56.0%	1.6	867,000	426,861	49.2%	-5.2
MARYLAND	2,383,000	973,099	40.8%	2,722,000	949,097	34.9%	-6.0	2,911,000	1,011,963	34.8%	-6.1	3,104,000	1,139,149	36.7%	-4.1	3,300,000	1,101,476	33.4%	-7.5
MASSACHUSETTS	3,539,000	1,867,906	52.8%	3,874,000	1,854,798	47.9%	-4.9	4,029,000	1,962,251	48.7%	-4.1	4,165,000	2,050,254	49.2%	-3.6	4,292,000	1,684,079	39.2%	-13.5
MICHIGAN	5,199,000	2,656,162	51.1%	5,928,000	2,657,017	44.8%	-6.3	6,272,000	2,867,212	45.7%	-5.4	6,466,000	3,040,008	47.0%	-4.1	6,591,000	2,396,564	36.4%	-14.7
MINNESOTA	2,238,000	1,365,443	61.0%	2,626,000	1,252,898	47.7%	-13.3	2,812,000	1,585,702	56.4%	-4.6	2,949,000	1,789,539	60.7%	-0.3	3,065,000	1,415,989	46.2%	-14.8
MISSISSIPPI																			
MISSOURI																			
MONTANA																			
NEBRASKA	898,000	461,619	51.4%	1,039,000	451,306	43.4%	-8.0	1,095,000	492,423	45.0%	-6.4	1,120,000	547,902	48.9%	-2.5	1,130,000	564,422	49.9%	-1.5
NEVADA	306,000	146,991	48.0%	431,000	169,358	39.3%	-8.7	530,000	192,445	36.3%	-11.7	642,000	239,751	37.3%	-10.7	759,000	260,375	34.3%	-13.7
NEW HAMPSHIRE	450,000	222,441	49.4%	558,000	226,665	40.6%	-8.8	629,000	269,587	42.9%	-6.6	696,000	282,588	40.6%	-8.8	761,000	251,107	33.0%	-16.4
NEW JERSEY																			
NEW MEXICO	559,000	290,375	51.9%	727,000	328,742	45.2%	-6.7	832,000	345,577	41.5%	-10.4	910,000	407,466	44.8%	-7.2	975,000	394,833	40.5%	-11.4
NEW YORK	11,599,000	6,013,064	51.8%	11,921,000	5,293,176	44.4%	-7.4	11,979,000	4,768,820	39.8%	-12.0	12,104,000	5,254,891	43.4%	-8.4	12,259,000	4,294,124	35.0%	-16.8

State Gubernatorial General Elections (continued)

Election Years 1970–1986 (continued)

State	1970 Voting-age population	1970 Turnout	1970 %	1974 Voting-age population	1974 Turnout	1974 %	1974 Difference from 1970	1978 Voting-age population	1978 Turnout	1978 %	1978 Difference from 1970	1982 Voting-age population	1982 Turnout	1982 %	1982 Difference from 1970	1986 Voting-age population	1986 Turnout	1986 %	1986 Difference from 1970
NORTH CAROLINA																			
NORTH DAKOTA																			
OHIO	6,402,000	3,184,133	49.7%	7,209,000	3,072,010	42.6%	-7.1	7,521,000	2,843,351	37.8%	-11.9	7,710,000	3,356,721	43.5%	-6.2	7,843,000	3,066,611	39.1%	-10.6
OKLAHOMA	1,597,000	698,790	43.8%	1,919,000	804,848	41.9%	-1.8	2,091,000	777,414	37.2%	-6.6	2,181,000	883,130	40.5%	-3.3	2,234,000	909,925	40.7%	-3.0
OREGON	1,301,000	666,394	51.2%	1,010,000	770,574	47.9%	-3.4	1,807,000	911,143	50.4%	-0.8	1,919,000	1,042,009	54.3%	3.1	1,990,000	1,059,630	53.2%	2.0
PENNSYLVANIA	7,387,000	3,700,060	50.1%	8,228,000	3,491,234	42.4%	-7.7	8,537,000	3,741,969	43.8%	-6.3	8,723,000	3,683,985	42.2%	-7.9	0,050,000	3,388,775	38.3%	-11.8
RHODE ISLAND	596,000	346,342	58.1%	651,000	321,660	49.4%	-8.7	669,000	314,363	47.0%	-11.1	690,000	337,259	48.9%	-9.2	714,000	322,724	45.2%	-12.9
SOUTH CAROLINA	1,482,000	484,857	32.7%	1,883,000	483,199	25.7%	-7.1	2,097,000	627,182	29.9%	-2.8	2,269,000	671,625	29.6%	-3.1	2,420,000	753,751	31.1%	-1.6
SOUTH DAKOTA	386,000	239,963	62.2%	452,000	278,228	61.6%	-0.6	475,000	259,795	54.7%	7.5	486,000	278,562	57.3%	-4.8	491,000	294,441	60.0%	-2.2
TENNESSEE	2,400,000	1,108,247	46.2%	2,914,000	1,040,714	35.7%	-10.5	3,187,000	1,189,695	37.3%	-8.8	3,373,000	1,238,927	36.7%	-9.4	3,516,000	1,210,339	34.4%	-11.8
TEXAS	6,658,000	2,235,847	33.6%	8,218,000	1,654,984	20.1%	-13.4	9,197,000	2,369,764	25.8%	-7.8	9,998,000	3,191,091	31.9%	-1.7	10,718,000	3,441,460	32.1%	-1.5
UTAH																			
VERMONT	264,000	153,528	58.2%	319,000	141,156	44.2%	-13.9	350,000	124,482	35.6%	-22.6	374,000	169,251	45.3%	-12.9	398,000	196,716	49.7%	-8.5
VIRGINIA																			
WASHINGTON																			
WEST VIRGINIA																			
WISCONSIN	2,613,000	1,343,160	51.4%	3,047,000	1,181,976	38.8%	-12.6	3,249,000	1,500,996	46.2%	-5.2	3,379,000	1,580,344	46.8%	-4.6	3,475,000	1,526,960	43.9%	-7.5
WYOMING	195,000	118,257	60.6%	263,000	128,386	48.8%	-11.8	307,000	137,567	44.8%	-15.8	319,000	168,555	52.8%	-7.8	317,000	164,720	52.0%	-8.7
Total	90,572,000	43,617,853	48.2%	104,053,000	41,866,871	40.2%	-7.9	119,804,000	47,894,618	40.0%	-8.2	126,400,000	54,540,657	43.1%	-5.0	132,219,000	51,770,905	39.2%	-9.0

*Percentage point difference between turnout in current year and initial year listed in chart. If data do not appear for a state in the initial year listed, the difference is calculated from the first year in which data do appear for that state.

STATE GUBERNATORIAL GENERAL ELECTIONS

Republican Turnout for Election Years 1970–1986

State	1970 Voting-age population	Turnout	%	1974 Voting-age population	Turnout	%	Difference from 1970*	1978 Voting-age population	Turnout	%	Difference from 1970	1982 Voting-age population	Turnout	%	Difference from 1970	1986 Voting-age population	Turnout	%	Difference from 1970
ALABAMA				2,449,000	88,381	3.6%		2,654,000	196,963	7.4%	3.8	2,785,000	440,815	15.8%	12.2	2,882,000	696,203	24.2%	20.5
ALASKA	179,000	37,264	20.8%	220,000	45,840	20.8%	0.0	255,000	49,580	19.4%	-1.4	294,000	72,291	24.6%	3.8	334,000	76,515	22.9%	2.1
ARIZONA	1,055,000	209,522	19.9%	1,463,000	273,674	18.7%	-1.2	1,767,000	241,093	13.6%	-6.2	2,050,000	235,877	11.5%	-8.4	2,324,000	343,913	14.8%	-5.1
ARKANSAS	1,179,000	197,418	16.7%	1,426,000	187,872	13.2%	-3.6	1,564,000	193,746	12.4%	-4.4	1,638,000	357,496	21.8%	5.1	1,682,000	248,427	14.8%	-2.0
CALIFORNIA	12,492,000	3,439,664	27.5%	13,878,000	2,952,954	21.3%	-6.3	15,085,000	2,526,534	16.7%	-10.8	16,246,000	3,881,014	23.9%	-3.6	17,387,000	4,506,601	25.9%	-1.6
COLORADO	1,324,000	350,690	26.5%	1,700,000	378,907	22.3%	-4.2	1,957,000	317,292	16.2%	-10.3	2,129,000	302,740	14.2%	-12.3	2,262,000	434,420	19.2%	-7.3
CONNECTICUT	1,895,000	582,160	30.7%	2,063,000	440,169	21.3%	-9.4	2,165,000	422,316	19.5%	-11.2	2,258,000	497,773	22.0%	-8.7	2,347,000	408,489	17.4%	-13.3
DELAWARE																			
DISTRICT OF COLUMBIA																			
FLORIDA	4,461,000	746,243	16.7%	5,661,000	709,438	12.5%	-4.2	6,657,000	1,123,888	16.9%	0.2	7,597,000	949,013	12.5%	-4.2	8,509,000	1,847,525	21.7%	5.0
GEORGIA	2,973,000	424,983	14.3%	3,336,000	289,113	8.7%	-5.6	3,675,000	128,139	3.5%	-10.8	4,022,000	434,496	10.8%	-3.5	4,373,000	346,512	7.9%	-6.4
HAWAII	436,000	101,249	23.2%	538,000	113,388	21.1%	-2.1	607,000	124,610	20.5%	-2.7	665,000	81,507	12.3%	-11.0	720,000	160,460	22.3%	-0.9
IDAHO	413,000	117,108	28.4%	532,000	68,731	12.9%	-15.4	605,000	114,149	18.9%	-9.5	643,000	161,157	25.1%	-3.3	666,000	189,794	28.5%	0.1
ILLINOIS								7,753,000	1,859,684	24.0%		7,891,000	1,816,101	23.0%	-1.0	7,965,000	1,655,849	20.8%	-3.2
INDIANA																			
IOWA	1,703,000	403,394	23.7%	1,951,000	534,518	27.4%	3.7	2,043,000	491,713	24.1%	0.4	2,063,000	548,313	26.6%	2.9	2,048,000	472,712	23.1%	-0.6
KANSAS	1,377,000	333,227	24.2%	1,588,000	387,792	24.4%	0.2	1,670,000	348,015	20.8%	-3.4	1,720,000	339,356	19.7%	-4.5	1,757,000	436,267	24.8%	0.6
KENTUCKY																			
LOUISIANA																			
MAINE	598,000	162,248	27.1%	709,000	84,176	11.9%	-15.3	771,000	126,862	16.5%	-10.7	822,000	172,949	21.0%	-6.1	867,000	170,312	19.6%	-7.5
MARYLAND	2,383,000	314,336	13.2%	2,722,000	346,449	12.7%	-0.5	2,911,000	293,635	10.1%	-3.1	3,104,000	432,826	13.9%	0.8	3,300,000	194,185	5.9%	-7.3
MASSACHUSETTS	3,539,000	1,058,623	29.9%	3,874,000	784,353	20.2%	-9.7	4,029,000	926,072	23.0%	-6.9	4,165,000	749,679	18.0%	-11.9	4,292,000	525,364	12.2%	-17.7
MICHIGAN	5,199,000	1,339,047	25.8%	5,928,000	1,356,865	22.9%	-2.9	6,272,000	1,628,485	26.0%	0.2	6,466,000	1,369,582	21.2%	-4.6	6,591,000	753,647	11.4%	-14.3
MINNESOTA	2,238,000	621,780	27.8%	2,626,000	367,722	14.0%	-13.8	2,812,000	830,019	29.5%	1.7	2,949,000	715,796	24.3%	-3.5	3,065,000	606,755	19.8%	-8.0
MISSISSIPPI																			
MISSOURI																			
MONTANA																			
NEBRASKA	898,000	201,994	22.5%	1,039,000	159,780	15.4%	-7.1	1,095,000	275,473	25.2%	2.7	1,120,000	270,203	24.1%	1.6	1,130,000	298,325	26.4%	3.9
NEVADA	306,000	64,400	21.0%	431,000	28,959	6.7%	-14.3	530,000	108,097	20.4%	-0.7	642,000	100,104	15.6%	-5.5	759,000	65,081	8.6%	-12.5
NEW HAMPSHIRE	450,000	102,298	22.7%	558,000	115,933	20.8%	-2.0	629,000	122,464	19.5%	-3.3	696,000	145,389	20.9%	-1.8	761,000	134,824	17.7%	-5.0
NEW JERSEY																			
NEW MEXICO	559,000	134,640	24.1%	727,000	160,430	22.1%	-2.0	832,000	170,848	20.5%	-3.6	910,000	191,626	21.1%	-3.0	975,000	209,455	21.5%	-2.6
NEW YORK	11,599,000	3,151,432	27.2%	11,921,000	2,219,667	18.6%	-8.6	11,979,000	2,156,404	18.0%	-9.2	12,104,000	2,494,827	20.6%	-6.6	12,259,000	1,363,810	11.1%	-16.0

State Gubernatorial General Elections (continued)

Republican Turnout for Election Years 1970–1986 (continued)

State	1970 Voting-age population	Turnout	%	1974 Voting-age population	Turnout	%	Difference from 1970	1978 Voting-age population	Turnout	%	Difference from 1970	1982 Voting-age population	Turnout	%	Difference from 1970	1986 Voting-age population	Turnout	%	Difference from 1970
NORTH CAROLINA																			
NORTH DAKOTA																			
OHIO	6,402,000	1,382,659	21.6%	7,209,000	1,493,679	20.7%	-0.9	7,521,000	1,402,167	18.6%	-3.0	7,710,000	1,303,962	16.9%	-4.7	7,843,000	1,207,264	15.4%	-6.2
OKLAHOMA	1,597,000	336,157	21.0%	1,919,000	290,459	15.1%	-5.9	2,091,000	367,055	17.6%	-3.5	2,181,000	332,207	15.2%	-5.8	2,234,000	431,762	19.3%	-1.7
OREGON	1,301,000	369,964	28.4%	1,610,000	324,751	20.2%	-8.3	1,807,000	498,452	27.6%	-0.9	1,919,000	639,841	33.3%	4.9	1,990,000	506,986	25.5%	-3.0
PENNSYLVANIA	7,387,000	1,542,854	20.9%	8,228,000	1,578,917	19.2%	-1.7	8,537,000	1,966,042	23.0%	2.1	8,723,000	1,872,784	21.5%	0.0	8,850,000	1,638,268	18.5%	-2.4
RHODE ISLAND	596,000	171,549	28.8%	651,000	69,224	10.6%	-18.1	669,000	96,596	14.4%	-14.3	690,000	79,602	11.5%	-17.2	714,000	208,822	29.2%	0.5
SOUTH CAROLINA	1,482,000	221,233	14.9%	1,883,000	226,109	12.0%	-2.9	2,097,000	236,946	11.3%	-3.6	2,269,000	202,806	8.9%	-6.0	2,420,000	384,565	15.9%	1.0
SOUTH DAKOTA	386,000	108,347	28.1%	452,000	129,077	28.6%	0.5	475,000	147,116	31.0%	2.9	486,000	197,426	40.6%	12.6	491,000	152,543	31.1%	3.0
TENNESSEE	2,400,000	575,777	24.0%	2,914,000	455,467	15.6%	-8.4	3,187,000	661,959	20.8%	-3.2	3,373,000	737,963	21.9%	-2.1	3,516,000	553,449	15.7%	-8.2
TEXAS	6,658,000	1,037,723	15.6%	8,218,000	514,725	6.3%	-9.3	9,197,000	1,183,839	12.9%	-2.7	9,998,000	1,465,937	14.7%	-0.9	10,718,000	1,813,779	16.9%	1.3
UTAH																			
VERMONT	264,000	87,458	33.1%	319,000	53,672	16.8%	-16.3	350,000	78,181	22.3%	-10.8	374,000	93,111	24.9%	-8.2	396,000	75,162	19.0%	-14.1
VIRGINIA																			
WASHINGTON																			
WEST VIRGINIA																			
WISCONSIN	2,613,000	602,617	23.1%	3,047,000	497,195	16.3%	-6.7	3,249,000	816,056	25.1%	2.1	3,379,000	662,838	19.6%	-3.4	3,475,000	805,090	23.2%	0.1
WYOMING	195,000	74,249	38.1%	263,000	56,645	21.5%	-16.5	307,000	67,595	22.0%	-16.1	319,000	62,128	19.5%	-18.6	317,000	75,841	23.9%	-14.2
Total	88,537,000	20,604,307	23.3%	104,053,000	17,785,031	17.1%	-6.2	119,804,000	22,298,085	18.6%	-4.7	126,400,000	24,411,535	19.3%	-4.0	132,219,000	23,998,976	18.2%	-5.1

Democratic Turnout for Election Years 1970–1986

State	1970 Voting-age population	Turnout	%	1974 Voting-age population	Turnout	%	Difference from 1970*	1978 Voting-age population	Turnout	%	Difference from 1970	1982 Voting-age population	Turnout	%	Difference from 1970	1986 Voting-age population	Turnout	%	Difference from 1970
ALABAMA	2,035,000	637,046	31.3%	2,449,000	497,574	20.3%	-11.0	2,654,000	551,886	20.8%	-10.5	2,785,000	650,538	23.4%	-7.9	2,882,000	537,163	18.6%	-12.7
ALASKA	179,000	42,309	23.6%	220,000	45,553	20.7%	-2.9	255,000	25,656	10.1%	-13.6	294,000	89,918	30.6%	6.9	334,000	84,943	25.4%	1.8
ARIZONA	1,055,000	201,887	19.1%	1,463,000	278,375	19.0%	-0.1	1,767,000	282,605	16.0%	-3.1	2,050,000	453,795	22.1%	3.0	2,324,000	298,986	12.9%	-6.3
ARKANSAS	1,179,000	375,648	31.9%	1,426,000	358,018	25.1%	-6.8	1,564,000	335,101	21.4%	-10.4	1,638,000	431,855	26.4%	-5.5	1,682,000	439,882	26.2%	-5.7
CALIFORNIA	12,492,000	2,938,607	23.5%	13,878,000	3,131,648	22.6%	-1.0	15,085,000	3,878,812	25.7%	2.2	16,246,000	3,787,669	23.3%	-0.2	17,387,000	2,781,714	16.0%	-7.5
COLORADO	1,324,000	302,432	22.8%	1,700,000	441,199	26.0%	3.1	1,957,000	483,985	24.7%	1.9	2,129,000	627,960	29.5%	6.7	2,262,000	616,325	27.2%	4.4
CONNECTICUT	1,895,000	500,561	26.4%	2,063,000	643,490	31.2%	4.8	2,165,000	613,109	28.3%	1.9	2,258,000	578,264	25.6%	-0.8	2,347,000	575,638	24.5%	-1.9
DELAWARE																			
DISTRICT OF COLUMBIA																			
FLORIDA	4,461,000	984,305	22.1%	5,661,000	1,118,954	19.8%	-2.3	6,657,000	1,406,580	21.1%	-0.9	7,597,000	1,739,553	22.9%	0.8	8,509,000	1,538,620	18.1%	-4.0

State Gubernatorial General Elections (continued)

State Gubernatorial General Elections *(continued)*

Democratic Turnout for Election Years 1970–1986 *(continued)*

State	1970 Voting-age population	Turnout	%	1974 Voting-age population	Turnout	%	Difference from 1970	1978 Voting-age population	Turnout	%	Difference from 1970	1982 Voting-age population	Turnout	%	Difference from 1970	1986 Voting-age population	Turnout	%	Difference from 1970
GEORGIA	2,973,000	620,419	20.9%	3,336,000	646,777	19.4%	-1.5	3,675,000	534,572	14.5%	-6.3	4,022,000	734,090	18.3%	-2.6	4,373,000	828,465	18.9%	-1.9
HAWAII	436,000	137,812	31.6%	538,000	136,262	25.3%	-6.3	607,000	153,394	25.3%	-6.3	665,000	141,043	21.2%	-10.4	720,000	173,655	24.1%	-7.5
IDAHO	413,000	128,004	31.0%	532,000	184,142	34.6%	3.6	605,000	169,540	28.0%	-3.0	643,000	165,365	25.7%	-5.3	666,000	193,429	29.0%	-2.0
ILLINOIS								7,753,000	1,263,134	16.3%		7,891,000	1,811,027	23.0%	6.7	7,965,000	208,830	2.6%	-13.7
INDIANA																			
IOWA	1,703,000	368,911	21.7%	1,951,000	377,553	19.4%	-2.3	2,043,000	345,519	16.9%	-4.8	2,063,000	483,291	23.4%	1.8	2,048,000	436,987	21.3%	-0.3
KANSAS	1,377,000	404,611	29.4%	1,588,000	384,115	24.2%	-5.2	1,670,000	363,835	21.8%	-7.6	1,720,000	405,772	23.6%	-5.8	1,757,000	404,338	23.0%	-6.4
KENTUCKY																			
LOUISIANA																			
MAINE	598,000	163,138	27.3%	709,000	132,219	18.6%	-8.6	771,000	176,493	22.9%	-4.4	822,000	281,066	34.2%	6.9	867,000	128,744	14.8%	-12.4
MARYLAND	2,383,000	639,579	26.8%	2,722,000	602,648	22.1%	-4.7	2,911,000	718,328	24.7%	-2.2	3,104,000	705,910	22.7%	-4.1	3,300,000	907,291	27.5%	0.7
MASSACHUSETTS	3,539,000	799,269	22.6%	3,874,000	992,284	25.6%	3.0	4,029,000	1,030,294	25.6%	3.0	4,165,000	1,219,109	29.3%	6.7	4,292,000	1,157,786	27.0%	4.4
MICHIGAN	5,199,000	1,294,638	24.9%	5,928,000	1,242,247	21.0%	-3.9	6,272,000	1,237,256	19.7%	-5.2	6,466,000	1,561,291	24.1%	-0.8	6,591,000	1,632,138	24.8%	-0.1
MINNESOTA	2,238,000	737,921	33.0%	2,626,000	786,787	30.0%	-3.0	2,812,000	718,244	25.5%	-7.4	2,949,000	1,049,104	35.6%	2.6	3,065,000	790,138	25.8%	-7.2
MISSISSIPPI																			
MISSOURI																			
MONTANA																			
NEBRASKA	898,000	248,552	27.7%	1,039,000	267,012	25.7%	-2.0	1,095,000	216,754	19.8%	-7.9	1,120,000	277,436	24.8%	-2.9	1,130,000	265,156	23.5%	-4.2
NEVADA	306,000	70,697	23.1%	431,000	114,114	26.5%	3.4	530,000	76,361	14.4%	-8.7	642,000	128,132	20.0%	-3.1	759,000	187,268	24.7%	1.6
NEW HAMPSHIRE	450,000	98,098	21.8%	558,000	110,591	19.8%	-2.0	629,000	133,133	21.2%	-0.6	696,000	132,317	19.0%	-2.8	761,000	116,142	15.3%	-6.5
NEW JERSEY																			
NEW MEXICO	559,000	148,835	26.6%	727,000	164,172	22.6%	-4.0	832,000	174,631	21.0%	-5.6	910,000	215,840	23.7%	-2.9	975,000	185,378	19.0%	-7.6
NEW YORK	11,599,000	2,421,426	20.9%	11,921,000	3,028,503	25.4%	4.5	11,979,000	2,429,272	20.3%	-0.6	12,104,000	2,675,213	22.1%	1.2	12,259,000	2,775,229	22.6%	1.8
NORTH CAROLINA																			
NORTH DAKOTA																			
OHIO	6,402,000	1,725,560	27.0%	7,209,000	1,482,191	20.6%	-6.4	7,521,000	1,354,631	18.0%	-8.9	7,710,000	1,981,882	25.7%	-1.2	7,843,000	1,858,372	23.7%	-3.3
OKLAHOMA	1,597,000	338,338	21.2%	1,919,000	514,389	26.8%	5.6	2,091,000	402,240	19.2%	-1.9	2,181,000	548,159	25.1%	3.9	2,234,000	405,295	18.1%	-3.0
OREGON	1,301,000	293,892	22.6%	1,610,000	444,812	27.6%	5.0	1,807,000	409,411	22.7%	0.1	1,919,000	374,316	19.5%	-3.1	1,990,000	549,456	27.6%	5.0
PENNSYLVANIA	7,387,000	2,043,029	27.7%	8,228,000	1,878,252	22.8%	-4.8	8,537,000	1,737,888	20.4%	-7.3	8,723,000	1,772,353	20.3%	-7.3	8,850,000	1,717,484	19.4%	-8.3
RHODE ISLAND	596,000	173,420	29.1%	651,000	252,436	38.8%	9.7	669,000	197,386	29.5%	0.4	690,000	247,208	35.8%	6.7	714,000	104,508	14.6%	-14.5
SOUTH CAROLINA	1,482,000	250,551	16.9%	1,883,000	248,938	13.2%	-3.7	2,097,000	384,898	18.4%	1.4	2,269,000	468,819	20.7%	3.8	2,420,000	361,325	14.9%	-2.0
SOUTH DAKOTA	386,000	131,616	34.1%	452,000	149,151	33.0%	-1.1	475,000	112,679	23.7%	-10.4	486,000	81,136	16.7%	-17.4	491,000	141,898	28.9%	-5.2
TENNESSEE	2,400,000	509,521	21.2%	2,914,000	576,833	19.8%	-1.4	3,187,000	523,495	16.4%	-4.8	3,373,000	500,937	14.9%	-6.4	3,516,000	656,602	18.7%	-2.6

State Gubernatorial General Elections (continued)

Democratic Turnout for Election Years 1970–1986 (continued)

State	1970 Voting-age population	Turnout	%	1974 Voting-age population	Turnout	%	Difference from 1970	1978 Voting-age population	Turnout	%	Difference from 1970	1982 Voting-age population	Turnout	%	Difference from 1970	1986 Voting-age population	Turnout	%	Difference from 1970
TEXAS	6,658,000	1,197,726	18.0%	8,218,000	1,016,334	12.4%	-5.6	9,197,000	1,166,979	12.7%	-5.3	9,998,000	1,697,870	17.0%	-1.0	10,718,000	1,584,515	14.8%	-3.2
UTAH																			
VERMONT	264,000	66,028	25.0%	319,000	79,842	25.0%	0.0	350,000	42,482	12.1%	-12.9	374,000	74,394	19.9%	-5.1	396,000	92,379	23.3%	-1.7
VIRGINIA																			
WASHINGTON																			
WEST VIRGINIA																			
WISCONSIN	2,613,000	728,403	27.9%	3,047,000	628,639	20.6%	-7.2	3,249,000	673,813	20.7%	-7.1	3,379,000	896,812	26.5%	-1.3	3,475,000	705,578	20.3%	-7.6
WYOMING	195,000	44,008	22.6%	263,000	71,741	27.3%	4.7	307,000	69,972	22.8%	0.2	319,000	106,427	33.4%	10.8	317,000	88,879	28.0%	5.5
Total	90,572,000	21,766,797	24.0%	104,053,000	23,027,795	22.1%	-1.9	119,804,000	24,394,368	20.4%	3.7	126,400,000	29,095,871	23.0%	-1.0	132,219,000	25,530,536	19.3%	-4.7

Other Turnout for Election Years 1970–1986

State	1970 Voting-age population	Turnout	%	1974 Voting-age population	Turnout	%	Difference from 1970*	1978 Voting-age population	Turnout	%	Difference from 1970	1982 Voting-age population	Turnout	%	Difference from 1970	1986 Voting-age population	Turnout	%	Difference from 1970
ALABAMA	2,035,000	217,906	10.7%	2,449,000	12,350	0.5%	-10.2	2,654,000	11,625	0.4%	-10.3	2,785,000	37,372	1.3%	-9.4	2,882,000	2,864	0.1%	-10.6
ALASKA	179,000	1,206	0.7%	220,000	4,770	2.2%	1.5	255,000	51,674	20.3%	19.6	294,000	32,676	11.1%	10.4	334,000	18,097	5.4%	4.7
ARIZONA				1,463,000	153	0.0%		1,767,000	14,858	0.8%	0.8	2,050,000	36,692	1.8%	1.8	2,324,000	224,085	9.6%	9.6
ARKANSAS	1,179,000	36,132	3.1%	1,426,000	84	0.0%	-3.1	1,564,000	65	0.0%	-3.1					1,682,000	242	0.0%	-3.1
CALIFORNIA	12,492,000	131,801	1.1%	13,878,000	163,468	1.2%	0.1	15,085,000	517,032	3.4%	2.4	16,246,000	208,015	1.3%	0.2	17,387,000	155,236	0.9%	-0.2
COLORADO	1,324,000	15,374	1.2%	1,700,000	8,862	0.5%	-0.6	1,957,000	22,530	1.2%	0.0	2,129,000	25,321	1.2%	0.0	2,262,000	8,183	0.4%	-0.8
CONNECTICUT	1,895,000	76	0.0%	2,063,000	19,114	0.9%	0.9	2,165,000	1,183	0.1%	0.1	2,258,000	8,119	0.4%	0.4	2,347,000	9,565	0.4%	0.4
DELAWARE																			
DISTRICT OF COLUMBIA																			
FLORIDA	4,461,000	265	0.0%													8,509,000	26	0.0%	0.0
GEORGIA	2,973,000	1,261	0.0%	3,336,000	548	0.0%	0.0	3,675,000	151	0.0%	0.0	4,022,000	455	0.0%	0.0	4,373,000	137	0.0%	0.0
HAWAII								607,000	3,583	0.6%		665,000	89,303	13.4%	12.8				
IDAHO				532,000	6,759	1.3%		605,000	4,877	0.8%	-0.5					666,000	4,203	0.6%	-0.6
ILLINOIS								7,753,000	27,277	0.4%		7,891,000	46,553	0.6%	0.2	7,965,000	1,279,299	16.1%	15.7
INDIANA																			
IOWA	1,703,000	18,936	1.1%	1,951,000	8,387	0.4%	-0.7	2,043,000	5,958	0.3%	-0.8	2,063,000	6,625	0.3%	-0.8	2,048,000	924	0.0%	-1.1
KANSAS	1,377,000	7,358	0.5%	1,588,000	11,968	0.8%	0.2	1,670,000	24,396	1.5%	0.9	1,720,000	18,135	1.1%	0.5				
KENTUCKY																			
LOUISIANA																			
MAINE				709,000	147,550	20.8%		771,000	66,903	8.7%	-12.1	822,000	6,280	0.8%	-20.0	867,000	127,805	14.7%	-6.1

State Gubernatorial General Elections (continued)

State Gubernatorial General Elections (continued)

Other Turnout for Election Years 1970–1986 (continued)

State	1970 Voting-age population	Turnout	%	1974 Voting-age population	Turnout	%	Difference from 1970	1978 Voting-age population	Turnout	%	Difference from 1970	1982 Voting-age population	Turnout	%	Difference from 1970	1986 Voting-age population	Turnout	%	Difference from 1970
MARYLAND	2,383,000	19,184	0.8%									3,104,000	413	0.0%	-0.8				
MASSACHUSETTS	3,539,000	10,014	0.3%	3,874,000	78,161	2.0%	1.7	4,029,000	5,885	0.1%	-0.1	4,165,000	81,466	2.0%	1.7	4,292,000	929	0.0%	-0.3
MICHIGAN	5,199,000	22,477	0.4%	5,928,000	57,905	1.0%	0.5	6,272,000	1,471	0.0%	-0.4	6,466,000	109,135	1.7%	1.3	6,591,000	10,779	0.2%	-0.3
MINNESOTA	2,238,000	5,742	0.3%	2,626,000	98,389	3.7%	3.5	2,812,000	37,439	1.3%	1.1	2,949,000	24,639	0.8%	0.6	3,065,000	19,096	0.6%	0.4
MISSISSIPPI																			
MISSOURI																			
MONTANA																			
NEBRASKA	898,000	11,073	1.2%	1,039,000	24,514	2.4%	1.1	1,095,000	196	0.0%	-1.2	1,120,000	263	0.0%	-1.2	1,130,000	941	0.1%	-1.1
NEVADA	306,000	11,894	3.9%	431,000	26,285	6.1%	2.2	530,000	7,987	1.5%	-2.4	642,000	11,515	1.8%	-2.1	759,000	8,026	1.1%	-2.8
NEW HAMPSHIRE	450,000	22,045	4.9%	558,000	141	0.0%	-4.9	629,000	13,990	2.2%	-2.7	696,000	4,882	0.7%	-4.2	761,000	141	0.0%	-4.9
NEW JERSEY																			
NEW MEXICO	559,000	6,900	1.2%	727,000	4,140	0.6%	-0.7	832,000	98	0.0%	-1.2								
NEW YORK	11,599,000	440,206	3.8%	11,921,000	45,006	0.4%	-3.4	11,979,000	183,144	1.5%	-2.3	12,104,000	84,851	0.7%	-3.1	12,259,000	155,085	1.3%	-2.5
NORTH CAROLINA																			
NORTH DAKOTA																			
OHIO	6,402,000	75,914	1.2%	7,209,000	96,140	1.3%	0.1	7,521,000	86,553	1.2%	0.0	7,710,000	70,877	0.9%	-0.3	7,843,000	975	0.0%	-1.2
OKLAHOMA	1,597,000	24,295	1.5%					2,091,000	8,119	0.4%	-1.1	2,181,000	2,764	0.1%	-1.4	2,234,000	72,868	3.3%	1.7
OREGON	1,301,000	2,538	0.2%	1,610,000	1,011	0.1%	-0.1	1,807,000	3,280	0.2%	0.0	1,919,000	27,852	1.5%	1.3	1,990,000	3,188	0.2%	0.0
PENNSYLVANIA	7,387,000	114,177	1.5%	8,228,000	34,065	0.4%	-1.1	8,537,000	38,039	0.4%	-1.1	8,723,000	38,848	0.4%	-1.1	8,850,000	32,523	0.4%	-1.2
RHODE ISLAND	596,000	1,373	0.2%					669,000	20,381	3.0%	2.8	690,000	10,449	1.5%	1.3	714,000	9,394	1.3%	1.1
SOUTH CAROLINA	1,482,000	13,073	0.9%	1,883,000	8,152	0.4%	-0.4	2,097,000	5,338	0.3%	-0.6					2,420,000	7,861	0.3%	-0.6
SOUTH DAKOTA																			
TENNESSEE	2,400,000	22,949	1.0%	2,914,000	8,414	0.3%	-0.7	3,187,000	4,241	0.1%	-0.8	3,373,000	27	0.0%	-1.0	3,516,000	288	0.0%	-0.9
TEXAS	6,658,000	398	0.0%	8,218,000	123,925	1.5%	1.5	9,197,000	18,946	0.2%	0.2	9,998,000	27,284	0.3%	0.3	10,718,000	43,166	0.4%	0.4
UTAH																			
VERMONT	264,000	42	0.0%	319,000	7,642	2.4%	2.4	350,000	3,819	1.1%	1.1	374,000	1,746	0.5%	0.5	396,000	29,175	7.4%	7.4
VIRGINIA																			
WASHINGTON																			
WEST VIRGINIA																			
WISCONSIN	2,613,000	12,140	0.5%	3,047,000	56,142	1.8%	1.4	3,249,000	11,127	0.3%	-0.1	3,379,000	20,694	0.6%	0.1	3,475,000	16,292	0.5%	0.0
WYOMING																			
Total	87,489,000	1,246,749	1.4%	91,847,000	1,054,045	1.1%	-0.3	109,454,000	1,202,165	1.1%	-0.3	112,538,000	1,033,251	0.9%	-0.5	124,659,000	2,241,393	1.8%	0.4

*Percentage point difference between turnout in current year and initial year listed in chart. If data do not appear for a state in the initial year listed, the difference is calculated from the first year in which data do appear for that state.

UNITED STATES SENATE GENERAL ELECTIONS

Election Years 1970–1986

State	1970 Voting-age population	Turnout	%	1974 Voting-age population	Turnout	%	Difference from 1970*	1978 Voting-age population	Turnout	%	Difference from 1970	1982 Voting-age population	Turnout	%	Difference from 1970	1986 Voting-age population	Turnout	%	Difference from 1970
ALABAMA				2,449,000	523,290	21.4%		2,654,000	582,025	21.9%	0.6					2,882,000	1,211,953	42.1%	20.7
ALASKA	179,000	80,364	44.9%	220,000	93,275	42.4%	-2.5	255,000	122,741	48.1%	3.2					334,000	180,801	54.1%	9.2
ARIZONA	1,055,000	407,796	38.7%	1,463,000	549,919	37.6%	-1.1					2,050,000	723,885	35.3%	-3.3	2,324,000	862,921	37.1%	-1.5
ARKANSAS				1,426,000	543,082	38.1%		1,564,000	522,239	33.4%	-4.7					1,682,000	695,487	41.3%	3.3
CALIFORNIA	12,492,000	6,402,167	52.0%	13,878,000	6,102,432	44.0%	-8.0					16,246,000	7,805,538	48.0%	-3.9	17,387,000	7,398,549	42.6%	-9.4
COLORADO				1,700,000	824,166	48.5%		1,957,000	819,150	41.9%	-6.6					2,262,000	1,060,765	46.9%	-1.6
CONNECTICUT	1,895,000	1,089,353	57.5%	2,063,000	1,084,918	52.6%	-4.9					2,258,000	1,083,613	48.0%	-9.5	2,347,000	976,933	41.6%	-15.9
DELAWARE	328,000	161,439	49.2%					413,000	162,072	39.2%	-10.0	442,000	190,960	43.2%	-6.0				
DISTRICT OF COLUMBIA																			
FLORIDA	4,461,000	1,675,378	37.6%	5,661,000	1,800,539	31.8%	-5.8					7,597,000	2,653,419	34.9%	-2.6	8,509,000	3,429,996	40.3%	2.8
GEORGIA				3,336,000	874,555	26.2%		3,675,000	645,164	17.6%	-8.7					4,373,000	1,225,008	28.0%	1.8
HAWAII	436,000	240,760	55.2%	538,000	250,221	46.5%	-8.7					665,000	306,410	46.1%	-9.1	720,000	328,797	45.7%	-9.6
IDAHO				532,000	258,847	48.7%		605,000	284,047	46.9%	-1.7					666,000	382,024	57.4%	8.7
ILLINOIS	6,804,000	3,599,272	52.9%	7,473,000	2,914,666	39.0%	-13.9	7,753,000	3,184,764	41.1%	-11.8					7,965,000	3,122,883	39.2%	-13.7
INDIANA	3,096,000	1,737,697	56.1%	3,571,000	1,752,978	49.1%	-7.0					3,895,000	1,817,287	46.7%	-9.5	3,979,000	1,545,563	38.8%	-17.3
IOWA				1,951,000	889,561	45.6%		2,043,000	824,654	40.4%	-5.2					2,048,000	891,762	43.5%	-2.1
KANSAS				1,588,000	794,437	50.0%		1,670,000	748,839	44.8%	-5.2					1,757,000	823,566	46.9%	-3.2
KENTUCKY				2,321,000	745,994	32.1%		2,507,000	476,783	19.0%	-13.1					2,665,000	677,280	25.4%	-6.7
LOUISIANA**				2,526,000	434,643	17.2%		2,766,000	839,669	30.4%	13.2					2,913,000	1,369,897	47.0%	29.8
MAINE	598,000	323,860	54.2%					771,000	375,172	48.7%	-5.5	822,000	459,715	55.9%	1.8				
MARYLAND	2,383,000	956,370	40.1%	2,722,000	877,786	32.2%	-7.9					3,104,000	1,114,690	35.9%	-4.2	3,300,000	1,112,637	33.7%	-6.4
MASSACHUSETTS	3,539,000	1,935,607	54.7%					4,029,000	1,985,700	49.3%	-5.4	4,165,000	2,050,769	49.2%	-5.5				
MICHIGAN	5,199,000	2,610,839	50.2%					6,272,000	2,846,630	45.4%	-4.8	6,466,000	2,994,334	46.3%	-3.9				
MINNESOTA	2,238,000	1,364,887	61.0%					2,812,000	1,580,778	56.2%	-4.8	2,949,000	1,804,675	61.2%	0.2				
MISSISSIPPI	1,248,000	324,215	26.0%					1,656,000	583,936	35.3%	9.3	1,729,000	645,026	37.3%	11.3				
MISSOURI	2,896,000	1,283,912	44.3%	3,306,000	1,224,303	37.0%	-7.3					3,593,000	1,543,521	43.0%	-1.4	3,690,000	1,477,327	40.0%	-4.3
MONTANA	406,000	247,869	61.1%					538,000	287,942	53.5%	-7.5	557,000	321,062	57.6%	-3.4				
NEBRASKA	898,000	458,966	51.1%					1,095,000	494,368	45.1%	-6.0	1,120,000	545,647	48.7%	-2.4				
NEVADA	306,000	147,768	48.3%	431,000	169,473	39.3%	-9.0					642,000	240,394	37.4%	-10.8	759,000	261,932	34.5%	-13.8
NEW HAMPSHIRE				558,000	223,363	40.0%		629,000	263,779	41.9%	1.9					761,000	244,797	32.2%	-7.9
NEW JERSEY	4,517,000	2,142,105	47.4%					5,049,000	1,957,515	38.8%	-8.7	5,219,000	2,193,945	42.0%	-5.4				
NEW MEXICO	559,000	289,906	51.9%					832,000	343,554	41.3%	-10.6	910,000	404,810	44.5%	-7.4				
NEW YORK	11,599,000	5,904,782	50.9%	11,921,000	5,163,600	43.3%	-7.6					12,104,000	4,967,729	41.0%	-9.9	12,259,000	4,179,447	34.1%	-16.8

United States Senate General Elections (continued)

United States Senate General Elections (continued)

Election Years 1970–1986 (continued)

State	1970			1974				1978				1982				1986			
	Voting-age population	Turnout	%	Voting-age population	Turnout	%	Difference from 1970	Voting-age population	Turnout	%	Difference from 1970	Voting-age population	Turnout	%	Difference from 1970	Voting-age population	Turnout	%	Difference from 1970
NORTH CAROLINA				3,730,000	1,020,367	27.4%		4,084,000	1,135,814	27.8%	0.5					4,713,000	1,591,330	33.8%	6.4
NORTH DAKOTA	356,000	219,560	61.7%	422,000	235,661	55.8%	-5.8					458,000	262,465	57.3%	-4.4	459,000	288,998	63.0%	1.3
OHIO	6,402,000	3,151,274	49.2%	7,209,000	2,987,951	41.4%	-7.8					7,710,000	3,395,463	44.0%	-5.2	7,843,000	3,121,189	39.8%	-9.4
OKLAHOMA				1,919,000	791,809	41.3%		2,091,000	754,264	36.1%	-5.2					2,234,000	893,666	40.0%	-1.3
OREGON				1,610,000	766,414	47.6%		1,807,000	892,518	49.4%	1.8					1,990,000	1,042,555	52.4%	4.8
PENNSYLVANIA	7,387,000	3,644,305	49.3%	8,228,000	3,477,812	42.3%	-7.1					8,723,000	3,604,108	41.3%	-8.0	8,850,000	3,378,226	38.2%	-11.2
RHODE ISLAND	596,000	341,222	57.3%					669,000	305,618	45.7%	-11.6	690,000	342,779	49.7%	-7.6				
SOUTH CAROLINA				1,883,000	512,397	27.2%		2,097,000	632,852	30.2%	3.0					2,420,000	737,962	30.5%	3.3
SOUTH DAKOTA				452,000	278,884	61.7%		475,000	255,599	53.8%	-7.9					491,000	295,830	60.3%	-1.4
TENNESSEE	2,400,000	1,097,041	45.7%					3,187,000	1,157,094	36.3%	-9.4	3,373,000	1,259,785	37.3%	-8.4				
TEXAS	6,658,000	2,231,671	33.5%					9,197,000	2,312,540	25.1%	-8.4	9,998,000	3,103,167	31.0%	-2.5				
UTAH	579,000	374,303	64.6%	756,000	420,642	55.6%	-9.0					947,000	530,802	56.1%	-8.6	1,014,000	435,111	42.9%	-21.7
VERMONT	264,000	154,899	58.7%	319,000	144,772	45.4%	-13.3					374,000	168,003	44.9%	-13.8	396,000	196,532	49.6%	-9.0
VIRGINIA	2,828,000	946,751	33.5%					3,702,000	1,222,256	33.0%	-0.5	3,998,000	1,415,622	35.4%	1.9				
WASHINGTON	2,087,000	1,066,807	51.1%	2,536,000	1,007,847	39.7%	-11.4					3,059,000	1,368,476	44.7%	-6.4	3,281,000	1,337,367	40.8%	-10.4
WEST VIRGINIA	1,069,000	445,623	41.7%					1,355,000	493,351	36.4%	-5.3	1,373,000	565,314	41.2%	-0.5				
WISCONSIN	2,613,000	1,338,967	51.2%	3,047,000	1,199,495	39.4%	-11.9					3,379,000	1,544,981	45.7%	-5.5	3,475,000	1,483,174	42.7%	-8.6
WYOMING	195,000	120,486	61.8%					307,000	133,364	43.4%	-18.3	319,000	167,191	52.4%	-9.4				
Total	100,566,000	48,608,211	48.3%	103,745,000	40,940,099	39.5%	-8.9	80,516,000	29,226,791	36.3%	-12.0	120,934,000	51,595,585	42.7%	-5.7	122,748,000	48,262,265	39.3%	-9.0

*Percentage point difference between turnout in current year and initial year listed in chart. If data do not appear for a state in the initial year listed, the difference is calculated from the first year in which data do appear for that state.

**In 1978 Louisiana eliminated the partisan primary for senator and instituted an open primary with candidates from all parties running on the same ballot. Any candidate who received a majority appeared in the general election unopposed. If no candidate received fifty percent, a runoff was held between the top two finishers. In 2008 Louisiana returned to a partisan primary system.

UNITED STATES SENATE GENERAL ELECTIONS

Republican Turnout for Election Years 1970–1986

State	1970 Voting-age population	Turnout	%	1974 Voting-age population	Turnout	%	Difference from 1970*	1978 Voting-age population	Turnout	%	Difference from 1970	1982 Voting-age population	Turnout	%	Difference from 1970	1986 Voting-age population	Turnout	%	Difference from 1970
ALABAMA																2,882,000	602,537	20.9%	20.9
ALASKA	179,000	47,908	26.8%	220,000	38,914	17.7%	-9.1	255,000	92,783	36.4%	9.6					334,000	97,674	29.2%	2.5
ARIZONA	1,055,000	228,284	21.6%	1,463,000	320,396	21.9%						2,050,000	291,749	14.2%	-7.4	2,324,000	521,850	22.5%	0.8
ARKANSAS				1,426,000	82,026	5.8%		1,564,000	84,722	5.4%	-0.3					1,682,000	262,313	15.6%	9.8
CALIFORNIA	12,492,000	2,877,617	23.0%	13,878,000	2,210,267	15.9%	-7.1					16,246,000	4,022,565	24.8%	1.7	17,387,000	3,541,804	20.4%	-2.7
COLORADO				1,700,000	325,508	19.1%		1,957,000	480,596	24.6%	5.4					2,262,000	512,994	22.7%	3.5
CONNECTICUT	1,895,000	454,721	24.0%	2,063,000	372,055	18.0%	-6.0					2,258,000	545,987	24.2%	0.2	2,347,000	340,438	14.5%	-9.5
DELAWARE	328,000	94,979	29.0%					413,000	66,479	16.1%	-12.9	442,000	105,357	23.8%	-5.1				
DISTRICT OF COLUMBIA																			
FLORIDA	4,461,000	772,817	17.3%	5,661,000	736,674	13.0%	-4.3					7,597,000	1,015,330	13.4%	-4.0	8,509,000	1,552,376	18.2%	0.9
GEORGIA				3,336,000	246,866	7.4%		3,675,000	108,808	3.0%	-4.4					4,373,000	601,241	13.7%	6.3
HAWAII	436,000	124,163	28.5%									665,000	52,071	7.8%	-20.6	720,000	86,910	12.1%	-16.4
IDAHO				532,000	109,072	20.5%		605,000	194,412	32.1%	11.6					666,000	196,958	29.6%	29.6
ILLINOIS	6,804,000	1,519,718	22.3%	7,473,000	1,084,884	14.5%	-7.8	7,753,000	1,698,711	21.9%	-0.4					7,965,000	1,053,734	13.2%	-9.1
INDIANA	3,096,000	866,707	28.0%	3,571,000	814,117	22.8%	-5.2					3,895,000	978,301	25.1%	-2.9	3,979,000	936,143	23.5%	-4.5
IOWA				1,951,000	420,546	21.6%		2,043,000	421,598	20.6%	-0.9					2,048,000	588,880	28.8%	28.8
KANSAS				1,588,000	403,983	25.4%		1,670,000	403,354	24.2%	-1.3					1,757,000	576,902	32.8%	7.4
KENTUCKY				2,321,000	328,982	14.2%		2,507,000	175,766	7.0%	-7.2					2,665,000	173,330	6.5%	6.5
LOUISIANA																2,913,000	646,311	22.2%	
MAINE	598,000	123,906	20.7%					771,000	212,294	27.5%	6.8	822,000	179,882	21.9%	1.2				
MARYLAND	2,383,000	484,960	20.4%	2,722,000	503,223	18.5%	-1.9					3,104,000	407,334	13.1%	-7.2	3,300,000	437,411	13.3%	-7.1
MASSACHUSETTS	3,539,000	715,978	20.2%					4,029,000	890,584	22.1%	1.9	4,165,000	784,602	18.8%	-1.4				
MICHIGAN	5,199,000	858,470	16.5%					6,272,000	1,362,165	21.7%	5.2	6,466,000	1,223,288	18.9%	2.4				
MINNESOTA	2,238,000	568,025	25.4%					2,812,000	894,092	31.8%	6.4	2,949,000	949,207	32.2%	6.8				
MISSISSIPPI								1,656,000	263,089	15.9%		1,729,000	230,927	13.4%	-2.5				
MISSOURI	2,896,000	617,903	21.3%	3,306,000	480,900	14.5%	-6.8					3,593,000	784,876	21.8%	0.5	3,690,000	777,612	21.1%	-0.3
MONTANA	406,000	97,809	24.1%					538,000	127,589	23.7%	-0.4	557,000	133,789	24.0%	-0.1				
NEBRASKA	898,000	240,894	26.8%					1,095,000	159,806	14.6%	-12.2	1,120,000	155,760	13.9%	-12.9				
NEVADA	306,000	60,838	19.9%	431,000	79,605	18.5%	-1.4					642,000	120,377	18.8%	-1.1	759,000	116,606	15.4%	-4.5
NEW HAMPSHIRE				558,000	110,926	19.9%		629,000	133,745	21.3%	1.4					761,000	154,090	20.2%	20.2
NEW JERSEY	4,517,000	903,026	20.0%					5,049,000	844,200	16.7%	-3.3	5,219,000	1,047,626	20.1%	0.1				
NEW MEXICO	559,000	135,004	24.2%					832,000	183,442	22.0%	-2.1	910,000	187,128	20.6%	-3.6				
NEW YORK	11,599,000	1,434,472	12.4%	11,921,000	2,340,188	19.6%	7.3					12,104,000	1,696,766	14.0%	1.7	12,259,000	2,378,197	19.4%	7.0

United States Senate General Elections (continued)

United States Senate General Elections *(continued)*

Republican Turnout for Election Years 1970–1986 *(continued)*

State	1970 Voting-age population	1970 Turnout	1970 %	1974 Voting-age population	1974 Turnout	1974 %	1974 Difference from 1970	1978 Voting-age population	1978 Turnout	1978 %	1978 Difference from 1970	1982 Voting-age population	1982 Turnout	1982 %	1982 Difference from 1970	1986 Voting-age population	1986 Turnout	1986 %	1986 Difference from 1970
NORTH CAROLINA				3,730,000	377,618	10.1%		4,084,000	619,151	15.2%	5.0					4,713,000	767,668	16.3%	16.3
NORTH DAKOTA	356,000	82,996	23.3%	422,000	114,117	27.0%	3.7					458,000	89,304	19.5%	-3.8	459,000	141,797	30.9%	7.6
OHIO	6,402,000	1,565,682	24.5%	7,209,000	918,133	12.7%	-11.7					7,710,000	1,396,790	18.1%	-6.3	7,843,000	1,171,893	14.9%	-9.5
OKLAHOMA				1,919,000	390,997	20.4%		2,091,000	247,857	11.9%	-8.5					2,234,000	493,436	22.1%	22.1
OREGON				1,610,000	420,984	26.1%		1,807,000	550,165	30.4%	4.3					1,990,000	656,317	33.0%	6.8
PENNSYLVANIA	7,387,000	1,874,106	25.4%	8,228,000	1,843,317	22.4%	-3.0					8,723,000	2,136,418	24.5%	-0.9	8,850,000	1,906,537	21.5%	-3.8
RHODE ISLAND	596,000	107,351	18.0%					669,000	76,061	11.4%	-6.6	690,000	175,495	25.4%	7.4				
SOUTH CAROLINA				1,883,000	146,645	7.8%		2,097,000	351,733	16.8%	9.0					2,420,000	262,886	10.9%	10.9
SOUTH DAKOTA				452,000	130,955	29.0%		475,000	170,832	36.0%	7.0					491,000	143,173	29.2%	29.2
TENNESSEE	2,400,000	562,645	23.4%					3,187,000	642,644	20.2%	-3.3	3,373,000	479,642	14.2%	-9.2				
TEXAS	6,658,000	1,035,794	15.6%					9,197,000	1,151,376	12.5%	-3.0	9,998,000	1,256,759	12.6%	-3.0				
UTAH	579,000	159,004	27.5%	756,000	210,299	27.8%	0.4					947,000	309,332	32.7%	5.2	1,014,000	314,608	31.0%	3.6
VERMONT	264,000	91,198	34.5%	319,000	66,223	20.8%	-13.8					374,000	84,450	22.6%	-12.0	396,000	67,798	17.1%	-17.4
VIRGINIA	2,828,000	145,031	5.1%					3,702,000	613,232	16.6%	11.4	3,998,000	724,571	18.1%	13.0				
WASHINGTON	2,087,000	170,790	8.2%	2,536,000	363,626	14.3%	6.2					3,059,000	332,273	10.9%	2.7	3,281,000	650,931	19.8%	11.7
WEST VIRGINIA	1,069,000	99,658	9.3%					1,355,000	244,317	18.0%	8.7	1,373,000	173,910	12.7%	3.3				
WISCONSIN	2,613,000	381,297	14.6%	3,047,000	429,327	14.1%	-0.5					3,379,000	527,355	15.6%	1.0	3,475,000	754,573	21.7%	7.1
WYOMING	195,000	53,279	27.3%					307,000	82,908	27.0%	-0.3	319,000	94,725	29.7%	2.4				
Total	99,318,000	19,557,030	19.7%	98,232,000	16,421,373	16.7%	-3.0	75,096,000	13,548,511	18.0%	-1.6	120,934,000	22,693,946	18.8%	-0.9	122,748,000	23,487,928	19.1%	-0.6

Democratic Turnout for Election Years 1970–1986

State	1970 Voting-age population	1970 Turnout	1970 %	1974 Voting-age population	1974 Turnout	1974 %	1974 Difference from 1970*	1978 Voting-age population	1978 Turnout	1978 %	1978 Difference from 1970	1982 Voting-age population	1982 Turnout	1982 %	1982 Difference from 1970	1986 Voting-age population	1986 Turnout	1986 %	1986 Difference from 1970
ALABAMA				2,449,000	501,541	20.5%		2,654,000	547,054	20.6%	0.1					2,882,000	609,360	21.1%	21.1
ALASKA	179,000	32,456	18.1%	220,000	54,361	24.7%	6.6	255,000	29,574	11.6%	-6.5					334,000	79,727	23.9%	5.7
ARIZONA	1,055,000	179,512	17.0%	1,463,000	229,523	15.7%	-1.3					2,050,000	411,970	20.1%	3.1	2,324,000	340,965	14.7%	-2.3
ARKANSAS				1,426,000	461,056	32.3%		1,564,000	399,916	25.6%	-6.8					1,682,000	433,122	25.8%	25.8
CALIFORNIA	12,492,000	3,496,558	28.0%	13,878,000	3,693,160	26.6%	-1.4					16,246,000	3,494,968	21.5%	-6.5	17,387,000	3,646,672	21.0%	-7.0
COLORADO				1,700,000	471,691	27.7%		1,957,000	330,247	16.9%	-10.9					2,262,000	529,449	23.4%	23.4
CONNECTICUT	1,895,000	368,111	19.4%	2,063,000	690,820	33.5%	14.1					2,258,000	499,146	22.1%	2.7	2,347,000	632,695	27.0%	7.5
DELAWARE	328,000	64,740	19.7%					413,000	93,930	22.7%	3.0	442,000	84,413	19.1%	-0.6				
DISTRICT OF COLUMBIA																			
FLORIDA	4,461,000	902,438	20.2%	5,661,000	781,031	13.8%	-6.4					7,597,000	1,637,667	21.6%	1.3	8,509,000	1,877,543	22.1%	1.8

United States Senate General Elections (continued)

Democratic Turnout for Election Years 1970–1986 (continued)

State	1970 Voting-age population	1970 Turnout	1970 %	1974 Voting-age population	1974 Turnout	1974 %	1974 Difference from 1970	1978 Voting-age population	1978 Turnout	1978 %	1978 Difference from 1970	1982 Voting-age population	1982 Turnout	1982 %	1982 Difference from 1970	1986 Voting-age population	1986 Turnout	1986 %	1986 Difference from 1970
GEORGIA				3,336,000	627,376	18.8%		3,675,000	536,320	14.6%	-4.2					4,373,000	623,707	14.3%	14.3
HAWAII	436,000	116,597	26.7%	538,000	207,454	38.6%	11.8					665,000	245,386	36.9%	10.2	720,000	241,887	33.6%	6.9
IDAHO				532,000	145,140	27.3%		605,000	89,635	14.8%	-12.5					666,000	185,066	27.8%	27.8
ILLINOIS	6,804,000	2,065,054	30.4%	7,473,000	1,811,496	24.2%	-6.1	7,753,000	1,448,187	18.7%	-11.7					7,965,000	2,033,783	25.5%	-4.8
INDIANA	3,096,000	870,990	28.1%	3,571,000	889,269	24.9%	-3.2					3,895,000	828,400	21.3%	-6.9	3,979,000	595,192	15.0%	-13.2
IOWA				1,951,000	462,947	23.7%		2,043,000	395,066	19.3%	-4.4					2,018,000	299,406	14.6%	-9.1
KANSAS				1,588,000	390,451	24.6%		1,670,000	317,602	19.0%	-5.6					1,757,000	246,664	14.0%	14.0
KENTUCKY				2,321,000	399,406	17.2%		2,507,000	290,730	11.6%	-5.6					2,665,000	503,775	18.9%	18.9
LOUISIANA**				2,526,000	434,643	17.2%		2,766,000	839,669	30.4%	13.2					2,913,000	723,586	24.8%	24.8
MAINE	598,000	199,954	33.4%					771,000	127,327	16.5%	-16.9	822,000	279,819	34.0%	0.6				
MARYLAND	2,383,000	460,422	19.3%	2,722,000	374,563	13.8%	-5.6					3,104,000	707,356	22.8%	3.5	3,300,000	675,225	20.5%	1.1
MASSACHUSETTS	3,539,000	1,202,856	34.0%					4,029,000	1,093,283	27.1%	-6.9	4,165,000	1,247,084	29.9%	-4.0				
MICHIGAN	5,199,000	1,744,716	33.6%					6,272,000	1,484,193	23.7%	-9.9	6,466,000	1,728,793	26.7%	-6.8				
MINNESOTA	2,238,000	788,256	35.2%					2,812,000	638,375	22.7%	-12.5	2,949,000	840,401	28.5%	-6.7				
MISSISSIPPI	1,248,000	286,622	23.0%					1,656,000	185,454	11.2%	-11.8	1,729,000	414,099	24.0%	1.0				
MISSOURI	2,896,000	655,431	22.6%	3,306,000	735,433	22.2%	-0.4					3,593,000	758,629	21.1%	-1.5	3,690,000	699,624	19.0%	-3.7
MONTANA	406,000	150,060	37.0%					538,000	160,353	29.8%	-7.2	557,000	174,861	31.4%	-5.6				
NEBRASKA	898,000	217,681	24.2%					1,095,000	334,276	30.5%	6.3	1,120,000	363,350	32.4%	8.2				
NEVADA	306,000	85,187	27.8%	431,000	78,981	18.3%	-9.5					642,000	114,720	17.9%	-10.0	759,000	130,955	17.3%	-10.6
NEW HAMPSHIRE				558,000	110,924	19.9%		629,000	127,945	20.3%	0.5					761,000	79,225	10.4%	10.4
NEW JERSEY	4,517,000	1,157,074	25.6%					5,049,000	1,082,960	21.4%	-4.2	5,219,000	1,117,549	21.4%	-4.2				
NEW MEXICO	559,000	151,486	27.1%					832,000	160,045	19.2%	-7.9	910,000	217,682	23.9%	-3.2				
NEW YORK	11,599,000	2,171,232	18.7%	11,921,000	1,973,781	16.6%	-2.2					12,104,000	3,232,146	26.7%	8.0	12,259,000	1,723,216	14.1%	-4.7
NORTH CAROLINA				3,730,000	633,775	17.0%		4,084,000	516,663	12.7%	-4.3					4,713,000	823,662	17.5%	17.5
NORTH DAKOTA	356,000	134,519	37.8%	422,000	113,931	27.0%	-10.8					458,000	164,873	36.0%	-1.8	459,000	143,932	31.4%	-6.4
OHIO	6,402,000	1,495,262	23.4%	7,209,000	1,930,670	26.8%	3.4					7,710,000	1,923,767	25.0%	1.6	7,843,000	1,949,208	24.9%	1.5
OKLAHOMA				1,919,000	387,162	20.2%		2,091,000	493,953	23.6%	3.4					2,234,000	400,230	17.9%	17.9
OREGON				1,610,000	338,591	21.0%		1,807,000	341,616	18.9%	-2.1					1,990,000	375,735	18.9%	18.9
PENNSYLVANIA	7,387,000	1,653,774	22.4%	8,228,000	1,596,121	19.4%	-3.0					8,723,000	1,412,965	16.2%	-6.2	8,850,000	1,448,219	16.4%	-6.0
RHODE ISLAND	596,000	230,469	38.7%					669,000	229,557	34.3%	-4.4	690,000	167,283	24.2%	-14.4				
SOUTH CAROLINA				1,883,000	356,126	18.9%		2,097,000	281,119	13.4%	-5.5					2,420,000	465,500	19.2%	0.3
SOUTH DAKOTA				452,000	147,929	32.7%		475,000	84,767	17.8%	-14.9					491,000	152,657	31.1%	-1.6
TENNESSEE	2,400,000	519,858	21.7%					3,187,000	466,228	14.6%	-7.0	3,373,000	780,113	23.1%	1.5				

United States Senate General Elections (continued)

United States Senate General Elections *(continued)*

Democratic Turnout for Election Years 1970–1986 *(continued)*

State	1970 Voting-age population	Turnout	%	1974 Voting-age population	Turnout	%	Difference from 1970	1978 Voting-age population	Turnout	%	Difference from 1970	1982 Voting-age population	Turnout	%	Difference from 1970	1986 Voting-age population	Turnout	%	Difference from 1970
TEXAS	6,658,000	1,194,069	**17.9%**					9,197,000	1,139,149	**12.4%**	-5.5	9,998,000	1,818,223	**18.2%**	0.3				
UTAH	579,000	210,207	**36.3%**	756,000	185,377	**24.5%**	-11.8					947,000	219,482	**23.2%**	-13.1	1,014,000	115,523	**11.4%**	-24.9
VERMONT	264,000	62,271	**23.6%**	319,000	72,629	**22.8%**	-0.8					374,000	79,340	**21.2%**	-2.4	396,000	124,123	**31.3%**	7.8
VIRGINIA	2,828,000	295,057	**10.4%**					3,702,000	608,511	**16.4%**	6.0	3,998,000	690,839	**17.3%**	6.8				
WASHINGTON	2,087,000	879,385	**42.1%**	2,536,000	611,811	**24.1%**	-18.0					3,059,000	943,655	**30.8%**	-11.3	3,281,000	677,471	**20.6%**	-21.5
WEST VIRGINIA	1,069,000	345,965	**32.4%**					1,355,000	249,034	**18.4%**	-14.0	1,373,000	387,170	**28.2%**	-4.2				
WISCONSIN	2,613,000	948,445	**36.3%**	3,047,000	740,700	**24.3%**	-12.0					3,379,000	983,311	**29.1%**	-7.2	3,475,000	702,963	**20.2%**	-16.1
WYOMING	195,000	67,207	**34.5%**					307,000	50,456	**16.4%**	-18.0	319,000	72,466	**22.7%**	-11.7				-34.5
Total	100,566,000	25,403,921	**25.3%**	103,745,000	22,639,869	**21.8%**	-3.4	80,516,000	15,173,194	**18.8%**	-6.4	120,934,000	28,041,926	**23.2%**	-2.1	122,748,000	24,290,067	**19.8%**	-5.5

Other Turnout for Election Years 1970–1986

State	1970 Voting-age population	Turnout	%	1974 Voting-age population	Turnout	%	Difference from 1970*	1978 Voting-age population	Turnout	%	Difference from 1970	1982 Voting-age population	Turnout	%	Difference from 1970	1986 Voting-age population	Turnout	%	Difference from 1970
ALABAMA				2,449,000	21,749	**0.9%**		2,654,000	34,971	**1.3%**	0.4					2,882,000	56	**0.0%**	0.0
ALASKA								255,000	384	**0.2%**		294,000				334,000	3,400	**1.0%**	0.9
ARIZONA												2,050,000	20,166	**1.0%**		2,324,000	106	**0.0%**	0.0
ARKANSAS								1,564,000	37,601	**2.4%**		1,638,000				1,682,000	52	**0.0%**	-2.4
CALIFORNIA	12,492,000	117,982	**0.9%**	13,878,000	199,005	**1.4%**	0.5					16,246,000	288,005	**1.8%**	0.8	17,387,000	210,073	**1.2%**	0.3
COLORADO				1,700,000	26,967	**1.6%**		1,957,000	8,307	**0.4%**	-1.2					2,262,000	18,322	**0.8%**	0.8
CONNECTICUT	1,895,000	266,521	**14.1%**	2,063,000	22,043	**1.1%**	-13.0					2,258,000	38,480	**1.7%**	-12.4	2,347,000	3,800	**0.2%**	-13.9
DELAWARE	328,000	1,720	**0.5%**					413,000	1,663	**0.4%**	-0.1	442,000	1,190	**0.3%**	-0.3				
DISTRICT OF COLUMBIA																			
FLORIDA	4,461,000	123	**0.0%**	5,661,000	282,834	**5.0%**	5.0					7,597,000	422	**0.0%**	0.0	8,509,000	77	**0.0%**	0.0
GEORGIA				3,336,000	313	**0.0%**		3,675,000	36	**0.0%**	0.0					4,373,000	60	**0.0%**	0.0
HAWAII				538,000	42,767	**7.9%**						665,000	8,953	**1.3%**	-6.6				
IDAHO				532,000	4,635	**0.9%**													
ILLINOIS	6,804,000	14,500	**0.2%**	7,473,000	18,286	**0.2%**	0.0	7,753,000	37,866	**0.5%**	0.3					7,965,000	35,366	**0.4%**	0.2
INDIANA				3,571,000	49,592	**1.4%**						3,895,000	10,586	**0.3%**	-1.1	3,979,000	14,228	**0.4%**	0.4
IOWA				1,951,000	6,068	**0.3%**		2,043,000	7,990	**0.4%**	0.1					2,048,000	3,476	**0.2%**	-0.1
KANSAS				1,588,000	3	**0.0%**		1,670,000	27,883	**1.7%**	1.7								
KENTUCKY				2,321,000	17,606	**0.8%**		2,507,000	10,287	**0.4%**	-0.3					2,665,000	175	**0.0%**	0.0
LOUISIANA**																			
MAINE								771,000	35,551	**4.6%**		822,000	14	**0.0%**	-4.6				

United States Senate General Elections (continued)

Other Turnout for Election Years 1970–1986 (continued)

State	1970 Voting-age population	Turnout	%	1974 Voting-age population	Turnout	%	Difference from 1970	1978 Voting-age population	Turnout	%	Difference from 1970	1982 Voting-age population	Turnout	%	Difference from 1970	1986 Voting-age population	Turnout	%	Difference from 1970
MARYLAND	2,383,000	10,988	0.5%													3,300,000	1	0.0%	-0.5
MASSACHUSETTS	3,539,000	16,773	0.5%					4,029,000	1,833	0.0%	-0.4	4,165,000	19,083	0.5%	0.0				
MICHIGAN	5,199,000	7,653	0.1%					6,272,000	272	0.0%	-0.1	6,466,000	42,253	0.7%	0.5				
MINNESOTA	2,238,000	8,606	0.4%					2,812,000	48,311	1.7%	1.3	2,949,000	15,067	0.5%	0.1				
MISSISSIPPI	1,248,000	37,593	3.0%					1,656,000	135,393	8.2%	5.2								
MISSOURI	2,896,000	10,578	0.4%	3,306,000	7,970	0.2%	-0.1					3,593,000	10	0.0%	0.4	3,690,000	91	0.0%	-0.4
MONTANA												557,000	12,412	2.2%					
NEBRASKA	898,000	391	0.0%					1,095,000	286	0.0%	0.0	1,120,000	26,537	2.4%	2.3				
NEVADA	306,000	1,743	0.6%	431,000	10,887	2.5%	2.0					642,000	5,297	0.8%	0.3	759,000	14,371	1.9%	1.3
NEW HAMPSHIRE				558,000	1,513	0.3%		629,000	2,089	0.3%	0.1					761,000	11,482	1.5%	1.2
NEW JERSEY	4,517,000	82,005	1.8%					5,049,000	30,355	0.6%	-1.2	5,219,000	28,770	0.6%	-1.3				
NEW MEXICO	559,000	3,416	0.6%					832,000	67	0.0%	-0.6								
NEW YORK	11,599,000	2,299,078	19.8%	11,921,000	849,631	7.1%	-12.7					12,104,000	38,817	0.3%	-19.5	12,259,000	78,034	0.6%	19.2
NORTH CAROLINA				3,730,000	8,974	0.2%													
NORTH DAKOTA	356,000	2,045	0.6%	422,000	7,613	1.8%	1.2					458,000	8,288	1.8%	1.2	459,000	3,269	0.7%	0.1
OHIO	6,402,000	90,330	1.4%	7,209,000	139,148	1.9%	0.5					7,710,000	74,906	1.0%	-0.4	7,843,000	88	0.0%	-1.4
OKLAHOMA				1,919,000	13,650	0.7%		2,091,000	12,454	0.6%	-0.1								
OREGON				1,610,000	6,839	0.4%		1,807,000	737	0.0%	-0.4					1,990,000	10,503	0.5%	0.5
PENNSYLVANIA	7,387,000	116,425	1.6%	8,228,000	38,374	0.5%	-1.1					8,723,000	54,725	0.6%	-0.9	8,850,000	23,470	0.3%	-1.3
RHODE ISLAND	596,000	3,402	0.6%									690,000	1	0.0%	-0.6				
SOUTH CAROLINA				1,883,000	9,626	0.5%										2,420,000	9,576	0.4%	0.4
SOUTH DAKOTA																			
TENNESSEE	2,400,000	14,538	0.6%					3,187,000	48,222	1.5%	0.9	3,373,000	30	0.0%	-0.6				
TEXAS	6,658,000	1,808	0.0%					9,197,000	22,015	0.2%	0.2	9,998,000	28,185	0.3%	0.3				
UTAH	579,000	5,092	0.9%	756,000	24,966	3.3%	2.4					947,000	1,988	0.2%	-0.7	1,014,000	4,980	0.5%	-0.4
VERMONT	264,000	1,430	0.5%	319,000	5,920	1.9%	1.3					374,000	4,213	1.1%	0.6	396,000	4,611	1.2%	0.6
VIRGINIA	2,828,000	506,663	17.9%					3,702,000	513	0.0%	-17.9	3,998,000	212	0.0%	-17.9				
WASHINGTON	2,087,000	16,632	0.8%	2,536,000	32,410	1.3%	0.5					3,059,000	92,548	3.0%	2.2	3,281,000	8,965	0.3%	-0.5
WEST VIRGINIA												1,373,000	4,234	0.3%					
WISCONSIN	2,613,000	9,225	0.4%	3,047,000	29,468	1.0%	0.6					3,379,000	34,315	1.0%	0.7	3,475,000	25,638	0.7%	0.4
WYOMING																			0.0
Total	93,532,000	3,647,260	3.9%	94,936,000	1,878,857	2.0%	-1.9	67,620,000	505,086	0.7%	-3.2	116,804,000	859,713	0.7%	-3.2	109,254,000	484,270	0.4%	-3.5

*Percentage point difference between turnout in current year and initial year listed in chart. If data do not appear for a state in the initial year listed, the difference is calculated from the first year in which data do appear for that state.

**In 1978 Louisiana eliminated the partisan primary for senator and instituted an open primary with candidates from all parties running on the same ballot. Any candidate who received a majority appeared in the general election unopposed. If no candidate received fifty percent, a runoff was held between the top two finishers. In 2008 Louisiana returned to a partisan primary system.

UNITED STATES HOUSE OF REPRESENTATIVES GENERAL ELECTIONS

Election Years 1970–1986

State	1970 Voting-age population	1970 Turnout	1970 %	1974 Voting-age population	1974 Turnout	1974 %	1974 Difference from 1970*	1978 Voting-age population	1978 Turnout	1978 %	1978 Difference from 1970	1982 Voting-age population	1982 Turnout	1982 %	1982 Difference from 1970	1986 Voting-age population	1986 Turnout	1986 %	1986 Difference from 1970
ALABAMA	2,035,000	742,072	36.5%	2,449,000	561,400	22.9%	-13.5	2,654,000	642,279	24.2%	-12.3	2,785,000	961,019	34.5%	-2.0	2,882,000	1,115,654	38.7%	2.2
ALASKA	179,000	80,084	44.7%	220,000	95,921	43.6%	-1.1	255,000	124,187	48.7%	4.0	294,000	181,084	61.6%	16.9	334,000	180,277	54.0%	9.2
ARIZONA	1,055,000	402,119	38.1%	1,463,000	543,823	37.2%	-0.9	1,767,000	518,982	29.4%	-8.7	2,050,000	711,011	34.7%	-3.4	2,324,000	803,730	34.6%	-3.5
ARKANSAS	1,179,000	173,211	14.7%	1,426,000	423,756	29.7%	15.0	1,564,000	293,259	18.8%	4.1	1,638,000	759,238	46.4%	31.7	1,682,000	665,645	39.6%	24.9
CALIFORNIA	12,492,000	6,321,394	50.6%	13,878,000	5,829,180	42.0%	-8.6	15,085,000	6,525,747	43.3%	-7.3	16,246,000	7,586,557	46.7%	-3.9	17,387,000	7,200,149	41.4%	-9.2
COLORADO	1,324,000	637,148	48.1%	1,700,000	784,543	46.1%	-2.0	1,957,000	785,175	40.1%	-8.0	2,129,000	946,423	44.5%	-3.7	2,262,000	1,018,257	45.0%	-3.1
CONNECTICUT	1,895,000	1,070,504	56.5%	2,063,000	1,078,533	52.3%	-4.2	2,165,000	1,021,021	47.2%	-9.3	2,258,000	1,070,675	47.4%	-9.1	2,347,000	979,655	41.7%	-14.8
DELAWARE	328,000	160,313	48.9%	382,000	160,328	42.0%	-6.9	413,000	157,566	38.2%	-10.7	442,000	188,064	42.5%	-6.3	471,000	160,757	34.1%	-14.7
DISTRICT OF COLUMBIA																			
FLORIDA	4,461,000	1,250,111	28.0%	5,661,000	1,061,620	18.8%	-9.3	6,657,000	1,619,987	24.3%	-3.7	7,597,000	2,211,594	29.1%	1.1	8,509,000	2,142,051	25.2%	-2.8
GEORGIA	2,973,000	879,241	29.6%	3,336,000	822,423	24.7%	-4.9	3,675,000	588,605	16.0%	-13.6	4,022,000	904,457	22.5%	-7.1	4,373,000	1,062,328	24.3%	-5.3
HAWAII	436,000	208,213	47.8%	538,000	259,427	48.2%	0.5	607,000	253,369	41.7%	-6.0	665,000	297,915	44.8%	-3.0	720,000	331,196	46.0%	-1.8
IDAHO	413,000	234,317	56.7%	532,000	250,278	47.0%	-9.7	605,000	285,283	47.2%	-9.6	643,000	321,146	49.9%	-6.8	666,000	375,759	56.4%	-0.3
ILLINOIS	6,804,000	3,494,984	51.4%	7,473,000	2,842,109	38.0%	-13.3	7,753,000	3,043,585	39.3%	-12.1	7,891,000	3,613,031	45.8%	-5.6	7,965,000	3,017,210	37.9%	-13.5
INDIANA	3,096,000	936,626	30.3%	3,571,000	1,730,834	48.5%	18.2	3,774,000	1,448,863	38.4%	8.1	3,895,000	1,796,060	46.1%	15.9	3,979,000	1,555,507	39.1%	8.8
IOWA	1,703,000	779,691	45.8%	1,951,000	903,515	46.3%	0.5	2,043,000	811,555	39.7%	-6.1	2,063,000	1,004,763	48.7%	2.9	2,048,000	889,595	43.4%	-2.3
KANSAS	1,377,000	719,671	52.3%	1,588,000	775,558	48.8%	-3.4	1,670,000	675,940	40.5%	-11.8	1,720,000	756,345	44.0%	-8.3	1,757,000	787,370	44.8%	-7.5
KENTUCKY	2,115,000	473,663	22.4%	2,321,000	679,225	29.3%	6.9	2,507,000	477,461	19.0%	-3.4	2,606,000	700,322	26.9%	4.5	2,665,000	629,796	23.6%	1.2
LOUISIANA	2,061,000	363,048	17.6%	2,526,000	546,042	21.6%	4.0	2,766,000	771,072	27.9%	10.3	2,870,000	516,957	18.0%	0.4	2,913,000	825,414	28.3%	10.7
MAINE	598,000	318,031	53.2%	709,000	353,280	49.8%	-3.4	771,000	369,552	47.9%	-5.3	822,000	452,141	55.0%	1.8	867,000	421,630	48.6%	-4.6
MARYLAND	2,383,000	885,541	37.2%	2,722,000	874,089	32.1%	-5.0	2,911,000	924,057	31.7%	-5.4	3,104,000	1,091,161	35.2%	-2.0	3,300,000	1,063,065	32.2%	-4.9
MASSACHUSETTS	3,539,000	1,800,498	50.9%	3,874,000	1,698,701	43.8%	-7.0	4,029,000	1,809,394	44.9%	-6.0	4,165,000	1,890,366	45.4%	-5.5	4,292,000	1,503,168	35.0%	-15.9
MICHIGAN	5,199,000	2,562,398	49.3%	5,928,000	2,519,420	42.5%	-6.8	6,272,000	2,707,714	43.2%	-6.1	6,466,000	2,808,416	43.4%	-5.9	6,591,000	2,327,176	35.3%	-14.0
MINNESOTA	2,238,000	1,340,626	59.9%	2,626,000	1,219,002	46.4%	-13.5	2,812,000	1,525,880	54.3%	-5.6	2,949,000	1,749,931	59.3%	-0.6	3,065,000	1,392,973	45.4%	-14.5
MISSISSIPPI	1,248,000	312,357	25.0%	1,525,000	305,909	20.1%	-5.0	1,656,000	518,961	31.3%	6.3	1,729,000	641,132	37.1%	12.1	1,778,000	523,563	29.4%	4.4
MISSOURI	2,896,000	1,197,407	41.3%	3,306,000	1,209,042	36.6%	-4.8	3,474,000	1,545,827	44.5%	3.2	3,593,000	1,528,416	42.5%	1.2	3,690,000	1,430,127	38.8%	-2.6
MONTANA	406,000	249,397	61.4%	493,000	254,146	51.6%	-9.9	538,000	283,355	52.7%	-8.8	557,000	316,539	56.8%	-4.6	565,000	317,862	56.3%	-5.2
NEBRASKA	898,000	448,099	49.9%	1,039,000	447,691	43.1%	-6.8	1,095,000	494,838	45.2%	-4.7	1,120,000	519,081	46.3%	-3.6	1,130,000	555,437	49.2%	-0.7
NEVADA	306,000	137,643	45.0%	431,000	167,966	39.0%	-6.0	530,000	190,643	36.0%	-9.0	642,000	234,072	36.5%	-8.5	759,000	257,229	33.9%	-11.1
NEW HAMPSHIRE	450,000	213,662	47.5%	558,000	219,542	39.3%	-8.1	629,000	258,316	41.1%	-6.4	696,000	268,918	38.6%	-8.8	761,000	240,747	31.6%	-15.8
NEW JERSEY	4,517,000	2,101,409	46.5%	4,852,000	2,083,557	42.9%	-3.6	5,049,000	1,933,923	38.3%	-8.2	5,219,000	2,146,090	41.1%	-5.4	5,376,000	1,553,545	28.9%	-17.6
NEW MEXICO	559,000	285,358	51.0%	727,000	316,372	43.5%	-7.5	832,000	284,682	34.2%	-16.8	910,000	394,906	43.4%	-7.7	975,000	385,655	39.6%	-11.5
NEW YORK	11,599,000	5,446,208	47.0%	11,921,000	4,894,349	41.1%	-5.9	11,979,000	4,379,028	36.6%	-10.4	12,104,000	4,681,377	38.7%	-8.3	12,259,000	3,903,611	31.8%	-15.1

United States House of Representatives General Elections *(continued)*

Election Years 1970–1986 *(continued)*

State	1970 Voting-age population	Turnout	%	1974 Voting-age population	Turnout	%	Difference from 1970	1978 Voting-age population	Turnout	%	Difference from 1970	1982 Voting-age population	Turnout	%	Difference from 1970	1986 Voting-age population	Turnout	%	Difference from 1970
NORTH CAROLINA	3,038,000	929,948	30.6%	3,730,000	988,340	26.5%	-4.1	4,084,000	1,019,956	25.0%	-5.6	4,406,000	1,321,080	30.0%	-0.6	4,713,000	1,572,505	33.4%	2.8
NORTH DAKOTA	356,000	210,160	59.0%	422,000	233,688	55.4%	-3.7	450,000	220,348	49.0%	-10.1	458,000	260,499	56.9%	-2.2	459,000	286,361	62.4%	3.4
OHIO	6,402,000	3,042,011	47.5%	7,209,000	2,944,925	40.9%	-6.7	7,521,000	2,779,945	37.0%	-10.6	7,710,000	3,326,098	43.1%	-4.4	7,843,000	3,066,852	39.1%	-8.4
OKLAHOMA	1,597,000	562,998	35.3%	1,919,000	506,312	26.4%	-8.9	2,091,000	589,112	28.2%	-7.1	2,181,000	856,324	39.3%	4.0	2,234,000	725,007	32.5%	-2.8
OREGON	1,301,000	652,990	50.2%	1,610,000	753,195	46.8%	-3.4	1,807,000	873,623	48.3%	-1.8	1,919,000	1,014,892	52.9%	2.7	1,990,000	1,031,544	51.8%	1.6
PENNSYLVANIA	7,387,000	3,613,245	48.9%	8,228,000	3,377,277	41.0%	-7.9	8,537,000	3,541,658	41.5%	-7.4	8,723,000	3,628,718	41.6%	-7.3	8,850,000	3,306,377	37.4%	-11.6
RHODE ISLAND	596,000	325,613	54.6%	651,000	303,871	46.7%	-8.0	669,000	307,802	46.0%	-8.6	690,000	333,182	48.3%	-6.3	714,000	305,663	42.8%	-11.8
SOUTH CAROLINA	1,482,000	426,965	28.8%	1,883,000	517,212	27.5%	-1.3	2,097,000	577,201	27.5%	-1.3	2,269,000	657,456	29.0%	0.2	2,420,000	716,866	29.6%	0.8
SOUTH DAKOTA	386,000	234,983	60.9%	452,000	272,470	60.3%	-0.6	475,000	255,523	53.8%	-7.1	486,000	275,652	56.7%	-4.2	491,000	289,723	59.0%	-1.9
TENNESSEE	2,400,000	988,698	41.2%	2,914,000	901,829	30.9%	-10.2	3,187,000	1,062,195	33.3%	-7.9	3,373,000	1,175,683	34.9%	-6.3	3,516,000	1,105,229	31.4%	-9.8
TEXAS	6,658,000	1,833,224	27.5%	8,218,000	1,488,819	18.1%	-9.4	9,197,000	2,182,380	23.7%	-3.8	9,998,000	2,849,034	28.5%	1.0	10,718,000	3,010,406	28.1%	0.6
UTAH	579,000	372,900	64.4%	756,000	412,962	54.6%	-9.8	868,000	379,160	43.7%	-20.7	947,000	489,651	51.7%	-12.7	1,014,000	428,795	42.3%	-22.1
VERMONT	264,000	152,557	57.8%	319,000	140,899	44.2%	-13.6	350,000	120,502	34.4%	-23.4	374,000	164,951	44.1%	-13.7	396,000	188,964	47.7%	-10.1
VIRGINIA	2,828,000	905,540	32.0%	3,396,000	924,186	27.2%	-4.8	3,702,000	1,056,565	28.5%	-3.5	3,998,000	1,335,386	33.4%	1.4	4,289,000	1,043,352	24.3%	-7.7
WASHINGTON	2,087,000	1,022,124	49.0%	2,536,000	980,925	38.7%	-10.3	2,818,000	978,574	34.7%	-14.2	3,059,000	1,307,499	42.7%	-6.2	3,281,000	1,294,836	39.5%	9.5
WEST VIRGINIA	1,069,000	440,883	41.2%	1,266,000	415,514	32.8%	-8.4	1,355,000	442,845	32.7%	-8.6	1,373,000	546,403	39.8%	-1.4	1,356,000	395,820	29.2%	-12.1
WISCONSIN	2,613,000	1,326,024	50.7%	3,047,000	1,196,571	39.3%	-11.5	3,249,000	1,450,482	44.6%	-6.1	3,379,000	1,450,932	42.9%	-7.8	3,475,000	1,383,141	39.8%	-10.9
WYOMING	195,000	116,304	59.6%	263,000	126,933	48.3%	-11.4	307,000	129,377	42.1%	-17.5	319,000	159,277	49.9%	-9.7	317,000	159,787	50.4%	-9.2
Total	124,000,000	53,382,211	43.1%	142,608,000	52,397,509	36.7%	-6.3	153,258,000	55,237,354	36.0%	-7.0	161,552,000	64,401,924	39.9%	-3.2	168,768,000	59,927,356	35.5%	-7.5

*Percentage point difference between turnout in current year and initial year listed in chart. If data do not appear for a state in the initial year listed, the difference is calculated from the first year in which data do appear for that state.

UNITED STATES HOUSE OF REPRESENTATIVES GENERAL ELECTIONS

Republican Turnout for Election Years 1970–1986

State	1970 Voting-age population	Turnout	%	1974 Voting-age population	Turnout	%	Difference from 1970*	1978 Voting-age population	Turnout	%	Difference from 1970	1982 Voting-age population	Turnout	%	Difference from 1970	1986 Voting-age population	Turnout	%	Difference from 1970
ALABAMA	2,035,000	189,050	9.3%	2,449,000	169,304	6.9%	-2.4	2,654,000	197,176	7.4%	-1.9	2,785,000	272,510	9.8%	0.5	2,882,000	436,357	15.1%	5.9
ALASKA	179,000	35,947	20.1%	220,000	51,641	23.5%	3.4	255,000	68,811	27.0%	6.9	294,000	128,274	43.6%	23.5	334,000	101,799	30.5%	10.4
ARIZONA	1,055,000	218,506	20.7%	1,463,000	266,117	18.2%	-2.5	1,767,000	230,573	13.0%	-7.7	2,050,000	394,872	19.3%	-1.4	2,324,000	539,940	23.2%	2.5
ARKANSAS	1,179,000	115,532	9.8%	1,426,000	156,183	11.0%	1.2	1,564,000	195,371	12.5%	2.7	1,638,000	361,772	22.1%	12.3	1,682,000	268,291	16.0%	6.2
CALIFORNIA	12,492,000	3,095,405	24.8%	13,878,000	2,369,389	17.1%	-7.7	15,085,000	3,105,933	20.6%	-4.2	16,246,000	3,536,658	21.8%	-3.0	17,387,000	3,328,119	19.1%	-5.6
COLORADO	1,324,000	317,696	24.0%	1,700,000	364,372	21.4%	-2.6	1,957,000	402,274	20.6%	-3.4	2,129,000	484,947	22.8%	-1.2	2,262,000	566,236	25.0%	1.0
CONNECTICUT	1,895,000	524,953	27.7%	2,063,000	440,207	21.3%	-6.4	2,165,000	423,474	19.6%	-8.1	2,258,000	485,491	21.5%	-6.2	2,347,000	433,977	18.5%	-9.2
DELAWARE	328,000	86,125	26.3%	382,000	93,826	24.6%	-1.7	413,000	91,689	22.2%	-4.1	442,000	87,153	19.7%	-6.5	471,000	53,767	11.4%	-14.8
DISTRICT OF COLUMBIA																			
FLORIDA	4,461,000	568,718	12.7%	5,661,000	580,975	10.3%	-2.5	6,657,000	671,942	10.1%	-2.7	7,597,000	900,203	11.8%	-0.9	8,509,000	986,780	11.6%	-1.2
GEORGIA	2,973,000	225,632	7.6%	3,336,000	233,769	7.0%	-0.6	3,675,000	116,301	3.2%	-4.4	4,022,000	225,215	5.6%	-2.0	4,373,000	289,068	6.6%	-1.0
HAWAII	436,000	31,764	7.3%	538,000	100,959	18.8%	11.5	607,000	40,167	6.6%	-0.7					720,000	135,054	18.8%	11.5
IDAHO	413,000	143,943	34.9%	532,000	142,678	26.8%	-8.0	605,000	167,271	27.6%	-7.2	643,000	170,150	26.5%	-8.4	666,000	208,153	31.3%	-3.6
ILLINOIS	6,804,000	1,680,861	24.7%	7,473,000	1,218,921	16.3%	-8.4	7,753,000	1,576,522	20.3%	-4.4	7,891,000	1,508,308	19.1%	-5.6	7,965,000	1,393,103	17.5%	-7.2
INDIANA	3,096,000	848,785	27.4%	3,571,000	770,154	21.6%	-5.8	3,774,000	680,513	18.0%	-9.4	3,895,000	909,731	23.4%	-4.1	3,979,000	756,135	19.0%	-8.4
IOWA	1,703,000	388,428	22.8%	1,951,000	413,230	21.2%	-1.6	2,043,000	406,248	19.9%	-2.9	2,063,000	475,356	23.0%	0.2	2,048,000	461,455	22.5%	-0.3
KANSAS	1,377,000	407,264	29.6%	1,588,000	417,956	26.3%	-3.3	1,670,000	440,586	26.4%	-3.2	1,720,000	400,837	23.3%	-6.3	1,757,000	474,570	27.0%	-2.6
KENTUCKY	2,115,000	222,813	10.5%	2,321,000	238,637	10.3%	-0.3	2,507,000	207,568	8.3%	-2.3	2,606,000	280,352	10.8%	0.2	2,665,000	252,849	9.5%	-1.0
LOUISIANA	2,061,000	19,703	1.0%	2,526,000	140,008	5.5%	4.6	2,766,000	320,010	11.6%	10.6	2,870,000	142,371	5.0%	4.0	2,913,000	208,665	7.2%	6.2
MAINE	598,000	122,313	20.5%	709,000	212,357	30.0%	9.5	771,000	208,730	27.1%	6.6	822,000	260,925	31.7%	11.3	867,000	249,030	28.7%	8.3
MARYLAND	2,383,000	430,300	18.1%	2,722,000	347,280	12.8%	-5.3	2,911,000	312,974	10.8%	-7.3	3,104,000	348,561	11.2%	-6.8	3,300,000	394,393	12.0%	-6.1
MASSACHUSETTS	3,539,000	718,052	20.3%	3,874,000	401,300	10.4%	-9.9	4,029,000	471,755	11.7%	-8.6	4,165,000	561,091	13.5%	-6.8	4,292,000	250,385	5.8%	-14.5
MICHIGAN	5,199,000	1,241,474	23.9%	5,928,000	1,019,544	17.2%	-6.7	6,272,000	1,150,495	18.3%	-5.5	6,466,000	1,093,425	16.9%	-7.0	6,591,000	977,122	14.8%	-9.1
MINNESOTA	2,238,000	628,583	28.1%	2,626,000	491,912	18.7%	-9.4	2,812,000	712,270	25.3%	-2.8	2,949,000	777,584	26.4%	-1.7	3,065,000	557,741	18.2%	-9.9
MISSISSIPPI	1,248,000	28,847	2.3%	1,525,000	130,999	8.6%	6.3	1,656,000	236,274	14.3%	12.0	1,729,000	259,553	15.0%	12.7	1,778,000	208,037	11.7%	9.4
MISSOURI	2,896,000	493,557	17.0%	3,306,000	396,617	12.0%	-5.0	3,474,000	575,578	16.6%	-0.5	3,593,000	653,468	18.2%	1.1	3,690,000	599,520	16.2%	-0.8
MONTANA	406,000	108,140	26.6%	493,000	105,162	21.3%	-5.3	538,000	139,859	26.0%	-0.6	557,000	142,370	25.6%	-1.1	565,000	145,778	25.8%	-0.8
NEBRASKA	898,000	242,507	27.0%	1,039,000	236,076	22.7%	-4.3	1,095,000	310,919	28.4%	1.4	1,120,000	402,167	35.9%	8.9	1,130,000	358,326	31.7%	4.7
NEVADA	306,000	24,147	7.9%	431,000	61,182	14.2%	6.3	530,000	44,425	8.4%	0.5	642,000	115,863	18.0%	10.2	759,000	133,821	17.6%	9.7
NEW HAMPSHIRE	450,000	146,389	32.5%	558,000	122,678	22.0%	-10.5	629,000	133,666	21.3%	-11.3	696,000	153,974	22.1%	-10.4	761,000	156,218	20.5%	-12.0
NEW JERSEY	4,517,000	984,728	21.8%	4,852,000	794,698	16.4%	-5.4	5,049,000	837,783	16.6%	-5.2	5,219,000	915,472	17.5%	-4.3	5,376,000	738,901	13.7%	-8.1
NEW MEXICO	559,000	152,261	27.2%	727,000	149,313	20.5%	-6.7	832,000	118,075	14.2%	-13.0	910,000	191,946	21.1%	-6.1	975,000	206,815	21.2%	-6.0
NEW YORK	11,599,000	2,447,752	21.1%	11,921,000	1,929,983	16.2%	-4.9	11,979,000	1,982,507	16.5%	-4.6	12,104,000	1,940,104	16.0%	-5.1	12,259,000	1,664,604	13.6%	-7.5

United States House of Representatives General Elections *(continued)*

Republican Turnout for Election Years 1970–1986 *(continued)*

State	1970 Voting-age population	1970 Turnout	1970 %	1974 Voting-age population	1974 Turnout	1974 %	1974 Difference from 1970	1978 Voting-age population	1978 Turnout	1978 %	1978 Difference from 1970	1982 Voting-age population	1982 Turnout	1982 %	1982 Difference from 1970	1986 Voting-age population	1986 Turnout	1986 %	1986 Difference from 1970
NORTH CAROLINA	3,038,000	410,742	13.5%	3,730,000	347,603	9.3%	-4.2	4,084,000	406,076	9.9%	-3.6	4,406,000	579,817	13.2%	-0.4	4,713,000	682,447	14.5%	1.0
NORTH DAKOTA	356,000	122,056	34.3%	422,000	130,184	30.8%	-3.4	450,000	147,746	32.8%	-1.5	458,000	72,241	15.8%	-18.5	459,000	66,989	14.6%	-19.7
OHIO	6,402,000	1,706,205	26.7%	7,209,000	1,458,222	20.2%	-6.4	7,521,000	1,471,860	19.6%	-7.1	7,710,000	1,456,712	18.9%	-7.8	7,843,000	1,536,105	19.6%	-7.1
OKLAHOMA	1,597,000	245,216	15.4%	1,919,000	208,243	10.9%	-4.5	2,091,000	258,160	12.3%	-3.0	2,181,000	310,186	14.2%	-1.1	2,234,000	291,098	13.0%	-2.3
OREGON	1,301,000	314,724	24.2%	1,610,000	270,319	16.8%	-7.4	1,807,000	258,140	14.3%	-9.9	1,919,000	436,754	22.8%	-1.4	1,990,000	446,462	22.4%	-1.8
PENNSYLVANIA	7,387,000	1,611,801	21.8%	8,228,000	1,421,944	17.3%	-4.5	8,537,000	1,711,318	20.0%	-1.8	8,723,000	1,651,922	18.9%	-2.9	9,050,000	1,575,803	17.2%	-4.6
RHODE ISLAND	596,000	114,781	19.3%	651,000	73,824	11.3%	-7.9	669,000	133,637	20.0%	0.7	690,000	157,535	22.8%	3.6	714,000	176,000	24.6%	5.4
SOUTH CAROLINA	1,482,000	115,531	7.8%	1,883,000	212,893	11.3%	3.5	2,097,000	183,369	8.7%	0.9	2,269,000	295,160	13.0%	5.2	2,420,000	261,489	10.8%	3.0
SOUTH DAKOTA	386,000	107,422	27.8%	452,000	167,012	36.9%	9.1	475,000	135,324	28.5%	0.7	486,000	133,530	27.5%	-0.4	491,000	118,261	24.1%	-3.7
TENNESSEE	2,400,000	403,233	16.8%	2,914,000	363,502	12.5%	-4.3	3,187,000	448,825	14.1%	-2.7	3,373,000	469,527	13.9%	-2.9	3,516,000	448,987	12.8%	-4.0
TEXAS	6,658,000	476,824	7.2%	8,218,000	406,744	4.9%	-2.2	9,197,000	888,215	9.7%	2.5	9,998,000	934,863	9.4%	2.2	10,718,000	1,263,413	11.8%	4.6
UTAH	579,000	186,818	32.3%	756,000	163,066	21.6%	-10.7	868,000	206,520	23.8%	-8.5	947,000	312,003	32.9%	0.7	1,014,000	229,717	22.7%	-9.6
VERMONT	264,000	103,806	39.3%	319,000	74,561	23.4%	-15.9	350,000	90,688	25.9%	-13.4	374,000	114,191	30.5%	-8.8	396,000	168,403	42.5%	3.2
VIRGINIA	2,828,000	414,275	14.6%	3,396,000	361,302	10.6%	-4.0	3,702,000	594,915	16.1%	1.4	3,998,000	690,167	17.3%	2.6	4,289,000	466,747	10.9%	-3.8
WASHINGTON	2,087,000	403,946	19.4%	2,536,000	400,557	15.8%	-3.6	2,818,000	450,847	16.0%	-3.4	3,059,000	603,916	19.7%	0.4	3,281,000	527,158	16.1%	-3.3
WEST VIRGINIA	1,069,000	152,877	14.3%	1,266,000	125,368	9.9%	-4.4	1,355,000	151,918	11.2%	-3.1	1,373,000	202,380	14.7%	0.4	1,356,000	96,864	7.1%	-7.2
WISCONSIN	2,613,000	576,575	22.1%	3,047,000	475,292	15.6%	-6.5	3,249,000	675,953	20.8%	-1.3	3,379,000	667,193	19.7%	-2.3	3,475,000	668,708	19.2%	-2.8
WYOMING	195,000	57,848	29.7%	263,000	57,499	21.9%	-7.8	307,000	75,855	24.7%	-5.0	319,000	113,236	35.5%	5.8	317,000	111,007	35.0%	5.4
Total	124,000,000	24,414,855	19.7%	142,608,000	21,285,562	14.9%	-4.8	153,258,000	24,867,105	16.2%	-3.5	160,887,000	27,782,036	17.3%	-2.4	168,768,000	26,620,667	15.8%	-3.9

Democratic Turnout for Election Years 1970–1986

State	1970 Voting-age population	1970 Turnout	1970 %	1974 Voting-age population	1974 Turnout	1974 %	1974 Difference from 1970*	1978 Voting-age population	1978 Turnout	1978 %	1978 Difference from 1970	1982 Voting-age population	1982 Turnout	1982 %	1982 Difference from 1970	1986 Voting-age population	1986 Turnout	1986 %	1986 Difference from 1970
ALABAMA	2,035,000	475,095	23.3%	2,449,000	375,976	15.4%	-8.0	2,654,000	439,564	16.6%	-6.8	2,785,000	676,584	24.3%	0.9	2,882,000	678,716	23.6%	0.2
ALASKA	179,000	44,137	24.7%	220,000	44,280	20.1%	-4.5	255,000	55,176	21.6%	-3.0	294,000	52,011	17.7%	-7.0	334,000	74,053	22.2%	-2.5
ARIZONA	1,055,000	182,256	17.3%	1,463,000	269,489	18.4%	1.1	1,767,000	261,567	14.8%	-2.5	2,050,000	300,493	14.7%	-2.6	2,324,000	260,144	11.2%	-6.1
ARKANSAS	1,179,000	57,679	4.9%	1,426,000	267,573	18.8%	13.9	1,564,000	97,888	6.3%	1.4	1,638,000	397,466	24.3%	19.4	1,682,000	386,672	23.0%	18.1
CALIFORNIA	12,492,000	3,124,147	25.0%	13,878,000	3,312,449	23.9%	-1.1	15,085,000	3,335,332	22.1%	-2.9	16,246,000	3,815,205	23.5%	-1.5	17,387,000	3,743,542	21.5%	-3.5
COLORADO	1,324,000	310,117	23.4%	1,700,000	413,434	24.3%	0.9	1,957,000	369,455	18.9%	-4.5	2,129,000	448,295	21.1%	-2.4	2,262,000	449,683	19.9%	-3.5
CONNECTICUT	1,895,000	531,523	28.0%	2,063,000	620,029	30.1%	2.0	2,165,000	592,396	27.4%	-0.7	2,258,000	577,340	25.6%	-2.5	2,347,000	544,938	23.2%	-4.8
DELAWARE	328,000	71,429	21.8%	382,000	63,490	16.6%	-5.2	413,000	64,863	15.7%	-6.1	442,000	98,533	22.3%	0.5	471,000	106,351	22.6%	0.8
DISTRICT OF COLUMBIA																			
FLORIDA	4,461,000	681,393	15.3%	5,661,000	477,121	8.4%	-6.8	6,657,000	948,045	14.2%	-1.0	7,597,000	1,311,342	17.3%	2.0	8,509,000	1,153,710	13.6%	-1.7

United States House of Representatives General Elections (continued)

United States House of Representatives General Elections (continued)

Democratic Turnout for Election Years 1970–1986 (continued)

State	1970 Voting-age population	1970 Turnout	1970 %	1974 Voting-age population	1974 Turnout	1974 %	1974 Difference from 1970	1978 Voting-age population	1978 Turnout	1978 %	1978 Difference from 1970	1982 Voting-age population	1982 Turnout	1982 %	1982 Difference from 1970	1986 Voting-age population	1986 Turnout	1986 %	1986 Difference from 1970
GEORGIA	2,973,000	653,513	22.0%	3,336,000	588,538	17.6%	-4.3	3,675,000	472,210	12.8%	-9.1	4,022,000	670,110	16.7%	-5.3	4,373,000	772,986	17.7%	-4.3
HAWAII	436,000	176,449	40.5%	538,000	158,468	29.5%	-11.0	607,000	202,824	33.4%	-7.1	665,000	266,851	40.1%	-0.3	720,000	186,891	26.0%	-14.5
IDAHO	413,000	87,615	21.2%	532,000	107,600	20.2%	-1.0	605,000	118,012	19.5%	-1.7	643,000	150,996	23.5%	2.3	666,000	162,758	24.4%	3.2
ILLINOIS	6,804,000	1,814,064	26.7%	7,473,000	1,601,152	21.4%	-5.2	7,753,000	1,464,688	18.9%	-7.8	7,891,000	2,093,272	26.5%	-0.1	7,965,000	1,622,759	20.4%	-6.3
INDIANA	3,096,000	87,841	2.8%	3,571,000	956,675	26.8%	24.0	3,774,000	751,940	19.9%	17.1	3,895,000	882,378	22.7%	19.8	3,979,000	788,419	19.8%	17.0
IOWA	1,703,000	387,510	22.8%	1,951,000	488,214	25.0%	2.3	2,043,000	403,365	19.7%	-3.0	2,063,000	528,726	25.6%	2.9	2,048,000	428,022	20.9%	-1.9
KANSAS	1,377,000	303,988	22.1%	1,588,000	325,400	20.5%	-1.6	1,670,000	233,001	14.0%	-8.1	1,720,000	345,507	20.1%	-2.0	1,757,000	312,800	17.8%	-4.3
KENTUCKY	2,115,000	247,585	11.7%	2,321,000	425,272	18.3%	6.6	2,507,000	264,798	10.6%	-1.1	2,606,000	413,286	15.9%	4.2	2,665,000	374,742	14.1%	2.4
LOUISIANA	2,061,000	330,464	16.0%	2,526,000	396,581	15.7%	-0.3	2,766,000	442,651	16.0%	0.0	2,870,000	336,275	11.7%	-4.3	2,913,000	608,367	20.9%	4.9
MAINE	598,000	195,718	32.7%	709,000	140,923	19.9%	-12.9	771,000	141,039	18.3%	-14.4	822,000	186,970	22.7%	-10.0	867,000	165,462	19.1%	-13.6
MARYLAND	2,383,000	452,546	19.0%	2,722,000	526,809	19.4%	0.4	2,911,000	604,457	20.8%	1.8	3,104,000	742,600	23.9%	4.9	3,300,000	668,669	20.3%	1.3
MASSACHUSETTS	3,539,000	1,019,657	28.8%	3,874,000	1,168,252	30.2%	1.3	4,029,000	1,249,311	31.0%	2.2	4,165,000	1,300,344	31.2%	2.4	4,292,000	1,198,143	27.9%	-0.9
MICHIGAN	5,199,000	1,314,448	25.3%	5,928,000	1,465,259	24.7%	-0.6	6,272,000	1,538,922	24.5%	-0.7	6,466,000	1,669,522	25.8%	0.5	6,591,000	1,342,034	20.4%	-4.9
MINNESOTA	2,238,000	709,635	31.7%	2,626,000	705,139	26.9%	-4.9	2,812,000	779,286	27.7%	-4.0	2,949,000	956,321	32.4%	0.7	3,065,000	831,715	27.1%	-4.6
MISSISSIPPI	1,248,000	269,193	21.6%	1,525,000	156,119	10.2%	-11.3	1,656,000	251,558	15.2%	-6.4	1,729,000	368,403	21.3%	-0.3	1,778,000	315,526	17.7%	-3.8
MISSOURI	2,896,000	692,026	23.9%	3,306,000	809,719	24.5%	0.6	3,474,000	966,553	27.8%	3.9	3,593,000	871,682	24.3%	0.4	3,690,000	828,403	22.4%	-1.4
MONTANA	406,000	141,257	34.8%	493,000	148,984	30.2%	-4.6	538,000	143,496	26.7%	-8.1	557,000	165,902	29.8%	-5.0	565,000	172,084	30.5%	-4.3
NEBRASKA	898,000	164,558	18.3%	1,039,000	211,496	20.4%	2.0	1,095,000	183,817	16.8%	-1.5	1,120,000	116,107	10.4%	-8.0	1,130,000	196,691	17.4%	-0.9
NEVADA	306,000	113,496	37.1%	431,000	93,665	21.7%	-15.4	530,000	132,513	25.0%	-12.1	642,000	114,166	17.8%	-19.3	759,000	121,263	16.0%	-21.1
NEW HAMPSHIRE	450,000	67,256	14.9%	558,000	96,851	17.4%	2.4	629,000	122,243	19.4%	4.5	696,000	114,187	16.4%	1.5	761,000	84,475	11.1%	-3.8
NEW JERSEY	4,517,000	1,098,788	24.3%	4,852,000	1,240,933	25.6%	1.3	5,049,000	1,043,747	20.7%	-3.7	5,219,000	1,206,416	23.1%	-1.2	5,376,000	802,762	14.9%	-9.4
NEW MEXICO	559,000	129,116	23.1%	727,000	162,095	22.3%	-0.8	832,000	166,471	20.0%	-3.1	910,000	202,802	22.3%	-0.8	975,000	178,822	18.3%	-4.8
NEW YORK	11,599,000	2,721,338	23.5%	11,921,000	2,807,472	23.6%	0.1	11,979,000	2,274,866	19.0%	-4.5	12,104,000	2,616,758	21.6%	-1.8	12,259,000	2,131,745	17.4%	-6.1
NORTH CAROLINA	3,038,000	513,905	16.9%	3,730,000	637,833	17.1%	0.2	4,084,000	607,324	14.9%	-2.0	4,406,000	708,279	16.1%	-0.8	4,713,000	890,058	18.9%	2.0
NORTH DAKOTA	356,000	88,104	24.7%	422,000	103,504	24.5%	-0.2	450,000	68,016	15.1%	-9.6	458,000	186,534	40.7%	16.0	459,000	216,258	47.1%	22.4
OHIO	6,402,000	1,323,271	20.7%	7,209,000	1,396,530	19.4%	-1.3	7,521,000	1,278,151	17.0%	-3.7	7,710,000	1,807,305	23.4%	2.8	7,843,000	1,512,037	19.3%	-1.4
OKLAHOMA	1,597,000	316,248	19.8%	1,919,000	294,704	15.4%	-4.4	2,091,000	330,952	15.8%	-4.0	2,181,000	539,413	24.7%	4.9	2,234,000	430,454	19.3%	-0.5
OREGON	1,301,000	337,998	26.0%	1,610,000	482,462	30.0%	4.0	1,807,000	587,445	32.5%	6.5	1,919,000	577,949	30.1%	4.1	1,990,000	584,763	29.4%	3.4
PENNSYLVANIA	7,387,000	1,945,360	26.3%	8,228,000	1,937,154	23.5%	-2.8	8,537,000	1,804,598	21.1%	-5.2	8,723,000	1,910,988	21.9%	-4.4	8,850,000	1,762,935	19.9%	-6.4
RHODE ISLAND	596,000	207,987	34.9%	651,000	230,047	35.3%	0.4	669,000	174,165	26.0%	-8.9	690,000	174,023	25.2%	-9.7	714,000	129,663	18.2%	-16.7
SOUTH CAROLINA	1,482,000	309,487	20.9%	1,883,000	301,516	16.0%	-4.9	2,097,000	378,888	18.1%	-2.8	2,269,000	353,111	15.6%	-5.3	2,420,000	453,232	18.7%	-2.2
SOUTH DAKOTA	386,000	127,561	33.0%	452,000	105,458	23.3%	-9.7	475,000	120,199	25.3%	-7.7	486,000	142,122	29.2%	-3.8	491,000	171,462	34.9%	1.9
TENNESSEE	2,400,000	579,783	24.2%	2,914,000	533,402	18.3%	-5.9	3,187,000	580,617	18.2%	-5.9	3,373,000	697,823	20.7%	-3.5	3,516,000	636,374	18.1%	-6.1

United States House of Representatives General Elections *(continued)*

Democratic Turnout for Election Years 1970–1986 *(continued)*

State	1970 Voting-age population	1970 Turnout	1970 %	1974 Voting-age population	1974 Turnout	1974 %	1974 Difference from 1970	1978 Voting-age population	1978 Turnout	1978 %	1978 Difference from 1970	1982 Voting-age population	1982 Turnout	1982 %	1982 Difference from 1970	1986 Voting-age population	1986 Turnout	1986 %	1986 Difference from 1970
TEXAS	6,658,000	1,339,012	20.1%	8,218,000	1,075,346	13.1%	-7.0	9,197,000	1,285,348	14.0%	-6.1	9,998,000	1,847,048	18.5%	-1.6	10,718,000	1,716,978	16.0%	-4.1
UTAH	579,000	182,499	31.5%	756,000	230,532	30.5%	-1.0	868,000	162,791	18.8%	-12.8	947,000	144,987	15.3%	-16.2	1,014,000	196,683	19.4%	-12.1
VERMONT	264,000	44,415	16.8%	319,000	56,342	17.7%	0.8	350,000	23,228	6.6%	-10.2	374,000	38,296	10.2%	-6.6				
VIRGINIA	2,828,000	465,418	16.5%	3,396,000	506,838	14.9%	-1.5	3,702,000	444,049	12.0%	-4.5	3,998,000	629,656	15.7%	-0.7	4,289,000	544,951	12.7%	-3.8
WASHINGTON	2,087,000	608,508	29.2%	2,536,000	574,055	22.6%	-6.5	2,818,000	507,252	18.0%	-11.2	3,059,000	689,811	22.6%	-6.6	3,281,000	767,678	23.4%	-5.8
WEST VIRGINIA	1,069,000	288,006	26.9%	1,266,000	290,146	22.9%	-4.0	1,355,000	290,927	21.5%	-5.5	1,373,000	343,236	25.0%	-1.9	1,356,000	298,956	22.0%	-4.9
WISCONSIN	2,613,000	740,485	28.3%	3,047,000	703,992	23.1%	-5.2	3,249,000	768,536	23.7%	-4.7	3,379,000	768,616	22.7%	-5.6	3,475,000	704,113	20.3%	-8.1
WYOMING	195,000	58,456	30.0%	263,000	69,434	26.4%	-3.6	307,000	53,522	17.4%	-12.5	319,000	46,041	14.4%	-15.5	317,000	48,780	15.4%	-14.6
Total	124,000,000	28,132,340	22.7%	142,608,000	30,154,752	21.1%	-1.5	153,258,000	29,582,062	19.3%	-3.4	161,552,000	35,602,088	22.0%	-0.6	168,372,000	32,758,722	19.5%	-3.2

Other Turnout for Election Years 1970–1986

State	1970 Voting-age population	1970 Turnout	1970 %	1974 Voting-age population	1974 Turnout	1974 %	1974 Difference from 1970*	1978 Voting-age population	1978 Turnout	1978 %	1978 Difference from 1970	1982 Voting-age population	1982 Turnout	1982 %	1982 Difference from 1970	1986 Voting-age population	1986 Turnout	1986 %	1986 Difference from 1970
ALABAMA	2,035,000	77,927	3.8%	2,449,000	16,120	0.7%	-3.2	2,654,000	5,539	0.2%	-3.6	2,785,000	11,925	0.4%	-3.4	2,882,000	581	0.0%	-3.8
ALASKA								255,000	200	0.1%		294,000	799	0.3%	0.2	334,000	4,425	1.3%	1.2
ARIZONA	1,055,000	1,357	0.1%	1,463,000	8,217	0.6%	0.4	1,767,000	26,842	1.5%	1.4	2,050,000	15,646	0.8%	0.6	2,324,000	3,646	0.2%	0.0
ARKANSAS																1,682,000	10,682	0.6%	
CALIFORNIA	12,492,000	101,842	0.8%	13,878,000	147,342	1.1%	0.2	15,085,000	84,482	0.6%	-0.3	16,246,000	234,694	1.4%	0.6	17,387,000	128,488	0.7%	-0.1
COLORADO	1,324,000	9,335	0.7%	1,700,000	6,737	0.4%	-0.3	1,957,000	13,446	0.7%	0.0	2,129,000	13,181	0.6%	-0.1	2,262,000	2,338	0.1%	-0.6
CONNECTICUT	1,895,000	14,028	0.7%	2,063,000	18,297	0.9%	0.1	2,165,000	5,151	0.2%	-0.5	2,258,000	7,844	0.3%	-0.4	2,347,000	740	0.0%	-0.7
DELAWARE	328,000	2,759	0.8%	382,000	3,012	0.8%	-0.1	413,000	1,014	0.2%	-0.6	442,000	2,378	0.5%	-0.3	471,000	639	0.1%	-0.7
DISTRICT OF COLUMBIA																			
FLORIDA				5,661,000	3,524	0.1%						7,597,000	49	0.0%	0.1	8,509,000	1,561	0.0%	0.0
GEORGIA	2,973,000	96	0.0%	3,336,000	116	0.0%	0.0	3,675,000	94	0.0%	0.0	4,022,000	9,132	0.2%	0.2	4,373,000	274	0.0%	0.0
HAWAII								607,000	10,378	1.7%		665,000	31,064	4.7%	3.0	720,000	9,251	1.3%	-0.4
IDAHO	413,000	2,759	0.7%													666,000	4,848	0.7%	0.1
ILLINOIS	6,804,000	59	0.0%	7,473,000	22,036	0.3%	0.3	7,753,000	2,375	0.0%	0.0	7,891,000	11,451	0.1%	0.1	7,965,000	1,348	0.0%	0.0
INDIANA				3,571,000	4,005	0.1%		3,774,000	16,410	0.4%	0.3	3,895,000	3,951	0.1%	0.0	3,979,000	10,953	0.3%	0.2
IOWA	1,703,000	3,753	0.2%	1,951,000	2,071	0.1%	-0.1	2,043,000	1,942	0.1%	-0.1	2,063,000	681	0.0%	-0.2	2,048,000	118	0.0%	-2.4
KANSAS	1,377,000	8,419	0.6%	1,588,000	32,202	2.0%	1.4	1,670,000	2,353	0.1%	-0.5	1,720,000	10,001	0.6%	0.0				
KENTUCKY	2,115,000	3,265	0.2%	2,321,000	15,316	0.7%	0.5	2,507,000	5,095	0.2%	0.0	2,606,000	6,684	0.3%	0.1	2,665,000	2,205	0.1%	-0.1
LOUISIANA	2,061,000	12,881	0.6%	2,526,000	9,453	0.4%	-0.3	2,766,000	8,411	0.3%	-0.3	2,870,000	38,311	1.3%	0.7	2,913,000	8,382	0.3%	-0.3
MAINE								771,000	19,783	2.6%		822,000	4,246	0.5%	-2.0	867,000	7,138	0.8%	-1.7

United States House of Representatives General Elections (continued)

Other Turnout for Election Years 1970–1986 (continued)

State	1970 Voting-age population	Turnout	%	1974 Voting-age population	Turnout	%	Difference from 1970	1978 Voting-age population	Turnout	%	Difference from 1970	1982 Voting-age population	Turnout	%	Difference from 1970	1986 Voting-age population	Turnout	%	Difference from 1970
MARYLAND	2,383,000	2,695	0.1%					2,911,000	6,626	0.2%	0.1					3,300,000	3	0.0%	-0.1
MASSACHUSETTS	3,539,000	62,789	1.8%	3,874,000	129,149	3.3%	1.6	4,029,000	88,328	2.2%	0.4	4,165,000	28,931	0.7%	-1.1	4,292,000	54,640	1.3%	-0.5
MICHIGAN	5,199,000	6,476	0.1%	5,928,000	34,617	0.6%	0.5	6,272,000	18,297	0.3%	0.2	6,466,000	45,469	0.7%	0.6	6,591,000	8,020	0.1%	0.0
MINNESOTA	2,238,000	2,408	0.1%	2,626,000	21,951	0.8%	0.7	2,812,000	34,324	1.2%	1.1	2,949,000	16,026	0.5%	0.4	3,065,000	3,517	0.1%	0.0
MISSISSIPPI	1,248,000	14,317	1.1%	1,525,000	18,791	1.2%	0.1	1,656,000	31,129	1.9%	0.7	1,729,000	13,176	0.8%	-0.4				
MISSOURI	2,896,000	11,824	0.4%	3,306,000	2,706	0.1%	-0.3	3,474,000	3,696	0.1%	-0.3	3,593,000	3,266	0.1%	-0.3	3,690,000	2,204	0.1%	-0.3
MONTANA												557,000	8,267	1.5%					
NEBRASKA	898,000	41,034	4.6%	1,039,000	119	0.0%	-4.6	1,095,000	102	0.0%	-4.6	1,120,000	807	0.1%	-4.5	1,130,000	420	0.0%	-4.5
NEVADA				431,000	13,119	3.0%		530,000	13,705	2.6%	-0.5	642,000	4,043	0.6%	-2.4	759,000	2,145	0.3%	-2.8
NEW HAMPSHIRE	450,000	17	0.0%	558,000	13	0.0%	0.0	629,000	2,407	0.4%	0.4	696,000	757	0.1%	0.1	761,000	54	0.0%	0.0
NEW JERSEY	4,517,000	17,893	0.4%	4,852,000	47,926	1.0%	0.6	5,049,000	52,393	1.0%	0.6	5,219,000	24,202	0.5%	0.1	5,376,000	11,882	0.2%	-0.2
NEW MEXICO	559,000	3,981	0.7%	727,000	4,964	0.7%	0.0	832,000	136	0.0%	-0.7	910,000	158	0.0%	-0.7	975,000	18	0.0%	-0.7
NEW YORK	11,599,000	277,118	2.4%	11,921,000	156,894	1.3%	-1.1	11,979,000	121,655	1.0%	-1.4	12,104,000	124,515	1.0%	-1.4	12,259,000	107,262	0.9%	-1.5
NORTH CAROLINA	3,038,000	5,301	0.2%	3,730,000	2,904	0.1%	-0.1	4,084,000	6,556	0.2%	0.0	4,406,000	32,984	0.7%	0.6				
NORTH DAKOTA								450,000	4,586	1.0%		458,000	1,724	0.4%	-0.6	459,000	3,114	0.7%	-0.3
OHIO	6,402,000	12,535	0.2%	7,209,000	90,173	1.3%	1.1	7,521,000	29,934	0.4%	0.2	7,710,000	62,081	0.8%	0.6	7,843,000	18,710	0.2%	0.0
OKLAHOMA	1,597,000	1,534	0.1%	1,919,000	3,365	0.2%	0.1					2,181,000	6,725	0.3%	0.2	2,234,000	3,455	0.2%	0.1
OREGON	1,301,000	268	0.0%	1,610,000	414	0.0%	0.0	1,807,000	28,038	1.6%	1.5	1,919,000	189	0.0%	0.0	1,990,000	319	0.0%	0.0
PENNSYLVANIA	7,387,000	56,084	0.8%	8,228,000	18,179	0.2%	-0.5	8,537,000	25,742	0.3%	-0.5	8,723,000	65,808	0.8%	0.0	8,850,000	17,639	0.2%	-0.6
RHODE ISLAND	596,000	2,845	0.5%									690,000	1,624	0.2%	-0.2				
SOUTH CAROLINA	1,482,000	1,947	0.1%	1,883,000	2,803	0.1%	0.0	2,097,000	14,944	0.7%	0.6	2,269,000	9,185	0.4%	0.3	2,420,000	2,145	0.1%	0.0
SOUTH DAKOTA																			
TENNESSEE	2,400,000	5,682	0.2%	2,914,000	4,925	0.2%	-0.1	3,187,000	32,753	1.0%	0.8	3,373,000	8,333	0.2%	0.0	3,516,000	19,868	0.6%	0.3
TEXAS	6,658,000	17,388	0.3%	8,218,000	6,729	0.1%	-0.2	9,197,000	8,817	0.1%	-0.2	9,998,000	67,123	0.7%	0.4	10,718,000	30,015	0.3%	0.0
UTAH	579,000	3,583	0.6%	756,000	19,364	2.6%	1.9	868,000	9,849	1.1%	0.5	947,000	32,661	3.4%	2.8	1,014,000	2,395	0.2%	-0.4
VERMONT	264,000	4,336	1.6%	319,000	9,996	3.1%	1.5	350,000	6,586	1.9%	0.2	374,000	12,464	3.3%	1.7	396,000	20,551	5.2%	3.5
VIRGINIA	2,828,000	25,847	0.9%	3,396,000	56,046	1.7%	0.7	3,702,000	17,601	0.5%	-0.4	3,998,000	15,563	0.4%	-0.5	4,289,000	31,654	0.7%	-0.2
WASHINGTON	2,087,000	9,670	0.5%	2,536,000	6,313	0.2%	-0.2	2,818,000	20,475	0.7%	0.3	3,059,000	13,772	0.5%	0.0				
WEST VIRGINIA												1,373,000	787	0.1%					
WISCONSIN	2,613,000	8,964	0.3%	3,047,000	17,287	0.6%	0.2	3,249,000	5,993	0.2%	-0.2	3,379,000	15,123	0.4%	0.1	3,475,000	10,320	0.3%	0.0
WYOMING																			
Total	111,333,000	835,016	0.8%	132,914,000	957,195	0.7%	0.0	138,997,000	788,187	0.6%	-0.2	155,362,000	1,017,800	0.7%	-0.1	153,796,000	547,967	0.4%	-0.4

*Percentage point difference between turnout in current year and initial year listed in chart. If data do not appear for a state in the initial year listed, the difference is calculated from the first year in which data do appear for that state.

TOTAL HIGHEST STATEWIDE GENERAL ELECTIONS

Election Years 1970–1986

State	1970 Voting-age population	Turnout	%	1974 Voting-age population	Turnout	%	Difference from 1970*	1978 Voting-age population	Turnout	%	Difference from 1970	1982 Voting-age population	Turnout	%	Difference from 1970	1986 Voting-age population	Turnout	%	Difference from 1970
ALABAMA	2,035,000	854,952	42.0%	2,449,000	598,305	24.4%	-17.6	2,654,000	760,474	28.7%	-13.4	2,785,000	1,128,725	40.5%	-1.5	2,882,000	1,236,230	42.9%	0.9
ALASKA	179,000	80,779	45.1%	220,000	96,163	43.7%	-1.4	255,000	126,910	49.8%	4.6	294,000	194,885	66.3%	21.2	334,000	180,801	54.1%	9.0
ARIZONA	1,055,000	411,409	39.0%	1,463,000	552,202	37.7%	-1.3	1,767,000	538,556	30.5%	-8.5	2,050,000	726,364	35.4%	-3.6	2,324,000	866,984	37.3%	-1.7
ARKANSAS	1,179,000	609,198	51.7%	1,426,000	545,974	38.3%	-13.4	1,564,000	528,912	33.8%	-17.9	1,638,000	789,351	48.2%	-3.5	1,682,000	695,487	41.3%	-10.3
CALIFORNIA	12,492,000	6,510,072	52.1%	13,878,000	6,248,070	45.0%	-7.1	15,085,000	6,922,378	45.9%	-6.2	16,246,000	7,876,698	48.5%	-3.6	17,387,000	7,443,551	42.8%	-9.3
COLORADO	1,324,000	668,496	50.5%	1,700,000	828,968	48.8%	-1.7	1,957,000	823,807	42.1%	-8.4	2,129,000	958,021	44.0%	-5.6	2,262,000	1,060,765	46.9%	-3.6
CONNECTICUT	1,895,000	1,089,353	57.5%	2,063,000	1,102,773	53.5%	-4.0	2,165,000	1,036,608	47.9%	-9.6	2,258,000	1,084,156	48.0%	-9.5	2,347,000	993,692	42.3%	-15.1
DELAWARE	328,000	161,439	49.2%	382,000	160,328	42.0%	-7.2	413,000	162,072	39.2%	-10.0	442,000	190,960	43.2%	-6.0	471,000	160,757	34.1%	-15.1
DISTRICT OF COLUMBIA																			
FLORIDA	4,461,000	1,730,813	38.8%	5,661,000	1,828,392	32.3%	-6.5	6,657,000	2,530,468	38.0%	-0.8	7,597,000	2,688,566	35.4%	-3.4	8,509,000	3,429,996	40.3%	1.5
GEORGIA	2,973,000	1,046,663	35.2%	3,336,000	936,438	28.1%	-7.1	3,675,000	662,862	18.0%	-17.2	4,022,000	1,169,041	29.1%	-6.1	4,373,000	1,225,008	28.0%	-7.2
HAWAII	436,000	240,760	55.2%	538,000	259,427	48.2%	-7.0	607,000	281,587	46.4%	-8.8	665,000	311,853	46.9%	-8.3	720,000	334,115	46.4%	-8.8
IDAHO	413,000	245,112	59.3%	532,000	259,632	48.8%	-10.5	605,000	288,566	47.7%	-11.7	643,000	326,522	50.8%	-0.6	666,000	387,426	58.2%	-1.2
ILLINOIS	6,804,000	3,599,272	52.9%	7,473,000	2,914,666	39.0%	-13.9	7,753,000	3,184,764	41.1%	-11.8	7,891,000	3,673,681	46.6%	-6.3	7,965,000	3,143,978	39.5%	-13.4
INDIANA	3,096,000	1,737,697	56.1%	3,571,000	1,752,978	49.1%	-7.0	3,774,000	1,448,863	38.4%	-17.7	3,895,000	1,817,287	46.7%	-9.5	3,979,000	1,555,507	39.1%	-17.0
IOWA	1,703,000	791,241	46.5%	1,951,000	920,458	47.2%	0.7	2,043,000	843,190	41.3%	-5.2	2,063,000	1,038,229	50.3%	3.9	2,048,000	910,623	44.5%	-2.0
KANSAS	1,377,000	745,196	54.1%	1,588,000	794,437	50.0%	-4.1	1,670,000	748,839	44.8%	-9.3	1,720,000	763,263	44.4%	-9.7	1,757,000	840,605	47.8%	-6.3
KENTUCKY	2,115,000	473,663	22.4%	2,321,000	745,994	32.1%	9.7	2,507,000	477,461	19.0%	-3.4	2,606,000	700,322	26.9%	4.5	2,665,000	677,280	25.4%	3.0
LOUISIANA	2,061,000	363,048	17.6%	2,526,000	546,042	21.6%	4.0	2,766,000	839,669	30.4%	12.7	2,870,000	516,957	18.0%	0.4	2,913,000	1,369,897	47.0%	29.4
MAINE	598,000	325,386	54.4%	709,000	363,945	51.3%	-3.1	771,000	375,172	48.7%	-5.8	822,000	460,295	56.0%	1.6	867,000	426,861	49.2%	-5.2
MARYLAND	2,383,000	973,099	40.8%	2,722,000	949,097	34.9%	-6.0	2,911,000	1,011,963	34.8%	-6.1	3,104,000	1,139,149	36.7%	-4.1	3,300,000	1,112,637	33.7%	-7.1
MASSACHUSETTS	3,539,000	1,935,607	54.7%	3,874,000	1,854,798	47.9%	-6.8	4,029,000	1,985,700	49.3%	-5.4	4,165,000	2,050,769	49.2%	-5.5	4,292,000	1,684,079	39.2%	-15.5
MICHIGAN	5,199,000	2,656,162	51.1%	5,928,000	2,657,017	44.8%	-6.3	6,272,000	2,867,212	45.7%	-5.4	6,466,000	3,040,008	47.0%	-4.1	6,591,000	2,396,564	36.4%	-14.7
MINNESOTA	2,238,000	1,365,443	61.0%	2,626,000	1,252,898	47.7%	-13.3	2,812,000	1,585,702	56.4%	-4.6	2,949,000	1,804,675	61.2%	0.2	3,065,000	1,415,989	46.2%	-14.8
MISSISSIPPI	1,248,000	324,215	26.0%	1,525,000	305,909	20.1%	-5.9	1,656,000	583,936	35.3%	9.3	1,729,000	645,026	37.3%	11.3	1,778,000	523,563	29.4%	3.5
MISSOURI	2,896,000	1,283,912	44.3%	3,306,000	1,224,303	37.0%	-7.3	3,474,000	1,545,827	44.5%	0.2	3,593,000	1,543,521	43.0%	-1.4	3,690,000	1,477,327	40.0%	-4.3
MONTANA	406,000	249,397	61.4%	493,000	254,146	51.6%	-9.9	538,000	287,942	53.5%	-7.9	557,000	321,062	57.6%	-3.8	565,000	317,862	56.3%	-5.2
NEBRASKA	898,000	461,619	51.4%	1,039,000	451,306	43.4%	-8.0	1,095,000	494,838	45.2%	-6.2	1,120,000	547,902	48.9%	-2.5	1,130,000	564,422	49.9%	-1.5
NEVADA	306,000	147,768	48.3%	431,000	169,473	39.3%	-9.0	530,000	192,445	36.3%	-12.0	642,000	240,394	37.4%	-10.8	759,000	261,932	34.5%	-13.8
NEW HAMPSHIRE	450,000	222,441	49.4%	558,000	226,665	40.6%	-8.8	629,000	269,587	42.9%	-6.6	696,000	282,588	40.6%	-8.8	761,000	251,107	33.0%	-16.4
NEW JERSEY	4,517,000	2,142,105	47.4%	4,852,000	2,083,557	42.9%	-4.5	5,049,000	1,957,515	38.8%	-8.7	5,219,000	2,193,945	42.0%	-5.4	5,376,000	1,553,545	28.9%	-18.5
NEW MEXICO	559,000	290,375	51.9%	727,000	328,742	45.2%	-6.7	832,000	345,577	41.5%	-10.4	910,000	407,466	44.8%	-7.2	975,000	394,833	40.5%	-11.4
NEW YORK	11,599,000	6,013,064	51.8%	11,921,000	5,293,176	44.4%	-7.4	11,979,000	4,768,820	39.8%	-12.0	12,104,000	5,254,891	43.4%	-8.4	12,259,000	4,294,124	35.0%	-16.8

Total Highest Statewide General Elections (continued)

Total Highest Statewide General Elections (continued)

Election Years 1970–1986 (continued)

State	1970 Voting-age population	Turnout	%	1974 Voting-age population	Turnout	%	Difference from 1970	1978 Voting-age population	Turnout	%	Difference from 1970	1982 Voting-age population	Turnout	%	Difference from 1970	1986 Voting-age population	Turnout	%	Difference from 1970
NORTH CAROLINA	3,038,000	929,948	30.6%	3,730,000	1,020,367	27.4%	-3.3	4,084,000	1,135,814	27.8%	-2.8	4,406,000	1,321,080	30.0%	-0.6	4,713,000	1,591,330	33.8%	3.2
NORTH DAKOTA	356,000	219,560	61.7%	422,000	235,661	55.8%	-5.8	450,000	220,348	49.0%	-12.7	458,000	262,465	57.3%	-4.4	459,000	288,998	63.0%	1.3
OHIO	6,402,000	3,184,133	49.7%	7,209,000	3,072,010	42.6%	-7.1	7,521,000	2,843,351	37.8%	-11.9	7,710,000	3,395,463	44.0%	-5.7	7,843,000	3,121,189	39.8%	-9.9
OKLAHOMA	1,597,000	698,790	43.8%	1,919,000	804,848	41.9%	-1.8	2,091,000	777,414	37.2%	-6.6	2,181,000	883,130	40.5%	-3.3	2,234,000	909,925	40.7%	-3.0
OREGON	1,301,000	666,394	51.2%	1,610,000	770,574	47.9%	-3.4	1,807,000	911,143	50.4%	-0.8	1,919,000	1,042,009	54.3%	3.1	1,990,000	1,059,630	53.2%	2.0
PENNSYLVANIA	7,387,000	3,700,060	50.1%	8,228,000	3,491,234	42.4%	-7.7	8,537,000	3,741,969	43.8%	-6.3	8,723,000	3,683,985	42.2%	-7.9	8,850,000	3,388,275	38.3%	-11.8
RHODE ISLAND	596,000	346,342	58.1%	651,000	321,660	49.4%	-8.7	669,000	314,363	47.0%	-11.1	690,000	342,779	49.7%	-8.4	714,000	322,724	45.2%	-12.9
SOUTH CAROLINA	1,482,000	484,857	32.7%	1,883,000	517,212	27.5%	-5.2	2,097,000	632,852	30.2%	-2.5	2,269,000	671,625	29.6%	-3.1	2,420,000	753,751	31.1%	-1.6
SOUTH DAKOTA	386,000	239,963	62.2%	452,000	278,884	61.7%	-0.5	475,000	259,795	54.7%	-7.5	486,000	278,562	57.3%	-4.8	491,000	295,830	60.3%	-1.9
TENNESSEE	2,400,000	1,108,247	46.2%	2,914,000	1,040,714	35.7%	-10.5	3,187,000	1,189,695	37.3%	-8.8	3,373,000	1,259,785	37.3%	-8.8	3,516,000	1,210,339	34.4%	-11.8
TEXAS	6,658,000	2,235,847	33.6%	8,218,000	1,654,984	20.1%	-13.4	9,197,000	2,369,764	25.8%	-7.8	9,998,000	3,191,091	31.9%	-1.7	10,718,000	3,441,460	32.1%	-1.5
UTAH	579,000	374,303	64.6%	756,000	420,642	55.6%	-9.0	868,000	379,160	43.7%	-21.0	947,000	530,802	56.1%	-8.6	1,014,000	435,111	42.9%	-21.7
VERMONT	264,000	154,899	58.7%	319,000	144,772	45.4%	-13.3	350,000	124,482	35.6%	-23.1	374,000	169,251	45.3%	-13.4	396,000	196,716	49.7%	-9.0
VIRGINIA	2,828,000	946,751	33.5%	3,396,000	924,186	27.2%	-6.3	3,702,000	1,222,256	33.0%	-0.5	3,998,000	1,415,622	35.4%	1.9	4,289,000	1,043,352	24.3%	-9.2
WASHINGTON	2,087,000	1,066,807	51.1%	2,536,000	1,007,847	39.7%	-11.4	2,818,000	978,574	34.7%	-16.4	3,059,000	1,368,476	44.7%	-6.4	3,281,000	1,337,367	40.8%	-10.4
WEST VIRGINIA	1,069,000	445,623	41.7%	1,266,000	415,514	32.8%	-8.9	1,355,000	493,351	36.4%	-5.3	1,373,000	565,314	41.2%	-0.5	1,356,000	395,820	29.2%	-12.5
WISCONSIN	2,613,000	1,343,160	51.4%	3,047,000	1,199,495	39.4%	-12.0	3,249,000	1,500,996	46.2%	-5.2	3,379,000	1,580,344	46.8%	-4.6	3,475,000	1,526,960	43.9%	-7.5
WYOMING	195,000	120,486	61.8%	263,000	128,386	48.8%	-13.0	307,000	137,567	44.8%	-17.0	319,000	168,555	52.8%	-8.9	317,000	164,720	52.0%	-9.8
Total	124,000,000	58,015,926	46.8%	142,608,000	55,955,269	39.2%	-7.5	153,258,000	59,711,116	39.0%	-7.8	161,552,000	68,014,910	42.1%	-4.7	168,768,000	64,671,044	38.3%	-8.5

*Percentage point difference between turnout in current year and initial year listed in chart. If data do not appear for a state in the initial year listed, the difference is calculated from the first year in which data do appear for that state.

TOTAL HIGHEST STATEWIDE GENERAL ELECTIONS
Republican Turnout for Election Years 1970–1986

State	1970 Voting-age population	1970 Turnout	1970 %	1974 Voting-age population	1974 Turnout	1974 %	1974 Difference from 1970*	1978 Voting-age population	1978 Turnout	1978 %	1978 Difference from 1970	1982 Voting-age population	1982 Turnout	1982 %	1982 Difference from 1970	1986 Voting-age population	1986 Turnout	1986 %	1986 Difference from 1970
ALABAMA	2,035,000	189,050	9.3%	2,449,000	169,304	6.9%	-2.4	2,654,000	197,176	7.4%	-1.9	2,785,000	440,815	15.8%	6.5	2,882,000	696,203	24.2%	14.9
ALASKA	179,000	47,908	26.8%	220,000	51,641	23.5%	-3.3	255,000	92,783	36.4%	9.6	294,000	128,274	43.6%	16.9	334,000	101,799	30.5%	3.7
ARIZONA	1,055,000	228,284	21.6%	1,463,000	320,396	21.9%	0.3	1,767,000	241,093	13.6%	-8.0	2,050,000	394,872	19.3%	-2.4	2,324,000	539,940	23.2%	1.6
ARKANSAS	1,179,000	197,418	16.7%	1,426,000	187,872	13.2%	-3.6	1,564,000	195,371	12.5%	-4.3	1,638,000	361,772	22.1%	5.3	1,682,000	268,291	16.0%	-0.8
CALIFORNIA	12,492,000	3,430,004	27.6%	13,878,000	2,952,954	21.3%	-6.3	15,085,000	3,105,933	20.6%	-6.9	16,246,000	4,022,565	24.8%	-2.8	17,387,000	4,506,601	25.9%	-1.6
COLORADO	1,324,000	350,690	26.5%	1,700,000	378,907	22.3%	-4.2	1,957,000	480,596	24.6%	-1.9	2,129,000	404,047	22.8%	-3.7	2,262,000	566,236	25.0%	-1.5
CONNECTICUT	1,895,000	582,160	30.7%	2,063,000	440,207	21.3%	-9.4	2,165,000	423,474	19.6%	-11.2	2,258,000	545,987	24.2%	-6.5	2,347,000	433,977	18.5%	-12.2
DELAWARE	328,000	94,979	29.0%	382,000	93,826	24.6%	-4.4	413,000	91,689	22.2%	-6.8	442,000	105,357	23.8%	-5.1	471,000	53,767	11.4%	-17.5
DISTRICT OF COLUMBIA																			
FLORIDA	4,461,000	772,817	17.3%	5,661,000	736,674	13.0%	-4.3	6,657,000	1,123,888	16.9%	-0.4	7,597,000	1,015,330	13.4%	-4.0	8,509,000	1,847,525	21.7%	4.4
GEORGIA	2,973,000	424,983	14.3%	3,336,000	289,113	8.7%	-5.6	3,675,000	128,139	3.5%	-10.8	4,022,000	434,496	10.8%	-3.5	4,373,000	601,241	13.7%	-0.5
HAWAII	436,000	124,163	28.5%	538,000	113,388	21.1%	-7.4	607,000	124,610	20.5%	-7.9	665,000	81,507	12.3%	-16.2	720,000	160,460	22.3%	-6.2
IDAHO	413,000	143,943	34.9%	532,000	142,678	26.8%	-8.0	605,000	194,412	32.1%	-2.7	643,000	170,150	26.5%	8.4	666,000	200,153	31.3%	-3.6
ILLINOIS	6,804,000	1,680,861	24.7%	7,473,000	1,218,921	16.3%	-8.4	7,753,000	1,859,684	24.0%	-0.7	7,891,000	1,816,101	23.0%	-1.7	7,965,000	1,655,849	20.8%	-3.9
INDIANA	3,096,000	866,707	28.0%	3,571,000	814,117	22.8%	-5.2	3,774,000	680,513	18.0%	-10.0	3,895,000	978,301	25.1%	-2.9	3,979,000	936,143	23.5%	4.5
IOWA	1,703,000	403,394	23.7%	1,951,000	534,518	27.4%	3.7	2,043,000	491,713	24.1%	0.4	2,063,000	548,313	26.6%	2.9	2,048,000	588,880	28.8%	5.1
KANSAS	1,377,000	407,264	29.6%	1,588,000	417,956	26.3%	-3.3	1,670,000	440,586	26.4%	-3.2	1,720,000	400,837	23.3%	-6.3	1,757,000	576,902	32.8%	3.3
KENTUCKY	2,115,000	222,813	10.5%	2,321,000	328,982	14.2%	3.6	2,507,000	207,568	8.3%	-2.3	2,606,000	280,352	10.8%	0.2	2,665,000	252,849	9.5%	-1.0
LOUISIANA	2,061,000	19,703	1.0%	2,526,000	140,008	5.5%	4.6	2,766,000	320,010	11.6%	10.6	2,870,000	142,371	5.0%	4.0	2,913,000	646,311	22.2%	21.2
MAINE	598,000	162,248	27.1%	709,000	212,357	30.0%	2.8	771,000	212,294	27.5%	0.4	822,000	260,925	31.7%	4.6	867,000	249,030	28.7%	1.6
MARYLAND	2,383,000	484,960	20.4%	2,722,000	503,223	18.5%	-1.9	2,911,000	312,974	10.8%	-9.6	3,104,000	432,826	13.9%	-6.4	3,300,000	437,411	13.3%	-7.1
MASSACHUSETTS	3,539,000	1,058,623	29.9%	3,874,000	784,353	20.2%	-9.7	4,029,000	926,072	23.0%	-6.9	4,165,000	784,602	18.8%	-11.1	4,292,000	525,364	12.2%	-17.7
MICHIGAN	5,199,000	1,339,047	25.8%	5,928,000	1,356,865	22.9%	-2.9	6,272,000	1,628,485	26.0%	0.2	6,466,000	1,369,582	21.2%	-4.6	6,591,000	977,122	14.8%	-10.9
MINNESOTA	2,238,000	628,583	28.1%	2,626,000	491,912	18.7%	-9.4	2,812,000	894,092	31.8%	3.7	2,949,000	949,207	32.2%	4.1	3,065,000	606,755	19.8%	-8.3
MISSISSIPPI	1,248,000	28,847	2.3%	1,525,000	130,999	8.6%	6.3	1,656,000	263,089	15.9%	13.6	1,729,000	259,553	15.0%	12.7	1,778,000	208,037	11.7%	9.4
MISSOURI	2,896,000	617,903	21.3%	3,306,000	480,900	14.5%	-6.8	3,474,000	575,578	16.6%	-4.8	3,593,000	784,876	21.8%	0.5	3,690,000	777,612	21.1%	-0.3
MONTANA	406,000	108,140	26.6%	493,000	105,162	21.3%	-5.3	538,000	139,859	26.0%	-0.6	557,000	142,370	25.6%	-1.1	565,000	145,778	25.8%	-0.8
NEBRASKA	898,000	242,507	27.0%	1,039,000	236,076	22.7%	-4.3	1,095,000	310,919	28.4%	1.4	1,120,000	402,167	35.9%	8.9	1,130,000	358,326	31.7%	4.7
NEVADA	306,000	64,400	21.0%	431,000	79,605	18.5%	-2.6	530,000	108,097	20.4%	-0.7	642,000	120,377	18.8%	-2.3	759,000	133,821	17.6%	-3.4
NEW HAMPSHIRE	450,000	146,389	32.5%	558,000	122,678	22.0%	-10.5	629,000	133,745	21.3%	-11.3	696,000	153,974	22.1%	-10.4	761,000	156,218	20.5%	-12.0
NEW JERSEY	4,517,000	984,728	21.8%	4,852,000	794,698	16.4%	-5.4	5,049,000	844,200	16.7%	-5.1	5,219,000	1,047,626	20.1%	-1.7	5,376,000	738,901	13.7%	-8.1
NEW MEXICO	559,000	152,261	27.2%	727,000	160,430	22.1%	-5.2	832,000	183,442	22.0%	-5.2	910,000	191,946	21.1%	-6.1	975,000	209,455	21.5%	-5.8
NEW YORK	11,599,000	3,151,432	27.2%	11,921,000	2,340,188	19.6%	-7.5	11,979,000	2,156,404	18.0%	-9.2	12,104,000	2,494,827	20.6%	-6.6	12,259,000	2,378,197	19.4%	-7.8

Total Highest Statewide General Elections (continued)

Total Highest Statewide General Elections (continued)

Republican Turnout for Election Years 1970–1986 (continued)

State	1970 Voting-age population	1970 Turnout	1970 %	1974 Voting-age population	1974 Turnout	1974 %	1974 Difference from 1970	1978 Voting-age population	1978 Turnout	1978 %	1978 Difference from 1970	1982 Voting-age population	1982 Turnout	1982 %	1982 Difference from 1970	1986 Voting-age population	1986 Turnout	1986 %	1986 Difference from 1970
NORTH CAROLINA	3,038,000	410,742	13.5%	3,730,000	377,618	10.1%	-3.4	4,084,000	619,151	15.2%	1.6	4,406,000	579,817	13.2%	-0.4	4,713,000	767,668	16.3%	2.8
NORTH DAKOTA	356,000	122,056	34.3%	422,000	130,184	30.8%	-3.4	450,000	147,746	32.8%	-1.5	458,000	89,304	19.5%	-14.8	459,000	141,797	30.9%	-3.4
OHIO	6,402,000	1,706,205	26.7%	7,209,000	1,493,679	20.7%	-5.9	7,521,000	1,471,860	19.6%	-7.1	7,710,000	1,456,712	18.9%	-7.8	7,843,000	1,536,105	19.6%	-7.1
OKLAHOMA	1,597,000	336,157	21.0%	1,919,000	390,997	20.4%	-0.7	2,091,000	367,055	17.6%	-3.5	2,181,000	332,207	15.2%	-5.8	2,234,000	493,436	22.1%	1.0
OREGON	1,301,000	369,964	28.4%	1,610,000	420,984	26.1%	-2.3	1,807,000	550,165	30.4%	2.0	1,919,000	639,841	33.3%	4.9	1,990,000	656,317	33.0%	4.5
PENNSYLVANIA	7,387,000	1,874,106	25.4%	8,228,000	1,843,317	22.4%	-3.0	8,537,000	1,966,042	23.0%	-2.3	8,723,000	2,136,418	24.5%	-0.9	8,850,000	1,906,537	21.5%	-3.8
RHODE ISLAND	596,000	171,549	28.8%	651,000	73,824	11.3%	-17.4	669,000	133,637	20.0%	-8.8	690,000	175,495	25.4%	-3.3	714,000	208,822	29.2%	0.5
SOUTH CAROLINA	1,482,000	221,233	14.9%	1,883,000	226,109	12.0%	-2.9	2,097,000	351,733	16.8%	1.8	2,269,000	295,160	13.0%	-1.9	2,420,000	384,565	15.9%	1.0
SOUTH DAKOTA	386,000	108,347	28.1%	452,000	167,012	36.9%	8.9	475,000	170,832	36.0%	7.9	486,000	197,426	40.6%	12.6	491,000	152,543	31.1%	3.0
TENNESSEE	2,400,000	575,777	24.0%	2,914,000	455,467	15.6%	-8.4	3,187,000	661,959	20.8%	-3.2	3,373,000	737,963	21.9%	-2.1	3,516,000	553,449	15.7%	-8.2
TEXAS	6,658,000	1,037,723	15.6%	8,218,000	514,725	6.3%	-9.3	9,197,000	1,183,839	12.9%	-2.7	9,998,000	1,465,937	14.7%	-0.9	10,718,000	1,813,779	16.9%	1.3
UTAH	579,000	186,818	32.3%	756,000	210,299	27.8%	-4.4	868,000	206,520	23.8%	-8.5	947,000	312,003	32.9%	0.7	1,014,000	314,608	31.0%	-1.2
VERMONT	264,000	103,806	39.3%	319,000	74,561	23.4%	-15.9	350,000	90,688	25.9%	-13.4	374,000	114,191	30.5%	-8.8	396,000	168,403	42.5%	3.2
VIRGINIA	2,828,000	414,275	14.6%	3,396,000	361,302	10.6%	-4.0	3,702,000	613,232	16.6%	1.9	3,998,000	724,571	18.1%	3.5	4,289,000	466,747	10.9%	-3.8
WASHINGTON	2,087,000	403,946	19.4%	2,536,000	400,557	15.8%	-3.6	2,818,000	450,847	16.0%	-3.4	3,059,000	603,916	19.7%	0.4	3,281,000	650,931	19.8%	0.5
WEST VIRGINIA	1,069,000	152,877	14.3%	1,266,000	125,368	9.9%	-4.4	1,355,000	244,317	18.0%	3.7	1,373,000	202,380	14.7%	0.4	1,356,000	96,864	7.1%	-7.2
WISCONSIN	2,613,000	602,617	23.1%	3,047,000	497,195	16.3%	-6.7	3,249,000	816,056	25.1%	2.1	3,379,000	667,193	19.7%	-3.3	3,475,000	805,090	23.2%	0.1
WYOMING	195,000	74,249	38.1%	263,000	57,499	21.9%	-16.2	307,000	82,908	27.0%	-11.1	319,000	113,236	35.5%	-2.6	317,000	111,007	35.0%	-3.1
Total	124,000,000	28,239,316	22.8%	142,608,000	24,951,605	17.5%	-5.3	153,258,000	29,217,075	19.1%	-3.7	161,552,000	32,590,975	20.2%	-2.6	168,768,000	33,771,822	20.0%	-2.8

Democratic Turnout for Election Years 1970–1986

State	1970 Voting-age population	1970 Turnout	1970 %	1974 Voting-age population	1974 Turnout	1974 %	1974 Difference from 1970*	1978 Voting-age population	1978 Turnout	1978 %	1978 Difference from 1970	1982 Voting-age population	1982 Turnout	1982 %	1982 Difference from 1970	1986 Voting-age population	1986 Turnout	1986 %	1986 Difference from 1970
ALABAMA	2,035,000	637,046	31.3%	2,449,000	501,541	20.5%	-10.8	2,654,000	551,886	20.8%	-10.5	2,785,000	676,584	24.3%	-7.0	2,882,000	678,716	23.6%	-7.8
ALASKA	179,000	44,137	24.7%	220,000	54,361	24.7%	0.1	255,000	55,176	21.6%	-3.0	294,000	89,918	30.6%	5.9	334,000	84,943	25.4%	0.8
ARIZONA	1,055,000	201,887	19.1%	1,463,000	278,375	19.0%	-0.1	1,767,000	282,605	16.0%	-3.1	2,050,000	453,795	22.1%	3.0	2,324,000	340,965	14.7%	-4.5
ARKANSAS	1,179,000	375,648	31.9%	1,426,000	461,056	32.3%	0.5	1,564,000	399,916	25.6%	-6.3	1,638,000	431,855	26.4%	-5.5	1,682,000	439,882	26.2%	-5.7
CALIFORNIA	12,492,000	3,496,558	28.0%	13,878,000	3,693,160	26.6%	-1.4	15,085,000	3,878,812	25.7%	-2.3	16,246,000	3,815,205	23.5%	-4.5	17,387,000	3,743,542	21.5%	-6.5
COLORADO	1,324,000	310,117	23.4%	1,700,000	471,691	27.7%	4.3	1,957,000	483,985	24.7%	1.3	2,129,000	627,960	29.5%	6.1	2,262,000	616,325	27.2%	3.8
CONNECTICUT	1,895,000	531,523	28.0%	2,063,000	690,820	33.5%	5.4	2,165,000	613,109	28.3%	0.3	2,258,000	578,264	25.6%	-2.4	2,347,000	632,695	27.0%	-1.1
DELAWARE	328,000	71,429	21.8%	382,000	63,490	16.6%	-5.2	413,000	93,930	22.7%	1.0	442,000	98,533	22.3%	0.5	471,000	106,351	22.6%	0.8
DISTRICT OF COLUMBIA																			
FLORIDA	4,461,000	984,305	22.1%	5,661,000	1,118,954	19.8%	-2.3	6,657,000	1,406,580	21.1%	-0.9	7,597,000	1,739,553	22.9%	0.8	8,509,000	1,877,543	22.1%	0.0

Total Highest Statewide General Elections *(continued)*

Democratic Turnout for Election Years 1970–1986 *(continued)*

State	1970 Voting-age population	Turnout	%	1974 Voting-age population	Turnout	%	Difference from 1970	1978 Voting-age population	Turnout	%	Difference from 1970	1982 Voting-age population	Turnout	%	Difference from 1970	1986 Voting-age population	Turnout	%	Difference from 1970
GEORGIA	2,973,000	653,513	22.0%	3,336,000	646,777	19.4%	-2.6	3,675,000	536,320	14.6%	-7.4	4,022,000	734,090	18.3%	-3.7	4,373,000	828,465	18.9%	-3.0
HAWAII	436,000	176,449	40.5%	538,000	207,454	38.6%	-1.9	607,000	202,824	33.4%	-7.1	665,000	266,851	40.1%	-0.3	720,000	241,887	33.6%	-6.9
IDAHO	413,000	128,004	31.0%	532,000	184,142	34.6%	3.6	605,000	169,540	28.0%	-3.0	643,000	165,365	25.7%	-5.3	666,000	193,429	29.0%	-2.0
ILLINOIS	6,804,000	2,065,054	30.4%	7,473,000	1,811,496	24.2%	-6.1	7,753,000	1,464,688	18.9%	-11.5	7,891,000	2,093,272	26.5%	-3.8	7,965,000	2,033,783	25.5%	-4.8
INDIANA	3,096,000	870,990	28.1%	3,571,000	956,675	26.8%	-1.3	3,774,000	751,940	19.9%	-8.2	3,895,000	882,378	22.7%	-5.5	3,979,000	788,419	19.8%	-8.3
IOWA	1,703,000	387,510	22.8%	1,951,000	488,214	25.0%	2.3	2,043,000	403,365	19.7%	-3.0	2,063,000	528,726	25.6%	2.9	2,048,000	436,987	21.3%	-1.4
KANSAS	1,377,000	404,611	29.4%	1,588,000	390,451	24.6%	-4.8	1,670,000	363,835	21.8%	-7.6	1,720,000	405,772	23.6%	-5.8	1,757,000	404,338	23.0%	-6.4
KENTUCKY	2,115,000	247,585	11.7%	2,321,000	425,272	18.3%	6.6	2,507,000	290,730	11.6%	-0.1	2,606,000	413,286	15.9%	4.2	2,665,000	503,775	18.9%	7.2
LOUISIANA	2,061,000	330,464	16.0%	2,526,000	434,643	17.2%	1.2	2,766,000	839,669	30.4%	14.3	2,870,000	336,275	11.7%	-4.3	2,913,000	723,586	24.8%	8.8
MAINE	598,000	199,954	33.4%	709,000	140,923	19.9%	-13.6	771,000	176,493	22.9%	-10.5	822,000	281,066	34.2%	0.8	867,000	165,462	19.1%	-14.4
MARYLAND	2,383,000	639,579	26.8%	2,722,000	602,648	22.1%	-4.7	2,911,000	718,328	24.7%	-2.2	3,104,000	742,600	23.9%	-2.9	3,300,000	907,291	27.5%	0.7
MASSACHUSETTS	3,539,000	1,202,856	34.0%	3,874,000	1,168,252	30.2%	-3.8	4,029,000	1,249,311	31.0%	-3.0	4,165,000	1,300,344	31.2%	-2.8	4,292,000	1,198,143	27.9%	-6.1
MICHIGAN	5,199,000	1,744,716	33.6%	5,928,000	1,465,259	24.7%	-8.8	6,272,000	1,538,922	24.5%	-9.0	6,466,000	1,728,793	26.7%	-6.8	6,591,000	1,632,138	24.8%	-8.8
MINNESOTA	2,238,000	788,256	35.2%	2,626,000	786,787	30.0%	-5.3	2,812,000	779,286	27.7%	-7.5	2,949,000	1,049,104	35.6%	0.4	3,065,000	831,715	27.1%	-8.1
MISSISSIPPI	1,248,000	286,622	23.0%	1,525,000	156,119	10.2%	-12.7	1,656,000	251,558	15.2%	-7.8	1,729,000	414,099	24.0%	1.0	1,778,000	315,526	17.7%	-5.2
MISSOURI	2,896,000	692,026	23.9%	3,306,000	809,719	24.5%	0.6	3,474,000	966,553	27.8%	3.9	3,593,000	871,682	24.3%	0.4	3,690,000	828,403	22.4%	-1.4
MONTANA	406,000	150,060	37.0%	493,000	148,984	30.2%	-6.7	538,000	160,353	29.8%	-7.2	557,000	174,861	31.4%	-5.6	565,000	172,084	30.5%	-6.5
NEBRASKA	898,000	248,552	27.7%	1,039,000	267,012	25.7%	-2.0	1,095,000	334,276	30.5%	2.8	1,120,000	363,350	32.4%	4.8	1,130,000	265,156	23.5%	-4.2
NEVADA	306,000	113,496	37.1%	431,000	114,114	26.5%	-10.6	530,000	132,513	25.0%	-12.1	642,000	128,132	20.0%	-17.1	759,000	187,268	24.7%	-12.4
NEW HAMPSHIRE	450,000	98,098	21.8%	558,000	110,924	19.9%	-1.9	629,000	133,133	21.2%	-0.6	696,000	132,317	19.0%	-2.8	761,000	116,142	15.3%	-6.5
NEW JERSEY	4,517,000	1,157,074	25.6%	4,852,000	1,240,933	25.6%	0.0	5,049,000	1,082,960	21.4%	-4.2	5,219,000	1,206,416	23.1%	-2.5	5,376,000	802,762	14.9%	-10.7
NEW MEXICO	559,000	151,486	27.1%	727,000	164,172	22.6%	-4.5	832,000	174,631	21.0%	-6.1	910,000	217,682	23.9%	-3.2	975,000	185,378	19.0%	-8.1
NEW YORK	11,599,000	2,721,338	23.5%	11,921,000	3,028,503	25.4%	1.9	11,979,000	2,429,272	20.3%	-3.2	12,104,000	3,232,146	26.7%	3.2	12,259,000	2,775,229	22.6%	-0.8
NORTH CAROLINA	3,038,000	513,905	16.9%	3,730,000	637,833	17.1%	0.2	4,084,000	607,324	14.9%	-2.0	4,406,000	708,279	16.1%	-0.8	4,713,000	890,058	18.9%	2.0
NORTH DAKOTA	356,000	134,519	37.8%	422,000	113,931	27.0%	-10.8	450,000	68,016	15.1%	-22.7	458,000	186,534	40.7%	2.9	459,000	216,258	47.1%	9.3
OHIO	6,402,000	1,725,560	27.0%	7,209,000	1,930,670	26.8%	-0.2	7,521,000	1,354,631	18.0%	-8.9	7,710,000	1,981,882	25.7%	-1.2	7,843,000	1,949,208	24.9%	-2.1
OKLAHOMA	1,597,000	338,338	21.2%	1,919,000	514,389	26.8%	5.6	2,091,000	493,953	23.6%	2.4	2,181,000	548,159	25.1%	3.9	2,234,000	430,454	19.3%	-1.9
OREGON	1,301,000	337,998	26.0%	1,610,000	482,462	30.0%	4.0	1,807,000	587,445	32.5%	6.5	1,919,000	577,949	30.1%	4.1	1,990,000	584,763	29.4%	3.4
PENNSYLVANIA	7,387,000	2,043,029	27.7%	8,228,000	1,937,154	23.5%	-4.1	8,537,000	1,804,598	21.1%	-6.5	8,723,000	1,910,988	21.9%	-5.7	8,850,000	1,762,935	19.9%	-7.7
RHODE ISLAND	596,000	230,469	38.7%	651,000	252,436	38.8%	0.1	669,000	229,557	34.3%	-4.4	690,000	247,208	35.8%	-2.8	714,000	129,663	18.2%	-20.5
SOUTH CAROLINA	1,482,000	309,487	20.9%	1,883,000	356,126	18.9%	-2.0	2,097,000	384,898	18.4%	-2.5	2,269,000	468,819	20.7%	-0.2	2,420,000	465,500	19.2%	-1.6
SOUTH DAKOTA	386,000	131,616	34.1%	452,000	149,151	33.0%	-1.1	475,000	120,199	25.3%	-8.8	486,000	142,122	29.2%	-4.9	491,000	171,462	34.9%	0.8
TENNESSEE	2,400,000	579,783	24.2%	2,914,000	576,833	19.8%	-4.4	3,187,000	580,617	18.2%	-5.9	3,373,000	780,113	23.1%	-1.0	3,516,000	656,602	18.7%	-5.5

Total Highest Statewide General Elections (continued)

Total Highest Statewide General Elections (continued)

Democratic Turnout for Election Years 1970–1986 (continued)

State	1970 Voting-age population	Turnout	%	1974 Voting-age population	Turnout	%	Difference from 1970	1978 Voting-age population	Turnout	%	Difference from 1970	1982 Voting-age population	Turnout	%	Difference from 1970	1986 Voting-age population	Turnout	%	Difference from 1970
TEXAS	6,658,000	1,339,012	20.1%	8,218,000	1,075,346	13.1%	-7.0	9,197,000	1,285,348	14.0%	-6.1	9,998,000	1,847,048	18.5%	-1.6	10,718,000	1,716,978	16.0%	-4.1
UTAH	579,000	210,207	36.3%	756,000	230,532	30.5%	-5.8	868,000	162,791	18.8%	-17.6	947,000	219,482	23.2%	-13.1	1,014,000	196,683	19.4%	-16.9
VERMONT	264,000	66,028	25.0%	319,000	79,842	25.0%	0.0	350,000	42,482	12.1%	-12.9	374,000	79,340	21.2%	-3.8	396,000	124,123	31.3%	6.3
VIRGINIA	2,828,000	465,418	16.5%	3,396,000	506,838	14.9%	-1.5	3,702,000	608,511	16.4%	0.0	3,998,000	690,839	17.3%	0.8	4,289,000	544,951	12.7%	-3.8
WASHINGTON	2,087,000	879,385	42.1%	2,536,000	611,811	24.1%	-18.0	2,818,000	507,252	18.0%	-24.1	3,059,000	943,655	30.8%	-11.3	3,281,000	767,678	23.4%	-18.7
WEST VIRGINIA	1,069,000	345,965	32.4%	1,266,000	290,146	22.9%	-9.4	1,355,000	290,927	21.5%	-10.9	1,373,000	387,170	28.2%	-4.2	1,356,000	298,956	22.0%	-10.3
WISCONSIN	2,613,000	948,445	36.3%	3,047,000	740,700	24.3%	-12.0	3,249,000	768,536	23.7%	-12.6	3,379,000	983,311	29.1%	-7.2	3,475,000	705,578	20.3%	-16.0
WYOMING	195,000	67,207	34.5%	263,000	71,741	27.3%	-7.2	307,000	69,972	22.8%	-11.7	319,000	106,427	33.4%	-1.1	317,000	88,879	28.0%	-6.4
Total	124,000,000	32,777,314	26.4%	142,608,000	33,640,862	23.6%	-2.8	153,258,000	32,883,556	21.5%	-5.0	161,552,000	38,989,599	24.1%	-2.3	168,768,000	36,759,057	21.8%	-4.7

Other Turnout for Election Years 1970–1986

State	1970 Voting-age population	Turnout	%	1974 Voting-age population	Turnout	%	Difference from 1970*	1978 Voting-age population	Turnout	%	Difference from 1970	1982 Voting-age population	Turnout	%	Difference from 1970	1986 Voting-age population	Turnout	%	Difference from 1970
ALABAMA	2,035,000	217,906	10.7%	2,449,000	21,749	0.9%	-9.8	2,654,000	34,971	1.3%	-9.4	2,785,000	37,372	1.3%	-9.4	2,882,000	2,864	0.1%	-10.6
ALASKA	179,000	1,206	0.7%	220,000	4,770	2.2%	1.5	255,000	51,674	20.3%	19.6	294,000	32,676	11.1%	10.4	334,000	18,097	5.4%	4.7
ARIZONA	1,055,000	1,357	0.1%	1,463,000	8,217	0.6%	0.4	1,767,000	26,842	1.5%	1.4	2,050,000	36,692	1.8%	1.7	2,324,000	224,085	9.6%	9.5
ARKANSAS	1,179,000	36,132	3.1%	1,426,000	84	0.0%	-3.1	1,564,000	37,601	2.4%	-0.7					1,682,000	10,682	0.6%	-2.4
CALIFORNIA	12,492,000	131,801	1.1%	13,878,000	199,005	1.4%	0.4	15,085,000	517,032	3.4%	2.4	16,246,000	288,005	1.8%	0.7	17,387,000	210,073	1.2%	0.2
COLORADO	1,324,000	15,374	1.2%	1,700,000	26,967	1.6%	0.4	1,957,000	22,530	1.2%	0.0	2,129,000	25,321	1.2%	0.0	2,262,000	18,322	0.8%	-0.4
CONNECTICUT	1,895,000	266,521	14.1%	2,063,000	22,043	1.1%	-13.0	2,165,000	5,151	0.2%	-13.8	2,258,000	38,480	1.7%	-12.4	2,347,000	9,565	0.4%	-13.7
DELAWARE	328,000	2,759	0.8%	382,000	3,012	0.8%	-0.1	413,000	1,663	0.4%	-0.4	442,000	2,378	0.5%	-0.3	471,000	639	0.1%	-0.7
DISTRICT OF COLUMBIA																			
FLORIDA	4,461,000	265	0.0%	5,661,000	282,834	5.0%	5.0					7,597,000	422	0.0%	0.0	8,509,000	1,561	0.0%	0.0
GEORGIA	2,973,000	1,261	0.0%	3,336,000	548	0.0%	0.0	3,675,000	151	0.0%	0.0	4,022,000	9,132	0.2%	0.2	4,373,000	274	0.0%	0.0
HAWAII				538,000	42,767	7.9%		607,000	10,378	1.7%	-6.2	665,000	89,303	13.4%	5.5	720,000	9,251	1.3%	-6.7
IDAHO	413,000	2,759	0.7%	532,000	6,759	1.3%	0.6	605,000	4,877	0.8%	-0.5					666,000	4,848	0.7%	0.1
ILLINOIS	6,804,000	14,500	0.2%	7,473,000	22,036	0.3%	0.1	7,753,000	37,866	0.5%	0.3	7,891,000	46,553	0.6%	0.4	7,965,000	1,279,299	16.1%	15.8
INDIANA				3,571,000	49,592	1.4%		3,774,000	16,410	0.4%	-1.0	3,895,000	10,586	0.3%	-1.1	3,979,000	14,228	0.4%	-1.0
IOWA	1,703,000	18,936	1.1%	1,951,000	8,387	0.4%	-0.7	2,043,000	7,990	0.4%	-0.7	2,063,000	6,625	0.3%	-0.8	2,048,000	3,476	0.2%	-0.9
KANSAS	1,377,000	8,419	0.6%	1,588,000	32,202	2.0%	1.4	1,670,000	27,883	1.7%	1.1	1,720,000	18,135	1.1%	0.4				
KENTUCKY	2,115,000	3,265	0.2%	2,321,000	17,606	0.8%	0.6	2,507,000	10,287	0.4%	0.3	2,606,000	6,684	0.3%	0.1	2,665,000	2,205	0.1%	-0.1
LOUISIANA	2,061,000	12,881	0.6%	2,526,000	9,453	0.4%	-0.3	2,766,000	8,411	0.3%	-0.3	2,870,000	38,311	1.3%	0.7	2,913,000	8,382	0.3%	-0.3
MAINE				709,000	147,550	20.8%		771,000	66,903	8.7%	-12.1	822,000	6,280	0.8%	-20.0	867,000	127,805	14.7%	-6.1

Total Highest Statewide General Elections (continued)

Other Turnout for Election Years 1970–1986 (continued)

State	1970 Voting-age population	1970 Turnout	1970 %	1974 Voting-age population	1974 Turnout	1974 %	1974 Difference from 1970	1978 Voting-age population	1978 Turnout	1978 %	1978 Difference from 1970	1982 Voting-age population	1982 Turnout	1982 %	1982 Difference from 1970	1986 Voting-age population	1986 Turnout	1986 %	1986 Difference from 1970
MARYLAND	2,383,000	19,184	0.8%					2,911,000	6,626	0.2%	-0.6	3,104,000	413	0.0%	-0.8	3,300,000	3	0.0%	-0.8
MASSACHUSETTS	3,539,000	62,789	1.8%	3,874,000	129,149	3.3%	1.6	4,029,000	88,328	2.2%	0.4	4,165,000	81,466	2.0%	0.2	4,292,000	54,640	1.3%	-0.5
MICHIGAN	5,199,000	22,477	0.4%	5,928,000	57,905	1.0%	0.5	6,272,000	18,297	0.3%	-0.1	6,466,000	109,135	1.7%	1.3	6,591,000	10,779	0.2%	-0.3
MINNESOTA	2,238,000	8,606	0.4%	2,626,000	98,389	3.7%	3.4	2,812,000	48,311	1.7%	1.3	2,949,000	24,639	0.8%	0.5	3,065,000	19,096	0.6%	0.2
MISSISSIPPI	1,248,000	37,503	3.0%	1,525,000	18,791	1.2%	-1.8	1,656,000	135,393	8.2%	5.2	1,729,000	13,176	0.8%	-2.3				
MISSOURI	2,896,000	11,824	0.4%	3,306,000	7,970	0.2%	-0.2	3,474,000	3,696	0.1%	-0.3	3,593,000	3,288	0.1%	0.3	3,690,000	2,204	0.1%	-0.3
MONTANA												557,000	12,412	2.2%					
NEBRASKA	898,000	41,034	4.6%	1,039,000	24,514	2.4%	-2.2	1,095,000	286	0.0%	-4.5	1,120,000	26,537	2.4%	-2.2	1,130,000	941	0.1%	-4.5
NEVADA	306,000	11,894	3.9%	431,000	26,285	6.1%	2.2	530,000	13,705	2.6%	-1.3	642,000	11,515	1.8%	-2.1	759,000	14,371	1.9%	-2.0
NEW HAMPSHIRE	450,000	22,045	4.9%	558,000	1,513	0.3%	-4.6	629,000	13,990	2.2%	-2.7	696,000	4,882	0.7%	-4.2	761,000	11,482	1.5%	-3.4
NEW JERSEY	4,517,000	82,005	1.8%	4,852,000	47,926	1.0%	-0.8	5,049,000	52,393	1.0%	-0.8	5,219,000	28,770	0.6%	-1.3	5,376,000	11,882	0.2%	-1.6
NEW MEXICO	559,000	6,900	1.2%	727,000	4,964	0.7%	0.6	832,000	136	0.0%	-1.2	910,000	158	0.0%	-1.2	975,000	18	0.0%	-1.2
NEW YORK	11,599,000	2,299,078	19.8%	11,921,000	849,631	7.1%	12.7	11,979,000	183,144	1.5%	-18.3	12,104,000	124,515	1.0%	-18.8	12,259,000	155,085	1.3%	-18.6
NORTH CAROLINA	3,038,000	5,301	0.2%	3,730,000	8,974	0.2%	0.1	4,084,000	6,556	0.2%	0.0	4,406,000	32,984	0.7%	0.6				
NORTH DAKOTA	356,000	2,045	0.6%	422,000	7,613	1.8%	1.2	450,000	4,586	1.0%	0.4	458,000	8,288	1.8%	1.2	459,000	3,269	0.7%	0.1
OHIO	6,402,000	90,330	1.4%	7,209,000	139,148	1.9%	0.5	7,521,000	86,553	1.2%	-0.3	7,710,000	74,906	1.0%	-0.4	7,843,000	18,710	0.2%	-1.2
OKLAHOMA	1,597,000	24,295	1.5%	1,919,000	13,650	0.7%	-0.8	2,091,000	12,454	0.6%	-0.9	2,181,000	6,725	0.3%	-1.2	2,234,000	72,868	3.3%	1.7
OREGON	1,301,000	2,538	0.2%	1,610,000	6,839	0.4%	0.2	1,807,000	28,038	1.6%	1.4	1,919,000	27,852	1.5%	1.3	1,990,000	10,503	0.5%	0.3
PENNSYLVANIA	7,387,000	116,425	1.6%	8,228,000	38,374	0.5%	-1.1	8,537,000	38,039	0.4%	-1.1	8,723,000	65,808	0.8%	-0.8	8,850,000	32,523	0.4%	-1.2
RHODE ISLAND	596,000	3,402	0.6%					669,000	20,381	3.0%	2.5	690,000	10,449	1.5%	0.9	714,000	9,394	1.3%	0.7
SOUTH CAROLINA	1,482,000	13,073	0.9%	1,883,000	9,626	0.5%	-0.4	2,097,000	14,944	0.7%	-0.2	2,269,000	9,185	0.4%	-0.5	2,420,000	9,576	0.4%	-0.5
SOUTH DAKOTA																			
TENNESSEE	2,400,000	22,949	1.0%	2,914,000	8,414	0.3%	-0.7	3,187,000	48,222	1.5%	0.6	3,373,000	8,333	0.2%	-0.7	3,516,000	19,868	0.6%	-0.4
TEXAS	6,658,000	17,388	0.3%	8,218,000	123,925	1.5%	1.2	9,197,000	22,015	0.2%	0.0	9,998,000	67,123	0.7%	0.4	10,718,000	43,166	0.4%	0.1
UTAH	579,000	5,092	0.9%	756,000	24,966	3.3%	2.4	868,000	9,849	1.1%	0.3	947,000	32,661	3.4%	2.6	1,014,000	4,980	0.5%	-0.4
VERMONT	264,000	4,336	1.6%	319,000	9,996	3.1%	1.5	350,000	6,586	1.9%	0.2	374,000	12,464	3.3%	1.7	396,000	29,175	7.4%	5.7
VIRGINIA	2,828,000	506,663	17.9%	3,396,000	56,046	1.7%	-16.3	3,702,000	17,601	0.5%	-17.4	3,998,000	15,563	0.4%	-17.5	4,289,000	31,654	0.7%	-17.2
WASHINGTON	2,087,000	16,632	0.8%	2,536,000	32,410	1.3%	0.5	2,818,000	20,475	0.7%	-0.1	3,059,000	92,548	3.0%	2.2	3,281,000	8,965	0.3%	-0.5
WEST VIRGINIA												1,373,000	4,234	0.3%					
WISCONSIN	2,613,000	12,140	0.5%	3,047,000	56,142	1.8%	1.4	3,249,000	11,127	0.3%	-0.1	3,379,000	34,315	1.0%	0.6	3,475,000	25,638	0.7%	0.3
WYOMING																			
Total	117,814,000	4,203,380	3.6%	136,761,000	2,708,741	2.0%	-1.6	143,926,000	1,800,351	1.3%	-2.3	158,466,000	1,637,277	1.0%	-2.5	157,791,000	2,546,446	1.6%	-1.9

*Percentage point difference between turnout in current year and initial year listed in chart. If data do not appear for a state in the initial year listed, the difference is calculated from the first year in which data do appear for that state.

STATE GUBERNATORIAL PRIMARY ELECTIONS

Election Years 1970–1986

State*	1970 Voting-age population	Turnout	%	1974 Voting-age population	Turnout	%	Difference from 1970**	1978 Voting-age population	Turnout	%	Difference from 1970	1982 Voting-age population	Turnout	%	Difference from 1970	1986 Voting-age population	Turnout	%	Difference from 1970
ALABAMA								2,624,000	925,767	35.3%						2,868,000	969,282	33.8%	-1.5
ALASKA	176,000	71,380	40.6%	214,000	82,977	38.8%	-1.8	249,000	106,372	42.7%	2.2	287,000	137,047	47.8%	7.2	328,000	147,490	45.0%	4.4
ARIZONA				1,419,000	320,877	22.6%		1,723,000	256,415	14.9%	-7.7	2,010,000	342,296	17.0%	-5.6	2,284,000	436,984	19.1%	-3.5
ARKANSAS	1,172,000	490,763	41.9%	1,406,000	587,903	41.8%	-0.1					1,632,000	580,472	35.6%	-6.3	1,676,000	542,974	32.4%	-9.5
CALIFORNIA				13,703,000	4,724,937	34.5%		14,909,000	5,828,398	39.1%	4.6	16,079,000	5,108,463	31.8%	-2.7	17,220,000	4,228,038	24.6%	-9.9
COLORADO				1,662,000	361,273	21.7%													
CONNECTICUT																			
DELAWARE								409,000	99,447	24.3%		438,000	119,678	27.3%	3.0				
DISTRICT OF COLUMBIA																			
FLORIDA	4,380,000	1,118,180	25.5%					6,513,000	1,420,364	21.8%	-3.7	7,463,000	1,369,982	18.4%	-7.2	8,376,000	1,561,325	18.6%	-6.9
GEORGIA	2,942,000	906,217	30.8%	3,286,000	902,655	27.5%	-3.3	3,626,000	722,516	19.9%	-10.9	3,972,000	972,434	24.5%	-6.3				
HAWAII	431,000	196,685	45.6%	528,000	227,931	43.2%	-2.5	596,000	281,894	47.3%	1.7	657,000	251,847	38.3%	-7.3	712,000	272,561	38.3%	-7.4
IDAHO	411,000	143,122	34.8%																
ILLINOIS																7,953,000	1,289,162	16.2%	
INDIANA																			
IOWA								2,029,000	260,636	12.8%									
KANSAS								1,657,000	334,712	20.2%		1,715,000	367,393	21.4%	1.2				
KENTUCKY																			
LOUISIANA																			
MAINE	596,000	133,976	22.5%	700,000	185,571	26.5%	4.0	762,000	147,575	19.4%	-3.1	815,000	159,003	19.5%	-3.0	860,000	234,565	27.3%	4.8
MARYLAND	2,352,000	589,595	25.1%	2,695,000	494,947	18.4%	-6.7	2,883,000	705,139	24.5%	-0.6	3,076,000	725,238	23.6%	-1.5				
MASSACHUSETTS				3,852,000	967,253	25.1%		4,007,000	1,117,947	27.9%	2.8	4,146,000	1,360,104	32.8%	7.7				
MICHIGAN	5,159,000	1,098,193	21.3%									6,448,000	1,451,561	22.5%	1.2	6,573,000	1,039,424	15.8%	-5.5
MINNESOTA								2,785,000	693,521	24.9%		2,933,000	847,895	28.9%	4.0	3,048,000	702,648	23.1%	-1.8
MISSISSIPPI																			
MISSOURI																			
MONTANA																			
NEBRASKA	895,000	316,016	35.3%					1,087,000	328,359	30.2%	-5.1	1,118,000	309,098	27.6%	-7.7	1,129,000	337,908	29.9%	-5.4
NEVADA	299,000	96,101	32.1%	416,000	110,582	26.6%	-5.6	516,000	135,166	26.2%	-5.9	626,000	177,222	28.3%	-3.8	742,000	158,196	21.3%	-10.8
NEW HAMPSHIRE	444,000	121,827	27.4%	547,000	129,735	23.7%	-3.7	619,000	111,442	18.0%	-9.4					751,000	94,214	12.5%	-14.9
NEW JERSEY																			
NEW MEXICO	555,000	184,437	33.2%	712,000	199,535	28.0%	-5.2	817,000	198,370	24.3%	-9.0	900,000	243,089	27.0%	-6.2				
NEW YORK												12,082,000	1,873,301	15.5%					

State Gubernatorial Primary Elections (continued)

Election Years 1970–1986 (continued)

State	1970 Voting-age population	Turnout	%	1974 Voting-age population	Turnout	%	Difference from 1970	1978 Voting-age population	Turnout	%	Difference from 1970	1982 Voting-age population	Turnout	%	Difference from 1970	1986 Voting-age population	Turnout	%	Difference from 1970
NORTH CAROLINA																			
NORTH DAKOTA																			
OHIO	6,367,000	1,845,703	29.0%	7,163,000	1,625,326	22.7%	-6.3	7,475,000	1,161,014	15.5%	-13.5	7,690,000	1,703,982	22.2%	-6.8				
OKLAHOMA				1,894,000	783,927	41.4%		2,066,000	662,306	32.1%	-9.3	2,173,000	572,882	26.4%	-15.0	2,226,000	676,209	30.4%	-11.0
OREGON	1,288,000	523,756	40.7%	1,582,000	557,000	35.2%	-5.5	1,779,000	532,892	30.0%	-10.7	1,907,000	566,174	29.7%	-11.0	1,980,000	602,454	30.4%	-10.2
PENNSYLVANIA				8,183,000	1,730,865	21.2%		8,492,000	2,279,309	26.8%	5.7								
RHODE ISLAND																			
SOUTH CAROLINA				1,852,000	353,954	19.1%		2,066,000	404,434	19.6%	0.5								
SOUTH DAKOTA				448,000	159,325	35.6%		4/1,000	160,816	34.1%	-1.4					490,000	188,092	38.4%	2.8
TENNESSEE	2,383,000	835,108	35.0%	2,875,000	900,432	31.3%	-3.7	3,148,000	1,051,559	33.4%	-1.6					3,495,000	976,610	27.9%	-7.1
TEXAS				8,075,000	1,590,407	19.7%		9,054,000	1,971,193	21.8%	2.1	9,893,000	1,583,665	16.0%	-3.7	10,612,000	1,641,271	15.5%	-4.2
UTAH																			
VERMONT	261,000	72,772	27.9%	314,000	64,905	20.7%	-7.2												
VIRGINIA																			
WASHINGTON																			
WEST VIRGINIA																			
WISCONSIN	2,598,000	515,399	19.8%					3,220,000	700,600	21.8%	1.9	3,365,000	920,474	27.4%	7.5	3,461,000	569,287	16.4%	-3.4
WYOMING				257,000	101,347	39.4%		300,000	111,801	37.3%	-2.2	319,000	122,783	38.5%	-0.9	317,000	135,333	42.7%	3.3
Total	32,709,000	9,259,230	28.3%	63,783,000	17,163,664	26.9%	-1.4	85,882,000	22,709,964	26.4%	-1.9	91,744,000	21,866,083	23.8%	-4.5	77,101,000	16,804,027	21.8%	-6.5

*Overall primary turnout reflects only states with primaries in both parties. To find single party primary results, see partisan primary charts.

**Percentage point difference between turnout in current year and initial year listed in chart. If data do not appear for a state in the initial year listed, the difference is calculated from the first year in which data do appear for that state.

STATE GUBERNATORIAL PRIMARY ELECTIONS

Republican Turnout for Election Years 1970–1986

State	1970 Voting-age population	Turnout	%	1974 Voting-age population	Turnout	%	Difference from 1970*	1978 Voting-age population	Turnout	%	Difference from 1970	1982 Voting-age population	Turnout	%	Difference from 1970	1986 Voting-age population	Turnout	%	Difference from 1970
ALABAMA								2,624,000	25,850	1.0%						2,868,000	29,194	1.0%	0.0
ALASKA	176,000	35,844	20.4%	214,000	60,607	28.3%	8.0	249,000	81,682	32.8%	12.4	287,000	81,732	28.5%	8.1	328,000	84,004	25.6%	5.2
ARIZONA				1,419,000	149,370	10.5%		1,723,000	115,082	6.7%	-3.8	2,010,000	176,245	8.8%	-1.8	2,284,000	226,296	9.9%	-0.6
ARKANSAS	1,172,000	60,130	5.1%	1,406,000	4,513	0.3%	-4.8					1,632,000	13,347	0.8%	-4.3	1,676,000	22,346	1.3%	-3.8
CALIFORNIA				13,703,000	1,848,825	13.5%		14,909,000	2,517,480	16.9%	3.4	16,079,000	2,281,115	14.2%	0.7	17,220,000	2,059,413	12.0%	-1.5
COLORADO				1,662,000	156,025	9.4%		1,920,000	147,845	7.7%	-1.7					2,242,000	187,820	8.4%	-1.0
CONNECTICUT	1,874,000	130,802	7.0%													2,334,000	94,536	4.1%	-2.9
DELAWARE								409,000	4,658	1.1%		438,000	5,349	1.2%	0.1				
DISTRICT OF COLUMBIA																			
FLORIDA	4,380,000	358,997	8.2%					6,513,000	382,831	5.9%	-2.3	7,463,000	376,448	5.0%	-3.2	8,376,000	554,663	6.6%	-1.6
GEORGIA	2,942,000	107,557	3.7%	3,286,000	48,022	1.5%	-2.2	3,626,000	26,605	0.7%	-2.9	3,972,000	61,410	1.5%	-2.1				
HAWAII	431,000	41,803	9.7%	528,000	30,830	5.8%	-3.9	596,000	22,416	3.8%	-5.9	657,000	12,395	1.9%	-7.8	712,000	41,001	5.8%	-3.9
IDAHO	411,000	80,053	19.5%					594,000	117,555	19.8%	0.3	640,000	99,554	15.6%	-3.9				
ILLINOIS												7,880,000	606,446	7.7%		7,953,000	497,982	6.3%	-1.4
INDIANA																			
IOWA								2,029,000	156,010	7.7%									
KANSAS	1,371,000	233,651	17.0%	1,577,000	207,937	13.2%	-3.9	1,657,000	205,452	12.4%	-4.6	1,715,000	235,828	13.8%	-3.3	1,751,000	276,126	15.8%	-1.3
KENTUCKY																			
LOUISIANA																			
MAINE	596,000	81,658	13.7%	700,000	96,794	13.8%	0.1	762,000	73,823	9.7%	-4.0	815,000	84,794	10.4%	-3.3	860,000	116,129	13.5%	-0.2
MARYLAND	2,352,000	124,525	5.3%	2,695,000	107,513	4.0%	-1.3	2,883,000	131,760	4.6%	-0.7	3,076,000	134,590	4.4%	-0.9				
MASSACHUSETTS				3,852,000	196,232	5.1%		4,007,000	252,088	6.3%	1.2	4,146,000	178,683	4.3%	-0.8	4,274,000	64,373	1.5%	-3.6
MICHIGAN	5,159,000	562,562	10.9%									6,448,000	641,377	9.9%	-1.0	6,573,000	582,337	8.9%	-2.0
MINNESOTA	2,223,000	240,694	10.8%					2,785,000	209,205	7.5%	-3.3	2,933,000	309,292	10.5%	-0.3	3,048,000	192,153	6.3%	-4.5
MISSISSIPPI																			
MISSOURI																			
MONTANA																			
NEBRASKA	895,000	193,255	21.6%					1,087,000	197,197	18.1%	-3.5	1,118,000	185,245	16.6%	-5.0	1,129,000	192,851	17.1%	-4.5
NEVADA	299,000	36,212	12.1%	416,000	34,532	8.3%	-3.8	516,000	48,567	9.4%	-2.7	626,000	68,986	11.0%	-1.1	742,000	68,236	9.2%	-2.9
NEW HAMPSHIRE	444,000	85,833	19.3%	547,000	86,053	15.7%	-3.6	619,000	75,537	12.2%	-7.1	686,000	83,434	12.2%	-7.2	751,000	58,105	7.7%	-11.6
NEW JERSEY																			
NEW MEXICO	555,000	56,278	10.1%	712,000	50,927	7.2%	-3.0	817,000	47,604	5.8%	-4.3	900,000	65,599	7.3%	-2.9	965,000	89,107	9.2%	-0.9
NEW YORK												12,082,000	576,045	4.8%					

State Gubernatorial Primary Elections *(continued)*

Republican Turnout for Election Years 1970–1986 *(continued)*

State	1970 Voting-age population	1970 Turnout	1970 %	1974 Voting-age population	1974 Turnout	1974 %	1974 Difference from 1970	1978 Voting-age population	1978 Turnout	1978 %	1978 Difference from 1970	1982 Voting-age population	1982 Turnout	1982 %	1982 Difference from 1970	1986 Voting-age population	1986 Turnout	1986 %	1986 Difference from 1970
NORTH CAROLINA																			
NORTH DAKOTA																			
OHIO	6,367,000	928,131	14.6%	7,163,000	614,506	8.6%	-6.0	7,475,000	581,176	7.8%	-6.8	7,690,000	673,564	8.8%	-5.8	7,823,000	730,946	9.3%	-5.2
OKLAHOMA				1,894,000	150,782	8.0%		2,066,000	107,866	5.2%	-2.7	2,173,000	113,846	5.2%	-2.7	2,226,000	158,899	7.1%	-0.8
OREGON	1,288,000	246,417	19.1%	1,582,000	238,004	15.0%	-4.1	1,779,000	249,329	14.0%	-5.1	1,907,000	252,798	13.3%	-5.9	1,980,000	284,937	14.4%	-4.7
PENNSYLVANIA				8,183,000	695,577	8.5%		8,492,000	998,486	11.8%	3.3								
RHODE ISLAND	592,000	12,320	2.1%																
SOUTH CAROLINA				1,852,000	34,954	1.9%		2,066,000	23,671	1.1%	-0.7	2,246,000	20,944	0.9%	-1.0				
SOUTH DAKOTA	386,000	83,413	21.6%	448,000	89,926	20.1%	-1.5	471,000	91,223	19.4%	-2.2					490,000	116,098	23.7%	2.1
TENNESSEE	2,383,000	244,999	10.3%	2,875,000	249,112	8.7%	-1.6	3,148,000	268,620	8.5%	-1.7					3,495,000	236,141	6.8%	-3.5
TEXAS	6,589,000	109,021	1.7%	8,075,000	69,101	0.9%	-0.8	9,054,000	158,403	1.7%	0.1	9,893,000	265,851	2.7%	1.0	10,612,000	544,719	5.1%	3.5
UTAH																			
VERMONT	261,000	39,772	15.2%	314,000	42,784	13.6%	-1.6												
VIRGINIA																			
WASHINGTON																			
WEST VIRGINIA																			
WISCONSIN	2,799,000	222,607	8.0%					3,220,000	340,640	10.6%	2.6	3,365,000	334,347	9.9%	2.0	3,461,000	301,118	8.7%	0.7
WYOMING				257,000	58,421	22.7%		300,000	68,284	22.8%	0.0	319,000	70,667	22.2%	-0.6	317,000	94,068	29.7%	6.9
Total	45,945,000	4,316,534	9.4%	65,360,000	5,321,347	8.1%	-1.3	88,396,000	7,726,945	8.7%	-0.7	103,196,000	8,009,931	7.8%	-1.6	96,490,000	7,903,598	8.2%	-1.2

Democratic Turnout for Election Years 1970–1986

State	1970 Voting-age population	1970 Turnout	1970 %	1974 Voting-age population	1974 Turnout	1974 %	1974 Difference from 1970*	1978 Voting-age population	1978 Turnout	1978 %	1978 Difference from 1970	1982 Voting-age population	1982 Turnout	1982 %	1982 Difference from 1970	1986 Voting-age population	1986 Turnout	1986 %	1986 Difference from 1970
ALABAMA	2,024,000	1,019,680	50.4%	2,418,000	828,311	34.3%	-16.1	2,624,000	899,917	34.3%	-16.1	2,771,000	1,000,295	36.1%	-14.3	2,868,000	940,088	32.8%	-17.6
ALASKA	176,000	35,536	20.2%	214,000	22,370	10.5%	-9.7	249,000	24,690	9.9%	-10.3	287,000	55,315	19.3%	-0.9	328,000	63,486	19.4%	-0.8
ARIZONA	1,035,000	121,749	11.8%	1,419,000	171,507	12.1%	0.3	1,723,000	141,333	8.2%	-3.6	2,010,000	166,051	8.3%	-3.5	2,284,000	210,688	9.2%	-2.5
ARKANSAS	1,172,000	430,633	36.7%	1,406,000	583,390	41.5%	4.7	1,543,000	571,812	37.1%	0.3	1,632,000	567,125	34.8%	-2.0	1,676,000	520,628	31.1%	-5.7
CALIFORNIA	12,305,000	2,502,861	20.3%	13,703,000	2,876,112	21.0%	0.6	14,909,000	3,310,918	22.2%	1.9	16,079,000	2,827,348	17.6%	-2.8	17,220,000	2,168,625	12.6%	-7.7
COLORADO				1,662,000	205,248	12.3%													
CONNECTICUT								2,150,000	204,828	9.5%									
DELAWARE				378,000	93,240	24.7%		409,000	94,789	23.2%	-1.5	438,000	114,329	26.1%	1.4	466,000	74,711	16.0%	-8.6
DISTRICT OF COLUMBIA																			
FLORIDA	4,380,000	759,183	17.3%	5,515,000	841,460	15.3%	-2.1	6,513,000	1,037,533	15.9%	-1.4	7,463,000	993,534	13.3%	-4.0	8,376,000	1,006,662	12.0%	-5.3

State Gubernatorial Primary Elections (continued)

State Gubernatorial Primary Elections (continued)

Democratic Turnout for Election Years 1970–1986 (continued)

State	1970 Voting-age population	Turnout	%	1974 Voting-age population	Turnout	%	Difference from 1970	1978 Voting-age population	Turnout	%	Difference from 1970	1982 Voting-age population	Turnout	%	Difference from 1970	1986 Voting-age population	Turnout	%	Difference from 1970
GEORGIA	2,942,000	798,660	27.1%	3,286,000	854,633	26.0%	-1.1	3,626,000	695,911	19.2%	-8.0	3,972,000	911,024	22.9%	-4.2	4,322,000	611,463	14.1%	-13.0
HAWAII	431,000	154,882	35.9%	528,000	197,101	37.3%	1.4	596,000	259,478	43.5%	7.6	657,000	239,452	36.4%	0.5	712,000	231,560	32.5%	-3.4
IDAHO	411,000	63,069	15.3%																
ILLINOIS								7,712,000	725,459	9.4%						7,953,000	791,180	9.9%	0.5
INDIANA																			
IOWA	1,698,000	103,787	6.1%	1,937,000	133,516	6.9%	0.8	2,029,000	104,626	5.2%	-1.0	2,064,000	196,071	9.5%	3.4	2,051,000	134,191	6.5%	0.4
KANSAS								1,657,000	129,260	7.8%		1,715,000	131,565	7.7%	-0.1				
KENTUCKY																			
LOUISIANA																			
MAINE	596,000	52,318	8.8%	700,000	88,777	12.7%	3.9	762,000	73,752	9.7%	0.9	815,000	74,209	9.1%	0.3	860,000	118,436	13.8%	5.0
MARYLAND	2,352,000	465,070	19.8%	2,695,000	387,434	14.4%	-5.4	2,883,000	573,379	19.9%	0.1	3,076,000	590,648	19.2%	-0.6	3,272,000	639,964	19.6%	-0.2
MASSACHUSETTS	3,514,000	674,577	19.2%	3,852,000	771,021	20.0%	0.8	4,007,000	865,859	21.6%	2.4	4,146,000	1,181,421	28.5%	9.3				
MICHIGAN	5,159,000	535,631	10.4%	5,877,000	726,478	12.4%	2.0	6,222,000	604,861	9.7%	-0.7	6,448,000	810,184	12.6%	2.2	6,573,000	457,087	7.0%	-3.4
MINNESOTA				2,599,000	325,542	12.5%		2,785,000	484,316	17.4%	4.9	2,933,000	538,603	18.4%	5.8	3,048,000	510,495	16.7%	4.2
MISSISSIPPI																			
MISSOURI																			
MONTANA																			
NEBRASKA	895,000	122,761	13.7%	1,030,000	143,811	14.0%	0.2	1,087,000	131,162	12.1%	-1.6	1,118,000	123,853	11.1%	-2.6	1,129,000	145,057	12.8%	-0.9
NEVADA	299,000	59,889	20.0%	416,000	76,050	18.3%	-1.7	516,000	86,599	16.8%	-3.2	626,000	108,236	17.3%	-2.7	742,000	89,960	12.1%	-7.9
NEW HAMPSHIRE	444,000	35,994	8.1%	547,000	43,682	8.0%	-0.1	619,000	35,905	5.8%	-2.3					751,000	36,109	4.8%	-3.3
NEW JERSEY																			
NEW MEXICO	555,000	128,159	23.1%	712,000	148,608	20.9%	-2.2	817,000	150,766	18.5%	-4.6	900,000	177,490	19.7%	-3.4				
NEW YORK	11,530,000	944,998	8.2%	11,912,000	987,652	8.3%	0.1	11,970,000	724,188	6.1%	-2.1	12,082,000	1,297,256	10.7%	2.5				
NORTH CAROLINA																			
NORTH DAKOTA																			
OHIO	6,367,000	917,572	14.4%	7,163,000	1,010,820	14.1%	-0.3	7,475,000	579,838	7.8%	-6.7	7,690,000	1,030,418	13.4%	-1.0				
OKLAHOMA	1,587,000	402,283	25.3%	1,894,000	633,145	33.4%	8.1	2,066,000	554,440	26.8%	1.5	2,173,000	459,036	21.1%	-4.2	2,226,000	517,310	23.2%	-2.1
OREGON	1,288,000	277,339	21.5%	1,582,000	318,996	20.2%	-1.4	1,779,000	283,563	15.9%	-5.6	1,907,000	313,376	16.4%	-5.1	1,980,000	317,517	16.0%	-5.5
PENNSYLVANIA	7,365,000	1,056,298	14.3%	8,183,000	1,035,288	12.7%	-1.7	8,492,000	1,280,823	15.1%	0.7	8,703,000	756,818	8.7%	-5.6	8,831,000	973,210	11.0%	-3.3
RHODE ISLAND																710,000	57,244	8.1%	
SOUTH CAROLINA				1,852,000	319,000	17.2%		2,066,000	380,763	18.4%	1.2					2,398,000	329,496	13.7%	-3.5
SOUTH DAKOTA				448,000	69,399	15.5%		471,000	69,593	14.8%	-0.7	485,000	41,017	8.5%	-7.0	490,000	71,994	14.7%	-0.8
TENNESSEE	2,383,000	590,109	24.8%	2,875,000	651,320	22.7%	-2.1	3,148,000	782,939	24.9%	0.1	3,351,000	635,830	19.0%	-5.8	3,495,000	740,469	21.2%	-3.6

State Gubernatorial Primary Elections *(continued)*

Democratic Turnout for Election Years 1970–1986 *(continued)*

State	1970 Voting-age population	Turnout	%	1974 Voting-age population	Turnout	%	Difference from 1970	1978 Voting-age population	Turnout	%	Difference from 1970	1982 Voting-age population	Turnout	%	Difference from 1970	1986 Voting-age population	Turnout	%	Difference from 1970
TEXAS				8,075,000	1,521,306	18.8%		9,054,000	1,812,790	20.0%	1.2	9,893,000	1,317,814	13.3%	-5.5	10,612,000	1,096,552	10.3%	-8.5
UTAH																			
VERMONT	261,000	33,000	12.6%	314,000	22,121	7.0%	-5.6	345,000	13,278	3.8%	-8.8	371,000	17,645	4.8%	-7.9				
VIRGINIA																			
WASHINGTON																			
WEST VIRGINIA																			
WISCONSIN	2,598,000	292,792	11.3%	3,019,000	331,114	11.0%	-0.3	3,220,000	359,960	11.2%	-0.1	3,365,000	586,127	17.4%	6.1	3,461,000	268,169	7.7%	-3.5
WYOMING				257,000	42,926	16.7%		300,000	43,517	14.5%	-2.2	319,000	52,116	16.3%	-0.4	317,000	41,265	13.0%	-3.7
Total	73,767,000	12,578,830	17.1%	98,468,000	16,461,378	16.7%	-0.3	115,824,000	18,092,845	15.6%	-1.4	109,489,000	17,314,206	15.8%	-1.2	99,151,000	13,163,616	13.3%	-3.8

*Percentage point difference between turnout in current year and initial year listed in chart. If data do not appear for a state in the initial year listed, the difference is calculated from the first year in which data do appear for that state.

UNITED STATES SENATE PRIMARY ELECTIONS

Election Years 1970–1986

State*	1970			1974				1978				1982				1986			
	Voting-age population	Turnout	%	Voting-age population	Turnout	%	Difference from 1970**	Voting-age population	Turnout	%	Difference from 1970	Voting-age population	Turnout	%	Difference from 1970	Voting-age population	Turnout	%	Difference from 1970
ALABAMA																2,868,000	852,249	29.7%	
ALASKA	176,000	69,870	39.7%	214,000	82,050	38.3%	-1.4									328,000	141,045	43.0%	3.3
ARIZONA												2,010,000	343,003	17.1%					
ARKANSAS																			
CALIFORNIA	12,305,000	4,491,957	36.5%	13,703,000	4,351,343	31.8%	-4.8					16,079,000	4,409,635	27.4%	-9.1	17,220,000	4,225,621	24.5%	-12.0
COLORADO																			
CONNECTICUT	1,874,000	309,511	16.5%																
DELAWARE																			
DISTRICT OF COLUMBIA																			
FLORIDA	4,380,000	1,082,935	24.7%	5,515,000	1,069,577	19.4%	-5.3									8,376,000	1,555,810	18.6%	-6.1
GEORGIA								3,626,000	681,979	18.8%						4,322,000	704,994	16.3%	-2.5
HAWAII																			
IDAHO				521,000	125,853	24.2%													
ILLINOIS				7,433,000	1,502,852	20.2%		7,712,000	1,171,744	15.2%	-5.0					7,953,000	1,333,989	16.8%	-3.4
INDIANA																			
IOWA								2,029,000	261,637	12.9%									
KANSAS								1,657,000	351,209	21.2%						1,751,000	386,041	22.0%	0.9
KENTUCKY				2,293,000	201,880	8.8%		2,479,000	148,255	6.0%	-2.8								
LOUISIANA***																2,908,000	1,185,711	40.8%	
MAINE																			
MARYLAND	2,352,000	580,320	24.7%	2,695,000	429,580	15.9%	-8.7					3,076,000	675,180	21.9%	-2.7	3,272,000	759,998	23.2%	-1.4
MASSACHUSETTS								4,007,000	1,109,968	27.7%									
MICHIGAN								6,222,000	994,341	16.0%									
MINNESOTA	2,223,000	663,564	29.8%					2,785,000	742,526	26.7%	-3.2	2,933,000	827,904	28.2%	-1.6				
MISSISSIPPI								1,636,000	452,064	27.6%		1,722,000	235,451	13.7%	-14.0				
MISSOURI	2,883,000	668,270	23.2%	3,281,000	647,519	19.7%	-3.4					3,579,000	881,530	24.6%	1.5	3,676,000	748,823	20.4%	-2.8
MONTANA								531,000	190,999	36.0%		555,000	178,680	32.2%	-3.8				
NEBRASKA	895,000	312,531	34.9%																
NEVADA	299,000	97,102	32.5%	416,000	117,771	28.3%	-4.2					626,000	178,148	28.5%	-4.0	742,000	159,494	21.5%	-11.0
NEW HAMPSHIRE				547,000	124,938	22.8%		619,000	109,779	17.7%	-5.1								
NEW JERSEY	4,473,000	521,154	11.7%					5,021,000	602,890	12.0%	0.4	5,196,000	759,787	14.6%	3.0				
NEW MEXICO	555,000	172,283	31.0%																
NEW YORK												12,082,000	1,593,977	13.2%					

United States Senate Primary Elections *(continued)*

Election Years 1970–1986 *(continued)*

State	1970 Voting-age population	Turnout	%	1974 Voting-age population	Turnout	%	Difference from 1970	1978 Voting-age population	Turnout	%	Difference from 1970	1982 Voting-age population	Turnout	%	Difference from 1970	1986 Voting-age population	Turnout	%	Difference from 1970
NORTH CAROLINA				3,678,000	681,183	18.5%										4,669,000	889,312	19.0%	0.5
NORTH DAKOTA																			
OHIO	6,367,000	1,868,461	29.3%	7,163,000	1,578,447	22.0%	-7.3					7,690,000	1,585,892	20.6%	-8.7				
OKLAHOMA				1,894,000	745,872	39.4%													
OREGON								1,779,000	503,283	28.3%						1,980,000	596,290	30.1%	1.8
PENNSYLVANIA																8,831,000	1,484,928	16.8%	
RHODE ISLAND																			
SOUTH CAROLINA																			
SOUTH DAKOTA								471,000	158,242	33.6%									
TENNESSEE	2,383,000	764,751	32.1%					3,148,000	814,678	25.9%	-6.2	3,351,000	799,098	23.8%	-8.2				
TEXAS	6,589,000	1,651,228	25.1%									9,893,000	1,526,332	15.4%	-9.6				
UTAH																			
VERMONT				314,000	69,627	22.2%						371,000	73,838	19.9%	2.3				
VIRGINIA																			
WASHINGTON	2,064,000	679,611	32.9%	2,496,000	481,343	19.3%	-13.6					3,026,000	633,666	20.9%	-12.0	3,249,000	627,100	19.3%	-13.6
WEST VIRGINIA								1,342,000	325,291	24.2%									
WISCONSIN												3,365,000	811,243	24.1%					
WYOMING	195,000	87,159	44.7%					300,000	109,993	36.7%	-8.0								
Total	50,013,000	14,020,707	28.0%	52,163,000	12,209,835	23.4%	-4.6	45,364,000	8,728,878	19.2%	-8.8	75,554,000	15,513,364	20.5%	-7.5	72,145,000	15,651,405	21.7%	-6.3

*Overall primary turnout reflects only states with primaries in both parties. To find single party primary results, see partisan primary charts.

**Percentage point difference between turnout in current year and initial year listed in chart. If data do not appear for a state in the initial year listed, the difference is calculated from the first year in which data do appear for that state.

***In 1978 Louisiana eliminated the partisan primary for senator and instituted an open primary with candidates from all parties running on the same ballot. Any candidate who received a majority appeared in the general election unopposed. If no candidate received fifty percent, a runoff was held between the top two finishers. In 2008 Louisiana returned to a partisan primary system.

UNITED STATES SENATE PRIMARY ELECTIONS

Republican Turnout for Election Years 1970–1986

State	1970 Voting-age population	Turnout	%	1974 Voting-age population	Turnout	%	Difference from 1970*	1978 Voting-age population	Turnout	%	Difference from 1970	1982 Voting-age population	Turnout	%	Difference from 1970	1986 Voting-age population	Turnout	%	Difference from 1970
ALABAMA																2,868,000	33,659	1.2%	
ALASKA	176,000	40,411	23.0%	214,000	40,003	18.7%	-4.3									328,000	91,705	28.0%	5.0
ARIZONA												2,010,000	176,766	8.8%					
ARKANSAS																			
CALIFORNIA	12,305,000	2,061,105	16.8%	13,703,000	1,643,021	12.0%	-4.8					16,079,000	2,018,837	12.6%	-4.2	17,220,000	1,986,374	11.5%	-5.2
COLORADO								1,920,000	147,820	7.7%									
CONNECTICUT	1,874,000	127,714	6.8%																
DELAWARE								409,000	22,529	5.5%									
DISTRICT OF COLUMBIA																			
FLORIDA	4,380,000	352,781	8.1%	5,515,000	276,946	5.0%	-3.0					7,463,000	370,795	5.0%	-3.1	8,376,000	554,427	6.6%	-1.4
GEORGIA								3,626,000	24,693	0.7%						4,322,000	78,654	1.8%	1.1
HAWAII												657,000	9,421	1.4%		712,000	30,089	4.2%	2.8
IDAHO				521,000	63,290	12.1%													
ILLINOIS	6,768,000	704,397	10.4%	7,433,000	510,942	6.9%	-3.5	7,712,000	476,432	6.2%	-4.2					7,953,000	483,940	6.1%	-4.3
INDIANA																			
IOWA				1,937,000	130,676	6.7%		2,029,000	152,446	7.5%	0.8								
KANSAS								1,657,000	220,142	13.3%						1,751,000	270,538	15.5%	2.2
KENTUCKY				2,293,000	40,986	1.8%		2,479,000	30,114	1.2%	-0.6					2,657,000	41,592	1.6%	-0.2
LOUISIANA**																2,908,000	531,926	18.3%	
MAINE	596,000	75,577	12.7%																
MARYLAND	2,352,000	119,400	5.1%	2,695,000	105,335	3.9%	-1.2					3,076,000	121,264	3.9%	-1.1	3,272,000	138,074	4.2%	-0.9
MASSACHUSETTS	3,514,000	190,701	5.4%					4,007,000	274,817	6.9%	1.4								
MICHIGAN	5,159,000	540,024	10.5%					6,222,000	411,935	6.6%	-3.8	6,448,000	550,200	8.5%	-1.9				
MINNESOTA	2,223,000	236,150	10.6%					2,785,000	206,920	7.4%	-3.2	2,933,000	308,052	10.5%	-0.1				
MISSISSIPPI								1,636,000	74,161	4.5%		1,722,000	41,287	2.4%	-2.1				
MISSOURI	2,883,000	228,447	7.9%	3,281,000	166,614	5.1%	-2.8					3,579,000	293,829	8.2%	0.3	3,676,000	269,861	7.3%	-0.6
MONTANA								531,000	57,537	10.8%		555,000	56,311	10.1%	-0.7				
NEBRASKA	895,000	185,684	20.7%					1,087,000	162,615	15.0%	-5.8	1,118,000	158,350	14.2%	-6.6				
NEVADA	299,000	36,272	12.1%	416,000	41,396	10.0%	-2.2					626,000	68,898	11.0%	-1.1	742,000	69,694	9.4%	-2.7
NEW HAMPSHIRE				547,000	80,419	14.7%		619,000	70,378	11.4%	-3.3								
NEW JERSEY	4,473,000	230,417	5.2%					5,021,000	233,637	4.7%	-0.5	5,196,000	356,828	6.9%	1.7				
NEW MEXICO	555,000	55,617	10.0%																
NEW YORK												12,082,000	510,906	4.2%					

United States Senate Primary Elections *(continued)*

Republican Turnout for Election Years 1970–1986 *(continued)*

State	1970 Voting-age population	Turnout	%	1974 Voting-age population	Turnout	%	Difference from 1970	1978 Voting-age population	Turnout	%	Difference from 1970	1982 Voting-age population	Turnout	%	Difference from 1970	1986 Voting-age population	Turnout	%	Difference from 1970
NORTH CAROLINA				3,678,000	95,857	2.6%										4,669,000	209,825	4.5%	1.9
NORTH DAKOTA																			
OHIO	6,367,000	939,152	14.8%	7,163,000	526,420	7.3%	-7.4					7,690,000	607,329	7.9%	-6.9				
OKLAHOMA				1,894,000	152,621	8.1%													
OREGON								1,779,000	243,086	13.7%						1,980,000	298,466	15.1%	1.4
PENNSYLVANIA																8,831,000	570,296	6.5%	
RHODE ISLAND																			
SOUTH CAROLINA																2,398,000	51,859	2.2%	
SOUTH DAKOTA				448,000	94,974	21.2%		471,000	90,539	19.2%	-2.0					490,000	116,388	23.8%	2.6
TENNESSEE	2,383,000	236,046	9.9%					3,148,000	246,499	7.8%	-2.1	3,351,000	224,550	6.7%	-3.2				
TEXAS	6,589,000	110,465	1.7%									9,893,000	262,865	2.7%	1.0				
UTAH																			
VERMONT				314,000	46,026	14.7%						371,000	56,920	15.3%	0.7	393,000	28,595	7.3%	-7.4
VIRGINIA																			
WASHINGTON	2,064,000	89,594	4.3%	2,496,000	169,867	6.8%	2.5					3,026,000	159,051	5.3%	0.9	3,249,000	313,815	9.7%	5.3
WEST VIRGINIA								1,342,000	99,820	7.4%		1,375,000	91,046	6.6%	-0.8				
WISCONSIN				3,019,000	153,237	5.1%						3,365,000	268,771	8.0%	2.9				
WYOMING	195,000	45,755	23.5%					300,000	68,303	22.8%	-0.7	319,000	76,193	23.9%	0.4				
Total	66,050,000	6,605,709	10.0%	57,567,000	4,338,630	7.5%	-2.5	48,780,000	3,314,423	6.8%	-3.2	92,934,000	6,788,469	7.3%	-2.7	78,795,000	6,169,777	7.8%	-2.2

Democratic Turnout for Election Years 1970–1986

State	1970 Voting-age population	Turnout	%	1974 Voting-age population	Turnout	%	Difference from 1970*	1978 Voting-age population	Turnout	%	Difference from 1970	1982 Voting-age population	Turnout	%	Difference from 1970	1986 Voting-age population	Turnout	%	Difference from 1970
ALABAMA				2,418,000	691,432	28.6%		2,624,000	853,453	32.5%	3.9					2,868,000	818,590	28.5%	-0.1
ALASKA	176,000	29,459	16.7%	214,000	42,047	19.6%	2.9	249,000	19,251	7.7%	-9.0					328,000	49,340	15.0%	-1.7
ARIZONA	1,035,000	119,568	11.6%	1,419,000	147,936	10.4%	-1.1					2,010,000	166,237	8.3%	-3.3				
ARKANSAS				1,406,000	585,378	41.6%		1,543,000	577,868	37.5%	-4.2								
CALIFORNIA	12,305,000	2,430,852	19.8%	13,703,000	2,708,322	19.8%	0.0					16,079,000	2,390,798	14.9%	-4.9	17,220,000	2,239,247	13.0%	-6.8
COLORADO				1,662,000	203,319	12.2%													
CONNECTICUT	1,874,000	181,797	9.7%																
DELAWARE																			
DISTRICT OF COLUMBIA																			
FLORIDA	4,380,000	730,154	16.7%	5,515,000	792,631	14.4%	-2.3									8,376,000	1,001,383	12.0%	-4.7

United States Senate Primary Elections (continued)

United States Senate Primary Elections (continued)

Democratic Turnout for Election Years 1970–1986 (continued)

State	1970 Voting-age population	Turnout	%	1974 Voting-age population	Turnout	%	Difference from 1970	1978 Voting-age population	Turnout	%	Difference from 1970	1982 Voting-age population	Turnout	%	Difference from 1970	1986 Voting-age population	Turnout	%	Difference from 1970
GEORGIA				3,286,000	642,144	19.5%		3,626,000	657,286	18.1%	-1.4					4,322,000	626,340	14.5%	-5.0
HAWAII	431,000	126,422	29.3%																
IDAHO				521,000	62,563	12.0%													
ILLINOIS				7,433,000	991,910	13.3%		7,712,000	695,312	9.0%	-4.3					7,953,000	850,049	10.7%	-2.7
INDIANA												3,883,000	441,346	11.4%		3,967,000	351,164	8.9%	-2.5
IOWA								2,029,000	109,191	5.4%						2,051,000	105,334	5.1%	-0.2
KANSAS				1,577,000	147,743	9.4%		1,657,000	131,067	7.9%	-1.5					1,751,000	115,503	6.6%	-2.8
KENTUCKY				2,293,000	160,894	7.0%		2,479,000	118,141	4.8%	-2.3								
LOUISIANA**				2,491,000	696,487	28.0%		2,731,000	839,669	30.7%	2.8					2,908,000	653,785	22.5%	-5.5
MAINE																			
MARYLAND	2,352,000	460,920	19.6%	2,695,000	324,245	12.0%	-7.6					3,076,000	553,916	18.0%	-1.6	3,272,000	621,924	19.0%	-0.6
MASSACHUSETTS								4,007,000	835,151	20.8%									
MICHIGAN								6,222,000	582,406	9.4%									
MINNESOTA	2,223,000	427,414	19.2%					2,785,000	535,606	19.2%	0.0	2,933,000	519,852	17.7%	-1.5				
MISSISSIPPI								1,636,000	377,903	23.1%		1,722,000	194,164	11.3%	-11.8				
MISSOURI	2,883,000	439,823	15.3%	3,281,000	480,905	14.7%	-0.6					3,579,000	587,701	16.4%	1.2	3,676,000	478,962	13.0%	-2.2
MONTANA	405,000	88,263	21.8%					531,000	133,462	25.1%	3.3	555,000	122,369	22.0%	0.3				
NEBRASKA	895,000	126,847	14.2%																
NEVADA	299,000	60,830	20.3%	416,000	76,375	18.4%	-2.0					626,000	109,250	17.5%	-2.9	742,000	89,800	12.1%	-8.2
NEW HAMPSHIRE				547,000	44,519	8.1%		619,000	39,401	6.4%	-1.8					751,000	33,617	4.5%	-3.7
NEW JERSEY	4,473,000	290,737	6.5%					5,021,000	369,253	7.4%	0.9	5,196,000	402,959	7.8%	1.3				
NEW MEXICO	555,000	116,666	21.0%									900,000	168,844	18.8%	-2.3				
NEW YORK	11,530,000	925,885	8.0%	11,912,000	863,653	7.3%	-0.8					12,082,000	1,083,071	9.0%	0.9	12,237,000	496,752	4.1%	-4.0
NORTH CAROLINA				3,678,000	585,326	15.9%		4,032,000	650,942	16.1%	0.2					4,669,000	679,487	14.6%	-1.4
NORTH DAKOTA				418,000	66,555	15.9%													
OHIO	6,367,000	929,309	14.6%	7,163,000	1,052,027	14.7%	0.1					7,690,000	978,563	12.7%	-1.9	7,823,000	774,480	9.9%	-4.7
OKLAHOMA				1,894,000	593,251	31.3%		2,066,000	551,018	26.7%	-4.7					2,226,000	482,048	21.7%	-9.7
OREGON				1,582,000	317,968	20.1%		1,779,000	260,197	14.6%	-5.5					1,980,000	297,824	15.0%	-5.1
PENNSYLVANIA	7,365,000	887,190	12.0%	8,183,000	1,031,279	12.6%	0.6					8,703,000	745,334	8.6%	-3.5	8,831,000	914,632	10.4%	-1.7
RHODE ISLAND	592,000	61,422	10.4%					666,000	80,135	12.0%	1.7	687,000	68,959	10.0%	-0.3				
SOUTH CAROLINA								2,066,000	367,033	17.8%									
SOUTH DAKOTA								471,000	67,703	14.4%									
TENNESSEE	2,383,000	528,705	22.2%					3,148,000	568,179	18.0%	-4.1	3,351,000	574,548	17.1%	-5.0				

United States Senate Primary Elections (continued)

Democratic Turnout for Election Years 1970–1986 (continued)

State	1970 Voting-age population	Turnout	%	1974 Voting-age population	Turnout	%	Difference from 1970	1978 Voting-age population	Turnout	%	Difference from 1970	1982 Voting-age population	Turnout	%	Difference from 1970	1986 Voting-age population	Turnout	%	Difference from 1970
TEXAS	6,589,000	1,540,763	23.4%					9,054,000	1,561,198	17.2%	-6.1	9,893,000	1,263,467	12.8%	-10.6				
UTAH																1,003,000	29,033	2.9%	
VERMONT	261,000	33,134	12.7%	314,000	23,601	7.5%	-5.2					371,000	16,918	4.6%	-8.1				
VIRGINIA	2,799,000	128,959	4.6%																
WASHINGTON	2,064,000	590,017	28.6%	2,496,000	311,476	12.5%	-16.1					3,026,000	474,615	15.7%	-12.9	3,249,000	313,285	9.6%	-18.9
WEST VIRGINIA	1,069,000	220,011	20.6%					1,342,000	225,471	16.8%	-3.8								
WISCONSIN												3,365,000	542,472	16.1%		3,461,000	265,639	7.7%	-8.4
WYOMING	195,000	41,404	21.2%					300,000	41,690	13.9%	-7.3								
Total	75,500,000	11,516,551	15.3%	88,517,000	13,643,986	15.4%	0.2	70,395,000	11,247,986	16.0%	0.7	89,727,000	11,405,383	12.7%	-2.5	105,664,000	12,288,218	11.6%	-3.6

*Percentage point difference between turnout in current year and initial year listed in chart. If data do not appear for a state in the initial year listed, the difference is calculated from the first year in which data do appear for that state.

**In 1978 Louisiana eliminated the partisan primary for Senator and instituted an open primary with candidates from all parties running on the same ballot. Any candidate who received a majority appeared in the general election unopposed. If no candidate received fifty percent, a runoff was held between the top two finishers. In 2008 Louisiana returned to a partisan primary system.

STATE GUBERNATORIAL GENERAL ELECTIONS

Election Years 1971–1989

State	1971 Voting-age population	Turnout	%	1973 Voting-age population	Turnout	%	1975 Voting-age population	Turnout	%	Difference from 1971*	1977 Voting-age population	Turnout	%	Difference from 1971	1979 Voting-age population	Turnout	%	Difference from 1971
KENTUCKY	2,181,000	883,373	40.5%				2,367,000	748,157	31.6%	-8.9					2,553,000	939,366	36.8%	-3.7
LOUISIANA**							2,586,000	430,095	16.6%						2,826,000	1,371,825	48.5%	31.9
MISSISSIPPI	1,427,000	773,984	54.2%				1,558,000	689,200	44.2%	-10.0					1,688,000	677,322	40.1%	-14.1
NEW JERSEY				4,803,000	2,073,848	43.2%					5,000,000	2,073,444	41.5%	-1.7				
VIRGINIA				3,319,000	1,035,178	31.2%					3,626,000	1,240,621	34.2%	3.0				

State	1981 Voting-age population	Turnout	%	Difference from 1971	1983 Voting-age population	Turnout	%	Difference from 1971	1985 Voting-age population	Turnout	%	Difference from 1971	1987 Voting-age population	Turnout	%	Difference from 1971	1989 Voting-age population	Turnout	%	Difference from 1971
KENTUCKY					2,621,000	1,016,324	38.8%	-1.7					2,681,000	777,402	29.0%	-11.5				
LOUISIANA**					2,882,000	1,594,925	55.3%	38.7												
MISSISSIPPI					1,741,000	697,973	40.1%	-14.1					1,790,000	720,331	40.2%	-14.0				
NEW JERSEY	5,180,000	2,290,201	44.2%	1.0					5,337,000	1,951,033	36.6%	-6.6					5,098,000	2,218,490	43.5%	0.3
VIRGINIA	3,926,000	1,419,755	36.2%	5.0					4,216,000	1,343,090	31.9%	-4.3					4,361,000	1,787,131	41.0%	9.8

*Percentage point difference between turnout in current year and initial year listed in chart. If data do not appear for a state in the initial year listed, the difference is calculated from the first year in which data do appear for that state.

**In 1978 Louisiana eliminated the partisan primary for senator and instituted an open primary with candidates from all parties running on the same ballot. Any candidate who received a majority appeared in the general election unopposed. If no candidate received fifty percent, a runoff was held between the top two finishers. In 2008 Louisiana returned to a partisan primary system.

STATE GUBERNATORIAL GENERAL ELECTIONS

Republican Turnout for Election Years 1971–1989

State	1971 Voting-age population	Turnout	%	1973 Voting-age population	Turnout	%	1975 Voting-age population	Turnout	%	Difference from 1971*	1977 Voting-age population	Turnout	%	Difference from 1971	1979 Voting-age population	Turnout	%	Difference from 1971
KENTUCKY	2,181,000	412,653	18.9%				2,367,000	277,998	11.7%	-7.2					2,553,000	381,278	14.9%	-4.0
LOUISIANA**															2,826,000	690,691	24.4%	
MISSISSIPPI							1,558,000	319,632	20.5%						1,688,000	263,702	15.6%	-4.9
NEW JERSEY				4,803,000	676,235	14.1%					5,000,000	888,880	17.8%	3.7				
VIRGINIA				3,319,000	525,075	15.8%					3,626,000	699,302	19.3%	3.5				

State	1981 Voting-age population	Turnout	%	Difference from 1971	1983 Voting-age population	Turnout	%	Difference from 1971	1985 Voting-age population	Turnout	%	Difference from 1971	1987 Voting-age population	Turnout	%	Difference from 1971	1989 Voting-age population	Turnout	%	Difference from 1971
KENTUCKY					2,621,000	454,650	17.3%	-1.6					2,681,000	273,035	10.2%	-8.7				
LOUISIANA**					2,882,000	586,643	20.4%	-4.1												
MISSISSIPPI					1,741,000	288,764	16.6%	-3.9					1,790,000	332,985	18.6%	-1.9				
NEW JERSEY	5,180,000	1,145,999	22.1%	8.0					5,337,000	1,372,631	25.7%	11.6					5,415,000	838,553	15.5%	1.4
VIRGINIA	3,926,000	659,398	16.8%	1.0					4,216,000	601,652	14.3%	-2.5					4,361,000	890,195	20.4%	4.6

Democratic Turnout for Election Years 1971–1989

State	1971 Voting-age population	Turnout	%	1973 Voting-age population	Turnout	%	1975 Voting-age population	Turnout	%	Difference from 1971*	1977 Voting-age population	Turnout	%	Difference from 1971	1979 Voting-age population	Turnout	%	Difference from 1971
KENTUCKY	2,181,000	470,720	21.6%				2,367,000	470,159	19.9%	-1.7					2,553,000	558,088	21.9%	0.3
LOUISIANA**							2,586,000	430,095	16.6%						2,826,000	681,134	24.1%	7.5
MISSISSIPPI	1,427,000	601,222	42.1%				1,558,000	369,568	23.7%	-18.4					1,688,000	413,620	24.5%	-17.6
NEW JERSEY				4,803,000	1,397,613	29.1%					5,000,000	1,184,564	23.7%	-5.4				
VIRGINIA											3,626,000	541,319	14.9%					

State	1981 Voting-age population	Turnout	%	Difference from 1971	1983 Voting-age population	Turnout	%	Difference from 1971	1985 Voting-age population	Turnout	%	Difference from 1971	1987 Voting-age population	Turnout	%	Difference from 1971	1989 Voting-age population	Turnout	%	Difference from 1971
KENTUCKY					2,621,000	561,674	21.4%	-0.2					2,681,000	504,367	18.8%	-2.8				
LOUISIANA**					2,882,000	1,008,282	35.0%	18.4												
MISSISSIPPI					1,741,000	409,209	23.5%	-18.6					1,790,000	387,346	21.6%	-20.5				
NEW JERSEY	5,180,000	1,144,202	22.1%	-7.0					5,337,000	578,402	10.8%	-18.3					5,415,000	1,379,937	25.5%	-3.6
VIRGINIA	3,926,000	760,357	19.4%	4.4					4,216,000	741,438	17.6%	2.7					4,361,000	896,936	20.6%	5.6

State Gubernatorial General Elections (continued)

State Gubernatorial General Elections *(continued)*

Other Turnout for Election Years 1971–1989

State	1971 Voting-age population	Turnout	%	1973 Voting-age population	Turnout	%	1975 Voting-age population	Turnout	%	Difference from 1971*	1977 Voting-age population	Turnout	%	Difference from 1971	1979 Voting-age population	Turnout	%	Difference from 1971
MISSISSIPPI	1,427,000	172,762	**12.1%**															
VIRGINIA				3,319,000	510,103	**15.4%**												

State	1981 Voting-age population	Turnout	%	Difference from 1971	1983 Voting-age population	Turnout	%	Difference from 1971	1985 Voting-age population	Turnout	%	Difference from 1971	1987 Voting-age population	Turnout	%	Difference from 1971	1989 Voting-age population	Turnout	%	Difference from 1971
MISSISSIPPI																				
VIRGINIA																				

*Percentage point difference between turnout in current year and initial year listed in chart. If data do not appear for a state in the initial year listed, the difference is calculated from the first year in which data do appear for that state.

**In 1975 Louisiana eliminated the partisan primary for governor and instituted an open primary with candidates from all parties running on the same ballot. Any candidate who received a majority appeared in the general election unopposed. If no candidate received fifty percent, a runoff was held between the top two finishers. In 2008 Louisiana returned to a partisan primary system.

STATE GUBERNATORIAL PRIMARY ELECTIONS

Republican Turnout for Election Years 1971–1989*

State	1971 Voting-age population	Turnout	%	1973 Voting-age population	Turnout	%	Difference % from 1971**	1975 Voting-age population	Turnout	%	Difference from 1971	1977 Voting-age population	Turnout	%	Difference from 1971	1979 Voting-age population	Turnout	%	Difference from 1971
KENTUCKY	2,154,000	96,711	4.5%					2,340,000	74,268	3.2%	-1.3					2,526,000	124,520	4.9%	0.4
LOUISIANA***	2,312,000	10,571	0.5%													2,791,000	297,674	10.7%	10.2
MISSISSIPPI																1,670,000	32,452	1.9%	
NEW JERSEY				4,774,000	357,691	7.5%						4,971,000	347,435	7.0%	-0.5				
VIRGINIA																			

State	1981 Voting-age population	Turnout	%	Difference from 1971	1983 Voting-age population	Turnout	%	Difference from 1971	1985 Voting-age population	Turnout	%	Difference from 1971	1987 Voting-age population	Turnout	%	Difference from 1971	1989 Voting-age population	Turnout	%	Difference from 1971
KENTUCKY					2,612,000	90,786	3.5%	-1.0					2,672,000	90,370	3.4%	-1.1				
LOUISIANA													2,918,000	287,780	9.9%	9.4				
MISSISSIPPI													1,783,000	18,855	1.1%	-0.9				
NEW JERSEY	5,157,000	361,584	7.0%	-0.5													5,471,000	378,711	6.9%	-0.6
VIRGINIA																	4,464,000	401,887	9.0%	

Democratic Turnout for Election Years 1971–1989

State	1971 Voting-age population	Turnout	%	1973 Voting-age population	Turnout	%	Difference % from 1971**	1975 Voting-age population	Turnout	%	Difference from 1971	1977 Voting-age population	Turnout	%	Difference from 1971	1979 Voting-age population	Turnout	%	Difference from 1971
KENTUCKY	2,154,000	433,493	20.1%					2,340,000	377,250	16.1%	-4.0					2,526,000	552,611	21.9%	1.8
LOUISIANA***	2,312,000	1,102,641	47.7%					2,551,000	1,188,695	46.6%	-1.1					2,791,000	1,051,154	37.7%	-10.0
MISSISSIPPI	1,408,000	728,204	51.7%					1,538,000	770,559	50.1%	-1.6					1,670,000	687,913	41.9%	-10.5
NEW JERSEY				4,774,000	404,910	8.5%						4,971,000	556,090	11.2%	2.7				
VIRGINIA												3,581,000	493,108	13.8%					

State	1981 Voting-age population	Turnout	%	Difference from 1971	1983 Voting-age population	Turnout	%	Difference from 1971	1985 Voting-age population	Turnout	%	Difference from 1971	1987 Voting-age population	Turnout	%	Difference from 1971	1989 Voting-age population	Turnout	%	Difference from 1971
KENTUCKY					2,612,000	642,647	24.6%	4.5					2,672,000	625,531	23.4%	3.3				
LOUISIANA													2,918,000	1,246,181	42.7%	-5.0				
MISSISSIPPI					1,734,000	782,178	45.1%	-6.6					1,783,000	796,582	44.7%	-7.0				
NEW JERSEY	5,157,000	552,284	10.7%	2.2					5,314,000	321,019	6.0%	-2.4					5,471,000	369,323	6.8%	-1.7
VIRGINIA																				

*Due to the paucity of data, no overall primary chart is included for this time period.

**Percentage point difference between turnout in current year and initial year listed in chart. If data do not appear for a state in the initial year listed, the difference is calculated from the first year in which data do appear for that state.

***In 1975 Louisiana eliminated the partisan primary for governor and instituted an open primary with candidates from all parties running on the same ballot. Any candidate who received a majority appeared in the general election unopposed. If no candidate received fifty percent, a runoff was held between the top two finishers. In 2008 Louisiana returned to a partisan primary system.

CHAPTER 11
1990–2009

Chronology of Major Events, 1990–2009

1990   East and West Germany are reunified. Iraq invades Kuwait; in response, the United States stations troops in Saudi Arabia. Congress passes the Clean Air Act; it also passes an updated Immigration Act, increasing quotas for both family reunion and employment. The twenty-first census counts the U.S. population at 249.6 million people.

1991   With United Nations approval, the United States and allies drive Iraq out of Kuwait. Dissident elements of the former Soviet military stage initially successful anti-Gorbachev coup. Mayor of Moscow Boris Yeltsin leads successful effort to end the coup and restore Gorbachev government. Later Gorbachev resigns and Yeltsin is chosen Russian president. Lithuania, Estonia and Latvia leave the Soviet Union, which becomes a commonwealth of eleven independent states, marking the end of the cold war.

1992   Yugoslavia is divided among Serbs, Croats, and Bosnians under Serb rule, with much ethnic violence. Los Angeles riots protest the acquittal of policemen who beat Rodney King. Independent Ross Perot runs a populist presidential campaign in protest against expanding national debt. Perot briefly leads in pre-election polls and his message has influence on the national agenda. Democrat Bill Clinton is elected president, defeating Perot and incumbent George H. W. Bush.

1993   The United States and Russia sign a nuclear arms reduction treaty. Congress, without one Republican vote, enacts a Clinton-backed economic plan that sharply reduces the budget deficit through slightly higher taxation. Clinton unsuccessfully pushes Congress to overhaul the health care system. Congress passes the North American Free Trade Agreement (NAFTA), increasing economic ties to Canada and Mexico.

1994   Anti-Clinton sentiment propels Republicans to their first two-house majority since 1946. House Minority Leader Newt Gingrich unites the GOP during the campaign with a "Contract with America," a number of reformist proposals.

1995   Timothy McVeigh bombs a government building in Oklahoma City, killing 168. Budget disputes between Gingrich and Clinton lead to two government shutdowns; the public takes Clinton's side because Gingrich overreaches beyond the mandate of the 1994 election.

1996   Clinton is reelected president by a landslide. Full-scale civil war erupts in former Yugoslavia; the Serbs and Croats are accused of ethnic cleansing. Congress passes landmark welfare reform, encouraging welfare recipients to gain employment but reducing the economic safety net.

1997   Madeleine Albright becomes the first female secretary of state. A climate change conference in Kyoto, Japan, produces a plan to reduce greenhouse gases, but the United States is one of several advanced industrial nations not to sign on.

1998   President Clinton denies charges of sexual involvement with a White House intern. The House impeaches him on a straight party-line vote, but despite the fact that his denials were shown to be false, the Senate fails to convict him. U.S. embassies in Uganda and Tanzania are attacked by Islamic terrorists affiliated with al-Qaida. Rivals India and Pakistan become nuclear powers, heightening the possibility of nuclear warfare.

1999   A U.S.-led NATO force enters the former Yugoslavia, effectively protecting Kosovo and Bosnians from Serbs and Croats.

2000   Republican George W. Bush is elected president, defeating Vice President Al Gore in the electoral college, although Gore narrowly wins a popular vote plurality. The election is in doubt during a thirty-seven-day litigious struggle over recounting votes in Florida, which is finally concluded by the U.S. Supreme Court in a 5–4 decision that effectively hands the election to Bush. The twenty-second census counts the U.S. population at 281.4 million people.

Chronology of Major Events, 1990–2009 *(continued)*

2001	Congress passes a massive Bush-proposed tax cut with the aid of Democratic Senate Finance Committee Chairman Max Baucus. On September 11th, al-Qaida terrorists hijack four planes, crashing one into the Pentagon and two into World Trade Center, killing thousands. With U.N. approval, a NATO force led by American and British troops invade Afghanistan, ultimately driving much of the Taliban and al-Qaida leaders into Pakistan, but allowing Osama Bin Laden to escape the mountains of Tora Bora.
2002	Based on erroneous intelligence alleging weapons of mass destruction in Iraq, Congress approves a resolution authorizing the United States to use force against Iraq. Democrats briefly gain control of the Senate with the defection of former Republican Vermont Sen. James Jeffords. In the 2002 midterm election, Republicans, riding a wave of national unity and support for President Bush in the aftermath of the 9/11 attacks, regain control of the Senate and expand their majority in the House.
2003	The United States invades Iraq, toppling Saddam Hussein. No weapons of mass destruction are found, but a civil war begins.
2004	The Central Intelligence Agency acknowledges that there were no weapons of mass destruction in Iraq prior to the United States' launching the war. Internal strife within Iraq intensifies. Photos reveal the abuse of prisoners by U.S. soldiers at Abu Ghraib camp. Despite a low popularity rating and public opposition to the war in Iraq, Bush is reelected president.
2005	Massive Hurricane Katrina devastates the southern gulf coast, especially New Orleans; the slow government response creates a furor. The U.S. death toll in Iraq exceeds 2,000 as insurgency continues.
2006	Democrats regain majorities in both houses of Congress.
2007	Nancy Pelosi becomes first female speaker of the U.S. House of Representatives. President Bush announces troop surge in Iraq aimed at stabilizing the country. The U.S. war dead exceed 4,000.
2008	Stock markets plunge as the United States and the world fall into most severe recession since the Great Depression of the 1930s. Congress passes a $700 billion bailout of the troubled financial industry, with a promise to guarantee up to $2.8 trillion more in debt. After a tightly contested race, Senator Hillary Clinton concedes the Democratic nomination for president to Barack Obama. Obama is elected president, becoming the first African American to hold the office.
2009	To counteract the recession, Congress authorizes a stimulus package of $787 billion, including $25 billion for the auto industry. President Obama announces a timeline for withdrawal of American troops from Iraq, but later in the year also announces plans for a troop surge in Afghanistan with a similar timeline for troop drawdown.

State and Federal Laws Chronology, 1990–2009

1991   *Chisom v. Roemer, United States v. Roemer*, 501 U.S. 380 (1991). The Supreme Court finds that the 1965 Voting Rights Act applies to judicial elections.[1]

1992   *Burdick v. Takushi*, 504 U.S. 428 (1992). The Supreme Court holds that states can prohibit write-in voting.

1993   *Shaw v. Reno*, 509 U.S. 630 (1993). In a 5–4 decision, the Supreme Court rules that while racial considerations can be a factor in redistricting, bizarrely-shaped districts constitute a form of segregation that violates the Fourteenth Amendment. Irregularly shaped districts require a compelling government interest. In the majority opinion, Justice Sandra Day O'Connor expresses concern about a racial "balkanization" of the country.

       Congress passes the National Voter Registration Act of 1993 (NVRA), also known as the "Motor-Voter Act." The law requires Departments of Motor Vehicles to actively offer to register citizens to vote, permits citizens in every state to register by mail, and mandates that social service agencies offer registration materials to their clients. The Act also provided a bi-partisanly supported set of rules for registration confirmation, cleaning the registration lists of names that should not be on them and reducing the possibility of fraud based on inaccurate lists.

1994   *Holder v. Hall*, 512 U.S. 874 (1994). In a 5–4 decision, the Supreme Court holds that the size of a governing body is not subject to constitutional challenge under the Voting Rights Act, even though a very small governing body decreases the likelihood of minority candidates taking office. This decision sidesteps the holding of *Thornburg v. Gingles* (1986) that de facto discrimination invalidates a voting system.

1995   *Miller v. Johnson*, 515 U.S. 900 (1995). In a 5–4 decision, the Supreme Court requires federal judges to use "strict scrutiny" in cases of redistricting with racial motivations to insure that the equal protection rights of whites are not violated.

1996   *Bush v. Vera*, 517 U.S. 952 (1996) and *Shaw v. Hunt*, 517 U.S. 899 (1996). In both cases, the Supreme Court by a 5–4 vote holds as unconstitutional districts drawn for the purpose of establishing an ethnic minority as the majority in those districts. In both cases, the Court finds that the state lacks a compelling interest for drawing districts along racial lines. It rejects arguments based on past discrimination.

2001   *Hunt/Easley v. Cromartie*, 532 U.S. 234 at 257 (2001). In a 5–4 vote, the Supreme Court finds that redistricting that happens to favor racial minorities is acceptable if the motivation is primarily political, not racial. This ruling gives greater leeway to state legislatures. Justice O'Connor again casts the deciding vote.

2002   Help America Vote Act (HAVA) is passed by Congress in response to voting irregularities in the 2000 presidential election. HAVA contains a number of provisions to enhance electoral participation, including funds to encourage states to upgrade their voting technology, the establishment of the Election Assistance Commission, the requirement of "provisional" ballots for those whose eligibility to vote is challenged at a polling place, the opportunity to review ballots prior to casting, and the centralization of state voter registration systems. HAVA also contains new identification requirements for first-time voters who register by mail.

2004   *Vieth v. Jubelier*, 541 U.S. 267 (2004). In a 5–4 vote, The Supreme Court upholds an instance of political gerrymandering in Pennsylvania due to a lack of a clear standard for judging when political gerrymandering is unconstitutional.

2006   Congress renews the Voting Rights Act for another twenty-five years.

League of United Latin American Citizens v. Perry, Governor of Texas, 548 U.S. 399 (2006). In a 5–4 vote, the Supreme Court upholds the highly political redistricting of Texas as permissible, but a different 5–4 majority rules that one of the new district boundaries is in violation of the Voting Rights Act for diluting a Latino majority. Justice Anthony Kennedy is the swing vote on the two rulings, offering no clear guidelines as to whether and under what conditions the court would intervene in cases involving the drawing of district lines.

2008   *Crawford v. Marion County Election Board*, 553 U.S. 181 (2008). The Supreme Court upholds Indiana's voter identification law requiring voters to provide picture identification (available for free but at a very limited number of locations) to vote or cast a provisional ballot, but for those who do not have a picture identification card at the polls, they must provide proof of their eligibility within ten days after an election. Indiana's voter ID law was the strictest of many such laws.

2009   *Northwest Austin Municipal Utilities District No. 1 v. Holder* (2009). The Supreme Court rules that any political subdivision, not only states and counties, is eligible for an exemption from the federal "preclearance" of district changes as required by the Voting Rights Act. The justices defer from ruling on the constitutionality of the preclearance provision, leaving open the possibility of voiding it in the future.

[1] For Supreme Court cases, see CQ Press Electronic Library, Guide to the U.S. Supreme Court Online Edition, "Chronology of Major Decisions of the Court, 1797–2007." Originally published in David G. Savage, *Guide to the U.S. Supreme Court,* 4th ed. (Revised), (Washington, D.C.: CQ Press, 2008). http://library.cqpress.com/supremecourtguide/search.php (accessed June 18th, 2010).

National Count of Popular Vote for President, 1992–2008

YEAR	NAME	PARTY	TOTAL	PERCENTAGE[1]
1992	Bill Clinton	Democratic	44,909,426	25.0%
	George H. W. Bush	Republican	39,103,882	21.7%
	Ross Perot	Reform	19,743,821	11.0%
1996	Bill Clinton	Democratic	47,402,357	25.3%
	Bob Dole	Republican	39,198,755	20.9%
	Ross Perot	Reform	8,085,402	4.3%
2000	**George W. Bush[2]**	**Republican**	**50,455,156**	**26.0%**
	Al Gore	Democratic	50,992,335	26.2%
	Ralph Nader	Green	2,882,955	1.5%
2004	George W. Bush	Republican	62,028,719	30.7%
	John Kerry	Democratic	59,028,550	29.3%
2008	Barack Obama	Democratic	69,494,351	33.2%
	John McCain	Republican	59,944,395	28.6%

[1] The percentage figures in this chart are based on the votes cast divided by the eligible voting-age population at the time of the election.

[2] George W. Bush gained the presidency with an electoral college count of 271 to 266, despite narrowly losing the popular vote to Vice President Al Gore. The outcome hinged on a few hundred votes in Florida, and a thirty-seven day legal dispute over manually recounting ballots was settled by the U.S. Supreme Court in *Bush v. Gore*. In a 5–4 decision, the Court ended the recount and effectively gave Bush the election.

United States Presidential Turnout, Election Years 1992–2008

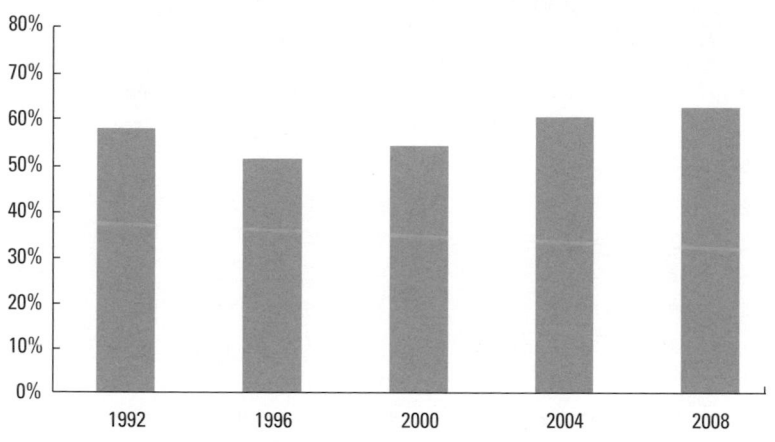

YEAR	VOTING-AGE POPULATION	TOTAL	%
1992	180,116,000	104,425,014	58.0%
1996	187,437,000	96,277,872	51.4%
2000	194,327,000	105,396,627	54.2%
2004	201,780,000	122,265,430	60.6%
2008	209,332,000	131,300,047	62.7%

Partisan Turnout Presidential Years Based on Aggregate House Turnout, Election Years 1992–2008

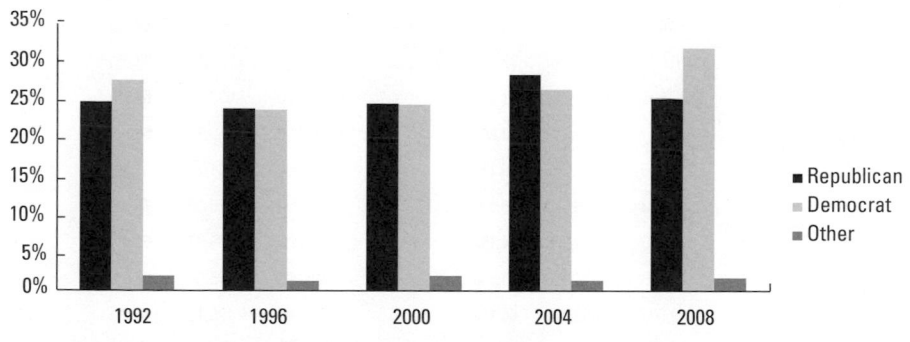

■ Republican
■ Democrat
■ Other

YEAR	VOTING-AGE POPULATION	REPUBLICAN TURNOUT	%	DEMOCRAT TURNOUT	%	OTHER TURNOUT	%
1992	180,116,000	43,806,043	24.3%	48,846,568	27.1%	3,437,963	1.9%
1996	187,437,000	43,965,860	23.5%	43,680,193	23.3%	2,334,105	1.2%
2000	194,327,000	46,860,119	24.1%	46,608,240	24.0%	3,756,420	1.9%
2004	201,780,000	56,223,235	27.9%	52,339,515	25.9%	2,670,807	1.3%
2008	209,332,000	51,844,289	24.8%	65,533,826	31.3%	3,484,135	1.7%

UNITED STATES PRESIDENTIAL GENERAL ELECTIONS

Election Years 1992–2008

	1992			1996				2000				2004				2008			
State	Voting-age population	Turnout	%	Voting-age population	Turnout	%	Difference from 1992*	Voting-age population	Turnout	%	Difference from 1992	Voting-age population	Turnout	%	Difference from 1992	Voting-age population	Turnout	%	Difference from 1992
ALABAMA	3,048,000	1,688,060	55.4%	3,174,000	1,534,349	48.3%	-7.0	3,284,000	1,666,272	50.7%	-4.6	3,343,000	1,883,415	56.3%	1.0	3,402,000	2,099,819	61.7%	6.3
ALASKA	383,000	258,506	67.5%	405,000	241,620	59.7%	-7.8	425,000	285,560	67.2%	-0.3	453,000	312,598	69.0%	1.5	480,000	326,197	68.0%	0.5
ARIZONA	2,778,000	1,486,975	53.5%	3,114,000	1,404,405	45.1%	-8.4	3,437,000	1,532,016	44.6%	-9.0	3,800,000	2,012,585	53.0%	-0.6	4,166,000	2,293,475	55.1%	1.5
ARKANSAS	1,782,000	950,653	53.3%	1,876,000	884,262	47.1%	-6.2	1,959,000	921,781	47.1%	-6.3	2,015,000	1,054,945	52.4%	-1.0	2,073,000	1,086,617	52.4%	-0.9
CALIFORNIA	18,781,000	11,131,721	59.3%	19,460,000	10,019,484	51.5%	-7.8	20,154,000	10,965,856	54.4%	-4.9	21,306,000	12,419,857	58.3%	-1.0	22,475,000	13,561,900	60.3%	1.1
COLORADO	2,541,000	1,569,180	61.8%	2,791,000	1,510,704	54.1%	-7.6	3,007,000	1,741,368	57.9%	-3.8	3,118,000	2,129,630	68.3%	6.5	3,233,000	2,401,349	74.3%	12.5
CONNECTICUT	2,414,000	1,616,332	67.0%	2,408,000	1,392,614	57.8%	-9.1	2,408,000	1,459,525	60.6%	-6.3	2,466,000	1,578,769	64.0%	-2.9	2,525,000	1,649,399	65.3%	-1.6
DELAWARE	515,000	289,735	56.3%	544,000	271,084	49.8%	-6.4	571,000	327,622	57.4%	1.1	603,000	375,190	62.2%	6.0	634,000	412,398	65.0%	8.8
DISTRICT OF COLUMBIA	441,000	227,572	51.6%	425,000	185,726	43.7%	-7.9	408,000	201,894	49.5%	-2.1	388,000	227,586	58.7%	7.1	367,000	265,853	72.4%	20.8
FLORIDA	9,754,000	5,314,392	54.5%	10,487,000	5,303,794	50.6%	-3.9	11,205,000	5,963,110	53.2%	-1.3	12,124,000	7,609,810	62.8%	8.3	13,051,000	8,390,744	64.3%	9.8
GEORGIA	4,938,000	2,321,125	47.0%	5,345,000	2,299,071	43.0%	-4.0	5,718,000	2,596,645	45.4%	-1.6	6,028,000	3,298,790	54.7%	7.7	6,344,000	3,924,454	61.9%	14.9
HAWAII	786,000	372,842	47.4%	817,000	360,120	44.1%	-3.4	847,000	367,951	43.4%	-4.0	885,000	429,013	48.5%	1.0	923,000	453,165	49.1%	1.7
IDAHO	741,000	482,142	65.1%	824,000	491,719	59.7%	-5.4	900,000	501,621	55.7%	-9.3	967,000	598,376	61.9%	-3.2	1,034,000	655,032	63.3%	-1.7
ILLINOIS	8,124,000	5,050,157	62.2%	8,269,000	4,311,391	52.1%	-10.0	8,393,000	4,742,123	56.5%	-5.7	8,466,000	5,275,415	62.3%	0.1	8,546,000	5,523,051	64.6%	2.5
INDIANA	4,146,000	2,305,871	55.6%	4,292,000	2,135,842	49.8%	-5.9	4,421,000	2,199,302	49.7%	-5.9	4,509,000	2,468,002	54.7%	-0.9	4,599,000	2,751,054	59.8%	4.2
IOWA	2,067,000	1,354,607	65.5%	2,109,000	1,234,075	58.5%	-7.0	2,147,000	1,315,563	61.3%	-4.3	2,175,000	1,506,908	69.3%	3.7	2,205,000	1,537,123	69.7%	4.2
KANSAS	1,818,000	1,157,335	63.7%	1,865,000	1,074,300	57.6%	-6.1	1,906,000	1,072,218	56.3%	-7.4	1,939,000	1,187,756	61.3%	-2.4	1,972,000	1,235,872	62.7%	-1.0
KENTUCKY	2,793,000	1,492,900	53.5%	2,909,000	1,388,708	47.7%	-5.7	3,013,000	1,544,187	51.3%	-2.2	3,085,000	1,795,860	58.2%	4.8	3,158,000	1,826,508	57.8%	4.4
LOUISIANA	3,017,000	1,790,017	59.3%	3,117,000	1,783,959	57.2%	-2.1	3,207,000	1,765,656	55.1%	-4.3	3,278,000	1,943,106	59.3%	-0.1	3,349,000	1,960,761	58.5%	-0.8
MAINE	920,000	679,499	73.9%	942,000	605,897	64.3%	-9.5	965,000	651,817	67.5%	-6.3	1,010,000	740,748	73.3%	-0.5	1,054,000	731,163	69.4%	-4.5
MARYLAND	3,524,000	1,985,046	56.3%	3,621,000	1,780,870	49.2%	-7.1	3,723,000	2,020,480	54.3%	-2.1	3,906,000	2,384,214	61.0%	4.7	4,090,000	2,630,994	64.3%	8.0
MASSACHUSETTS	4,416,000	2,773,700	62.8%	4,446,000	2,556,785	57.5%	-5.3	4,479,000	2,702,984	60.3%	-2.5	4,556,000	2,905,360	63.8%	1.0	4,635,000	3,080,985	66.5%	3.7
MICHIGAN	6,807,000	4,274,673	62.8%	6,972,000	3,848,844	55.2%	-7.6	7,131,000	4,232,711	59.4%	-3.4	7,323,000	4,839,252	66.1%	3.3	7,517,000	5,001,766	66.5%	3.7
MINNESOTA	3,252,000	2,347,948	72.2%	3,390,000	2,192,640	64.7%	-7.5	3,525,000	2,438,685	69.2%	-3.0	3,685,000	2,828,370	76.8%	4.6	3,847,000	2,910,369	75.7%	3.5
MISSISSIPPI	1,881,000	981,793	52.2%	1,974,000	893,857	45.3%	-6.9	2,056,000	994,184	48.4%	-3.8	2,107,000	1,139,826	54.1%	1.9	2,158,000	1,289,872	59.8%	7.6
MISSOURI	3,858,000	2,391,565	62.0%	3,989,000	2,158,065	54.1%	-7.9	4,110,000	2,359,892	57.4%	-4.6	4,227,000	2,731,364	64.6%	2.6	4,345,000	2,925,205	67.3%	5.3
MONTANA	598,000	410,611	68.7%	635,000	407,261	64.1%	-4.5	671,000	410,997	61.3%	-7.4	703,000	450,434	64.1%	-4.6	736,000	490,109	66.6%	-2.1
NEBRASKA	1,160,000	737,546	63.6%	1,193,000	677,415	56.8%	-6.8	1,221,000	697,019	57.1%	-6.5	1,233,000	778,186	63.1%	-0.5	1,244,000	801,281	64.4%	0.8
NEVADA	982,000	506,318	51.6%	1,168,000	464,279	39.7%	-11.8	1,339,000	608,970	45.5%	-6.1	1,500,000	829,587	55.3%	3.7	1,664,000	967,848	58.2%	6.6
NEW HAMPSHIRE	838,000	537,943	64.2%	873,000	499,175	57.2%	-7.0	910,000	569,081	62.5%	-1.7	968,000	677,662	70.0%	5.8	1,025,000	710,970	69.4%	5.2
NEW JERSEY	5,543,000	3,343,594	60.3%	5,599,000	3,075,807	54.9%	-5.4	5,659,000	3,187,226	56.3%	-4.0	5,787,000	3,611,691	62.4%	2.1	5,918,000	3,868,237	65.4%	5.0
NEW MEXICO	1,084,000	569,986	52.6%	1,165,000	556,074	47.7%	-4.9	1,238,000	598,605	48.4%	-4.2	1,296,000	756,204	58.3%	5.8	1,354,000	830,158	61.3%	8.7
NEW YORK	12,410,000	6,926,925	55.8%	12,447,000	6,316,129	50.7%	-5.1	12,474,000	6,821,999	54.7%	-1.1	12,563,000	7,391,036	58.8%	3.0	12,659,000	7,637,318	60.3%	4.5

United States Presidential General Elections (continued)

Election Years 1992–2008 (continued)

State	1992 Voting-age population	Turnout	%	1996 Voting-age population	Turnout	%	Difference from 1992	2000 Voting-age population	Turnout	%	Difference from 1992	2004 Voting-age population	Turnout	%	Difference from 1992	2008 Voting-age population	Turnout	%	Difference from 1992
NORTH CAROLINA	5,199,000	2,611,850	50.2%	5,542,000	2,515,807	45.4%	-4.8	5,862,000	2,911,262	49.7%	-0.6	6,161,000	3,501,007	56.8%	6.6	6,464,000	4,310,789	66.7%	16.5
NORTH DAKOTA	464,000	308,133	66.4%	470,000	266,411	56.7%	-9.7	476,000	288,256	60.6%	-5.8	481,000	312,833	65.0%	-1.4	485,000	316,621	65.3%	-1.1
OHIO	8,053,000	4,939,967	61.3%	8,201,000	4,534,434	55.3%	-6.1	8,337,000	4,701,998	56.4%	-4.9	8,458,000	5,627,903	66.5%	5.2	8,579,000	5,698,260	66.4%	5.1
OKLAHOMA	2,335,000	1,390,359	59.5%	2,420,000	1,206,713	49.9%	-9.7	2,491,000	1,234,229	49.5%	-10.0	2,528,000	1,463,758	57.9%	-1.6	2,566,000	1,462,661	57.0%	-2.5
OREGON	2,150,000	1,402,043	68.0%	2,297,000	1,377,760	60.0%	-8.0	2,428,000	1,533,968	63.2%	-4.9	2,528,000	1,836,782	72.7%	4.6	2,628,000	1,827,864	69.6%	1.5
PENNSYLVANIA	9,007,000	4,959,810	55.1%	9,085,000	4,506,118	49.6%	-5.5	9,166,000	4,913,119	53.6%	-1.5	9,318,000	5,765,764	61.9%	6.8	9,471,000	6,013,560	63.5%	8.4
RHODE ISLAND	737,000	453,477	61.5%	742,000	390,284	52.6%	-8.9	749,000	409,047	54.6%	-6.9	771,000	437,134	56.7%	-4.8	794,000	469,767	59.2%	-2.4
SOUTH CAROLINA	2,652,000	1,202,527	45.3%	2,810,000	1,151,689	41.0%	-4.4	2,960,000	1,382,717	46.7%	1.4	3,102,000	1,617,730	52.2%	6.8	3,244,000	1,920,969	59.2%	13.9
SOUTH DAKOTA	508,000	336,254	66.2%	529,000	323,826	61.2%	-5.0	547,000	316,269	57.8%	-8.4	562,000	388,215	69.1%	2.9	576,000	381,975	66.3%	0.1
TENNESSEE	3,790,000	1,982,638	52.3%	4,018,000	1,894,105	47.1%	-5.2	4,224,000	2,076,181	49.2%	-3.2	4,378,000	2,437,319	55.7%	3.4	4,534,000	2,599,749	57.3%	5.0
TEXAS	11,852,000	6,154,018	51.9%	12,650,000	5,611,644	44.4%	-7.6	13,404,000	6,407,637	47.8%	-4.1	14,189,000	7,410,749	52.2%	0.3	14,988,000	8,077,795	53.9%	2.0
UTAH	1,166,000	743,999	63.8%	1,309,000	665,629	50.9%	-13.0	1,435,000	770,754	53.7%	-10.1	1,511,000	927,844	61.4%	-2.4	1,588,000	952,370	60.0%	-3.8
VERMONT	424,000	289,701	68.3%	440,000	258,449	58.7%	-9.6	456,000	294,308	64.5%	-3.8	477,000	312,309	65.5%	2.9	499,000	325,046	65.1%	-3.2
VIRGINIA	4,669,000	2,558,665	54.8%	4,880,000	2,416,642	49.5%	5.3	5,086,000	2,739,447	53.9%	-0.9	5,339,000	3,198,360	59.9%	5.1	5,595,000	3,723,260	66.5%	11.7
WASHINGTON	3,635,000	2,288,230	62.9%	3,885,000	2,253,837	58.0%	-4.9	4,114,000	2,487,433	60.5%	-2.5	4,313,000	2,859,084	66.3%	3.3	4,516,000	3,036,878	67.2%	4.3
WEST VIRGINIA	1,359,000	683,762	50.3%	1,381,000	636,459	46.1%	-4.2	1,400,000	648,124	46.3%	-4.0	1,415,000	755,659	53.4%	3.1	1,430,000	713,362	49.9%	-0.4
WISCONSIN	3,649,000	2,531,114	69.4%	3,788,000	2,196,169	58.0%	-11.4	3,919,000	2,598,607	66.3%	-3.1	4,061,000	2,998,007	73.8%	4.5	4,203,000	2,983,417	71.0%	1.6
WYOMING	327,000	200,598	61.3%	345,000	211,571	61.3%	0.0	362,000	218,351	60.3%	-1.0	376,000	243,428	64.7%	3.4	390,000	254,658	65.3%	4.0
Total	180,116,000	104,425,014	58.0%	187,437,000	96,277,872	51.4%	-6.6	194,327,000	105,396,627	54.2%	-3.7	201,780,000	122,265,430	60.6%	2.6	209,332,000	131,300,047	62.7%	4.7

*Percentage point difference between turnout in current year and initial year listed in chart. If data do not appear for a state in the initial year listed, the difference is calculated from the first year in which data do appear for that state.

UNITED STATES PRESIDENTIAL GENERAL ELECTIONS

Republican Turnout for Election Years 1992–2008

State	1992 Voting-age population	1992 Turnout	1992 %	1996 Voting-age population	1996 Turnout	1996 %	1996 Difference from 1992*	2000 Voting-age population	2000 Turnout	2000 %	2000 Difference from 1992	2004 Voting-age population	2004 Turnout	2004 %	2004 Difference from 1992	2008 Voting-age population	2008 Turnout	2008 %	2008 Difference from 1992
ALABAMA	3,048,000	804,283	26.4%	3,174,000	769,044	24.2%	-2.2	3,284,000	941,173	28.7%	2.3	3,343,000	1,176,394	35.2%	8.8	3,402,000	1,266,546	37.2%	10.8
ALASKA	383,000	102,000	26.6%	405,000	122,746	30.3%	3.7	425,000	167,398	39.4%	12.8	453,000	190,889	42.1%	15.5	480,000	193,841	40.4%	13.8
ARIZONA	2,778,000	572,086	20.6%	3,114,000	622,073	20.0%	-0.6	3,437,000	781,652	22.7%	2.1	3,800,000	1,104,294	29.1%	8.5	4,166,000	1,230,111	29.5%	8.9
ARKANSAS	1,782,000	337,324	18.9%	1,876,000	325,416	17.3%	-1.6	1,959,000	472,940	24.1%	5.2	2,015,000	572,898	28.4%	9.5	2,073,000	638,017	30.8%	11.8
CALIFORNIA	18,781,000	3,630,574	19.3%	19,460,000	3,828,380	19.7%	0.3	20,154,000	4,567,429	22.7%	3.3	21,306,000	5,509,826	25.9%	6.5	22,475,000	5,011,781	22.3%	3.0
COLORADO	2,541,000	562,850	22.2%	2,791,000	691,848	24.8%	2.6	3,007,000	883,748	29.4%	7.2	3,118,000	1,101,255	35.3%	13.2	3,233,000	1,073,584	33.2%	11.1
CONNECTICUT	2,414,000	578,313	24.0%	2,408,000	483,109	20.1%	-3.9	2,408,000	561,094	23.3%	-0.7	2,466,000	693,826	28.1%	4.2	2,525,000	628,873	24.9%	0.9
DELAWARE	515,000	102,313	19.9%	544,000	99,062	18.2%	-1.7	571,000	137,288	24.0%	4.2	603,000	171,660	28.5%	8.6	634,000	152,373	24.0%	4.2
DISTRICT OF COLUMBIA	441,000	20,698	4.7%	425,000	17,339	4.1%	-0.6	408,000	18,073	4.4%	-0.3	388,000	21,256	5.5%	0.8	367,000	17,367	4.7%	0.0
FLORIDA	9,754,000	2,173,310	22.3%	10,487,000	2,244,536	21.4%	-0.9	11,205,000	2,912,790	26.0%	3.7	12,124,000	3,964,522	32.7%	10.4	13,051,000	4,045,624	31.0%	8.7
GEORGIA	4,938,000	995,252	20.2%	5,345,000	1,080,843	20.2%	0.1	5,718,000	1,419,720	24.8%	4.7	6,028,000	1,914,254	31.8%	11.6	6,344,000	2,048,744	32.3%	12.1
HAWAII	786,000	136,822	17.4%	817,000	113,943	13.9%	-3.5	847,000	137,845	16.3%	-1.1	885,000	194,191	21.9%	4.5	923,000	120,446	13.0%	-4.4
IDAHO	741,000	202,645	27.3%	824,000	256,595	31.1%	3.8	900,000	336,937	37.4%	10.1	967,000	409,235	42.3%	15.0	1,034,000	403,012	39.0%	11.6
ILLINOIS	8,124,000	1,734,096	21.3%	8,269,000	1,587,021	19.2%	-2.2	8,393,000	2,019,421	24.1%	2.7	8,466,000	2,346,608	27.7%	6.4	8,546,000	2,031,527	23.8%	2.4
INDIANA	4,146,000	989,375	23.9%	4,292,000	1,006,693	23.5%	-0.4	4,421,000	1,245,836	28.2%	4.3	4,509,000	1,479,438	32.8%	8.9	4,599,000	1,345,648	29.3%	5.4
IOWA	2,067,000	504,891	24.4%	2,109,000	492,644	23.4%	-1.1	2,147,000	634,373	29.5%	5.1	2,175,000	751,957	34.6%	10.1	2,205,000	682,379	30.9%	6.5
KANSAS	1,818,000	449,951	24.7%	1,865,000	583,245	31.3%	6.5	1,906,000	622,332	32.7%	7.9	1,939,000	736,456	38.0%	13.2	1,972,000	699,655	35.5%	10.7
KENTUCKY	2,793,000	617,178	22.1%	2,909,000	623,283	21.4%	-0.7	3,013,000	872,492	29.0%	6.9	3,085,000	1,069,439	34.7%	12.6	3,158,000	1,048,462	33.2%	11.1
LOUISIANA	3,017,000	733,386	24.3%	3,117,000	712,586	22.9%	-1.4	3,207,000	927,871	28.9%	4.6	3,278,000	1,102,169	33.6%	9.3	3,349,000	1,148,275	34.3%	10.0
MAINE	920,000	206,504	22.4%	942,000	186,378	19.8%	-2.7	965,000	286,616	29.7%	7.3	1,010,000	330,201	32.7%	10.2	1,054,000	295,273	28.0%	5.6
MARYLAND	3,524,000	707,094	20.1%	3,621,000	681,530	18.8%	-1.2	3,723,000	813,797	21.9%	1.8	3,906,000	1,024,703	26.2%	6.2	4,090,000	959,694	23.5%	3.4
MASSACHUSETTS	4,416,000	805,049	18.2%	4,446,000	718,107	16.2%	-2.1	4,479,000	878,502	19.6%	1.4	4,556,000	1,071,109	23.5%	5.3	4,635,000	1,108,854	23.9%	5.7
MICHIGAN	6,807,000	1,554,940	22.8%	6,972,000	1,481,212	21.2%	-1.6	7,131,000	1,953,139	27.4%	4.5	7,323,000	2,313,746	31.6%	8.8	7,517,000	2,048,639	27.3%	4.4
MINNESOTA	3,252,000	747,841	23.0%	3,390,000	766,476	22.6%	-0.4	3,525,000	1,109,659	31.5%	8.5	3,685,000	1,346,695	36.5%	13.5	3,847,000	1,275,409	33.2%	10.2
MISSISSIPPI	1,881,000	487,793	25.9%	1,974,000	439,838	22.3%	-3.7	2,056,000	572,844	27.9%	1.9	2,107,000	672,660	31.9%	6.0	2,158,000	724,597	33.6%	7.6
MISSOURI	3,858,000	811,159	21.0%	3,989,000	890,016	22.3%	1.3	4,110,000	1,189,924	29.0%	7.9	4,227,000	1,455,713	34.4%	13.4	4,345,000	1,445,814	33.3%	12.2
MONTANA	598,000	144,207	24.1%	635,000	179,652	28.3%	4.2	671,000	240,178	35.8%	11.7	703,000	266,063	37.8%	13.7	736,000	242,763	33.0%	8.9
NEBRASKA	1,160,000	343,678	29.6%	1,193,000	363,467	30.5%	0.8	1,221,000	433,862	35.5%	5.9	1,233,000	512,814	41.6%	12.0	1,244,000	452,979	36.4%	6.8
NEVADA	982,000	175,828	17.9%	1,168,000	199,244	17.1%	-0.8	1,339,000	301,575	22.5%	4.6	1,500,000	418,690	27.9%	10.0	1,664,000	412,827	24.8%	6.9
NEW HAMPSHIRE	838,000	202,484	24.2%	873,000	196,532	22.5%	-1.7	910,000	273,559	30.1%	5.9	968,000	331,237	34.2%	10.1	1,025,000	316,534	30.9%	6.7
NEW JERSEY	5,543,000	1,356,865	24.5%	5,599,000	1,103,078	19.7%	-4.8	5,659,000	1,284,173	22.7%	-1.8	5,787,000	1,670,003	28.9%	4.4	5,918,000	1,613,207	27.3%	2.8
NEW MEXICO	1,084,000	212,824	19.6%	1,165,000	232,751	20.0%	0.3	1,238,000	286,417	23.1%	3.5	1,296,000	376,930	29.1%	9.5	1,354,000	346,832	25.6%	6.0
NEW YORK	12,410,000	2,346,649	18.9%	12,447,000	1,933,492	15.5%	-3.4	12,474,000	2,403,374	19.3%	0.4	12,563,000	2,962,567	23.6%	4.7	12,659,000	2,752,771	21.7%	2.8

Republican Turnout for Election Years 1992-2008 (continued)

State	1992			1996				2000				2004				2008			
	Voting-age population	Turnout	%	Voting-age population	Turnout	%	Difference from 1992*	Voting-age population	Turnout	%	Difference from 1992	Voting-age population	Turnout	%	Difference from 1992	Voting-age population	Turnout	%	Difference from 1992
NORTH CAROLINA	5,199,000	1,134,661	21.8%	5,542,000	1,225,938	22.1%	0.3	5,862,000	1,631,163	27.8%	6.0	6,161,000	1,961,166	31.8%	10.0	6,464,000	2,128,474	32.9%	11.1
NORTH DAKOTA	464,000	136,244	29.4%	470,000	125,050	26.6%	-2.8	476,000	174,852	36.7%	7.4	481,000	196,651	40.9%	11.5	485,000	168,601	34.8%	5.4
OHIO	8,053,000	1,894,310	23.5%	8,201,000	1,859,883	22.7%	-0.8	8,337,000	2,350,363	28.2%	4.7	8,458,000	2,859,764	33.8%	10.3	8,579,000	2,674,491	31.2%	7.7
OKLAHOMA	2,335,000	592,929	25.4%	2,420,000	582,315	24.1%	-1.3	2,491,000	744,337	29.9%	4.5	2,528,000	959,792	38.0%	12.6	2,566,000	960,165	37.4%	12.0
OREGON	2,150,000	475,757	22.1%	2,297,000	538,152	23.4%	1.3	2,428,000	713,577	29.4%	7.3	2,528,000	868,831	34.3%	12.2	2,628,000	738,475	28.1%	6.0
PENNSYLVANIA	9,007,000	1,791,841	19.9%	9,085,000	1,801,169	19.8%	-0.1	9,166,000	2,281,127	24.9%	5.0	9,318,000	2,793,847	30.0%	10.1	9,471,000	2,655,885	28.0%	8.1
RHODE ISLAND	737,000	131,601	17.9%	742,000	104,683	14.1%	-3.7	749,000	130,555	17.4%	-0.4	771,000	169,046	21.9%	4.1	794,000	165,391	20.8%	3.0
SOUTH CAROLINA	2,652,000	577,507	21.8%	2,810,000	573,458	20.4%	-1.4	2,960,000	785,937	26.6%	4.8	3,102,000	937,974	30.2%	8.5	3,244,000	1,034,896	31.9%	10.1
SOUTH DAKOTA	508,000	136,718	26.9%	529,000	150,543	28.5%	1.5	547,000	190,700	34.9%	7.9	565,000	232,584	41.4%	14.5	576,000	203,054	35.3%	8.3
TENNESSEE	3,790,000	841,300	22.2%	4,018,000	863,530	21.5%	-0.7	4,224,000	1,061,949	25.1%	2.9	4,378,000	1,384,375	31.6%	9.4	4,534,000	1,479,178	32.6%	10.4
TEXAS	11,852,000	2,496,071	21.1%	12,650,000	2,736,167	21.6%	0.6	13,404,000	3,799,639	28.3%	7.3	14,189,000	4,526,917	31.9%	10.8	14,988,000	4,479,328	29.9%	8.8
UTAH	1,166,000	322,632	27.7%	1,309,000	361,911	27.6%	0.0	1,435,000	515,096	35.9%	8.2	1,511,000	663,742	43.9%	16.3	1,588,000	596,030	37.5%	9.9
VERMONT	424,000	88,122	20.8%	440,000	80,352	18.3%	-2.5	456,000	119,775	26.3%	5.5	477,000	121,180	25.4%	4.6	499,000	98,974	19.8%	-0.9
VIRGINIA	4,669,000	1,150,517	24.6%	4,880,000	1,138,350	23.3%	-1.3	5,080,000	1,437,490	28.3%	3.6	5,339,000	1,716,959	32.2%	7.5	5,595,000	1,725,005	30.8%	6.2
WASHINGTON	3,635,000	731,234	20.1%	3,885,000	840,712	21.6%	1.5	4,114,000	1,108,864	27.0%	6.8	4,313,000	1,304,894	30.3%	10.1	4,516,000	1,229,216	27.2%	7.1
WEST VIRGINIA	1,359,000	241,974	17.8%	1,381,000	233,946	16.9%	-0.9	1,400,000	336,475	24.0%	6.2	1,415,000	423,550	29.9%	12.1	1,430,000	397,466	27.8%	10.0
WISCONSIN	3,649,000	930,855	25.5%	3,788,000	845,029	22.3%	-3.2	3,919,000	1,237,279	31.6%	6.1	4,061,000	1,478,120	36.4%	10.9	4,203,000	1,262,393	30.0%	4.5
WYOMING	327,000	79,347	24.3%	345,000	105,388	30.5%	6.3	362,000	147,947	40.9%	16.6	376,000	167,629	44.6%	20.3	390,000	164,958	42.3%	18.0
Total	180,116,000	39,103,882	21.7%	187,437,000	39,198,755	20.9%	-0.8	194,327,000	50,455,156	26.0%	4.3	201,780,000	62,028,719	30.7%	9.0	209,332,000	59,944,438	28.6%	6.9

Democratic Turnout for Election Years 1992-2008

State	1992			1996				2000				2004				2008			
	Voting-age population	Turnout	%	Voting-age population	Turnout	%	Difference from 1992*	Voting-age population	Turnout	%	Difference from 1992	Voting-age population	Turnout	%	Difference from 1992	Voting-age population	Turnout	%	Difference from 1992
ALABAMA	3,048,000	690,080	22.6%	3,174,000	662,165	20.9%	-1.8	3,284,000	692,611	21.1%	-1.5	3,343,000	693,933	20.8%	-1.9	3,402,000	813,479	23.9%	1.3
ALASKA	383,000	78,294	20.4%	405,000	80,380	19.8%	-0.6	425,000	79,004	18.6%	-1.9	453,000	111,025	24.5%	4.1	480,000	123,594	25.7%	5.3
ARIZONA	2,778,000	543,050	19.5%	3,114,000	653,288	21.0%	1.4	3,437,000	685,341	19.9%	0.4	3,800,000	893,524	23.5%	4.0	4,166,000	1,034,707	24.8%	5.3
ARKANSAS	1,782,000	505,823	28.4%	1,876,000	475,171	25.3%	-3.1	1,959,000	422,768	21.6%	-6.8	2,015,000	469,953	23.3%	-5.1	2,073,000	422,310	20.4%	-8.0
CALIFORNIA	18,781,000	5,121,325	27.3%	19,460,000	5,119,835	26.3%	-1.0	20,154,000	5,861,203	29.1%	1.8	21,306,000	6,745,485	31.7%	4.4	22,475,000	8,274,473	36.8%	9.5
COLORADO	2,541,000	629,681	24.8%	2,791,000	671,152	24.0%	-0.7	3,007,000	738,227	24.6%	-0.2	3,118,000	1,001,732	32.1%	7.3	3,233,000	1,288,568	39.9%	15.1
CONNECTICUT	2,414,000	682,318	28.3%	2,408,000	735,740	30.6%	2.3	2,408,000	816,015	33.9%	5.6	2,466,000	857,488	34.8%	6.5	2,525,000	1,000,994	39.6%	11.4
DELAWARE	515,000	126,054	24.5%	544,000	140,355	25.8%	1.3	571,000	180,068	31.5%	7.1	603,000	200,152	33.2%	8.7	634,000	255,446	40.3%	15.8
DISTRICT OF COLUMBIA	441,000	192,619	43.7%	425,000	158,220	37.2%	-6.4	408,000	171,923	42.1%	-1.5	388,000	202,970	52.3%	8.6	367,000	245,800	67.0%	23.3
FLORIDA	9,754,000	2,072,798	21.3%	10,487,000	2,546,870	24.3%	3.0	11,205,000	2,912,253	26.0%	4.7	12,124,000	3,583,544	29.6%	8.3	13,051,000	4,282,074	32.8%	11.6

United States Presidential General Elections (continued)

United States Presidential General Elections (continued)

Democratic Turnout for Election Years 1992–2008 (continued)

State	1992 Voting-age population	Turnout	%	1996 Voting-age population	Turnout	%	Difference from 1992	2000 Voting-age population	Turnout	%	Difference from 1992	2004 Voting-age population	Turnout	%	Difference from 1992	2008 Voting-age population	Turnout	%	Difference from 1992
GEORGIA	4,938,000	1,008,966	20.4%	5,345,000	1,053,849	19.7%	-0.7	5,718,000	1,116,230	19.5%	-0.9	6,028,000	1,366,149	22.7%	2.2	6,344,000	1,844,137	29.1%	8.6
HAWAII	786,000	179,310	22.8%	817,000	205,012	25.1%	2.3	847,000	205,286	24.2%	1.4	885,000	231,708	26.2%	3.4	923,000	325,588	35.3%	12.5
IDAHO	741,000	137,013	18.5%	824,000	165,443	20.1%	1.6	900,000	138,637	15.4%	-3.1	967,000	181,098	18.7%	0.2	1,034,000	236,440	22.9%	4.4
ILLINOIS	8,124,000	2,453,350	30.2%	8,269,000	2,341,744	28.3%	-1.9	8,393,000	2,589,026	30.8%	0.6	8,466,000	2,891,989	34.2%	4.0	8,546,000	3,419,673	40.0%	9.8
INDIANA	4,146,000	848,420	20.5%	4,292,000	887,424	20.7%	0.2	4,421,000	901,980	20.4%	-0.1	4,509,000	969,011	21.5%	1.0	4,599,000	1,374,039	29.9%	9.4
IOWA	2,067,000	586,353	28.4%	2,109,000	620,258	29.4%	1.0	2,147,000	638,517	29.7%	1.4	2,175,000	741,898	34.1%	5.7	2,205,000	828,940	37.6%	9.2
KANSAS	1,818,000	390,434	21.5%	1,865,000	387,659	20.8%	-0.7	1,906,000	399,276	20.9%	-0.5	1,939,000	434,993	22.4%	1.0	1,972,000	514,765	26.1%	4.6
KENTUCKY	2,793,000	665,104	23.8%	2,909,000	636,614	21.9%	-1.9	3,013,000	638,898	21.2%	-2.6	3,085,000	712,733	23.1%	-0.7	3,158,000	751,985	23.8%	0.0
LOUISIANA	3,017,000	815,971	27.0%	3,117,000	927,837	29.8%	2.7	3,207,000	792,344	24.7%	-2.3	3,278,000	820,299	25.0%	-2.0	3,349,000	782,989	23.4%	-3.7
MAINE	920,000	263,420	28.6%	942,000	312,788	33.2%	4.6	965,000	319,951	33.2%	4.5	1,010,000	396,842	39.3%	10.7	1,054,000	421,923	40.0%	11.4
MARYLAND	3,524,000	988,571	28.1%	3,621,000	966,207	26.7%	-1.4	3,723,000	1,140,782	30.6%	2.6	3,906,000	1,334,493	34.2%	6.1	4,090,000	1,628,995	39.8%	11.8
MASSACHUSETTS	4,416,000	1,318,662	29.9%	4,446,000	1,571,763	35.4%	5.5	4,479,000	1,616,487	36.1%	6.2	4,556,000	1,803,800	39.6%	9.7	4,635,000	1,904,097	41.1%	11.2
MICHIGAN	6,807,000	1,871,281	27.5%	6,972,000	1,989,653	28.5%	1.0	7,131,000	2,170,418	30.4%	2.9	7,323,000	2,479,183	33.9%	6.4	7,517,000	2,872,579	38.2%	10.7
MINNESOTA	3,252,000	1,020,997	31.4%	3,390,000	1,170,438	33.1%	1.7	3,525,000	1,168,266	33.1%	1.7	3,685,000	1,445,014	39.2%	7.8	3,847,000	1,573,354	40.9%	9.5
MISSISSIPPI	1,881,000	400,258	21.3%	1,974,000	394,022	20.0%	-1.3	2,056,000	404,614	19.7%	-1.6	2,107,000	457,760	21.7%	0.4	2,158,000	554,669	25.7%	4.4
MISSOURI	3,888,000	1,053,873	27.3%	3,989,000	1,025,935	25.7%	-1.6	4,110,000	1,111,138	27.0%	-0.3	4,227,000	1,259,171	29.8%	2.5	4,345,000	1,441,911	33.2%	5.9
MONTANA	586,000	154,507	25.8%	635,000	167,922	26.4%	0.6	671,000	137,126	20.4%	-5.4	703,000	173,710	24.7%	-1.1	736,000	231,667	31.5%	5.6
NEBRASKA	1,160,000	216,864	18.7%	1,193,000	236,761	19.8%	1.2	1,221,000	231,780	19.0%	0.3	1,233,000	254,328	20.6%	1.9	1,244,000	333,319	26.8%	8.1
NEVADA	982,000	189,148	19.3%	1,168,000	203,974	17.5%	-1.8	1,339,000	279,978	20.9%	1.6	1,500,000	397,190	26.5%	7.2	1,664,000	533,736	32.1%	12.8
NEW HAMPSHIRE	838,000	209,040	24.9%	873,000	246,214	28.2%	3.3	910,000	266,348	29.3%	4.3	968,000	340,511	35.2%	10.2	1,025,000	384,826	37.5%	12.6
NEW JERSEY	5,543,000	1,436,206	25.9%	5,599,000	1,662,320	29.7%	3.6	5,659,000	1,788,850	31.6%	5.7	5,787,000	1,911,430	33.0%	7.1	5,918,000	2,215,422	37.4%	11.5
NEW MEXICO	1,084,000	261,617	24.1%	1,165,000	273,495	23.5%	-0.7	1,238,000	288,783	23.2%	-1.0	1,296,000	370,942	28.0%	4.6	1,354,000	472,422	34.9%	10.8
NEW YORK	12,410,000	3,444,450	27.8%	12,447,000	3,756,177	30.2%	2.4	12,474,000	4,107,697	32.9%	5.2	12,563,000	4,314,280	34.3%	6.6	12,659,000	4,804,945	38.0%	10.2
NORTH CAROLINA	5,199,000	1,114,042	21.4%	5,542,000	1,107,849	20.0%	-1.4	5,862,000	1,257,692	21.5%	0.0	6,161,000	1,525,849	24.8%	3.3	6,464,000	2,142,651	33.1%	11.7
NORTH DAKOTA	464,000	99,168	21.4%	470,000	106,905	22.7%	1.4	476,000	95,284	20.0%	-1.4	481,000	111,052	23.1%	1.7	485,000	141,278	29.1%	7.8
OHIO	8,053,000	1,984,942	24.6%	8,201,000	2,148,222	26.2%	1.5	8,337,000	2,183,628	26.2%	1.5	8,458,000	2,741,165	32.4%	7.8	8,579,000	2,933,388	34.2%	9.5
OKLAHOMA	2,335,000	473,066	20.3%	2,420,000	488,105	20.2%	-0.1	2,491,000	474,276	19.0%	-1.2	2,528,000	503,966	19.9%	-0.3	2,566,000	502,496	19.6%	-0.7
OREGON	2,150,000	621,314	28.9%	2,297,000	649,641	28.3%	-0.6	2,428,000	720,342	29.7%	0.8	2,528,000	943,163	37.3%	8.4	2,628,000	1,037,291	39.5%	10.6
PENNSYLVANIA	9,007,000	2,239,164	24.9%	9,085,000	2,215,819	24.4%	-0.5	9,166,000	2,485,967	27.1%	2.3	9,318,000	2,938,095	31.5%	6.7	9,471,000	3,276,363	34.6%	9.7
RHODE ISLAND	737,000	213,299	28.9%	742,000	233,050	31.4%	2.5	749,000	249,508	33.3%	4.4	771,000	259,760	33.7%	4.7	794,000	296,571	37.4%	8.4
SOUTH CAROLINA	2,652,000	479,514	18.1%	2,810,000	506,283	18.0%	-0.1	2,960,000	565,561	19.1%	1.0	3,102,000	661,699	21.3%	3.3	3,244,000	862,449	26.6%	8.5
SOUTH DAKOTA	508,000	124,888	24.6%	529,000	139,333	26.3%	1.8	547,000	118,804	21.7%	-2.9	562,000	149,244	26.6%	2.0	576,000	170,924	29.7%	5.1
TENNESSEE	3,790,000	933,521	24.6%	4,018,000	909,146	22.6%	-2.0	4,224,000	981,720	23.2%	-1.4	4,378,000	1,036,477	23.7%	-1.0	4,534,000	1,087,437	24.0%	-0.6

United States Presidential General Elections (continued)

Democratic Turnout for Election Years 1992-2008 (continued)

State	1992 Voting-age population	1992 Turnout	1992 %	1996 Voting-age population	1996 Turnout	1996 %	1996 Difference from 1992*	2000 Voting-age population	2000 Turnout	2000 %	2000 Difference from 1992	2004 Voting-age population	2004 Turnout	2004 %	2004 Difference from 1992	2008 Voting-age population	2008 Turnout	2008 %	2008 Difference from 1992
TEXAS	11,852,000	2,281,815	19.3%	12,650,000	2,459,683	19.4%	0.2	13,404,000	2,433,746	18.2%	-1.1	14,189,000	2,832,704	20.0%	0.7	14,988,000	3,528,633	25.5%	4.3
UTAH	1,166,000	183,429	15.7%	1,309,000	221,633	16.9%	1.2	1,435,000	203,053	14.2%	-1.6	1,511,000	241,199	16.0%	0.2	1,588,000	327,670	20.6%	4.9
VERMONT	424,000	133,592	31.5%	440,000	137,894	31.3%	-0.2	456,000	149,022	32.7%	1.2	477,000	184,067	38.6%	7.1	499,000	219,262	43.9%	12.4
VIRGINIA	4,669,000	1,038,650	22.2%	4,880,000	1,091,060	22.4%	0.1	5,080,000	1,217,290	23.9%	1.7	5,339,000	1,454,742	27.2%	5.0	5,595,000	1,959,532	35.0%	12.8
WASHINGTON	3,635,000	993,037	27.3%	3,885,000	1,123,323	28.9%	1.6	4,114,000	1,247,652	30.3%	3.0	4,313,000	1,510,201	35.0%	7.7	4,516,000	1,750,848	38.8%	11.5
WEST VIRGINIA	1,359,000	331,001	24.4%	1,381,000	327,812	23.7%	-0.6	1,400,000	295,497	21.1%	-3.2	1,415,000	326,541	23.1%	-1.3	1,430,000	303,857	21.2%	-3.1
WISCONSIN	3,649,000	1,041,066	28.5%	3,788,000	1,071,971	28.3%	-0.2	3,919,000	1,242,987	31.7%	3.2	4,061,000	1,489,504	36.7%	8.1	4,203,000	1,677,211	39.9%	11.4
WYOMING	327,000	68,160	20.8%	345,000	77,934	22.6%	1.7	362,000	60,481	16.7%	-4.1	376,000	70,776	18.8%	-2.0	390,000	82,868	21.2%	0.4
Total	180,116,000	44,909,426	24.9%	187,437,000	47,402,357	25.3%	0.4	194,327,000	50,992,335	26.2%	1.3	201,780,000	59,028,550	29.3%	4.3	209,332,000	69,494,595	33.2%	8.3

United States Presidential General Elections (continued)

Other Turnout for Election Years 1992-2008

State	1992 Voting-age population	1992 Turnout	1992 %	1996 Voting-age population	1996 Turnout	1996 %	1996 Difference from 1992*	2000 Voting-age population	2000 Turnout	2000 %	2000 Difference from 1992	2004 Voting-age population	2004 Turnout	2004 %	2004 Difference from 1992	2008 Voting-age population	2008 Turnout	2008 %	2008 Difference from 1992
ALABAMA	3,048,000	193,697	6.4%	3,174,000	103,140	3.2%	-3.1	3,284,000	32,488	1.0%	-5.4	3,343,000	13,088	0.4%	-6.0	3,402,000	19,794	0.6%	-5.8
ALASKA	383,000	78,212	20.4%	405,000	38,494	9.5%	-10.9	425,000	39,158	9.2%	-11.2	453,000	10,684	2.4%	-18.1	480,000	8,762	1.8%	-18.6
ARIZONA	2,778,000	371,839	13.4%	3,114,000	129,044	4.1%	-9.2	3,437,000	65,023	1.9%	-11.5	3,800,000	14,767	0.4%	-13.0	4,166,000	28,657	0.7%	-12.7
ARKANSAS	1,782,000	107,506	6.0%	1,876,000	83,675	4.5%	-1.6	1,959,000	26,073	1.3%	-4.7	2,015,000	12,094	0.6%	-5.4	2,073,000	26,290	1.3%	-4.8
CALIFORNIA	18,781,000	2,379,822	12.7%	19,460,000	1,071,269	5.5%	-7.2	20,154,000	537,224	2.7%	-10.0	21,306,000	164,546	0.8%	-11.9	22,475,000	275,646	1.2%	-11.4
COLORADO	2,541,000	376,649	14.8%	2,791,000	147,704	5.3%	-9.5	3,007,000	119,393	4.0%	-10.9	3,118,000	26,643	0.9%	-14.0	3,233,000	39,197	1.2%	-13.6
CONNECTICUT	2,414,000	355,701	14.7%	2,408,000	173,765	7.2%	-7.5	2,408,000	82,416	3.4%	-11.3	2,466,000	27,455	1.1%	-13.6	2,525,000	19,532	0.8%	-14.0
DELAWARE	515,000	61,368	11.9%	544,000	31,667	5.8%	-6.1	571,000	10,266	1.8%	-10.1	603,000	3,378	0.6%	-11.4	634,000	4,579	0.7%	-11.2
DISTRICT OF COLUMBIA	441,000	14,255	3.2%	425,000	10,167	2.4%	-0.8	408,000	11,898	2.9%	-0.3	388,000	3,360	0.9%	-2.4	367,000	2,686	0.7%	-2.5
FLORIDA	9,754,000	1,068,284	11.0%	10,487,000	512,388	4.9%	-6.1	11,205,000	138,067	1.2%	-9.7	12,124,000	61,744	0.5%	-10.4	13,051,000	63,046	0.5%	-10.5
GEORGIA	4,938,000	316,907	6.4%	5,345,000	164,379	3.1%	-3.3	5,718,000	60,695	1.1%	-5.4	6,028,000	18,387	0.3%	-6.1	6,344,000	31,573	0.5%	-5.9
HAWAII	786,000	56,710	7.2%	817,000	41,165	5.0%	-2.2	847,000	24,820	2.9%	-4.3	885,000	3,114	0.4%	-6.9	923,000	7,131	0.8%	-6.4
IDAHO	741,000	142,484	19.2%	824,000	69,681	8.5%	-10.8	900,000	26,047	2.9%	-16.3	967,000	8,043	0.8%	-18.4	1,033,000	15,580	1.5%	-17.7
ILLINOIS	8,124,000	862,711	10.6%	8,269,000	382,626	4.6%	-6.0	8,393,000	133,676	1.6%	-9.0	8,466,000	36,818	0.4%	-10.2	8,546,000	71,851	0.8%	-9.8
INDIANA	4,146,000	468,076	11.3%	4,292,000	241,725	5.6%	-5.7	4,421,000	51,486	1.2%	-10.1	4,509,000	19,553	0.4%	-10.9	4,599,000	31,367	0.7%	-10.6
IOWA	2,067,000	263,363	12.7%	2,109,000	121,173	5.7%	-7.0	2,147,000	42,673	2.0%	-10.8	2,175,000	13,053	0.6%	-12.1	2,205,000	25,804	1.2%	-11.6
KANSAS	1,818,000	316,950	17.4%	1,865,000	103,396	5.5%	-11.9	1,906,000	50,610	2.7%	-14.8	1,939,000	16,307	0.8%	-16.6	1,972,000	21,452	1.1%	-16.3
KENTUCKY	2,793,000	210,618	7.5%	2,909,000	128,811	4.4%	-3.1	3,013,000	32,797	1.1%	-6.5	3,085,000	13,688	0.4%	-7.1	3,158,000	26,061	0.8%	-6.7
LOUISIANA	3,017,000	240,660	8.0%	3,117,000	143,536	4.6%	-3.4	3,207,000	45,441	1.4%	-6.6	3,278,000	20,638	0.6%	-7.3	3,349,000	29,497	0.9%	-7.1
MAINE	920,000	209,575	22.8%	942,000	106,731	11.3%	-11.4	965,000	45,250	4.7%	-18.1	1,010,000	14,705	1.4%	-21.4	1,054,000	13,967	1.3%	-21.5

Other Turnout for Election Years 1992–2008 (continued)

State	1992 Voting-age population	1992 Turnout	1992 %	1996 Voting-age population	1996 Turnout	1996 %	1996 Difference from 1992	2000 Voting-age population	2000 Turnout	2000 %	2000 Difference from 1992	2004 Voting-age population	2004 Turnout	2004 %	2004 Difference from 1992	2008 Voting-age population	2008 Turnout	2008 %	2008 Difference from 1992
MARYLAND	3,524,000	289,381	8.2%	3,621,000	133,133	3.7%	-4.5	3,723,000	65,901	1.8%	-6.4	3,906,000	25,018	0.6%	-7.6	4,090,000	42,305	1.0%	-7.2
MASSACHUSETTS	4,416,000	649,989	14.7%	4,446,000	266,915	6.0%	-8.7	4,479,000	207,995	4.6%	-10.1	4,556,000	30,451	0.7%	-14.1	4,635,000	68,034	1.5%	-13.3
MICHIGAN	6,807,000	848,551	12.5%	6,972,000	377,979	5.4%	-7.0	7,131,000	109,154	1.5%	-10.9	7,323,000	46,323	0.6%	-11.8	7,517,000	80,548	1.1%	-11.4
MINNESOTA	3,252,000	579,110	17.8%	3,390,000	305,726	9.0%	-8.8	3,525,000	160,760	4.6%	-13.2	3,685,000	36,661	1.0%	-16.8	3,847,000	61,606	1.6%	-16.2
MISSISSIPPI	1,881,000	93,742	5.0%	1,974,000	59,997	3.0%	-1.9	2,056,000	16,726	0.8%	-4.2	2,107,000	9,398	0.4%	-4.5	2,158,000	10,606	0.5%	-4.5
MISSOURI	3,858,000	525,533	13.6%	3,989,000	242,114	6.1%	-7.6	4,110,000	58,830	1.4%	-12.2	4,227,000	16,480	0.4%	-13.3	4,345,000	37,480	0.9%	-12.8
MONTANA	598,000	111,897	18.7%	635,000	59,687	9.4%	-9.3	671,000	33,693	5.0%	-13.7	703,000	10,661	1.5%	-17.2	736,000	15,679	2.1%	-16.6
NEBRASKA	1,160,000	177,004	15.3%	1,193,000	77,187	6.5%	-8.8	1,221,000	31,377	2.6%	-12.7	1,233,000	11,044	0.9%	-14.4	1,244,000	14,983	1.2%	-14.1
NEVADA	986,000	141,342	14.4%	1,168,000	61,061	5.2%	-9.2	1,339,000	27,417	2.0%	-12.3	1,500,000	13,707	0.9%	-13.5	1,664,000	21,285	1.3%	-13.1
NEW HAMPSHIRE	838,000	126,419	15.1%	873,000	56,429	6.5%	-8.6	910,000	29,174	3.2%	-11.9	968,000	5,914	0.6%	-14.5	1,025,000	9,610	0.9%	-14.1
NEW JERSEY	5,543,000	550,523	9.9%	5,659,000	320,400	5.7%	-4.2	5,659,000	114,203	2.0%	-7.9	5,787,000	30,258	0.5%	-9.4	5,918,000	39,608	0.7%	-9.3
NEW MEXICO	1,084,000	96,545	8.8%	1,165,000	49,828	4.3%	-4.5	1,238,000	25,405	2.1%	-6.8	1,296,000	8,332	0.6%	-8.2	1,354,000	10,904	0.8%	-8.0
NEW YORK	12,410,000	1,135,826	9.2%	12,447,000	626,460	5.0%	-4.1	12,474,000	310,928	2.5%	-6.7	12,563,000	114,189	0.9%	-8.2	12,659,000	79,602	0.6%	-8.5
NORTH CAROLINA	5,199,000	363,147	7.0%	5,542,000	182,020	3.3%	-3.7	5,862,000	22,407	0.4%	-6.6	6,161,000	13,992	0.2%	-6.8	6,464,000	39,664	0.6%	-6.4
NORTH DAKOTA	464,000	72,721	15.7%	470,000	34,456	7.3%	-8.3	476,000	18,170	3.8%	-11.9	481,000	5,130	1.1%	-14.6	485,000	6,742	1.4%	-14.3
OHIO	8,053,000	1,060,715	13.2%	8,201,000	526,329	6.4%	-6.8	8,337,000	168,007	2.0%	-11.2	8,458,000	26,974	0.3%	-12.9	8,579,000	90,301	1.1%	-12.1
OKLAHOMA	2,335,000	324,364	13.9%	2,420,000	136,293	5.6%	-8.3	2,491,000	15,616	0.6%	-13.3								
OREGON	2,150,000	365,572	17.0%	2,297,000	189,967	8.3%	-8.7	2,428,000	100,049	4.1%	-12.9	2,528,000	26,788	1.1%	-15.9	2,628,000	52,098	2.0%	-15.0
PENNSYLVANIA	9,007,000	928,805	10.3%	9,085,000	489,130	5.4%	-4.9	9,166,000	146,025	1.6%	-8.7	9,318,000	33,822	0.4%	-9.9	9,471,000	81,312	0.9%	-9.5
RHODE ISLAND	737,000	108,577	14.7%	742,000	52,551	7.1%	-7.6	749,000	28,984	3.9%	-10.9	771,000	8,328	1.1%	-13.7	794,000	7,805	1.0%	-13.7
SOUTH CAROLINA	2,652,000	145,506	5.5%	2,810,000	71,948	2.6%	-2.9	2,960,000	31,219	1.1%	-4.4	3,102,000	18,057	0.6%	-4.9	3,244,000	23,624	0.7%	-4.8
SOUTH DAKOTA	508,000	74,648	14.7%	529,000	33,350	6.4%	-8.3	547,000	6,765	1.2%	-13.5	562,000	6,387	1.1%	-13.6	576,000	7,997	1.4%	-13.3
TENNESSEE	3,790,000	207,817	5.5%	4,018,000	121,429	3.0%	-2.5	4,224,000	32,512	0.8%	-4.7	4,378,000	16,467	0.4%	-5.1	4,634,000	33,134	0.7%	-4.8
TEXAS	11,852,000	1,376,132	11.6%	12,650,000	415,769	3.3%	-8.3	13,404,000	174,252	1.3%	-10.3	14,189,000	51,128	0.4%	-11.3	14,988,000	69,834	0.5%	-11.1
UTAH	1,166,000	237,938	20.4%	1,309,000	82,085	6.3%	-14.1	1,435,000	52,605	3.7%	-16.7	1,511,000	22,903	1.5%	-18.9	1,588,000	28,670	1.8%	-18.6
VERMONT	424,000	67,987	16.0%	440,000	40,203	9.1%	-6.9	456,000	25,511	5.6%	-10.4	477,000	7,062	1.5%	-14.6	499,000	6,810	1.4%	-14.7
VIRGINIA	4,669,000	369,498	7.9%	4,880,000	187,232	3.8%	-4.1	5,080,000	84,667	1.7%	-6.2	5,339,000	26,659	0.5%	-7.4	5,595,000	38,723	0.7%	-7.2
WASHINGTON	3,635,000	563,959	15.5%	3,885,000	289,802	7.5%	-8.1	4,114,000	130,917	3.2%	-12.3	4,313,000	43,989	1.0%	-14.5	4,516,000	56,814	1.3%	-14.3
WEST VIRGINIA	1,359,000	110,787	8.2%	1,381,000	74,701	5.4%	-2.7	1,400,000	16,152	1.2%	-7.0	1,415,000	5,568	0.4%	-7.8	1,430,000	12,039	0.8%	-7.3
WISCONSIN	3,649,000	559,193	15.3%	3,788,000	279,169	7.4%	-8.0	3,919,000	118,341	3.0%	-12.3	4,061,000	30,383	0.7%	-14.6	4,203,000	43,813	1.0%	-14.3
WYOMING	327,000	53,091	16.2%	345,000	28,249	8.2%	-8.0	362,000	9,923	2.7%	-13.5	376,000	5,023	1.3%	-14.9	390,000	6,832	1.8%	-14.5
Total	180,116,000	20,411,706	11.3%	187,437,000	9,676,760	5.2%	-6.2	194,327,000	3,949,136	2.0%	-9.3	193,252,000	1,208,161	0.6%	-10.7	206,766,000	1,861,014	0.9%	-10.4

*Percentage point difference between turnout in current year and initial year listed in chart. If data do not appear for a state for a given year listed, the difference is calculated from the first year in which data do appear for that state.

State Gubernatorial General Elections (continued)

State	1992 Voting-age population	1992 Turnout	1992 %	1996 Voting-age population	1996 Turnout	1996 %	1996 Difference from 1992*	2000 Voting-age population	2000 Turnout	2000 %	2000 Difference from 1992	2004 Voting-age population	2004 Turnout	2004 %	2004 Difference from 1992	2008 Voting-age population	2008 Turnout	2008 %	2008 Difference from 1992
ALABAMA																			
ALASKA																			
ARIZONA																			
ARKANSAS																			
CALIFORNIA																			
COLORADO																			
CONNECTICUT																			
DELAWARE	515,000	277,034	53.8%	544,000	271,122	49.8%	-4.0	571,000	323,569	56.7%	2.9	603,000	365,008	60.5%	6.7	634,000	395,200	62.3%	8.5
DISTRICT OF COLUMBIA																			
FLORIDA																			
GEORGIA																			
HAWAII																			
IDAHO																			
ILLINOIS																			
INDIANA	4,146,000	2,229,116	53.8%	4,292,000	2,110,047	49.2%	-4.6	4,421,000	2,179,268	49.3%	-4.5	4,509,000	2,448,503	54.3%	0.5	4,599,000	2,703,751	58.8%	5.0
IOWA																			
KANSAS																			
KENTUCKY																			
LOUISIANA																			
MAINE																			
MARYLAND																			
MASSACHUSETTS																			
MICHIGAN																			
MINNESOTA																			
MISSISSIPPI																			
MISSOURI	3,858,000	2,343,999	60.8%	3,989,000	2,142,518	53.7%	-7.0	4,110,000	2,346,830	57.1%	-3.7	4,227,000	2,719,599	64.3%	3.6	4,345,000	2,877,778	66.2%	5.5
MONTANA	598,000	407,822	68.2%	635,000	405,175	63.8%	-4.4	671,000	410,192	61.1%	-7.1	703,000	446,146	63.5%	-4.7	736,000	486,734	66.1%	-2.1
NEBRASKA																			
NEVADA																			
NEW HAMPSHIRE	838,000	516,170	61.6%	873,000	497,040	56.9%	-4.7	910,000	564,340	62.0%	0.4	968,000	661,543	68.3%	6.7	1,025,000	679,784	66.3%	4.7
NEW JERSEY																			
NEW MEXICO																			
NEW YORK																			

Election Years 1992–2008 (continued)

State	1992 Voting-age population	1992 Turnout	1992 %	1996 Voting-age population	1996 Turnout	1996 %	1996 Difference from 1992	2000 Voting-age population	2000 Turnout	2000 %	2000 Difference from 1992	2004 Voting-age population	2004 Turnout	2004 %	2004 Difference from 1992	2008 Voting-age population	2008 Turnout	2008 %	2008 Difference from 1992
NORTH CAROLINA	5,199,000	2,595,184	49.9%	5,542,000	2,556,185	46.3%	-3.6	5,862,000	2,942,062	50.2%	0.3	6,161,000	3,486,688	56.6%	6.7	6,464,000	4,268,941	66.0%	16.1
NORTH DAKOTA	464,000	304,861	65.7%	470,000	264,298	56.2%	-9.5	476,000	289,412	60.8%	-4.9	481,000	309,873	64.4%	-1.3	485,000	315,692	65.1%	-0.6
OHIO																			
OKLAHOMA																			
OREGON																			
PENNSYLVANIA																			
RHODE ISLAND	737,000	424,818	57.6%																
SOUTH CAROLINA																			
SOUTH DAKOTA																			
TENNESSEE																			
TEXAS																			
UTAH	1,166,000	762,536	65.4%	1,309,000	671,879	51.3%	-14.1	1,435,000	761,806	53.1%	-12.3	1,511,000	919,960	60.9%	-4.5	1,588,000	946,525	59.6%	-5.8
VERMONT	424,000	285,728	67.4%	440,000	254,648	57.9%	-9.5	456,000	293,473	64.4%	-3.0	477,000	309,285	64.8%	-2.5	499,000	319,085	63.9%	-3.4
VIRGINIA																			
WASHINGTON	3,635,000	2,270,531	62.5%	3,885,000	2,237,030	57.6%	-4.9	4,114,000	2,469,852	60.0%	-2.4	4,313,000	2,010,058	65.2%	2.7	4,516,000	3,002,862	66.5%	4.0
WEST VIRGINIA	1,359,000	657,182	48.4%	1,381,000	628,559	45.5%	-2.8	1,400,000	648,047	46.3%	-2.1	1,415,000	734,274	51.9%	3.5	1,430,000	706,502	49.4%	1.0
WISCONSIN																			
WYOMING																			
Total	22,939,000	13,074,981	57.0%	23,360,000	12,048,501	51.6%	-5.4	24,426,000	13,228,851	54.2%	-2.8	25,368,000	15,210,937	60.0%	3.0	26,321,000	16,702,854	63.5%	6.5

*Percentage point difference between turnout in current year and initial year listed in chart. If data do not appear for a state in the initial year listed, the difference is calculated from the first year in which data do appear for that state.

STATE GUBERNATORIAL GENERAL ELECTIONS

Republican Turnout for Election Years 1992–2008

State	1992 Voting-age population	1992 Turnout	1992 %	1996 Voting-age population	1996 Turnout	1996 %	1996 Difference from 1992*	2000 Voting-age population	2000 Turnout	2000 %	2000 Difference from 1992	2004 Voting-age population	2004 Turnout	2004 %	2004 Difference from 1992	2008 Voting-age population	2008 Turnout	2008 %	2008 Difference from 1992
ALABAMA																			
ALASKA																			
ARIZONA																			
ARKANSAS																			
CALIFORNIA																			
COLORADO																			
CONNECTICUT																			
DELAWARE	515,000	90,725	17.6%	544,000	82,654	15.2%	-2.4	571,000	128,603	22.5%	4.9	603,000	167,115	27.7%	10.1	634,000	126,661	20.0%	2.4
DISTRICT OF COLUMBIA																			
FLORIDA																			
GEORGIA																			
HAWAII																			
IDAHO																			
ILLINOIS																			
INDIANA	4,146,000	822,533	19.8%	4,292,000	986,982	23.0%	3.2	4,421,000	908,285	20.5%	0.7	4,509,000	1,302,907	28.9%	9.1	4,599,000	1,563,885	34.0%	14.2
IOWA																			
KANSAS																			
KENTUCKY																			
LOUISIANA																			
MAINE																			
MARYLAND																			
MASSACHUSETTS																			
MICHIGAN																			
MINNESOTA																			
MISSISSIPPI																			
MISSOURI	3,858,000	968,574	25.1%	3,989,000	866,268	21.7%	-3.4	4,110,000	1,131,307	27.5%	2.4	4,227,000	1,382,419	32.7%	7.6	4,345,000	1,136,364	26.2%	1.0
MONTANA	598,000	209,401	35.0%	635,000	320,768	50.5%	15.5	671,000	209,135	31.2%	-3.8	703,000	205,313	29.2%	-5.8	736,000	158,268	21.5%	-13.5
NEBRASKA																			
NEVADA																			
NEW HAMPSHIRE	838,000	289,170	34.5%	873,000	196,321	22.5%	-12.0	910,000	246,952	27.1%	-7.4	968,000	325,614	33.6%	-0.9	1,025,000	187,388	18.3%	-16.2
NEW JERSEY																			
NEW MEXICO																			
NEW YORK																			

State Gubernatorial General Elections (continued)

Republican Turnout for Election Years 1992-2008 (continued)

State	1992				1996				2000				2004				2008			
	Voting-age population	Turnout	%		Voting-age population	Turnout	%	Difference from 1992	Voting-age population	Turnout	%	Difference from 1992	Voting-age population	Turnout	%	Difference from 1992	Voting-age population	Turnout	%	Difference from 1992
NORTH CAROLINA	5,199,000	1,121,955	21.6%		5,542,000	1,097,053	19.8%	-1.8	5,862,000	1,360,960	23.2%	1.6	6,161,000	1,495,021	24.3%	2.7	6,464,000	2,001,168	31.0%	9.4
NORTH DAKOTA	464,000	176,398	38.0%		470,000	174,937	37.2%	-0.8	476,000	159,255	33.5%	-4.6	481,000	220,803	45.9%	7.9	485,000	235,009	48.5%	10.4
OHIO																				
OKLAHOMA																				
OREGON																				
PENNSYLVANIA																				
RHODE ISLAND	737,000	145,590	19.8%																	
SOUTH CAROLINA																				
SOUTH DAKOTA																				
TENNESSEE																				
TEXAS																				
UTAH	1,166,000	321,713	27.6%		1,309,000	503,693	38.5%	10.9	1,435,000	424,837	29.6%	2.0	1,588,000	531,190	35.2%	7.6	1,588,000	735,049	46.3%	18.7
VERMONT	424,000	65,837	15.5%		440,000	57,161	13.0%	-2.5	456,000	111,359	24.4%	8.9	477,000	181,540	38.1%	22.5	499,000	170,492	34.2%	18.6
VIRGINIA																				
WASHINGTON	3,635,000	1,086,216	29.9%		3,885,000	940,538	24.2%	-5.7	4,114,000	980,060	23.8%	6.1	4,313,000	1,373,232	31.8%	2.0	4,516,000	1,404,124	31.1%	1.2
WEST VIRGINIA	1,359,000	240,390	17.7%		1,381,000	324,518	23.5%	5.8	1,400,000	305,926	21.9%	4.2	1,415,000	250,172	17.7%	0.0	1,430,000	181,908	12.7%	-5.0
WISCONSIN																				
WYOMING																				
Total	22,939,000	5,538,502	24.1%		23,360,000	5,550,893	23.8%	-0.4	24,426,000	5,966,679	24.4%	0.3	25,368,000	7,435,326	29.3%	5.2	26,321,000	7,900,316	30.0%	5.9

Democratic Turnout for Election Years 1992-2008

State	1992				1996				2000				2004				2008			
	Voting-age population	Turnout	%		Voting-age population	Turnout	%	Difference from 1992*	Voting-age population	Turnout	%	Difference from 1992	Voting-age population	Turnout	%	Difference from 1992	Voting-age population	Turnout	%	Difference from 1992
ALABAMA																				
ALASKA																				
ARIZONA																				
ARKANSAS																				
CALIFORNIA																				
COLORADO																				
CONNECTICUT																				
DELAWARE	515,000	179,365	34.8%		544,000	188,300	34.6%	-0.2	571,000	191,695	33.6%	-1.3	603,000	185,687	30.8%	-4.0	634,000	266,858	42.1%	7.3
DISTRICT OF COLUMBIA																				
FLORIDA																				

Democratic Turnout for Election Years 1992–2008 (continued)

State Gubernatorial General Elections (continued)

State	1992 Voting-age population	1992 Turnout	1992 %	1996 Voting-age population	1996 Turnout	1996 %	1996 Difference from 1992	2000 Voting-age population	2000 Turnout	2000 %	2000 Difference from 1992	2004 Voting-age population	2004 Turnout	2004 %	2004 Difference from 1992	2008 Voting-age population	2008 Turnout	2008 %	2008 Difference from 1992
GEORGIA																			
HAWAII																			
IDAHO																			
ILLINOIS																			
INDIANA	4,146,000	1,382,151	33.3%	4,292,000	1,087,128	25.3%	-8.0	4,421,000	1,232,525	27.9%	-5.5	4,509,000	1,113,879	24.7%	-8.6	4,599,000	1,082,463	23.5%	-9.8
IOWA																			
KANSAS																			
KENTUCKY																			
LOUISIANA																			
MAINE																			
MARYLAND																			
MASSACHUSETTS																			
MICHIGAN																			
MINNESOTA																			
MISSISSIPPI																			
MISSOURI	3,858,000	1,375,425	35.7%	3,989,000	1,224,801	30.7%	-4.9	4,110,000	1,152,752	28.0%	-7.6	4,227,000	1,301,442	30.8%	-4.9	4,345,000	1,680,611	38.7%	3.0
MONTANA	589,000	198,421	33.2%	635,000	84,407	13.3%	-19.9	671,000	193,131	28.8%	-4.4	703,000	225,016	32.0%	-1.2	736,000	318,670	43.3%	10.1
NEBRASKA																			
NEVADA																			
NEW HAMPSHIRE	838,000	206,232	24.6%	873,000	284,175	32.6%	7.9	910,000	275,038	30.2%	5.6	968,000	335,929	34.7%	10.1	1,025,000	477,146	46.6%	21.9
NEW JERSEY																			
NEW MEXICO																			
NEW YORK																			
NORTH CAROLINA	5,199,000	1,368,246	26.3%	5,542,000	1,436,638	25.9%	-0.4	5,862,000	1,530,324	26.1%	-0.2	6,161,000	1,939,154	31.5%	5.2	6,464,000	2,146,189	33.2%	6.9
NORTH DAKOTA	464,000	123,845	26.7%	470,000	89,349	19.0%	-7.7	476,000	130,144	27.3%	0.7	481,000	84,877	17.6%	-9.0	485,000	74,279	15.3%	-11.4
OHIO																			
OKLAHOMA																			
OREGON																			
PENNSYLVANIA																			
RHODE ISLAND	737,000	261,484	35.5%																
SOUTH CAROLINA																			
SOUTH DAKOTA																			
TENNESSEE																			

State Gubernatorial General Elections (continued)

Democratic Turnout for Election Years 1992–2008 (continued)

State	1992 Voting-age population	1992 Turnout	1992 %	1996 Voting-age population	1996 Turnout	1996 %	1996 Difference from 1992	2000 Voting-age population	2000 Turnout	2000 %	2000 Difference from 1992	2004 Voting-age population	2004 Turnout	2004 %	2004 Difference from 1992	2008 Voting-age population	2008 Turnout	2008 %	2008 Difference from 1992
TEXAS																			
UTAH	1,166,000	177,181	15.2%	1,309,000	156,616	12.0%	-3.2	1,435,000	321,979	22.4%	7.2	1,511,000	380,359	25.2%	10.0	1,588,000	186,503	11.7%	-3.5
VERMONT	424,000	213,523	50.4%	440,000	179,544	40.8%	-9.6	456,000	148,059	32.5%	-17.9	477,000	117,327	24.6%	-25.8	499,000	69,534	13.9%	-36.4
VIRGINIA																			
WASHINGTON	3,635,000	1,184,315	32.6%	3,885,000	1,296,492	33.4%	0.8	4,114,000	1,441,973	35.1%	2.5	4,313,000	1,373,361	31.8%	-0.7	4,516,000	1,598,738	35.4%	2.8
WEST VIRGINIA	1,359,000	368,302	27.1%	1,381,000	287,870	20.8%	-6.3	1,400,000	324,822	23.2%	-3.9	1,415,000	466,025	32.9%	5.8	1,430,000	493,246	34.5%	7.4
WISCONSIN																			
WYOMING																			
Total	22,939,000	7,038,490	30.7%	23,360,000	6,315,320	27.0%	-3.6	24,426,000	6,942,442	28.4%	-2.3	25,368,000	7,523,056	29.7%	-1.0	26,321,000	8,394,237	31.9%	1.2

Other Turnout for Election Years 1992–2008

State	1992 Voting-age population	1992 Turnout	1992 %	1996 Voting-age population	1996 Turnout	1996 %	1996 Difference from 1992	2000 Voting-age population	2000 Turnout	2000 %	2000 Difference from 1992*	2004 Voting-age population	2004 Turnout	2004 %	2004 Difference from 1992	2008 Voting-age population	2008 Turnout	2008 %	2008 Difference from 1992
DELAWARE	515,000	6,944	1.3%	544,000	168	0.0%	-1.3	571,000	3,271	0.6%	-0.8	603,000	12,206	2.0%	0.7	634,000	1,681	0.3%	-1.1
INDIANA	4,146,000	24,432	0.6%	4,292,000	35,937	0.8%	0.2	4,421,000	38,458	0.9%	0.3	4,509,000	31,717	0.7%	0.1	4,599,000	57,403	1.2%	0.7
MISSOURI	3,989,000	51,449	1.3%					4,110,000	62,771	1.5%	0.2	4,227,000	35,738	0.8%	-0.4	4,345,000	60,803	1.4%	0.1
MONTANA								671,000	7,926	1.2%		703,000	15,817	2.2%	1.1	736,000	9,796	1.3%	0.1
NEW HAMPSHIRE	838,000	20,768	2.5%	873,000	16,544	1.9%	-0.6	910,000	42,350	4.7%	2.2					1,025,000	15,250	1.5%	-1.0
NORTH CAROLINA	5,199,000	104,983	2.0%	5,542,000	32,494	0.6%	-1.4	5,862,000	50,778	0.9%	-1.2	6,161,000	52,513	0.9%	-1.2	6,404,000	121,584	1.9%	-0.1
NORTH DAKOTA	464,000	4,618	1.0%	470,000	12	0.0%	-1.0	476,000	13	0.0%	-1.0	481,000	4,193	0.9%	-0.1	485,000	6,404	1.3%	0.3
RHODE ISLAND	737,000	17,744	7.4%																
UTAH	1,166,000	263,642	22.6%	1,309,000	11,570	0.9%	-21.7	1,435,000	14,990	1.0%	-21.6	1,511,000	8,411	0.6%	-22.1	1,588,000	24,973	1.6%	-21.0
VERMONT	424,000	6,368	1.5%	440,000	17,943	4.1%	2.6	456,000	34,055	7.5%	6.0	477,000	10,418	2.2%	0.7	499,000	79,059	15.8%	14.3
WASHINGTON								4,114,000	47,819	1.2%		4,313,000	63,465	1.5%	0.3				
WEST VIRGINIA	1,359,000	48,490	3.6%	1,381,000	16,171	1.2%	-2.4	1,400,000	17,299	1.2%	-2.3	1,415,000	18,077	1.3%	-2.3	1,430,000	31,348	2.2%	-1.4
Total	14,848,000	497,989	3.4%	18,840,000	182,288	1.0%	-2.4	24,426,000	319,730	1.3%	-2.0	24,400,000	252,555	1.0%	-2.3	21,805,000	408,301	1.9%	-1.5

*Percentage point difference between current year and initial year listed in chart. If data do not appear for a state in the initial year listed, the difference is calculated from the first year in which data do appear for that state.

UNITED STATES SENATE GENERAL ELECTIONS

Election Years 1992–2008

State	1992			1996				2000				2004				2008			
	Voting-age population	Turnout	%	Voting-age population	Turnout	%	Difference from 1992*	Voting-age population	Turnout	%	Difference from 1992	Voting-age population	Turnout	%	Difference from 1992	Voting-age population	Turnout	%	Difference from 1992
ALABAMA	3,048,000	1,577,799	51.8%	3,174,000	1,499,393	47.2%	-4.5	3,343,000	1,838,066	55.0%	3.2					3,402,000	2,060,191	60.6%	8.8
ALASKA	383,000	239,714	62.6%	405,000	231,916	57.3%	-5.3	453,000	307,371	67.9%	5.3					480,000	317,723	66.2%	3.6
ARIZONA	2,778,000	1,382,051	49.7%					3,437,000	1,397,076	40.6%	-9.1	3,800,000	1,961,677	51.6%	1.9				
ARKANSAS	1,782,000	920,008	51.6%	1,876,000	846,183	45.1%	-6.5	2,015,000	1,038,377	51.5%	-0.1					2,073,000	1,087,340	52.5%	0.8
CALIFORNIA	18,781,000	10,799,363	57.5%					20,154,000	10,623,614	52.7%	-4.8	21,306,000	12,053,293	56.6%	-0.9				
COLORADO	2,541,289	1,552,289	61.1%	2,791,000	1,469,611	52.7%	-8.4					3,118,000	2,107,472	67.6%	6.5	3,233,000	2,331,607	72.1%	11.0
CONNECTICUT	2,414,000	1,500,709	62.2%					2,408,000	1,311,261	54.5%	-7.7	2,466,000	1,424,726	57.8%	-4.4				
DELAWARE	544,000	275,605	50.7%	571,000	326,993	57.3%	6.6									634,000	398,125	62.8%	12.1
DISTRICT OF COLUMBIA																			
FLORIDA	9,754,000	4,962,290	50.9%					11,205,000	5,856,731	52.3%	1.4	12,124,000	7,263,252	59.9%	9.0				
GEORGIA	4,938,000	2,251,587	45.6%	5,345,000	2,259,232	42.3%	-3.3	5,718,000	2,428,242	42.5%	-3.1	6,028,000	3,220,943	53.4%	7.8	6,344,000	3,752,579	59.2%	13.6
HAWAII	786,000	363,662	46.3%					847,000	345,623	40.8%	-5.5	885,000	415,347	46.9%	0.7				
IDAHO	741,000	478,522	64.6%	824,000	497,233	60.3%	-4.2					967,000	503,932	52.1%	-12.5	1,034,000	644,777	62.4%	-2.2
ILLINOIS	8,124,000	4,939,558	60.8%	8,269,000	4,250,722	51.4%	-9.4					8,466,000	5,142,721	60.7%	-0.1	8,546,000	5,330,543	62.4%	1.6
INDIANA	4,146,000	2,211,426	53.3%					4,421,000	2,145,209	48.5%	-4.8	4,509,000	2,428,233	53.9%	0.5				
IOWA	2,067,000	1,292,494	62.5%	2,109,000	1,224,054	58.0%	-4.5					2,175,000	1,479,228	68.0%	5.5	2,205,000	1,501,671	68.1%	5.6
KANSAS	1,818,000	1,126,447	62.0%	1,865,000	1,064,716	57.1%	-4.9					1,939,000	1,129,022	58.2%	-3.7	1,972,000	1,210,690	61.4%	-0.6
KENTUCKY	2,793,000	1,330,858	47.6%	2,909,000	1,307,046	44.9%	-2.7					3,085,000	1,724,362	55.9%	8.2	3,158,000	1,800,821	57.0%	9.4
LOUISIANA**	3,017,000	843,037	27.9%	3,117,000	1,700,102	54.5%	26.6					3,278,000	1,848,056	56.4%	28.4	3,349,000	1,896,574	56.6%	28.7
MAINE				942,000	606,777	64.4%		965,000	634,872	65.8%	1.4					1,054,000	724,430	68.7%	4.3
MARYLAND	3,524,000	1,841,735	52.3%					3,723,000	1,946,898	52.3%	0.0	3,906,000	2,296,908	58.8%	6.5				
MASSACHUSETTS	4,446,000	2,555,886	57.5%					4,479,000	2,599,420	58.0%	0.5	4,635,000	2,994,247	64.6%	7.1				
MICHIGAN	6,972,000	3,762,575	54.0%					7,131,000	4,167,685	58.4%	4.5	7,517,000	4,848,620	64.5%	10.5				
MINNESOTA				3,390,000	2,183,062	64.4%		3,525,000	2,419,520	68.6%	4.2	3,847,000	2,424,946	63.0%	-1.4				
MISSISSIPPI				1,974,000	878,662	44.5%		2,056,000	994,144	48.4%	3.8					2,158,000	1,247,026	57.8%	13.3
MISSOURI	3,858,000	2,354,925	61.0%					4,110,000	2,361,586	57.5%	-3.6	4,227,000	2,706,402	64.0%	3.0				
MONTANA				635,000	407,490	64.2%		671,000	411,601	61.3%	-2.8					736,000	477,658	64.9%	0.7
NEBRASKA	1,193,000	676,789	56.7%					1,221,000	692,350	56.7%	0.0					1,244,000	792,511	63.7%	7.0
NEVADA	982,000	495,887	50.5%					1,339,000	600,250	44.8%	-5.7	1,500,000	810,068	54.0%	3.5				
NEW HAMPSHIRE	838,000	518,423	61.9%	873,000	492,598	56.4%	-5.4					968,000	658,069	68.0%	6.1	1,025,000	691,193	67.4%	5.6
NEW JERSEY	5,599,000	2,884,106	51.5%					5,659,000	3,015,662	53.3%	1.8					5,918,000	3,482,445	58.8%	7.3
NEW MEXICO	1,165,000	551,821	47.4%					1,238,000	589,526	47.6%	0.3					1,354,000	823,650	60.9%	13.5
NEW YORK	12,410,000	6,458,826	52.0%					12,474,000	6,779,839	54.4%	2.3	12,563,000	6,702,875	53.4%	1.3				

United States Senate General Elections (continued)

Election Years 1992–2008 (continued)

State	1992 Voting-age population	1992 Turnout	1992 %	1996 Voting-age population	1996 Turnout	1996 %	1996 Difference from 1992	2000 Voting-age population	2000 Turnout	2000 %	2000 Difference from 1992	2004 Voting-age population	2004 Turnout	2004 %	2004 Difference from 1992	2008 Voting-age population	2008 Turnout	2008 %	2008 Difference from 1992
NORTH CAROLINA	5,199,000	2,577,891	49.6%	5,542,000	2,556,456	46.1%	-3.5					6,161,000	3,472,072	56.4%	6.8	6,464,000	4,272,000	66.1%	16.5
NORTH DAKOTA	464,000	303,957	65.5%					481,000	310,396	64.5%	-1.0	476,000	287,539	60.4%	-5.1				
OHIO	8,053,000	4,803,954	59.7%					8,337,000	4,452,139	53.4%	-6.3	8,458,000	5,425,342	64.1%	4.5				
OKLAHOMA	2,335,000	1,294,423	55.4%	2,420,000	1,183,150	48.9%	-6.5					2,528,000	1,446,846	57.2%	1.8	2,566,000	1,346,819	52.5%	-2.9
OREGON	2,150,000	1,376,033	64.0%	2,297,000	1,360,230	59.2%	-4.8					2,528,000	1,780,550	70.4%	6.4	2,628,000	1,767,504	67.3%	3.3
PENNSYLVANIA	9,007,000	4,802,410	53.3%					9,166,000	4,735,116	51.7%	-1.7	9,318,000	5,593,354	60.0%	6.7				
RHODE ISLAND				742,000	363,378	49.0%		749,000	391,353	52.3%	3.3					794,000	436,818	55.0%	6.0
SOUTH CAROLINA	2,652,000	1,180,438	44.5%	2,810,000	1,161,372	41.3%	-3.2					3,102,000	1,597,231	51.5%	7.0	3,244,000	1,871,431	57.7%	13.2
SOUTH DAKOTA	508,000	334,495	65.8%	529,000	324,487	61.3%	-4.5					576,000	380,673	66.1%	0.2	562,000	391,188	69.6%	3.8
TENNESSEE				4,018,000	1,778,664	44.3%		4,224,000	1,928,613	45.7%	1.4					4,534,000	2,424,585	53.5%	9.2
TEXAS				12,650,000	5,527,441	43.7%		13,404,000	6,276,652	46.8%	3.1					14,988,000	7,912,075	52.8%	9.1
UTAH	1,166,000	758,479	65.0%					1,435,000	769,704	53.6%	-11.4	1,511,000	911,726	60.3%	-4.7				
VERMONT	424,000	285,739	67.4%					456,000	288,500	63.3%	-4.1	477,000	307,208	64.4%	-3.0				
VIRGINIA				4,880,000	2,354,715	48.3%	*	5,080,000	2,718,301	53.4%	5.2					5,595,000	3,643,294	65.1%	16.9
WASHINGTON	3,635,000	2,218,802	61.0%					4,114,000	2,461,379	59.8%	-1.2	4,313,000	2,818,651	65.4%	4.3				
WEST VIRGINIA				1,381,000	595,614	43.1%		1,400,000	603,477	43.1%	0.0					1,430,000	703,059	49.2%	6.0
WISCONSIN	3,649,000	2,455,124	67.3%					3,919,000	2,540,083	64.8%	-2.5	4,061,000	2,949,743	72.6%	5.4				
WYOMING				345,000	211,077	61.2%		362,000	213,659	59.0%	-2.2					390,000	256,033	65.6%	4.5
Total	130,765,000	71,833,355	54.9%	98,031,000	49,042,163	50.0%	-4.9	150,480,000	79,314,617	52.7%	-2.2	146,621,000	86,065,707	58.7%	3.8	109,127,000	65,853,658	60.3%	5.4

*Percentage point difference between turnout in current year and initial year listed in chart. If data do not appear for a state in the first year listed, the difference is calculated from the initial year in which data do appear for that state.

**In 1978 Louisiana eliminated the partisan primary for senator and instituted an open primary from all parties running on the same ballot. Any candidate who received a majority appeared in the general election unopposed. If no candidate received fifty percent, a runoff was held between the top two finishers. In 2008 Louisiana returned to a partisan primary system.

UNITED STATES SENATE GENERAL ELECTIONS

Republican Turnout for Election Years 1992–2008

United States Senate General Elections (continued)

State	1992			1996				2000				2004				2008			
	Voting-age population	Turnout	%	Voting-age population	Turnout	%	Difference from 1992*	Voting-age population	Turnout	%	Difference from 1992	Voting-age population	Turnout	%	Difference from 1992	Voting-age population	Turnout	%	Difference from 1992
ALABAMA	3,048,000	522,015	17.1%	3,174,000	786,436	24.8%	7.7					3,343,000	1,242,200	37.2%	20.0	3,402,000	1,305,383	38.4%	21.2
ALASKA	383,000	127,163	33.2%	405,000	177,893	43.9%	10.7	453,000	149,446	33.0%	-0.2					480,000	147,814	30.8%	-2.4
ARIZONA	2,778,000	771,395	27.8%					3,437,000	1,108,196	32.2%	4.5	3,800,000	1,505,372	39.6%	11.8				
ARKANSAS				1,876,000	445,942	23.8%	3.2					2,015,000	458,501	22.8%	2.2				
CALIFORNIA	18,781,000	4,644,139	24.7%					20,154,000	3,886,853	19.3%	-5.4	21,306,000	4,555,922	21.4%	-3.3				
COLORADO	2,541,000	662,893	26.1%	2,791,000	750,325	26.9%	0.8					3,118,000	986,699	31.5%	5.4	3,233,000	990,751	30.6%	4.6
CONNECTICUT	2,414,000	572,036	23.7%					2,408,000	448,077	18.6%	-5.1	2,466,000	457,749	18.6%	-5.1				
DELAWARE				544,000	105,088	19.3%		571,000	142,891	25.0%	5.7					634,000	140,593	22.2%	2.9
DISTRICT OF COLUMBIA																			
FLORIDA	9,754,000	1,716,505	17.6%					11,205,000	2,705,348	24.1%	6.5	12,124,000	3,672,864	30.3%	12.7				
GEORGIA	4,938,000	1,073,282	21.7%	5,345,000	1,073,969	20.1%	-1.6	5,718,000	920,478	16.1%	-5.6	6,028,000	1,864,202	30.9%	9.2	6,344,000	1,867,090	29.4%	7.7
HAWAII	786,000	97,928	12.5%					847,000	84,701	10.0%	-2.5	885,000	87,172	9.8%	-2.6				
IDAHO	741,000	270,468	36.5%	824,000	283,532	34.4%	-2.1					967,000	499,796	51.7%	15.2	1,034,000	371,744	36.0%	-0.5
ILLINOIS	8,124,000	2,126,833	26.2%	8,269,000	1,728,824	20.9%	-5.3					8,466,000	1,391,030	16.4%	-9.7	8,546,000	1,520,896	17.8%	-8.4
INDIANA	4,146,000	1,267,972	30.6%					4,421,000	1,427,944	32.3%	1.7	4,509,000	903,913	20.0%	-10.5				
IOWA	2,067,000	899,761	43.5%	2,109,000	571,807	27.1%	-16.4					2,175,000	1,038,175	47.7%	4.2	2,205,000	560,006	25.4%	-18.1
KANSAS	1,818,000	706,246	38.8%	1,865,000	574,021	30.8%	-8.1					1,939,000	780,863	40.3%	1.4	1,972,000	727,121	36.9%	-2.0
KENTUCKY	2,793,000	476,604	17.1%	2,909,000	724,794	24.9%	7.9					3,085,000	873,507	28.3%	11.3	3,158,000	953,816	30.2%	13.1
LOUISIANA**	3,017,000	106,392	3.5%	3,117,000	847,157	27.2%	23.7					3,278,000	943,014	28.8%	25.2	3,349,000	867,177	25.9%	22.4
MAINE	942,000	298,422	31.7%					965,000	437,689	45.4%	13.7					1,054,000	444,300	42.2%	10.5
MARYLAND	3,524,000	533,688	15.1%					3,723,000	715,178	19.2%	4.1	3,906,000	783,055	20.0%	4.9				
MASSACHUSETTS				4,446,000	1,142,837	25.7%		4,479,000	334,341	7.5%	-18.2					4,635,000	926,044	20.0%	-5.7
MICHIGAN				6,972,000	1,500,106	21.5%		7,131,000	1,994,693	28.0%	6.5					7,517,000	1,641,070	21.8%	0.3
MINNESOTA				3,390,000	901,282	26.6%		3,525,000	1,047,474	29.7%	3.1					3,847,000	1,212,317	31.5%	4.9
MISSISSIPPI				1,974,000	624,154	31.6%		2,056,000	654,941	31.9%	0.2					2,158,000	766,111	35.5%	3.9
MISSOURI	3,858,000	1,221,901	31.7%					4,110,000	1,142,852	27.8%	-3.9	4,227,000	1,518,089	35.9%	4.2				
MONTANA				635,000	182,111	28.7%		671,000	208,082	31.0%	2.3					736,000	129,369	17.6%	-11.1
NEBRASKA				1,193,000	379,933	31.8%		1,221,000	337,977	27.7%	-4.2					1,244,000	455,854	36.6%	4.8
NEVADA	982,000	199,413	20.3%					1,339,000	330,687	24.7%	4.4	1,500,000	284,640	19.0%	-1.3				
NEW HAMPSHIRE	838,000	249,591	29.8%	873,000	242,304	27.8%	-2.0					968,000	435,846	45.0%	15.2	1,025,000	312,601	30.5%	0.7
NEW JERSEY				5,599,000	1,227,817	21.9%		5,659,000	1,420,267	25.1%	3.2					5,918,000	1,461,025	24.7%	2.8
NEW MEXICO				1,165,000	357,171	30.7%		1,238,000	225,517	18.2%	-12.4					1,354,000	318,522	23.5%	-7.1
NEW YORK	12,410,000	3,166,994	25.5%					12,474,000	2,915,730	23.4%	-2.1	12,563,000	1,625,069	12.9%	-12.6				

United States Senate General Elections (continued)

Republican Turnout for Election Years 1992–2008 (continued)

State	1992 Voting-age population	1992 Turnout	1992 %	1996 Voting-age population	1996 Turnout	1996 %	1996 Difference from 1992*	2000 Voting-age population	2000 Turnout	2000 %	2000 Difference from 1992	2004 Voting-age population	2004 Turnout	2004 %	2004 Difference from 1992	2008 Voting-age population	2008 Turnout	2008 %	2008 Difference from 1992
NORTH CAROLINA	5,199,000	1,297,892	25.0%	5,542,000	1,345,833	24.3%	-0.7					6,161,000	1,791,450	29.1%	4.1	6,464,000	1,887,510	29.2%	4.2
NORTH DAKOTA	464,000	118,162	25.5%					476,000	111,069	23.3%	-2.1	481,000	98,553	20.5%	-5.0				
OHIO	8,053,000	2,028,434	25.2%					8,337,000	2,666,739	32.0%	6.8	8,458,000	3,464,044	41.0%	15.8				
OKLAHOMA	2,335,000	757,876	32.5%	2,420,000	670,610	27.7%	-4.7	2,528,000	763,433	30.2%	-2.3					2,566,000	763,375	29.7%	-2.7
OREGON	2,150,000	717,455	33.4%	2,297,000	677,336	29.5%	-3.9	2,528,000	565,254	22.4%	-11.0					2,628,000	805,159	30.6%	-2.7
PENNSYLVANIA	9,007,000	2,358,125	26.2%					9,166,000	2,481,962	27.1%	0.9	9,318,000	2,959,609	31.8%	5.6				
RHODE ISLAND	742,000	127,368	17.2%					749,000	222,588	29.7%	12.6					794,000	116,174	14.6%	-2.5
SOUTH CAROLINA	2,652,000	554,175	20.9%	2,810,000	619,859	22.1%	1.2					3,102,000	857,167	27.6%	6.7	3,244,000	1,076,534	33.2%	12.3
SOUTH DAKOTA	508,000	108,733	21.4%	529,000	157,954	29.9%	8.5					562,000	197,848	35.2%	13.8	576,000	142,784	24.8%	3.4
TENNESSEE	4,018,000	1,091,554	27.2%					4,224,000	1,255,444	29.7%	2.6					4,534,000	1,579,477	34.8%	7.7
TEXAS	12,650,000	3,027,680	23.9%					13,404,000	4,082,091	30.5%	6.5					14,988,000	4,337,469	28.9%	5.0
UTAH	1,166,000	420,069	36.0%					1,435,000	504,803	35.2%	-0.8	1,511,000	626,640	41.5%	5.4				
VERMONT	424,000	123,854	29.2%					456,000	189,133	41.5%	12.3	477,000	75,398	15.8%	-13.4				
VIRGINIA	4,000,000	1,235,744	25.3%					5,080,000	1,420,460	27.9%	2.6					5,595,000	1,228,830	22.0%	-3.4
WASHINGTON	3,635,000	1,020,829	28.1%					4,114,000	1,197,208	29.1%	1.0	4,313,000	1,204,584	27.9%	-0.7				
WEST VIRGINIA	1,381,000	139,088	10.1%					1,400,000	121,635	8.7%	-1.4					1,430,000	255,074	17.8%	7.8
WISCONSIN	3,649,000	1,129,599	31.0%					3,919,000	940,744	24.0%	-7.0	4,061,000	1,301,183	32.0%	1.1				
WYOMING	345,000	114,116	33.1%					362,000	157,622	43.5%	10.5					390,000	189,046	48.5%	15.4
Total	130,765,000	32,414,795	24.8%	98,031,000	24,133,067	24.6%	-0.2	150,480,000	37,841,414	25.1%	0.4	146,621,000	39,956,556	27.3%	2.5	107,054,000	29,501,036	27.6%	2.0

Democratic Turnout for Election Years 1992–2008

State	1992 Voting-age population	1992 Turnout	1992 %	1996 Voting-age population	1996 Turnout	1996 %	1996 Difference from 1992*	2000 Voting-age population	2000 Turnout	2000 %	2000 Difference from 1992	2004 Voting-age population	2004 Turnout	2004 %	2004 Difference from 1992	2008 Voting-age population	2008 Turnout	2008 %	2008 Difference from 1992
ALABAMA	3,048,000	1,022,698	33.6%	3,174,000	681,651	21.5%	-12.1					3,343,000	595,018	17.8%	-15.8	3,402,000	752,391	22.1%	-11.4
ALASKA	383,000	92,065	24.0%	405,000	23,977	5.9%	-18.1					453,000	139,878	30.9%	6.9	480,000	151,767	31.6%	7.6
ARIZONA	2,778,000	436,321	15.7%									3,800,000	404,507	10.6%	-5.1				
ARKANSAS	1,782,000	553,635	31.1%	1,876,000	400,241	21.3%	-9.7					2,015,000	579,534	28.8%	-2.3	2,073,000	804,678	38.8%	7.7
CALIFORNIA	18,781,000	5,173,443	27.5%					20,154,000	5,932,522	29.4%	1.9	21,306,000	6,955,728	32.6%	5.1				
COLORADO	2,541,000	803,725	31.6%	2,791,000	677,600	24.3%	-7.4	3,118,000	1,081,188	34.7%	3.0					3,233,000	1,230,984	38.1%	6.4
CONNECTICUT	2,414,000	882,569	36.6%					2,408,000	828,902	34.4%	-2.1	2,466,000	945,347	38.3%	1.8				
DELAWARE	544,000	165,465	30.4%					571,000	181,566	31.8%	1.4					634,000	257,532	40.6%	10.2
DISTRICT OF COLUMBIA																			
FLORIDA	9,754,000	3,245,565	33.3%					11,205,000	2,989,487	26.7%	-6.6	12,124,000	3,590,201	29.6%	-3.7				

United States Senate General Elections (continued)

Democratic Turnout for Election Years 1992–2008 (continued)

State	1992 Voting-age population	1992 Turnout	1992 %	1996 Voting-age population	1996 Turnout	1996 %	1996 Difference from 1992	2000 Voting-age population	2000 Turnout	2000 %	2000 Difference from 1992	2004 Voting-age population	2004 Turnout	2004 %	2004 Difference from 1992	2008 Voting-age population	2008 Turnout	2008 %	2008 Difference from 1992
GEORGIA	4,938,000	1,108,416	22.4%	5,345,000	1,103,993	20.7%	-1.8	5,718,000	1,413,224	24.7%	2.3	6,028,000	1,287,690	21.4%	-1.1	6,344,000	1,757,419	27.7%	5.3
HAWAII	786,000	207,266	26.5%					847,000	251,215	29.7%	3.2	885,000	313,629	35.4%	8.9				
IDAHO	741,000	208,036	28.1%	824,000	198,422	24.1%	-4.0					967,000	4,136	0.4%	-27.6	1,034,000	219,903	21.3%	-6.8
ILLINOIS	8,124,000	2,631,229	32.4%	8,269,000	2,384,028	28.8%	-3.6					8,466,000	3,598,277	42.5%	10.1	8,546,000	3,616,210	42.3%	9.9
INDIANA	4,146,000	900,148	21.7%					4,421,000	683,273	15.5%	-6.3	4,509,000	1,496,976	33.2%	11.5				
IOWA	2,067,000	351,561	17.0%	2,109,000	634,166	30.1%	13.1					2,175,000	412,365	19.0%	2.0	2,205,000	941,665	42.7%	25.7
KANSAS	1,818,000	349,525	19.2%	1,865,000	461,344	24.7%	5.5					1,939,000	310,337	16.0%	-3.2	1,972,000	441,399	22.4%	3.2
KENTUCKY	2,793,000	836,888	30.0%	2,909,000	560,012	19.3%	-10.7					3,085,000	850,855	27.6%	-2.4	3,158,000	847,005	26.8%	-3.1
LOUISIANA**	3,017,000	661,860	21.9%	3,117,000	852,945	27.4%	5.4					3,278,000	877,482	26.8%	4.8	3,349,000	988,298	29.5%	7.6
MAINE				942,000	266,226	28.3%		965,000	197,183	20.4%	-7.8					1,054,000	279,510	26.5%	-1.7
MARYLAND	3,524,000	1,307,610	37.1%					3,723,000	1,230,013	33.0%	-4.1	3,906,000	1,504,691	38.5%	1.4				
MASSACHUSETTS				4,446,000	1,334,345	30.0%		4,479,000	1,889,494	42.2%	12.2					4,635,000	1,971,974	42.5%	12.5
MICHIGAN				6,972,000	2,195,738	31.5%		7,131,000	2,061,952	28.9%	-2.6					7,517,000	3,038,386	40.4%	8.9
MINNESOTA				3,390,000	1,098,493	32.4%		3,525,000	1,181,553	33.5%	1.1					3,847,000	1,212,629	31.5%	-0.9
MISSISSIPPI				1,974,000	240,647	12.2%		2,056,000	314,090	15.3%	3.1					2,158,000	480,915	22.3%	10.1
MISSOURI	3,858,000	1,057,967	27.4%					4,110,000	1,191,812	29.0%	1.6	4,227,000	1,158,261	27.4%	0.0				
MONTANA				635,000	201,935	31.8%		671,000	194,430	29.0%	-2.8					736,000	348,289	47.3%	15.5
NEBRASKA				1,193,000	281,904	23.6%		1,221,000	353,093	28.9%	5.3					1,244,000	317,456	25.5%	1.9
NEVADA	982,000	253,150	25.8%					1,339,000	238,260	17.8%	-8.0	1,500,000	494,805	33.0%	7.2				
NEW HAMPSHIRE	838,000	234,982	28.0%	873,000	227,397	26.0%	-2.0					968,000	221,544	22.9%	-5.2	1,025,000	357,153	34.8%	6.8
NEW JERSEY				5,599,000	1,519,328	27.1%		5,659,000	1,511,237	26.7%	-0.4					5,918,000	1,951,218	33.0%	5.8
NEW MEXICO				1,165,000	164,356	14.1%		1,238,000	363,744	29.4%	15.3					1,354,000	505,128	37.3%	23.2
NEW YORK	12,410,000	3,086,200	24.9%					12,474,000	3,747,310	30.0%	5.2	12,563,000	4,769,824	38.0%	13.1				
NORTH CAROLINA	5,199,000	1,194,015	23.0%	5,542,000	1,173,875	21.2%	-1.8					6,161,000	1,632,527	26.5%	3.5	6,464,000	2,249,311	34.8%	11.8
NORTH DAKOTA	464,000	179,347	38.7%					476,000	176,470	37.1%	-1.6	481,000	211,843	44.0%	5.4				
OHIO	8,053,000	2,444,397	30.4%					8,337,000	1,597,122	19.2%	-11.2	8,458,000	1,961,002	23.2%	-7.2				
OKLAHOMA	2,335,000	494,350	21.2%	2,420,000	474,162	19.6%	-1.6					2,528,000	596,750	23.6%	2.4	2,566,000	527,736	20.6%	-0.6
OREGON	2,150,000	639,851	29.8%	2,297,000	624,370	27.2%	-2.6					2,528,000	1,128,728	44.6%	14.9	2,628,000	864,392	32.9%	3.1
PENNSYLVANIA	9,007,000	2,224,966	24.7%					9,166,000	2,154,908	23.5%	-1.2	9,318,000	2,334,126	25.0%	0.3				
RHODE ISLAND				742,000	230,676	31.1%		749,000	161,023	21.5%	-9.6					794,000	320,644	40.4%	9.3
SOUTH CAROLINA	2,652,000	591,030	22.3%	2,810,000	510,951	18.2%	-4.1					3,102,000	704,384	22.7%	0.4	3,244,000	790,621	24.4%	2.1
SOUTH DAKOTA	508,000	217,095	42.7%	529,000	166,533	31.5%	-11.3					562,000	193,340	34.4%	-8.3	576,000	237,889	41.3%	-1.4
TENNESSEE				4,018,000	654,937	16.3%		4,224,000	621,152	14.7%	-1.6					4,534,000	767,236	16.9%	0.6

Democratic Turnout for Election Years 1992–2008 (continued)

State	1992 Voting-age population	1992 Turnout	1992 %	1996 Voting-age population	1996 Turnout	1996 %	1996 Difference from 1992*	2000 Voting-age population	2000 Turnout	2000 %	2000 Difference from 1992	2004 Voting-age population	2004 Turnout	2004 %	2004 Difference from 1992	2008 Voting-age population	2008 Turnout	2008 %	2008 Difference from 1992
TEXAS	12,650,000	2,428,776	19.2%					13,404,000	2,030,315	15.1%	-4.1					14,988,000	3,389,365	22.6%	3.4
UTAH	1,166,000	301,228	25.8%					1,435,000	242,569	16.9%	-8.9	1,511,000	258,955	17.1%	-8.7				
VERMONT	424,000	154,762	36.5%					456,000	73,352	16.1%	-20.4	477,000	216,972	45.5%	9.0				
VIRGINIA	4,880,000	1,115,982	22.9%	5,080,000	1,296,093	25.5%	2.6									5,595,000	2,369,327	42.3%	19.5
WASHINGTON	3,635,000	1,197,973	33.0%					4,114,000	1,199,437	29.2%	-3.8	4,313,000	1,549,708	35.9%	3.0				
WEST VIRGINIA	1,381,000	456,526	33.1%					1,400,000	469,215	33.5%	0.5					1,430,000	447,985	31.3%	-1.7
WISCONSIN	3,649,000	1,290,662	35.4%					3,919,000	1,563,238	39.9%	4.5	4,061,000	1,632,697	40.2%	4.8				
WYOMING	345,000	89,103	25.8%					362,000	47,087	13.0%	-12.8					390,000	60,631	15.5%	-10.3
Total	130,765,000	36,335,535	27.8%	98,031,000	23,600,104	24.1%	-3.7	147,043,000	38,386,341	26.1%	-1.7	146,621,000	44,013,305	30.0%	2.2	109,127,000	34,497,046	31.6%	3.8

Other Turnout for Election Years 1992–2008

State	1992 Voting-age population	1992 Turnout	1992 %	1996 Voting-age population	1996 Turnout	1996 %	1996 Difference from 1992*	2000 Voting-age population	2000 Turnout	2000 %	2000 Difference from 1992	2004 Voting-age population	2004 Turnout	2004 %	2004 Difference from 1992	2008 Voting-age population	2008 Turnout	2008 %	2008 Difference from 1992
ALABAMA	3,048,000	33,080	1.1%	3,174,000	31,306	1.0%	-0.1					3,343,000	1,848	0.1%	-1.0	3,402,000	2,417	0.1%	-1.0
ALASKA	383,000	20,486	5.3%	405,000	30,046	7.4%	2.1					453,000	18,047	4.0%	-1.4	480,000	18,142	3.8%	-1.6
ARIZONA	2,778,000	174,335	6.3%					3,437,000	288,880	8.4%	2.1	3,800,000	51,798	1.4%	-4.9				
ARKANSAS												2,015,000	342	0.0%		2,073,000	282,662	13.6%	13.6
CALIFORNIA	18,781,000	981,781	5.2%					20,154,000	804,239	4.0%	-1.2	21,306,000	541,643	2.5%	-2.7				
COLORADO	2,541,000	85,671	3.4%	2,791,000	41,686	1.5%	-1.9					3,118,000	45,616	1.5%	-1.9	3,233,000	108,872	3.4%	0.0
CONNECTICUT	2,414,000	46,104	1.9%					2,408,000	34,282	1.4%	-0.5	2,466,000	21,630	0.9%	-1.0				
DELAWARE				544,000	5,052	0.9%		571,000	2,536	0.4%	-0.5								
DISTRICT OF COLUMBIA																			
FLORIDA	9,754,000	220	0.0%					11,205,000	161,896	1.4%	1.4	12,124,000	187	0.0%	0.0				
GEORGIA	4,938,000	69,889	1.4%	5,345,000	81,270	1.5%	0.1	5,718,000	94,540	1.7%	0.2	6,028,000	69,051	1.1%	-0.3	6,344,000	128,070	2.0%	0.6
HAWAII	786,000	57,468	7.3%					847,000	9,707	1.1%	-6.2	885,000	14,546	1.6%	-5.7				
IDAHO	741,000	18	0.0%	824,000	15,279	1.9%	1.9									1,034,000	53,130	5.1%	5.1
ILLINOIS	8,124,000	181,496	2.2%	8,269,000	137,870	1.7%	-0.6					8,466,000	153,414	1.8%	-0.4	8,546,000	193,437	2.3%	0.0
INDIANA	4,146,000	43,306	1.0%					4,421,000	33,992	0.8%	-0.3	4,509,000	27,344	0.6%	-0.4				
IOWA	2,067,000	41,172	2.0%	2,109,000	18,081	0.9%	-1.1					2,175,000	28,688	1.3%	-0.7				
KANSAS	1,818,000	70,676	3.9%	1,865,000	29,351	1.6%	-2.3	1,939,000	37,822	2.0%	-1.9					1,972,000	42,170	2.1%	-1.7
KENTUCKY	2,793,000	17,366	0.6%	2,909,000	22,240	0.8%	0.1												
LOUISIANA**	3,017,000	74,785	2.5%									3,278,000	27,560	0.8%	-1.6	3,349,000	41,099	1.2%	-1.3
MAINE				942,000	42,129	4.5%										1,054,000	620	0.1%	-4.4

United States Senate General Elections *(continued)*

Other Turnout for Election Years 1992–2008 *(continued)*

State	1992 Voting-age population	Turnout	%	1996 Voting-age population	Turnout	%	Difference from 1992	2000 Voting-age population	Turnout	%	Difference from 1992	2004 Voting-age population	Turnout	%	Difference from 1992	2008 Voting-age population	Turnout	%	Difference from 1992
MARYLAND	3,524,000	437	0.0%					3,723,000	1,707	0.0%	0.0	3,906,000	9,162	0.2%	0.2				
MASSACHUSETTS				4,446,000	78,704	1.8%		4,479,000	375,585	8.4%	6.6					4,635,000	96,229	2.1%	0.3
MICHIGAN				6,972,000	66,731	1.0%		7,131,000	111,040	1.6%	0.6					7,517,000	169,164	2.3%	1.3
MINNESOTA				3,390,000	183,287	5.4%		3,525,000	190,493	5.4%	0.0								
MISSISSIPPI				1,974,000	13,861	0.7%		2,056,000	25,113	1.2%	0.5								
MISSOURI	3,858,000	75,057	1.9%					4,110,000	26,922	0.7%	-1.3	4,227,000	30,052	0.7%	-1.2				
MONTANA				635,000	23,444	3.7%		671,000	9,089	1.4%	2.3								
NEBRASKA				1,193,000	14,952	1.3%		1,221,000	1,280	0.1%	-1.1					1,244,000	19,201	1.5%	0.3
NEVADA	982,000	43,324	4.4%					1,339,000	31,303	2.3%	-2.1	1,500,000	30,623	2.0%	-2.4				
NEW HAMPSHIRE	838,000	33,850	4.0%	873,000	22,897	2.6%	-1.4					968,000	679	0.1%	-4.0	1,025,000	21,439	2.1%	-1.9
NEW JERSEY				5,599,000	136,961	2.4%		5,659,000	84,158	1.5%	-1.0					5,918,000	70,202	1.2%	-1.3
NEW MEXICO				1,165,000	30,294	2.6%		1,238,000	265	0.0%	-2.6								
NEW YORK	12,410,000	205,632	1.7%					12,474,000	116,799	0.9%	-0.7	12,563,000	307,982	2.5%	0.8				
NORTH CAROLINA	5,199,000	85,984	1.7%	5,542,000	36,748	0.7%	-1.0					6,161,000	48,095	0.8%	-0.9	6,464,000	135,179	2.1%	0.4
NORTH DAKOTA	464,000	6,448	1.4%																
OHIO	8,053,000	331,123	4.1%					8,337,000	188,278	2.3%	-1.9	8,458,000	296	0.0%	-4.1				
OKLAHOMA	2,335,000	42,197	1.8%	2,420,000	38,378	1.6%	-0.2					2,528,000	86,663	3.4%	1.6	2,566,000	55,708	2.2%	0.4
OREGON	2,150,000	18,727	0.9%	2,297,000	58,524	2.5%	1.7					2,528,000	86,568	3.4%	2.6	2,628,000	97,953	3.7%	2.9
PENNSYLVANIA	9,007,000	219,319	2.4%					9,166,000	98,246	1.1%	-1.4	9,318,000	299,319	3.2%	0.8				
RHODE ISLAND				742,000	5,334	0.7%		749,000	7,742	1.0%	0.3								
SOUTH CAROLINA	2,652,000	35,233	1.3%	2,810,000	30,562	1.1%	-0.2					3,102,000	35,680	1.2%	-0.2	3,244,000	4,276	0.1%	-1.2
SOUTH DAKOTA	508,000	8,667	1.7%																
TENNESSEE				4,018,000	32,173	0.8%		4,224,000	52,017	1.2%	0.4					4,534,000	77,872	1.7%	0.9
TEXAS				12,650,000	70,985	0.6%		13,404,000	164,246	1.2%	0.7					14,988,000	185,241	1.2%	0.7
UTAH	1,166,000	37,182	3.2%					1,435,000	22,332	1.6%	-1.6	1,511,000	26,131	1.7%	-1.5				
VERMONT	424,000	7,123	1.7%					456,000	26,015	5.7%	4.0	477,000	14,838	3.1%	1.4				
VIRGINIA				4,880,000	2,989	0.1%		5,086,000	1,748	0.0%	0.0					5,595,000	45,137	0.8%	0.7
WASHINGTON								4,114,000	64,734	1.6%		4,313,000	64,359	1.5%	-0.1				
WEST VIRGINIA								1,400,000	12,627	0.9%									
WISCONSIN	3,649,000	34,863	1.0%					3,919,000	36,101	0.9%	0.0	4,061,000	15,863	0.4%	-0.6				
WYOMING				345,000	7,858	2.3%		362,000	8,950	2.5%	0.2					390,000	6,356	1.6%	-0.6
Total	125,348,000	3,083,025	2.5%	91,128,000	1,308,992	1.4%	-1.0	149,039,000	3,086,862	2.1%	-0.4	141,526,000	2,095,846	1.5%	-1.0	92,235,000	1,855,576	2.0%	-0.4

*Percentage point difference between turnout in current year and initial year listed in chart. If data do not appear for a state in the initial year listed, the difference is calculated from the first year in which data do appear for that state.

**In 1978 Louisiana eliminated the partisan primary for senator and instituted an open primary with candidates from all parties running on the same ballot. Any candidate who received a majority appeared in the general election unopposed. If no candidate received fifty percent, a runoff was held between the top two finishers. In 2008 Louisiana returned to a partisan primary system.

UNITED STATES HOUSE OF REPRESENTATIVES GENERAL ELECTIONS

Election Years 1992–2008

State	1992 Voting-age population	1992 Turnout	1992 %	1996 Voting-age population	1996 Turnout	1996 %	1996 Difference from 1992*	2000 Voting-age population	2000 Turnout	2000 %	2000 Difference from 1992	2004 Voting-age population	2004 Turnout	2004 %	2004 Difference from 1992	2008 Voting-age population	2008 Turnout	2008 %	2008 Difference from 1992
ALABAMA	3,048,000	1,602,536	52.6%	3,174,000	1,468,693	46.3%	-6.3	3,284,000	1,438,994	43.8%	-8.8	3,343,000	1,792,759	53.6%	1.1	3,402,000	1,855,268	54.5%	2.0
ALASKA	383,000	239,116	62.4%	405,000	233,700	57.7%	-4.7	425,000	274,393	64.6%	2.1	453,000	299,996	66.2%	3.8	480,000	316,978	66.0%	3.6
ARIZONA	2,778,000	1,408,921	50.7%	3,114,000	1,356,446	43.6%	-7.2	3,437,000	1,465,656	42.6%	-8.1	3,800,000	1,871,433	49.2%	-1.5	4,166,000	2,155,685	51.7%	1.0
ARKANSAS	1,782,000	888,521	49.9%	1,876,000	863,318	46.0%	-3.8	1,959,000	632,765	32.3%	-17.6	2,015,000	848,878	42.1%	-7.7	2,073,000	842,227	40.6%	-9.2
CALIFORNIA	18,781,000	10,535,065	56.1%	19,460,000	9,481,525	48.7%	-7.4	20,154,000	10,437,665	51.8%	-4.3	21,306,000	11,623,753	54.6%	-1.5	22,475,000	12,321,500	54.8%	-1.3
COLORADO	2,541,000	1,479,209	58.2%	2,791,000	1,461,249	52.4%	-5.9	3,007,000	1,623,882	54.0%	-4.2	3,118,000	2,039,011	65.4%	7.2	3,233,000	2,283,832	70.6%	12.4
CONNECTICUT	2,414,000	1,435,163	59.5%	2,408,000	1,294,335	53.8%	-5.7	2,408,000	1,313,490	54.5%	-4.9	2,466,000	1,428,738	57.9%	-1.5	2,525,000	1,526,782	60.5%	1.0
DELAWARE	515,000	276,157	53.6%	544,000	266,836	49.1%	-4.6	571,000	313,126	54.8%	1.2	603,000	356,045	59.0%	5.4	634,000	385,454	60.8%	7.2
DISTRICT OF COLUMBIA																			
FLORIDA	9,754,000	4,914,833	50.4%	10,487,000	4,692,118	44.7%	-5.6	11,205,000	5,011,372	44.7%	-5.7	12,124,000	5,627,494	46.4%	-4.0	13,051,000	7,421,172	56.9%	6.5
GEORGIA	4,938,000	2,213,987	44.8%	5,345,000	2,163,186	40.5%	-4.4	5,718,000	2,416,442	42.3%	-2.6	6,028,000	2,960,686	49.1%	4.3	6,344,000	3,654,892	57.6%	12.8
HAWAII	786,000	358,431	45.6%	817,000	353,169	43.2%	-2.4	847,000	340,424	40.2%	-5.4	885,000	416,570	47.1%	1.5	923,000	417,447	45.2%	-0.4
IDAHO	741,000	472,747	63.8%	824,000	494,026	60.0%	-3.8	900,000	492,835	54.8%	-9.0	967,000	572,426	59.2%	-4.6	1,034,000	637,240	61.6%	-2.2
ILLINOIS	8,124,000	4,830,941	59.5%	8,269,000	4,127,606	49.9%	-9.5	8,393,000	4,393,352	52.3%	-7.1	8,466,000	4,986,848	58.9%	-0.6	8,546,000	5,243,883	61.4%	1.9
INDIANA	4,146,000	2,218,976	53.5%	4,292,000	2,105,033	49.0%	-4.5	4,421,000	2,156,744	48.8%	-4.7	4,509,000	2,416,251	53.6%	0.1	4,599,000	2,676,850	58.2%	4.7
IOWA	2,067,000	1,242,436	60.1%	2,109,000	1,200,758	56.9%	-3.2	2,147,000	1,275,934	59.4%	-0.7	2,175,000	1,458,161	67.0%	6.9	2,205,000	1,529,536	69.4%	9.3
KANSAS	1,818,000	1,124,915	61.9%	1,865,000	1,048,878	56.2%	-5.6	1,906,000	1,031,719	54.1%	-7.7	1,939,000	1,156,383	59.6%	-2.2	1,972,000	1,208,302	61.3%	-0.6
KENTUCKY	2,793,000	1,360,911	48.7%	2,909,000	1,238,181	42.6%	-6.2	3,013,000	1,435,409	47.6%	-1.1	3,085,000	1,635,042	53.0%	4.3	3,158,000	1,749,835	55.4%	6.7
LOUISIANA	3,017,000	683,589	22.7%	3,117,000	777,680	24.9%	2.3	3,207,000	1,202,171	37.5%	14.8	3,278,000	1,545,982	47.2%	24.5	3,349,000	1,277,936	38.2%	15.5
MAINE	920,000	669,581	72.8%	942,000	599,800	63.7%	-9.1	965,000	638,399	66.2%	-6.6	1,010,000	710,176	70.3%	-2.5	1,054,000	710,101	67.4%	-5.4
MARYLAND	3,524,000	1,807,507	51.3%	3,621,000	1,639,245	45.3%	-6.0	3,723,000	1,926,764	51.8%	0.5	3,906,000	2,253,428	57.7%	6.4	4,090,000	2,414,328	59.0%	7.7
MASSACHUSETTS	4,416,000	2,614,229	59.2%	4,446,000	2,409,352	54.2%	-5.0	4,479,000	2,347,375	52.4%	-6.8	4,556,000	1,733,178	38.0%	-21.2	4,635,000	2,605,214	56.2%	-3.0
MICHIGAN	6,807,000	3,884,403	57.1%	6,972,000	3,699,567	53.1%	-4.0	7,131,000	4,069,736	57.1%	0.0	7,323,000	4,631,057	63.2%	6.2	7,517,000	4,724,852	62.9%	5.8
MINNESOTA	3,252,000	2,274,413	69.9%	3,390,000	2,141,375	63.2%	-6.8	3,525,000	2,363,738	67.1%	-2.9	3,685,000	2,721,652	73.9%	3.9	3,847,000	2,802,614	72.9%	2.9
MISSISSIPPI	1,881,000	965,401	51.3%	1,974,000	904,151	45.8%	-5.5	2,056,000	986,139	48.0%	-3.4	2,107,000	1,116,103	53.0%	1.6	2,158,000	1,264,747	58.6%	7.3
MISSOURI	3,858,000	2,348,560	60.9%	3,989,000	2,115,844	53.0%	-7.8	4,110,000	2,325,788	56.6%	-4.3	4,227,000	2,667,023	63.1%	2.2	4,345,000	2,821,484	64.9%	4.1
MONTANA	598,000	403,735	67.5%	635,000	404,426	63.7%	-3.8	671,000	410,521	61.2%	-6.3	703,000	444,230	63.2%	-4.3	736,000	480,900	65.3%	-2.2
NEBRASKA	1,160,000	710,835	61.3%	1,193,000	661,644	55.5%	-5.8	1,221,000	683,071	55.9%	-5.3	1,233,000	764,972	62.0%	0.8	1,244,000	775,398	62.3%	1.1
NEVADA	982,000	491,949	50.1%	1,168,000	449,785	38.5%	-11.6	1,339,000	585,204	43.7%	-6.4	1,500,000	791,433	52.8%	2.7	1,664,000	905,941	54.4%	4.3
NEW HAMPSHIRE	838,000	511,040	61.0%	873,000	491,323	56.3%	-4.7	910,000	556,417	61.1%	0.2	968,000	650,560	67.2%	6.2	1,025,000	674,975	65.9%	4.9
NEW JERSEY	5,543,000	2,991,739	54.0%	5,599,000	2,823,159	50.4%	-3.6	5,659,000	2,988,233	52.8%	-1.2	5,787,000	3,284,595	56.8%	2.8	5,918,000	3,437,330	58.1%	4.1
NEW MEXICO	1,084,000	555,601	51.3%	1,165,000	548,355	47.1%	-4.2	1,238,000	587,514	47.5%	-3.8	1,296,000	743,080	57.3%	6.1	1,354,000	814,566	60.2%	8.9
NEW YORK	12,410,000	5,933,653	47.8%	12,447,000	5,551,053	44.6%	-3.2	12,474,000	5,823,850	46.7%	-1.1	12,563,000	6,221,418	49.5%	1.7	12,659,000	6,384,146	50.4%	2.6

United States House of Representatives General Elections *(continued)*

Election Years 1992–2008 *(continued)*

State	1992 Voting-age population	1992 Turnout	1992 %	1996 Voting-age population	1996 Turnout	1996 %	1996 Difference from 1992	2000 Voting-age population	2000 Turnout	2000 %	2000 Difference from 1992	2004 Voting-age population	2004 Turnout	2004 %	2004 Difference from 1992	2008 Voting-age population	2008 Turnout	2008 %	2008 Difference from 1992
NORTH CAROLINA	5,199,000	2,567,011	49.4%	5,542,000	2,513,549	45.4%	-4.0	5,862,000	2,779,800	47.4%	-2.0	6,161,000	3,413,071	55.4%	6.0	6,464,000	4,215,093	65.2%	15.8
NORTH DAKOTA	464,000	297,898	64.2%	470,000	263,010	56.0%	-8.2	476,000	285,658	60.0%	-4.2	481,000	310,814	64.6%	0.4	485,000	313,965	64.7%	0.5
OHIO	8,053,000	4,576,934	56.8%	8,201,000	4,388,395	53.5%	-3.3	8,337,000	4,517,838	54.2%	-2.6	8,458,000	5,345,379	63.2%	6.4	8,579,000	5,365,668	62.5%	5.7
OKLAHOMA	2,335,000	1,275,696	54.6%	2,420,000	1,180,144	48.8%	-5.9	2,491,000	1,087,515	43.7%	-11.0	2,528,000	1,374,610	54.4%	-0.3	2,566,000	1,336,927	52.1%	-2.5
OREGON	2,150,000	1,390,754	64.7%	2,297,000	1,335,061	58.1%	-6.6	2,428,000	1,440,002	59.3%	-5.4	2,528,000	1,771,915	70.1%	5.4	2,628,000	1,682,509	64.0%	-0.7
PENNSYLVANIA	9,007,000	4,590,519	51.0%	9,085,000	4,316,403	47.5%	-3.5	9,166,000	4,558,010	49.7%	-1.2	9,318,000	5,151,135	55.3%	4.3	9,471,000	5,787,904	61.1%	10.1
RHODE ISLAND	737,000	398,502	54.1%	742,000	359,750	48.5%	-5.6	749,000	383,862	51.2%	-2.8	771,000	402,175	52.2%	-1.9	794,000	437,551	55.1%	1.0
SOUTH CAROLINA	2,652,000	1,115,450	42.1%	2,810,000	1,057,384	37.6%	-4.4	2,960,000	1,321,312	44.6%	2.6	3,102,000	1,439,118	46.4%	4.3	3,244,000	1,873,890	57.8%	15.7
SOUTH DAKOTA	508,000	332,902	65.5%	529,000	323,203	61.1%	-4.4	547,000	314,761	57.5%	-8.0	562,000	389,468	69.3%	3.8	576,000	379,007	65.8%	0.3
TENNESSEE	3,790,000	1,725,674	45.5%	4,018,000	1,783,543	44.4%	-1.1	4,224,000	1,854,378	43.9%	-1.6	4,378,000	2,218,738	50.7%	5.1	4,534,000	2,298,747	50.7%	5.2
TEXAS	11,852,000	5,622,472	47.4%	12,650,000	5,219,343	41.3%	-6.2	13,404,000	5,985,763	44.7%	-2.8	14,189,000	6,913,603	48.7%	1.3	14,988,000	7,527,712	50.2%	2.8
UTAH	1,166,000	727,284	62.4%	1,300,000	663,815	50.7%	-11.7	1,435,000	758,754	52.9%	-9.5	1,511,000	908,857	60.1%	-2.2	1,588,000	936,839	59.0%	-3.4
VERMONT	424,000	281,626	66.4%	440,000	254,706	57.9%	-8.5	456,000	283,366	62.1%	-4.3	477,000	305,000	63.9%	-2.5	499,000	298,151	59.7%	-6.7
VIRGINIA	4,669,000	2,368,047	50.7%	4,880,000	2,199,097	45.1%	-5.7	5,086,000	2,421,729	47.6%	-3.1	5,339,000	3,004,007	56.3%	5.5	5,595,000	3,495,141	62.5%	11.8
WASHINGTON	3,635,000	2,223,014	61.2%	3,885,000	2,174,261	56.0%	-5.2	4,114,000	2,382,411	57.9%	-3.2	4,313,000	2,729,995	63.3%	2.1	4,516,000	2,914,463	64.5%	3.4
WEST VIRGINIA	1,359,000	562,736	41.4%	1,381,000	522,368	37.8%	-3.6	1,400,000	579,872	41.4%	0.0	1,415,000	725,656	51.3%	9.9	1,430,000	646,061	45.2%	3.8
WISCONSIN	3,649,000	2,387,930	65.4%	3,788,000	2,150,327	56.8%	-8.7	3,919,000	2,506,314	64.0%	-1.5	4,061,000	2,821,613	69.5%	4.0	4,203,000	2,775,174	66.0%	0.6
WYOMING	327,000	197,025	60.3%	345,000	209,983	60.9%	0.6	362,000	214,312	59.2%	-1.1	376,000	239,034	63.6%	3.3	390,000	256,033	65.6%	5.4
Total	179,675,000	96,090,574	53.5%	187,012,000	89,980,158	48.1%	-5.4	193,919,000	97,224,779	50.1%	-3.3	201,392,000	111,233,557	55.2%	1.8	208,965,000	120,802,250	57.8%	4.4

*Percentage point difference between turnout in current year and initial year listed in chart. If data do not appear for a state in the initial year listed, the difference is calculated from the first year in which data do appear for that state.

UNITED STATES HOUSE OF REPRESENTATIVES GENERAL ELECTIONS

Republican Turnout for Election Years 1992–2008

State	1992 Voting-age population	1992 Turnout	1992 %	1996 Voting-age population	1996 Turnout	1996 %	1996 Difference from 1992*	2000 Voting-age population	2000 Turnout	2000 %	2000 Difference from 1992	2004 Voting-age population	2004 Turnout	2004 %	2004 Difference from 1992	2008 Voting-age population	2008 Turnout	2008 %	2008 Difference from 1992
ALABAMA	3,048,000	643,150	21.1%	3,174,000	785,513	24.7%	3.6	3,284,000	849,229	25.9%	4.8	3,343,000	1,079,657	32.3%	11.2	3,402,000	1,120,903	32.9%	11.8
ALASKA	383,000	111,849	29.2%	405,000	138,834	34.3%	5.1	425,000	190,862	44.9%	15.7	453,000	213,216	47.1%	17.9	480,000	158,939	33.1%	3.9
ARIZONA	2,778,000	740,047	26.6%	3,114,000	800,917	25.7%	-0.9	3,437,000	854,715	24.9%	-1.8	3,800,000	1,127,591	29.7%	3.0	4,166,000	1,021,798	24.5%	-2.1
ARKANSAS	1,782,000	356,900	20.0%	1,876,000	456,033	24.3%	4.3	1,959,000	277,146	14.1%	-5.9	2,015,000	357,990	17.8%	-2.3	2,073,000	215,196	10.4%	-9.6
CALIFORNIA	18,781,000	4,365,155	23.2%	19,460,000	4,291,647	22.1%	-1.2	20,154,000	4,446,295	22.1%	-1.2	21,306,000	5,030,821	23.6%	0.4	22,475,000	4,381,391	19.5%	-3.7
COLORADO	2,541,000	757,666	29.8%	2,791,000	832,763	29.8%	0.0	3,007,000	968,651	32.2%	2.4	3,118,000	991,835	31.8%	2.0	3,233,000	990,831	30.6%	0.8
CONNECTICUT	2,414,000	699,155	29.0%	2,408,000	547,084	22.7%	-6.2	2,408,000	590,689	24.5%	-4.4	2,466,000	629,934	25.5%	-3.4	2,525,000	504,804	20.0%	-9.0
DELAWARE	515,000	153,037	29.7%	544,000	185,576	34.1%	4.4	571,000	211,797	37.1%	7.4	603,000	245,978	40.8%	11.1	634,000	235,435	37.1%	7.4
DISTRICT OF COLUMBIA																			
FLORIDA	9,754,000	2,510,702	25.7%	10,487,000	2,639,657	25.2%	-0.6	11,205,000	2,851,623	25.4%	-0.3	12,124,000	3,319,296	27.4%	1.6	13,051,000	3,792,167	29.1%	3.3
GEORGIA	4,938,000	999,182	20.2%	5,345,000	1,151,993	21.6%	1.3	5,718,000	1,498,337	26.2%	6.0	6,028,000	1,819,817	30.2%	10.0	6,344,000	1,796,566	28.3%	8.1
HAWAII	786,000	81,645	10.4%	817,000	135,782	16.6%	6.2	847,000	110,895	13.1%	2.7	885,000	148,443	16.8%	6.4	923,000	82,465	8.9%	-1.5
IDAHO	741,000	230,766	31.1%	824,000	289,990	35.2%	4.1	900,000	242,992	27.0%	-4.1	967,000	401,366	41.5%	10.4	1,034,000	377,464	36.5%	5.4
ILLINOIS	8,124,000	2,096,717	25.8%	8,269,000	1,812,673	21.9%	-3.9	8,393,000	1,907,306	22.7%	-3.1	8,466,000	2,270,757	26.8%	1.0	8,546,000	1,961,425	23.0%	-2.9
INDIANA	4,146,000	998,334	24.1%	4,292,000	1,118,533	26.1%	2.0	4,421,000	1,140,554	25.8%	1.7	4,509,000	1,381,699	30.6%	6.6	4,599,000	1,169,351	25.4%	1.3
IOWA	2,067,000	729,496	35.3%	2,109,000	649,959	30.8%	-4.5	2,147,000	717,322	33.4%	-1.9	2,175,000	822,653	37.8%	2.5	2,205,000	638,412	29.0%	-6.3
KANSAS	1,818,000	591,712	32.5%	1,865,000	591,146	31.7%	-0.9	1,906,000	655,620	34.4%	1.9	1,939,000	723,794	37.3%	4.8	1,972,000	690,005	35.0%	2.4
KENTUCKY	2,793,000	638,166	22.8%	2,909,000	730,739	25.1%	2.3	3,013,000	824,915	27.4%	4.5	3,085,000	1,017,379	33.0%	10.1	3,158,000	955,182	30.2%	7.4
LOUISIANA	3,017,000	398,679	13.2%	3,117,000	461,761	14.8%	1.6	3,207,000	747,115	23.3%	10.1	3,278,000	936,801	28.6%	15.4	3,349,000	594,090	17.7%	4.5
MAINE	920,000	278,258	30.2%	942,000	211,210	22.4%	-7.8	965,000	203,437	21.1%	-9.2	1,010,000	283,210	28.0%	-2.2	1,054,000	278,198	26.4%	-3.9
MARYLAND	3,524,000	842,789	23.9%	3,621,000	762,163	21.0%	-2.9	3,723,000	856,306	23.0%	-0.9	3,906,000	896,232	22.9%	-1.0	4,090,000	762,428	18.6%	-5.3
MASSACHUSETTS	4,416,000	894,210	20.2%	4,446,000	780,729	17.6%	-2.7	4,479,000	343,498	7.7%	-12.6	4,556,000	431,212	9.5%	-10.8	4,635,000	318,561	6.9%	-13.4
MICHIGAN	6,807,000	1,855,241	27.3%	6,972,000	1,678,735	24.1%	-3.2	7,131,000	1,786,991	25.1%	-2.2	7,323,000	2,288,594	31.3%	4.0	7,517,000	2,036,470	27.1%	-0.2
MINNESOTA	3,252,000	930,814	28.6%	3,390,000	895,003	26.4%	-2.2	3,525,000	993,371	28.2%	-0.4	3,685,000	1,236,095	33.5%	4.9	3,847,000	1,069,015	27.8%	-0.8
MISSISSIPPI	1,881,000	273,234	14.5%	1,974,000	487,988	24.7%	10.2	2,056,000	468,483	22.8%	8.3	2,107,000	658,589	31.3%	16.7	2,158,000	527,330	24.4%	9.9
MISSOURI	3,858,000	1,036,268	26.9%	3,989,000	833,190	20.9%	-6.0	4,110,000	1,135,724	27.6%	0.8	4,227,000	1,429,767	33.8%	7.0	4,345,000	1,313,018	30.2%	3.4
MONTANA	598,000	189,570	31.7%	635,000	211,975	33.4%	1.7	671,000	211,418	31.5%	-0.2	703,000	286,076	40.7%	9.0	736,000	308,470	41.9%	10.2
NEBRASKA	1,160,000	427,398	36.8%	1,193,000	450,067	37.7%	0.9	1,221,000	486,513	39.8%	3.0	1,233,000	515,115	41.8%	4.9	1,244,000	510,513	41.0%	4.2
NEVADA	982,000	213,792	21.8%	1,168,000	248,782	21.3%	-0.5	1,339,000	330,884	24.7%	2.9	1,500,000	420,711	28.0%	6.3	1,664,000	382,802	23.0%	1.2
NEW HAMPSHIRE	838,000	227,063	27.1%	873,000	246,940	28.3%	1.2	910,000	303,190	33.3%	6.2	968,000	396,023	40.9%	13.8	1,025,000	294,560	28.7%	1.6
NEW JERSEY	5,543,000	1,503,145	27.1%	5,599,000	1,398,900	25.0%	-2.1	5,659,000	1,384,170	24.5%	-2.7	5,787,000	1,514,784	26.2%	-0.9	5,918,000	1,461,818	24.7%	-2.4
NEW MEXICO	1,084,000	277,833	25.6%	1,165,000	260,961	22.4%	-3.2	1,238,000	274,017	22.1%	-3.5	1,296,000	358,159	27.6%	2.0	1,354,000	321,083	23.7%	-1.9
NEW YORK	12,410,000	2,686,420	21.6%	12,447,000	2,357,553	18.9%	-2.7	12,474,000	2,465,640	19.8%	-1.9	12,563,000	2,447,345	19.5%	-2.2	12,659,000	2,034,740	16.1%	-5.6

United States House of Representatives General Elections *(continued)*

Republican Turnout for Election Years 1992–2008 *(continued)*

State	1992 Voting-age population	Turnout	%	1996 Voting-age population	Turnout	%	Difference from 1992	2000 Voting-age population	Turnout	%	Difference from 1992	2004 Voting-age population	Turnout	%	Difference from 1992	2008 Voting-age population	Turnout	%	Difference from 1992
NORTH CAROLINA	5,199,000	1,235,799	23.8%	5,542,000	1,339,515	24.2%	0.4	5,862,000	1,514,806	25.8%	2.1	6,161,000	1,743,131	28.3%	4.5	6,464,000	1,901,517	29.4%	5.6
NORTH DAKOTA	464,000	117,442	25.3%	470,000	113,684	24.2%	-1.1	476,000	127,251	26.7%	1.4	481,000	125,684	26.1%	0.8	485,000	119,388	24.6%	-0.7
OHIO	8,053,000	2,154,080	26.7%	8,201,000	2,191,974	26.7%	0.0	8,337,000	2,203,086	26.4%	-0.3	8,458,000	2,770,144	32.8%	6.0	8,579,000	2,488,784	29.0%	2.3
OKLAHOMA	2,335,000	504,133	21.6%	2,420,000	722,998	29.9%	8.3	2,491,000	701,820	28.2%	6.6	2,528,000	875,033	34.6%	13.0	2,566,000	802,530	31.3%	9.7
OREGON	2,150,000	553,101	26.7%	2,297,000	557,525	24.3%	-1.5	2,428,000	607,098	25.0%	-0.7	2,528,000	761,366	30.1%	4.4	2,628,000	435,920	16.6%	-9.1
PENNSYLVANIA	9,007,000	2,271,239	25.2%	9,085,000	2,037,508	22.4%	-2.8	9,166,000	2,229,057	24.3%	-0.9	9,310,000	2,666,077	27.5%	2.3	9,471,000	2,520,805	26.6%	1.4
RHODE ISLAND	737,000	185,980	25.2%	742,000	107,657	14.5%	-10.7	749,000	89,454	11.9%	-13.3	771,000	112,958	14.7%	-10.6	794,000	118,773	15.0%	-10.3
SOUTH CAROLINA	2,652,000	581,159	21.9%	2,810,000	682,563	24.3%	2.4	2,960,000	729,799	24.7%	2.7	3,102,000	913,168	29.4%	7.5	3,244,000	939,703	29.0%	7.1
SOUTH DAKOTA	508,000	89,375	17.6%	529,000	186,393	35.2%	17.6	547,000	231,083	42.2%	24.7	562,000	178,823	31.8%	14.2	576,000	122,966	21.3%	3.8
TENNESSEE	3,790,000	737,690	19.5%	4,018,000	888,546	22.1%	2.7	4,224,000	991,984	23.5%	4.0	4,378,000	1,160,821	26.5%	7.1	4,534,000	976,682	21.5%	2.1
TEXAS	11,852,000	2,685,973	22.7%	12,650,000	2,784,875	22.0%	-0.6	13,404,000	2,932,411	21.9%	-0.8	14,189,000	4,012,534	28.3%	5.6	14,988,000	4,208,586	28.1%	5.4
UTAH	1,166,000	362,363	31.1%	1,309,000	386,309	29.5%	-1.6	1,435,000	426,648	29.7%	-1.3	1,511,000	520,403	34.4%	3.4	1,588,000	503,917	31.7%	0.7
VERMONT	424,000	86,901	20.5%	440,000	83,021	18.9%	-1.6	456,000	51,977	11.4%	-9.1	477,000	74,271	15.6%	-4.9				
VIRGINIA	4,669,000	1,142,649	24.5%	4,880,000	1,117,187	22.9%	-1.6	5,086,000	1,131,999	22.3%	-2.2	5,339,000	1,817,422	34.0%	9.6	5,595,000	1,590,571	28.4%	4.0
WASHINGTON	3,635,000	911,913	25.1%	3,885,000	1,020,553	26.3%	1.2	4,114,000	997,877	24.3%	-0.8	4,313,000	1,095,493	25.4%	0.3	4,516,000	1,189,147	26.3%	1.2
WEST VIRGINIA	1,359,000	123,144	9.1%	1,381,000	63,933	4.6%	-4.4	1,400,000	108,769	7.8%	-1.3	1,415,000	303,042	21.4%	12.4	1,430,000	213,339	14.9%	5.9
WISCONSIN	3,649,000	1,210,827	33.2%	3,788,000	1,120,819	29.6%	-3.6	3,919,000	1,311,447	33.5%	0.3	4,061,000	1,380,819	34.0%	0.8	4,203,000	1,274,987	30.3%	-2.8
WYOMING	327,000	113,882	34.8%	345,000	116,004	33.6%	-1.2	362,000	143,848	39.7%	4.9	376,000	132,107	35.1%	0.3	390,000	131,244	33.7%	-1.2
Total	179,675,000	43,806,043	24.4%	187,012,000	43,965,860	23.5%	-0.9	193,919,000	46,860,119	24.2%	-0.2	201,392,000	56,223,235	27.9%	3.5	208,466,000	51,844,289	24.9%	0.5

Democratic Turnout for Election Years 1992–2008

State	1992 Voting-age population	Turnout	%	1996 Voting-age population	Turnout	%	Difference from 1992*	2000 Voting-age population	Turnout	%	Difference from 1992	2004 Voting-age population	Turnout	%	Difference from 1992	2008 Voting-age population	Turnout	%	Difference from 1992
ALABAMA	3,048,000	895,601	29.4%	3,174,000	656,047	20.7%	-8.7	3,284,000	485,660	14.8%	-14.6	3,343,000	708,425	21.2%	-8.2	3,402,000	718,367	21.1%	-8.3
ALASKA	383,000	102,378	26.7%	405,000	85,114	21.0%	-5.7	425,000	45,372	10.7%	-16.1	453,000	67,074	14.8%	-11.9	480,000	142,560	29.7%	3.0
ARIZONA	2,778,000	582,317	21.0%	3,114,000	521,345	16.7%	-4.2	3,437,000	557,849	16.2%	-4.7	3,800,000	597,526	15.7%	-5.2	4,166,000	1,055,305	25.3%	4.4
ARKANSAS	1,782,000	525,197	29.5%	1,876,000	395,506	21.1%	-8.4	1,959,000	355,366	18.1%	-11.3	2,015,000	483,627	24.0%	-5.5	2,073,000	415,481	20.0%	-9.4
CALIFORNIA	18,781,000	5,446,965	29.0%	19,460,000	4,706,819	24.2%	-4.8	20,154,000	5,407,163	26.8%	-2.2	21,306,000	6,223,698	29.2%	0.2	22,475,000	7,556,391	33.6%	4.6
COLORADO	2,541,000	691,479	27.2%	2,791,000	596,575	21.4%	-5.8	3,007,000	496,045	16.5%	-10.7	3,118,000	995,283	31.9%	4.7	3,233,000	1,259,714	39.0%	11.8
CONNECTICUT	2,414,000	644,424	26.7%	2,408,000	723,504	30.0%	3.4	2,408,000	699,237	29.0%	2.3	2,466,000	785,747	31.9%	5.2	2,525,000	911,009	36.1%	9.4
DELAWARE	515,000	117,426	22.8%	544,000	73,253	13.5%	-9.3	571,000	96,488	16.9%	-5.9	603,000	105,716	17.5%	-5.3	634,000	146,433	23.1%	0.3
DISTRICT OF COLUMBIA																			
FLORIDA	9,754,000	2,256,708	23.1%	10,487,000	2,036,620	19.4%	-3.7	11,205,000	1,976,189	17.6%	-5.5	12,124,000	2,212,324	18.2%	-4.9	13,051,000	3,434,831	26.3%	3.2

United States House of Representatives General Elections (continued)

United States House of Representatives General Elections *(continued)*

Democratic Turnout for Election Years 1992–2008 *(continued)*

State	1992 Voting-age population	1992 Turnout	1992 %	1996 Voting-age population	1996 Turnout	1996 %	1996 Difference from 1992	2000 Voting-age population	2000 Turnout	2000 %	2000 Difference from 1992	2004 Voting-age population	2004 Turnout	2004 %	2004 Difference from 1992	2008 Voting-age population	2008 Turnout	2008 %	2008 Difference from 1992
GEORGIA	4,938,000	1,214,792	24.6%	5,345,000	1,011,190	18.9%	-5.7	5,718,000	918,085	16.1%	-8.5	6,028,000	1,140,869	18.9%	-5.7	6,344,000	1,858,123	29.3%	4.7
HAWAII	786,000	260,786	33.2%	817,000	195,910	24.0%	-9.2	847,000	221,373	26.1%	-7.0	885,000	261,884	29.6%	-3.6	923,000	319,660	34.6%	1.5
IDAHO	741,000	222,435	30.0%	824,000	193,524	23.5%	-6.5	900,000	232,008	25.8%	-4.2	967,000	171,060	17.7%	-12.3	1,034,000	259,776	25.1%	-4.9
ILLINOIS	8,124,000	2,677,685	33.0%	8,269,000	2,267,369	27.4%	-5.5	8,393,000	2,453,674	29.2%	-3.7	8,466,000	2,674,375	31.6%	-1.4	8,546,000	3,171,615	37.1%	4.2
INDIANA	4,146,000	1,205,869	29.1%	4,292,000	944,469	22.0%	-7.1	4,421,000	953,167	21.6%	-7.5	4,509,000	999,082	22.2%	-6.9	4,599,000	1,388,963	30.2%	1.1
IOWA	2,067,000	492,843	23.8%	2,109,000	532,815	25.3%	1.4	2,147,000	531,642	24.8%	0.9	2,175,000	624,620	28.7%	4.9	2,205,000	819,289	37.2%	13.3
KANSAS	1,818,000	488,386	26.9%	1,865,000	424,984	22.8%	-4.1	1,906,000	328,174	17.2%	-9.6	1,939,000	386,970	20.0%	-6.9	1,972,000	470,031	23.8%	-3.0
KENTUCKY	2,793,000	721,747	25.8%	2,909,000	507,431	17.4%	-8.4	3,013,000	561,752	18.6%	-7.2	3,085,000	602,085	19.5%	-6.3	3,158,000	761,209	24.1%	-1.7
LOUISIANA	3,017,000	284,910	9.4%	3,117,000	315,919	10.1%	0.7	3,207,000	359,668	11.2%	1.8	3,278,000	609,181	18.6%	9.1	3,349,000	636,802	19.0%	9.6
MAINE	920,000	363,520	39.5%	942,000	379,184	40.3%	0.7	965,000	422,606	43.8%	4.3	1,010,000	418,380	41.4%	1.9	1,054,000	431,903	41.0%	1.5
MARYLAND	3,524,000	955,952	27.1%	3,621,000	876,658	24.2%	-2.9	3,723,000	1,060,857	28.5%	1.4	3,906,000	1,310,784	33.6%	6.4	4,090,000	1,593,735	39.0%	11.8
MASSACHUSETTS	4,416,000	1,480,570	33.5%	4,446,000	1,585,374	35.7%	2.1	4,479,000	1,967,942	43.9%	10.4	4,556,000	1,227,799	26.9%	-6.6	4,635,000	2,245,778	48.5%	14.9
MICHIGAN	6,807,000	1,913,175	28.1%	6,972,000	1,945,116	27.9%	-0.2	7,131,000	2,177,678	30.5%	2.4	7,323,000	2,242,435	30.6%	2.5	7,517,000	2,516,640	33.5%	5.4
MINNESOTA	3,252,000	1,178,072	36.2%	3,390,000	1,179,926	34.8%	-1.4	3,525,000	1,234,204	35.0%	-1.2	3,685,000	1,399,629	38.0%	1.8	3,847,000	1,612,480	41.9%	5.7
MISSISSIPPI	1,881,000	669,582	35.6%	1,974,000	397,410	20.1%	-15.5	2,056,000	495,687	24.1%	-11.5	2,107,000	334,505	15.9%	-19.7	2,158,000	731,805	33.9%	-1.7
MISSOURI	3,858,000	1,269,486	32.9%	3,989,000	1,116,201	28.0%	-4.9	4,110,000	1,136,020	27.6%	-5.3	4,227,000	1,192,674	28.2%	-4.7	4,345,000	1,413,016	32.5%	-0.4
MONTANA	598,000	203,711	34.1%	635,000	174,516	27.5%	-6.6	671,000	189,971	28.3%	-5.8	703,000	145,606	20.7%	-13.4	736,000	155,930	21.2%	-12.9
NEBRASKA	1,160,000	283,278	24.4%	1,193,000	204,432	17.1%	-7.3	1,221,000	178,071	14.6%	-9.8	1,233,000	230,697	18.7%	-5.7	1,244,000	264,885	21.3%	-3.1
NEVADA	982,000	245,477	25.0%	1,168,000	172,823	14.8%	-10.2	1,339,000	224,848	16.8%	-8.2	1,500,000	333,912	22.3%	-2.7	1,664,000	455,963	27.4%	2.4
NEW HAMPSHIRE	838,000	265,906	31.7%	873,000	221,329	25.4%	-6.4	910,000	238,754	26.2%	-5.5	968,000	242,501	25.1%	-6.7	1,025,000	364,767	35.6%	3.9
NEW JERSEY	5,543,000	1,354,915	24.4%	5,599,000	1,351,762	24.1%	-0.3	5,659,000	1,532,240	27.1%	2.6	5,787,000	1,721,392	29.7%	5.3	5,918,000	1,911,827	32.3%	7.9
NEW MEXICO	1,084,000	272,607	25.1%	1,165,000	271,144	23.3%	-1.9	1,238,000	299,841	24.2%	-0.9	1,296,000	384,921	29.7%	4.6	1,354,000	457,135	33.8%	8.6
NEW YORK	12,410,000	3,059,738	24.7%	12,447,000	3,040,840	24.4%	-0.2	12,474,000	3,189,626	25.6%	0.9	12,563,000	3,681,789	29.3%	4.7	12,659,000	4,279,747	33.8%	9.2
NORTH CAROLINA	5,199,000	1,284,720	24.7%	5,542,000	1,135,731	20.5%	-4.2	5,862,000	1,193,600	20.4%	-4.3	6,161,000	1,669,864	27.1%	2.4	6,464,000	2,293,971	35.5%	10.8
NORTH DAKOTA	464,000	169,273	36.5%	470,000	144,833	30.8%	-5.7	476,000	151,173	31.8%	-4.7	481,000	185,130	38.5%	2.0	485,000	194,577	40.1%	3.6
OHIO	8,053,000	2,198,039	27.3%	8,201,000	2,031,028	24.8%	-2.5	8,337,000	2,067,441	24.8%	-2.5	8,458,000	2,556,462	30.2%	2.9	8,579,000	2,746,283	32.0%	4.7
OKLAHOMA	2,335,000	764,249	32.7%	2,420,000	430,480	17.8%	-14.9	2,491,000	336,955	13.5%	-19.2	2,528,000	389,029	15.4%	-17.3	2,566,000	503,614	19.6%	-13.1
OREGON	2,150,000	824,796	38.4%	2,297,000	724,496	31.5%	-6.8	2,428,000	790,365	32.6%	-5.8	2,528,000	951,491	37.6%	-0.7	2,628,000	1,036,171	39.4%	1.1
PENNSYLVANIA	9,007,000	2,230,574	24.8%	9,085,000	2,222,863	24.5%	-0.3	9,166,000	2,279,227	24.9%	0.1	9,318,000	2,478,239	26.6%	1.8	9,471,000	3,209,168	33.9%	9.1
RHODE ISLAND	737,000	192,542	26.1%	742,000	240,608	32.4%	6.3	749,000	247,247	33.0%	6.9	771,000	279,315	36.2%	10.1	794,000	303,670	38.2%	12.1
SOUTH CAROLINA	2,652,000	505,887	19.1%	2,810,000	345,010	12.3%	-6.8	2,960,000	523,144	17.7%	-1.4	3,102,000	486,479	15.7%	-3.4	3,244,000	919,529	28.3%	9.3
SOUTH DAKOTA	508,000	230,070	45.3%	529,000	119,547	22.6%	-22.7	547,000	78,321	14.3%	-31.0	562,000	207,837	37.0%	-8.3	576,000	256,041	44.5%	-0.8
TENNESSEE	3,790,000	882,973	23.3%	4,018,000	856,487	21.3%	-2.0	4,224,000	819,100	19.4%	-3.9	4,378,000	1,031,959	23.6%	0.3	4,534,000	1,193,758	26.3%	3.0

United States House of Representatives General Elections (continued)

Democratic Turnout for Election Years 1992–2008 (continued)

State	1992 Voting-age population	Turnout	%	1996 Voting-age population	Turnout	%	Difference from 1992	2000 Voting-age population	Turnout	%	Difference from 1992	2004 Voting-age population	Turnout	%	Difference from 1992	2008 Voting-age population	Turnout	%	Difference from 1992
TEXAS	11,852,000	2,806,044	23.7%	12,650,000	2,322,729	18.4%	-5.3	13,404,000	2,799,051	20.9%	-2.8	14,189,000	2,683,968	18.9%	-4.8	14,988,000	2,972,888	19.8%	-3.8
UTAH	1,166,000	331,479	28.4%	1,309,000	264,327	20.2%	-8.2	1,435,000	304,797	21.2%	-7.2	1,511,000	361,628	23.9%	-4.5	1,588,000	393,761	24.8%	-3.6
VERMONT	424,000	22,279	5.3%	440,000	23,830	5.4%	0.2	456,000	14,918	3.3%	-2.0	477,000	21,684	4.5%	-0.7	499,000	248,203	49.7%	44.5
VIRGINIA	4,669,000	1,148,570	24.6%	4,880,000	1,027,020	21.0%	-3.6	5,086,000	1,060,484	20.9%	-3.7	5,339,000	1,023,187	19.2%	-5.4	5,595,000	1,852,690	33.1%	8.5
WASHINGTON	3,635,000	1,230,005	34.0%	3,885,000	1,129,609	29.1%	-4.9	4,114,000	1,245,872	30.3%	-3.7	4,313,000	1,608,751	37.3%	3.3	4,516,000	1,725,316	38.2%	4.2
WEST VIRGINIA	1,359,000	439,191	32.3%	1,381,000	458,435	33.2%	0.9	1,400,000	420,784	30.1%	-2.3	1,415,000	410,306	29.6%	-2.7	1,430,000	432,722	30.3%	-2.1
WISCONSIN	3,649,000	1,153,862	31.6%	3,788,000	1,012,327	26.7%	-4.9	3,919,000	1,187,866	30.3%	-1.3	4,061,000	1,368,537	33.7%	2.1	4,203,000	1,383,536	32.9%	1.3
WYOMING	327,000	77,418	23.7%	345,000	85,724	24.8%	1.2	362,000	60,638	16.8%	-6.9	376,000	99,989	26.6%	2.9	390,000	106,758	27.4%	3.7
Total	179,675,000	48,846,568	27.2%	187,012,000	43,680,193	23.4%	-3.8	193,919,000	46,608,240	24.0%	-3.2	201,392,000	52,339,515	26.0%	-1.2	208,965,000	65,533,826	31.4%	4.2

Other Turnout for Election Years 1992–2008

State	1992 Voting-age population	Turnout	%	1996 Voting-age population	Turnout	%	Difference from 1992*	2000 Voting-age population	Turnout	%	Difference from 1992	2004 Voting-age population	Turnout	%	Difference from 1992	2008 Voting-age population	Turnout	%	Difference from 1992
ALABAMA	3,048,000	63,785	2.1%	3,174,000	27,133	0.9%	-1.2	3,284,000	104,105	3.2%	1.1	3,343,000	4,677	0.1%	-2.0	3,402,000	15,998	0.5%	-1.6
ALASKA	383,000	24,889	6.5%	405,000	9,752	2.4%	-4.1	425,000	38,159	9.0%	2.5	453,000	19,706	4.4%	-2.1	480,000	15,479	3.2%	-3.3
ARIZONA	2,778,000	86,557	3.1%	3,114,000	34,184	1.1%	-2.0	3,437,000	53,092	1.5%	-1.6	3,800,000	146,316	3.9%	0.7	4,166,000	78,582	1.9%	-1.2
ARKANSAS	1,782,000	6,424	0.4%	1,876,000	11,779	0.6%	0.3	1,959,000	253	0.0%	-0.3	2,015,000	7,261	0.4%	0.0	2,073,000	211,550	10.2%	9.8
CALIFORNIA	18,781,000	722,945	3.8%	19,460,000	483,059	2.5%	-1.4	20,154,000	584,207	2.9%	-1.0	21,306,000	369,234	1.7%	-2.1	22,475,000	383,718	1.7%	-2.1
COLORADO	2,541,000	30,064	1.2%	2,791,000	31,911	1.1%	0.0	3,007,000	159,186	5.3%	4.1	3,118,000	51,893	1.7%	0.5	3,233,000	33,287	1.0%	-0.2
CONNECTICUT	2,414,000	91,584	3.8%	2,408,000	23,747	1.0%	-2.8	2,408,000	23,564	1.0%	-2.8	2,466,000	13,057	0.5%	-3.3	2,525,000	110,969	4.4%	0.6
DELAWARE	515,000	5,694	1.1%	544,000	8,007	1.5%	0.4	571,000	4,841	0.8%	-0.3	603,000	4,351	0.7%	-0.4	634,000	3,586	0.6%	-0.5
DISTRICT OF COLUMBIA																			
FLORIDA	9,754,000	147,423	1.5%	10,487,000	15,841	0.2%	-1.4	11,205,000	183,560	1.6%	0.1	12,124,000	95,874	0.8%	-0.7	13,051,000	194,174	1.5%	0.0
GEORGIA	4,938,000	13	0.0%	5,345,000	3	0.0%	0.0	5,718,000	20	0.0%	0.0					6,344,000	203	0.0%	0.0
HAWAII	786,000	16,000	2.0%	817,000	21,477	2.6%	0.6	847,000	8,156	1.0%	-1.1	885,000	6,243	0.7%	-1.3	923,000	15,322	1.7%	-0.4
IDAHO	741,000	19,546	2.6%	824,000	10,512	1.3%	-1.4	900,000	17,835	2.0%	-0.7								
ILLINOIS	8,124,000	56,539	0.7%	8,269,000	47,564	0.6%	-0.1	8,393,000	32,372	0.4%	-0.3	8,466,000	41,716	0.5%	-0.2	8,546,000	110,843	1.3%	0.6
INDIANA	4,146,000	14,773	0.4%	4,292,000	42,031	1.0%	0.6	4,421,000	63,023	1.4%	1.1	4,509,000	35,470	0.8%	0.4	4,599,000	118,536	2.6%	2.2
IOWA	2,067,000	20,097	1.0%	2,109,000	17,984	0.9%	-0.1	2,147,000	26,970	1.3%	0.3	2,175,000	10,888	0.5%	-0.5	2,205,000	71,835	3.3%	2.3
KANSAS	1,818,000	44,817	2.5%	1,865,000	32,748	1.8%	-0.7	1,906,000	47,925	2.5%	0.0	1,939,000	45,619	2.4%	-0.1	1,972,000	48,266	2.4%	0.0
KENTUCKY	2,793,000	998	0.0%	2,909,000	11	0.0%	0.0	3,013,000	48,742	1.6%	1.6	3,085,000	15,578	0.5%	0.5	3,158,000	33,444	1.1%	1.0
LOUISIANA								3,207,000	95,388	3.0%						3,349,000	47,044	1.4%	-1.6
MAINE	920,000	27,803	3.0%	942,000	9,406	1.0%	-2.0	965,000	12,356	1.3%	-1.7	1,010,000	8,586	0.9%	-2.2				

United States House of Representatives General Elections (continued)

United States House of Representatives General Elections *(continued)*

Other Turnout for Election Years 1992–2008 *(continued)*

State	1992 Voting-age population	1992 Turnout	1992 %	1996 Voting-age population	1996 Turnout	1996 %	1996 Difference from 1992	2000 Voting-age population	2000 Turnout	2000 %	2000 Difference from 1992	2004 Voting-age population	2004 Turnout	2004 %	2004 Difference from 1992	2008 Voting-age population	2008 Turnout	2008 %	2008 Difference from 1992
MARYLAND	3,524,000	8,766	0.2%	3,621,000	424	0.0%	-0.2	3,723,000	9,601	0.3%	0.0	3,906,000	46,412	1.2%	0.9	4,090,000	58,165	1.4%	1.2
MASSACHUSETTS	4,416,000	239,449	5.4%	4,446,000	43,249	1.0%	-4.4	4,479,000	35,935	0.8%	-4.6	4,556,000	74,167	1.6%	-3.8	4,635,000	40,875	0.9%	-4.5
MICHIGAN	6,807,000	115,987	1.7%	6,972,000	75,716	1.1%	-0.6	7,131,000	105,067	1.5%	-0.2	7,323,000	100,028	1.4%	-0.3	7,517,000	171,742	2.3%	0.6
MINNESOTA	3,252,000	165,527	5.1%	3,390,000	66,446	2.0%	-3.1	3,525,000	136,163	3.9%	-1.2	3,685,000	85,928	2.3%	-2.8	3,847,000	121,119	3.1%	-1.9
MISSISSIPPI	1,881,000	22,585	1.2%	1,974,000	18,753	1.0%	-0.3	2,056,000	21,969	1.1%	-0.1	2,107,000	123,009	5.8%	4.6	2,158,000	5,612	0.3%	-0.9
MISSOURI	3,858,000	42,806	1.1%	3,989,000	166,453	4.2%	3.1	4,110,000	54,044	1.3%	0.2	4,227,000	44,582	1.1%	-0.1	4,345,000	95,450	2.2%	1.1
MONTANA	598,000	10,454	1.7%	635,000	17,935	2.8%	1.1	671,000	9,132	1.4%	-0.4	703,000	12,548	1.8%	0.0	736,000	16,500	2.2%	0.5
NEBRASKA	1,160,000	159	0.0%	1,193,000	7,145	0.6%	0.6	1,221,000	18,487	1.5%	1.5	1,233,000	19,160	1.6%	1.5				
NEVADA	982,000	32,680	3.3%	1,168,000	28,180	2.4%	-0.9	1,339,000	29,472	2.2%	-1.1	1,500,000	36,810	2.5%	-0.9	1,664,000	67,176	4.0%	0.7
NEW HAMPSHIRE	838,000	18,071	2.2%	873,000	23,054	2.6%	0.5	910,000	14,473	1.6%	-0.6	968,000	12,036	1.2%	-0.9	1,025,000	15,648	1.5%	-0.6
NEW JERSEY	5,543,000	133,679	2.4%	5,599,000	72,497	1.3%	-1.1	5,659,000	71,823	1.3%	-1.1	5,787,000	48,419	0.8%	-1.6	5,918,000	63,685	1.1%	-1.3
NEW MEXICO	1,084,000	5,161	0.5%	1,165,000	16,250	1.4%	0.9	1,238,000	13,656	1.1%	0.6					1,354,000	36,348	2.7%	2.2
NEW YORK	12,410,000	187,495	1.5%	12,447,000	152,660	1.2%	-0.3	12,474,000	168,584	1.4%	-0.2	12,563,000	92,284	0.7%	-0.8	12,659,000	69,659	0.6%	-1.0
NORTH CAROLINA	5,199,000	46,492	0.9%	5,542,000	38,303	0.7%	-0.2	5,862,000	71,394	1.2%	0.3	6,161,000	76	0.0%	-0.9	6,464,000	19,605	0.3%	-0.6
NORTH DAKOTA	464,000	11,183	2.4%	470,000	4,493	1.0%	-1.5	476,000	7,234	1.5%	-0.9								
OHIO	8,053,000	224,815	2.8%	8,201,000	165,393	2.0%	-0.8	8,337,000	247,311	3.0%	0.2	8,458,000	18,773	0.2%	-2.6	8,579,000	130,601	1.5%	-1.3
OKLAHOMA	2,335,000	7,314	0.3%	2,420,000	26,666	1.1%	0.8	2,491,000	48,740	2.0%	1.6	2,528,000	110,548	4.4%	4.1	2,566,000	30,783	1.2%	0.9
OREGON	2,150,000	12,857	0.6%	2,297,000	53,040	2.3%	1.7	2,428,000	42,539	1.8%	1.2	2,528,000	59,058	2.3%	1.7	2,628,000	210,418	8.0%	7.4
PENNSYLVANIA	9,007,000	88,706	1.0%	9,085,000	56,032	0.6%	-0.4	9,166,000	49,726	0.5%	-0.4	9,318,000	107,819	1.2%	0.2	9,471,000	57,931	0.6%	-0.4
RHODE ISLAND	737,000	19,980	2.7%	742,000	11,485	1.5%	-1.2	749,000	47,161	6.3%	3.6	771,000	9,902	1.3%	-1.4	794,000	15,108	1.9%	-0.8
SOUTH CAROLINA	2,652,000	28,404	1.1%	2,810,000	29,811	1.1%	0.0	2,960,000	68,369	2.3%	1.2	3,102,000	39,471	1.3%	0.2	3,244,000	14,658	0.5%	-0.6
SOUTH DAKOTA	508,000	13,457	2.6%	529,000	17,263	3.3%	0.6	547,000	5,357	1.0%	-1.7	562,000	2,808	0.5%	-2.1				
TENNESSEE	3,790,000	105,011	2.8%	4,018,000	38,510	1.0%	-1.8	4,224,000	43,294	1.0%	-1.7	4,378,000	25,958	0.6%	-2.2	4,534,000	128,307	2.8%	0.1
TEXAS	11,852,000	130,455	1.1%	12,650,000	111,739	0.9%	-0.2	13,404,000	254,301	1.9%	0.8	14,189,000	217,101	1.5%	0.4	14,988,000	346,238	2.3%	1.2
UTAH	1,166,000	33,442	2.9%	1,309,000	13,179	1.0%	-1.9	1,435,000	27,309	1.9%	-1.0	1,511,000	26,826	1.8%	-1.1	1,588,000	39,161	2.5%	-0.4
VERMONT	424,000	172,446	40.7%	440,000	147,855	33.6%	-7.1	456,000	216,471	47.5%	6.8	477,000	209,053	43.8%	3.2	499,000	49,948	10.0%	-30.7
VIRGINIA	4,669,000	76,828	1.6%	4,880,000	54,890	1.1%	-0.5	5,086,000	229,246	4.5%	2.9	5,339,000	163,398	3.1%	1.4	5,595,000	51,880	0.9%	-0.7
WASHINGTON	3,635,000	74,436	2.0%	3,885,000	24,099	0.6%	-1.4	4,114,000	138,662	3.4%	1.3	4,313,000	25,751	0.6%	-1.5				
WEST VIRGINIA	1,359,000	401	0.0%					1,400,000	50,319	3.6%	3.6	1,415,000	3,218	0.2%	0.2				
WISCONSIN	3,649,000	23,241	0.6%	3,788,000	17,181	0.5%	-0.2	3,919,000	7,001	0.2%	-0.5	4,061,000	72,257	1.8%	1.1	4,203,000	116,651	2.8%	2.1
WYOMING	327,000	5,725	1.8%	345,000	8,255	2.4%	0.6	362,000	9,826	2.7%	1.0	376,000	6,938	1.8%	0.1	390,000	18,031	4.6%	2.9
Total	176,658,000	3,437,963	1.9%	182,514,000	2,334,105	1.3%	-0.7	193,919,000	3,756,420	1.9%	0.0	189,342,000	2,670,807	1.4%	-0.5	198,626,000	3,484,135	1.8%	-0.2

*Percentage point difference between turnout in current year and initial year listed in chart. If data do not appear for a state in the initial year listed, the difference is calculated from the first year in which data do appear for that state.

UNITED STATES PRESIDENTIAL PRIMARY ELECTIONS

Election Years 1992–2008

State*	1992 Voting-age population	Turnout	%	1996 Voting-age population	Turnout	%	Difference from 1992**	2000 Voting-age population	Turnout	%	Difference from 1992	2004 Voting-age population	Turnout	%	Difference from 1992	2008 Voting-age population	Turnout	%	Difference from 1992
ALABAMA	3,029,000	616,020	20.3%	3,156,000	513,971	16.3%	-4.1	3,276,000	481,606	14.7%	-5.6	3,335,000	420,061	12.6%	-7.7	3,394,000	1,088,781	32.1%	11.7
ALASKA																			
ARIZONA								3,384,000	409,337	12.1%						4,117,000	996,670	24.2%	12.1
ARKANSAS	1,769,000	554,758	31.4%	1,861,000	358,479	19.3%	-12.1	1,950,000	291,473	14.9%	-16.4	2,008,000	305,211	15.2%	-16.2	2,065,000	544,954	26.4%	-5.0
CALIFORNIA	18,681,000	5,058,878	27.1%	19,360,000	5,042,487	26.0%	-1.0	19,983,000	7,425,986	37.2%	10.1	21,152,000	5,358,621	25.3%	-1.7	22,319,000	8,104,947	36.3%	9.2
COLORADO	2,505,000	435,333	17.4%	2,754,000	302,406	11.0%	-6.4	2,990,000	269,385	9.0%	-8.4								
CONNECTICUT	2,416,000	272,592	11.3%					2,399,000	359,479	15.0%	3.7					2,518,000	506,143	20.1%	8.8
DELAWARE				539,000	43,513	8.1%		567,000	41,201	7.3%	-0.8					630,000	146,613	23.3%	15.2
DISTRICT OF COLUMBIA	444,000	67,139	15.1%	427,000	23,946	5.6%	-9.5	410,000	21,850	5.3%	-9.8					371,000	130,726	35.2%	20.1
FLORIDA	9,647,000	2,017,320	20.9%					11,070,000	1,251,233	11.3%	-9.6					12,923,000	3,699,418	28.6%	7.7
GEORGIA	4,878,000	908,621	18.6%	5,285,000	654,170	12.4%	-6.2	5,672,000	927,619	16.4%	-2.3	5,987,000	788,112	13.2%	-5.5	6,302,000	2,024,392	32.1%	13.5
HAWAII																			
IDAHO	729,000	170,626	23.4%	812,000	158,943	19.6%	-3.8	890,000	194,134	21.8%	-1.6	957,000	155,270	16.2%	-7.2	1,024,000	167,710	16.4%	-7.0
ILLINOIS	8,103,000	2,335,270	28.8%	8,248,000	1,620,768	19.7%	-9.2	8,381,000	1,546,505	18.5%	-10.4					8,540,000	2,932,211	34.3%	5.5
INDIANA	4,126,000	944,464	22.9%	4,270,000	807,549	18.9%	-4.0	4,408,000	699,836	15.9%	-7.0	4,497,000	786,739	17.5%	-5.4	4,586,000	1,690,987	36.9%	14.0
IOWA																			
KANSAS	1,812,000	373,447	20.6%																
KENTUCKY	2,777,000	471,697	17.0%	2,892,000	379,858	13.1%	-3.9	3,002,000	311,602	10.4%	-6.6	3,075,000	347,295	11.3%	-5.7	3,147,000	898,921	28.6%	11.6
LOUISIANA	3,003,000	519,506	17.3%	3,103,000	232,490	7.5%	-9.8	3,197,000	260,463	8.1%	-9.2	3,267,000	233,663	7.2%	-10.1	3,338,000	545,515	16.3%	-1.0
MAINE				939,000	94,307	10.0%		959,000	160,903	16.8%	6.7								
MARYLAND	3,510,000	807,264	23.0%	3,607,000	548,075	15.2%	-7.8	3,695,000	883,496	23.9%	0.9	3,880,000	624,892	16.1%	-6.9	4,064,000	1,199,163	29.5%	6.5
MASSACHUSETTS	4,412,000	1,063,971	24.1%	4,442,000	441,173	9.9%	-14.2	4,467,000	1,055,689	23.6%	-0.5	4,547,000	686,574	15.1%	-9.0	4,625,000	1,765,761	38.2%	14.1
MICHIGAN	6,783,000	1,035,105	15.3%	6,948,000	666,911	9.6%	-5.7									7,490,000	1,465,625	19.6%	4.3
MINNESOTA	3,232,000	336,926	10.4%																
MISSISSIPPI	1,867,000	346,065	18.5%	1,961,000	244,839	12.5%	-6.1	2,048,000	203,581	9.9%	-8.6					2,151,000	577,315	26.8%	8.3
MISSOURI								4,094,000	740,852	18.1%		4,210,000	543,392	12.9%	-5.2	4,328,000	1,413,219	32.7%	14.6
MONTANA	592,000	208,446	35.2%	630,000	210,139	33.4%	-1.9	666,000	201,538	30.3%	-4.9	698,000	206,290	29.6%	-5.7	731,000	278,151	38.1%	2.8
NEBRASKA	1,156,000	342,685	29.6%	1,189,000	264,767	22.3%	-7.4	1,219,000	291,029	23.9%	-5.8	1,231,000	228,412	18.6%	-11.1	1,243,000	231,335	18.6%	-11.0
NEVADA																			
NEW HAMPSHIRE	833,000	345,371	41.5%	869,000	288,445	33.2%	-8.3	902,000	392,855	43.6%	2.1	960,000	283,125	29.5%	-12.0	1,016,000	527,386	51.9%	10.4
NEW JERSEY	5,534,000	702,896	12.7%	5,591,000	485,552	8.7%	-4.0	5,640,000	619,082	11.0%	-1.7	5,771,000	356,556	6.2%	-6.5	5,904,000	1,707,400	28.9%	16.2
NEW MEXICO	1,072,000	268,410	25.0%	1,153,000	189,490	16.4%	-8.6	1,229,000	207,510	16.9%	-8.2	1,288,000	49,788	3.9%	-21.2				
NEW YORK								12,460,000	1,625,596	13.0%						12,653,000	2,590,221	20.5%	7.4

United States Presidential Primary Elections (continued)

United States Presidential Primary Elections (continued)

Election Years 1992–2008 (continued)

State	1992 Voting-age population	Turnout	%	1996 Voting-age population	Turnout	%	Difference from 1992	2000 Voting-age population	Turnout	%	Difference from 1992	2004 Voting-age population	Turnout	%	Difference from 1992	2008 Voting-age population	Turnout	%	Difference from 1992
NORTH CAROLINA	5,149,000	975,446	18.9%	5,492,000	856,374	15.6%	-3.4	5,817,000	867,439	14.9%	-4.0					6,423,000	2,098,309	32.7%	13.7
NORTH DAKOTA	463,000	80,594	17.4%	469,000	65,318	13.9%	-3.5												
OHIO	8,031,000	1,902,788	23.7%	8,180,000	1,736,155	21.2%	-2.5	8,319,000	2,336,594	28.1%	4.4	8,441,000	1,998,986	23.7%	0.0	8,562,000	3,450,638	40.3%	16.6
OKLAHOMA	2,322,000	633,850	27.3%	2,407,000	631,146	26.2%	-1.1	2,485,000	259,659	10.4%	-16.8	2,523,000	368,583	14.6%	-12.7	2,561,000	752,261	29.4%	2.1
OREGON	2,128,000	658,491	30.9%	2,275,000	776,692	34.1%	3.2	2,414,000	704,425	29.2%	-1.8	2,515,000	678,050	27.0%	-4.0	2,615,000	994,975	38.0%	7.1
PENNSYLVANIA	8,996,000	2,274,272	25.3%	9,073,000	1,372,273	15.1%	-10.2	9,144,000	1,347,235	14.7%	-10.5	9,296,000	1,645,524	17.7%	-7.6	9,450,000	3,148,856	33.3%	8.0
RHODE ISLAND	736,000	66,345	9.0%	741,000	23,179	3.1%	-5.9	746,000	82,964	11.1%	2.1	768,000	38,294	5.0%	-4.0	790,000	213,435	27.0%	18.0
SOUTH CAROLINA	2,629,000	265,254	10.1%													3,224,000	977,650	30.3%	20.2
SOUTH DAKOTA	505,000	104,174	20.6%													573,000	158,761	27.7%	7.1
TENNESSEE	3,757,000	564,135	15.0%	3,984,000	426,831	10.7%	-4.3	4,201,000	464,015	11.0%	-4.0	4,357,000	468,446	10.8%	-4.3	4,512,000	1,178,399	26.1%	11.1
TEXAS	11,736,000	2,280,121	19.4%	12,534,000	1,941,088	15.5%	-3.9	13,287,000	1,913,647	14.4%	-5.0	14,086,000	1,526,846	10.8%	-8.6	14,886,000	4,237,707	28.5%	9.0
UTAH								1,423,000	106,740	7.5%									
VERMONT				437,000	89,781	20.5%		452,000	130,638	28.9%	8.4	474,000	110,789	23.4%	2.8	495,000	194,803	39.4%	18.8
VIRGINIA																5,560,000	1,475,455	26.5%	
WASHINGTON	3,597,000	277,636	7.7%	3,848,000	664,249	17.3%	9.5	4,084,000	1,309,365	32.1%	24.3					4,489,000	1,221,313	27.2%	19.5
WEST VIRGINIA	1,356,000	431,023	31.8%	1,378,000	424,575	30.8%	-1.0	1,398,000	362,714	25.9%	-5.8	1,413,000	363,948	25.8%	-6.0	1,428,000	478,866	33.5%	1.7
WISCONSIN	3,629,000	1,254,844	34.6%	3,768,000	932,743	24.8%	-9.8	3,899,000	866,965	22.2%	-12.3	4,041,000	989,765	24.5%	-10.1	4,183,000	1,517,767	36.3%	1.7
WYOMING																			
Total	147,944,000	31,971,783	21.6%	134,622,000	23,512,682	17.5%	-4.1	166,627,000	31,626,240	19.0%	-2.6	114,777,000	19,563,240	17.0%	-4.6	189,230,000	57,332,759	30.3%	8.7

*Overall primary turnout reflects only states with primaries in both parties. To find single party primary results, see partisan primary charts.

**Percentage point difference between turnout in current year and initial year listed in chart. If data do not appear for a state in the initial year listed, the difference is calculated from the first year in which data do appear for that state.

UNITED STATES PRESIDENTIAL PRIMARY ELECTIONS

Republican Turnout for Election Years 1992–2008

State	1992 Voting-age population	Turnout	%	1996 Voting-age population	Turnout	%	Difference from 1992*	2000 Voting-age population	Turnout	%	Difference from 1992	2004 Voting-age population	Turnout	%	Difference from 1992	2008 Voting-age population	Turnout	%	Difference from 1992
ALABAMA	3,029,000	165,121	5.5%	3,156,000	211,933	6.7%	1.3	3,276,000	203,079	6.2%	0.7	3,335,000	201,487	6.0%	0.6	3,394,000	552,155	16.3%	10.8
ALASKA																			
ARIZONA				3,065,000	353,839	11.5%		3,384,000	322,430	9.5%	-2.0					4,117,000	541,035	13.1%	1.6
ARKANSAS	1,769,000	52,141	2.9%	1,861,000	42,976	2.3%	-0.6	1,950,000	44,573	2.3%	-0.7	2,008,000	38,363	1.9%	-1.0	2,065,000	229,882	11.1%	8.2
CALIFORNIA	18,681,000	2,150,464	11.5%	19,360,000	2,452,312	12.7%	1.1	19,983,000	4,153,963	20.8%	9.2	21,152,000	2,216,351	10.5%	-1.1	22,319,000	2,932,801	13.1%	1.6
COLORADO	2,505,000	195,690	7.8%	2,754,000	247,770	9.0%	1.2	2,990,000	180,650	6.0%	-1.8								
CONNECTICUT	2,416,000	99,473	4.1%	2,408,000	130,418	5.4%	1.3	2,399,000	179,175	7.5%	3.4					2,518,000	151,604	6.0%	1.9
DELAWARE				539,000	32,773	6.1%		567,000	30,060	5.3%	-0.8					630,000	50,239	8.0%	1.9
DISTRICT OF COLUMBIA	444,000	5,235	1.2%	427,000	2,987	0.7%	-0.5	410,000	2,433	0.6%	-0.6					371,000	6,211	1.7%	0.5
FLORIDA	9,647,000	893,463	9.3%	10,380,000	898,070	8.7%	-0.6	11,070,000	699,317	6.3%	-2.9					12,923,000	1,949,498	15.1%	5.8
GEORGIA	4,878,000	453,990	9.3%	5,285,000	559,067	10.6%	1.3	5,672,000	643,188	11.3%	2.0	5,987,000	161,374	2.7%	-6.6	6,302,000	963,541	15.3%	6.0
HAWAII																			
IDAHO	729,000	115,502	15.8%	812,000	118,715	14.6%	-1.2	890,000	158,446	17.8%	2.0	957,000	123,793	12.9%	-2.9	1,024,000	124,908	12.2%	-3.6
ILLINOIS	8,103,000	831,140	10.3%	8,248,000	818,364	9.9%	-0.3	8,381,000	736,857	8.8%	-1.5					8,540,000	899,422	10.5%	0.3
INDIANA	4,126,000	467,615	11.3%	4,270,000	510,653	12.0%	0.6	4,408,000	406,664	9.2%	-2.1	4,497,000	469,528	10.4%	-0.9	4,586,000	412,673	9.0%	-2.3
IOWA																			
KANSAS	1,812,000	213,196	11.8%																
KENTUCKY	2,777,000	101,119	3.6%	2,892,000	103,839	3.6%	-0.1	3,002,000	91,323	3.0%	-0.6	3,075,000	117,379	3.8%	0.2	3,147,000	197,153	6.3%	2.6
LOUISIANA	3,003,000	135,109	4.5%	3,103,000	77,789	2.5%	-2.0	3,197,000	102,912	3.2%	-1.3	3,267,000	72,010	2.2%	-2.3	3,338,000	161,169	4.8%	0.3
MAINE				939,000	67,280	7.2%		959,000	96,624	10.1%	2.9								
MARYLAND	3,510,000	240,021	6.8%	3,607,000	254,246	7.0%	0.2	3,695,000	376,034	10.2%	3.3	3,880,000	151,943	3.9%	-2.9	4,064,000	320,989	7.9%	1.1
MASSACHUSETTS	4,412,000	269,701	6.1%	4,442,000	284,833	6.4%	0.3	4,467,000	495,231	11.1%	5.0	4,547,000	69,278	1.5%	-4.6	4,625,000	501,997	10.9%	4.7
MICHIGAN	6,783,000	449,133	6.6%	6,948,000	524,161	7.5%	0.9	7,103,000	1,392,023	19.6%	13.0					7,490,000	869,169	11.6%	5.0
MINNESOTA	3,232,000	132,756	4.1%																
MISSISSIPPI	1,867,000	154,708	8.3%	1,961,000	151,925	7.7%	-0.5	2,048,000	114,979	5.6%	-2.7					2,151,000	143,286	6.7%	-1.6
MISSOURI								4,094,000	475,363	11.6%		4,210,000	123,086	2.9%	-8.7	4,328,000	588,427	13.6%	2.0
MONTANA	592,000	90,975	15.4%	630,000	117,746	18.7%	3.3	666,000	113,671	17.1%	1.7	698,000	112,747	16.2%	0.8	731,000	95,730	13.1%	-2.3
NEBRASKA	1,156,000	192,098	16.6%	1,189,000	170,591	14.3%	-2.3	1,219,000	185,758	15.2%	-1.4	1,231,000	136,014	11.0%	-5.6	1,243,000	136,648	11.0%	-5.6
NEVADA				1,141,000	140,637	12.3%													
NEW HAMPSHIRE	833,000	174,165	20.9%	869,000	205,903	23.7%	2.8	902,000	238,206	26.4%	5.5	960,000	63,338	6.6%	-14.3	1,016,000	236,884	23.3%	2.4
NEW JERSEY	5,534,000	310,270	5.6%	5,591,000	218,812	3.9%	-1.7	5,640,000	240,810	4.3%	-1.3	5,771,000	141,752	2.5%	-3.2	5,904,000	566,201	9.6%	4.0
NEW MEXICO	1,072,000	86,967	8.1%	1,153,000	67,841	5.9%	-2.2	1,229,000	75,230	6.1%	-2.0	1,288,000	49,165	3.8%	-4.3	1,346,000	110,939	8.2%	0.1
NEW YORK				12,441,000	1,088,324	8.7%		12,460,000	704,077	5.7%	-3.1					12,653,000	699,078	5.5%	-3.2

United States Presidential Primary Elections (continued)

United States Presidential Primary Elections (continued)

Republican Turnout for Election Years 1992–2008 (continued)

State	1972 Voting-age population	Turnout	%	1996 Voting-age population	Turnout	%	Difference from 1992	2000 Voting-age population	Turnout	%	Difference from 1992	2004 Voting-age population	Turnout	%	Difference from 1992	2008 Voting-age population	Turnout	%	Difference from 1992
NORTH CAROLINA	5,149,000	283,571	5.5%	5,492,000	284,214	5.2%	-0.3	5,817,000	322,517	5.5%	0.0					6,423,000	517,583	8.1%	2.6
NORTH DAKOTA	463,000	47,808	10.3%	469,000	63,734	13.6%	3.3												
OHIO	8,031,000	860,453	10.7%	8,180,000	959,625	11.7%	1.0	8,319,000	1,397,528	16.8%	6.1	8,441,000	777,972	9.2%	-1.5	8,562,000	1,095,917	12.8%	2.1
OKLAHOMA	2,322,000	217,721	9.4%	2,407,000	264,542	11.0%	1.6	2,485,000	124,809	5.0%	-4.4	2,523,000	66,198	2.6%	-6.8	2,561,000	335,054	13.1%	3.7
OREGON	2,128,000	304,159	14.3%	2,275,000	407,514	17.9%	3.6	2,414,000	349,831	14.5%	0.2	2,515,000	309,506	12.3%	-2.0	2,615,000	353,476	13.5%	-0.8
PENNSYLVANIA	8,996,000	1,008,777	11.2%	9,073,000	648,204	7.1%	-4.1	9,144,000	643,085	7.0%	-4.2	9,296,000	858,490	9.2%	-2.0	9,450,000	815,394	8.6%	-2.6
RHODE ISLAND	736,000	15,636	2.1%	741,000	14,427	1.9%	-0.2	746,000	36,120	4.8%	2.7	768,000	2,535	0.3%	-1.8	790,000	26,996	3.4%	1.3
SOUTH CAROLINA	2,629,000	148,840	5.7%	2,788,000	276,741	9.9%	4.3	2,939,000	573,101	19.5%	13.8					3,224,000	445,499	13.8%	8.2
SOUTH DAKOTA	505,000	44,671	8.8%	526,000	69,170	13.2%	4.3	545,000	45,386	8.3%	-0.5					573,000	60,964	10.6%	1.8
TENNESSEE	3,757,000	245,653	6.5%	3,984,000	289,043	7.3%	0.7	4,201,000	250,792	6.0%	-0.6	4,357,000	99,061	2.3%	-4.3	4,512,000	553,635	12.3%	5.7
TEXAS	11,736,000	797,146	6.8%	12,534,000	1,019,832	8.1%	1.3	13,287,000	1,126,757	8.5%	1.7	14,086,000	687,615	4.9%	-1.9	14,886,000	1,362,322	9.2%	2.4
UTAH								1,423,000	91,053	6.4%									
VERMONT				437,000	58,113	13.3%		452,000	81,355	18.0%	4.7	474,000	27,673	5.8%	-7.5	495,000	39,843	8.0%	-5.2
VIRGINIA								5,049,000	666,365	13.2%						5,560,000	489,252	8.8%	-4.4
WASHINGTON	3,597,000	129,655	3.6%	3,848,000	335,023	8.7%	5.1	4,084,000	833,658	20.4%	16.8					4,489,000	529,932	11.8%	8.2
WEST VIRGINIA	1,356,000	124,157	9.2%	1,378,000	127,454	9.2%	0.1	1,398,000	109,404	7.8%	-1.3	1,413,000	111,109	7.9%	-1.3	1,428,000	119,012	8.3%	-0.8
WISCONSIN	3,629,000	482,248	13.3%	3,768,000	578,109	15.3%	2.1	3,899,000	495,769	12.7%	-0.6	4,041,000	160,072	4.0%	-9.3	4,183,000	404,482	9.7%	-3.6
WYOMING																			
Total	147,944,000	12,696,547	8.6%	167,371,000	15,249,549	9.1%	0.5	182,263,000	19,610,606	10.8%	2.2	114,777,000	7,347,839	6.4%	-2.2	190,576,000	20,591,000	10.8%	2.2

Democratic Turnout for Election Years 1992–2008

State	1992 Voting-age population	Turnout	%	1996 Voting-age population	Turnout	%	Difference from 1992*	2000 Voting-age population	Turnout	%	Difference from 1992	2004 Voting-age population	Turnout	%	Difference from 1992	2008 Voting-age population	Turnout	%	Difference from 1992
ALABAMA	3,029,000	450,899	14.9%	3,156,000	302,038	9.6%	-5.3	3,276,000	278,527	8.5%	-6.4	3,335,000	218,574	6.6%	-8.3	3,394,000	536,626	15.8%	0.9
ALASKA																			
ARIZONA								3,384,000	86,907	2.6%		3,750,000	239,340	6.4%	3.8	4,117,000	455,635	11.1%	8.5
ARKANSAS	1,769,000	502,617	28.4%	1,861,000	315,503	17.0%	-11.5	1,950,000	246,900	12.7%	-15.8	2,008,000	266,848	13.3%	-15.1	2,065,000	314,234	15.2%	-13.2
CALIFORNIA	18,681,000	2,863,609	15.3%	19,360,000	2,523,062	13.0%	-2.3	19,983,000	3,272,023	16.4%	1.0	21,152,000	3,048,283	14.4%	-0.9	22,319,000	5,066,978	22.7%	7.4
COLORADO	2,505,000	239,643	9.6%	2,754,000	54,636	2.0%	-7.6	2,990,000	88,735	3.0%	-6.6								
CONNECTICUT	2,416,000	173,119	7.2%					2,399,000	180,304	7.5%	0.4	2,458,000	131,844	5.4%	-1.8	2,518,000	354,539	14.1%	6.9
DELAWARE				539,000	10,740	2.0%		567,000	11,141	2.0%	0.0	598,000	33,291	5.6%	3.6	630,000	96,374	15.3%	13.3
DISTRICT OF COLUMBIA	444,000	61,904	13.9%	427,000	20,959	4.9%	-9.0	410,000	19,417	4.7%	-9.2	391,000	42,516	10.9%	-3.1	371,000	123,994	33.4%	19.5
FLORIDA	9,647,000	1,123,857	11.6%					11,070,000	551,916	5.0%	-6.7	11,996,000	753,762	6.3%	-5.4	12,923,000	1,749,920	13.5%	1.9

United States Presidential Primary Elections (continued)

Democratic Turnout for Election Years 1992–2008 (continued)

State	1992 Voting-age population	1992 Turnout	1992 %	1996 Voting-age population	1996 Turnout	1996 %	1996 Difference from 1992	2000 Voting-age population	2000 Turnout	2000 %	2000 Difference from 1992	2004 Voting-age population	2004 Turnout	2004 %	2004 Difference from 1992	2008 Voting-age population	2008 Turnout	2008 %	2008 Difference from 1992
GEORGIA	4,878,000	454,631	9.3%	5,285,000	95,103	1.8%	-7.5	5,672,000	284,431	5.0%	-4.3	5,987,000	626,738	10.5%	1.1	6,302,000	1,060,851	16.8%	7.5
HAWAII																			
IDAHO	729,000	55,124	7.6%	812,000	40,228	5.0%	-2.6	890,000	35,688	4.0%	-3.6	957,000	31,485	3.3%	-4.3	1,024,000	42,802	4.2%	-3.4
ILLINOIS	8,103,000	1,504,130	18.6%	8,248,000	800,676	9.7%	-8.9	8,381,000	809,648	9.7%	-8.9	8,461,000	1,217,515	14.4%	-4.2	8,540,000	2,030,117	23.8%	5.2
INDIANA	4,128,000	470,040	11.6%	4,270,000	296,896	7.0%	-4.6	4,408,000	293,172	6.7%	-4.9	4,497,000	317,211	7.1%	-4.5	4,586,000	1,278,314	27.9%	16.3
IOWA																			
KANSAS	1,812,000	160,251	8.8%																
KENTUCKY	2,777,000	370,578	13.3%	2,892,000	276,019	9.5%	-3.8	3,002,000	220,279	7.3%	-6.0	3,075,000	229,916	7.5%	-5.9	3,147,000	701,768	22.3%	9.0
LOUISIANA	3,003,000	384,397	12.8%	3,103,000	154,701	5.0%	-7.8	3,197,000	157,551	4.9%	-7.9	3,267,000	161,653	4.9%	-7.9	3,338,000	384,346	11.5%	-1.3
MAINE				939,000	27,027	2.9%		959,000	64,279	6.7%	3.8								
MARYLAND	3,510,000	567,243	16.2%	3,607,000	293,829	8.1%	-8.0	3,695,000	507,462	13.7%	-2.4	3,880,000	472,949	12.2%	-4.0	4,064,000	878,174	21.6%	5.4
MASSACHUSETTS	4,412,000	792,885	18.0%	4,442,000	155,470	3.5%	14.5	4,467,000	560,458	12.5%	-5.4	4,547,000	617,296	13.6%	-4.4	4,625,000	1,263,764	27.3%	9.4
MICHIGAN	6,783,000	585,972	8.6%	6,948,000	142,750	2.1%	-6.6									7,490,000	594,398	7.9%	-0.7
MINNESOTA	3,232,000	204,170	6.3%																
MISSISSIPPI	1,867,000	191,357	10.2%	1,961,000	92,914	4.7%	-5.5	2,048,000	88,602	4.3%	-5.9	2,100,000	76,298	3.6%	-6.6	2,151,000	434,029	20.2%	9.9
MISSOURI								4,094,000	265,489	6.5%		4,210,000	418,339	9.9%	3.5	4,328,000	822,734	19.0%	12.5
MONTANA	592,000	117,471	19.8%	630,000	91,725	14.6%	-5.3	666,000	87,867	13.2%	-6.6	698,000	93,543	13.4%	-6.4	731,000	182,421	25.0%	5.1
NEBRASKA	1,156,000	150,587	13.0%	1,189,000	94,176	7.9%	-5.1	1,219,000	105,271	8.6%	-4.4	1,231,000	79,993	6.5%	-6.5	1,243,000	94,535	7.6%	-5.4
NEVADA																			
NEW HAMPSHIRE	833,000	167,819	20.1%	869,000	82,542	9.5%	-10.6	902,000	154,649	17.1%	-3.0	960,000	219,787	22.9%	2.7	1,016,000	290,005	28.5%	8.4
NEW JERSEY	5,534,000	392,626	7.1%	5,591,000	266,740	4.8%	-2.3	5,640,000	378,272	6.7%	-0.4	5,771,000	214,804	3.7%	-3.4	5,904,000	1,141,199	19.3%	12.2
NEW MEXICO	1,072,000	181,443	16.9%	1,153,000	120,267	10.4%	-6.5	1,229,000	132,280	10.8%	-6.2								
NEW YORK	12,405,000	1,007,726	8.1%					12,460,000	921,519	7.4%	-0.7	12,557,000	720,179	5.7%	-2.4	12,653,000	1,891,143	14.9%	6.8
NORTH CAROLINA	5,149,000	691,875	13.4%	5,492,000	572,160	10.4%	-3.0	5,817,000	544,922	9.4%	-4.1					6,423,000	1,580,726	24.6%	11.2
NORTH DAKOTA	463,000	32,786	7.1%	469,000	1,584	0.3%	-6.7												
OHIO	8,031,000	1,042,335	13.0%	8,180,000	776,530	9.5%	-3.5	8,319,000	939,066	11.3%	-1.7	8,441,000	1,221,014	14.5%	1.5	8,562,000	2,354,721	27.5%	14.5
OKLAHOMA	2,322,000	416,129	17.9%	2,407,000	366,604	15.2%	-2.7	2,485,000	134,850	5.4%	-12.5	2,523,000	302,385	12.0%	-5.9	2,561,000	417,207	16.3%	-1.6
OREGON	2,128,000	354,332	16.7%	2,275,000	369,178	16.2%	-0.4	2,414,000	354,594	14.7%	-2.0	2,515,000	368,544	14.7%	-2.0	2,615,000	641,499	24.5%	7.9
PENNSYLVANIA	8,996,000	1,265,495	14.1%	9,073,000	724,069	8.0%	-6.1	9,144,000	704,150	7.7%	-6.4	9,296,000	787,034	8.5%	-5.6	9,450,000	2,333,462	24.7%	10.6
RHODE ISLAND	736,000	50,709	6.9%	741,000	8,752	1.2%	-5.7	746,000	46,844	6.3%	-0.6	768,000	35,759	4.7%	-2.2	790,000	186,439	23.6%	16.7
SOUTH CAROLINA	2,629,000	116,414	4.4%									3,082,000	293,843	9.5%	5.1	3,224,000	532,151	16.5%	12.1
SOUTH DAKOTA	505,000	59,503	11.8%									560,000	84,405	15.1%	3.3	573,000	97,797	17.1%	5.3
TENNESSEE	3,757,000	318,482	8.5%	3,984,000	137,788	3.5%	-5.0	4,201,000	213,223	5.1%	-3.4	4,357,000	369,385	8.5%	0.0	4,512,000	624,764	13.8%	5.4

United States Presidential Primary Elections (continued)

United States Presidential Primary Elections (continued)

Democratic Turnout for Election Years 1992–2008 (continued)

State	1992 Voting-age population	Turnout	%	1996 Voting-age population	Turnout	%	Difference from 1992	2000 Voting-age population	Turnout	%	Difference from 1992	2004 Voting-age population	Turnout	%	Difference from 1992	2008 Voting-age population	Turnout	%	Difference from 1992
TEXAS	11,736,000	1,482,975	12.6%	12,534,000	921,256	7.4%	-5.3	13,287,000	786,890	5.9%	-6.7	14,086,000	839,231	6.0%	-6.7	14,886,000	2,874,986	19.3%	6.7
UTAH								1,423,000	15,687	1.1%		1,501,000	34,584	2.3%	1.2				
VERMONT				437,000	30,838	7.1%		452,000	49,283	10.9%	3.8	474,000	83,116	17.5%	10.5	495,000	154,960	31.3%	24.2
VIRGINIA								5,304,000	396,181	7.5%						5,560,000	986,203	17.7%	10.3
WASHINGTON	3,597,000	147,981	4.1%	3,848,000	329,226	8.6%	4.4	4,084,000	475,707	11.6%	7.5					4,489,000	691,381	15.4%	11.3
WEST VIRGINIA	1,356,000	306,866	22.6%	1,378,000	297,121	21.6%	-1.1	1,398,000	253,310	18.1%	-4.5	1,413,000	252,839	17.9%	-4.7	1,428,000	359,854	25.2%	2.6
WISCONSIN	3,629,000	772,596	21.3%	3,768,000	354,634	9.4%	-11.9	3,899,000	371,196	9.5%	-11.8	4,041,000	826,250	20.4%	-0.8	4,183,000	1,113,285	26.6%	5.3
WYOMING																			
Total	160,349,000	20,239,385	12.6%	134,622,000	11,147,741	8.3%	-4.3	166,627,000	14,692,509	8.8%	-3.8	166,247,000	16,126,734	9.7%	-2.9	189,230,000	36,738,335	19.4%	6.8

Other Turnout for Election Years 1992–2008

State	1992 Voting-age population	Turnout	%	1996 Voting-age population	Turnout	%	Difference from 1992*	2000 Voting-age population	Turnout	%	Difference from 1992	2004 Voting-age population	Turnout	%	Difference from 1992	2008 Voting-age population	Turnout	%	Difference from 1992
ARKANSAS																2,065,000	838	0.0%	
CALIFORNIA	18,681,000	38,805	0.2%	19,360,000	67,113	0.3%	0.1					21,152,000	93,987	0.4%	0.2	22,319,000	105,168	0.5%	0.3
DISTRICT OF COLUMBIA																371,000	521	0.1%	
ILLINOIS				8,248,000	1,728	0.0%										8,540,000	2,672	0.0%	0.0
MASSACHUSETTS	4,412,000	1,385	0.0%	4,442,000	870	0.0%	0.0												
MICHIGAN																7,490,000	2,058	0.0%	
MISSOURI												4,210,000	1,967	0.0%		4,328,000	2,058	0.0%	0.0
MONTANA				630,000	668	0.1%													
NEBRASKA												1,231,000	12,405	1.0%		1,243,000	152	0.0%	-1.0
NEVADA																			
NEW HAMPSHIRE	833,000	3,387	0.4%													1,016,000	497	0.0%	-0.4
NEW MEXICO				1,153,000	1,382	0.1%						1,288,000	623	0.0%	-0.1				
SOUTH DAKOTA				526,000	497	0.1%													
TEXAS																14,886,000	399	0.0%	
VERMONT				437,000	830	0.2%													
WISCONSIN												4,041,000	3,443	0.1%					
Total	23,926,000	43,577	0.2%	34,796,000	73,088	0.2%	0.0					31,922,000	112,425	0.4%	0.2	62,258,000	114,363	0.2%	0.0

*Percentage point difference between turnout in current year and initial year listed in chart. If data do not appear for a state in the initial year listed, the difference is calculated from the first year in which data do appear for that state.

STATE GUBERNATORIAL PRIMARY ELECTIONS
Election Years 1992–2008

State*	1992 Voting-age population	Turnout	%	1996 Voting-age population	Turnout	%	Difference from 1992**	2000 Voting-age population	Turnout	%	Difference from 1992	2004 Voting-age population	Turnout	%	Difference from 1992	2008 Voting-age population	Turnout	%	Difference from 1992
ALABAMA																			
ALASKA																			
ARIZONA																			
ARKANSAS																			
CALIFORNIA																			
COLORADO																			
CONNECTICUT																			
DELAWARE	510,000	70,374	13.8%					567,000	27,740	4.9%	-8.9	598,000	21,670	3.6%	-10.2	630,000	102,933	16.3%	2.5
DISTRICT OF COLUMBIA																			
FLORIDA																			
GEORGIA																			
HAWAII																			
IDAHO																			
ILLINOIS																			
INDIANA	4,126,000	848,184	20.6%	4,270,000	857,171	20.1%	-0.5	4,408,000	666,713	15.1%	-5.4	4,497,000	789,682	17.6%	-3.0	4,586,000	1,502,341	32.8%	12.2
IOWA																			
KANSAS																			
KENTUCKY																			
LOUISIANA																			
MAINE																			
MARYLAND																			
MASSACHUSETTS																			
MICHIGAN																			
MINNESOTA																			
MISSISSIPPI																			
MISSOURI	3,839,000	1,121,133	29.2%	3,969,000	710,636	17.9%	-11.3	4,094,000	712,971	17.4%	-11.8	4,210,000	1,445,083	34.3%	5.1	4,328,000	755,630	17.5%	-11.7
MONTANA	592,000	231,327	39.1%	630,000	195,197	31.0%	-8.1	666,000	209,372	31.4%	-7.6	698,000	204,993	29.4%	-9.7	731,000	256,371	35.1%	-4.0
NEBRASKA																			
NEVADA																			
NEW HAMPSHIRE	833,000	204,546	24.6%	869,000	163,926	18.9%	-5.7	902,000	179,286	19.9%	-4.7	960,000	125,312	13.1%	-11.5	1,016,000	102,244	10.1%	-14.5
NEW JERSEY																			
NEW MEXICO																			
NEW YORK																			

State Gubernatorial Primary Elections (continued)

State Gubernatorial Primary Elections (continued)

Election Years 1992–2008 (continued)

State	1992			1996				2000				2004				2008			
	Voting-age population	Turnout	%	Voting-age population	Turnout	%	Difference from 1992	Voting-age population	Turnout	%	Difference from 1992	Voting-age population	Turnout	%	Difference from 1992	Voting-age population	Turnout	%	Difference from 1992
NORTH CAROLINA	5,149,000	964,569	18.7%					5,817,000	875,995	15.1%	-3.7	6,120,000	808,979	13.2%	-5.5	6,423,000	1,681,641	26.2%	7.4
NORTH DAKOTA	463,000	125,068	27.0%	469,000	94,754	20.2%	-6.8	475,000	75,159	15.8%	-11.2	481,000	77,732	16.2%	-10.9	485,000	89,028	18.4%	-8.7
OHIO																			
OKLAHOMA																			
OREGON																			
PENNSYLVANIA																			
RHODE ISLAND																			
SOUTH CAROLINA																			
SOUTH DAKOTA																			
TENNESSEE																			
TEXAS																			
UTAH	1,144,000	369,370	32.3%																
VERMONT	421,000	53,530	12.7%	437,000	39,067	8.9%	-3.8	452,000	117,740	26.0%	13.3	474,000	41,220	8.7%	-4.0	495,000	31,127	6.3%	-6.4
VIRGINIA																			
WASHINGTON	3,597,000	1,155,160	32.1%	3,848,000	1,216,668	31.6%	-0.5	4,084,000	1,270,116	31.1%	-1.0	4,287,000	1,303,024	30.4%	-1.7	4,489,000	1,442,457	32.1%	0.0
WEST VIRGINIA	1,356,000	453,846	33.5%	1,378,000	463,030	33.6%	0.1	1,398,000	384,495	27.5%	-6.0	1,413,000	394,138	27.9%	-5.6				
WISCONSIN																			
WYOMING																			
Total	22,030,000	5,597,107	25.4%	15,870,000	3,740,449	23.6%	-1.8	22,863,000	4,519,587	19.8%	-5.6	23,738,000	5,211,833	22.0%	-3.5	23,183,000	5,963,772	25.7%	0.3

*Overall primary turnout reflects only states with primaries in both parties. To find single party primary results, see partisan primary charts.

**Percentage point difference between turnout in current year and initial year listed in chart. If data do not appear for a state in the initial year listed, the difference is calculated from the first year in which data do appear for that state.

STATE GUBERNATORIAL PRIMARY ELECTIONS

Republican Turnout for Election Years 1992–2008

State	1992 Voting-age population	Turnout	%	1996 Voting-age population	Turnout	%	Difference from 1992*	2000 Voting-age population	Turnout	%	Difference from 1992	2004 Voting-age population	Turnout	%	Difference from 1992	2008 Voting-age population	Turnout	%	Difference from 1992
ALABAMA																			
ALASKA																			
ARIZONA																			
ARKANSAS																			
CALIFORNIA																			
COLORADO																			
CONNECTICUT																			
DELAWARE	510,000	29,340	5.8%					567,000	27,740	4.9%	-0.9	598,000	21,670	3.6%	-2.1	630,000	28,972	4.6%	-1.2
DISTRICT OF COLUMBIA																			
FLORIDA																			
GEORGIA																			
HAWAII																			
IDAHO																			
ILLINOIS																			
INDIANA	4,126,000	457,246	11.1%	4,270,000	551,582	12.9%	1.8	4,408,000	394,500	8.9%	-2.1	4,497,000	505,758	11.2%	0.2	4,586,000	350,390	7.6%	-3.4
IOWA																			
KANSAS																			
KENTUCKY																			
LOUISIANA																			
MAINE																			
MARYLAND																			
MASSACHUSETTS																			
MICHIGAN																			
MINNESOTA																			
MISSISSIPPI																			
MISSOURI	3,839,000	420,145	10.9%	3,969,000	282,313	7.1%	-3.8	4,094,000	350,514	8.6%	-2.4	4,210,000	595,392	14.1%	3.2	4,328,000	395,885	9.1%	-1.8
MONTANA	592,000	99,051	16.7%	630,000	121,316	19.3%	2.5	666,000	113,016	17.0%	0.2	698,000	110,198	15.8%	-0.9	731,000	81,328	11.1%	-5.6
NEBRASKA																			
NEVADA																			
NEW HAMPSHIRE	833,000	115,312	13.8%	869,000	102,052	11.7%	-2.1	902,000	104,385	11.6%	-2.3	960,000	66,350	6.9%	-6.9	1,016,000	49,284	4.9%	-9.0
NEW JERSEY																			
NEW MEXICO																			
NEW YORK																			

State Gubernatorial Primary Elections (continued)

State Gubernatorial Primary Elections (continued)

Republican Turnout for Election Years 1992–2008 (continued)

State	1992 Voting-age population	1992 Turnout	1992 %	1996 Voting-age population	1996 Turnout	1996 %	1996 Difference from 1992	2000 Voting-age population	2000 Turnout	2000 %	2000 Difference from 1992	2004 Voting-age population	2004 Turnout	2004 %	2004 Difference from 1992	2008 Voting-age population	2008 Turnout	2008 %	2008 Difference from 1992
NORTH CAROLINA	5,149,000	262,963	5.1%	5,492,000	279,610	5.1%	0.0	5,817,000	314,055	5.4%	0.3	6,120,000	364,420	6.0%	0.8	6,423,000	186,643	2.9%	-2.2
NORTH DAKOTA	463,000	47,300	10.2%	469,000	48,412	10.3%	0.1	475,000	40,308	8.5%	-1.7	481,000	42,135	8.8%	-1.5	485,000	50,226	10.4%	0.1
OHIO																			
OKLAHOMA																			
OREGON																			
PENNSYLVANIA																			
RHODE ISLAND																			
SOUTH CAROLINA																			
SOUTH DAKOTA																			
TENNESSEE																			
TEXAS																			
UTAH	1,144,000	256,528	22.4%					1,423,000	198,008	13.9%	-8.5	1,501,000	152,015	10.1%	-12.3				
VERMONT	421,000	28,026	6.7%	437,000	20,292	4.6%	-2.0	452,000	80,571	17.8%	11.2	474,000	16,008	3.4%	-3.3	495,000	11,798	2.4%	-4.3
VIRGINIA																			
WASHINGTON	3,597,000	661,124	18.4%	3,848,000	581,709	15.1%	-3.3	4,084,000	539,609	13.2%	-5.2	4,287,000	521,889	12.2%	-6.2	4,489,000	695,116	15.5%	-2.9
WEST VIRGINIA	1,356,000	120,519	8.9%	1,378,000	133,972	9.7%	0.8	1,398,000	108,519	7.8%	-1.1	1,413,000	110,876	7.8%	-1.0				
WISCONSIN																			
WYOMING																			
Total	22,030,000	2,497,554	11.3%	21,362,000	2,121,258	9.9%	-1.4	24,286,000	2,271,225	9.4%	-2.0	25,239,000	2,506,711	9.9%	-1.4	23,183,000	1,849,642	8.0%	-3.4

Democratic Turnout for Election Years 1992–2008

State	1992 Voting-age population	1992 Turnout	1992 %	1996 Voting-age population	1996 Turnout	1996 %	1996 Difference from 1992*	2000 Voting-age population	2000 Turnout	2000 %	2000 Difference from 1992	2004 Voting-age population	2004 Turnout	2004 %	2004 Difference from 1992	2008 Voting-age population	2008 Turnout	2008 %	2008 Difference from 1992
ALABAMA																			
ALASKA																			
ARIZONA																			
ARKANSAS																			
CALIFORNIA																			
COLORADO																			
CONNECTICUT																			
DELAWARE	510,000	41,034	8.0%													630,000	73,961	11.7%	3.7
DISTRICT OF COLUMBIA																			
FLORIDA																			

State Gubernatorial Primary Elections *(continued)*

Democratic Turnout for Election Years 1992–2008 *(continued)*

State	1992 Voting-age population	Turnout	%	1996 Voting-age population	Turnout	%	Difference from 1992	2000 Voting-age population	Turnout	%	Difference from 1992	2004 Voting-age population	Turnout	%	Difference from 1992	2008 Voting-age population	Turnout	%	Difference from 1992
GEORGIA																			
HAWAII																			
IDAHO																			
ILLINOIS																			
INDIANA	4,126,000	390,938	9.5%	4,270,000	305,589	7.2%	-2.3	4,408,000	272,213	6.2%	-3.3	4,497,000	283,924	6.3%	-3.2	4,586,000	1,151,951	25.1%	15.6
IOWA																			
KANSAS																			
KENTUCKY																			
LOUISIANA																			
MAINE																			
MARYLAND																			
MASSACHUSETTS																			
MICHIGAN																			
MINNESOTA																			
MISSISSIPPI																			
MISSOURI	3,839,000	700,988	18.3%	3,969,000	425,770	10.7%	-7.5	4,094,000	362,457	8.9%	-9.4	4,210,000	846,090	20.1%	1.8	4,328,000	358,016	8.3%	-10.0
MONTANA	592,000	132,276	22.3%	630,000	73,881	11.7%	-10.6	666,000	96,356	14.5%	-7.9	698,000	94,795	13.6%	-8.8	731,000	175,043	23.9%	1.6
NEBRASKA																			
NEVADA																			
NEW HAMPSHIRE	833,000	87,591	10.5%	869,000	61,042	7.0%	-3.5	902,000	74,901	8.3%	-2.2	960,000	58,962	6.1%	-4.4	1,016,000	52,388	5.2%	-5.4
NEW JERSEY																			
NEW MEXICO																			
NEW YORK																			
NORTH CAROLINA	5,149,000	701,606	13.6%					5,817,000	561,940	9.7%	-4.0	6,120,000	444,559	7.3%	-6.4	6,423,000	1,494,998	23.3%	9.6
NORTH DAKOTA	463,000	77,768	16.8%	469,000	46,049	9.8%	-7.0	475,000	34,851	7.3%	-9.5	481,000	35,597	7.4%	-9.4	485,000	38,784	8.0%	-8.8
OHIO																			
OKLAHOMA																			
OREGON																			
PENNSYLVANIA																			
RHODE ISLAND																			
SOUTH CAROLINA																			
SOUTH DAKOTA																			
TENNESSEE																			

State Gubernatorial Primary Elections (continued)

Democratic Turnout for Election Years 1992–2008 (continued)

State	1992			1996				2000				2004				2008			
	Voting-age population	Turnout	%	Voting-age population	Turnout	%	Difference from 1992	Voting-age population	Turnout	%	Difference from 1992	Voting-age population	Turnout	%	Difference from 1992	Voting-age population	Turnout	%	Difference from 1992
TEXAS																			
UTAH	1,144,000	112,842	9.9%																
VERMONT	421,000	25,504	6.1%	437,000	18,518	4.2%	-1.8	452,000	37,169	8.2%	2.2	474,000	24,531	5.2%	-0.9	495,000	18,851	3.8%	-2.2
VIRGINIA																			
WASHINGTON	3,597,000	481,768	13.4%	3,848,000	631,217	16.4%	3.0	4,084,000	730,507	17.9%	4.5	4,287,000	768,066	17.9%	4.5	4,489,000	712,952	15.9%	2.5
WEST VIRGINIA	1,356,000	333,327	24.6%	1,378,000	329,058	23.9%	-0.7	1,398,000	275,976	19.7%	-4.8	1,413,000	283,262	20.0%	-4.5				
WISCONSIN																			
WYOMING																			
Total	22,030,000	3,085,642	14.0%	15,870,000	1,891,124	11.9%	-2.1	22,296,000	2,446,370	11.0%	-3.0	23,140,000	2,839,786	12.3%	-1.7	23,183,000	4,076,944	17.6%	3.6

Other Turnout for Election Years 1992–2008

State	1992			1996				2000				2004				2008			
	Voting-age population	Turnout	%	Voting-age population	Turnout	%	Difference from 1992*	Voting-age population	Turnout	%	Difference from 1992	Voting-age population	Turnout	%	Difference from 1992	Voting-age population	Turnout	%	Difference from 1992
MISSOURI				3,969,000	2,553	0.1%						4,210,000	3,601	0.1%	0.0	4,328,000	1,729	0.0%	0.0
NEW HAMPSHIRE	833,000	1,643	0.2%	869,000	832	0.1%	-0.1									1,016,000	572	0.1%	-0.1
NORTH DAKOTA				469,000	293	0.1%										485,000	18	0.0%	-0.1
VERMONT				437,000	257	0.1%						474,000	681	0.1%	0.1	495,000	478	0.1%	0.0
WASHINGTON	3,597,000	12,268	0.3%	3,848,000	3,742	0.1%	-0.2					4,287,000	13,069	0.3%	0.0	4,489,000	34,389	0.8%	0.4
Total	4,430,000	13,911	0.3%	9,592,000	7,677	0.1%	-0.2					8,971,000	17,351	0.2%	-0.1	10,813,000	37,186	0.3%	0.0

*Percentage point difference between turnout in current year and initial year listed in chart. If data do not appear for a state in the initial year listed, the difference is calculated from the first year in which data do appear for that state.

UNITED STATES SENATE PRIMARY ELECTIONS

Election Years 1992–2008

State*	1992 Voting-age population	Turnout	%	1996 Voting-age population	Turnout	%	Difference from 1992**	2000 Voting-age population	Turnout	%	Difference from 1992	2004 Voting-age population	Turnout	%	Difference from 1992	2008 Voting-age population	Turnout	%	Difference from 1992
ALABAMA				3,156,000	527,770	16.7%										3,394,000	392,297	11.6%	-5.2
ALASKA	380,000	120,552	31.7%	401,000	120,677	30.1%	-1.6					449,000	127,731	28.4%	-3.3	476,000	181,109	38.0%	6.3
ARIZONA	2,729,000	420,545	15.4%					3,384,000	260,449	7.7%	-7.7	3,750,000	508,016	13.5%	-1.9				
ARKANSAS	1,769,000	551,969	31.2%									2,008,000	332,088	16.5%	-14.7				
CALIFORNIA	18,681,000	5,611,115	30.0%					19,983,000	6,962,363	34.8%	4.8	21,152,000	4,827,805	22.8%	-7.2				
COLORADO	2,505,000	381,078	15.2%	2,754,000	334,461	12.1%	-3.1					3,104,000	572,571	18.4%	3.2	3,219,000	433,439	13.5%	-1.7
CONNECTICUT																			
DELAWARE																			
DISTRICT OF COLUMBIA																			
FLORIDA	9,647,000	1,885,882	19.5%					11,070,000	1,707,494	15.4%	-4.1	11,996,000	2,318,444	19.3%	-0.2				
GEORGIA	4,878,000	953,217	19.5%	5,285,000	963,263	18.2%	-1.3					5,987,000	1,276,107	21.3%	1.8	6,302,000	886,171	14.1%	-5.5
HAWAII	781,000	234,870	30.1%					841,000	238,463	28.4%	-1.7	879,000	213,941	24.3%	-5.7				
IDAHO	729,000	172,620	23.7%	812,000	141,368	17.4%	-6.3									1,024,000	163,691	16.0%	-7.7
ILLINOIS	8,103,000	2,064,347	25.5%	8,248,000	1,583,406	19.2%	-6.3					8,461,000	1,904,800	22.5%	-3.0	8,540,000	2,364,409	27.7%	2.2
INDIANA	4,126,000	709,851	17.2%					4,408,000	549,419	12.5%	-4.7	4,497,000	639,482	14.2%	-3.0				
IOWA	2,061,000	209,600	10.2%	2,103,000	264,817	12.6%	2.4					2,171,000	131,753	6.1%	-4.1	2,201,000	162,531	7.4%	-2.8
KANSAS	1,812,000	464,500	25.6%	1,858,000	513,517	27.6%	2.0					1,935,000	438,904	22.7%	-3.0	1,968,000	313,716	15.9%	-9.7
KENTUCKY				2,892,000	367,980	12.7%						3,075,000	333,909	10.9%	-1.9	3,147,000	815,201	25.9%	13.2
LOUISIANA***	3,003,000	843,037	28.1%	3,103,000	1,228,596	39.6%	11.5												
MAINE				939,000	181,380	19.3%		959,000	61,300	6.4%	-12.9					1,048,000	138,050	13.2%	-6.1
MARYLAND	3,510,000	699,067	19.9%					3,695,000	772,111	20.9%	1.0	3,880,000	593,731	15.3%	-4.6				
MASSACHUSETTS				4,442,000	293,613	6.6%		4,467,000	279,146	6.2%	-0.4								
MICHIGAN				6,948,000	1,088,818	15.7%		7,103,000	944,781	13.3%	-2.4					7,490,000	1,057,143	14.1%	-1.6
MINNESOTA				3,370,000	425,791	12.6%		3,502,000	559,462	16.0%	3.3					3,824,000	405,975	10.6%	-2.0
MISSISSIPPI				1,961,000	226,394	11.5%		2,048,000	182,129	8.9%	-2.7								
MISSOURI	3,839,000	1,040,688	27.1%					4,094,000	779,637	19.0%	-8.1	4,210,000	1,358,702	32.3%	5.2				
MONTANA				630,000	198,656	31.5%		666,000	191,556	28.8%	-2.8					731,000	239,214	32.7%	1.2
NEBRASKA				1,189,000	268,411	22.6%		1,219,000	303,409	24.9%	2.3					1,243,000	239,702	19.3%	-3.3
NEVADA	955,000	224,804	23.5%																
NEW HAMPSHIRE	833,000	197,738	23.7%	869,000	149,916	17.3%	-6.5					960,000	113,823	11.9%	-11.9	1,016,000	117,277	11.5%	-12.2
NEW JERSEY				5,591,000	438,328	7.8%		5,640,000	709,111	12.6%	4.7					5,904,000	529,317	9.0%	1.1
NEW MEXICO				1,153,000	186,007	16.1%		1,229,000	197,378	16.1%	-0.1					1,346,000	254,621	18.9%	2.8
NEW YORK																			

United States Senate Primary Elections (continued)

United States Senate Primary Elections (continued)

Election Years 1992–2008 (continued)

State	1992 Voting-age population	Turnout	%	1996 Voting-age population	Turnout	%	Difference from 1992	2000 Voting-age population	Turnout	%	Difference from 1992	2004 Voting-age population	Turnout	%	Difference from 1992	2008 Voting-age population	Turnout	%	Difference from 1992
NORTH CAROLINA																6,423,000	1,847,123	28.8%	
NORTH DAKOTA	463,000	113,724	24.6%					475,000	74,463	15.7%	-8.9	481,000	78,965	16.4%	-8.1				
OHIO	8,031,000	1,690,052	21.0%					8,319,000	2,150,725	25.9%	4.8	8,441,000	1,786,268	21.2%	0.1				
OKLAHOMA				2,407,000	490,325	20.4%						2,523,000	591,187	23.4%	3.1	2,561,000	329,023	12.8%	-7.5
OREGON	2,128,000	662,216	31.1%	2,275,000	592,468	26.0%	-5.1					2,515,000	585,451	23.3%	-7.8	2,615,000	896,924	34.3%	3.2
PENNSYLVANIA	8,996,000	2,292,062	25.5%					9,144,000	1,280,262	14.0%	-11.5	9,296,000	1,619,968	17.4%	-8.1				
RHODE ISLAND								746,000	92,271	12.4%						790,000	56,383	7.1%	-5.2
SOUTH CAROLINA				2,788,000	383,797	13.8%						3,082,000	462,459	15.0%	1.2	3,224,000	428,148	13.3%	-0.5
SOUTH DAKOTA																			
TENNESSEE				3,984,000	529,918	13.3%		4,201,000	376,667	9.0%	-4.3					4,512,000	426,946	9.5%	-3.8
TEXAS				12,534,000	1,876,825	15.0%		13,287,000	1,573,065	11.8%	-3.1					14,886,000	3,401,117	22.8%	7.9
UTAH	1,144,000	384,385	33.6%																
VERMONT	421,000	61,395	14.6%					452,000	112,846	25.0%	10.4	474,000	43,525	9.2%	-5.4				
VIRGINIA																			
WASHINGTON	3,597,000	1,121,763	31.2%					4,084,000	1,270,991	31.1%	-0.1	4,287,000	1,304,553	30.4%	-0.8				
WEST VIRGINIA				1,378,000	407,386	29.6%		1,398,000	333,138	23.8%	-5.7					1,428,000	433,283	30.3%	0.8
WISCONSIN	3,629,000	774,240	21.3%					3,899,000	404,920	10.4%	-10.9	4,041,000	686,550	17.0%	-4.3				
WYOMING				343,000	120,992	35.3%		360,000	93,724	26.0%	-9.2					388,000	92,494	23.8%	-11.4
Total	98,750,000	23,885,317	24.2%	83,413,000	13,904,880	16.7%	-7.5	120,673,000	22,461,280	18.6%	-5.6	113,654,000	22,850,733	20.1%	-4.1	89,700,000	16,605,304	18.5%	-5.7

*Overall primary turnout reflects only states with primaries in both parties. To find single party primary results, see partisan primary charts.

**Percentage point difference between turnout in current year and initial year listed in chart. If data do not appear for a state in the initial year listed, the difference is calculated from the first year in which data do appear for that state.

***In 1978 Louisiana eliminated the partisan primary for senator and instituted an open primary with candidates from all parties running on the same ballot. Any candidate who received a majority appeared in the general election unopposed. If no candidate received fifty percent, a runoff was held between the top two finishers. In 2008 Louisiana returned to a partisan primary system.

UNITED STATES SENATE PRIMARY ELECTIONS

Republican Turnout for Election Years 1992–2008

State	1992 Voting-age population	Turnout	%	1996 Voting-age population	Turnout	%	Difference from 1992*	2000 Voting-age population	Turnout	%	Difference from 1992	2004 Voting-age population	Turnout	%	Difference from 1992	2008 Voting-age population	Turnout	%	Difference from 1992
ALABAMA				3,156,000	212,046	6.7%										3,394,000	216,408	6.4%	-0.3
ALASKA	380,000	46,551	12.3%	401,000	104,879	26.2%	13.9					449,000	78,628	17.5%	5.3	476,000	105,326	22.1%	9.9
ARIZONA	2,729,000	201,500	7.4%					3,384,000	255,659	7.6%	0.2	3,750,000	331,720	8.8%	1.5				
ARKANSAS	1,769,000	52,238	3.0%									2,008,000	54,041	2.7%	-0.3				
CALIFORNIA	18,681,000	2,500,442	13.4%					19,983,000	3,021,699	15.1%	1.7	21,152,000	2,235,733	10.6%	-2.8				
COLORADO	2,505,000	122,427	4.9%	2,754,000	202,458	7.4%	2.5					3,104,000	336,431	10.8%	5.9	3,219,000	239,212	7.4%	2.5
CONNECTICUT	2,416,000	90,847	3.8%																
DELAWARE	510,000	29,340	5.8%	539,000	22,662	4.2%	-1.5												
DISTRICT OF COLUMBIA																			
FLORIDA	9,647,000	736,859	7.6%					11,070,000	814,205	7.4%	-0.3	11,996,000	1,165,931	9.7%	2.1				
GEORGIA	4,878,000	269,943	5.5%	5,285,000	445,566	8.4%	2.9					5,987,000	650,992	10.9%	5.3	6,302,000	392,928	6.2%	0.7
HAWAII	781,000	44,848	5.7%					841,000	61,180	7.3%	1.5	879,000	43,956	5.0%	-0.7				
IDAHO	729,000	116,660	16.0%	812,000	106,817	13.2%	-2.8									1,024,000	123,574	12.1%	-3.9
ILLINOIS	8,103,000	608,079	7.5%	8,248,000	791,645	9.6%	2.1					8,461,000	661,804	7.8%	0.3	8,540,000	710,576	8.3%	0.8
INDIANA	4,126,000	389,119	9.4%					4,408,000	356,888	8.1%	-1.3	4,497,000	335,215	7.5%	-2.0				
IOWA	2,061,000	109,273	5.3%	2,103,000	165,270	7.9%	2.6					2,171,000	79,037	3.6%	-1.7	2,201,000	70,672	3.2%	-2.1
KANSAS	1,812,000	304,069	16.8%	1,858,000	342,779	18.4%	1.7					1,935,000	329,719	17.0%	0.3	1,968,000	214,911	10.9%	-5.9
KENTUCKY	2,777,000	81,972	3.0%	2,892,000	100,030	3.5%						3,075,000	114,940	3.7%	0.3	3,147,000	195,297	6.2%	3.3
LOUISIANA**	3,003,000	106,392	3.5%	3,103,000	670,716	21.6%	18.1												
MAINE				939,000	96,107	10.2%		959,000	34,757	3.6%	-6.6					1,048,000	56,323	5.4%	-4.9
MARYLAND	3,510,000	208,590	5.9%					3,695,000	309,877	8.4%	2.4	3,880,000	138,855	3.6%	-2.4				
MASSACHUSETTS				4,442,000	72,600	1.6%		4,467,000	236,883	5.3%	3.7								
MICHIGAN				6,948,000	682,894	9.8%		7,103,000	527,278	7.4%	-2.4					7,490,000	495,467	6.6%	-3.2
MINNESOTA				3,370,000	196,904	5.8%		3,502,000	433,399	12.4%	6.5					3,824,000	143,429	3.8%	-2.1
MISSISSIPPI				1,961,000	145,575	7.4%		2,048,000	107,127	5.2%	-2.2								
MISSOURI	3,839,000	408,421	10.6%					4,094,000	365,545	8.9%	-1.7	4,210,000	615,352	14.6%	4.0				
MONTANA				630,000	111,313	17.7%		666,000	102,125	15.3%	-2.3					731,000	74,164	10.1%	-7.5
NEBRASKA				1,189,000	174,923	14.7%		1,219,000	188,708	15.5%	0.8					1,243,000	143,751	11.6%	-3.1
NEVADA	955,000	102,061	10.7%					1,315,000	108,939	8.3%	-2.4	1,479,000	120,791	8.2%	-2.5				
NEW HAMPSHIRE	833,000	114,737	13.8%	869,000	87,577	10.1%	-3.7					960,000	66,164	6.9%	-6.9	1,016,000	68,171	6.7%	-7.1
NEW JERSEY				5,591,000	214,884	3.8%		5,640,000	275,683	4.9%	1.0					5,904,000	184,785	3.1%	-0.7
NEW MEXICO				1,153,000	66,770	5.8%		1,229,000	72,491	5.9%	0.1					1,346,000	112,992	8.4%	2.6
NEW YORK																			

United States Senate Primary Elections (continued)

United States Senate Primary Elections (continued)

Republican Turnout for Election Years 1992–2008 (continued)

State	1992 Voting-age population	1992 Turnout	1992 %	1996 Voting-age population	1996 Turnout	1996 %	1996 Difference from 1992	2000 Voting-age population	2000 Turnout	2000 %	2000 Difference from 1992	2004 Voting-age population	2004 Turnout	2004 %	2004 Difference from 1992	2008 Voting-age population	2008 Turnout	2008 %	2008 Difference from 1992
NORTH CAROLINA	5,149,000	270,568	5.3%									6,120,000	343,875	5.6%	0.4	6,423,000	512,071	8.0%	2.7
NORTH DAKOTA	463,000	45,611	9.9%					475,000	37,878	8.0%	-1.9	481,000	39,329	8.2%	-1.7				
OHIO	8,031,000	830,430	10.3%					8,319,000	1,295,264	15.6%	5.2	8,441,000	835,558	9.9%	-0.4				
OKLAHOMA				2,407,000	154,285	6.4%						2,523,000	238,391	9.4%	3.0	2,561,000	138,247	5.4%	-1.0
OREGON	2,128,000	299,411	14.1%	2,275,000	287,500	12.6%	-1.4					2,515,000	236,845	9.4%	-4.7	2,615,000	346,958	13.3%	-0.8
PENNSYLVANIA	8,996,000	1,049,726	11.7%					9,144,000	545,687	6.0%	-5.7	9,296,000	1,037,403	11.2%	-0.5				
RHODE ISLAND	736,000	14,460	2.0%					746,000	2,221	0.3%	-1.7					790,000	1,068	0.1%	-1.8
SOUTH CAROLINA	2,629,000	160,924	6.1%	2,788,000	218,015	7.8%	1.7					3,082,000	294,669	9.6%	3.4	3,224,000	280,861	8.7%	0.9
SOUTH DAKOTA																573,000	52,628	9.2%	
TENNESSEE				3,984,000	283,287	7.1%		4,201,000	187,227	4.5%	-2.7					4,512,000	244,222	5.4%	-1.7
TEXAS				12,534,000	986,202	7.9%		13,287,000	955,033	7.2%	-0.7					14,886,000	1,223,865	8.2%	0.4
UTAH	1,144,000	263,639	23.0%																
VERMONT	421,000	36,674	8.7%					452,000	77,429	17.1%	8.4	474,000	14,170	3.0%	-5.7				
VIRGINIA				4,850,000	493,535	10.2%													
WASHINGTON	3,597,000	540,813	15.0%					4,084,000	601,113	14.7%	-0.3	4,287,000	522,094	12.2%	-2.9				
WEST VIRGINIA				1,378,000	90,446	6.6%		1,398,000	81,700	5.8%	-0.7					1,428,000	81,189	5.7%	-0.9
WISCONSIN	3,629,000	245,371	6.8%					3,899,000	198,939	5.1%	-1.7	4,041,000	432,872	10.7%	4.0				
WYOMING				343,000	83,328	24.3%		360,000	68,132	18.9%	-5.4					388,000	68,194	17.6%	-6.7
Total	112,967,000	10,401,995	9.2%	88,802,000	7,611,013	8.6%	-0.6	121,988,000	11,323,066	9.3%	0.1	121,253,000	11,353,515	9.4%	0.2	90,273,000	6,497,289	7.2%	-2.0

Democratic Turnout for Election Years 1992–2008

State	1992 Voting-age population	1992 Turnout	1992 %	1996 Voting-age population	1996 Turnout	1996 %	1996 Difference from 1992*	2000 Voting-age population	2000 Turnout	2000 %	2000 Difference from 1992	2004 Voting-age population	2004 Turnout	2004 %	2004 Difference from 1992	2008 Voting-age population	2008 Turnout	2008 %	2008 Difference from 1992
ALABAMA	3,029,000	496,181	16.4%	3,156,000	315,724	10.0%	-6.4									3,394,000	175,889	5.2%	-4.8
ALASKA	380,000	68,012	17.9%	401,000	12,047	3.0%	-14.9					449,000	43,006	9.6%	-8.3	476,000	70,192	14.7%	-3.2
ARIZONA	2,729,000	218,500	8.0%					3,384,000	4,790	0.1%	-7.9	3,750,000	173,540	4.6%	-3.4				
ARKANSAS	1,769,000	499,731	28.2%	1,861,000	328,369	17.6%	-10.6					2,008,000	278,047	13.8%	-14.4				
CALIFORNIA	18,681,000	3,064,648	16.4%					19,983,000	3,940,664	19.7%	3.3	21,152,000	2,532,621	12.0%	-4.4				
COLORADO	2,505,000	258,651	10.3%	2,754,000	132,003	4.8%	-5.5					3,104,000	237,140	7.6%	-2.7	3,219,000	194,227	6.0%	-4.3
CONNECTICUT																			
DELAWARE	510,000	41,034	8.0%																
DISTRICT OF COLUMBIA																			
FLORIDA	9,647,000	1,149,023	11.9%					11,070,000	893,289	8.1%	-3.8	11,996,000	1,152,513	9.6%	-2.3				

United States Senate Primary Elections (continued)

Democratic Turnout for Election Years 1992–2008 (continued)

State	1992 Voting-age population	1992 Turnout	1992 %	1996 Voting-age population	1996 Turnout	1996 %	1996 Difference from 1992	2000 Voting-age population	2000 Turnout	2000 %	2000 Difference from 1992	2004 Voting-age population	2004 Turnout	2004 %	2004 Difference from 1992	2008 Voting-age population	2008 Turnout	2008 %	2008 Difference from 1992
GEORGIA	4,878,000	683,274	14.0%	5,285,000	517,697	9.8%	-4.2					5,987,000	625,115	10.4%	-3.6	6,302,000	493,243	7.8%	-6.2
HAWAII	781,000	185,778	23.8%					841,000	177,283	21.1%	-2.7	879,000	167,855	19.1%	-4.7				
IDAHO	729,000	55,960	7.7%	812,000	34,551	4.3%	-3.4									1,024,000	40,117	3.9%	-3.8
ILLINOIS	8,103,000	1,456,268	18.0%	8,248,000	790,055	9.6%	-8.4					8,461,000	1,242,996	14.7%	-3.3	8,540,000	1,653,833	19.4%	1.4
INDIANA	4,126,000	320,732	7.0%					4,408,000	192,531	4.4%	-3.4	4,497,000	304,267	6.8%	-1.0				
IOWA	2,061,000	99,696	4.8%	2,103,000	99,547	4.7%	-0.1					2,171,000	52,710	2.4%	-2.4	2,201,000	91,859	4.2%	-0.7
KANSAS	1,812,000	160,431	8.9%	1,858,000	170,738	9.2%	0.3					1,935,000	109,185	5.6%	-3.2	1,968,000	98,805	5.0%	-3.8
KENTUCKY				2,892,000	267,950	9.3%						3,075,000	218,969	7.1%	-2.1	3,147,000	619,904	19.7%	10.4
LOUISIANA**	3,003,000	661,860	22.0%	3,103,000	534,887	17.2%	-4.8												
MAINE				939,000	85,273	9.1%		959,000	26,543	2.8%	-6.3					1,048,000	81,727	7.8%	-1.3
MARYLAND	3,510,000	490,477	14.0%					3,695,000	462,234	12.5%	-1.5	3,880,000	454,876	11.7%	-2.3				
MASSACHUSETTS				4,442,000	221,013	5.0%		4,467,000	42,263	0.9%	-4.0					4,625,000	493,561	10.7%	5.7
MICHIGAN				6,948,000	405,924	5.8%		7,103,000	417,503	5.9%	0.0					7,490,000	561,676	7.5%	1.7
MINNESOTA				3,370,000	225,334	6.7%		3,502,000	126,063	3.6%	-3.1					3,824,000	251,205	6.6%	-0.1
MISSISSIPPI				1,961,000	80,819	4.1%		2,048,000	75,002	3.7%	-0.5					2,151,000	359,099	16.7%	12.6
MISSOURI	3,839,000	632,267	16.5%					4,094,000	414,092	10.1%	-6.4	4,210,000	739,434	17.6%	1.1				
MONTANA				630,000	85,976	13.6%		666,000	89,431	13.4%	-0.2					731,000	165,050	22.6%	8.9
NEBRASKA				1,189,000	93,488	7.9%		1,219,000	114,701	9.4%	1.5					1,243,000	95,619	7.7%	-0.2
NEVADA	955,000	122,743	12.9%																
NEW HAMPSHIRE	833,000	83,001	10.0%	869,000	61,568	7.1%	-2.9					960,000	47,659	5.0%	-5.0	1,016,000	48,769	4.8%	-5.2
NEW JERSEY				5,591,000	223,444	4.0%		5,640,000	433,428	7.7%	3.7					5,904,000	344,532	5.8%	1.8
NEW MEXICO				1,153,000	117,794	10.2%		1,229,000	124,887	10.2%	-0.1					1,346,000	141,629	10.5%	0.3
NEW YORK	12,405,000	1,153,245	9.3%					12,460,000	689,668	5.5%	-3.8								
NORTH CAROLINA				5,492,000	588,963	10.7%										6,423,000	1,335,052	20.8%	10.1
NORTH DAKOTA	463,000	68,113	14.7%					475,000	36,585	7.7%	-7.0	481,000	39,636	8.2%	-6.5				
OHIO	8,031,000	859,622	10.7%					8,319,000	855,461	10.3%	-0.4	8,441,000	950,710	11.3%	0.6				
OKLAHOMA				2,407,000	336,040	14.0%						2,523,000	352,796	14.0%	0.0	2,561,000	190,776	7.4%	-6.5
OREGON	2,128,000	362,805	17.0%	2,275,000	304,968	13.4%	-3.6					2,515,000	348,606	13.9%	-3.2	2,615,000	549,966	21.0%	4.0
PENNSYLVANIA	8,996,000	1,242,336	13.8%					9,144,000	734,575	8.0%	-5.8	9,296,000	582,565	6.3%	-7.5				
RHODE ISLAND	736,000	150,746	20.5%					746,000	90,050	12.1%	-8.4					790,000	55,315	7.0%	-13.5
SOUTH CAROLINA				2,788,000	165,782	5.9%						3,082,000	167,790	5.4%	-0.5	3,224,000	147,287	4.6%	-1.4
SOUTH DAKOTA																			
TENNESSEE				3,984,000	246,631	6.2%		4,201,000	189,440	4.5%	-1.7					4,512,000	182,724	4.0%	-2.1

United States Senate Primary Elections (continued)

United States Senate Primary Elections *(continued)*

Democratic Turnout for Election Years 1992–2008 *(continued)*

State	1992 Voting-age population	Turnout	%	1996 Voting-age population	Turnout	%	Difference from 1992	2000 Voting-age population	Turnout	%	Difference from 1992	2004 Voting-age population	Turnout	%	Difference from 1992	2008 Voting-age population	Turnout	%	Difference from 1992
TEXAS				12,534,000	890,623	7.1%		13,287,000	618,032	4.7%	-2.5					14,886,000	2,177,252	14.6%	7.5
UTAH	1,144,000	120,746	10.6%																
VERMONT	421,000	24,721	5.9%					452,000	35,417	7.8%	2.0	474,000	29,113	6.1%	0.3				
VIRGINIA																			
WASHINGTON	3,597,000	561,588	15.6%					4,084,000	669,878	16.4%	0.8	4,287,000	769,514	17.9%	2.3				
WEST VIRGINIA				1,378,000	316,940	23.0%		1,398,000	251,438	18.0%	-5.0					1,428,000	352,094	24.7%	1.7
WISCONSIN	3,629,000	527,844	14.5%					3,899,000	205,981	5.3%	-9.3	4,041,000	252,777	6.3%	-8.3				
WYOMING				343,000	37,664	11.0%		360,000	25,592	7.1%	-3.9					388,000	24,300	6.3%	-4.7
Total	115,430,000	15,820,033	13.7%	90,766,000	7,691,812	8.5%	-5.2	133,133,000	11,936,821	9.0%	-4.7	113,654,000	11,873,446	10.4%	-3.3	96,476,000	10,995,702	11.4%	-2.3

Other Turnout for Election Years 1992–2008

State	1992 Voting-age population	Turnout	%	1996 Voting-age population	Turnout	%	Difference from 1992*	2000 Voting-age population	Turnout	%	Difference from 1992	2004 Voting-age population	Turnout	%	Difference from 1992	2008 Voting-age population	Turnout	%	Difference from 1992
ALASKA	380,000	5,989	1.6%	401,000	3,751	0.9%	-0.6					449,000	6,097	1.4%	-0.2	476,000	5,591	1.2%	-0.4
ARIZONA	2,729,000	545	0.0%									3,750,000	2,756	0.1%	0.1				
CALIFORNIA	18,681,000	46,025	0.2%									21,152,000	59,451	0.3%	0.0				
HAWAII	781,000	4,244	0.5%									879,000	2,130	0.2%	-0.3				
ILLINOIS				8,248,000	1,706	0.0%													
IOWA	2,061,000	631	0.0%																
LOUISIANA**	3,003,000	74,785	2.5%	3,103,000	22,993	0.7%	-1.7												
MINNESOTA				3,370,000	3,553	0.1%										3,824,000	11,341	0.3%	0.2
MISSOURI												4,210,000	3,916	0.1%					
MONTANA				630,000	1,367	0.2%													
NEBRASKA																1,243,000	332	0.0%	
NEW HAMPSHIRE				869,000	771	0.1%										1,016,000	337	0.0%	-0.1
NEW MEXICO				1,153,000	1,443	0.1%													
VERMONT												474,000	242	0.1%					
WASHINGTON	3,597,000	19,362	0.5%									4,287,000	12,945	0.3%	-0.2				
WISCONSIN	3,629,000	1,025	0.0%									4,041,000	901	0.0%	0.0				
Total	34,861,000	152,606	0.4%	17,774,000	35,584	0.2%	-0.2					39,242,000	88,438	0.2%	-0.2	6,559,000	17,601	0.3%	-0.2

*Percentage point difference between turnout in current year and initial year listed in chart. If data do not appear for a state in the initial year listed, the difference is calculated from the first year in which data do appear for that state.

**In 1978 Louisiana eliminated the partisan primary for senator and instituted an open primary with candidates from all parties running on the same ballot. Any candidate who received a majority appeared in the general election unopposed. If no candidate received fifty percent, a runoff was held between the top two finishers. In 2008 Louisiana returned to a partisan primary system.

Midterm Turnout Election Based on Highest Statewide Turnout, Election Years 1990–2006

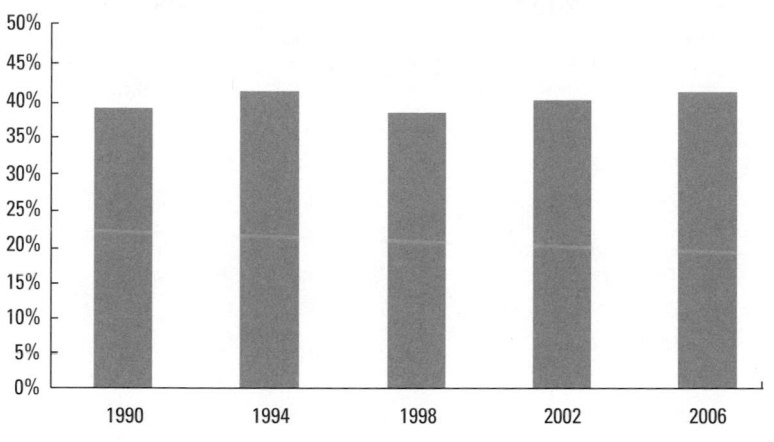

YEAR	VOTING-AGE POPULATION	TOTAL	%
1990	175,699,000	67,701,128	38.5%
1994	183,341,000	74,931,073	40.9%
1998	190,676,000	72,311,312	37.9%
2002	197,598,000	78,358,099	39.7%
2006	205,178,000	83,636,298	40.8%

Partisan Turnout Midterm Election Based on Aggregate House of Representatives Turnout, Election Years 1990–2006

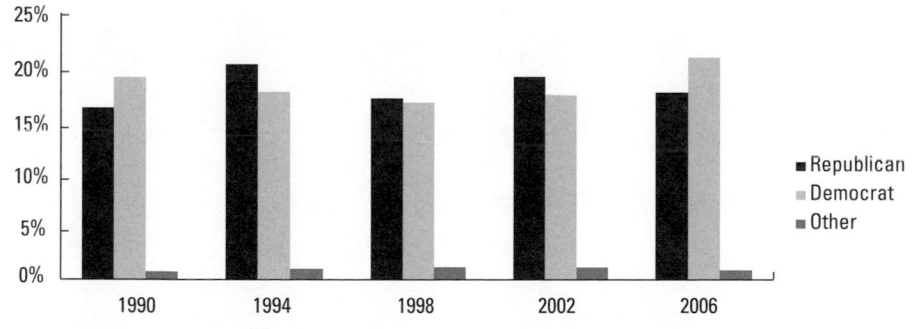

■ Republican
■ Democrat
■ Other

YEAR	VOTING-AGE POPULATION	REPUBLICAN TURNOUT	%	DEMOCRAT TURNOUT	%	OTHER TURNOUT	%
1990	175,699,000	28,056,339	16.0%	33,047,166	18.8%	1,310,734	0.7%
1994	183,341,000	36,753,202	20.0%	32,008,039	17.5%	1,843,274	1.0%
1998	190,676,000	32,149,162	16.9%	31,391,128	16.5%	2,213,599	1.2%
2002	197,598,000	37,305,165	18.9%	33,935,196	17.2%	2,255,479	1.1%
2006	205,178,000	35,733,764	17.4%	42,451,999	20.7%	1,819,858	0.9%

STATE GUBERNATORIAL GENERAL ELECTIONS

Election Years 1990–2006

State	1990 Voting-age population	Turnout	%	1994 Voting-age population	Turnout	%	Difference from 1990*	1998 Voting-age population	Turnout	%	Difference from 1990	2002 Voting-age population	Turnout	%	Difference from 1990	2006 Voting-age population	Turnout	%	Difference from 1990
ALABAMA	2,980,000	1,216,250	40.8%	3,111,000	1,201,969	38.6%	-2.2	3,238,000	1,317,842	40.7%	-0.1	3,313,000	1,367,053	41.3%	0.4	3,373,000	1,250,401	37.1%	-3.7
ALASKA	371,000	194,750	52.5%	394,000	213,435	54.2%	1.7	415,000	220,177	53.1%	0.6	439,000	231,484	52.7%	0.2	467,000	237,322	50.8%	-1.7
ARIZONA	2,596,000	1,055,406	40.7%	2,946,000	1,129,607	38.3%	-2.3	3,283,000	1,017,616	31.0%	-9.7	3,616,000	1,226,111	33.9%	-6.7	3,983,000	1,533,645	38.5%	-2.2
ARKANSAS	1,732,000	696,412	40.2%	1,829,000	716,840	39.2%	-1.0	1,921,000	706,011	36.8%	-3.5	1,987,000	805,856	40.6%	0.3	2,044,000	773,552	37.8%	-2.4
CALIFORNIA	18,412,000	7,699,467	41.8%	19,120,000	8,665,375	45.3%	3.5	19,799,000	8,381,871	42.3%	0.5	20,722,000	7,476,311	36.1%	-5.7	21,891,000	8,679,048	39.6%	-2.2
COLORADO	2,406,000	1,011,272	42.0%	2,666,000	1,116,184	41.9%	-0.2	2,916,000	1,321,307	45.3%	3.3	3,061,000	1,412,601	46.1%	4.1	3,176,000	1,558,405	49.1%	7.0
CONNECTICUT	2,418,000	1,141,122	47.2%	2,411,000	1,147,084	47.6%	0.4	2,403,000	999,537	41.6%	-5.6	2,436,000	1,022,582	42.0%	-5.2	2,496,000	1,122,887	45.0%	-2.2
DELAWARE	498,000	169,066	33.9%	529,000	183,649	34.7%	0.8					586,000	131,722	22.5%	-11.5	618,000	120,620	19.5%	-14.4
DISTRICT OF COLUMBIA																			
FLORIDA	9,357,000	3,530,871	37.7%	10,120,000	4,206,659	41.6%	3.8	10,853,000	3,965,751	36.5%	-1.2	11,661,000	5,100,581	43.7%	6.0	12,588,000	4,829,270	38.4%	0.6
GEORGIA	4,717,000	1,449,682	30.7%	5,141,000	1,545,327	30.1%	-0.7	5,548,000	1,792,808	32.3%	1.6	5,871,000	2,025,021	34.5%	3.8	6,186,000	2,122,258	34.3%	3.6
HAWAII	768,000	340,132	44.3%	801,000	369,013	46.1%	1.8	833,000	407,556	48.9%	4.6	866,000	382,110	44.1%	-0.2	904,000	344,315	38.1%	-6.2
IDAHO	696,000	320,610	46.1%	783,000	413,346	52.8%	6.7	865,000	381,248	44.1%	-2.0	933,000	411,477	44.1%	-2.0	1,000,000	450,822	45.1%	-1.0
ILLINOIS	8,044,000	3,257,410	40.5%	8,196,000	3,106,566	37.9%	-2.6	8,342,000	3,358,705	40.3%	-0.2	8,426,000	3,538,891	42.0%	1.5	8,507,000	3,486,671	41.0%	0.5
INDIANA																			
IOWA	2,043,000	971,224	47.5%	2,088,000	986,371	47.2%	-0.3	2,130,000	956,415	44.9%	-2.6	2,160,000	1,024,740	47.4%	-0.1	2,190,000	1,048,033	47.9%	0.3
KANSAS	1,793,000	783,325	43.7%	1,841,000	820,887	44.6%	0.9	1,888,000	742,665	39.3%	-4.4	1,922,000	835,692	43.5%	-0.2	1,956,000	849,700	43.4%	-0.2
KENTUCKY																			
LOUISIANA																			
MAINE	908,000	522,492	57.5%	931,000	511,308	54.9%	-2.6	953,000	421,009	44.2%	-13.4	987,000	505,191	51.2%	-6.4	1,032,000	550,865	53.4%	-4.2
MARYLAND	3,473,000	1,111,088	32.0%	3,573,000	1,410,300	39.5%	7.5	3,669,000	1,535,978	41.9%	9.9	3,813,000	1,706,179	44.7%	12.8	3,998,000	1,787,046	44.7%	12.7
MASSACHUSETTS	4,399,000	2,342,927	53.3%	4,431,000	2,164,278	48.8%	-4.4	4,462,000	1,903,336	42.7%	-10.6	4,517,000	2,194,179	48.6%	-4.7	4,595,000	2,219,779	48.3%	-5.0
MICHIGAN	6,717,000	2,564,563	38.2%	6,890,000	3,089,077	44.8%	6.7	7,055,000	3,027,104	42.9%	4.7	7,227,000	3,177,565	44.0%	5.8	7,420,000	3,801,274	51.2%	13.0
MINNESOTA	3,178,000	1,806,777	56.9%	3,321,000	1,765,581	53.2%	-3.7	3,459,000	2,091,766	60.5%	3.6	3,604,000	2,252,473	62.5%	5.6	3,766,000	2,202,937	58.5%	1.6
MISSISSIPPI																			
MISSOURI																			
MONTANA																			
NEBRASKA	1,143,000	586,542	51.3%	1,177,000	579,561	49.2%	-2.1	1,210,000	545,238	45.1%	-6.3	1,227,000	480,991	39.2%	-12.1	1,239,000	593,357	47.9%	-3.4
NEVADA	882,000	320,743	36.4%	1,074,000	379,676	35.4%	-1.0	1,260,000	433,630	34.4%	-2.0	1,419,000	504,079	35.5%	-0.8	1,583,000	582,158	36.8%	0.4
NEW HAMPSHIRE	819,000	295,018	36.0%	856,000	311,882	36.4%	0.4	892,000	318,940	35.8%	-0.3	939,000	442,976	47.2%	11.2	996,000	403,680	40.5%	4.5
NEW JERSEY																			
NEW MEXICO	1,040,000	411,236	39.5%	1,125,000	467,621	41.6%	2.0	1,205,000	498,703	41.4%	1.8	1,266,000	484,229	38.2%	-1.3	1,325,000	559,170	42.2%	2.7
NEW YORK	12,391,000	4,056,896	32.7%	12,429,000	5,203,762	41.9%	9.1	12,464,000	4,735,236	38.0%	5.3	12,514,000	4,579,078	36.6%	3.9	12,610,000	4,437,220	35.2%	2.4

State Gubernatorial General Elections *(continued)*

Election Years 1990–2006 *(continued)*

State	1990 Voting-age population	Turnout	%	1994 Voting-age population	Turnout	%	Difference from 1990	1998 Voting-age population	Turnout	%	Difference from 1990	2002 Voting-age population	Turnout	%	Difference from 1990	2006 Voting-age population	Turnout	%	Difference from 1990
NORTH CAROLINA																			
NORTH DAKOTA																			
OHIO	7,972,000	3,477,650	43.6%	8,127,000	3,346,238	41.2%	-2.4	8,276,000	3,354,213	40.5%	-3.1	8,396,000	3,228,992	38.5%	-5.2	8,518,000	4,022,681	47.2%	3.6
OKLAHOMA	2,289,000	911,314	39.8%	2,377,000	995,012	41.9%	2.0	2,461,000	873,585	35.5%	-4.3	2,509,000	1,035,620	41.3%	1.5	2,547,000	926,462	36.4%	-3.4
OREGON	2,071,000	1,112,847	53.7%	2,223,000	1,221,010	54.9%	1.2	2,370,000	1,113,098	47.0%	-6.8	2,477,000	1,260,497	50.9%	-2.8	2,578,000	1,379,475	53.5%	-0.2
PENNSYLVANIA	8,965,000	3,052,760	34.1%	9,045,000	3,585,526	39.6%	5.6	9,123,000	3,025,152	33.2%	-0.9	9,241,000	3,545,431	38.4%	4.3	9,394,000	4,092,652	43.6%	9.5
RHODE ISLAND	734,000	356,672	48.6%	740,000	361,377	48.8%	0.2	745,000	297,255	39.9%	-8.7	760,000	331,834	43.7%	-4.9	782,000	386,112	49.4%	0.8
SOUTH CAROLINA	2,566,000	760,965	29.7%	2,732,000	934,886	34.2%	4.6	2,890,000	1,064,317	36.8%	7.2	3,030,000	1,099,910	36.3%	6.6	3,173,000	1,091,963	34.4%	4.8
SOUTH DAKOTA	497,000	256,723	51.7%	518,000	311,613	60.2%	8.5	539,000	260,187	48.3%	-3.4	554,000	334,559	60.4%	8.7	569,000	335,508	59.0%	7.3
TENNESSEE	3,667,000	790,441	21.6%	3,904,000	1,487,130	38.1%	16.5	4,131,000	976,236	23.6%	2.1	4,301,000	1,653,042	38.4%	16.9	4,456,000	1,810,140	40.6%	19.1
TEXAS	11,419,000	3,892,746	34.1%	12,251,000	4,393,418	35.9%	1.8	13,051,000	3,738,078	28.6%	-5.4	13,790,000	4,527,068	32.8%	-1.3	14,589,000	4,399,068	30.2%	-3.9
UTAH																			
VERMONT	415,000	211,422	50.9%	431,000	212,046	49.2%	-1.7	447,000	218,120	48.8%	-2.1	466,000	225,980	48.5%	-2.5	400,000	262,524	53.8%	2.9
VIRGINIA																			
WASHINGTON																			
WEST VIRGINIA																			
WISCONSIN	3,574,000	1,379,727	38.6%	3,719,000	1,563,835	42.0%	3.4	3,857,000	1,756,016	45.5%	6.9	3,990,000	1,775,349	44.5%	5.9	4,131,000	2,161,700	52.3%	13.7
WYOMING	318,000	160,109	50.3%	337,000	200,990	59.6%	9.3	355,000	174,888	49.3%	-1.1	369,000	185,459	50.3%	-0.1	383,000	193,892	50.6%	0.3
Total	138,268,000	54,218,657	39.2%	144,187,000	60,318,439	41.8%	2.6	149,308,000	57,931,594	38.8%	-0.4	155,395,000	62,522,913	40.2%	1.0	161,551,000	66,606,612	41.2%	2.0

*Percentage point difference between turnout in current year and initial year listed in chart. If data do not appear for a state in the initial year listed, the difference is calculated from the first year in which data do appear for that state.

STATE GUBERNATORIAL GENERAL ELECTIONS

Republican Turnout for Election Years 1990–2006

State	1990 Voting-age population	1990 Turnout	1990 %	1994 Voting-age population	1994 Turnout	1994 %	1994 Difference from 1990*	1998 Voting-age population	1998 Turnout	1998 %	1998 Difference from 1990	2002 Voting-age population	2002 Turnout	2002 %	2002 Difference from 1990	2006 Voting-age population	2006 Turnout	2006 %	2006 Difference from 1990
ALABAMA	2,980,000	633,519	21.3%	3,111,000	604,926	19.4%	-1.8	3,238,000	554,746	17.1%	-4.1	3,313,000	672,225	20.3%	-1.0	3,373,000	718,327	21.3%	0.0
ALASKA	371,000	50,991	13.7%	394,000	87,157	22.1%	8.4	415,000	39,331	9.5%	-4.3	439,000	129,279	29.4%	15.7	467,000	114,697	24.6%	10.8
ARIZONA	2,596,000	523,984	20.2%	2,946,000	593,492	20.1%	0.0	3,283,000	620,188	18.9%	-1.3	3,616,000	554,465	15.3%	-4.9	3,983,000	543,528	13.6%	-6.5
ARKANSAS	1,732,000	295,925	17.1%	1,829,000	287,904	15.7%	-1.3	1,921,000	421,989	22.0%	4.9	1,987,000	427,189	21.5%	4.4	2,044,000	314,630	15.4%	-1.7
CALIFORNIA	18,412,000	3,791,904	20.6%	19,120,000	4,781,766	25.0%	4.4	19,799,000	3,216,749	16.2%	-4.3	20,722,000	3,169,801	15.3%	-5.3	21,891,000	4,850,157	22.2%	1.6
COLORADO	2,406,000	358,403	14.9%	2,666,000	432,042	16.2%	1.3	2,916,000	648,202	22.2%	7.3	3,061,000	884,583	28.9%	14.0	3,176,000	625,886	19.7%	4.8
CONNECTICUT	2,418,000	427,840	17.7%	2,411,000	415,201	17.2%	-0.5	2,403,000	628,707	26.2%	8.5	2,436,000	573,598	23.5%	5.9	2,496,000	709,987	28.4%	10.8
DELAWARE	498,000	19,764	4.0%	529,000	76,902	14.5%	10.6					586,000	45,407	7.7%	3.8	618,000	7,517	1.2%	-2.8
DISTRICT OF COLUMBIA																			
FLORIDA	9,357,000	1,535,068	16.4%	10,120,000	2,071,068	20.5%	4.1	10,853,000	2,192,105	20.2%	3.8	11,661,000	2,856,845	24.5%	8.1	12,588,000	2,519,845	20.0%	3.6
GEORGIA	4,717,000	645,625	13.7%	5,141,000	756,371	14.7%	1.0	5,548,000	790,201	14.2%	0.6	5,871,000	1,040,001	17.7%	4.0	6,186,000	1,229,724	19.9%	6.2
HAWAII	768,000	131,310	17.1%	801,000	107,908	13.5%	-3.6	833,000	198,952	23.9%	6.8	866,000	197,009	22.7%	5.7	904,000	215,313	23.8%	6.7
IDAHO	696,000	101,937	14.6%	783,000	216,123	27.6%	13.0	865,000	258,095	29.8%	15.2	933,000	231,566	24.8%	10.2	1,000,000	237,437	23.7%	9.1
ILLINOIS	8,044,000	1,653,126	20.6%	8,196,000	1,984,318	24.2%	3.7	8,342,000	1,714,094	20.5%	0.0	8,426,000	1,594,960	18.9%	-1.6	8,507,000	1,368,682	16.1%	-4.5
INDIANA																			
IOWA	2,043,000	591,852	29.0%	2,088,000	562,918	27.0%	-2.0	2,130,000	444,787	20.9%	-8.1	2,160,000	456,615	21.1%	-7.8	2,190,000	466,823	21.3%	-7.7
KANSAS	1,793,000	333,589	18.6%	1,841,000	526,113	28.6%	10.0	1,888,000	544,882	28.9%	10.3	1,922,000	376,830	19.6%	1.0	1,956,000	343,586	17.6%	-1.0
KENTUCKY																			
LOUISIANA																			
MAINE	908,000	243,766	26.8%	931,000	117,990	12.7%	-14.2	953,000	79,716	8.4%	-18.5	987,000	209,496	21.2%	-5.6	1,032,000	166,425	16.1%	-10.7
MARYLAND	3,473,000	446,980	12.9%	3,573,000	702,101	19.7%	6.8	3,669,000	688,357	18.8%	5.9	3,813,000	879,592	23.1%	10.2	3,998,000	825,464	20.6%	7.8
MASSACHUSETTS	4,399,000	1,175,817	26.7%	4,431,000	1,533,390	34.6%	7.9	4,462,000	967,160	21.7%	-5.1	4,517,000	1,091,988	24.2%	-2.6	4,595,000	784,342	17.1%	-9.7
MICHIGAN	6,717,000	1,276,134	19.0%	6,890,000	1,899,101	27.6%	8.6	7,055,000	1,883,005	26.7%	7.7	7,227,000	1,506,104	20.8%	1.8	7,420,000	1,608,086	21.7%	2.7
MINNESOTA	3,178,000	895,988	28.2%	3,321,000	1,094,156	32.9%	4.8	3,459,000	717,350	20.7%	-7.5	3,604,000	999,473	27.7%	-0.5	3,766,000	1,028,568	27.3%	-0.9
MISSISSIPPI																			
MISSOURI																			
MONTANA																			
NEBRASKA	1,143,000	288,741	25.3%	1,177,000	148,230	12.6%	-12.7	1,210,000	293,910	24.3%	-1.0	1,227,000	330,349	26.9%	1.7	1,239,000	435,507	35.1%	9.9
NEVADA	882,000	95,789	10.9%	1,074,000	156,875	14.6%	3.7	1,260,000	223,892	17.8%	6.9	1,419,000	344,001	24.2%	13.4	1,583,000	279,003	17.6%	6.8
NEW HAMPSHIRE	819,000	177,773	21.7%	856,000	218,134	25.5%	3.8	892,000	98,473	11.0%	-10.7	939,000	259,663	27.7%	5.9	996,000	104,288	10.5%	-11.2
NEW JERSEY																			
NEW MEXICO	1,040,000	185,692	17.9%	1,125,000	232,945	20.7%	2.9	1,205,000	271,948	22.6%	4.7	1,266,000	189,090	14.9%	-2.9	1,325,000	174,364	13.2%	-4.7
NEW YORK	12,391,000	865,948	7.0%	12,429,000	2,538,702	20.4%	13.4	12,464,000	2,571,991	20.6%	13.6	12,514,000	2,262,255	18.1%	11.1	12,610,000	1,274,335	10.1%	3.1

State Gubernatorial General Elections *(continued)*

Republican Turnout for Election Years 1990–2006 *(continued)*

State	1990 Voting-age population	1990 Turnout	1990 %	1994 Voting-age population	1994 Turnout	1994 %	1994 Difference from 1990	1998 Voting-age population	1998 Turnout	1998 %	1998 Difference from 1990	2002 Voting-age population	2002 Turnout	2002 %	2002 Difference from 1990	2006 Voting-age population	2006 Turnout	2006 %	2006 Difference from 1990
NORTH CAROLINA																			
NORTH DAKOTA																			
OHIO	7,972,000	1,938,103	24.3%	8,127,000	2,401,572	29.6%	5.2	8,276,000	1,678,721	20.3%	-4.0	8,396,000	1,865,007	22.2%	-2.1	8,518,000	1,474,285	17.3%	-7.0
OKLAHOMA	2,289,000	297,584	13.0%	2,377,000	466,740	19.6%	6.6	2,461,000	505,498	20.5%	7.5	2,509,000	441,277	17.6%	4.6	2,547,000	310,327	12.2%	-0.8
OREGON	2,071,000	444,646	21.5%	2,223,000	517,874	23.3%	1.8	2,370,000	334,001	14.1%	-7.4	2,477,000	581,785	23.5%	2.0	2,578,000	589,748	22.9%	1.4
PENNSYLVANIA	8,965,000	987,516	11.0%	9,045,000	1,627,976	18.0%	7.0	9,123,000	1,736,844	19.0%	8.0	9,241,000	1,566,567	17.0%	5.9	9,394,000	1,622,135	17.3%	6.3
RHODE ISLAND	734,000	92,177	12.6%	740,000	171,194	23.1%	10.6	745,000	151,602	20.3%	7.8	760,000	181,687	23.9%	11.3	782,000	197,013	25.2%	12.6
SOUTH CAROLINA	2,566,000	528,831	20.6%	2,732,000	470,756	17.2%	-3.4	2,890,000	486,373	16.8%	-3.8	3,030,000	580,459	19.2%	-1.5	3,173,000	601,871	19.0%	-1.6
SOUTH DAKOTA	497,000	151,198	30.4%	518,000	172,515	33.3%	2.9	539,000	166,621	30.9%	0.5	554,000	189,920	34.3%	3.9	569,000	206,990	36.4%	6.0
TENNESSEE	3,667,000	289,348	7.9%	3,904,000	807,104	20.7%	12.8	4,131,000	669,973	16.2%	8.3	4,301,000	786,683	18.3%	10.4	4,456,000	538,508	12.1%	4.2
TEXAS	11,419,000	1,826,431	16.0%	12,251,000	2,350,493	19.2%	3.2	13,051,000	2,550,821	19.5%	3.6	13,790,000	2,617,106	19.0%	3.0	14,589,000	1,716,803	11.8%	-4.2
UTAH																			
VERMONT	415,000	109,540	26.4%	431,000	40,292	9.3%	-17.0	447,000	89,726	20.1%	-6.3	466,000	101,738	21.8%	-4.6	488,000	148,014	30.3%	3.9
VIRGINIA																			
WASHINGTON																			
WEST VIRGINIA																			
WISCONSIN	3,574,000	802,321	22.4%	3,719,000	1,051,326	28.3%	5.8	3,857,000	1,047,718	27.2%	4.7	3,990,000	734,779	18.4%	-4.0	4,131,000	979,427	23.7%	1.3
WYOMING	318,000	55,471	17.4%	337,000	118,016	35.0%	17.6	355,000	97,235	27.4%	9.9	369,000	88,873	24.1%	6.6	383,000	58,100	15.2%	-2.3
Total	138,268,000	24,270,631	17.6%	144,187,000	32,341,691	22.4%	4.9	149,308,000	29,583,963	19.8%	2.3	155,395,000	31,018,265	20.0%	2.4	161,551,000	29,389,742	18.2%	0.6

Democratic Turnout for Election Years 1990–2006

State	1990 Voting-age population	1990 Turnout	1990 %	1994 Voting-age population	1994 Turnout	1994 %	1994 Difference from 1990*	1998 Voting-age population	1998 Turnout	1998 %	1998 Difference from 1990	2002 Voting-age population	2002 Turnout	2002 %	2002 Difference from 1990	2006 Voting-age population	2006 Turnout	2006 %	2006 Difference from 1990
ALABAMA	2,980,000	582,106	19.5%	3,111,000	594,169	19.1%	-0.4	3,238,000	760,155	23.5%	3.9	3,313,000	669,105	20.2%	0.7	3,373,000	519,827	15.4%	-4.1
ALASKA	371,000	60,201	16.2%	394,000	87,693	22.3%	6.0	415,000	112,879	27.2%	11.0	439,000	94,216	21.5%	5.2	467,000	97,238	20.8%	4.6
ARIZONA	2,596,000	519,691	20.0%	2,946,000	500,702	17.0%	-3.0	3,283,000	361,552	11.0%	-9.0	3,616,000	566,284	15.7%	-4.4	3,983,000	959,830	24.1%	4.1
ARKANSAS	1,732,000	400,386	23.1%	1,829,000	428,936	23.5%	0.3	1,921,000	272,923	14.2%	-8.9	1,987,000	378,303	19.0%	-4.1	2,044,000	430,090	21.0%	-2.1
CALIFORNIA	18,412,000	3,525,197	19.1%	19,120,000	3,519,799	18.4%	-0.7	19,799,000	4,858,817	24.5%	5.4	20,722,000	3,533,490	17.1%	-2.1	21,891,000	3,376,732	15.4%	-3.7
COLORADO	2,406,000	626,032	26.0%	2,666,000	619,205	23.2%	-2.8	2,916,000	639,905	21.9%	-4.1	3,061,000	475,372	15.5%	-10.5	3,176,000	888,095	28.0%	1.9
CONNECTICUT	2,418,000	236,641	9.8%	2,411,000	375,133	15.6%	5.8	2,403,000	354,187	14.7%	5.0	2,436,000	448,984	18.4%	8.6	2,496,000	397,745	15.9%	6.1
DELAWARE	498,000	144,701	29.1%	529,000	102,884	19.4%	-9.6					586,000	79,841	13.6%	-15.4	618,000	106,848	17.3%	-11.8
DISTRICT OF COLUMBIA																			
FLORIDA	9,357,000	1,995,206	21.3%	10,120,000	2,135,008	21.1%	-0.2	10,853,000	1,773,054	16.3%	-5.0	11,661,000	2,201,427	18.9%	-2.4	12,588,000	2,178,289	17.3%	-4.0

State Gubernatorial General Elections (continued)

State Gubernatorial General Elections (continued)

Democratic Turnout for Election Years 1990–2006 (continued)

State	1990 Voting-age population	Turnout	%	1994 Voting-age population	Turnout	%	Difference from 1990	1998 Voting-age population	Turnout	%	Difference from 1990	2002 Voting-age population	Turnout	%	Difference from 1990	2006 Voting-age population	Turnout	%	Difference from 1990
GEORGIA	4,717,000	766,662	16.3%	5,141,000	788,926	15.3%	-0.9	5,548,000	941,076	17.0%	0.7	5,871,000	937,057	16.0%	-0.3	6,186,000	811,049	13.1%	-3.1
HAWAII	768,000	203,491	26.5%	801,000	134,978	16.9%	-9.6	833,000	204,206	24.5%	-2.0	866,000	179,647	20.7%	-5.8	904,000	121,717	13.5%	-13.0
IDAHO	696,000	218,673	31.4%	783,000	181,363	23.2%	-8.3	865,000	110,815	12.8%	-18.6	933,000	171,711	18.4%	-13.0	1,000,000	198,845	19.9%	-11.5
ILLINOIS	8,044,000	1,569,217	19.5%	8,196,000	1,069,850	13.1%	-6.5	8,342,000	1,594,191	19.1%	-0.4	8,426,000	1,847,040	21.9%	2.4	8,507,000	1,736,219	20.4%	0.9
INDIANA																			
IOWA	2,043,000	379,372	18.6%	2,088,000	411,495	19.7%	1.1	2,130,000	500,231	23.5%	4.9	2,160,000	540,449	25.0%	6.5	2,190,000	565,898	25.8%	7.3
KANSAS	1,793,000	380,609	21.2%	1,841,000	294,733	16.0%	-5.2	1,888,000	168,243	8.9%	-12.3	1,922,000	441,858	23.0%	1.8	1,956,000	491,993	25.2%	3.9
KENTUCKY																			
LOUISIANA																			
MAINE	908,000	230,038	25.3%	931,000	172,951	18.6%	-6.8	953,000	50,506	5.3%	-20.0	987,000	238,179	24.1%	-1.2	1,032,000	209,927	20.3%	-5.0
MARYLAND	3,473,000	664,015	19.1%	3,573,000	708,094	19.8%	0.7	3,669,000	846,972	23.1%	4.0	3,813,000	813,422	21.3%	2.2	3,998,000	942,279	23.6%	4.4
MASSACHUSETTS	4,399,000	1,099,878	25.0%	4,431,000	611,650	13.8%	-11.2	4,462,000	901,843	20.2%	-4.8	4,517,000	985,981	21.8%	-3.2	4,595,000	1,234,984	26.9%	1.9
MICHIGAN	6,717,000	1,258,539	18.7%	6,890,000	1,188,438	17.2%	-1.5	7,055,000	1,143,574	16.2%	-2.5	7,227,000	1,633,796	22.6%	3.9	7,420,000	2,142,513	28.9%	10.1
MINNESOTA	3,178,000	836,218	26.3%	3,321,000	589,344	17.7%	-8.6	3,459,000	587,528	17.0%	-9.3	3,604,000	821,268	22.8%	-3.5	3,766,000	1,007,460	26.8%	0.4
MISSISSIPPI																			
MISSOURI																			
MONTANA																			
NEBRASKA	1,143,000	292,771	25.6%	1,177,000	423,270	36.0%	10.3	1,210,000	250,678	20.7%	-4.9	1,227,000	132,348	10.8%	-14.8	1,239,000	145,115	11.7%	-13.9
NEVADA	882,000	207,878	23.6%	1,074,000	200,026	18.6%	-4.9	1,260,000	182,281	14.5%	-9.1	1,419,000	110,935	7.8%	-15.8	1,583,000	255,684	16.2%	-7.4
NEW HAMPSHIRE	819,000	101,923	12.4%	856,000	79,686	9.3%	-3.1	892,000	210,769	23.6%	11.2	939,000	169,277	18.0%	5.6	996,000	298,761	30.0%	17.6
NEW JERSEY																			
NEW MEXICO	1,040,000	224,564	21.6%	1,125,000	186,686	16.6%	-5.0	1,205,000	226,755	18.8%	-2.8	1,266,000	268,674	21.2%	-0.4	1,325,000	384,806	29.0%	7.4
NEW YORK	12,391,000	2,157,087	17.4%	12,429,000	2,364,904	19.0%	1.6	12,464,000	1,570,317	12.6%	-4.8	12,514,000	1,534,064	12.3%	-5.1	12,610,000	3,086,709	24.5%	7.1
NORTH CAROLINA																			
NORTH DAKOTA																			
OHIO	7,972,000	1,539,416	19.3%	8,127,000	835,849	10.3%	-9.0	8,276,000	1,498,956	18.1%	-1.2	8,396,000	1,236,924	14.7%	-4.6	8,518,000	2,435,384	28.6%	9.3
OKLAHOMA	2,289,000	523,196	22.9%	2,377,000	294,936	12.4%	-10.4	2,461,000	357,552	14.5%	-8.3	2,509,000	448,143	17.9%	-5.0	2,547,000	616,135	24.2%	1.3
OREGON	2,071,000	508,749	24.6%	2,223,000	622,083	28.0%	3.4	2,370,000	717,061	30.3%	5.7	2,477,000	618,004	24.9%	0.4	2,578,000	699,786	27.1%	2.6
PENNSYLVANIA	8,965,000	2,065,244	23.0%	9,045,000	1,430,099	15.8%	-7.2	9,123,000	938,745	10.3%	-12.7	9,241,000	1,899,518	20.6%	-2.5	9,394,000	2,470,517	26.3%	3.3
RHODE ISLAND	734,000	264,411	36.0%	740,000	157,361	21.3%	-14.8	745,000	124,862	16.8%	-19.3	760,000	150,147	19.8%	-16.3	782,000	189,099	24.2%	-11.8
SOUTH CAROLINA	2,566,000	212,034	8.3%	2,732,000	447,002	16.4%	8.1	2,890,000	574,112	19.9%	11.6	3,030,000	518,288	17.1%	8.8	3,173,000	489,084	15.4%	7.2
SOUTH DAKOTA	497,000	105,525	21.2%	518,000	126,273	24.4%	3.1	539,000	85,473	15.9%	-5.4	554,000	140,263	25.3%	4.1	569,000	121,226	21.3%	0.1
TENNESSEE	3,667,000	480,885	13.1%	3,904,000	664,252	17.0%	3.9	4,131,000	287,750	7.0%	-6.1	4,301,000	837,280	19.5%	6.4	4,456,000	1,241,606	27.9%	14.7

State Gubernatorial General Elections (continued)

Democratic Turnout for Election Years 1990–2006 (continued)

State	1990 Voting-age population	1990 Turnout	1990 %	1994 Voting-age population	1994 Turnout	1994 %	1994 Difference from 1990	1998 Voting-age population	1998 Turnout	1998 %	1998 Difference from 1990	2002 Voting-age population	2002 Turnout	2002 %	2002 Difference from 1990	2006 Voting-age population	2006 Turnout	2006 %	2006 Difference from 1990
TEXAS	11,419,000	1,925,670	16.9%	12,251,000	2,014,399	16.4%	-0.4	13,051,000	1,165,592	8.9%	-7.9	13,790,000	1,809,915	13.1%	-3.7	14,589,000	1,310,353	9.0%	-7.9
UTAH																			
VERMONT	415,000	97,321	23.5%	431,000	145,661	33.8%	10.3	447,000	121,425	27.2%	3.7	466,000	95,370	20.5%	-3.0	488,000	108,090	22.1%	-1.3
VIRGINIA																			
WASHINGTON																			
WEST VIRGINIA																			
WISCONSIN	3,574,000	576,280	16.1%	3,719,000	482,850	13.0%	-3.1	3,857,000	679,553	17.6%	1.5	3,990,000	800,515	20.1%	3.9	4,131,000	1,139,115	27.6%	11.5
WYOMING	318,000	104,638	32.9%	337,000	80,747	24.0%	-8.9	355,000	70,754	19.9%	-13.0	369,000	92,662	25.1%	-7.8	383,000	135,516	35.4%	2.5
Total	138,268,000	27,084,465	19.6%	144,187,000	25,071,435	17.4%	-2.2	149,308,000	25,245,292	16.9%	-2.7	155,395,000	27,919,757	18.0%	-1.6	161,551,000	33,544,564	20.8%	1.2

Other Turnout for Election Years 1990–2006

State	1990 Voting-age population	1990 Turnout	1990 %	1994 Voting-age population	1994 Turnout	1994 %	1994 Difference from 1990*	1998 Voting-age population	1998 Turnout	1998 %	1998 Difference from 1990	2002 Voting-age population	2002 Turnout	2002 %	2002 Difference from 1990	2006 Voting-age population	2006 Turnout	2006 %	2006 Difference from 1990
ALABAMA	2,980,000	625	0.0%	3,111,000	2,874	0.1%	0.1	3,238,000	2,941	0.1%	0.1	3,313,000	25,723	0.8%	0.8	3,373,000	12,247	0.4%	0.3
ALASKA	371,000	83,558	22.5%	394,000	38,585	9.8%	-12.7	415,000	67,967	16.4%	-6.1	439,000	7,989	1.8%	-20.7	467,000	25,387	5.4%	17.1
ARIZONA	2,596,000	11,731	0.5%	2,946,000	35,413	1.2%	0.8	3,283,000	35,876	1.1%	0.6	3,616,000	105,362	2.9%	2.5	3,983,000	30,287	0.8%	0.3
ARKANSAS	1,732,000	101	0.0%					1,921,000	11,099	0.6%	0.6	1,987,000	364	0.0%	0.0	2,044,000	28,832	1.4%	1.4
CALIFORNIA	18,412,000	382,366	2.1%	19,120,000	363,810	1.9%	-0.2	19,799,000	306,305	1.5%	-0.5	20,722,000	773,020	3.7%	1.7	21,891,000	452,159	2.1%	0.0
COLORADO	2,406,000	26,837	1.1%	2,666,000	64,937	2.4%	1.3	2,916,000	33,200	1.1%	0.0	3,061,000	52,646	1.7%	0.6	3,176,000	44,424	1.4%	0.3
CONNECTICUT	2,418,000	476,641	19.7%	2,411,000	356,750	14.8%	-4.9	2,403,000	16,643	0.7%	-19.0					2,496,000	15,155	0.6%	-19.1
DELAWARE	498,000	4,601	0.9%	529,000	3,863	0.7%	-0.2					586,000	6,474	1.1%	0.2	618,000	6,255	1.0%	0.1
DISTRICT OF COLUMBIA																			
FLORIDA	9,357,000	597	0.0%	10,120,000	583	0.0%	0.0	10,853,000	592	0.0%	0.0	11,661,000	42,309	0.4%	0.4	12,588,000	131,136	1.0%	1.0
GEORGIA	4,717,000	37,395	0.8%	5,141,000	30	0.0%	-0.8	5,548,000	61,531	1.1%	0.3	5,871,000	47,963	0.8%	0.0	6,186,000	81,485	1.3%	0.5
HAWAII	768,000	5,331	0.7%	801,000	126,127	15.7%	15.1	833,000	4,398	0.5%	-0.2	866,000	5,454	0.6%	-0.1	904,000	7,285	0.8%	0.1
IDAHO				783,000	15,860	2.0%		865,000	12,338	1.4%	-0.6	933,000	8,200	0.9%	-1.1	1,000,000	14,540	1.5%	-0.6
ILLINOIS	8,044,000	35,067	0.4%	8,196,000	52,398	0.6%	0.2	8,342,000	50,420	0.6%	0.2	8,426,000	96,891	1.1%	0.7	8,507,000	381,770	4.5%	4.1
INDIANA																			
IOWA				2,088,000	11,958	0.6%		2,130,000	11,397	0.5%	0.0	2,160,000	27,676	1.3%	0.7	2,190,000	15,312	0.7%	0.1
KANSAS	1,793,000	69,127	3.9%	1,841,000	41	0.0%	-3.9	1,888,000	29,540	1.6%	-2.3	1,922,000	17,004	0.9%	-3.0	1,956,000	14,121	0.7%	-3.1
KENTUCKY																			
LOUISIANA																			
MAINE	908,000	48,688	5.4%	931,000	220,367	23.7%	18.3	953,000	290,787	30.5%	25.2	987,000	57,516	5.8%	0.5	1,032,000	174,513	16.9%	11.5

State Gubernatorial General Elections (continued)

State Gubernatorial General Elections (continued)

Other Turnout for Election Years 1990–2006 (continued)

State	1990 Voting-age population	Turnout	%	1994 Voting-age population	Turnout	%	Difference from 1990	1998 Voting-age population	Turnout	%	Difference from 1990	2002 Voting-age population	Turnout	%	Difference from 1990	2006 Voting-age population	Turnout	%	Difference from 1990
MARYLAND	3,473,000	93	0.0%	3,573,000	105	0.0%	0.0	3,669,000	649	0.0%	0.0	3,813,000	13,165	0.3%	0.3	3,998,000	19,303	0.5%	0.5
MASSACHUSETTS	4,399,000	67,232	1.5%	4,431,000	19,238	0.4%	-1.1	4,462,000	34,333	0.8%	-0.8	4,517,000	116,210	2.6%	1.0	4,595,000	200,453	4.4%	2.8
MICHIGAN	6,717,000	29,890	0.4%	6,890,000	1,538	0.0%	-0.4	7,055,000	525	0.0%	-0.4	7,227,000	37,665	0.5%	0.1	7,420,000	50,675	0.7%	0.2
MINNESOTA	3,178,000	74,571	2.3%	3,321,000	82,081	2.5%	0.1	3,459,000	786,888	22.7%	20.4	3,604,000	431,732	12.0%	9.6	3,766,000	166,909	4.4%	2.1
MISSISSIPPI																			
MISSOURI																			
MONTANA																			
NEBRASKA	1,143,000	5,030	0.4%	1,177,000	8,061	0.7%	0.2	1,210,000	650	0.1%	-0.4	1,227,000	18,294	1.5%	1.1	1,239,000	12,735	1.0%	0.6
NEVADA	882,000	17,076	1.9%	1,074,000	22,775	2.1%	0.2	1,260,000	27,457	2.2%	0.2	1,419,000	49,143	3.5%	1.5	1,583,000	47,471	3.0%	1.1
NEW HAMPSHIRE	819,000	15,322	1.9%	856,000	14,062	1.6%	-0.2	892,000	9,698	1.1%	-0.8	939,000	14,036	1.5%	-0.4	996,000	631	0.1%	-1.8
NEW JERSEY																			
NEW MEXICO	1,040,000	980	0.1%	1,125,000	47,990	4.3%	4.2					1,266,000	26,465	2.1%	2.0				
NEW YORK	12,391,000	1,033,861	8.3%	12,429,000	300,156	2.4%	-5.9	12,464,000	592,928	4.8%	-3.6	12,514,000	782,759	6.3%	-2.1	12,610,000	76,176	0.6%	-7.7
NORTH CAROLINA																			
NORTH DAKOTA																			
OHIO	7,972,000	131	0.0%	8,127,000	108,817	1.3%	1.3	8,276,000	176,536	2.1%	2.1	8,396,000	127,061	1.5%	1.5	8,518,000	113,012	1.3%	1.3
OKLAHOMA	2,289,000	90,534	4.0%	2,377,000	233,336	9.8%	5.9	2,461,000	10,535	0.4%	-3.5	2,509,000	146,200	5.8%	1.9				
OREGON	2,071,000	159,452	7.7%	2,223,000	81,053	3.6%	-4.1	2,370,000	62,036	2.6%	-5.1	2,477,000	60,708	2.5%	-5.2	2,578,000	89,941	3.5%	-4.2
PENNSYLVANIA				9,045,000	527,451	5.8%		9,123,000	349,563	3.8%	-2.0	9,241,000	79,346	0.9%	-5.0				
RHODE ISLAND	734,000	84	0.0%	740,000	32,822	4.4%	4.4	745,000	20,791	2.8%	2.8								
SOUTH CAROLINA	2,566,000	20,100	0.8%	2,732,000	17,128	0.6%	-0.2	2,890,000	3,832	0.1%	-0.7	3,030,000	1,163	0.0%	-0.7	3,173,000	1,008	0.0%	-0.8
SOUTH DAKOTA				518,000	12,825	2.5%		539,000	8,093	1.5%	-1.0	554,000	4,376	0.8%	-1.7	569,000	7,292	1.3%	-1.2
TENNESSEE	3,667,000	20,208	0.6%	3,904,000	15,774	0.4%	-0.1	4,131,000	18,513	0.4%	-0.1	4,301,000	29,079	0.7%	0.1	4,456,000	30,026	0.7%	0.1
TEXAS	11,419,000	140,645	1.2%	12,251,000	28,526	0.2%	-1.0	13,051,000	21,665	0.2%	-1.1	13,790,000	100,047	0.7%	-0.5	14,589,000	1,371,912	9.4%	8.2
UTAH																			
VERMONT	415,000	4,561	1.1%	431,000	26,093	6.1%	5.0	447,000	6,969	1.6%	0.5	466,000	28,872	6.2%	5.1	488,000	6,420	1.3%	0.2
VIRGINIA																			
WASHINGTON																			
WEST VIRGINIA																			
WISCONSIN	3,574,000	1,126	0.0%	3,719,000	29,659	0.8%	0.8	3,857,000	28,745	0.7%	0.7	3,990,000	240,055	6.0%	6.0	4,131,000	43,158	1.0%	1.0
WYOMING				337,000	2,227	0.7%		355,000	6,899	1.9%	1.3	369,000	3,924	1.1%	0.4	383,000	276	0.1%	-0.6
Total	125,749,000	2,863,561	2.3%	142,358,000	2,905,313	2.0%	-0.2	148,103,000	3,102,339	2.1%	-0.2	152,199,000	3,584,891	2.4%	0.1	147,503,000	3,672,306	2.5%	0.2

*Percentage point difference between turnout in current year and initial year listed in chart. If data do not appear for a state in the initial year listed, the difference is calculated from the first year in which data do appear for that state.

UNITED STATES SENATE GENERAL ELECTIONS

Election Years 1990–2006

State	1990 Voting-age population	Turnout	%	1994 Voting-age population	Turnout	%	Difference from 1990*	1998 Voting-age population	Turnout	%	Difference from 1990	2002 Voting-age population	Turnout	%	Difference from 1990	2006 Voting-age population	Turnout	%	Difference from 1990
ALABAMA	2,980,000	1,185,563	39.8%					3,238,000	1,293,405	39.9%	0.2	3,313,000	1,350,323	40.8%	1.0				
ALASKA	371,000	189,957	51.2%					415,000	221,807	53.4%	2.2	439,000	229,548	52.3%	1.1				
ARIZONA				2,946,000	1,119,060	38.0%		3,283,000	1,013,280	30.9%	-7.1					3,983,000	1,526,782	38.3%	0.3
ARKANSAS	1,732,000	494,735	28.6%					1,921,000	700,644	36.5%	7.9	1,987,000	804,121	40.5%	11.9				
CALIFORNIA				19,120,000	8,514,089	44.5%		19,799,000	8,311,905	42.0%	-2.5					21,891,000	8,541,476	39.0%	-5.5
COLORADO	2,406,000	1,022,027	42.5%					2,916,000	1,327,235	45.5%	3.0	3,061,000	1,416,093	46.3%	3.8				
CONNECTICUT				2,411,000	1,079,767	44.8%		2,403,000	964,457	40.1%	-4.6					2,496,000	1,134,762	45.5%	0.7
DELAWARE	498,000	180,152	36.2%	529,000	199,029	37.6%	1.4					586,000	232,304	39.6%	3.5	618,000	234,980	38.0%	1.8
DISTRICT OF COLUMBIA																			
FLORIDA				10,120,000	4,106,176	40.6%		10,853,000	3,899,261	35.9%	-4.6					12,588,000	4,793,534	38.1%	-2.5
GEORGIA	4,717,000	1,033,517	21.9%					5,548,000	1,753,911	31.6%	9.7	5,871,000	2,031,350	34.6%	12.7				
HAWAII	768,000	349,666	45.5%	801,000	356,902	44.6%	-1.0	833,000	398,124	47.8%	2.3					904,000	342,842	37.9%	-7.6
IDAHO	696,000	315,936	45.4%					865,000	378,174	43.7%	-1.7	933,000	408,544	43.8%	-1.6				
ILLINOIS	8,044,000	3,250,965	40.4%					8,342,000	3,394,521	40.7%	0.3	8,426,000	3,486,851	41.4%	1.0				
INDIANA	4,068,000	1,504,302	37.0%	4,220,000	1,543,559	36.6%	-0.4	4,364,000	1,588,617	36.4%	-0.6					4,554,000	1,341,162	29.5%	-7.5
IOWA	2,043,000	983,933	48.2%					2,130,000	947,907	44.5%	-3.7	2,160,000	1,023,075	47.4%	-0.8				
KANSAS	1,793,000	786,235	43.9%					1,888,000	727,236	38.5%	-5.3	1,922,000	776,850	40.4%	-3.4				
KENTUCKY	2,731,000	916,010	33.5%					2,967,000	1,145,414	38.6%	5.1	3,048,000	1,131,313	37.1%	3.6				
LOUISIANA**	2,963,000	1,396,113	47.1%					3,167,000	969,165	30.6%	-16.5	3,243,000	1,246,333	38.4%	-8.7				
MAINE	908,000	520,320	57.3%	931,000	511,733	55.0%	-2.3					987,000	504,899	51.2%	-6.1	1,032,000	543,981	52.7%	-4.6
MARYLAND				3,573,000	1,369,104	38.3%		3,669,000	1,507,447	41.1%	2.8					3,998,000	1,781,139	44.6%	6.2
MASSACHUSETTS	4,309,000	2,316,212	52.7%	4,431,000	2,179,964	49.2%	-3.5					4,517,000	2,006,758	44.4%	-8.2	4,595,000	2,165,490	47.1%	-5.5
MICHIGAN	6,717,000	2,560,494	38.1%	6,890,000	3,043,385	44.2%	6.1					7,227,000	3,129,287	43.3%	5.2	7,420,000	3,780,142	50.9%	12.8
MINNESOTA	3,178,000	1,808,045	56.9%	3,321,000	1,772,929	53.4%	-3.5					3,604,000	2,254,639	62.6%	5.7	3,766,000	2,197,912	58.4%	1.5
MISSISSIPPI	1,830,000	274,244	15.0%	1,927,000	608,085	31.6%	16.6					2,081,000	630,495	30.3%	15.3	2,132,000	605,921	28.4%	13.4
MISSOURI				3,923,000	1,775,116	45.2%		4,054,000	1,576,857	38.9%	-6.4	4,168,000	1,877,620	45.0%	-0.2	4,286,000	2,128,459	49.7%	4.4
MONTANA	577,000	319,336	55.3%	617,000	350,387	56.8%	1.4					687,000	323,537	47.1%	-8.3	719,000	406,505	56.5%	1.2
NEBRASKA	1,143,000	593,828	52.0%	1,177,000	579,205	49.2%	-2.7					1,227,000	480,217	39.1%	-12.8	1,239,000	592,316	47.8%	-4.1
NEVADA				1,074,000	380,530	35.4%		1,260,000	435,864	34.6%	-0.8					1,583,000	582,572	36.8%	1.4
NEW HAMPSHIRE	819,000	291,393	35.6%					892,000	314,956	35.3%	-0.3	939,000	447,135	47.6%	12.0				
NEW JERSEY	5,512,000	1,938,454	35.2%	5,571,000	2,054,887	36.9%	1.7					5,721,000	2,112,604	36.9%	1.8	5,852,000	2,250,070	38.4%	3.3
NEW MEXICO	1,040,000	406,938	39.1%	1,125,000	463,196	41.2%	2.0					1,266,000	483,056	38.2%	-1.0	1,325,000	558,560	42.2%	3.0
NEW YORK				12,429,000	4,790,336	38.5%		12,464,000	4,670,805	37.5%	-1.1					12,610,000	4,345,353	34.5%	-4.1

United States Senate General Elections (continued)

United States Senate General Elections *(continued)*

Election Years 1990–2006 *(continued)*

State	1990 Voting-age population	Turnout	%	1994 Voting-age population	Turnout	%	Difference from 1990	1998 Voting-age population	Turnout	%	Difference from 1990	2002 Voting-age population	Turnout	%	Difference from 1990	2006 Voting-age population	Turnout	%	Difference from 1990
NORTH CAROLINA	5,013,000	2,069,585	41.3%					5,714,000	2,012,143	35.2%	-6.1	6,010,000	2,331,181	38.8%	-2.5				
NORTH DAKOTA				468,000	236,547	50.5%		474,000	213,358	45.0%	-5.5					483,000	218,152	45.2%	-5.4
OHIO				8,127,000	3,436,884	42.3%		8,276,000	3,404,351	41.1%	-1.2					8,518,000	4,019,236	47.2%	4.9
OKLAHOMA	2,289,000	884,498	38.6%	2,377,000	982,430	41.3%	2.7	2,461,000	859,713	34.9%	-3.7	2,509,000	1,018,424	40.6%	1.9				
OREGON	2,071,000	1,099,255	53.1%					2,370,000	1,117,747	47.2%	-5.9	2,477,000	1,267,221	51.2%	-1.9				
PENNSYLVANIA				9,045,000	3,513,361	38.8%		9,123,000	2,957,772	32.4%	-6.4					9,394,000	4,077,762	43.4%	4.6
RHODE ISLAND	734,000	364,062	49.6%	740,000	345,388	46.7%	-2.9					760,000	323,582	42.6%	-7.0	782,000	370,109	47.3%	-2.3
SOUTH CAROLINA	2,566,000	750,716	29.3%					2,890,000	1,069,063	37.0%	7.7	3,030,000	1,095,157	36.1%	6.9				
SOUTH DAKOTA	497,000	258,976	52.1%					539,000	262,111	48.6%	-3.5	554,000	337,508	60.9%	8.8				
TENNESSEE	3,667,000	783,922	21.4%	3,904,000	1,480,391	37.9%	16.5					4,301,000	1,642,432	38.2%	16.8	4,456,000	1,833,695	41.2%	19.8
TEXAS	11,419,000	3,822,157	33.5%	12,251,000	4,279,940	34.9%	1.5					13,790,000	4,513,590	32.7%	-0.7	14,589,000	4,314,663	29.6%	-3.9
UTAH				1,237,000	519,323	42.0%		1,381,000	494,909	35.8%	-6.1					1,549,000	571,252	36.9%	-5.1
VERMONT				431,000	211,672	49.1%		447,000	214,036	47.9%	-1.2					488,000	262,419	53.8%	4.7
VIRGINIA	4,556,000	1,083,690	23.8%	4,774,000	2,057,463	43.1%	19.3					5,211,000	1,489,422	28.6%	4.8	5,467,000	2,370,445	43.4%	19.6
WASHINGTON				3,760,000	1,700,173	45.2%		4,009,000	1,888,561	47.1%	1.9					4,415,000	2,083,732	47.2%	2.0
WEST VIRGINIA	1,347,000	404,305	30.0%	1,369,000	420,936	30.7%	0.7					1,407,000	436,183	31.0%	1.0	1,423,000	460,334	32.3%	2.3
WISCONSIN				3,719,000	1,565,628	42.1%		3,857,000	1,761,740	45.7%	3.6					4,131,000	2,138,297	51.8%	9.7
WYOMING	318,000	157,632	49.6%	337,000	201,710	59.9%	10.3					369,000	183,280	49.7%	0.1	383,000	193,136	50.4%	0.9
Total	96,410,000	36,317,173	37.7%	139,675,000	57,749,285	41.3%	3.7	138,812,000	53,796,496	38.8%	1.1	107,831,000	43,024,932	39.9%	2.2	153,669,000	62,767,190	40.8%	3.2

*Percentage point difference between turnout in current year and initial year listed in chart. If data do not appear for a state in the initial year listed, the difference is calculated from the first year in which data do appear for that state.

**In 1978 Louisiana eliminated the partisan primary for senator and instituted an open primary with candidates from all parties running on the same ballot. Any candidate who received a majority appeared in the general election unopposed. If no candidate received fifty percent, a runoff was held between the top two finishers. In 2008 Louisiana returned to a partisan primary system.

UNITED STATES SENATE GENERAL ELECTIONS

Republican Turnout for Election Years 1990–2006

	1990			1994				1998				2002				2006			
State	Voting-age population	Turnout	%	Voting-age population	Turnout	%	Difference from 1990*	Voting-age population	Turnout	%	Difference from 1990	Voting-age population	Turnout	%	Difference from 1990	Voting-age population	Turnout	%	Difference from 1990
ALABAMA	2,980,000	467,190	15.7%					3,238,000	817,973	25.3%	9.6	3,313,000	792,561	23.9%	8.2				
ALASKA	371,000	125,806	33.9%					415,000	165,227	39.8%	5.9	439,000	179,438	40.9%	7.0				
ARIZONA				2,946,000	600,999	20.4%		3,283,000	696,577	21.2%	0.8					3,983,000	814,398	20.4%	0.0
ARKANSAS								1,921,000	292,906	15.2%		1,987,000	370,735	18.7%	3.4				
CALIFORNIA				19,120,000	3,817,025	20.0%		19,799,000	3,575,078	18.1%	-1.9					21,891,000	2,990,822	13.7%	-6.3
COLORADO	2,406,000	425,746	17.7%					2,916,000	829,370	28.4%	10.7	3,061,000	717,892	23.5%	5.8				
CONNECTICUT				2,411,000	334,833	13.9%		2,403,000	312,177	13.0%	-0.9					2,496,000	109,196	4.4%	-9.5
DELAWARE	498,000	64,554	13.0%	529,000	111,088	21.0%	8.0					586,000	94,783	16.2%	3.2	618,000	66,942	10.8%	-2.1
DISTRICT OF COLUMBIA																			
FLORIDA				10,120,000	2,894,726	28.6%		10,853,000	1,463,245	13.5%	-15.1					12,588,000	1,826,127	14.5%	-14.1
GEORGIA								5,548,000	918,540	16.6%		5,871,000	1,071,281	18.2%	1.7				
HAWAII	768,000	155,970	20.3%	801,000	86,320	10.8%	-9.5	833,000	70,964	8.5%	-11.8					904,000	126,097	13.9%	-6.4
IDAHO	696,000	193,641	27.8%					865,000	262,966	30.4%	2.6	933,000	266,215	28.5%	0.7				
ILLINOIS	8,044,000	1,135,628	14.1%					8,342,000	1,709,041	20.5%	6.4	8,426,000	1,325,703	15.7%	1.6				
INDIANA	4,068,000	806,048	19.8%	4,220,000	1,039,624	24.6%	4.8	4,364,000	552,732	12.7%	-7.1					4,554,000	1,171,596	25.7%	5.9
IOWA	2,043,000	446,869	21.9%					2,130,000	648,480	30.4%	8.6	2,160,000	447,892	20.7%	-1.1				
KANSAS	1,793,000	578,605	32.3%					1,888,000	474,639	25.1%	-7.1	1,922,000	641,075	33.4%	1.1				
KENTUCKY	2,731,000	478,034	17.5%					2,967,000	569,817	19.2%	1.7	3,048,000	731,679	24.0%	6.5				
LOUISIANA**	2,963,000	607,391	20.5%					3,167,000	306,616	9.7%	-10.8	3,243,000	631,035	19.5%	-1.0				
MAINE	908,000	319,167	35.2%	931,000	308,244	33.1%	-2.0					987,000	295,041	29.9%	-5.3	1,032,000	402,598	39.0%	3.9
MARYLAND				3,573,000	559,908	15.7%		3,669,000	444,637	12.1%	-3.6					3,998,000	787,182	19.7%	4.0
MASSACHUSETTS	4,399,000	1,321,712	30.0%	4,431,000	894,005	20.2%	-9.9									4,595,000	661,532	14.4%	-15.6
MICHIGAN	6,717,000	1,055,695	15.7%	6,890,000	1,578,770	22.9%	7.2					7,227,000	1,185,545	16.4%	0.7	7,420,000	1,559,597	21.0%	5.3
MINNESOTA	3,178,000	864,375	27.2%	3,321,000	869,653	26.2%	-1.0					3,604,000	1,116,697	31.0%	3.8	3,766,000	835,653	22.2%	-5.0
MISSISSIPPI	1,830,000	274,244	15.0%	1,927,000	418,333	21.7%	6.7					2,081,000	533,269	25.6%	10.6	2,132,000	383,399	18.0%	3.0
MISSOURI				3,923,000	1,060,149	27.0%		4,054,000	830,625	20.5%	-6.5	4,168,000	935,032	22.4%	-4.6	4,286,000	1,006,941	23.5%	-3.5
MONTANA	577,000	93,836	16.3%	617,000	218,542	35.4%	19.2					687,000	103,611	15.1%	-1.2	719,000	196,283	27.3%	11.0
NEBRASKA	1,143,000	243,013	21.3%	1,177,000	260,668	22.1%	0.9					1,227,000	397,438	32.4%	11.1	1,239,000	213,928	17.3%	-4.0
NEVADA				1,074,000	156,020	14.5%		1,260,000	208,220	16.5%	2.0					1,583,000	322,501	20.4%	5.8
NEW HAMPSHIRE	819,000	189,792	23.2%					892,000	213,477	23.9%	0.8	939,000	227,229	24.2%	1.0				
NEW JERSEY	5,512,000	918,874	16.7%	5,571,000	966,244	17.3%	0.7					5,721,000	928,439	16.2%	-0.4	5,852,000	997,775	17.1%	0.4
NEW MEXICO	1,040,000	296,712	28.5%	1,125,000	213,025	18.9%	-9.6					1,266,000	314,193	24.8%	-3.7	1,325,000	163,826	12.4%	-16.2
NEW YORK				12,429,000	1,988,308	16.0%		12,464,000	2,058,988	16.5%	0.5					12,610,000	1,392,189	11.0%	-5.0

United States Senate General Elections (continued)

United States Senate General Elections (continued)

Republican Turnout for Election Years 1990–2006 (continued)

State	1990 Voting-age population	Turnout	%	1994 Voting-age population	Turnout	%	Difference from 1990	1998 Voting-age population	Turnout	%	Difference from 1990	2002 Voting-age population	Turnout	%	Difference from 1990	2006 Voting-age population	Turnout	%	Difference from 1990
NORTH CAROLINA	5,013,000	1,087,331	21.7%					5,714,000	945,943	16.6%	-5.1	6,010,000	1,248,664	20.8%	-0.9				
NORTH DAKOTA				468,000	99,390	21.2%		474,000	75,013	15.8%	-5.4					483,000	64,417	13.3%	-7.9
OHIO				8,127,000	1,836,556	22.6%		8,276,000	1,922,087	23.2%	0.6					8,518,000	1,761,037	20.7%	-1.9
OKLAHOMA	2,289,000	148,814	6.5%	2,377,000	542,390	22.8%	16.3	2,461,000	570,682	23.2%	16.7	2,509,000	583,579	23.3%	16.8				
OREGON	2,071,000	590,095	28.5%					2,370,000	377,739	15.9%	-12.6	2,477,000	712,287	28.8%	0.3				
PENNSYLVANIA				9,045,000	1,735,691	19.2%		9,123,000	1,814,180	19.9%	0.7					9,394,000	1,684,778	17.9%	-1.3
RHODE ISLAND	734,000	138,947	18.9%	740,000	222,856	30.1%	11.2					760,000	69,808	9.2%	-9.7	782,000	171,765	22.0%	3.0
SOUTH CAROLINA	2,566,000	482,032	18.8%					2,890,000	488,238	16.9%	-1.9	3,030,000	595,218	19.6%	0.9				
SOUTH DAKOTA	497,000	135,682	27.3%					539,000	95,431	17.7%	-9.6	554,000	166,957	30.1%	2.8				
TENNESSEE	3,667,000	233,703	6.4%	3,904,000	834,226	21.4%	15.0					4,301,000	891,498	20.7%	14.4	4,456,000	929,911	20.9%	14.5
TEXAS	11,419,000	2,302,357	20.2%	12,251,000	2,604,218	21.3%	1.1					13,790,000	2,497,243	18.1%	-2.1	14,589,000	2,661,789	18.2%	-1.9
UTAH				1,237,000	357,297	28.9%		1,381,000	316,652	22.9%	-6.0					1,549,000	356,238	23.0%	-5.9
VERMONT				431,000	106,505	24.7%		447,000	48,051	10.7%	-14.0					488,000	84,924	17.4%	-7.3
VIRGINIA	4,556,000	876,782	19.2%	4,774,000	882,213	18.5%	-0.8					5,211,000	1,229,894	23.6%	4.4	5,467,000	1,166,277	21.3%	2.1
WASHINGTON				3,760,000	947,821	25.2%		4,009,000	785,377	19.6%	-5.6					4,415,000	832,106	18.8%	-6.4
WEST VIRGINIA	1,347,000	128,071	9.5%	1,369,000	130,441	9.5%	0.0					1,407,000	160,902	11.4%	1.9	1,423,000	155,043	10.9%	1.4
WISCONSIN				3,719,000	636,989	17.1%		3,857,000	852,272	22.1%	5.0					4,131,000	630,299	15.3%	-1.9
WYOMING	318,000	100,784	31.7%	337,000	118,754	35.2%	3.5					369,000	133,710	36.2%	4.5	383,000	135,174	35.3%	3.6
Total	89,961,000	17,287,508	19.2%	139,675,000	29,431,831	21.1%	1.9	138,812,000	25,713,960	18.5%	-0.7	103,314,000	21,596,543	20.9%	1.7	153,669,000	26,662,340	17.4%	-1.9

Democratic Turnout for Election Years 1990–2006

State	1990 Voting-age population	Turnout	%	1994 Voting-age population	Turnout	%	Difference from 1990*	1998 Voting-age population	Turnout	%	Difference from 1990	2002 Voting-age population	Turnout	%	Difference from 1990	2006 Voting-age population	Turnout	%	Difference from 1990
ALABAMA	2,980,000	717,814	24.1%					3,238,000	474,568	14.7%	-9.4	3,313,000	538,878	16.3%	-7.8				
ALASKA	371,000	61,152	16.5%					415,000	43,743	10.5%	-5.9	439,000	24,133	5.5%	-11.0				
ARIZONA				2,946,000	442,510	15.0%		3,283,000	275,224	8.4%	-6.6					3,983,000	664,141	16.7%	1.7
ARKANSAS	1,732,000	493,910	28.5%					1,921,000	385,878	20.1%	-8.4	1,987,000	433,386	21.8%	-6.7				
CALIFORNIA				19,120,000	3,979,152	20.8%		19,799,000	4,410,056	22.3%	1.5					21,891,000	5,076,289	23.2%	2.4
COLORADO	2,406,000	569,048	23.7%					2,916,000	464,754	15.9%	-7.7	3,061,000	648,129	21.2%	-2.5				
CONNECTICUT				2,411,000	723,842	30.0%		2,403,000	628,306	26.1%	-3.9					2,496,000	450,837	18.1%	-12.0
DELAWARE	498,000	112,918	22.7%	529,000	84,554	16.0%	-6.7					586,000	135,253	23.1%	0.4	618,000	165,421	26.8%	4.1
DISTRICT OF COLUMBIA																			
FLORIDA				10,120,000	1,210,412	12.0%		10,853,000	2,436,016	22.4%	10.5					12,588,000	2,890,548	23.0%	11.0

United States Senate General Elections *(continued)*

Democratic Turnout for Election Years 1990–2006 *(continued)*

State	1990 Voting-age population	Turnout	%	1994 Voting-age population	Turnout	%	Difference from 1990	1998 Voting-age population	Turnout	%	Difference from 1990	2002 Voting-age population	Turnout	%	Difference from 1990	2006 Voting-age population	Turnout	%	Difference from 1990
GEORGIA	4,717,000	1,033,439	21.9%					5,548,000	791,904	14.3%	-7.6	5,871,000	932,242	15.9%	-6.0				
HAWAII	768,000	188,901	24.6%	801,000	256,189	32.0%	7.4	833,000	315,252	37.8%	13.2					904,000	210,330	23.3%	-1.3
IDAHO	696,000	122,295	17.6%					865,000	107,375	12.4%	-5.2	933,000	132,975	14.3%	-3.3				
ILLINOIS	8,044,000	2,115,337	26.3%					8,342,000	1,610,496	19.3%	-7.0	8,426,000	2,103,766	25.0%	-1.3				
INDIANA	4,068,000	696,639	17.1%	4,220,000	470,796	11.2%	-6.0	4,364,000	1,012,244	23.2%	6.1								
IOWA	2,043,000	535,975	26.2%					2,130,000	289,049	13.6%	-12.7	2,160,000	554,270	25.7%	-0.6				
KANSAS	1,793,000	207,491	11.6%					1,888,000	229,718	12.2%	0.6								
KENTUCKY	2,731,000	437,976	16.0%					2,967,000	563,051	19.0%	2.9	3,048,000	399,634	13.1%	-2.9				
LOUISIANA**	2,963,000	788,722	26.6%					3,167,000	620,502	19.6%	-7.0	3,243,000	573,347	17.7%	-8.9				
MAINE	908,000	201,053	22.1%	931,000	186,042	20.0%	-2.2					987,000	209,858	21.3%	-0.9	1,032,000	111,984	10.9%	-11.3
MARYLAND				3,573,000	809,125	22.6%		3,669,000	1,062,810	29.0%	6.3					3,998,000	965,477	24.1%	1.5
MASSACHUSETTS	4,399,000	992,917	22.6%	4,431,000	1,266,011	28.6%	6.0					4,517,000	1,605,976	35.6%	13.0	4,595,000	1,500,738	32.7%	10.1
MICHIGAN	6,717,000	1,471,753	21.9%	6,890,000	1,300,960	18.9%	-3.0					7,227,000	1,896,614	26.2%	4.3	7,470,000	2,151,278	29.0%	7.1
MINNESOTA	3,178,000	911,999	28.7%	3,321,000	781,860	23.5%	-5.2					3,604,000	1,078,627	29.9%	1.2	3,766,000	1,278,849	34.0%	5.3
MISSISSIPPI				1,927,000	189,752	9.8%										2,132,000	213,000	10.0%	0.1
MISSOURI				3,923,000	633,697	16.2%		4,054,000	690,208	17.0%	0.9	4,168,000	913,778	21.9%	5.8	4,286,000	1,055,255	24.6%	8.5
MONTANA	577,000	217,563	37.7%	617,000	131,845	21.4%	-16.3					687,000	204,853	29.8%	-7.9	719,000	199,845	27.8%	-9.9
NEBRASKA	1,143,000	349,779	30.6%	1,177,000	317,297	27.0%	-3.6					1,227,000	70,290	5.7%	-24.9	1,239,000	378,388	30.5%	-0.1
NEVADA				1,074,000	193,804	18.0%		1,260,000	208,621	16.6%	-1.5					1,583,000	238,796	15.1%	-3.0
NEW HAMPSHIRE	819,000	91,299	11.1%					892,000	88,883	10.0%	-1.2	939,000	207,478	22.1%	10.9				
NEW JERSEY	5,512,000	977,810	17.7%	5,571,000	1,033,487	18.6%	0.8					5,721,000	1,138,193	19.9%	2.2	5,052,000	1,200,843	20.5%	2.8
NEW MEXICO	1,040,000	110,033	10.6%	1,125,000	249,989	22.2%	11.6					1,266,000	168,863	13.3%	2.8	1,325,000	394,365	29.8%	19.2
NEW YORK				12,429,000	2,646,541	21.3%		12,464,000	2,551,065	20.5%	-0.8					12,610,000	2,863,728	22.7%	1.4
NORTH CAROLINA	5,013,000	981,573	19.6%					5,714,000	1,029,237	18.0%	-1.6	6,010,000	1,047,983	17.4%	-2.1				
NORTH DAKOTA				468,000	137,157	29.3%		474,000	134,747	28.4%	-0.9					483,000	150,146	31.1%	1.8
OHIO				8,127,000	1,348,213	16.6%		8,276,000	1,482,054	17.9%	1.3					8,518,000	2,257,369	26.5%	9.9
OKLAHOMA	2,289,000	735,684	32.1%	2,377,000	392,488	16.5%	-15.6	2,461,000	268,898	10.9%	-21.2	2,509,000	369,789	14.7%	-17.4				
OREGON	2,071,000	507,743	24.5%					2,370,000	682,425	28.8%	4.3	2,477,000	501,898	20.3%	-4.3				
PENNSYLVANIA				9,045,000	1,648,481	18.2%		9,123,000	1,028,839	11.3%	-6.9					9,394,000	2,392,984	25.5%	7.2
RHODE ISLAND	734,000	225,105	30.7%	740,000	122,532	16.6%	-14.1					760,000	253,774	33.4%	2.7	782,000	198,344	25.4%	-5.3
SOUTH CAROLINA	2,566,000	244,112	9.5%					2,890,000	563,377	19.5%	10.0	3,030,000	484,422	16.0%	6.5				
SOUTH DAKOTA	497,000	116,727	23.5%					539,000	162,884	30.2%	6.7	554,000	167,481	30.2%	6.7				
TENNESSEE	3,667,000	530,898	14.5%	3,904,000	623,164	16.0%	1.5					4,301,000	728,232	16.9%	2.5	4,456,000	879,976	19.7%	5.3

United States Senate General Elections (continued)

United States Senate General Elections *(continued)*

Democratic Turnout for Election Years 1990–2006 *(continued)*

State	1990 Voting-age population	Turnout	%	1994 Voting-age population	Turnout	%	Difference from 1990	1998 Voting-age population	Turnout	%	Difference from 1990	2002 Voting-age population	Turnout	%	Difference from 1990	2006 Voting-age population	Turnout	%	Difference from 1990
TEXAS	11,419,000	1,429,986	12.5%	12,251,000	1,639,615	13.4%	0.9					13,790,000	1,955,758	14.2%	1.7	14,589,000	1,555,202	10.7%	-1.9
UTAH				1,237,000	146,938	11.9%		1,381,000	163,172	11.8%	-0.1					1,549,000	177,459	11.5%	-0.4
VERMONT				431,000	85,868	19.9%		447,000	154,567	34.6%	14.7								
VIRGINIA				4,774,000	938,376	19.7%										5,467,000	1,175,606	21.5%	1.8
WASHINGTON				3,760,000	752,352	20.0%		4,009,000	1,103,184	27.5%	7.5					4,415,000	1,184,657	26.8%	6.8
WEST VIRGINIA	1,347,000	276,234	20.5%	1,369,000	290,495	21.2%	0.7					1,407,000	275,281	19.6%	-0.9	1,423,000	296,726	20.9%	0.3
WISCONSIN				3,719,000	912,662	24.5%		3,857,000	890,059	23.1%	-1.5					4,131,000	1,439,214	34.8%	10.3
WYOMING	318,000	56,848	17.9%	337,000	79,287	23.5%	5.7					369,000	49,570	13.4%	-4.4	383,000	57,671	15.1%	-2.8
Total	90,024,000	18,510,733	20.6%	139,675,000	26,025,493	18.6%	-1.9	138,812,000	26,923,166	19.4%	-1.2	98,617,000	19,804,739	20.1%	-0.5	148,627,000	33,775,466	22.7%	2.2

Other Turnout for Election Years 1990–2006

State	1990 Voting-age population	Turnout	%	1994 Voting-age population	Turnout	%	Difference from 1990*	1998 Voting-age population	Turnout	%	Difference from 1990	2002 Voting-age population	Turnout	%	Difference from 1990	2006 Voting-age population	Turnout	%	Difference from 1990
ALABAMA	2,980,000	559	0.0%					3,238,000	864	0.0%	0.0	3,313,000	18,884	0.6%	0.6				
ALASKA	371,000	2,999	0.8%					415,000	12,837	3.1%	2.3	439,000	25,977	5.9%	5.1				
ARIZONA				2,946,000	75,551	2.6%		3,283,000	41,479	1.3%	-1.3					3,983,000	48,243	1.2%	-1.4
ARKANSAS	1,732,000	825	0.0%					1,921,000	21,860	1.1%	1.1								
CALIFORNIA				19,120,000	717,912	3.8%		19,799,000	326,771	1.7%	-2.1					21,891,000	474,365	2.2%	-1.6
COLORADO	2,406,000	27,233	1.1%					2,916,000	33,111	1.1%	0.0	3,061,000	50,072	1.6%	0.5				
CONNECTICUT				2,411,000	21,092	0.9%		2,403,000	23,974	1.0%	0.1					2,496,000	574,729	23.0%	22.2
DELAWARE	498,000	2,680	0.5%	529,000	3,387	0.6%	0.1					586,000	2,268	0.4%	-0.2	618,000	2,617	0.4%	-0.1
DISTRICT OF COLUMBIA																			
FLORIDA				10,120,000	1,038	0.0%										12,588,000	76,859	0.6%	0.6
GEORGIA	4,717,000	78	0.0%					5,548,000	43,467	0.8%	0.8	5,871,000	27,827	0.5%	0.5				
HAWAII	768,000	4,787	0.6%	801,000	14,393	1.8%	1.2	833,000	11,908	1.4%	0.8					904,000	6,415	0.7%	0.1
IDAHO								865,000	7,833	0.9%		933,000	9,354	1.0%	0.1				
ILLINOIS								8,342,000	74,984	0.9%		8,426,000	57,382	0.7%	-0.2				
INDIANA	4,068,000	1,615	0.0%	4,220,000	33,139	0.8%	0.7	4,364,000	23,641	0.5%	0.5					4,554,000	169,566	3.7%	3.7
IOWA	2,043,000	1,089	0.1%					2,130,000	10,378	0.5%	0.4	2,160,000	20,905	1.0%	0.9				
KANSAS	1,793,000	139	0.0%					1,888,000	22,879	1.2%	1.2	1,922,000	135,775	7.1%	7.1				
KENTUCKY								2,967,000	12,546	0.4%									
LOUISIANA**								3,167,000	42,047	1.3%		3,243,000	41,951	1.3%	0.0				
MAINE	908,000	100	0.0%	931,000	17,447	1.9%	1.9									1,032,000	29,399	2.8%	2.8

United States Senate General Elections (continued)

Other Turnout for Election Years 1990–2006 (continued)

State	1990 Voting-age population	Turnout	%	1994 Voting-age population	Turnout	%	Difference from 1990	1998 Voting-age population	Turnout	%	Difference from 1990	2002 Voting-age population	Turnout	%	Difference from 1990	2006 Voting-age population	Turnout	%	Difference from 1990
MARYLAND				3,573,000	71	0.0%										3,998,000	28,480	0.7%	0.7
MASSACHUSETTS	4,399,000	1,583	0.0%	4,431,000	19,948	0.5%	0.4					4,517,000	400,782	8.9%	8.8	4,595,000	3,220	0.1%	0.0
MICHIGAN	6,717,000	33,046	0.5%	6,890,000	163,655	2.4%	1.9					7,227,000	47,128	0.7%	0.2	7,420,000	69,267	0.9%	0.4
MINNESOTA	3,178,000	31,671	1.0%	3,321,000	121,416	3.7%	2.7					3,604,000	59,315	1.6%	0.6	3,766,000	83,410	2.2%	1.2
MISSISSIPPI												2,081,000	97,226	4.7%		2,132,000	9,522	0.4%	-4.2
MISSOURI				3,923,000	81,270	2.1%		4,054,000	56,024	1.4%	-0.7	4,168,000	28,810	0.7%	-1.4	4,286,000	66,263	1.5%	-0.5
MONTANA	577,000	7,937	1.4%									687,000	15,073	2.2%	0.8	719,000	10,377	1.4%	0.1
NEBRASKA	1,143,000	1,036	0.1%	1,177,000	1,240	0.1%	0.0					1,227,000	12,489	1.0%	0.9				
NEVADA				1,074,000	30,706	2.9%		1,260,000	19,023	1.5%	-1.3					1,583,000	21,275	1.3%	-1.5
NEW HAMPSHIRE	819,000	10,302	1.3%					892,000	12,596	1.4%	0.2	939,000	12,428	1.3%	0.1				
NEW JERSEY	5,512,000	41,770	0.8%	5,571,000	55,156	1.0%	0.2					5,721,000	45,972	0.8%	0.0	5,852,000	51,452	0.9%	0.1
NEW MEXICO	1,040,000	193	0.0%	1,125,000	102	0.0%	0.0									1,325,000	369	0.0%	0.0
NEW YORK				12,429,000	155,487	1.3%		12,464,000	60,752	0.5%	-0.8					12,610,000	89,436	0.7%	0.5
NORTH CAROLINA	5,013,000	681	0.0%					5,714,000	36,963	0.6%	0.6	6,010,000	34,534	0.6%	0.6				
NORTH DAKOTA								474,000	3,598	0.8%						483,000	3,589	0.7%	0.0
OHIO				8,127,000	252,115	3.1%		8,276,000	210	0.0%	-3.1					8,518,000	830	0.0%	-3.1
OKLAHOMA				2,377,000	47,552	2.0%		2,461,000	20,133	0.8%	-1.2	2,509,000	65,056	2.6%	1.8				
OREGON	2,071,000	1,417	0.1%					2,370,000	57,583	2.4%	2.4	2,477,000	53,036	2.1%	2.1				
PENNSYLVANIA				9,045,000	129,189	1.4%		9,123,000	114,753	1.3%	-0.2								
RHODE ISLAND	734,000	10	0.0%																
SOUTH CAROLINA	2,566,000	24,572	1.0%					2,890,000	17,448	0.6%	-0.4	3,030,000	15,517	0.5%	-0.4				
SOUTH DAKOTA	497,000	6,567	1.3%					539,000	3,796	0.7%	-0.6	554,000	3,070	0.6%	-0.8				
TENNESSEE	3,667,000	19,321	0.5%	3,904,000	23,001	0.6%	0.1					4,301,000	22,702	0.5%	0.0	4,456,000	23,808	0.5%	0.0
TEXAS	11,419,000	89,814	0.8%	12,251,000	36,107	0.3%	-0.5					13,790,000	60,589	0.4%	-0.3	14,589,000	97,672	0.7%	-0.1
UTAH				1,237,000	15,088	1.2%		1,381,000	15,085	1.1%	-0.1					1,549,000	37,555	2.4%	1.2
VERMONT				431,000	19,299	4.5%		447,000	11,418	2.6%	-1.9					488,000	177,495	36.4%	31.9
VIRGINIA	4,556,000	206,908	4.5%	4,774,000	236,874	5.0%	0.4					5,211,000	259,528	5.0%	0.4	5,467,000	28,562	0.5%	-4.0
WASHINGTON																4,415,000	66,969	1.5%	
WEST VIRGINIA																1,423,000	8,565	0.6%	
WISCONSIN				3,719,000	15,977	0.4%		3,857,000	19,409	0.5%	0.1					4,131,000	68,784	1.7%	1.2
WYOMING				337,000	3,669	1.1%										383,000	291	0.1%	-1.0
Total	76,192,000	518,932	0.7%	130,794,000	2,291,961	1.8%	1.1	120,281,000	1,159,370	1.0%	0.3	98,007,000	1,623,650	1.7%	1.0	142,254,000	2,329,384	1.6%	1.0

*Percentage point difference between turnout in current year and initial year listed in chart. If data do not appear for a state in the initial year listed, the difference is calculated from the first year in which data do appear for that state.

**In 1978 Louisiana eliminated the partisan primary for senator and instituted an open primary with candidates from all parties running on the same ballot. Any candidate who received a majority appeared in the general election unopposed. If no candidate received fifty percent, a runoff was held between the top two finishers. In 2008 Louisiana returned to a partisan primary system.

UNITED STATES HOUSE OF REPRESENTATIVES GENERAL ELECTIONS

Election Years 1990–2006

State	1990 Voting-age population	1990 Turnout	1990 %	1994 Voting-age population	1994 Turnout	1994 %	1994 Difference from 1990*	1998 Voting-age population	1998 Turnout	1998 %	1998 Difference from 1990	2002 Voting-age population	2002 Turnout	2002 %	2002 Difference from 1990	2006 Voting-age population	2006 Turnout	2006 %	2006 Difference from 1990
ALABAMA	2,980,000	1,016,863	34.1%	3,111,000	1,115,019	35.8%	1.7	3,238,000	1,215,179	37.5%	3.4	3,313,000	1,268,321	38.3%	4.2	3,373,000	1,140,152	33.8%	-0.3
ALASKA	371,000	191,647	51.7%	394,000	208,240	52.9%	1.2	415,000	223,300	53.8%	2.2	439,000	227,725	51.9%	0.2	467,000	234,645	50.2%	-1.4
ARIZONA	2,596,000	966,347	37.2%	2,946,000	1,099,389	37.3%	0.1	3,283,000	1,003,766	30.6%	-6.6	3,616,000	1,194,400	33.0%	-4.2	3,983,000	1,493,150	37.5%	0.3
ARKANSAS	1,732,000	665,071	38.4%	1,829,000	709,012	38.8%	0.4	1,921,000	525,308	27.3%	-11.1	1,987,000	688,434	34.6%	-3.8	2,044,000	761,891	37.3%	-1.1
CALIFORNIA	18,412,000	7,286,826	39.6%	19,120,000	8,334,440	43.6%	4.0	19,799,000	7,985,216	40.3%	0.8	20,722,000	7,248,417	35.0%	-4.6	21,891,000	8,295,816	37.9%	-1.7
COLORADO	2,406,000	1,000,551	41.6%	2,666,000	1,055,588	39.6%	-2.0	2,916,000	1,274,149	43.7%	2.1	3,061,000	1,397,027	45.6%	4.1	3,176,000	1,539,009	48.5%	6.9
CONNECTICUT	2,418,000	1,036,892	42.9%	2,411,000	1,069,167	44.3%	1.5	2,403,000	954,459	39.7%	-3.2	2,436,000	989,280	40.6%	-2.3	2,496,000	1,074,736	43.1%	0.2
DELAWARE	498,000	177,432	35.6%	529,000	195,037	36.9%	1.2	559,000	178,781	32.0%	-3.6	586,000	228,405	39.0%	3.3	618,000	251,694	40.7%	5.1
DISTRICT OF COLUMBIA																			
FLORIDA	9,357,000	2,378,435	25.4%	10,120,000	2,851,792	28.2%	2.8	10,853,000	1,108,621	10.2%	-15.2	11,661,000	3,766,535	32.3%	6.9	12,588,000	3,851,939	30.6%	5.2
GEORGIA	4,717,000	1,393,660	29.5%	5,141,000	1,497,536	29.1%	-0.4	5,548,000	1,631,715	29.4%	-0.1	5,871,000	1,917,749	32.7%	3.1	6,186,000	2,070,309	33.5%	3.9
HAWAII	768,000	340,999	44.4%	801,000	354,102	44.2%	-0.2	833,000	397,442	47.7%	3.3	866,000	359,984	41.6%	-2.8	904,000	337,944	37.4%	-7.0
IDAHO	696,000	314,512	45.2%	783,000	393,083	50.2%	5.0	865,000	378,829	43.8%	-1.4	933,000	405,023	43.4%	-1.8	1,000,000	445,306	44.5%	-0.7
ILLINOIS	8,044,000	3,077,167	38.3%	8,196,000	3,043,950	37.1%	-1.1	8,342,000	3,273,534	39.2%	1.0	8,426,000	3,429,046	40.7%	2.4	8,507,000	3,436,465	40.4%	2.1
INDIANA	4,068,000	1,514,006	37.2%	4,220,000	1,543,526	36.6%	-0.6	4,364,000	1,575,871	36.1%	-1.1	4,464,000	1,521,353	34.1%	-3.1	4,554,000	1,666,922	36.6%	-0.6
IOWA	2,043,000	792,140	38.8%	2,088,000	977,406	46.8%	8.0	2,130,000	900,701	42.3%	3.5	2,160,000	1,012,622	46.9%	8.1	2,190,000	1,032,981	47.2%	8.4
KANSAS	1,793,000	780,998	43.6%	1,841,000	817,396	44.4%	0.8	1,888,000	727,448	38.5%	-5.0	1,922,000	829,890	43.2%	-0.4	1,956,000	845,127	43.2%	-0.4
KENTUCKY	2,731,000	763,706	28.0%	2,851,000	784,299	27.5%	-0.5	2,967,000	1,098,862	37.0%	9.1	3,048,000	1,114,242	36.6%	8.6	3,122,000	1,253,526	40.2%	12.2
LOUISIANA	2,963,000	1,166,386	39.4%	3,067,000	826,837	27.0%	-12.4	3,167,000	303,971	9.6%	-29.8	3,243,000	1,152,356	35.5%	-3.8	3,313,000	902,496	27.2%	-12.1
MAINE	908,000	517,394	57.0%	931,000	502,663	54.0%	-3.0	953,000	414,553	43.5%	-13.5	987,000	495,294	50.2%	-6.8	1,032,000	535,935	51.9%	-5.1
MARYLAND	3,473,000	1,090,543	31.4%	3,573,000	1,345,073	37.6%	6.2	3,669,000	1,481,945	40.4%	9.0	3,813,000	1,660,965	43.6%	12.2	3,998,000	1,701,202	42.6%	11.2
MASSACHUSETTS	4,399,000	2,051,171	46.6%	4,431,000	1,976,374	44.6%	-2.0	4,462,000	1,744,015	39.1%	-7.5	4,517,000	1,840,871	40.8%	-5.9	4,595,000	1,923,657	41.9%	-4.8
MICHIGAN	6,717,000	2,433,629	36.2%	6,890,000	3,003,074	43.6%	7.4	7,055,000	2,985,233	42.3%	6.1	7,227,000	3,055,897	42.3%	6.1	7,420,000	3,648,502	49.2%	12.9
MINNESOTA	3,178,000	1,780,918	56.0%	3,321,000	1,748,385	52.6%	-3.4	3,459,000	2,039,603	59.0%	2.9	3,604,000	2,201,383	61.1%	5.0	3,766,000	2,178,974	57.9%	1.8
MISSISSIPPI	1,830,000	368,502	20.1%	1,927,000	620,319	32.2%	12.1	2,021,000	550,453	27.2%	7.1	2,081,000	677,366	32.6%	12.4	2,132,000	600,697	28.2%	8.0
MISSOURI	3,787,000	1,352,686	35.7%	3,923,000	1,765,509	45.0%	9.3	4,054,000	1,572,117	38.8%	3.1	4,168,000	1,853,563	44.5%	8.8	4,286,000	2,097,292	48.9%	13.2
MONTANA	577,000	317,434	55.0%	617,000	352,133	57.1%	2.1	654,000	331,551	50.7%	-4.3	687,000	331,321	48.2%	-6.8	719,000	406,125	56.5%	1.5
NEBRASKA	1,143,000	586,746	51.3%	1,177,000	570,763	48.5%	-2.8	1,210,000	525,959	43.5%	-7.9	1,227,000	473,814	38.6%	-12.7	1,239,000	596,087	48.1%	-3.2
NEVADA	882,000	313,061	35.5%	1,074,000	376,099	35.0%	-0.5	1,260,000	409,845	32.5%	-3.0	1,419,000	499,908	35.2%	-0.3	1,583,000	574,827	36.3%	0.8
NEW HAMPSHIRE	819,000	290,631	35.5%	856,000	309,395	36.1%	0.7	892,000	317,745	35.6%	0.1	939,000	443,382	47.2%	11.7	996,000	402,669	40.4%	4.9
NEW JERSEY	5,512,000	1,826,524	33.1%	5,571,000	2,005,116	36.0%	2.9	5,628,000	1,815,489	32.3%	-0.9	5,721,000	2,006,059	35.1%	1.9	5,852,000	2,136,842	36.5%	3.4
NEW MEXICO	1,040,000	359,334	34.6%	1,125,000	461,604	41.0%	6.5	1,205,000	497,690	41.3%	6.8	1,266,000	437,495	34.6%	0.0	1,325,000	561,084	42.3%	7.8
NEW YORK	12,391,000	3,661,888	29.6%	12,429,000	4,611,071	37.1%	7.5	12,464,000	4,267,360	34.2%	4.7	12,514,000	3,821,087	30.5%	1.0	12,610,000	4,070,349	32.3%	2.7

United States House of Representatives General Elections *(continued)*

Election Years 1990–2006 *(continued)*

State	1990 Voting-age population	Turnout	%	1994 Voting-age population	Turnout	%	Difference from 1990	1998 Voting-age population	Turnout	%	Difference from 1990	2002 Voting-age population	Turnout	%	Difference from 1990	2006 Voting-age population	Turnout	%	Difference from 1990
NORTH CAROLINA	5,013,000	2,011,394	40.1%	5,370,000	1,588,190	29.6%	-10.5	5,714,000	1,903,766	33.3%	-6.8	6,010,000	2,244,149	37.3%	-2.8	6,312,000	1,940,808	30.7%	-9.4
NORTH DAKOTA	460,000	233,979	50.9%	468,000	235,389	50.3%	-0.6	474,000	212,888	44.9%	-6.0	479,000	231,030	48.2%	-2.6	483,000	217,621	45.1%	-5.8
OHIO	7,972,000	3,418,298	42.9%	8,127,000	3,298,514	40.6%	-2.3	8,276,000	3,374,941	40.8%	-2.1	8,396,000	3,158,383	37.6%	-5.3	8,518,000	3,961,195	46.5%	3.6
OKLAHOMA	2,289,000	856,637	37.4%	2,377,000	969,046	40.8%	3.3	2,461,000	858,648	34.9%	-2.5	2,509,000	991,383	39.5%	2.1	2,547,000	905,194	35.5%	-1.9
OREGON	2,071,000	1,052,701	50.8%	2,223,000	1,192,957	53.7%	2.8	2,370,000	1,117,747	47.2%	-3.7	2,477,000	1,240,315	50.1%	-0.8	2,578,000	1,357,434	52.7%	1.8
PENNSYLVANIA	8,965,000	2,850,987	31.8%	9,045,000	3,371,572	37.3%	5.5	9,123,000	2,893,596	31.7%	-0.1	9,241,000	3,309,075	35.8%	4.0	9,394,000	4,011,205	42.7%	10.9
RHODE ISLAND	734,000	346,865	47.3%	740,000	341,908	46.2%	-1.1	745,000	284,073	38.1%	-9.1	760,000	328,238	43.2%	-4.1	782,000	373,148	47.7%	0.5
SOUTH CAROLINA	2,566,000	670,039	26.1%	2,732,000	867,593	31.8%	5.6	2,890,000	974,110	33.7%	7.6	3,030,000	978,843	32.3%	6.2	3,173,000	1,086,218	34.2%	8.1
SOUTH DAKOTA	497,000	257,298	51.8%	518,000	305,922	59.1%	7.3	539,000	258,590	48.0%	-3.8	554,000	336,807	60.8%	9.0	569,000	333,562	58.6%	6.9
TENNESSEE	3,667,000	716,872	19.5%	3,904,000	1,416,502	36.3%	16.7	4,131,000	913,681	22.1%	2.6	4,301,000	1,529,390	35.6%	16.0	4,456,000	1,715,420	38.5%	18.9
TEXAS	11,419,000	3,278,258	28.7%	12,251,000	4,120,060	33.6%	4.9	13,051,000	3,461,255	26.5%	-2.2	13,790,000	4,345,310	31.5%	2.8	14,589,000	4,141,765	28.4%	-0.3
UTAH	1,088,000	442,213	40.6%	1,237,000	504,349	40.8%	0.1	1,381,000	470,849	34.1%	-6.5	1,472,000	557,153	37.9%	-2.8	1,549,000	569,690	36.8%	-3.9
VERMONT	415,000	209,856	50.6%	431,000	211,449	49.1%	-1.5	447,000	215,133	48.1%	-2.4	466,000	221,965	47.6%	-2.9	400,000	262,726	53.8%	3.3
VIRGINIA	4,556,000	1,152,874	25.3%	4,774,000	1,908,754	40.0%	14.7	4,985,000	1,148,861	23.0%	-2.3	5,211,000	1,516,212	29.1%	3.8	5,467,000	2,297,236	42.0%	16.7
WASHINGTON	3,499,000	1,313,217	37.5%	3,760,000	1,687,085	44.9%	7.3	4,009,000	1,758,048	43.9%	6.3	4,212,000	1,739,118	41.3%	3.8	4,415,000	2,054,056	46.5%	9.0
WEST VIRGINIA	1,347,000	374,609	27.8%	1,369,000	406,564	29.7%	1.9	1,391,000	351,277	25.3%	-2.6	1,407,000	399,949	28.4%	0.6	1,423,000	454,813	32.0%	4.2
WISCONSIN	3,574,000	1,255,988	35.1%	3,719,000	1,459,067	39.2%	4.1	3,857,000	1,671,497	43.3%	8.2	3,990,000	1,637,156	41.0%	5.9	4,131,000	2,061,811	49.9%	14.8
WYOMING	318,000	158,055	49.7%	337,000	196,197	58.2%	8.5	355,000	174,219	49.1%	-0.6	369,000	182,152	49.4%	-0.3	383,000	193,369	50.5%	0.8
Total	175,699,000	62,414,239	35.5%	183,341,000	70,604,515	38.5%	3.0	190,676,000	65,753,889	34.5%	-1.0	197,598,000	73,495,840	37.2%	1.7	205,178,000	80,005,621	39.0%	3.5

*Percentage point difference between turnout in current year and initial year listed in chart. If data do not appear for a state in the initial year listed, the difference is calculated from the first year in which data do appear for that state.

UNITED STATES HOUSE OF REPRESENTATIVES GENERAL ELECTIONS

Republican Turnout for Election Years 1990–2006

State	1990 Voting-age population	1990 Turnout	1990 %	1994 Voting-age population	1994 Turnout	1994 %	1994 Difference from 1990*	1998 Voting-age population	1998 Turnout	1998 %	1998 Difference from 1990	2002 Voting-age population	2002 Turnout	2002 %	2002 Difference from 1990	2006 Voting-age population	2006 Turnout	2006 %	2006 Difference from 1990
ALABAMA	2,980,000	314,735	10.6%	3,111,000	558,437	18.0%	7.4	3,238,000	665,625	20.6%	10.0	3,313,000	694,606	21.0%	10.4	3,373,000	627,501	18.6%	8.0
ALASKA	371,000	99,003	26.7%	394,000	118,537	30.1%	3.4	415,000	139,676	33.7%	7.0	439,000	169,685	38.7%	12.0	467,000	132,743	28.4%	1.7
ARIZONA	2,596,000	620,906	23.9%	2,946,000	652,831	22.2%	-1.8	3,283,000	573,651	17.5%	-6.4	3,616,000	681,922	18.9%	-5.1	3,983,000	771,246	19.4%	-4.6
ARKANSAS	1,732,000	295,877	17.1%	1,829,000	372,889	20.4%	3.3	1,921,000	319,863	16.7%	-0.4	1,987,000	283,807	14.3%	-2.8	2,044,000	306,082	15.0%	-2.1
CALIFORNIA	18,412,000	3,346,692	18.2%	19,120,000	4,088,792	21.4%	3.2	19,799,000	3,509,530	17.7%	-0.5	20,722,000	3,225,666	15.6%	-2.6	21,891,000	3,314,398	15.1%	-3.0
COLORADO	2,406,000	487,326	20.3%	2,666,000	687,070	25.8%	5.5	2,916,000	715,820	24.5%	4.3	3,061,000	752,996	24.6%	4.3	3,176,000	623,785	19.6%	-0.6
CONNECTICUT	2,418,000	545,751	22.6%	2,411,000	516,134	21.4%	-1.2	2,403,000	442,066	18.4%	-4.2	2,436,000	465,982	19.1%	-3.4	2,496,000	419,888	16.8%	-5.7
DELAWARE	498,000	58,037	11.7%	529,000	137,960	26.1%	14.4	559,000	120,605	21.6%	9.9	586,000	164,605	28.1%	16.4	618,000	143,897	23.3%	11.6
DISTRICT OF COLUMBIA																			
FLORIDA	9,357,000	1,163,048	12.4%	10,120,000	1,693,874	16.7%	4.3	10,853,000	580,526	5.3%	-7.1	11,661,000	2,161,349	18.5%	6.1	12,588,000	2,182,853	17.3%	4.9
GEORGIA	4,717,000	538,865	11.4%	5,141,000	816,484	15.9%	4.5	5,548,000	1,039,711	18.7%	7.3	5,871,000	1,103,649	18.8%	7.4	6,186,000	1,138,048	18.4%	7.0
HAWAII	768,000	117,607	15.3%	801,000	119,514	14.9%	-0.4	833,000	119,328	14.3%	-1.0	866,000	116,693	13.5%	-1.8	904,000	118,134	13.1%	-2.2
IDAHO	696,000	131,450	18.9%	783,000	255,321	32.6%	13.7	865,000	204,568	23.6%	4.8	933,000	256,348	27.5%	8.6	1,000,000	248,105	24.8%	5.9
ILLINOIS	8,044,000	1,349,079	16.8%	8,196,000	1,576,655	19.2%	2.5	8,342,000	1,624,560	19.5%	2.7	8,426,000	1,657,093	19.7%	2.9	8,507,000	1,442,526	17.0%	0.2
INDIANA	4,068,000	682,593	16.8%	4,220,000	872,670	20.7%	3.9	4,364,000	861,951	19.8%	3.0	4,464,000	840,694	18.8%	2.1	4,554,000	831,785	18.3%	1.5
IOWA	2,043,000	385,003	18.8%	2,088,000	560,117	26.8%	8.0	2,130,000	551,767	25.9%	7.1	2,160,000	546,382	25.3%	6.5	2,190,000	522,388	23.9%	5.0
KANSAS	1,793,000	387,180	21.6%	1,841,000	519,127	28.2%	6.6	1,888,000	450,025	23.8%	2.2	1,922,000	536,026	27.9%	6.3	1,956,000	459,267	23.5%	1.9
KENTUCKY	2,731,000	397,388	14.6%	2,851,000	450,640	15.8%	1.3	2,967,000	637,091	21.5%	6.9	3,048,000	703,860	23.1%	8.5	3,122,000	611,780	19.6%	5.0
LOUISIANA	2,963,000	450,867	15.2%	3,067,000	400,607	13.1%	-2.2	3,167,000	107,743	3.4%	-11.8	3,243,000	707,923	21.8%	6.6	3,313,000	579,702	17.5%	2.3
MAINE	908,000	232,540	25.6%	931,000	234,070	25.1%	-0.5	953,000	124,834	13.1%	-12.5	987,000	205,780	20.8%	-4.8	1,032,000	163,165	15.8%	-9.8
MARYLAND	3,473,000	517,386	14.9%	3,573,000	682,578	19.1%	4.2	3,669,000	689,532	18.8%	3.9	3,813,000	752,944	19.7%	4.8	3,998,000	546,862	13.7%	-1.2
MASSACHUSETTS	4,399,000	566,923	12.9%	4,431,000	592,762	13.4%	0.5	4,462,000	412,508	9.2%	-3.6	4,517,000	290,484	6.4%	-6.5	4,595,000	198,550	4.3%	-8.6
MICHIGAN	6,717,000	1,089,299	16.2%	6,890,000	1,532,084	22.2%	6.0	7,055,000	1,438,283	20.4%	4.2	7,227,000	1,474,178	20.4%	4.2	7,420,000	1,624,865	21.9%	5.7
MINNESOTA	3,178,000	736,497	23.2%	3,321,000	846,950	25.5%	2.3	3,459,000	862,972	24.9%	1.8	3,604,000	1,029,612	28.6%	5.4	3,766,000	924,636	24.6%	1.4
MISSISSIPPI	1,830,000	69,216	3.8%	1,927,000	256,424	13.3%	9.5	2,021,000	232,415	11.5%	7.7	2,081,000	338,817	16.3%	12.5	2,132,000	304,308	14.3%	10.5
MISSOURI	3,787,000	624,666	16.5%	3,923,000	834,456	21.3%	4.8	4,054,000	748,432	18.5%	2.0	4,168,000	985,905	23.7%	7.2	4,286,000	1,049,346	24.5%	8.0
MONTANA	577,000	160,286	27.8%	617,000	148,715	24.1%	-3.7	654,000	175,748	26.9%	-0.9	687,000	214,100	31.2%	3.4	719,000	239,124	33.3%	5.5
NEBRASKA	1,143,000	309,106	27.0%	1,177,000	365,402	31.0%	4.0	1,210,000	392,736	32.5%	5.4	1,227,000	386,869	31.5%	4.5	1,239,000	334,177	27.0%	-0.1
NEVADA	882,000	150,885	17.1%	1,074,000	215,971	20.1%	3.0	1,260,000	275,163	21.8%	4.7	1,419,000	301,100	21.2%	4.1	1,583,000	260,317	16.4%	-0.7
NEW HAMPSHIRE	819,000	148,909	18.2%	856,000	180,138	21.0%	2.9	892,000	190,170	21.3%	3.1	939,000	254,797	27.1%	9.0	996,000	189,615	19.0%	0.9
NEW JERSEY	5,512,000	910,931	16.5%	5,571,000	1,091,251	19.6%	3.1	5,628,000	858,367	15.3%	-1.3	5,721,000	933,964	16.3%	-0.2	5,852,000	903,176	15.4%	-1.1
NEW MEXICO	1,040,000	213,803	20.6%	1,125,000	263,477	23.4%	2.9	1,205,000	246,127	20.4%	-0.1	1,266,000	175,342	13.9%	-6.7	1,325,000	247,825	18.7%	-1.9
NEW YORK	12,391,000	1,662,206	13.4%	12,429,000	1,992,633	16.0%	2.6	12,464,000	1,857,572	14.9%	1.5	12,514,000	1,770,532	14.1%	0.7	12,610,000	1,331,336	10.6%	-2.9

United States House of Representatives General Elections *(continued)*

Republican Turnout for Election Years 1990–2006 *(continued)*

State	1990 Voting-age population	Turnout	%	1994 Voting-age population	Turnout	%	Difference from 1990	1998 Voting-age population	Turnout	%	Difference from 1990	2002 Voting-age population	Turnout	%	Difference from 1990	2006 Voting-age population	Turnout	%	Difference from 1990
NORTH CAROLINA	5,013,000	935,054	18.7%	5,370,000	907,093	16.9%	-1.8	5,714,000	1,014,010	17.7%	-0.9	6,010,000	1,209,033	20.1%	1.5	6,312,000	913,893	14.5%	-4.2
NORTH DAKOTA	460,000	81,443	17.7%	468,000	105,988	22.6%	4.9	474,000	87,511	18.5%	0.8	479,000	109,957	23.0%	5.3	483,000	74,687	15.5%	-2.2
OHIO	7,972,000	1,590,381	19.9%	8,127,000	1,925,452	23.7%	3.7	8,276,000	1,742,025	21.0%	1.1	8,396,000	1,650,369	19.7%	-0.3	8,518,000	1,870,390	22.0%	2.0
OKLAHOMA	2,289,000	337,590	14.7%	2,377,000	554,800	23.3%	8.6	2,461,000	538,194	21.9%	7.1	2,509,000	546,832	21.8%	7.0	2,547,000	518,025	20.3%	5.6
OREGON	2,071,000	342,246	16.5%	2,223,000	400,020	22.4%	5.9	2,370,000	377,739	15.9%	-0.6	2,477,000	528,997	21.4%	4.8	2,578,000	557,491	21.6%	5.1
PENNSYLVANIA	8,965,000	1,552,475	17.3%	9,045,000	1,830,779	20.2%	2.9	9,123,000	1,472,161	16.1%	-1.2	9,241,000	1,859,270	20.1%	2.0	9,304,000	1,732,163	18.4%	1.1
RHODE ISLAND	734,000	164,916	22.5%	740,000	132,417	17.9%	-4.6	745,000	74,113	9.9%	-12.5	760,000	97,056	12.8%	-9.7	782,000	41,836	5.3%	-17.1
SOUTH CAROLINA	2,566,000	274,650	10.7%	2,732,000	552,085	20.2%	9.5	2,890,000	580,096	20.1%	9.4	3,030,000	564,223	18.6%	7.9	3,173,000	599,619	18.9%	8.2
SOUTH DAKOTA	497,000	83,484	16.8%	518,000	112,054	21.6%	4.8	539,000	194,157	36.0%	19.2	554,000	180,023	32.5%	15.7	569,000	97,864	17.2%	0.4
TENNESSEE	3,667,000	288,633	7.9%	3,904,000	775,843	19.9%	12.0	4,131,000	469,551	11.4%	3.5	4,301,000	770,510	17.9%	10.0	4,456,000	799,547	17.9%	10.1
TEXAS	11,419,000	1,498,096	13.1%	12,251,000	2,294,222	18.7%	5.6	13,051,000	1,786,731	13.7%	0.6	13,790,000	2,290,723	16.6%	3.5	14,589,000	2,183,833	15.0%	1.8
UTAH	1,088,000	191,067	17.6%	1,237,000	252,300	20.4%	2.8	1,381,000	304,256	22.0%	4.5	1,472,000	321,986	21.9%	4.3	1,549,000	292,235	18.9%	1.3
VERMONT	415,000	82,938	20.0%	431,000	98,523	22.9%	2.9	447,000	70,740	15.8%	-4.2	466,000	71,375	15.3%	-4.7	488,000	117,023	24.0%	4.0
VIRGINIA	4,556,000	410,941	9.0%	4,774,000	1,089,242	22.8%	13.8	4,985,000	542,216	10.9%	1.9	5,211,000	1,007,749	19.3%	10.3	5,467,000	1,222,790	22.4%	13.3
WASHINGTON	3,499,000	596,407	17.0%	3,760,000	853,712	22.7%	5.7	4,009,000	718,552	17.9%	0.9	4,212,000	778,922	18.5%	1.4	4,415,000	798,005	18.1%	1.0
WEST VIRGINIA	1,347,000	123,311	9.2%	1,369,000	137,663	10.1%	0.9	1,391,000	29,136	2.1%	-7.1	1,407,000	135,505	9.6%	0.5	1,423,000	190,893	13.4%	4.3
WISCONSIN	3,574,000	651,569	18.2%	3,719,000	893,405	24.0%	5.8	3,857,000	878,322	22.8%	4.5	3,990,000	888,696	22.3%	4.0	4,131,000	838,704	20.3%	2.1
WYOMING	318,000	87,078	27.4%	337,000	104,426	31.0%	3.6	355,000	100,687	28.4%	1.0	369,000	110,229	29.9%	2.5	383,000	93,336	24.4%	-3.0
Total	175,699,000	28,056,339	16.0%	183,341,000	36,753,202	20.0%	4.1	190,676,000	32,149,162	16.9%	0.9	197,598,000	37,305,165	18.9%	2.9	205,178,000	35,733,764	17.4%	1.4

Democratic Turnout for Election Years 1990–2006

State	1990 Voting-age population	Turnout	%	1994 Voting-age population	Turnout	%	Difference from 1990*	1998 Voting age population	Turnout	%	Difference from 1990	2002 Voting-age population	Turnout	%	Difference from 1990	2006 Voting-age population	Turnout	%	Difference from 1990
ALABAMA	2,980,000	689,987	23.2%	3,111,000	554,154	17.8%	-5.3	3,238,000	545,465	16.8%	-6.3	3,313,000	507,117	15.3%	-7.8	3,373,000	502,046	14.9%	-8.3
ALASKA	371,000	91,677	24.7%	394,000	68,172	17.3%	-7.4	415,000	77,232	18.6%	-6.1	439,000	39,357	9.0%	-15.7	467,000	93,879	20.1%	-4.6
ARIZONA	2,596,000	344,604	13.3%	2,946,000	409,672	13.9%	0.6	3,283,000	406,860	12.4%	-0.9	3,616,000	472,135	13.1%	-0.2	3,983,000	627,259	15.7%	2.5
ARKANSAS	1,732,000	369,194	21.3%	1,829,000	336,123	18.4%	-2.9	1,921,000	168,528	8.8%	-12.5	1,987,000	392,176	19.7%	-1.6	2,044,000	455,809	22.3%	1.0
CALIFORNIA	18,412,000	3,567,775	19.4%	19,120,000	3,959,574	20.7%	1.3	19,799,000	4,038,054	20.4%	1.0	20,722,000	3,721,081	18.0%	-1.4	21,891,000	4,720,164	21.6%	2.2
COLORADO	2,406,000	503,549	20.9%	2,666,000	364,391	13.7%	-7.3	2,916,000	533,297	18.3%	-2.6	3,061,000	589,412	19.3%	-1.7	3,176,000	832,987	26.2%	5.3
CONNECTICUT	2,418,000	489,206	20.2%	2,411,000	506,272	21.0%	0.8	2,403,000	495,557	20.6%	0.4	2,436,000	509,036	20.9%	0.7	2,496,000	642,863	25.8%	5.5
DELAWARE	498,000	116,274	23.3%	529,000	51,803	9.8%	-13.6	559,000	57,847	10.3%	-13.0	586,000	61,011	10.4%	-12.9	618,000	97,565	15.8%	-7.6
DISTRICT OF COLUMBIA																			
FLORIDA	9,357,000	1,212,978	13.0%	10,120,000	1,155,503	11.4%	-1.5	10,853,000	453,289	4.2%	-8.8	11,661,000	1,537,124	13.2%	0.2	12,588,000	1,599,968	12.7%	-0.3

United States House of Representatives General Elections (continued)

United States House of Representatives General Elections *(continued)*

Democratic Turnout for Election Years 1990–2006 *(continued)*

State	1990			1994				1998				2002				2006			
	Voting-age population	Turnout	%	Voting-age population	Turnout	%	Difference from 1990	Voting-age population	Turnout	%	Difference from 1990	Voting-age population	Turnout	%	Difference from 1990	Voting-age population	Turnout	%	Difference from 1990
GEORGIA	4,717,000	854,784	18.1%	5,141,000	681,051	13.2%	-4.9	5,548,000	592,004	10.7%	-7.5	5,871,000	814,100	13.9%	-4.3	6,186,000	932,143	15.1%	-3.1
HAWAII	768,000	215,777	28.1%	801,000	219,185	27.4%	-0.7	833,000	260,947	31.3%	3.2	866,000	232,344	26.8%	-1.3	904,000	219,810	24.3%	-3.8
IDAHO	696,000	183,062	26.3%	783,000	137,762	17.6%	-8.7	865,000	169,389	19.6%	-6.7	933,000	138,038	14.8%	-11.5	1,000,000	177,376	17.7%	-8.6
ILLINOIS	8,044,000	1,646,340	20.5%	8,196,000	1,459,928	17.8%	-2.7	8,342,000	1,565,998	18.8%	-1.7	8,426,000	1,740,541	20.7%	0.2	8,507,000	1,970,314	23.2%	2.7
INDIANA	4,068,000	830,500	20.4%	4,220,000	667,454	15.8%	-4.6	4,364,000	673,322	15.4%	-5.0	4,464,000	640,568	14.3%	-6.1	4,554,000	812,496	17.8%	-2.6
IOWA	2,043,000	400,852	19.6%	2,088,000	407,309	19.5%	-0.1	2,130,000	338,431	15.9%	-3.7	2,160,000	453,550	21.0%	1.4	2,190,000	492,937	22.5%	2.9
KANSAS	1,793,000	393,671	22.0%	1,841,000	298,269	16.2%	-5.8	1,888,000	272,252	14.4%	-7.5	1,922,000	259,911	13.5%	-8.4	1,956,000	369,191	18.9%	-3.1
KENTUCKY	2,731,000	353,439	12.9%	2,851,000	316,037	11.1%	-1.9	2,967,000	456,218	15.4%	2.4	3,048,000	360,924	11.8%	-1.1	3,122,000	601,723	19.3%	6.3
LOUISIANA	2,963,000	686,137	23.2%	3,067,000	375,539	12.2%	-10.9	3,167,000	196,228	6.2%	-17.0	3,243,000	361,471	11.1%	-12.0	3,313,000	295,762	8.9%	-14.2
MAINE	908,000	284,421	31.3%	931,000	235,988	25.3%	-6.0	953,000	280,537	29.4%	-1.9	987,000	289,514	29.3%	-2.0	1,032,000	350,721	34.0%	2.7
MARYLAND	3,473,000	565,669	16.3%	3,573,000	662,312	18.5%	2.2	3,669,000	792,280	21.6%	5.3	3,813,000	904,412	23.7%	7.4	3,998,000	1,099,441	27.5%	11.2
MASSACHUSETTS	4,399,000	1,420,422	32.3%	4,431,000	1,362,585	30.8%	-1.5	4,462,000	1,306,281	29.3%	-3.0	4,517,000	1,528,634	33.8%	1.6	4,595,000	1,632,307	35.5%	3.2
MICHIGAN	6,717,000	1,321,449	19.7%	6,890,000	1,418,142	20.6%	0.9	7,055,000	1,469,111	20.8%	1.2	7,227,000	1,507,174	20.9%	1.2	7,420,000	1,923,485	25.9%	6.2
MINNESOTA	3,178,000	1,042,201	32.8%	3,321,000	883,905	26.6%	-6.2	3,459,000	1,090,488	31.5%	-1.3	3,604,000	1,097,911	30.5%	-2.3	3,766,000	1,152,621	30.6%	-2.2
MISSISSIPPI	1,830,000	299,286	16.4%	1,927,000	354,487	18.4%	2.0	2,021,000	262,635	13.0%	-3.4	2,081,000	319,887	15.4%	-1.0	2,132,000	260,330	12.2%	-4.1
MISSOURI	3,787,000	728,020	19.2%	3,923,000	893,783	22.8%	3.6	4,054,000	787,655	19.4%	0.2	4,168,000	829,177	19.9%	0.7	4,286,000	992,258	23.2%	3.9
MONTANA	577,000	157,148	27.2%	617,000	171,372	27.8%	0.5	654,000	147,073	22.5%	-4.7	687,000	108,233	15.8%	-11.5	719,000	158,916	22.1%	-5.1
NEBRASKA	1,143,000	276,724	24.2%	1,177,000	203,062	17.3%	-7.0	1,210,000	104,548	8.6%	-15.6	1,227,000	46,843	3.8%	-20.4	1,239,000	261,910	21.1%	-3.1
NEVADA	882,000	144,231	16.4%	1,074,000	137,723	12.8%	-3.5	1,260,000	79,315	6.3%	-10.1	1,419,000	171,160	12.1%	-4.3	1,583,000	287,879	18.2%	1.8
NEW HAMPSHIRE	819,000	141,042	17.2%	856,000	116,724	13.6%	-3.6	892,000	124,000	13.9%	-3.3	939,000	175,905	18.7%	1.5	996,000	209,434	21.0%	3.8
NEW JERSEY	5,512,000	836,944	15.2%	5,571,000	879,855	15.8%	0.6	5,628,000	902,374	16.0%	0.8	5,721,000	1,030,204	18.0%	2.8	5,852,000	1,207,784	20.6%	5.5
NEW MEXICO	1,040,000	145,531	14.0%	1,125,000	187,532	16.7%	2.7	1,205,000	228,084	18.9%	4.9	1,266,000	262,071	20.7%	6.7	1,325,000	313,124	23.6%	9.6
NEW YORK	12,391,000	1,829,508	14.8%	12,429,000	2,146,180	17.3%	2.5	12,464,000	2,278,407	18.3%	3.5	12,514,000	1,924,769	15.4%	0.6	12,610,000	2,731,415	21.7%	6.9
NORTH CAROLINA	5,013,000	1,076,340	21.5%	5,370,000	681,064	12.7%	-8.8	5,714,000	827,078	14.5%	-7.0	6,010,000	970,716	16.2%	-5.3	6,312,000	1,026,915	16.3%	-5.2
NORTH DAKOTA	460,000	152,530	33.2%	468,000	123,134	26.3%	-6.8	474,000	119,668	25.2%	-7.9	479,000	121,073	25.3%	-7.9	483,000	142,934	29.6%	-3.6
OHIO	7,972,000	1,806,626	22.7%	8,127,000	1,327,955	16.3%	-6.3	8,276,000	1,604,291	19.4%	-3.3	8,396,000	1,457,160	17.4%	-5.3	8,518,000	2,081,737	24.4%	1.8
OKLAHOMA	2,289,000	519,047	22.7%	2,377,000	368,063	15.5%	-7.2	2,461,000	314,358	12.8%	-9.9	2,509,000	391,927	15.6%	-7.1	2,547,000	372,888	14.6%	-8.0
OREGON	2,071,000	667,258	32.2%	2,223,000	646,589	29.1%	-3.1	2,370,000	682,425	28.8%	-3.4	2,477,000	676,920	27.3%	-4.9	2,578,000	765,853	29.7%	-2.5
PENNSYLVANIA	8,965,000	1,292,717	14.4%	9,045,000	1,491,859	16.5%	2.1	9,123,000	1,379,834	15.1%	0.7	9,241,000	1,348,665	14.6%	0.2	9,394,000	2,229,091	23.7%	9.3
RHODE ISLAND	734,000	181,949	24.8%	740,000	209,491	28.3%	3.5	745,000	197,653	26.5%	1.7	760,000	224,545	29.5%	4.8	782,000	264,949	33.9%	9.1
SOUTH CAROLINA	2,566,000	382,939	14.9%	2,732,000	313,043	11.5%	-3.5	2,890,000	370,381	12.8%	-2.1	3,030,000	344,972	11.4%	-3.5	3,173,000	461,608	14.5%	-0.4
SOUTH DAKOTA	497,000	173,814	35.0%	518,000	183,036	35.3%	0.4	539,000	64,433	12.0%	-23.0	554,000	153,656	27.7%	-7.2	569,000	230,468	40.5%	5.5
TENNESSEE	3,667,000	369,294	10.1%	3,904,000	614,512	15.7%	5.7	4,131,000	412,478	10.0%	-0.1	4,301,000	708,375	16.5%	6.4	4,456,000	860,861	19.3%	9.2

United States House of Representatives General Elections (continued)

Democratic Turnout for Election Years 1990–2006 (continued)

State	1990 Voting-age population	Turnout	%	1994 Voting-age population	Turnout	%	Difference from 1990	1998 Voting-age population	Turnout	%	Difference from 1990	2002 Voting-age population	Turnout	%	Difference from 1990	2006 Voting-age population	Turnout	%	Difference from 1990
TEXAS	11,419,000	1,763,432	15.4%	12,251,000	1,734,163	14.2%	-1.3	13,051,000	1,531,234	11.7%	-3.7	13,790,000	1,935,278	14.0%	-1.4	14,589,000	1,852,613	12.7%	-2.7
UTAH	1,088,000	233,821	21.5%	1,237,000	216,080	17.5%	-4.0	1,381,000	126,505	9.2%	-12.3	1,472,000	221,401	15.0%	-6.5	1,549,000	244,483	15.8%	-5.7
VERMONT	415,000	6,315	1.5%													488,000	139,815	28.7%	27.1
VIRGINIA	4,556,000	662,800	14.5%	4,774,000	752,701	15.8%	1.2	4,985,000	514,435	10.3%	-4.2	5,211,000	440,208	8.4%	-6.1	5,467,000	947,103	17.3%	2.8
WASHINGTON	3,499,000	696,275	19.9%	3,760,000	826,753	22.0%	2.1	4,009,000	980,157	24.4%	4.5	4,212,000	907,440	21.5%	1.6	4,415,000	1,244,095	28.2%	8.3
WEST VIRGINIA	1,347,000	251,298	18.7%	1,369,000	268,901	19.6%	1.0	1,391,000	283,272	20.4%	1.7	1,407,000	264,124	18.8%	0.1	1,423,000	203,022	18.5%	-0.1
WISCONSIN	3,574,000	597,332	16.7%	3,719,000	547,825	14.7%	-2.0	3,857,000	761,821	19.8%	3.0	3,990,000	676,985	17.0%	0.3	4,131,000	1,204,523	29.2%	12.4
WYOMING	318,000	70,977	22.3%	337,000	81,022	24.0%	1.7	355,000	67,399	19.0%	-3.3	369,000	65,961	17.9%	-4.4	383,000	92,324	24.1%	1.8
Total	175,699,000	33,047,166	18.8%	182,910,000	32,008,039	17.5%	-1.3	190,229,000	31,391,128	16.5%	-2.3	197,132,000	33,935,196	17.2%	-1.6	205,178,000	42,451,999	20.7%	1.9

Other Turnout for Election Years 1990–2006

State	1990 Voting-age population	Turnout	%	1994 Voting-age population	Turnout	%	Difference from 1990*	1998 Voting-age population	Turnout	%	Difference from 1990	2002 Voting-age population	Turnout	%	Difference from 1990	2006 Voting-age population	Turnout	%	Difference from 1990
ALABAMA	2,980,000	12,141	0.4%	3,111,000	2,428	0.1%	-0.3	3,238,000	4,089	0.1%	-0.3	3,313,000	66,598	2.0%	1.6	3,373,000	10,605	0.3%	-0.1
ALASKA	371,000	967	0.3%	394,000	21,531	5.5%	5.2	415,000	6,392	1.5%	1.3	439,000	18,683	4.3%	4.0	467,000	8,023	1.7%	1.5
ARIZONA	2,596,000	837	0.0%	2,946,000	36,886	1.3%	1.2	3,283,000	23,255	0.7%	0.7	3,616,000	40,343	1.1%	1.1	3,983,000	94,645	2.4%	2.3
ARKANSAS								1,921,000	36,917	1.9%		1,987,000	12,451	0.6%	-1.3				
CALIFORNIA	18,412,000	372,359	2.0%	19,120,000	286,074	1.5%	-0.5	19,799,000	437,632	2.2%	0.2	20,722,000	301,670	1.5%	-0.6	21,891,000	261,254	1.2%	-0.8
COLORADO	2,406,000	9,676	0.4%	2,666,000	4,127	0.2%	-0.2	2,916,000	25,032	0.9%	0.5	3,061,000	54,619	1.8%	1.4	3,176,000	82,237	2.6%	2.2
CONNECTICUT	2,418,000	1,935	0.1%	2,411,000	46,761	1.9%	1.9	2,403,000	16,836	0.7%	0.6	2,436,000	14,262	0.6%	0.5	2,496,000	11,985	0.5%	0.4
DELAWARE	498,000	3,121	0.6%	529,000	5,274	1.0%	0.4	559,000	329	0.1%	-0.6	586,000	2,789	0.5%	-0.2	618,000	10,232	1.7%	1.0
DISTRICT OF COLUMBIA																			
FLORIDA	9,357,000	2,409	0.0%	10,120,000	2,415	0.0%	0.0	10,853,000	74,806	0.7%	0.7	11,661,000	68,062	0.6%	0.6	12,588,000	69,118	0.5%	0.5
GEORGIA	4,717,000	11	0.0%	5,141,000	1	0.0%	0.0									6,186,000	118	0.0%	0.0
HAWAII	768,000	7,615	1.0%	801,000	15,403	1.9%	0.9	833,000	17,167	2.1%	1.1	866,000	10,947	1.3%	0.3				
IDAHO								865,000	4,872	0.6%		933,000	10,637	1.1%	1.7	1,000,000	19,825	2.0%	1.4
ILLINOIS	8,044,000	81,748	1.0%	8,196,000	7,367	0.1%	-0.9	8,342,000	82,976	1.0%	0.0	8,426,000	31,412	0.4%	-0.6	8,507,000	23,625	0.3%	-0.7
INDIANA	4,068,000	913	0.0%	4,220,000	3,402	0.1%	0.1	4,364,000	40,598	0.9%	0.9	4,464,000	40,091	0.9%	0.9	4,554,000	22,641	0.5%	0.5
IOWA	2,043,000	6,285	0.3%	2,088,000	9,980	0.5%	0.2	2,130,000	10,503	0.5%	0.2	2,160,000	12,690	0.6%	0.3	2,190,000	17,656	0.8%	0.5
KANSAS	1,793,000	147	0.0%					1,888,000	5,171	0.3%	0.3	1,922,000	33,953	1.8%	1.8	1,956,000	16,669	0.9%	0.8
KENTUCKY	2,731,000	12,879	0.5%	2,851,000	17,622	0.6%	0.1	2,967,000	5,553	0.2%	-0.3	3,048,000	49,458	1.6%	1.2	3,122,000	40,023	1.3%	0.8
LOUISIANA	2,963,000	29,382	1.0%	3,067,000	50,691	1.7%	0.7					3,243,000	82,962	2.6%	1.6	3,313,000	27,032	0.8%	-0.2
MAINE	908,000	433	0.0%	931,000	32,605	3.5%	3.5	953,000	9,182	1.0%	0.9					1,032,000	22,049	2.1%	2.1

United States House of Representatives General Elections (continued)

United States House of Representatives General Elections (continued)

Other Turnout for Election Years 1990–2006 (continued)

State	1990 Voting-age population	Turnout	%	1994 Voting-age population	Turnout	%	Difference from 1990	1998 Voting-age population	Turnout	%	Difference from 1990	2002 Voting-age population	Turnout	%	Difference from 1990	2006 Voting-age population	Turnout	%	Difference from 1990
MARYLAND	3,473,000	7,488	0.2%	3,573,000	183	0.0%	-0.2	3,669,000	133	0.0%	-0.2	3,813,000	3,609	0.1%	-0.1	3,998,000	54,899	1.4%	1.2
MASSACHUSETTS	4,399,000	63,826	1.5%	4,431,000	21,027	0.5%	-1.0	4,462,000	25,226	0.6%	-0.9	4,517,000	21,753	0.5%	-1.0	4,595,000	92,800	2.0%	0.6
MICHIGAN	6,717,000	22,881	0.3%	6,890,000	52,848	0.8%	0.4	7,055,000	77,839	1.1%	0.8	7,227,000	74,545	1.0%	0.7	7,420,000	100,152	1.3%	1.0
MINNESOTA	3,178,000	2,220	0.1%	3,321,000	17,530	0.5%	0.5	3,459,000	86,143	2.5%	2.4	3,604,000	73,860	2.0%	2.0	3,766,000	101,717	2.7%	2.6
MISSISSIPPI				1,927,000	9,408	0.5%		2,021,000	55,403	2.7%	2.3	2,081,000	18,662	0.9%	0.4	2,132,000	36,059	1.7%	1.2
MISSOURI				3,923,000	37,270	1.0%		4,054,000	36,030	0.9%	-0.1	4,168,000	38,481	0.9%	0.0	4,286,000	55,688	1.3%	0.3
MONTANA				617,000	32,046	5.2%		654,000	8,730	1.3%	-3.9	687,000	8,988	1.3%	-3.9	719,000	8,085	1.1%	-4.1
NEBRASKA	1,143,000	916	0.1%	1,177,000	2,299	0.2%	0.1	1,210,000	28,675	2.4%	2.3	1,227,000	40,102	3.3%	3.2				
NEVADA	882,000	17,945	2.0%	1,074,000	22,405	2.1%	0.1	1,260,000	55,367	4.4%	2.4	1,419,000	27,648	1.9%	-0.1	1,583,000	26,631	1.7%	-0.4
NEW HAMPSHIRE	819,000	680	0.1%	856,000	12,533	1.5%	1.4	892,000	3,575	0.4%	0.3	939,000	12,680	1.4%	1.3	996,000	3,620	0.4%	0.3
NEW JERSEY	5,512,000	78,649	1.4%	5,571,000	34,010	0.6%	-0.8	5,628,000	54,748	1.0%	-0.5	5,721,000	41,891	0.7%	-0.7	5,852,000	25,882	0.4%	-1.0
NEW MEXICO				1,125,000	10,595	0.9%		1,205,000	23,479	1.9%	1.0	1,266,000	82	0.0%	-0.9	1,325,000	135	0.0%	-0.9
NEW YORK	12,391,000	170,174	1.4%	12,429,000	472,258	3.8%	2.4	12,464,000	131,381	1.1%	-0.3	12,514,000	125,786	1.0%	-0.4	12,610,000	7,598	0.1%	-1.3
NORTH CAROLINA				5,370,000	33	0.0%		5,714,000	62,678	1.1%	1.1	6,010,000	64,400	1.1%	1.1				
NORTH DAKOTA	460,000	6	0.0%	468,000	6,267	1.3%	1.3	474,000	5,709	1.2%	1.2								
OHIO	7,972,000	21,291	0.3%	8,127,000	45,107	0.6%	0.3	8,276,000	28,625	0.3%	0.1	8,396,000	50,854	0.6%	0.3	8,518,000	9,068	0.1%	-0.2
OKLAHOMA				2,377,000	46,183	1.9%		2,461,000	6,096	0.2%	-1.7	2,509,000	52,624	2.1%	0.2	2,547,000	14,281	0.6%	-1.4
OREGON	2,071,000	43,197	2.1%	2,223,000	47,740	2.1%	0.1	2,370,000	57,583	2.4%	0.3	2,477,000	34,398	1.4%	-0.7	2,578,000	34,090	1.3%	-0.8
PENNSYLVANIA	8,965,000	5,795	0.1%	9,045,000	48,934	0.5%	0.5	9,123,000	41,601	0.5%	0.4	9,241,000	101,140	1.1%	1.0	9,394,000	49,951	0.5%	0.5
RHODE ISLAND								745,000	12,307	1.7%		760,000	6,637	0.9%	-0.8	782,000	66,363	8.5%	6.8
SOUTH CAROLINA	2,566,000	12,450	0.5%	2,732,000	2,465	0.1%	-0.4	2,890,000	23,633	0.8%	0.3	3,030,000	69,648	2.3%	1.8	3,173,000	24,991	0.8%	0.3
SOUTH DAKOTA				518,000	10,832	2.1%						554,000	3,128	0.6%	-1.5	569,000	5,230	0.9%	-1.2
TENNESSEE	3,667,000	58,945	1.6%	3,904,000	26,147	0.7%	-0.9	4,131,000	31,652	0.8%	-0.8	4,301,000	50,505	1.2%	-0.4	4,456,000	55,012	1.2%	-0.4
TEXAS	11,419,000	16,730	0.1%	12,251,000	91,675	0.7%	0.6	13,051,000	143,290	1.1%	1.0	13,790,000	119,309	0.9%	0.7	14,589,000	105,319	0.7%	0.6
UTAH	1,088,000	17,325	1.6%	1,237,000	35,969	2.9%	1.3	1,381,000	40,088	2.9%	1.3	1,472,000	13,766	0.9%	-0.7	1,549,000	32,972	2.1%	0.5
VERMONT	415,000	120,603	29.1%	431,000	112,926	26.2%	-2.9	447,000	144,393	32.3%	3.2	466,000	150,590	32.3%	3.3	488,000	5,888	1.2%	-27.9
VIRGINIA	4,556,000	79,133	1.7%	4,774,000	66,811	1.4%	-0.3	4,985,000	92,210	1.8%	0.1	5,211,000	68,255	1.3%	-0.4	5,467,000	127,343	2.3%	0.6
WASHINGTON	3,499,000	20,535	0.6%	3,760,000	6,620	0.2%	-0.4	4,009,000	59,339	1.5%	0.9	4,212,000	52,754	1.3%	0.7	4,415,000	11,956	0.3%	-0.3
WEST VIRGINIA								1,391,000	38,869	2.8%		1,407,000	320	0.0%	-2.8	1,423,000	98	0.0%	-2.8
WISCONSIN	3,574,000	7,087	0.2%	3,719,000	17,837	0.5%	0.3	3,857,000	31,354	0.8%	0.6	3,990,000	71,475	1.8%	1.6	4,131,000	18,584	0.4%	0.3
WYOMING				337,000	10,749	3.2%		355,000	6,133	1.7%	-1.5	369,000	5,962	1.6%	-1.6	383,000	7,709	2.0%	-1.2
Total	155,839,000	1,310,734	0.8%	176,779,000	1,843,274	1.0%	0.2	181,422,000	2,213,599	1.2%	0.4	190,261,000	2,255,479	1.2%	0.3	194,196,000	1,819,858	0.9%	0.1

*Percentage point difference between turnout in current year and initial year listed in chart. If data do not appear for a state in the initial year listed, the difference is calculated from the first year in which data do appear for that state.

TOTAL HIGHEST STATEWIDE GENERAL ELECTIONS
Election Years 1990–2006

State	1990 Voting-age population	1990 Turnout	1990 %	1994 Voting-age population	1994 Turnout	1994 %	1994 Difference from 1990*	1998 Voting-age population	1998 Turnout	1998 %	1998 Difference from 1990	2002 Voting-age population	2002 Turnout	2002 %	2002 Difference from 1990	2006 Voting-age population	2006 Turnout	2006 %	2006 Difference from 1990
ALABAMA	2,980,000	1,216,250	40.8%	3,111,000	1,201,969	38.6%	-2.2	3,238,000	1,317,842	40.7%	-0.1	3,313,000	1,367,053	41.3%	0.4	3,373,000	1,250,401	37.1%	-3.7
ALASKA	371,000	194,750	52.5%	394,000	213,435	54.2%	1.7	415,000	223,300	53.8%	1.3	439,000	231,484	52.7%	0.2	467,000	237,322	50.8%	-1.7
ARIZONA	2,596,000	1,055,406	40.7%	2,946,000	1,129,607	38.3%	-2.3	3,283,000	1,017,616	31.0%	-9.7	3,616,000	1,226,111	33.9%	-6.7	3,983,000	1,533,645	38.5%	-2.2
ARKANSAS	1,732,000	696,412	40.2%	1,829,000	716,840	39.2%	-1.0	1,921,000	706,011	36.8%	-3.5	1,987,000	805,856	40.6%	0.3	2,044,000	773,552	37.8%	-2.4
CALIFORNIA	18,412,000	7,699,467	41.8%	19,120,000	8,665,375	45.3%	3.5	19,799,000	8,381,871	42.3%	0.5	20,722,000	7,476,311	36.1%	-5.7	21,891,000	8,679,048	39.6%	-2.2
COLORADO	2,406,000	1,022,027	42.5%	2,666,000	1,116,184	41.9%	-0.6	2,916,000	1,327,235	45.5%	3.0	3,061,000	1,416,093	46.3%	3.8	3,176,000	1,558,405	49.1%	6.6
CONNECTICUT	2,418,000	1,141,122	47.2%	2,411,000	1,147,084	47.6%	0.4	2,403,000	999,537	41.6%	-5.6	2,436,000	1,022,582	42.0%	-5.2	2,496,000	1,134,762	45.5%	-1.7
DELAWARE	498,000	180,152	36.2%	529,000	199,029	37.6%	1.4	559,000	178,781	32.0%	-4.2	586,000	232,304	39.6%	3.5	618,000	251,694	40.7%	4.6
DISTRICT OF COLUMBIA																			
FLORIDA	9,357,000	3,530,871	37.7%	10,120,000	4,206,659	41.6%	3.8	10,853,000	3,965,751	36.5%	-1.2	11,661,000	5,100,581	43.7%	6.0	12,588,000	4,829,270	38.4%	0.6
GEORGIA	4,717,000	1,449,682	30.7%	5,141,000	1,545,327	30.1%	-0.7	5,548,000	1,792,808	32.3%	1.6	5,871,000	2,031,350	34.6%	3.9	6,186,000	2,122,258	34.3%	3.6
HAWAII	760,000	348,666	45.5%	801,000	369,013	46.1%	0.5	833,000	407,556	48.9%	3.4	866,000	382,110	44.1%	-1.4	904,000	344,315	38.1%	-7.4
IDAHO	696,000	320,610	46.1%	783,000	413,346	52.8%	6.7	865,000	381,248	44.1%	-2.0	933,000	411,477	44.1%	2.0	1,000,000	450,822	45.1%	-1.0
ILLINOIS	8,044,000	3,257,410	40.5%	8,196,000	3,106,566	37.9%	-2.6	8,342,000	3,394,521	40.7%	0.2	8,426,000	3,538,891	42.0%	1.5	8,507,000	3,486,671	41.0%	0.5
INDIANA	4,068,000	1,514,006	37.2%	4,220,000	1,543,559	36.6%	-0.6	4,364,000	1,588,617	36.4%	-0.8	4,464,000	1,521,353	34.1%	-3.1	4,554,000	1,666,922	36.6%	-0.6
IOWA	2,043,000	983,933	48.2%	2,088,000	986,371	47.2%	-0.9	2,130,000	956,415	44.9%	-3.3	2,160,000	1,024,740	47.4%	-0.7	2,190,000	1,048,033	47.9%	-0.3
KANSAS	1,793,000	786,235	43.9%	1,841,000	820,887	44.6%	0.7	1,888,000	742,665	39.3%	-4.5	1,922,000	835,692	43.5%	-0.4	1,956,000	849,700	43.4%	-0.4
KENTUCKY	2,731,000	916,010	33.5%	2,851,000	784,299	27.5%	-6.0	2,967,000	1,145,414	38.6%	5.1	3,048,000	1,131,313	37.1%	3.6	3,122,000	1,253,526	40.2%	6.6
LOUISIANA	2,963,000	1,396,113	47.1%	3,067,000	826,837	27.0%	-20.2	3,167,000	969,165	30.6%	-16.5	3,243,000	1,246,333	38.4%	-8.7	3,313,000	902,496	27.2%	-19.9
MAINE	908,000	522,492	57.5%	931,000	511,733	55.0%	-2.6	953,000	421,009	44.2%	-13.4	987,000	505,191	51.2%	-6.4	1,032,000	550,865	53.4%	-4.2
MARYLAND	3,473,000	1,111,088	32.0%	3,573,000	1,410,300	39.5%	7.5	3,669,000	1,535,978	41.9%	9.9	3,813,000	1,706,179	44.7%	12.8	3,998,000	1,787,046	44.7%	12.7
MASSACHUSETTS	4,399,000	2,342,927	53.3%	4,431,000	2,179,964	49.2%	-4.1	4,462,000	1,903,336	42.7%	-10.6	4,517,000	2,194,179	48.6%	-4.7	4,595,000	2,219,779	48.3%	-5.0
MICHIGAN	6,717,000	2,564,563	38.2%	6,890,000	3,089,077	44.8%	6.7	7,055,000	3,027,104	42.9%	4.7	7,227,000	3,177,565	44.0%	5.8	7,420,000	3,801,274	51.2%	13.0
MINNESOTA	3,178,000	1,808,045	56.9%	3,321,000	1,772,929	53.4%	-3.5	3,459,000	2,091,766	60.5%	3.6	3,604,000	2,254,639	62.6%	5.7	3,766,000	2,202,937	58.5%	1.6
MISSISSIPPI	1,830,000	368,502	20.1%	1,927,000	620,319	32.2%	12.1	2,021,000	550,453	27.2%	7.1	2,081,000	677,366	32.6%	12.4	2,132,000	605,921	28.4%	8.3
MISSOURI	3,787,000	1,352,686	35.7%	3,923,000	1,775,116	45.2%	9.5	4,054,000	1,576,857	38.9%	3.2	4,168,000	1,877,620	45.0%	9.3	4,286,000	2,128,459	49.7%	13.9
MONTANA	577,000	319,336	55.3%	617,000	352,133	57.1%	1.7	654,000	331,551	50.7%	-4.6	687,000	331,321	48.2%	-7.1	719,000	406,505	56.5%	1.2
NEBRASKA	1,143,000	593,828	52.0%	1,177,000	579,561	49.2%	-2.7	1,210,000	545,238	45.1%	-6.9	1,227,000	480,991	39.2%	-12.8	1,239,000	596,087	48.1%	-3.8
NEVADA	882,000	320,743	36.4%	1,074,000	380,530	35.4%	-0.9	1,260,000	435,864	34.6%	-1.8	1,419,000	504,079	35.5%	-0.8	1,583,000	582,872	36.8%	0.5
NEW HAMPSHIRE	819,000	295,018	36.0%	856,000	311,882	36.4%	0.4	892,000	318,940	35.8%	-0.3	939,000	447,135	47.6%	11.6	996,000	403,680	40.5%	4.5
NEW JERSEY	5,512,000	1,938,454	35.2%	5,571,000	2,054,887	36.9%	1.7	5,628,000	1,815,489	32.3%	-2.9	5,721,000	2,112,604	36.9%	1.8	5,852,000	2,250,070	38.4%	3.3
NEW MEXICO	1,040,000	411,236	39.5%	1,125,000	467,621	41.6%	2.0	1,205,000	498,703	41.4%	1.8	1,266,000	484,229	38.2%	-1.3	1,325,000	561,084	42.3%	2.8
NEW YORK	12,391,000	4,052,896	32.7%	12,429,000	5,203,762	41.9%	9.2	12,464,000	4,735,236	38.0%	5.3	12,514,000	4,579,078	36.6%	3.9	12,610,000	4,437,220	35.2%	2.5

Total Highest Statewide General Elections (continued)

Total Highest Statewide General Elections *(continued)*

Election Years 1990–2006 *(continued)*

State	1990			1994				1998				2002				2006			
	Voting-age population	Turnout	%	Voting-age population	Turnout	%	Difference from 1990	Voting-age population	Turnout	%	Difference from 1990	Voting-age population	Turnout	%	Difference from 1990	Voting-age population	Turnout	%	Difference from 1990
NORTH CAROLINA	5,013,000	2,069,585	41.3%	5,370,000	1,588,190	29.6%	-11.7	5,714,000	2,012,143	35.2%	-6.1	6,010,000	2,331,181	38.8%	-2.5	6,312,000	1,940,808	30.7%	-10.5
NORTH DAKOTA	460,000	233,979	50.9%	468,000	236,547	50.5%	-0.3	474,000	213,358	45.0%	-5.9	479,000	231,030	48.2%	-2.6	483,000	218,152	45.2%	-5.7
OHIO	7,972,000	3,477,650	43.6%	8,127,000	3,436,884	42.3%	-1.3	8,276,000	3,404,351	41.1%	-2.5	8,396,000	3,228,992	38.5%	-5.2	8,518,000	4,022,681	47.2%	3.6
OKLAHOMA	2,289,000	911,314	39.8%	2,377,000	995,012	41.9%	2.0	2,461,000	873,585	35.5%	-4.3	2,509,000	1,035,620	41.3%	1.5	2,547,000	926,462	36.4%	-3.4
OREGON	2,071,000	1,112,847	53.7%	2,223,000	1,221,010	54.9%	1.2	2,370,000	1,117,747	47.2%	-6.6	2,477,000	1,267,221	51.2%	-2.6	2,578,000	1,379,475	53.5%	-0.2
PENNSYLVANIA	8,965,000	3,052,760	34.1%	9,045,000	3,585,526	39.6%	5.6	9,123,000	3,025,152	33.2%	-0.9	9,241,000	3,545,431	38.4%	4.3	9,394,000	4,092,652	43.6%	9.5
RHODE ISLAND	734,000	364,062	49.6%	740,000	361,377	48.8%	-0.8	745,000	297,255	39.9%	-9.7	760,000	331,834	43.7%	-5.9	782,000	386,112	49.4%	-0.2
SOUTH CAROLINA	2,566,000	760,965	29.7%	2,732,000	934,886	34.2%	4.6	2,890,000	1,069,063	37.0%	7.3	3,030,000	1,099,910	36.3%	6.6	3,173,000	1,091,963	34.4%	4.8
SOUTH DAKOTA	497,000	258,976	52.1%	518,000	311,613	60.2%	8.0	539,000	262,111	48.6%	-3.5	554,000	337,508	60.9%	8.8	569,000	335,508	59.0%	6.9
TENNESSEE	3,667,000	790,441	21.6%	3,904,000	1,487,130	38.1%	16.5	4,131,000	976,236	23.6%	2.1	4,301,000	1,653,042	38.4%	16.9	4,456,000	1,833,695	41.2%	19.6
TEXAS	11,419,000	3,892,746	34.1%	12,251,000	4,393,418	35.9%	1.8	13,051,000	3,738,078	28.6%	-5.4	13,790,000	4,527,068	32.8%	-1.3	14,589,000	4,399,068	30.2%	-3.9
UTAH	1,088,000	442,213	40.6%	1,237,000	519,323	42.0%	1.3	1,381,000	494,909	35.8%	-4.8	1,472,000	557,153	37.9%	-2.8	1,549,000	571,252	36.9%	-3.8
VERMONT	415,000	211,422	50.9%	431,000	212,046	49.2%	-1.7	447,000	218,120	48.8%	-2.1	466,000	225,980	48.5%	-2.5	488,000	262,726	53.8%	2.9
VIRGINIA	4,556,000	1,152,874	25.3%	4,774,000	2,057,463	43.1%	17.8	4,985,000	1,148,861	23.0%	-2.3	5,211,000	1,516,212	29.1%	3.8	5,467,000	2,370,445	43.4%	18.1
WASHINGTON	3,499,000	1,313,217	37.5%	3,760,000	1,700,173	45.2%	7.7	4,009,000	1,888,561	47.1%	9.6	4,212,000	1,739,116	41.3%	3.8	4,415,000	2,083,732	47.2%	9.7
WEST VIRGINIA	1,347,000	404,305	30.0%	1,369,000	420,936	30.7%	0.7	1,391,000	351,277	25.3%	-4.8	1,407,000	436,183	31.0%	1.0	1,423,000	460,334	32.3%	2.3
WISCONSIN	3,574,000	1,379,727	38.6%	3,719,000	1,565,628	42.1%	3.5	3,857,000	1,761,740	45.7%	7.1	3,990,000	1,775,349	44.5%	5.9	4,131,000	2,161,700	52.3%	13.7
WYOMING	318,000	160,109	50.3%	337,000	201,710	59.9%	9.5	355,000	174,888	49.3%	-1.1	369,000	185,459	50.3%	-0.1	383,000	192,892	50.4%	0.0
Total	175,699,000	67,701,128	38.5%	183,341,000	74,931,073	40.9%	2.3	190,676,000	72,311,312	37.9%	-0.6	197,598,000	78,358,099	39.7%	1.1	205,178,000	83,636,298	40.8%	2.2

*Percentage point difference between turnout in current year and initial year listed in chart. If data do not appear for a state in the initial year listed, the difference is calculated from the first year in which data do appear for that state.

TOTAL HIGHEST STATEWIDE GENERAL ELECTIONS

Republican Turnout for Election Years 1990–2006

State	1990 Voting-age population	1990 Turnout	1990 %	1994 Voting-age population	1994 Turnout	1994 %	1994 Difference from 1990*	1998 Voting-age population	1998 Turnout	1998 %	1998 Difference from 1990	2002 Voting-age population	2002 Turnout	2002 %	2002 Difference from 1990	2006 Voting-age population	2006 Turnout	2006 %	2006 Difference from 1990
ALABAMA	2,980,000	633,519	21.3%	3,111,000	604,926	19.4%	-1.8	3,238,000	817,973	25.3%	4.0	3,313,000	792,561	23.9%	2.7	3,373,000	718,327	21.3%	0.0
ALASKA	371,000	125,806	33.9%	394,000	118,537	30.1%	-3.8	415,000	165,227	39.8%	5.9	439,000	179,438	40.9%	7.0	467,000	132,743	28.4%	-5.5
ARIZONA	2,596,000	620,906	23.9%	2,946,000	652,831	22.2%	-1.8	3,283,000	696,577	21.2%	-2.7	3,616,000	681,922	18.9%	-5.1	3,983,000	814,398	20.4%	-3.5
ARKANSAS	1,732,000	295,925	17.1%	1,829,000	372,889	20.4%	3.3	1,921,000	421,989	22.0%	4.9	1,987,000	427,189	21.5%	4.4	2,044,000	314,630	15.4%	-1.7
CALIFORNIA	18,412,000	3,791,904	20.6%	19,120,000	4,781,766	25.0%	4.4	19,799,000	3,575,078	18.1%	-2.5	20,722,000	3,225,666	15.6%	-5.0	21,891,000	4,850,157	22.2%	1.6
COLORADO	2,406,000	487,326	20.3%	2,666,000	687,070	25.8%	5.5	2,916,000	829,370	28.4%	8.2	3,061,000	884,583	28.9%	8.6	3,176,000	625,886	19.7%	-0.5
CONNECTICUT	2,418,000	545,751	22.6%	2,411,000	516,134	21.4%	-1.2	2,403,000	628,707	26.2%	3.6	2,436,000	573,598	23.5%	1.0	2,496,000	709,987	28.4%	5.9
DELAWARE	498,000	64,554	13.0%	529,000	137,960	26.1%	13.1	559,000	120,605	21.6%	8.6	586,000	164,605	28.1%	15.1	618,000	143,897	23.3%	10.3
DISTRICT OF COLUMBIA																			
FLORIDA	9,357,000	1,535,068	16.4%	10,120,000	2,894,726	28.6%	12.2	10,853,000	2,192,105	20.2%	3.8	11,661,000	2,856,845	24.5%	8.1	12,588,000	2,519,845	20.0%	3.6
GEORGIA	4,717,000	645,625	13.7%	5,141,000	816,484	15.9%	2.2	5,548,000	1,039,711	18.7%	5.1	5,871,000	1,103,649	18.8%	5.1	6,186,000	1,229,724	19.9%	6.2
HAWAII	768,000	155,978	20.3%	801,000	119,614	14.9%	-5.4	833,000	198,952	23.9%	3.6	866,000	197,009	22.7%	2.4	904,000	215,313	23.8%	3.5
IDAHO	696,000	193,641	27.8%	783,000	255,321	32.6%	4.8	865,000	262,966	30.4%	2.6	933,000	266,215	28.5%	0.7	1,000,000	248,105	24.8%	-3.0
ILLINOIS	8,044,000	1,653,126	20.6%	8,196,000	1,984,318	24.2%	3.7	8,342,000	1,714,094	20.5%	0.0	8,426,000	1,657,093	19.7%	-0.9	8,507,000	1,442,526	17.0%	-3.6
INDIANA	4,068,000	806,048	19.8%	4,220,000	1,039,624	24.6%	4.8	4,364,000	861,951	19.8%	-0.1	4,464,000	840,694	18.8%	-1.0	4,554,000	1,171,596	25.7%	5.9
IOWA	2,043,000	591,852	29.0%	2,088,000	562,918	27.0%	-2.0	2,130,000	648,480	30.4%	1.5	2,160,000	546,382	25.3%	-3.7	2,190,000	522,388	23.9%	-5.1
KANSAS	1,793,000	578,605	32.3%	1,841,000	526,113	28.6%	-3.7	1,888,000	544,882	28.9%	-3.4	1,922,000	641,075	33.4%	1.1	1,956,000	459,267	23.5%	-8.8
KENTUCKY	2,731,000	478,034	17.5%	2,851,000	450,640	15.8%	-1.7	2,967,000	637,091	21.5%	4.0	3,048,000	731,679	24.0%	6.5	3,122,000	611,780	19.6%	2.1
LOUISIANA	2,963,000	607,391	20.5%	3,067,000	400,607	13.1%	-7.4	3,167,000	306,616	9.7%	-10.8	3,243,000	707,923	21.8%	1.3	3,313,000	579,702	17.5%	-3.0
MAINE	908,000	319,167	35.2%	931,000	308,244	33.1%	-2.0	953,000	124,834	13.1%	-22.1	987,000	295,041	29.9%	-5.3	1,032,000	402,598	39.0%	3.9
MARYLAND	3,473,000	517,386	14.9%	3,573,000	702,101	19.7%	4.8	3,669,000	689,532	18.8%	3.9	3,813,000	879,592	23.1%	8.2	3,998,000	825,464	20.6%	5.7
MASSACHUSETTS	4,309,000	1,321,712	30.0%	4,431,000	1,533,390	34.6%	4.6	4,462,000	967,160	21.7%	-8.4	4,517,000	1,091,988	24.2%	-5.9	4,595,000	784,342	17.1%	-13.0
MICHIGAN	6,717,000	1,276,134	19.0%	6,890,000	1,899,101	27.6%	8.6	7,055,000	1,883,005	26.7%	7.7	7,227,000	1,506,104	20.8%	1.8	7,420,000	1,624,865	21.9%	2.9
MINNESOTA	3,178,000	895,988	28.2%	3,321,000	1,094,156	32.9%	4.8	3,459,000	862,972	24.9%	-3.2	3,604,000	1,116,697	31.0%	2.8	3,766,000	1,028,568	27.3%	-0.9
MISSISSIPPI	1,830,000	274,244	15.0%	1,927,000	418,333	21.7%	6.7	2,021,000	232,415	11.5%	-3.5	2,081,000	985,905	47.4%	32.4	2,132,000	383,399	18.0%	3.0
MISSOURI	3,787,000	624,666	16.5%	3,923,000	1,060,149	27.0%	10.5	4,054,000	830,625	20.5%	4.0	4,168,000	533,269	12.8%	-3.7	4,286,000	1,049,346	24.5%	8.0
MONTANA	577,000	160,286	27.8%	617,000	218,542	35.4%	7.6	654,000	175,748	26.9%	-0.9	687,000	214,100	31.2%	3.4	719,000	239,124	33.3%	5.5
NEBRASKA	1,143,000	309,106	27.0%	1,177,000	365,402	31.0%	4.0	1,210,000	392,736	32.5%	5.4	1,227,000	397,438	32.4%	5.3	1,239,000	435,507	35.1%	8.1
NEVADA	882,000	150,885	17.1%	1,074,000	215,971	20.1%	3.0	1,260,000	275,163	21.8%	4.7	1,419,000	344,001	24.2%	7.1	1,583,000	322,501	20.4%	3.3
NEW HAMPSHIRE	819,000	189,792	23.2%	856,000	218,134	25.5%	2.3	892,000	213,477	23.9%	0.8	939,000	259,663	27.7%	4.5	996,000	189,615	19.0%	-4.1
NEW JERSEY	5,512,000	918,874	16.7%	5,571,000	1,091,251	19.6%	2.9	5,628,000	858,367	15.3%	-1.4	5,721,000	933,964	16.3%	-0.3	5,852,000	997,775	17.1%	0.4
NEW MEXICO	1,040,000	296,712	28.5%	1,125,000	263,477	23.4%	-5.1	1,205,000	271,948	22.6%	-6.0	1,266,000	314,193	24.8%	-3.7	1,325,000	247,825	18.7%	-9.8
NEW YORK	12,391,000	1,662,206	13.4%	12,429,000	2,538,702	20.4%	7.0	12,464,000	2,571,991	20.6%	7.2	12,514,000	2,262,255	18.1%	4.7	12,610,000	1,392,189	11.0%	-2.4

Total Highest Statewide General Elections (continued)

Total Highest Statewide General Elections (continued)

Republican Turnout for Election Years 1990–2006 (continued)

State	1990 Voting-age population	1990 Turnout	1990 %	1994 Voting-age population	1994 Turnout	1994 %	1994 Difference from 1990	1998 Voting-age population	1998 Turnout	1998 %	1998 Difference from 1990	2002 Voting-age population	2002 Turnout	2002 %	2002 Difference from 1990	2006 Voting-age population	2006 Turnout	2006 %	2006 Difference from 1990
NORTH CAROLINA	5,013,000	1,087,331	21.7%	5,370,000	907,093	16.9%	-4.8	5,714,000	1,014,010	17.7%	-3.9	6,010,000	1,248,664	20.8%	-0.9	6,312,000	913,893	14.5%	-7.2
NORTH DAKOTA	460,000	81,443	17.7%	468,000	105,988	22.6%	4.9	474,000	87,511	18.5%	0.8	479,000	109,957	23.0%	5.3	483,000	74,687	15.5%	-2.2
OHIO	7,972,000	1,938,103	24.3%	8,127,000	2,401,572	29.6%	5.2	8,276,000	1,922,087	23.2%	-1.1	8,396,000	1,865,007	22.2%	-2.1	8,518,000	1,870,390	22.0%	-2.4
OKLAHOMA	2,289,000	337,590	14.7%	2,377,000	554,800	23.3%	8.6	2,461,000	570,682	23.2%	8.4	2,509,000	583,579	23.3%	8.5	2,547,000	518,025	20.3%	5.6
OREGON	2,071,000	590,095	28.5%	2,223,000	517,874	23.3%	-5.2	2,370,000	377,739	15.9%	-12.6	2,477,000	712,287	28.8%	0.3	2,578,000	589,748	22.9%	-5.6
PENNSYLVANIA	8,965,000	1,552,475	17.3%	9,045,000	1,830,779	20.2%	2.9	9,123,000	1,814,180	19.9%	2.6	9,241,000	1,859,270	20.1%	2.8	9,394,000	1,732,163	18.4%	1.1
RHODE ISLAND	734,000	164,916	22.5%	740,000	222,856	30.1%	7.6	745,000	151,602	20.3%	-2.1	760,000	181,687	23.9%	1.4	782,000	197,013	25.2%	2.7
SOUTH CAROLINA	2,566,000	528,831	20.6%	2,732,000	552,085	20.2%	-0.4	2,890,000	580,096	20.1%	-0.5	3,030,000	595,218	19.6%	-1.0	3,173,000	601,871	19.0%	-1.6
SOUTH DAKOTA	497,000	151,198	30.4%	518,000	172,515	33.3%	2.9	539,000	194,157	36.0%	5.6	554,000	189,920	34.3%	3.9	569,000	206,990	36.4%	6.0
TENNESSEE	3,667,000	289,348	7.9%	3,904,000	834,226	21.4%	13.5	4,131,000	669,973	16.2%	8.3	4,301,000	891,498	20.7%	12.8	4,456,000	929,911	20.9%	13.0
TEXAS	11,419,000	2,302,357	20.2%	12,251,000	2,604,218	21.3%	1.1	13,051,000	2,550,821	19.5%	-0.6	13,790,000	2,617,106	19.0%	-1.2	14,589,000	2,661,789	18.2%	-1.9
UTAH	1,088,000	191,067	17.6%	1,237,000	357,297	28.9%	11.3	1,381,000	316,652	22.9%	5.4	1,472,000	321,986	21.9%	4.3	1,549,000	356,238	23.0%	5.4
VERMONT	415,000	109,540	26.4%	431,000	106,505	24.7%	-1.7	447,000	89,726	20.1%	-6.3	466,000	101,738	21.8%	-4.6	488,000	148,014	30.3%	3.9
VIRGINIA	4,556,000	876,782	19.2%	4,774,000	1,089,242	22.8%	3.6	4,985,000	542,216	10.9%	-8.4	5,211,000	1,229,894	23.6%	4.4	5,467,000	1,222,790	22.4%	3.1
WASHINGTON	3,499,000	596,407	17.0%	3,760,000	947,821	25.2%	8.2	4,009,000	785,377	19.6%	2.5	4,212,000	778,922	18.5%	1.4	4,415,000	832,106	18.8%	1.8
WEST VIRGINIA	1,347,000	128,071	9.5%	1,369,000	137,663	10.1%	0.5	1,391,000	29,136	2.1%	-7.4	1,407,000	160,902	11.4%	1.9	1,423,000	190,893	13.4%	3.9
WISCONSIN	3,574,000	802,321	22.4%	3,719,000	1,051,326	28.3%	5.8	3,857,000	1,047,718	27.2%	4.7	3,990,000	888,696	22.3%	-0.2	4,131,000	979,427	23.7%	1.3
WYOMING	318,000	100,784	31.7%	337,000	118,754	35.2%	3.5	355,000	100,687	28.4%	-3.3	369,000	133,710	36.2%	4.5	383,000	135,174	35.3%	3.6
Total	175,699,000	34,556,876	19.7%	183,341,000	43,361,945	23.7%	4.0	190,676,000	38,856,717	20.4%	0.7	197,598,000	42,082,377	21.3%	1.6	205,178,000	41,394,511	20.2%	0.5

Democratic Turnout for Election Years 1990–2006

State	1990 Voting-age population	1990 Turnout	1990 %	1994 Voting-age population	1994 Turnout	1994 %	1994 Difference from 1990*	1998 Voting-age population	1998 Turnout	1998 %	1998 Difference from 1990	2002 Voting-age population	2002 Turnout	2002 %	2002 Difference from 1990	2006 Voting-age population	2006 Turnout	2006 %	2006 Difference from 1990
ALABAMA	2,980,000	717,814	24.1%	3,111,000	594,169	19.1%	-5.0	3,238,000	760,155	23.5%	-0.6	3,313,000	669,105	20.2%	-3.9	3,373,000	519,827	15.4%	-8.7
ALASKA	371,000	91,677	24.7%	394,000	87,693	22.3%	-2.5	415,000	112,879	27.2%	2.5	439,000	94,216	21.5%	-3.2	467,000	97,238	20.8%	-3.9
ARIZONA	2,596,000	519,691	20.0%	2,946,000	500,702	17.0%	-3.0	3,283,000	406,860	12.4%	-7.6	3,616,000	566,284	15.7%	-4.4	3,983,000	959,830	24.1%	4.1
ARKANSAS	1,732,000	493,910	28.5%	1,829,000	428,936	23.5%	-5.1	1,921,000	385,878	20.1%	-8.4	1,987,000	433,386	21.8%	-6.7	2,044,000	455,809	22.3%	-6.2
CALIFORNIA	18,412,000	3,567,775	19.4%	19,120,000	3,979,152	20.8%	1.4	19,799,000	4,858,817	24.5%	5.2	20,722,000	3,721,081	18.0%	-1.4	21,891,000	5,076,289	23.2%	3.8
COLORADO	2,406,000	626,032	26.0%	2,666,000	619,205	23.2%	-2.8	2,916,000	639,905	21.9%	-4.1	3,061,000	648,129	21.2%	-4.8	3,176,000	888,095	28.0%	1.9
CONNECTICUT	2,418,000	489,206	20.2%	2,411,000	723,842	30.0%	9.8	2,403,000	628,306	26.1%	5.9	2,436,000	509,036	20.9%	0.7	2,496,000	642,863	25.8%	5.5
DELAWARE	498,000	116,274	23.3%	529,000	84,554	16.0%	-7.4	559,000	57,847	10.3%	-13.0	586,000	135,253	23.1%	-0.3	618,000	165,421	26.8%	3.4
DISTRICT OF COLUMBIA																			
FLORIDA	9,357,000	1,995,206	21.3%	10,120,000	2,135,008	21.1%	-0.2	10,853,000	2,436,016	22.4%	1.1	11,661,000	2,201,427	18.9%	-2.4	12,588,000	2,890,548	23.0%	1.6

Total Highest Statewide General Elections *(continued)*

Democratic Turnout for Election Years 1990–2006 *(continued)*

State	1990 Voting-age population	1990 Turnout	1990 %	1994 Voting-age population	1994 Turnout	1994 %	1994 Difference from 1990	1998 Voting-age population	1998 Turnout	1998 %	1998 Difference from 1990	2002 Voting-age population	2002 Turnout	2002 %	2002 Difference from 1990	2006 Voting-age population	2006 Turnout	2006 %	2006 Difference from 1990
GEORGIA	4,717,000	1,033,439	21.9%	5,141,000	788,926	15.3%	-6.6	5,548,000	941,076	17.0%	-4.9	5,871,000	937,057	16.0%	-5.9	6,186,000	932,143	15.1%	-6.8
HAWAII	768,000	215,777	28.1%	801,000	256,189	32.0%	3.9	833,000	315,252	37.8%	9.7	866,000	232,344	26.8%	-1.3	904,000	219,810	24.3%	-3.8
IDAHO	696,000	218,673	31.4%	783,000	181,363	23.2%	-8.3	865,000	169,389	19.6%	-11.8	933,000	171,711	18.4%	-13.0	1,000,000	198,845	19.9%	-11.5
ILLINOIS	8,044,000	2,115,337	26.3%	8,196,000	1,459,928	17.8%	-8.5	8,342,000	1,610,496	19.3%	-7.0	8,426,000	2,103,766	25.0%	-1.3	8,507,000	1,970,314	23.2%	-3.1
INDIANA	4,068,000	830,500	20.4%	4,220,000	667,454	15.8%	-4.6	4,364,000	1,012,244	23.2%	2.8	4,464,000	640,568	14.3%	-6.1	4,554,000	812,496	17.8%	-2.6
IOWA	2,043,000	535,975	26.2%	2,088,000	411,495	19.7%	-6.5	2,130,000	500,231	23.5%	-2.7	2,160,000	554,278	25.7%	-0.6	2,190,000	565,898	25.8%	-0.4
KANSAS	1,793,000	393,671	22.0%	1,841,000	298,269	16.2%	-5.8	1,888,000	272,252	14.4%	-7.5	1,922,000	441,858	23.0%	1.0	1,956,000	491,993	25.2%	3.2
KENTUCKY	2,731,000	437,976	16.0%	2,851,000	316,037	11.1%	-5.0	2,967,000	563,051	19.0%	2.9	3,048,000	399,634	13.1%	-2.9	3,122,000	601,723	19.3%	3.2
LOUISIANA	2,963,000	788,722	26.6%	3,067,000	375,539	12.2%	-14.4	3,167,000	620,502	19.6%	-7.0	3,243,000	573,347	17.7%	-8.9	3,313,000	295,762	8.9%	-17.7
MAINE	908,000	284,421	31.3%	931,000	235,988	25.3%	-6.0	953,000	280,537	29.4%	-1.9	987,000	289,514	29.3%	-2.0	1,032,000	350,721	34.0%	2.7
MARYLAND	3,473,000	664,015	19.1%	3,573,000	809,125	22.6%	3.5	3,669,000	1,062,810	29.0%	9.8	3,813,000	904,412	23.7%	4.6	3,998,000	1,099,441	27.5%	8.4
MASSACHUSETTS	4,399,000	1,420,422	32.3%	4,431,000	1,362,505	30.8%	-1.5	4,462,000	1,306,281	29.3%	-3.0	4,517,000	1,605,976	35.6%	3.3	4,595,000	1,632,307	35.5%	3.2
MICHIGAN	6,717,000	1,471,753	21.9%	6,890,000	1,418,142	20.6%	-1.3	7,055,000	1,469,111	20.8%	-1.1	7,227,000	1,896,614	26.2%	4.3	7,420,000	2,151,278	29.0%	7.1
MINNESOTA	3,178,000	1,042,201	32.8%	3,321,000	883,905	26.6%	-6.2	3,459,000	1,090,488	31.5%	-1.3	3,604,000	1,097,911	30.5%	-2.3	3,766,000	1,278,849	34.0%	1.2
MISSISSIPPI	1,830,000	299,286	16.4%	1,927,000	354,487	18.4%	2.0	2,021,000	262,635	13.0%	-3.4	2,081,000	319,887	15.4%	-1.0	2,132,000	260,330	12.2%	-4.1
MISSOURI	3,787,000	728,020	19.2%	3,923,000	893,783	22.8%	3.6	4,054,000	787,655	19.4%	0.2	4,168,000	913,778	21.9%	2.7	4,286,000	1,055,255	24.6%	5.4
MONTANA	577,000	217,563	37.7%	617,000	171,372	27.8%	-9.9	654,000	147,073	22.5%	-15.2	687,000	204,853	29.8%	-7.9	719,000	199,845	27.8%	-9.9
NEBRASKA	1,143,000	349,779	30.6%	1,177,000	423,270	36.0%	5.4	1,210,000	250,670	20.7%	-9.9	1,227,000	132,348	10.8%	-19.8	1,239,000	378,388	30.5%	-0.1
NEVADA	882,000	207,878	23.6%	1,074,000	200,026	18.6%	-4.9	1,260,000	208,621	16.6%	-7.0	1,419,000	171,160	12.1%	-11.5	1,583,000	287,879	18.2%	-5.4
NEW HAMPSHIRE	819,000	141,042	17.2%	856,000	116,724	13.6%	-3.6	892,000	210,769	23.6%	6.4	939,000	207,478	22.1%	4.9	996,000	298,761	30.0%	12.8
NEW JERSEY	5,512,000	977,810	17.7%	5,571,000	1,033,487	18.6%	0.8	5,628,000	902,374	16.0%	-1.7	5,721,000	1,138,193	19.9%	2.2	5,852,000	1,207,784	20.6%	2.9
NEW MEXICO	1,040,000	224,564	21.6%	1,125,000	249,989	22.2%	0.6	1,205,000	228,084	18.9%	-2.7	1,266,000	268,674	21.2%	-0.4	1,325,000	394,365	29.8%	8.2
NEW YORK	12,391,000	2,157,087	17.4%	12,429,000	2,646,541	21.3%	3.9	12,464,000	2,551,065	20.5%	3.1	12,514,000	1,924,769	15.4%	-2.0	12,610,000	3,086,709	24.5%	7.1
NORTH CAROLINA	5,013,000	1,076,340	21.5%	5,370,000	681,064	12.7%	-8.8	5,714,000	1,029,237	18.0%	-3.5	6,010,000	1,047,983	17.4%	-4.0	6,312,000	1,026,915	16.3%	-5.2
NORTH DAKOTA	460,000	152,530	33.2%	468,000	137,157	29.3%	-3.9	474,000	134,747	28.4%	-4.7	479,000	121,073	25.3%	-7.9	483,000	150,146	31.1%	-2.1
OHIO	7,972,000	1,806,626	22.7%	8,127,000	1,348,213	16.6%	-6.1	8,276,000	1,604,291	19.4%	-3.3	8,396,000	1,457,160	17.4%	-5.3	8,518,000	2,435,384	28.6%	5.9
OKLAHOMA	2,289,000	735,684	32.1%	2,377,000	392,488	16.5%	-15.6	2,461,000	357,552	14.5%	-17.6	2,509,000	448,143	17.9%	-14.3	2,547,000	616,135	24.2%	-7.9
OREGON	2,071,000	667,258	32.2%	2,223,000	646,589	29.1%	-3.1	2,370,000	717,061	30.3%	-2.0	2,477,000	676,920	27.3%	-4.9	2,578,000	765,853	29.7%	-2.5
PENNSYLVANIA	8,965,000	2,065,244	23.0%	9,045,000	1,648,481	18.2%	-4.8	9,123,000	1,379,834	15.1%	-7.9	9,241,000	1,899,518	20.6%	-2.5	9,394,000	2,470,517	26.3%	3.3
RHODE ISLAND	734,000	264,411	36.0%	740,000	209,491	28.3%	-7.7	745,000	197,653	26.5%	-9.5	760,000	253,774	33.4%	-2.6	782,000	264,949	33.9%	-2.1
SOUTH CAROLINA	2,566,000	382,939	14.9%	2,732,000	447,002	16.4%	1.4	2,890,000	574,112	19.9%	4.9	3,030,000	518,288	17.1%	2.2	3,173,000	489,084	15.4%	0.5
SOUTH DAKOTA	497,000	173,814	35.0%	518,000	183,036	35.3%	0.4	539,000	162,884	30.2%	-4.8	554,000	167,481	30.2%	-4.7	569,000	230,468	40.5%	5.5
TENNESSEE	3,667,000	530,898	14.5%	3,904,000	664,252	17.0%	2.5	4,131,000	412,478	10.0%	-4.5	4,301,000	837,280	19.5%	5.0	4,456,000	1,241,606	27.9%	13.4

Total Highest Statewide General Elections (continued)

Total Highest Statewide General Elections (continued)

Democratic Turnout for Election Years 1990–2006 (continued)

State	1990 Voting-age population	Turnout	%	1994 Voting-age population	Turnout	%	Difference from 1990	1998 Voting-age population	Turnout	%	Difference from 1990	2002 Voting-age population	Turnout	%	Difference from 1990	2006 Voting-age population	Turnout	%	Difference from 1990
TEXAS	11,419,000	1,925,670	16.9%	12,251,000	2,014,399	16.4%	-0.4	13,051,000	1,531,234	11.7%	-5.1	13,790,000	1,955,758	14.2%	-2.7	14,589,000	1,852,613	12.7%	-4.2
UTAH	1,088,000	233,821	21.5%	1,237,000	216,080	17.5%	-4.0	1,381,000	163,172	11.8%	-9.7	1,472,000	221,401	15.0%	-6.5	1,549,000	244,483	15.8%	-5.7
VERMONT	415,000	97,321	23.5%	431,000	145,661	33.8%	10.3	447,000	154,567	34.6%	11.1	466,000	95,370	20.5%	-3.0	488,000	139,815	28.7%	5.2
VIRGINIA	4,556,000	662,800	14.5%	4,774,000	938,376	19.7%	5.1	4,985,000	514,435	10.3%	-4.2	5,211,000	440,208	8.4%	-6.1	5,467,000	1,175,606	21.5%	7.0
WASHINGTON	3,499,000	696,275	19.9%	3,760,000	826,753	22.0%	2.1	4,009,000	1,103,184	27.5%	7.6	4,212,000	907,440	21.5%	1.6	4,415,000	1,244,095	28.2%	8.3
WEST VIRGINIA	1,347,000	276,234	20.5%	1,369,000	290,495	21.2%	0.7	1,391,000	283,272	20.4%	-0.1	1,407,000	275,281	19.6%	-0.9	1,423,000	296,726	20.9%	0.3
WISCONSIN	3,574,000	597,332	16.7%	3,719,000	912,662	24.5%	7.8	3,857,000	890,059	23.1%	6.4	3,990,000	800,515	20.1%	3.3	4,131,000	1,439,214	34.8%	18.1
WYOMING	318,000	104,638	32.9%	337,000	81,022	24.0%	-8.9	355,000	70,754	19.9%	-13.0	369,000	92,662	25.1%	-7.8	383,000	135,516	35.4%	2.5
Total	175,699,000	37,823,331	21.5%	183,341,000	36,491,106	19.9%	-1.6	190,676,000	38,329,863	20.1%	-1.4	197,598,000	38,324,302	19.4%	-2.1	205,178,000	47,685,941	23.2%	1.7

Other Turnout for Election Years 1990–2006

State	1990 Voting-age population	Turnout	%	1994 Voting-age population	Turnout	%	Difference from 1990*	1998 Voting-age population	Turnout	%	Difference from 1990	2002 Voting-age population	Turnout	%	Difference from 1990	2006 Voting-age population	Turnout	%	Difference from 1990
ALABAMA	2,980,000	12,141	0.4%	3,111,000	2,874	0.1%	-0.3	3,238,000	4,089	0.1%	-0.3	3,313,000	66,598	2.0%	1.6	3,373,000	12,247	0.4%	0.0
ALASKA	371,000	83,558	22.5%	394,000	38,585	9.8%	-12.7	415,000	67,967	16.4%	-6.1	439,000	25,977	5.9%	-16.6	467,000	25,387	5.4%	-17.1
ARIZONA	2,596,000	11,731	0.5%	2,946,000	75,551	2.6%	2.1	3,283,000	41,479	1.3%	0.8	3,616,000	105,362	2.9%	2.5	3,983,000	94,645	2.4%	1.9
ARKANSAS	1,732,000	825	0.0%					1,921,000	36,917	1.9%	1.9	1,987,000	12,451	0.6%	0.6	2,044,000	28,832	1.4%	1.4
CALIFORNIA	18,412,000	382,366	2.1%	19,120,000	717,912	3.8%	1.7	19,799,000	437,632	2.2%	0.1	20,722,000	773,020	3.7%	1.7	21,891,000	474,365	2.2%	0.1
COLORADO	2,406,000	27,233	1.1%	2,666,000	64,937	2.4%	1.3	2,916,000	33,200	1.1%	0.0	3,061,000	54,619	1.8%	0.7	3,176,000	82,237	2.6%	1.5
CONNECTICUT	2,418,000	476,641	19.7%	2,411,000	356,750	14.8%	-4.9	2,403,000	23,974	1.0%	-18.7	2,436,000	14,262	0.6%	-19.1	2,496,000	574,729	23.0%	3.3
DELAWARE	498,000	3,121	0.6%	529,000	5,274	1.0%	0.4	559,000	329	0.1%	-0.6	586,000	2,789	0.5%	-0.2	618,000	10,232	1.7%	1.0
DISTRICT OF COLUMBIA																			
FLORIDA	9,357,000	2,409	0.0%	10,120,000	2,415	0.0%	0.0	10,853,000	74,806	0.7%	0.7	11,661,000	68,062	0.6%	0.6	12,588,000	131,136	1.0%	1.0
GEORGIA	4,717,000	37,395	0.8%	5,141,000	30	0.0%	-0.8	5,548,000	61,531	1.1%	0.3	5,871,000	47,963	0.8%	0.0	6,186,000	81,485	1.3%	0.5
HAWAII	768,000	7,615	1.0%	801,000	126,127	15.7%	14.8	833,000	17,167	2.1%	1.1	866,000	10,947	1.3%	0.3	904,000	7,285	0.8%	-0.2
IDAHO				783,000	15,860	2.0%		865,000	12,338	1.4%	-0.6	933,000	10,637	1.1%	-0.9	1,000,000	19,825	2.0%	0.0
ILLINOIS	8,044,000	81,748	1.0%	8,196,000	52,398	0.6%	-0.4	8,342,000	82,976	1.0%	0.0	8,426,000	96,891	1.1%	0.1	8,507,000	381,770	4.5%	3.5
INDIANA	4,068,000	1,615	0.0%	4,220,000	33,139	0.8%	0.7	4,364,000	40,598	0.9%	0.9	4,464,000	40,091	0.9%	0.9	4,554,000	169,566	3.7%	3.7
IOWA	2,043,000	6,285	0.3%	2,088,000	11,958	0.6%	0.3	2,130,000	11,397	0.5%	0.2	2,160,000	27,676	1.3%	1.0	2,190,000	17,656	0.8%	0.5
KANSAS	1,793,000	69,127	3.9%	1,841,000	41	0.0%	-3.9	1,888,000	29,540	1.6%	-2.3	1,922,000	135,775	7.1%	3.2	1,956,000	16,669	0.9%	-3.0
KENTUCKY	2,731,000	12,879	0.5%	2,851,000	17,622	0.6%	0.1	2,967,000	12,546	0.4%	0.0	3,048,000	49,458	1.6%	1.2	3,122,000	40,023	1.3%	0.8
LOUISIANA	2,963,000	29,382	1.0%	3,067,000	50,691	1.7%	0.7	3,167,000	42,047	1.3%	0.3	3,243,000	82,962	2.6%	1.6	3,313,000	27,032	0.8%	-0.2
MAINE	908,000	48,688	5.4%	931,000	220,367	23.7%	18.3	953,000	290,787	30.5%	25.2	987,000	57,516	5.8%	0.5	1,032,000	174,513	16.9%	11.5

Total Highest Statewide General Elections (continued)

Other Turnout for Election Years 1990–2006 (continued)

State	1990 Voting-age population	1990 Turnout	1990 %	1994 Voting-age population	1994 Turnout	1994 %	1994 Difference from 1990	1998 Voting-age population	1998 Turnout	1998 %	1998 Difference from 1990	2002 Voting-age population	2002 Turnout	2002 %	2002 Difference from 1990	2006 Voting-age population	2006 Turnout	2006 %	2006 Difference from 1990
MARYLAND	3,473,000	7,488	0.2%	3,573,000	183	0.0%	-0.2	3,669,000	649	0.0%	-0.2	3,813,000	13,165	0.3%	0.1	3,998,000	54,899	1.4%	1.2
MASSACHUSETTS	4,399,000	67,232	1.5%	4,431,000	21,027	0.5%	-1.1	4,462,000	34,333	0.8%	-0.8	4,517,000	400,782	8.9%	7.3	4,595,000	200,453	4.4%	2.8
MICHIGAN	6,717,000	33,046	0.5%	6,890,000	163,655	2.4%	1.9	7,055,000	77,839	1.1%	0.6	7,227,000	74,545	1.0%	0.5	7,420,000	100,152	1.3%	0.9
MINNESOTA	3,178,000	74,571	2.3%	3,321,000	121,416	3.7%	1.3	3,459,000	786,888	22.7%	20.4	3,604,000	431,732	12.0%	9.6	3,766,000	166,909	4.4%	2.1
MISSISSIPPI				1,927,000	9,408	0.5%		2,021,000	55,403	2.7%	2.3	2,081,000	97,226	4.7%	4.2	2,132,000	36,059	1.7%	1.2
MISSOURI				3,923,000	81,270	2.1%		4,054,000	56,024	1.4%	-0.7	4,168,000	38,481	0.9%	-1.1	4,286,000	66,263	1.5%	-0.5
MONTANA	577,000	7,937	1.4%	617,000	32,046	5.2%	3.8	654,000	8,730	1.3%	0.0	687,000	15,073	2.2%	0.8	719,000	10,377	1.4%	0.1
NEBRASKA	1,143,000	5,030	0.4%	1,177,000	8,061	0.7%	0.2	1,210,000	28,675	2.4%	1.9	1,227,000	40,102	3.3%	2.8	1,239,000	12,735	1.0%	0.6
NEVADA	882,000	17,945	2.0%	1,074,000	30,706	2.9%	0.8	1,260,000	55,367	4.4%	2.4	1,419,000	49,143	3.5%	1.4	1,583,000	47,471	3.0%	1.0
NEW HAMPSHIRE	819,000	15,322	1.9%	856,000	14,062	1.6%	-0.2	892,000	12,596	1.4%	-0.5	939,000	14,036	1.5%	-0.4	996,000	3,620	0.4%	-1.5
NEW JERSEY	5,512,000	78,649	1.4%	5,571,000	55,156	1.0%	-0.4	5,628,000	54,748	1.0%	-0.5	5,721,000	45,972	0.8%	-0.6	5,852,000	51,452	0.9%	-0.5
NEW MEXICO	1,040,000	980	0.1%	1,125,000	47,990	4.3%	4.2	1,205,000	23,479	1.9%	1.9	1,266,000	26,465	2.1%	2.0	1,325,000	369	0.0%	-0.1
NEW YORK	12,391,000	1,033,861	8.3%	12,429,000	472,258	3.8%	-4.5	12,464,000	592,928	4.8%	-3.6	12,514,000	782,759	6.3%	-2.1	12,610,000	89,438	0.7%	-7.6
NORTH CAROLINA	5,013,000	681	0.0%	5,370,000	33	0.0%	0.0	5,714,000	62,678	1.1%	1.1	6,010,000	64,400	1.1%	1.1				
NORTH DAKOTA	460,000	6	0.0%	468,000	6,267	1.3%	1.3	474,000	5,709	1.2%	1.2					483,000	3,589	0.7%	0.7
OHIO	7,972,000	21,291	0.3%	8,127,000	252,115	3.1%	2.8	8,276,000	176,536	2.1%	1.9	8,396,000	127,061	1.5%	1.2	8,518,000	113,012	1.3%	1.1
OKLAHOMA	2,289,000	90,534	4.0%	2,377,000	233,336	9.8%	5.9	2,461,000	20,133	0.8%	-3.1	2,509,000	146,200	5.8%	1.9	2,547,000	14,281	0.6%	-3.4
OREGON	2,071,000	159,452	7.7%	2,223,000	81,053	3.6%	-4.1	2,370,000	62,036	2.6%	-5.1	2,477,000	60,708	2.5%	-5.2	2,578,000	89,941	3.5%	-4.2
PENNSYLVANIA	8,965,000	5,795	0.1%	9,045,000	527,451	5.8%	5.8	9,123,000	349,563	3.8%	3.8	9,241,000	101,140	1.1%	1.0	9,394,000	49,951	0.5%	0.5
RHODE ISLAND	734,000	84	0.0%	740,000	32,822	4.4%	4.4	745,000	20,791	2.8%	2.8	760,000	6,637	0.9%	0.9	782,000	66,363	8.5%	8.5
SOUTH CAROLINA	2,566,000	24,572	1.0%	2,732,000	17,128	0.6%	-0.3	2,890,000	23,633	0.8%	-0.1	3,030,000	69,648	2.3%	1.3	3,173,000	24,991	0.8%	-0.2
SOUTH DAKOTA	497,000	6,567	1.3%	518,000	12,825	2.5%	1.2	539,000	8,093	1.5%	0.2	554,000	4,376	0.8%	-0.5	569,000	7,292	1.3%	0.0
TENNESSEE	3,667,000	58,945	1.6%	3,904,000	26,147	0.7%	-0.9	4,131,000	31,652	0.8%	-0.8	4,301,000	50,505	1.2%	-0.4	4,456,000	55,012	1.2%	-0.4
TEXAS	11,419,000	140,645	1.2%	12,251,000	91,675	0.7%	-0.5	13,051,000	143,290	1.1%	-0.1	13,790,000	119,309	0.9%	-0.4	14,589,000	1,371,912	9.4%	8.2
UTAH	1,088,000	17,325	1.6%	1,237,000	35,969	2.9%	1.3	1,381,000	40,088	2.9%	1.3	1,472,000	13,766	0.9%	-0.7	1,549,000	37,555	2.4%	0.8
VERMONT	415,000	120,603	29.1%	431,000	112,926	26.2%	-2.9	447,000	144,393	32.3%	3.2	466,000	150,590	32.3%	3.3	488,000	177,495	36.4%	7.3
VIRGINIA	4,556,000	206,908	4.5%	4,774,000	236,874	5.0%	0.4	4,985,000	92,210	1.8%	-2.7	5,211,000	259,528	5.0%	0.4	5,467,000	127,343	2.3%	-2.2
WASHINGTON	3,499,000	20,535	0.6%	3,760,000	6,620	0.2%	-0.4	4,009,000	59,339	1.5%	0.9	4,212,000	52,754	1.3%	0.7	4,415,000	66,969	1.5%	0.9
WEST VIRGINIA								1,391,000	38,869	2.8%		1,407,000	320	0.0%	-2.8	1,423,000	8,565	0.6%	-2.2
WISCONSIN	3,574,000	7,087	0.2%	3,719,000	29,659	0.8%	0.6	3,857,000	31,354	0.8%	0.6	3,990,000	240,055	6.0%	5.8	4,131,000	68,784	1.7%	1.5
WYOMING				337,000	10,749	3.2%		355,000	6,899	1.9%	-1.2	369,000	5,962	1.6%	-1.6	383,000	7,709	2.0%	-1.2
Total	167,721,000	3,517,850	2.1%	180,143,000	4,563,418	2.5%	0.4	190,676,000	4,426,245	2.3%	0.2	197,119,000	5,185,496	2.6%	0.5	198,866,000	5,500,593	2.8%	0.7

*Percentage point difference between turnout in current year and initial year listed in chart. If data do not appear for a state in the initial year listed, the difference is calculated from the first year in which data do appear for that state.

STATE GUBERNATORIAL PRIMARY ELECTIONS

Election Years 1990–2006

State*	1990 Voting-age population	1990 Turnout	1990 %	1994 Voting-age population	1994 Turnout	1994 %	1994 Difference from 1990**	1998 Voting-age population	1998 Turnout	1998 %	1998 Difference from 1990	2002 Voting-age population	2002 Turnout	2002 %	2002 Difference from 1990	2006 Voting-age population	2006 Turnout	2006 %	2006 Difference from 1990*
ALABAMA	2,966,000	866,827	29.2%	3,093,000	916,038	29.6%	0.4	3,218,000	818,539	25.4%	-3.8	3,305,000	792,807	24.0%	-5.2	3,364,000	926,556	27.5%	-1.7
ALASKA	369,000	138,100	37.4%	391,000	114,344	29.2%	-8.2	412,000	109,026	26.5%	-11.0	436,000	110,247	25.3%	-12.1	462,000	155,682	33.7%	-3.7
ARIZONA	2,560,000	625,381	24.4%	2,897,000	564,744	19.5%	-4.9	3,234,000	342,540	10.6%	-13.8	3,567,000	538,531	15.1%	-9.3	3,933,000	538,975	13.7%	-10.7
ARKANSAS	1,722,000	578,123	33.6%									1,979,000	371,334	18.8%	-14.8				
CALIFORNIA	18,341,000	4,726,581	25.8%	19,021,000	4,412,154	23.2%	-2.6	19,700,000	5,950,524	30.2%	4.4	20,567,000	4,540,756	22.1%	-3.7	21,736,000	4,422,360	20.3%	-5.4
COLORADO				2,629,000	239,860	9.1%		2,879,000	357,955	12.4%	3.3	3,047,000	295,862	9.7%	0.6	3,161,000	336,390	10.6%	1.5
CONNECTICUT				2,412,000	285,467	11.8%													
DELAWARE																			
DISTRICT OF COLUMBIA																			
FLORIDA	9,281,000	1,742,237	18.8%	10,013,000	1,737,651	17.4%	-1.4									12,460,000	1,843,800	14.8%	-4.0
GEORGIA	4,675,000	1,170,433	25.0%	5,082,000	757,000	14.9%	-10.1	5,488,000	905,383	16.5%	-8.5	5,829,000	946,355	16.2%	-8.8	6,144,000	901,371	14.7%	-10.4
HAWAII	765,000	245,851	32.1%	796,000	290,848	36.5%	4.4	828,000	269,918	32.6%	0.5	860,000	266,289	31.0%	-1.2	898,000	271,072	30.2%	-2.0
IDAHO				770,000	176,688	22.9%		853,000	154,963	18.2%	-4.8	923,000	184,738	20.0%	-2.9	990,000	167,618	16.9%	-6.0
ILLINOIS	8,029,000	1,579,024	19.7%	8,175,000	1,794,357	21.9%	2.3	8,320,000	1,658,296	19.9%	0.3	8,420,000	2,170,344	25.8%	6.1	8,501,000	1,680,207	19.8%	0.1
INDIANA																			
IOWA				2,081,000	439,594	21.1%		2,124,000	277,543	13.1%	-8.1	2,156,000	280,076	13.0%	-8.1	2,186,000	372,056	17.0%	-4.1
KANSAS	1,787,000	481,788	27.0%	1,835,000	427,365	23.3%	-3.7	1,882,000	413,631	22.0%	-5.0	1,918,000	382,003	19.9%	-7.0	1,951,000	270,341	13.9%	-13.1
KENTUCKY																			
LOUISIANA																			
MAINE	906,000	108,191	11.9%	928,000	189,829	20.5%	8.5	950,000	103,050	10.8%	-1.1	981,000	152,131	15.5%	3.6	1,026,000	123,219	12.0%	0.1
MARYLAND	3,463,000	586,381	16.9%	3,558,000	784,405	22.0%	5.1	3,655,000	640,304	17.5%	0.6	3,788,000	791,017	20.9%	3.9	3,972,000	738,415	18.6%	1.7
MASSACHUSETTS	4,396,000	1,499,424	34.1%	4,426,000	660,767	14.9%	-19.2	4,458,000	871,343	19.5%	-14.6	4,507,000	979,926	21.7%	-12.4	4,585,000	983,778	21.5%	-12.7
MICHIGAN	6,700,000	845,195	12.6%	6,865,000	1,237,855	18.0%	5.4	7,031,000	1,262,746	18.0%	5.3	7,200,000	1,630,058	22.6%	10.0	7,393,000	1,112,845	15.1%	2.4
MINNESOTA	3,163,000	736,450	23.3%	3,301,000	864,927	26.2%	2.9	3,439,000	651,362	18.9%	-4.3	3,582,000	465,606	13.0%	-10.3	3,744,000	482,582	12.9%	-10.4
MISSISSIPPI																			
MISSOURI																			
MONTANA																			
NEBRASKA	1,139,000	358,050	31.4%	1,172,000	297,748	25.4%	-6.0	1,205,000	328,231	27.2%	-4.2	1,225,000	209,066	17.1%	-14.4	1,237,000	349,238	28.2%	-3.2
NEVADA	863,000	164,325	19.0%	1,047,000	236,908	22.6%	3.6	1,233,000	237,176	19.2%	0.2	1,398,000	206,499	14.8%	-4.3	1,560,000	259,552	16.6%	-2.4
NEW HAMPSHIRE	815,000	135,371	16.6%	850,000	107,018	12.6%	-4.0	886,000	103,609	11.7%	-4.9	931,000	215,507	23.1%	6.5	988,000	87,312	8.8%	-7.8
NEW JERSEY																			
NEW MEXICO	1,032,000	262,211	25.4%	1,113,000	288,875	26.0%	0.5	1,194,000	255,062	21.4%	-4.0	1,259,000	241,979	19.2%	-6.2	1,317,000	161,057	12.2%	-13.2
NEW YORK				12,423,000	1,075,113	8.7%													

State Gubernatorial Primary Elections (continued)

Election Years 1990–2006 (continued)

State	1990 Voting-age population	Turnout	%	1994 Voting-age population	Turnout	%	Difference from 1990	1998 Voting-age population	Turnout	%	Difference from 1990	2002 Voting-age population	Turnout	%	Difference from 1990	2006 Voting-age population	Turnout	%	Difference from 1990
NORTH CAROLINA																			
NORTH DAKOTA																			
OHIO	7,957,000	1,460,720	18.4%	8,105,000	1,445,213	17.8%	-0.5	8,254,000	1,355,778	16.4%	-1.9	8,379,000	1,020,063	12.2%	-6.2	8,502,000	1,626,334	19.1%	0.8
OKLAHOMA	2,280,000	732,456	32.1%	2,365,000	648,170	27.4%	-4.7					2,504,000	556,265	22.2%	-9.9	2,542,000	446,603	17.6%	-14.6
OREGON	2,056,000	539,942	26.3%	2,202,000	556,446	25.3%	-1.0	2,349,000	524,310	22.3%	-3.9	2,464,000	686,859	27.9%	1.6	2,564,000	619,731	24.2%	-2.1
PENNSYLVANIA	8,957,000	1,410,758	15.8%	9,034,000	2,107,230	23.3%	7.6	9,112,000	1,021,234	11.2%	-4.5	9,220,000	1,700,003	19.3%	3.6	9,374,000	1,238,643	13.2%	-2.5
RHODE ISLAND	734,000	178,717	24.3%	738,000	142,155	19.3%	-5.1					757,000	145,269	19.2%	-5.2	779,000	119,162	15.3%	-9.1
SOUTH CAROLINA				2,708,000	515,165	19.0%										3,153,000	385,624	12.2%	-6.8
SOUTH DAKOTA				516,000	158,422	30.7%						553,000	179,301	32.4%	1.7				
TENNESSEE	3,643,000	652,016	17.9%	3,870,000	1,001,493	25.9%	8.0	4,098,000	686,326	16.7%	-1.1	4,279,000	1,073,651	25.1%	7.2	4,434,000	765,432	17.3%	0.6
TEXAS	11,335,000	2,342,491	20.7%	12,135,000	1,594,284	13.1%	-7.5					13,687,000	1,623,851	11.9%	-8.8	14,486,000	1,174,521	8.1%	-12.6
UTAH																			
VERMONT	414,000	61,794	14.9%	429,000	53,492	12.5%	-2.5	445,000	70,479	15.8%	0.9	463,000	51,828	11.2%	-3.8	485,000	67,030	13.8%	-1.1
VIRGINIA																			
WASHINGTON																			
WEST VIRGINIA																			
WISCONSIN				3,698,000	446,882	12.1%		3,837,000	497,463	13.0%	0.9	3,970,000	803,447	20.2%	8.2	4,112,000	554,802	13.5%	1.4
WYOMING	316,000	119,549	37.8%	334,000	128,437	38.5%	0.6	352,000	117,681	33.4%	-4.4	366,000	127,484	34.8%	-3.0	381,000	81,415	21.4%	-16.5
Total	110,664,000	24,348,386	22.0%	141,012,000	26,696,944	18.9%	-3.1	101,436,000	19,984,472	19.7%	-2.3	124,520,000	23,819,942	19.1%	-2.9	142,420,000	23,263,723	16.3%	-5.7

*Overall primary turnout reflects only states with primaries in both parties. To find single party primary results, see partisan primary charts.

**Percentage point difference between turnout in current year and initial year listed in chart. If data do not appear for a state in the initial year listed, the difference is calculated from the first year in which data do appear for that state.

STATE GUBERNATORIAL PRIMARY ELECTIONS

Republican Turnout for Election Years 1990–2006

State	1990 Voting-age population	Turnout	%	1994 Voting-age population	Turnout	%	Difference from 1990*	1998 Voting-age population	Turnout	%	Difference from 1990	2002 Voting-age population	Turnout	%	Difference from 1990	2006 Voting-age population	Turnout	%	Difference from 1990
ALABAMA	2,966,000	125,117	4.2%	3,093,000	212,471	6.9%	2.7	3,218,000	460,360	14.3%	10.1	3,305,000	357,497	10.8%	6.6	3,364,000	460,019	13.7%	9.5
ALASKA	369,000	73,839	20.0%	391,000	49,924	12.8%	-7.2	412,000	60,166	14.6%	-5.4	436,000	72,248	16.6%	-3.4	462,000	101,695	22.0%	2.0
ARIZONA	2,560,000	372,324	14.5%	2,897,000	297,328	10.3%	-4.3	3,234,000	231,733	7.2%	-7.4	3,567,000	310,885	8.7%	-5.8	3,933,000	308,094	7.8%	-6.7
ARKANSAS	1,722,000	86,977	5.1%	1,815,000	47,353	2.6%	-2.4	1,908,000	57,623	3.0%	-2.0	1,979,000	92,237	4.7%	-0.4				
CALIFORNIA	18,341,000	2,121,728	11.6%	19,021,000	2,061,828	10.8%	-0.7	19,700,000	2,147,268	10.9%	-0.7	20,567,000	2,285,452	11.1%	-0.5	21,736,000	1,916,099	8.8%	-2.8
COLORADO				2,629,000	171,975	6.5%		2,879,000	213,882	7.4%	0.9	3,047,000	191,753	6.3%	-0.2	3,161,000	193,804	6.1%	-0.4
CONNECTICUT				2,412,000	115,061	4.8%													
DELAWARE																			
DISTRICT OF COLUMBIA																			
FLORIDA	9,281,000	668,181	7.2%	10,013,000	901,237	9.0%	1.8									12,460,000	985,986	7.9%	0.7
GEORGIA	4,675,000	118,118	2.5%	5,082,000	297,221	5.8%	3.3	5,488,000	418,542	7.6%	5.1	5,829,000	511,463	8.8%	6.2	6,144,000	419,254	6.8%	4.3
HAWAII	765,000	43,104	5.6%	796,000	54,075	6.8%	1.2	828,000	158,070	19.1%	13.5	860,000	78,868	9.2%	3.5	898,000	32,669	3.6%	-2.0
IDAHO	688,000	101,725	14.8%	770,000	118,891	15.4%	0.7	853,000	127,990	15.0%	0.2	923,000	145,549	15.8%	1.0	990,000	137,175	13.9%	-0.9
ILLINOIS	8,029,000	767,695	9.6%	8,175,000	695,332	8.5%	-1.1	8,320,000	707,406	8.5%	-1.1	8,420,000	917,828	10.9%	1.3	8,501,000	735,810	8.7%	-0.9
INDIANA																			
IOWA				2,081,000	311,277	15.0%		2,124,000	162,200	7.6%	-7.3	2,156,000	199,234	9.2%	-5.7	2,186,000	74,554	3.4%	-11.5
KANSAS	1,787,000	309,560	17.3%	1,835,000	268,211	14.6%	-2.7	1,882,000	310,150	16.5%	-0.8	1,918,000	294,504	15.4%	-2.0	1,951,000	194,295	10.0%	-7.4
KENTUCKY																			
LOUISIANA																			
MAINE	906,000	48,225	5.3%	928,000	89,623	9.7%	4.3	950,000	57,832	6.1%	0.8	981,000	78,783	8.0%	2.7	1,026,000	70,044	6.8%	1.5
MARYLAND	3,463,000	127,031	3.7%	3,558,000	237,002	6.7%	3.0	3,655,000	216,759	5.9%	2.3	3,788,000	247,529	6.5%	2.9	3,972,000	213,744	5.4%	1.7
MASSACHUSETTS	4,396,000	446,992	10.2%	4,426,000	211,917	4.8%	-5.4	4,458,000	237,424	5.3%	-4.8	4,507,000	229,794	5.1%	-5.1	4,585,000	71,430	1.6%	-8.6
MICHIGAN	6,700,000	473,233	7.1%	6,865,000	549,565	8.0%	0.9	7,031,000	533,081	7.6%	0.5	7,200,000	583,385	8.1%	1.0	7,393,000	581,523	7.9%	0.8
MINNESOTA	3,163,000	342,879	10.8%	3,301,000	482,754	14.6%	3.8	3,439,000	140,124	4.1%	-6.8	3,582,000	195,099	5.4%	-5.4	3,744,000	166,112	4.4%	-6.4
MISSISSIPPI																			
MISSOURI																			
MONTANA																			
NEBRASKA	1,139,000	190,941	16.8%	1,172,000	182,633	15.6%	-1.2	1,205,000	220,315	18.3%	1.5	1,225,000	147,718	12.1%	-4.7	1,237,000	274,975	22.2%	5.5
NEVADA	863,000	76,028	8.8%	1,047,000	116,717	11.1%	2.3	1,233,000	132,353	10.7%	1.9	1,398,000	117,528	8.4%	-0.4	1,560,000	140,515	9.0%	0.2
NEW HAMPSHIRE	815,000	86,486	10.6%	850,000	77,787	9.2%	-1.5	886,000	71,231	8.0%	-2.6	931,000	153,047	16.4%	5.8	988,000	43,656	4.4%	-6.2
NEW JERSEY																			
NEW MEXICO	1,032,000	80,971	7.8%	1,113,000	93,071	8.4%	0.5	1,194,000	78,191	6.5%	-1.3	1,259,000	94,161	7.5%	-0.4	1,317,000	53,113	4.0%	-3.8
NEW YORK				12,423,000	361,922	2.9%													

State Gubernatorial Primary Elections (continued)

Republican Turnout for Election Years 1990–2006 (continued)

State	1990 Voting-age population	Turnout	%	1994 Voting-age population	Turnout	%	Difference from 1990	1998 Voting-age population	Turnout	%	Difference from 1990	2002 Voting-age population	Turnout	%	Difference from 1990	2006 Voting-age population	Turnout	%	Difference from 1990
NORTH CAROLINA																			
NORTH DAKOTA																			
OHIO	7,957,000	645,224	8.1%	8,105,000	750,779	9.3%	1.2	8,254,000	691,946	8.4%	0.3	8,379,000	552,491	6.6%	-1.5	8,502,000	825,967	9.7%	1.6
OKLAHOMA	2,280,000	189,450	8.3%	2,365,000	205,947	8.7%	0.4					2,504,000	205,876	8.2%	-0.1	2,542,000	182,136	7.2%	-1.1
OREGON	2,056,000	288,040	14.0%	2,202,000	273,310	12.4%	-1.6	2,349,000	207,055	8.8%	-5.2	2,464,000	332,575	13.5%	-0.5	2,564,000	300,554	11.7%	-2.3
PENNSYLVANIA	8,957,000	589,799	6.6%	9,034,000	996,784	11.0%	4.4	9,112,000	501,532	5.5%	-1.1	9,220,000	538,757	5.8%	-0.7	9,374,000	583,658	6.2%	-0.4
RHODE ISLAND	734,000	10,801	1.5%	738,000	43,023	5.8%	4.4					757,000	25,745	3.4%	1.9	779,000	51,650	6.6%	5.2
SOUTH CAROLINA				2,708,000	253,719	9.4%		2,867,000	158,049	5.5%	-3.9	3,010,000	316,255	10.5%	1.1	3,153,000	247,281	7.8%	-1.5
SOUTH DAKOTA				516,000	105,975	20.5%						553,000	111,264	20.1%	-0.4				
TENNESSEE	3,643,000	172,001	4.7%	3,870,000	464,447	12.0%	7.3	4,098,000	387,860	9.5%	4.7	4,279,000	534,213	12.5%	7.8	4,434,000	321,378	7.2%	2.5
TEXAS	11,335,000	855,231	7.5%	12,135,000	557,340	4.6%	-3.0					13,687,000	620,463	4.5%	-3.0	14,486,000	665,919	4.6%	-2.9
UTAH																			
VERMONT	414,000	44,869	10.8%	429,000	27,670	6.4%	-4.4	445,000	52,531	11.8%	1.0	463,000	24,155	5.2%	-5.6	485,000	34,280	7.1%	-3.8
VIRGINIA																			
WASHINGTON																			
WEST VIRGINIA																			
WISCONSIN	3,560,000	217,723	6.1%	3,698,000	321,487	8.7%	2.6	3,837,000	275,509	7.2%	1.1	3,970,000	230,232	5.8%	-0.3	4,112,000	234,020	5.7%	-0.4
WYOMING	316,000	76,076	24.1%	334,000	88,613	26.5%	2.5	352,000	84,179	23.9%	-0.2	366,000	90,685	24.8%	0.7	381,000	51,803	13.6%	-10.5
Total	114,912,000	9,750,368	8.5%	142,827,000	12,094,269	8.5%	0.0	106,211,000	9,101,361	8.6%	0.1	127,530,000	10,887,273	8.5%	0.1	142,420,000	10,673,212	7.5%	-1.0

Democratic Turnout for Election Years 1990–2006

State	1990 Voting-age population	Turnout	%	1994 Voting-age population	Turnout	%	Difference from 1990*	1998 Voting-age population	Turnout	%	Difference from 1990	2002 Voting-age population	Turnout	%	Difference from 1990	2006 Voting-age population	Turnout	%	Difference from 1990
ALABAMA	2,966,000	741,710	25.0%	3,093,000	703,567	22.7%	-2.3	3,218,000	358,179	11.1%	-13.9	3,305,000	435,310	13.2%	-11.8	3,364,000	466,537	13.9%	-11.1
ALASKA	369,000	64,261	17.4%	391,000	56,658	14.5%	-2.9	412,000	43,668	10.6%	-6.8	436,000	32,547	7.5%	-9.9	462,000	53,987	11.7%	-5.7
ARIZONA	2,560,000	253,057	9.9%	2,897,000	262,364	9.1%	-0.8	3,234,000	109,044	3.4%	-6.5	3,567,000	224,874	6.3%	-3.6	3,933,000	230,881	5.9%	-4.0
ARKANSAS	1,722,000	491,146	28.5%									1,979,000	279,097	14.1%	-14.4				
CALIFORNIA	18,341,000	2,604,853	14.2%	19,021,000	2,295,226	12.1%	-2.1	19,700,000	3,596,683	18.3%	4.1	20,567,000	2,169,555	10.5%	-3.7	21,736,000	2,506,261	11.5%	-2.7
COLORADO				2,629,000	67,885	2.6%		2,879,000	144,073	5.0%	2.4	3,047,000	104,109	3.4%	0.8	3,161,000	142,586	4.5%	1.9
CONNECTICUT	2,419,000	131,065	5.4%	2,412,000	170,406	7.1%	1.6					2,488,000	266,689						
DELAWARE																			
DISTRICT OF COLUMBIA																			
FLORIDA	9,281,000	1,074,056	11.6%	10,013,000	836,414	8.4%	-3.2					11,533,000	1,357,017	11.8%	0.2	12,460,000	857,814	6.9%	-4.7

State Gubernatorial Primary Elections (continued)

State Gubernatorial Primary Elections (continued)

Democratic Turnout for Election Years 1990–2006 (continued)

State	1990 Voting-age population	Turnout	%	1994 Voting-age population	Turnout	%	Difference from 1990	1998 Voting-age population	Turnout	%	Difference from 1990	2002 Voting-age population	Turnout	%	Difference from 1990	2006 Voting-age population	Turnout	%	Difference from 1990
GEORGIA	4,675,000	1,052,315	22.5%	5,082,000	459,779	9.0%	-13.5	5,488,000	486,841	8.9%	-13.6	5,829,000	434,892	7.5%	-15.0	6,144,000	482,117	7.8%	-14.7
HAWAII	765,000	202,747	26.5%	796,000	201,286	25.3%	-1.2	828,000	111,123	13.4%	-13.1	860,000	185,951	21.6%	-4.9	898,000	238,403	26.5%	0.0
IDAHO				770,000	57,797	7.5%		853,000	26,973	3.2%	-4.3	923,000	38,083	4.1%	-3.4	990,000	30,443	3.1%	-4.4
ILLINOIS	8,029,000	811,329	10.1%	8,175,000	1,099,025	13.4%	3.3	8,320,000	950,307	11.4%	1.3	8,420,000	1,252,516	14.9%	4.8	8,501,000	944,397	11.1%	1.0
INDIANA																			
IOWA				2,081,000	128,317	6.2%		2,124,000	115,080	5.4%	-0.7	2,156,000	80,443	3.7%	-2.4	2,186,000	297,502	13.6%	7.4
KANSAS	1,787,000	172,228	9.6%	1,835,000	159,154	8.7%	-1.0	1,882,000	103,481	5.5%	-4.1	1,918,000	87,499	4.6%	-5.1	1,951,000	76,046	3.9%	-5.7
KENTUCKY																			
LOUISIANA																			
MAINE	906,000	59,966	6.6%	928,000	100,206	10.8%	4.2	950,000	45,218	4.8%	-1.9	981,000	71,735	7.3%	0.7	1,026,000	53,175	5.2%	-1.4
MARYLAND	3,463,000	459,350	13.3%	3,558,000	547,403	15.4%	2.1	3,655,000	423,545	11.6%	-1.7	3,788,000	543,488	14.3%	1.1	3,972,000	524,671	13.2%	-0.1
MASSACHUSETTS	4,396,000	1,052,432	23.9%	4,426,000	448,850	10.1%	-13.8	4,458,000	633,919	14.2%	-9.7	4,507,000	747,303	16.6%	-7.4	4,585,000	912,348	19.9%	-4.0
MICHIGAN	6,700,000	371,962	5.6%	6,865,000	688,290	10.0%	4.5	7,031,000	729,665	10.4%	4.8	7,200,000	1,046,673	14.5%	9.0	7,393,000	531,322	7.2%	1.6
MINNESOTA	3,163,000	393,571	12.4%	3,301,000	382,173	11.6%	-0.9	3,439,000	494,069	14.4%	1.9	3,582,000	224,238	6.3%	-6.2	3,744,000	316,470	8.5%	-4.0
MISSISSIPPI																			
MISSOURI																			
MONTANA																			
NEBRASKA	1,139,000	167,109	14.7%	1,172,000	115,115	9.8%	-4.8	1,205,000	107,916	9.0%	-5.7	1,225,000	61,312	5.0%	-9.7	1,237,000	74,263	6.0%	-8.7
NEVADA	863,000	88,297	10.2%	1,047,000	120,191	11.5%	1.2	1,233,000	104,823	8.5%	-1.7	1,398,000	88,971	6.4%	-3.9	1,560,000	119,037	7.6%	-2.6
NEW HAMPSHIRE	815,000	48,885	6.0%	850,000	28,020	3.3%	-2.7	886,000	32,262	3.6%	-2.4	931,000	62,460	6.7%	0.7	988,000	43,656	4.4%	-1.6
NEW JERSEY																			
NEW MEXICO	1,032,000	181,240	17.6%	1,113,000	195,804	17.6%	0.0	1,194,000	176,011	14.7%	-2.8	1,259,000	147,818	11.7%	-5.8	1,317,000	107,944	8.2%	-9.4
NEW YORK				12,423,000	690,680	5.6%		12,459,000	737,083	5.9%	0.4	12,508,000	633,708	5.1%	-0.5	12,604,000	762,947	6.1%	0.5
NORTH CAROLINA																			
NORTH DAKOTA																			
OHIO	7,957,000	815,496	10.2%	8,105,000	694,434	8.6%	-1.7	8,254,000	663,832	8.0%	-2.2	8,379,000	467,572	5.6%	-4.7	8,502,000	800,367	9.4%	-0.8
OKLAHOMA	2,280,000	543,006	23.8%	2,365,000	442,223	18.7%	-5.1	2,449,000	284,062	11.6%	-12.2	2,504,000	350,389	14.0%	-9.8	2,542,000	264,467	10.4%	-13.4
OREGON	2,056,000	251,902	12.3%	2,202,000	283,136	12.9%	0.6	2,349,000	307,584	13.1%	0.8	2,464,000	354,284	14.4%	2.1	2,564,000	319,177	12.4%	0.2
PENNSYLVANIA	8,957,000	820,959	9.2%	9,034,000	1,110,446	12.3%	3.1	9,112,000	519,702	5.7%	-3.5	9,220,000	1,242,236	13.5%	4.3	9,374,000	654,985	7.0%	-2.2
RHODE ISLAND	734,000	167,916	22.9%	738,000	99,132	13.4%	-9.4	744,000	64,575	8.7%	-14.2	757,000	119,524	15.8%	-7.1	779,000	67,512	8.7%	-14.2
SOUTH CAROLINA	2,550,000	193,900	7.6%	2,708,000	261,446	9.7%	2.1									3,153,000	138,343	4.4%	-3.2
SOUTH DAKOTA				516,000	52,447	10.2%						553,000	68,037	12.3%	2.1	567,000	36,389	6.4%	-3.7
TENNESSEE	3,643,000	480,015	13.2%	3,870,000	537,046	13.9%	0.7	4,098,000	298,466	7.3%	-5.9	4,279,000	539,438	12.6%	-0.6	4,434,000	444,054	10.0%	-3.2

State Gubernatorial Primary Elections (continued)

Democratic Turnout for Election Years 1990–2006 (continued)

State	1990 Voting-age population	1990 Turnout	1990 %	1994 Voting-age population	1994 Turnout	1994 %	1994 Difference from 1990	1998 Voting-age population	1998 Turnout	1998 %	1998 Difference from 1990	2002 Voting-age population	2002 Turnout	2002 %	2002 Difference from 1990	2006 Voting-age population	2006 Turnout	2006 %	2006 Difference from 1990
TEXAS	11,335,000	1,487,260	13.1%	12,135,000	1,036,944	8.5%	-4.6					13,687,000	1,003,388	7.3%	-5.8	14,486,000	508,602	3.5%	-9.6
UTAH																			
VERMONT	414,000	16,925	4.1%	429,000	25,544	6.0%	1.9	445,000	17,948	4.0%	-0.1	463,000	25,754	5.6%	1.5	485,000	32,750	6.8%	2.7
VIRGINIA																5,432,000	155,784	2.9%	
WASHINGTON																			
WEST VIRGINIA																			
WISCONSIN				3,698,000	121,916	3.3%		3,837,000	219,273	5.7%	2.4	3,970,000	553,634	13.9%	10.6	4,112,000	320,782	7.8%	4.5
WYOMING	316,000	43,473	13.8%	334,000	39,824	11.9%	-1.8	352,000	33,502	9.5%	-4.2	366,000	36,799	10.1%	-3.7	381,000	29,612	7.8%	-6.0
Total	115,633,000	15,242,431	13.2%	141,012,000	14,519,148	10.3%	-2.9	117,088,000	11,938,907	10.2%	-3.0	148,561,000	15,070,654	10.1%	-3.0	163,511,000	13,812,320	8.4%	-4.7

Other Turnout for Election Years 1990–2006

State	1990 Voting-age population	1990 Turnout	1990 %	1994 Voting-age population	1994 Turnout	1994 %	1994 Difference from 1990*	1998 Voting-age population	1998 Turnout	1998 %	1998 Difference from 1990	2002 Voting-age population	2002 Turnout	2002 %	2002 Difference from 1990	2006 Voting-age population	2006 Turnout	2006 %	2006 Difference from 1990
ALASKA				391,000	7,762	2.0%		412,000	5,192	1.3%	-0.7	436,000	5,452	1.3%	-0.7				
ARIZONA				2,897,000	5,052	0.2%		3,234,000	1,763	0.1%	-0.1	3,567,000	2,772	0.1%	-0.1				
CALIFORNIA				19,021,000	55,100	0.3%		19,700,000	206,573	1.0%	0.8	20,567,000	85,749	0.4%	0.1				
HAWAII				796,000	35,487	4.5%		828,000	725	0.1%	-4.4	860,000	1,470	0.2%	-4.3				
IDAHO												923,000	1,106	0.1%					
ILLINOIS								8,320,000	583	0.0%									
IOWA								2,124,000	263	0.0%		2,156,000	399	0.0%	0.0				
MAINE												981,000	1,613	0.2%					
MASSACHUSETTS												4,507,000	2,829	0.1%					
MINNESOTA								3,439,000	17,169	0.5%		3,582,000	46,269	1.3%	0.8				
NEBRASKA												1,225,000	36	0.0%					
NEW HAMPSHIRE				850,000	1,211	0.1%		886,000	116	0.0%	-0.1								
NEW MEXICO								1,194,000	860	0.1%									
NEW YORK				12,423,000	22,511	0.2%						12,508,000	39,534	0.3%	0.1				
OREGON								2,349,000	9,671	0.4%									
VERMONT				429,000	278	0.1%						463,000	1,719	0.4%	0.3				
WISCONSIN				3,698,000	3,479	0.1%		3,837,000	2,681	0.1%	0.0	3,970,000	19,581	0.5%	0.4				
Total				40,505,000	130,880	0.3%		46,323,000	245,596	0.5%	0.2	55,745,000	208,529	0.4%	0.1				

*Percentage point difference between turnout in current year and initial year listed in chart. If data do not appear for a state in the initial year listed, the difference is calculated from the first year in which data do appear for that state.

UNITED STATES SENATE PRIMARY ELECTIONS

Election Years 1990–2006

State*	1990 Voting-age population	1990 Turnout	1990 %	1994 Voting-age population	1994 Turnout	1994 %	1994 Difference from 1990**	1998 Voting-age population	1998 Turnout	1998 %	1998 Difference from 1990	2002 Voting-age population	2002 Turnout	2002 %	2002 Difference from 1990	2006 Voting-age population	2006 Turnout	2006 %	2006 Difference from 1990
ALABAMA																			
ALASKA	369,000	138,492	37.5%					412,000	106,785	25.9%	-11.6	436,000	104,625	24.0%	-13.5				
ARIZONA				2,897,000	493,980	17.1%		3,234,000	309,581	9.6%	-7.5					3,933,000	512,246	13.0%	-4.0
ARKANSAS								1,908,000	373,578	19.6%									
CALIFORNIA				19,021,000	4,192,801	22.0%		19,700,000	5,851,574	29.7%	7.7					21,736,000	4,063,841	18.7%	-3.3
COLORADO	2,380,000	382,419	16.1%					2,879,000	365,526	12.7%	-3.4	3,047,000	308,566	10.1%	-5.9				
CONNECTICUT																			
DELAWARE																			
DISTRICT OF COLUMBIA																			
FLORIDA																			
GEORGIA								5,488,000	734,135	13.4%		5,829,000	946,345	16.2%	2.9				
HAWAII	765,000	245,097	32.0%	796,000	209,602	26.3%	-5.7	828,000	214,297	25.9%	-6.2					898,000	270,697	30.1%	-1.9
IDAHO	688,000	158,304	23.0%					853,000	148,783	17.4%	-5.6								
ILLINOIS								8,320,000	1,386,694	16.7%									
INDIANA	4,054,000	619,204	15.3%	4,198,000	747,889	17.8%	2.5	4,342,000	719,921	16.6%	1.3								
IOWA	2,040,000	294,451	14.4%					2,124,000	236,007	11.1%	-3.3	2,156,000	281,258	13.0%	-1.4				
KANSAS	1,787,000	458,894	25.7%					1,882,000	354,669	18.8%	-6.8								
KENTUCKY	2,719,000	382,480	14.1%					2,951,000	773,583	26.2%	12.1								
LOUISIANA***	2,953,000	1,396,113	47.3%																
MAINE				928,000	162,525	17.5%						981,000	134,375	13.7%	-3.8	1,026,000	104,253	10.2%	-7.4
MARYLAND				3,558,000	701,830	19.7%		3,655,000	591,812	16.2%	-3.5					3,972,000	737,061	18.6%	-1.2
MASSACHUSETTS				4,426,000	625,631	14.1%						4,507,000	633,972	14.1%	-0.1	4,585,000	70,776	1.5%	-12.6
MICHIGAN				6,865,000	1,219,103	17.8%						7,200,000	1,335,393	18.5%	0.8	7,393,000	1,108,937	15.0%	-2.8
MINNESOTA	3,163,000	712,808	22.5%	3,301,000	847,663	25.7%	3.1					3,582,000	481,446	13.4%	-9.1	3,744,000	481,487	12.9%	-9.7
MISSISSIPPI				1,914,000	210,863	11.0%													
MISSOURI				3,905,000	839,845	21.5%		4,035,000	549,631	13.6%	-7.9	4,151,000	881,360	21.2%	-0.3	4,269,000	675,722	15.8%	-5.7
MONTANA	573,000	186,097	32.5%	611,000	206,493	33.8%	1.3					683,000	146,786	21.5%	-11.0	714,000	205,680	28.8%	-3.7
NEBRASKA	1,139,000	353,269	31.0%	1,172,000	282,855	24.1%	-6.9					1,225,000	201,581	16.5%	-14.6	1,237,000	222,144	18.0%	-13.1
NEVADA																1,560,000	258,268	16.6%	
NEW HAMPSHIRE	815,000	132,704	16.3%					886,000	98,558	11.1%	-5.2	931,000	214,025	23.0%	6.7				
NEW JERSEY	5,506,000	325,955	5.9%	5,563,000	375,345	6.7%	0.8					5,705,000	399,768	7.0%	1.1	5,837,000	361,566	6.2%	0.3
NEW MEXICO				1,113,000	254,884	22.9%						1,259,000	232,345	18.5%	-4.4	1,317,000	173,172	13.1%	-9.8
NEW YORK																12,604,000	954,976	7.6%	

United States Senate Primary Elections (continued)

Election Years 1990–2006 (continued)

State	1990 Voting-age population	1990 Turnout	1990 %	1994 Voting-age population	1994 Turnout	1994 %	1994 Difference from 1990	1998 Voting-age population	1998 Turnout	1998 %	1998 Difference from 1990	2002 Voting-age population	2002 Turnout	2002 %	2002 Difference from 1990	2006 Voting-age population	2006 Turnout	2006 %	2006 Difference from 1990
NORTH CAROLINA	4,977,000	880,091	17.7%					5,663,000	805,319	14.2%	-3.5	5,969,000	1,065,134	17.8%	0.2				
NORTH DAKOTA				467,000	115,758	24.8%		473,000	80,598	17.0%	-7.7					482,000	98,878	20.5%	-4.3
OHIO				8,105,000	1,746,549	21.5%		8,254,000	1,432,470	17.4%	-4.2					8,502,000	1,536,148	18.1%	-3.5
OKLAHOMA				2,365,000	640,822	27.1%													
OREGON	2,050,000	535,023	26.0%					2,349,000	526,228	22.4%	-3.6	2,464,000	635,682	25.8%	-0.2				
PENNSYLVANIA				9,034,000	1,533,014	17.0%		9,112,000	1,036,398	11.4%	-5.0					9,374,000	1,305,700	13.9%	-3.0
RHODE ISLAND				738,000	86,141	11.7%						757,000	101,356	13.4%	1.7	779,000	146,978	18.9%	7.2
SOUTH CAROLINA																			
SOUTH DAKOTA																			
TENNESSEE				3,870,000	848,353	21.9%						4,279,000	1,057,357	24.7%	2.8	4,434,000	903,043	20.4%	-1.6
TEXAS				12,135,000	1,583,247	13.0%						13,687,000	1,573,957	11.5%	-1.5	14,486,000	1,127,948	7.8%	-5.3
UTAH																			
VERMONT				429,000	57,630	13.4%		445,000	72,333	16.3%	2.8					485,000	73,777	15.2%	1.8
VIRGINIA																			
WASHINGTON				3,723,000	929,603	25.0%		3,973,000	1,037,344	26.1%	1.1					4,387,000	1,091,648	24.9%	-0.1
WEST VIRGINIA	1,344,000	299,467	22.3%	1,366,000	300,032	22.0%	-0.3					1,406,000	299,191	21.3%	-1.0	1,421,000	267,088	18.8%	-3.5
WISCONSIN				3,698,000	484,495	13.1%										4,112,000	554,945	13.5%	0.4
WYOMING	316,000	116,431	36.8%	334,000	120,944	36.2%	-0.6					366,000	122,091	33.4%	-3.5	381,000	103,135	27.1%	-9.8
Total	37,644,000	7,617,299	20.2%	106,532,000	19,817,897	18.6%	-1.6	93,766,000	17,805,824	19.0%	-1.2	70,620,000	11,156,613	15.8%	-4.4	123,668,000	17,410,114	14.1%	-6.2

*Overall primary turnout reflects only states with primaries in both parties. To find single party primary results, see partisan primary charts.

**Percentage point difference between turnout in current year and initial year listed in chart. If data do not appear for a state in the initial year listed, the difference is calculated from the first year in which data do appear for that state.

***In 1978 Louisiana eliminated the partisan primary for senator and instituted an open primary with candidates from all parties running on the same ballot. Any candidate who received a majority appeared in the general election unopposed. If no candidate received fifty percent, a runoff was held between the top two finishers. In 2008 Louisiana returned to a partisan primary system.

UNITED STATES SENATE PRIMARY ELECTIONS

Republican Turnout for Election Years 1990–2006

State	1990 Voting-age population	Turnout	%	1994 Voting-age population	Turnout	%	Difference from 1990*	1998 Voting-age population	Turnout	%	Difference from 1990	2002 Voting-age population	Turnout	%	Difference from 1990	2006 Voting-age population	Turnout	%	Difference from 1990
ALABAMA																			
ALASKA	369,000	116,792	31.7%					412,000	82,947	20.1%	-11.5	436,000	72,312	16.6%	-15.1				
ARIZONA				2,897,000	233,523	8.1%		3,234,000	207,058	6.4%	-1.7					3,933,000	297,791	7.6%	-0.5
ARKANSAS								1,908,000	54,777	2.9%		1,979,000	92,122	4.7%	1.8				
CALIFORNIA				19,021,000	1,934,891	10.2%		19,700,000	2,854,776	14.5%	4.3					21,736,000	1,560,472	7.2%	-3.0
COLORADO	2,380,000	184,152	7.7%					2,879,000	219,049	7.6%	-0.1	3,047,000	192,305	6.3%	-1.4				
CONNECTICUT				2,412,000	104,705	4.3%													
DELAWARE																			
DISTRICT OF COLUMBIA																			
FLORIDA								10,746,000	550,633	5.1%						12,460,000	960,654	7.7%	2.6
GEORGIA								5,488,000	323,350	5.9%		5,829,000	491,612	8.4%	2.5				
HAWAII	765,000	46,435	6.1%	796,000	40,725	5.1%	-1.0	828,000	96,252	11.6%	5.6					898,000	32,661	3.6%	-2.4
IDAHO	688,000	111,563	16.2%					853,000	126,280	14.8%	-1.4	923,000	130,126	14.1%	-2.1				
ILLINOIS								8,320,000	719,522	8.6%		8,420,000	825,231	9.8%	1.2				
INDIANA	4,054,000	348,133	8.6%	4,198,000	398,111	9.5%	0.9	4,342,000	394,998	9.1%	0.5								
IOWA	2,040,000	94,253	4.6%					2,124,000	149,943	7.1%	2.4	2,156,000	197,096	9.1%	4.5				
KANSAS	1,787,000	307,325	17.2%					1,882,000	255,747	13.6%	-3.6	1,918,000	279,133	14.6%	-2.6				
KENTUCKY	2,719,000	72,373	2.7%					2,951,000	205,291	7.0%	4.3								
LOUISIANA**	2,953,000	607,391	20.6%																
MAINE				928,000	80,046	8.6%						981,000	74,643	7.6%	-1.0	1,026,000	59,652	5.8%	-2.8
MARYLAND				3,558,000	217,626	6.1%		3,655,000	177,652	4.9%	-1.3					3,972,000	204,895	5.2%	-1.0
MASSACHUSETTS	4,396,000	400,942	9.1%	4,426,000	229,178	5.2%	-3.9					4,507,000	12,945	0.3%	-8.8	4,585,000	70,047	1.5%	-7.6
MICHIGAN	6,700,000	453,035	6.8%	6,865,000	562,905	8.2%	1.4					7,200,000	445,876	6.2%	-0.6	7,393,000	595,481	8.1%	1.3
MINNESOTA	3,163,000	337,821	10.7%	3,301,000	464,033	14.1%	3.4					3,582,000	207,308	5.8%	-4.9	3,744,000	163,057	4.4%	-6.3
MISSISSIPPI				1,914,000	76,019	4.0%													
MISSOURI				3,905,000	312,648	8.0%		4,035,000	245,843	6.1%	-1.9	4,151,000	435,702	10.5%	2.5	4,269,000	325,782	7.6%	-0.4
MONTANA	573,000	87,421	15.3%	611,000	82,827	13.6%	-1.7					683,000	80,073	11.7%	-3.5	714,000	97,473	13.7%	-1.6
NEBRASKA	1,139,000	195,310	17.1%	1,172,000	169,586	14.5%	-2.7					1,225,000	144,160	11.8%	-5.4	1,237,000	129,643	10.5%	-6.7
NEVADA				1,047,000	115,982	11.1%		1,233,000	130,646	10.6%	-0.5					1,560,000	140,426	9.0%	-2.1
NEW HAMPSHIRE	815,000	84,035	10.3%					886,000	74,787	8.4%	-1.9	931,000	153,542	16.5%	6.2				
NEW JERSEY	5,506,000	112,214	2.0%	5,563,000	188,300	3.4%	1.3					5,705,000	218,300	3.8%	1.8	5,837,000	171,622	2.9%	0.9
NEW MEXICO				1,113,000	89,736	8.1%						1,259,000	91,960	7.3%	-0.8	1,317,000	57,974	4.4%	-3.7
NEW YORK																12,604,000	189,022	1.5%	

United States Senate Primary Elections *(continued)*

Republican Turnout for Election Years 1990–2006 *(continued)*

State	1990 Voting-age population	1990 Turnout	1990 %	1994 Voting-age population	1994 Turnout	1994 %	1994 Difference from 1990	1998 Voting-age population	1998 Turnout	1998 %	1998 Difference from 1990	2002 Voting-age population	2002 Turnout	2002 %	2002 Difference from 1990	2006 Voting-age population	2006 Turnout	2006 %	2006 Difference from 1990
NORTH CAROLINA	4,977,000	186,595	3.7%					5,663,000	265,288	4.7%	0.9	5,969,000	426,106	7.1%	3.4				
NORTH DAKOTA				467,000	49,493	10.6%		473,000	36,770	7.8%	-2.8					482,000	40,647	8.4%	-2.2
OHIO				8,105,000	811,661	10.0%		8,254,000	751,844	9.1%	-0.9					8,502,000	788,744	9.3%	-0.7
OKLAHOMA				2,365,000	204,360	8.6%													
OREGON	2,056,000	281,586	13.7%					2,349,000	213,756	9.1%	-4.6	2,464,000	309,943	12.6%	-1.1				
PENNSYLVANIA				9,034,000	818,084	9.1%		9,112,000	559,610	6.1%	-2.9					9,374,000	561,952	6.0%	-3.1
RHODE ISLAND				738,000	40,423	5.5%						757,000	16,041	2.1%	-3.4	779,000	64,483	8.3%	2.8
SOUTH CAROLINA								2,867,000	154,193	5.4%									
SOUTH DAKOTA								536,000	51,032	9.5%									
TENNESSEE	3,643,000	139,775	3.8%	3,870,000	445,651	11.5%	7.7					4,279,000	548,482	12.8%	9.0	4,434,000	481,117	10.9%	7.0
TEXAS				12,135,000	555,338	4.6%						13,687,000	619,302	4.5%	-0.1	14,486,000	627,163	4.3%	-0.2
UTAH																			
VERMONT				429,000	27,080	6.3%		445,000	52,813	11.9%	5.6					485,000	35,591	7.3%	1.0
VIRGINIA				4,744,000	266,944	5.6%													
WASHINGTON				3,723,000	530,282	14.2%		3,973,000	496,090	12.5%	-1.8					4,387,000	462,894	10.6%	-3.7
WEST VIRGINIA	1,344,000	63,170	4.7%	1,366,000	77,533	5.7%	1.0					1,406,000	78,513	5.6%	0.9	1,421,000	81,325	5.7%	1.0
WISCONSIN				3,698,000	331,512	9.0%										4,112,000	195,163	4.7%	-4.2
WYOMING	316,000	81,920	25.9%	334,000	81,381	24.4%	-1.6					366,000	91,543	25.0%	-0.9	381,000	78,211	20.5%	-5.4
Total	52,383,000	4,312,241	8.2%	114,735,000	9,540,583	8.3%	0.1	109,148,000	9,450,947	8.7%	0.4	83,860,000	6,234,376	7.4%	-0.8	136,128,000	8,473,942	6.2%	-2.0

Democratic Turnout for Election Years 1990–2006

State	1990 Voting-age population	1990 Turnout	1990 %	1994 Voting-age population	1994 Turnout	1994 %	1994 Difference from 1990*	1998 Voting-age population	1998 Turnout	1998 %	1998 Difference from 1990	2002 Voting-age population	2002 Turnout	2002 %	2002 Difference from 1990	2006 Voting-age population	2006 Turnout	2006 %	2006 Difference from 1990
ALABAMA	2,966,000	664,384	22.4%									3,305,000	397,919	12.0%	-10.4				
ALASKA	369,000	21,700	5.9%					412,000	17,059	4.1%	-1.7	436,000	27,548	6.3%	0.4				
ARIZONA				2,897,000	255,033	8.8%		3,234,000	100,822	3.1%	-5.7					3,933,000	214,455	5.5%	-3.4
ARKANSAS								1,908,000	318,801	16.7%									
CALIFORNIA				19,021,000	2,204,580	11.6%		19,700,000	2,793,514	14.2%	2.6					21,736,000	2,503,369	11.5%	-0.1
COLORADO	2,380,000	198,267	8.3%					2,879,000	146,477	5.1%	-3.2	3,047,000	116,261	3.8%	-4.5				
CONNECTICUT																2,488,000	282,870	11.4%	
DELAWARE																			
DISTRICT OF COLUMBIA																			
FLORIDA				10,013,000	756,663	7.6%													

United States Senate Primary Elections *(continued)*

Democratic Turnout for Election Years 1990–2006 *(continued)*

State	1990 Voting-age population	Turnout	%	1994 Voting-age population	Turnout	%	Difference from 1990	1998 Voting-age population	Turnout	%	Difference from 1990	2002 Voting-age population	Turnout	%	Difference from 1990	2006 Voting-age population	Turnout	%	Difference from 1990
GEORGIA								5,488,000	410,785	7.5%		5,829,000	454,733	7.8%	0.3				
HAWAII	765,000	198,662	26.0%	796,000	168,877	21.2%	-4.8	828,000	117,612	14.2%	-11.8					898,000	238,036	26.5%	0.5
IDAHO	688,000	46,741	6.8%					853,000	22,503	2.6%	-4.2	923,000	37,158	4.0%	-2.8				
ILLINOIS								8,320,000	666,419	8.0%		8,420,000	918,467	10.9%	2.9				
INDIANA	4,054,000	271,071	6.7%	4,198,000	349,778	8.3%	1.6	4,342,000	324,923	7.5%	0.8								
IOWA	2,040,000	200,198	9.8%					2,124,000	86,064	4.1%	-5.8	2,156,000	84,060	3.9%	-5.9				
KANSAS	1,787,000	151,569	8.5%					1,882,000	98,922	5.3%	-3.2								
KENTUCKY	2,719,000	310,107	11.4%					2,951,000	568,292	19.3%	7.9	3,039,000	461,068	15.2%	3.8				
LOUISIANA**	2,953,000	788,722	26.7%																
MAINE				928,000	82,479	8.9%						981,000	59,732	6.1%	-2.8	1,026,000	44,601	4.3%	-4.5
MARYLAND				3,558,000	484,204	13.6%		3,655,000	414,160	11.3%	-2.3					3,972,000	532,166	13.4%	-0.2
MASSACHUSETTS				4,426,000	391,637	8.8%						4,507,000	619,496	13.7%	4.9	4,585,000	729	0.0%	-8.8
MICHIGAN				6,865,000	656,198	9.6%						7,200,000	889,517	12.4%	2.8	7,393,000	513,456	6.9%	-2.6
MINNESOTA	3,163,000	374,987	11.9%	3,301,000	383,630	11.6%	-0.2					3,582,000	240,775	6.7%	-5.1	3,744,000	318,430	8.5%	-3.4
MISSISSIPPI				1,914,000	134,844	7.0%						2,074,000	58,984	2.8%	-4.2	2,125,000	104,486	4.9%	-2.1
MISSOURI				3,905,000	524,895	13.4%		4,035,000	301,123	7.5%	-6.0	4,151,000	442,386	10.7%	-2.8	4,269,000	349,940	8.2%	-5.2
MONTANA	573,000	98,676	17.2%	611,000	123,666	20.2%	3.0					683,000	66,713	9.8%	-7.5	714,000	108,207	15.2%	-2.1
NEBRASKA	1,139,000	157,959	13.9%	1,172,000	104,860	8.9%	-4.9					1,225,000	57,193	4.7%	-9.2	1,237,000	92,501	7.5%	-6.4
NEVADA																1,560,000	117,842	7.6%	
NEW HAMPSHIRE	815,000	48,669	6.0%					886,000	23,771	2.7%	-3.3	931,000	60,483	6.5%	0.5				
NEW JERSEY	5,506,000	213,741	3.9%	5,563,000	187,045	3.4%	-0.5					5,705,000	181,468	3.2%	-0.7	5,837,000	189,944	3.3%	-0.6
NEW MEXICO				1,113,000	165,148	14.8%						1,259,000	140,385	11.2%	-3.7	1,317,000	115,198	8.7%	-6.1
NEW YORK				12,423,000	704,997	5.7%		12,459,000	764,638	6.1%	0.5					12,604,000	765,954	6.1%	0.4
NORTH CAROLINA	4,977,000	693,496	13.9%					5,663,000	540,031	9.5%	-4.4	5,969,000	639,028	10.7%	-3.2				
NORTH DAKOTA				467,000	66,265	14.2%		473,000	43,494	9.2%	-5.0					482,000	58,231	12.1%	-2.1
OHIO				8,105,000	934,888	11.5%		8,254,000	680,626	8.2%	-3.3					8,502,000	747,404	8.8%	-2.7
OKLAHOMA	2,280,000	529,047	23.2%	2,365,000	436,462	18.5%	-4.7	2,449,000	263,208	10.7%	-12.5	2,504,000	346,387	13.8%	-9.4				
OREGON	2,056,000	253,437	12.3%					2,349,000	309,110	13.2%	0.8	2,464,000	325,739	13.2%	0.9				
PENNSYLVANIA				9,034,000	714,930	7.9%		9,112,000	476,788	5.2%	-2.7					9,374,000	743,748	7.9%	0.0
RHODE ISLAND				738,000	45,718	6.2%						757,000	85,315	11.3%	5.1	779,000	82,495	10.6%	4.4
SOUTH CAROLINA																			
SOUTH DAKOTA												553,000	68,996	12.5%					
TENNESSEE				3,870,000	402,702	10.4%						4,279,000	508,875	11.9%	1.5	4,434,000	421,926	9.5%	-0.9

United States Senate Primary Elections (continued)

Democratic Turnout for Election Years 1990–2006 (continued)

State	1990 Voting-age population	Turnout	%	1994 Voting-age population	Turnout	%	Difference from 1990	1998 Voting-age population	Turnout	%	Difference from 1990	2002 Voting-age population	Turnout	%	Difference from 1990	2006 Voting-age population	Turnout	%	Difference from 1990
TEXAS	11,335,000	1,015,729	9.0%	12,135,000	1,027,909	8.5%	-0.5					13,687,000	954,655	7.0%	-2.0	14,486,000	500,785	3.5%	-5.5
UTAH																			
VERMONT				429,000	30,229	7.0%		445,000	19,290	4.3%	-2.7					485,000	38,186	7.9%	0.8
VIRGINIA																5,432,000	155,784	2.9%	
WASHINGTON				3,723,000	386,773	10.4%		3,973,000	525,344	13.2%	2.8					4,387,000	628,754	14.3%	3.9
WEST VIRGINIA	1,344,000	236,297	17.6%	1,366,000	222,499	16.3%	-1.3					1,406,000	220,678	15.7%	-1.9	1,421,000	185,763	13.1%	-4.5
WISCONSIN				3,698,000	151,561	4.1%										4,112,000	359,782	8.7%	4.7
WYOMING	316,000	34,511	10.9%	334,000	39,563	11.8%	0.9					366,000	30,548	8.3%	-2.6	381,000	24,924	6.5%	-4.4
Total	54,225,000	6,507,970	12.0%	128,968,000	12,138,033	9.4%	-2.6	108,674,000	10,033,776	9.2%	-2.8	91,438,000	8,494,567	9.3%	-2.7	133,713,000	10,439,966	7.8%	-4.2

Other Turnout for Election Years 1990–2006

State	1990 Voting-age population	Turnout	%	1994 Voting-age population	Turnout	%	Difference from 1990*	1998 Voting-age population	Turnout	%	Difference from 1990	2002 Voting-age population	Turnout	%	Difference from 1990	2006 Voting-age population	Turnout	%	Difference from 1990
ALASKA								412,000	6,779	1.6%		436,000	4,765	1.1%	-0.6				
ARIZONA				2,897,000	5,424	0.2%		3,234,000	1,701	0.1%	-0.1								
CALIFORNIA				19,021,000	53,330	0.3%		19,700,000	203,284	1.0%	0.8								
HAWAII				796,000	351	0.0%		828,000	433	0.1%	0.0								
ILLINOIS								8,320,000	753	0.0%									
IOWA												2,156,000	102	0.0%					
MASSACHUSETTS				4,426,000	4,816	0.1%						4,507,000	1,531	0.0%	-0.1				
MINNESOTA												3,582,000	33,363	0.9%					
MISSOURI				3,905,000	2,302	0.1%		4,035,000	2,665	0.1%	0.0	4,151,000	3,272	0.1%	0.0				
NEBRASKA				1,172,000	8,409	0.7%						1,225,000	228	0.0%	-0.7				
NEW YORK				12,423,000	19,551	0.2%		12,459,000	10,436	0.1%	-0.1								
NORTH DAKOTA								473,000	334	0.1%									
OREGON								2,349,000	3,362	0.1%									
UTAH				1,217,000	1,438	0.1%													
VERMONT				429,000	321	0.1%		445,000	230	0.1%	0.0								
WASHINGTON				3,723,000	12,548	0.3%		3,973,000	15,910	0.4%	0.1								
WISCONSIN				3,698,000	1,422	0.0%													
Total				50,009,000	108,490	0.2%		56,228,000	245,887	0.4%	0.2								

*Percentage point difference between turnout in current year and initial year listed in chart. If data do not appear for a state in the initial year listed, the difference is calculated from the first year in which data do appear for that state.

**In 1978 Louisiana eliminated the partisan primary for senator and instituted an open primary with candidates from all parties running on the same ballot. Any candidate who received a majority appeared in the general election unopposed. If no candidate received fifty percent, a runoff was held between the top two finishers. In 2008 Louisiana returned to a partisan primary system.

STATE GUBERNATORIAL GENERAL ELECTIONS

Election Years 1991–2009

State	1991 Voting-age population	Turnout	%	1993 Voting-age population	Turnout	%	Difference from 1991*	1995 Voting-age population	Turnout	%	Difference from 1991	1997 Voting-age population	Turnout	%	Difference from 1991	1999 Voting-age population	Turnout	%	Difference from 1991
KENTUCKY	2,764,000	834,920	30.2%					2,881,000	980,014	34.0%	3.8					2,996,000	580,074	19.4%	-10.8
LOUISIANA**	2,992,000	1,728,040	57.8%					3,092,000	1,550,360	50.1%	-7.6					3,192,000	1,295,205	40.6%	-17.2
MISSISSIPPI	1,858,000	699,935	37.7%					1,950,000	819,471	42.0%	4.4					2,043,000	749,725	36.7%	-1.0
NEW JERSEY				5,557,000	2,446,155	44.0%						5,614,000	2,241,362	39.9%	-4.1				
VIRGINIA				4,722,000	1,778,846	37.7%						4,933,000	1,708,033	34.6%	-3.0				

State	2001 Voting-age population	Turnout	%	Difference from 1991	2003 Voting-age population	Turnout	%	Difference from 1991	2005 Voting-age population	Turnout	%	Difference from 1991	2007 Voting-age population	Turnout	%	Difference from 1991	2009 Voting-age population	Turnout	%	Difference from 1991
KENTUCKY					3,066,000	1,083,433	35.3%	5.1					3,140,000	1,055,325	33.6%	3.4				
LOUISIANA					3,260,000	1,407,842	43.2%	-14.6					3,331,000	1,297,943	39.0%	-18.8				
MISSISSIPPI					2,094,000	894,487	42.7%	5.0					2,145,000	715,590	33.4%	-4.3				
NEW JERSEY	5,688,000	2,227,165	39.2%	-4.9					5,819,000	2,290,099	39.4%	-4.7					5,951,000	2,423,792	40.7%	-3.3
VIRGINIA	5,148,000	1,886,721	36.6%	-1.0					5,403,000	1,983,778	36.7%	-1.0					5,659,000	1,982,432	35.0%	-2.6

*Percentage point difference between turnout in current year and initial year listed in chart. If data do not appear for a state in the initial year listed, the difference is calculated from the first year in which data do appear for that state.

**In 1975 Louisiana eliminated the partisan primary for governor and instituted an open primary with candidates from all parties running on the same ballot. Any candidate who received a majority appeared in the general election unopposed. If no candidate received fifty percent, a runoff was held between the top two finishers. In 2008 Louisiana returned to a partisan primary system.

STATE GUBERNATORIAL GENERAL ELECTIONS

Republican Turnout for Election Years 1991–2009

State	1991 Voting-age population	Turnout	%	1993 Voting-age population	Turnout	%	Difference from 1991*	1995 Voting-age population	Turnout	%	Difference from 1991	1997 Voting-age population	Turnout	%	Difference from 1991	1999 Voting-age population	Turnout	%	Difference from 1991
KENTUCKY	2,764,000	294,452	10.7%					2,881,000	479,227	16.6%	6.0					2,996,000	217,718	7.3%	-3.4
LOUISIANA**	2,992,000	671,009	22.4%					3,092,000	984,499	31.8%	9.4					3,192,000	840,637	26.3%	3.9
MISSISSIPPI	1,858,000	361,500	19.5%					1,950,000	455,261	23.3%	3.9					2,043,000	370,691	18.1%	-1.3
NEW JERSEY				5,557,000	1,236,124	22.2%						5,614,000	1,123,534	20.0%	-2.2				
VIRGINIA				4,722,000	733,527	15.5%						4,933,000	969,062	19.6%	4.1				

State	2001 Voting-age population	Turnout	%	Difference from 1991	2003 Voting-age population	Turnout	%	Difference from 1991	2005 Voting-age population	Turnout	%	Difference from 1991	2007 Voting-age population	Turnout	%	Difference from 1991	2009 Voting-age population	Turnout	%	Difference from 1991
KENTUCKY					3,066,000	596,284	19.4%	8.8					3,140,000	435,773	13.9%	3.2				
LOUISIANA					3,260,000	676,484	20.8%	-1.7					3,331,000	699,275	21.0%	-1.4				
MISSISSIPPI					2,094,000	409,787	19.6%	0.1					2,145,000	430,807	20.1%	0.6				
NEW JERSEY	5,608,000	928,174	16.3%	-5.9					5,819,000	985,271	16.9%	-5.3					5,951,000	1,174,445	19.7%	-2.5
VIRGINIA	5,148,000	984,177	19.1%	3.6					5,403,000	1,025,942	19.0%	3.5					5,659,000	1,163,523	20.6%	5.0

Democratic Turnout for Election Years 1991–2009

State	1991 Voting-age population	Turnout	%	1993 Voting-age population	Turnout	%	Difference from 1991*	1995 Voting-age population	Turnout	%	Difference from 1991	1997 Voting-age population	Turnout	%	Difference from 1991	1999 Voting-age population	Turnout	%	Difference from 1991
KENTUCKY	2,764,000	540,468	19.6%					2,881,000	500,605	17.4%	-2.2					2,996,000	352,099	11.8%	-7.8
LOUISIANA**	2,992,000	1,057,031	35.3%					3,092,000	565,861	18.3%	-17.0					3,192,000	438,975	13.8%	-21.6
MISSISSIPPI	1,858,000	338,435	18.2%					1,950,000	364,210	18.7%	0.5					2,043,000	379,034	18.6%	0.3
NEW JERSEY				5,557,000	1,210,031	21.8%						5,614,000	1,096,581	19.5%	-2.2				
VIRGINIA				4,722,000	1,045,319	22.1%						4,933,000	738,971	15.0%	-7.2				

State	2001 Voting-age population	Turnout	%	Difference from 1991	2003 Voting-age population	Turnout	%	Difference from 1991	2005 Voting-age population	Turnout	%	Difference from 1991	2007 Voting-age population	Turnout	%	Difference from 1991	2009 Voting-age population	Turnout	%	Difference from 1991
KENTUCKY					3,066,000	487,159	15.9%	-3.7					3,140,000	619,552	19.7%	0.2				
LOUISIANA					3,260,000	731,358	22.4%	-12.9					3,331,000	397,755	11.9%	-23.4				
MISSISSIPPI					2,094,000	470,404	22.5%	4.2					2,145,000	313,232	14.6%	-3.6				
NEW JERSEY	5,688,000	1,256,853	22.1%	0.3					5,819,000	1,224,551	21.0%	-0.7					5,951,000	1,087,731	18.3%	-3.5
VIRGINIA	5,148,000	887,234	17.2%	-4.9					5,403,000	912,327	16.9%	-5.3					5,659,000	818,909	14.5%	-7.7

State Gubernatorial General Elections (continued)

State Gubernatorial General Elections (continued)

Other Turnout for Election Years 1991–2009

State	1991 Voting-age population	Turnout	%		1993 Voting-age population	Turnout	%	Difference from 1991*	1995 Voting-age population	Turnout	%	Difference from 1991	1997 Voting-age population	Turnout	%	Difference from 1991	1999 Voting-age population	Turnout	%	Difference from 1991
KENTUCKY									2,881,000	3,965	0.1%	0.1					2,996,000	6,934	0.2%	0.2
LOUISIANA**																	3,192,000	15,593	0.5%	
MISSISSIPPI																				
NEW JERSEY					5,557,000	58,578	1.1%						5,614,000	166,586	3.0%	1.9				
VIRGINIA					4,722,000	15,070	0.3%						4,933,000	27,921	0.6%	0.2				

State	2001 Voting-age population	Turnout	%	Difference from 1991	2003 Voting-age population	Turnout	%	Difference from 1991	2005 Voting-age population	Turnout	%	Difference from 1991	2007 Voting-age population	Turnout	%	Difference from 1991	2009 Voting-age population	Turnout	%	Difference from 1991
KENTUCKY																				
LOUISIANA													3,331,000	200,810	6.0%	6.0				
MISSISSIPPI					2,094,000	14,296	0.7%	0.7												
NEW JERSEY	5,688,000	42,102	0.7%	-0.3					5,819,000	80,277	1.4%	0.3					5,951,000	161,616	2.7%	1.7
VIRGINIA	5,148,000	15,210	0.3%	0.0					5,403,000	45,509	0.8%	0.5					5,659,000	2,502	0.0%	-0.3

*Percentage point difference between turnout in current year and initial year listed in chart. If data do not appear for a state in the initial year listed, the difference is calculated from the first year in which data do appear for that state.

**In 1975 Louisiana eliminated the partisan primary for governor and instituted an open primary with candidates from all parties running on the same ballot. Any candidate who received a majority appeared in the general election unopposed. If no candidate received fifty percent, a runoff was held between the top two finishers. In 2008 Louisiana returned to a partisan primary system.

STATE GUBERNATORIAL PRIMARY ELECTIONS

Republican Turnout for Election Years 1991–2009*

State	1991 Voting-age population	Turnout	%	1993 Voting-age population	Turnout	%	Difference from 1991**	1995 Voting-age population	Turnout	%	Difference from 1991	1997 Voting-age population	Turnout	%	Difference from 1991	1999 Voting-age population	Turnout	%	Difference from 1991
KENTUCKY	2,748,000	161,107	5.9%					2,863,000	114,153	4.0%	-1.9					2,979,000	37,543	1.3%	-4.6
LOUISIANA***	2,978,000	984,715	33.1%					3,078,000	648,597	21.1%	-12.0								
MISSISSIPPI	1,843,000	790,026	42.9%					1,937,000	632,556	32.7%	-10.2					2,030,000	153,142	7.5%	-35.3
NEW JERSEY				5,549,000	399,825	7.2%						5,605,000	147,731	2.6%	-4.6				
VIRGINIA																			

State	2001 Voting-age population	Turnout	%	Difference from 1991	2003 Voting-age population	Turnout	%	Difference from 1991	2005 Voting-age population	Turnout	%	Difference from 1991	2007 Voting-age population	Turnout	%	Difference from 1991	2009 Voting-age population	Turnout	%	Difference from 1991
KENTUCKY					3,057,000	158,528	5.2%	-0.7					3,129,000	202,339	6.5%	0.6				
LOUISIANA																				
MISSISSIPPI					2,087,000	190,223	9.1%	-33.8					2,138,000	197,647	9.2%	-33.6				
NEW JERSEY	5,673,000	336,948	5.9%	-1.3					5,804,000	510,171	8.8%	1.6					5,936,000	534,335	9.0%	1.8
VIRGINIA									5,369,000	175,170	3.3%									

Democratic Turnout for Election Years 1991–2009

State	1991 Voting-age population	Turnout	%	1993 Voting-age population	Turnout	%	Difference from 1991**	1995 Voting-age population	Turnout	%	Difference from 1991	1997 Voting-age population	Turnout	%	Difference from 1991	1999 Voting-age population	Turnout	%	Difference from 1991
KENTUCKY	2,748,000	491,949	17.9%					2,863,000	334,334	11.7%	-6.2								
LOUISIANA***	2,978,000	523,195	17.6%					3,078,000	686,130	22.3%	4.7								
MISSISSIPPI	1,843,000	63,561	3.4%					1,937,000	117,907	6.1%	2.6					2,030,000	545,555	26.9%	23.4
NEW JERSEY				5,549,000	200,420	3.6%						5,605,000	365,485	6.5%	2.9				
VIRGINIA																			

State	2001 Voting-age population	Turnout	%	Difference from 1991	2003 Voting-age population	Turnout	%	Difference from 1991	2005 Voting-age population	Turnout	%	Difference from 1991	2007 Voting-age population	Turnout	%	Difference from 1991	2009 Voting-age population	Turnout	%	Difference from 1991
KENTUCKY					3,057,000	285,149	9.3%	-8.6					3,129,000	348,238	11.1%	-6.8				
LOUISIANA																				
MISSISSIPPI					2,087,000	517,345	24.8%	21.3					2,138,000	446,722	20.9%	17.4				
NEW JERSEY	5,673,000	262,086	4.6%	1.0					5,804,000	235,778	4.1%	0.5					5,936,000	534,335	9.0%	5.4
VIRGINIA									5,369,000	175,170	3.3%						5,623,000	319,168	5.7%	2.4

*Due to the paucity of data, no overall primary chart is included for this time period.

**Percentage point difference between turnout in current year and initial year listed in chart. If data does not appear for a state in the initial year listed, the difference is calculated from the first year in which data does appear for that state.

***In 1975 Louisiana eliminated the partisan primary for governor and instituted an open primary with candidates from all parties running on the same ballot. Any candidate who received a majority appeared in the general election unopposed. If no candidate received fifty percent, a runoff was held between the top two finishers. In 2008 Louisiana returned to a partisan primary system.

APPENDIX

Voter Turnout
1920–1964

ADJUSTED FOR THE DISENFRANCHISEMENT OF
AFRICAN AMERICANS IN THE SOUTHERN UNITED STATES

OVERVIEW

PRESIDENTIAL-YEAR GENERAL ELECTIONS

MIDTERM GENERAL ELECTIONS

ABOUT THE APPENDIX

In 1870, the Fifteenth Amendment to the U.S. Constitution was ratified, prohibiting governments from infringing citizens' right to vote on the basis of "race, color, or previous condition of servitude." Federal troops, stationed in the south to promote reconstruction after the Civil War, enforced this amendment. African Americans were able to vote and played a key role in Republican victories in the South. However, after federal troops were withdrawn in 1877 following the contested election of President Rutherford B. Hayes, southern states gradually found numerous ways to reduce African American voter turnout. Poll taxes, literacy tests, intimidation, and fear kept African Americans from that basic act of citizenship and influence. By a certain point, virtually every electoral decision of consequence was decided in the region by a one-party (Democratic) whites-only primary with minimal turnout.

By 1920, although African Americans living in the South were counted by the Census Bureau as citizens and eligible voters, in reality they were denied the vote. To reflect that reality, the charts in this appendix provide turnout data for all general election races from 1920 through 1964 based on a denominator that does not include African American citizens residing in the South during those years. It may provide a more realistic picture of actual turnout nationally and in the southern states of Alabama, Arkansas, Florida, Georgia, Kentucky, Louisiana, Mississippi, North Carolina, South Carolina, Tennessee, Texas, Virginia, and West Virginia (those south of the Mason-Dixon line).

Gradually in the 1950s and early 1960s (especially in states which were not deep in the south), a combination of Supreme Court decisions and congressional action enabled more African Americans to vote, although still in modest numbers. When Martin Luther King Jr. led a "Walk for Freedom" in Selma, Alabama, in March of 1965, only 383 African American voters were previously registered in that county out of a pool of over fifteen thousand. Only the passage of the Voting Rights Act in 1965 finally enforced the constitutional right of African Americans to vote. African American voter registration increased dramatically in the years after the act's passage, but it should be noted that, according to the Census Bureau's biennial Current Population Survey on reported registration and voting, the general election of 2008 was the first in which the percentage of eligible African American citizens who voted approximated parity with the voting rate of whites.

United States Presidential Turnout, Adjusted versus Unadjusted, 1920–1964

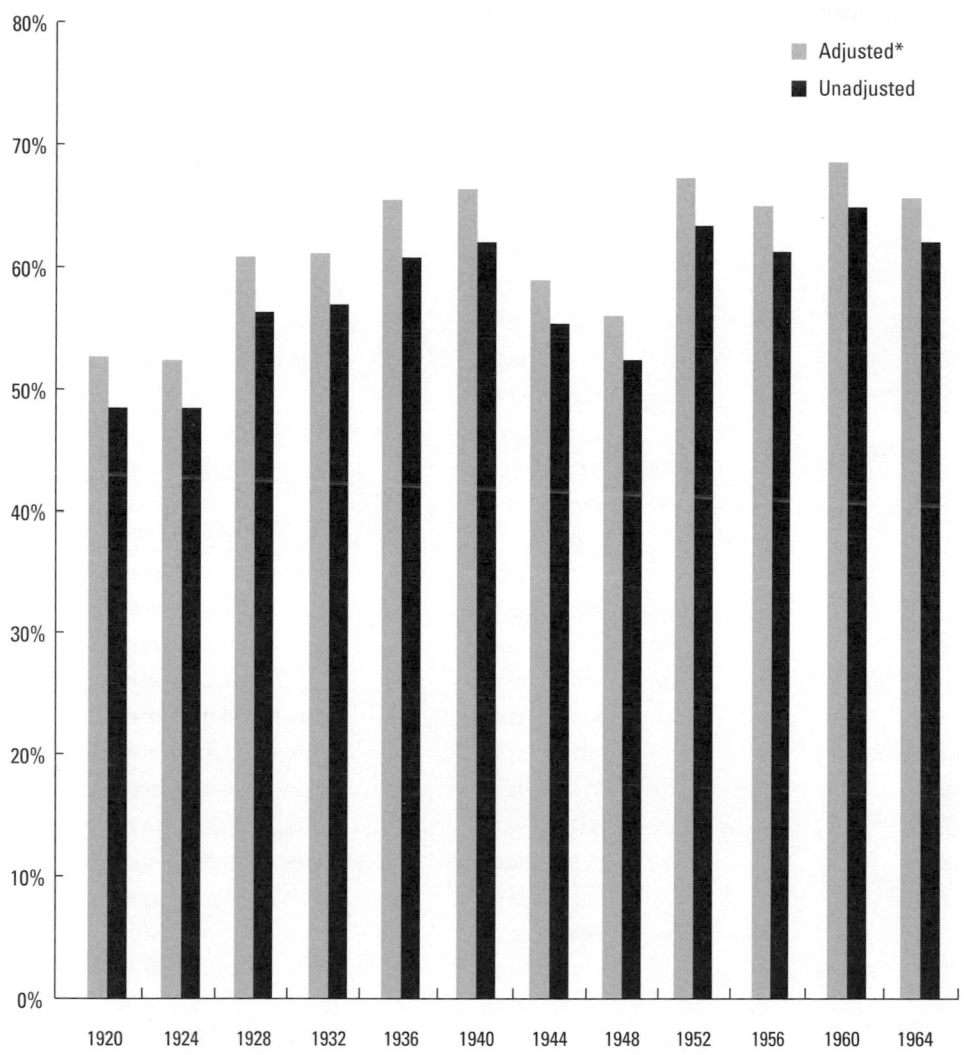

■ Adjusted*
■ Unadjusted

YEAR	UNADJUSTED VOTING-AGE POPULATION	ADJUSTED VOTING-AGE POPULATION*	TURNOUT	UNADJUSTED NATIONAL TURNOUT %	ADJUSTED NATIONAL TURNOUT %
1920	55,442,000	51,262,000	26,768,613	48.3%	52.2%
1924	60,351,000	56,038,000	29,095,023	48.2%	51.9%
1928	65,267,000	60,820,000	36,805,951	56.4%	60.5%
1932	70,022,000	65,390,000	39,758,759	56.8%	60.8%
1936	75,005,000	70,155,000	45,654,763	60.9%	65.1%
1940	80,471,000	75,541,000	49,900,418	62.0%	66.1%
1944	86,671,000	81,658,000	47,976,670	55.4%	58.8%
1948	92,869,000	87,521,000	48,690,956	52.4%	55.6%
1952	97,344,000	92,181,000	61,550,918	63.2%	66.8%
1956	101,295,000	96,246,000	62,033,908	61.2%	64.5%
1960	106,188,000	101,043,000	68,838,219	64.8%	68.1%
1964	113,979,000	108,785,000	70,644,592	62.0%	64.9%

*The African American population of states south of the Mason-Dixon line (Alabama, Arkansas, Florida, Georgia, Kentucky, Louisiana, Mississippi, North Carolina, South Carolina, Tennessee, Texas, Virginia, and West Virginia) was largely excluded from voting by poll taxes, literacy tests, intimidation, and fear. Therefore, this adjusted voting-age population subtracts the number of African Americans in the population. This is an imprecise formulation, as a few African Americans could vote in a few locales, but it is, in the main, a much more accurate portrayal of turnout percentages in the South and nation.

UNITED STATES PRESIDENTIAL GENERAL ELECTIONS

Election Years 1920–1928
(Population Adjusted for Disenfranchisement of African Americans in South)*

State	1920 Voting-age population	Turnout	%	1924 Voting-age population	Turnout	%	Difference from 1920**	1928 Voting-age population	Turnout	%	Difference from 1920
ALABAMA	710,000	233,951	**33.0%**	777,000	164,563	**21.2%**	-11.8	845,000	248,981	**29.5%**	-3.5
ALASKA											
ARIZONA	145,000	66,803	**46.1%**	153,000	73,961	**48.3%**	2.3	161,000	91,254	**56.7%**	10.6
ARKANSAS	628,000	183,871	**29.3%**	663,000	138,540	**20.9%**	-8.4	698,000	197,726	**28.3%**	-1.0
CALIFORNIA	2,110,000	943,463	**44.7%**	2,603,000	1,281,778	**49.2%**	4.5	3,096,000	1,796,656	**58.0%**	13.3
COLORADO	526,000	292,053	**55.5%**	546,000	342,261	**62.7%**	7.2	564,000	392,242	**69.5%**	14.0
CONNECTICUT	648,000	365,518	**56.4%**	714,000	400,396	**56.1%**	-0.3	780,000	553,118	**70.9%**	14.5
DELAWARE	128,000	94,875	**74.1%**	134,000	90,885	**67.8%**	-6.3	140,000	104,602	**74.7%**	0.6
DISTRICT OF COLUMBIA											
FLORIDA	357,000	145,684	**40.8%**	460,000	109,158	**40.8%**	-17.1	562,000	252,068	**40.8%**	4.0
GEORGIA	852,000	149,558	**17.6%**	901,000	166,635	**18.5%**	0.9	952,000	231,592	**24.3%**	6.8
HAWAII											
IDAHO	223,000	138,281	**62.0%**	228,000	147,690	**64.8%**	2.8	233,000	151,541	**65.0%**	3.0
ILLINOIS	3,553,000	2,094,714	**59.0%**	3,938,000	2,470,067	**62.7%**	3.8	4,322,000	3,107,489	**71.9%**	12.9
INDIANA	1,725,000	1,262,974	**73.2%**	1,822,000	1,272,390	**69.8%**	-3.4	1,918,000	1,421,314	**74.1%**	0.9
IOWA	1,377,000	894,959	**65.0%**	1,419,000	976,770	**68.8%**	3.8	1,461,000	1,009,189	**69.1%**	4.1
KANSAS	995,000	570,243	**57.3%**	1,042,000	662,456	**63.6%**	6.3	1,091,000	713,200	**65.4%**	8.1
KENTUCKY	1,148,000	918,636	**80.0%**	1,204,000	813,843	**67.6%**	-12.4	1,260,000	940,521	**74.6%**	-5.4
LOUISIANA	553,000	126,397	**22.9%**	619,000	121,951	**19.7%**	-3.2	684,000	215,833	**31.6%**	8.7
MAINE	423,000	197,840	**46.8%**	430,000	192,192	**44.7%**	-2.1	437,000	262,170	**60.0%**	13.2
MARYLAND	832,000	428,443	**51.5%**	888,000	358,630	**40.4%**	-11.1	943,000	528,348	**56.0%**	4.5
MASSACHUSETTS	1,895,000	993,718	**52.4%**	2,031,000	1,129,837	**55.6%**	3.2	2,166,000	1,577,823	**72.8%**	20.4
MICHIGAN	1,947,000	1,048,411	**53.8%**	2,221,000	1,160,419	**52.2%**	-1.6	2,497,000	1,372,082	**54.9%**	1.1
MINNESOTA	1,257,000	735,838	**58.5%**	1,345,000	822,146	**61.1%**	2.6	1,432,000	970,976	**67.8%**	9.3
MISSISSIPPI	427,000	82,351	**19.3%**	468,000	112,442	**24.0%**	4.7	507,000	151,568	**29.9%**	10.6
MISSOURI	1,993,000	1,332,140	**66.8%**	2,093,000	1,310,095	**62.6%**	-4.2	2,194,000	1,500,845	**68.4%**	1.6
MONTANA	291,000	179,006	**61.5%**	292,000	174,425	**59.7%**	-1.8	292,000	194,108	**66.5%**	5.0
NEBRASKA	696,000	382,743	**55.0%**	734,000	463,559	**63.2%**	8.2	772,000	547,128	**70.9%**	15.9

Election Years 1920–1928 *(continued)*
(Population Adjusted for Disenfranchisement of African Americans in South)

State	1920			1924				1928			
	Voting-age population	Turnout	%	Voting-age population	Turnout	%	Difference from 1920	Voting-age population	Turnout	%	Difference from 1920
NEVADA	45,000	27,194	**60.4%**	47,000	26,921	**57.3%**	-3.2	50,000	32,417	**64.8%**	4.4
NEW HAMPSHIRE	237,000	159,092	**67.1%**	246,000	164,769	**67.0%**	-0.1	255,000	196,757	**77.2%**	10.0
NEW JERSEY	1,588,000	910,251	**57.3%**	1,849,000	1,088,054	**58.8%**	1.5	2,110,000	1,549,381	**73.4%**	16.1
NEW MEXICO	170,000	105,412	**62.0%**	172,000	112,830	**65.6%**	3.6	174,000	118,077	**67.9%**	5.9
NEW YORK	5,294,000	2,898,513	**54.8%**	5,965,000	3,263,939	**54.7%**	0.0	6,635,000	4,405,626	**66.4%**	11.6
NORTH CAROLINA	887,000	538,649	**60.7%**	987,000	481,608	**48.8%**	-11.9	1,086,000	635,150	**58.5%**	-2.2
NORTH DAKOTA	297,000	205,786	**69.3%**	314,000	199,081	**63.4%**	-5.9	332,000	239,845	**72.2%**	3.0
OHIO	3,289,000	2,021,653	**61.5%**	3,551,000	2,016,296	**56.8%**	-4.7	3,811,000	2,508,346	**65.8%**	4.4
OKLAHOMA	1,026,000	485,678	**47.3%**	1,118,000	527,828	**47.2%**	-0.1	1,211,000	618,427	**51.1%**	3.7
OREGON	467,000	238,522	**51.1%**	514,000	279,488	**54.4%**	3.3	563,000	319,942	**56.8%**	5.8
PENNSYLVANIA	4,412,000	1,851,248	**42.0%**	4,766,000	2,144,850	**45.0%**	3.0	5,121,000	3,150,612	**61.5%**	19.6
RHODE ISLAND	296,000	167,981	**56.8%**	323,000	210,115	**65.1%**	8.3	351,000	237,194	**67.6%**	10.8
SOUTH CAROLINA	407,000	66,808	**16.4%**	436,000	50,755	**11.6%**	-4.8	465,000	68,605	**14.8%**	-1.7
SOUTH DAKOTA	326,000	182,237	**55.9%**	342,000	203,868	**59.6%**	3.7	359,000	261,857	**72.9%**	17.0
TENNESSEE	980,000	428,036	**43.7%**	1,051,000	301,030	**28.6%**	-15.0	1,122,000	353,192	**31.5%**	-12.2
TEXAS	1,912,000	486,109	**25.4%**	2,131,000	657,054	**30.8%**	5.4	2,351,000	717,733	**30.5%**	5.1
UTAH	213,000	145,828	**68.5%**	227,000	156,990	**69.2%**	0.7	243,000	176,603	**72.7%**	4.2
VERMONT	199,000	89,961	**45.2%**	201,000	102,917	**51.2%**	6.0	203,000	135,191	**66.6%**	21.4
VIRGINIA	854,000	231,000	**27.0%**	902,000	223,603	**24.8%**	-2.3	951,000	305,364	**32.1%**	5.1
WASHINGTON	774,000	398,715	**51.5%**	833,000	421,549	**50.6%**	-0.9	892,000	500,840	**56.1%**	4.6
WEST VIRGINIA	673,000	509,936	**75.8%**	732,000	583,662	**79.7%**	4.0	791,000	642,752	**81.3%**	5.5
WISCONSIN	1,371,000	701,281	**51.2%**	1,493,000	840,827	**56.3%**	5.2	1,617,000	1,016,831	**62.9%**	11.7
WYOMING	106,000	56,253	**53.1%**	113,000	79,900	**70.7%**	17.6	120,000	82,835	**69.0%**	16.0
Total	51,262,000	26,768,613	**52.2%**	56,038,000	29,095,023	**51.9%**	-0.3	60,820,000	36,805,951	**60.5%**	8.3

*The African American population of states south of the Mason-Dixon line (Alabama, Arkansas, Florida, Georgia, Kentucky, Louisiana, Mississippi, North Carolina, South Carolina, Tennessee, Texas, Virginia, and West Virginia) was largely excluded from voting by poll taxes, literacy tests, intimidation, and fear. Therefore, this adjusted voting-age population subtracts the number of African Americans in the population. This is an imprecise formulation, as a few African Americans could vote in a few locales, but it is, in the main, a much more accurate portrayal of turnout percentages in the South and nation.

**Percentage point difference between turnout in current year and initial year listed in chart. If data do not appear for a state in the initial year listed, the difference is calculated from the first year in which data do appear for that state.

UNITED STATES PRESIDENTIAL GENERAL ELECTIONS

Election Years 1932–1948
(Population Adjusted for Disenfranchisement of African Americans in South)*

State	1932 Voting-age population	Turnout	%	1936 Voting-age population	Turnout	%	Difference from 1932**	1940 Voting-age population	Turnout	%	Difference from 1932	1944 Voting-age population	Turnout	%	Difference from 1932	1948 Voting-age population	Turnout	%	Difference from 1932
ALABAMA	911,000	245,303	26.9%	979,000	275,744	28.2%	1.2	1,045,000	294,219	28.2%	1.2	1,121,000	244,743	21.8%	-5.1	1,193,000	214,980	18.0%	-8.9
ALASKA																			
ARIZONA	184,000	118,251	64.3%	213,000	124,163	58.3%	-6.0	272,000	150,039	55.2%	-9.1	338,000	137,634	40.7%	-23.5	402,000	177,065	44.0%	-20.2
ARKANSAS	741,000	216,569	29.2%	788,000	179,431	22.8%	-6.5	831,000	200,429	24.1%	-5.1	852,000	212,954	25.0%	-4.2	871,000	242,475	27.8%	-1.4
CALIFORNIA	3,535,000	2,266,972	64.1%	3,979,000	2,638,882	66.3%	2.2	4,595,000	3,268,791	71.1%	7.0	5,592,000	3,520,875	63.0%	-1.2	6,547,000	4,021,538	61.4%	-2.7
COLORADO	601,000	457,696	76.2%	649,000	488,685	75.3%	-0.9	697,000	549,004	78.8%	2.6	754,000	505,039	67.0%	-9.2	809,000	515,237	63.7%	-12.5
CONNECTICUT	857,000	594,183	69.3%	942,000	690,723	73.3%	4.0	1,029,000	781,502	75.9%	6.6	1,147,000	831,990	72.5%	3.2	1,262,000	883,518	70.0%	0.7
DELAWARE	151,000	112,901	74.8%	162,000	127,603	78.8%	4.0	174,000	136,374	78.4%	3.6	188,000	125,361	66.7%	-8.1	203,000	139,073	68.5%	-6.3
DISTRICT OF COLUMBIA																			
FLORIDA	667,000	276,943	40.8%	780,000	327,436	40.8%	0.5	904,000	485,640	40.8%	12.2	1,135,000	482,803	42.5%	1.0	1,357,000	577,643	42.6%	1.0
GEORGIA	1,027,000	255,590	24.9%	1,116,000	293,170	26.3%	1.4	1,401,000	312,686	22.3%	-2.6	1,485,000	328,129	22.1%	-2.8	1,567,000	418,764	26.7%	1.8
HAWAII																			
IDAHO	254,000	186,520	73.4%	280,000	199,617	71.3%	-2.1	307,000	235,168	76.6%	3.2	324,000	208,321	64.3%	-9.1	339,000	214,816	63.4%	-10.1
ILLINOIS	4,615,000	3,407,926	73.8%	4,891,000	3,956,522	80.9%	7.0	5,160,000	4,217,935	81.7%	7.9	5,444,000	4,036,061	74.1%	0.3	5,717,000	3,984,046	69.7%	-4.2
INDIANA	2,014,000	1,576,927	78.3%	2,116,000	1,650,897	78.0%	-0.3	2,218,000	1,782,747	80.4%	2.1	2,357,000	1,672,091	70.9%	-7.4	2,490,000	1,656,214	66.5%	-11.8
IOWA	1,510,000	1,036,687	68.7%	1,564,000	1,142,737	73.1%	4.4	1,612,000	1,215,432	75.4%	6.7	1,641,000	1,052,599	64.1%	-4.5	1,668,000	1,038,264	62.2%	-6.4
KANSAS	1,115,000	791,978	71.0%	1,131,000	865,507	76.5%	5.5	1,150,000	860,297	74.8%	3.8	1,186,000	733,776	61.9%	-9.2	1,220,000	788,819	64.7%	-6.4
KENTUCKY	1,335,000	983,059	73.6%	1,422,000	926,214	65.1%	-8.5	1,637,000	970,163	59.3%	-14.4	1,682,000	867,924	51.6%	-22.0	1,725,000	822,658	47.7%	-25.9
LOUISIANA	754,000	268,804	35.7%	829,000	329,778	39.8%	4.1	903,000	372,305	41.2%	5.6	992,000	349,383	35.2%	-0.4	1,076,000	416,326	38.7%	3.0
MAINE	454,000	298,444	65.7%	475,000	304,240	64.1%	-1.7	497,000	320,840	64.6%	-1.2	521,000	296,400	56.9%	-8.8	544,000	264,787	48.7%	-17.1
MARYLAND	1,012,000	511,054	50.5%	1,090,000	624,896	57.3%	6.8	1,174,000	660,104	56.2%	5.7	1,319,000	608,439	46.1%	-4.4	1,457,000	596,708	41.0%	-9.5
MASSACHUSETTS	2,305,000	1,580,114	68.6%	2,454,000	1,840,357	75.0%	6.4	2,603,000	2,026,993	77.9%	9.3	2,796,000	1,960,665	70.1%	1.6	2,981,000	2,107,146	70.7%	2.1
MICHIGAN	2,724,000	1,664,765	61.1%	2,947,000	1,805,098	61.3%	0.1	3,180,000	2,085,929	65.6%	4.5	3,527,000	2,205,223	62.5%	1.4	3,859,000	2,109,609	54.7%	-6.4
MINNESOTA	1,529,000	1,002,843	65.6%	1,637,000	1,129,975	69.0%	3.4	1,738,000	1,251,188	72.0%	6.4	1,799,000	1,125,504	62.6%	-3.0	1,855,000	1,212,226	65.3%	-0.2
MISSISSIPPI	548,000	146,034	26.6%	594,000	162,142	27.3%	0.6	636,000	175,824	27.6%	1.0	668,000	180,234	27.0%	0.3	699,000	192,190	27.5%	0.8
MISSOURI	2,287,000	1,609,894	70.4%	2,384,000	1,828,635	76.7%	6.3	2,473,000	1,833,729	74.1%	3.8	2,538,000	1,571,697	61.9%	-8.5	2,600,000	1,578,628	60.7%	-9.7
MONTANA	304,000	216,479	71.2%	321,000	230,502	71.8%	0.6	344,000	247,873	72.1%	0.8	353,000	207,355	58.7%	-12.5	361,000	224,278	62.1%	-9.1
NEBRASKA	792,000	570,135	72.0%	805,000	608,023	75.5%	3.5	819,000	615,878	75.2%	3.2	831,000	563,126	67.8%	-4.2	842,000	488,940	58.1%	-13.9

United States Presidential General Elections (continued)

Election Years 1932–1948 (continued)
(Population Adjusted for Disenfranchisement of African Americans in South)

State	1932 Voting-age population	1932 Turnout	1932 %	1936 Voting-age population	1936 Turnout	1936 %	1936 Difference from 1932	1940 Voting-age population	1940 Turnout	1940 %	1940 Difference from 1932	1944 Voting-age population	1944 Turnout	1944 %	1944 Difference from 1932	1948 Voting-age population	1948 Turnout	1948 %	1948 Difference from 1932
NEVADA	55,000	41,430	**75.3%**	62,000	43,848	**70.7%**	-4.6	72,000	53,174	**73.9%**	-1.5	86,000	54,234	**63.1%**	-12.3	99,000	62,117	**62.7%**	-12.6
NEW HAMPSHIRE	268,000	205,520	**76.7%**	283,000	218,114	**77.1%**	0.4	298,000	235,419	**79.0%**	2.3	315,000	229,625	**72.9%**	-3.8	332,000	231,440	**69.7%**	-7.0
NEW JERSEY	2,294,000	1,630,063	**71.1%**	2,459,000	1,820,437	**74.0%**	3.0	2,630,000	1,972,552	**75.0%**	3.9	2,889,000	1,963,761	**68.0%**	-3.1	3,139,000	1,949,555	**62.1%**	-9.0
NEW MEXICO	197,000	151,006	**77.0%**	231,000	169,135	**73.2%**	-3.7	281,000	183,258	**65.2%**	-11.7	319,000	152,225	**47.7%**	-29.2	356,000	186,853	**52.5%**	-24.5
NEW YORK	7,228,000	4,688,614	**64.9%**	7,826,000	5,596,398	**71.5%**	6.6	8,418,000	6,301,596	**74.9%**	10.0	9,028,000	6,310,790	**70.0%**	5.1	9,613,000	6,177,337	**64.3%**	-0.6
NORTH CAROLINA	1,199,000	711,498	**59.3%**	1,322,000	839,475	**63.5%**	4.2	1,452,000	822,648	**56.7%**	2.7	1,597,000	790,554	**49.5%**	-9.8	1,734,000	791,209	**45.6%**	-13.7
NORTH DAKOTA	341,000	256,290	**75.2%**	348,000	273,716	**78.7%**	3.5	358,000	280,775	**78.4%**	3.3	358,000	220,182	**61.5%**	-13.7	358,000	220,716	**61.7%**	-13.5
OHIO	4,025,000	2,609,728	**64.8%**	4,234,000	3,012,660	**71.2%**	6.3	4,449,000	3,319,912	**74.6%**	9.8	4,773,000	3,153,056	**66.1%**	1.2	5,084,000	2,936,071	**57.8%**	-7.1
OKLAHOMA	1,263,000	704,633	**55.8%**	1,301,000	749,740	**57.6%**	1.8	1,363,000	826,212	**60.6%**	4.8	1,369,000	722,636	**52.8%**	-3.0	1,374,000	721,599	**52.5%**	-3.3
OREGON	612,000	368,751	**60.3%**	667,000	414,021	**62.1%**	1.8	732,000	481,240	**65.7%**	5.5	842,000	480,147	**57.0%**	-3.2	947,000	524,080	**55.3%**	-4.9
PENNSYLVANIA	5,441,000	2,859,021	**52.5%**	5,766,000	4,138,105	**71.8%**	19.2	6,078,000	4,078,714	**67.1%**	14.6	6,411,000	3,794,793	**59.2%**	6.6	6,729,000	3,735,148	**55.5%**	3.0
RHODE ISLAND	377,000	266,170	**70.6%**	403,000	310,278	**77.0%**	6.4	430,000	321,152	**74.7%**	4.1	468,000	299,276	**63.9%**	-6.7	503,000	327,702	**65.1%**	-5.5
SOUTH CAROLINA	510,000	104,407	**20.5%**	563,000	115,437	**20.5%**	0.0	615,000	99,830	**16.2%**	-4.2	678,000	103,382	**15.2%**	-5.2	739,000	142,571	**19.3%**	-1.2
SOUTH DAKOTA	364,000	288,438	**79.2%**	366,000	296,452	**81.0%**	1.8	380,000	308,427	**81.2%**	1.9	387,000	232,076	**60.0%**	-19.3	395,000	250,105	**63.3%**	-15.9
TENNESSEE	1,211,000	390,273	**32.2%**	1,312,000	477,086	**36.4%**	4.1	1,410,000	522,823	**37.1%**	4.9	1,518,000	510,692	**33.6%**	1.4	1,623,000	550,283	**33.9%**	1.7
TEXAS	2,615,000	874,382	**33.4%**	2,919,000	849,701	**29.1%**	-4.3	3,219,000	1,124,437	**34.9%**	1.5	3,567,000	1,150,334	**32.2%**	-1.2	3,902,000	1,147,245	**29.4%**	-4.0
UTAH	260,000	206,578	**79.5%**	279,000	216,679	**77.7%**	-1.8	303,000	247,819	**81.8%**	2.3	337,000	248,319	**73.7%**	-5.8	370,000	276,305	**74.7%**	-4.8
VERMONT	207,000	136,980	**66.2%**	211,000	143,689	**68.1%**	1.9	216,000	143,062	**66.2%**	0.1	222,000	125,361	**56.5%**	-9.7	227,000	123,382	**54.4%**	-11.8
VIRGINIA	1,023,000	297,942	**29.1%**	1,110,000	334,590	**30.1%**	1.0	1,206,000	346,608	**28.7%**	-0.4	1,377,000	388,485	**28.2%**	-0.9	1,542,000	419,256	**27.2%**	-1.9
WASHINGTON	962,000	614,814	**63.9%**	1,042,000	692,338	**66.4%**	2.5	1,146,000	793,833	**69.3%**	5.4	1,306,000	856,328	**65.6%**	1.7	1,459,000	905,059	**62.0%**	-1.9
WEST VIRGINIA	854,000	743,774	**87.1%**	921,000	829,945	**90.1%**	3.0	979,000	868,076	**88.7%**	1.6	1,003,000	715,596	**71.3%**	-15.7	1,026,000	748,750	**73.0%**	-14.1
WISCONSIN	1,729,000	1,114,814	**64.5%**	1,842,000	1,258,560	**68.3%**	3.8	1,955,000	1,405,522	**71.9%**	7.4	2,056,000	1,339,152	**65.1%**	0.7	2,154,000	1,276,800	**59.3%**	-5.2
WYOMING	129,000	96,962	**75.2%**	140,000	103,382	**73.8%**	-1.3	152,000	112,240	**73.8%**	-1.3	162,000	101,340	**62.6%**	-12.6	172,000	101,425	**59.0%**	-16.2
Total	65,390,000	39,758,759	**60.8%**	70,155,000	45,654,763	**65.1%**	4.3	75,541,000	49,900,418	**66.1%**	5.3	81,658,000	47,976,670	**58.8%**	-2.0	87,521,000	48,690,956	**55.6%**	-5.2

*The African American population of states south of the Mason-Dixon line (Alabama, Arkansas, Florida, Georgia, Kentucky, Louisiana, Mississippi, North Carolina, South Carolina, Tennessee, Texas, Virginia, and West Virginia) was largely excluded from voting by poll taxes, literacy tests, intimidation, and fear. Therefore, this adjusted voting-age population subtracts the number of African Americans in the population. This is an imprecise formulation, as a few African Americans could vote in a few locales, but it is, in the main, a much more accurate portrayal of turnout percentages in the South and nation.

**Percentage point difference between turnout in current year and initial year listed in chart. If data do not appear for a state in the initial year listed, the difference is calculated from the first year in which data do appear for that state.

UNITED STATES PRESIDENTIAL GENERAL ELECTIONS

Election Years 1952–1964
(Population Adjusted for Disenfranchisement of African Americans in South)*

State	1952			1956				1960				1964			
	Voting-age population	Turnout	%	Voting-age population	Turnout	%	Difference from 1952**	Voting-age population	Turnout	%	Difference from 1952	Voting-age population	Turnout	%	Difference from 1952
ALABAMA	1,253,000	426,120	34.0%	1,305,000	496,861	38.1%	4.1	1,361,000	570,225	41.9%	7.9	1,452,000	689,818	47.5%	13.5
ALASKA								135,000	60,762	45.0%		153,000	67,259	44.0%	-1.0
ARIZONA	501,000	260,570	52.0%	615,000	290,173	47.2%	-4.8	728,000	398,491	54.7%	2.7	863,000	480,770	55.7%	3.7
ARKANSAS	870,000	404,800	46.5%	856,000	406,572	47.5%	1.0	855,000	428,509	50.1%	3.6	916,000	560,426	61.2%	14.7
CALIFORNIA	7,453,000	5,141,849	69.0%	8,335,000	5,466,355	65.6%	-3.4	9,239,000	6,506,578	70.4%	1.4	10,572,000	7,057,586	66.8%	-2.2
COLORADO	875,000	630,103	72.0%	946,000	664,074	70.2%	-1.8	1,020,000	736,236	72.2%	0.2	1,145,000	776,986	67.9%	-4.2
CONNECTICUT	1,358,000	1,096,911	80.8%	1,445,000	1,117,121	77.3%	-3.5	1,537,000	1,222,883	79.6%	-1.2	1,683,000	1,218,578	72.4%	-8.4
DELAWARE	221,000	174,025	78.7%	241,000	177,988	73.9%	-4.9	261,000	196,683	75.4%	-3.4	289,000	201,320	69.7%	-9.1
DISTRICT OF COLUMBIA												497,000	198,597	40.0%	
FLORIDA	1,722,000	989,337	57.5%	2,152,000	1,125,762	52.3%	-5.1	2,578,000	1,544,176	59.9%	2.4	3,132,000	1,854,481	59.2%	1.8
GEORGIA	1,661,000	655,785	39.5%	1,761,000	669,655	38.0%	-1.5	1,870,000	733,349	39.2%	-0.3	2,075,000	1,139,335	54.9%	15.4
HAWAII								345,000	184,705	53.5%		383,000	207,271	54.1%	0.6
IDAHO	350,000	276,254	78.9%	360,000	272,989	75.8%	-3.1	371,000	300,450	81.0%	2.1	388,000	292,477	75.4%	-3.5
ILLINOIS	5,889,000	4,481,058	76.1%	6,016,000	4,407,407	73.3%	-2.8	6,155,000	4,757,409	77.3%	1.2	6,422,000	4,702,841	73.2%	-2.9
INDIANA	2,593,000	1,955,049	75.4%	2,682,000	1,974,607	73.6%	-1.8	2,773,000	2,135,360	77.0%	1.6	2,906,000	2,091,606	72.0%	-3.4
IOWA	1,669,000	1,268,773	76.0%	1,659,000	1,234,564	74.4%	-1.6	1,654,000	1,273,810	77.0%	1.0	1,674,000	1,184,539	70.8%	-5.3
KANSAS	1,253,000	896,166	71.5%	1,286,000	866,243	67.4%	-4.2	1,316,000	928,825	70.6%	-0.9	1,341,000	857,901	64.0%	-7.5
KENTUCKY	1,755,000	993,148	56.6%	1,762,000	1,053,805	59.8%	3.2	1,779,000	1,124,462	63.2%	6.6	1,866,000	1,046,105	56.1%	-0.5
LOUISIANA	1,151,000	651,952	56.6%	1,220,000	617,544	50.6%	-6.0	1,292,000	807,891	62.5%	5.9	1,388,000	896,293	64.6%	7.9
MAINE	555,000	351,786	63.4%	560,000	351,706	62.8%	-0.6	565,000	421,767	74.6%	11.3	578,000	380,965	65.9%	2.5
MARYLAND	1,586,000	902,074	56.9%	1,711,000	932,827	54.5%	-2.4	1,842,000	1,055,349	57.3%	0.4	2,064,000	1,116,457	54.1%	-2.8
MASSACHUSETTS	3,056,000	2,383,398	78.0%	3,082,000	2,348,506	76.2%	-1.8	3,126,000	2,469,480	79.0%	1.0	3,296,000	2,344,798	71.1%	-6.9
MICHIGAN	4,099,000	2,798,592	68.3%	4,297,000	3,080,468	71.7%	3.4	4,498,000	3,318,097	73.8%	5.5	4,786,000	3,203,102	66.9%	-1.3
MINNESOTA	1,901,000	1,379,483	72.6%	1,942,000	1,340,005	69.0%	-3.6	1,988,000	1,541,887	77.6%	5.0	2,091,000	1,554,462	74.3%	1.8
MISSISSIPPI	719,000	285,532	39.7%	733,000	248,104	33.8%	-5.9	752,000	298,171	39.7%	-0.1	800,000	409,146	51.1%	11.4
MISSOURI	2,636,000	1,892,062	71.8%	2,658,000	1,832,562	68.9%	-2.8	2,687,000	1,934,422	72.0%	0.2	2,772,000	1,817,879	65.6%	-6.2
MONTANA	370,000	265,037	71.6%	378,000	271,171	71.7%	0.1	386,000	277,579	71.9%	0.3	394,000	278,628	70.7%	-0.9
NEBRASKA	847,000	609,660	72.0%	848,000	577,137	68.1%	-3.9	851,000	613,095	72.0%	0.1	870,000	584,154	67.1%	-4.8

Election Years 1952–1964 *(continued)*
(Population Adjusted for Disenfranchisement of African Americans in South)

State	1952 Voting-age population	1952 Turnout	1952 %	1956 Voting-age population	1956 Turnout	1956 %	1956 Difference from 1952	1960 Voting-age population	1960 Turnout	1960 %	1960 Difference from 1952	1964 Voting-age population	1964 Turnout	1964 %	1964 Difference from 1952
NEVADA	122,000	82,190	67.4%	148,000	96,689	65.3%	-2.0	177,000	107,267	60.6%	-6.8	230,000	135,433	58.9%	-8.5
NEW HAMPSHIRE	344,000	272,950	79.3%	353,000	266,994	75.6%	-3.7	365,000	295,761	81.0%	1.7	400,000	288,093	72.0%	-7.3
NEW JERSEY	3,354,000	2,418,554	72.1%	3,552,000	2,484,312	69.9%	-2.2	3,758,000	2,773,111	73.8%	1.7	4,069,000	2,847,663	70.0%	-2.1
NEW MEXICO	402,000	238,608	59.4%	452,000	253,926	56.2%	-3.2	497,000	311,107	62.6%	3.2	522,000	328,645	63.0%	3.6
NEW YORK	9,944,000	7,128,239	71.7%	10,159,000	7,095,971	69.8%	-1.8	10,402,000	7,291,079	70.1%	-1.0	10,003,000	7,166,275	65.8%	-5.9
NORTH CAROLINA	1,839,000	1,210,910	65.8%	1,926,000	1,165,592	60.5%	-5.3	2,023,000	1,368,556	67.6%	1.8	2,206,000	1,424,983	64.6%	-1.3
NORTH DAKOTA	356,000	270,127	75.9%	353,000	253,991	72.0%	-3.9	350,000	278,431	79.6%	3.7	352,000	258,389	73.4%	-2.5
OHIO	5,339,000	3,700,758	69.3%	5,567,000	3,702,205	66.5%	-2.8	5,790,000	4,161,859	71.9%	2.6	6,040,000	3,969,196	65.7%	-3.6
OKLAHOMA	1,385,000	948,984	68.5%	1,399,000	859,350	61.4%	-7.1	1,420,000	903,150	63.6%	-4.9	1,493,000	932,499	62.5%	-6.1
OREGON	1,000,000	695,059	69.5%	1,030,000	736,132	71.5%	2.0	1,068,000	776,421	72.7%	3.2	1,164,000	786,305	67.6%	-2.0
PENNSYLVANIA	6,870,000	4,580,969	66.7%	6,928,000	4,576,503	66.1%	-0.6	6,998,000	5,006,541	71.5%	4.9	7,157,000	4,822,690	67.4%	0.7
RHODE ISLAND	516,000	414,498	80.3%	518,000	387,609	74.8%	-5.5	524,000	405,535	77.4%	-2.9	554,000	390,091	70.4%	-9.9
SOUTH CAROLINA	795,000	341,087	42.9%	848,000	300,583	35.4%	-7.5	903,000	386,688	42.8%	-0.1	986,000	524,779	53.2%	10.3
SOUTH DAKOTA	395,000	294,283	74.5%	392,000	293,857	75.0%	0.5	388,000	306,487	79.0%	4.5	388,000	293,118	75.5%	1.0
TENNESSEE	1,688,000	892,553	52.9%	1,735,000	939,404	54.1%	1.3	1,790,000	1,051,792	58.8%	5.9	1,908,000	1,143,946	60.0%	7.1
TEXAS	4,208,000	2,075,946	49.3%	4,504,000	1,955,168	43.4%	-5.9	4,808,000	2,311,084	48.1%	-1.3	5,265,000	2,626,811	49.9%	0.6
UTAH	400,000	329,554	82.4%	429,000	333,995	77.9%	-4.5	461,000	374,709	81.3%	-1.1	510,000	401,413	78.7%	-3.7
VERMONT	228,000	153,557	67.3%	226,000	152,978	67.7%	0.3	226,000	167,324	74.0%	6.7	241,000	163,089	67.7%	0.3
VIRGINIA	1,666,000	619,689	37.2%	1,771,000	697,978	39.4%	2.2	1,885,000	771,449	40.9%	3.7	2,084,000	1,042,267	50.0%	12.8
WASHINGTON	1,553,000	1,102,708	71.0%	1,617,000	1,150,889	71.2%	0.2	1,692,000	1,241,572	73.4%	2.4	1,854,000	1,258,556	67.9%	-3.1
WEST VIRGINIA	1,032,000	873,548	84.6%	1,028,000	830,831	80.8%	-3.8	1,027,000	837,781	81.6%	-3.1	1,029,000	792,040	77.0%	-7.7
WISCONSIN	2,223,000	1,607,370	72.3%	2,278,000	1,550,558	68.1%	-4.2	2,338,000	1,729,082	74.0%	1.6	2,452,000	1,691,815	69.0%	-3.3
WYOMING	179,000	129,253	72.2%	183,000	124,127	67.8%	-4.4	189,000	140,782	74.5%	2.3	192,000	142,716	74.3%	2.1
Total	92,181,000	61,550,918	66.8%	96,246,000	62,033,908	64.5%	-2.3	101,043,000	68,838,219	68.1%	1.4	108,785,000	70,644,592	64.9%	-1.8

*The African American population of states south of the Mason-Dixon line (Alabama, Arkansas, Florida, Georgia, Kentucky, Louisiana, Mississippi, North Carolina, South Carolina, Tennessee, Texas, Virginia, and West Virginia) was largely excluded from voting by poll taxes, literacy tests, intimidation, and fear. Therefore, this adjusted voting-age population subtracts the number of African Americans in the population. This is an imprecise formulation, as a few African Americans could vote in a few locales, but it is, in the main, a much more accurate portrayal of turnout percentages in the South and nation.

**Percentage point difference between turnout in current year and initial year listed in chart. If data do not appear for a state in the initial year listed, the difference is calculated from the first year in which data do appear for that state.

Total Highest Statewide Turnout, Adjusted versus Unadjusted, 1922–1962

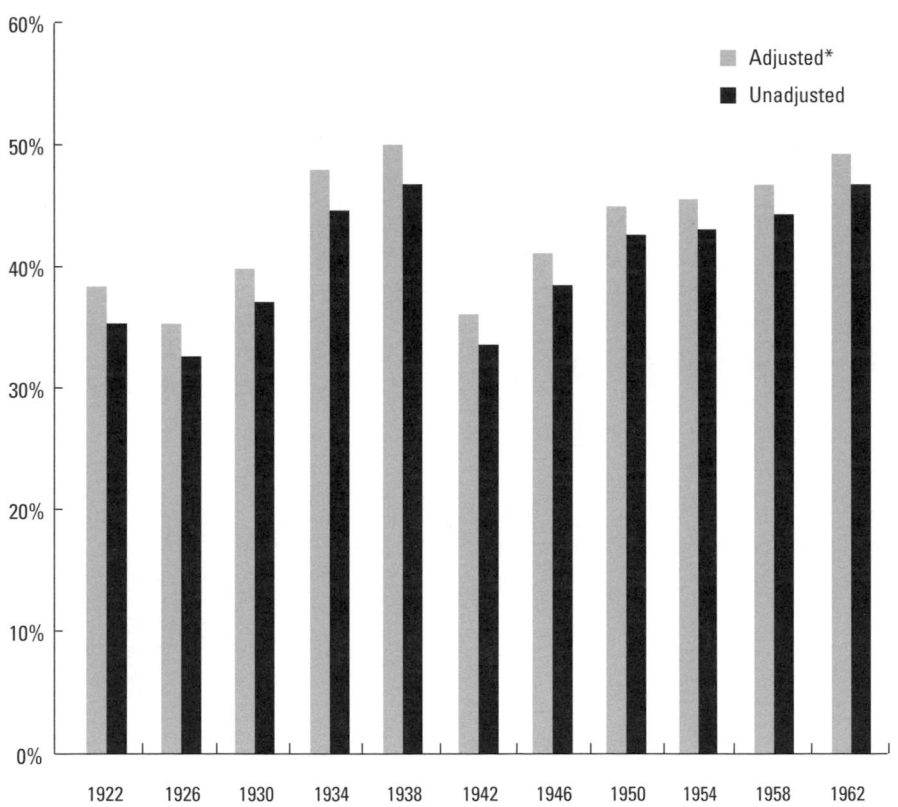

YEAR	UNADJUSTED VOTING-AGE POPULATION	ADJUSTED VOTING-AGE POPULATION*	TURNOUT	UNADJUSTED NATIONAL TURNOUT %	ADJUSTED NATIONAL TURNOUT %
1922	57,897,000	53,654,000	20,410,828	35.3%	38.0%
1926	62,807,000	58,427,000	20,398,829	32.5%	34.9%
1930	67,322,000	62,809,000	24,800,840	36.8%	39.5%
1934	72,507,000	67,768,000	32,279,984	44.5%	47.6%
1938	77,495,000	72,535,000	36,128,468	46.6%	49.8%
1942	83,574,000	78,728,000	28,077,247	33.6%	35.7%
1946	89,772,000	84,598,000	34,364,954	38.3%	40.6%
1950	94,998,000	89,969,000	40,311,778	42.4%	44.8%
1954	99,232,000	94,214,000	42,585,072	42.9%	45.2%
1958	103,892,000	98,749,000	45,816,549	44.1%	46.4%
1962	109,984,000	104,808,000	51,350,966	46.7%	49.0%

*The African American population of states south of the Mason-Dixon line (Alabama, Arkansas, Florida, Georgia, Kentucky, Louisiana, Mississippi, North Carolina, South Carolina, Tennessee, Texas, Virginia, and West Virginia) was largely excluded from voting by poll taxes, literacy tests, intimidation, and fear. Therefore, this adjusted voting-age population subtracts the number of African Americans in the population. This is an imprecise formulation, as a few African Americans could vote in a few locales, but it is, in the main, a much more accurate portrayal of turnout percentages in the South and nation.

TOTAL HIGHEST STATEWIDE GENERAL ELECTIONS

Election Years 1922–1926
(Population Adjusted for Disenfranchisement of
African Americans in South)*

State	1922 Voting-age Population	Turnout	%	1926 Voting-age Population	Turnout	%	Difference from 1922**
ALABAMA	744,000	139,792	18.8%	811,000	107,095	13.2%	-5.6
ALASKA							
ARIZONA	148,000	51,863	35.0%	157,000	68,227	43.5%	8.4
ARKANSAS	646,000	34,581	5.4%	681,000	33,712	5.0%	-0.4
CALIFORNIA	2,357,000	781,889	33.2%	2,850,000	954,418	33.5%	0.3
COLORADO	536,000	265,636	49.6%	555,000	291,275	52.5%	2.9
CONNECTICUT	680,000	323,590	47.6%	746,000	301,458	40.4%	7.2
DELAWARE	131,000	72,611	55.4%	137,000	68,333	49.9%	-5.6
DISTRICT OF COLUMBIA							
FLORIDA	408,000	50,883	40.8%	511,000	64,684	40.8%	0.2
GEORGIA	877,000	78,679	9.0%	927,000	47,003	5.1%	-3.9
HAWAII							
IDAHO	226,000	121,143	53.6%	231,000	114,740	49.7%	-3.9
ILLINOIS	3,746,000	1,679,173	44.8%	4,130,000	1,630,610	39.5%	-5.3
INDIANA	1,773,000	1,082,088	61.0%	1,870,000	1,027,407	54.9%	-6.1
IOWA	1,398,000	585,590	41.9%	1,439,000	504,925	35.1%	-6.8
KANSAS	1,019,000	524,858	51.5%	1,067,000	480,161	45.0%	-6.5
KENTUCKY	1,176,000	352,858	30.0%	1,232,000	503,216	40.8%	10.8
LOUISIANA	587,000	44,198	7.5%	652,000	54,192	8.3%	0.8
MAINE	427,000	175,351	41.1%	433,000	173,039	40.0%	-1.1
MARYLAND	860,000	303,859	35.3%	915,000	336,098	36.7%	1.4
MASSACHUSETTS	1,963,000	824,713	42.0%	2,099,000	933,091	44.5%	2.4
MICHIGAN	2,084,000	546,333	26.2%	2,359,000	561,713	23.8%	-2.4
MINNESOTA	1,302,000	636,896	48.9%	1,389,000	658,762	47.4%	-1.5
MISSISSIPPI	447,000	68,152	15.2%	488,000	26,917	5.5%	-9.7
MISSOURI	2,043,000	976,529	47.8%	2,143,000	987,831	46.1%	-1.7
MONTANA	292,000	149,795	51.3%	292,000	153,452	52.6%	1.3
NEBRASKA	715,000	375,541	52.5%	754,000	389,400	51.6%	-0.9

Total Highest Statewide General Elections (continued)

Election Years 1922–1926 (continued)
(Population Adjusted for Disenfranchisement of
African Americans in South)

State	1922 Voting-age Population	Turnout	%	1926 Voting-age Population	Turnout	%	Difference from 1922
NEVADA	46,000	28,075	61.0%	48,000	30,508	63.6%	2.5
NEW HAMPSHIRE	242,000	127,037	52.5%	251,000	124,151	49.5%	-3.0
NEW JERSEY	1,718,000	792,271	46.1%	1,980,000	791,603	40.0%	-6.1
NEW MEXICO	170,000	109,760	64.6%	173,000	107,805	62.3%	-2.2
NEW YORK	5,630,000	2,427,949	43.1%	6,300,000	2,789,657	44.3%	1.2
NORTH CAROLINA	937,000	364,443	38.9%	1,037,000	358,917	34.6%	-4.3
NORTH DAKOTA	306,000	150,492	49.2%	323,000	146,183	45.3%	-3.9
OHIO	3,420,000	1,589,363	46.5%	3,680,000	1,286,478	35.0%	11.5
OKLAHOMA	1,072,000	469,827	43.8%	1,165,000	362,544	31.1%	-12.7
OREGON	491,000	180,292	36.7%	538,000	208,259	38.7%	2.0
PENNSYLVANIA	4,589,000	1,446,417	31.5%	4,943,000	1,468,782	29.7%	-1.8
RHODE ISLAND	310,000	155,450	50.1%	337,000	164,080	48.7%	-1.5
SOUTH CAROLINA	421,000	35,130	8.3%	451,000	14,322	3.2%	-5.2
SOUTH DAKOTA	334,000	159,776	47.8%	350,000	168,001	48.0%	0.2
TENNESSEE	1,015,000	219,494	21.6%	1,086,000	102,679	9.5%	-12.2
TEXAS	2,022,000	400,403	19.8%	2,241,000	237,026	10.6%	-9.2
UTAH	220,000	119,613	54.4%	234,000	141,546	60.5%	6.1
VERMONT	200,000	70,351	35.2%	202,000	72,426	35.9%	0.7
VIRGINIA	877,000	166,234	19.0%	926,000	107,893	11.7%	-7.3
WASHINGTON	804,000	260,085	32.3%	862,000	270,757	31.4%	-0.9
WEST VIRGINIA	703,000	381,490	54.3%	761,000	427,463	56.2%	1.9
WISCONSIN	1,432,000	452,373	31.6%	1,554,000	481,216	31.0%	-0.6
WYOMING	110,000	57,902	52.6%	117,000	64,774	55.4%	2.7
Total	53,654,000	20,410,828	38.0%	58,427,000	20,398,829	34.9%	-3.1

*The African American population of states south of the Mason-Dixon line (Alabama, Arkansas, Florida, Georgia, Kentucky, Louisiana, Mississippi, North Carolina, South Carolina, Tennessee, Texas, Virginia, and West Virginia) was largely excluded from voting by poll taxes, literacy tests, intimidation, and fear. Therefore, this adjusted voting-age population subtracts the number of African Americans in the population. This is an imprecise formulation, as a few African Americans could vote in a few locales, but it is, in the main, a much more accurate portrayal of turnout percentages in the South and nation.

**Percentage point difference between turnout in current year and initial year listed in chart. If data do not appear for a state in the initial year listed, the difference is calculated from the first year in which data do appear for that state.

TOTAL HIGHEST STATEWIDE GENERAL ELECTIONS

Midterm Election Years 1930–1946
(Population Adjusted for Disenfranchisement of African Americans in South)*

State	1930 Voting-age population	1930 Turnout	1930 %	1934 Voting-age population	1934 Turnout	1934 %	1934 Difference from 1930**	1938 Voting-age population	1938 Turnout	1938 %	1938 Difference from 1930	1942 Voting-age population	1942 Turnout	1942 %	1942 Difference from 1930	1946 Voting-age population	1946 Turnout	1946 %	1946 Difference from 1930
ALABAMA	874,000	198,433	22.7%	945,000	164,890	17.4%	-5.3	1,012,000	123,876	12.2%	-10.5	1,084,000	69,131	6.4%	-16.3	1,157,000	179,488	15.5%	-7.2
ALASKA																			
ARIZONA	168,000	52,342	31.2%	198,000	96,044	48.5%	17.4	228,000	104,058	45.6%	14.5	307,000	79,747	26.0%	-5.2	370,000	112,812	30.5%	-0.7
ARKANSAS	715,000	145,124	20.3%	765,000	139,895	18.3%	-2.0	813,000	143,956	17.7%	-2.6	842,000	98,346	11.7%	-8.6	862,000	151,333	17.6%	-2.7
CALIFORNIA	3,295,000	1,096,598	33.3%	3,756,000	2,028,658	54.0%	20.7	4,201,000	2,389,227	56.9%	23.6	5,113,000	1,899,109	37.1%	3.9	6,070,000	2,334,522	38.5%	5.2
COLORADO	577,000	314,643	54.5%	624,000	395,698	63.4%	8.9	672,000	449,537	66.9%	12.4	727,000	342,396	47.1%	-7.4	782,000	331,982	42.5%	-12.1
CONNECTICUT	810,000	428,179	52.9%	899,000	551,778	61.4%	8.5	985,000	630,132	64.0%	11.1	1,091,000	569,005	52.2%	-0.7	1,205,000	679,766	56.4%	3.6
DELAWARE	143,000	87,011	60.8%	156,000	98,857	63.4%	2.5	168,000	108,571	64.6%	3.8	182,000	84,726	46.6%	-14.3	196,000	112,621	57.5%	-3.4
DISTRICT OF COLUMBIA																			
FLORIDA	606,000	95,943	15.8%	724,000	125,263	17.3%	1.5	836,000	153,061	18.3%	2.5	1,025,000	91,120	8.9%	-6.9	1,246,000	186,763	15.0%	-0.8
GEORGIA	979,000	56,458	5.8%	1,072,000	52,683	4.9%	-0.9	1,161,000	68,065	5.9%	0.1	1,445,000	61,879	4.3%	-1.5	1,527,000	161,539	10.6%	4.8
HAWAII																			
IDAHO	239,000	126,528	52.9%	267,000	163,376	61.2%	8.2	294,000	178,684	60.8%	7.8	316,000	139,287	44.1%	-8.9	331,000	178,758	54.0%	1.1
ILLINOIS	4,466,000	2,065,436	46.2%	4,753,000	2,750,326	57.9%	11.6	5,029,000	3,054,847	60.7%	14.5	5,308,000	2,887,632	54.4%	8.2	5,580,000	3,458,882	62.0%	15.7
INDIANA	1,960,000	1,214,387	62.0%	2,065,000	1,456,301	70.5%	8.6	2,167,000	1,572,649	72.6%	10.6	2,291,000	1,286,734	56.2%	-5.8	2,424,000	1,332,634	55.0%	-7.0
IOWA	1,480,000	530,250	35.8%	1,536,000	829,427	54.0%	18.2	1,592,000	802,637	50.4%	14.6	1,627,000	664,747	40.9%	5.0	1,655,000	593,031	35.8%	0.0
KANSAS	1,106,000	565,252	51.1%	1,123,000	757,234	67.4%	16.3	1,139,000	737,021	64.7%	13.6	1,169,000	493,692	42.2%	-8.9	1,203,000	554,860	46.1%	-5.0
KENTUCKY	1,289,000	548,582	42.6%	1,379,000	469,470	34.0%	-8.5	1,465,000	533,968	36.4%	-6.1	1,660,000	342,605	20.6%	-21.9	1,703,000	583,302	34.3%	-8.3
LOUISIANA	713,000	132,293	18.6%	791,000	186,112	23.5%	5.0	867,000	152,410	17.6%	-1.0	949,000	84,987	9.0%	-9.6	1,034,000	106,009	10.3%	-8.3
MAINE	442,000	143,541	32.5%	464,000	279,295	60.2%	27.7	486,000	281,619	57.9%	25.5	509,000	160,841	31.6%	-0.9	533,000	174,248	32.7%	0.2
MARYLAND	970,000	466,056	48.0%	1,052,000	455,630	43.3%	-4.7	1,129,000	486,473	43.1%	-5.0	1,250,000	337,436	27.0%	-21.1	1,388,000	444,955	32.1%	-16.0
MASSACHUSETTS	2,224,000	1,176,585	52.9%	2,379,000	1,381,425	58.1%	5.2	2,527,000	1,719,677	68.1%	15.1	2,703,000	1,327,242	49.1%	-3.8	2,888,000	1,617,314	56.0%	3.1
MICHIGAN	2,604,000	744,429	28.6%	2,836,000	1,212,526	42.8%	14.2	3,058,000	1,547,211	50.6%	22.0	3,361,000	1,170,694	34.8%	6.2	3,693,000	1,604,732	43.5%	14.9
MINNESOTA	1,471,000	759,763	51.6%	1,583,000	995,605	62.9%	11.2	1,690,000	1,070,927	63.4%	11.7	1,770,000	761,274	43.0%	-8.6	1,827,000	875,005	47.9%	-3.8
MISSISSIPPI	524,000	34,897	6.7%	571,000	57,327	10.0%	3.4	616,000	35,439	5.8%	-0.9	652,000	51,698	7.9%	1.3	684,000	49,957	7.3%	0.6
MISSOURI	2,234,000	947,063	42.4%	2,336,000	1,320,343	56.5%	14.1	2,432,000	1,245,034	51.2%	8.8	2,506,000	925,319	36.9%	-5.5	2,569,000	1,084,276	42.2%	-0.2
MONTANA	295,000	170,147	57.7%	312,000	196,739	63.1%	5.4	329,000	208,710	63.4%	5.8	349,000	169,508	48.6%	-9.1	357,000	190,088	53.2%	-4.4
NEBRASKA	785,000	415,601	52.9%	798,000	519,339	65.1%	12.1	812,000	477,715	58.8%	5.9	825,000	357,569	43.3%	-9.6	837,000	372,040	44.4%	-8.5

Total Highest Statewide General Elections (continued)

Election Years 1930–1946 (continued)
(Population Adjusted for Disenfranchisement of African Americans in South)

State	1930 Voting-age population	1930 Turnout	1930 %	1934 Voting-age population	1934 Turnout	1934 %	1934 Difference from 1930	1938 Voting-age population	1938 Turnout	1938 %	1938 Difference from 1930	1942 Voting-age population	1942 Turnout	1942 %	1942 Difference from 1930	1946 Voting-age population	1946 Turnout	1946 %	1946 Difference from 1930
NEVADA	51,000	33,622	65.9%	58,000	41,683	71.9%	5.9	65,000	45,441	69.9%	4.0	79,000	39,389	49.9%	-16.1	93,000	49,046	52.7%	-13.2
NEW HAMPSHIRE	260,000	123,829	47.6%	276,000	170,213	61.7%	14.0	291,000	181,273	62.3%	14.7	308,000	156,215	50.7%	3.1	324,000	161,092	49.7%	2.1
NEW JERSEY	2,205,000	990,834	44.9%	2,376,000	1,328,407	55.9%	11.0	2,540,000	1,531,121	60.3%	15.3	2,765,000	1,203,455	43.5%	-1.4	3,014,000	1,381,993	45.9%	0.9
NEW MEXICO	179,000	117,398	05.6%	216,000	148,268	69.0%	3.4	249,000	155,157	62.3%	-3.3	300,000	105,947	35.3%	-30.3	338,000	126,939	37.6%	-28.0
NEW YORK	6,904,000	3,025,182	43.8%	7,527,000	3,613,973	48.0%	4.2	8,124,000	4,511,005	55.5%	11.7	8,735,000	3,953,789	45.3%	1.4	9,321,000	4,712,410	50.6%	6.7
NORTH CAROLINA	1,132,000	532,686	47.1%	1,260,000	493,703	39.2%	-7.9	1,384,000	479,267	34.6%	-12.4	1,527,000	314,827	20.6%	-26.4	1,666,000	452,222	27.1%	-19.9
NORTH DAKOTA	338,000	182,500	54.0%	345,000	276,680	80.2%	26.2	351,000	216,340	61.6%	7.6	358,000	182,380	50.9%	-3.0	359,000	144,394	40.2%	-13.8
OHIO	3,913,000	1,880,085	48.0%	4,130,000	1,981,089	48.0%	-0.1	4,338,000	2,246,090	51.8%	3.7	4,618,000	1,663,687	36.0%	-12.0	4,929,000	2,153,524	43.7%	-4.4
OKLAHOMA	1,242,000	456,730	36.8%	1,281,000	530,356	41.4%	4.6	1,319,000	445,824	33.8%	-3.0	1,367,000	351,727	25.7%	-11.0	1,372,000	492,141	35.9%	-0.9
OREGON	584,000	228,525	39.1%	640,000	285,389	44.6%	5.5	693,000	365,943	52.8%	13.7	790,000	276,425	35.0%	-4.1	894,000	334,670	37.4%	-1.7
PENNSYLVANIA	5,264,000	2,019,307	38.4%	5,803,000	2,926,338	52.2%	13.9	5,928,000	3,783,751	63.8%	25.5	6,251,000	2,489,357	39.8%	1.5	6,570,000	3,111,987	47.4%	9.0
RHODE ISLAND	362,000	219,322	60.6%	389,000	244,560	62.9%	2.3	417,000	300,220	72.0%	11.4	450,000	236,604	52.6%	-8.0	485,000	272,450	56.2%	-4.4
SOUTH CAROLINA	481,000	16,163	3.4%	536,000	22,156	4.1%	0.8	589,000	46,190	7.8%	4.5	647,000	23,356	3.6%	0.2	708,000	26,358	3.7%	0.4
SOUTH DAKOTA	364,000	170,073	46.7%	365,000	277,593	76.1%	29.3	367,000	274,425	74.8%	28.1	384,000	178,111	46.4%	-0.3	391,000	162,804	41.6%	-5.1
TENNESSEE	1,156,000	197,870	17.1%	1,262,000	275,242	21.8%	4.7	1,363,000	264,404	19.4%	2.3	1,466,000	156,211	10.7%	-6.5	1,571,000	193,444	12.3%	-4.8
TEXAS	2,449,000	293,733	12.0%	2,767,000	445,883	16.1%	4.1	3,073,000	366,541	11.9%	-0.1	3,399,000	278,419	8.2%	-3.8	3,735,000	349,659	9.4%	-2.6
UTAH	249,000	154,754	62.2%	269,000	179,977	66.9%	4.8	289,000	102,532	63.2%	1.0	321,000	150,493	46.9%	-15.3	353,000	196,672	55.7%	-6.4
VERMONT	204,000	72,822	35.7%	208,000	129,725	62.4%	26.7	213,000	114,473	53.7%	18.0	219,000	58,070	26.5%	-9.2	224,000	73,066	32.6%	-3.1
VIRGINIA	977,000	164,832	16.9%	1,067,000	148,124	13.9%	-3.0	1,153,000	126,043	10.9%	-5.9	1,295,000	90,014	7.0%	-9.9	1,460,000	253,855	17.4%	0.5
WASHINGTON	920,000	289,378	31.5%	1,002,000	479,365	47.8%	16.4	1,081,000	586,493	54.3%	22.8	1,230,000	428,186	34.8%	3.4	1,383,000	644,930	46.6%	15.2
WEST VIRGINIA	817,000	537,836	65.8%	888,000	619,947	69.8%	4.0	955,000	622,821	65.2%	-0.6	992,000	460,287	46.4%	-19.4	1,015,000	537,357	52.9%	-12.9
WISCONSIN	1,666,000	509,409	30.6%	1,785,000	885,689	49.6%	19.0	1,899,000	912,302	48.0%	17.5	2,009,000	748,717	37.3%	6.7	2,105,000	983,566	46.7%	16.1
WYOMING	123,000	68,409	55.6%	135,000	91,383	67.7%	12.1	146,000	94,500	64.7%	9.1	157,000	74,857	47.7%	-7.9	167,000	79,458	47.6%	-8.0
Total	62,809,000	24,800,840	39.5%	67,768,000	32,279,984	47.6%	8.1	72,535,000	36,128,468	49.8%	10.3	78,728,000	28,077,247	35.7%	-3.8	84,598,000	34,364,954	40.6%	1.1

*The African American population of states south of the Mason-Dixon line (Alabama, Arkansas, Florida, Georgia, Kentucky, Louisiana, Mississippi, North Carolina, South Carolina, Tennessee, Texas, Virginia, and West Virginia) was largely excluded from voting by poll taxes, literacy tests, intimidation, and fear. Therefore, this adjusted voting-age population subtracts the number of African Americans in the population. This is an imprecise formulation, as a few African Americans could vote in a few locales, but it is, in the main, a much more accurate portrayal of turnout percentages in the South and nation.

**Percentage point difference between turnout in current year and initial year listed in chart. If data do not appear for a state in the initial year listed, the difference is calculated from the first year in which data do appear for that state.

TOTAL HIGHEST STATEWIDE GENERAL ELECTIONS

Midterm Election Years 1950–1962
(Population Adjusted for Disenfranchisement of African Americans in South)*

State	1950			1954				1958				1962			
	Voting-age population	Turnout	%	Voting-age population	Turnout	%	Difference from 1950**	Voting-age population	Turnout	%	Difference from 1950	Voting-age population	Turnout	%	Difference from 1950
ALABAMA	1,224,000	152,192	12.4%	1,279,000	279,789	21.9%	9.4	1,332,000	237,162	17.8%	5.4	1,409,000	477,858	33.9%	21.5
ALASKA								127,000	48,644	38.3%		144,000	58,591	40.7%	2.4
ARIZONA	438,000	177,667	40.6%	559,000	223,402	40.0%	-0.6	673,000	277,566	41.2%	0.7	798,000	349,024	43.7%	3.2
ARKANSAS	876,000	295,802	33.8%	863,000	280,274	32.5%	-1.3	850,000	60,222	7.1%	-26.7	887,000	181,592	20.5%	-13.3
CALIFORNIA	6,975,000	3,357,704	48.1%	7,895,000	3,873,075	49.1%	0.9	8,777,000	4,953,137	56.4%	8.3	9,933,000	5,573,346	56.1%	8.0
COLORADO	838,000	442,892	52.9%	910,000	480,054	52.8%	-0.1	981,000	534,019	54.4%	1.6	1,086,000	596,596	54.9%	2.1
CONNECTICUT	1,311,000	878,388	67.0%	1,401,000	932,410	66.6%	-0.4	1,488,000	967,767	65.0%	-2.0	1,612,000	1,032,244	64.0%	-3.0
DELAWARE	210,000	129,404	61.6%	231,000	144,236	62.4%	0.8	251,000	152,896	60.9%	-0.7	275,000	153,356	55.8%	-5.9
DISTRICT OF COLUMBIA															
FLORIDA	1,489,000	253,049	17.0%	1,937,000	326,287	16.8%	-0.1	2,365,000	494,361	20.9%	3.9	2,866,000	940,839	32.8%	15.8
GEORGIA	1,608,000	290,008	18.0%	1,711,000	352,743	20.6%	2.6	1,810,000	158,638	8.8%	-9.3	1,977,000	333,374	16.9%	-1.2
HAWAII								337,000	163,717	48.6%		364,000	194,529	53.4%	4.9
IDAHO	345,000	200,084	58.0%	355,000	226,012	63.7%	5.7	365,000	239,028	65.5%	7.5	380,000	254,329	66.9%	8.9
ILLINOIS	5,820,000	3,509,695	60.3%	5,953,000	3,257,722	54.7%	-5.6	6,079,000	3,229,864	53.1%	-7.2	6,295,000	3,625,309	57.6%	-2.7
INDIANA	2,545,000	1,587,309	62.4%	2,638,000	1,586,631	60.1%	-2.2	2,727,000	1,721,464	63.1%	0.8	2,842,000	1,790,709	63.0%	0.6
IOWA	1,675,000	819,959	49.0%	1,664,000	817,253	49.1%	0.2	1,654,000	829,916	50.2%	1.2	1,665,000	802,847	48.2%	-0.7
KANSAS	1,236,000	604,746	48.9%	1,269,000	614,989	48.5%	-0.5	1,302,000	717,694	55.1%	6.2	1,329,000	625,282	47.0%	-1.9
KENTUCKY	1,751,000	488,614	27.9%	1,758,000	668,488	38.0%	10.1	1,765,000	475,818	27.0%	-0.9	1,825,000	631,453	34.6%	6.7
LOUISIANA	1,113,000	227,075	20.4%	1,186,000	216,323	18.2%	-2.2	1,256,000	182,124	14.5%	-5.9	1,341,000	346,232	25.8%	5.4
MAINE	553,000	237,632	43.0%	557,000	241,443	43.3%	0.4	561,000	274,962	49.0%	6.0	572,000	285,501	49.9%	6.9
MARYLAND	1,519,000	572,927	37.7%	1,648,000	638,875	38.8%	1.0	1,772,000	712,126	40.2%	2.5	1,958,000	718,772	36.7%	-1.0
MASSACHUSETTS	3,042,000	1,859,396	61.1%	3,070,000	1,782,659	58.1%	-3.1	3,095,000	1,776,218	57.4%	-3.7	3,214,000	1,970,481	61.3%	0.2
MICHIGAN	3,992,000	1,804,724	45.2%	4,199,000	2,133,390	50.8%	5.6	4,396,000	2,253,810	51.3%	6.1	4,648,000	2,679,253	57.6%	12.4
MINNESOTA	1,879,000	1,018,267	54.2%	1,922,000	1,131,492	58.9%	4.7	1,962,000	1,131,127	57.7%	3.5	2,041,000	1,204,753	59.0%	4.8
MISSISSIPPI	710,000	87,756	12.4%	725,000	99,342	13.7%	1.3	740,000	61,464	8.3%	-4.1	777,000	161,615	20.8%	8.4
MISSOURI	2,623,000	1,250,150	47.7%	2,646,000	1,184,813	44.8%	-2.9	2,669,000	1,166,817	43.7%	-3.9	2,731,000	1,212,324	44.4%	-3.3
MONTANA	365,000	210,527	57.7%	374,000	224,587	60.1%	2.4	382,000	228,470	59.8%	2.1	390,000	248,441	63.7%	6.0
NEBRASKA	846,000	436,330	51.6%	847,000	406,690	48.0%	-3.6	849,000	415,590	49.0%	-2.6	861,000	445,032	51.7%	0.1

Total Highest Statewide General Elections *(continued)*

Midterm Election Years 1950–1962 *(continued)*
(Population Adjusted for Disenfranchisement of African Americans in South)

State	1950 Voting-age population	1950 Turnout	1950 %	1954 Voting-age population	1954 Turnout	1954 %	1954 Difference from 1950	1958 Voting-age population	1958 Turnout	1958 %	1958 Difference from 1950	1962 Voting-age population	1962 Turnout	1962 %	1962 Difference from 1950
NEVADA	107,000	60,328	56.4%	136,000	77,639	57.1%	0.7	162,000	82,328	50.8%	-5.6	205,000	93,324	45.5%	-10.9
NEW HAMPSHIRE	339,000	185,247	54.6%	348,000	191,818	55.1%	0.5	357,000	197,501	55.3%	0.7	383,000	221,252	57.8%	3.1
NEW JERSEY	3,246,000	1,571,263	48.4%	3,453,000	1,786,853	51.7%	3.3	3,652,000	1,906,452	52.2%	3.8	3,920,000	1,958,960	50.0%	1.6
NEW MEXICO	375,000	172,634	46.0%	427,000	188,862	44.2%	-1.8	477,000	197,846	41.5%	-4.6	509,000	244,913	48.1%	2.1
NEW YORK	9,827,000	5,051,889	51.4%	10,051,000	5,002,181	49.8%	-1.6	10,266,000	5,522,916	53.8%	2.4	10,057,000	5,550,064	62.2%	0.8
NORTH CAROLINA	1,790,000	522,200	29.2%	1,882,000	604,179	32.1%	2.9	1,970,000	608,853	30.9%	1.7	2,119,000	818,529	38.6%	9.5
NORTH DAKOTA	358,000	181,369	50.7%	354,000	188,934	53.4%	2.7	351,000	197,424	56.2%	5.6	351,000	216,282	61.6%	11.0
OHIO	5,214,000	2,684,563	51.5%	5,454,000	2,498,837	45.8%	-5.7	5,682,000	3,110,579	54.7%	3.3	5,920,000	3,000,610	50.7%	-0.8
OKLAHOMA	1,378,000	606,786	44.0%	1,392,000	545,789	39.2%	-4.8	1,406,000	529,775	37.7%	-6.4	1,457,000	624,613	42.9%	-1.2
OREGON	985,000	499,489	50.7%	1,016,000	564,494	55.6%	4.9	1,045,000	595,111	56.9%	6.2	1,117,000	630,865	56.5%	5.8
PENNSYLVANIA	6,838,000	3,511,889	51.4%	6,899,000	3,695,910	53.6%	2.2	6,958,000	3,961,198	56.9%	5.6	7,081,000	4,354,207	61.5%	10.1
RHODE ISLAND	514,000	295,591	57.5%	517,000	326,059	63.1%	5.6	520,000	340,642	65.5%	8.0	540,000	318,658	59.0%	1.5
SOUTH CAROLINA	766,000	50,400	6.6%	821,000	213,335	26.0%	19.4	875,000	76,647	8.8%	2.2	947,000	262,554	27.7%	21.1
SOUTH DAKOTA	396,000	248,426	62.7%	393,000	231,167	58.8%	-3.9	390,000	257,989	66.2%	3.4	388,000	252,731	65.1%	2.4
TENNESSEE	1,662,000	262,608	15.8%	1,711,000	344,796	20.2%	4.4	1,758,000	371,803	21.1%	5.3	1,850,000	605,907	32.8%	17.0
TEXAS	4,049,000	360,442	8.9%	4,357,000	630,918	14.5%	5.6	4,652,000	768,847	16.5%	7.6	5,045,000	1,551,699	30.8%	21.9
UTAH	384,000	263,847	68.7%	415,000	263,031	63.4%	-5.3	445,000	286,323	64.3%	-4.4	486,000	317,010	65.2%	-3.5
VERMONT	229,000	88,822	38.8%	227,000	114,284	50.3%	11.6	225,000	122,667	54.5%	15.7	234,000	121,381	51.9%	13.1
VIRGINIA	1,610,000	211,830	13.2%	1,719,000	342,344	19.9%	6.8	1,824,000	431,609	23.7%	10.5	1,988,000	448,952	22.6%	9.4
WASHINGTON	1,518,000	723,605	47.7%	1,584,000	809,795	51.1%	3.5	1,650,000	876,826	53.1%	5.5	1,777,000	881,150	49.6%	1.9
WEST VIRGINIA	1,033,000	662,836	64.2%	1,030,000	591,402	57.4%	-6.7	1,027,000	615,787	60.0%	-4.2	1,027,000	613,018	59.7%	-4.5
WISCONSIN	2,192,000	1,110,069	50.6%	2,250,000	1,140,695	50.7%	0.1	2,306,000	1,181,025	51.2%	0.6	2,397,000	1,244,331	51.9%	1.3
WYOMING	176,000	93,348	53.0%	181,000	108,771	60.1%	7.1	186,000	111,780	60.1%	7.1	190,000	116,474	61.3%	8.3
Total	89,969,000	40,311,778	44.8%	94,214,000	42,585,072	45.2%	0.4	98,749,000	45,816,549	46.4%	1.6	104,808,000	51,350,966	49.0%	4.2

*The African American population of states south of the Mason-Dixon line (Alabama, Arkansas, Florida, Georgia, Kentucky, Louisiana, Mississippi, North Carolina, South Carolina, Tennessee, Texas, Virginia, and West Virginia) was largely excluded from voting by poll taxes, literacy tests, intimidation, and fear. Therefore, this adjusted voting-age population subtracts the number of African Americans in the population. This is an imprecise formulation, as a few African Americans could vote in a few locales, but it is, in the main, a much more accurate portrayal of turnout percentages in the South and nation.

**Percentage point difference between turnout in current year and initial year listed in chart. If data do not appear for a state in the initial year listed, the difference is calculated from the first year in which data do appear for that state.